J	Japan	susp.	suspension
KIU	1000 international units	tabl.	tablets
L	Luxembourg	TEA	triethylamine
LD$_{50}$	lethal dose 50%	TEBA	triethylbenzylammonium
LDA	lithium diisopropylamide		chloride
Leu	leucine	temp.	temperature
LHRH	luteinizing hormone-releasing	TEA	triethylamine
	hormone	THF	tetrahydrofuran
liq.	liquid	Thr	threonine
LUX	Luxembourg	Tos	tosyl, 4-methylphenylsulfonyl
lyo.	lyophilizate	TosOH	4-methylbenzenesulfonic acid
Lys	lysine	Trp	tryptophan
M	mouse	Tyr	tyrosine
Me	CH$_3$ (in structural formulas)	USA	United States of America
Met	Methionine	Val	valine
MEX	Mexico	wfm	withdrawn from the market
MF	molecular formula		(for commercial products)
Mf	mouse, female	YU	Yugoslavia
ml	milliliter (cubic centimeter)	Z	benzyloxycarbonyl
Mm	mouse, male		
MTBE	methyl *tert*-butyl ether		
MW	molecular weight	**Country codes in patent descriptions**	
N	Norway	AT	Austria
NBS	*N*-bromosuccinimide	AU	Australia
NZ	New Zealand	BE	Belgium
ophth.	ophthalmic	CA	Canada
P	Portugal	CH	Switzerland
p.	page	DAS	Deutsche Auslegungsschrift
p.o.	per os (orally)	DD	German Democratic Republic
prior.	priority (patent)	DE	Federal Republic of Germany
Pro	proline	DOS	Deutsche Offenlegungsschrift
psi	pounds per square inch	DRP	Deutsches Reichspatent
q. v.	quod vide (which see)	EP	European Patent
R	rat	ES	Spain
Rf	rat, female	GB	Great Britain
Rm	rat, male	HU	Hungary
RN	Chemical Abstracts Registry	IL	Israel
	Number	IN	India
	Note: CA Registry numbers are	NL	Netherlands
	subject to change without notice	IT	Italia
s. r.	sustained release	JP	Japan
s.c.	subcutaneously	LU	Luxemburg
Ser	serine	SE	Sweden
SF	Finland	SU	Soviet Union
SIE	saccharose inhibitory unit	US	United States of America
sol.	solution	WO	World Patent
suppos.	suppositories	ZA	South Africa

Pharmaceutical Substances

Syntheses, Patents, Applications

N–Z
and Indexes (A–Z)

Axel Kleemann and
Jürgen Engel

Bernhard Kutscher and
Dietmar Reichert

4th Edition

Thieme
Stuttgart · New York

Prof. Dr. Axel Kleemann
Amselstr. 2
D-63454 Hanau

Dr. Dietmar Reichert
Degussa-Hüls
FC-FEA1
Postfach 13 45
D-63403 Hanau

Prof. Dr. Jürgen Engel
ASTA Medica AG
Weismüllerstr. 45
D-60314 Frankfurt

Prof. Dr. Bernhard Kutscher
ASTA Medica AG
Weismüllerstr. 45
D-60314 Frankfurt

Die Deutsche Bibliothek –
CIP-Einheitsaufnahme

Kleemann, Axel:
Pharmaceutical substances : syntheses, patents,
applications / Axel Kleemann and
Jürgen Engel. Bernhard Kutscher and
Dietmar Reichert. – 4th ed. – Stuttgart ;
New York : Thieme, 2001
  Einheitssacht.: Pharmazeutische Wirkstoffe
<engl.>

© 2001 Georg Thieme Verlag
Rüdigerstraße 14
D-70469 Stuttgart
http://www.thieme.de
electronic documents and indexes:
FIZ CHEMIE BERLIN
Franklinstr. 11
D-10587 Berlin
http: //www.fiz-chemie.de

Coverdesign: Thieme Marketing

Printed in Germany
by Konrad Triltsch, 97199 Ochsenfurt-Hohestadt

Some of the product names, patents and registered designs referred to in this book are in fact
registered trademarks or proprietary names even
though specific reference to this fact is not always
made in the text. Therefore, the appearance of a
name without designation as proprietary is not to
be construed as a representation by the publisher
that it is in the public domain.

ISBN 3-13-558404-6 (GTV, Stuttgart)
ISBN 1-58890-031-2 (TNY, New York)

1 2 3 4 5 6

Table of Contents

Preface to the fourth edition

The third edition of this book was a great success. Within less than 18 months it was more or less sold out, the printed version as well as the electronic one. So the publishers plagued the authors to prepare the next edition. Again, our "junior authors", Prof. Dr. Bernhard Kutscher and Dr. Dietmar Reichert, were doing an excellent job in elaborating the manuscript of about 100 new drug monographs. Furthermore we took the chance to carry out numerous additions and corrections. As a consequence of this extension it was no longer possible to stay with a "one volume edition" and we now have the fourth edition with two volumes.

This fourth edition contains 2267 active pharmaceutical ingredients ("API's") including those which were launched only recently. No fundamental changes were made in comparison to the third edition, which means that the preface, the acknowledgements and the introduction to the third edition are also still valid for the new edition.

We are very grateful to the many readers who kindly provided us with proposals for corrections. Again, the authors are deeply indebted to Dr. Hans-Georg Scharnow and his excellent team from the FIZ CHEMIE BERLIN, for their contributions to the preparation process of this book. We also would like to thank Dr. Elisabeth Hillen and Dr. Guido Herrmann from the Georg Thieme Verlag for the good cooperation. Finally the authors are very grateful to the colleagues of the experienced "ASTA Medica team", who were already mentioned in the "Acknowledgements" to the third edition. In the meantime Dr. Knut Eis joined this team.

Frankfurt a. M., Autumn 2000   Axel Kleemann
Jürgen Engel

Preface to the third edition

For many years, the second edition of "Pharmazeutische Wirkstoffe" has been out of print and colleagues and friends have asked and plagued us to publish a new edition. Everyone who has ever prepared a similar reference book knows how much energy and enthusiasm has to be put into such a task besides the "daily job" in industry. After some hesitation we finally decided to prepare the new edition, in English. Two fortunate circumstances made things a lot easier.

Firstly, Mr. Willi Plein brought us into contact with Dr. H.-G. Scharnow of the FIZ CHEMIE BERLIN[1], who was interested in preparing the new edition as an electronic version by making use of their specialised know-how and self-developed software. With this technology we were able to transform greater parts of the second edition, especially the formula drawings, into the new electronic version – thereby establishing an innovative method of book production, making future new editions much easier to prepare, and also enabling the publisher to offer a CD-ROM version. The FIZ CHEMIE team was successful in attracting the BMBF[2] for this interesting project and luckily received generous financial support.

Secondly, we persuaded the young colleagues Prof. Dr. Bernhard Kutscher and Dr. Dietmar Reichert to take responsibility as "junior authors" for this book. About a quarter of the workload for this volume was done by them and furthermore they have the capability and talent to contribute to future editions – if hopefully necessary.

The purpose and object of this book are to establish a link between INN's[3], structure, synthesis and production processes, patent (and literature) situation, medical use and trade names of important pharmaceuticals.

This volume contains a collection of 2171 active pharmaceutical ingredients, which are listed alphabetically according to their INN's. Often there are still other Generic Names in use, for example BAN[4], DCF[5], USAN[6], which are added in brackets under the INN's and are listed in the index. In addition to the foregoing editions, we have added the molecular formulas and molecular weights as well as the CAS Registry Numbers[7] and – where available – the ATC Code Numbers[8], the EINECS numbers[9], and data for acute toxicology as well as pharmaceutical dosage forms. In the last section of each monograph, the trade names in the six most important markets are listed. The trade names were taken from the relevant reference books on pharmaceutical specialities[10] [11] [12].

Within the 16 years since the second edition, respectively 11 years since the supplement volumes were published, many changes have occurred. Companies disappeared or were acquired and the trade names of many products were changed. Some products were withdrawn from the market, either as mono drugs or combinations. In such cases, we added "w f m" behind the trade name, when we felt that we should not eliminate

---

[1] FIZ CHEMIE BERLIN, Fachinformationszentrum Chemie GmbH, Franklinstraße 11, D-10587 Berlin
[2] Bundesministerium für Bildung, Wissenschaft, Forschung und Technologie, Bonn
[3] INN = International Nonproprietary Names; synonymous with "Generic Names"
[4] BAN = British Approved Name
[5] DCF = Dénomination Commune Française
[6] USAN = United States Adopted Name
[7] CAS = Chemical Abstracts Service
[8] ATC = Anatomic Therapeutic Chemical (Classification of Drugs)
  a) ATC Index, WHO Collaborating Center for Drug Statistics Methodology, Oslo 1997
  b) European Drug Index, N. F. Miller, R. P. Dessing, 4th ed., Deutscher Apotheker Verlag Stuttgart 1997
[9] EINECS = European Inventory of Existing Chemical Substances
[10] "WDI, World Drug Index" – database, Derwent Information, 1998
[11] "MDDR"-database, Drug Data Report, Prous Science, MDL, San Leandro, 1998
[12] Speciality lists for
  D: "Rote Liste 2000", Hrsg. Bundesverband der Pharmazeutischen Industrie e.V., Frankfurt/M.
  "List of Pharmaceutical Substances", 10. edition, ABDATA Pharma-Daten-Service, Eschborn, March 1997
  F: "Dictionnaire VIDAL 1998" OUP, Paris
  GB: "MIMS" (Monthly Index of Medical Specialities), Haymarket Publishing Services Ltd., London 1998
  I: "L'Informatore Farmaceutico", 58. edit., Organizzazione Editoriale Medico Farmaceutico srl, Milano 1998
  J: a) "Japta List" 1987, Japanese Drug Directory, 3rd ed., Tokyo 1987
  b) Drugs in Japan/Ethical Drugs 1970, 10, ed. by Japan Pharmaceutical Information Center, Tokyo, Japan
  USA: "PDR, Physicians Desk Reference", 52. edition, 1998; Medical Economics Comp., Montvale, N. J.

the monograph or its former trade name because the drug is still in use in other countries or in numerous combinations – even if not listed here – or is of historical interest. The given trade names are normally representing the mono drug product. In some cases, we listed the year of market introduction behind the name of the company.

It was the intention of the authors to present the synthesis routes in broad details. In many cases, we describe different synthesis routes, especially for the economically most important drugs – but also when we are not completely sure which particular route is applied technically. The practicability of such a reference book is to a great extent dependent on clearly arranged and in-depth indexes. The reader will find appropriate and comprehensive indexes for

1. Trade Names
2. Intermediates
3. Enzymes, Microorganisms, Plants, Animal Tissues
4. Substance classes.

As many abbreviations are used in this book, a separate "list of abbreviations" has been added, see front and back endpapers. Concerning abbreviations for chemicals and reagents we adhered to the "Standard List of Abbreviations", published in J. Org. Chem., Vol. **68**, No. 1, 1998, p. 19A.

We have had many discussions regarding the inclusion of the newer biopharmaceuticals ("Pharmaproteins") which are produced by recombinant DNA methods (e.g., Interferons, human Insulin, Erythropoietin etc.). After several trials, we dropped this plan because we could not find a concept consistent with the original character of the book, which predominantly contains synthetic drugs as well as some antibiotics made by conventional fermentation and some plant ingredients that are produced by extraction. A borderline case exists with many synthethic peptides. It is often practically impossible to find out the applied technical synthesis process among the manifold routes described in the literature. So, we more or less stayed with the peptide drugs that were already included in the 2nd edition and supplement volume.

The book is designed to serve the needs of not only the specialists in drug synthesis but also of a broad usergroup in the chemical, intermediates and pharmaceutical industry, pharmacists, universities and other research institutes. So, it is important for everybody who has to deal with pharmaceuticals or their raw materials and intermediates and would like to have a quick survey. For the analytical chemist, knowledge about the synthesis route of an active ingredient is essential in order to recognize contaminations with intermediates or possible byproducts. Often, also the allergologist has a need for information regarding the synthesis of a drug in order to localize allergic byproducts or intermediates. The synthetic chemist will be provided with stimulating suggestions for his work.

We hope that this book will prove to be a standard reference for everyone who is interested in pharmaceuticals.

Frankfurt a. M., Autumn 1998   Axel Kleemann
                                     Jürgen Engel

Acknowledgements

Preparing a reference book of this kind is by no means feasible without the contributions of numerous dedicated colleagues who bring in their special expertise and knowledge.

The authors are deeply indebted to Dr. Hans-Georg Scharnow, Ingo Adamczyk, Gerhard Fabian, Martin Holberg, Gudrun Lippmann, Ulrich Quandt, Karin Raatsch and Dr. Katrin Seemeyer from FIZ CHEMIE BERLIN, for providing their computer know-how and software expertise. This FIZ CHEMIE team has taken a decisive part in the preparation of the book, also in reminding the authors regularly of their obligation to deliver the manuscripts on time. It was always a reliable, fruitful and pleasant cooperation. We also wish to extend our gratefulness to the BMBF (Bundesministerium für Bildung, Wissenschaft, Forschung und Technologie) for generous support of this project.

It is the authors special desire to express their gratitude to the many co-workers of the Chemical Research Department of ASTA Medica AG, who willingly agreed to assist and support the process of manuscript preparation and correction. For their assistance in patent and literature searching, we wish to thank Dr. Ilona Fleischhauer, Dieter Heiliger, Christa Krehmer, Thomas Kynast, Horst Mai, Dr. Ulf Niemeyer, Wolfgang Paul, Horst Rauer, Jürgen Schael and Norbert Schulmeyer. Important contributions in the search for and correction of trade names have been made by Dr. Thomas Arnold, Dr. Gerhard Nößner, Dr. Klaus Paulini and Dr. Heinz Weinberger and the trade name searching process was greatly supported by Dr. Patricia Charpentier, Dr. Stefan Eils, Anja Heddrich, Dr. Gilbert Müller, Sandra Nemetz, Sven-Oliver Schmidt, Anita Storch and Silvia Werner.

Important advice concerning the pharmaceutical specialities on the Japanese market was provided by our Japanese colleague Nobuo Kumagai, whom we wish to thank sincerely.

A word of thanks has also to be addressed to Dr. Elisabeth Hillen and Dr. Rolf Hoppe from the Georg Thieme Verlag for the always good cooperation and acceptance of many special suggestions concerning the production of this book and its CD-ROM version.

Finally, we would like to express our gratitude to the many readers and users of the foregoing editions who took the time to provide us with comments, corrections and suggestions.

The authors

Introduction

This reference book describes the production/isolation processes of 2267 active pharmaceutical substances (including the syntheses of their intermediates) that are or have been marketed. In order to illustrate what particular information can be drawn from the book a typical monograph is depicted below and labelled. It is self-explanatory.

The frequently-used abbreviations are explained in a separate list, q.v. see front and back endpapers.

With respect to the names of reagents and intermediates in the course of the syntheses the authors tried to use the names found in the catalogues of the commercial providers of fine chemicals, e.g. Sigma-Aldrich, otherwise the Chemical Abstracts Names are given.

In addition to the respective patents and publications in journals several standard reference books for Pharmaceuticals and Fine Chemicals were used and sometimes also cited. The most important sources are given here:

- The Merck Index, 12 ed., Merck & Co., Inc.; NJ 1996
  abbrev.: Merck Index
- Z. Budesinsky and M. Protiva, Synthetische Arzneimittel, Akademie-Verlag, Berlin 1961
  abbrev.: Budesinsky-Protiva
- G. Ehrhart, H. Ruschig, Arzneimittel, vols. 1–5, Verlag Chemie, Weinheim 1972
  abbrev.: Ehrhart-Ruschig

- Index Nominum, international drug directory, ed. by Swiss Pharmaceutical Society, 1992/93
- A. Kleemann, E. Lindner, J. Engel, Arzneimittel-Fortschritte 1972–1985, VCH Verlagsgesellschaft mbH, Weinheim 1987
- D. Lednicer, L. A. Mitscher, The Organic Chemistry of Drug Synthesis, vols. 1–6, John Wiley & Sons, New York 1977–1999
- Ullmanns Encyclopädie der technischen Chemie, 3. and 4. edition, Verlag Chemie Weinheim;
- Ullmann's Encyclopedia of Industrial Chemistry, 5. ed., vols. A1–A28, B1–B8, VCH Verlagsgesellschft mbH, Weinheim 1985–1997 abbrev.: Ullmanns Encycl. Techn. Chem.
- Ullmann's Encyclopedia of Industrial Chemistry, 6. ed., on CD-ROM, 1999 and 2000
- M. Negwer, Organic-chemical drugs and their synonyms, Akademie-Verlag, Berlin 1994
- USP Dictionary of USAN and International Drug Names, US Pharmacopeia, Rockville, MD 1998

The acute toxicity data were in most cases taken from different data banks or other secondary sources, so no guarantee can be given for validity.

For information regarding pharmaceutical dosage forms see preface, footnote 12.

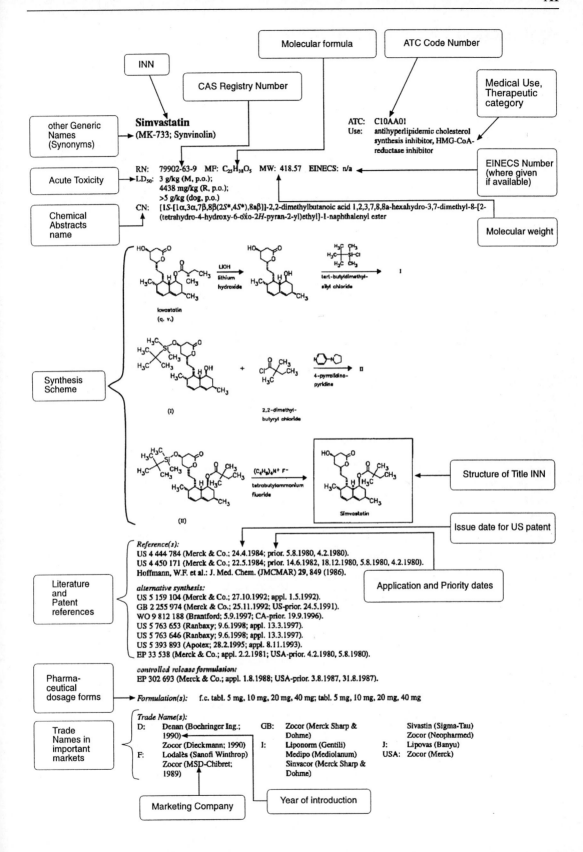

INN

CAS Registry Number

Molecular formula

ATC Code Number

Medical Use, Therapeutic category

other Generic Names (Synonyms)

Simvastatin
(MK-733; Synvinolin)

ATC: C10AA01
Use: antihyperlipidemic cholesterol synthesis inhibitor, HMG-CoA-reductase inhibitor

EINECS Number (where given if available)

Acute Toxicity

RN: 79902-63-9 MF: $C_{25}H_{38}O_5$ MW: 418.57 EINECS: n/a
LD$_{50}$: 3 g/kg (M, p.o.);
4438 mg/kg (R, p.o.);
>5 g/kg (dog, p.o.)

Chemical Abstracts name

CN: [1S-[1α,3α,7β,8β(2S*,4S*),8aβ]]-2,2-dimethylbutanoic acid 1,2,3,7,8,8a-hexahydro-3,7-dimethyl-8-[2-(tetrahydro-4-hydroxy-6-oxo-2H-pyran-2-yl)ethyl]-1-naphthalenyl ester

Molecular weight

Synthesis Scheme

lovastatin (q. v.)

LiOH lithium hydroxide

tert-butyldimethyl-silyl chloride

I

(I)

2,2-dimethyl-butyryl chloride

4-pyrrolidino-pyridine

II

$(C_4H_9)_4N^+ F^-$ tetrabutylammonium fluoride

Simvastatin

(II)

Structure of Title INN

Issue date for US patent

Reference(s):
US 4 444 784 (Merck & Co.; 24.4.1984; prior. 5.8.1980, 4.2.1980).
US 4 450 171 (Merck & Co.; 22.5.1984; prior. 14.6.1982, 18.12.1980, 5.8.1980, 4.2.1980).
Hoffmann, W.F. et al.: J. Med. Chem. (JMCMAR) 29, 849 (1986).

alternative synthesis:
US 5 159 104 (Merck & Co.; 27.10.1992; appl. 1.5.1992).
GB 2 255 974 (Merck & Co.; 25.11.1992; US-prior. 24.5.1991).
WO 9 812 188 (Brantford; 5.9.1997; CA-prior. 19.9.1996).
US 5 763 653 (Ranbaxy; 9.6.1998; appl. 13.3.1997).
US 5 763 646 (Ranbaxy; 9.6.1998; appl. 13.3.1997).
US 5 393 893 (Apotex; 28.2.1995; appl. 8.11.1993).
EP 33 538 (Merck & Co.; appl. 2.2.1981; USA-prior. 4.2.1980, 5.8.1980).

controlled release formulation:
EP 302 693 (Merck & Co.; appl. 1.8.1988; USA-prior. 3.8.1987, 31.8.1987).

Literature and Patent references

Application and Priority dates

Pharma-ceutical dosage forms

Formulation(s): f.c. tabl. 5 mg, 10 mg, 20 mg, 40 mg; tabl. 5 mg, 10 mg, 20 mg, 40 mg

Trade Names in important markets

Trade Name(s):
D: Denan (Boehringer Ing.; 1990)
     Zocor (Dieckmann; 1990)
F: Lodalès (Sanofi Winthrop)
     Zocor (MSD-Chibret; 1989)

GB: Zocor (Merck Sharp & Dohme)
I: Liponorm (Gentili)
     Medipo (Mediolanum)
     Sinvacor (Merck Sharp & Dohme)

Sivastin (Sigma-Tau)
Zocor (Neopharmed)
J: Lipovas (Banyu)
USA: Zocor (Merck)

Marketing Company

Year of introduction

Alphabetical List of Drug Monographs

Mazindol 1210
McN-4853 2079
McN-A-2833 1600
MCNU 1788
MDL-14042 1180
MDL-16455A 856
MDL-73147EF 700
ME-1207 381
ME-3255 1408
ME-3737 2040
Mebendazole 1211
Mebeverine 1212
Mebhydrolin 1213
Mebumalum 1589
Mebutamate 1214
Mecamylamine 1215
Mecillinam 1215
Meclastine 496
Meclizine 1218
Meclofenamic acid 1216
Meclofenoxate 1217
Mecloqualone 1217
Meclozine 1218
Mecobalamin 1218
Mecoffaminum 314
Mecysteine hydrochloride
    1220
Medazepam 1221
Medibazine 1222
Medifoxamine 1223
Medigoxin 1308
Medrogestone 1224
Medroxyprogesterone acetate
    1225
Medrylamine 1227
Medrysone 1227
Mefenamic acid 1228
Mefenorex 1229
Mefexamide 1229
Mefloquine 1230
Mefruside 1231
Megalocin 862
Megestrol acetate 1232
Meglutol 1233
Melengestrol acetate 1234
Melitracen 1235
Meloxicam 1235
Melperone 1236
Melphalan 1237
Memantine 1238
ME-MPA 1378
Menadiol diacetate 1239
Menadiol sodium diphosphate
    1239
Menadione 1240
Menadione sodium bisulfite
    1241
Menaphthone 1240
Menaphthone sodium
    bisulfite 1241
Menaquinone 1240
(−)-Menthol 1241
Mepacrine 1243
Meparfynol 1298
Mepartricin 1244
Mepazine 1570
Mepenicycline 1580
Mepenzolate bromide 1245

Meperidine 1603
Mephenesin 1245
Mephenytoin 1246
Mephobarbital 1299
Mepindolol 1247
Mepirizole 753
Mepirodipine hydrochloride
    180
Mepirzepine 1343
Mepitiostane 1248
Mepivacaine 1249
Meprednisone 1250
Meprobamate 1251
Meproscillaridin 1252
Meproscillarin 1252
Meprylcaine 1253
Meptazinol 1253
Mepyramine 1254
Mequitazine 1255
Meractinomycin 571
Merbromin 1256
Mercamidum 2051
Mercaptopurine 1256
Mercurochrome 1256
Mercurothiolate sodique 2020
Meropenem 1257
Mesalamine 1259
Mesalazine 1259
Mesna 1261
Mesoridazine 1262
Mestanolone 1263
Mesterolone 1264
Mestranol 1265
Mesulfen 1266
Mesuximide 1266
Metaclazepam 1267
Metacycline 1268
Metahexamide 1269
Metamizole sodium 1270
Metampicillin 1271
Metandienone 1271
Metapramine 1272
Metaproterenol 1492
Metaraminol 1273
Metaxalone 1274
Metenamine 1283
Metenolone acetate 1275
Metformin 1276
Methacycline 1268
Methadone 1277
Methallenestril 1278
Methallenoestril 1278
Methallenoestrol 1278
Methamphetamine 1279
Methandienone 1271
Methandriol 1279
Methandrostenediolone 1531
Methandrostenolone 1271
Methapyrilene 1281
Methaqualone 1281
Methazolamide 1282
Methdilazine 1283
Methenamine 1283
Methenolone acetate 1275
Methestrol dipropionate 1284
Methicillin 1306
Methimazole 2014
Methioninyl adenylate 40

Methiosulfonii chloridum
    1297
Methixene 1311
Methocarbamol 1285
Methohexital 1286
Methohexitone 1286
Methoin 1246
Methonitrate d'atropine 152
D-Methorphan 615
Methotrexate 1287
Methotrimeprazine 1168
Methoxamine 1289
Methoxsalen 1289
Methoxyflurane 1291
Methoxypsoralen 1289
Methoxysalen 1289
Methscopolamine bromide
    1291
Methscopolamine nitrate
    1291
Methsuximide 1266
Methyclothiazide 1292
Methylatropine Nitrate 152
Methylcatechol 983
Methylcobalamin 1218
Methylcoffanolamine 314
β-Methyldigoxin 1308
Methyldopa 1293
Methyldopate 1295
Methylenblau 1303
Methylene blue 1303
Méthylènecycline 1268
Methylergometrine 1295
Methylergonovine 1295
Methylestrenolone 1296
Methylhomatropine bromide
    1017
Methylmethionine sulfonium
    bromide 1297
Methylmethionine sulfonium
    chloride 1297
Methyloxazepam 1981
Methylpartricin 1244
Methylpentynol 1298
Methylperidol 1362
Methylperone 1236
Methylphenidate 1299
Methylphenobarbital 1299
Methylphenobarbitone 1299
Methylprednisolone 1300
Methylsulfadiazine 1928
Methylsynephrine 1520
Methyltestosterone 1302
Methylthioninium chloride
    1303
Methylthiouracil 1304
α-Methyltyrosine 1310
Methyprylon 1304
Methysergide 1305
Metiazinic acid 1306
Meticillin 1306
Meticrane 1307
Metildigoxin 1308
Metipranolol 1309
Metirosine 1310
Metixene 1311
Metoclopramide 1312
Metocurine chloride 667

Metolazone 1314
Metopimazine 1315
Metoprolol 1315
Metrizamide 1316
Metrizoic acid 1317
Metronidazole 1318
Metuclazepam 1267
Metylperon 1236
Metyrapone 1318
Metyrosine 1310
Mevinolin 1198
Mexazolam 1319
Mexenone 1320
Mexiletine 1320
Mezlocillin 1321
MF 934 1843
Mianserin 1322
Mibefradil hydrochloride
    1323
Mibolerone 1325
Micinicate 1325
Miconazole 1326
Micronomicin 1327
Midalcipran hydrochloride
    1335
Midazolam 1328
Midecamicin 1329
Midecamycin 1329
Midecamycin acetate 1330
Midodrine 1331
Midoriamin 1332
Mifepristone 1333
Miglitol 1334
Milnacipran hydrochloride
    1335
Milrinone 1338
Miltefosine 1339
Minaprine 1340
Minocycline 1341
Minoxidil 1342
Miokamycin 1330
Mirtazapine 1343
Misoprostol 1344
Mitobronitol 1346
Mitomycin 1347
Mitopodozide 1347
Mitotane 1348
Mitoxantrone 1348
Mizolastine 1349
Mizoribine 1350
MJ-13754-1 1411
MK 383 2057
MK-462 1827
MK-476 1359
MK-507 707
MK-521 1176
MK-639 1067
MK-733 1877
MK 803 1198
MK-954 1193
MK-966 1830
MK-0476 1359
MKC-431 1349
MMS 1297
Moclobemide 1351
Modafinil 1352
Moexipril 1353
Mofebutazone 1354

S-1991 1866
S-3341 1815
S-6059 1143
6315-S 864
S-9490 1600
SA-96 277
Saccharin 1847
Salacetamide 1848
Salazosulfapyridine 1849
Salbutamol 1849
Salicylamide 1851
Salicylate de choline 455
Salicylazosulfapyridine 1849
Salicylic acid 1852
Salmaterol 1853
Salmeterol 1853
Salsalate 1854
SAM 40
Saquinavir 1854
Saralasin acetate 1858
SB-1 763
SB-75 418
SB-205312 1682
SC-58635 409
Sch-16134 1765
Sch-21420 1097
Sch-29851 1188
Sch-33844 1892
Sch-34117 592
Sch-60936 763
Schizophyllan 1880
Scopolamine 1859
Scopolamine butyl bromide
    311
(–)sddc 1136
SDT-DJN 608 1406
SDZ 212-713 1826
SDZ-205502 1768
Secbutabarbital 1860
Secbutobarbitone 1860
Secnidazole 1860
Secobarbital 1861
Secretin 1862
SED-9490 (as erbumine)
    1600
Selegiline 1863
Seratrodast 1864
Sertaconazole 1865
Sertindole 1866
Sertraline 1868
Serum-Tryptase 858
Setastine 1869
Setiptiline 1870
Sevoflurane 1871
SF-86327 1991
SH-401 1048
SHB 331 960
Sibutramine hydrochloride
    1872
Sildenafil 1873
Silibinin 1876
Simethicone 665
Simfibrate 1876
Simvastatin 1877
Sisomicin 1878
β-Sitosterin 1879
β-Sitosterol 1879
Sizofiran 1880

SK & F-96022 1554
SK & F-101468 1837
SK & F-101468A 1837
SK & F-S 104864-A 2080
SKB 108566 758
SKF 108566 758
SKF 82526-J 844
SL-85.0324 1349
SL-80-0750-23N 2207
SM-7338 1257
SM-3997 (as citrate) 1971
SN-305 1133
SND-919Y 1679
Sobrerol 1881
Sobuzoxane 1881
Sodium aurothiomalate 1882
Sodium Butabarbital 1860
Sodium dioctyl sulfosuccinate
    1882
Sodium picosulfate 1884
Sodium picosulphate 1884
Sofalcone 1884
Sorbitol 1885
Sorivudine 1886
Sotalol 1888
Sparfloxacin 1889
Spectinomycin 1890
Spiperone 1891
Spiramycin 1891
Spirapril 1892
Spironolactone 1895
Spiroylsäure 1852
Spirsäure 1852
Spizofurone 1897
SPM-925 1353
SQ-28555 937
SR-41319 2040
SR-47436 1095
SR-41319B 2040
SR-25990C 526
SRI-62320 921
SS-717 1419
ST-1396 409
Stallimycin 1897
Stanazol 1899
Stanolone 122
Stanozolol 1899
Stavudine 1900
Stepronin 1904
Streptokinase 1905
Streptomycin 1905
Streptoniazid 1906
Streptonicozid 1906
Streptozocin 1907
Streptozotocin 1907
g-Strophanthin 1908
k-Strophanthin 1909
k-Strophanthin-α 1910
k-Strophanthin-β 1909
k-Strophanthin-β + k-
    Strophanthoside 1909
k-Strophanthoside 1909
g-Strophantoside 1908
Styramate 1911
SU-88 1884
SU 101 1148
Succinylcholine chloride
    1952

Succinylsulfathiazole 1911
Sucralfate 1912
Sufentanil 1913
Sulbactam 1913
Sulbenicillin 1914
Sulbentine 1915
Sulconazole 1915
Sulfabenzamide 1916
Sulfacarbamide 1917
Sulfacetamide 1918
Sulfachlorpyridazine 1919
Sulfacitine 1919
Sulfacytine 1919
Sulfadiazine 1920
Sulfadicramide 1921
Sulfadimethoxine 1922
Sulfadoxine 1923
Sulfaethidole 1924
Sulfafurazole 1924
Sulfaguanidine 1925
Sulfaguanole 1926
Sulfalene 1926
Sulfaloxic acid 1927
Sulfamerazine 1928
Sulfameter 1932
Sulfamethizole 1929
Sulfamethoxazole 1930
Sulfamethoxypyridazine 1931
Sulfametopyrazine 1926
Sulfametoxydiazine 1932
Sulfametrole 1933
Sulfamoxole 1933
Sulfanilamide 1934
Sulfanylurea 1917
Sulfaperin 1935
Sulfaphenazole 1936
Sulfaproxyline 1937
Sulfasalazine 1849
Sulfathiazole 1938
Sulfatolamide 1204
Sulfinpyrazone 1938
Sulfisomidine 1939
Sulfisoxazole 1924
Sulfisoxazole Acetyl 29
Sulforidazine 1940
Sulformethoxine 1923
Sulformetoxinum 1923
Sulforthomidine 1923
Sulfoxone sodium 1941
Sulindac 1941
Sulmetozin 1942
Suloctidil 1943
Sulphabenzamide 1916
Sulphacetamide 1918
Sulphadiazine 1920
Sulphafurazole 1924
Sulphaguanidine 1925
Sulphaloxate 1927
Sulphaloxic Acid 1927
Sulphamethizole 1929
Sulphamethoxazole 1930
Sulphamethoxypyridazine
    1931
Sulphamoxole 1933
Sulphanilamide 1934
Sulphaphenazole 1936
Sulphasalazine 1849
Sulphasomidine 1939

Sulphathiazole 1938
Sulphaurea 1917
Sulphinpyrazone 1938
Sulpiride 1944
Sultamicillin 1945
Sulthiame 1946
Sultiame 1946
Sultopride 1947
Sultroponium 1948
Sumatriptan 1948
SUN-1165 1635
SUN 5555 828
Suplatast tosilate 1950
Suprofen 1951
Surfactant TA 1952
Suxamethonium chloride
    1952
Suxibuzone 1953
Synephrine 1953
Synvinolin 1877
Syrosingopine 1954

T

TA-058 141
TA-064 587
TA-167 1980
TA-870 689
TA-903 193
TA-2711 727
TA-6366 1051
TA-8704 689
Tacalcitol 1956
Tacrine 1957
Tacrolimus 1958
Talampicillin 1964
Talinolol 1965
Talipexole 1966
Tamoxifen 1967
Tamsulosin hydrochloride
    1969
Tandospirone 1971
Tazanolast 1972
Tazarotene 1973
3 TC 1136
TC-80 1094
TCV-116 329
Teciptiline 1870
Teclothiazide 1974
TECZA 2107
Tegafur 1974
Tegafur-Uracil 1976
Teichomycin 1976
Teicoplanin 1976
Telmesteine 1978
Telmisartan 1978
Temafloxacin 1980
Temazepam 1981
Temocapril 1981
Temocillin 1984
Teniposide 1987
Tenoglicine 1904
Tenonitrozole 1988
Tenoxicam 1988
Tenylidone 1989
Teofyllamin 2012
Terazosin 1990

ATC
Anatomical Therapeutic Chemical Classification

In 1981, the WHO[1] Regional Office for Europe recommended the *Anatomical Therapeutic Chemical* (ATC) classification system. In the ATC system drugs are classified in groups at 5 different levels. The drugs are divided into main groups (1st level), with two therapeutic/pharmacological subgroups (2nd and 3rd levels). Level 4 is a therapeutic/pharmacological/chemical subgroup and level 5 is the chemical substance.

The complete classification of *simvastatin* illustrates the structure of the code:

C	Cardiovascular System
C10	Serum Lipid Reducing Agents
C10A	Cholesterol And Triglyceride Reducers
C10AA	HMG CoA reductase inhibitors
C10AA01	Simvastatin

The ATC classification system was originally based on the same main principles as the *Anatomical Classification* (AC-system)[2] developed by the *European Pharmaceutical Market Research Association* (EPhMRA) and the *Pharmaceutical Business Intelligence and Research Group* (PBIRG)[3].

---

[1] WHO Collaborating Centre for Drug Statistics Methodology, c/o Norsk Medisinaldepot AS, P. O. Box 100, Veltvet, N-0518 Oslo, Norway, Telephone: (47) 22169810/22169801, Telefax: (47) 22169818
[2] http://www.ephmra.org/6_001
[3] Formerly called International Pharmaceutical Market Research Group (IPMRG)

A01AB	Antiinfectives for local oral treatment
A01AC	Corticosteroids for local oral treatment
A01AD	Other agents for local oral treatment
A02	Antacids, drugs for treatment of peptic ulcer and flatulence
A02A	Antacids
A02AB	Aluminum compounds
A02AD	Combinations and complexes of aluminium, calcium and magnesium compounds
A02B	Drugs for treatment of peptic ulcer
A02BA	H_2-receptor antagonists
A02BB	Prostaglandins
A02BC	Proton pump inhibitors
A02BD	Proton pump inhibitors
A02BO	Antiulcerants
A02BX	Other drugs for treatment of peptic ulcer
A03	Antispasmodic and anticholinergic agents and propulsives
A03A	Synthetic antispasmodic and anticholinergic agents
A03AA	Synthetic anticholinergics, esters with tertiary amino group
A03AB	Synthetic anticholinergics, quaternary ammonium compounds
A03AC	Synthetic antispasmodics, amides with tertiary amines
A03AX	Other synthetic anticholinergic agents
A03BA	Belladonna alkaloids, tertiary amines
A03BB	Belladonna alkaloids semisynthetic, quaternary ammonium compounds
A03CA	Synthetic anticholinergic agents in combination with psycholeptics
A03DA	Synthetic anticholinergic agents in combination with analgesics
A03E	Antispasmodics and anticholinergics in combination with other drugs
A03FA	Propulsives
A04	Antiemetics and antinauseants
A04A	Antiemetics and antinauseants
A04AA	Serotonin (5HT3) antagonists
A04AD	Other antiemetics
A05	Bile and liver therapy
A05A1	Bile therapy
A05AA	Bile acid preparations
A05AB	Preparations for biliary tract therapy
A05AX	Other drugs for bile therapy
A05B	Liver therapy, lipotropics
A05BA	Liver therapy
A06A	Laxatives
A06AB	Contact laxatives
A06AD	Osmotically acting laxatives
A06AG	Enemas

A07	Antidiarrheals, intestinal antiinflammatory and antiinfective agents	B04AA	Cholesterol- and triglyceride reducers
A07AA	Antibiotics	B04AB	HMG Co-A-reductase inhibitors
A07AB	Suflonamides	B04AC	Fibrates
A07AC	Imidazole derivatives	B05A	Blood and related products
A07AX	Other intestinal antiinfectives	B05BB	Solutions affecting the electrolyte balance
A07DA	Antipropulsives	B05CA	Antiinfectives
A07EA	Corticosteroids for local use	B05CX	Other irrigating solutions
A07EB	Antiallergic agents, excl. corticosteroids	B05XX	Other i.v. solution additives
A07EC	Aminosalicylic acid and similar agents	B06A	Other hematological agents
A07XA	All other antidiarrhoeals	B06AA	Enzymes
A08A	Antiobesity preparations, excl. diet products	C01	Cardiac therapy
A08AA	Centrally acting antiobesity products	C01A	Cardiac glycosides
A08AB	Peripherally acting antiobesity products	C01AA	Digitalis glycosides
A09A	digestives, incl. Enzymes	C01AB	Scilla glycosides
A09AB	Acid preparations	C01AC	Strophantus glycosides
A10	Drugs use in diabetes	C01AX	Other cardiac glycosides
A10BA	Biguanides	C01B	Antiarrhythmics, class I and II
A10BB	Sulfonamides, urea derivatives	C01BA	Antiarrhythmics, class IA
A10BC	Sulfonamides (heterocyclic)	C01BB	Antiarrhythmics, class IB
A10BF	glycosidase inhibitors	C01BC	Antiarrhythmics, class IC
A10BG	Thiazolinediones	C01BD	Antiarrhythmics, class III
A10BX	Other oral blood glucose lowering drugs	C01BG	Other class I antiarrhythmics
A10XA	Aldose reductase inhibitors	C01CA	Adrenergic and dopaminergic agents
A11	Vitamins	C01CE	Phosphodiesterase inhibitors
A11CA	Vitamin A, plain	C01CX	Other cardiac stimulants
A11CC	Vitamin D and analogues	C01D	Vasodilators used in cardiac diseases
A11DA	Vitamin B_1, plain	C01DA	Organic nitrates
A11DB	Vitamin B_1 in comb. with vitamin B_6 and/or vitamin B_{12}	C01DB	Quinolone vasodilators
		C01DX	Other vasodilators used in cardiac diseases
A11GA	Ascorbic acid (vit C), plain	C01EB	Other cardiac preparations
A11HA	Other plain vitamin preparations	C02	Antihypertensives
A11JC	Vitamins, other combinations	C02AA	Rauwolfia alkaloids
A12AX	Calcium, combinations with other drugs	C02AB	Methyldopa
A12BA	Potassium	C02AC	Imidazoline receptor agonists
A13A	Tonics	C02BB	Secondary and tertiary amines
A14	Anabolic agents for systemic use	C02CA	α-adrenoceptor blocking agents
A14A	Anabolic steroids	C02CB	α- and β-adrenoceptor blocking agent
A14AA	Androstan derivatives	C02CC	Guanidine derivatives
A14AB	Estren derivatives	C02DA	Thiazide derivatives
A14B	Other anabolic agents	C02DB	Hydrazinophthalazine derivatives
A16AA	Amino acids and derivatives	C02DC	Pyrimidine derivatives
A16AX	Various alimentary tract and metabolism products	C02DE	Calcium channel blockers
		C02DG	Guanidine derivatives
		C02KB	Tyrosine hydroxylase inhibitors
		C02KC	MAO inhibitors
B01AA	Vitamin K antagonists	C02KD	Serotonin antagonists
B01AB	Heparin group	C02L	Antihypertensives and diuretics in combination
B01AC	Platelet aggregation inhibitors excl. heparin	C02LA	Rauwolfia alkaloids and diuretics in combination
B01AD	Enzymes		
B01AX	Other antithrombotic agents	C02LX	Other antihypertensives and diuretics
B02AA	amino acids	C03	Diuretics
B02AB	Proteinase inhibitors	C03AA	Thiazides, plain
B02BA	Vitamin K	C03AX	Thiazides, combinations with other drugs
B02BC	Local hemostatics	C03BA	Sulfonamides, plain
B02BX	Other systemic hemostatics	C03BD	Xanthine derivatives
B03BA	Vitamin B_{12} (cyanocobalamin and derivatives)	C03BX	Other low-ceiling diuretics
		C03CA	Sulfonamides, plain
B03BB	Folic acid and derivatives	C03CC	Aryloxyacetic acid derivatives

C03CD	Pyrazolone derivatives
C03CX	Other high-ceiling diuretics
C03DA	Aldosterone antagonists
C03DB	Other potassium-sparing agents
C03E	Diuretics and potassium-sparing agents in combination
C03EA	Low-ceiling diuretics and potassium-sparing agents
C04	Peripheral vasodilators
C04A	Peripheral vasodilators
C04AA	2-amino-1-phenylethanol derivatives
C04AB	Imidazoline derivatives
C04AC	Nicotinic acid and derivatives
C04AD	Purine derivatives
C04AE	Ergot alkaloids
C04AX	Other peripheral vasodilators
C05	Vasoprotectives
C05AA	Products containing corticosteroids
C05AD	Products containing local anesthetics
C05AX	Other antihemorrhoidals for topical use
C05BA	Preparations with heparin for topical use
C05BB	Sclerosing agents for local injection
C05BX	Other sclerosing agents
C05C	Capillary stabilizing agents
C05CA	Bioflavonoids
C05CX	Other capillary stabilizing agents
C07A	Beta blocking agents
C07AA	β blocking agents, non-selective
C07AB	β blocking agents, selective
C07AG	α and β blocking agents
C07BA	β blocking agents, non-selective, and thiazides
C07BB	β blocking agents, selective, and thiazides
C07DA	β blocking agents, non-selective, thiazides and other diuretics
C07EA	β blocking agents, non-selective, and vasodilators
C08CA	Dihydropyridine derivatives
C08CX	Other selective calcium channel blockers with mainly vascular effects
C08DA	Phenylalkylamine derivatives
C08DB	Benzothiazepine derivatives
C08EA	Phenylalkylamine derivatives
C08EX	Other non-selective calcium channel blockers
C09	Agents acting on the Renin-Angiotensin System
C09A	ACE inhibitors, plain
C09AA	ACE inhibitors, plain
C09BA	ACE inhibitors and diuretics
C09CA	Angiotensin II antagonists, plain
C10A	Cholesterol and triglyceride reducers
C10AA	HMG CoA reductase inhibitors
C10AB	Fibrates
C10AD	Nicotinic acid and derivatives
C10AX	Other cholesterol and triglyceride reducers
D01	Antifungal for dermatological use
D01A	Antifungals for topical use
D01AA	Antibiotics

D01AC	Imidazole derivatives
D01AE	Other antifungals for topical use
D01BA	Antifungals for systemic use
D02B	Protectives against UV-radiation
D02BB	Protectives against UV-radiation for systemic use
D03	Preparations for treatment of wounds and ulcers
D03A	Cicatrizants
D03AX	Other cicatrizants
D04	Antipruritics, incl. antihistamines, anesthetics, etc.
D04AA	Antihistamines for topical use
D04AB	Anesthetics for topical use
D05	Antipsoriatics
D05AC	Antracen derivatives
D05AD	Psoralens for topical use
D05AX	Other antipsoriatics for topical use
D05B	Antipsoriatics for systemic use
D05BA	Psoralens for systemic use
D05BB	Retinoids for treatment of psoriasis
D06A	Antibiotics for topical use
D06AA	Tetracycline and derivatives
D06AX	Other antibiotics for topical use
D06BA	Sulfonamides
D06BB	Antivirals
D06BX	Other chemotherapeutics
D07A	Corticosteroids, plain
D07AA	Corticosteroids, weak (group I)
D07AB	Corticosteroids, moderately potent (group II)
D07AC	Corticosteroids, potent (group III)
D07AD	Corticosteroids, very potent (group IV)
D07BB	Corticosteroids, moderately potent, combinations with antiseptics
D07BC	Corticosteroids, potent, combinations with antiseptics
D07CB	Corticosteroids, moderately potent, combinations with antibiotics
D07CC	Corticosteroids, potent, combinations with antibiotics
D07XA	Corticosteroids, weak, other combinations
D07XB	Corticosteroids, moderately potent, other combinations
D07XC	Corticosteroids, potent, other combinations
D08	Antiseptics and disinfectants
D08A	Antiseptics and disinfectants
D08AA	Acridine derivatives
D08AC	Biguanides and amidines
D08AE	Phenol and derivatives
D08AF	Furan derivatives
D08AG	Iodine products
D08AH	Quinoline derivatives
D08AJ	Quaternary ammonium compounds
D08AK	Mercurial products
D08AX	Other antiseptic and disinfectants
D09AA	Ointment dressings with antiinfectives
D10AA	Corticosteroids, combinations for treatment of acne

D10AB	Preparations containing sulfur
D10AD	Retinoids for topical use in acne
D10AE	Peroxides
D10AF	Antiinfectives for treatment of acne
D10AX	Other anti-acne preparations for topical use
D10BA	Retinoids for treatment of acne
D11AA	Antihidrotics
D11AE	Androgens for topical use
D11AX	Other dermatologicals
G01AA	Antibiotics
G01AB	Arsenic compounds
G01AC	Quinoline derivatives
G01AE	Sulfonamides
G01AF	Imidazole derivatives
G01AG	Triazole derivatives
G01AX	Other antiinfectives and antiseptics
G02AB	Ergot alkaloids
G02AD	Prostaglandins
G02B	Contraceptives for topical use
G02BB	Intravaginal contraceptives
G02CA	Sympathomimetics, labour repressants
G02CB	Prolactine inhibitors
G02CC	Antiinflammatory products for vaginal administration
G03	Sex hormones and modulators of the genital system
G03A	Hormonal contraceptives for systemic use
G03AA	Progestogens and estrogens, fixed combinations
G03AB	Progestogens and estrogens, sequential preparations
G03AC	Progestogens
G03B	Androgens
G03BA	3-oxoandrosten-4 derivatives
G03BB	5-androstanon-3 derivatives
G03C	Estrogens
G03CA	Natural and semisynthetic estrogens, plain
G03CB	Synthetic estrogens, plain
G03CC	Estrogens, combinations with other drugs
G03D	Progestogens
G03DA	Pregnen-4 derivatives
G03DB	Pregnadien derivatives
G03DC	Estren derivatives
G03EA	Androgens and estrogens
G03EB	Androgen, progestogen and estrogen in combination
G03EK	Androgens and female sex hormones
G03FA	Progestogens and estrogens, fixed combinations
G03FB	Progestogens and estrogens, sequential preparations
G03GB	Ovulation stimulants, synthetic
G03H	Antiandrogens
G03HA	Antiandrogens, plain preparations
G03HB	Antiandrogens and estrogens
G03X	Other sex hormones and modulators of the genital system
G03XA	Antigonadotropins and similar agents
G03XB	Antiprogestogens

G04A	Urinary antiseptives and antiinfectives
G04AA	Methenamine preparations
G04AB	Quinolone derivatives (excl. J01M)
G04AC	Nitrofuran derivatives
G04AG	Other urinary antiseptics and antiinfectives
G04BD	Urinary antispasmodics
G04BE	Papaverine and derivatives
G04BX	Other urologicals
G04C	Drugs used in benign prostatic hypertrophy
G04CA	α-adrenoreceptor antagonists
G04CB	Testosterone-5-α-reductase inhibitors
H01BA	Vasopressin and analogues
H01BB	Oxytocin and derivatives
H01C	Hypothalamic hormones
H01CA	Gonadotropin-releasing hormones
H02AA	Mineralocortocoides
H02AB	Glucocorticoides
H02CA	Anticorticosteroids
H03AA	Thyroid hormones
H03BA	Thiouracils
H03BB	Sulfur-containing imidazole derivatives
H03CA	Iodine therapy
J01	Antibacterials for systemic use
J01AA	Tetracyclines
J01BA	Amphenicols
J01C	β-lactam antibacterials, penicillins
J01CA	Penicillin with extended spectrum
J01CE	β-lactamase sensitive penicillins
J01CF	β-lactamase resistent penicillins
J01CG	β-lactamase inhibitors
J01CR	Combinations of penicillins, incl. beta-lactamase inhibitors
J01DA	Cephalosporins and related substances
J01DF	Monobactams
J01DH	Carbapenems
J01E	Sulfonamides and trimethoprim
J01EA	Trimethoprim and derivatives
J01EB	Short-acting sulfonamides
J01EC	Intermediate-acting sulfonamides
J01ED	Long-acting sulfonamides
J01FA	Macrolides
J01FF	Lincosamides
J01G	Aminoglycoside antibacterials
J01GA	Streptomycins
J01GB	Other aminoglycosides
J01HA	Penicillinase sensitive penicillins
J01KD	Aminoglycoside antibiotics
J01M	Quinolone antibacterials
J01MA	Fluoroquinolones
J01MB	Other quinolones excl. G04AB
J01XA	Glycopeptide antibacterials
J01XB	Polymyxins
J01XD	Imidazole derivatives
J01XX	Other antibacterials
J02AA	Antibiotics
J02AB	Imidazole derivatives
J02AC	Triazole derivatives
J02AX	Other antimycotics for systemic use
J04A	Drugs for treatment of tuberculosis

J04AA	Aminosalicylic acid and derivatives
J04AB	Antibiotics
J04AC	Hydrazides
J04AD	Thiocarbamide derivatives
J04AK	Other drugs for treatment of tuberculosis
J04BA	Drugs for treatment of lepra
J05	Antivirals for systemic use
J05A	Direct acting antivirales
J05AB	Nucleosides and nucleotides
J05AC	Cyclic amines
J05AE	HIV-proteinase inhibitors
J05AF	Nucleosides and nucleotides excl. reverse transcriptase inhibitors
J05AG	Non-nucleoside reverse transcriptase inhibitors
J05AX	Other antivirals
L01	Antineoplastic agents
L01AA	Nitrogen mustard analogues
L01AB	Alkyl sulfonates
L01AC	Ethylene imines
L01AD	Nitrosoureas
L01AX	Other alkylating agents
L01BA	Folic acid analogues
L01BB	Purine analogues
L01BC	Pyrimidine analogues
L01C	Plant alkaloids and other natural products
L01CA	Vinca alkaloids and analogues
L01CB	Podophyllotoxin derivatives
L01CD	Taxanes
L01DA	Actinomycines
L01DB	Anthracyclines and related substances
L01DC	Other cytotoxic antibiotics
L01XA	Platinum compounds
L01XB	Methylhydrazines
L01XX	Other antineoplastic agents
L02A	Hormones and related agents
L02AA	Estrogens
L02AB	Progestogens
L02AE	Gonadotropin releasing hormone analogues
L02AX	Other hormones
L02B	Hormone antagonists and related agents
L02BA	Anti-estrogens
L02BB	Anti-androgens
L02BG	Enzyme inhibitors
L03A	Immunostimulating agents
L03AX	Other immunostimulating agents
L04	Immunosuppressive agents
L04AA	Selective immunosuppressive agents
L04AX	Other immunosuppressive agents
M01	Antiinflammatory and antirheumatic products
M01A	Antiinflammatory and antirheumatic agents, non steroids
M01AA	Butylpyrazolidines
M01AB	Acetic acid derivatives and related substances
M01AC	Oxicams
M01AE	Propionic acid derivatives
M01AG	Fenamates
M01AH	Cycloxygenase-2-inhibitors
M01AX	Other antiinflammatory and antirheumatic agents, non-steroids
M01BA	Antiinflammatory and antirheumatic agents in combination with corticosteroids
M01CB	Gold preparations
M01CC	Penicillamine and similar agents
M02A	Topical products for joint and muscular pain
M02AA	Antiinflammatory preparations, non-steroids for topical use
M02AC	Preparations with salicylic acid derivatives
M02AX	Other topical products for joint and muscular pain
M03	Muscle relaxants
M03A	Muscle relaxants, peripherally acting agents
M03AA	Curare alkaloids
M03AB	Choline derivatives
M03AC	Other quaternary ammonium compounds
M03B	Muscle relaxants, centrally acting agents
M03BA	Carbamic acid esters
M03BB	Oxazol, thiazine, triazine derivatives
M03BC	Ethers, chemically close to antihistamines
M03BX	Other centrally acting agents
M03CA	Dantrolene and derivatives
M04	Antigout preparations
M04AA	Preparations inhibiting uric acid production
M04AB	Preparations increasing uric acid excretion
M05BA	Bisphosphonates
M05BX	Other drugs affecting mineralization
M09AB	Enzymes
N01A	Anesthetics, general
N01AA	Ethers
N01AB	Halogenated hydrocarbons
N01AF	Barbiturates, plain
N01AH	Opioid anesthetics
N01AX	Other general anesthetics
N01B	Anesthetics, local
N01BA	Esters of aminobenzoic acid
N01BB	Amides
N01BC	Esters of benzoic acid
N01BX	Other local anesthetics
N02	Analgesics
N02A	Opioids
N02AA	Natural opium alkaloids
N02AB	Phenylpiperidine derivatives
N02AC	Diphenylpropylamine derivatives
N02AD	Benzomorphan derivatives
N02AE	Oripavine derivatives
N02AF	Morphinan derivatives
N02AX	Other opioids
N02B	Other analgesics and antipyretics
N02BA	Salicylic acid and derivatives
N02BB	Pyrazolones
N02BE	Anilides
N02BG	Other analgesics and antipyretics
N02CA	Ergot alkaloids
N02CB	Corticosteroid derivatives
N02CC	Selective 5HT1-receptor agonists

N02CX	Other antimigraine preparations
N03AA	Barbiturates and derivatives
N03AB	Hydantoin derivatives
N03AC	Oxazolidine derivatives
N03AD	Succinimide derivatives
N03AE	Benzodiazepine derivatives
N03AF	Carboxamide derivatives
N03AG	Fatty acid derivatives
N03AX	Other antiepileptics
N04	Anti-parkinson drugs
N04A	Anticholinergic agents
N04AA	Tertiary amines
N04AB	Ethers chemically close to antihistamines
N04AC	Ethers of tropine or tropine derivatives
N04B	Dopaminergic agents
N04BA	Dopa and dopa derivatives
N04BB	Adamantane derivatives
N04BC	Dopamine agonists
N04BD	Monoamine oxidase Type B inhibitors
N05	Psycholeptics
N05A	Antipsychotics
N05AA	Phenothiazines with aliphatic side-chain
N05AB	Phenothiazines with piperazine structure
N05AC	Phenothiazines with piperidine structure
N05AD	Butyrophenone derivatives
N05AE	Indole derivatives
N05AF	Thioxanthene derivatives
N05AG	Diphenylbutylpiperidine derivatives
N05AH	Diazepines and oxazepines
N05AK	Neuroleptics, in tardive dyskinesia
N05AL	Benzamides
N05AX	Other antipsychotics
N05B	Anxiolytics
N05BA	Benzodiazepine derivatives
N05BB	Diphenylmethane derivatives
N05BC	Carbamates
N05BD	Dibenzo-bicyclo-octadiene derivatives
N05BE	Azaspirodecanedione derivatives
N05BX	Other anxiolytics
N05C	Hypnotics and sedatives
N05CA	Barbiturates, plain
N05CC	Aldehydes and derivatives
N05CD	Benzodiazepine derivatives
N05CE	Piperidinedione derivatives
N05CF	Cyclopyrrolones
N05CG	Imidazopyridines
N05CM	Other hypnotics and sedatives
N06	Psychoanaleptics
N06A	Antidepressants
N06AA	Non-selective monoamine reuptake inhibitors
N06AB	Selective serotonin reuptake inhibitors
N06AE	Monocyclic derivatives
N06AF	Monoamine oxidase inhibitors, nonselective
N06AG	Monoamine oxidase type A inhibitors
N06AX	Other antidepressants
N06B	Psychostimulants and nootropics
N06BA	Centrally acting sympathomimetics
N06BC	Xanthine derivatives
N06BX	Other psychostimulants and nootropics
N07	Other nervous system drugs
N07A	Parasympathomimetics
N07AA	Anticholinesterases
N07AB	Choline esters
N07AX	Other parasympathomimetics
N07CA	Antivertigo preparations
N07X	Other nervous system drugs
N07XX	Other nervous system drugs
P01AA	Hydroxyquinoline derivatives
P01AB	Nitroimidazole derivatives
P01AC	Dichloroacetamide derivatives
P01AX	Other agents against amoebiasis and other protozoal diseases
P01BA	Aminoquinolines
P01BB	Biguanides
P01BC	Quinine alkaloids
P01BD	Diaminopyrimidines
P01BX	Other antimalarials
P01C	Agents against Leishmaniasis and Trypanosomiasis
P01CC	Nitrofurane derivatives
P01CD	Arsenic compounds
P01CX	Other agents against leishmaniasis and trypanosomiasis
P02	Anthelmintics
P02BA	Quinoline derivatives and related substances
P02BX	Other antitrematodal agents
P02CA	Benzimidazole derivatives
P02CB	Piperazine and derivatives
P02CC	Tetrahydropyrimidine derivatives
P02CE	Imidazothiazole derivatives
P02CX	Other antinematodals
P02DA	Salicylic acid derivatives
P02DX	Other anticestodals
P03A	Ectoparasiticides, incl. scabicides
P03AA	Sulphur containing products
P03AX	Other ectoparasiticides, incl. scabicides
R01A	Decongestants and other nasal preparations for topical use
R01AA	Sympathomimetics, plain
R01AB	Sympathomimetics, combinations excl. corticosteroids
R01AC	Antiallergic agents, excl. corticosteroids
R01AD	Corticosteroids
R01AX	Other nasal preparations
R01BA	Sympathomimetics
R02AA	Antiseptics
R02AB	Antibiotics
R02AD	Anesthetics, local
R03	Anti-asthmatics
R03A	Adrenergics, inhalants
R03AA	α and β-adrenoceptor agonists
R03AB	Non-selective β-adrenoceptor agonists
R03AC	Selective β-2-adrenoceptor agonists
R03AK	Adrenergics and other anti-asthmatics
R03B	Other anti-asthmatics, inhalants
R03BA	Glucocorticoids

R03BB	Anticholinergics		S01FB	Sympathomimetics excl. antiglaucoma preparations
R03BC	Antiallergic agents, excl. corticosteroids		S01GA	Sympathomimetics used as decongestants
R03BX	Other anti-asthmatics, inhalants		S01GX	Other antiallergics
R03CA	α and β-adrenoceptor agonists		S01HA	Local anesthetics
R03CB	Non-selective β-adrenoceptor agonists		S01JA	Colouring agents
R03CC	Selective β-2-adrenoceptor agonists		S01KK	Other surgical acids
R03D	Other anti-asthmatics for systemic use		S01XA	Other ophthalmologicals
R03DA	Xanthines		S02	otologicals
R03DC	Leukotriene receptor antagonists		S02AA	Antiinfectives
R03DX	Other anti-asthmatics for systemic use		S02BA	Corticosteroids
R05CA	Expectorants		S02CA	Corticosteroids and antiinfectives in combination
R05CB	Mucolytics		S02DA	Analgesics and anesthetics
R05DA	Opium alkaloids and derivatives		S03	Ophthalmological and otological preparations
R05DB	Other cough suppressants		S03AA	Antiinfectives
R06	Antihistamines for systemic use		S03BA	Corticosteroids
R06A	Antihistamines for systemic use		S03CA	Corticosteroids and antiinfectives in combination
R06AA	Aminoalkyl ethers		V03A	All other therapeutic products
R06AB	Substituted alkylamines		V03AA	Drugs for treatment of chronic alcoholism
R06AC	Substituted ethylene diamines		V03AB	Antidotes
R06AD	Phenothiazine derivatives		V03AC	Iron chelating agents
R06AE	Piperazine derivatives		V03AF	Detoxifying agents for antineoplastic treatment
R06AX	Other antihistamines for systemic use		V03AG	Drugs for treatment of hypercalcemia
R07A	Other respiratory system products		V03AH	Drugs for treatment of hypoglycemia
R07AA	Lung surfactants		V04CA	Tests for diabetes
R07AB	Respiratory stimulants		V04CC	Tests for bile duct patency
S01AA	Antibiotics		V04CD	Tests for pituitary function
S01AB	Sulfonamides		V04CG	Tests for gastric secretion
S01AD	Antivirals		V04CJ	Tests for thyreoidea function
S01AX	Other antiinfectives		V04CK	Tests for pancreatic function
S01B	Antiinflammatory agents		V08	Contrast media
S01BA	Corticosteroids, plain		V08AA	Watersoluble, nephrotropic, high osmolar X-ray contrast media
S01BC	Antiinflammatory agents, non-steroids		V08AB	Watersoluble, nephrotropic, low osmolar X-ray contrast media
S01CA	Corticosteroids and antiinfectives in combination		V08AC	Watersoluble, hepatotropic X-ray contrast media
S01CB	Corticosteroids, antiinfectives and mydriatics in combination		V08AD	Non-watersoluble X-ray contrast media
S01EA	Sympathomimetics in glaucoma therapy		V09D	Hepatic and reticulo endothelial system
S01EB	Parasympathomimetics			
S01EC	Carbonic anhydrase inhibitors			
S01ED	β blocking agents			
S01EX	Other antiglaucoma preparations			
S01FA	Anticholinergics			

Nabilone

ATC: A04
Use: anti-emetic, controlled substance

RN: 51022-71-0   MF: $C_{24}H_{36}O_3$ MW: 372.55
LD$_{50}$:   >1000 mg/kg (M, p.o.);
>1000 mg/kg (R, p.o.);
>1 mg/kg (dog, i.v.); >5 mg/kg (dog, p.o.)
CN: *trans*-(±)-3-(1,1-dimethylheptyl)-6,6a7,8,10,10a-hexahydro-1-hydroxy-6,6-dimethyl-9*H*-dibenzo[*b,d*]pyran-9-one

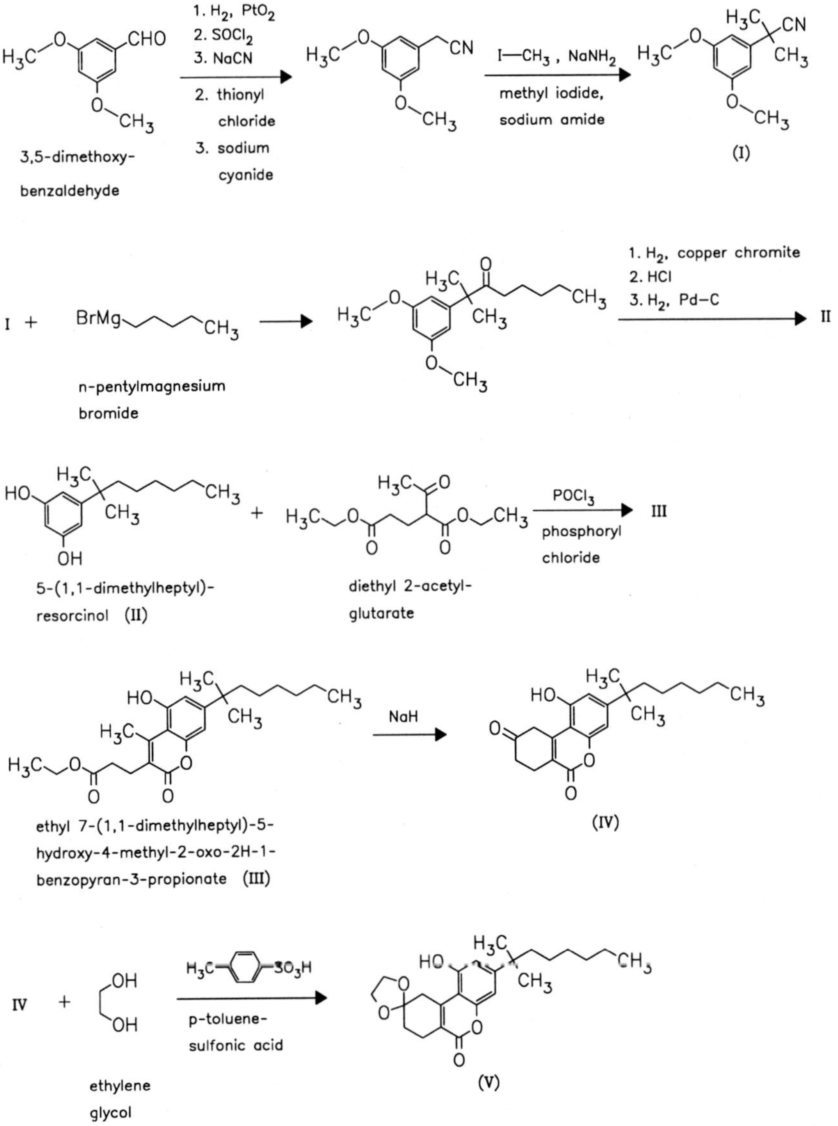

3,5-dimethoxy-benzaldehyde

1. H_2, PtO_2
2. $SOCl_2$
3. NaCN

2. thionyl chloride
3. sodium cyanide

$I-CH_3$, $NaNH_2$

methyl iodide, sodium amide

(I)

I +   BrMg⌒⌒⌒CH$_3$

n-pentylmagnesium bromide

1. H_2, copper chromite
2. HCl
3. H_2, Pd–C

II

5-(1,1-dimethylheptyl)-resorcinol (II)

+   diethyl 2-acetyl-glutarate

$POCl_3$

phosphoryl chloride

III

ethyl 7-(1,1-dimethylheptyl)-5-hydroxy-4-methyl-2-oxo-2H-1-benzopyran-3-propionate (III)

NaH

(IV)

IV   +

ethylene glycol

H_3C—⬡—SO_3H

p-toluene-sulfonic acid

(V)

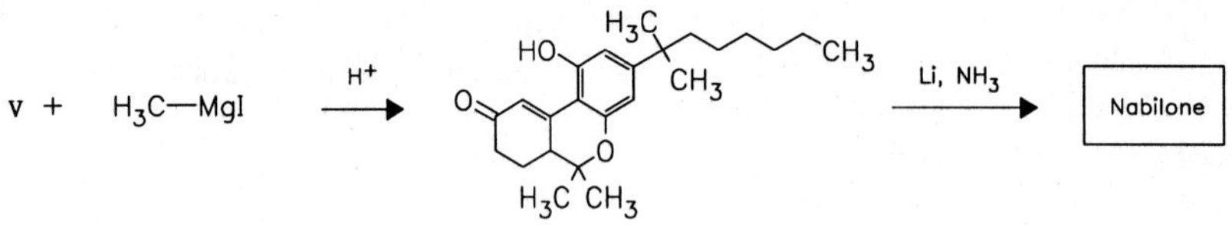

v + H₃C—MgI →(H⁺) [structure] →(Li, NH₃) [Nabilone]

methylmagnesium
iodide

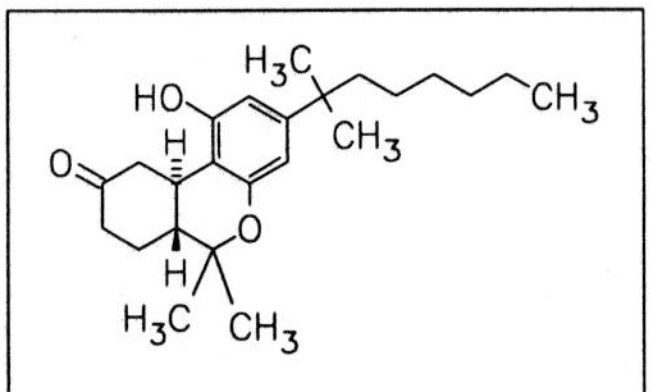

[structure]

Nabilone

Reference(s):
DOS 2 451 934 (Eli Lilly; appl. 31.10.1974; USA-prior. 5.11.1973).
DOS 2 451 932 (Eli Lilly; appl. 31.10.1974; USA-prior. 5.11.1973).
US 3 944 673 (Eli Lilly; 16.3.1976; prior. 23.5.1975, 5.11.1973).
US 3 928 598 (Eli Lilly; 23.12.1975; prior. 5.11.1973).
US 3 953 603 (Eli Lilly; 27.4.976; prior. 5.11.1973, 1.5.1974).

synthesis of 5-(1,1-dimethylheptyl)resorcinol:
Adams, R. et al.: J. Am. Chem. Soc. (JACSAT) **70**, 664 (1948).

Formulation(s):   cps. 1 mg

Trade Name(s):
GB: Cesamet (Lilly); wfm

Nabumetone

ATC: M01AX01
Use: analgesic, anti-inflammatory (NSAI)

RN: 42924-53-8   MF: $C_{15}H_{16}O_2$ MW: 228.29
LD$_{50}$:   2380 mg/kg (M, i.p.); 4290 mg/kg (M, p.o.);
          1520 mg/kg (R, i.p.); 3880 mg/kg (R, p.o.)
CN: 4-(6-methoxy-2-naphthalenyl)-2-butanone

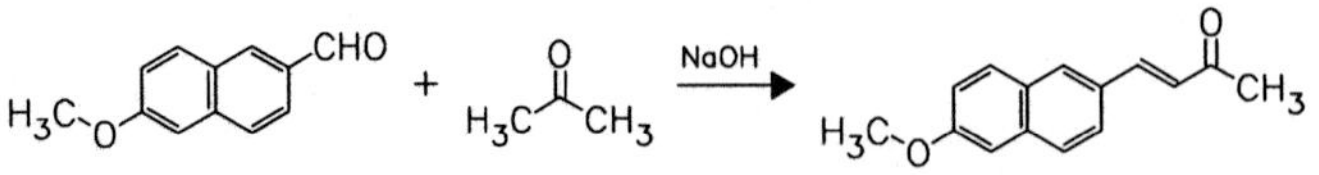

[reaction scheme]

6-methoxy-2-   acetone   4-(6-methoxy-2-naphthyl)-
naphthaldehyde   3-buten-2-one   (I)

I →(H₂, Pd–C) [Nabumetone structure]

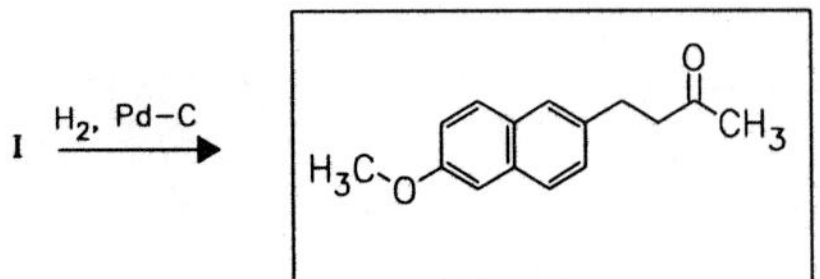

Nabumetone

Reference(s):
DE 2 463 219 (Beecham; appl. 4.9.1974; GB-prior. 11.9.1973).
DE 2 442 305 (Beecham; appl. 4.9.1974; GB-prior. 11.9.1973).
US 4 061 779 (Beecham; 6.12.1977; GB-prior. 11.9.1973).
US 4 420 639 (Beecham; 13.12.1983; GB-prior. 11.9.1973).

alternative syntheses:
EP 376 516 (Hoechst Celanese; appl. 7.12.1989; USA-prior. 8.12.1988).
JP 2 101 038 (Beecham; appl. 19.12.1988; GB-prior. 10.7.1988, 19.12.1987).
ES 8 507 452 (Bioiberica; appl. 28.9.1984).
Govdic, A.C. et al.: J. Med. Chem. (JMCMAR) **21**, 1260 (1978).
Prabhakar, C. et al.: Org. Process Res. Dev. (OPRDFK) **3**, 121 (1999).

topical formulation:
EP 167 062 (Beecham; appl. 19.6.1985; GB-prior. 29.6.1984).

Formulation(s):   susp. 500 mg/5 ml; f. c. tabl. 500 mg, 750 mg

Trade Name(s):

D:	Arthaxan (SmithKline Beecham; 1987); wfm	I:	Artaxan (SmithKline Beecham)	J:	Relifen (Fujisawa; 1990)
GB:	Relifex (Bencard; 1987)		Nabuser (Procter & Gamble)	USA:	Relafen (SmithKline Beecham)

Nadolol

ATC: C07AA12; C07BA
Use: beta blocking agent, antihypertensive

RN: 42200-33-9   MF: $C_{17}H_{27}NO_4$ MW: 309.41   EINECS: 255-706-3
LD$_{50}$:   47.1 mg/kg (M, i.v.); 3800 mg/kg (M, p.o.);
        59.2 mg/kg (R, i.v.); 5300 mg/kg (R, p.o.);
        >500 mg/kg (dog, p.o.)
CN: *cis*-5-[3-[(1,1-dimethylethyl)amino]-2-hydroxypropoxy]-2-hydroxypropoxy]-1,2,3,4-tetrahydro-2,3-naphthalenediol

5,8-dihydro-1-naphthol

cis-1,6,7-tri-hydroxy-5,6,7,8-tetrahydro-naphthalene

epichloro-hydrin

(I)   +   tert-butyl-amine   →   Nadolol

Reference(s):
Condon, M.E. et al.: J. Med. Chem. (JMCMAR) **21**, 913 (1978).
US 3 935 267 (Squibb; 27.1.1976; prior. 22.6.1970, 1.12.1971).
US 3 982 021 (Squibb; 21.9.1976; prior. 22.6.1970, 1.12.1971, 9.10.1975).
US 4 156 789 (Squibb; 29.5.1979; prior. 22.6.1970, 1.12.1971, 9.10.1975).
DOS 2 258 995 (Squibb; appl. 1.12.1972; USA-prior. 1.12.1971).
DAS 2 130 393 (Squibb; appl. 18.6.1971; USA-prior. 22.6.1970).
DOS 2 421 549 (Squibb; appl. 3.5.1974; USA-prior. 3.5.1973).

starting material:
Gutsche, C.D. et al.: Org. Synth. (ORSYAT), Coll. Vol. IV, 887.

Formulation(s):   tabl. 20 mg, 40 mg, 60 mg, 80 mg, 120 mg

Trade Name(s):

D:	Solgol (Bristol-Myers Squibb; 1978)		Corgaretic (Sanofi Winthrop)-comb.	USA:	Corgard (Bristol-Myers Squibb; 1979); wfm
F:	Corgard (Sanofi Winthrop; 1982)	I:	Corgard (Bristol-Myers Squibb)		Corgard (Squibb); wfm Corzide (Squibb); wfm
GB:	Corgard (Sanofi Winthrop; 1979)	J:	Nadic (Dainippon) Nadolol (Squibb)		Nadolol (Mydal) generic

---

Nadoxolol

ATC: C01B
Use: antiarrhythmic

RN: 54063-51-3   MF: $C_{14}H_{16}N_2O_3$ MW: 260.29
CN: N,3-dihydroxy-4-(1-naphthalenyloxy)butanimidamide

monohydrochloride
RN: 35991-93-6   MF: $C_{14}H_{16}N_2O_3 \cdot HCl$ MW: 296.75   EINECS: 252-825-2
LD_{50}:   180 mg/kg (M, i.v.); 1 g/kg (M, p.o.)

1-naphthol   epichloro-   2,3-epoxy-1-
                    hydrin   (1-naphthyloxy)-
                                        propane

3-hydroxy-4-
(1-naphthyloxy)-
butyronitrile (I)

(II)   Nadoxolol

Reference(s):
DOS 2 166 869 (Orsymonde; appl. 28.6.1971; F-prior. 29.6.1970, 1.4.1971).

Formulation(s):   tabl. 250 mg (as hydrochloride)

Trade Name(s):
F: Bradyl 250 (Lafon)

Nafamostat
(FUT-175; Nafamstat)

ATC: V03A
Use: protease inhibitor, treatment of acute pancreatitis

RN: 81525-10-2   MF: $C_{19}H_{17}N_5O_2$ MW: 347.38
CN: 4-[(aminoiminomethyl)amino]benzoic acid 6-(aminoiminoethyl)-2-naphthalenyl ester

dihydrochloride
RN: 80251-32-7   MF: $C_{19}H_{17}N_5O_2 \cdot 2HCl$ MW: 420.30
dimesylate
RN: 82956-11-4   MF: $C_{19}H_{17}N_5O_2 \cdot 2CH_4O_3S$ MW: 539.59
LD_{50}:   24.4 mg/kg (M, i.v.); 4600 mg/kg (M, p.o.);
        162 mg/kg (R, i.p.); 16.4 mg/kg (R, i.v.); 3050 mg/kg (R, p.o.); 9200 mg/kg (R, s.c.)

4-amino-benzoic acid   cyanamide   4-guanidinobenzoic acid (I)   4-guanidinobenzoyl chloride (II)

6-amidino-2-naphthol methanesulfonate (III)   Nafamostat

I + III →(DCC)→ Nafamostat

Reference(s):
EP 48 433 (Torii; appl. 15.9.1981; J-prior. 28.4.1981, 16.9.1980).
US 4 454 338 (Torii; 12.6.1984; appl. 9.9.1981; J-prior. 28.4.1981, 16.9.1980).
US 4 532 255 (Torii; 30.7.1985; appl. 20.1.1984; prior. 9.9.1981; J-prior. 28.4.1981, 16.9.1980).
Aoyama, T. et al.: Chem. Pharm. Bull. (CPBTAL) **33**, 1485 (1985).

synthesis of 4-guanidinobenzoic acid:
DE 950 552 (Hoechst; appl. 1956).

synthesis of 6-amidino-2-naphthol methanesulfonate:
JP 50 123 649 (Kyowa Hakko; appl. 15.3.1974).
Wagner, G. et al.: Pharmazie (PHARAT) **32**, 761 (1977).

Formulation(s):   vial 10 mg, 50 mg (as dimesylate)

Nafcillin

ATC: J01C
Use: antibiotic

RN: 147-52-4   MF: $C_{21}H_{22}N_2O_5S$ MW: 414.48   EINECS: 205-690-9
CN: [2S-(2α,5α,6β)]-6-[[(2-ethoxy-1-naphthalenyl)carbonyl]amino]-3,3-dimethyl-7-oxo-4-thia-1-azabicyclo[3.2.0]heptane-2-carboxylic acid

monosodium salt
RN: 985-16-0   MF: $C_{21}H_{21}N_2NaO_5S$ MW: 436.46   EINECS: 213-574-4
LD_{50}: 1 g/kg (M, i.v.);
       633 mg/kg (dog, i.v.)
monosodium salt monohydrate
RN: 7177-50-6   MF: $C_{21}H_{21}N_2NaO_5S \cdot H_2O$ MW: 454.48

2-ethoxy-1-
naphthoyl chloride

6-amino-
penicillanic acid

Nafcillin

Reference(s):
US 3 157 639 (Beecham; 17.11.1964; GB-prior. 19.8.1959).
GB 880 400 (Beecham; appl. 15.7.1959; 19.8.1959; addition to GB 870 395 from 15.7.1958).
US 3 248 386 (American Home Products; 26.4.1966; appl. 30.12.1960).

Formulation(s):   cps. 250 mg; vial 500 mg, 1 g, 2 g (as monosodium salt monohydrate)

Naftidrofuryl
(Nafronyl)

ATC: C04AX21
Use: vasodilator

RN: 31329-57-4   MF: $C_{24}H_{33}NO_3$ MW: 383.53   EINECS: 250-572-2
LD_{50}: 23 mg/kg (M, i.v.); 365 mg/kg (M, p.o.);
       1890 mg/kg (R, p.o.)
CN: tetrahydro-α-(1-naphthalenylmethyl)-2-furanpropanoic acid 2-(diethylamino)ethyl ester

hydrogen oxalate
RN: 3200-06-4   MF: $C_{24}H_{33}NO_3 \cdot C_2H_2O_4$ MW: 473.57   EINECS: 221-703-0
LD_{50}: 18.4 mg/kg (M, i.v.); 567 mg/kg (M, p.o.);
       11.08 mg/kg (R, i.v.); 711 mg/kg (R, p.o.)

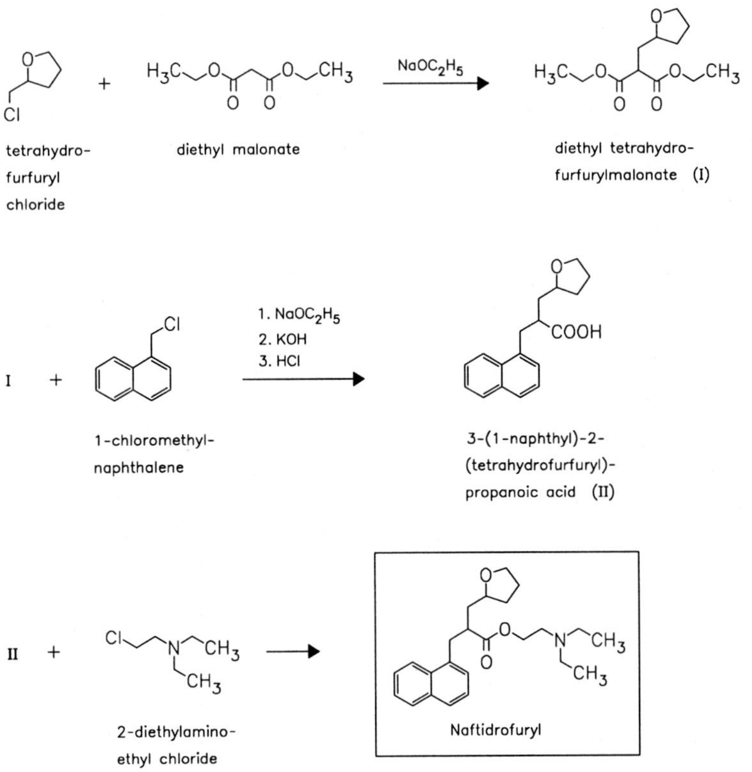
tetrahydrofurfuryl chloride
diethyl malonate
$NaOC_2H_5$
diethyl tetrahydrofurfurylmalonate (I)
I
1-chloromethylnaphthalene
1. $NaOC_2H_5$
2. KOH
3. HCl
3-(1-naphthyl)-2-(tetrahydrofurfuryl)-propanoic acid (II)
II
2-diethylaminoethyl chloride
Naftidrofuryl

Reference(s):

DAS 1 543 741 (Lipha; appl. 24.3.1964; F-prior. 28.3.1963).
FR 1 363 948 (Lipha; appl. 28.3.1963).
FR-M 3 843 (Lipha; appl. 17.3.1964).
US 3 334 096 (Lipha; 1.8.1967; F-prior. 28.3.1963).

pharmaceutical formulation for retard form:
DOS 2 800 654 (Lipha; appl. 7.1.1978; F-prior. 13.1.1977).

Formulation(s): amp. 200 mg; cps. 100 mg; f. c. tabl. 200 mg; s. r. drg. 100 mg

Trade Name(s):

D:	Artocoron (Knoll)
	Azunaftil (Azupharma)
	Dusodril (Lipha)
	Luctor (Sanofi Winthrop)
	nafti (ct-Arzneimittel)
	Nafti (Isis Puren; ratiopharm)
	Naftilong (Hexal)
F:	Di-Actane (Menarini)
	Gévatran (Lipha Santé)
	Naftilux (Lucien)
	Praxiléne (Lipha Santé)
GB:	Praxilene (Lipha; as oxalate)
I:	Esdedril (Lipha)
	Praxilene (Formenti)

Naftifine

(Naftifungin)

ATC: D01AE22
Use: antifungal

RN: 65472-88-0 MF: $C_{21}H_{21}N$ MW: 287.41
CN: (*E*)-*N*-methyl-*N*-(3-phenyl-2-propenyl)-1-naphthalenemethanamine

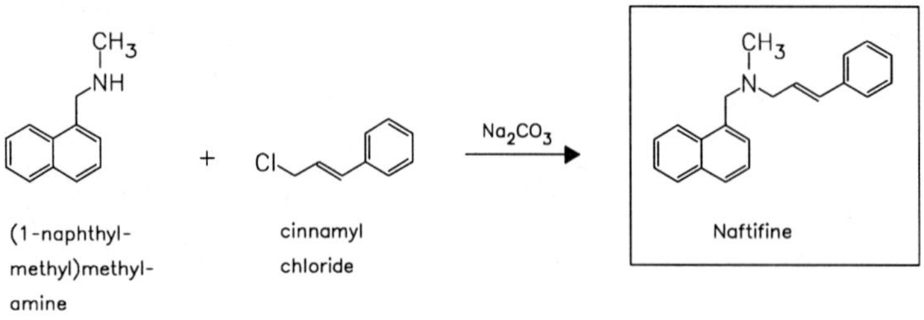

(1-naphthyl-methyl)methyl-amine
+ cinnamyl chloride
→ [Na₂CO₃]
Naftifine

Reference(s):

DOS 2 716 943 (Sandoz; appl. 16.4.1977; CH-prior. 28.4.1976).
DOS 2 809 211 (Sandoz; appl. 3.3.1978).
US 4 282 251 (Sandoz; CH-prior. 28.4.1976).

Formulation(s):   cream 10 mg/g; gel 10 mg/g; sol. 10 mg/ml

Trade Name(s):
D: Exoderil (Rentschler; 1985)   I: Suadian (Schering)   USA: Naftin (Allergan)

Naftopidil
(BM-15275; KT-611)

Use: α_1-antagonist, treatment of dysuria/BPH, antihypertensive

RN: 57149-07-2   MF: $C_{24}H_{28}N_2O_3$ MW: 392.50
CN: 4-(2-Methoxyphenyl)-α-[(1-naphthalenyloxy)methyl]-1-piperazineethanol

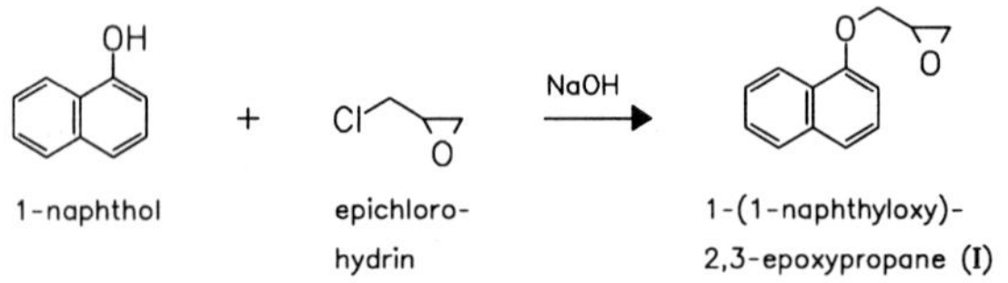

1-naphthol
+ epichloro-hydrin
→ [NaOH]
1-(1-naphthyloxy)-2,3-epoxypropane (I)

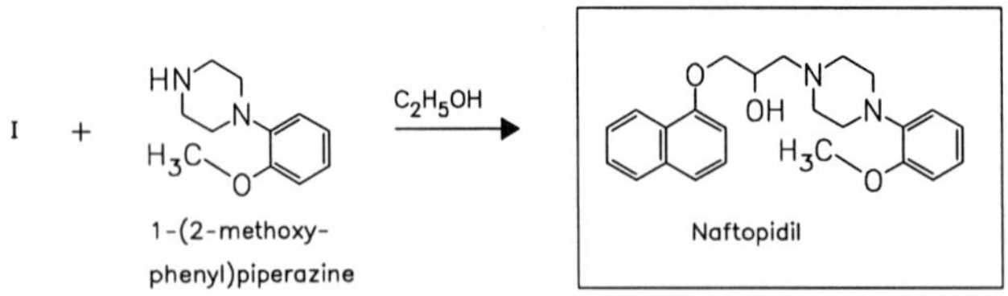

I +
1-(2-methoxy-phenyl)piperazine
→ [C₂H₅OH]
Naftopidil

Reference(s):
DE 2 408 804 (Boehringer Mannheim; D-prior. 23.2.1974)

synthesis of potential metabolites:
Kutscher, B. et al.: Arch. Pharm. (Weinheim, Ger.) (ARPMAS) 326 (10), 803-806 (1993).

use for the treatment of dysuria caused by BPH:
EP 401 653 (Boehringer Mannheim; appl. 30.5.1990; D-prior. 7.6.1989).

combination for the treatment of impotence:
WO 9 930 697 (Pfizer; appl. 29.10.1998; USA-prior. 16.12.1997).

Formulation(s):   tabl. 25 mg, 50 mg

Trade Name(s):
J: Flivas (Asahi Chemical)

Nalbuphine

ATC: N02AF02
Use: morphine antagonist, analgesic

RN: 20594-83-6   MF: $C_{21}H_{27}NO_4$ MW: 357.45   EINECS: 243-901-6
CN: (5α,6α)-17-(cyclobutylmethyl)-4,5-epoxymorphinan-3,6,14-triol

hydrochloride
RN: 23277-43-2   MF: $C_{21}H_{27}NO_4 \cdot HCl$ MW: 393.91   EINECS: 245-549-9
LD_{50}:   140 mg/kg (dog, i.v.); 1100 mg/kg (dog, p.o.)

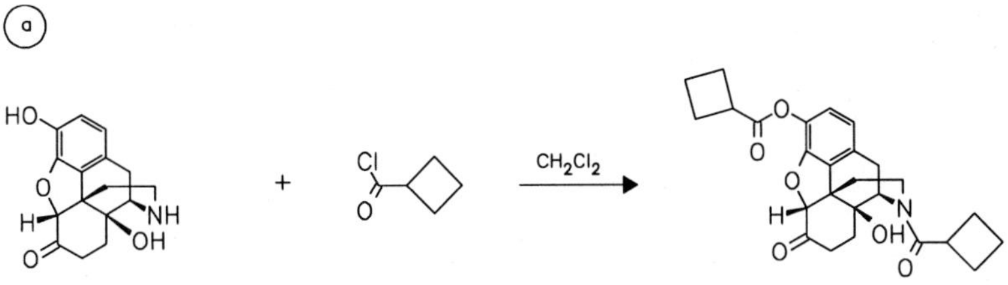

ⓐ

14-hydroxydihydro-
normorphinone (I)
(cf. naloxone synthesis)

cyclobutane-
carbonyl
chloride

(II)

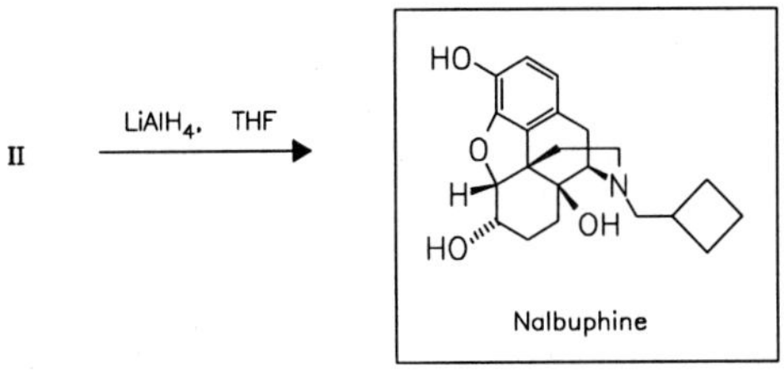

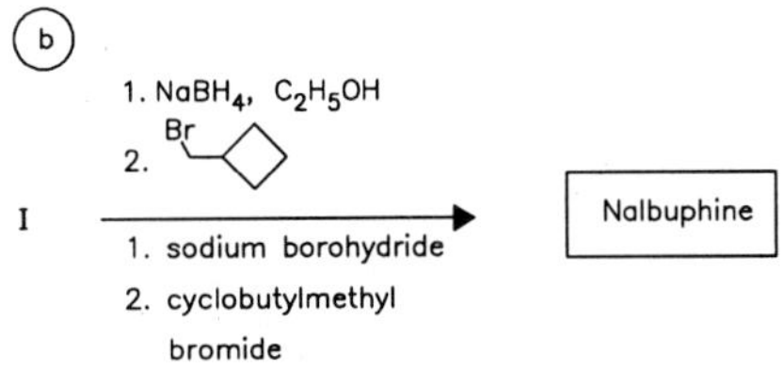

II $\xrightarrow{\text{LiAlH}_4,\ \text{THF}}$

Nalbuphine

ⓑ

1. NaBH$_4$, C$_2$H$_5$OH
2.

I $\longrightarrow$ Nalbuphine

1. sodium borohydride
2. cyclobutylmethyl
   bromide

Reference(s):
GB 1 119 270 (Endo; valid from 16.12.1966; USA-prior. 19.1.1966).
US 3 332 950 (Endo; 25.7.1967; prior. 6.12.1966, 15.5.1963, 23.3.1963).

Formulation(s):   amp. 10 mg/ml, 20 mg/2 ml (as hydrochloride)

Trade Name(s):
D: Nubain (Du Pont Pharma)   GB: Nubain (Du Pont)
F: Nubain (Du Pont)   USA: Nubain (Endo)

Nalidixic acid

ATC: G04AB01
Use: chemotherapeutic (urinary tract infections)

RN: 389-08-2   MF: $C_{12}H_{12}N_2O_3$ MW: 232.24   EINECS: 206-864-7
LD$_{50}$: 101 mg/kg (M, i.v.); 572 mg/kg (M, p.o.);
88.4 mg/kg (R, i.v.); 2040 mg/kg (R, p.o.)
CN: 1-ethyl-1,4-dihydro-7-methyl-4-oxo-1,8-naphthyridine-3-carboxylic acid

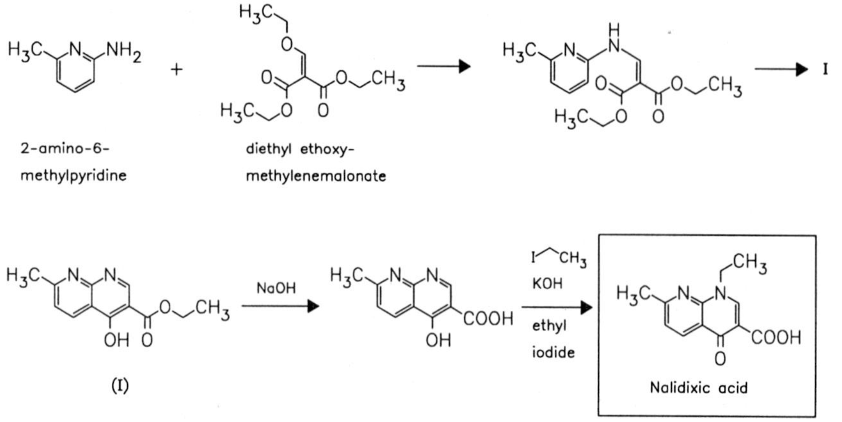

2-amino-6-
methylpyridine

diethyl ethoxy-
methylenemalonate

(I)

Nalidixic acid

Reference(s):

US 3 149 104 (Sterling Drug; 15.9.1964; prior. 3.1.1961).
Lesher, G.Y. et al.: J. Med. Pharm. Chem. (JMPCAS) 5, 1063 (1962).

alternative synthesis:
GB 1 338 023 (Koli Chem. Comp.; appl. 19.4.1971; J-prior. 20.2.1970).

Formulation(s):   aq. susp. 60 ml/ml; gran. 660 mg; tabl. 250 mg, 500 mg, 1 g

Trade Name(s):
D: Nogacit (Winthrop); wfm
Nogram (Winthrop); wfm
F: Négram (Sanofi Winthrop)
GB: Mictral (Sanofi Winthrop)
Negram (Sanofi Winthrop)-
comb.
Uriben (Rosemont)-comb.
I: Betaxina (Terapeutico
M.R.)
Nalidixin (Nuovo Cons.
Sanit. Naz.)
Naligram (Geymonat)

Nalissina (Rhône-Poulenc
Rorer)
Neg-Gram (Sanofi
Winthrop)
Uralgin (Ceccarelli)
Uri-Flor (AGIPS)
Urogram (Firma)
numerous generics
J: Entolon (Sawai)
Innoxalon (Sanko)
Kusnarin (Kodama)
Mirtolor (Zensei)
Mytacin (Fuji)

Nalidicron (San-a)
Narigix (Taiyo)
Oxoranil (Mohan)
Poleon (Sumitomo)
Restelon (Maruishi)
Uicelate (Toyo Jozo)
Urologin N (Takata)
Wintomylon (Daiichi)
Wintron (Tobishi)
generic
USA: NegGram (Sanofi
Winthrop)

Nalmefene

(NIH-10365; Nalmetrene (base); JF-1; ORF-11676)

ATC: V03AB3O
Use: cognition disorders therapeutic, antagonist to narcotics, neuronal injury inhibitor

RN: 55096-26-9   MF: $C_{21}H_{25}NO_3$ MW: 339.44
CN: (5α)-17-(cyclopropylmethyl)-4,5-epoxy-6-methylenemorphinan-3,14-diol

monohydrochloride
RN: 58895-64-0   MF: $C_{21}H_{25}NO_3 \cdot HCl$ MW: 375.90
(+)-base
RN: 131378-67-1   MF: $C_{21}H_{25}NO_3$ MW: 339.44
(+)-monohydrochloride
RN: 131712-55-5   MF: $C_{21}H_{25}NO_3 \cdot HCl$ MW: 375.90

naltrexone
(q. v.)

Nalmefene hydrochloride

Reference(s):
Hahn, F.E. et al.: J. Med. Chem. (JMCMAR) **18**, 259 (1975).

synthesis of nalmefene *from* naltrexone:
US 7 421 900 (Nat. Inst. of Health; appl. 28.8.1990; USA-prior. 26.10.1989).
US 4 322 426 (Du Pont de N.; appl. 30.3.1982; USA-prior. 28.4.1980).
US 4 751 307 (Mallinckrodt, Inc.; appl. 27.2.1987; USA-prior. 17.1.1985).
EP 140 367 (Key Pharm. Inc.; appl. 8.5.1985; USA-prior. 1.11.1983).

use of nalmefene:
US 4 880 813 (Baker Cummins Pharm.; appl. 14.11.1989; USA-prior. 22.7.1988).
WO 8 910 125 (Baker Cummins Pharm.; appl. 2.11.1989; USA-prior. 27.4.1988).
WO 8 702 586 (Key Pharmaceuticals; appl. 7.5.1987; 29.1.1985).
US 4 639 455 (Key Pharmaceuticals; appl. 27.1.1987; USA-prior. 2.1.1984).
US 4 863 928 (Baker Cummins Pharm.; appl. 5.9.1989; USA-prior. 4.1.1989).
US 4 877 791 (Baker Cummins Pharm.; appl. 31.10.1989; USA-prior. 1.11.1988).
US 4 923 875 (Baker Cummins Pharm.; appl. 8.5.1990; 10.7.1989).
WO 9 218 126 (Baker Cummins Pharm.; appl. 29.10.1992; USA-prior. 10.4.1991).
WO 9 118 605 (Finland; appl. 12.12.1991; USA-prior. 4.6.1990).

formulation:
US 4 511 570 (Key Pharmaceuticals; appl. 16.4.1985; 28.3.1983).

combination:
WO 9 531 985 (Italy; appl. 30.11.1995; I-prior. 24.5.1994).

Formulation(s):   amp. 100 µg/ml, 2 mg/2 ml; syringe 2 mg/2 ml (as hydrochloride)

Trade Name(s):
USA: Revex (Ohmeda)

Nalorphine

ATC: V03AB02
Use: morphine antagonist

RN: 62-67-9   MF: $C_{19}H_{21}NO_3$ MW: 311.38   EINECS: 200-546-1
LD_{50}:   127 mg/kg (M, i.v.); 1140 mg/kg (M, p.o.);
          226 mg/kg (R, i.v.)
CN: (5α,6α)-7,8-didehydro-4,5-epoxy-17-(2-propenyl)morphinan-3,6-diol

hydrochloride
RN: 57-29-4   MF: $C_{19}H_{21}NO_3 \cdot HCl$ MW: 347.84   EINECS: 200-321-8
LD_{50}:   63 mg/kg (M, i.v.);
            1150 mg/kg (R, p.o.);
            120 mg/kg (dog, i.v.)
hydrobromide
RN: 1041-90-3   MF: $C_{19}H_{21}NO_3 \cdot HBr$ MW: 392.29   EINECS: 213-868-2
LD_{50}:   260 mg/kg (M, i.p.); 921 mg/kg (M, s.c.)

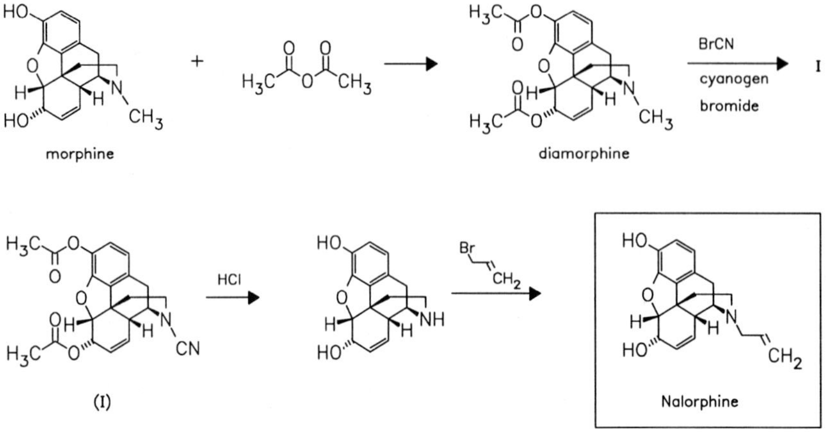

morphine

diamorphine

(I)

Nalorphine

Reference(s):
US 2 364 833 (Merck & Co.; 1944; prior. 1941).
US 2 891 954 (Merck & Co.; 1959; prior. 1951).

Formulation(s):   amp. 1 mg, 5 mg, 10 mg (as hydrobromide)

Trade Name(s):
D: Lethidrone (Wellcome);   GB: Lethidrone (Burroughs   USA: Nalline (Merck Sharp &
      wfm   Wellcome); wfm   Dohme); wfm
F: Nalorphine Serb   I: Norfin (Lusofarmaco); wfm
      (L'Arguenon)

Naloxone

ATC: V03AB15
Use: narcotic antagonist

RN: 465-65-6   MF: $C_{19}H_{21}NO_4$ MW: 327.38   EINECS: 207-365-7
LD_{50}:   260 mg/kg (M, s.c.)
CN: (5α)-4,5-epoxy-3,14-dihydroxy-17-(2-propenyl)morphinan-6-one

hydrochloride
RN: 357-08-4   MF: $C_{19}H_{21}NO_4 \cdot HCl$ MW: 363.84   EINECS: 206-611-0
LD_{50}:   90 mg/kg (M, i.v.); >1 g/kg (M, p.o.);
            107 mg/kg (R, i.v.); >1 g/kg (R, p.o.)

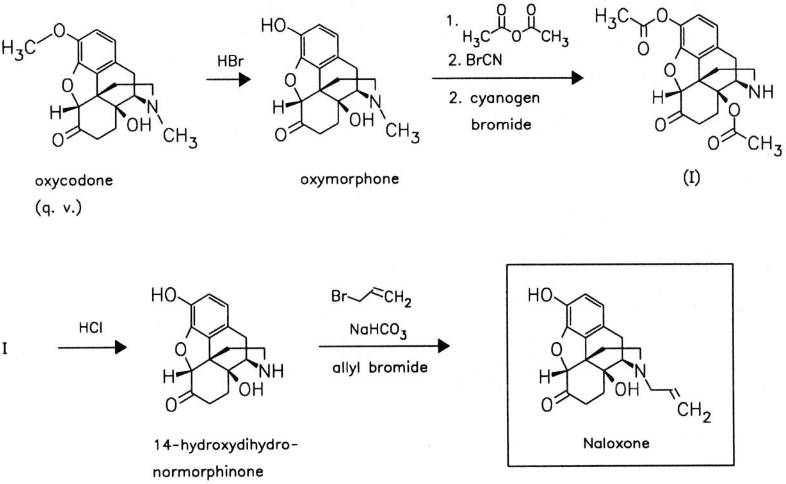

oxycodone
(q. v.)

oxymorphone

(I)

14-hydroxydihydro-
normorphinone

Naloxone

Reference(s):

US 3 254 088 (M. J. Lewenstein; 31.5.1966; appl. 14.3.1961).
DE 1 183 508 (M. J. Lewenstein; appl. 7.3.1962; USA-prior. 14.3.1961).
GB 929 287 (Sankyo; appl. 9.3.1962; J-prior. 14.3.1961).

Formulation(s):   amp. 0.04 mg/2 ml, 0.4 mg/ml; cps. 4 mg in comb. with tilidine (as hydrochloride);
tabl. 0.5 mg in comb. with pentazocine.HCl (as hydrochloride); vial 0.4 mg/ml, 1 mg/ml,
10 mg/ml

Trade Name(s):

D:	Findol (Mundipharma)-comb. with tilidine	Valomerck (Merck)-comb. with tilidine		generics
	Gruntin (Grünenthal)-comb. with tilidine	Valoron (Gödecke)-comb. with tilidine	J:	Naloxone Hydrochloride (Sankyo)
	Narcanti (Du Pont Pharma)	F:	Nalone (Serb)	USA: Narcan (Endo; as
	Tilador (Hexal)-comb. with tilidine		Narcan (Du Pont)	hydrochloride)
	Tilidin (Isis Puren;	GB:	Narcan (Du Pont; as	Talwin Nx (Sanofi)
	Heumann; Stada; BASF;		hydrochloride)	generics and combination
	ratiopharm; Saar)-comb.	I:	Narcan (Crinos)	preparations
			Narcan neonatal (Crinos)	

Naltrexone

ATC: V03AB30
Use: narcotic antagonist

RN: 16590-41-3   MF: $C_{20}H_{23}NO_4$ MW: 341.41   EINECS: 240-649-9
LD$_{50}$:   551 mg/kg (M, s.c.)
CN: (5α)-17-(cyclopropylmethyl)-4,5-epoxy-3,14-dihydroxymorphinan-6-one

hydrochloride
RN: 16676-29-2   MF: $C_{20}H_{23}NO_4 \cdot HCl$ MW: 377.87   EINECS: 240-723-0
LD$_{50}$:   1100 mg/kg (M, p.o.);
1450 mg/kg (R, p.o.)

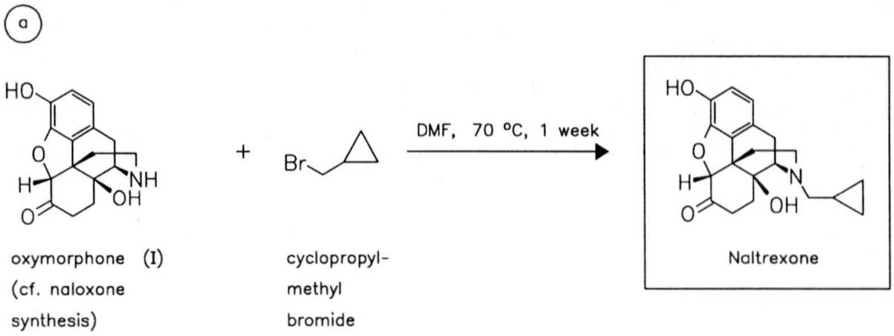

(a)

oxymorphone (I)
(cf. naloxone
synthesis)

cyclopropyl-
methyl
bromide

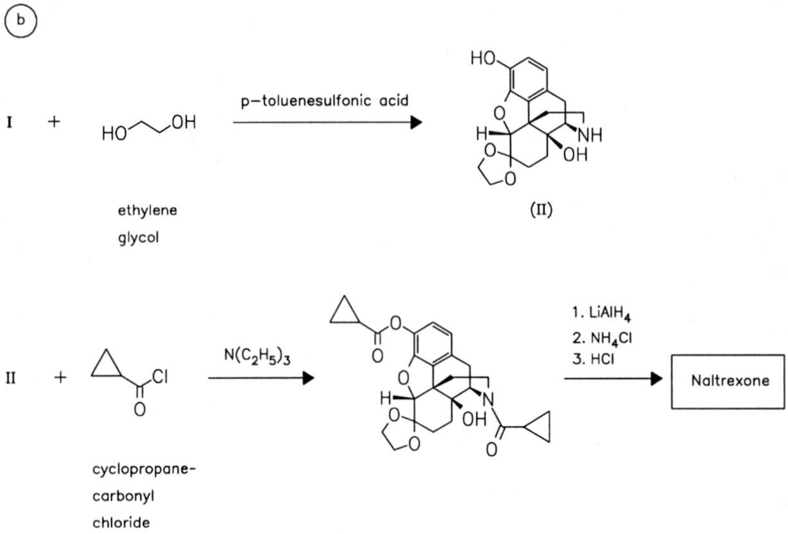

DMF, 70 °C, 1 week

Naltrexone

(b)

I +

ethylene
glycol

p—toluenesulfonic acid

(II)

II +

cyclopropane-
carbonyl
chloride

N(C₂H₅)₃

1. LiAlH₄
2. NH₄Cl
3. HCl

Naltrexone

Reference(s):
DAS 1 795 707 (Endo; appl. 19.12.1966; USA-prior. 19.1.1966).
FR-M 6 358 (Endo; appl. 24.2.1967).
US 3 332 950 (Endo; 25.7.1967; prior. 23.3.1963, 15.5.1963, 6.12.1966).

Formulation(s):   tabl. 50 mg (as hydrochloride)

Trade Name(s):
D: Nemexin (Du Pont Pharma)   GB: Nalorex (Du Pont)   Narcoral (Crinos)
F: Nalorex (Du Pont)   I: Antaxone (Zambon Italia)   USA: ReVia (Du Pont)
     Revia (Du Pont)   Nalorex (Du Pont Pharma)

Nandrolone

ATC: A14AB01; S01XA11
Use: anabolic

RN: 434-22-0   MF: C₁₈H₂₆O₂   MW: 274.40   EINECS: 207-101-0
CN: (17β)-17-hydroxyestr-4-en-3-one

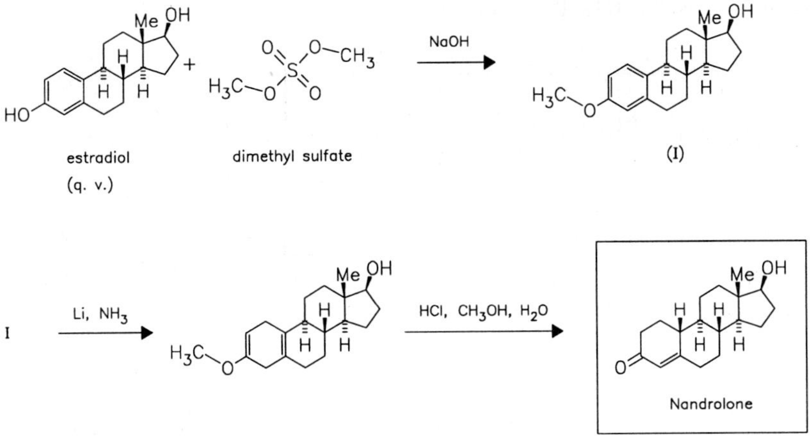

estradiol
(q. v.)

dimethyl sulfate

(I)

Nandrolone

Reference(s):

US 2 698 855 (Organics; 1955; prior. 1953).
US 2 774 777 (Syntex; 1956; prior. 1952).
Wilds, A.L.; Nelson, N.A.: J. Am. Chem. Soc. (JACSAT) **75**, 5366 (1953).
Djerassi, C. et al.: J. Am. Chem. Soc. (JACSAT) **76**, 4092 (1954).

Formulation(s):   eye drops 10 mg/ml (as monosodium sulfate)

Trade Name(s):

D:	Keratyl (Chauvin ankerpharm)	I:	Dynabolon (Crinos); wfm	USA:	Nortestonate (Upjohn); wfm
F:	Keratyl (Chauvin)	J:	Andol (Tokyo Tanabe; as cyclohexylpropionate)		

Nandrolone decanoate

ATC: A14AB01
Use: anabolic

RN: 360-70-3   MF: $C_{28}H_{44}O_3$ MW: 428.66   EINECS: 206-639-3
LD$_{50}$: >566 mg/kg (M, i.p.)
CN: (17β)-17-[(1-oxodecyl)oxy]estr-4-en-3-one

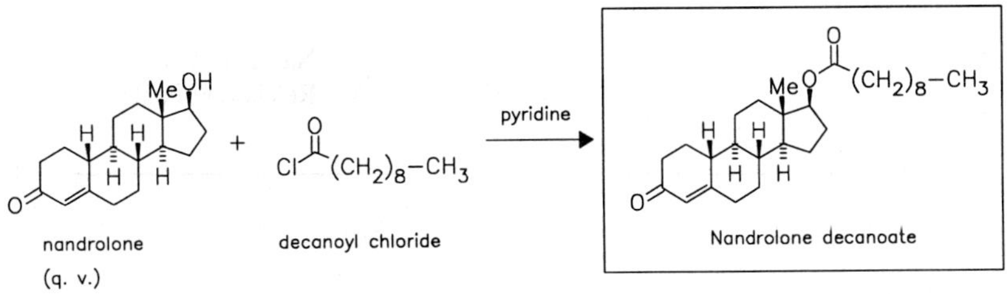

nandrolone
(q. v.)

decanoyl chloride

Nandrolone decanoate

Reference(s):

US 2 998 423 (Organon; 29.8.1961; appl. 2.2.1959; NL-prior. 25.2.1958).

Formulation(s):   amp.. 25 mg/ml, 50 mg/ml

Trade Name(s):

D:	Deca-Durabolin (Organon) Keratyl (Chauvin ankerpharm)	F:	Deca-Durabolin (Organon); wfm	I:	Deca-Durabolin (Organon Italia)
		GB:	Deca-Durabolin (Organon)		

J:　Deca-Durabolin (Organon-　USA:　Deca-Durabolin (Organon)
　　Sankyo)

Nandrolone hexyloxyphenylpropionate

ATC:　A14AB01
Use:　anabolic

RN:　52279-57-9　MF: $C_{33}H_{46}O_4$　MW: 506.73　EINECS: 257-810-4
CN:　(17β)-17-[3-[4-(hexyloxy)phenyl]-1-oxopropoxy]estr-4-en-3-one

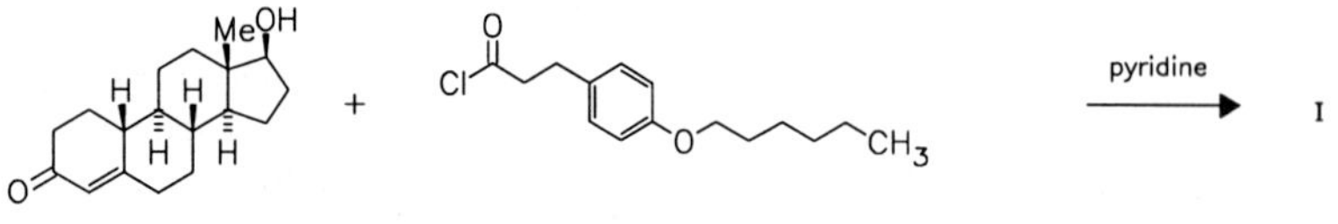

nandrolone
(q. v.)

3-(4-hexyloxyphenyl)-
propionyl chloride

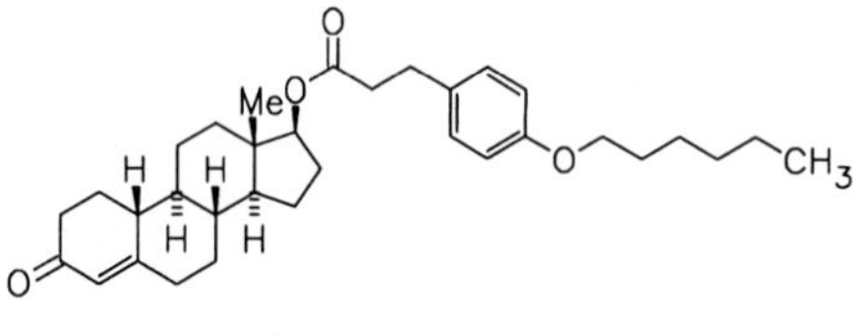

pyridine

I

Nandrolone hexyloxyphenylpropionate　(I)

Reference(s):
US 2 904 562 (Leo; 15.9.1959; appl. 20.1.1958).

Formulation(s):　amp. 50 mg; susp. 50 mg/2 ml

Trade Name(s):
D:　Anadur (Bastian-Werk);　F:　Anador (Logeais); wfm
　　wfm

Nandrolone phenylpropionate
(Nandrolone phenpropionate)

ATC:　A14AB01
Use:　anabolic

RN:　62-90-8　MF: $C_{27}H_{34}O_3$　MW: 406.57　EINECS: 200-551-9
LD$_{50}$:　>1 g/kg (M, i.p.);
　　595 mg/kg (R, i.p.)
CN:　(17β)-17-(1-oxo-3-phenylpropoxy)estr-4-en-3-one

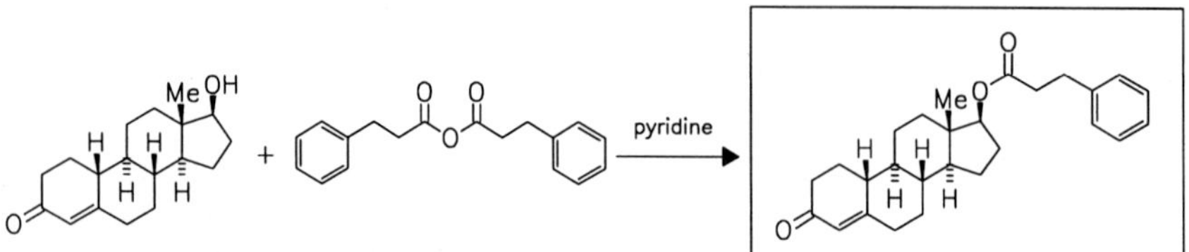

nandrolone
(q. v.)

3-phenylpropionic
anhydride

pyridine

Nandrolone phenylpropionate

Reference(s):
GB 826 028 (Organon; appl. 1956; NL-prior. 1955).
US 2 868 809 (Upjohn; 1959; prior. 1953).

Formulation(s):   amp. 25 mg

Trade Name(s):

D:	Docabolin (Nourypharma)-comb.; wfm	I:	Anticatabolin (Falorni); wfm		Stenabolin (AFI); wfm
	Durabolin (Organon); wfm		Anticatabolin (Nativelle); wfm		Strabolene (Isola-Ibi); wfm
	Hepa-Obaton (Nourypharma)-comb.; wfm		Durabolin (Ravasini); wfm		Superbolin (Labif); wfm
			Norandrol (Panther-Osfa Chemie); wfm	J:	Durabolin (Organon-Sankyo)
F:	Durabolin (Organon); wfm		Norbalin (Bieffe); wfm	USA:	Durabolin (Organon); wfm
GB:	Durabolin (Organon); wfm		Sintabolin (AFI); wfm		Nandrolin (Tutag); wfm
					generics; wfm

Nandrolone undecylate

(Nandrolone undecanoate)

ATC: A14AB01
Use: anabolic

RN: 862-89-5   MF: $C_{29}H_{46}O_3$ MW: 442.68   EINECS: 212-729-3
CN: (17β)-17-[(1-oxoundecyl)oxy]estr-4-en-3-one

nandrolone
(q. v.)   undecanoyl chloride   Nandrolone undecylate

Reference(s):
BE 659 440 (N. Gueritee; appl. 9.2.1965; GB-prior. 21.2.1964).

use as anabolic in combination with estradiol esters:
FR-M 3 424 (N. Gueritee; appl. 27.1.1964).

alternative synthesis and combination with mineral corticoids:
DOS 2 638 507 (Akzo; appl. 26.8.1976; NL-prior. 27.8.1975).

use in combination with vitamin E:
FR-M 7 284 (J. M. Gastand; appl. 7.3.1968).

Formulation(s):   inj. sol. 80.5 mg/1 ml

Trade Name(s):

F:	Dynabolon (Théramex); wfm		Trophoboléne (Théramex)-comb.; wfm	I:	Dynabolon (Fournier Pierrel)

Naphazoline

ATC: R01AA08; R01AB02; S01GA01
Use: vasoconstrictor, rhinological
      therapeutic

RN: 835-31-4 MF: $C_{14}H_{14}N_2$ MW: 210.28 EINECS: 212-641-5
LD$_{50}$: 170 mg/kg (M, i.v.); 270 mg/kg (M, p.o.)
CN: 4,5-dihydro-2-(1-naphthalenylmethyl)-1H-imidazole

monohydrochloride
RN: 550-99-2 MF: $C_{14}H_{14}N_2 \cdot HCl$ MW: 246.74 EINECS: 208-989-2
mononitrate
RN: 5144-52-5 MF: $C_{14}H_{14}N_2 \cdot HNO_3$ MW: 273.29 EINECS: 225-915-4
LD$_{50}$: 13.2 mg/kg (M, i.v.); 265 mg/kg (M, p.o.);
          1260 mg/kg (R, p.o.)

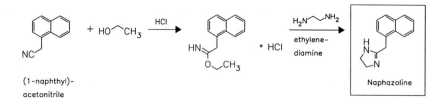

(1-naphthyl)-
acetonitrile

Naphazoline

Reference(s):
US 2 161 938 (Ciba; 1939; D-prior. 1934).

Formulation(s):   eye drops 0.3 mg/ml, 1 mg/ml; nasal spray

Trade Name(s):

D: Antistin-Privin (CIBA
    Vision)-comb.
    Piniol (Spitzner; as
    hydrochloride)
    Privin (Novartis Pharma; as
    nitrate)
    Proculin (Chauvin
    ankerpharm)
    Rhinex (Pharma
    Wernigerode)
    Vistalbalon (Pharm-
    Allergan)
    numerous generics and
    combination preparations
F: Collyres bleus Laiter
    (Leurquin)-comb.
    Dérinox (Thérabel Lucien
    pharma)-comb.

Frazoline (Bouchara)-
comb.
Soframycyne (Roussel)-
comb.
Xylocaïne naphthazoline
(Astra)-comb.
GB: Antistin-Privine (Ciba)-
comb.; wfm
Murine (Abbott); wfm
Nomaze (Fisons); wfm
Vasocon A (Cooper
Vision)-comb.; wfm
Vasocon A (Knox)-comb.;
wfm
I: Citroftalmina (SIFI)-comb.
Collirio Alfa (Bracco)
Deltarinolo (Hoechst
Marion Roussel)-comb.

Desamin Same (Savoma)
Imidazyl (Recordati)
Imizol (Farmigea)
Naftazolina (Bruschettini)
Pupilla (Alfa Wassermann)
Rinazina (Maggioni)
Rinazina Senza Sulfamide
(Maggioni)
Virginiana Gocce Verdi
(Kelemata)
numerous combination
preparations
J: Privina (Ciba-Geigy-
Takeda; as nitrate)
USA: Naphcon (Alcon; as
hydrochloride)

Naproxen

ATC: G02CC02; M01AE02; M02AA12
Use: anti-inflammatory, antirheumatic, analgesic

RN: 22204-53-1   MF: $C_{14}H_{14}O_3$ MW: 230.26   EINECS: 244-838-7
LD$_{50}$:   435 mg/kg (M, i.v.); 360 mg/kg (M, p.o.);
248 mg/kg (R, p.o.);
>1 g/kg (dog, p.o.)
CN: (S)-6-methoxy-α-methyl-2-naphthaleneacetic acid

sodium salt
RN: 26159-34-2   MF: $C_{14}H_{13}NaO_3$ MW: 252.25

(a)   Original process:

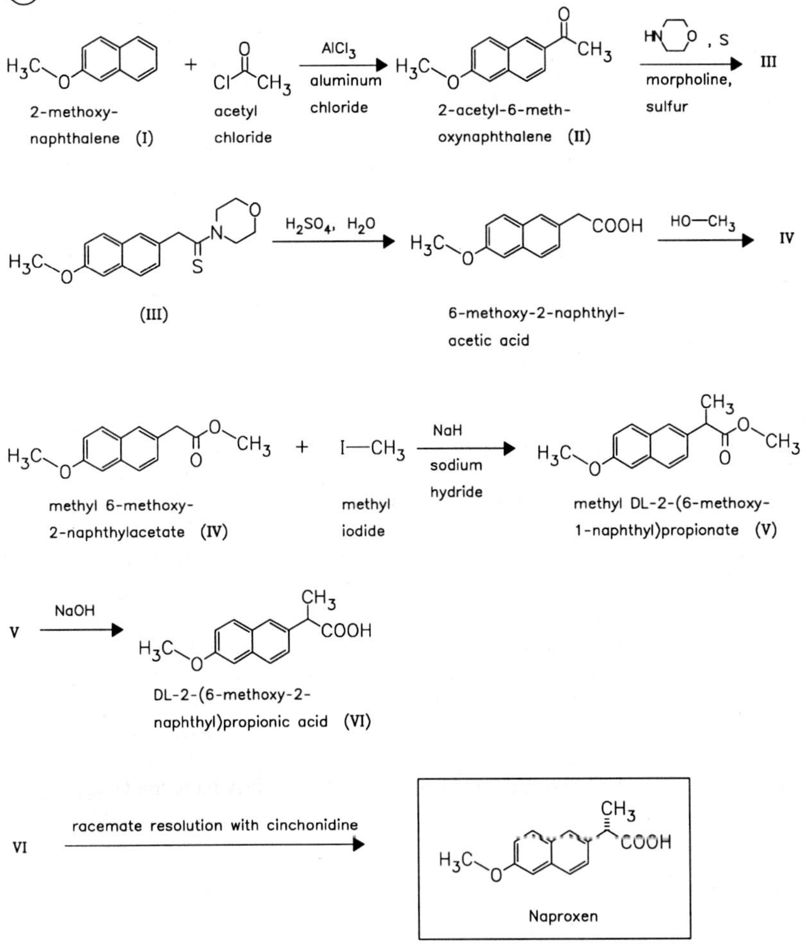

2-methoxy-
naphthalene (I)

acetyl
chloride

2-acetyl-6-meth-
oxynaphthalene (II)

morpholine,
sulfur

(III)

6-methoxy-2-naphthyl-
acetic acid

methyl 6-methoxy-
2-naphthylacetate (IV)

methyl
iodide

methyl DL-2-(6-methoxy-
1-naphthyl)propionate (V)

DL-2-(6-methoxy-2-
naphthyl)propionic acid (VI)

Naproxen

(b)   First large-scale manufacturing process of Syntex:

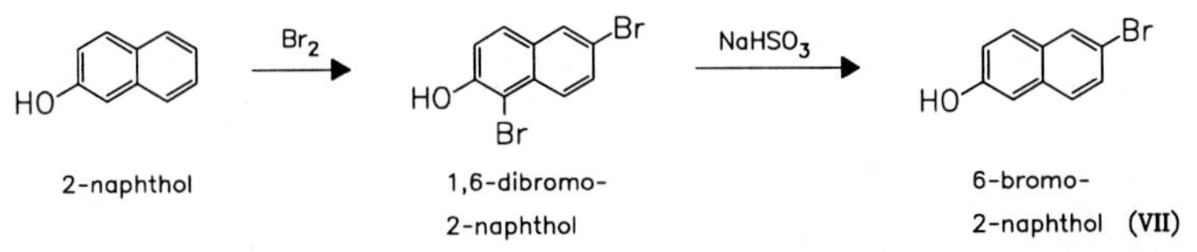

2-naphthol

1,6-dibromo-
2-naphthol

6-bromo-
2-naphthol (VII)

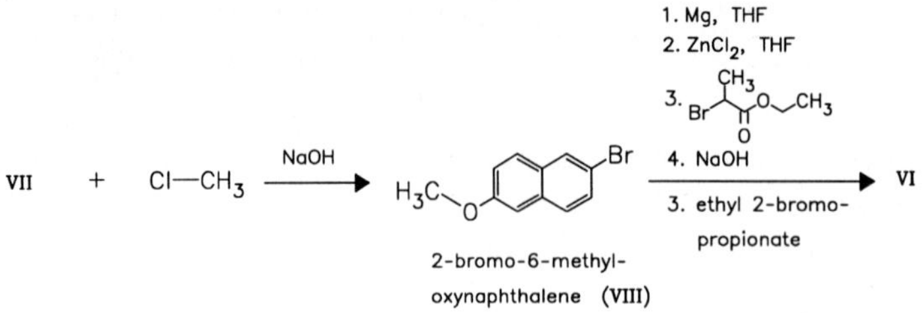

VII + Cl—CH₃ →(NaOH) **2-bromo-6-methyl-oxynaphthalene (VIII)**

1. Mg, THF
2. ZnCl₂, THF
3. (CH₃ Br ... O CH₃)
4. NaOH

3. ethyl 2-bromo-propionate

→ VI

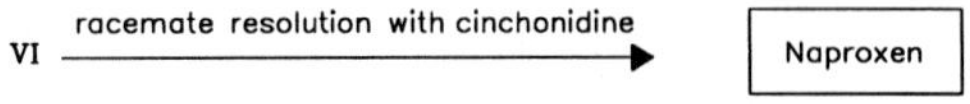

VI →(racemate resolution with cinchonidine)→ Naproxen

(c) Second large-scale manufacturing process of Syntex:

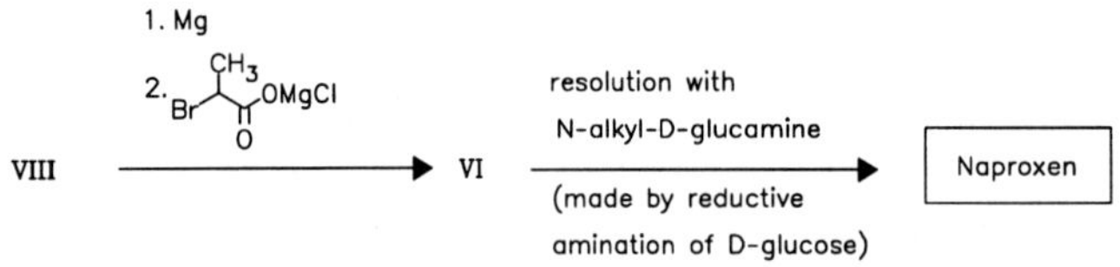

1. Mg
2. (CH₃ Br ... OMgCl)

VIII ──────→ VI

resolution with N-alkyl-D-glucamine (made by reductive amination of D-glucose) → Naproxen

(d) Asymmetric hydrogenation:

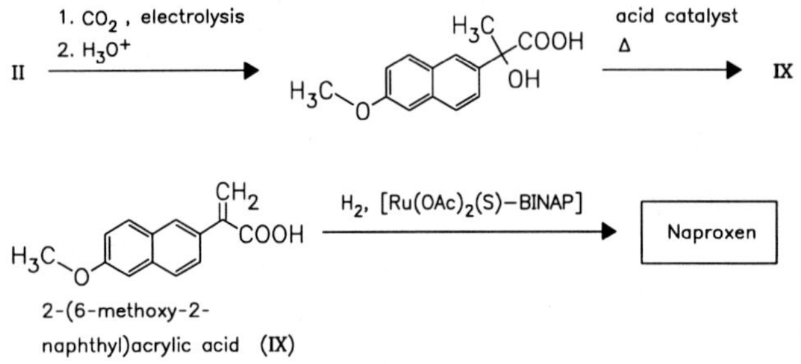

II →(1. CO₂, electrolysis / 2. H₃O⁺)→ (H₃C COOH OH structure)

→(acid catalyst, Δ)→ IX

2-(6-methoxy-2-naphthyl)acrylic acid (IX)

→(H₂, [Ru(OAc)₂(S)–BINAP])→ Naproxen

(e) Zambon process:

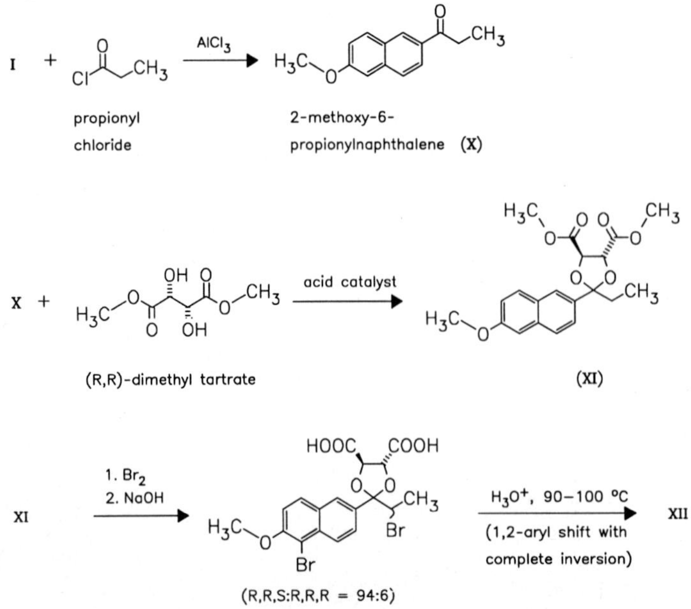

I + (propionyl chloride) →(AlCl₃)→ **2-methoxy-6-propionylnaphthalene (X)**

X + (R,R)-dimethyl tartrate →(acid catalyst)→ (XI)

XI →(1. Br₂ / 2. NaOH)→ (R,R,S:R,R,R = 94:6)

→(H₃O⁺, 90–100 °C) (1,2-aryl shift with complete inversion)→ XII

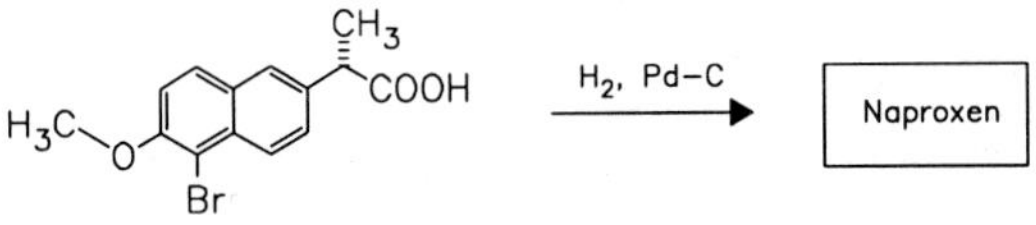

(S)-2-(5-bromo-6-
methoxy-2-naphthyl)-
propanoic acid (XII)

H₂, Pd–C → Naproxen

(f) Stereospecific Syntex process:

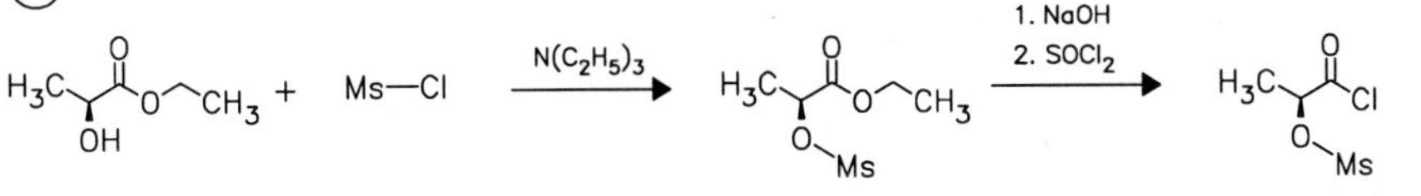

ethyl (S)-lactate + mesyl chloride

$N(C_2H_5)_3$ →

1. NaOH
2. $SOCl_2$ →

(XIII)

Ms: —S(=O)(=O)—CH₃

+ XIII

THF, −40 °C →

(XIV)

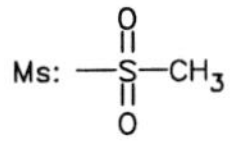

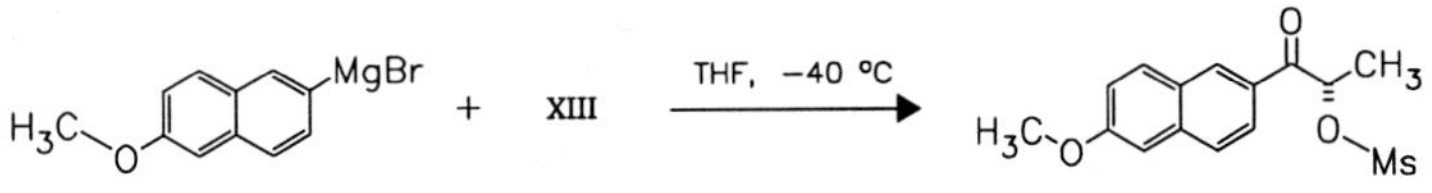

XIV 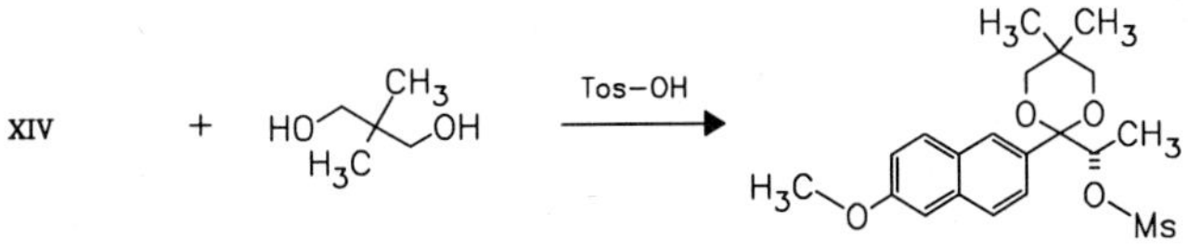 + 2,2-dimethyl-1,3-propanediol

Tos–OH →

(XV)

XV

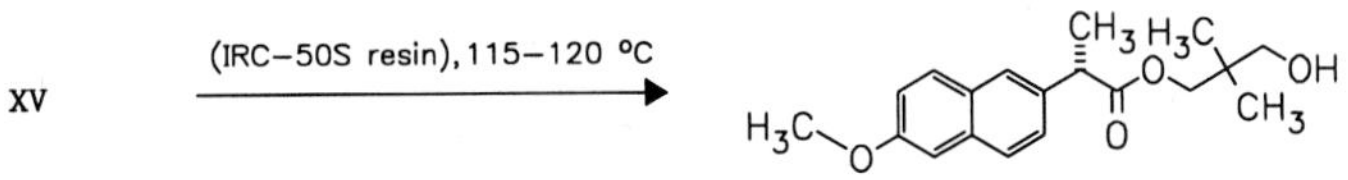

(IRC–50S resin), 115–120 °C →

(XVI)

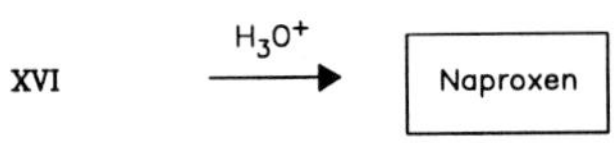

XVI

H_3O^+ → Naproxen

Reference(s):

process review:
Harrington, P.J.; Lodewijk, E.: Organic Process Res. & Dev. **1**, 72 (1997).
Harrison, J.T. et al.: J. Med. Chem. (JMCMAR) **13**, 203 (1970).
a US 3 896 157 (Syntex; 22.7.1975; prior. 13.1.1967, 7.12.1967, 4.11.1971).
   US 3 904 682 (Syntex; 9.9.1975; prior. 13.1.1967, 7.12.1967, 24.3.1969, 31.8.1971, 21.6.1973).
   US 3 978 116 (Syntex; 31.8.1976; prior. 13.1.1967, 7.12.1967, 4.11.1971).
   US 3 978 124 (Syntex; 31.8.1976; prior. 13.1.1967, 7.12.1967, 4.11.1971).
   US 3 998 966 (Syntex; prior. 4.11.1971).
   US 4 001 301 (Syntex; 4.1.1977; prior. 4.11.1971).
   US 4 009 197 (Syntex; 22.2.1977; prior. 13.1.1967).
   DAS 1 668 654 (Syntex; appl. 8.1.1968; USA-prior. 13.1.1967; 7.12.1967).
   improved racemate resolution with cinchonidine:
   DAS 2 319 245 (Syntex; appl. 16.4.1973; USA-prior. 21.4.1972, 11.4.1973).

racemization:
DAS 2 008 272 (Syntex; appl. 23.2.1970; USA-prior. 24.3.1969).
b US 3 663 584 (Syntex; 16.5.1972; appl. 4.12.1970).
similar process with Cu-compound:
US 3 658 863 (Syntex; 25.4.1972; appl. 30.9.1969).
similar process with Cd-compound:
US 3 694 476 (Syntex; 26.9.1972; appl. 4.12.1970).
c DOS 2 805 488 (Syntex; appl. 9.2.1978; USA-prior. 16.2.1977, 19.12.1977).
resolution with N-alkyl-D-glucamines:
US 4 515 811 (Syntex; 7.5.1985; USA-prior. 6.7.1979, 26.11.1979).
EP 7 116 (Syntex; appl. 17.7.1979; CH-prior. 19.7.1978).
DOS 3 025 448 (Syntex; appl. 4.7.1980; USA-prior. 6.7.1979, 26.11.1979).
d Ohta, T. et al.: J. Org. Chem. (JOCEAH) **52**, 3174 (1987).
DOS 2 919 919 (Montedison; appl. 17.5.1979; I-prior. 22.5.1978).
US 4 239 914 (Montedison; 16.12.1980; I-prior. 22.5.1978).
electrocarboxylation of 2-acetyl-6-methoxynaphthalene:
Chan, A.S. et al.: J. Org. Chem. (JOCEAH) **60**, 742 (1995).
naphthacrylic acid via corresponding cyanohydrins:
US 3 637 767 (Syntex; 25.1.1972; appl. 30.7.1968).
e Giordano, C. et al.: Tetrahedron (TETRAB) **45**, 4243 (1989).
US 4 579 968 (Zambon; 1.4.1986; I-prior. 24.2.1984).
US 4 697 036 (Zambon; 29.9.1987; I-prior. 6.8.1984).
US 4 810 819 (Zambon; 7.3.1989; appl. 5.8.1987; USA-prior. 5.4.1985).
US 4 855 464 (Zambon; 29.9.1987; I-prior. 6.8.1984).
US 4 888 433 (Zambon; 29.9.1987; I-prior. 6.8.1984).
preparation of 2-propionylnaphthalene:
EP 176 142 (Blaschim; appl. 16.9.1985; I-prior. 24.9.1984, 17.5.1985).
EP 301 311 (Zambon; appl. 12.7.1988; I-prior. 28.7.1987).
f US 4 605 758 (Syntex; 12.8.1986; prior. 11.12.1981, 23.4.1984).
US 4 749 804 (Syntex; 7.6.1988; prior. 11.12.1981, 23.4.1984, 10.6.1986).
US 4 912 254 (Syntex; 27.3.1990; prior. 11.12.1981, 23.4.1984, 10.6.1986, 6.5.1988).

alternative syntheses:
DAS 1 934 460 (Syntex; appl. 8.7.1969; USA-prior. 30.7.1968).
US 3 637 767 (Syntex; 25.1.1972; appl. 30.7.1968).
DAS 1 793 825 (Syntex; appl. 8.1.1968; USA-prior. 13.1.1967, 7.12.1967).

resolution with dehydroabietylamine:
DAS 2 339 765 (Syntex; appl. 6.8.1973; USA-prior. 10.8.1972).

resolution with (S)-α-phenylethylamine:
US 4 546 201 (Blaschim; 8.10.1985; I-prior. 27.7.1983).

enzymatic cleavage of esters of racemic naproxen:
US 4 857 462 (Boehringer Mannh.; 15.8.1989; D-prior. 16.12.1983).
EP 195 717 (Montedison; appl. 17.3.1986; I-prior. 22.3.1985).
EP 233 656 (Gist-Brocades; appl. 6.1.1987; GB-prior. 7.1.1986).
EP 330 217 (Ist. Guido Donegani; appl. 24.2.1989; I-prior. 25.2.1988, 29.7.1988).

Formulation(s):   f. c. tabl. 250 mg, 500 mg, 1000 mg; suppos. 250 mg, 500 mg; susp. 125 mg/5 ml, 250 mg/5 ml; tabl. 250 mg, 375 mg, 500 mg, 750 mg (as acid); f. c. tabl. 550 mg; tabl. 275 mg, 550 mg, 375 mg, 500 mg (as sodium salt)

Trade Name(s):

D:	Apranax (Roche; Syntex)	Naprosyne (Cipharm;	I: Aperdan (ABC
	Dysmenalgit (Krewel	1975)	Farmaceutici)-comb.
	Meuselbach)	GB: Napratec (Searle)	Artroxen (Errekappa
	Proxen (Roche; Syntex;	Naprosyn (Roche; 1973)	Euroter.)
	1975)	Nycopren (Ardern)	
F:	Apranax (Roche)	Synflex (Roche)	

Axer Alfa (Alfa Wassermann; as sodium salt)
Floginax (Teofarma)
Flogogin (Angelini; as sodium salt)
Floxalin (Salus Research; as sodium salt)
Gibinap (Metafarm)
Gibixen (Metafarm)
Laser (Tosi-Novara)
Leniartril (Sancarlo)

Naprius (Aesculapius-Bs)
Naprorex (Lampugnani)
Naprosyn (Recordati)
Neoblimon (Guidotti)
Nitens (Pulitzer)-comb.
Numidan (Therabel Pharma)-comb.
Piproxen (Nuovo ISM)-comb.
Prexan (Lafare)
Primeral (Master Pharma; as sodium salt)

Proxine (Del Saz & Filippini)
Synalgo (Geymonat)
Synflex (Recordati; as sodium salt)
Ticoflex (Farma Uno)
Xenar (Alfa Wassermann)

J: Naixan (Tanabe)
USA: Anaprox (Roche)
      Naprosyn (Roche; 1976)
      generics

Naratriptan
(GR-85548)

ATC: N02CC02
Use: antimigraine agent, 5-HT$_1$-agonist

RN: 121679-13-8   MF: C$_{17}$H$_{25}$N$_3$O$_2$S   MW: 335.47
CN: N-methyl-3-(1-methyl-4-piperidinyl)-1H-indole-5-ethanesulfonamide

hydrochloride
RN: 121679-19-4   MF: C$_{17}$H$_{25}$N$_3$O$_2$S · xHCl   MW: unspecified
monohydrochloride
RN: 143388-64-1   MF: C$_{17}$H$_{25}$N$_3$O$_2$S · HCl   MW: 371.93

5-bromo-indole (I)   +   1-methyl-4-piperidone (II)   → [KOH, CH$_3$OH, 20 °C]   5-bromo-3-(4-hydroxy-1-methyl-4-piperidinyl)-1H-indole (III)

III   +   N-methylvinyl-sulfonamide (IV)   → [Pd(OCOCH$_3$)$_2$, tri-p-tolylphosphine, DMF, 110 °C, palladium acetate (V), tri-p-tolylphosphine (VI)]   (E)-N-methyl-2-[3-(1-methyl-1,2,3,6-tetrahydro-4-pyridinyl)-1H-indol-5-yl]vinylsulfonamide (VII)

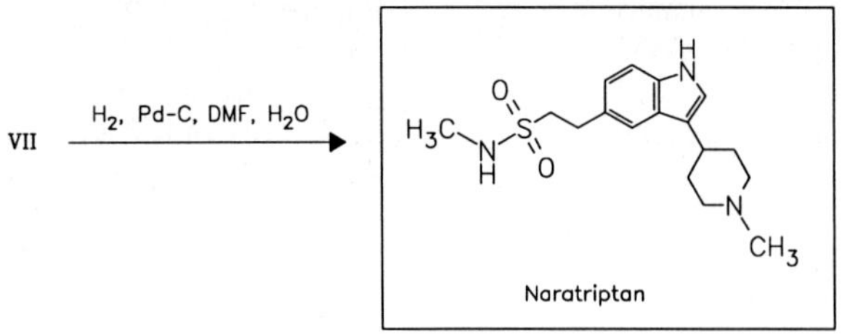

Naratriptan

VII → (H₂, Pd-C, DMF, H₂O)

b

I + II → (KOH, CH₃OH, Δ) →

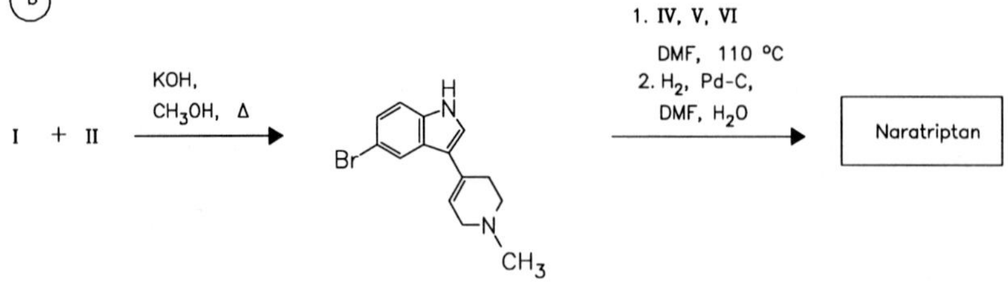

5-bromo-3-(1-methyl-
1,2,3,6-tetrahydro-4-
pyridinyl)-1H-indole (VIII)

1. IV, V, VI
   DMF, 110 °C
2. H₂, Pd-C,
   DMF, H₂O

→ Naratriptan

or:

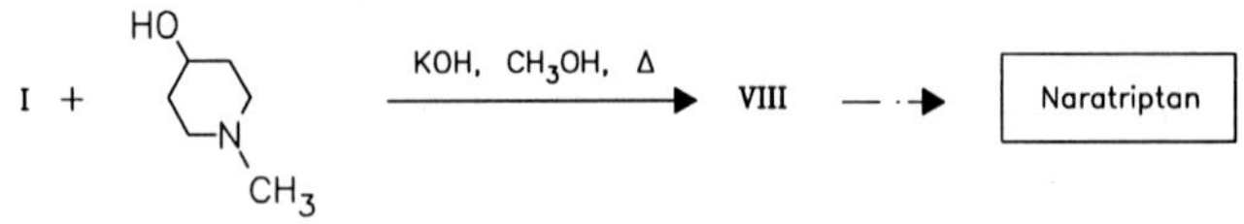

I + (4-hydroxy-
1-methyl-
piperidine) → (KOH, CH₃OH, Δ) → VIII — ⤍ Naratriptan

c

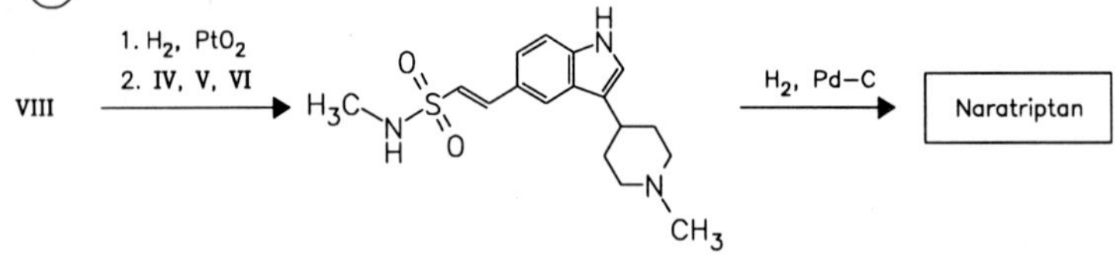

VIII → (1. H₂, PtO₂ 2. IV, V, VI) → → (H₂, Pd-C) → Naratriptan

d

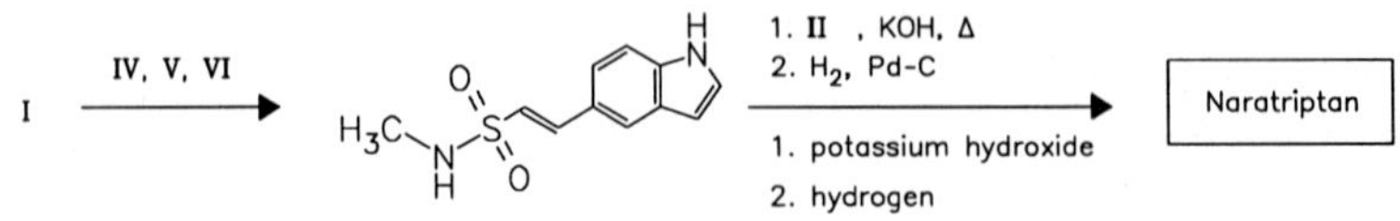

I → (IV, V, VI) → → (1. II , KOH, Δ 2. H₂, Pd-C) → Naratriptan

1. potassium hydroxide
2. hydrogen

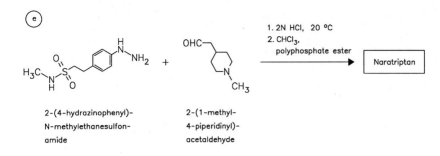

2-(4-hydrazinophenyl)-
N-methylethanesulfon-
amide

2-(1-methyl-
4-piperidinyl)-
acetaldehyde

Reference(s):
WO 9 509 166 (Glaxo; appl. 6.4.1995; GB-prior. 29.9.1993).
EP 303 507 (Glaxo; appl. 15.2.1989; GB-prior. 13.8.1987, 14.6.1988, 17.6.1988).

Formulation(s):   tabl. 2.5 mg (as monohydrochloride)

Trade Name(s):
D: Naramig (Glaxo Wellcome/
       Cascan)

Natamycin
(Pimaricin)

ATC: A01AB10; A07AA03; D01AA02;
         G01AA02; S01AA10
Use: fungicidal antibiotic

RN: 7681-93-8   MF: $C_{33}H_{47}NO_{13}$ MW: 665.73   EINECS: 231-683-5
LD$_{50}$:   >5 g/kg (M, i.v.); 1500 mg/kg (M, p.o.);
              36 mg/kg (R, i.v.); 2730 mg/kg (R, p.o.);
              18 mg/kg (dog, i.v.); >300 mg/kg (dog, p.o.)
CN: [1R-(1R*,3S*,5R*,7R*,8E,12R*,14E,16E,18E,20E,22R*,24S*,25R*,26S*)]-22-[(3-amino-3,6-dideoxy-β-
        D-mannopyranosyl)oxy]-1,3,26-trihydroxy-12-methyl-10-oxo-6,11,28-trioxatricyclo[22.3.1.0^{5,7}]octacosa-
        8,14,16,18,20-pentaene-25-carboxylic acid

Natamycin

From fermentation solutions of *Streptomyces natalensis*.

Reference(s):
GB 844 289 (Königl. Niederl. Gist- & Spiritusfabr.; appl. 1957; NL-prior. 1956).
GB 846 933 (American Cyanamid; appl. 1957; USA-prior. 1956).

Formulation(s):   cream 2 g/100 g; drg. 100 mg; ointment 10 mg/g; tabl. 10 mg

Trade Name(s):
D: Deronga (Galderma)
       Pima Biciron (S & K
       Pharma)

       Pimafucin (Galderma)
       Pimafucort (Yamanouchi)-
       comb.

F: Pimafucine (Beytout); wfm
       Pimafucine (Duphar); wfm
       Pimafucort (Beytout); wfm

GB:	Pimafucin (Brocades); wfm	I:	Natafucin (Yamanouchi Pharma)	J:	Pimafucin (Torii)-comb.
				USA:	Myprozine (Lederle); wfm

Nateglinide

(A 4166; Ay 416; SDT-DJN 608)

Use: hypoglycemic agent

RN: 105816-04-4 MF: $C_{19}H_{27}NO_3$ MW: 317.43
CN: trans-*N*-[[4-(1-Methylethyl)cyclohexyl]-carbonyl]-D-phenylalanine

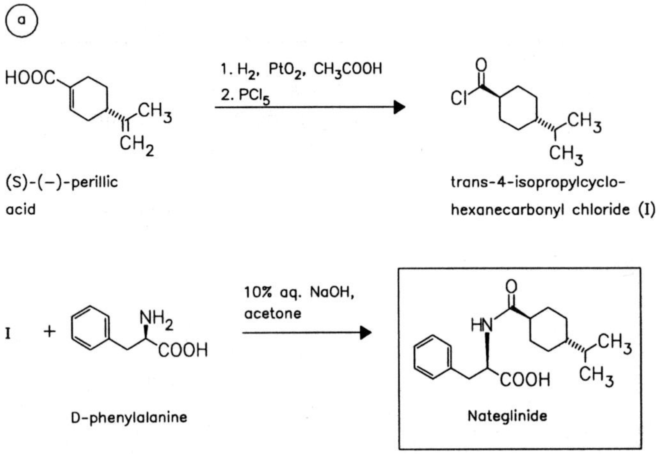

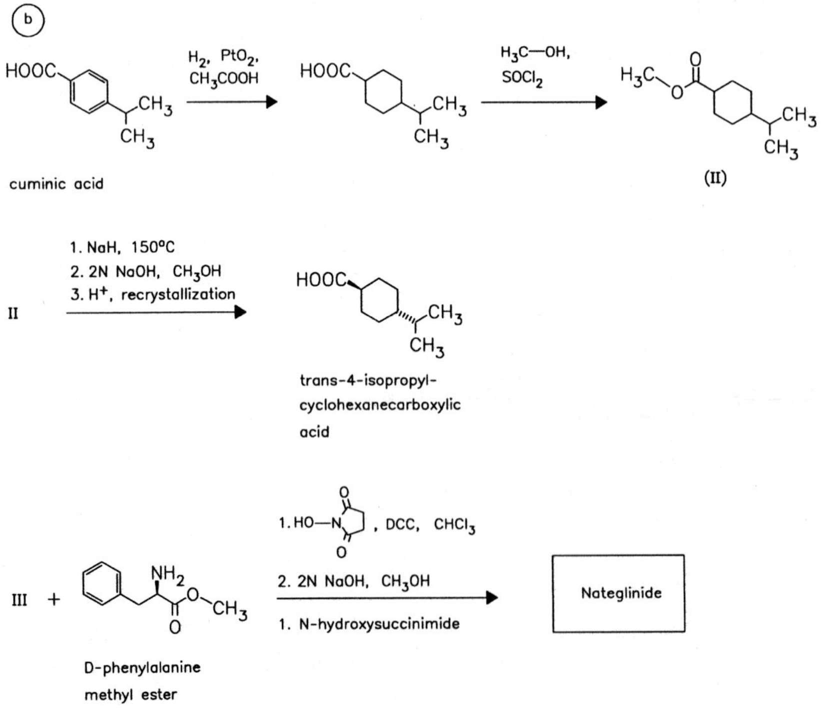

Reference(s):
EP 196 222 (Ajinomoto; appl. 26.3.1986; J-prior. 27.3.1985).

preparation of I:
JP 7 017 899 (Ajinomoto; appl. 1.7.1993).

stable crystals:
US 5 463 116 (Ajinomoto; 31.10.1999; J-prior. 30.7.1991).

tablet formulation:
WO 9 822 105 (Ajinomoto; appl. 14.11.1997; J-prior. 15.11.1996).

Formulation(s):   tabl. 30 mg

Trade Name(s):
J: Starlix (Ajinomoto, 1999)

Nazasetron
(Y-25130)

ATC: A04AA
Use: anti-emetic, 5-HT$_3$-antagonist

RN: 123040-69-7   MF: $C_{17}H_{20}ClN_3O_3$ MW: 349.82
CN: (±)-*N*-1-azabicyclo[2.2.2]oct-3-yl-6-chloro-3,4-dihydro-4-methyl-3-oxo-2*H*-1,4-benzoxazine-8-carboxamide

monohydrochloride
RN: 141922-90-9   MF: $C_{17}H_{20}ClN_3O_3 \cdot HCl$ MW: 386.28
(–)-enantiomer
RN: 123040-95-9   MF: $C_{17}H_{20}ClN_3O_3$ MW: 349.82
(–)-enantiomer monohydrochloride
RN: 123040-96-0   MF: $C_{17}H_{20}ClN_3O_3 \cdot HCl$ MW: 386.28
(+)-enantiomer
RN: 123040-93-7   MF: $C_{17}H_{20}ClN_3O_3$ MW: 349.82
(+)-enantiomer hydrochloride
RN: 123040-94-8   MF: $C_{17}H_{20}ClN_3O_3 \cdot HCl$ MW: 386.28

methyl 5-chloro-
salicylate

HNO_3, H_2SO_4

methyl 5-chloro-3-
nitrosalicylate

Fe, NH_4Cl

methyl 3-amino-
5-chlorosalicylate   (I)

I + bromoacetyl chloride

$N(C_2H_5)_3$, $CHCl_3$

methyl 3-(2-bromo-
acetylamino)-5-chloro-
salicylate

1. K_2CO_3, DMF
2. H_3C—I, KOtBu

II

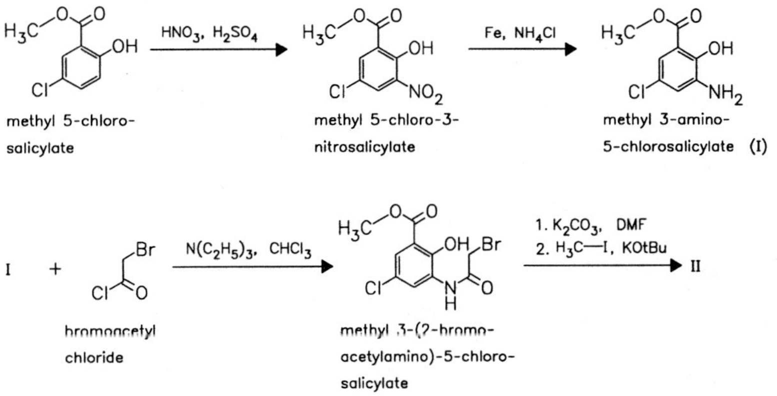

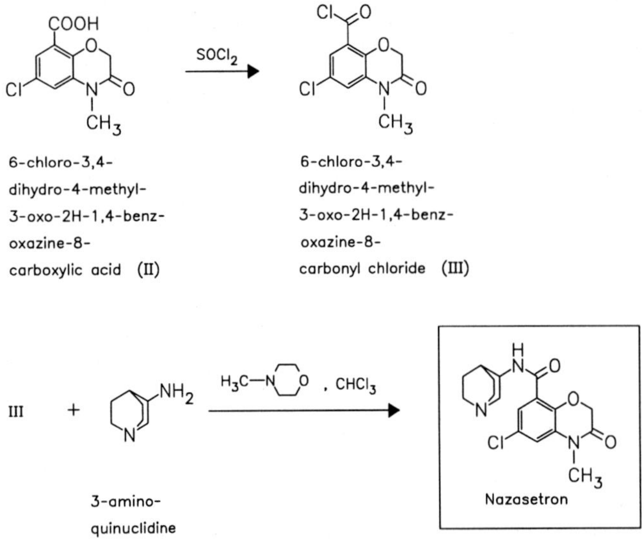
COOH
SOCl2
6-chloro-3,4-dihydro-4-methyl-3-oxo-2H-1,4-benzoxazine-8-carboxylic acid (II)
6-chloro-3,4-dihydro-4-methyl-3-oxo-2H-1,4-benzoxazine-8-carbonyl chloride (III)
III
3-amino-quinuclidine
H3C—N O , CHCl3
Nazasetron

Reference(s):
EP 313 393 (Yoshitomi; appl. 21.10.1988; J-prior. 22.10.1987, 25.12.1987, 13.1.1988).

stable crystalline structure of (+)-enantiomer:
JP 07 070 120 (Yoshitomi; appl. 5.7.1994; J-prior. 5.7.1993).

medical use:
JP 08 027 001 (Yoshitomi; J-prior. 13.7.1994).
JP 08 027 000 (Yoshitomi; J-prior. 13.7.1994).
JP 08 026 999 (Yoshitomi; J-prior. 12.7.1994).
WO 9 601 630 (Yoshitomi; appl. 7.7.1995; J-prior. 12.7.1994).

suppository formulation:
JP 06 305 969 (Yoshitomi; appl. 27.4.1993; J-prior. 27.4.1993).

light-stabilized injection solution:
WO 9 425 032 (Yoshitomi; appl. 25.4.1995; J-prior. 28.4.1994).

Formulation(s): amp. for injection 10 mg/2 ml

Trade Name(s):
J: Serotone (Yoshitomi; Tobacco/Green Cross)

Nebivolol
(ME-3255; R-65824; R-67555 as hydrochloride)

ATC: C07AB12
Use: antihypertensive, β_1-adrenergic blocker

RN: 118457-14-0 MF: $C_{22}H_{25}F_2NO_4$ MW: 405.44
CN: [2*R**[*R**[*R**(*S**)]]]-α,α'-[iminobis(methylene)]bis[6-fluoro-3,4-dihydro-2*H*-1-benzopyran-2-methanol]

hydrochloride
RN: 152520-56-4 MF: $C_{22}H_{25}F_2NO_4 \cdot HCl$ MW: 441.90

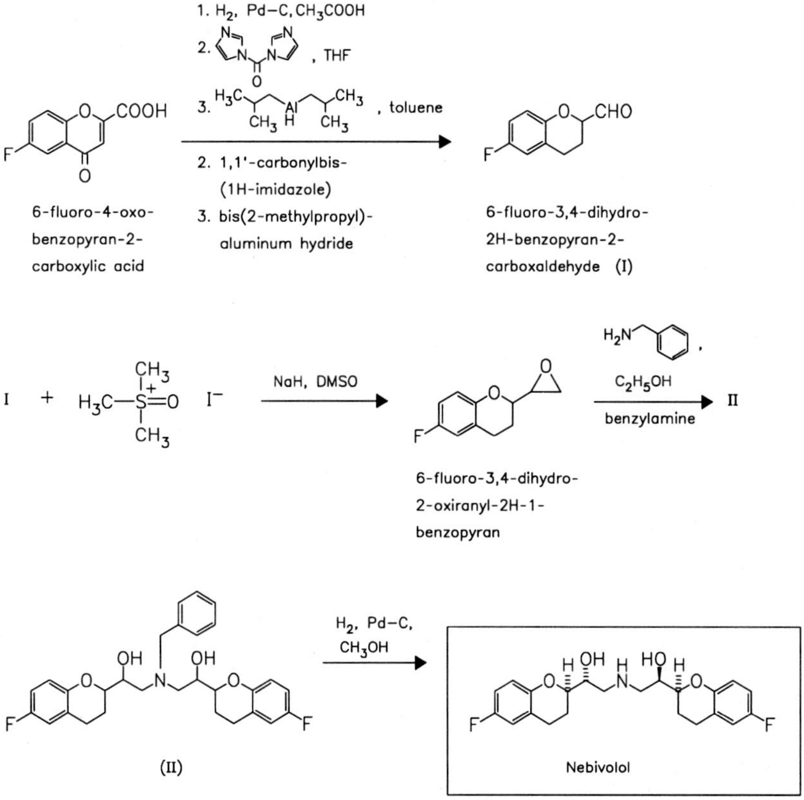

1. H_2, Pd–C, CH_3COOH

2. [imidazole carbonyl structure] , THF

3. [aluminum reagent] , toluene

2. 1,1'-carbonylbis-
(1H-imidazole)
3. bis(2-methylpropyl)-
aluminum hydride

6-fluoro-4-oxo-
benzopyran-2-
carboxylic acid

6-fluoro-3,4-dihydro-
2H-benzopyran-2-
carboxaldehyde (I)

I + $H_3C-\overset{+}{\underset{CH_3}{S}}=O$ I⁻   → (NaH, DMSO)

6-fluoro-3,4-dihydro-
2-oxiranyl-2H-1-
benzopyran

H_2N [benzyl], C_2H_5OH
benzylamine
→ II

(II)

H_2, Pd–C,
CH_3OH
→

Nebivolol

Reference(s):
EP 145 067 (Janssen Pharm.; appl. 22.11.1984; USA-prior. 5.12.1983).

Formulation(s):   tabl. 5 mg (as hydrochloride)

Trade Name(s):
D: Nebilet (Berlin-Chemie)

Nedaplatin
(S 254)

Use: antineoplastic platinum complex

RN: 95734-82-0   MF: $C_2H_8N_2O_3Pt$ MW: 303.18
LD$_{50}$: 20 mg/kg (R, i. v.);
       44.1 mg/kg (M, i. v.);
       4 mg/kg (dog, i. v.)
CN: (SP-4-3)-Diammine[hydroxyacetato(2–)-O¹,O²]platinum

CN: (SP-4-3)-Diammine[hydroxyacetato(2–)-O^1,O^2]platinum

[cisplatin structure] AgNO₃ → [diammineplatinum nitrate structure] anion exchange resin → (I)

cisplatin (q. v.)

diammineplatinum
nitrate

(I)

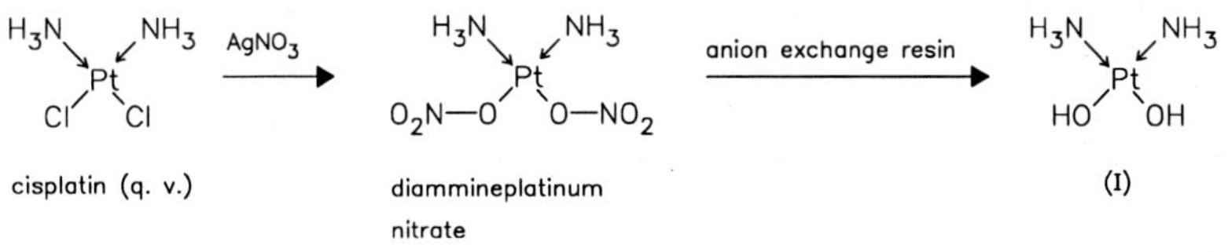

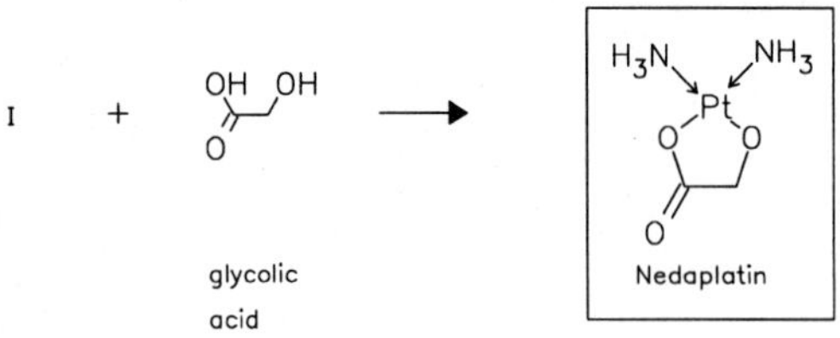

I + glycolic acid → Nedaplatin

Reference(s):

JP 59 222 497 (Shionogi & Co.; appl. 1.6.1983).
US 4 575 550 (Shionogi & Co.; J-prior. 11.3.1986; appl. 14.4.1983; J-prior. 23.10.1981; USA-prior. 6.1.1982).
Totani, T.; Aono, K.; Komura, M.; Adachi, Y.: Chem. Lett. (CMLTAG) **1986** (3), 429.

Formulation(s):   powder 10 mg, 50 mg, 100 mg; vials 10 mg, 50 mg, 100 mg

Trade Name(s):
J: Aqupla (Shionogi)

Nedocromil

ATC: R01AC07; R03BC03; S01GX04
Use: antiallergic, antiasthmatic

RN: 69049-73-6   MF: $C_{19}H_{17}NO_7$ MW: 371.35
CN: 9-ethyl-6,9-dihydro-4,6-dioxo-10-propyl-4H-pyrano[3,2-g]quinoline-2,8-dicarboxylic acid

disodium salt
RN: 69049-74-7   MF: $C_{19}H_{15}NNa_2O_7$ MW: 415.31
LD_{50}:   2000-4000 mg/kg (R, dog, i.v.); >5000 mg/kg (R, dog, p.o., s.c.)

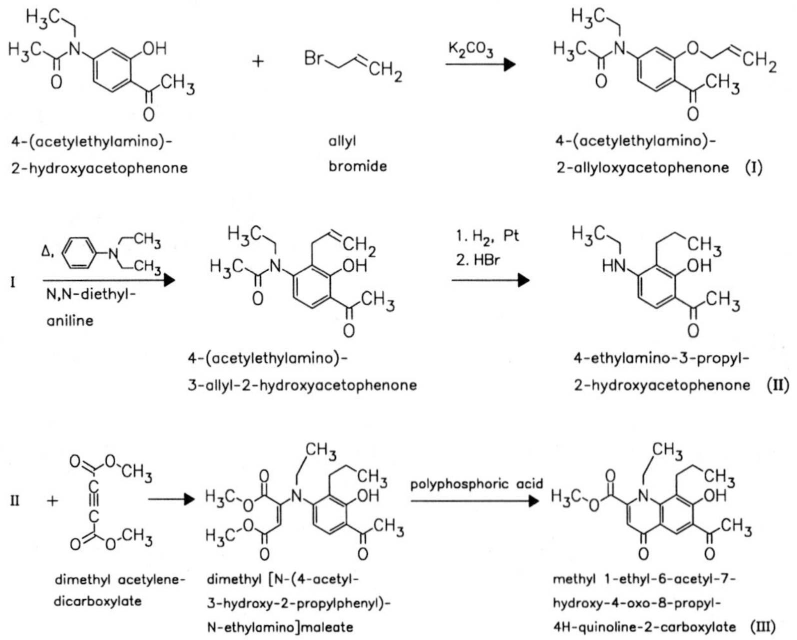

4-(acetylethylamino)-2-hydroxyacetophenone + allyl bromide $\xrightarrow{K_2CO_3}$ 4-(acetylethylamino)-2-allyloxyacetophenone (I)

I $\xrightarrow[\text{aniline}]{\Delta, \text{ N,N-diethyl-}}$ 4-(acetylethylamino)-3-allyl-2-hydroxyacetophenone $\xrightarrow[\text{2. HBr}]{\text{1. } H_2, \text{ Pt}}$ 4-ethylamino-3-propyl-2-hydroxyacetophenone (II)

II + dimethyl acetylenedicarboxylate → dimethyl [N-(4-acetyl-3-hydroxy-2-propylphenyl)-N-ethylamino]maleate $\xrightarrow{\text{polyphosphoric acid}}$ methyl 1-ethyl-6-acetyl-7-hydroxy-4-oxo-8-propyl-4H-quinoline-2-carboxylate (III)

III + [diethyl oxalate structure] —NaH, DMF / sodium hydride→ [structure]

diethyl
oxalate

diethyl 9-ethyl-6,9-dihydro-10-
propyl-4,6-dioxo-4H-pyrano[3,2-g]-
quinoline-2,8-dicarboxylate (IV)

IV —NaHCO₃, C₂H₅OH / sodium hydrogen carbonate→ [structure]

Nedocromil

Reference(s):
US 4 474 787 (Fisons, 2.10.1984; GB-prior. 4.11.1977).
DE 2 819 215 (Fisons; appl. 2.5.1978; GB-prior. 4.5.1977, 4.11.1977).
GB 2 022 078 (Fisons; appl. 6.6.1978; prior. 4.5.1977).
Cairns, H. et al.: J. Med. Chem. (JMCMAR) **28**, 1832 (1985).

synthesis of ²H, ³H, ¹⁴C-labelled nedochromil sodium:
Wilkinson, D.J.; Lockley, W.J.S.: J. Labelled Compd. Radiopharm. (JLCRD4) **22**, 883 (1985).

combination with anticholinergics:
GB 2 204 790 (Fisons; appl. 23.5.1987).

Formulation(s): aerosol 2 mg/puff; eye drops 20 mg/ml (as sodium salt); spray 1.3 mg/0.13 ml

Trade Name(s):
D: Halamid (ASTA Medica AWD)
Irtan (Fisons; Rhône-Poulenc Rorer)
Tilade (Fisons; Rhône-Poulenc Rorer; 1988)
F: Tilade (Spécia; 1988)

Tilade Syncroner (Spécia)
Tivalist (Spécia)
GB: Rapitil (Rhône-Poulenc Rorer)
Tilade Syncroner (Rhône-Poulenc Rorer; 1986)

Tilarin (Rhône-Poulenc Rorer)
I: Kovilen (Mediolanum)
Tilade (Italchimici)
USA: Tilade (Rhône-Poulenc Rorer)

Nefazodone hydrochloride
(BMY-13754; MJ-13754-1)

ATC: N06AX06
Use: antidepressant, 5-HT₂A-antagonist

RN: 82752-99-6 MF: C₂₅H₃₂ClN₅O₂ · HCl MW: 506.48
CN: 2-[3-[4-(3-chlorophenyl)-1-piperazinyl]propyl]-5-ethyl-2,4-dihydro-4-(2-phenoxyethyl)-3H-1,2,4-triazol-3-one hydrochloride

base
RN: 83366-66-9 MF: C₂₅H₃₂ClN₅O₂ MW: 470.02

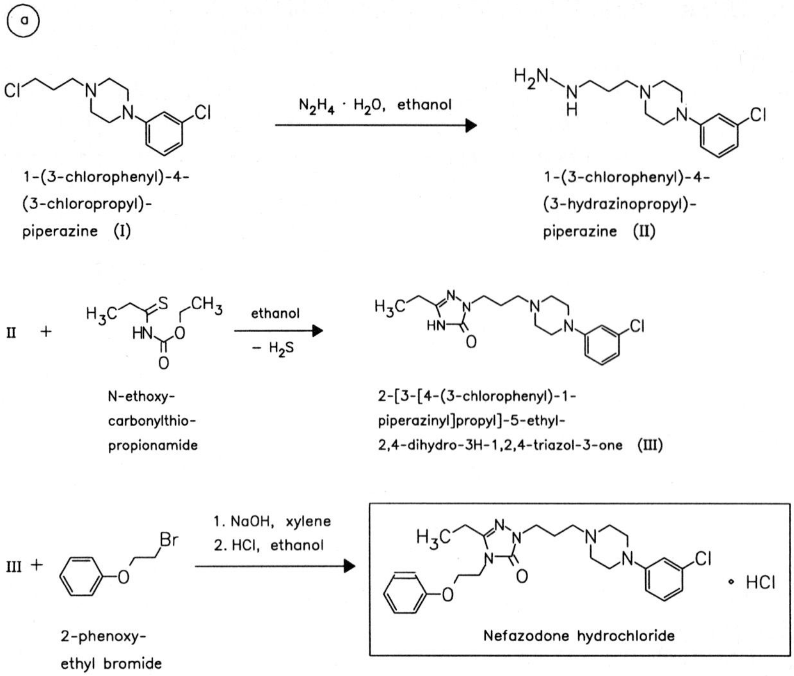

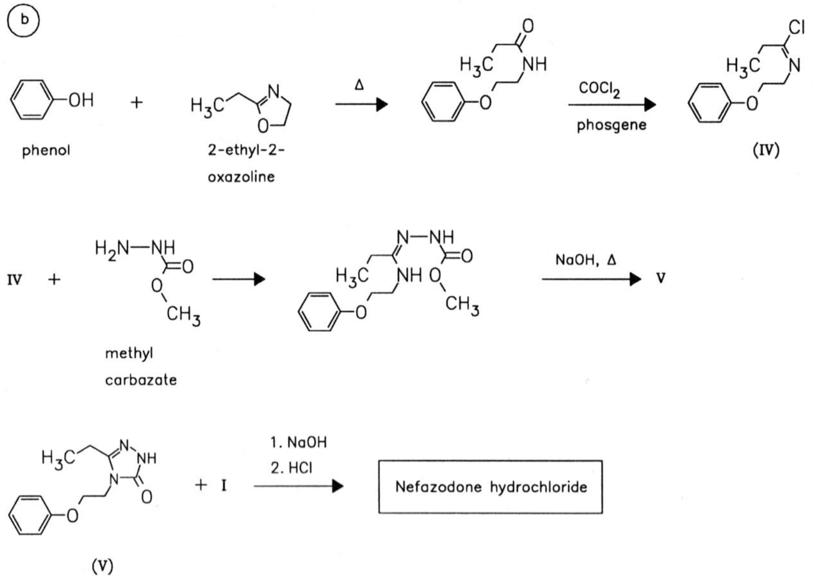

ⓐ

1-(3-chlorophenyl)-4-
(3-chloropropyl)-
piperazine (I)

N₂H₄ · H₂O, ethanol →

1-(3-chlorophenyl)-4-
(3-hydrazinopropyl)-
piperazine (II)

II + N-ethoxy-
carbonylthio-
propionamide

ethanol
− H₂S

2-[3-[4-(3-chlorophenyl)-1-
piperazinyl]propyl]-5-ethyl-
2,4-dihydro-3H-1,2,4-triazol-3-one (III)

III + 2-phenoxy-
ethyl bromide

1. NaOH, xylene
2. HCl, ethanol

Nefazodone hydrochloride   • HCl

ⓑ

phenol   +   2-ethyl-2-
oxazoline

Δ →

COCl₂
phosgene →

(IV)

IV +   methyl
carbazate

→   NaOH, Δ →   V

(V)   + I

1. NaOH
2. HCl

Nefazodone hydrochloride

Reference(s):
a US 4 338 317 (Bristol-Myers Squibb; appl. 16.3.1981; USA-prior. 16.3.1981).
b Madding, G.D. et al.: J. Heterocycl. Chem. (JHTCAD) **22**, 1121 (1985).

use for treatment of sleep disorders:
US 5 116 852 (Bristol-Myers Squibb; appl. 3.12.1990; USA-prior. 3.12.1990).

improved administration:
EP 428 272 (Ellinwood; appl. 17.10.1990; USA-prior. 17.10.1989).

controlled release preparation:
US 5 169 638 (Squibb & Sous; appl. 23.10.1991; USA-prior. 23.10.1991).

Formulation(s):   tabl. 100 mg, 150 mg, 200 mg, 250 mg, 300 mg (as hydrochloride)

Trade Name(s):

D: Nefadar (Bristol-Myers Squibb)

GB: Dutonin (Bristol-Myers Squibb)

USA: Serzone (Bristol-Myers Squibb)

Nefopam

ATC: N02BG06
Use: analgesic, muscle relaxant

RN: 13669-70-0   MF: $C_{17}H_{19}NO$ MW: 253.35   EINECS: 237-148-2
LD_{50}:   180 mg/kg (M, p.o.)
CN: 3,4,5,6-tetrahydro-5-methyl-1-phenyl-1H-2,5-benzoxazocine

hydrochloride
RN: 23327-57-3   MF: $C_{17}H_{19}NO \cdot HCl$ MW: 289.81

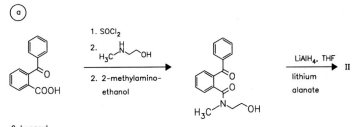

IV —LiAlH$_4$→ Nefopam

Reference(s):

a US 3 487 153 (Rexall; 30.12.1969; appl. 19.1.1968).
b US 3 830 803 (Riker; 20.8.1974; appl. 10.5.1965).
   DAS 1 620 198 (Riker; appl. 5.5.1966; USA-prior. 10.5.1965).

Formulation(s):   amp. 20 mg; f. c. tabl. 30 mg; tabl. 30 mg (as hydrochloride)

Trade Name(s):

D:	Ajan (3M Medica)	GB:	Acupan (3M Health Care;
	Silentan (Krewel		as hydrochloride)
	Meuselbach)	I:	Nefadol (Zilliken)
F:	Acupan (Biocodex)		Nefam (Farma-Biagini)

Oxadol (ISI)
USA: Acupan (Riker); wfm

Nelfinavir mesylate

(AG-1343; LY-312857)

ATC: J05AE04
Use: antiviral, HIV-protease inhibitor

RN: 159989-65-8 MF: C$_{32}$H$_{45}$N$_3$O$_4$S · CH$_4$O$_3$S MW: 663.90
CN: [3S-[2(2S*,3S*),3α,4aβ,8aβ]]-N-(1,1-dimethylethyl)decahydro-2-[2-hydroxy-3-[(3-hydroxy-2-methylbenzoyl)amino]-4-(phenylthio)butyl]-3-isoquinolinecarboxamide monomethanesulfonate (salt)

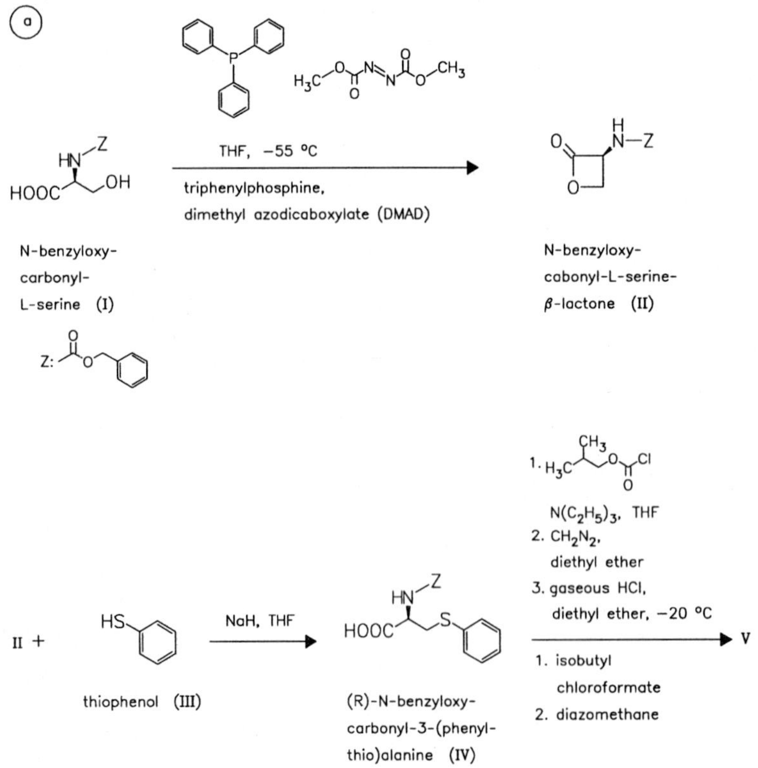

(a)

N-benzyloxy-
carbonyl-
L-serine (I)

THF, −55 °C
triphenylphosphine,
dimethyl azodicaboxylate (DMAD)

N-benzyloxy-
cabonyl-L-serine-
β-lactone (II)

Z:

II + thiophenol (III) —NaH, THF→ (R)-N-benzyloxy-
carbonyl-3-(phenyl-
thio)alanine (IV)

1. H$_3$C—O—Cl (CH$_3$)
   N(C$_2$H$_5$)$_3$, THF
2. CH$_2$N$_2$,
   diethyl ether
3. gaseous HCl,
   diethyl ether, −20 °C
   —→ V
1. isobutyl
   chloroformate
2. diazomethane

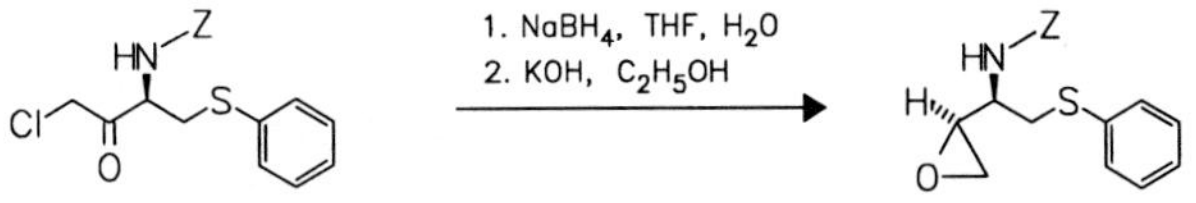

(R)-phenylmethyl
[3-chloro-2-oxo-1-
[(phenylthio)methyl]-
propyl]carbamate (V)

[S-(R*,S*)]-phenyl-
methyl [1-oxiranyl-
2-(phenylthio)ethyl]-
carbamate (VI)

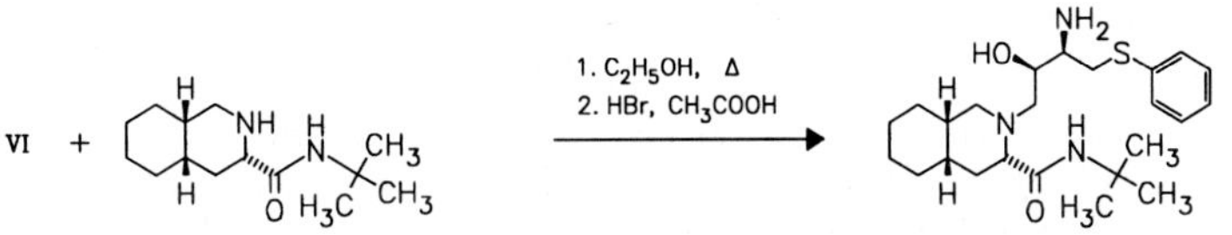

VI +

[3S-(3α,4aβ,8aβ)]-N-(1,1-
dimethylethyl)decahydro-
3-isoquinolinecarboxamide (VII)
(cf. saquinavir synthesis)

[3S-[2(2S*,3S*),3α,4aβ,8aβ]]-2-
[3-amino-2-hydroxy-4-(phenylthio)-
butyl]-N-(1,1-dimethylethyl)deca-
hydro-3-isoquinolinecarboxamide (VIII)

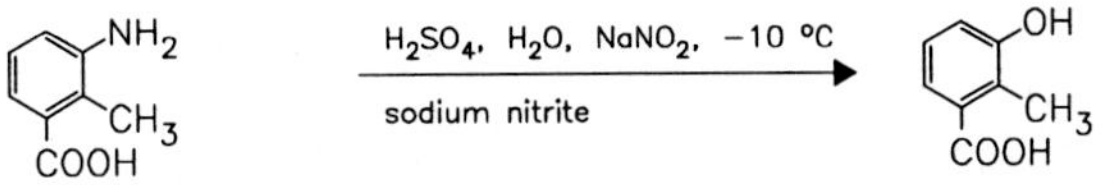

3-amino-2-methyl-
benzoic acid

3-hydroxy-2-methyl-
benzoic acid (IX)

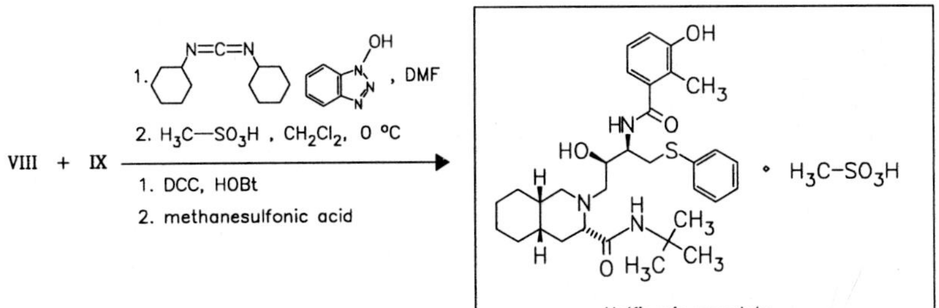

VIII + IX

Nelfinavir mesylate

alternative synthesis of intermediate IX:

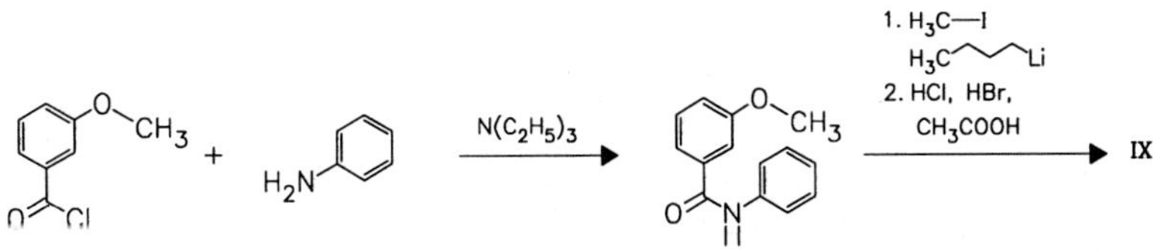

3-methoxy-
benzoyl chloride

aniline

IX

(b)

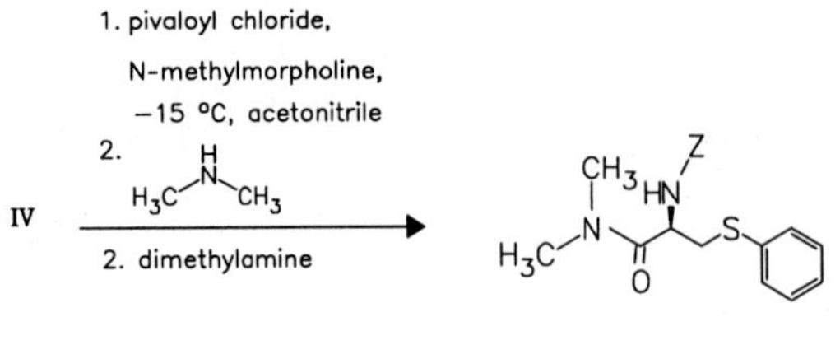

1. pivaloyl chloride,
   N-methylmorpholine,
   −15 °C, acetonitrile
2.

IV

2. dimethylamine

(X)

1. H$_3$C⌒⌒Li , THF, −10 °C
2. NaBH$_4$, CH$_3$OH/THF, 4 °C

X   +   1,3-dithiane

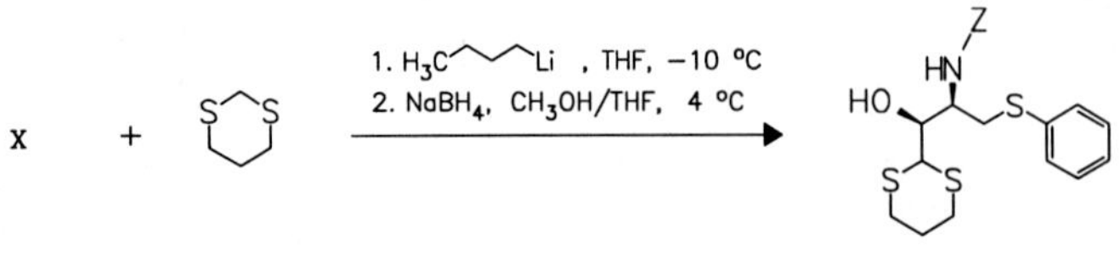

(1S,2R)-2-(benzyloxy-
carbonylamino)-1-(1,3-di-
thian-2-yl)-3-(phenylthio)-
1-propanol (XI)

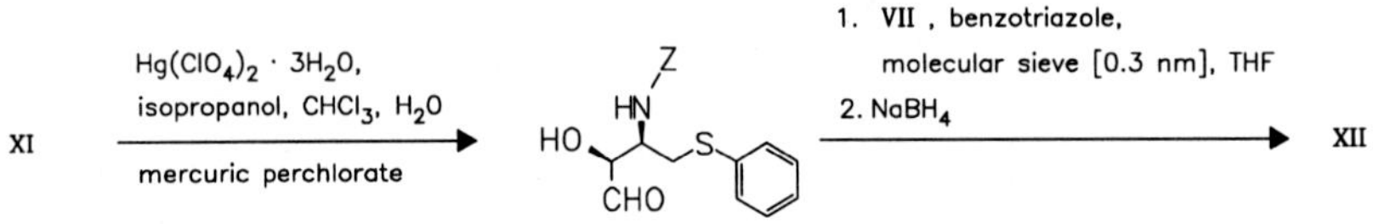

Hg(ClO$_4$)$_2$ · 3H$_2$O,
isopropanol, CHCl$_3$, H$_2$O

XI

mercuric perchlorate

1. VII , benzotriazole,
    molecular sieve [0.3 nm], THF
2. NaBH$_4$ XII

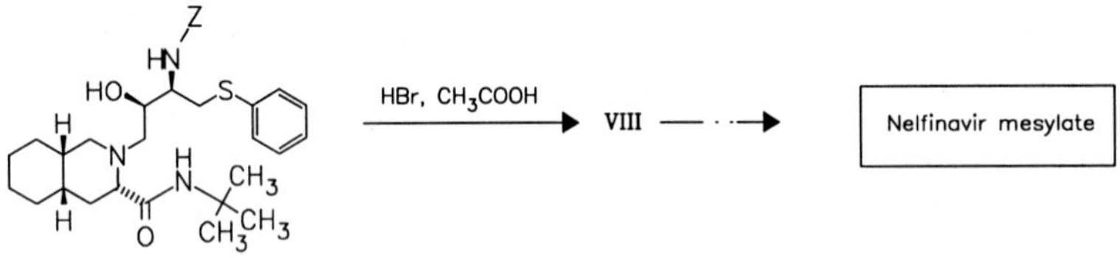

(XII)

HBr, CH$_3$COOH   VIII ---·-▶   Nelfinavir mesylate

(ba)   synthesis of the starting material IV:

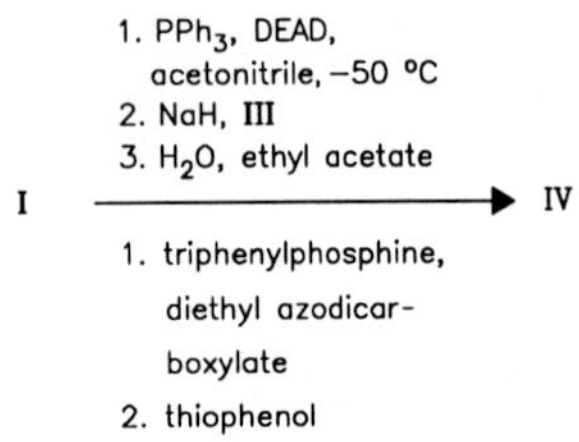

1. PPh$_3$, DEAD,
   acetonitrile, −50 °C
2. NaH, III
3. H$_2$O, ethyl acetate

I   IV

1. triphenylphosphine,
   diethyl azodicar-
   boxylate
2. thiophenol

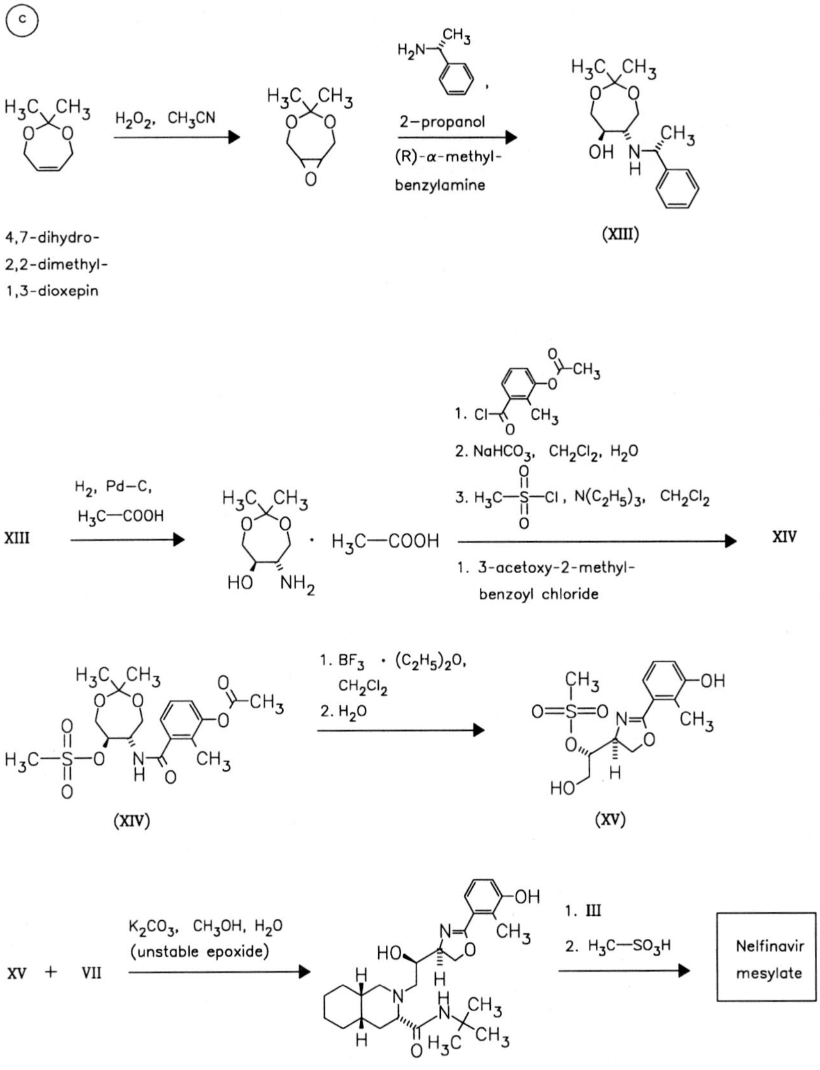

c

4,7-dihydro-
2,2-dimethyl-
1,3-dioxepin

(XIII)

XIII

XIV

(XIV)

(XV)

XV + VII

Nelfinavir
mesylate

Reference(s):

Kaldar, S.W. et al.: J. Med. Chem. (JMCMAR) **40**, 3979-3985 (1997).

WO 9 509 843 (Agouron Pharm.; appl. 7.10.1994; USA-prior. 7.10.1993, 2.2.1994).

WO 9 521 164 (Eli Lilly; prior. 2.2.1994).

Inaba, T. et al.: J. Org. Chem. (JOCEAH) **63**, 7582-7583 (1998).

b   Rieger, D.L.: J. Org. Chem. (JOCEAH) **62**, 8546-8548 (1997).

ba Marzoni, G. et al.: Synth. Commun. (SYNCAV) **25**, 2475 (1995).

c   Inaba, T. et al.: J. Org. Chem. (JOCEAH) **63**, 7582-7583 (1998).

alternative synthesis of VI:

Inaba, T. et al.: J.Org. Chem. (JOCEAH) **65**, 1623-1628 (2000).

Formulation(s):   oral powder 50 mg/g; tabl. 250 mg

Trade Name(s):

D: Viracept (Roche)   GB: Viracept (Roche)   USA: Viracept (Agouron)

Nemonapride

(Emonapride)

ATC: N05AH; N04B
Use: antipsychotic, selective D_2-antagonist

RN: 75272-39-8   MF: $C_{21}H_{26}ClN_3O_2$ MW: 387.91
LD$_{50}$:   24.5 mg/kg (M, i.v.); 604 mg/kg (M, p.o.); >320 mg/kg (M, s.c.);
17 mg/kg (R, i.v.); >367 mg/kg (R, p.o.); >320 mg/kg (R, s.c.)
>200 mg/kg (dog, p.o.)
CN: cis-5-chloro-2-methoxy-4-(methylamino)-N-[2-methyl-1-(phenylmethyl)-3-pyrrolidinyl]benzamide

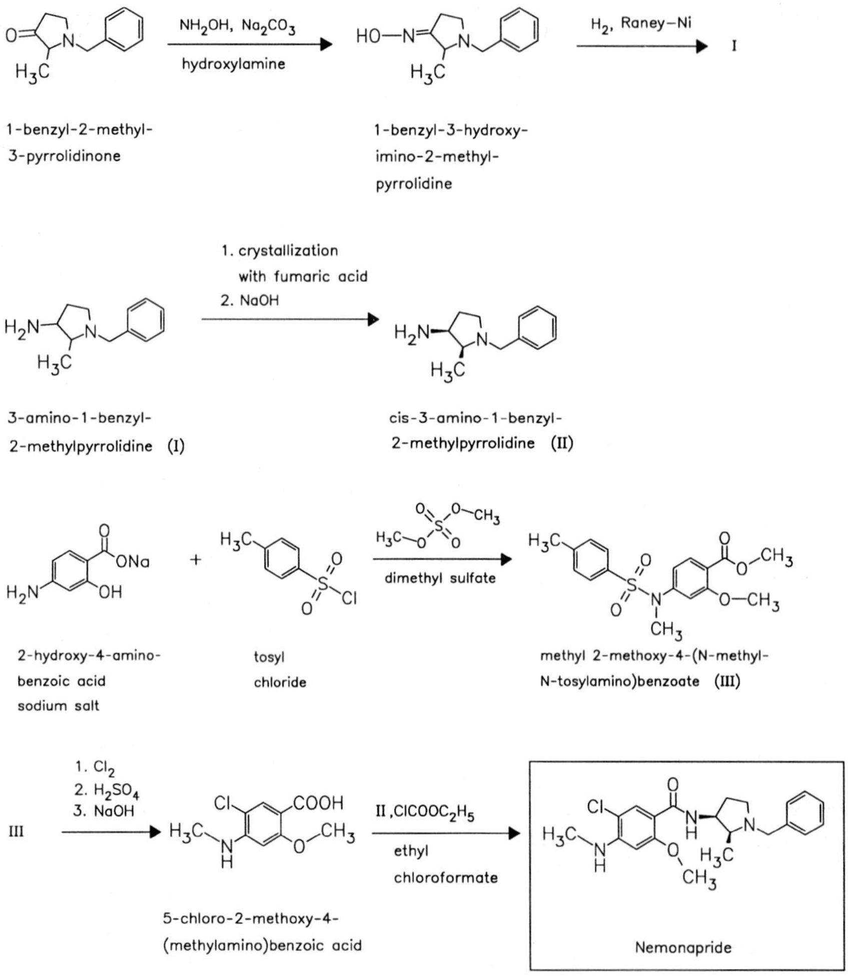

1-benzyl-2-methyl-
3-pyrrolidinone

1-benzyl-3-hydroxy-
imino-2-methyl-
pyrrolidine

3-amino-1-benzyl-
2-methylpyrrolidine   (I)

cis-3-amino-1-benzyl-
2-methylpyrrolidine   (II)

2-hydroxy-4-amino-
benzoic acid
sodium salt

tosyl
chloride

methyl 2-methoxy-4-(N-methyl-
N-tosylamino)benzoate   (III)

5-chloro-2-methoxy-4-
(methylamino)benzoic acid

Nemonapride

Reference(s):

DE 2 855 853 (Yamanouchi; appl. 22.12.1978; J-prior. 1.7.1977).
US 4 210 660 (Yamanouchi; appl. 20.12.1978; J-prior. 1.7.1977).
Iwanami, S. et al.: J. Med. Chem. (JMCMAR) 24, 1224 (1981).
JP 54 014 965 (Yamanouchi Pharm. Co. Ltd; J-prior. 1.7.1977, 30.6.1978).

Formulation(s):   tabl. 3 mg, 10 mg

Trade Name(s):
J: Emirace (Yamanouchi;
      1991)

Neostigmine methylsulfate

ATC: N07AA01; S01EB06
Use: parasympathomimetic, vagotonic,
        cholinesterase inhibitor

RN: 51-60-5   MF: $C_{12}H_{19}N_2O_2 \cdot CH_3O_4S$ MW: 334.39   EINECS: 200-109-5
LD_{50}:   160 µg/kg (M, i.v.); 7500 µg/kg (M, p.o.)
CN: 3-[[(dimethylamino)carbonyl]oxy]-*N,N,N*-trimethylbenzenaminium methyl sulfate

bromide
RN: 114-80-7   MF: $C_{12}H_{19}BrN_2O_2$ MW: 303.20   EINECS: 204-054-8

3-dimethyl-   dimethyl-
aminophenol   carbamoyl
                     chloride

dimethyl
sulfate

Neostigmine
methylsulfate

Reference(s):
US 1 905 990 (Roche; 1933; prior. 1931).

Formulation(s):   amp. 0.5 mg/ml (as methyl sulfate); eye drops 30 mg/ml; ointment 10 mg/g; tabl. 15 mg (as
                     bromide)

Trade Name(s):
D: Neostigmin-Stulln (Pharma   GB: Prostigmin (Roche); wfm   Prostigmina (Roche)
      Stulln)   Robinul Neostigmine   J: Vagostigmin (Shionogi)
      Neostig-Reu (Reusch)   (Anpharm)-comb.   USA: Prostigmin (Roche); wfm
      Syncarpin (Winzer)-comb.   I: Intrastigmina   generics; wfm
F: Prostigmine (Roche)   (Lusofarmaco)

Neticonazole hydrochloride

(SS-717)

Use: antifungal

RN: 130773-02-3   MF: $C_{17}H_{22}N_2OS \cdot HCl$ MW: 338.90
CN: (*E*)-1-[2-(Methylthio)-1-[2-(pentyloxy)phenyl]ethenyl]-1*H*-imidazole monohydrochloride

base
RN: 130726-68-0   MF: $C_{17}H_{22}N_2OS$ MW: 302.44
undefined isomer
RN: 111788-99-9   MF: $C_{17}H_{22}N_2OS$ MW: 302.44

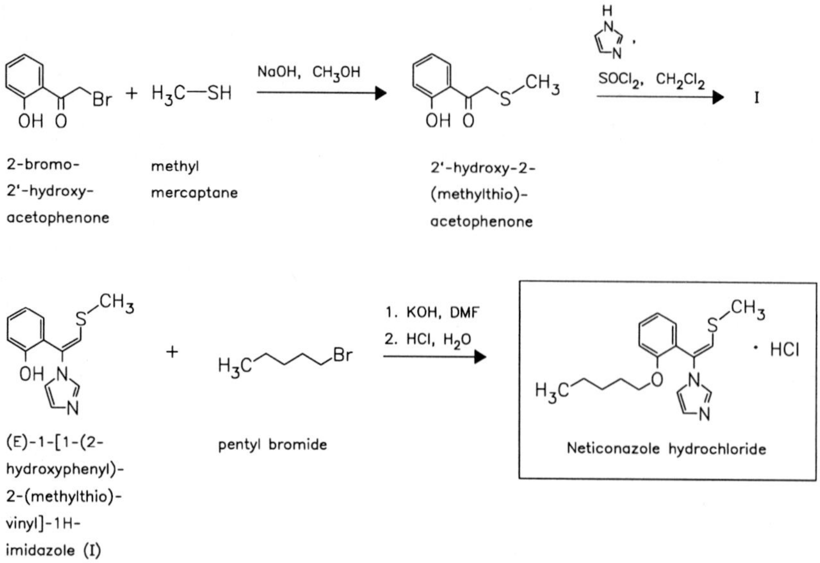
NaOH, CH3OH
SOCl2, CH2Cl2
I
2-bromo-2'-hydroxy-acetophenone
methyl mercaptane
2'-hydroxy-2-(methylthio)-acetophenone
1. KOH, DMF
2. HCl, H2O
(E)-1-[1-(2-hydroxyphenyl)-2-(methylthio)-vinyl]-1H-imidazole (I)
pentyl bromide
Neticonazole hydrochloride

Reference(s):

Ogawa, M. et al.: Chem. Pharm. Bull. (CPBTAL) **39** (9), 2301 (1991).
EP 227 011 (SS Pharm.; appl. 16.12.1986; J-prior. 23.12.1983).

Formulation(s): cream 1%, sol. 1% (as hydrochloride)

Trade Name(s):

J: Atolant (Green Cross; SS Pharm.)

Netilmicin

ATC: J01GB07; S01AA23
Use: antibiotic

RN: 56391-56-1 MF: $C_{21}H_{41}N_5O_7$ MW: 475.59 EINECS: 260-146-8
LD_{50}: 40 mg/kg (M, i.v.);
25.2 mg/kg (R, i.v.)
CN: *O*-3-deoxy-4-*C*-methyl-3-(methylamino)-β-L-arabinopyranosyl-(1→6)-*O*-[2,6-diamino-2,3,4,6-tetradeoxy-α-D-*glycero*-hex-4-enopyranosyl-(1→4)]-2-deoxy-N^1-ethyl-D-streptamine

sulfate (2:5)

RN: 56391-57-2 MF: $C_{21}H_{41}N_5O_7 \cdot 5/2H_2SO_4$ MW: 1441.56 EINECS: 260-147-3
LD_{50}: 22 mg/kg (M, i.v.);
40.7 mg/kg (R, i.v.); >10 g/kg (R, p.o.)

(a)

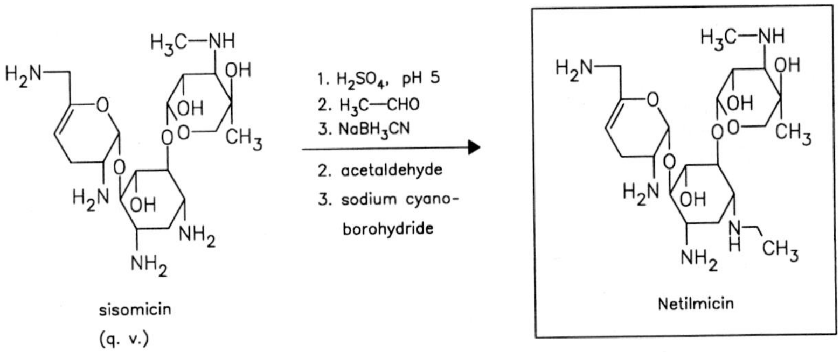
H₂N
H₃C—NH
OH
O
OH
O
O
CH₃
O
H₂N
OH
NH₂
NH₂
sisomicin
(q. v.)
1. H₂SO₄, pH 5
2. H₃C—CHO
3. NaBH₃CN
2. acetaldehyde
3. sodium cyano-
borohydride
Netilmicin

(b) from 1-N-ethyl-α-deoxy-D-streptamin by fermentation with Micromonospora inyoensis 1550F-1G

Reference(s):

DOS 2 462 485 (Scherico; appl. 1.8.1974; USA-prior. 6.8.1973, 19.3.1974).
DOS 2 437 160 (Scherico; appl. 1.8.1974; USA-prior. 6.8.1973, 19.3.1974) - (also further methods).
US 4 002 742 (Scherico; 11.1.1977; prior. 19.3.1974).

Formulation(s): amp. 15 mg/1.5 ml, 50 mg /ml, 100 mg/ml, 150 mg/ml, 200 mg/2 ml (as sulfate)

Trade Name(s):

D:	Certomycin (Essex Pharma; 1980)	GB:	Netillin (Schering-Plough; 1981)	J:	Netilyn (Sankyo; 1985) Vectacin (Essex)
F:	Netromicine (Schering-Plough; 1983)	I:	Nettacin (Schering-Plough; 1982) Zetamicin (Menarini; 1982)	USA:	Netromycin (Schering; 1983)

Nevirapine

(BI-RG-587)

ATC: J05AG01
Use: antiviral, anti-AIDS therapeutic, reverse transcriptase inhibitor

RN: 129618-40-2 MF: $C_{15}H_{14}N_4O$ MW: 266.30
CN: 11-cyclopropyl-5,11-dihydro-4-methyl-6*H*-dipyrido[3,2-*b*:2',3'-*e*][1,4]diazepin-6-one

(a)

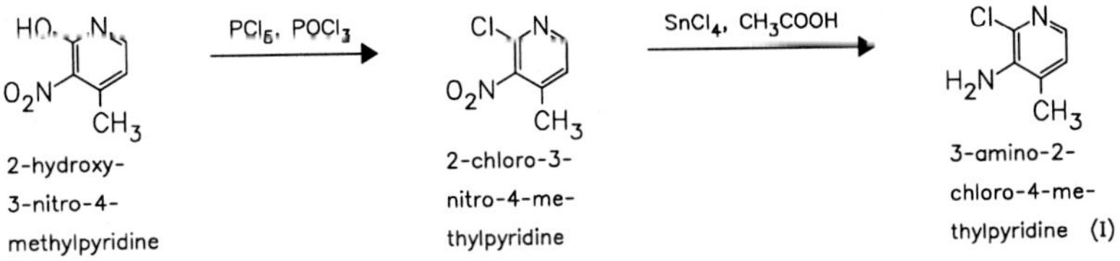
HO
N
O₂N
CH₃
2-hydroxy-
3-nitro-4-
methylpyridine
PCl₅, POCl₃
Cl
N
O₂N
CH₃
2-chloro-3-
nitro-4-me-
thylpyridine
SnCl₄, CH₃COOH
Cl
N
H₂N
CH₃
3-amino-2-
chloro-4-me-
thylpyridine (I)

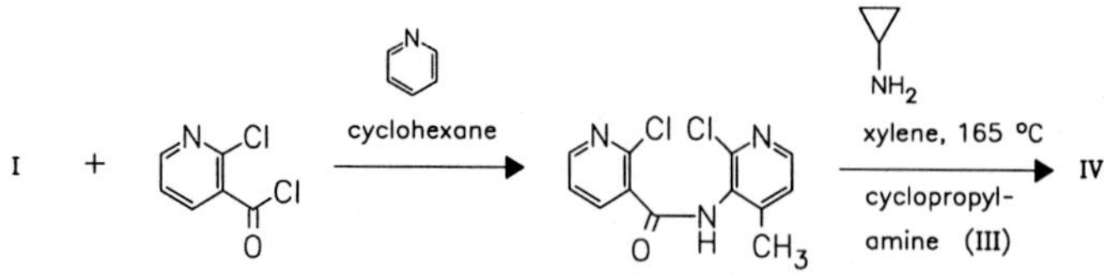

I + 2-chloro-nicotinoyl chloride (II) → cyclohexane → 2-chloro-N-(2-chloro-4-methyl-3-pyridinyl)-3-pyridinecarboxamide → NH₂ / xylene, 165 °C / cyclopropyl-amine (III) → IV

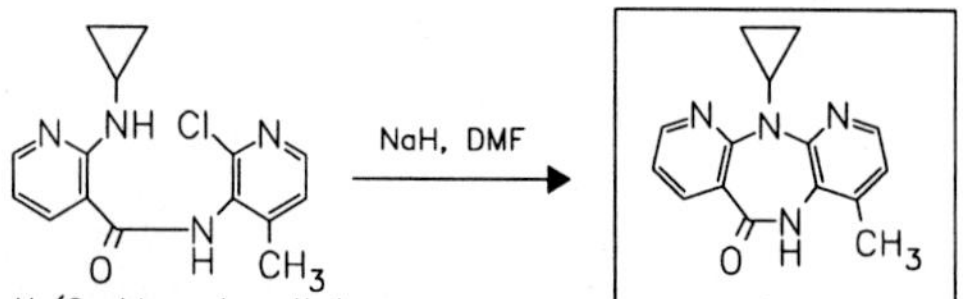

N-(2-chloro-4-methyl-3-pyridyl)-2-cyclopro-pylamino-3-pyridine-carboxamide (IV) → NaH, DMF → Nevirapine

b)

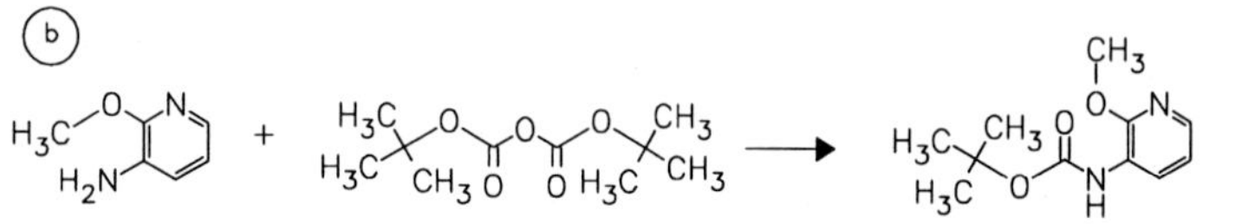

2-methoxy-3-aminopyridine + di-tert-butyl dicarbonate → 3-(tert-butoxy-carbonylamino)-2-methoxy-pyridine (V)

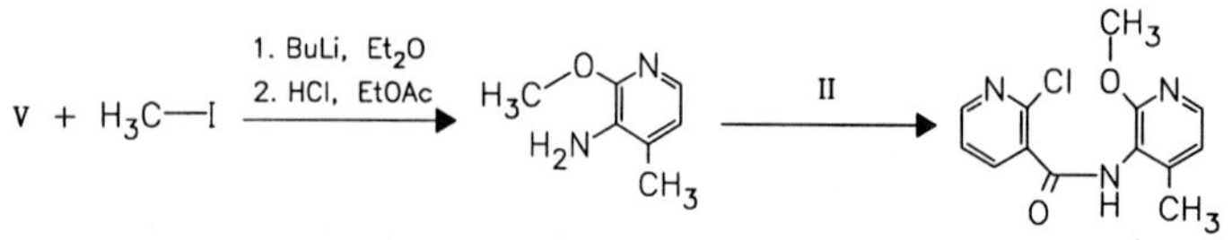

V + H₃C—I → 1. BuLi, Et₂O / 2. HCl, EtOAc → 3-amino-2-methoxy-4-methylpyridine → II → 2-chloro-N-(2-methoxy-4-methyl-3-pyridinyl)-3-pyridinecarbox-amide (VI)

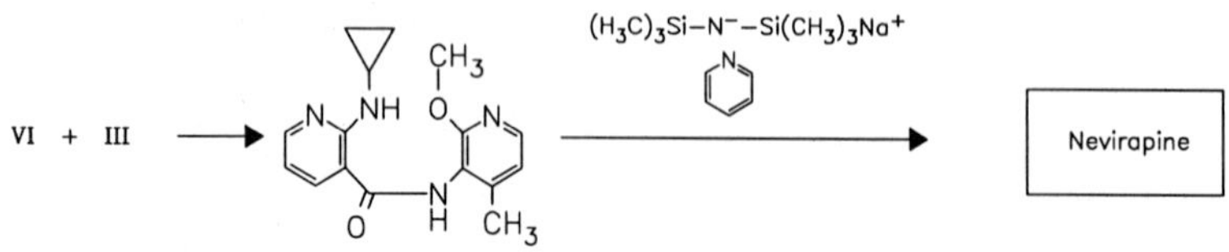

VI + III → (H₃C)₃Si—N⁻—Si(CH₃)₃Na⁺ → Nevirapine

c)

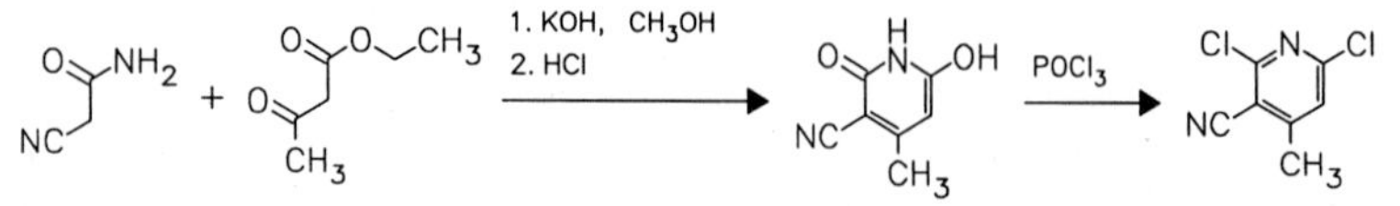

cyano-acetamide + ethyl acetoacetate → 1. KOH, CH₃OH / 2. HCl → POCl₃ → 2,6-dichloro-4-methyl-3-pyridine-carbonitrile (VII)

II, (pyridine),

VII →(H₂SO₄, 150–170°C)→ 2,6-dichloro-4-methyl-3-pyridine-carboxamide →(NaOH, Br₂)→ 3-amino-2,6-dichloro-4-methylpyridine →(cyclohexane)→ VIII

2,6-dichloro-3-(2-chloronicotinoyl-amino)-4-methyl-pyridine (VIII)

III → [intermediate] →(1. NaH 2. H₂, Pd)→ Nevirapine

Reference(s):

review:

Pedersen, O.S.; Pedersen, E.B.: Synthesis (SYNTBF) ,(4), 479 (2000).

a EP 429 987 (Boehringer Ing.; USA-prior. 19.10.1990).

b US 5 532 358 (Boehringer Ing.; 2.7.1996; USA-prior. 12.10.1994).

c EP 482 481 (Boehringer Ing.; appl. 16.10.1991; USA-prior. 19.10.1990).

process for IV avoiding excess of cyclopropylamine:
DE 4 403 311 (Boehringer Ing.; D-prior. 3.2.1994).

combination with HIV-protease inhibitors:
WO 9 600 068 (Merck & Co.; appl. 23.6.1995; USA-prior. 27.6.1994).

osmotic dosage forms:
US 5 358 721 (Alza Corp.; appl. 4.12.1992; USA-prior. 4.12.1994).

Formulation(s):   tabl. 200 mg

Trade Name(s):

D:	Viramune (Boehringer Ingelh.; 1998)	GB: Viramune (Boehringer Ingelh.; 1998) USA: Viramune (Roxane; 1998)

Nialamide

ATC: N06AF02
Use: psychoanaleptic, antidepressant

RN: 51-12-7   MF: C₁₆H₁₈N₄O₂   MW: 298.35   EINECS: 200-079-3
LD₅₀: 120 mg/kg (M, i.v.); 590 mg/kg (M, p.o.);
    1700 mg/kg (R, p.o.)
CN: 4-pyridinecarboxylic acid 2-[3-oxo-3-[(phenylmethyl)amino]propyl]hydrazide

isoniazid (q. v.)   +   methyl acrylate   →   (I)

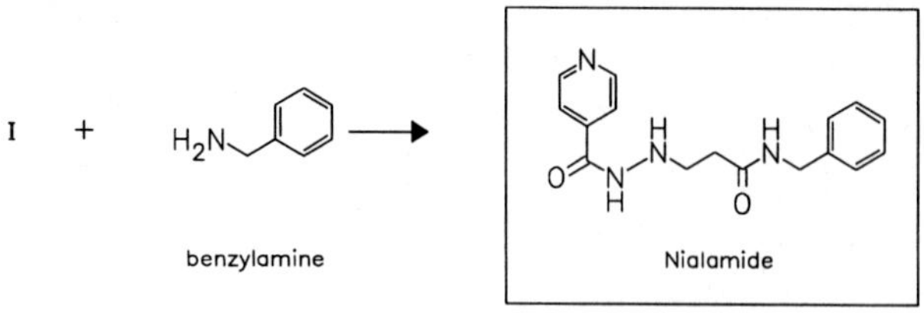
I +
H2N
benzylamine
Nialamide

Reference(s):
US 2 894 972 (Pfizer; 14.7.1959; prior. 31.12.1958).
US 3 040 061 (Pfizer; 19.6.1962; prior. 27.4.1959, 1.6.1961).

Formulation(s): cps. 25 mg, 100 mg

Trade Name(s):
F: Niamide (Pfizer); wfm GB: Niamid (Pfizer); wfm J: Niamid (Taito Pfizer)

Niaprazine

ATC: N05CM16
Use: antiallergic, bronchodilator, sedative

RN: 27367-90-4 MF: $C_{20}H_{25}FN_4O$ MW: 356.45 EINECS: 248-431-5
LD_{50}: 145 mg/kg (M, i.v.); 890 mg/kg (M, p.o.)
CN: *N*-[3-[4-(4-fluorophenyl)-1-piperazinyl]-1-methylpropyl]-3-pyridinecarboxamide

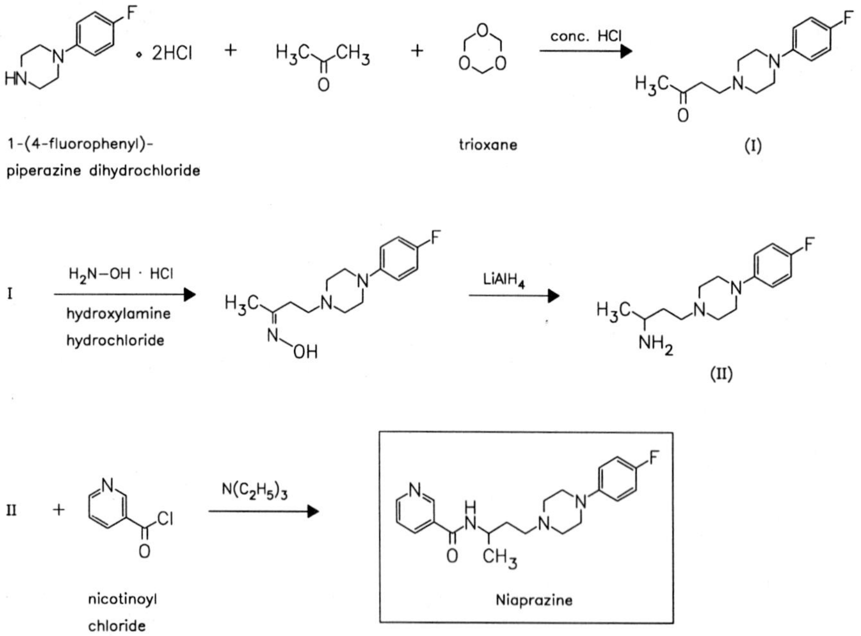
• 2HCl
+
+
conc. HCl
1-(4-fluorophenyl)-
piperazine dihydrochloride
trioxane
(I)
I
H2N–OH · HCl
hydroxylamine
hydrochloride
LiAlH4
(II)
II +
N(C2H5)3
nicotinoyl
chloride
Niaprazine

Reference(s):
DOS 1 957 371 (Mauvernay; appl. 14.11.1969; F-prior. 14.11.1968).
US 3 712 893 (Mauvernay; 23.1.1973; F-prior. 14.11.1968).

Formulation(s): syrup 0.3 g/100 ml

Trade Name(s):
F: Nopron (Synthélabo)   I: Nopron (Sanofi Winthrop)

Nicardipine

ATC: C08CA04
Use: calcium antagonist

RN: 55985-32-5   MF: $C_{26}H_{29}N_3O_6$ MW: 479.53   EINECS: 259-932-3
LD_{50}:   9.7 mg/kg (M, i.v.); 480 mg/kg (M, p.o.);
320 mg/kg (R, p.o.)
CN: 1,4-dihydro-2,6-dimethyl-4-(3-nitrophenyl)-3,5-pyridinedicarboxylic acid methyl 2-[methyl(phenylmethyl)amino]ethyl ester

monohydrochloride
RN: 54527-84-3   MF: $C_{26}H_{29}N_3O_6 \cdot HCl$ MW: 515.99   EINECS: 259-198-4
LD_{50}:   19.9 mg/kg (M, i.v.); 322 mg/kg (M, p.o.);
15.5 mg/kg (R, i.v.); 184 mg/kg (R, p.o.);
5 mg/kg (dog, i.v.)

methyl 3-aminocrotonate

3-nitrobenzaldehyde

2-(methylbenzylamino)-ethyl acetoacetate

Nicardipine

Reference(s):
US 3 985 758 (Yamanouchi; 12.10.1976; J-prior. 20.2.1973).
DOS 2 407 115 (Yamanouchi; appl. 15.2.1974; J-prior. 20.2.1973, 3.3.1973, 20.4.1973, 11.5.1973, 17.5.1973, 24.7.1973, 29.11.1973).
Iwanami, M. et al.: Chem. Pharm. Bull. (CPBTAL) **27**, 1426 (1979).
(alternative syntheses are described).

synthesis of enantiomers:
Shibanuma, T. et al.: Chem. Pharm. Bull. (CPBTAL) **28**, 2809 (1980).

Formulation(s):   cps. 20 mg, 30 mg; s. r. cps. 30 mg, 45 mg, 60 mg (as hydrochloride)

Trade Name(s):
D: Antagonil (Novartis Pharma)
F: Loxen (Novartis; 1986)
GB: Cardene (Yamanouchi; 1986)
I: Bionicard (Bioindustria)
     Cardioten (OFF)
     Cardip (Francia Farm.)
Cardipinen (Farmaceutica Pr.)
Lisanirc (Lisapharma)
Neucor (CT)
Nicapress (Benedetti)
Nicardal (Italfarmaco)
Nicarpin (Sancarlo)
Nimicor (Formenti)
Niven (Pulitzer)
Perdipina (Novartis Farma)
Ranvil (Gentili)
Vasodin (Teofarma)
Vasonorm (NCSN)
J: Nicodel (Mitsui; 1981)
     Perdipine (Yamanouchi; 1981)

USA: Cardene (Roche; Wyeth-
      Ayerst)

Nicergoline

ATC: C04AE02
Use: vasodilator

RN: 27848-84-6   MF: $C_{24}H_{26}BrN_3O_3$ MW: 484.39   EINECS: 248-694-6
LD$_{50}$: 46 mg/kg (M, i.v.); 633 mg/kg (M, p.o.);
      42 mg/kg (R, i.v.); 1193 mg/kg (R, p.o.);
      20 mg/kg (dog, i.v.); 790 mg/kg (dog, p.o.)
CN: (8β)-10-methoxy-1,6-dimethylergoline-8-methanol 5-bromo-3-pyridinecarboxylate (ester)

tartrate
RN: 32222-75-6   MF: $C_{24}H_{26}BrN_3O_3 \cdot xC_4H_6O_6$ MW: unspecified   EINECS: 250-964-3

methyl lysergate

methyl 10-O-
methyl-lumilysergate

lumilysergol
10-methyl ether (I)

5-bromonico-
tinoyl chloride

lumilysergol 10-methyl
ether 8-O-(5-bromo-
nicotinate) (II)

II + H_3C—I   KNH₂ potassium amide

methyl
iodide

Nicergoline

lysergol
[by extraction from
Kaladana seeds
(Calonyction-Ipomoea
(Choisy) Hallier f.
nova species)]

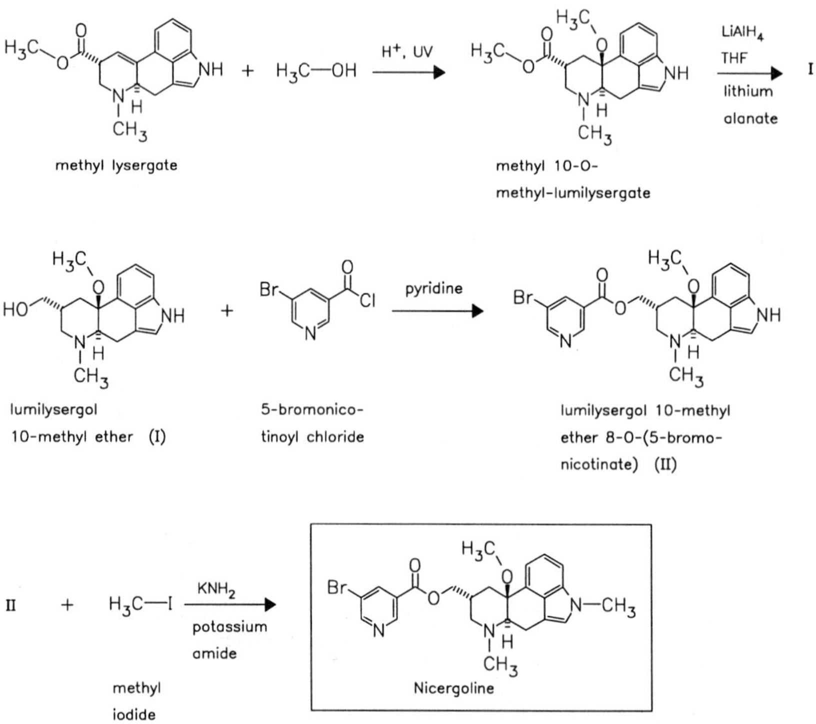

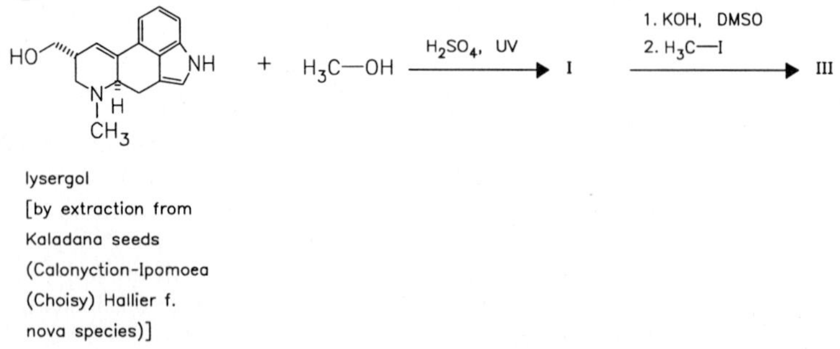

1-methyl-10α-meth-
oxylumilysergol   (III)

5-bromonicotinic
acid

Reference(s):
US 3 879 554 (Soc. Farmaceutici Italia; 22.4.1975; I-prior. 20.3.1970).
a   US 3 228 943 (Soc. Farmaceutici Italia; 11.1.1966; I-prior. 11.6.1962).
   DOS 2 022 926 (Soc. Farmaceutici Italia; appl. 11.5.1970; I-prior. 13.5.1969).
   DOS 2 112 273 (Soc. Farmaceutici Italia; appl. 15.3.1971; I-prior. 20.3.1970).
   Arcari, G. et al.: Experientia (EXPEAM) **28**, 819 (1972).
   Bernardi, L.: Arzneim.-Forsch. (ARZNAD) **29** (II), 1204 (1979).
   alternative method for esterification with 5-bromonicotinic acid *(imidazolide method):*
   DOS 2 752 533 (LEK; appl. 24.11.1977; YU-prior. 22.12.1976).
   GB 1 557 506 (LEK; appl. 6.12.1977; YU-prior. 22.12.1976).
b   a)   *isolation of* lysergol *from kaladana seeds:*
   Abou-Chaar, C.I.; Digenis, G.A.: Nature (London) (NATUAS) **212**, 618 (1966).
   DOS 2 240 266 (Simes; appl. 16.8.1972; B-prior. 17.8.1971, 14.1.1972).
   DOS 2 834 703 (Simes; appl. 8.8.1978; CH-prior. 12.8.1977).
b   b)   *method:*
   GB 2 018 245 (E. Corvi Mora; appl. 4.4.1979; I-prior. 5.4.1978).

Formulation(s):   cps. 5 mg, 10 mg, 15 mg, 30 mg; f. c. tabl. 5 mg, 10 mg, 20 mg, 30 mg; drg. 5 mg, 10 mg;
                      tabl. 10 mg, 20 mg; vial 4 mg/4 ml (as tartrate)

Trade Name(s):

D:	Circo-Maren (Krewel Meuselbach)	F:	Sermion (Specia; 1975)		Sermion (Pharmacia & Upjohn)
	ergobel (Hormosan)	I:	Cebran (Garant)		
	Memoq (Parke Davis)		Ergolin (Boniscontro & Gazzone)	J:	Sermion (Farmitalia-Tanabe)
	Nicerium (Neuro Hexal)		Nicer (Ist. Chim. Inter.)		
	Sermion (Pharmacia & Upjohn; 1978)		Sermidrina (Farmitalia)-comb.		

Niceritrol

ATC: C10AD01
Use: cholesterol depressant,
       antiarteriosclerotic

RN: 5868-05-3   MF: $C_{29}H_{24}N_4O_8$ MW: 556.53   EINECS: 227-519-7
CN: 3-pyridinecarboxylic acid 2,2-bis[[(3-pyridinylcarbonyl)oxy]methyl]-1,3-propanediyl ester

pentaerythritol   nicotinoyl
                         chloride

Niceritrol

Reference(s):
GB 1 022 880 (Bofors; appl. 18.11.1964; S-prior. 13.10.1964).

Formulation(s):   tabl. 500 mg

Trade Name(s):
I: Perycit (Tosi); wfm   J: Perycit (Sanwa Kagaku)

Niclosamide

ATC: P02DA01
Use: anthelmintic

RN: 50-65-7   MF: $C_{13}H_8Cl_2N_2O_4$ MW: 327.12   EINECS: 200-056-8
LD_{50}: 7500 µg/kg (M, i.v.); 1 g/kg (M, p.o.);
       2500 mg/kg (R, p.o.)
CN: 5-chloro-*N*-(2-chloro-4-nitrophenyl)-2-hydroxybenzamide

5-chlorosali-   2-chloro-4-   Niclosamide
cylic acid   nitroaniline

Reference(s):
US 3 079 297 (Bayer; 26.2.1963; prior. 26.9.1956, 21.10.1959; 31.5.1960).

new formulations:
GB 1 527 638 (Bayer; appl. 14.12.1976; D-prior. 20.12.1975).

Formulation(s):   tabl. 500 mg

Trade Name(s):
D: Yomesan (Bayer Vital)   GB: Yomesan (Bayer)   USA: Niclocide (Miles Pharm.);
F: Trédémine (Roger Bellon)   I: Yomesan (Bayer Italia)   wfm

Nicoclonate

ATC: C10AD
Use: antiarteriosclerotic, hyperlipidemic

RN: 10571-59-2   MF: $C_{16}H_{16}ClNO_2$ MW: 289.76   EINECS: 234-156-8
LD_{50}: 2.27 g/kg (M, i.p.)
CN: 3-pyridinecarboxylic acid 1-(4-chlorophenyl)-2-methylpropyl ester

4-chloro-   isopropyl-   1-(4-chlorophenyl)-   Nicoclonate
benzaldehyde   magnesium   2-methyl-1-propanol
                 bromide

Reference(s):
FR-M 3 454 (Établ. Kuhlmann; appl. 10.4.1964).
US 3 367 939 (Établ. Kuhlmann; 6.2.1968; F-prior. 10.4.1964).

Formulation(s):   cps. 250 mg

Trade Name(s):
F: Lipidium-Sedaph   I: Lipidium (Rorer)
     (Sedaph)-comb.; wfm

Nicofuranose
(Tetranicotinoylfructose)

ATC: C10AD03
Use: vasodilator

RN: 15351-13-0   MF: $C_{30}H_{24}N_4O_{10}$ MW: 600.54   EINECS: 239-385-7
CN: β-D-fructofuranose 1,3,4,6-tetra-3-pyridinecarboxylate

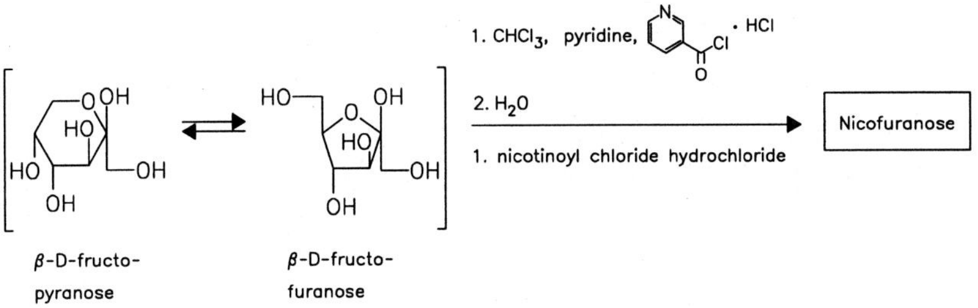

β-D-fructo-
pyranose

β-D-fructo-
furanose

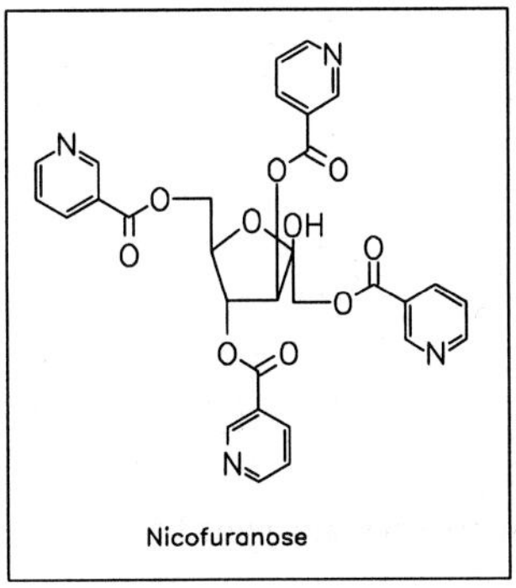

1. CHCl₃, pyridine,

2. H₂O

1. nicotinoyl chloride hydrochloride

Nicofuranose

Nicofuranose

Reference(s):
CH 366 523 (Eprova; appl. 1958).

Formulation(s):   drg. 250 mg

Trade Name(s):
D: Bradilan (Mundipharma);   GB: Bradilan (Napp); wfm
     wfm

Nicorandil

ATC: C01DX16
Use: coronary vasodilator

RN: 65141-46-0   MF: $C_8H_{10}N_2O_2$ MW: 166.18
LD_{50}: 626 mg/kg (M, p.o.);
       502 mg/kg (R, i.v.); 1220 mg/kg (R, p.o.);
       62.5 mg/kg (dog, p.o.)
CN: N-[2-(nitrooxy)ethyl]-3-pyridinecarboxamide

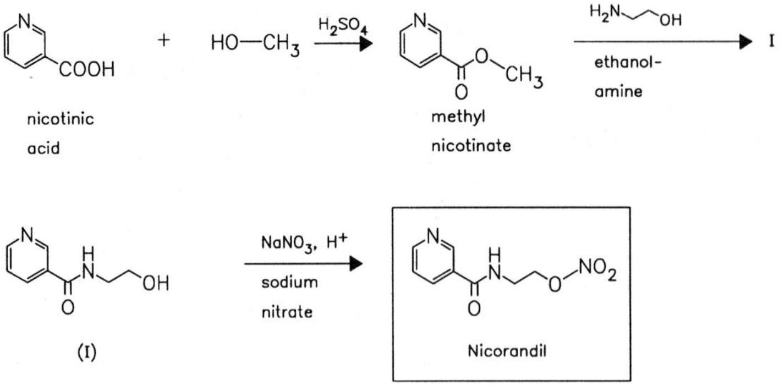

nicotinic acid

methyl nicotinate

(I)

Nicorandil

Reference(s):
Masayoshi, S.: Yakugaku Zasshi (YKKZAJ) **80**, 1706 (1960).
DE 2 714 713 (Chugai; prior. 1.4.1977).

medical use:
US 4 200 640 (Chugai; 29.4.1980; J-prior. 2.4.1976).
JP-appl. 58/85 819 (Chugai; appl. 17.11.1981).

transdermal application system:
JP-appl. 59/10 513 (Nitto; appl. 12.7.1982).

Formulation(s):   tabl. 2.5 mg, 5 mg, 10 mg, 20 mg

Trade Name(s):
F: Adancor (Lipha Santé)   GB: Ikorel (Rhône-Poulenc   J: Perisalol (Mitsubishi;
      Ikorel (Bellon)   Rorer)   1984)
                                                                             Sigmart (Chugai; 1984)

Nicotafuryl

ATC: M01
Use: antirheumatic (extern), rubefacient

(Thurfyl nicotinate)

RN: 70-19-9   MF: $C_{11}H_{13}NO_3$ MW: 207.23   EINECS: 200-727-5
CN: 3-pyridinecarboxylic acid (tetrahydro-2-furanyl)methyl ester

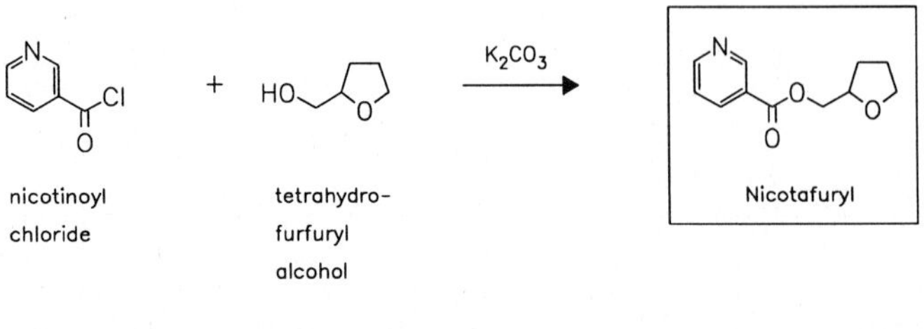

nicotinoyl chloride

tetrahydro-furfuryl alcohol

Nicotafuryl

Reference(s):
DE 839 036 (Ciba; appl. 1948; CH-prior. 1947).
US 2 485 152 (Ciba; 1949; CH-prior. 1947).

Formulation(s):   tabl. 5 mg, 10 mg

Trade Name(s):
F: Trafuril (Ciba); wfm   I: Balsamo Di Trasalen   Trafuril (Ciba); wfm
                                             (Ciba)-comb.; wfm

---

Nicotinamide
(Niacinamide)

ATC: A11HA01
Use: vitamin B_3, antipellagra agent

RN: 98-92-0   MF: $C_6H_6N_2O$ MW: 122.13   EINECS: 202-713-4
LD_{50}:   1.68 g/kg (R, s.c.)
CN: 3-pyridinecarboxamide

nicotinic
acid

NH_3, >200 °C

Nicotinamide

nicotinonitrile

H_2O, NaOH or $CaCO_3$

Nicotinamide

Reference(s):
a   US 2 280 040 (SMA Corp.; 1942; appl. 1939).
       US 2 314 843 (American Cyanamid; 1943; appl. 1941).
       US 2 993 051 (Cowles Chem. Comp.; 18.7.1961; appl. 26.2.1958).
b   US 2 904 552 (Distillers; 15.9.1959; appl. 21.7.1958).
       DAS 2 539 435 (Showa Denko; appl. 4.9.1975; J-prior. 11.9.1974).

Formulation(s):   amp. 100 mg; tabl. 200 mg

Trade Name(s):
D: Nicobion (Merck)   I: Eparolo (Bonomelli)-comb.   Vitabil composto (IBP)-
      numerous combination   Farmobion Pp   comb.
      preparations   (Farmochimica Ital.)   Vit. PP (Angelini)
F: Nicobion 500 (Astra)   Ietepar (Rottapharm)-   generic and polyvitaminous
      further combination   comb.   combination preparations
      preparations   Nicospasmolo   J: numerous generic and
GB: Papulex (Euroderma)   (Italfarmaco)-comb.   combination preparations
      generic and combination   Nicotinamide (Dynacren)   USA: Mega-B (Arco)-comb.
      preparations   Nicotinamide (IDI)

Nicotinic acid

(Acide nicotinique; Acidum nicotinicum; Niacin)

ATC: A11HA01
Use: vasodilator (peripheral), antipellagra effect, antihyperlipidemic

RN: 59-67-6   MF: $C_6H_5NO_2$ MW: 123.11   EINECS: 200-441-0
LD_{50}:   5 g/kg (M, i.v.); 3720 mg/kg (M, p.o.);
        7 g/kg (R, p.o.)
CN: 3-pyridinecarboxylic acid

magnesium salt
RN: 7069-06-9   MF: $C_{12}H_8MgN_2O_4$ MW: 268.51   EINECS: 230-361-1
LD_{50}:   9 g/kg (M, p.o.)
sodium salt
RN: 54-86-4   MF: $C_6H_4NNaO_2$ MW: 145.09   EINECS: 200-215-1
LD_{50}:   2900 mg/kg (M, i.v.)

paraldehyde → 5-ethyl-2-methyl-pyridine → Nicotinic acid

NH₃, 220–280 °C, 100 bar ; HNO₃

Reference(s):
DOS 2 046 556 (Lonza; appl. 22.9.1970; CH-prior. 24.9.1969).
US 2 905 688 (Abbott; 1959; appl. 1954).

continuous process:
DAS 2 256 508 (Nippon Soda; appl. 17.11.1972; J-prior. 17.11.1971).

5-ethyl-2-methylpyridine:
Nenz, A.; Pieroni, M.: Hydrocarbon Process. (HYPRAX) **47**, (11), 139 (1968).

Formulation(s):   s. r. tabl. 250 mg, 500 mg, 750 mg; tabl. 500 mg

Trade Name(s):
D: Antisklerosin
      (Medopharm)-comb.
      Merz Spezial Dragees
      (Merz & Co.)-comb.
      Niconacid (Wander); wfm
F: Algipan (Darcy)-comb.
      Sedartryl (Oberlin)-comb.

      numerous combination
      preparations
GB: Equivert (Pfizer)-comb.;
      wfm
      Pernivit (Duncan,
      Flockhart)-comb.; wfm
      Tonivitan (Medo)-comb.;
      wfm

I: Enzimina (Menarini); wfm
      Enzycol (Ausonia); wfm
      Otophon (SIT); wfm
J: generic
USA: Niacor (Upsher-Smith)
      Nicolar (Rhône-Poulenc
      Rorer)

Nicotinic acid benzyl ester

(Benzyl nicotinate)

ATC: C05
Use: rubefacient (for external use)

RN: 94-44-0   MF: $C_{13}H_{11}NO_2$ MW: 213.24   EINECS: 202-332-3
LD_{50}:   100 mg/kg (M, i.v.); 2188 mg/kg (M, p.o.)
CN: 3-pyridinecarboxylic acid phenylmethyl ester

nicotinic acid (q. v.) + benzyl alcohol → toluene, 165–170 °C → Nicotinic acid benzyl ester

Reference(s):
GB 817 103 (Nordmark-Werke; appl. 1956; D-prior. 1955).

Formulation(s):   gel 300 mg/100 g; ointment 40 mg/100 g

Trade Name(s):
D: Lomazell (Lomapharm)-
     comb.
     Pernionin (Krewel
     Meuselbach)

     Pykaryl (Rodleben)
     further combination
     preparations
F: Bayoline (Bayer)-comb.

     Lumbalgine (RPR Cooper)

Nicotinyl alcohol
(Pyridylcarbinol; Pyridylmethanol)

ATC: C04AC02; C10AD05
Use: vasodilator (peripheral)

RN: 100-55-0   MF: C_6H_7NO MW: 109.13   EINECS: 202-864-6
LD_{50}:   1 g/kg (M, i.v.)
CN: 3-pyridinemethanol

tartrate (1:1)
RN: 6164-87-0   MF: $C_6H_7NO \cdot C_4H_6O_6$ MW: 259.21   EINECS: 228-199-1
LD_{50}:   1600 mg/kg (M, i.v.); 3300 mg/kg (M, p.o.);
      1540 mg/kg (R, i.v.); 5790 mg/kg (R, p.o.)

nicotino-nitrile → H_2, Pd–C → 3-(aminomethyl)-pyridine → $NaNO_2$ → Nicotinyl alcohol

Reference(s):
US 2 615 896 (Hoffmann-La Roche; 1952; prior. 1950).
US 2 547 048 (Hoffmann-La Roche; 1951; prior. 1946).

alternative syntheses:
US 2 509 171 (Ciba; 1950, CH-prior. 1946).
US 2 520 037 (Roche; 1950; GB-prior. 1947).

Formulation(s):   amp. 100 mg/2 ml, 500 mg/10 ml; drg. 150 mg; tabl. 25 mg, 100 mg, 150 mg, 200 mg (as
      tartrate)

Trade Name(s):
D: Radecol (ASTA Medica
     AWD)
F: Ronicol (Roche); wfm
     Ronicol-retard (Roche);
     wfm

GB: Ronicol (Tillomed)
I: Ronicol retard (Roche);
     wfm
     Selcarbinol (Sella); wfm

J: Ronicol Timespan (Nippon
     Roche-Shionogi)
USA: Roniacol (Roche); wfm

Nifedipine

ATC: C08CA05
Use: coronary vasodilator, calcium antagonist

RN: 21829-25-4   MF: $C_{17}H_{18}N_2O_6$ MW: 346.34   EINECS: 244-598-3
CN: 1,4-dihydro-2,6-dimethyl-4-(2-nitrophenyl)-3,5-pyridinedicarboxylic acid dimethyl ester

methyl
acetoacetate

2-nitro-
benzaldehyde

Nifedipine

Reference(s):
US 3 485 847 (Bayer; 23.12.1969; D-prior. 20.3.1967).
US 3 488 359 (Bayer; 13.4.1971; D-prior. 20.3.1967).
US 3 644 627 (Bayer; 22.2.1972; D-prior. 20.3.1967).
GB 1 173 862 (Bayer; appl. 20.3.1968; D-prior. 20.3.1967).

formulation for perlingual application:
US 3 784 684 (Bayer; 8.1.1974; D-prior. 24.8.1971, 29.2.1972).
DOS 2 209 526 (Bayer; appl. 29.2.1972).
DE 1 670 827 (Bayer; appl. 20.3.1967).

improved pharmaceutical formulation:
DOS 2 822 882 (Yamanouchi; appl. 26.5.1978; J-prior. 7.6.1977, 14.7.1977).

Formulation(s):   cps. 5 mg, 10 mg, 20 mg; inf. sol. 5 mg/50 ml; s. r. tabl. 10 mg, 20 mg, 40 mg;
sol. 1 mg/0.4 ml; syringe 0.2 mg; tabl. 10 mg, 20 mg, 30 mg, 60 mg

Trade Name(s):
D: Adalat (Bayer Vital; 1975)
      Aprical (Rentschler)
      Aprical long (Rentschler)-comb.
      Cordicant (Mundipharma)
      Corinfar (ASTA Medica AWD)
      Corotrend (Kytta-Siegfried)
      Dignokonstant (Sankyo)
      Duranifin (durachemie)
      Nifeclair (Hennig)
      Nifedipat (Azuchemie)

      numerous generics
F: Adalate (Bayer-Pharma; 1979)
      Beta-Adalate (Bayer-Pharma)-comb.
      Chronadalate (Bayer-Pharma)
      Tenordate (Zeneca)
GB: Adalat (Bayer; 1977)
      Beta-Adalat (Bayer)-comb.
      numerous generics and combination preparations

I: Adalat (Bayer Italia; 1976)
      Anifed (Farmac. Formenti)
      Citilat (CT)
      Coral (Drug Research)
      Nifedicor (Monsanto)
      Nifedin (Benedetti)
J: Adalat (Bayer; 1976)
USA: Adalat (Bayer; 1986)
      Procardia (Pfizer; 1982)
      Procardia XL (Pfizer)
      generic

Nifenalol
(INPEA)

ATC: C01B; C07A
Use: beta blocking agent, antianginal, antiarrhythmic

RN: 7413-36-7   MF: $C_{11}H_{16}N_2O_3$ MW: 224.26   EINECS: 231-023-6
CN: (±)-α-[[(1-methylethyl)amino]methyl]-4-nitrobenzenemethanol

monohydrochloride
RN: 5704-60-9 MF: $C_{11}H_{16}N_2O_3 \cdot HCl$ MW: 260.72 EINECS: 227-194-1
LD_{50}: 70 mg/kg (M, i.v.)

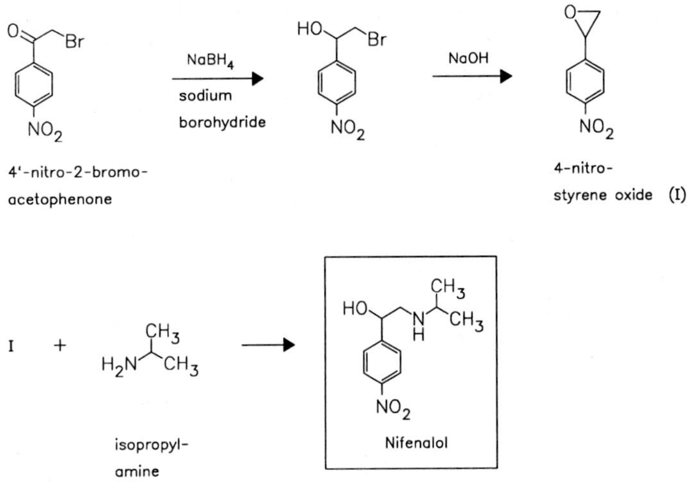

NaBH4
sodium
borohydride
NaOH
4'-nitro-2-bromo-
acetophenone
4-nitro-
styrene oxide (I)
I +
isopropyl-
amine
Nifenalol

Reference(s):
GB 950 682 (Lab. Bioterapico Milanese; appl. 30.6.1961).

Formulation(s): cps. 100 mg (as hydrochloride) in comb.

Trade Name(s):
D: Beta-Intensain (Cassella-Riedel)-comb.; wfm
I: Inpea (Selvi); wfm
Inpea (Selvi/3M); wfm
Nifepam (Selvi/3M)-comb.; wfm

Nifenazone

ATC: N02BB05
Use: antirheumatic, analgesic, antipyretic

RN: 2139-47-1 MF: $C_{17}H_{16}N_4O_2$ MW: 308.34 EINECS: 218-387-1
LD_{50}: 7890 mg/kg (M, p.o.)
CN: *N*-(2,3-dihydro-1,5-dimethyl-3-oxo-2-phenyl-1*H*-pyrazol-4-yl)-3-pyridinecarboxamide

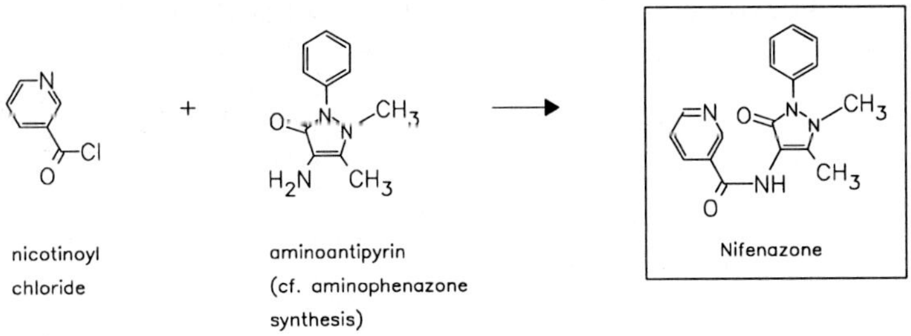

nicotinoyl
chloride
aminoantipyrin
(cf. aminophenazone
synthesis)
Nifenazone

Reference(s):
DE 897 407 (Dr. W. Heid; appl. 1951).

method:
DE 1 046 058 (P. Stoltenberg Chem. Fabr.; appl. 8.2.1957).

Formulation(s):   drg. 250 mg, ointment 5 %; suppos. 200 mg, 400 mg; tabl. 200 mg

Trade Name(s):
D:	Nicopyron (Trommsdorff); wfm	I:	Neopiran (Panthox & Burck)	Nicazolidin (Kissei)
F:	Pro-Dol (Meram)-comb.; wfm		Reumatosil (Saba)	Nicotinoyl (Nissin)
		J:	Bontoram (Sanwa)	Rhyumapirine N (Nichiiko)
GB:	Thylin (Sinclair); wfm		Chillos-N (Kotani)	Sausal (Tokyo Hosei)
			Niapyrine (Iwaki)	Seberin (Mohan)
				Tromrheuman (Maruko)

Niflumic acid
(Nifluril)

ATC: M01AX02; M02AA17
Use: anti-inflammatory, antirheumatic

RN: 4394-00-7   MF: $C_{13}H_9F_3N_2O_2$ MW: 282.22   EINECS: 224-516-2
LD_{50}:   152 mg/kg (M, i.v.); 350 mg/kg (M, p.o.);
          250 mg/kg (R, p.o.)
CN: 2-[[3-(trifluoromethyl)phenyl]amino]-3-pyridinecarboxylic acid

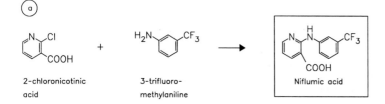

a

2-chloronicotinic acid   +   3-trifluoro-methylaniline   →   Niflumic acid

b

2-amino-nicotinic acid   +   1-bromo-3-trifluoromethyl-benzene $\xrightarrow{K_2CO_3,\ Cu}$ Niflumic acid

Reference(s):
a   DE 1 470 014 (Labs. U.P.S.A.; appl. 10.12.1964; GB-prior. 19.12.1963, 25.3.1964).
      BE 657 266 (Labs. U.P.S.A.; Am. 19.12.1964; GB-prior. 19.12.1963; 25.3.1964).
      US 3 415 834 (U.P.S.A.; 10.12.1968; GB-prior. 19.12.1963, 25.3.1964).
b   US 3 337 570 (Schering Corp.; 22.8.1967; prior. 23.10.1965).

Formulation(s):   cps. 250 mg

Trade Name(s):
D:	Actol (Fournier Pharma)		Nifluril (UPSA)	I:	Niflam (Upsamedica)
F:	Flunir (Oberlin)		Nifluril gel gingival		
	Niflugel (UPSA)		(UPSA)-comb.		

Nifuratel

ATC: G01AX05
Use: chemotherapeutic (trichomonas), antibacterial, antifungal, antiprotozoal

RN: 4936-47-4   MF: $C_{10}H_{11}N_3O_5S$ MW: 285.28   EINECS: 225-576-2
LD$_{50}$:   >4.5 g/kg (M, p.o.)
CN: 5-[(methylthio)methyl]-3-[[(5-nitro-2-furanyl)methylene]amino]-2-oxazolidinone

methyl mercaptan   epichloro-hydrin   1-chloro-3-methyl-thio-2-propanol   (3-methylthio-2-hydroxypropyl)-hydrazine (I)

diethyl carbonate   3-amino-5-(methyl-thiomethyl)-2-oxazolidone (II)

5-nitrofurfural   Nifuratel

Reference(s):
BE 635 608 (Polichimica SAP; appl. 30.7.1963; I-prior. 1.8.1962).
GB 969 126 (Polichimica; appl. 25.10.1962; I-prior. 1.8.1962).

Formulation(s):   drg. 200 mg; ointment 100 mg/g; pessaries 250 mg

Trade Name(s):
D: Inimur (Taurus Pharma)
F: Mycomnes (Fumouze)-comb.
GB: Magmilor (Calmic); wfm
I: Emorril (Poli)-comb.
       Macmiror (Poli)
       Macmiror Complex (Poli)-comb.

Nifuroxazide

ATC: A07AX03
Use: chemotherapeutic, intestinal antiseptic

RN: 965-52-6   MF: $C_{12}H_9N_3O_5$ MW: 275.22   EINECS: 213-521-5
LD$_{50}$:   100 mg/kg (M, i.p.)
CN: 4-hydroxybenzoic acid [(5-nitro-2-furanyl)methylene]hydrazide

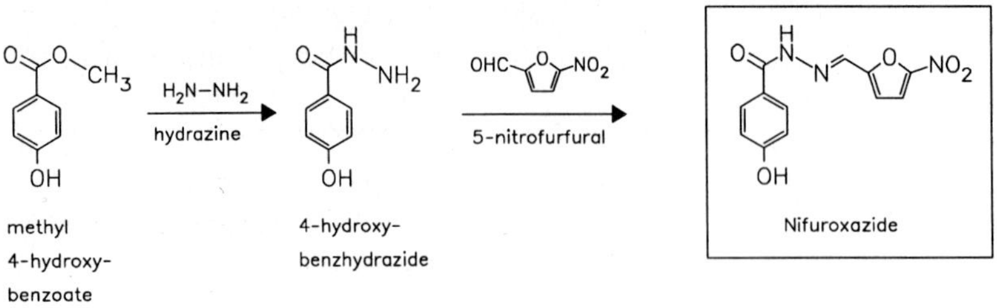
H₂N–NH₂
hydrazine
5-nitrofurfural
methyl 4-hydroxy-benzoate
4-hydroxy-benzhydrazide
Nifuroxazide

Reference(s):
FR 1 327 840 (Lab. Robert et Carrière; appl. 10.4.1962).
FR-M 1 427 (Lab. Robert et Carrière; appl. 12.7.1961).

Formulation(s): cps. 200 mg; syrup 100 mg

Trade Name(s):
D: Pentofuryl (Karlspharma); wfm
F: Ambatrol (SmithKline Beecham)
Antinal (Roques)
Ercéfuryl (Synthélabo)
Lumifurex (Irex)
Panfurex (Bouchara)
I: Diarret (Geymonat)
Ercefuryl (Sanko Pharma)

Nifurprazine

ATC: J01
Use: topical antibacterial

RN: 1614-20-6 MF: $C_{10}H_8N_4O_3$ MW: 232.20 EINECS: 216-563-2
CN: 6-[2-(5-nitro-2-furanyl)ethenyl]-3-pyridazinamine

monohydrochloride
RN: 50832-74-1 MF: $C_{10}H_8N_4O_3 \cdot HCl$ MW: 268.66

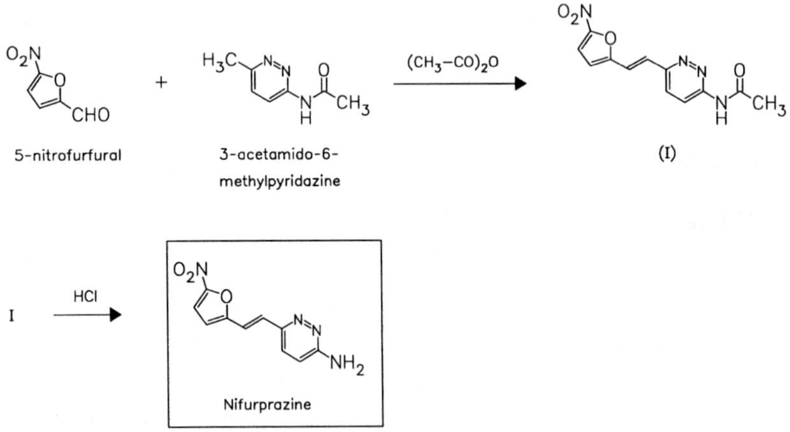
(CH₃–CO)₂O
5-nitrofurfural
3-acetamido-6-methylpyridazine
(I)
I
HCl
Nifurprazine

Reference(s):
DE 1 273 535 (Boehringer Mannh.; appl. 28.3.1962).

Formulation(s): ointment 0.1 % (as hydrochloride)

Trade Name(s):
D: Carofur (Boehringer
        Mannh.); wfm

Nifurtimox

ATC: P01CC01
Use: chemotherapeutic (trypanosomiasis),
        antiprotozoal

RN: 23256-30-6   MF: $C_{10}H_{13}N_3O_5S$ MW: 287.30   EINECS: 245-531-0
LD$_{50}$:   2291 mg/kg (M, p.o.);
        4050 mg/kg (R, p.o.);
        >2 g/kg (dog, p.o.)
CN: 3-methyl-*N*-[(5-nitro-2-furanyl)methylene]-4-thiomorpholinamine 1,1-dioxide

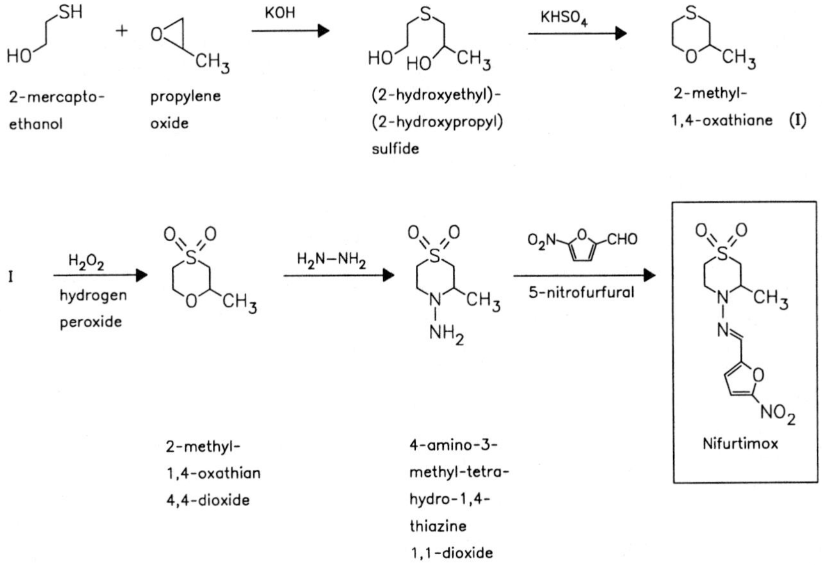

2-mercapto-   propylene   (2-hydroxyethyl)-   2-methyl-
ethanol   oxide   (2-hydroxypropyl)   1,4-oxathiane   (I)
                            sulfide

2-methyl-   4-amino-3-   Nifurtimox
1,4-oxathian   methyl-tetra-
4,4-dioxide   hydro-1,4-
                   thiazine
                   1,1-dioxide

Reference(s):
DE 1 170 957 (Bayer; appl. 23.11.1962).

Formulation(s):   tabl. 30 mg, 120 mg

Trade Name(s):
D: Lampit (Bayer); wfm

Nifurtoinol

ATC: G04AC02
Use: chemotherapeutic, antibacterial

RN: 1088-92-2   MF: $C_9H_8N_4O_6$ MW: 268.19   EINECS: 214-126-0
CN: 3-(hydroxymethyl)-1-[[(5-nitro-2-furanyl)methylene]amino]-2,4-imidazolidinedione

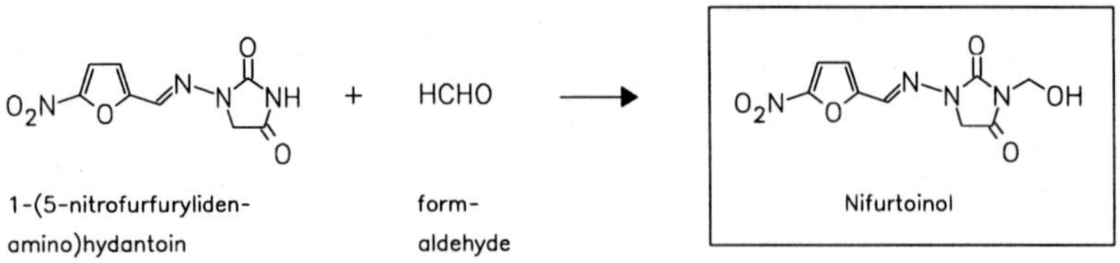

1-(5-nitrofurfuryliden-
amino)hydantoin

form-
aldehyde

Nifurtoinol

Reference(s):
GB 988 374 (Norwich; appl. 6.12.1961; USA-prior. 27.12.1960).

Formulation(s):　tabl. 40 mg

Trade Name(s):
D:　Urfadyne (Inpharzam);　　I:　Fultrexin (Zambon Farm.)-　　Urfadyn (Zambon Farm.);
　　wfm　　　　　　　　　　　　comb.; wfm　　　　　　　　　wfm
F:　Urfadyn (Arsac); wfm

Nifurzide

ATC:　A07AX04
Use:　chemotherapeutic, antiinfective

RN:　39978-42-2　MF: $C_{12}H_8N_4O_6S$　MW: 336.28　EINECS: 254-728-0
LD_{50}:　3200 mg/kg (M, p.o.)
CN:　5-nitro-2-thiophenecarboxylic acid [3-(5-nitro-2-furanyl)-2-propylidene]hydrazide

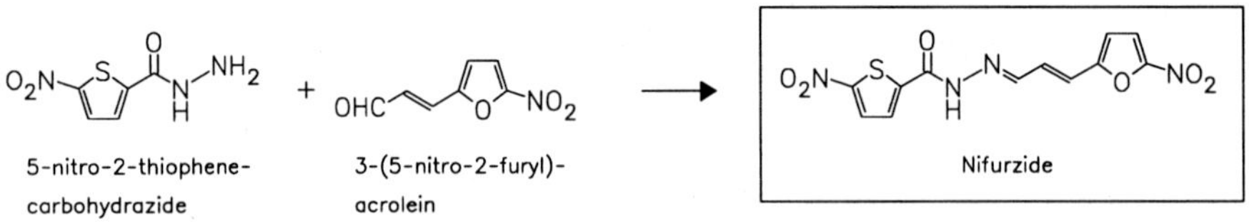

5-nitro-2-thiophene-
carbohydrazide

3-(5-nitro-2-furyl)-
acrolein

Nifurzide

Reference(s):
DOS 2 200 375 (Lipha; appl. 5.1.1972; F-prior. 7.1.1971).
Szarvasi, E.; Fontaine, L.; Betbeder-Matibet, A.: J. Med. Chem. (JMCMAR) **16**, 281 (1973).

starting material:
Carrara, G.; Chiancone, F.M.; d'Amato, V.: Gazz. Chim. Ital. (GCITA9) **82**, 652 (1952).

Formulation(s):　cps. 150 mg; susp. 40 mg/ml

Trade Name(s):
F:　Ricridène (Lipha Santé)　　　Ricridène (Lipha)

Nikethamide

(Nicethamide)

ATC:　R07AB02
Use:　respiratory analeptic

RN:　59-26-7　MF: $C_{10}H_{14}N_2O$　MW: 178.24　EINECS: 200-418-5
LD_{50}:　180 mg/kg (M, i.v.); 188 mg/kg (M, p.o.);
　　191 mg/kg (R, i.v.)
CN:　*N,N*-diethyl-3-pyridinecarboxamide

calcium thiocyanate
RN:　179799-22-5　MF: $C_{22}H_{28}CaN_6O_2S_2$　MW: 512.72

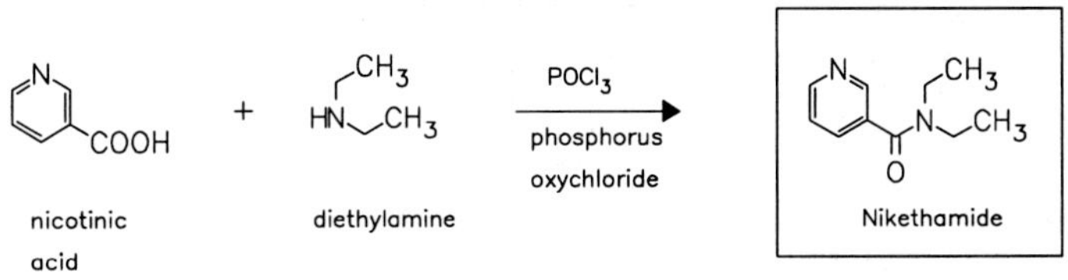

nicotinic acid + diethylamine → (POCl₃ / phosphorus oxychloride) → Nikethamide

Reference(s):
DRP 351 085 (Ciba; 1920).
DRP 441 707 (Ciba; 1924).

Formulation(s): drg. 50 mg in comb. (as calcium thiocyanate); powder 150 mg; sol. 250 mg/ml

Trade Name(s):
D: Felsol (Roland)-comb.
Zellaforte Plus (Eurim
Pharma)-comb.
F: Coramine (Ciba); wfm

GB: Coramine (Ciba); wfm
I: Miocardina (Croce
Bianca); wfm

J: Coramin (Ciba-Geigy-
Takeda)
USA: Coramine (Ciba); wfm

Nilutamide
(RU-23908)

ATC: G03H; L02BB02
Use: non-steroidal antiandrogen (for
treatment of prostatic carcinoma)

RN: 63612-50-0 MF: $C_{12}H_{10}F_3N_3O_4$ MW: 317.22
LD$_{50}$: 200 mg/kg (M, p.o.);
195 mg/kg (R, p.o.)
CN: 5,5-dimethyl-3-[4-nitro-3-(trifluoromethyl)phenyl]-2,4-imidazolidinedione

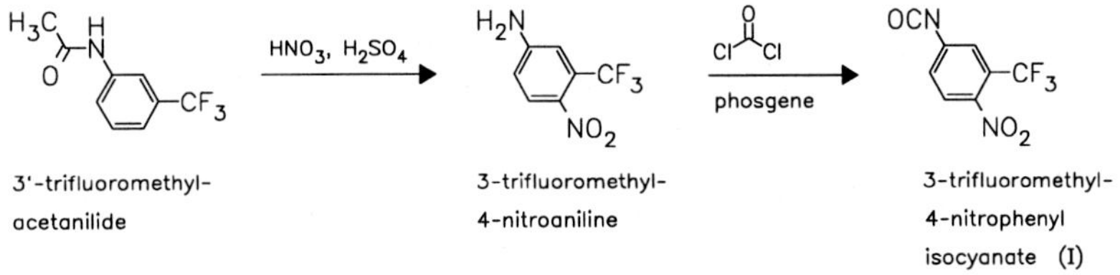

3'-trifluoromethyl-acetanilide → (HNO₃, H₂SO₄) → 3-trifluoromethyl-4-nitroaniline → (phosgene) → 3-trifluoromethyl-4-nitrophenyl isocyanate (I)

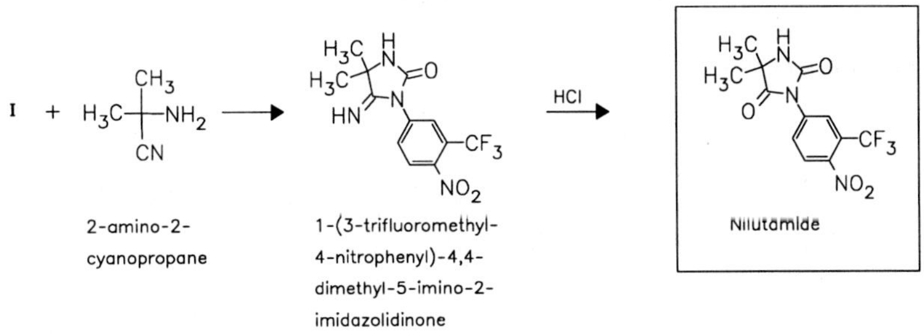

I + 2-amino-2-cyanopropane → 1-(3-trifluoromethyl-4-nitrophenyl)-4,4-dimethyl-5-imino-2-imidazolidinone → (HCl) → Nilutamide

Reference(s):
DOS 2 649 925 (Roussel-Uclaf; appl. 29.10.1976; F-prior. 29.10.1975).
US 4 097 578 (Roussel-Uclaf; 28.6.1978; F-prior. 29.10.1975).

synthesis of 3-trifluoromethyl-4-nitrophenyl isocyanate:
Rouche, H.: Bull. Cl. Sci., Acad. R. Belg. (BCSAAF) 13, 346 (1927).
JP 6 725 067 (Japan Bureau of Ind. Techn.; appl. 15.3.1966).

medical use for the treatment of hormone dependent cancer other than prostatic cancer:
WO 8 803 404 (Roussel-Uclaf; appl. 3.11.1987; I-prior. 4.11.1986).

Formulation(s):   tabl. 50 mg

Trade Name(s):
F: Anandron (Cassenne)   USA: Nilandron (Hoechst Marion
                                                      Roussel)

Nilvadipine
(FR-34235; Niprodipine)

ATC: C08CA10
Use: calcium antagonist, antihypertensive, antianginal

RN: 75530-68-6   MF: $C_{19}H_{19}N_3O_6$ MW: 385.38
LD$_{50}$:   9150 µg/kg (M, i.v.); 1300 mg/kg (M, p.o.);
       9650 µg/kg (R, i.v.); 1560 mg/kg (R, p.o.);
       3850 µg/kg (dog, i.v.); 510 mg/kg (dog, p.o.)
CN: 2-cyano-1,4-dihydro-6-methyl-4-(3-nitrophenyl)-3,5-pyridinedicarboxylic acid 3-methyl 5-(1-methylethyl) ester

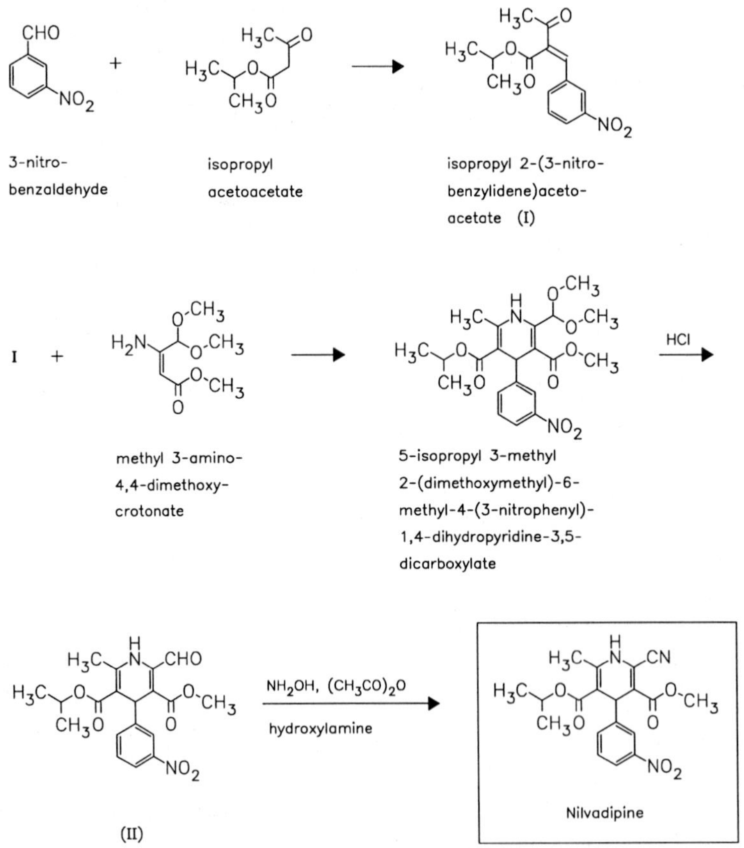

3-nitro-
benzaldehyde

isopropyl
acetoacetate

isopropyl 2-(3-nitro-
benzylidene)aceto-
acetate (I)

methyl 3-amino-
4,4-dimethoxy-
crotonate

5-isopropyl 3-methyl
2-(dimethoxymethyl)-6-
methyl-4-(3-nitrophenyl)-
1,4-dihydropyridine-3,5-
dicarboxylate

NH$_2$OH, (CH$_3$CO)$_2$O
hydroxylamine

(II)

Nilvadipine

Reference(s):

DE 2 940 833 (Fujisawa; appl. 9.10.1979; GB-prior. 10.10.1978).
US 4 338 322 (Fujisawa; 6.7.1982; GB-prior. 10.10.1978).
US 4 525 478 (Fujisawa; 25.6.1985; GB-prior. 10.10.1978).
Migamal, A. et al.: Chem. Pharm. Bull. (CPBTAL) **34**, 3071 (1986).

medical use for treatment of arteriosclerosis:
EP 185 283 (Fujisawa; appl. 7.12.1985; GB-prior. 10.12.1984).

medical use for treatment of cerebral dysfunction:
EP 253 173 (Fujisawa; appl. 26.6.1987; J-prior. 1.7.1986, 29.6.1987).

Formulation(s):   s. r. cps. 8 mg, 16 mg

Trade Name(s):
D: Escor (Merck)   Nivadil (Klinge)   J: Nivadil (Fujisawa; 1989)

Nimesulide

ATC: M01AX17
Use: anti-inflammatory

RN: 51803-78-2   MF: $C_{13}H_{12}N_2O_5S$ MW: 308.31   EINECS: 257-431-4
LD_{50}:   392 mg/kg (M, p.o.);
      200 mg/kg (R, p.o.)
CN: N-(4-nitro-2-phenoxyphenyl)methanesulfonamide

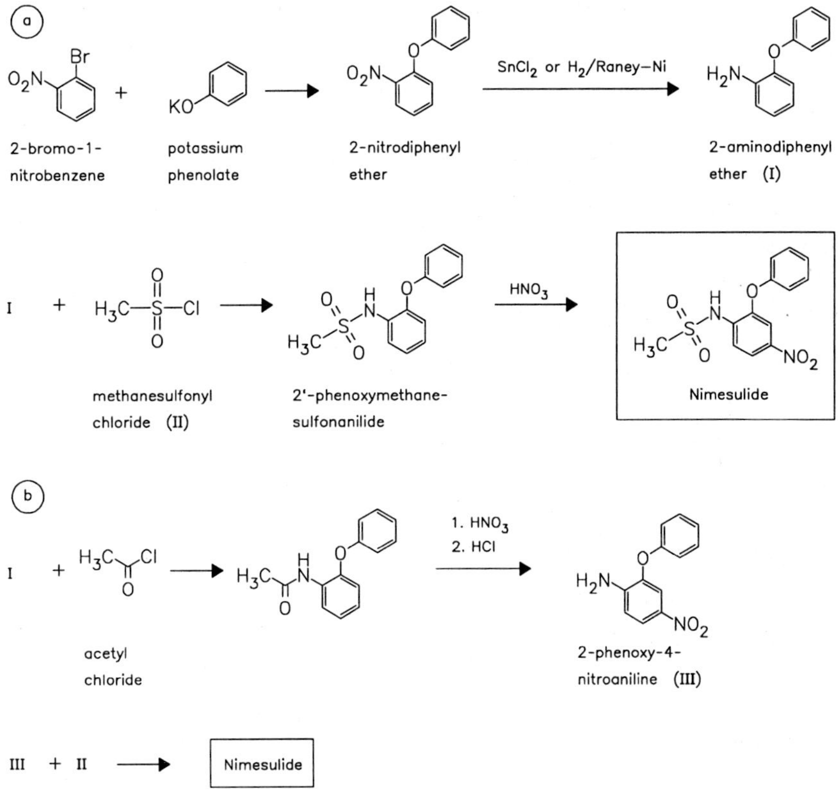

2-bromo-1-
nitrobenzene

potassium
phenolate

2-nitrodiphenyl
ether

$SnCl_2$ or H_2/Raney–Ni

2-aminodiphenyl
ether (I)

methanesulfonyl
chloride (II)

2'-phenoxymethane-
sulfonanilide

HNO_3

Nimesulide

acetyl
chloride

1. HNO_3
2. HCl

2-phenoxy-4-
nitroaniline (III)

III + II ⟶ Nimesulide

Reference(s):
US 3 840 597 (Riker; 8.10.1974; prior. 3.7.1972; 24.2.1971, 13.4.1970).
DOS 2 333 643 (Riker; appl. 2.7.1973; USA-prior. 3.7.1972).

synthesis of 2-phenoxy-4-nitroaniline:
DOS 2 842 186 (BASF; appl. 28.9.1978).
McCombie, H. et al.: J. Chem. Soc. (JCSOA9) **1931**, 529.

synthesis of 2-nitrodiphenyl ether:
Suter, C.M.: J. Am. Chem. Soc. (JACSAT) **51**, 2581 (1929).
Lock, G.: Monatsh. Chem. (MOCMB7) **55**, 167 (1930).

Formulation(s):   gran. 100 mg; suppos. 200 mg; tabl. 100 mg, 200 mg

Trade Name(s):
I: Algolide (Garant)   Folid (CT)   Nimesil (Lucofarmaco)
     Aulin (Boehringer Mannh.;   Laider (Esseti)   Remov (Piam)
     1985)   Mesid (Janssen-Cilag)   generics
     Eudolene (Savio IBN)   Mesulid (Novartis Farma;
     Fansidol (NCSN)   1985)

Nimetazepam

ATC: N05CD
Use: hypnotic, tranquilizer, anticonvulsant, skeletal muscle relaxant

RN: 2011-67-8   MF: $C_{16}H_{13}N_3O_3$ MW: 295.30   EINECS: 217-931-5
LD_{50}:   750 mg/kg (M, p.o.);
      970 mg/kg (R, p.o.)
CN: 1,3-dihydro-1-methyl-7-nitro-5-phenyl-2*H*-1,4-benzodiazepin-2-one

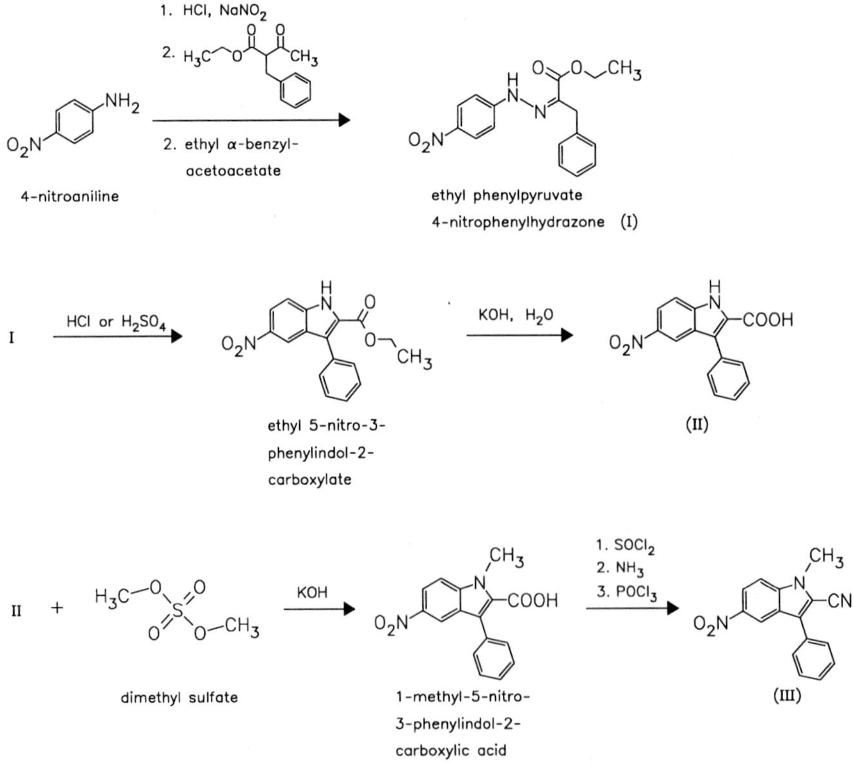

1. HCl, $NaNO_2$
2. H_3C-O ... CH_3

4-nitroaniline

2. ethyl α-benzyl-acetoacetate

ethyl phenylpyruvate 4-nitrophenylhydrazone   (I)

I $\xrightarrow{\text{HCl or } H_2SO_4}$

ethyl 5-nitro-3-phenylindol-2-carboxylate

KOH, H_2O

(II)

II +   dimethyl sulfate

KOH

1-methyl-5-nitro-3-phenylindol-2-carboxylic acid

1. $SOCl_2$
2. NH_3
3. $POCl_3$

(III)

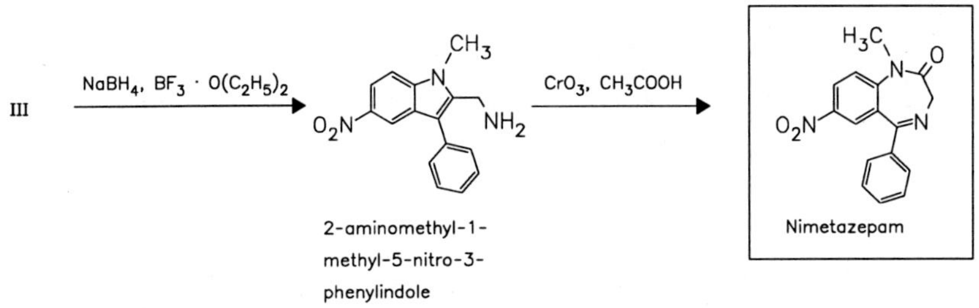
III
NaBH4, BF3 · O(C2H5)2
CrO3, CH3COOH
2-aminomethyl-1-methyl-5-nitro-3-phenylindole
Nimetazepam

Reference(s):

US 3 652 551 (Sumitomo; 28.3.1972; J-prior. 1.12.1967, 9.12.1967, 14.12.1967, 15.12.1967, 21.12.1967, 28.12.1967, 10.1.1968, 11.3.1968).

DOS 1 811 830 (Sumitomo; appl. 29.11.1968; J-prior. 1.12.1967, 9.12.1967, 14.12.1967, 15.12.1967, 21.12.1967, 28.12.1967, 10.1.1968, 11.3.1968).

DOS 1 816 046 (Sumitomo; appl. 20.12.1968; J-prior. 25.12.1967, 9.4.1968).

DOS 1 817 761 (Sumitomo; appl. 29.11.1968; J-prior. 1.12.1967, 9.12.1967, 14.12.1967, 15.12.1967, 21.12.1967, 28.12.1967, 10.1.1968, 11.3.1968).

DOS 1 817 794 (Sumitomo; appl. 20.12.1968; J-prior. 25.12.1967).

Ihizumi, K. et al.: J. Org. Chem. (JOCEAH) **37**, 4111 (1972).

indole precursor:

US 3 770 767 (Sumitomo; 6.11.1973; J-prior. 28.12.1967).

Formulation(s): tabl. 3 mg, 5 mg

Trade Name(s):

J: Erimin (Sumitomo)

Nimodipine

ATC: C08CA06
Use: calcium antagonist, cerebral vasodilator

RN: 66085-59-4 MF: $C_{21}H_{26}N_2O_7$ MW: 418.45 EINECS: 266-127-0

LD_{50}: 26.2 mg/kg (M, i.v.); 940 mg/kg (M, p.o.);
5 mg/kg (R, i.v.); 2738 mg/kg (R, p.o.);
4 mg/kg (dog, i.v.); 1 g/kg (dog, p.o.)

CN: 1,4-dihydro-2,6-dimethyl-4-(3-nitrophenyl)-3,5-pyridinedicarboxylic acid 2-methoxyethyl 1-methylethyl ester

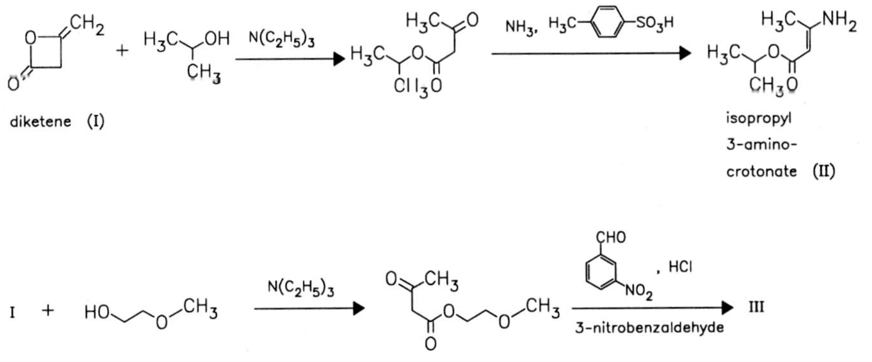
N(C2H5)3
NH3, H3C–C6H4–SO3H
diketene (I)
isopropyl 3-aminocrotonate (II)
I +
N(C2H5)3
, HCl
3-nitrobenzaldehyde
III

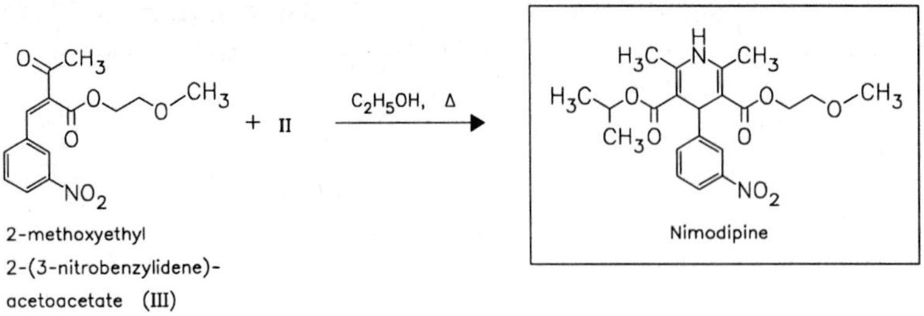

2-methoxyethyl
2-(3-nitrobenzylidene)-
acetoacetate (III)

Nimodipine

Reference(s):

DOS 2 117 571 (Bayer; appl. 10.4.1971).
DE 2 117 573 (Bayer; prior. 10.4.1971).
US 3 799 934 (Bayer; 26.3.1974; D-prior. 10.4.1971).
US 3 932 645 (Bayer; 13.1.1976; D-prior. 10.4.1971).
Meyer, H. et al.: Arzneim.-Forsch. (ARZNAD) **31**, 407 (1981); **33**, 106 (1983).

Formulation(s):   cps. 30 mg; f. c. tabl. 30 mg; vial 10 mg/50 ml

Trade Name(s):

D:	Nimotop (Bayer Vital; 1985)	GB:	Nimotop (Bayer; 1988)	USA:	Nimotop (Bayer)
F:	Nimotop (Bayer)	I:	Nimotop (Bayer Italia) Periplum (Italfarmaco)		

Nimorazole

(Nitrimidazine)

ATC: P01AB06
Use: chemotherapeutic (trichomonas), antiprotozoal

RN: 6506-37-2   MF: $C_9H_{14}N_4O_3$ MW: 226.24   EINECS: 229-394-4
LD_{50}:   1530 mg/kg (M, p.o.);
      1540 mg/kg (R, p.o.)
CN: 4-[2-(5-nitro-1*H*-imidazol-1-yl)ethyl]morpholine

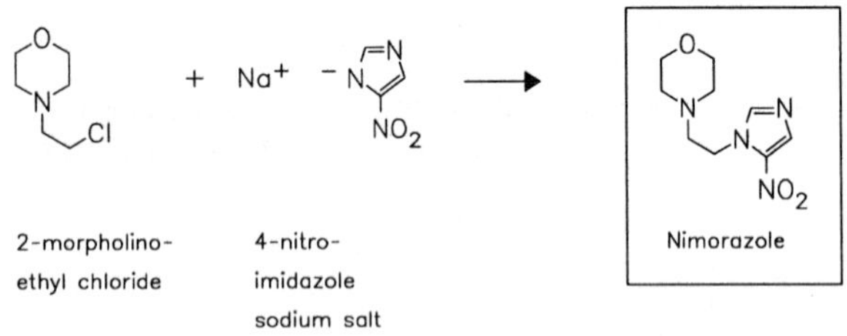

2-morpholino-
ethyl chloride

4-nitro-
imidazole
sodium salt

Nimorazole

Reference(s):

US 3 399 193 (Carlo Erba; 27.8.1968; prior. 4.8.1965).
US 3 458 528 (Merck & Co.; 29.7.1969; prior. 7.7.1965, 18.5.1966).
US 3 646 027 (Merck & Co.; 29.2.1972; prior. 7.7.1965, 18.5.1966).

Formulation(s):   tabl. 500 mg

Trade Name(s):

D:	Esclama (Pharmacia & Upjohn)	F:	Naxogyn (Pharmacia & Upjohn)	GB:	Naxogin (Carlo Erba); wfm Nulogyl (Bristol); wfm

I: Naxogin (Erba)   Sirledi (Cansyth)   Sirledi (Inverni della Beffa)

Nimustine
(ACNU)

ATC: L01AD06
Use: antineoplastic

RN: 42471-28-3   MF: $C_9H_{13}ClN_6O_2$ MW: 272.70   EINECS: 255-838-1
CN: N'-[(4-amino-2-methyl-5-pyrimidinyl)methyl]-N-(2-chloroethyl)-N-nitrosourea

2-chloroethyl   4-amino-5-   (I)
isocyanate   aminomethyl-
                         2-methylpyrimidine

Nimustine

Reference(s):
DOS 2 257 360 (Sankyo; appl. 20.11.1972; J-prior. 20.11.1971, 4.12.1971, 26.7.1972).
US 4 003 901 (Sankyo; 18.1.1977; J-prior. 20.11.1971, 4.12.1971, 26.7.1972).

Formulation(s):   vial 25 mg, 50 mg

Trade Name(s):
D: ACNU 50 (ASTA Medica   J: Nidran (Sankyo)
       AWD)

Nipradilol
(Nipradolol)

ATC: C07A; C04A
Use: β-antagonist with vasodilating
         activity, antihypertensive, antianginal

RN: 81486-22-8   MF: $C_{15}H_{22}N_2O_6$ MW: 326.35
LD$_{50}$:   68 mg/kg (M, i.v.); 461 mg/kg (M, p.o.);
         144 mg/kg (R, i.p.); 78 mg/kg (R, i.v.); 1040 mg/kg (R, p.o.); 850 mg/kg (R, s.c.);
         20 mg/kg (dog, i.v.); >400 mg/kg (dog, p.o.)
CN: 3,4 dihydro 8 [2 hydroxy-3-[(1-methylethyl)amino]propoxy]-2H-1-benzopyran-3-ol 3-nitrate

2-hydroxy-3-   acrylo-   (I)
methoxybenz-   nitrile
aldehyde

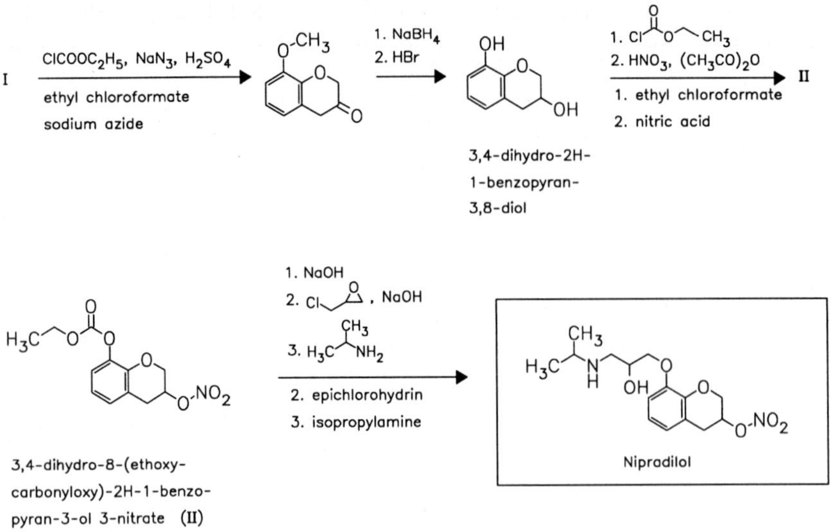

I → [reaction scheme with CICOOC₂H₅, NaN₃, H₂SO₄ (ethyl chloroformate, sodium azide) → intermediate → 1. NaBH₄ 2. HBr → 3,4-dihydro-2H-1-benzopyran-3,8-diol → 1. ClCOOC₂H₅ 2. HNO₃, (CH₃CO)₂O; 1. ethyl chloroformate, 2. nitric acid → II]

3,4-dihydro-8-(ethoxy-
carbonyloxy)-2H-1-benzo-
pyran-3-ol 3-nitrate (II)

→ 1. NaOH 2. Cl epoxide, NaOH 3. H₃C-NH₂ (isopropylamine); 2. epichlorohydrin 3. isopropylamine → Nipradilol

Reference(s):

EP 42 299 (Kowa; appl. 16.6.1981; J-prior. 25.12.1980, 17.6.1980).
US 4 394 382 (Kowa; 19.7.1983; appl. 9.6.1981; J-prior. 25.12.1980, 17.6.1980).
Shiratsuchi, M. et al.: Chem. Pharm. Bull. (CPBTAL) **35**, 632 (1987).

separation of diastereomeric racemates:
EP 154 511 (Kowa; appl. 27.2.1985; J-prior. 29.2.1984).
US 4 727 085 (Kowa; 23.2.1988; appl. 28.8.1985; J-prior. 29.2.1984).

synthesis of enantiomers:
Shiratsuchi, M. et al.: Chem. Pharm. Bull. (CPBTAL), **33**, 2735 (1985); **35**, 3691 (1987).

synthesis of 3,4-dihydro-2H-1-benzopyran-3,8-diol:
JP 59 029 681 (Kowa; appl. 12.8.1982).
Kawamura, K. et al.: Chem. Pharm. Bull. (CPBTAL) **38**, 2088 (1990).

Formulation(s):   tabl. 3 mg, 6 mg

Trade Name(s):
J: Hypadil (Kowa; 1988)

Niridazole

ATC: P02BX02
Use: chemotherapeutic (antischistosomal)

RN: 61-57-4   MF: $C_6H_6N_4O_3S$ MW: 214.21   EINECS: 200-512-6
LD$_{50}$:   2500 mg/kg (M, p.o.);
            900 mg/kg (R, p.o.)
CN: 1-(5-nitro-2-thiazolyl)-2-imidazolidinone

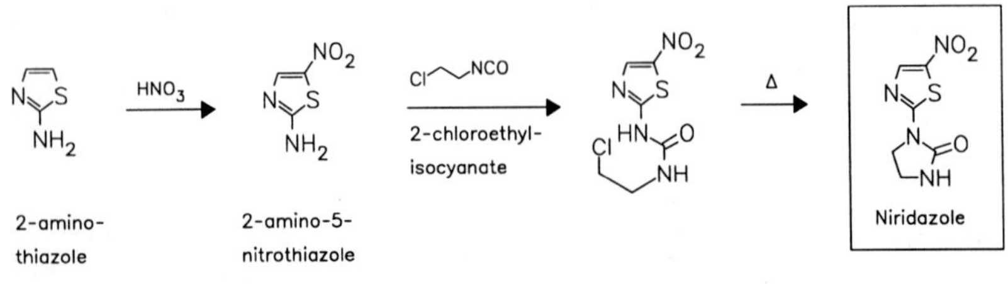

[reaction scheme: 2-aminothiazole → HNO₃ → 2-amino-5-nitrothiazole → 2-chloroethyl-isocyanate → intermediate → Δ → Niridazole]

2-amino-
thiazole

2-amino-5-
nitrothiazole

2-chloroethyl-
isocyanate

Niridazole

Reference(s):
Lambert, C.R. et al.: Experientia (EXPEAM) **20**, 452 (1964).
GB 986 562 (Ciba; appl. 22.5.1963; CH-prior. 30.5.1962, 23.4.1963).

alternative syntheses:
DAS 2 033 611 (Egyt; appl. 7.7.1970; H-prior. 7.7.1969).
DAS 2 117 050 (Egyt; appl. 7.4.1971; H-prior. 16.4.1970).

Formulation(s):   tabl. 100 mg, 500 mg

Trade Name(s):
F: Ambilhar (Ciba); wfm

Nisoldipine

(Bay-K 5552)

ATC: C02DE; C08CA07
Use: calcium antagonist, antihypertensive, antianginal

RN: 63675-72-9   MF: $C_{20}H_{24}N_2O_6$ MW: 388.42   EINECS: 264-407-7
LD$_{50}$:   360 µg/kg (M, i.v.); 411 mg/kg (M, p.o.); 384 mg/kg (M, s.c.);
1120 µg/kg (R, i.v.); 1257 mg/kg (R, p.o.); 654 mg/kg (R, s.c.);
2 mg/kg (dog, i.v.); 400 mg/kg (dog, p.o.)
CN: 1,4-dihydro-2,6-dimethyl-4-(2-nitrophenyl)-3,5-pyridinedicarboxylic acid methyl 2-methylpropyl ester

2-nitro-
benzaldehyde

isobutyl
acetoacetate

isobutyl 2-(2-nitro-
benzylidene)acetoacetate   (I)

methyl 3-amino-
crotonate

Nisoldipine

Reference(s):
DOS 2 549 568 (Bayer; appl. 5.11.1975).
US 4 154 839 (Bayer, 15.5.1979; appl. 8.5.1978; D-prior. 5.11.1975).

additional synthesis:
ES 539 113 (Ind. y Comercial Quimica; appl. 27.12.1984).
ES 549 302 (Mora Ruedas; appl. 26.11.1985).
ES 546 423 (Inke; appl. 31.7.1985).
ES 546 784 (Sune Coma; appl. 9.9.1985).
CS 243 591 (P. Cupka et al.; appl. 25.1.1985).

medical use for treatment of alcoholism:
DOS 3 806 277 (Tropon; appl. 27.2.1988).

medical use for inhibition of opioid tolerance:
JP 61 260 025 (Miles; appl. 12.5.1986; USA-prior. 13.5.1985).

medical use as saluretic:
DOS 3 212 736 (Bayer; appl. 6.4.1982).

medical use as antiarteriosclerotic:
DOS 3 222 367 (Bayer; appl. 15.6.1982).

Formulation(s):　　f. c. tabl. 5 mg, 10 mg, 20 mg, 30 mg, 40 mg

Trade Name(s):

D:	Baymycard (Bayer Vital/ Zeneca; 1990)	I:	Syscor (Bayer Italia) Zadipina (SmithKline Beecham)
GB:	Syscor MR (Bayer)		

J:　　Baymycard (Bayer; 1990)
USA:　Sular (Zeneca)

Nitrazepam

ATC:　N05CD02
Use:　hypnotic, anticonvulsant

RN:　146-22-5　MF: C$_{15}$H$_{11}$N$_3$O$_3$　MW: 281.27　EINECS: 205-665-2
LD$_{50}$:　130 mg/kg (M, i.v.); 550 mg/kg (M, p.o.);
　　　825 mg/kg (R, p.o.)
CN:　1,3-dihydro-7-nitro-5-phenyl-2*H*-1,4-benzodiazepin-2-one

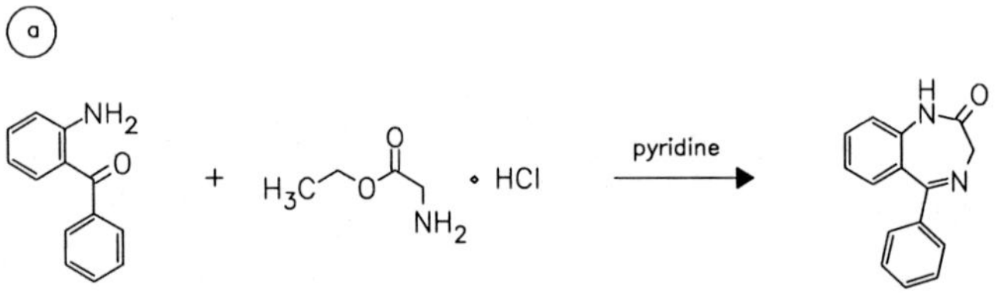

2-amino-
benzophenone

glycine ethyl
ester hydrochloride　(I)

2-oxo-5-phenyl-
2,3-dihydro-1H-
1,4-benzodiazepine　(II)

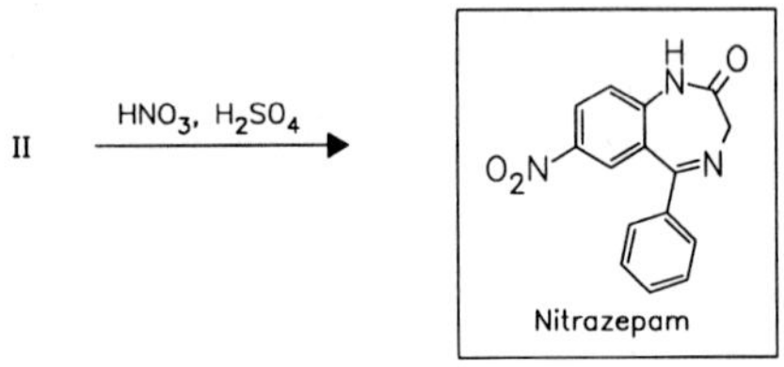

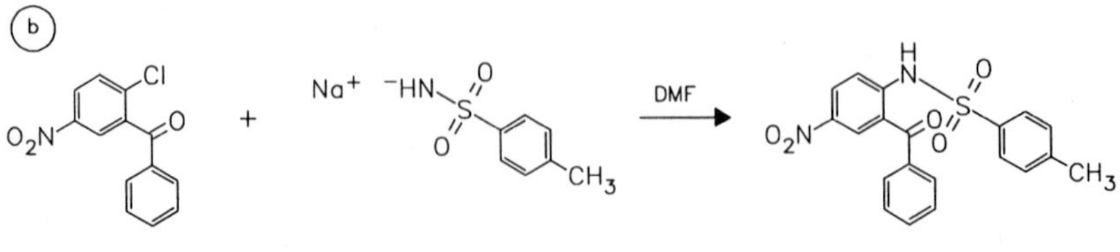

II　$\xrightarrow{\text{HNO}_3,\ \text{H}_2\text{SO}_4}$

Nitrazepam

2-chloro-5-
nitrobenzo-
phenone

p-toluene-
sulfamide
sodium salt

(III)

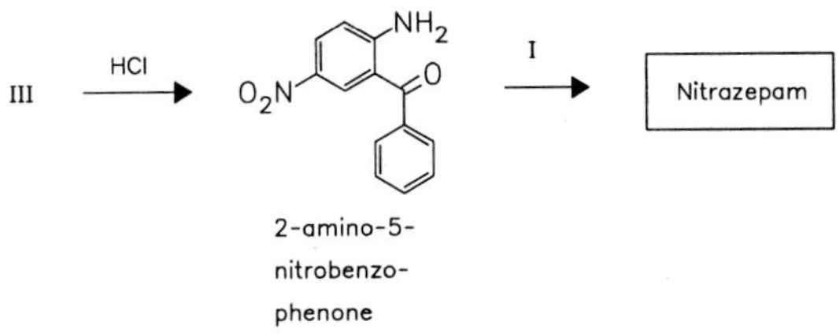

III $\xrightarrow{\text{HCl}}$ 2-amino-5-nitrobenzophenone $\xrightarrow{\text{I}}$ Nitrazepam

Reference(s):

US 3 109 843 (Hoffmann-La Roche; 5.11.1963; appl. 21.6.1962; prior. 28.7.1961, 4.12.1961).
US 3 116 203 (Hoffman-La Roche; 31.12.1963; prior. 14.3.1962).
US 3 123 529 (Hoffman-La Roche; 3.3.1964; prior. 9.3.1962).
DE 1 136 709 (Hoffman-La Roche; appl. 7.12.1960; USA-prior. 10.12.1959, 27.6.1960).
DE 1 145 626 (Hoffman-La Roche; appl. 7.12.1960; USA-prior. 10.12.1959, 15.1.1960, 26.4.1960, 27.6.1960).
Sternbach, L.H. et al.: J. Med. Chem. (JMCMAR) 6, 261 (1963).
DAS 1 811 785 (Delmar Chemicals; appl. 29.11.1968; CDN-prior. 29.11.1967).

condensation of 2-aminobenzophenone *with* glycine *and* POCl$_3$/nitrobenzene *and following nitration with* KNO$_3$/H$_2$SO$_4$:
DOS 2 252 378 (Roche; appl. 25.10.1972; CH-prior. 18.11.1971).

Formulation(s):   drops 0.5 g/100 g; tabl. 5 mg, 10 mg

Trade Name(s):

D:	Dormalon (Pharma Wernigerode)	
	Dormo-Puren (Isis Puren)	
	Eatan N (Desitin)	F:
	Imeson (Desitin)	
	Mogadan Roche (Roche)	GB:

Novanox/-forte (Pfleger)
Radedorm (ASTA Medica AWD)
Mogadon (Roche)
Rohypnol (Roche)
Mogadon (Roche)

generics
I: Mogadon (Roche)
J: Benzalin (Shionogi)
    Nelbon (Sankyo)
USA: Mogadon (Roche); wfm

Nitrefazole

ATC: V03AA
Use: alcohol deterrent

RN: 21721-92-6   MF: C$_{10}$H$_8$N$_4$O$_4$ MW: 248.20   EINECS: 244-542-8
LD$_{50}$:   5.501 g/kg (M, p.o.);
    4.813 g/kg (R, p.o.);
    >6.4 g/kg (dog, p.o.)
CN: 2-methyl-4-nitro-1-(4-nitrophenyl)-1*H*-imidazole

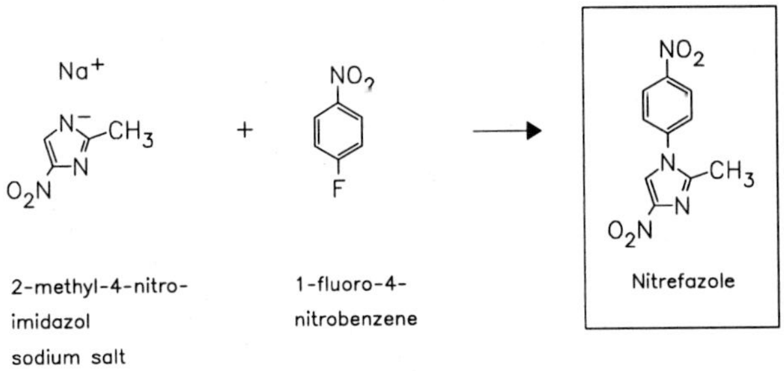

2-methyl-4-nitro-imidazol sodium salt   +   1-fluoro-4-nitrobenzene   →   Nitrefazole

Reference(s):

DE 1 620 043 (Merck AG; appl. 15.10.1966).
DOS 2 145 651 (Merck AG; appl. 13.9.1971).

medical use:
DOS 2 645 709 (Merck AG; appl. 9.10.1976).

Formulation(s): cps. 0.2 g

Trade Name(s):
D: Altimol (Merck); wfm

Nitrendipine

ATC: C08CA08
Use: calcium antagonist, antihypertensive

RN: 39562-70-4 MF: $C_{18}H_{20}N_2O_6$ MW: 360.37 EINECS: 254-513-1
LD_{50}: 34.5 mg/kg (M, i.v.); 2540 mg/kg (M, p.o.);
12.6 mg/kg (R, i.v.); 15.37 g/kg (R, p.o.);
>2.5 mg/kg (dog, i.v.); >100 mg/kg (dog, p.o.)
CN: 1,4-dihydro-2,6-dimethyl-4-(3-nitrophenyl)-3,5-pyridinedicarboxylic acid ethyl methyl ester

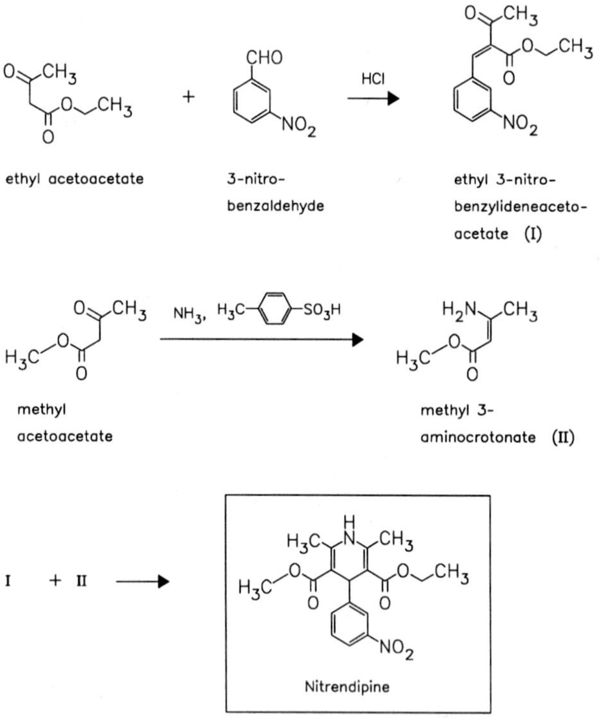
HCl
ethyl acetoacetate
3-nitrobenzaldehyde
ethyl 3-nitrobenzylideneacetoacetate (I)
NH_3, H_3C–C_6H_4–SO_3H
methyl acetoacetate
methyl 3-aminocrotonate (II)
I + II
Nitrendipine

Reference(s):
US 3 799 934 (Bayer; 26.3.1974; appl. 7.4.1972; D-prior. 10.4.1971).
US 3 932 645 (Bayer; 13.1.1976; D-prior. 10.4.1971).
DOS 2 117 571 (Bayer; appl. 10.4.1971).
Meyer, H. et al.: Arzneim.-Forsch. (ARZNAD) **31**, 407 (1981).

Formulation(s): sol. 5 mg/ml; tabl. 10 mg, 20 mg

D: Bayotensin (Bayer Vital;   I: Baypress (Bayer Italia)   J: Baylotensin (Bayer-
      1985)   Deiten (ABC Farmaceutici)   Yoshitomi)
      numerous generics

Nitrofural
(Nitrofurazone)

ATC: B05CA03; D08AF01; D09AA03;
        P01CC02; S01AX04; S02AA02
Use: antiseptic, topical antibacterial

RN: 59-87-0   MF: $C_6H_6N_4O_4$ MW: 198.14   EINECS: 200-443-1
LD_{50}:   249 mg/kg (M, p.o.);
       590 mg/kg (R, p.o.)
CN: 2-[(5-nitro-2-furanyl)methylene]hydrazinecarboxamide

5-nitrofurfural   +   semicarbazide hydrochloride   →   Nitrofural

Reference(s):
US 2 416 234 (Eaton Labs.; 1947; prior. 1945).
US 2 927 110 (Norwich Pharmacal; 1.3.1960; appl. 23.1.1958).

Formulation(s):   cream 0.2 g/100 g; ointment 0.2 g/100 g; sol. 0.2 g/100 g

Trade Name(s):
D: Furacin (Procter &   I: Furanvit (SIFI)-comb.   J: Monafuracin (Dainippon)
      Gamble)   Furotricina (Biomedica   USA: Furacin (Eaton); wfm
GB: Furacin (Eaton); wfm   Foscama)-comb.

Nitrofurantoin

ATC: G04AC01
Use: chemotherapeutic (urinary tract
        infections)

RN: 67-20-9   MF: $C_8H_6N_4O_5$ MW: 238.16   EINECS: 200-646-5
LD_{50}:   360 mg/kg (M, p.o.);
       604 mg/kg (R, p.o.)
CN: 1-[[(5-nitro-2-furanyl)methylene]amino]-2,4-imidazolidinedione

hydrazine   chloroacetic   2-hydrazinoacetic
(hydrate)   acid   acid   (I)

potassium   semicarbazidoacetic   1-aminohydantoin   (II)
cyanate   acid

II　　+

2-diacetoxymethyl-
5-nitrofuran

Nitrofurantoin

Reference(s):
US 2 610 181 (Eaton Labs.; 1950; prior. 1950).
US 2 779 786 (Norwich; 29.1.1957; prior. 17.4.1953).
US 2 898 335 (Norwich; 4.8.1959; prior. 28.2.1958).
US 2 927 110 (Norwich; 1.3.1960; prior. 23.1.1958).

special pharmaceutical formulations:
US 3 401 221 (Norwich Pharmacal; 10.9.1968; prior. 25.8.1964).
US 4 122 157 (Richardson-Merrell; 24.10.1978; appl. 4.3.1977).

sustained release formulation:
DOS 2 749 745 (Chem. Fabrik von Heyden; appl. 7.11.1977; F-prior. 15.9.1977).

Formulation(s):　cps. 25 mg, 50 mg, 100 mg, 150 mg; drg. 20 mg, 100 mg; s. r. cps. 100 mg; susp. 25 mg/5 ml; tabl. 50 mg

Trade Name(s):

D:	Cystit (Bristol-Myers Squibb)	GB:	Furadantin (Procter & Gamble)		Nitrofurin (IFI)
	Furadantin/retard (Procter & Gamble)		Macrobid (Procter & Gamble)	J:	Furadantin (Yamanouchi)
	Uro-Tablinen (Sanorania)		Macrodantin (Procter & Gamble)		Parfuran (Parke Davis)
	numerous generics and combination preparations				Trantoin (McKesson)
		I:	Cistofuran (Crosara)		Uretoin (Azusa-Tokyo Tanabe)
F:	Furadantine (Lipha Santé)		Furadantin (Formenti)	USA:	Furadantin (Dura)
	Furadoïne (Lipha Santé)		Furedan (Scharper)		Macrodantin (Procter & Gamble)
	Microdoïne (Gomenol)		Furil (OFF)		

Nitroxoline

ATC:　　G04AG06
Use:　　urinary antiseptic, antifungal

RN:　　4008-48-4　MF: C$_9$H$_6$N$_2$O$_3$　MW: 190.16　EINECS: 223-662-4
LD$_{50}$:　8300 µg/kg (M, i.v.); 104 mg/kg (M, p.o.);
　　　510 mg/kg (R, p.o.)
CN:　　5-nitro-8-quinolinol

oxyquinoline
(q. v.)

8-hydroxy-
5-nitroso-
quinoline

Nitroxoline

Reference(s):
Kostanecki, St. v.: Ber. Dtsch. Chem. Ges. (BDCGAS) **24**, 150 (1891).
Petrow, V.; Sturgeon, B.: J. Chem. Soc. (JCSOA9) **1954**, 570.

Formulation(s):   cps. 50 mg, 80 mg, 150 mg, 250 mg; susp. 1 %

Trade Name(s):
D: Nitroxolin (Cephasaar)   I: Urocoli (Roussel-
F: Nibiol (Débat)   Maestretti); wfm

Nizatidine

ATC: A02BA04
Use: ulcer therapeutic, H_2-receptor
antagonist

RN: 76963-41-2   MF: $C_{12}H_{21}N_5O_2S_2$ MW: 331.47
LD_{50}:   265 mg/kg (M, i.v.); 1685 mg/kg (M, p.o.);
301 mg/kg (R, i.v.); 1680 mg/kg (R, p.o.);
>75 mg/kg (dog, i.v.); >800 mg/kg (dog, p.o.)
CN: N-[2-[[[2-[(dimethylamino)methyl]-4-thiazolyl]methyl]thio]ethyl]-N'-methyl-2-nitro-1,1-ethenediamine

ethyl bromo-
pyruvate

dimethylamino-
thioacetamide

ethyl 2-(dimethylamino-
methyl)-4-thiazole-
carboxylate

$LiB(C_2H_5)_3H$,
THF

lithium triethyl-
borohydride

(I)

cysteamine

2-(dimethylaminomethyl)-
4-(2-aminoethylthiomethyl)-
thiazole (II)

1-(methylthio)-2-nitro-
N-methylethylenamine

(cf. ranitidine synthesis)

Nizatidine

Reference(s):
EP 49 618 (Lilly; appl. 2.10.1981; USA-prior. 2.10.1980).
US 4 375 547 (Lilly; 1.3.1983; prior. 2.10.1980).
DE 3 171 819 (Lilly; appl. 14.4.1982; USA-prior. 2.10.1980).
US 4 382 090 (Lilly; 3.5.1983; prior. 2.10.1980).

preparation of ethyl 2-(dimethylaminomethyl)-4-thiazolecarboxylate *from* ethyl bromopyruvate *and*
dimethylaminothioacetamide:
Trumm, K.A. et al.: Arzneim.-Forsch. (ARZNAD) **35** (3), 573 (1985).

alternative synthesis:
GB 2 134 521 (Lilly; appl. 6.2.1984; USA-prior. 7.2.1983).

Formulation(s):   amp. 100 mg, 150 mg, 300 mg; cps. 150 mg, 300 mg

Trade Name(s):
D:	Gastrax (Asche; 1989)	F:	Nizaxid (Norgine Pharma)		Nizax (Lilly; 1988)
	Gastrax mite (Asche; 1989)	GB:	Axid (Lilly; 1987)		Zanizal (Italfarmaco; 1988)
	Nizax (Lilly; 1989)		Zinga (Ashbourne)	J:	Acinon (Zeria; Lilly; 1990)
	Nizax mite (Lilly; 1989)	I:	Cronizat (Farmitalia; 1988)	USA:	Axid (Lilly)

Nizofenone

(Y-9179)

ATC: N06BX10
Use: antianoxic, nootropic

RN: 54533-85-6   MF: $C_{21}H_{21}ClN_4O_3$ MW: 412.88
CN: (2-chlorophenyl)[2-[2-[(diethylamino)methyl]-1*H*-imidazol-1-yl]-5-nitrophenyl]methanone

fumarate (1:1)
RN: 54533-86-7   MF: $C_{21}H_{21}ClN_4O_3 \cdot C_4H_4O_4$ MW: 528.95
LD_{50}:   70 mg/kg (M, i.v.); 495 mg/kg (Mm, p.o.); 504 mg/kg (Mf, p.o.); 270 mg/kg (M, s.c.);
65 mg/kg (R, i.v.); 1711 mg/kg (Rm, p.o.); 1580 mg/kg (Rf, p.o.); 1830 mg/kg (R, s.c.)

2-amino-5-nitro-
2'-chlorobenzo-
phenone

1. HCl, NaNO$_2$
2. CuCl

2,2'-dichloro-5-nitro-
benzophenone (I)

I + 2-(diethylamino-
methyl)imidazole

NaH

Nizofenone

Reference(s):
US 3 915 981 (Yoshitomi; 28.10.1975; J-prior. 16.3.1973, 20.3.1973).
DE 2 403 416 (Yoshitomi; appl. 24.1.1974; J-prior. 24.1.1973, 16.3.1973, 20.3.1973, 14.5.1973, 16.6.1973, 7.7.1973).

Formulation(s):   amp. 5 mg/2 ml

Trade Name(s):
J: Ekonal (Yoshitomi; 1989)

Nomegestrol acetate

ATC: G03DB04
Use: synthetic progestogen for treatment
of gynecological disturbances

RN: 58652-20-3   MF: C$_{23}$H$_{30}$O$_4$ MW: 370.49   EINECS: 261-379-8
LD$_{50}$: >2 g/kg (M, p.o.);
        >2 g/kg (R, p.o.)
CN: 17-(acetyloxy)-6-methyl-19-norpregna-4,6-diene-3,20-dione

nomegestrol
RN: 58691-88-6   MF: C$_{21}$H$_{28}$O$_3$ MW: 328.45

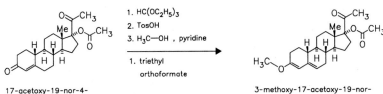

17-acetoxy-19-nor-4-
pregnene-3,20-dione

1. HC(OC$_2$H$_5$)$_3$
2. TosOH
3. H$_3$C—OH , pyridine

1. triethyl
orthoformate

3-methoxy-17-acetoxy-19-nor-
3,5-pregnadien-20-one (I)

I + OHC—N(CH$_3$)CH$_3$ →[POCl$_3$]

6-formyl-3-methoxy-17-
acetoxy-19-nor-3,5-
pregnadien-20-one (II)

II →
1. NaBH$_4$
2. HCl
3. H$_2$, Pd—C, NaOAc

Nomegestrol acetate

Reference(s):
DOS 2 522 533 (J. M. Gastaud; 21.5.1975; GB-prior. 21.5.1974).

alternative synthesis:
EP 157 842 (Théramex; appl. 4.10.1984; F-prior. 4.10.1983).

medical use for i.m. treatment of luteal deficiency:
US 4 544 555 (J. M. Gastaud; 1.10.1985; appl. 27.9.1982; prior. 28.4.1980, 13.5.1975).

Formulation(s):   tabl. 5 mg

Trade Name(s):
F: Lutenyl (Théramex; 1985)   I: Lutenyl (Schering)

Nomifensine

ATC: N06AX04
Use: antidepressant

RN: 24526-64-5   MF: $C_{16}H_{18}N_2$ MW: 238.33
LD$_{50}$: 260 mg/kg (M, p.o.)
CN: 1,2,3,4-tetrahydro-2-methyl-4-phenyl-8-isoquinolinamine

maleate (1:1)
RN: 32795-47-4   MF: $C_{16}H_{18}N_2 \cdot C_4H_4O_4$ MW: 354.41   EINECS: 251-223-7
LD$_{50}$: 68 mg/kg (M, i.v.); 300 mg/kg (M, p.o.);
       66 mg/kg (R, i.v.); 430 mg/kg (R, p.o.)

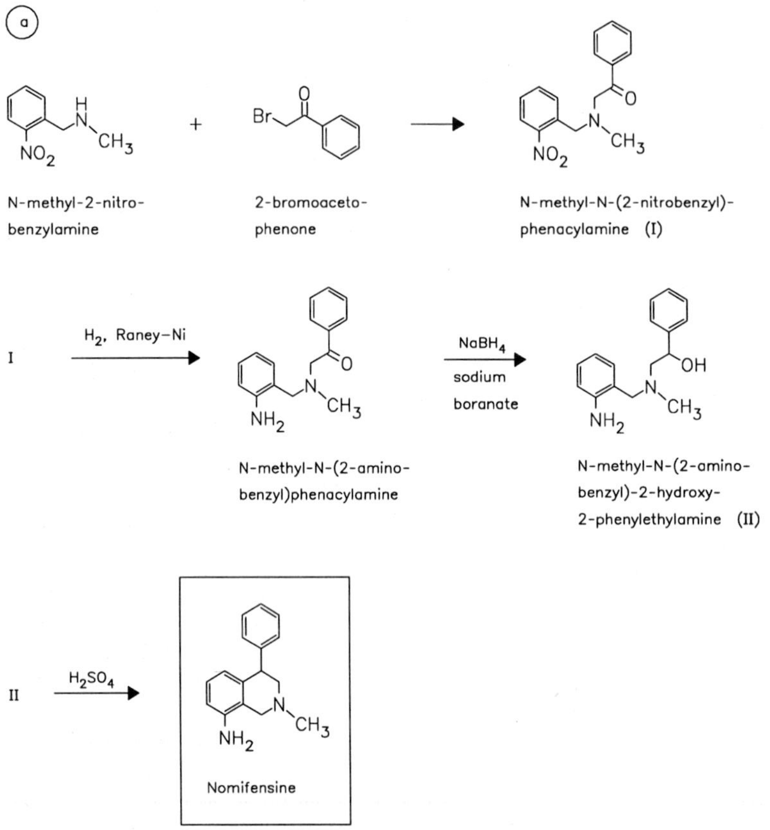

a)

N-methyl-2-nitro-
benzylamine

2-bromoaceto-
phenone

N-methyl-N-(2-nitrobenzyl)-
phenacylamine (I)

I → H$_2$, Raney–Ni

NaBH$_4$
sodium
boranate

N-methyl-N-(2-amino-
benzyl)phenacylamine

N-methyl-N-(2-amino-
benzyl)-2-hydroxy-
2-phenylethylamine   (II)

II → H$_2$SO$_4$

Nomifensine

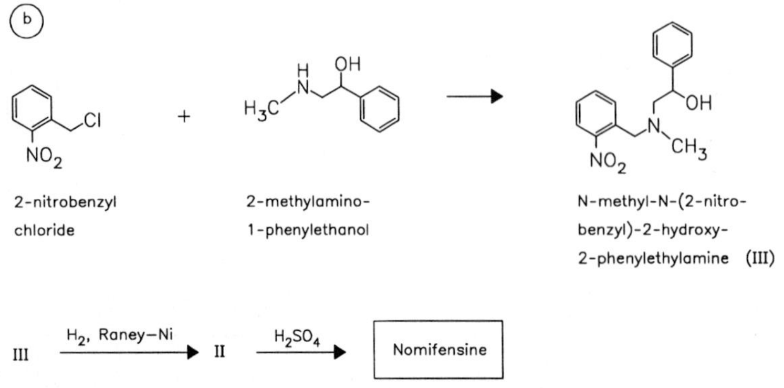

b)

2-nitrobenzyl
chloride

2-methylamino-
1-phenylethanol

N-methyl-N-(2-nitro-
benzyl)-2-hydroxy-
2-phenylethylamine   (III)

III → H$_2$, Raney–Ni → II → H$_2$SO$_4$ → Nomifensine

Reference(s):
DE 1 670 694 (Hoechst; appl. 5.5.1966).
DAS 1 795 830 (Hoechst; appl. 12.8.1966).
US 3 577 424 (Hoechst; 4.5.1971; D-prior. 5.5.1966, 12.8.1966, 15.4.1967).
GB 1 164 192 (Hoechst; appl. 5.5.1967; D-prior. 5.5.1966, 12.8.1966, 14.4.1967).
Hoffmann, J. et al.: Arzneim.-Forsch. (ARZNAD) 21, 1045 A (1971).

Formulation(s):   cps. 25 mg, 50 mg (as hydrogen maleate)

Trade Name(s):
D: Alival (Hoechst); wfm   GB: Merital 25 (Hoechst); wfm   I: Psicronizer (Albert-Farma);
F: Alival (Hoechst); wfm   wfm

Nonoxinol 9
(Nonoxynol 9)

ATC: G02BB
Use: spermatocide

RN: 26027-38-3   MF: [C_2H_4O]x$C_{15}H_{24}O$ MW: unspecified
CN: α-(4-nonylphenyl)-ω-hydroxypoly(oxy-1,2-ethanediyl)

H₃C–(CH₂)₈– ⬡ –OH + (ethylene oxide) → H₃C–(CH₂)₈– ⬡ –(O–CH₂–CH₂)ₓ–OH

4-nonylphenol   ethylene oxide   Nonoxinol 9

Reference(s):
US 2 313 477 (GAF; 1940).

Formulation(s):   foam 12.5 %; suppos. 0.075 g; vaginal gel 2 g/100 g

Trade Name(s):
D: Ortho-Creme (Janssen-Cilag)   Double Check (Family Planning Sales)   Staycept (Syntex)
      Patentex Oral (Patentex)   Gynol II (Janssen-Cilag)   I: Florigien (Schering)-comb.
F: Patentex (Lab. C.C.D.)   Ortho-Creme (Janssen-Cilag)   Koromex (Sanico)
      Semicid (Théraplix)   USA: Ramses (Schmid Prod.);
GB: Delfen (Janssen-Cilag)   Ortho-Forms (Janssen-Cilag)   wfm
                                                                                 Semicid (Whitehall); wfm

Norboletone
(Norbolethone)

ATC: A14AB
Use: anabolic

RN: 1235-15-0   MF: $C_{21}H_{32}O_2$ MW: 316.49
LD$_{50}$:   >5010 mg/kg (M, p.o.)
CN: (17α)-(±)-13-ethyl-17-hydroxy-18,19-dinorpregn-4-en-3-one

(±)-17α-ethyl-17β-hydroxy-
3-oxo-18-homo-5(10)-estrene

Norboletone

Reference(s):
GB 1 041 280 (G. A. Hughes, H. Smith; valid from 8.10.1962; prior. 19.10.1961).

total synthesis and synthesis of enantiomers:
GB 1 096 761 (Roussel-Uclaf; valid from 17.12.1964; F-prior. 20.2.1964, 14.1.1964, 17.12.1963);
US 3 959 322 (H. Smith; 25.5.1976; prior. 15.1.1964, 4.10.1962, 16.5.1962, 15.5.1962, 12.9.1961, 24.2.1961, 23.9.1960).
US 3 850 911 (G. A. Hughes, H. Smith; 26.11.1974; GB-prior. 22.9.1960).
US 3 519 714 (G. A. Hughes; H. Smith; 7.7.1970; prior. 15.3.1966, 16.5.1962, 15.5.1962, 4.10.1962, 12.9.1961, 24.2.1961, 23.9.1960).
Smith, H. et al.: J. Chem. Soc. (JCSOA9) **1964**, 4472.

Trade Name(s):
USA: Genabol (Wyeth); wfm

Nordazepam

(Nordiazepam)

ATC: N05BA16
Use: anxiolytic, benzodiazepine

RN: 1088-11-5   MF: $C_{15}H_{11}ClN_2O$ MW: 270.72   EINECS: 214-123-4
LD$_{50}$: >400 mg/kg (M, i.p.); 670 mg/kg (M, p.o.);
>5200 mg/kg (R, p.o.)
CN: 7-chloro-1,3-dihydro-5-phenyl-2*H*-1,4-benzodiazepin-2-one

| 2-amino-5-chlorobenzo-phenone | chloroacetyl chloride | 2-chloroacetamido-5-chlorobenzo-phenone | Nordazepam |

Reference(s):
DE 1 136 709 (Hoffmann-La Roche; appl. 1960).
Sternbach, L.H.; Reeder, E.: J. Org. Chem. (JOCEAH) **26**, 4936 (1961).
Bell, S.C. et al.: J. Org. Chem. (JOCEAH) **27**, 562 (1962).

Formulation(s):   drops 5 mg/g; tabl. 7.5 mg, 10 mg, 15 mg

Trade Name(s):
D: Tranxilium N (Sanofi
     Winthrop)
F: Nordaz (Bouchara)
I: Madar Notte (Ravizza)

Norethandrolone

ATC: A14AA09
Use: anabolic

RN: 52-78-8 MF: $C_{20}H_{30}O_2$ MW: 302.46 EINECS: 200-153-5
CN: (17α)-17-hydroxy-19-norpregn-4-en-3-one

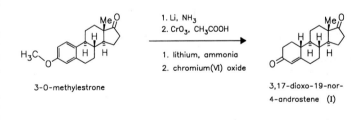

norethisterone (q. v.)   Norethandrolone

Reference(s):
US 2 721 871 (Searle; 1955; appl. 1954).

alternative synthesis:
US 2 691 028 (Searle; 1954; prior. 1952).
Colton, F.B. et al.: J. Am. Chem. Soc. (JACSAT) **79**, 1123 (1957).

Formulation(s):   tabl. 10 mg

Trade Name(s):
F: Nilevar (Laphal)   GB: Nilevar (Searle); wfm   USA: Nilevar (Coastal); wfm

Norethisterone
(Norethindrone)

ATC: G03AC01; G03DC02
Use: progestogen

RN: 68-22-4 MF: $C_{20}H_{26}O_2$ MW: 298.43 EINECS: 200-681-6
LD$_{50}$: 6 g/kg (M, p.o.)
CN: (17α)-17-hydroxy-19-norpregn-4-en-20-yn-3-one

3-0-methylestrone

1. Li, NH$_3$
2. CrO$_3$, CH$_3$COOH

1. lithium, ammonia
2. chromium(VI) oxide

3,17-dioxo-19-nor-4-androstene (I)

I + orthoformic acid triethyl ester

pyridine·HCl

3-ethoxy-17-oxo-19-nor-3,5-androstadiene (II)

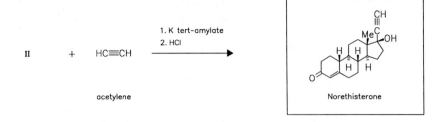

II + HC≡CH

acetylene

1. K tert-amylate
2. HCl

Norethisterone

Reference(s):

US 2 774 122 (Syntex; 1956; MEX-prior. 1951).
US 2 774 777 (Syntex; 1956; prior. 1952).
Djerassi, C. et al.: J. Am. Chem. Soc. (JACSAT) **76**, 4092 (1954).

alternative syntheses:

US 2 849 462 (P. de Ruggieri; 1958; appl. 1957).
Ringold, H.J. et al.: J. Am. Chem. Soc. (JACSAT) **78**, 2477 (1956).
Ringold, H.J. et al.: Ann. N. Y. Acad. Sci. (ANYAA9) **71**, 500 (1958).
Ueberwasser, H. et al.: Helv. Chim. Acta (HCACAV) **34**, 344 (1963).
Ullmanns Encykl. Tech. Chem., 4. Aufl., Vol. **13**, 31.
Onken, D.; Meublein, D.: Pharmazie (PHARAT) **25**, 3 (1970).

total synthesis of 3,17-dioxo-19-nor-4-androstene:

DE 1 958 600 (Hoffmann-La Roche; appl. 21.11.1969; USA-prior. 22.11.1968).

Formulation(s): tabl. 0.35 mg, 0.5 mg (also in comb.)

Trade Name(s):

D:	Conceplan (Grünenthal)-comb.	Noriday (Searle)	Micronor (Ortho-McNeil)

D: Conceplan (Grünenthal)-
     comb.
     Micronovum (Janssen-
     Cilag)
     TriNovum (Janssen-Cilag)-
     comb.
     numerous generics
F: Norluten (SmithKline
     Beecham)
     Ortho-Novum 1/35
     (Janssen-Cilag)-comb.
     Triella (Cilag)-comb.
GB: Micronor (Janssen-Cilag)

Noriday (Searle)
Primolut N (Schering)
Utovlan (Searle)
numerous combination
preparations
I: Trinovum (Janssen-Cilag)-
     comb.
J: Norluten D (Shionogi)
     Primosiston Tab. (Nihon
     Schering)-comb.
     Sophia-A, C (Teikoku
     Zoki)-comb.
USA: Brevicon (Searle)-comb.

Micronor (Ortho-McNeil)
Modicon (Ortho-McNeil)-
comb.
Nelova (Warner Chilcott)-
comb.
Norinyl (Searle)-comb.
Ortho-Novum (Ortho-
McNeil)-comb.
generic and combination
preparations

Norethisterone acetate

(Norethindrone acetate)

ATC: G03D
Use: progestogen

RN: 51-98-9 MF: C$_{22}$H$_{28}$O$_3$ MW: 340.46 EINECS: 200-132-0
CN: (17α)-17-(acetyloxy)-19-norpregn-4-en-20-yn-3-one

norethisterone
(q. v.)

acetic anhydride

19-norpregna-3,5-dien-20-yne-
3,17β-diol diacetate (I)

Norethisterone acetate

Reference(s):
US 2 964 437 (Schering AG; 13.12.1960; appl. 11.6.1957; D-prior. 16.6.1956).
Djerassi, C. et al.: J. Am. Chem. Soc. (JACSAT) **81**, 436 (1959).
DE 1 017 166 (Schering AG; appl. 16.6.1956).

alternative synthesis:
DD 136 502 (VEB Jenapharm; appl. 11.5.1978).

Formulation(s):   f. c. tabl. 1 mg; tabl. 1 mg, 5 mg, 10 mg

Trade Name(s):
D: Gestakadin (Kade)
      Neorlest 21 (Parke Davis)-
      comb.
      Norethisteron (Jenapharm)
      Primolut-Nor (Schering)
      Primosiston (Schering)-
      comb.
      Prosiston (Schering)-comb.
      Sinovula (Asche)-comb.
      Sovel (Novartis Pharma)-
      comb.
      Trisequens (Novo Nordisk;
      Rhône-Poulenc Rorer)-
      comb.
F: Kliogest (Specia)-comb.

      Milli-Anovlar (Schering)-
      comb.
      Milligynon (Schering)
      Miniphase (Schering)-
      comb.
      Primolut-Nor (Schering)-
      comb.
GB: Elleste Deret (Searle)-
      comb.
      Estra combi (Novartis)-
      comb.
      Evorel combi (Janssen-
      Cilag)-comb.
      Klimofem (Novo Nordisk)-
      comb.

      Loestrin (Parke Davis)-
      comb.
      S.H. 420 (Schering
      Chemicals)
      Trisequens (Novo
      Nordisk)-comb.
I: Primolut-Nor (Schering)
J: Anovlar (Nihon Schering)-
      comb.
      Norluten A (Shionogi)
USA: Aygestin (ESI Lederle)
      Estrostep (Parke Davis)-
      comb.

Norethisterone enanthate

ATC: G03DB
Use: progestogen

RN: 3836-23-5   MF: $C_{27}H_{38}O_3$ MW: 410.60   EINECS: 223-326-7
CN: (17α)-17-[(1-oxoheptyl)oxy]-19-norpregn-4-en-20-yn-3-one

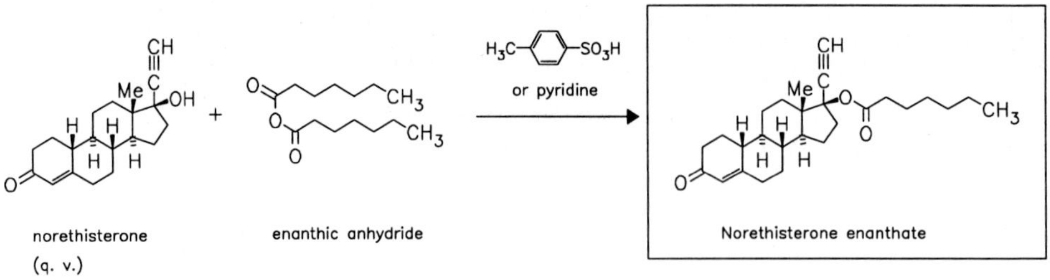
norethisterone
(q. v.)
enanthic anhydride
H_3C–C6H4–SO_3H
or pyridine
Norethisterone enanthate

Reference(s):
DE 1 017 166 (Schering AG; appl. 16.6.1956).

alternative synthesis:
FR 1 349 991 (Parke Davis; appl. 29.11.1962; GB-prior. 1.12.1961).

use as progestogen depot preparation:
DOS 2 548 413 (Schering AG; appl. 27.10.1975).

Formulation(s): amp. 200 mg/ml

Trade Name(s):

D:	Noristerat (Schering)	F:	Noristerat (Schering)	GB:	Noristerat (Schering)

Noretynodrel
(Norethynodrel)

ATC: G03D
Use: progestogen

RN: 68-23-5 MF: $C_{20}H_{26}O_2$ MW: 298.43 EINECS: 200-682-1
CN: (17α)-17-hydroxy-19-norpregn-5(10)-en-20-yn-3-one

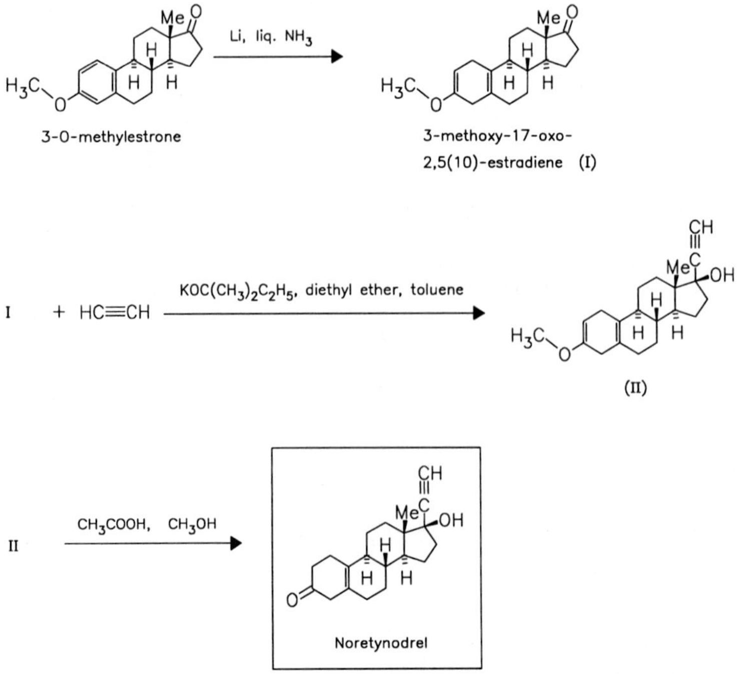
Li, liq. NH3
3-O-methylestrone
3-methoxy-17-oxo-
2,5(10)-estradiene (I)
I + HC≡CH
KOC(CH3)2C2H5, diethyl ether, toluene
(II)
II
CH3COOH, CH3OH
Noretynodrel

Reference(s):
US 2 691 028 (Searle; 1954; prior. 1953, 1952).
US 2 725 389 (Searle; 1955; prior. 1953).

starting material:
US 2 655 518 (Searle; 1953; appl. 1952).

alternative synthesis:
FR 1 421 476 (Roussel-Uclaf; appl. 2.11.1964).

Formulation(s): tabl. 2.5 mg, 5 mg, 9.85 mg in comb. with metranol

Trade Name(s):

D:	Kontrazeptivum 63 (ratiopharm)-comb.; wfm Zyklustabletten IB 2 (Ce-Ka-Ce)-comb.; wfm	I:	Ebionel (Panther-Osfa Chemie)-comb.; wfm Elan (Valeas)-comb.; wfm Singestol (Caber)-comb.; wfm	USA:	Enovid (Searle)-comb.; wfm Enovid E (Searle)-comb.; wfm
GB:	Enavid (Searle)-comb.; wfm	J:	Enavid (Dainippon)-comb.		

Norfenefrine

ATC: C01CA05
Use: sympathomimetic, circulatory analeptic, adrenergic

RN: 536-21-0 MF: $C_8H_{11}NO_2$ MW: 153.18 EINECS: 208-626-8
LD_{50}: 4.9 mg/kg (M, i.v.); 263 mg/kg (M, p.o.);
17.4 mg/kg (R, i.v.); 390 mg/kg (R, p.o.)
CN: α-(aminomethyl)-3-hydroxybenzenemethanol

hydrochloride
RN: 4779-94-6 MF: $C_8H_{11}NO_2 \cdot HCl$ MW: 189.64 EINECS: 225-323-6
LD_{50}: 113 mg/kg (M, i.v.); 3300 mg/kg (M, p.o.);
17.4 mg/kg (R, i.v.); 390 mg/kg (R, p.o.)

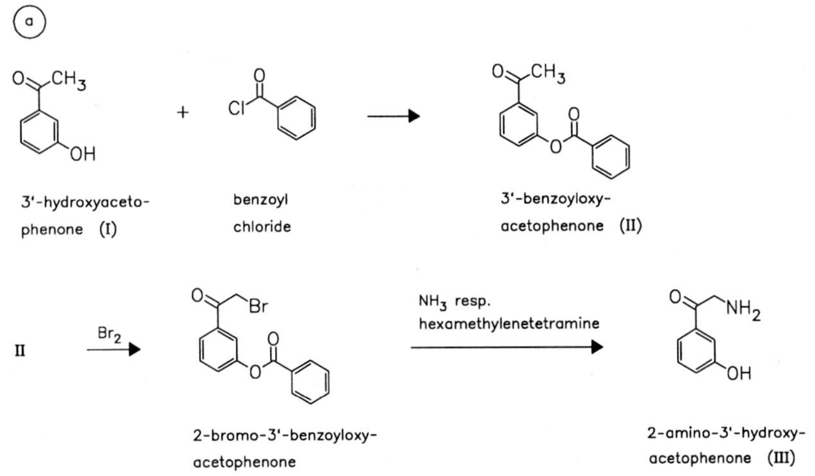
a
3'-hydroxyacetophenone (I)
benzoyl chloride
3'-benzoyloxyacetophenone (II)
II
Br2
2-bromo-3'-benzoyloxyacetophenone
NH3 resp. hexamethylenetetramine
2-amino-3'-hydroxyacetophenone (III)

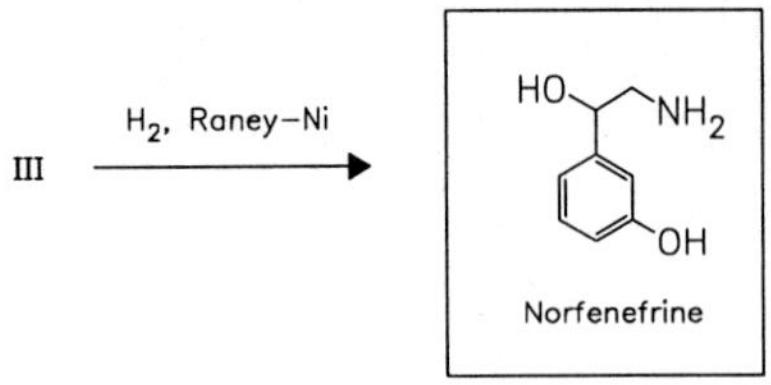

Norfenefrine

b

2-hydroxyimino-
3'-hydroxyacetophenone

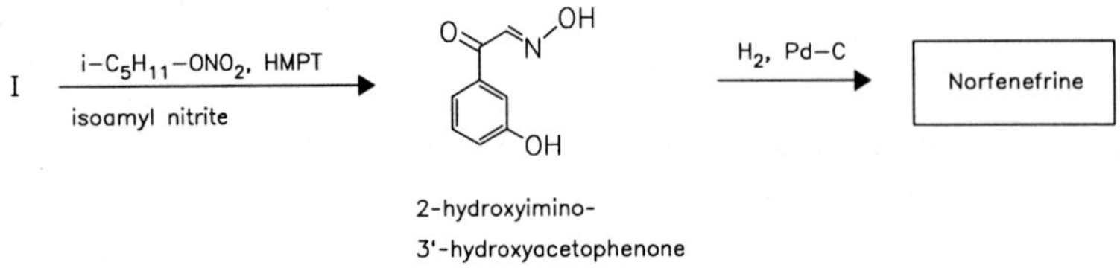

Reference(s):
a FR 851 296 (R. Sachs; 1938).
    FR 866 569 (R. Sachs; 1939).
b DE 2 130 710 (Gödecke; appl. 21.6.1971).

Formulation(s):   amp. 50 mg/5 ml; cps. 6 mg; drg. 15 mg, 45 mg; drops 6 mg/ml; sol. 6 mg/ml; s. r. tabl. 50 mg;
            tabl. 45 mg (as hydrochloride)

Trade Name(s):
D: Energona (Maurer)   Norfenefrin Ziethen   Normetolo (Selvi); wfm
    Esbuphon (Schaper &   (Ziethen)   J: Coritat (Green Cross)
    Brümmer)   Novadral (Gödecke)   Tonolift (Teisan)
    Norfenefrin retard forte-   generic and numerous   Zondel (Grelan; as
    ratiopharm (ratiopharm)   combination preparations   hydrochloride)
                  I: Euro-Cir (Virgiliano); wfm

Norfloxacin

ATC: J01MA06; S01AX12
Use: antibiotic (gyrase inhibitor)

RN: 70458-96-7   MF: $C_{16}H_{18}FN_3O_3$ MW: 319.34   EINECS: 274-614-4
LD$_{50}$:   220 mg/kg (M, i.v.); 4 g/kg (M, p.o.);
    245 mg/kg (R, i.v.); >4 g/kg (R, p.o.)
CN: 1-ethyl-6-fluoro-1,4-dihydro-4-oxo-7-(1-piperazinyl)-3-quinolinecarboxylic acid

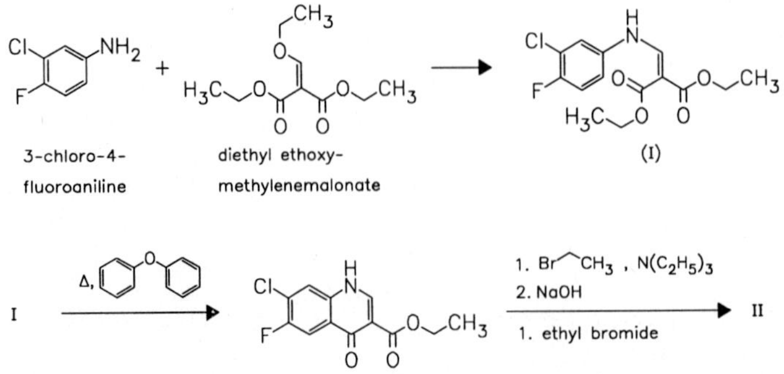

3-chloro-4-   diethyl ethoxy-   (I)
fluoroaniline   methylenemalonate

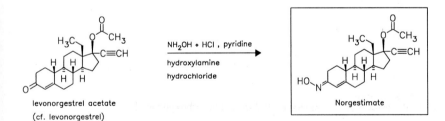

1-ethyl-6-fluoro-7-
chloro-1,4-dihydro-
4-oxoquinoline-3-
carboxylic acid (II)

piperazine

Norfloxacin

Reference(s):
DE 2 804 097 (Kyorin; appl. 31.1.1978; J-prior. 16.5.1977).
US 4 146 719 (Kyorin; 27.3.1979; J-prior. 16.2.1977).

synthesis of 1-ethyl-6-fluoro-7-chloro-1,4-dihydro-4-oxoquinoline-3-carboxylic acid:
Koga, H. et al.: J. Med. Chem. (JMCMAR) **23**, 1358 (1980).

Formulation(s):   eye drops 3 mg/ml; f. c. tabl. 400 mg

Trade Name(s):
D:	Barazan (Dieckmann; 1984)		Noroxine (MSD-Chibret; 1986)	J:	Sebercim (ISF) Baccidal (Kyorin)
	Chibroxin (Chibret)	GB:	Utinor (Merck Sharp & Dohme)	USA:	Chibroxin (Merck)
F:	Chibroxine (Merck Sharp & Dohme-Chibret)	I:	Fulgram (ABC) Noroxin (MSD)		Noroxin (Merck; 1986) Noroxin (Roberts)

Norgestimate

ATC: G03AA
Use: progestogen, oral contraceptive

RN: 35189-28-7   MF: $C_{23}H_{31}NO_3$ MW: 369.51
CN: (17α)-17-(acetyloxy)-13-ethyl-18,19-dinorpregn-4-en-20-yn-3-one oxime

levonorgestrel acetate
(cf. levonorgestrel)

$NH_2OH \cdot HCl$, pyridine
hydroxylamine
hydrochloride

Norgestimate

Reference(s):
GB 1 123 104 (Ortho; appl. 2.9.1966; USA-prior. 22.10.1965).
DE 1 620 102 (Ortho; appl. 9.9.1966; USA-prior. 22.10.1965).

medical use for suppression of fertility:
US 4 027 019 (Ortho; 31.5.1977; appl. 23.1.1976; prior. 24.7.1975).

Formulation(s):   tabl. 0.25 mg in comb. with ethinylestradiole

Trade Name(s):
D:	Cilest (Janssen-Cilag)-comb.	F:	Cilest (Janssen-Cilag)-comb.	GB:	Cilest (Janssen-Cilag)-comb.
	Pramino (Janssen-Cilag)-comb.		Effiprev (Effik)-comb.	I:	Cilest (Cilag)-comb.

USA: Ortho-Cyclen (Ortho-   Ortho-Tri-Cyclen (Ortho-
       McNeil)   McNeil)

Norgestrel

ATC: G03AA06; G03FA10; G03FB01
Use: progestogen

RN: 6533-00-2   MF: $C_{21}H_{28}O_2$ MW: 312.45   EINECS: 229-433-5
LD_{50}:   5010 mg/kg (M, p.o.);
       5010 mg/kg (R, p.o.)
CN: (17α)-(±)-13-ethyl-17-hydroxy-18,19-dinorpregn-4-en-20-yn-3-one

(±)-3-methoxy-18-methyl-   acetylene
17-oxo-2,5(10)-estradiene

(±)-3-methoxy-18-methyl-
19-norpregna-2,5(10)-
dien-20-yne-17β-ol (I)

Norgestrel

Reference(s):
GB 1 041 279 (H. Smith; appl. 19.10.1961).
GB 1 041 280 (H. Smith; appl. 19.10.1961).
DOS 2 030 056 (Schering AG; appl. 13.6.1970).
Buzby, G.C. et al.: J. Med. Chem. (JMCMAR) **9**, 782 (1966).

starting material:
Smith, H. et al.: J. Chem. Soc. (JCSOA9) **1964**, 4472.

total synthesis:
NL-appl. 6 414 702 (Roussel-Uclaf; appl. 17.12.1964; F-prior. 17.12.1963).
Smith, H. et al.: Experientia (EXPEAM) **19**, 394 (1963).
Smith, H. et al.: J. Chem. Soc. (JCSOA9) **1963**, 5072.
Blickenstaff, R.T.; Ghosh, A.C.; Wolf, G.C.: Total Synthesis of Steroids (Organic Chemistry Vol. **30**) p. 270,
Academic Press, New York, London 1974.

Formulation(s):   drg. 0.5 mg in comb. with ethinylestradiole

Trade Name(s):
D: Cyclo-Progynova   Minidril (Wyeth-Lederle)-   GB: Cyclo Progynova (ASTA
       (Schering)-comb.   comb.   Medica)-comb.
       Stediril (Wyeth)-comb.   Stédiril (Wyeth-Lederle)-   Eugynon (Schering)-comb.
F: Adepal (Wyeth-Lederle)-   comb.   Neogest (Schering)
       comb.   Trinordiol (Wyeth-   Prempak C (Wyeth)
       Microval (Wyeth-Lederle) Lederle)-comb.   Schering PC4 (Schering)-
                                                                       comb.

I: Eugynon (Schering)-comb.   USA: Lo/Ovral (Wyeth-Ayerst)-   Ovral (Wyeth-Ayerst)-
J: Duoluton (Schering)   comb.   comb.
                                                                                                     Ovrette (Wyeth-Ayerst)

Norgestrienone

ATC: G03AC07
Use: progestogen

RN: 848-21-5   MF: $C_{20}H_{22}O_2$ MW: 294.39   EINECS: 212-698-6
CN: (17α)-17-hydroxy-19-norpregna-4,9,11-trien-20-yn-3-one

17β-hydroxy-3-oxo-
4,9,11-estratriene

1. hydroxylamine
2. cyclohexanone, aluminum
   isopropylate

4,9,11-estratrien-3,17-dione
3-oxime (I)

ethynylmagnesium
bromide

17β-hydroxy-19-norpregna-
4,9,11-trien-20-yn-3-one
oxime (II)

Norgestrienone

Reference(s):
US 3 257 278 (Roussel-Uclaf; 21.6.1966; F-prior. 5.7.1963, 4.10.1963, 15.5.1964, 14.8.1964, 1.6.1965).
FR-M 3 060 (Roussel-Uclaf; appl. 4.10.1963).
NL 6 401 555 (Roussel-Uclaf; appl. 20.2.1964; F-prior. 20.2.1963, 5.7.1963, 4.10.1963).
Nominé, G. et al.: C. R. Hebd. Seances Acad. Sci. (COREAF) **260**, 4545 (1965).

starting material:
BE 631 298 (Roussel-Uclaf; appl. 19.4.1963; F-prior. 20.4.1962).
NL 6 414 702 (Roussel-Uclaf; appl. 17.12.1964; F-prior. 17.12.1963, 14.1.1964, 20.2.1964).
NL 6 517 141 (Roussel-Uclaf; appl. 30.12.1965; F-prior. 31.12.1964, 26.2.1965, 24.3.1965, 14.6.1965, 3.9.1965,
17.9.1965).
Velluz, L. et al.: C. R. Hebd. Seances Acad. Sci. (COREAF) **257**, 569 (1963).

total synthesis:
Ullmanns Encykl. Tech. Chem., 4. Aufl., Vol. **13**, 34.
Velluz, L. et al.: C. R. Hebd. Seances Acad. Sci. (COREAF) **257**, 3086 (1963).

Formulation(s):   tabl. 0.35 mg

Normethadone

ATC: R05DA06
Use: antitussive, analgesic

RN: 467-85-6   MF: $C_{20}H_{25}NO$ MW: 295.43   EINECS: 207-401-1
LD_{50}: 31 mg/kg (M, i.v.)
CN: 6-(dimethylamino)-4,4-diphenyl-3-hexanone

hydrochloride
RN: 847-84-7   MF: $C_{20}H_{25}NO \cdot HCl$ MW: 331.89   EINECS: 212-694-4
LD_{50}: 45 mg/kg (M, i.v.)

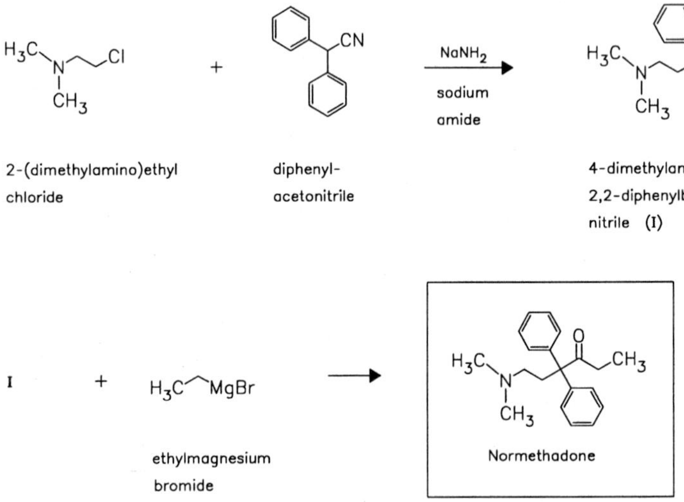

2-(dimethylamino)ethyl
chloride

diphenyl-
acetonitrile

4-dimethylamino-
2,2-diphenylbutyro-
nitrile (I)

ethylmagnesium
bromide

Normethadone

Reference(s):
DE 865 314 (Hoechst; appl. 1941).
DE 870 700 (Hoechst; appl. 1942).
Bockmühl, M.; Ehrhart, G.: Justus Liebigs Ann. Chem. (JLACBF) **561**, 52 (1948).

Formulation(s):   drops 10 mg/ml

Normolaxol

ATC: A06A
Use: laxative

RN: 18831-34-0   MF: $C_{22}H_{17}NO_2$ MW: 327.38
CN: 4,4'-(2-quinolinylmethylene)bis[phenol]

hydrochloride
RN: 19035-45-1   MF: $C_{22}H_{17}NO_2 \cdot HCl$ MW: 363.84

quinoline-2-
carboxaldehyde

phenol

Normolaxol

Reference(s):
US 2 753 351 (Dr. K. Thomae; 1956; D-prior. 1952).
US 3 627 893 (Boehringer Ing.; 14.12.1971; prior. 11.1.1967, 2.1.1970).

Trade Name(s):
D: Normolaxol (Boehringer
      Ing.); wfm

D-Norpseudoephedrine

(D-Pseudonorephedrine; Norisoephedrine)

ATC: N06B
Use: appetite depressant

RN: 492-39-7   MF: $C_9H_{13}NO$ MW: 151.21   EINECS: 207-754-1
LD_{50}:   275 mg/kg (M, s.c.)
CN: [S-(R^*,R^*)]-α-(1-aminoethyl)benzenemethanol

hydrochloride
RN: 2153-98-2   MF: $C_9H_{13}NO \cdot HCl$ MW: 187.67   EINECS: 218-446-1
LD_{50}:   161 mg/kg (M, i.p.)

L-norephedrine

1. $SOCl_2$
2. HCl, H_2O, Δ

1. thionyl chloride

D-Norpseudoephedrine

Reference(s):
DD 13 785 (H. Pfanz, H. Wieduwilt; appl. 1956).

starting material:
DE 1 014 553 (Knoll; appl. 1954).

alternative syntheses:
DD 43 989 (H. Müller, H. Baborowski; appl. 30.1.1965).
Rebstock, M.C. et al.: J. Am. Chem. Soc. (JACSAT) **73**, 3668 (1951).
DOS 3 408 850 (Knoll; appl. 10.3.1984; D-prior. 12.3.1983).

review:
Heacock, R.A.; Forrest, J.E.: Can. J. Pharm. Sci. (JPMSAE) **9**, 64 (1974).
Pfanz, H.; Wieduwilt, H.: Arch. Pharm. Ber. Dtsch. Pharm. Ges. (APBDAJ) **288**, 563 (1955).

Formulation(s):   cps. 20 mg (as base); drg. 15 mg; drops 4 g/100 ml; sol. 3.5 g/100 ml (as hydrochloride)

Trade Name(s):
D: Antiadipositum (Hänseler)   Mirapront N (Mack)-on   Vita Schlanktropfen
      Fasupond (Eu Rho Arznei)   ion-exchanger   (Schuck)

Nortriptyline
(Desitriptyline)

ATC:　N06AA10
Use:　antidepressant

RN:　72-69-5　MF: $C_{19}H_{21}N$　MW: 263.38　EINECS: 200-788-8
LD_{50}:　17 mg/kg (M, i.v.); 370 mg/kg (M, p.o.);
　　　22 mg/kg (R, i.v.); 502 mg/kg (R, p.o.)
CN:　3-(10,11-dihydro-5H-dibenzo[a,d]cyclohepten-5-ylidene)-N-methyl-1-propanamine

hydrochloride
RN:　894-71-3　MF: $C_{19}H_{21}N \cdot HCl$　MW: 299.85　EINECS: 212-973-0
LD_{50}:　18.7 mg/kg (M, i.v.); 260 mg/kg (M, p.o.);
　　　13 mg/kg (R, i.v.); 405 mg/kg (R, p.o.)

amitriptyline (I)　　　　methyl iodide　　　amitriptyline methiodide (II)
(q. v.)

II　$\xrightarrow{CH_3NH_2,\ 140\ °C}$

Nortriptyline

I　+　chloroformic acid ethyl ester　→　ethyl nortriptyline-N-carboxylate　$\xrightarrow{KOH}$　Nortriptyline

5-(3-bromopropylidene)-10,11-dihydro-5H-dibenzo[a,d]cycloheptene　+　H_3C-NH_2 methylamine　→　Nortriptyline

Reference(s):
a   FR 1 345 936 (Kefalas; appl. 21.1.1963; GB-prior. 26.1.1962).
b   DE 1 288 599 (Geigy; appl. 13.3.1962; CH-prior. 14.3.1961, 30.3.1961).
c   Hoffsommer, R.D. et al.: J. Org. Chem. (JOCEAH) **27**, 4134 (1962).

alternative syntheses:
DE 1 266 755 (Kefalas; appl. 6.10.1961).
BE 628 904 (Eli Lilly; appl. 26.2.1963; USA-prior. 26.2.1963).
DE 1 269 614 (Hoffman-La Roche; appl. 15.1.1962).
CH 407 990 (Hoffman-La Roche; appl. 1.2.1962).
CH 407 993 (Hoffman-La Roche; appl. 1.2.1962).
US 3 281 469 (Eli Lilly; appl. 10.8.1962; prior. 26.2.1962).
DAS 1 468 138 (Kefalas; appl. 12.3.1963; GB-prior. 23.3.1962, 9.11.1962).
DOS 1 918 739 (Egyesült; appl. 12.4.1969; H-prior. 12.4.1968).
US 3 215 739 (Kefalas; 2.11.1965; appl. 10.10.1961; DK-prior. 12.10.1960).
US 3 372 196 (Merck & Co.; 5.3.1968; prior. 25.7.1963, 25.11.1966).

Formulation(s):   drg. 10 mg, 25 mg, 50 mg, 75 mg (as hydrochloride)

Trade Name(s):

D:	Nortrilen (Promonta Lundbeck)		Motipress (Sanofi Winthrop)-comb.		Noritren (Lundbeck) Vividyl (Lilly)
F:	Motival (Norgine Pharma)-comb.		Motival (Sanofi Winthrop)-comb.	J:	Noritren (Dainippon)
GB:	Allegron (King; as hydrochloride)	I:	Dominans (Recordati)-comb. Nodal (Squibb)-comb.	USA:	Aventyl (Lilly) Pamelor (Novartis) generics

---

Novobiocin

ATC: J01
Use: antibiotic

RN: 303-81-1   MF: $C_{31}H_{36}N_2O_{11}$ MW: 612.63   EINECS: 206-146-3
LD$_{50}$:   407 mg/kg (M, i.v.); 1500 mg/kg (M, p.o.)
CN: N-[7-[[3-O-(aminocarbonyl)-6-deoxy-5-C-methyl-4-O-methyl-β-L-*lyxo*-hexopyranosyl]oxy]-4-hydroxy-8-methyl-2-oxo-2H-1-benzopyran-3-yl]-4-hydroxy-3-(3-methyl-2-butenyl)benzamide

monosodium salt
RN: 1476-53-5   MF: $C_{31}H_{35}N_2NaO_{11}$ MW: 634.61   EINECS: 216-023-6
LD$_{50}$:   407 mg/kg (M, i.v.); 962 mg/kg (M, p.o.);
385 mg/kg (R, i.v.); 3500 mg/kg (R, p.o.)

Novobiocin

From cultures of *Streptomyces niveus* or *Streptomyces spheroides*.

Reference(s):
US 2 925 411 (C. H. Stammer; 16.2.1960; prior. 29.4.1958).
US 2 966 484 (Merck & Co.; 27.12.1960; appl. 26.12.1957; prior. 19.4.1956).
US 2 983 723 (Upjohn; 9.5.1961; prior. 17.7.1957).
US 3 000 873 (Merck & Co.; 19.9.1961; prior. 21.5.1957).
US 3 049 475 (Merck & Co.; 14.8.1962; prior. 19.4.1956).
US 3 049 476 (Merck & Co.; 14.8.1962; prior. 19.4.1956).
US 3 049 534 (Merck & Co.; 14.8.1962; appl. 7.3.1956; prior. 21.4.1955).
US 3 068 221 (Upjohn; 11.12.1962; prior. 18.3.1960).
Kaczka, E.A. et al.: J. Am. Chem. Soc. (JACSAT) **77**, 6404 (1955).
Hoeksema, H. et al.: J. Am. Chem. Soc. (JACSAT) **77**, 6711 (1955).

Formulation(s):   cps. 250 mg (as sodium salt); vial 500 mg

Trade Name(s):

D:	Inamycin (Hoechst); wfm	GB:	Albamycin (Upjohn); wfm	J:	Albiocin (Upjohn)
F:	Albacycline (Upjohn)-	I:	Robiocina (San Carlo);		Cathomycin (Meiji)
	comb.; wfm		wfm	USA:	Albacycline (Upjohn)-
	Cathomycine (Théraplix);		Stilbiocina (Donatello);		comb.; wfm
	wfm		wfm		Albamycin (Upjohn); wfm

Noxiptiline

ATC: N06A
Use: antidepressant

RN: 3362-45-6   MF: $C_{19}H_{22}N_2O$ MW: 294.40
CN: 10,11-dihydro-5*H*-dibenzo[*a,d*]cyclohepten-5-one *O*-[2-(dimethylamino)ethyl]oxime

monohydrochloride
RN: 4985-15-3   MF: $C_{19}H_{22}N_2O \cdot HCl$ MW: 330.86   EINECS: 225-638-9
LD_{50}:   21.3 mg/kg (M, i.v.); 275 mg/kg (M, p.o.);
       12 mg/kg (R, i.v.); 607 mg/kg (R, p.o.);
       800 mg/kg (dog, p.o.)

dibenzosuberone → (NH$_2$OH, pyridine / hydroxylamine) → dibenzosuberone oxime (I)

I → (1. NaOC$_2$H$_5$ 2. Cl-CH$_2$CH$_2$-N(CH$_3$)$_2$ / 2. 2-(dimethylamino)ethyl chloride) → Noxiptiline

Reference(s):
DE 1 198 353 (H. Engelhard; appl. 29.7.1964).
DE 1 225 169 (Bayer; appl. 26.11.1964).
US 3 963 778 (Bayer; 15.6.1976; appl. 14.7.1969; D-prior. 10.11.1965).
GB 1 045 911 (Pfizer; appl. 22.2.1963; valid from 6.2.1964).

Formulation(s):   tabl. 25 mg (as monohydrochloride)

Trade Name(s):
D: Agedal (Bayer); wfm   F: Nogédal (Théraplix); wfm   I: Agedal (Bayer); wfm

---

Noxytiolin
(Noxitiolinum; Noxythiolin)

ATC: B05CA07
Use: bactericide (external)

RN: 15599-39-0   MF: $C_3H_8N_2OS$ MW: 120.18   EINECS: 239-679-5
LD_{50}:   >3 g/kg (M, p.o.)
CN: *N*-(hydroxymethyl)-*N*'-methylthiourea

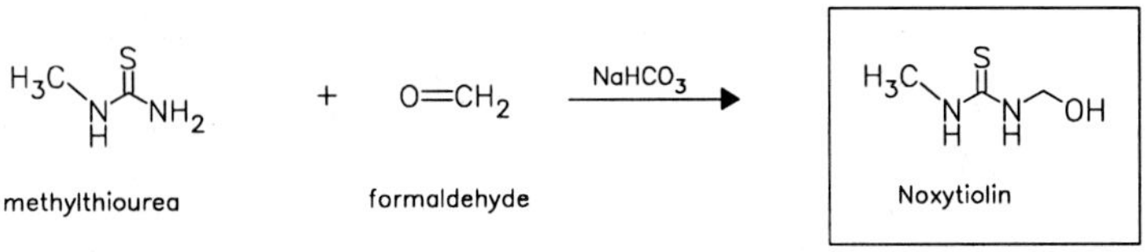

methylthiourea   formaldehyde   Noxytiolin

Reference(s):
GB 970 414 (Ed. Geistlich Söhne; appl. 12.1.1960; valid from 4.1.1961).

Formulation(s):   powder 2.5 g

Trade Name(s):
F: Noxyflex (Innothéra)   GB: Noxyflex (Geistlich)

Nystatin

ATC: A07AA02; D01AA01; G01AA01
Use: fungicidal antibiotic, antimycotic

RN: 1400-61-9   MF: unspecified   MW: unspecified   EINECS: 215-749-0
LD_{50}:   3 mg/kg (M, i.v.); 8 g/kg (M, p.o.);
          10 g/kg (R, p.o.)
CN: nystatin

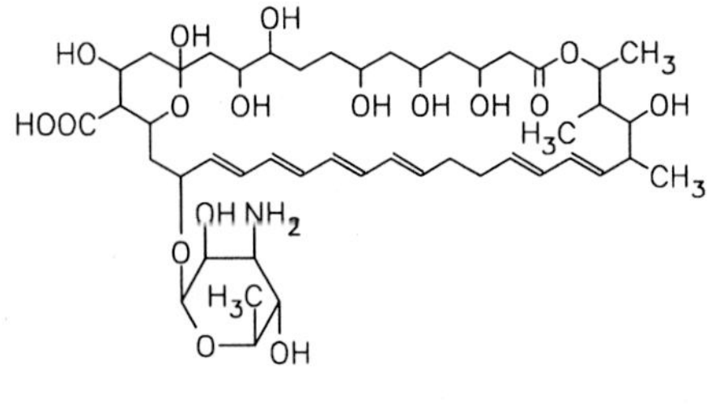

Nystatin A₁ (component of Nystatin)

From fermentation solutions of *Streptomyces noursei*.

Reference(s):

US 2 786 781 (Olin Mathieson; 1957; prior. 1954).
US 2 797 183 (Research Corp. 1957; prior. 1952).
US 2 832 719 (Olin Mathieson; 1958; prior. 1956).
US 3 517 100 (American Cyanamid; 23.6.1970; appl. 2.7.1968).

preliposomal powder:

EP 567 582 (Argus Pharmac.; appl. 10.1.1992; USA-prior. 14.1.1991).

Formulation(s):   cream 100000 iu/g; drg. 500000 iu; f. c. tabl. 500000 iu/g; gel 100000 iu/g;
                     ointment 100000 iu; pessaries 100000 iu; susp. 100000 iu/ml

Trade Name(s):

D: Adiclair (Ardeypharm)
    Aureomycin (Lederle)-
    comb. with
    chlortetracycline
    Biofanal (Pfleger)
    Candio-Hermal (Hermal)
    Candio-Hermal (Hermal)-
    comb. with
    chlortetracycline
    Fungireduct (Azupharma)
    Halog (Bristol-Myers
    Squibb)-comb.
    Jellin (Grünenthal)-comb.
    Lokalisation
    (Dermapharm)-comb.
    Moronal (Bristol-Myers
    Squibb)
    Moronal (Bristol-Myers
    Squibb)-comb.
    Mykoderm (Engelhard)
    Mykoproct (Bristol-Myers
    Squibb)-comb.
    Mykundex (Biocur)-comb.
    Nystaderm (Dermapharm)-
    comb.

    Penanyst (Johnson &
    Johnson)-comb.
    Polygynax (UCB)-comb.
    Topsym (Grünenthal)-
    comb.
    Volonimat (Bristol-Myers
    Squibb)-comb.
    generic and numerous
    combination preparations
F: Auricularum (Sérolam)-
    comb.
    Mycolog (Bristol-Myers
    Squibb)-comb.
    Mycomnès (Fumouze)-
    comb.
    Mycostatine (Bristol-Myers
    Squibb)
    Myco-ultralan (Schering)-
    comb.
    Polygynax /-virgo
    (Innothéra)-comb.
    Tergynan (Bouchara)-
    comb.
GB: Dermovate (Glaxo
    Wellcome)-comb.

    Flagyl Compak (Rhône-
    Poulenc Rorer)-comb.
    Gregoderm (Unigreg)-
    comb.
I: Fasigin (Pfizer)-comb.
    Halciderm Combi (Squibb;
    as sulfate)-comb.
    Macmiror Complex (Poli)-
    comb.
    Mycocur (Schering)-comb.
    Mycostatin (Bristol-Myers
    Squibb)
J: Mycostatin (Squibb-
    Sankyo)
USA: Mycostatin (Westwood-
    Squibb)
    Myco-Triacet II (Teva)
    Mytrex (Savage)
    Nystop (Paddock)
    Pedi-Dri (Pedinol)
    generics

Obidoxime chloride

ATC: V03AB13
Use: antidote (poisoning with phosphoric acid esters (e. g. E 605))

RN: 114-90-9   MF: $C_{14}H_{16}Cl_2N_4O_3$ MW: 359.21   EINECS: 204-059-5
LD$_{50}$:   70 mg/kg (M, i.v.); >2.24 g/kg (M, p.o.);
133 mg/kg (R, i.v.); >4 g/kg (R, p.o.);
>70 mg/kg (dog, i.v.)
CN: 1,1'-[oxybis(methylene)]bis[4-[(hydroxyimino)methyl]pyridinium] dichloride

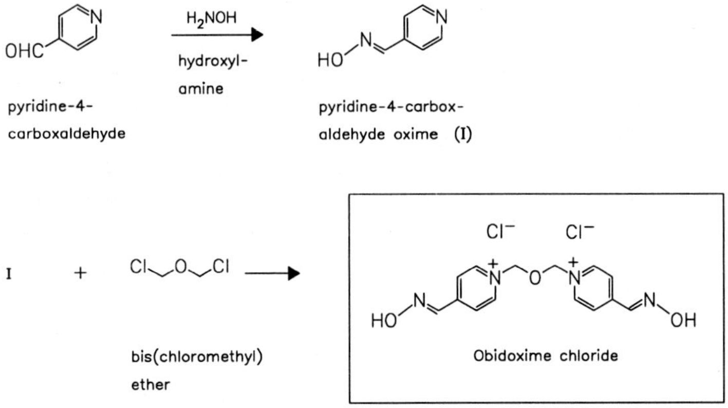

pyridine-4-
carboxaldehyde

pyridine-4-carbox-
aldehyde oxime (I)

bis(chloromethyl)
ether

Obidoxime chloride

Reference(s):
US 3 137 702 (E. Merck AG; 16.6.1964; D-prior. 13.8.1960).
Lüttringhaus, A.; Hagedorn, I.: Arzneim.-Forsch. (ARZNAD) **14**, 1 (1964).

Formulation(s):   amp. 250 mg/ml

Trade Name(s):
D: Toxogonin (Merck)

Octatropine methylbromide
(Anisotropine methylbromide)

ATC: A03AB
Use: anticholinergic, gastric and intestinal antispasmodic

RN: 80-50-2   MF: $C_{17}H_{32}BrNO_2$ MW: 362.35   EINECS: 201-285-6
LD$_{50}$:   6300 µg/kg (M, i.v.); 850 mg/kg (M, p.o.);
705 mg/kg (R, p.o.)
CN: *endo*-8,8-dimethyl-3-[(1-oxo-2-propylpentyl)oxy]-8-azoniabicyclo[3.2.1]octane bromide

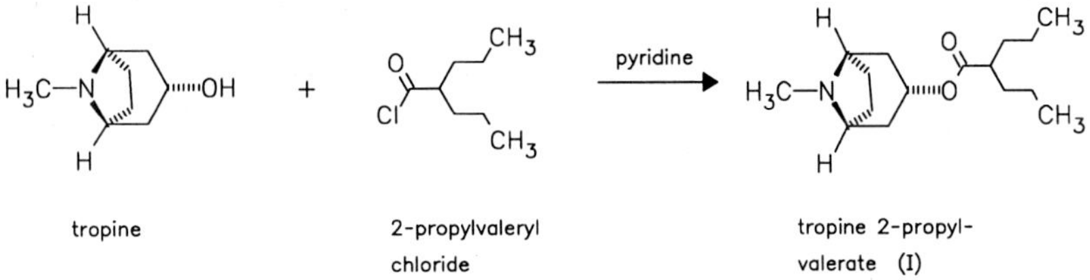

tropine

2-propylvaleryl
chloride

tropine 2-propyl-
valerate (I)

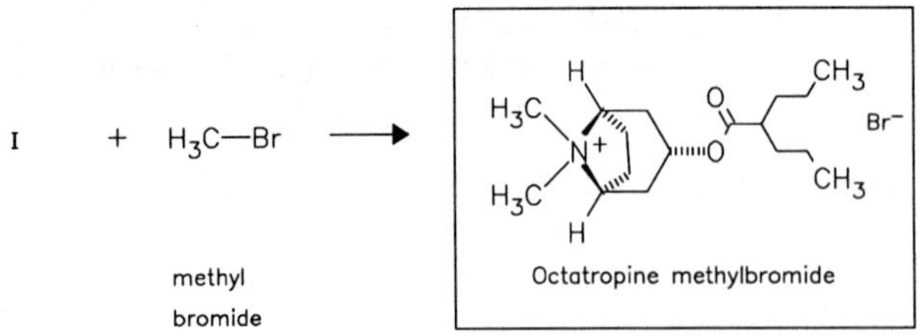

$$I \quad + \quad H_3C-Br \quad \longrightarrow$$

methyl
bromide

Octatropine methylbromide

Reference(s):

US 2 962 499 (Endo Labs.; 29.11.1960; prior. 3.7.1957).

Formulation(s):   amp. 1 %; gran. 10 %; tabl. 10 mg

Trade Name(s):

I: Valpinax (Crinos)-comb.   USA: Valpin (Du Pont); wfm
J: Valpin (Sankyo)   Valpin (Endo); wfm

Octopamine

(*p*-Norsynephrine)

ATC: C01CA18
Use: sympathomimetic, circulatory
            stimulant

RN: 104-14-3   MF: $C_8H_{11}NO_2$ MW: 153.18   EINECS: 203-179-5
LD_{50}:   75 mg/kg (M, i.v.); 4200 mg/kg (M, p.o.);
            1240 mg/kg (R, p.o.)
CN: α-(aminomethyl)-4-hydroxybenzenemethanol

hydrochloride
RN: 770-05-8   MF: $C_8H_{11}NO_2 \cdot HCl$ MW: 189.64   EINECS: 212-216-4

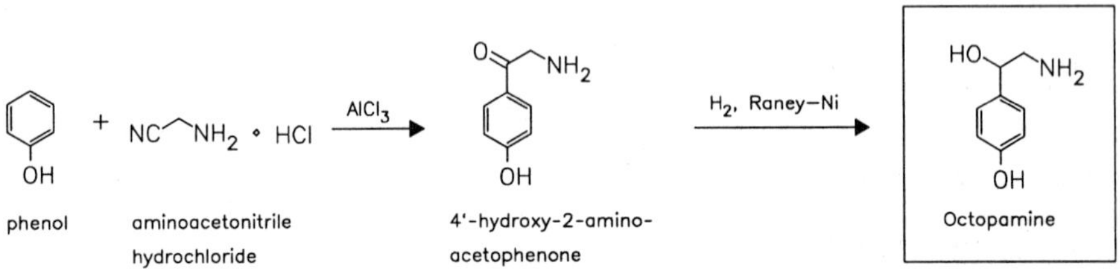

phenol   aminoacetonitrile   4'-hydroxy-2-amino-   Octopamine
                  hydrochloride   acetophenone

Reference(s):

US 2 585 988 (Hartford National Bank; 1952; NL-prior. 1948).

Formulation(s):   cps. 60 mg (as hydrogen tartrate); drg. 150 mg (as hydrochloride); sol. 150 mg/ml (as
                          hydrochloride)

Trade Name(s):

D: Depot-Norphen (Byk   Norphen (Byk Gulden);   I: Norden (Byk Gulden); wfm
        Gulden); wfm   wfm   J: Norfen (Morishita)

Octotiamine

ATC: A11
Use: neurotropic analgesic (thiamine derivative)

RN: 137-86-0   MF: $C_{23}H_{36}N_4O_5S_3$ MW: 544.76
LD$_{50}$: 399 mg/kg (M, i.v.); 2590 mg/kg (M, p.o.)
CN: 6-(acetylthio)-8-[[2-[[(4-amino-2-methyl-5-pyrimidinyl)methyl]formylamino]-1-(2-hydroxyethyl)-1-propenyl]dithio]octanoic acid methyl ester

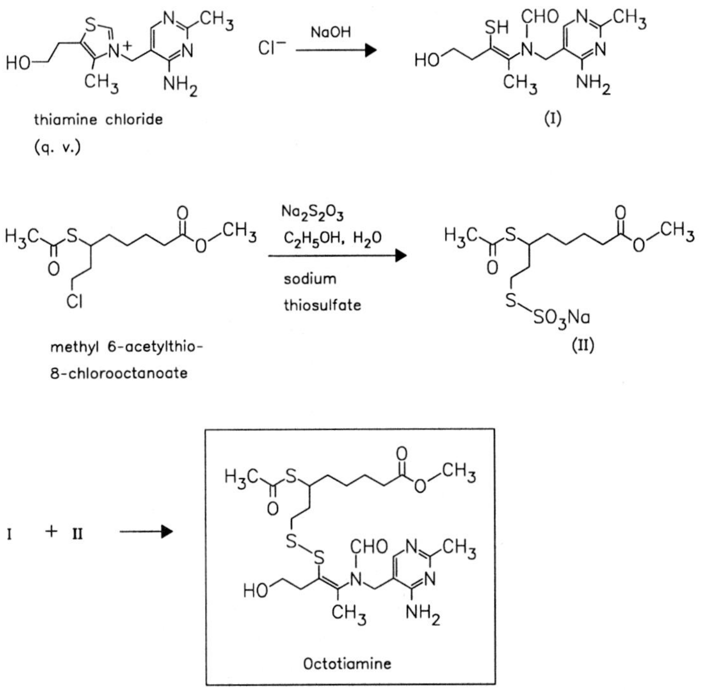

thiamine chloride
(q. v.)

(I)

methyl 6-acetylthio-
8-chlorooctanoate

sodium
thiosulfate

(II)

I + II

Octotiamine

Reference(s):
US 3 098 856 (Fujisawa; 1963; J-prior. 1960).

Formulation(s):   tabl. 5 mg, 25 mg, 50 mg

Trade Name(s):
D: Clinit-N (Hormosan)-
        comb.; wfm
        Jasivita (Bolder)-comb.;
        wfm

Neuro-Elmedal
(Thiemann)-comb.; wfm
Neuro-Europan
(Hormosan)-comb., wfm

J: Neurovitan (Fujisawa)-
        comb.
        Neuvita (Fujisawa)

Ofloxacin

ATC: J01MA01; S01AX11
Use: antibiotic (gyrase inhibitor)

RN: 82419-36-1   MF: $C_{18}H_{20}FN_3O_4$ MW: 361.37
CN: (±)-9-fluoro-2,3-dihydro-3-methyl-10-(4-methyl-1-piperazinyl)-7-oxo-7H-pyrido[1,2,3-de]-1,4-benzoxazine-6-carboxylic acid

hydrochloride
RN: 118120-51-7   MF: $C_{18}H_{20}FN_3O_4 \cdot HCl$ MW: 397.83

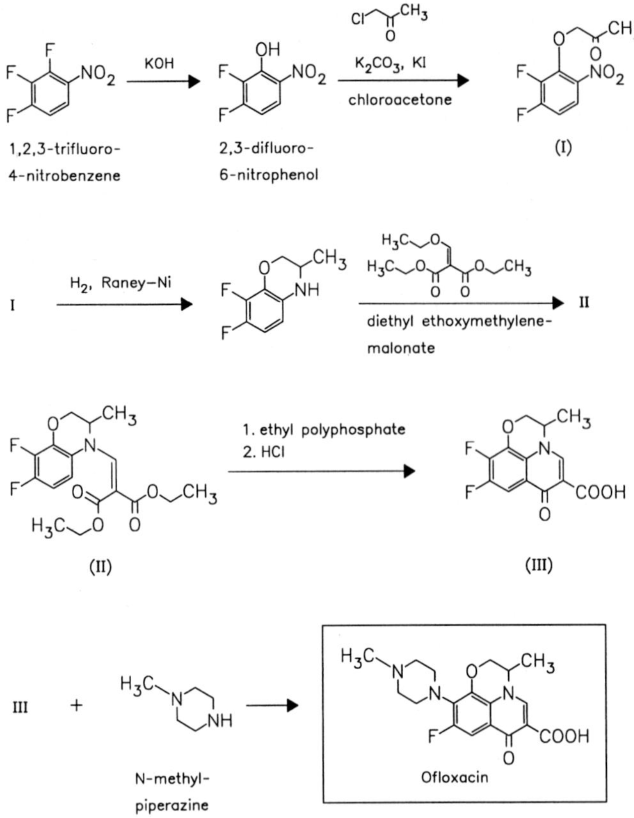

1,2,3-trifluoro-4-nitrobenzene → **2,3-difluoro-6-nitrophenol** → (I)

I → II

(II) → (III)

III + N-methyl-piperazine → Ofloxacin

Reference(s):

EP 47 005 (Daiichi Seiyaku; appl. 28.8.1981; J-prior. 2.9.1980).
US 4 382 892 (Daiichi Seiyaku; 10.5.1983, appl. 2.9.1981; J-prior. 2.9.1980).

preparation of 1,2,3-trifluoro-4-nitrobenzene:
Finger et al.: J. Am. Chem. Soc. (JACSAT) **81**, 94, 99 (1959).
Yoshida, Y.; Kimura, Y.; Tomoi, M.: Tetrahedron Lett. (TELEAY) **30** (51), 7199 (1989).

Formulation(s):　　cream 3 mg/g; eye drops 3 mg/ml; f. c. tabl. 100 mg, 200 mg, 400 mg; tabl. 200 mg, 400 mg; vial 100 mg/50 ml, 200 mg/100 ml, 400 mg/200 ml (as hydrochloride)

Trade Name(s):

D:	Floxal (Mann)		Oflocet (Roussel)		Oflocin (Glaxo Wellcome;
	Tarivid (Hoechst; 1985)	GB:	Exocin (Allergan)		1987)
	Uro-Tarivid (Hoechst)		Tarivid (Hoechst)	J:	Tarivid (Daiichi Seiyaku)
F:	Exocine (Allergan)	I:	Exocin (Allergan)	USA:	Floxin (Ortho-McNeil)
	Monoflocet (Roussel)		Flobacin (Sigma-Tau)		Ocuflox (Allergan)

Olanzapine
(LY-170053)

ATC:　N05AH03
Use:　antipsychotic

RN:　132539-06-1　MF: $C_{17}H_{20}N_4S$　MW: 312.44
CN:　2-methyl-4-(4-methyl-1-piperazinyl)-10H-thieno[2,3-b][1,5]benzodiazepine

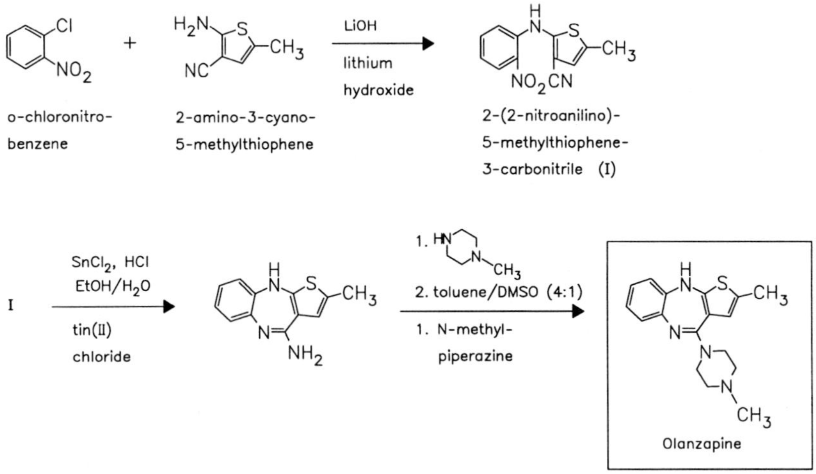

o-chloronitro-benzene + 2-amino-3-cyano-5-methylthiophene → (LiOH, lithium hydroxide) → 2-(2-nitroanilino)-5-methylthiophene-3-carbonitrile (I)

I → (SnCl₂, HCl, EtOH/H₂O, tin(II) chloride) → intermediate → (1. HN-piperazine-CH₃; 2. toluene/DMSO (4:1); 1. N-methyl-piperazine) → Olanzapine

Reference(s):

EP 454 436 (Lilly; appl. 30.10.1991; GB-prior. 25.4.1990).
EP 733 634 (Lilly; appl. 25.9.1996; USA-prior. 24.3.1995).
US 5 229 382 (Lilly; 20.7.1993; GB-prior. 25.4.1990).
EP 733 367 (Lilly & Co.; appl. 25.9.1996).
Chakrabati, J.K. et al.: J. Med. Chem. (JMCMAR) 23, 878, 884 (1980).
Hagopian, G.S.; Meyers, D.B.; Markham, J.K.: Teratology (TJADAB) 35(2), Abst. P65 (1987).

intermediates and process for preparing olanzapine:
EP 831 098 (Eli Lilly; appl. 22.9.1997; USA-prior. 23.9.1996).

pharmaceutical compositions:
US 5 919 485 (Eli Lilly; 6.7.1999; appl. 20.9.1996; USA-prior. 24.3.1995).
EP 830 864 (Eli Lilly; appl. 22.9.1997; USA-prior. 23.9.1996).

crystalline olanzapine:
EP 733 635 (Eli Lilly; appl. 22.3.1996; USA-prior. 24.3.1995).

Formulation(s):   f. c. tabl. 2.5 mg, 5 mg, 7.5 mg, 10 mg

Trade Name(s):
D: ZYPREXA (Lilly)   I: Zyprexa (Lilly)
GB: Zyprexa (Lilly; 1996)   USA: Zyprexa (Lilly)

Oleandomycin

(Troleandomycin)

ATC: J01FA05
Use: antibiotic

RN: 3922-90-5   MF: $C_{35}H_{61}NO_{12}$ MW: 687.87   EINECS: 223-495-7
LD$_{50}$:   460 mg/kg (M, i.v.); 8200 mg/kg (M, p.o.);
     440 mg/kg (R, i.v.); 6700 mg/kg (R, p.o.)
CN: [3R-(3R*,5R*,6S*,7R*,8R*,11R*,12R*,13R*,14S*,15S*)]-12-[(2,6-dideoxy-3-O-methyl-α-L-arabino-hexopyranosyl)oxy]-6-hydroxy-5,7,8,11,13,15-hexamethyl-14-[[3,4,6-trideoxy-3-(dimethylamino)-β-D-xylo-hexopyranosyl]oxy]-1,9-dioxaspiro[2.13]hexadecane-4,10-dione

phosphate (1:1)
RN: 7060-74-4   MF: $C_{35}H_{61}NO_{12} \cdot H_3PO_4$ MW: 785.86   EINECS: 230-351-7
LD$_{50}$:   400 mg/kg (M, i.v.); 4 g/kg (M, p.o.);
     480 mg/kg (R, i.v.)

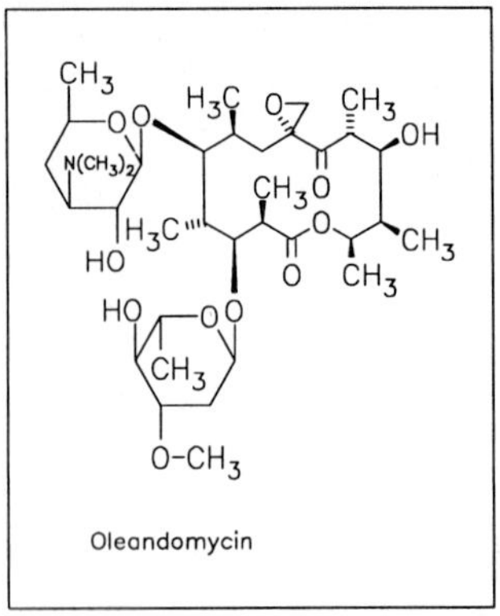

Oleandomycin

From fermentation solutions of *Streptomyces antibioticus*.

Reference(s):
US 2 757 123 (Pfizer; 31.7.1956; prior. 1.6.1953, 29.6.1955).
US 2 842 481 (Pfizer; 8.7.1958; prior. 12.3.1957).

Formulation(s):   cps. 250 mg; tabl. 100 mg; vial 500 mg (as phosphate)

Trade Name(s):

D:	Oleandocyn (Pfizer); wfm	I:	Boramycina (Benvegna)-comb.; wfm	J:	Matromycin (Taito Pfizer)
F:	Sigmamycine (Rosa-Phytopharma)-comb.; wfm		Olmicina (Morgan); wfm		Sigmamycin (Pfizer)-comb.
	generic; wfm		Triolmicina (Ripari-Gero); wfm		Taocin-O (Sankyo)
				USA:	TAO (Pfizer)

Olprinone hydrochloride
(E-1020; Loprinone)

ATC: C01D
Use: cardiotonic, vasodilator, PDE III-inhibitor

RN: 119615-63-3   MF: $C_{14}H_{10}N_4O \cdot HCl$ MW: 286.72
LD$_{50}$:   242 mg/kg (M, i.v.); >10 g/kg (M, p.o.);
176 mg/kg (R, i.v.); 7804 mg/kg (R, p.o.);
>100 mg/kg (dog, i.v.)
CN: 1,2-dihydro-5-imidazo[1,2-a]pyridin-6-yl-6-methyl-2-oxo-3-pyridinecarbonitrile monohydrochloride

olprinone
RN: 106730-54-5   MF: $C_{14}H_{10}N_4O$ MW: 250.26

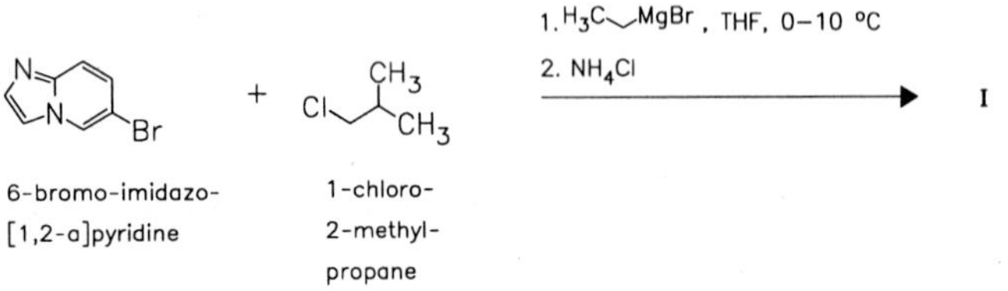

6-bromo-imidazo-
[1,2-a]pyridine

1-chloro-
2-methyl-
propane

1. H_3C⌒MgBr , THF, 0–10 °C
2. NH_4Cl

I

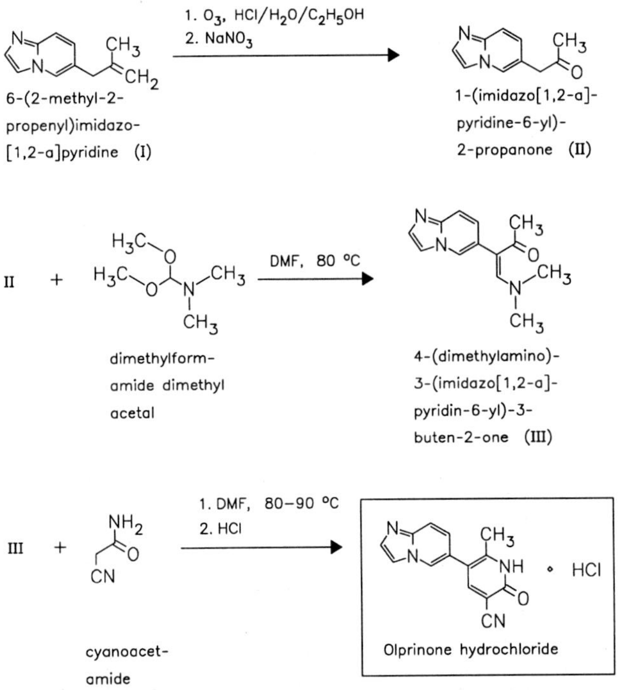

6-(2-methyl-2-propenyl)imidazo-[1,2-a]pyridine (I)

1. O₃, HCl/H₂O/C₂H₅OH
2. NaNO₃

1-(imidazo[1,2-a]-pyridine-6-yl)-2-propanone (II)

II + dimethylform-amide dimethyl acetal

DMF, 80 °C

4-(dimethylamino)-3-(imidazo[1,2-a]-pyridin-6-yl)-3-buten-2-one (III)

III + cyanoacet-amide

1. DMF, 80–90 °C
2. HCl

Olprinone hydrochloride

Reference(s):

preparation of intermediate II:
JP 63 077 879 (Eisai; appl. 22.9.1986; J-prior. 22.9.1986).
Yamanaka, M. et al.: Chem. Pharm. Bull. (CPBTAL) **40** (6), 1486 (1992).

preparation of olprinone *from II:*
EP 199 127 (Eisai; appl. 25.3.1986; J-prior. 26.3.1985).
Yamanaka, M. et al.: Chem. Pharm. Bull. (CPBTAL) **39** (6), 1556 (1991).

Formulation(s):   vial 5 mg/5 ml

Trade Name(s):
J: Coretec (Eisai)

Olsalazine sodium

(Di-5-ASA)

ATC: A07EC03
Use: therapeutic (ulcerative colitis)

RN: 6054-98-4   MF: C₁₄H₈N₂Na₂O₆   MW: 346.21
CN: 3,3'-azobis[6-hydroxybenzoic acid] disodium salt

free acid
RN: 15722-48-2   MF: C₁₄H₁₀N₂O₆   MW: 302.24   EINECS: 227-975-7

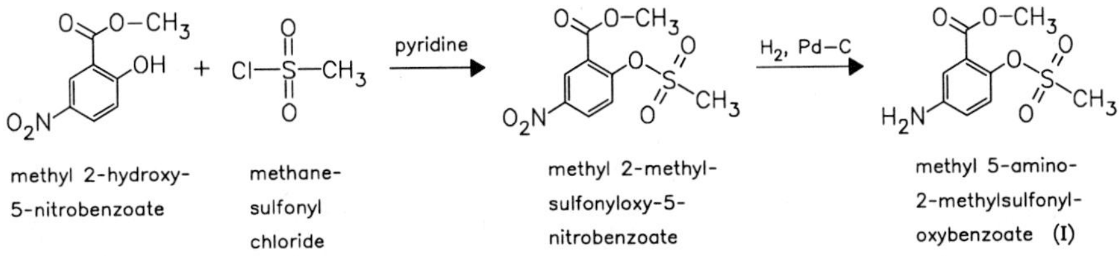

methyl 2-hydroxy-5-nitrobenzoate

methane-sulfonyl chloride

pyridine

methyl 2-methyl-sulfonyloxy-5-nitrobenzoate

H₂, Pd–C

methyl 5-amino-2-methylsulfonyl-oxybenzoate (I)

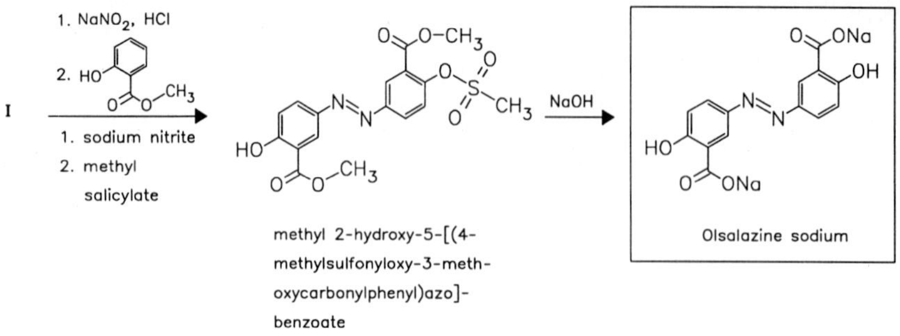

I

1. NaNO₂, HCl
2. HO—

1. sodium nitrite
2. methyl salicylate

methyl 2-hydroxy-5-[(4-methylsulfonyloxy-3-methoxycarbonylphenyl)azo]-benzoate

NaOH →

Olsalazine sodium

Reference(s):
EP 36 636 (Pharmacia; appl. 19.3.1981; S-prior. 26.3.1980).
US 4 528 367 (Pharmacia; 9.7.1985; S-prior. 26.3.1980).

preparation of methyl 2-hydroxy-5-nitrobenzoate:
Kakigami, T.; Baba, K.; Usui, T.: Heterocycles (HTCYAM) **48** (12), 2611 (1998).
Baker et al.: J. Chem. Soc. (JCSOA9) **1950**, 170.
Barany; Pianka: J. Chem. Soc. (JCSOA9) **1946**, 965.

Formulation(s): cps. 250 mg; tabl. 500 mg

Trade Name(s):

D:	Dipentum (Pharmacia & Upjohn; 1989)	GB:	Dipentum (Pharmacia & Upjohn; 1989)
F:	Dipentum (Pharmacia & Upjohn)	I:	Dipentum (Pharmacia & Upjohn; 1991)

USA: Dipentum (Pharmacia & Upjohn)

Omapatrilat
(BMS-186716)

Use: antihypertensive, dual ACE and NEP (neutral endopeptidase) inhibitor

RN: 167305-00-2 MF: $C_{19}H_{24}N_2O_4S_2$ MW: 408.54
CN: (4S,7S,10aS)-Octahydro-4-[[(2S)-2-mercapto-1-oxo-3-phenylpropyl]amino]-5-oxo-7H-pyrido[2,1-b][1,3]thiazepine-7-carboxylic acid

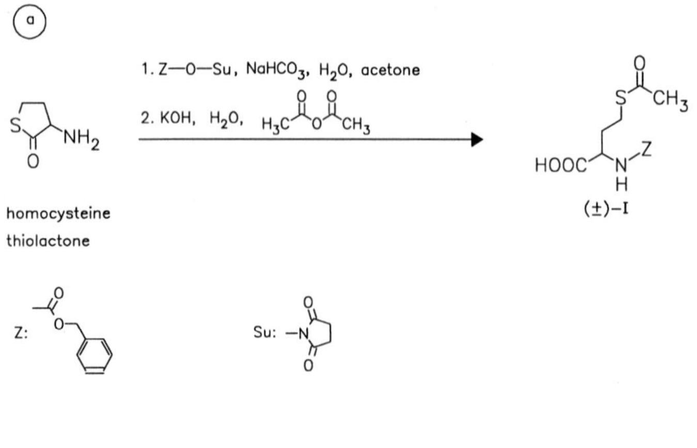

(a)

1. Z—O—Su, NaHCO₃, H₂O, acetone
2. KOH, H₂O, H₃C—CO—O—CO—CH₃

homocysteine thiolactone

(±)-I

Z:

Su: —N

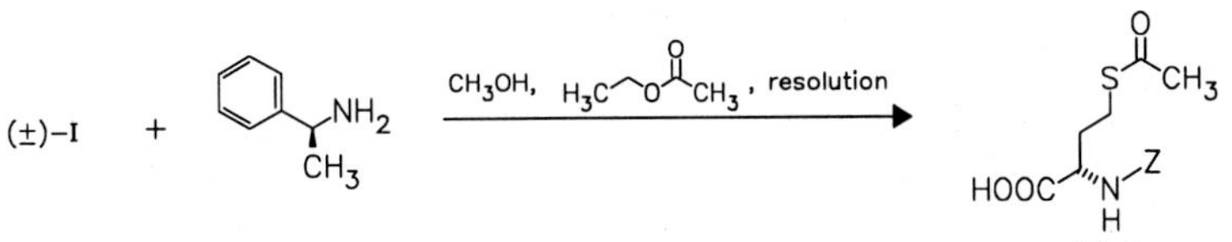

(±)−I   +   (S)-α-methyl-benzylamine

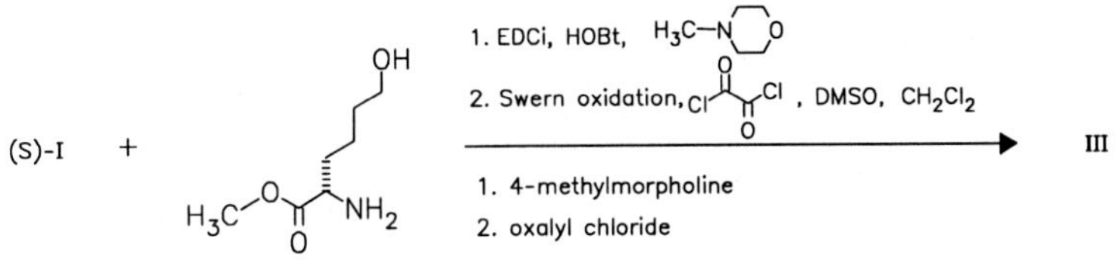

CH₃OH, H₃C—O—C(O)—CH₃ , resolution

→   (S)−I

(S)-I   +   L-ε-hydroxynorleucine methyl ester (II)

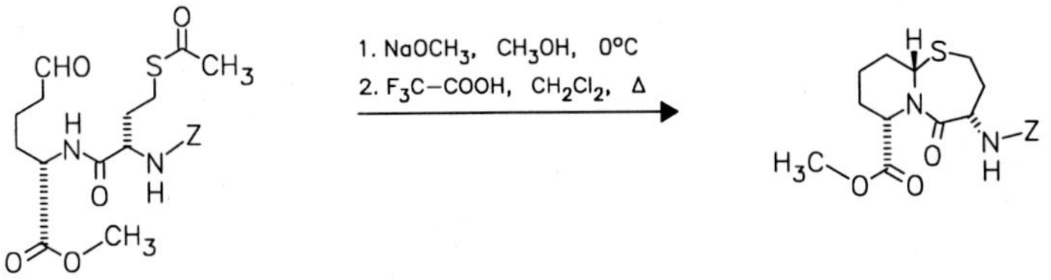

1. EDCi, HOBt, H₃C—N(morpholine)O

2. Swern oxidation, Cl—C(O)—C(O)—Cl , DMSO, CH₂Cl₂

1. 4-methylmorpholine

2. oxalyl chloride

→   III

1. NaOCH₃, CH₃OH, 0°C

2. F₃C—COOH, CH₂Cl₂, Δ

→

[S-(R*,R*)]-2-[[4-(acetylthio)-1-oxo-2-[[(phenylmethoxy)-carbonyl]amino]butyl]-amino]-6-oxohexanoic acid methyl ester (III)

[4S-(4α,7α,10aβ)]-octa-hydro-4-[[(phenylmethoxy)-carbonyl]amino]-5-oxo-7H-pyrido[2,1-b][1,3]-thiazepine-7-carboxylic acid methyl ester (IV)

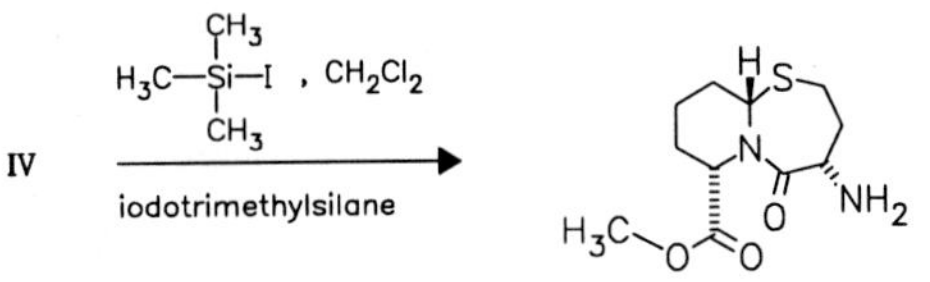

IV

H₃C—Si(CH₃)₂—I , CH₂Cl₂

iodotrimethylsilane

→   (V)

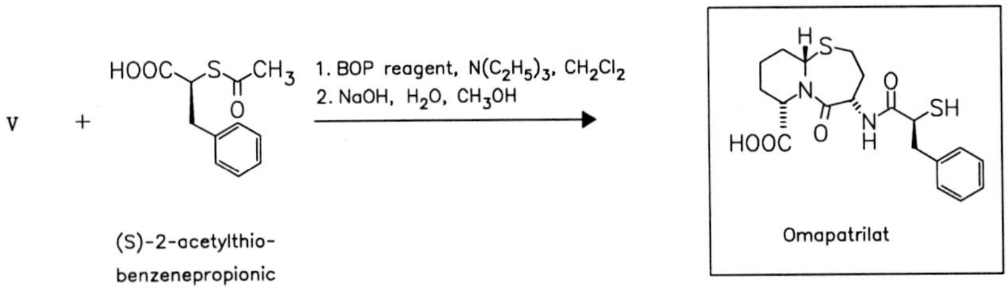

V   +   (S)-2-acetylthio-benzenepropionic acid (VI)

1. BOP reagent, N(C₂H₅)₃, CH₂Cl₂

2. NaOH, H₂O, CH₃OH

→

Omapatrilat

BOP reagent: (benzotriazol-1-yloxy)tris(dimethylamino)phosphonium PF₆⁻

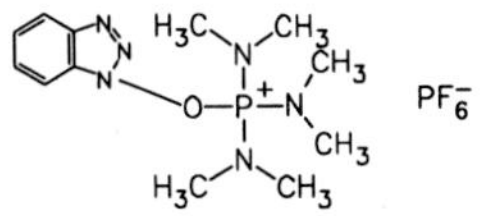

aa synthesis of L-ε-hydroxynorleucine methyl ester (II)

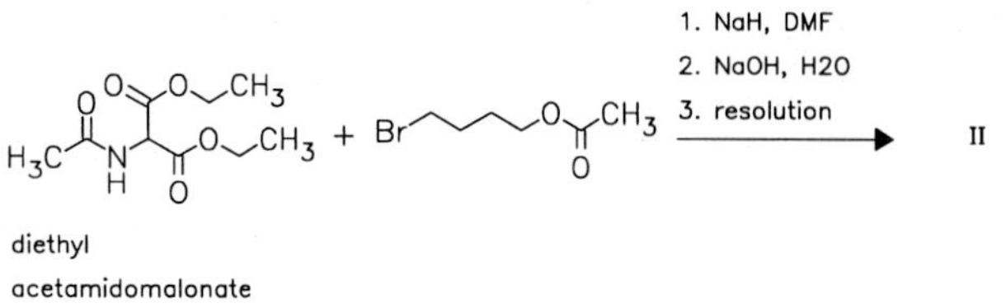

1. NaH, DMF
2. NaOH, H2O
3. resolution

diethyl
acetamidomalonate

→ II

ab synthesis of (S)-2-(acetylthio)benzenepropionic acid (VI)

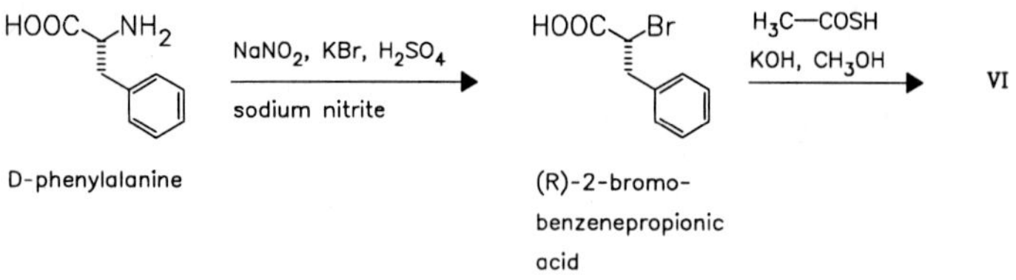

HOOC NH2

NaNO2, KBr, H2SO4
─────────────────
sodium nitrite

HOOC Br

H3C—COSH
KOH, CH3OH
──────────── VI

D-phenylalanine

(R)-2-bromo-
benzenepropionic
acid

Reference(s):
EP 629 627 (Bristol-Myers Squibb; appl. 13.6.1994; USA-prior. 15.6.1993).
US 5 508 272 (Bristol-Myers Squibb; 16.4.1996; USA-prior. 15.6.1993).
Robl, J.A. et al.: J. Med. Chem. (JMCMAR) **40**, 1570-1577 (1997).
WO 9 935 145 (Bristol-Myers Squibb; appl. 11.12.1998; USA-prior. 6.1.1998).

Trade Name(s):
D: Vanlev (Bristol-Myers
     Squibb)

Omeprazole
(H-168/68)

ATC: A02BD01
Use: H^+/K^+-ATPase-inhibitory ulcer
       therapeutic (Zollinger-Ellison
       Syndrom, reflux oesophagitis)

RN: 73590-58-6   MF: $C_{17}H_{19}N_3O_3S$ MW: 345.42
LD$_{50}$: 82.8 mg/kg (M, i.v.); >4 g/kg (M, p.o.);
      >50 mg/kg (R, i.v.); 2210 mg/kg (R, p.o.)
CN: 5-methoxy-2-[[(4-methoxy-3,5-dimethyl-2-pyridinyl)methyl]sulfinyl]-1*H*-benzimidazole

monosodium salt
RN: 95510-70-6   MF: $C_{17}H_{18}N_3NaO_3S$ MW: 367.41
LD$_{50}$: 278 mg/kg (R, i.v.)

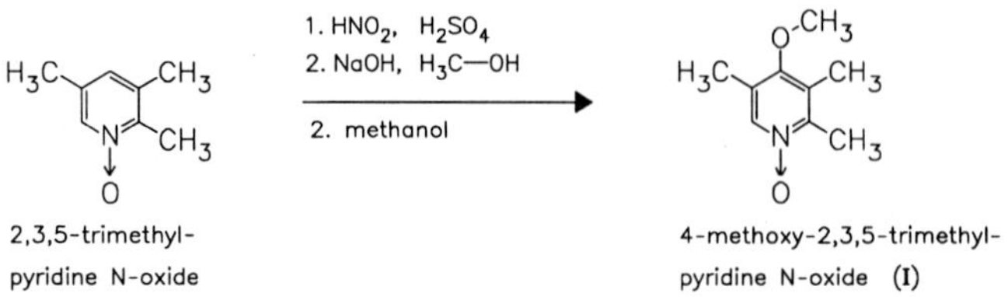

1. HNO2, H2SO4
2. NaOH, H3C—OH

2. methanol

2,3,5-trimethyl-
pyridine N-oxide

4-methoxy-2,3,5-trimethyl-
pyridine N-oxide (I)

4-methoxy-3,5-dimethyl-
2-pyridinemethanol acetate   (II)

2-(hydroxymethyl)-3,5-
dimethyl-4-methoxy-
pyridine

2-(chloromethyl)-3,5-
dimethyl-4-methoxy-
pyridine   (III)

4-methoxy-o-
phenylenediamine

potassium ethyl-
xanthogenate

5-methoxy-2-mercapto-
benzimidazole   (IV)

Omeprazole

Reference(s):
EP 5 129 (Hässle; appl. 3.4.1979; S-prior. 14.4.1978).
US 4 255 431 (Hässle; 10.3.1981; S-prior. 14.4.1978).

alternative synthesis of III:
EP 103 553 (Hässle; appl. 30.6.1983; S-prior. 26.8.1982).

alternative synthesis of omeprazole:
WO 9 809 962 (Slovakofarma 13.3.1998; appl. 8.9.1997; SK-prior. 9.9.1996).
WO 9 729 103 (PDI Res.; 14.8.1994; appl. 5.2.1997; CA-prior. 6.2.1996, 10.4.1996).
WO 9 722 603 (Astra; 26.6.1997; appl. 5.12.1996; S-prior. 15.12.1995).
US 5 374 730 (Torcan; 20.12.1994; appl. 4.11.1993).
EP 533 264 (Merck & Co.; 24.3.1993; appl. 12.9.1992; USA-prior. 20.9.1991, 15.10.1991).
WO 9 118 895 (Astra; 12.12.1991; appl. 5.6.1991; S-prior. 7.6.1990).
EP 484 265 (Centro Genesis para la Inv.; appl. 24.10.1991; E-prior. 31.10.1990).
WO 9 850 361 (PDI Research; appl. 21.4.1998; CA-prior. 6.5.1997).
WO 9 840 378 (Bristol-Myers Squibb; appl. 16.2.1998; DK-prior. 7.3.1997).
WO 9 947 514 (Knoll AG; appl. 11.3.1999; GB-prior. 17.3.1998).
EP 302 720 (Takeda Chem. Ind.; appl. 3.8.1988; J-prior. 4.8.1987).

synthesis of intermediates:
EP 226 558 (Hässle; appl. 8.9.1986; S-prior. 24.9.1985).
ES 2 035 767 (Centro Genesis; 16.4.1993; appl. 5.4.1991)

alkaline salts:
EP 124 495 (Hässle; appl. 28.2.1984; S-prior. 4.3.1983).
ES 2 023 778 (Centro Genesis; 1.2.1992).
WO 9 900 380 (Astra; appl. 11.6.1998; S-prior. 27.6.1997).

cyclodextrin complexes:
EP 190 239 (Byk Gulden Lomberg; appl. 24.7.1985; D-prior. 27.7.1984).

oral composition:
EP 247 983 (Yoshitomi; appl. 16.4.1987; GB-prior. 30.4.1986).
WO 9 601 623 (Astra; 25.1.1996; appl. 7.6.1995; S-prior. 8.7.1994).
US 5 232 706 (Esteve; 3.8.1993; E-prior. 31.12.1990, 24.6.1991).
WO 9 850 019 (Sage Pharm; appl. 8.5.1998; USA-prior. 9.5.1997; 15.10.1997).

new crystalline form of omeprazole:
WO 9 908 500 (Astra; appl. 10.11.1998).

transdermal application:
WO 9 000 054 (Upjohn; appl. 1.5.1989; USA-prior. 30.6.1988).

treatment of osteoporosis:
EP 338 066 (Hässle; appl. 27.10.1988; S-prior. 30.10.1987).

Formulation(s):   cps. 10 mg, 20 mg, 40 mg; vial 40 mg (as sodium salt)

Trade Name(s):

D:	Antra (Astra; 1989)	I:	Anthra (Astra Farmaceutici)	J:	Omepral (Fujisawa-Astra; 1991)
	Gastroloc (pharma-stern; 1989)		Losec (Plough; 1990)		Omeprazon (Yoshitomi)
F:	Mopral (Astra; 1989)		Mepral (Bracco; 1990)	USA:	Prilosec (Astra Merck)
GB:	Losec (Astra; 1989)		Omeprazen (Malesci; 1990)		

Omoconazole nitrate

ATC: D01AC13; G01AF16
Use: topical antifungal, antimycotic

RN: 83621-06-1   MF: $C_{20}H_{17}Cl_3N_2O_2 \cdot HNO_3$ MW: 486.74
CN: (Z)-1-[2-[2-(4-chlorophenoxy)ethoxy]-2-(2,4-dichlorophenyl)-1-methylethenyl]-1*H*-imidazole mononitrate

omoconazole
RN: 74512-12-2   MF: $C_{20}H_{17}Cl_3N_2O_2$ MW: 423.73

1,3-dichloro-benzene   2-chloro-propionyl chloride   2,2',4'-trichloro-propiophenone   imidazole   (I)

I + (structure) Br〜O〜Cl

1-bromo-2-(4-chloro-
phenoxy)ethane

1. NaOH, $(C_4H_9)_4N^+$ OH^-,
   benzene
2. HNO_3

→

· HNO_3

Omoconazole nitrate

Reference(s):
US 4 210 657 (Siegfried AG; 1.7.1980; D-prior. 11.9.1978).
US 4 554 356 (Siegfried AG; 19.11.1985; CH-prior. 23.1.1981).
EP 8 804 (Siegfried AG; appl. 7.9.1979; D-prior. 11.9.1978).
EP 69 754 (Siegfried AG; appl. 21.1.1982; CH-prior. 23.1.1981).
Thiele, K. et al.: Helv. Chim. Acta (HCACAV) **70**, 441 (1987).

preparation of 2,2',4'-trichloropropiophenone:
Konosu, T. et al.: Chem. Pharm. Bull. (CPBTAL) **38** (5), 1258 (1990).

Formulation(s):   cream 10 mg/1 g

Trade Name(s):
D: Fungisan (Galderma)   Fongarex (Besins-   I: Afongan (Galderma)
F: Fongamil (Biorga)   Iscovesco)

Ondansetron

ATC: A04AA01
Use: 5-HT$_3$-antagonist, anti-emetic

RN: 99614-02-5   MF: $C_{18}H_{19}N_3O$ MW: 293.37
CN: 1,2,3,9-tetrahydro-9-methyl-3-[(2-methyl-1*H*-imidazol-1-yl)methyl]-4*H*-carbazol-4-one

monohydrochloride
RN: 99614-01-4   MF: $C_{18}H_{19}N_3O \cdot HCl$ MW: 329.83
LD$_{50}$:   20.2 mg/kg (R, i.v.); 94.897 mg/kg (R, p.o.);
           >15 mg/kg (dog, i.v.); >45 mg/kg (dog, p.o.)
monohydrochloride dihydrate
RN: 103639-04-9   MF: $C_{18}H_{19}N_3O \cdot HCl \cdot 2H_2O$ MW: 365.86

ⓐ

(structure) NH$_2$ / Br   +   cyclohexane-1,3-dione   →   3-(2-bromoanilino)-cyclohex-2-en-1-one

1. CH$_3$I (I), NaH
2. Pd(OAc)$_2$, PPh$_3$, NaHCO$_3$

II

2. palladium acetate,
   triphenylphosphine

2-bromo-
aniline

cyclohexane-
1,3-dione

3-(2-bromoanilino)-
cyclohex-2-en-1-one

1. H₂C=O ,

2. I

CH₃

1,2,3,9-tetrahydro-
9-methyl-4H-
carbazol-4-one   (II)

2,3,4,9-tetrahydro-N,N,N,9-
tetramethyl-4-oxo-1H-
carbazole-3-methan-
aminium iodide   (III)

III   +   2-methyl-
imidazole   (IV)

Ondansetron

b

3-(dimethylaminomethyl)-
1,2,3,9-tetrahydro-4H-
carbazol-4-one

1. CH₃I
2. IV

, NaH

Ondansetron

Reference(s):
DOS 3 502 508 (Glaxo; appl. 25.1.1985; GB-prior. 25.1.1984, 15.10.1984).
US 4 695 578 (Glaxo; 22.9.1987; appl. 17.11.1986; prior. 22.1.1986; GB-prior. 25.1.1984).

(R)-(+)-enantiomer:
US 5 470 868 (Sepracor; 28.11.1995; prior. 26.6.1991; 27.8.1991)

synthesis of intermediate II:
Iida, H. et al.: J. Org. Chem. (JOCEAH) **45**, 2938 (1980).

alternative syntheses:
US 4 739 072 (Glaxo; appl. 23.7.1986; GB-prior. 24.7.1985).
US 4 957 609 (Glaxo; 18.9.1990; GB-prior. 24.7.1985).
US 4 725 615 (Glaxo; appl. 23.7.1986; GB-prior. 24.7.1985).
Kim, M.Y. et al.: Heterocycles (HTCYAM) **45** (10), 2041 (1997).

antiemetic compositions:
DOS 3 906 883 (Glaxo; appl. 3.3.1989; GB-prior. 4.3.1988).
US 4 983 621 (Glaxo; 8.1.1991; appl. 6.7.1989; GB-prior. 7.7.1988).

medical use for treating panic disorders:
WO 9 012 569 (Sandoz; appl. 1.11.1990).

medical use for treating dementia:
EP 275 668 (Glaxo; appl. 16.12.1987; GB-prior. 17.12.1986).

medical use for treatment of withdrawal syndrome:
WO 8 803 801 (Glaxo; appl. 20.11.1987; GB-prior. 21.11.1986).

Formulation(s):   amp. 4 mg/2 ml, 8 mg/4 ml; f. c. tabl. 4 mg, 8 mg; sol. (inj.) 4 mg/ml (as hydrochloride
dihydrate)

Opipramol

ATC: N06AA05
Use: thymoleptic, antidepressant

RN: 315-72-0   MF: $C_{23}H_{29}N_3O$ MW: 363.51   EINECS: 206-254-0
LD_{50}:   45 mg/kg (M, i.v.); 400 mg/kg (M, p.o.);
         32 mg/kg (R, i.v.); 1110 mg/kg (R, p.o.)
CN: 4-[3-(5H-dibenz[b,f]azepin-5-yl)propyl]-1-piperazineethanol

dihydrochloride
RN: 909-39-7   MF: $C_{23}H_{29}N_3O \cdot 2HCl$ MW: 436.43   EINECS: 213-000-2
LD_{50}:   45 mg/kg (M, i.v.); 443 mg/kg (M, p.o.);
         32 mg/kg (R, i.v.); 900 mg/kg (R, p.o.)

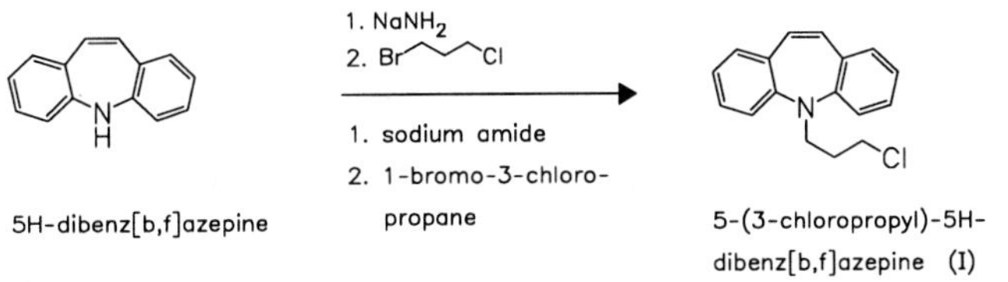

5H-dibenz[b,f]azepine

1. NaNH₂
2. Br⌒⌒Cl

1. sodium amide
2. 1-bromo-3-chloro-
   propane

5-(3-chloropropyl)-5H-
dibenz[b,f]azepine (I)

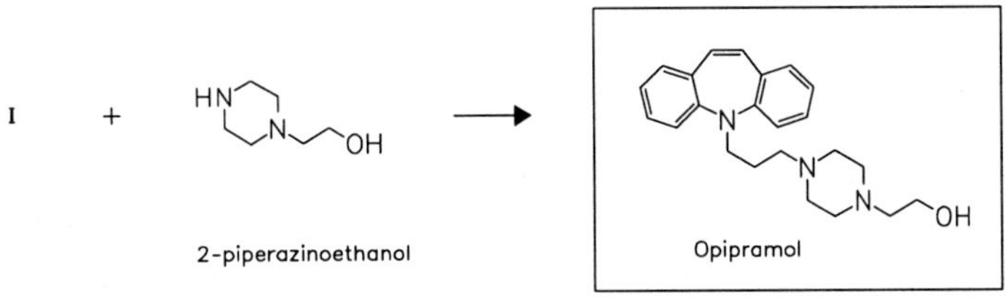

I + 2-piperazinoethanol → Opipramol

Reference(s):
GB 862 297 (Geigy; appl. 8.5.1958; CH-prior. 9.5.1957).
FR 1 271 971 (Geigy; appl. 12.8.1959; CH-prior. 13.8.1958).
GB 881 398 (Rhône-Poulenc, appl. 29.9.1958; valid from 7.9.1959).
DE 1 132 556 (Geigy; appl. 12.8.1959; CH-prior. 13.8.1958).
DE 1 133 729 (Geigy; appl. 8.5.1958; CH-prior. 9.5.1957).

Formulation(s):   drg. 50 mg (as dihydrochloride)

Orazamide
(AICA-Orotate)

ATC: A05B
Use: liver therapeutic

RN: 2574-78-9   MF: $C_5H_4N_2O_4 \cdot C_4H_6N_4O$ MW: 282.22   EINECS: 219-923-7
LD_{50}:   600 mg/kg (M, i.p.)
CN: 5-amino-1H-imidazole-4-carboxamide orotate (1:1)

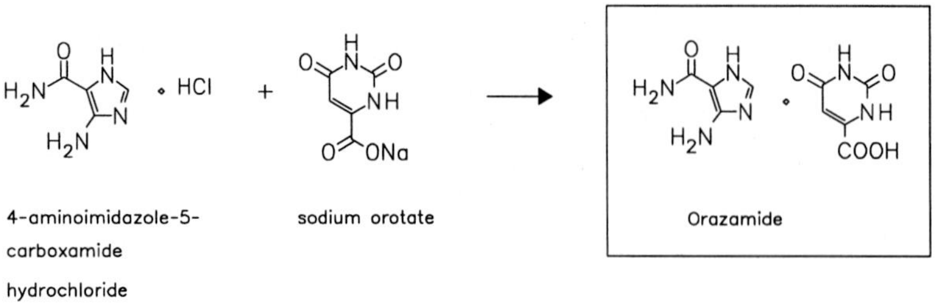
· HCl
+
Orazamide
4-aminoimidazole-5-carboxamide hydrochloride
sodium orotate

Reference(s):
GB 1 018 117 (Fujisawa; appl. 13.3.1963; J-prior. 15.3.1962).
US 3 271 398 (Fujisawa; 6.9.1966; J-prior. 15.3.1962).

newer method for AICA:
DE 2 160 674 (Sagami; appl. 29.12.1971; J-prior. 9.12.1970).

Formulation(s): tabl. 100 mg

Trade Name(s):

D:	Aicorat (Mack, Illert.); wfm	F:	Aicamine (Labaz); wfm	J:	Aicamin (Fujisawa)
		I:	Aicamin (Crinos); wfm		

Orciprenaline
(Metaproterenol)

ATC: R03AB03; R03CB03
Use: bronchodilator, antiasthmatic

RN: 586-06-1 MF: $C_{11}H_{17}NO_3$ MW: 211.26 EINECS: 209-569-1
LD_{50}: 86 mg/kg (M, i.v.); >8130 mg/kg (M, p.o.);
67.2 mg/kg (R, i.v.); 3370 mg/kg (R, p.o.);
30 mg/kg (dog, i.v.); 125 mg/kg (dog, p.o.)
CN: 5-[1-hydroxy-2-[(1-methylethyl)amino]ethyl]-1,3-benzenediol

sulfate (2:1)
RN: 5874-97-5 MF: $C_{11}H_{17}NO_3 \cdot 1/2H_2SO_4$ MW: 520.60 EINECS: 227-539-6
LD_{50}: 114 mg/kg (M, i.v.); 4800 mg/kg (M, p.o.);
5538 mg/kg (R, p.o.)

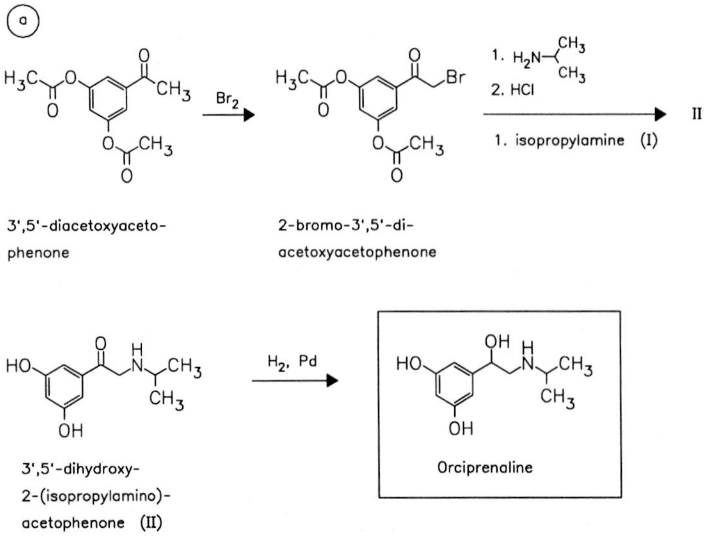
a
Br_2
1. $H_2N-CH(CH_3)_2$
2. HCl
1. isopropylamine (I)
II
3',5'-diacetoxyacetophenone
2-bromo-3',5'-diacetoxyacetophenone
H_2, Pd
3',5'-dihydroxy-2-(isopropylamino)-acetophenone (II)
Orciprenaline

b)

3',5'-dimethoxyaceto-
phenone

2-bromo-3',5'-di-
methoxyacetophenone

2-isopropylamino-3',5'-di-
methoxyacetophenone (III)

III $\xrightarrow{\text{HBr}}$ II $\xrightarrow{\text{H}_2, \text{ Raney-Ni}}$ Orciprenaline

Reference(s):
DE 1 275 069 (Boehringer Ing.; appl. 15.2.1960).
US 3 341 594 (Boehringer Ing.; 12.9.1967; D-prior. 15.2.1960).

Formulation(s):   amp. 0.5 mg; doses aerosol 1.5 mg, 0.75 mg; drops 2 %; inhalation aerosol 750 µg/metered
inhalation; syrup 10 mg/5 ml; sol. 15 mg; tabl. 20 mg (as sulfate)

Trade Name(s):
D: Alupent (Boehringer Ing.)   I: Alupent (Boehringer Ing.)   USA: Alupent (Boehringer Ing.)
F: Alupent (Boehringer Ing.)   J: Alotec (Boehringer-   generics
GB: Alupent (Boehringer Ing.)   Tanabe)

Orgotein

ATC: M01AX14
Use: anti-inflammatory

RN: 9054-89-1   MF: unspecified   MW: unspecified   EINECS: 232-771-6
CN: dismutase superoxide

Water soluble protein with a relative molecular mass of ca. 32600, which particularly contains copper and zinc
bound like chelate (ca. 4 gram atoms) and has superoxide-dismutase-activity. It is isolated from bovine liver or
from hemolyzed, plasma free erythrocytes obtained from bovine blood. Purification by manyfold fractionated
precipitation and solvolyse methods and definitive separation of the residual foreign proteins by denaturizing
heating of the orgotein concentrate in buffer solution to ca. 65-70 ºC and gel filtration and/or dialysis.

Reference(s):
DE 2 101 866 (Diagnostic Data; appl. 15.1.1971; USA-prior. 16.1.1970).
US 3 579 495 (Diagnostic Data; 18.5.1971; prior. 13.5.1968, 10.4.1969, 24.4.1970).
US 3 624 251 (Diagnostic Data; 30.11.1971; appl. 16.1.1970).
US 3 687 927 (Diagnostic Data; 29.8.1972; prior. 31.8.1966, 2.8.1967, 7.6.1971).

Formulation(s):   vial 4 mg, 8 mg

Trade Name(s):
D: Peroxinorm (Grünenthal);   Interceptor (Isnardi); wfm   Oxinorm (Zambeletti);
       wfm   Orgo-M (Max Farma); wfm   wfm
I: Artrolasi (Ausonia); wfm   Orgoten (Serono); wfm

Orlistat

(Tetrahydrolipstatin; Orlipastat; Ro-18-0647)

ATC: A08AB01
Use: antiobesity, pancreatic lipase inhibitor

RN: 96829-58-2 MF: $C_{29}H_{53}NO_5$ MW: 495.75
CN: *N*-Formyl-L-leucine [2*S*-[2α(*R**),3.beta.]]-1-[[3-hexyl-4-oxo-2-oxetanyl]methyl]dodecyl ester

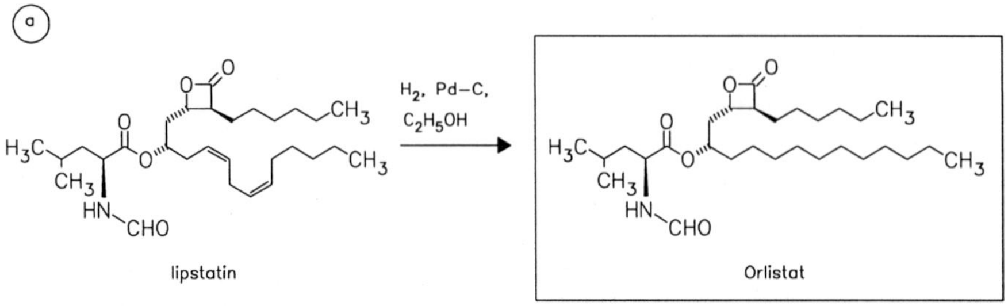
a
H2, Pd-C, C2H5OH
lipstatin
Orlistat

lipstatin is produced by fermentation of Streptomyces toxytricini.

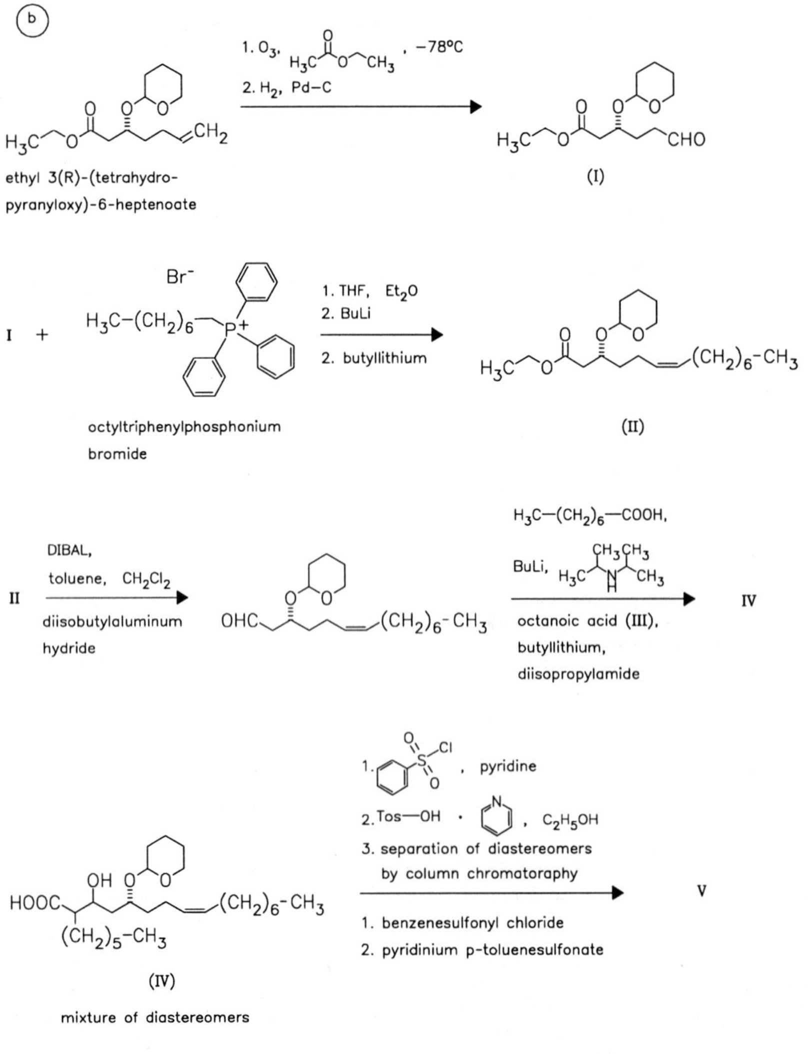
b
1. O3, H3C-C(O)-O-CH2CH3, −78°C
2. H2, Pd−C
ethyl 3(R)-(tetrahydro-pyranyloxy)-6-heptenoate
(I)
I +
octyltriphenylphosphonium bromide
1. THF, Et2O
2. BuLi
2. butyllithium
(II)
II
DIBAL, toluene, CH2Cl2
diisobutylaluminum hydride
H3C−(CH2)6—COOH, BuLi,
octanoic acid (III), butyllithium, diisopropylamide
IV
(IV)
mixture of diastereomers
1. pyridine
2. Tos—OH · C2H5OH
3. separation of diastereomers by column chromatoraphy
1. benzenesulfonyl chloride
2. pyridinium p-toluenesulfonate
V

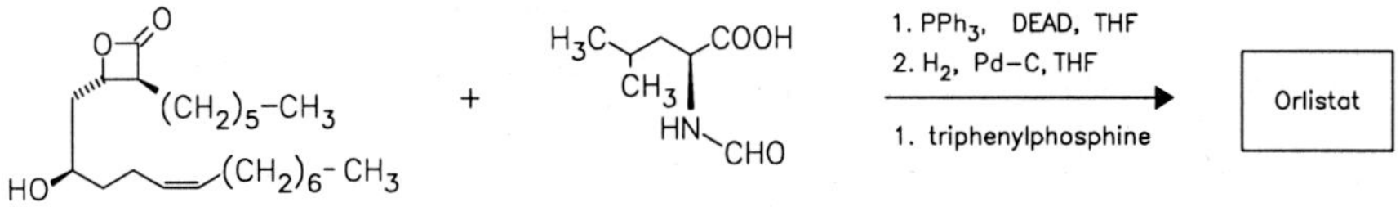
O
(CH2)5-CH3
HO
(CH2)6-CH3
H3C
COOH
CH3
HN
CHO
+
1. PPh3, DEAD, THF
2. H2, Pd-C, THF
1. triphenylphosphine
Orlistat

(V)

(S)-N-formyl-
leucine (VI)

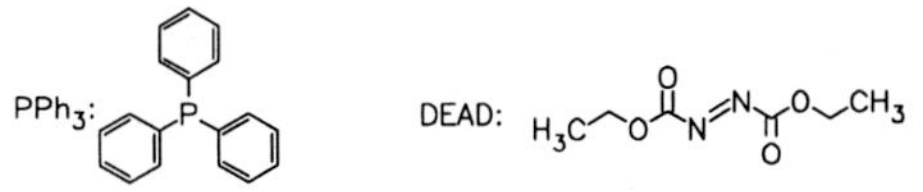
PPh3:
P
DEAD:
H3C
O
N
CH3

(c)

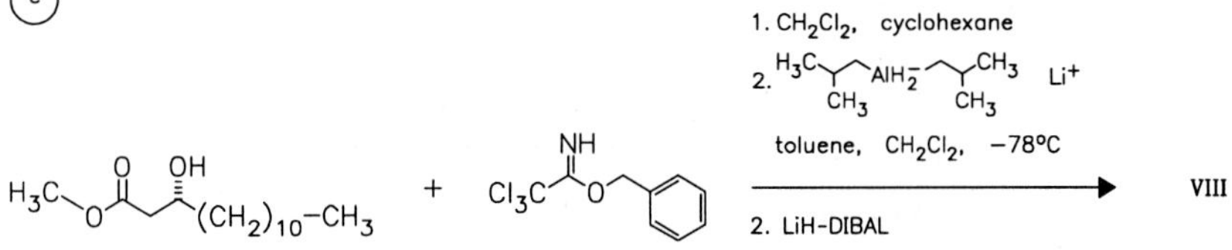
1. CH2Cl2, cyclohexane
2. H3C AlH2 CH3 Li+
CH3 CH3
toluene, CH2Cl2, −78°C
2. LiH-DIBAL
H3C
O
OH
(CH2)10-CH3
+
NH
Cl3C
VIII

methyl (R)-3-hydroxy-
tetradecanoate

benzyl trichloro-
acetimidate (VII)

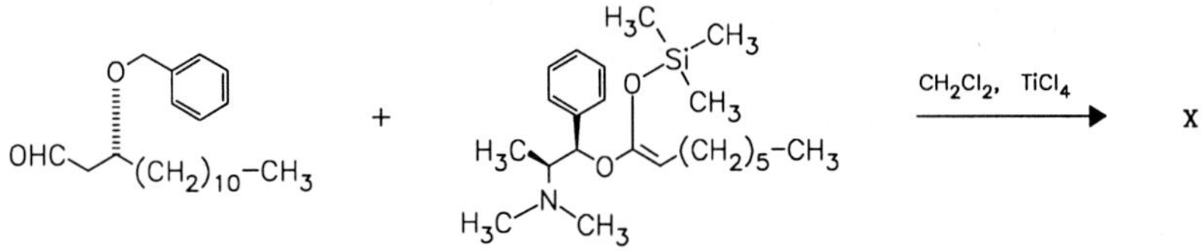
OHC
(CH2)10-CH3
+
H3C
CH3
Si
CH3
(CH2)5-CH3
N
CH3
CH2Cl2, TiCl4
X

(VIII)

(IX)

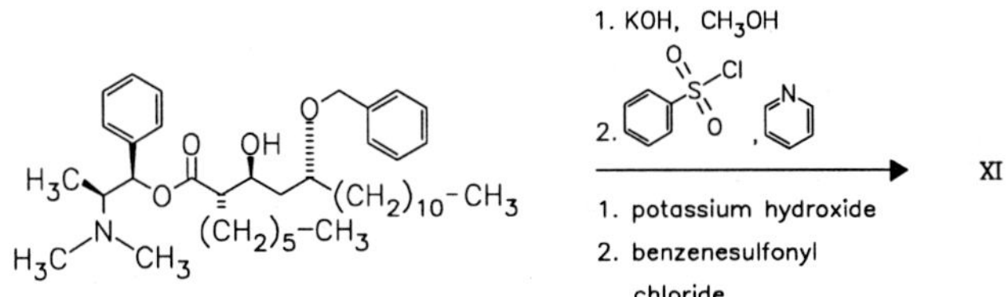
H3C
OH
(CH2)10-CH3
(CH2)5-CH3
N
CH3
1. KOH, CH3OH
Cl
2.
1. potassium hydroxide
2. benzenesulfonyl
chloride
XI

(X)

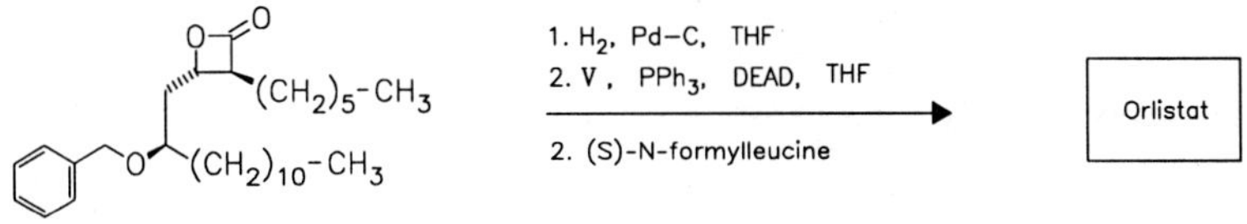
(CH2)5-CH3
(CH2)10-CH3
1. H2, Pd-C, THF
2. V, PPh3, DEAD, THF
2. (S)-N-formylleucine
Orlistat

(XI)

preparation of intermediate IX

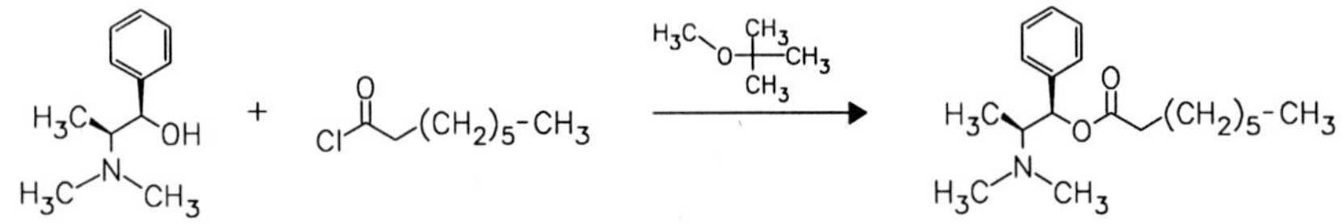
H3C
OH
N
CH3
+
Cl
(CH2)5-CH3
H3C
CH3
CH3
CH3
(CH2)5-CH3

(−)-N-methyl-
ephedrine

octanoyl chloride

(XII)

XII

1. BuLi, THF, $H_3C\overset{CH_3}{\underset{H}{\overset{|}{N}}}\overset{CH_3}{\underset{CH_3}{}}$

2. $Cl-\overset{CH_3}{\underset{CH_3}{\overset{|}{Si}}}-CH_3$

→ IX

1. butyllithium, diisopropylamine
2. trimethylsilyl chloride

(d)

HOOC$\overset{OH}{\underset{}{\curvearrowright}}$COOH + cyclohexanone $\xrightarrow[\text{boron trifluoride etherate}]{BF_3 \cdot OEt_2}$ HOOC$\cdots$ (XIII)

(S)-malic acid

XIII $\xrightarrow[\substack{\text{1. borane} \\ \text{2. tert-butyl-} \\ \text{diphenylsilyl} \\ \text{chloride}}]{\substack{\text{1. BH}_3, \text{ THF} \\ \text{2. Cl}-\text{SiPh}_2\text{tBu}}}$ tBuPh$_2$Si$\overset{OH}{\underset{}{\curvearrowright}}O-CH_3$ $\xrightarrow[\substack{\text{1. borane} \\ \text{2. 2-naphthylsulfonyl} \\ \text{chloride}}]{\substack{\text{1. BH}_3, \text{ THF} \\ \text{2.}}}$ XIV

SiPh2tBu: $-\overset{}{\underset{}{Si}}\overset{CH_3}{\underset{CH_3}{\overset{|}{-}}}CH_3$

tBuPh$_2$Si$\overset{OH}{\underset{}{\curvearrowright}}O\overset{O}{\underset{O}{\overset{\|}{S}}}$ $\xrightarrow{NaOCH_3, \ CH_3OH}$ tBuPh$_2$Si$\curvearrowright$O$\triangleleft$

(XIV) (XV)

XV $\xrightarrow[\substack{\text{1. decyllithium} \\ \text{2. benzyl} \\ \text{trichloroacetimidate}}]{\substack{\text{1. Li}-(CH_2)_9-CH_3 \\ \text{2. VII}}}$ tBuPh$_2$Si$\curvearrowright$O$(CH_2)_{10}-CH_3$

(XVI)

XVI $\xrightarrow[\substack{\text{2. pyridinium} \\ \text{dichromate}}]{\substack{\text{1. HF, } CH_3CN \\ \text{2. Py}_2 \cdot H_2Cr_2O_7}}$ OHC$\curvearrowright$$(CH_2)_{10}-CH_3$

3(R)-benzyloxy-tetradecanal (XVII)

XVII + $H_3C\overset{CH_3}{\underset{H_3C}{\overset{|}{Si}}}\curvearrowright(CH_2)_5-CH_3$ $\xrightarrow{TiCl_4}$ XVIII + XIX

(E)-1-trimethylsilyl-2-nonene

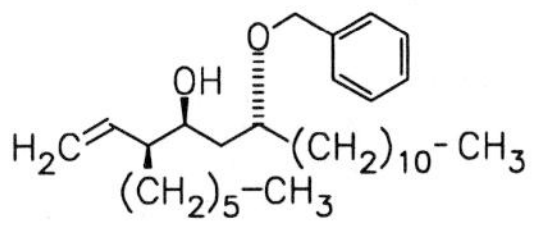

(XVIII) 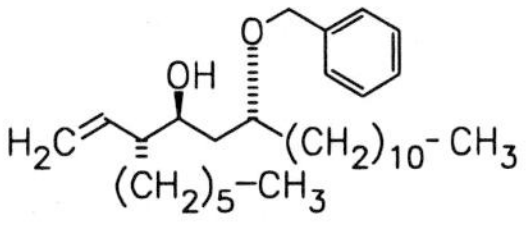   (XIX)

the diastereomers are separated by column chromatography

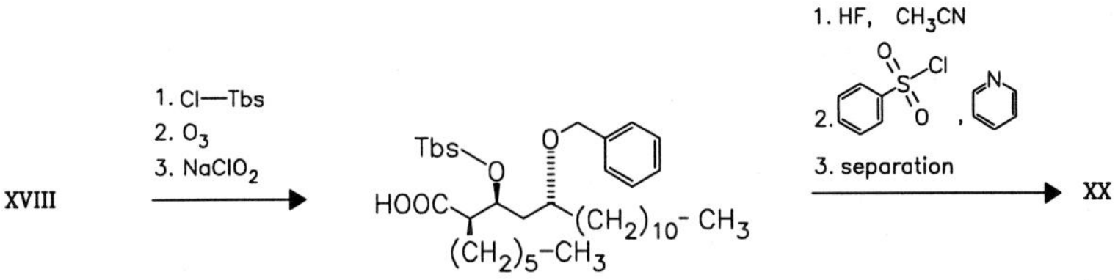

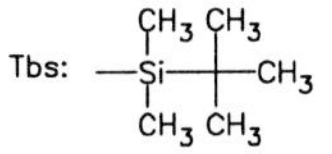

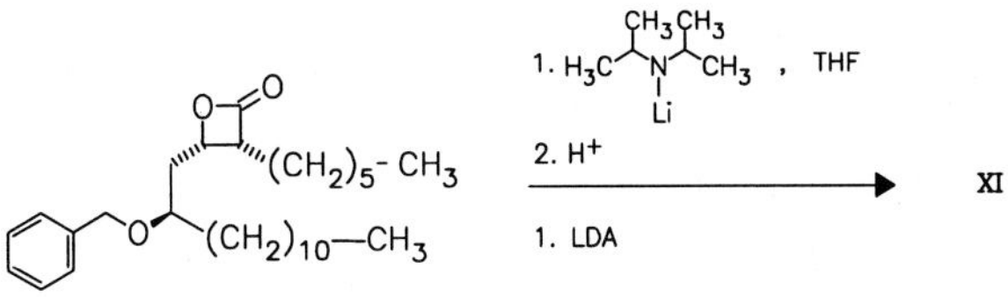

XVIII

1. Cl—Tbs
2. O$_3$
3. NaClO$_2$

1. HF, CH$_3$CN

2.

3. separation

XX

Tbs:

(XX)

1. H$_3$C—N(CH$_3$)CH$_3$, THF (Li)

2. H$^+$

1. LDA

XI

XI

1. H$_2$, Pd—C
2. VI, PPh$_3$, DEAD

2. (S)-formylleucine,
   triphenylphosphine

Orlistat

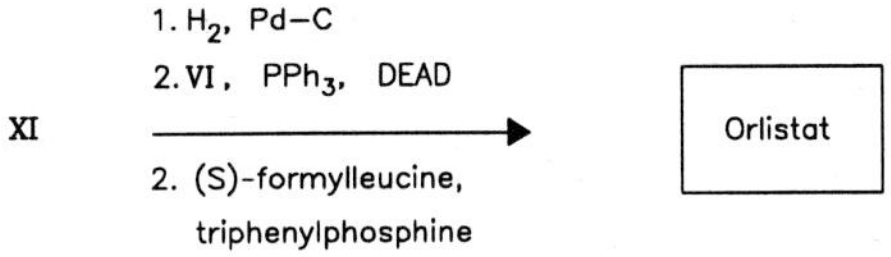

finalization of synthesis from the stereoisomer XIX

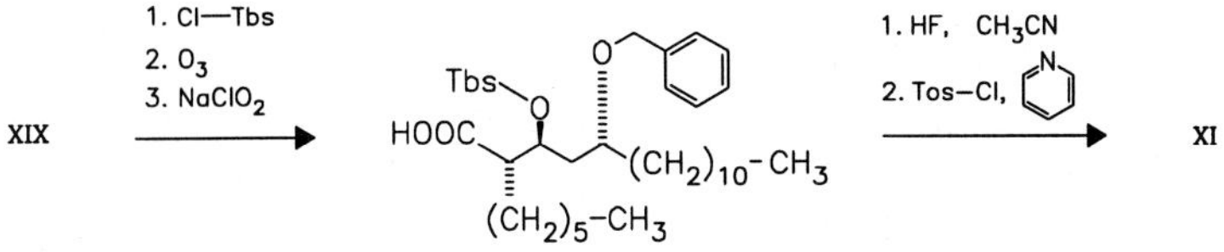

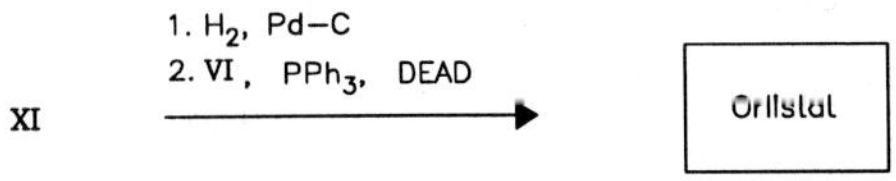

XIX

1. Cl—Tbs
2. O$_3$
3. NaClO$_2$

1. HF, CH$_3$CN

2. Tos—Cl,

XI

XI

1. H$_2$, Pd—C
2. VI, PPh$_3$, DEAD

Orlistat

alternative synthesis of 3(R)-benzyloxytetradecanal XVII

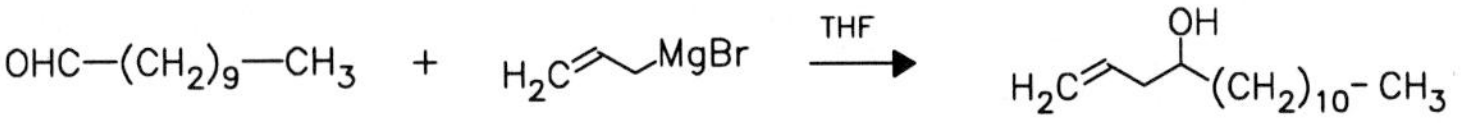

OHC—(CH$_2$)$_9$—CH$_3$ + H$_2$C—MgBr

allylmagnesium
bromide

THF

(RS)-1-pentadecen-4-ol (XXI)

XXI + [2(R)-acetoxy-2-phenylacetic acid structure with COOH and O-C(=O)-CH₃]

2(R)-acetoxy-2-
phenylacetic acid

DCC, DMAP →

[structures XXII and XXIII, the diastereomers are separated by column chromatography]

(XXII)

+

(XXIII)

the diastereomers are separated by column
chromatography

XXII

1. KOH, CH₃OH
2. KH, [Br—benzyl], THF
2. benzyl bromide (XXIII)

→ [benzyl ether structure H₂C=...(CH₂)₁₀-CH₃]

O_3, CH₃OH,
CH_2Cl_2 → XVII

XXIII

1. KOH, CH₃OH
2. O_2N—⟨⟩—COOH, PPh₃, DEAD, K_2CO_3

isomerization of unwanted stereoisomer

→ [structure with OH, H₂C=...(CH₂)₁₀-CH₃]

(XXV)

XXV

1. XXIV, KH, THF
2. O_3, CH₃OH, CH_2Cl_2

1. benzyl bromide
2. ozone

→ XVII

(e)

XVII + III

LDA, THF

lithium
diisopropyl-
amide

→ [structure HOOC...OH OH...(CH₂)₁₀-CH₃, (CH₂)₅-CH₃]

(XXVI)

mixture of diastereomers

XXVI

1. H_2, Pd–C, THF
2. Tos–OH, CHCl₃

→ [lactone structure (XXVII) with (CH₂)₁₀-CH₃, H₃C-(CH₂)₅, OH]

(XXVII)

mixture of diastereomers

CrO_3, H_2SO_4,

[H₃C-C(=O)-CH₃]

(Jones oxidation)

→ XXVIII

[structure XXVIII lactone with (CH₂)₁₀-CH₃, H₃C-(CH₂)₅, O]

(XXVIII)

⇌

[structure XXIX lactone with (CH₂)₁₀-CH₃, H₃C-(CH₂)₅, OH]

(XXIX)

H_2, PtO_2,

[H₃C-O-C(=O)-CH₃], 50 bar

→ XXX

[structure XXX lactone with (CH₂)₁₀-CH₃, H₃C-(CH₂)₅, OH]

(XXX)

1. VII, F₃C–SO₃H, CH_2Cl_2
2. 1 N NaOH

1. benzyl
trichloroacetimidate

→ [structure XXXI with benzyl, OH, (CH₂)₁₀-CH₃, (CH₂)₅-CH₃, NaO-C(=O)]

(XXXI)

XXXI

1. XXIII, THF, HMPT

2. [tetrahydropyran structure], Tos—OH, CH$_2$Cl$_2$

1. benzyl bromide
2. 3,4-dihydro-2H-pyran (**XXXII**)

$\longrightarrow$

HOOC—[structure with OBn and O-THP groups]—(CH$_2$)$_{10}$—CH$_3$
(CH$_2$)$_5$—CH$_3$

(**XXXIII**)

XXXIII

1. [benzenesulfonyl chloride structure], pyridine

2. Tos—OH · [pyridine], C$_2$H$_5$OH

1. benzenesulfonyl chloride
2. pyridinium p-toluenesulfonate

$\longrightarrow$

[β-lactone structure]—(CH$_2$)$_5$—CH$_3$
HO—(CH$_2$)$_{10}$—CH$_3$

(**XXXIV**)

XXXIV + **VI** $\xrightarrow{\text{PPh}_3, \ \text{DEAD}}$ Orlistat

(f)

H$_3$C—C(CH$_3$)(CH$_3$)—O—CO—CH$_2$—CH(OH)—(CH$_2$)$_{10}$—CH$_3$ +   **XXXII**

tert-butyl (R)-3-hydroxy-
tetradecanoate

1. CH$_2$Cl$_2$, Tos—OH
2. DIBAL, toluene

$\longrightarrow$ **VIII**

2. diisobutylaluminum
hydride

VIII + H$_3$C—C(CH$_3$)(CH$_3$)—O—CO—CH$_2$—S(=O)—[C$_6$H$_4$]—CH$_3$

tert-butyl (S)-p-toluene-
sulfinylacetate

$\xrightarrow[\text{THF, } -78°C]{\text{Et}_2\text{O, } \ \text{H}_3\text{C—C(CH}_3\text{)}_2\text{—MgBr}}$

H$_3$C—C(CH$_3$)(CH$_3$)—O—CO—CH(S(=O)[C$_6$H$_4$]CH$_3$)—CH(OH)—[O-THP]—(CH$_2$)$_{10}$—CH$_3$

(**XXXV**)

XXXV

1. Hg—Al, THF, H$_2$O
2. Br—(CH$_2$)$_5$—CH$_3$, BuLi,

H$_3$C—N(CH(CH$_3$)(CH$_3$))(CH(CH$_3$)(CH$_3$))H , —50°C

2. hexyl bromide, butyllithium

$\longrightarrow$

H$_3$C—C(CH$_3$)(CH$_3$)—O—CO—CH( )—CH(OH)—[O-THP]—(CH$_2$)$_{10}$—CH$_3$
(CH$_2$)$_5$—CH$_3$

(**XXXVI**)

XXXVI

1. KOH, CH$_3$OH

2. [benzenesulfonyl chloride structure] · [pyridine]

$\longrightarrow$

[THP-O structure with β-lactone]—(CH$_2$)$_5$—CH$_3$
(CH$_2$)$_{10}$—CH$_3$

(**XXXVII**)

1. Tos—OH · [pyridine], C$_2$H$_5$OH, 60°C

2. VI, PPh$_3$, DEAD, THF

XXXVII ⟶ Orlistat

(g)

H$_3$C—O ... OH ...(CH$_2$)$_{10}$—CH$_3$ +   Cl—(C=O)—(CH$_2$)$_5$—CH$_3$ / Br   pyridine ⟶   Br—(CH$_2$)$_5$—CH$_3$ ... H$_3$C—O ...(CH$_2$)$_{10}$—CH$_3$ (XXXIX)

methyl (R)-3-hydroxy-
tetradecanoate (XXXVIII)

α-bromooctanoyl
chloride

or

XXXVIII + HOOC—(CH$_2$)$_5$—CH$_3$ / Br   NaH, DCC, DMAP ⟶ XXXIX

α-bromooctanoic acid

XXXIX   Zn, Et$_2$O, Cl—Si(CH$_3$)$_3$ ⟶   XXIX   analogously to method (e) ⟶   Orlistat

zinc, trimethyl-
silyl chloride

Reference(s):
a   EP 129 748 (Hoffmann-La Roche & Co. AG; appl. 2.1.1985; CH-prior. 22.6.1983).
b   Schneider, F.; Barbier, P.: Helv. Chim. Acta (HCACAV) **70**,196 (1987).
    synthesis of 3(R)-(tetrahydropyranyloxy)-6-heptenoic acid ethyl ester:
    Hirama, M.; Nei, M.: J. Am. Chem. Soc. (JACSAT) **104**, 4251 (1982).
c   Widmer, U.; Schneider, F.; Barbier, P.: Helv. Chim. Acta (HCACAV) **70**,1412 (1987).
d   Hanessian, S.; Tehim, A.; Chen., P.: J. Org. Chem. (JOCEAH) **58** (27), 7768 (1993).
e   Barbier, P.; Schneider, F.: J. Org. Chem. (JOCEAH) **53**, 1218 (1988).
f   EP 189 577 (Hoffmann-La Roche & Co. AG; appl. 6.8.1986; CH-prior. 21.12.1984).
g   EP 524 495 (Hoffmann-La Roche & Co. AG; appl. 27.1.1993; USA-prior. 23.7.1991; 12.3.1992).

further syntheses of orlistat:
Kocieski, P.; Pons, J.M.: Tetrahedron Lett. (TELEAY) **30**, 1833 (1989).
Fleming, I.; Lawrence, N.J.: Tetrahedron Lett. (TELEAY) **31** (25), 3645 (1990).
Casc-Green, S.C.; Davies, S.G.; Hedgecock, C.J.R.: Synlett (SYNLES) **1991**, 781
Uskovic, M.R.; Chadka, N.K.; Batcho, A.D.; Tang P.C.; Courtney, L.F.; Cook C.M.; Wovliulich, P.M.: J. Org. Chem. (JOCEAH) **56**, 4714 (1991).

Formulation(s):   cps. 120 mg

Trade Name(s):
D: Xenical (Roche; 1999)   GB: Xenical (Roche; 1998)
F: Xenical (Roche; 1998)   USA: Xenical (Roche; 1998)

Ornipressin
(Ornipresina; Orpressin)

ATC: H01BA05
Use: vasoconstrictor

RN: 3397-23-7   MF: C$_{45}$H$_{63}$N$_{13}$O$_{12}$S$_2$ MW: 1042.21   EINECS: 222-253-8
CN: 8-L-ornithinevasopressin

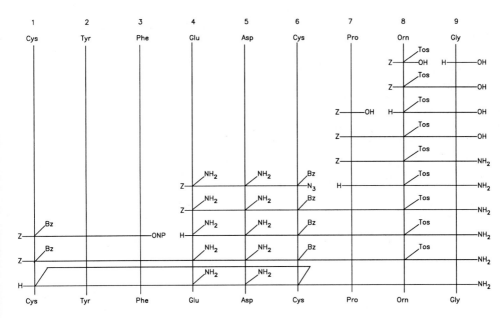

Reference(s):

FR 1 396 607 (Sandoz; appl. 3.4.1964; CH-prior. 5.4.1963).
Huguenin, R.L.; Boissonnas, R.A.: Helv. Chim. Acta (HCACAV) **46**, 1669 (1963).
Bodanszky, M. et al.: J. Am. Chem. Soc. (JACSAT) **86**, 4452 (1964).

Formulation(s): amp. 2.5 iu/0.5 ml, 2.5 iu/5 ml

Trade Name(s):
D: Por 8 Sandoz (Novartis Pharma)

Orotic acid
(Acide orotique)

ATC: A14B
Use: metabolic therapeutic, electrolyte carrier

RN: 65-86-1 MF: $C_5H_4N_2O_4$ MW: 156.10 EINECS: 200-619-8
LD_{50}: 770 mg/kg (M, i.v.); 2 g/kg (M, p.o.)
CN: 1,2,3,6-tetrahydro-2,6-dioxo-4-pyrimidinecarboxylic acid

potassium salt
RN: 24598-73-0 MF: $C_5H_3KN_2O_4$ MW: 194.19 EINECS: 246-341-0
LD_{50}: 10.9 g/kg (R, p.o.)
magnesium salt
RN: 34717-03-8 MF: $C_{10}H_6MgN_4O_8$ MW: 334.48
zinc salt
RN: 60388-02-5 MF: $C_{10}H_6N_4O_8Zn$ MW: 375.57 EINECS: 262-207-4
choline orotate
RN: 24381-49-5 MF: $C_5H_{14}NO \cdot C_5H_3N_2O_4$ MW: 259.26 EINECS: 246-213-4
L-lysine orotate
RN: 28003-86-3 MF: $C_6H_{14}N_2O_2 \cdot C_5H_4N_2O_4$ MW: 302.29 EINECS: 248-771-4

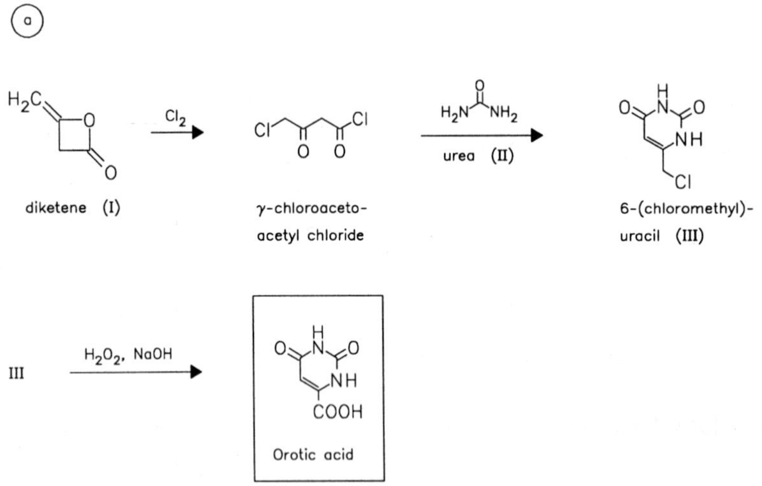
a
Cl2
H2N NH2
urea (II)
diketene (I)
γ-chloroaceto-acetyl chloride
6-(chloromethyl)-uracil (III)
III
H2O2, NaOH
COOH
Orotic acid

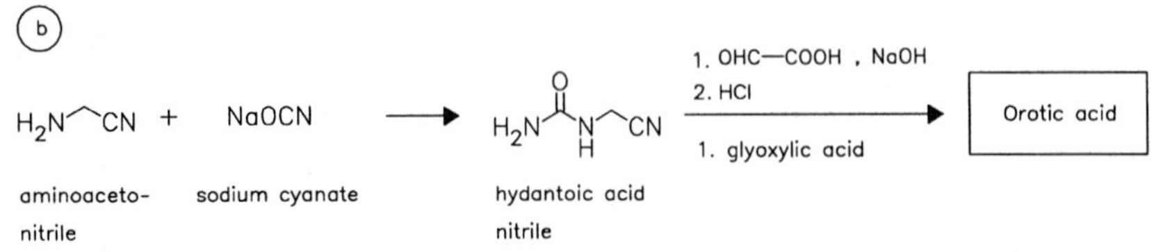
b
H2N CN + NaOCN
1. OHC—COOH , NaOH
2. HCl
1. glyoxylic acid
Orotic acid
aminoaceto-nitrile
sodium cyanate
hydantoic acid nitrile

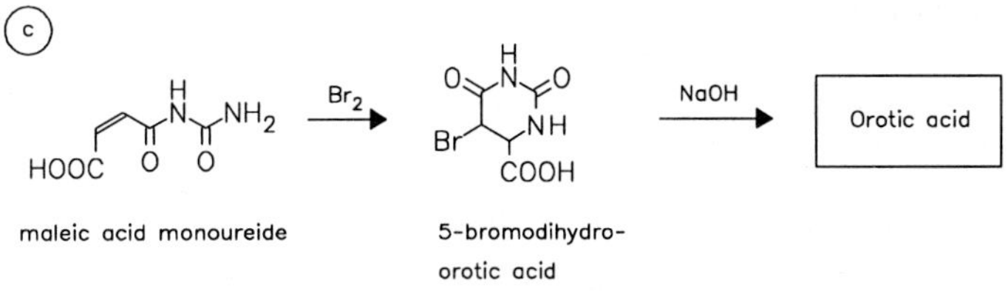

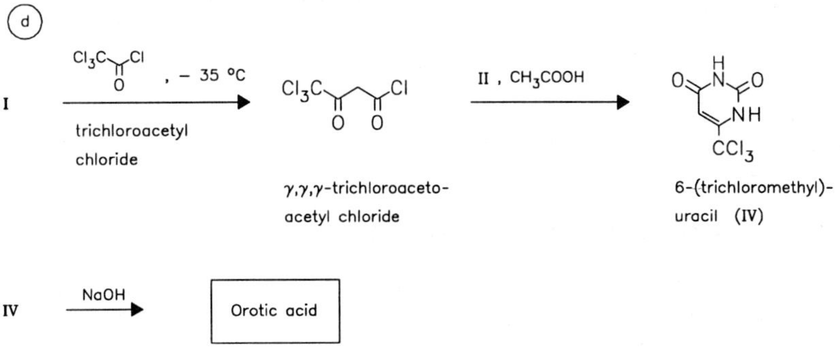

c

maleic acid monoureide → 5-bromodihydro-orotic acid → Orotic acid

d

I → trichloroacetyl chloride → γ,γ,γ-trichloroaceto-acetyl chloride → 6-(trichloromethyl)-uracil (IV)

IV → NaOH → Orotic acid

Reference(s):

a   DAS 1 770 117 (Diamalt; appl. 2.4.1968).
     DAS 2 025 247 (Lonza; appl. 23.5.1970; CH-prior. 28.5.1969).
b   DAS 2 502 951 (Diamalt; appl. 24.1.1975).
     US 4 113 950 (Diamalt; 12.9.1978; D-prior. 24.1.1975).
c   CH 595 351 (Lonza; appl. 7.5.1975).
d   US 4 064 126 (Lonza; 20.12.1977; CH-prior. 11.8.1975).
     DOS 2 540 275 (Lonza; appl. 24.2.1977; CH-prior. 11.8.1975).

alternative syntheses:
from oxalacetic acid ester *and* urea:
Müller: J. Prakt. Chem. (JPCEAO) **56**, 488 (1897).
Behrend: Justus Liebigs Ann. Chem. (JLACBF) **378**, 165 (1910).
US 2 937 175 (Rhône-Poulenc; 17.5.1960; F-prior. 18.1.1956).
DE 1 034 640 (Rhône-Poulenc; appl. 1956).

from aspartic acid:
Nye, F. et al.: J. Am. Chem. Soc. (JACSAT) **69**, 1382 (1947).

from glyoxylic acid *and* hydantoin:
US 4 062 847 (Diamalt; 13.12.1977; D-prior. 24.1.1975).

fermentatively:
US 3 086 917 (Kyowa Hakko; 23.4.1963; J-prior. 15.6.1960).

lithium orotate:
DOS 2 410 181 (Nadrol-Chemie; appl. 4.3.1974).

Formulation(s):   cps. 250 mg (as hydrochloride); cps. 60 mg in comb. with α-tocopherol acetate; tabl. 20 mg (as zinc salt), 40 mg (as zinc salt), 500 mg (as choline orotate)

Trade Name(s):
D: Vigodana N (Loges)-comb.
       Zinkorotat (Nadrol; as zinc
       salt)
       Zinkorotat (Ursapharm; as
       zinc salt)

       numerous combination
       preparations
F: Lysortine (Théraplix; as
       lysine orotate); wfm
       Oroturic (Grémy-Longuet);
       wfm

       Orotyl (Porcher-Lavril);
       wfm
I: Oro B$_{12}$ (Ripari-Gero)-
       comb.
J: Orodine (Takeda)
       Orosan (Maruishi)

Orotics (Nippon Shinyaku)	Orotopin (Fuso)	Vita-thirteen (Sumitomo)
Orotonsan (Ono)	Urabon (Nissin)	generic

Orphenadrine

ATC: M03BC01; N04AB02
Use: antiparkinsonian, muscle relaxant

RN: 83-98-7   MF: $C_{18}H_{23}NO$ MW: 269.39   EINECS: 201-509-2
LD_{50}:   33 mg/kg (M, i.v.); 125 mg/kg (M, p.o.)
CN: N,N-dimethyl-2-[(2-methylphenyl)phenylmethoxy]ethanamine

hydrochloride
RN: 341-69-5   MF: $C_{18}H_{23}NO \cdot HCl$ MW: 305.85   EINECS: 206-435-4
LD_{50}:   20 mg/kg (M, i.v.); 100 mg/kg (M, p.o.);
         27.5 mg/kg (R, i.v.); 255 mg/kg (R, p.o.)
citrate (1:1)
RN: 4682-36-4   MF: $C_{18}H_{23}NO \cdot C_6H_8O_7$ MW: 461.51   EINECS: 225-137-5

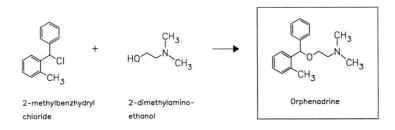

2-methylbenzhydryl chloride   +   2-dimethylamino-ethanol   →   Orphenadrine

Reference(s):
US 2 567 351 (Parke Davis; 1951; prior. 1946).
US 2 991 225 (Brocades-Stheeman; 4.7.1961; NL-prior. 1952).
Bijlsma, U.G. et al.: Arzneim.-Forsch. (ARZNAD) **5**, 72 (1955).

Formulation(s):   amp. 60 mg/2 ml; s. r. tabl. 100 mg; tabl. 100 mg (as citrate)

Trade Name(s):
D:	Norflex (3M Medica)	GB:	Biorphen (Bioglan; as	J:	Delenar (Schering-
	Norgesic (3M Medica)-		hydrochloride)		Shionogi)-comb.
	comb.		Disipal (Yamanouchi; as	USA:	Norflex (3M; as citrate)
F:	Disipal (Beytout); wfm		hydrochloride)		Norgesic (3M; as citrate)
	Estomul (Jean Roy-	I:	Disipal (Yamanouchi)		
	Freyssinge)-comb.; wfm				

Oseltamivir
(GS 4104)

ATC: J01AH02
Use: antiviral, anti-influenza, neuramidase inhibitor

RN: 196618-13-0   MF: $C_{16}H_{28}N_2O_4$ MW: 312.41
CN: (3R,4R,5S)-4-(Acetylamino)-5-amino-3-(1-ethylpropoxy)-1-cyclohexene-1-carboxylic acid ethyl ester

phosphate
RN: 204255-11-8   MF: $C_{16}H_{28}N_2O_4 \cdot H_3O_4P$ MW: 410.40
hydrochloride
RN: 204255-09-4   MF: $C_{16}H_{28}N_2O_4 \cdot HCl$ MW: 348.87
citrate
RN: 209965-30-0   MF: $C_{16}H_{28}N_2O_4 \cdot C_6H_8O_7$ MW: 504.53

a

(−)-quinic acid   2,2-dimethoxy-   3,4-0-isopropylidene-
                                   propane   1,5-quinic lactone (I)

1. H$_3$C—ONa , C$_2$H$_5$OH

2. H$_3$C—S—Cl

I   SO$_2$Cl$_2$, −20°C,
                                                                    pyridine, CH$_2$Cl$_2$ II

                                                                    sulfuryl chloride

ethyl 3,4-0-isopropylidene-   3-pentanone (III)   ethyl 3,4-0-(1-ethylpropylidene)-
5-0-(methanesulfonyl)-   5-0-(methanesulfonyl)-
shikimate (II)   shikimate (IV)

70% HClO$_4$

perchloric
acid

1. H$_3$C—Si—O—S—CF$_3$, BF$_3$ · H$_3$C—S—CH$_3$

2. KHCO$_3$, aq. C$_2$H$_5$OH

IV

1. trimethylsilyl triflate

ethyl (3R,4R,5S)-4,5-
epoxy-3-(1-ethylpropoxy)-
1-cyclohexene-1-carboxylate (V)

1. NaN$_3$, NH$_4$Cl, aq. C$_2$H$_5$OH

2.

V   1. NaN$_3$, NH$_4$Cl, DMF

                                                                   2. H$_3$C—O—CH$_3$,

                                                                   CH$_2$Cl$_2$, NaHCO$_3$ VI

1. sodium azide

2. triphenylphosphine   2. acetic anhydride

1. H$_2$, Raney—Ni, C$_2$H$_5$OH

2. 85% H$_3$PO$_4$

(VI)   Oseltamivir

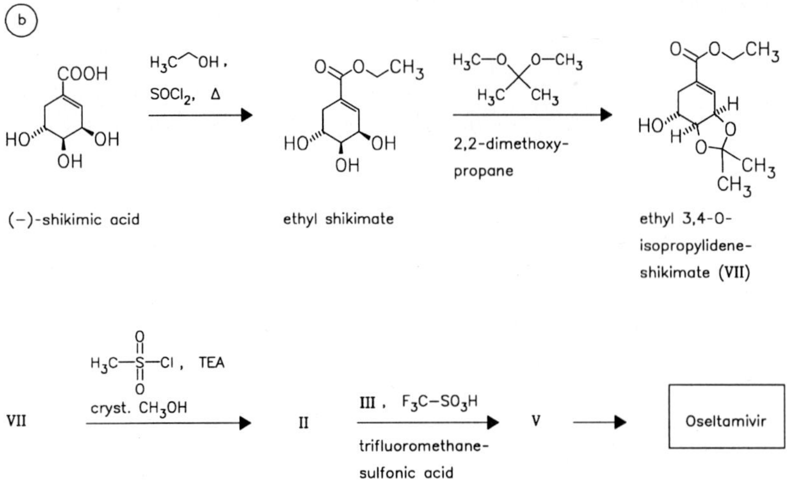

(b)

(−)-shikimic acid → ethyl shikimate → ethyl 3,4-O-isopropylidene-shikimate (VII)

H₃C—OH, SOCl₂, Δ

2,2-dimethoxy-propane

VII

H₃C—S(=O)₂—Cl , TEA

cryst. CH₃OH

→ II

III , F₃C—SO₃H

trifluoromethane-sulfonic acid

→ V → Oseltamivir

Reference(s):
a Rohloff, J.C. et al.: J. Org. Chem. (JOCEAH) **63**, 4545-4550 (1998)
   WO 9 626 933 (Gilead Sciences; appl. 26.2.1996; USA-prior. 27.2.1995)
   US 5 886 213 (Gilead Sciences; 23.3.1999; USA-prior. 22.8.1997)
   US 5 859 284 (Gilead Sciences; 12.1.1999; USA-prior. 23.8.1996)
b Federspiel, M. et al.: Org. Process Res. Dev. (OPRDFK) **3** (4), 266-274 (1999)

Trade Name(s):
CH: Tamiflu (Roche; 1999)

Otilonium bromide

ATC: A03AB06
Use: antispasmodic

RN: 26095-59-0   MF: C$_{29}$H$_{43}$BrN$_2$O$_4$ MW: 563.58   EINECS: 247-457-4
LD$_{50}$: 46.5 mg/kg (M, i.v.); >1500 mg/kg (M, p.o.);
        14.1 mg/kg (R, i.v.); >1650 mg/kg (R, p.o.)
CN: N,N-diethyl-N-methyl-2-[[4-[[2-(octyloxy)benzoyl]amino]benzoyl]oxy]ethanaminium bromide

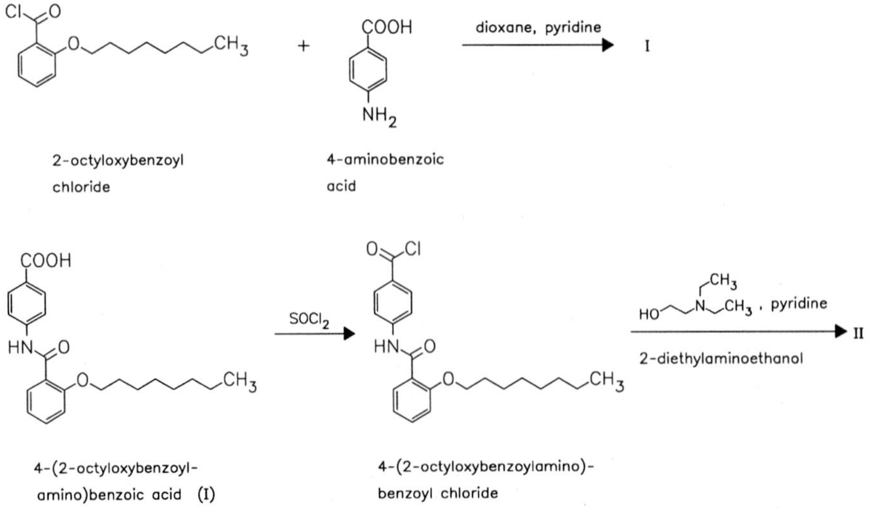

2-octyloxybenzoyl chloride   +   4-aminobenzoic acid

dioxane, pyridine → I

4-(2-octyloxybenzoyl-amino)benzoic acid (I)

SOCl₂ →

4-(2-octyloxybenzoylamino)-benzoyl chloride

HO—N(CH₃)(CH₃) , pyridine

2-diethylaminoethanol

→ II

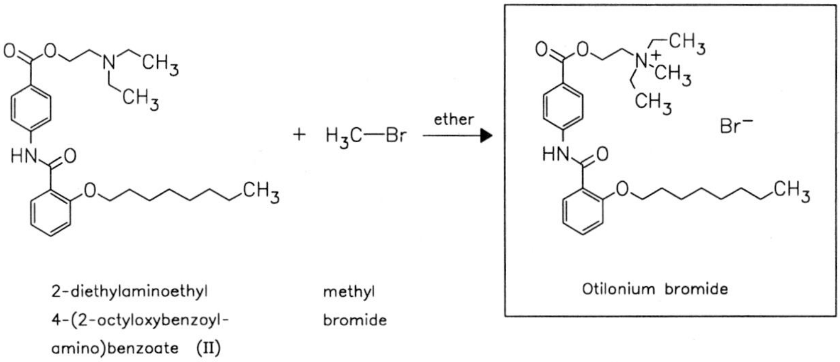

2-diethylaminoethyl
4-(2-octyloxybenzoyl-
amino)benzoate (II)

methyl
bromide

Otilonium bromide

Reference(s):
DOS 1 643 458 (Menarini; appl. 15.9.1967; I-prior. 17.9.1966).
US 3 536 723 (Menarini; 27.10.1970; I-prior. 27.9.1966).
Ghelardoni, M. et al.: J. Med. Chem. (JMCMAR) **16**, 1063 (1973).

Formulation(s):   amp. 150 mg; drg. 40 mg; suppos. 20 mg; tabl. 40 mg

Trade Name(s):
I: Spasen (Firma)   Spasmomen (Menarini)
      Spasen Somatico (Firma)-   Spasmomen Somatico
      comb.   (Menarini)-comb.

Oxaceprol
(Aceprolinum; *N*-Acetyl-4-hydroxy-L-proline)

ATC: D11AX09; M01AX24
Use: connective tissue therapeutic,
       antirheumatic

RN: 33996-33-7   MF: $C_7H_{11}NO_4$ MW: 173.17   EINECS: 251-780-6
CN: *trans*-1-acetyl-4-hydroxy-L-proline

trans-L-hydroxy-
proline

acetic anhydride

Oxaceprol

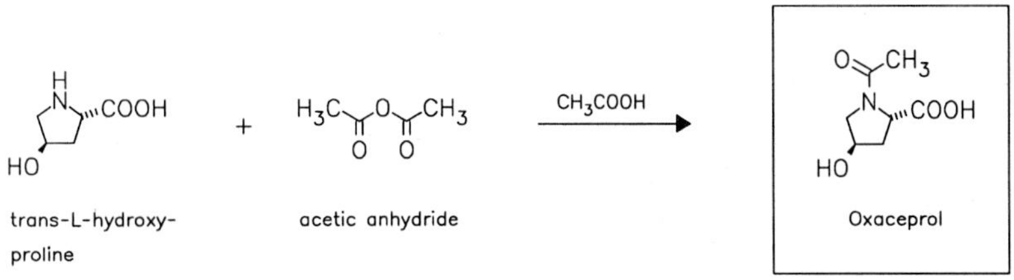

Reference(s):
GB 1 246 141 (P. and B. Coirre; appl. 30.8.1968; F-prior. 14.9.1967, 16.5.1968).
DAS 1 795 327 (S.A.R.L. Franco-Chimie; appl. 13.9.1968; F-prior. 14.9.1967, 16.5.1968).
DOS 2 139 476 (P. and B. Coirre; appl. 6.8.1971).

Formulation(s):   f. c. tabl. 200 mg

Trade Name(s):
D: AHP 200 (Chephasaar)   F: Jonctum (Marion Merrell)

Oxacillin

ATC: J01CF04
Use: antibiotic

RN: 66-79-5   MF: C$_{19}$H$_{19}$N$_3$O$_5$S   MW: 401.44   EINECS: 200-635-5
LD$_{50}$: 1490 mg/kg (M, i.v.); 6500 mg/kg (M, p.o.)
CN: [2S-(2α,5α,6β)]-3,3-dimethyl-6-[[(5-methyl-3-phenyl-4-isoxazolyl)carbonyl]amino]-7-oxo-4-thia-1-azabicyclo[3.2.0]heptane-2-carboxylic acid

monosodium salt monohydrate
RN: 7240-38-2   MF: C$_{19}$H$_{18}$N$_3$NaO$_5$S · H$_2$O   MW: 441.44

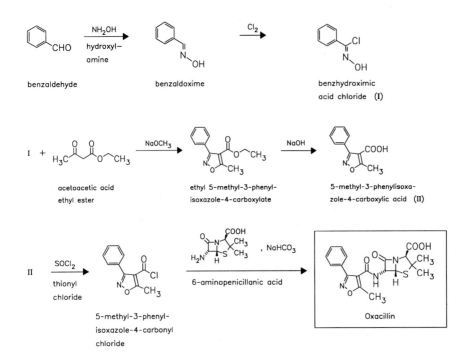

benzaldehyde → benzaldoxime → benzhydroximic acid chloride (I)

acetoacetic acid ethyl ester → ethyl 5-methyl-3-phenyl-isoxazole-4-carboxylate → 5-methyl-3-phenylisoxazole-4-carboxylic acid (II)

5-methyl-3-phenyl-isoxazole-4-carbonyl chloride

6-aminopenicillanic acid

Oxacillin

Reference(s):
US 2 996 501 (Beecham; 15.8.1961; GB-prior. 31.3.1960).
GB 905 778 (Beecham; appl. 31.3.1960; valid from 14.3.1961).
GB 958 478 (Beecham; appl. 28.2.1963; USA-prior. 13.3.1962).

Formulation(s):   cps. 250 mg, 500 mg; vial 0.5 g, 1 g (as sodium salt)

Trade Name(s):
D:	Optocillin (Bayer Vital)-comb.	I:	Penstapho (Bristol-Myers Squibb)
	Stapenor (Bayer Vital)	J:	Staphcillin V (Banyu)
F:	Bristopen (Bristol-Myers Squibb)	USA:	Bactocill (Beecham-Massengill); wfm

Oxacillin (Teva)
Prostaphlin (Bristol); wfm

Oxaflozane

ATC: N06AX10
Use: antidepressant

RN: 26629-87-8   MF: C$_{14}$H$_{18}$F$_3$NO   MW: 273.30   EINECS: 247-855-8
CN: 4-(1-methylethyl)-2-[3-(trifluoromethyl)phenyl]morpholine

hydrochloride
RN: 26629-86-7   MF: $C_{14}H_{18}F_3NO \cdot HCl$ MW: 309.76   EINECS: 247-854-2
LD$_{50}$:   80 mg/kg (M, i.v.); 365 mg/kg (M, p.o.)

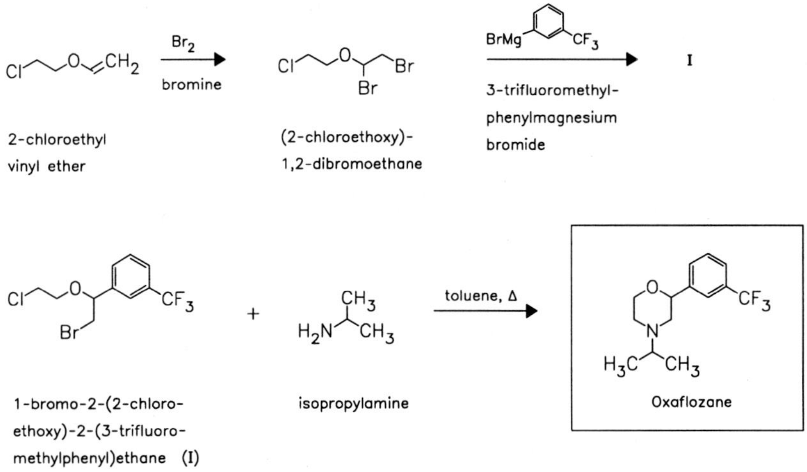

2-chloroethyl
vinyl ether

(2-chloroethoxy)-
1,2-dibromoethane

3-trifluoromethyl-
phenylmagnesium
bromide

I

1-bromo-2-(2-chloro-
ethoxy)-2-(3-trifluoro-
methylphenyl)ethane   (I)

isopropylamine

Oxaflozane

Reference(s):
DOS 1 910 477 (CERM; appl. 1.3.1969; F-prior. 4.3.1968, 29.5.1968 18.6.1968, 27.8.1968, 15.11.1968, 19.2.1969).
US 3 637 680 (CERM; 25.1.1972; F-prior. 4.3.1968, 29.5.1968, 18.6.1968, 27.8.1968, 15.11.1968, 19.2.1969).
Busch, N. et al.: Eur. J. Med. Chem.-Chim. Ther. (EJMCA5) **11**, 201 (1976).

Formulation(s):   drops 2 %

Trade Name(s):
F: Conflictan (Solvay Pharma)   I: Conflictan (Riom); wfm

Oxaflumazine

ATC: N05AB
Use: psychosedative

RN: 16498-21-8   MF: $C_{26}H_{32}F_3N_3O_2S$ MW: 507.62
CN: 10-[3-[4-[2-(1,3-dioxan-2-yl)ethyl]-1-piperazinyl]propyl]-2-(trifluoromethyl)-10*H*-phenothiazine

hydrogen succinate (1:1)
RN: 41761-40-4   MF: $C_{26}H_{32}F_3N_3O_2S \cdot C_4H_6O_4$ MW: 625.71

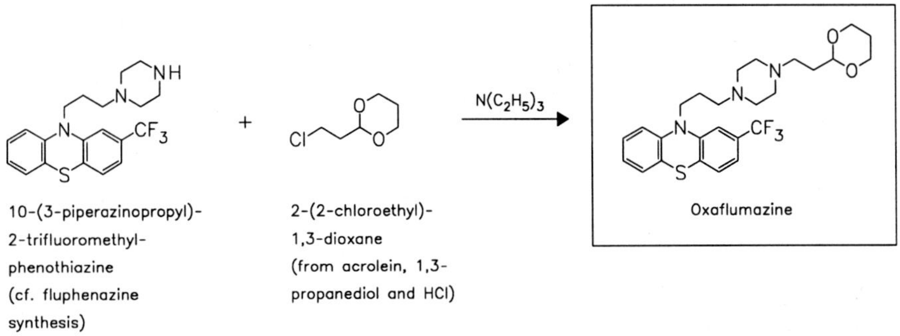

10-(3-piperazinopropyl)-
2-trifluoromethyl-
phenothiazine
(cf. fluphenazine
synthesis)

2-(2-chloroethyl)-
1,3-dioxane
(from acrolein, 1,3-
propanediol and HCl)

Oxaflumazine

Reference(s):
DAS 1 620 281 (Roussel-Uclaf; appl. 28.6.1965; F-prior. 29.6.1964, 28.9.1964).
Ratouis, R.; Boissier, J.R.: Bull. Soc. Chim. Fr. (BSCFAS) **1966**, 2963.

alternative synthesis:
DOS 1 911 719 (S.I.F.A.; appl. 7.3.1969; F-prior. 8.3.1968).

Trade Name(s):
F: Oxaflumine (Diamant);
       wfm

Oxaliplatin

(1-OHP; NSC-266046; RP-54780)

ATC: L01XA03
Use: antitumor

RN: 61825-94-3   MF: $C_8H_{14}N_2O_4Pt$ MW: 397.29
LD_{50}:   19.8 mg/kg (M, i.p.);
       14.3-15.6 mg/kg (R, i.p.)
CN: [*SP*-4-2-(1*R-trans*)](1,2-cyclohexanediamine-*N,N'*)[ethanedioato(2–)-*O,O'*]platinum

1(R),2(R)-di-
aminocyclohexane

(I)

Oxaliplatin

Reference(s):
Kidani, Y. et al.: J. Clin. Hematol. Oncol. (JCHODP) **7**, 197 (1977).
JP 53 031 648 (Kidani; appl. 25.3.1978; J-prior. 6.9.1976).
JP 09 132 583 (Tanaku Kihinzobo Kogyo; appl. 20.5.1997; J-prior. 10.11.1995).

as stable aqueous formulation:
WO 9 604 904 (Debiopharm SA; appl. 22.2.1996; CH-prior. 8.8.1994).

in combination with cisplatin:
WO 9 412 193 (Debiopharm SA; appl. 9.6.1994; CH-prior. 24.11.1992).

Formulation(s):   vial 50 mg, 100 mg

Trade Name(s):
F: Eloxatin (Sanofi Winthrop)   Transplatin (Debiopharm)

Oxametacin

ATC: M01AB13
Use: anti-inflammatory, analgesic

RN: 27035-30-9   MF: $C_{19}H_{17}ClN_2O_4$ MW: 372.81   EINECS: 248-179-6
LD_{50}:   92 mg/kg (M, p.o.);
       78 mg/kg (R, p.o.)
CN: 1-(4-chlorobenzoyl)-*N*-hydroxy-5-methoxy-2-methyl-1*H*-indole-3-acetamide

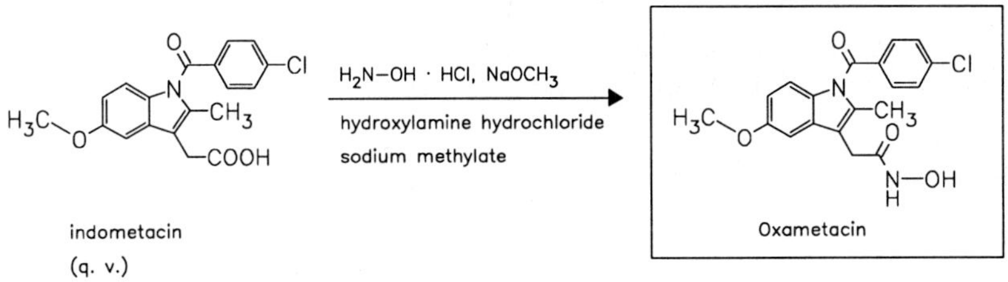

indometacin
(q. v.)

H₂N–OH · HCl, NaOCH₃
hydroxylamine hydrochloride
sodium methylate

Oxametacin

Reference(s):
FR 1 579 495 (R. Aries; appl. 22.1.1968).

Formulation(s):   tabl. 100 mg

Trade Name(s):
F: Dinulcid (Lab.   I: Flogan (ABC); wfm
        Pharmascience); wfm   Restid (UCB); wfm

Oxandrolone

ATC: A14AA08
Use: anabolic

RN: 53-39-4   MF: $C_{19}H_{30}O_3$ MW: 306.45   EINECS: 200-172-9
LD_{50}:   1832 mg/kg (M, p.o.);
        >10 g/kg (R, p.o.)
CN: (5α,17β)-17-hydroxy-17-methyl-2-oxaandrostan-3-one

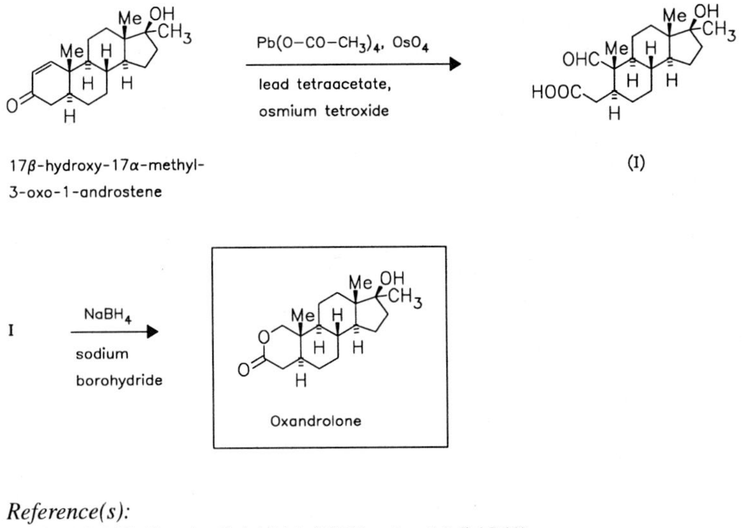

17β-hydroxy-17α-methyl-
3-oxo-1-androstene

Pb(O–CO–CH₃)₄, OsO₄
lead tetraacetate,
osmium tetroxide

(I)

I   NaBH₄
    sodium
    borohydride

Oxandrolone

Reference(s):
US 3 128 283 (Searle; 7.4.1964; MEX-prior. 10.5.1961).
Pappo, R.; Jung, C.J.: Tetrahedron Lett. (TELEAY) **1962**, 365.

starting material:
Counsell, R.E. et al.: J. Org. Chem. (JOCEAH) **27**, 248 (1962).

Formulation(s):   tabl. 2.5 mg

Oxaprozin

ATC: M01AE12
Use: anti-inflammatory

RN: 21256-18-8   MF: $C_{18}H_{15}NO_3$ MW: 293.32   EINECS: 244-296-1
LD$_{50}$: 93 mg/kg (M, i.v.); 1210 mg/kg (M, p.o.);
       82 mg/kg (R, i.v.); 4470 mg/kg (R, p.o.);
       124 mg/kg (dog, i.v.); >2 g/kg (dog, p.o.)
CN: 4,5-diphenyl-2-oxazolepropanoic acid

benzoin   succinic   Oxaprozin
           anhydride

Reference(s):
DE 1 670 005 (Wyeth; prior. 17.11.1967).
US 3 578 671 (Wyeth; 11.5.1971; prior. 6.11.1967).
Brown, K. et al.: Nature (London) (NATUAS) **219**, 164 (1968).

Formulation(s):   f. c. tabl. 600 mg

Oxatomide

ATC: R06AE06
Use: antiallergic

RN: 60607-34-3   MF: $C_{27}H_{30}N_4O$ MW: 426.56   EINECS: 262-320-9
LD$_{50}$: 25 mg/kg (M, i.v.); 9596 mg/kg (M, p.o.);
       29 mg/kg (R, i.v.); 1410 mg/kg (R, p.o.);
       >2 g/kg (dog, p.o.)
CN: 1-[3-[4-(diphenylmethyl)-1-piperazinyl]propyl]-1,3-dihydro-2H-benzimidazol-2-one

2-benz-   1-bromo-3-   1-(3-chloropropyl)-
imidazolone   chloropropane   2-benzimidazolone   (I)

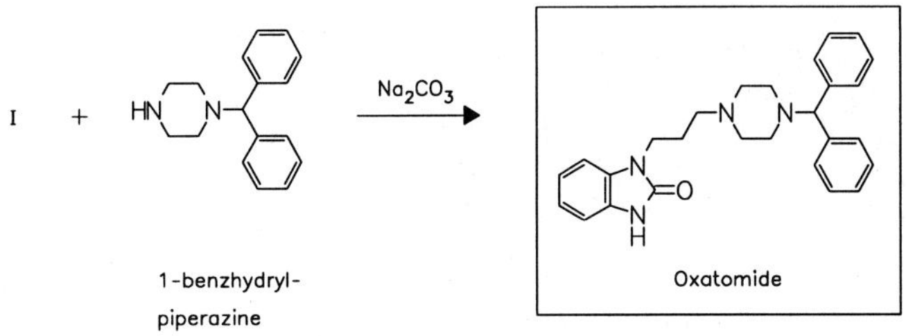
I
Na₂CO₃
1-benzhydryl-piperazine
Oxatomide

Reference(s):
BE 852 405 (Janssen; appl. 14.3.1977; USA-prior. 21.12.1976, 2.4.1976).
US 4 250 176 (Janssen; 10.2.1981; prior. 6.2.1978).

Formulation(s): susp. 2.6 mg/ml; tabl. 30 mg

Trade Name(s):

D:	Tinset (Janssen-Cilag; 1982)	GB:	Tinset (Janssen; 1982)	J:	Celtect (Kyowa Hakko; 1987)
F:	Tinset (Janssen-Cilag)	I:	Tinset (Formenti; 1985)		

Oxazepam

ATC: N05BA04
Use: tranquilizer

RN: 604-75-1 MF: $C_{15}H_{11}ClN_2O_2$ MW: 286.72 EINECS: 210-076-9
LD_{50}: 3700 mg/kg (M, p.o.);
>8 g/kg (R, p.o.)
CN: 7-chloro-1,3-dihydro-3-hydroxy-5-phenyl-2*H*-1,4-benzodiazepin-2-one

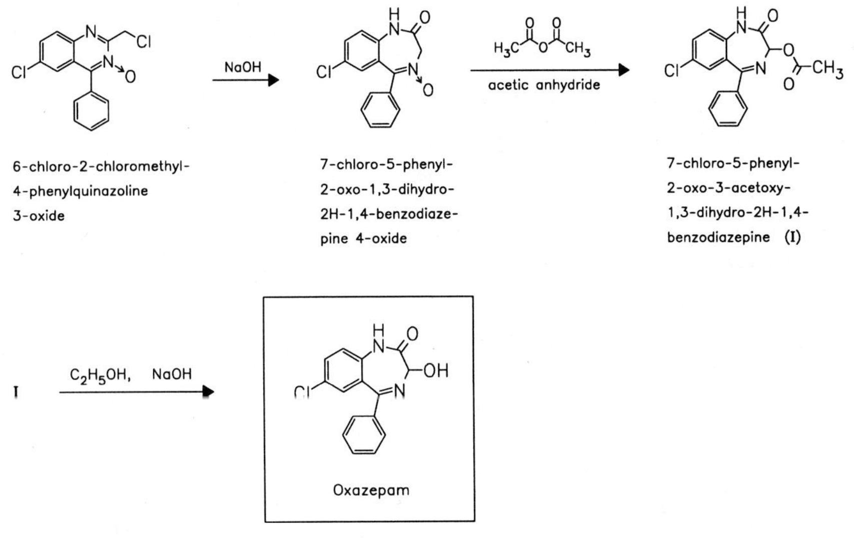
NaOH
acetic anhydride
6-chloro-2-chloromethyl-4-phenylquinazoline 3-oxide
7-chloro-5-phenyl-2-oxo-1,3-dihydro-2H-1,4-benzodiazepine 4-oxide
7-chloro-5-phenyl-2-oxo-3-acetoxy-1,3-dihydro-2H-1,4-benzodiazepine (I)
I
C₂H₅OH, NaOH
Oxazepam

Reference(s):
DE 1 645 904 (American Home Products; prior. 17.8.1962).
US 3 176 009 (American Home Products; 30.3.1965; prior. 5.3.1962).
US 3 296 249 (American Home Products; 3.1.1967; appl. 4.6.1963; prior. 29.8.1961, 5.3.1962).
DE 1 445 412 (American Home Products; appl. 17.8.1962; USA-prior. 29.8.1961, 5.3.1962).
DE 1 795 509 (American Home Products; appl. 17.8.1962; USA-prior. 29.8.1961, 5.3.1962).
Bell, S.C. et al.: J. Org. Chem. (JOCEAH) **27**, 562 (1962).
Bell, S.C.; Childress, S.J.: J. Org. Chem. (JOCEAH) **27**, 1691 (1962).

alternative synthesis:
DE 1 295 563 (American Home Products; appl. 21.5.1964; USA-prior. 29.5.1963, 13.8.1963).
DE 1 300 114 (American Home Products; appl. 21.5.1964; USA-prior. 29.5.1963, 13.8.1963, 3.12.1963, 7.5.1964).
DE 1 543 325 (American Home Products; appl. 21.5.1964; USA-prior. 29.5.1963, 31.8.1963, 3.12.1963, 7.5.1964).
DAS 1 795 231 (American Home Products; appl. 21.5.1964; USA-prior. 29.5.1963, 13.8.1963, 3.12.1963, 7.5.1964).
Bell, S.C. et al.: J. Org. Chem. (JOCEAH) **33**, 216 (1968).

Formulation(s): s. r. cps. 30 mg; tabl. 10 mg, 50 mg

Trade Name(s):

D:	Adumbran (Boehringer Ing.; 1965)		Praxiten (Wyeth; 1965)	I:	Limbial (Chiesi)
	Azutranquil (Azuchemie)		Sigacalm (Kytta-Siegfried)		Persumbrax (Boehringer Ing.)-comb.
	Durazepam /-forte (durachemie)		Uskan (Desitin) generics		Serpax (Wyeth-Lederle)
	Milfudorm (Merckle)	F:	Seresta (Wyeth-Lederle; 1966)	J:	Hilong (Banyu)
	Noctazepam (Brenner-Efeka)	GB:	Oxanid (Steinhard); wfm		Wakazepam (Wakamoto)
	Oxahexal (Neuro-Hexal)		Serenid-D (Wyeth); wfm generics	USA:	Serax (Wyeth-Ayerst) generics

---

Oxcarbazepine
(GP-47680)

ATC: N03AF02
Use: anticonvulsant

RN: 28721-07-5 MF: $C_{15}H_{12}N_2O_2$ MW: 252.27 EINECS: 249-188-8
CN: 10,11-Dihydro-10-oxo-5H-dibenz[*b*,*f*]azepine-5-carboxamide

iminostilbene (I)
(c.f. Carbamazepine)

10-methoxy-5H-dibenz[b,f]azepine (II)

10-methoxy-5H-dibenz[b,f]azepine-5-carboxamide (III)

Oxcarbazepine

b

1. Cl—CN

2. NaNO$_2$, H$_3$C—CO—O—CO—CH$_3$, CH$_3$COOH

I →

1. cyanogen chloride

5-cyano-10-nitro-
5H-dibenz[b,f]azepine

→ BF$_3$, Fe, CH$_3$COOH →

Oxcarbazepine

c

carbamazepine (IV)

1. H$_3$C—CO—O—OH, CH$_2$Cl$_2$, NaOAc

2. LiI, CHCl$_3$

1. peracetic acid

→ Oxcarbazepine

d

IV →

1. Cl$_2$, CHCl$_3$

2. DMF

10-chloro-5H-
dibenz[b,f]azepine-
5-carboxamide

→ H$_2$SO$_4$, 25°C →

Oxcarbazepine

Reference(s):

a DE 2 011 087 (Geigy AG; appl. 4.3.1970; CH-prior. 10.3.1969).
   HU 63 389 (Alkaloida; appl. 27.12.1991).
   WO 9 621 649 (Trifarma; appl. 3.1.1996; I-prior. 13.1.1995).
b EP 29 409 (Ciba-Geigy AG; appl. 24.10.1980; CH-prior. 30.10.1979).
   EP 28 028 (Ciba-Geigy AG; appl. 27.10.1980; CH-prior. 30.10.1979).
c CH 633 271 (Ciba-Geigy Ag; appl. 18.4.1978; CH-prior. 18.4.1978).
d CH 642 950 (Ciba-Geigy AG; appl. 30.10.1979; CH-prior. 30.10.1979).

Formulation(s):   tabl. 300 mg, 600 mg

Trade Name(s):
A: Trileptal (Novartis)   CH: Trileptal (Novartis)   NL: Trileptal (Novartis)

Oxeladin

ATC: R05DB09
Use: antitussive

RN: 468-61-1   MF: C$_{20}$H$_{33}$NO$_3$ MW: 335.49   EINECS: 207-418-4
LD$_{50}$: 13 mg/kg (M, i.v.); 130 mg/kg (M, p.o.);
       183 mg/kg (R, p.o.)
CN: α,α-diethylbenzeneacetic acid 2-[2-(diethylamino)ethoxy]ethyl ester

citrate (1:1)
RN: 52432-72-1   MF: C$_{20}$H$_{33}$NO$_3$ · C$_6$H$_8$O$_7$ MW: 527.61   EINECS: 257-910-8
LD$_{50}$: 13 mg/kg (M, i.v.); 130 mg/kg (M, p.o.);
       183 mg/kg (R, p.o.)

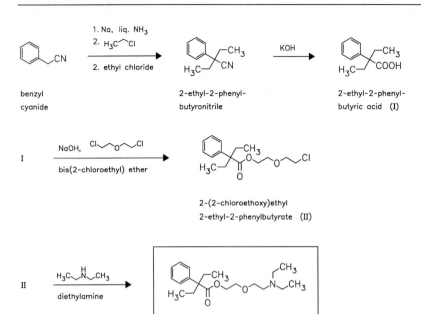

benzyl
cyanide

2-ethyl-2-phenyl-
butyronitrile

2-ethyl-2-phenyl-
butyric acid (I)

2-(2-chloroethoxy)ethyl
2-ethyl-2-phenylbutyrate (II)

Oxeladin

Reference(s):

US 2 885 404 (British Drug Houses; 5.5.1959; GB-prior. 4.1.1956).
Petrow, V. et al.: J. Pharm. Pharmacol. (JPPMAB) **10**, 40 (1958).

Formulation(s):   cps. 40 mg (as hydrogen citrate)

Trade Name(s):

D: Bronchisan (Atmos)-
       comb.; wfm
       dorex-retard (ICN); wfm
       dorex-retard (Woelm); wfm
       Kontagripp (Azuchemie)-
       comb.; wfm
       Mirfusot (Merckle)-comb.;
       wfm
       Pectischöll (Hestia)-comb.;
       wfm
       Piniol (Spitzner)-comb.;
       wfm

Silopentol (Hormosan);
wfm
Stas (Stada)-comb.; wfm
Toramin (Athenstaedt)-
comb.

F: Paxéladine (Beaufour)
       Paxéladine noctée
       (Beaufour)

I: Neobex (Lampugnani);
       wfm
       Notox (Medici)-comb.;
       wfm

Pectamol (Malesci); wfm
Tussiflex (Italsuisse)-
comb.; wfm
Tussilisin (Ibirn); wfm

J: Ethochlon (Hokuriku)
       Hustopan (Ohta)
       Neoasdrin (Toa)
       Neusedan (Nichizo)
       Tarmina (Mochida)

Oxetacaine

(Oxethazaine)

ATC: C05AD06
Use: gastric mucous membrane anesthetic

RN: 126-27-2   MF: $C_{28}H_{41}N_3O_3$ MW: 467.65   EINECS: 204-780-5
LD$_{50}$:   27 mg/kg (M, i.p.); 58 mg/kg (M, s.c.);
       30 mg/kg (R, i.p.)
CN: 2,2'-[(2-hydroxyethyl)imino]-bis[*N*-(1,1-dimethyl-2-phenylethyl)-*N*-methylacetamide]

monohydrochloride
RN: 13930-31-9   MF: $C_{28}H_{41}N_3O_3 \cdot HCl$ MW: 504.12   EINECS: 237-698-3
LD$_{50}$:   3881 µg/kg (M, i.v.); 431 mg/kg (M, p.o.);
       1400 µg/kg (R, i.v.); 675 mg/kg (R, p.o.)

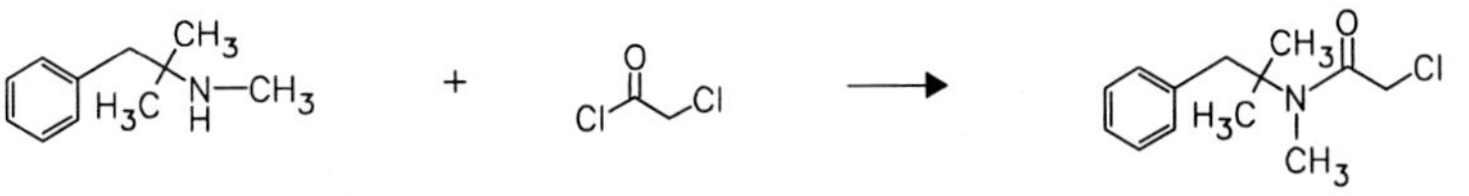

(1,1-dimethyl-2-phenyl-ethyl)methylamine

chloroacetyl chloride

2-chloro-N-methyl-N-(phenyl-tert-butyl)acetamide (I)

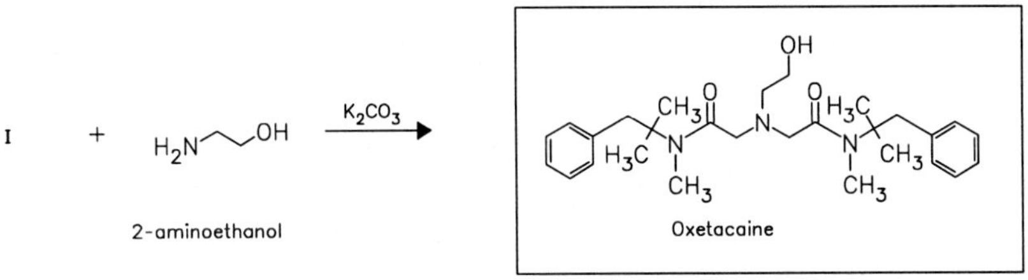

2-aminoethanol

Oxetacaine

Reference(s):

US 2 780 646 (American Home Products; 1957; prior. 1955).

Freed, M.E. et al.: J. Org. Chem. (JOCEAH) **26**, 2378 (1961).

Formulation(s):   susp. (in comb.) 10 mg/5 ml; tabl. 5 mg

Trade Name(s):

D:	Tepilta (Wyeth)-comb.		Mucoxin (Wyeth-Lederle)-	Strocain (Eisai)
F:	Mutésa (Wyeth-Lederle)-comb.		comb.	Topicain (Chugai)
			Mucoxin os sosp. (Wyeth-	USA: Oxaine (Wyeth)-comb.;
GB:	Mucaine (Wyeth)-comb.		Lederle)-comb.	wfm
I:	Emoren (IFI)	J:	Stomacain (Teisan-Pfizer)	

Oxetorone

ATC: N02CX06

Use: antimigraine agent

RN: 26020-55-3   MF: $C_{21}H_{21}NO_2$ MW: 319.40   EINECS: 247-411-3

CN: 3-benzofuro[3,2-c][1]benzoxepin-6-(12H)-ylidene-N,N-dimethyl-1-propanamine

hydrogen fumarate (1:1)

RN: 34522-46-8   MF: $C_{21}H_{21}NO_2 \cdot C_4H_4O_4$ MW: 435.48

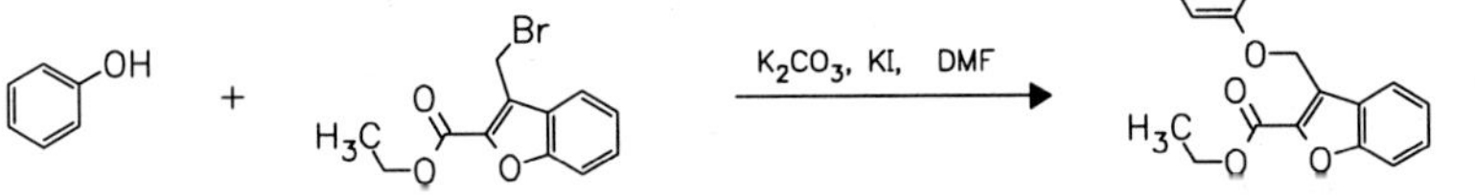

phenol

3-bromomethylcoumarilic acid ethyl ester

(from 3-methylcoumarilic acid ethyl ester)

3-phenoxymethylcoumarilic acid ethyl ester (I)

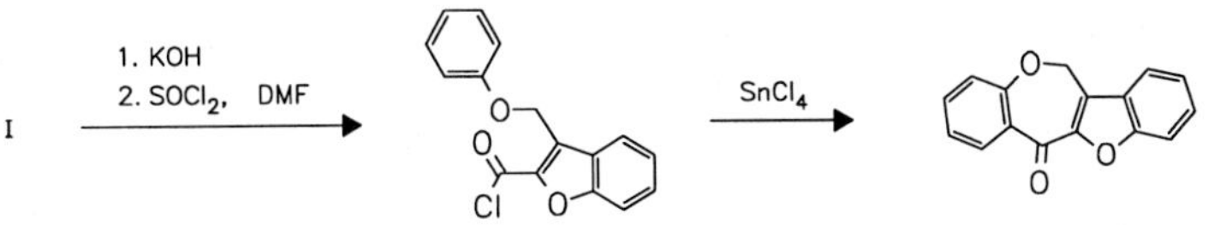

3-phenoxymethyl-coumariloyl chloride

6-oxo-6,12-dihydrobenzo-furo[3,2-c][1]benzoxepin (II)

II +   3-dimethylaminopropyl-magnesium chloride → 6-hydroxy-6-(3-dimethyl-aminopropyl)-6,12-dihydro-benzofuro[3,2-c][1]benzoxepin → (H₂SO₄) Oxetorone

Reference(s):
DOS 1 963 205 (Labaz; appl. 17.12.1969; GB-prior. 20.12.1968).
FR-appl. 2 026 686 (Labaz; appl. 19.12.1969; GB-prior. 20.12.1968).

Formulation(s):   tabl. 60 mg (as hydrogen fumarate)

Trade Name(s):
D: Nocertone (Labaz); wfm   F: Nocertone (Sanofi Winthrop)

Oxfendazole

ATC: P02CA
Use: anthelmintic

RN: 53716-50-0   MF: $C_{15}H_{13}N_3O_3S$ MW: 315.35   EINECS: 258-714-5
LD$_{50}$:   >6.4 g/kg (M, route unreported);
>6.4 g/kg (R, route unreported);
>1.6 g/kg (dog, route unreported)
CN: [5-(phenylsulfinyl)-1H-benzimidazol-2-yl]carbamic acid methyl ester

2-amino-4-chloro-nitrobenzene + sodium phenylmercaptide → (DMF) → 2-amino-4-phenylthio-nitrobenzene (I)

I →
1. H_3C acetic anhydride
2. H_3C peracetic acid , CH_3OH
→ 2-acetamido-4-phenyl-sulfinylnitrobenzene →
1. NaOH
2. H_2, Pd-C
→ 1,2-diamino-4-phenyl-sulfinylbenzene (II)

II + H_3C N,N'-bis(methoxycarbonyl)-S-methylisothiourea → C_2H_5OH, H_2O, CH_3COOH → Oxfendazole

Reference(s):
DOS 2 363 351 (Syntex; appl. 21.11.1973; USA-prior. 29.12.1972).
Averkin, G.A. et al.: J. Med. Chem. (JMCMAR) **18**, 1164 (1975).

Trade Name(s):
GB: Synanthic (Syntex); wfm   Systamex (Wellcome); wfm

Oxiconazole

ATC: D01AC11; G01AF17
Use: antifungal

RN: 64211-45-6   MF: $C_{18}H_{13}Cl_4N_3O$ MW: 429.13
CN: (Z)-1-(2,4-dichlorophenyl)-2-(1H-imidazol-1-yl)ethanone O-[(2,4-dichlorophenyl)methyl]oxime

mononitrate
RN: 64211-46-7   MF: $C_{18}H_{13}Cl_4N_3O \cdot HNO_3$ MW: 492.15   EINECS: 264-730-3
LD$_{50}$:   2.63 g/kg (M, p.o.);
        >2.458 g/kg (R, p.o.)

2,2',4'-tri-   imidazole   1-(2,4-dichloro-
chloroaceto-   phenacyl)-
phenone   imidazole

(I)   Oxiconazole

Reference(s):
DOS 2 657 578 (Siegfried AG; appl. 18.12.1976; CH-prior. 24.12.1975).
US 4 124 767 (Siegfried AG; 7.11.1978; CH-prior. 24.12.1975).
GB 1 514 870 (Siegfried AG; appl. 23.12.1976; CH-prior. 24.12.1975).
FR 2 336 129 (Siegfried AG; appl. 23.12.1976; CH-prior. 24.12.1975).

Formulation(s):   cream 10 mg/g; pessaries 600 mg (as mononitrate); powder 10 mg/g; sol. 10 mg/ml

Trade Name(s):
D: Myfungar (Brenner-Efeka;   F: Fonx (Yamanouchi   Okinazole (Tokyo Tanabe)
      1984)   Pharma)   USA: Oxistat (Glaxo Wellcome;
      Oceral (Yamanouchi; 1984)   J: Derimine (Kaken)   as nitrate)

Oxilofrine
(*p*-Hydroxyephedrine; Methylsynephrine; Oxyephedrine)

ATC: N07A
Use: circulatory analeptic, sympathomimetic

RN: 365-26-4 MF: C₁₀H₁₅NO₂ MW: 181.24 EINECS: 206-672-3

RN: 365-26-4 MF: $C_{10}H_{15}NO_2$ MW: 181.24 EINECS: 206-672-3

CN: (*R**,*S**)-4-hydroxy-α-[1-(methylamino)ethyl]benzenemethanol

hydrochloride
RN: 942-51-8 MF: $C_{10}H_{15}NO_2 \cdot HCl$ MW: 217.70 EINECS: 213-392-5

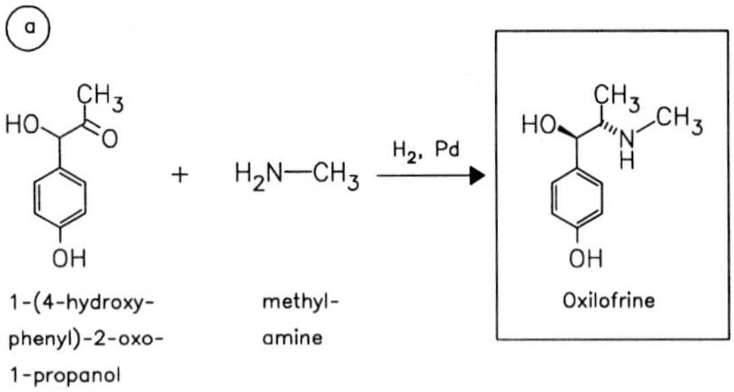

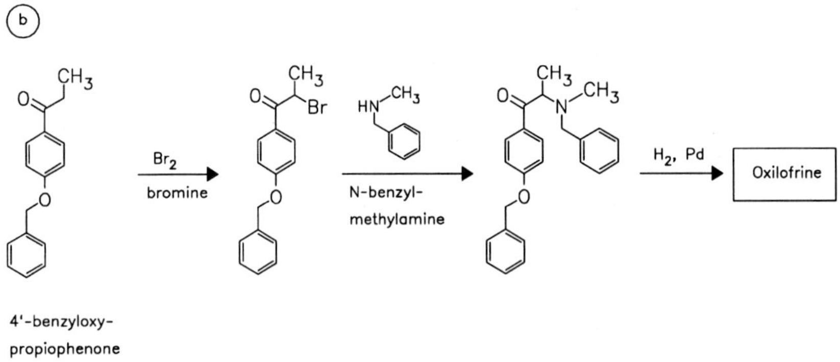

1-(4-hydroxy-
phenyl)-2-oxo-
1-propanol

methyl-
amine

Oxilofrine

4'-benzyloxy-
propiophenone

bromine

N-benzyl-
methylamine

Oxilofrine

Reference(s):
a DRP 571 229 (I. G. Farben; appl. 1930).
   starting material:
   DRP 555 404 (I. G. Farben; appl. 1930).
b US 1 877 756 (M. Bockmühl et al.; 1932; D-prior. 1929).
   US 1 878 021 (Winthrop; 1932; D-prior. 1928).

alternative syntheses:
DRP 526 393 (I. G. Farben; appl. 1928).
DRP 597 123 (I. G. Farben; appl. 1928).

review:
Ehrhart, Ruschig, Vol. **2**, 154.

Formulation(s): drg. 16 mg, 32 mg; drops 20 mg/ml, 40 mg/ml (as hydrochloride)

Trade Name(s):
D: Carnigen (Albert-Roussel,
   Hoechst)

Oxitefonium bromide

ATC: A03AB
Use: anticholinergic, antispasmodic

RN: 17692-63-6   MF: $C_{19}H_{26}BrNO_3S$ MW: 428.39   EINECS: 241-688-4
LD$_{50}$:   27.5 mg/kg (M, i.v.); 1050 mg/kg (M, p.o.)
CN: N,N-diethyl-2-[(hydroxyphenyl-2-thienylacetyl)oxy]-N-methylethanaminium bromide

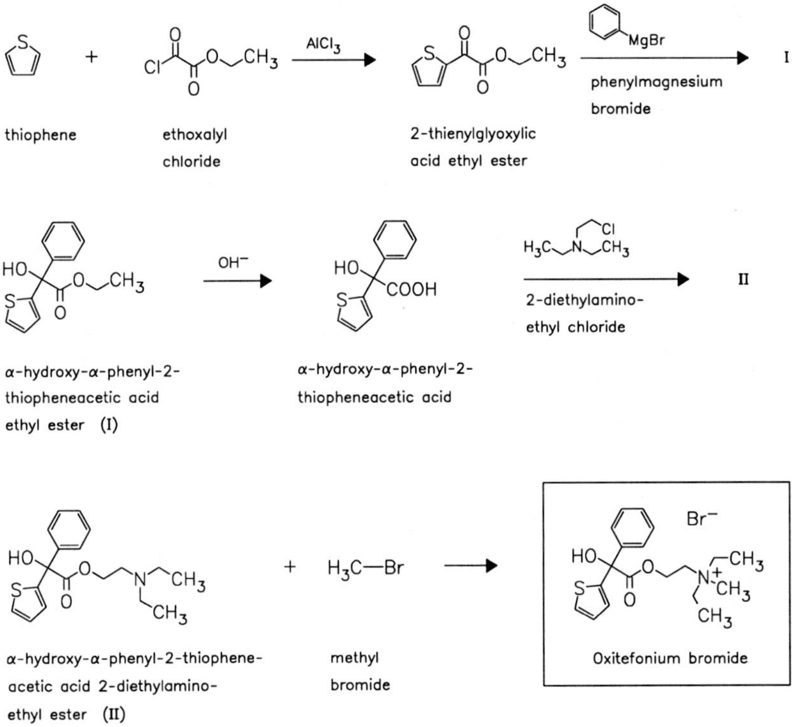

thiophene   ethoxalyl
chloride

2-thienylglyoxylic
acid ethyl ester

phenylmagnesium
bromide

I

α-hydroxy-α-phenyl-2-
thiopheneacetic acid
ethyl ester   (I)

α-hydroxy-α-phenyl-2-
thiopheneacetic acid

2-diethylamino-
ethyl chloride

II

α-hydroxy-α-phenyl-2-thiophene-
acetic acid 2-diethylamino-
ethyl ester   (II)

methyl
bromide

Oxitefonium bromide

Reference(s):
US 2 541 024 (F. F. Blicke; 1951; prior. 1946).
Blicke, F.F.; Tsao, M.U.: J. Am. Chem. Soc. (JACSAT) **66**, 1645 (1944).

Trade Name(s):
F: Bismutran (ISH)-comb.;   Nibitor (ISH); wfm   Védrénan (ISH)-comb.;
     wfm   wfm

Oxitriptan

(5-Hydroxy-L-tryptophan; Oxytriptanum)

ATC: N06AB
Use: antidepressant (psysiological
       serotonin precursor)

RN: 4350-09-8   MF: $C_{11}H_{12}N_2O_3$ MW: 220.23   EINECS: 224-411-1
LD$_{50}$:   375 mg/kg (M, i.v.); 1708 mg/kg (M, p.o.);
       27 mg/kg (R, i.v.); 243 mg/kg (R, p.o.)
CN: 5-hydroxy-L-tryptophan

(a) 5-benzyloxy-DL-tryptophan

(a1)

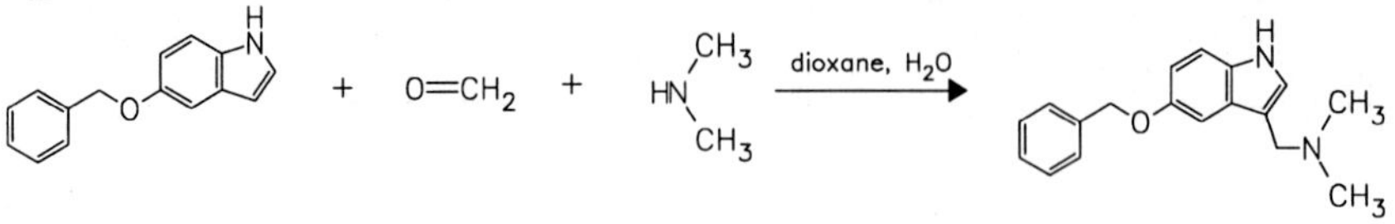
dioxane, H_2O

5-benzyloxyindole

5-benzyloxygramine (I)

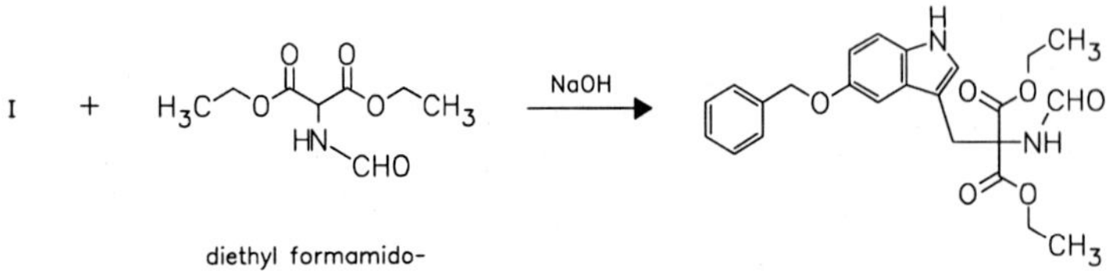
I
NaOH

diethyl formamido-malonate

(II)

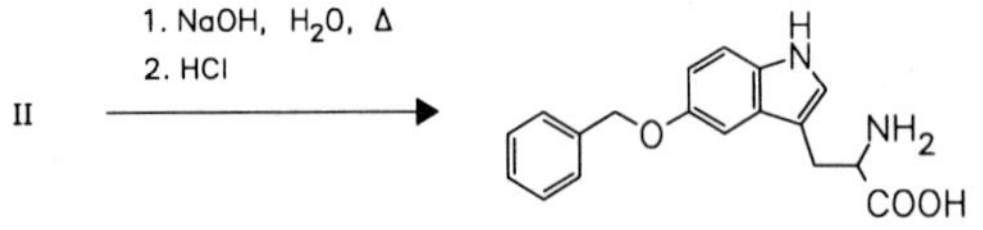
II
1. NaOH, H_2O, Δ
2. HCl

5-benzyloxy-DL-tryptophan (III)

(a2)

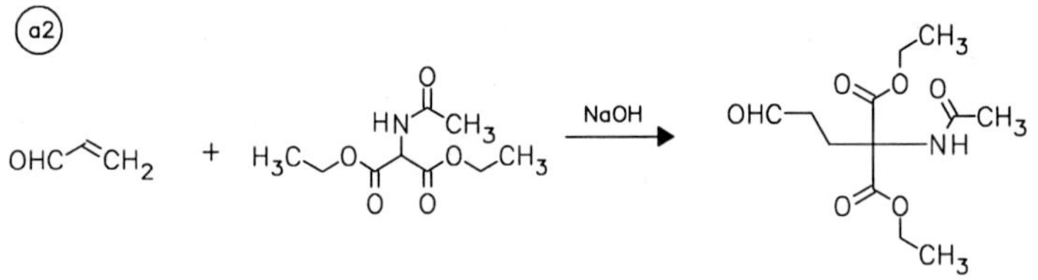
NaOH

acrolein

diethyl acetamido-malonate

(IV)

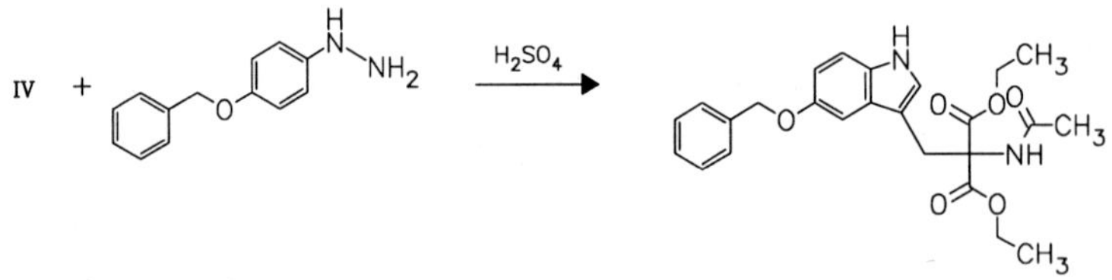
IV
H_2SO_4

(V)

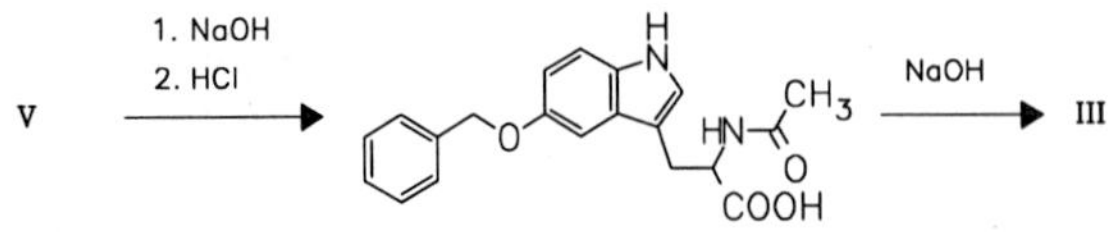
V
1. NaOH
2. HCl
NaOH
III

N-acetyl-5-benzyloxy-DL-tryptophan

(b) optical resolution

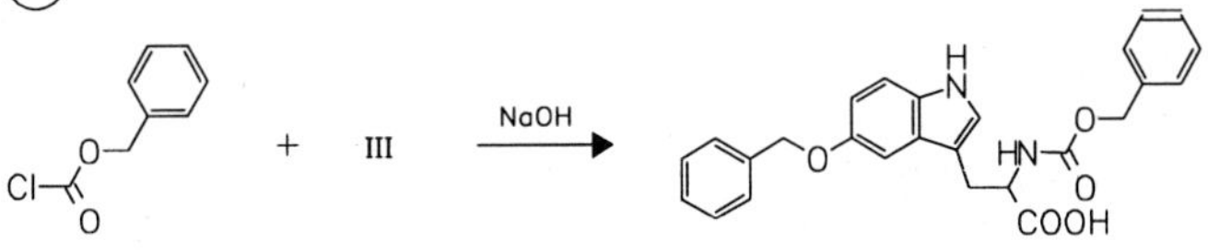
Cl
O
O
+ III
NaOH
H
N
O
HN
O
O
COOH

benzyl chloroformate

(VI)

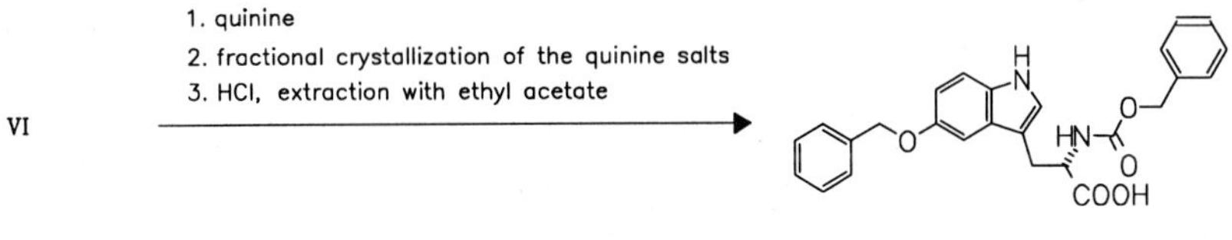
VI
1. quinine
2. fractional crystallization of the quinine salts
3. HCl, extraction with ethyl acetate
H
N
O
HN
O
O
COOH

(VII)

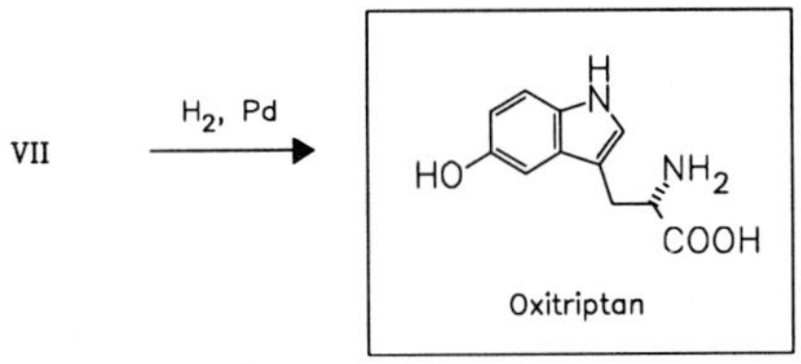
VII
H2, Pd
H
N
HO
NH2
COOH
Oxitriptan

(c) microbiological oxidation of L-tryptophan

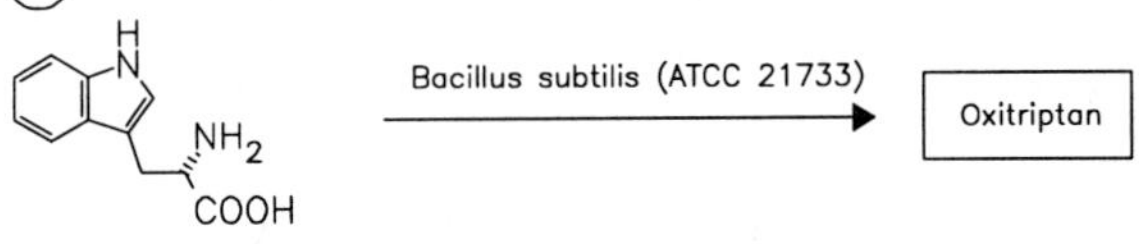
H
N
NH2
COOH
Bacillus subtilis (ATCC 21733)
Oxitriptan

L-tryptophan

(d) microbiological coupling with tryptophanase producing strains

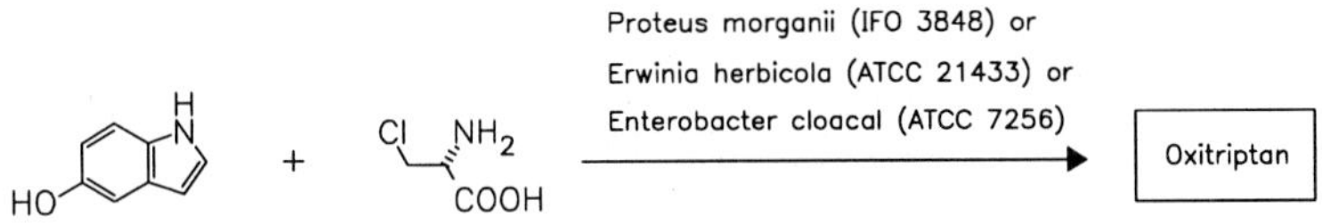
Proteus morganii (IFO 3848) or
Erwinia herbicola (ATCC 21433) or
Enterobacter cloacal (ATCC 7256)
H
N
HO
+
Cl
NH2
COOH
Oxitriptan

5-hydroxy-indole (VIII)

β-chloro-L-alanine

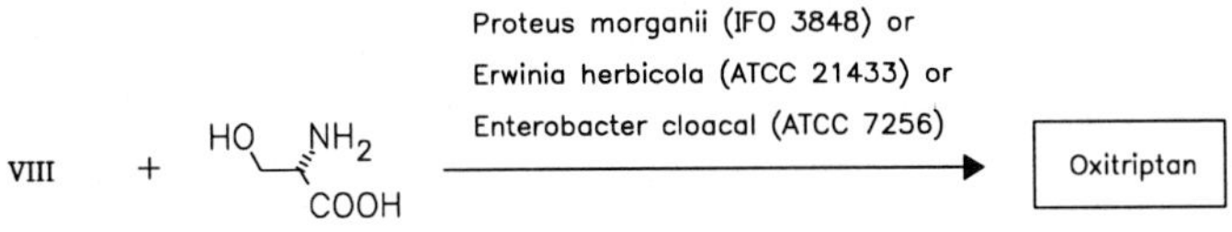
Proteus morganii (IFO 3848) or
Erwinia herbicola (ATCC 21433) or
Enterobacter cloacal (ATCC 7256)
VIII
+
HO
NH2
COOH
Oxitriptan

L-serine

Reference(s):

a1 Ek, A.; Witkop, B.: J. Am. Chem. Soc. (JACSAT) **76**, 5579 (1954).
preparation of 5-benzyloxyindole:
Shaw, N.F. et al.: Biochem. Prep. (BIPRAP) **9**, 12 (1962).
a2 GB 845 034 (May & Baker; appl. 1957).
b Morris, A.J.; Armstrong, M.D.: J. Org. Chem. (JOCEAH) **22**, 306 (1957).
c DOS 2 150 535 (Schering AG; appl. 6.10.1971).
d DE 2 461 188 (Ajinomoto; appl. 23.12.1974; J-prior. 29.12.1973).

alternative syntheses:
DOS 2 151 088 (Kyowa Hakko; appl. 19.10.1971; J-prior. 26.10.1970).
DAS 2 409 675 (Sagami; appl. 28.2.1974; J-prior. 1.3.1973).

combination with benserazide:
DOS 2 327 636 (Hoffmann-La Roche; appl. 30.5.1973; CH-prior. 30.6.1972).

Formulation(s):   cps. 100 mg

Trade Name(s):
D:	Levothym (Promonta Lundbeck)	F:	Lévotonine (Panpharma)
		I:	Oxyfan (Coli)

Tript-OH (Sigma-Tau)

Oxitropium bromide

ATC: R03BB02
Use: anticholinergic, antiasthmatic

RN: 30286-75-0   MF: $C_{19}H_{26}BrNO_4$ MW: 412.32   EINECS: 250-113-6
LD_{50}:   25.7 mg/kg (M, i.v.); 1.6 g/kg (M, p.o.);
        19 mg/kg (R, i.v.); 2.25 g/kg (R, p.o.);
        40 mg/kg (dog, i.v.); 3 g/kg (dog, p.o.)
CN: [7(S)-(1α,2β,4β,5α,7β)]-9-ethyl-7-(3-hydroxy-1-oxo-2-phenylpropoxy)-9-methyl-3-oxa-9-azoniatricyclo[3.3.1.0^{2,4}]nonane bromide

(−)-scopolamine   phosgene
(q. v.)

(I)   methyl bromide   Oxitropium bromide

Reference(s):
US 3 472 861 (Boehringer Ing.; 19.1.1971; D-prior. 26.1.1966).
DOS 1 670 048 (Boehringer Ing.; appl. 26.1.1966).
DE 1 795 818 (Boehringer Ing.; prior. 26.1.1966).

Formulation(s):   doses aerosol 0.1 mg; cps. 0.1 mg; inhalation sol. 1.5 mg; powder cps.0.1 mg/5 mg; sol. 1.5 mg/ml

Trade Name(s):
D:	Ventilate (Boehringer Ing.; 1983)	F:	Tersigat (3M Santé; 1984)

Oxolamine

ATC: R05DB07
Use: antitussive

RN: 959-14-8   MF: $C_{14}H_{19}N_3O$ MW: 245.33   EINECS: 213-493-4
LD_{50}:   679 mg/kg (M, p.o.);
       >2 g/kg (R, p.o.)
CN: N,N-diethyl-3-phenyl-1,2,4-oxadiazole-5-ethanamine

citrate (1:1)
RN: 1949-20-8   MF: $C_{14}H_{19}N_3O \cdot C_6H_8O_7$ MW: 437.45   EINECS: 217-760-6
LD_{50}:   650 mg/kg (M, p.o.);
       1650 mg/kg (R, p.o.)

benzamidoxime   3-chloro-   O-(3-chloro-1-oxopropyl)-   diethylamine   Oxolamine
propionyl   benzamidoxime
chloride

Reference(s):
DE 1 097 998 (Angelini Francesco; appl. 30.9.1959).

Formulation(s):   syrup 1 %; tabl. 100 mg

Trade Name(s):
F: Prilon (Cassenne); wfm
      Proxybron (Cassenne)-
      comb.; wfm
I: Gantrimex (Geymonat)-
      comb.
      Gantrimex ad scir
      (Angelini; as phosphate)

Perebron /-Ciclina
(Angelini)
Tussibron (Sella)
J: Flogobron (Intersint)
      Oxamin (Violani-
      Farmavigor)
      Oxarmin (Daiichi)

Oxolev (Barlocco)
Perebron (Angelini)
Tussibron (Sella)
numerous combination
preparations

Oxolinic acid
(Acide oxolinique)

ATC: G04AB04
Use: chemotherapeutic (Proteus bacteria
        infections, gyrase inhibitor)

RN: 14698-29-4   MF: $C_{13}H_{11}NO_5$ MW: 261.23   EINECS: 238-750-8
LD_{50}:   1890 mg/kg (M, p.o.);
       525 mg/kg (R, p.o.);
       >1 g/kg (dog, p.o.)
CN: 5-ethyl-5,8-dihydro-8-oxo-1,3-dioxolo[4,5-g]quinoline-7-carboxylic acid

1,2-methylene-   3,4-methylenedioxy-   3,4-methylene-
dioxybenzene   1-nitrobenzene   dioxyaniline (I)

ethoxymethylenemalonic
acid diethyl ester

[(1,3-benzodioxol-5-ylamino)-
methylene]malonic acid
diethyl ester

1. NaOH, DMF
2. H₃C—I

2. ethyl iodide

4-hydroxy-6,7-methylene-
dioxyquinoline-3-carboxylic
acid ethyl ester (II)

Oxolinic acid

Reference(s):
US 3 287 458 (Warner-Lambert; 22.11.1966; appl. 27.4.1966; prior. 12.12.1963).

alternative synthesis:
DAS 2 103 805 (Sumitomo; appl. 27.1.1971; J-prior. 28.1.1970, 18.2.1970, 23.2.1970, 24.2.1970).

Formulation(s):   tabl. 0.75 g

Trade Name(s):

D:	Nidantin (Gödecke/Sasse); wfm	Oxolina (Rorer); wfm		Uroxol (Ausonia); wfm
		Pelvis (Coli); wfm		Uroxol mite (Ausonia); wfm
F:	Urotrate (Parke Davis)	Tilvis (Scharper); wfm		
GB:	Prodoxol (Warner); wfm	Tiurasin (Bouty)	USA:	Utibid (Warner); wfm
I:	Decme (Poli); wfm	Uritrate (Parke Davis); wfm		
	Ossian (Bioindustria); wfm	Uroxin (Von Boch); wfm		

Oxomemazine

ATC: R06AD08
Use: antiallergic, antipruritic, sedative

RN: 3689-50-7   MF: $C_{18}H_{22}N_2O_2S$ MW: 330.45   EINECS: 222-996-8
LD$_{50}$:   35 mg/kg (M, i.v.); 140 mg/kg (M, p.o.)
CN: N,N,β-trimethyl-10H-phenothiazine-10-propanamine 5,5-dioxide

monohydrochloride
RN: 4784-40-1   MF: $C_{18}H_{22}N_2O_2S \cdot HCl$ MW: 366.91   EINECS: 225-330-4

phenothiazine

3-dimethylamino-2-
methylpropyl chloride

NaNH₂

sodium
amide

10-(3-dimethylamino-2-
methylpropyl)phenothiazine (I)

I $\xrightarrow{\text{H}_2\text{O}_2, \text{ CH}_3\text{COOH}}$

Oxomemazine

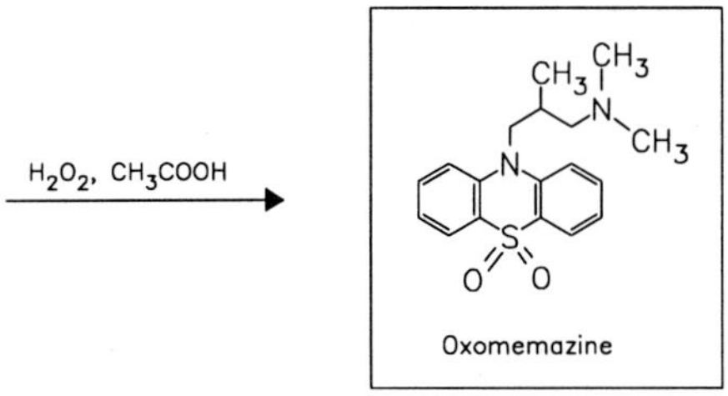

Reference(s):
US 2 972 612 (Rhône-Poulenc; 21.2.1961; GB-prior. 13.5.1955).

Formulation(s):   syrup 150 mg/150 ml; tabl. 10 mg

Trade Name(s):
D: Aplexil (Rhône-Poulenc)-
     comb.; wfm
     Imakol (Rhodia Pharma);
     wfm

Imakol (Rhône-Poulenc);
wfm
F: Rectoplexil (Théraplix)-
     comb.

J:

Toplexil (Théraplix)-comb.
Dysedon (Meiji)

Oxprenolol

ATC: C07AA02
Use: beta blocking agent

RN: 6452-71-7   MF: $C_{15}H_{23}NO_3$ MW: 265.35   EINECS: 229-257-9
LD$_{50}$:   20 mg/kg (M, i.v.); 375 mg/kg (M, p.o.)
CN: 1-[(1-methylethyl)amino]-3-[2-(2-propenyloxy)phenoxy]-2-propanol

hydrochloride
RN: 6452-73-9   MF: $C_{15}H_{23}NO_3 \cdot HCl$ MW: 301.81   EINECS: 229-260-5
LD$_{50}$:   20 mg/kg (M, i.v.);
     33 mg/kg (R, i.v.); 214 mg/kg (R, p.o.);
     15 mg/kg (dog, i.v.)

(a)

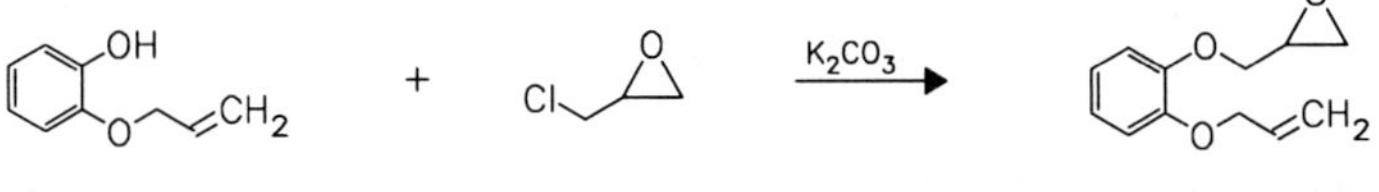

2-allyloxyphenol (I)   +   epichloro-
hydrin (II) $\xrightarrow{\text{K}_2\text{CO}_3}$ 3-(2-allyloxyphenoxy)-
1,2-epoxypropane (III)

III   + H_2N—CH$_3$ / CH$_3$ isopropylamine (IV) $\longrightarrow$ Oxprenolol

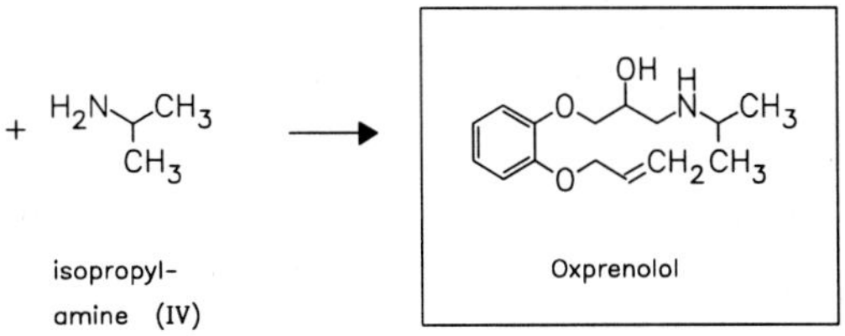

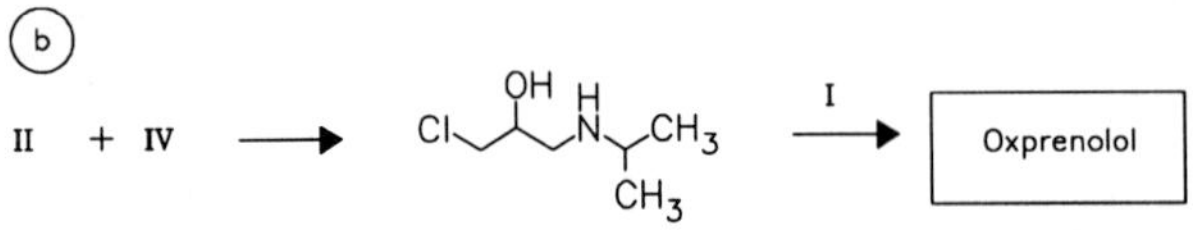

(b)

II + IV ⟶

OH H
Cl⌃⌃N⌃CH₃
    |
    CH₃

⟶ [Oxprenolol] I

1-chloro-3-isopropyl-
amino-2-propanol

Reference(s):

DE 1 242 596 (Ciba; prior. 19.8.1965).
US 3 483 221 (Ciba; 9.12.1969; CH-prior. 10.9.1964).
CH 451 144 (Ciba; appl. 10.9.1964).
CH 451 115 (Ciba; appl. 10.9.1964).
CH 451 915 (Ciba; appl. 10.9.1964).
GB 1 077 603 (Ciba; appl. 23.8.1965; CH-prior. 10.9.1964).

Formulation(s):   f. c. tabl. 20 mg, 40 mg, 80 mg, 160 mg (as hydrochloride)

Trade Name(s):

D:	Trasicor (Novartis) numerous generics and combination preparations		Trasitensine (Novartis; as hydrochloride)-comb.	Trasicor (Ciba) Trasitensin Retard (Ciba)-comb.
		GB:	Slow Trasicor (Novartis)	
F:	Trasicor (Novartis; 1975) Trasipressol (Novartis; 1977)-comb.		Trasicor (Novartis; 1970) Trasidrex (Novartis Farma; 1978)-comb.	J: Trasacor (Ciba-Geigy-Takeda)
		I:	Tensilene (Caber)-comb.	USA: Trasicor (Ciba-Geigy); wfm

Oxybuprocaine

(Benoxinate)

ATC: D04AB03; S01HA02
Use: local anesthetic

RN: 99-43-4   MF: $C_{17}H_{28}N_2O_3$ MW: 308.42
LD$_{50}$: 7800 µg/kg (M, i.v.)
CN: 4-amino-3-butoxybenzoic acid 2-(diethylamino)ethyl ester

monohydrochloride

RN: 5987-82-6   MF: $C_{17}H_{28}N_2O_3 \cdot HCl$ MW: 344.88   EINECS: 227-808-8
LD$_{50}$: >6.8 mg/kg (M, i.v.); >5.6 mg/kg (R, i.v.)

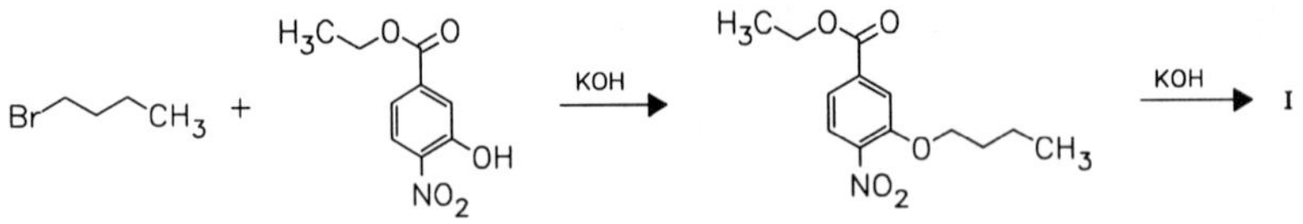

H₃C⌃O⌃O

Br⌃⌃CH₃ +

H₃C⌃O⌃O

⟶ KOH ⟶

H₃C⌃O⌃O

⟶ KOH ⟶ I

| butyl bromide | 3-hydroxy-4-nitro-benzoic acid ethyl ester | 3-butyloxy-4-nitrobenzoic acid ethyl ester |

3-butyloxy-4-nitro-
benzoic acid   (I)

3-butyloxy-4-nitro-
benzoyl chloride

2-diethylamino-
ethanol

3-butyloxy-4-nitrobenzoic acid
2-diethylaminoethyl ester   (II)

Oxybuprocaine

Reference(s):
GB 654 484 (Dr. A. Wander AG; appl. 1948; CH-prior. 1947).

Formulation(s):   eye drops 2 mg, 4 mg/ml; sol. 10 mg/ml (as hydrochloride)

Trade Name(s):
D: Benoxinat 0,4 % Thilo
      (Alcon)
      Conjuncain EDO (Mann)
      Novesine (CIBA Vision)
      Novesine Wander (Novartis
      Pharma)
      Oxbarukain (Chauvin
      ankerpharm)

F: Thilorbin (Thilo)-comb.
      Cébésine (Chauvin-Blache)
      Novésine (Merck Sharp &
      Dohme-Chibret)

GB: Minims Benoxinate
      (Chauvin; as
      hydrochloride)

I: Opulets Benoxinate
      (Alcon)
      Novesina (Novartis Farma)
J: Benoxil (Santen)
      Lacrimin (Santen)
      Primacaine (Hori-Morita)
USA: Dorsacaine (Dorsey); wfm

Oxybutynin

ATC: G04BD04
Use: anticholinergic, antispasmodic

RN: 5633-20-5   MF: $C_{22}H_{31}NO_3$ MW: 357.49
CN: α-cyclohexyl-α-hydroxybenzeneacetic acid 4-(diethylamino)-2-butynyl ester

hydrochloride
RN: 1508-65-2   MF: $C_{22}H_{31}NO_3 \cdot HCl$ MW: 393.96   EINECS: 216-139-7
LD$_{50}$: 42 mg/kg (M, i.v.); 725 mg/kg (M, p.o.);
       61 mg/kg (R, i.v.); 460 mg/kg (R, p.o.);
       >400 mg/kg (dog, p.o.)

α-cyclohexylphenylglycolic
acid propargyl ester

paraform-
aldehyde

diethylamine

Oxybutynin

(b)

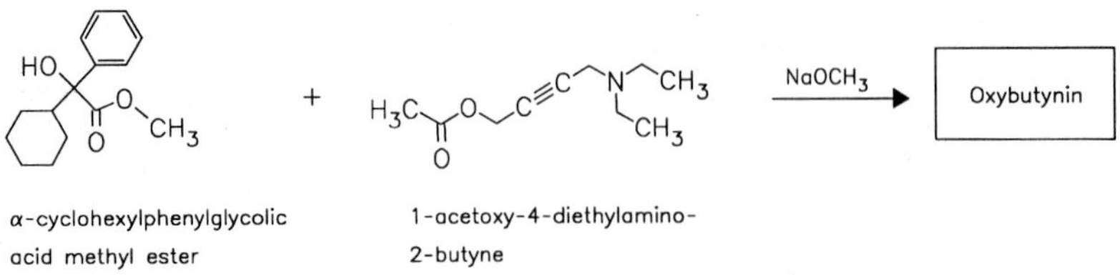
HO
O
CH3
O
+
H3C
O
C
C
N
CH3
CH3
O
NaOCH3
Oxybutynin
α-cyclohexylphenylglycolic
acid methyl ester
1-acetoxy-4-diethylamino-
2-butyne

Reference(s):
GB 940 540 (Mead Johnson; appl. 25.7.1961; USA-prior. 26.7.1960, 20.6.1961).

Formulation(s): syrup 2.5 mg/5 ml; tabl. 2.5 mg, 5 mg (as hydrochloride)

Trade Name(s):
F: Ditropan (Synthélabo)
Dxiptane (Débat)
GB: Cystrin (Pharmacia & Upjohn)
Ditropan (Lorex)
I: Ditropan (Synthelabo)
J: Pollakisu (Kodama)
USA: Ditropan (Hoechst Marion Roussel)

Oxycodone

ATC: N02AA05
Use: analgesic

RN: 76-42-6 MF: $C_{18}H_{21}NO_4$ MW: 315.37 EINECS: 200-960-2
LD_{50}: 320 mg/kg (M, i.p.); 426 mg/kg (M, s.c.)
CN: (5α)-4,5-epoxy-14-hydroxy-3-methoxy-17-methylmorphinan-6-one

hydrochloride
RN: 124-90-3 MF: $C_{18}H_{21}NO_4 \cdot HCl$ MW: 351.83 EINECS: 204-717-1

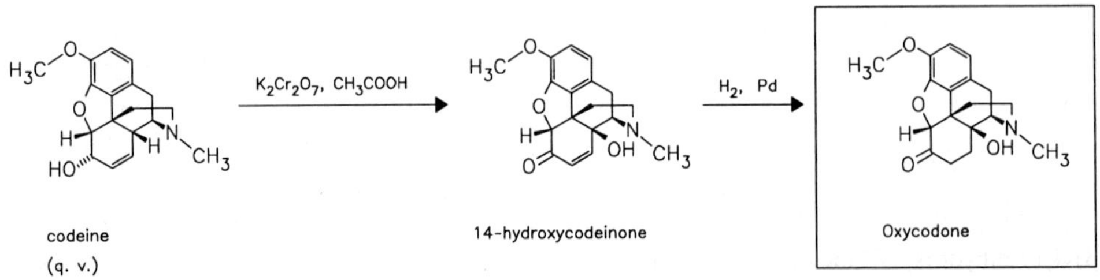
H3C
O
O
H
HO
H
N
CH3
K2Cr2O7, CH3COOH
OH
H2, Pd
codeine
(q. v.)
14-hydroxycodeinone
Oxycodone

Reference(s):
Ehrhart-Ruschig **I**, 118.
DRP 411 530 (E. Merck AG; 1925).

controlled release composition:
US 5 266 331 (Euroceltique; 30.11.1993; appl. 27.11.1991).

Formulation(s): cps. 5 mg; s. r. tabl. 10 mg, 20 mg, 40 mg, 80 mg

Trade Name(s):
D: Eubine (Chemipharm); wfm
Eukodal (Merck); wfm
Scophedal (Merck)-comb.; wfm
F: Eubine (Promedica)
GB: Proladone (Boots); wfm

Oxyfedrine

ATC: C01DX03
Use: coronary therapeutic

RN: 15687-41-9   MF: $C_{19}H_{23}NO_3$ MW: 313.40
CN: [R-(R*,S*)]-3-[(2-hydroxy-1-methyl-2-phenylethyl)amino]-1-(3-methoxyphenyl)-1-propanone

hydrochloride
RN: 16777-42-7   MF: $C_{19}H_{23}NO_3 \cdot HCl$ MW: 349.86   EINECS: 240-828-1
LD_{50}:   23 mg/kg (M, i.v.); 510 mg/kg (M, p.o.);
       46 mg/kg (R, i.v.); 500 mg/kg (R, p.o.);
       50 mg/kg (dog, i.v.); 200 mg/kg (dog, p.o.)

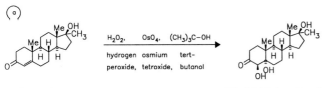

3-methoxyaceto-   paraform-   L-norephedrine   Oxyfedrine
phenone   aldehyde

Reference(s):
DE 1 493 574 (Degussa; appl. 31.3.1962).
US 3 225 095 (Degussa; 21.12.1965; D-prior. 31.3.1962).

Formulation(s):   amp. 4 mg/2 ml; f. c. tabl. 8 mg, 24 mg (as hydrochloride)

Trade Name(s):
D: Ildamen (ASTA Medica   F: Modacor (I.S.H.); wfm   Ildamen (Sir); wfm
      AWD)   I: Ildamen (Farmades); wfm   J: Ildamen (Chugai)

Oxymesterone
(Oxymestrone; Methandrostenediolone)

ATC: G03B
Use: anabolic

RN: 145-12-0   MF: $C_{20}H_{30}O_3$ MW: 318.46   EINECS: 205-646-9
CN: (17β)-4,17-dihydroxy-17-methylandrost-4-en-3-one

(a)

        H_2O_2, OsO_4, $(CH_3)_3C-OH$

        hydrogen   osmium   tert-
        peroxide,   tetroxide, butanol

methyltestosterone   4β,5α,17β-trihydroxy-17-methyl-3-
(q. v.)   androstanone (I)

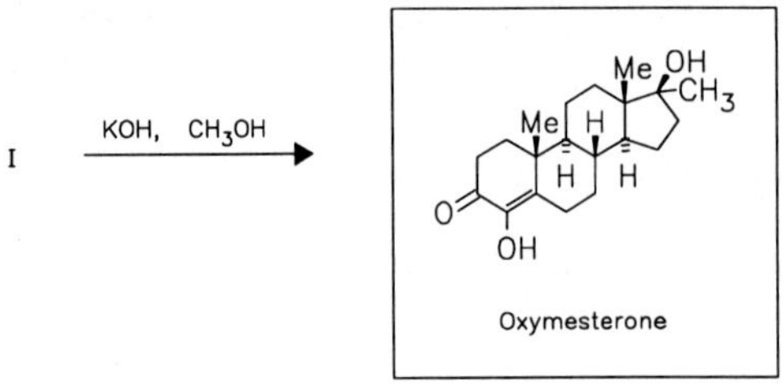

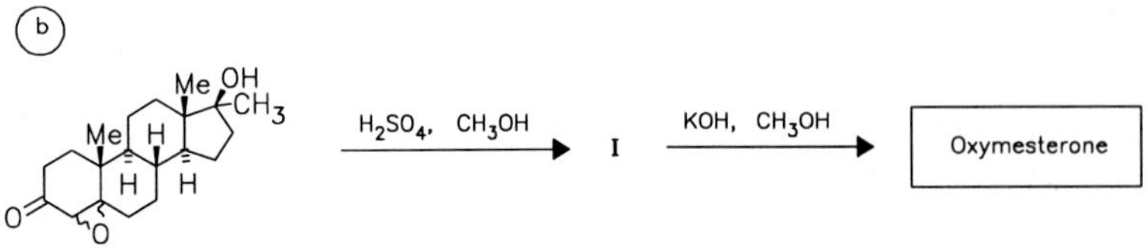

I $\xrightarrow{\text{KOH, CH}_3\text{OH}}$

Oxymesterone

(b)

17α-methyltestosterone
4,5-epoxide

$\xrightarrow{\text{H}_2\text{SO}_4,\ \text{CH}_3\text{OH}}$ I $\xrightarrow{\text{KOH, CH}_3\text{OH}}$ Oxymesterone

Reference(s):
US 3 060 201 (Farmitalia; 23.10.1962; GB-prior. 6.6.1958).

Formulation(s):   tabl. 5 mg

Trade Name(s):
D: Olocortina (Montedison   Oranabol (Montedison   J: Anamidol (Iwaki)
     Farma)-comb.; wfm   Farma); wfm   Oranabol (Sumitomo)
                              I: Anamidol (Iwaki); wfm

Oxymetazoline

ATC: R01AA05; R01AB07; S01GA04
Use: rhinological therapeutic
       (vasoconstrictor)

RN: 1491-59-4   MF: C$_{16}$H$_{24}$N$_2$O   MW: 260.38   EINECS: 216-079-1
LD$_{50}$:   2700 µg/kg (M, i.v.);
       800 µg/kg (R, p.o.)
CN: 3-[(4,5-dihydro-1H-imidazol-2-yl)methyl]-6-(1,1-dimethylethyl)-2,4-dimethylphenol

monohydrochloride
RN: 2315-02-8   MF: C$_{16}$H$_{24}$N$_2$O · HCl   MW: 296.84   EINECS: 219-015-0
LD$_{50}$:   4700 µg/kg (M, p.o.);
       1070 µg/kg (R, i.v.); 680 µg/kg (R, p.o.)

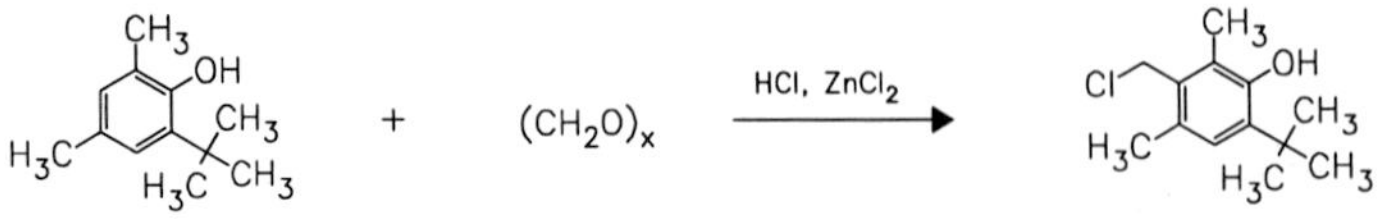

6-tert-butyl-2,4-
dimethylphenol

+   (CH$_2$O)$_x$

paraform-
aldehyde

$\xrightarrow{\text{HCl, ZnCl}_2}$

6-tert-butyl-3-chloromethyl-
2,4-dimethylphenol   (I)

Reference(s):
US 3 147 275 (E. Merck AG; 1.9.1964; D-prior. 30.9.1960).

Formulation(s):   doses spray 0.5 mg; drops 10 mg/100 ml; gel 0.5 mg; nasal drops 10mg/100 ml,
25 mg/100 ml, 50 mg/100 ml; spray 50 mg/100 ml (as hydrochloride)

Trade Name(s):
D:	Nasivin (Merck)		Atomol (Allen &	J:	Nasivin (Merck-Chugai)
	Nasivinetten (Merck)		Hanburys); wfm	USA:	4-Way Long Acting Nasal
	Vistoxyn (Pharm-Allergan)		Iliadin-Mini (Merck); wfm		Spray (Bristol-Myers);
	Wick Sinex (Wick Pharma)		Oxilin (Allergan)		wfm
F:	Aturgyl (Synthélabo)		Rino Calyptol (Rhône-		Afrin (Schering); wfm
	Sinex Lachartre (Lachartre)		Poulenc Rorer)		Dristan Long Lasting Nasal
GB:	Actifed Nasale (Warner-	I:	Nasivin (Bracco)		Spray (Whitehall); wfm
	Lambert)		Triaminic Nasale (Novartis		Neo-Synephrine
	Afrazine (Kirby-Warrick);		Consumer Health)		(Winthrop); wfm
	wfm		Vicks Simex Spray (Procter		
			& Gamble)-comb.		

Oxymetholone

(Hydroxymetholone)

ATC: A14AA05
Use: anabolic

RN: 434-07-1   MF: $C_{21}H_{32}O_3$ MW: 332.48   EINECS: 207-098-6
LD$_{50}$:   >1 g/kg (R, i.p.)
CN: (5α,17β)-17-hydroxy-2-(hydroxymethylene)-17-methylandrostan-3-one

Reference(s):
DE 1 070 632 (Syntex; appl. 30.1.1957; MEX-prior. 7.2.1956).
Ringold, H.J. et al.: J. Am. Chem. Soc. (JACSAT) **81**, 427 (1959).

Formulation(s):   tabl. 50 mg

Trade Name(s):
D:	Pardroyd (Parke Davis);		Plenastril (Grünenthal);	F:	Nastenon (Syntex-Daltan);
	wfm		wfm		wfm

GB:	Anapolon (Syntex)	J:	Adroyd (Parke Davis-Sankyo)		Anadrol (Shionogi)
				USA:	Anadrol (Unimed)

Oxymorphone
(Oxydimorphone)

ATC: A14AA05
Use: analgesic

RN: 76-41-5   MF: $C_{17}H_{19}NO_4$ MW: 301.34   EINECS: 200-959-7
LD_{50}:   172 mg/kg (M, i.v.)
CN: (5α)-4,5-epoxy-3,14-dihydroxy-17-methylmorphinan-6-one

hydrochloride
RN: 357-07-3   MF: $C_{17}H_{19}NO_4 \cdot HCl$ MW: 337.80

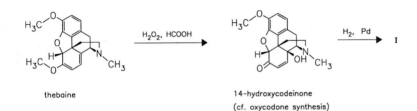

thebaine

H_2O_2, HCOOH →

14-hydroxycodeinone
(cf. oxycodone synthesis)

H_2, Pd → I

oxycodone (I)
(alternative synthesis,
cf. oxycodone synthesis)

HBr, 120 °C →

Oxymorphone

Reference(s):
US 2 806 033 (M. J. Lewenstein and U. Weiss; 1957; appl. 1955).

Formulation(s):   amp. 1 mg/ml, 1.5 mg/ml; suppos. 5 mg (as hydrochloride)

Trade Name(s):
USA: Numorphan (Endo)

Oxypendyl

ATC: A04
Use: anti-emetic

RN: 5585-93-3   MF: $C_{20}H_{26}N_4OS$ MW: 370.52
CN: 4-[3-(10H-pyrido[3,2-b][1,4]benzothiazin-10-yl)propyl]-1-piperazineethanol

dihydrochloride
RN: 17297-82-4   MF: $C_{20}H_{26}N_4OS \cdot 2HCl$ MW: 443.44   EINECS: 241-326-5
LD_{50}:   75 mg/kg (M, i.v.); 735 mg/kg (M, p.o.);
        1610 mg/kg (R, p.o.)

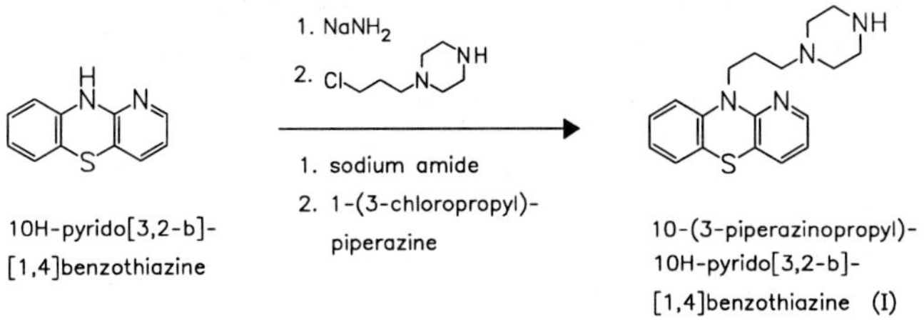

10H-pyrido[3,2-b]-
[1,4]benzothiazine

1. NaNH₂

2. Cl⌇⌇N⌇NH

1. sodium amide
2. 1-(3-chloropropyl)-
   piperazine

10-(3-piperazinopropyl)-
10H-pyrido[3,2-b]-
[1,4]benzothiazine (I)

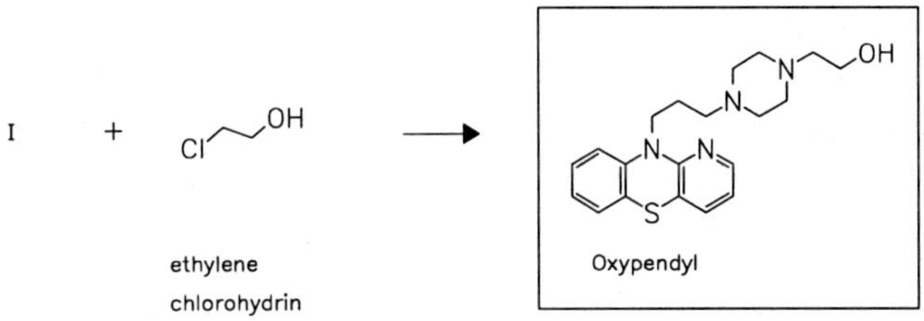

I   +   Cl⌇⌇OH

ethylene
chlorohydrin

Oxypendyl

Reference(s):
DE 1 063 603 (Degussa; appl. 3.12.1957).

Formulation(s):   vial 25 mg

Trade Name(s):
D: Pervetral (Homburg); wfm

Oxypertine

ATC: N05AE01
Use: neuroleptic, antipsychotic

RN: 153-87-7   MF: $C_{23}H_{29}N_3O_2$ MW: 379.50   EINECS: 205-818-3
LD$_{50}$:   2300 mg/kg (M, p.o.);
1 g/kg (R, p.o.)
CN: 5,6-dimethoxy-2-methyl-3-[2-(4-phenyl-1-piperazinyl)ethyl]-1*H*-indole

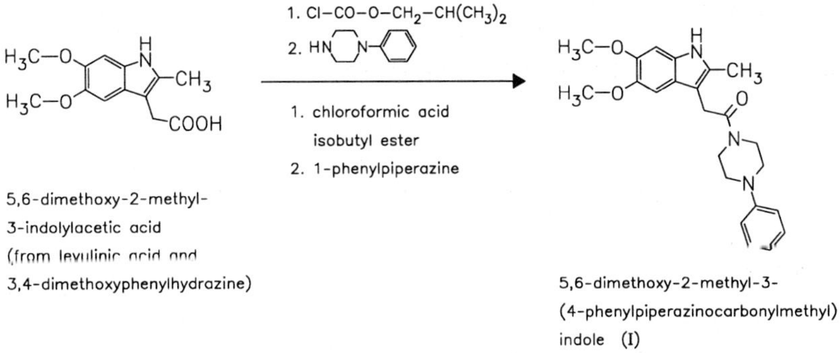

5,6-dimethoxy-2-methyl-
3-indolylacetic acid
(from levulinic acid and
3,4-dimethoxyphenylhydrazine)

1. Cl–CO–O–CH₂–CH(CH₃)₂

2. HN⌇N⌇phenyl

1. chloroformic acid
   isobutyl ester
2. 1-phenylpiperazine

5,6-dimethoxy-2-methyl-3-
(4-phenylpiperazinocarbonylmethyl)
indole (I)

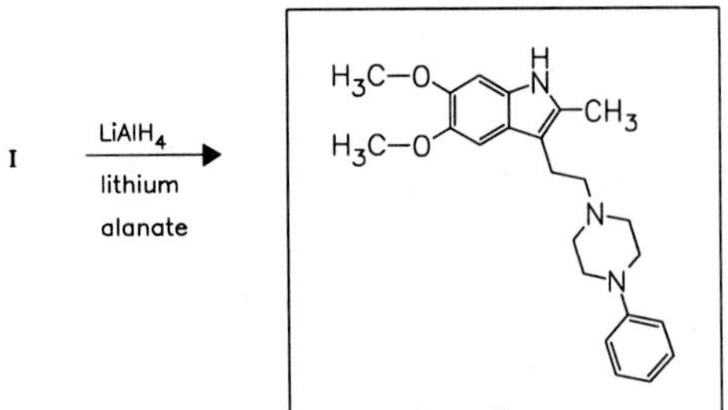

I $\xrightarrow{\text{LiAlH}_4}$ lithium alanate

Oxypertine

Reference(s):
DE 1 445 151 (Sterling Drug; appl. 23.9.1960; USA-prior. 25.9.1959).
BE 595 341 (Sterling Drug; appl. 23.9.1960; USA-prior. 25.9.1959).

Formulation(s):   tabl. 40 mg

Trade Name(s):
D: Forit (Winthrop); wfm
F: Equipertine (Winthrop); wfm
GB: Integrin (Winthrop); wfm
J: Forit (Daiichi)
USA: Forit (Sterling Winthrop); wfm

Oxyphenbutazone

ATC: M01AA03; M02AA04; S01BC02
Use: anti-inflammatory

RN: 129-20-4   MF: $C_{19}H_{20}N_2O_3$ MW: 324.38   EINECS: 204-936-2
LD$_{50}$:   52 mg/kg (M, i.v.); 330 mg/kg (M, p.o.);
68 mg/kg (R, i.v.); 329 mg/kg (R, p.o.);
178 mg/kg (dog, i.v.)
CN: 4-butyl-1-(4-hydroxyphenyl)-2-phenyl-3,5-pyrazolidinedione

monohydrate
RN: 7081-38-1   MF: $C_{19}H_{20}N_2O_3 \cdot H_2O$ MW: 342.40

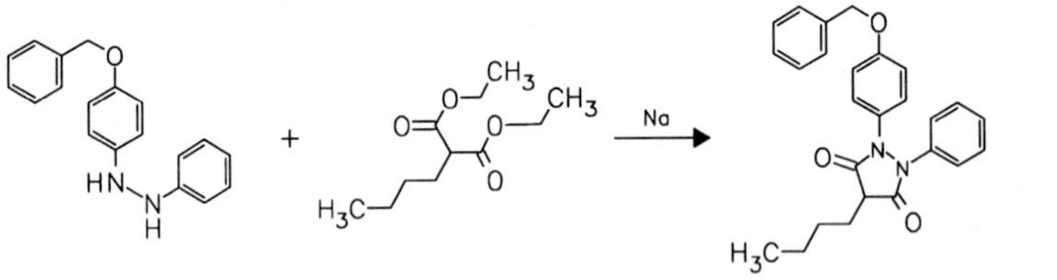

4-benzyloxyhydrazo-
benzene

butylmalonic acid
diethyl ester

O-benzyloxyphenbutazone (I)

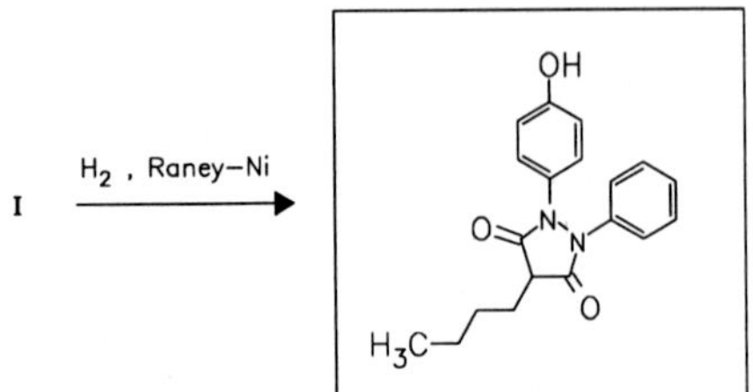

Oxyphenbutazone

Reference(s):
US 2 745 783 (Geigy; 1956; CH-prior. 1950).

Formulation(s):   suppos. 250 mg, 500 mg

Trade Name(s):

D: Californit (Merckle); wfm
     Dolo-Phlogase
     (Adenylchemie)-comb.;
     wfm
     Imbun (Merckle); wfm
     Oxyphenbutazon-
     ratiopharm (ratiopharm);
     wfm
     Oxyphenbutazon Stada
     (Stada Chemie); wfm
     Phlogase (Adenylchemie)-
     comb.; wfm
     Phlogistol (Helopharm);
     wfm
     Phlogont (Azuchemie);
     wfm
     Tanderil (Geigy); wfm
F: Tandéril (Geigy); wfm

GB: Tandacote (Geigy); wfm
     Tanderil (Geigy); wfm
     Tanderil (Zyma); wfm
     Tanderil Chloramphenicol
     (Zyma); wfm
I: Artroflog (Magis); wfm
     Butaflogin (Chimipharma);
     wfm
     Butaspirone (Brocchieri);
     wfm
     Butilene (Francia Farm.);
     wfm
     Difmedol Gel (UCM-
     Difme)-comb.; wfm
     Flogistin (Scharper); wfm
     Flogitolo (Isnardi); wfm
     Flogodin (Firma); wfm
     Iridil (Farmila); wfm

     Isobutil (Panther-Osfa
     Chemie); wfm
     Neo-Farmadol
     (Ottolenghi); wfm
     Pirabutina (Ellea); wfm
     Piraflogin (Jamco); wfm
     Poliflogil
     (Farmacobiologico); wfm
     Tanderil (Geigy); wfm
     Validil (Von Boch); wfm
J: Tanderil (Ciba-Geigy-
     Fujisawa)
     Tantal (Sawai)
USA: Oxalid (USV); wfm
     Oxyphenbutazone Tablets
     (Bolar; Bioline); wfm
     Tandearil (Geigy); wfm

Oxyphencyclimine

ATC: A03AA01
Use: anticholinergic

RN: 125-53-1   MF: $C_{20}H_{28}N_2O_3$ MW: 344.46   EINECS: 204-743-3
CN: α-cyclohexyl-α-hydroxybenzeneacetic acid (1,4,5,6-tetrahydro-1-methyl-2-pyrimidinyl)methyl ester

monohydrochloride
RN: 125-52-0   MF: $C_{20}H_{28}N_2O_3 \cdot HCl$ MW: 380.92   EINECS: 204-742-8
LD$_{50}$: 80 mg/kg (M, i.v.); 860 mg/kg (M, p.o.);
          88 mg/kg (R, i.v.); 1370 mg/kg (R, p.o.);
          47 mg/kg (dog, i.v.); 1 g/kg (dog, p.o.)

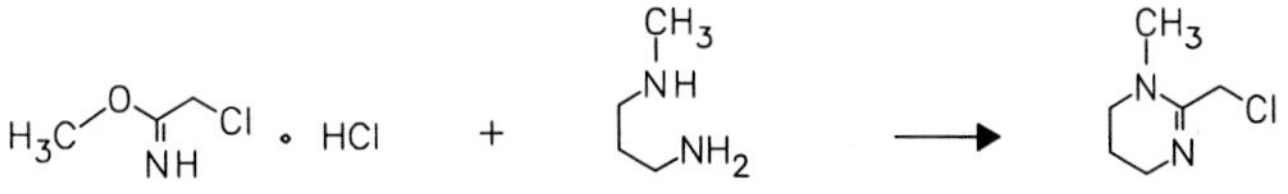

2-chloroacetimidic acid
methyl ester
hydrochloride

3-methylamino-
propylamine

2-chloromethyl-1-methyl-
1,4,5,6-tetrahydropyrimidine (I)

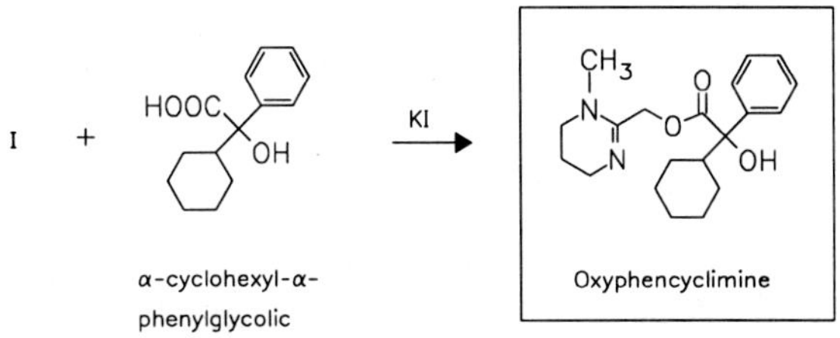

α-cyclohexyl-α-
phenylglycolic
acid

Oxyphencyclimine

Reference(s):
GB 795 758 (Pfizer; appl. 1956; USA-prior. 1955).
DE 1 058 515 (Pfizer; appl. 1956; USA-prior. 1955).

Formulation(s):   drg. 5 mg (as hydrochloride)

Trade Name(s):
D: Orbigastril (Roerig); wfm
     Orbigastril (Roerig)-comb.
     with meprobamate
F: Daritran (Opodex)-comb.;
     wfm
     Manir (Valpan); wfm
GB: Daricon (Pfizer); wfm
I: Gastrised (Benvegna)-
     comb.; wfm
     Madil (Beolet); wfm
     Ulcelac (Sigurtà)-comb.;
     wfm

J: Vagogastrin (Benvegna);
     wfm
     combination preparations;
     wfm
     Daricon (Taito Pfizer)
     Inomaru-S (Sawai)
     Norma (Sankyo)
USA: Daricon (Beecham-
     Massengill); wfm
     Daricon (SmithKline
     Beecham; as
     hydrochloride); wfm

Daricon PB (Beecham-
Massengill)-comb. with
phenobarbital; wfm
Enarax (Roerig)-comb.
with hydroxyzine; wfm
Gastrix (Rowell); wfm
Gastrix W/Phenobarbital
(Rowell)-comb. with
phenobarbital; wfm
Vistrax (Pfizer)-comb. with
hydroxyzine

Oxyphenisatin acetate
(Diphesatine; Acetphenolisatin)

ATC: A06A
Use: laxative

RN: 115-33-3   MF: $C_{24}H_{19}NO_5$ MW: 401.42   EINECS: 204-083-6
CN: 3,3-bis[4-(acetyloxy)phenyl]-1,3-dihydro-2H-indol-2-one

isatin   phenol   oxyphenisatin   (I)

I   +   acetic anhydride   →   Oxyphenisatin acetate

Reference(s):
DRP 406 210 (Hoffmann-La Roche; appl. 1923; CH-prior. 1922).
DRP 447 539 (Hoffmann-La Roche; appl. 1924; CH-prior. 1924).
DRP 482 435 (Hoffmann-La Roche; appl. 1928).

Formulation(s):   tabl. 5 mg

Trade Name(s):
D: Bisco-Zitron (Biscova);
     wfm

Darmoletten (Omegin);
wfm

Laxatan forte
(Divapharma); wfm
Obstilax (Zirkulin); wfm

Schokolax (Dallmann);
wfm
Vinco-Abführperlen
(Krehayn); wfm

F: numerous combination
preparations; wfm
Laxénia (Dumesny)-comb.;
wfm
GB: Bydolax (Moore); wfm

USA: Veripaque (Winthrop); wfm
Isocrin (Warner Chilcott);
wfm
Lavema (Winthrop); wfm

Oxyphenonium bromide

ATC: A03AB03
Use: anticholinergic, antispasmodic

RN: 50-10-2   MF: $C_{21}H_{34}BrNO_3$ MW: 428.41   EINECS: 200-010-7
LD_{50}:   30 mg/kg (M, i.v.); 400 mg/kg (M, p.o.);
13.2 mg/kg (R, i.v.); 995 mg/kg (R, p.o.)
CN: 2-[(cyclohexylhydroxyphenylacetyl)oxy]-N,N-diethyl-N-methylethanaminium bromide

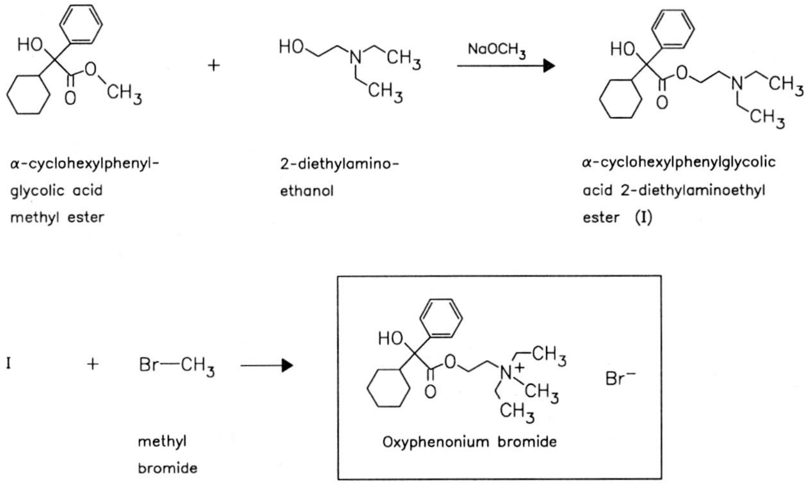

α-cyclohexylphenyl-
glycolic acid
methyl ester

2-diethylamino-
ethanol

α-cyclohexylphenylglycolic
acid 2-diethylaminoethyl
ester (I)

methyl
bromide

Oxyphenonium bromide

Reference(s):
CH 259 958 (Ciba; appl. 1944).

Formulation(s):   drg. 10 mg; tabl. 5 mg

Trade Name(s):
D: Antrenyl (Ciba); wfm
GB: Antrenyl (Ciba); wfm
I: Antrenil (Ciba); wfm

Ossitetra Sciroppo
(Pierrel); wfm
USA: Antrenyl (Ciba); wfm

Oxypyrronium bromide

ATC: A03AB
Use: anticholinergic, antispasmodic

RN: 561-43-3   MF: $C_{21}H_{32}BrNO_3$ MW: 426.40   EINECS: 209-219-8
LD_{50}:   18 mg/kg (M, i.v.); 1040 mg/kg (M, p.o.);
27.5 mg/kg (R, i.v.); 780 mg/kg (R, p.o.)
CN: 2-[[(cyclohexylhydroxyphenylacetyl)oxy]methyl]-1,1-dimethylpyrrolidinium bromide

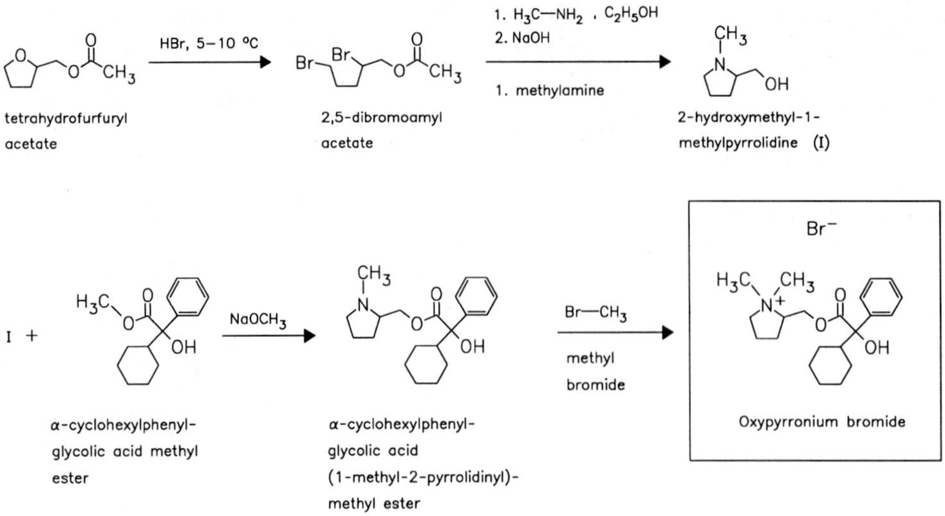

tetrahydrofurfuryl acetate

2,5-dibromoamyl acetate

2-hydroxymethyl-1-methylpyrrolidine (I)

1. H₃C—NH₂, C₂H₅OH
2. NaOH
1. methylamine

I +

α-cyclohexylphenyl-glycolic acid methyl ester

NaOCH₃

α-cyclohexylphenyl-glycolic acid (1-methyl-2-pyrrolidinyl)-methyl ester

Br—CH₃
methyl bromide

Br⁻

Oxypyrronium bromide

Reference(s):
GB 859 260 (Beecham; appl. 1957; valid from 1958).

2-hydroxymethyl-1-methylpyrrolidine:
GB 820 503 (Beecham; appl. 1956; valid from 1957).

Formulation(s):　3 mg, 6 mg

Trade Name(s):
F:　Immetropan (Dausse); wfm　J:　Immetro (Fujisawa)

Oxyquinoline
(Oxine)

ATC:　A01AB07; D08AH03; G01AC30; R02AA14
Use:　antiseptic, disinfectant

RN:　148-24-3　MF: C₉H₇NO　MW: 145.16　EINECS: 205-711-1
LD₅₀:　20 g/kg (M, p.o.);
　　　　1200 mg/kg (R, p.o.)
CN:　8-quinolinol

hydrochloride
RN:　16862-11-6　MF: C₉H₇NO · HCl　MW: 181.62　EINECS: 240-884-7
sulfate (2:1)
RN:　134-31-6　MF: C₉H₇NO · 1/2H₂SO₄　MW: 388.40　EINECS: 205-137-1
LD₅₀:　280 mg/kg (M, p.o.);
　　　　1200 mg/kg (R, p.o.)

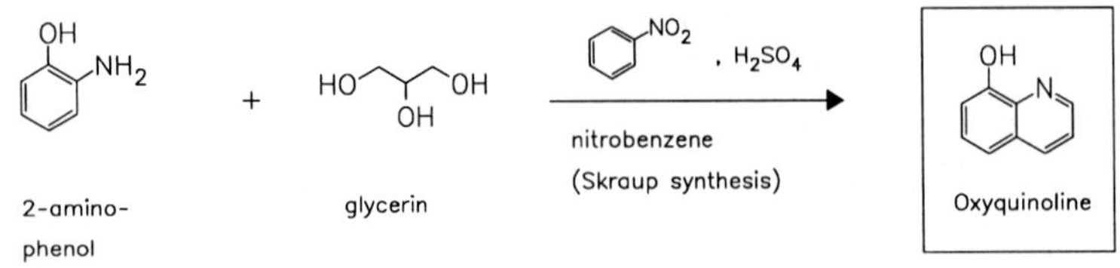

2-amino-phenol

glycerin

nitrobenzene
(Skraup synthesis)

Oxyquinoline

Reference(s):
DRP 14 976 (Z. H. Skraup; 1881).

Formulation(s):   vaginal jelly 0.025 % (as sulfate)

Trade Name(s):
D: Antimycoticum Stulln
    (Stulln)-comb.; wfm
    Aperisan Gel (Dentinox)-
    comb.; wfm
    Brand-u. Wundgel Herit
    (Engelhard)-comb.; wfm
    Chinomint Plus
    (Chinosolfabrik)-comb.;
    wfm
    Chinosol (Chinosolfabrik)-
    comb.; wfm
    Fungiderm (Terra-Bio)-
    comb.; wfm

    Nasalgon (Labopharma)-
    comb.; wfm
    Onychofissan (Fink)-
    comb.; wfm
    Ovis (Warner)-comb.; wfm
    Robumycon (Robugen)-
    comb.; wfm
    Semori (Luitpold); wfm
    Trachiform-V (Starke)-
    comb.; wfm
F: Chromargon (Richard)-
    comb.
    Dermacide (Labs. CS)-
    comb.

    Quinocarbine (GNR-
    pharma)-comb.
    Uvéline (Crinex)
GB: Aci-jel (Ortho-Cilag)-
    comb.; wfm
I: Anticolitico Roberts
    (Manetti Roberts); wfm
    Cortanol (Schiapparelli
    Farm.)-comb.; wfm
    Foille (Isnardi)-comb.; wfm
    Leucorsan (Zilliken)-comb.
    Viderm (Gerassini)-comb.
USA: Aci-jel (Ortho-McNeil)-
    comb.

Oxytetracycline

ATC: D06AA03; G01AA07; J01AA06;
      S01AA04
Use: antibiotic

RN: 79-57-2   MF: $C_{22}H_{24}N_2O_9$ MW: 460.44   EINECS: 201-212-8
LD_{50}: 140 mg/kg (M, i.v.); 2240 mg/kg (M, p.o.);
      260 mg/kg (R, i.v.); 4800 mg/kg (R, p.o.)
CN: [4S-(4α,4aα,5α,5aα,6β,12aα)]-4-(dimethylamino)-1,4,4a,5,5a,6,11,12a-octahydro-3,5,6,10,12,12a-
      hexahydroxy-6-methyl-1,11-dioxo-2-naphthacenecarboxamide

monohydrochloride
RN: 2058-46-0   MF: $C_{22}H_{24}N_2O_9 \cdot HCl$ MW: 496.90   EINECS: 218-161-2
LD_{50}: 100 mg/kg (M, i.v.); 6696 mg/kg (M, p.o.);
      302 mg/kg (R, i.v.)

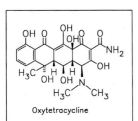
Oxytetracycline

From fermentation solutions of *Streptomyces rimosus.*

Reference(s):
US 2 516 080 (Pfizer; 1950; prior. 1949).
Finlay, A.C. et al.: Science (Washington, D.C.) (SCIEAS) **111**, 85 (1950).

stabilized formulations:
US 3 017 323 (Pfizer; 16.1.1962; prior. 1952).
US 3 026 248 (Pfizer; 20.3.1962; prior. 11.9.1959).
BE 861 855 (Philips; appl. 14.12.1977; GB-prior. 16.12.1976).

Formulation(s):   cps. 250 mg, 500 mg; eye ointment 10 mg/g; ointment 10 mg/g; vial 5 ml (as hydrochloride)

Trade Name(s):

D: Bisolvomycin (Boehringer
    Ing.)-comb. with
    bromhexine
    Corti Biciron (S & K
    Pharma)-comb. with
    tramazoline
    Corti Biciron Augensalbe
    (S & K Pharma)-comb.
    with dexamethasone 21-
    isonicotinate
    Dura Tetracyclin
    (durachemie)
    Macocyn (Mack)
    Oxytetracyclin Augensalbe
    Jenapharm (Alcon;
    Jenapharm)
    Oxytetracyclinsalbe (Leyh)
    Terracortil (Pfizer)-comb.
    with hydrocortisone

    Terramycin (Pfizer)-comb.
    Terramycin/Depot (Pfizer)
    Terravenös (Pfizer)
    Tetracycletten (Voigt)
    Tetra-Gelomyrtol (Pohl)-
    comb.
    Tetra-Tablinen (Beiersdorf-
    Tablinen)
    Tetra-Tablinen (Sanorania)
    Vendarcin (Schering)
    numerous combination
    preparations
F: Auricularum (Sérolam)-
    comb.
    Posicycline (Alcon)
    Primxyine (Thera France)-
    comb.
    Ster-Dex (CIBA Vision
    Ophthalmics)-comb.

    Terramycine (Pfizer)
    Tetranase (Rottapharm)-
    comb.
GB: Stecsolin (Squibb)
    Terra-cortril (Pfizer)-comb.
    Terramycin (Pfizer)-comb.
    Trimovate (Glaxo
    Wellcome)-comb.
I: Cosmiciclina (Alfa Intes)-
    comb.
J: Geomycin (Otsuka)
    Oxeten (Mochida)
    Terramycin (Taito Pfizer)
USA: Terra-Cortril (Pfizer)
    Terramycin (Pfizer)
    Urobiotic-250 (Pfizer)

Oxytocin

ATC: H01BB02
Use: posterior lobe of pituitary gland
      hormone

RN: 50-56-6   MF: $C_{43}H_{66}N_{12}O_{12}S_2$ MW: 1007.21   EINECS: 200-048-4
LD$_{50}$: 5800 µg/kg (M, i.v.); >514 mg/kg (M, p.o.);
      2275 µg/kg (R, i.v.); >20.52 mg/kg (R, p.o.)
CN: L-cysteinyl-L-tyrosyl-L-isoleucyl-L-glutaminyl-L-asparaginyl-L-cysteinyl-L-prolyl-L-leucylglycinamide
     cyclic (1→6)-disulfide

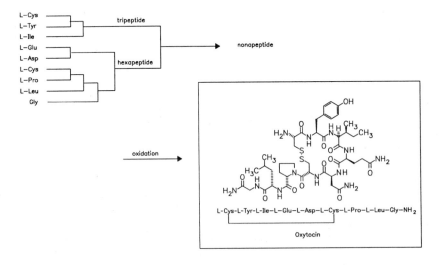

L-Cys-L-Tyr-L-Ile-L-Glu-L-Asp-L-Cys-L-Pro-L-Leu-Gly-NH$_2$

Oxytocin

(only schematic)
In each case by use of *S*- and *N*-trityl groups.

Reference(s):
US 2 938 891 (Roussel-Uclaf; 31.5. 1960; F-prior. 30.3.1956).
US 3 076 797 (Roussel-Uclaf; 5.2.1963; F-prior. 22.7.1957).

Formulation(s):   amp. 3 iu/ml, 5 iu/ml, 10 iu/ml; spray 40 iu/ml

Trade Name(s):
D:	Orasthin (Hoechst)	F:	Synthocinon (Novartis)		Pitocin (Sankyo)
	Oxytocin Hexal (Hexal)	GB:	Syntocinon (Novartis)		Pituitan (Nippon Zoki)
	Oxytocin-Noury		Syntometrine (Novartis)-		Syntocinon (Sandoz-
	(Nourypharma)		comb.		Sankyo)
	Syntocinon (Novartis	I:	Syntocinon (Novartis	USA:	Pitocin (Parke Davis)
	Pharma)		Farma)		
	Syntometrin (Novartis	J:	Atonin-O (Teikoku Zoki)		
	Pharma)-comb.		Orasthin (Hoechst)		

Ozagrel
(OKY-046)

ATC: B01AC
Use: thromboxane synthetase inhibitor,
platelet aggregation inhibitor

RN: 82571-53-7   MF: $C_{13}H_{12}N_2O_2$ MW: 228.25
LD$_{50}$:   1940 mg/kg (Mm, i.v.); 1580 mg/kg (Mf, i.v.); 3800 mg/kg (M, p.o.);
1150 mg/kg (Rm, i.v.); 1300 mg/kg (Rf, i.v.); 5900 mg/kg (R, p.o.)
CN: (E)-3-[4-(1H-imidazol-1-ylmethyl)phenyl]-2-propenoic acid

monohydrochloride monohydrate
RN: 83993-01-5   MF: $C_{13}H_{12}N_2O_2 \cdot HCl \cdot H_2O$ MW: 282.73
monohydrochloride
RN: 78712-43-3   MF: $C_{13}H_{12}N_2O_2 \cdot HCl$ MW: 264.71

Reference(s):
US 4 226 878 (Kissei, Ono; 7.10.1980; J-prior. 13.6.1978).
DOS 2 923 815 (Ono; appl. 12.6.1979; J-prior. 13.6.1978).
Iizuka, K. et al.: J. Med. Chem. (JMCMAR) **24**, 1139 (1981).

synthesis of ethyl 4-(bromomethyl)cinnamate:
DOS 2 755 759 (Merck & Co.; appl. 14.12.1977; USA-prior. 17.12.1976).

Formulation(s):   amp. 20 mg

Trade Name(s):
J: Cataclot (Ono; 1988)   Xanbon (Kissei; 1988)

Paclitaxel

(BMS-181339; NSC-125973)

ATC: L01CD01
Use: antineoplastic

RN: 33069-62-4 MF: $C_{47}H_{51}NO_{14}$ MW: 853.92
CN: [2a*R*-[2aα,4β,4aβ,6β,9α(α*R**,β*S**),11α,12α,12aα,12bα]]-β-(benzoylamino)-α-hydroxybenzenepropanoic acid 6,12b-bis(acetyloxy)-12-(benzyloxy)-2a,3,4,4a,5,6,9,10,11,12,12a,12b-dodecahydro-4,11-dihydroxy-4a,8,13,13-tetramethyl-5-oxo-7,11-methano-1*H*-cyclodeca[3,4]benz[1,2-*c*]oxet-9-yl ester

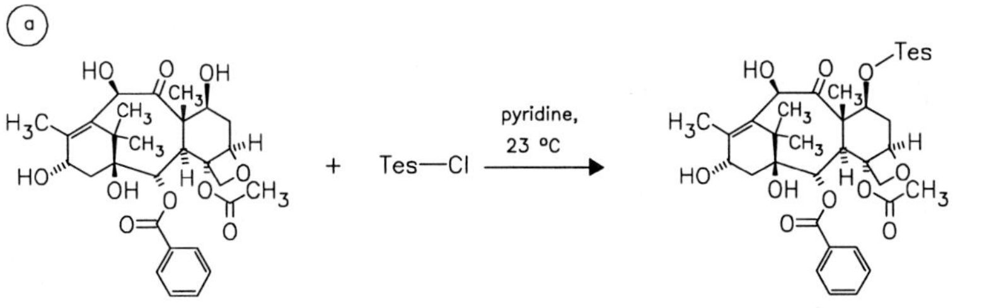
a
+
Tes—Cl
pyridine,
23 °C

10-deacetylbaccatin III (I) (isolated from the leaves of Taxus baccata L.)

triethylsilyl chloride

7-O-triethylsilyl-10-deacetylbaccatin III (II)

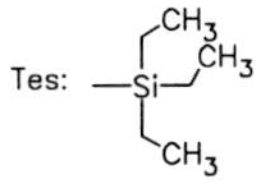
Tes:

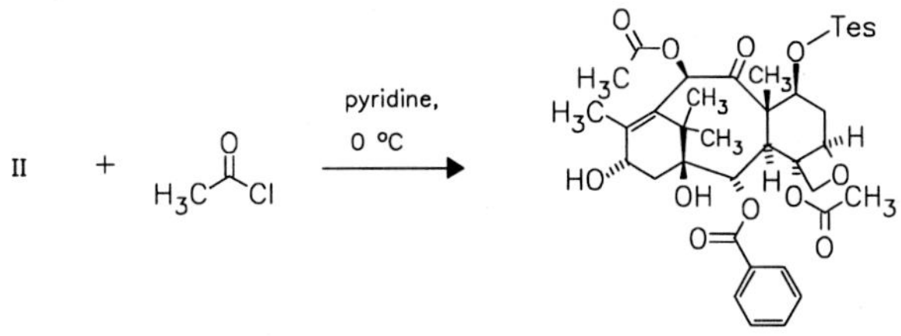
II
+
pyridine,
0 °C

acetyl chloride

7-O-triethylsilylbaccatin III (III)

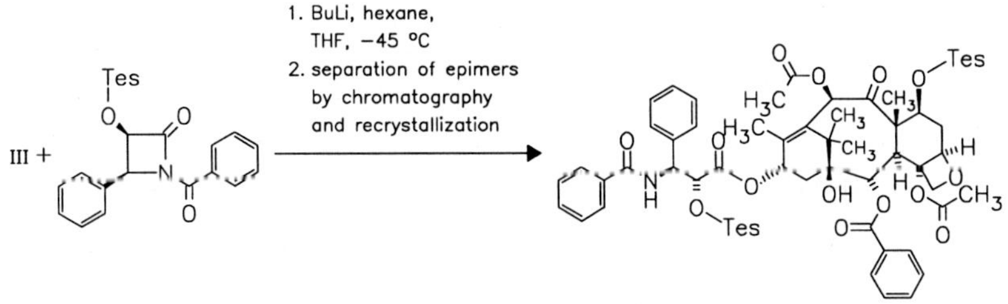
III +
1. BuLi, hexane, THF, −45 °C
2. separation of epimers by chromatography and recrystallization

cis-1-benzoyl-3-(triethylsilyloxy)-4-phenyl-2-azetidinone (IV)

2',7-bis(triethylsilyl)paclitaxel (V)

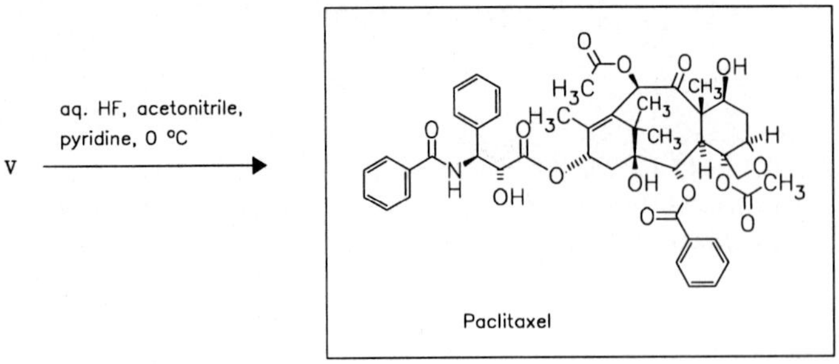

aq. HF, acetonitrile,
pyridine, 0 °C

V ⟶

Paclitaxel

(aa) synthesis of IV:

HO⌒O⌒CH3   +   Tes—Cl   ⟶   Tes⌒O⌒O⌒CH3
     ‖O   ‖O

ethyl glycolate   triethyl-   (VII)
                   silyl
                   chloride (VI)

VII + benzaldehyde imine with Tms

H_3C⌒N⌒CH_3 with Li, CH_3CH_3
THF, −50 °C
lithium diiso-
propylamide
⟶
Tes-O azetidinone with NH

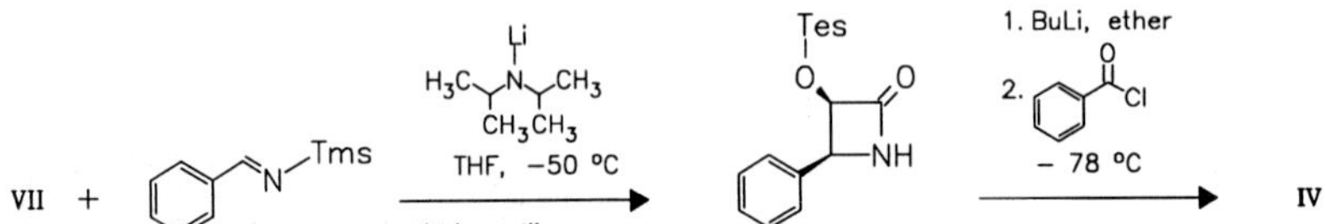

1. BuLi, ether
2. benzoyl chloride
   − 78 °C
2. benzoyl
   chloride (VIII)
⟶ IV

N-(trimethyl-
silyl)benz-
aldehyde imine

cis-3-(triethyl-
silyloxy)-4-
phenyl-2-
azetidinone

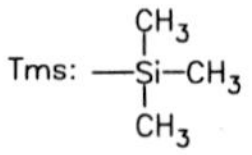

Tms: —$\overset{\underset{CH_3}{|}}{\underset{|}{Si}}$—$CH_3$
           CH_3

(ab)

benzaldehyde CHO   + H_2N⌒O⌒CH_3 p-methoxy-aniline   ⟶   benzylidene-N⌒O⌒CH_3 (IX)

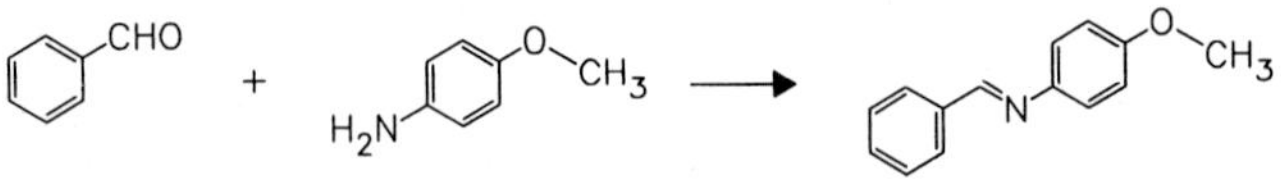

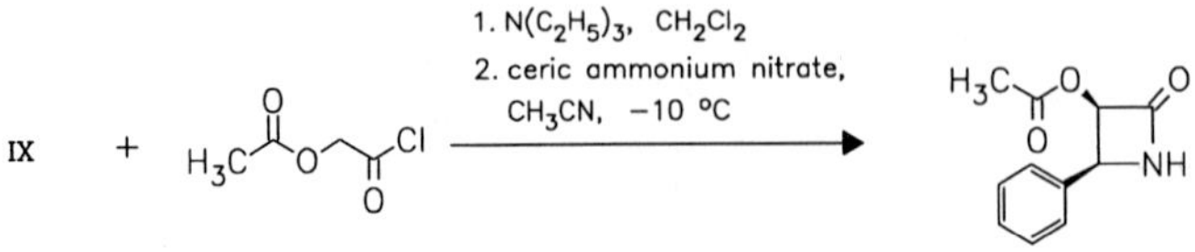

benzaldehyde   p-methoxy-
                  aniline

IX + H_3C⌒O⌒⌒Cl
            ‖O ‖O

1. $N(C_2H_5)_3$, CH_2Cl_2
2. ceric ammonium nitrate,
   CH_3CN, −10 °C
⟶
H_3C⌒O azetidinone with NH

2-acetoxyacetyl
chloride (X)

cis-3-acetyloxy-
4-phenyl-2-
azetidinone (XI)

XI
$\xrightarrow{\begin{array}{c}\text{KOH, } H_2O, \text{ THF}\\ 0\ ^\circ C\end{array}}$

(3R,4S)-3-
hydroxy-4-
phenyl-2-
azetidinone   (XII)

$\xrightarrow{\begin{array}{c}\text{1. VI , pyridine}\\ \text{2. BuLi, VIII}\end{array}}$ IV

(b)

XII + H$_2$C≈O CH$_3$

ethyl vinyl ether   (XIII)

$\xrightarrow{\begin{array}{c}\text{1. THF, H}^+\\ \text{2. BuLi, ether,}\\ \text{VIII , } -78\ ^\circ C\end{array}}$

$\xrightarrow{\begin{array}{c}\text{1. KOH}\\ \text{2. KOtBu,} \quad H_3C-S-Cl\\ \text{2. methanesulfo-}\\ \text{nyl chloride}\end{array}}$ XIV

(−)-cis-2,4-diphenyl-
5-(1-ethoxyethoxy)-
4,5-dihydro-1,3-
oxazin-6-one   (XIV)

+ III

$\xrightarrow{\begin{array}{c}\text{1. BuLi, THF, } -45\ ^\circ C\\ \text{2. HCl, } C_2H_5OH, \ 0\ ^\circ C\end{array}}$ Paclitaxel

(c)

III +

(2R,3S)-N-benzoyl-
0-(1-ethoxyethyl)-
3-phenylisoserine   (XV)

$\xrightarrow{\begin{array}{c}\text{1.} \quad \text{(di(2-pyridyl) carbonate)}\\ \text{(4-dimethylamino-pyridine)}\\ \text{toluene, 73}\ ^\circ C\\ \text{2. HCl, } C_2H_5OH, H_2O\end{array}}$ Paclitaxel

1. di(2-pyridyl) carbonate
   4-dimethylamino-
   pyridine

(ca)   synthesis of intermediate XV (or unprotected analogues)
(for more 3-phenylisoserine syntheses see Docetaxel)

tert-butyl
3-phenylglycidate

$\xrightarrow{\begin{array}{c}\text{1. NaN}_3, C_2H_5OH\\ \text{2. HCl, } C_2H_5OH\\ \text{3. H}_2, \text{ Pd-C, } C_2H_5OH\\ \text{1. sodium azide}\end{array}}$

threo-ethyl
2-hydroxy-3-
amino-3-phenyl-
propionate   (XVI)

XVI

1. VIII
2. XIII
3. LiOH, C₂H₅OH → XV

(cb)

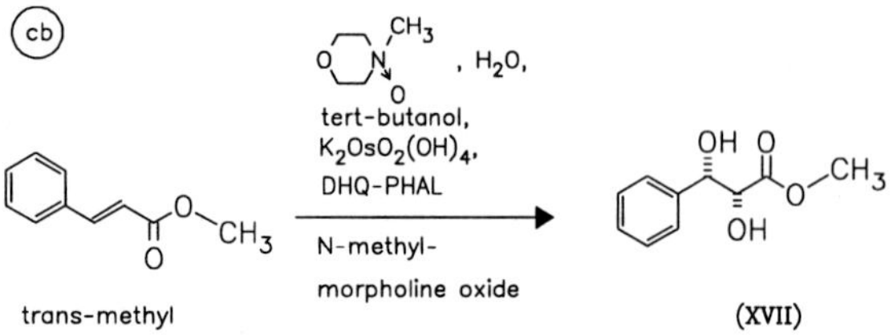

trans-methyl cinnamate

CH₃
O—N , H₂O,
O
tert-butanol,
K₂OsO₂(OH)₄,
DHQ-PHAL
N-methyl-
morpholine oxide

OH O
O—CH₃
OH

(XVII)

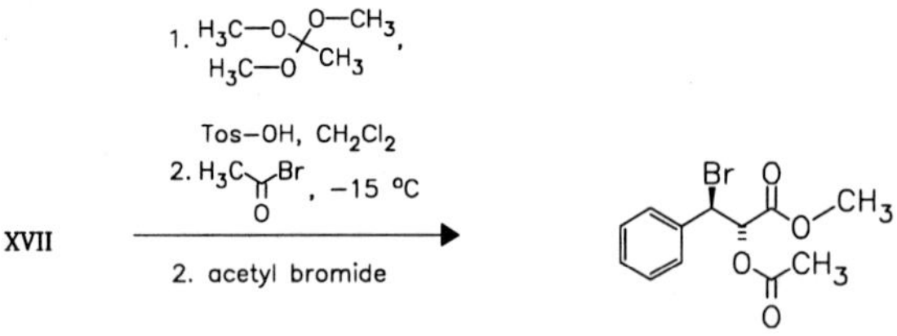

XVII

1. H₃C—O O—CH₃
      H₃C—O CH₃

Tos—OH, CH₂Cl₂
2. H₃C Br , −15 °C
         O

2. acetyl bromide

Br O
O—CH₃
O CH₃
O

(XVIII)

XVIII

1. NaN₃, DMF, 50 °C
2. H₂, Pd-C
3. 10% aq. HCl
4. VIII, 2N NaOH

HN O

COOH
OH

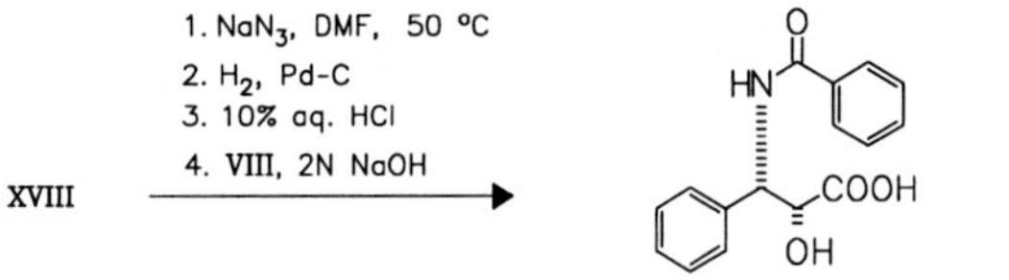

(2R,3S)-N-benzoyl-
3-phenylisoserine   (XIX)

(cc)

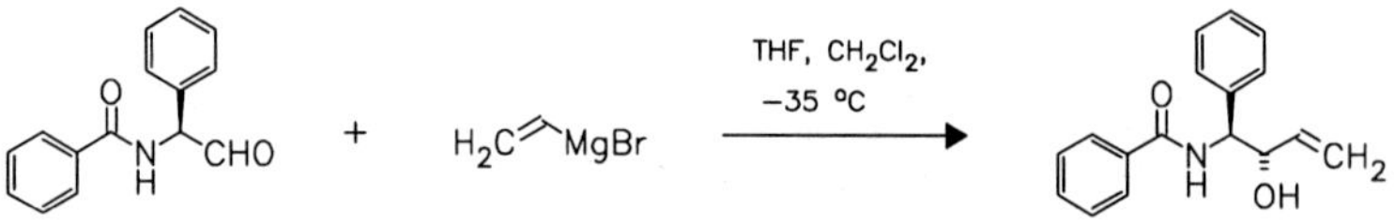

N-benzoyl-L-
phenylglycinal

+

H₂C MgBr

vinylmagnesium
bromide

THF, CH₂Cl₂,
−35 °C →

CH₂
OH

(−)-(1S,2S)-N-(2-
hydroxy-1-phenyl-
3-butenyl)benz-
amide (XX)

XX

1. XIII
   Tos-OH, CH₃CN
2. RuCl₃, NaIO₄,
   CH₃CN, NaHCO₃
3. (+)-ephedrine,
   acetone → XV

(cd)

cis-methyl cinnamate

N→O

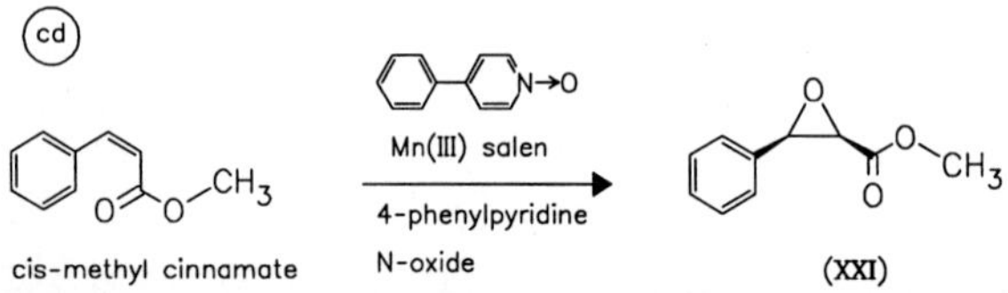

Mn(III) salen
4-phenylpyridine
N-oxide

O
O—CH₃
O

(XXI)

XXI $\xrightarrow{\begin{array}{l}\text{1. NH}_3\\\text{2. VIII}\end{array}}$ XIX

(ce)

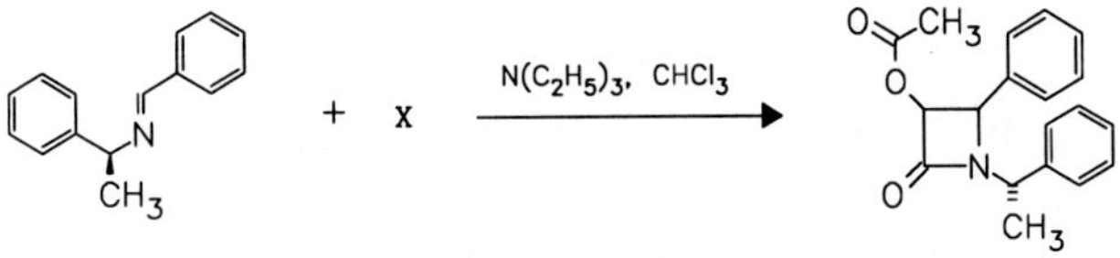

(S)-N-benzylidene-
1-phenylethylamine

N(C₂H₅)₃, CHCl₃

3-acetoxy-4-phenyl-
1-[(S)-1-phenylethyl]-
2-azetidinone (XXII)

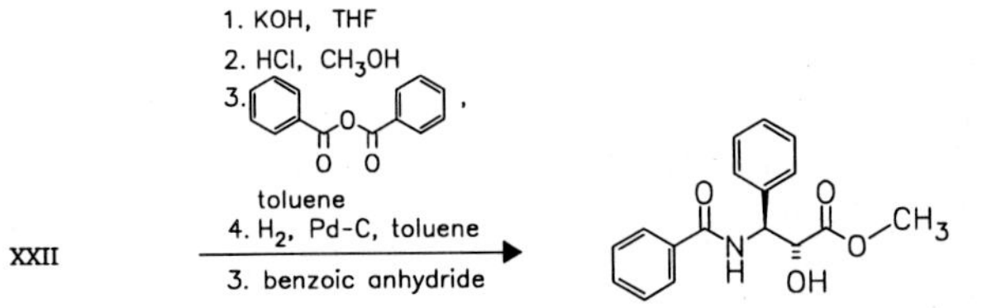

XXII $\xrightarrow{\begin{array}{l}\text{1. KOH, THF}\\\text{2. HCl, CH}_3\text{OH}\\\text{3.}\\\text{toluene}\\\text{4. H}_2\text{, Pd-C, toluene}\\\text{3. benzoic anhydride}\end{array}}$

methyl (2R,3S)-benzoylamino-
2-hydroxy-3-phenylpropionate

(cf)

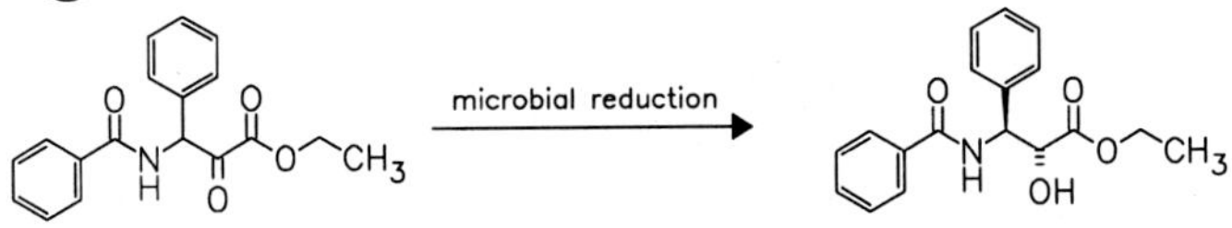

(±)-ethyl 2-oxo-3-
benzoylamino-3-
phenylpropionate

microbial reduction

(2R,3S)-N-benzoyl-
3-phenylisoserine
ethyl ester

(cg)

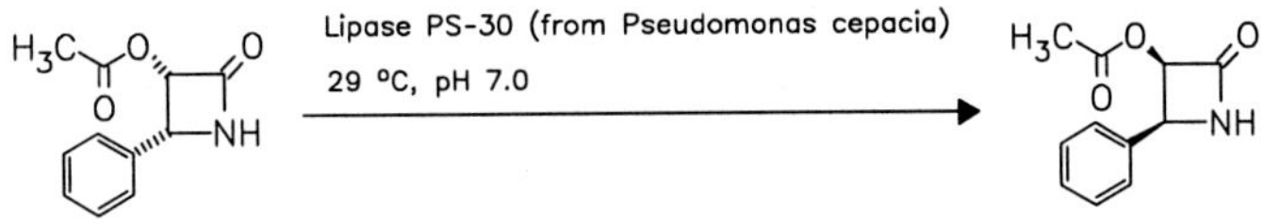

rac-(XI)

Lipase PS-30 (from Pseudomonas cepacia)
29 °C, pH 7.0

(3R,4S)-(XI)

Reference(s):
a   Denis, J.N. et al.: J. Am. Chem. Soc. (JACSAT) **110**, 5917-5919 (1988).
    WO 9 306 094 (Florida State Univ.; appl. 22.9.1992; USA-prior. 3.4.1992, 23.9.1991).
    George, G.I. et al.: J. Med. Chem. (JMCMAR) **35**, 4230-4237 (1992).
aa US 5 015 744 (Florida State Univ.; appl. 14.11.1989).
    Georg, G.I. et al.: Bioorg. Med. Chem. Lett. (BMCLE8) **3**, 2467-2470 (1993).
ab WO 9 418 164 (Univ. New York State; appl. 28.1.1994; USA-prior. 1.2.1993).
    Ojima, I. et al.: J. Org. Chem. (JOCEAH) **56**, 1681-1683 (1991).
    Holton, R.A. et al.: Bioorg. Med. Chem. Lett. (BMCLE8) **3**, 2475 (1993).
b   US 5 254 703 (Florida State Univ.; appl. 6.4.1992; USA-prior. 6.4.1992).
    EP 428 376 (Florida State Univ.; appl. 13.11.1990; USA-prior. 14.11.1989).
c   Denis, J.N. et al.: J. Am. Chem. Soc. (JACSAT) **110**, 5917-5919 (1988).
ca Denis, J.N. et al.: J. Org. Chem. (JOCEAH) **51**, 46-50 (1986).
cb Sharpless, B. et al.: J. Org. Chem. (JOCEAH) **59**, 5104 (1994).
cc Denis, J.N. et al.: J. Org. Chem. (JOCEAH) **56**, 6939 (1991).
    EP 528 729 (Rhône-Poulenc Rorer; appl. 17.8.1992; F-prior. 19.8.1991).
cd Deng, L. et al.: J. Org. Chem. (JOCEAH) **57**, 4320-4323 (1992).
    Denis, J.N. et al.: J. Org. Chem. (JOCEAH) **55**, 1957 (1990).
ce WO 9 317 997 (Rhône-Poulenc Rorer; appl. 16.9.1993; F-prior. 10.3.1992).
    WO 9 422 813 (Rhône-Poulenc Rorer; appl. 25.3.1994; F-prior. 29.3.1993).
cf Pabel, R.N. et al.: Tetrahedron: Asymmetry (TASYE3) **33**, 5185-5188 (1993).
cg Pabel, R.N. et al.: Biotechnol. Appl. Biochem. (BABIEC) **20**, 23-33 (1994).

further chemoenzymatic resolutions:
Hoenig, H. et al.: Tetrahedron (TETRAB) **46**, 3841-50 (1990).
Gonet, D.-M. et al.: J. Org. Chem. (JOCEAH) **58**, 1287-1289 (1993).
Brieva, R. et al.: J. Org. Chem. (JOCEAH) **58**, 1068 (1993).

esterification:
Commercon, A. et al.: Tetrahedron Lett. (TELEAY) **33**, 5185 (1992).

reviews:
Hepperle, M.; Georg, G.I.: Drugs Future (DRFUD4) **19**, 573-584 (1994).
Georg, G.I. et al.: Expert Opin. Ther. Pat. (EOTPEG) **4**, 109-120 (1994).
Nicolaou, K.C. et al.: Angew. Chem. (ANCEAD) **107**, 2247-2259 (1995).

total synthesis of taxanes:
Holton, R.A. et al.: J. Am. Chem. Soc. (JACSAT) **116**, 1599-1600 (1994).
Masters, J.J. et al.: Angew. Chem. (ANCEAD) **107**, 1883 (1995).
Nicolaou, K.C. et al.: Nature (London) (NATUAS) **367**, 630-634 (1994).
US 5 274 137 (K. C. Nicolaou et al.; appl. 23.6.1992; USA-prior. 23.6.1992).
Wessjohann, L.: Angew. Chem. (ANCEAD) **106**, 1011 (1994).

purification of 10-deacetylbaccatin III:
WO 9 421 622 (Rhône-Poulenc Rorer; appl. 18.3.1994; F-prior. 22.3.1993).

production of taxanes from explant tissue:
EP 568 821 (Squibb; appl. 6.4.1993; USA-prior. 7.4.1992).

liposome formulation:
US 5 415 869 (Univ. New York State; appl. 12.11.1993; USA-prior. 12.11.1993).

cyclodextrine complexes:
WO 9 426 728 (Chinoin; appl. 9.5.1994; HU-prior. 12.5.1993).

use against protozoa:
WO 9 412 172 (Th. Jefferson Univ.; appl. 2.12.1993; USA-prior. 2.12.1992, 26.1.1993).

Formulation(s):   vial 30 mg/5 ml

Pamidronic acid
(APD)

ATC: M05BA03
Use: calcium metabolism regulator (treatment of Paget's disease, hypercalcemia of malignancy)

RN: 40391-99-9 MF: $C_3H_{11}NO_7P_2$ MW: 235.07 EINECS: 254-905-2
CN: (3-amino-1-hydroxypropylidene)bis(phosphonic acid)

disodium salt
RN: 57248-88-1 MF: $C_3H_9NNa_2O_7P_2$ MW: 279.03 EINECS: 260-647-1

β-aminopropionic acid phosphite → phosphorous trichloride → Pamidronic acid

Reference(s):
a DOS 2 130 794 (Benckiser; appl. 22.6.1971).
b DOS 2 658 961 (Benckiser; appl. 24.12.1976).
   DOS 2 943 498 (Henkel; appl. 27.10.1981).
c EP 82 472 (Henkel; appl. 15.12.1982; D-prior. 23.12.1981).

crystalline disodium salt:
JP 61 043 196 (Ciba-Geigy; appl. 6.8.1984).

controlled-release granule:
CA 2 024 631 (Ciba-Geigy; appl. 7.9.1989).

pharmaceutical formulation of disodium pamidronate *for controlling calcium deposition and treatment of calcium metabolism disorders:*
DOS 2 405 254 (Henkel; appl. 4.2.1974).
DOS 2 553 963 (Henkel; appl. 1.12.1975).
AT 538 311 (Henkel; appl. 2.1.1981).

topical pharmaceutical formulation:
EP 407 345 (Ciba-Geigy, Henkel; appl. 28.6.1990; CH-prior. 7.7.1989).

synergistic combination with cytostatics:
DOS 3 804 686 (Henkel, DKFZ; appl. 15.2.1988).

Formulation(s):　amp. 15 mg/5 ml, 30 mg/5 ml, 60 mg/5 ml, 90 mg/5 ml, 15 mg/10 ml, 30 mg/10 ml,
　　　　　　　　　60 mg/10 ml, 90 mg/10 ml (as disodium salt)

Trade Name(s):
GB:　Aredia (Novartis; 1989)　　J:　　Aredia (Ciba-Geigy)
I:　　Aredia (Novartis Farma)　　USA:　Aredia (Novartis)

Pancuronium bromide

ATC:　M03AC01
Use:　ganglionic blocker, anticonvulsant

RN:　15500-66-0　MF: $C_{35}H_{60}Br_2N_2O_4$　MW: 732.68　EINECS: 239-532-5
LD$_{50}$:　13 µg/kg (M, i.v.); 21.2 mg/kg (M, p.o.);
　　　153 µg/kg (R, i.v.); 202 mg/kg (R, p.o.)
CN:　1,1'-[(2β,3α,5α,16β,17β)-3,17-bis(acetyloxy)androstane-2,16-diyl]bis[1-methylpiperidinium] dibromide

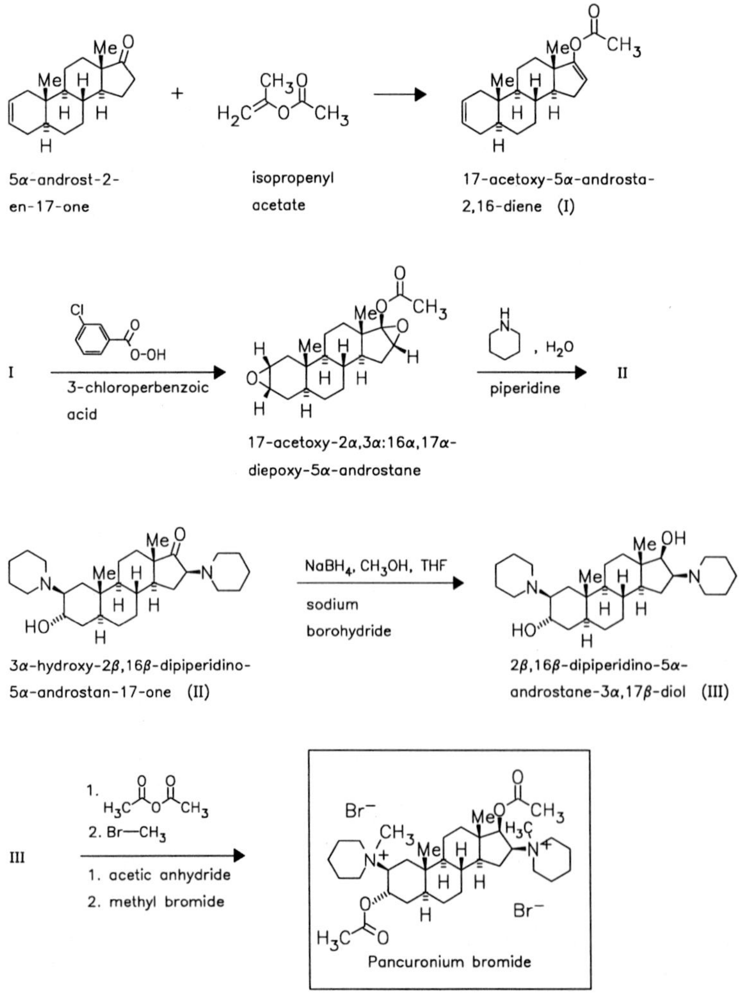

5α-androst-2-
en-17-one

isopropenyl
acetate

17-acetoxy-5α-androsta-
2,16-diene　(I)

I → 3-chloroperbenzoic acid →

17-acetoxy-2α,3α:16α,17α-
diepoxy-5α-androstane

piperidine, H_2O → II

3α-hydroxy-2β,16β-dipiperidino-
5α-androstan-17-one　(II)

NaBH$_4$, CH$_3$OH, THF
sodium
borohydride

2β,16β-dipiperidino-5α-
androstane-3α,17β-diol　(III)

III

1. H_3C—CO—O—CO—CH$_3$
2. Br—CH$_3$

1. acetic anhydride
2. methyl bromide

Pancuronium bromide

Reference(s):
NL-appl. 6 602 098 (Organon; appl. 17.2.1966; GB-prior. 19.2.1965).
US 4 177 190 (Richter Gedeon; 4.12.1979; H-prior. 1.8.1975).

Formulation(s):   amp. 1 mg/ml, 4 mg/2 ml, 8 mg4 ml; vial 10 mg

Trade Name(s):

D:	Pancuronium Curamed (Schwabe-Curamed)		Pancuronium ratiopharm (ratiopharm)	GB: Pavulon (Organon Teknika)
	Pancuronium "Organon" Amp. (Organon Teknika)	F:	Pavulon (Organon Teknika); wfm	I: Pavulon (Organon Teknika) J: Myoblock (Sankyo) USA: Pavulon (Organon)

Pantethine

ATC: A11HA32
Use: growth factor

RN: 16816-67-4   MF: $C_{22}H_{42}N_4O_8S_2$ MW: 554.73   EINECS: 240-842-8
LD_{50}:   3400 mg/kg (M, i.v.); >10 g/kg (M, p.o.);
3410 mg/kg (R, i.v.); >10 g/kg (R, p.o.)
CN: [R-(R*,R*)]-N,N'-[dithiobis[2,1-ethanediylimino(3-oxo-3,1-propanediyl)]]bis[2,4-dihydroxy-3,3-dimethylbutanamide]

D-pantothenic acid methyl ester → H₂N—NH₂·H₂O hydrazine hydrate → D-pantothenic hydrazide (I)

I → 1. HCl, NaNO₂ / 2. H₂N~S-S~NH₂ / 2. cystamine → Pantethine

calcium D-pantothenate   +   cystamine dihydrochloride · 2HCl

1. [benzotriazole] , pyridine
2. dicyclohexylcarbodiimide
3. purification by ion exchange
1. 1-hydroxybenzotriazole
→ Pantethine

Reference(s):
a   US 2 625 565 (Parke Davis; 1953; appl. 1951).
b   DAS 2 638 555 (Sago Pharmaceutical; appl. 26.8.1976; J-prior. 25.5.1976).

alternative syntheses:
Wieland; Bokelmann: Naturwissenschaften (NATWAY) **38**, 384 (1950).
Wittle et al.: J. Am. Chem. Soc. (JACSAT) **75**, 1694 (1953).
Viscontini et al.: Helv. Chim. Acta (HCACAV) **37**, 375 (1954).
Bowman; Cavalla: J. Chem. Soc. (JCSOA9) **1954**, 1171.
Shimizu et al.: Chem. Pharm. Bull. (CPBTAL) **13**, 180 (1965).

Formulation(s):   cps. 300 mg; tabl. 60 mg

Trade Name(s):
I: Analip (Iketon)   Pantetina (Sanofi
       Carpantin (Sanofi   Winthrop)
       Winthrop)-comb.   J: Pantosin (Daiichi)

Pantoprazole sodium
(BY-1023; B 8510-29; SK & F-96022)

ATC: A02BC02; A02BD04
Use: antisecretory, gastric H$^+$/K$^+$-ATPase
       inhibitor

RN: 138786-67-1   MF: $C_{16}H_{14}F_2N_3NaO_4S$ MW: 405.36
LD$_{50}$: 1000 mg/kg (M, p.o.)
CN: 5-(difluoromethoxy)-2-[[(3,4-dimethoxy-2-pyridinyl)methyl]sulfinyl]-1H-benzimidazole sodium salt

hydrate
RN: 164579-32-2   MF: $C_{16}H_{14}F_2N_3NaO_4S \cdot 3/2H_2O$ MW: 864.76
(+)-isomer
RN: 160098-11-3   MF: $C_{16}H_{14}F_2N_3NaO_4S$ MW: 405.36
(–)-isomer
RN: 160488-53-9   MF: $C_{16}H_{14}F_2N_3NaO_4S$ MW: 405.36
racemate
RN: 142678-34-0   MF: $C_{16}H_{14}F_2N_3NaO_4S$ MW: 405.36

intermediate **II**

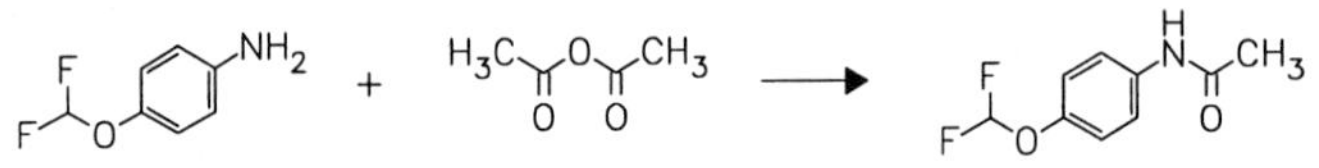

4-(difluoromethoxy)-
aniline

(I)

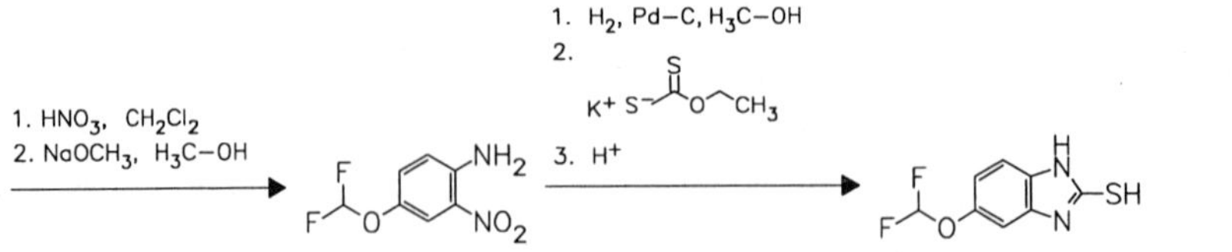

5-(difluoromethoxy)-
2-mercaptobenzimidazole (**II**)

intermediate **IV**

H₃C—(pyridine N-oxide with Cl, OCH₃) + Na⁺ O⁻—CH₃ ⟶ H₃C—(pyridine N-oxide with O—CH₃, OCH₃) → 1. (CH₃CO)₂O 2. NaOH → **III**

4-chloro-3-methoxy-
2-methylpyridine
N-oxide

HO—(2-hydroxymethyl pyridine, OCH₃, OCH₃) SOCl₂ → Cl—(2-chloromethyl pyridinium, OCH₃, OCH₃) · HCl

2-hydroxymethyl-   2-chloromethyl-
3,4-dimethoxypyridine (**III**)   3,4-dimethoxy-
                                    pyridinium chloride (**IV**)

Pantoprazole sodium

II + **IV** NaOH → (benzimidazole structure V)

(**V**)

V 1. NaOCl 2. NaOH → Na⁺ (pantoprazole sodium structure)

Pantoprazole sodium

Reference(s):
preparation of pantoprazole:
EP 134 400 (Byk Gulden Lomberg; appl. 1.5.1984; CH-prior. 3.5.1983).

inhibitors of gastric acid secretion useful for treating and preventing ulcers:
EP 166 287 (Byk Gulden Lomberg; CH-prior. 16.6.1984).
US 4 758 579 (Byk Gulden Lomberg; 19.7.1988; CH-prior. 16.6.1984).

nonhygroscopic monohydrate salt:
DE 4 018 642 (Byk Gulden Lomberg; appl. 12.12.1991; D-prior. 11.6.1990).

pantoprazole sodium sesquihydrate lyophilisates:
DE 4 324 014 (Byk Gulden Lomberg; D-prior. 17.7.1993).

oral multiple-unit tablet for treatment of gastrointestinal inflammation:
WO 9 601 624 (Astra; appl. 25.1.1996; S-prior. 8.7.1994).

pharmaceutical compositions for inhibition of gastric acid secretion in animals:
WO 9 425 070 (Astra; appl. 10.11.1994; S-prior. 30.4.1993).

new pantoprazole *tablets and pellets:*
EP 519 365 (Byk Gulden Lomberg; appl. 23.12.1992; CH-prior. 17.6.1991; HU-prior. 13.6.1992).

treating viral infections such as herpes infections by H⁺/K⁺- or ATPase-inhitiors:
WO 9 529 897 (Searle & Co.; appl. 9.11.1995; USA-prior. 29.4.1994).

use of (−)-pantoprazole for treating gastric disorders:
WO 9 424 867 (Sepracor Inc.; appl. 10.11.1994; USA-prior. 27.4.1993).

use of (+)-pantoprazole for treating gastric disorders:
WO 9 425 028 (Sepracor Inc.; appl. 10.11.1994; prior. 27.4.1993).

rectal antiulcer composition containing benzimidazole derivatives:
EP 645 140 (Takeda Chem. Ind.; appl. 29.3.1995; J-prior. 30.3.1994, 31.8.1995).

synthesis of 3,4-dialkoxypyridines:
AT 394 368 (Byk Gulden Lomberg; appl. 25.3.1992; A-prior. 4.8.1990).

Formulation(s):   amp. 40 mg; tabl. 40 mg

Trade Name(s):
| D: | Pantozol (Byk Gulden) | F: | Inipaup (Synthélabo) |
| | Rifun (Sanol, Schwarz Pharma) | USA: | Protonix (American Home Products) |

Papaverine

ATC: G04BE02; G04BE52
Use: antispasmodic, vasodilator

RN: 58-74-2   MF: $C_{20}H_{21}NO_4$ MW: 339.39   EINECS: 200-397-2
LD_{50}:   25 mg/kg (M, i.v.); 162 mg/kg (M, p.o.);
       13.3 mg/kg (R, i.v.); 325 mg/kg (R, p.o.)
CN: 1-[(3,4-dimethoxyphenyl)methyl]-6,7-dimethoxyisoquinoline

hydrochloride
RN: 61-25-6   MF: $C_{20}H_{21}NO_4 \cdot HCl$ MW: 375.85   EINECS: 200-502-1
LD_{50}:   14.4 mg/kg (M, i.v.); 130 mg/kg (M, p.o.);
       20 mg/kg (R, i.v.); 68.8 mg/kg (R, p.o.)

veratrole   form-   3,4-dimethoxybenzyl   homoveratronitrile (I)
                aldehyde   chloride

homoveratrylamine (II)

homoveratric acid   N-homoveratrylhomoveratramide (III)

III $\xrightarrow{\text{POCl}_3}$

phosphoryl chloride

3,4-dihydropapaverine

$\xrightarrow{\text{Pd, 250 °C, tetralin}}$

Papaverine

Reference(s):
Budesinsky-Protiva, 87.

combination with adenosin monophosphate:
US 3 823 234 (C.E.R.M.; 9.7.1974; F-prior. 16.5.1971).

Formulation(s): amp. 60 mg/2 ml; multiple-dose vial 30 mg/ml

Trade Name(s):

D:	Artegodan (Artesan); wfm		Vascleran (Klinge)-comb.; wfm	I:	Antispasmina (Recordati)-comb.

D: Artegodan (Artesan); wfm
Atropaverin (Saemann); wfm
Nyxanthan (Abbott)-comb.; wfm
Optenyl (Stroschein); wfm
Panergon (Mack); wfm
Papaverin Hameln (Hameln); wfm
Paveron (Karlspharma); wfm
Spastretten (Tropon); wfm

Vascleran (Klinge)-comb.; wfm
numerous combination preparations

F: Acticarbine (Warner-Lambert)-comb.
Albatran (Beaufour)
Oxadiléne (Evans Medical)-comb.
Papavérine Aguettant (Aguettant)

GB: Aspace (Hoechst)-comb.

I: Antispasmina (Recordati)-comb.
Monotrean (Sankyo Pharma)-comb.
generics

J: Papermin Inj. (Sanwa)-comb.
numerous generic preparations

USA: Papaverine Hydrochloride (Lilly; as hydrochloride)

Paracetamol

(Acetaminophenol)

ATC: N02BE01
Use: analgesic, antipyretic

RN: 103-90-2　MF: $C_8H_9NO_2$　MW: 151.17　EINECS: 203-157-5
LD_{50}: 338 mg/kg (M, p.o.);
2404 mg/kg (R, p.o.)
CN: *N*-(4-hydroxyphenyl)acetamide

(a) classical route:

phenol (I) $\xrightarrow[\text{nitric acid}]{\text{HNO}_3}$ 4-nitrophenol $\xrightarrow{\text{H}_2, \text{ Raney–Ni}}$ 4-aminophenol $\xrightarrow[\text{acetic anhydride (II)}]{}$ Paracetamol

(b) Hoechst-Celanese process:

I + II $\xrightarrow{\text{H}_2\text{F}_2}$ 4'-hydroxy-acetophenone $\xrightarrow[\text{hydroxylamine sulfate}]{\text{H}_2\text{NOH} \cdot 0.5 \text{ H}_2\text{SO}_4}$ $\xrightarrow[\text{2. KI, 50 °C}]{\text{1. EtOAc, SOCl}_2}$ Paracetamol

Reference(s):
Ullmanns Encykl. Tech. Chem., 3. Aufl., Vol. **13**, 297.
Ullmanns Encykl. Tech. Chem., 4. Aufl., Vol. **7**, 543.
US 2 998 450 (Warner-Lambert; 1961; appl. 1958).
DAS 2 121 164 (Howard Hall; appl. 29.4.1971; USA-prior. 29.4.1970).

acetylation with ketene:
DRP 453 577 (M. Bergmann; appl. 1925).

pharmaceutical formulations:
US 4 097 606 (Bristol-Myers; 27.6.1978; appl. 8.10.1975).

combination with phenyltoloxamine:
US 3 173 835 (Endo; 16.3.1965; appl. 19.3.1963).

Formulation(s):   cps. 500 mg; powder 500 mg, 600 mg; sol. 200 mg/5 ml; suppos. 125 mg, 250 mg, 500 mg,
1 g; susp. 125 mg, 250 mg, 500 mg, 1000 mg; syrup 120 mg/5 ml, 200 mg/5 ml, 2 g/100 ml;
tabl. 200 mg, 270 mg, 350 mg, 500 mg

Trade Name(s):
D: Ben-u-ron (bene-
        Arzneimittel)
        Captin (Krewel
        Meuselbach)
        Doregrippin (Rentschler)-
        comb.
        Enelfa (Dolorgiet)
        Mono Praecimed
        (Molimin)
        nilnOcen (Zeppenfeldt)
        Paedialgon (Cephasaar)
        Paracetamol (Hexal;
        Heumann; Stada)
        Paracetamol-ratiopharm
        (ratiopharm)
        Pyromed (Sanofi Winthrop)
        RubieMol (RubiePharm)
        Togal (Togal)
        Treupel P (ASTA Medica
        AWD)
        numerous combination
        preparations
F: Aféradol Oberlin (Oberlin)
        Dafalgan (UPSA)
        Doliprane (Théraplix)
        Efferalgan 500 /-
        pédiatrique (UPSA)

        Paracétamol SmithKline
        Beecham (SmithKline
        Beecham)
        combination preparations
GB: Alvedon (Novex)
        Calpol (Warner-Lambert)
        Disprol (Reckitt &
        Colman)
        Medinol (Seton)
        Panaleve (Pinewood)
        Salzone (Wallace)
        further combination
        preparations
I: Acetamol (Abiogen
        Pharma)
        Alsogil (Also)-comb.
        Antiflu (Byk Gulden)-
        comb.
        Antinevralgico Penegal
        (Fama)-comb.
        Baby Rinolo (Lepetit)-
        comb.
        Doloflex (Byk Gulden)-
        comb.
        Efferalgan (Ursamedica)
        Fluciwas (IFI)-comb.

        Fluental (Camillo Corvi)-
        comb.
        Fluvaleas (Valeas)-comb.
        Lonarid (Boehringer Ing.)-
        comb.
        Migranet (Ogna)
        Neofepramol (Istoria)
        Neouniplus (Angelini)-
        comb.
        Neoneoral (Hoechst
        Marion Roussel)-comb.
        Omniadol (Montefarmaco)-
        comb.
        Panadol (Maggioni)
        Saridon (Roche)-comb.
        Tachipirina (Angelini)
        Verdal (Falqui)-comb.
        Zerinol (Fher)-comb.
        numerous generics and
        combination preparations
J: Pyrinazin (Yamanouchi)
USA: Phrenilin (Carnrick)-comb.
        Tylenol with Codeine
        (Ortho-McNeil)-comb.
        numerous combination
        preparations and generics

Paraflutizide

ATC: C03
Use: diuretic

RN: 1580-83-2   MF: $C_{14}H_{13}ClFN_3O_4S_2$ MW: 405.86   EINECS: 216-426-7
CN: 6-chloro-3-[(4-fluorophenyl)methyl]-3,4-dihydro-2*H*-1,2,4-benzothiadiazine-7-sulfonamide 1,1-dioxide

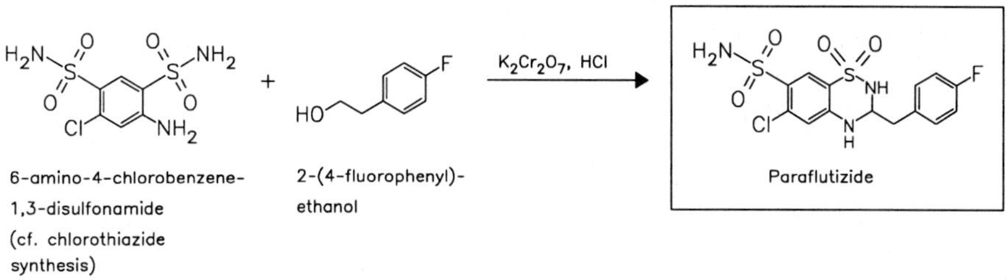

H2N O O NH2
S S
O O
Cl NH2
+
HO F
K2Cr2O7, HCl
H2N O O O
S S NH F
O
Cl N H
6-amino-4-chlorobenzene-1,3-disulfonamide (cf. chlorothiazide synthesis)
2-(4-fluorophenyl)-ethanol
Paraflutizide

Reference(s):
GB 961 641 (Lab. Dausse; appl. 31.7.1962; F-prior. 31.7.1961).

Formulation(s): drg. 2.5 mg

Trade Name(s):

D:	Detensitral (Karlspharma)-comb.; wfm	F:	Divimax (Dausse)-comb.; wfm	Tensitral (Dausse)-comb.; wfm

Paramethadione

(Isoethadione)

ATC: N03AC01
Use: antiepileptic

RN: 115-67-3 MF: $C_7H_{11}NO_3$ MW: 157.17 EINECS: 204-098-8
LD$_{50}$: 1 g/kg (M, p.o.)
CN: 5-ethyl-3,5-dimethyl-2,4-oxazolidinedione

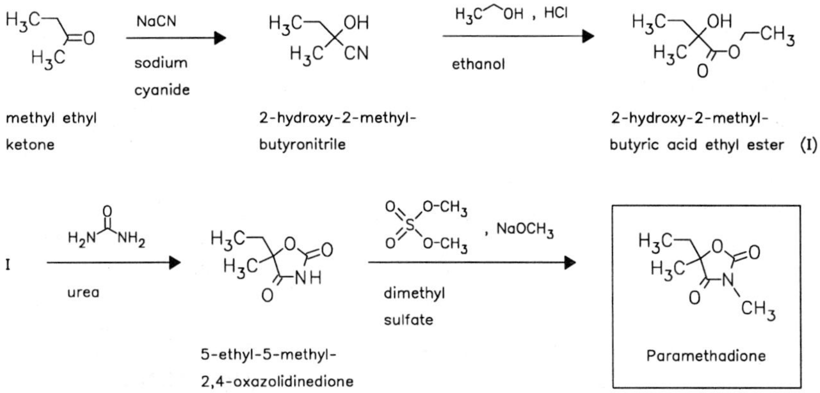

NaCN
sodium cyanide
H3C OH, HCl
ethanol
methyl ethyl ketone
2-hydroxy-2-methyl-butyronitrile
2-hydroxy-2-methyl-butyric acid ethyl ester (I)
urea
dimethyl sulfate
NaOCH3
5-ethyl-5-methyl-2,4-oxazolidinedione
Paramethadione

Reference(s):
US 2 575 693 (Abbott; 1951; appl. 1949).

Formulation(s): cps. 150 mg, 300 mg; drops 300 mg

Trade Name(s):

F:	Paradione (Abbott); wfm	GB:	Paradione (Abbott); wfm	USA:	Paradione (Abbott); wfm

Paramethasone

ATC: H02AB05
Use: glucocorticoid

RN: 53-33-8 MF: $C_{22}H_{29}FO_5$ MW: 392.47 EINECS: 200-169-2
CN: (6α,11β,16α)-6-fluoro-11,17,21-trihydroxy-16-methylpregna-1,4-diene-3,20-dione

disodium phosphate
RN: 2145-14-4 MF: C_{22}H_{28}FNa_2O_8P MW: 516.41 EINECS: 218-410-5
acetate
RN: 1597-82-6 MF: C_{24}H_{31}FO_6 MW: 434.50 EINECS: 216-486-4
LD_{50}: >1 g/kg (M, p.o.)

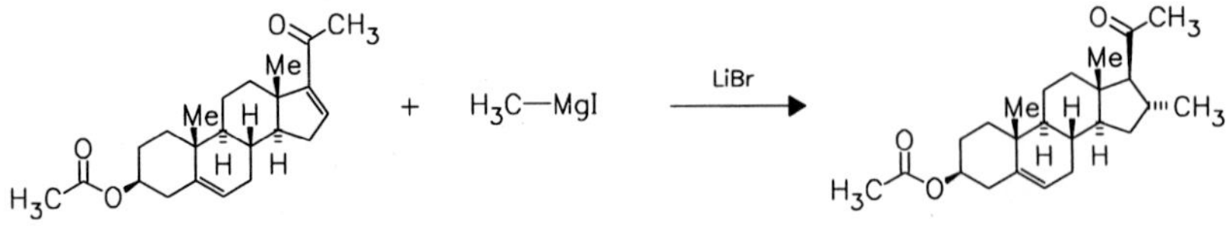

16-dehydropregnenolone
acetate

methylmagnesium
iodide

16α-methylpregnenolone
3β-acetate (I)

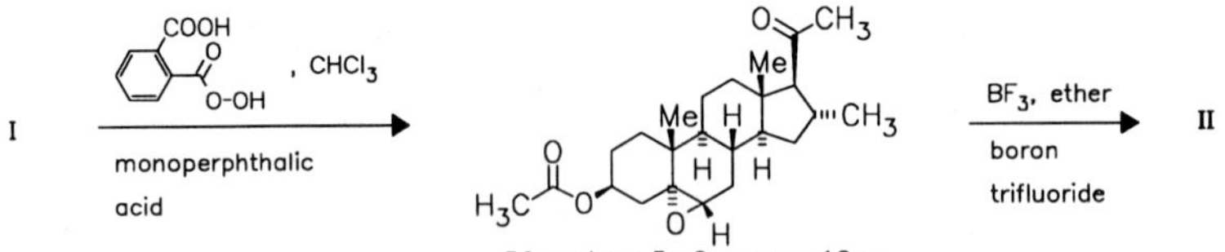

monoperphthalic
acid

3β-acetoxy-5α,6α-epoxy-16α-
methylpregnan-20-one

BF_3, ether
boron
trifluoride

II

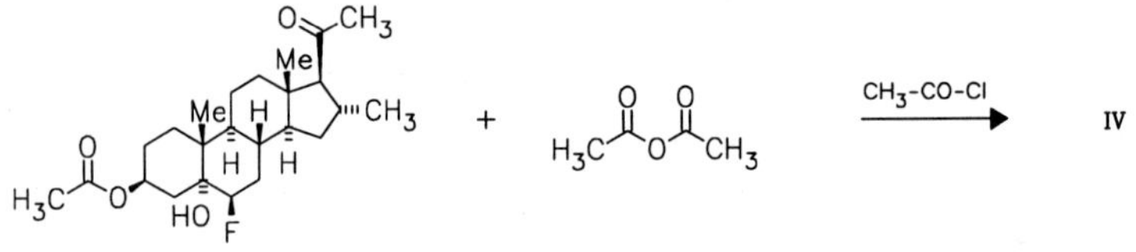

3β-acetoxy-6β-fluoro-5α-hydroxy-
16α-methylpregnan-20-one (II)

acetic
anhydride (III)

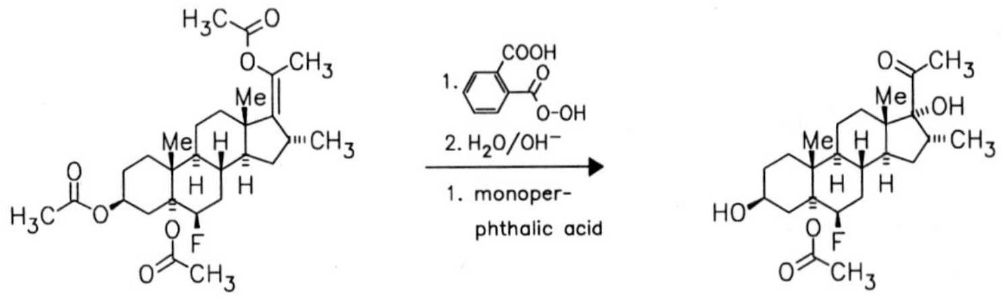

CH_3-CO-Cl

IV

6β-fluoro-16α-methylpregn-17(20)-
ene-3β,5α,20-triol triacetate (IV)

1. monoper-
phthalic acid

5α-acetoxy-6β-fluoro-
3β,17-dihydroxy-16α-
methylpregnan-20-one (V)

V

1. Br_2
2. NaI
3. KO-CO-CH_3

1. bromine
3. potassium
acetate

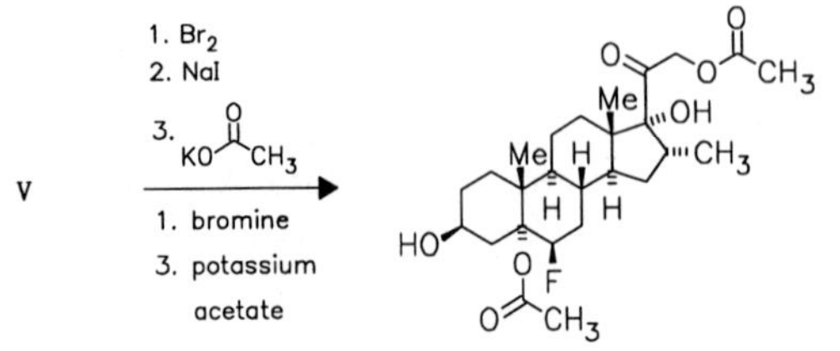

5α,21-diacetoxy-6β-fluoro-
3β,17-dihydroxy-16α-methyl-
pregnan-20-one (VI)

VI

1. CrO₃, H₂SO₄
2. CH₃COOK,
   C₂H₅OH

1. chromium(VI)
   oxide

21-acetoxy-6β-fluoro-17-hydroxy-
16α-methylpregn-4-ene-3,20-dione

1. HCl, CH₃COOH
2. KOH,
   CH₃OH, N₂

6α-fluoro-17,21-dihydroxy-
16α-methylpregn-4-ene-
3,20-dione (VII)

VII

1. microbiological
   hydroxylation
2. III

21-acetoxy-6α-fluoro-11β,17-
dihydroxy-16α-methylpregn-4-
ene-3,20-dione

SeO₂

selenium
dioxide

Paramethasone acetate

disodium phosphate:

1. ... N—P—N ... ,
     Cl
     O
   pyridine
2. acidic ion exchanger,
   NaHCO₃
3. NaOH, pH 8

1. dimorpholino-
   phosphinic chloride

paramethasone

Paramethasone 21-disodium phosphate

Reference(s):
US 2 671 752 (Syntex; 1954; appl. 1951).
Djerassi, C. et al.: J. Am. Chem. Soc. (JACSAT) **82**, 2318 (1960).

starting material:
Marker, R.E.; Crooks, H.M.: J. Am. Chem. Soc. (JACSAT) **64**, 1280 (1942).

alternative syntheses:
US 3 557 158 (Upjohn; 19.1.1971; appl. 22.1.1962; prior. 4.8.1958).
Schneider, P. et al.: J. Am. Chem. Soc. (JACSAT) **81**, 3167 (1959).
GB 850 263 (Organon; appl. 30.4.1959; NL-prior. 12.5.1958).
US 4 041 055 (Upjohn; 9.8.1977; appl. 17.11.1975).

disodium phosphate:
DE 1 134 075 (Merck AG; appl. 26.11.1959).

Formulation(s):   amp.. 20 mg/ml (as acetate); tabl. 2 mg, 6 mg (as acetate)

Trade Name(s):

D:	Monocortin (Grünenthal); wfm	GB:	Haldrate (Lilly); wfm
	Monocortin S (Grünenthal); wfm		Metilar (Syntex); wfm
		I:	Alfa-6 (Sam)
F:	Dilar (Cassenne); wfm		Luxazone XP (Allergan)-comb.

Paramezone (Recordati)
J: Haldron (Dainippon)
Parame A (Syntex-Tanabe)-comb.

| | | Paramesone (Syntex-Tanabe) | USA: | Haldrone (Lilly); wfm
Stemex (Syntex); wfm | Stero-Darvon (Lilly)-comb.; wfm |

Parethoxycaine

ATC: N01BC
Use: local anesthetic

RN: 94-23-5　MF: C₁₅H₂₃NO₃　MW: 265.35
CN: 4-ethoxybenzoic acid 2-(diethylamino)ethyl ester

hydrochloride
RN: 136-46-9　MF: C₁₅H₂₃NO₃ · HCl　MW: 301.81　EINECS: 205-246-4
LD₅₀: 300 mg/kg (M, i.p.); 430 mg/kg (M, s.c.)

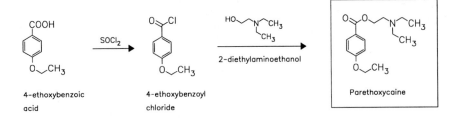

4-ethoxybenzoic acid　　4-ethoxybenzoyl chloride　　2-diethylaminoethanol　　Parethoxycaine

Reference(s):
US 2 404 691 (Squibb; 1946; prior. 1937, 1944).

Formulation(s):　tabl. 0.75 mg (as hydrochloride)

Trade Name(s):
F:　　Maxicaine (Synthélabo)

Pargyline

ATC: C02KC01
Use: MAO-inhibitor, antihypertensive

RN: 555-57-7　MF: C₁₁H₁₃N　MW: 159.23　EINECS: 209-101-6
LD₅₀: 56 mg/kg (M, i.v.); 680 mg/kg (M, p.o.);
　　　300 mg/kg (R, p.o.)
CN: *N*-methyl-*N*-2-propynylbenzenemethanamine

hydrochloride
RN: 306-07-0　MF: C₁₁H₁₃N · HCl　MW: 195.69　EINECS: 206-175-1
LD₅₀: 99 mg/kg (M, i.v.); 680 mg/kg (M, p.o.);
　　　175 mg/kg (R, i.v.); 250 mg/kg (R, p.o.);
　　　175 mg/kg (dog, p.o.)

N-benzylmethyl-amine　　+　　propargyl bromide　　Na₂CO₃　　Pargyline

Reference(s):
US 3 155 584 (Abbott; 3.11.1964; prior. 3.12.1962).

Formulation(s):   tabl. 10 mg, 25 mg (as hydrochloride)

Trade Name(s):

F:	Euditron (Abbott)-comb.; wfm	GB:	Eutonyl (Abbott); wfm	Eutron (Abbott)-comb.; wfm
		USA:	Eutonyl (Abbott)	

Paricalcitol
(Paracalcin)

Use: vitamin D-analog, treatment for hyperparathyroidism

RN: 131918-61-1   MF: $C_{27}H_{44}O_3$ MW: 416.65

CN: (1α,3β,7E,22E)-19-Nor-9,10-secoergosta-5,7,22-triene-1,3,25-triol

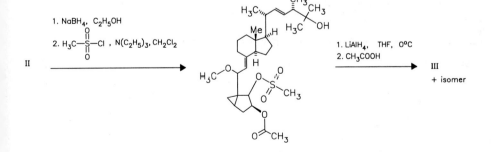

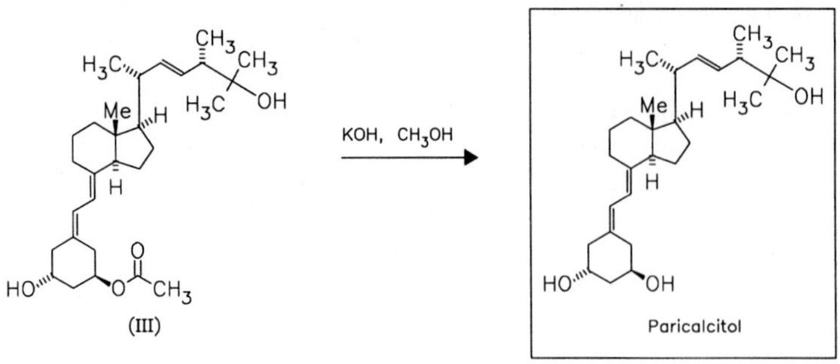

KOH, CH₃OH

(III)

Paricalcitol

Reference(s):

EP 387 077 (Wisconsin Alumni Res. Found.; 12.9.1990; appl. 9.3.1990; USA-prior. 16.2.1990).
WO 9 729 740 (Wisconsin Alumni Res. Found.; appl. 5.9.1996; USA-prior. 13.2.1996).
Paaren, H.E. et al.: J. Org. Chem. (JOCEAH) **45**, 3253-3258 (1980).
Paaren, H.E. et al.: J. Org. Chem. (JOCEAH) **48**, 3819-3820 (1983).

treatment of osteoporosis in comb. with growth hormone secretagogue:
WO 9 853 827 (Ramoz Univ.; appl. 22.5.1998; IL-prior. 30.5.1997).

Formulation(s):　　amp. 5 µg/ml; 1 ml, 2 ml, 5 ml

Trade Name(s):
USA:　Zemplar (Abbott; 1998)

Paromomycin
(Aminosidine)

ATC:　A07AA06
Use:　antibiotic

RN:　7542-37-2　MF: $C_{23}H_{45}N_5O_{14}$　MW: 615.63　EINECS: 231-423-0
LD₅₀:　2.275 g/kg (M, p.o.);
　　　21.62 g/kg (R, p.o.)
CN:　*O*-2-amino-2-deoxy-α-D-glucopyranosyl-(1→4)-*O*-[*O*-2,6-diamino-2,6-dideoxy-β-l-idopyranosyl(1→3)-β-D-ribofuranosyl-(1→5)]-2-deoxy-D-streptamine

sulfate
RN:　1263-89-4　MF: $C_{23}H_{45}N_5O_{14} \cdot xH_2SO_4$　MW: unspecified　EINECS: 215-031-7
LD₅₀:　90 mg/kg (M, i.v.); 23.5 g/kg (M, p.o.);
　　　181 mg/kg (R, i.v.); 21.62 g/kg (R, p.o.)

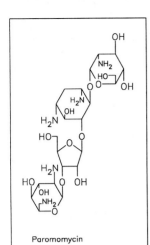

Paromomycin

From fermentation solutions of *Streptomyces rimosus forma paromomycinus* or *Streptomyces krestomyceticus* N.C.I.B. 8995.

Reference(s):
US 2 916 485 (Parke Davis; 8.12.1959; prior. 12.1.1959).
GB 880 035 (Soc. Farmaceutici Italia; appl. 31.3.1959; valid from 18.2.1960).

Formulation(s):   cps. 250 mg; powder 1 g; syrup 125 mg/5 ml

Trade Name(s):

D:	Humatin (Parke Davis)	GB: Humatin (Parke Davis);
F:	Humagel (Parke Davis);	wfm
	wfm	I: Aminoxidin (Farmalabor)
	Humatin (Parke Davis);	Gabbroral (Carlo Erba)
	wfm	Gabbroral (Farmalabor)
		Humatin (Parke Davis)

Paramicina (Ragionieri)
Sinosid (SIFI)
J: Humatin (Parke Davis-Sankyo)
USA: Humatin (Parke Davis); wfm

Paroxetine
(BRL 29060; FG 7051)

ATC: N06AB05; N06AE
Use: antidepressant, selective 5-HT-uptake inhibitor

RN: 61869-08-7   MF: $C_{19}H_{20}FNO_3$ MW: 329.37
LD$_{50}$: 374 mg/kg (R, p.o.)
CN: (3S-trans)-(–)-3-[(1,3-benzodioxol-5-yloxy)methyl]-4-(4-fluorophenyl)piperidine

hydrochloride
RN: 78246-49-8   MF: $C_{19}H_{20}FNO_3 \cdot HCl$ MW: 365.83
LD$_{50}$: 42 mg/kg (M, i.v.); 378 mg/kg (M, p.o.);
        30 mg/kg (R, i.v.); 415 mg/kg (R, p.o.)
hydrochloride hydrate (2:1)
RN: 110429-35-1   MF: $C_{19}H_{20}FNO_3 \cdot HCl \cdot 1/2H_2O$ MW: 749.68
maleate
RN: 64006-44-6   MF: $C_{19}H_{20}FNO_3 \cdot xC_4H_4O_4$ MW: unspecified
LD$_{50}$: 500 mg/kg (M, p.o.); 845 mg/kg (M. s.c.)
acetate
RN: 72471-80-8   MF: $C_{19}H_{20}FNO_3 \cdot C_2H_4O_2$ MW: 389.42

a

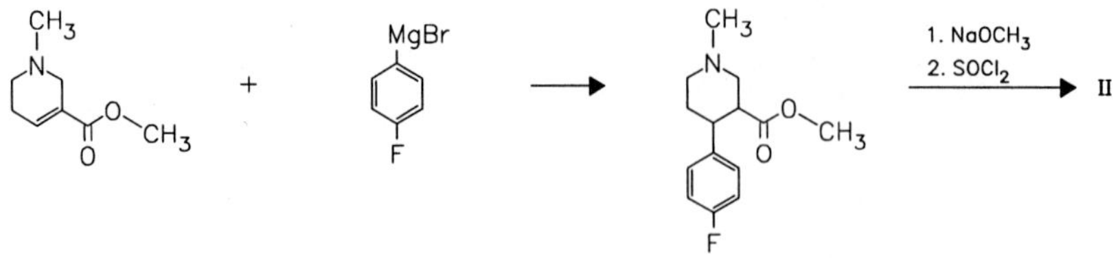

arecoline	4-fluorophenyl-magnesium bromide (I)	methyl cis/trans-4-(4-fluorophenyl)-N-methylnipecotate

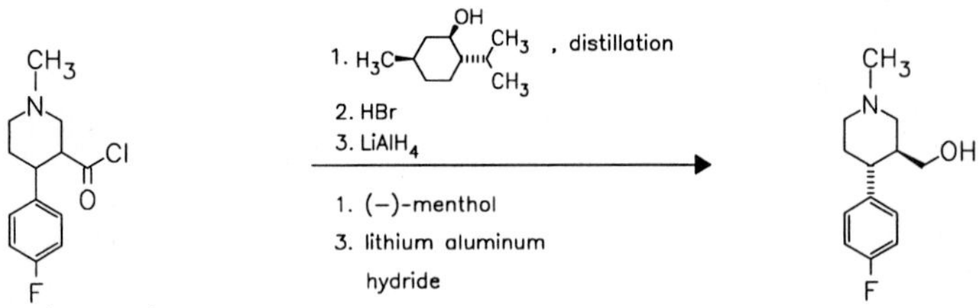

1. (−)-menthol
3. lithium aluminum hydride

cis/trans-4-(4-fluorophenyl)-N-methylnipecotoyl chloride (II)	(−)-trans-4-(4-fluorophenyl)-N-methyl-3-hydroxymethylpiperidine (III)

b

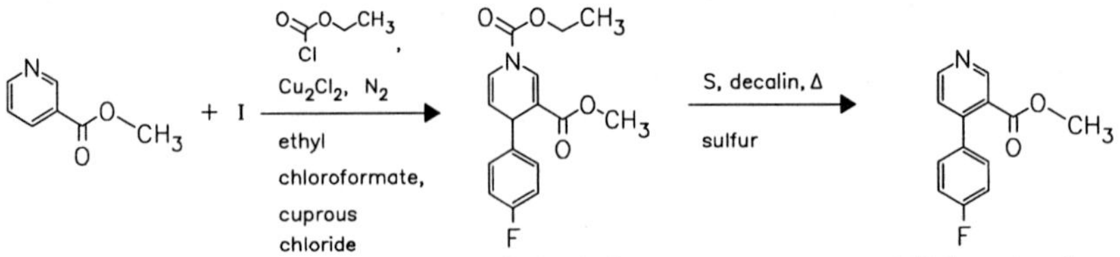

methyl nicotinate	1,4-dihydro-1-ethoxycarbonyl-4-(4-fluorophenyl)-3-methoxycarbonylpyridine	4-(4-fluorophenyl)-3-methoxycarbonylpyridine (IV)

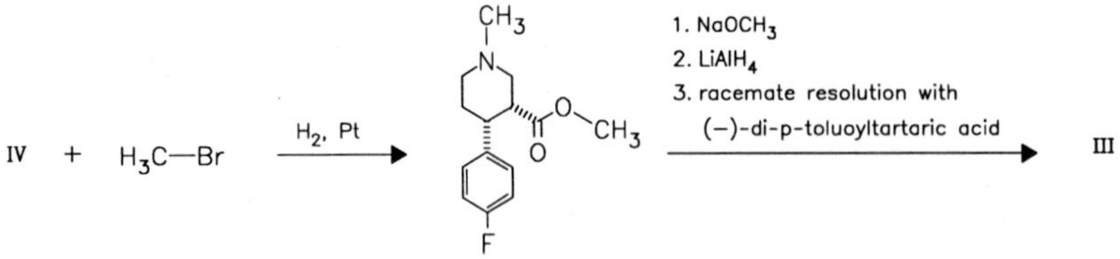

IV + H$_3$C—Br

methyl bromide	(±)-cis-4-(4-fluorophenyl)-3-methoxycarbonyl-1-methylpiperidine

c)

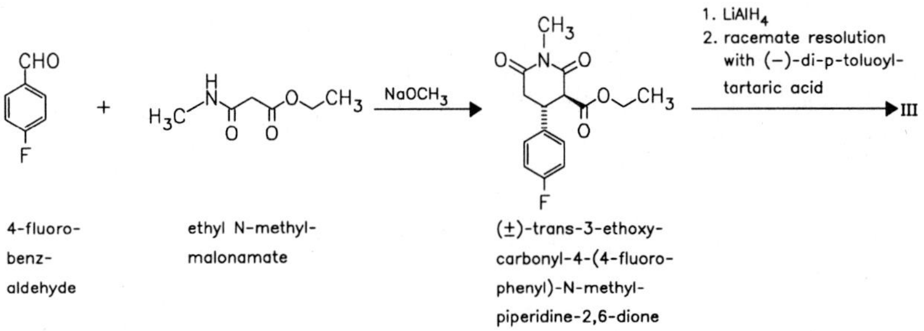

4-fluoro-
benz-
aldehyde

ethyl N-methyl-
malonamate

NaOCH₃

(±)-trans-3-ethoxy-
carbonyl-4-(4-fluoro-
phenyl)-N-methyl-
piperidine-2,6-dione

1. LiAlH₄
2. racemate resolution
   with (−)-di-p-toluoyl-
   tartaric acid

III

d)

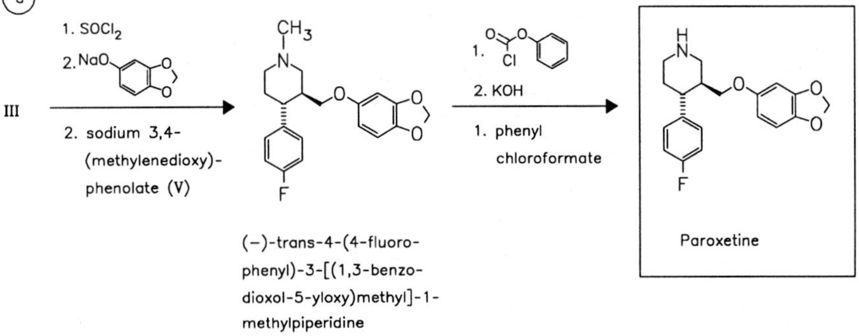

III

1. SOCl₂
2. NaO...

2. sodium 3,4-
   (methylenedioxy)-
   phenolate (V)

(−)-trans-4-(4-fluoro-
phenyl)-3-[(1,3-benzo-
dioxol-5-yloxy)methyl]-1-
methylpiperidine

1. phenyl
   chloroformate
2. KOH

Paroxetine

e)

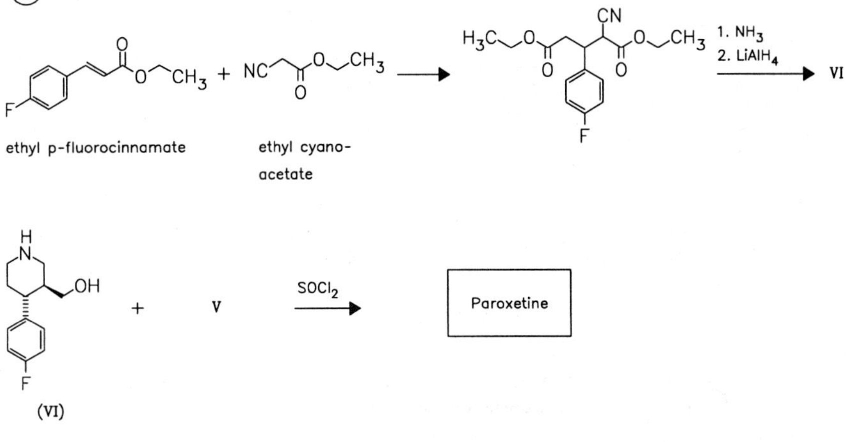

ethyl p-fluorocinnamate

ethyl cyano-
acetate

1. NH₃
2. LiAlH₄

VI

(VI)

+   V

SOCl₂

Paroxetine

f)

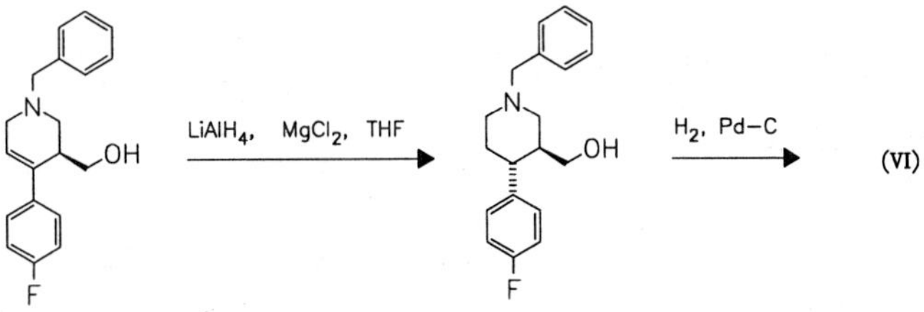

LiAlH₄, MgCl₂, THF

H₂, Pd–C

(VI)

3-pyridine-
carboxaldehyde

Reference(s):
US 3 912 743 (Ferrosan, 14.10.1975; GB-prior. 30.1.1973).
a,d US 4 007 196 (AIS Ferrosan; 8.2.1977; appl. 23.7.1975; prior. 21.1.1974; GB-prior. 30.1.1973).
    DE 2 404 113 (AIS Ferrosan; appl. 29.1.1974; GB-prior. 30.1.1973).
    GB 1 422 263 (AIS Ferrosan; appl. 30.1.1973).
b   EP 219 934 (Beecham; appl. 6.8.1986; GB-prior. 10.8.1985).
c   EP 223 334 (Beecham; appl. 6.8.1986; GB-prior. 10.8.1985, 23.5.1986).
e   WO 9 853 824 (SmithKline Beecham; appl. 29.5.1998; GB-prior. 29.5.1997).
f   WO 9 852 920 (Knoll; appl. 13.5.1998; GB-prior. 17.5.1997).
g   WO 9 724 323 (Chiroscience; appl. 30.12.1996; GB-prior. 29.12.1995).

alternative synthesis of III:
EP 300 617 (Beecham; appl. 17.6.1988; GB-prior. 23.6.1987).

synthesis of arecoline:
The Merck Index, 11th Ed., 803 (Rahway 1989).

optically pure precursors:
US 52 582 517 (Sepracor; 2.11.1993; appl. 6.8.1992).

crystalline hydrochloride hemihydrate:
EP 223 403 (Beecham; appl. 14.10.1986; GB-prior. 25.10.1985).
US 4 721 723 (Beecham; 26.1.1988; appl. 23.10.1986; GB-prior. 25.10.1985).

medical use for treatment of pain:
EP 269 303 (Beecham; appl. 9.11.1986; GB-prior. 11.11.1985).

medical use for treatment of obesity:
EP 188 081 (Ferrosan; appl. 2.12.1985; GB-prior. 4.12.1984).

preparation of easily soluble paroxetine:
WO 9 831 365 (SmithKline Beecham; appl. 12.1.1998; GB-prior. 15.1.1997).

new polymorph of anhydrous paroxetine:
CA 2 187 128 (Brabtfort Chem.; appl. 4.10.1996).

method of producing amorphous paroxetine:
EP 810 224 (Asahi Glass; appl. 30.5.1997; J-prior. 30.5.1996).
US 5 672 612 (Pentech Pharm; USA-prior. 9.9.1996).

controlled-release pharmaceutical compositions:
WO 9 703 670 (SmithKline Beecham; appl. 19.7.1996; GB-prior. 20.7.1995).

Formulation(s):   tabl., 20 mg, 30 mg (as hydrochloride)

Trade Name(s):
D: Seroxat (SmithKline   F: Dexorat (SmithKline   GB: Seroxat (SmithKline
         Beecham)   Beecham)   Beecham; 1991)
         Tagonis (Janssen-Cilag)

I: Sereupin (Ravizza)	Seroxat (SmithKline Beecham)	USA:	Paxil (SmithKline Beecham)

Parsalmide

ATC: N02
Use: anti-inflammatory

RN: 30653-83-9 MF: $C_{14}H_{18}N_2O_2$ MW: 246.31 EINECS: 250-274-2
LD_{50}: 148 mg/kg (M, i.v.); 428 mg/kg (M, p.o.); 864 mg/kg (R, p.o.)
CN: 5-amino-*N*-butyl-2-(2-propynyloxy)benzamide

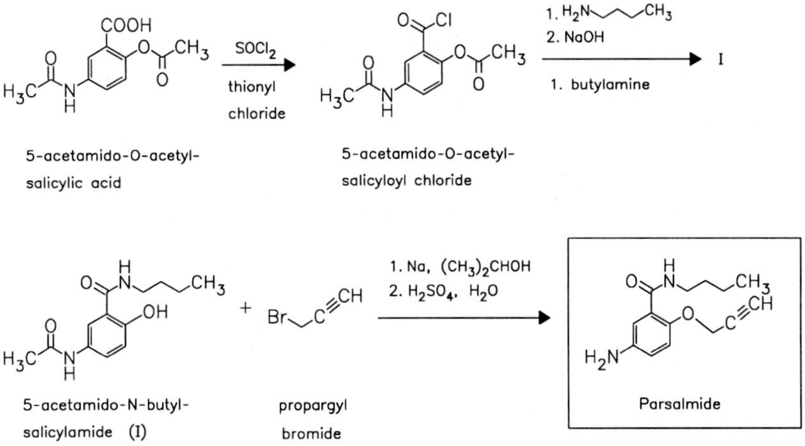
COOH
SOCl2
thionyl chloride
5-acetamido-O-acetyl-salicylic acid
1. H2N CH3
2. NaOH
1. butylamine
I
5-acetamido-O-acetyl-salicyloyl chloride
1. Na, (CH3)2CHOH
2. H2SO4, H2O
5-acetamido-N-butyl-salicylamide (I)
propargyl bromide
Parsalmide

Reference(s):
DOS 2 029 991 (E.R.A.S.M.E.; appl. 18.6.1970; GB-prior. 20.6.1969).
US 3 739 030 (E.R.A.S.M.E.; 12.6.1973; GB-prior. 20.6.1969).
Pedrazzoli, A. et al.: Chim. Ther. (CHTPBA) **3**, 200 (1968).

alternative synthesis:
GB 1 539 007 (C. M. Ind.; valid from 26.10.1977; F-prior. 8.11.1976).

Formulation(s): drg. 200 mg, 400 mg; f. c. tabl. 600 mg; s. r. tabl. 800 mg

Trade Name(s):
I: Parsal (Midy); wfm

Pasiniazid

ATC: J04AA
Use: tuberculostatic, antibacterial

RN: 2066-89-9 MF: $C_7H_7NO_3 \cdot C_6H_7N_3O$ MW: 290.28 EINECS: 218-183-2
CN: 4-pyridinecarboxylic acid hydrazide mono(4-amino-2-hydroxybenzoate)

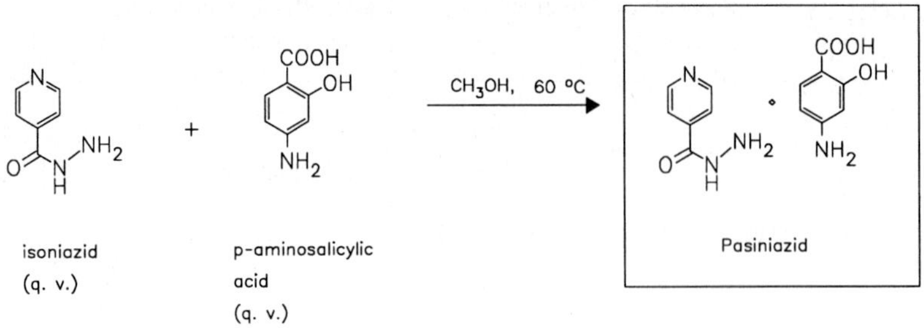

| isoniazid (q. v.) | p-aminosalicylic acid (q. v.) | | Pasiniazid |

Reference(s):
CH 303 085 (Roche; appl. 1952).

Formulation(s):   tabl. 100 mg

Trade Name(s):
D: Dipasic (Gewo); wfm
F: Paraniazide (L'Hépatrol);
     wfm

Pasiniazide Rolland
(L'Hépatrol); wfm
I: Dipasic (Farmerid); wfm

Pecazine
(Mepazine)

ATC: N05A
Use: neuroleptic

RN: 60-89-9   MF: $C_{19}H_{22}N_2S$ MW: 310.47   EINECS: 200-490-8
LD_{50}:   70 mg/kg (M, i.v.)
CN: 10-[(1-methyl-3-piperidinyl)methyl]-10H-phenothiazine

monoacetate
RN: 24360-97-2   MF: $C_{19}H_{22}N_2S \cdot C_2H_4O_2$ MW: 370.52   EINECS: 246-207-1
monohydrochloride
RN: 2975-36-2   MF: $C_{19}H_{22}N_2S \cdot HCl$ MW: 346.93   EINECS: 221-020-8
LD_{50}:   62 mg/kg (M, i.v.); 155 mg/kg (M, p.o.);
     20 mg/kg (R, i.v.); 1 g/kg (R, p.o.)

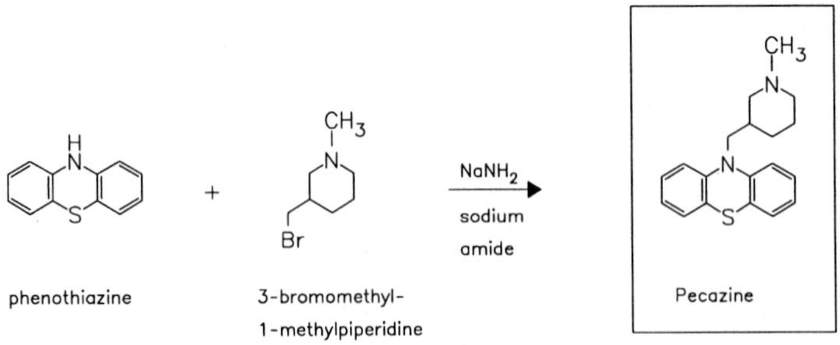

| phenothiazine | 3-bromomethyl-1-methylpiperidine | | Pecazine |

Reference(s):
US 2 784 185 (Promonta; 1957; D-prior. 1953).

Formulation(s):   tabl. 50 mg, 400 mg (as hydrochloride)

Trade Name(s):
D: Pacatal (Promonta); wfm

Pecilocin

ATC: D01AA04
Use: fungicidal antibiotic

RN: 19504-77-9   MF: $C_{17}H_{25}NO_3$ MW: 291.39   EINECS: 243-116-9
LD_{50}:   320 mg/kg (M, i.p.)
CN: [*R-(E,E,E)*]-1-(8-hydroxy-6-methyl-1-oxo-2,4,6-dodecatrienyl)-2-pyrrolidinone

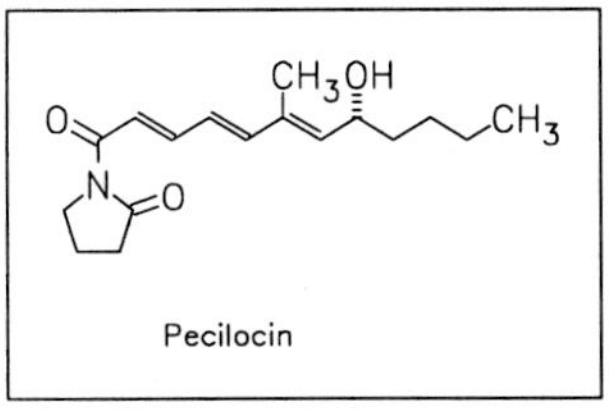

Pecilocin

From culture of *Paecilomyces varioti* Bainier *var. antibioticus*.

Reference(s):
GB 866 425 (Japan Antibiotics Research Assoc.; appl. 7.4.1959).

Formulation(s):   ointment 3000 iu/g; topical sol. 1500 iu/ml

Trade Name(s):
D: Supral (Basotherm); wfm   GB: Variotin (Leo); wfm
F: Leofungine (Leo); wfm   J: Variotin (Nippon Kayaku)

Pefloxacin

ATC: J01MA03
Use: antibiotic (gyrase inhibitor)

RN: 70458-92-3   MF: $C_{17}H_{20}FN_3O_3$ MW: 333.36   EINECS: 274-611-8
LD_{50}:   225 mg/kg (M, i.v.); >4 g/kg (M, p.o.)
CN: 1-ethyl-6-fluoro-1,4-dihydro-7-(4-methyl-1-piperazinyl)-4-oxo-3-quinolinecarboxylic acid

monomesylate
RN: 70458-95-6   MF: $C_{17}H_{20}FN_3O_3 \cdot CH_4O_3S$ MW: 429.47   EINECS: 274-613-9
LD_{50}:   225 mg/kg (M, i.v.); 1 g/kg (M, p.o.);
          2500 mg/kg (R, p.o.)

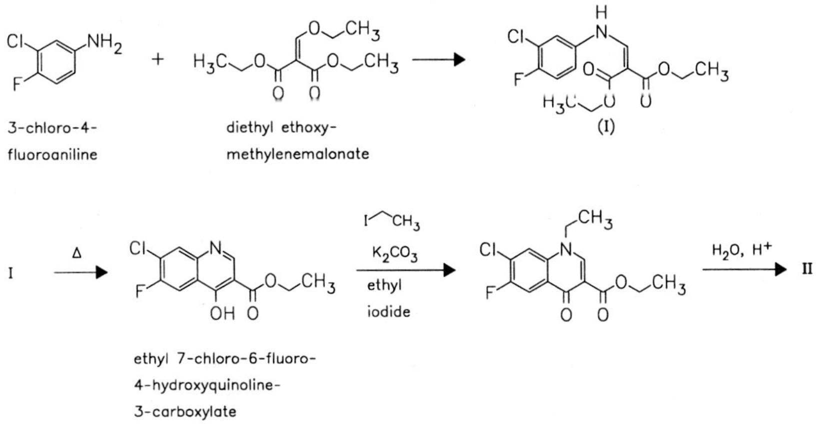

3-chloro-4-
fluoroaniline

diethyl ethoxy-
methylenemalonate

(I)

ethyl 7-chloro-6-fluoro-
4-hydroxyquinoline-
3-carboxylate

ethyl
iodide

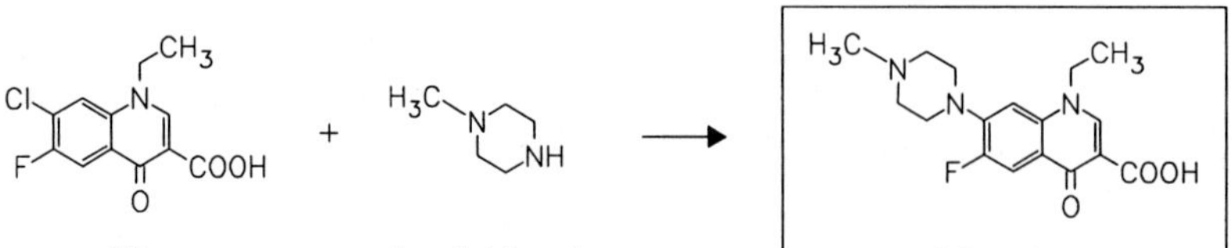

(II)   +   N-methylpiperazine   →   Pefloxacin

Reference(s):

US 4 292 317 (Roger Bellon; 29.9.1981; appl. 15.9.1978; GB-prior. 20.9.1977).
DOS 2 840 910 (Lab. Roger Bellon; appl. 20.9.1978; GB-prior. 20.9.1977).
Gouffon, G. et al.: C. R. Hebd. Seances Acad. Sci. (COREAF) 292 (1981).

Formulation(s):   f. c. tabl. 400 mg; inj. sol. 400 mg/125 ml, 400 mg/5 ml (as mesylate)

Trade Name(s):

D: Peflacin (Rhône-Poulenc Rorer)   F: Peflazine (Bellon; Rhône-Poulenc; 1985)   I: Peflacin (Rhône-Poulenc Pharma)
Peflox (Formenti)

Pemirolast

ATC: R03
Use: antiallergic

RN: 69372-19-6   MF: $C_{10}H_8N_6O$ MW: 228.22
CN: 9-methyl-3-(1*H*-tetrazol-5-yl)-4*H*-pyrido[1,2-*a*]pyrimidin-4-one

potassium salt
RN: 100299-08-9   MF: $C_{10}H_7KN_6O$ MW: 266.31
LD_{50}:   220 mg/kg (M, i.v.); 1185 mg/kg (M, p.o.);
372 mg/kg (R, i.v.); 687 mg/kg (R, p.o.)

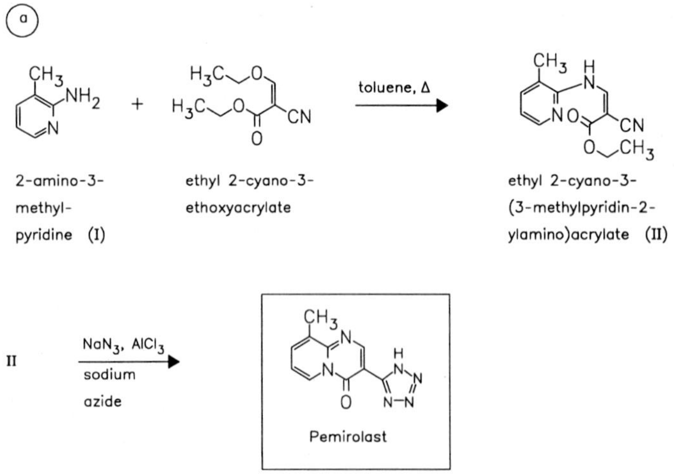

2-amino-3-methyl-pyridine (I)   +   ethyl 2-cyano-3-ethoxyacrylate   —toluene, Δ→   ethyl 2-cyano-3-(3-methylpyridin-2-ylamino)acrylate (II)

II   —NaN₃, AlCl₃ / sodium azide→   Pemirolast

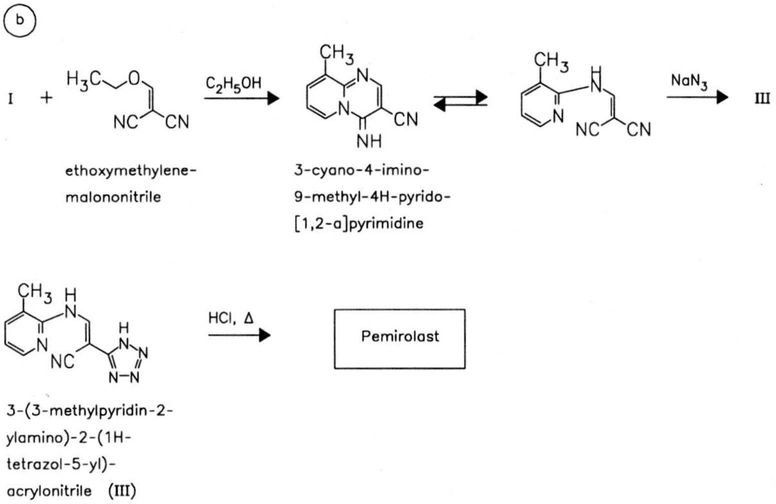

(b)

I + ethoxymethylenemalononitrile (H₃C-O, NC-CN) →(C₂H₅OH) 3-cyano-4-imino-9-methyl-4H-pyrido-[1,2-a]pyrimidine ⇌ →(NaN₃) III

3-(3-methylpyridin-2-ylamino)-2-(1H-tetrazol-5-yl)-acrylonitrile (III) →(HCl, Δ) Pemirolast

Reference(s):
a   DE 2 822 544 (Bristol-Myers; appl. 23.5.1978; USA-prior. 25.5.1977).
    US 4 122 274 (Bristol-Myers; 24.10.1978; appl. 25.5.1977).
b   EP 385 634 (Wako, Tokyo Tanabe; appl. 20.2.1990; J-prior. 27.2.1989).

medical use for treatment of gastrointestinal diseases:
US 4 457 932 (Bristol-Myers; 3.7.1984; appl. 22.7.1983).
DOS 3 424 324 (Bristol-Myers; appl. 2.7.1984; USA-prior. 22.7.1983).

Formulation(s):   tabl. 10 mg (as potassium salt); ophth. sol. 0.1%

Trade Name(s):
J: Alegysal (Santen; Tokyo   Pemilaston (Bristol-Myers   USA: Alamast (Santen)
        Tanabe; 1991)   Squibb; 1991)

Pemoline
(Phenoxazole)

ATC: N06BA05
Use: psychoenergetic

RN: 2152-34-3   MF: $C_9H_8N_2O_2$ MW: 176.18   EINECS: 218-438-8
LD$_{50}$: 365 mg/kg (M, p.o.);
        436 mg/kg (R, p.o.)
CN: 2-amino-5-phenyl-4(5H)-oxazolone

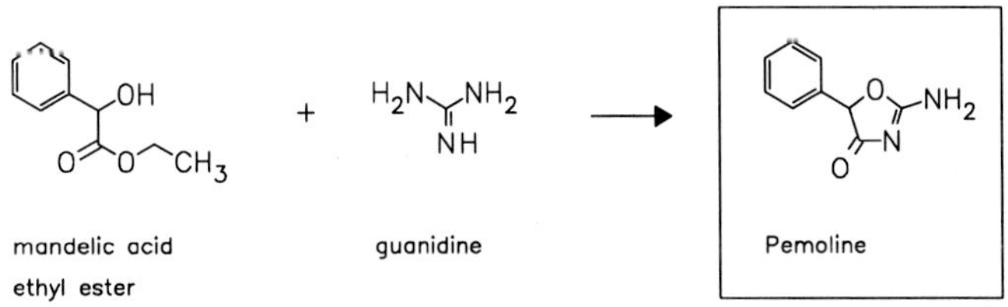

mandelic acid   guanidine   Pemoline
ethyl ester

Reference(s):
US 2 892 753 (Boehringer Ing.; 30.6.1959; prior. 26.2.1957).

Formulation(s):   tabl. (USA) 18.75 mg, 20 mg, 37.5 mg, 70 mg

D: Senior (Strathmann)   Ronyl (Rona); wfm   Sigmadyn (Spemsa); wfm
      Tradon (Beiersdorf-Lilly)   Volital (L.A.B.); wfm   J: Antimeran (Nichiiko)
F: Deltamine (Aron); wfm   I: Deadyn (De Angeli)-   USA: Cylert (Abbott)
GB: Cylert (Abbott); wfm   comb.; wfm
      Kethamed (Medo); wfm   Psicodelta (Chiesi); wfm

Penbutolol

ATC: C07AA23
Use: beta blocking agent

RN: 38363-40-5   MF: $C_{18}H_{29}NO_2$ MW: 291.44
LD_{50}:   18 mg/kg (M, i.v.); 1230 mg/kg (M, p.o.);
       22 mg/kg (R, i.v.); 1265 mg/kg (R, p.o.);
       >20 mg/kg (dog, i.v.)
CN: (S)-1-(2-cyclopentylphenoxy)-3-[(1,1-dimethylethyl)amino]-2-propanol

2-cyclopentyl-   epichlorohydrin   1,2-epoxy-3-(2-cyclo-
phenol   pentylphenoxy)propane (I)

1. C_2H_5OH
2. racemate resolution
   with D-(−)-mandelic
   acid

tert-butylamine   Penbutolol

Reference(s):
DE 1 668 055 (Hoechst; prior. 8.12.1967).
US 3 551 493 (Hoechst; 29.12.1970; appl. 7.3.1968; D-prior. 10.3.1967).
ZA 687 915 (Hoechst; appl. 15.11.1968; D-prior. 8.12.1967).

preparation of 2-cyclopentylphenol:
DE 615 448 (Hoffmann La Roche; 1932).
Pajeau, B.: Bull. Soc. Chim. Fr. (BSCFAS) **1962**, 1923, 1926.
Bader: J. Am. Chem. Soc. (JACSAT) **75**, 5967 (1953)

alternative synthesis:
DOS 2 503 222 (Boehringer Mannh.; appl. 27.1.1975).

Formulation(s):   f. c. tabl. 20 mg, 40 mg (as sulfate)

D: Betapressin (Hoechst;   F: Betapressine (Roussel;   Betasemid (Hoechst Italia
      1981)   1984)   Sud)-comb.; wfm
      Betarelix (Hoechst; 1985)- GB: Lasipressin (Hoechst)-   Ipobar (Mida); wfm
      comb.   comb.; wfm   J: Betapressin (Hoechst;
      Betasemid (Hoechst;   I: Betapressin (Hoechst Italia   1985)
      1982)-comb.   Sud); wfm   USA: Levatol (Schwarz)

Penciclovir
(BRL-39123)

ATC: J05AB13
Use: topical antiviral

RN: 39809-25-1   MF: $C_{10}H_{15}N_5O_3$ MW: 253.26
CN: 2-amino-1,9-dihydro-9-[4-hydroxy-3-(hydroxymethyl)butyl]-6H-purin-6-one

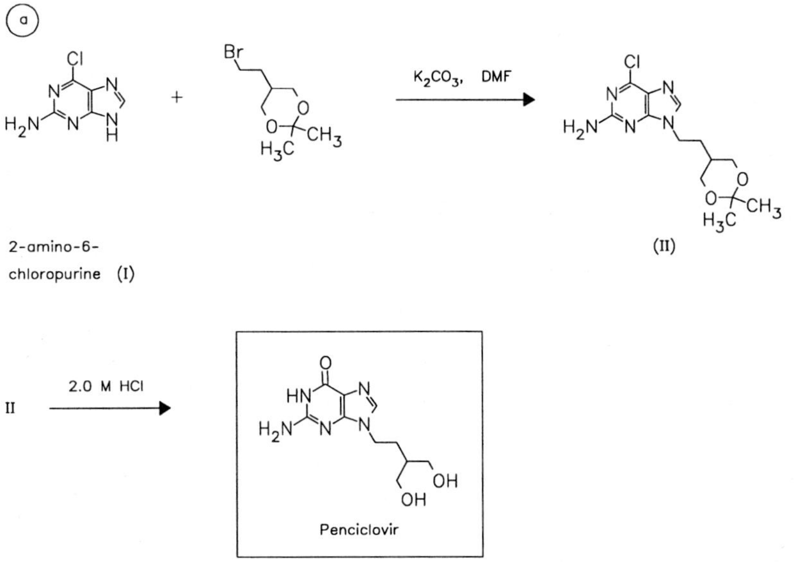

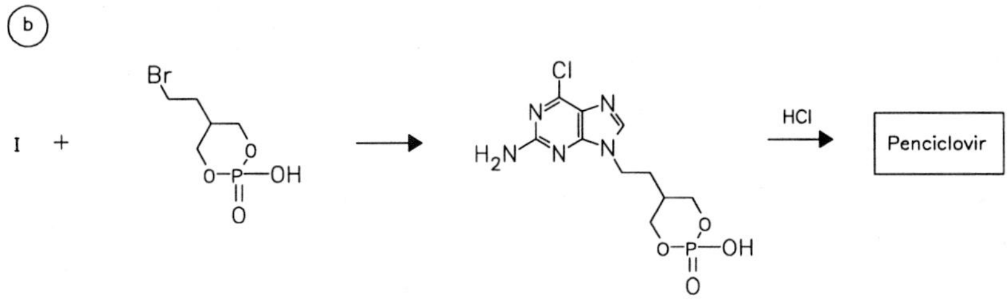

2-amino-6-
chloropurine (I)

(II)

Penciclovir

Reference(s):
a   EP 141 927 (Beecham; appl. 22.5.1985; GB-prior. 18.8.1983).
b   EP 152 316 (Merck & Co.; appl. 21.8.1985; USA-prior. 26.1.1984).

synthesis of 2-amino-6-chloropurine:
WO 9 407 892 (SmithKline Beecham; appl. 28.9.1993; GB-prior. 30.9.1992).

synergistic combination with interferon:
EP 271 270 (Beecham Group; appl. 15.6.1988; GB-prior. 2.12.1986).
WO 9 513 074 (SmithKline Beecham; appl. 18.5.1995; GB-prior. 12.11.1993).

combination with anti-inflammatory glucocorticoide:
WO 9 624 355 (Astra; appl. 15.8.1996; WO-prior. 6.2.1995).

topical formulations:
WO 9 624 354 (Astra; appl. 15.8.1996; WO-prior. 6.2.1995).
WO 9 300 905 (SmithKline Beecham; appl. 21.1.1993; GB-prior. 11.7.1991).

stable crystalline monohydrate:
EP 216 459 (Beecham Group; appl. 1.4.1987; GB-prior. 27.7.1985).

Formulation(s):   cream 10 mg/g (1 %)

Trade Name(s):
D: Vectavir (SmithKline
    Beecham)
GB: Vectavir (SmithKline
    Beecham)

I: Vectavir (SmithKline
    Beecham)
USA: Denavir (SmithKline
    Beecham)

Penfluridol

ATC: N05AG03
Use: neuroleptic

RN: 26864-56-2   MF: $C_{28}H_{27}ClF_5NO$ MW: 523.97   EINECS: 248-074-5
LD$_{50}$:   87 mg/kg (M, p.o.);
    160 mg/kg (R, p.o.)
CN: 1-[4,4-bis(4-fluorophenyl)butyl]-4-[4-chloro-3-(trifluoromethyl)phenyl]-4-piperidinol

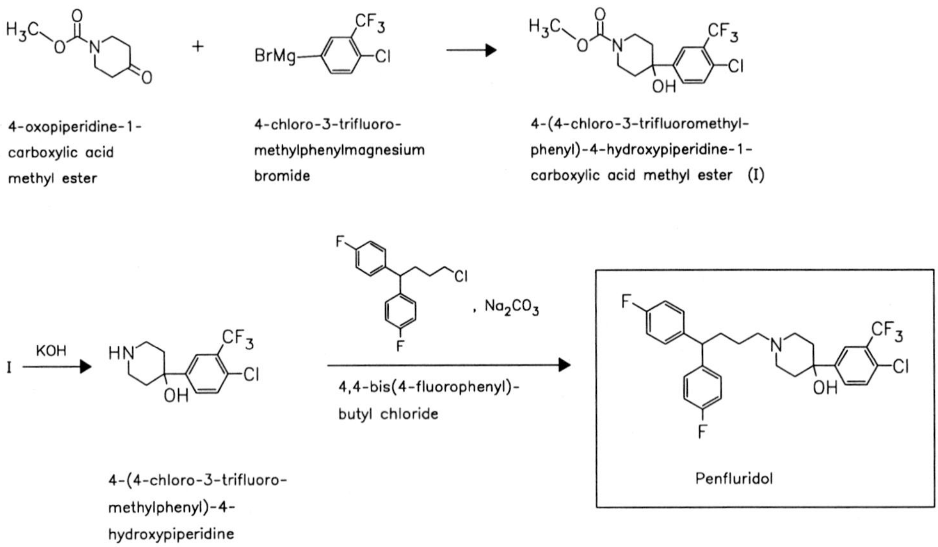

4-oxopiperidine-1-
carboxylic acid
methyl ester

4-chloro-3-trifluoro-
methylphenylmagnesium
bromide

4-(4-chloro-3-trifluoromethyl-
phenyl)-4-hydroxypiperidine-1-
carboxylic acid methyl ester   (I)

4-(4-chloro-3-trifluoro-
methylphenyl)-4-
hydroxypiperidine

4,4-bis(4-fluorophenyl)-
butyl chloride

Penfluridol

Reference(s):
US 3 575 990 (Janssen; 20.4.1971; appl. 3.9.1969).
DOS 2 040 231 (Janssen; appl. 13.8.1970; USA-prior. 3.9.1969).

alternative synthesis:
FR-appl. 2 161 007 (Janssen; appl. 23.11.1972; J-prior. 25.11.1971).

Formulation(s):   tabl. 20 mg

Trade Name(s):
D: Semap (Janssen); wfm

F: Semap (Janssen-Cilag)

Pengitoxin

ATC: C01AA
Use: cardiac glycoside

RN: 7242-04-8   MF: $C_{51}H_{74}O_{19}$ MW: 991.13   EINECS: 230-645-5
LD_{50}:   21 mg/kg (R, i.v.)
CN: (3β,5β,16β)-16-(acetyloxy)-3-[(*O*-3,4-di-*O*-acetyl-2,6-dideoxy-β-D-*ribo*-hexopyranosyl-(1→4)-*O*-3-*O*-
acetyl-2,6-dideoxy-β-D-*ribo*-hexopyranosyl-(1→4)-3-*O*-acetyl-2,6-dideoxy-β-D-*ribo*-
hexopyranosyl)oxy]-14-hydroxycard-20(22)-enolide

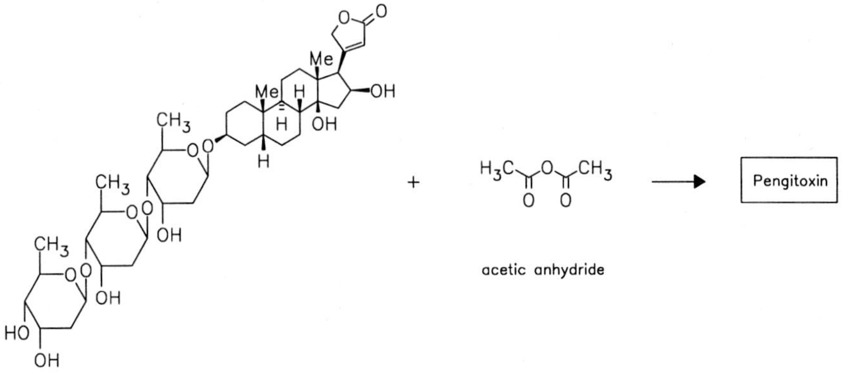

gitoxin

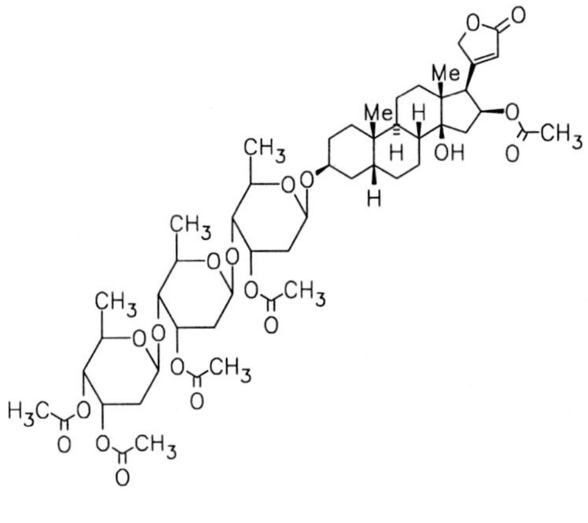

acetic anhydride

Pengitoxin

Pengitoxin

Reference(s):
DE 1 252 202 (Deutsche Akad. der Wissenschaften; appl. 4.11.1963).
GB 1 043 029 (Arzneimittelwerk Dresden; appl. 15.6.1965).
JP-appl. 6 982 ('60) (Shionogi; appl. 15.6.1960).

Formulation(s):   tabl. 0.4 mg

Trade Name(s):
D: Carnacid-Cor (TAD); wfm

D-Penicillamine

ATC: M01CC01
Use: antidote (heavy metal poisonings), antirheumatic (PCA and Morbus Wilson)

RN: 52-67-5 MF: $C_5H_{11}NO_2S$ MW: 149.21 EINECS: 200-148-8
LD_{50}: 3840 mg/kg (M, i.v.); 720 mg/kg (M, p.o.);
2 g/kg (R, i.v.); 6170 mg/kg (R, p.o.)
CN: 3-mercapto-D-valine

hydrochloride
RN: 2219-30-9 MF: $C_5H_{11}NO_2S \cdot HCl$ MW: 185.68 EINECS: 218-727-9
LD_{50}: 2170 mg/kg (M, i.v.); 3670 mg/kg (M, p.o.)

from penicillin G

(a)

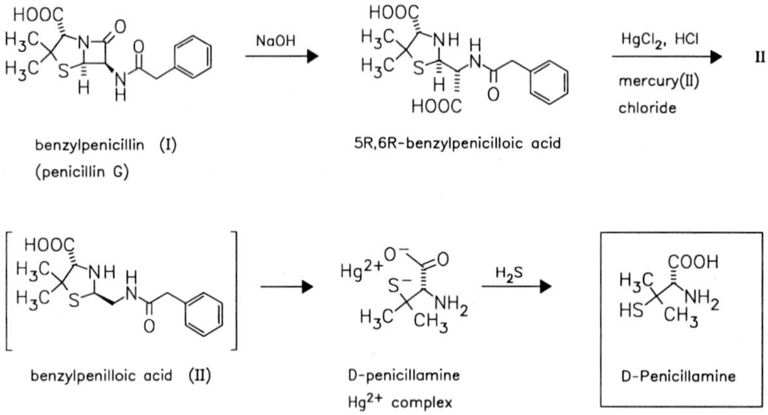
NaOH
HgCl2, HCl
mercury(II) chloride
II
benzylpenicillin (I)
(penicillin G)
5R,6R-benzylpenicilloic acid
benzylpenilloic acid (II)
H2S
D-penicillamine Hg2+ complex
D-Penicillamine

(b)

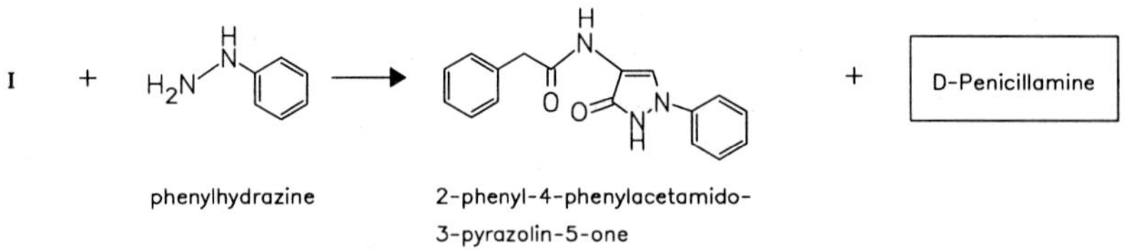
I
phenylhydrazine
2-phenyl-4-phenylacetamido-3-pyrazolin-5-one
D-Penicillamine

total synthetic

(c)

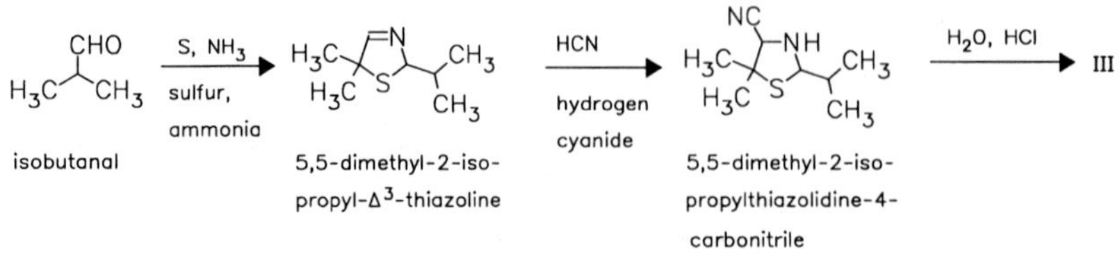
S, NH3
sulfur, ammonia
HCN
hydrogen cyanide
H2O, HCl
III
isobutanal
5,5-dimethyl-2-isopropyl-Δ3-thiazoline
5,5-dimethyl-2-isopropylthiazolidine-4-carbonitrile

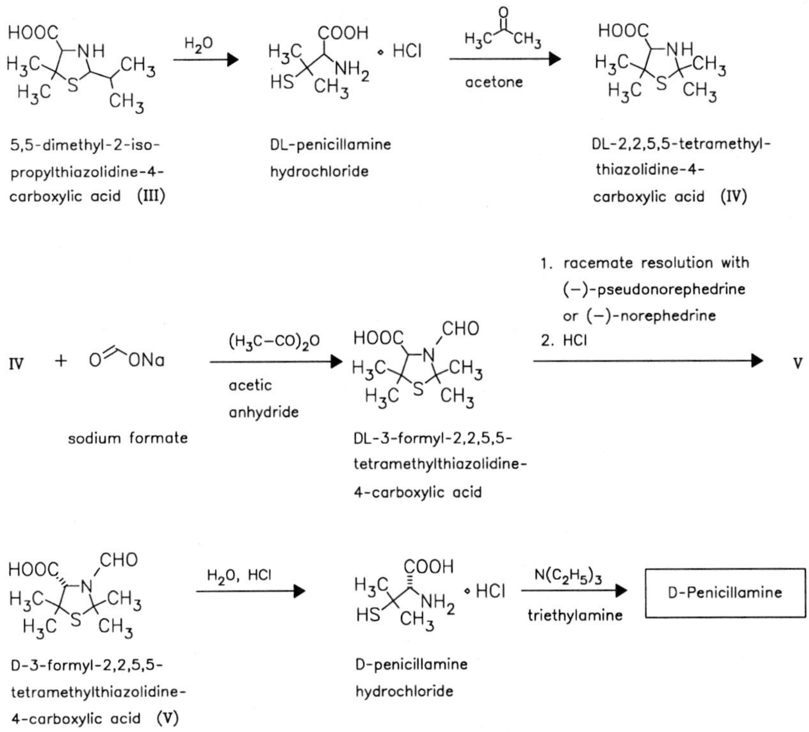

HOOC, H$_3$C—NH, H$_3$C—S, CH$_3$, CH$_3$ (5,5-dimethyl-2-isopropylthiazolidine-4-carboxylic acid (III))

$\xrightarrow{H_2O}$

COOH, H$_3$C, NH$_2$, HS CH$_3$ · HCl (DL-penicillamine hydrochloride)

$\xrightarrow[\text{acetone}]{H_3C\text{-CO-}CH_3}$

HOOC, H$_3$C—NH, H$_3$C—S, CH$_3$, CH$_3$ (DL-2,2,5,5-tetramethyl-thiazolidine-4-carboxylic acid (IV))

IV + O ONa (sodium formate)

$\xrightarrow[\substack{\text{acetic}\\ \text{anhydride}}]{(H_3C\text{-CO})_2O}$

HOOC, CHO, N, H$_3$C, CH$_3$, H$_3$C—S—CH$_3$ (DL-3-formyl-2,2,5,5-tetramethylthiazolidine-4-carboxylic acid)

1. racemate resolution with (−)-pseudonorephedrine or (−)-norephedrine
2. HCl

$\longrightarrow$ V

HOOC, CHO, N, H$_3$C, CH$_3$, H$_3$C—S—CH$_3$ (D-3-formyl-2,2,5,5-tetramethylthiazolidine-4-carboxylic acid (V))

$\xrightarrow{H_2O,\ HCl}$

COOH, H$_3$C, NH$_2$, HS CH$_3$ · HCl (D-penicillamine hydrochloride)

$\xrightarrow[\text{triethylamine}]{N(C_2H_5)_3}$

D-Penicillamine

Reference(s):

a GB 854 339 (Distillers Co.; appl. 22.8.1957; valid from 23.7.1958).
US 3 281 461 (Squibb; 25.10.1966; appl. 7.11.1963).
DAS 2 114 329 (Heyl & Co., appl. 24.3.1971).
DOS 2 413 185 (Heyl & Co., appl. 19.3.1974).
similar process (with N,N'-diphenylethylenediamine):
DOS 2 728 870 (Taisho; appl. 27.6.1977; J-prior. 10.7.1976, 30.12.1976).
US 4 150 240 (Taisho; 17.4.1979; J-prior. 10.7.1976).
b DOS 2 512 608 (Pliva; appl. 21.3.1975; YU-prior. 8.4.1974).
DOS 2 605 563 (Pliva; appl. 12.2.1976; YU-prior. 14.2.1975).
c DOS 1 795 299 (Degussa; appl. 6.9.1968).
DOS 1 795 297 (Degussa; appl. 6.9.1968).
DOS 2 032 952 (Degussa; appl. 3.7.1970).
DOS 2 123 232 (Degussa; appl. 11.5.1971).
DOS 2 156 601 (Degussa; appl. 15.11.1971).
DOS 2 335 990 (Degussa; appl. 14.7.1973).
DOS 2 138 122 (Degussa; appl. 30.7.1971).
DOS 2 258 411 (Degussa; appl. 29.11.1972).
DOS 2 304 055 (Degussa; appl. 27.1.1973).

Formulation(s):   cps. 300 mg; f. c. tabl. 150 mg, 300 mg

Trade Name(s):

D:	Metalcaptase (Heyl)	GB: Distamine (Dista)
	Trisorcin (Merckle)	Pendramine (ASTA
	Trolovol (ASTA Medica	Medica)
	AWD)	I: Pemine (Lilly)
F:	Trolovol (Bayer-Pharma)	J: D-Penicillamine (Takeda)

USA: Cuprimine (Merck Sharp & Dohme)
Depen (Wallace)

Penimepicycline
(Mepenicycline)

ATC: J01AA10
Use: antibiotic

RN: 4599-60-4   MF: $C_{29}H_{38}N_4O_9 \cdot C_{16}H_{18}N_2O_5S$ MW: 937.04   EINECS: 225-002-0
LD$_{50}$:   342 mg/kg (M, i.v.); 3 g/kg (M, p.o.);
345 mg/kg (R, i.v.); 3990 mg/kg (R, p.o.)
CN: [2S-(2α,5α,6β)]-3,3-dimethyl-7-oxo-6-[(phenoxyacetyl)amino]-4-thia-1-azabicyclo[3.2.0]heptane-2-carboxylic acid compd. with [4S-(4α,4aα,5aα,6β,12aα)]-4-(dimethylamino)-1,4,4a,5,5a,6,11,12a-octahydro-3,6,10,12,12a-pentahydroxy-N-[[4-(2-hydroxyethyl)-1-piperazinyl]methyl]-6-methyl-1,11-dioxo-2-naphthacenecarboxamide (1:1)

Pipacycline

RN: 1110-80-1   MF: $C_{29}H_{38}N_4O_9$ MW: 586.64   EINECS: 214-176-3
LD$_{50}$:   188 mg/kg (M, i.v.)
CN: [4S-(4α,4aα,5aα,6β,12aα)]-4-(dimethylamino)-1,4,4a,5,5a,6,11,12a-octahydro-3,6,10,12,12a-pentahydroxy-N-[[4-(2-hydroxyethyl)-1-piperazinyl]methyl]-6-methyl-1,11-dioxo-2-naphthacenecarboxamide

tetracycline   formaldehyde   1-(2-hydroxyethyl)-
piperazine   →   Pipacycline

Pipacycline   phenoxymethylpenicillin   →   Penimepicycline

Penimepicycline

Reference(s):
pipacycline:
GB 888 968 (E.R.A.S.M.E.; appl. 31.3.1959)

penimepicycline:
GB 891 004 (E.R.A.S.M.E.; appl. 31.3.1959)
GB 897 826 (Soc. d'Etudes de Recherches et d'Applications Scientifiques et Medicals E.R.A.S.M.E.; appl. 17.3.1960).

Trade Name(s):

F: Penetracyne Midy (Clin-
    Midy); wfm
I: Idrociclin (Biagini); wfm
    Lisomicina (Borromeo);
    wfm
    Nikeciclina (Panther-Osfa
    Chemie); wfm
    Penetracyn (Midy); wfm

Peniltetra 500 (Panther-
Osfa Chemie); wfm
Prestociclina (Chemil);
wfm
Singramicina (Mitim); wfm
pipacycline
Boniciclina (Boniscontro &
Gazzone); wfm

Sieromicin (Sierochimica);
wfm
Tetrasolvina (Nouvo Cons.
Sanit. Naz.); wfm
Valtomicina (Midy; as
guajacol glycolate)

Penmesterol
(Penmestrol)

ATC: G03B
Use: androgen

RN: 67-81-2 MF: $C_{25}H_{38}O_2$ MW: 370.58 EINECS: 200-670-6
CN: (17β)-3-(cyclopentyloxy)-17-methylandrosta-3,5-dien-17-ol

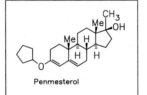

3,17-dioxo-4-androstene

1. HC(OC₂H₅)₃, H₃C-⟨⟩-SO₃H
2. ⟨⟩-OH

1. orthoformic acid triethyl ester
2. cyclopentyl alcohol

3-cyclopentyloxy-17-oxo-3,5-
androstadiene (I)

I + H₃C—MgBr →

methylmagnesium
bromide

Penmesterol

Reference(s):

FR-M 568 (Francesco Vismara; appl. 31.8.1960; D-prior. 4.5.1959; GB-prior. 15.10.1959).
US 3 019 241 (A. Ercoli; 30.1.1962; D-prior. 4.5.1959).

alternative synthesis:

DAS 1 159 940 (Francesco Vismara; appl. 10.7.1961; I-prior. 9.5.1961) addition to DE 1 119 264.

Trade Name(s):

F: Pandrocine (Spécia); wfm

Pentaerythrityl tetranitrate
(Pentanitrolum)

ATC: A06AD14
Use: coronary vasodilator

RN: 78-11-5 MF: $C_5H_8N_4O_{12}$ MW: 316.14 EINECS: 201-084-3
LD₅₀: >5 g/kg (M, i.p.)
CN: 2,2-bis[(nitrooxy)methyl]-1,3-propanediol dinitrate (ester)

pentaerythritol   94% HNO$_3$ Pentaerythrityl tetranitrate

Reference(s):
US 2 370 437 (Du Pont; 1945; prior. 1943).

Formulation(s):   drg. 40 mg; s. r. tabl. 80 mg; tabl. 50 mg, 80 mg

Trade Name(s):

D: Dilcoran 80 (Gödecke);
      wfm
      and following combination
      preparations:
      Adenolanat (Herbrand);
      wfm
      Adenopurin Herbrand
      (Herbrand); wfm
      Dilcoran 80 S Retard
      (Gödecke); wfm
      Gilucor (Giulini); wfm
      Govil (Stada); wfm
      Klimax-H Taeschner, -N
      Taeschner (Taeschner);
      wfm
      Nirason (Ravensberg); wfm
      Nitro-Crataegutt
      (Schwabe); wfm

F: Nitrodex (Dexo)
GB: Mycardol (Sanofi
      Winthrop)
I: Ajmetril (Inverni della
      Beffa)-comb.
      Peritrate Sincron.
      (Teofarma)

      Nitro-Novodigal
      (Beiersdorf); wfm
      Nitro-Sandolanid (Sandoz);
      wfm
      Opticardon (UCB); wfm
      Pentaneural (Wyeth); wfm
      Pentrium (Hoffmann-La
      Roche); wfm
      Pheracor (Kanoldt); wfm
      Stenoppressin (Efeka);
      wfm
      VisanoCor (Kade); wfm

J: Hasethrol (Shionogi)
      Hypothurol (Nissin)
      Pectolex (Shionogi)
USA: Duotrate (Marion); wfm
      Metranil Duracap (Meyer);
      wfm
      Neo-Corovas (Amfre-
      Grant); wfm
      Pentaerythritol Tetranitrate
      (Philips Roxane); wfm
      Pentritol (Armour); wfm
      Perispan (USV); wfm
      Peritrate (Parke Davis;
      Warner Chilcott); wfm
      SK-PETN (Smith Kline &
      French); wfm
      Vasitol (Rowell); wfm

Pentagastrin

ATC: V04CG04
Use: gastric secretion diagnostic

RN: 5534-95-2   MF: C$_{37}$H$_{49}$N$_7$O$_9$S   MW: 767.91   EINECS: 226-889-7
CN: *N*-[(1,1-dimethylethoxy)carbonyl]-β-alanyl-L-tryptophyl-L-methionyl-L-α-aspartyl-L-phenylalaninamide

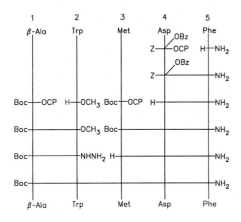

	1	2	3	4	5
	β-Ala	Trp	Met	Asp	Phe
				Z—⟨OBz / OCP	H—NH₂
				Z—⟨OBz	NH₂
	Boc—OCP	H—OCH₃	Boc—OCP	H—	NH₂
	Boc—	OCH₃	Boc—		NH₂
	Boc—	NHNH₂	H—		NH₂
	Boc—				NH₂
	β-Ala	Trp	Met	Asp	Phe

Boc:

Bz:

OCP:

Pentagastrin

Reference(s):
Davey, J.M. et al.: J. Chem. Soc. C (JSOOAX) **1966**, 555.
US 3 896 103 (ICI; 22.7.1975; GB-prior. 25.6.1964, 9.3.1965).

Formulation(s):   amp. 0.25 mg/2 ml

Trade Name(s):
D: Gastrodiagnost (Merck);   GB: Peptavlon (ICI); wfm   USA: Peptavlon (Wyeth-Ayerst)
     wfm   J: Pentagastrin (Sumitomo
F: Peptavlon (Zeneca)   Chem.)

Pentagestrone acetate

(Pentagestroni acetas)

ATC: G03
Use: progestogen

RN: 1178-60-5   MF: C₂₈H₄₀O₄   MW: 440.62
CN: 17-(acetyloxy)-3-(cyclopentyloxy)pregna-3,5-dien-20-one

17-acetoxyprogesterone   cyclopentanol   Pentagestrone acetate

Reference(s):
DAS 1 167 830 (Francesco Vismara; appl. 18.1.1961; I-prior. 6.2.1960).

alternative syntheses:
US 3 019 241 (A. Ercoli; 30.1.1962; D-prior. 4.5.1959).
DAS 1 159 940 (Francesco Vismara; appl. 10.7.1961; I-prior. 9.5.1961) addition to DE 1 119 264.

Trade Name(s):
I: Gestovis (Vister); wfm

Pentamidine

ATC: P01CX01
Use: chemotherapeutic (protozoal
        infections)

RN: 100-33-4   MF: $C_{19}H_{24}N_4O_2$ MW: 340.43   EINECS: 202-841-0
LD$_{50}$: 50 mg/kg (M, i.p.)
CN: 4,4'-[1,5-pentanediylbis(oxy)]bis[benzenecarboximidamide]

diisethionate
RN: 140-64-7   MF: $C_{19}H_{24}N_4O_2 \cdot 2C_2H_6O_4S$ MW: 592.69   EINECS: 205-424-1
LD$_{50}$: 15.1 mg/kg (M, i.v.)

4-hydroxybenzo-   1,5-dibromo-   1,5-bis(4-cyanophenoxy)-
nitrile   pentane   pentane (I)

Pentamidine

Reference(s):
GB 507 565 (May & Baker; appl. 1938).
Ashley, J.N. et al.: J. Chem. Soc. (JCSOA9) **1942**, 103.

Formulation(s):   vial 120 mg, 300 mg

Trade Name(s):

D:	Pentacarinat (Glaxo Wellcome; Rhône-Poulenc Rorer)		Pneumopent aerosol (Italchimici)		Pentam 300 (Lyphomed); wfm
F:	Pentacarinat (Bellon)	J:	Benambax (Rhône-Poulenc-Chugai)		Pneumopent (Rhône-Poulenc Rorer); wfm
GB:	Pentacarinat (GHC)	USA:	Pentacarinate (Rhône-Poulenc Rorer); wfm		
I:	Pentacarinat (Rhône-Poulenc Rorer)		Pentam (Fujisawa); wfm		

Pentapiperide

ATC: N04A
Use: antispasmodic, anticholinergic

RN: 7009-54-3   MF: $C_{18}H_{27}NO_2$ MW: 289.42   EINECS: 230-286-4
CN: α-(1-methylpropyl)benzeneacetic acid 1-methyl-4-piperidinyl ester

hydrogen fumarate (1:1)
RN: 635-32-5   MF: $C_{18}H_{27}NO_2 \cdot C_4H_4O_4$ MW: 405.49   EINECS: 211-233-4
methyl sulfate
RN: 7681-80-3   MF: $C_{19}H_{30}NO_2 \cdot CH_3O_4S$ MW: 415.55   EINECS: 231-678-8
LD_{50}:   7500 μg/kg (M, i.v.); 435 mg/kg (M, p.o.);
         720 mg/kg (R, p.o.)

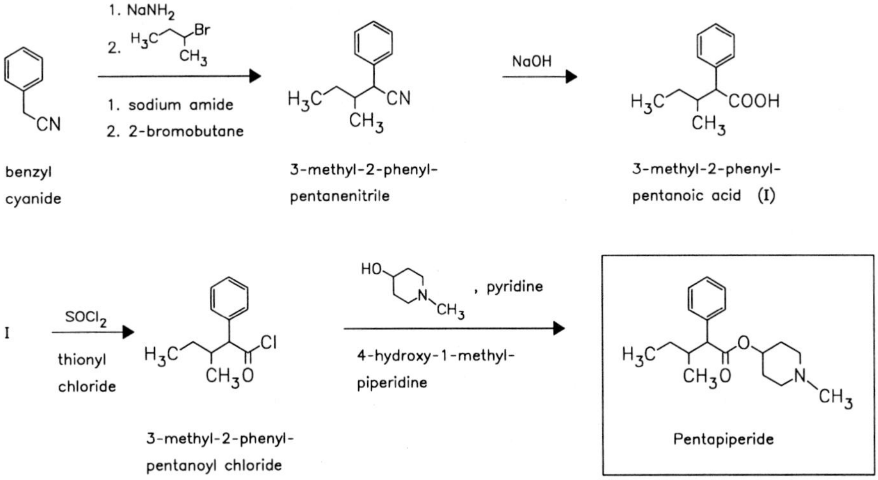

benzyl cyanide

3-methyl-2-phenyl-pentanenitrile

3-methyl-2-phenyl-pentanoic acid (I)

3-methyl-2-phenyl-pentanoyl chloride

4-hydroxy-1-methyl-piperidine

Pentapiperide

Reference(s):
US 2 987 517 (Cilag-Chemie AG; 6.6.1961; D-prior. 20.4.1954).

Trade Name(s):

F:	Cryléne (Auclair); wfm	Togestal (Biosedra)-comb.; wfm	I:	Crilin (Ayerst); wfm
			USA:	Perium (Rover); wfm

Pentazocine

ATC: N02AD01
Use: analgesic

RN: 359-83-1   MF: $C_{19}H_{27}NO$ MW: 285.43   EINECS: 206-634-6
LD_{50}: 19.8 mg/kg (M, i.v.); 205 mg/kg (M, p.o.);
21 mg/kg (R, i.v.); 1110 mg/kg (R, p.o.)
CN: (2α,6α,11R*)-1,2,3,4,5,6-hexahydro-6,11-dimethyl-3-(3-methyl-2-butenyl)-2,6-methano-3-benzazocin-8-ol

hydrochloride
RN: 2276-52-0   MF: $C_{19}H_{27}NO \cdot HCl$ MW: 321.89   EINECS: 218-896-9
LD_{50}: 126 mg/kg (M, s.c.)
lactate (1:1)
RN: 17146-95-1   MF: $C_{19}H_{27}NO \cdot C_3H_6O_3$ MW: 375.51   EINECS: 241-209-9
LD_{50}: 103 mg/kg (M, i.p.)

3,4-dimethyl-   methyl   1,3,4-trimethyl-   2-(4-methoxybenzyl)-
pyridine   iodide   pyridinium   1,3,4-trimethyl-1,2-
                               iodide   dihydropyridine (I)

2-(4-methoxybenzyl)-   2'-hydroxy-2,5,9-
1,3,4-trimethyl-1,2,5,6-   trimethylbenzo-
tetrahydropyridine   6-morphen

2'-hydroxy-5,9-   1-bromo-3-methyl-   Pentazocine
dimethylbenzo-   2-butene
6-morphen (II)

Reference(s):
BE 611 000 (Sterling Drug; appl. 30.11.1961; USA-prior. 1.12.1960).
Archer, S. et al.: J. Med. Chem. (JMCMAR) **7**, 123 (1964).

Formulation(s):   amp. 30 mg/ml; cps. 50 mg, 56.4 mg; suppos. 50 mg; tabl. 25 mg

Trade Name(s):
D: Fortal (Winthrop)   GB: Fortagesic (Sanofi   Fortral (Sterwin; as
F: Fortal (Sanofi Winthrop)   Winthrop; as   hydrochloride)
                                       hydrochloride)

I: Pentalgina (Pierrel)   Talwintab (Sanofi   Pentagin (Sankyo)
        Talwin (Pierrel)   Winthrop)   USA: Talacen (Sanofi)
        Talwin (Sanofi Winthrop)   J: Peltazon (Grelan)   Talwin (Sanofi)

Pentetrazol

(Pentylenetetrazol)

ATC: R07AB03
Use: analgesic, circulatory stimulant

RN: 54-95-5   MF: $C_6H_{10}N_4$ MW: 138.17   EINECS: 200-219-3
LD_{50}: 31.4 mg/kg (M, i.v.); 88 mg/kg (M, p.o.);
        45 mg/kg (R, i.v.); 140 mg/kg (R, p.o.)
CN: 6,7,8,9-tetrahydro-5H-tetrazolo[1,5-a]azepine

ε–capro-   dimethyl   2-methoxy-Δ¹-   2-hydrazino-Δ¹-
lactam   sulfate   tetrahydroazepine   tetrahydroazepine (I)

Pentetrazol

Reference(s):
Schmidt, K.F.: Ber. Dtsch. Chem. Ges. (BDCGAS) **57**, 704 (1924).
Stolle, R.: Ber. Dtsch. Chem. Ges. (BDCGAS) **63**, 1032 (1930).

alternative syntheses (azide method):
DRP 427 858 (Knoll; appl. 1923).
DRP 439 041 (Knoll; appl. 1924).
DRP 455 585 (Knoll; appl. 1925).
DRP 521 870 (Knoll; appl. 1929).
DRP 537 739 (Knoll; appl. 1928).
DRP 538 981 (Knoll; appl. 1926).
DRP 543 025 (Knoll; appl. 1927).
DRP 545 850 (Knoll; appl. 1927).
DRP 574 943 (Knoll; appl. 1932).
DRP 576 327 (Knoll; appl. 1930).
DRP 611 692 (Chinoin; appl. 1934).

Formulation(s):   drops 100 mg/g

Trade Name(s):
D: Afpred (Hefa-Frenon)-   Poikiloton (Lomapharm)-   Tetracor (Chinoin); wfm
        comb.; wfm   comb.; wfm   Tetrazol (Lisapharma);
        Cardaminol (Reinecke)-   Sympatocard (Boehringer   wfm
        comb.; wfm   Ing.)-comb.; wfm   J: Cardiazol (Sankyo)
        Cardiazol (Knoll); wfm   F: Désintex-Pentazol (M.   Pentazol (Yashima)
        Indovert (Dolorgiet)-comb.;   Richard); wfm   USA: Analeptone (Reed &
        wfm   I: Cardiazol (Knoll); wfm   Carnrick); wfm
        Jasivita (Bolder)-comb.;   Cardiazol Paracodina   Benizol (ICI)-comb. with
        wfm   (Knoll)-comb.; wfm   nicotinic acid; wfm

Geroniazol (Philips
Roxane)-comb. with
nicotinic acid; wfm
Metrazol (Knoll); wfm

Nico-Metrazol (Knoll)-
comb. with nicotinic acid;
wfm
Rovite Tonic (Rotex); wfm

Vita-Metrazol (Knoll)-
comb. with vitamin B
complex; wfm

Penthienate methobromide

(Penthienate bromide)

ATC: A03AB
Use: antispasmodic

RN: 60-44-6 MF: $C_{18}H_{30}BrNO_3S$ MW: 420.41 EINECS: 200-478-2
LD$_{50}$: 16 mg/kg (M, i.v.); 2080 mg/kg (M, p.o.)
CN: 2-[(cyclopentylhydroxy-2-thienylacetyl)oxy]-N,N-diethyl-N-methylethanaminium bromide

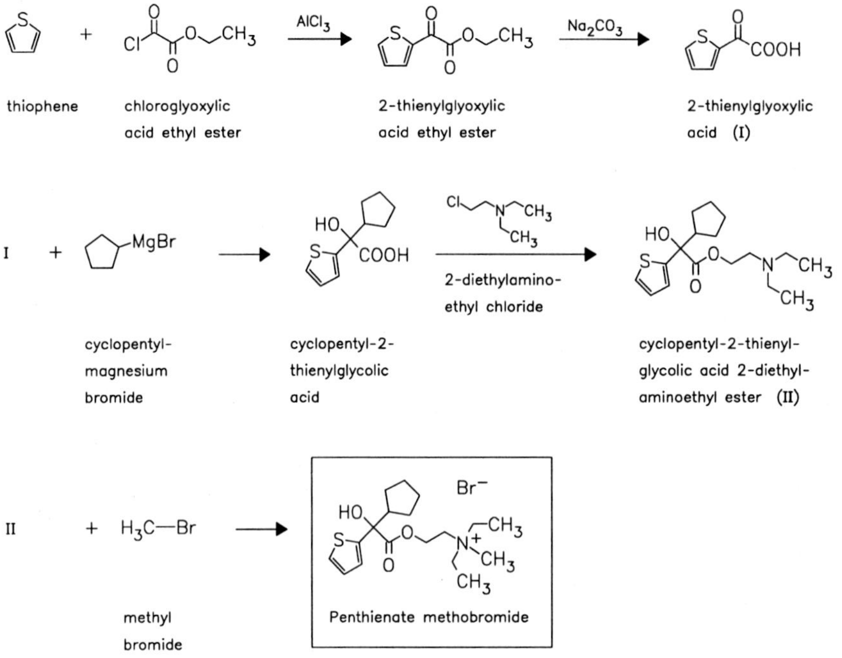

| thiophene | chloroglyoxylic acid ethyl ester | 2-thienylglyoxylic acid ethyl ester | 2-thienylglyoxylic acid (I) |

| cyclopentyl-magnesium bromide | cyclopentyl-2-thienylglycolic acid | 2-diethylamino-ethyl chloride | cyclopentyl-2-thienyl-glycolic acid 2-diethyl-aminoethyl ester (II) |

| methyl bromide | Penthienate methobromide |

Reference(s):
US 2 541 634 (Univ. of Michigan; 1951; prior. 1946).

Formulation(s):   tabl. 5 mg

Trade Name(s):
GB: Monodral (Winthrop); wfm   J: Monodral (Nakataki)   USA: Monodral (Winthrop); wfm

Pentifylline

(Hexyltheobromine)

ATC: C04AD01
Use: vasodilator

RN: 1028-33-7 MF: $C_{13}H_{20}N_4O_2$ MW: 264.33 EINECS: 213-842-0
LD$_{50}$: 1040 mg/kg (M, p.o.)
CN: 1-hexyl-3,7-dihydro-3,7-dimethyl-1H-purine-2,6-dione

theobromine   hexyl chloride   Pentifylline

Reference(s):
DE 860 217 (Chemische Werke Albert; appl. 1950).

alternative synthesis:
SU 202 152 (K. Chkhikoadze et al.; appl. 17.9.1966).

combination with inositol hexanicotinate:
GB 1 129 134 (Sterling Winthrop; valid from 3.11.1965; prior. 4.11.1964).

combination with nicotinic acid:
GB 815 969 (Chemische Werke Albert; valid from 1958; USA-prior. 1957).

use for stabilization of vitamins:
DOS 1 810 705 (Chemische Werke Albert; appl. 25.11.1968).

retard form:
DE 1 617 418 (Chemische Werke Albert; appl. 16.12.1967).

oral pharmaceutical formulation:
DOS 2 520 978 (Hoechst; appl. 10.5.1975).

Formulation(s):   s. r. drg. 400 mg

Trade Name(s):
D: Cosaldon (Albert-Roussel,   Cosaldon (Albert-Roussel,   J: Tonostan (Tokyo Tanabe)-
      Hoechst)-comb. with   Hoechst)   comb. with nicotinic acid
      retinol palmitate   F: Cosadon (Hoechst)-comb.
                                         with nicotinic acid; wfm

---

Pentobarbital
(Mebumalum; Pentobarbitone)

ATC: N05CA01
Use: hypnotic

RN: 76-74-4   MF: $C_{11}H_{18}N_2O_3$ MW: 226.28   EINECS: 200-983-8
LD_{50}:   65 mg/kg (M, i.v.); 170 mg/kg (M, p.o.);
      125 mg/kg (R, p.o.);
      50 mg/kg (dog, i.v.)
CN: 5-ethyl-5-(1-methylbutyl)-2,4,6(1*H*,3*H*,5*H*)-pyrimidinetrione

monosodium salt
RN: 57-33-0   MF: $C_{11}H_{17}N_2NaO_3$ MW: 248.26   EINECS: 200-323-9
LD_{50}:   81 mg/kg (M, i.v.); 239 mg/kg (M, p.o.);
      65 mg/kg (R, i.v.); 118 mg/kg (R, p.o.);
      65 mg/kg (dog, p.o.)
calcium salt
RN: 7563-42-0   MF: $C_{11}H_{18}N_2O_3 \cdot xCa$ MW: unspecified   EINECS: 231-460-2

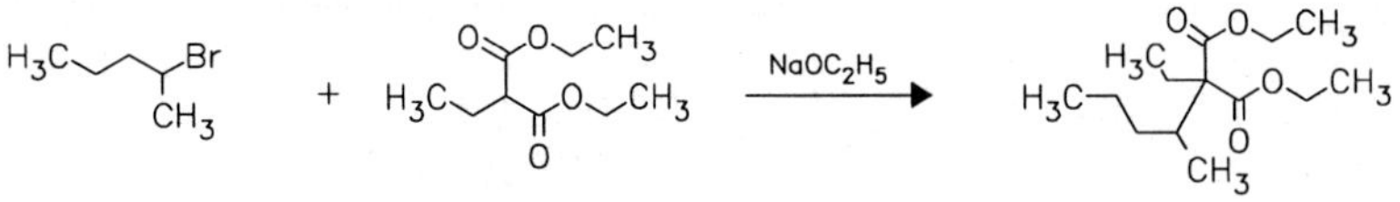

2-bromopentane

ethylmalonic acid
diethyl ester

ethyl(1-methylbutyl)-
malonic acid
diethyl ester (I)

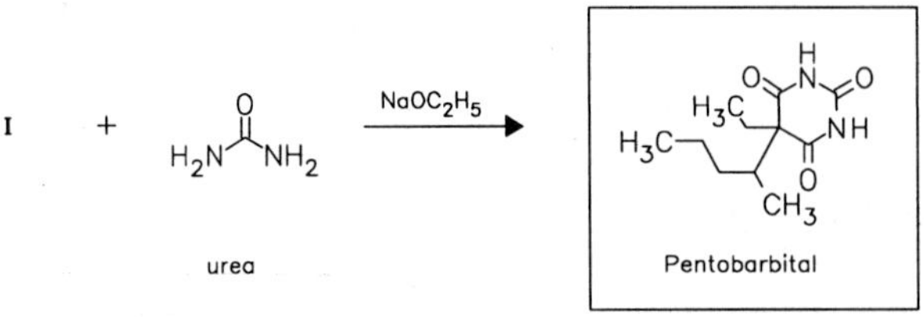

urea

Pentobarbital

Reference(s):
DRP 293 163 (Bayer; 1915).
GB 650 354 (Geigy; appl. 1948) - method.

Formulation(s):   cps. 50 mg, 100 mg; sol. 50 mg/ml; suppos. 60 mg, 120 mg (as sodium salt)

Trade Name(s):

D:	Isoptin S (Knoll)-comb.; wfm	
	Migrexa (Sanorania)-comb.; wfm	
	Nembutal (Abbott); wfm	
	Neodorm (Minden); wfm	
	Norkotral (Desitin)-comb.; wfm	

Omka-Nacht Tabletten
(Heyden)-comb.; wfm
Praecicalm (Molimin);
wfm
Priatan (Minden)-comb.;
wfm
Repocal (Desitin); wfm

F: Nembutal (Abbott); wfm
GB: Nembutal (Abbott); wfm

I: Isoptin S (Knoll)-comb.;
wfm
Nembutal (Abbott); wfm
J: Mintal (Tanabe)
Nembutal (Dainippon)
USA: Nembutal (Abbott)
Pentobarbital Sodium
(Wyeth-Ayerst)

Pentorex

(Phenpentermine)

ATC: A08A
Use: appetite depressant

RN: 434-43-5   MF: $C_{11}H_{17}N$ MW: 163.26   EINECS: 207-102-6
CN: α,α,β-trimethylbenzeneethanamine

hydrogen tartrate (2:1)
RN: 22876-60-4   MF: $C_{11}H_{17}N \cdot 1/2C_4H_6O_6$ MW: 476.61

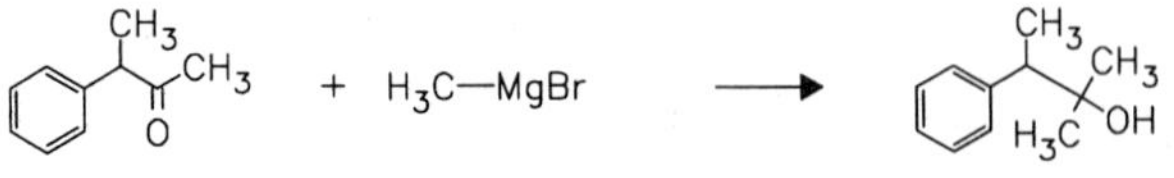

3-oxo-2-phenyl-
butane

methylmagnesium
bromide

3-methyl-2-phenyl-
3-butanol (I)

I + NaCN →[CH₃COOH, H₂SO₄] 3-formylamino-3-methyl-2-phenyl-butane →[1. HCl 2. NaOH] Pentorex

sodium
cyanide

3-formylamino-3-
methyl-2-phenyl-
butane

Pentorex

Reference(s):
FR-M 2 594 (Nordmark-Werke; appl. 17.4.1963; D-prior. 13.11.1962).

Trade Name(s):
D: Modatrop (Nordmark);   F: Liprodéne (Anphar); wfm
      wfm

Pentostatin

(Deoxycoformycin; Co-vidarabine)

ATC: L01XX08
Use: adenosine deaminase inhibitor (for
        hairy cell leucemia treatment)

RN: 53910-25-1   MF: $C_{11}H_{16}N_4O_4$ MW: 268.27
LD_{50}:   122 mg/kg (M, i.v.); 227 mg/kg (M, p.o.)
CN: (*R*)-3-(2-deoxy-β-D-*erythro*-pentofuranosyl)-3,6,7,8-tetrahydroimidazo[4,5-*d*][1,3]diazepin-8-ol

Fermentation of *streptomyces antibioticus* MRRL.

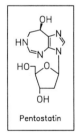

Pentostatin

Reference(s):
US 3 923 785 (Parke Davis; 2.12.1975; appl. 22.4.1974).
DE 2 517 596 (Parke Davis; appl. 30.10.1975; USA-prior. 22.4.1974).

Formulation(s):   vial 10 mg

Trade Name(s):
D: Nipent (Lederle)   J: Coforin (Kaketsuken-
F: Nipent (Wyeth-Lederle)   Nippon Kayaku)
GB: Nipent (Wyeth)   USA: Nipent (SuperGen)

Pentoxifylline

ATC: C04AD03
Use: vasodilator

RN: 6493-05-6   MF: $C_{13}H_{18}N_4O_3$ MW: 278.31   EINECS: 229-374-5
LD_{50}:   108 mg/kg (M, i.v.); 1225 mg/kg (M, p.o.);
        231 mg/kg (R, i.v.); 1170 mg/kg (R, p.o.)
CN: 3,7-dihydro-3,7-dimethyl-1-(5-oxohexyl)-1*H*-purine-2,6-dione

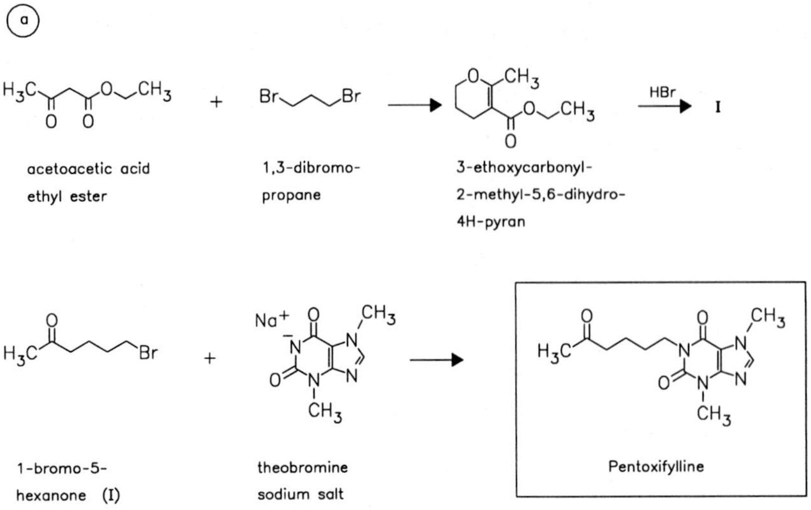

a

| acetoacetic acid ethyl ester | 1,3-dibromo-propane | 3-ethoxycarbonyl-2-methyl-5,6-dihydro-4H-pyran |

| 1-bromo-5-hexanone (I) | theobromine sodium salt | Pentoxifylline |

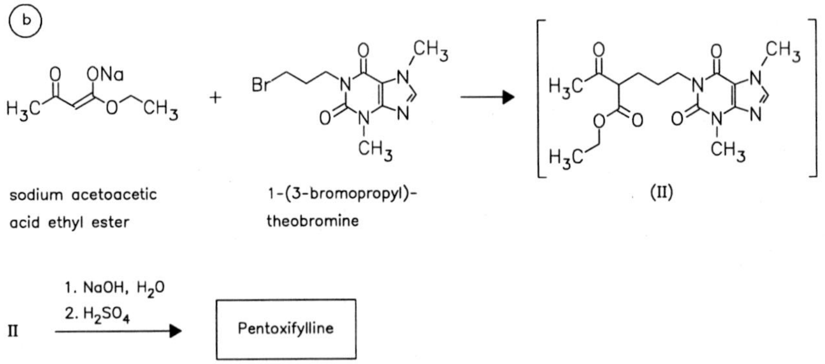

b

| sodium acetoacetic acid ethyl ester | 1-(3-bromopropyl)-theobromine | (II) |

II → Pentoxifylline

1. NaOH, H_2O
2. H_2SO_4

Reference(s):
DE 1 235 320 (Chemische Werke Albert; appl. 5.9.1964).
US 3 422 107 (Chemische Werke Albert; 14.1.1969; D-prior. 30.8.1965, 24.7.1965, 10.7.1965, 2.7.1965, 5.9.1964).
US 3 737 433 (Chemische Werke Albert; 5.6.1973; D-prior. 5.9.1964, 2.7.1965, 10.7.1965, 24.7.1965).
Mohler, W.; Söder, A.: Arzneim.-Forsch. (ARZNAD) **21**, 1159 (1971).
Mohler, W. et al.: Arch. Pharm. (Weinheim, Ger.) (ARPMAS) **299**, 448 (1966).

alternative syntheses:
DOS 2 330 741 (Chemische Werke Albert; appl. 16.6.1973).
DOS 2 302 772 (Chemische Werke Albert; appl. 20.1.1973).
DOS 2 234 202 (Chemische Werke Albert; appl. 12.7.1972).
JP-appl. 54 112 893 (Kohjin; appl. 21.2.1978).

pharmaceutical formulation:
DE 1 617 418 (Chemische Werke Albert; appl. 16.12.1967).
DOS 2 520 978 (Hoechst AG; appl. 10.5.1975).

use as dissolving intermediary:
DE 1 250 968 (Chemische Werke Albert; appl. 24.7.1965).

Formulation(s):　amp. 100 mg/5 ml, 300 mg/15 ml; drg. 100 mg; f. c. tabl. 400 mg; s. r. cps. 400 mg, 600 mg; s. r. drg. 400 mg; s. r. tabl. 400 mg, 600 mg

Trade Name(s):

D: Claudicat retard (Promonta Lundbeck)
Durapental 400 (durachemie)
Pento AbZ (AbZ-Pharma)
Pentohexal (Hexal)
pentox (ct-Arzneimittel)

Pentoxifyllin-ratiopharm 400 (ratiopharm)
Ralofekt (ASTA Medica AWD)
Rentylin (Rentschler)
Trental (Albert-Roussel, Hoechst)

F: Hatial (Wyeth-Lederle)

Pentoflux (Bouchara)
Torental (Hoechst)
GB: Trental (Hoechst)
I: Trental (Hoechst Marion)
J: Trental (Hoechst)
USA: Trental (Hoechst Marion Roussel)

Pentoxyverine
(Carbetapentane)

ATC: R05DB05
Use: antitussive

RN: 77-23-6   MF: $C_{20}H_{31}NO_3$ MW: 333.47   EINECS: 201-014-1
LD_{50}: 13 mg/kg (M, i.v.); 130 mg/kg (M, p.o.);
150 mg/kg (R, p.o.)
CN: 1-phenylcyclopentanecarboxylic acid 2-[2-(diethylamino)ethoxy]ethyl ester

citrate (1:1)
RN: 23142-01-0   MF: $C_{20}H_{31}NO_3 \cdot C_6H_8O_7$ MW: 525.60   EINECS: 245-449-5
LD_{50}: 38 mg/kg (M, i.v.); 230 mg/kg (M, p.o.);
34 mg/kg (R, i.v.); 810 mg/kg (R, p.o.)
hydrochloride
RN: 1045-21-2   MF: $C_{20}H_{31}NO_3 \cdot HCl$ MW: 369.93

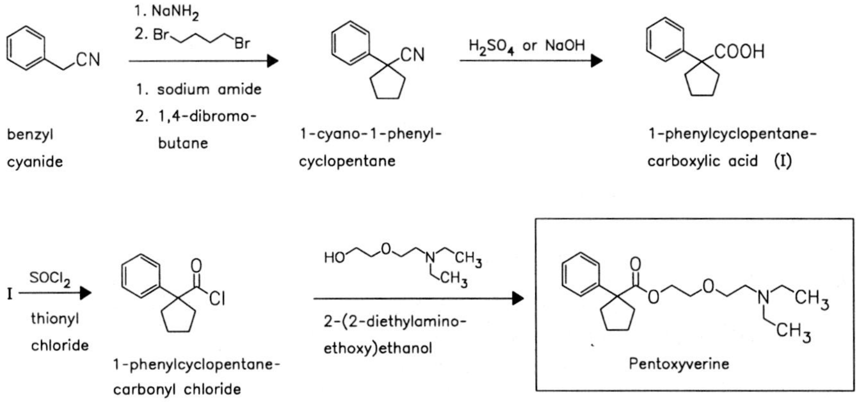

Reference(s):
GB 753 779 (H. Morren; appl. 1954; B-prior. 1953).

Formulation(s): f. c. tabl. 50 mg; cps. 75 mg; drops 30 mg/ml; suppos. 8 mg, 20 mg; syrup 213 mg/100 ml (as citrate); suppos. 8 mg, 20 mg (as base); syrup 150 mg/100 ml (as hydrochloride)

Trade Name(s):

D: Pertix (Hommel)
Sedotussin (Rodleben; UCB; Vedim)-comb. with chlorphenamine hydrogen maleate
Sedotussin (Rodleben; UCB; Vedim)

F: Pectosan Toux Séche (RPR Cooper)
I: Tuclase (UCB)
J: Aslos (Kotani)
Carbeten (Showa Yakuhin)
Culten (Towa)
Kaibohl (Sawai)

Milysted (Nissin Yakuhin)
Takabetane (Takata)
Toclase (Sumitomo)
USA: Rynatuss (Wallace)-comb.

Perazine

ATC: N05AB10
Use: psychosedative

RN: 84-97-9 MF: $C_{20}H_{25}N_3S$ MW: 339.51 EINECS: 201-578-9
LD$_{50}$: 75 mg/kg (M, i.v.); 640 mg/kg (M, p.o.);
80 mg/kg (R, i.v.); 500 mg/kg (R, p.o.)
CN: 10-[3-(4-methyl-1-piperazinyl)propyl]-10H-phenothiazine

dimalonate
RN: 14777-25-4 MF: $C_{20}H_{25}N_3S \cdot 2C_3H_4O_4$ MW: 547.63 EINECS: 238-842-8

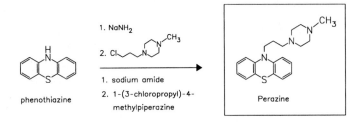

phenothiazine

1. sodium amide
2. 1-(3-chloropropyl)-4-methylpiperazine

Perazine

Reference(s):
DE 1 037 461 (Rhône-Poulenc; appl. 1955; GB-prior. 1954).
Hromatka, O.: Monatsh. Chem. (MOCMB7) **88**, 56 (1957).

Formulation(s): amp. 50 mg/2 ml; drg. 25 mg, 100 mg; f. c. tabl. 25 mg, 100 mg, 200 mg; sol. 44 mg/ml; tabl.
100 mg (as dimalonate)

Trade Name(s):
D: Taxilan (Promonta J: Taxilan (Morishita)
Lundbeck)

Perfluamine

ATC: B05A
Use: blood substitute in combination with
perflunafene

RN: 338-83-0 MF: $C_9F_{21}N$ MW: 521.06 EINECS: 206-420-2
CN: 1,1,2,2,3,3,3-heptafluoro-N,N-bis(heptafluoropropyl)-1-propanamine

mixture with perflunafene
RN: 75216-20-5 MF: unspecified MW: unspecified

HF, e$^-$
electrochemical
fluorination

Perfluamine

Reference(s):
US 2 616 927 (3M; 1952)

medical use as blood substitute:
DOS 2 630 586 (Green Cross; appl. 7.7.1976; USA-prior. 3.2.1976).
US 4 252 827 (Green Cross; 24.2.1981; appl. 3.2.1976).

reduction of tumor metastasis:
EP 201 275 (Alpha Therap. Corp.; appl. 30.4.1986; USA-prior. 9.5.1985).
WO 8 908 459 (Alpha Therap. Corp.; appl. 21.9.1989; USA-prior. 11.3.1988).

Formulation(s):   mixture of perfluamine, perflunafene (3:7), pluronic F-68, yolk phospholipids, glycerol (20 % emulsion)

Trade Name(s):

GB:	Fluosol (Alpha Therap.)- comb. with perflunafene; wfm	USA:	Fluosol (Alpha Therap.; 1990)-comb. with perflunafene; wfm

---

Perflunafene

(Perfluorodecaline)

ATC: B05A
Use: blood substitute in combination with perfluamine

RN: 306-94-5   MF: $C_{10}F_{18}$ MW: 462.07   EINECS: 206-192-4
LD_{50}:   50 mg/kg (M, i.v.)
CN: octadecafluorodecahydronaphthalene

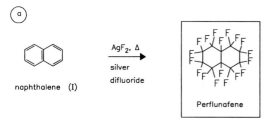

naphthalene   (I)   Perflunafene

Reference(s):
a   McBee, E.T.; Bechtol, L.D.: Ind. Eng. Chem. (IECHAD) **39**, 380 (1947).
      US 2 459 780 (Purdue Research Found.; 1949).
b   JP 1 186 828 (Tokuyama; appl. 16.1.1988).
      Sokolov, S.V. et al.: Zh. Prikl. Khim. (Leningrad) (ZPKHAB) **39**, 362 (1966) [CA (CHABA8) **64**, 19443 (1966)].

additional synthesis:
US 2 487 820 (Purdue Research Found.; 1949).
Sander, M.; Bloeche, W.: Chem.-Ing.-Tech. (CITEAH) **37**, 7 (1965).

Formulation(s):   cf. perfluamine

Pergolide

(LY-127809)

ATC: N04BC02
Use: long acting dopamine D_1 and D_2-
        agonist, antiparkinsonian, prolactin
        release inhibitor

RN: 66104-22-1   MF: $C_{19}H_{26}N_2S$ MW: 314.50
CN: (8β)-8-[(methylthio)methyl]-6-propylergoline

mesylate
RN: 66104-23-2   MF: $C_{19}H_{26}N_2S \cdot CH_4O_3S$ MW: 410.60
LD_{50}:   100 mg/kg (M, i.p.); 54 mg/kg (M, p.o.);
       15 mg/kg (R, p.o.)

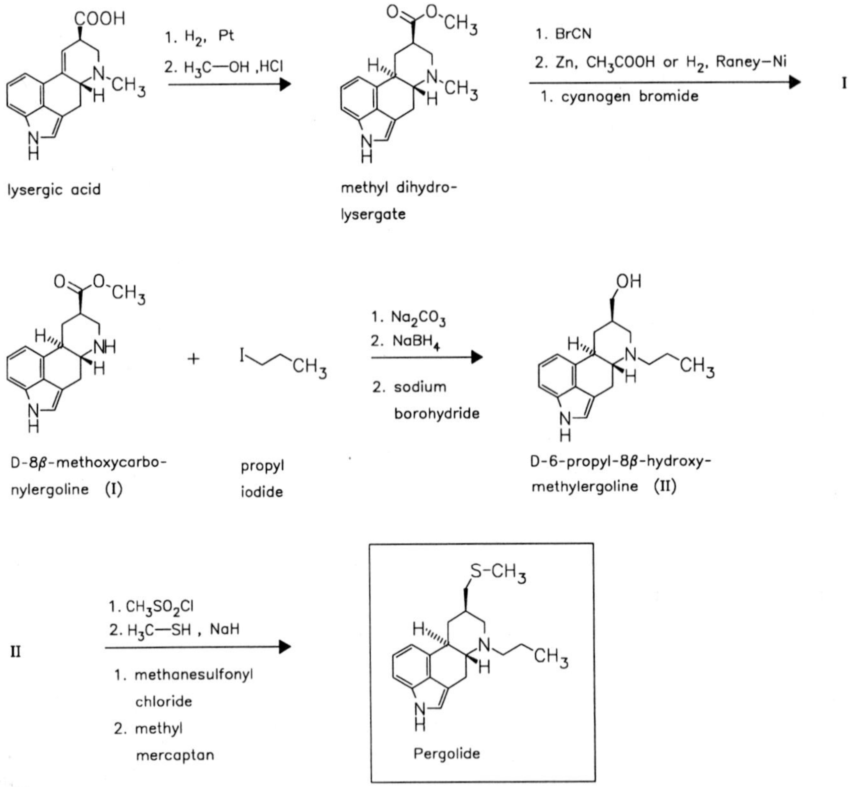

lysergic acid

1. H_2, Pt
2. H_3C—OH , HCl

methyl dihydro-
lysergate

1. BrCN
2. Zn, CH_3COOH or H_2, Raney—Ni

1. cyanogen bromide

I

D-8β-methoxycarbo-
nylergoline (I)

propyl
iodide

1. Na_2CO_3
2. $NaBH_4$

2. sodium
borohydride

D-6-propyl-8β-hydroxy-
methylergoline (II)

II

1. CH_3SO_2Cl
2. H_3C—SH , NaH

1. methanesulfonyl
chloride
2. methyl
mercaptan

Pergolide

Reference(s):
US 4 166 182 (Lilly; 28.8.1979; appl. 8.2.1978).
US 4 180 582 (Lilly; 25.12.1979; appl. 11.1.1979; prior. 8.2.1978).
US 4 202 979 (Lilly; 13.5.1980; appl. 11.1.1979; prior. 8.2.1978).
EP 3 667 (Lilly; appl. 5.2.1979; USA-prior. 8.2.1978).

synthesis of intermediates:
EP 213 850 (Lilly; appl. 14.8.1986; USA-prior. 16.8.1985).

light stabilised pergolide *formulation:*
US 4 797 405 (Lilly; 10.1.1989; appl. 26.10.1987).

Formulation(s):   tabl. 0.05 mg, 0.25 mg, 1 mg (as mesylate)

Trade Name(s):
D: Parkotil (Lilly)   I: Nopar (Lilly)   USA: Permax (Athera)
GB: Celance (Lilly)   J: Permax (Lilly)

Perhexiline

ATC: C08EX02
Use: coronary vasodilator

RN: 6621-47-2   MF: $C_{19}H_{35}N$ MW: 277.50   EINECS: 229-569-5
CN: 2-(2,2-dicyclohexylethyl)piperidine

maleate (1:1)
RN: 6724-53-4   MF: $C_{19}H_{35}N \cdot C_4H_4O_4$ MW: 393.57   EINECS: 229-775-5
LD_{50}:   2641 mg/kg (M, p.o.);
           2150 mg/kg (R, p.o.)

| formic acid ethyl ester | cyclohexyl-magnesium bromide | dicyclohexyl-carbinol | dicyclohexyl ketone (I) |

| 2-picoline (II) | butyl-lithium | 1,1-dicyclohexyl-2-(2-pyridyl)ethanol hydrochloride | 1,1-dicyclohexyl-2-(2-pyridyl)ethylene hydrochloride (III) |

Perhexiline

(b)

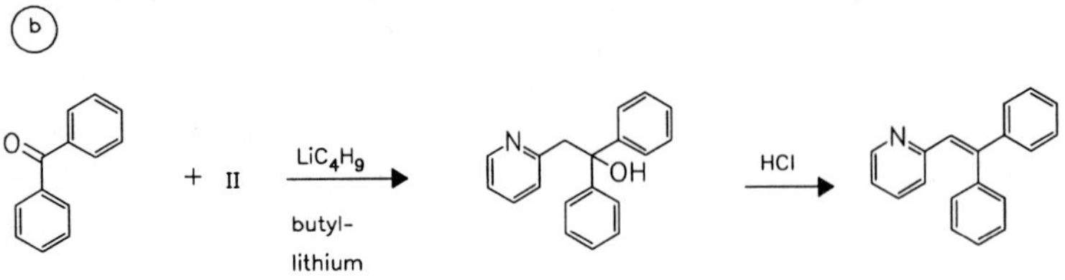

benzophenone   + II   →(LiC₄H₉, butyl-lithium)   1,1-diphenyl-2-(2-pyridyl)ethanol   →(HCl)   1,1-diphenyl-2-(2-pyridyl)ethylene   (IV)

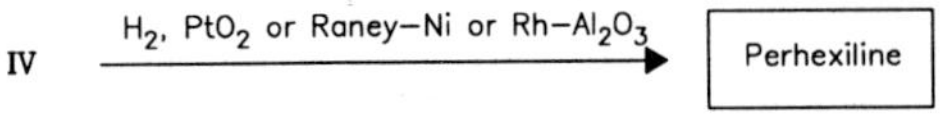

IV   →(H₂, PtO₂ or Raney-Ni or Rh-Al₂O₃)   Perhexiline

Reference(s):

a   US 3 038 905 (Richardson-Merrell; 12.6.1962; prior. 24.5.1960).
FR-M 4 474 (Richardson-Merrell; appl. 20.11.1964; USA-prior. 26.11.1963).
precursor:
GB 912 830 (Richardson-Merrell; appl. 16.5.1961; USA-prior. 24.5.1960).
b   DOS 2 643 473 (B.T.B. Industria Chimica S.p.A.; appl. 27.9.1976; I-prior. 29.9.1975, 7.11.1975).
DOS 2 713 500 (Richardson-Merrell; appl. 26.3.1977; USA-prior. 14.4.1976).
DOS 2 714 081 (Richardson-Merrell; appl. 30.3.1977; USA-prior. 14.4.1976).
US 4 069 222 (Richardson-Merrell; 17.1.1978; appl. 14.4.1976).

Formulation(s):   tabl. 100 mg

Trade Name(s):

D:	Pexid (Merrell); wfm	GB:	Pexid (Merrell); wfm
F:	Pexid (Merrell-Toraude); wfm	I:	Pexid (Merrell); wfm

USA: Pexid (Merrell-National); wfm

Periciazine
(Pericyazine; Propericiazine)

ATC: N05AC01
Use: antipsychotic, neuroleptic

RN: 2622-26-6   MF: $C_{21}H_{23}N_3OS$ MW: 365.50   EINECS: 220-071-3
LD$_{50}$: 27.7 mg/kg (M, i.v.); 530 mg/kg (M, p.o.);
35 mg/kg (R, i.v.); 395 mg/kg (R, p.o.)
CN: 10-[3-(4-hydroxy-1-piperidinyl)propyl]-10H-phenothiazine-2-carbonitrile

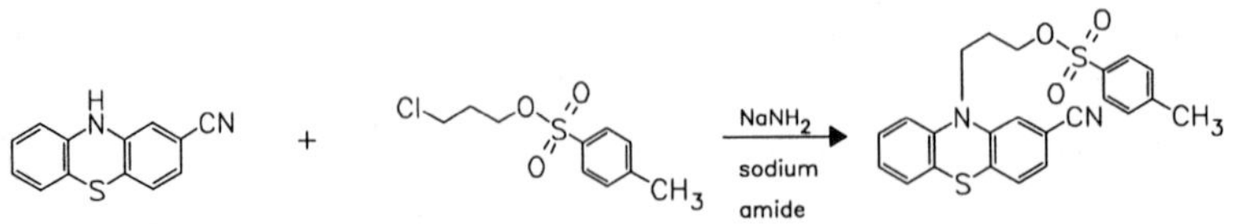

2-cyanophenothiazine   +   3-(p-toluenesulfonyl-oxy)propyl chloride   →(NaNH₂, sodium amide)   2-cyano-10-[3-(p-toluene-sulfonyloxy)propyl]phenothiazine   (I)

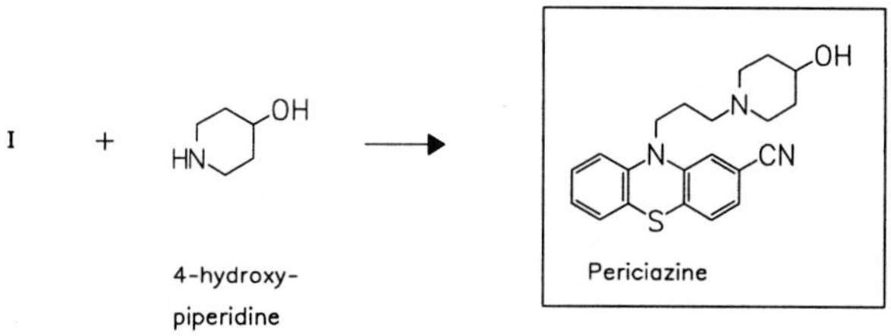

4-hydroxy-
piperidine

Periciazine

Reference(s):

FR 1 212 031 (Rhône-Poulenc; appl. 21.10.1957).

Formulation(s):   drops 1 mg/drop; tabl. 5 mg, 10 mg, 25 mg

Trade Name(s):

D: Aolept (Bayer); wfm
F: Neuleptil (Specia)
GB: Neulactil (May & Baker); wfm

I: Neuleptil (Rhône-Poulenc Rorer)
J: Apamin (Yoshitomi)
       Neuleptil (Shionogi)

Perimetazine

(Perimethazin)

ATC: N05A
Use: neuroleptic

RN: 13093-88-4   MF: $C_{22}H_{28}N_2O_2S$ MW: 384.54   EINECS: 236-009-3
CN: 1-[3-(2-methoxy-10H-phenothiazin-10-yl)-2-methylpropyl]-4-piperidinol

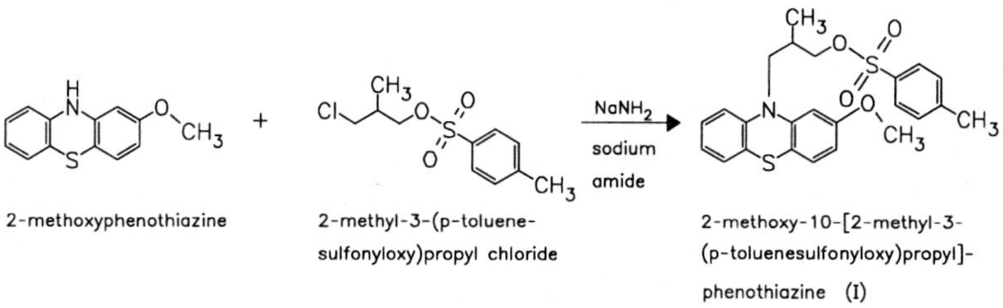

2-methoxyphenothiazine

2-methyl-3-(p-toluene-
sulfonyloxy)propyl chloride

NaNH₂
sodium amide

2-methoxy-10-[2-methyl-3-
(p-toluenesulfonyloxy)propyl]-
phenothiazine   (I)

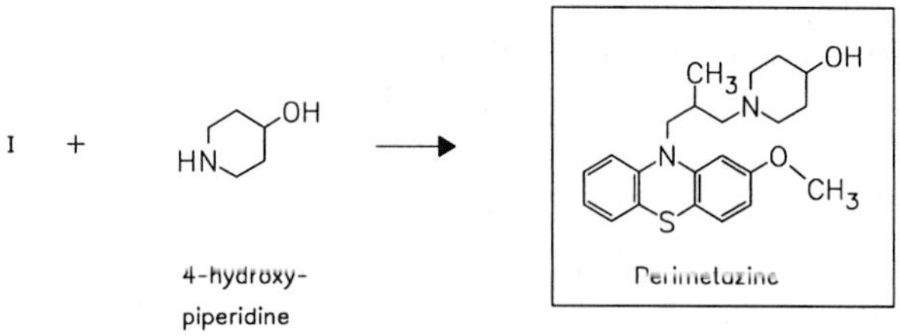

4-hydroxy-
piperidine

Perimetazine

Reference(s):

US 3 075 976 (Rhône-Poulenc; 29.1.1963; F-prior. 21.10.1957).

Trade Name(s):

F: Leptryl (Roger Bellon); wfm

Perindopril

(S-9490; McN-A-2833; SED-9490 (as erbumine); DW-7950 (as erbumine))

ATC: C09AA04
Use: antihypertensive (ACE inhibitor), cardiotonic

RN: 82834-16-0   MF: $C_{19}H_{32}N_2O_5$ MW: 368.47
CN: [2S-[1[R*(R*)],2α,3aβ,7aβ]]-1-[2-[[1-(ethoxycarbonyl)butyl]amino]-1-oxopropyl]octahydro-1H-indole-2-carboxylic acid

erbumine (compd. with tert-butylamine 1:1)
RN: 107133-36-8   MF: $C_{19}H_{32}N_2O_5 \cdot C_4H_{11}N$ MW: 441.61

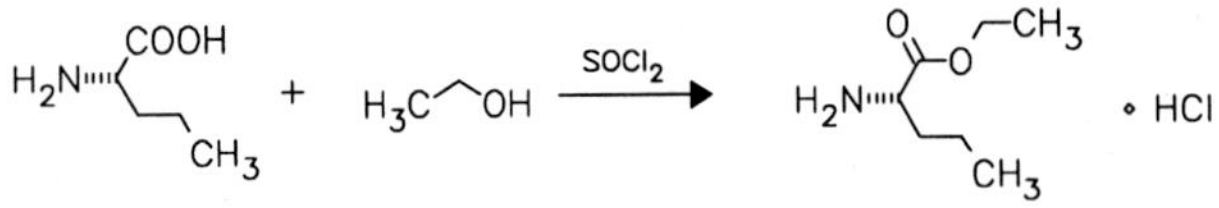

L-norvaline

ethyl L-norvalinate
hydrochloride (I)

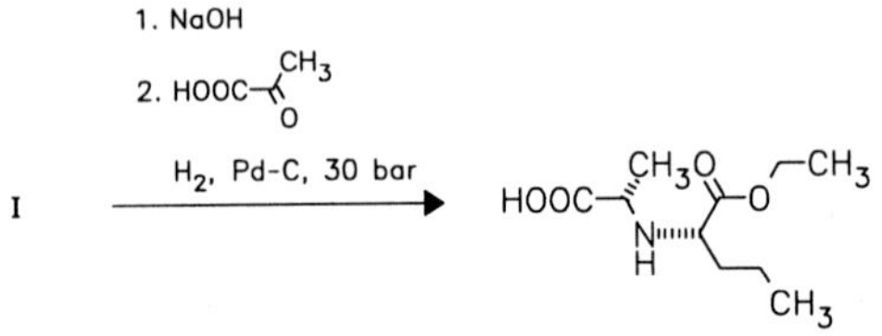

N-[(S)-1-ethoxycarbonyl-
butyl]-L-alanine (II)

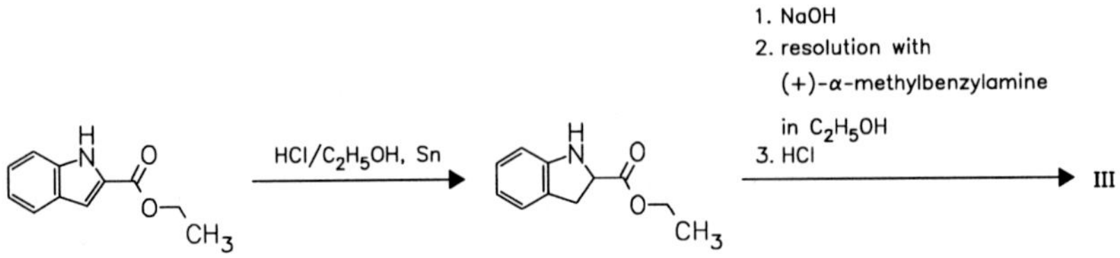

ethyl indole-
2-carboxylate

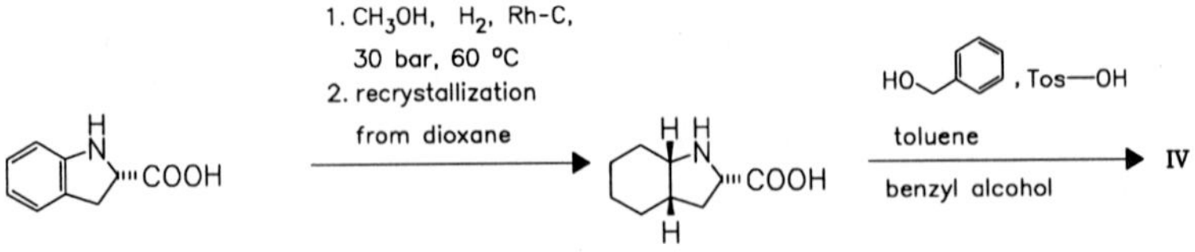

(S)-indoline-
2-carboxylic acid (III)

(2S,3aS,7aS)-
octahydroindole-
2-carboxylic acid

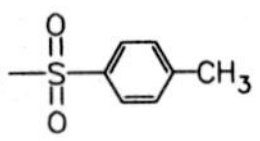

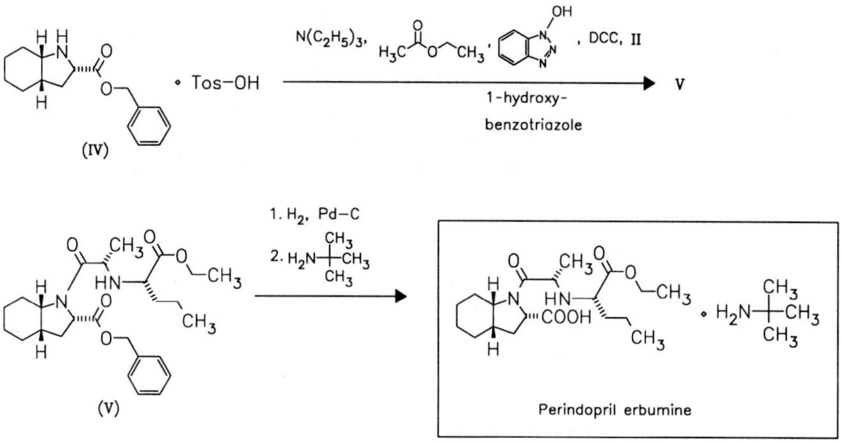

(IV)

(V)

Perindopril erbumine

Reference(s):
Vincent, M. et al.: Tetrahedron Lett. (TELEAY) **23**, 1677 (1982).
US 4 508 729 (ADIR).
EP 49 658 (ADIR; appl. 29.9.1981; F-prior. 2.10.1980, 7.4.1981).

industrial process:
US 4 914 214 (ADIR; 3.4.1990; F-prior. 17.9.1987).

Formulation(s):   tabl. 2 mg, 4 mg, 8 mg

Trade Name(s):
D: Coversum Cor (Servier)   I: Coversyl (Servier)   USA: Aceon (Rhône-Poulenc
F: Coversyl (Servier)   Procaptan (Stroder)   Rorer)
GB: Coversyl (Servier)

Perlapine

ATC: N05C
Use: hypnotic

RN: 1977-11-3   MF: $C_{19}H_{21}N_3$ MW: 291.40
LD_{50}:   61 mg/kg (M, i.v.); 270 mg/kg (M, p.o.);
        60 mg/kg (R, i.v.); 660 mg/kg (R, p.o.)
CN: 6-(4-methyl-1-piperazinyl)-11*H*-dibenz[*b,e*]azepine

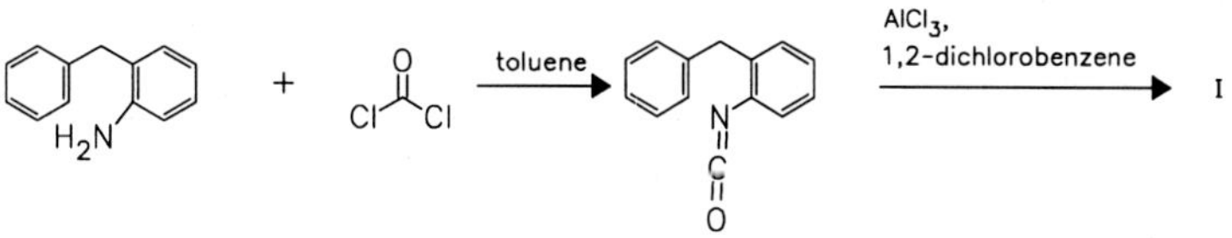

2-aminodiphenyl-   phosgene   2-isocyanatodi-
methane   phenylmethane

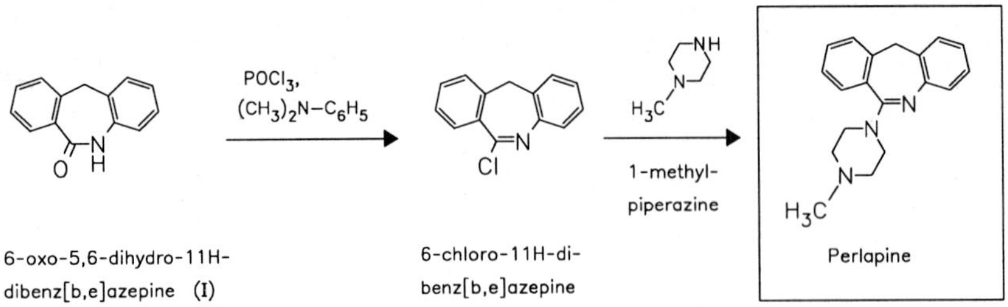

6-oxo-5,6-dihydro-11H-
dibenz[b,e]azepine (I)

POCl₃,
(CH₃)₂N−C₆H₅

6-chloro-11H-di-
benz[b,e]azepine

1-methyl-
piperazine

Perlapine

Reference(s):
US 3 389 139 (Dr. A. Wander; 18.6.1968; prior. 10.6.1964; 2.6.1966).

Formulation(s):   tabl. 2.5 mg

Trade Name(s):
J: Hypnodin (Takeda)

Perphenazine

ATC: N05AB03
Use: neuroleptic, anti-emetic

RN: 58-39-9   MF: C₂₁H₂₆ClN₃OS   MW: 403.98   EINECS: 200-381-5
LD₅₀: 19 mg/kg (M, i.v.); 120 mg/kg (M, p.o.);
       34 mg/kg (R, i.v.); 318 mg/kg (R, p.o.);
       51 mg/kg (dog, i.v.)
CN: 4-[3-(2-chloro-10H-phenothiazin-10-yl)propyl]-1-piperazineethanol

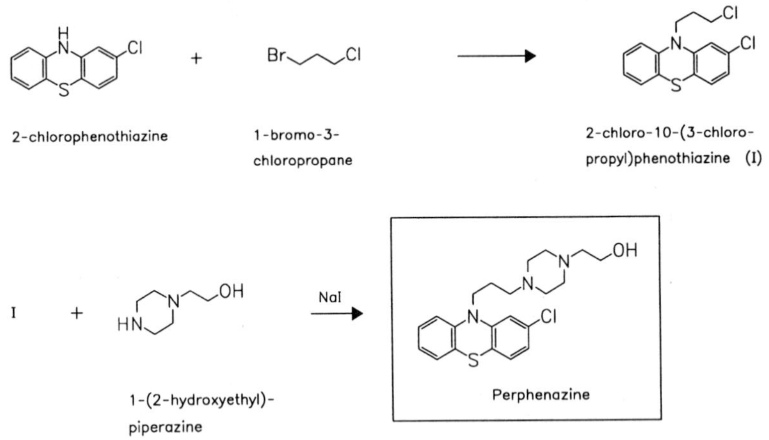

2-chlorophenothiazine   1-bromo-3-
                               chloropropane

2-chloro-10-(3-chloro-
propyl)phenothiazine (I)

I   +

1-(2-hydroxyethyl)-
piperazine

NaI

Perphenazine

Reference(s):
US 2 838 507 (Searle; 1958; appl. 1957; prior. 1955).

carbamate derivatives:
US 2 860 138 (Schering Corp.; 1958; appl. 1956).

acetate:
US 2 766 235 (J. W. Cusic; 1956; appl. 1956).

Formulation(s):   amp. 76 mg/ml; drops 4 mg/ml; inj. flask 1000 mg; tabl. 2 mg, 4 mg, 8mg, 16 mg

Peruvoside

ATC: C01AX02
Use: cardiac glycoside

RN: 1182-87-2   MF: $C_{30}H_{44}O_9$ MW: 548.67   EINECS: 214-659-9
LD$_{50}$: 145 µg/kg (cat, i.v.)
CN: (3β,5β)-3-[(6-deoxy-3-O-methyl-α-L-glucopyranosyl)oxy]-14-hydroxy-19-oxocard-20(22)-enolide

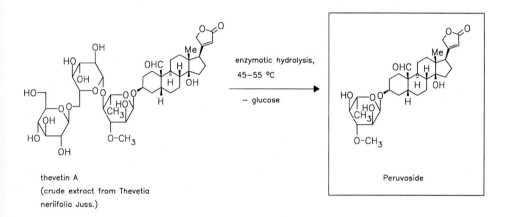

thevetin A
(crude extract from Thevetia neriifolia Juss.)

Peruvoside

From the seeds of *Thevetia peruviana*.

Reference(s):
DE 1 959 039 (Merck Patent GmbH; appl. 25.11.1969).
Ullmanns Encykl. Tech. Chem., 3. Aufl., Vol. **8**, 239.
Ullmanns Encykl. Tech. Chem., 4. Aufl., Vol. **12**, 617.

starting material:
Bloch et al.: Helv. Chim. Acta (HCACAV) **43**, 652 (1960).

Formulation(s):   drg. 0.3 mg; drops 0.3 mg/ml

Pethidine
(Meperidine)

ATC: N02AB02
Use: analgesic, antispasmodic

RN: 57-42-1   MF: $C_{15}H_{21}NO_2$ MW: 247.34   EINECS: 200-329-1
LD$_{50}$: 34.7 mg/kg (M, i.v.); 200 mg/kg (M, p.o.);
22.5 mg/kg (R, i.v.); 162 mg/kg (R, p.o.)
CN: 1-methyl-4-phenyl-4-piperidinecarboxylic acid ethyl ester

hydrochloride
RN: 50-13-5 MF: $C_{15}H_{21}NO_2 \cdot HCl$ MW: 283.80 EINECS: 200-013-3
LD_{50}: 32 mg/kg (M, i.v.); 178 mg/kg (M, p.o.);
30 mg/kg (R, i.v.); 170 mg/kg (R, p.o.);
68 mg/kg (dog, i.v.)

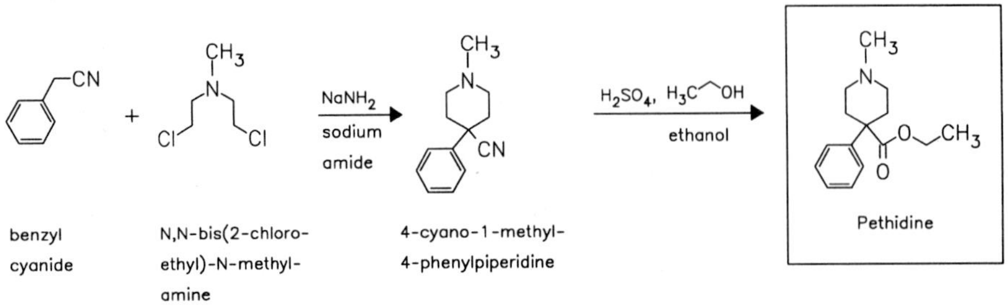

CN
CH3
N
Cl
Cl
NaNH2
sodium
amide
CH3
N
CN
H2SO4, H3C OH
ethanol
CH3
N
O
CH3
O
Pethidine
benzyl
cyanide
N,N-bis(2-chloro-
ethyl)-N-methyl-
amine
4-cyano-1-methyl-
4-phenylpiperidine

Reference(s):
US 2 167 351 (Winthrop; 1939; D-prior. 1937).
DE 679 281 (I. G. Farben; appl. 1937).

Formulation(s): drops 50 mg/ml; suppos. 100 mg; syrup 50 mg/5 ml; tabl. 50 mg, 100 mg; vial 20 ml (100 mg/ml), 30 ml (50 mg/ml) (as hydrochloride)

Trade Name(s):
D: Dolantin (Hoechst)
F: Dolosal (Specia)
GB: Pamergan P100 (Martindale)-comb.
J: Neomochin (Sumitomo)
USA: Demerol (Sanofi)
Mepergan (Wyeth-Ayerst)-comb.

Phanquinone

(Phanchinonum; Phanquone)

ATC: P01AX04
Use: amoebicide, bactericide

RN: 84-12-8 MF: $C_{12}H_6N_2O_2$ MW: 210.19 EINECS: 201-516-0
LD_{50}: 4 mg/kg (M, p.o.);
5 mg/kg (R, p.o.)
CN: 4,7-phenanthroline-5,6-dione

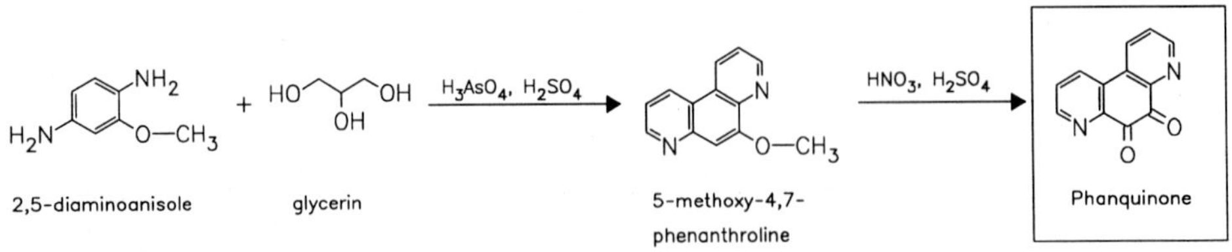

NH2
H2N
O—CH3
HO
OH
OH
H3AsO4, H2SO4
N
N
O—CH3
HNO3, H2SO4
N
N
O
O
Phanquinone
2,5-diaminoanisole
glycerin
5-methoxy-4,7-
phenanthroline

Reference(s):
GB 688 802 (Ciba; appl. 1951; CH-prior. 1950).
Druey, J. et al.: Helv. Chim. Acta (HCACAV) **33**, 1080 (1950).
Druey, J.: Angew. Chem. (ANCEAD) **72**, 677 (1960).

Formulation(s): drg. 10 mg, 20 mg; drops 0.3 mg/ml

Trade Name(s):
D: Mexaform plus/S (Ciba)-comb.; wfm
Mexase (Ciba)-comb.; wfm

Phenacaine

(Fenacaine)

ATC: N01B
Use: local anesthetic

RN: 101-93-9   MF: $C_{18}H_{22}N_2O_2$ MW: 298.39
CN: N,N'-bis(4-ethoxyphenyl)ethanimidamide

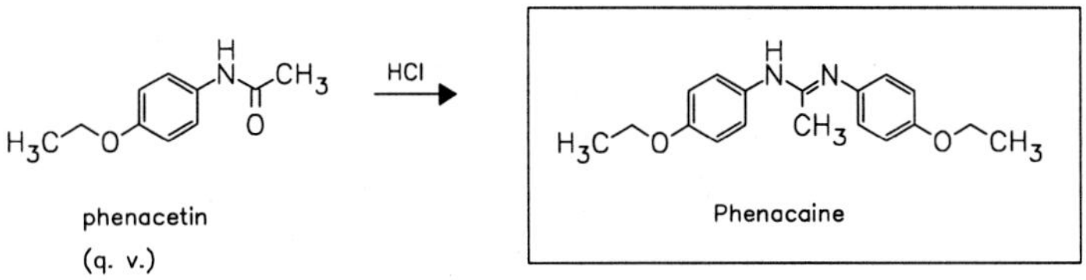

phenacetin
(q. v.)

Phenacaine

Reference(s):
DRP 79 868 (E. Täuber, appl. 1894); also further methods.

Trade Name(s):
USA: Holocaine (Lilly); wfm

Phenacemide

ATC: N03AX07
Use: antiepileptic

RN: 63-98-9   MF: $C_9H_{10}N_2O_2$ MW: 178.19   EINECS: 200-570-2
LD$_{50}$: 987 mg/kg (M, p.o.);
           1600 mg/kg (R, p.o.)
CN: N-(aminocarbonyl)benzeneacetamide

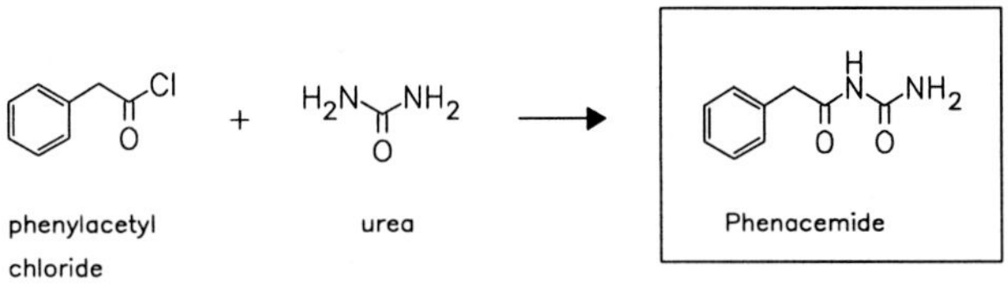

phenylacetyl
chloride

urea

Phenacemide

Reference(s):
Spielman, M.A. et al.. J. Am. Chem. Soc. (JACSAT) **70**, 4189 (1948).

Formulation(s):   tabl. 500 mg

Trade Name(s):
F: Epiclase (Roger Bellon);   USA: Phenurone (Abbott); wfm
        wfm

Phenacetin
(Acetophenetidin)

ATC: N02BE03
Use: analgesic, antipyretic

RN: 62-44-2   MF: $C_{10}H_{13}NO_2$ MW: 179.22   EINECS: 200-533-0
LD$_{50}$: 866 mg/kg (M, p.o.);
3600 mg/kg (R, p.o.)
CN: N-(4-ethoxyphenyl)acetamide

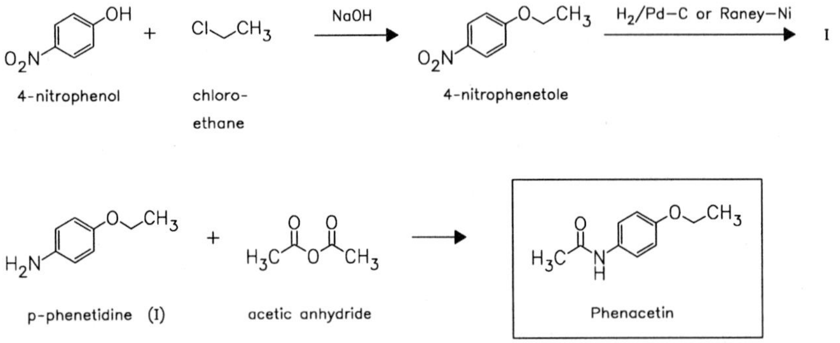

4-nitrophenol   chloro-   4-nitrophenetole
ethane

p-phenetidine (I)   acetic anhydride   Phenacetin

Reference(s):
Ullmanns Encykl. Tech. Chem., 3. Aufl., Vol. **13**, 296.
Ullmanns Encykl. Tech. Chem., 4. Aufl., Vol. **7**, 543.

Formulation(s):   f. c. tabl. 50 mg

Trade Name(s):
D: numerous combination
preparations; wfm
F: Polipirine (Lehning)
I: Cachets Lia (Arnaldi)-
comb.; wfm

Ciclergot (ITA)-comb.;
wfm
Neuroxin (Edmond)-comb.;
wfm
Novamon (Farge)-comb.;
wfm

Thomapirina N (Fher)-
comb.; wfm
J: numerous generic
preparations
USA: numerous combination
preparations; wfm

Phenaglycodol

ATC: N05C
Use: psychosedative, tranquilizer

RN: 79-93-6   MF: $C_{11}H_{15}ClO_2$ MW: 214.69   EINECS: 201-235-3
LD$_{50}$: 254 mg/kg (M, i.v.); 514 mg/kg (M, p.o.);
832 mg/kg (R, p.o.)
CN: 2-(4-chlorophenyl)-3-methyl-2,3-butanediol

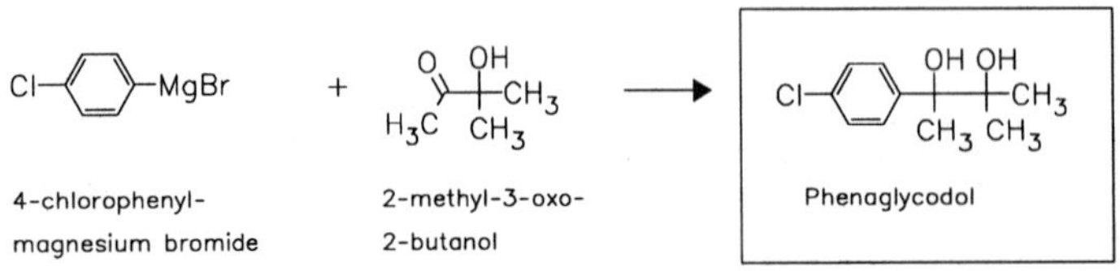

4-chlorophenyl-   2-methyl-3-oxo-   Phenaglycodol
magnesium bromide   2-butanol

Reference(s):
US 2 812 363 (Eli Lilly; 1957; prior. 1953).
DE 1 038 024 (Eli Lilly; appl. 1956).

Trade Name(s):

I:	Felixyn (Radiumfarma); wfm	USA:	Ultran (Lilly); wfm

Phenazocine

ATC: N02AD02
Use: analgesic

RN: 127-35-5 MF: $C_{22}H_{27}NO$ MW: 321.46 EINECS: 204-835-3
LD_{50}: 20 mg/kg (M, i.v.);
90 mg/kg (R, p.o.)
CN: 1,2,3,4,5,6-hexahydro-6,11-dimethyl-3-(2-phenylethyl)-2,6-methano-3-benzazocin-8-ol

hydrobromide
RN: 1239-04-9 MF: $C_{22}H_{27}NO \cdot HBr$ MW: 402.38 EINECS: 214-982-5
LD_{50}: 11 mg/kg (M, i.v.)

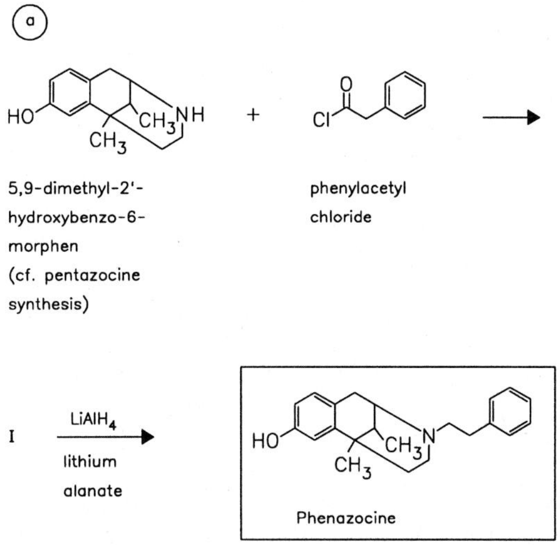
a
5,9-dimethyl-2'-hydroxybenzo-6-morphen (cf. pentazocine synthesis)
phenylacetyl chloride
5,9-dimethyl-2'-hydroxy-2-phenylacetylbenzo-6-morphen (I)
I
LiAlH4
lithium alanate
Phenazocine

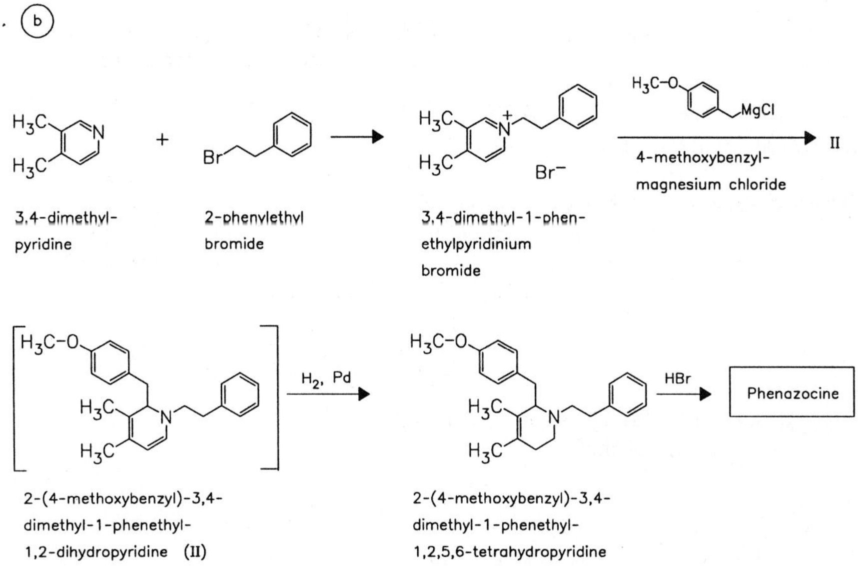
b
3,4-dimethylpyridine
2-phenylethyl bromide
3,4-dimethyl-1-phenethylpyridinium bromide
4-methoxybenzylmagnesium chloride
II
2-(4-methoxybenzyl)-3,4-dimethyl-1-phenethyl-1,2-dihydropyridine (II)
H2, Pd
2-(4-methoxybenzyl)-3,4-dimethyl-1-phenethyl-1,2,5,6-tetrahydropyridine
HBr
Phenazocine

Reference(s):
US 2 959 594 (Smith Kline & French; 8.11.1960; prior. 22.9.1958).
May, E.L. et al.: J. Org. Chem. (JOCEAH) **22**, 1366, 1369 (1957); **24**, 294, 1435 (1959); **25**, 984 (1960).

Formulation(s):   tabl. 5 mg (as hydrobromide)

Trade Name(s):
GB: Narphen (Napp)   USA: Primadol (Smith Kline &
    French); wfm

Phenazopyridine

ATC: G04BX06
Use: chemotherapeutic, antiseptic

RN: 94-78-0   MF: $C_{11}H_{11}N_5$ MW: 213.24   EINECS: 202-363-2
LD$_{50}$:   580 mg/kg (M, p.o.)
CN: 3-(phenylazo)-2,6-pyridinediamine

monohydrochloride
RN: 136-40-3   MF: $C_{11}H_{11}N_5 \cdot HCl$ MW: 249.71   EINECS: 205-243-8
LD$_{50}$:   180 mg/kg (M, i.v.);
    472 mg/kg (R, p.o.)

benzenediazonium   2,6-diamino-   Phenazopyridine
chloride   pyridine

Reference(s):
DRP 515 781 (Boehringer; 1927).
US 1 680 108, US 1 680 109, US 1 680 110, US 1 680 111 (Pyridium Corp.; 1928).
Chichibabin, A.F.; Zeide, O.A.: Zh. Russ. Fiz.-Khim. O-va (ZRKOAC) **46**, 1216 (1914).
Shreve, R.N. et al.: J. Am. Chem. Soc. (JACSAT) **65**, 2241 (1943).

Formulation(s):   cps. 50 mg (as hydrochloride) in comb.; f. c. tabl. 50 mg; tabl. 100 mg, 200 mg (as
    hydrochloride)

Trade Name(s):
D: Urospasmon (Heumann)-   GB: Pyridium (Parke Davis);   J: Fenason (Kanto)
    comb.   wfm   Uriseptin (Nissin)
F: Azocline (Bristol)-comb.;   Pyridium (Warner); wfm   Uropyridin (Eisai)
    wfm   Uromide (Consolidated)-   USA: Pyridium (Warner Chilcott)
    Pyridium (Servier); wfm   comb.; wfm   Urobiotic (Pfizer)-comb.

Phendimetrazine

ATC: A08AA49
Use: appetite depressant, psychostimulant

RN: 634-03-7   MF: $C_{12}H_{17}NO$ MW: 191.27   EINECS: 211-204-6
CN: (2S-*trans*)-3,4-dimethyl-2-phenylmorpholine

hydrochloride
RN: 7635-51-0   MF: $C_{12}H_{17}NO \cdot HCl$ MW: 227.74   EINECS: 231-566-9
LD$_{50}$:   92 mg/kg (M, i.v.); 340 mg/kg (M, p.o.);
         455 mg/kg (R, p.o.)
tartrate (1:1)
RN: 50-58-8   MF: $C_{12}H_{17}NO \cdot C_4H_6O_6$ MW: 341.36   EINECS: 200-051-0
LD$_{50}$:   210 mg/kg (M, i.p.)

propiophenone   α-bromopropio-   2-methylamino-   α-[N-(2-hydroxyethyl)-   Phendimetrazine
                 phenone   ethanol   methylamino]propio-
                                                     phenone

Reference(s):
US 2 997 469 (Boehringer Ing.; 22.8.1961; D-prior. 13.3.1958).

pamoate:
FR 1 461 407 (Sobio; appl. 9.6.1965).

Formulation(s):   cps. 105 mg; tabl. 35 mg (as tartrate)

Trade Name(s):
F: Fringanor (Sobio); wfm   USA: Bontril (Carnrick)   Prelu-2 (Roxane)
I: Plegine (Wyeth-Lederle)   Plegine (Wyeth-Ayerst)

Phenelzine

ATC: N06AF03
Use: antidepressant, MAO-inhibitor

RN: 51-71-8   MF: $C_8H_{12}N_2$ MW: 136.20   EINECS: 200-117-9
LD$_{50}$:   130 mg/kg (M, p.o.)
CN: (2-phenylethyl)hydrazine

dihydrogen sulfate
RN: 156-51-4   MF: $C_8H_{12}N_2 \cdot H_2SO_4$ MW: 234.28   EINECS: 205-856-0
LD$_{50}$:   157 mg/kg (M, i.v.); 156 mg/kg (M, p.o.);
         210 mg/kg (R, p.o.)
dihydrochloride
RN: 16904-30-6   MF: $C_8H_{12}N_2 \cdot 2HCl$ MW: 209.12
LD$_{50}$:   100 mg/kg (M, i.p.)

2-phenylethyl   hydrazine   Phenelzine
bromide

Reference(s):
US 3 000 903 (Lakeside Labs.; 19.9.1961; appl. 15.9.1959; prior. 23.8.1956).

Formulation(s):　tabl. 15 mg (as dihydrogen sulfate)

Trade Name(s):
F:	Nardelzine (Substantia); wfm	GB:	Nardil (Parke Davis)	USA:	Nardil (Parke Davis)
		I:	Nardil (Vister); wfm		

Pheneticillin
(Phenethicillin)

ATC:　J01CE05
Use:　antibiotic

RN:　147-55-7　MF: $C_{17}H_{20}N_2O_5S$　MW: 364.42　EINECS: 205-691-4
LD$_{50}$:　52.25 mg/kg (M, intracerebral)
CN:　[2S-(2α,5α,6β)]-3,3-dimethyl-7-oxo-6-[(1-oxo-2-phenoxypropyl)amino]-4-thia-1-azabicyclo[3.2.0]heptane-2-carboxylic acid

monopotassium salt
RN:　132-93-4　MF: $C_{17}H_{19}KN_2O_5S$　MW: 402.51　EINECS: 205-084-4
LD$_{50}$:　312 mg/kg (M, i.v.); >2 g/kg (M, p.o.);
　　　>103 mg/kg (dog, i.v.)

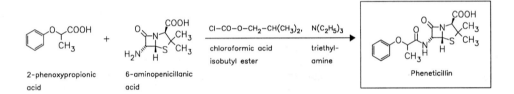

2-phenoxypropionic acid　+　6-aminopenicillanic acid　　chloroformic acid isobutyl ester　　triethyl-amine　　Pheneticillin

Reference(s):
GB 877 120 (Beecham; appl. 10.5.1960; USA-prior. 25.5.1959, 22.10.1959).
GB 958 478 (Beecham; appl. 28.2.1963; USA-prior. 13.3.1962).
GB 899 199 (Pfizer; appl. 7.1.1960; USA-prior. 28.9.1959).
GB 904 576 (Bayer; appl. 24.11.1960; D-prior. 4.12.1959).
DE 1 143 817 (Beecham; appl. 25.5.1960; USA-prior. 25.5.1959).
DE 1 159 449 (Grünenthal; appl. 22.3.1961).
DE 1 159 454 (Pfizer; appl. 18.3.1961; USA-prior. 24.6.1960).

Formulation(s):　tabl. 135 mg (as monopotassium salt)

Trade Name(s):
D:	Palliopen (Merck)-comb.; wfm Pen-200 (Pfizer); wfm	I:	Altocillin (Caber); wfm Metilpen (Boniscontro & Gazzone); wfm	J:	Maxipen (Taito Pfizer) Syncillin (Banyu) Synthepen (Meiji)
F:	Péniplus (Fumouze); wfm Synthécilline (Bristol); wfm		Penicilloral (Terapeutico M.R.); wfm Penorale (Lusofarmaco); wfm	USA:	Maxipen (Pfizer); wfm Syncillin (Bristol); wfm
GB:	Broxil (Beecham); wfm				

Pheneturide

ATC:　N03AX13
Use:　antiepileptic

RN:　90-49-3　MF: $C_{11}H_{14}N_2O_2$　MW: 206.25　EINECS: 201-998-2
LD$_{50}$:　910 mg/kg (M, p.o.);
　　　>2063 mg/kg (R, p.o.)
CN:　N-(aminocarbonyl)-α-ethylbenzeneacetamide

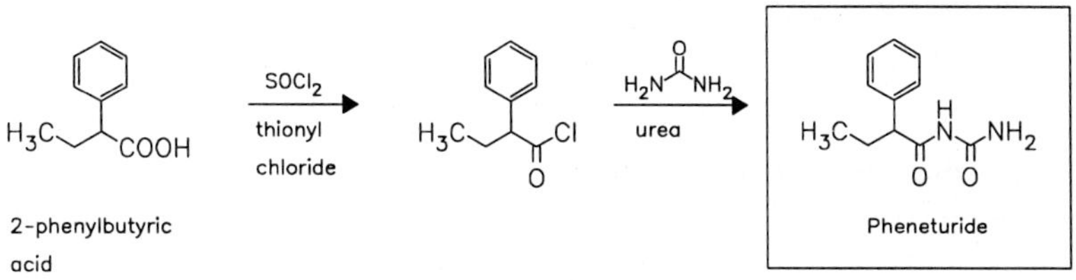

2-phenylbutyric
acid

Pheneturide

Reference(s):
DRP 249 241 (Bayer; 1910).
Kushner, S. et al.: J. Org. Chem. (JOCEAH) **16**, 1283 (1951).

optical active isomers:
CH 374 644 (Lab. Sapos; appl. 30.10.1958).

Trade Name(s):
F: Trinuride (Robert et   I: Lircapil (Lirca)-comb.;   generic
      Carrière)-comb.; wfm   wfm
GB: Benuride (Bengue); wfm   J: Sepotence Pulv. (Kanto)

Phenglutarimide

ATC: N04AA09
Use: antiparkinsonian

RN: 1156-05-4   MF: $C_{17}H_{24}N_2O_2$ MW: 288.39   EINECS: 214-587-8
LD$_{50}$:   1200 mg/kg (M, p.o.)
CN: 3-[2-(diethylamino)ethyl]-3-phenyl-2,6-piperidinedione

monohydrochloride
RN: 1674-96-0   MF: $C_{17}H_{24}N_2O_2 \cdot HCl$ MW: 324.85   EINECS: 216-819-3
LD$_{50}$:   1200 mg/kg (M, p.o.)

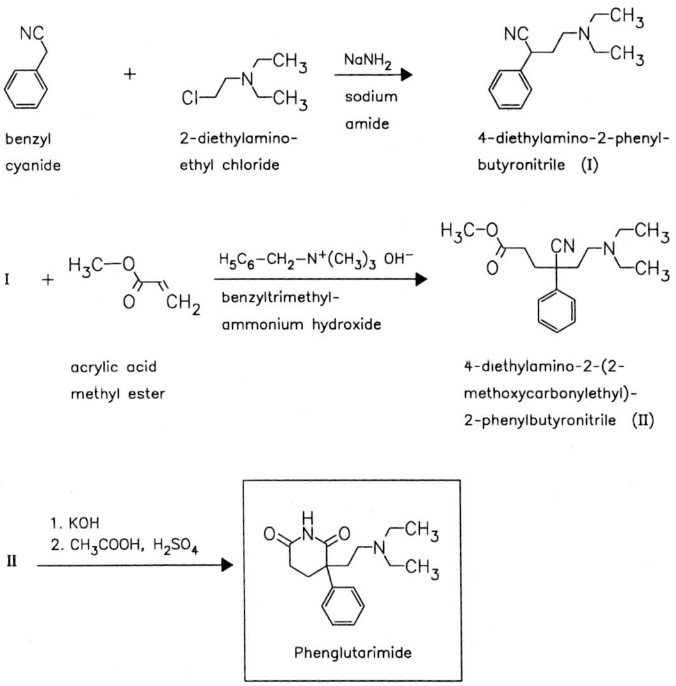

benzyl   2-diethylamino-   4-diethylamino-2-phenyl-
cyanide   ethyl chloride   butyronitrile (I)

4-diethylamino-2-(2-
methoxycarbonylethyl)-
2-phenylbutyronitrile (II)

acrylic acid
methyl ester

Phenglutarimide

Reference(s):
US 2 664 424 (Ciba; 1953; CH-prior. 1950).

Trade Name(s):
D: Aturbal (Ciba); wfm   GB: Aturbane (Ciba); wfm

Phenindamine

ATC: R06AX04
Use: antiallergic, antihistaminic

RN: 82-88-2   MF: $C_{19}H_{19}N$ MW: 261.37   EINECS: 201-443-4
LD_{50}:   265 mg/kg (M, p.o.)
CN: 2,3,4,9-tetrahydro-2-methyl-9-phenyl-1H-indeno[2,1-c]pyridine

tartrate (1:1)
RN: 569-59-5   MF: $C_{19}H_{19}N \cdot C_4H_6O_6$ MW: 411.45   EINECS: 209-320-7
LD_{50}:   18 mg/kg (M, i.v.); 265 mg/kg (M, p.o.);
        280 mg/kg (R, p.o.)

aceto-   methyl-   form-   β,β'-(methylimino)bis-   3-benzoyl-4-hydroxy-
phenone   amine   aldehyde   (propiophenone)   1-methyl-4-phenyl-
                                                                        piperidine (I)

2-methyl-9-phenyl-   Phenindamine
2,3-dihydro-1H-
indeno[2,1-c]pyridine

Reference(s):
US 2 470 108 (Roche; 1949; appl. 1947).

Formulation(s):   tabl. 25 mg (as tartrate)

Trade Name(s):
D: Fluprim (Roche)-comb.;   GB: Thephorin (Sinclair)   Nolamine (Carnrick)
      wfm   USA: Nolahist (Carnrick)

Pheniramine

ATC: R06AB05
Use: antihistaminic

RN: 86-21-5   MF: $C_{16}H_{20}N_2$ MW: 240.35   EINECS: 201-656-2
LD_{50}:   48 mg/kg (M, i.v.)
CN: N,N-dimethyl-γ-phenyl-2-pyridinepropanamine

maleate (1:1)
RN: 132-20-7   MF: $C_{16}H_{20}N_2 \cdot C_4H_4O_4$ MW: 356.42   EINECS: 205-051-4
LD$_{50}$:   268 mg/kg (M, p.o.);
        520 mg/kg (R, p.o.)
p-aminosalicylate (1:1)
RN: 3269-83-8   MF: $C_{16}H_{20}N_2 \cdot C_7H_7NO_3$ MW: 393.49   EINECS: 221-888-8
LD$_{50}$:   48 mg/kg (M, i.v.)

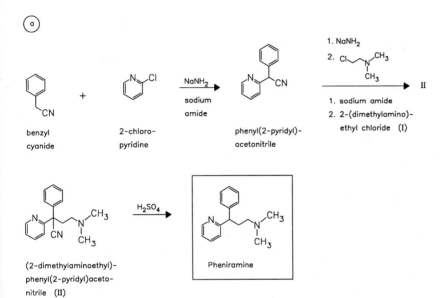

ⓐ

benzyl cyanide

2-chloro-pyridine

NaNH₂
sodium amide

phenyl(2-pyridyl)-acetonitrile

1. NaNH₂
2. 2-(dimethylamino)-ethyl chloride (I)

II

1. sodium amide
2. 2-(dimethylamino)-ethyl chloride (I)

(2-dimethylaminoethyl)-phenyl(2-pyridyl)aceto-nitrile (II)

H₂SO₄

Pheniramine

ⓑ

benzyl chloride

pyridine

Cu

2-benzylpyridine (along with 4-benzylpyridine)

1. NaNH₂
2. I

1. sodium amide

Pheniramine

Reference(s):
US 2 567 245 (Schering Corp.; 1951; prior. 1948).
US 2 676 964 (Schering Corp.; 1954; prior. 1950).
DE 830 193 (Farbw. Hoechst; appl. 1948).
DE 832 153 (Farbw. Hoechst; appl. 1948).

Formulation(s):   drg. 75 mg (as maleate)

Trade Name(s):
D: Avil (Albert-Roussel, Hoechst)
      Konjunktival Thilo Augentropfen (Alcon)-comb. with naphazoline hydrochloride

      Rhinosovil (Eu Rho Arznei)-comb. with naphazoline nitrate
F: Fervex Oberlin (Oberlin)-comb.
      Triaminic (Novartis)-comb.

GB: Daneral (Hoechst; as maleate)
I: Inhiston (Biomedica Foscama)
      Senodin-An (Bristol-Myers Squibb)-comb.

Tetramil (Farmigea)-comb.   USA: Naphcon A (Alcon)-comb.   Triaminic (Novartis
Triaminic (Novartis)-comb.   Poly-Histine D (Sanofi)-   Consumer)-comb.
J: Chlor-Trimeton (Schering)   comb.

Phenmetrazine

(Oxazimedrine)

ATC: N06B
Use: psychostimulant

RN: 134-49-6   MF: C$_{11}$H$_{15}$NO   MW: 177.25   EINECS: 205-143-4
LD$_{50}$:   125 mg/kg (M, p.o.);
        370 mg/kg (R, p.o.)
CN: 3-methyl-2-phenylmorpholine

hydrochloride
RN: 1707-14-8   MF: C$_{11}$H$_{15}$NO · HCl   MW: 213.71   EINECS: 216-950-6
LD$_{50}$:   71 mg/kg (M, i.v.); 165 mg/kg (M, p.o.);
        165 mg/kg (R, p.o.)

propiophenone   α-bromopropio-   α-[benzyl(2-hydroxyethyl)-
        phenone   amino]propiophenone   (I)

2-(2-hydroxyethyl-   Phenmetrazine
amino)-1-phenyl-1-
propanol

Reference(s):
US 2 835 669 (Boehringer Ing.; 1958; D-prior. 1952).

Formulation(s):   drg. 30 mg

Trade Name(s):
D: Cafilon (Ravensberg)-   J: Cafilon (Yamanouchi)-
    comb.; wfm   comb.
F: Cafilon (Merck-Clévenot)-   USA: Preludin (Boehringer Ing.);
    comb.; wfm   wfm

Phenobarbital

(Phenemalum; Phenobarbitone)

ATC: N03AA02
Use: hypnotic, sedative, anticonvulsant

RN: 50-06-6   MF: C$_{12}$H$_{12}$N$_2$O$_3$ MW: 232.24   EINECS: 200-007-0
LD$_{50}$:   218 mg/kg (M, i.v.); 137 mg/kg (M, p.o.);
        209 mg/kg (R, i.v.); 162 mg/kg (R, p.o.);
        150 mg/kg (dog, p.o.)
CN: 5-ethyl-5-phenyl-2,4,6(1H,3H,5H)-pyrimidinetrione

monosodium salt

RN: 57-30-7   MF: $C_{12}H_{11}N_2NaO_3$ MW: 254.22   EINECS: 200-322-3

LD$_{50}$:   226 mg/kg (M, i.v.); 200 mg/kg (M, p.o.);

83 mg/kg (R, i.v.); 150 mg/kg (R, p.o.)

calcium salt

RN: 7645-06-9   MF: $C_{12}H_{12}N_2O_3 \cdot xCa$ MW: unspecified   EINECS: 231-583-1

magnesium salt

RN: 7645-05-8   MF: $C_{12}H_{12}N_2O_3 \cdot xMg$ MW: unspecified

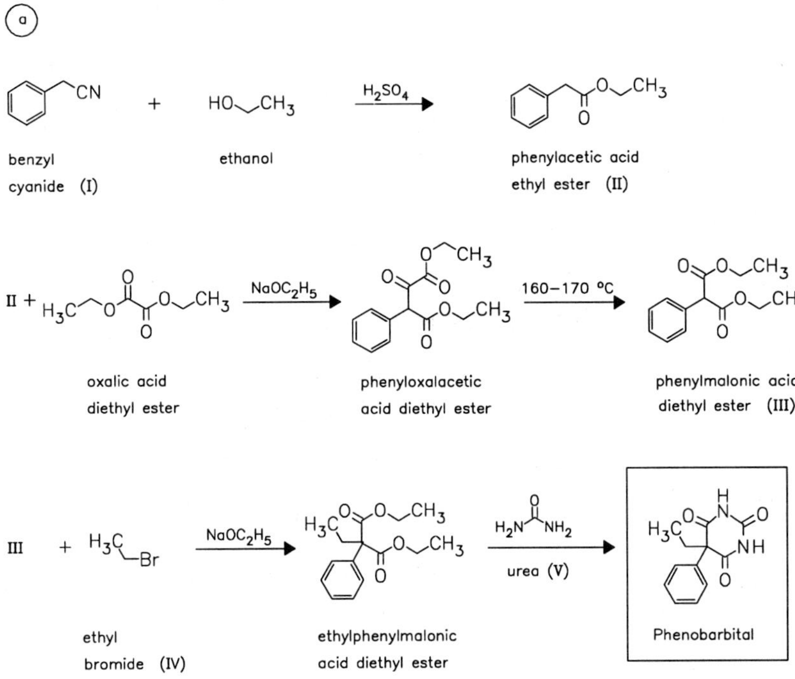

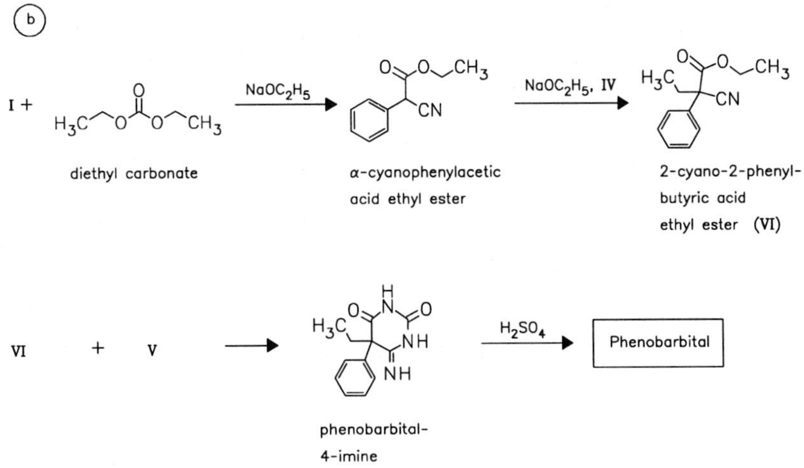

benzyl cyanide (I) + ethanol → phenylacetic acid ethyl ester (II)

II + oxalic acid diethyl ester → phenyloxalacetic acid diethyl ester → phenylmalonic acid diethyl ester (III)

III + ethyl bromide (IV) → ethylphenylmalonic acid diethyl ester → Phenobarbital (with urea (V))

I + diethyl carbonate → α-cyanophenylacetic acid ethyl ester → 2-cyano-2-phenyl-butyric acid ethyl ester (VI)

VI + V → phenobarbital-4-imine → Phenobarbital

Reference(s):

DRP 247 952 (Bayer; 1911).

US 2 358 072 (Kay-Fries; 1944; appl. 1941).

Formulation(s):   amp. 200 mg/ml (as monosodium salt); tabl. 15 mg, 100 mg

Phenolphthalein

(Dihydroxyphthalophenone; Fenolftalein)

ATC: A06AB04
Use: laxative

RN: 77-09-8   MF: $C_{20}H_{14}O_4$ MW: 318.33   EINECS: 201-004-7
CN: 3,3-bis(4-hydroxyphenyl)-1(3H)-isobenzofuranone

phthalic   phenol   Phenolphthalein
anhydride

Reference(s):
Baeyer, A. v.: Justus Liebigs Ann. Chem. (JLACBF) **202**, 68 (1880).

Formulation(s):   drg. 30 mg; emulsion 1.3 g/100 g

Purgestol (Zoja)-comb.;
wfm
Reolina (IFI)-comb.; wfm
Ricinagar (Ottolenghi)-
comb.; wfm

J: Eval (Nippon Shinyaku)-
comb.
Laxatol (Shionogi)-comb.
USA: Agoral (Warner-Lambert)-
comb.

Evac-Q-Kit (Savage)-comb.
Modane (Savage)

Phenoperidine
(Fenoperidine)

ATC: N01AH04
Use: analgesic

RN: 562-26-5 MF: $C_{23}H_{29}NO_3$ MW: 367.49 EINECS: 209-229-2
CN: 1-(3-hydroxy-3-phenylpropyl)-4-phenyl-4-piperidinecarboxylic acid ethyl ester

hydrochloride
RN: 3627-49-4 MF: $C_{23}H_{29}NO_3 \cdot HCl$ MW: 403.95 EINECS: 222-846-1
LD_{50}: 64 mg/kg (M, i.p.)

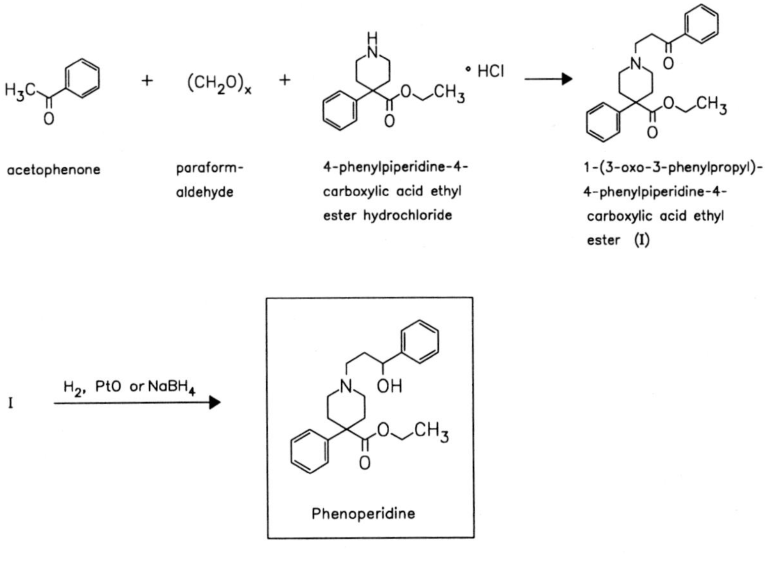

acetophenone paraform-
aldehyde

4-phenylpiperidine-4-
carboxylic acid ethyl
ester hydrochloride

1-(3-oxo-3-phenylpropyl)-
4-phenylpiperidine-4-
carboxylic acid ethyl
ester (I)

Phenoperidine

Reference(s):
US 2 951 080 (Eli Lilly; 30.8.1960; prior. 5.8.1957).
US 2 962 501 (Merck & Co.; 29.11.1960; prior. 19.9.1956).

Formulation(s): amp. 10 mg/10 ml, 2 mg/2 ml

Trade Name(s):
F: R. 1406 (Janssen); wfm   R. 1406 (LeBrun); wfm   GB: Operidine (Janssen); wfm

Phenoxybenzamine

ATC: C04AX02
Use: vasodilator, antihypertensive

RN: 59-96-1 MF: $C_{18}H_{22}ClNO$ MW: 303.83 EINECS: 200-446-8
LD_{50}: 1535 mg/kg (M, p.o.);
2500 mg/kg (R, p.o.)
CN: *N*-(2-chloroethyl)-*N*-(1-methyl-2-phenoxyethyl)benzenemethanamine

hydrochloride

RN: 63-92-3 MF: $C_{18}H_{22}ClNO \cdot HCl$ MW: 340.29 EINECS: 200-569-7
LD_{50}: 63.75 mg/kg (M, i.v.); 900 mg/kg (M, p.o.)

| phenol | propylene oxide | 1-phenoxy-2-propanol | 1-phenoxy-2-propyl chloride (I) |

| ethanolamine | N-(1-methyl-2-phenoxyethyl)-ethanolamine | |

| N-benzyl-N-(1-methyl-2-phenoxyethyl)ethanolamine (II) | | Phenoxybenzamine |

Reference(s):
US 2 599 000 (Smith Kline & French; 1952; prior. 1950).

Formulation(s): cps. 1 mg, 5 mg, 10 mg (as hydrochloride)

Trade Name(s):
D: Dibenzyran (Procter & Gamble)
GB: Dibenyline (Smith Kline & French); wfm
USA: Dibenzyline (SmithKline Beecham)

Phenoxymethylpenicillin
(Penicillin V)

ATC: J01CE02
Use: antibiotic

RN: 87-08-1 MF: $C_{16}H_{18}N_2O_5S$ MW: 350.40 EINECS: 201-722-0
LD_{50}: 6.578 g/kg (M, p.o.);
>1.775 g/kg (R, i.v.); >2.22 g/kg (R, p.o.)
CN: [2S-(2α,5α,6β)]-3,3-dimethyl-7-oxo-6-[(phenoxyacetyl)amino]-4-thia-1-azabicyclo[3.2.0]heptane-2-carboxylic acid

monopotassium salt

RN: 132-98-9 MF: $C_{16}H_{17}KN_2O_5S$ MW: 388.49 EINECS: 205-086-5
LD_{50}: 1 g/kg (M, i.v.); >4 g/kg (M, p.o.);
>1.04 g/kg (R, p.o.)

calcium salt (2:1)

RN: 147-48-8 MF: $C_{32}H_{34}CaN_4O_{10}S_2$ MW: 738.85 EINECS: 205-689-3

Phenoxymethylpenicillin

From fermentation solutions of *Penicillium notatum* Westling or *Penicillium chrysogenum* Thom by addition of phenoxyacetic acid as precursor substance.

Reference(s):
US 2 479 295 (Lilly; 1949; prior. 1946).
US 2 479 296 (Lilly; 1949; prior. 1946).
US 2 562 410 (Lilly; 1951; prior. 1946).
US 2 941 995 (Beecham; 1960; GB-prior. 1957).

partial synthesis:
US 3 159 617 (A. D. Little; 1.12.1964; prior. 1.3.1957, 1.5.1959).

Formulation(s):   f. c. tabl. 1000000 iu 1500000 iu; susp. 300000 iu/5 ml; syrup 250000 iu, 500000 iu; tabl. 664 mg (as potassium salt)

Trade Name(s):

D:	Arcasin (Engelhard)	F:	Oracilline (Schwarz)	Penagen (Genethic); wfm
	Isocillin (Hoechst)		Ospen (Novartis)	Stabilin V-K (Boots); wfm
	Ispenoral (Rosen Pharma)	GB:	Apsin VK (A.P.S.); wfm	Ticillin V-K (Ticen); wfm
	Megacillin oral		Bicillin (Yamanouchi)-	V-Cil-K (Lilly); wfm
	(Grünenthal)		comb.	I: Fenospen (Pharmacia &
	P-Mega-Tablinen		Crystapen V (Britannia)	Upjohn)
	(Sanorania)		Distaquaine V-K (Dista);	J: Newcillin (Takeda)
	V-Tablopen (ASTA Medica		wfm	USA: Pen Vee (Wyeth-Ayerst)
	AWD)		Econopen V (Berk); wfm	Pfizerpen (Pfizer)
	numerous generics		Icipen (ICI); wfm	

Phenprobamate

ATC: M03BA01
Use: muscle relaxant, tranquilizer

RN: 673-31-4   MF: $C_{10}H_{13}NO_2$ MW: 179.22   EINECS: 211-606-1
LD$_{50}$:   320 mg/kg (M, i.v.); 840 mg/kg (M, p.o.);
          1110 mg/kg (R, p.o.)
CN: benzenepropanol carbamate

3-phenyl-1-propanol

1. COCl$_2$
2. NH$_3$

1. phosgene

Phenprobamate

Reference(s):
GB 837 718 (Siegfried AG; appl. 6.5.1958; D-prior. 9.5.1957).

Formulation(s):   tabl. 200 mg

Phenprocoumon

ATC: B01AA04
Use: anticoagulant

RN: 435-97-2   MF: $C_{18}H_{16}O_3$ MW: 280.32   EINECS: 207-108-9
LD_{50}:   32 mg/kg (M, i.v.); 190 mg/kg (M, p.o.);
     200 mg/kg (R, p.o.)
CN: 4-hydroxy-3-(1-phenylpropyl)-2H-1-benzopyran-2-one

2-acetoxybenzoyl   (1-phenylpropyl)malonic   (2-acetoxybenzoyl)(1-phenyl-
chloride   acid diethyl ester   propyl)malonic acid
                          (sodium salt)   diethyl ester (I)

3,4-dihydro-2,4-dioxo-3-   Phenprocoumon
(1-phenylpropyl)-2H-1-benzo-
pyran-3-carboxylic acid
ethyl ester

Reference(s):
US 2 701 804 (Hoffmann-La Roche; 1955; CH-prior. 1952).

alternative synthesis:
US 2 872 457 (Wisconsin Alumni Research; 1959; appl. 1956).

resolution of racemate:
US 3 239 529 (Wisconsin Alumni Research; 8.3.1966; appl. 1.3.1962).

Formulation(s):   f. c. tabl. 3 mg; tabl. 3 mg

Phensuximide

ATC: N03AD02
Use: antiepileptic

RN: 86-34-0 MF: $C_{11}H_{11}NO_2$ MW: 189.21 EINECS: 201-664-6
LD$_{50}$: 700 mg/kg (M, p.o.)
CN: 1-methyl-3-phenyl-2,5-pyrrolidinedione

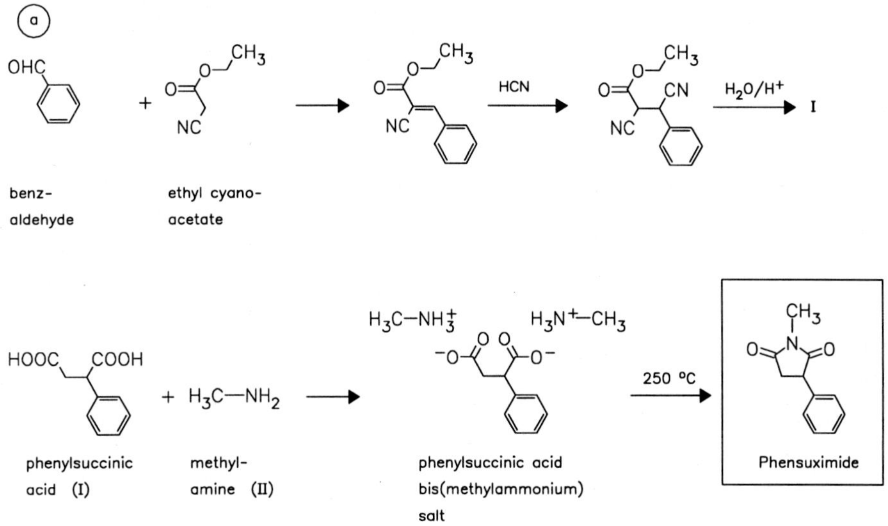
a
HCN
H_2O/H^+
I
benz-aldehyde
ethyl cyano-acetate
250 °C
phenylsuccinic acid (I)
methyl-amine (II)
phenylsuccinic acid bis(methylammonium) salt
Phensuximide

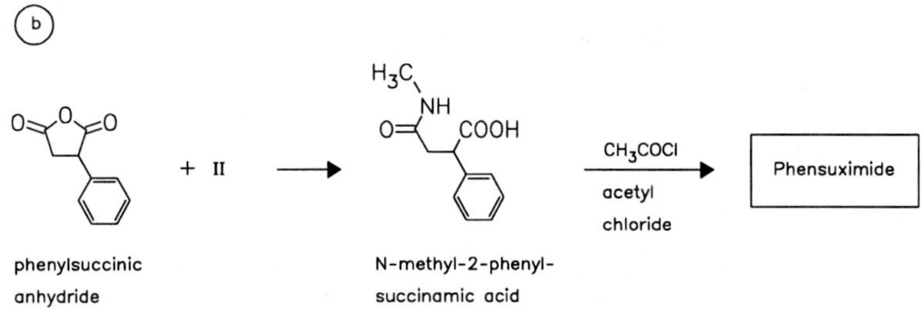
b
+ II
CH_3COCl
acetyl chloride
Phensuximide
phenylsuccinic anhydride
N-methyl-2-phenyl-succinamic acid

Reference(s):
US 2 643 258 (Parke Davis; 1953; prior. 1950).
Miller, C.A.; Long, L.M.: J. Am. Chem. Soc. (JACSAT) **73**, 4895 (1951); **75**, 373 (1953).

Formulation(s): cps. 0.5 g

Trade Name(s):
F: Liféne (Débat); wfm
GB: Milontin (Parke Davis); wfm
USA: Milontin (Parke Davis); wfm

Phentermine

ATC: A08AA01
Use: appetite depressant

RN: 122-09-8 MF: $C_{10}H_{15}N$ MW: 149.24 EINECS: 204-522-1
LD$_{50}$: 14 mg/kg (M, i.v.); 105 mg/kg (M, p.o.)
CN: α,α-dimethylbenzeneethanamine

hydrochloride

RN: 1197-21-3   MF: $C_{10}H_{15}N \cdot HCl$ MW: 185.70   EINECS: 214-821-9

LD_{50}:   154 mg/kg (M, p.o.);
            188 mg/kg (R, p.o.)

| benz– | 2-nitro– | 2-methyl-2-nitro- | 2-amino-2-methyl- |
| aldehyde | propane | 1-phenyl-1-propanol | 1-phenyl-1-propanol (I) |

2-amino-2-methyl-
1-phenylpropyl
chloride hydrochloride   Phentermine

Reference(s):

US 2 408 345 (Merrell; 1946; prior. 1942).

alternative syntheses:

US 2 590 079 (Wyeth; 1952; appl. 1947).

Formulation(s):   cps. 30 mg; tabl. 30 mg (as hydrochloride)

Trade Name(s):

D:	Netto Longcaps (Neda); wfm		Ionamin (Torbet)	Banobese (Seatrace)
		I:	Lipopill (Roussel-Maestretti); wfm	Fastin (SmithKline Beecham)
F:	Linyl (Roussel); wfm		Mirapront (Bracco); wfm	Oby-Cap (Richwood)
GB:	Duromine (3M Health Care)	USA:	Adipex-P (Gate)	Zantryl (Ion)

Phentolamine

ATC: C04AB01
Use: sympatholytic, antihypertensive, peripheral vasodilator

RN: 50-60-2   MF: $C_{17}H_{19}N_3O$ MW: 281.36   EINECS: 200-053-1
LD_{50}:   35 mg/kg (M, i.v.); 1 g/kg (M, p.o.)
CN: 3-[[(4,5-dihydro-1H-imidazol-2-yl)methyl](4-methylphenyl)amino]phenol

monohydrochloride

RN: 73-05-2   MF: $C_{17}H_{19}N_3O \cdot HCl$ MW: 317.82   EINECS: 200-793-5
LD_{50}:   75 mg/kg (R, i.v.); 1250 mg/kg (R, p.o.)

monomesylate

RN: 65-28-1   MF: $C_{17}H_{19}N_3O \cdot CH_4O_3S$ MW: 377.47   EINECS: 200-604-6
LD_{50}:   75 mg/kg (M, i.v.)

resorcinol   4-methyl-   3-(4-methyl-   Phentolamine
             aniline   anilino)phenol

2-chloromethyl-Δ^2-
imidazoline
hydrochloride

Reference(s):
US 2 503 059 (Ciba; 1950; CH-prior. 1947).
Urech, E. et al.: Helv. Chim. Acta (HCACAV) **33**, 1386 (1950).

Formulation(s):   vial 5 mg (as mesylate)

Trade Name(s):
D: Regitin (Ciba); wfm   J: Regitin (Ciba-Geigy-
GB: Rogitine (Novartis)   Takeda)
I: Regitine (Ciba); wfm   USA: Regitine (Novartis)

Phenylbutazone

ATC: M01AA01; M02AA01
Use: anti-inflammatory

RN: 50-33-9   MF: $C_{19}H_{20}N_2O_2$ MW: 308.38   EINECS: 200-029-0
LD$_{50}$:   90 mg/kg (M, i.v.); 238 mg/kg (M, p.o.);
              100 mg/kg (R, i.v.); 245 mg/kg (R, p.o.);
              121 mg/kg (dog, i.v.); 332 mg/kg (dog, p.o.)
CN: 4-butyl-1,2-diphenyl-3,5-pyrazolidinedione

sodium salt
RN: 129-18-0   MF: $C_{19}H_{18}N_2NaO_2$ MW: 329.36   EINECS: 204-935-7
LD$_{50}$:   94 mg/kg (M, i.v.); 476 mg/kg (M, p.o.);
              113 mg/kg (R, i.v.); 855 mg/kg (R, p.o.)

hydrazo-   butylmalonic acid   Phenylbutazone
benzene   diethyl ester

Reference(s):
US 2 562 830 (Geigy; 1951; CH-prior. 1948).

salt with procaine:
DAS 2 055 853 (Dr. Voigt; appl. 13.11.1970).

Formulation(s):   amp. 400 mg/2 ml (as sodium salt); drg. 200 mg; f. c. tabl. 200 mg; suppos. 300 mg (as acid)

Trade Name(s):
D: Ambene (Merckle)   Demoplas (Gödecke)-   F: Butazolidine (Pierre Fabre)
        Butazolidin (Novartis   comb.   Carudol (Boehringer Ing.)
        Pharma)-comb.   Exrheudon N (Optimed)

	Dextrarine Phenylbutazone (Synthélabo)-comb.	numerous combination preparations

Dextrarine Phenylbutazone
(Synthélabo)-comb.
Traumalgyl
(Pharmadéveloppement)-
comb.
GB: Butacote (Novartis)
I: Fenilbutazone (Ecobi; IFI)
     Kadol (Teofarma)

J: numerous combination
     preparations
     Acrizeal (S. S. Pharm.)
     Bulentan (Sanwa)
     Butazolidin (Ciba-Geigy-
     Fujisawa)
     Neuplus (Toyo Pharmar)
     Pilazon (Kobayashi Kako)

Reumazin (Mohan)
Schemergen (Azusa)
Sedazole (Toho)
Tokugen (Sawai)
USA: Azolid (USV); wfm
      Butazolidin (Geigy); wfm
      Sterazolidin (Geigy); wfm

Phenylmercuric borate

ATC: D08AK02
Use: antiseptic, antifungal, disinfectant

RN: 102-98-7   MF: $C_6H_7BHgO_3$ MW: 338.52   EINECS: 203-068-1
CN: dihydrogen[orthoborato(3-)-κO]phenylmercurate(2-)

benzene + mercuric diacetate → phenylmercuric acetate (I)

I → (KOH) phenylmercuric hydroxide → (B(OH)₃, boric acid) Phenylmercuric borate

Reference(s):
US 2 196 384 (Lever Bros.; 1940; prior. 1937).

Formulation(s):   sol. 0.066 %

Trade Name(s):
D: Aderman (Schülke & Mayr); wfm
     Chibro S Lösung (Chibret)-comb.; wfm
     Exomycol (Zyma); wfm
     Glycero-Merfen (Zyma); wfm
     Hydro-Merfen (Zyma); wfm
     Merfen (Zyma)-comb.; wfm
     Merfen-Orange/-Tabl. (Zyma)

Phenylpropanolamine
(DL-Norephedrine)

ATC: R01BA01
Use: sympathomimetic

RN: 14838-15-4   MF: $C_9H_{13}NO$ MW: 151.21   EINECS: 207-755-7
LD₅₀: 1060 mg/kg (M, p.o.);
      1538 mg/kg (R, p.o.)
CN: (R*,S*)-α-(1-aminoethyl)benzenemethanol

hydrochloride
RN: 154-41-6   MF: $C_9H_{13}NO \cdot HCl$ MW: 187.67   EINECS: 205-826-7
LD₅₀: 150 mg/kg (M, p.o.);
      1490 mg/kg (R, p.o.)

propiophenone	methyl nitrite (from CH$_3$OH, NaNO$_2$ and H$_2$SO$_4$)	α-isonitroso-propiophenone	Phenylpropanol-amine

Reference(s):

Nagai, W.N.; Kanao, S.: Justus Liebigs Ann. Chem. (JLACBF) **470**, 157 (1929).

US 3 028 429 (Nepera Chem. Co.; 3.4.1962; prior. 24.9.1959) – only hydrogenation process.

Hartung et al.: J. Am. Chem. Soc. (JACSAT) **74**, 5927 (1952).

Hartung et al.: J. Am. Chem. Soc. (JACSAT) **51**, 2262 (1929).

alternative synthesis (from benzaldehyde *and* nitroethane):

US 2 151 517 (J. Kamlet; 1939; prior. 1938).

resolution of racemate with pantothenic acid:

DAS 2 558 507 (Alps; appl. 24.12.1975; J-prior. 19.2.1975).

Formulation(s):   tabl. 25 mg (as hydrochloride)

Trade Name(s):

D:	Basoplex (RIAM)-comb.		Dénoral (Pharmuka)		Tempo Rinolo (Hoechst
	Contac (SmithKline		Humex (Fournier)		Marion)-comb.
	Beecham OTC Medicines)-		Rinurel (Substantia)		Triaminic (Novartis
	comb.		Rinutan (Substantia)		Consumer Health)-comb.
	Recatol (Woelm)-comb.		Rupton (Dexo)	USA:	Propagest (Carnrick; as
	Rhinopront (Mack, Illert.)-		Triaminic (Sandoz)		hydrochloride)
	comb.		Triatussic (Sandoz)		numerous combination
	Wick DayMed (Wick	GB:	Rinurel (Parke Davis)-		preparations
	Pharma)-comb.		comb.; wfm		
F:	only combination	I:	Denoral (Rhône-Poulenc		
	preparations:		Rorer)-comb.		

Phenyltoloxamine

ATC: R06AA
Use: antihistaminic

RN: 92-12-6   MF: C$_{17}$H$_{21}$NO   MW: 255.36   EINECS: 202-127-9

LD$_{50}$:   55 mg/kg (M, i.v.); 1127 mg/kg (M, p.o.);
        1400 mg/kg (R, p.o.)

CN: *N,N*-dimethyl-2-[2-(phenylmethyl)phenoxy]ethanamine

hydrochloride

RN: 6152-43-8   MF: C$_{17}$H$_{21}$NO · HCl   MW: 291.82

LD$_{50}$:   33 mg/kg (M, i.v.); 305 mg/kg (M, p.o.)

dihydrogen citrate (1:1)

RN: 1176-08-5   MF: C$_{17}$H$_{21}$NO · C$_6$H$_8$O$_7$ MW: 447.48   EINECS: 214-644-7

LD$_{50}$:   1472 mg/kg (R, p.o.)

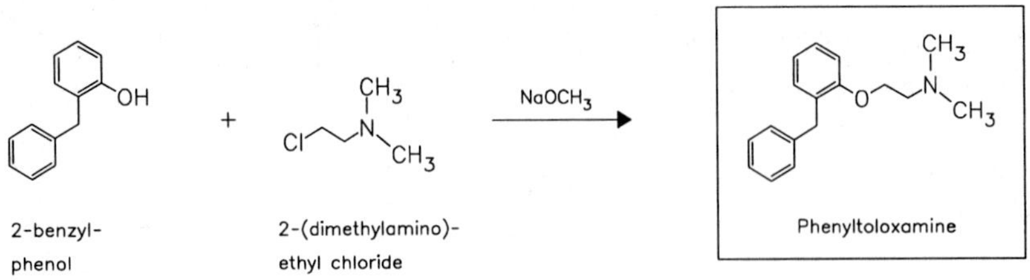

2-benzyl-
phenol

2-(dimethylamino)-
ethyl chloride

NaOCH₃

Phenyltoloxamine

Reference(s):

US 2 703 324 (Bristol; 1955; prior. 1947).

Cheney, L.C. et al.: J. Am. Chem. Soc. (JACSAT) **71**, 60 (1949).

Formulation(s):   drops 4 mg/g; s. r. cps. 10 mg; syrup 66 mg/90 ml

Trade Name(s):

D: Codipront (Mack, Illert.)-
     comb.
F: Biocidan O.R.L. (Menarini)
     Nétux (Nicholas)
     Rinurel (Warner-Lambert)
     Rinutan (Warner-Lambert)
GB: Pholtex (Riker)-comb.;
     wfm

Rinurel (Parke Davis)-
comb.; wfm
Rinurel (Warner)-comb.;
wfm
I: Codipront (Bracco)-comb.;
     wfm
     Neosyth (Inverni della
     Beffa)-comb.; wfm

J: Bristamine (Banyu)
     combination preparations
USA: only combination
     preparations:
     Kurtrase (Schwarz)
     Lobac (Seatrace)
     Nalex (Blansett)
     Poly-Histine-D (Sanofi)

Phenytoin

(Diphenylhydantoin)

ATC: N03AB02
Use: antiepileptic

RN: 57-41-0   MF: C₁₅H₁₂N₂O₂   MW: 252.27   EINECS: 200-328-6

LD_{50}:   92 mg/kg (M, i.v.); 150 mg/kg (M, p.o.);
       101 mg/kg (R, i.v.); 1635 mg/kg (R, p.o.);
       90 mg/kg (dog, i.v.)

CN: 5,5-diphenyl-2,4-imidazolidinedione

monosodium salt

RN: 630-93-3   MF: C₁₅H₁₁N₂NaO₂   MW: 274.26   EINECS: 211-148-2

LD_{50}:   98 mg/kg (M, i.v.); 165 mg/kg (M, p.o.);
       90 mg/kg (R, i.v.); 1530 mg/kg (R, p.o.)

benzil   urea   Phenytoin

benzophenone   Phenytoin

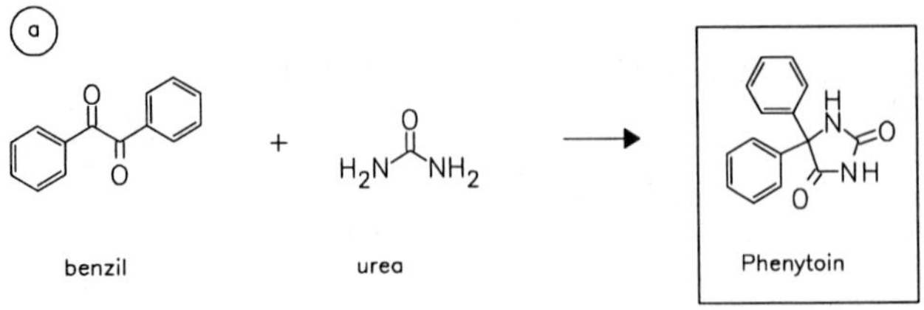

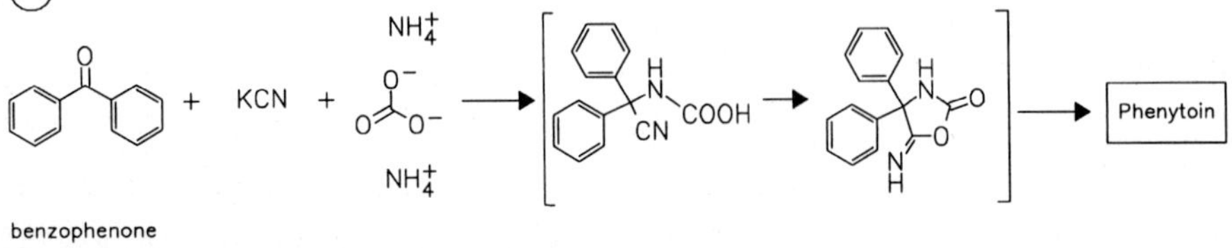

Reference(s):
a   Biltz, H.: Ber. Dtsch. Chem. Ges. (BDCGAS) **41**, 1391 (1908).
b   US 2 409 754 (Parke Davis; 1946).

infusion concentrate:
DE 1 617 433 (Desitin; appl. 9.11.1966).
DAS 2 213 275 (Desitin-Werk; appl. 18.3.1972).

Formulation(s):   amp. 250 mg/5 ml; cps. 30 mg, 100 mg; susp. 30 mg/5 ml; tabl. 100 mg (as sodium salt)

Trade Name(s):

D:	Epanutin (Parke Davis)	GB:	Epanutin (Parke Davis)	Metinal Idantoina (Bayer
	Phenhydan (Desitin)	I:	Aurantin (Parke Davis)	Italia)-comb.
	Phenytoin AWD (ASTA		Dintoina (Recordati)	J: Aleviatin (Dainippon)
	Medica AWD)-comb.		Dintoinale (Recordati)-	Hydantol (Fujinaga)
	Zentropil (Knoll)		comb.	USA: Dilantin (Parke Davis; as
F:	Dihydan (Synthélabo)		Dintospina (Recordati)-	sodium salt)
	Pyorédol (Roussel)		comb.	Dilantin (Parke Davis)

Pholcodine

ATC: R05DA08
Use: analgesic, tussive sedative

RN: 509-67-1   MF: $C_{23}H_{30}N_2O_4$ MW: 398.50   EINECS: 208-102-9
LD$_{50}$:   230 mg/kg (M, i.v.); 1 g/kg (M, p.o.)
CN: (5α,6α)-7,8-didehydro-4,5-epoxy-17-methyl-3-[2-(4-morpholinyl)ethoxy]morphinan-6-ol

2-morpholino-
ethyl chloride

morphine
(q. v.)

Pholcodine

Reference(s):
US 2 619 485 (Lab. Dausse; 1952; F-prior. 1949).

Formulation(s):   syrup 5 mg/5 ml, 15 mg/15 ml

Trade Name(s):

D:	Contrapect (Krewel)-		Eucalyptine pholcodine	Copholcoids (Radiol)-
	comb.; wfm		(Martin-Johnson &	comb.; wfm
F:	Biocalyptol pholcodine		Johnson-MSD)-comb.	Galenphol (Galen)
	(Laphal)-comb.		Hexapneumine (Doms-	Pavacol-D (Boehringer
	Bronchalène (Martin-		Adrian)-comb.	Ing.)
	Johnson & Johnson-MSD)-		Isomyrtine (Schwarz)-	Pholtex (Riker)-comb.;
	comb.		comb.	wfm
	Broncorinol (Roche;		Pholcones (RPR Cooper)-	Rinurel linctus (Parke
	Nicholas)-comb.		comb.	Davis)-comb.; wfm
	Dénoral (Théraplix)-comb.		Trophirès (Sanofi	USA: Ethnine (Purdue
	Dimétane expectorant		Winthrop)-comb.	Frederick); wfm
	(Whitehall)-comb.	GB:	Copholco (Radiol)-comb.;	Simplex (Purdue
			wfm	Frederick); wfm

Pholedrine

ATC: N06
Use: sympathomimetic, circulatory
stimulant, mydriatic

RN: 370-14-9   MF: $C_{10}H_{15}NO$ MW: 165.24   EINECS: 206-725-0
LD_{50}:   100 mg/kg (M, parenteral); 119 mg/kg (M, s.c.);
400 mg/kg (R, s.c.)
CN: 4-[2-(methylamino)propyl]phenol

sulfate (2:1)
RN: 6114-26-7   MF: $C_{10}H_{15}NO \cdot 1/2H_2SO_4$ MW: 428.55   EINECS: 228-083-0
LD_{50}:   180 mg/kg (M, i.v.)

4-hydroxyphenyl-   methylamine   Pholedrine
acetone

Reference(s):
Ehrhart-Ruschig, **II**, 155.
DRP 665 793 (Knoll; 1936).
DRP 674 753 (Knoll; 1936).
DRP 672 372 (Knoll; 1936).
DRP 675 361 (Knoll; 1936).

Formulation(s):   drg. 40 mg; drops 20 mg/ml

Trade Name(s):
D: Adyston (Krewel   Pholedrin-longo-Isis (Isis   I: Veritol (Knoll); wfm
Meuselbach)-comb.   Pharma)
Pholedrin liquidum   Zellaforte (Eurim Pharma)-
(Krewel Meuselbach)   comb.

Phthalylsulfathiazole

ATC: A07AB02
Use: chemotherapeutic

RN: 85-73-4   MF: $C_{17}H_{13}N_3O_5S_2$ MW: 403.44   EINECS: 201-627-4
LD_{50}:   920 mg/kg (M, i.p.)
CN: 2-[[[4-[(2-thiazolylamino)sulfonyl]phenyl]amino]carbonyl]benzoic acid

8-hydroxychinoline salt (1:1)
RN: 52310-12-0   MF: $C_{17}H_{13}N_3O_5S_2 \cdot C_9H_7NO$ MW: 548.60   EINECS: 257-837-1

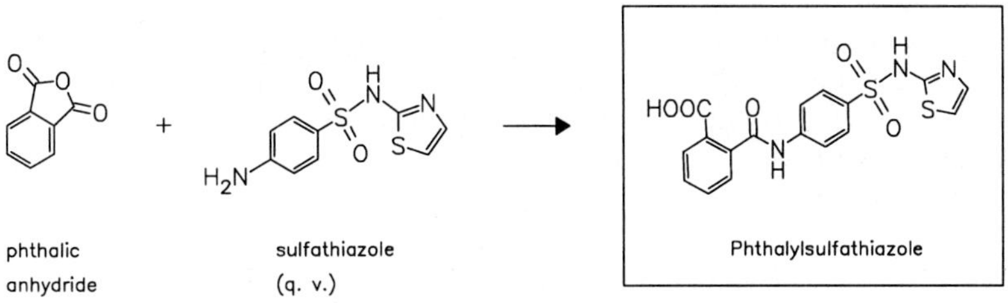

phthalic anhydride   +   sulfathiazole (q. v.)   →   Phthalylsulfathiazole

Reference(s):

US 2 324 013 (Sharp & Dohme; 1943; prior. 1941).
US 2 324 015 (Sharp & Dohme; 1943; prior. 1941).

Formulation(s):   tabl. 500 mg

Trade Name(s):

D:	Diarönt (Chephasaar)-comb.; wfm	GB:	Thalazole (May & Baker); wfm	Streptoguanidin (Lisapharma)-comb.; wfm
	Fluomycin (Fink)-comb.; wfm	I:	Colicitina (Panthox & Burck); wfm	Sulfenteral (Ogna); wfm combination preparations; wfm
F:	Gélotamide (Choay)-comb.; wfm		Enterosteril (Ripari-Gero); wfm	
	Lyantil (Syntex-Daltan)-comb.; wfm		Novosulfina (Medosan); wfm	USA: Neothalidine (Merck Sharp & Dohme)-comb.; wfm
	Talidine (Midy); wfm			Sulfathalidine (Merck Sharp & Dohme); wfm

Phytomenadione

(Phylloquinone; Phytonadione; Vitamin K_1)

ATC: B02BA01
Use: antihemorrhagic vitamin

RN: 84-80-0   MF: $C_{31}H_{46}O_2$ MW: 450.71   EINECS: 201-564-2

LD_{50}:   >6.57 g/kg (M, i.v.); 25 g/kg (M, p.o.);
>33.487 g/kg (R, p.o.)

CN: [R-[R*,R*-(E)]]-2-methyl-3-(3,7,11,15-tetramethyl-2-hexadecenyl)-1,4-naphthalenedione

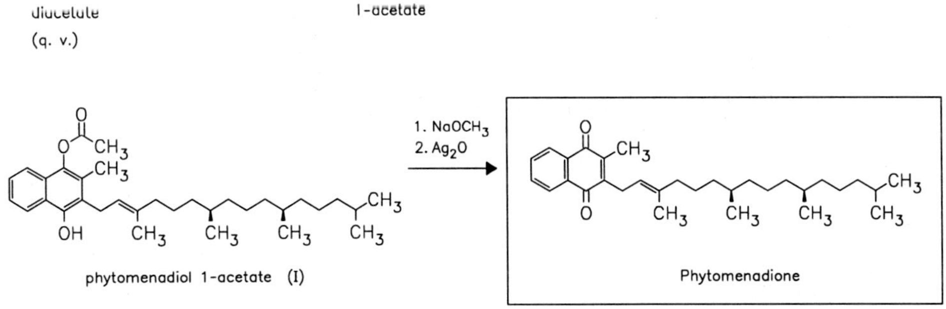

menadiol diacetate (q. v.)

menadiol 1-acetate

phytomenadiol 1-acetate (I)

Phytomenadione

Reference(s):
Fieser, L.F.: J. Am. Chem. Soc. (JACSAT) **61**, 2559, 3467 (1939).
Hirschmann, R. et al.: J. Am. Chem. Soc. (JACSAT) **76**, 4592 (1954).
Isler, O.; Doebel, K.: Helv. Chim. Acta (HCACAV) **22**, 945 (1939); **37**, 225 (1954).
US 2 325 681 (Roche; 1943; CH-prior. 1939).
US 2 683 176 (Roche; 1954; CH-prior. 1951).

direct synthesis from menadiol:
DOS 2 907 864 (Wakunaga Yakuhin; appl. 1.3.1979; J-prior. 4.3.1978).

Formulation(s):   amp. 1 mg/0.5 ml, 1 mg/ml, 10 mg/ml; chewing drg. 10 mg; sol. 2 mg/0.2 ml, 20 mg/ml; syrup
20 mg/ml; tabl. 5 mg

Trade Name(s):

D:	Konakion (Roche)	J:	Eleven K (Nippon		Keipole (Kyowa)

D: Konakion (Roche)   J: Eleven K (Nippon   Keipole (Kyowa)
      Konavit (medphano)   Shinyaku)   Kinadione (Chugai)
      combination preparations   Hymeron (Toa Eiyo-   Kephton (Toyo Jozo)
F: Lafenalac Mead Johnson   Yamanouchi)   Mephyton (Merck-Banyu)
      (Bristol-Myers Squibb;   Kativ N (Takeda)   Monodion (Maruko)
      Division Mead Johnson)-   Kayeine (Kanto)   Nichivita K$_1$ (Nichiiko)
      comb.   Kaywan (Eisai)   One Kay (Mohan)
      Vitalipide (Pharmacia &   K-Eine (Hokuriku)   Synthex P. (Tanabe)
      Upjohn SA)-comb.   Kennegin (Kowa)   USA: Aqua Mephyton (Merck
      Vitamine K$_1$ (Roche)   Kphy (Kobayashi)   Sharp & Dohme)
GB: Konakion (Roche)   Kisikonon (Kyorin)   Mephyton (Merck Sharp &
I: Konakion (Roche)   K-Top Wan (Sawai)   Dohme)

Picotamide

ATC: B01AC03
Use: anticoagulant, fibrinolytic

RN: 32828-81-2   MF: C$_{21}$H$_{20}$N$_4$O$_3$ MW: 376.42   EINECS: 251-245-7
LD$_{50}$: 1205 mg/kg (Mm, i.p.);
       3 g/kg (R, p.o.);
       3 g/kg (dog, p.o.)
CN: 4-methoxy-*N,N'*-bis(3-pyridinylmethyl)-1,3-benzenedicarboxamide

tartrate
RN: 86247-87-2   MF: C$_{21}$H$_{20}$N$_4$O$_3$ · xC$_4$H$_6$O$_6$ MW: unspecified
hydrate
RN: 80530-63-8   MF: C$_{21}$H$_{20}$N$_4$O$_3$ · H$_2$O   MW: 394.43

4-amino-1,3-
dimethyl-
benzene

4-methoxyiso-
phthaloyl
chloride (I)

1. (sulfonate reagent)
2. KMnO$_4$
3. SOCl$_2$

1. dimethyl sulfate
2. potassium permanganate
3. thionyl chloride

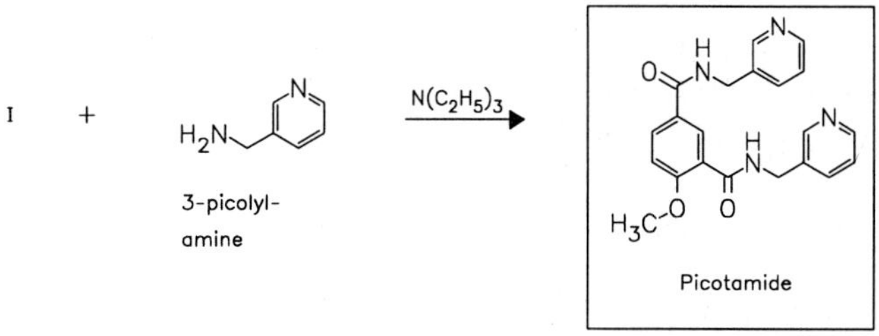

I   +   3-picolyl-amine $\xrightarrow{N(C_2H_5)_3}$ Picotamide

Reference(s):
FR 2 100 850 (Manetti Roberts; appl. 30.6.1971; I-prior. 1.7.1970).
DE 2 506 209 (Manetti Roberts; appl. 14.2.1975).
US 3 973 026 (Manetti Roberts; 3.8.1976; prior. 5.2.1975).
BE 851 967 (Manetti Roberts; appl. 1.3.1977).
Selleri, R. et al.: Chim. Ther. (CHTPBA) **6**, 203 (1971).

Formulation(s):   tabl. 300 mg (as hydrate)

Trade Name(s):
I: Plactidil (Samil)

Pifarnine

ATC: A02B
Use: peptic ulcer therapeutic, gastric acid
secretion inhibitor

RN: 56208-01-6   MF: $C_{27}H_{40}N_2O_2$ MW: 424.63
LD_{50}: 500 mg/kg (M, i.p.)
CN: 1-(1,3-benzodioxol-5-ylmethyl)-4-(3,7,11-trimethyl-2,6,10-dodecatrienyl)piperazine

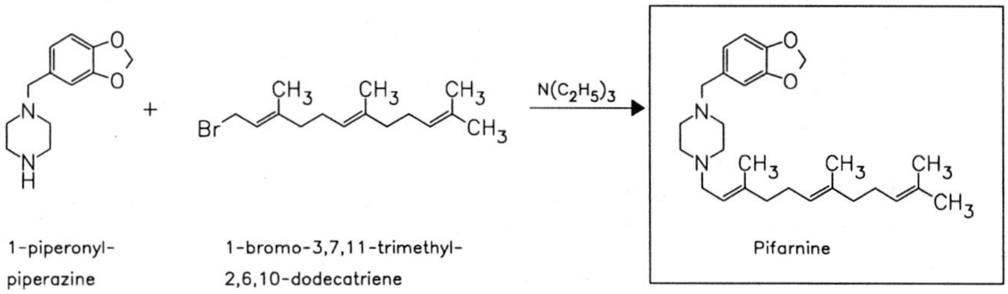

1-piperonyl-piperazine   +   1-bromo-3,7,11-trimethyl-2,6,10-dodecatriene $\xrightarrow{N(C_2H_5)_3}$ Pifarnine

Reference(s):
ES 452 269 (Boehringer Mannh.; appl. 12.11.1976).
Bianchetti, A. et al.: Eur. J. Med. Chem. (EJMCA5) **9**, 555 (1974); **10**, 585 (1975).

Formulation(s):   50 mg

Trade Name(s):
I: Pifazin (Pierrel); wfm

Pifoxime
(Pixifenidum)

ATC: M01AB
Use: anti-inflammatory

RN: 31224-92-7   MF: $C_{15}H_{20}N_2O_3$ MW: 276.34
LD$_{50}$: 1 g/kg (M, p.o.)
CN: 1-[[4-[1-(hydroxyimino)ethyl]phenoxy]acetyl]piperidine

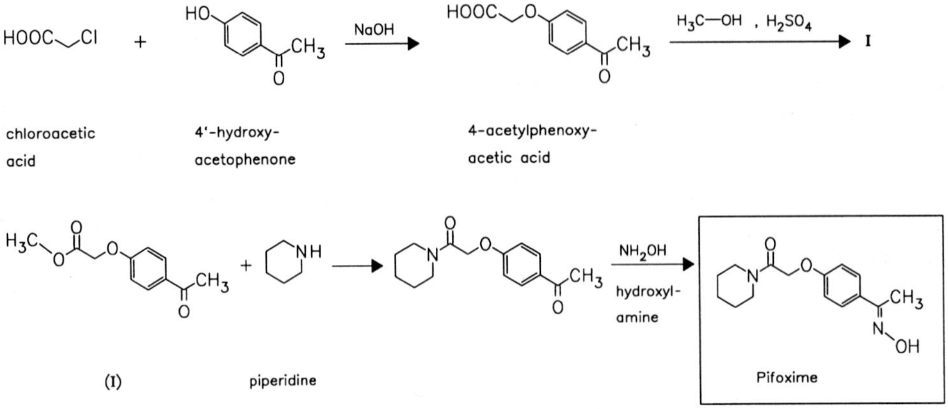

chloroacetic   4'-hydroxy-   4-acetylphenoxy-
acid   acetophenone   acetic acid

(I)   piperidine   Pifoxime

Reference(s):
US 3 907 792 (A. Mieville; 23.9.1975; CH-prior. 31.1.1969, 28.8.1969).

Trade Name(s):
F: Flamanil (Salvoxyl-
      Wander); wfm

Piketoprofen

ATC: M02AA
Use: topical non-steroidal anti-
       inflammatory and analgesic,
       ketoprofen derivative

RN: 60576-13-8   MF: $C_{22}H_{20}N_2O_2$ MW: 344.41
CN: 3-benzoyl-α-methyl-N-(4-methyl-2-pyridinyl)benzeneacetamide

monohydrochloride
RN: 59512-37-7   MF: $C_{22}H_{20}N_2O_2 \cdot$ HCl   MW: 380.88

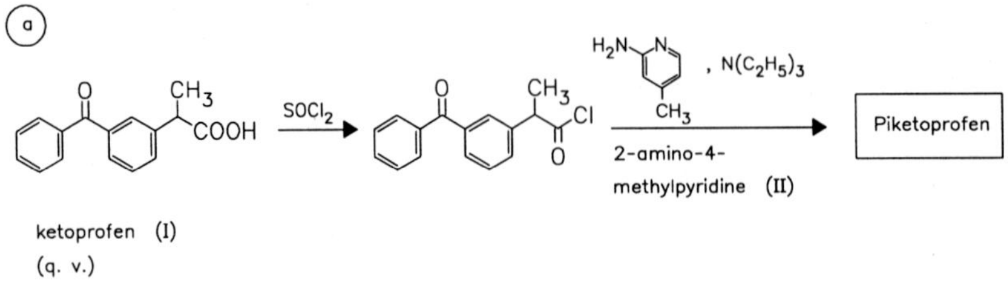

ketoprofen (I)
(q. v.)

2-amino-4-
methylpyridine (II)

Piketoprofen

b

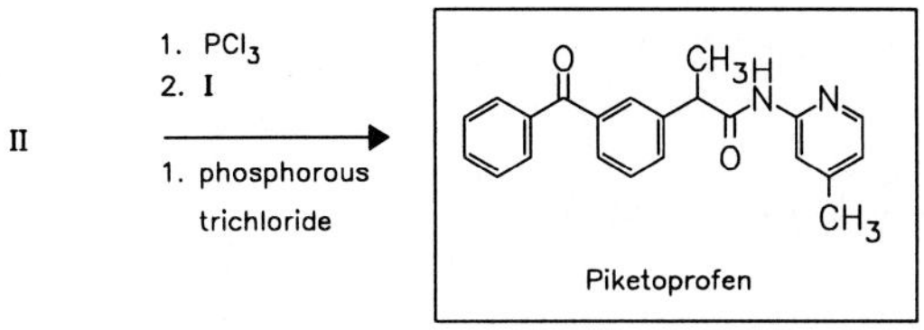

1. PCl₃
2. I

II
→

1. phosphorous
   trichloride

Piketoprofen

Reference(s):
a GB 1 436 502 (A. Gallardo SA; appl. 10.4.1974; E-prior. 10.4.1973).
b BE 882 711 (Fordonal SA; appl. 31.7.1980; E-prior. 25.2.1980).

Formulation(s):   aerosol 20 mg/ml

Trade Name(s):
E: Calmatel (Almirall; 1985)

Pildralazine

ATC: C01D
Use: hypotensive, vasodilator

RN: 64000-73-3   MF: $C_8H_{15}N_5O$ MW: 197.24
CN: 6-[(2-hydroxypropyl)methylamino]-3(2H)-pyridazinone hydrazone

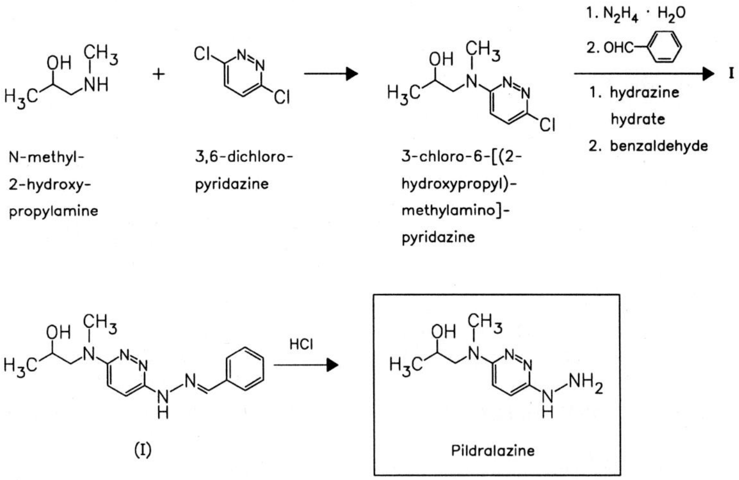

1. $N_2H_4 \cdot H_2O$
2. OHC—

1. hydrazine
   hydrate
2. benzaldehyde

→ I

N-methyl-   3,6-dichloro-   3-chloro-6-[(2-
2-hydroxy-   pyridazine   hydroxypropyl)-
propylamine   methylamino]-
                                      pyridazine

(I)

HCl
→

Pildralazine

Reference(s):
Pifferi, G.; Parravicini, F.; Carpi, C.; Dorigotti, L.: J. Med. Chem. (JMCMAR) **18**, 741 (1975).
DOS 2 154 245 (ISF; appl. 30.10.1971; I-prior. 15.12.1970).

Trade Name(s):
I: Atensil (ISF); wfm

Pilocarpine

ATC: N07AX01; S01EB01
Use: parasympathomimetic, miotic

RN: 92-13-7   MF: $C_{11}H_{16}N_2O_2$ MW: 208.26   EINECS: 202-128-4
LD_{50}:   61.9 mg/kg (M, i.v.); 119 mg/kg (M, p.o.);
        88.5 mg/kg (R, i.v.); 402 mg/kg (R, p.o.)
CN: (3S-cis)-3-ethyldihydro-4-[(1-methyl-1H-imidazol-5-yl)methyl]-2(3H)-furanone

monohydrochloride
RN: 54-71-7   MF: $C_{11}H_{16}N_2O_2 \cdot HCl$ MW: 244.72   EINECS: 200-212-5
LD_{50}:   150 mg/kg (M, i.v.); 200 mg/kg (M, p.o.)
borate
RN: 16509-56-1   MF: $C_{11}H_{16}N_2O_2 \cdot xBH_3O_3$ MW: unspecified
mononitrate
RN: 148-72-1   MF: $C_{11}H_{16}N_2O_2 \cdot HNO_3$ MW: 271.27   EINECS: 205-723-7
LD_{50}:   345 mg/kg (M, i.v.);
        911 mg/kg (R, p.o.)

Pilocarpine

By extraction of *Jaborandi* leaves (especially *Pilocarpus microphyllus* Stapf.) and isolation as hydrochloride.

Reference(s):
Ullmanns Encykl. Tech. Chem., 3. Aufl., Vol. **3**, 277.
BIOS Final Reports No. 766, 233.

pamoate:
DAS 2 462 081 (Merck & Co., appl. 16.12.1974; USA-prior. 17.12.1973, 31.10.1974).

Formulation(s):   eye drops 0.5 %, 1 %, 2 %, 3 %, 4 %; eye ointment 10 mg/g, 20 mg/g, 30 mg/g; gel 40 mg/g
        (as hydrochloride)

Trade Name(s):
D: Isopto-Pilocarpin (Alcon)
    Pilocarpol (Winzer)
    Pilomann (Mann)
    Spersa carpin (CIBA
    Vision)
    Vistacarpin (Pharm-
    Allergan)
    numerous generics and
    combination preparations
F: Chibro-Pilocarpine (Merck
    Sharp & Dohme-Chibret)

    Isopto-Pilocarpine (Alcon)
    Pilo (Chauvin)
    Pilocarpine Martinet (CIBA
    Vision Ophthalmics)
GB: Isoptocarpin (Alcon)
    Minims Pilocarpine
    (Chauvin; as nitrate)
    Ocusert Pilo (Dominion)
    Pilogel (Alcon)
    Salagen (Chiron)
    Sno-Pilo (Chauvin)

I: Dropilton (Bruschettini)
    Liocarpina (SIFI)
    Pilocarpina Lux (Allergan)
    Pilogel (Alcon)
    Pilotonina (Farmila)
    Salagen (Chiron Italia)
    generics
J: generic preparations
USA: Salagen (MGI)

Pilsicainide
(SUN-1165)

ATC: C01BC
Use: class Ic antiarrhythmic

RN: 88069-67-4   MF: $C_{17}H_{24}N_2O$ MW: 272.39
LD$_{50}$: 17 mg/kg (M, i.v.); 175 mg/kg (M, p.o.);
        18 mg/kg (R, i.v.); 255 mg/kg (R, p.o.);
        53 mg/kg (dog, p.o.)
CN: N-(2,6-dimethylphenyl)tetrahydro-1H-pyrrolizine-7a(5H)-acetamide

monohydrochloride
RN: 88069-49-2   MF: $C_{17}H_{24}N_2O \cdot HCl$ MW: 308.85
LD$_{50}$: 222 mg/kg (M, p.o.); 410 mg/kg (M, s.c.);
        260 mg/kg (R, p.o.);
        87 mg/kg (rabbit, p.o.);
        50 mg/kg (dog, p.o.)

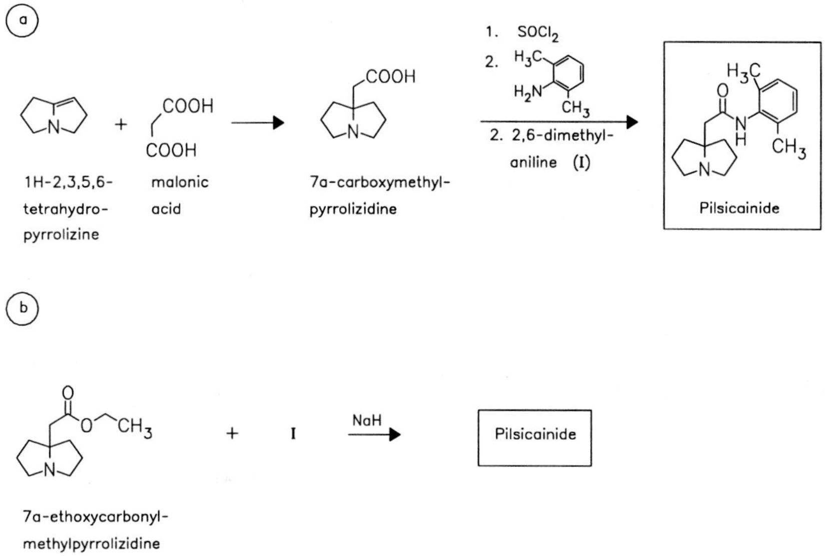

1H-2,3,5,6-
tetrahydro-
pyrrolizine

malonic
acid

7a-carboxymethyl-
pyrrolizidine

Pilsicainide

7a-ethoxycarbonyl-
methylpyrrolizidine

Pilsicainide

Reference(s):
EP 89 061 (Suntory; appl. 15.3.1983; J-prior. 16.3.1982).
US 4 564 624 (Suntory; 14.1.1986; appl. 10.3.1983; J-prior. 16.3.1982).
JP 9 167 591 (Suntory; appl. 11.3.1983).

Formulation(s):   cps. 25 mg, 50 mg (as hydrochloride)

Trade Name(s):
J: Sunrythm (Suntory; Daiichi
        Seiyaku; 1991)

Pimefylline

ATC: C01D
Use: vasodilator

RN: 10001-43-1   MF: $C_{15}H_{18}N_6O_2$ MW: 314.35
LD$_{50}$: 402 mg/kg (M, i.v.); 1900 mg/kg (M, p.o.)
CN: 3,7-dihydro-1,3-dimethyl-7-[2-[(3-pyridinylmethyl)amino]ethyl]-1H-purine-2,6-dione

nicotinate (1:1)

RN: 10058-07-8 MF: $C_{15}H_{18}N_6O_2 \cdot C_6H_5NO_2$ MW: 437.46 EINECS: 233-185-3
LD$_{50}$: 470 mg/kg (M, i.v.); 2530 mg/kg (M, p.o.);
3700 mg/kg (R, p.o.)

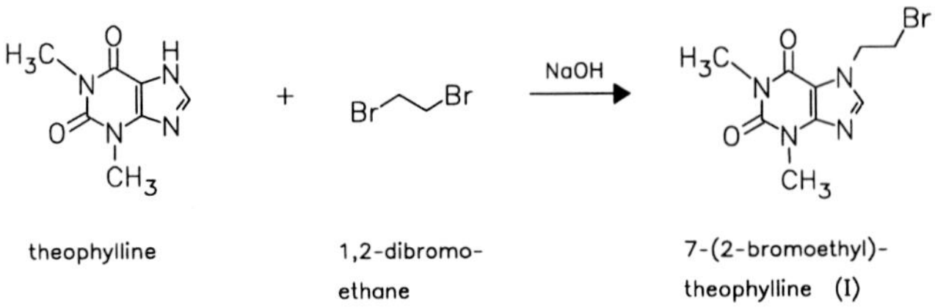

theophylline   1,2-dibromo-ethane   7-(2-bromoethyl)-theophylline (I)

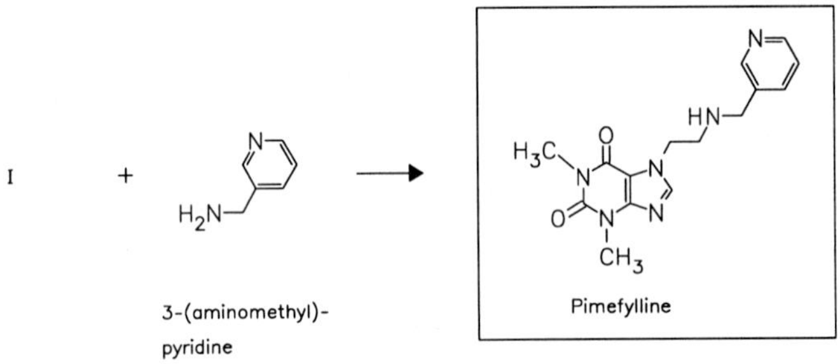

I +

3-(aminomethyl)-pyridine   Pimefylline

Reference(s):

US 3 350 400 (Eprova; 31.10.1967; CH-prior. 12.1.1965).

Trade Name(s):

I: Teonicon (Neopharmed);   J: Teonicon (Neopharmed)
wfm

Pimeprofen

(Ibuprofen piconol)

ATC: M01AE; M02AA
Use: anti-inflammatory

RN: 64622-45-3 MF: $C_{19}H_{23}NO_2$ MW: 297.40 EINECS: 264-979-8
LD$_{50}$: 1980 mg/kg (M, p.o.);
1440 mg/kg (R, p.o.);
>4 g/kg (dog, p.o.)
CN: α-methyl-4-(2-methylpropyl)benzeneacetic acid 2-pyridinylmethyl ester

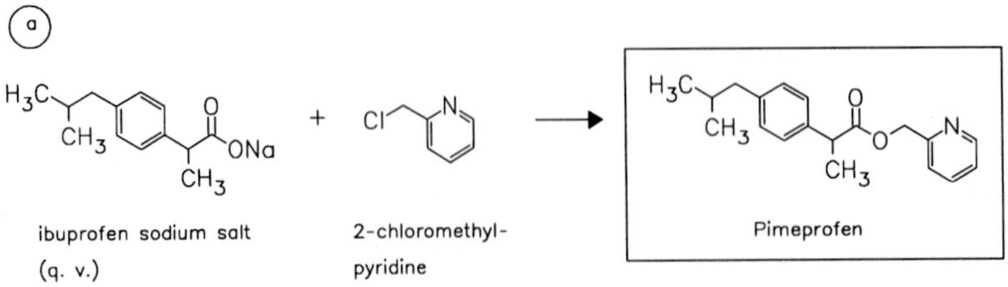

ibuprofen sodium salt   2-chloromethyl-pyridine   Pimeprofen
(q. v.)

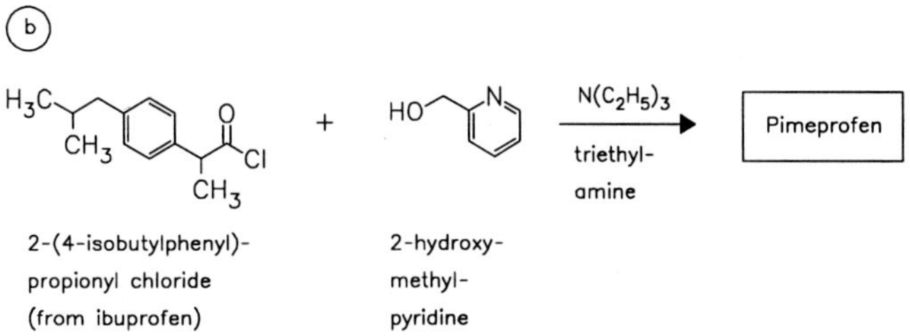

ⓑ

2-(4-isobutylphenyl)-
propionyl chloride
(from ibuprofen)

2-hydroxy-
methyl-
pyridine

Pimeprofen

N(C₂H₅)₃
triethyl-
amine

Reference(s):
DOS 2 658 610 (Hisamitsu; appl. 23.12.1976; J-prior. 24.12.1975).
US 4 150 137 (Hisamitsu; 17.4.1979; J-prior. 24.12.1975).

Formulation(s):   cream 5 %; ointment 5 %

Trade Name(s):
J: Staderm (Torii)   Vesicum (Hisamitsu)

Pimobendan
(UD-CG 115; UD-CG 115BS)

ATC: C01CE
Use: cardiotonic, PDE III-inhibitor,
         vasodilator

RN: 74150-27-9   MF: $C_{19}H_{18}N_4O_2$ MW: 334.38
LD$_{50}$: >2 g/kg (M, p.o.);
        72 mg/kg (R, i.v.); 950 mg/kg (R, p.o.)
CN: 4,5-dihydro-6-[2-(4-methoxyphenyl)-1H-benzimidazol-5-yl]-5-methyl-3(2H)-pyridazinone

hydrochloride
RN: 74149-75-0   MF: $C_{19}H_{18}N_4O_2 \cdot$ xHCl   MW: unspecified
monohydrochloride
RN: 77469-98-8   MF: $C_{19}H_{18}N_4O_2 \cdot$ HCl   MW: 370.84
racemate
RN: 118428-36-7   MF: $C_{19}H_{18}N_4O_2$ MW: 334.38
LD$_{50}$: 75 mg/kg (R, i.v.)
(–)-enantiomer
RN: 118428-37-8   MF: $C_{19}H_{18}N_4O_2$ MW: 334.38
LD$_{50}$: 100 mg/kg (R, i.v.)
(+)-enantiomer
RN: 118428-38-9   MF: $C_{19}H_{18}N_4O_2$ MW: 334.38
LD$_{50}$: 75 mg/kg (R, i.v.)

4-anisoyl
chloride

methyl 3-(4-amino-
3-nitrobenzoyl)-
butyrate

chloro-
benzene

methyl 3-[4-(4-methoxy-
benzoylamino)-3-nitro-
benzoyl]butyrate (I)

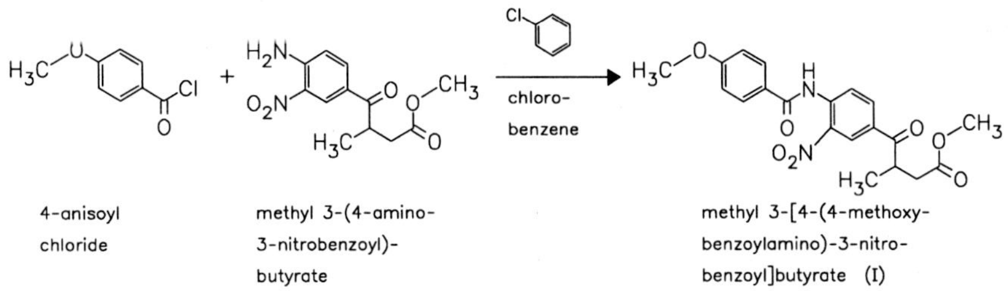

I

II

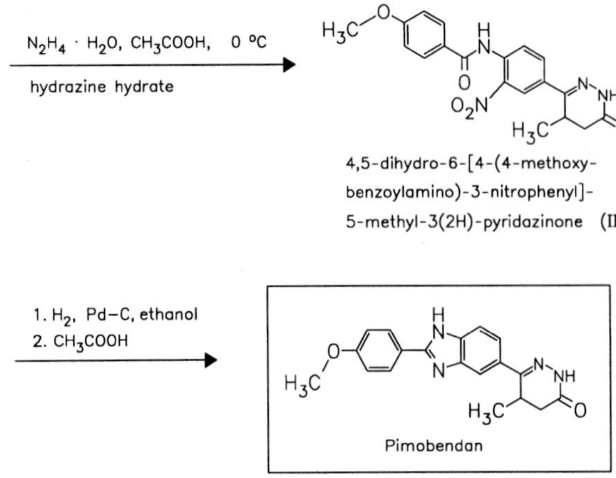

N2H4 · H2O, CH3COOH, 0 °C
hydrazine hydrate
4,5-dihydro-6-[4-(4-methoxy-benzoylamino)-3-nitrophenyl]-5-methyl-3(2H)-pyridazinone (II)
1. H2, Pd–C, ethanol
2. CH3COOH
Pimobendan

Reference(s):
EP 8 391 (Thomae GmbH; appl. 3.2.1980; D-prior. 25.8.1978, 1.6.1979).

separation of enantiomers:
DE 3 728 244 (Thomae GmbH; appl. 25.8.1987; D-prior. 25.8.1987).

oral formulation:
DE 4 001 622 (Thomae GmbH; appl. 20.1.1990; D-prior. 20.1.1990).

use for treatment of asthma:
DE 4 001 623 (Thomae GmbH; appl. 20.1.1990; D-prior. 20.1.1990).

combination with β-blockers:
EP 387 762 (Thomae GmbH; appl. 12.3.1990; D-prior. 16.3.1989).

use for treating erectile dysfunction:
DE 4 338 948 (J. Carlen; appl. 15.11.1993; D-prior. 15.11.1993).

Formulation(s): cps. 1.25 mg, 2.5 mg

Trade Name(s):
J: Acardi (Nippon Boehringer)

Pimozide

ATC: N05AG02
Use: neuroleptic

RN: 2062-78-4 MF: $C_{28}H_{29}F_2N_3O$ MW: 461.56 EINECS: 218-171-7
LD_{50}: 14 mg/kg (M, i.v.); 228 mg/kg (M, p.o.);
90 mg/kg (R, i.v.); 1100 mg/kg (R, p.o.);
32 mg/kg (dog, i.v.); 40 mg/kg (dog, p.o.)
CN: 1-[1-[4,4-bis(4-fluorophenyl)butyl]-4-piperidinyl]-1,3-dihydro-2*H*-benzimidazol-2-one

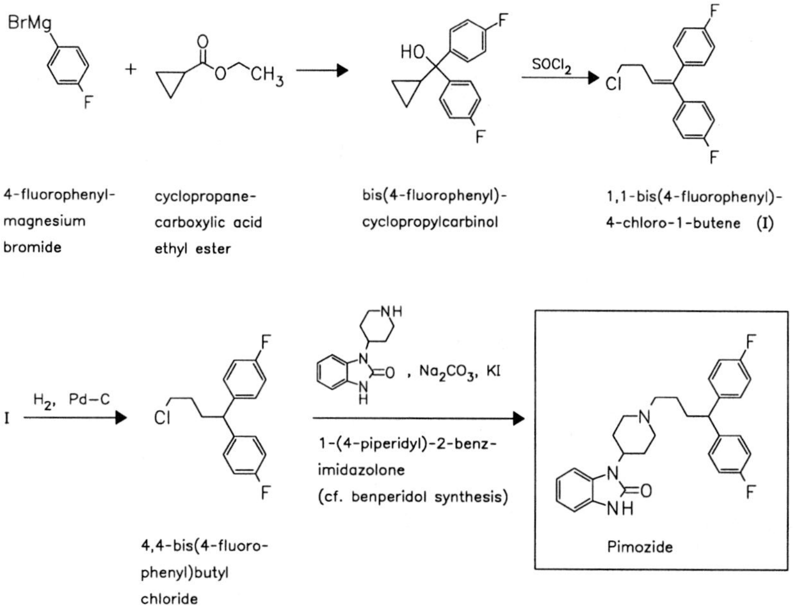

4-fluorophenyl-
magnesium
bromide

cyclopropane-
carboxylic acid
ethyl ester

bis(4-fluorophenyl)-
cyclopropylcarbinol

1,1-bis(4-fluorophenyl)-
4-chloro-1-butene   (I)

4,4-bis(4-fluoro-
phenyl)butyl
chloride

1-(4-piperidyl)-2-benz-
imidazolone
(cf. benperidol synthesis)

Pimozide

Reference(s):

DAS 1 470 124 (Janssen; appl. 12.6.1963; USA-prior. 13.6.1962, 11.6.1963).
FR-M 3 695 (Janssen; appl. 12.9.1963; USA-prior. 11.6.1963).
US 3 196 157 (Janssen; 20.7.1965; appl. 11.6.1963).
DD 243 284 (VEB Arzneimittelwerk Dresden; appl. 13.12.1985).

Formulation(s):   tabl. 1 mg, 2 mg, 4 mg

Trade Name(s):
D: Antalon (ASTA Medica   F: Orap (Janssen-Cilag)   J: Orap (Fujisawa)
        AWD)   GB: Orap (Janssen-Cilag)   USA: Orap (Gate)
        Orap (Janssen-Cilag)   I: Orap (Janssen-Cilag)

Pinacidil

(P-1134)

ATC: C02DG01
Use: antihypertensive, vasodilator,
        potassium channel activator

RN: 60560-33-0   MF: $C_{13}H_{19}N_5$ MW: 245.33   EINECS: 262-294-9
LD$_{50}$:   177 mg/kg (M, i.v.); 412 mg/kg (M, p.o.);
        155 mg/kg (R, i.v.); 210 mg/kg (R, p.o.)
CN: N-cyano-N'-4-pyridinyl-N''-(1,2,2-trimethylpropyl)guanidine

monohydrate
RN: 85371-64-8   MF: $C_{13}H_{19}N_5 \cdot H_2O$ MW: 263.35
LD$_{50}$:   600 mg/kg (M, p.o.);
        570 mg/kg (R, p.o.)

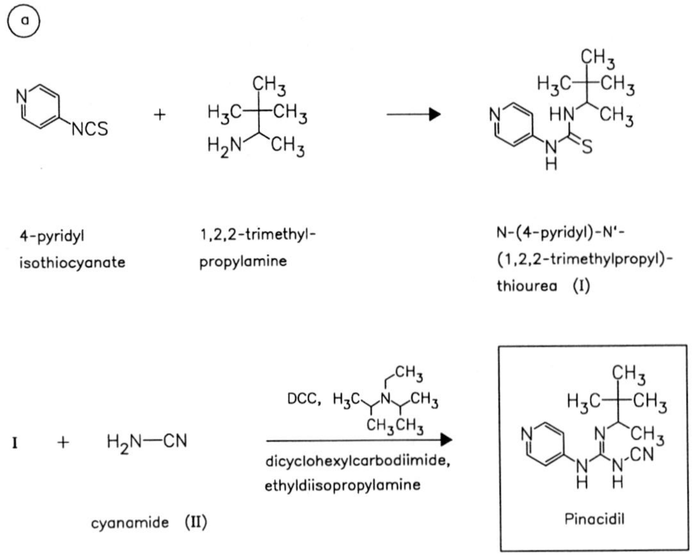

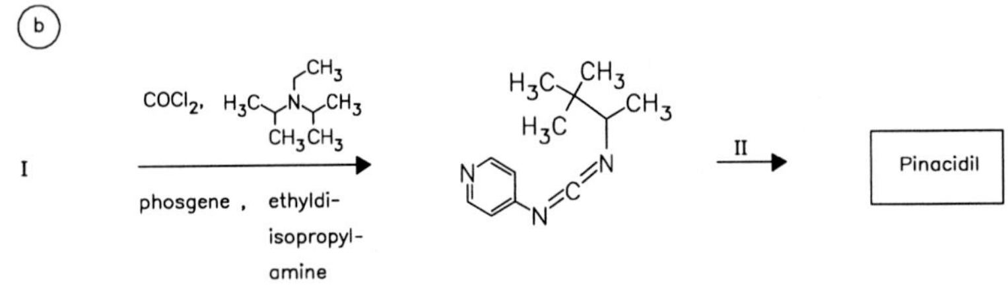

a

4-pyridyl
isothiocyanate

1,2,2-trimethyl-
propylamine

N-(4-pyridyl)-N'-
(1,2,2-trimethylpropyl)-
thiourea (I)

I + H₂N—CN

DCC, H₃C—N—CH₃ / CH₃CH₃
dicyclohexylcarbodiimide,
ethyldiisopropylamine

cyanamide (II)

Pinacidil

b

I

COCl₂, H₃C—N—CH₃ / CH₃CH₃
phosgene , ethyldi-
isopropyl-
amine

II

Pinacidil

Reference(s):
DE 2 557 438 (Leo; appl. 19.12.1975; GB-prior. 20.12.1974).
DE 2 560 633 (Leo; appl. 19.12.1975; GB-prior. 20.12.1974).
GB 1 489 879 (Leo; appl. 20.12.1974).
Petersen, H.J. et al.: J. Med. Chem. (JMCMAR) **21**, 773 (1978).
Hansen, E.T.; Petersen, H.J.: Synth. Commun. (SYNCAV) **14**, 537 (1984).

medical use for treatment of asthma:
EP 207 606 (Lilly; appl. 15.5.1986; USA-prior. 17.5.1985).

medical use for treatment of peripheral vascular disease:
EP 223 811 (Beecham; appl. 20.5.1986; GB-prior. 29.5.1985, 22.5.1985).

combination with ACE inhibitors:
EP 271 271 (Beecham; appl. 30.11.1987; GB-prior. 24.12.1986, 6.12.1986).

combination with β-blocker:
EP 323 745 (Beecham; appl. 23.12.1988; GB-prior. 6.1.1988).

sustained release formulation:
DOS 3 404 595 (Leo; appl. 9.2.1984; DK-prior. 11.2.1983).

Formulation(s):   cps. 12.5 mg, 25 mg

Trade Name(s):
DK: Pindac (Leo)

Pinazepam

ATC: N05BA14
Use: tranquilizer

RN: 52463-83-9   MF: $C_{18}H_{13}ClN_2O$ MW: 308.77   EINECS: 257-934-9
LD_{50}:   1302 mg/kg (M, p.o.);
5819 mg/kg (R, p.o.)
CN: 7-chloro-1,3-dihydro-5-phenyl-1-(2-propynyl)-2H-1,4-benzodiazepin-2-one

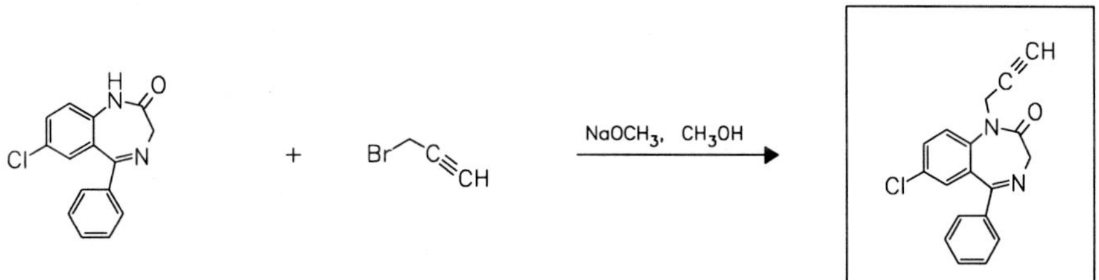

7-chloro-1,3-dihydro-
5-phenyl-2H-1,4-benzo-
diazepin-2-one
(cf. diazepam synthesis)

2-propynyl
bromide

Pinazepam

Reference(s):
DOS 2 339 790 (Zambeletti; appl. 6.8.1973; I-prior. 9.8.1972).
GB 1 406 946 (Zambeletti; valid from 28.6.1973; I-prior. 9.8.1972).

alternative synthesis:
US 3 842 094 (Delmar Chem.; 15.10.1974; prior. 31.8.1972).

Formulation(s):   cps. 2.5 mg, 5 mg, 10 mg

Trade Name(s):
I: Domar (Teofarma)

Pindolol

ATC: C07AA03
Use: beta blocking agent

RN: 13523-86-9   MF: $C_{14}H_{20}N_2O_2$ MW: 248.33   EINECS: 236-867-9
LD_{50}:   22.6 mg/kg (M, i.v.); 235 mg/kg (M, p.o.);
51 mg/kg (R, i.v.); 263 mg/kg (R, p.o.)
CN: 1-(1H-indol-4-yloxy)-3-[(1-methylethyl)amino]-2-propanol

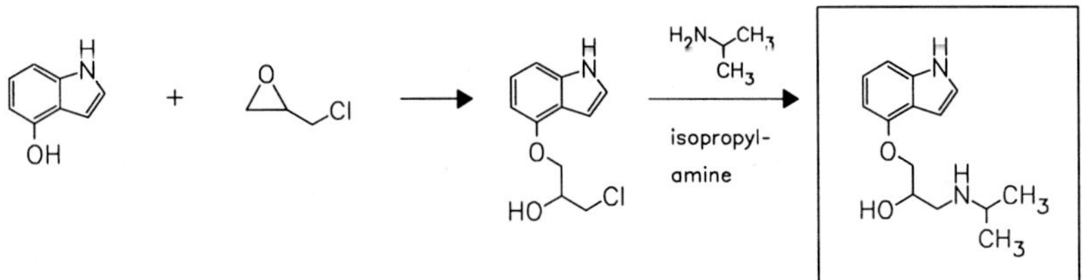

4-hydroxy-
indole

epichloro-
hydrin

3-chloro-1-
(4-indolyloxy)-
2-propanol

isopropyl-
amine

Pindolol

Reference(s):
DE 1 620 342 (Sandoz; prior. 26.1.1966).
US 3 471 515 (Sandoz; 7.10.1967; CH-prior. 1.2.1965).
CH 453 363 (Sandoz; appl. 1.2.1965).

Formulation(s):   amp. 0.4 mg/2 ml; eye drops 5 mg/ml, 10 mg/5 ml; s. r. tabl. 20 mg; tabl. 2.5 mg, 5 mg, 10 mg, 15 mg

Trade Name(s):

D:	Durapindol (durachemie)	Visken (Novartis Pharma;	I:	Visken (Novartis Farma;
	Glauco-Stulln (Pharma | 1971)		1973)
	Stulln)	F:	Viskaldix (Novartis)-comb.	J:	Carvisken (Sankyo)
	Pindoptan (Kanoldt)	Visken (Novartis; 1971)	USA:	Visken (Sandoz; 1982);
	Viskaldix (Novartis	GB:	Viskaldix (Novartis)-comb.		wfm
	Pharma)-comb.	Visken (Novartis; 1974)		generics

Pioglitazone
(AD-4833; U 72107)

ATC: A10BG03
Use: antidiabetic, insulinenhancer

RN: 111025-46-8   MF: $C_{19}H_{20}N_2O_3S$ MW: 356.45
CN: (±)-5-[[4-[2-(5-Ethyl-2-pyridinyl)ethoxy]phenyl]methyl]-2,4-thiazolidinedione

hydrochloride
RN: 112529-15-4   MF: $C_{19}H_{20}N_2O_3S \cdot HCl$ MW: 392.91

2-(5-ethyl-2-pyridyl)ethanol (I) + 4-fluoro-1-nitrobenzene → (NaH, DMF) → 4-[2-(5-ethyl-2-pyridyl)ethoxy]-1-nitrobenzene (II)

II → (H₂, Pd–C, CH₃OH) → amine → 1. NaNO₂, HBr, Cu₂O, H₂O; 2. H₂C=CH-COOCH₃ methyl acrylate → III

methyl 2-bromo-3-[4-[2-(5-ethyl-2-pyridyl)ethoxy]phenyl]-propionate (III) + thiourea → (H₃C—COONa, H₃C—OH sodium acetate) → IV

(IV) → (2N HCl) → Pioglitazone hydrochloride

(b)

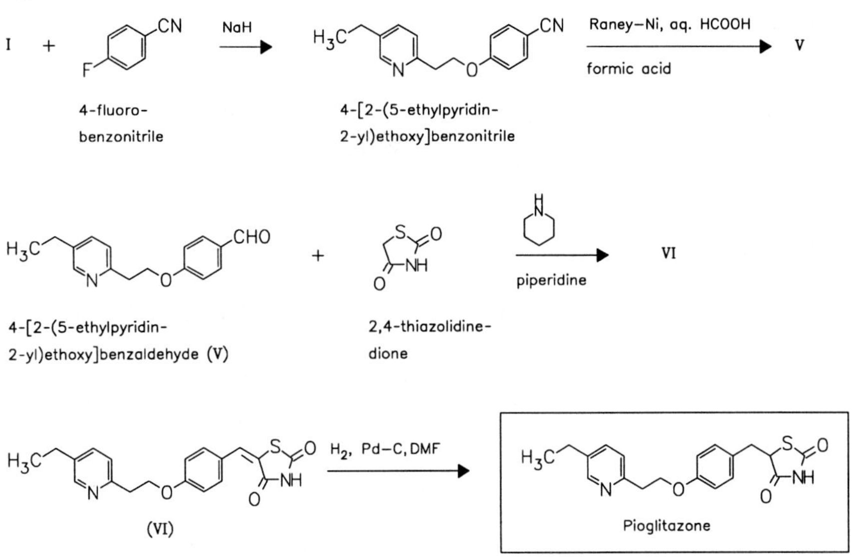

I + [4-fluoro-benzonitrile] →(NaH) [4-[2-(5-ethylpyridin-2-yl)ethoxy]benzonitrile] →(Raney—Ni, aq. HCOOH / formic acid) V

4-fluoro-
benzonitrile

4-[2-(5-ethylpyridin-
2-yl)ethoxy]benzonitrile

[4-[2-(5-ethylpyridin-2-yl)ethoxy]benzaldehyde (V)] + [2,4-thiazolidine-dione] →(piperidine) VI

4-[2-(5-ethylpyridin-
2-yl)ethoxy]benzaldehyde (V)

2,4-thiazolidine-
dione

(VI) →(H₂, Pd—C, DMF) Pioglitazone

(VI)

Pioglitazone

(c)

I + [Cl-SO₂-C₆H₄-CH₃] →(benzyltributyl-ammonium chloride (VII), Cl⁻, aq. NaOH) (VIII)

benzyltributyl-
ammonium chloride (VII)

(VIII)

VIII + [4-hydroxy-benzaldehyde] →(VII, aq. NaOH) V - - - → Pioglitazone

4-hydroxy-
benzaldehyde

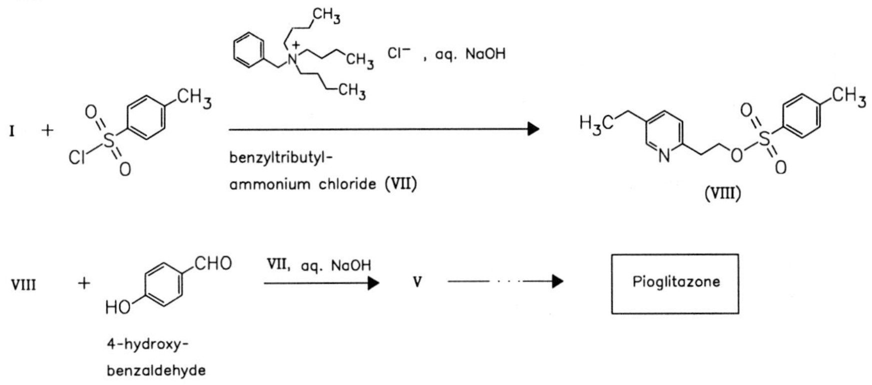

(d)

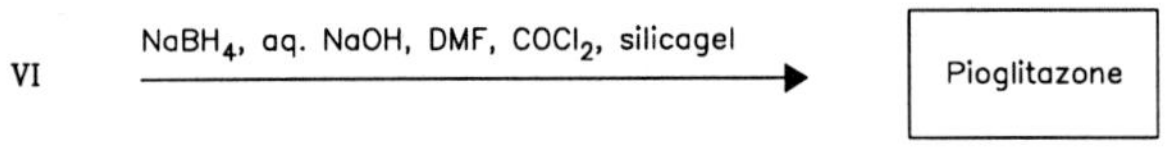

VI →(NaBH₄, aq. NaOH, DMF, COCl₂, silicagel) Pioglitazone

Reference(s):
a   Sohda, T. et al.: Arzneim.-Forsch. (ARZNAD) **40** (1), 37-42 (1990).
    EP 193 256 (Takeda; appl. 15.1.1986; J-prior. 19.1.1985).
b,c EP 506 273 (Takeda; appl. 16.3.1992; J-prior. 25.3.1991).
    Momose, Y. et al.: Chem. Pharm. Bull. (CPBTAL) **39** (6), 1440-1445 (1991).
c   EP 186 340 (Takeda; appl. 26.6.1997; J-prior. 27.6.1996).
d   WO 9 313 095 (Upjohn; appl. 4.12.1992; USA-prior. 20.12.1991).

synthesis of metabolites:
Tanis, S.P. et al.: J. Med. Chem. (JMCMAR) **39** (26), 5053-5063 (1996).
WO 9 322 445 (Upjohn; appl. 21.4.1993; USA-prior. 5.5.1992).

Formulation(s):   tabl. 15 mg, 30 mg, 45 mg (as hydrochloride)

Trade Name(s):
USA: Actos (Takeda/Lilly; 1999)

Pipamazine

ATC: A04
Use: anti-emetic

RN: 84-04-8   MF: $C_{21}H_{24}ClN_3OS$ MW: 401.96   EINECS: 201-512-9
LD_{50}:   370 mg/kg (M, p.o.);
          620 mg/kg (R, p.o.)
CN: 1-[3-(2-chloro-10*H*-phenothiazin-10-yl)propyl]-4-piperidinecarboxamide

2-chloro-
phenothiazine

1. NaNH₂
2. Br⌒⌒Cl

1. sodium amide
2. 1-bromo-3-chloro-
   propane

2-chloro-10-(3-chloro-
propyl)phenothiazine   (I)

I   +   piperidine-4-
carboxamide   →[K₂CO₃, NaI]   Pipamazine

Reference(s):
US 2 957 870 (Searle; 25.10.1960; prior. 5.11.1957).
DE 1 089 386 (Searle; appl. 8.11.1957; USA-prior. 15.11.1956).

Formulation(s):   5 mg

Trade Name(s):
F: Nausidol (Grémy-   USA: Mornidine (Searle); wfm
       Longuet); wfm

Pipamperone

(Floropipamide)

ATC: N05AD05
Use: neuroleptic

RN: 1893-33-0   MF: $C_{21}H_{30}FN_3O_2$ MW: 375.49
LD_{50}:   66 mg/kg (M, i.v.); 490 mg/kg (M, p.o.);
          48 mg/kg (R, i.v.); 160 mg/kg (R, p.o.)
CN: 1'-[4-(4-fluorophenyl)-4-oxobutyl][1,4'-bipiperidine]-4'-carboxamide

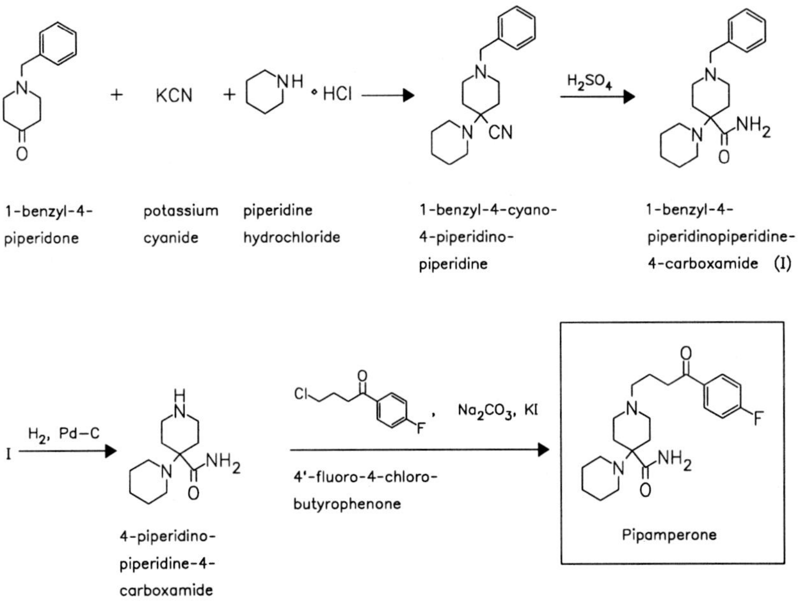
KCN
HCl
H2SO4
CN
NH2
1-benzyl-4-piperidone
potassium cyanide
piperidine hydrochloride
1-benzyl-4-cyano-4-piperidino-piperidine
1-benzyl-4-piperidinopiperidine-4-carboxamide (I)
H2, Pd–C
Na2CO3, KI
4'-fluoro-4-chloro-butyrophenone
4-piperidino-piperidine-4-carboxamide
Pipamperone

Reference(s):
US 3 041 344 (Janssen; 26.6.1962; prior. 1.12.1960).
DE 1 235 319 (Janssen; appl. 28.11.1961; USA-prior. 1.12.1960).
Westeringh, C. van de et al.: J. Med. Chem. (JMCMAR) **7**, 619 (1964).

Formulation(s): syrup 20 mg/5 ml; tabl. 40 mg (as dihydrochloride)

Trade Name(s):

D:	Dipiperon (Janssen-Cilag)	F:	Dipiperon (Janssen-Cilag; as dihydrochloride)	I:	Piperonil (Lusofarmaco)
				J:	Propitan (Eisai)

Pipazetate
(Pipazethate)

ATC: R05DB11
Use: antitussive

RN: 2167-85-3 MF: $C_{21}H_{25}N_3O_3S$ MW: 399.52 EINECS: 218-508-8
LD_{50}: 13.14 mg/kg (M, i.v.)
CN: 10*H*-pyrido[3,2-*b*][1,4]benzothiazine-10-carboxylic acid 2-[2-(1-piperidinyl)ethoxy]ethyl ester

monohydrochloride
RN: 6056-11-7 MF: $C_{21}H_{25}N_3O_3S \cdot HCl$ MW: 435.98 EINECS: 227-980-4
LD_{50}: 16 mg/kg (M, i.v.); 214 mg/kg (M, p.o.);
17 mg/kg (R, i.v.); 530 mg/kg (R, p.o.),
8 mg/kg (dog, i.v.); 80 mg/kg (dog, p.o.)

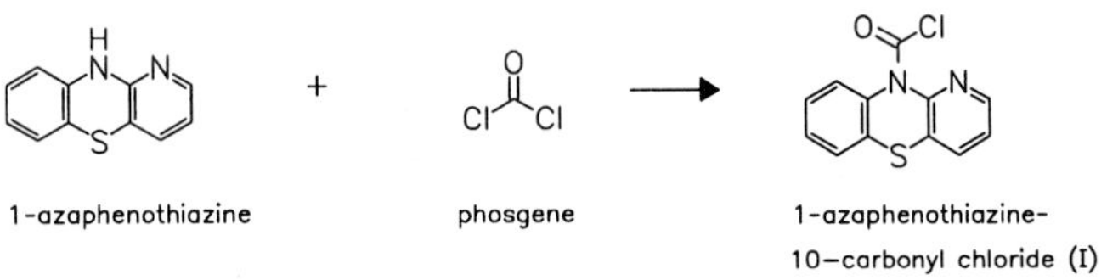
1-azaphenothiazine
phosgene
1-azaphenothiazine-10-carbonyl chloride (I)

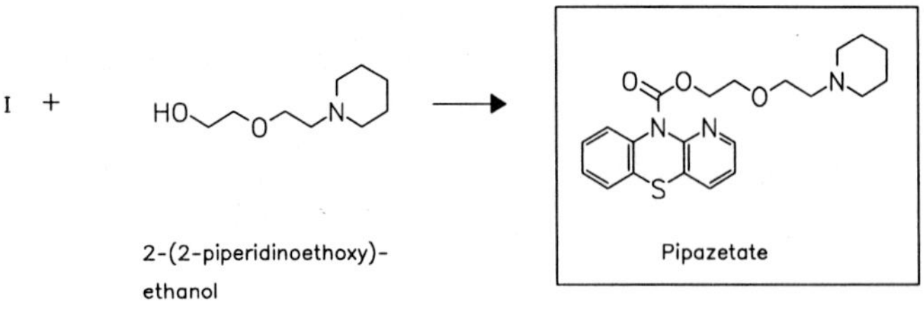

I +   HO⌣⌣O⌣⌣N◯

2-(2-piperidinoethoxy)-
ethanol

Pipazetate

Reference(s):
DE 1 055 538 (Degussa; appl. 15.6.1957).
US 2 989 529 (Degussa; 20.6.1961; D-prior. 15.6.1957).

Formulation(s):   drops 40 mg; suppos. 10 mg; syrup 10 mg/5 ml (as hydrochloride)

Trade Name(s):
D: Selvigon (ASTA Medica   GB: Selvigon (Smith Kline &   I: Selvigon (Rhône-Poulenc
        AWD)   French); wfm   Rorer)

Pipebuzone

ATC: M01AA; S01BC
Use: anti-inflammatory, antipyretic,
            analgesic

RN: 27315-91-9   MF: $C_{25}H_{32}N_4O_2$ MW: 420.56   EINECS: 248-398-7
CN: 4-butyl-4-[(4-methyl-1-piperazinyl)methyl]-1,2-diphenyl-3,5-pyrazolidinedione

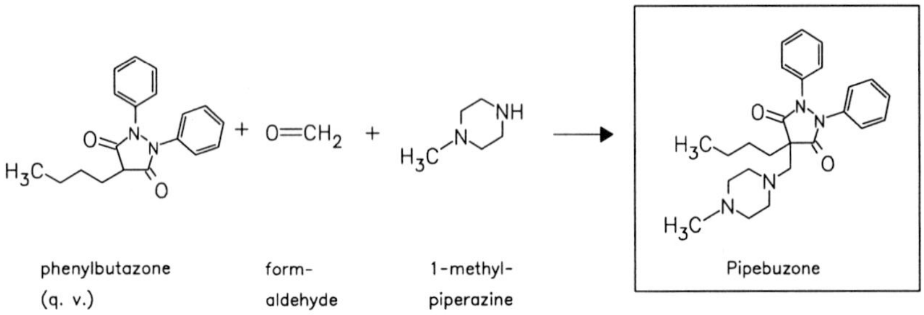

phenylbutazone   form-   1-methyl-   Pipebuzone
(q. v.)   aldehyde   piperazine

Reference(s):
DE 1 958 722 (Lab. Dausse; appl. 22.11.1969; F-prior. 25.11.1968, 19.2.1969).

Formulation(s):   cps. 150 mg; suppos. 300 mg

Trade Name(s):
F: Élarzone-Dausse (Dausse);
        wfm

Pipecuronium bromide

ATC: M03AC06
Use: muscle relaxant, non-depolarizing
        neuromuscular blocker

RN: 52212-02-9   MF: C$_{35}$H$_{62}$Br$_2$N$_4$O$_4$ MW: 762.71   EINECS: 257-740-4
LD$_{50}$:   55300 ng/kg (M, i.m.); 70600 ng/kg (M, i.p.); 29700 ng/kg (M, i.v.); 22 mg/kg (M, p.o.);
        60500 ng/kg (M, s.c.);
        450 μg/kg (R, i.p.); 173 μg (R, i.p.); 173 μg (R, i.v.)
CN: 4,4'-[(2β,3α,5α,16β,17β)-3,17-bis(acetyloxy)androstane-2,16-diyl]bis[1,1-dimethylpiperazinium]
       dibromide

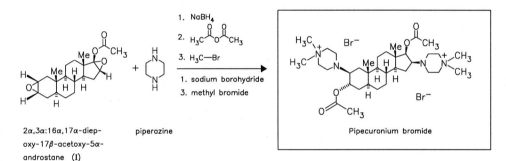

5α-androst-2-
en-17-one

isopropenyl
acetate

17-acetoxy-5α-
androsta-2,16-diene

perbenzoic
acid

I

2α,3α:16α,17α-diep-
oxy-17β-acetoxy-5α-
androstane (I)

piperazine

1. NaBH$_4$
2. (acetic anhydride)
3. H$_3$C—Br

1. sodium borohydride
3. methyl bromide

Pipecuronium bromide

Reference(s):
DE 2 337 882 (Richter Gedeon; appl. 26.7.1973; H-prior. 27.7.1972).
NL 7 310 389 (Richter Gedeon; appl. 26.7.1973; H-prior. 27.7.1972).
Tuba, Z.: Arzneim.-Forsch. (ARZNAD) **30**, 342 (1980).

Formulation(s):   vial 10 mg/10 ml

Trade Name(s):
USA: Arduan (Organon; 1990)

Pipemidic acid

(Acide pipemidique; Piperamic acid)

ATC: G04AB03
Use: chemotherapeutic (urinary tract
        infections), antibacterial

RN: 51940-44-4   MF: C$_{14}$H$_{17}$N$_5$O$_3$ MW: 303.32   EINECS: 257-530-2
LD$_{50}$:   300 mg/kg (M, i.v.); 5 g/kg (M, p.o.);
        529 mg/kg (R, i.v.); 16 g/kg (R, p.o.);
        >2 g/kg (dog, p.o.)
CN: 8-ethyl-5,8-dihydro-5-oxo-2-(1-piperazinyl)pyrido[2,3-*d*]pyrimidine-6-carboxylic acid

trihydrate
RN: 72571-82-5   MF: C$_{14}$H$_{17}$N$_5$O$_3$ · 3H$_2$O   MW: 357.37

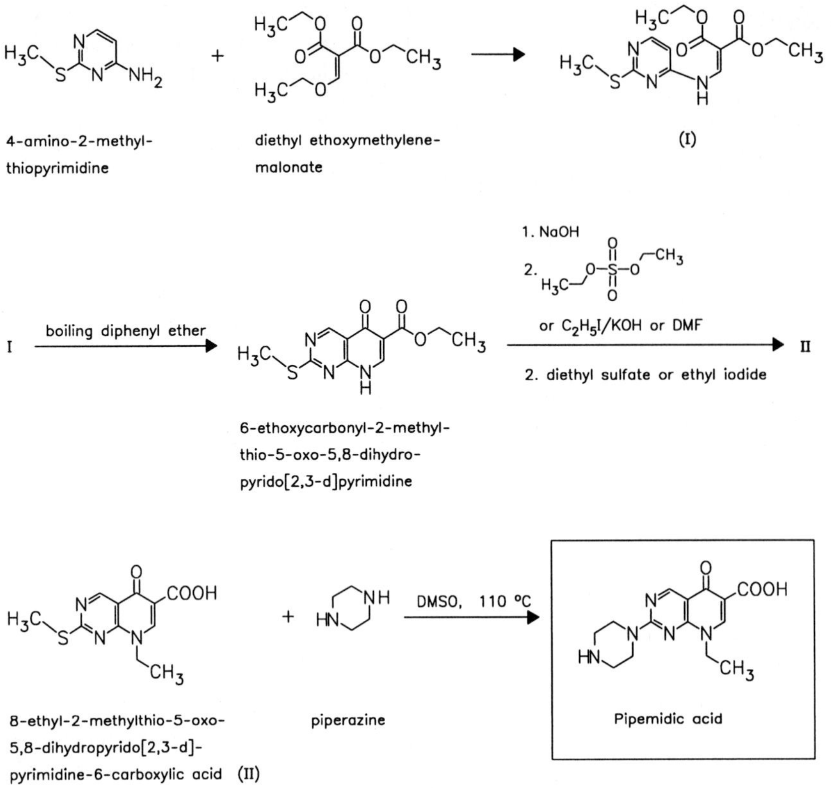

H₃C-S-...-NH₂   +   diethyl ethoxymethylene-malonate   →   (I)

4-amino-2-methyl-thiopyrimidine   diethyl ethoxymethylene-malonate

I   boiling diphenyl ether →   6-ethoxycarbonyl-2-methyl-thio-5-oxo-5,8-dihydro-pyrido[2,3-d]pyrimidine

1. NaOH
2. H₃C-O-S(=O)₂-O-CH₃
or C₂H₅I/KOH or DMF
2. diethyl sulfate or ethyl iodide
→ II

8-ethyl-2-methylthio-5-oxo-5,8-dihydropyrido[2,3-d]-pyrimidine-6-carboxylic acid (II)   +   piperazine   DMSO, 110 °C →   Pipemidic acid

Reference(s):

US 3 950 338 (Roger Bellon; 13.4.1976; appl. 31.7.1973; F-prior. 2.8.1972).
DE 2 338 325 (Roger Bellon; prior. 1.8.1973).
DOS 2 341 146 (Dainippon; appl. 14.8.1973; J-prior. 14.8.1972, 19.12.1972, 22.12.1972, 26.12.1972, 27.12.1972, 25.5.1973, 19.6.1973).
US 3 887 557 (Dainippon; 3.6.1975; J-prior. 14.8.1972).
US 3 962 443 (Dainippon; 8.6.1976; J-prior. 14.8.1972, 19.12.1972, 22.12.1972, 26.12.1972, 27.12.1972, 25.5.1973, 19.6.1973).
Matsumoto, J.; Minami, S.: J. Med. Chem. (JMCMAR) **18**, 74 (1975).

precursor (8-ethyl-2-methylthio-5-oxo-5,8-dihydropyrido[2,3-*d*]pyrimidine-6-carboxylic acid):
DOS 2 143 369 (Dainippon; appl. 30.8.1971; J-prior. 29.8.1970)
GB 1 129 358 (Dainippon; appl. 8.9.1966; J-prior. 8.9.1965, 10.9.1965).

alternative synthesis:
DOS 2 338 325 (Roger Bellon; appl. 1.8.1973; F-prior. 2.8.1972).

Formulation(s):   cps. 200 mg, 400 mg (as trihydrate)

Trade Name(s):

D:	Deblaston (Madaus; 1978)	Pipefort (Lampugnani)	Urosan (AGIPS)
F:	Pipram (Rhône-Poulenc	Pipemid (Gentili)	Urosetic (Finmedical)
	Rorer Bellon; 1975)	Pipram (Rhône-Poulenc	Urotractin (SmithKline
I:	Acipem (Caber)	Rorer; 1979)	Beecham)
	Diperpen (Francia Farm.)	Pipurin (NCSN)	Uroval (Firma)
	Filtrax (Ipso-Pharma)	Tractur (Damor)	J: Dolcol (Dainippon; 1979)
	Pipeacid (Tosi-Novara)	Urodene (O.F.F.)	
	Pipedac (Teofarma)	Uropimid (CT)	

Pipenzolate bromide

ATC: A03AB14
Use: anticholinergic, antispasmodic

RN: 125-51-9   MF: $C_{22}H_{28}BrNO_3$ MW: 434.37   EINECS: 204-741-2
LD_{50}:   18 mg/kg (M, i.v.); 1140 mg/kg (M, p.o.);
    18 mg/kg (R, i.v.); 916 mg/kg (R, p.o.)
CN: 1-ethyl-3-[(hydroxydiphenylacetyl)oxy]-1-methylpiperidinium bromide

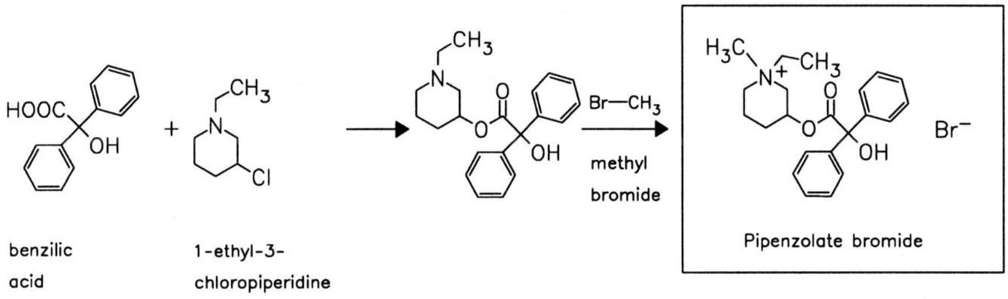

benzilic acid   1-ethyl-3-chloropiperidine   methyl bromide   Pipenzolate bromide

Reference(s):
US 2 918 406 (Lakeside Labs.; 22.12.1959; appl. 8.4.1957; prior. 18.8.1950).

Formulation(s):   tabl. 5 mg

Trade Name(s):
F: Piptal (Roger Bellon); wfm
GB: Piptal (M.C.P. Pharmaceuticals); wfm
    Piptalin (M.C.P. Pharmaceuticals)-comb.; wfm
I: Piper (Panthox & Burck); wfm
    Piptal (RBS Pharma); wfm
    Piptal (Roger Bellon); wfm
J: Piptal (Chugai)
USA: Piptal (Hoechst Marion Roussel; Merrell-National); wfm

Piperacetazine

ATC: N05AC
Use: neuroleptic, antihistaminic

RN: 3819-00-9   MF: $C_{24}H_{30}N_2O_2S$ MW: 410.58   EINECS: 223-312-0
LD_{50}:   575 mg/kg (M, p.o.);
    390 mg/kg (R, p.o.)
CN: 1-[10-[3-[4-(2-hydroxyethyl)-1-piperidinyl]propyl]-10H-phenothiazin-2-yl]ethanone

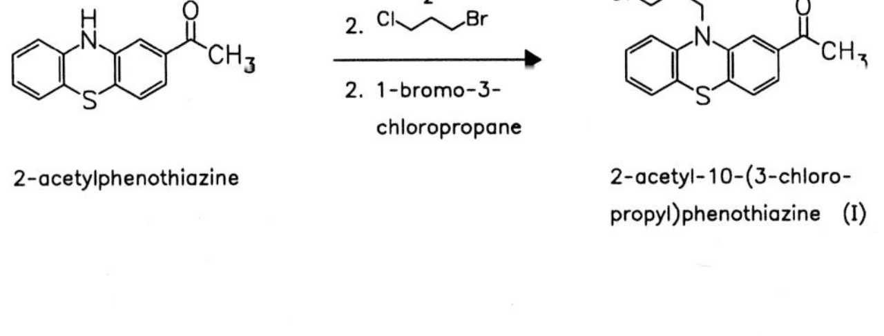

2-acetylphenothiazine   1. NaNH$_2$ or KOH   2. 1-bromo-3-chloropropane   2-acetyl-10-(3-chloropropyl)phenothiazine (I)

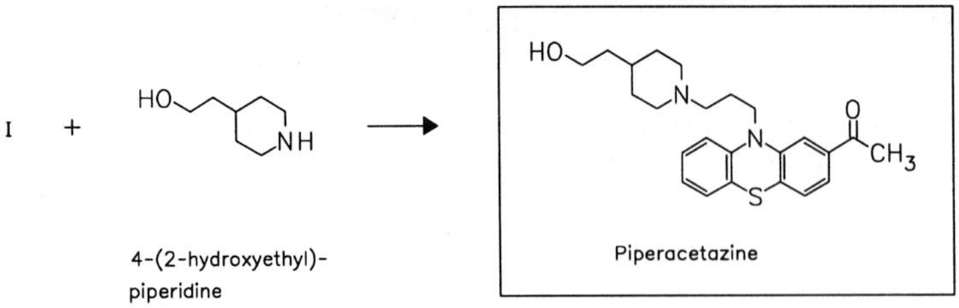

4-(2-hydroxyethyl)-
piperidine

Piperacetazine

Reference(s):
GB 861 807 (Searle; appl. 6.8.1959; USA-prior. 7.8.1958).

Formulation(s):   tabl. 10 mg

Trade Name(s):
USA: Quide (Dow); wfm

Piperacillin

ATC: J01CA12
Use: antibiotic

RN: 61477-96-1   MF: $C_{23}H_{27}N_5O_7S$ MW: 517.56   EINECS: 262-811-8
LD_{50}:   5 g/kg (M, i.v.)
CN: [2S-[2α,5α,6β(S*)]]-6-[[[[(4-ethyl-2,3-dioxo-1-piperazinyl)carbonyl]amino]phenylacetyl]amino]-3,3-
dimethyl-7-oxo-4-thia-1-azabicyclo[3.2.0]heptane-2-carboxylic acid

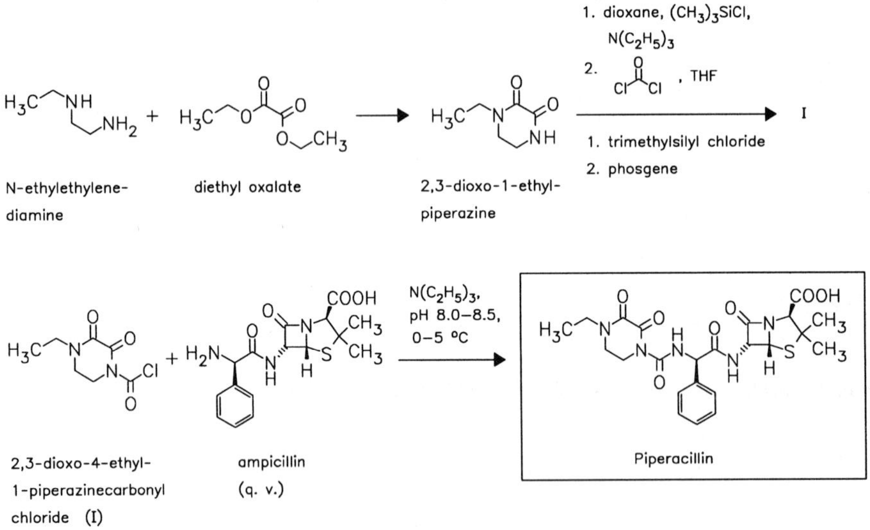

N-ethylethylene-
diamine

diethyl oxalate

2,3-dioxo-1-ethyl-
piperazine

1. trimethylsilyl chloride
2. phosgene

2,3-dioxo-4-ethyl-
1-piperazinecarbonyl
chloride (I)

ampicillin
(q. v.)

Piperacillin

Reference(s):
DOS 2 519 400 (Toyama; appl. 30.4.1975; J-prior. 9.5.1974, 13.5.1974, 31.5.1974, 13.8.1974, 26.9.1974,
13.12.1974, 27.3.1975).
DOS 2 824 610 (Toyama; appl. 5.6.1978; J-prior. 8.6.1977).
GB 1 508 062 (Toyama; appl. 28.4.1975; J-prior. 9.5.1974, 13.5.1974, 31.5.1974, 24.7.1974, 7.8.1974, 13.8.1974,
26.9.1974, 12.10.1974, 28.10.1974, 6.12.1974, 13.12.1974, 17.2.1975, 26.3.1975, 27.3.1975).
US 4 112 090 (Toyama; 5.9.1978; J-prior. 13.12.1974).

precursors:
US 4 087 424 (Toyama; 2.5.1978; J-prior. 9.5.1974).

Formulation(s):   amp. 1 g/10 ml, 2 g/20 ml; vial 1 g, 1.5 g, 2 g, 3 g, 4 g (as sodium salt)

Trade Name(s):

D: Pipril (Lederle; 1980)
F: Pipérilline (Wyeth-Lederle)   I:
     Tazocilline (Wyeth-
     Lederle)
GB: Pipril (Wyeth-Lederle;
     1982)

Tazocin (Wyeth)-comb.
Avocin (Wyeth-Lederle;
1982)
Eril (Savio IBN)
Tazocil (Wyeth-Lederle)-
comb.

J: Pentcillin (Sankyo; 1980)
USA: Pipracil (Lederle; 1982)
      Zasyn (Lederle)

Piperazine

ATC: P02CB01
Use: anthelmintic

RN: 110-85-0   MF: $C_4H_{10}N_2$ MW: 86.14   EINECS: 203-808-3
LD_{50}: 1180 mg/kg (M, i.v.); 600 mg/kg (M, p.o.);
      1340 mg/kg (R, i.v.); 1900 mg/kg (R, p.o.)
CN: piperazine

hexahydrate
RN: 142-63-2   MF: $C_4H_{10}N_2 \cdot 6H_2O$ MW: 194.23
LD_{50}: 11.2 g/kg (M, p.o.)
dihydrochloride
RN: 142-64-3   MF: $C_4H_{10}N_2 \cdot 2HCl$ MW: 159.06   EINECS: 205-551-2
LD_{50}: 4900 mg/kg (R, p.o.)
phosphate
RN: 1951-97-9   MF: $C_4H_{10}N_2 \cdot xH_3O_4P$ MW: unspecified   EINECS: 217-775-8
LD_{50}: 20 g/kg (M, p.o.)
tartrate (1:1)
RN: 133-36-8   MF: $C_4H_{10}N_2 \cdot C_4H_6O_6$ MW: 236.22   EINECS: 205-104-1
citrate (3:2)
RN: 144-29-6   MF: $C_6H_8O_7 \cdot 3/2C_4H_{10}N_2$ MW: 642.66   EINECS: 205-622-8
LD_{50}: 8500 mg/kg (M, p.o.);
      11200 mg/kg (R, p.o.)
citrate (3:2) hydrate
RN: 41372-10-5   MF: $C_6H_8O_7 \cdot 3/2C_4H_{10}N_2 \cdot xH_2O$ MW: unspecified
edetate calcium (1:1)
RN: 12002-30-1   MF: $C_{10}H_{14}CaN_2O_8 \cdot C_4H_{10}N_2$ MW: 416.44
edetate calcium (1:1) dihydrate
RN: 50322-15-1   MF: $C_{10}H_{14}CaN_2O_8 \cdot C_4H_{10}N_2 \cdot 2H_2O$ MW: 452.47
adipate (1:1)
RN: 142-88-1   MF: $C_6H_{10}O_4 \cdot C_4H_{10}N_2$ MW: 232.28   EINECS: 205-569-0
LD_{50}: 8 g/kg (M, p.o.);
      7900 mg/kg (R, p.o.)

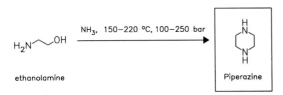

ethanolamine   Piperazine

NH₃, 150–220 °C, 100–250 bar

Reference(s):
Ullmanns Encykl. Tech. Chem., 4. Aufl., Vol. **7**, 385.

Formulation(s):   tabl. 10 mg

Piperidolate

ATC: A03AA30
Use: anticholinergic, antispasmodic

RN: 82-98-4   MF: $C_{21}H_{25}NO_2$ MW: 323.44   EINECS: 201-449-7
LD$_{50}$:   75 mg/kg (M, i.v.);
      100 mg/kg (R, i.v.)
CN: α-phenylbenzeneacetic acid 1-ethyl-3-piperidinyl ester

hydrochloride
RN: 129-77-1   MF: $C_{21}H_{25}NO_2 \cdot HCl$ MW: 359.90   EINECS: 204-964-5
LD$_{50}$:   26 mg/kg (M, i.v.); 1040 mg/kg (M, p.o.);
      19 mg/kg (R, i.v.);
      35 mg/kg (dog, i.v.)

furfural   ethylamine   N-ethyl-N-(tetrahydro-   1-ethyl-3-hydroxy-
                            furfuryl)amine   piperidine (I)

diphenylacetyl   Piperidolate
chloride

Reference(s):
US 2 918 407 (Lakeside Labs.; 22.12.1959; appl. 8.4.1957; prior. 18.8.1950).
Biel, J.H. et al.: J. Am. Chem. Soc. (JACSAT) **74**, 1485 (1952).

Formulation(s):   tabl. 50 mg (as hydrochloride)

Piperocaine

ATC: N01BC
Use: local anesthetic

RN: 136-82-3   MF: $C_{16}H_{23}NO_2$ MW: 261.37   EINECS: 205-262-1
CN: (±)-2-methyl-1-piperidinepropanol benzoate (ester)

hydrochloride
RN: 24561-10-2 MF: $C_{16}H_{23}NO_2 \cdot HCl$ MW: 297.83
LD_{50}: 18.2 mg/kg (M, i.v.);
20 mg/kg (R, i.v.)

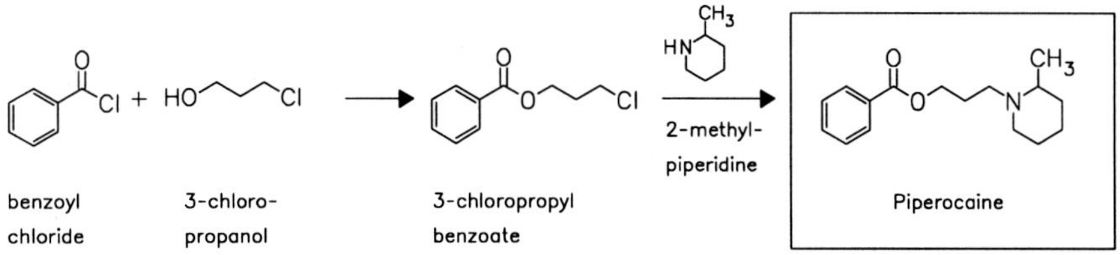

benzoyl chloride
3-chloropropanol
3-chloropropyl benzoate
2-methylpiperidine
Piperocaine

Reference(s):
US 1 784 903 (S. M. McElvain; 1930; prior. 1927).

Trade Name(s):
USA: Metycaine (Lilly); wfm

Piperylone

ATC: N02BB
Use: analgesic

RN: 2531-04-6 MF: $C_{17}H_{23}N_3O$ MW: 285.39 EINECS: 219-788-4
CN: 4-ethyl-1,2-dihydro-2-(1-methyl-4-piperidinyl)-5-phenyl-3*H*-pyrazol-3-one

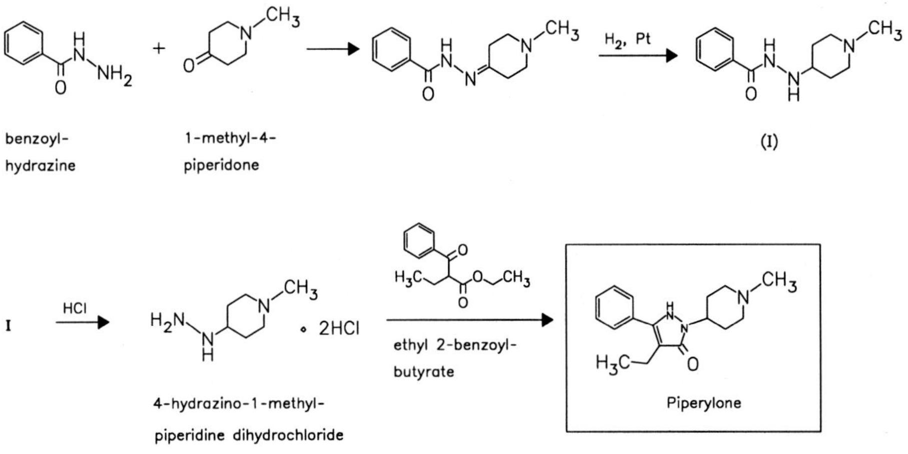

benzoylhydrazine
1-methyl-4-piperidone
H2, Pt
(I)
HCl
4-hydrazino-1-methylpiperidine dihydrochloride
ethyl 2-benzoylbutyrate
Piperylone

Reference(s):
US 2 903 460 (Sandoz; 8.9.1959; CH-prior. 7.4.1956).
Ebnöther, A. et al.: Helv. Chim. Acta (HCACAV) **42**, 1201 (1959).

Trade Name(s):
D: Pelerol (Sandoz)-comb.;
wfm

Pipobroman

ATC: L01AX02
Use: antineoplastic

RN: 54-91-1   MF: $C_{10}H_{16}Br_2N_2O_2$ MW: 356.06
LD$_{50}$:   382 mg/kg (M, p.o.);
        220 mg/kg (R, p.o.)
CN: 1,4-bis(3-bromo-1-oxopropyl)piperazine

3-bromopropionyl   piperazine   Pipobroman
chloride

Reference(s):
DE 1 138 781 (Abbott; appl. 10.10.1960; USA-prior. 11.7.1960).

Formulation(s):   tabl. 10 mg, 25 mg

Trade Name(s):
D: Vercyte (Abbott); wfm   I: Vercite 25 (Abbott)   USA: Vercyte (Abbott); wfm
F: Vercyte (Abbott)   J: Amedel (Marupi)

Pipotiazine

ATC: N05AC04
Use: neuroleptic

RN: 39860-99-6   MF: $C_{24}H_{33}N_3O_3S_2$ MW: 475.68   EINECS: 254-659-6
CN: 10-[3-[4-(2-hydroxyethyl)-1-piperidinyl]propyl]-*N,N*-dimethyl-10*H*-phenothiazine-2-sulfonamide

palmitate
RN: 37517-26-3   MF: $C_{40}H_{63}N_3O_4S_2$ MW: 714.09

2-dimethylaminosulfonyl-   3-(p-toluenesulfonyl-   (I)
phenothiazine   oxy)propyl chloride

I   +

4-(2-hydroxyethyl)-   Pipotiazine
piperidine

Reference(s):
DE 1 117 584 (Rhône-Poulenc; appl. 1958; F-prior. 1957).

Formulation(s): amp. 10 mg/2 ml, 100 mg/4 ml, 25 mg/1 ml; drops 4 % (as palmitate); tabl. 10 mg

Trade Name(s):
F: Piportil (Rhône-Poulenc Rorer Specia)
Piportil L4 (Rhône-Poulenc Rorer Specia; as palmitate)
GB: Piportil Depot (IHC; as palmitate)

Pipoxolan

ATC: A03AA
Use: antispasmodic

RN: 23744-24-3 MF: $C_{22}H_{25}NO_3$ MW: 351.45
CN: 5,5-diphenyl-2-[2-(1-piperidinyl)ethyl]-1,3-dioxolan-4-one

hydrochloride
RN: 18174-58-8 MF: $C_{22}H_{25}NO_3 \cdot HCl$ MW: 387.91
LD_{50}: 35 mg/kg (M, i.v.); 700 mg/kg (M, p.o.);
60 mg/kg (R, i.v.); 1500 mg/kg (R, p.o.)

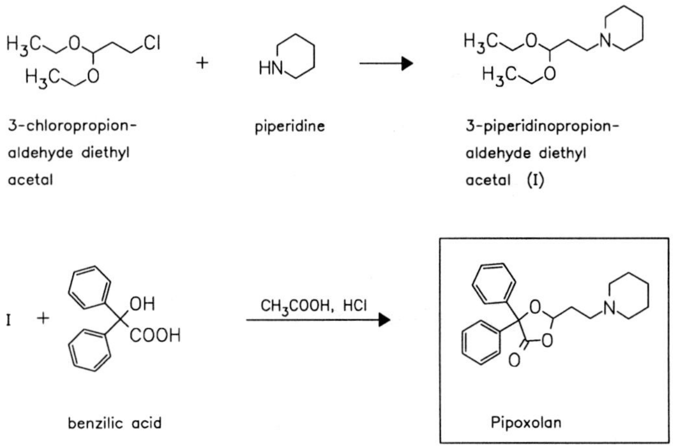
H3C O Cl
H3C O
+
HN
H3C O N
H3C O
3-chloropropionaldehyde diethyl acetal
piperidine
3-piperidinopropionaldehyde diethyl acetal (I)
I +
OH
COOH
CH3COOH, HCl
O
N
O
O
benzilic acid
Pipoxolan

Reference(s):
GB 1 109 959 (Rowa-Wagner; appl. 3.10.1966; A-prior. 5.10.1965).

Formulation(s): tabl. 10 mg

Trade Name(s):
D: Rowapraxin (Rowa-Wagner)

Pipradrol

ATC: N06BX15
Use: central stimulant

RN: 467-60-7 MF: $C_{18}H_{21}NO$ MW: 267.37 EINECS: 207-394-5
LD_{50}: 74 mg/kg (M, p.o.);
30 mg/kg (R, i.v.); 180 mg/kg (R, p.o.)
CN: α,α-diphenyl-2-piperidinemethanol

hydrochloride
RN: 71-78-3 MF: $C_{18}H_{21}NO \cdot HCl$ MW: 303.83 EINECS: 200-764-7
LD_{50}: 20 mg/kg (M, i.v.); 120 mg/kg (M, p.o.);
30 mg/kg (R, i.v.); 180 mg/kg (R, p.o.)

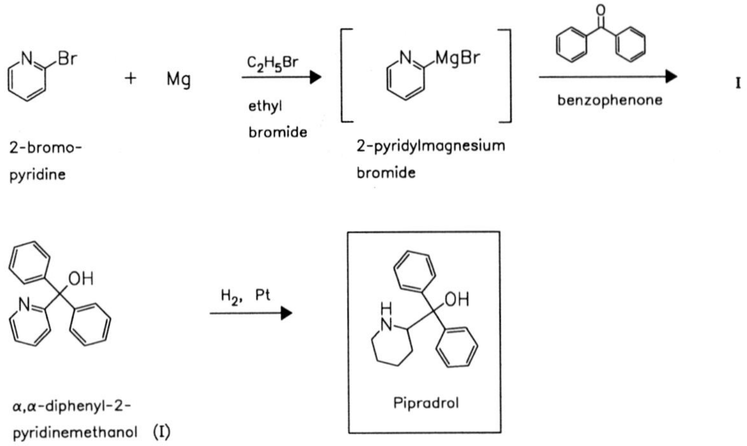

Br
Mg
C2H5Br
ethyl bromide
MgBr
benzophenone
I
2-bromo-pyridine
2-pyridylmagnesium bromide
OH
H2, Pt
α,α-diphenyl-2-pyridinemethanol (I)
Pipradrol

Reference(s):
Tilford, C.H. et al.: J. Am. Chem. Soc. (JACSAT) **70**, 4001 (1948).
US 2 624 739 (Merrell; 1953; appl. 1949).

Formulation(s): drg. 1 mg (as hydrochloride)

Trade Name(s):
D: Vitazell G forte (Tosse)-comb.; wfm
I: Detaril (Isom); wfm

Piprinhydrinate

ATC: R06
Use: antihistaminic, anti-emetic, antirhinitic

RN: 606-90-6 MF: $C_{19}H_{23}NO \cdot C_7H_7ClN_4O_2$ MW: 496.01 EINECS: 210-128-0
LD_{50}: 75 mg/kg (M, i.v.); 275 mg/kg (M, p.o.)
CN: 8-chloro-3,7-dihydro-1,3-dimethyl-1*H*-purine-2,6-dione compd. with 4-(diphenylmethoxy)-1-methylpiperidine (1:1)

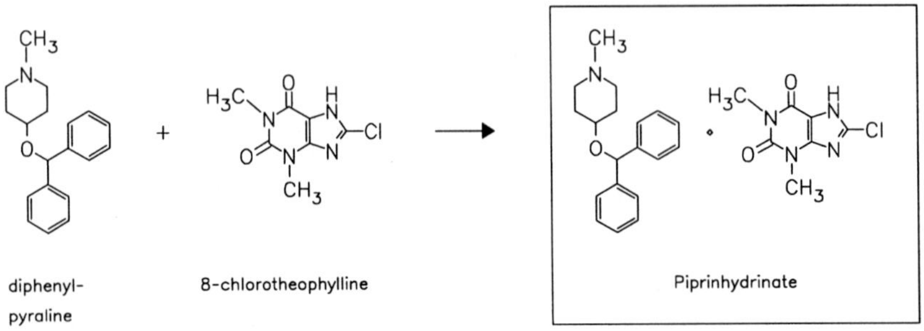

diphenyl-pyraline
8-chlorotheophylline
Piprinhydrinate

Reference(s):
DE 934 890 (Promonta; appl. 1951).

Piproxen
(Naproxen piperazine)

ATC: M01AE
Use: non-steroidal anti-inflammatory

RN: 70981-66-7   MF: $C_{14}H_{14}O_3 \cdot 1/2C_4H_{10}N_2$ MW: 546.66   EINECS: 275-083-1
CN: (S)-6-methoxy-α-methyl-2-naphthaleneacetic acid, compd. with piperazine (2:1)

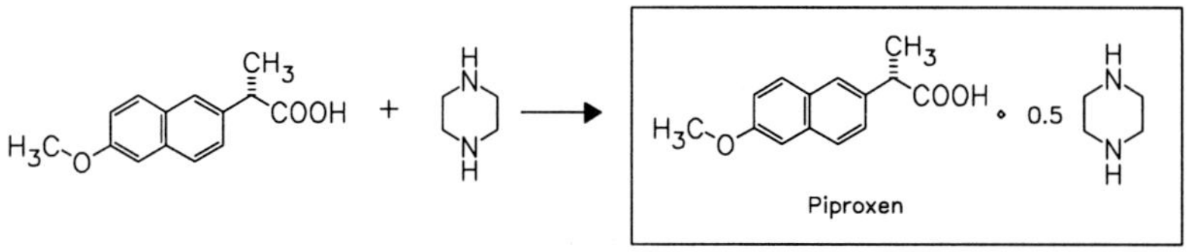

naproxen
(q. v.)

Reference(s):
ES 474 535 (Centro Inv. Farm.; appl. 16.3.1979).
EP 308 739 (Coop. Farm. Soc.; appl. 9.9.1989; I-prior. 22.9.1987).

Formulation(s):   suppos. 600 mg; tabl. 300 mg

Piprozolin

ATC: A05AX01
Use: choleretic

RN: 17243-64-0   MF: $C_{14}H_{22}N_2O_3S$ MW: 298.41   EINECS: 241-280-6
LD$_{50}$:   1310 mg/kg (M, p.o.);
        3256 mg/kg (R, p.o.)
CN: [3-ethyl-4-oxo-5-(1-piperidinyl)-2-thiazolidinylidene]acetic acid ethyl ester

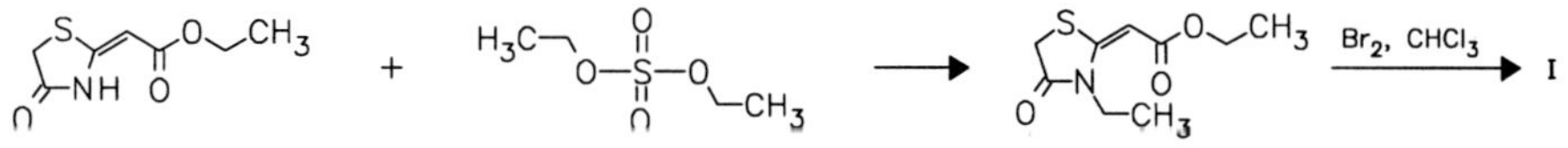

ethyl 4-oxothiazolidin-
2-ylideneacetate
(cf. etozolin synthesis)

diethyl sulfate

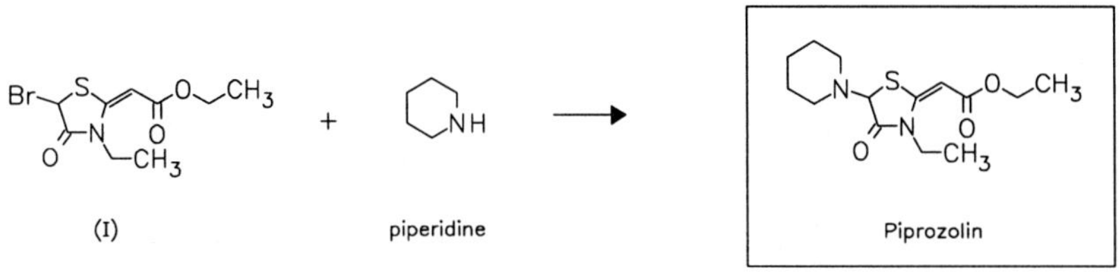

(I)   piperidine   Piprozolin

Reference(s):
DOS 2 414 345 (Gödecke; appl. 25.3.1974).

Formulation(s):   drg. 100 mg

Trade Name(s):
D: Probilin (Gödecke); wfm   I: Probilin (Parke Davis);   Secrebil (Isnardi); wfm
                                          wfm

Piracetam

ATC: N06BX03
Use: cerebrostimulant

RN: 7491-74-9   MF: $C_6H_{10}N_2O_2$ MW: 142.16   EINECS: 231-312-7
LD$_{50}$:   9200 mg/kg (M, i.v.); 2 g/kg (M, p.o.)
CN: 2-oxo-1-pyrrolidineacetamide

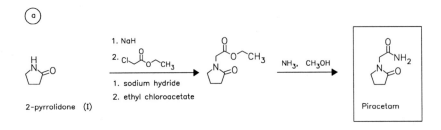

Reference(s):
US 3 459 738 (UCB; 5.8.1969; GB-prior. 6.8.1964).
DAS 1 620 608 (UCB; appl. 4.8.1965; GB-prior. 6.8.1964).

alternative synthesis (from N-(4-chlorobutyryl)glycinamide):
DAS 2 759 297 (Pliva; appl. 14.1.1977; YU-prior. 14.1.1976, 11.8.1976).
DOS 2 701 450 (Pliva; appl. 14.1.1977; YU-prior. 14.1.1976, 11.8.1976).

platelet aggregation inhibitory activity:
DOS 2 746 761 (UCB; appl. 18.10.1977; GB-prior. 19.10.1976).
US 4 115 579 (UCB; 19.9.1978; GB-prior. 19.10.1976).

Formulation(s):   amp. 1 g/5 ml; sol. 333 mg, 416.25 mg; cps. 400 mg, 1200 mg; drinking amp. 1 g; f. c. tabl.
                     800 mg, 1200 mg; gran. 1200 mg, 1600 mg; tabl. 400 mg, 1200 mg

Trade Name(s):
D: Avigilen (Brenner-Efeka)   Normabrain (Hoechst;   F: Axonyl (Parke Davis)
      Cerebroforte (Azuchemie)   1974)   Gabacet (Synthélabo)
      Cerepar (Merckle)   Pinacetrop (Holsten)   Geram (Vedim)
      Cuxabrain (TAD)   Sinapsan (Rodleben;   Nootropyl (UCB; 1972)
      Encetrop (Kytta-Siegfried)   Vedim)   GB: Nootropil (UCB)
      Nootrop (UCB; 1974)   generics   I: Cerebropan (Nuovo ISM)

Clevian (Aesculapius)   Nootropil (UCB)   Psycoton (Esseti)
Flavis (Pulitzer)   Norzetam (Vedim Pharma)

Pirarubicin
(Theprubicin; THP-ADM)

ATC: L01DB08
Use: antitumor anthracycline antibiotic

RN: 72496-41-4   MF: $C_{32}H_{37}NO_{12}$ MW: 627.64
LD_{50}:   27.8 mg/kg (M, i.v.)
CN: [8S-[8α,10α(S*)]]-10-[[3-amino-2,3,6-trideoxy-4-O-(tetrahydro-2H-pyran-2-yl)-α-L-lyxo-hexopyranosyl]oxy]-7,8,9,10-tetrahydro-6,8,11-trihydroxy-8-(hydroxyacetyl)-1-methoxy-5,12-naphthacenedione

monohydrochloride
RN: 95343-20-7   MF: $C_{32}H_{37}NO_{12} \cdot HCl$ MW: 664.10
LD_{50}:   14 mg/kg (M, i.v.); 420 mg/kg (M, p.o.);
        18.1 mg/kg (R, i.v.); >1.013 g/kg (R, p.o.)

14-O-acetyldoxorubicin

Pirarubicin

Reference(s):
EP 14 853 (Zaidan Hojin Biseibutsu Kagaku; appl. 23.1.1980; J-prior. 3.2.1979, 31.8.1979).
US 4 303 785 (Zaidan Hojin Biseibutsu Kagaku; 1.12.1981; J-prior. 5.8.1978, 3.2.1979, 31.8.1979).
Umezawa, H. et al.: J. Antibiot. (JANTAJ) **32**, 1082 (1979).

alternative synthesis:
EP 228 546 (Zaidan Hojin Biseibutsu Kagaku; appl. 14.11.1986; J-prior. 16.11.1985).

Formulation(s):   amp. 10 mg, 20 mg, 50 mg (as hydrochloride)

Trade Name(s):
F: Théprubicine (Rhône-   J: Pinorubicin (Nippon   Therarubicin (Meiji Seika;
       Poulenc Rorer; 1990)   Kayaku/Sanraku; 1988)   1988)

Pirbuterol

ATC: R03AC08; R03CC07
Use: bronchodilator

RN: 38677-81-5   MF: $C_{12}H_{20}N_2O_3$ MW: 240.30
CN: $α^6$-[[(1,1-dimethylethyl)amino]methyl]-3-hydroxy-2,6-pyridinedimethanol

dihydrochloride
RN: 38029-10-6   MF: $C_{12}H_{20}N_2O_3 \cdot 2HCl$ MW: 313.23   EINECS: 253-751-3
monoacetate
RN: 65652-44-0   MF: $C_{12}H_{20}N_2O_3 \cdot C_2H_4O_2$ MW: 300.36   EINECS: 265-862-4

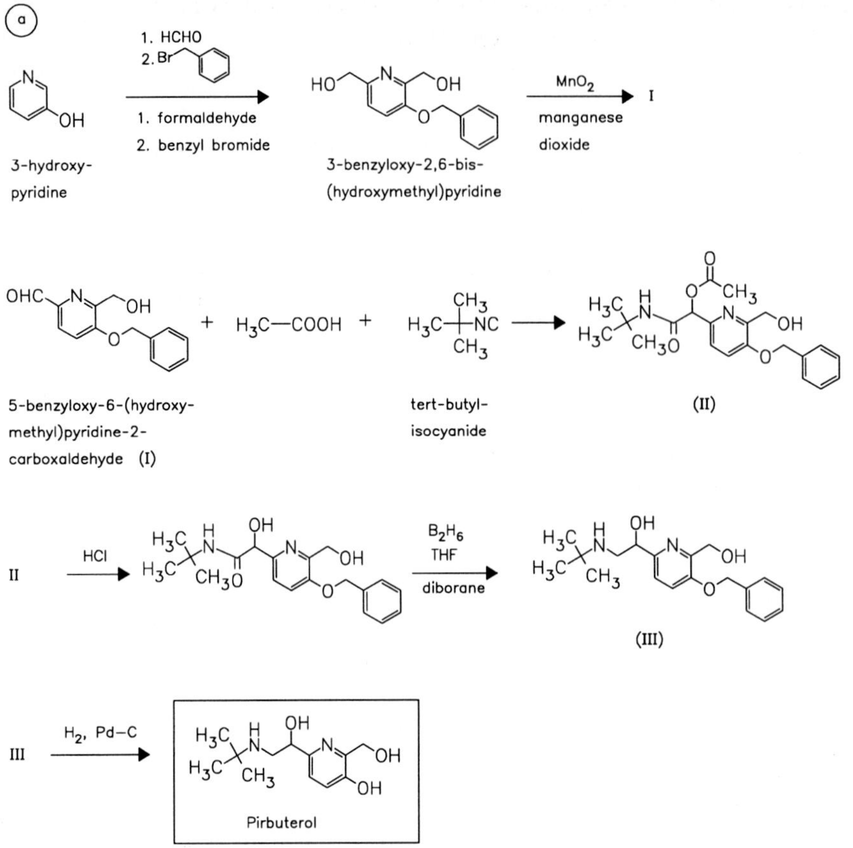

ⓐ

3-hydroxy-pyridine

1. HCHO
2. Br—CH₂—C₆H₅

1. formaldehyde
2. benzyl bromide

3-benzyloxy-2,6-bis-(hydroxymethyl)pyridine

MnO₂
manganese dioxide

→ I

5-benzyloxy-6-(hydroxy-methyl)pyridine-2-carboxaldehyde (I)

+ H₃C—COOH +

tert-butyl-isocyanide

→ (II)

II

HCl →

B₂H₆
THF
diborane

→ (III)

III

H₂, Pd–C →

Pirbuterol

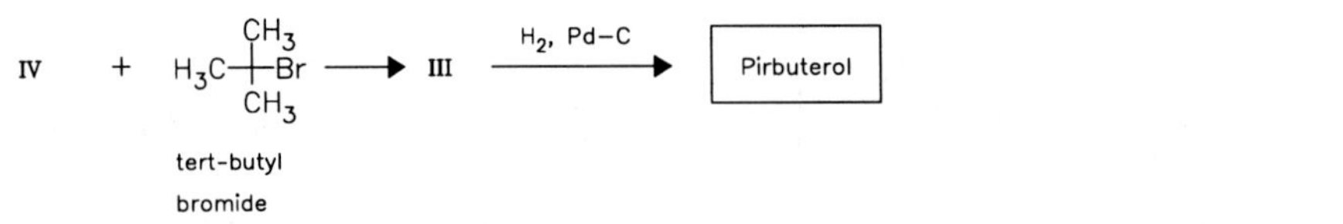

ⓑ

I + O₂N—CH₃ →

nitro-methane

H₂, Raney–Ni →

(IV)

IV + tert-butyl bromide

H₂, Pd–C →

III →

Pirbuterol

Reference(s):

US 3 700 681 (Pfizer; 24.10.1972; prior. 16.2.1971).
US 3 763 173 (Pfizer; 2.10.1973; pior. 25.5.1972, 16.2.1971).
US 3 772 314 (Pfizer; 13.11.1973; prior. 24.10.1972, 25.5.1972, 16.2.1971).
US 3 786 160 (Pfizer; 15.1.1974; prior. 25.5.1972, 24.10.1972, 16.2.1971).
DOS 2 204 195 (Pfizer; appl. 29.1.1972; USA-prior. 16.2.1971).

alternative syntheses:

EP 58 069 (Pfizer; appl. 8.2.1982; USA-prior. 9.2.1981).
US 3 948 919 (Pfizer; 6.4.1976; prior. 9.10.1974; 26.12.1973).
US 4 031 108 (Pfizer; 21.6.1977; prior. 14.7.1976, 22.9.1975, 9.10.1974, 26.12.1973).

Formulation(s):   cps. 10 mg, 15 mg (as dihydrochloride); doses aerosol 0.2 mg (as acetate)

Trade Name(s):
D: Zeisin (3M Medica)   J: Exirel (Taito Pfizer)
GB: Exirel (Pfizer); wfm   USA: Maxair (3M)

Pirenzepine

ATC: A02BX03
Use: peptic ulcer therapeutic

RN: 28797-61-7   MF: $C_{19}H_{21}N_5O_2$ MW: 351.41   EINECS: 249-228-4
LD_{50}:   156 mg/kg (M, i.v.); 3046 mg/kg (M, p.o.);
>5 g/kg (R, p.o.)
CN: 5,11-dihydro-11-[(4-methyl-1-piperazinyl)acetyl]-6H-pyrido[2,3-b][1,4]benzodiazepin-6-one

dihydrochloride
RN: 29868-97-1   MF: $C_{19}H_{21}N_5O_2 \cdot 2HCl$ MW: 424.33   EINECS: 249-907-5
LD_{50}:   96 mg/kg (M, i.v.); 2.6 g/kg (M, p.o.);
92 mg/kg (R, i.v.); 5 g/kg (R, p.o.);
62.5 mg/kg (dog, i.v.); >3.7 g/kg (dog, p.o.)

2-chloro-3-   2-nitrobenzoyl   (I)
aminopyridine   chloride

5,11-dihydro-6H-pyrido-   chloroacetyl chloride,   (II)
[2,3-b][1,4]benzo-   triethylamine
diazepin-6-one

1-methyl-   Pirenzepine
piperazine

Reference(s):
DE 1 795 183 (Thomae; appl. 20.8.1968).
Eberlein, W. et al.: Arzneim.-Forsch. (ARZNAD) **27**, 356 (1977).

5,11-dihydro-6H-pyrido[2,3-b][1,4]benzodiazepin-6-one:
DE 1 179 943 (Thomae; appl. 8.11.1962).

combination with anti-inflammatories:
DOS 2 708 520 (Thomae; appl. 26.2.1977).
US 4 154 833 (Boehringer Ing.; 15.5.1979; D-prior. 26.2.1977).

Formulation(s):   amp. 10 mg/2 ml; cps. 50 mg; tabl. 25 mg, 50 mg (as dihydrochloride)

Trade Name(s):

D:	Gastricur (Heumann)	GB:	Gastrozepin (Boots); wfm
	Gastrozepin (Boehringer	I:	Duogastral (Nuovo ISM)
	Ing.)		Frazim (Francia Farm.)
	Ulcoprotect-25/-50		Gastrol (Salus Research)
	(Azuchemie)		Gastropiren (AGIPS)
	generics		Gastrosed (Samil)
F:	Gastrozépine (Boehringer		Gastrozepin (Boehringer
	Ing.); wfm		Ing.)

Leblon (De Angeli)
Lulcus (Tosi-Novara)
Maghen (Caber)
Ulcin (Ibirn)
J: Gastrozepin (Boehringer
Ing.)
Gastrozepin (Boehringer-
Tablinen)

Piretanide

ATC: C03CA03
Use: diuretic

RN: 55837-27-9   MF: $C_{17}H_{18}N_2O_5S$ MW: 362.41   EINECS: 259-852-9
LD$_{50}$: 618 mg/kg (M, i.v.); 2 g/kg (M, p.o.);
        700 mg/kg (R, i.v.); 5601 mg/kg (R, p.o.);
        >1 g/kg (dog, p.o.)
CN: 3-(aminosulfonyl)-4-phenoxy-5-(1-pyrrolidinyl)benzoic acid

3-nitro-4-phen-
oxy-5-sulfamoyl-
benzoic acid
(cf. bumetanide
synthesis)

methyl 3-amino-
4-phenoxy-5-sulf-
amoylbenzoate

methyl 3-succinimido-
4-phenoxy-5-sulf-
amoylbenzoate (I)

Piretanide

Reference(s):
DOS 2 419 970 (Hoechst; appl. 25.4.1974).
Merkel, W. et al.: Eur. J. Med. Chem. (EJMCA5) **11**, 399 (1976).

Formulation(s):   amp. 6 mg/2 ml, 12 mg/5 ml; s. r. cps. 6 mg; tabl. 3 mg, 6 mg

Trade Name(s):

D: Arelix (Hoechst)   Arelix (Hoechst/Albert);   I: Tauliz (Hoechst Marion
      Betarelix (Hoechst)-comb.   wfm   Roussel)
GB: Arelix (Albert); wfm   J: Arelix (Hoechst)

Piribedil

ATC: C04AX13
Use: vasodilator

RN: 3605-01-4   MF: $C_{16}H_{18}N_4O_2$ MW: 298.35   EINECS: 222-764-6
LD_{50}:   88 mg/kg (M, i.v.); 1460 mg/kg (M, p.o.)
CN: 2-[4-(1,3-benzodioxol-5-ylmethyl)-1-piperazinyl]pyrimidine

monomesylate
RN: 52293-23-9   MF: $C_{16}H_{18}N_4O_2 \cdot CH_4O_3S$ MW: 394.45   EINECS: 257-818-8
LD_{50}:   510 mg/kg (M, i.p.)

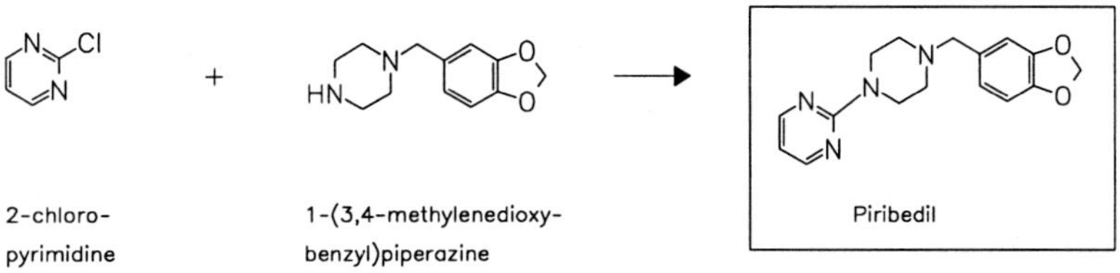

2-chloro-   1-(3,4-methylenedioxy-   Piribedil
pyrimidine   benzyl)piperazine

Reference(s):
US 3 299 067 (Science Union; 17.1.1967; GB-prior. 19.11.1963).
GB 1 101 425 (Science Union; appl. 19.11.1963; valid from 18.11.1964).
Regnier, G.J. et al.: J. Med. Chem. (JMCMAR) **11**, 1151 (1968).

Formulation(s):   amp. 3 mg/1 ml; drg. 20 mg; s. r. drg. 50 mg (as mesylate)

Trade Name(s):
D: Trivastal (Servier)   F: Trivastal (Euthérapie)   I: Trivastan (Stroder)

Pirisudanol

ATC: N06BX08
Use: psychotropic drug, cerebrostimulant

RN: 33605-94-6   MF: $C_{16}H_{24}N_2O_6$ MW: 340.38   EINECS: 251-591-9
CN: butanedioic acid 2-(dimethylamino)ethyl [5-hydroxy-4-(hydroxymethyl)-6-methyl-3-pyridinyl]methyl
       ester

dimaleate
RN: 33510-78-0   MF: $C_{16}H_{24}N_2O_6 \cdot C_4H_4O_4$ MW: 456.45   EINECS: 251-550-5

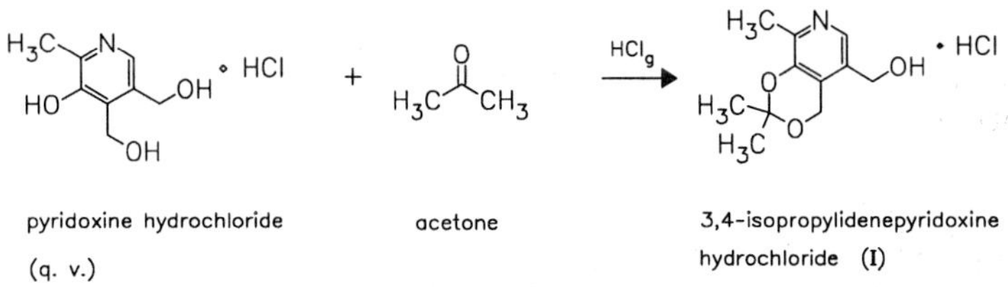

pyridoxine hydrochloride   acetone   3,4-isopropylidenepyridoxine
(q. v.)   hydrochloride (I)

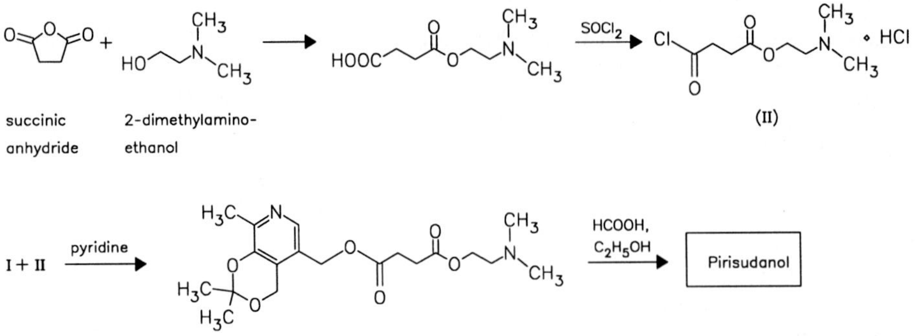

succinic anhydride

2-dimethylamino-ethanol

(II)

I + II   pyridine

HCOOH, C₂H₅OH → Pirisudanol

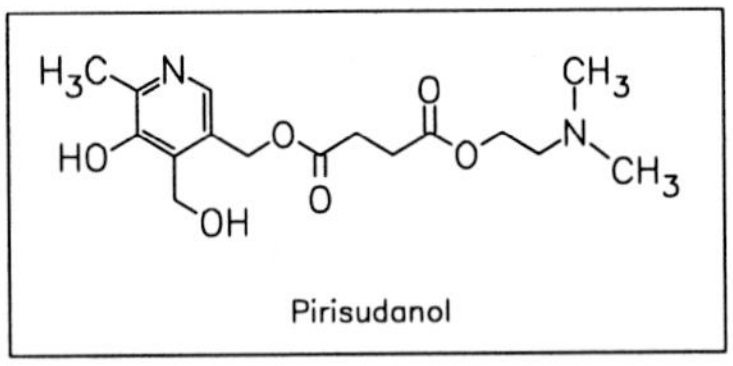

Pirisudanol

Reference(s):
US 3 717 636 (A. Esanu; 20.2.1973; GB-prior. 21.1.1970).
DE 2 102 831 (Soc. d'Etudes de Produits Chim.; appl. 21.1.1971; GB-prior. 21.1.1970).

Formulation(s):   cps. 300 mg (as maleate)

Trade Name(s):
F: Stivane (Beaufour)   I: Mentium (Guidotti)

Piritramide
(Pirinitramide)

ATC: N02AC03
Use: analgesic

RN: 302-41-0   MF: $C_{27}H_{34}N_4O$ MW: 430.60   EINECS: 206-124-3
LD$_{50}$:   30.7 mg/kg (M, i.v.); >320 mg/kg (M, p.o.);
13 mg/kg (R, i.v.); 320 mg/kg (R, p.o.)
CN: 1'-(3-cyano-3,3-diphenylpropyl)[1,4'-bipiperidine]-4'-carboxamide

3,3-diphenyl-3-cyano-propyl bromide

4-piperidinopiperidine-4-carboxamide
(cf. pipamperone synthesis)

Piritramide

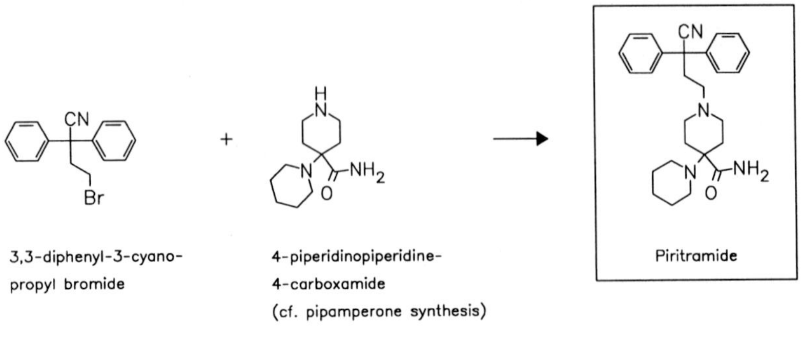

Reference(s):
DE 1 238 472 (Janssen; appl. 2.8.1961; USA-prior. 3.8.1960).

Formulation(s):   amp. 15 mg, 20 mg; vial 15 mg, 20 mg

Trade Name(s):

D:　　Dipidolor (Janssen-Cilag)-　　GB:　　Dipidolor (Janssen); wfm
　　　comb.

Pirmenol hydrochloride

(CI-845)

ATC:　C01B
Use:　antiarrhythmic

RN:　61477-94-9　MF: $C_{22}H_{30}N_2O \cdot HCl$　MW: 374.96
LD$_{50}$:　16 mg/kg (M, i.v.); 159 mg/kg (M, p.o.);
　　　7900 μg/kg (R, i.v.); 251 mg/kg (R, p.o.)
CN:　*cis*-(±)-α-[3-(2,6-dimethyl-1-piperidinyl)propyl]-α-phenyl-2-pyridinemethanol monohydrochloride

base
RN:　68252-19-7　MF: $C_{22}H_{30}N_2O$　MW: 338.50

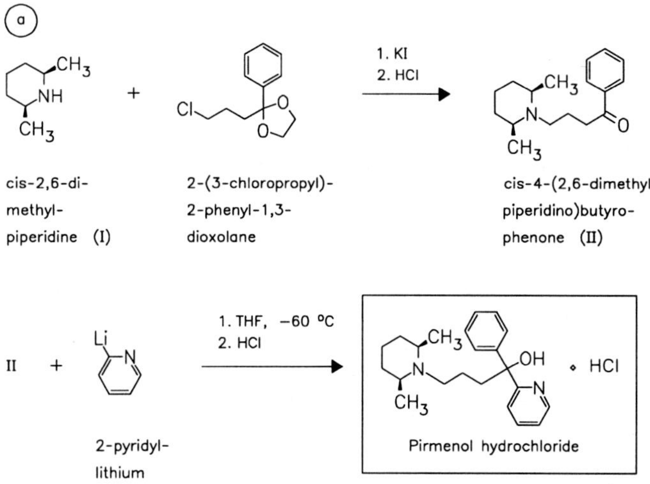

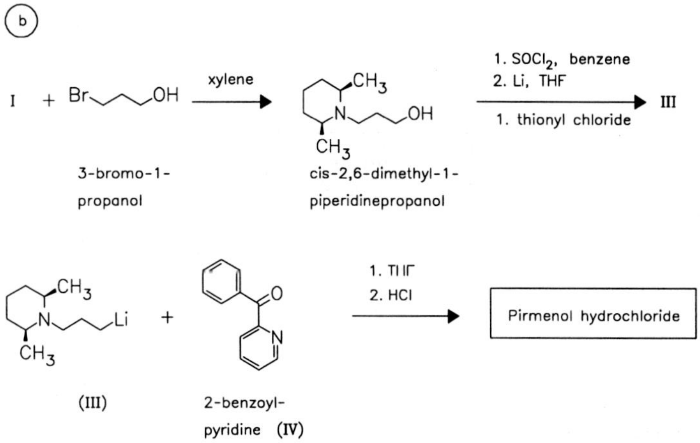

cis-2,6-di-
methyl-
piperidine (I)

2-(3-chloropropyl)-
2-phenyl-1,3-
dioxolane

cis-4-(2,6-dimethyl-
piperidino)butyro-
phenone (II)

2-pyridyl-
lithium

Pirmenol hydrochloride

3-bromo-1-
propanol

cis-2,6-dimethyl-1-
piperidinepropanol

(III)

2-benzoyl-
pyridine (IV)

Pirmenol hydrochloride

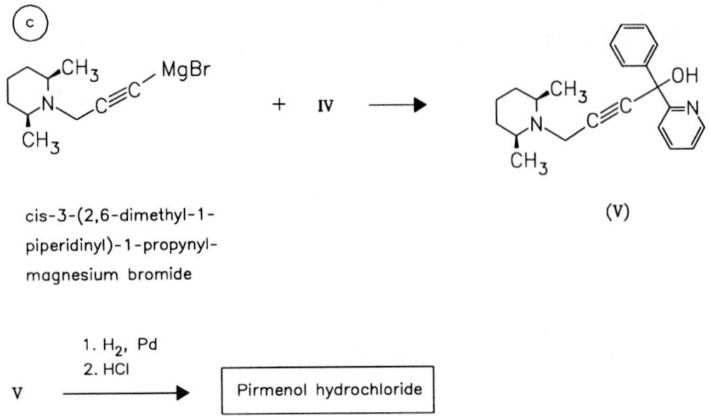

cis-3-(2,6-dimethyl-1-
piperidinyl)-1-propynyl-
magnesium bromide

(V)

Reference(s):
a,b BE 864 033 (Parke Davis; appl. 16.2.1978; USA-prior. 15.4.1976).
c JP 57 053 482 (Sumitomo Chem.; appl. 16.9.1980; J-prior. 16.9.1980).

Formulation(s): cps. 50 mg, 100 mg

Trade Name(s):
J: Pimenol (Warner-Lambert-
Dainippon)

Piromidic acid

ATC: G04AB02
Use: chemotherapeutic (gramnegative
bacteria)

RN: 19562-30-2 MF: $C_{14}H_{16}N_4O_3$ MW: 288.31 EINECS: 243-161-4
LD_{50}: 100 mg/kg (M, i.v.); 1500 mg/kg (M, p.o.);
158 mg/kg (R, i.v.); >5 g/kg (R, p.o.);
>2 g/kg (dog, p.o.)
CN: 8-ethyl-5,8-dihydro-5-oxo-2-(1-pyrrolidinyl)pyrido[2,3-d]pyrimidine-6-carboxylic acid

8-ethyl-2-methylthio-5-
oxo-5,8-dihydropyrido-
[2,3-d]pyrimidine-6-
carboxylic acid
(cf. pipemidic acid synthesis)

pyrrolidine

Piromidic acid

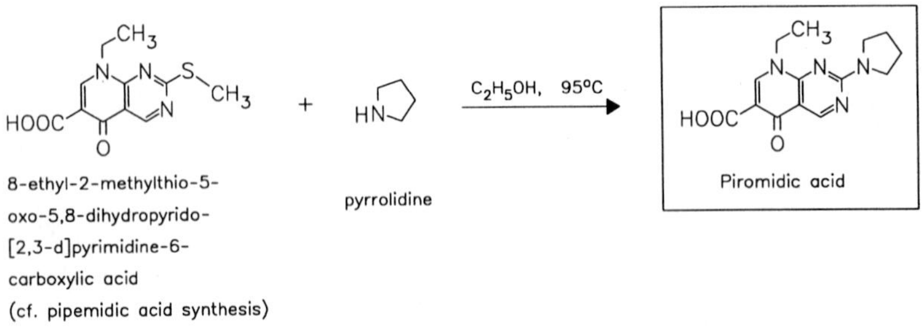

Reference(s):
DOS 2 143 369 (Dainippon; appl. 30.8.1971; J-prior. 29.8.1970).
US 3 673 184 (Dainippon; 27.6.1972; prior. 8.9.1966, 2.9.1970).
GB 1 129 358 (Dainippon; appl. 8.9.1966; J-prior. 8.9.1965, 10.8.1965).

alternative syntheses:
DOS 2 338 325 (Roger Bellon; appl. 1.8.1973; F-prior. 2.8.1972).
US 4 125 720 (Roger Bellon; 14.11.1978; F-prior. 16.4.1976).

Formulation(s): cps. 250 mg; tabl. 250 mg, 500 mg

Trade Name(s):
D: Septural (Grünenthal); wfm
F: Bactamyl (Carrion); wfm   I: Enteromix (Bioprogress)

Purim (Laphal); wfm   J: Panacid (Dainippon)

Piroxicam

ATC: M01AC01; M02AA07; S01BC06
Use: anti-inflammatory

RN: 36322-90-4   MF: $C_{15}H_{13}N_3O_4S$ MW: 331.35   EINECS: 252-974-3
LD$_{50}$:   250 mg/kg (M, p.o.);
        216 mg/kg (R, p.o.);
        108 mg/kg (dog, p.o.)
CN: 4-hydroxy-2-methyl-*N*-2-pyridinyl-2*H*-1,2-benzothiazine-3-carboxamide 1,1-dioxide

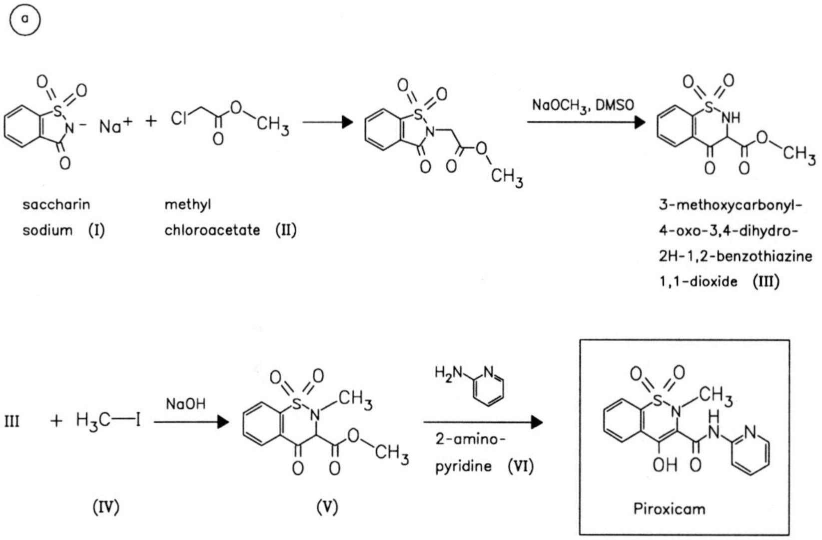

saccharin
sodium (I)

methyl
chloroacetate (II)

NaOCH$_3$, DMSO

3-methoxycarbonyl-
4-oxo-3,4-dihydro-
2H-1,2-benzothiazine
1,1-dioxide (III)

III   + H$_3$C—I   NaOH

(IV)   (V)

H$_2$N-   2-amino-
pyridine (VI)

Piroxicam

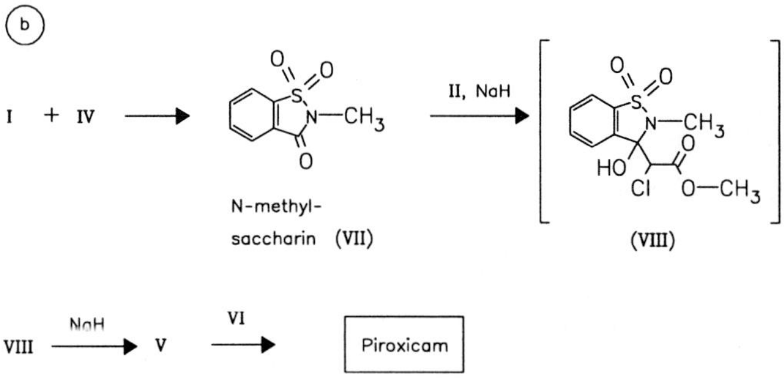

I   + IV   II, NaH

N-methyl-
saccharin (VII)

(VIII)

VIII   NaH   V   VI   Piroxicam

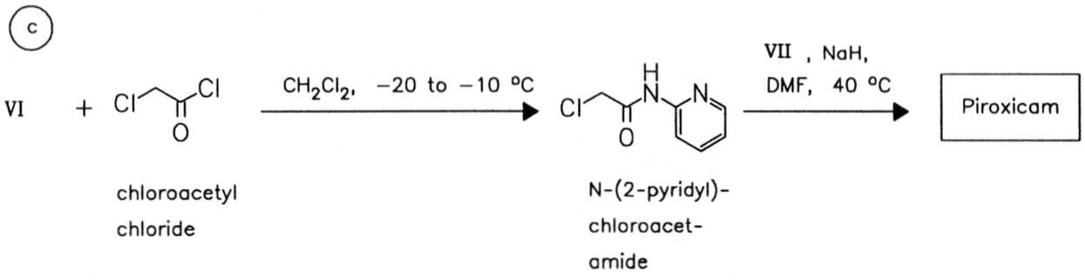

VI   + Cl   Cl   CH$_2$Cl$_2$,   −20 to −10 °C

chloroacetyl
chloride

N-(2-pyridyl)-
chloroacet-
amide

VII , NaH,
DMF, 40 °C

Piroxicam

Reference(s):
a   US 3 591 584 (Pfizer; 6.7.1971; appl. 27.8.1968).
    DOS 1 943 265 (Pfizer; appl. 26.8.1969; USA-prior. 27.8.1968).
    Lombardino, J.G. et al.: J. Med. Chem. (JMCMAR) **14**, 1171 (1971); **15**, 848 (1972); **16**, 493 (1973).
b,c US 4 483 982 (Pfizer; 20.11.1984; prior. 5.10.1981, 2.9.1982).
    EP 76 643 (Pfizer; appl. 29.9.1982; USA-prior. 5.10.1981, 2.9.1982).

alternative synthesis:
US 3 853 862 (Pfizer; 10.12.1974; appl. 23.4.1973).
US 3 891 637 (Pfizer; 24.6.1975; appl. 1.10.1974).
US 3 892 740 (Pfizer; 1.7.1975; appl. 15.10.1974).
US 4 100 347 (Pfizer; 11.7.1978; appl. 10.6.1976).
US 4 469 866 (Pfizer; 4.9.1984; USA-prior. 3.8.1981, 17.6.1982).
US 4 474 955 (V. Iannella; 2.10.1984; I-prior. 17.6.1981, 7.8.1981).
BE 900 758 (Orion; appl. 5.10.1984; Finnl.-prior. 6.10.1983).

pharmaceutical formulations:
polymorphic monoethanolamine salt:
US 4 582 831 (Pfizer; 15.4.1986; appl. 16.11.1984).
EP 182 572 (Pfizer; appl. 11.11.1985; USA-prior. 16.11.1984).

water soluble salts:
US 4 434 163 (Pfizer; 28.2.1984; prior. 1.6.1981, 13.4.1982).
US 4 434 164 (Pfizer; 28.2.1984; prior. 1.6.1981, 13.4.1982).
EP 66 458 (Pfizer; appl. 27.5.1982; USA-prior. 1.6.1981, 13.4.1982).
EP 66 459 (Pfizer; appl. 27.5.1982; USA-prior. 1.6.1981, 13.4.1982).

lyophilizates:
US 4 942 167 (Chiesi; 17.7.1990; I-prior. 1.4.1988).

stabilized injectable solutions of the salt with D(–)-*N*-methylglucamine:
US 4 628 053 (H. Mack; 9.12.1986; D-prior. 10.10.1984).
EP 177 870 (H. Mack; appl. 30.9.1985; D-prior. 10.10.1984).

deposition on carrier for rapid onset of action:
EP 123 520 (Pfizer; appl. 19.4.1984; USA-prior. 25.4.1983).

complex with β-cyclodextrin:
EP 153 998 (Chiesi; appl. 17.11.1984; I-prior. 22.4.1984).

topical compositions:
US 4 678 666 (Pfizer; 7.7.1987; J-prior. 13.7.1982).
EP 101 178 (Pfizer; appl. 7.7.1983; J-prior. 13.7.1982).

Formulation(s):   amp. 20 mg; cps. 10 mg, 20 mg; cream 5 mg/g; eff. tabl. 10 mg, 20 mg; gel 5 mg/g;
                     suppos. 20 mg; tabl. 10 mg, 20 mg

Trade Name(s):

D:	durapirox (durachemie)	Larapam (Lagap)	Polipirox (Bruschettini)
	Fasax (BASF Generics)	I: Antiflog (Firma)	Reucam (CT)
	Felden (Mack, Illert.; 1980)	Artroxicam (Coli)	Reudene (ABC
	Flexase (TAD)	Clevian (Aesculapius-Bs)	Farmaceutici)
	Reumitin (Krewel	Dexicam (O.F.F.)	Reumagil (Lenza)
	Meuselbach)	Feldene (Pfizer)	Riacen (Chiesi)
F:	Feldène (Pfizer; 1981)	Fladol (Farma Uno)	Roxene (Benedetti)
	Geldéne (Pfizer)	Flogobene (Ursamedica)	Roxenil (Caber)
	Inflaced (Biotherapie)	Lampoflex (Lampugnani)	Roxiden (Pulitzer)
	Olcam (Irex)	Nirox (Medici)	Zacam (Fournier Pierrel)
GB:	Feldene (Pfizer)	Piroftal (Bruschettini)	Zunden (Sankyo Pharma)

J: Baxo (Toyama)

Feldene (Pfizer Taito; 1982)

USA: Feldene (Pfizer; 1982)

Piroxicam cyclodextrin

ATC: M01AC
Use: non-steroidal anti-inflammatory

RN: 96684-40-1   MF: $C_{42}H_{70}O_{35} \cdot 2/5C_{15}H_{13}N_3O_4S$ MW: 6337.64
CN: β-cyclodextrin compd. with 4-hydroxy-2-methyl-N-2-pyridinyl-2H-1,2-benzothiazine-3-carboxamide 1,1-dioxide (5:2)

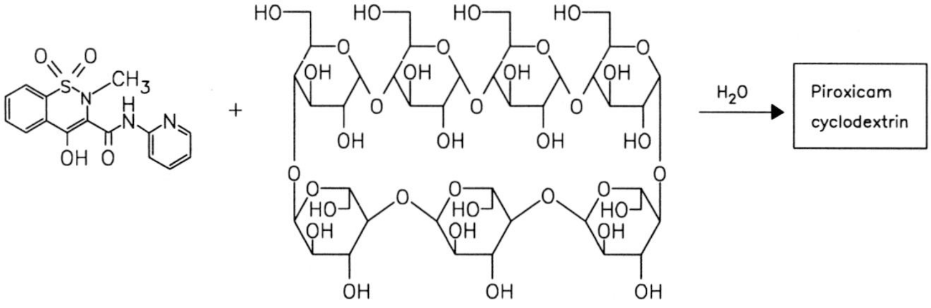

piroxicam
(q. v.)

β-cyclodextrin

Reference(s):
EP 153 998 (Chiesi; appl. 17.11.1984; I-prior. 22.2.1984).
US 4 603 123 (Chiesi; 29.7.1986; appl. 13.11.1984).

preparation by co-grinding in presence of steam:
EP 449 167 (Chiesi; appl. 25.3.1991; I-prior. 27.3.1990).

Formulation(s):   gran.. 20 mg/3 g; tabl. 20 mg

Trade Name(s):
D: Brexidol (Pharmacia & Upjohn)-comb.
F: Brexin (Robapharm)

I: Cycladol (Promedica)
     Brexin (Chiesi; 1989)

Cicladol (Master Pharma; 1989)

Pirprofen

ATC: M01AE08
Use: anti-inflammatory

RN: 31793-07-4   MF: $C_{13}H_{14}ClNO_2$ MW: 251.71   EINECS: 250-805-8
LD$_{50}$: 1350 mg/kg (M, p.o.);
         167 mg/kg (R, i.v.); 351 mg/kg (R, p.o.)
CN: 3-chloro-4-(2,5-dihydro-1H-pyrrol-1-yl)-α-methylbenzeneacetic acid

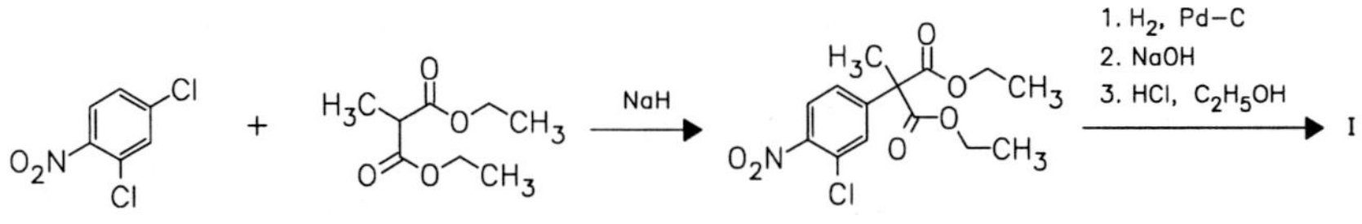

2,4-dichloro-1-
nitrobenzene

diethyl methyl-
malonate

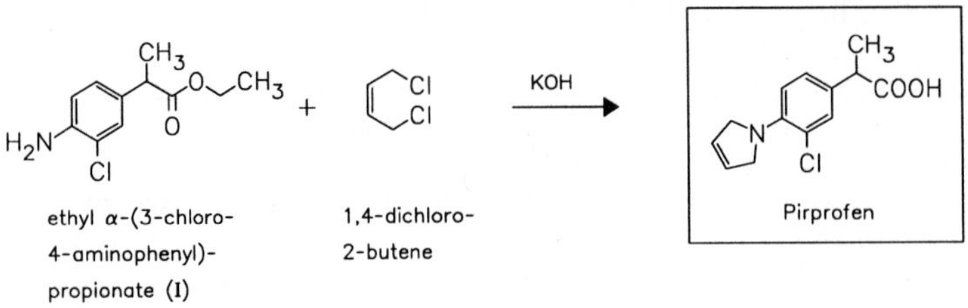

ethyl α-(3-chloro-
4-aminophenyl)-
propionate (I)

1,4-dichloro-
2-butene

Pirprofen

Reference(s):

Carney, R.W. et al.: Experientia (EXPEAM) **29**, 938 (1973).
US 3 641 040 (Ciba; 8.2.1972; F-prior. 8.7.1969, 18.3.1969, 13.1.1969, 3.9.1968, 27.3.1968).
US 3 868 391 (Ciba Geigy; 25.2.1972; prior. 3.9.1968).

Formulation(s):   amp. 400 mg/4 ml; cps. 200 mg, 400 mg

Trade Name(s):

D: Rengasil (Brunnengräber;   F: Rengasil (Ciba-Geigy);   I: Rengasil (Ciba); wfm
     1984); wfm   wfm

Pivampicillin

ATC: J01CA02
Use: antibiotic

RN: 33817-20-8   MF: $C_{22}H_{29}N_3O_6S$ MW: 463.56   EINECS: 251-688-6
LD$_{50}$:   148 mg/kg (R, i.v.); >6 g/kg (R, p.o.)
CN: [2S-[2α,5α,6β(S*)]]-6-[(aminophenylacetyl)amino]-3,3-dimethyl-7-oxo-4-thia-1-
azabicyclo[3.2.0]heptane-2-carboxylic acid (2,2-dimethyl-1-oxopropoxy)methyl ester

monohydrochloride
RN: 26309-95-5   MF: $C_{22}H_{29}N_3O_6S \cdot HCl$ MW: 500.02   EINECS: 247-604-2
LD$_{50}$:   150 mg/kg (M, i.v.); 2819 mg/kg (M, p.o.);
145 mg/kg (R, i.v.); >6 g/kg (R, p.o.)

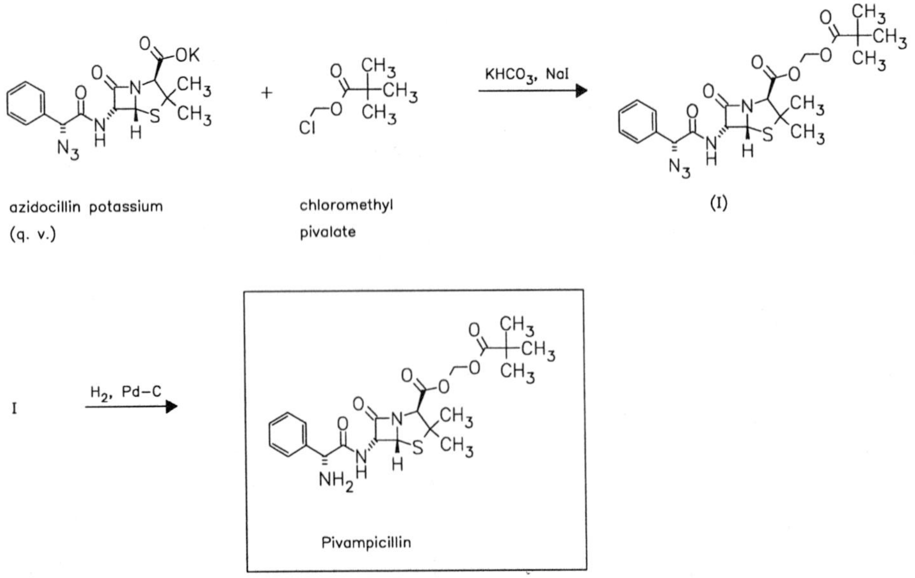

azidocillin potassium
(q. v.)

chloromethyl
pivalate

(I)

Pivampicillin

Reference(s):
DE 1 795 423 (Lovens; 2.5.1972; prior. 27.9.1968).
US 3 660 575 (Lovens; 2.5.1972; prior. 26.9.1968).
US 3 697 507 (Lovens Kem. Fabr.; 10.10.1972; appl. 26.9.1968; GB-prior. 29.9.1967).
GB 1 215 812 (Lovens Kem. Fabr.; appl. 29.9.1967; valid from 27.9.1968).
DAS 1 795 702 (Loevens; appl. 27.9.1968; GB-prior. 10.11.1967, 3.1.1968, 22.3.1968).
DAS 1 795 713 (Loevens; appl. 27.9.1968; GB-prior. 29.9.1967, 5.10.1967, 23.10.1967, 10.11.1967, 6.12.1967, 3.1.1968, 22.3.1968).

crystalline form:
US 3 956 279 (Leo; 11.5.1976; appl. 21.9.1973).
DAS 2 349 971 (Leo; appl. 4.10.1973; GB-prior. 6.10.1972).

Formulation(s):   susp. 175 mg; tabl. 350 mg, 500 mg (as hydrochloride)

Trade Name(s):

D:	Berocillin (Thomae; 1972); wfm	Miraxid/-K (Rorer)-comb.; wfm	I:	Pondocillina (Sigma-Tau); wfm
	Maxifen (Sharp & Dohme/ Boehringer Mannh.; 1972); wfm	Uro Berocillin (Thomae)-comb.; wfm		
		F:	Proampi (Leo)	

Pivmecillinam

ATC: J01CA08
Use: antibiotic

RN: 32886-97-8   MF: $C_{21}H_{33}N_3O_5S$ MW: 439.58   EINECS: 251-276-6
CN: [2S-(2α,5α,6β)]-6-[[(hexahydro-1H-azepin-1-yl)methylene]amino]-3,3-dimethyl-7-oxo-4-thia-1-azabicyclo[3.2.0]heptane-2-carboxylic acid (2,2-dimethyl-1-oxopropoxy)methyl ester

hydrochloride
RN: 32887-03-9   MF: $C_{21}H_{33}N_3O_5S \cdot HCl$ MW: 476.04

6-aminopenicillanic
acid sodium salt

chloromethyl
pivalate

pivaloyloxymethyl 6-amino-
penicillanate tosylate (I)

1. NaHCO₃
2. CHCl₃, N(C₂H₅)₃
3.

I

3. hexahydroazepine-1-carboxaldehyde,
oxalyl chloride

Pivmecillinam

Reference(s):
DOS 2 055 531 (Loevens; appl. 11.11.1970; GB-prior. 11.11.1969, 8.7.1970).
GB 1 293 590 (Loevens; appl. 11.11.1969, 8.7.1970; valid from 10.11.1970).
US 3 957 764 (Loevens; 18.5.1976; GB-prior. 11.11.1969, 8.7.1970).

combination with trimethoprim:
US 4 076 816 (Leo; 28.2.1978; GB-prior. 17.5.1974).

Formulation(s):   gran. 100 mg; tabl. 50 mg, 200 mg (as hydrochloride)

Trade Name(s):

D:	Miraxid/-K (Rorer; 1984)-comb.; wfm	F:	Selexid (Leo; 1984)		Selexid (Leo); wfm
		GB:	Miraxid (Leo)-comb.; wfm	J:	Melycin (Takeda; 1979)

Pizotifen

(Pizotyline)

ATC: N02CX01
Use: antimigraine agent

RN: 15574-96-6   MF: $C_{19}H_{21}NS$ MW: 295.45   EINECS: 239-632-9
LD$_{50}$:   410 mg/kg (R, p.o.)
CN: 4-(9,10-dihydro-4H-benzo[4,5]cyclohepta[1,2-b]thien-4-ylidene)-1-methylpiperidine

maleate (1:1)
RN: 5189-11-7   MF: $C_{19}H_{21}NS \cdot C_4H_6O_5$ MW: 429.54   EINECS: 225-970-4
LD$_{50}$:   43 mg/kg (M, i.v.);
        17 mg/kg (R, i.v.)

phthalic anhydride + 2-thienyl-acetic acid → (NaOCOCH₃, 1-methyl-2-pyrrolidone) → 3-(2-thienyl-methylene)-phthalide → (HI, P) → 2-[2-(2-thienyl)ethyl]-benzoic acid (I)

I → (polyphosphoric acid) → 4-oxo-9,10-dihydro-4H-benzo[4,5]cyclohepta[1,2-b]thiophene → (1-methyl-4-piperidyl-magnesium chloride) → (HCl, CH₃COOH) → Pizotifen

Reference(s):
BE 636 717 (Sandoz; appl. 28.8.1963; CH-prior. 31.8.1962, 8.7.1963).
US 3 272 826 (Sandoz; 13.9.1966; CH-prior. 31.8.1962).

Formulation(s):   drg. 0.5 mg, 1.5 mg; syrup 0.5 mg/10 ml (as maleate)

Trade Name(s):

D:	Mosegor (Novartis Pharma)	GB:	Sanomigran (Novartis)	USA:	Sandomigran (Sandoz); wfm
	Sandomigran (Novartis Pharma)	I:	Sandomigran (Novartis Farma)		
F:	Sanmigran (Novartis)				

Plaunotol

ATC: A02B
Use: peptic ulcer therapeutic

RN: 64218-02-6 MF: $C_{20}H_{34}O_2$ MW: 306.49
LD_{50}: 83 mg/kg (M, i.v.); 8.1 g/kg (M, p.o.);
10.9 g/kg (R, p.o.)
CN: (*Z,E,E*)-2-(4,8-dimethyl-3,7-nonadienyl)-6-methyl-2,6-octadiene-1,8-diol

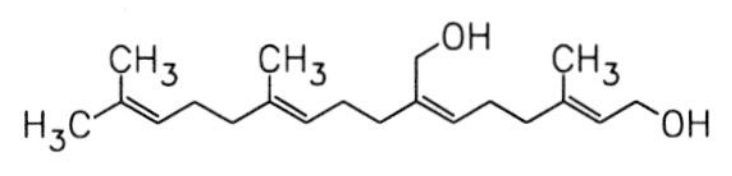

Plaunotol

Isolation by extraction of *Croton sublyratus* or *Croton columnaris* and purification on silica gel.

Reference(s):
Ogiso, A. et al.: Chem. Pharm. Bull. (CPBTAL) **26**, 3117 (1978).
US 4 059 641 (Sankyo; 22.11.1977; prior. 18.11.1975).

total synthesis:
CH 629 471 (Sankyo; appl. 18.11.1976; USA-prior. 18.11.1975).
US 4 151 357 (Sankyo; 24.4.1979; J-prior. 24.4.1976).

Formulation(s): cps. 50 mg

Trade Name(s):
J: Kelnac (Sankyo)

Polaprezinc

(CAZ; Z-103)

ATC: A02B
Use: hepatic protectant, ulcer therapeutic, anti-helicobacter pylori

RN: 107667-60-7 MF: $C_9H_{12}N_4O_3Zn$ MW: 289.61
LD_{50}: 1269 mg/kg (M, p.o.);
7375 mg/kg (R, p.o.)
CN: [*N* β alanyl L histidinato(2–)-*N*,N^N,$O^α$]zinc

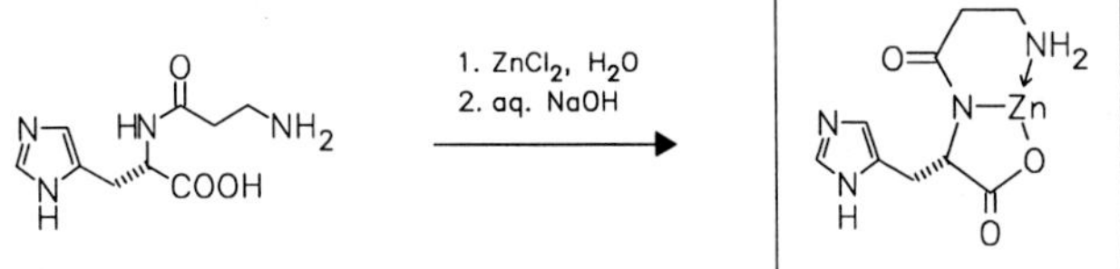

L-carnosine Polaprezinc

Reference(s):
Yoshikawa, T.; Naito, Y.; Tanigawa, T.; Yoneta, T.; Kondo, M.: Biochim. Biophys. Acta (BBACAQ) **1115** (1), 15 (1991).

synthesis:
WO 8 800 048 (Zeria Pharmaceutical Co.; appl. 14.1.1988; J-prior. 3.7.1986).
EP 303 380 (Hamari Chemicals; appl. 15.2.1989; J-prior. 10.8.1987).

pharmaceutical compositions with cyclodextrins:
WO 9 525 513 (Bellera Medical Products; appl. 28.9.1995; 18.3.1994).

oral pharmaceutical compositions:
WO 9 015 616 (Zeria Pharmaceutical Co.; 27.12.1990; J-prior. 15.6.1989).
EP 466 029 (Zeria Pharmaceutical Co.; appl. 15.1.1992; J-prior. 6.7.1990).

Formulation(s):　gran. 15 %

Trade Name(s):
J:　　Promac (Zeria)

Polidocanol

(Hydroxypolyethoxydodecane)

ATC:　C05BB02
Use:　local anesthetic, agent for sclerotherapy of varicose veins

RN:　3055-99-0　MF: $C_{30}H_{62}O_{10}$　MW: 582.82　EINECS: 221-284-4
CN:　3,6,9,12,15,18,21,24,27-nonaoxanonatriacontan-1-ol

$$H_3C-(CH_2)_{11}-OH + \triangle \xrightarrow{\Delta} \boxed{H_3C-(CH_2)_{11}-(O-CH_2-CH_2)_9-OH}$$

1-dodecanol　　ethylene oxide　　　　Polidocanol

Reference(s):
Schöller, C.: Angew. Chem. (ANCEAD) **62**, 7 (1950).
Pertsemlides, D.; Soehring, K.: Arzneim.-Forsch. (ARZNAD) **10**, 990 (1960).

Formulation(s):　amp. 0.5 %, 1 %, 2 %, 3 %, 4 %; cream 5 g/100 g; ointment 30 mg/g, 5 g/100 g; suppos. 10 mg

Trade Name(s):

D:	Aethoxysklerol (Kreussler)-comb.	numerous generics and combination preparations	GB: Alcos-Anal (Norgine)-comb.; wfm
	Recessan (Kreussler)	F: Aetoxisclérol (Dexo)	I: Atossisclerol (Also)

Polymyxin B

ATC:　A07AA05; J01XB02; S01AA18; S02AA11; S03AA03
Use:　antibiotic (macrocyclic peptide)

RN:　1404-26-8　MF: unspecified　MW: unspecified　EINECS: 215-768-4
LD_{50}:　3980 µg/kg (M, i.v.)
CN:　polymyxin B

sulfate
RN:　1405-20-5　MF: $H_2SO_4 \cdot x$ unspecified　MW: unspecified　EINECS: 215-774-7
LD_{50}:　5400 µg (M, i.v.); 790 mg (M, p.o.)

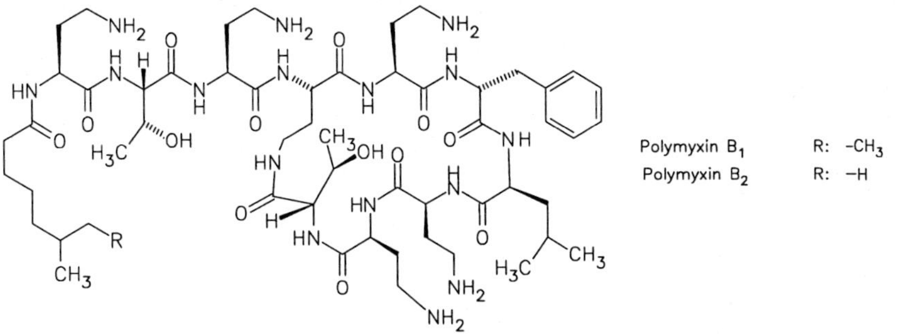

Polymyxin B

Polymyxin B$_1$ R: −CH$_3$
Polymyxin B$_2$ R: −H

Cyclopolypeptide antibiotic from cultures of *Bacillus polymyxa*.

Reference(s):

US 2 565 057 (Burroughs Wellcome; 1951; GB-prior. 1946).
US 2 595 605 (American Cyanamid; 1952; appl. 1948).
US 2 771 397 (US-Secretary of Agriculture; 1956; prior. 1930).

Formulation(s):   ophthalmic ointment 10000 iu/g; sol./drops 10000 iu; tabl. 20 mg (200000 iu), 25 mg (250000 iu) (as sulfate); vial 50 mg

Trade Name(s):

D: Polymyxin-B (Pfizer)
numerous generics and
combination preparations
F: Antibiotulle Lumière
(Solvay Pharma)-comb.
Maxidol (Alcon)-comb.
Primxyine (Thera France)-
comb.
Stérimycine (CIBA
Vision)-comb.
numerous combination
preparations
GB: Gregoderm (Unigreg)-
comb.
Maxitrol (Alcon)-comb.
Neosporin (Dominion)-
comb.

Otosporin (Glaxo
Wellcome)-comb.
Polyfax (Dominion)-comb.
Polytrim (Dominion)-
comb.
I: Anauran (Zambon Farm.)-
comb.
Localyn Oto (Recordati)-
comb.
Mixotone (Teofarma)-
comb.
Otosporia (Warner-
Lambert)-comb.
J: Polymyxin B sulfate
(Pfizer)
USA: Betadine (Purdue
Frederick) comb.

Cortisporin (Monarch)-
comb.
Lazersporin-C (Pedinol)-
comb.
Neosporin (Glaxo
Wellcome)-comb.
Pediotic (Monarch; as
sulfate)-comb.
Polysporin (Warner-
Lambert)-comb.
Polytrim (Allergan)-comb.
Terramycin (Pfizer; as
sulfate)-comb.

Polythiazide

ATC: C03AA05
Use: diuretic

RN: 346-18-9   MF: C$_{11}$H$_{13}$ClF$_3$N$_3$O$_4$S$_3$ MW: 439.89   EINECS: 206-468-4
LD$_{50}$:   >5 g/kg (M, p.o.);
>10 mg/kg (R, p.o.);
450 mg/kg (dog, p.o.)
CN: 6-chloro-3,4-dihydro-2-methyl-3-[[(2,2,2-trifluoroethyl)thio]methyl]-2*H*-1,2,4-benzothiadiazine-7-sulfonamide 1,1-dioxide

4-aminosulfonyl-5-chloro-   (2,2,2-trifluoroethyl-   Polythiazide
2-methylaminosulfonyl-   thio)acetaldehyde
aniline   dimethyl acetal

Reference(s):
US 3 009 911 (Pfizer; 21.11.1961; appl. 4.1.1961; prior. 3.6.1960).

Formulation(s):   cps 0.5 mg (in comb. with prazosin·HCl); tabl. 0.25 mg, 0.5 mg, 1 mg (as hydrochloride)

Trade Name(s):
D: Polypress/-forte (Pfizer)-   Rénèse (Pfizer); wfm   USA: Minizide (Pfizer)-comb.
     comb.   GB: Nephril (Pfizer)
F: Envarèse (Pfizer)-comb.;   J: Polyregulon (Yamanouchi)
     wfm   Renese (Taito Pfizer)

Potassium canrenoate

ATC: C03DA02
Use: aldosterone antagonist, diuretic

RN: 2181-04-6   MF: $C_{22}H_{29}KO_4$ MW: 396.57   EINECS: 218-554-9
LD$_{50}$:   125 mg/kg (M, i.v.); 740 mg/kg (M, p.o.);
      112 mg/kg (R, i.v.); 650 mg/kg (R, p.o.)
CN: (17α)-17-hydroxy-3-oxopregna-4,6-diene-21-carboxylic acid monopotassium salt

canrenone
RN: 976-71-6   MF: $C_{22}H_{28}O_3$ MW: 340.46   EINECS: 213-554-5
LD$_{50}$:   >5 g/kg (R, p.o.)

3-(17β-hydroxy-3-oxo-   canrenone   (I)
4-androsten-17-yl)-
propionic acid lactone
(cf. spironolactone
synthesis)

Potassium canrenoate

Reference(s):
US 3 013 012 (Searle; 12.12.1961; prior. 22.12.1960, 12.12.1958).
US 2 900 383 (Searle; 18.8.1959; appl. 18.12.1957).
Cella, J.A.; Tweit, R.C.: J. Org. Chem. (JOCEAH) **24**, 1109 (1959).

starting material:
Cella, J.A. et al.: J. Org. Chem. (JOCEAH) **24**, 743 (1959) (spironolactone, q. v.).

injection solutions:
US 4 088 759 (Boehringer Mannh.; 9.5.1978; D-prior. 12.12.1975).
Woog, M. et al.: Pharm. Ind. (PHINAN) 40, 1371 (1978).

Formulation(s):   amp. 200 mg/10 ml; tabl. 25 mg, 50 mg, 75 mg, 100 mg

Trade Name(s):

D:	Aldactone (Boehringer Mannh.)		Phanurane (Specia); wfm		Luvion (Gienne Pharma)
			Soludactone (Monsanto)		Venactone (Lepetit)
	Kalium-Can.-ratiopharm (ratiopharm)	GB:	Spiroctan-M (Boehringer Mannh.)	J:	Soldactone (Dainippon)
	Osyrol pro inj. (Hoechst)	I:	Kadiur (Gienne Pharma)-	USA:	Soldactone (Searle); wfm
F:	Aldatense (Searle)-comb.; wfm		comb.		
			Kanrenol (GNR)		

Prajmalium bitartrate

ATC: C01BA08
Use: antiarrhythmic

RN: 2589-47-1   MF: $C_{23}H_{33}N_2O_2 \cdot C_4H_5O_6$ MW: 518.61   EINECS: 219-975-0
LD$_{50}$: 1700 µg/kg (M, i.v.); 43 mg/kg (M, p.o.);
        3400 µg/kg (R, i.v.); 54 mg/kg (R, p.o.)
CN: (17R,21α)-17,21-dihydroxy-4-propylajmalanium salt with [R-(R*,R*)]-2,3-dihydroxybutanedioic acid (1:1)

ajmaline
(q. v.)

propyl
bromide

prajmalium bromide

prajmalium hydroxide
(aldehyde base) (I)

L-tartaric
acid

Prajmalium bitartrate

Reference(s):
DE 1 154 120 (Thomae; appl. 10.1.1962).
DE 1 196 207 (Thomae; appl. 5.7.1963; USA-prior. 17.12.1962).
US 3 414 577 (Boehringer Ing.; 3.12.1968; appl. 17.12.1962, 23.7.1964, 7.10.1965; D-prior. 10.1.1962).

Formulation(s):   f. c. tabl. 20 mg; tabl. 20 mg

Trade Name(s):
D: Neo-Gilurytmal (Solvay   I: Neoaritmina (Solvay
        Arzneimittel)   Pharma)

Pralidoxime iodide

ATC: V03AB04
Use: antidote (against anticholinesterase-
            alkylphosphate), cholinesterase
            reactivator

RN: 94-63-3   MF: $C_7H_9IN_2O$ MW: 264.07   EINECS: 202-349-6
LD_{50}:   145 mg/kg (M, i.v.); 1500 mg/kg (M, p.o.);
            178 mg/kg (R, i.v.)
CN: 2-[(hydroxyimino)methyl]-1-methylpyridinium iodide

hydroxide
RN: 495-94-3   MF: $C_7H_{10}N_2O_2$ MW: 154.17
mesylate
RN: 154-97-2   MF: $C_7H_9N_2O \cdot CH_3O_3S$ MW: 232.26   EINECS: 205-839-8
LD_{50}:   118 mg/kg (M, i.v.); 3700 mg/kg (M, p.o.);
            109 mg/kg (R, i.v.); 7 g/kg (R, p.o.)
chloride
RN: 51-15-0   MF: $C_7H_9ClN_2O$ MW: 172.62   EINECS: 200-080-9
LD_{50}:   90 mg/kg (M, i.v.); 4100 mg/kg (M, p.o.);
            96 mg/kg (R, i.v.)

pyridine-2-   pyridine-2-   Pralidoxime iodide
carboxaldehyde   carboxaldehyde
                                oxime

Reference(s):
US 2 816 113 (US-Secretary of the Army; 1957; appl. 1956).

alternative syntheses:
US 3 123 613 (Campbell Pharmac.; 3.3.1964; appl. 5.5.1961).
US 3 140 289 (US-Secretary of the Army; 7.7.1964; appl. 11.4.1962).
US 3 155 674 (Olin Mathieson; 3.11.1964; appl. 19.11.1962).

stabilization of aqueous solutions:
EP 46 685 (Survival Technology; appl. 25.8.1981; USA-prior. 26.8.1980).

Formulation(s):   amp. 200 mg/10 ml (as mesylate); vial 1 g/20 ml (as chloride)

Trade Name(s):
F: Contrathion (Serb; as   I: Contrathion (Rhône-   USA: Protopam (Wyeth-Ayerst;
      methyl sulfate)   Poulenc Rorer; as   as chloride)
                                            mesylate)

Pramipexole hydrochloride
(SND-919Y)

ATC: N04BC05
Use: dopamine D_2-agonist

RN: 104632-25-9   MF: $C_{10}H_{17}N_3S \cdot 2HCl$ MW: 284.26
CN: (S)-4,5,6,7-Tetrahydro-N^6-propyl-2,6-benzothiazolediamine dihydrochloride

(S)-base
RN: 104632-26-0   MF: $C_{10}H_{17}N_3S$ MW: 211.33
(S)-dihydrochloride hydrate
RN: 191217-81-9   MF: $C_{10}H_{17}N_3S \cdot 2HCl \cdot H_2O$ MW: 302.27
(±)-base
RN: 104617-86-9   MF: $C_{10}H_{17}N_3S$ MW: 211.33
(±)-dihydrochloride
RN: 104617-85-8   MF: $C_{10}H_{17}N_3S \cdot 2HCl$ MW: 284.26

phthalic   4-aminocyclo-   4-(phthalimido)-
anhydride   hexanol   cyclohexanol (I)
                  hydrochloride

I

$K_2Cr_2O_7$, H_2O,
H_2SO_4, $CHCl_3$

potassium
dichromate

4-(phthalimido)-
cyclohexanone

1. Br_2, HBr, CH_3COOH

2. H_2N NH_2 , CH_3COOH

1. bromine

2. thiourea

II

(±)-2-amino-6-phthal-
imido-4,5,6,7-tetra-
hydrobenzothiazole (II)

1. $H_2N-NH_2 \cdot H_2O$, C_2H_5OH
2. L-(+)-tartaric acid

1. hydrazine hydrate
2. racemate resolution

(S)-(−)-2,6 diamino
4,5,6,7-tetrahydro-
benzothiazole (III)

III   + H_3C CHO

propionaldehyde (IV)

1. DMF
2. $NaBH_4$
3. HCl

2. sodium
borohydride

Pramipexole hydrochloride

ⓑ

1. Br$_2$, CH$_3$COOH
2. [structure: H$_3$C—C(=S)—CH$_3$] , CH$_3$COOH
3. K$_2$CO$_3$, H$_2$O

[structure]

4-acetamido-
cyclohexanone

[structure]

(±)-6-acetamido-2-
amino-4,5,6,7-tetra-
hydrobenzothiazole (V)

1. IV, DMF
2. NaBH$_4$
3. HCl

or

1. [structure: H$_3$C—C(=O)—O—C(=O)—CH$_3$]
2. B$_2$H$_6$
3. HCl

1. HBr, H$_2$O
2. L-(+)-tartaric acid

V ⟶ III ⟶ [Pramipexole hydrochloride]

Reference(s):
EP 186 087 (Thomae GmbH; appl. 16.12.1985; D-prior. 22.12.1984).
Schneider, G.S.; Mierau, J.: J. Med. Chem. (JMCMAR) **30**, 494 (1987).

Formulation(s):   tabl. 0.088 mg, 0.125 mg, 0.18 mg, 0.25 mg, 0.7 mg, 1.0 (as dihydrochloride hydrate)

Trade Name(s):
D: Sifrol (Boehringer   USA: Mirapex (Boehringer
      Ingelheim)   Ingelheim; Pharmacia &
                                          Upjohn)

Pramiracetam hydrochloride

ATC: N06BX16
Use: nootropic

RN: 75733-50-5   MF: C$_{14}$H$_{27}$N$_3$O$_2$ · HCl   MW: 305.85
CN: N-[2-[Bis(1-methylethyl)amino]ethyl]-2-oxo-1-pyrrolidineacetamide hydrochloride

base
RN: 68497-62-1   MF: C$_{14}$H$_{27}$N$_3$O$_2$ MW: 269.39
sulfate
RN: 72869-16-0   MF: C$_{14}$H$_{27}$N$_3$O$_2$ · H$_2$SO$_4$ MW: 367.47

[structure] + [structure: Br—CH$_2$—C(=O)—O—CH$_3$] —NaH, THF→ [structure]

2-pyrroli-   **ethyl 2-bromo-**   **ethyl 2-oxo-1-**
dinone   **acetate**   **pyrrolidineacetate (I)**

Pramiracetam hydrochloride

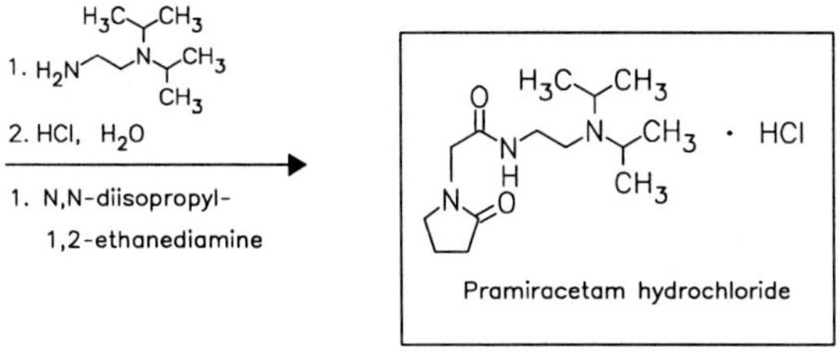

Reference(s):
BE 864 269 (Parke Davis & Co.; appl. 7.3.1978; USA-prior. 3.3.1977).
US 4 145 347 (Parke Davis & Co; 20.3.1979; USA-prior. 3.3.1977).
Butler, D.E.; Nordin, I.C.; L'Italien, Y.J.; Zweisler, L.; Poschel, P.H.; Marriott, J.G.: J. Med. Chem. (JMCMAR) **27**, 684 (1984).

Formulation(s):   tabl. 600 mg (as sulfate)

Trade Name(s):
I: Neupramir (Lusofarmaco)   Pramistar (Firma)   Remen (Parke Davis)

Pramiverine

ATC: A03A
Use: antispasmodic

RN: 14334-40-8   MF: $C_{21}H_{27}N$ MW: 293.45
CN: *N*-(1-methylethyl)-4,4-diphenylcyclohexanamine

hydrochloride
RN: 14334-41-9   MF: $C_{21}H_{27}N \cdot HCl$ MW: 329.92   EINECS: 238-284-5
LD$_{50}$:   25 mg/kg (M, i.v.); 346 mg/kg (M, p.o.);
       26 mg/kg (R, i.v.); 623 mg/kg (R, p.o.);
       20 mg/kg (dog, i.v.); 140 mg/kg (dog, p.o.)

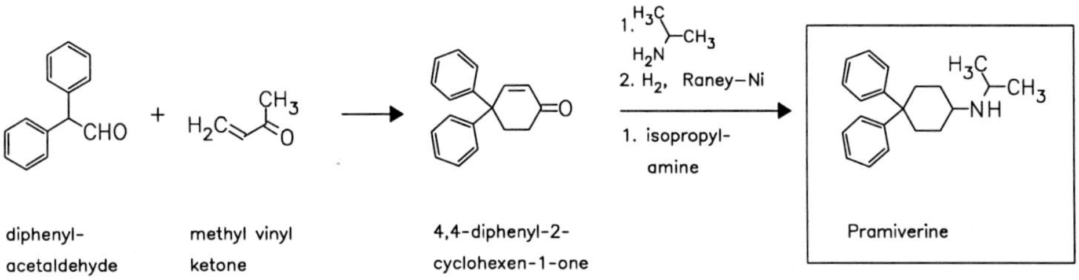

| diphenyl-acetaldehyde | methyl vinyl ketone | 4,4-diphenyl-2-cyclohexen-1-one | Pramiverine |

Reference(s):
DE 1 793 611 (Merck AG; appl. 15.12.1964).

Formulation(s):   amp. 2 mg/2 ml; drg. 2 mg; drops 2 mg/ml; suppos. 6 mg (as hydrochloride)

Trade Name(s):
D: Sistalgin (Cascan); wfm   I: Sistalgin (Bracco)-comb.;
                                           wfm

Pramocaine

(Pramoxine)

ATC: C05AD07
Use: local anesthetic

RN: 140-65-8   MF: $C_{17}H_{27}NO_3$ MW: 293.41   EINECS: 205-425-7
LD$_{50}$:   79 mg/kg (M, i.v.)
CN: 4-[3-(4-butoxyphenoxy)propyl]morpholine

hydrochloride
RN: 637-58-1   MF: $C_{17}H_{27}NO_3 \cdot HCl$ MW: 329.87   EINECS: 211-293-1
LD$_{50}$:   79.5 mg/kg (M, i.v.); 1050 mg/kg (M, p.o.)

4—butoxyphenol   3-morpholino-   Pramocaine
                        propyl chloride

Reference(s):
US 2 870 151 (Abbott; 1959; prior. 1954).
Wilson, J.W. et al.: J. Org. Chem. (JOCEAH) **16**, 792 (1951).

Formulation(s):   cream 1 g/100 g; gel 1 g/100 g (as hydrochloride)

Trade Name(s):
D: Proctofoam HC   Anusol (Warner-Lambert)   Prax (Ferndale)
       (Trommsdorff)-comb.; wfm   Caladryl (Warner-Lambert)   Proctofoam (Schwarz)
F: Tronothane (Abbott)   Cortane-B OTIC (Blansett)   Promasone (Ferndale)
I: Tronotene (Abbott)   Cortic (Everett)   Zoto-HC (Horizon)
USA: Analpram-HC (Ferndale)   Epifoam (Schwarz)

Pranlukast

(ONO-1078; RS-411; SB-205312)

ATC: R03DC02
Use: antiallergic, antiasthmatic,
        leukotriene D_4-antagonist

RN: 103177-37-3   MF: $C_{27}H_{23}N_5O_4$ MW: 481.51
CN: N-[4-oxo-2-(1H-tetrazol-5-yl)-4H-1-benzopyran-8-yl]-4-(4-phenylbutoxy)benzamide

hydrate (2:1)
RN: 150821-03-7   MF: $C_{27}H_{23}N_5O_4 \cdot 1/2H_2O$ MW: 981.04
monosodium salt
RN: 103180-28-5   MF: $C_{27}H_{22}N_5NaO_4$ MW: 503.49

ethyl 8-nitro-4-   2-cyano-8-   8-nitro-2-(tetra-
oxo-1-benzopyran-   nitro-1-benzo-   zol-5-yl)-1-benzo-
2-carboxylate   pyran-4-one   pyran-4-one (I)

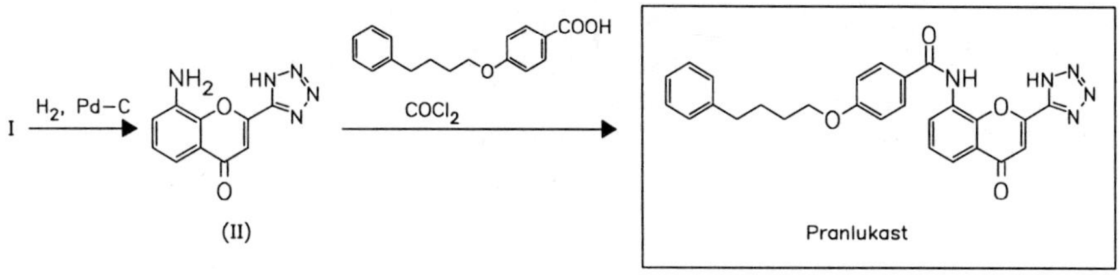

synthesis of II

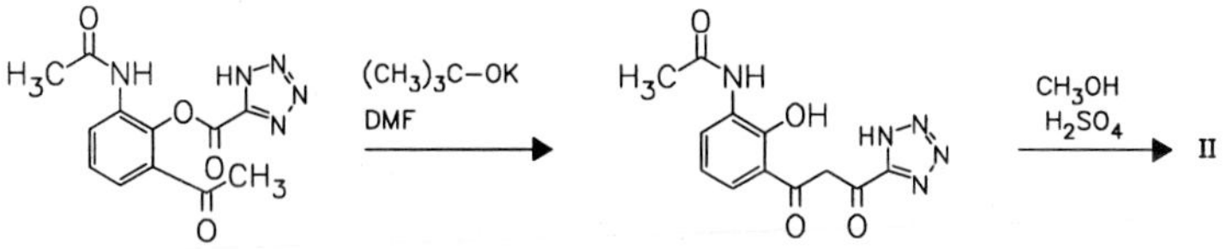

b

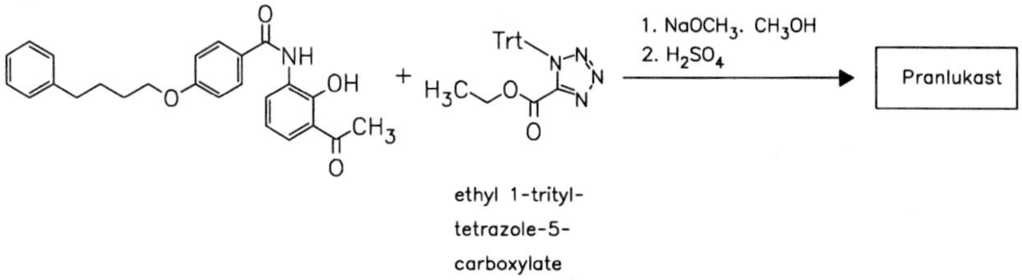

ethyl 1-trityl-
tetrazole-5-
carboxylate

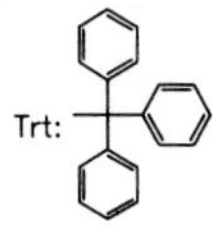

Trt:

Reference(s):
a EP 173 516 (Ono Pharm.; 1.12.1993; J-prior. 22.11.1984).
     Nakai, H. et al.: J. Med. Chem. (JMCMAR) **31**, 84-91 (1988).
b EP 0 716 088 (Sumitomo Chem.; appl. 23.6.1995; J-prior. 23.6.1994).

synthesis of intermediates type II:
WO 9 532 199 (SmithKline Beecham; appl. 30.11.1995; GB-prior. 21.5.1994).

combination with PAF-antagonists:
EP 469 477 (Hoffmann-La Roche; appl. 26.7.1991; USA-prior. 2.8.1990).

Formulation(s):   cps. 112.5 mg (as hydrate)

Trade Name(s):
J: Onon (Ono; 1995)

Pranoprofen

ATC: M01AE
Use: anti-inflammatory, analgesic

RN: 52549-17-4   MF: $C_{15}H_{13}NO_3$ MW: 255.27
LD_{50}:   447 mg/kg (M, p.o.);
        59.5 mg/kg (R, p.o.)
CN: α-methyl-5*H*-[1]benzopyrano[2,3-*b*]pyridine-7-acetic acid

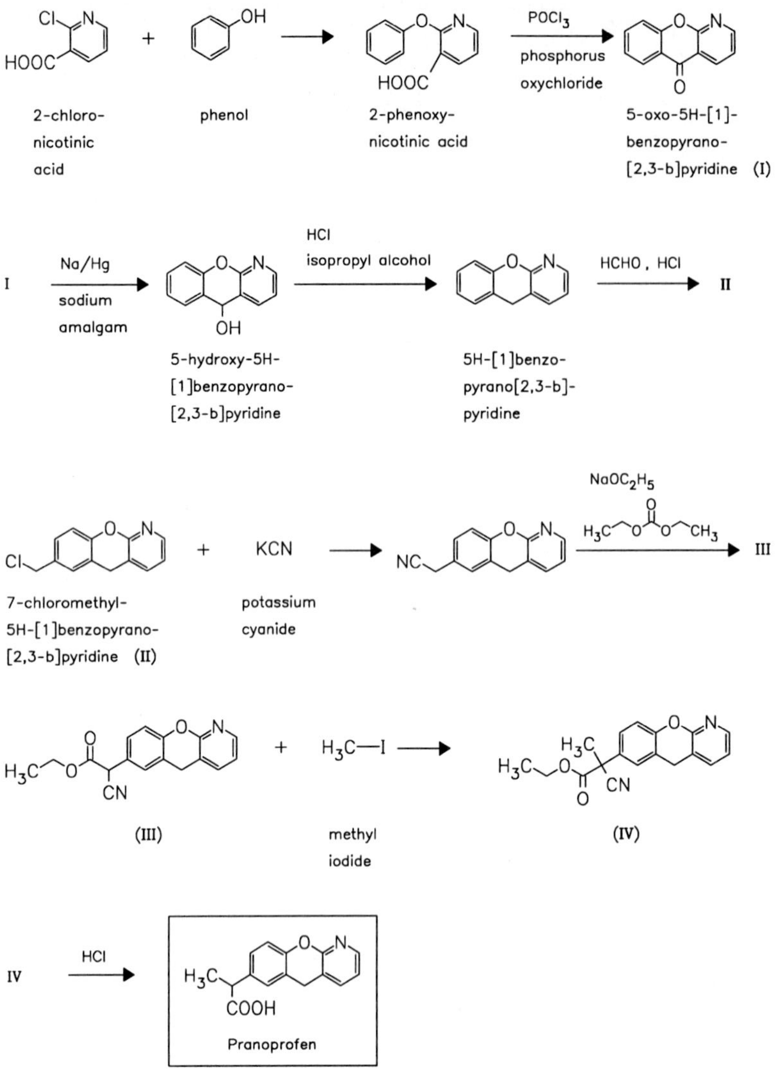

2-chloro-
nicotinic
acid

phenol

2-phenoxy-
nicotinic acid

POCl₃

phosphorus
oxychloride

5-oxo-5H-[1]-
benzopyrano-
[2,3-b]pyridine (I)

I

Na/Hg

sodium
amalgam

5-hydroxy-5H-
[1]benzopyrano-
[2,3-b]pyridine

HCl

isopropyl alcohol

5H-[1]benzo-
pyrano[2,3-b]-
pyridine

HCHO , HCl

II

7-chloromethyl-
5H-[1]benzopyrano-
[2,3-b]pyridine (II)

+   KCN

potassium
cyanide

NaOC₂H₅

III

(III)

+   H₃C—I

methyl
iodide

(IV)

IV

HCl

Pranoprofen

Reference(s):

FR 2 193 593 (Yoshitomi; appl. 19.7.1973; J-prior. 21.7.1972, 13.1.1973, 3.4.1973).
DOS 2 337 052 (Yoshitomi; appl. 20.7.1973; J-prior. 21.7.1972, 13.1.1973, 3.4.1973).
US 3 931 205 (Yoshitomi; 6.1.1976; appl. 18.7.1973; J-prior. 21.7.1972).

synthesis of 5-hydroxy-5H-[1]benzopyrano[2,3-b]pyridine:
Mann, F.G.; Reid, J.A.: J. Chem. Soc. (JCSOA9) 1952, 2057.

Formulation(s):   cps. 75 mg

Trade Name(s):
J: Niflan (Yoshitomi; 1981)

Prasterone

ATC: A14AA07
Use: anabolic, androgen

RN: 53-43-0   MF: $C_{19}H_{28}O_2$ MW: 288.43   EINECS: 200-175-5
LD_{50}: >10 g/kg (M, p.o.);
         >10 g/kg (R, p.o.)
CN: (3β)-3-hydroxyandrost-5-en-17-one

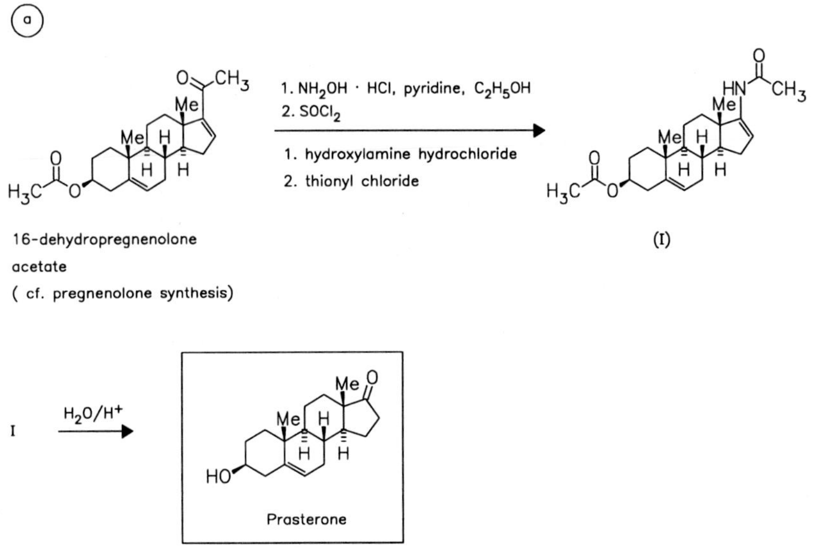

(a)

1. $NH_2OH \cdot HCl$, pyridine, C_2H_5OH
2. $SOCl_2$

1. hydroxylamine hydrochloride
2. thionyl chloride

16-dehydropregnenolone
acetate
(cf. pregnenolone synthesis)

(I)

I $\xrightarrow{H_2O/H^+}$

Prasterone

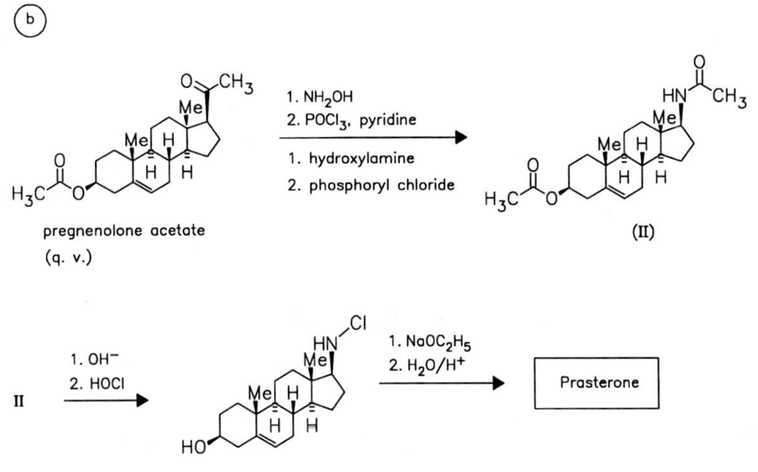

(b)

1. NH_2OH
2. $POCl_3$, pyridine

1. hydroxylamine
2. phosphoryl chloride

pregnenolone acetate
(q. v.)

(II)

II   1. OH^-
      2. HOCl

1. $NaOC_2H_5$
2. H_2O/H^+

Prasterone

Reference(s):
Ullmanns Encykl. Tech. Chem., 4. Aufl., Vol. **13**, 30.

from cholesterol:
Ullmanns Encykl. Tech. Chem., 3. Aufl., Vol. **8**, 648.
Rosenkranz, G. et al.: J. Org. Chem. (JOCEAH) **21**, 520 (1956).
US 2 335 616 (Parke Davis; 1943; prior. 1941).

Formulation(s):   amp. 200 mg/ml

Trade Name(s):
D: Gero Hormetten (Hormon-
      Chemie; as sulfate)-comb.;
      wfm

Gyno Hormetten (Hormon-
Chemie; as sulfate)-comb.;
wfm

I: Gynodian (Schering; as
      valerate)

GB: Diandrone (Organon); wfm

J: Mylis (Kanebo)

Prasterone enanthate

ATC: A14AA07; G03EA03
Use: androgen

RN: 23983-43-9   MF: $C_{26}H_{40}O_3$ MW: 400.60   EINECS: 245-970-8
CN: (3β)-3-[(1-oxoheptyl)oxy]androst-5-en-17-one

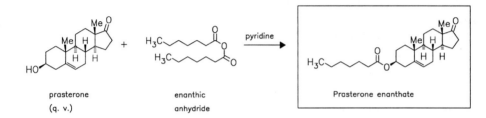

prasterone
(q. v.)

enanthic
anhydride

Prasterone enanthate

Reference(s):
BE 721 825 (Schering AG; appl. 4.10.1968; D-prior. 4.10.1967).
ZA 686 112 (Schering AG; appl. 20.9.1968; D-prior. 4.10.1967).
GB 1 246 639 (Schering AG; valid from 30.9.1968; D-prior. 4.10.1967).

alternative synthesis:
DOS 2 534 911 (Schering AG; appl. 1.8.1975).

use against psoriasis:
DOS 2 147 309 (Schering AG; appl. 17.9.1971).

Formulation(s):   amp. 200 mg in comb. with estradiol valerate

Trade Name(s):
D: Gynodian Depot
      (Schering)-comb.

F: Gynodian Depot
      (Schering)-comb.; wfm

I: Gynodian Depot
      (Schering)-comb.

Pravastatin
(Eptastatin)

ATC: C10AA03
Use: cholesterol depressant, HMG-CoA-
       reductase inhibitor

RN: 81093-37-0   MF: $C_{23}H_{36}O_7$ MW: 424.53
CN: [1S-[1α(βS*,δS*),2α,6α,8β(R*),8aα]]-1,2,6,7,8,8a-hexahydro-β,δ,6-trihydroxy-2-methyl-8-(2-methyl-1-
       oxobutoxy)-1-naphthaleneheptanoic acid

monosodium salt
RN: 81131-70-6   MF: $C_{23}H_{35}NaO_7$ MW: 446.52
LD_{50}: 2011 mg/kg (M, i.v.); 8939 mg/kg (M, p.o.);
       440 mg/kg (R, i.v.); >12 g/kg (R, p.o.)

mevastatin → Pravastatin

hydroxylation by Mucor hiemalis or P. coccineus, R. solani, Nocardia

Reference(s):
DE 3 122 499 (Sankyo; appl. 5.6.1981; J-prior. 6.6.1980, 8.9.1980, 19.9.1980, 22.8.1980).
US 4 346 227 (Sankyo; 24.8.1982; appl. 5.6.1981; J-prior. 6.6.1980, 22.8.1980, 11.3.1980).
Serizawa, N. et al.: J. Antibiot. (JANTAJ) **36**, 604 (1983).

asymmetric synthesis:
Daniewski, A.R. et al.: J. Org. Chem. (JOCEAH) **57**, 7133 (1992).

pharmaceutical formulation with increased stability:
EP 336 298 (Squibb; appl. 30.3.1989; USA-prior. 31.3.1988).

combination with coenzyme Q10:
US 4 933 165 (Merck & Co.; 12.6.1990; appl. 8.11.1989).
US 4 929 437 (Merck & Co.; 29.5.1990; appl. 2.2.1989).

mevastatin (compactin):
The Merck Index, 11th Ed., 6088 (Rahway 1989).
Endo, A.: J. Med. Chem. (JMCMAR) **28**, 401 (1985).

new production process:
EP 877 089 (Gist-Brocades, EP-prior. 7.5.1997).
WO 9 736 996 (Gist-Brocades; appl. 21.3.1997; EP-prior. 28.3.1996).
WO 9 845 410 (Yungjin; appl. 30.6.1997; KR-prior. 10.4.1997).
EP 776 974 (Sankyo; appl. 29.11.1996; J-prior. 29.11.1995).

conversion of compactin *by Actinomadura:*
WO 9 640 863 (MIT; appl. 4.6.1996; USA-prior. 7.6.1995).

hydroxylation by Saccharopolysopra hirsuta:
EP 649 907 (Bristo-Myers Squibb; appl. 18.10.1994; USA-prior. 22.10.1993).

use for slowing progression of atherosclerosis:
EP 671 170 (Bristol-Myers Squibb; appl. 21.2.1995; USA-prior. 11.3.1994).

use for preventing restinosis:
EP 459 453 (Squibb & Sons; appl. 29.5.1991; USA-prior. 31.5.1990).

Formulation(s):   tabl. 5 mg, 10 mg, 20 mg (as sodium salt)

Trade Name(s):

D:	Liprevil (Schwarz/Sanol)	GB:	Lipostat (Bristol-Myers		Selectin (Bristol-Myers
	Mevalotin (Sankyo)		Squibb)		Squibb; 1990)
	Pravasin (Bristol-Myers	I:	Aplactin (Mead Johnson)	J:	Mevalotin (Sankyo; 1989)
	Squibb; 1991)		Prasterol (Malesci)	USA:	Pravachol (Bristol-Myers
F:	Elisor (Bristol-Myers		Pravaselect (Menarini;		Squibb; 1991)
	Squibb; 1991)		1990)		
	Vasten (Specia; Rhône-		Sanaprav (Sankyo Pharma)		
	Poulenc Rorer; 1991)				

Prazepam

ATC: N05BA11
Use: tranquilizer

RN: 2955-38-6 MF: C$_{19}$H$_{17}$ClN$_2$O MW: 324.81 EINECS: 220-975-8
LD$_{50}$: 2300 mg/kg (M, p.o.);
>4 g/kg (R, p.o.);
>4 g/kg (dog, p.o.)
CN: 7-chloro-1-(cyclopropylmethyl)-1,3-dihydro-5-phenyl-2H-1,4-benzodiazepin-2-one

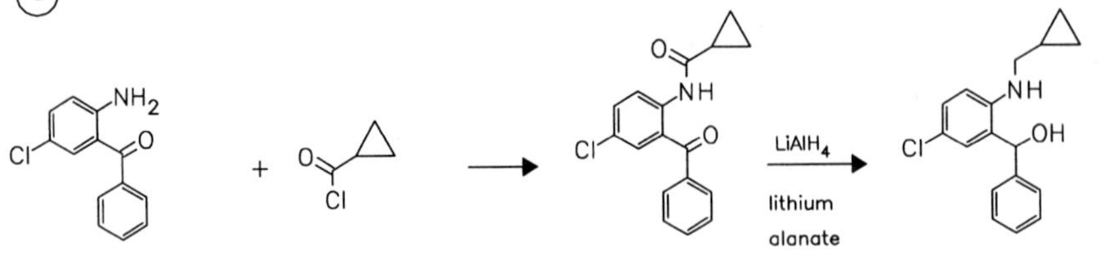

2-amino-5-chloro-
benzophenone

cyclopropane-
carbonyl chloride

(I)

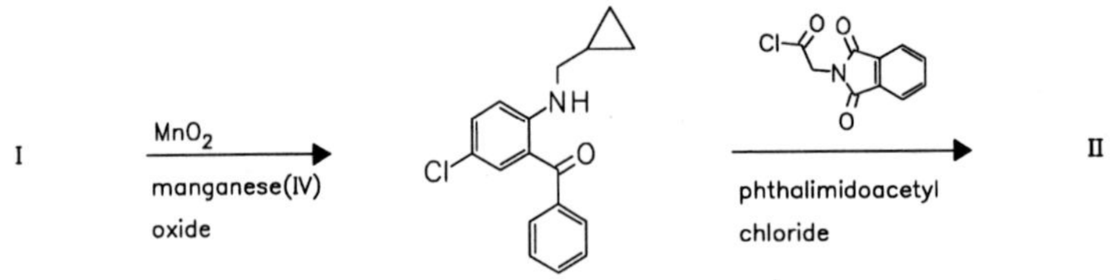

5-chloro-2-[(cyclo-
propylmethyl)amino]-
benzophenone

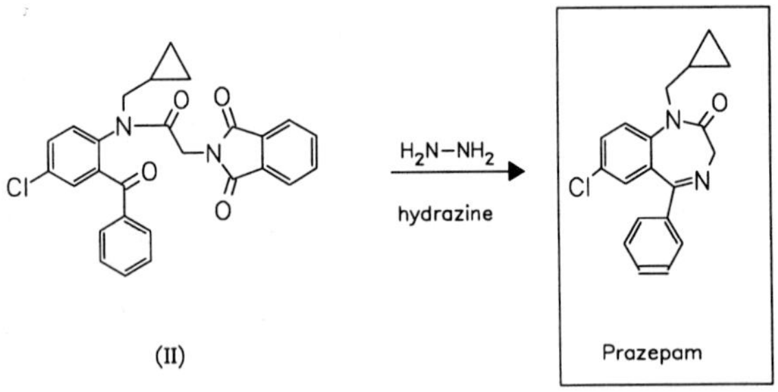

phthalimidoacetyl
chloride

II

(II)

hydrazine

Prazepam

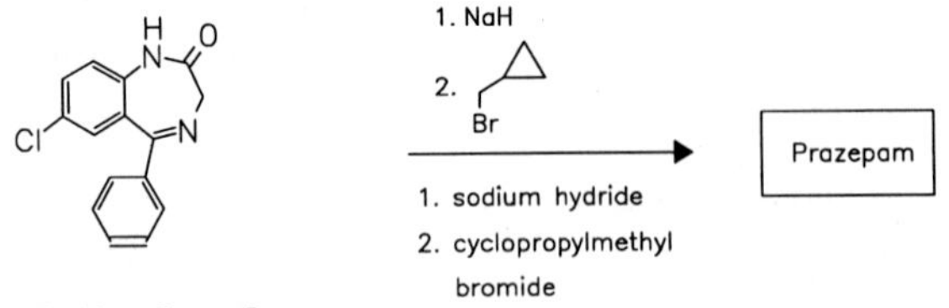

7-chloro-2-oxo-5-
phenyl-2,3-dihydro-
1H-1,4-benzodiazepine
(cf. diazepam synthesis)

1. NaH
2. [cyclopropylmethyl bromide]
   Br

1. sodium hydride
2. cyclopropylmethyl
   bromide

Prazepam

Reference(s):

a DAS 1 229 098 (Warner-Lambert; appl. 24.2.1964; USA-prior. 1.3.1963).
   US 3 192 199 (F. H. McMillan, J. Pattison; 29.6.1965; appl. 1.3.1963).
b US 3 192 200 (H. M. Wuest; 29.6.1965; prior. 5.3.1963).

alternative synthesis:
Inaba, S. et al.: Chem. Pharm. Bull. (CPBTAL) **17**, 1263 (1969).

Formulation(s):   drops 15 mg/ml; tabl. 10 mg, 20 mg, 40 mg

Trade Name(s):

D:	Demetrin (Gödecke; Parke Davis)	GB:	Centrax (Parke Davis); wfm	USA:	Centrax (Parke Davis); wfm
	Mono-Demetrin (Gödecke; Parke Davis)	I:	Prazene (Parke Davis) Trepidan (Max Farma)		Verstran (Parke Davis; Warner Chilcott); wfm
F:	Lysanxia (Parke Davis)	J:	Prazepam (Sumitomo Chem.)		

Praziquantel

ATC: P02BA01
Use: anthelmintic

RN: 55268-74-1   MF: $C_{19}H_{24}N_2O_2$ MW: 312.41   EINECS: 259-559-6
LD$_{50}$:   2454 mg/kg (M, p.o.);
   2840 mg/kg (R, p.o.);
   >200 mg/kg (dog, p.o.)
CN: 2-(cyclohexylcarbonyl)-1,2,3,6,7,11b-hexahydro-4*H*-pyrazino[2,1-*a*]isoquinolin-4-one

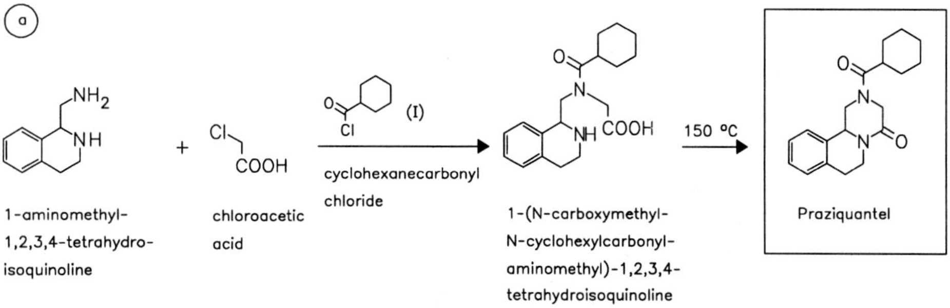

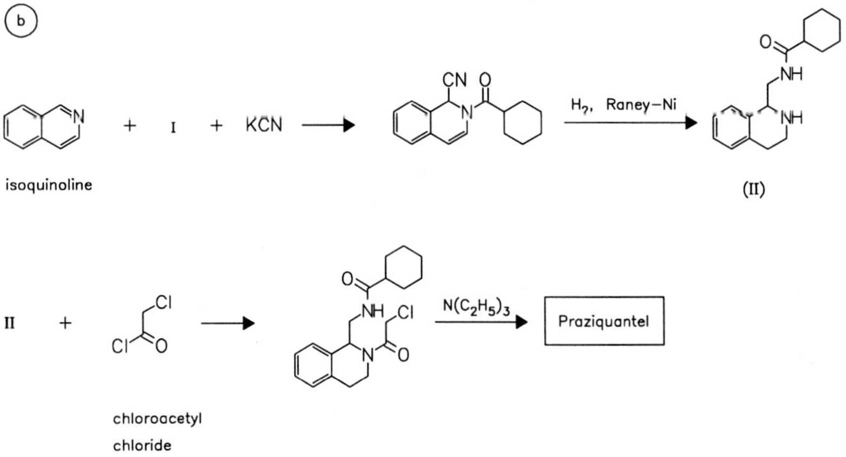

a

1-aminomethyl-
1,2,3,4-tetrahydro-
isoquinoline

chloroacetic
acid

cyclohexanecarbonyl
chloride

1-(N-carboxymethyl-
N-cyclohexylcarbonyl-
aminomethyl)-1,2,3,4-
tetrahydroisoquinoline

Praziquantel

b

isoquinoline

(II)

II + chloroacetyl chloride

Praziquantel

Reference(s):
DOS 2 457 971 (E. Merck Patent GmbH; appl. 7.12.1974).
DOS 2 362 539 (E. Merck Patent GmbH; appl. 17.12.1973).
DOS 2 504 250 (E. Merck Patent GmbH; appl. 1.2.1975).
DOS 3 011 156 (E. Merck Patent GmbH; appl. 22.3.1980).

Formulation(s):   f. c. tabl. 150 mg, 600 mg; tabl. 500 mg

Trade Name(s):
D: Biltricide (Bayer)   Cysticide (Merck)   J: Biltrizide (Bayer)
      Cesol (Merck)   F: Biltricide (Bayer Pharma)   USA: Biltricide (Bayer)

Prazosin

ATC: C02CA01
Use: antihypertensive, α_1-adrenergic blocker

RN: 19216-56-9   MF: $C_{19}H_{21}N_5O_4$ MW: 383.41   EINECS: 242-885-8
LD_{50}: >400 mg/kg (M, i.v.); >4 g/kg (M, p.o.)
CN: 1-(4-amino-6,7-dimethoxy-2-quinazolinyl)-4-(2-furanylcarbonyl)piperazine

monohydrochloride
RN: 19237-84-4   MF: $C_{19}H_{21}N_5O_4 \cdot HCl$ MW: 419.87   EINECS: 242-903-4
LD_{50}: 92 mg/kg (M, i.v.); 5 g/kg (M, p.o.);
      73 mg/kg (R, i.v.); 1950 mg/kg (R, p.o.);
      >700 mg/kg (dog, p.o.)

2-amino-4,5-di-   sodium   2,4-dihydroxy-6,7-   2,4-dichloro-6,7-
methoxybenzoic   cyanate   dimethoxyquinazoline   dimethoxyquinazoline (I)
acid

4-amino-2-chloro-   Prazosin
6,7-dimethoxy-
quinazoline

1-(2-furoyl)piperazine

Reference(s):
US 3 511 836 (Pfizer; 12.5.1970; appl. 13.12.1967; prior. 6.8.1965, 7.6.1966).
US 3 635 979 (Pfizer; 18.1.1972; prior. 6.8.1965, 7.6.1966, 13.12.1967).
US 3 663 706 (Pfizer; 16.5.1972; prior. 6.8.1965, 13.12.1967, 12.5.1970).
DAS 1 620 138 (Pfizer; appl. 2.7.1966; USA-prior. 6.7.1965, 7.6.1966).

alternative synthesis:
US 3 935 213 (Pfizer; 27.1.1976; prior. 5.12.1973).
DOS 2 457 911 (Pfizer; appl. 4.12.1974; USA-prior. 5.12.1973).
DOS 2 731 737 (Pfizer; appl. 11.7.1977; USA-prior. 6.8.1976).
US 4 062 844 (Pfizer; 13.12.1977; appl. 20.9.1976).
US 4 138 561 (Bristol-Myers; 6.2.1979; prior. 30.9.1977).
BE 861 821 (Fermion; appl. 14.12.1977; SF-prior. 15.12.1976).
BE 861 822 (Fermion; appl. 14.12.1977; SF-prior. 15.12.1976).

α-form:
US 4 092 315 (Pfizer; 30.5.1978; appl. 1.3.1976).
DAS 2 708 192 (Pfizer; appl. 25.2.1977; USA-prior. 1.3.1976).

anhydrous crystalline form:
DE 3 429 415 (Orion; appl. 9.8.1984; FL-prior. 25.6.1984).
US 4 816 455 (Heumann Pharma; 28.3.1989; appl. 3.3.1987; EP-prior. 21.3.1986).

Formulation(s):   s. r. cps. 1 mg, 2 mg, 4 mg, 6 mg; tabl. 0.5 mg, 1 mg, 2 mg, 5 mg (as hydrochloride)

Trade Name(s):

D:	Adversuten (ASTA Medica AWD)		Polypress/-forte (Pfizer)-comb.	GB:	Hypovase (Invicta; 1974)
	Duramipress (durachemie)		Prazosin-ratiopharm	I:	Minipress (Pfizer; 1978); wfm
	Eurex (Sanofi Winthrop)		(ratiopharm)		
	Minipress (Pfizer; 1977)	F:	Alpress LP (Pfizer)	J:	Minipress (Pfizer Taito; 1981)
			Minipress (Pfizer; 1979)	USA:	Minipress (Pfizer)

Prednicarbate
(Hoe 777)

ATC: D07AC18
Use: topical glucocorticoid, steroidal anti-inflammatory

RN: 73771-04-7   MF: $C_{27}H_{36}O_8$ MW: 488.58   EINECS: 277-590-3
CN: (11β)-17-[(ethoxycarbonyl)oxy]-11-hydroxy-21-(1-oxopropoxy)pregna-1,4-diene-3,20-dione

prednisolone (q. v.)   +   tetraethyl orthocarbonate   — Tos—OH, dioxane →   prednisolone 17,21-diethyl orthocarbonate (I)

I   — CH₃COOH, H₂O →   prednisolone 17-ethylcarbonate   — propionyl chloride / pyridine →   Prednicarbate

Reference(s):
Stache, U. et al.: Arzneim.-Forsch. (ARZNAD) **35** (II), 1753 (1985).
EP 742 (Hoechst; appl. 27.7.1978; D-prior. 4.8.1977).
DE 2 735 110 (Hoechst; appl. 4.8.1977).
US 4 242 334 (Hoechst; appl. 21.2.1979; D-prior. 4.8.1977).

Formulation(s):   cream 2.5 mg/1 g; ointment 2.5 mg/1 g; sol. (in aqueous ethanol, 20 %) 2.5 mg/1 g

Trade Name(s):
D: Dermatop (Hoechst)   I: Dermatop (Hoechst Marion   USA: Dermatop (Hoechst Marion
                                       Roussel)   Roussel)

Prednimustine

ATC: L01AA08
Use: antineoplastic

RN: 29069-24-7   MF: $C_{35}H_{45}Cl_2NO_6$ MW: 646.65   EINECS: 249-410-3
LD_{50}:   530 mg/kg (R, p.o.)
CN: (11β)-21-[4-[4-[bis(2-chloroethyl)amino]phenyl]-1-oxobutoxy]-11,17-dihydroxypregna-1,4-diene-3,20-dione

prednisolone   4-[4-[bis(2-chloroethyl)amino]phenyl]-
(q. v.)   butyric anhydride

Prednimustine   (**I**)

Reference(s):
DOS 2 001 305 (A B Leo; appl. 13.1.1970; GB-prior. 23.1.1969).

Formulation(s):   cps. 10 mg, 50 mg; tabl. 10 mg, 100 mg

Trade Name(s):
D: Sterecyt (Pharmaleo); wfm   F: Stéréocyt (Roger Bellon);
                                         wfm

Prednisolamate

ATC: H02AB06
Use: glucocorticoid

RN: 5626-34-6   MF: $C_{27}H_{39}NO_6$ MW: 473.61   EINECS: 227-064-4
CN: *N,N*-diethylglycine (11β)-11,17-dihydroxy-3,20-dioxopregna-1,4-dien-21-yl ester

hydrochloride
RN: 17140-01-1   MF: $C_{27}H_{39}NO_6 \cdot HCl$ MW: 510.07

prednisolone   chloroacetyl   (I)
                        chloride

diethyl-   Prednisolamate
amine

Reference(s):
GB 862 370 (Pfizer; valid from 1957; USA-prior. 1956).
DE 1 037 451 (Schering AG; appl. 1957).

alternative synthesis:
Pancrazio, G.; Sbarigia, G.: Farmaco, Ed. Prat. (FRPPAO) **16**, 190 (1961).

Formulation(s):   tabl. 5 mg

Trade Name(s):
D: Deltacortril-intravenös
          (Pfizer); wfm

Prednisolone

ATC: A07EA01; C05AA04; D07AA03;
        D07XA02; H02AB06; R01AD02;
        R01AD52; S01BA04; S01CB02;
        S02BA03; S03BA02
Use: glucocorticoid

RN: 50-24-8   MF: $C_{21}H_{28}O_5$ MW: 360.45   EINECS: 200-021-7
LD$_{50}$;   180 mg/kg (M, i.v.); 1680 mg/kg (M, p.o.);
          120 mg/kg (R, i.v.)
CN: (11β)-11,17,21-trihydroxypregna-1,4-diene-3,20-dione

acetate
RN: 52-21-1   MF: $C_{23}H_{30}O_6$ MW: 402.49   EINECS: 200-134-1
LD$_{50}$:   3500 mg/kg (M, s.c.);
          >240 mg/kg (R, s.c.)

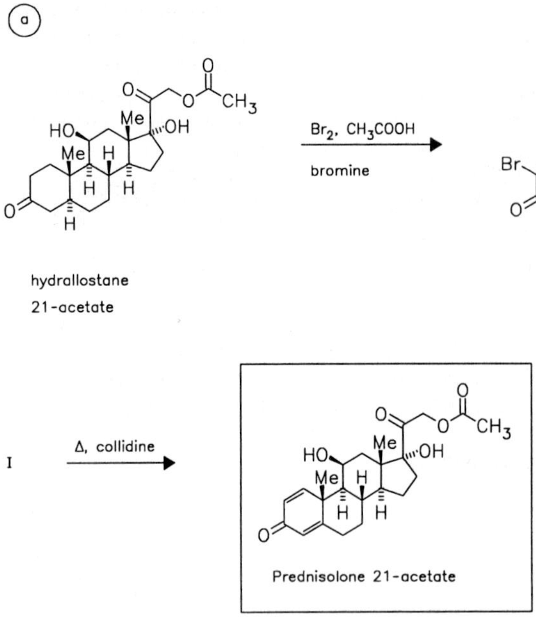

ⓐ

hydrallostane
21-acetate

(I)

I → Δ, collidine

Prednisolone 21-acetate

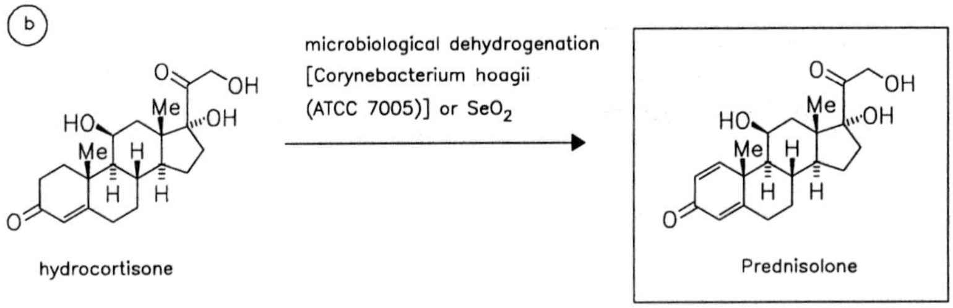

ⓑ

hydrocortisone

microbiological dehydrogenation
[Corynebacterium hoagii
(ATCC 7005)] or SeO₂

Prednisolone

Reference(s):
a US 2 897 216 (Schering Corp.; 1959; prior. 1952).
starting material:
The Merck Index, 12th Ed., 815 (1996).
b US 3 134 718 (Schering Corp.; 26.5.1964; appl. 12.12.1963; prior. 11.8.1954).
Wettstein, A. et al.: Helv. Chim. Acta (HCACAV) **39**, 734 (1956).
Nobile, A. et al.: J. Am. Chem. Soc. (JACSAT) **77**, 4184 (1955).
DAS 1 135 899 (Schering AG; appl. 20.5.1960).

alternative synthesis:
US 4 041 055 (Upjohn; 9.8.1977; appl. 17.11.1975).

Formulation(s):   amp. 10 mg/ml, 25 mg/ml, 50 mg/ml (as acetate); eye drops 1.2 mg/ml, 10 mg/ml (as acetate);
ointment 5 mg/g, 100 mg/g; suppos. 100 mg (as acetate); syrup 15 mg/5 ml; tabl. 1 mg, 5 mg,
20 mg

Trade Name(s):
D: Alferm (Schöning-Berlin)-
comb.
Decaprednil (Orion
Pharma)
Decortin H (Merck)
Dontisolan (Hoechst)
Dura Prednisolon
(durachemie)

Hefasolon (Hefa Pharma)
Inflanefran (Pharm-
Allergan)
Klismacort (bene-
Arzneimittel)
Linola (Wolff)
Prectal (Artesan; Cassella-
med)

Prednabene (Merckle)
Prednihexal (Hexal)
Predni-H-injekt
(Sanorania)
Predni-H-Tablinen
(Sanorania)
Predni-POS (Ursapharm)

Prednisolon "Ferring" (Ferring)
Prednisolon "Lentia" (Lentia)
Prednisolon Augensalbe Jenapharm (Jenapharm)
Prednisolut (Jenapharm)
Solu-Decortin (Merck)
Ultracortenol (CIBA Vision)
combination preparations

F:　Deliproct (Schering; as caproate)-comb.
Dérinox (Thérabel Lucien pharma)-comb.
combination preparations
GB:　Deltacortril (Pfizer)

Deltastab (Knoll)
Hydrocortancyl cp séc (Roussel)
Hydrocortancyl susp inj (Roussel)
Precortisyl forte (Hoechst)
Pred forte (Allergan)
Scheriproct (Schering; as hexanoate)-comb.
I:　Biodeltacortilen (SIFI)-comb.
Meticortelone (Schering-Plough)
Solprene (Farmigea)
J:　Codelcortone (Merck-Banyu)
Deltacortil (Taito Pfizer)

Delta Prenin (Sumitomo)
Donisolone (Sankyo)
Lavine (Tatsumi)
Prednisolone Cream (Toho)
Prednisolon Ophthalmic Oint (Nitten)
Predonine (Shionogi)
Scherisolon Inj. (Nihon Schering)
Scherisolon Tab. (Nihon Schering)
numerous combination preparations
USA:　Predniso (Roxane)
Prelone (Muro)

Prednisolone sodium phosphate

ATC:　H02AB06
Use:　glucocorticoid

RN:　125-02-0　MF: $C_{21}H_{27}Na_2O_8P$　MW: 484.39　EINECS: 204-722-9
LD$_{50}$:　360 mg/kg (rabbit, i.v.)
CN:　(11β)-11,17-dihydroxy-21-(phosphonooxy)pregna-1,4-diene-3,20-dione disodium salt

free acid
RN:　302-25-0　MF: $C_{21}H_{29}O_8P$　MW: 440.43　EINECS: 206-120-1

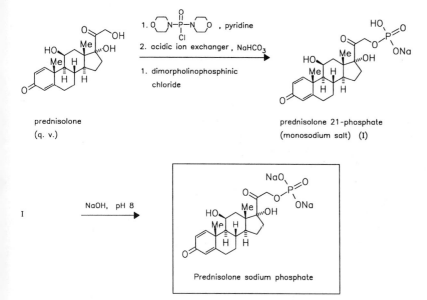

prednisolone
(q. v.)

prednisolone 21-phosphate
(monosodium salt)　(I)

Prednisolone sodium phosphate

Reference(s):
DE 1 134 075 (Merck AG; appl. 26.11.1959).

alternative syntheses:
US 2 789 117 (Merck & Co.; 1957; appl. 1957).
US 2 870 177 (Merck & Co.; 1959; appl. 1954).
US 2 932 657 (Merck k Co.; 12.4.1960; appl. 30.7.1957).
US 2 936 313 (Glaxo; 10.5.1960; appl. 18.11.1958; GB-prior. 19.11.1957).

Formulation(s):   amp. 33.6 mg/5 ml, 53.75 mg/5 ml; eye drops 0.5 g/100 ml; oral sol. 6.7 mg/5 ml

Trade Name(s):
D:	Hefasolon (Hefa Pharma)		Phortisolone (Fumouze);		Prednesol (Glaxo
	Prednabene		wfm		Wellcome)
	Injektionslösung (Merckle)		Solucort (Merck Sharp &		Predsol (Evans)
F:	Colicort (Merck Sharp &		Dohme-Chibret)	I:	Solprene (Farmigea)-comb.
	Dohme-Chibret)-comb.	GB:	Minims Prednisolone	J:	Prozorin (Takeda)
	Deturgylone (Synthélabo)-		(Chauvin)	USA:	Optimyd (Medeva)-comb.
	comb.				

Prednisolone sodium succinate

ATC: H02AB06
Use: glucocorticoid

RN: 1715-33-9   MF: $C_{25}H_{31}NaO_8$ MW: 482.51   EINECS: 216-995-1
LD$_{50}$:   1125 mg/kg (M, i.v.);
770 mg/kg (R, i.v.)
CN: (11β)-21-(3-carboxy-1-oxopropoxy)-11,17-dihydroxypregna-1,4-diene-3,20-dione monosodium salt

free acid
RN: 2920-86-7   MF: $C_{25}H_{32}O_8$ MW: 460.52   EINECS: 220-861-8

prednisolone   succinic   (I)
(q. v.)   anhydride

Prednisolone sodium succinate

Reference(s):
DAS 1 045 400 (Pfizer; appl. 1956; USA-prior. 1955)-withdrawn.
continuation of DE 1 013 648

Formulation(s):   amp. 10 mg, 25 mg, 100 mg (as free acid); amp. 10 mg/ml, 25 mg/ml, 50 mg/ml, 100 mg/ml,
250 mg/5 ml, 250 mg/10 ml, 500 mg/5 ml, 500 mg/10 ml, 1000 mg/5 ml, 1000 mg/10 ml

Prednisolone sodium sulfobenzoate

ATC: H02AB06
Use: glucocorticoid

RN: 630-67-1   MF: $C_{28}H_{31}NaO_9S$ MW: 566.60   EINECS: 211-141-4
CN: (11β)-11,17-dihydroxy-21-[(3-sulfobenzoyl)oxy]pregna-1,4-diene-3,20-dione monosodium salt

prednisolone   methanesulfonyl   (I)
(q. v.)   chloride

sodium 3-sulfo-   Prednisolone sodium 21-sulfobenzoate
benzoate

Reference(s):
US 3 037 034 (Roussel-Uclaf; 29.5.1962; appl. 21.4.1960; F-prior. 24.4.1959).

alternative synthesis:
US 3 032 568 (Roussel-Uclaf; 1.5.1962; appl. 15.3.1961; prior. 13.4.1959).

Formulation(s):   collutorium 22.5 mg/3 ml;clysma 20 mg; eye ointment 30 mg/4 g; foam 20 mg

Prednisolone steaglate

(Prednisolone stearoylglycolate)

ATC: H02AB06
Use: glucocorticoid

RN: 5060-55-9   MF: $C_{41}H_{64}O_8$ MW: 684.96   EINECS: 225-763-9
CN: (11β)-11,17-dihydroxy-21-[[[(1-oxooctadecyl)oxy]acetyl]oxy]pregna-1,4-diene-3,20-dione

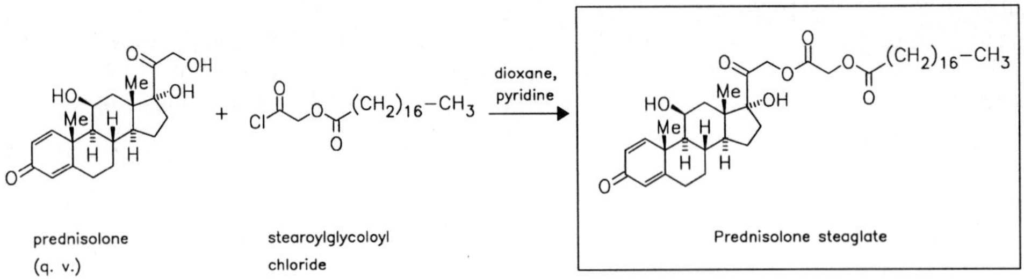

prednisolone
(q. v.)

stearoylglycoloyl
chloride

Prednisolone steaglate

Reference(s):
US 3 171 846 (Carlo Erba; 2.3.1965; I-prior. 10.7.1962).
Girardi, P.N. et al.: Arzneim.-Forsch. (ARZNAD) **16**, 162 (1966).

Formulation(s):   nasal drops 0.25 %

Trade Name(s):
F: Rollsone (Bellon); wfm
GB: Sintisone (Farmitalia Carlo
         Erba); wfm
I: Erbacort (Erba); wfm

Estilsona (Erba); wfm
Glistelone (Erba); wfm
Glitisone (Vis); wfm
Prenisei (Cifa); wfm

Siutisane (Erba); wfm
Verisone (Tiber); wfm

Prednisolone tebutate

ATC: H02AB06
Use: glucocorticoid

RN: 7681-14-3   MF: $C_{27}H_{38}O_6$ MW: 458.60   EINECS: 231-661-5
CN: (11β)-21-(3,3-dimethyl-1-oxobutoxy)-11,17-dihydroxypregna-1,4-diene-3,20-dione

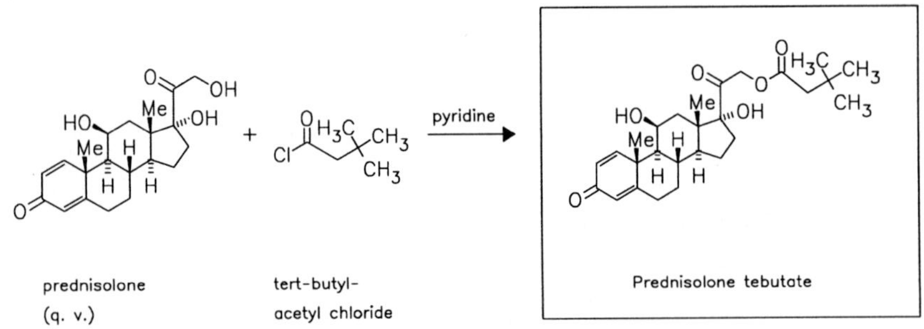

prednisolone
(q. v.)

tert-butyl-
acetyl chloride

Prednisolone tebutate

Reference(s):
US 2 736 734 (Merck & Co.; 1956; prior. 1955).
DE 1 135 904 (Merck & Co.; appl. 1956; USA-prior. 1955).

Formulation(s):   susp. 20 mg/ml

Trade Name(s):
USA: Hydeltra-TBA (Merck
          Sharp & Dohme)

Prednisolone 21-trimethylacetate
(Prednisolon 21-pivalate)

ATC: H02AB06
Use: glucocorticoid

RN: 1107-99-9   MF: $C_{26}H_{36}O_6$ MW: 444.57   EINECS: 214-172-1
CN: (11β)-21-(2,2-dimethyl-1-oxopropoxy)-11,17-dihydroxypregna-1,4-diene-3,20-dione

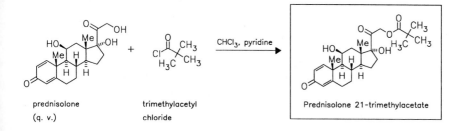

prednisolone (q. v.)   +   trimethylacetyl chloride   CHCl₃, pyridine →   Prednisolone 21-trimethylacetate

Reference(s):
CH 398 585 (Ciba; appl. 1956).

Formulation(s):   ophthalmic ointment 5 mg/ml (0.5 %)

Trade Name(s):
D: Ultracortenol (Ciba); wfm

Varecort (Zyma-Blaes)-
comb.; wfm

Prednisone

ATC: A07EA03; H02AB07
Use: glucocorticoid

RN: 53-03-2   MF: $C_{21}H_{26}O_5$ MW: 358.43   EINECS: 200-160-3
LD₅₀: 600 mg/kg (M, i.m.); 135 mg/kg (M, i.p.); 101 mg/kg (M, s.c.)
CN: 17,21-dihydroxypregna-1,4-diene-3,11,20-trione

ⓐ

dihydrocortisone 21-acetate

(cf. cortisone synthesis)

Br₂, CH₃COOH
bromine →

(I)

I

1. collidine, 3% 3,5-lutidine
2. KHCO₃
→

Prednisone

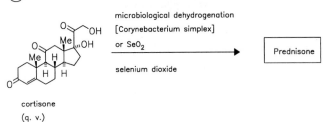

cortisone
(q. v.)

Reference(s):
a US 2 897 216 (Schering Corp.; 1959; prior. 1952).
   Applezweig, N.: Steroid Drugs, Vol. 1, 66 (New York, London, Toronto 1962).
   starting material:
   Applezweig, N.: Steroid Drugs, Vol. 1, 66 (New York, London, Toronto 1962).
b US 3 134 718 (Schering Corp.; 26.5.1964; appl. 12.12.1963; prior. 11.8.1954).
   Wettstein, A. et al.: Helv. Chim. Acta (HCACAV) 39, 734 (1956).

review:
Ullmanns Encykl. Tech. Chem., 4. Aufl., Vol. 13, 54.

Formulation(s):   cream 5 mg/g; eye drops 2 mg/g in comb. with chloramphenicole; suppos. 5 mg, 10 mg,
                   30 mg, 100 mg; syrup 5 mg/5 ml, 25 mg/ml, 50 mg/ml; tabl. 1 mg, 5 mg, 20 mg, 50 mg

Trade Name(s):

D:	Decortin (Merck)	Prednison "Sanhelios"	Delta-Butazolidin (Geigy)-
	Oleomycetin-Prednison	(Börner)	comb.; wfm
	Augentropfen (Winzer)-	Predni-Tablinen	J: Delta-Butazolidin (Ciba-
	comb.	(Beiersdorf-Tablinen)	Geigy-Fujisawa)-comb.
	Prednison "Dorsch" (Orion	Predni-Tablinen	USA: Liquid Pred (Muro)
	Pharma)	(Sanorania)	Lisacort (Fellows)
	Prednison "Ferring"	Rectodelt (Trommsdorff)	Sterapred (Merz)
	(Pharmagalen)	F: Cortancyl (Roussel)	generics
		GB: Decortisyl (Roussel); wfm	

Prednival acetate

(Prednisolone 17-O-valerate)

ATC: H02AB
Use: glucocorticoid

RN: 72064-79-0   MF: $C_{28}H_{38}O_7$ MW: 486.61   EINECS: 276-312-8
LD_{50}: >3 g/kg (M, p.o.);
        >4 g/kg (R, p.o.)
CN: (11β)-21-(acetyloxy)-11-hydroxy-17-[(1-oxopentyl)oxy]pregna-1,4-diene-3,20-dione

prednival
RN: 15180-00-4   MF: $C_{26}H_{36}O_6$ MW: 444.57   EINECS: 239-228-2
LD_{50}: 490 mg/kg (M, s.c.)

prednisolone
(q. v.)

trimethyl
orthovalerate

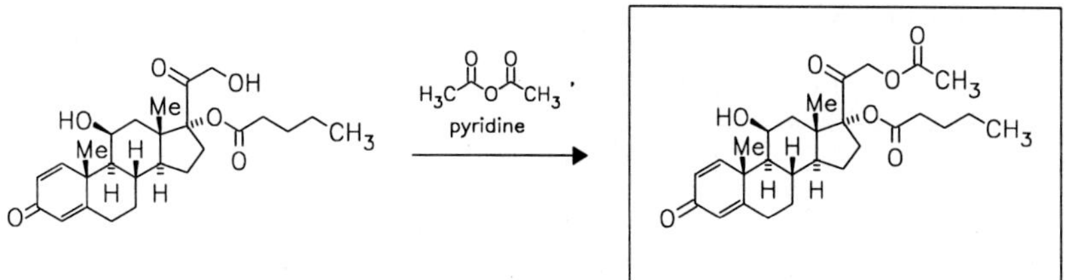

prednisolone 17-valerate (I) → Prednival acetate

Reference(s):
Gardi, R. et al.: Gazz. Chim. Ital. (GCITA9) **93**, 431 (1963).

prednisolone 17-valerate:
DE 1 214 677 (Francesco Vismara; appl. 1.6.1962; I-prior. 24.6.1961).
US 3 147 249 (Francesco Vismara; 1.9.1964; I-prior. 13.6.1961).
cf. hydrocortisone butyrate, betametasone valerate

Trade Name(s):
I: Acepreval (Parke Davis-
         Vister); wfm

Prednylidene

ATC: H02AB11
Use: glucocorticoid

RN: 599-33-7   MF: $C_{22}H_{28}O_5$ MW: 372.46   EINECS: 209-964-9
LD_{50}: 7450 mg/kg (M, p.o.)
CN: (11β)-11,17,21-trihydroxy-16-methylenepregna-1,4-diene-3,20-dione

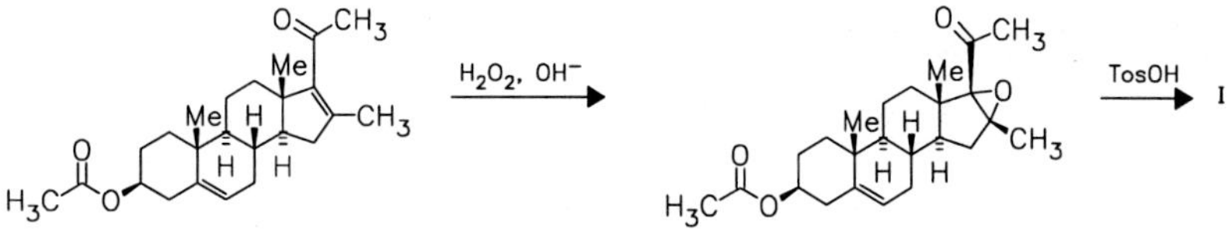

3β-acetoxy-16-methyl-20-
oxo-5,16-pregnadiene

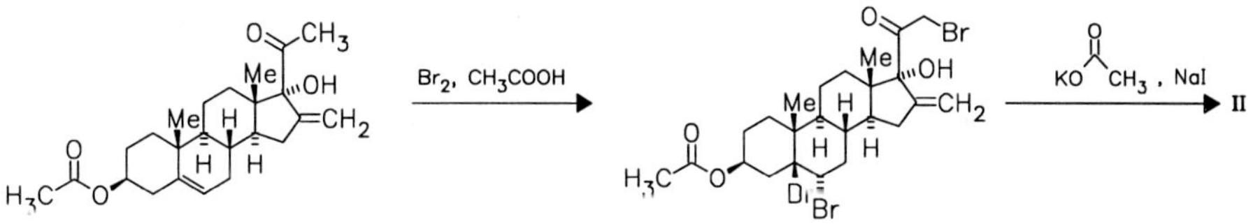

(I)

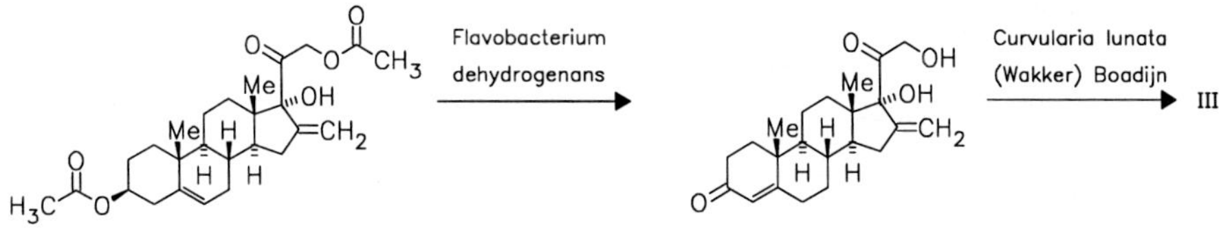

(II)

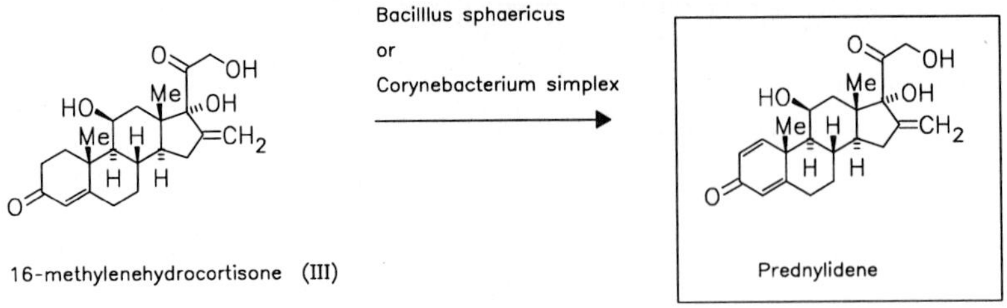

16-methylenehydrocortisone (III)

Bacilllus sphaericus
or
Corynebacterium simplex

Prednylidene

Reference(s):
DE 1 134 074 (E. Merck AG; appl. 31.1.1959).
Mannhardt, H.J. et al.: Tetrahedron Lett. (TELEAY) **1960**, 21.
Taub, D. et al.: J. Org. Chem. (JOCEAH) **25**, 2258 (1960).

alternative synthesis:
US 3 068 226 (Merck & Co.; 1962; prior. 1961, 1959).

Formulation(s):   tabl. 6 mg, 24 mg, 60 mg

Trade Name(s):
D: Decortilen (Merck)   I: Dacortilen Merck (Bracco);
F: Décortilène (Farmex); wfm   wfm

Prednylidene diethylaminoacetate

ATC: H02AB11
Use: glucocorticoid

RN: 6890-42-2   MF: $C_{28}H_{39}NO_6$ MW: 485.62
CN: *N,N*-diethylglycine (11β)-11,17-dihydroxy-16-methylene-3,20-dioxopregna-1,4-dien-21-yl ester

hydrochloride
RN: 22887-42-9   MF: $C_{28}H_{39}NO_6 \cdot HCl$ MW: 522.08   EINECS: 245-299-0

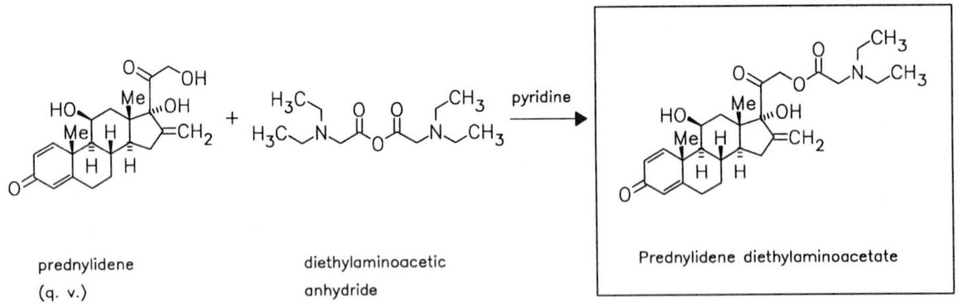

prednylidene
(q. v.)

diethylaminoacetic
anhydride

pyridine

Prednylidene diethylaminoacetate

Reference(s):
DE 1 134 074 (E. Merck AG; appl. 31.1.1959).

combination with quinoline derivatives:
BE 829 197 (Grosjean; appl. 16.5.1975).

Formulation(s):   amp. 30 mg/ml, 60 mg/ml

Trade Name(s):
D: Decortilen sol. (Merck)

Pregnenolone

ATC: L02BA
Use: glucocorticoid

RN: 145-13-1   MF: $C_{21}H_{32}O_2$ MW: 316.49   EINECS: 205-647-4
CN: (3β)-3-hydroxypregn-5-en-20-one

succinate
RN: 4598-67-8   MF: $C_{25}H_{36}O_5$ MW: 416.56   EINECS: 225-001-5
acetate
RN: 1778-02-5   MF: $C_{23}H_{34}O_3$ MW: 358.52   EINECS: 217-212-6

diosgenin   acetic anhydride   (I)

dehydropregnenolone
acetate (II)   Pregnenolone

Reference(s):
Ehrhart-Ruschig, **III**, 341.
Ullmanns Encykl. Tech. Chem., 3. Aufl., Vol. **8**, 664, and there cited literature.

alternative syntheses:
Ullmanns Encykl. Tech. Chem., 3. Aufl., Vol. **8**, 660.

Formulation(s):   cream 0.5 % (as acetate)

Trade Name(s):
F: Fadiamone Crème (Sauba;   USA: Formula 405 (Doak; as   Panzalone (Doak; as
      as acetate)-comb.; wfm   succinate); wfm   succinate); wfm
                                                                                  Prenolon (Schering); wfm

Prenalterol

ATC: C01CA13
Use: cardiotonic

RN: 57526-81-5   MF: $C_{12}H_{19}NO_3$ MW: 225.29   EINECS: 260-791-5
CN: (S)-4-[2-hydroxy-3-[(1-methylethyl)amino]propoxy]phenol

hydrochloride
RN: 61260-05-7 MF: $C_{12}H_{19}NO_3 \cdot HCl$ MW: 261.75

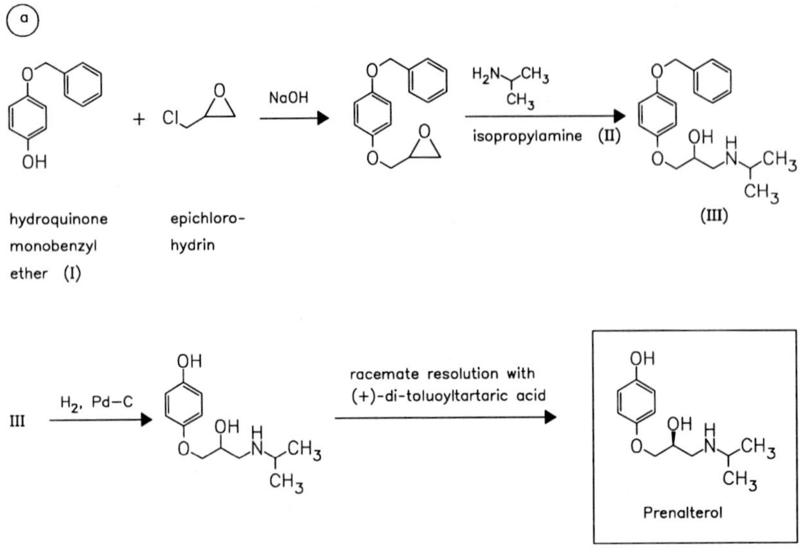
a
NaOH
H_2N CH_3 CH_3
isopropylamine (II)
hydroquinone monobenzyl ether (I)
epichlorohydrin
(III)
III
H_2, Pd–C
racemate resolution with (+)-di-toluoyltartaric acid
Prenalterol

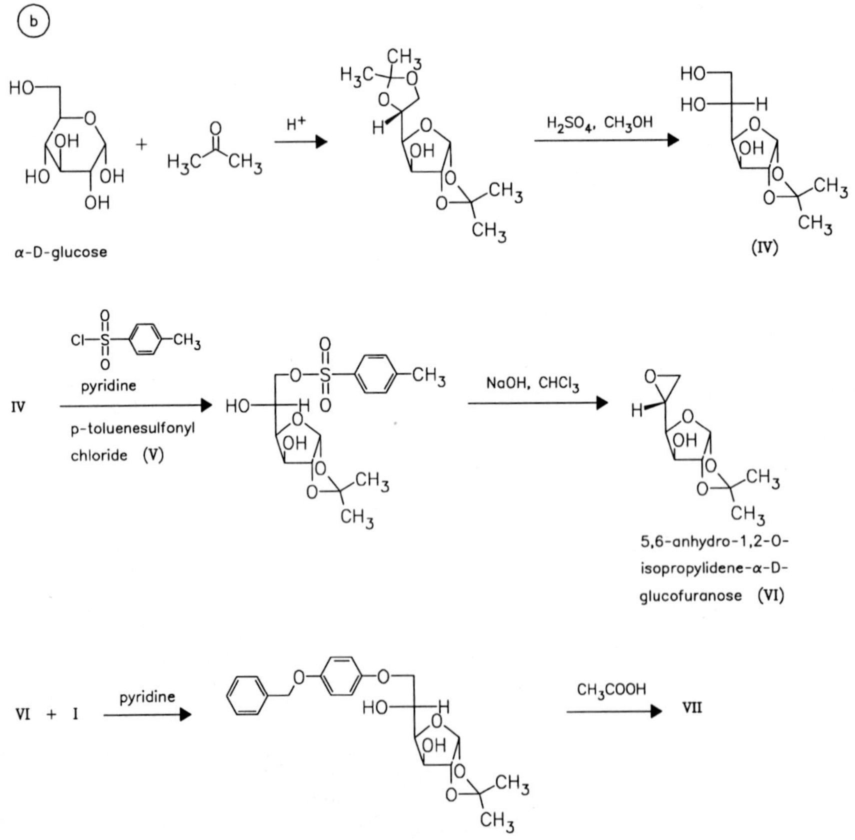
b
α-D-glucose
H+
H_2SO_4, CH_3OH
(IV)
IV
pyridine
p-toluenesulfonyl chloride (V)
NaOH, $CHCl_3$
5,6-anhydro-1,2-O-isopropylidene-α-D-glucofuranose (VI)
VI + I
pyridine
CH_3COOH
VII

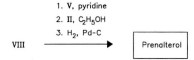

1. NaIO$_4$, CH$_3$OH, CH$_3$COOH
2. NaBH$_4$, CH$_3$OH

1. sodium periodate
2. sodium borohydride

(VII)

1-(4-benzyloxyphenyl)-
2(S),3-dihydroxypropane   (VIII)

1. V, pyridine
2. II, C$_2$H$_5$OH
3. H$_2$, Pd-C

VIII ────────▶ | Prenalterol |

Reference(s):
DOS 2 503 751 (Ciba-Geigy; appl. 30.1.1975; CH-prior. 8.2.1974).

racemate:
NL-appl. 7 501 785 (Hässle; appl. 14.2.1974).
US 4 080 471 (Hässle; 21.3.1978; prior. 25.6.1976).

synthesis of 5,6-anhydro-1,2-*O*-isopropylidene-α-D-glucofuranose:
Ohle, H.; Dickhäuser, E.: Chem. Ber. (CHBEAM) **58**, 2593 (1925).
Ohle, H.; Vargha, L. v.: Chem. Ber. (CHBEAM) **61**, 1203 (1928); **62**, 2435 (1929).
Schmidt, D. Th.: Methods Carbohydr. Chem. (MCACAI) **2**, 326 (1963).
Horton, D.; Tsai, J.: Methods Carbohydr. Chem. (MCACAI) **8**, 177 (1980).

Formulation(s):   amp. 5 mg (as hydrochloride)

Trade Name(s):
GB: Hyprenan (Astra); wfm   Varbian (Ciba Labs); wfm   I: Varbian (Ciba-Geigy); wfm

---

Prenylamine

ATC: C01DX02
Use: coronary vasodilator

RN: 390-64-7   MF: C$_{24}$H$_{27}$N   MW: 329.49   EINECS: 206-869-4
LD$_{50}$: 250 mg/kg (M, i.v.);
      11 mg/kg (R, i.v.); 250 mg/kg (R, p.o.)
CN: *N*-(1-methyl-2-phenylethyl)-γ-phenylbenzenepropanamine

lactate (1:1)
RN: 69-43-2   MF: C$_{24}$H$_{27}$N · C$_3$H$_6$O$_3$ MW: 419.57   EINECS: 200-705-5
LD$_{50}$: 250 mg/kg (M, p.o.);
      1 g/kg (R, p.o.);
      680 mg/kg (dog, p.o.)
gluconate (1:1)
RN: 21156-48-9   MF: C$_{24}$H$_{27}$N · C$_6$H$_{12}$O$_7$ MW: 525.64
LD$_{50}$: 14 mg/kg (M, i.v.);
      11 mg/kg (R, i.v.)

phenylacetone   3,3-diphenyl-   Prenylamine
propylamine

Reference(s):
DE 1 111 642 (Hoechst; appl. 7.5.1958).
DE 1 100 031 (Hoechst; appl. 7.5.1958).

Formulation(s):   drg. 15 mg, 30 mg, 60 mg; tabl. 4 mg, 15 mg, 30 mg, 60 mg (as lactate)

Trade Name(s):
D: Daxauten (Kettelhack-   I: Angiovigor (Violani-   J: Crepasin (Hoei)
      Riker); wfm   Farmavigor); wfm   Epocol (Teisan-Nagase)
      Daxauten (Woelm); wfm   Angorsan (Isola-Ibi); wfm   Herzcon (Sana)
      Segontin (Albert-Roussel);   Carditin-Same (Savoma);   Lactamine (Daisan)
      wfm   wfm   NP 30 (Sanken)
      Segontin (Hoechst); wfm   Eucardion (Vita); wfm   Onlemin (Ono)
      Segontin-Digoxin (Albert-   Incoran (ITA); wfm   Prectolact (Showa
      Roussel)-comb.; wfm   Irrorin (Alfa Farm.)   Yakuhin)
      Segontin-Digoxin   Reocorin (Farmochimica   Prenylamine Lactate
      (Hoechst)-comb.; wfm   Ital.); wfm   (Towa)
F: Clémodril (Hoechst)-   Segontin (Hoechst); wfm   Roinin (Mohan)
      comb.; wfm   Wasangor (IFI); wfm   Segontin (Hoechst)
      Segontine (Hoechst); wfm   Wasangor (Wassermann);
GB: Synadrin (Hoechst); wfm   wfm

Pridinol

ATC: M03BX03
Use: anticholinergic, antiparkinsonian

RN: 511-45-5   MF: $C_{20}H_{25}NO$ MW: 295.43   EINECS: 208-128-0
LD_{50}:   100 mg/kg (M, i.p.); 193 mg/kg (M, s.c.)
CN: α,α-diphenyl-1-piperidinepropanol

hydrochloride
RN: 968-58-1   MF: $C_{20}H_{25}NO \cdot HCl$ MW: 331.89   EINECS: 213-529-9
LD_{50}:   25 mg/kg (M, i.v.);
           33 mg/kg (R, i.v.)
mesylate
RN: 6856-31-1   MF: $C_{20}H_{25}NO \cdot CH_4O_3S$ MW: 391.53   EINECS: 229-953-2

phenylmagnesium   ethyl 3-piperidino-   Pridinol
bromide (I)   propionate

(b)

acetophenone   paraform-   piperidine   3-piperidino-
                aldehyde   propiophenone

Reference(s):
DE 875 660 (Hoechst; appl. 1941).

Formulation(s):   amp. 2 mg/ml; drg. 5 mg (as hydrochloride); tabl. 4 mg (as mesylate)

Trade Name(s):
D: Lyseen-Hommel (Hommel)   Lyseen (Novartis)   Mitanoline (Toyo Pharmar)
      Parks 12 (Hommel)   J: Hikicenon (Tatsumi)   Trilax (Toyo Seiyaku
F: Parks-12 (Laroze); wfm   Konlax (Nippon Shinyaku)   Kasei)
I: Algolisina (Celsius)-comb.   Loxeen (Maruko-Tobishi)

Prilocaine

ATC: N01BB04
Use: local anesthetic

RN: 721-50-6   MF: $C_{13}H_{20}N_2O$ MW: 220.32   EINECS: 211-957-0
LD$_{50}$:   59.9 mg/kg (M, i.v.)
CN: N-(2-methylphenyl)-2-(propylamino)propanamide

monohydrochloride
RN: 1786-81-8   MF: $C_{13}H_{20}N_2O \cdot HCl$ MW: 256.78   EINECS: 217-244-0
LD$_{50}$:   55 mg/kg (M, i.v.);
        56.6 mg/kg (R, i.v.)

o-toluidine   2-bromopropionyl   propylamine   Prilocaine
               bromide

Reference(s):
GB 839 943 (Astra; appl. 6.6.1958; S-prior. 26.6.1957).
Löfgren, N.; Tegner, C.: Acta Chem. Scand. (ACHSE7) **14**, 486, 490 (1960).

Formulation(s):   cream 25 mg/g in comb. with lidocaine; plaster 25 mg; vial 5 mg/ml, 10 mg/ml, 20 mg/ml,
        30 mg/ml

Trade Name(s):
D: EMLA Creme (Astra)-   Emlapatch (Astra)   Emla (Astra Farmaceutici)-
      comb. with lidocaine   GB: Citanest (Astra)   comb.
      Xylonest (Astra)   EMLA (Astra)-comb.   J: Citanest (Astra-Fujisawa)
      Xylonest (Astra)-comb.   I: Citanest 3 % Octapressin   USA: Emla (Astra)
F: Emla (Astra)-comb.   (Astra Farmaceutici)-comb.

Primaperone

ATC: C01D
Use: vasodilator, antihypotensive

RN: 1219-35-8　MF: $C_{15}H_{20}FNO$　MW: 249.33　EINECS: 214-941-1
CN: 1-(4-fluorophenyl)-4-(1-piperidyl)-1-butanone

hydrochloride
RN: 15847-48-0　MF: $C_{15}H_{20}FNO \cdot HCl$　MW: 285.79

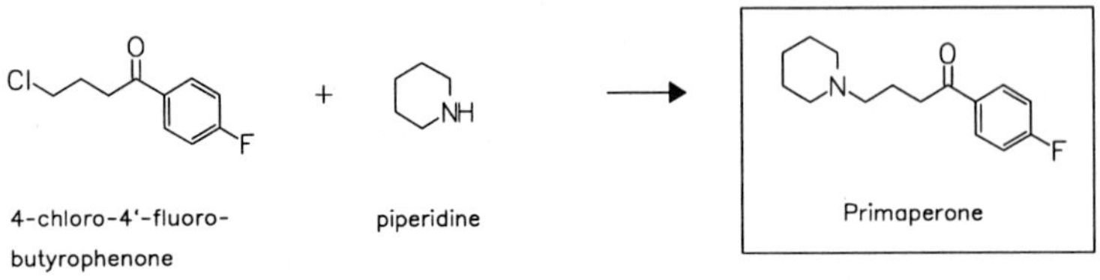

4-chloro-4'-fluoro-
butyrophenone

piperidine

Primaperone

Reference(s):
FR 1 301 863 (Science Union; appl. 29.6.1961).
FR 1 459 M (Science Union; appl. 18.8.1961; prior. 29.6.1961).

Trade Name(s):
F:　Diviator (Servier)-comb.;
　　wfm

Primaquine

(Primachin)

ATC: P01BA03
Use: antimalarial

RN: 90-34-6　MF: $C_{15}H_{21}N_3O$　MW: 259.35　EINECS: 201-987-2
LD_{50}: 15.9 mg/kg (M, i.v.); 100 mg/kg (M, p.o.)
CN: N^4-(6-methoxy-8-quinolinyl)-1,4-pentanediamine

phosphate (1:2)
RN: 63-45-6　MF: $C_{15}H_{21}N_3O \cdot 2H_3O_4P$　MW: 455.34　EINECS: 200-560-8
LD_{50}: 68 mg/kg (M, p.o.);
　　　　177 mg/kg (R, p.o.)

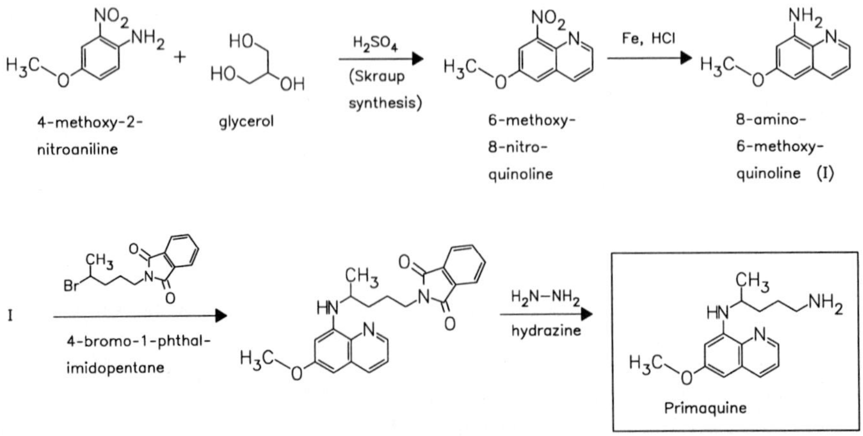

4-methoxy-2-
nitroaniline

glycerol

6-methoxy-
8-nitro-
quinoline

8-amino-
6-methoxy-
quinoline (I)

4-bromo-1-phthal-
imidopentane

H₂N—NH₂
hydrazine

Primaquine

Reference(s):
Elderfield, R.C. et al.: J. Am. Chem. Soc. (JACSAT) **68**, 1524 (1946).
Elderfield, R.C. et al.: J. Am. Chem. Soc. (JACSAT) **77**, 4816 (1955).

Formulation(s):   tabl. 15 mg

Trade Name(s):
D:	Primaquine Bayer (Bayer); wfm	GB:	Primaquine Phosphate (ICI); wfm	USA:	Primaquine Phosphate (Sanofi); wfm
		I:	Primachina fosfato (IFI)		

Primidone
(Primaclone)

ATC: N03AA03
Use: antiepileptic, anticonvulsant

RN: 125-33-7   MF: $C_{12}H_{14}N_2O_2$ MW: 218.26   EINECS: 204-737-0
LD_{50}:   280 mg/kg (M, p.o.);
          1500 mg/kg (R, p.o.)
CN: 5-ethyldihydro-5-phenyl-4,6(1H,5H)-pyrimidinedione

ethylphenyl-
malondiamide

formamide

Primidone

Reference(s):
US 2 578 847 (ICI; 1951; GB-prior. 1949).
DE 843 413 (ICI; appl. 1950; GB-prior. 1949).

Formulation(s):   susp. 250 mg/5 ml; syrup 125 mg/5 ml; tabl. 250 mg

Trade Name(s):
D:	Liskatin (Desitin)	F:	Mysoline (Zeneca)	J:	Mysoline (Dainippon; Marupi)
	Mylepsinum (Zeneca)	GB:	Mysoline (Zeneca)		Primron (Fujinaga)
	Resimatil (Sanofi Winthrop)	I:	Mysoline (SIT)	USA:	Mysoline (Wyeth-Ayerst)

Probenecid

ATC: M04AB01
Use: uricosuric agent

RN: 57-66-9   MF: $C_{13}H_{19}NO_4S$ MW: 285.36   EINECS: 200-344-3
LD_{50}:   1666 mg/kg (M, p.o.);
          1600 mg/kg (R, p.o.)
CN: 4-[(dipropylamino)sulfonyl]benzoic acid

dipropylamine   4-carboxybenzene-
                sulfonyl chloride   Probenecid

Reference(s):
US 2 608 507 (Sharp & Dohme; 1952; prior. 1949).

Formulation(s):   tabl. 500 mg

Trade Name(s):

D:	Probenecid (Weimer)		Colbenemid (Merck Sharp	USA:	Benemid (Merck Sharp &
F:	Bénémide (Théraplix);		& Dohme)-comb.; wfm		Dohme)
	wfm	I:	Probenecid (IFI)		ColBENEMID (Merck
	Prototapen (Bristol)-comb.;	J:	Benecid (Kaken)		Sharp & Dohme)-comb.
	wfm		Probenemid (Merck-		with colchidine
GB:	Benemid (Merck Sharp &		Banyu)		
	Dohme)				

Probucol

ATC: C10AX02
Use: antiarteriosclerotic (cholesterol
        depressant and antihyperlipidemic)

RN: 23288-49-5   MF: $C_{31}H_{48}O_2S_2$ MW: 516.86   EINECS: 245-560-9
LD$_{50}$: >5 g/kg (M, p.o.);
      >5 g/kg (R, p.o.)
CN: 4,4'-[(1-methylethylidene)bis(thio)]bis[2,6-bis(1,1-dimethylethyl)phenol]

2,6-di-tert-butyl-
4-mercaptophenol   Probucol

Reference(s):
US 3 576 883 (Consol. Coal; 27.4.1971; prior. 3.6.1969).
US 3 862 332 (Dow; 21.1.1975; prior. 11.5.1967, 19.11.1969).
DE 1 767 443 (Dow; appl. 10.5.1968; USA-prior. 11.5.1967).
DE 1 768 334 (Consol. Coal; prior. 2.5.1968).

starting material:
US 3 129 262 (Consolidation Coal Comp.; 14.4.1964; appl. 8.10.1962).

Formulation(s):   tabl. 250 mg, 500 mg

Procainamide

ATC: C01BA02
Use: antiarrhythmic

RN: 51-06-9   MF: $C_{13}H_{21}N_3O$ MW: 235.33   EINECS: 200-078-8
LD$_{50}$:   49 mg/kg (M, i.v.); 525 mg/kg (M, p.o.);
       110 mg/kg (R, i.v.); 1950 mg/kg (R, p.o.)
CN: 4-amino-*N*-[2-(diethylamino)ethyl]benzamide

monohydrochloride
RN: 614-39-1   MF: $C_{13}H_{21}N_3O \cdot HCl$ MW: 271.79   EINECS: 210-381-7
LD$_{50}$:   94.64 mg/kg (M, i.v.); 1.11 g/kg (M, p.o.);
       95 mg/kg (R, i.v.); >2 g/kg (R, p.o.)

4-nitro-   N,N-diethyl-   Procainamide
benzoyl chloride   ethylenediamine

Reference(s):
Ehrhart-Ruschig **II**, 38.
Baltzy, R. et al.: J. Am. Chem. Soc. (JACSAT) **64**, 2231 (1942).
Yamazaki, M.Y. et al.: Yakugaku Zasshi (YKKZAJ) **73**, 294 (1953).

Formulation(s):   s. r. tabl. 500 mg, 1000 mg (as hydrochloride)

Procaine

ATC: C05AD05; N01BA02; S01HA05
Use: local anesthetic, analgesic, geriatric

RN: 59-46-1   MF: $C_{13}H_{20}N_2O_2$ MW: 236.32   EINECS: 200-426-9
LD$_{50}$:   45 mg/kg (M, i.v.); 350 mg/kg (M, p.o.);
       42 mg/kg (R, i.v.)
CN: 4-aminobenzoic acid 2-(diethylamino)ethyl ester

monohydrochloride
RN: 51-05-8   MF: $C_{13}H_{20}N_2O_2 \cdot HCl$ MW: 272.78   EINECS: 200-077-2
LD$_{50}$:   33 mg/kg (M, i.v.); 175 mg/kg (M, p.o.);
       38 mg/kg (R, i.v.); 200 mg/kg (R, p.o.);
       63 mg/kg (dog, i.v.)

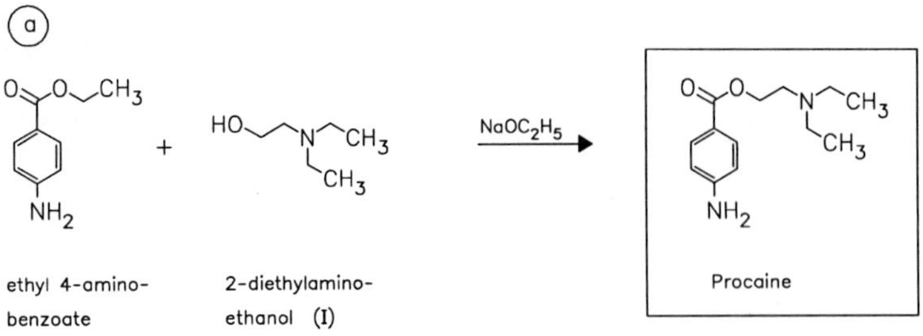
a
NaOC2H5
ethyl 4-amino-benzoate
2-diethylamino-ethanol (I)
Procaine

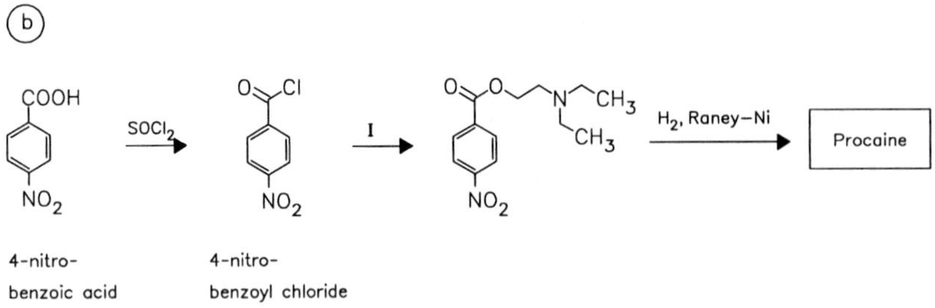
b
SOCl2
I
H2, Raney-Ni
Procaine
4-nitro-benzoic acid
4-nitro-benzoyl chloride

Reference(s):

Eichhorn, A.; Uhlfelder, E.: Justus Liebigs Ann. Chem. (JLACBF) **371**, 125, 131, 142, 162 (1909).
DRP 179 627 (Farbwerke Hoechst; appl. 1904).
DRP 180 291 (Farbwerke Hoechst; appl. 1905).
DRP 194 748 (Farbwerke Hoechst; appl. 1905).

salt with phenylbutazone *(anti-inflammatory):*
DAS 2 055 853 (Dr. Voigt; appl. 13.11.1970).

Formulation(s): amp. 5 mg/ml, 10 mg/ml, 20 mg/ml, 40 mg/2 ml, 100 mg/5 ml (as hydrochloride)

Trade Name(s):

D: Causat (Sanofi Winthrop)-comb.
Dodecatol (Heyl)-comb.
Impletol (Bayer Vital)-comb.
K.H. 3 Geriatricum Schwarzhaupt (Schwarzhaupt)-comb.
Lophakomp-Procain (Lomapharm)
Ney Chondrin (vitOrgan)
Novocain (Hoechst)
Pasconeural-Injektopas (Pascoe)-comb.
Procain (curasan; Jenapharm)
Röwo Procain (Pharmakon)
generics and circa 100 combination preparations

F: Antiseptique Calmante (Chauvin)-comb.
Otylol (Bridoux)-comb.
Procaine Aguettant (Aguettant)
Procaine Lavoisier (Chaix et du Marais)
numerous combination preparations

GB: Bicillin (Yamanouchi)-comb.

I: Citroftalmina /-V.C. (SIFI)-comb.
Dentosedina (Teofarma)-comb.
Lenident (Zeta)
Mios (Intes)-comb.
Neuroftal Fiale (Alfa Intes)-comb.
Oftalzina (SIT)-comb.
Otalgan Berna (Berna)-comb.
Otomidone (SIT)-comb.
Rinantipiol (Ottolenghi)-comb.

J: Bancain (Banyu)
Omnicain (Daiichi)

USA: Adrocaine (Parke Davis); wfm
Novocain (Winthrop); wfm
Procaine Hydrochloride (Abbott); wfm
Procaine Hydrochloride (Elkins-Sinn); wfm

Procarbazine

ATC: L01XB01
Use: antineoplastic

RN: 671-16-9 MF: $C_{12}H_{19}N_3O$ MW: 221.30 EINECS: 211-582-2
LD$_{50}$: 614 mg/kg (M, i.p.);
>400 mg/kg (R, i.p.); 350 mg/kg (R, route unreported)
CN: N-(1-methylethyl)-4-[(2-methylhydrazino)methyl]benzamide

monohydrochloride
RN: 366-70-1 MF: $C_{12}H_{19}N_3O \cdot HCl$ MW: 257.77 EINECS: 206-678-6
LD$_{50}$: 540 mg/kg (M, i.v.); 560 mg/kg (M, p.o.);
350 mg/kg (R, i.v.); 570 mg/kg (R, p.o.)

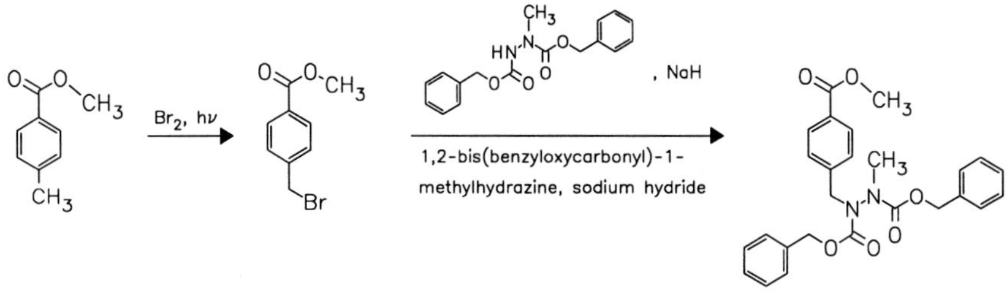

methyl 4-methyl-
benzoate

methyl 4-bromo-
methylbenzoate

(I)

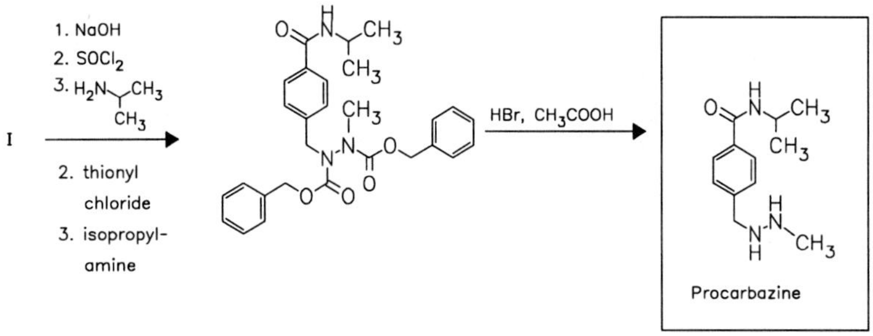

Procarbazine

Reference(s):
US 3 520 926 (Roche; 21.7.1970; CH-prior. 9.6.1961).
GB 968 460 (Roche; appl. 7.6.1962; CH-prior. 9.6.1961).
Zeller, P. et al.: Experientia (EXPEAM) **19**, 129 (1963).

Formulation(s): cps. 50 mg; inj. sol. 250 mg/5 ml; syrup 3030 mg (as hydrochloride)

Trade Name(s):
D: Natulan (Roche) GB: Natulan (Roche); wfm J: Natulan (Roche)
F: Natulan (Roche) I: Natulan (Roche) USA: Matulane (Roche)

Procaterol

ATC: R03AC16; R03CC08
Use: bronchodilator

RN: 72332-33-3 MF: $C_{16}H_{22}N_2O_3$ MW: 290.36 EINECS: 276-590-0
LD$_{50}$: 320 mg/kg (M, i.p.)
CN: (R*,S*)-8-hydroxy-5-[1-hydroxy-2-[(1-methylethyl)amino]butyl]-2(1H)-quinolinone

monohydrochloride
RN: 62929-91-3   MF: $C_{16}H_{22}N_2O_3 \cdot HCl$ MW: 326.82   EINECS: 263-763-0
LD_{50}: 70.3 mg/kg (M, i.v.); 3.2 g/kg (M, p.o.);
         80 mg/kg (R, i.v.); 2.6 g/kg (R, p.o.);
         100 mg/kg (dog, i.v.); >5 g/kg (dog, p.o.)

8-hydroxy-   2-bromo-
carbostyril   butyryl chloride

(I)   Procaterol

Reference(s):
DE 2 461 596 (Otsuka; appl. 27.11.1975; prior. 27.12.1974).
US 4 026 897 (Otsuka; 10.5.1977; prior. 26.12.1974).
BE 833 841 (Otsuka; appl. 16.4.1975; J-prior. 4.12.1974).
Yoshizaki, S. et al.: J. Med. Chem. (JMCMAR) **19**, 1138 (1976).
Yoshizaki, S. et al.: Chem. Pharm. Bull. (CPBTAL) **28**, 3441 (1980).

Formulation(s):   aerosol 0.01 mg; syrup 0.025 mg; tabl. 0.05 mg, 0.1 mg (as hydrochloride)

Trade Name(s):
D: Onsukil (Grünenthal;   I: Procadil (Recordati)   J: Meptin (Otsuka; 1980)
      1984); wfm   Propulm (Istoria)   Mucodin (Kyorin)

Prochlorperazine

ATC: N05AB04
Use: anti-emetic

RN: 58-38-8   MF: $C_{20}H_{24}ClN_3S$ MW: 373.95   EINECS: 200-379-4
LD_{50}: 85 mg/kg (M, i.v.); 400 mg/kg (M, p.o.);
         >20 mg/kg (R, i.v.); 1800 mg/kg (R, p.o.)
CN: 2-chloro-10-[3-(4-methyl-1-piperazinyl)propyl]-10H-phenothiazine

maleate (1:2)
RN: 84-02-6   MF: $C_{20}H_{24}ClN_3S \cdot 2C_4H_4O_4$ MW: 606.10   EINECS: 201-511-3
LD_{50}: 85 mg/kg (M, i.v.);
         750 mg/kg (R, p.o.)
dimesylate
RN: 51888-09-6   MF: $C_{20}H_{24}ClN_3S \cdot 2CH_4O_3S$ MW: 566.16   EINECS: 257-495-3

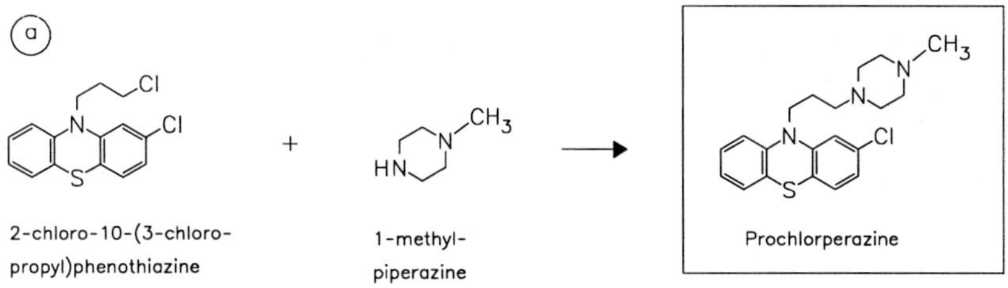

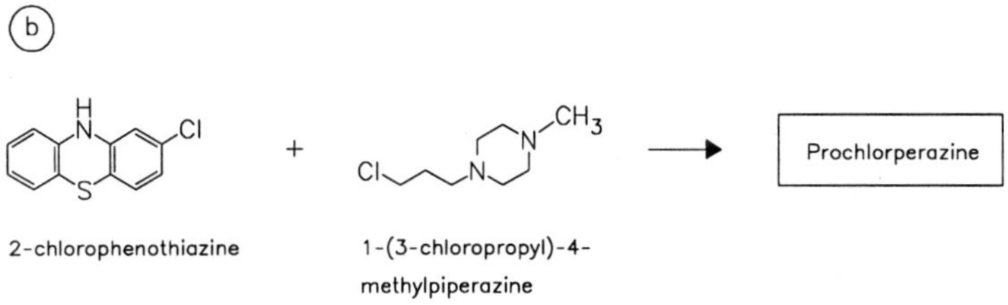

(a)

2-chloro-10-(3-chloro-propyl)phenothiazine   +   1-methyl-piperazine   →   Prochlorperazine

(b)

2-chlorophenothiazine   +   1-(3-chloropropyl)-4-methylpiperazine   →   Prochlorperazine

Reference(s):
US 2 902 484 (Rhône-Poulenc; 1.9.1959; GB-prior. 1954).
DE 1 037 461 (Rhône-Poulenc; appl. 1955; GB-prior. 1954).

Formulation(s):   cps. 10 mg, 15 mg; drg. 5 mg, 10 mg; suppos. 2 mg, 5 mg, 25 mg; vial 5 mg/5 ml, 10 mg/2 ml, 50 mg/10 ml

Trade Name(s):

F:	Témentil (Specia); wfm	I:	Stemetil (Rhône-Poulenc
GB:	Buccastem (Reckitt &		Rorer)
	Colman)	J:	Nibromin A (Maruko)
	Stemetil (Rhône-Poulenc		Novamin (Shionogi)
	Rorer)		Pasotomin (Yoshitomi)

USA: Compazine (SmithKline Beecham)

Procyclidine

ATC: N04AA04
Use: antiparkinsonian

RN: 77-37-2   MF: $C_{19}H_{29}NO$ MW: 287.45   EINECS: 201-023-0
LD_{50}: 60 mg/kg (M, i.v.)
CN: α-cyclohexyl-α-phenyl-1-pyrrolidinepropanol

hydrochloride
RN: 1508-76-5   MF: $C_{19}H_{29}NO \cdot HCl$ MW: 323.91   EINECS: 216-141-8
LD_{50}: 55 mg/kg (M, i.v.)

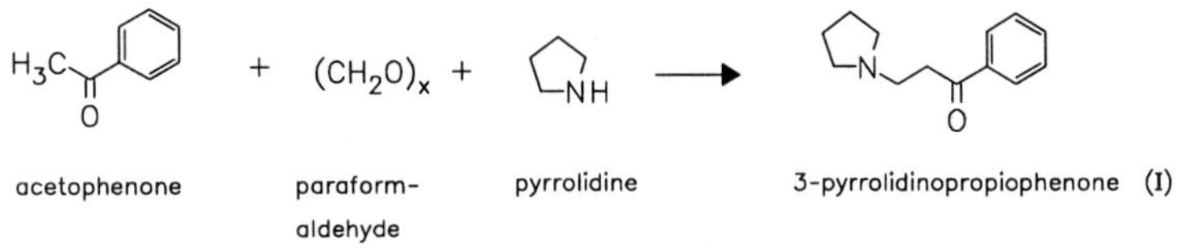

acetophenone   + $(CH_2O)_x$ +   pyrrolidine paraform-aldehyde   →   3-pyrrolidinopropiophenone (I)

phenylmagnesium
bromide

Procyclidine

Reference(s):
US 2 682 543 (Burroughs Wellcome; 1954; prior. 1951).
US 2 891 890 (Burroughs Wellcome; 1959; prior. 1952).

alternative syntheses:
US 2 826 590 (Lilly; 1958; appl. 1954).
US 2 842 555 (Burroughs Wellcome; 1958; appl. 1954).

Formulation(s):   tabl. 5 mg (as hydrochloride)

Trade Name(s):

D:	Osnervan (Glaxo Wellcome)		Kemadrin (Glaxo Wellcome)	USA:	Kemadrin (Glaxo Wellcome)
F:	Kémadrine (Wellcome); wfm	I:	Kemadrin (Glaxo Wellcome)		
GB:	Arpicolin (Rosemont)	J:	Kemadrin (Chugai)		

Profenamine
(Ethopropazine)

ATC: N04AA05
Use: neuroleptic, antiparkinsonian

RN: 522-00-9   MF: $C_{19}H_{24}N_2S$ MW: 312.48   EINECS: 208-320-4
LD_{50}:   50 mg/kg (M, i.v.); 300 mg/kg (M, p.o.);
        15 mg/kg (R, i.v.)
CN: *N,N*-diethyl-α-methyl-10*H*-phenothiazine-10-ethanamine

monohydrochloride
RN: 1094-08-2   MF: $C_{19}H_{24}N_2S \cdot HCl$ MW: 348.94   EINECS: 214-134-4
LD_{50}:   32 mg/kg (M, i.v.); 650 mg/kg (M, p.o.);
        1700 mg/kg (R, p.o.)

phenothiazine

1. NaNH₂
2. H₃C-N-CH₃, Cl-CH₃

(separation of isomers by crystallization)
1. sodium amide
2. 2-chloro-N,N-diethyl-
   1-propanamine

Profenamine

Reference(s):
US 2 526 118 (Rhône-Poulenc; 1950; F-prior. 1948).
US 2 607 773 (Rhône-Poulenc; 1952; GB-prior. 1949).

Formulation(s):   powder 10 %; tabl. 10 mg, 50 mg (as hydrochloride)

Trade Name(s):
F: Parsidol (Sevenet); wfm   J: Parkin (Yoshitomi-Takeda)   Parsidol (Warner Chilcott);
GB: Lysivane (May & Baker);   USA: Parsidol (Parke Davis);   wfm
      wfm   wfm

Progabide

ATC: N03AG05
Use: anticonvulsant

RN: 62666-20-0   MF: $C_{17}H_{16}ClFN_2O_2$ MW: 334.78   EINECS: 263-679-4
LD$_{50}$:   1350 mg/kg (M, p.o.);
      1350 mg/kg (R, p.o.)
CN: 4-[[(4-chlorophenyl)(5-fluoro-2-hydroxyphenyl)methylene]amino]butanamide

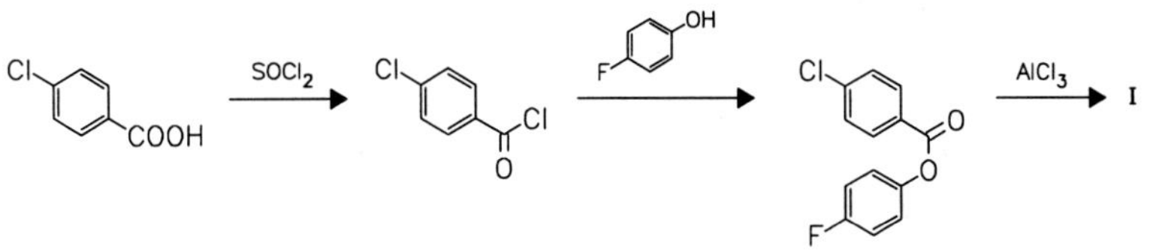

4-chlorobenzoic
acid

4-chlorobenzoyl
chloride

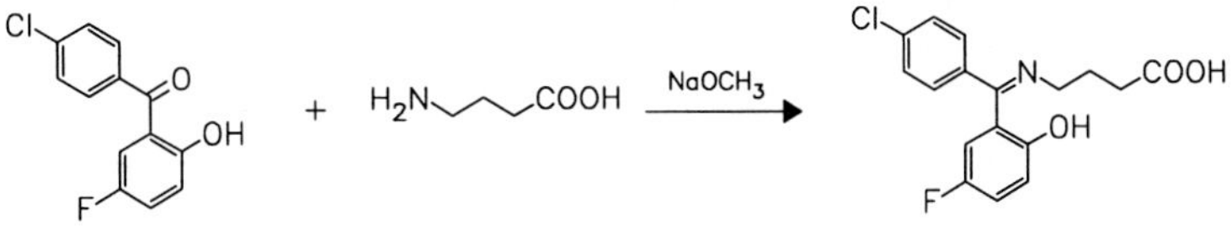

4-chloro-2'-
hydroxy-5'-fluoro-
benzophenone   (I)

4-aminobutyric
acid

(II)

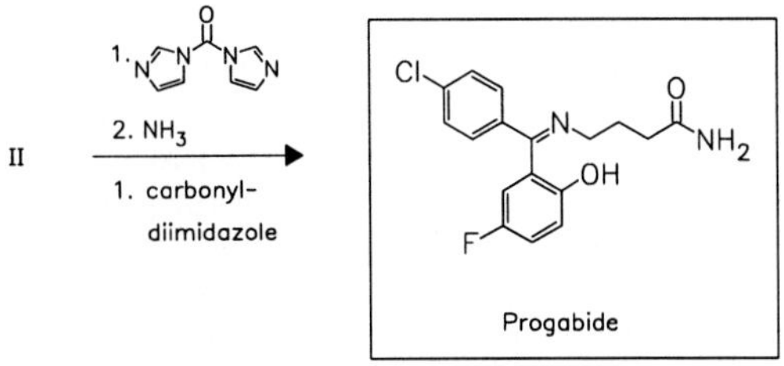

Progabide

Reference(s):
US 4 094 992 (Synthelabo; 13.6.1978; F-prior. 1.8.1975).
DOS 2 634 288 (Synthelabo; appl. 30.7.1976; F-prior. 1.8.1975).
DOS 2 830 034 (Synthelabo; appl. 7.7.1978; F-prior. 12.7.1977).
FR 2 319 338 (Synthelabo; appl. 1.8.1975).
GB 1 506 808 (Synthelabo; appl. 30.6.1976; F-prior. 1.8.1975).

Formulation(s):   powder 150 mg; tabl. 300 mg, 600 mg

Trade Name(s):
F: Gabrène (Synthélabo)

Progesterone

ATC: G03DA04
Use: progestogen

RN: 57-83-0   MF: $C_{21}H_{30}O_2$ MW: 314.47   EINECS: 200-350-6
CN: pregn-4-ene-3,20-dione

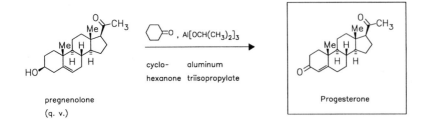

pregnenolone
(q. v.)

cyclo-   aluminum
hexanone   triisopropylate

Progesterone

Reference(s):
US 2 379 832 (Schering Corp.; 1945; D-prior. 1936).
Oppenauer, R.: Recl. Trav. Chim. Pays-Bas Belg. (RTCPB4) **56**, 137 (1937).

alternative syntheses:
US 2 232 438 (Schering Corp.; 1941; D-prior. 1934).
US 2 420 489 (Parke Davis; 1947; prior. 1941).
Heyl, F.W.; Herr, U.E.: J. Am. Chem. Soc. (JACSAT) **72**, 2617 (1950).
Slomp, G.; Johnson, J.L.: J. Am. Chem. Soc. (JACSAT) **80**, 915 (1953).
Ullmanns Encykl. Tech. Chem., 3. Aufl., Vol. **8**, 660, and patents cited there.
Ullmanns Encykl. Tech. Chem., 4. Aufl., Vol. **13**, 29.

Formulation(s):   amp. 20 mg in comb. with estradiolbenzoate; cps. 100 mg; gel 1 %, 4 %, 8 %

Trade Name(s):
D: Crinone (Wyeth)
    Jephagynon (Jenapharm)
    Progestogel (Kade)
    Utrogest (Kade)
F: Progestasert (Théraplix)
    Progestogel (Besins-
    Iscovesco)
    Progestosol (Besins-
    Iscovesco)
    Synergon (Lipha Santé)-
    comb.
    Tocogestan (Théramex)-
    comb.
    Trophigil (Sanofi
    Winthrop)-comb.

    Utrogestan (Besins-
    Iscovesco)
GB: Crinone (Wyeth)
    Cyclogest (Shire)
    Gestone (Ferring)
I: Biormon (Amsa)-comb.
    Esolut (Angelini)
    Menovis (Teofarma)-comb.
    Progestogel (Lusofarmaco)
    Progestol (Synthelabo)
    Prontagest (Amsa)
J: Duogynon (Nihon
    Schering)-comb.
    Estormon (Hokuriku)-
    comb.

    Lutes (Mochida)-comb.
    Luteum Depot (Teikoku
    Zoki)-comb.
    Oophormin Luteum
    (Teikoku Zoki)
    Prodiol (Santen-
    Yamanouchi)-comb.
    Progehormon (Mochida)
    Progenin (Santen-
    Yamanouchi)
    Proluton (Nihon Schering)
USA: Crinone (Wyeth-Ayerst)

Proglumetacin

ATC: M01AB14
Use: anti-inflammatory

RN: 57132-53-3   MF: $C_{46}H_{58}ClN_5O_8$ MW: 844.45
CN: (±)-1-(4-chlorobenzoyl)-5-methoxy-2-methyl-1*H*-indole-3-acetic acid 2-[4-[3-[[4-(benzoylamino)-5-
    (dipropylamino)-1,5-dioxopentyl]oxy]propyl]-1-piperazinyl]ethyl ester

dihydrochloride
RN: 59209-41-5   MF: $C_{46}H_{58}ClN_5O_8 \cdot 2HCl$ MW: 917.37

maleate (1:2)
RN: 59209-40-4   MF: $C_{46}H_{58}ClN_5O_8 \cdot 2C_4H_4O_4$ MW: 1076.59   EINECS: 261-656-3

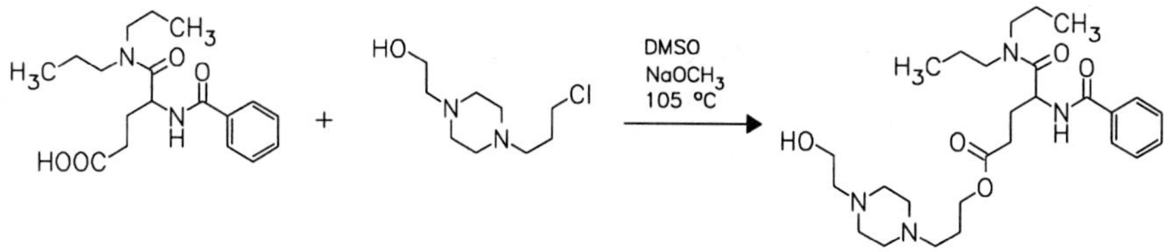

proglumide
(q. v.)

1-(3-chloropropyl)-
4-(2-hydroxyethyl)-
piperazine
(from 1-(2-hydroxy-
ethyl)piperazine
and 1-bromo-3-
chloropropane)

(I)

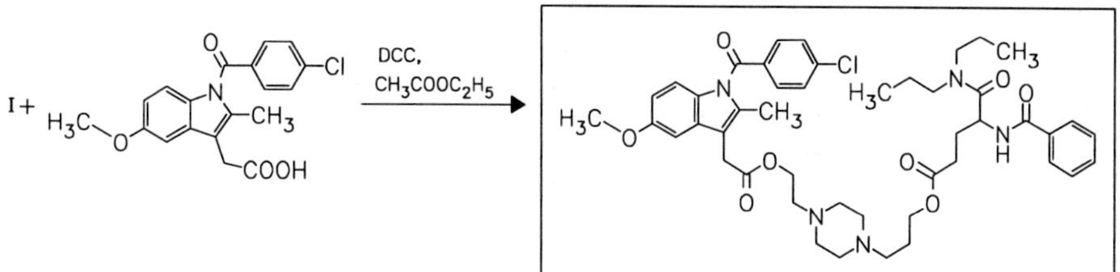

indometacin
(q. v.)

Proglumetacin

Reference(s):
DOS 2 535 799 (Rotta Research Lab.; appl. 11.8.1975; I-prior. 12.8.1974).
US 3 985 878 (Rotta Research Lab.; 12.10.1976; I-prior. 12.8.1974).

Formulation(s):   f. c. tabl. 300 mg; cps. 150 mg (as dimaleate)

Trade Name(s):

D:	Protaxon (Opfermann)	Proxil (Rottapharm)	J:	Miridacin (Taiho; as
I:	Afloxan (Rotta Research)			maleate)

Proglumide

ATC: A02BX06
Use: peptic ulcer therapeutic

RN: 6620-60-6   MF: $C_{18}H_{26}N_2O_4$ MW: 334.42   EINECS: 229-567-4
LD$_{50}$: 2250 mg/kg (M, i.v.), 8070 mg/kg (M, p.o.);
20 g/kg (R, p.o.)
CN: (±)-4-(benzoylamino)-5-(dipropylamino)-5-oxopentanoic acid

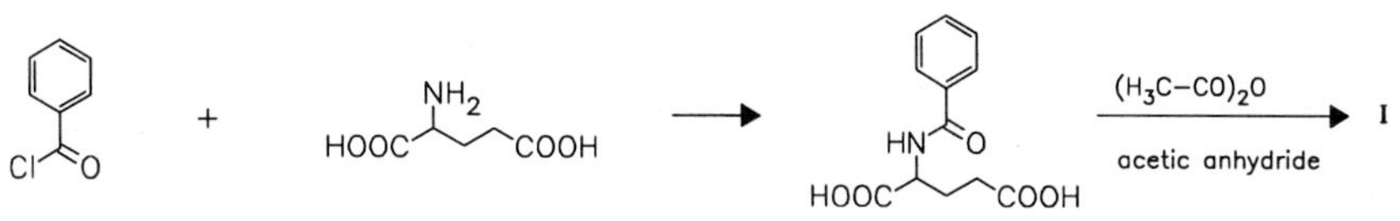

benzoyl
chloride

DL-glutamic acid

N-benzoyl-DL-
glutamic acid

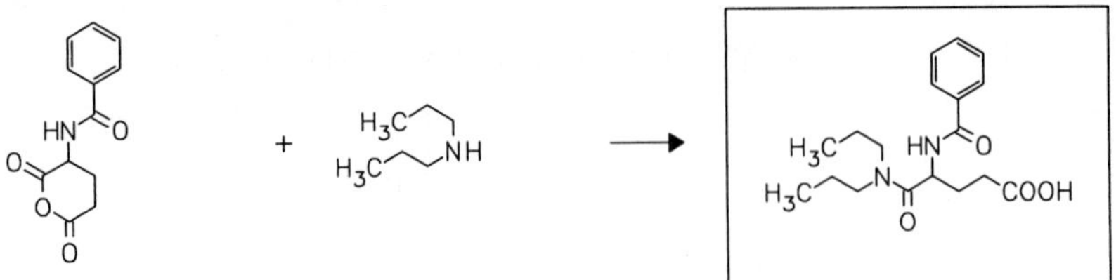

N-benzoyl-DL-
glutamic anhydride (I)

dipropylamine

Proglumide

Reference(s):
ZA 65/4 065 (Rotta Research; appl. 16.7.1965; I-prior. 31.7.1964).
DAS 1 518 125 (Rotta Research; appl. 30.7.1965; I-prior. 31.7.1964).

Formulation(s):   amp. 400 mg/5 ml; f. c. tabl. 400 mg; tabl. 200 mg, 400 mg

Trade Name(s):
D: Milid (Opfermann)   F: Milide (Fournier Frères);   I: Milid (Rottapharm)
      Promid (Opfermann); wfm   wfm   J: Promid (Kaken)

Proguanil
(Chlorguanide; Chloriguane; Chloroguanide)

ATC: P01BB01
Use: antimalarial

RN: 500-92-5   MF: $C_{11}H_{16}ClN_5$ MW: 253.74   EINECS: 207-915-6
LD_{50}:   22 mg/kg (M, i.v.)
CN: N-(4-chlorophenyl)-N'-(1-methylethyl)imidodicarbonimidic diamide

monohydrochloride
RN: 637-32-1   MF: $C_{11}H_{16}ClN_5 \cdot HCl$ MW: 290.20   EINECS: 211-283-7
LD_{50}:   23 mg/kg (M, i.v.); 27 mg/kg (M, p.o.);
           33 mg/kg (R, i.v.); 58 mg/kg (R, p.o.)

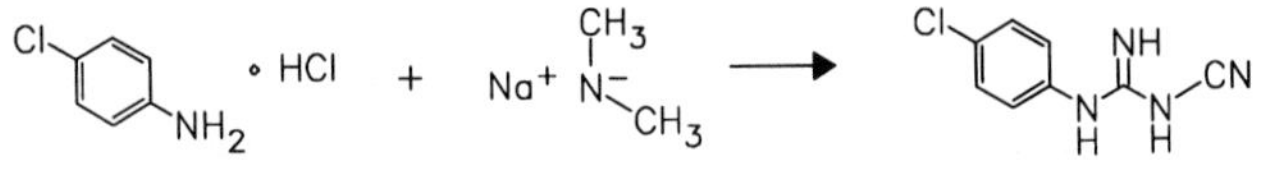

4-chloroaniline
hydrochloride

(4-chlorophenyl)-
dicyanodiamide (I)
(cf. chlorhexidine
synthesis)

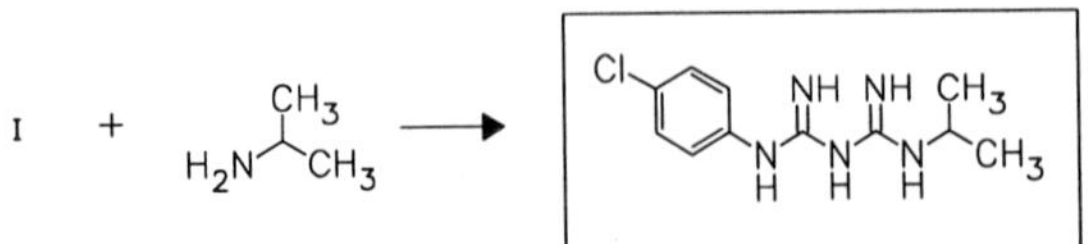

isopropyl-
amine

Proguanil

Reference(s):
Curd, F.H.S.; Rose, F.L.: J. Chem. Soc. (JCSOA9) **1946**, 729.
FR 1 001 548 (Rhône-Poulenc; appl. 1946).

Formulation(s):   tabl. 100 mg (as hydrochloride)

Trade Name(s):
D: Malarone (Glaxo
        Wellcome)
        Paludrine (Zeneca)
F: Paludrine (Zeneca)

GB: Savarine (Zeneca)-comb.
        Malarone (Glaxo
        Wellcome)-comb.
        Paludrine (Zeneca)

I: Paludrine (Zeneca)

Proligestone

ATC: G03DB
Use: progestogen

RN: 23873-85-0   MF: $C_{24}H_{34}O_4$ MW: 386.53   EINECS: 245-922-6
CN: 14,17-[propylidenebis(oxy)]pregn-4-ene-3,20-dione

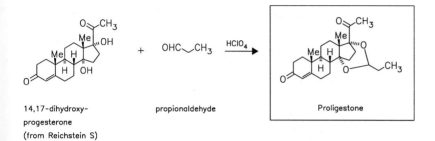

14,17-dihydroxy-
progesterone
(from Reichstein S)

propionaldehyde

Proligestone

Reference(s):
Sijde, D. van der et al.: J. Med. Chem. (JMCMAR) **15**, 909 (1972).
ZA 681 592 (Koninkl. Nederl. Gist & Spiritusfabriek; appl. 22.2.1968; NL-prior. 13.3.1967).

starting material:
Cooley, G. et al.: Tetrahedron Suppl. (TETSAE) **7**, 325 (1966).

Formulation(s):   vial 100 mg/ml

Trade Name(s):
GB: Delvosteron (Mycofarm);
        wfm

Prolintane

ATC: N06BX14
Use: analeptic, central stimulant,
        depressant

RN: 493-92-5   MF: $C_{15}H_{23}N$ MW: 217.36   EINECS: 207-784-5
LD$_{50}$:   157 mg/kg (R, p.o.)
CN: 1-[1-(phenylmethyl)butyl]pyrrolidine

hydrochloride
RN: 1211-28-5   MF: $C_{15}H_{23}N \cdot HCl$ MW: 253.82   EINECS: 214-917-0
LD$_{50}$:   25 mg/kg (M, i.v.); 230 mg/kg (M, p.o.);
        40 mg/kg (R, i.v.); 278 mg/kg (R, p.o.)

2-oxo-1-phenylpentane   pyrrolidine   Prolintane

Reference(s):
DE 1 088 962 (Thomae; appl. 1956).
DE 1 093 799 (Thomae; appl. 1957; addition to DE 1 088 962).

Formulation(s):   drg. 10 mg

Trade Name(s):
D: Katovit (Thomae)-comb.;   Promotil (Boehringer Ing.);   I: Villescon-Fher (Boehringer
      wfm   wfm   Ing.); wfm
F: Promotil (Badrial); wfm   GB: Villescon (Boehringer
                                       Ing.)-comb.; wfm

Prolonium iodide

ATC: H03CA
Use: thyroid therapeutic

RN: 123-47-7   MF: $C_9H_{24}I_2N_2O$ MW: 430.11   EINECS: 204-630-9
CN: 2-hydroxy-*N,N,N,N',N',N'*-hexamethyl-1,3-propanediaminium diiodide

trimethyl-   1,3-diiodo-2-   Prolonium iodide
amine   propanol

dimethyl-   epichlorohydrin   1,3-bis(dimethylamino)-   methyl
amine   2-propanol   iodide

Reference(s):
US 1 526 627 (Bayer; 1925; prior. 1924).

Formulation(s):   amp. 400 mg/2 ml; drg. 25 mg, 50 mg, 100 mg; drops 20 mg/ml; susp. 50 mg/5 ml; vial 50
                     mg/ml

Trade Name(s):
D: Endojodin (Bayer); wfm   Jodopropano   Trijodina (Lafare); wfm
I: Endojodo (Cozzolino);   (Farmochimica Ital.); wfm   USA: Entodon (Winthrop); wfm
      wfm   Neoiodorsolo os
      Intrajodina (Gentili); wfm   (Baldacci)-comb.; wfm

Promazine

ATC: N05AA03
Use: neuroleptic, anti-emetic,
       antipsychotic

RN: 58-40-2   MF: $C_{17}H_{20}N_2S$ MW: 284.43   EINECS: 200-382-0
LD$_{50}$:   45 mg/kg (M, i.v.); 401 mg/kg (M, p.o.);
       14.5 mg/kg (R, i.v.); 350 mg/kg (R, p.o.)
CN: N,N-dimethyl-10H-phenothiazine-10-propanamine

monohydrochloride
RN: 53-60-1   MF: $C_{17}H_{20}N_2S \cdot HCl$ MW: 320.89   EINECS: 200-179-7
LD$_{50}$:   38 mg/kg (M, i.v.);
       29 mg/kg (R, i.v.); 400 mg/kg (R, p.o.)
maleate (2:1)
RN: 4701-69-3   MF: $C_{17}H_{20}N_2S \cdot 1/2C_4H_4O_4$ MW: 684.93
phosphate
RN: 1508-27-6   MF: $C_{17}H_{20}N_2S \cdot xH_3O_4P$ MW: unspecified
LD$_{50}$:   60 mg/kg (M, i.v.);
       350 mg/kg (R, p.o.)

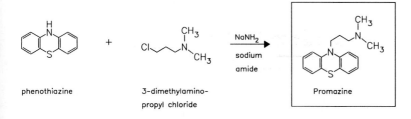

phenothiazine   3-dimethylamino-   Promazine
                       propyl chloride

Reference(s):
US 2 519 886 (Rhône-Poulenc; 1950; F-prior. 1945).
DE 824 944 (Rhône-Poulenc; appl. 1950; F-prior. 1945).
Wirth, W.: Arzneim.-Forsch. (ARZNAD) **8**, 507 (1958).

Formulation(s):   amp. 20 mg/ml, 50 mg/1 ml, 100 mg/2 ml; drg. 25 mg, 50 mg, 100 mg; f. c. tabl. 25 mg; susp.
                    50 mg/ml (as hydrochloride)

Trade Name(s):
D: Protactyl (Wyeth)   GB: Sparine (Wyeth)   J: Savamine (Banyu)
      Sinophenin (Rodleben)   I: Talofen (Fournier Pierrel) USA: Sparine (Wyeth); wfm

Promegestone

ATC: G03DB07
Use: progestogen

RN: 34184-77-5   MF: $C_{22}H_{30}O_2$ MW: 326.48
CN: (17β)-17-methyl-17-(1-oxopropyl)estra-4,9-dien-3-one

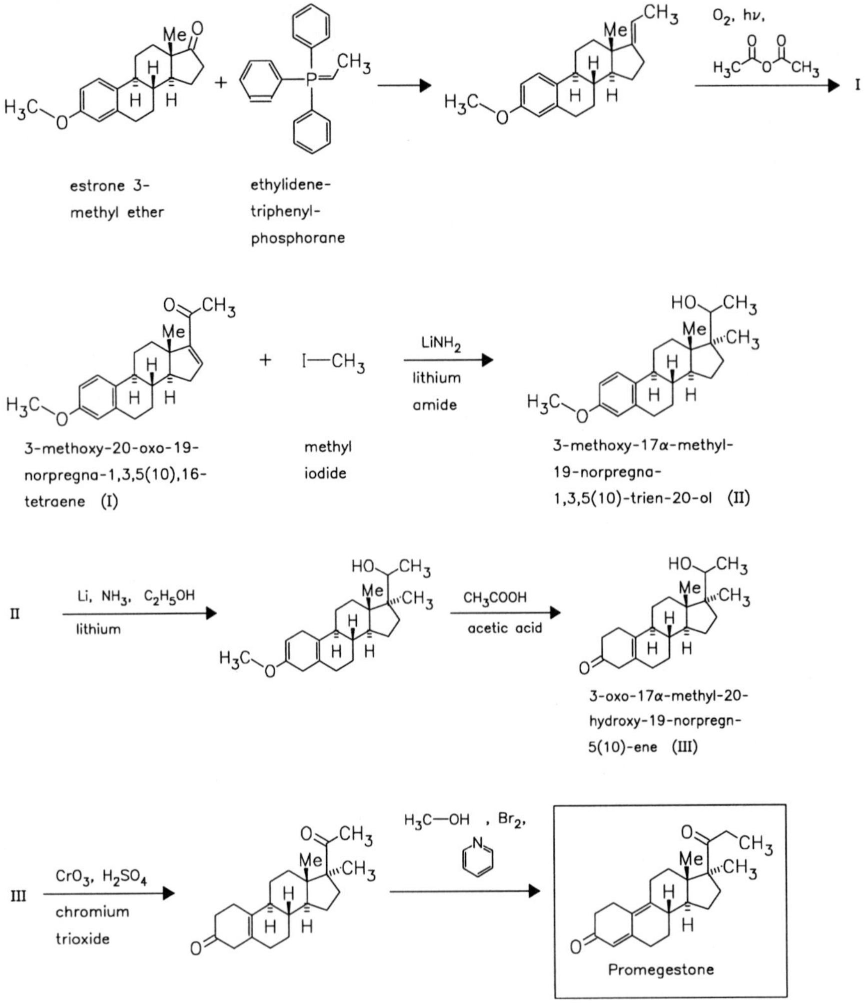

estrone 3-
methyl ether

ethylidene-
triphenyl-
phosphorane

3-methoxy-20-oxo-19-
norpregna-1,3,5(10),16-
tetraene (I)

methyl
iodide

3-methoxy-17α-methyl-
19-norpregna-
1,3,5(10)-trien-20-ol (II)

3-oxo-17α-methyl-20-
hydroxy-19-norpregn-
5(10)-ene (III)

Promegestone

Reference(s):

DOS 2 107 835 (Roussel-Uclaf; appl. 18.2.1971; F-prior. 20.2.1970).
US 3 679 714 (Roussel-Uclaf; 25.7.1972; F-prior. 20.2.1970).
US 3 761 591 (Roussel-Uclaf; 25.9.1973; F-prior. 20.2.1970).

synthesis of 3-methoxy-20-oxo-19-norpregna-1,3,5(10),16-tetraene:
Krubiner, A.M.; Oliveto, E.P.: J. Org. Chem. (JOCEAH) 31, 24 (1966).
Krubiner, A.M. et al.: J. Org. Chem. (JOCEAH) 34, 3502 (1969).

Formulation(s):   tabl. 0.125 mg, 0.25 mg, 0.5 mg

Trade Name(s):
F: Surgestone (Cassenne)

Promestriene

ATC: G03CA09
Use: estrogen

RN: 39219-28-8   MF: $C_{22}H_{32}O_2$ MW: 328.50   EINECS: 254-361-6
CN: (17β)-17-methoxy-3-propoxyestra-1,3,5(10)-triene

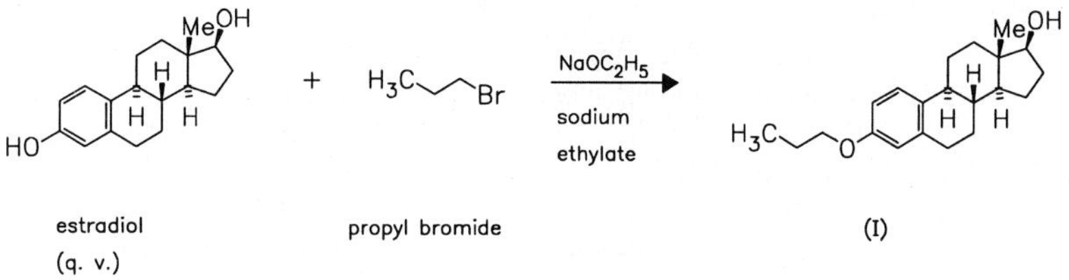

estradiol
(q. v.)

propyl bromide

(I)

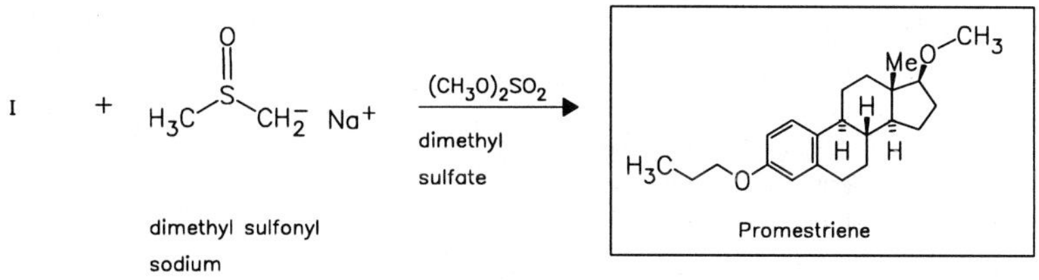

dimethyl sulfonyl
sodium

Promestriene

Reference(s):
DE 2 215 499 (Sogeras; appl. 29.3.1972; GB-prior. 21.4.1971).

Formulation(s):   cream 1 %; vaginal cps. 10 mg

Trade Name(s):
F: Colposeptine (Théramex)-   Colpotrophine (Théramex)
      comb.   I: Colpotrophine (Schering)

Promethazine

ATC: D04AA10; R06AD02
Use: antihistaminic, sedative

RN: 60-87-7   MF: $C_{17}H_{20}N_2S$ MW: 284.43   EINECS: 200-489-2
LD_{50}:   40 mg/kg (M, i.v.); 326 mg/kg (M, p.o.);
       45 mg/kg (R, i.v.)
CN: N,N,α-trimethyl-10H-phenothiazine-10-ethanamine

monohydrochloride
RN: 58-33-3   MF: $C_{17}H_{20}N_2S \cdot HCl$ MW: 320.89   EINECS: 200-375-2
LD_{50}:   50 mg/kg (M, i.v.); 255 mg/kg (M, p.o.);
       15 mg/kg (R, i.v.)

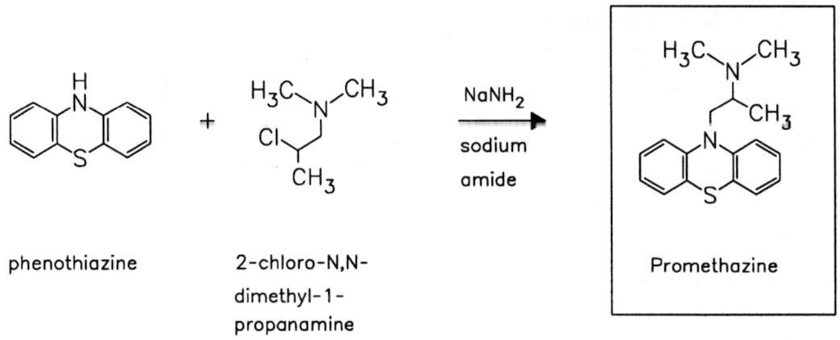

phenothiazine

2-chloro-N,N-
dimethyl-1-
propanamine

Promethazine

Reference(s):
US 2 530 451 (Rhône-Poulenc; 1950; F-prior. 1946).
US 2 607 773 (Rhône-Poulenc; 1952; GB-prior. 1949).

Formulation(s):   amp. 56 mg/2 ml; f. c. tabl. 25 mg; drg. 25 mg; drops 20 mg/ml; suppos. 12.5 mg, 25 mg,
                   50 mg; syrup 1 mg/ml, 5.65 mg; tabl. 12.5 mg, 25 mg, 50 mg (as hydrochloride)

Trade Name(s):

D: Atosil (Bayer Vital)
    Eusedon (Krewel
    Meuselbach)
    Promethawern (Pharma
    Wernigerode)
    Promethazin-neuraxpharm
    (neuraxpharm)
    Prothazin (Rodleben)
F: Algotropyl prométhazine
    (Thera France)-comb.
    Fluisédal (Elerté)-comb.
    Paxéladine noctée
    (Beaufour)-comb.
    Phénergan (Evans Medical)
    Rhinathiol prométhazine
    (Synthélabo)-comb.

Tussisèdal (Elerté)-comb.
GB: Avomine (Rhône-Poulenc
    Rorer)
    Parmergan P100
    (Martindale)-comb.
    Phenergan (Rhône-Poulenc
    Rorer)
    Sominex (Seton)
I: Allerfen (Sella)
    Duplamin (Bruschettini)-
    comb.
    Fargan (Carlo Erba)
    Farganesse (Pharmacia &
    Upjohn)
    Fenazil (Sella)
    Prometazina (Dynacren)

Prometazina Cloridrato
(Ecobi)
generics and combination
preparations
J: Hiberna (Yoshitomi)
    Pipolphen (Nakataki)
    Prothia (Kanto)
    Pyrethia (Shionogi)
USA: Mepergan (Wyeth-Ayerst)
    Phenergan (Wyeth-Ayerst)
    generics and combination
    preparations

Propacetamol

ATC: N02BE05
Use: analgesic (paracetamol prodrug)

RN: 66532-85-2   MF: $C_{14}H_{20}N_2O_3$ MW: 264.33   EINECS: 266-390-1
CN: *N,N*-diethylglycine 4-(acetylamino)phenyl ester

monohydrochloride
RN: 66532-86-3   MF: $C_{14}H_{20}N_2O_3 \cdot HCl$ MW: 300.79   EINECS: 266-391-7

4-hydroxyacet-   chloroacetyl   p-acetamidophenyl
anilide   chloride   chloroacetate (I)

I + diethyl-   Propacetamol
      amine

Reference(s):
BE 854 376 (Hexachimie, appl. 9.5.1977).
DE 2 721 987 (Hexachimie; appl. 14.5.1977).
US 4 127 671 (Hexachimie; 28.11.1978; prior. 26.5.1977).

synthesis of p-acetamidophenyl chloroacetate:
Dittert, L.W. et al.: J. Pharm. Sci. (JPMSAE) **57**, 774 (1968).

Formulation(s):   amp. 1 g (as hydrochloride)

Trade Name(s):
F: Pro-Dafalgan (UPSA)

Propafenone

ATC: C01BC03
Use: antiarrhythmic

RN: 54063-53-5   MF: $C_{21}H_{27}NO_3$ MW: 341.45   EINECS: 258-955-6
LD_{50}:   440 mg/kg (M, p.o.)
CN: 1-[2-[2-hydroxy-3-(propylamino)propoxy]phenyl]-3-phenyl-1-propanone

hydrochloride
RN: 34183-22-7   MF: $C_{21}H_{27}NO_3 \cdot HCl$ MW: 377.91   EINECS: 251-867-9
LD_{50}:   25 mg/kg (M, i.v.); 341 mg/kg (M, p.o.);
        18.8 mg/kg (R, i.v.); 700 mg/kg (R, p.o.);
        10 mg/kg (dog, i.v.)

1-(2-hydroxyphenyl)-3-   epichlorohydrin   (I)
phenyl-1-propanone

propylamine   Propafenone

Reference(s):
DE 2 001 431 (Helopharm; appl. 6.1.1970).
GB 1 307 455 (Helopharm; appl. 7.7.1971).
US 4 474 986 (BASF; 2.10.1984; appl. 18.3.1983; D-prior. 19.3.1982).

Formulation(s):   amp. 70 mg/20 ml; drg. 10 mg; f. c. tabl. 150 mg, 300 mg; USA: tabl. 150 mg, 225 mg,
        300 mg (as hydrochloride)

Trade Name(s):
D:	Cuxafenon (TAD)	Rytmonorm (Knoll; 1978)	F:	Rythmol (Knoll; 1985)

D: Cuxafenon (TAD)   Rytmonorm (Knoll; 1978)   F: Rythmol (Knoll; 1985)
        Propafen-BASF (BASF   Tachyfenon (ASTA Medica   I: Pro-effekalgan imiv
        Generics)   AWD)   (Upsamedica)
        Propa Sanorania   various generics and   J: Pronon (Yamanouchi)
        (Sanorania)   combination preparations   USA: Rythmol (Knoll)

Propallylonal

ATC: N05C
Use: hypnotic

RN: 545-93-7   MF: $C_{10}H_{13}BrN_2O_3$ MW: 289.13   EINECS: 208-896-7
LD_{50}:   90 mg/kg (R, s.c.)
CN: 5-(2-bromo-2-propenyl)-5-(1-methylethyl)-2,4,6(1H,3H,5H)-pyrimidinetrione

2,3-dibromo-   5-isopropyl-   Propallylonal
propene   barbituric acid

Reference(s):
US 1 622 129 (Riedel AG; 1927; D-prior. 1923).
DRP 481 733 (Riedel-deHaen; appl. 1923).
DRP 482 841 (Riedel-deHaen; appl. 1923).
DRP 485 832 (Riedel-deHaen; appl. 1923).

Formulation(s):   tabl. 200 mg

Trade Name(s):
D: Noctal (Cassella-Riedel);   Noctal (UCB); wfm
      wfm   J: Noctenal (Boehringer-Uji)

Propanidid

ATC: N01AX04
Use: anesthetic

RN: 1421-14-3   MF: $C_{18}H_{27}NO_5$ MW: 337.42   EINECS: 215-822-7
LD$_{50}$:   113 mg/kg (M, i.v.);
       81 mg/kg (R, i.v.); >10 g/kg (R, p.o.);
       80 mg/kg (dog, i.v.)
CN: 4-[2-(diethylamino)-2-oxoethoxy]-3-methoxybenzeneacetic acid propyl ester

N,N-diethylchloro-   propyl homovanillate   Propanidid
acetamide   sodium salt

Reference(s):
DE 1 134 981 (Bayer; appl. 6.5.1960).

Formulation(s):   amp. 1.5 g/30 ml, 500 mg/10 ml

Trade Name(s):
D: Epontol (Bayer); wfm   GB: Epontol (Bayer); wfm   J: Epontol (Bayer)
F: Epontol (Théraplix); wfm   I: Epontol (Bayer); wfm

Propantheline bromide

ATC: A03AB05
Use: antispasmodic, anticholinergic

RN: 50-34-0   MF: $C_{23}H_{30}BrNO_3$ MW: 448.40   EINECS: 200-030-6
LD$_{50}$:   6400 µg/kg (M, i.v.); 445 mg/kg (M, p.o.);
       4 mg/kg (R, i.v.); 370 mg/kg (R, p.o.)
CN: N-methyl-N-(1-methylethyl)-N-[2-[(9H-xanthen-9-ylcarbonyl)oxy]ethyl]-2-propanaminium bromide

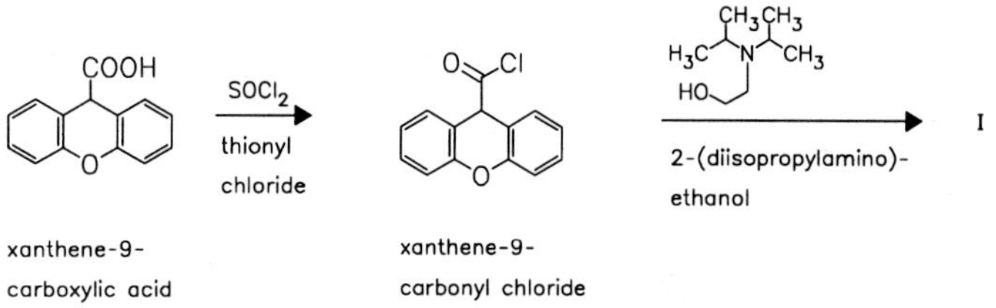
COOH
SOCl2
thionyl
chloride
O Cl
HO
2-(diisopropylamino)-
ethanol
I
xanthene-9-
carboxylic acid
xanthene-9-
carbonyl chloride

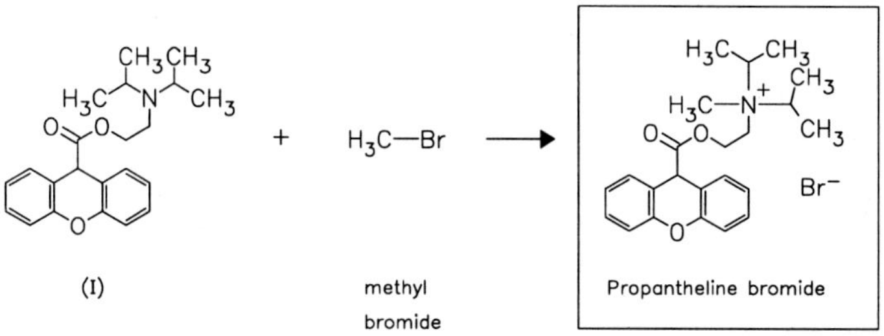
(I)
H3C—Br
methyl
bromide
Br⁻
Propantheline bromide

Reference(s):
US 2 659 732 (Searle; 1953; appl. 1952; prior. 1950).

Formulation(s): tabl. 7.5 mg, 15 mg

Trade Name(s):

D:	Corigast (Searle); wfm	F:	Pro-Banthine (Monsanto)	J:	Pro-Banthine (Dainippon)
	Hydonan (Hermal)-comb.; wfm	GB:	Pro-Banthine (Baker Norton)	USA:	Pro-Banthine (Roberts)
	Tensilan (Desitin); wfm	I:	Lexil (Roche)-comb.		

Propatyl nitrate
(Ettriol trinitrate)

ATC: C01DA07
Use: coronary vasodilator (angina pectoris)

RN: 2921-92-8 MF: $C_6H_{11}N_3O_9$ MW: 269.17 EINECS: 220-866-5
CN: 2-ethyl-2-[(nitrooxy)methyl]-1,3-propanediol dinitrate (ester)

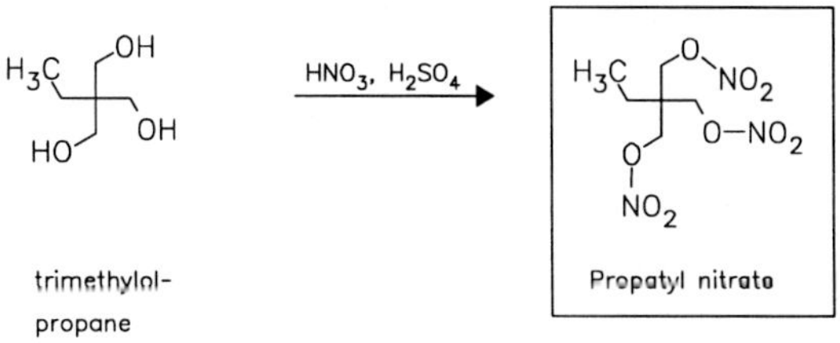
HNO3, H2SO4
trimethylol-
propane
Propatyl nitrate

Reference(s):
Médard: Meml. Poudres (MPOUAT) **35**, 113 (1953).
Bourjol: Meml. Poudres (MPOUAT) **36**, 79 (1954).

Formulation(s): tabl. 10 mg

Trade Name(s):

F:	Atrilon 5 (Winthrop); wfm	GB:	Gina (Winthrop); wfm	J:	Etrynit (Yoshitomi); wfm

Propentofylline
(HWA-285)

ATC: N06BC02
Use: vasodilator, cognition enhancer

RN: 55242-55-2   MF: $C_{15}H_{22}N_4O_3$ MW: 306.37
LD$_{50}$:   168 mg/kg (M, i.v.); 780 mg/kg (M, p.o.);
180 mg/kg (R, i.v.); 940 mg/kg (R, p.o.)
CN: 3,7-dihydro-3-methyl-1-(5-oxohexyl)-7-propyl-1H-purine-2,6-dione

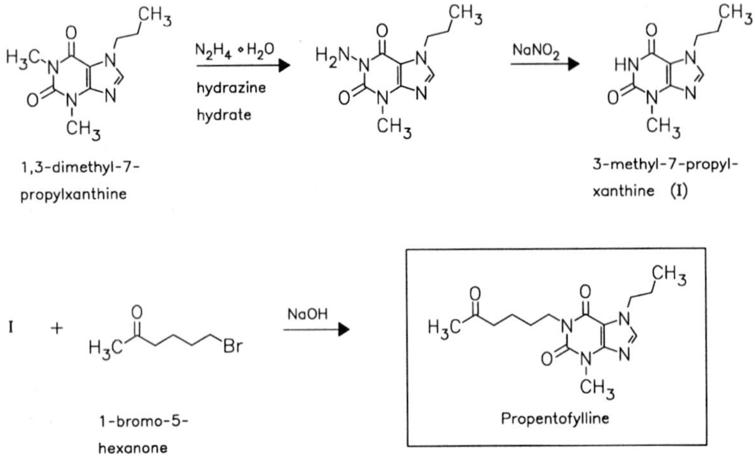

1,3-dimethyl-7-
propylxanthine

3-methyl-7-propyl-
xanthine   (I)

1-bromo-5-
hexanone

Propentofylline

Reference(s):
DE 2 330 742 (Albert; appl. 16.6.1973).
DE 2 366 501 (Albert; appl. 16.6.1973).
US 4 289 776 (Hoechst; 15.9.1981; D-prior. 16.6.1973).

synthesis of 3-methyl-7-propylxanthine:
Ohsaki, T. et al.: Chem. Pharm. Bull. (CPBTAL) **36**, 877 (1988).

Formulation(s):   tabl. 100 mg

Trade Name(s):
J: Hextol (Hoechst; 1988)

Propicillin

ATC: J01CE03
Use: antibiotic

RN: 551-27-9   MF: $C_{18}H_{22}N_2O_5S$ MW: 378.45   EINECS: 208-995-5
CN: [2S-(2α,5α,6β)]-3,3-dimethyl-7-oxo-6-[(1-oxo-2-phenoxybutyl)amino]-4-thia-1-
azabicyclo[3.2.0]heptane-2-carboxylic acid

monopotassium salt
RN: 1245-44-9   MF: $C_{18}H_{21}KN_2O_5S$ MW: 416.54   EINECS: 214-993-5
LD$_{50}$:   292 mg/kg (M, i.v.);
5 g/kg (R, p.o.)

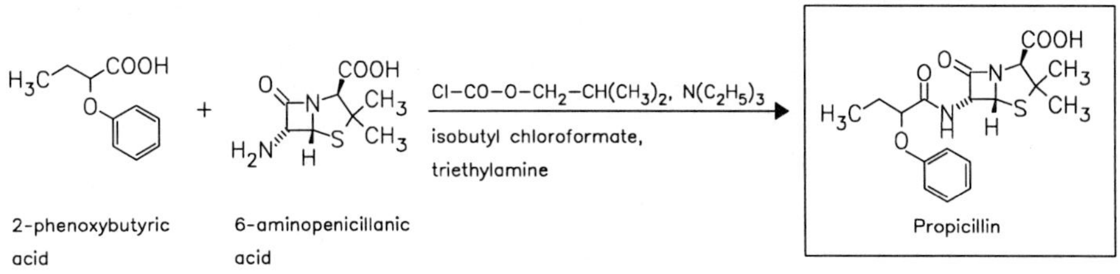

2-phenoxybutyric acid

6-aminopenicillanic acid

Propicillin

Reference(s):

GB 877 120 (Beecham; appl. 10.5.1960; USA-prior. 25.5.1959, 22.10.1959).
GB 899 199 (Pfizer; appl. 7.1.1960; USA-prior. 28.9.1959).
GB 904 576 (Bayer; appl. 24.11.1960; D-prior. 4.12.1959).
GB 958 478 (Beecham; appl. 28.2.1963; USA-prior. 13.3.1962).
DE 1 143 817 (Beecham; appl. 25.5.1960; USA-prior. 25.5.1959, 22.10.1959).
DE 1 154 805 (Bayer; appl. 24.10.1961).
DE 1 159 449 (Grünenthal; appl. 22.3.1961).

Formulation(s):   f. c. tabl. 280 mg, 700 mg; syrup 70 mg; tabl. 125 mg, 140 mg, 280 mg, 700 mg (as potassium salt)

Trade Name(s):

D:	Baycillin (Bayer Vital)		Ultrapen (Pfizer); wfm	Trescillin (Beecham-
	Pluscillin (Bayropharm)	I:	Bayercillin (Bayer); wfm	Fujisawa)
F:	Brocilline (Nativelle); wfm	J:	Oracillin (Takeda)	
GB:	Brocillin (Beecham); wfm		Synthepen-P (Meiji)	

Propiram

ATC: N02
Use: analgesic

RN: 15686-91-6   MF: $C_{16}H_{25}N_3O$ MW: 275.40   EINECS: 239-775-7
LD$_{50}$:   290 mg/kg (M, s.c.);
        366 mg/kg (R, s.c.)
CN: N-[1-methyl-2-(1-piperidinyl)ethyl]-N-2-pyridinylpropanamide

fumarate (1:1)
RN: 13717-04-9   MF: $C_{16}H_{25}N_3O \cdot C_4H_4O_4$ MW: 391.47   EINECS: 237-270-6
LD$_{50}$:   48.2 mg/kg (M, i.v.); 874 mg/kg (M, p.o.);
        63.8 mg/kg (R, i.v.); 1289 mg/kg (R, p.o.);
        1 g/kg (dog, p.o.)

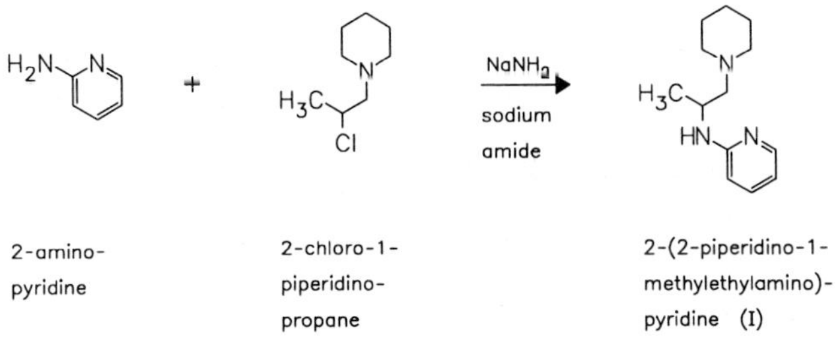

2-amino-pyridine

2-chloro-1-piperidino-propane

2-(2-piperidino-1-methylethylamino)-pyridine (I)

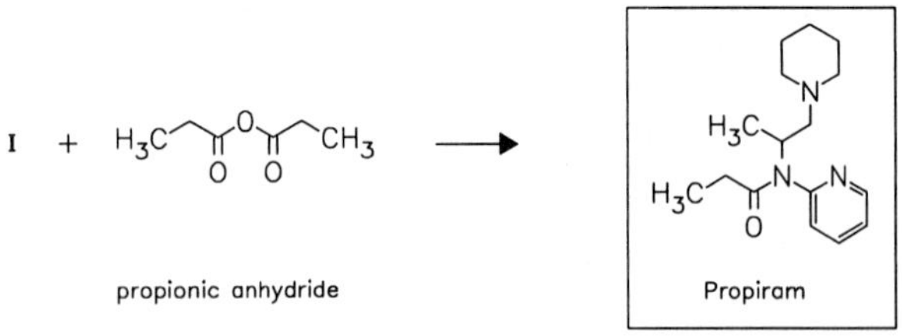

I + H₃C propionic anhydride → Propiram

Reference(s):
US 3 163 654 (Bayer; 29.12.1964; D-prior. 13.4.1961).
FR 1 492 761 (Bayer; appl. 13.4.1962; D-prior. 13.4.1961).

combinations:
US 4 479 956 (Analgesic Assoc.; 30.10.1984; appl. 26.4.1983).

Trade Name(s):
I: Algeril (Bayer); wfm

Propiverine
(P4)

ATC: G04BD06
Use: anticholinergic, treatment of incontinence

RN: 60569-19-9   MF: C$_{23}$H$_{29}$NO$_3$ MW: 367.49
CN: α-Phenyl-α-propoxybenzeneacetic acid 1-methyl-4-piperidinyl ester

hydrochloride
RN: 54556-98-8   MF: C$_{23}$H$_{29}$NO$_3$ · HCl   MW: 403.95

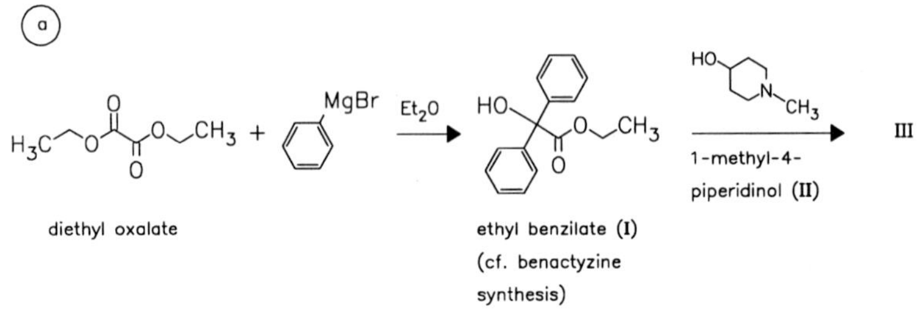

diethyl oxalate

ethyl benzilate (I)
(cf. benactyzine synthesis)

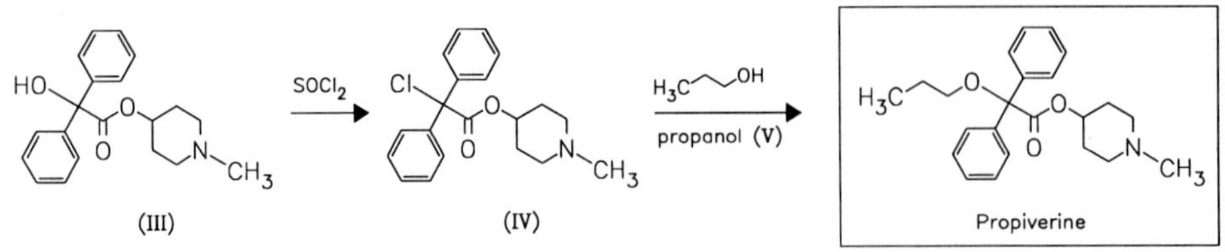

1-methyl-4-piperidinol (II)

III

(III)   (IV)   Propiverine

propanol (V)

(b)

II →[SOCl₂, benzene] Cl—[1-methyl-4-chloropiperidine with N-CH₃] →[isopropanol, benzilic acid (HO-C(C₆H₅)₂-COOH)] III →[SOCl₂] IV →[V] Propiverine

1-methyl-4-chloropiperidine

alternative synthesis of ethyl benzilate (I):

benzaldehyde →[CN⁻] benzoin (OH) →[HNO₃] benzil (O) →[1. NaOH, CH₃OH; 2. HO–CH₃, H⁺] I

benzaldehyde   benzoin   benzil

Reference(s):
a   DD 106 643 (C. Starke et al.; appl. 12.7.1973; DD-prior. 12.7.1973).
    Laphin, I.I. et al.: Khim. Khim. Tekhnol. (SSAKAG) **30** (7), 27-36 (1987).
b   Klosa, J.; Delmar, G.: J. Prakt. Chem. (JPCEAO) **16**, 71-82 (1962).

pharmaceutical preparation:
DE 2 937 489 (C. Starke, G. Schubert; appl. 17.9.1979; DD-prior. 9.10.1978).

transdermal formulation:
JP 04 266 821 (Rido Chem.; appl. 22.2.1991)

Formulation(s):   drg. 5 mg, 15 mg (as hydrochloride)

Trade Name(s):
D: Mictonetten (Apogepha)   Mictonorm (Apogepha)

Propofol
(Disoprofol; ICI-35868)

ATC: N01AX10
Use: anesthetic (injectible)

RN: 2078-54-8   MF: $C_{12}H_{18}O$ MW: 178.28   EINECS: 218-206-6
LD$_{50}$:   50 mg/kg (M, i.v.); 1100 mg/kg (M, p.o.);
       42 mg/kg (R, i.v.); 500 mg/kg (R, p.o.)
CN: 2,6-bis(1-methylethyl)phenol

phenol + H_2C=CH—CH₃ (propylene) →[Al, Δ, p] Propofol

phenol   propylene   Propofol

Reference(s):
US 2 831 898 (Ethyl Corp.; 1958).
Kolka, A.J. et al.: J. Org. Chem. (JOCEAH) **21**, 712 (1956); **22**, 642 (1957).
Kealy, T.J.; Coffman, D.D.: J. Org. Chem. (JOCEAH) **26**, 987 (1961).
Carlton, J.K.; Bradbury, W.C.: J. Am. Chem. Soc. (JACSAT) **78**, 1069 (1956).

Formulation(s):   amp. 10 mg/ml, 20 mg/ml; prefilled Syringe 10 mg/ml; vial 500 mg/50 ml, 1 g/100 ml

Trade Name(s):

D:	Disoprivan (Glaxo Wellcome; Zeneca) Klimofol (IVAmed) Propofol-Abbott (Abbott)	Propofol-Fresenius (Fresenius-Klinik) Propofol-Parke Davis (Parke Davis)	GB: Diprivan (Zeneca) I: Diprivan (Zeneca) J: Diprivan (Zeneca) USA: Diprivan (Zeneca)
		F: Diprivan (Zeneca)	

Propoxycaine

ATC: N01BA
Use: local anesthetic

RN: 86-43-1   MF: $C_{16}H_{26}N_2O_3$ MW: 294.40   EINECS: 201-670-9
LD_{50}: 9 mg/kg (M, i.v.)
CN: 4-amino-2-propoxybenzoic acid 2-(diethylamino)ethyl ester

monohydrochloride
RN: 550-83-4   MF: $C_{16}H_{26}N_2O_3 \cdot HCl$ MW: 330.86   EINECS: 208-988-7
LD_{50}: 7417 µg/kg (M, i.v.)

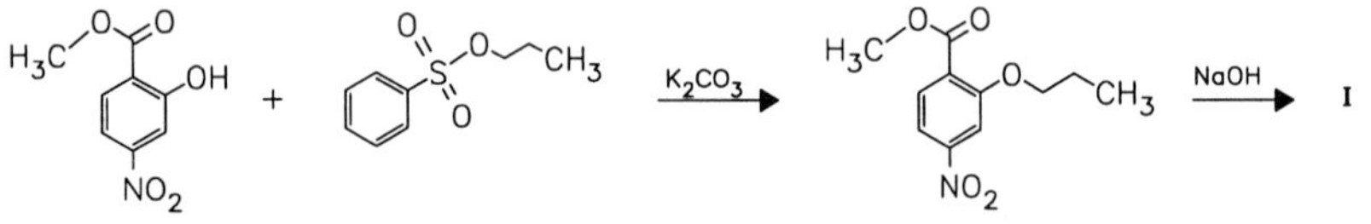

methyl 4-nitro-
salicylate

propyl benzene-
sulfonate

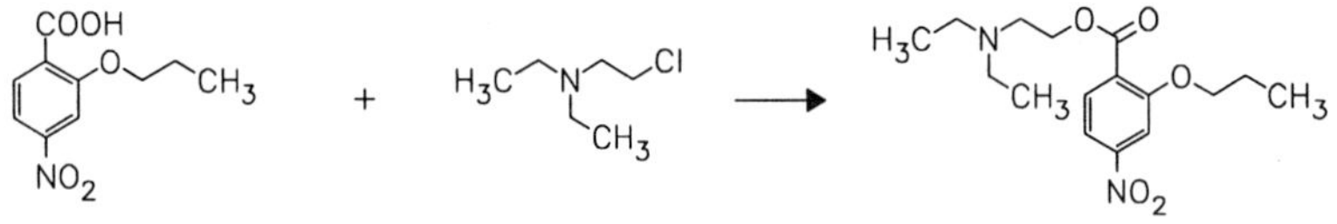

4-nitro-2-propoxy-
benzoic acid (I)

2-diethylamino-
ethyl chloride

(II)

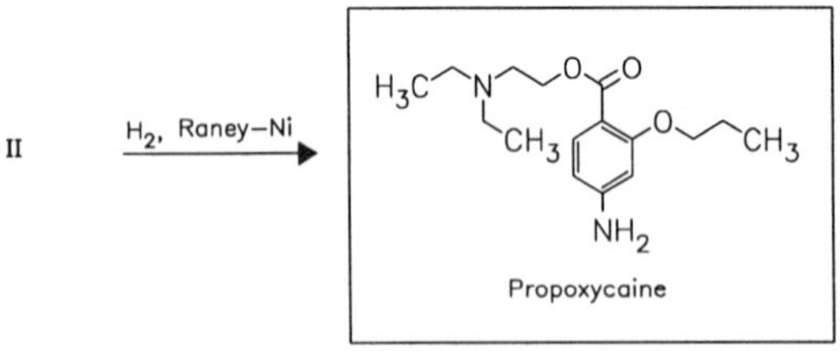

Propoxycaine

Reference(s):
US 2 689 248 (Sterling Drug; prior. 1950).

Trade Name(s):
USA: Blockain (Breon); wfm

Ravocaine (Cook-Waite)-
comb.; wfm

Propranolol

ATC: C07AA05
Use: beta blocking agent

RN: 525-66-6   MF: $C_{16}H_{21}NO_2$ MW: 259.35   EINECS: 208-378-0
LD_{50}:   28.1 mg/kg (M, i.v.); 289 mg/kg (M, p.o.);
        23 mg/kg (R, i.v.); 660 mg/kg (R, p.o.)
CN: 1-[(1-methylethyl)amino]-3-(1-naphthalenyloxy)-2-propanol

hydrochloride
RN: 318-98-9   MF: $C_{16}H_{21}NO_2 \cdot HCl$ MW: 295.81   EINECS: 206-268-7
LD_{50}:   18 mg/kg (M, i.v.); 320 mg/kg (M, p.o.);
        21 mg/kg (R, i.v.); 466 mg/kg (R, p.o.)

1-naphthol (I)   epichloro-   1-chloro-3-   isopropyl-   Propranolol
            hydrin (II)   (1-naphthoxy)-   amine (III)
                2-propanol

3-(1-naphthoxy)-
propylene oxide

Reference(s):
DE 1 493 847 (ICI; prior. 18.11.1963).
US 3 337 628 (ICI; 22.8.1967; GB-prior. 23.11.1962).
GB 994 918 (ICI; appl. 23.11.1962; valid from 28.10.1963).
GB 995 800 (ICI; appl. 23.11.1962; valid from 28.10.1963).

retard form:
US 4 138 475 (ICI; 6.2.1979; GB-prior. 1.6.1977).

Formulation(s):   amp. 5 mg/5 ml; f. c. tabl. 10 mg, 20 mg, 40 mg, 80 mg; s. r. cps. 60 mg, 80 mg, 120 mg,
            160 mg; tabl. 10 mg, 25 mg, 40 mg, 80 mg (as hydrochloride)

Trade Name(s):
D: Beta-Tablinen (Sanorania)
    Dociton (Rhein-Pharma;
    Zeneca)
    Efektolol (Brenner-Efeka)
    Elbrol (Pfleger)
    Indobloc (ASTA Medica
    AWD)
    Obsidian (Isis Pharma)
    Probabloc-40/-80
    (Azupharma)

    Propanur 20/40/80
    (Henning Berlin)
    Prophylux (Hennig)
    Propranolol-Gry (Gry)
    Sagittol 40/80/160
    (Sagitta); wfm
    various generics and
    combination preparations
F: Avlocardyl (Zeneca; 1967)
    Hémipralon (Urpac-Astier)
GB: Beta-Prograne (Tillomed)

    Inderal LA (Zeneca; 1965)
    Inderetic (Zeneca)-comb.
    Inderex (Zeneca)-comb.
    Probeta LA (Trinity)
    Propanix LA (Ashbourne)
I: Inderal (Zeneca; 1967)
J: Caridolol (Sankyo Zoki)
    Inderal (Sumitomo)
    Kemi (Otsuka)
    Pylapron (Kyorin)

USA: Inderal (Wyeth-Ayerst; 1967)　　Inderide (Wyeth-Ayerst)-comb. with hydrochlorothiazide　　generics

Propylhexedrine

ATC: A08A; N07A
Use: sympathomimetic, appetite depressant

RN: 101-40-6　MF: $C_{10}H_{21}N$　MW: 155.29　EINECS: 202-939-3
CN: N,α-dimethylcyclohexaneethanamine

hydrochloride
RN: 1007-33-6　MF: $C_{10}H_{21}N \cdot HCl$　MW: 191.75　EINECS: 213-753-7
(±)-base
RN: 3595-11-7　MF: $C_{10}H_{21}N$　MW: 155.29　EINECS: 222-741-0
(±)-hydrochloride
RN: 6192-98-9　MF: $C_{10}H_{21}N \cdot HCl$　MW: 191.75　EINECS: 228-246-6
LD_{50}: 70 mg/kg (M, i.p.)

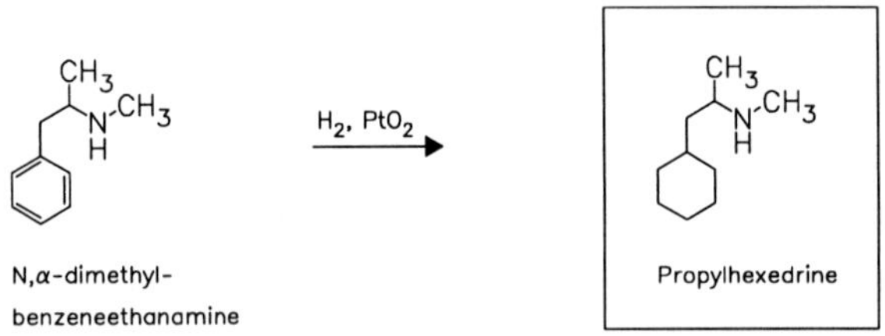

N,α-dimethyl-
benzeneethanamine

Propylhexedrine

Reference(s):
DE 949 657 (Knoll; appl. 1954).
DE 970 480 (Knoll; appl. 1940).
Zenitz, B.L. et al.: J. Am. Chem. Soc. (JACSAT) **69**, 1117 (1947).

alternative synthesis:
US 2 454 746 (Smith Kline & French; 1948; appl. 1947).

Formulation(s):　drg. 25 mg

Trade Name(s):
D:　Eventin (Minden); wfm
GB:　Benzedrex (Smith Kline & French); wfm
USA:　Benzedrex (Smith Kline & French); wfm

Propyliodone

ATC: V08AD03
Use: X-ray contrast medium

RN: 587-61-1　MF: $C_{10}H_{11}I_2NO_3$　MW: 447.01　EINECS: 209-603-5
LD_{50}: 300 mg/kg (M, i.v.); >18 g/kg (M, p.o.)
CN: 3,5-diiodo-4-oxo-1(4H)-pyridineacetic acid propyl ester

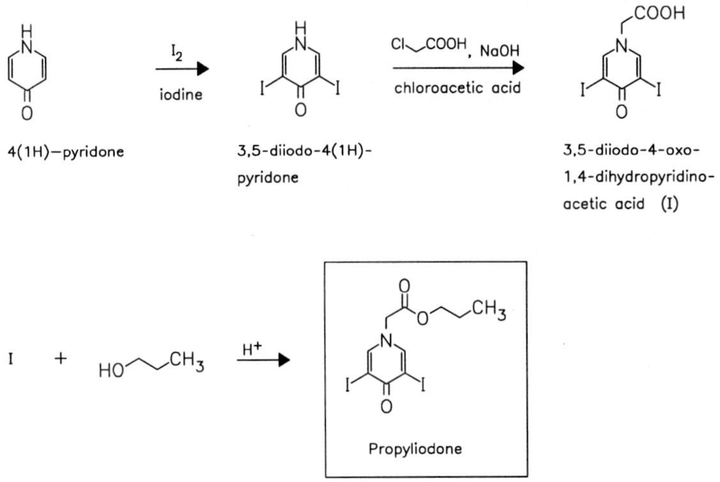
I2
iodine
Cl COOH, NaOH
chloroacetic acid
COOH
4(1H)–pyridone
3,5-diiodo-4(1H)-pyridone
3,5-diiodo-4-oxo-1,4-dihydropyridino-acetic acid (I)
I
HO CH3
H+
Propyliodone

Reference(s):
GB 517 382 (ICI; appl. 1938).
BE 516 687 (Glaxo; appl. 1953; GB-prior. 1952).

Formulation(s): susp. 10 g/20 ml, vial 50 %

Trade Name(s):
D: Dionosil (Glaxo); wfm
Propyliodon-Cilag (Cilag-Chemie); wfm
J: Dionosil (Torii)

Propylthiouracil

ATC: H03BA02
Use: antithyroid drug

RN: 51-52-5 MF: $C_7H_{10}N_2OS$ MW: 170.24 EINECS: 200-103-2
LD_{50}: 1250 mg/kg (R, p.o.)
CN: 2,3-dihydro-6-propyl-2-thioxo-4(1*H*)-pyrimidinone

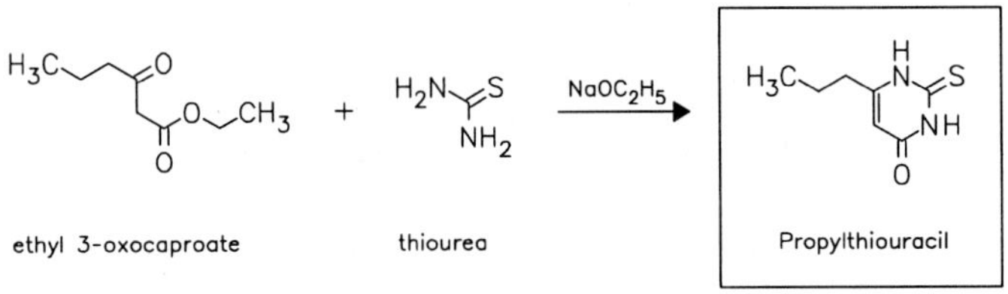
NaOC2H5
ethyl 3-oxocaproate
thiourea
Propylthiouracil

Reference(s):
Anderson, G.W. et al.: J. Am. Chem. Soc. (JACSAT) **67**, 2197 (1945).

Formulation(s): tabl. 25 mg, 50 mg

Trade Name(s):
D: Thyreostat II (Herbrand Hersteller/Berlin-Chemie Vertrieb)
F: Propylthiouracil Diamant (Diamant); wfm
I: Propycil (Sir); wfm
J: Propacil (Chugai)
Thiuragyl (Tokyo Tanabe)
USA: Propylthiouracil (Lederle)

Propyphenazone
(Isopropylantipyrin)

ATC: N02BB04
Use: analgesic, antipyretic

RN: 479-92-5 MF: $C_{14}H_{18}N_2O$ MW: 230.31 EINECS: 207-539-2
LD$_{50}$: 960 mg/kg (M, p.o.);
860 mg/kg (R, p.o.)
CN: 1,2-dihydro-1,5-dimethyl-4-(1-methylethyl)-2-phenyl-3H-pyrazol-3-one

ethyl acetoacetate

phenylhydrazine

3-methyl-1-phenyl-5-Δ²-pyrazolone

4-isopropyl-3-methyl-1-phenyl-5-Δ²-pyrazolone (I)

dimethyl sulfate

Propyphenazone

Reference(s):
DRP 565 799 (Hoffmann-La Roche; appl. 1931).
DE 962 254 (Riedel-deHaen; appl. 1954).

Formulation(s): cps. 400 mg; suppos. 100 mg, 200 mg, 300 mg, 400 mg; tabl. 500 mg

Trade Name(s):
D: Avamigran (ASTA Medica AWD)
Demex (Berlin-Chemie)
Eufibron (Berlin-Chemie)
Isoprochin (Merckle)
Saridon (Roche Nicholas)-comb.
and circa 150 more generics and combination preparations
F: Polypirine (Lehning)-comb.

I: Caffalgina (Home)-comb.
Flexidone (Poli)-comb.
Influvit (Recordati)-comb.
Micranet (Ogna)-comb.
Mindol (Merck-Bracco)-comb.
Neo-Optalidon (Novartis)-comb.
Omniadol (Montefarmaco)-comb.
Optalidon confetti (Novartis)-comb.

Ribelfan (Pharmacia & Upjohn)-comb.
Saridon (Roche)-comb.
Spasmocibalgina (Novartis)-comb.
Spasmoplus (Novartis)-comb.
Uniplus (Angelini)-comb.
Veramon (Sofar)-comb.
Vitialgin (Boots H.M. VITI)-comb.

Propyramazine bromide

ATC: A03
Use: antispasmodic

RN: 145-54-0 MF: $C_{20}H_{23}BrN_2OS$ MW: 419.39 EINECS: 205-657-9
LD$_{50}$: 80 mg/kg (M, i.p.)
CN: 1-methyl-1-[1-methyl-2-oxo-2-(10H-phenothiazin-10-yl)ethyl]pyrrolidinium bromide

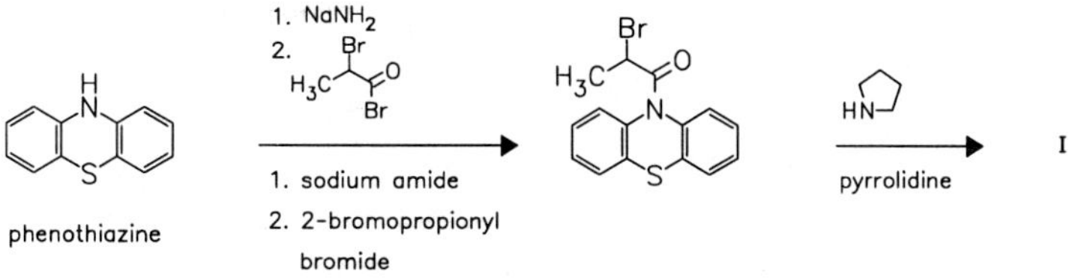

phenothiazine

1. sodium amide
2. 2-bromopropionyl bromide

pyrrolidine

I

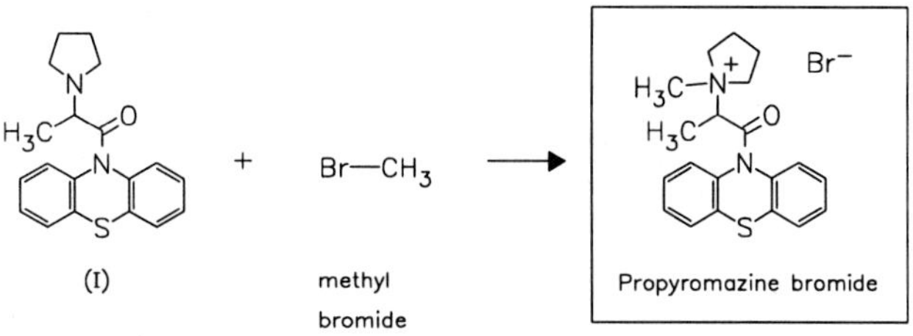

(I)   +   Br—CH₃   →   Propyromazine bromide

methyl bromide

Reference(s):
US 2 615 886 (Astra; 1952; prior. 1951).

Formulation(s):   tabl. 25 mg; vial 10 mg/ml

Trade Name(s):
F: Diaspasmyl (Diamant);
       wfm

Proquazone

ATC: M01AX13
Use: analgesic, anti-inflammatory

RN: 22760-18-5   MF: $C_{18}H_{18}N_2O$ MW: 278.36   EINECS: 245-203-7
LD$_{50}$: 930 mg/kg (M, p.o.);
       759 mg/kg (R, p.o.)
CN: 7-methyl-1-(1-methylethyl)-4-phenyl-2(1H)-quinazolinone

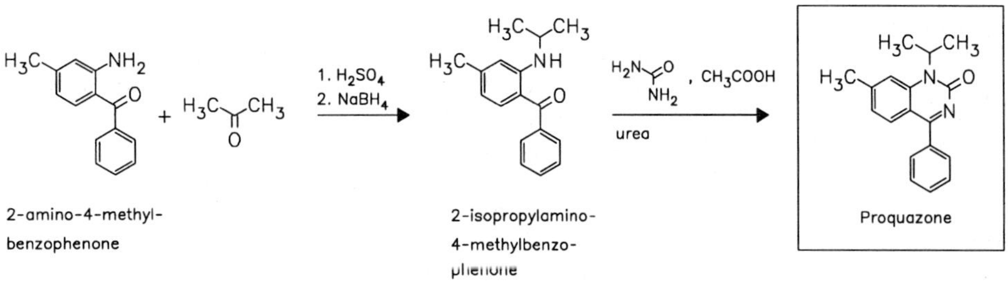

2-amino-4-methyl-
benzophenone

+   H₃C

1. H₂SO₄
2. NaBH₄

2-isopropylamino-
4-methylbenzo-
phenone

H₂N   , CH₃COOH

urea

Proquazone

Reference(s):
US 3 723 432 (Sandoz-Wander; 27.3.1973; prior. 29.8.1966, 4.5.1967, 4.10.1967, 26.2.1968, 1.7.1968, 12.11.1968).
DE 1 805 501 (Sandoz; appl. 26.10.1968; USA-prior. 30.10.1967, 26.2.1968, 1.7.1968).

alternative synthesis:
US 3 549 635 (Sandoz-Wander; 22.12.1970; prior. 26.2.1968, 1.7.1968).
DOS 1 909 110 (Sandoz; appl. 24.2.1969; USA-prior. 26.2.1968, 1.7.1968).

2-isopropylamino-4-methylbenzophenone:
US 3 845 128 (Sandoz; 29.10.1974; prior. 30.10.1967, 5.8.1970).
DOS 1 818 012 (Sandoz; appl. 26.10.1968; USA-prior. 30.10.1967, 26.2.1968, 1.7.1968).
US 4 071 557 (Sandoz; 31.1.1978; appl. 29.1.1976).

Formulation(s):   cps. 200 mg, 300 mg; suppos. 300 mg

Trade Name(s):
D: Biarison (Sandoz); wfm

Proscillaridin
(Proscillaridin A)

ATC: C01AB01
Use: cardiac glycoside

RN: 466-06-8   MF: $C_{30}H_{42}O_8$ MW: 530.66   EINECS: 207-370-4
LD_{50}: 4.7 mg/kg (M, i.v.); 30.5 mg/kg (M, p.o.);
        9 mg/kg (R, i.v.); 56 mg/kg (R, p.o.)
CN: (3β)-3-[(6-deoxy-α-L-mannopyranosyl)oxy]-14-hydroxybufa-4,20,22-trienolide

glucoscillaren A
(from Scilla maritima L.)

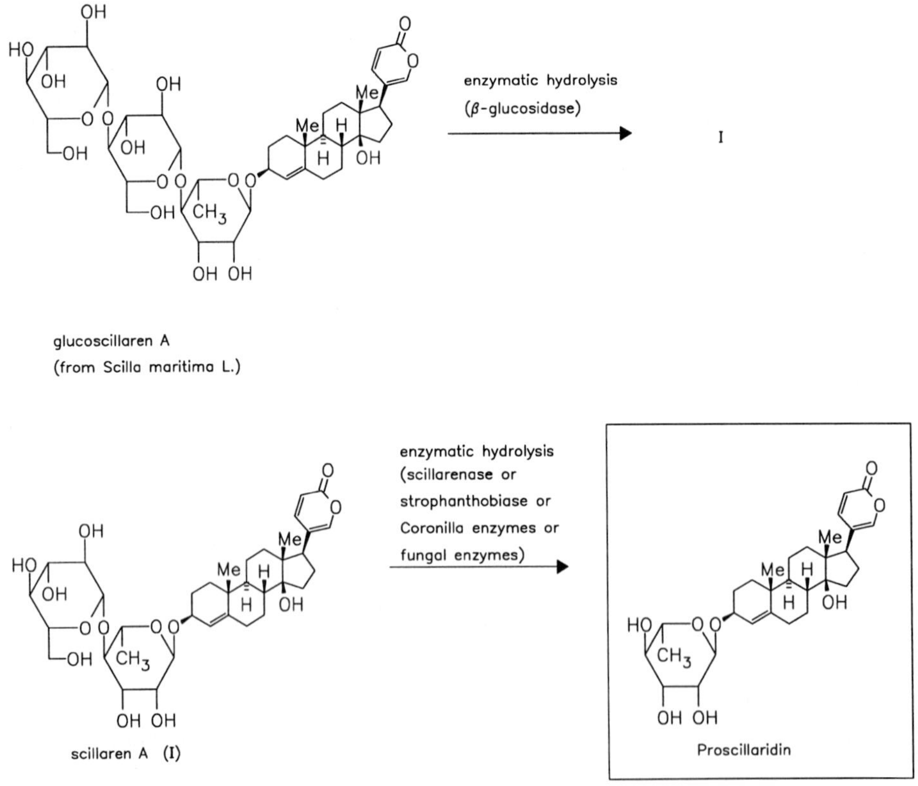

enzymatic hydrolysis
(β-glucosidase)

I

enzymatic hydrolysis
(scillarenase or
strophanthobiase or
Coronilla enzymes or
fungal enzymes)

scillaren A (I)

Proscillaridin

from Urginea burkei Baker

Reference(s):
a   Stoll, A. et al.: Helv. Chim. Acta (HCACAV) **16**, 703 (1933).
    Stoll, A.; Kreis, W.: Helv. Chim. Acta (HCACAV) **34**, 1431 (1951).
    Stoll, A. et al.: Helv. Chim. Acta (HCACAV) **35**, 2495 (1952).
    DRP 646 930 (Ciba; appl. 1933; CH-prior. 1932).
    US 3 361 630 (Knoll; 2.1.1968; appl. 30.10.1964; D-prior. 2.11.1963).
b   Louw, P.G.J: Nature (London) (NATUAS) **163**, 30 (1949).
    Zoller, P.; Tamm, Ch.: Helv. Chim. Acta (HCACAV) **36**, 1744 (1953).

Formulation(s):   drg. 0.25 mg, 0.5 mg

Trade Name(s):

D:	Talusin (Knoll)	J:	Apocerpin (Kotani)	Pros Tab. (Mita)
F:	Talusin (Biosedra); wfm		Bunosquin (Seiko)	Proscillar (Toyo Jozo)
I:	Caradrin (Boehringer Ing.);		Caradrin (Kowa)	Prosiladin (Sawai)
	wfm		Cardiolidin (Nichiiko)	Proslladin (Zeria)
	Neogratusminal (Simes)-		Cardion (Nippon	Proszin (Teisan)
	comb.; wfm		Chemiphar)	Scillaridin (Moroshita)
	Stellarid (Zambeletti); wfm		Cardon (Kanto)	Silamarin A (Wakamoto)
	Talusin (Knoll); wfm		Mitredin (Nippon Shoji)	Stellarid (Tobishi-Mochida)
	Teostellarid (Zambeletti)-		Procardin (Mohan)	Talusin (Dainippon)
	comb.; wfm		Procillan (Hokuriku)	USA: Talusin (Knoll); wfm
	Urgilan (Simes); wfm		Proherz (Shinshin)	Tradenal (Knoll); wfm

Protheobromine

ATC: C03BD
Use: diuretic, cardiotonic

RN: 50-39-5   MF: $C_{10}H_{14}N_4O_3$ MW: 238.25   EINECS: 200-034-8
LD_{50}:   580 mg/kg (M, s.c.)
CN: 3,7-dihydro-1-(2-hydroxypropyl)-3,7-dimethyl-1H-purine-2,6-dione

propylene oxide   theobromine   → NaOH →   Protheobromine

Reference(s):
DE 1 067 025 (Degussa; appl. 23.8.1955).

Formulation(s):   drg. 50 mg, 100 mg

Trade Name(s):

D:	Cordabromin-Digoxin	I:	Antelin (OFF)-comb.; wfm	Tebe (Simes); wfm
	(Homburg)-comb.; wfm		Idromin (Arnaldi); wfm	

Prothipendyl

ATC: N05AX07
Use: psychosedative, neuroleptic

RN: 303-69-5   MF: $C_{16}H_{19}N_3S$ MW: 285.42
LD_{50}:   415 mg/kg (M, p.o.);
        25 mg/kg (R, i.v.)
CN: N,N-dimethyl-10H-pyrido[3,2-b][1,4]benzothiazine-10-propanamine

monohydrochloride
RN: 1225-65-6   MF: $C_{16}H_{19}N_3S \cdot HCl$ MW: 321.88   EINECS: 214-958-4
LD_{50}:   110 mg/kg (R, i.v.); 610 mg/kg (R, p.o.)

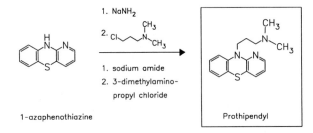

1-azaphenothiazine

1. NaNH₂
2. Cl...N(CH₃)CH₃

1. sodium amide
2. 3-dimethylamino-
   propyl chloride

Prothipendyl

Reference(s):
DE 1 001 684 (Degussa; appl. 1954).
US 2 974 139 (Degussa; 7.3.1961; D-prior. 2.10.1954).

Formulation(s):   amp. 40 mg/2 ml; drg. 40 mg; drops 25 mg/0.5 ml; f. c. tabl. 80 mg (as hydrochloride)

Trade Name(s):
D: Dominal /-forte (ASTA   GB: Tolnate (Smith Kline &   J: Prosyl (Kanto)
      Medica AWD)   French); wfm

Protionamide
(Prothionamide)

ATC: J04AD01
Use: tuberculostatic, antibacterial

RN: 14222-60-7   MF: $C_9H_{12}N_2S$ MW: 180.28   EINECS: 238-093-7
LD_{50}:   1 g/kg (M, p.o.);
        1320 mg/kg (R, p.o.)
CN: 2-propyl-4-pyridinecarbothioamide

diethyl oxalate   +   2-pentanone   NaOC₂H₅ →   ethyl 2,4-dioxo-heptanoate   2-cyano-acetamide →   I

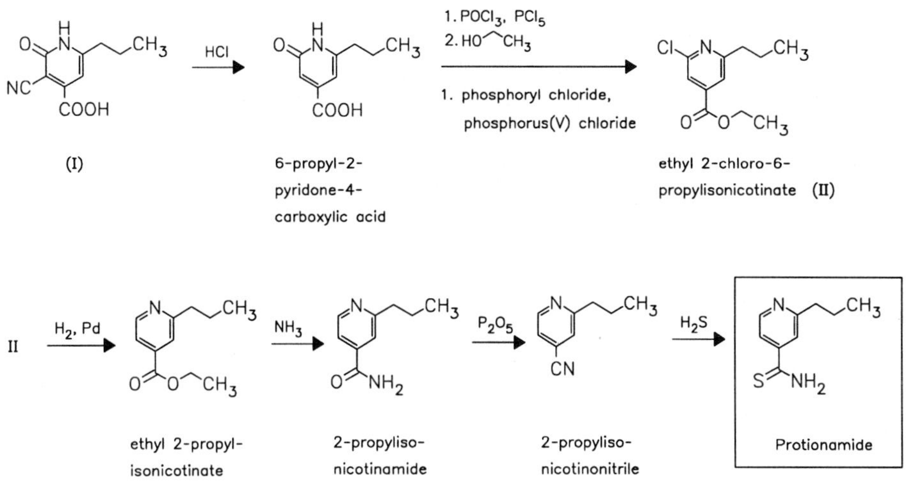

HCl
1. POCl3, PCl5
2. HO CH3
1. phosphoryl chloride, phosphorus(V) chloride
(I)
6-propyl-2-pyridone-4-carboxylic acid
ethyl 2-chloro-6-propylisonicotinate (II)
II
H2, Pd
NH3
P2O5
H2S
ethyl 2-propylisonicotinate
2-propylisonicotinamide
2-propylisonicotinonitrile
Protionamide

Reference(s):

GB 800 250 (Chimie et Atomistique; appl. 26.3.1957; F-prior. 27.3.1956, 19.4.1956, 6.8.1956, 7.12.1956).
Libermann, S. et al.: C. R. Hebd. Seances Acad. Sci. (COREAF) **242**, 2409, 2412 (1956).

Formulation(s): f. c. tabl. 250 mg; tabl. 125 mg, 250 mg

Trade Name(s):

D:	Ektebin (Hefa Pharma)	GB:	Trevintix (May & Baker); wfm	Tuberamin (Meiji)
	Isoprodion (Fatol)-comb.	J:	Entelohl (Kyowa)	Tuberex (Shionogi)
	Peteha Dragees (Fatol)		Protionamid (Lederle-Takeda)	Tubermide (Sankyo)
F:	Trévintix (Théraplix); wfm			

Protirelin

(TRH; Thyroliberin; Tyroliberin)

ATC: V04CJ02
Use: antidepressant, thyroid diagnostic

RN: 24305-27-9 MF: $C_{16}H_{22}N_6O_4$ MW: 362.39 EINECS: 246-143-4
LD_{50}: 921 mg/kg (M, i.v.); >10 g/kg (M, p.o.);
514 mg/kg (R, i.v.); >5 g/kg (R, p.o.)
CN: 5-oxo-L-prolyl-L-histidyl-L-prolinamide

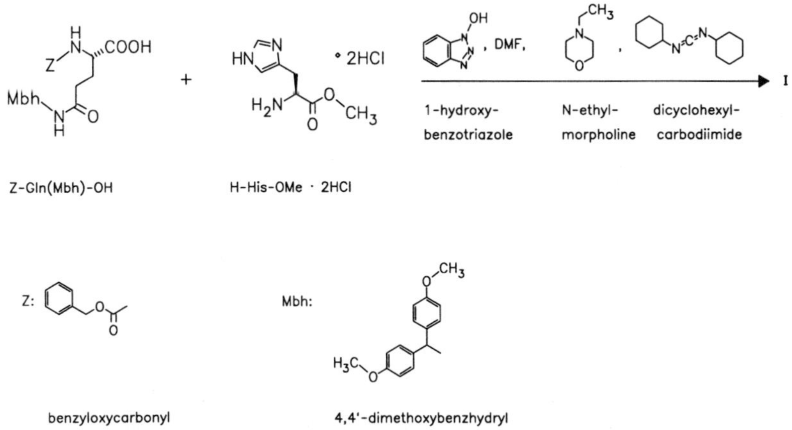

· 2HCl
, DMF,
1-hydroxybenzotriazole
N-ethylmorpholine
dicyclohexylcarbodiimide
I
Z-Gln(Mbh)-OH
H-His-OMe · 2HCl
Z:
Mbh:
benzyloxycarbonyl
4,4'-dimethoxybenzhydryl

Z-Gln(Mbh)-His-OMe (I)

NaOH, dioxane, H₂O →

Z-Gln(Mbh)-His-OH (II)

II + H-Pro-NH₂ · HCl

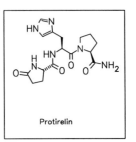

1-hydroxy-benzotriazole , DMF, N-ethyl-morpholine , dicyclohexyl-carbodiimide

→ III

Z-Gln(Mbh)-His-Pro-NH₂ (III)

trifluoroacetic acid/anisole (9:1), reflux, 1.5 h →

Protirelin

Reference(s):
synthesis:
König, W.; Geiger, R.: Chem. Ber. (CHBEAM) **105**, 2872 (1972).
US 3 746 697 (K. Folkers et al.; 17.7.1973; prior. 19.9.1969).
US 3 757 003 (K. Folkers et al.; 4.9.1973; prior. 18.12.1969).
US 3 753 969 (K. Folkers et al.; 21.8.1973; prior. 22.12.1969).
US 3 959 247 (Takeda; 25.5.1976; appl. 21.6.1974; J-prior. 2.7.1973).
DE 2 431 331 (Takeda; appl. 22.5.1975; prior. 29.6.1974).

starting material:
König, W.; Geiger, R.: Chem. Ber. (CHBEAM) **103**, 2041 (1970).
Flouret, G.: J. Med. Chem. (JMCMAR) **13**, 843 (1970).

use:
as antidepressant:
US 3 737 549 (Abbott; 5.6.1973; appl. 20.3.1972).
DOS 2 313 635 (Abbott; appl. 19.3.1973; USA-prior. 20.3.1972).

at impaired consciousness:
DOS 2 611 976 (Takeda; appl. 20.3.1976; GB-prior. 3.4.1975, 26.11.1975).
US 4 059 692 (Takeda; 22.11.1977; GB-prior. 3.4.1975, 26.11.1975).

for abolition of schizophrenia:
GB 1 540 574 (Takeda; appl. 23.5.1975; valid from 24.5.1976).

injectable solutions (by use of sugar alcohols):
DOS 2 743 586 (Takeda; appl. 28.9.1977; J-prior. 1.10.1976).

Formulation(s):   amp. 200 µg/2 ml, 400 µg/2 ml; nasal spray 1 mg/0.09 ml; tabl. 40 mg; USA: amp. 500 µg/ml

Trade Name(s):

D: Antepan (Henning Berlin;   TRH (Berlin-Chemie;   Xantium (Wyeth-Lederle)
     1980)   Ferring; 1974)   J: TRH (Tanabe)
     Relefact TRH (Hoechst;   F: Stimu-T.S.H. (Roussel)   USA: Thyrel TRH (Ferring)
     1975)   GB: Relefact (LH-RH/TRH
     Thyroliberin/TRF Merck   Hoechst; 1978); wfm
     (Merck; 1978)   I: Irtonin (Takeda)

Protizinic acid
(Acide protizinique)

ATC: M01AE
Use: anti-inflammatory

RN: 13799-03-6   MF: C$_{17}$H$_{17}$NO$_3$S   MW: 315.39   EINECS: 237-453-0
CN: 7-methoxy-α,10-dimethyl-10H-phenothiazine-2-acetic acid

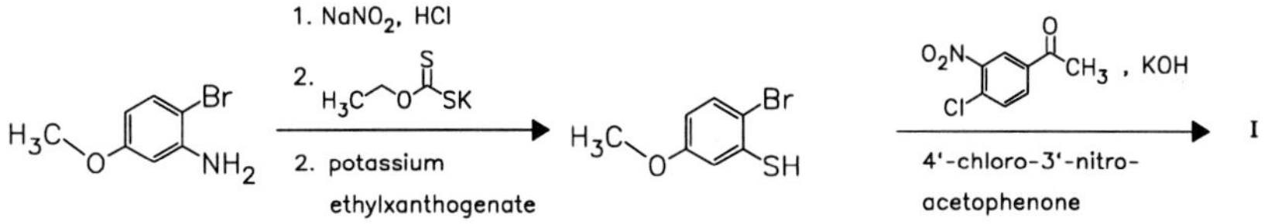

2-bromo-5-methoxy-
thiophenol

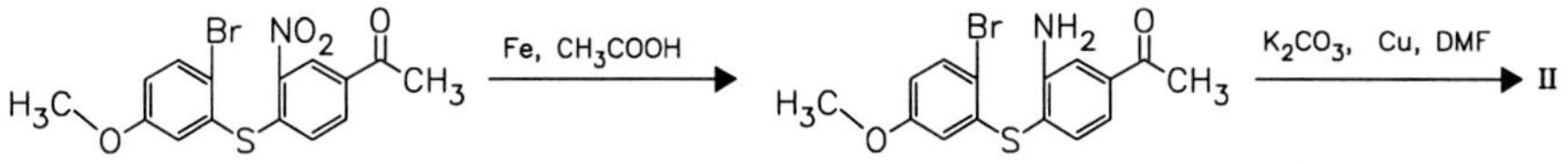

4'-chloro-3'-nitro-
acetophenone

3-amino-4-bromo-
anisole

(I)

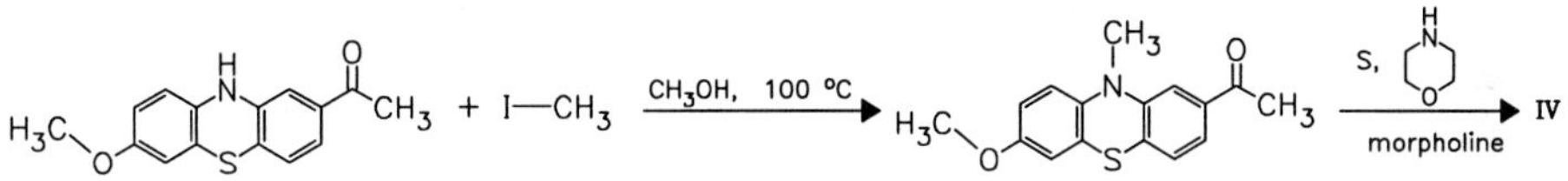

2-acetyl-7-methoxy-
phenothiazine (II)

methyl
iodide (III)

2-acetyl-7-methoxy-10-
methylphenothiazine

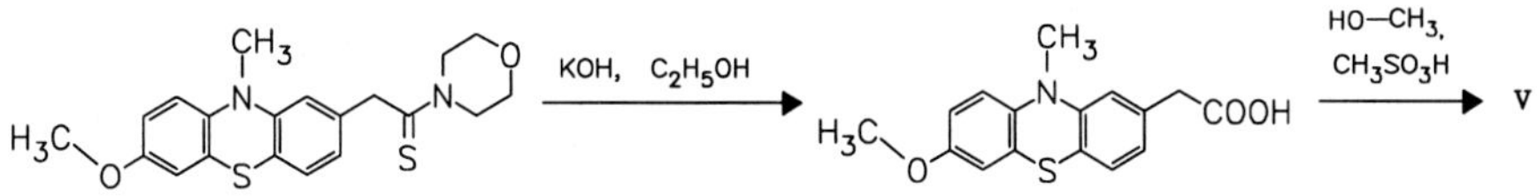

morpholine

(IV)

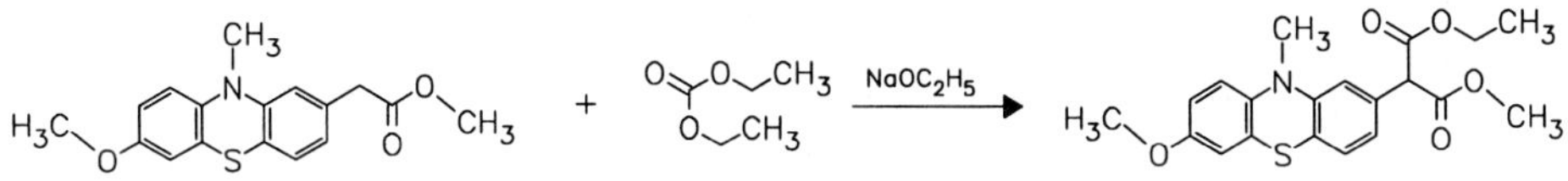

(V)

diethyl
carbonate

(VI)

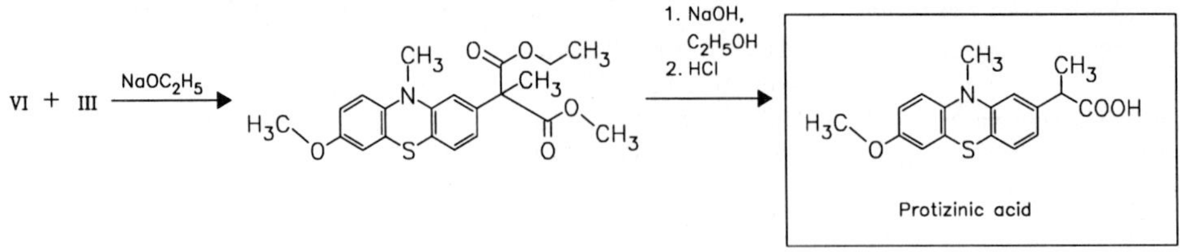

VI + III $\xrightarrow{\text{NaOC}_2\text{H}_5}$ [intermediate] $\xrightarrow{\begin{array}{l}1.\ \text{NaOH,}\\ \text{C}_2\text{H}_5\text{OH}\\ 2.\ \text{HCl}\end{array}}$ [Protizinic acid]

Protizinic acid

Reference(s):

US 3 450 698 (Rhône-Poulenc; 17.6.1969; F-prior. 29.10.1964).

Formulation(s):   cps. 200 mg

Trade Name(s):
F: Pirocrid (Théraplix); wfm   J: Piroarid (Mochidia)

Protokylol

ATC: R03A
Use: β-sympathomimetic, bronchodilator

RN: 136-70-9   MF: $C_{18}H_{21}NO_5$ MW: 331.37   EINECS: 205-255-3
CN: 4-[2-[[2-(1,2-benzodioxol-5-yl)-1-methylethyl]amino]-1-hydroxyethyl]-1,2-benzenediol

hydrochloride
RN: 136-69-6   MF: $C_{18}H_{21}NO_5 \cdot HCl$ MW: 367.83   EINECS: 205-254-8
LD$_{50}$:   86.5 mg/kg (M, i.v.); 785 mg/kg (M, p.o.);
71 mg/kg (R, i.v.); 865 mg/kg (R, p.o.)

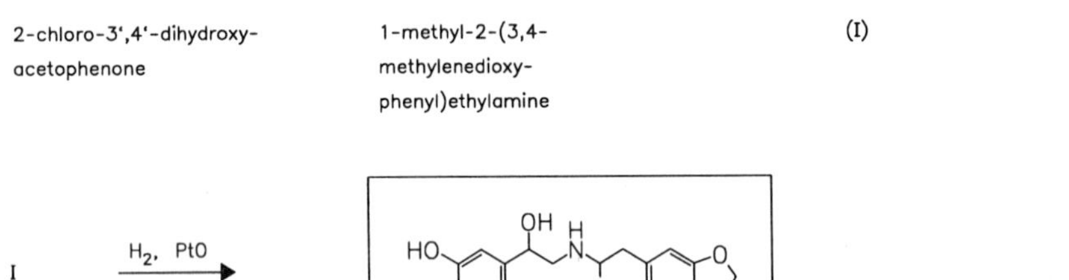

2-chloro-3',4'-dihydroxy-
acetophenone

1-methyl-2-(3,4-
methylenedioxy-
phenyl)ethylamine

(I)

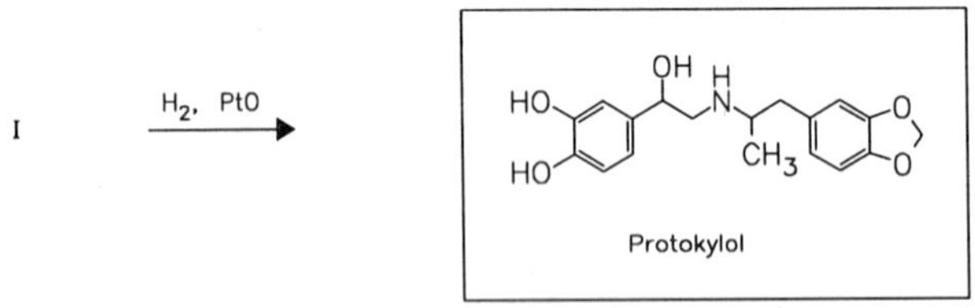

I $\xrightarrow{\text{H}_2,\ \text{PtO}}$ [Protokylol]

Protokylol

Reference(s):
US 2 900 415 (Lakeside Labs.; 1959; prior. 1954).

Formulation(s):   aerosol 0.01 mg; drg. 1 mg; tabl. 1 mg (as hydrochloride)

Trade Name(s):
D: atma-sanol (Sanol)-comb.;   I: Asmetil (Benvegna); wfm   J: Caytine (Chugai)
wfm   Beres (Simes); wfm   USA: Ventaire (Marion); wfm

Protriptyline

ATC: N06AA11
Use: antidepressant

RN: 438-60-8 MF: C$_{19}$H$_{21}$N MW: 263.38 EINECS: 207-119-9
LD$_{50}$: 30 mg/kg (M, i.v.); 269 mg/kg (M, p.o.);
240 mg/kg (R, p.o.)
CN: *N*-methyl-5*H*-dibenzo[*a,d*]cycloheptene-5-propanamine

hydrochloride
RN: 1225-55-4 MF: C$_{19}$H$_{21}$N · HCl MW: 299.85 EINECS: 214-956-3
LD$_{50}$: 49 mg/kg (M, i.v.); 211 mg/kg (M, p.o.);
299 mg/kg (R, p.o.)

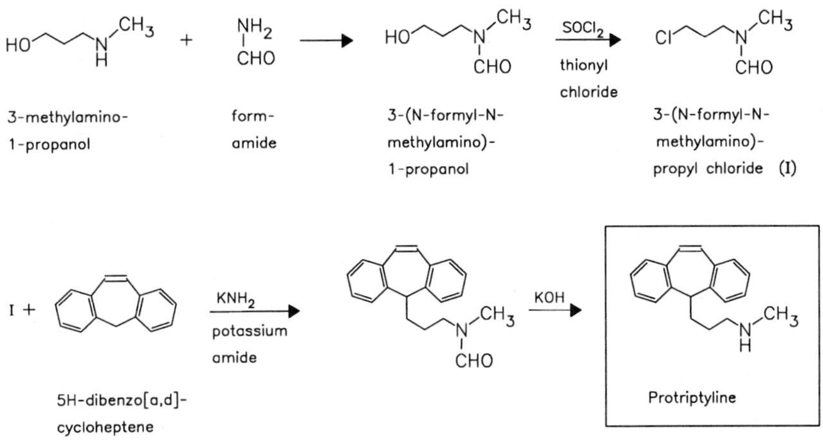

3-methylamino-
1-propanol

form-
amide

3-(N-formyl-N-
methylamino)-
1-propanol

3-(N-formyl-N-
methylamino)-
propyl chloride (I)

thionyl
chloride

5H-dibenzo[a,d]-
cycloheptene

potassium
amide

Protriptyline

Reference(s):
US 3 244 748 (Merck & Co.; 5.4.1966; prior. 3.7.1962).
US 3 271 451 (Merck & Co.; 6.9.1966; appl. 3.7.1962).
BE 617 967 (Merck & Co.; appl. 22.5.1962; USA-prior. 24.5.1961, 25.9.1961).
DE 1 287 573 (Merck & Co.; appl. 6.5.1963; USA-prior. 14.5.1962).
DE 1 468 212 (Merck & Co.; appl. 21.5.1962; USA-prior. 24.5.1961, 25.9.1961).

alternative syntheses:
DE 1 288 599 (Geigy; appl. 13.3.1962; CH-prior. 14.3.1961, 30.3.1961).
Engelhardt, E.L. et al.: J. Med. Chem. (JMCMAR) **11**, 325 (1968).

Formulation(s): tabl. 5 mg, 10 mg (as hydrochloride)

Trade Name(s):
D: Maximed (Sharp &
     Dohme); wfm
F: Concordine (Merck Sharp
     & Dohme); wfm

GB: Condordin (Merck Sharp &
     Dohme)
I: Concordin (Merck Sharp &
     Dohme); wfm

USA: Vivactil (Merck Sharp &
     Dohme)

Proxazole
(Propaxoline)

ATC: A03AX07
Use: analgesic, anti-inflammatory,
antitussive, antispasmodic, relaxant
(smooth muscle)

RN: 5696-09-3 MF: C$_{17}$H$_{25}$N$_3$O MW: 287.41
CN: *N,N*-diethyl-3-(1-phenylpropyl)-1,2,4-oxadiazole-5-ethanamine

citrate (1:1)
RN: 132-35-4 MF: $C_{17}H_{25}N_3O \cdot C_6H_8O_7$ MW: 479.53 EINECS: 205-059-8
LD_{50}: 68 mg/kg (M, i.v.); 1270 mg/kg (M, p.o.);
1400 mg/kg (R, p.o.)

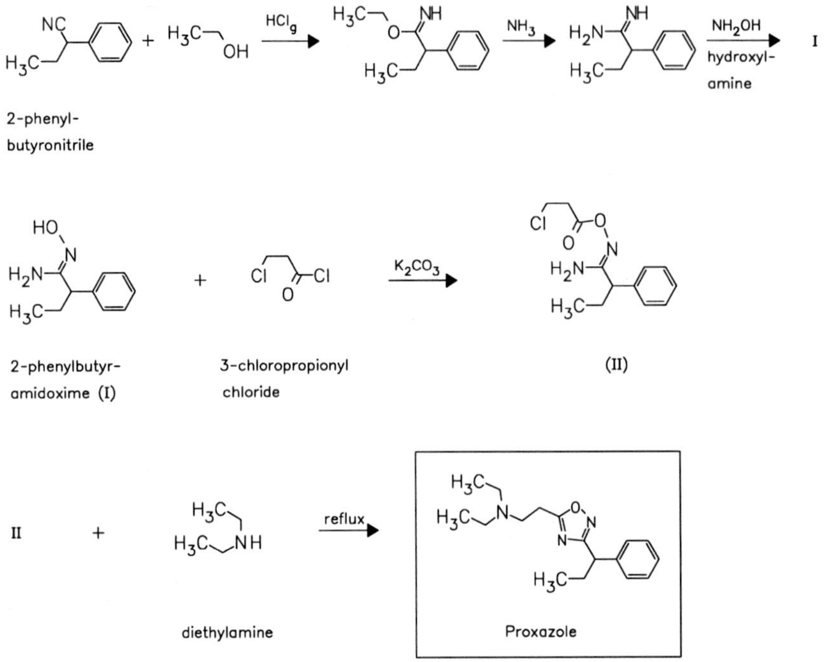
HCl
NH3
NH2OH
hydroxylamine
I
2-phenylbutyronitrile
K2CO3
2-phenylbutyramidoxime (I)
3-chloropropionyl chloride
(II)
II
reflux
diethylamine
Proxazole

Reference(s):
US 3 141 019 (Angelini Francesco; 14.7.1964; A-prior. 29.9.1959).

Formulation(s): drops 5 %; tabl. 100 mg (as citrate); vial 30 mg/5 ml

Trade Name(s):
F: Mendozal (Beaufour); wfm I: Toness (Angelini) J: Pirecin (Yoshitomi)

Proxymetacaine
(Proparacaine)

ATC: S01HA04
Use: local anesthetic

RN: 499-67-2 MF: $C_{16}H_{26}N_2O_3$ MW: 294.40 EINECS: 207-884-9
CN: 3-amino-4-propoxybenzoic acid 2-(diethylamino)ethyl ester

monohydrochloride
RN: 5875-06-9 MF: $C_{16}H_{26}N_2O_3 \cdot HCl$ MW: 330.86 EINECS: 227-541-7
LD_{50}: 3371 µg/kg (M, i.v.)

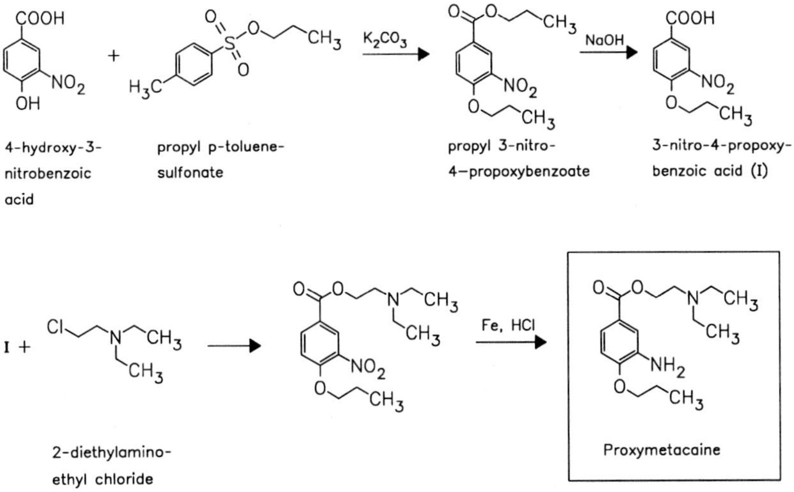
4-hydroxy-3-nitrobenzoic acid
propyl p-toluenesulfonate
K_2CO_3
propyl 3-nitro-4-propoxybenzoate
NaOH
3-nitro-4-propoxybenzoic acid (I)
2-diethylaminoethyl chloride
Fe, HCl
Proxymetacaine

Reference(s):
Clinton, R.O. et al.: J. Am. Chem. Soc. (JACSAT) **74**, 592 (1952).
US 1 317 250 (Parke Davis; 1919; appl. 1918).
DRP 522 064 (Schering-Kahlbaum AG; appl. 1928).
US 2 288 334 (Abbott; 1942; appl. 1940).

Formulation(s): eye drops 5 mg/ml (as hydrochloride)

Trade Name(s):

D:	Proparakain-POS (Ursapharm)	GB:	Mimius Proxymetacaine (Chauvin)	I:	Visuanestetico (ISF); wfm
F:	Keracaine (Merck Sharp & Dohme-Chibret); wfm		Ophthaine (Bristol-Myers Squibb)	USA:	Alcaine (Alcon); wfm Ophthaine (Squibb); wfm Ophthetic (Allergan); wfm

Proxyphylline

ATC: R03DA03
Use: cardiotonic, bronchodilator

RN: 603-00-9 MF: $C_{10}H_{14}N_4O_3$ MW: 238.25 EINECS: 210-028-7
LD_{50}: 510 mg/kg (M, i.v.); 1460 mg/kg (M, p.o.);
430 mg/kg (R, i.v.); 460 mg/kg (R, p.o.)
CN: 3,7-dihydro-7-(2-hydroxypropyl)-1,3-dimethyl-1*H*-purine-2,6-dione

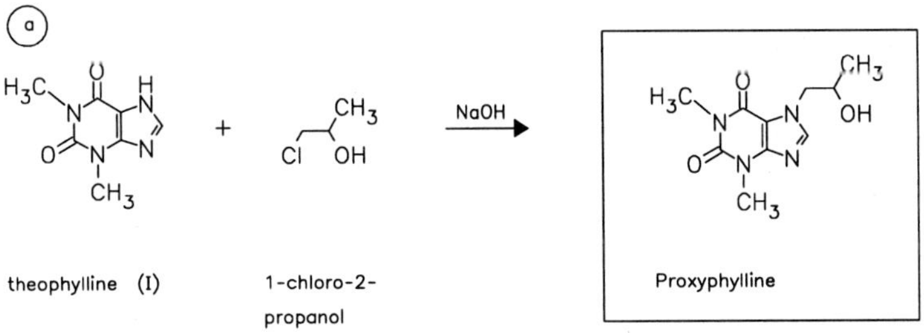
a
theophylline (I)
1-chloro-2-propanol
NaOH
Proxyphylline

(b)

I   +   propylene oxide [CH₃ epoxide structure] —NaOH→ [Proxyphylline]

propylene
oxide

Reference(s):
US 2 715 125 (Gane's Chem. Works; 1955; prior. 1953).

Formulation(s):   clysma 150 mg/5 ml, 300 mg/10 ml, 600 mg/20 ml; s. r. tabl. 200 mg, 300 mg; suppos. 500
mg; tabl. 300 mg

Trade Name(s):
D: Antihypertonicum   GB: Brontyl (Reckitt &   I: Pantafillina
      (Trommsdorff)-comb.   Colman); wfm   (Farmacobiologico); wfm
      Neobiphyllin-Clys   Thean (Astra); wfm   J: Monophyllin (Yoshitomi)
      (Trommsdorff)-comb.   Tomophyllin (Nichiiko)

Prozapine
(Hexadiphane)

ATC: A03BA
Use: choleretic, antispasmodic

RN: 3426-08-2   MF: $C_{21}H_{27}N$ MW: 293.45   EINECS: 222-325-9
CN: 1-(3,3-diphenylpropyl)hexahydro-1H-azepine

hydrochloride
RN: 13657-24-4   MF: $C_{21}H_{27}N \cdot HCl$ MW: 329.92   EINECS: 237-143-5

[reaction scheme]

ethylene   hexahydro—   1-(2-hydroxyethyl)-   1-(2-chloroethyl)-
oxide   1H-azepine   hexahydro-1H-   hexahydro-1H-
                                      azepine   azepine (I)

I + [structure] —NaNH₂→ [structure] —1. H₂SO₄ / 2. NaOH→ [Prozapine]

diphenyl—   2,2-diphenyl-4-   Prozapine
acetonitrile   (hexahydro-1H-azepino)-
                      butyronitrile

Reference(s):
US 2 881 165 (Janssen; 1959; NL-prior. 1956).

Formulation(s):   amp. 1 mg/5 ml, 2 mg/5 ml; syrup 1 mg (as hydrochloride)

Pyrantel

ATC: P02CC01
Use: anthelmintic (nematodes)

RN: 15686-83-6   MF: $C_{11}H_{14}N_2S$ MW: 206.31   EINECS: 239-774-1
LD$_{50}$:   175 mg/kg (M, p.o.);
        170 mg/kg (R, p.o.);
        2 g/kg (dog, p.o.)
CN: (E)-1,4,5,6-tetrahydro-1-methyl-2-[2-(2-thienyl)ethenyl]pyrimidine

tartrate (1:1)
RN: 33401-94-4   MF: $C_{11}H_{14}N_2S \cdot C_4H_6O_6$ MW: 356.40   EINECS: 251-501-8
LD$_{50}$:   2220 µg/kg (M, i.v.); 123 mg/kg (M, p.o.);
        170 mg/kg (R, p.o.)
pamoate (1:1)
RN: 22204-24-6   MF: $C_{11}H_{14}N_2S \cdot C_{23}H_{16}O_6$ MW: 594.69   EINECS: 244-837-1
LD$_{50}$:   620 mg/kg (M, i.p.);
        535 mg/kg (R, i.p.)

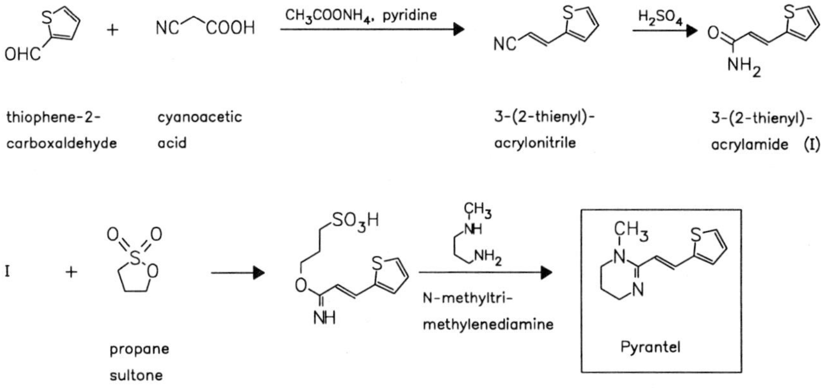

thiophene-2-   cyanoacetic   3-(2-thienyl)-   3-(2-thienyl)-
carboxaldehyde   acid   acrylonitrile   acrylamide (I)

propane
sultone

N-methyltri-
methylenediamine

Pyrantel

Reference(s):

BE 658 987 (Pfizer; appl. 28.1.1965; GB-prior. 28.1.1964, 13.8.1964, 26.9.1964).
US 3 502 661 (Pfizer; 24.3.1970; prior. 14.2.1967, 5.6.1967, 9.11.1967).
CH 404 677 (Dr. A. Wander; appl. 2.12.1960).
CH 398 620 (Dr. A. Wander; appl. 16.8.1960).
GD 980 853 (Dr. A. Wander; appl. 16.8.1961; CH-prior. 16.8.1960, 2.12.1960).
NL 147 426 (Dr. A. Wander; appl. 24.5.1963; CH-prior. 25.5.1962, 8.6.1962, 5.12.1962, 15.2.1963).
DE 1 280 879 (Wander; appl. 7.8.1961; CH-prior. 16.8.1960, 2.12.1960).
US 3 539 573 (Wander; 10.11.1970; CH-prior. 16.8.1960, 2.12.1960, 20.7.1961, 25.5.1962, 5.12.1962, 15.2.1963, 22.3.1967, 11.7.1967, 3.11.1967).
Hunziker, F. et al.: Helv. Chim. Acta (HCACAV) **50**, 1588 (1967).

Formulation(s):   chewing tabl. 250 mg; sol. 5 %; susp. 250 mg/5 ml, 720 mg; tabl. 125 mg, 250 mg (as pamoate)

USA: Antiminth (Pfizer); wfm Antiminth (Roerig); wfm Combantrin (Pfizer); wfm

Pyrazinamide

ATC: J04AK01
Use: tuberculostatic, antibacterial

RN: 98-96-4 MF: $C_5H_5N_3O$ MW: 123.12 EINECS: 202-717-6
LD_{50}: 1680 mg/kg (M, i.p.); 2793 mg/kg (M, s.c.)
CN: pyrazinecarboxamide

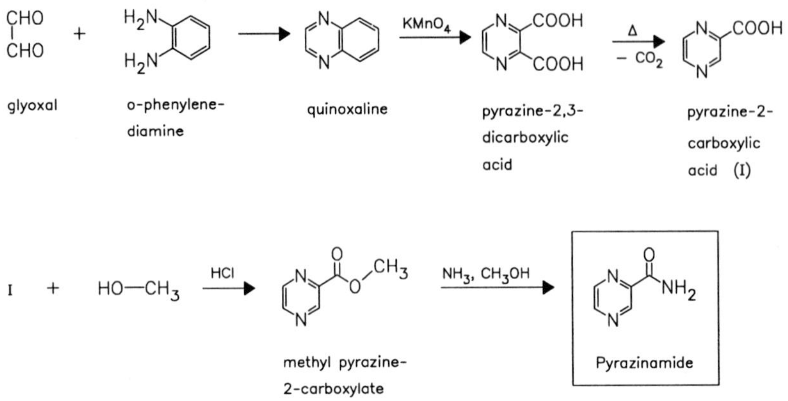

Reference(s):
DRP 632 257 (Merck; 1934).
Hall, S.A. et al.: J. Am. Chem. Soc. (JACSAT) **62**, 664 (1940).

alternative synthesis via 2-cyanopyrazine (*from* 2-chloropyrazine):
EP 122 355 (Servipharm; appl. 25.7.1983; CH-prior. 21.3.1983).

Formulation(s): cps. 500 mg; drg. 300 mg in comb. with rifapiam, isoniazide; f. c. tabl. 500 mg; tabl. 100 mg, 500 mg

Trade Name(s):

D:	Pyrafat (Fatol) Pyrazinamid (Hefa Pharma) Pyrazinamid "Lederle" (Lederle) Rifater (Grünenthal)-comb.	F:	Pirilène (Marion Merrell) Rifater (Marion Merrell)-comb.	I:	Piraldina (Bracco)
		GB:	Rifater (Hoechst)-comb. Zinamide (Merck Sharp & Dohme)	J:	Pyramide (Sankyo)
				USA:	Rifater (Hoechst Marion Merrell)-comb. generics

Pyridinol carbamate
(Pyricarbate)

ATC: C04AX49
Use: antiarteriosclerotic

RN: 1882-26-4 MF: $C_{11}H_{15}N_3O_4$ MW: 253.26 EINECS: 217-538-9
LD_{50}: 3100 mg/kg (M, p.o.);
1230 mg/kg (R, p.o.);
1 g/kg (dog, p.o.)
CN: 2,6-pyridinedimethanol bis(methylcarbamate)

starting product:

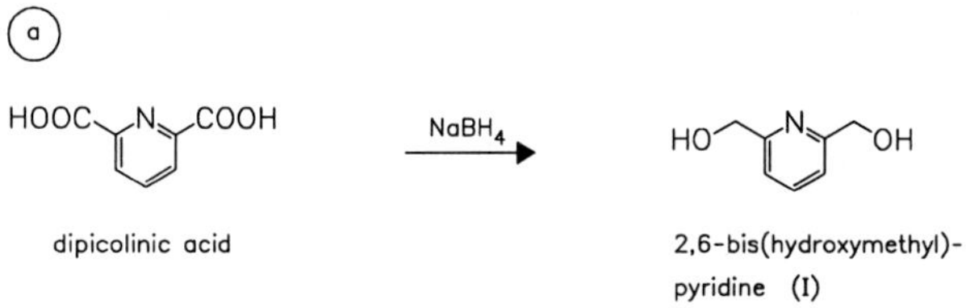

a

dipicolinic acid

2,6-bis(hydroxymethyl)-
pyridine (I)

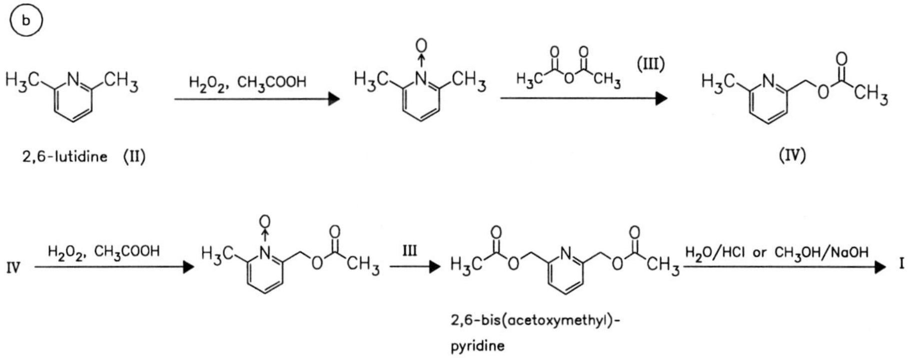

b

2,6-lutidine (II)

(IV)

2,6-bis(acetoxymethyl)-
pyridine

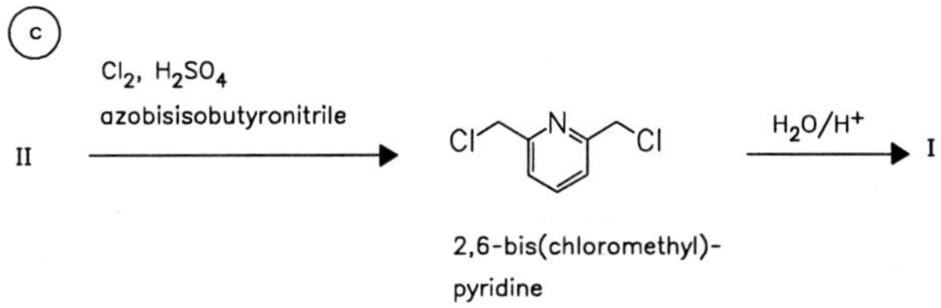

c

2,6-bis(chloromethyl)-
pyridine

final product:

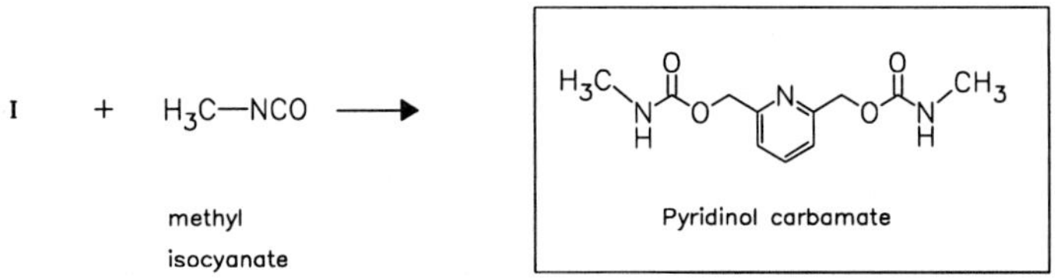

I + H₃C—NCO ⟶

methyl
isocyanate

Pyridinol carbamate

Reference(s):
FR 1 396 624 (M. Inoue; appl. 13.4.1964; J-prior. 13.4.1963).
AT 258 953 (M. Inoue; appl. 13.4.1964; J-prior. 13.4.1963).
AT 258 954 (M. Inoue; appl. 13.4.1964; J-prior. 13.4.1963).
AT 258 955 (M. Inoue; appl. 8.11.1965).

alternative syntheses [*from* 2,6-bis(hydroxymethyl)pyridine *and* N,N'-dimethylurea]:
DOS 2 263 812 (Rocador S. A.; appl. 28.12.1972; E-prior. 28.12.1971).

γ₁- *and* γ₂-*modifications:*
DOS 2 702 772 (Richter Gedeon; appl. 24.1.1977; H-prior. 24.1.1976).
GB 1 548 334 (Richter Gedeon; appl. 21.1.1977; H-prior. 24.1.1976).

2,6-bis(hydroxymethyl)pyridine:
a   FR 1 396 624 (M. Inoue; appl. 13.4.1964; J-prior. 13.4.1963).
b   Bockelheide, V.; Linn, W.J.: J. Am. Chem. Soc. (JACSAT) **76**, 1286 (1954).
c   FR 1 394 362 (Merck & Co.; appl. 31.3.1964; USA-prior. 2.4.1963).

alternative syntheses:
DAS 2 460 039 (Richter Gedeon; appl. 19.12.1974; H-prior. 29.12.1973).
DAS 2 614 400 (Richter Gedeon; appl. 2.4.1976; H-prior. 2.4.1975).

Formulation(s):   tabl. 250 mg

Trade Name(s):
F: Angioxine (Roussel); wfm   I: Cicloven (AGIPS)   J: Anginin (Banyu)

Pyridofylline

ATC: C01D
Use: coronary vasodilator

RN: 53403-97-7   MF: $C_9H_{12}N_4O_6S \cdot C_8H_{11}NO_3$ MW: 473.46   EINECS: 258-521-6
LD$_{50}$:   1 g/kg (M, i.v.); 1600 mg/kg (M, p.o.)
CN: 3,7-dihydro-1,3-dimethyl-7-[2-(sulfooxy)ethyl]-1H-purine-2,6-dione compd. with 5-hydroxy-6-methyl-3,4-pyridinedimethanol (1:1)

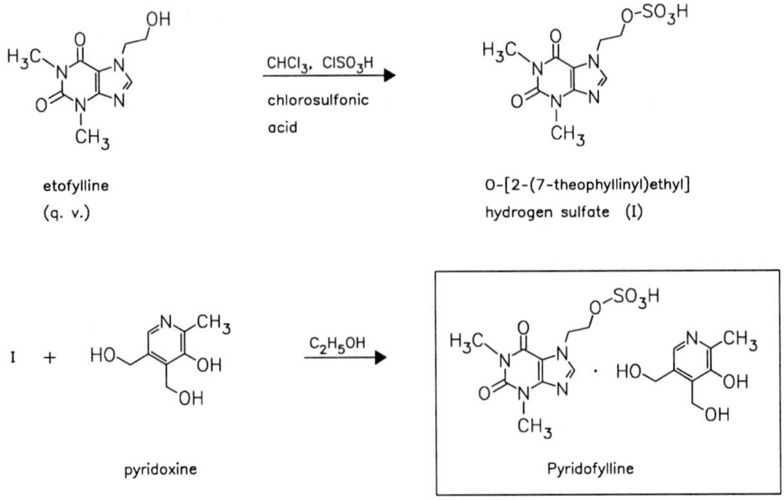

etofylline
(q. v.)

O-[2-(7-theophyllinyl)ethyl]
hydrogen sulfate (I)

pyridoxine

Pyridofylline

Reference(s):
FR-M 828 (J. Debarge; appl. 23.12.1960).

Trade Name(s):
F: Atherophylline (Merrell);
      wfm

Pyridostigmine bromide

ATC: N07AA02
Use: parasympathomimetic (cholinesterase blocker), antimyasthenic, vagotonic

RN: 101-26-8   MF: $C_9H_{13}BrN_2O_2$ MW: 261.12   EINECS: 202-929-9
LD$_{50}$:   1500 µg/kg (M, i.v.); 16 mg/kg (M, p.o.)
CN: 3-[[(dimethylamino)carbonyl]oxy]-1-methylpyridinium bromide

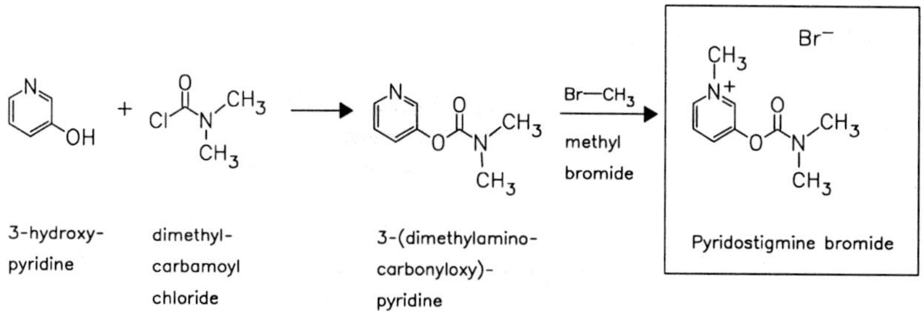
Br—CH3
methyl
bromide
Br−
3-hydroxy-
pyridine
dimethyl-
carbamoyl
chloride
3-(dimethylamino-
carbonyloxy)-
pyridine
Pyridostigmine bromide

Reference(s):
CH 246 834 (Roche; appl. 1945).
US 2 572 579 (Roche; 1951; CH-prior. 1945).

Formulation(s): amp. 1 mg/ml, 5 mg/ml; drg. 60 mg; s. r. tabl. 180 mg; syrup 60 mg/5 ml; tabl. 60 mg

Trade Name(s):

D:	Kalymin (ASTA Medica AWD)	F:	Mestinon (Roche)	J:	Mestinon (Nippon Roche)
	Mestinon (ICN)	GB:	Mestinon (Roche)	USA:	Mestinon (ICN)
		I:	Mestinon (Roche)		Regonol (Organon)

Pyridoxine
(Vitamin B_6)

ATC: A11HA02
Use: vitamin (enzym co-factor)

RN: 65-23-6 MF: $C_8H_{11}NO_3$ MW: 169.18 EINECS: 200-603-0
LD_{50}: 545 mg/kg (M, i.v.);
657 mg/kg (R, i.v.); 4 g/kg (R, p.o.)
CN: 5-hydroxy-6-methyl-3,4-pyridinedimethanol

hydrochloride
RN: 58-56-0 MF: $C_8H_{11}NO_3 \cdot HCl$ MW: 205.64 EINECS: 200-386-2
LD_{50}: 660 mg/kg (M, i.v.); 5500 mg/kg (M, p.o.);
530 mg/kg (R, i.v.); 4 g/kg (R, p.o.);
>500 mg/kg (dog, p.o.)

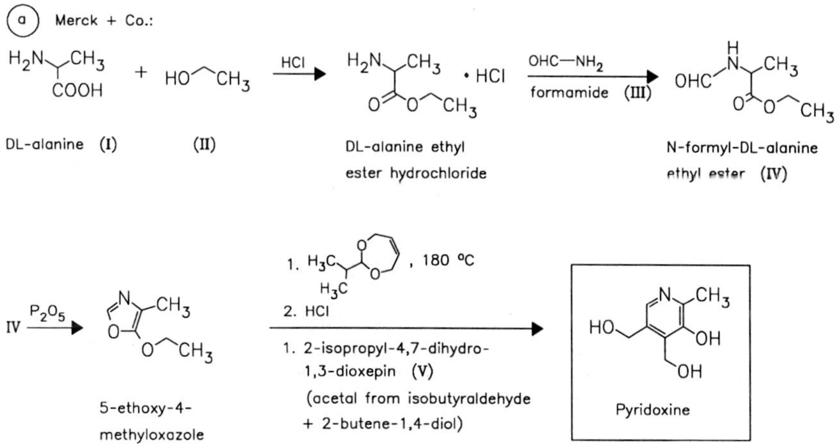
a
Merck + Co.:
HCl
OHC—NH2
formamide (III)
DL-alanine (I)
(II)
DL-alanine ethyl
ester hydrochloride
N-formyl-DL-alanine
ethyl ester (IV)
IV
P2O5
1. , 180 °C
2. HCl
5-ethoxy-4-
methyloxazole
1. 2-isopropyl-4,7-dihydro-
1,3-dioxepin (V)
(acetal from isobutyraldehyde
+ 2-butene-1,4-diol)
Pyridoxine

b   Roche:

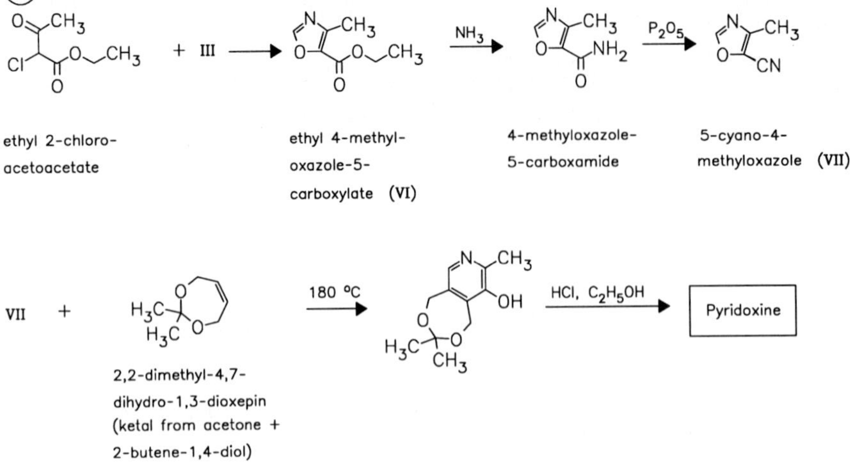

ethyl 2-chloro-
acetoacetate

+ III ⟶

ethyl 4-methyl-
oxazole-5-
carboxylate (VI)

NH₃ ⟶

4-methyloxazole-
5-carboxamide

P₂O₅ ⟶

5-cyano-4-
methyloxazole (VII)

VII   +

H₃C
H₃C

2,2-dimethyl-4,7-
dihydro-1,3-dioxepin
(ketal from acetone +
2-butene-1,4-diol)

180 °C ⟶

HCl, C₂H₅OH ⟶   Pyridoxine

c   BASF:

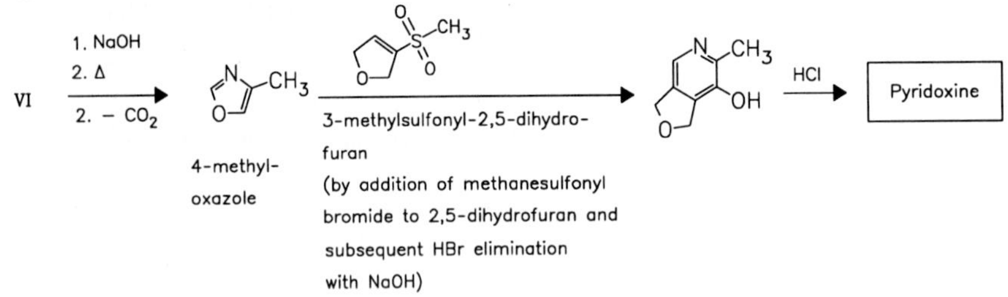

VI

1. NaOH
2. Δ
2. − CO₂
⟶

4-methyl-
oxazole

3-methylsulfonyl-2,5-dihydro-
furan
(by addition of methanesulfonyl
bromide to 2,5-dihydrofuran and
subsequent HBr elimination
with NaOH)

⟶

HCl ⟶   Pyridoxine

d

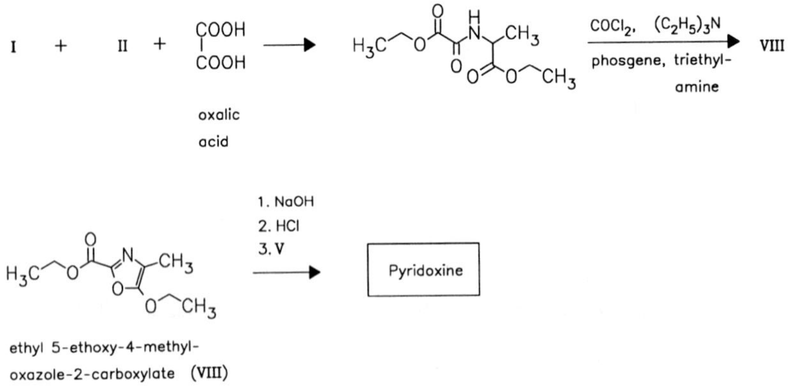

I   +   II   +

COOH
COOH

oxalic
acid

⟶

COCl₂, (C₂H₅)₃N ⟶   VIII
phosgene, triethyl-
amine

H₃C

ethyl 5-ethoxy-4-methyl-
oxazole-2-carboxylate (VIII)

1. NaOH
2. HCl
3. V
⟶

Pyridoxine

Reference(s):
review of pyridoxine syntheses:
König, H.; Böll, W.: Chem.-Ztg. (CMKZAT) **100**, 105 (1976).
a   Harris, E.E. et al.: J. Org. Chem. (JOCEAH) **27**, 2705 (1962).
     DAS 1 470 022 (Merck & Co.; appl. 10.5.1962; USA-prior. 15.5.1961, 16.1.1962).
     US 3 227 721 (Merck & Co.; 4.1.1966; prior. 15.5.1961, 16.1.1962, 24.5.1965).
     US 3 227 724 (Merck & Co.; 4.1.1966; prior. 15.5.1961, 16.1.1962, 16.6.1964).
b   US 3 222 374 (Roche; 7.12.1965; prior. 22.5.1963, 20.11.1964).
     US 3 250 778 (Roche; 10.5.1966; appl. 29.11.1962).
     US 4 026 901 (Roche; 31.5.1977; appl. 30.4.1975).
     DOS 2 616 349 (Roche; appl. 14.4.1976; USA-prior. 30.4.1975).
     5-cyano-4-methyloxazole:
     US 4 093 654 (Roche; 6.6.1978; appl. 31.3.1977).
c   DAS 2 143 989 (BASF; appl. 2.9.1971).
     3-methylsulfonyl-2,5-dihydrofuran:
     DOS 2 435 098 (BASF; 22.7.1974).
d   Maeda, J. et al.: Bull. Chem. Soc. Jpn. (BCSJA8) **42**, 1435 (1969).

alternative syntheses:
from 5-ethoxy-4-oxazolylacetic acid:
DAS 2 008 854 (Roche; appl. 25.2.1970; CH-prior. 25.3.1969).

4-methyloxazol *from formimino ester hydrochloride and* hydroxyacetone:
GB 1 515 737 (BASF; appl. 22.10.1975; D-prior. 31.10.1974).

Formulation(s):   amp. 25 mg/2 ml, 50 mg/2 ml, 100 mg/2 ml, 300 mg; drg. 100 mg, 300 mg; f. c. tabl. 40 mg; tabl. 1 mg, 25 mg, 40 mg, 50 mg, 100 mg, 300 mg (as hydrochloride)

Trade Name(s):

D: B$_6$-ASmedic (Dyckerhoff)
      B$_6$-Vicotrat (Heyl)
      BYK (Roche Nicholas)-comb.
      Bonasanit (Weimer)
      Hexobion (Merck)
      Vitamin B$_6$ ratiopharm (ratiopharm)
      generics and circa 500 combination preparations
F: Becilan (Specia)
      Dermo-6 (Pharmadéveloppement)
      Pyridoxine Aguettant (Aguettant)
      Vitamine B$_6$ Richard (Richard)
      numerous combination preparations
GB: Comploment Continus (Napp); wfm
      numerous combination preparations
I: Acutil Fosforo (SmithKline Beecham)
      Adenoplex (Lepetit)-comb.

Alcalosio (SIT)-comb.
Antemesyl (Molteni)-comb.
Antimicotico pom. derm. (IFI)-comb.
Benadon (Roche)
Benexol (Roche)-comb.
Coxanturenasi (Teofarma)-comb.
Detoxergon (Baldacci)-comb.
Dobetin (Angelini)-comb.
Emoferrina B$_{12}$ os (Piam)-comb.
Etanicozid (Piam)-comb.
Furanvit (SIFI)-comb.
Memosprint (Poli)-comb.
Menalgon (Menarini)-comb.
Miazide B$_6$ (Wyeth-Lederle)-comb.
Midium (Glaxo)-comb.
Mionevrasi forte (Boehringer Mannh.)-comb.

Neogeynevral (Geymonat)-comb.
Neuraben (Bioindustria)-comb.
Neurobionta (Bracco)-comb.
Sustenium (Menarini)-comb.
Triferon (Salus)-comb.
Trinevrina B$_6$ (Guidotti)-comb.
Xanturenasi (Teofarma)

J: Aderoxin (Sonybod-Torii)
      Pyridomin (Showa)
      Sandoxin (Sanko)
      numerous combination preparations
USA: Aminoxin (Tyson)
      Beelith (Beach)-comb.
      Lurline (Fielding)-comb.
      Marlyn Formula 50 (Marlyn)-comb.
      Mega-B (Arco)-comb.

Pyrimethamine

ATC: P01BD01
Use: chemotherapeutic (toxoplasmosis and malaria), antimalarial

RN: 58-14-0   MF: $C_{12}H_{13}ClN_4$ MW: 248.72   EINECS: 200-364-2
LD_{50}:   92 mg/kg (M, p.o.);
       440 mg/kg (R, p.o.)
CN: 5-(4-chlorophenyl)-6-ethyl-2,4-pyrimidinediamine

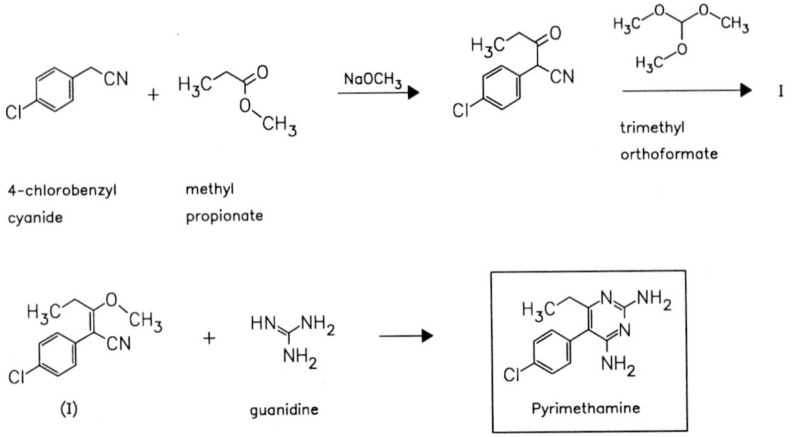

4-chlorobenzyl   methyl
cyanide   propionate

(I)   guanidine   Pyrimethamine

Reference(s):
US 2 576 939 (Burroughs Wellcome; 1951; prior. 1950).
US 2 602 794 (Burroughs Wellcome; 1952; appl. 1950).
US 2 680 740 (Rhône-Poulenc; 1954; F-prior. 1951).

Formulation(s):   tabl. 25 mg

Trade Name(s):
D: Daraprim (Glaxo
      Wellcome)
      Pyrimethamin-Heyl (Heyl)
F: Fansidar (Roche)-comb.
      Malocide (Specia)
GB: Daraprim (Burroughs
      Wellcome)

      Fansidar (Roche)-comb.
      Maloprim (Wellcome)-
      comb.
I: Metakelfin (Pharmacia &
      Upjohn)-comb.
J: Fansidar (Roche)-comb.

USA: Daraprim (Glaxo
      Wellcome)
      Fansidar (Roche)-comb.
      with sulfadioxine

Pyrithione zinc
(Zinc pyrithione)

ATC: D11AX
Use: antiseborrhoic, fungicide, bactericide

RN: 13463-41-7   MF: $C_{10}H_8N_2O_2S_2Zn$ MW: 317.71   EINECS: 236-671-3
LD_{50}:   160 mg/kg (M, p.o.);
       177 mg/kg (R, p.o.);
       600 mg/kg (dog, p.o.)
CN: (T-4)-bis(1-hydroxy-2(1H)-pyridinethionato-O,S)zinc

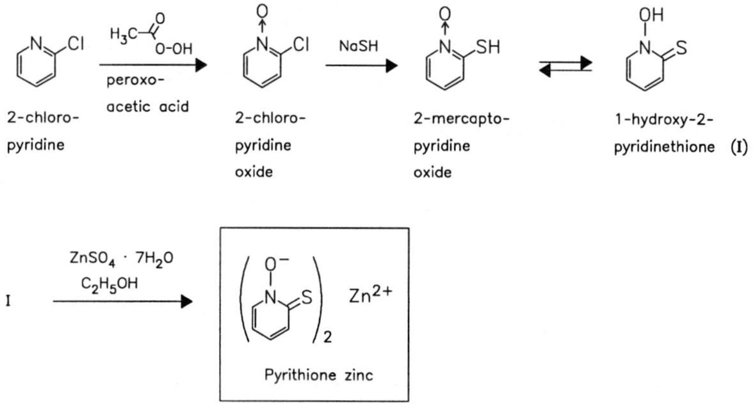

2-chloro-pyridine → 2-chloro-pyridine oxide → 2-mercapto-pyridine oxide ⇌ 1-hydroxy-2-pyridinethione (I)

Pyrithione zinc

Reference(s):
GB 761 171 (Olin Mathieson; appl. 19.5.1954; USA-prior. 29.5.1953).

pyrithione:
US 2 745 826 (Olin Mathieson; 15.5.1956; appl. 16.12.1953).
Shaw, E. et al.: J. Am. Chem. Soc. (JACSAT) **72**, 4362 (1950).

use:
US 3 236 733 (Procter & Gamble; 22.2.1966; prior. 5.9.1963, 1.4.1965).
US 3 281 366 (Procter & Gamble; 25.10.1966; prior. 25.8.1964, 4.11.1965).

Formulation(s): cream 1 g/100 g; shampoo 1 %, 2 %

Trade Name(s):
D:	de-squaman hermal (Hermal)		Ultrex antipelliculaire (Lab. Pharmaeurop); wfm
F:	Fonderma (Doms); wfm	GB:	Polystar AF (Stiefel)-comb.
		J:	Merit (Kao)

USA: DHS Zinc (Person & Covey)
Head & Shoulders (Procter & Gamble)

Pyrithyldione

ATC: N05CE03
Use: hypnotic, sedative

RN: 77-04-3 MF: $C_9H_{13}NO_2$ MW: 167.21 EINECS: 201-000-5
LD_{50}: 780 mg/kg (R, p.o.)
CN: 3,3-diethyl-2,4(1H,3H)-pyridinedione

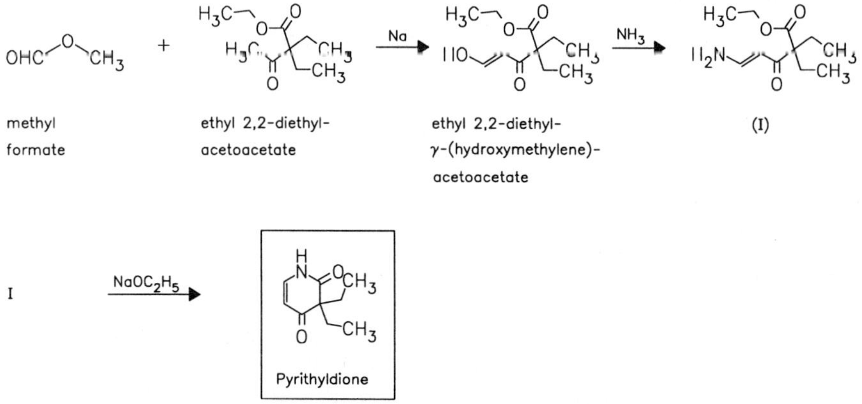

methyl formate + ethyl 2,2-diethyl-acetoacetate → ethyl 2,2-diethyl-γ-(hydroxymethylene)-acetoacetate → (I)

I → Pyrithyldione

Reference(s):
US 2 090 068 (Hoffmann-La Roche; 1937; D-prior. 1935).

Trade Name(s):

D:	Persedon Roche (Roche);	I:	Hibersulfan (Ecobi)-comb.;
	wfm		wfm

Pyritinol
(Pyrithioxine)

ATC: N06BX02
Use: neurotropic, nootropic

RN: 1098-97-1   MF: $C_{16}H_{20}N_2O_4S_2$ MW: 368.48   EINECS: 214-150-1
CN: 3,3'-[dithiobis(methylene)]bis[5-hydroxy-6-methyl-4-pyridinemethanol]

dihydrochloride monohydrate
RN: 10049-83-9   MF: $C_{16}H_{20}N_2O_4S_2 \cdot 2HCl \cdot H_2O$ MW: 459.42   EINECS: 233-178-5
LD_{50}:   221 mg/kg (M, i.v.); 5786 mg/kg (M, p.o.);
   300 mg/kg (R, i.v.); 6 g/kg (R, p.o.)

3,4-bis(bromomethyl)-
5-hydroxy-6-methyl-
pyridine hydrobromide
(from pyridoxine)

potassium ethyl-
xanthogenate

(I)

Pyritinol

Reference(s):
US 3 010 966 (E. Merck AG; 28.11.1961; D-prior. 21.3.1958).
DE 1 135 460 (E. Merck AG; appl. 21.3.1958).
DE 1 197 455 (E. Merck AG; appl. 27.8.1960).

alternative syntheses:
DAS 1 210 429 (E. Merck AG; appl. 3.8.1963).
DE 1 222 062 (E. Merck AG; appl. 8.2.1964).
DE 1 227 908 (E. Merck AG; appl. 8.2.1964).
DOS 1 695 402 (E. Merck AG; appl. 25.3.1967).

Formulation(s):   amp. 200 mg; drg. 100 mg, 200 mg; susp. 80.5 mg/5 ml, 100 mg; syrup 100 mg (as
   hydrochloride)

Trade Name(s):

D:	Ardeyceryl P	F:	Biontabol (Merck-	I:	Encefabol (Bracco)
	(Ardeypharm)		Clévenot)-comb.; wfm	J:	Chioebon (Kyowa
	Encephabol (Merck)		Encéphabol (Merck-		Yakuhin)
			Clévenot); wfm		Divalvon (Nippon Kayaku)

Enbol (Merck-Chugai)   Neuroxin (Yamanouchi)
Neurotin (Nakataki)   Piritiomin (Hishiyama)

Pyrovalerone

ATC: N06BA
Use: central stimulant

RN: 3563-49-3   MF: $C_{16}H_{23}NO$ MW: 245.37
CN: 1-(4-methylphenyl)-2-(1-pyrrolidinyl)-1-pentanone

hydrochloride
RN: 1147-62-2   MF: $C_{16}H_{23}NO \cdot HCl$ MW: 281.83   EINECS: 214-556-9
LD_{50}:   43 mg/kg (M, i.v.); 350 mg/kg (M, p.o.);
        47 mg/kg (R, i.v.); 620 mg/kg (R, p.o.)

4'-methylvalerophenone   2-bromo-4'-methyl-   Pyrovalerone
                              valerophenone

Reference(s):
GB 933 507 (Thomae; appl. 4.4.1961; D-prior. 7.4.1960).
GB 927 475 (Dr. A. Wander; appl. 18.5.1961; CH-prior. 24.5.1960).

Formulation(s):   cps. 20 mg

Trade Name(s):
F: Thymergix (Joullié); wfm

Pyrrobutamine

ATC: R06AX08
Use: antihistaminic

RN: 91-82-7   MF: $C_{20}H_{22}ClN$ MW: 311.86   EINECS: 202-101-7
CN: 1-[4-(4-chlorophenyl)-3-phenyl-2-butenyl]pyrrolidine

phosphate (1:2)
RN: 135-31-9   MF: $C_{20}H_{22}ClN \cdot 2H_3O_4P$ MW: 507.84   EINECS: 205-185-3
LD_{50}:   54 mg/kg (M, i.v.); 1116 mg/kg (M, p.o.)

acetophenone   paraform-   pyrrolidine   3-pyrrolidino-
                    aldehyde   propiophenone (I)

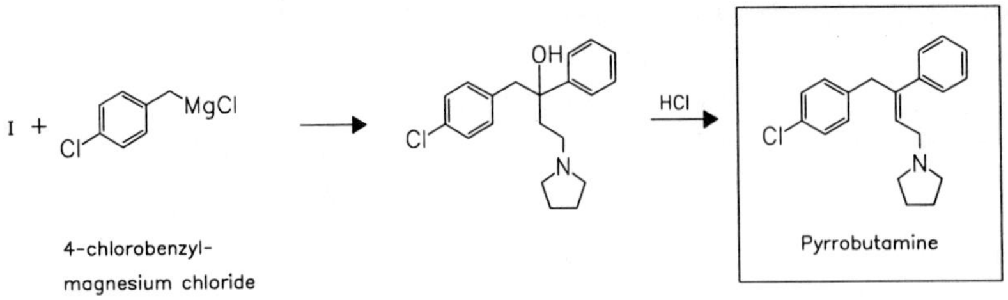

4-chlorobenzyl-
magnesium chloride

Pyrrobutamine

Reference(s):
US 2 655 509 (Eli Lilly; 1953; prior. 1951).

Formulation(s):   tabl. 15 mg

Trade Name(s):
D: Copyronilum (Lilly)-
      comb.; wfm
GB: Co-Pyronil (Lilly)-comb.;
      wfm

USA: Co-Pyronil (Dista)-comb.;
      wfm
      Co-Pyronil (Lilly)-comb.;
      wfm

Pyrrocaine

ATC: N01BB
Use: local anesthetic

RN: 2210-77-7   MF: $C_{14}H_{20}N_2O$ MW: 232.33
CN: N-(2,6-dimethylphenyl)-1-pyrrolidineacetamide

monohydrochloride
RN: 2210-64-2   MF: $C_{14}H_{20}N_2O \cdot HCl$ MW: 268.79   EINECS: 218-642-7

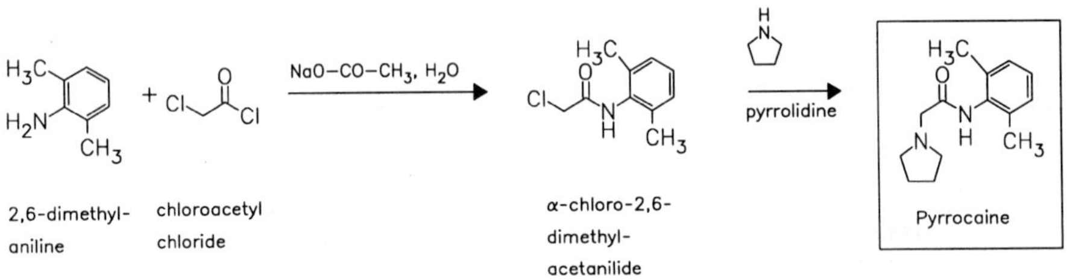

2,6-dimethyl-   chloroacetyl
aniline   chloride

α-chloro-2,6-
dimethyl-
acetanilide

Pyrrocaine

Reference(s):
Löfgren, N. et al.: Acta Chem. Scand. (ACHSE7) **11**, 1724 (1957).

Formulation(s):   vial 2 %

Trade Name(s):
USA: Dynacaine (Graham); wfm

Endocaine (Endo); wfm

Pyrrolnitrin

ATC: D01AA07
Use: antibiotic, antifungal

RN: 1018-71-9   MF: $C_{10}H_6Cl_2N_2O_2$ MW: 257.08   EINECS: 213-812-7
LD_{50}:   1 g/kg (M, p.o.);
        >2 g/kg (R, p.o.)
CN: 3-chloro-4-(3-chloro-2-nitrophenyl)-1H-pyrrole

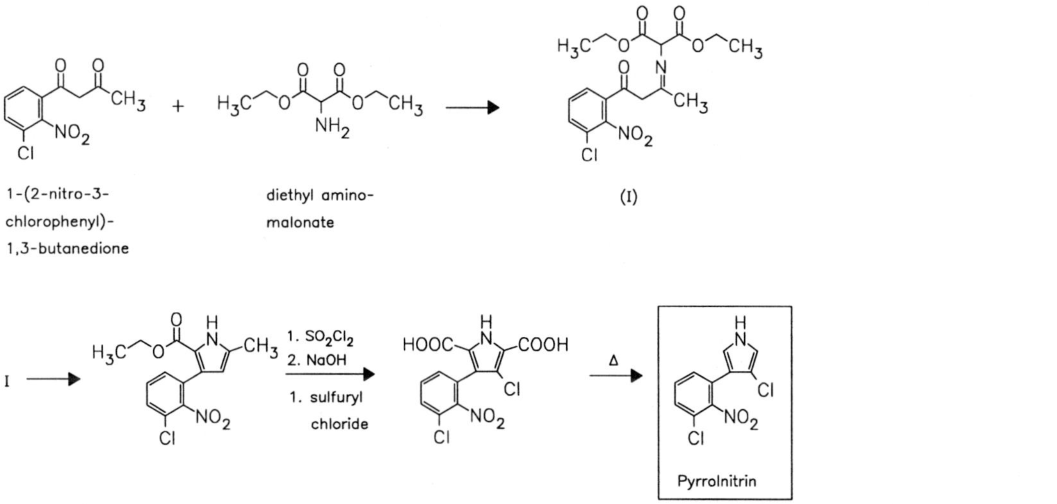

1-(2-nitro-3-
chlorophenyl)-
1,3-butanedione

diethyl amino-
malonate

(I)

1. SO₂Cl₂
2. NaOH

1. sulfuryl
   chloride

Δ

Pyrrolnitrin

Reference(s):
US 3 428 648 (Fujisawa; 18.2.1969; J-prior. 8.4.1965, 2.2.1965, 4.12.1964, 7.12.1964, 22.10.1964, 12.10.1964).
Nakano, H. et al.: Tetrahedron Lett. (TELEAY) **1966**, 737 (also further methods).

isolation from Pseudomonas:
Arina, K. et al.: Agric. Biol. Chem. (ABCHA6) **28**, 575 (1964).

Formulation(s):   cream 1 %

Trade Name(s):
D: Antimycoticum Klinger   Micutrin Beta (Monsanto)-
       (Dr. Klinger)-comb.; wfm   comb.
I: Micutrin (Monsanto)   J: Pyroace (Fujisawa)

Pyrvinium embonate
(Pyrvinium pamoate)

ATC: P02CX01
Use: anthelmintic

RN: 3546-41-6   MF: $C_{26}H_{28}N_3 \cdot 1/2C_{23}H_{14}O_6$ MW: 1151.42   EINECS: 222-596-3
LD$_{50}$:   200 mg/kg (M, s.c.)
CN: 6-(dimethylamino)-2-[2-(2,5-dimethyl-1-phenyl-1*H*-pyrrol-3-yl)ethenyl]-1-methylquinolinium 4,4'-
        methylenebis[3-hydroxy-2-naphthalenecarboxylate] (2:1)

chloride
RN: 548-84-5   MF: $C_{26}H_{28}ClN_3$ MW: 417.98

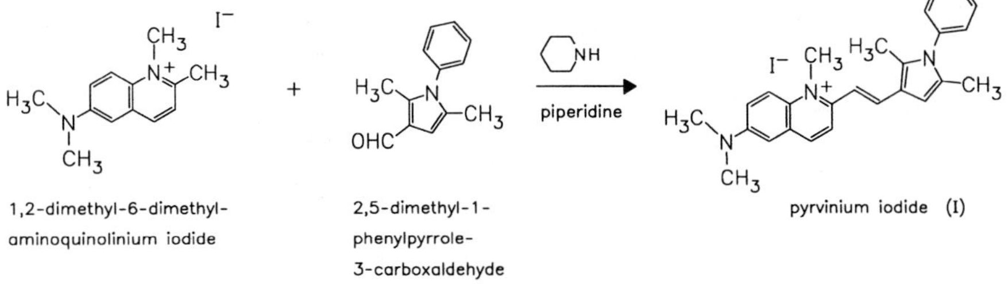

1,2-dimethyl-6-dimethyl-
aminoquinolinium iodide

2,5-dimethyl-1-
phenylpyrrole-
3-carboxaldehyde

piperidine

pyrvinium iodide   (I)

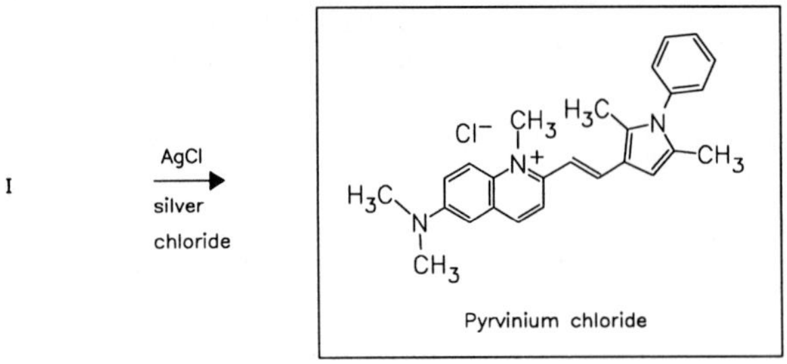

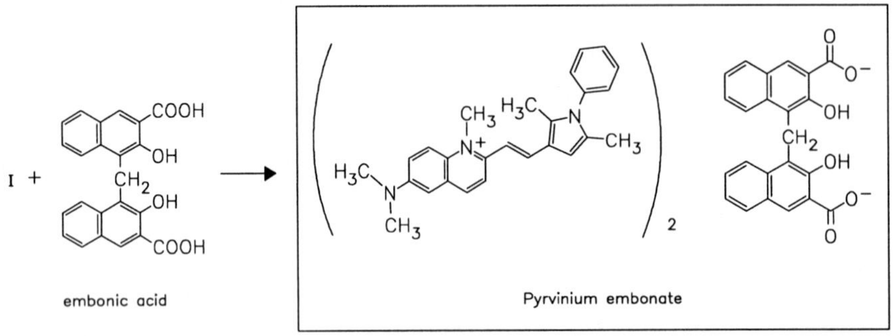

Pyrvinium chloride

embonic acid　　　　Pyrvinium embonate

Reference(s):

pyrvinium iodide *and* chloride:
US 2 515 912 (Eastman Kodak; 1950; prior. 1946).

pyrvinium embonate:
US 2 925 417 (Parke Davis; 16.2.1960; prior. 6.11.1957).

Formulation(s):　　drg. 75.25 mg; susp.75.25 mg/5 ml

Trade Name(s):
D:　　Molevac (Parke Davis)　　F:　Povanyl (Warner-Lambert)　J:　Poquil (Parke Davis-
　　　Pyrcen (Krewel　　　　　　I:　Vanquin (Parke Davis)　　　　Sankyo)
　　　Meuselbach)　　　　　　　　　　　　　　　　　　　　USA:　Povan (Parke Davis); wfm

Quazepam
(Sch-16134)

ATC: N05CD10
Use: benzodiazepine hypnotic

RN: 36735-22-5   MF: $C_{17}H_{11}ClF_4N_2S$ MW: 386.80   EINECS: 253-179-4
LD$_{50}$: 845 mg/kg (M, i.p.); >1370 mg/kg (M, i.v.); >5000 mg/kg (M, p.o.);
2749 mg/kg (R, i.p.); >5 g/kg (R, p.o.)
CN: 7-chloro-5-(2-fluorophenyl)-1,3-dihydro-1-(2,2,2-trifluoroethyl)-2H-1,4-benzodiazepine-2-thione

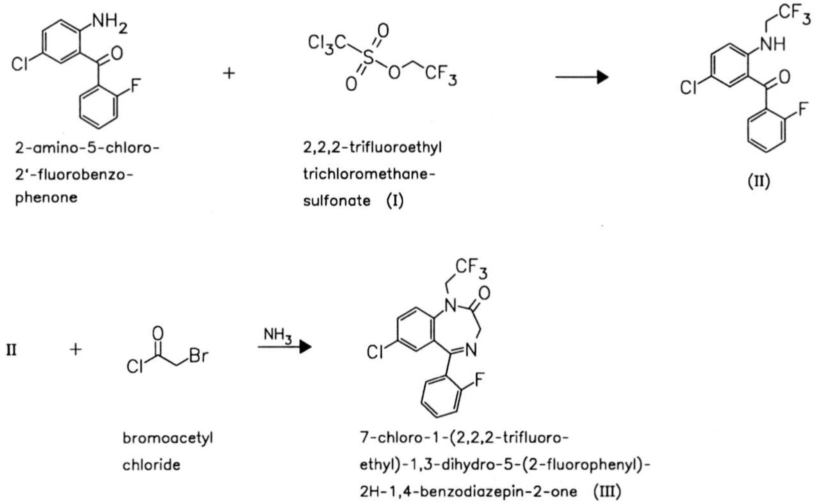

2-amino-5-chloro-
2'-fluorobenzo-
phenone

2,2,2-trifluoroethyl
trichloromethane-
sulfonate (I)

(II)

II + bromoacetyl chloride

NH$_3$

7-chloro-1-(2,2,2-trifluoro-
ethyl)-1,3-dihydro-5-(2-fluorophenyl)-
2H-1,4-benzodiazepin-2-one (III)

4-chloro-
aniline

4-chloro-N-(2,2,2-
trifluoroethyl)-
aniline

aziridine

(IV)

IV + 2-fluoro-
benzoyl
chloride

P$_2$O$_5$, POCl$_3$

7-chloro-1-(2,2,2-trifluoro-
ethyl)-2,3-dihydro-5-(2-fluoro-
phenyl)-1H-1,4-benzodiazepine

RuO$_4$
ruthenium
tetroxide

III

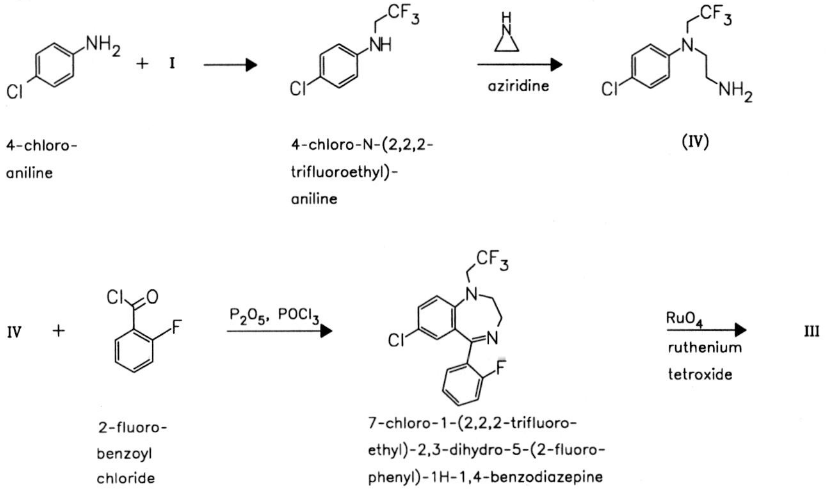

Quazepam

III →(P₂S₅, dioxane)→ Quazepam

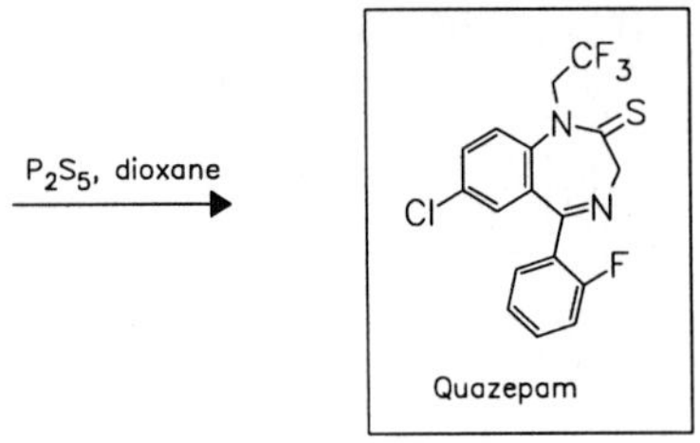

Reference(s):
US 3 845 039 (Schering Corp.; 29.10.1974; appl. 26.7.1972; prior. 7.8.1970).
US 3 920 818 (Schering Corp.; 18.11.1975; appl. 31.7.1974; prior. 26.7.1972, 24.1.1972, 7.8.1970).
DOS 2 138 773 (Scherico; appl. 3.8.1971; USA-prior. 7.8.1970).
Steinman, M. et al.: J. Med. Chem. (JMCMAR) **16**, 1354 (1973).

alternative synthesis:
DOS 2 106 175 (Scherico; appl. 10.2.1971; USA-prior. 13.2.1970).

Formulation(s):   tabl. 7.5 mg, 15 mg

Trade Name(s):
I: Quazium (Schering-   USA: Doral (Wallace)
      Plough; 1987)

Quetiapine fumarate
(ZD 5077; ZM 204636; ICI-204636)

ATC: N05AH04
Use: antipsychotic

RN: 111974-72-2 MF: $C_{21}H_{25}N_3O_2S \cdot 1/2C_4H_4O_4$ MW: 883.10
CN: 2-[2-(4-Dibenzo[b,f][1,4]thiazepin-11-yl-1-piperazinyl)ethoxy]ethanol fumarate (2:1)

base
RN: 111974-69-7 MF: $C_{21}H_{25}N_3O_2S$ MW: 383.52

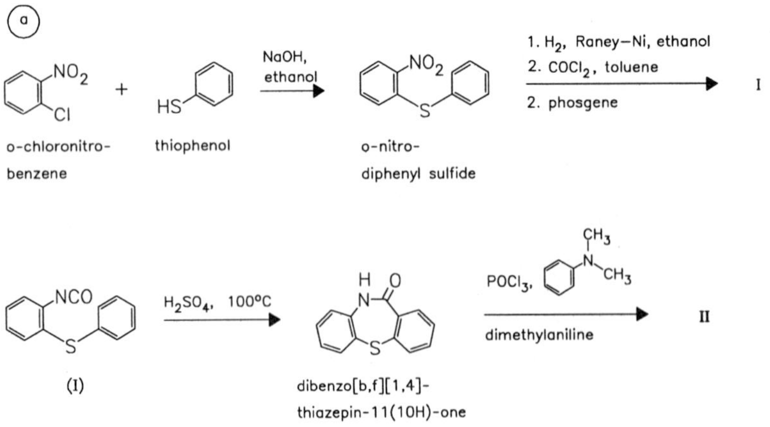

o-chloronitro-benzene + thiophenol →(NaOH, ethanol)→ o-nitro-diphenyl sulfide →(1. H₂, Raney–Ni, ethanol; 2. COCl₂, toluene; 2. phosgene)→ I

(I) →(H₂SO₄, 100°C)→ dibenzo[b,f][1,4]thiazepin-11(10H)-one →(POCl₃, dimethylaniline)→ II

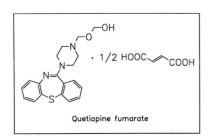

11-chlorodibenzo-
[b,f][1,4]thiazepine (II)

1-[2-(2-hydroxy-
ethoxy)ethyl]-
piperazine

1. NaOH, xylene, Δ
2. HOOC COOH (III),
   ethanol
2. fumaric acid

Quetiapine fumarate

· 1/2 HOOC COOH

Quetiapine fumarate

b

II + piperazine

toluene

11-piperazino-
dibenzo[b,f][1,4]-
thiazepine

1. Cl O OH ,
   Na₂CO₃, NaI, 1-propanol,
   O , Δ
2. III

Quetiapine fumarate

Reference(s):
a EP 240 228 (ICI; appl. 24.3.1987; GB-prior. 27.3.1986).
b EP 282 236 (ICI; appl. 4.3.1988; GB-prior. 10.3.1987).

synthesis of dibenzo[b,f][1,4]thiazepin-10(11H)-one:
Schmutze, J. et al.: Helv. Chim. Acta (HCACAV) **48**, 336 (1965).

sustained-release formulation:
WO 9 745 124 (Zeneca; appl. 27.5.1997; GB-prior. 31.5.1996).

pharmaceutical composition for treatment of psychoses:
EP 830 864 (Eli Lilly; appl. 22.9.1997; USA-prior. 23.9.1996).

Formulation(s):   tabl. 25 mg, 100 mg, 150 mg, 200 mg

Trade Name(s):
GB: Seroquel (Zeneca; 1997)   USA: Seroquel (Zeneca; 1997)

Quinagolide hydrochloride
(CV-205502; SDZ-205502)

ATC: G02CB04
Use: dopamine D$_2$-receptor agonist, antiparkinsonian, prolactin secretion inhibitor

RN: 94424-50-7   MF: C$_{20}$H$_{33}$N$_3$O$_3$S · HCl   MW: 432.03
CN: (3α,4aα,10aβ)-(±)-N,N-diethyl-N'-(1,2,3,4,4a,5,10,10a-octahydro-6-hydroxy-1-propylbenzo[g]quinolin-3-yl)sulfamide monohydrochloride

base (racemate)
RN: 87056-78-8   MF: C$_{20}$H$_{33}$N$_3$O$_3$S   MW: 395.57
all diastereomers
RN: 130793-78-1   MF: C$_{20}$H$_{33}$N$_3$O$_3$S · HCl   MW: 432.03
base (all diastereomers)
RN: 130793-77-0   MF: C$_{20}$H$_{33}$N$_3$O$_3$S   MW: 395.57
3β-diastereomers
RN: 132071-86-4   MF: C$_{20}$H$_{33}$N$_3$O$_3$S · HCl   MW: 432.03
base (3β-diastereomers)
RN: 132014-58-5   MF: C$_{20}$H$_{33}$N$_3$O$_3$S   MW: 395.57

5-methoxy-2-tetralone (I)   +   S-phenyl benzene-thiosulfonate

1. CH$_3$OH, NaOAc
2. n-BuLi, hexane, −70 °C
3. Br-CH$_2$ ... 2-bromomethyl-acrylate
2. butyllithium
3. tert-butyl

tert-butyl β-[1,2,3,4-tetrahydro-1,1-bis(phenyl-thio)-2-oxo-5-methoxy-3-naphthyl]-α-methylene-propionate (II)

II →

1. Al, Hg, THF
2. H$_2$N-O-CH$_3$ · HCl, Na$_2$HPO$_4$ · 2 H$_2$O, CH$_3$OH
3. NaBH$_3$CN, CH$_3$OH

(III)

III →

1. K$_2$HPO$_4$, cyclization
2. separation by HPLC

1. CF$_3$COOH
2. H$_2$C=N$_2$, Et$_2$O
3. Zn, CH$_3$COOH
→ IV

(IV) →

1. OHC-CH$_3$, CH$_3$CH$_2$CH$_2$OH
2. H$_2$, Pd–C
3. N$_2$H$_4$ · H$_2$O, CH$_3$OH
4. NOCl, −30 °C, THF

(V)

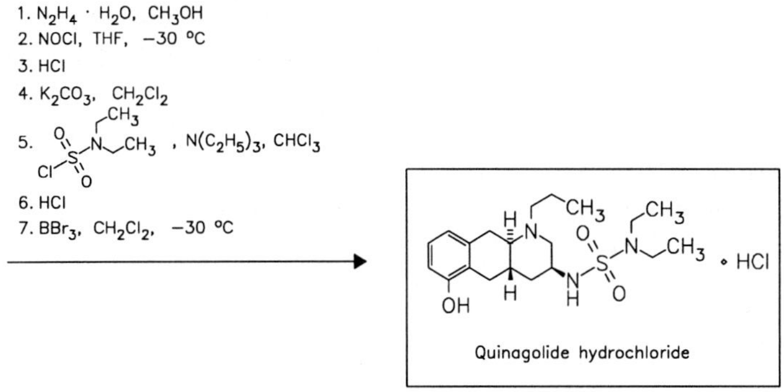

1. $N_2H_4 \cdot H_2O$, CH_3OH
2. NOCl, THF, $-30\ °C$
3. HCl
4. K_2CO_3, CH_2Cl_2
5. [structure], $N(C_2H_5)_3$, $CHCl_3$
6. HCl
7. BBr_3, CH_2Cl_2, $-30\ °C$

V   ⟶

Quinagolide hydrochloride

preparation of 5-methoxy-2-tetralone

H_3C—OH, H_2SO_4

or

H_3C-O-S(=O)(=O)-O-CH_3

1. Na, C_2H_5OH
2. HCl, H_2O

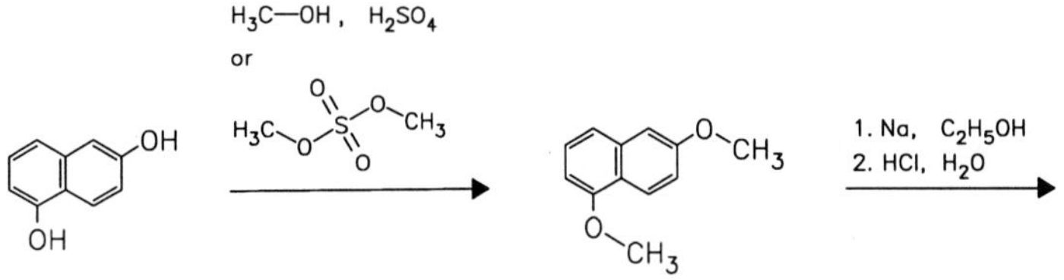

I

1,6-naphthalene-
diol

Reference(s):

EP 77 754 (Sandoz; appl. 27.4.1983; CH-prior. 16.10.1982, 25.6.1982).
US 4 565 818 (Sandoz; appl. 21.1.1986; CH-prior. 16.10.1981, 25.6.1982).

preparation of 5-methoxy-2-tetralone:
Abell, A.D. et al.: Aust. J. Chem. (AJCHAS) **51** (5), 398 (1998).
Copinga, S. et al.: J. Med. Chem. (JMCMAR) **36** (20), 2891 (1993).
Cornforth, Robinson: J. Chem. Soc. (JCSOA9) **1949** 1855, 1861.
Cornforth et al.: J. Chem. Soc. (JCSOA9) 689 (1942).

use for treatment of nicotine addiction:
FR 2 634 379 (Sandoz; appl. 26.1.1990; USA-prior. 22.7.1989).
WO 9 000 896 (Sandoz; appl. 8.2.1990; USA-prior. 22.7.1988).

use in cancer therapy:
EP 373 658 (Sandoz; appl. 20.6.1990; GB-prior. 16.12.1988).

Formulation(s):   tabl. (containing quinagolide hydrochloride base equivalent) 0.025 mg, 0.050 mg, 0.075 mg, 0.150 mg

Trade Name(s):
D: Norprolac (Novartis Pharma)
F: Norprolac (Novartis)
GB: Norprolac (Novartis)

Quinapril hydrochloride

ATC: C02EA; C09AA06
Use: non-sulfhydryl angiotensine
converting enzyme inhibitor,
antihypertensive

RN: 82586-55-8   MF: $C_{25}H_{30}N_2O_5 \cdot HCl$ MW: 474.99
LD$_{50}$:   504 mg/kg (M, i.v.); 1739 mg/kg (M, p.o.);
   107 mg/kg (Rf, i.v.); 158 mg/kg (Rm,i.v.); 3541 mg/kg (R, p.o.)
CN: [3S-[2[R*(R*)],3R*]]-2-[2-[[1-(ethoxycarbonyl)-3-phenylpropyl]amino]-1-oxopropyl]-1,2,3,4-tetrahydro-
3-isoquinolinecarboxylic acid monohydrochloride

monohydrate
RN: 90243-99-5   MF: $C_{25}H_{30}N_2O_5 \cdot HCl \cdot H_2O$ MW: 493.00
quinapril
RN: 85441-61-8   MF: $C_{25}H_{30}N_2O_5$ MW: 438.52

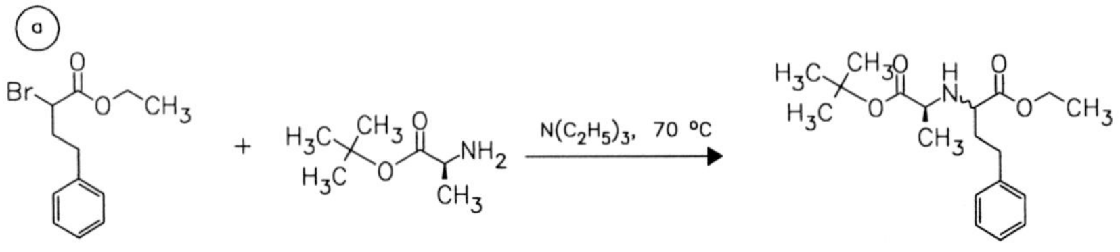

(±)-ethyl 2-bromo-
4-phenylbutanoate

L-alanine
tert-butyl ester

(I)

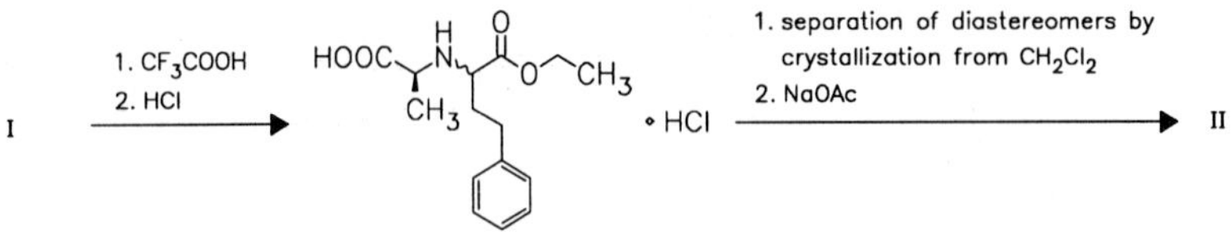

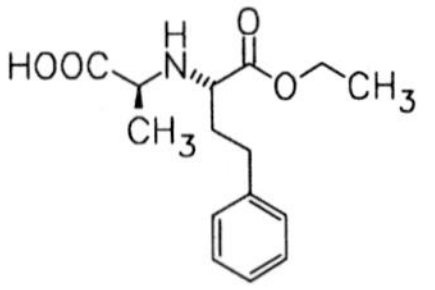

ethyl (S,S)-2-[(1-
carboxyethyl)amino]-
4-phenylbutanoate (II)

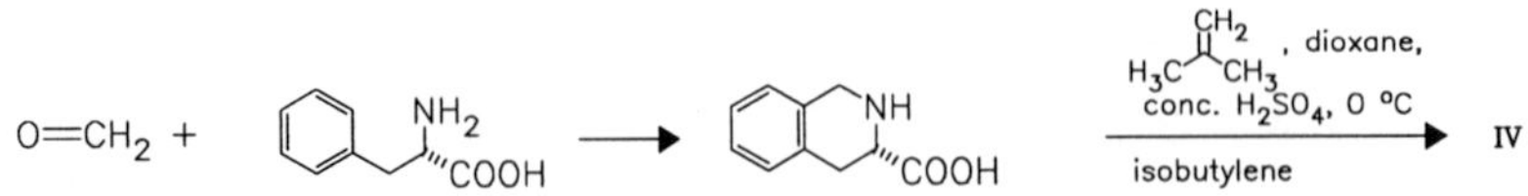

form-
aldehyde

L-phenyl-
alanine

(S)-1,2,3,4-tetrahydro-
3-isoquinoline-
carboxylic acid (III)

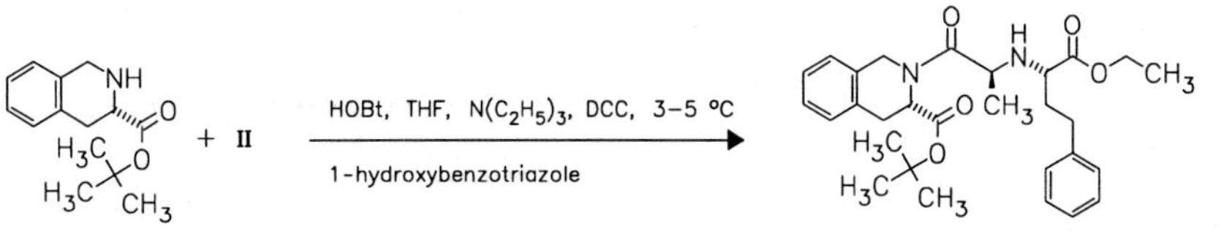

(IV)   + II → (V)

HOBt, THF, N(C$_2$H$_5$)$_3$, DCC, 3–5 °C

1-hydroxybenzotriazole

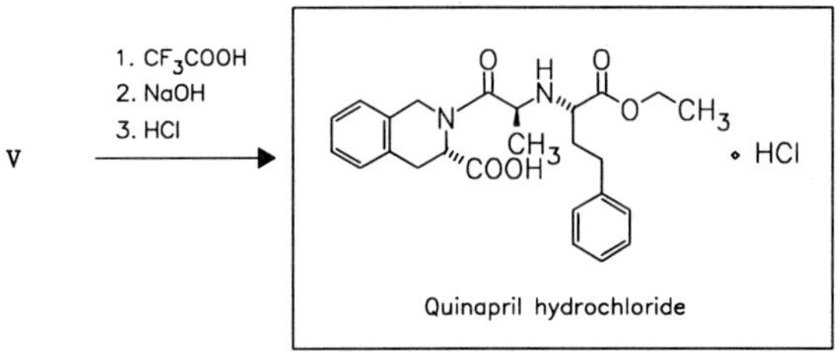

V →

1. CF$_3$COOH
2. NaOH
3. HCl

• HCl

Quinapril hydrochloride

(b)

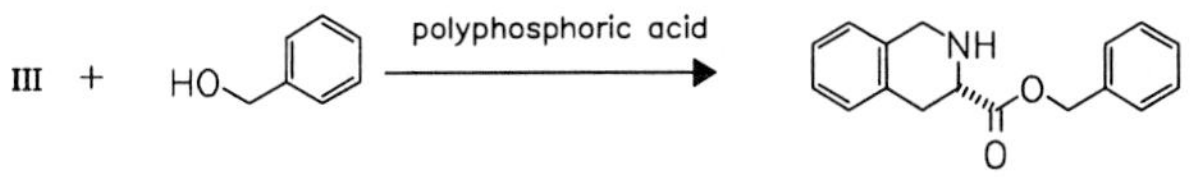

III + HO–CH$_2$–C$_6$H$_5$ →

polyphosphoric acid

benzyl alcohol

benzyl (S)-1,2,3,4-
tetrahydro-3-isoquinoline-
carboxylate (VI)

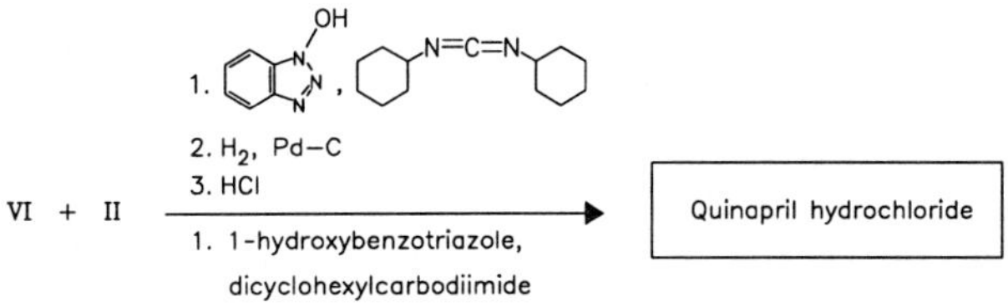

VI + II →

1. [1-hydroxybenzotriazole], dicyclohexylcarbodiimide
2. H$_2$, Pd–C
3. HCl

Quinapril hydrochloride

Reference(s):

a EP 49 605 (Warner-Lambert; appl. 1.10.1981; USA-prior. 20.2.1981, 3.10.1980).
   US 4 344 949 (Warner-Lambert; 17.8.1982; appl. 20.2.1981; prior. 3.10.1980).
   Klutchko, S. et al.: J. Med. Chem. (JMCMAR) 29, 1953 (1986).
b EP 49 605 (Warner-Lambert; appl. 1.10.1981; USA-prior. 20.2.1981, 3.10.1980).
   US 4 344 949 (Warner-Lambert; 17.8.1982; appl. 20.2.1981; prior. 3.10.1980).

crystalline quinapril hydrochloride:
EP 285 992 (Warner-Lambert; appl. 29.3.1988; USA-prior. 30.3.1987).
US 4 761 479 (Warner-Lambert; 2.8.1988; appl. 30.3.1987).

preparation of ethyl 2-bromo-4-phenylbutanoate and 2-bromo-4-phenylbutanoic acid:
Fischer, E.; Schmitz: Ber. Dtsch. Chem. Ges. (BDCGAS) 39, 2212 (1906).
Baxter, A.D. et al.: Bioorg. Med. Chem. Lett. (BMCLE8) 7 (21), 2765 (1997).
Iwasaki, G.; Kimura, R.; Numao, N.; Kondo, K.: Chem. Pharm. Bull. (CPBTAL) 37 (2), 280 (1989).
Coric, P. et al.: J. Med. Chem. (JMCMAR) 39 (6), 1210 (1996).
Goel, O.P.; Krolls, K.: Tetrahedron Lett. (TELEAY) 24 (2), 163 (1983).

stabilization of pharmaceutical formulations:
EP 264 887 (Warner-Lambert; appl. 19.10.1987; USA-prior. 20.10.1986).
EP 264 888 (Warner-Lambert; 19.10.1987; USA-prior. 20.10.1986).
EP 280 999 (Warner-Lambert; appl. 23.2.1988; USA-prior. 24.2.1987).

Formulation(s):   f. c. tabl. 5 mg, 10 mg, 20 mg, 40 mg

Trade Name(s):

D: Accupro (Gödecke/Parke Davis; 1991)
Accuzide (Gödecke; Parke Davis)-comb.
F: Acuilix (Parke Davis)-comb.
Acuitel (Parke Davis; 1990)
Korec (Sanofi Winthrop)
Koretic (Sanofi Winthrop)-comb.
GB: Accupro (Parke Davis)
I: Accuprin (Parke Davis; 1989)
Acequin (Recordati; 1989)
Quinazil (Malesci; 1989)
J: Conan (Yoshitomi-Green Cross)
USA: Accupril (Parke Davis; 1991)

Quinestrol

ATC: G03
Use: estrogen

RN: 152-43-2 MF: $C_{25}H_{32}O_2$ MW: 364.53 EINECS: 205-803-1
CN: (17α)-3-(cyclopentyloxy)-19-norpregna-1,3,5(10)-trien-20-yn-17-ol

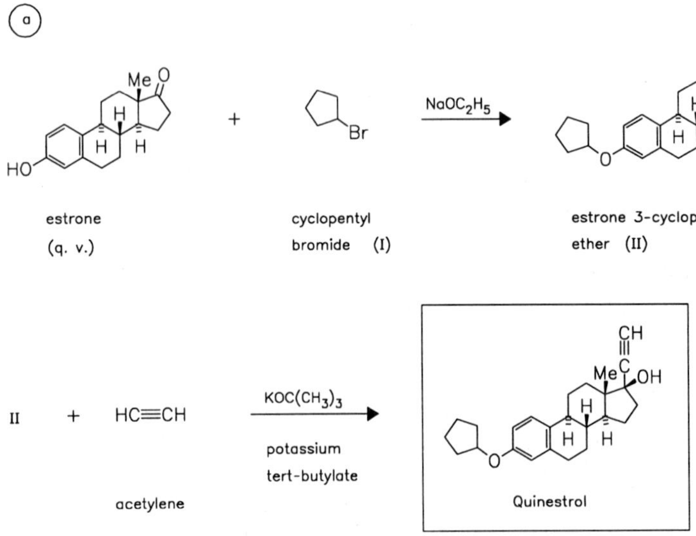
a
Me O
HO
H H H
estrone
(q. v.)
+
Br
cyclopentyl
bromide (I)
$NaOC_2H_5$
estrone 3-cyclopentyl
ether (II)
II + HC≡CH
acetylene
$KOC(CH_3)_3$
potassium
tert-butylate
CH
C
Me OH
Quinestrol

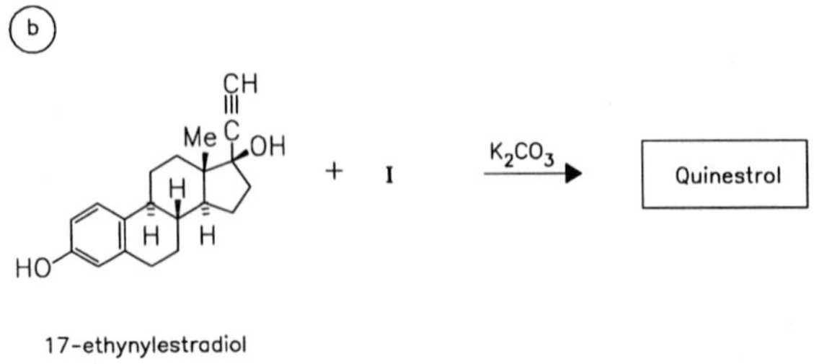
b
CH
C
Me OH
HO
17-ethynylestradiol
+ I
K_2CO_3
Quinestrol

Reference(s):
US 3 159 543 (F. Vismara S.p.A.; 1.12.1964; I-prior. 7.4.1961).
DAS 1 157 610 (F. Vismara S.p.A.; appl. 7.2.1961; I-prior. 8.2.1960, 13.12.1960).
Ercoli, A.; Gardi, R.: Chem. Ind. (London) (CHINAG) **1961**, 1037.

alternative syntheses:
US 3 231 567 (F. Vismara; 25.1.1966; I-prior. 16.12.1963).
BE 641 351 (F. Vismara; appl. 16.12.1963; I-prior. 19.12.1962, 30.9.1963).

Formulation(s): tabl. 0.025 mg, 0.1 mg

Quinethazone
(Chinethazonum)

ATC: C03BA02
Use: diuretic, antihypertensive

RN: 73-49-4   MF: $C_{10}H_{12}ClN_3O_3S$ MW: 289.74   EINECS: 200-801-7
LD$_{50}$: >10 g/kg (M, p.o.)
CN: 7-chloro-2-ethyl-1,2,3,4-tetrahydro-4-oxo-6-quinazolinesulfonamide

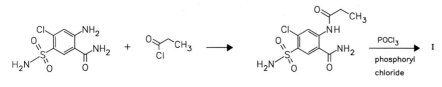

5-aminosulfonyl-   propionyl
4-chloroanthranil-   chloride
amide

6-aminosulfonyl-7-
chloro-2-ethyl-
4(3H)-quinazolinone (I)

AlCl$_3$,   NaBH$_4$
aluminum   sodium
chloride   borohydride

Quinethazone

Reference(s):
US 2 976 289 (American Cyanamid; 21.3.1961; prior. 30.6.1959).

Formulation(s):   tabl. 50 mg

Quingestanol acetate

ATC: G03AC04
Use: progestogen

RN: 3000-39-3   MF: $C_{27}H_{36}O_3$ MW: 408.58   EINECS: 221-078-4
CN: (17α)-3-(cyclopentyloxy)-19-norpregna-3,5-dien-20-yn-17-ol acetate

quingestanol
RN: 10592-65-1   MF: $C_{25}H_{34}O_2$ MW: 366.55   EINECS: 234-199-2

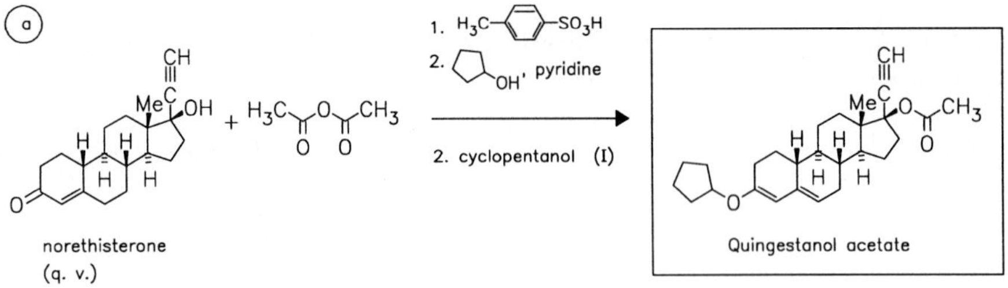
a
1. H_3C–⟨⟩–SO_3H
2. cyclopentanol–OH, pyridine
2. cyclopentanol (I)
norethisterone
(q. v.)
Quingestanol acetate

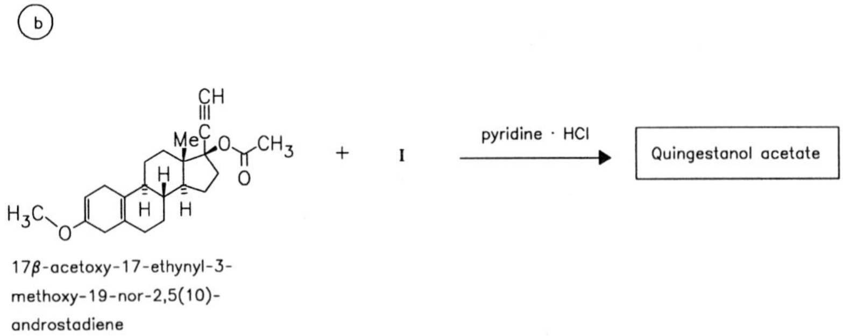
b
pyridine · HCl
I
Quingestanol acetate
17β-acetoxy-17-ethynyl-3-
methoxy-19-nor-2,5(10)-
androstadiene

Reference(s):

a DE 1 159 940 (F. Vismara; appl. 1961; I-prior. 1961).
addition to DE 1 119 264 (F. Vismara; appl. 1959).

b DE 1 228 608 (F. Vismara; appl. 1.6.1964; I-prior. 12.6.1963).
addition to DE 1 119 264 (F. Vismara; appl. 1959).

alternative synthesis:
US 3 159 620 (F. Vismara; 1.12.1964; I-prior. 22.5.1963).

Trade Name(s):

F: Délovis (Substantia); wfm I: Demovis (Vister); wfm

Quinidine

ATC: C01BA01
Use: antiarrhythmic

RN: 56-54-2 MF: $C_{20}H_{24}N_2O_2$ MW: 324.42 EINECS: 200-279-0
LD_{50}: 53.6 mg/kg (M, i.v.); 535 mg/kg (M, p.o.);
23 mg/kg (R, i.v.); 263 mg/kg (R, p.o.)
CN: (9*S*)-6'-methoxycinchonan-9-ol

sulfate (2:1)
RN: 50-54-4 MF: $C_{20}H_{24}N_2O_2 \cdot 1/2H_2SO_4$ MW: 746.93 EINECS: 200-046-3
LD_{50}: 54 mg/kg (M, i.v.); 505 mg/kg (M, p.o.);
55 mg/kg (R, i.v.); 456 mg/kg (R, p.o.)
gluconate
RN: 7054-25-3 MF: $C_{20}H_{24}N_2O_2 \cdot C_6H_{12}O_7$ MW: 520.58 EINECS: 230-333-9
polygalacturonate
RN: 58829-32-6 MF: $C_{20}H_{24}N_2O_2 \cdot$ x unspecified MW: unspecified

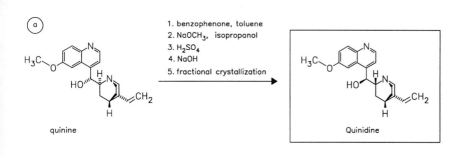

ⓐ

1. benzophenone, toluene
2. NaOCH₃, isopropanol
3. H₂SO₄
4. NaOH
5. fractional crystallization

quinine

Quinidine

ⓑ   from the mother liquors of the quinine production

Reference(s):
a DE 877 611 (Boehringer Mannh.; appl. 1950).
b Ullmanns Encykl. Tech. Chem., 3. Aufl., Vol. **3**, 212.

polygalacturonate:
US 2 878 252 (Synergistics; 1959; appl. 1957).

quinidine alginate:
DOS 2 156 725 (Lab. G.-A. Cochard; appl. 16.11.1971; B-prior. 19.11.1970, 8.11.1971).

Formulation(s):   f. c. tabl. 250 mg; s. r. tabl. 200 mg, 250 mg (as hydrogen sulfate); tabl. 166 mg, 275 mg (as polygalacturonate); s. r. tabl. 300 mg; tabl. 100 mg, 200 mg, 300 mg (as sulfate)

Trade Name(s):
D: Chinidin Duriles (Astra)
Chinidin-retard (Isis
Pharma)
Chinidinum Compretten
(Cascan); wfm
Chinidinum sulfuricum
"Buchler" (Buchler); wfm
Galactoquin
(Mundipharma; as
polygalacturonate); wfm
Optochinidin (Boehringer
Mannh.; as hydrogen
sulfate)
Quinitex Extentabs
(Brenner); wfm
Systodin "Buchler"
(Buchler); wfm
numerous combination
preparations

F: Cardioquine (ASTA
Medica; as
polygalacturonate)
Longacor (Procter &
Gamble; as
arabogalacturonate)
Quinidurule (Astra)
Quinimax (Sanofi
Winthrop)-comb.
GB: Kinidin Durules (Astra; as
bisulfate)
I: Chin el (Fadem)
Chinina cloridrato
(Biologici Italia)
Chinina solfato (Iema)
Chinteina (Lafare; as
sulfate)
Longachin (Teofarma)
Naticardina (ASTA
Medica)

Natisedina (Teofarma)
Nicoprive (IFI)-comb.
Ritmocor (Malesci; as
polygalacturonate)
numerous generics
J: Quinidine HCl (Nikken)
Quinidine Sulfate (Alps;
Hoei; Iwaki; Sanko;
Yamada)
generics
USA: Cardioquin (Purdue
Frederick; as
polygalacturonate)
Quinaglute Dura-Tabs'
(Berex; as gluconate)
Quinidex Extentabs
(Robins; as sulfate)
generics

Quinine

ATC: P01BC01
Use: chemotherapeutic, antipyretic,
stimulant

RN: 130-95-0   MF: C₂₀H₂₄N₂O₂   MW: 324.42   EINECS: 205-003-2
LD₅₀: 68 mg/kg (M, i.v.)
CN: (8α,9R)-6'-methoxycinchonan-9-ol

hydrochloride
RN: 7549-43-1   MF: $C_{20}H_{24}N_2O_2 \cdot xHCl$ MW: unspecified   EINECS: 231-437-7
sulfate (1:1)
RN: 549-56-4   MF: $C_{20}H_{24}N_2O_2 \cdot H_2SO_4$ MW: 422.50   EINECS: 208-970-9
iodobismutate
RN: 8048-94-0   MF: $C_{20}H_{24}N_2O_2 \cdot BiI_3 \cdot HI$ MW: 1042.03
acetylsalicylate (1:1)
RN: 130-93-8   MF: $C_{20}H_{24}N_2O_2 \cdot C_9H_8O_4$ MW: 504.58
monoformate
RN: 130-90-5   MF: $C_{20}H_{24}N_2O_2 \cdot CH_2O_2$ MW: 370.45   EINECS: 205-002-7
LD_{50}:   290 mg/kg (dog, i.m.)

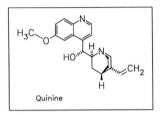

Quinine

By extraction of *Cinchona* bark with aromatic hydrocarbons, conversion of the crude alkaloids into the sulfates and fractional precipitation with NaOH as sulfate.

Reference(s):
Ullmanns Encykl. Tech. Chem., 3. Aufl., Vol. **3**, 213.
Ullmanns Encykl. Tech. Chem., 4. Aufl., Vol. **7**, 86.
BIOS Final Reports No. 1404, p. 20.
FR 1 279 901 (Omnium Chimique; appl. 1955).

combination of quinine sulfate *with* theophylline ethylenediamine:
US 2 985 558 (W. B. Rawls; 23.5.1961; appl. 27.2.1959).

Formulation(s):   amp. 245 mg/ml, 250 mg/ml (as dihydrochloride); tabl. 200 mg (as ethyl carbonate); tabl. 250 mg (as hydrochloride); tabl. 200 mg (as sulfate)

Trade Name(s):

D: Chininum aethylcarbonicum (Cassella-med)
Chininum dihydrochloricum (Cassella-med)
Chininum hydrochloricum (Merck)
Chininum hydrochloricum Compretten (Cascan); wfm
Chininum sulfuricum "Buchler" (Buchler); wfm
Limptar (Cassella-med; as sulfate)
Sagittaproct (BASF Generics)
numerous combination preparations and generics

F: Cequinyl (SmithKline Beecham)-comb.
Dinacode (Picot)-comb.
Hexaquine (Gomenol)-comb.
Kinuréa "H" (Fuca)
Nicoprive (Théranol-Deglaude)-comb.
Quinimax (Sanofi Winthrop)-comb.
Quinine Lafran (Lafran; as hydrochloride)
numerous combination preparations

GB: numerous combination preparations; wfm

I: Broncopulmin (Ecobi)-comb.
Nicoprive (IFI)-comb.

J: Quinine HCl (Alps; Hoei; Iwaki; Kotani; Sank; Takeda; Torii; Toyo S.-Ono; Yamada)
Quinine Sulfate (Alps; Hoei; Iwaki; Sanko; Yamada)
generics

USA: Quinine Sulfate (Watson)

Quinisocaine
(Dimethisoquin)

ATC: D04AB05
Use: local anesthetic

RN: 86-80-6 MF: $C_{17}H_{24}N_2O$ MW: 272.39 EINECS: 201-700-0
LD$_{50}$: 8 mg/kg (M, i.v.)
CN: 2-[(3-butyl-1-isoquinolinyl)oxy]-N,N-dimethylethanamine

monohydrochloride
RN: 2773-92-4 MF: $C_{17}H_{24}N_2O \cdot HCl$ MW: 308.85 EINECS: 220-468-1
LD$_{50}$: 45 mg/kg (R, i.p.)

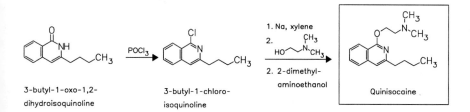

3-butyl-1-oxo-1,2-
dihydroisoquinoline

3-butyl-1-chloro-
isoquinoline

1. Na, xylene
2. CH$_3$ / HO—N-CH$_3$
2. 2-dimethyl-
aminoethanol

Quinisocaine

Reference(s):
US 2 612 503 (Smith Kline & French; 1952; CDN-prior. 1949).

Formulation(s): ointment 0.5 g/100 g (as hydrochloride)

Trade Name(s):
D: Haenal Salbe (Strathmann)
Isochinol (Schwarzhaupt)
Isochinol Salbe
(Chemipharm)

Pruralgan Salbe
(Pharmacia)
F: Quotane (Evans Medical)
Rectoquotane (Evans
Medical)-comb.

GB: Quotane (Smith Kline &
French); wfm
I: Pruralgin Pharmacia
(Importex); wfm

Quinupramine

ATC: N06AA23
Use: antidepressant

RN: 31721-17-2 MF: $C_{21}H_{24}N_2$ MW: 304.44 EINECS: 250-780-3
CN: 5-(1-azabicyclo[2.2.2]oct-3-yl)-10,11-dihydro-5H-dibenz[b,f]azepine

10,11-dihydro-5H-
dibenz[b,f]azepine

3-phenylsulfonyl-
oxyquinuclidine

NaNH$_2$, toluene
sodium amide

Quinupramine

Reference(s):
DOS 2 030 492 (Sogeras; appl. 20.6.1970; GB-prior. 20.6.1969).
GB 1 252 320 (Sogeras; valid from 29.5.1970; prior. 20.6.1969).

Formulation(s): vial 2.5 mg; tabl. 2.5 mg, 7.5 mg

Trade Name(s):
F: Kinupril (Bellon)

Rabeprazole sodium

ATC: A02BC04
Use: gastric antisecretory, H$^+$/K$^+$-ATPase
inhibitor

RN: 117976-90-6   MF: C$_{18}$H$_{20}$N$_3$NaO$_3$S   MW: 381.43
CN: (±)-2-[[[4-(3-Methoxypropoxy)-3-methyl-2-pyridinyl]-methyl]sulfinyl]-1H-benzimidazole sodium salt

acid
RN: 117976-89-3   MF: C$_{18}$H$_{21}$N$_3$O$_3$S   MW: 359.45

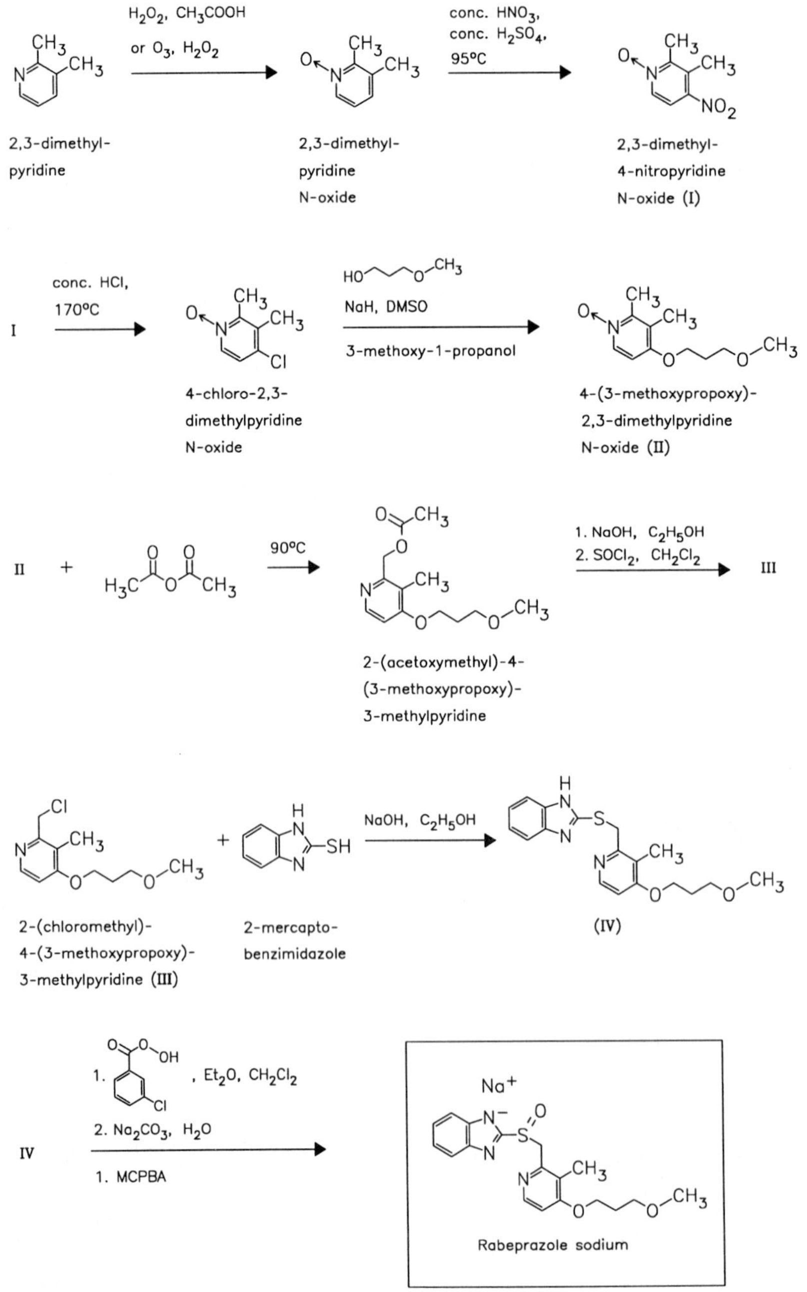

2,3-dimethyl-
pyridine

2,3-dimethyl-
pyridine
N-oxide

2,3-dimethyl-
4-nitropyridine
N-oxide (I)

4-chloro-2,3-
dimethylpyridine
N-oxide

4-(3-methoxypropoxy)-
2,3-dimethylpyridine
N-oxide (II)

2-(acetoxymethyl)-4-
(3-methoxypropoxy)-
3-methylpyridine

2-(chloromethyl)-
4-(3-methoxypropoxy)-
3-methylpyridine (III)

2-mercapto-
benzimidazole

(IV)

Rabeprazole sodium

Reference(s):
EP 268 956 (Eisai Co.; J-prior. 13.11.1986; 2.2.1987; 31.3.1987).
WO 8 910 927 (Eisai Co.; appl. 11.5.1989; J-prior. 12.5.1988).

preparation of 4-chloro-2,3-dimethylpyridine *N*-oxide:
Kuehler, T.C.; Fryklund, J.; Bergman, H.A.; Weilitz, J.; Lee, A.; Larsson, H.: J. Med. Chem. (JMCMAR) **38** (25), 4906 (1995).

pharmaceutical preparations:
WO 9 953 918 (Eisai Co.; appl. 20.4.1999; J-prior. 20.4.1998).
EP 585 722 (Eisai Co.; appl. 17.8.1993; J-prior. 21.8.1992).
WO 9 902 521 (Eisai Co.; appl. 10.7.1998; J-prior. 11.7.1997).

Formulation(s):   tabl. 10 mg, 20 mg (as sodium salt)

Trade Name(s):
D: Pariet (Eisai; Janssen-   J: Pariet (Eisai; 1998)
      Cilag; 1998)   USA: Aciphex (Eisai)

Racefemine

ATC: A03
Use: antispasmodic, coronary vasodilator

RN: 22232-57-1   MF: C$_{18}$H$_{23}$NO   MW: 269.39   EINECS: 244-856-5
CN: (*R**,*R**)-(±)-α-methyl-*N*-(1-methyl-2-phenoxyethyl)benzeneethanamine

hydrogen fumarate (1:1)
RN: 1590-35-8   MF: C$_{18}$H$_{23}$NO · C$_4$H$_4$O$_4$ MW: 385.46   EINECS: 216-462-3

(±)-amphetamine   phenoxyacetone   Racefemine

Reference(s):
NL-appl. 6 407 309 (Clin-Byla; appl. 26.6.1964; F-prior. 28.6.1963).

Formulation(s):   tabl. 50 mg; vial 50 mg/5 ml

Trade Name(s):
F: Dysmalgine (Clin-Comar-   Dysmalgine (Clin-Midy);
      Byla); wfm   wfm

Raloxifene hydrochloride
(LY-156758; Keoxifene)

ATC: G03XC01
Use: antiestrogen, prevention of
        osteoporosis

RN: 82640-04-8   MF: C$_{28}$H$_{27}$NO$_4$S · HCl   MW: 510.05
CN: [6-Hydroxy-2-(4-hydroxyphenyl)benzo[*b*]thien-3-yl][4-[2-(1-piperidinyl)ethoxy]phenyl]methanone hydrochloride

a

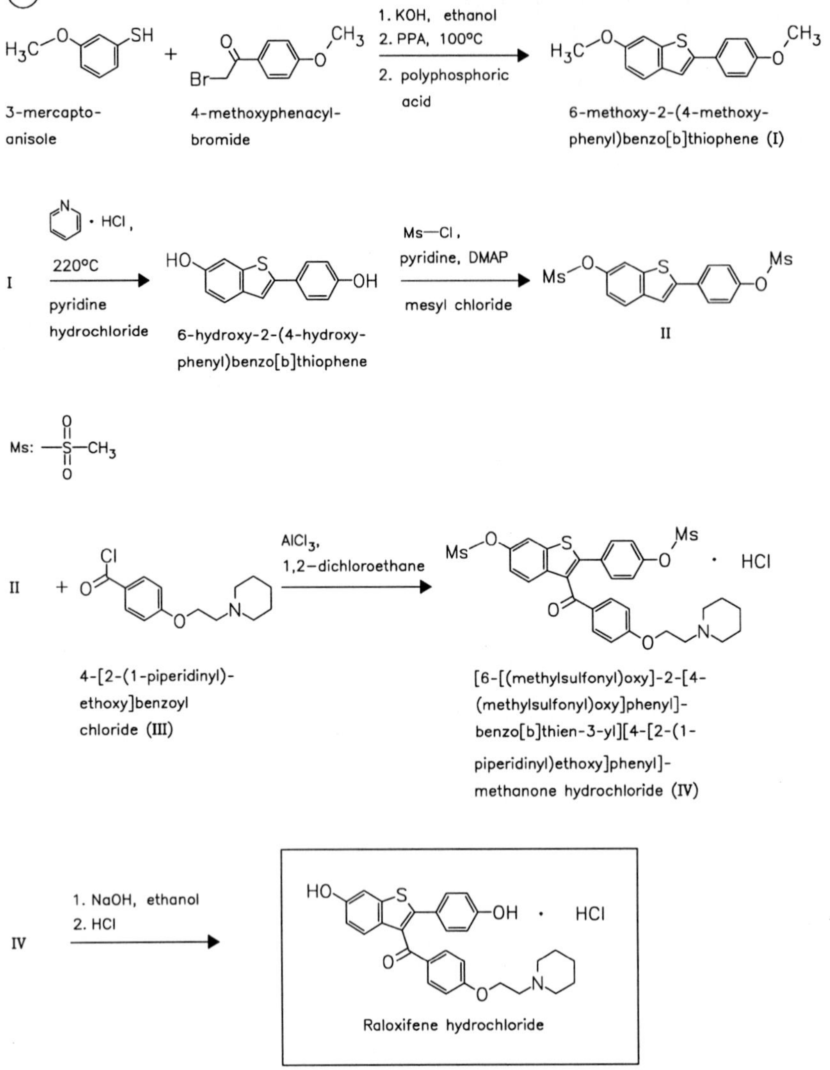

3-mercapto-anisole + 4-methoxyphenacyl-bromide

1. KOH, ethanol
2. PPA, 100°C
2. polyphosphoric acid

→ 6-methoxy-2-(4-methoxyphenyl)benzo[b]thiophene (I)

I →
pyridine hydrochloride
220°C

6-hydroxy-2-(4-hydroxyphenyl)benzo[b]thiophene

Ms—Cl, pyridine, DMAP
mesyl chloride

→ II

Ms: —S(=O)(=O)—CH₃

II + 4-[2-(1-piperidinyl)ethoxy]benzoyl chloride (III)

AlCl₃, 1,2-dichloroethane

→ [6-[(methylsulfonyl)oxy]-2-[4-(methylsulfonyl)oxy]phenyl]-benzo[b]thien-3-yl][4-[2-(1-piperidinyl)ethoxy]phenyl]-methanone hydrochloride (IV)

IV →
1. NaOH, ethanol
2. HCl

Raloxifene hydrochloride

aa starting material III can be synthesized from

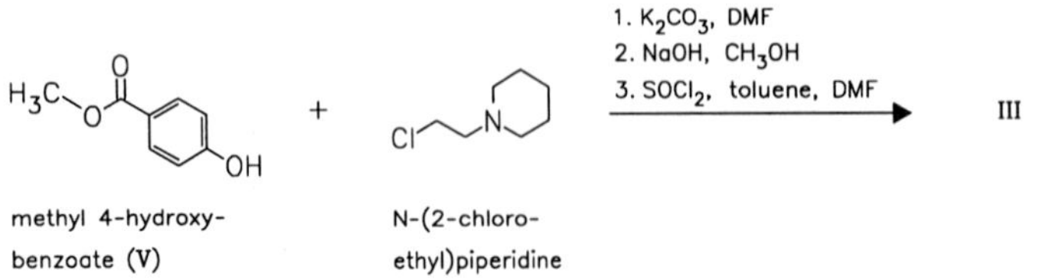

methyl 4-hydroxybenzoate (V) + N-(2-chloroethyl)piperidine

1. K₂CO₃, DMF
2. NaOH, CH₃OH
3. SOCl₂, toluene, DMF

→ III

ab

V + ethylene carbonate →

1. HN-piperidine (VI), SOCl₂
2. NaOH
3. SOCl₂
1. piperidine

→ III

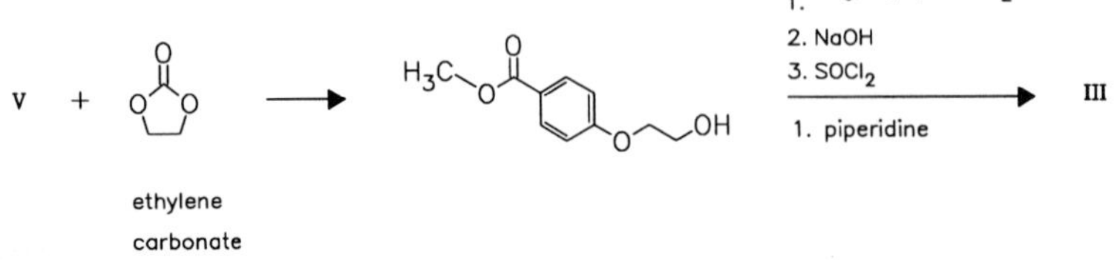

(b)

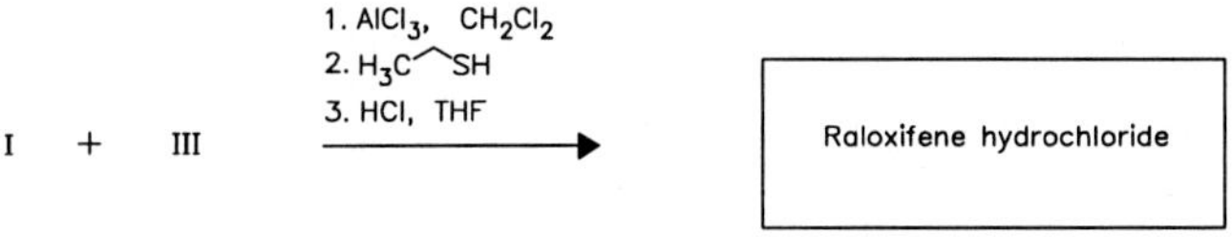

1. AlCl$_3$, CH$_2$Cl$_2$
2. H$_3$C$\diagup$SH
3. HCl, THF

I + III $\longrightarrow$ Raloxifene hydrochloride

(c)

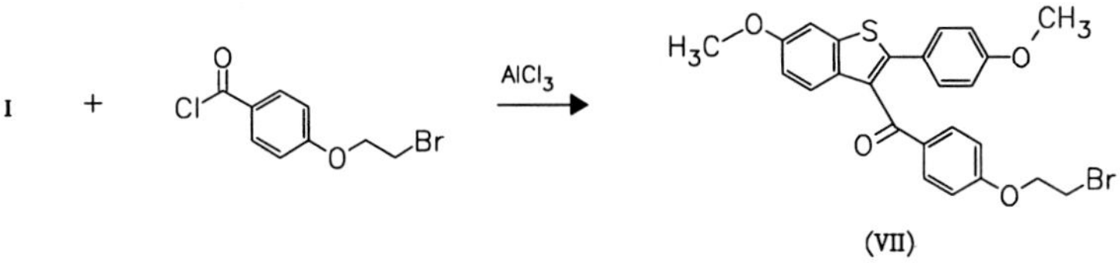

I + [structure: Cl—C(=O)—C$_6$H$_4$—O—CH$_2$CH$_2$—Br] $\xrightarrow{\text{AlCl}_3}$ [structure: (VII)]

(VII)

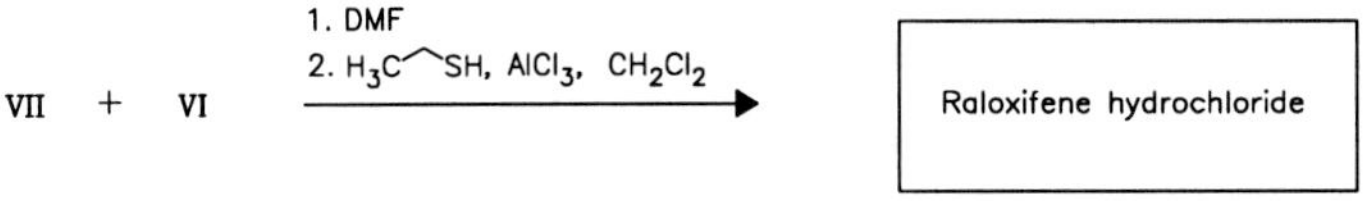

1. DMF
2. H$_3$C$\diagup$SH, AlCl$_3$, CH$_2$Cl$_2$

VII + VI $\longrightarrow$ Raloxifene hydrochloride

(d)

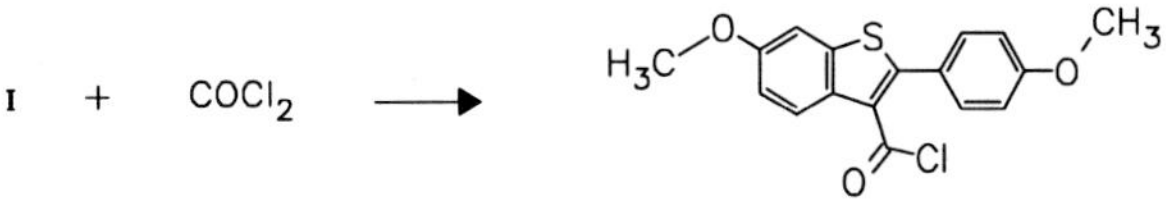

I + COCl$_2$ $\longrightarrow$ [structure]

phosgene

6-methoxy-2-(4-methoxy-
phenyl)-benzo[b]thiophene-
3-carbonyl chloride

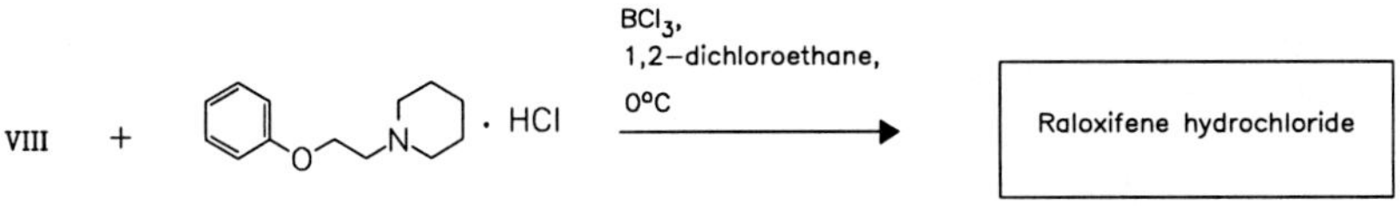

BCl$_3$,
1,2-dichloroethane,
0°C

VIII + [structure] · HCl $\longrightarrow$ Raloxifene hydrochloride

phenyl 2-piperidino-
ethyl ether hydrochloride

alternative regiospecific synthesis of I

(ea)

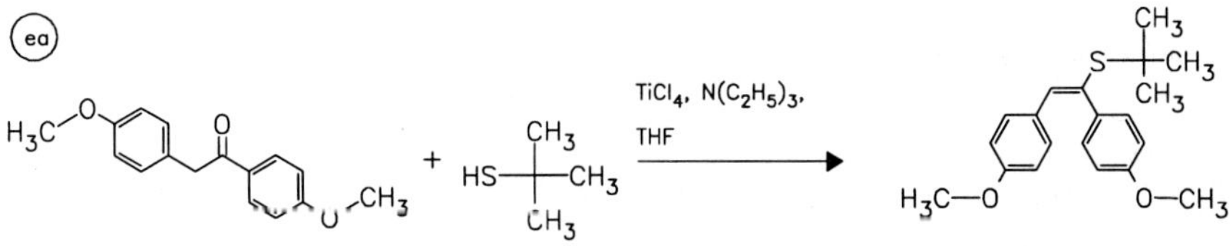

[structure: deoxyanisoin] + HS$-$C(CH$_3$)$_3$ $\xrightarrow{\text{TiCl}_4, \text{N(C}_2\text{H}_5)_3,}$ [structure: (X)]

deoxyanisoin

2-methyl-
2-propane-
thiol (IX)

tert-butyl 4,4'-di-
methoxy-α-stilbenyl
sulfide (X)

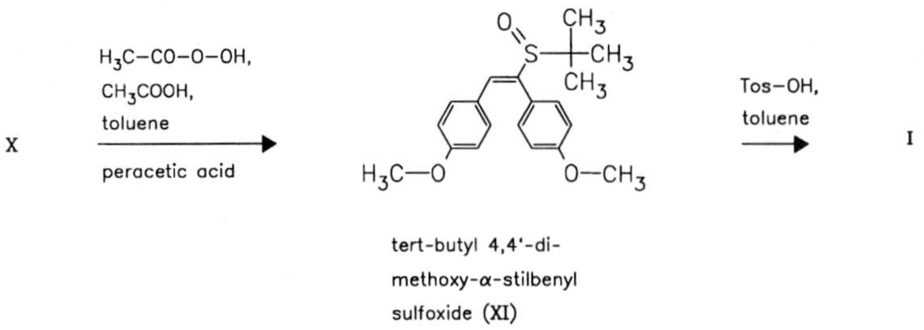

tert-butyl 4,4'-di-
methoxy-α-stilbenyl
sulfoxide (XI)

tert-butyl
4-methoxybenzyl
sulfide (XII)

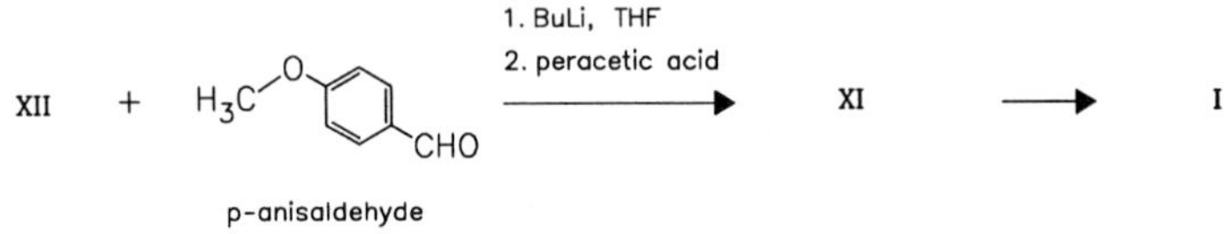

p-anisaldehyde

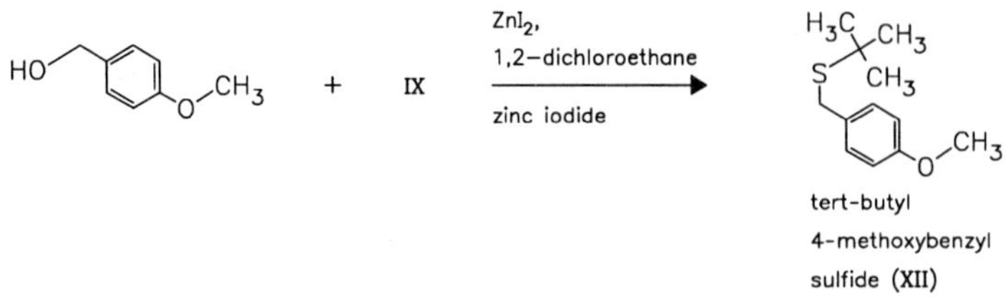

Reference(s):

a,b Jones, C.D. et al.: J. Med. Chem. (JMCMAR) **27**, 1057 (1984).
    EP 62 504 (Lilly + Co., appl. 1.4.1982; USA-prior. 3.4.1981).
    Vicenzi, J.T. et al.: Org. Process Res. Dev. (OPRDFK) **3**, 56-59 (1999).
a   US 4 418 068 (Lilly + Co.; 29.11.1983; USA-prior. 3.4.1981).
aa EP 699 672 (E. Lilly + Co.; appl. 30.8.1995; USA-prior. 31.8.1994).
b EP 693 488 (Lilly + Co.; appl. 20.7.1995; USA-prior. 22.7.1994).
    US 4 380 635 (Lilly + Co.; 19.4.1983; USA-prior. 3.4.1981).
c   EP 738 725 (E. Lilly + Co.; appl. 18.4.1996; USA-prior. 21.4.1995).
d WO 9 734 888 (E. Lilly + Co.; appl. 20.3.1996; USA-prior. 19.3.1996).
e   WO 9 640 691 (E. Lilly + Co.; appl. 4.6.1996; USA-prior. 7.6.1995).
    WO 9 640 693 (E. Lilly + Co.; appl. 4.6.1996; USA-prior. 7.6.1995).
    WO 9 640 677 (E. Lilly + Co.; appl. 4.6.1996; USA-prior. 7.6.1995).
    WO 9 640 676 (E. Lilly + Co.; appl. 4.6.1996; USA-prior. 7.6.1995).
    US 5 512 701 (E. Lilly + Co.; 30.4.1996; USA-prior. 7.6.1995).

preparation of an amorphous form and formulation:
WO 9 808 513 (E. Lilly + Co.; appl. 22.8.1997; USA-prior. 28.8.1996).

preparation of glucopyranosides (metabolites) as antihyperlibpidemics:
EP 683 170 (E. Lilly + Co.; appl. 16.5.1995; USA-prior. 20.5.1994).

treatment of hormone dependent cancers:
EP 62 503 (E. Lilly + Co.; appl. 1.4.1982; USA-prior. 3.4.1981).

method for lowering serum cholesterol:
US 5 464 845 (E. Lilly + Co.; 7.11.1995; USA-prior. 22.12.1992).

treatment of mammary cancer:
US 4 656 187 (E. Lilly + Co.; 7.4.1987; USA-prior. 3.8.1981).

pharmaceutical composition for inhibiting bone loss and lowering serum cholesterol:
CA 2 141 999 (E. Lilly + Co.; appl. 7.2.1995; USA-prior. 2.3.1994).

preparation of unsolvated crystalline form:
DE 19 534 744 (E. Lilly + Co.; appl. 19.9.1995; USA-prior. 19.9.1994).

Formulation(s):   f. c. tabl. 60 mg (as hydrochloride); tabl. 60 mg

Trade Name(s):
D: EVISTA (Eli Lilly; 1997)   USA: Evista (Eli Lilly; 1998)

Raltitrexed
(D-1694; ICI-D 1694; ZN-1694)

ATC: L01BA03
Use: antineoplastic, thymidylate synthetase inhibitor

RN: 112887-68-0   MF: $C_{21}H_{22}N_4O_6S$ MW: 458.50
CN: *N*-[[5-[[(1,4-dihydro-2-methyl-4-oxo-6-quinazolinyl)methyl]methylamino]-2-thienyl]carbonyl]-L-glutamic acid

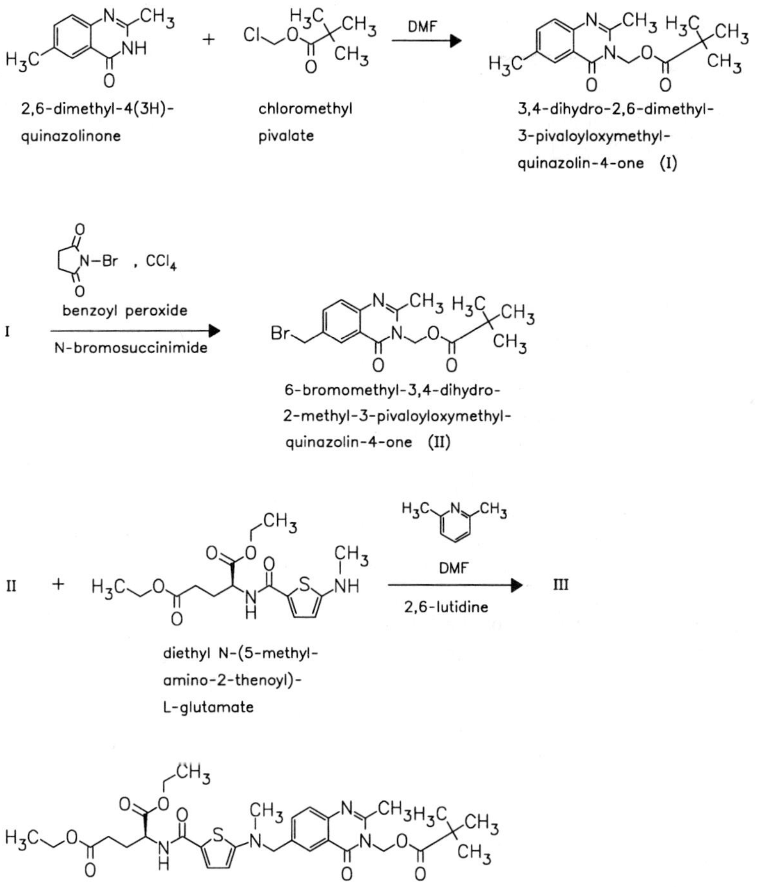

2,6-dimethyl-4(3H)-
quinazolinone

chloromethyl
pivalate

3,4-dihydro-2,6-dimethyl-
3-pivaloyloxymethyl-
quinazolin-4-one   (I)

6-bromomethyl-3,4-dihydro-
2-methyl-3-pivaloyloxymethyl-
quinazolin-4-one   (II)

diethyl N-(5-methyl-
amino-2-thenoyl)-
L-glutamate

(III)

III →

1. NaOH, C_2H_5OH
2. HCl

Raltitrexed

Reference(s):
EP 239 362 (ICI; appl. 24.3.1987; GB-prior. 27.3.1986).
Marsham, P.R. et al.: J. Med. Chem. (JMCMAR) **42** (19), 3809 (1999).
Marsham, P.R. et al.: J. Med. Chem. (JMCMAR) **34** (5), 1594 (1991).
Bisset, G.M.F. et al.: J. Med. Chem. (JMCMAR) **35** (5), 859 (1992).

preparation of 2,6-dimethyl-4(3H)-quinazolinone *from* 5-methylanthranilic acid:
Patil, S.D; Jones, C.; Nair, M.G.; Galivan, J.; Maley, F.: J. Med. Chem. (JMCMAR) **32** (6), 1284 (1989).
Battacharyya; Bose; Ray: J. Indian. Chem. Soc. (JICSAH) **6**, 283 (1929).
Bischler; Muntendam: Ber. Dtsch. Chem. Ges. (BDCGAS) **28**, 730 (1895).

Formulation(s):　amp. 2 mg

Trade Name(s):
F:　　Tomudex (Zeneca)　　　　　I:　　Tomudex (Zeneca)
GB:　　Tomudex (Zeneca)　　　　J:　　Tomudex (Zeneca)

Ramatroban
(Bay u 3405)

Use:　treatment of allergic rhinitis, thromboxane receptor antagonist

RN:　116649-85-5　MF: $C_{21}H_{21}FN_2O_4S$　MW: 416.47
CN:　(R)-3-[[(4-Fluorophenyl)sulfonyl]amino]-1,2,3,4-tetrahydro-9H-carbazole-9-propanoic acid

cyclo-
hexanone

4-methoxy-
phenylhydrazine

C_2H_5OH, CH_3COOH

3-methoxy-
carbazole (I)

I

1. Li, NH_3
2. H_2O, H^+

1,2,4,9-tetrahydro-
carbazol-3-one

1. H_2N—CH₃ , $NaBH_4$, N^+Bu_4 Br^-

2. H_2SO_4, crystallization

1. (S)-(−)-α-methylbenzylamine
(separation of diastereomers)

II

(II) · H_2SO_4

$HCOO^-$ NH_4^+, Pd–C
ammonium formate

(3R)-3-amino-1,2,3,4-
tetrahydrocarbazole (III)

III + [structure: 4-fluorobenzene-sulfonyl chloride] → [H₃C-O-CO-CH₃, N(C₂H₅)₃] → (IV)

4-fluorobenzene-
sulfonyl chloride

(IV)

IV + H₂C=CH-CN →

1. [structure with CH₃, K₂CO₃, benzyltrimethylammonium Cl⁻]
2. NaOH, H₂O

→ Ramatroban

Ramatroban

Reference(s):
DE 3 631 824 (Bayer AG; appl. 19.9.1986; prior. 21.2.1986).
EP 728 743 (Bayer AG; appl. 14.2.1996; D-prior. 27.2.1995).

thermodynamically stable form of ramatroban:
DE 19 757 983 (Bayer Yakuhin Ltd.; D-prior. 24.12.1997)

preparation of 1,2,4,9-tetrahydrocarbazol-3-one:
Bailey, A.S.; Vandrevala, M.H.: J. Chem. Soc., Perkin Trans. 1 (JCPRB4) 1980, 1512

preparation of 1,2,3,4-tetrahydrocarbazol-3-ol:
Gardner et al.: J. Org. Chem. (JOCEAH) 22, 1206, 1210 (1957)

oxidation of 1,2,3,4-tetrahydrocarbazol-3-ol:
Ritchie, R.; Saxton, J.E.: J. Chem. Res., Miniprint (JRMPDM) 1990 (2), 528.

Formulation(s):   tabl.

Trade Name(s):
J: Baynas (Bayer; 2000)

Ramipril

ATC: C09AA05
Use: antihypertensive (ACE inhibitor)

RN: 87333-19-5   MF: $C_{23}H_{32}N_2O_5$ MW: 416.52
LD$_{50}$:   1100 mg/kg (M, i.v.); 10.048 g/kg (M, p.o.);
          600 mg/kg (R, i.v.); >10 g/kg (R, p.o.);
          >250 mg/kg (dog, i.v.); >1 g/kg (dog, p.o.)
CN: [2S-[1[R*(R*)],2α,3aβ,6aβ]]-1-[2-[[1-(ethoxycarbonyl)-3-phenylpropyl]amino]-1-oxopropyl]octahydrocyclopenta[b]pyrrole-2-carboxylic acid

[structure: ethyl 3-benzoylacrylate] + [structure: L-alanine benzyl ester] → [N(C₂H₅)₃] → (I)

ethyl 3-benzoyl-   L-alanine   (I)
acrylate   benzyl ester

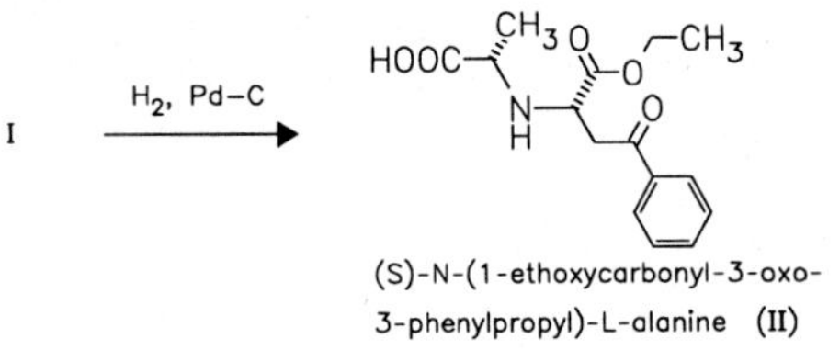

I → (S)-N-(1-ethoxycarbonyl-3-oxo-3-phenylpropyl)-L-alanine (II)

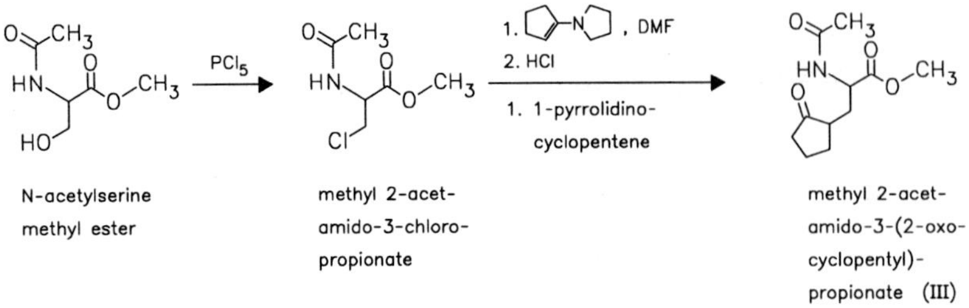

H₂, Pd–C

N-acetylserine methyl ester → PCl₅ → methyl 2-acetamido-3-chloropropionate

1. (pyrrolidinocyclopentene), DMF
2. HCl

1. 1-pyrrolidinocyclopentene

methyl 2-acetamido-3-(2-oxocyclopentyl)-propionate (III)

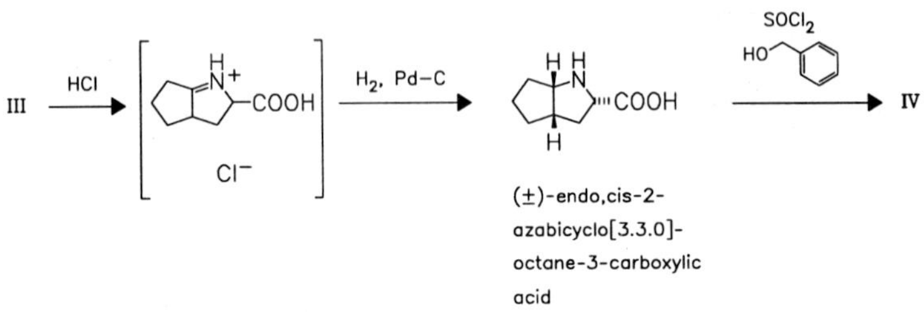

III → HCl → [cyclic ammonium chloride -COOH · Cl⁻] → H₂, Pd–C → (±)-endo,cis-2-azabicyclo[3.3.0]-octane-3-carboxylic acid

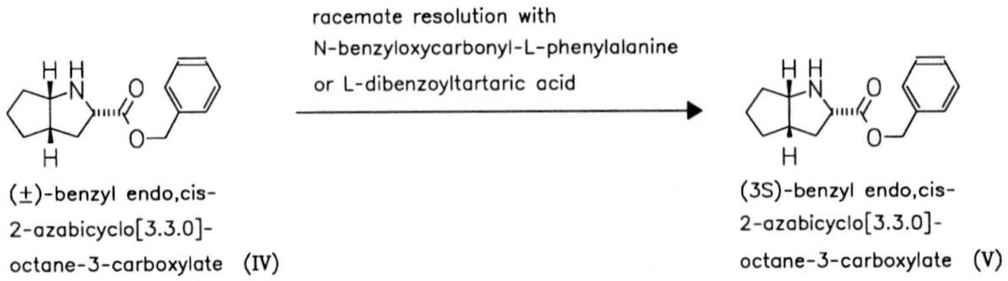

SOCl₂, HO-CH₂-C₆H₅ → IV

(±)-benzyl endo,cis-2-azabicyclo[3.3.0]-octane-3-carboxylate (IV)

racemate resolution with N-benzyloxycarbonyl-L-phenylalanine or L-dibenzoyltartaric acid →

(3S)-benzyl endo,cis-2-azabicyclo[3.3.0]-octane-3-carboxylate (V)

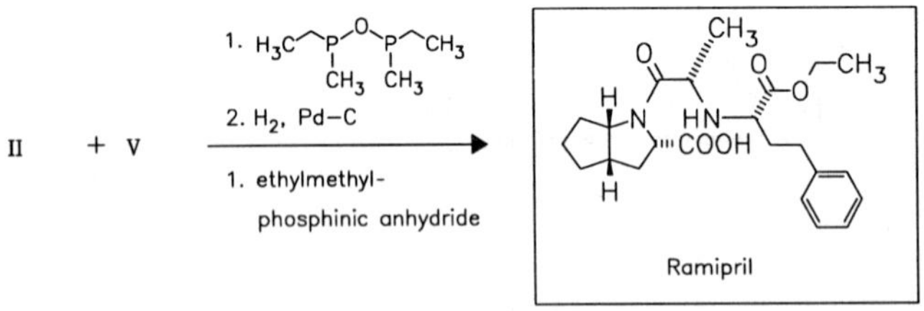

II + V

1. H₃C–P(CH₃)–O–P(CH₃)–CH₃
2. H₂, Pd–C

1. ethylmethylphosphinic anhydride

Ramipril

Reference(s):

Teetz, V. et al.: Arzneim.-Forsch. (ARZNAD) **34** (II), 1399 (1984).
EP 79 022 (Hoechst; appl. 2.11.1982; D-prior. 5.11.1981, 17.7.1982).
DOS 3 226 768 (Hoechst; appl. 5.11.1981).
EP 115 345 (Hoechst; appl. 27.1.1984; D-prior. 31.1.1983).
DOS 3 303 112 (Hoechst; appl. 31.1.1983).
DOS 3 303 139 (Hoechst; appl. 31.1.1983).

Formulation(s):   cps. 1.25 mg, 2.5 mg, 5 mg; tabl. 1.25 mg, 2.5 mg, 5 mg

Trade Name(s):
D: Arelix (Hoechst)-comb.   Delix (Hoechst)   Delix (Hoechst)-comb.

	Vesdil (Astra/Promed)	GB:	Tritace (Hoechst)	Unipril (Astra
	Vesdil (Astra/Promed)-	I:	Quark (Polifarma)	Farmaceutici)
	comb.		Triatec (Hoechst Marion	USA: Altace (Hoechst Marion
F:	Triatec (Hoechst Houdé)		Roussel)	Roussel)

Ramosetron hydrochloride
(YM-060)

ATC: A04AA
Use: anti-emetic, 5-HT$_3$-antagonist

RN: 132907-72-3   MF: C$_{17}$H$_{17}$N$_3$O · HCl   MW: 315.80
CN: (R)-(1-methyl-1H-indol-3-yl)(4,5,6,7-tetrahydro-1H-benzimidazol-5-yl)methanone monohydrochloride

ramosetron
RN: 132036-88-5   MF: C$_{17}$H$_{17}$N$_3$O   MW: 279.34

methyl benzimidazole-
5-carboxylate

(RS)-4,5,6,7-tetrahydro-
1H-benzimidazole-
5-carboxylic acid (I)

(RS)-5-pyrrolidinocarbonyl-
4,5,6,7-tetrahydro-1H-
benzimidazole hydrochloride (II)

1-methyl-
indole

Ramosetron hydrochloride

Reference(s):
EP 381 422 (Yamanouchi Pharm.; appl. 4.8.1994; J-prior. 2.2.1989).
Ohta, M. et al.: Chem. Pharm. Bull. (CPBTAL) **44** (9), 1707 (1996).

sustained release composition:
WO 9 933 491 (Yamanouchi Pharm.; appl. 25.12.1998; J-prior. 26.12.1977).
WO 9 933 489 (Yamanouchi Pharm.; appl. 25.12.1998; J-prior. 26.12.1977).

preparation of methyl benzimidazole-5-carboxylate *from* 3,4-diaminobenzoic acid:
Dellweg et al.: Biochem. Z. (BIZEA2) **327**, 422, 446 (1956).

drug composition:
WO 9 416 682 (Yamanouchi Pharm.; appl. 4.8.1994; J-prior. 21.1.1993).

Formulation(s):   amp. 0.3 mg/2 ml; tabl. 0.1 mg

Ranimustine
(MCNU; Ranomustine)

ATC: L01AD07
Use: antineoplastic, nitrosourea

RN: 58994-96-0   MF: $C_{10}H_{18}ClN_3O_7$ MW: 327.72
LD$_{50}$:   41.2 mg/kg (M, i.v.); 45.7 mg/kg (M, p.o.);
31.8 mg/kg (R, i.v.); 46.4 mg/kg (R, p.o.)
CN: methyl 6-[[[(2-chloroethyl)nitrosoamino]carbonyl]amino]-6-deoxy-α-D-glucopyranoside

methyl 6-amino-
6-deoxy-α-D-
glucopyranoside

2-chloroethyl
isocyanate

(I)

Ranimustine

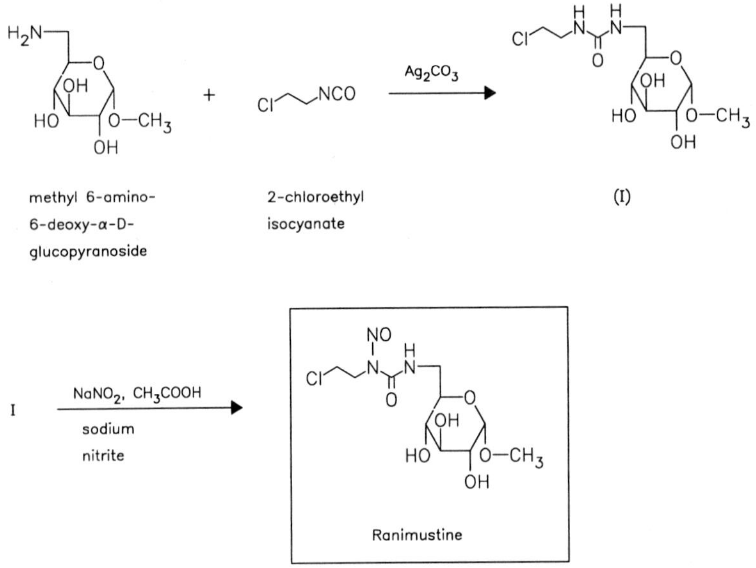

Reference(s):
DE 2 530 416 (Tokyo Tanabe; appl. 4.7.1975; J-prior. 5.7.1974).
GB 1 499 760 (Tokyo Tanabe; appl. 4.7.1975; J-prior. 5.7.1974).

alternative synthesis:
US 4 156 777 (Tokyo Tanabe; 29.5.1979; J-prior. 3.2.1977).
DE 2 805 185 (Tokyo Tanabe; appl. 3.2.1978; J-prior. 3.2.1977).

Formulation(s):   amp. 50 mg, 100 mg

Ranitidine

ATC: A02BA02
Use: peptic ulcer therapeutic (H$_2$-blocker)

RN: 66357-35-5   MF: $C_{13}H_{22}N_4O_3S$ MW: 314.41   EINECS: 266-332-5
LD$_{50}$:   80 mg/kg (M, i.v.); 884 mg/kg (M, p.o.);
93 mg/kg (R, i.v.); >5 g/kg (R, p.o.)
CN: N-[2-[[[5-[(dimethylamino)methyl]-2-furanyl]methyl]thio]ethyl]-N'-methyl-2-nitro-1,1-ethenediamine

monohydrochloride
RN: 66357-59-3   MF: $C_{13}H_{22}N_4O_3S \cdot HCl$ MW: 350.87   EINECS: 266-333-0
LD_{50}:   60 mg/kg (M, i.v.); 1100 mg/kg (M, p.o.);
        85 mg/kg (R, i.v.); 4190 mg/kg (R, p.o.)
bismuth citrate
RN: 128345-62-0   MF: $C_{19}H_{30}BiN_4O_{10}S$ MW: 715.51

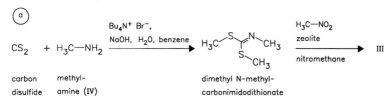

dimethylamine hydrochloride

paraformaldehyde

furfuryl alcohol

5-(dimethylaminomethyl)furfuryl alcohol (I)

cysteamine hydrochloride

(II)

N-methyl-1-methylthio-2-nitro-ethenamine (III)

Ranitidine

preparation of N-methyl-1-methylthio-2-nitroethenamine

(a)

CS_2 + H_3C-NH_2

carbon disulfide   methylamine (IV)

Bu_4N^+ Br^-, NaOH, H_2O, benzene

dimethyl N-methyl-carbonimidodithionate

H_3C-NO_2 zeolite nitromethane

III

(b)

$1,1$-bis(methylthio)-2-nitroethene   + IV C_2H_5OH III

Reference(s):
DOS 2 734 070 (Allen & Hanburys; appl. 28.7.1977; GB-prior. 4.8.1976, 6.12.1976, 13.5.1977).
US 4 128 658 (Glaxo; 5.12.1978; GB-prior. 4.8.1976, 6.12.1976, 13.5.1977).

"form 2":
US 4 521 431 (Glaxo; 4.6.1985; GB-prior. 1.10.1980).
US 4 672 133 (Glaxo; 4.6.1985; GB-prior. 1.10.1980).

alternative syntheses:
EP-appl. 59 082 (Glaxo; appl. 19.2.1982; GB-prior. 20.2.1981).
US 4 399 294 (Glaxo; 16.8.1983; GB-prior. 30.12.1980).
US 4 399 293 (Glaxo; 16.8.1983; GB-prior. 20.1.1981).
DOS 3 242 204 (Lab. Pharmamedical; appl. 15.11.1982; E-prior. 16.11.1981).
BE 888 747 (Ricerca Chimica; appl. 11.5.1981; I-prior. 13.5.1980, 7.10.1980, 21.11.1980).

synthesis of 5-(dimethylaminomethyl)furfuryl alcohol:
Gill, E.W.; Ing, H.R.: J. Chem. Soc. (JCSOA9) **1958**, 4728.

preparation of N-methyl-1-methylthio-2-nitroethenamine:
a IN 172 064 (Council Scient. Ind. Res.; 23.10.1993; prior. 3.1.1989).
   Deshmulek, A.R. et al.: J. Chem. Soc., Perkin Trans. 1 (JCPRB4) **1990** (4); 1217.
   Mohanalingam, K.; Nethaji, M.; Das, P.K.: J. Mol. Struct. (JMOSB4) **378** (3), 177 (1996).
b JP 7 157 465 (Nitto Chem. Ind. Co. Ltd.; 20.6.1995; prior. 3.12.1993).
   Sega, A. et al.: Gazz. Chim. Ital. (GCITA9) **111** (5/6), 217 (1981).
   Manjunatha, S.G.; Reddy, K.V.; Rajappa, S.: Tetrahedron Lett. (TELEAY) **31**, 1327 (1990).

stable aqueous formulations:
US 4 585 790 (Glaxo)

ranitidine bismuth citrate:
GB 2 220 937 (Glaxo; appl. 17.7.1989; prior. 18.7.1988; 1.3.1989).
DE 4 130 061 (Glaxo; appl. 10.9.1991; GB-prior. 11.9.1990).

Formulation(s):   amp. 50 mg/5 ml; eff. tabl. 150 mg, 300 mg; f. c. tabl. 150 mg, 300 mg; tabl. 150 mg, 300 mg
                (as hydrochloride); tabl. 400 mg (as bismuth citrate)

Trade Name(s):

D:	Sostril (Glaxo Wellcome/ Cascan; 1982)	GB:	Zantac (Glaxo Wellcome; 1981)		Ulcex (Guidotti) Zantac (Glaxo Wellcome; 1981)
	Zantic (Glaxo Wellcome; 1982) various generics and combination preparations	I:	Elicodil (Menarini; as bismuth citrate) Pylorid (Glaxo Wellcome; as bismuth citrate)	J:	Zantac (Glaxo; 1984) Zantac Glaxo (Nippon Glaxo)
F:	Azantac (Glaxo Wellcome; 1984) Raniplex (Fournier; 1984)		Raniben (Firma) Ranibloc (Glaxo Allen) Ranidil (Menarini; 1981)	USA:	Zantac Sankyo (Sankyo) Tritec (Glaxo Wellcome) Zantac (Glaxo; 1983)

Razoxane

ATC: V03AF
Use: antineoplastic

RN: 21416-87-5   MF: $C_{11}H_{16}N_4O_4$ MW: 268.27
LD_{50}:   861 mg/kg (M, i.p.)
CN: (±)-4,4'-(1-methyl-1,2-ethanediyl)bis[2,6-piperazinedione]

(±)-1,2-diaminopropane-
N,N,N',N'-tetraacetic acid

Razoxane

Reference(s):
DOS 1 910 283 (ICI; appl. 28.2.1969; USA-prior. 2.7.1968).

Formulation(s):   tabl. 125 mg

Trade Name(s):
GB: Razoxin (ICI); wfm

Rebamipide
(Proamipide)

ATC: A02BX
Use: ulcer therapeutic

RN: 90098-04-7   MF: $C_{19}H_{15}ClN_2O_4$ MW: 370.79
LD_{50}:   572 mg/kg (M, i.v.);
       700 mg/kg (R, i.v.);
       >2 g/kg (dog, p.o.)
CN: α-[(4-chlorobenzoyl)amino]-1,2-dihydro-2-oxo-4-quinolinepropanoic acid

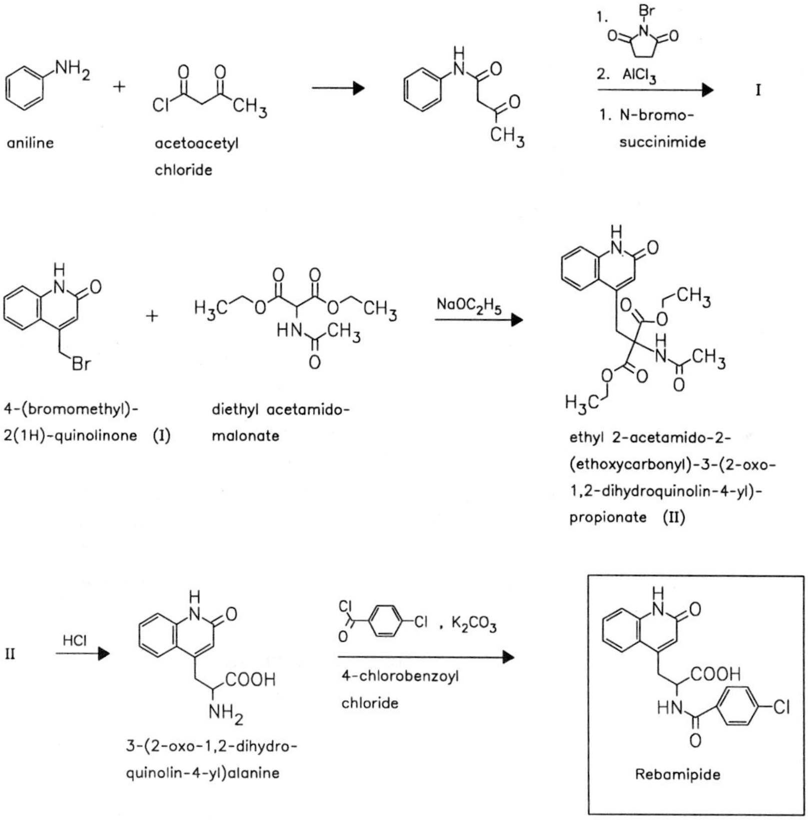

aniline   +   acetoacetyl chloride

1. N-bromo-succinimide
2. AlCl₃ → I

4-(bromomethyl)-2(1H)-quinolinone (I)   +   diethyl acetamido-malonate

$NaOC_2H_5$

ethyl 2-acetamido-2-(ethoxycarbonyl)-3-(2-oxo-1,2-dihydroquinolin-4-yl)-propionate (II)

II →[HCl] 3-(2-oxo-1,2-dihydro-quinolin-4-yl)alanine

4-chlorobenzoyl chloride , K_2CO_3

Rebamipide

Reference(s):
DOS 3 324 034 (Otsuka; appl. 7.4.1983; J-prior. 7.5.1982).
GB 2 123 825 (Otsuka, appl. 7.5.1983; J-prior. 7.5.1982).
Uchida, M. et al.: Chem. Pharm. Bull. (CPBTAL) **33**, 3775 (1985).

oral and parenteral formulations:
JP 60 019 767 (Otsuka; appl. 7.11.1983).

Formulation(s):   tabl. 100 mg

Trade Name(s):
J: Mucosta (Otsuka; 1990)

Reboxetine
(FCE-20124)

ATC: N06AX18
Use: antidepressant, selective
        norepinephrine reuptake inhibitor

RN: 98769-81-4   MF: C$_{19}$H$_{23}$NO$_3$ MW: 313.40
CN: (R*,R*)-2-[(2-Ethoxyphenoxy)phenylmethyl]morpholine

mesilate
RN: 98769-82-5   MF: C$_{19}$H$_{23}$NO$_3$ · CH$_4$O$_3$S   MW: 409.50

Reference(s):
racemic synthesis:
DE 2 901 032 (Farmitalia Carlo Erba; appl. 12.1.1979; I-prior. 20.1.1978).

synthesis of stereoisomers of reboxetine:
DE 3 540 093 (Farmitalia Carlo Erba; appl. 12.11.1985; GB-prior. 22.11.1984).

configurational studies on 2-[α-(2-ethoxyphenoxy)benzyl]morpholine:
Melloni, P.; Della Torre, A.; Lazzari, E.; Mazzini, G.; Meroni, M.: Tetrahedron (TETRAB) **41** (7), 1393 (1985).

Formulation(s):   tabl. 2 mg, 4 mg

Trade Name(s):
D: Edronax (Pharmacia &
      Upjohn)

GB: Edronax (Pharmacia &
      Upjohn; 1997)
I: Davedax (Carlo Erba)

Edronax (Pharmacia &
Upjohn)

Remifentanil
(GI-87084B)

ATC: N01AH06
Use: analgesic

RN: 132875-61-7   MF: $C_{20}H_{28}N_2O_5$ MW: 376.45
CN: 4-(methoxycarbonyl)-4-[(1-oxopropyl)phenylamino]-1-piperidinepropanoic acid methyl ester

monohydrochloride
RN: 132539-07-2   MF: $C_{20}H_{28}N_2O_5 \cdot HCl$ MW: 412.91
oxalate (1:1)
RN: 132875-62-8   MF: $C_{20}H_{28}N_2O_5 \cdot C_2H_2O_4$ MW: 466.49

4-methoxycarbonyl-
4-[(1-oxopropyl)-
phenylamino]-
piperidine

methyl
acrylate

Remifentanil

H_3C-CN, 50 °C

Reference(s):
EP 383 579 (Glaxo; appl. 14.2.1990; USA-prior. 11.12.1989).

preparation of 4-methoxycarbonyl-4-[(1-oxopropyl)phenylamino]piperidine:
DE 2 610 228 (Janssen Pharmaceutica; appl. 13.1.1976; prior. 14.3.1975).
Feldman, P.L., Brackeen, M.F.: J. Org. Chem. (JOCEAH) **55** (13), 4207 (1990).
Colapret, J.A.; Diamantidis, G.; Spencer, H.K.; Spaulding, T.C.; Rudo, F.G: J. Med. Chem. (JMCMAR) **32** (5), 968 (1989).

use as anesthetic:
US 5 466 700 (Glaxo Wellcome; USA-prior. 30.8.1993).

Formulation(s):   amp. 1 mg, 2 mg, 5 mg; vial 1 mg, 2 mg, 5 mg (as hydrochloride)

Trade Name(s):
D: Ultiva (Glaxo Wellcome;
      Zeneca)

F: Ultiva (Glaxo Wellcome)
GB: Ultiva (Glaxo Wellcome)

I: Ultiva (Glaxo Wellcome)
USA: Ultiva (Glaxo Wellcome)

Remoxipride

ATC: N05AL04
Use: neuroleptic with selective dopamine
       D_2-antagonistic activity

RN: 80125-14-0   MF: $C_{16}H_{23}BrN_2O_3$ MW: 371.28
CN: (S)-3-bromo-N-[(1-ethyl-2-pyrrolidinyl)methyl]-2,6-dimethoxybenzamide

hydrochloride

RN: 100288-39-9   MF: C$_{16}$H$_{23}$BrN$_2$O$_3$ · xHCl   MW: unspecified

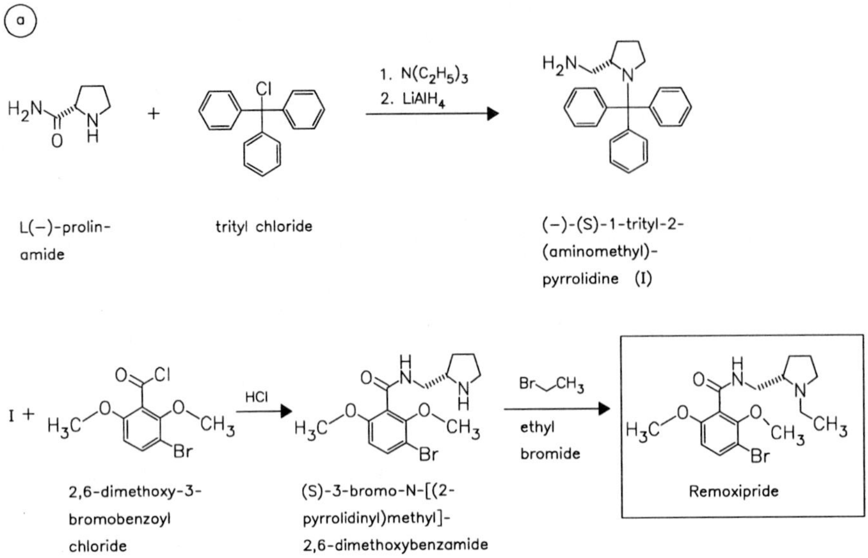

a

L(−)-prolin-
amide

trityl chloride

(−)-(S)-1-trityl-2-
(aminomethyl)-
pyrrolidine (I)

2,6-dimethoxy-3-
bromobenzoyl
chloride

(S)-3-bromo-N-[(2-
pyrrolidinyl)methyl]-
2,6-dimethoxybenzamide

Remoxipride

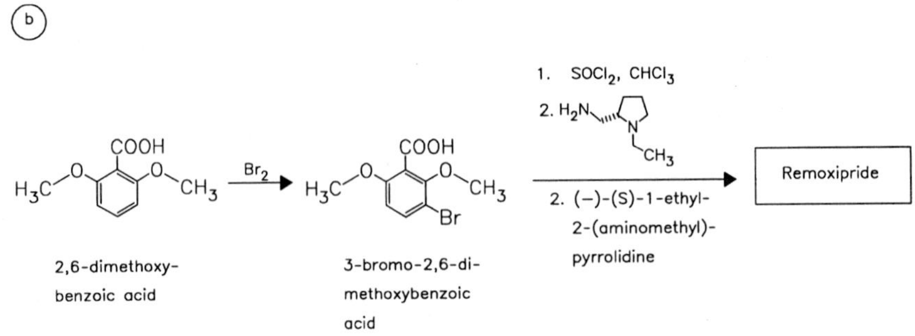

b

2,6-dimethoxy-
benzoic acid

3-bromo-2,6-di-
methoxybenzoic
acid

2. (−)-(S)-1-ethyl-
2-(aminomethyl)-
pyrrolidine

Remoxipride

Reference(s):
US 4 232 037 (Astra; 4.11.1980; S-prior. 23.3.1978).
DE 2 964 774 (Astra; appl. 5.3.1979; S-prior. 23.3.1978).
EP 4 831 (Astra; appl. 5.3.1979; S-prior. 23.3.1978).
EP 60 235 (Astra; appl. 5.3.1982; S-prior. 11.3.1981).
Florvall, L.; Ögren, S.-O.: J. Med. Chem. (JMCMAR) **25**, 1280 (1986).

synthesis of 2,6-dimethoxybenzoic acid:
Doyle, F.P. et al.: J. Chem. Soc. (JCSOA9) 497 (1963).

synthesis of (−)-(S)-1-ethyl-2-(aminomethyl)pyrrolidine:
FR 1 528 014 (Soc. d'Etudes Sci. et ind.; appl. 24.4.1967).

oral pharmaceutical formulation:
EP 273 890 (Astra; appl. 7.12.1987; S-prior. 22.12.1986).

Formulation(s):   amp. 200 mg/2 ml; s. r. cps. 150 mg, 300, mg; susp. 150 mg/6 ml (as hydrochloride)

Trade Name(s):
D: Psyloc (Astra; 1991); wfm   Roxiam (Astra; 1991); wfm

Repaglinide
(AG-EE-623ZW; AG-EE-388)

ATC: A10BX02
Use: antidiabetic

RN: 135062-02-1   MF: $C_{27}H_{36}N_2O_4$ MW: 452.60
CN: (S)-2-Ethoxy-4-[2-[[3-methyl-1-[2-(1-piperidinyl)-phenyl]butyl]amino]-2-oxoethyl]benzoic acid

(S)-(+)-Ca salt
RN: 172041-25-7   MF: $C_{44}H_{70}CaN_4O_8$ MW: 823.14
racemate
RN: 108157-53-5   MF: $C_{27}H_{36}N_2O_4$ MW: 452.60

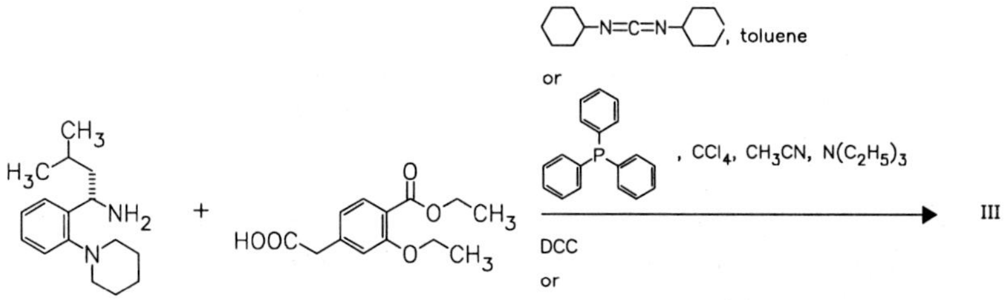

(S)-3-methyl-
1-[2-(1-piperidinyl)-
phenyl]butylamine (I)

2-[4-(ethoxycarbonyl)-
3-ethoxyphenyl]-
acetic acid

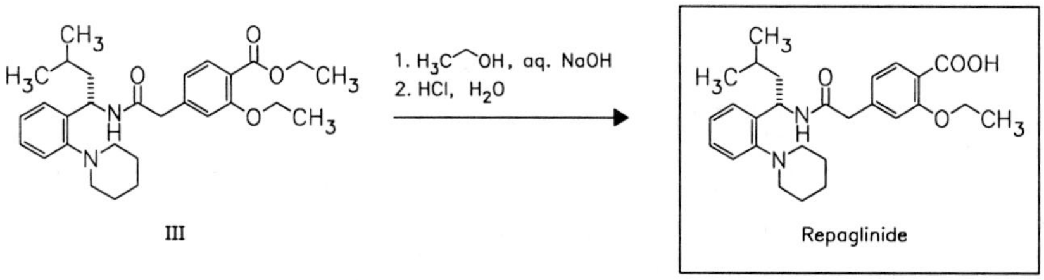

triphenylphosphine (II)

III

III

Repaglinide

synthesis of starting product I: (S)-3-methyl-1-[2-(1-piperidinyl)phenyl]butylamine

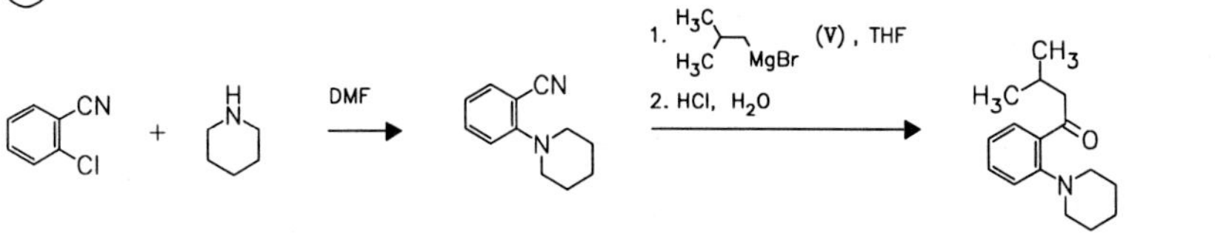

2-chloro-
benzonitrile

piperidine (IV)

2-(1-piperidinyl)-
benzonitrile

3-methyl-1-
[2-(1-piperidinyl)-
phenyl]-1-butanone (VI)

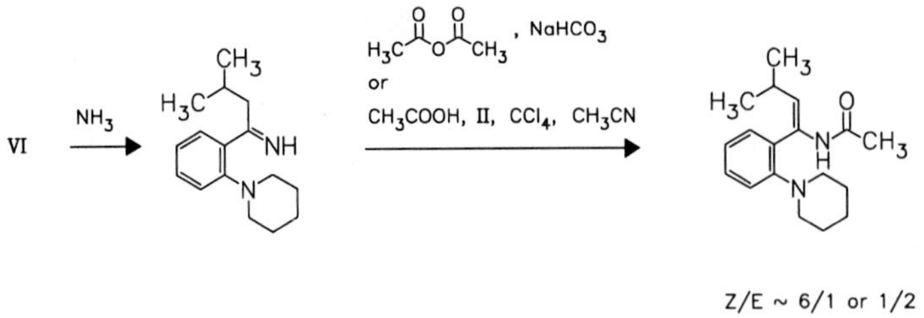

VI

Z/E ~ 6/1 or 1/2

3-methyl-1-
[2-(1-piperidinyl)-
phenyl]-1-
butanimine

N-[3-methyl-1-[2-(1-
piperidinyl)phenyl]-
1-butenyl]acetamide (VII)

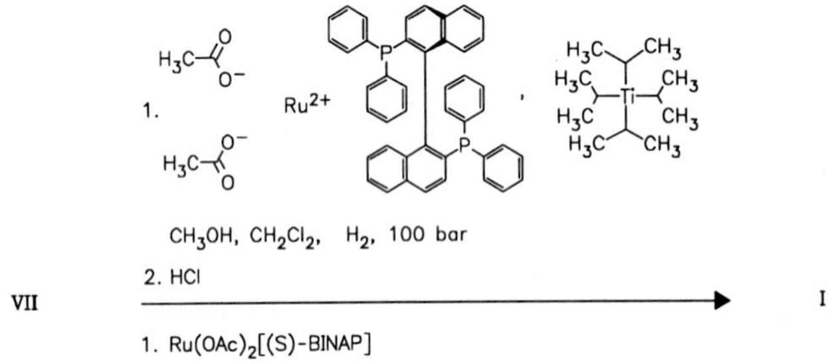

VII

1. Ru(OAc)$_2$[(S)-BINAP]

⓫ b

VI + H$_2$N (S)-1-phenyl-ethylamine → (VIII)

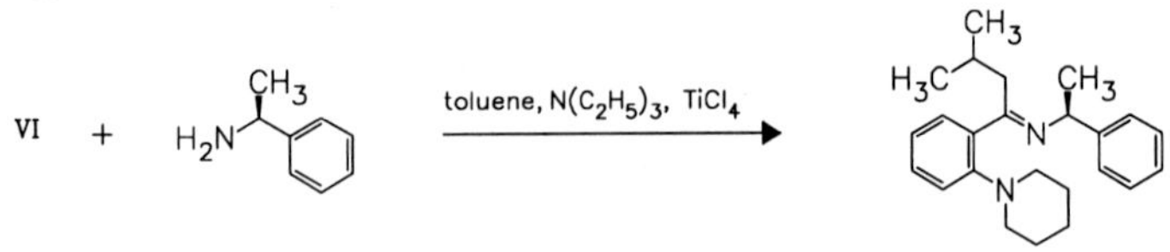

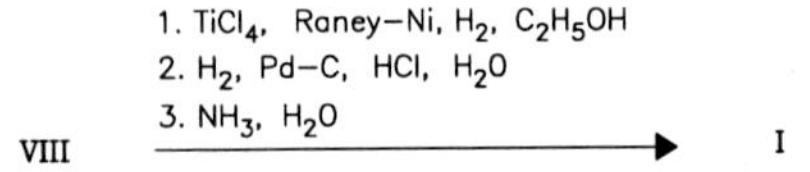

(S)-1-phenyl-
ethylamine

1. TiCl$_4$, Raney–Ni, H$_2$, C$_2$H$_5$OH
2. H$_2$, Pd–C, HCl, H$_2$O
3. NH$_3$, H$_2$O

VIII ——————————→ I

ⓒ c

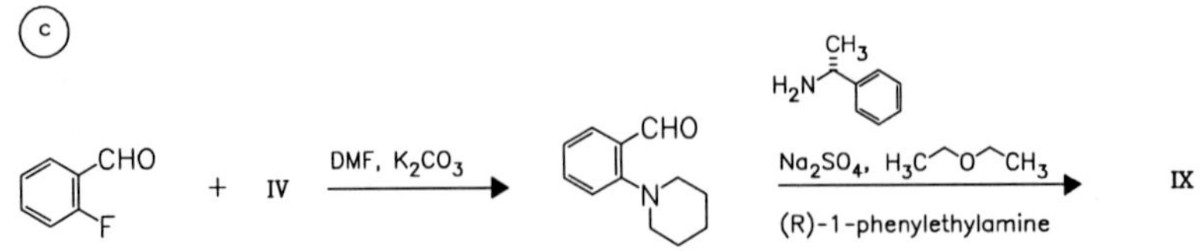

2-fluoro-
benzaldehyde

+ IV —DMF, K$_2$CO$_3$→ 2-(1-piperidinyl)-benzaldehyde

—Na$_2$SO$_4$, H$_3$C–O–CH$_3$, (R)-1-phenylethylamine→ IX

2-(1-piperidinyl)-
benzaldehyde

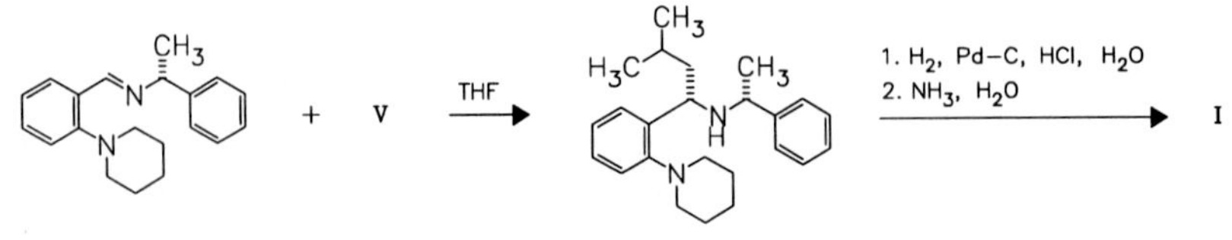

(VIII) + V —THF→ —1. H$_2$, Pd–C, HCl, H$_2$O 2. NH$_3$, H$_2$O→ I

(d) resolution of racemic mixture

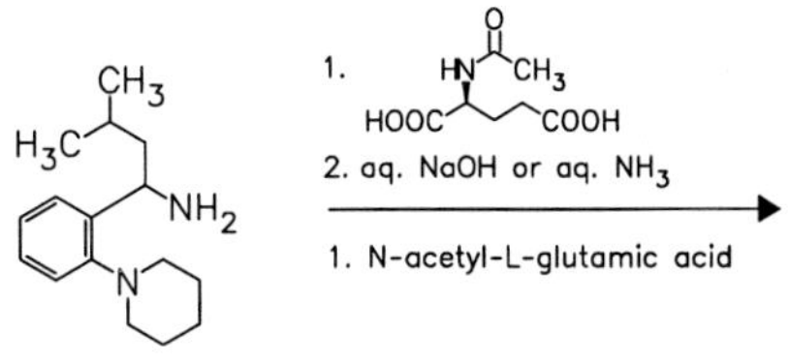
1.
HOOC COOH
2. aq. NaOH or aq. NH3
1. N-acetyl-L-glutamic acid
I

(±)-I

Reference(s):
WO 9 300 337 (Thomae GmbH; WO-prior. 21.6.1991).
Grell, W. et al.: Eur. J. Med. Chem. (EJMCA5) **41** (26), 5219 (1998)

racemic synthesis and solid forms of repaglinide:
EP 207 331 (Thomae GmbH; appl. 10.6.1986; D-prior. 25.6.1985)

preparation of 2-(1-piperidinyl)benzaldehyde:
GB 1 299 580 (Lilly Ind.; GB-prior. 15.10.1968)

Formulation(s): tabl. 0.5 mg, 1 mg, 2 mg

Trade Name(s):
D: NovoNorm (Novo Nordisk) USA: Prandin (Novo Nordisk; 1998)

Repirinast

ATC: R03D
Use: antiallergic, treatment of bronchial asthma

RN: 73080-51-0 MF: $C_{20}H_{21}NO_5$ MW: 355.39
LD_{50}: >5 g/kg (M, p.o., s.c.);
>5 g/kg (R, p.o., s.c.)
CN: 5,6-dihydro-7,8-dimethyl-4,5-dioxo-4*H*-pyrano[3,2-*c*]quinoline-2-carboxylic acid 3-methylbutyl ester

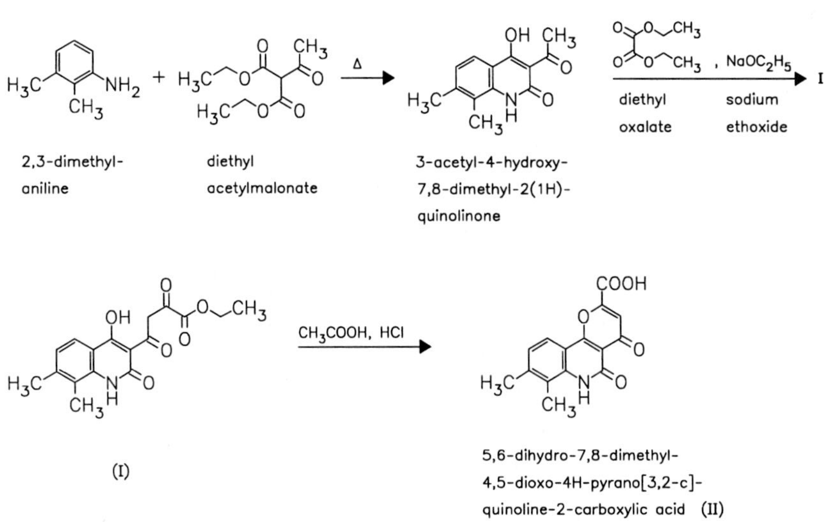
2,3-dimethyl-aniline
diethyl acetylmalonate
Δ
3-acetyl-4-hydroxy-7,8-dimethyl-2(1H)-quinolinone
, NaOC2H5
diethyl oxalate
sodium ethoxide
I
(I)
CH3COOH, HCl
5,6-dihydro-7,8-dimethyl-4,5-dioxo-4H-pyrano[3,2-c]-quinoline-2-carboxylic acid (II)

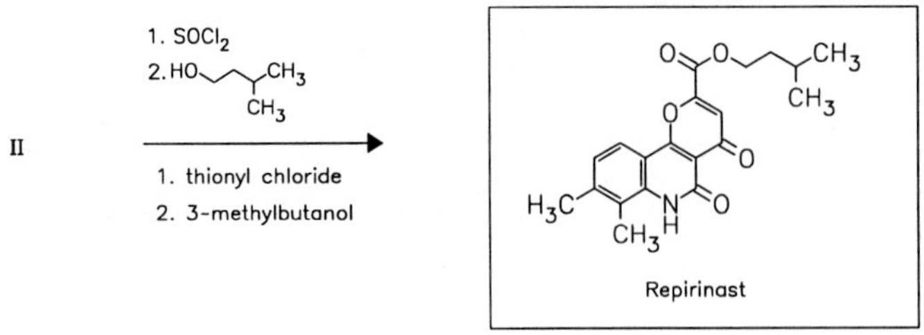
II
1. $SOCl_2$
2. HO
CH_3
CH_3
1. thionyl chloride
2. 3-methylbutanol
H_3C
CH_3
Repirinast

Reference(s):
DOS 2 922 231 (Mitsubishi; appl. 31.5.1979; J-prior. 5.6.1978).
US 4 298 610 (Mitsubishi; 3.11.1981; J-prior. 5.6.1978).
Morinaka, Y. et al.: Eur. J. Med. Chem. (EJMCA5) **16**, 251 (1981).

synthesis of ^{14}C-repirinast:
Esumi, A. et al.: Clin. Rep. **20**, 391 (1986).

Formulation(s): tabl. 150 mg

Trade Name(s):
J: Romet (Mitsubishi; 1989)

Reproterol

ATC: R03AC15; R03CC14
Use: bronchodilator

RN: 54063-54-6 MF: $C_{18}H_{23}N_5O_5$ MW: 389.41 EINECS: 258-956-1
LD_{50}: 145 mg/kg (M, i.v.)
CN: 7-[3-[[2-(3,5-dihydroxyphenyl)-2-hydroxyethyl]amino]propyl]-3,7-dihydro-1,3-dimethyl-1*H*-purine-2,6-dione

monohydrochloride
RN: 13055-82-8 MF: $C_{18}H_{23}N_5O_5 \cdot HCl$ MW: 425.87 EINECS: 235-942-3
LD_{50}: 148 mg/kg (M, i.v.); >10 g/kg (M, p.o.);
142 mg/kg (R, i.v.); >10 g/kg (R, p.o.);
160 mg/kg (dog, i.v.); 400 mg/kg (dog, p.o.)

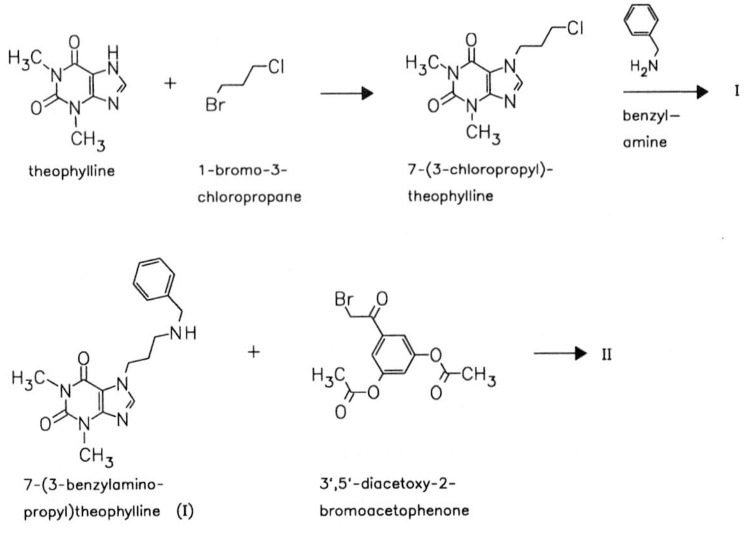
theophylline
1-bromo-3-chloropropane
7-(3-chloropropyl)-theophylline
benzyl-amine
I
7-(3-benzylamino-propyl)theophylline (I)
3',5'-diacetoxy-2-bromoacetophenone
II

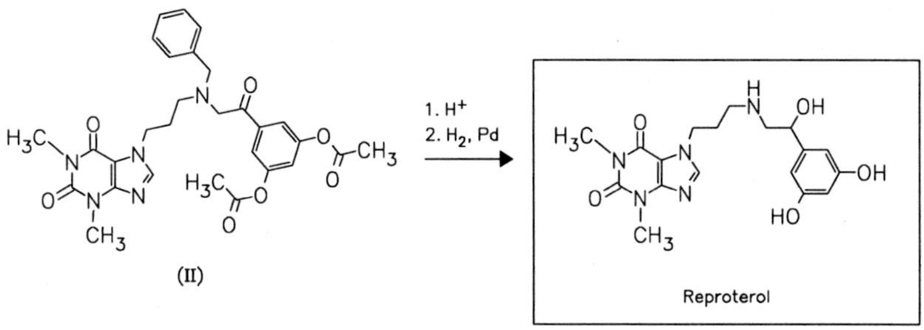

(II) → Reproterol

1. H⁺
2. H₂, Pd

Reference(s):
DE 1 545 725 (Degussa; appl. 16.1.1965).
DE 1 795 573 (Degussa; appl. 16.1.1965).

hydrogenation:
DOS 2 701 629 (Degussa; appl. 17.1.1977).
US 4 150 227 (Degussa; 17.4.1979; D-prior. 17.1.1977).

medical use:
US 3 544 685 (Degussa; 1.12.1970; prior. 26.7.1968).

starting material:
Priewe, H.; Poljak, A.: Chem. Ber. (CHBEAM) **90**, 1651 (1957).

review:
Klingler, K.H.: Arzneim.-Forsch. (ARZNAD) **27**, 1-76 (1a) (1977).

Formulation(s):   aerosol 0.5 mg/0.05 ml; amp. 0.09 mg/ml; f. c. tabl. 20 mg (as hydrochloride)

Trade Name(s):
D: Allergospasmin (ASTA Medica AWD)-comb.
Arane (Fisons; Rhône-Poulenc Rorer)-comb.

Bronchospasmin (ASTA Medica AWD)

GB: Bronchodil (ASTA Medica)

I: Broncospasmin (ASTA Medica)

J: Bronchospasmin (Farmades)

Rescimetol

ATC: C02AA
Use: antihypertensive

RN: 73573-42-9   MF: $C_{33}H_{38}N_2O_8$ MW: 590.67
LD$_{50}$:   >40 mg/kg (M, i.v.); >15 g/kg (M, p.o.);
       >20 mg/kg (R, i.v.); >15 g/kg (R, p.o.)
CN: [3β,16β,17α,18β(E),20α]-18-[[3-(4-hydroxy-3-methoxyphenyl)-1-oxo-2-propenyl]oxy]-11,17-dimethoxyyohimban-16-carboxylic acid methyl ester

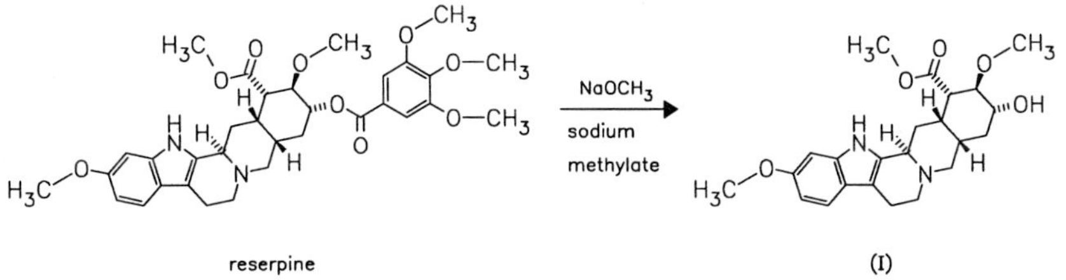

reserpine → (I)

NaOCH₃
sodium methylate

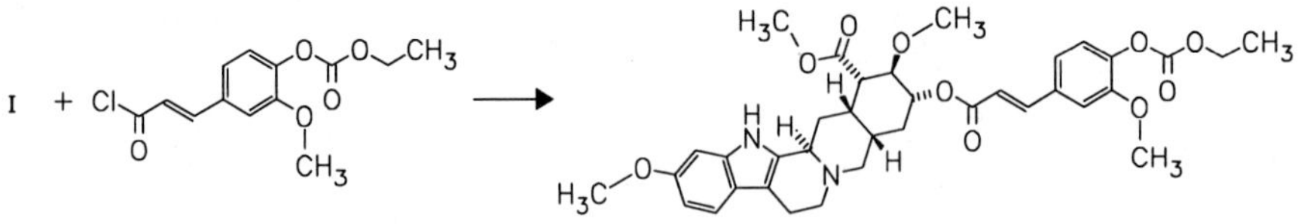

I + 3-methoxy-4-(ethoxy-carbonyloxy)cinnamoyl chloride → (II)

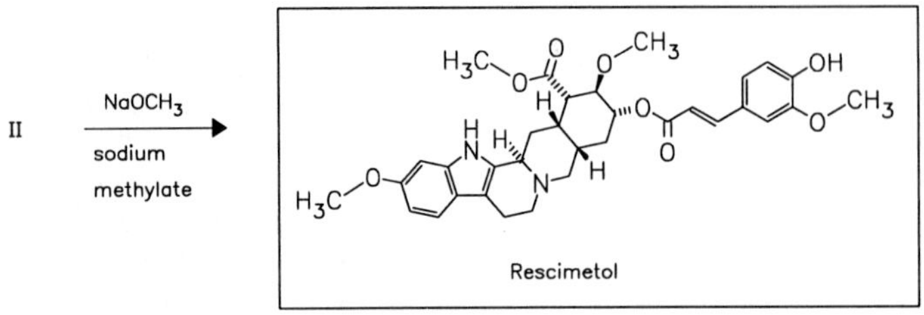

II → NaOCH₃ sodium methylate → Rescimetol

Reference(s):
DOS 2 221 123 (Nippon Chemiphar; appl. 28.8.1972; J-prior. 8.10.1971, 28.12.1971).
US 3 898 215 (Nippon Chemiphar; 5.8.1975; J-prior. 8.10.1971, 28.12.1971).
Kametami, T. et al.: J. Med. Chem. (JMCMAR) **15**, 686 (1972).
JP 7 619 799 (Nippon Chemiphar; appl. 7.8.1974).
JP 7 476 890 (Nippon Chemiphar; appl. 30.11.1972).

Formulation(s):　tabl. 1 mg

Trade Name(s):
J:　　Toscarna (Nippon
　　　Chemiphar)

Rescinnamine

ATC:　C02AA01
Use:　antihypertensive, sedative, tranquilizer

RN:　24815-24-5　MF: $C_{35}H_{42}N_2O_9$　MW: 634.73　EINECS: 246-471-8
LD$_{50}$:　56 mg/kg (M, i.v.); 1420 mg/kg (M, p.o.);
　　1 g/kg (R, p.o.)
CN:　(3β,16β,17α,18β,20α)-11,17-dimethoxy-18-[[1-oxo-3-(3,4,5-trimethoxyphenyl)-2-propenyl]oxy]yohimban-16-carboxylic acid methyl ester

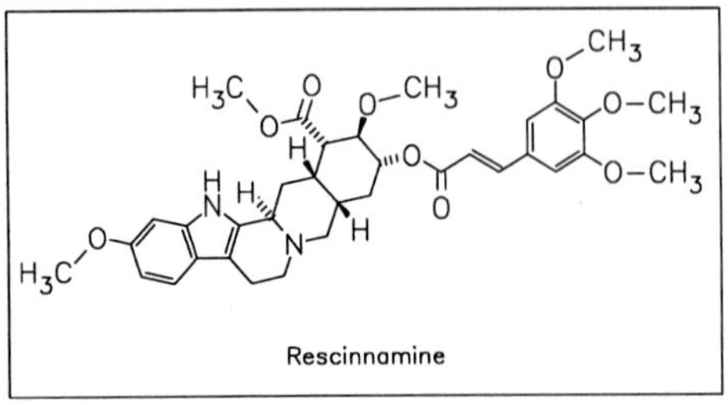

Rescinnamine

By extraction of the roots of *Rauwolfia serpentina* (L.) Beuth. and column chromatographic separation of reserpine.

Reference(s):
US 2 974 144 (Riker; 7.3.1961; appl. 1954; prior. 1953).
US 2 876 228 (Pfizer; 3.3.1959; appl. 1956).
Klohs, M.W. et al.: J. Am. Chem. Soc. (JACSAT) **77**, 2241 (1955).

partial synthesis from reserpic acid methyl ester:
US 2 854 454 (P. R. Ulshafer; 1958; appl. 1954).

Formulation(s):   tabl. 0.25 mg, 0.5 mg

Trade Name(s):

D:	Detensitral (Karlspharma)-comb.; wfm	Sarparel (Servier)-comb.; wfm		Caniramine (Hokuriku)
	Diuraupur (Guilini)-comb.; wfm	Tensid (Bayer Pharma)-comb.; wfm		Cinnaloid (Taito Pfizer)
	Rauwopur (Giulini)-comb.; wfm	Tensitral (Dausse)-comb.; wfm		Colstamin "Kowa" (Kowa)
F:	Aldatense (Searle)-comb.; wfm	Tensitral (Synthélabo)-comb.; wfm		Daisaloid (Mohan)
	Anaprel F (Servier)-comb.; wfm	Resertan (Perkins)-comb.; wfm	I:	Isocalsin (Kowa Yakuhin)
	Diviator (Servier)-comb.; wfm	Apolon (Toyama)	J:	Rescinate (Ohta)
		Aporecin (Kayaku)		Resiloid (Nippon Shoji)
		Atension (Santen)		Rozex (Teisan)

D:
- Detensitral (Karlspharma)-comb.; wfm
- Diuraupur (Guilini)-comb.; wfm
- Rauwopur (Giulini)-comb.; wfm

F:
- Aldatense (Searle)-comb.; wfm
- Anaprel F (Servier)-comb.; wfm
- Diviator (Servier)-comb.; wfm

- Sarparel (Servier)-comb.; wfm
- Tensid (Bayer Pharma)-comb.; wfm
- Tensitral (Dausse)-comb.; wfm
- Tensitral (Synthélabo)-comb.; wfm

I:
- Resertan (Perkins)-comb.; wfm

J:
- Apolon (Toyama)
- Aporecin (Kayaku)
- Atension (Santen)

- Caniramine (Hokuriku)
- Cinnaloid (Taito Pfizer)
- Colstamin "Kowa" (Kowa)
- Daisaloid (Mohan)
- Isocalsin (Kowa Yakuhin)
- Rescinate (Ohta)
- Resiloid (Nippon Shoji)
- Rozex (Teisan)
- Sciminan (Kotani)
- Seripinin (Fuji Zoki)
- Sinselpin (Kobayashi)

USA:
- Moderil (Pfizer); wfm

Reserpine

ATC: C02AA02
Use: antihypertensive, tranquilizer

RN: 50-55-5   MF: $C_{33}H_{40}N_2O_9$ MW: 608.69   EINECS: 200-047-9
LD_{50}:   21 mg/kg (M, i.v.); 200 mg/kg (M, p.o.);
15 mg/kg (R, i.v.); 420 mg/kg (R, p.o.);
500 µg/kg (dog, i.v.)
CN: (3β,16β,17α,18β,20α)-11,17-dimethoxy-18-[(3,4,5-trimethoxybenzoyl)oxy]yohimban-16-carboxylic acid methyl ester

Reserpine

By extraction of the roots of *Rauwolfia serpentina* (L.) Beuth.

Reference(s):
DE 967 469 (Boehringer Ing.; appl. 1954).
US 2 752 351 (Ciba; 1956; appl. 1953).
US 2 833 771 (Ciba; 1958; CH-Frior. 1954).
US 2 887 489 (Ciba; 1959; CH-prior. 1956).
US 2 938 906 (Ciba; 1960; CH-prior. 1952).
Dorfmann, L. et al.: Helv. Chim. Acta (HCACAV) **37**, 59 (1954).
Ullmanns Encykl. Tech. Chem., 4. Aufl., Vol. **7**, 178.
Ullmanns Encykl. Tech. Chem., 3. Aufl., Vol. **13**, 277.

total synthesis:
DAS 1 088 062 (Research Corp.; appl. 3.5.1957; USA-prior. 3.5.1956).
Hanessian, S et al.: J. Org. Chem. (JOCEAH) **62**, 465 (1997).

Formulation(s):   cps. 0.075 mg, 0.15 mg; drg. 0.05 mg, 0.07 mg, 0.1 mg; tabl. 0.1 mg, 0.125 mg, 0.25 mg

Trade Name(s):

D:	Adelphan-Esidrix (Novartis Pharma)-comb.	Resaltex (Procter & Gamble)-comb.	Serpasil Esidrex (Ciba)-comb.; wfm
	Barotonal (Brenner-Efeka)-comb.	Reserpin Hameln (Hameln); wfm	combination preparations; wfm
	Bendigon (Bayer Vital)-comb.	Reserpin Saar (Chephasaar); wfm	I: Brinerdina (Novartis)-comb.
	Brisarin (Novartis Pharma)-comb.	Sedaraupin (Boehringer Mannh.); wfm	Igroton (Novartis)-comb.
	Darebon (Novartis Pharma)-comb.	Serpasil (Ciba); wfm	J: numerous generic preparations
	Disalpin (ASTA Medica AWD)-comb.	Triniton (Apogepha)-comb.	Serpasil (Ciba-Geigy-Takeda)
	Durotan (Beiersdorf-Lilly)-comb.	Tri-Thiazid Reserpin (Stada)-comb. numerous combination preparations	USA: Diupres (Merck Sharp & Dohme)-comb.
	dysto-Loges (Loges)-comb.	F: Tensionorme (Leo)-comb.	Diutensen-R (Wallace)-comb.
	Modenol (Boehringer Mannh.)-comb.	GB: Abicol (Boots)-comb.; wfm Serpasil (Ciba); wfm	Hydropres (Merck Sharp & Dohme)-comb.

Retinol

(Axerophthol; Vitamin A)

ATC: A11CA01; D10AD02; R01AX02; S01XA02
Use: epithelial protective vitamin

RN: 68-26-8   MF: $C_{20}H_{30}O$ MW: 286.46   EINECS: 200-683-7
LD_{50}:   1510 mg/kg (M, p.o.);
          2 g/kg (R, p.o.)
CN: (all-E)-3,7-dimethyl-9-(2,6,6-trimethyl-1-cyclohexen-1-yl)-2,4,6,8-nonatetraen-1-ol

acetate
RN: 127-47-9   MF: $C_{22}H_{32}O_2$ MW: 328.50   EINECS: 204-844-2
LD_{50}:   432 mg/kg (M, i.v.); 4100 mg/kg (M, p.o.)
propionate
RN: 7069-42-3   MF: $C_{23}H_{34}O_2$ MW: 342.52   EINECS: 230-363-2
palmitate
RN: 79-81-2   MF: $C_{36}H_{60}O_2$ MW: 524.87   EINECS: 201-228-5
LD_{50}:   6060 mg/kg (M, p.o.);
          7910 mg/kg (R, p.o.)

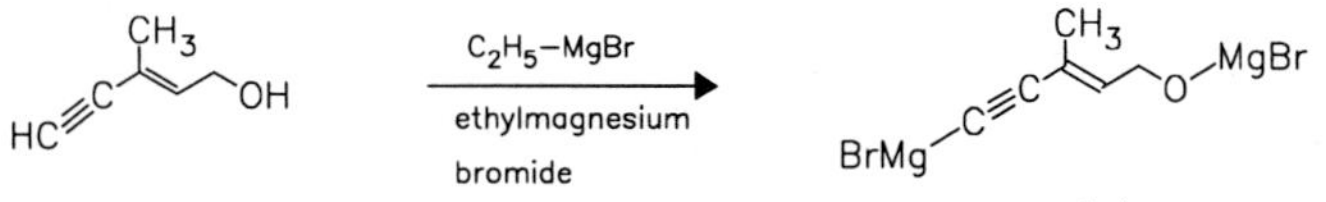

1-hydroxy-3-methyl-2-penten-4-yne (II)

(III)

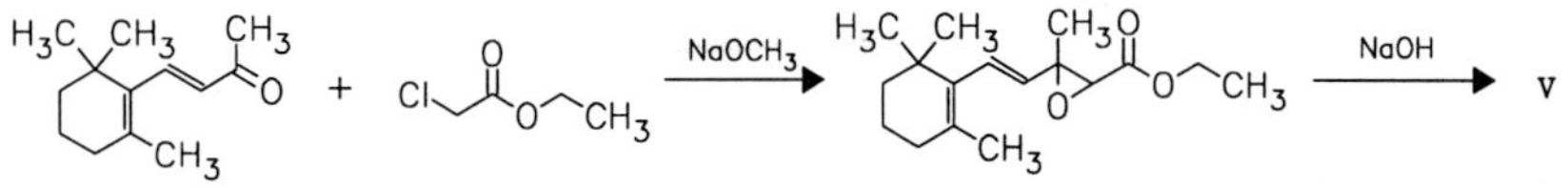

β-ionone (IV)

ethyl chloroacetate

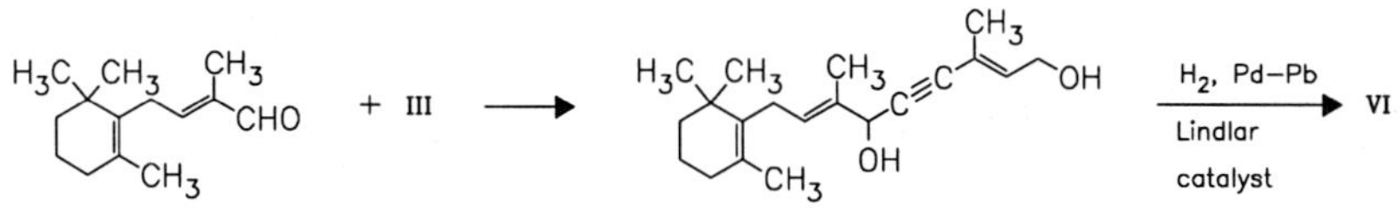

V

"aldehyde C₁₄" (V)

+ III

VI

H₂, Pd–Pb Lindlar catalyst

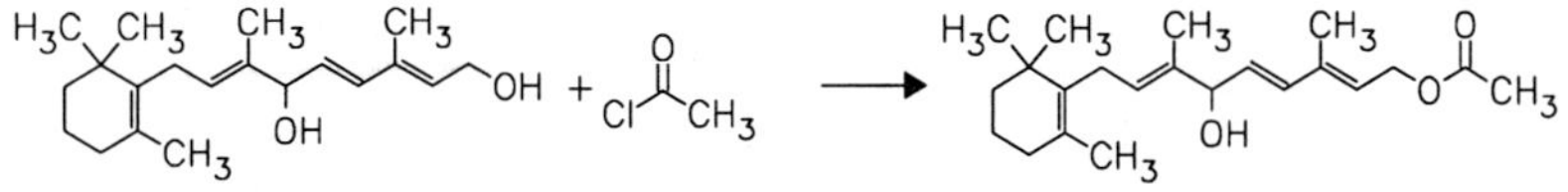

(VI)

acetyl chloride (VII)

(VIII)

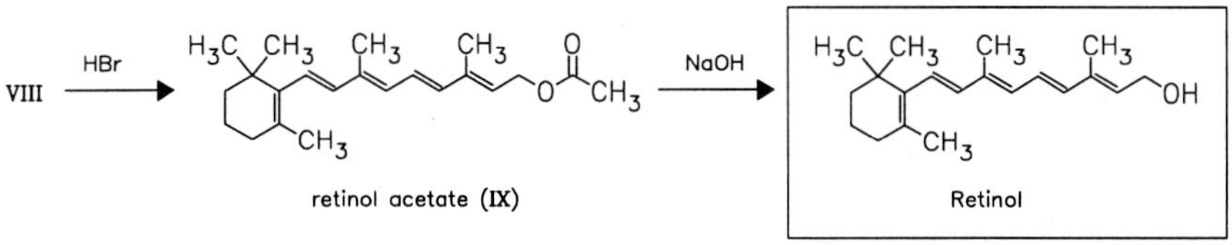

VIII

retinol acetate (IX)

Retinol

(b) BASF:

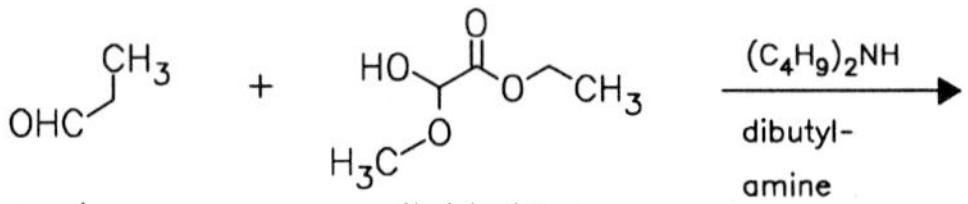

propion-aldehyde

ethyl hydroxy-methoxyacetate

ethyl 3-formyl-crotonate (X)

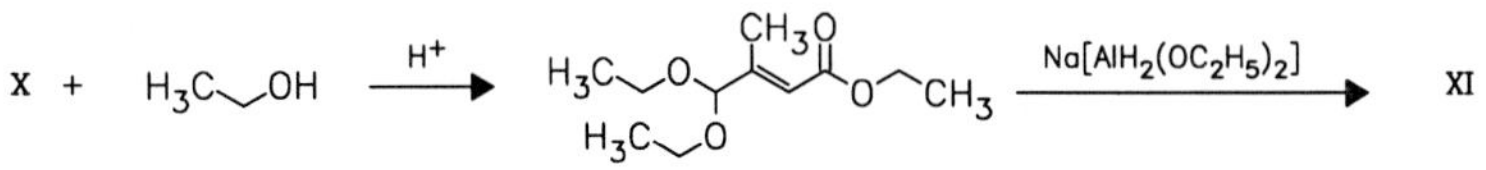

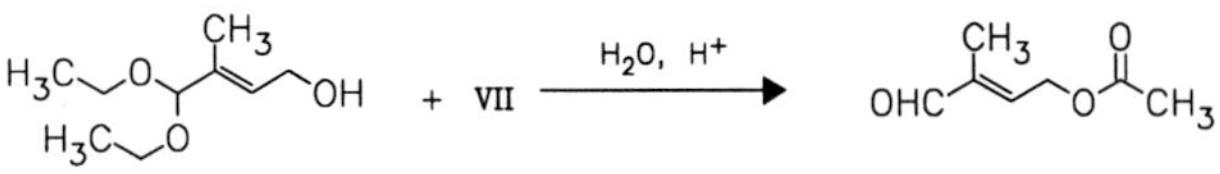

X + H₃C–OH

XI

4,4-diethoxy-3-methyl-crotyl alcohol (XI)

+ VII

3-formylcrotyl acetate (XII)

alternative synthesis:

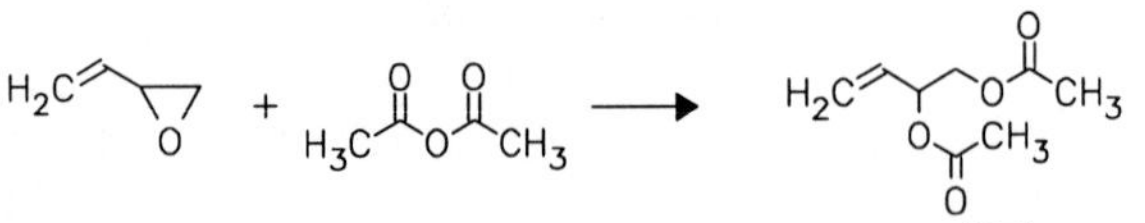

3,4-epoxy-
1-butene

(XIII)

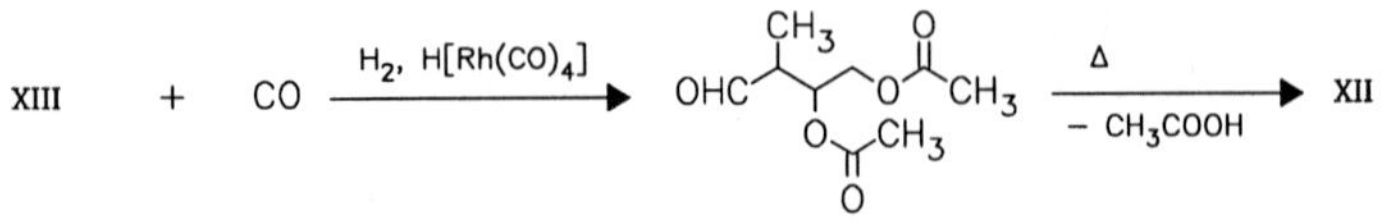

XIII + CO $\xrightarrow{H_2, H[Rh(CO)_4]}$ $\xrightarrow[- CH_3COOH]{\Delta}$ XII

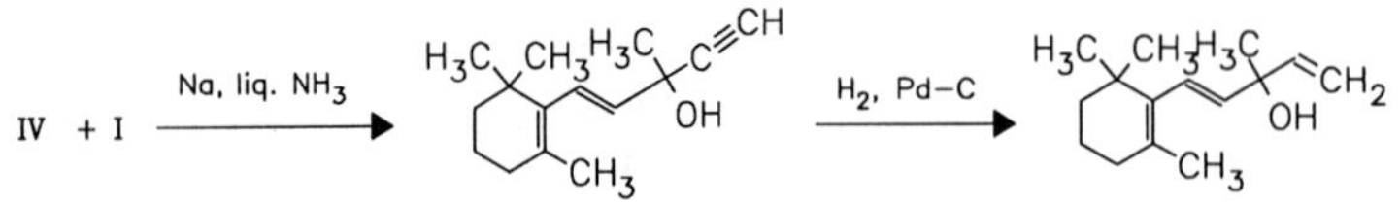

IV + I $\xrightarrow{Na, liq. NH_3}$ $\xrightarrow{H_2, Pd-C}$

vinyl-β-ionol (XIV)

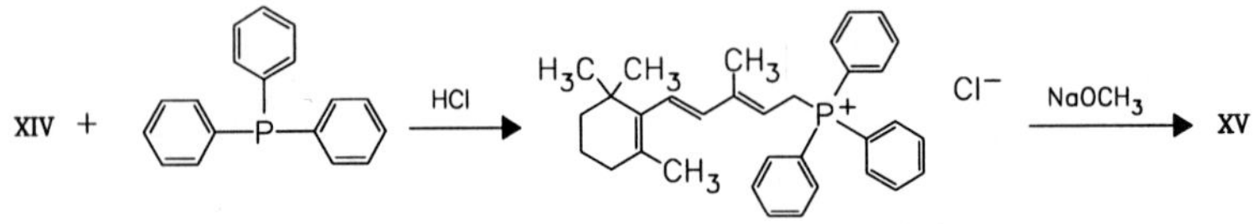

XIV + $\xrightarrow{HCl}$ $\xrightarrow{NaOCH_3}$ XV

triphenyl-
phosphine

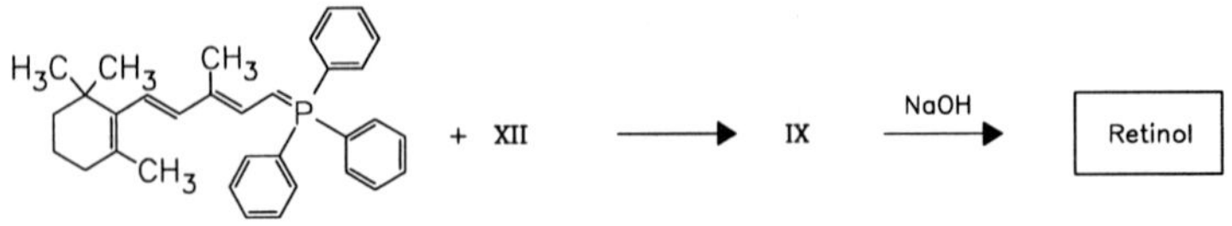

+ XII $\longrightarrow$ IX $\xrightarrow{NaOH}$ Retinol

(XV)

(c) A. E. C.:

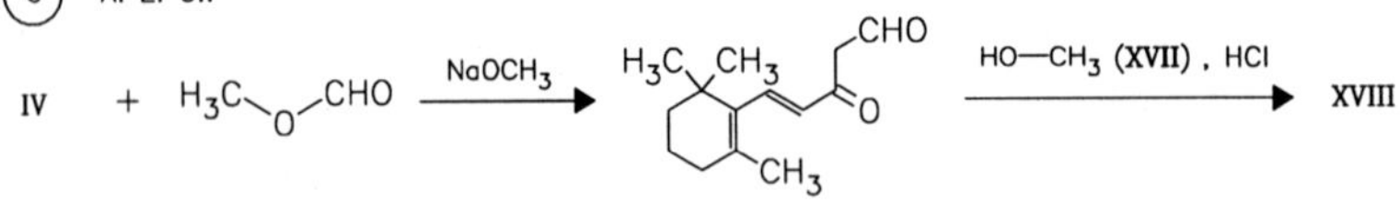

IV + $H_3C-O-CHO$ $\xrightarrow{NaOCH_3}$ $\xrightarrow{HO-CH_3 \ (XVII) \ , \ HCl}$ XVIII

methyl
formate (XVI)

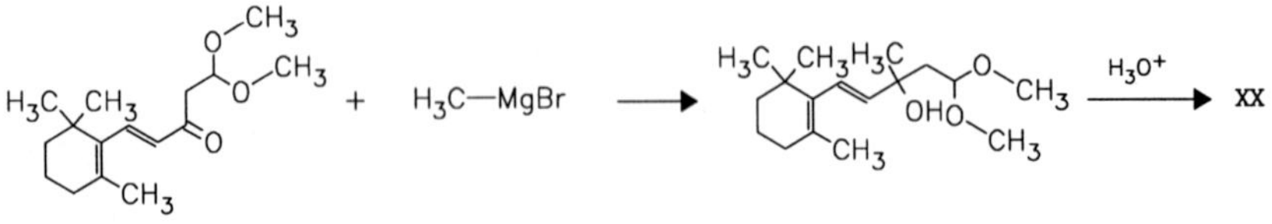

+ $H_3C-MgBr$ $\longrightarrow$ $\xrightarrow{H_3O^+}$ XX

(XVIII)   methylmagnesium
bromide (XIX)

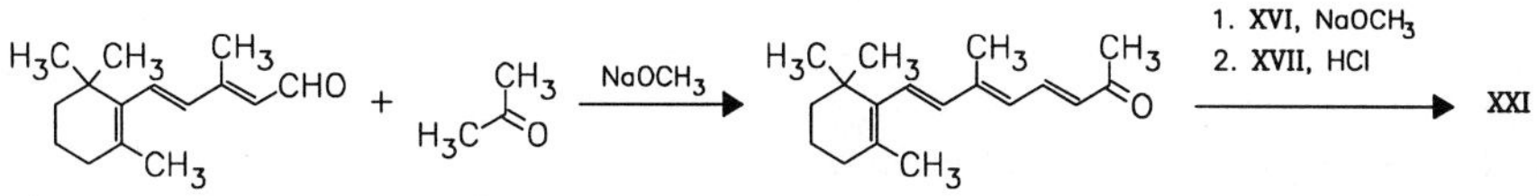

β-ionylidene-
acetaldehyde (XX)

acetone

"β-C₁₈-ketone"

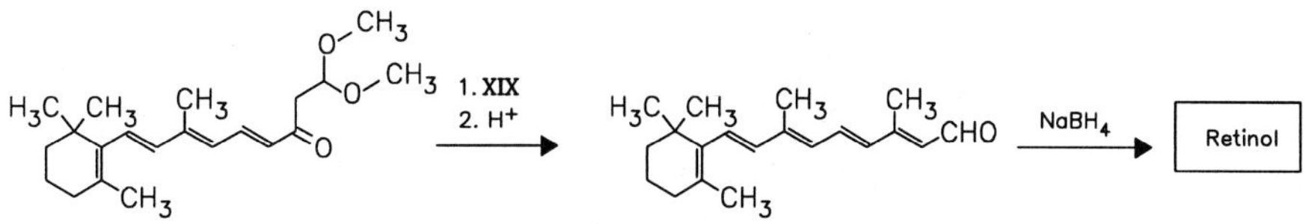

1. XVI, NaOCH₃
2. XVII, HCl

XXI

(XXI)

retinal

Retinol

d Rhone-Poulenc:

XIV +

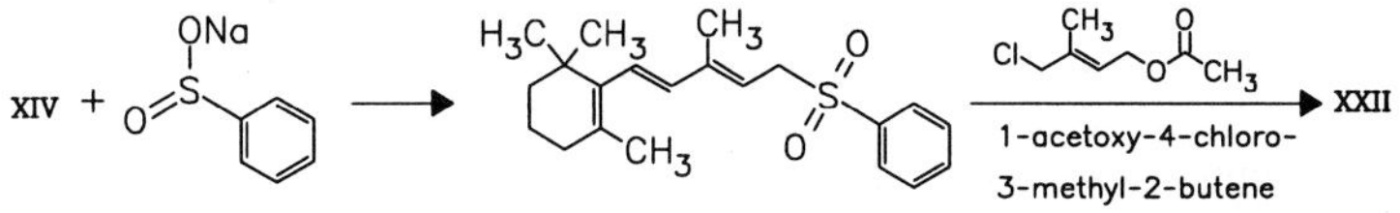

sodium
phenylsulfinate

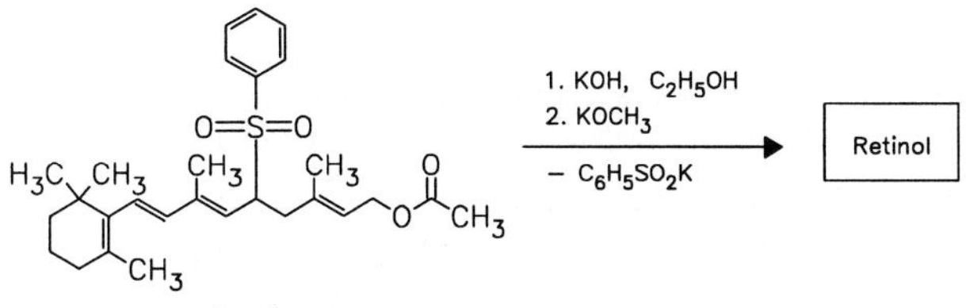

1-acetoxy-4-chloro-
3-methyl-2-butene

XXII

(XXII)

1. KOH, C₂H₅OH
2. KOCH₃

− C₆H₅SO₂K

Retinol

Retinol palmitate:

IX +

methyl palmitate

NaOCH₃

Retinol palmitate

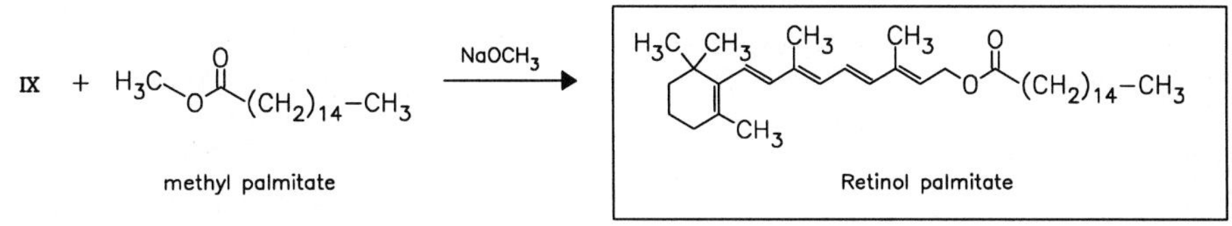

Reference(s):
reviews:
Isler, O.; Brubacher, G.: Vitamine I (Fat Soluble Vitamins), Thieme Verlag Stuttgart, New York 1982.
Ullmann's Encyclopedia of Industrial Chemistry, 5th Ed., Vol. **A27**, p. 453-469, VCH Verlagsges. m.b.H.,
Weinheim 1996.

older review:

Baxter, J.G.: Fortschr. Chem. Org. Naturst. (FCONAA) **9**, 41 (1952).

a Isler, O. et al.: Helv. Chim. Acta (HCACAV) **30**, 1911 (1947).

Isler, O. et al.: Helv. Chim. Acta (HCACAV) **32**, 489 (1949).

Isler, O.: Chimia (CHIMAD) **4**, 103 (1950).

Isler, O.: Angew. Chem. (ANCEAD) **68**, 547 (1956).

DE 839 495 (Roche; appl. 1949; CH-prior. 1945, 1947).

DE 844 596 (Roche; appl. 1949; CH-prior. 1947).

DE 842 190 (Roche; appl. 1949; CH-prior. 1946) ("C_{14}-*aldehyde*")

b Pommer, H.: Angew. Chem. (ANCEAD) **72**, 811, 911 (1960).

Pommer, H.: Angew. Chem. (ANCEAD) **89**, 437 (1977).

Reif, W.; Grassner, H.: Chem.-Ing.-Tech. (CITEAH) **45**, 646 (1973).

Freyschlag, H. et al.: Angew. Chem. (ANCEAD) **77**, 277 (1965).

DE 957 942 (BASF; appl. 1955).

DE 1 059 900 (BASF; appl. 1957).

DE 1 060 386 (BASF; appl. 1957).

DE 1 068 702 (BASF; appl. 1958).

ethinylation of β-ionone:

DE 1 081 883 (BASF; appl. 1958).

synthesis of 3-formylcrotyl acetate:

DAS 2 004 675 (BASF; appl. 1970).

EP 87 097 (BASF; appl. 14.2.1983; D-prior. 20.2.1982).

c FR 1 243 824 (A.E.C.).

d Julia, M.; Arnould, D.: Bull. Soc. Chim. Fr. (BSCFAS) **1973**, 743, 746.

DOS 2 305 267 (Rhône-Poulenc).

DAS 2 361 144 (Rhône-Poulenc; appl. 7.12.1973; F-prior. 7.12.1972, 22.12.1972).

DE 2 734 172 (Rhône-Poulenc; appl. 28.7.1977; F-prior. 28.7.1976).

Formulation(s): cps. 2500 iu, 30000 iu, 50000 iu; drg. 10000 iu (as acetate); drops 1000 iu/ml, 10000 iu/g, 40000 iu/ml; emulsion 30000 iu/ml, 300000 iu/g; gel 1000 iu/ml; ointment 250 iu/g, 10000 iu/g; tabl. 20000 iu.

Trade Name(s):

D: A-Mulsin (Mucos)
Arovit (Roche); wfm
A-Vicotrat (Heyl)
Oculotect Augentropfen (CIBA Vision)
Ophtosan Augentropfen (Winzer)
Retinol (Ursapharm)
Solan (Winzer)
Taxofit Vitamin A (Anasco); wfm
Vitamin A Dispersa (CIBA Vision)
Vitamin A Dispersa Baeschlin (Baeschlin); wfm
Vitamin-A-Kapseln "Extracta" (Extracta); wfm
Vitamin-A-POS (Ursapharm)
Vitamin-A-Saar (Chephasaar)
Vogan (Merck); wfm

generics and circa 300 combination preparations

F: A 313 (Pharmadéveloppement)
Arovit Roche (Roche)
Avibon (Théraplix)
Halivite (Whitehall)
Vitamine A Dulcis (Allergan)
Vitamine A Faure (Théa)
numerous combination preparations

GB: Abidec (Warner-Lambert)-comb.
Dalivit drops (Eastern)-comb.
numerous combination preparations

I: AD Pabyrn (Samil)-comb.
Adisterolo (Abiogen Pharma)-comb.
Arovit (Roche)

Euvitol (Bracco)
Euvitol Labra (Bracco)
Evitex (Alcon)
Haliborange (Eurospital)-comb.
Lasonil H Antiemorr. (Bayer)-comb.
Midium (Teofarma)-comb.
Repervit (IDI)
Rovigon (Roche)-comb.
Tocalfa (ASTA Medica)-comb.
Vitalipid (Pharmacia & Upjohn)

J: numerous combination preparations

USA: ACES (Carlson)-comb.
Aquasol A (Astra)
Lazer (Pedinol)-comb.
Materna (Lederle)-comb.
Megadose (Arco)-comb.
Vi-Daylin (Ross)-comb.

Ribavirin

ATC: J05AB04
Use: antiviral

RN: 36791-04-5   MF: $C_8H_{12}N_4O_5$ MW: 244.21
LD$_{50}$: 2700 mg/kg (R, p.o.)
CN: 1-β-D-ribofuranosyl-1H-1,2,4-triazole-3-carboxamide

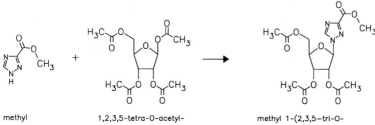

methyl   1,2,3,5-tetra-O-acetyl-   methyl 1-(2,3,5-tri-O-
1,2,4-triazole-   β-D-ribofuranose   acetyl-β-D-ribofuranosyl)-
3-carboxylate   1,2,4-triazole-3-carboxylate (I)

I   →[NH₃ CH₃OH]

Ribavirin

Reference(s):
Witkowski, J.T.: J. Med. Chem. (JMCMAR) **15**, 1150 (1972).

alternative syntheses:
DOS 2 220 246 (ICN; appl. 25.4.1972; USA-prior. 1.6.1971, 31.3.1972).
DOS 2 441 823 (ICN; appl. 12.3.1974; USA-prior. 12.3.1973).
DOS 2 511 828 (ICN; appl. 18.3.1975; USA-prior. 18.3.1974).
JP-appl. 75 123 883 (Kyowa; appl. 15.3.1974).
US 3 976 545 (ICN; 24.8.1976; prior. 1.6.1971).
US 4 138 547 (ICN; 6.2.1979; prior. 22.12.1977).

structure and conformation:
Kreishman, G.P. et al.: J. Am. Chem. Soc. (JACSAT) **94**, 5894 (1972).

Formulation(s):   powder 6 g (for preparation of inhalation solution)

Trade Name(s):
D: Virazole (ICN)   I: Viramid (Alfa   USA: Virazole (ICN)
                                Wassermann)

Riboflavin

(Lactoflavin; Vitamin B$_2$)

ATC: A11HA04
Use: vitamin

RN: 83-88-5   MF: $C_{17}H_{20}N_4O_6$ MW: 376.37   EINECS: 201-507-1
LD$_{50}$: 50 mg/kg (R, i.v.); >10 g/kg (R, p.o.)
CN: 1-deoxy-1-[3,4-dihydro-7,8-dimethyl-2,4-dioxobenzo[g]pteridin-10(2H)-yl]-D-ribitol

5'-phosphate monosodium salt
RN: 130-40-5   MF: $C_{17}H_{20}N_4NaO_9P$ MW: 478.33

N-(3,4-dimethylphenyl)-D-ribamine

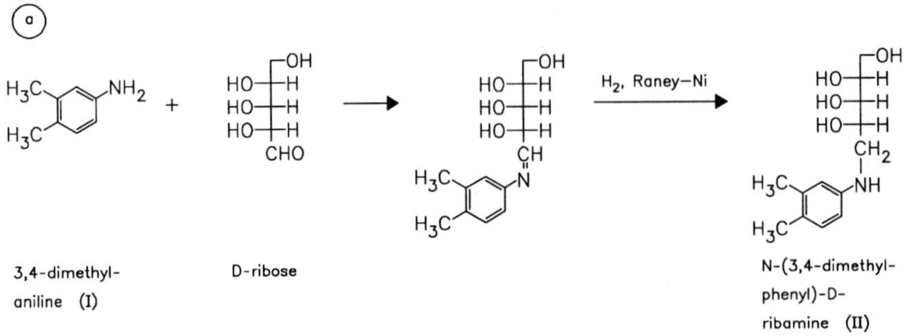

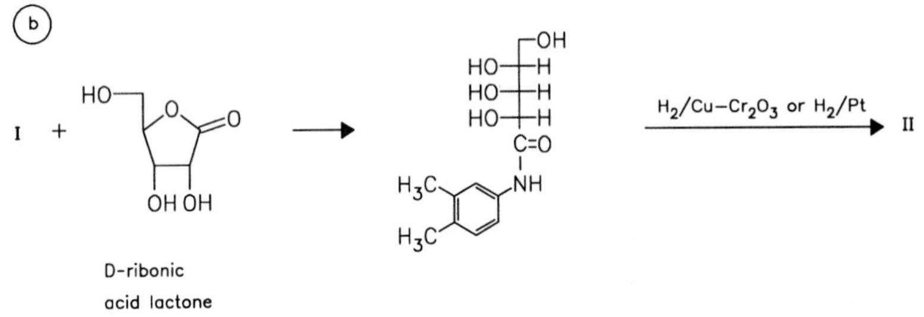

3,4-dimethyl-   D-ribose   N-(3,4-dimethyl-
aniline (I)   phenyl)-D-
                                                                               ribamine (II)

D-ribonic
acid lactone

riboflavin

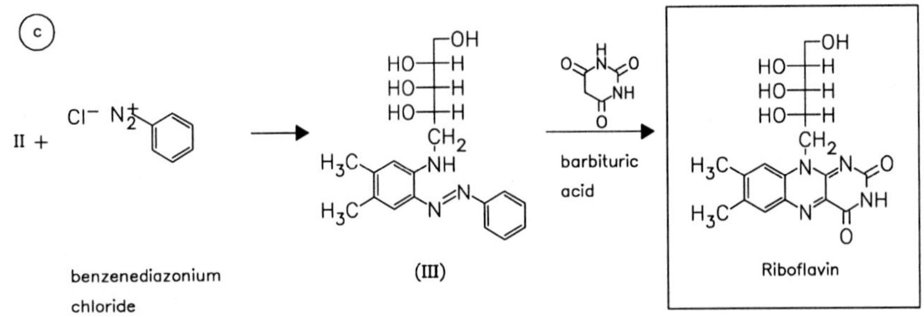

benzenediazonium   (III)   Riboflavin
chloride

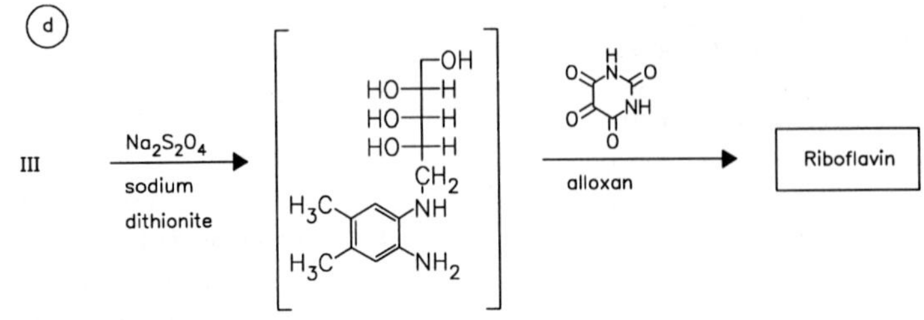

Reference(s):
a   US 2 384 105 (Roche; 1945; appl. 1943).
b   US 2 411 611 (Roche; 1946; GB-prior. 1941).
    US 2 422 997 (Roche; 1947; appl. 1944).
    DAS 2 558 515 (BASF; appl. 24.12.1975) – hydrogenation on Cu-Cr$_2$O$_3$.
    DAS 2 558 516 (BASF; appl. 24.12.1975) – hydrogenation on Cu- Cr$_2$O$_3$.

alternative syntheses (*from* 3,4-dimethylnitrobenzene):
DOS 2 650 830 (BASF; appl. 6.11.1976).
c Tishler, M. et al.: J. Am. Chem. Soc. (JACSAT) **69**, 1487 (1947).
US 2 350 376 (Merck & Co.; 1944; appl. 1941).
US 2 370 093 (Merck & Co.; 1945; appl. 1941).
similar processes:
Tishler, M. et al.: J. Am. Chem. Soc. (JACSAT) **67**, 2165 (1945).
US 2 807 611 (Merck & Co.; 1957; appl. 1955).
d Karrer, P.; Meerwein, H.: Helv. Chim. Acta (HCACAV) **18**, 1130 (1935).
Kuhn, R.; Weygand, F.: Ber. Dtsch. Chem. Ges. (BDCGAS) **68**, 1282 (1935).

fermentative methods:
US 2 445 128 (USA-Secret. Agriculture; 1948; Anm, 1946).
US 2 483 855 (Commercial Solvents Corp.; 1949; appl. 1942).
US 2 876 169 (Grain Process. Corp.; 1959; appl. 1956).
US 4 165 250 (Merck & Co.; 21.8.1979; prior. 29.8.1975, 22.3.1976, 14.11.1977).

isolation from fermentation liquors and purification:
US 2 387 023 (Commercial Solvents Corp.; 1945; appl. 1944).
US 2 421 142 (Commercial Solvents Corp.; 1947; appl. 1944).
US 2 367 646 (Commercial Solvents Corp.; 1945; appl. 1943).
US 2 571 896 (Merck & Co.; 1951; appl. 1945).
US 2 797 215 (Commercial Solvents Corp.; 1957; prior. 1951, 1955).
US 4 165 250 (Merck & Co.; 21.8.1979; prior. 29.8.1975, 22.3.1976, 14.11.1977).

Formulation(s):   amp. 10 mg/2 ml, 20 mg/ml (as 5'-phosphate monosodium salt); drg. 10 mg; tabl. 10 mg

Trade Name(s):

D: Biovital (Dr. Schieffer)-comb.
B-Komplex-Vicotrat (Heyl)
BVK Roche (Roche Nicholas)
Doppelherz (Quiesser Pharma)
Eunova (SmithKline Beecham OTC Medicines)
Kendural (Abbott)
Merz Spezial Dragees (Merz & Co.)
Multibionta (Merck Produkte)
Multi Sanostol (Roland)
Polybion (Merck)
Tai Ginseng (Dr. Poehlmann)
Vita Buerlecithin (Roland)-comb.
and circa 300 combination preparations
F: Alvityl (Solvay Pharma)-comb.
B-Chabre (ATC Pharma)-comb.
Bécozyme (Roche)-comb.
Beflavine (Roche)

Capsules Pharmaton (Boehringer Ing.)-comb.
Carencyl (Riom)-comb.
Glutamag Vitaminé (Euform)-comb.
Hydrosol polyvitaminé Labaz (Labaz)-comb.
Hydrosol polyvitaminé Roche (Roche)-comb.
Nutrigène (GNR-pharma)-comb.
Plurifactor (Gomenol)-comb.
Renutryl 500 (Nestlé clinical)-comb.
Survitine (Roche Nicholas)-comb.
Vitamine C-B$_2$ Lemoine (Lemoine)-comb.
Vivamyne (Whitehall)-comb.
numerous combination preparations
GB: only combination preparations:
Abidec (Warner-Lambert)
Dalivit Drops (Paines & Byrne)
Ketovite (Paines & Byrne)

Pabrinex (Link)
I: following vitaminous combination preparations:
Becozym (Roche)
Berocca (Roche)
Betacomplesso (Medosan)
Betotal (Pharmacia & Upjohn)
Diagran (Bristol-Myers Squibb)
Emazian (Bioindustria)
Emoantitossina (Piam)
Idropan B (Lisapharma)
Idroplurivit (Menarini)
Ipavit (IPA)
Katabios (SIT)
Neocromaton (Menarini)
Plexoton B12 (Coli)
Priovit (SIT)
Sincrivit (AGIPS)
Vinutro Drops (Bergamon)
Vitalerina (Polifarma)
Vitamax (Medosan)
Vitate (SIT)
Viterra (Pfizer)
J: numerous combination preparations
USA: Mega-B (Arco)

Ribostamycin

(Ribostamin)

ATC: J01GB10
Use: antibiotic

RN: 25546-65-0   MF: $C_{17}H_{34}N_4O_{10}$ MW: 454.48   EINECS: 247-091-5
LD$_{50}$:   300 mg/kg (M, i.v.); 7 g/kg (M, p.o.);
535 mg/kg (R, i.v.); >10 g/kg (R, p.o.)
CN: O-2,6-diamino-2,6-dideoxy-α-D-glucopyranosyl(1→4)-O-[β-D-ribofuranosyl-(1→5)]-2-deoxy-D-streptamine

sulfate
RN: 53797-35-6   MF: $C_{17}H_{34}N_4O_{10} \cdot xH_2SO_4$ MW: unspecified   EINECS: 258-783-1
LD$_{50}$:   210 mg/kg (M, i.v.); >7 g/kg (M, p.o.);
375 mg/kg (R, i.v.); >7 g/kg (R, p.o.)

ⓐ   by fermentation from Streptomyces ribosidicus (ATCC 21294)

ⓑ

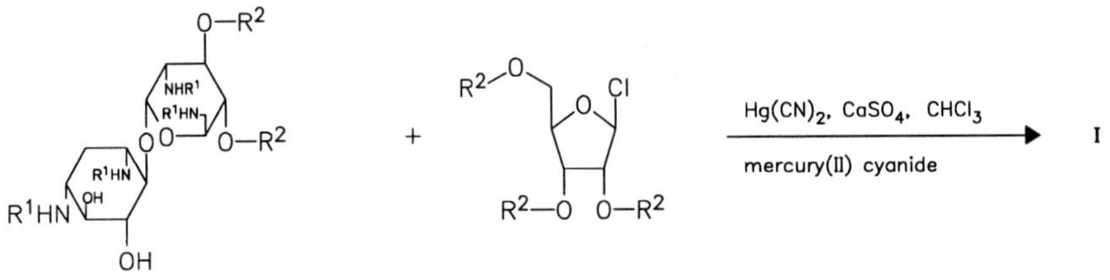

4-O-[2,6-bis(benzyloxycarbonyl-
amino)-3,4-di-O-benzyl-2,6-di-
deoxy-α-D-glucopyranosyl]-N,N'-
bis(benzyloxycarbonyl)-2-deoxy-
D-streptamine

2,3,5-tri-O-benzyl-
β-D-ribofuranosyl
chloride

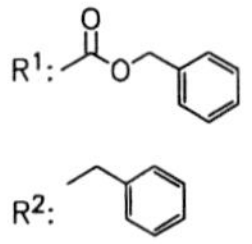

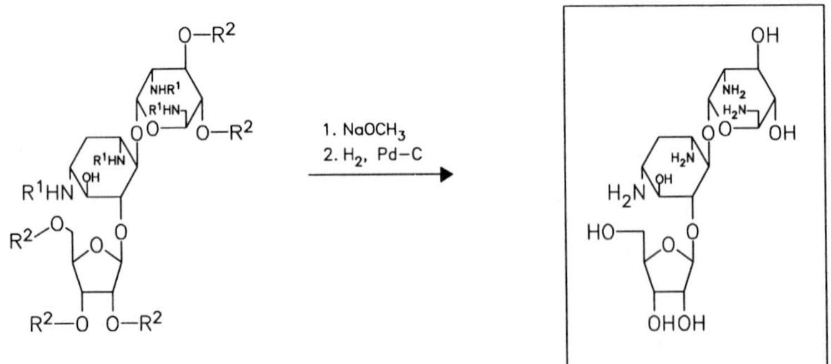

(I)

Ribostamycin

Reference(s):

a   DE 1 814 735 (Meiji Seika Kaisha; appl. 14.12.1968; J-prior. 15.10.1968, 18.12.1967).
Shomura, T. et al.: J. Antibiot. (JANTAJ) **23**, 155 (1970).
US 3 661 892 (Meiji Seika; appl. 3.12.1968; J-prior. 18.12.1967).
US 3 799 842 (Meiji Seika; USA-prior. 1.6.1970; J-prior. 15.10.1968, 18.12.1967).
b   DOS 2 104 129 (Meiji Seika Kaisha; appl. 29.1.1971; J-prior. 2.2.1970).

alternative syntheses:
DOS 2 537 688 (Hoechst; appl. 23.8.1975).
JP 54 008 792 (Shionogi; appl. 16.6.1977).
JP 53 201 155 (Suami; appl. 10.8.1976).
Suami, T. et al.: Carbohydr. Res. (CRBRAT) **56**, 415 (1977) and literature cited therein.

total synthesis:
Fukami, H. et al.: Agric. Biol. Chem. (ABCHA6) **41**, 1689 (1977).

Formulation(s): vial 0.5 g, 1 g (as sulfate)

Trade Name(s):

D:	Landamycine (Delalande; 1977); wfm	F:	Ribomycin (Delalande); wfm	I:	Ibistacin (IBI); wfm
				J:	Vistamycin (Meiji; 1972)

Rifampicin

ATC: J04AB02
Use: antibiotic (tuberculosis agent)

RN: 13292-46-1 MF: $C_{43}H_{58}N_4O_{12}$ MW: 822.95 EINECS: 236-312-0
LD_{50}: 260 mg/kg (M, i.v.); 500 mg/kg (M, p.o.);
1570 mg/kg (R, p.o.)
CN: 3-[[(4-methyl-1-piperazinyl)imino]methyl]rifamycin

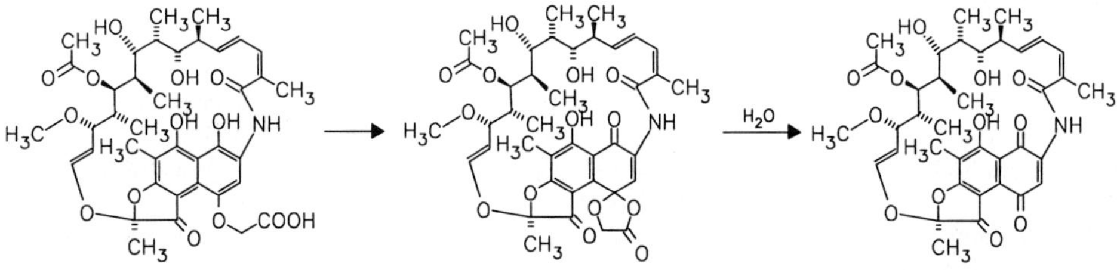
H2O

rifamycin B [from Streptomyces mediterranei (ATCC 13685)] — rifamycin O — rifamycin S (I)

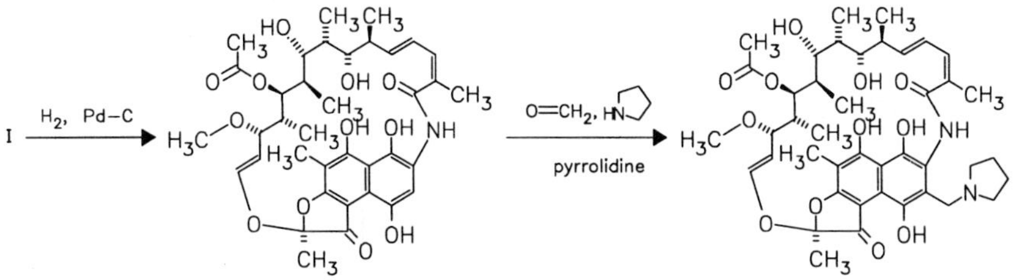
I
H2, Pd-C
O=CH2, HN
pyrrolidine

rifamycin SV — 3-pyrrolidinomethyl-rifamycin SV (II)

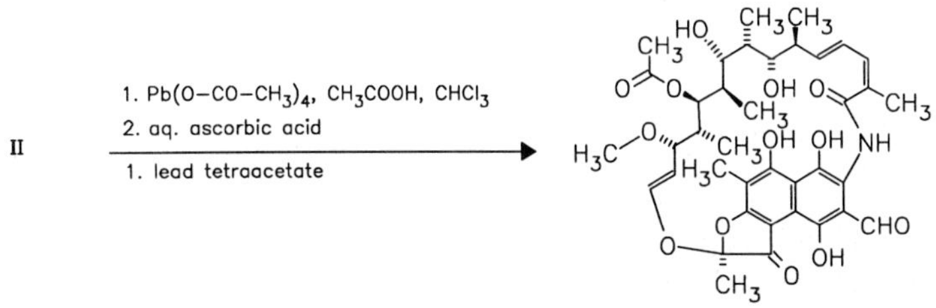
II
1. Pb(O-CO-CH3)4, CH3COOH, CHCl3
2. aq. ascorbic acid
1. lead tetraacetate

3-formylrifamycin SV (III)

III + 1-amino-4-methyl-piperazine

H_2N— [piperazine ring with N—CH₃]

THF →

Rifampicin

Reference(s):
Maggi, N. et al.: Chemotherapia (CMTRAG) **11**, 285 (1966).
US 3 342 810 (Lepetit; 19.9.1967; GB-prior. 31.7.1964).
DAS 1 795 567 (Lepetit; appl. 28.7.1965; GB-prior. 31.7.1964).

alternative syntheses:
DOS 2 846 321 (Holco; appl. 24.10.1978; GB-prior. 25.11.1977).

fermentative production of rifamycin B:
DE 1 089 513 (Lepetit; appl. 11.8.1959; GB-prior. 12.8.1958).

Formulation(s):   cps. 150 mg, 300 mg; drg. 150 mg, 300 mg, 450 mg, 600 mg; f. c. tabl. 150 mg, 300 mg,
                   450 mg, 600 mg; syrup 100 mg/5 ml; vial 600 mg

Trade Name(s):
D: Eremfat (Fatol)
      Rifa (Grünenthal; 1970)
      Rifampicin-Hefa (Hefa
      Pharma)
      Rifater (Grünenthal)-comb.
      Rifinah (Grünenthal)-comb.
F: Rifadine (Marion Merrell
      SA; 1969)
      Rifater (Marion Merrell
      SA)-comb.
      Rifinah (Marion Merrell
      SA)-comb.
      Rimactan (Novartis Pharma
      SA; 1969)

GB: Rifadin (Hoechst; 1969)
      Rifater (Hoechst)-comb.
      with isoniazid
      Rifinah (Hoechst)-comb.
      with isoniazid
      Rimactane (Ciba; 1969)
      Rimactazid (Ciba)-comb.
      with isoniazid
I: Rifadin (Lepetit)
      Rifapiam (Piam)
      Rifinah (Lepetit)-comb.
      with isoniazid
J: Rifadin (Daiichi)

      Rimactane (Ciba-Geigy-
      Fujisawa)
USA: Rifadin (Hoechst Marion
      Roussel; 1970)
      Rifamate (Hoechst Marion
      Roussel; 1976)-comb. with
      isoniazid
      Rifater (Hoechst Marion
      Roussel)
      Rimactazid (Ciba)-comb.
      with isoniazid

Rifapentine

Use: antibacterial

RN: 61379-65-5   MF: $C_{47}H_{64}N_4O_{12}$ MW: 877.05   EINECS: 262-743-9
CN: 3-[[(4-Cyclopentyl-1-piperazinyl)imino]methyl]rifamycin

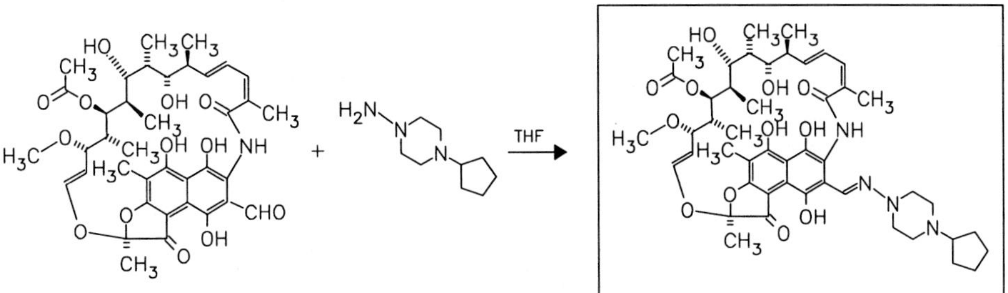

3-formylrifamycin
(cf. rifampicin synthesis)

1-amino-4-
cyclopentyl-
piperazine

Rifapentine

Reference(s):
DE 2 608 218 (Gruppo Lepetit; GB-prior. 5.3.1975).
Traxler, P.; Kümp, W.; Mueller, K.; Tosch, W.: J. Med. Chem. (JMCMAR) **33**, 552 (1990)

Formulation(s):   tabl 150 mg

Trade Name(s):
USA: Priftin (Hoechst Marion
         Roussel; 1998)

Rifaximin
(L-105)

ATC: A07AA11; D06AX11
Use: antibiotic, antibacterial

RN: 80621-81-4   MF: $C_{43}H_{51}N_3O_{11}$ MW: 785.89
LD$_{50}$: >2 g/kg (R, p.o.);
        >2 g/kg (dog, p.o.)
CN: [2S-(2R*,16Z,18E,20R*,21R*,22S*,23S*,24S*,25R*,26S*,27R*,28E)]-25-(acetyloxy)-5,6,21,23-
        tetrahydroxy-27-methoxy-2,4,11,16,20,22,24,26-octamethyl-2,7-
        (epoxypentadeca[1,11,13]trienimino)benzofuro[4,5-e]pyrido[1,2-a]benzimidazole-1,15(2H)-dione

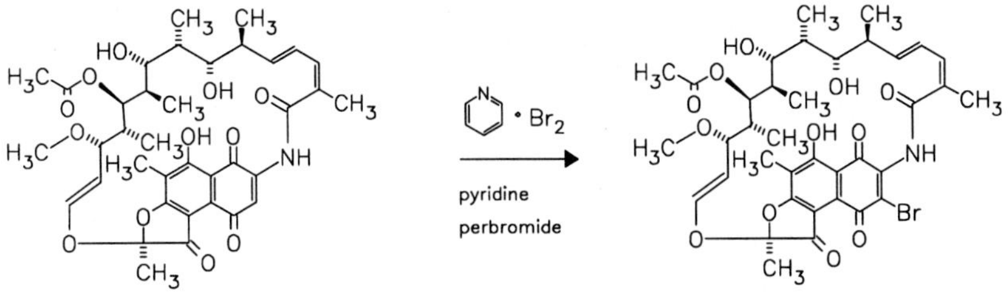

rifamycin S

pyridine
perbromide

3-bromorifamycin S (I)

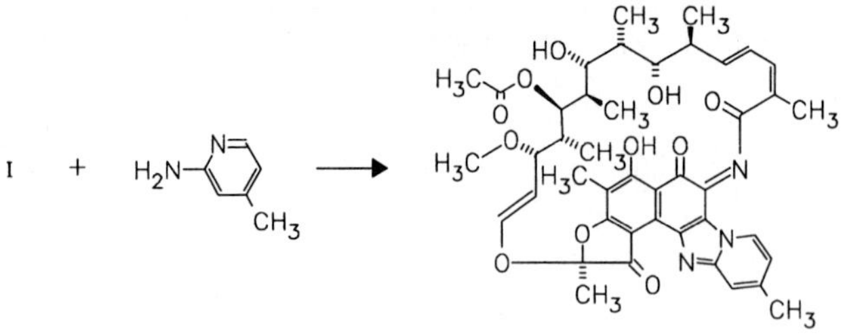

I + H₂N—(2-amino-4-methyl-pyridine) ⟶ (II)

2-amino-4-methyl-
pyridine

(II)

II ——L(+)-ascorbic acid——▶

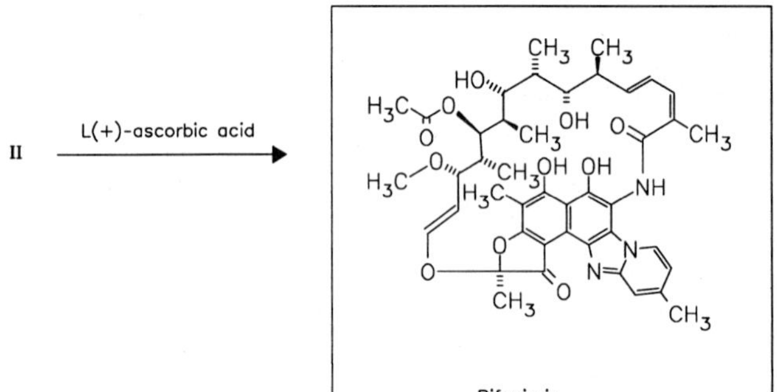

Rifaximin

Reference(s):
DE 3 120 460 (Alfa Farm.; appl. 22.5.1981; I-prior. 22.5.1980).
US 4 341 785 (Alfa Farm.; 27.7.1982; I-prior. 22.5.1980).
Marchi, E. et al.: J. Med. Chem. (JMCMAR) **28**, 960 (1985).

alternative synthesis:
EP 161 534 (Alfa Farm.; appl. 19.4.1985; I-prior. 15.5.1984).

synthesis of 3-bromorifamycin S:
US 4 179 438 (Alfa Farm.; 18.12.1979; I-prior. 29.11.1977).

Formulation(s):   ointment 5 %; susp. 2 %; tabl. 200 mg

Trade Name(s):
I: Dermadis (Farmades)   Redactiv (Alfa   Rifacol (Formenti)
       Normix (Alfa Wassermann)   Wassermann)

Rilmazafone

ATC: N05B; N05C
Use: hypnotic, anxiolytic, treatment of
       neurotic insomnia, ring-opened
       benzodiazepine

RN: 99593-25-6   MF: $C_{21}H_{20}Cl_2N_6O_3$ MW: 475.34
LD$_{50}$: 72 mg/kg (M, i.p.); 540 mg/kg (M, p.o.); 620 mg/kg (M, s.c.);
       91 mg/kg (R, i.p.); 680 mg/kg (R, p.o.); 1600 mg/kg (R, s.c.)
CN: 5-[[(aminoacetyl)amino]methyl]-1-[4-chloro-2-(2-chlorobenzoyl)phenyl]-*N,N*-dimethyl-1*H*-1,2,4-
       triazole-3-carboxamide

monohydrochloride
RN: 85815-37-8 MF: $C_{21}H_{20}Cl_2N_6O_3 \cdot HCl$ MW: 511.80

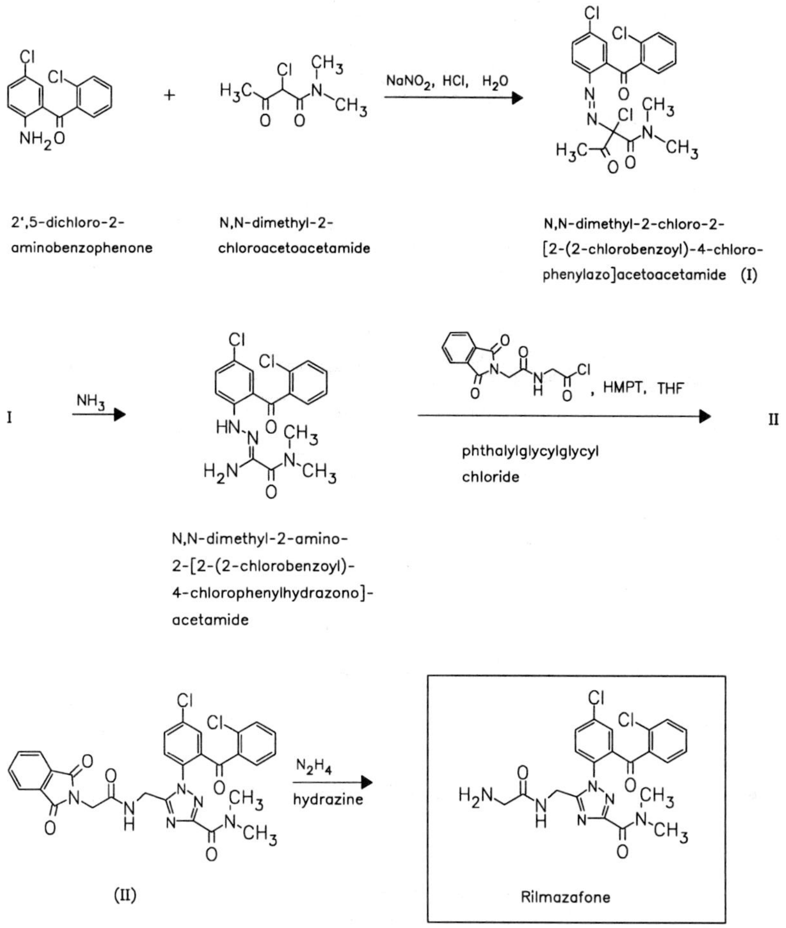
NaNO2, HCl, H2O
2',5-dichloro-2-aminobenzophenone
N,N-dimethyl-2-chloroacetoacetamide
N,N-dimethyl-2-chloro-2-[2-(2-chlorobenzoyl)-4-chlorophenylazo]acetoacetamide (I)
I
NH3
N,N-dimethyl-2-amino-2-[2-(2-chlorobenzoyl)-4-chlorophenylhydrazono]-acetamide
, HMPT, THF
phthalylglycylglycyl chloride
II
(II)
N2H4
hydrazine
Rilmazafone

Reference(s):
DE 2 725 164 (Shionogi; appl. 6.3.1977; J-prior. 6.4.1976).
US 4 159 374 (Shionogi; 26.6.1979; appl. 6.3.1977; J-prior. 6.4.1976).
Hirai, K. et al.: J. Heterocycl. Chem. (JHTCAD) **19**, 1363 (1982).

Formulation(s): tabl. 1 mg, 2 mg

Trade Name(s):
J: Rhythmy (Shionogi; 1989)

Rilmenidine
(Oxaminozolin; S-3341)

ATC: C02AC06
Use: antihypertensive, α_2-adrenoceptor agonist

RN: 54187-04-1 MF: $C_{10}H_{16}N_2O$ MW: 180.25 EINECS: 259-021-0
LD_{50}: 24 mg/kg (M, i.v.)
CN: *N*-(dicyclopropylmethyl)-4,5-dihydro-2-oxazolamine

(E)-2-butendioate (1:1)
RN: 54249-57-9 MF: $C_{10}H_{16}N_2O \cdot C_4H_4O_4$ MW: 296.32
dihydrogen phosphate
RN: 85409-38-7 MF: $C_{10}H_{16}N_2O \cdot H_3PO_4$ MW: 278.25

| 2-chloroethyl isocyanate | dicyclopropyl- methylamine | | Rilmenidine |

Reference(s):
DE 2 362 754 (Sci. Union et Cie., Soc. Franç. de Recherche Medicale; appl. 17.12.1973; GB-prior. 28.12.1972).
US 3 988 464 (Sci. Union et Cie., Soc. Franç. de Recherche Medicale; 26.10.1976; appl. 26.12.1973; F-prior. 28.12.1972).
US 4 102 890 (Sci. Union et Cie., Soc. Franç. de Recherche Medicale; 25.7.1978; appl. 11.8.1976; F-prior. 26.12.1973; prior. 28.12.1972).

synthesis of dicyclopropylmethylamine:
Corrodi, H.: Helv. Chim. Acta (HCACAV) **46**, 1059 (1963).
Timberlake, J.; Martin, J.C.: J. Org. Chem. (JOCEAH) **33**, 4054 (1968).

Formulation(s): tabl. 1 mg (as dihydrogen phosphate)

Trade Name(s):
F: Hyperium (Biopharma; Servier; 1988)

Riluzole
(PK-26124; RP-54274)

ATC: N07XX02
Use: anticonvulsant, glutamate release inhibitor

RN: 1744-22-5 MF: $C_8H_5F_3N_2OS$ MW: 234.20
LD$_{50}$: 67 mg/kg (M, p.o.)
CN: 6-(trifluoromethoxy)-2-benzothiazolamine

| 4-trifluoromethoxy- aniline | potassium thiocyanate | | Riluzole |

Reference(s):
EP 50 551 (Pharmindustrie; appl. 9.10.1981; F-prior. 17.10.1980).

use to treat mitochondrial disorders:
FR 2 714 828 (Rhône-Poulenc Rorer; F-prior. 12.1.1994).

use to treat neurological symptoms with HIV infections:
FR 2 702 148 (Rhône-Poulenc Rorer; F-prior. 5.3.1993).

use as radioprotector:
FR 2 700 116 (Rhône-Poulenc Rorer; F-prior. 7.1.1993).

use to treat Parkinson's disease:
FR 2 700 117 (Rhône-Poulenc Rorer; F-prior. 7.1.1993).

use to treat neurological disorders:
WO 9 413 288 (Rhône-Poulenc Rorer; appl. 10.12.1993; F-prior. 16.12.1992).

use to treat motor-neuron diseases:
EP 558 861 (Rhône-poulenc Rorer; appl. 22.10.1992; F-prior. 6.3.1992).

use to treat schizophrenia:
EP 305 276 (Rhône-Poulenc Rorer; appl. 18.8.1988; F-prior. 25.8.1987).

use to treat depression:
EP 3 052 277 (Rhône-Poulenc Rorer; appl. 18.8.1988; F-prior. 25.8.1987).

use to treat amyotrophic lateral sclerosis:
WO 9 715 304 (Sanofi; appl. 25.10.1996; F-prior. 13.6.1996).

Formulation(s):   f. c. tabl. 50 mg

Trade Name(s):

D:	Rilutek (Rhône-Poulenc Rorer)	GB:	Rilutek (Rhône-Poulenc Rorer)	USA:	Rilutek (Rhône-Poulenc Rorer)
F:	Rilutek (Specia; Rhône-Poulenc Rorer)	I:	Rilutek (Rhône-Poulenc Rorer)		

Rimantadine

ATC: J05AC02
Use: antiviral

RN: 13392-28-4   MF: $C_{12}H_{21}N$ MW: 179.31
CN: α-methyltricyclo[3.3.1.1^{3,7}]decane-1-methanamine

hydrochloride
RN: 1501-84-4   MF: $C_{12}H_{21}N \cdot HCl$ MW: 215.77
LD$_{50}$:   640 mg/kg (R, p.o.)

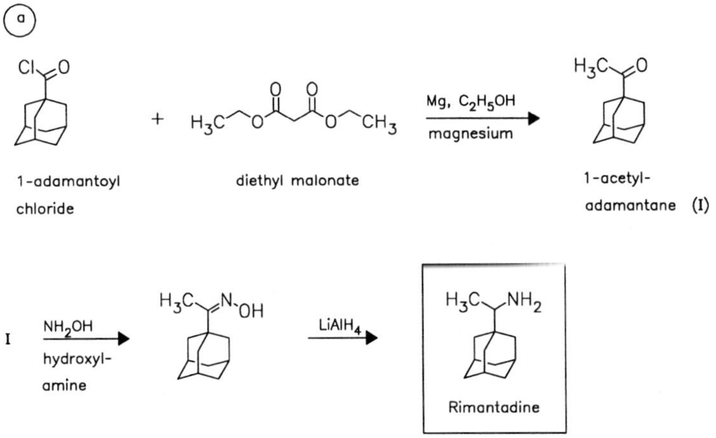

1-adamantoyl
chloride

diethyl malonate

1-acetyl-
adamantane (I)

hydroxyl-
amine

Rimantadine

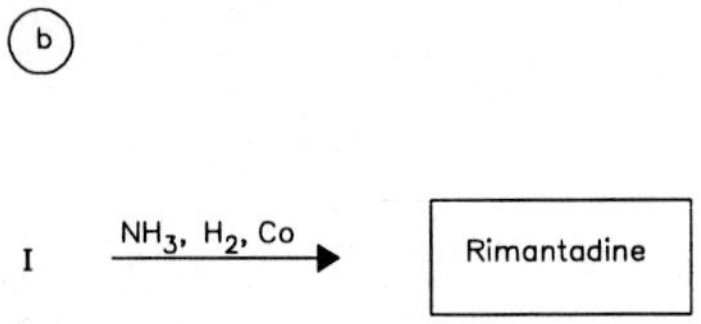
b
I
NH3, H2, Co
Rimantadine

Reference(s):
DE 1 468 769 (Du Pont; appl. 18.7.1964; USA-prior. 24.7.1963).
US 3 352 912 (Du Pont; 14.11.1967; prior. 18.6.1964, 24.7.1963).

alternative synthesis:
EP 178 668 (Du Pont; appl. 17.10.1985; USA-prior. 19.10.1984).

Formulation(s): syrup 50 mg/5 ml; tabl. 100 mg (as hydrochloride)

Trade Name(s):

F:	Roflual (Hoffmann-La Roche; 1988); wfm	USA:	Flumadine (Forest)

Rimiterol

ATC: R03AC05
Use: bronchodilator

RN: 32953-89-2 MF: $C_{12}H_{17}NO_3$ MW: 223.27 EINECS: 251-305-2
CN: (*R**,*S**)-4-(hydroxy-2-piperidinylmethyl)-1,2-benzenediol

hydrobromide
RN: 31842-61-2 MF: $C_{12}H_{17}NO_3 \cdot HBr$ MW: 304.18 EINECS: 250-834-6

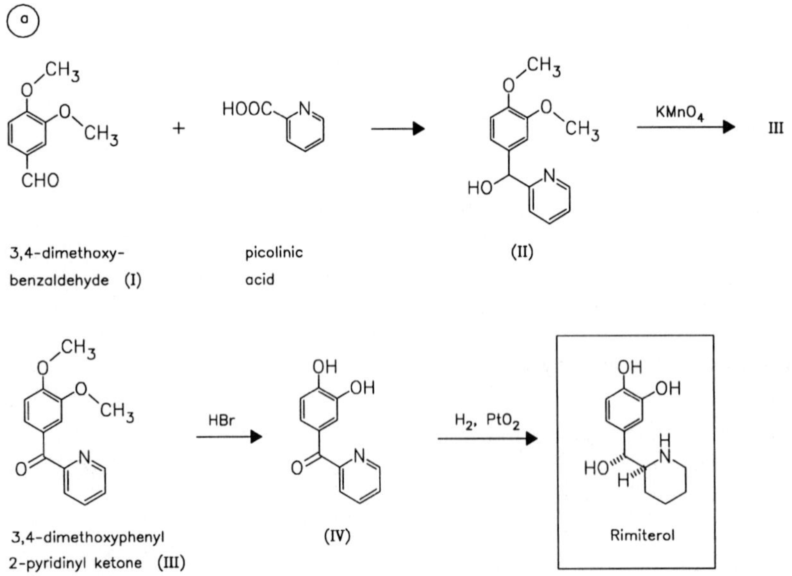
a
3,4-dimethoxy-
benzaldehyde (I)
picolinic
acid
(II)
KMnO4
III
3,4-dimethoxyphenyl
2-pyridinyl ketone (III)
HBr
(IV)
H2, PtO2
Rimiterol

b

I + 2-bromo-pyridine (Br–N) →[LiC₄H₉ / butyl-lithium] II →[KMnO₄] III →[HBr] IV →[H₂, PtO₂] Rimiterol

Reference(s):
a   DAS 2 024 049 (Minnesota 3M; appl. 16.5.1970; GB-prior. 20.5.1969).
b   US 3 705 169 (Smith Kline & French; 5.12.1972; prior. 8.10.1969, 5.11.1970).

Formulation(s):   inhalation aerosol 10 mg, 0.2 mg/dose (as hydrobromide)

Trade Name(s):
GB: Pulmadil (Riker); wfm

Risedronate sodium

Use: bone resorption inhibitor, bisphosphonate

RN: 115436-72-1   MF: $C_7H_{10}NNaO_7P_2$ MW: 305.10
CN: [1-Hydroxy-2-(3-pyridinyl)ethylidene]bis-[phosphonic acid] monosodium salt

acid
RN: 105462-24-6   MF: $C_7H_{11}NO_7P_2$ MW: 283.11

2-(3-pyridyl)-acetic acid (COOH) →[1. H_3PO_4, $POCl_3$, reflux / 2. NaOH, H_2O] Risedronate sodium

Reference(s):
EP 186 405 (Procter and Gamble Co.; appl. 16.12.1985; USA-prior. 21.12.1984).
WO 9 211 269 (Huhtamaki Oy; appl. 18.12.1991; FI-prior. 20.12.1990).

oral enteric-coated sustained-release compositions:
WO 9 309 785 (Procter and Gamble Pharm.; USA-prior. 22.11.1991).

Formulation(s):   tabl. 30 mg (as sodium hemipentahydrate)

Trade Name(s):
USA: Actonel (Procter & Gamble; 1998)

Risperidone

ATC: N05AX08
Use: antipsychotic, 5-HT$_2$-antagonist,
        dopamine-D$_2$-antagonist

RN: 106266-06-2   MF: C$_{23}$H$_{27}$FN$_4$O$_2$ MW: 410.49
LD$_{50}$: 34.3 mg/kg (R, i. v.); 56.6 mg/kg (R, p. o.);
        26.9 mg/kg (M, i. v.); 63.1 mg/kg (M, p. o.);
        14.1 mg/kg (dog, i. v.); 18.3 mg/kg (dog, p. o.)
CN: 3-[2-[4-(6-Fluoro-1,2-benzisoxazol-3-yl)-1-piperidinyl]ethyl]-6,7,8,9-tetrahydro-2-methyl-4H-
        pyrido[1,2-a]pyrimidin-4-one

1-acetyl-4-
piperidinecarboxylic
acid

1-acetyl-4-
piperidinecarbonyl
chloride

hydroxylamine
hydrochloride

N,N-diethyl-1,2-
ethanediamine

(II)

4-(2,4-difluorobenzoyl)-
piperidine hydrochloride

(III)

6-fluoro-3-(4-
piperidinyl)-1,2-
benzisoxazole (IV)

3-(2-chloroethyl)-
2-methyl-6,7,8,9-
tetrahydro-4H-pyrido-
[1,2-a]pyrimidin-4-one (V)

Risperidone

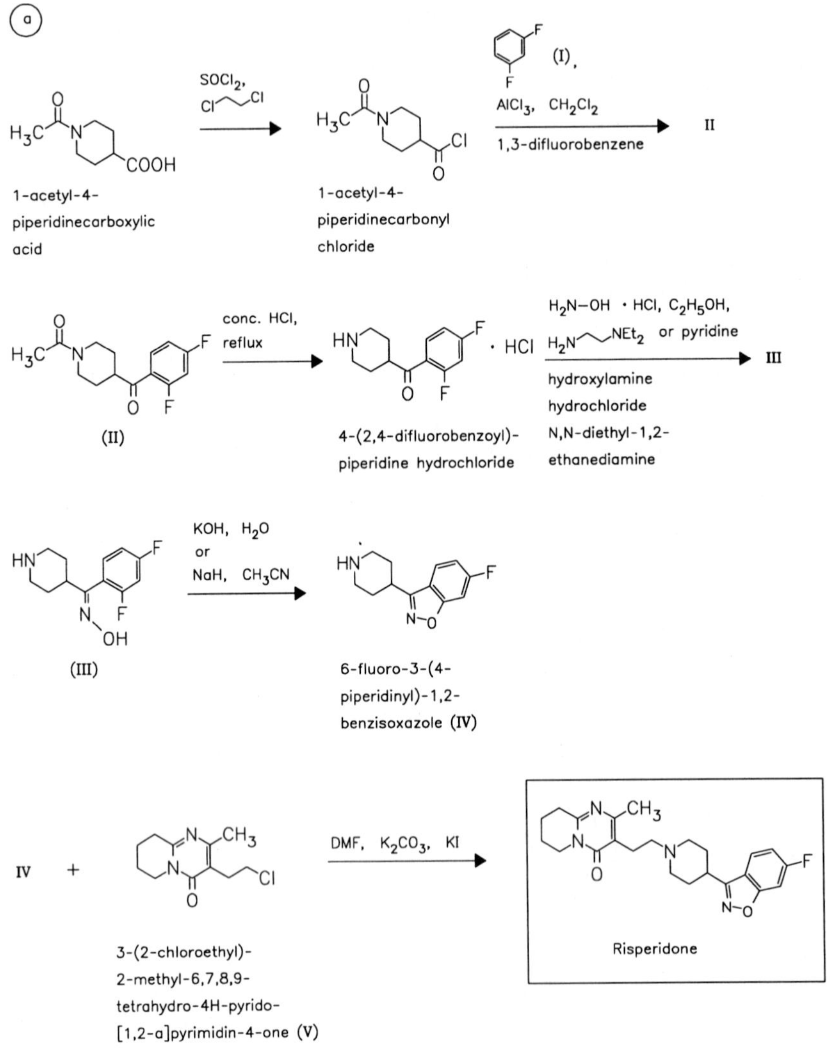

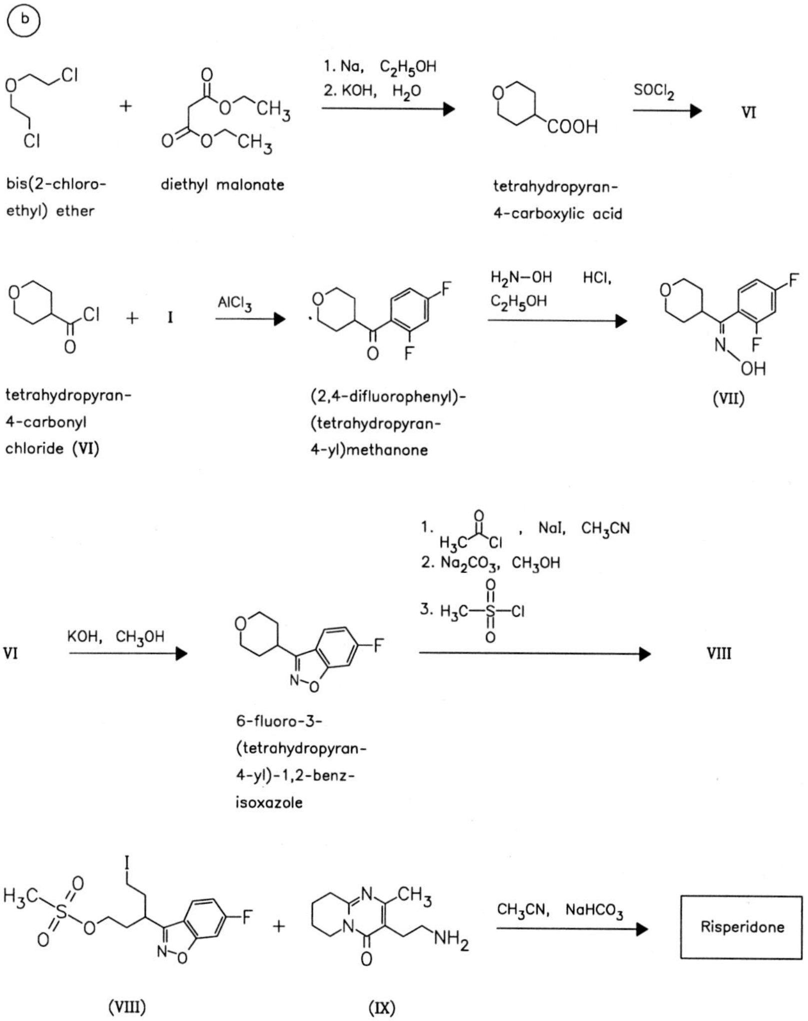
b
bis(2-chloro-ethyl) ether
diethyl malonate
1. Na, C_2H_5OH
2. KOH, H_2O
tetrahydropyran-4-carboxylic acid
$SOCl_2$
VI
tetrahydropyran-4-carbonyl chloride (VI)
I
$AlCl_3$
(2,4-difluorophenyl)-(tetrahydropyran-4-yl)methanone
H_2N-OH HCl, C_2H_5OH
(VII)
VI
KOH, CH_3OH
6-fluoro-3-(tetrahydropyran-4-yl)-1,2-benzisoxazole
1. NaI, CH_3CN
2. Na_2CO_3, CH_3OH
3.
VIII
(VIII)
(IX)
CH_3CN, $NaHCO_3$
Risperidone

preparation of intermediates V and IX

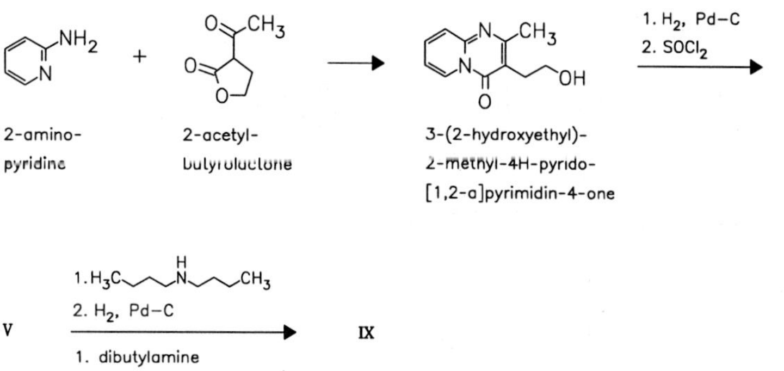
2-amino-pyridine
2-acetyl-butyrolactone
3-(2-hydroxyethyl)-2-methyl-4H-pyrido-[1,2-a]pyrimidin-4-one
1. H_2, Pd-C
2. $SOCl_2$
V
V
2. H_2, Pd-C
1. dibutylamine
IX

Reference(s):

a EP 196 132 (Janssen Pharmaceutica N. V.; appl. 13.3.1986; USA-prior. 27.3.1985; 5.2.1986).

b ES 2 074 966 (Vita-invest, S. A.; appl. 16.9.1995; E-prior. 11.2.1994).

preparation of 1-acetyl-4-piperidinecarbonylchloride:
Strupczewski, J.T.; Allen, R.C.; Gardner, B.A.; Schmid, B.L.; Stache, U.: J. Med. Chem. (JMCMAR) **28** (6), 761 (1985).

preparation of tetrahydropyran-4-carboxylic acid:
Radiszewski, J.G.; Kaszynski, P.; Littmann, D.; Balaji, V; Hess, B.A.; Michl, J.: J. Am. Chem. Soc. (JACSAT) **115** (18), 8401 (1993)
Straessler, C.; Linden, A.; Heimgartner, H.: Helv. Chim. Acta (HCACAV) **80** (5), 1528 (1997)
Angelastro, M.R.; Baugh, L.E; Bey, P.; Burkhardt, J.P; Chen Teng-Man: J. Med. Chem. (JMCMAR) **37** (26), 4538 (1994)

preparation of 3-(2-hydroxyethyl)-2-methylpyrido[1,2-*a*]pyrimidin-4-one:
Willenbrock et al.: Justus Liebigs Ann. Chem. (JLACBF) **1973**, 107, 108, 109

Formulation(s):   f. c. tabl. 1 mg, 2 mg, 3 mg, 4 mg; sol. 100 ml 1 mg/ml

Trade Name(s):
D:	Risperdal (Janssen-Cilag)	I:	Belivon (Organon)	USA: Risperdal (Janssen
	Risperdal (Organon)		Risperdal (Janssen-Cilag)	Pharmac.)
GB:	Risperdal (Janssen-Cilag)	J:	Risperdal (Janssen-Kyowa)	

Ritodrine

ATC: G02CA01
Use: uterus relaxant

RN: 26652-09-5   MF: $C_{17}H_{21}NO_3$ MW: 287.36   EINECS: 247-879-9
CN: (*R**,*S**)-4-hydroxy-α-[1-[[2-(4-hydroxyphenyl)ethyl]amino]ethyl]benzenemethanol

hydrochloride
RN: 23239-51-2   MF: $C_{17}H_{21}NO_3 \cdot HCl$ MW: 323.82   EINECS: 245-514-8
LD$_{50}$:   69 mg/kg (M, i.v.); 687 mg/kg (M, p.o.);
        83 mg/kg (R, i.v.); 1840 mg/kg (R, p.o.);
        128 mg/kg (dog, i.v.); 2458 mg/kg (dog, p.o.)

4'-benzyloxypropiophenone

4'-benzyloxy-2-bromo-propiophenone

2-(4-benzyloxyphenyl)ethylamine

(I)

Ritodrine

Reference(s):
US 3 410 944 (Philips; 12.11.1968; NL-prior. 27.2.1964).

Formulation(s):   amp. 50 mg/5 ml; s. r. cps. 40 mg; tabl. 10 mg (as hydrochloride)

Trade Name(s):

D:	Pre-par (Solvay Arzneimittel)	GB:	Yutopar (Solvay)	J:	Miolene (Lusofarmaco)
		I:	Miolene (Lusofarmaco)		Utemerin (Kissei)
F:	Pre-Par (Solvay Pharma)		Prepar (Solvay Pharma)	USA:	Yutopar (Astra)

Ritonavir

(A-84538; ABT-538)

ATC: J05AE03
Use: antiviral, HIV-1-protease inhibitor

RN: 155213-67-5 MF: $C_{37}H_{48}N_6O_5S_2$ MW: 720.96
CN: [5*S*-(5*R**,8*R**,10*R**,11*R**)]-10-hydroxy-2-methyl-5-(1-methylethyl)-1-[2-(1-methylethyl)-4-thiazolyl]-3,6-dioxo-8,11-bis(phenylmethyl)-2,4,7,12-tetraazatridecan-13-oic acid 5-thiazolylmethyl ester

(a)

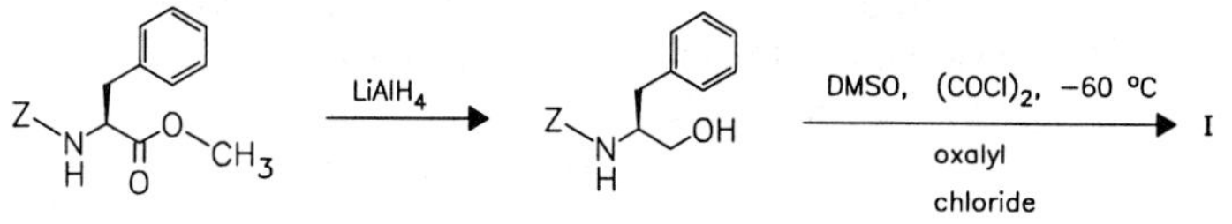

N-(benzyloxycarbonyl)-L-phenylalanine methyl ester

N-(benzyloxycarbonyl)-L-phenylalaninol

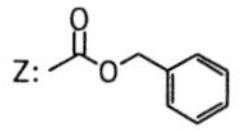

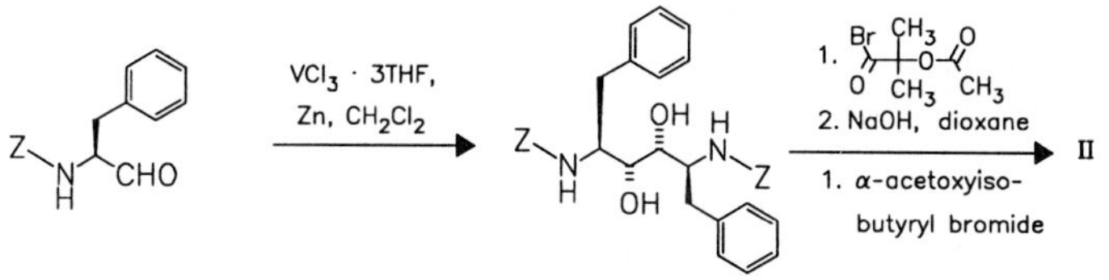

N-(benzyloxycarbonyl)-L-phenylalaninal (I)

(2S,3R,4R,5S)-2,5-bis[(benzyloxycarbonyl)amino]-3,4-dihydroxy-1,6-diphenylhexane

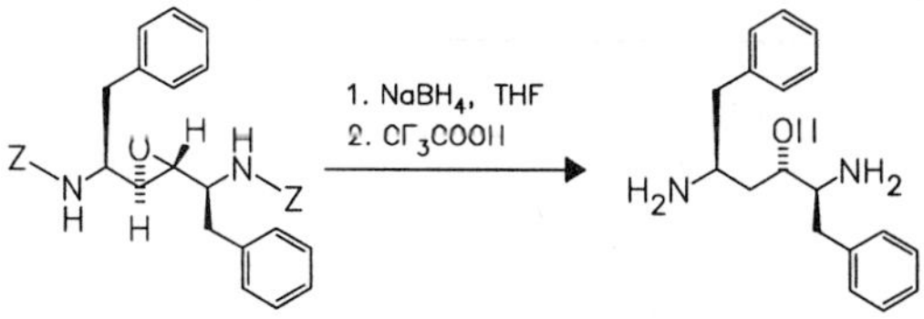

(2S,3R,4R,5S)-2,5-bis[(benzyloxycarbonyl)amino]-3,4-epoxy-1,6-diphenylhexane (II)

(2S,3S,5S)-2,5-diamino-3-hydroxy-1,6-diphenylhexane (III)

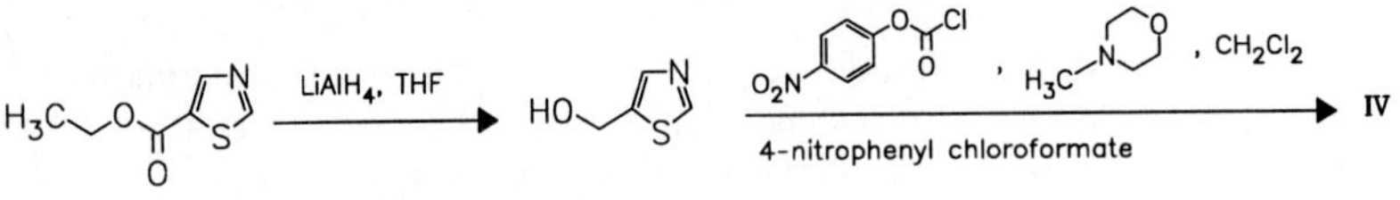

ethyl thiazole-
5-carboxylate

LiAlH$_4$, THF

5-(hydroxy-
methyl)-
thiazole

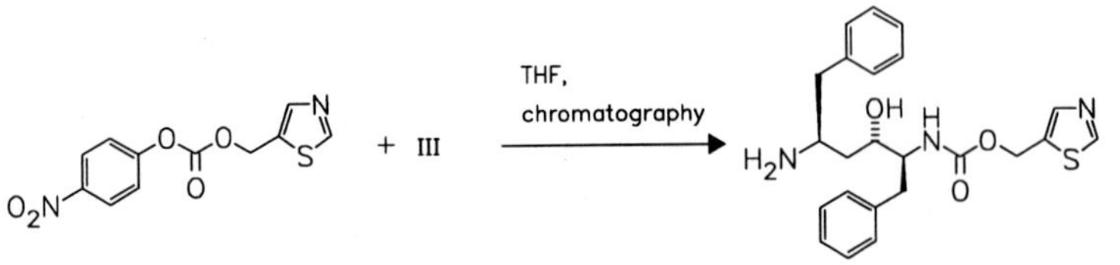

4-nitrophenyl chloroformate

, CH$_2$Cl$_2$

IV

+ III

THF,
chromatography

5-thiazolylmethyl
4-nitrophenyl
carbonate (IV)

(2S,3S,5S)-5-amino-2-
(5-thiazolylmethoxycarbonyl-
amino)-3-hydroxy-1,6-di-
phenylhexane (V)

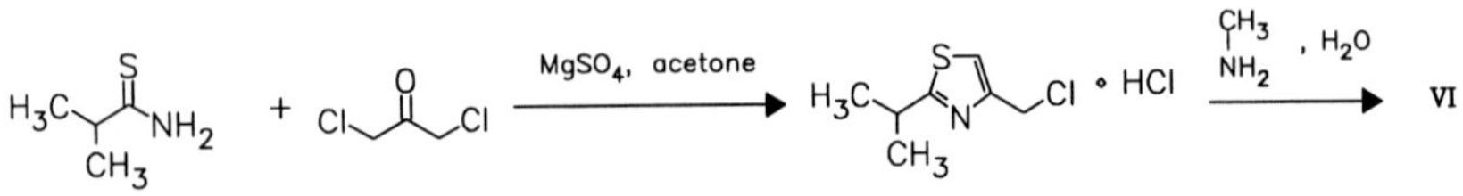

2-methyl-
propane-
thioamide

1,3-dichloro-
acetone

MgSO$_4$, acetone

4-(chloromethyl)-2-
isopropylthiazole
hydrochloride

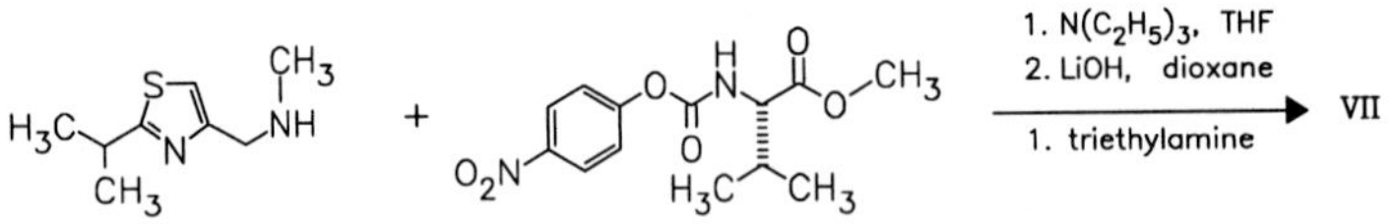

, H$_2$O

VI

2-isopropyl-4-
(methylamino-
methyl)thiazole (VI)

N-(4-nitrophenyloxy-
carbonyl)-L-valine
methyl ester

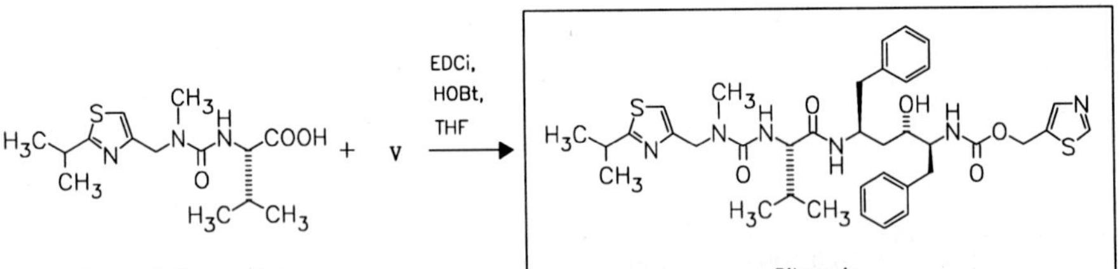

1. N(C$_2$H$_5$)$_3$, THF
2. LiOH, dioxane

1. triethylamine

VII

N-[methyl(2-isopropyl-4-
thiazolylmethyl)amino-
carbonyl]-L-valine (VII)

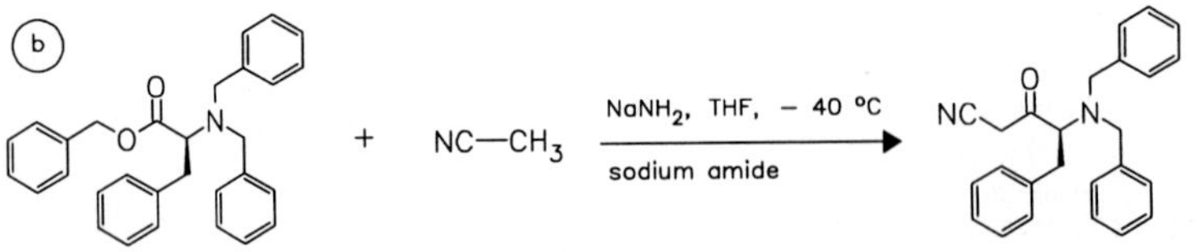

+ V

EDCi,
HOBt,
THF

Ritonavir

b

N,N-dibenzyl-L-
phenylalanine
benzyl ester

+ NC—CH$_3$

NaNH$_2$, THF, − 40 °C

sodium amide

4(S)-dibenzylamino-
3-oxo-5-phenyl-
pentanenitrile (VIII)

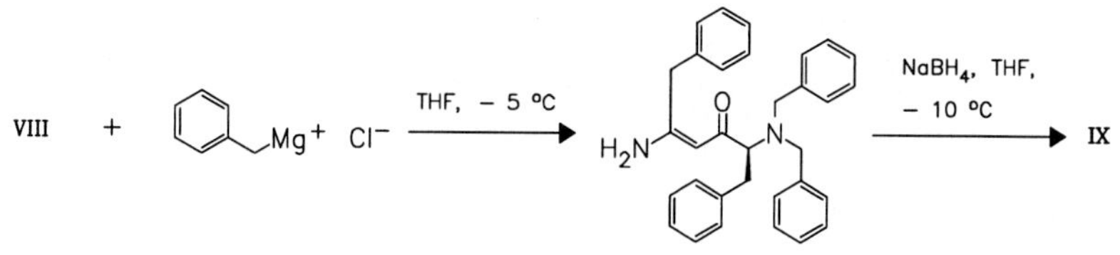

VIII + benzylmagnesium chloride $\xrightarrow{\text{THF, } -5 \text{ °C}}$ 2-amino-5(S)-dibenzylamino-4-oxo-1,6-diphenyl-2-hexene $\xrightarrow{\text{NaBH}_4, \text{ THF,} \\ -10 \text{ °C}}$ IX

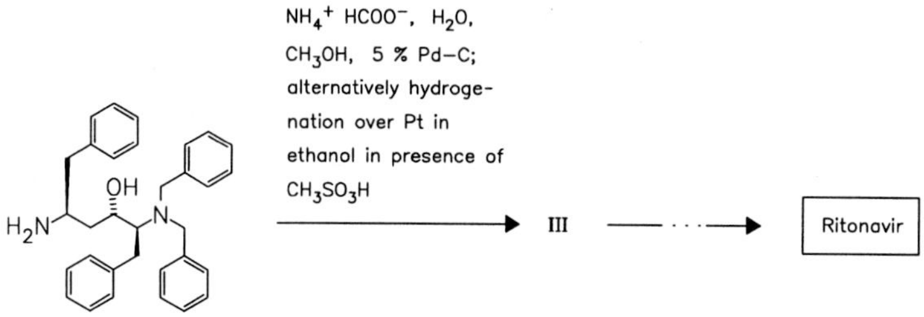

(2S,3S,5S)-5-amino-2-dibenzylamino-3-hydroxy-1,6-diphenyl-hexane (IX)

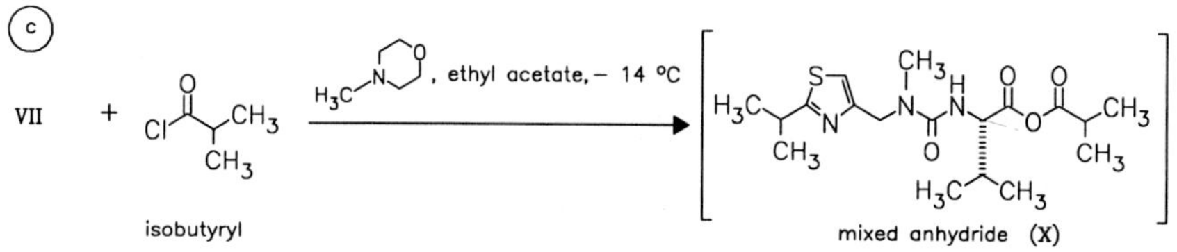

$\xrightarrow{\text{NH}_4^+ \text{ HCOO}^-, \text{ H}_2\text{O,} \\ \text{CH}_3\text{OH, } 5 \text{ % Pd-C;} \\ \text{alternatively hydroge-} \\ \text{nation over Pt in} \\ \text{ethanol in presence of} \\ \text{CH}_3\text{SO}_3\text{H}}$ III $\dashrightarrow$ Ritonavir

c

VII + isobutyryl chloride $\xrightarrow{\text{(morpholine), ethyl acetate, } -14 \text{ °C}}$ mixed anhydride (X)

X + V $\xrightarrow{\text{N-hydroxy-succinimide, } 0 \text{ °C}}$ Ritonavir

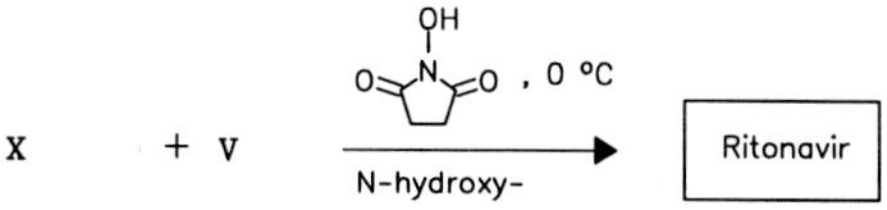

Reference(s):

a,b WO 9 414 436 (Abbott Labs.; appl. 16.12.1993; USA-prior. 29.12.1992, 2.12.1993).
b WO 9 511 224 (Abbott Labs.; appl. 26.9.1994; USA-prior. 22.10.1993, 27.7.1994).
WO 9 604 232 (Abbott Labs.; appl. 17.7.1995; USA-prior. 29.7.1994).
c US 5 567 823 (Abbott Labs; 22.10.1996; appl. 6.6.1995; USA-prior. 6.6.1995).
Kempf, D.J. et al.: J. Med. Chem. (JMCMAR) **41**, 602 (1998).

pharmaceutical composition in alcoholic/organic solvent:
WO 9 507 696 (Abbott Labs.; appl. 30.4.1994; USA-prior. 13.9.1993, 28.1.1994, 15.8.1994).
WO 9 520 384 (Abbott Labs.; appl. 3.1.1995; USA-prior. 29.7.1994, 28.1.1994, 12.5.1995).

use for treating HIV:
WO 9 701 349 (Abbott Labs.; appl. 28.6.1996; USA-prior. 15.9.1995, 29.6.1995).

combination with lamivudine:
WO 9 626 734 (Glaxo; appl. 22.2.1996; GB-prior. 25.2.1995).

combination of HIV protease inhibitors:
WO 9 604 913 (Merck & Co.; appl. 7.8.1995; USA-prior. 20.7.1995, 11.8.1994, 14.11.1994).
EP 691 345 (Bristol-Myers Squibb; appl. 5.7.1995; USA-prior. 17.5.1995, 5.7.1994, 31.7.1987).

pharmaceutical composition with improved oral bioavailability:
WO 9 509 614 (Abbott Labs.; appl. 9.9.1994; USA-prior. 31.8.1994).

Formulation(s):   cps. 100 mg wfm; sol. 600 mg/7.5 ml

Trade Name(s):

D:	Norvir (Abbott)	GB:	Norvir (Abbott)	USA:	Norvir (Abbott)
F:	Norvir (Abbott)	I:	Norvir (Abbott)		

Rivastigmine
(SDZ 212-713; ENA 713)

ATC: N06DA03
Use: cognition enhancer, alzheimer treatment, acetylcholinesterase inhibitor

RN: 123441-03-2   MF: $C_{14}H_{22}N_2O_2$ MW: 250.34
CN: (*S*)-Ethylmethylcarbamic acid 3-[1-(dimethylamino)-ethyl]phenyl ester

(±)-3-[1-(dimethyl-
amino)ethyl]phenol

N-ethyl-N-methyl-
carbamoyl chloride

NaH, THF

I

(±)-N-ethyl-N-methyl-
carbamic acid
3-[1-(dimethylamino)-
ethyl]phenyl ester (I)

1. D(+)-O,O'-di(p-toluoyl)tartaric acid,
   CH_3OH
2. 1N NaOH

Rivastigmine

Reference(s):
Amstutz, R. et al.: Helv. Chim. Acta (HCACAV) **73** (3), 739-753 (1990).
DE 3 805 744 (Sandoz; appl. 24.2.1988; D-prior. 4.3.1987).

systemic transdermal administration:
AT 392 587 (Sandoz; appl. 25.1.1989; A-prior. 3.3.1988).

Formulation(s):   cps. 1 mg, 1.5 mg, 3 mg, 4.5 mg, 6 mg (as tartrate)

Trade Name(s):

D:	Exelon (Novartis; 1998)	GB:	Exelon (Novartis)

Rizatriptan benzoate
(MK-462)

ATC: N02CC04
Use: antimigraine agent, selective 5-HT$_{1B/1D}$-agonist

RN: 145202-66-0   MF: C$_{15}$H$_{19}$N$_5$ · C$_7$H$_6$O$_2$ MW: 391.48
CN: N,N-Dimethyl-5-(1H-1,2,4-triazol-1-ylmethyl)-1H-indole-3-ethanamine benzoate

base
RN: 144034-80-0   MF: C$_{15}$H$_{19}$N$_5$ MW: 269.35

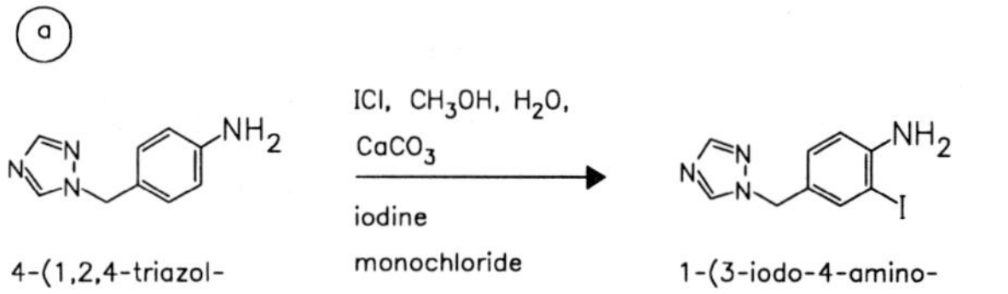

4-(1,2,4-triazol-1-ylmethyl)aniline (I)

ICl, CH$_3$OH, H$_2$O, CaCO$_3$

iodine monochloride

1-(3-iodo-4-amino-benzyl)-1,2,4-triazole (II)

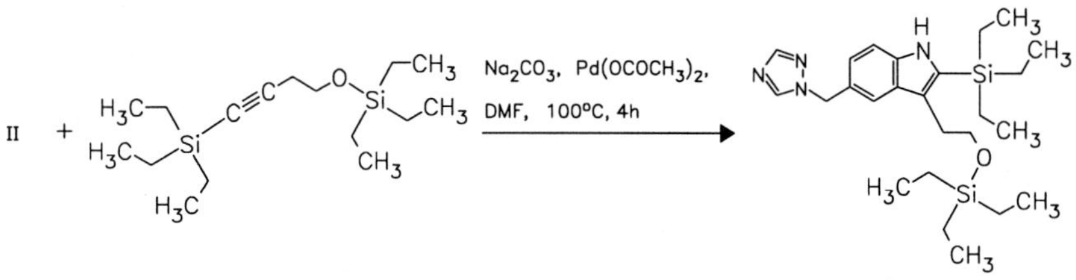

II +

4-triethylsilyl-3-butyn-1-ol triethylsilyl ether (III)

Na$_2$CO$_3$, Pd(OCOCH$_3$)$_2$, DMF, 100°C, 4h

(IV)

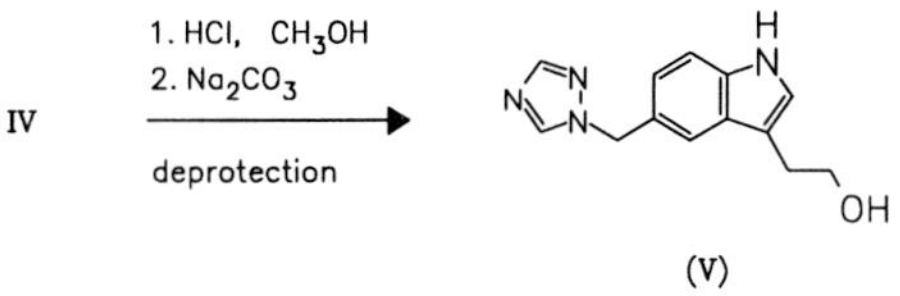

IV

1. HCl, CH$_3$OH
2. Na$_2$CO$_3$

deprotection

(V)

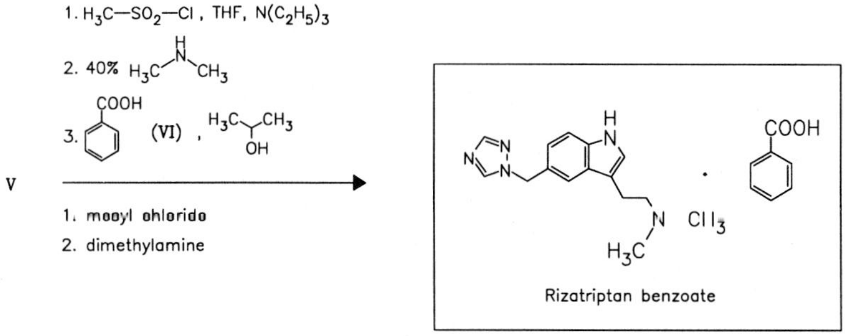

V

1. H$_3$C—SO$_2$—Cl, THF, N(C$_2$H$_5$)$_3$
2. 40% H$_3$C—NH—CH$_3$
3. COOH (VI), H$_3$C—CH$_3$ / OH

1. mesyl chloride
2. dimethylamine

Rizatriptan benzoate

preparation of the silyl reagent III

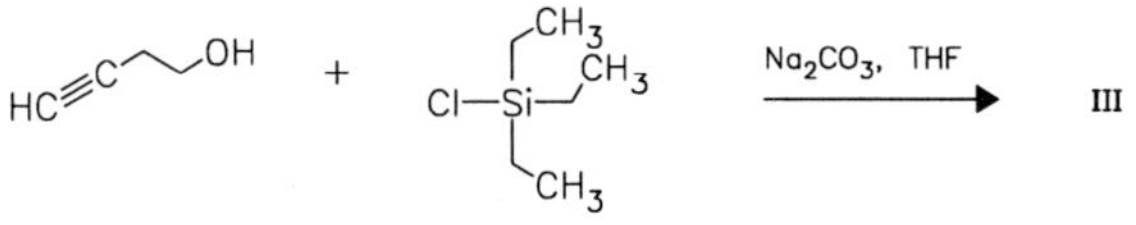

HC≡C—CH$_2$—CH$_2$—OH + Cl—Si(CH$_3$)... Na$_2$CO$_3$, THF → III

3-butyn-1-ol

(b)

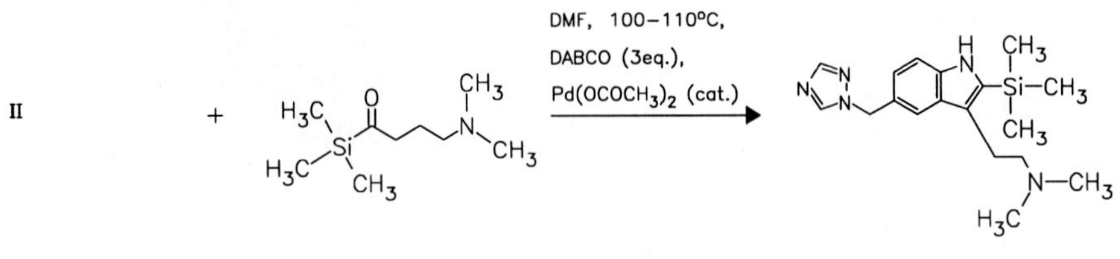

II   +   (VII)

DMF, 100–110°C,
DABCO (3eq.),
Pd(OCOCH₃)₂ (cat.)

→   (VIII)

(see method (a))   (VII)   (VIII)

DABCO:

VIII

1. 2n HCl, CH₃OH
2. Na₂CO₃
3. VI , H_3C CH_3 COOH

→   Rizatriptan benzoate

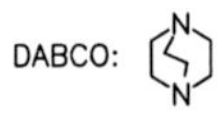

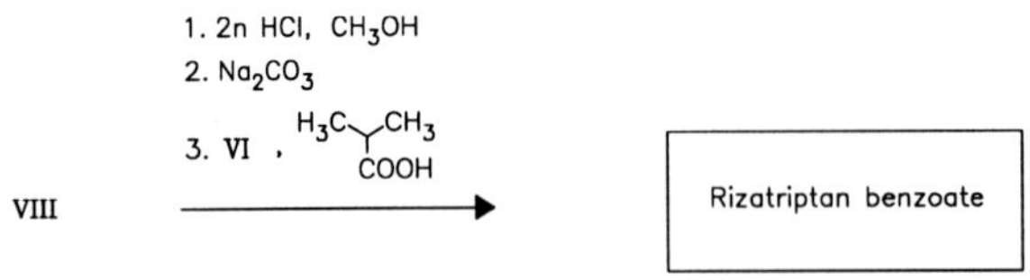

preparation of acyl silane VII

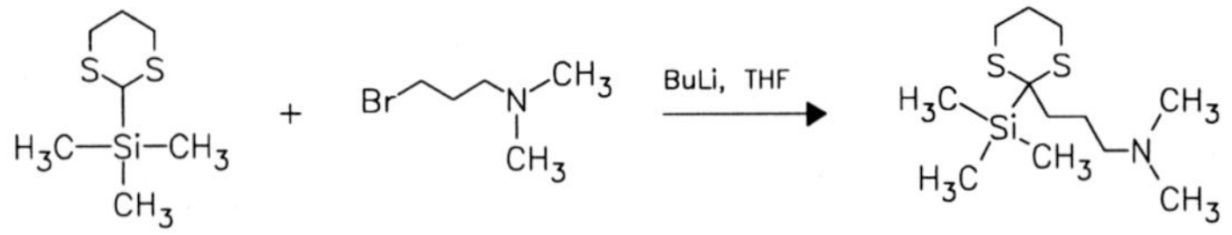

2-trimethylsilyl-
1,3-dithiane

+   Br $\sim$ N CH_3 / CH_3

BuLi, THF

→   (IX)

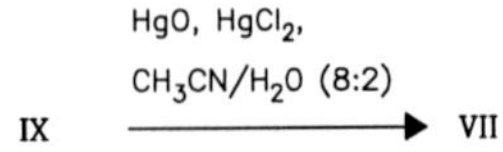

IX

HgO, HgCl₂,
CH₃CN/H₂O (8:2)

→   VII

(c)

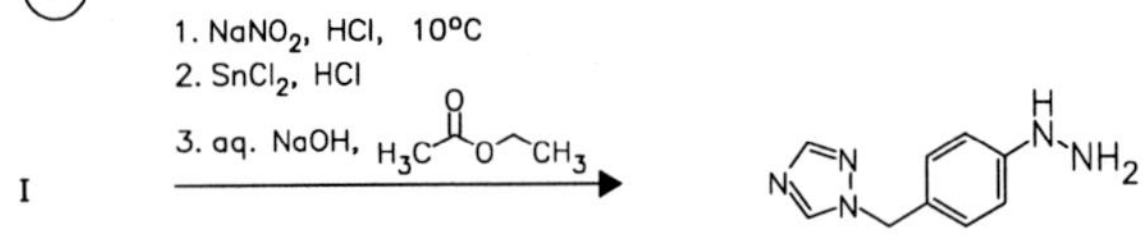

I

1. NaNO₂, HCl, 10°C
2. SnCl₂, HCl
3. aq. NaOH, H_3C O CH₃

→   (X)

X   +   H₃C O / H₃C O $\sim$ Cl

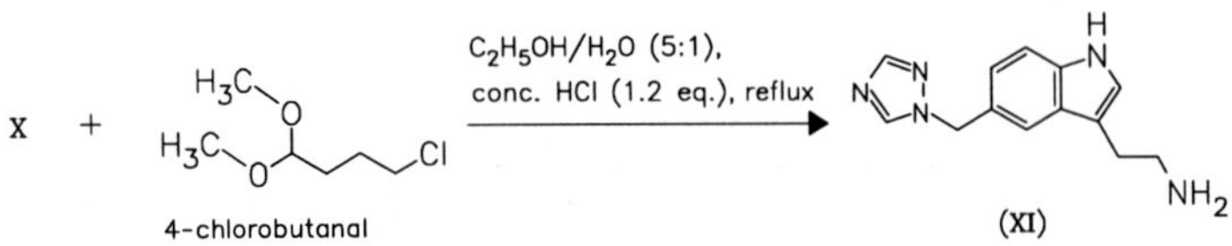

4-chlorobutanal
dimethyl acetal

C₂H₅OH/H₂O (5:1),
conc. HCl (1.2 eq.), reflux

→   (XI)

XI   +   HCHO

form-
aldehyde

1. NaBH₃CN, CH₃COOH, CH₃OH
2. VI

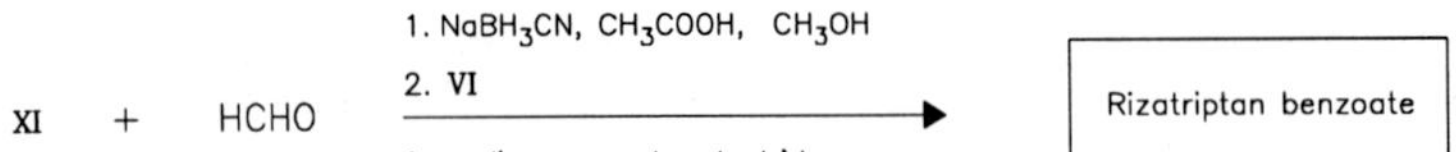

1. sodium cyanoborohydride
2. benzoic acid

→   Rizatriptan benzoate

(d)

preparation of 4-(1,2,4-triazol-1-ylmethyl)aniline I

(aa)

4-nitrobenzyl   1,2,4-triazole   1-(4-nitrobenzyl)-
bromide (XII)   sodium salt   1,2,4-triazole

(ab)

4-amino-   4-amino-1-(4-nitro-
1,2,4-triazole   benzyl)-1,2,4-
                                  triazolium bromide (XIII)

XIII $\xrightarrow{\text{HCOONH}_4, \text{ Pd-C}}$ I

Reference(s):
a WO 9 532 197 (Merck & Co.; appl. 19.5.1995; USA-prior. 24.5.1994).
   Chen, C.-Y.: Tetrahedron Lett. (TELEAY) **35** (38), 6981 (1994).
b WO 9 806 725 (Merck & Co.; appl. 8.8.1997; USA-prior. 13.8.1996; GB-prior. 12.9.1996).
c EP 497 512 (Merck & Co.; appl. 24.1.1992; GB-prior. 1.2.1991).
d EP 573 221 (Merck Sharp & Dohme, Ltd.; appl. 28.5.1993; GB-prior. 5.6.1992).

preparation of 4-(1,2,4-triazol-1-ylmethyl)aniline (I)
c,d Street, L.J. et al.: J. Med. Chem. (JMCMAR) **38**, 1799 (1995).

Formulation(s):   tabl. 5 mg, 10 mg (as benzoate)

Trade Name(s):
D: MAXALT (Merck Sharp &   GB: Maxalt (Merck Sharp &   USA: Maxalt (Merck Sharp &
      Dohme)   Dohme)   Dohme; 1998)

Rocuronium bromide
(Org-9426)

ATC: M03AC09
Use: neuromuscular blocker, non-
       depolarizing blocking drug

RN: 119302-91-9   MF: $C_{32}H_{53}BrN_2O_4$ MW: 609.69
CN: 1-[(2β,3α,5α,16β,17β)-17-(acetyloxy)-3-hydroxy-2-(4-morpholinyl)androstan-16-yl]-1-(2-propenyl)pyrrolidinium bromide

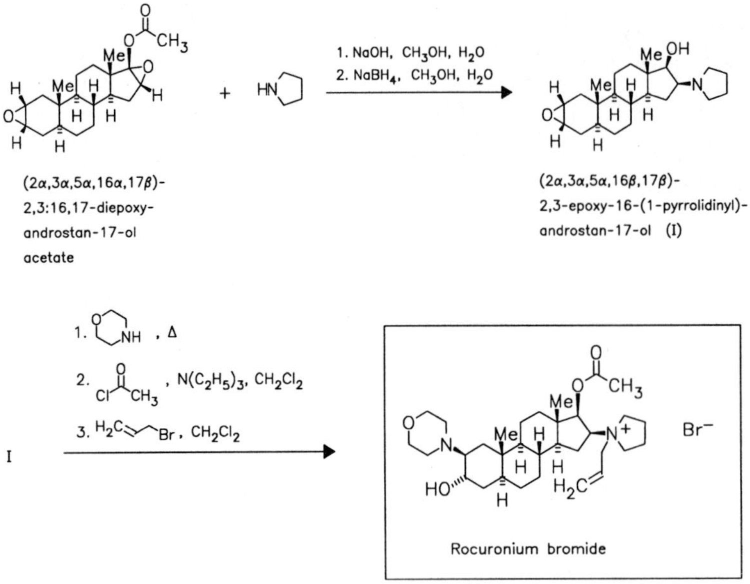

(2α,3α,5α,16α,17β)-
2,3:16,17-diepoxy-
androstan-17-ol
acetate

1. NaOH, CH₃OH, H₂O
2. NaBH₄, CH₃OH, H₂O

(2α,3α,5α,16β,17β)-
2,3-epoxy-16-(1-pyrrolidinyl)-
androstan-17-ol (I)

1. $\bigcirc$NH , Δ

2. Cl$\ce{-}$CH₃ , N(C₂H₅)₃, CH₂Cl₂
   O

3. H₂C$\ce{=}$Br , CH₂Cl₂

I →

Rocuronium bromide

Reference(s):
EP 287 150 (AKZO NV; appl. 19.10.1988; GB-prior. 14.4.1987).
Buckett, W.R. et al.: J. Med. Chem. (JMCMAR) **16**, 1116 (1973).
Meyer, M.; Doenicke, A.; Hofmann, A.; Angster, R.; Peter, K.: Anaesthesist (ANATAE) **40**(12), 668 (1991).

Formulation(s):   amp. 50 mg/5 ml; vial 100 mg/100 ml

Trade Name(s):
D: Esmeron (Organon   F: Esmeron (Organon   I: Esmeron (Organon
      Teknika)   Teknika)   Teknika)
                             GB: Esmeron (Organon)   USA: Zemuron (Organon)

Rofecoxib
(MK-966)

ATC: M01AH02
Use: anti-inflammatory, cyclooxygenase-2
        inhibitor

RN: 162011-90-7   MF: C₁₇H₁₄O₄S   MW: 314.36
CN: 4-[4-(Methylsulfonyl)phenyl]-3-phenyl-2(5H)-furanone

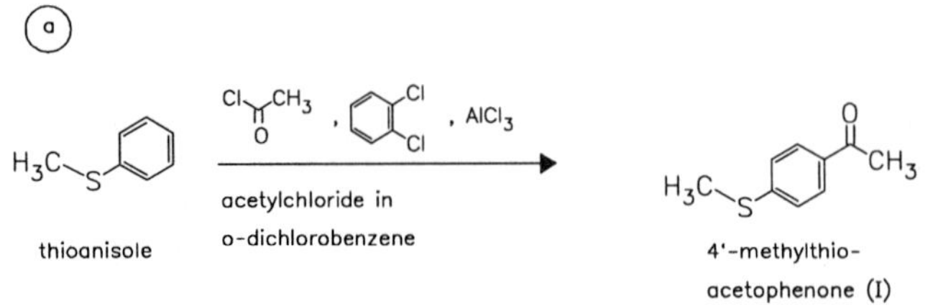

(a)

thioanisole

acetylchloride in
o-dichlorobenzene

Cl$\ce{-}$CH₃ , $\bigcirc$Cl Cl , AlCl₃
   O

4'-methylthio-
acetophenone (I)

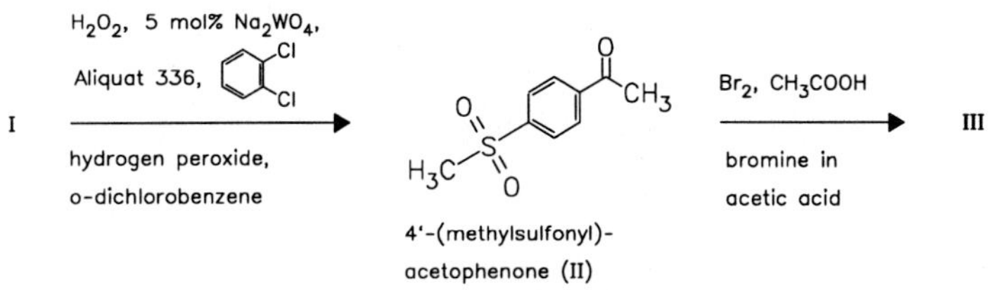

H₂O₂, 5 mol% Na₂WO₄,

Aliquat 336,

I →

hydrogen peroxide,
o-dichlorobenzene

4'-(methylsulfonyl)-
acetophenone (II)

Br₂, CH₃COOH   III

bromine in
acetic acid

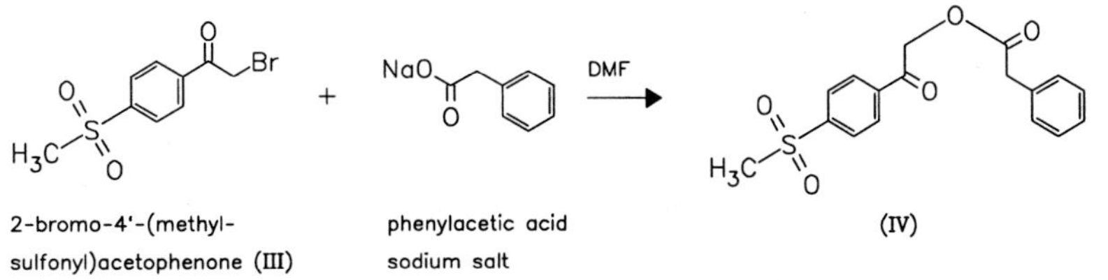

2-bromo-4'-(methyl-
sulfonyl)acetophenone (III)

+

phenylacetic acid
sodium salt

NaO   DMF →

(IV)

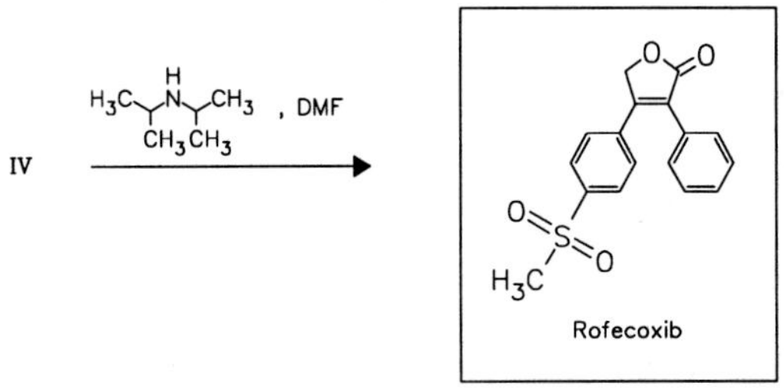

IV →

, DMF

Rofecoxib

(b)

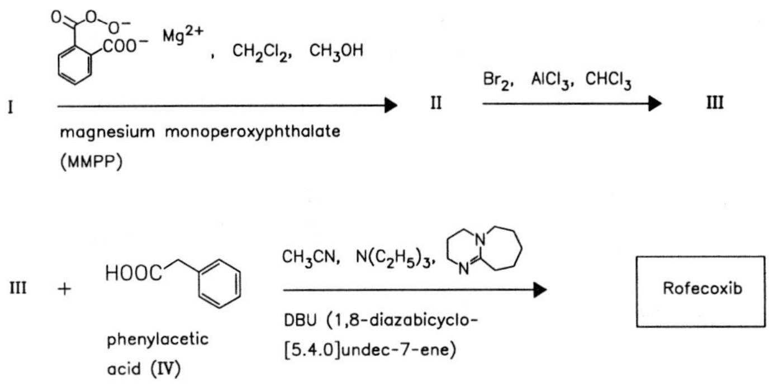

I →

magnesium monoperoxyphthalate
(MMPP)

, CH₂Cl₂, CH₃OH

II →

Br₂, AlCl₃, CHCl₃

III

III +

HOOC

phenylacetic
acid (IV)

CH₃CN, N(C₂H₅)₃,

DBU (1,8-diazabicyclo-
[5.4.0]undec-7-ene)

Rofecoxib

(c)

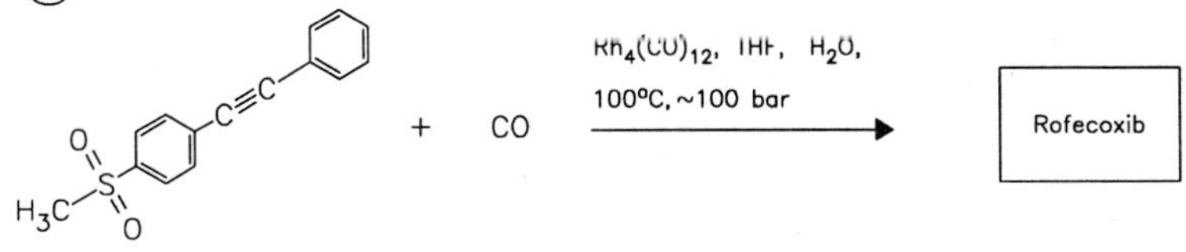

+   CO →

Rh₄(CO)₁₂, THF, H₂O,
100°C, ~100 bar

Rofecoxib

d

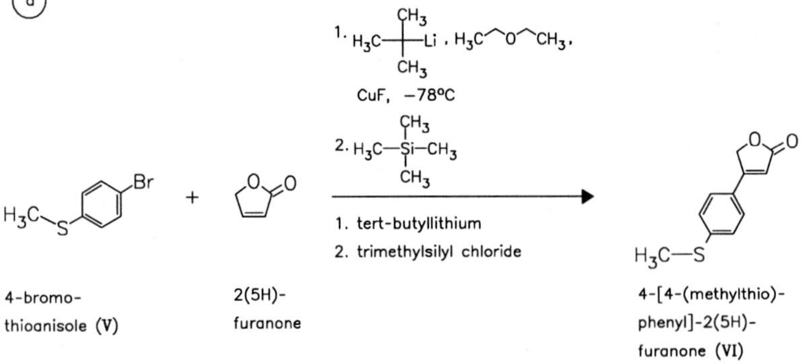

4-bromo-
thioanisole (V)

2(5H)-
furanone

4-[4-(methylthio)-
phenyl]-2(5H)-
furanone (VI)

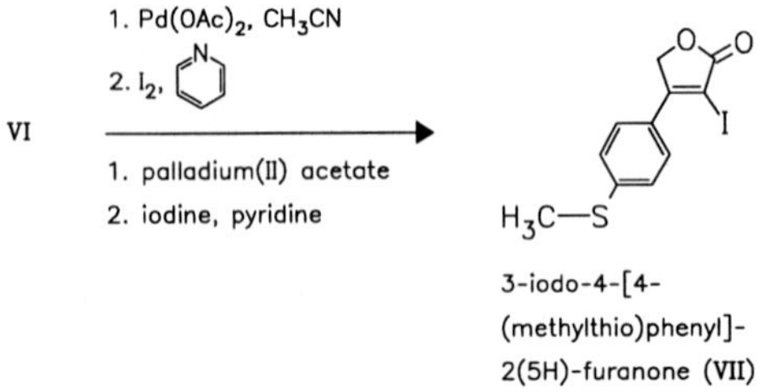

VI

1. Pd(OAc)$_2$, CH$_3$CN
2. I$_2$,
1. palladium(II) acetate
2. iodine, pyridine

3-iodo-4-[4-
(methylthio)phenyl]-
2(5H)-furanone (VII)

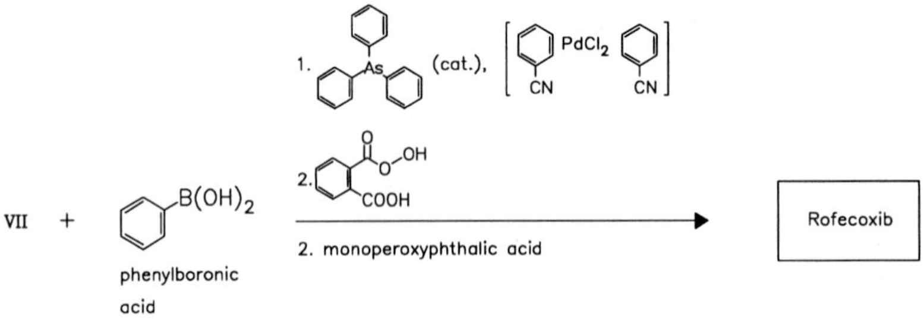

VII +

B(OH)$_2$

phenylboronic
acid

2. monoperoxyphthalic acid

Rofecoxib

e

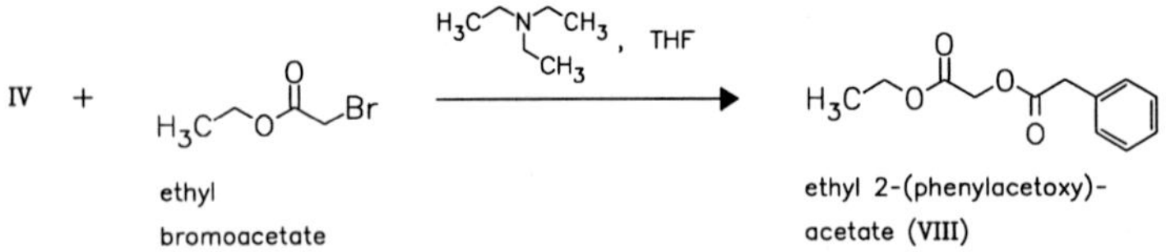

IV +

H$_3$C   O   Br

ethyl
bromoacetate

THF

ethyl 2-(phenylacetoxy)-
acetate (VIII)

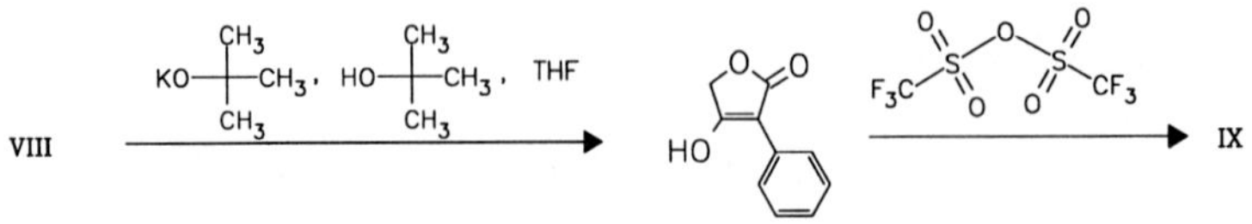

VIII

KO   CH$_3$, HO   CH$_3$,   THF

IX

synthesis of 4-(methylthio)phenylboronic acid

triisopropyl borate

Reference(s):
a   WO 9 800 416 (Merck & Co.; appl. 27.6.1997; GB-prior. 29.7.1996).
b   WO 9 613 483 (Merck Frosst Canada; appl. 2.10.1994; USA-prior. 27.10.1994)
e   WO 9 608 482 (Merck & Co.; appl. 12.9.1995; USA-prior. 16.9.1994).
a-e WO 9 500 501 (Merck Frosst Canada Inc.; appl. 15.5.1995; USA-prior. 24.6.1993, 10.1.1994).

The discovery of rofecoxib:
Prasit, P. et al.: Bioorg. Med. Chem. Lett. (BMCLE8) **9** (13), 1773 (1999).

alternative syntheses:
WO 9 636 623 (Merck Frosst Canada; appl. 15.5.1996; USA-prior. 18.5.1995).
GB 2 294 879 (Merck & Co.; appl. 9.10.1995; USA-prior. 19.10.1994).
WO 9 619 469 (Merck Frosst Canada; appl. 18.12.1995; USA-prior. 21.12.1994).

Formulation(s):   susp. 25 mg; tabl. 12.5 mg

Trade Name(s):
D: Vioxx (Merck Sharp &   GB: Vioxx (Merck Sharp &   USA: Vioxx (Merck Sharp &
      Dohme)   Dohme; 1999)   Dohme)

Rolitetracycline

ATC: J01AA09
Use: antibiotic, antibacterial

RN: 751-97-3   MF: $C_{27}H_{33}N_3O_8$ MW: 527.57   EINECS: 212-031-9
LD$_{50}$: 75 mg/kg (M, i.v.); 1320 mg/kg (M, p.o.);
      93 mg/kg (dog, i.v.)
CN: [4S-(4α,4aα,5aα,6β,12aα)]-4-(dimethylamino)-1,4,4a,5,5a,6,11,12a-octahydro-3,6,10,12,12a-
      pentahydroxy-6-methyl-1,11-dioxo-N-(1-pyrrolidinylmethyl)-2-naphthacenecarboxamide

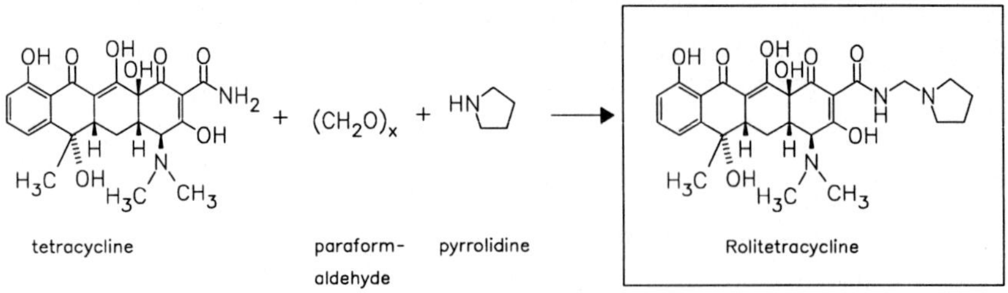

tetracycline + paraform- + pyrrolidine → Rolitetracycline
aldehyde

Reference(s):

DE 1 044 806 (Hoechst; appl. 3.10.1956).
DE 1 063 598 (Hoechst; appl. 14.2.1957).
US 3 104 240 (Bristol-Myers; 17.9.1963; prior. 18.8.1958).
Gottstein, W.J. et al.: J. Am. Chem. Soc. (JACSAT) **81**, 1198 (1959).

Formulation(s):   vial 275 mg

Trade Name(s):

D:	Reverin (Hoechst); wfm	I:	Colbiocin (SIFI)-comb.	Hostacyclin-PRM
F:	Transcycline (Hoechst); wfm		Iducol (SIFI)-comb.	(Hoechst)
			Vitecaf (SIFI)-comb.	Velacycline (Squibb)
GB:	Tetrex PMT (Bristol)-comb.; wfm	J:	Bristacin (Bristre-Banyu)	USA: Syntetrin (Bristol); wfm

---

Romurtide

(Muroctasin; Nomurtide)

ATC: L03AX
Use: immunostimulant, muramyldipeptide derivative, treatment of leukopenia associated with cancer radiotherapy

RN: 78113-36-7   MF: $C_{43}H_{78}N_6O_{13}$ MW: 887.13
LD_{50}:   >600 mg/kg (M, p.o.); 436 mg/kg (Mm, s.c.); 625 mg/kg (Mf, s.c.); >90 mg/kg (R, i.v.); >600 mg/kg (R, p.o.); 761 mg/kg (Rm, s.c.); 801 mg/kg (Rf, s.c.); >200 mg/kg (dog, s.c.)
CN: N^2-[N^2-[N-(N-acetylmuramoyl)-L-alanyl]-D-α-glutaminyl]-N^6-(1-oxooctadecyl)-L-lysine

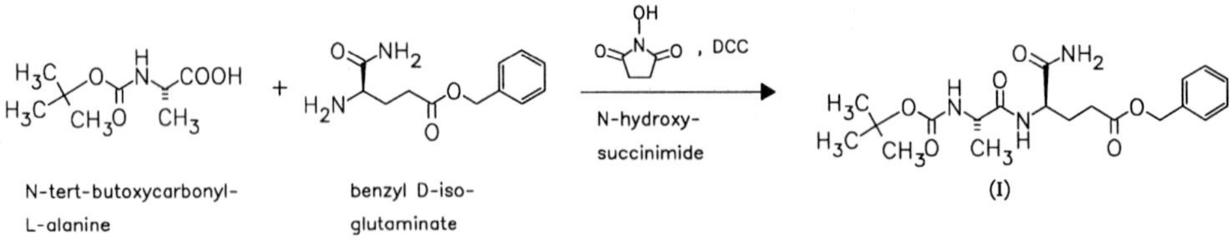

N-tert-butoxycarbonyl-L-alanine + benzyl D-iso-glutaminate → N-hydroxy-succinimide , DCC → (I)

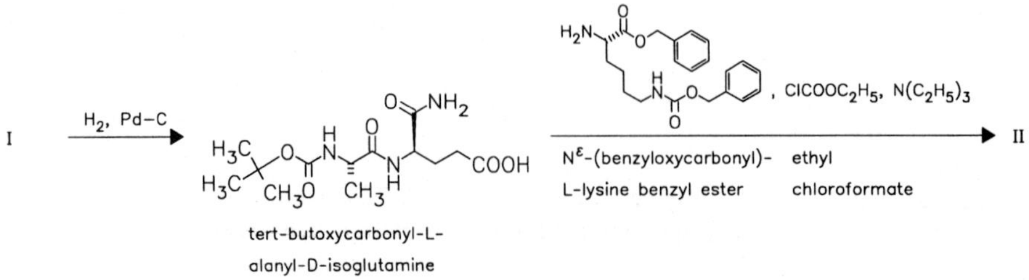

I →[H_2, Pd-C] tert-butoxycarbonyl-L-alanyl-D-isoglutamine → N^ε-(benzyloxycarbonyl)-L-lysine benzyl ester , $ClCOOC_2H_5$, $N(C_2H_5)_3$ ethyl chloroformate → II

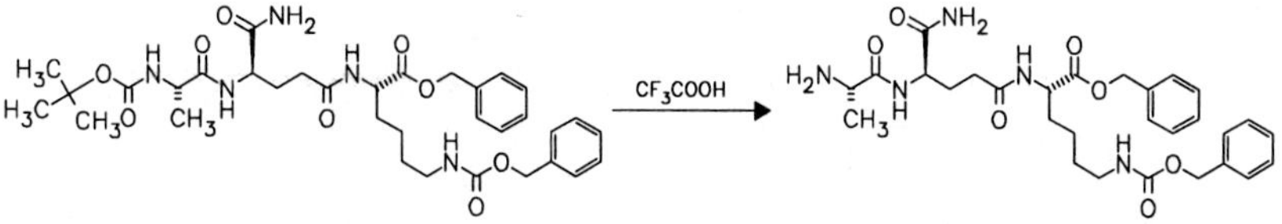

(II)

L-alanyl-D-isoglutaminyl-N$^\varepsilon$-(benzyloxycarbonyl)-L-lysine benzyl ester (III)

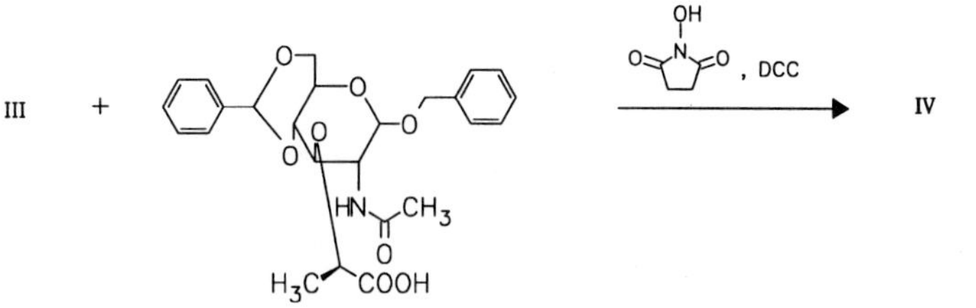

III +

1-O-benzyl-4,6-O-benzylidene-
N-acetylmuramic acid

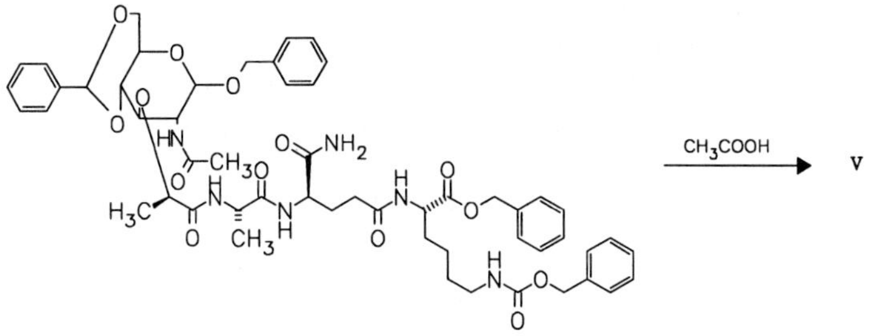

IV

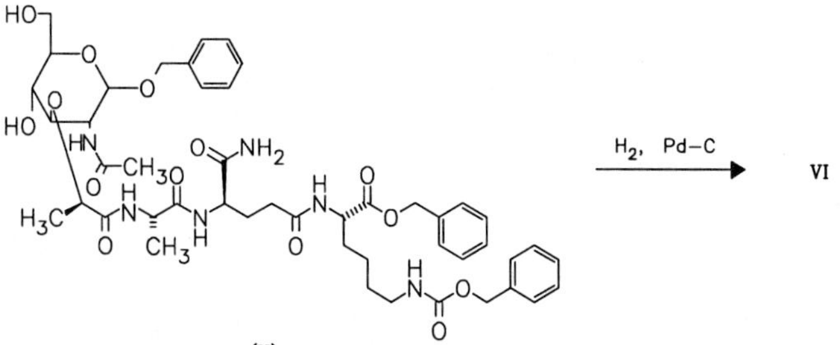

(IV)

(V)

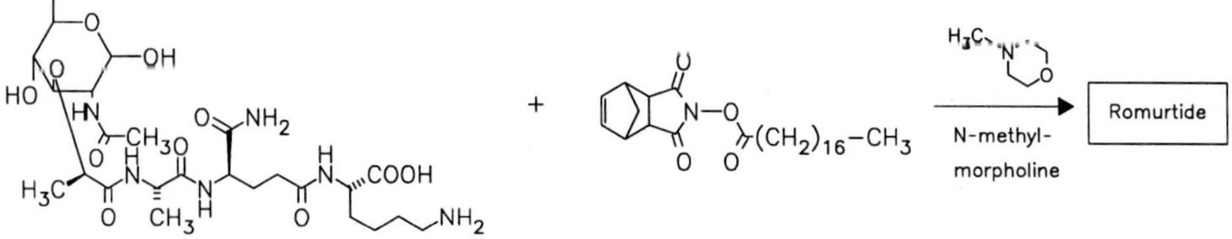

N$^\alpha$-(N-acetylmuramoyl-L-alanyl-
D-isoglutaminyl)-L-lysine (VI)

N-(stearoyloxy)-5-norbornene-
2,3-dicarboximide

N-methyl-
morpholine

Romurtide

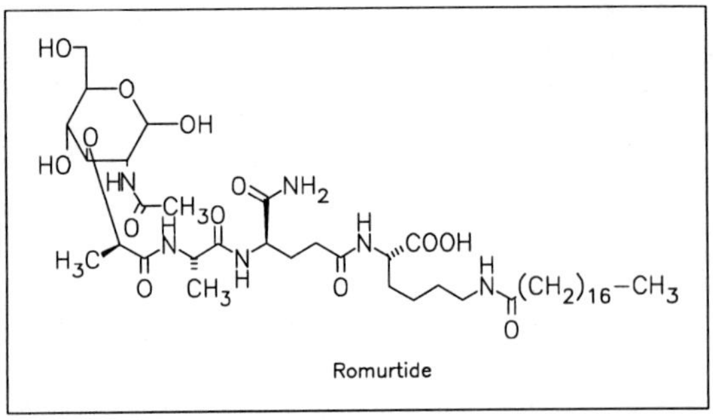

Romurtide

Reference(s):
EP 21 367 (Daiichi; appl. 20.6.1980; J-prior. 21.6.1979).
US 4 317 771 (Daiichi; 2.3.1982; appl. 23.6.1980; J-prior. 21.6.1979).

medical use for treatment of thrombopenia:
EP 331 756 (Daiichi; appl. 2.9.1988; J-prior. 2.9.1987).

medical use as analgesic/anti-inflammatory:
JP 63 093 724 (Daiichi; appl. 9.10.1986).

Formulation(s):   vial 200 μg

Trade Name(s):
J: Nopia (Daiichi; 1991)

Ronifibrate

ATC: C10AB07
Use: antihyperlipoproteinemic, fibrate
        serum antihyperlipidemic

RN: 42597-57-9   MF: $C_{19}H_{20}ClNO_5$ MW: 377.82
LD$_{50}$: 3100-4080 mg/kg (M, p.o.)
CN: 3-pyridinecarboxylic acid 3-[2-(4-chlorophenoxy)-2-methyl-1-oxopropoxy]propyl ester

hydrochloride
RN: 42749-78-0   MF: $C_{19}H_{20}ClNO_5 \cdot HCl$ MW: 414.29

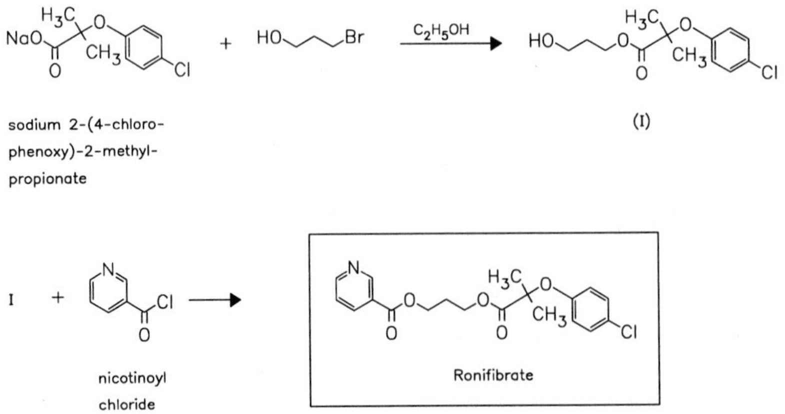

sodium 2-(4-chloro-
phenoxy)-2-methyl-
propionate

(I)

nicotinoyl
chloride

Ronifibrate

Reference(s):
JP 49 030 377 (Kowa; appl. 19.7.1972); C.A. (CHABA8) **81**, 135984s.
JP 4 840 777 (Yamanouchi; appl. 5.10.1971); C.A. (CHABA8) **79**, 66180w (1973).

Formulation(s):   cps. 250 mg, 500 mg

Trade Name(s):
I: Cloprane (Sankyo Pharma)

Ropinirole
(SK & F-101468; SK & F-101468A)

ATC: N04BC04
Use: dopamine-D$_2$-agonist,
            antiparkinsonian

RN: 91374-21-9   MF: C$_{16}$H$_{24}$N$_2$O   MW: 260.38
CN: 4-[2-(dipropylamino)ethyl]-1,3-dihydro-2-indol-2-one

hydrochloride
RN: 91374-20-8   MF: C$_{16}$H$_{24}$N$_2$O · HCl   MW: 296.84

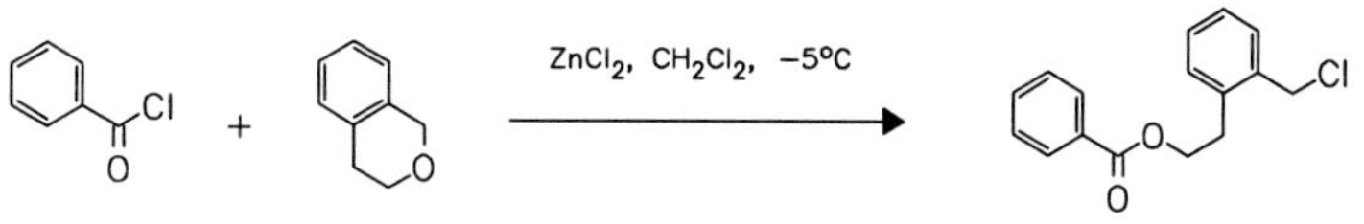

benzoyl
chloride

isochroman

2-chloromethylphenethyl
benzoate (I)

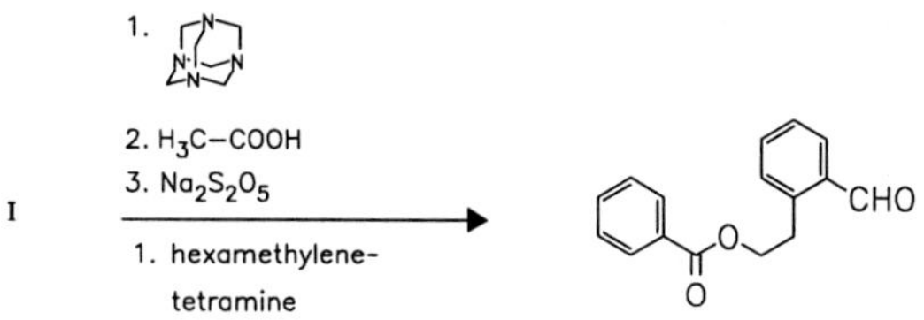

2-formylphenethyl
benzoate (II)

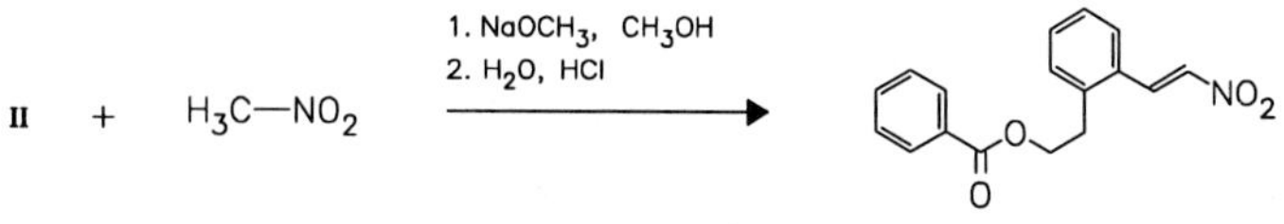

2-(2-benzoyloxyethyl)-
β-nitrostyrene (III)

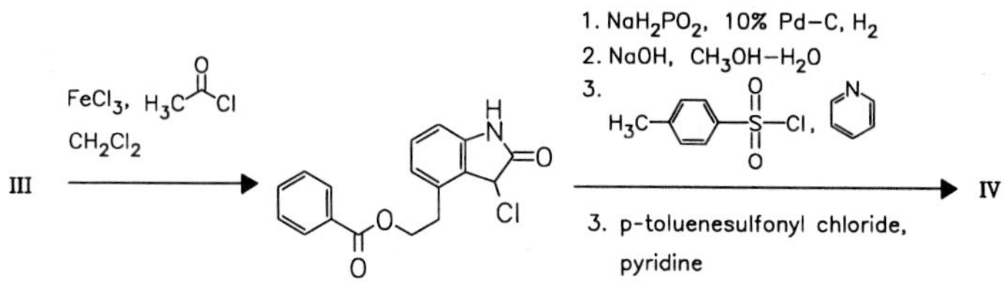

IV

(IV) + dipropylamine → Ropinirole

Reference(s):
synthesis of ropinirole:
WO 9 116 306 (Smith Kline & French; appl. 15.4.1991; GB-prior. 17.4.1990).
EP 113 964 (Smith Kline & French; appl. 30.11.1983; USA-prior. 7.12.1982).
Hayler, J.D. et al.: Org. Process Res. Dev. (OPRDFK) **2**, 3 (1998).

synthesis of 2-formylphenethyl benzoate:
Hayler, H.D.; Howie, S.L.B.; Negus, A.; Oxley, P.W.: J. Heterocycl. Chem. (JHTCAD) **32** (3), 875 (1995).

dihydroindolinones as cardiovascular agents:
US 4 997 954 (Smith Kline & French; 25.1.1989; GB-prior. 19.6.1987).
EP 300 614 (Smith Kline & French; appl. 16.6.1988; GB-prior. 19.6.1987).
AU 8 777 615 (Smith Kline & French; appl. 25.1.1989; GB-prior. 30.8.1986).
US 4 452 808 (Smith Kline & French; appl. 5.6.1984; USA-prior. 7.12.1982).
WO 9 415 918 (Smith Kline & French; appl. 21.7.1994; GB-prior. 8.1.1993).

use for treatment of Parkinson's disease:
EP 299 602 (Smith Kline & French; appl. 18.1.1989; GB-prior. 21.5.1987).
WO 9 711 696 (Cygnus Inc.; appl. 6.9.1996; USA-prior. 29.9.1995, 4.9.1996).
WO 9 639 136 (SmithKline Beecham; appl. 12.12.1996; GB-prior. 6.6.1995).
WO 9 323 035 (SmithKline Beecham; appl. 25.11.1993; GB-prior. 18.5.1992).
WO 9 200 735 (SmithKline Beecham; appl. 8.7.1991; GB-prior. 9.7.1990).
WO 9 706 786 (Scherer Ltd.; appl. 16.8.1996; GB-prior. 18.18.1995).

Formulation(s):   tabl. 0.25 mg, 0.5 mg, 1 mg, 2 mg, 3 mg, 4 mg, 5 mg (as hydrochloride)

Trade Name(s):

D:	Requib (SmithKline Beecham)	GB:	ReQuip (SmithKline Beecham; 1996)	USA:	Requib (SmithKline Beecham)
F:	Requib (SmithKline Beecham)	I:	Requib (SmithKline Beecham)		

Ropivacaine hydrochloride
(LEA-103)

ATC: N01BB09
Use: local anesthetic

RN: 98717-15-8   MF: $C_{17}H_{26}N_2O \cdot HCl$ MW: 310.87
CN: (*S*)-*N*-(2,6-dimethylphenyl)-1-propyl-2-piperidinecarboxamide monohydrochloride

monohydrate
RN: 132112-35-7   MF: $C_{17}H_{26}N_2O \cdot HCl \cdot H_2O$ MW: 328.88
base
RN: 84057-95-4   MF: $C_{17}H_{26}N_2O$ MW: 274.41

L-pipecolic acid → L-pipecoloyl chloride → 2,6-xylidine → (I)

I + H₃C–Br → Ropivacaine hydrochloride

Reference(s):
WO 8 500 599 (Apothekernes Lab., Astra; WO-prior. 1.8.1983).

preparation of optically-enriched pipecolic acid:
WO 9 611 185 (Chiroscience; appl. 9.10.1995; GB-prior. 7.10.1994).

storage stable optically pure hydrochloride monohydrate:
AU 8 666 449 (Astra, Nissan; appl. 12.12.1986; S-prior. 3.1.1986).
WO 9 636 606 (Astra; appl. 30.4.1996; S-prior. 16.5.1995).

composition with long/medium chain triglycerides:
EP 770 387 (Braun Melsungen; prior. 28.10.1995).

sustained release formulation:
WO 9 641 616 (Euroceltique; USA-prior. 9.6.1996).

combination with β-blocker:
WO 9 527 511 (Astra; appl. 24.3.1995; S-prior. 7.4.1994).

composition containing hydroxypropyl-β-cyclodextrin:
WO 9 505 198 (F. M. Borgbjerg; appl. 16.8.1994; DK-prior. 17.8.1993).

injection suspension:
WO 9 401 087 (Astra; appl. 24.6.1993; S-prior. 9.7.1992).

Formulation(s):   amp. 2 mg/ml, 5 mg/ml, 7.5 mg/ml, 10 mg/ml (as monohydrate)

Trade Name(s):
D: Naropin (Astra)   GB: Naropin (Astra)   USA: Naropin (Astra)
F: Naropeine (Astra)   I: Naropina (Astra)

Rosiglitazone
(BRL 49653)

ATC: A10BG02
Use: antidiabetic, insulin enhancer

RN: 122320-73-4   MF: $C_{18}H_{19}N_3O_3S$ MW: 357.43
CN: 5-[[4-[2-(Methyl-2-pyridinylamino)ethoxy]phenyl]methyl]-2,4-thiazolidinedione

(R)-(+)-form
RN: 163860-16-0   MF: $C_{18}H_{19}N_3O_3S$ MW: 357.43
maleate
RN: 155141-29-0   MF: $C_{18}H_{19}N_3O_3S \cdot C_4H_4O$ MW: 425.51

a

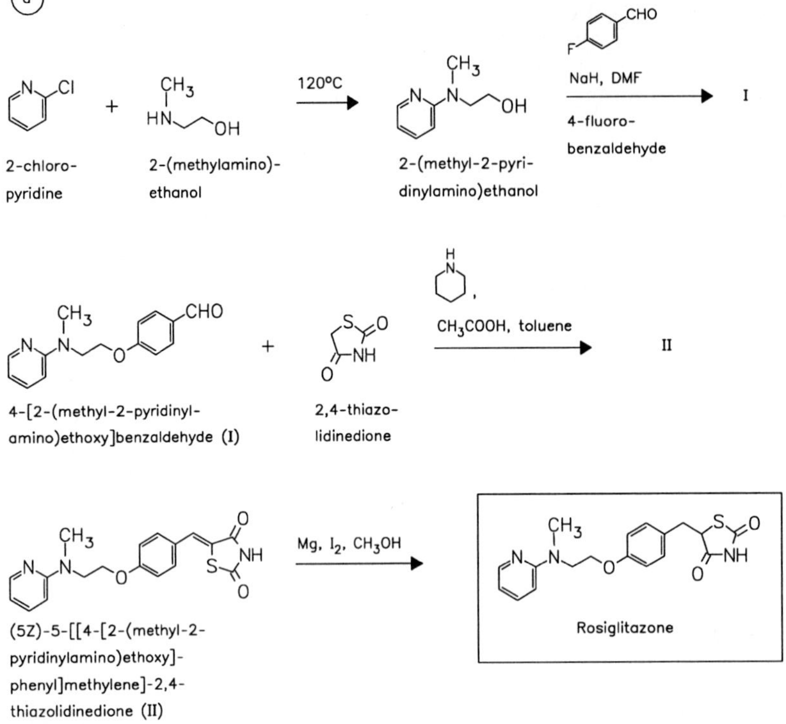

2-chloro-
pyridine

2-(methylamino)-
ethanol

2-(methyl-2-pyri-
dinylamino)ethanol

120°C

NaH, DMF

4-fluoro-
benzaldehyde

I

4-[2-(methyl-2-pyridinyl-
amino)ethoxy]benzaldehyde (I)

2,4-thiazo-
lidinedione

CH₃COOH, toluene

II

(5Z)-5-[[4-[2-(methyl-2-
pyridinylamino)ethoxy]-
phenyl]methylene]-2,4-
thiazolidinedione (II)

Mg, I₂, CH₃OH

Rosiglitazone

b   alternative biocatalytic reduction of II and synthesis of the (R)-(+)-enantiomer

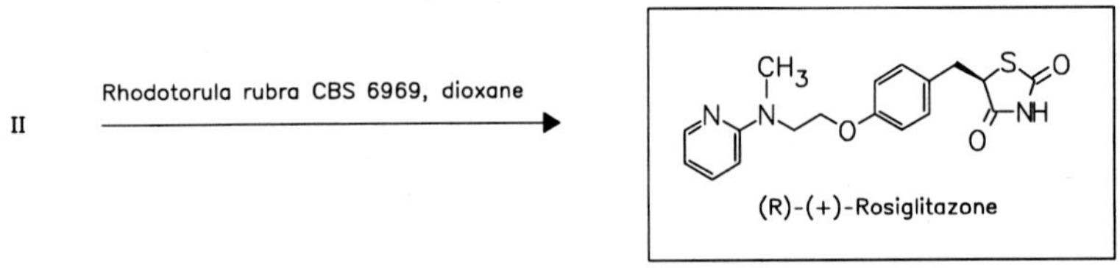

II   Rhodotorula rubra CBS 6969, dioxane

(R)-(+)-Rosiglitazone

c

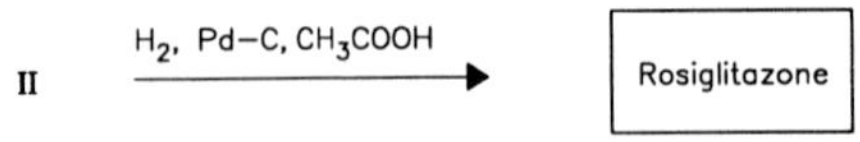

II   H₂, Pd—C, CH₃COOH   Rosiglitazone

d

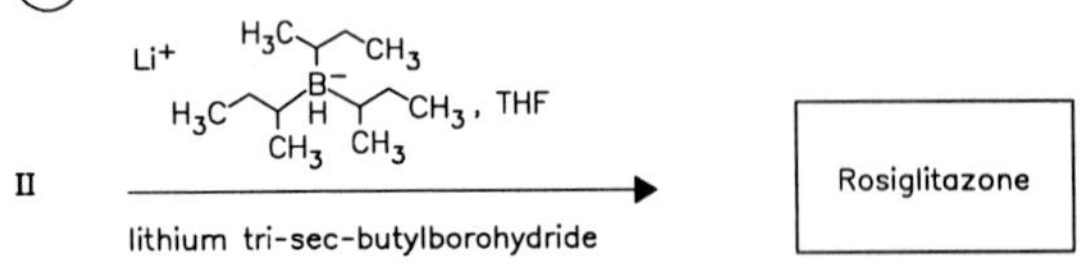

II   lithium tri-sec-butylborohydride   Rosiglitazone

Reference(s):

a Cantello, B.C.C. et al.: J. Med. Chem. (JMCMAR) **37**, 3977-3985 (1994).
Cantello, B.C.C. et al.: Bioorg. Med. Chem. Lett. (BMCLE8) **4** (1), 29. (1994).
EP 306 228 (Beecham; appl. 26.8.1988; GB-prior. 4.9.1987).

b Cantello, B.C.C. et al.: J. Chem. Soc., Perkin Trans. 1 (JCPRB4) **1994**, 3319.
Heath, C.M. et al.: J. Chem. Technol. Biotechnol. (JCTBED) **68** (3), 324-330 (1997).
WO 9 310 254 (SmithKline Beecham; appl. 19.11.1992; GB-prior. 19.11.1991).

c WO 9 923 095 (SmithKline Beecham; appl. 27.10.1998; GB-prior. 4.11.1997).

d WO 9 837 073 (SmithKline Beecham; appl. 13.2.1998; GB-prior. 18.2.1997).

maleate salt and other derivatives:
WO 9 405 659 (SmithKline Beecham; appl. 1.9.1993; GB-prior. 5.9.1992).

treatment of diabetes with insulin and rosiglitazone:
WO 9 837 073 (SmithKline Beecham; appl. 15.6.1998; GB-prior. 18.6.1997).

Formulation(s): tabl. 2 mg, 4 mg, 8 mg

Trade Name(s):
USA: Avandia (SmithKline Beecham; 1999)

Rosoxacin
(Acrosoxacin)

ATC: J01MB01
Use: antibiotic

RN: 40034-42-2 MF: $C_{17}H_{14}N_2O_3$ MW: 294.31 EINECS: 254-758-4
CN: 1-ethyl-1,4-dihydro-4-oxo-7-(4-pyridinyl)-3-quinolinecarboxylic acid

sodium salt
RN: 40035-08-3 MF: $C_{17}H_{13}N_2NaO_3$ MW: 316.29

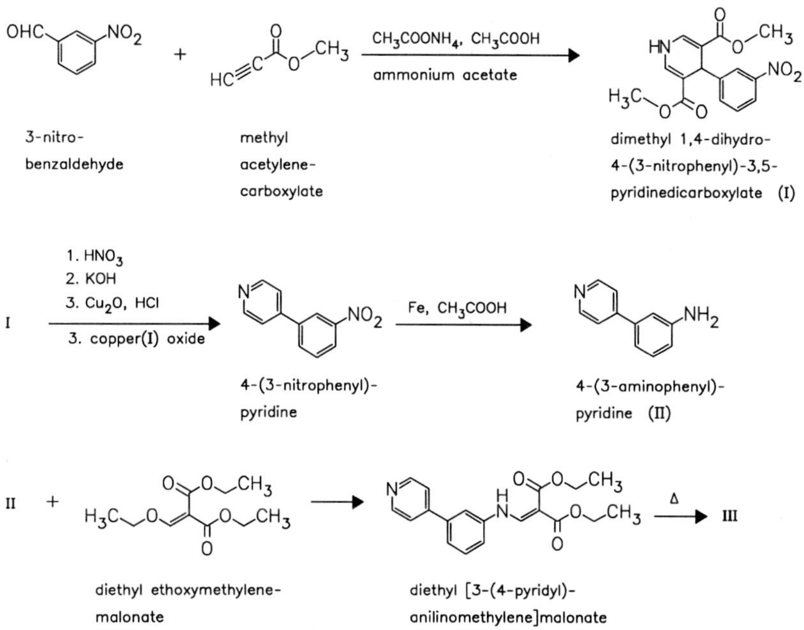
CH3COONH4, CH3COOH
ammonium acetate
3-nitrobenzaldehyde
methyl acetylenecarboxylate
dimethyl 1,4-dihydro-4-(3-nitrophenyl)-3,5-pyridinedicarboxylate (I)
I
1. HNO3
2. KOH
3. Cu2O, HCl
3. copper(I) oxide
Fe, CH3COOH
4-(3-nitrophenyl)-pyridine
4-(3-aminophenyl)-pyridine (II)
II
Δ
III
diethyl ethoxymethylenemalonate
diethyl [3-(4-pyridyl)-anilinomethylene]malonate

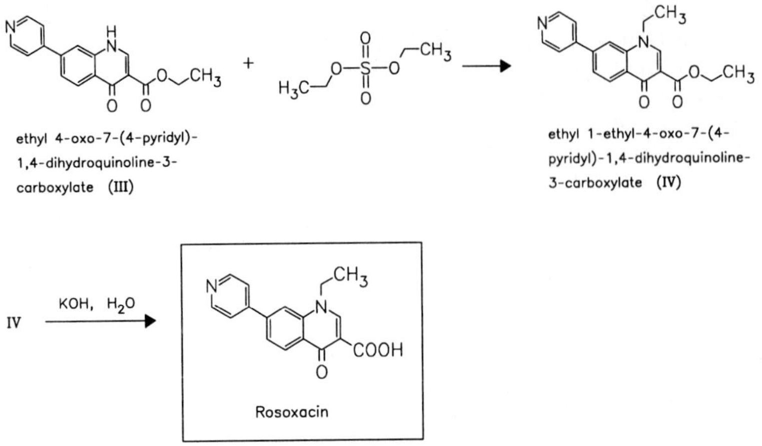

CH3
O
CH3
H3C
O
S
O
O
O
CH3
N
H
N
O
O
CH3
ethyl 4-oxo-7-(4-pyridyl)-1,4-dihydroquinoline-3-carboxylate (III)
ethyl 1-ethyl-4-oxo-7-(4-pyridyl)-1,4-dihydroquinoline-3-carboxylate (IV)
IV
KOH, H2O
COOH
Rosoxacin

Reference(s):
US 3 753 993 (Sterling Drug; 21.8.1973; prior. 17.5.1971).
US 3 907 808 (Sterling Drug; 23.9.1975; prior. 17.5.1971, 3.5.1973).
US 3 922 278 (Sterling Drug; 25.11.1975; prior. 12.6.1972).

alternative synthesis:
US 4 107 167 (Sterling Drug; 15.8.1978; prior. 17.6.1974).

Formulation(s): cps. 150 mg

Trade Name(s):

D:	Winuron (Winthrop); wfm	GB:	Eradacin (Sterling); wfm
F:	Ésacine (Sanofi Winthrop)	USA:	Eradocil (Winthrop); wfm

Roxatidine acetate

ATC: A02BA06
Use: histamine H_2-receptor antagonist, ulcer therapeutic

RN: 78628-28-1 MF: $C_{19}H_{28}N_2O_4$ MW: 348.44
LD_{50}: 1 g/kg (M, p.o.)
CN: 2-(acetyloxy)-*N*-[3-[3-(1-piperidinylmethyl)phenoxy]propyl]acetamide

monohydrochloride
RN: 93793-83-0 MF: $C_{19}H_{28}N_1O_4 \cdot HCl$ MW: 370.90
LD_{50}: 83 mg/kg (M, i.v.); 509 mg/kg (M, p.o.); 384 mg/kg (M, s.c.);
227 mg/kg (R, i.p.); 755 mg/kg (R, p.o.); 595 mg/kg (R, s.c.);
900 mg/kg (rabbit, p.o.);
75 mg/kg (dog, i.v.); 100 mg/kg (dog, p.o.);
50 mg/kg (monkey, p.o.)

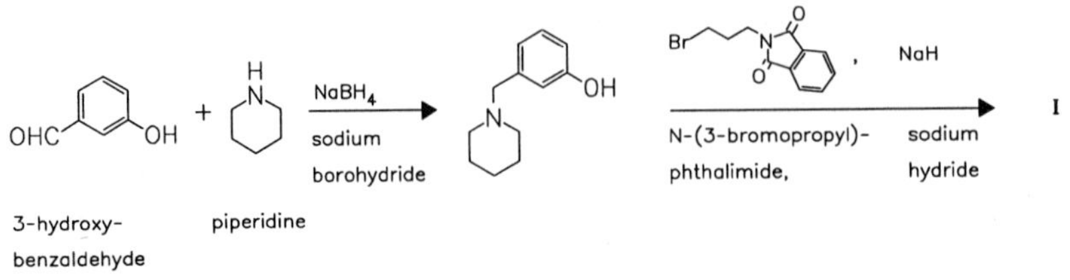

OHC
OH
H
N
NaBH4
sodium borohydride
OH
N
Br
N
O
O
NaH
N-(3-bromopropyl)-phthalimide,
sodium hydride
I
3-hydroxy-benzaldehyde
piperidine

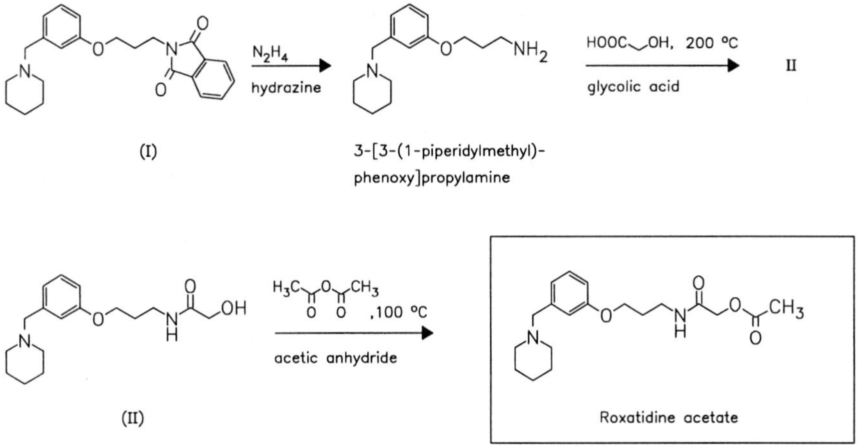

(I)   3-[3-(1-piperidylmethyl)-
phenoxy]propylamine

(II)   Roxatidine acetate

Reference(s):
EP 24 510 (Teikoku Hormone; appl. 1.7.1980; J-prior. 3.7.1979, 20.2.1980).
US 4 293 557 (Teikoku Hormone; 10.6.1981; appl. 30.6.1980; J-prior. 3.7.1979, 20.2.1980).

combination with serotonin antagonists:
EP 275 669 (Glaxo; appl. 16.12.1987; GB-prior. 17.12.1986).

Formulation(s):   s. r. cps. 75 mg, 150 mg; tabl. 75 mg, 150 mg (as hydrochloride)

Trade Name(s):
D: Roxit (Albert-Roussel;   I: Gastralgin (Ist. De Angeli)   J: Altat (Teikoku; Takeda;
      Hoechst Marion Roussel;   Neoh 2 (Boehringer Ing.)   Sumitomo; 1986)
      1989)   Roxit (Hoechst Marion)

Rufloxacin hydrochloride
(ISF-09334; MF 934)

ATC: J01MA10
Use: antibacterial

RN: 106017-08-7   MF: $C_{17}H_{18}FN_3O_3S \cdot HCl$ MW: 399.87
CN: 9-Fluoro-2,3-dihydro-10-(4-methyl-1-piperazinyl)-7-oxo-7H-pyrido[1,2,3-de]-1,4-benzothiazine-6-
       carboxylic acid monohydrochloride

base
RN: 101363-10-4   MF: $C_{17}H_{18}FN_3O_3S$ MW: 363.41

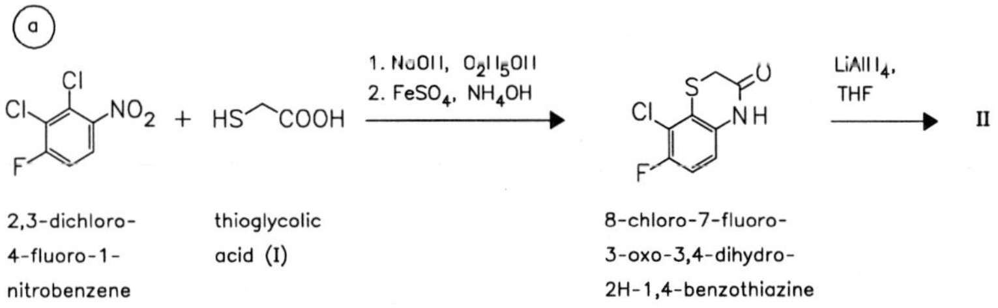

2,3-dichloro-   thioglycolic   8-chloro-7-fluoro-
4-fluoro-1-   acid (I)   3-oxo-3,4-dihydro-
nitrobenzene   2H-1,4-benzothiazine

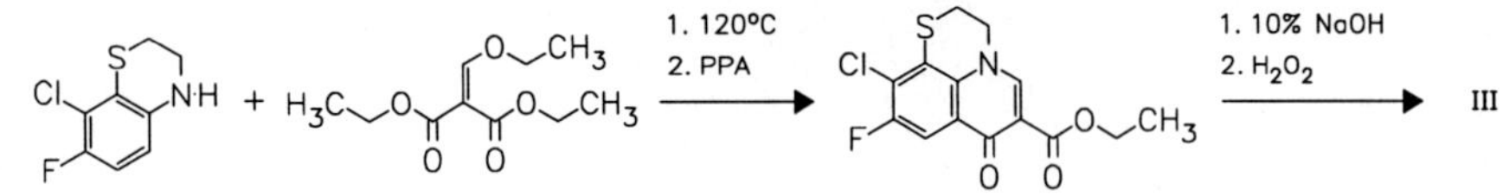

8-chloro-7-
fluoro-3,4-
dihydro-2H-
1,4-benzo-
thiazine (II)

diethyl ethoxymethylene-
malonate

ethyl 10-chloro-9-fluoro-
7-oxo-2,3-dihydro-7H-
pyrido[1,2,3-de]-1,4-benzo-
thiazine-6-carboxylate

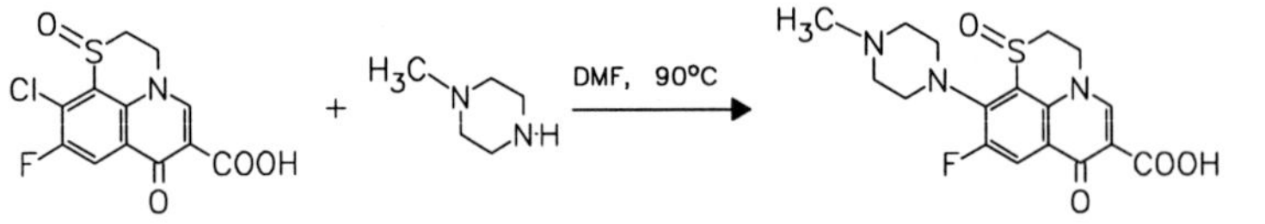

(III)

N-methyl-
piperazine (IV)

(V)

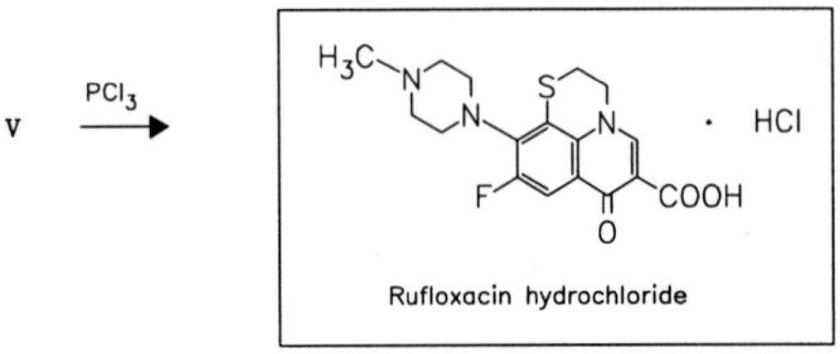

Rufloxacin hydrochloride

ⓑ

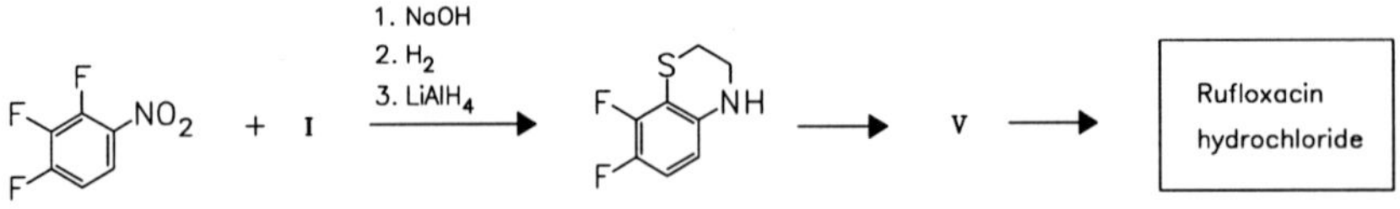

Rufloxacin
hydrochloride

ⓒ

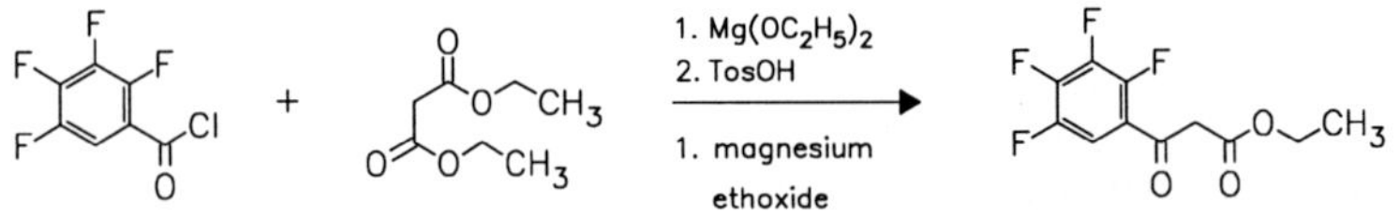

2,3,4,5-tetra-
fluorobenzoyl
chloride

diethyl
malonate

(VI)

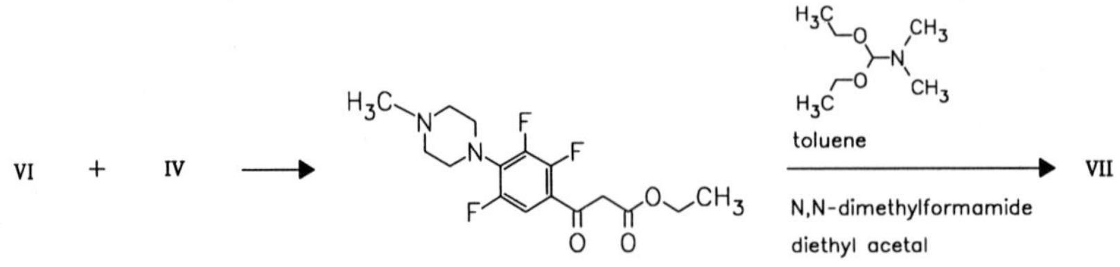

ethyl 2,3,5-trifluoro-4-(4-methyl-
1-piperazinyl)benzoylacetate

N,N-dimethylformamide
diethyl acetal

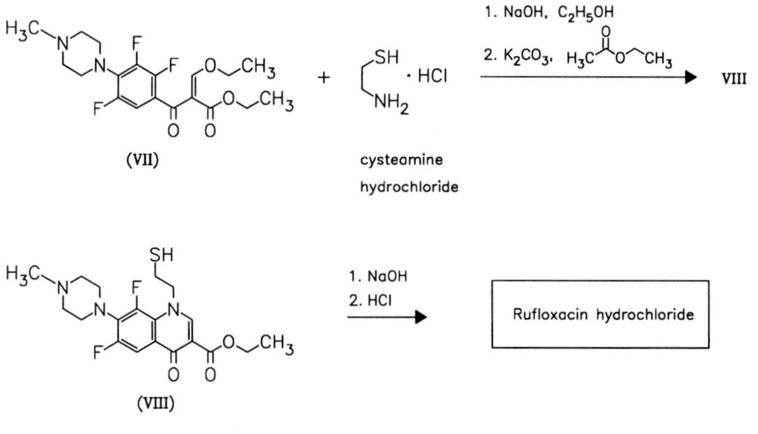

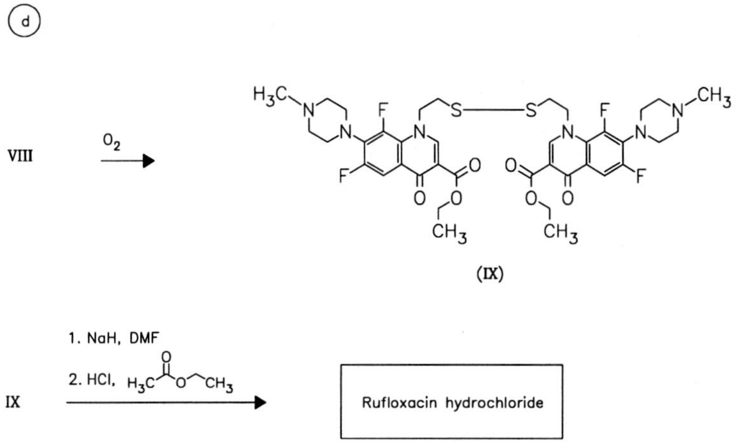

(VII)   +   cysteamine hydrochloride

1. NaOH, C$_2$H$_5$OH
2. K$_2$CO$_3$,   → VIII

(VIII)

1. NaOH
2. HCl
→ Rufloxacin hydrochloride

(d)

VIII $\xrightarrow{O_2}$

(IX)

IX   1. NaH, DMF   2. HCl,   → Rufloxacin hydrochloride

Reference(s):

a Cecchetti, V. et al.: J. Med. Chem. (JMCMAR) **30**, 465-473 (1987).
EP 165 375 (Mediolanum Farm.; appl. 21.2.1985; I-prior. 24.2.1984).
EP 252 352 (Mediolanum Farm.; appl. 22.6.1987; I-prior. 1.7.1986).
b Wang, E. et al.: Zhongguo Yaoke Daxue Xuebao (ZHXYE9) **28** (1), 5-8 (1997).
c EP 522 277 (Mediolanum Farm.; appl. 29.5.1992; I-prior. 7.6.1991).
Cecchetti, V. et al.: Synth. Commun. (SYNCAV) **21** (22), 2301-2308 (1991).
d WO 9 511 907 (Archimica; appl. 26.10.1994; I-prior. 27.10.1993).
WO 9 511 886 (Archimica; appl. 26.10.1994; I-prior. 27.10.1993).

Formulation(s):   cps. 150 mg, 200 mg; tabl 150 mg, 200 mg (as hydrochloride)

Trade Name(s):
I: Monos (SmithKline   Qari (Mediolanum)
          Beecham)   Tebraxin (Bracco)

Ruscogenin

ATC: C05AX
Use: vein therapeutic, hemorrhoidal therapeutic

RN: 472-11-7   MF: C$_{27}$H$_{42}$O$_4$ MW: 430.63   EINECS: 207-447-2
CN: (1β,3β,25R)-spirost-5-ene-1,3-diol

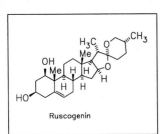

Ruscogenin

a Hydrolyzation of *Ruscus aculeatus*,
b hydrolyzation of *Tribulus terrestris*,
c hydrolyzation of *Ruscus hyrcanus*.

Reference(s):
Iskenderov, G.B.: Farmatsiya (Moscow) (FRMTAL) **38** (1), 42-46 (1989).
Panova, D.; Nikolov, St.; Minkov, Cr.: Farmatsiya (Sofia) (FMTYA2) **30** (4), 33-35 (1980).
Panova, D.; Nikolov, St.: Farmatsiya (Sofia) (FMTYA2) **29** (6), 25-29 (1979).
Ilarionov, J.; Panova, D.; Nikolov, St.: Farmatsiya (Sofia) (FMTYA2) **33** (1), 18-24 (1983).
a   Panova, D.; Nikolov, St.: Farmatsiya (Sofia) (FMTYA2) **21**, 43 (1971).
     Sannié, C.; Lapin, H.: Bull. Soc. Chim. Fr. (BSCFAS) **1957**, 301, 1237.
     Sannié, C.; Lapin, H.: C. R. Hebd. Seances Acad. Sci. (COREAF) **241**, 1498 (1955).
b   Iskenderov, G.B.: Khim. Prir. Soedin. (KPSUAR) **6**, 488 (1970); **3**, 216 (1967).
c   Iskenderov, G.B.: Farmatsiya (Moscow) (FRMTAL) **17**, 37 (1968).

use as anti-inflammatory:
FR-M 2 366 (C. P. Roux, D. R. Torossiar; appl. 3.4.1964).
FR 2 104 911 (Inv. Scientifiques Pharm.; appl. 3.9.1970).

structure:
Benn, W.R. et al.: J. Am. Chem. Soc. (JACSAT) **79**, 3920 (1957).
Burn, D. et al.: J. Chem. Soc. (JCSOA9) **1958**, 795.
Burn, D. et al.: Proc. Chem. Soc., London (PCSLAW) **1957**, 119.
Lapin, H.: C. R. Hebd. Seances Acad. Sci. (COREAF) **244**, 3065 (1957).

Formulation(s):   ointment 800 mg/100g; suppos. 8 mg

Trade Name(s):

D:	Ruscorectal (Heumann)	F:	Calmoroïde (Phygiène)	I:	Ruscoroid (Inverni della
	Venobiase (Fournier		Proctolog (Jouveinal)-		Beffa)-comb.
	Pharma)-comb.		comb.		

Saccharin

RN: 81-07-2   MF: $C_7H_5NO_3S$ MW: 183.19   EINECS: 201-321-0
LD$_{50}$:   17 g/kg (M, p.o.)
CN: 1,2-benzisothiazol-3(2H)-one 1,1-dioxide

calcium salt
RN: 6485-34-3   MF: $C_{14}H_8CaN_2O_6S_2$ MW: 404.44   EINECS: 229-349-9
calcium salt hydrate (4:7)
RN: 6381-91-5   MF: $C_{14}H_8CaN_2O_6S_2 \cdot 7/2H_2O$ MW: 934.98
sodium salt
RN: 128-44-9   MF: $C_7H_4NNaO_3S$ MW: 205.17   EINECS: 204-886-1
LD$_{50}$:   17.5 g/kg (M, p.o.);
        1.28 g/kg (R, p.o.)
sodium salt dihydrate
RN: 6155-57-3   MF: $C_7H_4NNaO_3S \cdot 2H_2O$ MW: 241.20
LD$_{50}$:   17.5 g/kg (M, i.p.)

Reference(s):
review:
Ullmanns Encykl. Tech. Chem., 4. Aufl., Vol. **22**, 356.
a   DRP 35 211 (Fahlberg-List; appl. 1884).
    US 1 601 505 (J. W. Orelup; 1926; appl. 1921).
    oxidation of 2-toluenesulfonamide *with oxygen*:
    US 3 759 936 (Rhône-Poulenc, ert. 18.9.1973; F-prior. 1.4.1970, 16.11.1970).
b   DOS 3 044 112 (BASF; appl. 24.11.1980).
    US 4 464 537 (BASF; 7.8.1984; D-prior. 24.11.1980).

other methods:
US 2 667 503 (Maumee Dev.; 1954; appl. 1951).

purification:
DOS 2 730 861 (Chimicasa; appl. 8.7.1977; LUX-prior. 2.8.1976).

Formulation(s):   tabl. 16.2 mg, 32.4 mg, 64.8 mg

Trade Name(s):
D: numerous combination   Saccar (Schiapparelli
     preparations   Farm.)
I: Diet Sucaryl (Abbott)   USA: Sweetaste (Purepac)

Salacetamide
(Acetsalicylamide)

ATC: N02B
Use: antipyretic, antirheumatic

RN: 487-48-9   MF: $C_9H_9NO_3$ MW: 179.18   EINECS: 207-656-9
LD_{50}: >5 g/kg (M, p.o.);
        2 g/kg (R, p.o.)
CN: *N*-acetyl-2-hydroxybenzamide

salicylamide   acetic anhydride   Salacetamide

Reference(s):
DRP 177 054 (Kalle; appl. 1905).
DAS 2 509 481 (Bayer; appl. 5.3.1975).

Formulation(s):   tabl. 100 mg

Trade Name(s):
D: Eu-Med (Novartis   Octadon (Thiemann)-
     Consumer Health)-comb.;   comb.; wfm
     wfm

Salazosulfapyridine

(Salicylazosulfapyridine; Sulphasalazine; Sulfasalazine)

ATC: A07EC01
Use: chemotherapeutic (colitis), intestinal anti-inflammatory (ulcerative colitis, Crohn's disease)

RN: 599-79-1   MF: $C_{18}H_{14}N_4O_5S$ MW: 398.40   EINECS: 209-974-3
LD$_{50}$: 1096 mg/kg (M, i.v.); 12500 mg/kg (M, p.o.);
1520 mg/kg (R, i.v.); 15600 mg/kg (R, p.o.)
CN: 2-hydroxy-5-[[4-[(2-pyridinylamino)sulfonyl]phenyl]azo]benzoic acid

sulfapyridine   Salazosulfapyridine

Reference(s):
US 2 396 145 (AB Pharmacia; 1946; S-prior. 1940).

Formulation(s):   drg. 500 mg; f. c. tabl. 500 mg; suppos. 500 mg; susp. 3 g/100 ml; tabl. 500 mg

Trade Name(s):
D: Azulfidine (Pharmacia & Upjohn)
Colo-Pleon (Henning Berlin)
Sulfasalazin-Heyl (Heyl)

F: Salazopyrine (Pharmacia)
GB: Salazopyrin (Pharmacia & Upjohn)
I: Salazopyrin (Pharmacia & Upjohn)

Salisulf gastroprotetto (Gipharmex)
USA: Azulfidine (Pharmacia & Upjohn)

Salbutamol

(Albuterol)

ATC: R03AC02; R03AK04; R03CC02
Use: bronchodilator

RN: 18559-94-9   MF: $C_{13}H_{21}NO_3$ MW: 239.32   EINECS: 242-424-0
LD$_{50}$: 48.7 mg/kg (M, i.v.); 2707 mg/kg (M, p.o.);
57.1 mg/kg (R, i.v.); 660 mg/kg (R, p.o.)
CN: α^1-[[(1,1-dimethylethyl)amino]methyl]-4-hydroxy-1,3-benzenedimethanol

sulfate (2:1)
RN: 51022-70-9   MF: $C_{13}H_{21}NO_3 \cdot 1/2H_2SO_4$ MW: 576.71   EINECS: 256-916-8
LD$_{50}$: 48.7 mg/kg (M, i.v.); 1950 mg/kg (M, p.o.);
59.1 mg/kg (R, i.v.); >2500 mg/kg (R, p.o.)

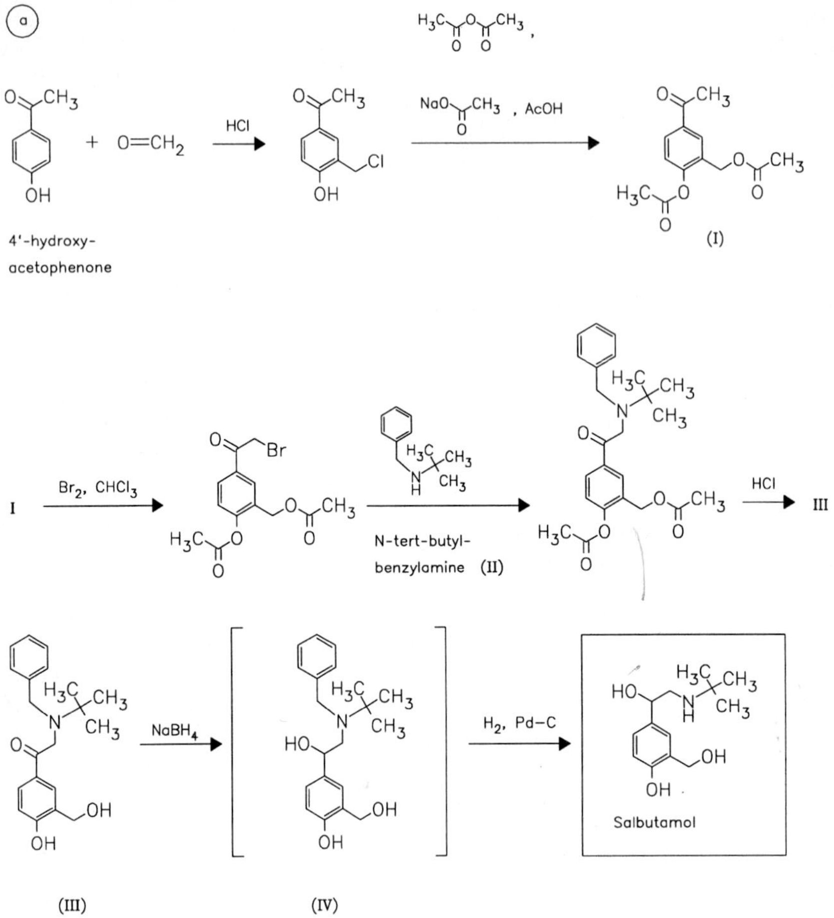
a
HCl
NaOAc, AcOH
4'-hydroxy-acetophenone
(I)
I
Br2, CHCl3
N-tert-butyl-benzylamine (II)
HCl
III
NaBH4
H2, Pd-C
Salbutamol
(III)
(IV)

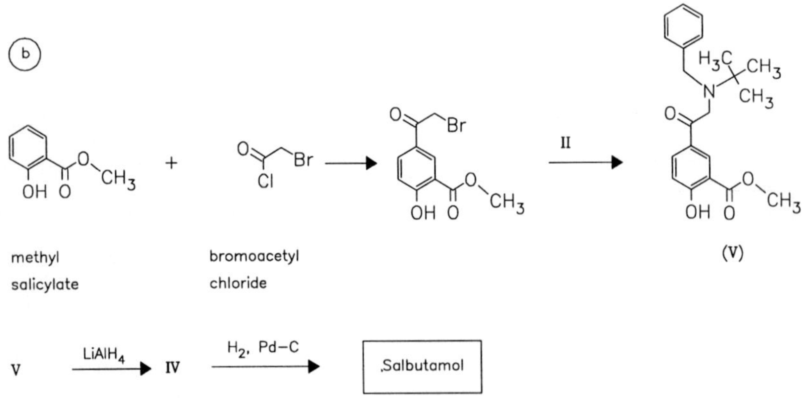
b
methyl salicylate
bromoacetyl chloride
II
(V)
V
LiAlH4
IV
H2, Pd-C
Salbutamol

Reference(s):
DE 1 643 224 (Allen & Hanburys; prior. 22.9.1967).
US 3 644 353 (Allen & Hanburys; 15.2.1972; prior. 23.9.1966).
Collin, D.T. et al.: J. Med. Chem. (JMCMAR) **13**, 674 (1970).
GB 1 200 886 (Allen & Hanburys; appl. 23.9.1966; valid from 21.4.1967).
a US 3 642 896 (Allen & Hanburys; 15.2.1972; GB-prior. 21.4.1967).
b US 3 705 233 (Allen & Hanburys; 5.12.1972; GB-prior. 23.9.1966).

alternative synthesis:
DAS 2 340 189 (Polfa; appl. 8.8.1973).

R(−)-enantiomer:
DE 2 128 258 (Allen & Hanburys; appl. 7.6.1971; GB-prior. 17.6.1970).
Effenberger, F., Jäger, J.: J. Org. Chem. (JOCEAH) **62**, 3867 (1997).

stable aqueous formulation:
DOS 3 319 356 (Glaxo; appl. 27.5.1983; GB-prior. 27.5.1982).

Formulation(s):   amp. 0.6 mg/ml, 1.5 mg/2.5 ml, 3 mg/2.5 ml, 6 mg/5 ml; metered-dose aerosol 0.1 mg; metered-dose aerosol 0.12 mg; powder 0.12 mg, 0.24 mg; sol. 6 mg/g, 6 mg/ml; s. r. tabl. 4.82 mg, 9.64 mg; syrup 2.4 mg/5 ml (as sulfate)tabl. 2.4 mg, 4.8 mg

Trade Name(s):

D: Apsomol (Farmasan)
      Arubendol (Farmasan)
      Bronchospray (Klinge)
      Epaq (ASTA Medica
      AWD; 3M Medica)
      Loftan (Glaxo Wellcome/
      Cascan)
      Salbulair (ASTA Medica
      AWD; 3M Medica)
      Sultanol (Glaxo; 1971)
      Volmac (Glaxo Wellcome)
F: Combivent (Boehringer
      Ing.)-comb.
      Salbumol (Glaxo
      Wellcome)

      Spréor (Inava)
      Ventodisks (Glaxo
      Wellcome)
      Ventoline (Glaxo
      Wellcome; 1971)
GB: Asmasal (Evans)
      Combivent (Boehringer
      Ing.)-comb.
      Salamol Steri-Neb (Baker)
      Ventide (A. & H.)-comb.
      Ventolin (Allen &
      Hanburys; 1969)
      Volmax (Allen &
      Hanburys)
I: Breva (Valeas)-comb.

      Broncovaleas (Valeas)
      Clenil (Chiesi)- comb.
      Perventil (Malesci)-comb.
      Salbutard (Lusofarmaco)
      Ventolin (Glaxo Wellcome)
      Volmax (Glaxo Allen)
J: Asmidon (Dainippon)
      Sultanol (Nippon Glaxo)
      Ventoli (Sankyo)
USA: Proventil (Schering; 1981)
      Ventolin (Glaxo Wellcome;
      1981)
      Volumax (Muro)

Salicylamide

ATC: N02BA05
Use: analgesic, antipyretic, antirheumatic

RN: 65-45-2   MF: $C_7H_7NO_2$ MW: 137.14   EINECS: 200-609-3
LD_{50}:   313 mg/kg (M, i.v.); 300 mg/kg (M, p.o.);
      980 mg/kg (R, p.o.)
CN: 2-hydroxybenzamide

methyl
salicylate

Salicylamide

Reference(s):
Ullmanns Encykl. Tech. Chem., 3. Aufl., Vol. **13**, 91.

Formulation(s):   gel 4 g/100 g; tabl. 200 mg, 400 mg

Trade Name(s):

D: Coffalon (Stark, Konstanz)-
      comb.
      Girheulit (Pflüger)-comb.

      Glutisal (Ravensberg)-
      comb.
      Salistoperm (Ursapharm)-
      comb.

      numerous combination
      preparations
F: Percutalgine (Besins-
      Iscovesco)-comb.

GB: Intralgin (3M Health Care)
I: Azerodol (Edmond)
     Tuscalman Berna (Berna)-
     comb.

J: Saliamin (Yoshitomi)
     Salimid (Yoshitomi)
     numerous combination
     preparations

USA: Lobac (Seatrace)-comb.

Salicylic acid
(Acidum salicylicum; Spiroylsäure; Spirsäure)

ATC: D01AE12
Use: keratolytic, antipyretic, antirheumatic

RN: 69-72-7 MF: $C_7H_6O_3$ MW: 138.12 EINECS: 200-712-3
LD_{50}: 184 mg/kg (M, i.v.); 480 mg/kg (M, p.o.);
     891 mg/kg (R, p.o.)
CN: 2-hydroxybenzoic acid

monosodium salt
RN: 54-21-7 MF: $C_7H_5NaO_3$ MW: 160.10 EINECS: 200-198-0
LD_{50}: 560 mg/kg (M, i.v.); 540 mg/kg (M, p.o.);
     930 mg/kg (R, p.o.);
     562 mg/kg (dog, i.v.)
calcium salt (2:1)
RN: 824-35-1 MF: $C_{14}H_{10}CaO_6$ MW: 314.31 EINECS: 212-525-4
magnesium salt
RN: 18917-89-0 MF: $C_{14}H_{10}MgO_6$ MW: 298.53 EINECS: 242-669-3

sodium phenolate + CO_2 → (150–160 °C, 5 bar) (Kolbe-Schmitt process) → H_2SO_4 → Salicylic acid

Reference(s):
Ullmanns Encykl. Tech. Chem., 4. Aufl., Vol. **20**, 300.

fluid bed process:
EP 89 565 (Bayer; appl. 11.3.1983; D-prior. 23.3.1982).

Formulation(s): cream 40 g/100 g; eye drops 1 mg/ml; gel 10 g/100 g; ointment 3 g/100 g, 2 g/100 g;
     plaster 4 mg, 23 mg, 32 mg, 0.81 g, 1.39 g; sol. 0.1 g/g, 10 g/100 g

Trade Name(s):
D: Gehwol (Gerlach)
     Guttaplast (Beiersdorf)
     Hansaplast Footcare
     (Beiersdorf)
     Mobilat (Sankyo)
     Squamasol Gel (Ichthyol)
     Urgo Hühneraugenpflaster
     (Fournier Pharma)
     numerous combination
     preparations
F: Algipan (Darcy)
     Betnesalic (Glaxo
     Wellcome)
     Coricide Le Diable (Sodia)

Diprosalic (Schering-
Plough)
Eau Précieuse (Phygiène)
Génésérine (Amido)
Pansoral (Pierre Fabre)
Verrucosal (Novartis)
numerous combination
preparations
GB: Acnisal (Euroderma)
     Aserbine (Goldshield)-
     comb.
     Capasal (Dermal)
     Cocois (Evans)
     Cuplex (S & N)-comb.

Diprosalic (Schering-
Plough)-comb.
Duofilm (Stiefel)-comb.
Gelcosal (Quinoderm)-
comb.
Ionil T (Galderma)-comb.
Meted (Euroderma)
Monphytol (L.A.B.)-comb.
Movelat (Sankyo)-comb.
Occlusal (Euroderma)
Phytex (Pharmax)-comb.
Posalfilin (Norgine)-comb.
Pragmatar (Bioglan)-comb.
Pyralvex (Norgine)-comb.
Salactol (Dermal)-comb.

Salmeterol

(Salmaterol)

ATC: R03AC12
Use: long acting β_2-adrenoceptor agonist

RN: 89365-50-4   MF: $C_{25}H_{37}NO_4$ MW: 415.57
CN: ($\pm$)-4-hydroxy-α^1-[[[6-(4-phenylbutoxy)hexyl]amino]methyl]-1,3-benzenedimethanol

xinafoate (1-hydroxy-2-naphthoate)
RN: 94749-08-3   MF: $C_{25}H_{37}NO_4 \cdot C_{11}H_8O_3$ MW: 603.76

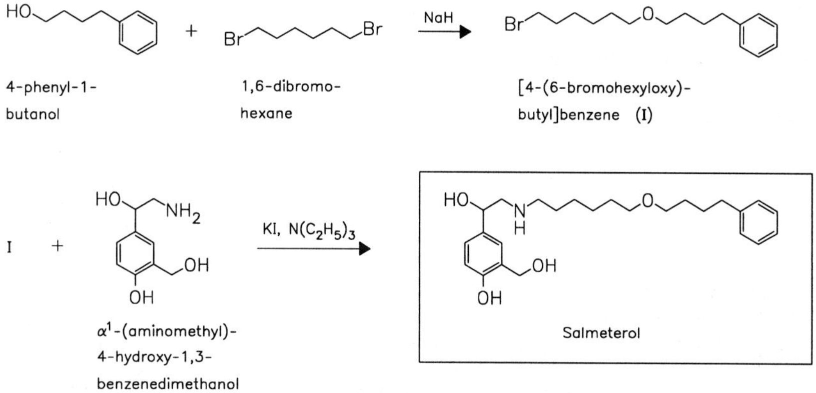

4-phenyl-1-
butanol

1,6-dibromo-
hexane

[4-(6-bromohexyloxy)-
butyl]benzene (I)

α^1-(aminomethyl)-
4-hydroxy-1,3-
benzenedimethanol

Salmeterol

Reference(s):
DOS 3 414 752 (Glaxo; appl. 23.8.1989; GB-prior. 18.4.1983, 23.6.1983, 4.11.1983, 25.1.1984).
US 4 992 474 (Glaxo; 12.2.1991; appl. 23.8.1989; GB-prior. 18.4.1984, 19.11.1986; GB-prior. 18.4.1983,
23.6.1983, 4.11.1983, 25.1.1984).

medical use for treatment of inflammation:
EP 416 925 (Glaxo; appl. 6.9.1990; GB-prior. 7.9.1989).

combination with beclometasone:
EP 416 950 (Glaxo; appl. 7.9.1990; GB-prior. 8.9.1989; 20.10.1989).

combination with fluticasone:
EP 416 951 (Glaxo; appl. 7.9.1990; GB-prior. 8.9.1989, 20.10.1989).

Formulation(s):   dose aerosol 0.025 mg/85 mg; powder for inhalation 0.05 mg/12.5 mg (as xinafoate)

Trade Name(s):
D: aeromax (Glaxo Wellcome/
      Cascan)

F: Serevent (Glaxo Wellcome)
      Serevent (Glaxo Wellcome)

GB: Serevent (Allen &
      Hanburys)

I: Arial (Dompe) Serevent (Glaxo Wellcome)
    Salmetedur (Menarini) USA: Serevent (Glaxo Wellcome)

Salsalate

ATC: N02BA
Use: analgesic, antirheumatic, urinary antiseptic

RN: 552-94-3 MF: $C_{14}H_{10}O_5$ MW: 258.23 EINECS: 209-027-4
LD_{50}: 1020 mg/kg (M, s.c.)
CN: 2-hydroxybenzoic acid 2-carboxyphenyl ester

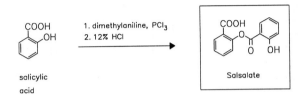

salicylic acid

1. dimethylaniline, PCl₃
2. 12% HCl

Salsalate

Reference(s):
DRP 211 403 (C. F. Boehringer Mannh.; appl. 1907).

Formulation(s): cps. 500 mg; tabl. 500 mg, 750 mg

Trade Name(s):
D: Disalgesic (Kettelhack-Riker); wfm   USA: Disalcid (3M)   generic
GB: Disalcid (Riker); wfm   Mono-Gesic (Schwarz)
                                         Salflex (Carnrick)

Saquinavir
(Ro-31-8959)

ATC: J05AE01
Use: antiviral, HIV-1-protease inhibitor

RN: 127779-20-8 MF: $C_{38}H_{50}N_6O_5$ MW: 670.86
CN: [3S-[2[1R*(R*),2S*],3α,4aβ,8aβ]]-N^1-[3-[3-[[(1,1-dimethylethyl)amino]carbonyl]octahydro-2(1H)-isoquinolinyl]-2-hydroxy-1-(phenylmethyl)propyl]-2-[(2-quinolinylcarbonyl)amino]butanediamide

monomesylate
RN: 149845-06-7 MF: $C_{38}H_{50}N_6O_5 \cdot CH_4O_3S$ MW: 766.96

Ⓐ

L-phenyl-alanine (I)

+ O=CH₂

1. HCl, H₂O
2. HO⟨benzyl⟩ H₃C⟨⟩SO₃H
2. benzyl alcohol

(II)

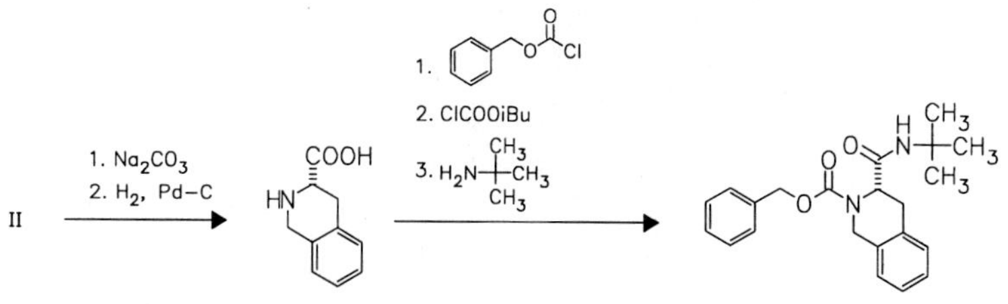

II → 1. Na₂CO₃
       2. H₂, Pd–C

1. (benzyl chloroformate)
2. ClCOOiBu
3. H₂N–C(CH₃)₃

(III)

III → H₂, 5% Rh–C, H₂O, 120 bar, 20 °C

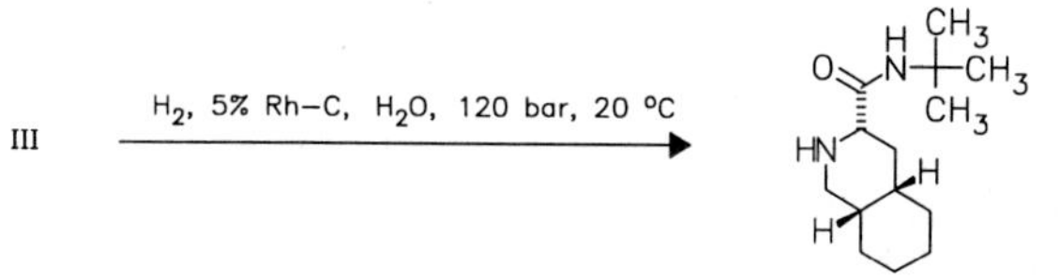

N-tert-butyldecahydro-
(4aS,8aS)-isoquinoline-
3(S)-carboxamide (IV)

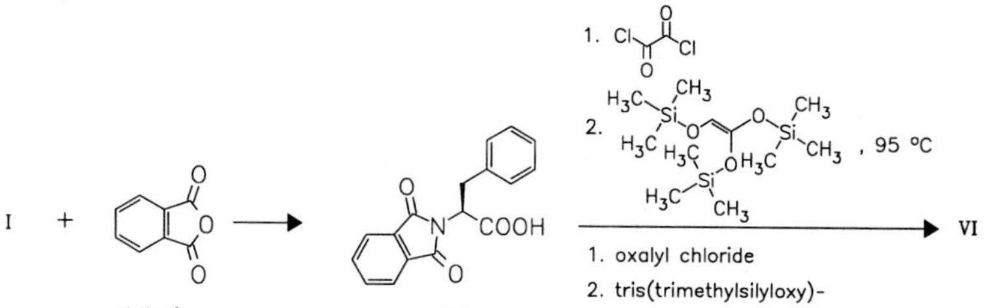

I + phthalic anhydride → (V)

1. Cl–CO–CO–Cl
2. tris(trimethylsilyloxy)-ethylene , 95 °C

1. oxalyl chloride
2. tris(trimethylsilyloxy)-ethylene

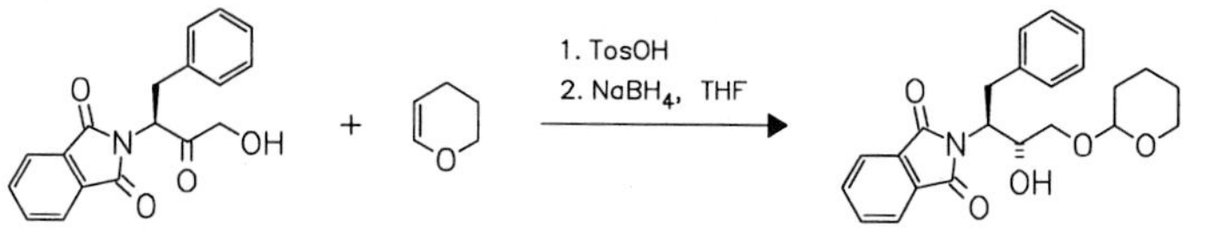

→ VI

(VI) + (dihydropyran)

1. TosOH
2. NaBH₄, THF

→ (VII)

VII →

1. CH₃SO₂Cl, pyridine
2. TosOH, C₂H₅OH
3. t-BuOK, THF

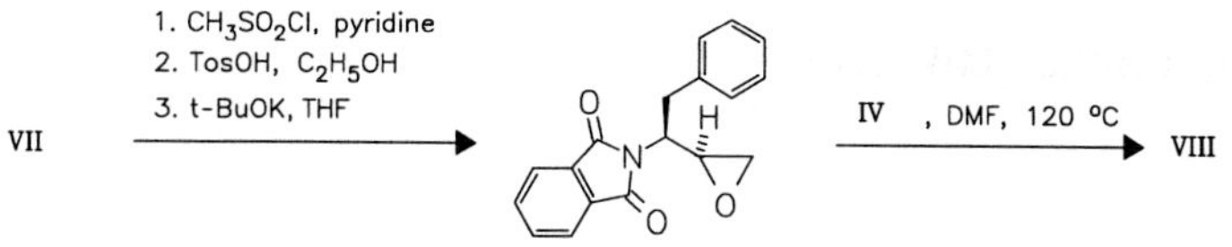

2(S)-[2-phenyl-1(S)-
phthalimidoethyl]-
oxirane

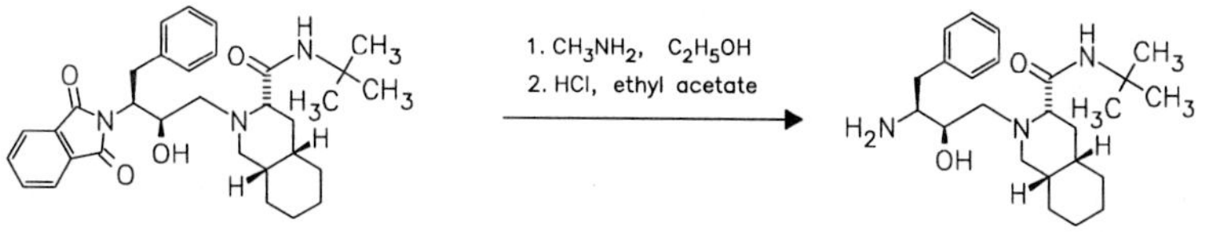

IV , DMF, 120 °C → VIII

N-tert-butyl-2-[2(R)-hydroxy-
4-phenyl-3(S)-phthalimido-
butyl]decahydro-(4aS,8aS)-iso-
quinoline-3(S)-carboxamide (VIII)

1. CH₃NH₂, C₂H₅OH
2. HCl, ethyl acetate

→ N-tert-butyl-2-[3(S)-amino-
2(R)-hydroxy-4-phenylbutyl]-
decahydro-(4aS,8aS)-iso-
quinoline-3(S)-carboxamide (IX)

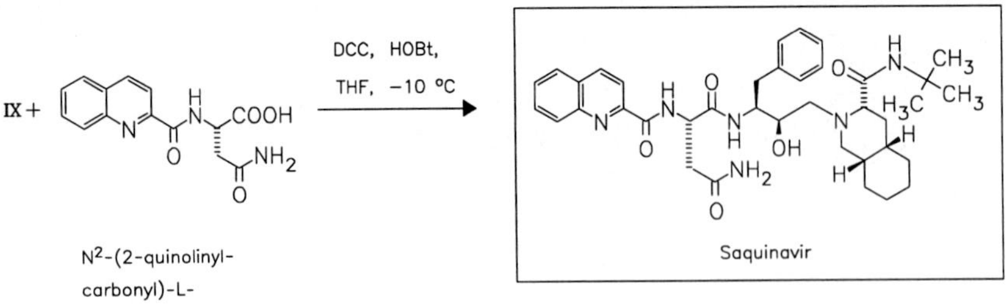

IX + N²-(2-quinolinyl-carbonyl)-L-asparagine

DCC, HOBt, THF, −10 °C → Saquinavir

b

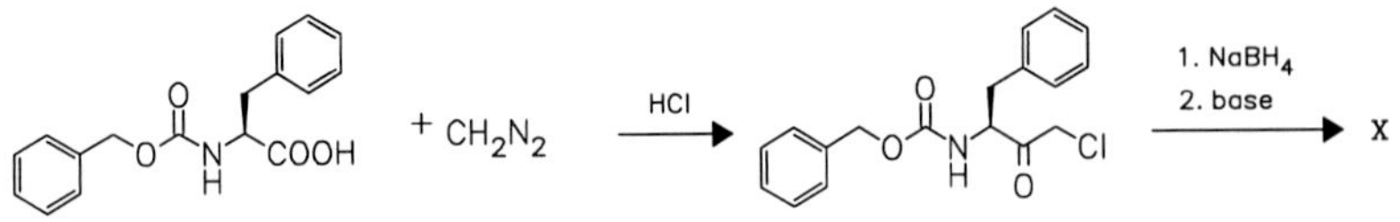

N-benzyloxycarbonyl-L-phenylalanine + CH₂N₂ diazo-methane

HCl →

1. NaBH₄
2. base → X

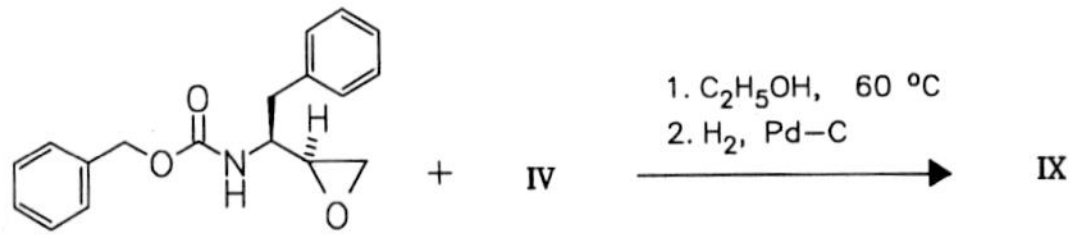

3(S)-benzyloxycarbonyl-amino-1,2(S)-epoxy-4-phenylbutane (X) + IV

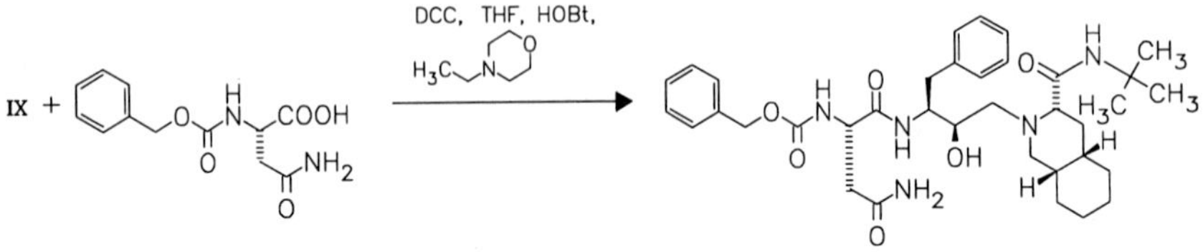

1. C₂H₅OH, 60 °C
2. H₂, Pd−C → IX

IX + N²-benzyloxycarbonyl-L-asparagine

DCC, THF, HOBt, H₃C−N(morpholine) → (XI)

XI

H₂, 10% Pd−C, C₂H₅OH →

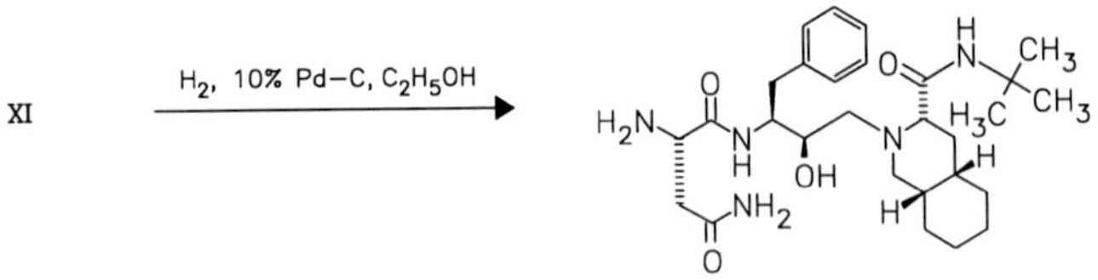

2-[3(S)-(L-asparaginylamino)-2(R)-hydroxy-4-phenylbutyl]-N-tert-butyldecahydro-(4aS,8aS)-isoquinoline-3(S)-carboxamide (XII)

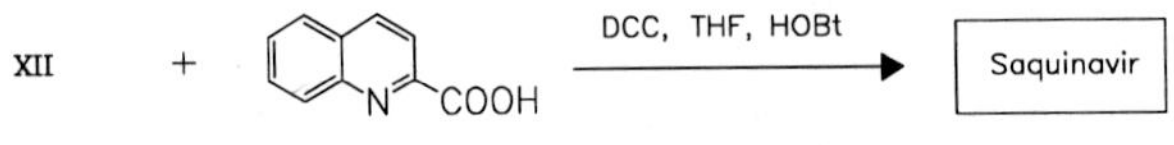

XII + quinaldic acid

DCC, THF, HOBt → Saquinavir

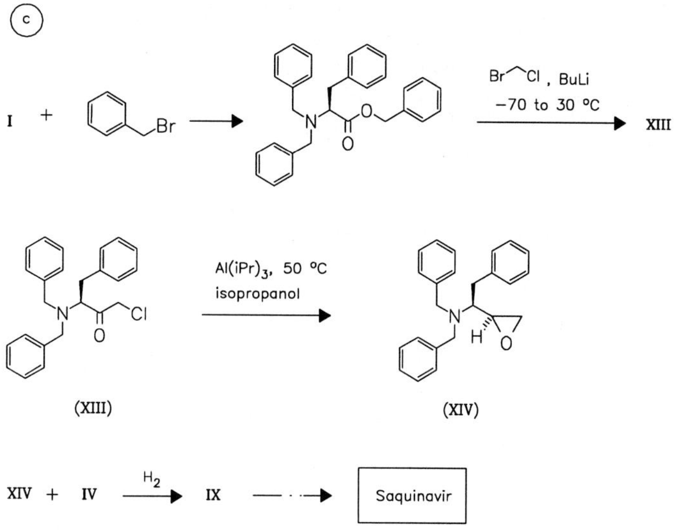

c

I + [benzyl bromide] → [structure] $\xrightarrow[\text{-70 to 30 °C}]{\text{Br}\frown\text{Cl , BuLi}}$ XIII

(XIII) $\xrightarrow[\text{isopropanol}]{\text{Al(iPr)}_3,\ 50\ °C}$ (XIV)

XIV + IV $\xrightarrow{\text{H}_2}$ IX ---→ Saquinavir

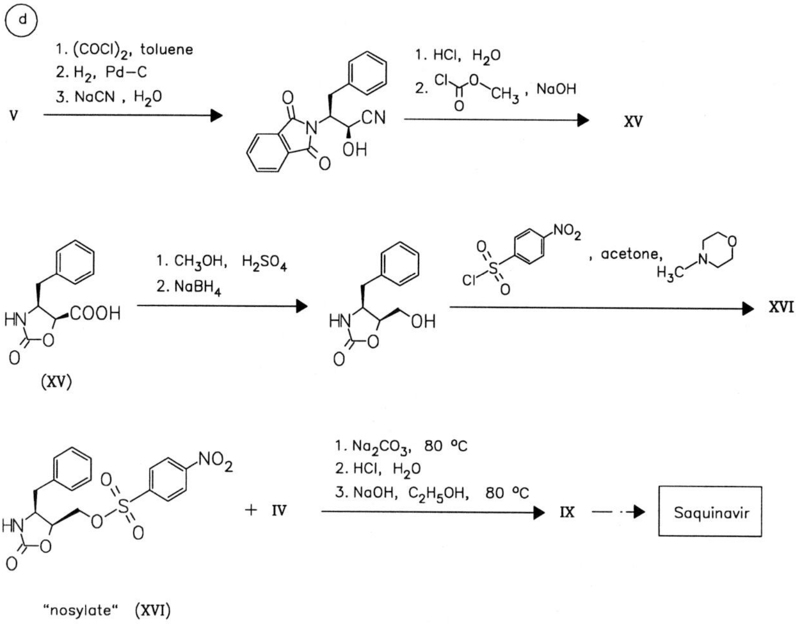

d

V $\xrightarrow{\substack{\text{1. (COCl)}_2\text{, toluene}\\ \text{2. H}_2\text{, Pd–C}\\ \text{3. NaCN , H}_2\text{O}}}$ [structure] $\xrightarrow{\substack{\text{1. HCl, H}_2\text{O}\\ \text{2. [ClCO}_2\text{CH}_3\text{] , NaOH}}}$ XV

(XV) $\xrightarrow{\substack{\text{1. CH}_3\text{OH, H}_2\text{SO}_4\\ \text{2. NaBH}_4}}$ [structure] $\xrightarrow{\text{[4-nitrobenzenesulfonyl chloride] , acetone, [methylmorpholine]}}$ XVI

"nosylate" (XVI) + IV $\xrightarrow{\substack{\text{1. Na}_2\text{CO}_3,\ 80\ °C\\ \text{2. HCl, H}_2\text{O}\\ \text{3. NaOH, C}_2\text{H}_5\text{OH,}\ 80\ °C}}$ IX ---→ Saquinavir

Reference(s):

a Parkes, K.E.B. et al.: J. Org. Chem. (JOCEAH) **59**, 3656 (1994).
     EP 346 847 (Hoffmann-La Roche; appl. 13.6.1989; GB-prior. 13.6.1988, 10.4.1989).
     EP 432 694 (Hoffmann-La Roche; appl. 10.12.1992; GB-prior. 11.12.1989).
b EP 432 695 (Hoffmann-La Roche; appl. 10.12.1990; GB-prior. 11.12.1989, 10.12.1990).

combinations:
WO 9 419 008 (Merrell Dow Pharm.; appl. 18.1.1994; GB-prior. 22.2.1993).
EP 513 917 (Glaxo; appl. 11.5.1992; GB-prior. 16.5.1991, 8.10.1991, 6.11.1991).
EP 691 345 (Bristol-Myers Squibb; appl. 5.7.1995; USA-prior. 17.5.1995, 5.7.1994).
WO 9 533 464 (Searle & Co.; appl. 2.6.1995; USA-prior. 3.6.1994).

Formulation(s):   cps. 200 mg (as mesylate)

Trade Name(s):
D: FORTOVASE (Roche)   GB: Fortovase (Roche)   USA: Invirase (Roche)
     Invirase (Roche)   Invirase (Roche; 1996)
F: Invirase (Roche; 1996)   I: Invirase (Roche)

Saralasin acetate

ATC: C09
Use: antihypertensive, diagnostic (renin-dependent hypertension)

RN: 39698-78-7   MF: $C_{42}H_{65}N_{13}O_{10} \cdot xC_2H_4O_2 \cdot xH_2O$ MW: unspecified
LD_{50}: 1171 mg/kg (M, i.v.)
CN: 1-(*N*-methylglycine)-5-L-valine-8-L-alanineangiotensin II acetate (salt) hydrate

saralasin
RN: 34273-10-4   MF: $C_{42}H_{65}N_{13}O_{10}$ MW: 912.06
monoacetate
RN: 60173-70-8   MF: $C_{42}H_{65}N_{13}O_{10} \cdot C_2H_4O_2$ MW: 972.12

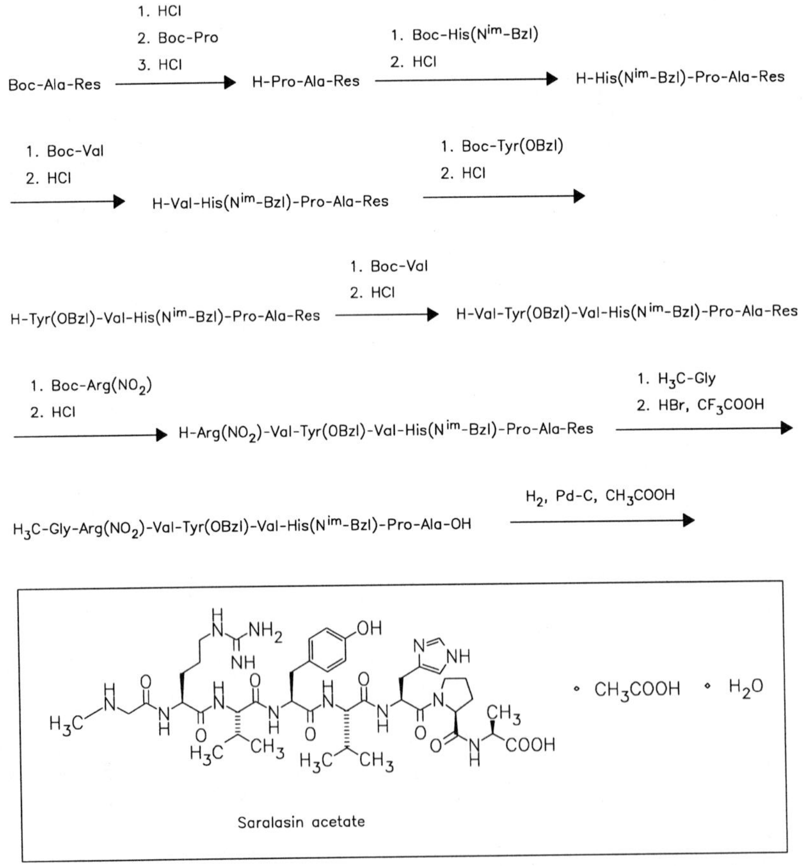

Boc-Ala-Res
   1. HCl
   2. Boc-Pro
   3. HCl
→ H-Pro-Ala-Res
   1. Boc-His(N^{im}-Bzl)
   2. HCl
→ H-His(N^{im}-Bzl)-Pro-Ala-Res

   1. Boc-Val
   2. HCl
→ H-Val-His(N^{im}-Bzl)-Pro-Ala-Res
   1. Boc-Tyr(OBzl)
   2. HCl
→

H-Tyr(OBzl)-Val-His(N^{im}-Bzl)-Pro-Ala-Res
   1. Boc-Val
   2. HCl
→ H-Val-Tyr(OBzl)-Val-His(N^{im}-Bzl)-Pro-Ala-Res

   1. Boc-Arg(NO_2)
   2. HCl
→ H-Arg(NO_2)-Val-Tyr(OBzl)-Val-His(N^{im}-Bzl)-Pro-Ala-Res
   1. H_3C-Gly
   2. HBr, CF_3COOH
→

H_3C-Gly-Arg(NO_2)-Val-Tyr(OBzl)-Val-His(N^{im}-Bzl)-Pro-Ala-OH
   H_2, Pd-C, CH_3COOH
→

Saralasin acetate

$\circ$ CH_3COOH $\circ$ H_2O

N^{im}-Bzl: N-benzylation in the imidazole ring

Res: resin ester

Reference(s):
DOS 2 127 393 (Norwich; appl. 2.6.1971; USA-prior. 12.2.1971).
GB 1 320 104 (Norwich; valid from 20.5.1971).
ZA 7 103 182 (Norwich; appl. 29.9.1971).

subcutaneously applicable pharmaceutical formulation:
US 3 932 624 (Morton-Norwich; 13.1.1976; prior. 17.6.1974).

Trade Name(s):

D:	Sarenin (Röhm Pharma); wfm	USA:	Sarenin (Norwich Pharm.); wfm

---

Scopolamine
(Hyoscine)

ATC: A04AD01; N05CM05; S01FA02
Use: mydriatic, parasympatholytic, sedative, antispasmodic

RN: 51-34-3   MF: $C_{17}H_{21}NO_4$ MW: 303.36   EINECS: 200-090-3
LD_{50}: 100 mg/kg (M, i.v.); 1275 mg/kg (M, p.o.);
2650 mg/kg (R, p.o.)
CN: [7(S)-(1α,2β,4β,5α,7β)]-α-(hydroxymethyl)benzeneacetic acid 9-methyl-3-oxa-9-azatricyclo[3.3.1.0^{2,4}]non-7-yl ester

hydrobromide
RN: 114-49-8   MF: $C_{17}H_{21}NO_4 \cdot HBr$ MW: 384.27   EINECS: 204-050-6
LD_{50}: 203 mg/kg (M, i.v.); 1880 mg/kg (M, p.o.);
1270 mg/kg (R, p.o.)
hydrobromide trihydrate
RN: 6533-68-2   MF: $C_{17}H_{21}NO_4 \cdot HBr \cdot 3H_2O$ MW: 438.32

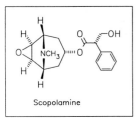
Scopolamine

a From mother liquors of hyoscyamine production (atropine, q. v.).
b By extraction of Scopolia drugs, as *Datura metel* and *Duboisia*.

Reference(s):
Ullmanns Encykl. Tech. Chem., 3. Aufl., Vol. **3**, 204.

Formulation(s):   amp. 0.3 mg/ml, 0.5 mg/ml, 1 mg/ml; eye drops 0.25 % (as hydrobromide trihydrate); eye drops 2.5 mg/g (as borate); plaster 1.5 mg/2.5 cm^2

Trade Name(s):

D:	Boro-Scopol (Winzer) Neurovegetalin (Verla)-comb. Scopoderm TTS (Novartis Pharma) Scopolamin. hydrobromic. Dispersa (Dispersa); wfm		Scopolamin. hydrobromic. Dispersa Baeschlin (Baeschlin); wfm		Scopolamina Bromidrato (Biologici Italia) Spasmeridan (UCB) Transcop 4 sistemi transderm (Recordati) combination preparations
		F:	Génoseopolamine (Amido) Scopoderm TTS (Novartis)		
		GB:	Buscopan (Boehringer Ing.) Hypal 2 (S & N)	J:	numerous generic
		I:	Buscopan (Boehringer Ing.)		preparations

USA:　Atrohist Plus (Medeva; as hydrobromide)

Bellatal (Richwood; as hydrobromide)

Donnatal (Robins; as hydrobromide)
Transderm Scop (Novartis)

Secbutabarbital

(Butabarbital; Secbutobarbitone; Sodium Butabarbital; Butethal)

ATC:　N05CA
Use:　sedative, hypnotic

RN:　125-40-6　MF: $C_{10}H_{16}N_2O_3$　MW: 212.25　EINECS: 204-738-6
LD$_{50}$:　175 mg/kg (M, i.v.)
CN:　5-ethyl-5-(1-methylpropyl)-2,4,6(1H,3H,5H)-pyrimidinetrione

monosodium salt
RN:　143-81-7　MF: $C_{10}H_{15}N_2NaO_3$　MW: 234.23　EINECS: 205-611-8
LD$_{50}$:　70 mg/kg (R, i.v.); 78 mg/kg (R, p.o.);
　　　90 mg/kg (dog, i.v.)

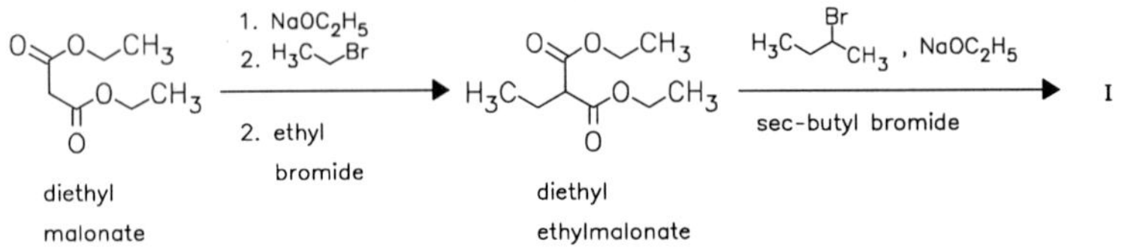

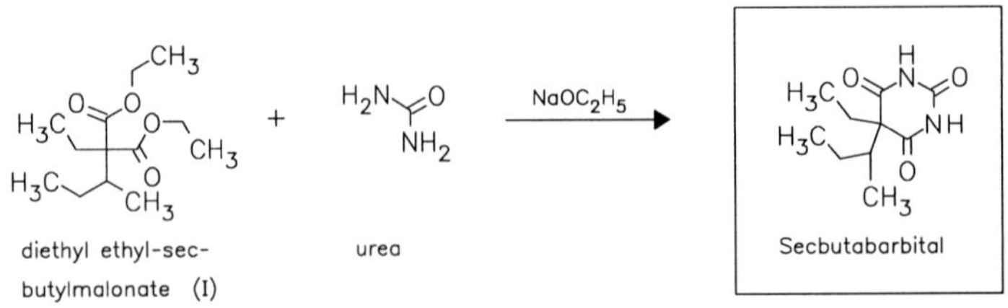

diethyl malonate

diethyl ethylmalonate

sec-butyl bromide

diethyl ethyl-sec-butylmalonate (I)

urea

Secbutabarbital

Reference(s):
US 1 856 792 (Eli Lilly; 1932; prior. 1929).

Formulation(s):　tabl. 15 mg, 30 mg, 50 mg, 100 mg (as sodium salt)

Trade Name(s):
D:　Dormilfo (Wachter)-comb.;
　　wfm
　　Nervolitan (Kettelhack)-comb.; wfm

　　Resedorm (Lappe)-comb.
　　with aprobarbital; wfm
F:　Butobarbital Dipharma (Amido)

Hypnasmine (Élerté)-comb.
GB:　Soneryl (Concord)
USA:　Barbased (Major)
　　　Butisol Sodium (Wallace)

Secnidazole

ATC:　P01AB07
Use:　chemotherapeutic, amoebicide

RN:　3366-95-8　MF: $C_7H_{11}N_3O_3$　MW: 185.18　EINECS: 222-134-0
CN:　α,2-dimethyl-5-nitro-1H-imidazole-1-ethanol

a

2-methyl-
imidazole (I)

H_2SO_4, HNO_3 →

2-methyl-5-
nitroimidazole

H_3C [propylene oxide], HCOOH [formic acid] →

Secnidazole

b

I + [chloro-acetone with Cl] →

K_2CO_3, acetone →

(2-methyl-1-
imidazolyl)-
acetone

1. HNO_3, P_2O_5
2. $NaBH_4$, CH_3OH

2. sodium
borohydride →

Secnidazole

Reference(s):
a   Cosar, C. et al.: Arzneim.-Forsch. (ARZNAD) **16**, 23 (1966).
     FR-M 3 270 (Rhône-Poulenc; appl. 30.12.1963).
     FR 1 427 627 (Rhône-Poulenc; appl. 10.10.1963).
b   DOS 2 107 423 (Rhône-Poulenc; appl. 16.2.1971; F-prior. 16.2.1970).
     GB 1 278 758 (Rhône-Poulenc; valid from 19.4.1971; F-prior. 16.2.1970).
     GB 1 265 466 (Rhône-Poulenc; valid from 15.7.1970; F-prior. 16.2.1970).

alternative syntheses:
DOS 2 107 405 (Rhône-Poulenc; appl. 16.2.1971; F-prior. 16.2.1970).
GB 1 278 757 (Rhône-Poulenc; valid from 19.4.1971; F-prior. 16.2.1970).

Formulation(s):   tabl. 500 mg

Trade Name(s):
F: Flagentyl (Specia; Rhône-
          Poulenc)

Secobarbital
(Quinalbarbitone)

ATC: N05CA06
Use: hypnotic

RN: 76-73-3   MF: $C_{12}H_{18}N_2O_3$ MW: 238.29   EINECS: 200-982-2
LD_{50}:   145 mg/kg (M, p.o.);
          80 mg/kg (R, i.v.)
CN;   5-(1-methylbutyl)-5-(2-propenyl)-2,4,6(1H,3H,5H)-pyrimidinetrione

monosodium salt
RN: 309-43-3   MF: $C_{12}H_{17}N_2NaO_3$ MW: 260.27   EINECS: 206-218-4
LD_{50}:   110 mg/kg (M, i.v.);
          65 mg/kg (R, i.v.); 125 mg/kg (R, p.o.);
          48 mg/kg (dog, i.v.); 85 mg/kg (dog, p.o.)

Reference(s):
US 1 954 429 (Eli Lilly; 1934; CDN-prior. 1930).

Formulation(s):   cps. 50 mg, 100 mg; powder 50 mg (as sodium salt)

Trade Name(s):
D: Dormilfo (Wachter)-comb.;   F: Binoctal (Houdé)-comb.;   Supponoctal (Houdé)-
      wfm   wfm   comb.; wfm
      Medinox (Pfleger)-comb.;   Dinoctin (Spret-   combination preparations;
      wfm   Mauchant)-comb.; wfm   wfm
      Optipyrin (Pfleger)-comb.;   Divinoctal (I.S.H.)-comb.;   GB: Seconal Sodium (Lilly)
      wfm   wfm   I: Immenox (Roussel-
      Solamin (Ardeypharm)-   Imménoctal (Houdé); wfm   Maestretti); wfm
      comb.; wfm   Imménoctal (I.S.H.); wfm   Neogratusminal (Simes)-
      Tempidorm (Roland)-   Insomnyl (Elerté)-comb.;   comb.; wfm
      comb.; wfm   wfm   Vesparax (UCB)-comb.;
      Tempidorm N (Roland)-   Noctadiol (Millot-Solac)-   wfm
      comb.; wfm   comb.; wfm   J: Ional Sodium (Yoshitomi)
      Trisomin (Asche)-comb.;   Reposal (Martinet)-comb.;   USA: Seconal Sodium (Lilly)
      wfm   wfm   Tuinal (Lilly)-comb.
      Vesparax (UCB)-comb.;   Sonuctane (Bottu)-comb.;
      wfm   wfm

Secretin

ATC: V04CK01
Use: diagnostic, hormon (pancreatic)

RN: 1393-25-5   MF: unspecified   MW: unspecified   EINECS: 215-733-3
LD$_{50}$: >5000 iu/kg (M, i.v.); >5000 iu/kg (M, p.o.);
      >5000 iu/kg (R, i.v.); >5000 iu/kg (R, p.o.)
CN: secretin

```
H-L-His-L-Ser-L-Asp-Gly-L-Thr-L-Phe-L-Thr-L-Ser-L-Glu-L-Leu-

L-Ser-L-Arg-L-Leu-L-Arg-L-Asp-L-Ser-L-Ala-L-Arg-L-Leu-L-Gln-

L-Arg-L-Leu-L-Leu-L-Gln-Gly-L-Leu-L-Val-NH₂


      Secretin
```

From hog duodenummucosa.

Reference(s):
Jorpes, J.E.; Mutt, V.: Acta Chem. Scand. (ACHSE7) **15**, 1790 (1961).

synthesis:
US 3 767 639 (Squibb; 23.10.1973; prior. 12.4.1968, 17.4.1970).
Bodanszky, M. et al.: J. Am. Chem. Soc. (JACSAT) **89**, 685; 6753 (1967).
Ondetti, M.A. et al.: J. Am. Chem. Soc. (JACSAT) **90**, 4711 (1968).
Wuensch, E. et al.: Chem. Ber. (CHBEAM) **104**, 2430, 2445, 3854 (1971); **105**, 2508 (1972).

purification:
Wuensch, E. et al.: Chem. Ber. (CHBEAM) **105**, 2515 (1972).

structure:
Mutt, V.; Jorpes, J.E.: Eur. J. Biochem. (EJBCAI) **15**, 513 (1970).

Formulation(s):   amp. 0.029 mg (as hydrochloride)

Trade Name(s):
D: Sekretolin (Hoechst)   F: Sécrétine Sinbio (Fimex);   J: Secrepan (Eisai)
      wfm   USA: Secretin-Ferring (Ferring)

Selegiline
(L-Deprenil; L-Deprenyl)

ATC: N04BD01
Use: antiparkinsonian

RN: 14611-51-9   MF: $C_{13}H_{17}N$ MW: 187.29
CN: (*R*)-*N*,α-dimethyl-*N*-2-propynylbenzeneethanamine

hydrochloride
RN: 14611-52-0   MF: $C_{13}H_{17}N \cdot HCl$ MW: 223.75

(±)-methamphetamine   L-tartaric acid   →   (−)-methamphetamine (+)-tartrate (I)

I   →(NaOH, H₂O)   (−)-methamphetamine   →(Br-CH₂-C≡CH, NaOH)   Selegiline

Reference(s):
DOS 1 568 277 (Chinoin; appl. 30.4.1966; H-prior. 3.5.1965).

alternative syntheses:
GB 1 031 425 (Chinoin; Complete Specification 26.3.1963; H-prior. 30.3.1962).
EP 344 675 (Farmakon; appl. 29.5.1989; CS-prior. 30.5.1988).

methamphetamine *racemate resolution:*
Li Chiang: J. Chin. Chem. Soc. (Peking) (JCCOAV) **18**, 161 (1951).
Jung et al.: J. Am. Chem. Soc. (JACSAT) **75**, 4664 (1953).

Formulation(s):   tabl. 5 mg, 10 mg (as hydrochloride)

Trade Name(s):

D: Amindan (Desitin)
     Antiparkin (ASTA Medica
     AWD)
     Deprenyl (Sanofi
     Winthrop)
     Movergan (Orion Pharma)
     Selegam (Neuro Hexal)

     Selepark (betapharm)
     Seletop (Azupharma)
F: Déprényl (Schering-
     Plough)
GB: Eldepryl (Orion)
     Vivapryl (ASTA Medica)
I: Egibren (Chiesi)

     Jumex (Chiesi)
     Seledat (Master Pharma)
     Selpar (Therabel Pharma)
USA: Atapryl (Athena)
     Eldepryl (Somerset)
     generics

Seratrodast
(AA-2414; A-73001; ABT-001)

ATC: R03DC
Use: antiallergic, antiasthmatic,
      thromboxane A_2/leukotriene
      antagonist

RN: 112665-43-7   MF: $C_{22}H_{26}O_4$ MW: 354.45
LD_{50}: 1520 mg/kg (M, p.o.);
      3750 mg/kg (R, p.o.)
CN: ζ-(2,4,5-trimethyl-3,6-dioxo-1,4-cyclohexadien-1-yl)benzeneheptanoic acid

(+)-*R*-enantiomer
RN: 103187-09-3   MF: $C_{22}H_{26}O_4$ MW: 354.45
(−)-*S*-enantiomer
RN: 103196-89-0   MF: $C_{22}H_{26}O_4$ MW: 354.45

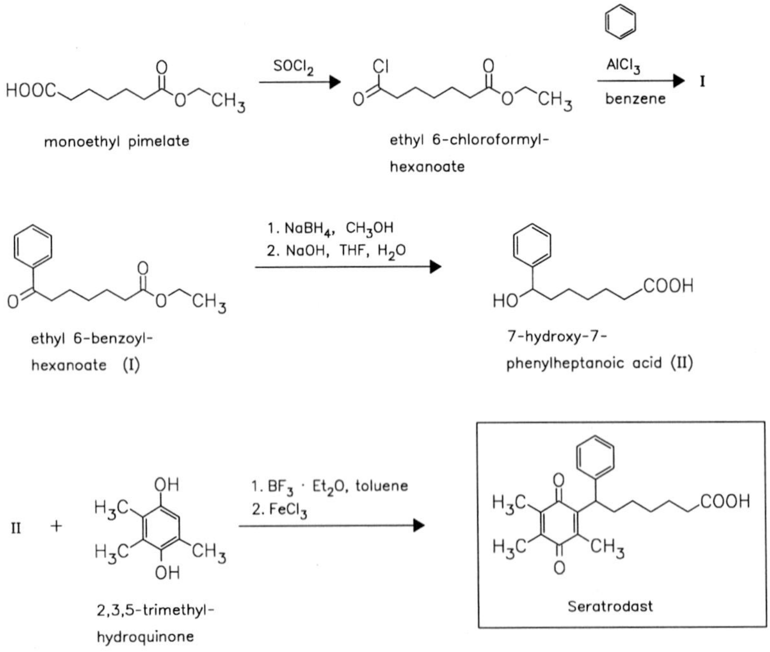

monoethyl pimelate

ethyl 6-chloroformyl-
hexanoate

ethyl 6-benzoyl-
hexanoate (I)

7-hydroxy-7-
phenylheptanoic acid (II)

2,3,5-trimethyl-
hydroquinone

Seratrodast

Reference(s):
Shiraishi, M. et al.: J. Med. Chem. (JMCMAR) **32** (9), 2214-2221 (1989).
EP 171 251 (Takeda Chem.; appl. 30.7.1985; prior. 1.8.1984).

medical use as thromboxane A_2 antagonist:
EP 645 137 (Takeda Chem.; appl. 19.9.1994; J-prior. 21.9.1993).
EP 719 552 (Takeda Chem.; appl. 22.12.1995; J-prior. 26.12.1994).
JP 02 273 625 (Takeda Chem.; J-prior. 14.4.1989).

composition for treatment/prophylaxis of circulatory disorders:
JP 63 101 322 (Takeda Chem.; J-prior. 17.10.1986).

Formulation(s):   gran. 100 mg/g (10 %); tabl. 40 mg, 80 mg

Trade Name(s):
J: Bronica (Takeda; Grelan)

Sertaconazole

ATC: D01AC
Use: antifungal

RN: 99592-32-2   MF: $C_{20}H_{15}Cl_3N_2OS$ MW: 437.78
CN: 1-[2-[(7-chlorobenzo[*b*]thien-3-yl)methoxy]-2-(2,4-dichlorophenyl)ethyl]-1*H*-imidazole

mononitrate
RN: 99592-39-9   MF: $C_{20}H_{15}Cl_3N_2OS \cdot HNO_3$ MW: 500.79

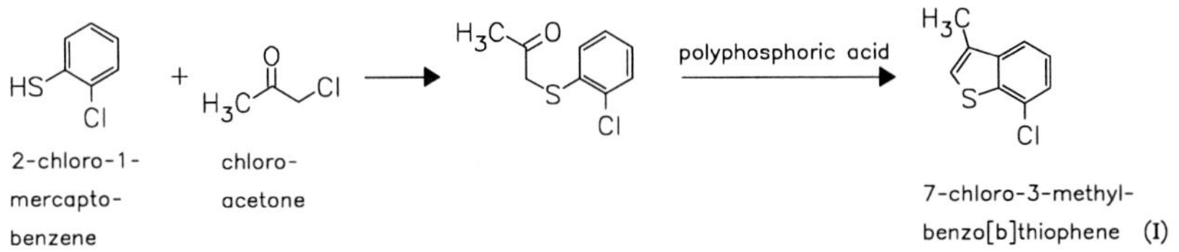

2-chloro-1-
mercapto-
benzene

chloro-
acetone

polyphosphoric acid

7-chloro-3-methyl-
benzo[b]thiophene   (I)

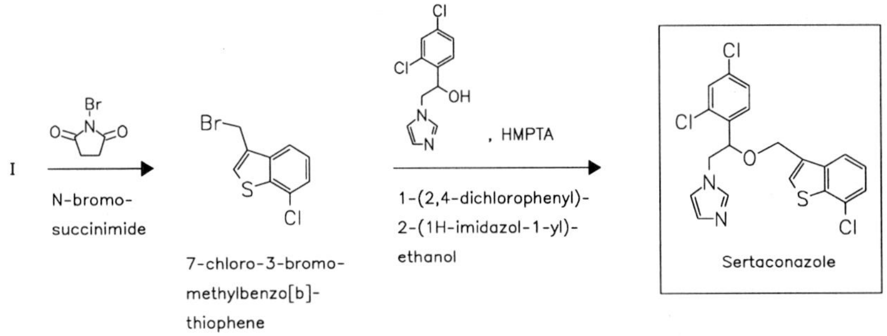

N-bromo-
succinimide

7-chloro-3-bromo-
methylbenzo[b]-
thiophene

1-(2,4-dichlorophenyl)-
2-(1H-imidazol-1-yl)-
ethanol

, HMPTA

Sertaconazole

Reference(s):
EP 151 477 (Ferrer; appl. 2.1.1985; E-prior. 8.6.1984, 2.2.1984, 6.1.1984).
Raga, M.M. et al.: Arzneim.-Forsch. (ARZNAD) **42**, 691 (1992).

Formulation(s):   cream 20 mg/g

Trade Name(s):
D: Zalain (Trommsdorff)

Sertindole
(LU-23-174; S-1991)

ATC: N05AE03
Use: antipsychotic, dopamine D_2-antagonist, 5-HT_2-antagonist

RN: 106516-24-9　MF: $C_{24}H_{26}ClFN_4O$　MW: 440.95
CN: 1-[2-[4-[5-chloro-1-(4-fluorophenyl)-1H-indol-3-yl]-1-piperidinyl]ethyl]-2-imidazolidinone

maleate
RN: 106516-25-0　MF: $C_{24}H_{26}ClFN_4O \cdot C_4H_4O_4$　MW: 557.02

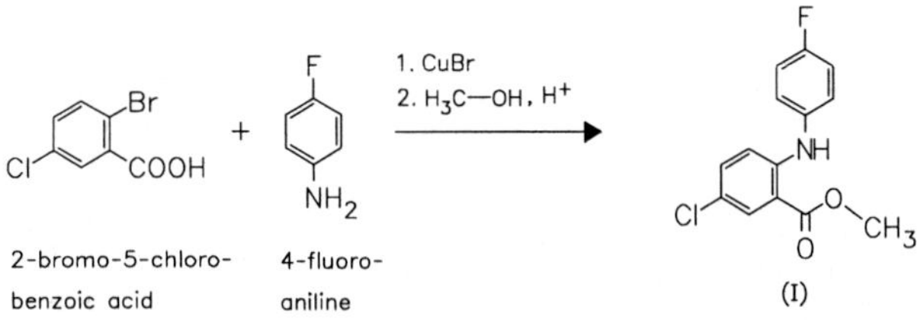

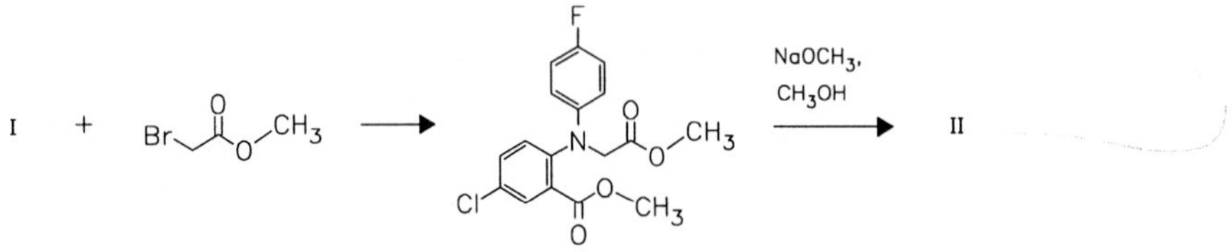

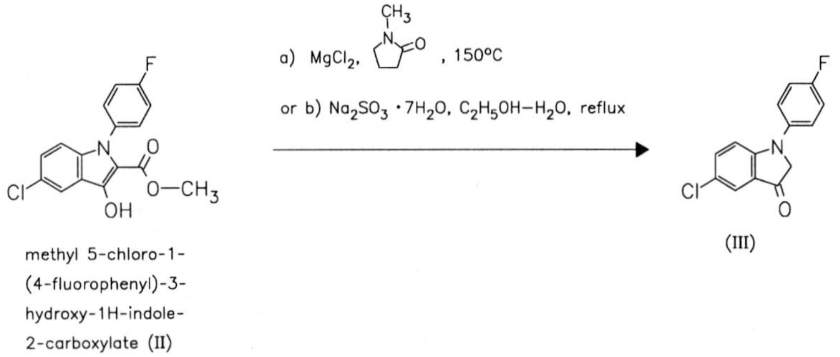

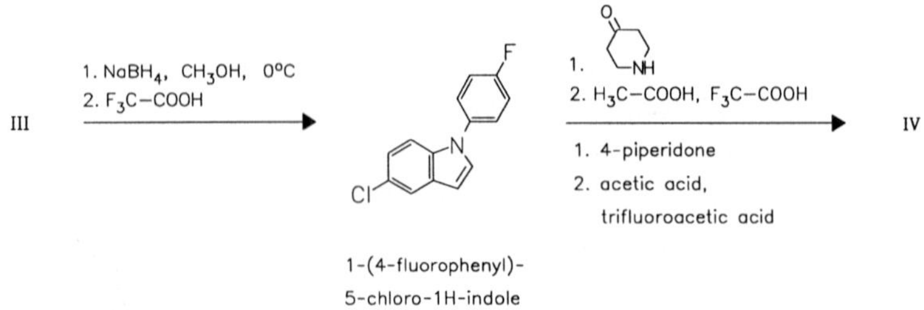

2-bromo-5-chloro-benzoic acid + 4-fluoroaniline

1. CuBr
2. H_3C—OH, H+

(I)

I + Br—CH₂—CO—O—CH₃

NaOCH₃, CH_3OH

II

methyl 5-chloro-1-(4-fluorophenyl)-3-hydroxy-1H-indole-2-carboxylate (II)

a) $MgCl_2$, N-methyl-2-pyrrolidinone, 150°C

or b) $Na_2SO_3 \cdot 7H_2O$, $C_2H_5OH–H_2O$, reflux

(III)

III

1. $NaBH_4$, CH_3OH, 0°C
2. F_3C—COOH

1-(4-fluorophenyl)-5-chloro-1H-indole

1. 4-piperidone
2. H_3C—COOH, F_3C—COOH

1. 4-piperidone
2. acetic acid, trifluoroacetic acid

IV

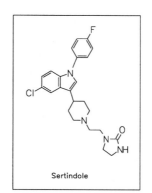

5-chloro-1-(4-fluoro-
phenyl)-3-(1,2,3,6-
tetrahydropyridin-
4-yl)-1H-indole (IV)

1-(2-chloroethyl)-
2-imidazolidinone

1. PtO$_2$, C$_2$H$_5$OH
2. H$_2$

1. platinum oxide,
   ethanol
2. hydrogen

(V)

Sertindole

Reference(s):
EP 200 322 (Lundbeck; appl. 5.11.1986; GB-prior. 10.4.1985).

synthesis of 1-(4-fluorophenyl)-5-chloro-1*H*-indole:
Perregaard, J.K. et al.: J. Med. Chem. (JMCMAR) **35**, 1092 (1992).
Anderssen, K. et al.: J. Med. Chem. (JMCMAR) **39**, 3723 (1996).
WO 9 200 070 (Lundbeck; appl. 9.1.1992; DK-prior. 22.6.1990).

use of sertindole *for the treatment of schizophrenia:*
EP 392 959 (Lundbeck; appl. 17.10.1990; GB-prior. 11.4.1989).

use of sertindole *as serotonin-2/dopamine-2-receptor-blocking agent for the treatment of mental disorders:*
EP 730 865 (Sumitomo Pharm.; appl. 11.9.1996; J-prior. 12.1.1995).

use of sertindole *for the treatment of cognitive disorders, for the treatment of addiction and alleviating, relieving or suppressing cocaine, diazepame, nicotine or alcohol addictions:*
WO 9 215 303 (Lundbeck; appl. 17.9.1992; DK-prior. 1.3.1991).

use of sertindole *for treating of hypertension and peripheral vascular diseases:*
WO 9 215 301 (Lundbeck; appl. 17.9.1992; J-prior. 1.3.1991).

Formulation(s):   f. c. tabl. 4 mg, 12 mg, 16 mg, 20 mg

Trade Name(s):
D: Serdolect (Promonta   GB: Serdolect (Lundbeck)
      Lundbeck)

Sertraline

ATC: N06AB06
Use: antidepressant, selective competitive inhibitor of synaptosomal serotonin-uptake

RN: 79617-96-2   MF: $C_{17}H_{17}Cl_2N$ MW: 306.24
CN: (1S-cis)-4-(3,4-dichlorophenyl)-1,2,3,4-tetrahydro-N-methyl-1-naphthalenamine

hydrochloride
RN: 79559-97-0   MF: $C_{17}H_{17}Cl_2N \cdot HCl$ MW: 342.70

Cl   O
3,4-dichloro-benzoyl chloride

+   benzene $\xrightarrow{AlCl_3}$ 3,4-dichloro-benzophenone

$\xrightarrow[\text{tert-butoxide}]{\substack{\text{diethyl succinate,} \\ \text{potassium}}}$ $KOC(CH_3)_3$ I

COOH   3-ethoxycarbonyl-4-(3,4-dichlorophenyl)-4-phenylbut-3-enoic acid (I)

$\xrightarrow{HBr, HOAc}$ COOH   4-(3,4-dichlorophenyl)-4-phenylbut-3-enoic acid

$\xrightarrow{H_2, Pd-C}$ COOH   (±)-4-(3,4-dichlorophenyl)-4-phenylbutanoic acid (II)

II $\xrightarrow[\text{2. AlCl}_3]{\text{1. SOCl}_2}$ (±)-4-(3,4-dichlorophenyl)-3,4-dihydro-1(2H)-naphthalenone

$\xrightarrow[\substack{\text{1. methylamine,} \\ \text{titanium tetra-} \\ \text{chloride}}]{\substack{\text{1. H}_2\text{N—CH}_3\,,\ \text{TiCl}_4 \\ \text{2. H}_2,\ \text{Pd—C} \\ \text{3. crystallization}}}$ HN-CH₃   (±)-cis-N-methyl-4-(3,4-di-chlorophenyl)-1,2,3,4-tetra-hydro-1-naphthalenamine (III)

III $\xrightarrow{\substack{\text{HO} \\ \text{D(−)-mandelic acid}}}$ HN-CH₃   Sertraline

Reference(s):
EP 30 081 (Pfizer; appl. 28.10.1980; USA-prior. 1.11.1979).
US 4 536 518 (Pfizer; 20.8.1985; appl. 1.11.1979).
Welch, W.M. et al.: J. Med. Chem. (JMCMAR) **27**, 1508 (1984).

alternative synthesis:
US 4 839 104 (Pfizer; 13.6.1989; appl. 16.6.1988; prior. 11.6.1987).
EP 295 050 (Pfizer; appl. 7.6.1988; USA-prior. 11.6.1987).
Lautens, M.; Rovis, T.: J. Org. Chem. (JOCEAH) **62**, 5246 (1977)
WO 9 827 050 (Richter Gedeon Vegyeszeti Gyar Rt.; appl. 15.12.1997; HU-prior. 18.12.1996).
WO 9 815 516 (Egis Gyogyszergyar Rt.; appl. 8.10.1997; HU-prior. 9.10.1996).
Corey, E.J., Gant, T.G.: Tetrahedron Lett. (TELEAY) **35** (30), 5373 (1994).
WO 9 515 299 (Pfizer; appl. 2.9.1994; USA-prior. 30.11.1993).
WO 9 301 162 (Pfizer; appl. 3.9.1992; GB-prior. 11.7.1991).
Williams, M.; Quallich, G.: Chem. Ind. (London) (CHINAG) **1990** (10), 315

synthesis of trans-isomer:
US 4 556 676 (Pfizer; 3.12.1985; appl. 1.11.1979).
EP 28 901 (Pfizer; appl. 28.10.1980; USA-prior. 1.11.1979, 5.9.1980).

preparation of sertraline intermediates:
WO 9 312 062 (Pfizer; appl. 15.9.1992; USA-prior. 13.12.1991).
WO 9 301 161 (Pfizer; appl. 3.7.1992; GB-prior. 11.7.1991).
Quallich, G.J.; Williams, M.T; Friedmann, R.C.: J. Org. Chem. (JOCEAH) **55** (16), 4971 (1990).

process for converting trans to cis isomer:
US 5 082 970 (Pfizer; 21.1.1992; USA-prior. 6.3.1991).

sertraline *polymorphism:*
US 5 248 699 (Pfizer; 28.9.1993; USA-prior. 13.8.1992).
US 5 734 083 (Torcan Chemical Ltd.; 31.3.1998; USA-prior. 17.5.1996).

controlled-release formulation:
EP 259 113 (Pfizer; appl. 28.8.1987; USA-prior. 4.9.1986).
EP 357 369 (Pfizer; appl. 29.8.1989; USA-prior. 30.8.1988).

medical use for treatment of anxiety:
US 4 962 128 (Pfizer; 9.10.1990; appl. 2.11.1989).
EP 429 189 (Pfizer; appl. 29.10.1990; USA-prior. 2.11.1989).

medical use for treatment of psychosis:
US 4 981 870 (Pfizer; 1.1.1991; appl. 7.3.1989).
EP 386 997 (Pfizer; appl. 6.3.1990; USA-prior. 7.3.1989).

medical use for treatment of dependency:
EP 415 612 (Pfizer; appl. 17.8.1990; USA-prior. 30.8.1989).

Formulation(s):   f. c. tabl. 50 mg, 100 mg (as hydrochloride)

Trade Name(s):

D:	Gladem (Boehringer Ing.)	GB:	Lustral (Invicta; Pfizer;		Tatig (Bioindustria)
	Zoloft (Pfizer)		1990)		Zoloft (Roerig)
F:	Zoloft (Pfizer)	I:	Serad (Boehringer Mannh.)	USA:	Zoloft (Pfizer; 1991)

Setastine

ATC: R06AB
Use: antihistaminic

RN: 64294-95-7   MF: $C_{22}H_{28}ClNO$ MW: 357.93
CN: 1-[2-[1-(4-chlorophenyl)-1-phenylethoxy]ethyl]hexahydro-1*H*-azepine

hydrochloride
RN: 59767-13-4   MF: $C_{22}H_{28}ClNO \cdot HCl$ MW: 394.39
LD_{50}:   510 mg/kg (M, p.o.)

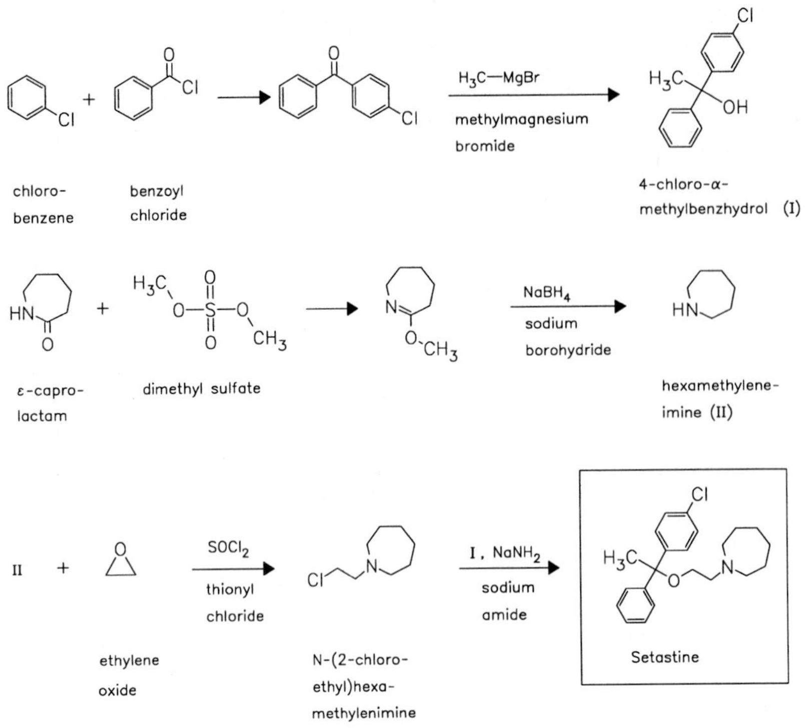

chloro-   benzoyl
benzene   chloride

4-chloro-α-
methylbenzhydrol   (I)

ε-capro-   dimethyl sulfate
lactam

hexamethylene-
imine (II)

II   +

ethylene
oxide

N-(2-chloro-
ethyl)hexa-
methylenimine

Setastine

Reference(s):
DE 2 528 194 (Egyt; appl. 24.6.1975; H-prior. 24.6.1974).
GB 1 463 038 (Egyt; appl. 24.6.1975; H-prior. 24.6.1974).

Formulation(s):   tabl. 1 mg (as hydrochloride)

Trade Name(s):
H: Loderix (EGIS; 1988)

Setiptiline
(Teciptiline)

ATC: N06AX
Use: antidepressant, mianserin analog

RN: 57262-94-9   MF: $C_{19}H_{19}N$ MW: 261.37   EINECS: 260-653-4
LD$_{50}$:   423 mg/kg (M, p.o.);
554 mg/kg (R, p.o.)
CN: 2,3,4,9-tetrahydro-2-methyl-1H-dibenzo[3,4:6,7]cyclohepta[1,2-c]pyridine

maleate (1:1)
RN: 85650-57-3   MF: $C_{19}H_{19}N \cdot C_4H_4O_4$ MW: 377.44   EINECS: 288-065-3

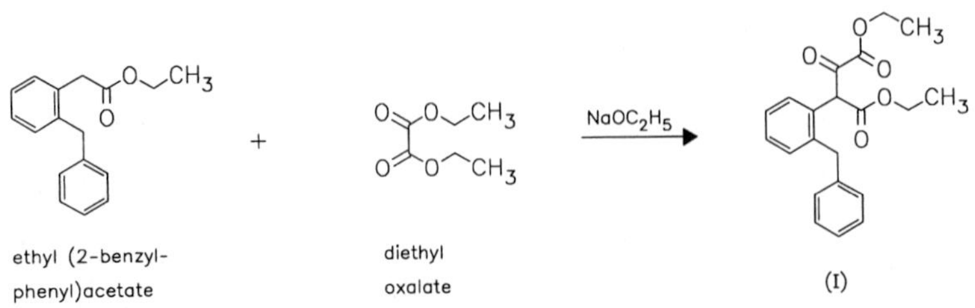

ethyl (2-benzyl-   diethyl
phenyl)acetate   oxalate

(I)

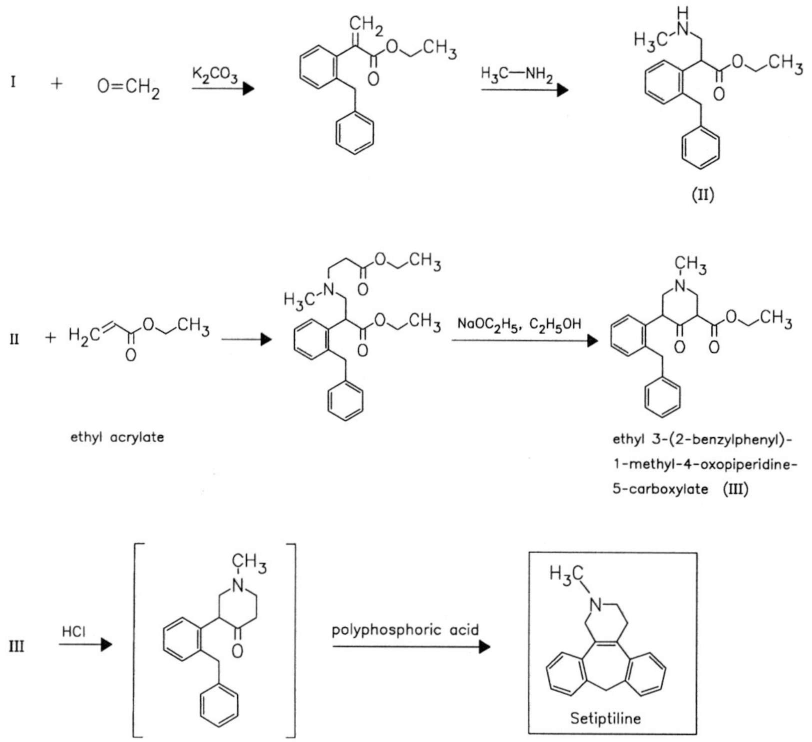

(II)

ethyl acrylate

ethyl 3-(2-benzylphenyl)-
1-methyl-4-oxopiperidine-
5-carboxylate (III)

Setiptiline

Reference(s):
DE 2 503 407 (Akzo; appl. 28.1.1975; NL-prior. 31.1.1974).
US 4 002 632 (Akzo; 11.1.1977; appl. 22.1.1975; NL-prior. 31.1.1974).

preparation of ethyl (2-benzylphenyl)acetate:
Kenyon, W.G. et al.: J. Org. Chem. (JOCEAH) **28**, 3108 (1963).
Yoshioka, M.; Osawa, H.; Fukuzawa, S.: Bull. Chem. Soc. Jpn. (BCSJA8) **55** (3), 877 (1982).
Weizmann et al.: J. Org. Chem. (JOCEAH) **15**, 918, 920, 926 (1950).
McElvain; Kent; Stevens: J. Am. Chem. Soc. (JACSAT) **68**, 1922 (1946).
Meyer: Ber. Dtsch. Chem. Ges. (BDCGAS) **21**, 1313 (1888).

medical use for treatment of gastric ulcers:
US 4 447 437 (Mochida; 8.5.1984; appl. 24.5.1982; J-prior. 3.6.1981).

Formulation(s):   tabl. 1 mg

Trade Name(s):
J: Tecipul (Mochida; 1989)

Sevoflurane

ATC: N01AB08
Use: anesthetic (inhalation)

RN: 28523-86-6   MF: $C_4H_3F_7O$ MW: 200.05
LD$_{50}$: 18.2 g/kg (M, p.o.); 28300 ppm/3H (M, inhal.);
        10.8 g/kg (R, p.o.); 28800 ppm/3H (R, inhal.)
CN: 1,1,1,3,3,3-hexafluoro-2-(fluoromethoxy)propane

(a)

H₃C–O CF₃
    CF₃   Cl₂, hν →   Cl O CF₃
                                           CF₃   KF →   F O CF₃
                                                                    CF₃

1,1,1,3,3,3-hexa-   1,1,1,3,3,3-hexa-   Sevoflurane
fluoro-2-methoxy-   fluoro-2-(chloro-
propane   methoxy)propane (I)

(b)

I   BrF₃ or ClF₃ →   Sevoflurane

Reference(s):
a   DE 1 954 268 (Baxter; appl. 28.10.1969; USA-prior. 29.10.1968).
    US 3 683 092 (Baxter; 8.8.1972; appl. 31.7.1970; prior. 28.10.1968).
    EP 341 005 (BOC; appl. 28.4.1989; USA-prior. 6.5.1988).
    US 4 874 901 (BOC; 17.10.1989; appl. 6.5.1988).
b   US 4 874 902 (BOC; 17.10.1989; appl. 20.5.1988).

alternative synthesis:
EP 42 412 (Baxter Travenol; appl. 10.12.1980; USA-prior. 26.12.1979).

Formulation(s):   inhalation sol. 1 ml

Trade Name(s):
D: Sevorane (Abbott)   J: Sevofrane (Maruishi; 1990)   Ultane (Abbott)
I: Sevorane (Abbott)   USA: Sevorane (Abbott)

Sibutramine hydrochloride
(BTS-54524)

ATC: A08AA
Use: antidepressant, anorexic

RN: 125494-59-9   MF: $C_{17}H_{26}ClN \cdot HCl \cdot H_2O$ MW: 334.33
CN: (±)-1-(4-chlorophenyl)-*N,N*-dimethyl-α-(2-methylpropyl)cyclobutanemethanamine hydrochloride
      monohydrate

(±)-base
RN: 106650-56-0   MF: $C_{17}H_{26}ClN$ MW: 279.86
(±)-anhydrous hydrochloride
RN: 84485-00-7   MF: $C_{17}H_{26}ClN \cdot HCl$ MW: 316.32
(+)-base
RN: 154752-44-0   MF: $C_{17}H_{26}ClN$ MW: 279.86
(+)-hydrochloride
RN: 154752-45-1   MF: $C_{17}H_{26}ClN \cdot HCl$ MW: 316.32
(−)-base
RN: 153341-22-1   MF: $C_{17}H_{26}ClN$ MW: 279.86
(−)-hydrochloride
RN: 153341-23-2   MF: $C_{17}H_{26}ClN \cdot HCl$ MW: 316.32

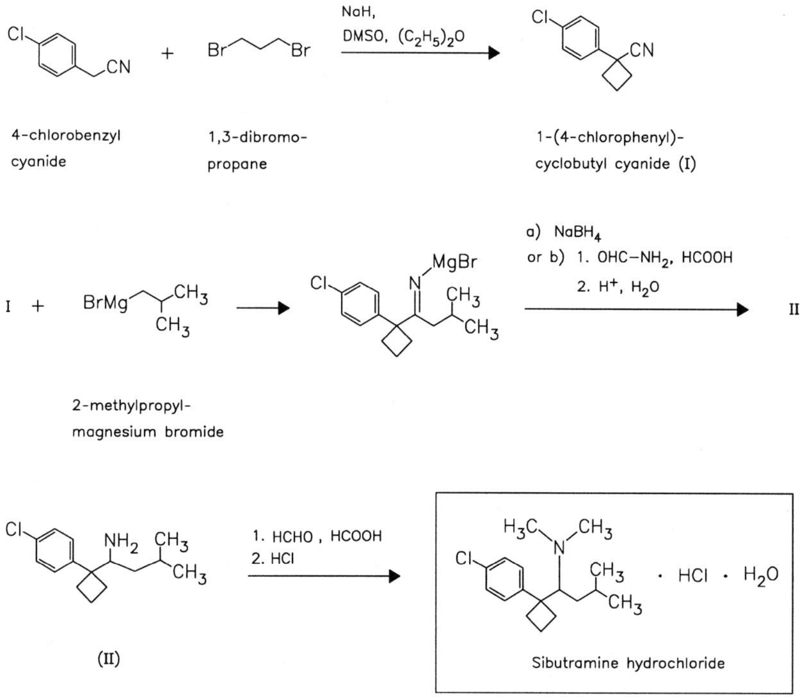

4-chlorobenzyl cyanide + 1,3-dibromo-propane → 1-(4-chlorophenyl)-cyclobutyl cyanide (I)

NaH, DMSO, $(C_2H_5)_2O$

I + 2-methylpropyl-magnesium bromide (BrMg) →
a) $NaBH_4$ or b) 1. OHC—NH$_2$, HCOOH 2. H$^+$, H$_2$O → II

(II)
1. HCHO, HCOOH
2. HCl
→ Sibutramine hydrochloride · HCl · H$_2$O

Reference(s):
DE 3 212 682 (Boots; appl. 21.10.1982; GB-prior. 6.4.1981).
WO 9 720 810 (Knoll AG; appl. 12.6.1997; GB-prior. 2.12.1996).
US 4 929 629 (Boots; 29.5.1990; GB-prior. 17.12.1985).

synthesis of 1-(4-chlorophenyl)cyclobutyl cyanide:
Butler, D.E.; Pollatz, J.C.: J. Org. Chem. (JOCEAH) 36, 1308 (1971).

use for treating depression:
GB 2 184 122 (Boots; appl. 17.6.1987; GB-prior. 17.12.1985).

use for treatment of Parkinson's disease:
WO 8 806 444 (Boots; appl. 7.9.1988; GB-prior. 28.2.1987).

use for treatment of obesity:
WO 9 006 110 (Boots; appl. 14.6.1990; USA-prior. 29.11.1988).

use to lower lipid levels:
WO 9 813 034 (Knoll AG; appl. 2.4.1998; GB-prior. 25.9.1996).

Formulation(s):   cps. 5 mg, 10 mg, 15 mg

Trade Name(s):
D: Reductil (Knoll; 1999)   USA: Meridia (Knoll; 1998)

Sildenafil
(UK-92480)

ATC: G04C
Use: male erectile dysfunction, PDE 5-inhibitor

RN: 139755-83-2   MF: $C_{22}H_{30}N_6O_4S$ MW: 474.59
CN: 1-[[3-(4,7-dihydro-1-methyl-7-oxo-3-propyl-1H-pyrazolo [4,3-d]pyrimidin-5-yl)-4-ethoxyphenyl]sulfonyl]-4-methylpiperazine

citrate
RN: 171599-83-0 MF: $C_{22}H_{30}N_6O_4S \cdot C_6H_8O_7$ MW: 666.71

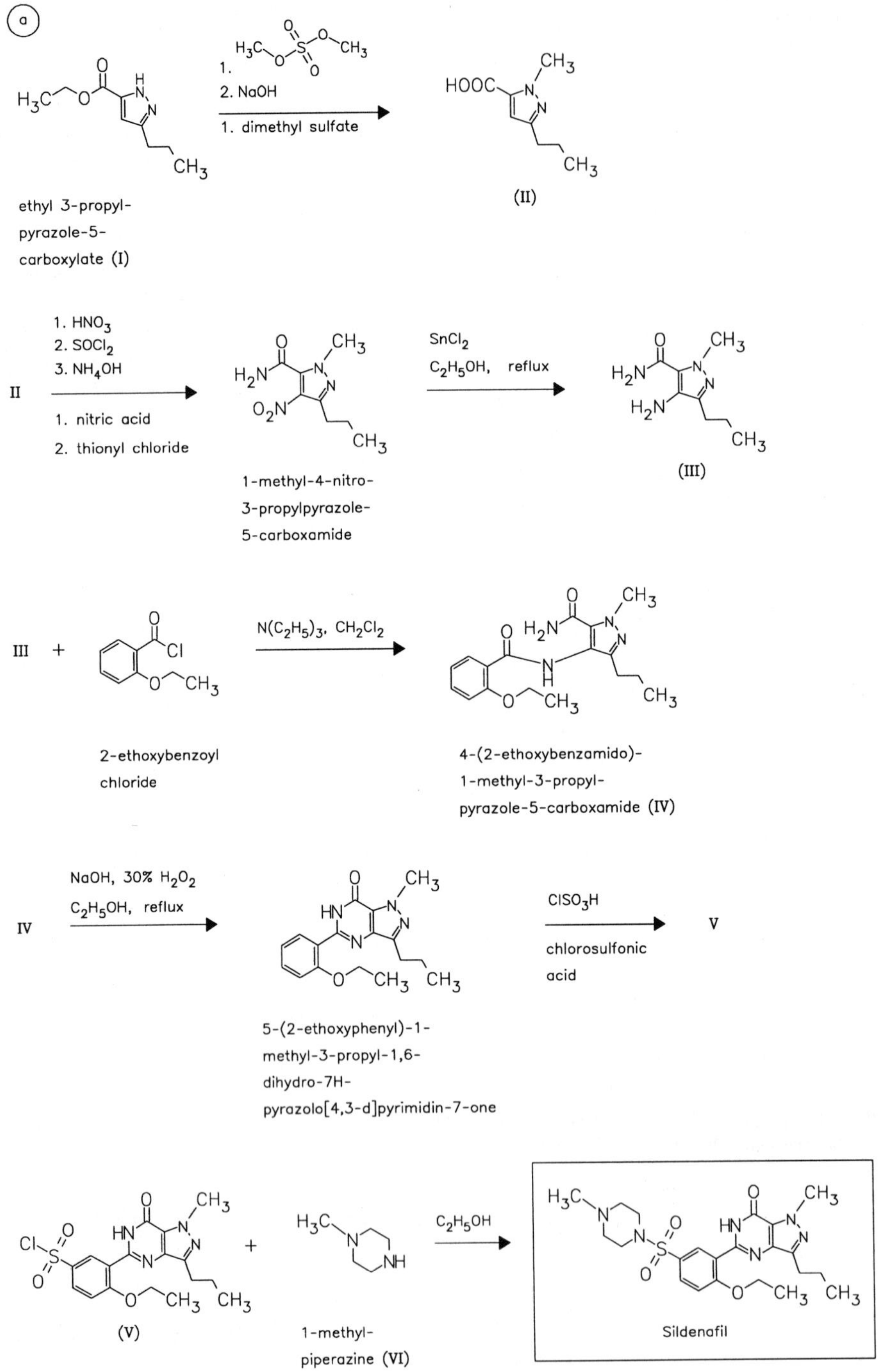
a
1. dimethyl sulfate
2. NaOH
ethyl 3-propyl-pyrazole-5-carboxylate (I)
(II)
1. HNO3
2. SOCl2
3. NH4OH
1. nitric acid
2. thionyl chloride
1-methyl-4-nitro-3-propylpyrazole-5-carboxamide
SnCl2
C2H5OH, reflux
(III)
N(C2H5)3, CH2Cl2
2-ethoxybenzoyl chloride
4-(2-ethoxybenzamido)-1-methyl-3-propyl-pyrazole-5-carboxamide (IV)
NaOH, 30% H2O2
C2H5OH, reflux
5-(2-ethoxyphenyl)-1-methyl-3-propyl-1,6-dihydro-7H-pyrazolo[4,3-d]pyrimidin-7-one
ClSO3H
chlorosulfonic acid
(V)
1-methyl-piperazine (VI)
C2H5OH
Sildenafil

b

2-ethoxy-
benzoic acid

SOCl₂, ClSO₃H
thionyl chloride,
chlorosulfonic acid

5-chlorosulfonyl-
2-ethoxybenzoic acid (VII)

VII + VI   H₂O, 10–20°C

2-ethoxy-5-(4-methyl-
piperazin-1-ylsulfonyl)-
benzoic acid (VIII)

III + VIII   , ethyl acetate, 55°C

N,N'-carbonyldiimidazole

(IX)

IX   K⁺O⁻–C(CH₃)₃, HO–C(CH₃)₃, Δ   Sildenafil

potassium tert-butoxide

preparation of ethyl 3-propylpyrazole-5-carboxylate

2-pentanone   diethyl oxalate   NaOC₂H₅,
C₂H₅OH

ethyl 2,4-dioxo-
heptanoate

N₂H₄ · H₂O,
C₂H₅OH   I

hydrazine
hydrate

Reference(s):
a   EP 463 756 (Pfizer Inc.; appl. 7.6.1991; GB-prior. 20.6.1990).
Terrett, N.K. et al.: Bioorg. Med. Chem. Lett. (BMCLE8) **6**, 1819-1824 (1996).
Palmer, E.: Chem. Brit. (CHMBAY) **1999**, 24
b   EP 812 845 (Pfizer Corp.; appl. 4.6.1997; GB-prior. 14.6.1996).
Dale, D.J. et al.: Org. Process Res. Dev. (OPRDFK) **4**, 17-22 (2000).

preparation of ethyl 3-propylpyrazole-5-carboxylate:
Terrett, N.K; Bell, A.S.; Brown, D.; Ellis, P.: Bioorg. Med. Chem. Lett. (BMCLE8) **6** (15), 1819 (1996).

preparation of ethyl 2,4-dioxoheptanoate:
Lapworth; Hann: J. Chem. Soc. (JCSOA9) **81**, 1490 (1902).
Libermann et al.: Bull. Soc. Chim. Fr. (BSCFAS) **1958**, 687, 690.
Burch, H.A.; Gray, J.E.: J. Med. Chem. (JMCMAR) **15**, 429 (1972).

use for treatment of impotence:
WO 9 428 902 (Pfizer Inc; appl. 13.5.1994; GB-prior. 9.6.1993).

Formulation(s):   f. c. tabl. 25 mg, 50 mg, 100 mg (as citrate)

Silibinin

ATC:　A05
Use:　liver therapeutic

RN:　22888-70-6　MF: $C_{25}H_{22}O_{10}$　MW: 482.44　EINECS: 245-302-5
LD_{50}:　1056 mg/kg (M, i.v.)
CN:　[2R-[2α,3β,6(2R*,3R*)]]-2-[2,3-dihydro-3-(4-hydroxy-3-methoxyphenyl)-2-(hydroxymethyl)-1,4-benzodioxin-6-yl]-2,3-dihydro-3,5,7-trihydroxy-4H-1-benzopyran-4-one

Silibinin

By extraction of the fruits of *Silybum marianum* Gaertn. (milk thistle) and column chromatographic purification.

Reference(s):
Wagner, H. et al.: Arzneim.-Forsch. (ARZNAD) **18**, 688 (1968); **24**, 466 (1974).
DOS 1 767 666 (Madaus; appl. 1.6.1968)
DAS 1 923 082 (Madaus; appl. 6.5.1969)
DOS 3 537 656 (Madaus; appl. 23.10.1985; D-prior. 22.11.1984).

derivatives and salts:
DRP 1 963 318 (ATO Investment; appl. 17.12.1969).
DAS 2 302 593 (Madaus; appl. 19.1.1973).

Formulation(s):　cps. 35 mg, 70 mg, 140 mg, 150 mg, 200 mg; f. c. tabl. 70 mg, 140 mg; gran. 200 mg; susp. 0.43 g/100 g

Simfibrate

ATC:　C01AB06
Use:　antiarteriosclerotic (hypolipemic)

RN:　14929-11-4　MF: $C_{23}H_{26}Cl_2O_6$　MW: 469.36　EINECS: 238-998-7
LD_{50}:　3300 mg/kg (M, p.o.);
　　　　7300 mg/kg (R, p.o.)
CN:　2-(4-chlorophenoxy)-2-methylpropanoic acid 1,3-propanediyl ester

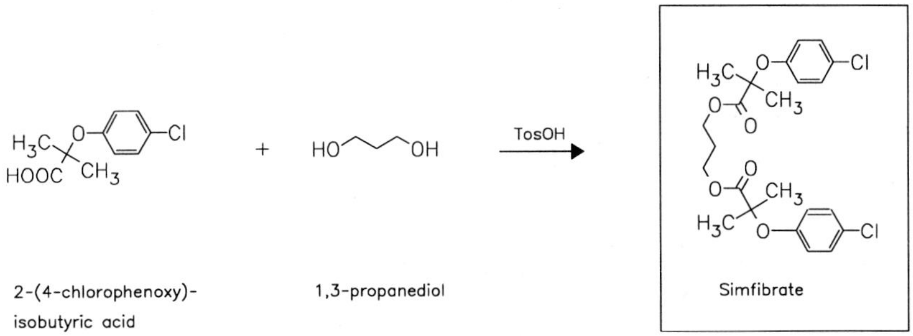

2-(4-chlorophenoxy)-   1,3-propanediol   Simfibrate
isobutyric acid
(cf. clofibrate
synthesis)

Reference(s):
US 3 494 957 (Yoshitomi; 10.2.1970; J-prior. 5.1.1965).

Formulation(s):   cps. 250 mg

Trade Name(s):

I:	Cholesolvin (Cyanamid); wfm	Liposolvin (Tosi-Novara); wfm	Sinfibrex (Isnardi); wfm
		J:	Cholesorbin (Takeda)

Simvastatin
(MK-733; Synvinolin)

ATC: C10AA01
Use: antihyperlipidemic cholesterol
synthesis inhibitor, HMG-CoA-
reductase inhibitor

RN: 79902-63-9   MF: $C_{25}H_{38}O_5$ MW: 418.57
LD$_{50}$:   3 g/kg (M, p.o.);
4438 mg/kg (R, p.o.);
>5 g/kg (dog, p.o.)
CN: [1S-[1α,3α,7β,8β(2S*,4S*),8aβ]]-2,2-dimethylbutanoic acid 1,2,3,7,8,8a-hexahydro-3,7-dimethyl-8-[2-
(tetrahydro-4-hydroxy-6-oxo-2H-pyran-2-yl)ethyl]-1-naphthalenyl ester

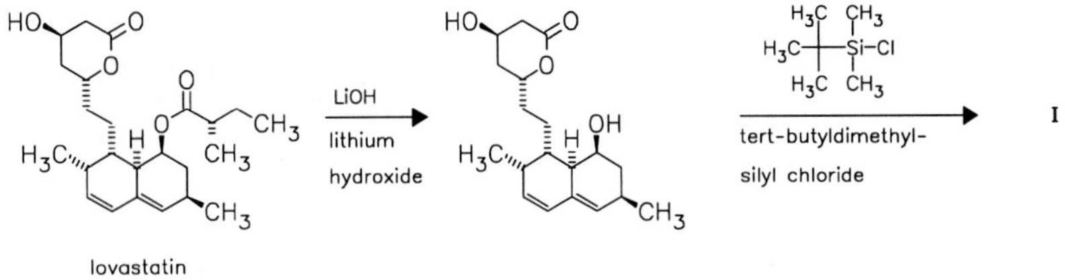

lovastatin
(q. v.)

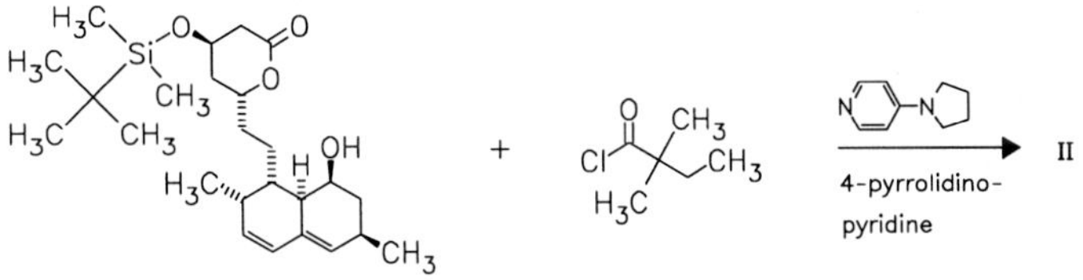

(I)   2,2-dimethyl-
butyryl chloride

(II)

Simvastatin

Reference(s):
US 4 444 784 (Merck & Co.; 24.4.1984; prior. 5.8.1980, 4.2.1980).
US 4 450 171 (Merck & Co.; 22.5.1984; prior. 14.6.1982, 18.12.1980, 5.8.1980, 4.2.1980).
Hoffmann, W.F. et al.: J. Med. Chem. (JMCMAR) **29**, 849 (1986).

alternative syntheses:
US 5 159 104 (Merck & Co.; 27.10.1992; appl. 1.5.1991).
GB 2 255 974 (Merck & Co.; 25.11.1992; USA-prior. 24.5.1991).
WO 9 812 188 (Brantford; 5.9.1996; CA-prior. 19.9.1996).
US 5 763 653 (Ranbaxy; 9.6.1998; appl. 13.3.1997).
US 5 763 646 (Ranbaxy; 9.6.1998; appl. 13.3.1997).
US 5 393 893 (Apotex; 28.2.1995; appl. 8.11.1993).
EP 33 538 (Merck & Co.; appl. 2.2.1981; USA-prior. 4.2.1980, 5.8.1980).
Thaper, R.K. et al.: Org. Process Res. Dev. (OPRDFK) **3**, 476-479 (1999).

controlled-release formulation:
EP 302 693 (Merck & Co.; appl. 1.8.1988; USA-prior. 3.8.1987, 31.8.1987).

Formulation(s):   f. c. tabl. 5 mg, 10 mg, 20 mg, 40 mg; tabl. 5 mg, 10 mg, 20 mg, 40 mg

Trade Name(s):

D:	Denan (Boehringer Ing.; 1990)	GB:	Zocor (Merck Sharp & Dohme; 1989)		Sivastin (Sigma-Tau)
	Zocor (Dieckmann; 1990)	I:	Liponorm (Gentili)		Zocor (Neopharmed)
F:	Lodalès (Sanofi Winthrop)		Medipo (Mediolanum)	J:	Lipovas (Banyu)
	Zocor (MSD-Chibret; 1989)		Sinvacor (Merck Sharp & Dohme)	USA:	Zocor (Merck)

Sisomicin

ATC: J01GB08
Use: antibiotic

RN: 32385-11-8   MF: $C_{19}H_{37}N_5O_7$ MW: 447.53   EINECS: 251-018-2
LD_{50}:   34 mg/kg (M, i.v.); >5 g/kg (M, p.o.);
         32 mg/kg (R, i.v.); >5 g/kg (R, p.o.)
CN: *O*-3-deoxy-4-*C*-methyl-3-(methylamino)-β-L-arabinopyrasoyl-(1→6)-*O*-[2,6-diamino-2,3,4,6-tetradeoxy-α-D-*glycero*-hex-4-enopyranosyl-(1→4)]-2-deoxy-D-streptamine

sulfate (2:5)
RN: 53179-09-2   MF: $C_{19}H_{37}N_5O_7 \cdot 5/2H_2SO_4$ MW: 1385.46   EINECS: 258-414-4
LD_{50}:   34 mg/kg (M, i.v.); >5 g/kg (M, p.o.);
         49 mg/kg (R, i.v.); >5 g/kg (R, p.o.)

Sisomicin

From fermentation solutions of *Micromonospora inyoensis* (NRRL 3292).

Reference(s):
DOS 1 932 309 (Scherico; appl. 26.6.1969; USA-prior. 27.6.1968, 16.12.1968).
US 3 832 286 (Schering Corp.; 27.8.1974; prior. 16.12.1968, 27.6.1968, 26.6.1973).
US 3 907 771 (Schering Corp.; 23.9.1975; prior. 3.2.1971, 16.12.1968, 27.6.1968).
US 4 009 328 (Scherico; 22.2.1977; prior. 2.5.1975).
Wagman, G.H. et al.: J. Antibiot. (JANTAJ) **23**, 551, 555 (1970).
Schmidt-Kastner, G.; Reimann, H.: Infection (Munich) (IFTNAL) **4**, (Suppl. 4), 292 (1976).

structure:
Reimann, H. et al.: J. Org. Chem. (JOCEAH) **39**, 1451 (1974).
Cleophax, J. et al.: J. Chem. Soc., Chem. Commun. (JCCCAT) **1975**, 11.

synthesis:
Davis, D.H. et al.: J. Med. Chem. (JMCMAR) **21**, 189 (1978).

Formulation(s):   amp. 20 mg/2 ml, 100 mg/2 ml, 75 mg/1.5 ml (as sulfate)

Trade Name(s):

D:	Extramycin (Bayer; 1976); wfm	F:	Sisolline (Schering Plough); wfm	I:	Mensiso (Menarini) Sisomin (Max)
	Pathomycin (Byk Essex; 1976); wfm		Sisolline (Unilabo-Cétrane); wfm	USA:	Siseptin (Schering); wfm

---

β-Sitosterin
(β-Sitosterol; α-Phytosterol)

ATC: C10AX; G04C
Use: prostata adenoma therapeutic (benign prostate hypertrophy, BPH), antihypercholesterolemic

RN: 83-46-5   MF: $C_{29}H_{50}O$ MW: 414.72   EINECS: 201-480-6
CN: (3β)-stigmast-5-en-3-ol

β-Sitosterin

From wheat seeds, soybeans etc.

Reference(s):
The Merck Index, 12th Ed., 1467 (1996).
US 4 153 622 (Medipolar Oy; 8.5.1979; prior. 18.5.1978).

use in combination with chenodeoxycholic acid *for disintegration of gallstones:*
DOS 2 618 854 (Fresenius; appl. 29.4.1976).

Formulation(s):   cps. 10 mg, 65 mg; gran. 1.76 g/2 g; tabl. 75 mg, 100 mg

Trade Name(s):
D: Azuprostat Kapseln   Liposit Merz (Merz & Co.)   Triastonal (Intermuti)
      (Azuchemie)-comb.   LP-Truw (Truw)   F: Sitostérol Delalande
      Cinchol Kapseln (Evers);   Prostasal Kapseln (TAD)   (Delalande); wfm
      wfm   Sito-Lande (Synthelabo)   USA: Cytellin (Lilly); wfm
      Flemun (Intermuti)   Sitosterin Prostata Kapseln
      Harzol (Hoyer)   (Intermuti)

Sizofiran

(Schizophyllan)

ATC: A06A; L03A
Use: antineoplastic, immunomodulator

RN: 9050-67-3   MF: $[C_{24}H_{40}O_{20}]x$ MW: unspecified
LD_{50}: >300 mg/kg (M, i.v.); >1 g/kg (M, p.o.);
        >300 mg/kg (R, i.v.); >500 mg/kg (R, p.o.);
        >100 mg/kg (dog, i.v.)
CN: poly[3→[O-β-D-glucopyranosyl-(1→3)-O-[β-D-glucopyranosyl-(1→6)-O-β-D-glucopyranosyl-(1→3)]-
       O-β-D-glucopyranosyl]→1]

Sizofiran

Preparation by fermentation of *Schizophyllum commune.*

Reference(s):
JP 71/37 873 (Taito; appl. 20.7.1968).
Kozima, T. et al.: Int. J. Immunopharmacol. (IJIMDS) **2** (3), 49 (1980).

Formulation(s):   amp. 40 mg

Trade Name(s):
J: Sonifilan (Taito Pfizer)

Sobrerol
(Pinolhydrat)

ATC: R05CB07
Use: respiratory stimulant, secretolytic, mucolytic

RN: 498-71-5   MF: $C_{10}H_{18}O_2$ MW: 170.25   EINECS: 207-868-1
LD$_{50}$:   580 mg/kg (M, i.v.)
CN: 5-hydroxy-α,α,4-trimethyl-3-cyclohexene-1-methanol

(±)-α-pinene   (±)-α-pinene   Sobrerol
                      oxide

Reference(s):
US 2 815 378 (Glidden; 3.12.1957; appl. 12.6.1953).
DE 1 096 348 (FMC; appl. 26.10.1959).
DE 2 114 138 (C. Corvi; appl. 24.3.1971; I-prior. 17.4.1970).

medical use:
DE 2 166 355 (Camillo Corvi; appl. 24.3.1971; I-prior. 17.4.1970).
GB 1 176 817 (C. Corvi; appl. 8.12.1967; NL-prior. 9.12.1966).

Formulation(s):   cps. 200 mg; gran. 100 mg, 300 mg; suppos. 20 mg, 100 mg, 200 mg; syrup 0.8 %

Trade Name(s):
I: Fluental (Corvi)-comb.   Sobrepin (Roche)
       Polimucil (Poli)-comb.   Sopulmin (Scharper)

Sobuzoxane
(MST 16)

ATC: L01
Use: antineoplastic, topoisomerase II-inhibitor

RN: 98631-95-9   MF: $C_{22}H_{34}N_4O_{10}$ MW: 514.53
LD$_{50}$:   >1 g/kg (M, p.o.);
       >5 g/kg (R, p.o.);
       >3 g/kg (dog, p.o.)
CN: carbonic acid 1,2-ethanediylbis[(2,6-dioxo-4,1-piperazinediyl)methylene] bis(2-methylpropyl) ester

1,2-bis(3,5-dioxo-
piperazin-1-yl)-
ethane
(from ethylenediamine-
tetraacetic acid)

1,2-bis(4-hydroxymethyl-
3,5-dioxopiperazin-1-yl)-
ethane   (I)

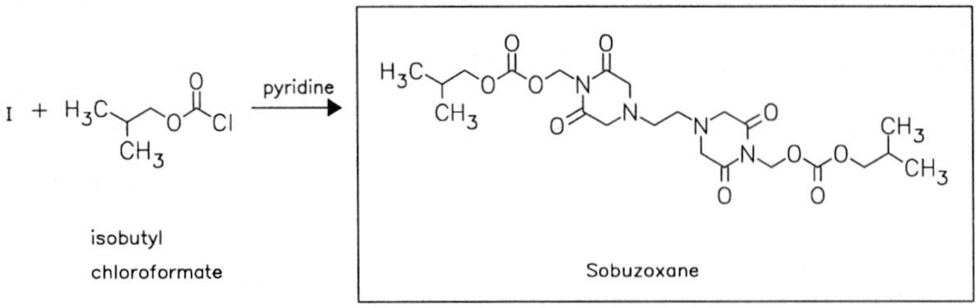

isobutyl
chloroformate

Sobuzoxane

Reference(s):

EP 140 327 (Zenyaku Koguo Co.; appl. 23.10.1984; J-prior. 31.10.1983).

Formulation(s):   sachets containing gran. 400 mg, 800 mg, 1200 mg, 1600 mg

Trade Name(s):
J: Perazolin (Zenyaku Koguo)

Sodium aurothiomalate

(Gold Sodium Thiomalate)

ATC: M01CB01
Use: gold therapeutic (antirheumatic, antiarthritic)

RN: 12244-57-4   MF: $C_4H_5AuO_4S \cdot xNa$ MW: unspecified   EINECS: 235-479-7
CN: sodium [mercaptobutanedioato(2–)]aurate(2–)

free acid
RN: 24145-43-5   MF: $C_4H_5AuO_4S$ MW: 346.14   EINECS: 246-034-1

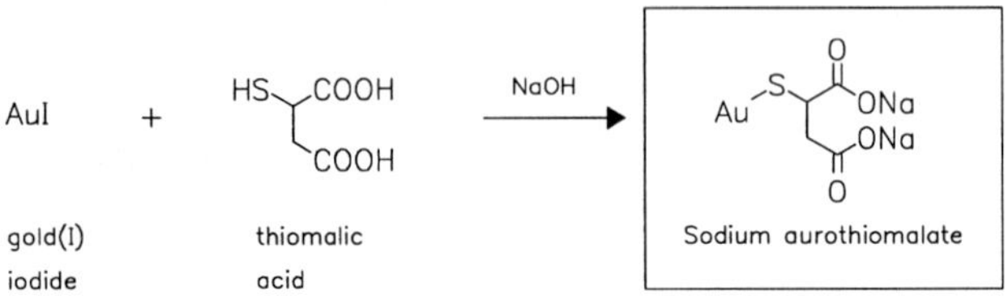

gold(I)   thiomalic   Sodium aurothiomalate
iodide   acid

Reference(s):

US 1 994 213 (Rhône-Poulenc; 1935; GB-prior. 1933).

Formulation(s):   amp. 10 mg, 20 mg, 50 mg

Trade Name(s):
D: Tauredon (Byk Gulden;   GB: Myocrisin (IHC)   USA: Myochrysine (Merck)
        Byk Tosse)   J: Kidon (Ono)

Sodium dioctyl sulfosuccinate

(Dioctyl sodium sulfosuccinate; Docusate sodium)

ATC: A06A
Use: laxative, detergent, emulgator, cerumenolytic

RN: 577-11-7   MF: $C_{20}H_{37}NaO_7S$ MW: 444.57   EINECS: 209-406-4
CN: sulfobutanedioic acid 1,4-bis(2-ethylhexyl) ester sodium salt

free acid
RN: 10041-19-7   MF: $C_{20}H_{38}O_7S$ MW: 422.58   EINECS: 233-124-0

calcium salt
RN: 128-49-4   MF: $C_{40}H_{74}CaO_{14}S_2$ MW: 883.23   EINECS: 204-889-8
potassium salt
RN: 7491-09-0   MF: $C_{20}H_{37}KO_7S$ MW: 460.67   EINECS: 231-308-5

fumaric acid   2-ethyl-1-hexanol   bis(2-ethylhexyl) fumarate (I)

Sodium dioctyl sulfosuccinate

Reference(s):
US 2 028 091 (American Cyanamid; 1936; appl. 1933).
US 2 176 423 (American Cyanamid; 1939; appl. 1936).

calcium salt:
US 3 035 973 (Lloyd Brothers Inc.; 1962; appl. 1958).

Formulation(s):   drg. 5 mg; drinking amp. 50 mg, 100 mg; suppos. 10 mg; syrup 20 mg/5 ml; tabl. 2.5 mg, 5 mg, 50 mg

Trade Name(s):
D: Agaroletten (Warner-
        Lambert)-comb.
        Florisan (Boehringer Ing.)-
        comb.
        Laxagetten (ct-
        Arzneimittel)-comb.
        Otowaxol (Norgine)-comb.
        Potsilo (Stark, Konstanz)-
        comb.
        Tirgon (Woelm)-comb.
        further combination
        preparations
F: Jamylène (Expanpharm)

GB: Norgalax (Norgine Pharma)
        Klyx (Ferring); wfm
        Solivax (Concept); wfm
        numerous combination
        preparations
I: Dorbantyl (Robins)-comb.;
        wfm
        Fisiolax (Manetti Roberts)-
        comb.; wfm
        Ikelax (Iketon)-comb.; wfm
        Lambanol (Zilliken)-
        comb.; wfm

        Sorbiclis (Pharkos)-comb.;
        wfm
        Tipicol (Biomedica
        Foscama)-comb.; wfm
J: Bulkosol (Eisai)
USA: Colace (Roberts)
        Modane Plus (Savage)
        Modane Soft (Savage)
        Peri-Colace (Roberts)
        Senokot-S (Purdue
        Frederick)
        generics and further
        combination preparations

Sodium picosulfate

(Natrium-picosulfat; Picosulfate sodium; Sodium
  picosulphate)

ATC: A06AB08
Use: laxative

RN: 10040-45-6   MF: $C_{18}H_{13}NNa_2O_8S_2$ MW: 481.41   EINECS: 233-120-9
LD$_{50}$: 1600 mg/kg (M, i.v.); 14.5 g/kg (M, p.o.);
      1450 mg/kg (R, i.v.); 17 g/kg (R, p.o.)
CN: 4,4'-(2-pyridinylmethylene)bisphenol bis(hydrogen sulfate)(ester) disodium salt

2-(4,4'-dihydroxybenz-
hydryl)pyridine
(cf. bisacodyl)

1. ClSO$_3$H, pyridine
2. NaOH

1. chlorosulfonic acid

Sodium picosulfate

Reference(s):
US 3 528 986 (De Angeli; 15.9.1970; appl. 22.8.1966).

alternative synthesis (with amidosulfonic acid *or pyridine sulfur trioxide adduct):*
DOS 1 904 322 (Dr. K. Thomae; appl. 29.1.1969).

Formulation(s):   drg. 5 mg; drops 7.5 mg/ml; tabl. 1.25 mg, 5 mg

Trade Name(s):
D: Agiolax (Madaus)   Regulax (Krewel   Gocce Antonetto
      Dalcolax (Boehringer Ing.)   Meuselbach)   (Antonetto)
      Laxoberal (Boehringer   GB: Laxoberal (Windsor)   Gocce Lassative Aicardi
      Ing.)   Picolax (Ferring)-comb.   (SIT)
      Mandrolax Pico (Dolorgiet)   I: Falquigut (Falqui)   Guttalax (Fher)
      Midro (Midro)

Sofalcone

(SU-88)

ATC: A02B
Use: ulcer therapeutic

RN: 64506-49-6   MF: $C_{27}H_{30}O_6$ MW: 450.53
LD$_{50}$: 131 mg/kg (M, i.v.); >10 g/kg (M, p.o.);
      105 mg/kg (R, i.v.); >10 g/kg (R, p.o.);
      >20 g/kg (dog, p.o.)
CN: [5-[(3-methyl-2-butenyl)oxy]-2-[3-[4-[(3-methyl-2-butenyl)oxy]phenyl]-1-oxo-2-
      propenyl]phenoxy]acetic acid

2',4'-dihydroxy-
acetophenone

prenyl bromide

KOH or K$_2$CO$_3$/acetone

2'-hydroxy-4'-(3-methyl-
2-butenyloxy)acetophenone (I)

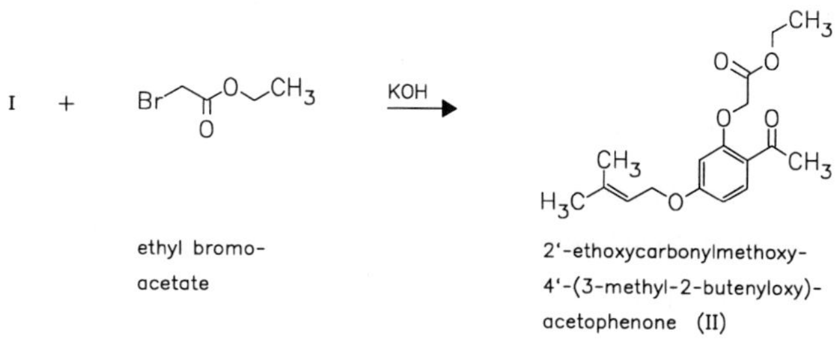

I + ethyl bromo-acetate (Br-CH2-CO-O-CH3) → KOH → 2'-ethoxycarbonylmethoxy-4'-(3-methyl-2-butenyloxy)-acetophenone (II)

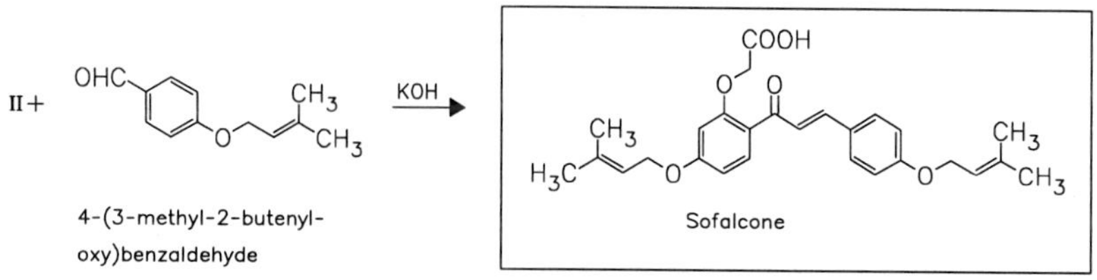

II + 4-(3-methyl-2-butenyl-oxy)benzaldehyde → KOH → Sofalcone

Reference(s):

DE 2 705 603 (Taisho; appl. 10.2.1977; J-prior. 13.2.1976).

US 4 085 135 (Taisho; 18.4.1978; appl. 11.2.1977; J-prior. 13.2.1976).

synthesis of intermediate I:

Kyogoku, K. et al.: Chem. Pharm. Bull. (CPBTAL) **27**, 2943 (1979).

Formulation(s):   cps. 50 mg, 100 mg; gran. 10 %

Trade Name(s):

J: Solon (Taisho; 1984); wfm

Sorbitol

(D-Glucitol)

ATC: A06AG07; B05CX02; V04CC01
Use: osmotic, laxative

RN: 50-70-4   MF: $C_6H_{14}O_6$ MW: 182.17   EINECS: 200-061-5
CN: D-glucitol

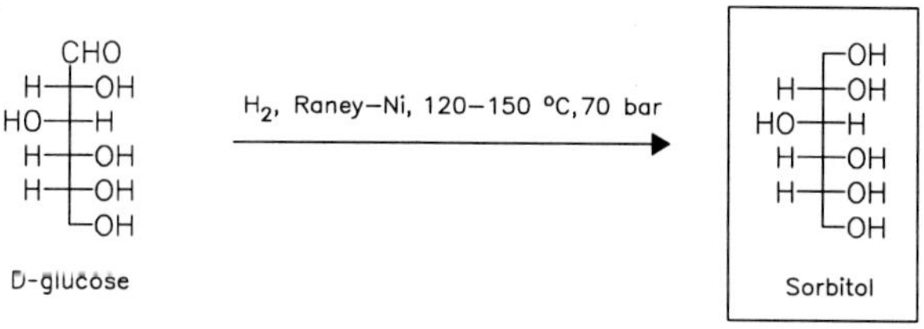

D-glucose → H_2, Raney-Ni, 120–150 °C, 70 bar → Sorbitol

Reference(s):

Ullmanns Encykl. Tech. Chem., 4. Aufl., Vol. **24**, 772.

Formulation(s):   sol. 13.4 g/67.5 ml, 400 g/1000 ml; clysma 200 g/1000 ml; susp. 48 g/120 ml, 96 g/240 ml

Trade Name(s):

D: 1 x klysma Sorbit Klistier (Pharmacia & Upjohn) Mikroklist (Pharmacia & Upjohn)-comb.

Sorbitol-Infusionslösung 40 (Braun Melsungen) Yal (Trommsdorff)

numerous combination preparations

F: Arnilose (ATC Pharma)

Hépagrume (Rosa-
Phytopharma)
Hépargitol (Elerté)
Sorbitol Aguettant
(Aguettant)
Sorbitol Delalande
(Synthelabo)
numerous combination
preparations

GB: Glandosane (Fresenius)-
comb.
Relaxit (Crawford)-comb.
combination preparations
only

I: Sorbilande (Delalande)
numerous combination
preparations

J: Sorbit Inj. (Nikken
Kagaku)
D-Sorbitol Solution
(Maruishi)
Sorbit TS Inj. (Termo)

USA: Actidose (Paddock)-comb.
Sorbitol Sodium
(Pharmaceutical
Associates)

Sorivudine
(BVAU)

Use: antiviral

RN: 77181-69-2   MF: $C_{11}H_{13}BrN_2O_6$ MW: 349.14
LD$_{50}$:   >8 g/kg (R, p. o.); >2 g/kg (R, s. c.);
>10 g/kg (M, p. o.); >5 g/kg (M, s. c.);
>5 g/kg (dog, p. o.)
CN: (E)-1-β-D-Arabinofuranosyl-5-(2-bromoethenyl)-2,4(1H,3H)-pyrimidinedione

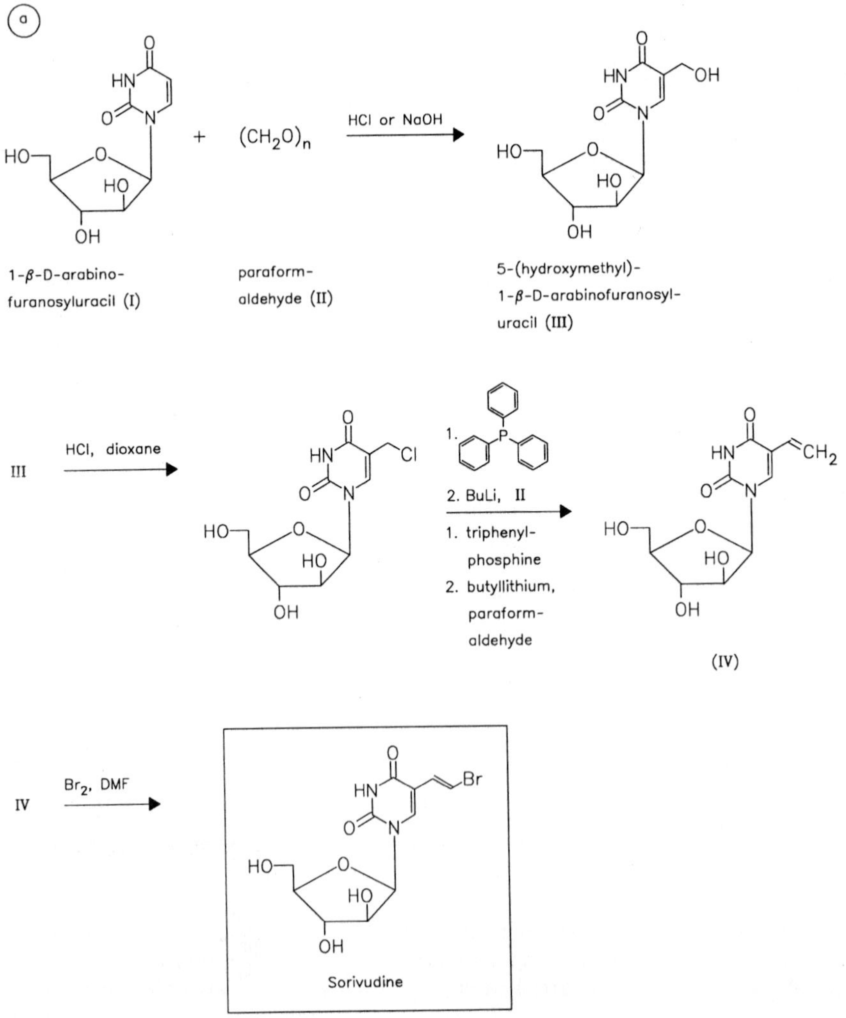

1-β-D-arabino-
furanosyluracil (I)

paraform-
aldehyde (II)

5-(hydroxymethyl)-
1-β-D-arabinofuranosyl-
uracil (III)

III → HCl, dioxane

1. triphenyl-
phosphine
2. butyllithium,
paraform-
aldehyde

(IV)

IV → Br$_2$, DMF

Sorivudine

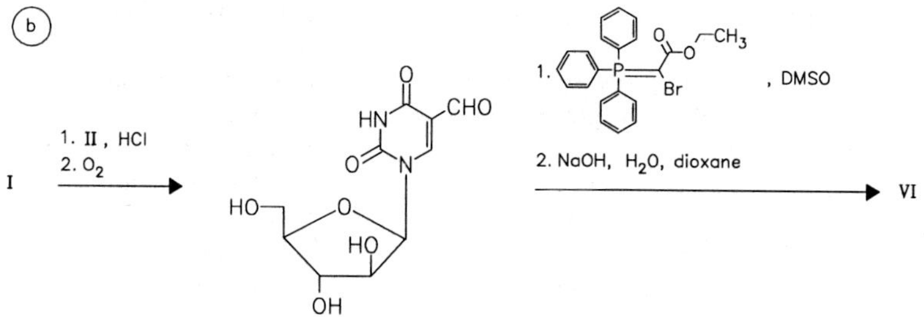

(b)

5-formyl-1-β-D-
arabinofuranosyl-
uracil (V)

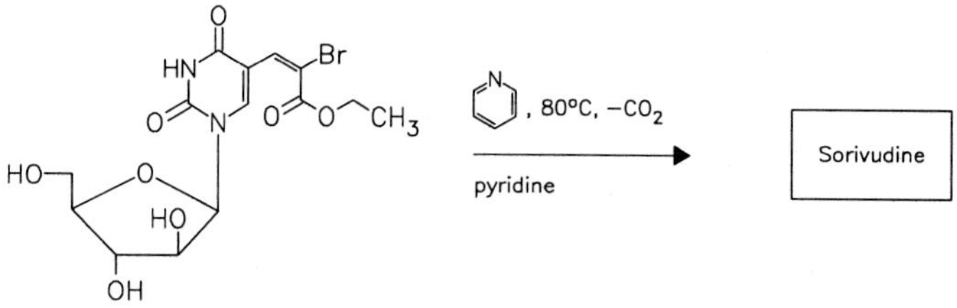

(VI)

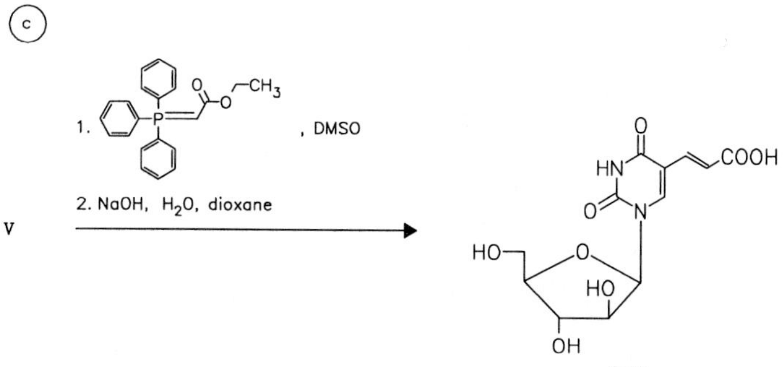

(c)

(VII)

(d)

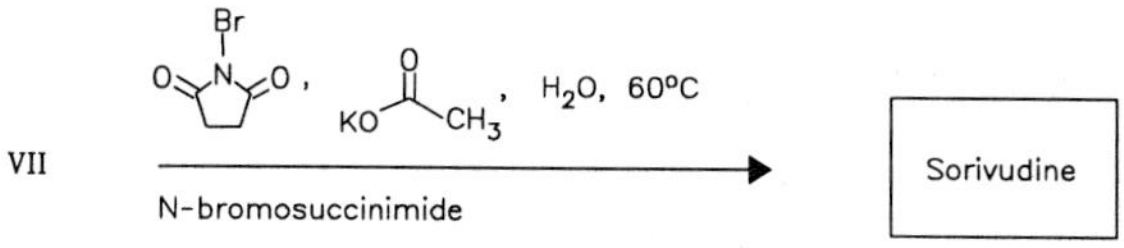

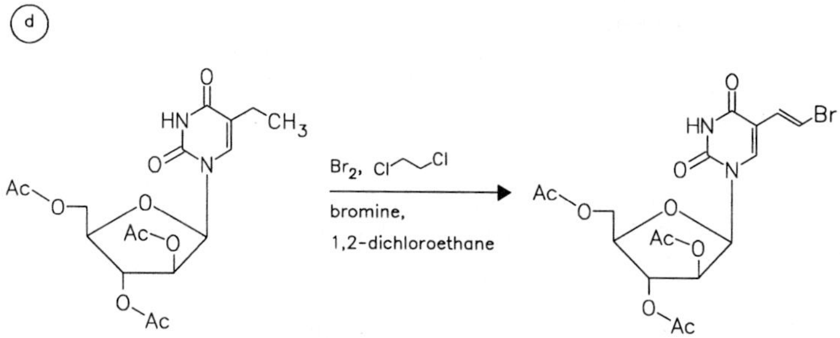

1-(2,3,5-tri-O-acetyl-β-D-
arabinofuranosyl)-5-ethyl-
uracil

VIII

VIII →[1. NaOCH$_3$, CH$_3$OH 2. Dowex 50WX8]→ Sorivudine

Reference(s):
a EP 031 128 (Yamasa Shoyu; appl. 1.7.1981; J-prior. 19.12.1979).
b JP 59 163 395 (Yamasa Shoyu Co.; appl. 14.9.1984; J-prior. 8.3.1983).
c JP 58 062 195 (Yamasa Shoyu Co.; appl. 14.4.1983; J-prior. 8.10.1981).
d DD 280 763 (Akademie der Wissenschaften der DDR; appl. 18.7.1990; DD-prior. 4.8.1981).

nucleic acid related compounds:
Robins, M.J.; Manfredini, S.: Tetrahedron Lett. (TELEAY) **31** (39), 5633 (1990).

facile access to 2'-O-acetyl prodrugs of 1-(β-D-arabinofuranosyl)-5(E)-(2-bromovinyl)uracil:
Baraldi, P.G.; Bazzanini, R.; Manfredini, S.; Simoni, D.; Robins, M.J.: Tetrahedron Lett. (TELEAY) **34** (19), 3177 (1993).

synthesis and antiviral activity of (E)-5-(2-bromovinyl)uracil:
De Clercq, E. et al.: J. Med. Chem. (JMCMAR) **29**, 213 (1986).

Formulation(s): tabl. 50 mg

Trade Name(s):
J: Usevir (Nippon Shoji
   Kaisha/Eisai; 1993); wfm

Sotalol

ATC: C07AA07
Use: beta blocking agent, antianginal, antihypertensive

RN: 3930-20-9 MF: $C_{12}H_{20}N_2O_3S$ MW: 272.37
LD$_{50}$: 166 mg/kg (M, i.v.)
CN: N-[4-[1-hydroxy-2-[(1-methylethyl)amino]ethyl]phenyl]methanesulfonamide

monohydrochloride
RN: 959-24-0 MF: $C_{12}H_{20}N_2O_3S \cdot HCl$ MW: 308.83 EINECS: 213-496-0
LD$_{50}$: 2600 mg/kg (M, p.o.);
   3450 mg/kg (R, p.o.)

methanesulfonyl chloride + aniline → methanesulfonanilide →[Br⌒Br , AlCl$_3$, CS$_2$ / bromoacetyl bromide]→ 4-(bromoacetyl)methanesulfonanilide (I)

I + H$_2$N-CH(CH$_3$)$_2$ (isopropylamine) → (intermediate) →[H$_2$, Pd–C or NaBH$_4$]→ Sotalol

Reference(s):
Uloth, R.H. et al.: J. Med. Chem. (JMCMAR) **9**, 88 (1966).

Formulation(s): amp. 20 mg/2 ml, 40 mg/4 ml; tabl. 40 mg, 80 mg, 160 mg, 240 mg

Trade Name(s):

D: CorSotalol (durachemie)
Darob (Knoll)
Gilucor (Solvay
Arzneimittel)
Sotalex (Bristol-Myers
Squibb)
Sotaziden (Bristol)-comb.
Tachytalol (ASTA Medica
AWD)

F: various generics
Sotalex (Bristol-Myers
Squibb)
GB: Beta-Cardone (Evans)
Sotacor (Bristol-Myers
Squibb)
Sotazide (Bristol-Myers)-
comb.; wfm

Tolerzide (Bristol-Myers)-
comb.; wfm
I: Betades (Farmades)
Sotalex (Bristol-Myers
Squibb)
USA: Betapace (Berlex; as
hydrochloride)

Sparfloxacin

(AT-4140; Ci-978; CP 103826; PD-131501; RP-64206)

ATC: J01MA09
Use: antibacterial

RN: 110871-86-8 MF: $C_{19}H_{22}F_2N_4O_3$ MW: 392.41
LD$_{50}$: >5 g/kg (R, p. o.); >2 g/kg (R, s. c.);
>2 g/kg (M, p. o.); >2 g/kg (M, s. c.);
> 600 mg/kg (dog, p. o.)
CN: *cis*-5-Amino-1-cyclopropyl-7-(3,5-dimethyl-1-piperazinyl)-6,8-difluoro-1,4-dihydro-4-oxo-3-
quinolinecarboxylic acid

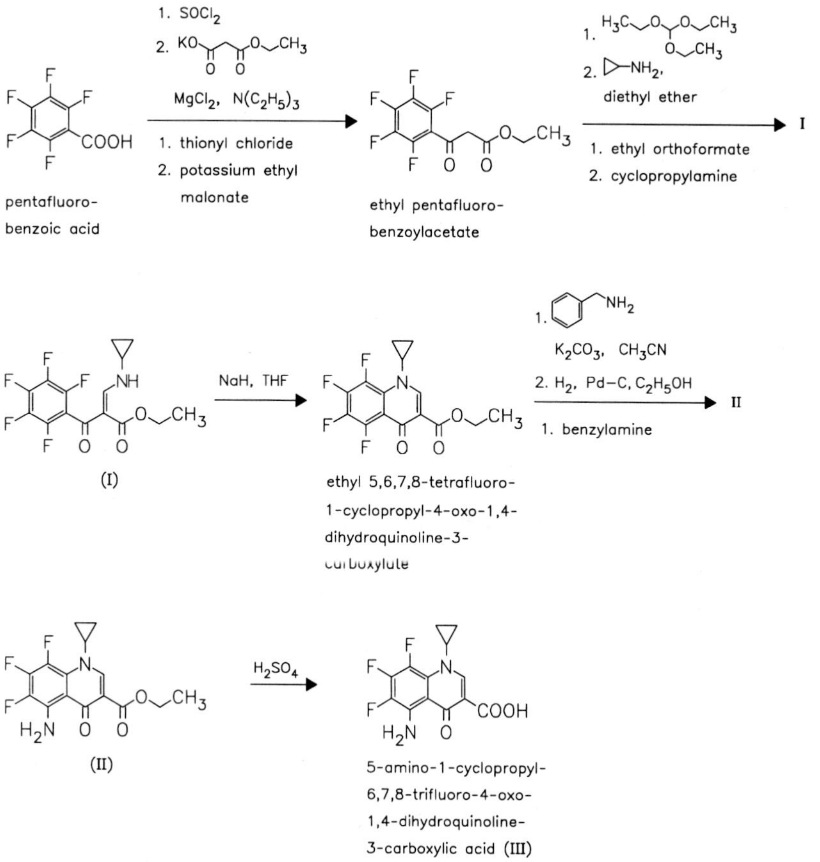

pentafluoro-
benzoic acid

ethyl pentafluoro-
benzoylacetate

(I)

ethyl 5,6,7,8-tetrafluoro-
1-cyclopropyl-4-oxo-1,4-
dihydroquinoline-3-
carboxylate

(II)

5-amino-1-cyclopropyl-
6,7,8-trifluoro-4-oxo-
1,4-dihydroquinoline-
3-carboxylic acid (III)

III + cis-2,6-dimethyl-piperazine → (pyridine, 110°C) → Sparfloxacin

Reference(s):
Miyamoto, T. et al.: J. Med. Chem. (JMCMAR) **33**, 1645-1656 (1990).
EP 221 463 (Dainippon; appl. 23.10.1986; J-prior. 29.10.1985).

synthesis of ethyl pentafluorobenzoylacetate:
Clay, R.J.; Collom, T.A.; Karride, G.L.; Wemple, J.: Synthesis (SYNTBF) **3**, 290 (1993)

Formulation(s):   f. c. tabl. 200 mg; tabl. 100 mg, 150 mg

Trade Name(s):
D: Zagam (Rhône-Poulenc   J: Spara (Dainippon)   USA: Zagam (Rhône-Poulenc
      Rorer)   Zagam (Dainippon)   Rorer)
F: Zagam (Specia)

Spectinomycin
(Actinospectacin)

ATC: J01XX04
Use: antibiotic

RN: 1695-77-8   MF: $C_{14}H_{24}N_2O_7$ MW: 332.35   EINECS: 216-911-3
LD$_{50}$: 2 g/kg (M, i.v.);
         >5 g/kg (R, p.o.)
CN: [2R-(2α,4aβ,5aβ,6β,7β,8β,9α,9aα,10aβ)]-decahydro-4a,7,9-trihydroxy-2-methyl-6,8-bis(methylamino)-
       4H-pyrano[2,3-b][1,4]benzodioxin-4-one

dihydrochloride pentahydrate
RN: 22189-32-8   MF: $C_{14}H_{24}N_2O_7 \cdot 2HCl \cdot 5H_2O$ MW: 495.35
LD$_{50}$: >10 mg/kg (M, p.o.);
         >5 g/kg (R, p.o.)

Spectinomycin

From culture of *Streptomyces spectabilis.*

Reference(s):
US 3 206 360 (Upjohn; 14.9.1965; prior. 18.6.1962).
US 3 234 092 (Upjohn; 8.2.1966; prior. 20.10.1959).
US 3 272 706 (Upjohn; 13.9.1966; prior. 2.8.1961).
US 3 819 485 (Abbott; 25.6.1974; appl. 3.7.1972).

Formulation(s):   vial 3 g (as dihydrochloride pentahydrate)

Trade Name(s):
D: Stanilo (Pharmacia &   GB: Trobicin (Pharmacia &   J: Trobicin (Nihon Upjohn)
       Upjohn)   Upjohn)   USA: Trobicin (Upjohn); wfm
F: Trobicine (Pharmacia &   I: Trobicin (Pharmacia &
       Upjohn)   Upjohn)

Spiperone

ATC: N05C
Use: neuroleptic

RN: 749-02-0   MF: $C_{23}H_{26}FN_3O_2$ MW: 395.48   EINECS: 212-024-0
LD$_{50}$:   25.5 mg/kg (M, i.v.); 600 mg/kg (M, p.o.);
         14 mg/kg (R, i.v.); >1 g/kg (R, p.o.);
         >20 mg/kg (dog, i.v.); >100 mg/kg (dog, p.o.)
CN: 8-[4-(4-fluorophenyl)-4-oxobutyl]-1-phenyl-1,3,8-triazaspiro[4.5]decan-4-one

4-chloro-4'-fluoro-
butyrophenone

(cf. haloperidol synthesis)

4-oxo-1-phenyl-
1,3,8-triazaspiro-
[4.5]decane
(cf. fluspirilene
synthesis)

Spiperone

Reference(s):
US 3 155 669 (Janssen; 3.11.1964; appl. 22.6.1962).
US 3 155 670 (Janssen; 3.11.1964; appl. 22.6.1962).
US 3 161 644 (Janssen; 15.12.1964; appl. 22.6.1962).

Formulation(s):   tabl. 0.25 mg; vial 3 mg

Trade Name(s):
J: Spiropitan (Eisai)

Spiramycin

ATC: J01FA02
Use: antibiotic

RN: 8025-81-8   MF: unspecified   MW: unspecified   EINECS: 232-429-6
LD$_{50}$:   130 mg/kg (M, i.v.); 2900 mg/kg (M, p.o.);
         170 mg/kg (R, i.v.); 3550 mg/kg (R, p.o.);
         5200 mg/kg (dog, p.o.)
CN: spiramycin

Spiramycin

Spiramycin I   R: —H

Spiramycin II   R: (acetyl group) CH₃

Spiramycin III   R: (propionyl group) CH₃

From culture of *Streptomyces ambofaciens*.

Reference(s):
US 2 943 023 (Rhône-Poulenc; 28.6.1960; F-prior. 30.5.1956).
US 2 978 380 (Rhône-Poulenc; 4.4.1961; F-prior. 30.11.1955).
US 3 000 785 (Rhône-Poulenc; 19.9.1961; F-prior. 31.7.1953).
US 3 011 947 (Rhône-Poulenc; 5.12.1961; F-prior. 30.11.1955).
Pinnert-Sindico, S. et al.: Antibiot. Annu. (ABANAE) **1954-1955**, 724.

Formulation(s):   f. c. tabl. 187.5 mg, 250 mg, 375 mg, 500 mg

Trade Name(s):
D: Rovamycine (Rhône-
       Poulenc Rorer)
       Selectomycin (Grünenthal)
F: Rodogyl (Specia)-comb.

       Rovamycine (Specia)
GB: Rovamycin (May &
       Baker); wfm

I: Rovamicina (Rhône-
       Poulenc Rorer)

Spirapril
(Sch-33844)

ATC: C09AA11
Use: antihypertensive (ACE inhibitor)

RN: 83647-97-6   MF: $C_{22}H_{30}N_2O_5S_2$ MW: 466.62
LD₅₀: >2500 mg/kg (M, p.o.);
        >2500 mg/kg (R, p.o.)
CN: [8S-[7[R*(R*)],8R*]]-7-[2-[[1-(ethoxycarbonyl)-3-phenylpropyl]amino]-1-oxopropyl]-1,4-dithia-7-azaspiro[4.4]nonane-8-carboxylic acid

monohydrochloride
RN: 94841-17-5   MF: $C_{22}H_{30}N_2O_5S_2 \cdot HCl$ MW: 503.08
maleate (2:1)
RN: 94799-76-5   MF: $C_{22}H_{30}N_2O_5S_2 \cdot 1/2C_4H_4O_4$ MW: 1049.32

N-benzyloxycarbonyl-
4-hydroxy-L-proline

N-benzyloxycarbonyl-
4-oxo-L-proline

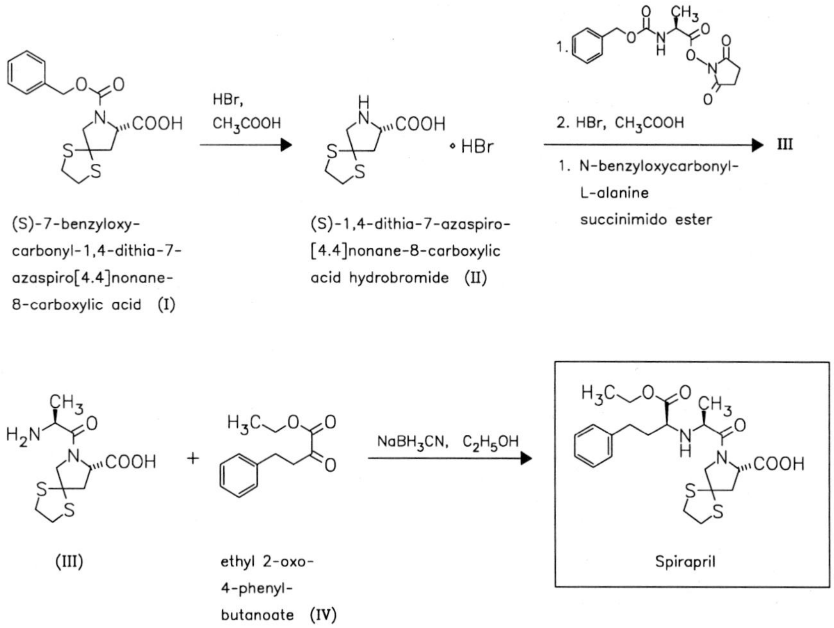

(S)-7-benzyloxy-
carbonyl-1,4-dithia-7-
azaspiro[4.4]nonane-
8-carboxylic acid (I)

(S)-1,4-dithia-7-azaspiro-
[4.4]nonane-8-carboxylic
acid hydrobromide (II)

1. N-benzyloxycarbonyl-
L-alanine
succinimido ester

2. HBr, CH₃COOH

1. N-benzyloxycarbonyl-
L-alanine
succinimido ester

(III)

ethyl 2-oxo-
4-phenyl-
butanoate (IV)

Spirapril

b

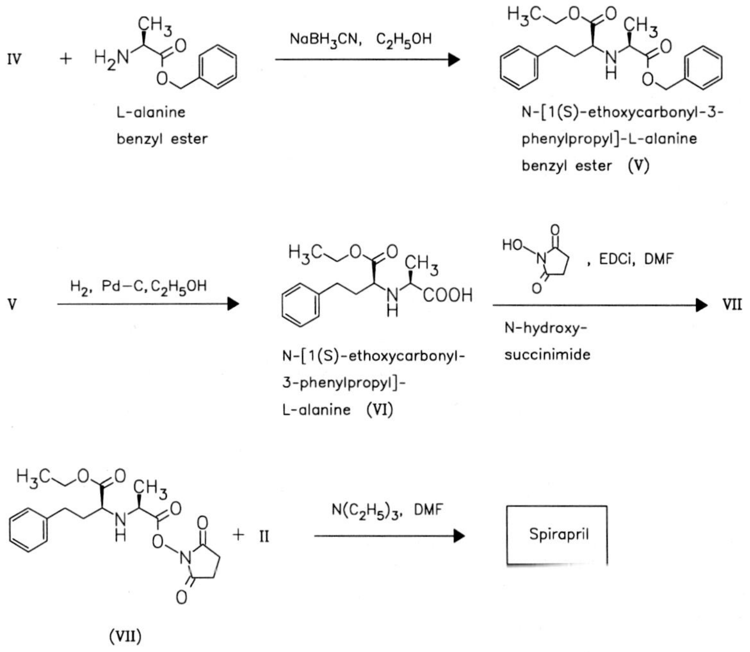

IV + H₂N ... L-alanine
benzyl ester

NaBH₃CN, C₂H₅OH

N-[1(S)-ethoxycarbonyl-3-
phenylpropyl]-L-alanine
benzyl ester (V)

V → H₂, Pd–C, C₂H₅OH

N-[1(S)-ethoxycarbonyl-
3-phenylpropyl]-
L-alanine (VI)

HO-N-succinimide , EDCi, DMF

N-hydroxy-
succinimide

VII

(VII) + II → N(C₂H₅)₃, DMF → Spirapril

c

VI + benzothiazolyl-S-S-benzothiazolyl → N(C₂H₅)₃, (CH₃CH₂O)₃P, CH₂Cl₂, 0 °C

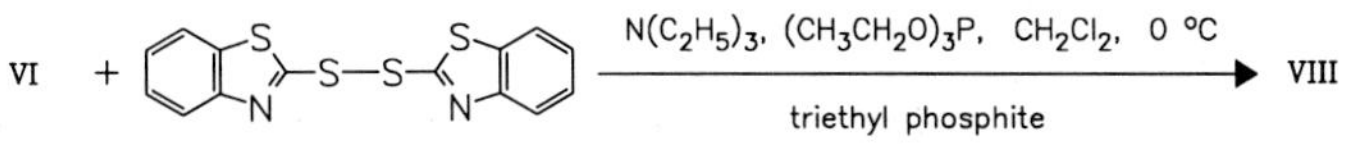

triethyl phosphite

VIII

N-[1(S)-ethoxycarbonyl-3-
phenylpropyl]-L-alanine
benzothiazol-2-yl thioester (VIII)

Spirapril hydrochloride

(d)

II   + H₃C—OH   methanol

methyl (S)-1,4-dithia-
7-azaspiro[4.4]nonane-
8-carboxylate
hydrochloride (IX)

IX   + VI

1. diphenylphosphoryl azide, DMF
2. NaOH, C₂H₅OH

Spirapril

Reference(s):
a,b US 4 470 972 (Schering Corp.; appl. 6.12.1982; USA-prior. 23.10.1980).
c   US 4 847 384 (Sandoz Pharm.; appl. 12.3.1987; USA-prior. 12.3.1987).
d   US 4 462 943 (Squibb & Sons; appl. 28.9.1981; USA-prior. 24.11.1980).

topical composition for reducing intraocular pressure:
EP 114 333 (Schering Corp.; appl. 19.12.1983; USA-prior. 27.12.1982, 23.7.1986).
WO 8 702 585 (Schering Corp.; appl. 31.10.1986; USA-prior. 1.11.1985).

combinations:
EP 254 032 (Schering Corp.; appl. 17.6.1987; USA-prior. 20.6.1986, 27.3.1987, 11.5.1988).
DE 3 736 505 (Sandoz; appl. 28.10.1987; GB-prior. 3.11.1986, 8.6.1987).
DE 4 020 133 (Sandoz; appl. 25.6.1990; GB-prior. 4.7.1989).

formulations:
EP 468 929 (Sandoz; appl. 23.7.1991; USA-prior. 25.7.1990).
US 5 403 593 (Sandoz; appl. 4.3.1991; USA-prior. 4.3.1991).
US 5 178 867 (Alza Corp.; appl. 19.8.1991; USA-prior. 19.8.1991).
Patchett, A.A.; Witkop, B.: J. Am. Chem. Soc. (JACSAT) **79**, 185 (1957).

alternative oxidation reagents:
Blanco, M.J. et al.: Tetrahedron Lett. (TELEAY) **35** (45), 8493-8496 (1994).
Dornoy, J.R. et al.: Synthesis (SYNTBF) **1986**, 81.
Barraclough, P. et al.: Tetrahedron (TETRAB) **51** (14), 4195-4212 (1995).

Formulation(s):   tabl. 6 mg (as hydrochloride)

Trade Name(s):
D: Quadropril (ASTA Medica   I: Setrilan (Essex Italia)
       AWD; as hydrochloride)

Spironolactone

ATC: C03DA01
Use: diuretic (aldosterone antagonist)

RN: 52-01-7   MF: $C_{24}H_{32}O_4S$ MW: 416.58   EINECS: 200-133-6
LD$_{50}$:   >1 g/kg (M, p.o.);
    >1 g/kg (R, p.o.)
CN: (7α,17α)-7-(acetylthio)-17-hydroxy-3-oxopregn-4-ene-21-carboxylic acid γ-lactone

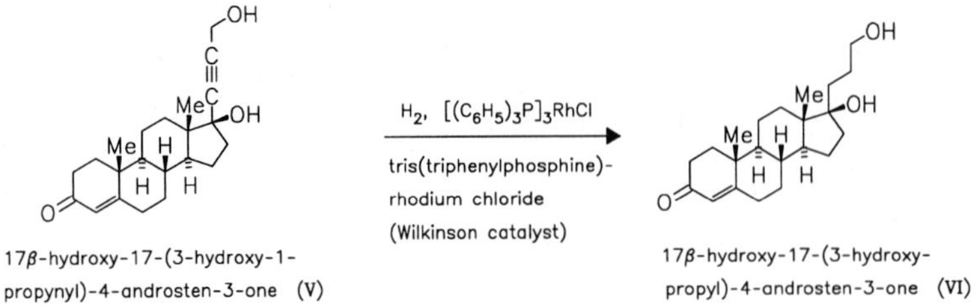

17β-hydroxy-17-(3-hydroxy-1-
propynyl)-4-androsten-3-one (V)

H_2, $[(C_6H_5)_3P]_3RhCl$

tris(triphenylphosphine)-
rhodium chloride
(Wilkinson catalyst)

17β-hydroxy-17-(3-hydroxy-
propyl)-4-androsten-3-one (VI)

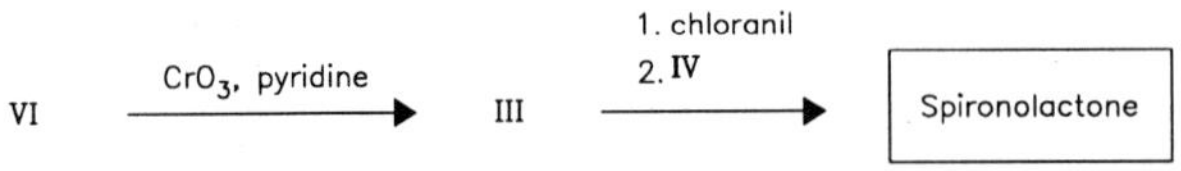

VI →[CrO_3, pyridine] III →[1. chloranil 2. **IV**] Spironolactone

Reference(s):

a US 3 013 012 (Searle; 12.12.1961; appl. 22.12.1960; prior. 12.12.1958).
DE 1 121 610 (Searle; appl. 10.12.1959; USA-prior. 12.12.1958).
Cella, J.A. et al.: J. Org. Chem. (JOCEAH) **24**, 1109 (1959).
Dodson, R.M. et al.: J. Am. Chem. Soc. (JACSAT) **81**, 1224 (1959).
US 3 137 690 (Searle; 16.6.1964; appl. 26.9.1963).
improved methods for precursors:
US 3 270 008 (Searle; 30.8.1966; GB-prior. 1.10.1963).
US 3 738 983 (Searle; 12.6.1973; appl. 6.8.1971).
improved thioacetic acid *addition*:
DOS 2 809 838 (Mitsubishi Chemical; appl. 7.3.1978; J-prior. 17.3.1977).
b DE 2 327 448 (Schering AG; appl. 25.5.1973).

alternative syntheses:
GB 1 444 272 (Hoechst; appl. 27.7.1973; D-prior. 28.7.1972).
GB 1 447 247 (Hoechst; appl. 22.10.1973; D-prior. 20.10.1972).
GB 1 450 425 (Hoechst; appl. 4.10.1973; D-prior. 5.10.1972).
GB 1 450 693 (Hoechst; appl. 4.10.1973; D-prior. 5.10.1972).
DAS 1 250 818 (Searle; appl. 30.9.1964; GB-prior. 1.10.1963).
DOS 2 852 145 (Searle; appl. 1.12.1978; USA-prior. 2.12.1977).
GB 1 548 259 (Ciba-Geigy; appl. 11.6.1976; CH-prior. 13.6.1975).

Formulation(s):   cps. 100 mg; drg. 25 mg, 50 mg; tabl. 25 mg, 50 mg, 100 mg

Trade Name(s):

D: Aldactone (Boehringer
Mannh.)
Aldactone (Boehringer
Mannh.-Searle)
Aldactone-Saltucin
(Boehringer Mannh.)-
comb.
Aquareduct (Azupharma)
Duraspiron (durachemie)
Osyrol (Hoechst)
Risicordin (Heumann)-
comb.
Sali-Aldopur (Hormosan)-
comb.
Spiro comp. forte
(ratiopharm)-comb.
Spironolacton (ratiopharm;
Stada)

Spironothiazid (Henning
Berlin)-comb.
Spirostada (Stada)-comb.
various generics and
combination preparations

F: Aldactazine (Monsanto)-
comb.
Aldactone (Monsanto)
Aldalix (Monsanto)-comb.
Flumach (Mayoly-
Spindler)
Practazin (Cardel)-comb.
Practon 50 (Cardel)
Prinactizide (Dakota)-
comb.
Spiroctan (Boehringer
Mannh.)
Spiroctazine (Boehringer
Mannh.)-comb.

Spironolactone (GNR-
pharma)
Spironone Microfine (EG
Labo)

GB: Aldactide 50 (Searle)-
comb.
Lasilactone (Hoechst)-
comb.
Spiroctan (Boehringer
Mannh.)

I: Aldactone (Lepetit)
Lasitone (Hoechst Marion
Roussel)-comb.
Spiridazide (SIT)-comb.
Spiroderm (Monsanto)
Spirofur (Bruno
Farmaceutici)-comb.
Spirolang (SIT)
Uractone (SPA)

J: Aldactone-A (Dainippon; Searle-Marupi)
     Alexan (Sanwa)
     Almatol (Fujisawa)
     Alpamed (Sawai)

     Apolasnon (Nihon Iyakuhin)
     Dairopeal (Daito Koeki)
     Dira (Kakenyaku Kako)
     Lacalmin (Tatsumi)
     Nefurofan (Maruko)

     Osyrol (Hoechst)
     Suracton (Toho Iyaku)
USA: Aldactazide (Searle)-comb.
     Aldactone (Searle)
     generics and combination preparations

Spizofurone
(AG-629)

ATC: A02B
Use: ulcer therapeutic

RN: 72492-12-7   MF: $C_{12}H_{10}O_3$ MW: 202.21
LD$_{50}$:   1740 mg/kg (M, p.o.);
        5440 mg/kg (R, p.o.)
CN: 5-acetylspiro[benzofuran-2(3H),1'-cyclopropan]-3-one

methyl 5-acetyl-salicylate

α-bromo-γ-butyrolactone

α-[(2-carboxy-4-acetylphenyl)oxy]-γ-butyrolactone   (I)

I → (CH$_3$CO)$_2$O acetic anhydride → 155°C, DMSO dimethyl sulfoxide → Spizofurone

Reference(s):
US 4 284 644 (Takeda; 18.8.1981; J-prior. 6.11.1978).
EP 3 084 (Takeda; appl. 27.12.1978; J-prior. 27.12.1977, 19.6.1978, 6.11.1978).
DE 2 861 651 (Takeda; 25.7.1979; J. prior. 27.12.1977, 19.6.1978, 6.11.1978).
Kawada, M. et al.: Chem. Pharm. Bull. (CPBTAL) **32**, 3532 (1984).

one step synthesis:
Watanabe, M. et al.: Chem. Pharm. Bull. (CPBTAL) **32**, 3373 (1984).

Formulation(s):   tabl. 80 mg

Trade Name(s):
J: Maon (Takeda; 1987)

Stallimycin
(Distamycin A)

ATC: D06BB
Use: antibiotic, antiviral

RN: 636-47-5   MF: $C_{22}H_{27}N_9O_4$ MW: 481.52
LD$_{50}$:   75 mg/kg (M, i.v.)
CN: N-[5-[[(3-amino-3-iminopropyl)amino]carbonyl]-1-methyl-1H-pyrrol-3-yl]-4-[[[4-(formylamino)-1-methyl-1H-pyrrol-2-yl]carbonyl]amino]-1-methyl-1H-pyrrole-2-carboxamide

monohydrochloride
RN: 6576-51-8   MF: $C_{22}H_{27}N_9O_4 \cdot HCl$ MW: 517.98   EINECS: 229-505-6
LD_{50}: 75 mg/kg (M, i.v.)

(a)   isolation from fermentation solutions of Streptomyces distallicus

(b)

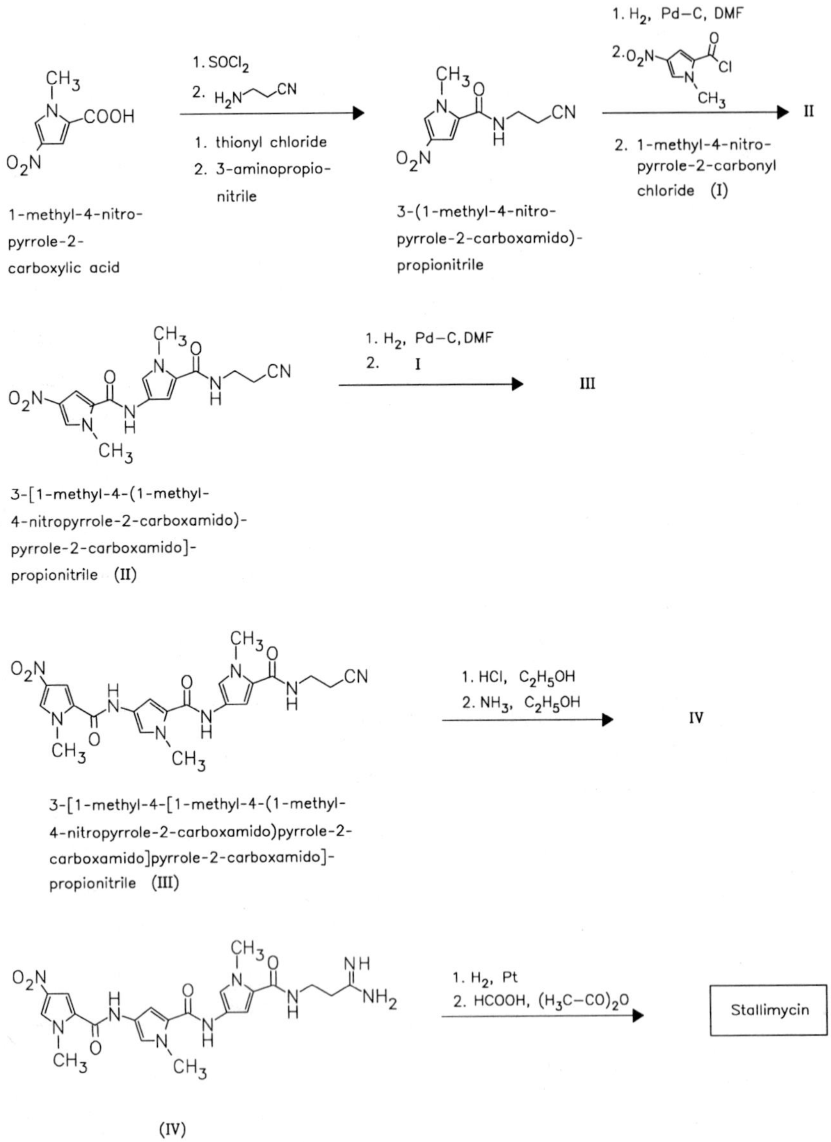

1. SOCl₂
2. H₂N—CN

1. thionyl chloride
2. 3-aminopropio-
   nitrile

1. H₂, Pd—C, DMF
2. O₂N—⎓⎓Cl
   (I)
2. 1-methyl-4-nitro-
   pyrrole-2-carbonyl
   chloride (I)

1-methyl-4-nitro-
pyrrole-2-
carboxylic acid

3-(1-methyl-4-nitro-
pyrrole-2-carboxamido)-
propionitrile

II

1. H₂, Pd—C, DMF
2.   I

III

3-[1-methyl-4-(1-methyl-
4-nitropyrrole-2-carboxamido)-
pyrrole-2-carboxamido]-
propionitrile (II)

1. HCl, C₂H₅OH
2. NH₃, C₂H₅OH

IV

3-[1-methyl-4-[1-methyl-4-(1-methyl-
4-nitropyrrole-2-carboxamido)pyrrole-2-
carboxamido]pyrrole-2-carboxamido]-
propionitrile (III)

1. H₂, Pt
2. HCOOH, (H₃C—CO)₂O

Stallimycin

(IV)

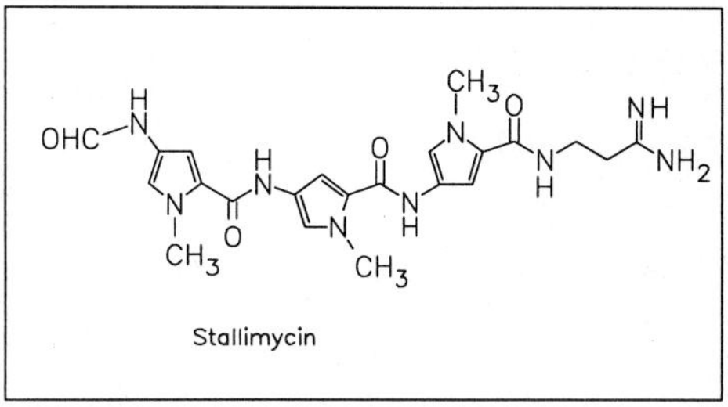
Stallimycin

Reference(s):

a US 3 190 801 (Farmitalia; 22.6.1965; I-prior. 12.12.1956).
Arcamone, F. et al.: Gazz. Chim. Ital. (GCITA9) **97**, 1097 (1967).

b DE 1 470 284 (Farmitalia; appl. 22.7.1964; I-prior. 26.7.1963).
US 3 420 844 (Farmitalia; 7.1.1969; I-prior. 26.7.1963).
Arcamone, F. et al.: Nature (London) (NATUAS) **203**, 1064 (1964).

starting material:
Weiss, M.J. et al.: J. Am. Chem. Soc. (JACSAT) **79**, 1266 (1957).

Trade Name(s):
I: Herperal (Carlo Erba); wfm

Stanozolol
(Stanazol)

ATC: A14AA02
Use: anabolic steroid

RN: 10418-03-8 MF: $C_{21}H_{32}N_2O$ MW: 328.50 EINECS: 233-894-8
CN: (5α,17β)-17-methyl-2'*H*-androst-2-eno[3,2-*c*]pyrazol-17-ol

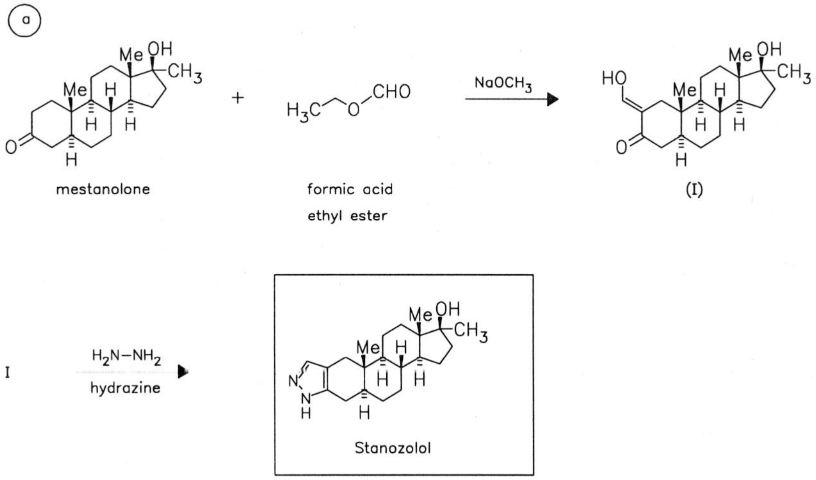
a
NaOCH3
mestanolone
formic acid ethyl ester
(I)
I
H2N–NH2
hydrazine
Stanozolol

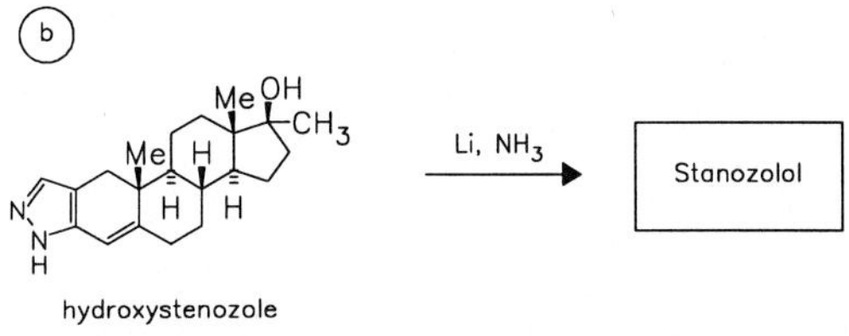
b
Li, NH3
Stanozolol
hydroxystenozole

Reference(s):

a   Clinton, R.O. et al.: J. Am. Chem. Soc. (JACSAT) **81**, 1513 (1959).
    Clinton, R.O. et al.: J. Am. Chem. Soc. (JACSAT) **83**, 1478 (1961).
b   US 3 030 358 (Sterling Drug; 17.4.1962; appl. 11.5.1961; prior. 16.2.1959).

starting material:
Clinton, R.O.: J. Am. Chem. Soc. (JACSAT) **83**, 1478 (1961).

Formulation(s):   tabl. 2 mg, 5 mg, 15 mg

Trade Name(s):

D:	Stromba (Winthrop); wfm			Winstrol (Zambon); wfm
	Strombaject (Winthrop);		Strombaject (Winthrop)-	J: Winstrol (Yamanouchi)
	wfm		comb.; wfm	USA: Winstrol (Sanofi Winthrop)
F:	Stromba (Winthrop); wfm	GB:	Stromba (Sanofi Winthrop)	
		I:	Anasyth (Causyth); wfm	

Stavudine

(BMY-27857; dde Thd; DTH; D4T)

ATC: J05AF04
Use: anti-AIDS therapeutic

RN: 3056-17-5   MF: $C_{10}H_{12}N_2O_4$ MW: 224.22
CN: 2',3'-didehydro-3'-deoxythymidine

Intermediates II and III:

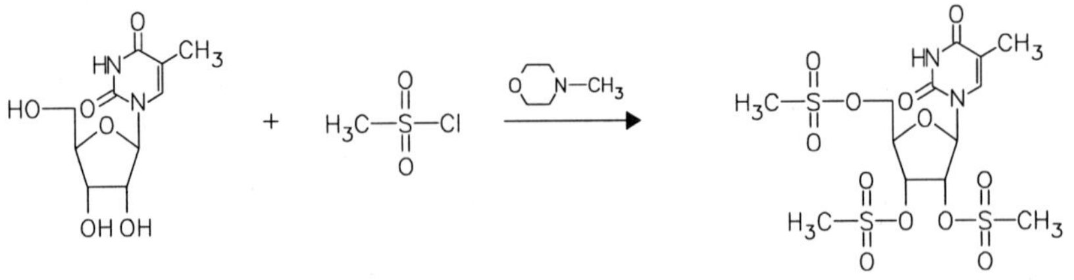

5-methyluridine   (I)   2',3',5'-tris(methane-
                                                  sulfonyl)-5-methyl-
                                                  uridine (II)

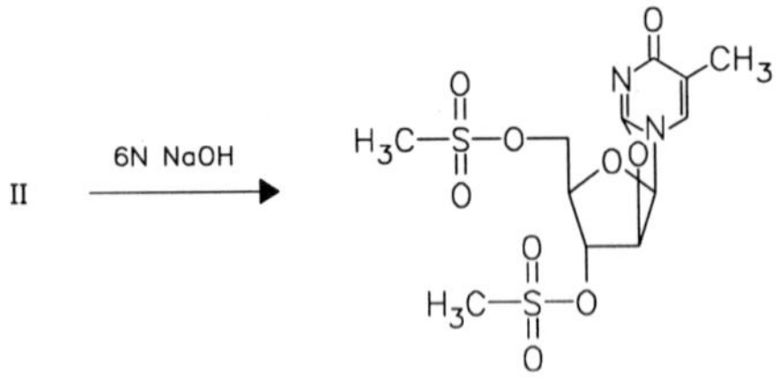

3',5'-bis(methane-
sulfonyl)-2,2'-anhydro-
5-methyluridine (III)

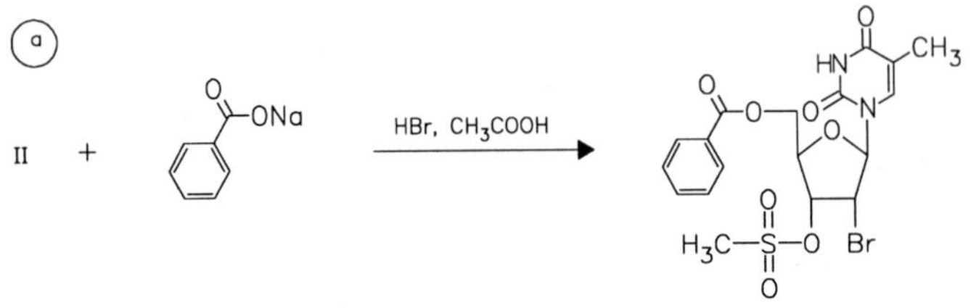

sodium
benzoate (IV)   (V)

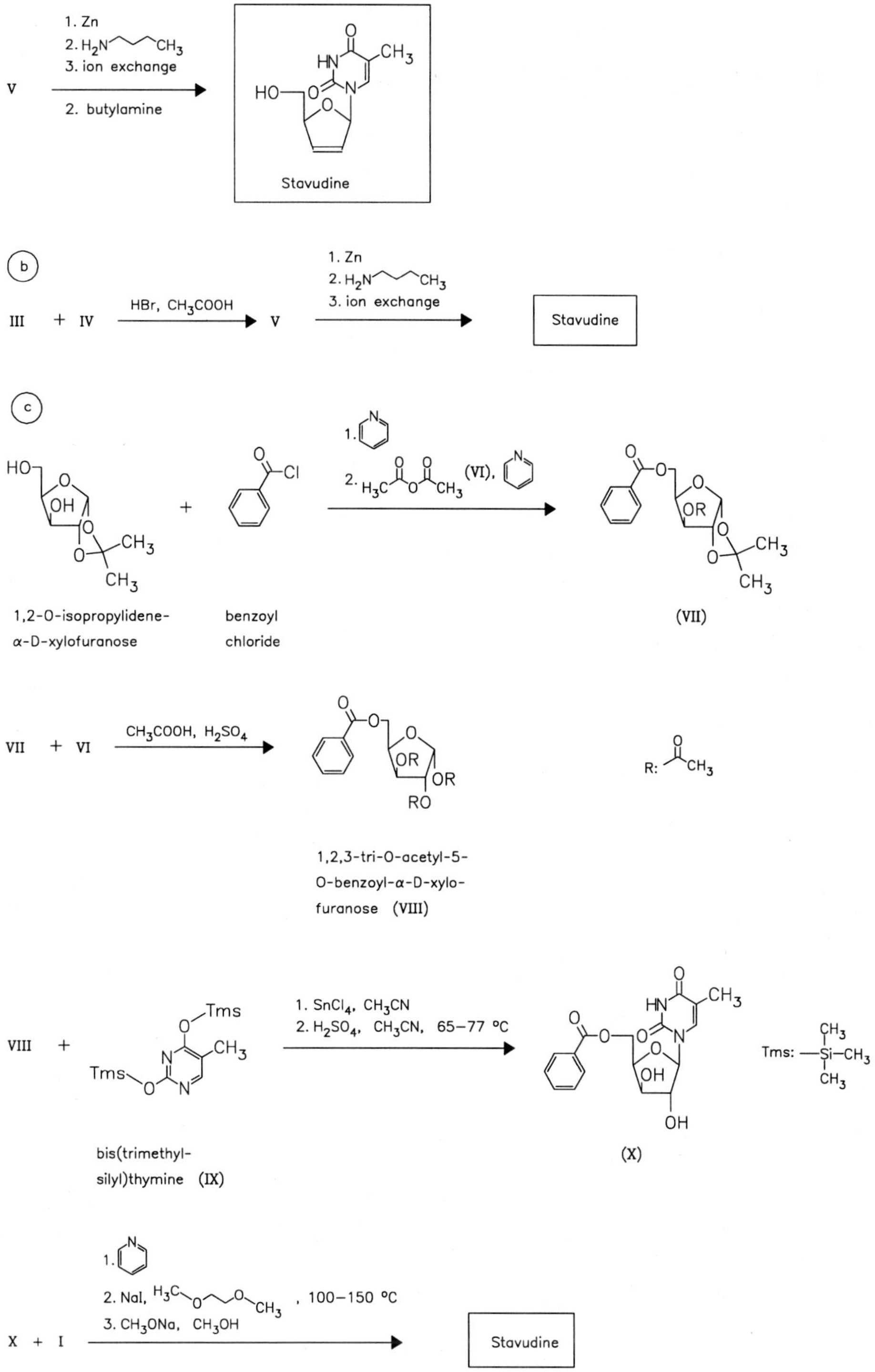

1. Zn
2. H_2N ~~~ CH_3
3. ion exchange

V ————————————→

2. butylamine

Stavudine

b

III + IV $\xrightarrow{\text{HBr, CH}_3\text{COOH}}$ V $\xrightarrow[\substack{\text{1. Zn} \\ \text{2. } H_2N\text{~}CH_3 \\ \text{3. ion exchange}}]{}$ Stavudine

c

HO——[O, OH, O—C(CH_3)CH_3]   +   benzoyl chloride [O=C—Cl, benzene]

$\xrightarrow[\substack{\text{2. } H_3C\text{-CO-O-CO-}CH_3 \text{ (VI),} \\ \text{pyridine}}]{\text{1. pyridine}}$

(VII)

1,2-O-isopropylidene-
α-D-xylofuranose

benzoyl
chloride

VII + VI $\xrightarrow{\text{CH}_3\text{COOH, H}_2\text{SO}_4}$

1,2,3-tri-O-acetyl-5-
O-benzoyl-α-D-xylo-
furanose (VIII)

R: —CO—CH_3

VIII + bis(trimethyl-silyl)thymine (IX) $\xrightarrow[\substack{\text{2. } H_2SO_4, \text{ CH}_3\text{CN, } 65-77 \text{ °C}}]{\text{1. SnCl}_4, \text{ CH}_3\text{CN}}$

(X)

Tms: —Si(CH_3)_3

X + I $\xrightarrow[\substack{\text{2. NaI, } H_3C\text{-O-}\sim\sim\text{-O-}CH_3 \text{ , } 100-150 \text{ °C} \\ \text{3. CH}_3\text{ONa, CH}_3\text{OH}}]{\text{1. pyridine}}$ Stavudine

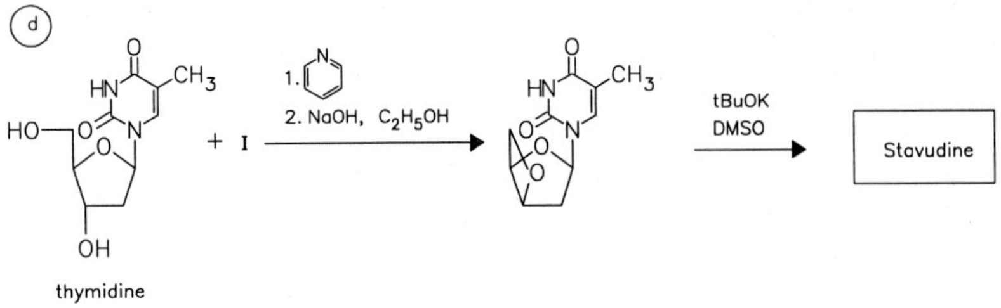

(d)

thymidine　+ I

1. [pyridine]
2. NaOH, C_2H_5OH

$\xrightarrow{}$

$\xrightarrow[\text{DMSO}]{\text{tBuOK}}$ Stavudine

(e)

thymine　+　2,3,5-tri-O-benzoyl-α-D-ribofuranosyl acetate

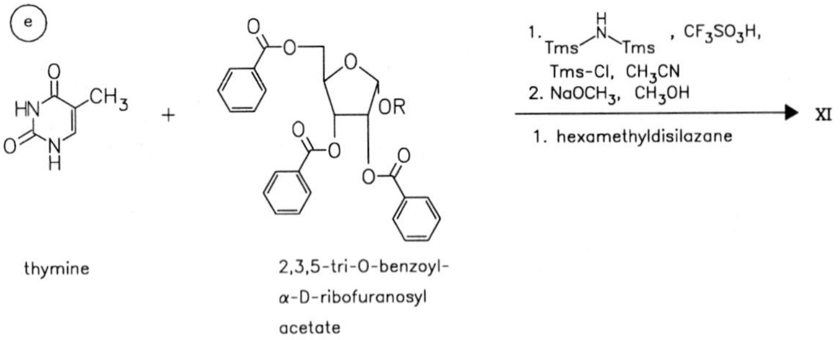

1. Tms–N(H)–Tms , CF_3SO_3H, Tms-Cl, CH_3CN
2. $NaOCH_3$, CH_3OH
1. hexamethyldisilazane

$\xrightarrow{}$ XI

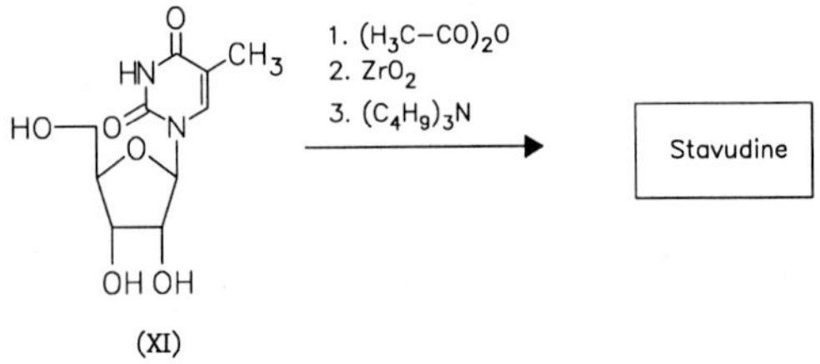

(XI)

1. $(H_3C-CO)_2O$
2. ZrO_2
3. $(C_4H_9)_3N$

$\xrightarrow{}$ Stavudine

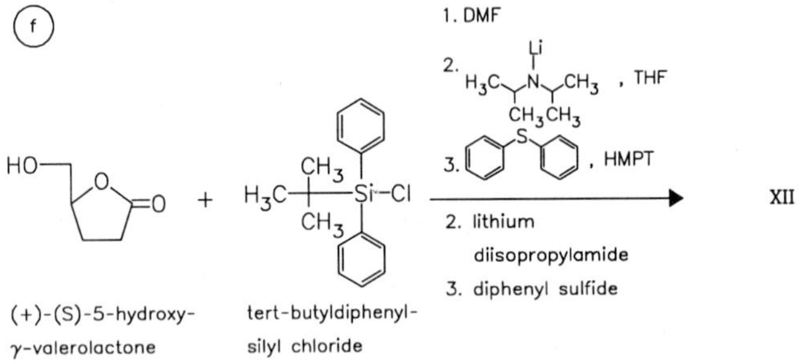

(f)

(+)-(S)-5-hydroxy-γ-valerolactone　+　tert-butyldiphenyl-silyl chloride

1. DMF
2. H_3C–N(Li)–CH_3 with CH_3CH_3 , THF
3. diphenyl sulfide , HMPT
2. lithium diisopropylamide
3. diphenyl sulfide

$\xrightarrow{}$ XII

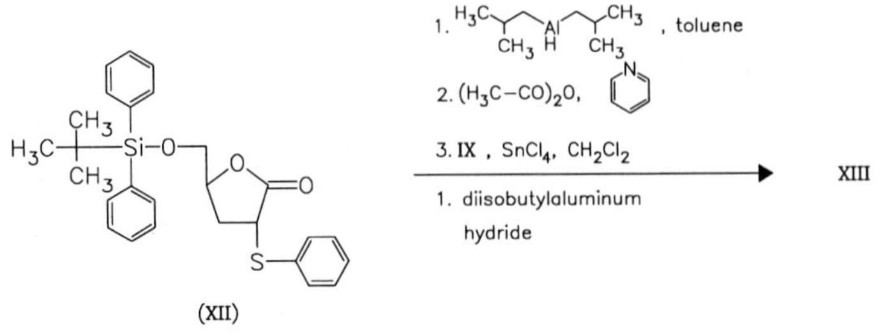

(XII)

1. H_3C–Al–CH_3 , toluene
2. $(H_3C-CO)_2O$, [pyridine]
3. IX , $SnCl_4$, CH_2Cl_2
1. diisobutylaluminum hydride

$\xrightarrow{}$ XIII

(XIII)

Reference(s):
synthesis:
EP 334 368 (Bristol-Myers Squibb; appl. 27.9.1989; USA-prior. 24.3.1988).
EP 653 436 (Bristol-Myers Squibb; appl. 17.5.1995; USA-prior. 15.11.1993, 3.11.1994, 23.9.1994).
RU 2 047 619 (Institut Organicheskoj Khimii Ufimskogo Nauchnogo Tsentra Ran.; appl. 10.11.1995; RU-prior. 14.4.1993).
JP 07 278 178 (Nippon Tobacco Sangyo; appl. 24.1.1995; J-prior. 1.4.1994).
EP 501 511 (Bristol-Myers Squibb; appl. 2.9.1992; USA-prior. 2.9.1992).
JP 04 054 193 (Nippon Tobacco Sangyo; appl. 20.2.1992; J-prior. 25.5.1990).
WO 9 202 516 (Japan Tobacco Inc.; appl. 26.6.1991; J-prior. 27.7.1990, 30.11.1990).
WO 9 209 599 (Yamasa Shoyu; appl. 11.6.1992; J-prior. 30.11.1990).
EP 519 464 (Ajinomoto Co.; appl. 23.12.1992; J-prior. 19.6.1991).
JP 04 226 976 (Japan Tobacco Inc.; appl. 17.8.1992; J-prior. 5.6.1990).
US 5 175 267 (University of Georgia Res. Found.; appl. 29.12.1992; USA-prior. 2.3.1990).
Horwitz, J.P. et al.: J. Org. Chem. (JOCEAH) 31, 205 (1966).
Herdewijn, P. et al.: J. Med. Chem. (JMCMAR) 30 (8), 1270 (1987).
Lin, T.-S. et al.: J. Med. Chem. (JMCMAR) 30 (2), 440 (1987).

pharmaceutical compositions:
EP 273 277 (Yale University; appl. 6.7.1988; USA-prior. 17.12.1986).
JP 63 107 924 (Yamasa Shoyu Co.; appl. 12.5.1988; J-prior. 25.10.1986).
JP 04 038 727 (Yamasa Shoyu Co.; appl. 25.6.1992; J-prior. 25.10.1986).

in combination with
porphyrin and phthalocyanine:
WO 8 911 277 (Georgia State Univ. Found.; appl. 30.11.1989; USA-prior. 23.5.1988).

nucleoside derivatives:
WO 9 011 081 (Oncogene; appl. 16.3.1990; USA-prior. 22.3.1989, 17.3.1989).
EP 631 783 (Mitsubishi Kasei; appl. 31.5.1994; J-prior. 3.6.1993).

quinoxalines:
EP 657 166 (Hoechst AG; appl. 5.12.1992; D-prior. 9.12.1993).

aminopyridones:
EP 484 071 (Merck & Co.; appl. 6.5.1992; USA-prior. 1.11.1990, 25.1.1991).

Formulation(s):   cps. 15 mg, 20 mg, 30 mg 40 mg; powder 200 mg (oral sol.)

Trade Name(s):
D:	Zerit (Bristol-Myers Squibb)	GB:	Zerit (Bristol-Myers Squibb)	USA:	Zerit (Bristol-Myers Squibb)
F:	Zerit (Bristol-Myers Squibb)	J:	Zerit (Green Cross)		

Stepronin
(Prostenoglycine; Tenoglicine; Tiofacic)

ATC: R05CB11
Use: mucolytic, hepatic protectant

RN: 72324-18-6　MF: $C_{10}H_{11}NO_4S_2$　MW: 273.33　EINECS: 276-587-4
LD$_{50}$: >1250 mg/kg (M, i.v.); 3336 mg/kg (M, p.o.);
　　　1801 mg/kg (R, i.m.); >1250 mg/kg (R, i.v.); >2500 mg/kg (R, p.o.)
CN: N-[1-oxo-2-[(2-thienylcarbonyl)thio]propyl]glycine

sodium salt
RN: 78126-10-0　MF: $C_{10}H_{10}NNaO_4S_2$　MW: 295.32

α-bromopropionyl-glycine + thiobenzoic acid → α-(benzoylthio)-propionylglycine (I)

I $\xrightarrow{NH_3, H_2O}$ α-mercaptopropionyl-glycine + 2-thenoyl chloride (II) → Stepronin

2-mercapto-propionic acid + II $\xrightarrow{K_2CO_3}$ 2-(2-thenoylthio)-propionic acid $\xrightarrow[\text{2. glycine}]{\text{1. SOCl}_2 \text{ 2. } H_2N-COOH}$ Stepronin

II $\xrightarrow[\text{sodium hydrosulfide}]{NaHS}$ → α-chloropropionyl-glycine → Stepronin

Reference(s):
a　DE 2 913 211 (Mediolanum; appl. 3.4.1979; I-prior. 11.4.1978).
　　US 4 242 354 (Mediolanum; 30.12.1980; appl. 4.4.1979; I-prior. 11.4.1978, 12.2.1979).
b　DOS 3 120 592 (BTB Ind. Chimica; appl. 23.5.1981; I-prior. 3.6.1980).
c　IT 1 193 195 (Mediolanum; appl. 20.7.1979).

synthesis of α-mercaptopropionylglycine:
JP 11 616 (Santen; appl. 1961); C.A. (CHABA8) **61**, 16155 (1962).
US 3 246 025 (Santen; 1965; appl. 1962; J-prior. 1961).

Formulation(s):　cps. 420 mg; gran. 180 mg, 360 mg (as sodium salt); suppos. 180 mg, 360 mg, 720 mg (as sodium salt); vial 335 mg

Streptokinase

ATC: B01AD01
Use: fibrinolytic (plasminogen activator)

RN: 9002-01-1   MF: unspecified   MW: unspecified   EINECS: 232-647-1
LD$_{50}$: 3700 mg/kg (M, i.v.); >10 g/kg (M, p.o.);
       2 g/kg (R, i.v.)
CN: streptokinase (enzyme-activating)

Co-enzyme obtained from cultures of various strains *of Streptococcus haemolyticus* and capable of changing plasminogen into plasmin (complex enzyme mixture of streptokinase, streptodornase and streptolysin "O"). From fermentation liquors of hemolytic streptococci species (*Streptococcus haemolyticus*), e. g. H 46 A.

Reference(s):
US 2 666 729 (Merck & Co.; 1954; appl. 1951).
US 2 701 227 (American Cyanamid; 1955; appl. 1951).
US 3 063 913 (Behringwerke; 13.11.1962; D-prior. 29.12.1959).
US 3 063 914 (Behringwerke; 13.11.1962; D-prior. 22.12.1959).

purification:
US 2 753 291 (American Cyanamid; 1956; appl. 1954).
US 3 016 337 (Ortho Pharmac. Corp.; 9.1.1962; appl. 27.4.1959).
US 3 042 586 (Merck & Co.; 3.7.1962; appl. 29.9.1959).
US 3 107 203 (Merck & Co.; 15.10.1963; appl. 24.11.1961).
US 3 138 542 (Behringwerke; 23.6.1964; D-prior. 31.12.1959).

Formulation(s):   vial 100000 iu, 250000 iu, 600000 iu, 750000 iu, 1500000 iu.

Streptomycin

ATC: A07AA04; J01GA01
Use: antibiotic

RN: 57-92-1   MF: C$_{21}$H$_{39}$N$_7$O$_{12}$ MW: 581.58   EINECS: 200-355-3
LD$_{50}$: 90.2 mg/kg (M, i.v.); 500 mg/kg (M, p.o.);
       175 mg/kg (R, i.v.); 9 g/kg (R, p.o.)
CN: *O*-2-deoxy-2-(methylamino)-α-L-glucopyranosyl(1→2)-*O*-5-deoxy-3-*C*-formyl-α-L-
       lyxofuranosyl(1→4)-*N*,*N*'-bis(aminoiminomethyl)-D-streptamine

sulfate (2:3)
RN: 3810-74-0　MF: $C_{21}H_{39}N_7O_{12} \cdot 3/2H_2SO_4$　MW: 1457.39　EINECS: 223-286-0
LD_{50}: 90.2 mg/kg (M, i.v.); 430 mg/kg (M, p.o.);
　　　430 mg/kg (R, p.o.)

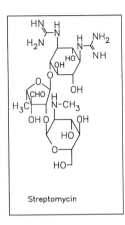

Streptomycin

From fermentation solutions of *Streptomyces griseus*.

Reference(s):
US 2 449 866 (Rutgers Res. Found; 1948; prior. 1945).
Ehrhart, Ruschig **IV**, 317.

purification:
US 2 765 302 (Olin Mathieson; 1956; appl. 1953).
US 2 868 779 (Olin Mathieson; 1959; appl. 1956).

Formulation(s):　amp. 1 g (as sulfate)

Trade Name(s):
D:	Strepto-Fatol (Fatol)	GB:	Orastrep (Dista); wfm	J:	Streptomycin Sulfate
	Streptomycin-Hefa (Hefa		Streptaguaine (Dista); wfm		(Banyu; Dainippon; Kaken;
	Pharma)		Streptotriad (May &		Kyowa; Meiji; Nikken;
	generics		Baker)-comb.; wfm		Sankyo; Sanwa; Taito
F:	Streptomycine Diamant	I:	Streptocol (Molteni)		Pfizer; Takeda; Toyo Jozo)
	(Diamant); wfm		Streptomicina Solfato	USA:	Streptomycin Sulfate
	generics; wfm		(Fisiopharma; ISF)		(Pfizer)

Streptoniazid
(Streptonicozid)

ATC: D08; J04A
Use: tuberculostatic

RN: 4480-58-4　MF: $C_{27}H_{44}N_{10}O_{12}$　MW: 700.71
LD_{50}: 81.9 mg/kg (M, route unreported)
CN: 4-pyridinecarboxylic acid hydrazide, hydrazone with *O*-2-deoxy-2-(methylamino)-α-L-glucopyranosyl-
　　(1→2)-*O*-5-deoxy-3-*C*-formyl-α-L-lyxofuranosyl-1(1→4)-*N*,*N*'-bis(aminoiminomethyl)-D-streptamine

sulfate (2:3)
RN: 5667-71-0　MF: $C_{27}H_{44}N_{10}O_{12} \cdot 3/2H_2SO_4$　MW: 1695.65　EINECS: 227-128-1

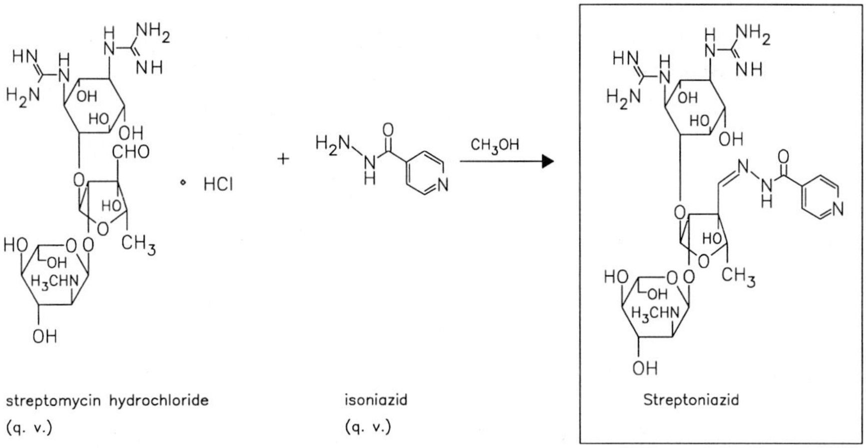

streptomycin hydrochloride
(q. v.)

isoniazid
(q. v.)

Streptoniazid

Reference(s):
Pennington, F.C. et al.: J. Am. Chem. Soc. (JACSAT) **75**, 2261 (1953).
DE 1 069 618 (Pfizer; appl. 1953; USA-prior. 1953, 1952).

use as tuberculostatic:
US 3 035 044 (Olin Mathieson; 15.5.1962; prior. 4.5.1956, 1.3.1952).

alternative synthesis:
FR 1 058 441 (Rhône-Poulenc; appl. 1952).

Trade Name(s):

F:	Streptoniacide "LeBrun" (LeBrun); wfm	I:	Nicostreptil Atral (Mastroeni); wfm	USA:	Streptohydrazid (Pfizer); wfm

Streptozocin

(Streptozotocin)

ATC: L01AD04
Use: antineoplastic

RN: 72521-89-2   MF: $C_8H_{15}N_3O_7$ MW: 265.22
CN: 2-deoxy-2-[[(methylnitrosoamino)carbonyl]amino]-D-glucopyranose

open-chain tautomer
RN: 18883-66-4   MF: $C_8H_{15}N_3O_7$ MW: 265.22   EINECS: 242-646-8
LD_{50}: 275 mg/kg (M, i.v.);
       138 mg/kg (R, i.v.);
       50 mg/kg (dog, i.v.).

From cultures of *Streptomyces achromogenes var. streptozoticus.*

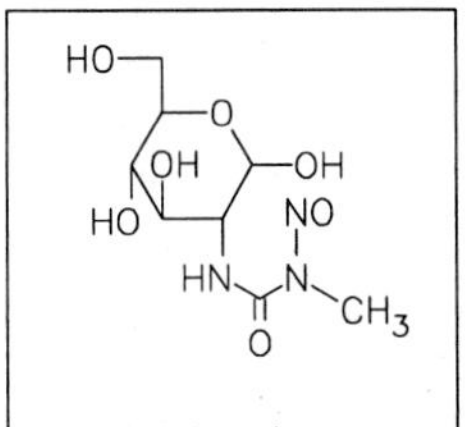

Streptozocin

Reference(s):
Vavra, J.J. et al.: Antibiot. Annu. (ABANAE). **1959-60**, 230.
DE 1 090 823 (Upjohn; appl. 29.7.1960; USA-prior. 1.8.1958).
US 3 027 300 (Upjohn; 27.3.1962; prior. 1.8.1958).

Formulation(s):   vial 1 g

Trade Name(s):
F: Zanosar (Pharmacia &   USA: Zanosar (Pharmacia &
        Upjohn)   Upjohn)

---

g-Strophanthin
(*g*-Strophantoside; Ouabain)

ATC: C01AC01
Use: cardiac glycoside

RN: 630-60-4   MF: $C_{29}H_{44}O_{12}$ MW: 584.66   EINECS: 211-139-3
LD_{50}: 2200 µg/kg (M, i.v.); 5 mg/kg (M, p.o.);
        14 mg/kg (R, i.v.)
CN: (1β,3β,5β,11α)-3-[(6-deoxy-α-L-mannopyranosyl)oxy]-1,5,11,14,19-pentahydroxycard-20(22)-enolide

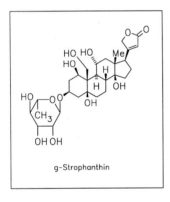

g-Strophanthin

a From *Strophantus gratus*.
b From *Acokanthera ouabaio* Cathel.

Reference(s):
a   Arnaud, A.: C. R. Hebd. Seances Acad. Sci. (COREAF) **106**, 1011 (1888); **107**, 1162 (1888).
        Mannich, C.; Siewert, G.: Ber. Dtsch. Chem. Ges. (BDCGAS) **75**, 737 (1942).
        Reichstein, T. et al.: Helv. Chim. Acta (HCACAV) **50**, 179 (1967).
b   Arnaud, A.: C. R. Hebd. Seances Acad. Sci. (COREAF) **106**, 1011 (1888); **107**, 1162 (1888).

review:
Podolsky, E.: Am. Prof. Pharm. (APPTAZ) **8**, 293 (1942).
Fieser, L.F.; Fieser, M.: Steroide, 845 (Weinheim 1961).
Ullmanns Encykl. Tech. Chem., 4. Aufl., Vol. **12**, 617.

Formulation(s):   cps. 3 mg, 6 mg

Trade Name(s):
D: Strodival (Herbert)   Ouabaïne Aguettant   GB: Oubaine Arnaud (Wilcox);
F: Antally Ouabaïne (Bailly)-   (Aguettant); wfm   wfm
        comb.; wfm   Ouabaïne-Arnaud   J: Uabanin (Takeda)
        Digibaïne (Deglaude)-   (Nativelle); wfm
        comb.; wfm

k-Strophanthin
(*k*-Strophanthin-β + *k*-Strophanthoside)

ATC: C01AC
Use: cardiac glycoside

RN: 11005-63-3   MF: unspecified   MW: unspecified
CN: strophanthin

k-Strophanthin-β

RN: 560-53-2   MF: $C_{36}H_{54}O_{14}$ MW: 710.81   EINECS: 209-210-9
LD_{50}:   1071 µg/kg (M, i.p.); 213 µg/kg (M, s.c.)
CN: (3β,5β)-3-[(2,6-dideoxy-4-*O*-β-D-glucopyranosyl-3-*O*-methyl-β-D-*ribo*-hexopyranosyl)oxy]-5,14-dihydroxy-19-oxocard-20(22)-enolide

k-Strophanthoside

RN: 33279-57-1   MF: $C_{42}H_{64}O_{19}$ MW: 872.96
CN: (3β,5β)-3-[(*O*-β-D-glucopyranosyl-(1→6)-*O*-β-D-glucopyranosyl-(1→4)-2,6-dideoxy-3-*O*-methyl-β-D-*ribo*-hexopyranosyl)oxy]-5,14-dihydroxy-19-oxocard-20(22)-enolide

From *Strophanthus kombé* and other Strophanthus species (preparation of *k*-strophanthin-α, q. v.).

Reference(s):
DRP 721 001 (Sandoz; appl. 1937; CH-prior. 1937).
DRP 737 540 (Sandoz; appl. 1937; CH-prior. 1937).
Ullmanns Encykl. Tech. Chem., 3. Aufl., Vol. **8**, 232.
Ullmanns Encykl. Tech. Chem., 4. Aufl.; Vol. **12**, 617.

Formulation(s):   amp. 0.125 mg, 0.25 mg

Trade Name(s):

| D: | Kombetin (Boehringer Mannh.) | I: | Kombetin (Boehringer Biochemia) | USA: | Pasanol (Tilden Yates)-comb.; wfm |

k-Strophanthin-α
(Cymarin)

ATC: C01AC03
Use: cardiac glycoside

RN: 508-77-0 MF: $C_{30}H_{44}O_9$ MW: 548.67 EINECS: 208-087-9
LD$_{50}$: 2800 µg/kg (M, i.v.);
20 mg/kg (R, i.v.)
CN: (3β,5β)-3-[(2,6-dideoxy-3-*O*-methyl-β-D-*ribo*-hexopyranosyl)oxy]-5,14-dihydroxy-19-oxocard-20(22)-enolide

a From *Strophanthus kombé*.

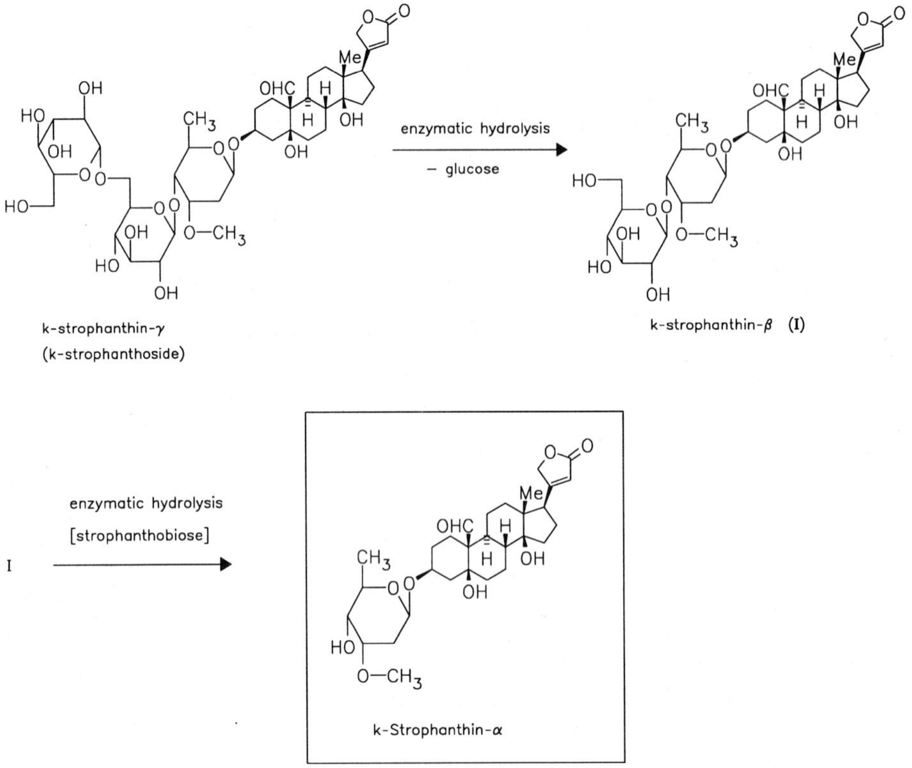

k-strophanthin-γ
(k-strophanthoside)

enzymatic hydrolysis
− glucose

k-strophanthin-β (I)

enzymatic hydrolysis
[strophanthobiose]

I

k-Strophanthin-α

b From *Castilloa elastica* Cerv.
c From *Apocynum cannabium*.

Reference(s):
a Stoll, A. et al.: Helv. Chim. Acta (HCACAV) **20**, 1484 (1937).
   DRP 721 001 (Sandoz; appl. 1937; CH-prior. 1937).
   DRP 737 540 (Sandoz; appl. 1937; CH-prior. 1937).
   Ullmanns Encykl. Tech. Chem., 3. Aufl., Vol. **8**, 232.
   DE 1 920 177 (Gödecke; appl. 21.4.1969).
   DOS 2 050 457 (Gödecke; appl. 14.10.1972).
b GB 972 917 (Wellcome Foundation; appl. 20.4.1961).
c DD 35 688 (W. Grundmann, R. Giessner; appl. 26.3.1964).
   DD 43 401 (W. Grundmann; R. Giessner; appl. 25.1.1965).

alternative syntheses:
The Merck Index, 12th Ed., 1512 (1996).

Formulation(s):   amp. 0.125 mg, 0.25 mg

Trade Name(s):
D: Alvonal MR (Gödecke);   Stabilocard (Gödecke);   Theo-Alvonal (Gödecke);
      wfm   wfm   wfm

Styramate

ATC: M03BA04
Use: muscle relaxant, antispasmodic

RN: 94-35-9   MF: $C_9H_{11}NO_3$ MW: 181.19   EINECS: 202-326-0
LD_{50}:   1240 mg/kg (M, p.o.)
CN: 1-phenyl-1,2-ethanediol 2-carbamate

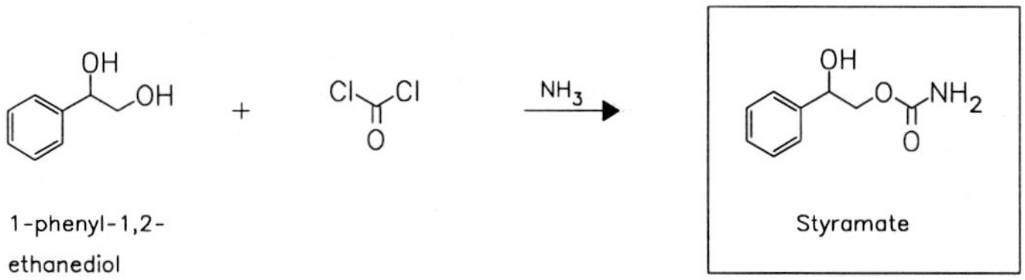

1-phenyl-1,2-
ethanediol

Styramate

Reference(s):
GB 841 626 (Armour; appl. 1956; USA-prior. 1955).

Formulation(s):   tabl. 200 mg

Trade Name(s):
GB: Sinaxar (Armour); wfm   J: Menfula (Taisho)-comb.   Sinaxar (Tokyo Tanabe)

Succinylsulfathiazole

ATC: A07AB04
Use: chemotherapeutic, antibacterial

RN: 116-43-8   MF: $C_{13}H_{13}N_3O_5S_2$ MW: 355.40   EINECS: 204-141-0
LD_{50}:   10 g/kg (M, i.v.)
CN: 4-oxo-4-[[4-[(2-thiazolylamino)sulfonyl]phenyl]amino]butanoic acid

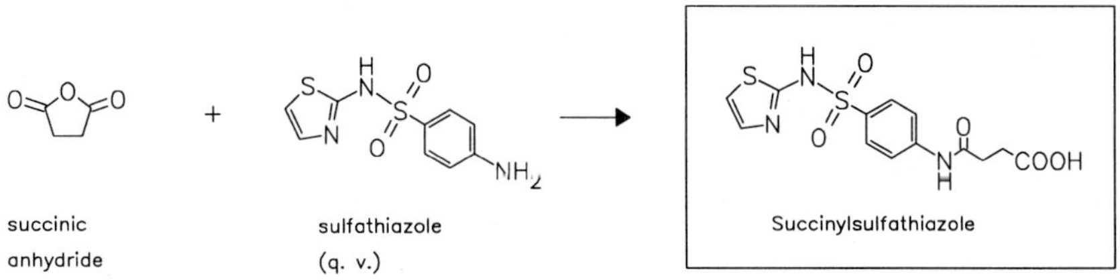

succinic
anhydride

sulfathiazole
(q. v.)

Succinylsulfathiazole

Reference(s):
US 2 324 013 (Sharp & Dohme; 1943; appl. 1941).
US 2 324 014 (Sharp & Dome; 1943; appl. 1941).

Formulation(s):   tabl. 500 mg

Trade Name(s):
F: Thiacyl (Théraplix); wfm   GB: Cremomycin (Merck Sharp   Cremostrep (Merck Sharp
                                         & Dohme)-comb.; wfm   & Dohme)-comb.; wfm

Cremosuxidine (Merck Sharp & Dohme); wfm	I:	Cremosulfa strept. (Angelini)-comb.; wfm
Sulfasuxidine (Merck Sharp & Dohme); wfm		Streptoguanidin (Lisapharma)-comb.; wfm

Sucralfate

ATC: A02BX02
Use: ulcer therapeutic

RN: 54182-58-0   MF: $C_{12}H_{54}Al_{16}O_{75}S_8$ MW: 2086.73   EINECS: 259-018-4
LD$_{50}$:   >8 g/kg (M, p.o.);
    >12 g/kg (R, p.o.)
CN: hexadeca-μ-hydroxytetracosahydroxy[μ$_8$-[[1,3,4,6-tetra-O-sulfo-β-D-fructofuranosyl α-D-glucopyranoside tetrakis(sulfato-κO')](8-)]]hexadecaaluminum

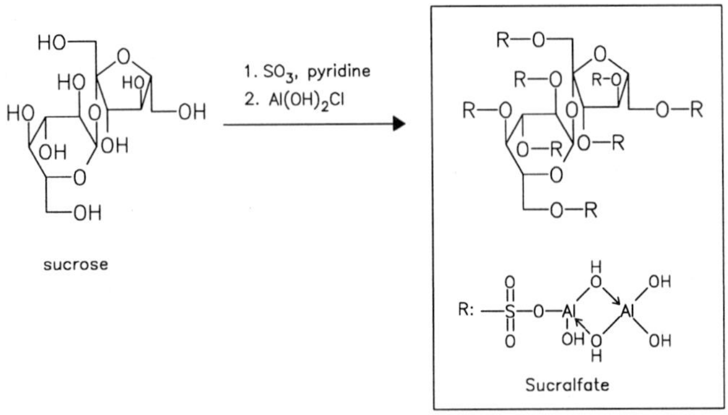

sucrose

1. SO$_3$, pyridine
2. Al(OH)$_2$Cl

Sucralfate

Reference(s):

DE 1 568 346 (Chugai; appl. 31.10.1966; J-prior. 5.11.1965).
US 3 432 489 (Chugai; 11.3.1969; J-prior. 5.11.1965).
FR 1 500 571 (Chugai; appl. 3.11.1966; S-prior. 5.11.1965).
Nagashima, R.; Yoshida, N.: Arzneim.-Forsch. (ARZNAD) **29**, 1668 (1979).

formulations with amino acids:
EP 107 209 (Chugai; appl. 26.10.1983; J-prior. 27.10.1982).

Formulation(s):   chewing tabl. 1 g; gran. 1 g; susp. 1 g/5 ml; tabl. 0.5 g, 1 g

Trade Name(s):

D:	Sucrabest (Hexal)		Sucrager (Ripari-Gero)	Ritaalumin (Hotta)
	Sucralfat-ratiopharm (ratiopharm)		Sucral (Bioprogress)	Shualmin (Rorer-Funai)
			Sucralfin (Inverni della	Sibonarl (Mohan-
	Sucraphil (Philopharm)		Beffa)	Wakamoto)
	Ulcogant (Lipha; Merck)		Sucramal (Sanofi	Tredol (Kaigai-Nippon
F:	Kéal (EG Labo)		Winthrop)	Kayaku)
	Sucralfate (GNR-pharma)		Sucrate (Lisapharma)	Ulban-A (Toho)
	Ulcar (Houdé)		Suril (Ibirn)	Ulcerlmin (Chugai)
GB:	Antepsin (Wyeth)	J:	Adopilon (Kantoishi)	Yuwan-S (Sawai-Meiji)
I:	Antepsin (Baldacci)		Altsamin (Taiyo-Sanwa)	USA: Carafate (Hoechst Marion
	Crafilm (Francia Farm.)		Bingast (Maruko)	Roussel)
	Gastrogel (Giuliani)		Bisma (Sana)	generics

Sufentanil

ATC: N01AH03
Use: narcotic, analgesic

RN: 56030-54-7   MF: $C_{22}H_{30}N_2O_2S$ MW: 386.56
CN: N-[4-(methoxymethyl)-1-[2-(2-thienyl)ethyl]-4-piperidinyl]-N-phenylpropanamide

citrate (1:1)
RN: 60561-17-3   MF: $C_{22}H_{30}N_2O_2S \cdot C_6H_8O_7$ MW: 578.68   EINECS: 262-295-4
LD_{50}:   18.7 mg/kg (M, i.v.);
        17.9 mg/kg (R, i.v.);
        14.1 mg/kg (dog, i.v.)

2-thiophene-   methane-   (I)
ethanol   sulfonyl
        chloride

N-(4-methoxymethyl-   Sufentanil
4-piperidyl)propionanilide
(cf. alfentanil synthesis)

Reference(s):
DE 2 610 228 (Janssen; prior. 11.3.1976).
US 3 998 834 (Janssen; 21.12.1976; prior. 14.3.1975, 13.1.1976, 13.9.1976).
Daele, P.G.H. van et al.: Arzneim.-Forsch. (ARZNAD) **26**, 1521 (1976).

Formulation(s):   amp. 50 µg/ml, 100 µg/2 ml, 500 µg/5 ml (as citrate)

Trade Name(s):
D: Sulfenta (Janssen-Cilag)   F: Sulfenta (Janssen-Cilag; as   I: Fentatienil (Angelini)
                citrate)   USA: Sufenta (Janssen; 1984)

Sulbactam

(CP-45899-2)

ATC: J01CG01
Use: antibacterial in combination with β
        lactam antibiotics, semisynthetic β-
        lactamase inhibitor

RN: 68373-14-8   MF: $C_8H_{11}NO_5S$ MW: 233.24   EINECS: 269-878-2
CN: (2S-cis)-3,3-dimethyl-7-oxo-4-thia-1-azabicyclo[3.2.0]heptane-2-carboxylic acid 4,4-dioxide

sodium salt
RN: 69388-84-7   MF: $C_8H_{10}NNaO_5S$ MW: 255.23   EINECS: 273-984-4

6-aminopeni-
cillanic acid

Br$_2$, CH$_2$Cl$_2$,
H$_2$SO$_4$, NaNO$_2$

6,6-dibromo-
penicillanic acid

KMnO$_4$, H$_3$PO$_4$
potassium
permanganate
I

6,6-dibromo-
penicillanic acid
S,S-dioxide (I)

1. NaHCO$_3$, H$_2$, Pd-C
2. HCl

Sulbactam

Reference(s):
Volkmann, R.A. et al.: J. Org. Chem. (JOCEAH) **47**, 3344 (1982).
US 4 234 579 (Pfizer; 18.11.1980; appl. 5.3.1979; USA-prior. 7.6.1977, 21.2.1978, 29.3.1978).
US 4 420 426 (Pfizer; 13.12.1983; appl. 9.12.1980; USA-prior. 5.3.1979).
DE 2 824 535 (Pfizer; appl. 5.6.1978; USA-prior. 7.6.1977, 21.2.1978).
DE 2 912 511 (Pfizer; appl. 29.3.1979; USA-prior. 29.3.1978, 27.11.1978).

combination with cefoperazone:
US 4 276 285 (Pfizer; 30.6.1981; appl. 5.3.1978; USA-prior. 7.6.1977, 21.2.1978, 29.3.1978, 27.11.1978).

Formulation(s):   vial 750 mg, 1 g, 1.5 g, 3 g (as sodium sulfate)

Trade Name(s):
D: Combactam 1,0 g (Pfizer)
      Unacid (Pfizer; 1987)-
      comb. with ampicillin
F: Bétamaze (Pfizer; as
      sodium salt)

      Unacim (Jouveinal; as
      sodium salt)-comb. with
      ampicillin
I: Bethacil (Bioindustria)-
      comb. with ampicillin
      Loricin (Sigma-Tau)-comb.
      with ampicillin

      Unasyn (Pfizer)-comb. with
      ampicillin
J: Sulperazone (Pfizer Taito;
      1986)-comb.
USA: Unasyn (Pfizer; 1987)-
      comb. with ampicillin

Sulbenicillin

ATC: J01CA16
Use: antibiotic

RN: 34779-28-7   MF: C$_{16}$H$_{18}$N$_2$O$_7$S$_2$ MW: 414.46   EINECS: 252-209-3
CN: [2S-(2α,5α,6β)]-3,3-dimethyl-7-oxo-6-[(phenylsulfoacetyl)amino]-4-thia-1-azabicyclo[3.2.0]heptane-2-
       carboxylic acid

disodium salt
RN: 28002-18-8   MF: C$_{16}$H$_{16}$N$_2$Na$_2$O$_7$S$_2$ MW: 458.42   EINECS: 248-769-3
LD$_{50}$: 7900 mg/kg (M, i.v.); >15 g/kg (M, p.o.);
       6 g/kg (R, i.v.); >15 g/kg (R, p.o.)

phenylacetic
acid

SO$_3$, dichloroethane

α-sulfophenyl-
acetic acid

SOCl$_2$

(I)

6-aminopeni-
cillanic acid

Sulbenicillin

Reference(s):
DE 1 933 629 (Takeda; prior. 2.7.1969).
DOS 1 948 943 (Takeda; appl. 27.9.1969; J-prior. 28.9.1968).
DAS 1 966 850 (Takeda; appl. 27.9.1969; J-prior. 28.9.1968).
US 3 660 379 (Takeda; 2.5.1972; appl. 29.9.1969; J-prior. 28.9.1968).
US 3 891 763 (Takeda; 24.6.1975; prior. 18.1.1972).

Formulation(s):   vial 1 g, 2 g, 4 g (as disodium salt)

Trade Name(s):
I: Kedacillina (Bracco; 1982)   J: Kedacillin (Takeda)   Lilacillin (Takeda)

Sulbentine
(Dibenzthione)

ATC: D01AE09
Use: antifungal

RN: 350-12-9   MF: $C_{17}H_{18}N_2S_2$ MW: 314.48   EINECS: 206-497-2
LD$_{50}$:   1100 mg/kg (M, i.p.)
CN: tetrahydro-3,5-bis(phenylmethyl)-2H-1,3,5-thiadiazine-2-thione

benzylamine   form-
aldehyde   carbon
disulfide   Sulbentine

Reference(s):
DD 20 634 (appl. 17.8.1958).

Formulation(s):   gel 3 g/100 g; ointment 3 g/100 g; sol. 3 g/100 g

Trade Name(s):
D: Fungiplex (Hermal); wfm   I: Fungiplex (Bruschettini);   J: Dampa D (Nippon
wfm   Shinyaku)

Sulconazole

ATC: N01AH03
Use: antifungal

RN: 61318-90-9   MF: $C_{18}H_{15}Cl_3N_2S$ MW: 397.76
CN: (±)-1-[2-[[(4-chlorophenyl)methyl]thio]-2-(2,4-dichlorophenyl)ethyl]-1H-imidazole

mononitrate
RN: 61318-91-0   MF: $C_{18}H_{15}Cl_3N_2S \cdot HNO_3$ MW: 460.77
LD$_{50}$:   2475 mg/kg (M, p.o.);
1741 mg/kg (R, p.o.)

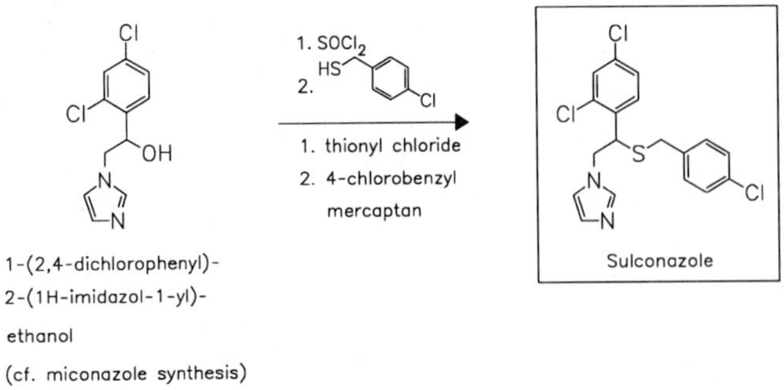
1. SOCl2
2. HS
Cl
1. thionyl chloride
2. 4-chlorobenzyl mercaptan
Cl
OH
N
N
1-(2,4-dichlorophenyl)-2-(1H-imidazol-1-yl)-ethanol
(cf. miconazole synthesis)
S
Sulconazole

Reference(s):
DOS 2 541 833 (Syntex; appl. 19.9.1975; USA-prior. 23.9.1974, 7.7.1975).
US 4 055 652 (Syntex; 25.10.1977; appl. 8.3.1976; prior. 7.7.1975).

Formulation(s): cream 1 %; sol. 1 % (as nitrate)

Trade Name(s):

F:	Myk (Cassenne)	I:	Exelderm (Schwarz)	USA:	Exelderm (Westwood-Squibb)
GB:	Exelderm (Zeneca; 1985)	J:	Exelderm (Tanabe; 1986)		

Sulfabenzamide

(Benzoylsulfanilamide; Sulphabenzamide)

ATC: D08; J01E
Use: chemotherapeutic (sulfonamide), antibacterial

RN: 127-71-9 MF: $C_{13}H_{12}N_2O_3S$ MW: 276.32 EINECS: 204-859-4
LD_{50}: 320 mg/kg (M, i.v.)
CN: *N*-[(4-aminophenyl)sulfonyl]benzamide

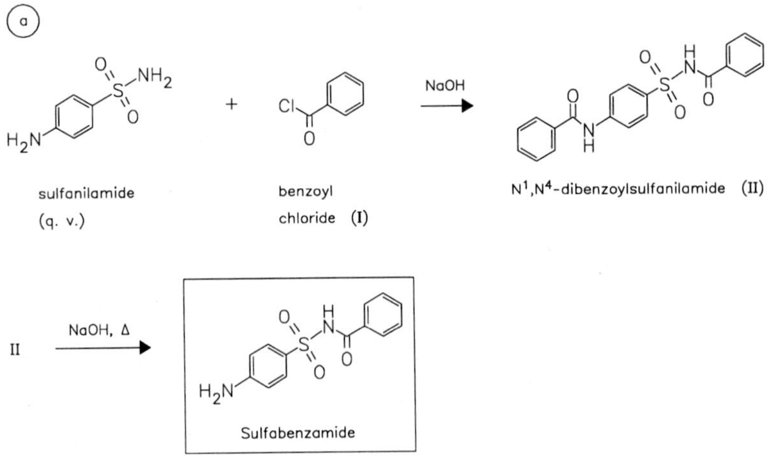
a
NH2
H2N
sulfanilamide
(q. v.)
+
Cl
benzoyl
chloride (I)
NaOH
N1,N4-dibenzoylsulfanilamide (II)
II
NaOH, Δ
Sulfabenzamide

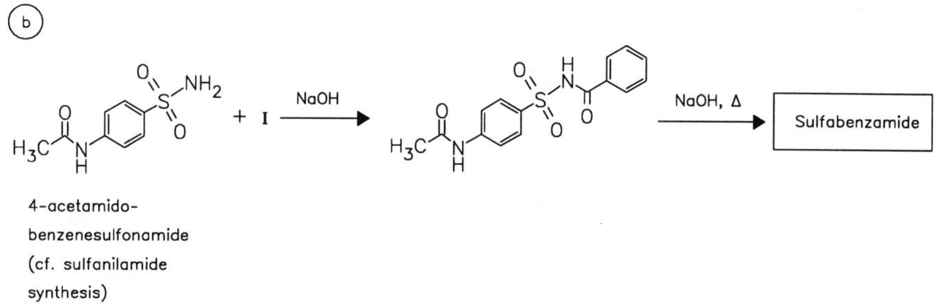

(b)

4-acetamido-
benzenesulfonamide
(cf. sulfanilamide
synthesis)

Reference(s):
a   Siebenmann, C.; Schnitzer, R.J.: J. Am. Chem. Soc. (JACSAT) **65**, 2126 (1943).
b   US 2 240 496 (Monsanto; 1941; appl. 1939).
    GB 541 958 (Schering AG; appl. 1938; D-prior. 1938).

Formulation(s):   pessaries 185 mg; vaginal cream 37 mg/g

Trade Name(s):
D: Neosultrin (Cilag)-comb.;   GB: Sultrin (Janssen-Cilag)-   USA: Sultrin (Ortho-McNeil
        wfm   comb.   Pharmaceutical)-comb.

Sulfacarbamide
(Sulphaurea; Sulfanylurea)

ATC: D08; J01E
Use: chemotherapeutic, antibacterial

RN: 547-44-4   MF: $C_7H_9N_3O_3S$ MW: 215.23   EINECS: 208-922-7
LD_{50}:   405 mg/kg (M, i.p.)
CN: 4-amino-N-(aminocarbonyl)benzenesulfonamide

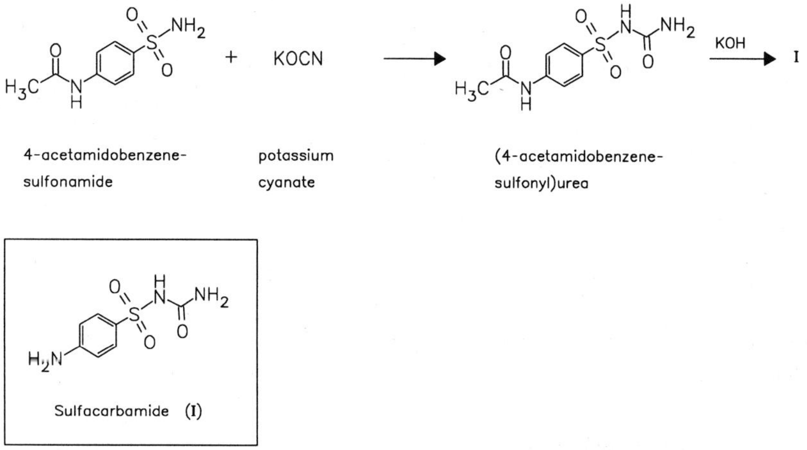

4-acetamidobenzene-   potassium   (4-acetamidobenzene-
sulfonamide   cyanate   sulfonyl)urea

Sulfacarbamide   (I)

Reference(s):
US 2 411 661 (Geigy; 1946; CH-prior. 1939).

Formulation(s):   drg. 0.5 g; syrup 0.1 g/ml

Sulfacetamide
(N'-acetylsulfanilamide; Sulphacetamide)

ATC: S01AB04
Use: chemotherapeutic (eye infection), antibacterial

RN: 144-80-9   MF: $C_8H_{10}N_2O_3S$ MW: 214.25   EINECS: 205-640-6
LD$_{50}$:   16.5 g/kg (M, p.o.);
     6.6 g/kg (R, i.v.)
CN: N-[(4-aminophenyl)sulfonyl]acetamide

monosodium salt
RN: 127-56-0   MF: $C_8H_9N_2NaO_3S$ MW: 236.23   EINECS: 204-848-4
LD$_{50}$:   6 g/kg (M, s.c.)

4-aminobenzene-
sulfonyl chloride   acetamide   Sulfacetamide

4-aminobenzene-
sulfonamide   acetic anhydride   Sulfacetamide

Reference(s):
US 2 411 495 (Schering Corp.; 1946; D-prior. 1938).

Formulation(s):   eye drops 100 mg/ml; ophthalmic ointment 2 mg/g, 100 mg/g (as sodium salt); pessaries
                  143.75 mg

J: Neo-Gerison (Yamanouchi)   Sultrin (Ortho-McNeil
USA: Blephamide (Allergan)   Pharmaceutical)-comb.

Sulfachlorpyridazine

ATC: D08; J01ED
Use: chemotherapeutic (urogenital tract
        infections), antibacterial

RN: 80-32-0   MF: $C_{10}H_9ClN_4O_2S$ MW: 284.73   EINECS: 201-269-9
CN: 4-amino-N-(6-chloro-3-pyridazinyl)benzenesulfonamide

4-aminobenzene-   3,6-dichloro-   Sulfachlorpyridazine
sulfonamide   pyridazine

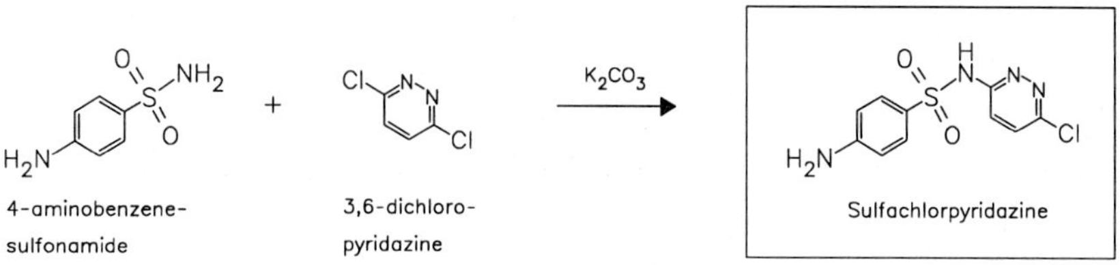

Reference(s):
US 2 790 798 (American Cyanamid; 1957; prior. 1955).

Formulation(s):   tabl. 500 mg

Trade Name(s):
I: Durasulf (Dessy); wfm   USA: Consulid (Ciba-Geigy);   Sonilyn (Mallinckrodt);
        Sulfaclorazina (Ellem);   wfm   wfm
        wfm   Nefrosul (Riker); wfm

Sulfacitine
(Sulfacytine)

ATC: J01E
Use: chemotherapeutic (depot
        sulfonamide), antibacterial

RN: 17784-12-2   MF: $C_{12}H_{14}N_4O_3S$ MW: 294.34
CN: 4-amino-N-(1-ethyl-1,2-dihydro-2-oxo-4-pyrimidinyl)benzenesulfonamide

3-ethylamino-   potassium   1-(2-cyanoethyl)-
propionitrile   cyanate   1-ethylurea

1-ethyl-5,6-dihydro-   1-ethylcytosine   4-acetamidobenzene-
cytosine hydrobromide   (I)   sulfonyl chloride

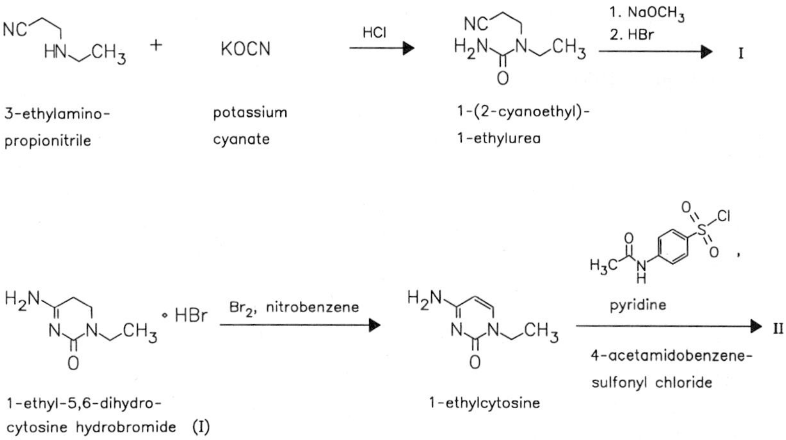

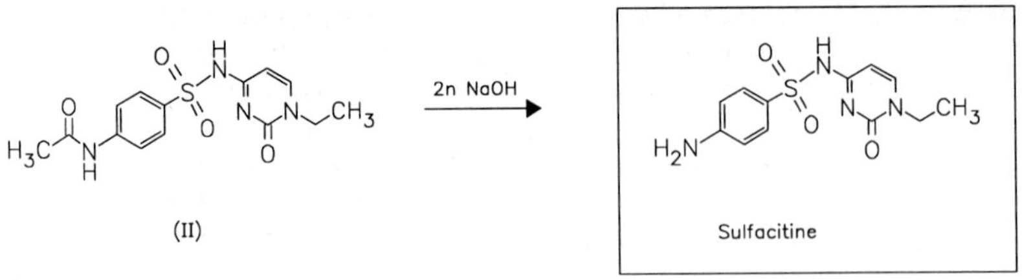

(II)

Sulfacitine

Reference(s):
US 3 375 247 (Parke Davis; 26.3.1968; appl. 2.8.1965).
DE 1 620 140 (Parke Davis; appl. 1.8.1966; USA-prior. 2.8.1965).
Doub, L. et al.: J. Med. Chem. (JMCMAR) **13**, 242 (1970).

Formulation(s):   tabl. 250 mg

Trade Name(s):
USA: Renoquid (Parke Davis);
      wfm

Sulfadiazine
(Sulphadiazine)

ATC: J01EC02
Use: chemotherapeutic

RN: 68-35-9   MF: $C_{10}H_{10}N_4O_2S$ MW: 250.28   EINECS: 200-685-8
LD$_{50}$: 180 mg/kg (M, i.v.); 1500 mg/kg (M, p.o.);
       880 mg/kg (R, i.v.)
CN: 4-amino-N-2-pyrimidinylbenzenesulfonamide

silver salt
RN: 22199-08-2   MF: $C_{10}H_9AgN_4O_2S$ MW: 357.14

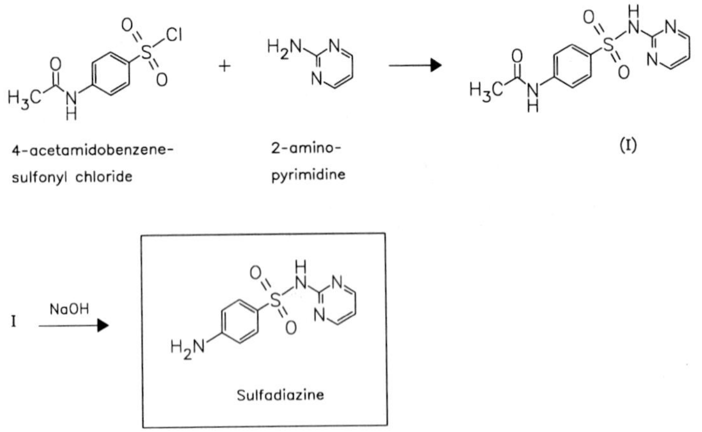

4-acetamidobenzene-
sulfonyl chloride

2-amino-
pyrimidine

(I)

Sulfadiazine

Reference(s):
US 2 407 966 (Sharp & Dohme; 1946).
US 2 410 793 (American Cyanamid; 1946).

Formulation(s):   cream 1 %; tabl. 500 mg (as silver salt)

Trade Name(s):
D: Brandiazine (medphano)   Flammazine (Solvay   Arzneimittel)

Sterinor (Heumann)-comb.
with textroprim
Sulfadiazin (Heyl)
Urospasmon (Heumann)-
comb.
F: Adiazine (Doms-Adrian)
Antrima (Doms-Adrian)-
comb.
Flamenacerium (Solvay
Pharma; as silver salt)-
comb.
Flammazine (Solvay
Pharma; as silver salt)
Sicazine (Smith &
Nephew; as silver salt)
GB: Flamazine (Smith &
Nephew; as silver salt);
wfm

Streptotriad (M. & B.)-
comb.; wfm
I: Connettivina (Fidia; as
silver salt)
Kombinax (Bracco)-comb.
Oxosint (Medivis)-comb.
Sofargen (Sofar; as silver
salt)
Sterinor (ABC
Farmaceutici)-comb.
Sulfadiazina (Ecobi; IFI)
Sulfadiazina Sodica (Salf;
as sodium salt)
J: Theradia (Daiichi)
Theradiazine (Daiichi)
USA: Coco-Diazine (Lilly); wfm
Neotrizine (Lilly)-comb.;
wfm

Silvadene (Marion Labs.;
as silver salt); wfm
Sodium Sulfadiazine (City
Chem.); wfm
Sodium Sulfadiazine
(Lederle); wfm
Sulfonamides Duplex
(Lilly); wfm
Sulfose (Wyeth)-comb.;
wfm
Terfonyl (Squibb)-comb.;
wfm
Triple Sulfas (Lederle)-
comb.; wfm
Trisem (Beecham)-comb.;
wfm
further combination
preparations; wfm

Sulfadicramide

ATC: S01AB03
Use: chemotherapeutic

RN: 115-68-4   MF: $C_{11}H_{14}N_2O_3S$ MW: 254.31   EINECS: 204-099-3
CN: N-[(4-aminophenyl)sulfonyl]-3-methyl-2-butenamide

3-methyl-
crotonamide

sodium
amide

4-acetamidobenzene-
sulfonyl chloride

(I)

Sulfadicramide

Reference(s):
US 2 417 005 (Geigy; 1947; CH-prior. 1943).

Formulation(s):   ophthalmic ointment 150 mg/g

Trade Name(s):
D: Irgamid Augensalbe
(Dispersa); wfm

Irgamid Augensalbe
(Zyma-Blaes); wfm

Sulfadimethoxine

ATC: J01ED01
Use: chemotherapeutic

RN: 122-11-2 MF: $C_{12}H_{14}N_4O_4S$ MW: 310.33 EINECS: 204-523-7
LD$_{50}$: 844 mg/kg (M, i.v.);
>3200 mg/kg (dog, p.o.)
CN: 4-amino-N-(2,6-dimethoxy-4-pyrimidinyl)benzenesulfonamide

a

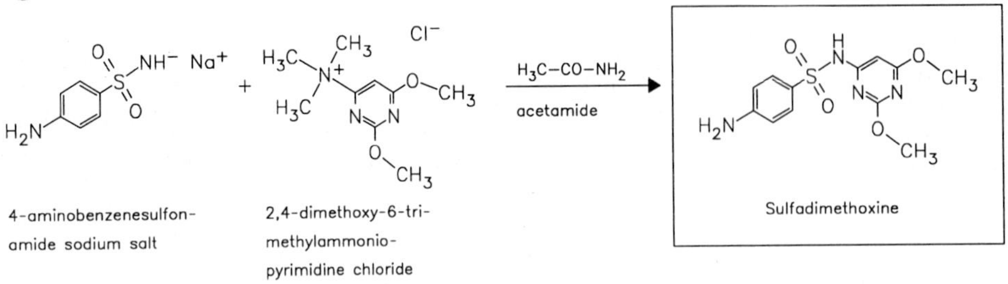

4-aminobenzenesulfon-
amide sodium salt

2,4-dimethoxy-6-tri-
methylammonio-
pyrimidine chloride

Sulfadimethoxine

b

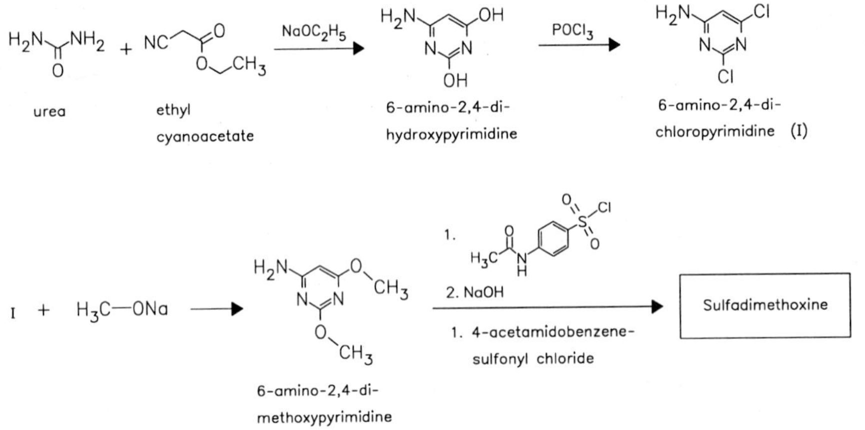

urea ethyl
cyanoacetate

6-amino-2,4-di-
hydroxypyrimidine

6-amino-2,4-di-
chloropyrimidine (I)

1. 4-acetamidobenzene-
sulfonyl chloride

6-amino-2,4-di-
methoxypyrimidine

Sulfadimethoxine

Reference(s):
a US 2 703 800 (Österr. Stickstoffwerke; 1955; A-prior. 1951).
b Bretschneider, H. et al.: Monatsh. Chem. (MOCMB7) **87**, 136 (1956); **92**, 75 (1961); **92**, 128 (1961).

Formulation(s): drops 200 mg/ml; syrup 250 mg/5 ml; tabl. 250 mg, 500 mg

Trade Name(s):
D: Madribon (Roche); wfm
F: Madribon (Roche); wfm
GB: Madribon (Roche); wfm
I: Sulfadimetossina (IFI)
J: Abcid (Daiichi)
Asthoxin (Kobayashi)
Dimetoxin (Nissin)

Dimexin (Fuso)
Hachimetoxin (Toyo S.-
Ono)
Melfa (Tanabe)
Mition-D (Taisho)
Omunibon (Yamanouchi)
Sulfalon (Sumitomo)

Sulmethon (Mohan)
Sulmetoxyn (Nichiiko)
Sulxin (Chugai)
Sumetamin (Samva)
USA: Albon (Roche); wfm

Sulfadoxine

(Sulformetoxinum; Sulforthomidine; Sulformethoxine)

ATC: P01BD51
Use: chemotherapeutic (sulfonamide)

RN: 2447-57-6   MF: $C_{12}H_{14}N_4O_4S$ MW: 310.33   EINECS: 219-504-9
LD$_{50}$: 5200 mg/kg (M, p.o.)
CN: 4-amino-N-(5,6-dimethoxy-4-pyrimidinyl)benzenesulfonamide

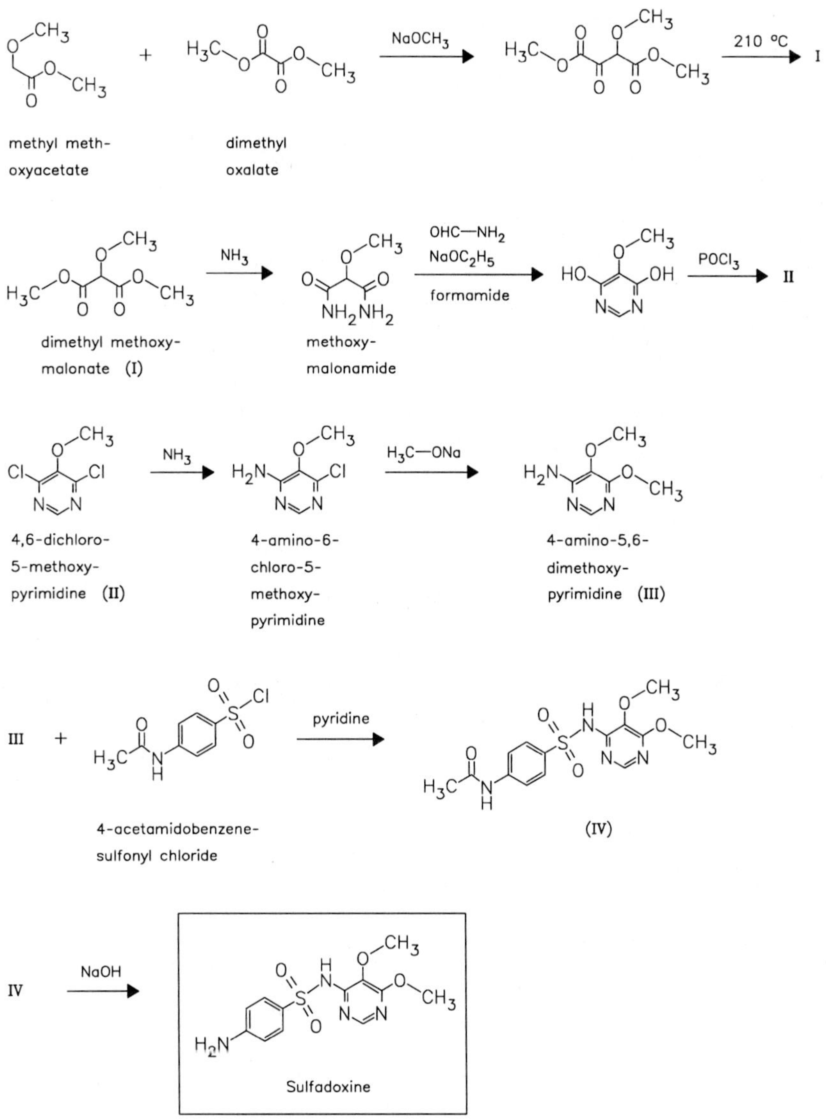

methyl meth-
oxyacetate

dimethyl
oxalate

dimethyl methoxy-
malonate (I)

methoxy-
malonamide

4,6-dichloro-
5-methoxy-
pyrimidine (II)

4-amino-6-
chloro-5-
methoxy-
pyrimidine

4-amino-5,6-
dimethoxy-
pyrimidine (III)

4-acetamidobenzene-
sulfonyl chloride

(IV)

Sulfadoxine

Reference(s):
US 3 132 139 (Roche; 1964; CH-prior. 1961).
Grüssner, A. et al.: Monatsh. Chem. (MOCMB7) **96**, 1676 (1965).
Bretschneider, H. et al.: Monatsh. Chem. (MOCMB7) **96**, 1661 (1965).

Formulation(s):   amp. 400 mg; tabl. 500 mg (in comb. with 25 mg pyrimethamine)

Trade Name(s):
D: Fansidar (Roche)-comb.;   GB: Fansidar (Roche)-comb.   USA: Fansidar (Roche)
     wfm   I: Fanasil (Roche); wfm
F: Fansidar (Roche)-comb.   J: Fansidar (Roche)-comb.

Sulfaethidole

ATC: G04A
Use: chemotherapeutic

RN: 94-19-9   MF: $C_{10}H_{12}N_4O_2S_2$ MW: 284.36   EINECS: 202-312-4
LD$_{50}$:   1300 mg/kg (R, i.v.)
CN: 4-amino-*N*-(5-ethyl-1,3,4-thiadiazol-2-yl)benzenesulfonamide

(a)

4-nitrobenzene-   5-amino-2-ethyl-
sulfonyl chloride   1,3,4-thiadiazole   Fe   Sulfaethidole

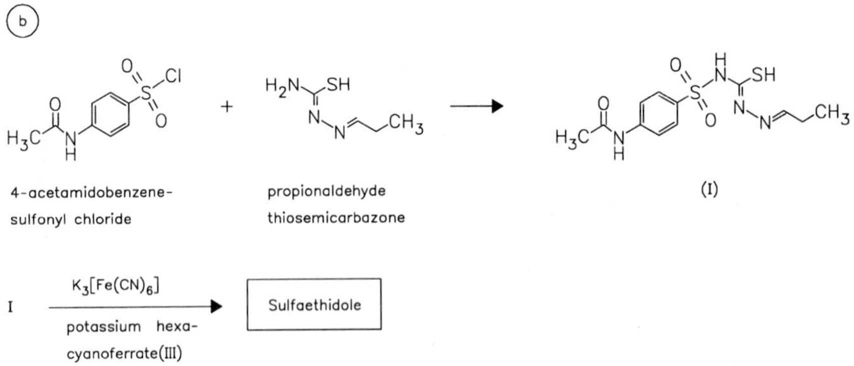

(b)

4-acetamidobenzene-   propionaldehyde
sulfonyl chloride   thiosemicarbazone   (I)

I $\xrightarrow{K_3[Fe(CN)_6]}$ Sulfaethidole
     potassium hexa-
     cyanoferrate(III)

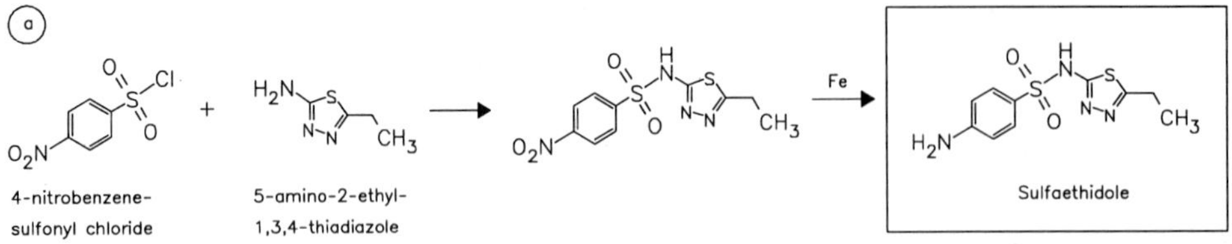

Reference(s):
a   US 2 358 031 (American Cyanamid; 1944; prior. 1940).
     DE 957 841 (Schering AG; appl. 1940).
b   US 2 447 702 (Lundbeck; 1948; DK-prior. 1942).

Formulation(s):   drg. 150 mg (in comb. with 350 mg sulfamethiozole)

Trade Name(s):
D: Harnosal (TAD)-comb.

Sulfafurazole
(Sulfisoxazole; Sulphafurazole)

ATC: J01EB05; S01AB02
Use: chemotherapeutic

RN: 127-69-5   MF: $C_{11}H_{13}N_3O_3S$ MW: 267.31   EINECS: 204-858-9
LD$_{50}$:   2500 mg/kg (M, i.v.); 6800 mg/kg (M, p.o.);
     10 g/kg (R, p.o.)
CN: 4-amino-*N*-(3,4-dimethyl-5-isoxazolyl)benzenesulfonamide

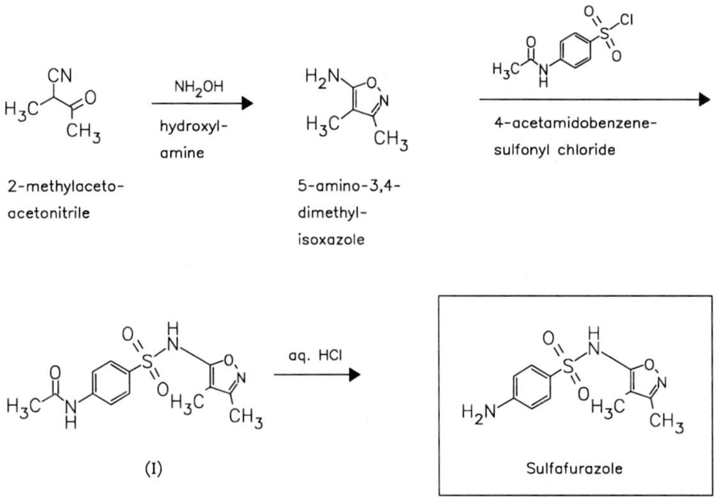

2-methylaceto-
acetonitrile

5-amino-3,4-
dimethyl-
isoxazole

4-acetamidobenzene-
sulfonyl chloride

(I)

Sulfafurazole

Reference(s):

US 2 430 094 (Hoffmann-La Roche; 1947; prior. 1944).
DE 819 855 (Hoffmann-La Roche; USA-prior. 1944).

Formulation(s):   amp. 4 mg/ml; eye drops 4 %; tabl. 500 mg

Trade Name(s):

D:	Gantrisin (Roche); wfm	Thiasin (Yamanouchi)	Koro-Sulf (Holland-
F:	Gantrisine (Roche); wfm	USA: Azo-Gantrisin (Roche)-	Rantos); wfm
	Pédiazole (Abbott)-comb.	comb.; wfm	SK-Soxazole (Smith Kline
	with erythromycine	Dow-Sulfisoxazole (Dow);	& French); wfm
GB:	Gantrisin (Roche); wfm	wfm	Sosol (McKesson); wfm
I:	Fultrexin (Zambon)-comb.;	Erythromycin	Soxomide (Upjohn); wfm
	wfm	Ethylsuccinate /	Sulfalar (Parke Davis);
	Pancid (Lister); wfm	Sulfisoxazole Acetate	wfm
J:	Isoxamin (Fuso)	(Warner Chilcott)	combination preparations
	Sulfazin (Shionogi)	Gantrisin (Roche); wfm	and generics

Sulfaguanidine

(Sulphaguanidine)

ATC: A07AB03
Use: chemotherapeutic

RN: 57-67-0   MF: C$_7$H$_{10}$N$_4$O$_2$S   MW: 214.25   EINECS: 200-345-9
CN: 4-amino-*N*-(aminoiminomethyl)benzenesulfonamide

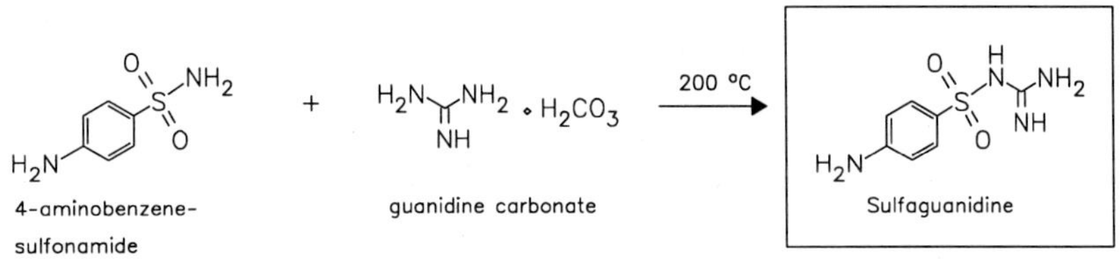

4-aminobenzene-
sulfonamide

guanidine carbonate

Sulfaguanidine

Reference(s):

US 2 218 490 (American Cyanamid; 1940; appl. 1940).
US 2 229 784 (American Cyanamid; 1941; appl. 1940).
US 2 233 569 (American Cyanamid; 1941; appl. 1940).

Formulation(s):   tabl. 0.5 g (as hydrate)

Trade Name(s):

D: Diarönt (Chephasaar)-
     comb.; wfm
     Enterastrept (Heyl)-comb.;
     wfm
     Guabeta (OTW); wfm
     Jacosulfon (Giulini)-comb.;
     wfm

     Resulfon-S (Nordmark);
     wfm
F: Litoxol (SmithKline
     Beecham)
I: Aseptil-Guanidina
     (Wassermann); wfm
     Kinol (Lafare)-comb.; wfm

     Streptoguanidin
     (Lisapharma)-comb.; wfm
     combination preparations;
     wfm
J: Aterian (Takeda)

Sulfaguanole

ATC: D08
Use: chemotherapeutic (depot
       sulfonamide)

RN: 27031-08-9   MF: C$_{12}$H$_{15}$N$_5$O$_3$S   MW: 309.35   EINECS: 248-175-4
CN: 4-amino-*N*-[[(4,5-dimethyl-2-oxazolyl)amino]iminomethyl]benzenesulfonamide

N^1-(4-aminophenylsulfonyl)-
N^3-cyanoguanidine

acetoin

Sulfaguanole

Reference(s):
US 3 562 258 (Nordmark; 9.2.1971; prior. 10.2.1969).
GB 1 185 139 (Nordmark; appl. 13.2.1969).

Formulation(s):   drg. 400 mg

Trade Name(s):

D: Enterocura (Nordmark);
     wfm
I: Asorec (Radiumfarma);
     wfm
     Enterocura (De Angeli);
     wfm

Sulfalene
(Sulfametopyrazine)

ATC: J01ED02
Use: chemotherapeutic (depot
       sulfonamide)

RN: 152-47-6   MF: C$_{11}$H$_{12}$N$_4$O$_3$S   MW: 280.31   EINECS: 205-804-7
LD$_{50}$:   893 mg/kg (M, i.v.); 1292 mg/kg (M, p.o.);
             1790 mg/kg (R, i.v.); 2739 mg/kg (R, p.o.)
CN: 4-amino-*N*-(3-methoxypyrazinyl)benzenesulfonamide

starting product:

Br₂ / CH₃COOH → H₃C—ONa (I) → H₂, Pd–C

2-amino-
pyrazine

3-amino-2-
methoxy-
pyrazine (II)

b)

3-hydroxypyrazine-
2-carboxamide

POCl₃ →

3-chloro-2-
cyanopyrazine

I →

2-cyano-3-
methoxy-
pyrazine (III)

III   H₂O₂, NaOH →   NaOCl →   II

3-methoxypyrazine-
2-carboxamide

final product:

II +

4-acetamidobenzene-
sulfonyl chloride

NaOH →

Sulfalene

Reference(s):
US 3 098 069 (Carlo Erba; 16.7.1963; GB-prior. 14.7.1959).

Formulation(s):   tabl. 2 g

Trade Name(s):
D: Longum (Pharmacia &   I: Kelfiprim (Pharmacia &
      Upjohn)   Upjohn)-comb.
GB: Kelfizine-W (Pharmacia &   Kelfizina (Pharmacia &
      Upjohn)   Upjohn)

Sulfaloxic acid

(Sulphaloxate; Sulphaloxic Acid)

ATC: D08
Use: chemotherapeutic (sulfonamide),
        antibacterial

RN: 14376-16-0   MF: C₁₆H₁₅N₃O₇S   MW: 393.38   EINECS: 238-348-2
CN: 2-[[[4-[[[[(hydroxymethyl)amino]carbonyl]amino]sulfonyl]phenyl]amino]carbonyl]benzoic acid

calcium salt
RN: 97259-91-1   MF: $C_{32}H_{28}CaN_6O_{14}S_2$ MW: 824.81

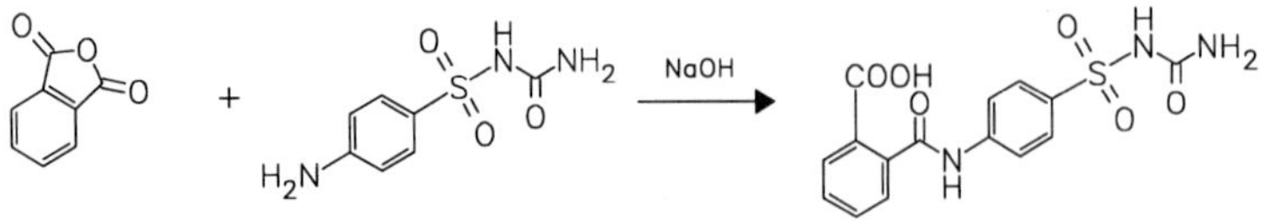

phthalic anhydride + sulfacarbamide (q. v.) →(NaOH)→ (I)

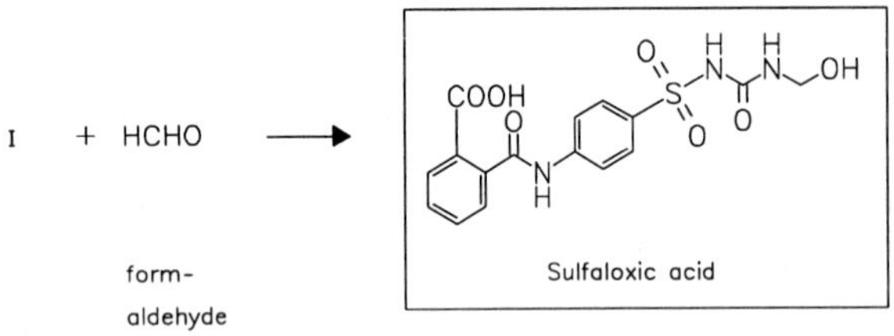

I + HCHO → Sulfaloxic acid

form-aldehyde

Reference(s):
DE 960 190 (Chem. Fabrik von Heyden; appl. 1954).
DAS 1 002 319 (Chem. Fabrik von Heyden; appl. 15.6.1954).

Formulation(s):   tabl. 0.55 g (as calcium salt)

Trade Name(s):
D: Intestin-Euvernil (Heyden)   Sulfa-Adsorgan   GB: Enteromide (Consolidated;
      Myacine (Schur)-comb.;   (Combustin); wfm   as calcium salt); wfm
      wfm

Sulfamerazine
(Methylsulfadiazine)

ATC: J01ED07
Use: chemotherapeutic, antibacterial

RN: 127-79-7   MF: $C_{11}H_{12}N_4O_2S$ MW: 264.31   EINECS: 204-866-2
LD_{50}:   25 g/kg (M, p.o.);
             1100 mg/kg (R, i.v.)
CN: 4-amino-N-(4-methyl-2-pyrimidinyl)benzenesulfonamide

sodium salt
RN: 127-58-2   MF: $C_{11}H_{11}N_4NaO_2S$ MW: 286.29

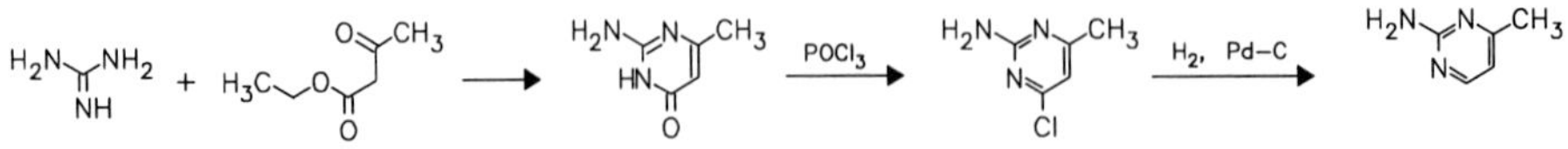

guanidine + ethyl acetoacetate → ... →(POCl₃)→ ... →(H₂, Pd–C)→ 2-amino-4-methyl-pyrimidine (I)

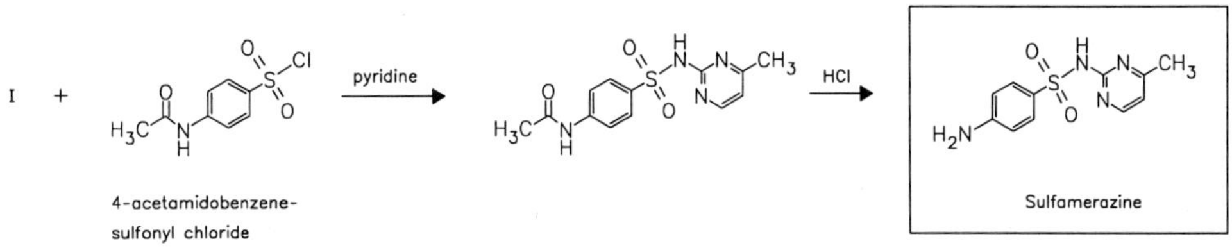

4-acetamidobenzene-
sulfonyl chloride

Sulfamerazine

Reference(s):
US 2 407 966 (Sharp & Dohme; 1946; appl. 1940).

Formulation(s):   susp. 60 mg/5 ml; tabl. 120 mg (as sodium salt)

Trade Name(s):
D: Dosulfin (Geigy)-comb.;   F: Dosulfine (Gomenol)-   I: Polagin (De Angeli)-comb.;
      wfm   comb.; wfm   wfm
                                        Solumedine (Specia); wfm   J: Romezin (Tanabe)

Sulfamethizole
(Sulphamethizole)

ATC: B05CA04; D06BA04; J01EB02;
        S01AB01
Use: chemotherapeutic, antibacterial

RN: 144-82-1   MF: $C_9H_{10}N_4O_2S_2$ MW: 270.34   EINECS: 205-641-1
LD_{50}:   1820 mg/kg (M, i.v.); >10 g/kg (M, p.o.);
       2710 mg/kg (R, i.v.); 3500 mg/kg (R, p.o.)
CN: 4-amino-*N*-(5-methyl-1,3,4-thiadiazol-2-yl)benzenesulfonamide

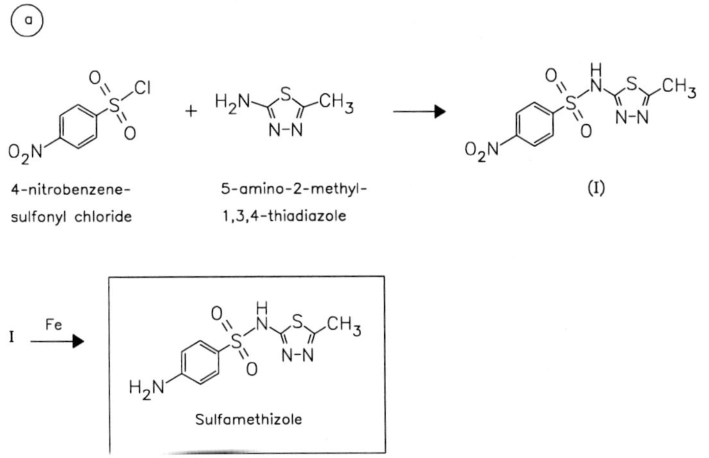

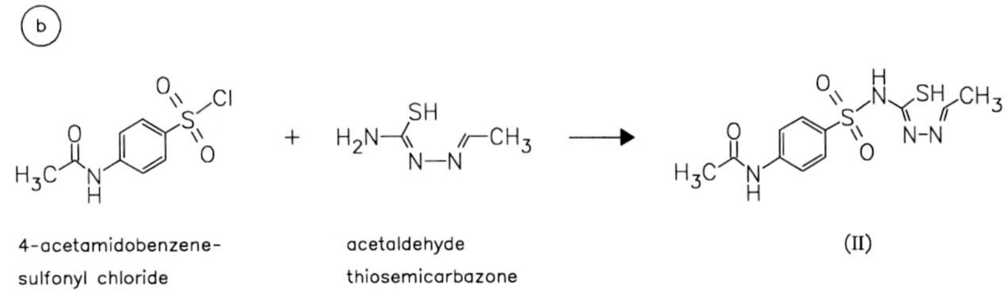

(a)

4-nitrobenzene-   5-amino-2-methyl-   (I)
sulfonyl chloride   1,3,4-thiadiazole

Sulfamethizole

(b)

4-acetamidobenzene-   acetaldehyde   (II)
sulfonyl chloride   thiosemicarbazone

II $\xrightarrow{\text{K}_3[\text{Fe(CN)}_6]}$ [Sulfamethizole]

potassium
hexacyano-
ferrate(III)

Reference(s):
a US 2 358 031 (American Cyanamid; 1944; prior. 1940).
b US 2 447 702 (Lundbeck & Co.; 1948; DK-prior. 1942).

Formulation(s): cps. 250 mg in comb. with oxytetracycline.HCl (250 mg) and phenazopyridine.HCl (50 mg); drg. 350 mg in comb. with sulfaethidiole

Trade Name(s):
D: Harnosal (TAD)-comb. Thiosulfil (Ayerst); wfm Urosol (Kanto)
F: Rufol (Débat) J: Harnway (Nichiiko) Urosul (Mohan)
GB: Urolucosil (Warner); wfm Salimol (Maruishi-Kanebo) USA: Urobiotic-250 (Pfizer)-
I: Rufol (Roussel-Maestretti); Urokinon (Chugai) comb.
 wfm Urokizol (Chugai)

Sulfamethoxazole
(Sulphamethoxazole)

ATC: J01EC01
Use: antipneumocystis, chemotherapeutic (urogenital tract infections)

RN: 723-46-6 MF: $C_{10}H_{11}N_3O_3S$ MW: 253.28 EINECS: 211-963-3
LD$_{50}$: 1460 mg/kg (M, i.v.); 2300 mg/kg (M, p.o.);
 6200 mg/kg (R, p.o.)
CN: 4-amino-N-(5-methyl-3-isoxazolyl)benzenesulfonamide

4-acetamidobenzene-
sulfonyl chloride

3-amino-5-
methylisoxazole

(I)

I $\xrightarrow{\text{NaOH}}$

Sulfamethoxazole

Reference(s):
US 2 888 455 (Shionogi; 26.5.1959; J-prior. 4.9.1956).

Formulation(s): amp. 400 mg/5 ml, 800 mg/3 ml; susp. 200 mg/5 ml; syrup 200 mg/5 ml, 400 mg/5 ml; tabl. 100 mg, 400 mg, 800 mg, 960 mg

Trade Name(s):
D: Bactoreduct (Azupharma)- Bactrim/forte (Roche)- Berlocid (Berlin-Chemie)-
 comb. with trimethoprim comb. with trimethoprim comb. with trimethoprim

Cotrim (Heumann; ct-Arzneimittel; Holsten; BASF; Hefa; PUREN; ratiopharm; Hexal)-comb. with trimethoprim
Cotrim-Diolan/-forte (Engelhard)-comb. with trimethoprim
Cotrim-EuRho (Eu Rho Arznei)-comb. with trimethoprim
Cotrimoxazol (Aluid Pharma)-comb. with trimethoprim
Cotrimoxazol/-forte (Fatol)-comb. with trimethoprim
Cotrimox-Wolff (Wolff)-comb. with trimethoprim

Drylin (Merckle)-comb. with trimethoprim
Eusaprine (Glaxo Wellcome)-comb. with trimethoprim
Jenamoxazol (Jenapharm)-comb. with trimethoprim
Kepinol (Pfleger)-comb. with trimethoprim
Microtrim (Rosen Pharma)-comb.
Sijaprim (Kytta-Siegfried)-comb.

F: Bactrim (Roche)
Cotrimazol Forte Ratiopharm (Lafon-ratiopharm)
Eusaprim (Glaxo Wellcome)
Gantanol (Roche)

GB: Chemotrim (Rosemont)-comb.
Gantanol (Roche)
Septrin (Glaxo Wellcome)-comb.

I: Abacin (Benedetti)-comb.
Bacterial (CT)-comb.
Bactrim (Dompé)-comb.
Chemitrim (Biomedica Foscama)-comb.
Eusaprim (Glaxo Wellcome)-comb.
Gantrim (Geymonat)-comb.
Isotrim (Ghimas)-comb.

J: Sinomin (Shionogi)
USA: Bactrim (Roche)-comb.
Gantanol (Roche)
Septra (Glaxo Wellcome)-comb.
generics

Sulfamethoxypyridazine
(Sulphamethoxypyridazine)

ATC: J01ED05
Use: chemotherapeutic

RN: 80-35-3   MF: $C_{11}H_{12}N_4O_3S$ MW: 280.31   EINECS: 201-272-5
LD_{50}:   1 g/kg (M, i.v.); 1700 mg/kg (M, p.o.); 2739 mg/kg (R, p.o.)
CN: 4-amino-N-(6-methoxy-3-pyridazinyl)benzenesulfonamide

sulfachlorpyridazine (q. v.)   +   sodium methylate   →   Sulfamethoxypyridazine

Reference(s):
US 2 712 012 (American Cyanamid; 1955; prior. 1954).

N'-acetyl derivative:
US 2 833 761 (American Cyanamid; 1958; appl. 1957).

Formulation(s):   cps. 120 mg in comb. with trimethoprim; suppos. 60 mg, 200 mg, 400 mg in comb. with trimethoprim; syrup 75 mg in comb. with trimethoprim; tabl. 250 mg, 500 mg;

Trade Name(s):
D: Davosin (Parke Davis); wfm
Lederkyn (Novalis Arzn.); wfm

F: Sulmidal (Roger Bellon)-comb.; wfm
Sultiréne (Specia); wfm

GB: Lederkyn (Lederle); wfm
Midicel (Parke Davis); wfm

I: Velaten (Camillo Corvi)-comb.
J: Lederkyn (Lederle)
Oroxin (Otsuka)
USA: Midicel (Parke Davis); wfm

Sulfametoxydiazine

(Sulfameter)

ATC: D08; J01ED
Use: chemotherapeutic (depot sulfonamide)

RN: 651-06-9 MF: $C_{11}H_{12}N_4O_3S$ MW: 280.31 EINECS: 211-480-8
LD_{50}: 1 g/kg (M, i.v.); 16 g/kg (M, p.o.);
1 g/kg (R, i.v.); 6 g/kg (R, p.o.);
1 g/kg (dog, p.o.)
CN: 4-amino-*N*-(5-methoxy-2-pyrimidinyl)benzenesulfonamide

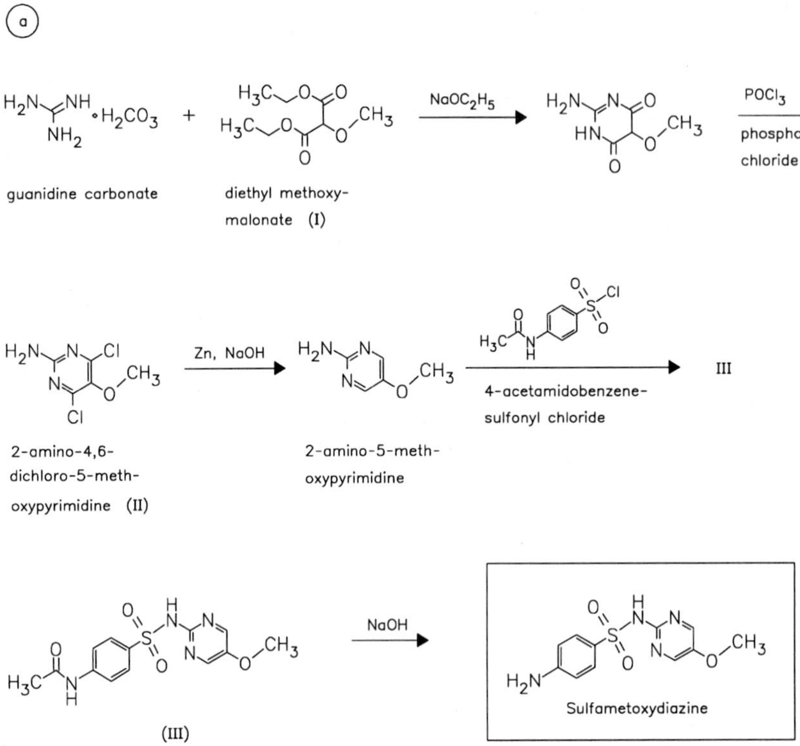
a
guanidine carbonate
diethyl methoxy-malonate (I)
NaOC2H5
POCl3
phosphoryl chloride
II
Zn, NaOH
4-acetamidobenzene-sulfonyl chloride
III
2-amino-4,6-dichloro-5-meth-oxypyrimidine (II)
2-amino-5-meth-oxypyrimidine
NaOH
(III)
Sulfametoxydiazine

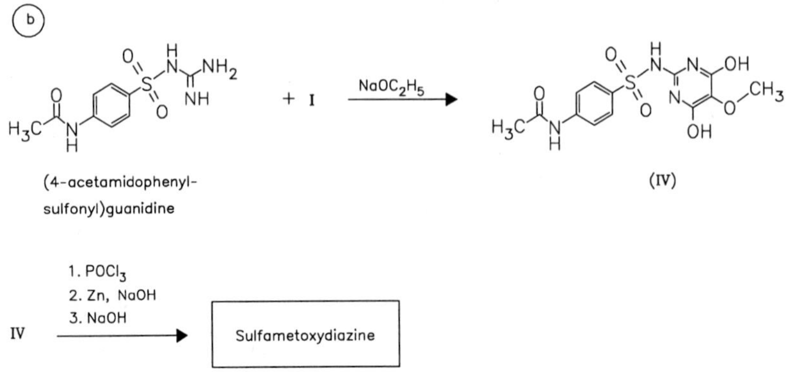
b
+ I
NaOC2H5
(4-acetamidophenyl-sulfonyl)guanidine
(IV)
IV
1. POCl3
2. Zn, NaOH
3. NaOH
Sulfametoxydiazine

Reference(s):
DE 1 101 428 (Schering AG; appl. 8.7.1959).

Formulation(s): syrup 200 mg/5 ml; tabl. 0.5 g

Trade Name(s):
D: Durenat (Bayer-Schering); wfm
F: Bayrena (Bayer-Pharma); wfm
GB: Durenate (Bayer); wfm
I: Kiron (Schering); wfm
USA: Sulla (Robins); wfm

Sulfametrole

ATC: J01EA
Use: chemotherapeutic (in combination with trimethoprim)

RN: 32909-92-5   MF: $C_9H_{10}N_4O_3S_2$ MW: 286.34   EINECS: 251-288-1
CN: 4-amino-*N*-(4-methoxy-1,2,5-thiadiazol-3-yl)benzenesulfonamide

dicyanogen

3-chloro-4-methoxy-1,2,5-thiadiazole (I)

sulfanilamide

Sulfametrole

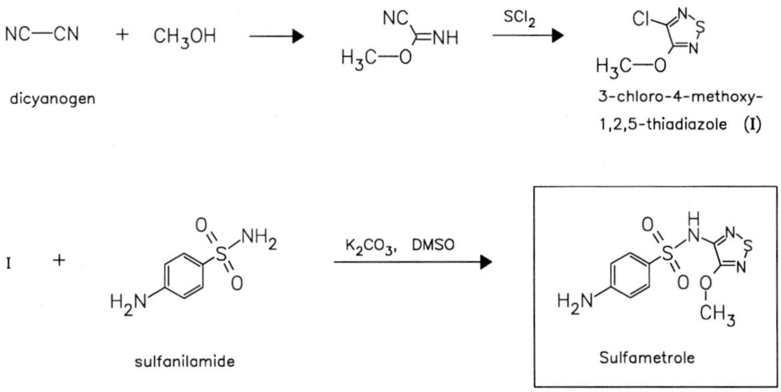

Reference(s):
BE 862 952 (Chemie Linz; appl. 16.1.1978; D-prior. 17.1.1977).
DOS 2 701 632 (Lentia; appl. 17.1.1977).
US 4 151 164 (Chemie Linz; 24.4.1979; D-prior. 17.1.1977).

alternative syntheses:
US 3 247 193 (Österr. Stickstoffwerke; 19.4.1966; A-prior. 14.3.1962).
US 3 636 209 (Merck & Co.; 18.1.1972; prior. 15.10.1965, 16.9.1966, 1.8.1969, 11.4.1965).

Formulation(s):   f. c. tabl. 800 mg; vial 800 mg; tabl. 400 mg

Trade Name(s):
D: Lidaprim (Hormon-Chemie)-comb. with trimethoprim; wfm
I: Lidaprim (Lisapharma)-comb. with trimethoprim

Sulfamoxole

(Sulphamoxole)

ATC: J01EC03
Use: chemotherapeutic

RN: 729-99-7   MF: $C_{11}H_{13}N_3O_3S$ MW: 267.31   EINECS: 211-982-7
LD$_{50}$: 1 g/kg (M, i.v.); 15.2 g/kg (M, p.o.);
        >12.5 g/kg (R, p.o.)
CN: 4-amino-*N*-(4,5-dimethyl-2-oxazolyl)benzenesulfonamide

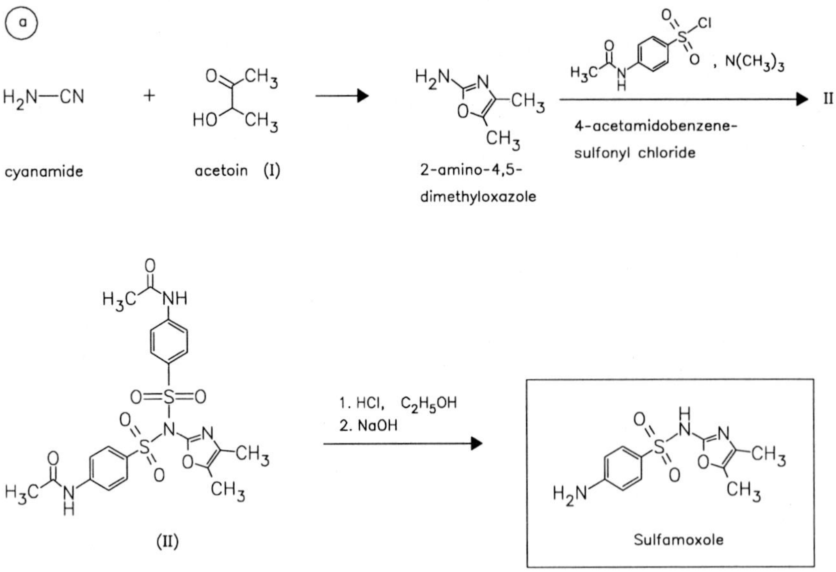

a

cyanamide + acetoin (I) → 2-amino-4,5-dimethyloxazole

4-acetamidobenzene-sulfonyl chloride → II

(II)

1. HCl, C_2H_5OH
2. NaOH

Sulfamoxole

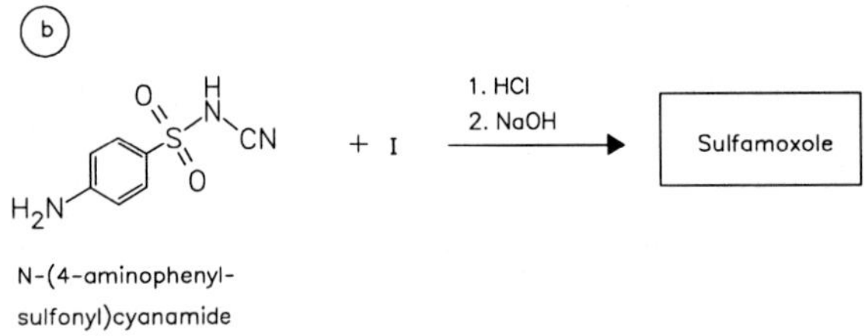

b

N-(4-aminophenyl-sulfonyl)cyanamide + I

1. HCl
2. NaOH

Sulfamoxole

Reference(s):

a   DE 1 003 737 (Nordmark; appl. 28.7.1955).
    US 2 809 966 (Nordmark; 1957; D-prior. 1955).
b   DE 1 121 052 (Nordmark; appl. 1.2.1960).
    DE 1 128 429 (Nordmark; appl. 19.5.1960; addition to DE 1 121 052).

Formulation(s):   susp. 200 mg; tabl. 400 mg

Trade Name(s):

D: Sulfuno (Nordmark); wfm
      Tardamide (Grünenthal);
      wfm
F: Justamil (Hépatrol); wfm

      Supristol (Gallier)-comb.
      with trimethoprim; wfm
I: Oxasulfa (Trinum); wfm

      Sulmen (Menarini)-comb.
      with trimethoprim; wfm
USA: Naprin (Upjohn); wfm

Sulfanilamide

(Sulphanilamide)

ATC: J01EB06
Use: chemotherapeutic

RN: 63-74-1   MF: $C_6H_8N_2O_2S$ MW: 172.21   EINECS: 200-563-4
LD_{50}:   500 mg/kg (M, i.v.); 3 g/kg (M, p.o.);
      1400 mg/kg (R, i.v.); 3900 mg/kg (R, p.o.);
      2 g/kg (dog, p.o.)
CN: 4-aminobenzenesulfonamide

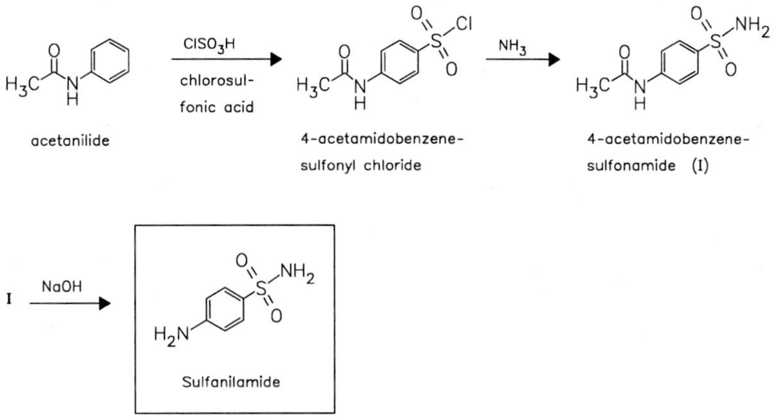

acetanilide → (CISO₃H, chlorosulfonic acid) → 4-acetamidobenzene-sulfonyl chloride → (NH₃) → 4-acetamidobenzene-sulfonamide (I)

I → (NaOH) → Sulfanilamide

Reference(s):
US 2 132 178 (Mietzsch, Klarer; 1938).
US 2 276 664 (Mietzsch, Klarer; 1942).

Formulation(s):   vaginal ointment 15 %; vaginal suppos. 1.05 g

Trade Name(s):

D: Pyodental (Artesan); wfm
    Sulfonamid-Spuman
    (Luitpold); wfm
    combination preparations;
    wfm
F: Anafluose (Techni-
    Pharma)-comb.; wfm

Exoseptoplix (Théraplix);
wfm
Pulvi-bactéramide (Bailly);
wfm
Rhinamide (Bailly)-comb.;
wfm
Tablamide (Bureau)

I: Chemiovis (SIT)-comb.;
    wfm
    Rinocorfene (Ottolenghi)-
    comb.; wfm
J: Neo-Gerison (Yamanouchi)
USA: AVC (Hoechst Marion
    Roussel)-comb.
    generic

Sulfaperin

ATC: J01ED06
Use: chemotherapeutic

RN: 599-88-2   MF: C₁₁H₁₂N₄O₂S   MW: 264.31   EINECS: 209-976-4
LD₅₀: >8 g/kg (M, s.c.)
CN: 4-amino-*N*-(5-methyl-2-pyrimidinyl)benzenesulfonamide

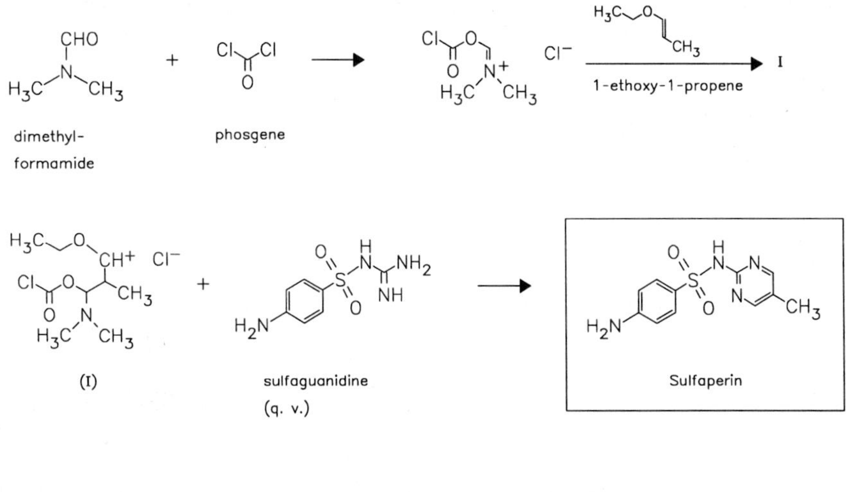

dimethylformamide + phosgene → → (1-ethoxy-1-propene) → I

(I) + sulfaguanidine (q. v.) → Sulfaperin

Reference(s):
DE 1 117 587 (BASF; appl. 25.10.1958)-method.

Formulation(s):   styl. 1 g

Trade Name(s):
D: Pallidin (Merck); wfm
    Palliopen (Merck)-comb.
I: Ipersulfidin (Francia
    Farm.); wfm
    Palidin (Bracco); wfm
    Retardsulf (Virgiliano);
    wfm

Rexulfa (Medici); wfm
Sintosulfa (AFI); wfm
Sulfalest (Farmochimica
Ital.); wfm
Sulfapenta (Savoma); wfm
Sulfatreis (Ecobi); wfm

Sulfixone (Ital. Suisse);
wfm
Sulfopiran (Panthox &
Burck); wfm
Sulfopirimidina
(Terapeutico M.R.); wfm

Sulfaphenazole
(Sulphaphenazole)

ATC: J01ED08
Use: chemotherapeutic

RN: 526-08-9   MF: $C_{15}H_{14}N_4O_2S$ MW: 314.37   EINECS: 208-384-3
LD_{50}:   470 mg/kg (M, i.v.); 3016 mg/kg (M, p.o.);
    525 mg/kg (R, i.v.)
CN: 4-amino-N-(1-phenyl-1H-pyrazol-5-yl)benzenesulfonamide

phenyl-   acrylo-
hydrazine   nitrile

3-amino-2-
phenylpyrazole   (I)

4-(ethoxycarbonylamino)-
benzenesulfonyl chloride

Sulfaphenazole

Reference(s):
DE 1 049 384 (Ciba; appl. 30.4.1957; CH-prior. 7.5.1956).
US 2 858 309 (Ciba; 28.10.1958; CH-prior. 7.5.1956).

3-amino-2-phenylpyrazole:
DE 1 065 850 (Ciba; appl. 26.3.1958; CH-prior. 5.4.1957, 29.8.1957).

Formulation(s):   tabl. 500 mg

Trade Name(s):
D: Orisul (Ciba); wfm
GB: Orisulf (Ciba); wfm
I: Fenazolo (Sam); wfm
    Sulfapadil (Padil); wfm

Sulfapirina (Biopharma)-
comb.; wfm
Sulforal (Farber-Ref); wfm

Temoxa (Chinoin)-comb.;
wfm
combination preparations;
wfm

J: Merian (Dainippon)   Sulphena (Nisshin)   USA: Sulfabid (Purdue
      Sulfenal (Kanto)   Frederick); wfm

Sulfaproxyline

ATC: D08; J01ED
Use: chemotherapeutic (sulfonamide)

RN: 116-42-7   MF: C$_{16}$H$_{18}$N$_2$O$_4$S   MW: 334.40   EINECS: 204-140-5
CN: N-[(4-aminophenyl)sulfonyl]-4-(1-methylethoxy)benzamide

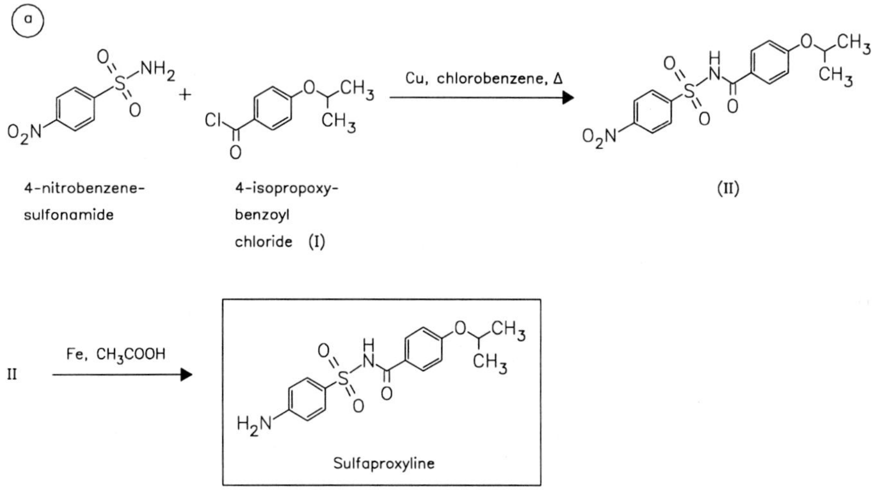

4-nitrobenzene-
sulfonamide

4-isopropoxy-
benzoyl
chloride (I)

Cu, chlorobenzene, Δ

(II)

II   Fe, CH$_3$COOH

Sulfaproxyline

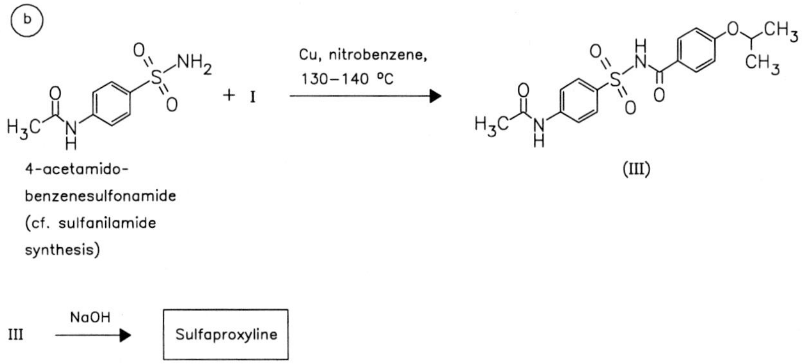

4-acetamido-
benzenesulfonamide
(cf. sulfanilamide
synthesis)

Cu, nitrobenzene,
130–140 °C

(III)

III   NaOH → Sulfaproxyline

Reference(s):
US 2 503 820 (Geigy; 1950; CH-prior. 1947).

Trade Name(s):
F: Dosulfine (Gomenol)-
      comb.; wfm

Sulfathiazole

(Sulphathiazole)

ATC: D06BA02; J01EB07
Use: chemotherapeutic

RN: 72-14-0   MF: $C_9H_9N_3O_2S_2$ MW: 255.32   EINECS: 200-771-5
LD$_{50}$:   990 mg/kg (M, i.v.); 4500 mg/kg (M, p.o.);
        1370 mg/kg (R, i.v.)
CN: 4-amino-N-2-thiazolylbenzenesulfonamide

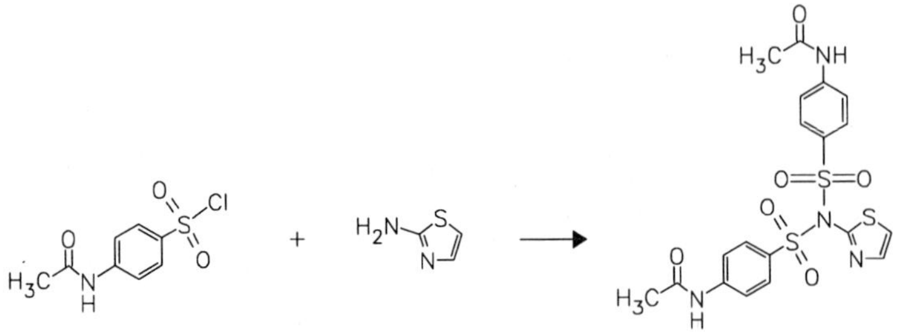

4-acetamidobenzene-
sulfonyl chloride

2-amino-
thiazole

(I)

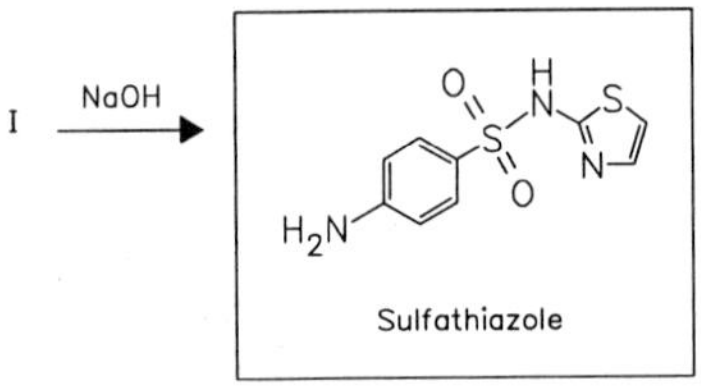

Sulfathiazole

Reference(s):
DRP 742 753 (Ciba; appl. 1938; CH-prior. 1938).

soluble form:
US 4 070 356 (MBH Chemical Corp.; 24.1.1978; appl. 22.1.1976).

Formulation(s):   cream 3.42 %; pessaries 172.5 mg (in comb. with sulfacetamide, sulfabenzamide)

Trade Name(s):
D: Cibazol (Ciba); wfm
      Neosultrin (Cilag)-comb.;
      wfm
      Peniazol (Winzer)-comb.;
      wfm

F: Tampovagan (AGM)-
      comb.; wfm
      Thiazomide (Specia); wfm
GB: Thiazamide (May &
      Baker); wfm

I: Streptosil Neomicina
      (Fher)-comb.
J: Sulzol (Yoshitomi)
USA: Sultrin (Ortho-McNeil)-
      comb.

Sulfinpyrazone

(Sulphinpyrazone)

ATC: M04AB02
Use: antiarthritic, uricosuric agent, platelet
        aggregation inhibitor (for descent of
        postinfarct mortality)

RN: 57-96-5   MF: $C_{23}H_{20}N_2O_3S$ MW: 404.49   EINECS: 200-357-4
LD$_{50}$:   240 mg/kg (M, i.v.); 298 mg/kg (M, p.o.);
        154 mg/kg (R, i.v.); 358 mg/kg (R, p.o.)
CN: 1,2-diphenyl-4-[2-(phenylsulfinyl)ethyl]-3,5-pyrazolidinedione

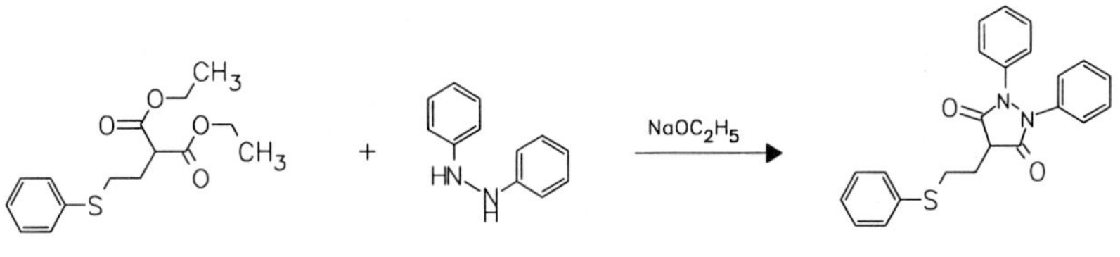

diethyl 2-phenyl-
thioethylmalonate

hydrazo-
benzene

(I)

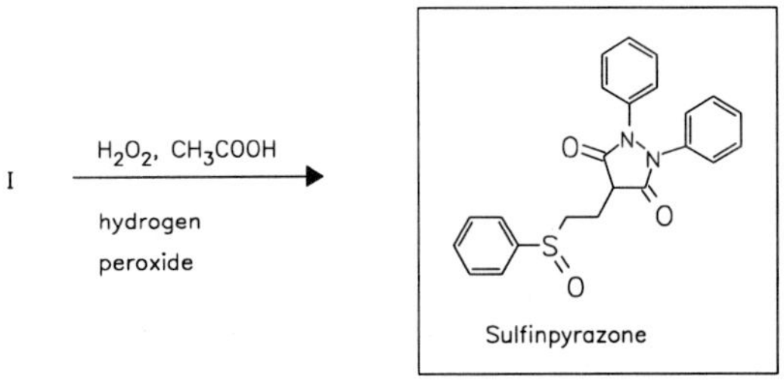

I → H₂O₂, CH₃COOH

hydrogen
peroxide

Sulfinpyrazone

Reference(s):
DE 903 578 (Geigy; appl. 1951; CH-prior. 1950).
US 2 700 671 (Geigy; 1955; CH-prior. 1950).
CH 303 938 (Geigy; appl. 1950).
Pfister, R.; Häfliger, F.: Helv. Chim. Acta (HCACAV) **44**, 232 (1961).

Formulation(s):   drg. 200 mg; tabl. 100 mg

Trade Name(s):
D: Anturano (Geigy); wfm   I: Enturen (CIBA Vision)   USA: Anturane (Geigy); wfm
F: Anturan (Geigy); wfm   J: Anturan (Ciba-Geigy-
GB: Anturan (Novartis)   Fujisawa)

Sulfisomidine
(Sulphasomidine)

ATC: J01E
Use: chemotherapeutic

RN: 515-64-0   MF: $C_{12}H_{14}N_4O_2S$ MW: 278.34   EINECS: 208-204-3
LD$_{50}$:   50 g/kg (M, p.o.)
CN: 4-amino-*N*-(2,6-dimethyl-4-pyrimidinyl)benzenesulfonamide

sodium salt hydrate
RN: 2462-17-1   MF: $C_{12}H_{13}N_4NaO_2S \cdot H_2O$ MW: 318.33

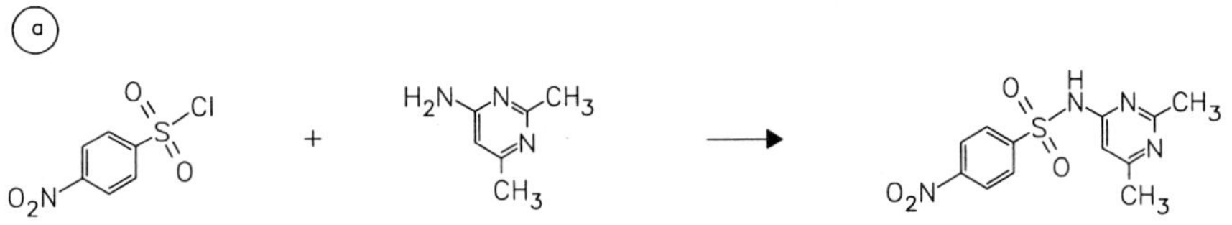

ⓐ

4-nitrobenzene-
sulfonyl chloride

6-amino-2,4-di-
methylpyrimidine (I)

(II)

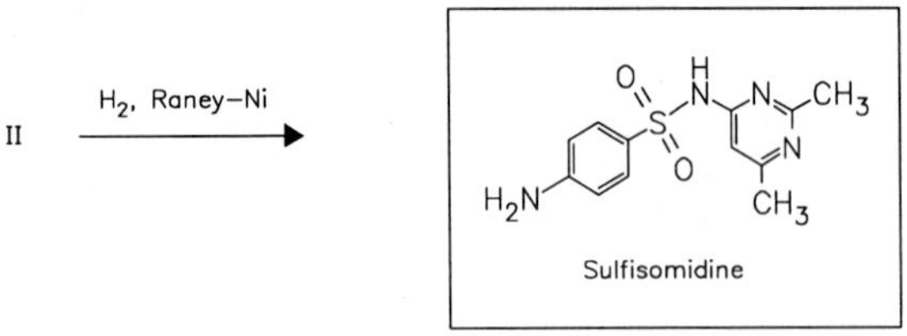

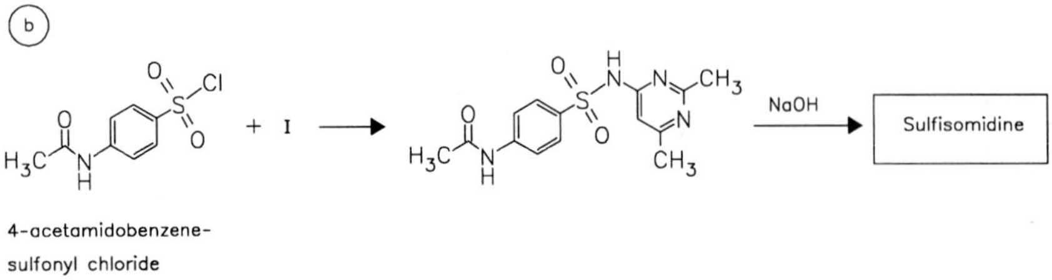

Sulfisomidine

4-acetamidobenzene-
sulfonyl chloride

Reference(s):
US 2 351 333 (Geigy; 1944; CH-prior. 1940).

Formulation(s):   eye drops 114.4 mg; ophthalmic ointment 100 mg (as sodium salt hydrate)

Trade Name(s):
D:	Aristamid (Nordmark); wfm	F:	Elcosine (Ciba); wfm	USA:	Elkosin (Ciba); wfm
		J:	Domian (Dainippon)		Elkosin (Ciba-Geigy); wfm
	Elkosin (Ciba); wfm		Entamidine (Nippon Shoji)		

Sulforidazine

ATC: N05C
Use: neuroleptic

RN: 14759-06-9   MF: $C_{21}H_{26}N_2O_2S_2$ MW: 402.58   EINECS: 238-818-7
LD$_{50}$:   29 mg/kg (M, i.v.); 520 mg/kg (M, p.o.);
        24 mg/kg (R, i.v.)
CN: 10-[2-(1-methyl-2-piperidinyl)ethyl]-2-(methylsulfonyl)-10H-phenothiazine

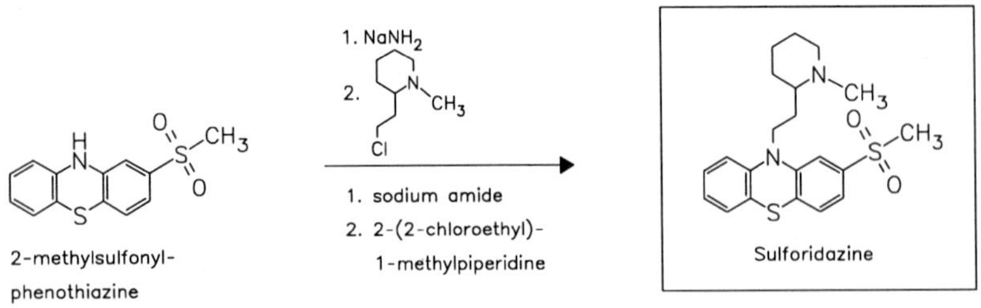

2-methylsulfonyl-
phenothiazine

1. sodium amide
2. 2-(2-chloroethyl)-
    1-methylpiperidine

Sulforidazine

Reference(s):
FR 1 459 476 (Sandoz; appl. 30.11.1965; CH-prior. 15.9.1965).

alternative synthesis:
FR 1 363 683 (Sandoz; appl. 17.7.1963; CH-prior. 19.7.1962, 23.10.1962).

Formulation(s):   drg. 50 mg

Sulfoxone sodium
(Aldesulfon Natrium)

ATC: D08
Use: chemotherapeutic (leprosy)

RN: 144-75-2   MF: C$_{14}$H$_{14}$N$_2$Na$_2$O$_6$S$_3$ MW: 448.45
LD$_{50}$:   10 g/kg (M, p.o.)
CN: [sulfonylbis(4,1-phenyleneimino)]bis[methanesulfinic acid] disodium salt

free acid
RN: 144-76-3   MF: C$_{14}$H$_{16}$N$_2$O$_6$S$_3$ MW: 404.49

dapsone   sodium form-   Sulfoxone sodium
(q. v.)   aldehydesulfoxylate

Reference(s):
US 2 234 981 (US-Secretary of the Treasury; 1941; appl. 1938).

Formulation(s):   tabl. 330 mg

Trade Name(s):
J: Diazon (Joshitomi)   USA: Diasone Sodium (Abbott);
                                           wfm

Sulindac

ATC: M01AB02
Use: anti-inflammatory, analgesic,
        antipyretic

RN: 38194-50-2   MF: C$_{20}$H$_{17}$FO$_3$S   MW: 356.42   EINECS: 253-819-2
LD$_{50}$:   507 mg/kg (M, p.o.);
        264 mg/kg (R, p.o.)
CN: (Z)-5-fluoro-2-methyl-1-[[4-(methylsulfinyl)phenyl]methylene]-1H-indene-3-acetic acid

4-fluorobenz-   propionic   4-fluoro-α-methyl-
aldehyde   anhydride   cinnamic acid

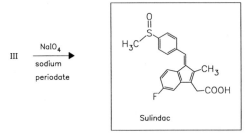

4-fluoro-α-methyl-dihydrocinnamic acid (I)

polyphosphoric acid 95 °C

5-fluoro-2-methyl-3-indanone

1. $NC-COOH$, CH_3COOH, CH_3COONH_4
2. KOH
3. HCl

1. cyanoacetic acid

II

5-fluoro-2-methyl-indene-3-acetic acid (II)

+

4-methylthio-benzaldehyde

$NaOCH_3$

5-fluoro-2-methyl-1-(4-methylthiobenzylidene)-indene-3-acetic acid (III)

III

$NaIO_4$

sodium periodate

Sulindac

Reference(s):
DE 2 039 426 (Merck & Co.; appl. 7.8.1970; USA-prior. 8.8.1969, 1.5.1970).
US 3 654 349 (Merck & Co.; 4.4.1972; prior. 8.8.1969, 1.5.1970).
US 3 647 858 (Merck & Co.; 7.3.1972; prior. 19.11.1969, 1.5.1970).
US 3 725 548 (Merck & Co.; 3.4.1973; prior. 6.10.1971).
US 3 882 239 (Merck & Co.; 6.5.1975; prior. 21.1.1971, 6.9.1972, 13.6.1974).

Formulation(s):   tabl. 150 mg, 200 mg

Trade Name(s):
D: Imbaral (Merck Sharp & Dohme; 1977); wfm
F: Arthrocine (Merck Sharp & Dohme-Chibret; 1977)
GB: Clinoril (Merck Sharp & Dohme; 1977)
I: Algocetil (Francia Farm.)

Citereuma (CT)
Clinoril (Neopharmed)
Lyndac (Eurofarmaco)
Sulartrene (NGSN)
Sulen (Farmacologico Milanese)
Sulic (Crosara)

Sulinol (ICT)
J: Chinoril (Merck-Banyu)
USA: Clinoril (Merck Sharp & Dohme; 1978)

Sulmetozin
(Trithiozine)

ATC: A02BX
Use: gastric acid secretion inhibitor, peptic ulcer therapeutic

RN: 35619-65-9 MF: $C_{14}H_{19}NO_4S$ MW: 297.38 EINECS: 252-645-4
LD$_{50}$: 3 g/kg (M, p.o.);
     670 mg/kg (R, p.o.)
CN: 4-[thioxo(3,4,5-trimethoxyphenyl)methyl]morpholine

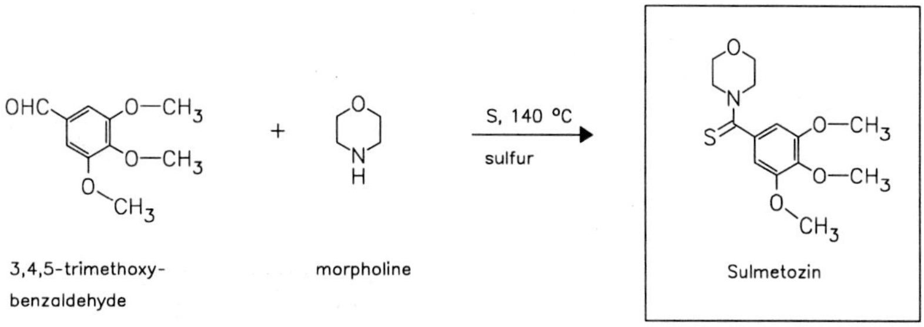

3,4,5-trimethoxy-
benzaldehyde   morpholine   Sulmetozin

Reference(s):

DOS 2 102 246 (ISF; appl. 19.1.1971; I-prior. 31.7.1970).
Banfi, S. et al.: Chim. Ther. (CHTPBA) **4**, 462 (1973).

Trade Name(s):
I: Tresanil (Italseber); wfm

Suloctidil

ATC: C01DX
Use: vasodilator

RN: 54767-75-8   MF: $C_{20}H_{35}NOS$ MW: 337.57   EINECS: 259-332-1
CN: (R*,S*)-4-[(1-methylethyl)thio]-α-[1-(octylamino)ethyl]benzenemethanol

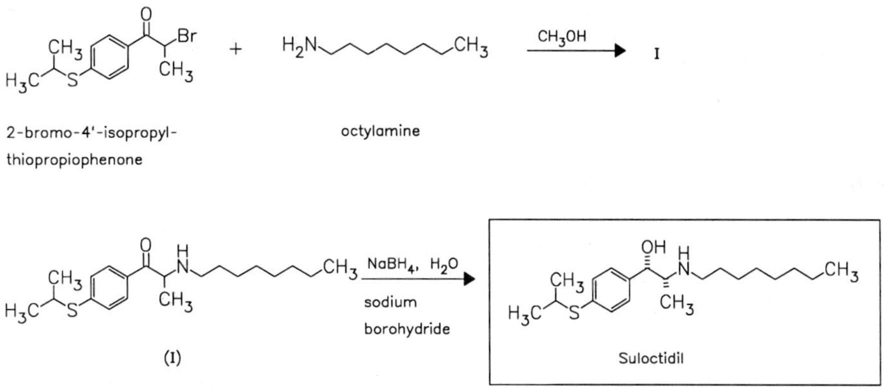

2-bromo-4'-isopropyl-
thiopropiophenone   octylamine

(I)   Suloctidil

Reference(s):

DOS 2 334 404 (Continental Pharma; appl. 6.7.1973; GB-prior. 9.4.1973).
US 4 228 187 (Continental Pharma; 14.10.1980; appl. 30.8.1976; GB-prior. 9.4.1973).

alternative syntheses.

ES 460 766 (Lab. F. Bonet; appl. 14.7.1977).
JP 54 005 928 (Mitsubishi; appl. 15.6.1977).
JP 54 005 929 (Mitsubishi; appl. 15.6.1977).
JP 54 005 930 (Mitsubishi; appl. 15.6.1977).
JP 54 019 927 (Zambeletti; appl. 11.7.1977).

use as vasodilator:

JP 54 005 930 (Mitsubishi; appl. 1979).

Formulation(s):   cps. 100 mg, tabl. 100 mg

Trade Name(s):

D: Fluversin (Searle; 1980);   Euvasal (Selvi); wfm   Polivasol (Coli); wfm
     wfm   Llangene (Farmochimica
GB: Duloctil (Searle); wfm   Ital.); wfm
I: Cerebro (Sidus); wfm   Locton (Lepetit); wfm

Sulpiride

ATC: N05AL01
Use: psychotropic drug, antispasmodic, anti-emetic, antidepressant, antipsychotic

RN: 15676-16-1   MF: $C_{15}H_{23}N_3O_4S$ MW: 341.43   EINECS: 239-753-7
LD$_{50}$: 48 mg/kg (M, i.v.); 1700 mg/kg (M, p.o.);
         40 mg/kg (R, i.v.); 9800 mg/kg (R, p.o.);
         137 mg/kg (dog, i.v.); 2 g/kg (dog, p.o.)
CN: 5-(aminosulfonyl)-*N*-[(1-ethyl-2-pyrrolidinyl)methyl]-2-methoxybenzamide

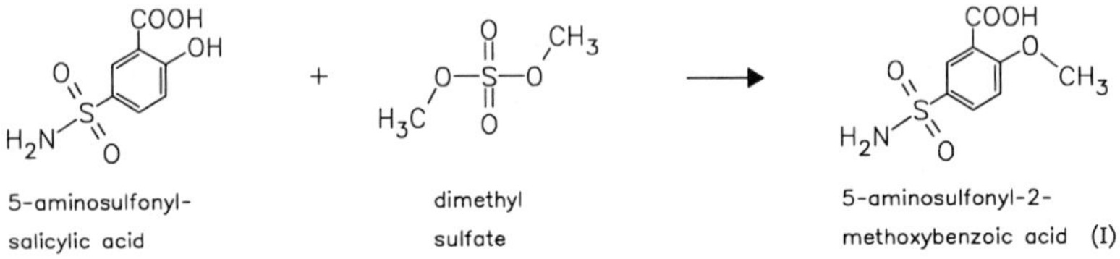

5-aminosulfonyl-salicylic acid   +   dimethyl sulfate   →   5-aminosulfonyl-2-methoxybenzoic acid   (I)

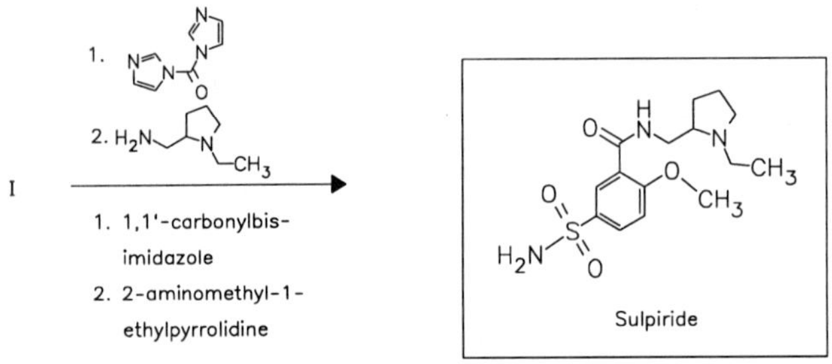

I →

1. 1,1'-carbonylbis-imidazole
2. 2-aminomethyl-1-ethylpyrrolidine

Sulpiride

Reference(s):
DOS 1 595 915 (Soc. d'Etudes Scientif. et Ind. de l'Ile-de-France; appl. 8.1.1965; USA-prior. 13.1.1964).
DOS 1 795 723 (Soc. d'Etudes Scientif. et Ind. de l'Ile-de-France; appl. 8.1.1965; USA-prior. 13.1.1964).
US 3 342 826 (Soc. d'Etudes Scientif. et Ind. de l'Ile-de-France; 19.9.1967; appl. 13.1.1964).

alternative synthesis via the enamine from 2-aminomethyl-1-ethylpyrrolidine *and* acetylacetic acid methyl ester:
US 4 077 976 (Soc. d'Etudes Scientif. et Ind. de l'Ile-de-France; 7.3.1978; F-prior. 12.6.1975).

alternative synthesis:
GB 1 492 166 (Alkaloida Vegyeszetigyar; appl. 26.3.1976; H-prior. 28.3.1975).

preparation of 2-aminomethyl-1-ethylpyrrolidine *from* 1-ethyl- *resp.* 1-vinyl-2-pyrrolidinone *via* 1-ethyl-2-nitromethylpyrrolidine:
DAS 1 941 536 (Soc. d'Etudes Scientif. et Ind. de l'Ile-de-France; appl. 14.8.1969; J-prior. 19.8.1968, 20.5.1969, 9.6.1969).
DAS 1 966 195 (Soc. d'Etudes Scientif. et Ind. de l'Ile-de-France; appl. 14.8.1969; J-prior. 19.8.1968, 20.5.1969, 9.6.1969).

optically active "Levo"-sulpiride:
DOS 2 903 891 (Ravizza; appl. 1.2.1979; I-prior. 16.2.1978).

Formulation(s):   amp. 100 mg/2 ml, 100 mg/3 ml; cps. 50 mg; tabl. 50 mg, 200 mg

Trade Name(s):

D: Arminol (Krewel
    Meuselbach)
    Desulpid (Desitin)
    Dogmatil (Synthelabo;
    1972)
    Meresa (Dolorgiet)
    Neogama (Hormosan)
    Sulp (Neuro Hexal)
    Sulpirid-ratiopharm
    (ratiopharm)
    Sulpivert (Hennig)

    vertigo-neogama
    (Hormosan)
F: Aiglonyl (Fumouze)
    Dogmatil (Synthélabo;
    1969)
    Synédil (Yamanouchi
    Pharma)
GB: Dolmatil (Delalande; 1983)
    Sulparex (Bristol-Myers
    Squibb)

    Sulpitil (Pharmacia &
    Upjohn)
I: Championyl (Synthelabo)
    Dobren (Ravizza)
    Equilid (Bruno
    Farmaceutici)
J: Abilit (Sumitomo)
    Coolspan (Hishiyama)
    Dogmatyl (Fujisawa)
    Miradol (Mitsui)
    Omperan (Taiho)

Sultamicillin
(CP-49952; VD-1827)

ATC: J01CR04
Use: antibacterial, semisynthetic β-lactam
      antibiotic (double ester of ampicillin
      and sulbactam)

RN: 76497-13-7   MF: $C_{25}H_{30}N_4O_9S_2$ MW: 594.67
CN: [2S-[2α(2R*,5S*),5α,6β(S*)]]-6-[(aminophenylacetyl)amino]-3,3-dimethyl-7-oxo-4-thia-1-
     azabicyclo[3.2.0]heptane-2-carboxylic acid [[(3,3-dimethyl-7-oxo-4-thia-1-azabicyclo[3.2.0]hept-2-
     yl)carbonyl]oxy]methyl ester S,S-dioxide

monotosylate
RN: 83105-70-8   MF: $C_{25}H_{30}N_4O_9S_2 \cdot C_7H_8O_3S$ MW: 766.87

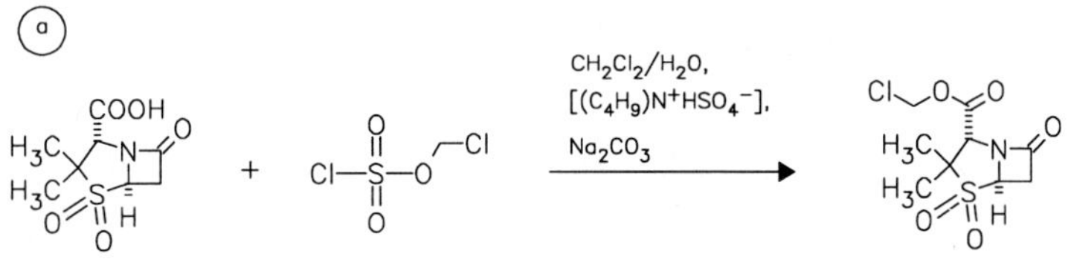

sulbactam
(q. v.)

(I)

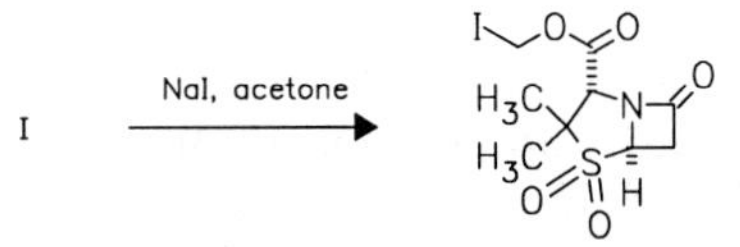

iodomethyl
penicillanate
S,S-dioxide (II)

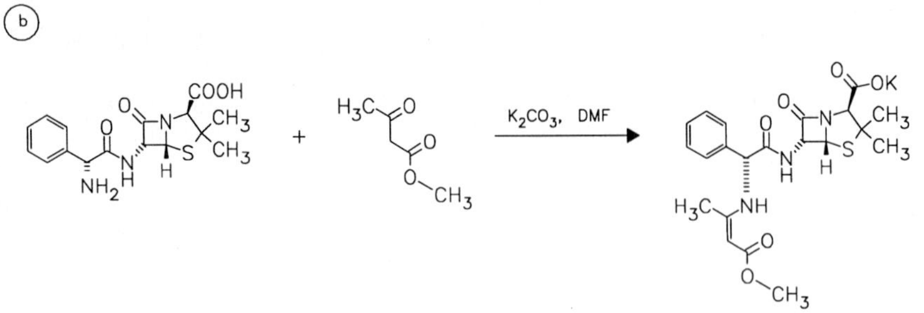

b)

ampicillin	methyl	Dane salt
(q. v.)	acetoacetate	of ampicillin (III)

c)

II + III

1. DMF, 5–10 °C
2. H₂O, HCl

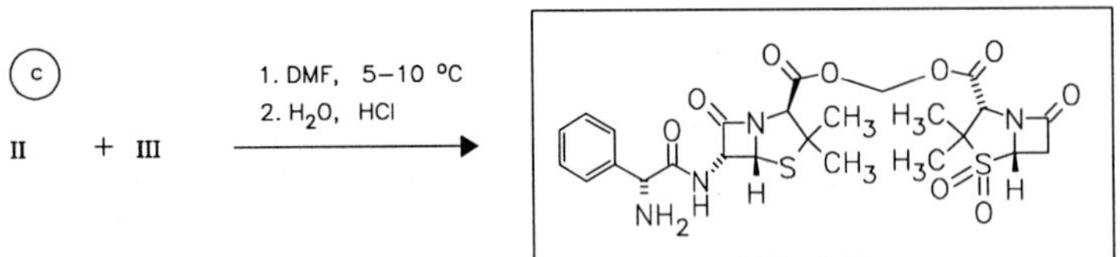

Sultamicillin

Reference(s):
Baltzer, B. et al.: J. Antibiot. (JANTAJ) **33**, 1183 (1980).
US 4 342 772 (Leo; 3.8.1982; UK-prior. 13.2.1979, 19.6.1979, 9.8.1979, 14.11.1979).
US 4 407 751 (Leo; 4.10.1983; UK-prior. 13.2.1979, 19.6.1979, 9.8.1979, 14.11.1979, 25.1.1980).
DOS 3 005 164 (Leo; appl. 12.2.1980; UK-prior. 13.2.1979, 19.6.1979, 9.8.1979, 14.11.1979).

Formulation(s):　f. c. tabl. 375 mg (as tosylate); vial 375 mg

Trade Name(s):
D:　Unacid P Doral (Pfizer)　　J:　Unasyn (Pfizer Taito; 1987)　USA:　Unasyn (Pfizer); wfm

Sultiame
(Sulthiame)

ATC:　N03AX03
Use:　anticonvulsant, antiepileptic

RN:　61-56-3　MF: C₁₀H₁₄N₂O₄S₂　MW: 290.36　EINECS: 200-511-0
LD₅₀:　4852 mg/kg (M, p.o.);
　　　>5 g/kg (R, p.o.)
CN:　4-(tetrahydro-2H-1,2-thiazin-2-yl)benzenesulfonamide S,S-dioxide

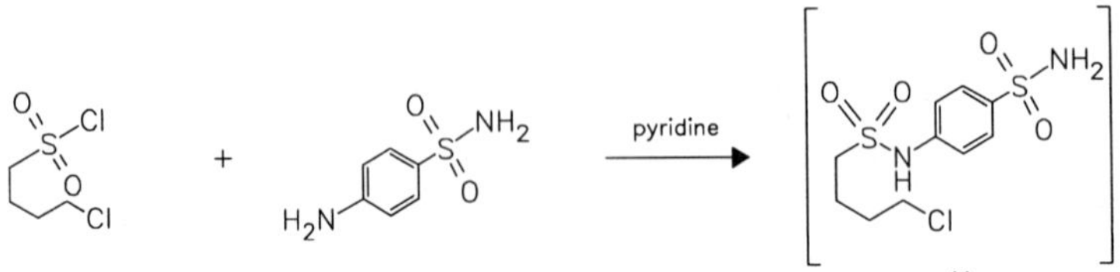

4-chloro-1-butanesulfonyl chloride	4-aminobenzene-sulfonamide	pyridine	(I)

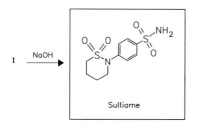

Sultiame

Reference(s):
DE 1 111 191 (Bayer; appl. 28.3.1959).

Formulation(s):   f. c. tabl. 50 mg, 200 mg

Trade Name(s):
D:	Ospolot/mite (Bayer)	I:	Ospolot (Bayer); wfm	J:	Ospolot (Bayer)	
F:	Elisal (Specia); wfm		Ospolot (Bayropharm);	USA:	Conadil (Riker); wfm	
GB:	Ospolot (Bayer); wfm		wfm		Trolone (Riker); wfm	

Sultopride

ATC: N05AL02
Use: anti-emetic, psychotropic drug,
        antidepressant

RN: 53583-79-2   MF: $C_{17}H_{26}N_2O_4S$ MW: 354.47   EINECS: 258-641-9
LD_{50}:   665 mg/kg (M, p.o.)
CN: *N*-[(1-ethyl-2-pyrrolidinyl)methyl]-5-(ethylsulfonyl)-2-methoxybenzamide

hydrochloride
RN: 23694-17-9   MF: $C_{17}H_{26}N_2O_4S \cdot HCl$ MW: 390.93

5-ethylsulfonyl-2-
methoxybenzoic acid

1. isobutyl chloroformate
2. 2-aminomethyl-1-ethyl-
   pyrrolidine

Sultopride

Reference(s):
DOS 2 327 192 (Soc. d'Etudes Scientifique et Industrielles de l'Ile-de-France; appl. 28.5.1973; F-prior. 1.6.1972, 12.6.1972, 3.4.1973).
DOS 2 327 193 (Soc. d'Etudes Scientifique et Industrielles de l'Ile-de-France; appl. 28.5.1973; F-prior. 1.6.1972, 2.6.1972).
FR 2 187 309 (Soc. d'Etudes Scientifique et Industrielles de l'Ile-de-France; appl. 1.6.1972).

Formulation(s):   amp. 200 mg/2 ml; tabl. 400 mg (as hydrochloride)

Sultroponium

ATC: A03
Use: anticholinergic, antispasmodic

RN: 15130-91-3   MF: $C_{20}H_{29}NO_6S$ MW: 411.52
CN: endo-(±)-3-(3-hydroxy-1-oxo-2-phenylpropoxy)-8-methyl-8-(3-sulfopropyl)-8-
      azoniabicyclo[3.2.1]octane hydroxide inner salt

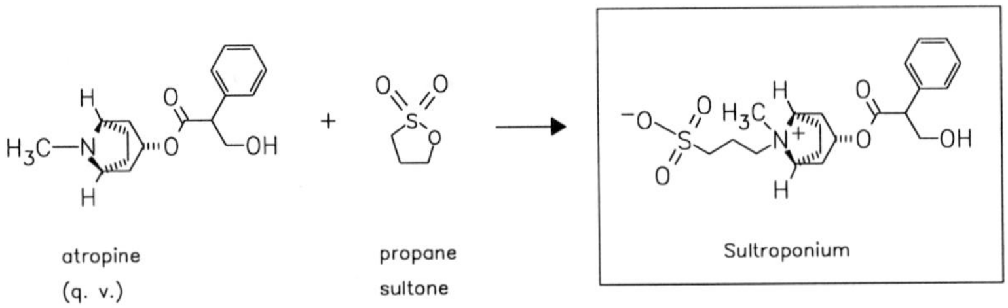

atropine   propane   Sultroponium
(q. v.)   sultone

Reference(s):
GB 1 082 445 (J. P. M. Raudnitz, H. Wahl; appl. 2.12.1965; F-prior. 3.12.1964).

Formulation(s):   amp. 5 mg; suppos. 25 mg; tabl. 15 mg

Sumatriptan

ATC: N02CC01
Use: antimigraine agent, selective 5-HT$_1$-
       receptor agonist

RN: 103628-46-2   MF: $C_{14}H_{21}N_3O_2S$ MW: 295.41
CN: 3-[2-(dimethylamino)ethyl]-N-methyl-1H-indole-5-methanesulfonamide

succinate (1:1)
RN: 103628-48-4   MF: $C_{14}H_{21}N_3O_2S \cdot C_4H_6O_4$ MW: 413.50
LD$_{50}$:   43.112 mg/kg (R, i.v.); >2.939 g/kg (R, p.o.)

1. H_2, Pd–C
2. $NaNO_2$, HCl
3. $SnCl_2$

4-chlorobutanal
dimethyl acetal

4-nitrophenyl-N-methyl-
methanesulfonamide

4-hydrazinophenyl-N-methyl-
methanesulfonamide   (I)

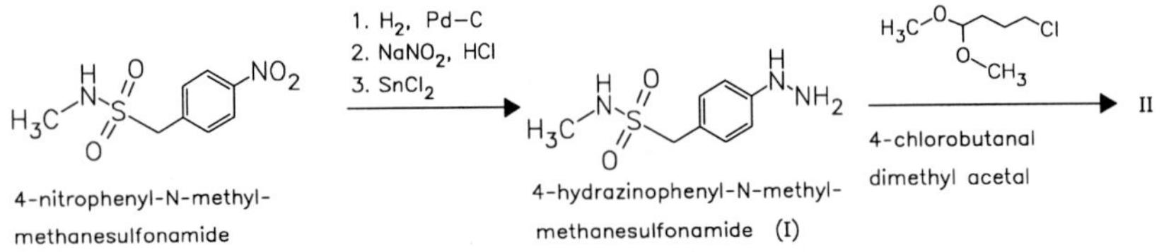

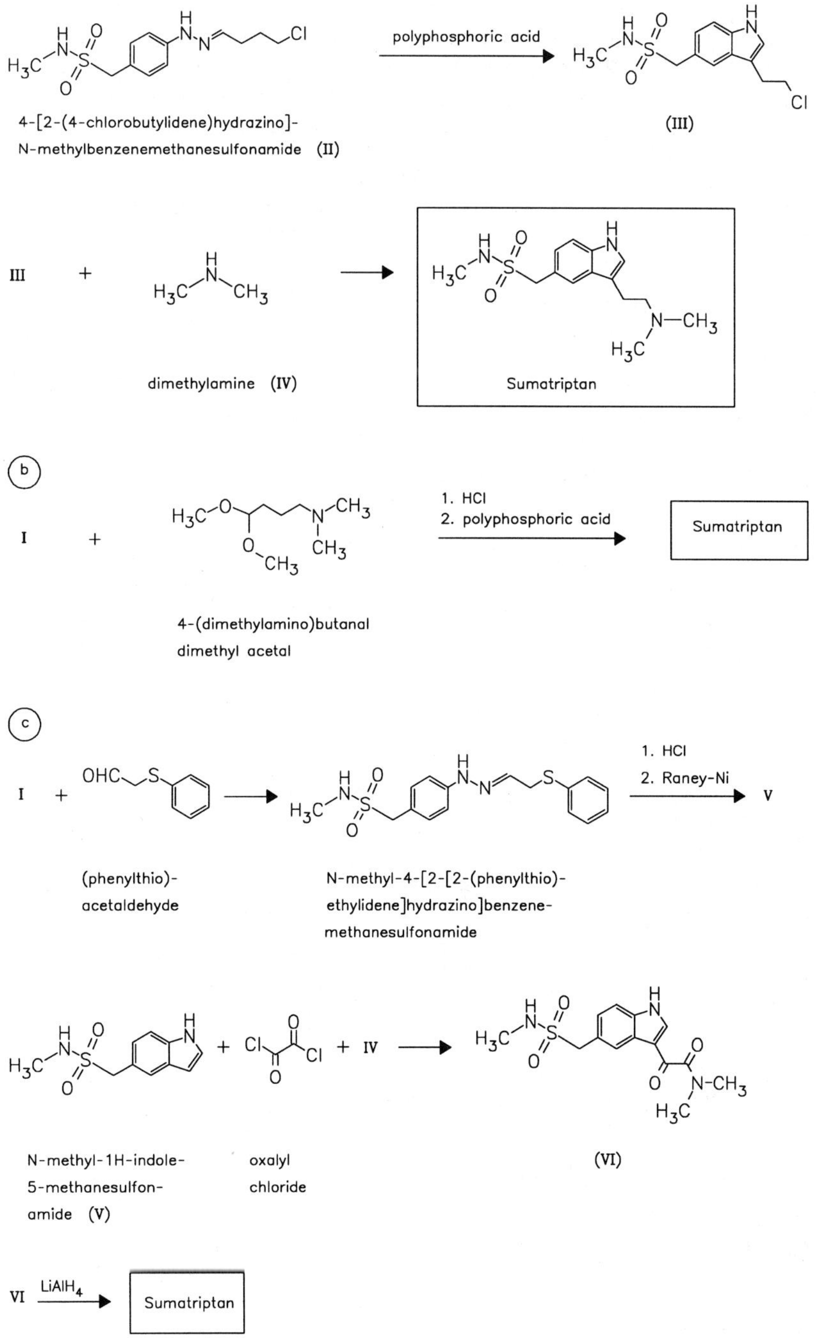

4-[2-(4-chlorobutylidene)hydrazino]-
N-methylbenzenemethanesulfonamide (II)

(III)

III +

dimethylamine (IV)

Sumatriptan

b

I +

1. HCl
2. polyphosphoric acid

Sumatriptan

4-(dimethylamino)butanal
dimethyl acetal

c

I +

(phenylthio)-
acetaldehyde

1. HCl
2. Raney-Ni

V

N-methyl-4-[2-[2-(phenylthio)-
ethylidene]hydrazino]benzene-
methanesulfonamide

N-methyl-1H-indole-
5-methanesulfon-
amide (V)

oxalyl
chloride

+ IV →

(VI)

VI —LiAlH₄→ Sumatriptan

Reference(s):
a   DOS 3 320 521 (Glaxo; appl. 6.7.1983; GB-prior. 6.7.1982).
   GB 2 124 210 (Glaxo; appl. 7-6-1982).
b,c DOS 3 527 648 (Glaxo; appl. 8.1.1985; GB-prior. 8.1.1984).
   GB 2 162 522 (Glaxo; appl. 8.1.1984).

Formulation(s):   f. c. tabl. 50 mg, 100 mg; nasal spray 10 mg/0.1 ml, 20 mg/0.1 ml; suppos. 25 mg;
   syringe 6 mg; tabl. 25 mg, 50 mg; vial 6 mg/0.5 ml (as succinate)

Trade Name(s):
D: Imigran (Glaxo Wellcome/
      Cascan)
F: Imigrane (Glaxo
      Wellcome)

Imijekt (Glaxo Wellcome)
GB: Imigran (Glaxo Wellcome;
      1991)
I: Imigran (Glaxo Wellcome)

USA: Imitrex (Glaxo Wellcome)

Suplatast tosilate
(IPD-1151T)

ATC: R03
Use: antiallergic, antiasthmatic

RN: 94055-76-2   MF: $C_{16}H_{26}NO_4S \cdot C_7H_7O_3$ MW: 467.58
LD_{50}: 81 mg/kg (M, i.v.); >12.5 g/kg (M, p.o.);
      93 mg/kg (R, i.v.); >10 g/kg (R, p.o.);
      2124 mg/kg (dog, p.o.)
CN: [3-[[4-(3-ethoxy-2-hydroxypropoxy)phenyl]amino]-3-oxopropyl]dimethylsulfonium p-toluenesulfonate
      (1:1)

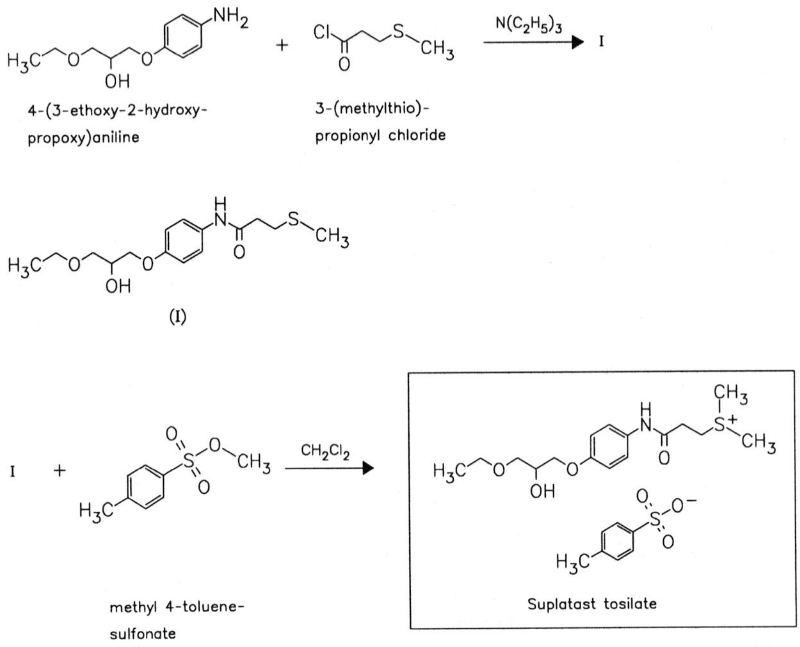

4-(3-ethoxy-2-hydroxy-
propoxy)aniline

3-(methylthio)-
propionyl chloride

(I)

methyl 4-toluene-
sulfonate

Suplatast tosilate

Reference(s):
DE 3 408 708 (Taiho Pharm.; 13.9.1984; J-prior. 11.3.1983).

resolution:
JP 07 252 213 (Taiho Pharm. 3.1.1995; J-prior. 27.1.1994).

topical application:
EP 624 367 (Senju/Taiho Pharm.; 17.11.1994; J-prior. 14.5.1993).

Formulation(s):   cps. 50 mg, 100 mg

Trade Name(s):
J: IPD (Taiho)   MPD (Taiho)

Suprofen

ATC: M01AE07
Use: anti-inflammatory, analgesic

RN: 40828-46-4   MF: $C_{14}H_{12}O_3S$ MW: 260.31   EINECS: 255-096-9
LD$_{50}$:   185 mg/kg (M, i.v.); 590 mg/kg (M, p.o.);
226 mg/kg (R, i.v.); 70.6 mg/kg (R, p.o.);
>160 mg/kg (dog, p.o.)
CN: α-methyl-4-(2-thienylcarbonyl)benzeneacetic acid

Reference(s):
DOS 2 353 357 (Janssen; appl. 24.10.1973; USA-prior. 24.10.1972, 10.9.1973, 23.3.1974).
Daele, P.G.H. van et al.: Arzneim.-Forsch. (ARZNAD) 25, 1495 (1975).

Formulation(s):   cps. 200 mg

Trade Name(s):
GB: Suprol (Cilag); wfm   Sufenide (Italfarmaco);   Lindrax (Taiho)
I: Erdol (Herdel); wfm   wfm   Mexaron (Toyo Yozo)
      Masterfin (Dompé); wfm   Suprol (Cilag); wfm   Sulplotin (Ichikawa Labs)
                            J: Lindral (Taiho)   USA: Suprol (Ortho); wfm

Surfactant TA

(Beractant)

ATC: R07A
Use: surfactant (for treatment of respiratory distress syndrome)

RN: 108778-82-1   MF: unspecified   MW: unspecified
LD$_{50}$:   2000 mg/kg (M, i.p.); 3000 mg/kg (M, p.o.)
CN: beractant

Production comprises (a) extracting mammalian lung slices with an electrolyte soln. (NaCl), (b) centrifuging the extract to collect a crude precipitation, (c) suspending the precipitate in water, adjusting specific gravity of the suspension with CaCl$_2$ and centrifuging the suspension to separate upper emulsion layer, (d) dialysing the emulsion and freeze-drying the dialysed soln., (e) treating the resultant powder with ethyl acetate, collecting the insoluble material and extracting the insoluble material with an organic solvent (CH$_3$OH, CHCl$_3$) and (f) concentrating the extract to give a solid.

Reference(s):
DE 3 021 006 (Tokyo Tanabe; appl. 30.5.1980; J-prior. 2.6.1979).
US 4 397 839 (Tokyo Tanabe; 9.8.1983; J-prior. 10.9.1981).

Formulation(s):   vial 120 mg (lyo.)

Trade Name(s):
J: Surfacten (Tokyo Tanabe; 1987)

Suxamethonium chloride

(Succinylcholine chloride)

ATC: M03AB01
Use: muscle relaxant

RN: 71-27-2   MF: C$_{14}$H$_{30}$Cl$_2$N$_2$O$_4$ MW: 361.31   EINECS: 200-747-4
LD$_{50}$:   430 µg/kg (M, i.v.)
CN: 2,2'-[(1,4-dioxo-1,4-butanediyl)bis(oxy)]bis[*N,N,N*-trimethylethanaminium] dichloride

succinyl
chloride

2-dimethyl-
aminoethanol

bis(2-dimethylaminoethyl)
succinate (I)

methyl
chloride

Suxamethonium chloride

Reference(s):
Tammelin, L.E.: Acta Chem. Scand. (ACHSE7) **7**, 185 (1953).
Walker, J.: J. Chem. Soc. (JCSOA9) **1950**, 193.

suxamethonium-chloride – *dry ampules:*
US 2 957 501 (Burroughs Wellcome; 1960; appl. 1958).
US 2 957 609 (Burroughs Wellcome; 1960; appl. 1958).

Formulation(s):   amp. 50 mg/5 ml, 100 mg/5 ml; vial 100 mg/10 ml, 200 mg/10 ml

Trade Name(s):

D:	Lysthenon (Nycomed)	GB:	Anecthine (Glaxo	J:	Relaxin (Kyorin)
	Pantolax (Schwabe-		Wellcome)		Succin (Yamanouchi)
	Curamed)	I:	Midarine (Glaxo	USA:	Anecthine (Glaxo
	Succicuran (Rodleben)		Wellcome)		Wellcome)
F:	Célocurine (Pharmacia &		Myotenlis (Pharmacia &		
	Upjohn)		Upjohn)		

Suxibuzone

ATC: M02AA22
Use: antirheumatic

RN: 27470-51-5   MF: $C_{24}H_{26}N_2O_6$ MW: 438.48   EINECS: 248-477-6
LD$_{50}$:   285 mg/kg (M, i.v.); 1200 mg/kg (M, p.o.);
          305 mg/kg (R, i.v.); 1700 mg/kg (R, p.o.);
          373 mg/kg (dog, p.o.)
CN: butanedioic acid mono[(4-butyl-3,5-dioxo-1,2-diphenyl-4-pyrazolidinyl)methyl] ester

phenylbutazone   form-   Suxibuzone
(q. v.)   aldehyde

Reference(s):
DE 1 936 747 (Lab. Dr. Esteve; appl. 18.7.1969; E-prior. 20.7.1968).

Formulation(s):   cream 7 %

Trade Name(s):

D:	Solurol (Delalande); wfm	F:	Calibene (Carrion); wfm	J:	Danicon (Taiho-Fujisawa)

Synephrine

(Oxedrine)

ATC: C01CA08
Use: sympathomimetic, adrenergic,
         vasopressor

RN: 94-07-5   MF: $C_9H_{13}NO_2$ MW: 167.21   EINECS: 202-300-9
LD$_{50}$:   270 mg/kg (M, i.v.)
CN: 4-hydroxy-α-[(methylamino)methyl]benzenemethanol

tartrate (2:1)
RN: 16589-24-5   MF: $C_9H_{13}NO_2 \cdot 1/2C_4H_6O_6$ MW: 484.50   EINECS: 240-647-8

phenol   (methylamino)-   4'-hydroxy-2-methyl-
                acetonitrile   aminoacetophenone (I)

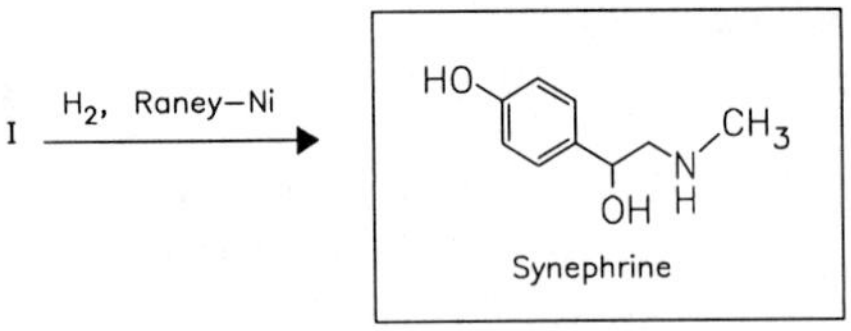

Synephrine

Reference(s):

US 2 585 988 (Hartford Nat. Bank; 1952; NL-prior. 1948).
DRP 522 790 (H. Legerlotz; 1929).
DRP 566 578 (Boehringer Ing.; 1927).
DRP 569 149 (Boehringer Ing.; 1928).

Formulation(s):　drg. 12.5 mg in comb.; eye drops 0.5 mg/ml, 1 mg/ml in comb.; nasal drops 1.5 mg/ml in comb.; sol. 100 mg/g

Trade Name(s):

D:	Corpivas (Pascoe)-comb. Dacrin (Chibret)-comb. Ophtalmin (Winzer)-comb. Pasgensin (Pascoe)-comb. Solupen (Winzer) Sympatol (Boehringer Ing.)	F:	Antalyre (Boehringer Ing.)-comb. Dacryne (Martin-Johnson & Johnson-MSD)-comb. Dacryoboraline (Martin-Johnson & Johnson-MSD)-comb.	GB: I:	Posine (Alcon)-comb. Sédacollyre (Rhône-Poulenc Rorer Cooper)-comb. Sympatol (Lewis); wfm Sympatol (Boehringer Ing.)

Syrosingopine

ATC:　C02LA09
Use:　antihypertensive

RN:　84-36-6　MF: $C_{35}H_{42}N_2O_{11}$　MW: 666.72　EINECS: 201-527-0
LD$_{50}$:　1293 mg/kg (M, p.o.);
　　　50 mg/kg (R, i.v.); >2 g/kg (R, p.o.)
CN:　(3β,16β,17α,18β,20α)-18[[4-[(ethoxycarbonyl)oxy]-3,5-dimethoxybenzoyl]oxy]-11,17-dimethoxyyohimban-16-carboxylic acid methyl ester

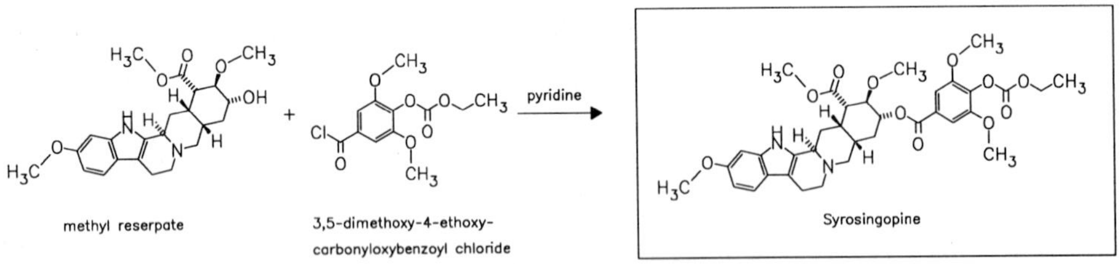

methyl reserpate

3,5-dimethoxy-4-ethoxy-carbonyloxybenzoyl chloride

Syrosingopine

Reference(s):

US 2 813 871 (Ciba 1957; appl. 1954).
Lucas, R.A. et al.: J. Am. Chem. Soc. (JACSAT) 81, 1928 (1959).

Formulation(s):　tabl. 1 mg in comb. with hydrochlorothiazide (25 mg); tabl. 0.5 mg

Trade Name(s):

I: Flurizin (Savio IBN)-
comb.; wfm
Ipodiuril (Ceccarelli)-
comb.; wfm
Neoreserpan (Panthox &
Burck); wfm

Novoserpina (Ghimas);
wfm
Raunova (Zambeletti); wfm
Raunova Plus (Zambeletti)-
comb.; wfm

J: Elumonon (Tatsumi)

Rosidil (Nippon
Chemiphar)
Tesamurin (Zensei)

USA: Singoserp-Esidrix (Ciba);
wfm

Tacalcitol
(TV-02)

ATC: D05AX04
Use: antipsoriatic

RN: 57333-96-7 MF: $C_{27}H_{44}O_3$ MW: 416.65
CN: (1α,3β,5Z,7E,24R)-9,10-Secocholesta-5,7,10(19)-triene-1,3,24-triol

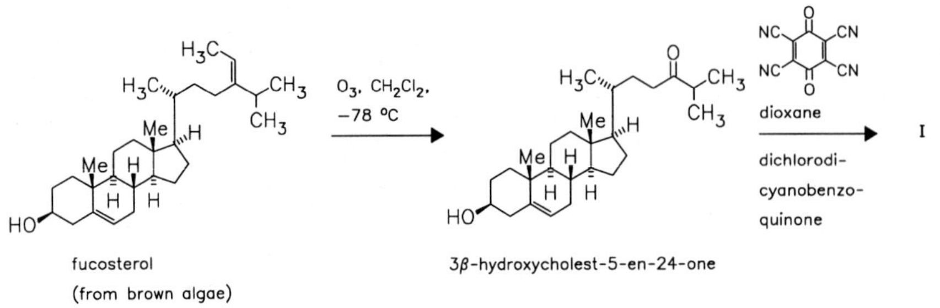

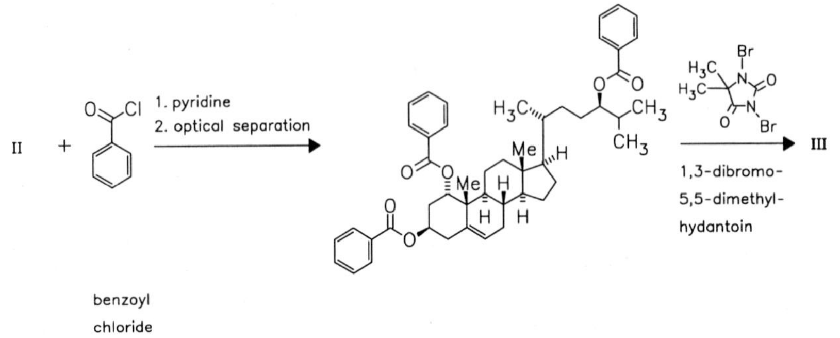

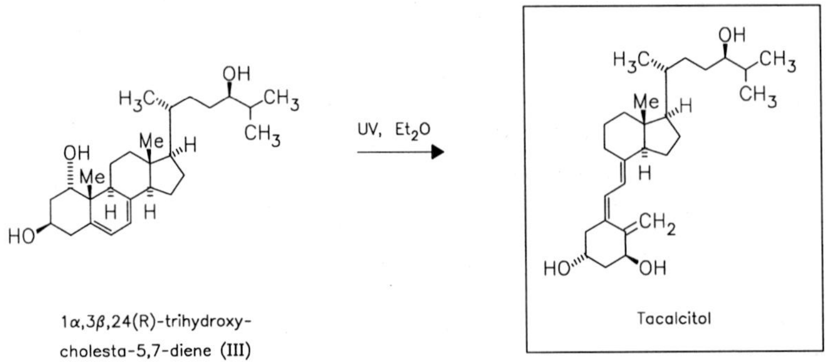

fucosterol
(from brown algae)

O_3, CH_2Cl_2,
−78 °C

3β-hydroxycholest-5-en-24-one

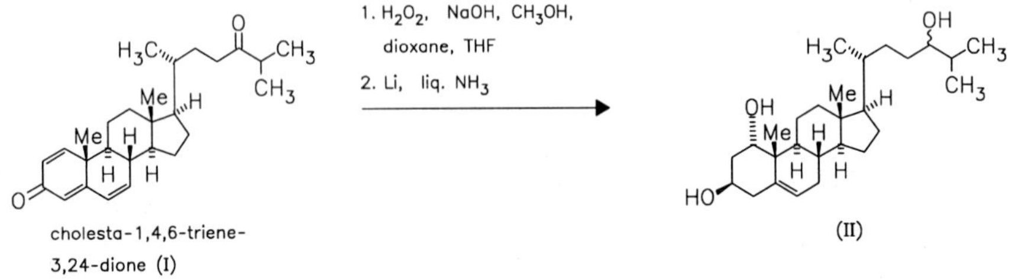

NC, CN
NC, CN
dioxane
dichlorodi-
cyanobenzo-
quinone

I

cholesta-1,4,6-triene-
3,24-dione (I)

1. H_2O_2, NaOH, CH_3OH,
   dioxane, THF
2. Li, liq. NH_3

(II)

II +

benzoyl
chloride

1. pyridine
2. optical separation

1,3-dibromo-
5,5-dimethyl-
hydantoin

III

1α,3β,24(R)-trihydroxy-
cholesta-5,7-diene (III)

UV, Et_2O

Tacalcitol

Reference(s):
DE 2 526 981 (Teijin; 18.6.1975; J-prior. 18.6.1974).
Synform (SNFMDF) **5** (1), 1-8 (1987).
Morisaki, M. et al.: J. Chem. Soc., Perkin Trans. 1 (JCPRB4) **1975**, 1421-1424.

Formulation(s):   ointment 4.17 μg/g (as hydrate); ointment 0.0002%, 0.0004%

Trade Name(s):
D: Curatoderm (Hermal)   J: Bonalfa (Teijin)
GB: Curatoderm (Merck)   Bonealfa (Fujisawa)

Tacrine

ATC: N06DA01
Use: acetylcholinesterase inhibitor, nootropic, antidementia

RN: 321-64-2   MF: $C_{13}H_{14}N_2$ MW: 198.27   EINECS: 206-291-2
LD_{50}: 20 mg/kg (R, i. v.); 70 mg/kg (R, p. o.);
        39.8 mg/kg (M, p. o.); 25 mg/kg (M, s. c.)
CN: 1,2,3,4-Tetrahydro-9-acridinamine

hydrochloride
RN: 1684-40-8   MF: $C_{13}H_{14}N_2 \cdot HCl$ MW: 234.73   EINECS: 216-867-5
hydrochloride monohydrate
RN: 7149-50-0   MF: $C_{13}H_{14}N_2 \cdot HCl \cdot H_2O$ MW: 252.75

aniline + ethyl 2-oxo-cyclohexane-carboxylate → (HCl, benzene) 1,2,3,4-tetra-hydro-9-acridone → (1. POCl₃ 2. NH₃, p-cresol) Tacrine

2-amino-benzonitrile + cyclo-hexanone (I) → (ZnCl₂) Tacrine

2-amino-banzamide + I + 4-methylaniline hydrochloride → Tacrine

(d)

isatin   +   I   →[aq. NH₃, 150°C, pressure vessel]   1,2,3,4-tetrahydro-acridine-9-carboxamide   →[Br₂, NaOCH₃ or aq. H₂SO₄, Δ]   Tacrine

(e)

1,2,3,4-tetrahydro-acridine   →[H₂O₂, CH₃COOH]   1,2,3,4-tetrahydro-acridine N-oxide   →[HNO₃, H₂SO₄]   1,2,3,4-tetrahydro-9-nitroacridine N-oxide (II)

II   →[Fe, CH₃COOH]   Tacrine

Reference(s):
a   US 3 232 945 (S. E. Massengill Co.; 1.2.1966; USA-prior. 13.8.1962).
    Albert; Gledhill: J. Soc. Chem. Ind., London (JSCIAN) **64**, 169 (1945).
b   Moore, J.A.; Kornreich, L.D.: Tetrahedron (TETRAB) **20**, 127 (1963).
    Goncharenko, S.B; Kaganskii, M.M.; Portnov, Yu.N.; Granik V.G.: Pharm. Chem. J. (Engl. Transl.)
    (PCJOAU) **26**, 769 (1992).
c   Girgis, N.S.; Pedersen, E.B.: Synthesis (SYNTBF) **5**, 547 (1985).
d   Ettel, V.; Neumann: Collect. Czech. Chem. Commun. (CCCCAK) **23**, 1319 (1958).
e   SU 319 596 (Klimov, G.A.; Makar'eva, T.N.; Tilchenko, M.N.)

Formulation(s):   cps. 10 mg, 20 mg, 30 mg, 40 mg (as hydrochloride)

Trade Name(s):
D: Cognex (Parke Davis)   F: Cognex (Parke Davis)   USA: Cognex (Parke Davis)

Tacrolimus
(FK-506; FR-900506; Fujimycin; L-679934)

ATC: L04AA05
Use: immunosuppressant

RN: 104987-11-3   MF: C₄₄H₆₉NO₁₂   MW: 804.03
CN: [3S-[3R*[E(1S*,3S*,4S*)],4S*,5R*,8S*,9E,12R*,14R*,15S*,16R*,18S*,19S*,26aR*]]-
    5,6,8,11,12,13,14,15,16,17,18,19,24,25,26,26a-hexadecahydro-5,19-dihydroxy-3-[2-(4-hydroxy-3-
    methoxycyclohexyl)-1-methylethenyl]-14,16-dimethoxy-4,10,12,18-tetramethyl-8-(2-propenyl)-15,19-
    epoxy-3H-pyrido[2,1-c][1,4]oxaazacyclotricosine-1,7,20,21(4H,23H)-tetrone

Isolation:
A fermentation broth of *Streptomyces tsukubaensis* No. 9993 is filtered and the mycelial cake is extracted with
acetone. The filtrate is combined with the acetone extract and passed through a column of Diaion HP-20. The
dilution with 75 % aqueous acetone, by evaporation gives an oily residue that is extracted with ethyl acetate and
submitted to column chromatography over silica gel.

synthesis
intermediate V:

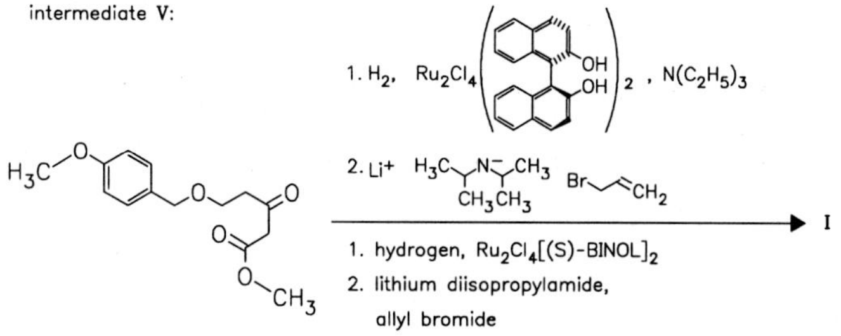

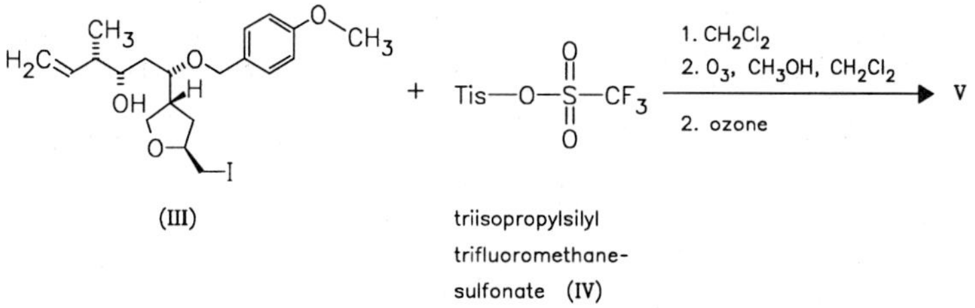

1. H₂, Ru₂Cl₄ (... OH / OH)₂ , N(C₂H₅)₃

2. Li⁺ H₃C N CH₃ Br CH₂
        CH₃ CH₃

1. hydrogen, Ru₂Cl₄[(S)-BINOL]₂
2. lithium diisopropylamide,
   allyl bromide

→ I

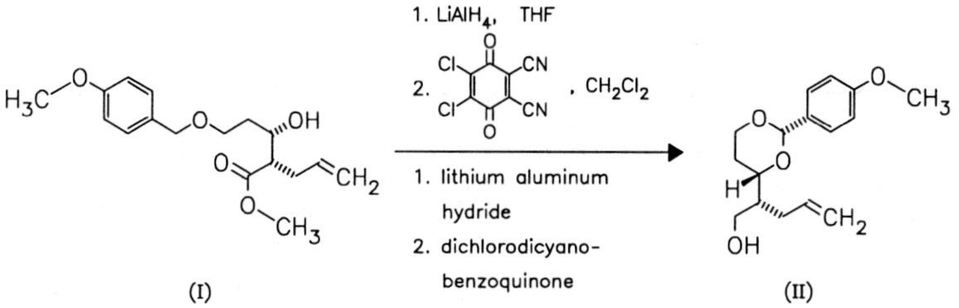

1. LiAlH₄, THF

2. Cl CN / Cl CN , CH₂Cl₂

1. lithium aluminum
   hydride
2. dichlorodicyano-
   benzoquinone

(I)   (II)

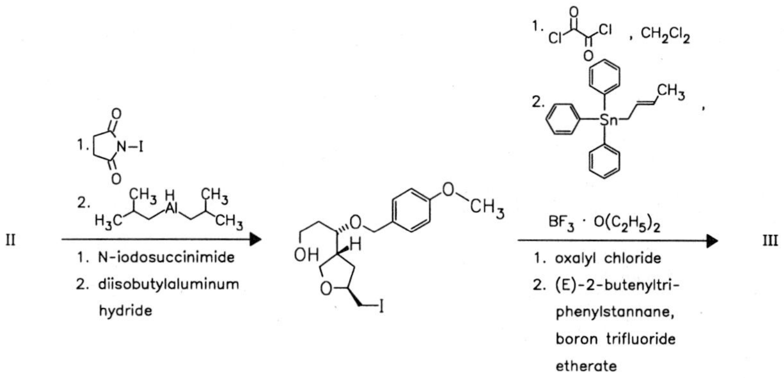

1. N-I (succinimide)

2. CH₃ H CH₃
   H₃C Al CH₃

1. N-iodosuccinimide
2. diisobutylaluminum
   hydride

1. Cl–C(O)–C(O)–Cl , CH₂Cl₂

2. (phenyl)₃Sn CH₃

BF₃ · O(C₂H₅)₂

1. oxalyl chloride
2. (E)-2-butenyltri-
   phenylstannane,
   boron trifluoride
   etherate

II → III

(III) + Tis—O—S(O)(O)—CF₃

triisopropylsilyl
trifluoromethane-
sulfonate (IV)

1. CH₂Cl₂
2. O₃, CH₃OH, CH₂Cl₂

2. ozone

→ V

Tis: H₃C CH₃ / CH₃ —Si— CH₃ / H₃C CH₃

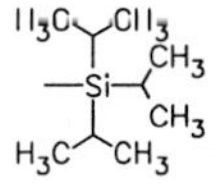

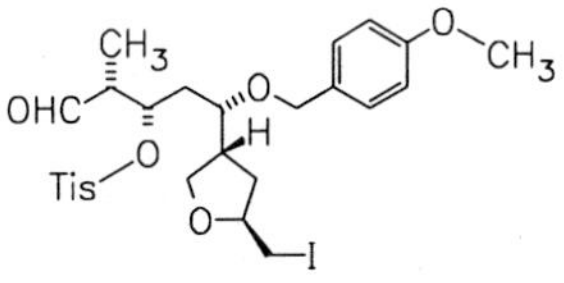

(V)

intermediate XI:

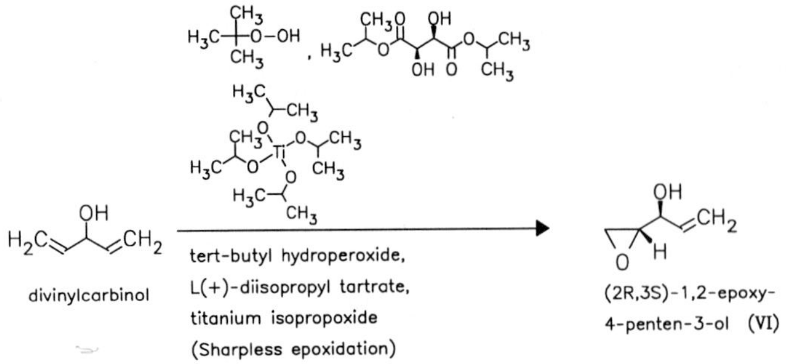

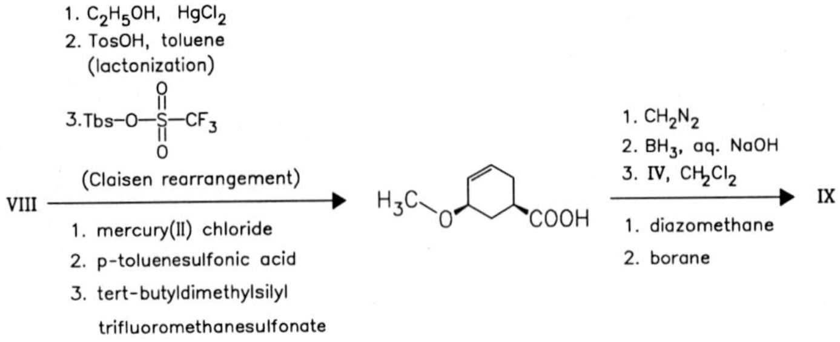

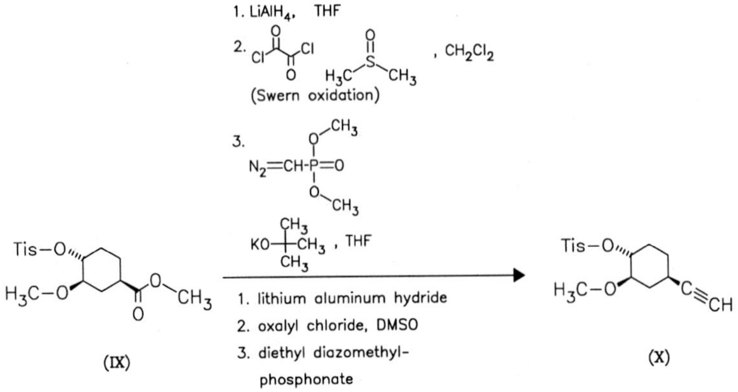

divinylcarbinol

tert-butyl hydroperoxide,
L(+)-diisopropyl tartrate,
titanium isopropoxide
(Sharpless epoxidation)

(2R,3S)-1,2-epoxy-
4-penten-3-ol (VI)

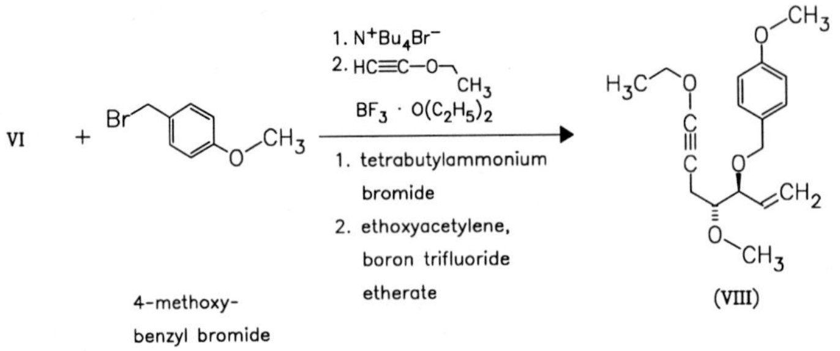

VI +

4-methoxy-
benzyl bromide

1. N$^+$Bu$_4$Br$^-$
2. HC≡C–O–CH$_3$
   BF$_3$ · O(C$_2$H$_5$)$_2$

1. tetrabutylammonium
   bromide
2. ethoxyacetylene,
   boron trifluoride
   etherate

(VIII)

1. C$_2$H$_5$OH, HgCl$_2$
2. TosOH, toluene
   (lactonization)

3. Tbs–O–S(=O)$_2$–CF$_3$

(Claisen rearrangement)

VIII

1. mercury(II) chloride
2. p-toluenesulfonic acid
3. tert-butyldimethylsilyl
   trifluoromethanesulfonate

1. CH$_2$N$_2$
2. BH$_3$, aq. NaOH
3. IV, CH$_2$Cl$_2$

1. diazomethane
2. borane

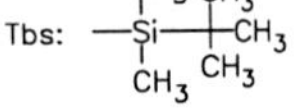

IX

Tbs: –Si(CH$_3$)$_2$–C(CH$_3$)$_3$

1. LiAlH$_4$, THF

2. Cl–C(=O)–C(=O)–Cl , H$_3$C–S(=O)–CH$_3$, CH$_2$Cl$_2$
   (Swern oxidation)

3. N$_2$=CH-P(=O)(O–CH$_3$)$_2$

(IX)

KO–C(CH$_3$)$_3$, THF

1. lithium aluminum hydride
2. oxalyl chloride, DMSO
3. diethyl diazomethyl-
   phosphonate

(X)

1. Li⌢⌢CH₃ H₃C—I

2. (imide)N—Br , benzene

X ⟶ (XI)

Tis—O⳽⳽⳽ / H₃C—O with CH₃ / Br group

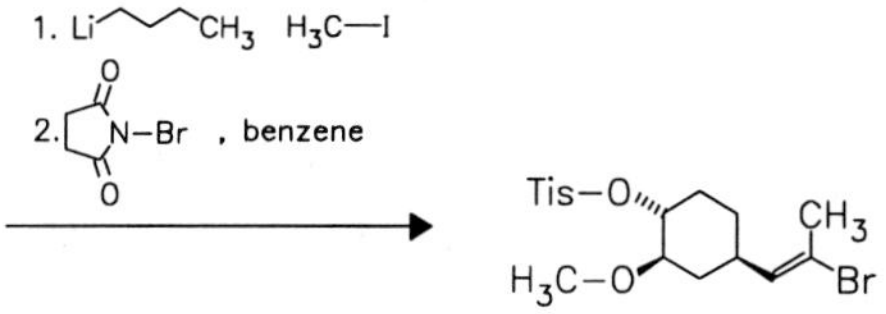

(XI)

intermediate XIX:

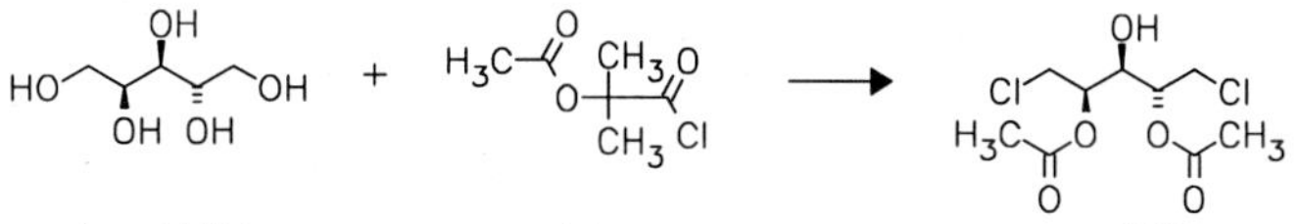

HO⌢(OH)⌢(OH OH)⌢OH L-arabinitol

+ H₃C—C(=O)—O—C(CH₃)(CH₃)—C(=O)—Cl α-acetoxy-isobutyryl chloride

⟶ Cl⌢(OH)⌢Cl with H₃C—O—C(=O) and (=O)C—O—CH₃

(XII)

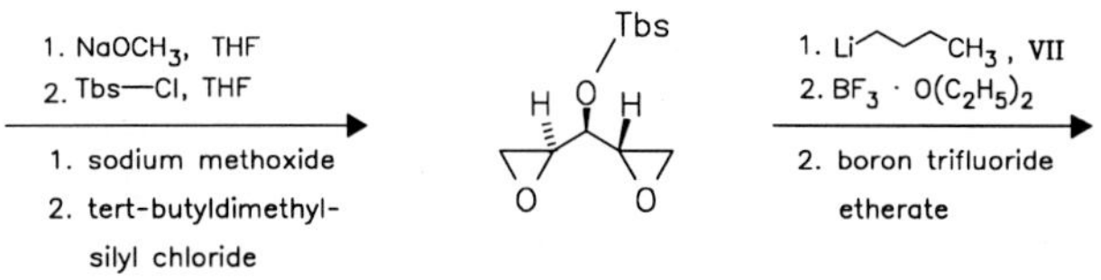

1. NaOCH₃, THF
2. Tbs—Cl, THF
—————————————
1. sodium methoxide
2. tert-butyldimethyl-
   silyl chloride

XII ⟶ Tbs—O epoxide diepoxide structure with H, O, H

1. Li⌢⌢CH₃ , VII
2. BF₃ · O(C₂H₅)₂
—————————————
2. boron trifluoride
   etherate ⟶ XIII

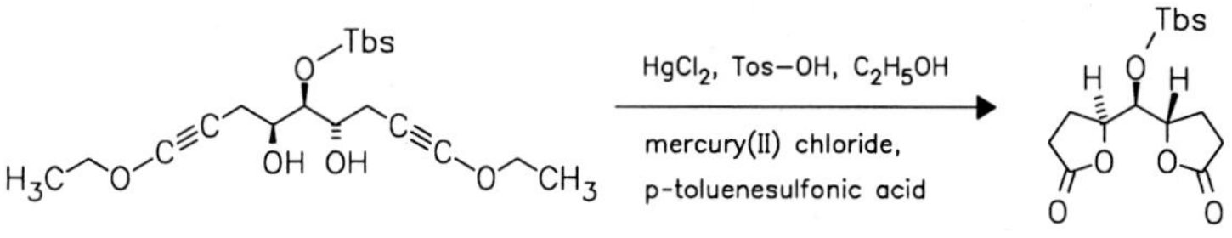

H₃C—O—C≡C⌢(OH)(OH)⌢C≡C—O⌢CH₃ with O—Tbs

(XIII)

HgCl₂, Tos—OH, C₂H₅OH
—————————————————
mercury(II) chloride,
p-toluenesulfonic acid ⟶

(XIV) bicyclic lactone structure with Tbs, H, O, H

XIV

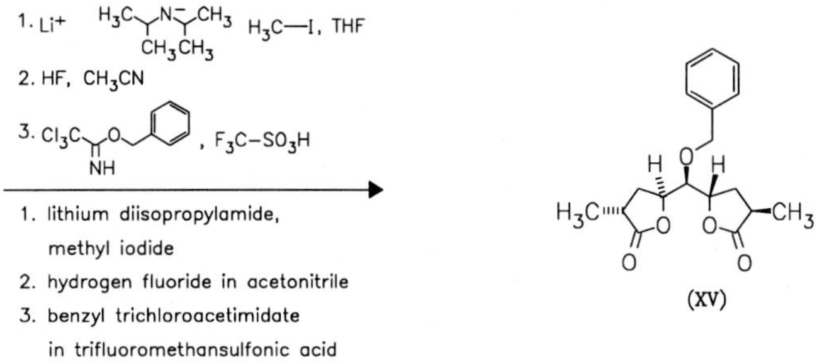

1. Li+ H₃C—C(N⁻)(CH₃)(CH₃CH₃) H₃C—I, THF

2. HF, CH₃CN

3. Cl₃C—C(=O)(NH)—O—CH₂—phenyl , F₃C—SO₃H

—————————————————
1. lithium diisopropylamide,
   methyl iodide
2. hydrogen fluoride in acetonitrile
3. benzyl trichloroacetimidate
   in trifluoromethansulfonic acid ⟶

(XV) bicyclic structure with benzyl (OBn), H, O, H, H₃C⳽⳽, CH₃

XV

1. CH₃OH, NaH
2. H₃C—I, DMF
3. H₂, Pd-C
—————————————
1. methanol,
   sodium hydride
2. methyl iodide
3. hydrogen ⟶

H₃C—O—C(=O)⌢(CH₃O)⌢(O)(OH)⌢(CH₃)⌢C(=O)—O—CH₃ with CH₃CH₃

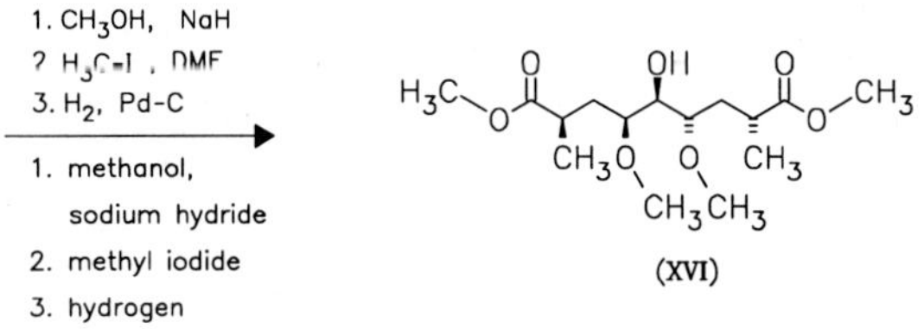

(XVI)

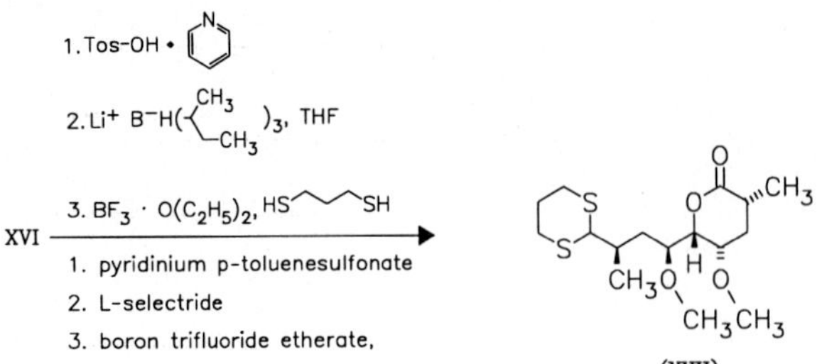

1. Tos-OH · (pyridine)

2. Li⁺ B⁻H(-CH(CH₃)CH₃)₃, THF

3. BF₃ · O(C₂H₅)₂, HS~~~SH

XVI ─────────────────────────►

1. pyridinium p-toluenesulfonate
2. L-selectride
3. boron trifluoride etherate,
   1,3-propanedithiol

(XVII)

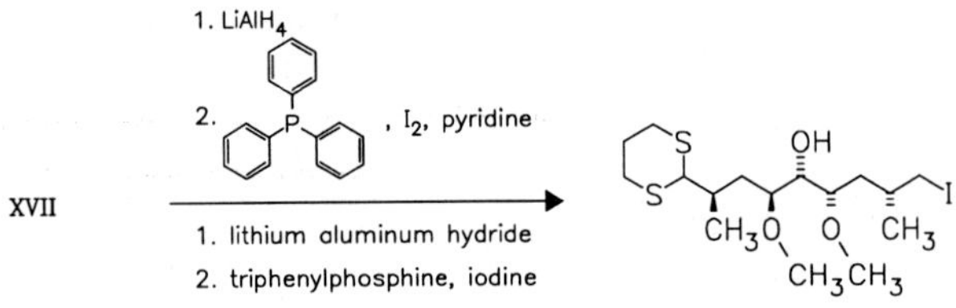

1. LiAlH₄

2. (Ph)₃P , I₂, pyridine

XVII ─────────────────────────►

1. lithium aluminum hydride
2. triphenylphosphine, iodine

(XVIII)

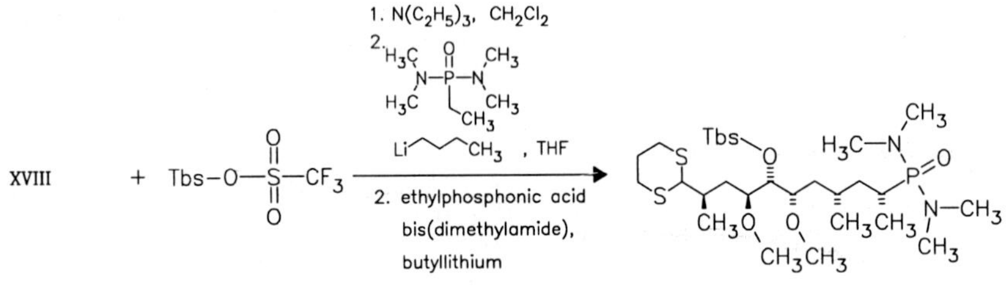

1. N(C₂H₅)₃, CH₂Cl₂

2. H₃C–N–P(=O)–N(CH₃)₂ ... Li~~~CH₃ , THF

2. ethylphosphonic acid
   bis(dimethylamide),
   butyllithium

XVIII   +   Tbs–O–S(=O)₂–CF₃

tert-butyldimethyl-
silyl trifluoro-
methanesulfonate

(XIX)

Tacrolimus:

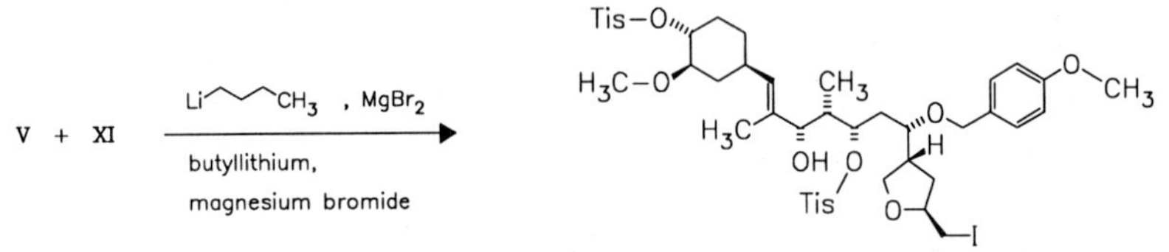

Li~~~CH₃ , MgBr₂

V + XI ─────────────────────────►

butyllithium,
magnesium bromide

(XX)

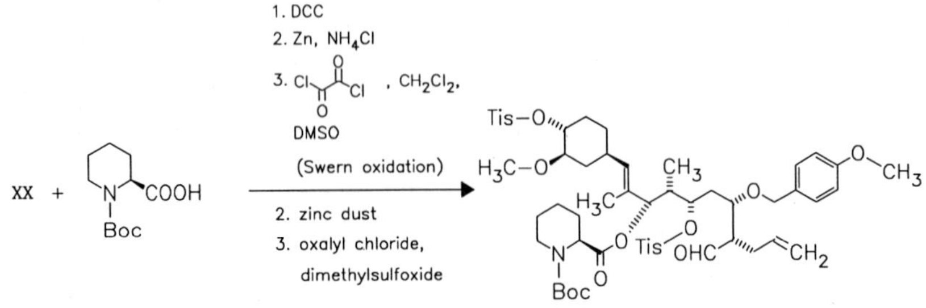

1. DCC
2. Zn, NH₄Cl
3. Cl–C(=O)–C(=O)–Cl , CH₂Cl₂,
   DMSO
   (Swern oxidation)

XX + (N-Boc piperidine-COOH)

2. zinc dust
3. oxalyl chloride,
   dimethylsulfoxide

N-tert-butoxycarbo-
nylpiperidine-2(S)-
carboxylic acid

(XXI)

Boc: (=O)–O–C(CH₃)₃

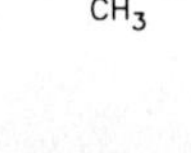

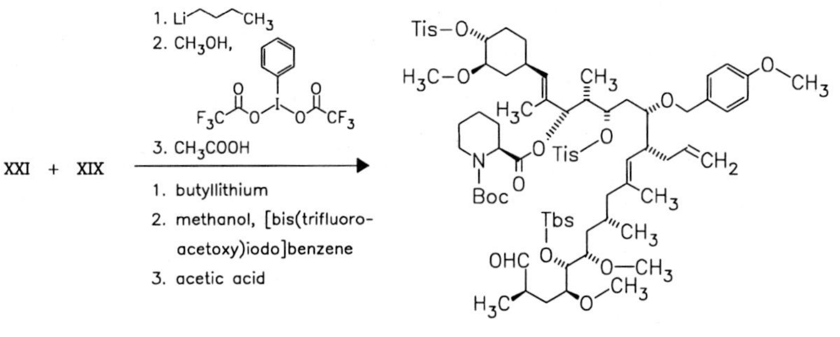

1. Li-CH₃ (with CH₃ chain)
2. CH₃OH,

F_3C ... I ... Phenyl ... CF_3 (bis(trifluoroacetoxy)iodobenzene)

3. CH₃COOH

XXI + XIX →

1. butyllithium
2. methanol, [bis(trifluoroacetoxy)iodo]benzene
3. acetic acid

(XXII)

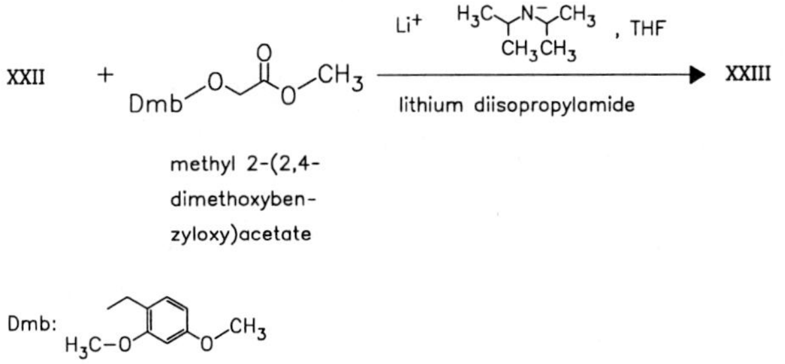

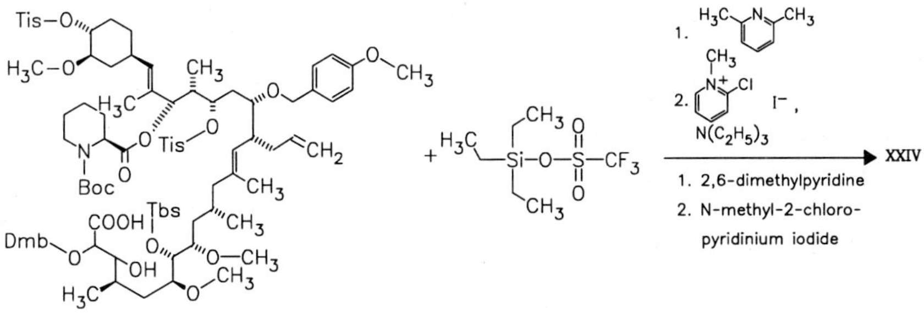

XXII + Dmb-O....O-CH₃

methyl 2-(2,4-
dimethoxyben-
zyloxy)acetate

Li⁺ H₃C-N-CH₃ (with CH₃CH₃), THF

lithium diisopropylamide

→ XXIII

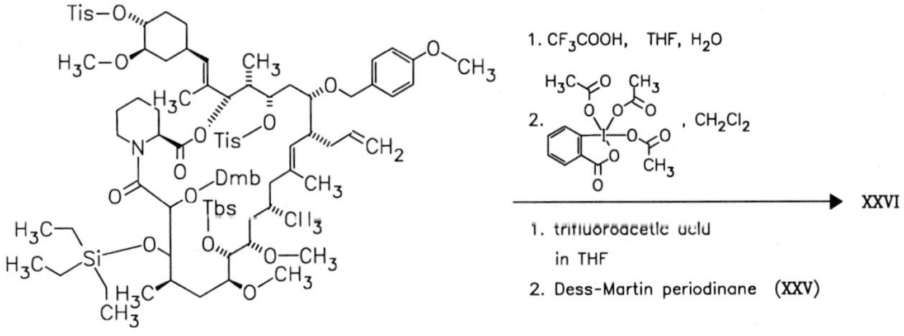

Dmb: H₃C-O....O-CH₃

(XXIII)

+ H₃C-Si-O-S-CF₃ (CH₃ groups, O)

1. H₃C-N-CH₃ (pyridine, CH₃)

2. CH₃ N⁺-Cl I⁻, N(C₂H₅)₃

1. 2,6-dimethylpyridine
2. N-methyl-2-chloro-
   pyridinium iodide

→ XXIV

(XXIV)

1. CF₃COOH, THF, H₂O

2. H₃C-O...CH₃ ... O ... CH₃ , CH₂Cl₂

1. trifluoroacetic acid
   in THF
2. Dess-Martin periodinane (XXV)

→ XXVI

(XXVI)

1. [structure] , CH₂Cl₂
   (selective deprotection)
2. XXV
3. HF, CH₃CN

→ Tacrolimus

1. dichlorodicyanobenzoquinone
2. Dess-Martin periodinane
3. HF in acetonitrile

Tacrolimus

Reference(s):
production and a pharmaceutical composition; isolation:
EP 184 162 (Fujisawa Pharmaceutical; appl. 11.6.1986; GB-prior. 5.2.1985, 1.4.1985).

synthesis of FK-506:
EP 378 318 (Fujisawa Pharmaceutical; appl. 18.7.1990; USA-prior. 11.1.1989, 30.6.1989).
Ireland, R. et al.: J. Org. Chem. (JOCEAH) **61**, 6856 (1996).

synthesis of intermediates:
Danishefsky, S.J. et al.: J. Org. Chem. (JOCEAH) **55** (9), 2786 (1990).
Schreiber, S.L. et al.: J. Am. Chem. Soc. (JACSAT) **112** (4), 5583 (1990).
US 4 940 797 (Fujisawa Pharmaceutical; 10.7.1990; USA-prior. 23.3.1989).

alternative synthesis:
Shinkai, I. et al.: J. Am. Chem. Soc. (JACSAT) **111** (3), 1157 (1989).
Shinkai, I. et al.: Tetrahedron Lett. (TELEAY) **29** (3), 281 (1988).

Formulation(s):   amp. 5 mg/ml; cps. 1 mg, 5 mg

Trade Name(s):
D: Prograf (Fujisawa)   GB: Prograf (Fujisawa)   USA: Prograf (Fujisawa)
F: Prograf (Fujisawa)   J: Prograf (Fujisawa)

Talampicillin

ATC: J01CA15
Use: antibiotic, antibacterial

RN: 47747-56-8   MF: C₂₄H₂₃N₃O₆S   MW: 481.53   EINECS: 256-332-3
CN: [2S-[2α,5α,6β(S*)]]-6-[(aminophenylacetyl)amino]-3,3-dimethyl-7-oxo-4-thia-1-
       azabicyclo[3.2.0]heptane-2-carboxylic acid 1,3-dihydro-3-oxo-1-isobenzofuranyl ester

monohydrochloride
RN: 39878-70-1   MF: $C_{24}H_{23}N_3O_6S \cdot HCl$ MW: 517.99
LD_{50}:   >1 g/kg (M, i.v.); >4 g/kg (M, p.o.);
786 mg/kg (R, i.v.); >1 g/kg (R, p.o.)

ampicillin potassium salt   methyl aceto-   (I)
(q. v.)   acetate

I   +   pH 2.5

3-bromo-   Talampicillin
phthalide

Reference(s):
US 3 860 579 (Beecham; 14.1.1975; GB-prior. 9.6.1971).
DAS 2 228 012 (Beecham; appl. 8.6.1972; GB-prior. 9.6.1971).
DOS 2 228 255 (Beecham; appl. 9.6.1972; GB-prior. 9.6.1971).
US 3 951 954 (Yamanouchi; 20.4.1976; J-prior. 5.6.1971, 15.6.1971, 25.6.1971, 10.8.1971, 11.3.1972).
DOS 2 225 149 (Yamanouchi; appl. 24.5.1972; J-prior. 5.6.1971, 15.6.1971, 25.6.1971, 10.8.1971, 11.3.1972).

Formulation(s):   cps. 125 mg, 250 mg; tabl. 250 mg, 500 mg, 750 mg, 1 g (as hydrochloride)

Trade Name(s):
GB: Talpen (Beecham; 1975);   Precillin (Edmond); wfm   Talat (Polifarma); wfm
       wfm   Talampicillina (Midy);   J: Yamacillin (Beecham-
I: Ausotal (Ausonia); wfm   wfm   Yamanouchi)

Talinolol

ATC: C07AA
Use: β-adrenoceptor antagonist,
        antihypertensive

RN: 57460-41-0   MF: $C_{20}H_{33}N_3O_3$ MW: 363.50
LD_{50}:   30 mg/kg (R, i.v.)
CN: (±)-*N*-cyclohexyl-*N'*-[4-[3-[(1,1-dimethylethyl)amino]-2-hydroxypropoxy]phenyl]urea

monohydrochloride
RN: 38652-10-7   MF: $C_{20}H_{33}N_3O_3 \cdot HCl$ MW: 399.96

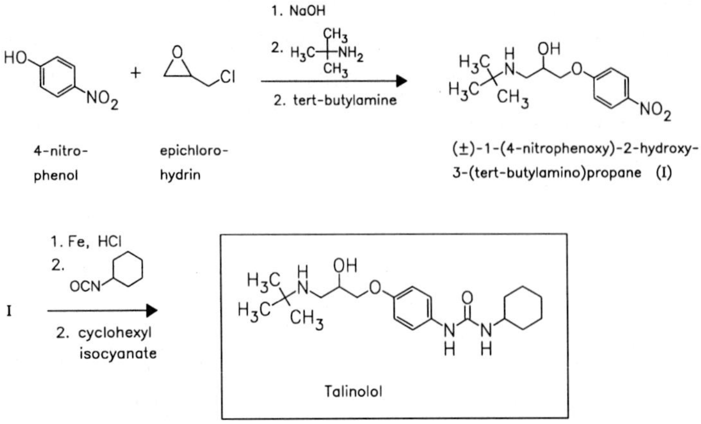
1. NaOH
2. tert-butylamine
4-nitro-
phenol
epichloro-
hydrin
(±)-1-(4-nitrophenoxy)-2-hydroxy-
3-(tert-butylamino)propane (I)
1. Fe, HCl
2. cyclohexyl
isocyanate
Talinolol

Reference(s):

DE 2 100 323 (VEB Arzneimittelwerk Dresden, Ciba-Geigy; appl. 5.1.1971; CH-prior. 8.10.1970, 13.11.1970).
US 4 120 978 (VEB Arzneimittelwerk Dresden, Ciba-Geigy; 17.10.1978).
DD 283 501 (VEB Arzneimittelwerk Dresden; appl. 29.7.1988).
DD 283 499 (VEB Arzneimittelwerk Dresden; appl. 29.7.1988).
DD 283 498 (VEB Arzneimittelwerk Dresden; appl. 29.7.1988).
DD 283 496 (VEB Arzneimittelwerk Dresden; appl. 29.7.1988).
DD 264 114 (VEB Arzneimittelwerk Dresden; appl. 25.5.1987).

synthesis of enantiomers:
DD 285 343 (VEB Arzneimittelwerk Dresden; appl. 29.6.1989).

Formulation(s): amp. 10 mg/5 ml; drg. 50 mg, 100 mg

Trade Name(s):
D: Cordanum (ASTA Medica AWD)

Talipexole
(B-HT-920)

Use: antiparkinsonian

RN: 101626-70-4 MF: $C_{10}H_{15}N_3S$ MW: 209.32
CN: 5,6,7,8-tetrahydro-6-(2-propenyl)-4*H*-thiazolo[4,5-*d*]azepin-2-amine

dihydrochloride
RN: 36085-73-1 MF: $C_{10}H_{15}N_3S \cdot 2HCl$ MW: 282.24
LD_{50}: 455 mg/kg (M, p.o.);
66 mg/kg (R, i.v.); 403 mg/kg (R, p.o.)

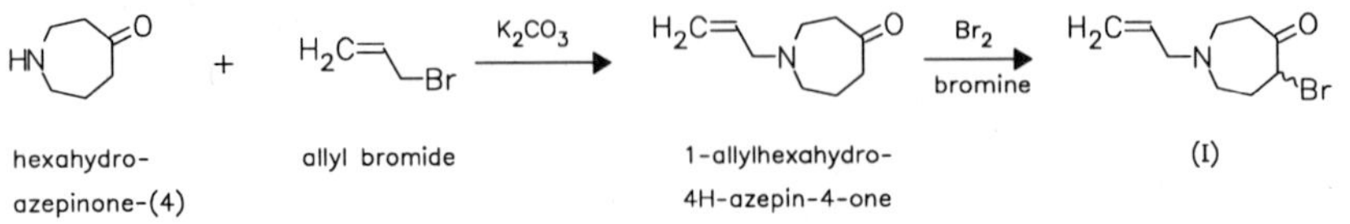
bromine
hexahydro-
azepinone-(4)
allyl bromide
1-allylhexahydro-
4H-azepin-4-one
(I)

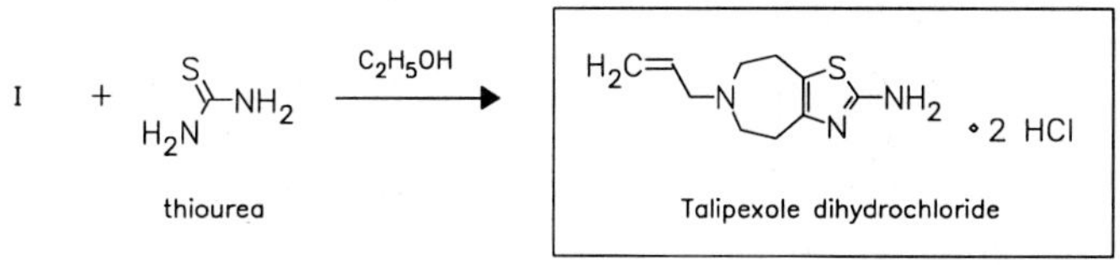

I + [thiourea structure: S, NH₂, H₂N] $\xrightarrow{C_2H_5OH}$ [Talipexole dihydrochloride structure] • 2 HCl

thiourea   Talipexole dihydrochloride

Reference(s):

EP 195 888 (Thomae GmbH; appl. 1.10.1986; D-prior. 25.1.1985).
DE 2 040 510 (Thomae GmbH, prior. 14.8.1970).
DE 3 642 066 (Boehringer Ing., appl. 19.6.1987; prior. 9.12.1986).
Anden, N.-E.; Grabowska-Anden, M.: J. Neural. Transm. (JNTMAH) **79** (3), 209-214 (1990).

Formulation(s):   tabl. 0.4 mg

Trade Name(s):

J: Domin (Boehringer Ing.)

Tamoxifen

ATC: L02BA01
Use: antineoplastic, antiestrogen
         (palliative treatment of breast cancer)

RN: 10540-29-1   MF: $C_{26}H_{29}NO$ MW: 371.52   EINECS: 234-118-0
LD$_{50}$: 2150 mg/kg (M, p.o.);
         4100 mg/kg (R, p.o.)
CN: (Z)-2-[4-(1,2-diphenyl-1-butenyl)phenoxy]-*N*,*N*-dimethylethanamine

citrate (1:1)
RN: 54965-24-1   MF: $C_{26}H_{29}NO \cdot C_6H_8O_7$ MW: 563.65   EINECS: 259-415-2
LD$_{50}$: 62.5 mg/kg (M, i.v.); 3100 mg/kg (M, p.o.);
         62.5 mg/kg (R, i.v.); 1190 mg/kg (R, p.o.)

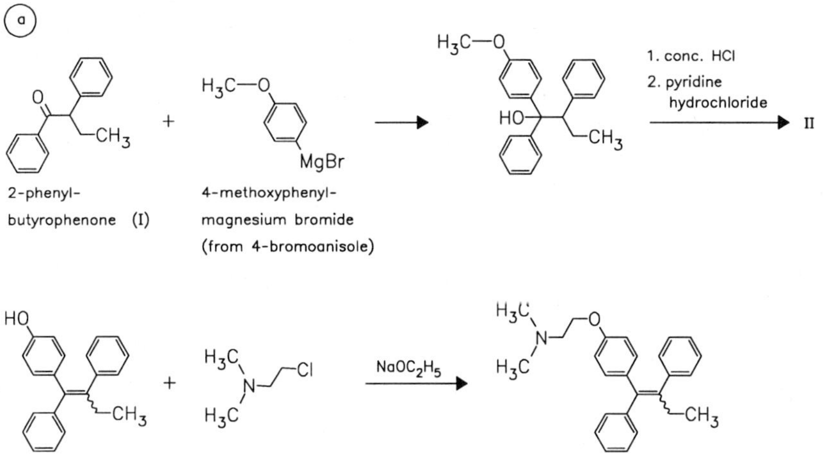

2-phenyl-   4-methoxyphenyl-
butyrophenone (I)   magnesium bromide
                        (from 4-bromoanisole)

1. conc. HCl
2. pyridine
   hydrochloride
→ II

(II)   2-(dimethylamino)-   cis,trans-tamoxifen (IV)
                        ethyl chloride (III)

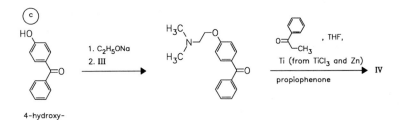

IV → crystallization from petroleum ether →

Tamoxifen

b

I + 4-(2-dimethylamino-
ethoxy)phenyl-
magnesium bromide

→

conc. HCl, C$_2$H$_5$OH → IV

IV → crystallization from petroleum ether → Tamoxifen

c

4-hydroxy-
benzophenone

1. C$_2$H$_5$ONa
2. III

→

, THF,

Ti (from TiCl$_3$ and Zn)

propiophenone

→ IV

IV → crystallization from petroleum ether → Tamoxifen

Reference(s):
US 4 536 516 (ICI)
a,b Harper, M.J.K.; Walpole, A.L.: Nature (London) (NATUAS) **212**, 87 (1966).
    GB 1 013 907 (ICI; appl. 13.9.1962).
    GB 1 064 629 (ICI; appl. 20.7.1965).

separation of isomers:
Bedford, G.R.; Richardson, D.N.: Nature (London) (NATUAS) **212**, 733 (1966).
DE 1 468 088 (ICI; appl. 5.9.1963; GB-prior. 13.9.1962, 21.8.1963).
  c EP 126 470 (Bristol-Myers; appl. 18.5.1984; USA-prior. 19.5.1983, 22.2.1984).

similar process:
EP 168 175 (Nat. Res. Dev. Corp.; appl. 19.11.1987; GB-prior. 12.6.1984, 11.6.1985).

polymorphs of tamoxifen citrate:
Goldberg, I.; Becker, Y.: J. Pharm. Sci. (JPMSAE) **76**, 259 (1987).

percutaneous administration:
WO 85/03 228 (P. Mauvais-Jarvis and F. Kuttenn; appl. 21.12.1984; F-prior. 20.1.1984).
GB 1 013 907 (ICI; appl. 13.9.1962; valid from 21.8.1963).
GB 1 064 629 (ICI; appl. 20.7.1965; valid from 4.3.1966).
DE 1 468 088 (ICI; appl. 5.9.1963; GB-prior. 13.9.1962, 21.8.1963).

separation of isomers:
Bedford, G.R.; Richardson, D.N.: Nature (London) (NATUAS) **212**, 733 (1966).

Formulation(s):   f. c. tabl. 10 mg, 20 mg, 30 mg, 40 mg; tabl. 10 mg, 20 mg, 30 mg, 40 mg (as citrate)

Trade Name(s):

D:	duratamoxifen (durachemie)	Tamoxasta (ASTA Medica AWD)
	Jenoxifen (Jenapharm)	Tamoxifen (Hexal;
	Kessar (Farmitalia)	Heumann; ct-Arzneimittel;
	Nolvadex (ICI-Pharma; 1976)	cell pharm; Aliud Pharma; biosyn; ratiopharm)
	Nourytan (Nourypharma)	F: Kessar (Pharmacia &
	Tamobeta (betapharm)	Upjohn)
	Tamofen (Rhône-Poulenc Rorer)	Nolvadex (Zeneca; 1977) Oncotam (Mayoly-
	Tamox-GRY (Gry)	Spindler)
	Tamox-PUREN (Isis Puren)	Tamofine (Rhône-Poulenc Rorer)

GB:	Nolvadex (Zeneca; 1973) Tamofen (Pharmacia & Upjohn; as citrate)
I:	Nolvadex (Zeneca)
J:	Nolvadex (Zeneca-Sumitomo Chem.; 1981)
USA:	Kessar (Pharmacia & Upjohn) Ledertam (Wyeth-Lederle) Nolvadex (Zeneca; 1978)

Tamsulosin hydrochloride

((–)-LY 253352; LY 253351; (–)-YM 12617; (*R*)-(–)-YM 12617)

ATC: G04BX08
Use: antihypertensive, BPH, α-blocker

RN: 106463-17-6   MF: $C_{20}H_{28}N_2O_5S \cdot HCl$ MW: 444.98
CN: (*R*)-5-[2-[[2-(2-Ethoxyphenoxy)ethyl]amino]propyl]-2-methoxybenzenesulfonamide monohydrochloride

base
RN: 106133-20-4   MF: $C_{20}H_{28}N_2O_5S$ MW: 408.52
(+)-hydrochloride
RN: 106463-19-8   MF: $C_{20}H_{28}N_2O_5S \cdot HCl$ MW: 444.98
(±)-hydrochloride
RN: 80223-99-0   MF: $C_{20}H_{28}N_2O_5S \cdot HCl$ MW: 444.98

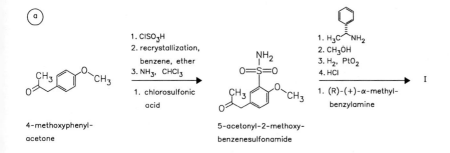

4-methoxyphenyl-acetone

1. ClSO₃H
2. recrystallization, benzene, ether
3. NH₃, CHCl₃

1. chlorosulfonic acid

5-acetonyl-2-methoxy-benzenesulfonamide

1. H₃C–NH₂
2. CH₃OH
3. H₂, PtO₂
4. HCl

1. (R)-(+)-α-methyl-benzylamine

I

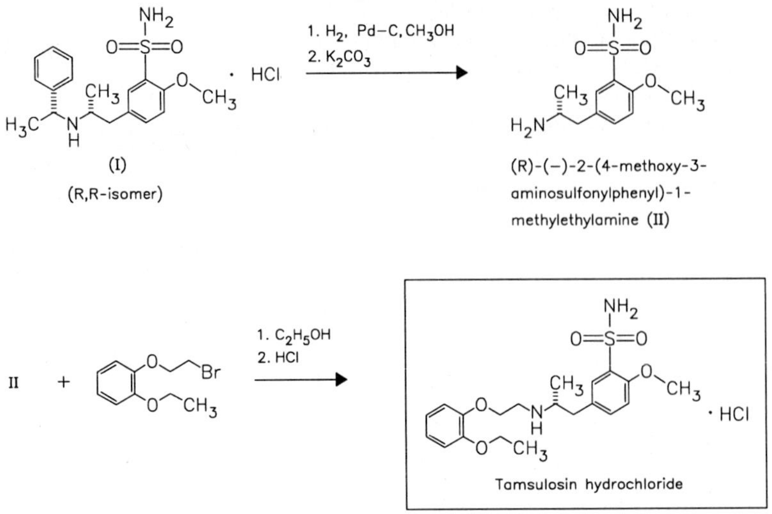

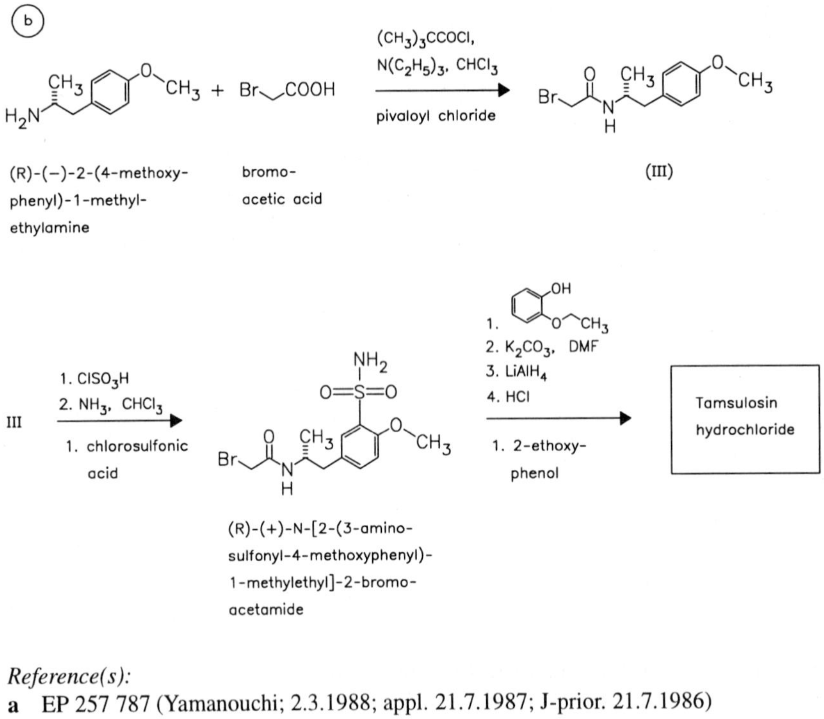

(I)

(R,R-isomer)

1. H₂, Pd–C, CH₃OH
2. K₂CO₃

(R)-(−)-2-(4-methoxy-3-
aminosulfonylphenyl)-1-
methylethylamine (II)

II +

1. C₂H₅OH
2. HCl

Tamsulosin hydrochloride

b

(R)-(−)-2-(4-methoxy-
phenyl)-1-methyl-
ethylamine

bromo-
acetic acid

(CH₃)₃CCOCl,
N(C₂H₅)₃, CHCl₃

pivaloyl chloride

(III)

III

1. CISO₃H
2. NH₃, CHCl₃

1. chlorosulfonic
acid

(R)-(+)-N-[2-(3-amino-
sulfonyl-4-methoxyphenyl)-
1-methylethyl]-2-bromo-
acetamide

1.
2. K₂CO₃, DMF
3. LiAlH₄
4. HCl

1. 2-ethoxy-
phenol

Tamsulosin
hydrochloride

Reference(s):
a EP 257 787 (Yamanouchi; 2.3.1988; appl. 21.7.1987; J-prior. 21.7.1986)
b JP 02 306 958 (Hokuriku; appl. 22.5.1988)

synthesis of racemic YM 12617:
EP 34 432 (Yamanouchi, 26.8.1981; appl. 2.2.1981; J-prior. 8.2.1980)

Formulation(s):   cps. 0.1 mg, 0.2 mg, 0.4 mg

Trade Name(s):
D: Alna (Boehringer   F: Josir (Boehringer   GB: Flomax (Boehringer
       Ingelheim)   Ingelheim)   Ingelheim)
       OMNIC (Yamanouchi)   Omix (Yamanouchi)

I:	Omnic (Yamanouchi)	USA:	Flomax (Boehringer Ingelheim; 1997)
J:	Harnal (Yamanouchi)		

Tandospirone
(SM-3997 (as citrate))

ATC: N05BX
Use: anxiolytic, antidepressant

RN: 87760-53-0 MF: $C_{21}H_{29}N_5O_2$ MW: 383.50
CN: (3aα,4β,7β,7aα)-hexahydro-2-[4-[4-(2-pyrimidinyl)-1-piperazinyl]butyl]-4,7-methano-1*H*-isoindole-1,3(2*H*)-dione

citrate
RN: 112457-95-1 MF: $C_{21}H_{29}N_5O_2 \cdot C_6H_8O_7$ MW: 575.62

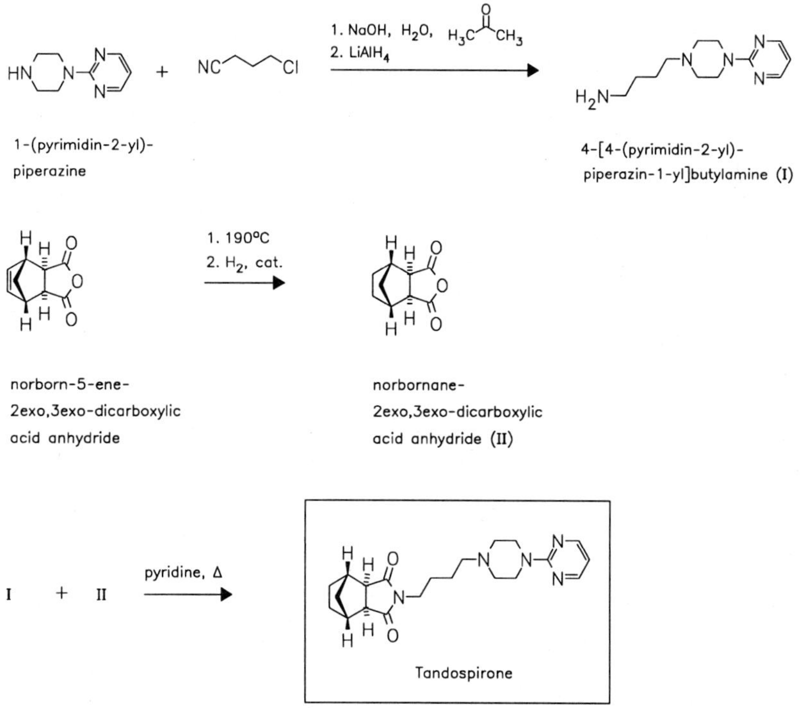
1. NaOH, H2O, H3C(CO)CH3
2. LiAlH4
1-(pyrimidin-2-yl)-piperazine
4-[4-(pyrimidin-2-yl)-piperazin-1-yl]butylamine (I)
1. 190°C
2. H2, cat.
norborn-5-ene-2exo,3exo-dicarboxylic acid anhydride
norbornane-2exo,3exo-dicarboxylic acid anhydride (II)
I + II
pyridine, Δ
Tandospirone

Reference(s):
EP 82 402 (Sumitomo Chem.; appl. 29.6.1983; J-prior. 22.12.1981, 3.6.1982).
JP 60 087 262 (Sumitomo Chem.; appl. 16.5.1985; USA-prior. 19.1.1983).
JP 63 010 760 (Sumitomo Chem.; appl. 18.1.1988; J-prior. 1.7.1986).

use of tandospirone*:*
a) *treating depression:*
US 5 011 841 (Pfizer; appl. 30.4.1991; USA-prior. 14.11.1989).

b) *as psychotropic agents:*
US 5 521 313 (Bristol-Myers Squibb; appl. 28.5.1996; USA-prior. 5.5.1994).

c) *as 5-HT$_1$A-receptor agonist:*
WO 9 605 817 (Medinova SF; appl. 29.2.1996; GB-prior. 23.8.1994).

dosage forms:
US 5 330 762 (Alza Corp.; appl. 19.7.1994; USA-prior. 27.1.1993).
US 5 246 711 (Alza Corp.; appl. 21.9.1993; USA-prior. 27.2.1992, 10.9.1992).
US 5 246 710 (Alza Corp.; appl. 22.9.1993; USA-prior. 27.2.1992, 10.9.1992).
US 5 185 158 (Alza Corp.; appl. 9.2.1993; USA-prior. 27.2.1992).

synergistic compositions with 8-hydroxy-2-(dipropylamino)tetraline *and* idazoxan:
US 5 124 346 (Pfizer; appl. 23.6.1992; USA-prior. 23.4.1991).

synthesis of I:
Kikuo, I. et al.: Chem. Pharm. Bull. (CPBTAL) **39**, 2288 (1991).
Wu et al.: J. Med. Chem. (JMCMAR) **15**, 477 (1972).

Formulation(s):   tabl. 5 mg, 10 mg

Trade Name(s):
J: Sediel (Sumitomo)

Tazanolast

ATC: R03DX
Use: antiallergic, antiasthmatic

RN: 82989-25-1   MF: $C_{13}H_{15}N_5O_3$ MW: 289.30
LD$_{50}$: 1121 mg/kg (M, i.v.); >4 g/kg (M, p.o.);
         1119 mg/kg (R, i.v.); >4 g/kg (R, p.o.);
         >4 g/kg (dog, p.o.)
CN: oxo[[3-(1*H*-tetrazol-5-yl)phenyl]amino]acetic acid butyl ester

3-nitro-
benzonitrile

5-(3-nitrophenyl)-
tetrazole

3-(5-tetrazolyl)-
aniline (I)

oxalic acid monochloride
butyl ester

Tazanolast

Reference(s):
JP 82 011 975 (Wakamoto; appl. 21.1.1982; J-prior. 25.6.1980).
JP 57 011 975 (Wakamoto; appl. 21.1.1982; J-prior. 21.1.1982; prior. 25.6.1980).

synthesis of 3-(5-tetrazolyl)aniline I:
McManus, J.M.; Herbst, R.M.: J. Org. Chem. (JOCEAH) **24**, 1044 (1959).

medical use as inhibitor of SRS-A-release:
DOS 3 530 780 (Wakamoto; appl. 28.8.1985; J-prior. 24.12.1984, 29.3.1985).
US 4 778 816 (Wakamoto; 18.10.1988; appl. 17.9.1985; J-prior. 24.12.1984, 29.3.1985).

Formulation(s):   cps. 75 mg

Trade Name(s):
J: Tazalest (Wakamoto;   Tazanol (Torii; 1990).
      1990).

Tazarotene
(AGN-190168)

ATC: D05B
Use: antipsoriatic, acne therapeutic,
        retinoid

RN: 118292-40-3   MF: $C_{21}H_{21}NO_2S$ MW: 351.47
CN: 6-[(3,4-dihydro-4,4-dimethyl-2*H*-1-benzothiopyran-6-yl)ethynyl]-3-pyridinecarboxylic acid ethyl ester

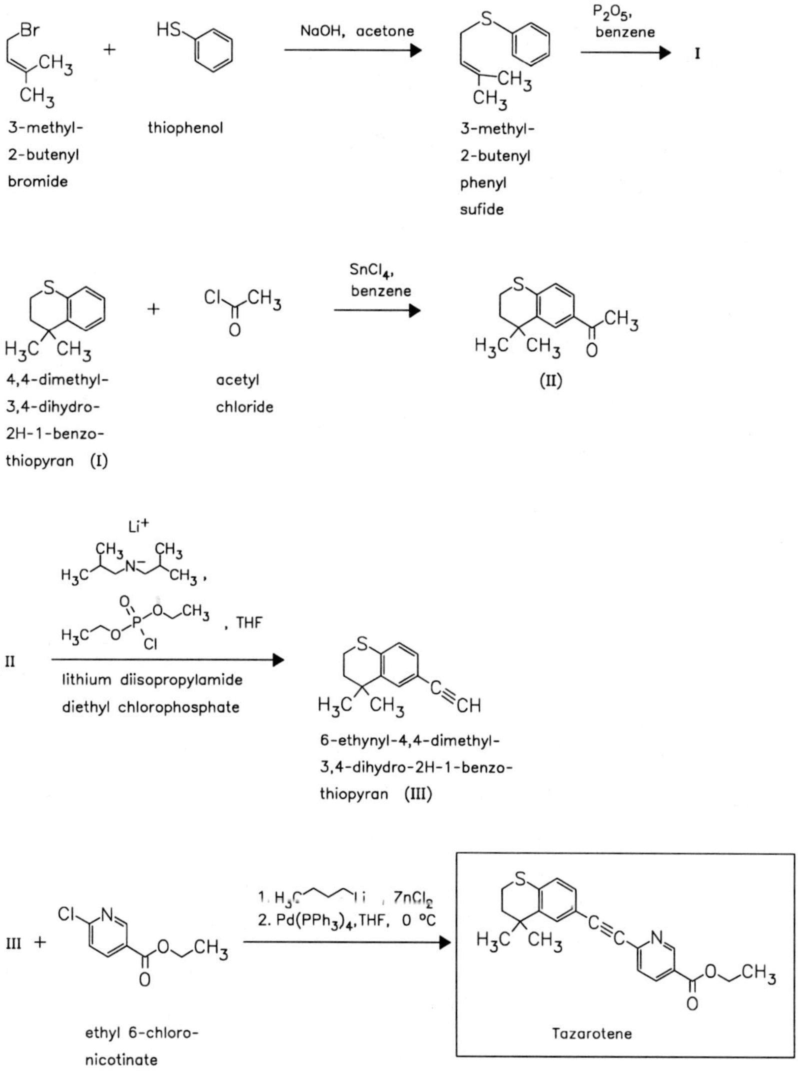

3-methyl-   thiophenol   3-methyl-
2-butenyl   2-butenyl
bromide   phenyl
                                         sufide

4,4-dimethyl-   acetyl   (II)
3,4-dihydro-   chloride
2H-1-benzo-
thiopyran (I)

II → lithium diisopropylamide / diethyl chlorophosphate , THF

6-ethynyl-4,4-dimethyl-
3,4-dihydro-2H-1-benzo-
thiopyran (III)

III + ethyl 6-chloro-nicotinate

1. H_3C ⌒ li , $ZnCl_2$
2. $Pd(PPh_3)_4$, THF, 0 °C

Tazarotene

Reference(s):
EP 284 261 (Allergan Inc.; USA-prior. 13.3.1987).
EP 284 288 (Allergan Inc.; USA-prior. 20.3.1987).
US 5 089 509 (Allergan Inc.; USA-prior. 20.3.1989).

Formulation(s):   gel 0.5 mg/g, 1 mg/g

Trade Name(s):
D: Zorac (Pharm-Allergan)   GB: Zorac (Allergan)   USA: Tazorac (Allergan)

Teclothiazide

(Tetrachlormethiazide;
  Trichlormethylhydrochlorothiazide)

ATC: C03AX
Use: diuretic

RN: 4267-05-4   MF: $C_8H_7Cl_4N_3O_4S_2$ MW: 415.11   EINECS: 224-253-3
CN: 6-chloro-3,4-dihydro-3-(trichloromethyl)-2H-1,2,4-benzothiadiazine-7-sulfonamide 1,1-dioxide

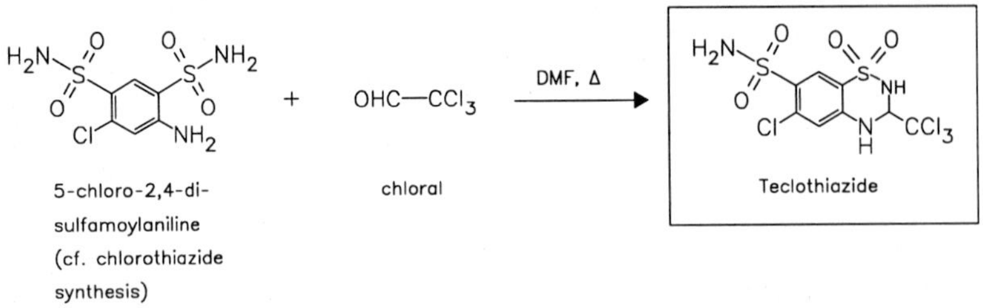

5-chloro-2,4-di-
sulfamoylaniline
(cf. chlorothiazide
synthesis)

chloral

Teclothiazide

Reference(s):
Novello, F.C. et al.: J. Org. Chem. (JOCEAH) **25**, 970 (1960).
Close, W.J. et al.: J. Am. Chem. Soc. (JACSAT) **82**, 1132 (1960).

Formulation(s):   tabl. 18 mg

Trade Name(s):
F: Chymodrex (Pharmuka)-
      comb.; wfm

Tegafur

(Ftorafur)

ATC: L01BC03
Use: antineoplastic

RN: 17902-23-7   MF: $C_8H_9FN_2O_3$ MW: 200.17   EINECS: 241-846-2
LD_{50}: 800 mg/kg (M, i.v.); 775 mg/kg (M, p.o.);
        685 mg/kg (R, i.v.); 930 mg/kg (R, p.o.);
        34 mg/kg (dog, p.o.)
CN: 5-fluoro-1-(tetrahydro-2-furanyl)-2,4(1H,3H)-pyrimidinedione

monosodium salt
RN: 28721-46-2   MF: $C_8H_8FN_2NaO_3$ MW: 222.15

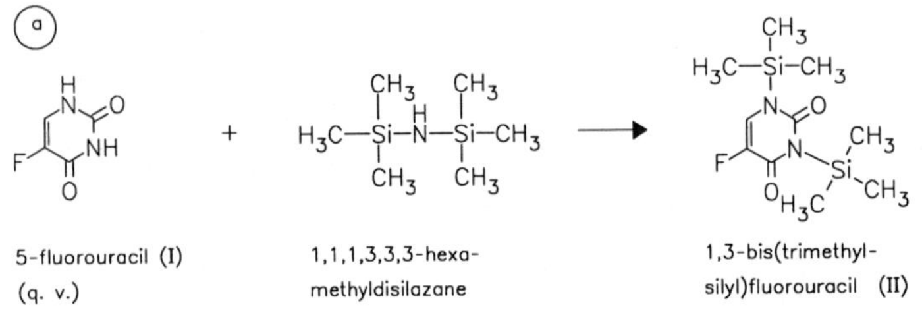

5-fluorouracil (I)
(q. v.)

1,1,1,3,3,3-hexa-
methyldisilazane

1,3-bis(trimethyl-
silyl)fluorouracil (II)

a

1. [2-chlorotetrahydrofuran structure] , CH₂Cl₂

2. NH₃, CH₃OH

II ⟶ Tegafur

1. 2-chlorotetrahydrofuran

b

I + [2,3-dihydrofuran structure] ──pyridine, CaCl₂, 105–110 °C──▶ Tegafur

2,3-dihydro-
furan

Reference(s):
a US 3 635 946 (S. A. Giller et al.; 18.1.1972; appl. 21.12.1967, 22.7.1969).
   US 3 912 734 (S. A. Giller et al.; 14.10.1975; appl. 1.6.1973; SU-prior. 20.11.1972).
   GB 1 168 391 (Inst. Organitschesk. sinteza, Riga; appl. 8.1.1968).
   DAS 1 695 297 (Inst. Organitschesk. sinteza, Riga; appl. 10.1.1968).
   US 4 039 546 (S. A. Giller et al.; 2.8.1977; appl. 28.4.1975).
   GB 1 503 614 (Univ. of Utah; appl. 14.4.1975; USA-prior. 6.5.1974).
   US 4 107 162 (Asahi; 15.8.1978; J-prior. 10.11.1975).
   with dimethyldichlorosilane:
   DOS 2 834 698 (Toshin Chemical; appl. 8.8.1978; J-prior. 19.9.1977, 14.12.1977).
b DOS 2 653 398 (Takeda; appl. 24.11.1976; J-prior. 28.11.1975; 19.1.1976; 13.7.1976).
   DOS 2 657 709 (Takeda; appl. 20.12.1976; J-prior. 25.12.1975).
   DOS 2 709 838 (Nikken Chemical; appl. 7.3.1977; J-prior. 26.6.1976, 28.8.1976).
   US 4 121 037 (Nikken Chemical; 17.10.1978; J-prior. 26.6.1976, 28.8.1976).
   DOS 2 709 839 (Nikken Chemical; appl. 7.3.1977; J-prior. 23.6.1976).
   GB 1 522 860 (Mitsui Toatsu; appl. 7.12.1976; J-prior. 24.12.1975, 9.1.1976, 22.1.1976, 20.5.1976).
   DOS 2 744 956 (ABIC; appl. 6.10.1977; IL-prior. 12.10.1976).
   US 4 159 378 (Toshin Chemical; 26.6.1979; J-prior. 19.9.1977, 14.12.1977).

alternative synthesis (also suitable for optical antipodes):
DOS 2 723 450 (Roche; appl. 24.5.1977; A-prior. 28.5.1976).

further syntheses:
Yasumoto, M. et al.: J. Med. Chem. (JMCMAR) **21**, 738 (1978).
DOS 2 648 239 (Rikagaku Kenkyusho; appl. 25.10.1976; J-prior. 24.10.1975, 4.12.1975, 5.1.1976, 15.3.1976, 11.5.1976).

Formulation(s):   tabl. 2.5 mg, 5 mg, 10 mg

Trade Name(s):

I:	Citofur (Lusofarmaco)	Franroze (Hishiyama)	Helpa (Teikoku)

I: Citofur (Lusofarmaco)

J: Coparogin (Nippon
      Chemiphar)
      Daiyalose (Daito)
      Exonal (Toyama)
      Fental (Kanebo)
      FH (Mitsui)
      Filacul (Torii)
      Flopholin (Tsuruhara)

Franroze (Hishiyama)
FTR (Tenyosha)
Fulaid (Takeda)
Fulfeel (Kyorin)
Furofluor (Green Cross)
Furofutran (Taiyo)
Futol-P (Teisan)
Futraful (Taiho)
Geen (Tatumi)

Helpa (Teikoku)
Helpa Taito (Pfizer)
Icalus (Isei)
Lamar (Tokyo Tanabe)
Natira U (Mohan)
Neberk (Fuji)
Nitobanil (Kyowa)
Pharmic (Toyo Pharmar)
Rescrel (Nikken)

Rial (Toa Eiyo)
Richina (Takata)

Sinoflurol (Kaken)
Sunfural (Toyo Jozo)

Tefsiel C (Towa)
Youfural (Showa)

Tegafur-Uracil

ATC: L01BC03
Use: antineoplastic

RN: 74578-38-4　MF: $C_8H_9FN_2O_3 \cdot C_4H_4N_2O_2$　MW: 312.26
LD$_{50}$: 1275 mg/kg (M, p.o.);
　　　1580 mg/kg (R, p.o.);
　　　150 mg/kg (dog, p.o.)
CN: 5-fluoro-1-(tetrahydro-2-furanyl)-2,4(1H,3H)-pyrimidinedione mixt. with 2,4(1H,3H)-pyrimidinedione

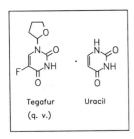

Tegafur
(q. v.)

Uracil

Reference(s):
JP 56 046 813 (Taiho; appl. 27.9.1979).
Yamamoto, J. et al.: Arzneim.-Forsch. (ARZNAD) **31**, 1276 (1981).

Formulation(s): cps. 100 mg; drg. 100 mg in comb. with 224 mg uracil

Trade Name(s):
J: UFT (Miguel-Otsuka)

Teicoplanin
(Teichomycin)

ATC: J01XA02
Use: antibacterial, antibiotic

RN: 61036-62-2　MF: $C_{41\text{-}43}H_{51\text{-}53}ClN_4O_{17}$　MW: unspecified
LD$_{50}$: 715 mg/kg (M, i.v.);
　　　160 mg/kg (R, i.v.);
　　　>900 mg/kg (dog, i.m.); 750 mg/kg (dog, i.v.)
CN: teicoplanin

Teichomycin A$_1$
RN: 61036-63-3　MF: unspecified　MW: unspecified
Teichomycin A$_2$
RN: 61036-64-4　MF: unspecified　MW: unspecified
LD$_{50}$: 275 mg/kg (M, i.v.); >1 g/kg (M, p.o.)

Teicoplanin

compound	R	formula
Teicoplanin A 2−1		$C_{88}H_{95}Cl_2N_9O_{33}$
Teicoplanin A 2−2		$C_{88}H_{97}Cl_2N_9O_{33}$
Teicoplanin A 2−3		$C_{88}H_{97}Cl_2N_9O_{33}$
Teicoplanin A 2−4		$C_{89}H_{99}Cl_2N_9O_{33}$
Teicoplanin A 2−5		$C_{89}H_{99}Cl_2N_9O_{33}$

Reference(s):
DE 2 608 216 (Lepetit; appl. 28.2.1976; GB-prior. 5.3.1975).
US 4 239 751 (Lepetit; 16.12.1980; GB-prior. 5.3.1975).
Parenti, F. et al.: J. Antibiot. (JANTAJ) **31**, 276 (1978).
Bardone, M.R. et al.: J. Antibiot. (JANTAJ) **31**, 170 (1978).
Coronelli, C. et al.: J. Antibiot. (JANTAJ) **37**, 621 (1984).
Borghi, A. et al.: J. Antibiot. (JANTAJ) **37**, 615 (1984).

isolation of teichomycin A₂ factors:
US 4 542 018 (Lepetit; 17.9.1985; appl. 7.6.1983; GB-prior. 8.6.1982).

Formulation(s):   vial 100 mg, 200 mg, 400 mg (lyo.)

Trade Name(s):
D: Targocid (Hoechst; 1989)   GB: Targocid (Hoechst; 1990)   I: Targosid (Hoechst Marion
F: Targocid (Marion Merrell)   Roussel)

Telmesteine

ATC: R05CB
Use: mucolytic agent

RN: 122946-43-4   MF: $C_7H_{11}NO_4S$ MW: 205.23
LD_{50}:   415 mg/kg (R, i.p.); >4000 mg/kg (R, p.o.)
CN: (R)-3,4-thiazolidinedicarboxylic acid 3-ethyl ester

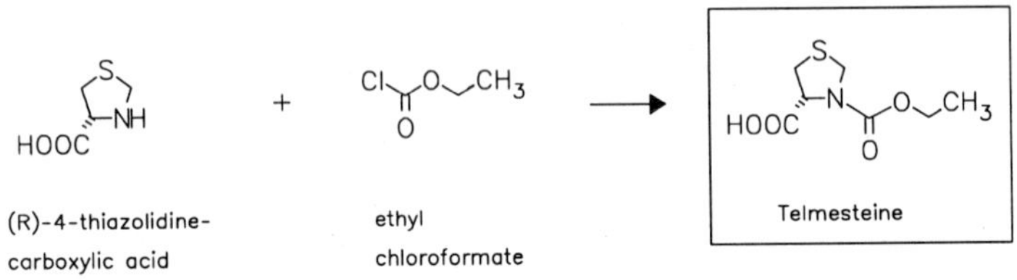

(R)-4-thiazolidine-   ethyl
carboxylic acid   chloroformate

Telmesteine

Reference(s):
US 4 874 776 (Yason; 17.10.1989; appl. 11.7.1988).

lysine salt:
EP 348 541 (Yason; appl. 29.6.1988).

Formulation(s):   sachets 300 mg; syrup 3 %

Trade Name(s):
I: Muconorm (Prospa Italia)   Reolase (Pulitzer)

Telmisartan
(BIBR 277; BIBR 277SE)

ATC: C09CA07
Use: antihypertensive, angiotensin II
            receptor blocker

RN: 144701-48-4   MF: $C_{33}H_{30}N_4O_2$ MW: 514.63
CN: 4'-[(1,4'-Dimethyl-2'-propyl[2,6'-bi-1*H*-benzimidazol]-1'-yl)methyl][1,1'-biphenyl]-2-carboxylic acid

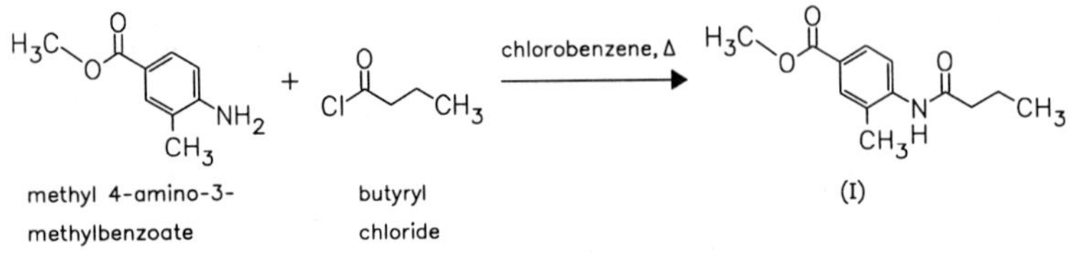

methyl 4-amino-3-   butyryl
methylbenzoate   chloride

(I)

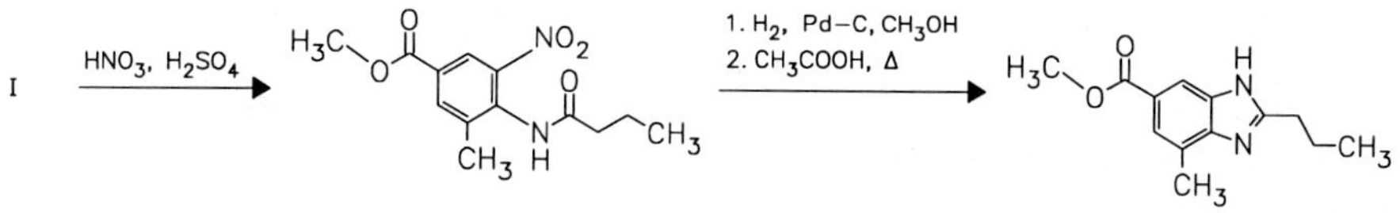

methyl 4-butyramido-
3-methyl-5-nitrobenzoate

methyl 2-propyl-4-
methylbenzimidazole-
6-carboxylate (II)

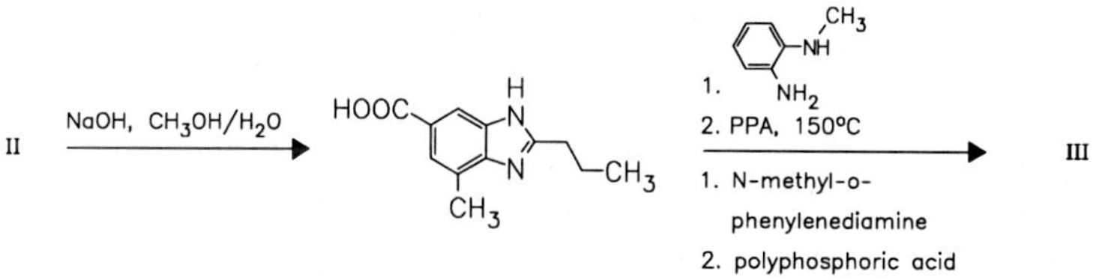

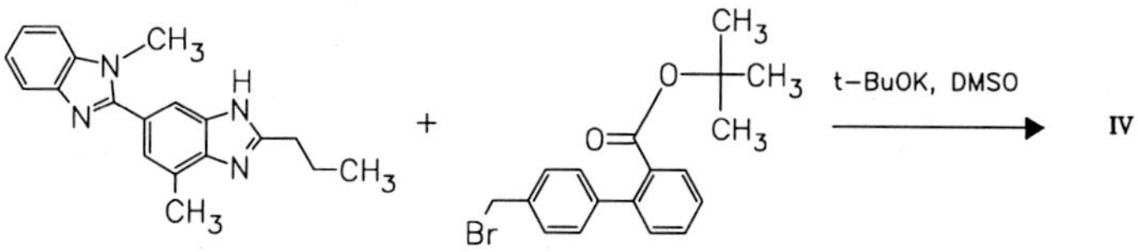

1. N-methyl-o-
phenylenediamine
2. polyphosphoric acid

4-methyl-6-(1-methyl-
benzimidazol-2-yl)-2-
propylbenzimidazole (III)

tert-butyl 4'-(bromo-
methyl)biphenyl-2-
carboxylate

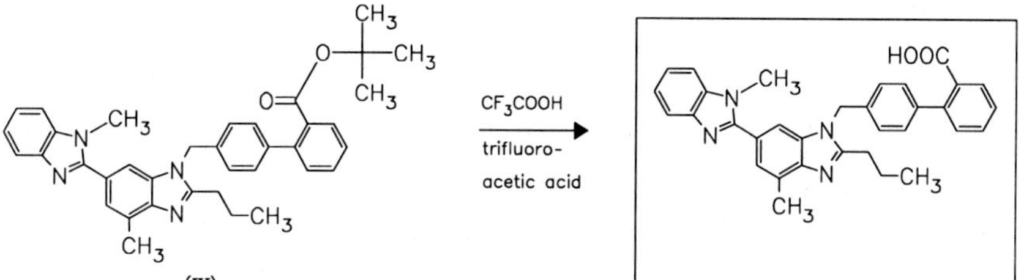

(IV)

Telmisartan

Reference(s):
Ries, U. et al.: J. Med. Chem. (JMCMAR) **36**, 4040-4051 (1993)
EP 502 314 (Thomae; 9.9.1992; appl. 31.1.1992; D-prior. 6.2.1991)
DE 4 408 497 (Thomae; 21.9.1995; appl. 14.3.1994; D-prior. 14.3.1994)

use for the treatment of a condition associated with hypoxia or unpaired metabolic function:
WO 9 920 260 (Eurogene Ltd.; appl. 19.10.1998, GB-prior. 17.10.1997)

use to treat symptomatic heart failure:
WO 9 830 216 (Merck + Co.; appl. 7.1.1998; USA-prior. 10.1.1997)

method to treat cardiofibrosis with a combination of an ATII-antagonist and spironolactone:
WO 9 640 256 (G. D. Searle; appl. 5.6.1996; USA-prior. 7.6.1995)

Formulation(s):   tabl. 40 mg, 80 mg

Trade Name(s):
D: Micardis (Boehringer
       Ingelheim; 1998)

Temafloxacin
(TA-167)

ATC: J01MA05
Use: quinolone antibacterial, gyrase inhibitor

RN: 108319-06-8   MF: $C_{21}H_{18}F_3N_3O_3$ MW: 417.39
CN: 1-(2,4-difluorophenyl)-6-fluoro-1,4-dihydro-7-(3-methyl-1-piperazinyl)-4-oxo-3-quinolinecarboxylic acid

monohydrochloride
RN: 105784-61-0   MF: $C_{21}H_{18}F_3N_3O_3 \cdot HCl$ MW: 453.85

2,4-dichloro-5-fluoroacetophenone   +   diethyl carbonate   → (NaH) →   (I)

I   +   triethyl orthoformate   →
(1. Ac$_2$O; 2. H$_2$N-; 2. 2,4-difluoro-aniline)
ethyl 2-(2,4-dichloro-5-fluoro-benzoyl)-3-(2,4-difluoro-anilino)-2-propenoate
→ (1. NaH; 2. NaOH) →   II

7-chloro-1-(2,4-difluoro-phenyl)-6-fluoro-1,4-dihydro-4-oxo-3-quinoline-carboxylic acid (II)
+   N^1-ethoxycarbonyl-2-methylpiperazine
→ (1. ; 2. NaOH) →   Temafloxacin

Reference(s):
EP 131 839 (Abbott; appl. 3.7.1984; USA-prior. 18.7.1983).
US 4 730 000 (Abbott; 8.3.1988; prior. 18.7.1983; 9.4.1984, 6.12.1984, 7.10.1985, 4.8.1987).
EP 350 950 (Abbott; appl. 14.7.1989; USA-prior. 15.7.1988).

medical use for treatment of AIDS related infections:
EP 437 128 (Rhône-Poulenc; appl. 10.12.1990; F-prior. 11.12.1989).

i.v. formulation with improved tolerability:
WO 9 109 525 (Abbott; appl. 20.12.1990; USA-prior. 29.12.1989).

Formulation(s):   tabl. 300 mg, 400 mg, 600 mg (as hydrochloride)

Trade Name(s):
GB: Teflox (Abbott; ICI; 1991);   USA: Omniflox (Abbott-Zeneca);
      wfm   wfm

Temazepam

(Methyloxazepam)

ATC: N05CD07
Use: tranquilizer, anticonvulsant, sedative, hypnotic

RN: 846-50-4   MF: $C_{16}H_{13}ClN_2O_2$ MW: 300.75   EINECS: 212-688-1
LD$_{50}$: 370 mg/kg (M, p.o.);
2 g/kg (R, p.o.);
3620 mg/kg (dog, p.o.)
CN: 7-chloro-1,3-dihydro-3-hydroxy-1-methyl-5-phenyl-2H-1,4-benzodiazepin-2-one

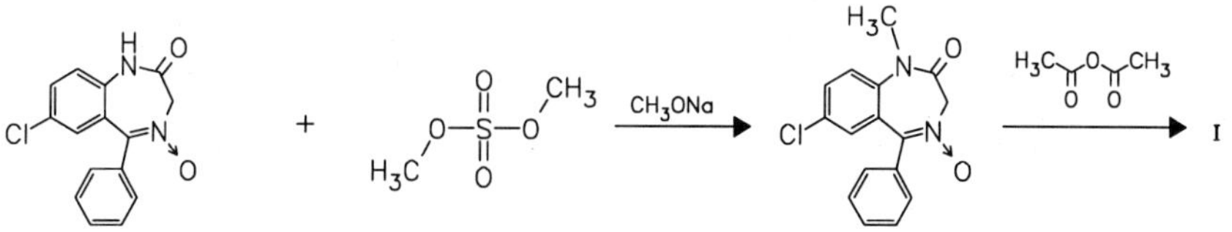

7-chloro-5-phenyl-
2-oxo-1,3-dihydro-
2H-1,4-benzodiazepine
4-oxide

(cf. oxazepam synthesis)

dimethyl
sulfate

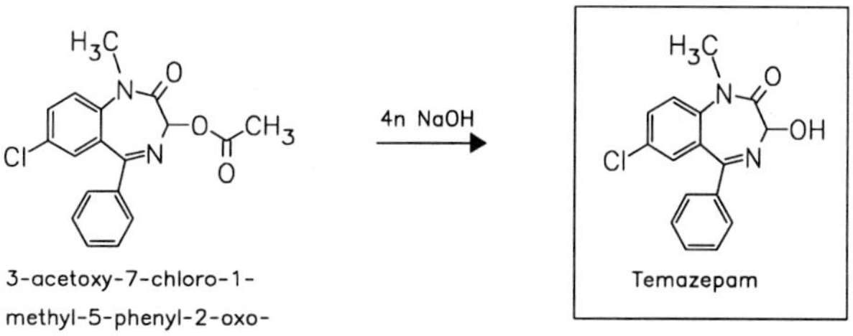

3-acetoxy-7-chloro-1-
methyl-5-phenyl-2-oxo-
1,3-dihydro-2H-1,4-
benzodiazepine (I)

Temazepam

Reference(s):
GB 1 022 642 (American Home; appl. 28.8.1962; USA-prior. 29.8.1961, 5.3.1962).
GB 1 022 645 (American Home; appl. 28.8.1962; USA-prior. 29.8.1961, 5.3.1962).

Formulation(s):   cps. 7.5 mg, 10 mg, 15 mg, 20 mg, 30 mg

Trade Name(s):
D: Neodorm (Knoll)
Norkotral (Desitin)
Planum /-mite (Pharmacia
& Upjohn)
Pronervon (Produpharm
Lappe)

Remestan /-mite (Wyeth)
temazep (ct-Arzneimittel)
F: Normison (Wyeth)
GB: Euhypnos (Montedison)
Normison (Wyeth)

I: Evipnos (Pharmacia &
Upjohn)
Levanxol (Carlo Erba);
wtm
Normison (Wyeth-Lederle)
USA: Restoril (Novartis)

Temocapril

(RS-5142; CS 622)

ATC: C09AA
Use: antihypertensive (ACE inhibitor)

RN: 111902-57-9   MF: $C_{23}H_{28}N_2O_5S_2$ MW: 476.62
CN: [2S-[2α,6β(R*)]]-6-[[1-(ethoxycarbonyl)-3-phenylpropyl]amino]tetrahydro-5-oxo-2-(2-thienyl)-1,4-thiazepine-4(5H)-acetic acid

monohydrochloride
RN: 110221-44-8   MF: $C_{23}H_{28}N_2O_5S_2 \cdot HCl$ MW: 513.08
LD_{50}: >5 g/kg (M, p.o.);
>5 g/kg (R, p.o.)

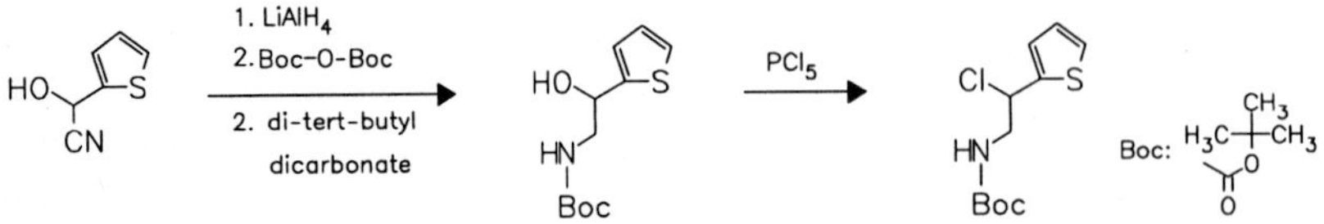

α-hydroxy-2-
thiophene-
acetonitrile

2-tert-butoxy-
carbonylamino-
1-(2-thienyl)-
ethanol

2-tert-butoxy-
carbonylamino-
1-chloro-1-(2-
thienyl)ethane (I)

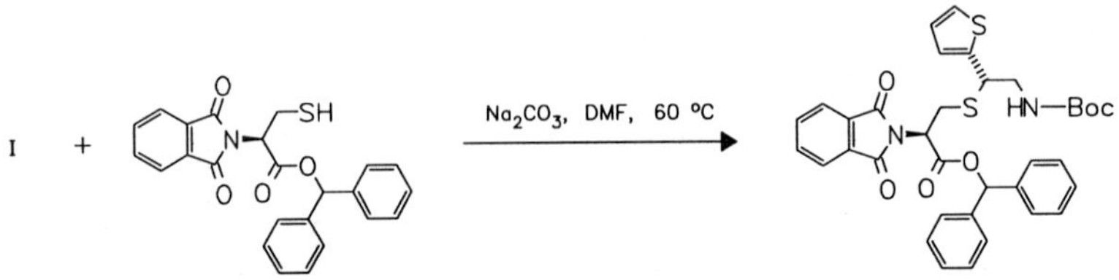

N-phthaloyl-L-cysteine
benzhydryl ester

S-[2-tert-butoxycarbonyl-
amino-1(S)-(2-thienyl)ethyl]-
N-phthaloyl-L-cysteine
benzhydryl ester (II)

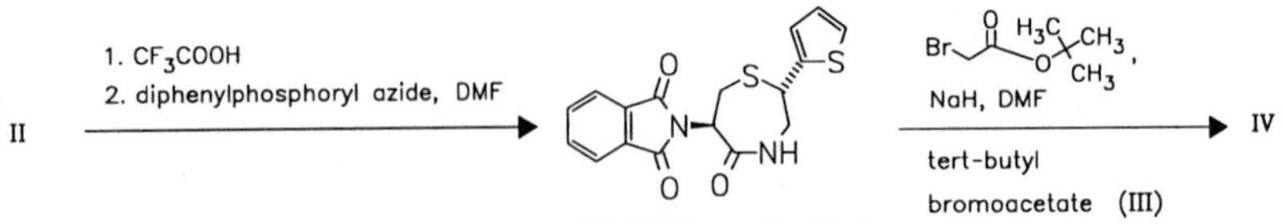

(2S,6R)-5-oxo-6-phthal-
imido-2-(2-thienyl)per-
hydro-1,4-thiazepine

tert-butyl
bromoacetate (III)

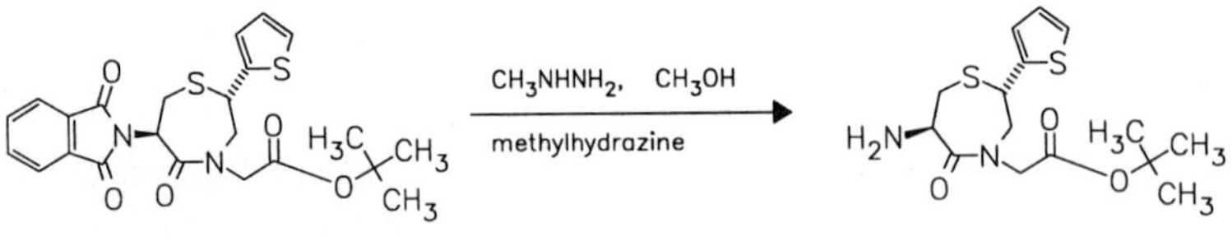

tert-butyl (2S,6R)-5-oxo-6-
phthalimido-2-(2-thienyl)-
perhydro-1,4-thiazepine-
4-acetate (IV)

tert-butyl (2S,6R)-6-amino-
5-oxo-2-(2-thienyl)-
perhydro-1,4-thiazepine-
4-acetate (V)

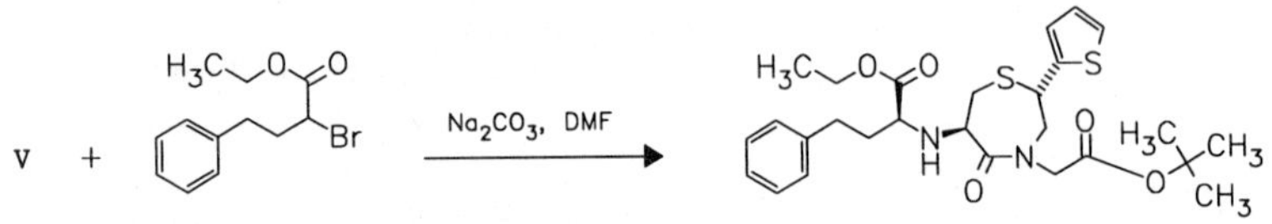

ethyl 2-bromo-
4-phenylbutyrate

(VI)

VI

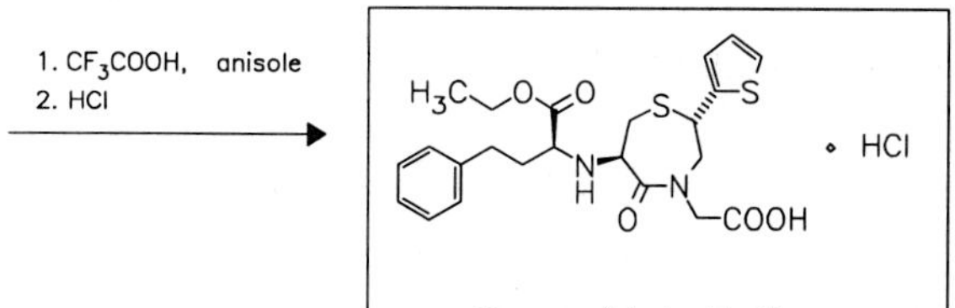

1. CF$_3$COOH, anisole
2. HCl

Temocapril hydrochloride

b)

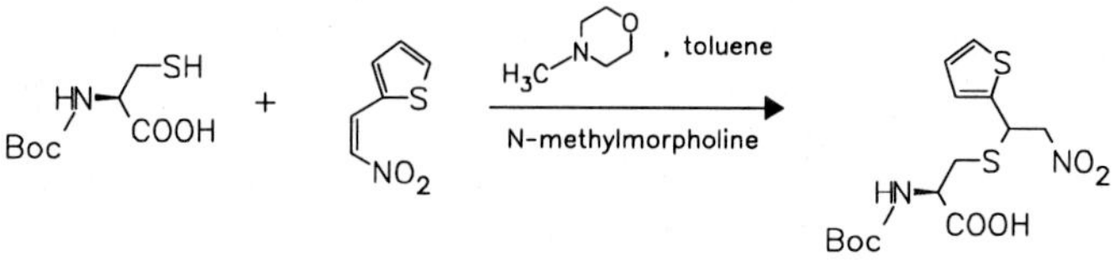

N-tert-butoxy-
carbonyl-L-
cysteine

2-(2-nitro-
ethenyl)-
thiophene

, toluene

N-methylmorpholine

S-[2-nitro-1-(2-
thienyl)ethyl]-N-
tert-butoxycarbonyl-
L-cysteine (VII)

VII

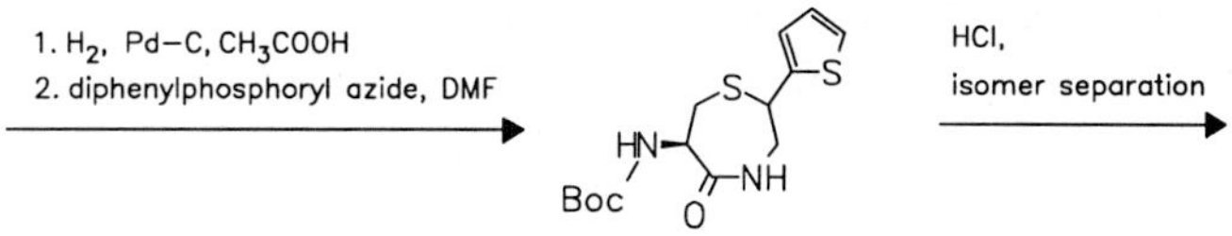

1. H$_2$, Pd–C, CH$_3$COOH
2. diphenylphosphoryl azide, DMF

HCl,
isomer separation

VIII

(2RS,6R)-6-tert-
butoxycarbonylamino-
2-(2-thienyl)-5-
oxoperhydro-1,4-
thiazepine

(2S,6R)-6-amino-
5-oxo-2-(2-
thienyl)perhydro-
1,4-thiazepine (VIII)

ethyl 2(R)-tri-
fluoromethylsulfo-
nyloxy-4-phenyl-
butyrate

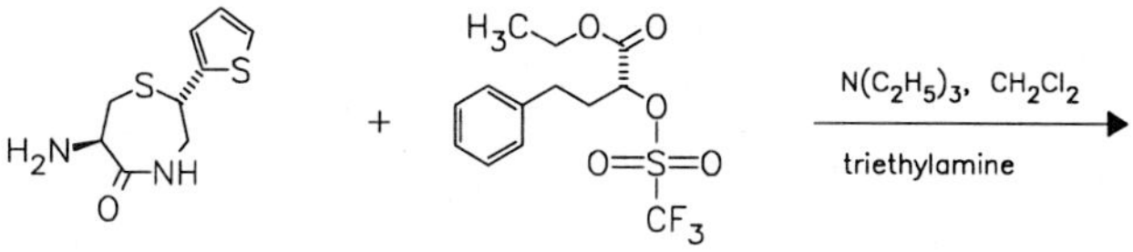

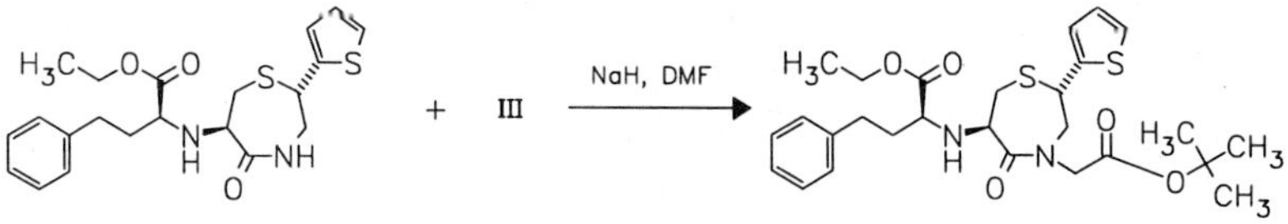

N(C$_2$H$_5$)$_3$, CH$_2$Cl$_2$

triethylamine

IX

(2S,6R)-6-[[1(S)-ethoxy-
carbonyl-3-phenylpropyl]-
amino]-5-oxo-2-(2-
thienyl)perhydro-1,4-
thiazepine (IX)

+   III

NaH, DMF

(X)

X

HCl, dioxane

Temocapril hydrochloride

Reference(s):
Yanagisawa, H. et al.: J. Med. Chem. (JMCMAR) **30**, 1984-1991 (1987).
EP 161 801 (Sankyo; 21.11.1985; J-prior. 10.4.1984).

process patent:
JP 62 161 775 (Sankyo; 17.7.1987; J-prior. 12.9.1985).

synergistic combination with thromboxane A2 inhibitors:
WO 9 206 713 (Farmitalia; appl. 16.10.1991; I-prior. 16.10.1990).

combination with diuretics:
WO 9 317 685 (Merck & Co.; appl. 3.3.1993; USA-prior. 11.3.1992).

Formulation(s):   tabl. 1 mg, 2 mg, 4 mg (as hydrochloride)

Trade Name(s):
J: Acecol (Sankyo/Nippon
        Boehringer Ing.)

Temocillin

ATC: J01CA17
Use: β-lactam antibiotic (penicillin
        derivative)

RN: 66148-78-5   MF: $C_{16}H_{18}N_2O_7S_2$ MW: 414.46   EINECS: 266-184-1
CN: [2S-(2α,5α,6α)]-6-[(carboxy-3-thienylacetyl)amino]-6-methoxy-3,3-dimethyl-7-oxo-4-thia-1-
       azabicyclo[3.2.0]heptane-2-carboxylic acid

disodium salt
RN: 61545-06-0   MF: $C_{16}H_{16}N_2Na_2O_7S_2$ MW: 458.42   EINECS: 262-835-9

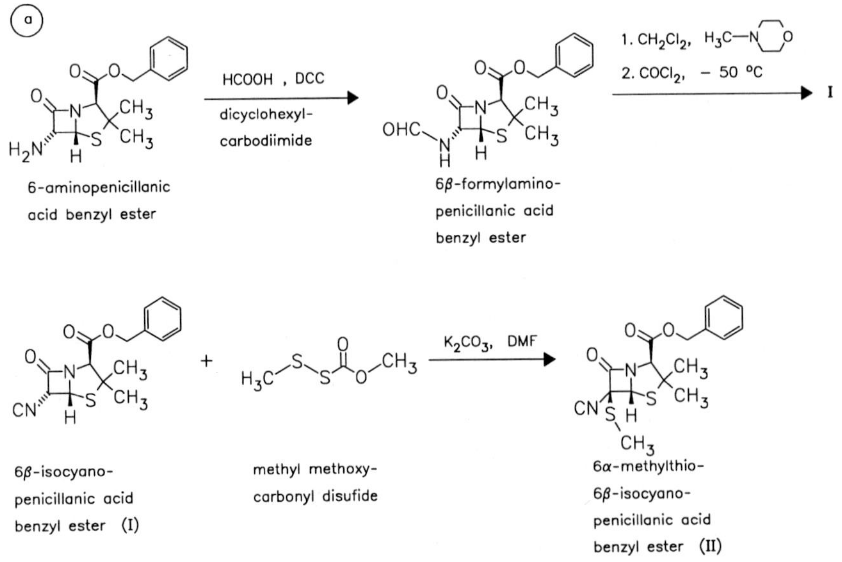

6-aminopenicillanic
acid benzyl ester

6β-formylamino-
penicillanic acid
benzyl ester

6β-isocyano-
penicillanic acid
benzyl ester   (I)

methyl methoxy-
carbonyl disufide

6α-methylthio-
6β-isocyano-
penicillanic acid
benzyl ester   (II)

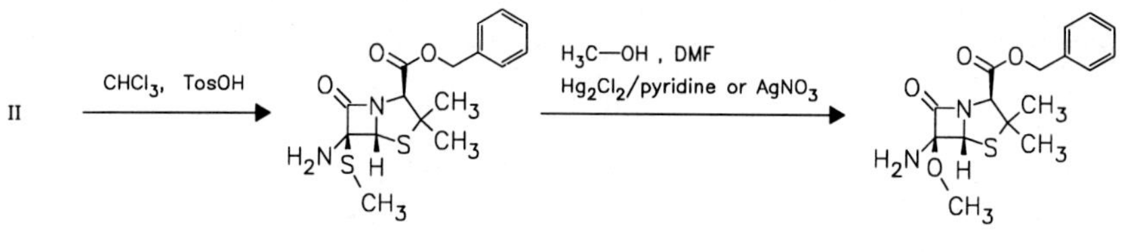

II

$\xrightarrow{\text{CHCl}_3,\ \text{TosOH}}$

6α-methylthio-6β-
aminopenicillanic
acid benzyl ester

$\xrightarrow[\text{Hg}_2\text{Cl}_2/\text{pyridine or AgNO}_3]{\text{H}_3\text{C}-\text{OH}\ ,\ \text{DMF}}$

6α-methoxy-6β-
aminopenicillanic
acid benzyl ester   (III)

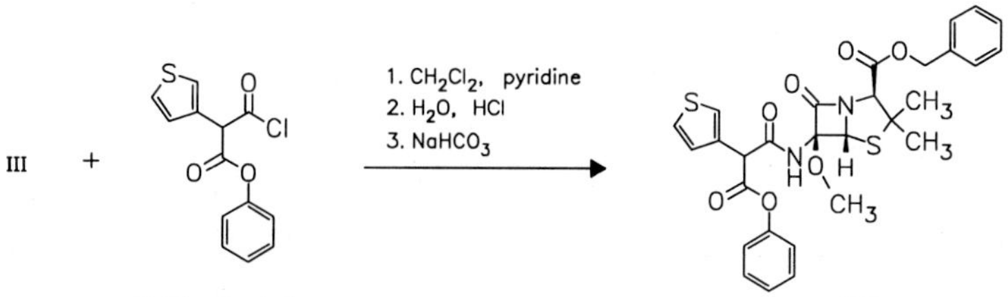

III +

3-thienylmalonic
acid monophenyl
ester monochloride

1. CH$_2$Cl$_2$, pyridine
2. H$_2$O, HCl
3. NaHCO$_3$

(IV)

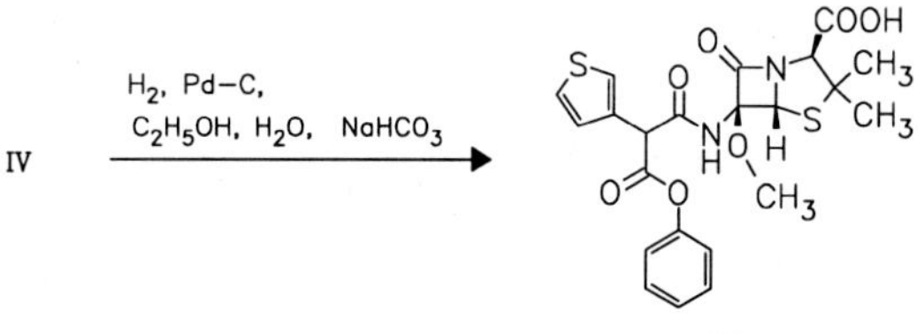

IV

$\xrightarrow[\text{C}_2\text{H}_5\text{OH},\ \text{H}_2\text{O},\ \text{NaHCO}_3]{\text{H}_2,\ \text{Pd}-\text{C},}$

(V)

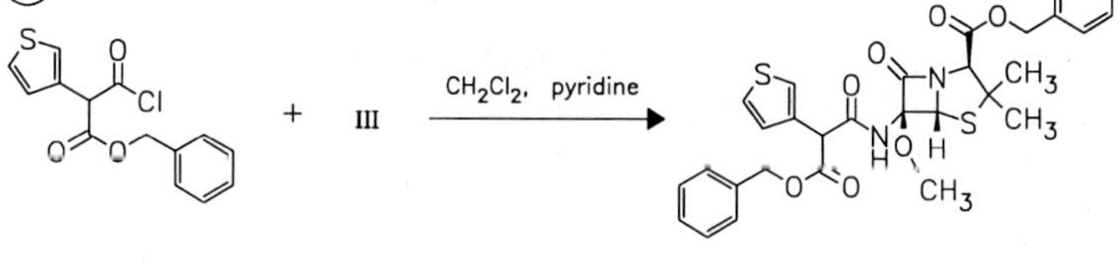

V

$\xrightarrow[\text{H}_2\text{O},\ 20\ ^\circ\text{C}]{\text{Na}_2\text{B}_4\text{O}_7\ \cdot\ 10\ \text{H}_2\text{O},}$

Temocillin disodium

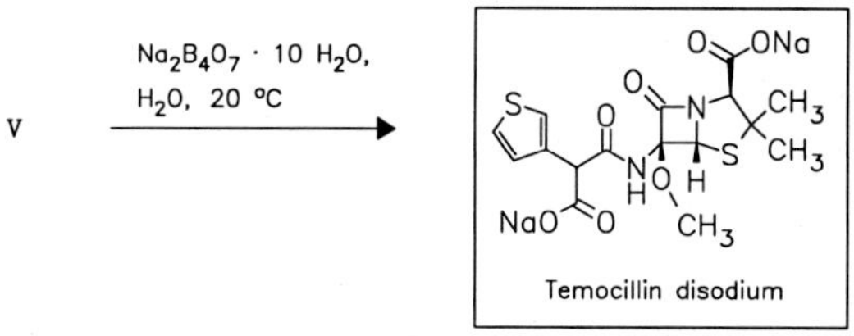

b

3-thienylmalonic
acid monobenzyl
ester monochloride

+ III

$\xrightarrow{\text{CH}_2\text{Cl}_2,\ \text{pyridine}}$

(VI)

VI

$\xrightarrow[\text{C}_2\text{H}_5\text{OH},\ \text{H}_2\text{O},\ \text{NaHCO}_3]{\text{H}_2,\ \text{Pd}-\text{C},}$

Temocillin disodium

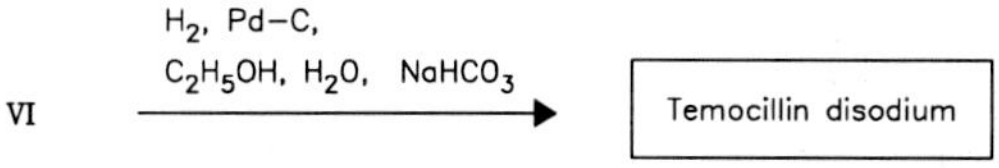

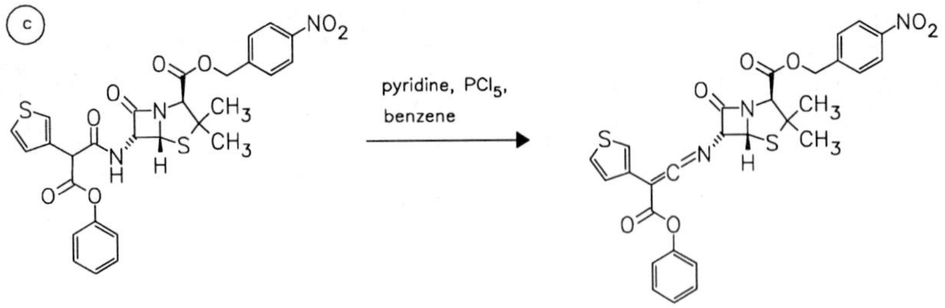

ⓒ

pyridine, PCl$_5$,
benzene

6β-[2-(3-thienyl)-2-(phenoxycarbonyl)acetamido]penicillanic
acid 4-nitrobenzyl ester
(from Ticarcillin, q. v.)

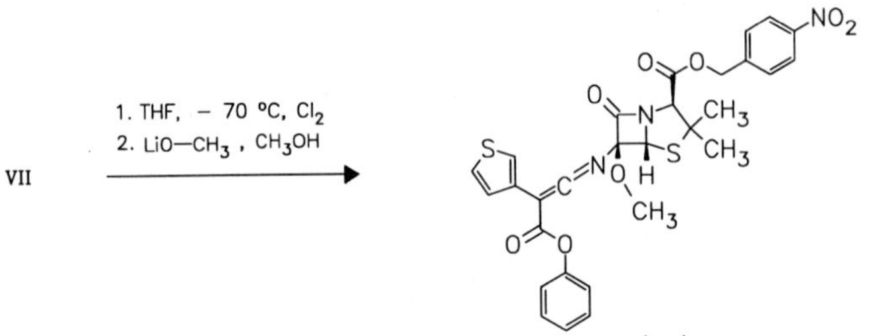

(VII)

1. THF, − 70 °C, Cl$_2$
2. LiO—CH$_3$, CH$_3$OH

VII

(VIII)

THF, H$_2$O, H$_3$PO$_4$

VIII

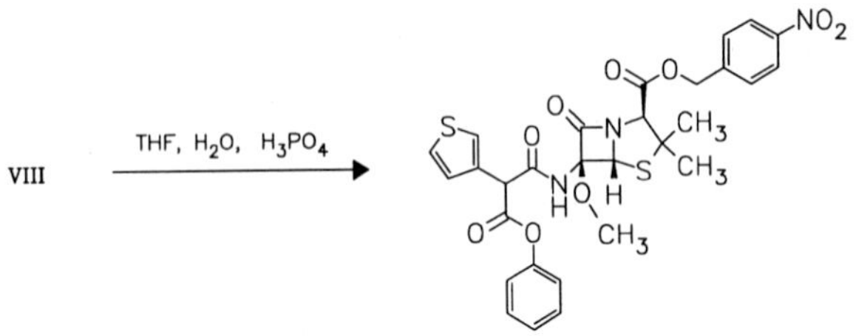

(IX)

H$_2$, Pd–C,
C$_2$H$_5$OH, THF

IX ──────────→ V

Na$_2$B$_4$O$_7$ · 10 H$_2$O

H$_2$O, 20 °C

Temocillin disodium

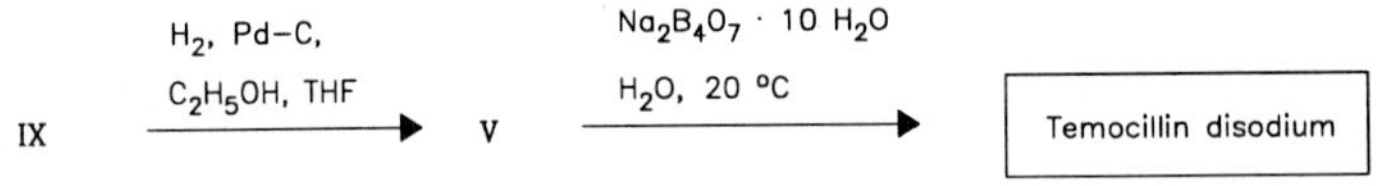

Reference(s):
a,b DOS 2 600 866 (Beecham; appl. 12.1.1976; GB-prior. 17.1.1975, 17.6.1975, 16.8.1975).
　　US 4 048 320 (Beecham; 13.9.1977; GB-prior. 17.1.1975, 17.6.1975, 16.8.1975).
　　6α-methylthio- resp. 6α-methoxy-6β-aminopenicillanic acid ester:
　　DOS 2 407 000 (Beecham; appl. 14.2.1974).
　　Jen, T. et al: J. Org. Chem. (JOCEAH) **38**, 2857 (1973).
　　Slusarchyk, W.A. et al.: J. Org. Chem. (JOCEAH) **38**, 943 (1973).
　　Baldwin, J.E. et al.: J. Am. Chem. Soc. (JACSAT) **95**, 2401 (1973).
　　6-isocyanopenicillanic acid derivatives:
　　Bentley, P.H. et al.: J. Chem. Soc., Perkin Trans. 1 (JCPRB4) **1979**, 2455.
c　DOS 2 728 601 (Beecham; appl. 24.8.1977; GB-prior. 26.6.1976).
　　US 41 82-710 (Beecham; 8.1.1980; GB-prior. 26.6.1976).
　　US 4 185 014 (Beecham; 22.1.1980; GB-prior. 26.6.1976).

Formulation(s):　　vial 500 mg, 1 g, 2 g (as disodium salt)

Trade Name(s):

D: Temopen (Beecham-Wülfing); wfm

GB: Temopen (Bencard)

Teniposide

ATC: L01CB02
Use: antineoplastic (leucemia)

RN: 29767-20-2 MF: $C_{32}H_{32}O_{13}S$ MW: 656.66 EINECS: 249-831-2
LD_{50}: 29.57 mg/kg (M, i.p.); 31.56 mg/kg (M, s.c.)
CN: [5*R*-[5α,5aβ,8aα,9β(*R**)]]-5,8,8a,9-tetrahydro-5-(4-hydroxy-3,5-dimethoxyphenyl)-9-[[4,6-*O*-(2-thienylmethylene)-β-D-glucopyranosyl]oxy]furo[3',4':6,7]naphtho[2,3-*d*]-1,3-dioxol-6(5a*H*)-one

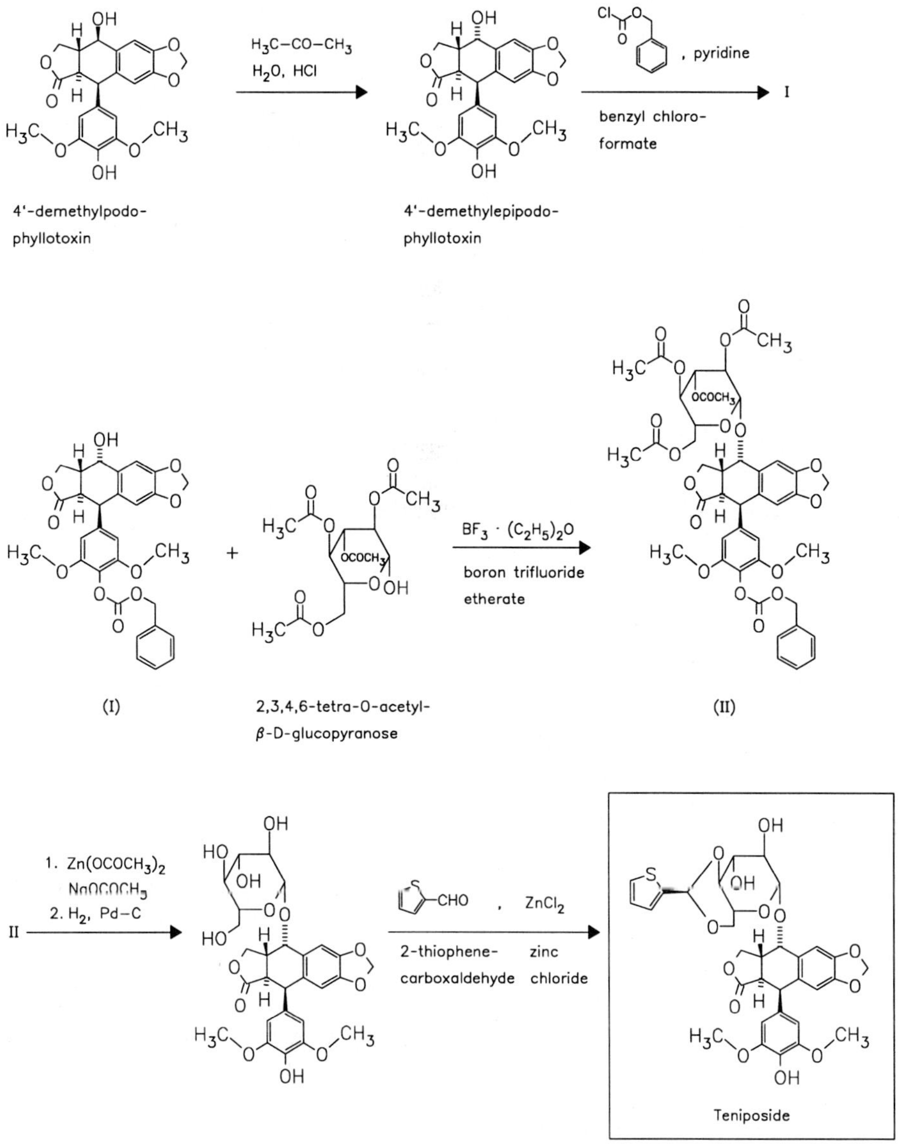

H3C–CO–CH3
H2O, HCl
, pyridine
benzyl chloroformate
I
4'-demethylpodophyllotoxin
4'-demethylepipodophyllotoxin
+
BF3 · (C2H5)2O
boron trifluoride etherate
(I)
2,3,4,6-tetra-O-acetyl-β-D-glucopyranose
(II)
II
1. Zn(OCOCH3)2
NaOCOCH3
2. H2, Pd–C
CHO
, ZnCl2
2-thiophenecarboxaldehyde
zinc chloride
Teniposide

Reference(s):
DOS 1 543 890 (Sandoz; appl. 10.12.1966; CH-prior. 14.12.1966, 12.10.1966, 14.12.1965).
Keller-Juslen, C. et al.: J. Med. Chem. (JMCMAR) **14**, 936 (1971).
FR 1 518 706 (Sandoz AG; appl. 15.6.1967; CH-prior. 12.10.1966, 14.12.1965).

toxicity reduction by addition of lithium carbonate:
FR 2 320 104 (Sandoz; appl. 6.8.1975).

Formulation(s):　amp. 50 mg

Trade Name(s):

D:	VM-26-Bristol (Bristol-Myers Squibb)	I:	Vumon (Bristol-Myers Squibb)	USA:	Vumon (Bristol-Myers Squibb)
F:	Véhem-Sandoz (Novartis)				

Tenonitrozole

(Thenitrazolum)

ATC:　P01AX08
Use:　antiparasitic agent, antifungal, chemotherapeutic (trichomonas), antiprotozoal

RN:　3810-35-3　MF: $C_8H_5N_3O_3S_2$　MW: 255.28　EINECS: 223-282-9
CN:　*N*-(5-nitro-2-thiazolyl)-2-thiophenecarboxamide

2-amino-5-nitro-thiazole	2-thenoyl chloride	Tenonitrozole

Reference(s):
FR-M 715 (H. R. Chantereau; appl. 1961).

Formulation(s):　drg. 100 mg

Trade Name(s):

D:	Moniflagon (Schur); wfm	F:	Atrican (Innotech International)	I:	Atrican (Bouty); wfm

---

Tenoxicam

ATC:　M01AC02
Use:　anti-inflammatory, analgesic analog of piroxicam

RN:　59804-37-4　MF: $C_{13}H_{11}N_3O_4S_2$　MW: 337.38
LD$_{50}$:　297 mg/kg (M, p.o.);
　　　79 mg/kg (R, p.o.);
　　　>128 mg/kg (dog, p.o.)
CN:　4-hydroxy-2-methyl-*N*-2-pyridinyl-2*H*-thieno[2,3-*e*]-1,2-thiazine-3-carboxamide 1,1-dioxide

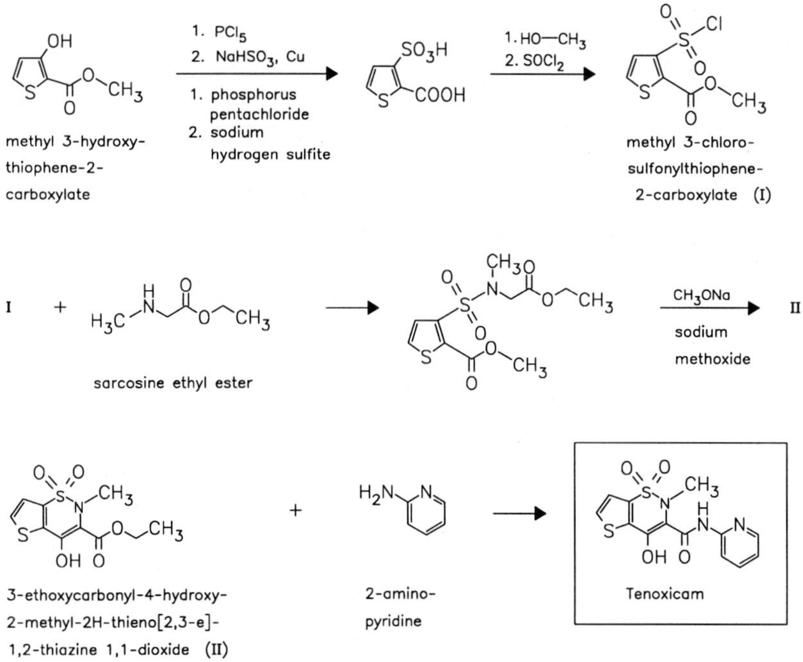

methyl 3-hydroxy-
thiophene-2-
carboxylate

1. PCl5
2. NaHSO3, Cu

1. phosphorus
pentachloride
2. sodium
hydrogen sulfite

1. HO—CH3
2. SOCl2

methyl 3-chloro-
sulfonylthiophene-
2-carboxylate (I)

I + sarcosine ethyl ester

CH3ONa

sodium
methoxide

II

3-ethoxycarbonyl-4-hydroxy-
2-methyl-2H-thieno[2,3-e]-
1,2-thiazine 1,1-dioxide (II)

+

2-amino-
pyridine

Tenoxicam

Reference(s):
DOS 2 537 070 (Hoffmann-La Roche; appl. 20.8.1975; CH-prior. 26.8.1974, 9.9.1974).
GB 1 519 812 (Hoffmann-La Roche; appl. 22.8.1975).
GB 1 519 811 (Hoffmann-La Roche; appl. 22.8.1975; CH-prior. 9.9.1974).
US 4 076 709 (Roche; 28.2.1978; appl. 21.8.1975; CH-prior. 9.9.1974).

Formulation(s): amp. 20 mg; powder 20 mg; suppos. 20 mg; tabl. 10 mg, 20 mg

Trade Name(s):
D: Liman (Solvay
Arzneimittel; 1990)
Tilcotil (Roche; 1990)
F: Tilcotil (Roche; 1988)

GB: Mobiflex (Roche; 1988)
I: Dolmen (Sigma-Tau; 1989)
Rexalgan (Dompé)
Tilcotil (Roche; 1989)

J: Tilcotil (Nihon Roche-
Kyorin)

Tenylidone

ATC: A05BA
Use: liver therapeutic

RN: 893-01-6 MF: $C_{16}H_{14}OS_2$ MW: 286.42 EINECS: 212-969-9
CN: 2,6-bis(2-thienylmethylene)cyclohexanone

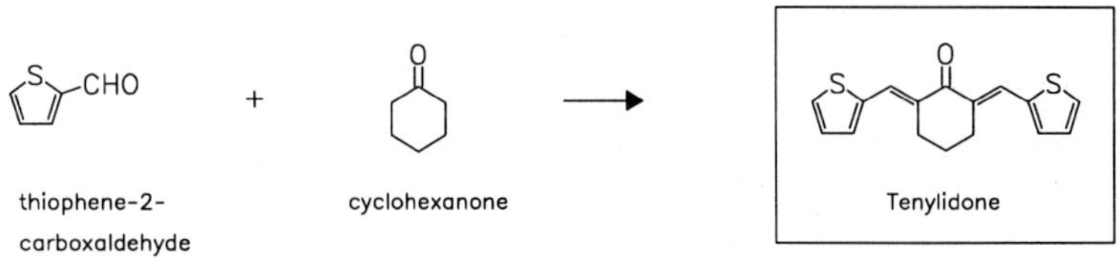

thiophene-2-
carboxaldehyde

+

cyclohexanone

Tenylidone

Reference(s):
FR-M 64 (R. Blaise; appl. 1960).

Formulation(s):   gran. 50 %

Trade Name(s):
F: Margéryl (Marinier); wfm   Thiofantile (Ana); wfm   Vanitile (Ana); wfm

Terazosin

ATC: G04CA03
Use: antihypertensive, α-blocker

RN: 63590-64-7   MF: $C_{19}H_{25}N_5O_4$ MW: 387.44
CN: 1-(4-amino-6,7-diethoxy-2-quinazolinyl)-4-[(tetrahydro-2-furanyl)carbonyl]piperazine

hydrochloride
RN: 63074-08-8   MF: $C_{19}H_{25}N_5O_4 \cdot HCl$ MW: 423.90
monohydrochloride dihydrate
RN: 70024-40-7   MF: $C_{19}H_{25}N_5O_4 \cdot HCl \cdot 2H_2O$ MW: 459.93
LD_{50}:   237 mg/kg (M, i.v.); >8 g/kg (M, p.o.);
    255 mg/kg (R, i.v.); 5500 mg/kg (R, p.o.)

piperazine   furan-2-carbonyl chloride   1-(2-furoyl)-piperazine   N-(2-tetrahydro-furoyl)piperazine (I)

4-amino-2-chloro-6,7-dimethoxyquinazoline
(cf. prazosin synthesis)   Terazosin

Reference(s):
DOS 2 646 186 (Abbott; appl. 13.10.1976; USA-prior. 14.10.1975).
US 4 026 894 (Abbott; 31.5.1977; prior. 14.10.1975).
US 4 112 097 (Abbott; 5.9.1978; prior. 21.1.1977).

hydrochloride hydrate:
DOS 2 831 112 (Abbott; appl. 14.7.1978; USA-prior. 4.8.1977).

dihydrate via form IV:
US 5 504 207 (Abbott; 2.4.1996; USA-prior. 18.10.1994).

dihydrate:
WO 9 925 715 (Teva; appl. 12.11.1998; USA-prior. 14.11.1997).

manufacture of form I:
EP 845 461 (Alfa Chem; appl. 17.10.1997; I-prior. 29.11.1996).
EP 845 462 (Alfa Chem; appl. 17.10.1997; I-prior. 29.11.1996).

form III:
US 5 412 905 (Abbott; appl. 20.5.1994; USA-prior. 29.4.1993).

process for a polymorph:
CA 2 173 407 (Acic; appl. 3.4.1993).
WO 9 721 705 (Uetikon; appl. 12.12.1996; D-prior. 13.12.1995).
US 5 587 377 (Invamed; USA-prior. 24.10.1995).

capsules:
WO 9 805 308 (Novartis; appl. 31.7.1997; USA-prior. 1.8.1996).

pharmaceutical composition for treating glaucoma:
WO 9 531 200 (Senju Pharm.; appl. 15.5.1995; J-prior. 18.5.1994).

(R)-(+)-terazosin:
WO 9 200 073 (Abbott; appl. 26.6.1991; USA-prior. 29.6.1990).

Formulation(s):   cps. (USA) 1 mg, 2 mg, 5 mg, 10 mg; tabl. 1 mg, 2 mg, 5 mg, 10 mg (as monohydrochloride dihydrate)

Trade Name(s):

D:	Flotrin Start (Abbott)		Hytrine (Abbott)		Vasomet (Mitsubishi)
	Heitrin (Abbott; 1985)	GB:	Hytrin (Abbott; 1987)	USA:	Hytrine (Abbott; 1987)
F:	Dysalfa (Débat)	J:	Hytracin (Dainabot)		

Terbinafine

(SF-86327)

ATC: D01AE15; D01BA02; J02AX
Use: orally and topically active antifungal

RN: 91161-71-6   MF: $C_{21}H_{25}N$ MW: 291.44
LD_{50}:   393 mg/kg (M, i.v.); 4000 mg/kg (M, p.o.); >2 g/kg (M, s.c.);
    213 mg/kg (R, i.v.); 4000 mg/kg (R, p.o.); >2 g/kg (R, s.c.); >2 g/kg (R, skin)
CN: (E)-N-(6,6-dimethyl-2-hepten-4-ynyl)-N-methyl-1-naphthalenemethanamine

hydrochloride
RN: 78628-80-5   MF: $C_{21}H_{25}N \cdot HCl$ MW: 327.90
LD_{50}:   >2 g/kg (M, s.c.);
    >2 g/kg (R, s.c.); >2 g/kg (R, skin)

Reference(s):
EP 24 587 (Sandoz; appl. 6.8.1980; CH-prior. 22.8.1979).
Stütz, A.; Petranyi, G.: J. Med. Chem. (JMCMAR) **27**, 1539 (1984).

Formulation(s):   cream 10 mg/g; tabl. 250 mg (as hydrochloride)

Trade Name(s):

D:	Lamisil (Novartis; 1991)	I:	Daskil (LPB)	J:	Lamisil (Toko Yakuhin-
F:	Lamisil (Novartis)		Lamisil (Novartis)		Sandoz)
GB:	Lamisil (Novartis; 1990)			USA:	Lamisil (Novartis)

Terbutaline

ATC: R03AC03; R03CC03
Use: bronchodilator, tocolytic

RN: 23031-25-6   MF: $C_{12}H_{19}NO_3$ MW: 225.29   EINECS: 245-385-8
CN: 5-[2-[(1,1-dimethylethyl)amino]-1-hydroxyethyl]-1,3-benzenediol

sulfate (2:1)
RN: 23031-32-5   MF: $C_{12}H_{19}NO_3 \cdot 1/2H_2SO_4$ MW: 548.65   EINECS: 245-386-3
LD_{50}:   36 mg/kg (M, i.v.); 205 mg/kg (M, p.o.);
        69 mg/kg (R, i.v.); 8700 mg/kg (R, p.o.);
        116 mg/kg (dog, i.v.); 1520 mg/kg (dog, p.o.)

Reference(s):
DE 1 643 296 (Draco; prior. 17.10.1967).
GB 1 199 630 (Draco; Lund; appl. 18.10.1967; S-prior. 19.10.1966).
US 3 937 838 (Draco; 10.2.1976; prior. 18.10.1967).
US 4 011 258 (Draco; 8.3.1977; prior. 21.6.1973).

Formulation(s):   amp. 0.5 mg/ml, 1 mg/ml; powder inhaler 0.5 mg/puff; sol. for inhalation 10 mg/ml (as
        sulfate); s. r. cps. 7.5 mg; s. r. tabl. 7.5 mg; tabl. 2.5 mg, 5 mg

Trade Name(s):

D:	Aerodur (Astra/pharma-stern)	Bricanyl (pharma-stern; 1971)		Terbul (Hexal)
	ARUBENDOL (Isis Pharma)	Bricanyl (Astra)-comb. with guaifenesin		Terbutalin (Mundipharma; Stada; Aluid Pharma; ratiopharm)
	Asthmo (Krewel Meuselbach)	Butaliret (Fatol)		Terbuturmant (Desitin)
	Asthmoprotect (Azupharma)	Butalitab (Fatol)Contimit (Lindopharm)	F:	Bricanyl (Astra; 1973)
		Eudur (Astra)-comb. with theophyllin	GB:	Bricanyl Turbohaler (Astra)
			GB:	Bricanyl (Astra; 1971)
			I:	Bricanyl (Astra)

J: Bricanyl (Astra-Fujisawa;   Bristurin (Bristol)   Brinacyl (Hoechst Marion
      1974)   USA: Brethine (Novartis; 1975)   Roussel; 1974)

Terconazole

(Triconazole)

ATC: G01AG02
Use: antifungal

RN: 67915-31-5   MF: $C_{26}H_{31}Cl_2N_5O_3$ MW: 532.47   EINECS: 267-751-6
LD_{50}:   1741 mg/kg (Rm, p.o.); 849 mg/kg (Rf, p.o.)
CN: *cis*-1-[4-[[2-(2,4-dichlorophenyl)-2-(1*H*-1,2,4-triazol-1-ylmethyl)-1,3-dioxolan-4-yl]methoxy]phenyl]-4-
       (1-methylethyl)piperazine

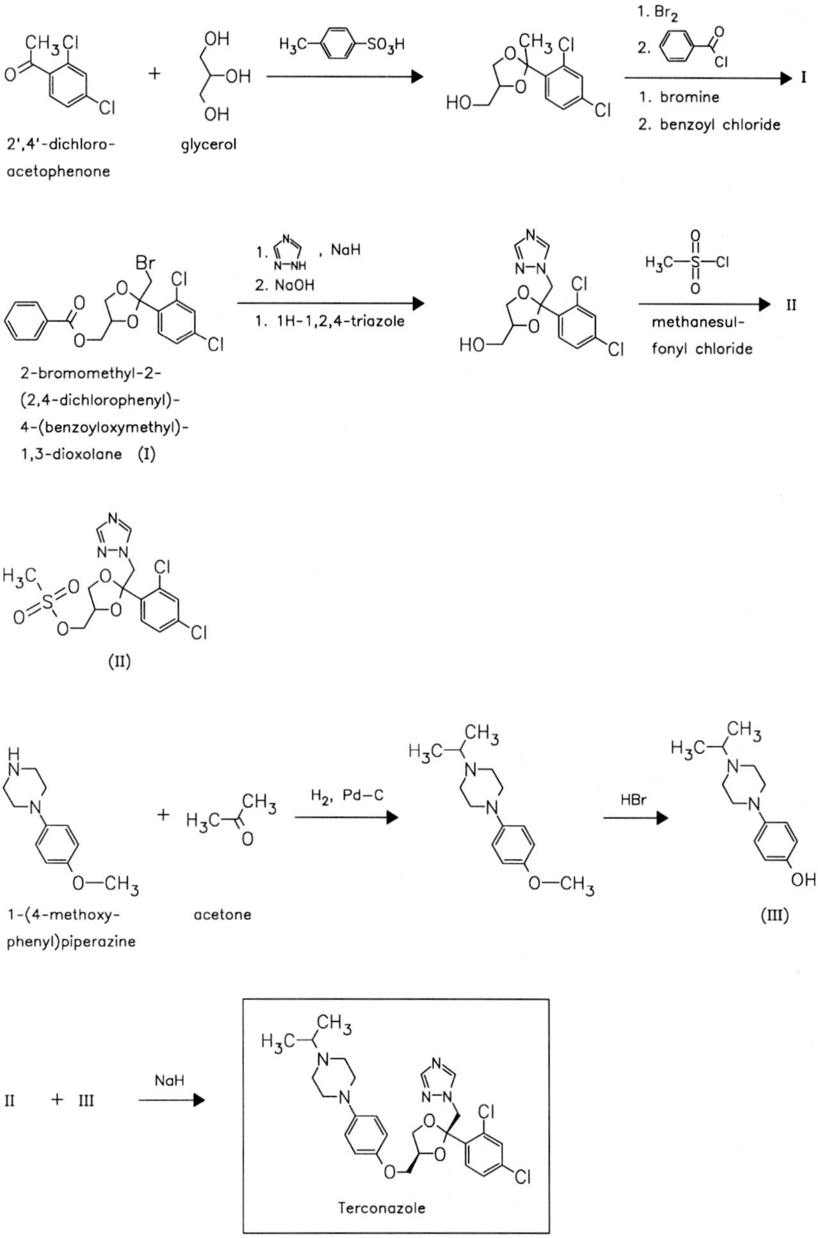

2',4'-dichloro-
acetophenone

glycerol

1. bromine
2. benzoyl chloride

2-bromomethyl-2-
(2,4-dichlorophenyl)-
4-(benzoyloxymethyl)-
1,3-dioxolane (I)

1. 1H-1,2,4-triazole

methanesul-
fonyl chloride

(II)

1-(4-methoxy-
phenyl)piperazine

acetone

(III)

II + III $\xrightarrow{\text{NaH}}$

Terconazole

Reference(s):
DE 2 804 096 (Janssen; appl. 3.8.1978; prior. 31.1.1978).
US 4 358 449 (Janssen; 9.11.1982; prior. 21.11.1977).
US 4 144 346 (Janssen; 13.3.1979; prior. 21.11.1977, 31.1.1977).
US 4 223 036 (Janssen; 16.9.1980; prior. 8.1.1979, 21.11.1977, 31.1.1977).
Heeres, J. et al.: J. Med. Chem. (JMCMAR) **26**, 611 (1983).

synthesis of 2-bromomethyl-2-(2,4-dichlorophenyl)-4-(benzoyloxymethyl)-1,3-dioxolane:
Heeres, J. et al.: J. Med. Chem. (JMCMAR) **22**, 1003 (1979).

Formulation(s):   suppos. 80 mg; vaginal cream 0.4 %, 0.8 %; vaginal tabl. 80 mg

Trade Name(s):
D: Tercospor (Cilag; 1985);   I: Terconal (Italchimici)   USA: Terazol (Ortho-McNeil;
        wfm   1988)

Terfenadine

ATC: R06AX12
Use: antihistaminic, antiallergic

RN: 50679-08-8   MF: $C_{32}H_{41}NO_2$ MW: 471.69   EINECS: 256-710-8
LD$_{50}$: 5 g/kg (M, p.o.);
        5 g/kg (R, p.o.)
CN: α-[4-(1,1-dimethylethyl)phenyl]-4-(hydroxydiphenylmethyl)-1-piperidinebutanol

azacyclonol (I)   1-(4-tert-butylphenyl)-   Terfenadine
(q. v.)   4-chloro-1-butanol

1-(4-tert-butylphenyl)-
4-chloro-1-butanone

Reference(s):
DOS 2 303 305 (Richardson-Merrell; appl. 24.1.1973; USA-prior. 28.1.1972).
DOS 2 503 362 (Richardson-Merrell; appl. 28.1.1975; USA-prior. 8.2.1974).
addition to DOS 2 303 306 (Richardson-Merrell; appl. 28.1.1975; USA-prior. 8.2.1974).
GB 1 412 605 (Richardson-Merrell; valid from 15.12.1972; USA-prior. 28.1.1972).
US 3 878 217 (Richardson-Merrell; 15.4.1975; appl. 12.7.1973; prior. 28.1.1972).

Formulation(s):   susp. 30 mg/5 ml; s. r. tabl. 60 mg in comb. with pseudoephedrine.HCl; tabl. 60 mg, 120 mg

Terodiline

ATC: G04BD05
Use: antianginal, calcium antagonist,
      anticholinergic, treatment of urinary
      frequency and incontinence

RN: 15793-40-5   MF: $C_{20}H_{27}N$ MW: 281.44
CN: N-(1,1-dimethylethyl)-α-methyl-γ-phenylbenzenepropanamine

hydrochloride
RN: 7082-21-5   MF: $C_{20}H_{27}N \cdot HCl$ MW: 317.90
LD_{50}: 28 mg/kg (M, i.v.); 330 mg/kg (M, p.o.); 170 mg/kg (M, s.c.)
      27 mg/kg (R, i.v.); 465 mg/kg (R, p.o.); 370 mg/kg (R, s.c.)
      63.3 g/kg (dog, p.o.)

β,β-diphenylethyl methyl ketone (I) + tert-butyl-amine (II) → Terodiline

I + II →(1. AlCl₃; 2. H₂, Pd–C) Terodiline

Reference(s):
a   DE 1 170 417 (Aktiebolaget Recip.; appl. 8.11.1961; GB-prior. 8.11.1960).
b   HU T32 331 (Richter Gedeon Vegyeszeti Gyar; appl. 30.7.1984, HU-prior. 21.9.1982).

Formulation(s):   f. c. tabl. 12.5 mg, 25 mg (as hydrochloride)

Tertatolol

ATC: C07AA16
Use: β-adrenoceptor antagonist, antihypertensive

RN: 34784-64-0   MF: $C_{16}H_{25}NO_2S$ MW: 295.45
CN: (±)-1-[(3,4-dihydro-2H-1-benzothiopyran-8-yl)oxy]-3-[(1,1-dimethylethyl)amino]-2-propanol

hydrochloride
RN: 33580-30-2   MF: $C_{16}H_{25}NO_2S \cdot HCl$ MW: 331.91   EINECS: 251-578-8
LD_{50}:   120 mg/kg (M, i.p.); 37 mg/kg (M, i.v.);
        90 mg/kg (R, i.p.); 40 mg/kg (R, i.v.)

2-methoxy-   β-chloro-   3-(2-methoxyphenyl-   8-hydroxy-
thiophenol   propionic acid   thio)propionic acid   thiochroman   (I)

1. PPA
2. N_2H_4, KOH
1. polyphosphoric acid
2. hydrazine

epichloro-   tert-butyl-   Tertatolol
hydrin   amine

Reference(s):
DE 2 115 201 (Science Union et Cie.; appl. 29.3.1971; GB-prior. 6.4.1970).
US 3 960 891 (Science Union et Cie.; 1.6.1976; GB-prior. 6.4.1970).
US 4 032 648 (Science Union et Cie.; 28.6.1977; GB-prior. 6.4.1970).

alternative synthesis:
GB 1 561 153 (Science Union et Cie.; appl. 23.8.1976).

Formulation(s):   f. c. tabl. 5 mg (as hydrochloride)

Trade Name(s):
D: Prenalex (Servier; 1990)   F: Artex (Servier; Therval; 1990)

Testolactone

ATC: L02AX
Use: antineoplastic (mamma carcinoma)

RN: 968-93-4   MF: $C_{19}H_{24}O_3$ MW: 300.40   EINECS: 213-534-6
CN: D-homo-17a-oxaandrosta-1,4-diene-3,17-dione

microbiologically
Cylindrocarpon radicola (ATCC 11011)

progesterone   Testolactone

Reference(s):
US 2 744 120 (Olin Mathieson; 1956; appl. 1953).

Formulation(s):   tabl. 50 mg

Trade Name(s):
D: Fludestrin (Bristol-Myers   I: Teslac (Squibb); wfm   USA: Teslac (Bristol-Myers
      Squibb)   Squibb)

Testosterone

ATC: G03BA03
Use: androgen

RN: 58-22-0   MF: $C_{19}H_{28}O_2$ MW: 288.43   EINECS: 200-370-5
LD_{50}: >5 g/kg (M, p.o.)
CN: (17β)-17-hydroxyandrost-4-en-3-one

undecanoate
RN: 5949-44-0   MF: $C_{30}H_{48}O_3$ MW: 456.71

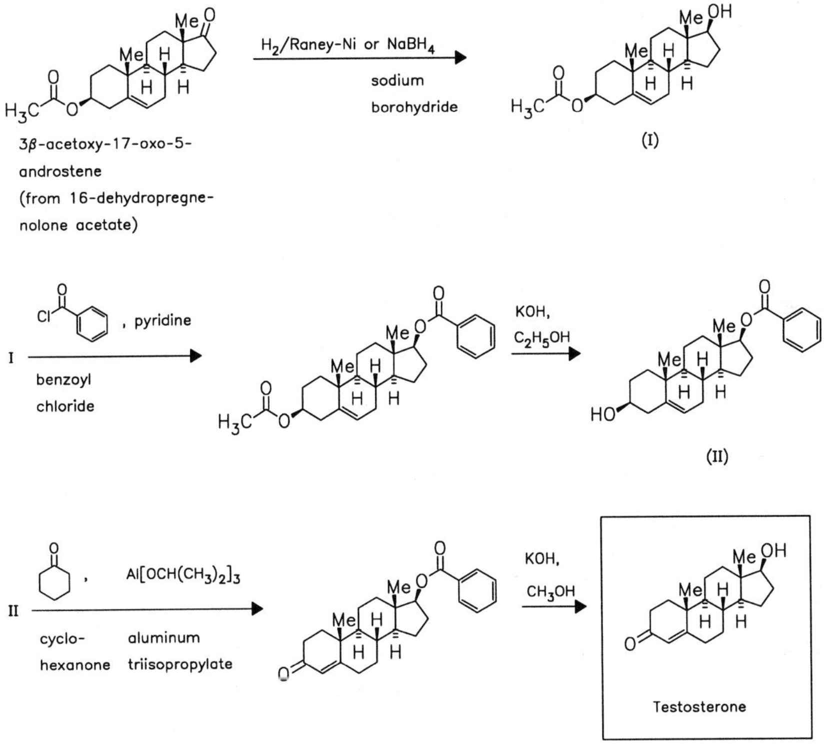

3β-acetoxy-17-oxo-5-
androstene
(from 16-dehydropregne-
nolone acetate)

(I)

(II)

Testosterone

Reference(s):
US 2 308 833 (Ciba; 1943; CH-prior. 1935).
US 2 308 834 (Ciba; 1943; CH-prior. 1935).
US 2 379 832 (Schering Corp.; D-prior. 1936).
US 2 387 469 (Ciba; 1945; CH-prior. 1935).

starting material:
The Merck Index, 12th Ed., 1569 (1996).

alternative syntheses:
US 2 236 574 (Schering Corp.; 1941, D-prior. 1937).
US 2 341 110 (Schering Corp.; 1944, CS-prior. 1939).

Formulation(s):   cps. 40 mg (as undecanoate); plaster 2.5 mg/37 cm², 4 mg/40 cm², 5 mg/44 cm², 6 mg/60 cm²

Trade Name(s):

D: Andriol (Organon)
F: Pantestone (Organon SA)
     Trotoseptine (Boehringer
     Ing.)-comb.
GB: Menopax (Nicholas)-
     comb.; wfm
     Testoral (Organon); wfm

I: Mydrotest (Ayerst); wfm
     Testosterone Tarrico
     (Mitim); wfm
J: Androgen Depot (Santen-
     Yamanouchi)
     Enarmon (Teikoku Zoki)
     Tes-Hol "Z" (Nippon Zoki)

Testoviron Depot (Nihon
Schering)-comb.
USA: Androderm (SmithKline
      Beecham)
      Testoderm (Alza)

Testosterone cypionate
(Testosterone cyclopentylpropionate)

ATC: G03EA02
Use: depot androgen

RN: 58-20-8   MF: $C_{27}H_{40}O_3$ MW: 412.61   EINECS: 200-368-4
LD_{50}: >1 g/kg (M, i.p.)
CN: (17β)-17-(3-cyclopentyl-1-oxopropoxy)androst-4-en-3-one

testosterone   3-cyclopentyl-   Testosterone cypionate
(q. v.)   propionyl chloride

Reference(s):
US 2 566 358 (Upjohn; 1951; prior. 1949).
DE 896 805 (Upjohn; appl. 1951).
Gould, D. et al.: J. Am. Chem. Soc. (JACSAT) **79**, 4472 (1957).

alternative syntheses:
US 2 625 556 (Upjohn; 1953; prior. 1949).
ES 241 206 (Alter; appl. 1958).
US 2 742 485 (Francesco Vismara; 1956; prior. 1954).

Formulation(s):   vial 200 mg/ml (10 ml)

Trade Name(s):

D: Femovirin Amp. (Albert-
     Roussel)-comb.; wfm
F: Ch. P. T. Théramex
     (Théramex); wfm
     Testostérone retard
     Théramex (Théramex; as
     cyclohexylpropionate);
     wfm

Trioestrine-Retard
Théramex (Théramex)-
comb.; wfm
Trioestrine-Retard
Théramex (Théramex; as
cyclohexylpropionate)-
comb.; wfm
I: Ciclosterone (Farmigea)

Clym depositum (Poli)-
comb.
Ginandrolo Depositum
(Lusofarmaco)-comb.
Pertestis-Dep. (Orma)
Testorit-Dep. (Gallo)
Testosterone Depositum
(Lusofarmaco)

J: Depo Testosteron   USA: Virilon (Star)
      (Upjohn); wfm

Testosterone enanthate

ATC: G03EB
Use: androgen

RN: 315-37-7   MF: $C_{26}H_{40}O_3$ MW: 400.60   EINECS: 206-253-5
LD_{50}:   4 mg/kg (M, i.p.);
       2 g/kg (R, i.p.)
CN: (17β)-17-[(1-oxoheptyl)oxy]androst-4-en-3-one

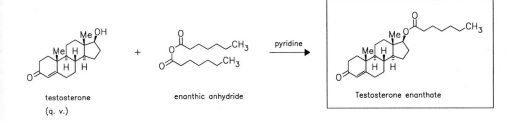

testosterone   enanthic anhydride   Testosterone enanthate
(q. v.)

Reference(s):
US 2 840 508 (Schering AG; 1958; D-prior. 1951).

Formulation(s):   amp. 250 mg/ml; vial 200 mg/ml, 1 g/5 ml

Trade Name(s):
D: Testosteron-Depot   F: Androtardyl (Schering)   Primodian Depot (Nihon
      Jenapharm (Jenapharm)   GB: Primoteston Depot   Schering)-comb.
      Testosteron Depot-   (Schering Chemicals); wfm   Testoviron Depot (Nihon
      Rotexmedica   I: Testo Enant (Geymonat)   Schering)-comb.
      (Rotexmedica)   J: Enarmon Depot (Teikoku USA: Delatestryl (Bio-
      Testoviron Depot   Zoki)   Technology)
      (Schering)-comb.

Testosterone propionate

ATC: G03BA03
Use: androgen

RN: 57-85-2   MF: $C_{22}H_{32}O_3$ MW: 344.50   EINECS: 200-351-1
LD_{50}:   1350 mg/kg (M, p.o.);
       1 g/kg (R, p.o.)
CN: (17β)-17-(1-oxopropoxy)androst-4-en-3-one

ⓐ

testosterone   propionic anhydride   Testosterone propionate
(q. v.)

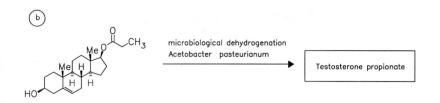

androstenediol 17-propionate

Reference(s):
a   CH 206 119 (Ciba; appl. 1936) addition to CH 203 257.
    DRP 661 384 (Ciba; appl. 1936; CH-prior. 1935).
b   US 2 236 574 (Schering Corp; 1941; D-prior. 1937).

starting material:
The Merck Index, 12th Ed., 107 (1996).

alternative syntheses:
US 2 311 067 (Ciba; 1943; CH-prior. 1939).
US 2 374 369 (Ciba; 1945; CH-prior. 1939).
US 2 374 370 (Ciba; 1945; CH-prior. 1939).

Formulation(s):   amp. 10 mg, 25 mg, 50 mg, 100 mg; amp. 50 mg/ml, 100 mg/ml (in comb.);
                    ointment 80 mg/100 mg (in comb.)

Trade Name(s):
D: Tachynerg (Eberth)-comb.
      Testosteron Propionat
      "Eifelfango" (Eifelfango)
      Testoviron (Schering)-
      comb.
F: Fadiamone (CS)-comb.
GB: Sustanon (Organon)-comb.
      Virormone (Ferring)
I: Testovis (SIT)
J: Enarmon Susp. (Teikoku
      Zoki)
      Forton (Shionogi)

      Primodian Inj. (Nihon
      Schering)
      Sonybod M Inj. (Sonybod-
      Torii)
      Testinon (Mochida)
USA: Androlan (Lannett); wfm
      Androlin (Lincoln); wfm
      Andrusol-P (Smith, Miller
      & Patch); wfm
      Gynetone (Schering)-
      comb.; wfm
      Neo-Hombreol (Organon);
      wfm

      Neutron (Myers-Carter)-
      comb.; wfm
      Oreton Propionate
      (Schering); wfm
      Synandrol (Pfizer); wfm
      Synerone (Dow); wfm
      Testex (Pasadena Res.);
      wfm
      Testodet (Merck Sharp &
      Dohme); wfm
      Testonate (Kay); wfm

Tetracaine
(Amethocaine)

ATC: C05AD02; D04AB06; N01BA03;
       S01HA03
Use: local anesthetic

RN: 94-24-6   MF: $C_{15}H_{24}N_2O_2$ MW: 264.37   EINECS: 202-316-6
LD$_{50}$: 6 mg/kg (M, i.v.); 300 mg/kg (M, p.o.);
      6 mg/kg (R, i.v.)
CN: 4-(butylamino)benzoic acid 2-(dimethylamino)ethyl ester

monohydrochloride
RN: 136-47-0   MF: $C_{15}H_{24}N_2O_2 \cdot HCl$ MW: 300.83   EINECS: 205-248-5
LD$_{50}$: 6600 µg/kg (M, i.v.); 160 mg/kg (M, p.o.);
      4500 µg/kg (R, i.v.)

(a)

butyl bromide   4-amino-   4-butylamino-
                 benzoic acid   benzoic acid

2-dimethyl-
amino-
ethanol (I)

Tetracaine

(b)

ethyl 4-amino-   2-dimethylamino-
benzoate   ethyl 4-amino-
                        benzoate

Tetracaine

1. butyraldehyde

Reference(s):
US 1 889 645 (Winthrop; 1932; CH-prior. 1930).

Formulation(s):   ear drops 5 mg/g; in combination preparations: eye drops 6 mg/g; sol. 1 g/100 g;
                     spray 5 mg/ml, 2 % (as hydrochloride)

Trade Name(s):
D: Acoin (Combustinwerk)-   Cantalène (RPR Cooper)   I: only combination
     comb.   Eludril (Inava)   preparations:
     Gingicain M Spray   Hexomédine (Théraplix)   Corizzina (SIT)
     (Hoechst)-comb.   Lysofon (L. Laton)   Donalg (Dinacren)
     Herviros (Hermal)-comb.   Oromédine (Sanofi   J: Butylcain (Tanabe)
     Ophtocain (Winzer)-comb.   Winthrop)   Recto-reparil (Naturwaren
     Oto-Flexiole (Mann)   Otylol (Bridoux)   Madaus)
F: only combination   Solutricine Tétracaïne   Ruscoroid (Inverni della
     preparations: (Théraplix SA)   Beffa)
     Amygdospray (Merck-   Tyrcine (Oberlin)   Tetocaine (Kyorin)
     Clévenot)   GB: Eludril (Chefaro)-comb.   USA: Cetacaine (Cetylite)
     Broncorinol Maux de gorge   Minims amethocaine
     (Roche Nicholas SA)   (Chauvin)

Tetracycline

ATC: A01AB13; D06AA04; J01AA07;
       S01AA09; S02AA08; S03AA02
Use: antibiotic, antibacterial, antiamebic,
       antitrichettisal

RN: 60-54-8   MF: $C_{22}H_{24}N_2O_8$ MW: 444.44   EINECS: 200-481-9
LD$_{50}$:   157 mg/kg (M, i.v.); 678 mg/kg (M, p.o.);
      129 mg/kg (R, i.v.); 807 mg/kg (R, p.o.)
CN: [4S-(4α,4aα,5aα,6β,12aα)]-4-(dimethylamino)-1,4,4a,5,5a,6,11,12a-octahydro-3,6,10,12,12a-
      pentahydroxy-6-methyl-1,11-dioxo-2-naphthacene carboxamide

monohydrochloride
RN: 64-75-5   MF: $C_{22}H_{24}N_2O_8 \cdot HCl$ MW: 480.90   EINECS: 200-593-8
LD$_{50}$:   157 mg/kg (M, i.v.); 2759 mg/kg (M, p.o.);
       128 mg/kg (R, i.v.); 6443 mg/kg (R, p.o.)
phosphate
RN: 1336-20-5   MF: unspecified   MW: unspecified   EINECS: 215-646-0

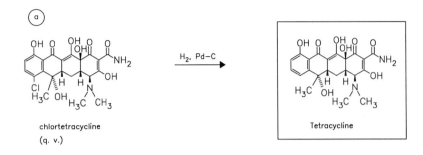

chlortetracycline
(q. v.)

Tetracycline

ⓑ   from fermentation solutions of Streptomyces viridifaciens or aureofaciens

Reference(s):
a   US 2 699 054 (L. H. Conover; 1955; prior. 1953).
       US 3 005 023 (American Cyanamid; 17.10.1961; appl. 5.4.1957).
       Boothe, J.H. et al.: J. Am. Chem. Soc. (JACSAT) **75**, 4621 (1953).
       Conover, L.H. et al.: J. Am. Chem. Soc. (JACSAT) **75**, 4622 (1963).
b   US 2 734 018 (American Cyanamid; 1956; prior. 1953).
       US 2 712 517 (Bristol; 1955; appl. 1954).
       US 2 886 595 (Bristol; 1959; appl. 1958).
       US 3 019 173 (American Cyanamid; 30.1.1962; appl. 4.6.1956).

purification:
US 3 301 899 (Bristol-Myers; 31.1.1967; appl. 27.11.1963).

synthesis of pure tetracycline hydrochloride:
DE 2 504 347 (DSO, Pharmachim, Sofia; appl. 3.2.1975).

complex with metaphosphoric acid:
US 3 053 892 (American Cyanamid; 11.9.1962; appl. 27.4.1960).

Formulation(s):   cps. 250 mg, 500 mg; cream 30 mg/g; f. c. tabl. 500 mg; ointment 30 mg/g; vial 500 mg

Trade Name(s):

D: Achromycin (Lederle)	Tetralution (Merckle)	Deteclo (Wyeth)-comb.
Imex (Merz & Co.)	F: Amphocycline (Squibb)-	Topicycline (Monmouth)
Mysteclin (Bristol-Myers	comb.	I: Ambramicina (Scharper)
Squibb)-comb. with	Colicort (Merck Sharp &	Calociclina (ISI)
amphotericine	Dohme-Chibret)-comb.	Pensulvit (SIFI)-comb.
Polcorton (mephano)-	Florocycline (SmithKline	Spaciclina (SPA)
comb. with triamcinolone	Beecham)-comb.	combination preparations
acetonide	Tétracycline Diamant	J: Achromycin (Lederle)
Supramycin N	(Diamant)	Cosa-Tetracyn (Taito
(Grünenthal)	numerous combination	Pfizer)
Tefilin (Hermal)	preparations	Cytome (Tokyo Tanabe)
Tetracyclin (Heyl;	GB: Achromycin (Wyeth; as	Junmycin V (Tanabe)
ratiopharm; Wolff)	hydrochloride)	Neocycline (Meiji)

USA: Achromycin (Lederle)   Helidac (Procter &
                                     Gamble)-comb.

Tetrazepam
(Tetrahydrodiazepam)

ATC: M03BX07
Use: tranquilizer, skeletal muscle relaxant

RN: 10379-14-3   MF: $C_{16}H_{17}ClN_2O$ MW: 288.78   EINECS: 233-837-7
LD_{50}:   2 g/kg (M, p.o.)
CN: 7-chloro-5-(1-cyclohexen-1-yl)-1,3-dihydro-1-methyl-2H-1,4-benzodiazepin-2-one

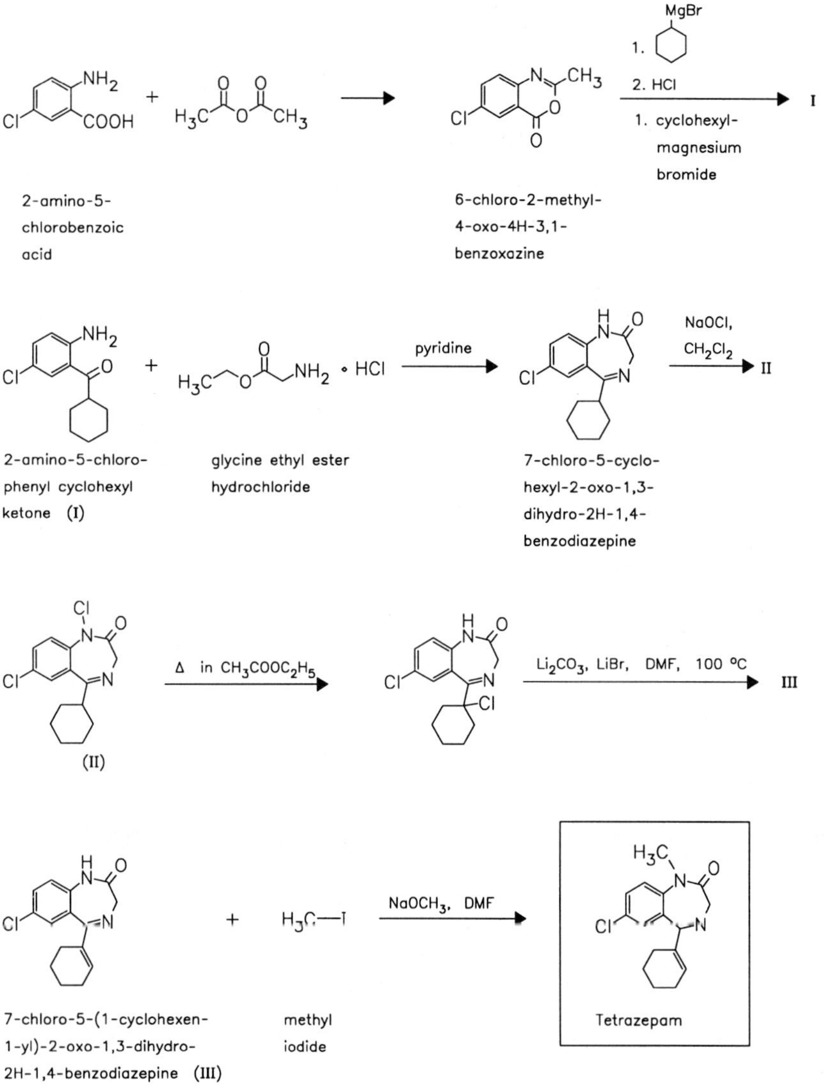

2-amino-5-
chlorobenzoic
acid

6-chloro-2-methyl-
4-oxo-4H-3,1-
benzoxazine

2-amino-5-chloro-
phenyl cyclohexyl
ketone (I)

glycine ethyl ester
hydrochloride

7-chloro-5-cyclo-
hexyl-2-oxo-1,3-
dihydro-2H-1,4-
benzodiazepine

(II)

7-chloro-5-(1-cyclohexen-
1-yl)-2-oxo-1,3-dihydro-
2H-1,4-benzodiazepine (III)

methyl
iodide

Tetrazepam

Reference(s):
DE 1 670 620 (Clin-Byla; prior. 5.1.1966).
US 3 426 014 (Clin-Byla; 4.2.1969; F-prior. 9.1.1965, 9.4.1965).
US 3 551 412 (Clin-Byla; 29.12.1970; F-prior. 8.8.1967).

intermediate (7-chloro-5-cyclohexyl-2-oxo-1,3-dihydro-2*H*-1,4-benzodiazepine):
US 3 268 586 (Roche; 23.8.1966; prior. 23.8.1960, 16.8.1961).

Formulation(s):   f. c. tabl. 25 mg, 50 mg; tabl. 50 mg

Trade Name(s):

D:	Mobiforton (Sanofi Winthrop)	Muskelat (Azupharma)		Tetramdura (durachemie)
		Myospasmal (TAD)		tetrazep (ct-Arzneimittel)
	Musapam (Krewel Meuselbach)	Rilex (Lindopharm)	F:	Myolastan (Sanofi
		Tepam-BASF (BASF)		Winthrop; 1969)
	Musaril (Sanofi Winthrop; 1981)	Tethexal (Hexal)		Panos (Lederle)
		Tetra-saar (Chephasaar)		

Tetroxoprim

ATC: J01
Use: chemotherapeutic, antibacterial

RN: 53808-87-0   MF: $C_{16}H_{22}N_4O_4$ MW: 334.38   EINECS: 258-789-4
LD$_{50}$:   192 mg/kg (M, i.v.); 1060 mg/kg (M, p.o.);
300 mg/kg (R, i.v.); 1172 mg/kg (R, p.o.)
CN: 5-[[3,5-dimethoxy-4-(2-methoxyethoxy)phenyl]methyl]-2,4-pyrimidinediamine

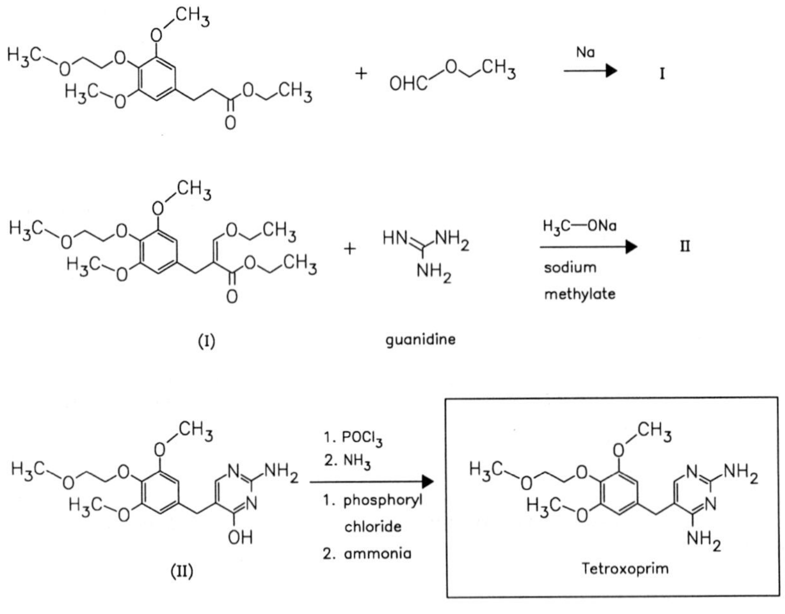

(I)   guanidine

(II)   Tetroxoprim

Reference(s):
DOS 2 313 361 (Heumann; appl. 17.3.1973).
(also further methods)
Liebenow, W.; Prikryl, J.: J. Antimicrob. Chemother. (JACHDX) **5**, (Suppl. B), 15 (1979).

Formulation(s):   sol. 25 mg/5 ml, 100 mg/5 ml; tabl. 100 mg (in comb. with sulfadiazine)

Trade Name(s):

D:	Sterinor (Heumann)-comb.	I:	Oxosint (Medivis)-comb.	Sterinor (ABC)-comb.

Tetryzoline
(Tetrahydrozoline)

ATC: R01AA06; R01AB03; S01GA02
Use: vasoconstrictor

RN: 84-22-0   MF: $C_{13}H_{16}N_2$ MW: 200.29   EINECS: 201-522-3
LD_{50}:   48.1 mg/kg (M, i.v.); 335 mg/kg (M, p.o.)
CN: 4,5-dihydro-2-(1,2,3,4-tetrahydro-1-naphthalenyl)-1H-imidazole

monohydrochloride
RN: 522-48-5   MF: $C_{13}H_{16}N_2 \cdot HCl$ MW: 236.75   EINECS: 208-329-3
LD_{50}:   39 mg/kg (M, i.v.); 345 mg/kg (M, p.o.);
       35 mg/kg (R, i.v.); 785 mg/kg (R, p.o.)

1-cyano-
tetralin
    ethylene-
diamine
    Tetryzoline

Reference(s):
US 2 731 471 (Sahyun Labs.; 1956; prior. 1954).

Formulation(s):   eye drops 0.5 mg/ml; nasal drops/nasal spray 5 mg/10 ml, 10 mg/10 ml, 100 mg/100 ml

Trade Name(s):
D: Allergopos (Ursapharm)
    Berberil (Mann)
    Caltheon (Cephasaar)
    Diabenyl (Chauvin
    ankerpharm)
    Efemolin (CIBA Vision)-
    comb. with flurometholone
    Exrhinin (Pharma
    Wernigerode)
    Rhinopront Spray/
    Nasentropfen (Mack,
    Illert.)
    Spersadeloxin (CIBA
    Vision)-comb.
    Spersallerg (CIBA Vision)-
    comb. with antazoline
    hydrochloride

    Tetrilin (MIP Pharma)
    Tyzine (Pfizer)
    Vasapos (Ursapharm)
    Vidiseptal (Mann)
    Yxin (Pfizer)
F: Constrilia (Alcon SA)
I: Demetil (Farmila)-comb.
    Flumetol (Farmila)-comb.
    Ischemol A (Farmila)-
    comb.
    Stilla (Angelini)
    Tetramil (Farmigea)-comb.
    Vasorinil (Farmila)
    Vasosterone (Angelini)-
    comb.
    Visine (Pfizer)

    Visublefarite (Pharmec)-
    comb.
    Visumetazone (Pharmec)-
    comb.
    Visumicina (Pharmec)-
    comb.
    Visustrin (Merck Sharp &
    Dohme)-comb.
J: Narbel (Chugai)
USA: Collirium Wyeth (Wyeth)-
    comb.; wfm
    Murine (Ross)-comb.; wfm
    Tyzine (Key Pharm.); wfm
    Tyzine (Pfizer); wfm

Thalidomide
(K-17; NSC-66847)

Use: anti-inflammatory,
immunomodulator, blocker of TNF-
production, sedative, treatment of
erythema nodosum leprosum

RN: 50-35-1   MF: $C_{13}H_{10}N_2O_4$ MW: 258.23   EINECS: 200-031-1
LD_{50}:   >5000 mg/kg (M, p. o.)
CN: 2-(2,6-Dioxo-3-piperidinyl)-1H-isoindole-1,3(2H)-dione

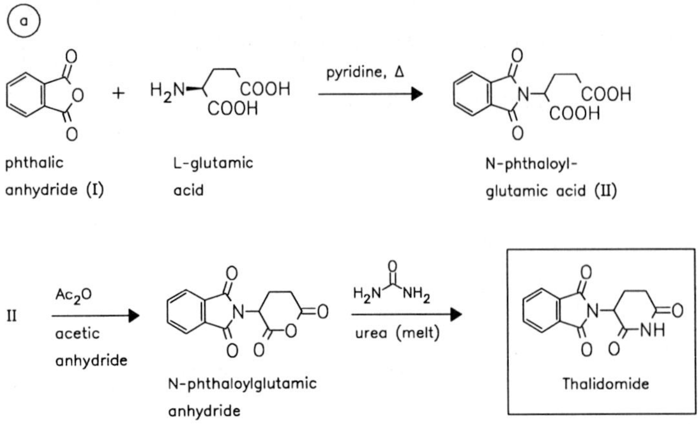

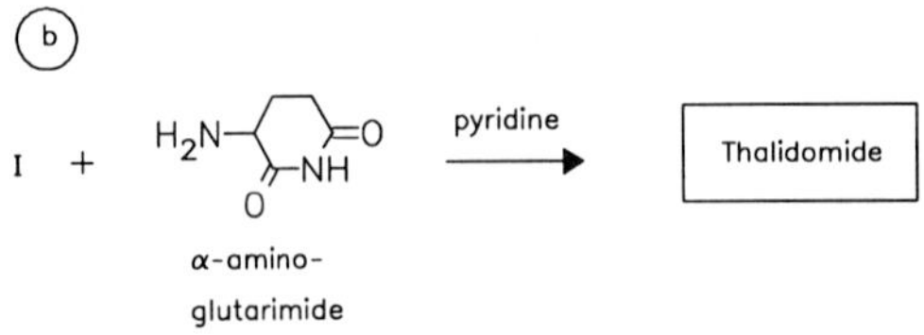

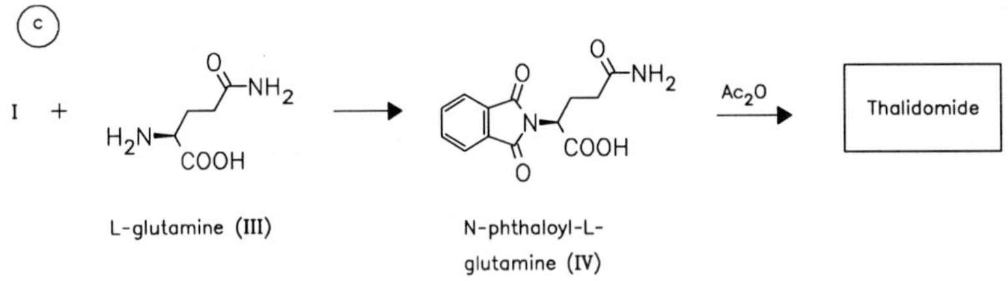

a

phthalic anhydride (I) + L-glutamic acid →[pyridine, Δ] N-phthaloyl-glutamic acid (II)

II →[Ac₂O / acetic anhydride] N-phthaloylglutamic anhydride →[H₂N-NH₂ / urea (melt)] Thalidomide

b

I + α-amino-glutarimide →[pyridine] Thalidomide

c

I + L-glutamine (III) → N-phthaloyl-L-glutamine (IV) →[Ac₂O] Thalidomide

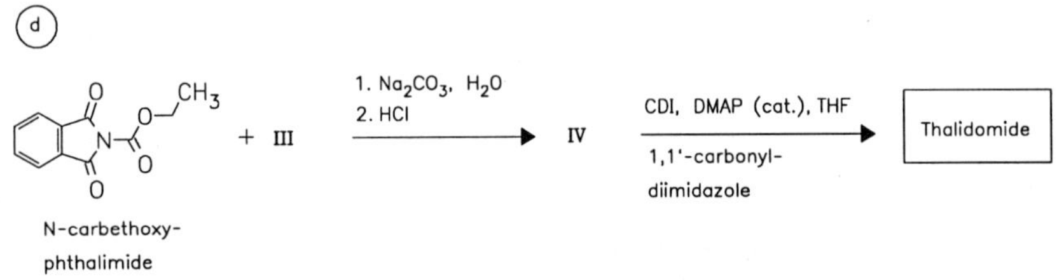

d

N-carbethoxy-phthalimide + III →[1. Na₂CO₃, H₂O 2. HCl] IV →[CDI, DMAP (cat.), THF / 1,1'-carbonyl-diimidazole] Thalidomide

Reference(s):
a GB 768 821 (Chemie Grünenthal; 20.2.1957).
     Kunz, W. et al.: Arzneim.-Forsch. (ARZNAD) **6**, 426-430 (1956).
b JP 5 071 (Dainippon; 13.5.1960).
c King, F.E. et al.: J. Chem. Soc. (JCSOA9) **1957**, 873-880
d Muller, G.W. et al.: Org. Process Res. Dev. (OPRDFK) **3**, 139-140 (1999)

intravenous administration form for treatment of immunologic diseases:
EP 908 176 (Grünenthal; appl. 18.9.1998; D-prior. 6.10.1997)

pharmaceutical comp. for the treatment of melanomas:
US 5 731 325 (Andrulis Pharm.; 24.3.1998; USA-prior. 6.6.1995).

use for treating neurocognitive disorders:
WO 9 517 154 (Andrulis Pharm.; appl. 22.12.1994; USA-prior. 23.12.1993).

treatment of rheumatoid arthritis:
WO 9 504 533 (Andrulis Pharm.; appl. 3.8.1994; USA-prior. 4.8.1993).

controlling abnormal concentration of TNF-α:
WO 9 214 455 (Rockefeller Univ.; appl. 14.2.1992; USA-prior. 14.2.1991).

Formulation(s):   cps. 50 mg

Trade Name(s):
USA: Thalomid (Celgene; 1998)

Thebacon

(Acethydrocodone)

ATC: R05DA10
Use: narcotic, analgesic

RN: 466-90-0   MF: $C_{20}H_{23}NO_4$ MW: 341.41   EINECS: 207-377-2
LD_{50}: 81 mg/kg (M, s.c.)
CN: (5α)-6,7-didehydro-4,5-epoxy-3-methoxy-17-methylmorphinan-6-ol acetate (ester)

hydrochloride
RN: 20236-82-2   MF: $C_{20}H_{23}NO_4 \cdot HCl$ MW: 377.87   EINECS: 243-623-5

hydrocodone
(q. v.)

acetic anhydride

Thebacon

Reference(s):
a   Ehrhart-Ruschig **I**, 120.
b   US 1 731 152 (C. Schopf; 1929).

Formulation(s):   tabl 5 mg (as hydrochloride)

Trade Name(s):
D: Acedicon (Boehringer   I: Acedicon (Boehringer
       Ing.); wfm   Ing.); wfm

Thenalidine

(Thenaldine)

ATC: D04AA03; R06AX03
Use: antihistaminic

RN: 86-12-4   MF: $C_{17}H_{22}N_2S$ MW: 286.44   EINECS: 201-651-5
LD_{50}: 42 mg/kg (M, i.v.); 165 mg/kg (M, p.o.);
       42 mg/kg (R, i.v.); 1060 mg/kg (R, p.o.)
CN: 1-methyl-*N*-phenyl-*N*-(2-thienylmethyl)-4-piperidinamine

tartrate (1:1)
RN: 2784-55-6   MF: $C_{17}H_{22}N_2S \cdot C_4H_6O_6$ MW: 436.53   EINECS: 220-493-8

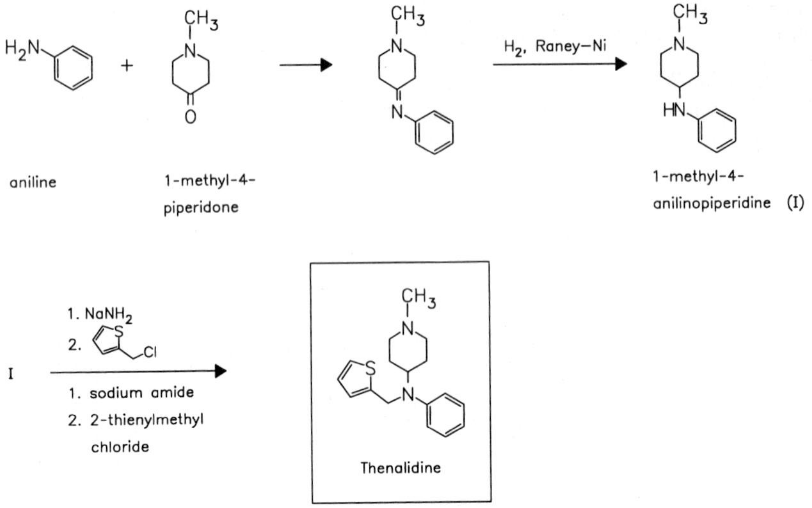
H2N
CH3
N
O
CH3
N
N
H2, Raney–Ni
CH3
N
HN
aniline
1-methyl-4-
piperidone
1-methyl-4-
anilinopiperidine (I)
1. NaNH2
2.
S
Cl
I
1. sodium amide
2. 2-thienylmethyl
chloride
CH3
N
S
N
Thenalidine

Reference(s):
US 2 717 251 (Sandoz; 1955; CH-prior. 1951).

Formulation(s): drg. 25 mg (as tartrate)

Trade Name(s):
D: Sandosten-Calcium (Sandoz); wfm
F: Sandosténe (Sandoz); wfm

Thenium closilate

(Theniumclosylat)

ATC: P02
Use: anthelmintic

RN: 4304-40-9 MF: $C_{15}H_{20}NOS \cdot C_6H_4ClO_3S$ MW: 454.01 EINECS: 224-318-6
CN: *N,N*-dimethyl-*N*-(2-phenoxyethyl)-2-thiophenemethanaminium salt with 4-chlorobenzenesulfonic acid (1:1)

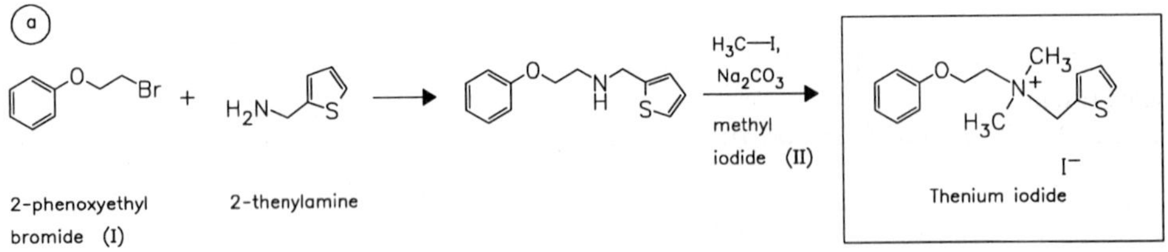
a
O
Br
H2N
S
O
N
H
S
H3C—I,
Na2CO3
methyl
iodide (II)
O
CH3
N+
H3C
S
I−
Thenium iodide
2-phenoxyethyl
bromide (I)
2-thenylamine

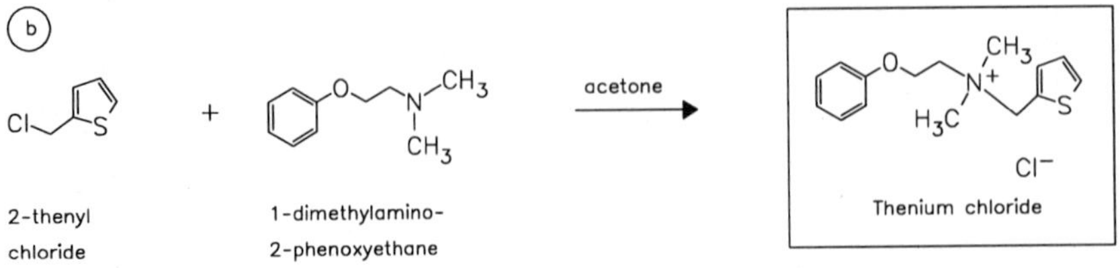
b
Cl
S
O
N
CH3
CH3
acetone
O
CH3
N+
H3C
S
Cl−
Thenium chloride
2-thenyl
chloride
1-dimethylamino-
2-phenoxyethane

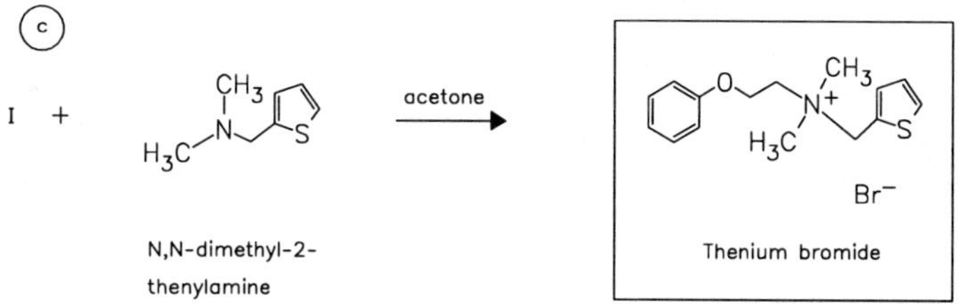

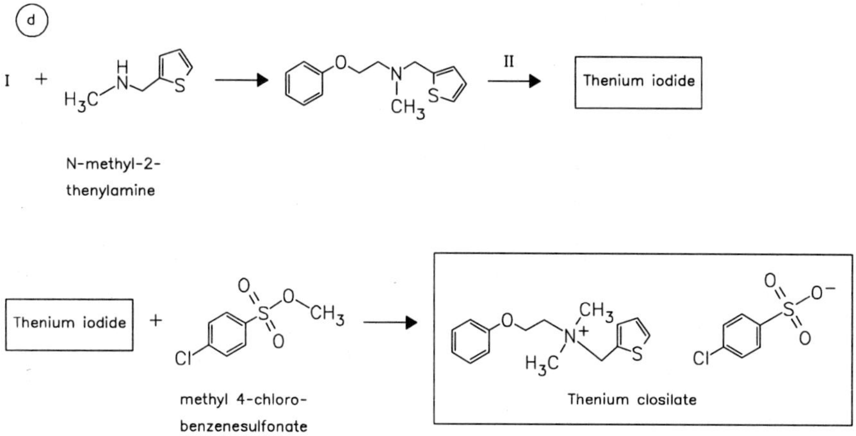

c

I +

N,N-dimethyl-2-
thenylamine

acetone →

Thenium bromide

d

I +

N-methyl-2-
thenylamine

→ II → Thenium iodide

Thenium iodide +

methyl 4-chloro-
benzenesulfonate

→

Thenium closilate

Reference(s):
GB 864 885 (Wellcome Found.; valid from 1958; prior. 1957).

use:
GB 994 742 (Wellcome Found.; valid from 1961; prior. 1960).

Trade Name(s):
USA: Bancaris (Burroughs
         Wellcome); wfm

Thenyldiamine

ATC: R06
Use: antihistaminic

RN: 91-79-2   MF: $C_{14}H_{19}N_3S$ MW: 261.39   EINECS: 202-098-2
LD$_{50}$: 77 mg/kg (M, i.p.)
CN: N,N-dimethyl-N'-2-pyridinyl-N'-(3-thienylmethyl)-1,2-ethanediamine

monohydrochloride
RN·   958-93-0   MF: $C_{14}H_{19}N_3S \cdot$ HCl   MW: 297.85   EINECS: 213-490-8
LD$_{50}$: 12.2 mg/kg (M, i.v.); 277 mg/kg (M, p.o.);
            15 mg/kg (R, i.v.); 525 mg/kg (R, p.o.);
            10 mg/kg (dog, i.v.); 60 mg/kg (dog, p.o.)

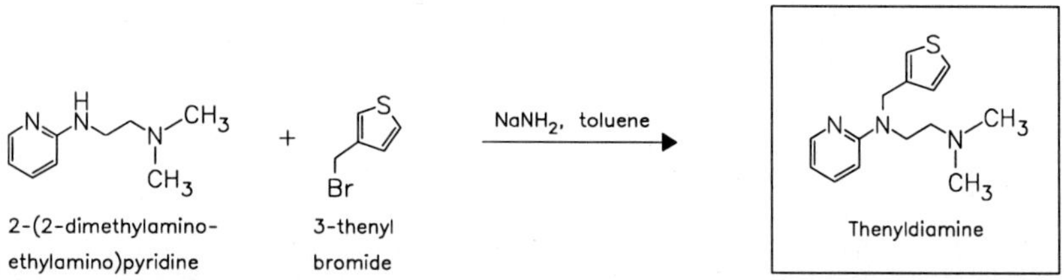

2-(2-dimethylamino-
ethylamino)pyridine

+

3-thenyl
bromide

NaNH$_2$, toluene →

Thenyldiamine

Reference(s):
Campaigne, E.; Le Suer, W.M.: J. Am. Chem. Soc. (JACSAT) **71**, 333 (1949).

starting material:
US 2 581 868 (Monsanto; 1952; prior. 1946).

Formulation(s):   drops 1 mg/ml (as hydrochloride)

Trade Name(s):

D:	Nebdosator (Winthrop); wfm	GB:	Bronchilator (Izal)-comb.; wfm	I:	N.T.R. (Teofarma)-comb.
F:	Arhumyl (Sterling Winthrop)-comb.; wfm		Haphryn (Winthrop)-comb.; wfm	USA:	Thenfadil (Winthrop Stearns); wfm

Theodrenaline

ATC: C01CA23
Use: circulatory analeptic, diuretic, cardiotonic

RN: 13460-98-5   MF: $C_{17}H_{21}N_5O_5$ MW: 375.39
LD$_{50}$:   1140 mg/kg (M, i.p.)
CN: 7-[2-[[2-(3,4-dihydroxyphenyl)-2-hydroxyethyl]amino]ethyl]-3,7-dihydro-1,3-dimethyl-1H-purine-2,6-dione

monohydrochloride
RN: 2572-61-4   MF: $C_{17}H_{21}N_5O_5 \cdot HCl$ MW: 411.85   EINECS: 219-920-0

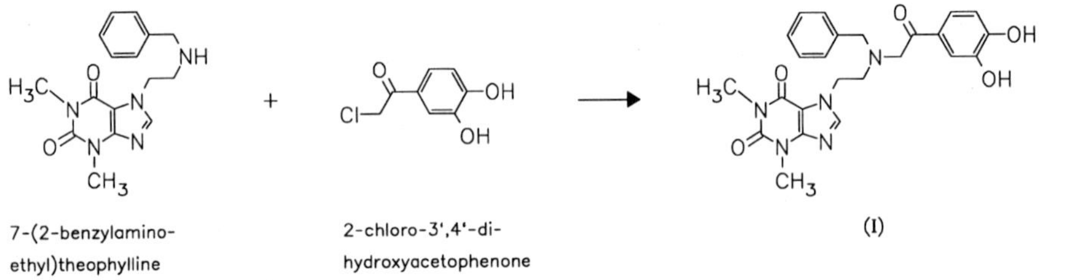

7-(2-benzylamino-ethyl)theophylline

2-chloro-3',4'-di-hydroxyacetophenone

(I)

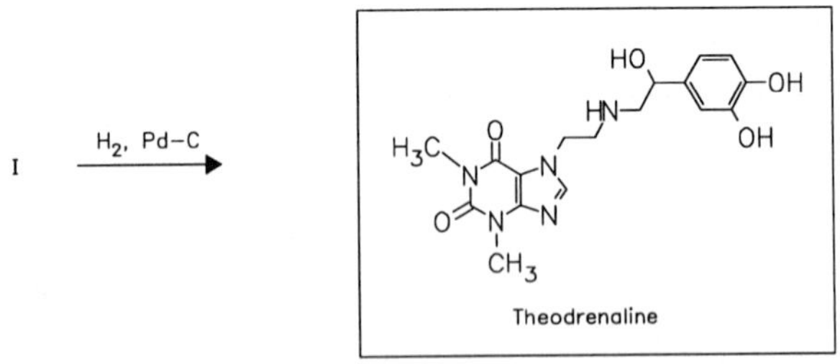

Theodrenaline

Reference(s):
DE 1 119 868 (Degussa; appl. 5.5.1959).
US 3 112 313 (Degussa; 26.11.1963; D-prior. 5.5.1959).

Formulation(s):   amp. 10 mg/2 ml, 50 mg/10 ml; f. c. tabl. 5 mg (as hydrochloride in comb. with cafedrine hydrochloride)

Theophylline

ATC: R03DA04
Use: cardiotonic, diuretic

RN: 58-55-9   MF: $C_7H_8N_4O_2$ MW: 180.17   EINECS: 200-385-7
LD_{50}:   136 mg/kg (M, i.v.); 235 mg/kg (M, p.o.);
      225 mg/kg (R, p.o.)
CN: 3,7-dihydro-1,3-dimethyl-1H-purine-2,6-dione

monohydrate
RN: 5967-84-0   MF: $C_7H_8N_4O_2 \cdot H_2O$ MW: 198.18

N,N'-dimethyl-   ethyl cyano-   6-amino-1,3-
urea   acetate   dimethyluracil (I)

5,6-diamino-1,3-
dimethyluracil   Theophylline

Reference(s):
DE 834 105 (Boehringer Ing.; appl. 1949).

Formulation(s):   amp. 104 mg/ml, 200 mg/10 ml, 208 mg/5 ml, 420 mg/60 ml, 500 mg/20 ml;
      drops 104 mg/ml; s. r. cps. 125 mg, 200 mg, 250 mg, 300 mg, 375 mg, 400 mg, 500 mg;
      s. r. tabl. 200 mg, 300 mg, 600 mg; suppos. 50 mg

GB: Franol (Sanofi Winthrop)-
      comb.
      Labophylline (Labs. for
      Applied Biology)
      Lasma (Pharmax)
      Nuelin (3M Health Care)
      Slo-Phyllin (Lipha)
      Theo-Dur (Astra)
      Uniphyllin Continus
      (Napp)

          numerous combination
          preparations
I: Aminomal (Malesci)
      Diffumal (Malesci)
      Euphyllina (Byk Gulden)
      Respicur (Byk Gulden)
      Tefamin (Recordati)
      Teobid (Vita)
      Teonova (Camillo Corvi)
      Theo-dur (Recordati)

J: Theolair (Synthelabo)
      Theophyllol (Sanko)
      generic and numerous
      combination preparations
USA: Aerolate (Fleming)
      Elixophyllin (Forest)
      Theolair (3M)

Theophylline ethylenediamine
(Aminophylline; Teofyllamin; Theophyllamin)

ATC: R03DA04
Use: cardiotonic, diuretic, bronchodilator

RN: 317-34-0 MF: $C_7H_8N_4O_2 \cdot 1/2C_2H_8N_2$ MW: 420.43 EINECS: 206-264-5
LD_{50}: 125 mg/kg (M, i.v.); 150 mg/kg (M, p.o.);
      104 mg/kg (R, i.v.); 243 mg/kg (R, p.o.)
CN: 3,7-dihydro-1,3-dimethyl-1H-purine-2,6-dione compd. with 1,2-ethanediamine (2:1)

dihydrate
RN: 5897-66-5 MF: $C_{14}H_{16}N_4O_2 \cdot C_6H_8N_2 \cdot 2H_2O$ MW: 416.48

theophylline   ethylenediamine   Theophylline ethylenediamine

Reference(s):
DRP 223 695 (Byk; appl. 1907).

stabilized solutions:
US 4 073 907 (Abbott; 14.2.1978; appl. 1.6.1976).

Formulation(s):   amp. 120 mg/ml, 240 mg/10 ml; s. r. tabl. 225 mg, 350 mg; tabl. 125 mg (as dihydrate)

Trade Name(s):
D: Afonilum (Knoll)
      Aminophyllin (OPW)
      Limptar (Cassella-med)-
      comb.
      Phyllotemp
      (Mundipharma)
      Theophyllin-
      Aethylendiamin ratiopharm
      (ratiopharm)
F: Aminophylline Lobica
      (Opodex); wfm
      Campho-pneumine
      aminophylline (Merrell)-
      comb.; wfm

      Cardiophylline (Lefranca)-
      comb.; wfm
      Inophyline (Millot); wfm
      Eusédyl aminophylline
      (Chanteau)-comb.; wfm
      Inophyline (Millot-Solac);
      wfm
      Planphylline (Plantier);
      wfm
      Sédo-caréna (Delagrange)-
      comb.; wfm
      combination preparations;
      wfm
GB: Cardophylin (Fisons); wfm

      Delaminoph (BM Labs.);
      wfm
      Phyllocontin (Napp); wfm
      Theodrox (Riker)-comb.;
      wfm
I: Aminomal (Malesci); wfm
      Amminophilline (Farber-
      Ref); wfm
      Asmarectal (Serpero)-
      comb.; wfm
      Euphyllina (Byk Gulden);
      wfm
      Tefamin (Recordati); wfm
      numerous combination
      preparations; wfm

Thevetin A

(Tevosid)

ATC: C01A
Use: cardiac glycoside

RN: 37933-66-7   MF: $C_{42}H_{64}O_{19}$ MW: 872.96   EINECS: 253-722-5
LD_{50}:   85 µg/kg (cat, i.v.)
CN: (3β,5β)-3-[(O-β-D-glucopyranosyl-(1→6)-O-D-glucopyranosyl(1→4)-6-deoxy-3-O-methyl-α-L-
       glucopyranosyl)oxy]-14-hydroxy-19-oxocard-20(22)-enolide

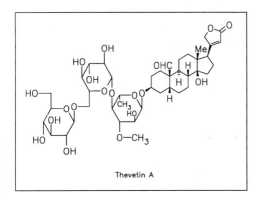

Thevetin A

From *Thevetia neriifolia* Juss., *Apocynaceae*, separation from thevetin B by extraction.

Reference(s):
Bloch, R. et al.: Helv. Chim. Acta (HCACAV) **43**, 652 (1960).
US 3 030 355 (M. Delalande, J. Baisse; 17.4.1962; prior. 16.5.1960).
US 3 043 829 (M. Delalande, J. Baisse; 10.7.1962; prior. 31.5.1960).

Trade Name(s):
I: Tevosid (Zanardi); wfm

Thiadrine

Use: antitussive

RN: 14007-67-1   MF: $C_{11}H_{14}N_2S$ MW: 206.31
CN: 3,4-dimethyl-5-phenyl-2-thiazolidinimine

L-ephedrine
SOCl₂
thionyl
chloride
NH₄⁺ SCN⁻
ammonium
rhodanide
Thiadrine

Reference(s):
US 2 558 068 (Knoll; 1951; prior. 1949).
GB 690 238 (Knoll; appl. 1950; USA-prior. 1949).

Formulation(s):   tabl.

Thiamazole

(Methimazole)

ATC: H03BB02
Use: thyreostatic, antihyperthyroid

RN: 60-56-0   MF: $C_4H_6N_2S$ MW: 114.17   EINECS: 200-482-4
LD_{50}:   860 mg/kg (M, p.o.);
        2250 mg/kg (R, p.o.)
CN: 1,3-dihydro-1-methyl-$2H$-imidazole-2-thione

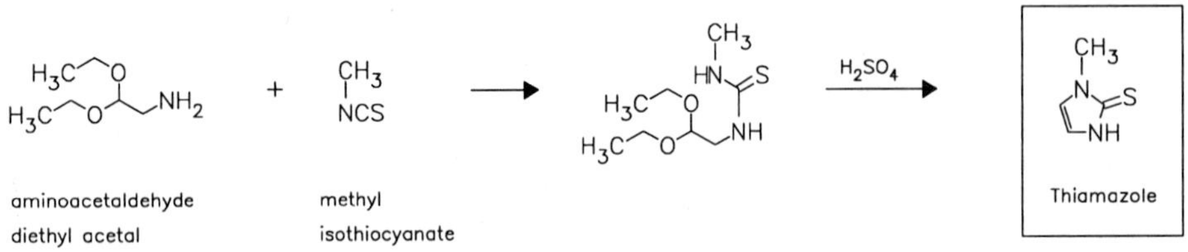

aminoacetaldehyde   methyl   Thiamazole
diethyl acetal   isothiocyanate

Reference(s):
Wohl, A. et al.: Ber. Dtsch. Chem. Ges. (BDCGAS) **22**, 1354 (1889).
Jones, R.G. et al.: J. Am. Chem. Soc. (JACSAT) **71**, 4000 (1949).

Formulation(s):   amp. 40 mg/ml; tabl. 5 mg, 10 mg, 20 mg

Thiamine

(Aneurine; Vitamin B_1)

ATC: A11DA01
Use: vitamin

RN: 59-43-8   MF: $C_{12}H_{17}ClN_4OS$ MW: 300.81   EINECS: 200-425-3
LD_{50}:   301 mg/kg (M, s.c.)
CN: 3-[(4-amino-2-methyl-5-pyrimidinyl)methyl]-5-(2-hydroxyethyl)-4-methylthiazolium chloride

monohydrochloride
RN: 67-03-8   MF: $C_{12}H_{17}ClN_4OS \cdot HCl$ MW: 337.28   EINECS: 200-641-8
LD_{50}:   74 mg/kg (M, i.v.); 8224 mg/kg (M, p.o.);
        118 mg/kg (R, i.v.); 3710 mg/kg (R, p.o.)
nitrate
RN: 532-43-4   MF: $C_{12}H_{16}N_4OS \cdot HNO_3$ MW: 327.37

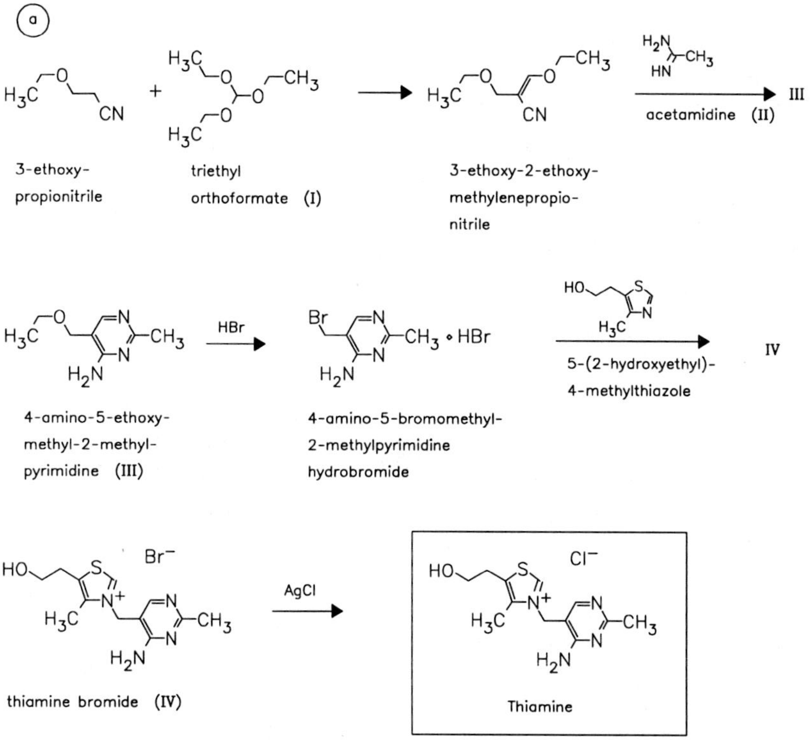

a)

3-ethoxy-
propionitrile

triethyl
orthoformate (I)

3-ethoxy-2-ethoxy-
methylenepropio-
nitrile

acetamidine (II)

III

4-amino-5-ethoxy-
methyl-2-methyl-
pyrimidine (III)

4-amino-5-bromomethyl-
2-methylpyrimidine
hydrobromide

5-(2-hydroxyethyl)-
4-methylthiazole

IV

thiamine bromide (IV)

Thiamine

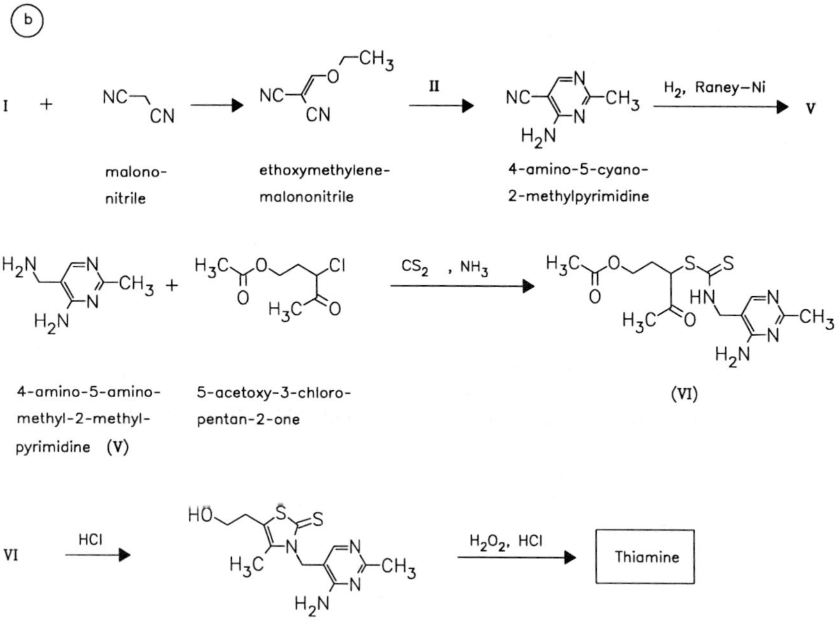

b)

I +

malono-
nitrile

ethoxymethylene-
malononitrile

4-amino-5-cyano-
2-methylpyrimidine

H_2, Raney–Ni

V

4-amino-5-amino-
methyl-2-methyl-
pyrimidine (V)

5-acetoxy-3-chloro-
pentan-2-one

CS_2, NH_3

(VI)

VI

HCl

H_2O_2, HCl

Thiamine

Reference(s):

a Williams, R.R.; Cline, J.K.: J. Am. Chem. Soc. (JACSAT) **58**, 1504 (1936).
   US 2 216 574 (Research Corp.; 1938).
   US 2 166 233 (Research Corp.; 1938).
   US 2 184 964 (Research Corp.; 1937).
b Grewe, R.: Hoppe-Seyler's Z. Physiol. Chem. (HSZPAZ) **242**, 89 (1936).
   DRP 671 787 (I. G. Farben; appl. 1936).
   US 2 592 930 (Takeda; 1952; J-prior. 1950).

synthesis of 5-(2-hydroxyethyl)-4-methylthiazole *and* 5-acetoxy-3-chloropentan-2-one:
Buchman, E.R.: J. Am. Chem. Soc. (JACSAT) **58**, 1803 (1936).
DRP 678 153 (Roche; appl. 1938; CH-prior. 1937).

full review of patent literature up to 1952 for thiamine synthesis:
Vogel, H.: Chemie und Technik der Vitamine, 3. Aufl., Vol. **2**, I. Part, p. 96 ff; F. Enke Verlag, Stuttgart 1955.

Formulation(s):   amp. 25 mg/2 ml, 25 mg/ml, 100 mg/ml, 100 mg/2 ml, 200 mg/2 ml; drg. 100 mg; f. c. tabl.
500 mg; tabl. 10 mg, 250 mg, 300 mg (as hydrochloride); tabl. 100 mg (as nitrate)

Trade Name(s):

D: Aneurin A.S. (A.S.)
   Betabion (Merck)
   Lophakomp (Lomapharm)
   Vitamin B$_1$ Hevert (Hevert)
   Vitamin B$_1$-Injektopas
   (Pascoe)
   Vitamin B$_1$ JENAPHARM
   (Jenapharm)
   Vitamin B$_1$ Kattwiga
   (Kattwiga)
   Vitamin B$_1$-ratiopharm
   (ratiopharm)

   numerous combination
   preparations
F: Bénerva (Roche)
   Bévitine (Specia)
   and circa 70 combination
   preparations
GB: Benerva (Roche)
   numerous combination
   preparations: multivitamins
I: Benexol B$_{12}$ (Roche)-comb.
   Dobetin (Angelini)-comb.
   Fibronevrina (Ceccarelli)-
   comb.

   Fosfoutipi Vit. (Terapeutico
   M.R.)-comb.
   Neurobionta (Bracco)-
   comb.
   Neuroftal (Alfa Intes)-
   comb.
   Triferon (Salus)-comb.
   Trinevrina (Guidotti)-
   comb.
USA: Mega-B (Arco; as
   mononitrate)-comb.

Thiamphenicol

ATC: J01BA02; J01BA52
Use: antibiotic

RN: 15318-45-3   MF: C$_{12}$H$_{15}$Cl$_2$NO$_5$S   MW: 356.23   EINECS: 239-355-3
LD$_{50}$:   368 mg/kg (M, i.v.); >7 g/kg (M, p.o.);
   339 mg/kg (R, i.v.); >7 g/kg (R, p.o.)
CN: [R-(R*,R*)]-2,2-dichloro-N-[2-hydroxy-1-(hydroxymethyl)-2-[4-(methylsulfonyl)phenyl]ethyl]acetamide

glycinate hydrochloride
RN: 2611-61-2   MF: C$_{14}$H$_{18}$Cl$_2$NO$_6$S · HCl   MW: 435.73

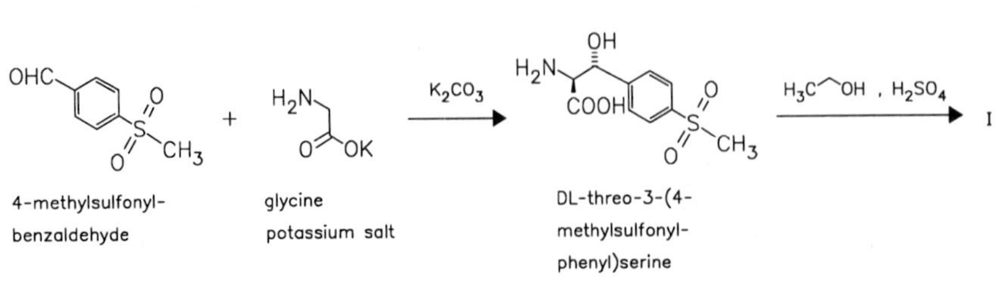

4-methylsulfonyl-   glycine   DL-threo-3-(4-
benzaldehyde   potassium salt   methylsulfonyl-
      phenyl)serine

Reference(s):
DE 1 938 513 (Sumitomo; appl. 29.7.1969) - only methods.

older methods:
US 2 721 207 (Parke Davis; 1955; prior. 1952).
US 2 726 266 (Du Pont; 1955; prior. 1951).
US 2 759 927 (Sterling Drug; 1956; prior. 1951, 1955).
US 2 759 970 (Sterling Drug; 1956; appl. 1956).
US 2 759 971 (Sterling Drug; 1956; appl. 1951).
US 2 816 915 (Du Pont; 1957; prior. 1951).
Cutler, R.A. et al.: J. Am. Chem. Soc. (JACSAT) **74**, 5475 (1952).
Suter, C.M. et al.: J. Am. Chem. Soc. (JACSAT) **75**, 4330 (1953).

Formulation(s):   amp. 500 mg, 750 mg; cps. 125 mg, 250 mg, 500 mg; suppos. 125 mg, 250 mg, 500 mg; vial 500 mg (as glycinate hydrochloride)

Trade Name(s):

D:	Urfamicina (Inpharzam); wfm	J:	Chlomic S (Kowa Shinyaku)	Roseramin (Takata)
F:	Fluimucil antibiotic 750 (Zambon)		Efnicol (Nichizo)	Synticol (Nisshin)
	Thiophénicol (Sanofi Winthrop)		Fricol (SS)	Thiamcol (Morishita)
I:	Flogotisol (Zambon)		Hyrazin (Kowa Yakuhin)	Thiancol (Kakenyaku)
	Fluimucil Antib. (Zambon)-comb.		Igralin (Kotobuki Seiyaku-Zeria)	Thiofact (Showa Yakuhin)
	Glitisol (Zambon)		Neomyson (Eisai)	Thionicol (Mohan)
			Racenicol (Kissei)	Thiophenicol (Hishiyama)
			Rigelon (Dojin)	Thiotal (Sumitomo)
			Rincrol (Tokyo Tanabe)	Tiozon (Mitsui)
				Unaseran-D (Isei)
				Urophenil (Iwaki)

Thiamylal

ATC: N01AF
Use: ultrashort narcotic, anesthetic (intravenous)

RN: 77-27-0   MF: C_{12}H_{18}N_2O_2S   MW: 254.35   EINECS: 201-018-3
CN: dihydro-5-(1-methylbutyl)-5-(2-propenyl)-2-thioxo-4,6(1H,5H)-pyrimidinedione

monosodium salt

RN: 337-47-3 MF: $C_{12}H_{17}N_2NaO_2S$ MW: 276.34 EINECS: 206-415-5
LD_{50}: 85 mg/kg (M, i.v.); 180 mg/kg (M, p.o.);
51 mg/kg (R, i.v.);
32 mg/kg (dog, i.v.); 134 mg/kg (dog, p.o.)

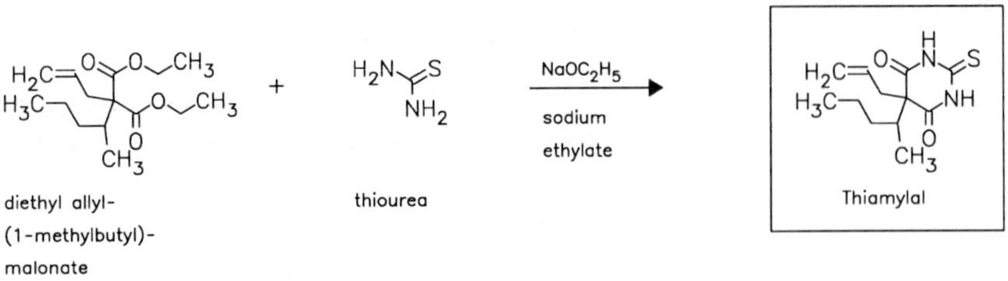
diethyl allyl-(1-methylbutyl)-malonate
thiourea
$NaOC_2H_5$
sodium ethylate
Thiamylal

Reference(s):
US 2 153 729 (Abbott; 1939; prior. 1934).
US 2 876 225 (Abbott; 1959; appl. 1956).

Formulation(s): vial 1 g, 5 g (as sodium salt)

Trade Name(s):

J:	Citosol (Kyorin)	Isozol (Yoshitomi)	USA:	Surital (Parke Davis); wfm

Thiethylperazine

ATC: R06AD03
Use: anti-emetic, antivertignosant

RN: 1420-55-9 MF: $C_{22}H_{29}N_3S_2$ MW: 399.63 EINECS: 215-819-0
LD_{50}: 71.6 mg/kg (M, i.v.); 680 mg/kg (M, p.o.)
CN: 2-(ethylthio)-10-[3-(4-methyl-1-piperazinyl)propyl]-10*H*-phenothiazine

dimaleate

RN: 1179-69-7 MF: $C_{22}H_{29}N_3S_2 \cdot 2C_4H_4O_4$ MW: 631.77 EINECS: 214-648-9
LD_{50}: 93 mg/kg (M, i.v.); 680 mg/kg (M, p.o.);
90 mg/kg (R, i.v.); 1260 mg/kg (R, p.o.)

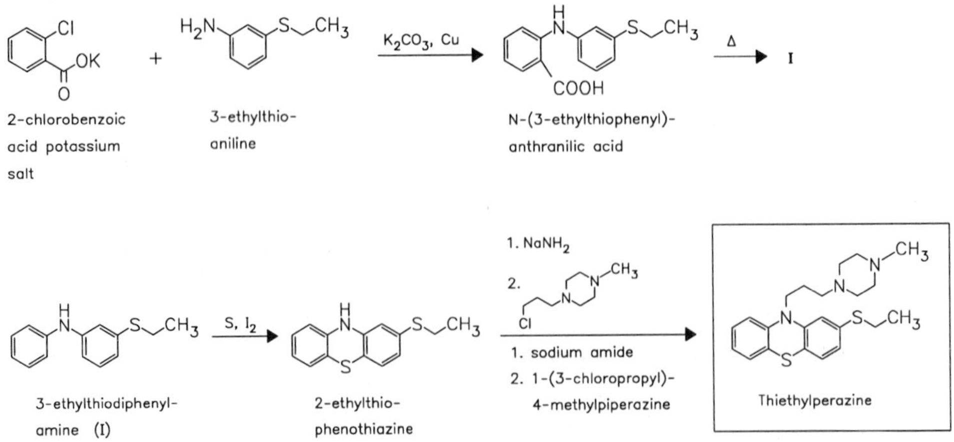
2-chlorobenzoic acid potassium salt
3-ethylthio-aniline
K_2CO_3, Cu
N-(3-ethylthiophenyl)-anthranilic acid
Δ
I
3-ethylthiodiphenyl-amine (I)
S, I_2
2-ethylthio-phenothiazine
1. $NaNH_2$
2.
1. sodium amide
2. 1-(3-chloropropyl)-4-methylpiperazine
Thiethylperazine

Reference(s):

US 3 336 197 (Sandoz; 15.8.1967; CH-prior. 19.4.1956).
Bourquin, J.P. et al.: Helv. Chim. Acta (HCACAV) **41**, 1072 (1958).

Formulation(s): amp. 10 mg/2 ml; drg. 6.5 mg; tabl. 10 mg (as dimaleate)

Trade Name(s):

D:	Torecan (Novartis Pharma)	GB:	Torecan (Sandoz); wfm	J:	Toresten (Sandoz-Sankyo)
F:	Torécan (Sandoz); wfm	I:	Torecan (Lpd)	USA:	Torecan (Roxane)

Thioctic acid

(Thioctacid; α-Lipoic acid)

ATC: N07XX
Use: detoxicant, liver protective drug, lipotropic, growth factor

RN: 62-46-4 MF: $C_8H_{14}O_2S_2$ MW: 206.33 EINECS: 200-534-6
LD_{50}: 197 mg/kg (M, i.v.); 502 mg/kg (M, p.o.);
180 mg/kg (R, i.v.); 1130 mg/kg (R, p.o.)
CN: 1,2-dithiolane-3-pentanoic acid

sodium salt
RN: 2319-84-8 MF: $C_8H_{13}NaO_2S_2$ MW: 228.31
LD_{50}: 197 mg/kg (M, i.v.)

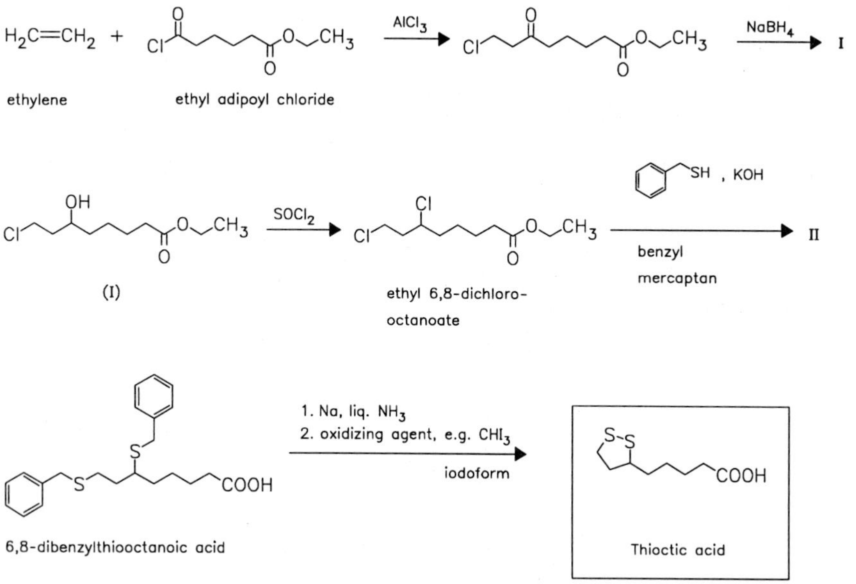
H2C=CH2
ethylene
ethyl adipoyl chloride
AlCl3
NaBH4
I
(I)
SOCl2
ethyl 6,8-dichloro-octanoate
SH , KOH
benzyl mercaptan
II
6,8-dibenzylthiooctanoic acid
1. Na, liq. NH3
2. oxidizing agent, e.g. CHI3
iodoform
COOH
Thioctic acid

Reference(s):

Bullock et al.: J. Am. Chem. Soc. (JACSAT) **74**, 3455 (1952).
US 2 980 716 (Research Corp.; 1961; appl. 1954).

alternative method:
US 2 752 373 (Du Pont; 1956; appl. 1952).
US 2 752 374 (Du Pont; 1956; appl. 1952).
US 2 792 406 (Du Pont; 1957; appl. 1954).
US 3 049 549 (Research Corp. ert. 1962; appl. 1954).
US 3 223 712 (Yamanouchi; 14.12.1965; J-prior. 18.7.1960, 25.7.1960, 29.7.1960, 18.8.1960, 1.9.1960, 12.10.1960, 26.12.1960, 12.6.1961).
Tsuji, J. et al.: J. Org. Chem. (JOCEAH) **43**, 3606 (1978).
Bullock et al.: J. Am. Chem. Soc. (JACSAT) **74**, 1868 (1952).

Formulation(s):   amp. 150 mg, 300 mg, 600 mg; cps. 200mg, 250 mg, 300 mg; drg. 20 mg, 25 mg; f. c. tabl. 100 mg, 200 mg, 300 mg, 600 mg

Trade Name(s):

D: Alpha-Lipon Stada (Stada)
     alpha-Vibolex (Chephasaar)
     Azulipont (Azupharma)
     Berlithion (Berlin-Chemie)
     biomolipon (biomo)
     duralipon (durachemie)
     espalipon (esparma)
     Fenint (Pharmacia & Upjohn)

     Liponsäure-ratiopharm (ratiopharm)
     Neurium (Hexal)
     Pleomix-Alpha (Illa)
     Thioctacid (ASTA Medica AWD)
     Thiogamma (Wörwag)
     Verla-Lipon (Verla)
     Zeel (Heel)-comb.

I: Atoxan (Lagap)-comb.; wfm

     Hepatosten (Chimipharma); wfm
     Lipoatox (Salus); wfm
     Piruvasi (Bruco)-comb.; wfm
     Tioctamina (Morgan); wfm
     Tioctidasi (ISI); wfm
     Trofepar (Malesci)-comb.; wfm

J: Thioctsan (Otsuka)

Thiomersal
(Mercurothiolate sodique; Thimerosal)

ATC: D08AK06
Use: antiseptic

RN: 148-61-8   MF: $C_9H_{10}HgO_2S$ MW: 382.83   EINECS: 205-719-5
CN: ethyl(2-mercaptobenzoato-S)mercury

sodium salt
RN: 54-64-8   MF: $C_9H_9HgNaO_2S$ MW: 404.82   EINECS: 200-210-4
LD_{50}:   45 mg/kg (M, i.v.); 91 mg/kg (M, p.o.); 75 mg/kg (R, p.o.)

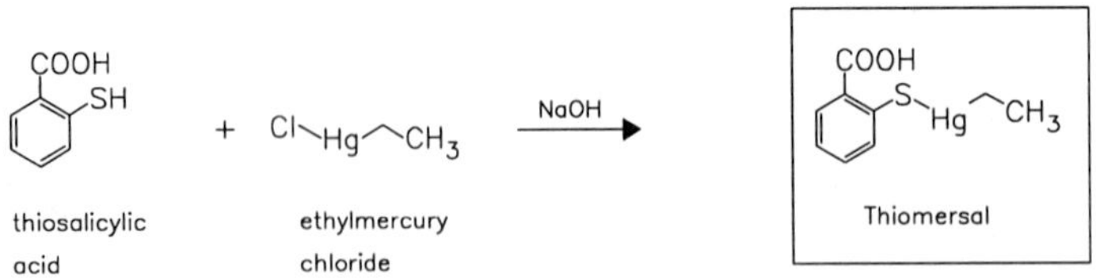

thiosalicylic acid   +   ethylmercury chloride   →(NaOH)→   Thiomersal

Reference(s):
US 1 672 615 (M. S. Kharasch; 1928; appl. 1927).

stabilization:
US 1 862 896 (M. S. Kharasch; 1932; appl. 1931).
US 2 012 820 (Lilly; 1935; appl. 1934).

with EDTA:
US 2 864 844 (Lilly; 1958; appl. 1955).

use in ophthalmic preparations:
US 3 767 788 (Burton, Parsons Chemicals; 23.10.1973; prior. 6.11.1968, 1.12.1969, 8.6.1970).

topical use for herpes infections:
US 4 083 991 (Burton, Parsons & Comp.; 11.4.1978; appl. 6.5.1977).

Formulation(s):   sol. 0.01 mg/ml

Trade Name(s):
D: Oxysept (Pharm-Allergan)-
     comb.
F: Collyrex (SmithKline
     Beecham)-comb.
     Constrilia (Alcon SA)-
     comb.

Dermachrome
(Synthélabo)-comb.
Polyclean (Alcon SA)-
comb.
Soaclens (Alcon SA)
Vitaseptol (CIBA Vital
Ophthalmics)

GB: Merthiolate (Lilly); wfm
     Otopred (Typharm); wfm
I: Lacrigel (Farmigea)-comb.
J: Merzonin (Takeda)
USA: Merthiolate (Lilly); wfm

Thiopental

ATC: N01AF03; N05CA19
Use: narcotic

RN: 76-75-5   MF: $C_{11}H_{18}N_2O_2S$ MW: 242.34   EINECS: 200-984-3
LD_{50}: 70 mg/kg (M, i.v.); 600 mg/kg (M, p.o.)
CN: 5-ethyldihydro-5-(1-methylbutyl)-2-thioxo-4,6(1H,5H)-pyrimidinedione

monosodium salt
RN: 71-73-8   MF: $C_{11}H_{17}N_2NaO_2S$ MW: 264.33   EINECS: 200-763-1
LD_{50}: 57 mg/kg (M, i.v.); 208 mg/kg (M, p.o.);
      43.6 mg/kg (R, i.v.); 117 mg/kg (R, p.o.);
      36 mg/kg (dog, i.v.)

2-bromo-
pentane

diethyl ethyl-
malonate

diethyl ethyl-
(1-methylbutyl)-
malonate (I)

thiourea

Thiopental

Reference(s):
US 2 153 729 (Abbott; 1939; appl. 1934).
US 2 876 225 (Abbott; 1959; appl. 1956).

Formulation(s):   vial 0.5 g/20 ml, 1 g/20 ml, 2.5 g/100 ml, 5 g/200 ml

Trade Name(s):
D: Thiopental "Hycomed"
     (Hycomed)
     Trapanal (Byk Gulden)
F: Nesdonal (Specia); wfm

Penthiobarbital Sodique
Adrian (Adrian-Marinier);
wfm
Pentothal (Abbott); wfm

GB: Intraval (May & Baker);
     wfm
     Pentothal (Abbott); wfm
I: Farmotal (Pharmacia &
     Upjohn; as sodium salt)

	J:		USA:	
Pentothal (Abbott; as sodium salt)		Ravonal (Tanabe) Thiobal (Daiichi)		Pentothal Sodium (Ohmeda)

2-Thiophenecarboxylic acid

ATC: R01AX10
Use: antiallergic

RN: 527-72-0 MF: $C_5H_4O_2S$ MW: 128.15 EINECS: 208-423-4
LD_{50}: 1670 mg/kg (M, i.v.)
CN: 2-thiophenecarboxylic acid

lithium salt
RN: 59753-16-1 MF: $C_5H_3LiO_2S$ MW: 134.08 EINECS: 261-914-5
sodium salt
RN: 25112-68-9 MF: $C_5H_3NaO_2S$ MW: 150.13
potassium salt
RN: 33311-43-2 MF: $C_5H_3KO_2S$ MW: 166.24
magnesium salt
RN: 36292-28-1 MF: $C_{10}H_6MgO_4S_2$ MW: 278.59

thiophene (I) + carbamoyl chloride → 2-thiophene-carboxamide → 2-Thiophene-carboxylic acid

I + acetic anhydride → (HClO₄) 2-acetyl-thiophene → (NaOBr, sodium hypobromite) 2-Thiophene-carboxylic acid

Reference(s):
a DD 13 495 (VEB Hydrierwerk Zeitz; appl. 15.7.1957).
b Sy, M.; de Malleray, B.: Bull. Soc. Chim. Fr. (BSCFAS) **1963**, 1276.

alternative syntheses:
Gross, H. et al.: Chem. Ber. (CHBEAM) **96**, 1382 (1963).
DE 1 146 055 (Deutsche Akademie der Wissenschaft; appl. 10.3.1961; DDR-prior. 10.3.1961).
Voerman, M.G.L.: Recl. Trav. Chim. Pays-Bas (RTCPA3) **26**, 293 (1907).

use of the magnesium salt as liver protective drug:
FR 2 043 477 (Invest. Scientif. Pharmac.; appl. 20.5.1969).

Formulation(s): cps. 300 mg (as sodium salt); nasal drops 2.3 % (as sodium salt); tabl. 200 mg (as lithium salt)

Trade Name(s):
F: Soufrane (Roland-Marie)-
comb.; wfm

Thiophéol (Biogalénique);
wfm
Thiophéol (Inava); wfm

Trophirés (Roland-Marie)-
comb.; wfm

Thiopropazate

ATC: N05AB05
Use: neuroleptic

RN: 84-06-0 MF: C$_{23}$H$_{28}$ClN$_3$O$_2$S MW: 446.02 EINECS: 201-513-4
LD$_{50}$: 1100 mg/kg (M, s.c.)
CN: 4-[3-(2-chloro-10H-phenothiazin-10-yl)propyl]-1-piperazineethanol acetate (ester)

dihydrochloride
RN: 146-28-1 MF: C$_{23}$H$_{28}$ClN$_3$O$_2$S · 2HCl MW: 518.94 EINECS: 205-666-8
LD$_{50}$: 279 mg/kg (M, p.o.)

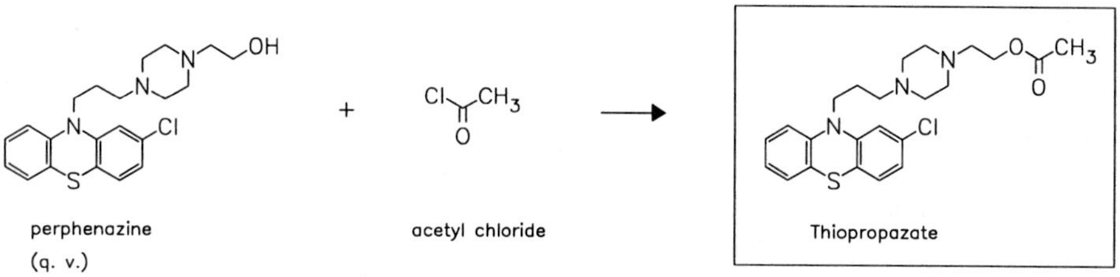

perphenazine
(q. v.)

acetyl chloride

Thiopropazate

Reference(s):
US 2 766 235 (J. W. Cusic; 1956; prior. 1956).

Formulation(s):   tabl. 5 mg, 10 mg (as dihydrochloride)

Trade Name(s):
D: Vesitan (Boehringer   GB: Dartalan (Searle); wfm
      Mannh.); wfm

Thioproperazine
(Thioperazine)

ATC: N05AB08
Use: neuroleptic, anti-emetic

RN: 316-81-4 MF: C$_{22}$H$_{30}$N$_4$O$_2$S$_2$ MW: 446.64 EINECS: 206-262-4
LD$_{50}$: 70 mg/kg (M, i.v.); 830 mg/kg (M, p.o.);
      25 mg/kg (R, i.v.)
CN: N,N-dimethyl-10-[3-(4-methyl-1-piperazinyl)propyl]-10H-phenothiazine-2-sulfonamide

dimesylate
RN: 2347-80-0 MF: C$_{22}$H$_{30}$N$_4$O$_2$S$_2$ · 2CH$_4$O$_3$S MW: 638.85 EINECS: 219-074-2
LD$_{50}$: 70 mg/kg (M, i.v.); 800 mg/kg (M, p.o.);
      45 mg/kg (R, i.v.); 750 mg/kg (R, p.o.)

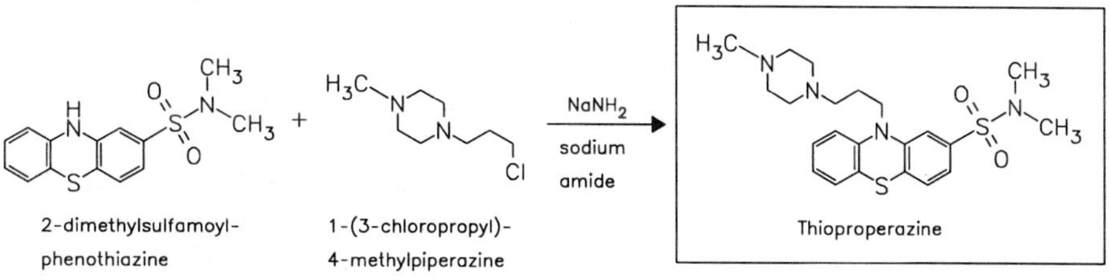

2-dimethylsulfamoyl-
phenothiazine

1-(3-chloropropyl)-
4-methylpiperazine

NaNH$_2$
sodium amide

Thioproperazine

Reference(s):
GB 814 512 (Rhône-Poulenc; appl. 15.7.1957; F-prior. 1.8.1956, 18.12.1956).
DE 1 088 964 (Rhône-Poulenc; appl. 17.7.1957; F-prior. 1.8.1956, 18.12.1956).

Formulation(s):   drops 1 mg/drop; tabl. 10 mg, 25 mg (as bismethanesulfonate)

Trade Name(s):
D: Mayeptil (Rhodia Pharma);   GB: Majeptil (May & Baker);   USA: Vontil (Smith Kline &
      wfm   wfm   French); wfm
F: Majeptil (Rhône-Poulenc   J: Cephalmin (Shionogi)
      Rorer Specia)

Thioridazine

ATC: N05AC02
Use: neuroleptic

RN: 50-52-2   MF: $C_{21}H_{26}N_2S_2$ MW: 370.59   EINECS: 200-044-2
LD$_{50}$:   385 mg/kg (M, p.o.);
       71 mg/kg (R, i.v.); 995 mg/kg (R, p.o.)
CN: 10-[2-(1-methyl-2-piperidinyl)ethyl]-2-(methylthio)-10H-phenothiazine

monohydrochloride
RN: 130-61-0   MF: $C_{21}H_{26}N_2S_2 \cdot HCl$ MW: 407.05   EINECS: 204-992-8
LD$_{50}$:   33 mg/kg (M, i.v.); 360 mg/kg (M, p.o.);
       71 mg/kg (R, i.v.); 1060 mg/kg (R, p.o.);
       160 mg/kg (dog, p.o.)
tartrate
RN: 1257-76-7   MF: $C_{21}H_{26}N_2S_2 \cdot xC_4H_6O_6$ MW: unspecified

2-chloro-
benzoic acid

3-methylthio-
aniline

N-(3-methylthiophenyl)-
anthranilic acid

3-methylthiodi-
phenylamine (I)

2-methylthio-
phenothiazine

1. sodium amide
2. 2-(2-chloroethyl)-
1-methylpiperidine

Thioridazine

Reference(s):
US 3 239 514 (Sandoz; 8.3.1966; CH-prior. 19.4.1956).
Bourquin, J.P. et al.: Helv. Chim. Acta (HCACAV) **41**, 1072 (1958).

Formulation(s):   drg. 10 mg, 25 mg, 100 mg; f. c. tabl. 100 mg, 200 mg; s. r. tabl. 30 mg, 200 mg (as
                   hydrochloride); USA: sol. 30 mg/ml (as free base); tabl. 10 mg, 15 mg, 25 mg, 50 mg, 100 mg,
                   150 mg, 200 mg (as hydrochloride)

Trade Name(s):
D: Melleretten (ASTA Medica   Melleril (Novartis Pharma)   Thioridazine-neuraxpharm
      AWD)   (neuraxpharm)

F:	Melleril (Sandoz)	I:	Mellerette (Novartis)	J:	Melleril (Sandoz-Sankyo)
GB:	Melleril (Novartis)		Melleril (Novartis)	USA:	Thioridazine HCl (Geneva)

Thiotepa

ATC: L01AC01
Use: antineoplastic

RN: 52-24-4   MF: $C_6H_{12}N_3PS$ MW: 189.22   EINECS: 200-135-7
LD$_{50}$: 14500 μg/kg (M, i.v.); 38 mg/kg (M, p.o.);
9400 μg/kg (R, i.v.)
CN: 1,1',1''-phosphinothioylidynetrisaziridine

aziridine   thiophosphoryl chloride   Thiotepa

Reference(s):
US 2 670 347 (American Cyanamid; 1954; prior. 1952).

Formulation(s):   vial 15 mg

Trade Name(s):

D:	Thiotepa "Lederle" (Lederle)	GB:	Thio-Tepa (Lederle); wfm	J:	Tespamin (Sumitomo)
F:	Thiotépa Lederle (Lederle)	I:	Onco-Tiotepa (Simes); wfm	USA:	Thioplex (Immunex)

Tiabendazole

(Thiabendazole)

ATC: D01AC06; P02CA02
Use: anthelmintic

RN: 148-79-8   MF: $C_{10}H_7N_3S$ MW: 201.25   EINECS: 205-725-8
LD$_{50}$: 1300 mg/kg (M, p.o.);
2080 mg/kg (R, p.o.)
CN: 2-(4-thiazolyl)-1H-benzimidazole

o-phenylene-diamine   4-thiazole-carboxylic acid   Tiabendazole

Reference(s):
US 3 017 415 (Merck & Co.; 16.1.1962; prior. 18.1.1960).

alternative methods:
US 3 262 939 (Merck & Co.; 26.7.1966; prior. 2.8.1961, 4.6.1965).
US 3 274 208 (Merck & Co.; 20.9.1966; prior. 18.7.1961, 17.1.1964, 30.8.1965).

use as fungicide:
US 3 370 957 (Merck & Co.; 27.2.1968; prior. 23.5.1963, 12.5.1964).

hypophosphite salt:
US 3 535 331 (Merck & Co.; 20.10.1970; appl. 26.7.1967).

lactate salt:
US 3 658 827 (Merck Sharp & Dohme; 25.4.1972; prior. 26.6.1967, 15.6.1970).

glycolate:
US 4 160 029 (Merck & Co.; 3.7.1979; NL-prior. 10.5.1976).

thiazole-4-carboxylic acid:
US 3 274 207 (Merck & Co.; 20.9.1966; appl. 2.10.1961).

Formulation(s):   chewing tabl. 500 mg; susp. 500 mg/5 ml

Trade Name(s):

D:	Minzolum (Sharp & Dohme); wfm	GB:	Mintezol (Merck Sharp & Dohme)	J:	Mintezol (Banyu)
		I:	Tiabendazolo (IFI)	USA:	Mintezol (Merck Sharp & Dohme)

Tiadenol

ATC: C10AX03
Use: antihyperlipidemic

RN: 6964-20-1   MF: $C_{14}H_{30}O_2S_2$ MW: 294.52   EINECS: 230-165-6
CN: 2,2'-[1,10-decanediylbis(thio)]bis[ethanol]

1,10-dibromo-
decane or
1,10-dichloro-
decane

2-mercapto-
ethanol

Tiadenol

R: −Cl, −Br

Reference(s):
DOS 2 038 836 (Orsymonde; appl. 5.8.1970; GB-prior. 8.8.1969).

Formulation(s):   tabl. 400 mg, 600 mg, 800 mg

Trade Name(s):

F:	Fonlipol (Lafon)	Tiabrenolo (NCSN)
I:	Eulip (SIT)	Tiaden (Malesci)

Tiagabine
(ABT-569; NO-05-0328)

ATC: N03AG06
Use: anticonvulsant, GABA uptake inhibitor

RN: 115103-54-3   MF: $C_{20}H_{25}NO_2S_2$ MW: 375.56
CN: (R)-1-[4,4-bis(3-methyl-2-thienyl)-3-butenyl]-3-piperidinecarboxylic acid

hydrochloride
RN: 145821-59-6   MF: $C_{20}H_{25}NO_2S_2 \cdot HCl$ MW: 412.02
hydrochloride monohydrate
RN: 145821-57-4   MF: $C_{20}H_{25}NO_2S_2 \cdot HCl \cdot H_2O$ MW: 430.03
S-enantiomer
RN: 115103-55-4   MF: $C_{20}H_{25}NO_2S_2$ MW: 375.56

S-enantiomer hydrochloride
RN: 145264-34-2   MF: C$_{20}$H$_{25}$NO$_2$S$_2$ · HCl   MW: 412.02
racemate
RN: 127254-36-8   MF: C$_{20}$H$_{25}$NO$_2$S$_2$ MW: 375.56

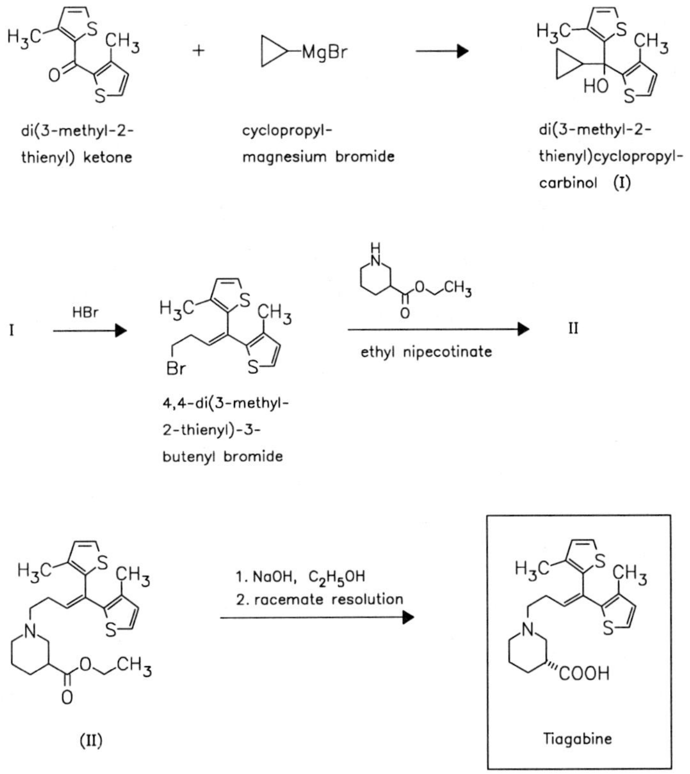

di(3-methyl-2-
thienyl) ketone

cyclopropyl-
magnesium bromide

di(3-methyl-2-
thienyl)cyclopropyl-
carbinol (I)

ethyl nipecotinate

4,4-di(3-methyl-
2-thienyl)-3-
butenyl bromide

(II)

1. NaOH, C$_2$H$_5$OH
2. racemate resolution

Tiagabine

Reference(s):
WO 8 700 171 (Novo Industri; appl. 26.6.1986; DK-prior. 26.6.1985).

preparation of crystalline R-isomer:
WO 9 217 473 (Novo Nordisk; appl. 23.3.1992; DK-prior. 4.2.1991).

composition with improved stability:
WO 96 344 606 (Novo Nordisk; appl. 29.4.1996; DK-prior. 5.5.1995).

transdermal delivery system:
WO 9 531 976 (Novo Nordisk; appl. 17.5.1995; DK-prior. 20.5.1994).

slow release formulation:
WO 9 529 665 (Alza Corp.; appl. 14.4.1995; USA-prior. 28.4.1994).

Formulation(s):   cps. 4 mg, 12 mg, 16 mg, 20 mg; tabl. 5 mg, 10 mg, 15 mg (as hydrochloride)

Trade Name(s):
D: Gabitril (Novo Nordisk)   F: Gabitril (Novo Nordisk)   USA: Gabitril (Abbott)

Tiamenidine

ATC: C02AC
Use: antihypertensive

RN: 31428-61-2 MF: $C_8H_{10}ClN_3S$ MW: 215.71
CN: N-(2-chloro-4-methyl-3-thienyl)-4,5-dihydro-1H-imidazol-2-amine

monohydrochloride
RN: 51274-83-0 MF: $C_8H_{10}ClN_3S \cdot HCl$ MW: 252.17 EINECS: 257-100-4
LD$_{50}$: 45 mg/kg (M, i.v.); 400 mg/kg (M, p.o.); 170 mg/kg (M, s.c.);
40 mg/kg (R, i.v.)

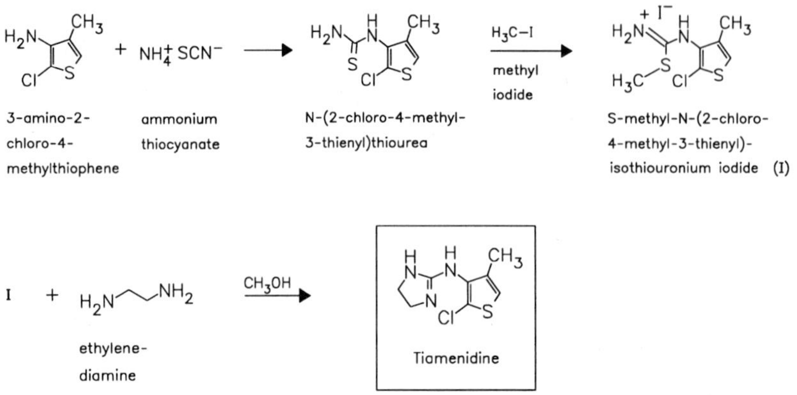

3-amino-2-
chloro-4-
methylthiophene

ammonium
thiocyanate

N-(2-chloro-4-methyl-
3-thienyl)thiourea

methyl
iodide

S-methyl-N-(2-chloro-
4-methyl-3-thienyl)-
isothiouronium iodide (I)

ethylene-
diamine

Tiamenidine

Reference(s):
DE 1 941 761 (Hoechst AG; appl. 16.8.1969).
US 3 758 476 (Hoechst AG; 11.9.1973; D-prior. 16.8.1969).

Formulation(s): tabl. 0.5 mg, 1 mg (as hydrochloride)

Trade Name(s):
D: Sundralen (Delalande;
1988)

Tianeptine sodium

ATC: N06AX14
Use: tricyclic antidepressant

RN: 30123-17-2 MF: $C_{21}H_{24}ClN_2NaO_4S$ MW: 458.94 EINECS: 250-059-3
LD$_{50}$: 450 mg/kg (M, i.p.); 900 mg/kg (M, p.o.)
CN: 7-[(3-chloro-6,11-dihydro-6-methyl-5,5-dioxidodibenzo[c,f][1,2]thiazepin-11-yl)amino]heptanoic acid
monosodium salt

free acid
RN: 66981-73-5 MF: $C_{21}H_{25}ClN_2O_4S$ MW: 436.96

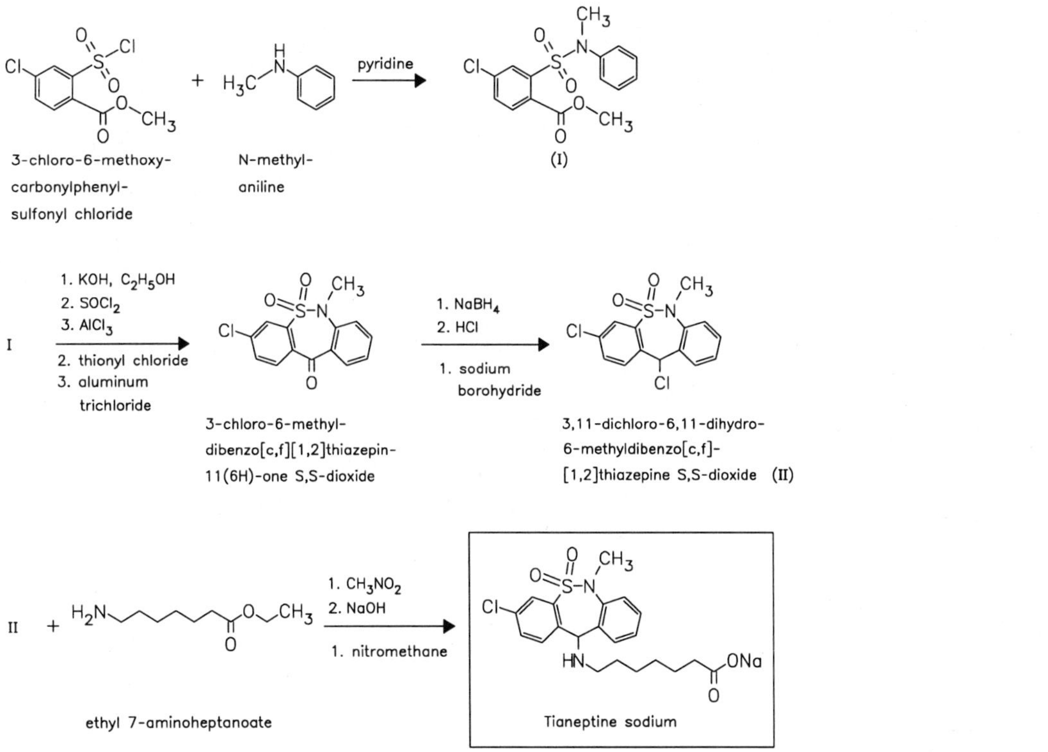

3-chloro-6-methoxy-
carbonylphenyl-
sulfonyl chloride

N-methyl-
aniline

(I)

I →

1. KOH, C₂H₅OH
2. SOCl₂
3. AlCl₃

2. thionyl chloride
3. aluminum
   trichloride

3-chloro-6-methyl-
dibenzo[c,f][1,2]thiazepin-
11(6H)-one S,S-dioxide

1. NaBH₄
2. HCl

1. sodium
   borohydride

3,11-dichloro-6,11-dihydro-
6-methyldibenzo[c,f]-
[1,2]thiazepine S,S-dioxide (II)

II + ethyl 7-aminoheptanoate

1. CH₃NO₂
2. NaOH

1. nitromethane

Tianeptine sodium

Reference(s):

DOS 2 011 806 (Science Union et Cie.; appl. 12.3.1970; GB-prior. 27.3.1969).
DE 2 065 635 (Science Union et Cie.; appl. 12.3.1970; GB-prior. 27.3.1969).
US 3 758 528 (Science Union et Cie.; 11.9.1973; appl. 13.3.1970; GB-prior. 27.3.1969).
DE 2 065 636 (Science Union et Cie.; appl. 12.3.1970; GB-prior. 27.3.1969).
US 3 821 249 (Science Union et Cie.; 28.6.1974; appl. 30.10.1972).

synthesis of 3-chloro-6-methyldibenzo[c,f][1,2]thiazepin-11(6H)-one S,S-dioxide:
GB 1 179 109 (Science Union et Cie.; appl. 19.12.1966).

medical use for treatment of stress:
FR 2 635 461 (ADIR; appl. 18.8.1988).

Formulation(s):   tabl. 12.5 mg

Trade Name(s):
F: Stablon (Ardix; 1988)

Tiapride

ATC: N05AL03
Use: anti-emetic, neuroleptic,
         antidyskinetic

RN: 51012-32-9   MF: C₁₅H₂₄N₂O₄S   MW: 328.43   EINECS: 256-907-9
CN: N-[2-(diethylamino)ethyl]-2-methoxy-5-(methylsulfonyl)benzamide

monohydrochloride
RN: 51012-33-0   MF: C₁₅H₂₄N₂O₄S · HCl   MW: 364.89   EINECS: 256-908-4
LD₅₀: 189 mg/kg (M, i.v.); 1340 mg/kg (M, p.o.);
        254 mg/kg (R, i.v.); 4840 mg/kg (R, p.o.);
        240 mg/kg (dog, p.o.)

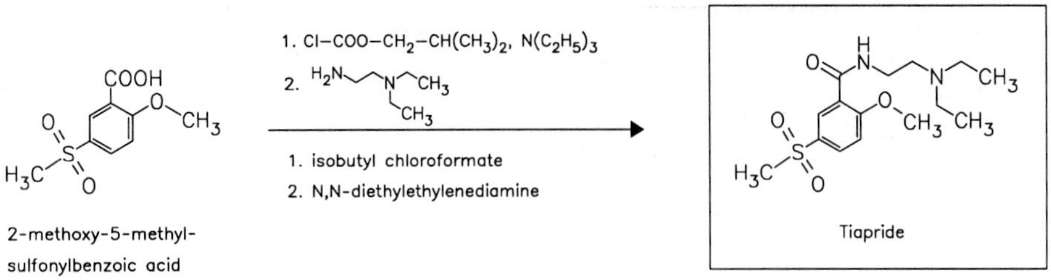

2-methoxy-5-methyl-
sulfonylbenzoic acid

Tiapride

Reference(s):

DOS 2 327 192 (Soc. d'Etudes Scientif. et Industrielle de l'Ile-de-France; appl. 28.5.1973; F-prior. 1.6.1972, 12.6.1972, 3.4.1973).

DOS 2 327 193 (Soc. d'Etudes Scientif. et Industrielle de l'Ile-de-France; appl. 28.5.1973; F-prior. 1.6.1972, 2.6.1972).

FR 2 188 601 (Soc. d'Etudes Scientif. et Industrielle de l'Ile-de-France; appl. 2.6.1972).

2-methoxy-5-methylsulfonylbenzoic acid:
US 3 342 826 (Soc. d'Etudes Scientif. et Industrielle d l'Ile-de-France; 19.9.1967; appl. 13.1.1964).

Formulation(s):   amp. 100 mg/2 ml; tabl. 100 mg (as hydrochloride)

Trade Name(s):

D:	Tiapridex (Synthelabo; 1978)		Tiapridal (Synthélabo; 1977)		Luxoben (ASTA Medica) Sereprile (Synthelabo)
F:	Equilium (Fumouze)	I:	Italprid (Teofarma)	J:	Gramalil (Fujisawa)

Tiaprofenic acid

ATC: M01AE11
Use: anti-inflammatory

RN: 33005-95-7   MF: $C_{14}H_{12}O_3S$ MW: 260.31   EINECS: 251-329-3
LD$_{50}$:   690 mg/kg (M, p.o.);
    181 mg/kg (R, p.o.)
CN: 5-benzoyl-α-methyl-2-thiopheneacetic acid

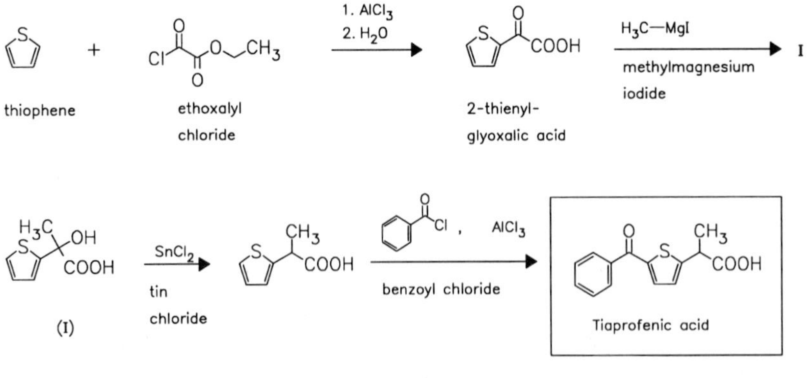

thiophene   ethoxalyl   2-thienyl-
                   chloride   glyoxalic acid

(I)   tin   benzoyl chloride   Tiaprofenic acid
       chloride

Reference(s):

DOS 2 055 264 (Roussel-Uclaf; appl. 10.11.1970; F-prior. 12.11.1969).
BE 758 741 (Roussel-Uclaf; appl. 10.5.1971; F-prior. 12.11.1969).
FR 2 112 111 (Roussel-Uclaf; appl. 4.11.1970).
US 4 159 986 (Roussel-Uclaf; 3.7.1979; prior. 25.2.1972).

calcium salt:
FR 2 268 522 (Roussel-Uclaf; appl. 12.11.1969).
Clémence, F. et al.: Eur. J. Med. Chem. (EJMCA5) **9**, 390 (1974).

salt with dibasic amino acids:
ES 460 926 (Lab. Cusi; appl. 21.7.1977).

Formulation(s):   s. r. cps. 300 mg; suppos. 300 mg; tabl. 200 mg, 300 mg

Trade Name(s):
D:	Surgam (Albert-Roussel, Hoechst; 1981)	GB:	Surgam (Florizel; 1982)		Tioprofen (Scharper); wfm
		I:	Surgamyl (Roussel-Maestretti); wfm	J:	Surgam (Roussel)
F:	Surgam (Roussel; 1975)				

Tiaramide

ATC: M01; N02
Use: anti-inflammatory, analgesic, antipyretic

RN: 32527-55-2   MF: $C_{15}H_{18}ClN_3O_3S$ MW: 355.85   EINECS: 251-083-7
LD$_{50}$:   564 mg/kg (M, p.o.);
3600 mg/kg (R, p.o.)
CN: 4-[(5-chloro-2-oxo-3(2H)-benzothiazolyl)acetyl]-1-piperazineethanol

monohydrochloride
RN: 35941-71-0   MF: $C_{15}H_{18}ClN_3O_3S \cdot HCl$ MW: 392.31   EINECS: 252-802-7
LD$_{50}$:   178 mg/kg (M, i.v.); 564 mg/kg (M, p.o.);
203 mg/kg (R, i.v.); 2300 mg/kg (R, p.o.);
157 mg/kg (dog, i.v.); >4 g/kg (dog, p.o.)

5-chloro-2(3H)-benzothiazolone   ethyl chloro-acetate   (I)

1-(2-hydroxy-ethyl)piperazine   Tiaramide

Reference(s):
DE 1 770 571 (Fujisawa; prior. 5.6.1968).
US 3 661 921 (Fujisawa; 9.5.1972; J-prior. 5.6.1967, 30.9.1967).
US 3 755 327 (Fujisawa; 28.8.1973; J-prior. 5.6.1967).

Formulation(s):   tabl. 50 mg, 100 mg (as hydrochloride)

Trade Name(s):
I: Ventaval (Crinos); wfm   J: Solantal (Fujisawa; 1975)

Tibezonium iodide
(Tiabenzazoniumjodid)

ATC: A01AB15
Use: chemotherapeutic, antiseptic, antibacterial

RN: 54663-47-7   MF: $C_{28}H_{32}IN_3S_2$ MW: 601.62   EINECS: 259-284-1
LD_{50}:   9 g/kg (M, p.o.);
        >10 g/kg (R, p.o.)
CN: N,N-diethyl-N-methyl-2-[[4-[4-(phenylthio)phenyl]-3H-1,5-benzodiazepin-2-yl]thio]ethanaminium iodide

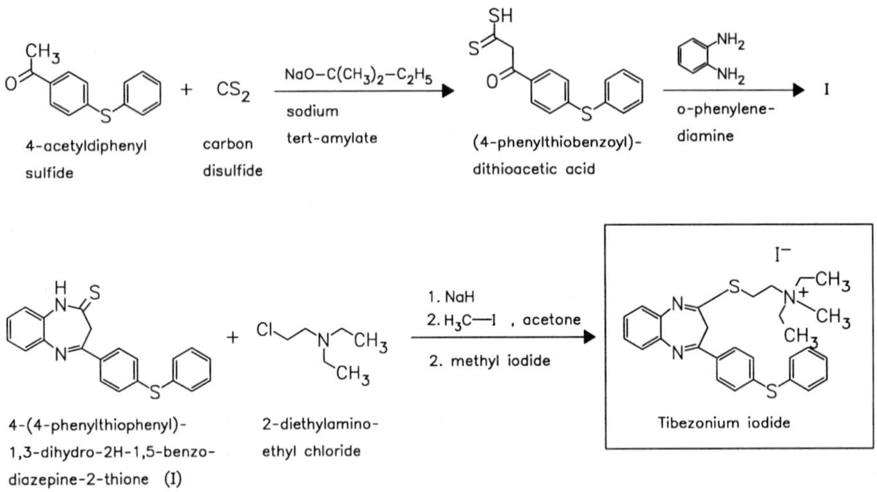

4-acetyldiphenyl sulfide + carbon disulfide → (4-phenylthiobenzoyl)-dithioacetic acid → o-phenylene-diamine → I

NaO–C(CH₃)₂–C₂H₅ sodium tert-amylate

4-(4-phenylthiophenyl)-1,3-dihydro-2H-1,5-benzo-diazepine-2-thione (I) + 2-diethylamino-ethyl chloride

1. NaH
2. H₃C—I, acetone
2. methyl iodide

Tibezonium iodide

Reference(s):
US 3 933 793 (Recordati; 20.1.1976; I-prior. 19.10.1971, 18.5.1972).
GB 1 412 008 (Recordati; valid from 11.10.1972; I-prior. 19.10.1971, 18.5.1972).
GB 1 412 009 (Recordati; valid from 11.10.1972; I-prior. 19.10.1971, 18.5.1972), (addition to GB 1 412 008).

Formulation(s):   collutorium 0.05 %; lozenge 5 mg

Trade Name(s):
I: Antoral (Recordati)

Tibolone

ATC: G03DC05
Use: anabolic, immunomodulating steroid, treatment of postmenopausal vasomotor symptoms

RN: 5630-53-5   MF: $C_{21}H_{28}O_2$ MW: 312.45   EINECS: 227-069-1
CN: (7α,17α)-17-hydroxy-7-methyl-19-norpregn-5(10)-en-20-yn-3-one

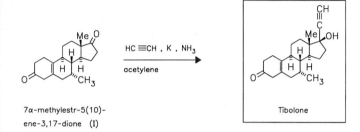

3-methoxy-7α-methyl-
estra-1,3,5(10)-trien-17-one

7α-methylestr-5(10)-
ene-3,17-dione (I)

Tibolone

Reference(s):
DOS 1 618 747 (Organon; appl. 23.6.1967; NL-prior. 24.6.1966).
US 3 340 279 (Organon; 5.9.1967; NL-prior. 16.6.1964).
US 3 475 465 (Organon; 28.10.1969; NL-prior. 24.6.1966).

alternative synthesis:
DE 1 543 273 (Organon; appl. 15.6.1965; NL-prior. 16.6.1964).

synthesis of 7α-methylestr-5(10)-ene-3,17-dione:
Anner, G. et al.: Chimia (CHIMAD) **20**, 434 (1966).

medical use as immunomodulator:
EP 159 739 (Akzo; appl. 20.3.1985; NL-prior. 21.3.1984).

combination with fluoride salts:
WO 8 909 058 (Akzo; appl. 17.3.1989; NL-prior. 25.3.1988).

Formulation(s):   tabl 2.5 mg

Trade Name(s):
GB: Livial (Organon; 1991)   I: Livial (Organon)

Ticarcillin

ATC: J01CA13
Use: antibiotic, antibacterial

RN: 34787-01-4   MF: $C_{15}H_{16}N_2O_6S_2$ MW: 384.43   EINECS: 252-213-5
CN: [2S-(2α,5α,6β(S^*))]-6-[(carboxy-3-thienylacetyl)amino]-3,3-dimethyl-7-oxo-4-thia-1-azabicyclo[3.2.0]heptane-2-carboxylic acid

disodium salt
RN: 29457-07-6   MF: $C_{15}H_{14}N_2Na_2O_6S_2$ MW: 428.40   EINECS: 249-642-5
LD$_{50}$:   5200 mg/kg (M, i.v.); >16 g/kg (M, p.o.);
        5350 mg/kg (R, i.v.); 16 g/kg (R, p.o.);
        >4 g/kg (dog, i.v.)

3-thienyl-
malonic acid

(I)

6-aminopenicillanic
acid

Ticarcillin

Reference(s):
DE 1 295 558 (Beecham; appl. 23.4.1964; GB-prior. 23.4.1963).
US 3 282 926 (Beecham; 1.11.1966; GB-prior. 23.4.1963).
GB 1 004 670 (Beecham; appl. 23.4.1963; valid from 20.4.1964).
US 3 492 291 (Beecham; 27.1.1970; prior. 17.4.1964, 3.5.1966).
GB 1 197 973 (Beecham; appl. 18.4.1967; valid from 18.4.1968).
DAS 2 244 556 (Pfizer; appl. 11.9.1972; USA-prior. 1.10.1971).

ticarcillin α-benzyl ester *from the monobenzyl ester of 3-thienylmalonic acid (can be hydrogenated on Pd-C to ticarcillin)*:
DAS 1 670 222 (Beecham; appl. 12.5.1967; GB-prior. 13.5.1966).
GB 1 125 557 (Beecham; appl. 13.5.1966; valid from 9.5.1967).

acylation via 3-thienylmalonic acid monophenyl ester monochloride:
GB 1 133 886 (Beecham; appl. 5.11.1966, 27.1.1967; valid from 30.10.1967).

alternative method (*via* 2,2-dimethyl-5-(3-thienyl)-1,3-dioxan-4,6-dione):
US 4 066 664 (Recherche et Industrie Thérapeutiques, Belg.; 3.1.1978; prior. 8.4.1975, 27.9.1976).

new method for 3-thienylmalonic acid (*resp.* 3-thienylacetic acid) *based on* 2,5-dichlorothiophene:
DOS 2 157 540 (Beecham; appl. 19.11.1971; GB-prior. 25.11.1970).

synthesis of 3-thienylmalonic acid monoalkyl esters by carboxylation of 3-thienylacetic acid esters:
GB 1 426 557 (Beecham; appl. 5.10.1972; valid from 10.9.1973).
DOS 2 348 473 (Beecham; appl. 26.9.1973; GB-prior. 5.10.1972).

from aliphatic precursors:
EP-appl. 633 (Beecham; appl. 12.7.1978; GB-prior. 23.7.1977).

from 3-halothiophenes:
GB 2 009 158 (Oce-Andeno; appl. 6.12.1977).

Formulation(s):   amp. 1.5 g, 3 g, 5 g; vial 1 g, 3 g, 6 g

Trade Name(s):
D: Betabactyl (SmithKline
      Beecham)-comb.
F: Claventin (SmithKline
      Beecham)-comb.
      Ticarpen (SmithKline
      Beecham)

GB: Ticar (Beecham)
      Timentin (SmithKline
      Beecham)-comb.
J: Monapen (Fujisawa)
      Ticarpenin (Beecham-Meiji
      Seika)

USA: Ticar (SmithKline
      Beecham)
      Timentin (SmithKline
      Beecham)-comb.

Ticlopidine

ATC: B01AC05
Use: platelet aggregation inhibitor

RN: 55142-85-3   MF: $C_{14}H_{14}ClNS$ MW: 263.79   EINECS: 259-498-5
LD$_{50}$: 88 mg/kg (M, i.v.); 600 mg/kg (M, p.o.);
        70 mg/kg (R, i.v.); 1780 mg/kg (R, p.o.)
CN: 5-[(2-chlorophenyl)methyl]-4,5,6,7-tetrahydrothieno[3,2-c]pyridine

hydrochloride

RN: 53885-35-1   MF: $C_{14}H_{14}ClNS \cdot HCl$ MW: 300.25   EINECS: 258-837-4
LD$_{50}$: 55 mg/kg (M, i.v.); 600 mg/kg (M, p.o.);
        70 mg/kg (R, i.v.); 1780 mg/kg (R, p.o.)

4,5,6,7-tetra-
hydrothieno-
[3,2-c]pyridine

2-chlorobenzyl
chloride (I)

Ticlopidine

thieno[3,2-c]-
pyridine

ethylene
oxide

1. THF
2. H_3C—⬡—SO_2Cl
3. 2-chlorobenzylamine

2. p-toluenesulfonyl
   chloride
3. 2-chlorobenzyl-
   amine

Ticlopidine

Reference(s):
DE 2 404 308 (Centre Etud. Ind. Pharm.; prior. 30.1.1974).
US 4 051 141 (Centre Etud. Ind. Pharm.; 27.9.1977; F-prior. 1.2.1973).
a,b Maffrand, J.P.; Eloy, F.: Eur. J. Med. Chem. (EJMCA5) **9**, 483 (1974).
    starting material:
    DOS 2 530 516 (Parcor; appl. 9.7.1975; F-prior. 16.7.1974).
c US 4 127 580 (Parcor; 28.11.1978; F-prior. 30.7.1975, 7.2.1975).

alternative syntheses:
US 4 174 448 (Parcor; 13.11.1979; F-prior. 6.6.1978).

use as cytostatic:
BE 873 326 (Sopharma; appl. 5.1.1979; J-prior. (Daiichi Seiyaku) 6.1.1978).

ticlopidine-aspirin-*combination:*
US 4 080 447 (Cent. Etud. Ind. Pharm.; 21.3.1978; F-prior. 29.3.1976).

use as antithrombotic:
JP 54 086 626 (Sopharma; appl. 21.12.1977).
JP 54 105 236 (Sopharma; appl. 6.2.1978).

Formulation(s):　cps. 250 mg; drg. 250 mg; f. c. tabl. 250 mg (as hydrochloride); tabl. 250 mg

Trade Name(s):

D:	Tiklyd (Sanofi Winthrop; 1980)	Clox (Caber) Fluilast (Boniscontro &		Ticlopidine Dorom (Dorom)
F:	Ticlid (Sanofi Winthrop; 1978)	Gazzone) Klodin (Savio IBN)		Ticloproge (Proge Farm) Tiklid (Sanofi Winthrop)
I:	Anagregal (Gentili)	Opteron (Therabel Pharma)	J:	Panaldin (Daiichi)
	Antigreg (Piam)	Parsilid (Crinos)	USA:	Ticlid (Roche)
	Aplaket (Rottapharm)	Ticlodone (Sigma-Tau)		

Tiemonium iodide

ATC:　A03AB17
Use:　antispasmodic, analgesic, anticholinergic

RN:　144-12-7　MF: $C_{18}H_{24}INO_2S$　MW: 445.37　EINECS: 205-616-5
LD$_{50}$:　30 mg/kg (M, i.v.); 1800 mg/kg (M, p.o.);
　　　30 mg/kg (R, i.v.); 2295 mg/kg (R, p.o.)
CN:　4-[3-hydroxy-3-phenyl-3-(2-thienyl)propyl]-4-methylmorpholinium iodide

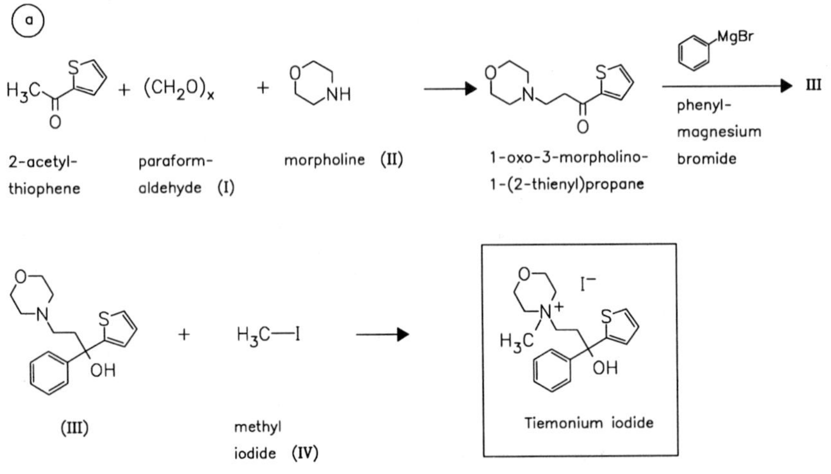

2-acetyl-thiophene　paraform-aldehyde (I)　morpholine (II)　1-oxo-3-morpholino-1-(2-thienyl)propane　phenyl-magnesium bromide

(III)　methyl iodide (IV)　Tiemonium iodide

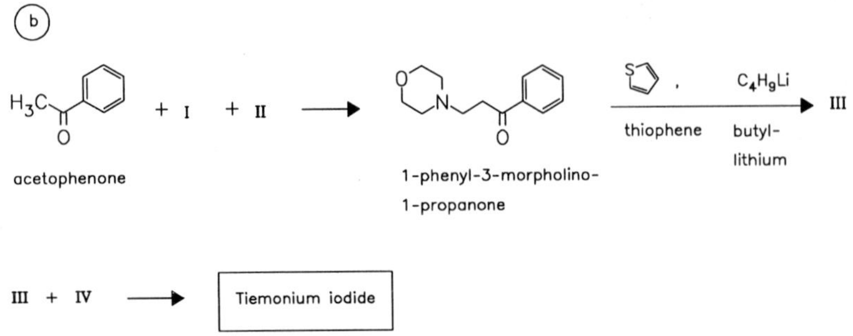

acetophenone　+ I + II　1-phenyl-3-morpholino-1-propanone　thiophene　butyl-lithium

III + IV　⟶　Tiemonium iodide

Reference(s):

a GB 953 386 (Mauvernay; appl. 3.3.1961; F-prior. 17.8.1960).
  FR-M 387 (Mauvernay; appl. 17.8.1960; prior. 4.3.1960).
b DOS 2 609 923 (Ravensberg; appl. 10.3.1976).

Formulation(s): syrup 0.2 %; tabl. 5 mg as combination preparation

Trade Name(s):

D:	Coffalon (Stark, Konstanz)-comb.		Viscéralgine (Riom) combination preparations		Ottimal (ICT-Lodi); wfm Visceralgina (Lirca); wfm
F:	Colchimax (Houdé)-comb. with colchicine	I:	Ottimal (Fardeco; as methyl sulfate); wfm	J:	Visceralgina (SIT); wfm Visceralgine (Nippon Zoki)

Tienilic acid

ATC: C03CC02
Use: diuretic, uricosuric agent

RN: 40180-04-9 MF: $C_{13}H_8Cl_2O_4S$ MW: 331.18 EINECS: 254-826-3
LD_{50}: 225 mg/kg (M, i.v.); 1275 mg/kg (M, p.o.)
CN: [2,3-dichloro-4-(2-thienylcarbonyl)phenoxy]acetic acid

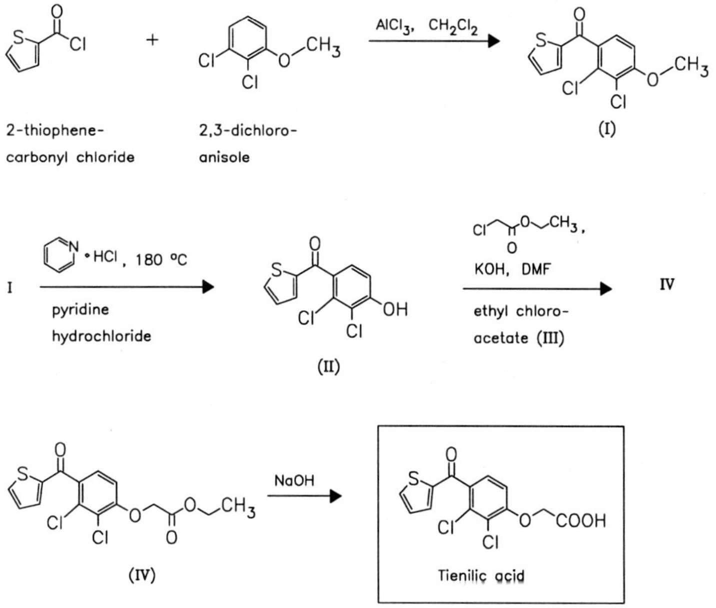

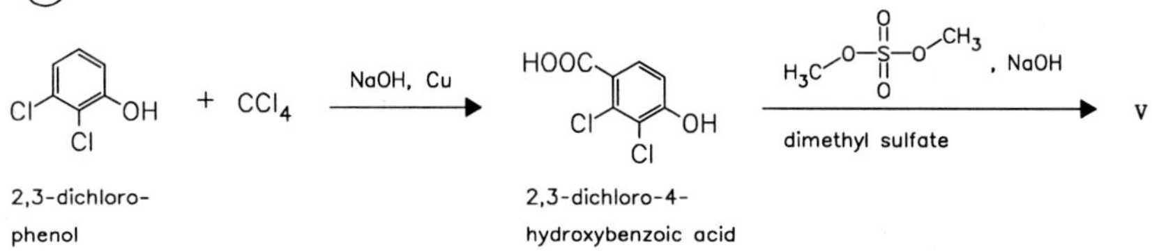

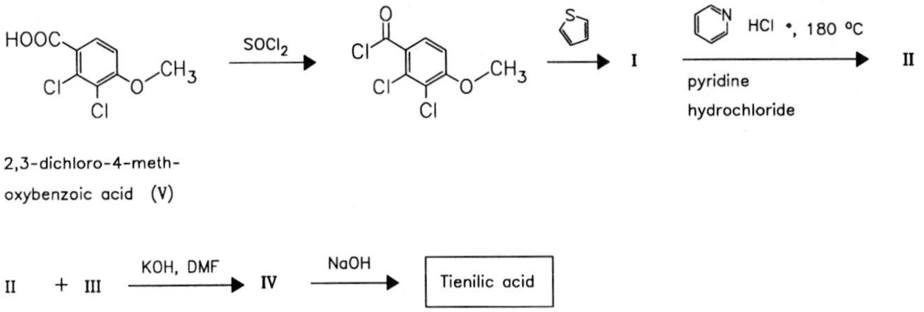

2,3-dichloro-4-meth-

oxybenzoic acid (V)

Reference(s):

a DE 2 048 372 (CERPHA; appl. 1.10.1970; F-prior. 10.10.1969).
   US 3 758 506 (CERPHA; 11.9.1973; F-prior. 10.10.1969).
   US 4 107 179 (Smith Kline; 15.8.1978; prior. 22.8.1977).
   Thuillier, G. et al.: Eur. J. Med. Chem. (EJMCA5) **9**, 625 (1974).
   new method for 2,3-dichloroanisole:
   FR-appl. 2 363 539 (Albert Rolland; appl. 31.8.1976).
b DOS 2 743 469 (Smith Kline; appl. 27.9.1977; USA-prior. 4.10.1976).
   GB 1 545 639 (Smith Kline; appl. 26.9.1977; USA-prior. 4.10.1976).

acylation of thiophene *with* 4-carboxy-2,3-dichlorophenoxyacetic acid ethyl ester *in presence of* polyphosphoric acid:
BE 858 848 (Albert Rolland; appl. 19.9.1977; F-prior. 21.9.1976).

alternative syntheses:
FR 2 407 925 (Smith Kline; appl. 27.9.1978; USA-prior. 2.11.1977).
US 4 166 061 (Smith Kline; 28.8.1979; appl. 2.11.1977).

use as antihyperlipidemic:
US 3 969 508 (Smith Kline Corp.; 13.7.1976; appl. 27.11.1974).

Formulation(s):   tabl. 250 mg

Trade Name(s):
F: Diflurex (Anphar); wfm

Tilidine

(Tilidate)

ATC: N02AX01
Use: analgesic, narcotic

RN: 51931-66-9 MF: $C_{17}H_{23}NO_2$ MW: 273.38 EINECS: 243-774-7
CN: *trans*-2-(dimethylamino)-1-phenyl-3-cyclohexene-1-carboxylic acid ethyl ester

hydrochloride
RN: 27107-79-5 MF: $C_{17}H_{23}NO_2 \cdot HCl$ MW: 309.84 EINECS: 248-226-0
LD$_{50}$: 52 mg/kg (M, i.v.); 437 mg/kg (M, p.o.);
       74 mg/kg (R, i.v.); 418 mg/kg (R, p.o.);
       500 mg/kg (dog, p.o.)

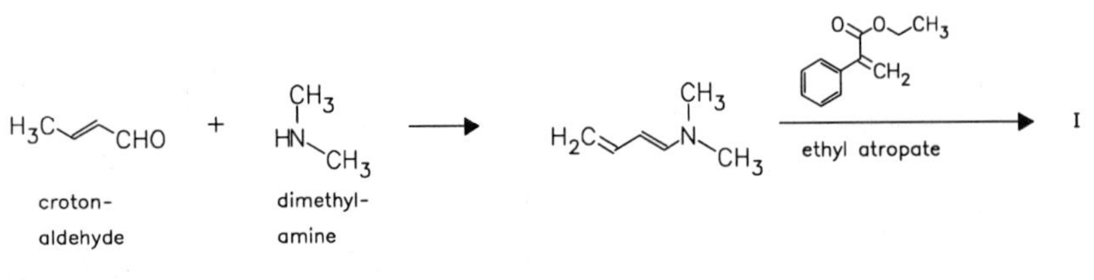

croton-
aldehyde

dimethyl-
amine

ethyl atropate

"cis,trans-tilidine" (I)

separation of isomers via ZnCl₂ complexes

Tilidine

Reference(s):
DE 1 518 959 (Gödecke; appl. 19.11.1965).
DE 1 618 476 (Gödecke; appl. 3.6.1967).
DE 1 618 482 (Gödecke; appl. 23.6.1967).
DE 1 768 704 (Gödecke; appl. 21.6.1968).
DAS 1 793 571 (Gödecke; appl. 19.11.1965).
DAS 1 907 909 (Gödecke; appl. 17.2.1969).
DOS 1 907 911 (Gödecke; appl. 17.2.1969).
DE 1 923 620 (Gödecke; appl. 8.5.1969).
US 3 557 126 (Warner-Lambert; 19.1.1971; D-prior. 19.11.1965, 8.6.1967, 23.6.1967, 21.6.1968, 17.2.1969).
Satzinger, G.: Justus Liebigs Ann. Chem. (JLACBF) **728**, 64 (1962).

Formulation(s):   cps. 50 mg; inj. sol. 100 mg; sol./drops 50 mg/0.72 ml; suppos. 75 mg (as hydrochloride in comb. with naloxone)

Trade Name(s):
D: Findol (Mundipharma)-comb.
Grüntin (Grünenthal)-comb.
Tilidalor (Hexal)-comb.

Tiligetic-saar (Azupharma)-comb.
TIW-Puren (Isis Puren)-comb.
Valomerck (Merck Generika)-comb.

Valoron N (Gödecke)-comb. with naloxone
I: Analgesic (Isom); wfm
Lucayan (Corvi); wfm

Tilisolol hydrochloride
(N-696)

Use: antihypertensive and antiangina, β-adrenergic blocker

RN: 155346-82-0   MF: C₁₇H₂₄N₂O₃ · HCl   MW: 340.85
CN: (±)-4-[3-[(1,1-Dimethylethyl)amino]-2-hydroxypropoxy]-2-methyl-1(2*H*)-isoquinolinone hydrochloride

(±)-base
RN: 85136-71-6   MF: C₁₇H₂₄N₂O₃   MW: 304.39

1. acetone, 55°C, 2h

2. H₃C—O—S(O)₂—O—CH₃, K₂CO₃, 50°C

phthalic anhydride

methyl N-methyl-glycinate

methyl 2-[[(methoxy-carbonylmethyl)methyl-amino]carbonyl]benzoate (I)

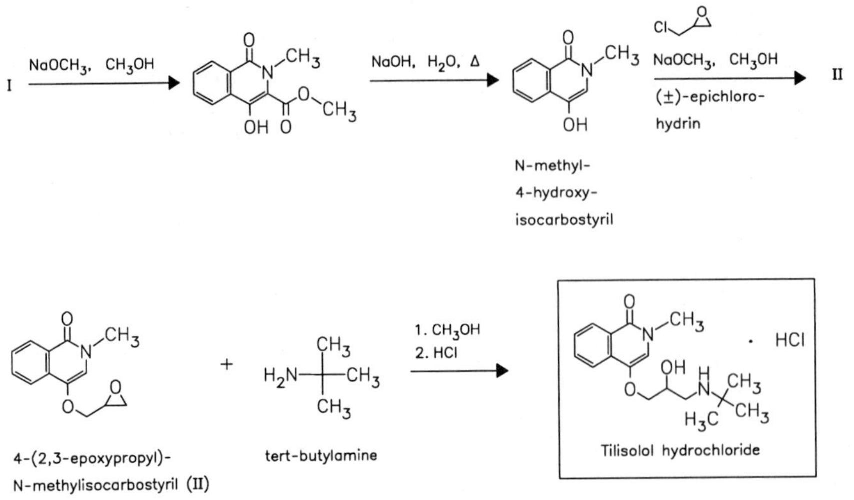

N-methyl-
4-hydroxy-
isocarbostyril

4-(2,3-epoxypropyl)-
N-methylisocarbostyril (II)

tert-butylamine

Tilisolol hydrochloride

Reference(s):
GB 1 501 150 (Nisshin Flour Milling Co.; GB-prior. 11.7.1975)
DE 2 631 080 (Nisshin Flour Milling Co.; appl. 9.7.1976; GB-prior. 11.7.1975).

synthetic preparation of N-methyl-4-hydroxyisocarbostyril:
Lombardino, J.G.: J. Heterocycl. Chem. (JHTCAD) **7** (5), 1057 (1970).

synthetic preparation of phthalic acid monoamide diethyl esters:
JP 57 054 152 (Nisshin Flour Milling Co.; J-prior. 18.9.1980).
JP 0 108 595 (Nisshin Flour Milling Co.; J-prior. 2.9.1988).

Formulation(s):   tabl. 10 mg, 20 mg (as hydrochloride)

Trade Name(s):
J: Daim (Nisshin Flour   Selecal (Toyama)
      Milling/Maruho)

Tiludronate disodium

(CI-TMBP; ME-3737; SR-41319; SR-41319B)

ATC: M05BA05
Use: calcium regulator, antiarthritic,
        treatment of osteoporosis,
        bisphosphonate bone resorption
        inhibitor

RN: 149845-07-8   MF: $C_7H_7ClNa_2O_6P_2S$ MW: 362.57
CN: [[(4-chlorophenyl)thio]methylene]bis [phosphonic acid] disodium salt

monohydrate
RN: 155453-09-1   MF: $C_7H_7ClNa_2O_6P_2S \cdot H_2O$ MW: 380.59
hemihydrate
RN: 155453-10-4   MF: $C_7H_7ClNa_2O_6P_2S \cdot 1/2H_2O$ MW: 743.16
free acid
RN: 89987-06-4   MF: $C_7H_9ClO_6P_2S$ MW: 318.61

tetraisopropyl
methylenedi-
phosphonate

tetraisopropyl (4-chloro-
phenylthio)methylenedi-
phosphonate (I)

Tiludronate disodium

Reference(s):
Ohnishi, H.; Nakamura, T.; Tsurukami, H.; Murakami, H.; Abe, M.; Barbier, A.: Bone Miner. (BOMIET) **25** (Suppl. 1), Abstr. 11 (1994).

synthesis:
EP 100 718 (Sanofi; appl. 25.7.1983; F-prior. 29.7.1982).

monohydrate of the disodium salt:
EP 582 515 (Elf Sanofi; appl. 3.8.1993; F-prior. 5.8.1992).

pharmaceutical preparations:
WO 9 617 616 (Sanofi; appl. 5.12.1995; F-prior. 6.12.1994).
WO 9 641 618 (Sanofi Winthrop; appl. 4.6.1996; USA-prior. 8.6.1995).

pharmaceutical compositions:
WO 9 530 421 (Ciba-Geigy AG; appl. 16.11.1995; GB-prior. 4.5.1994).
JP 05 105 632 (Meiji Seika Kaisha; appl. 27.4.1993; J-prior. 6.6.1991).
EP 336 851 (Sanofi; appl. 11.10.1989; F-prior. 7.4.1988).

combinations:
with estrogenes for treatment of osteoporosis:
WO 9 214 474 (Norwich Easton Pharmaceuticals; appl. 3.9.1992; USA-prior. 26.2.1991).
WO 9 414 455 (Merck & Co.; appl. 7.7.1994; USA-prior. 23.12.1992).

with parathyroid hormone for treatment of osteoporosis:
WO 9 607 418 (Procter and Gamble Company; appl. 14.3.1996; USA-prior. 9.9.1994).
WO 9 607 417 (Procter and Gamble Company; appl. 14.3.1996; USA-prior. 9.9.1994).

with growth hormone secretagogues for treatment of osteoporosis:
WO 9 511 029 (Merck & Co.; appl. 27.4.1995; USA-prior. 19.10.1993).

Formulation(s):   tabl. 200 mg, 240 mg (as sodium salt hemihydrate)

Trade Name(s):
D: Skelid (Sanofi Winthrop)   F: Skelid (Sanofi Winthrop)   USA: Skelid (Sanofi)

Timepidium bromide

ATC: A03
Use: antispasmodic, anticholinergic

RN: 35035-05-3   MF: $C_{17}H_{22}BrNOS_2$ MW: 400.41
LD$_{50}$:   12 mg/kg (M, i.v.); 713 mg/kg (M, p.o.);
        7 mg/kg (R, i.v.); 1213 mg/kg (R, p.o.)
CN: 3-(di-2-thienylmethylene)-5-methoxy-1,1-dimethylpiperidinium bromide

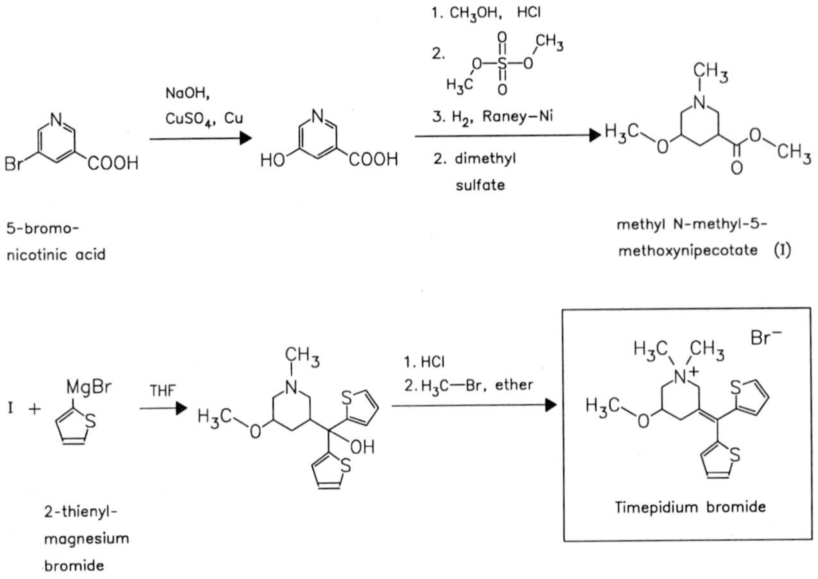

5-bromo-
nicotinic acid

methyl N-methyl-5-
methoxynipecotate   (I)

2-thienyl-
magnesium
bromide

Timepidium bromide

Reference(s):
US 3 764 607 (Tanabe Seiyaku; 9.10.1973; appl. 3.6.1971; J-prior. 11.6.1970).
FR 2 100 750 (Tanabe Seiyaku; appl. 28.4.1972; J-prior. 11.6.1970).
DOS 2 128 808 (Tanabe Seiyaku; appl. 9.6.1971; J-prior. 11.6.1970).
Kawazu, M. et al.: J. Med. Chem. (JMCMAR) **15**, 914 (1972).

Formulation(s):   cps. 30 mg; vial 7.5 mg

Trade Name(s):
I: Mepidium (Recordati;   J: Sesden (Tanabe Seiyaku;
        1987); wfm   1976)

Timiperone

ATC: N05AK
Use: neuroleptic, antipsychotic

RN: 57648-21-2   MF: $C_{22}H_{24}FN_3OS$ MW: 397.52   EINECS: 260-880-9
LD$_{50}$:   500 mg/kg (M, p.o.);
        >12.1 mg/kg (R, i.v.); 232 mg/kg (R, p.o.);
        20 mg/kg (dog, i.v.); 85 mg/kg (dog, p.o.)
CN: 4-[4-(2,3-dihydro-2-thioxo-1*H*-benzimidazol-1-yl)-1-piperidinyl]-1-(4-fluorophenyl)-1-butanone

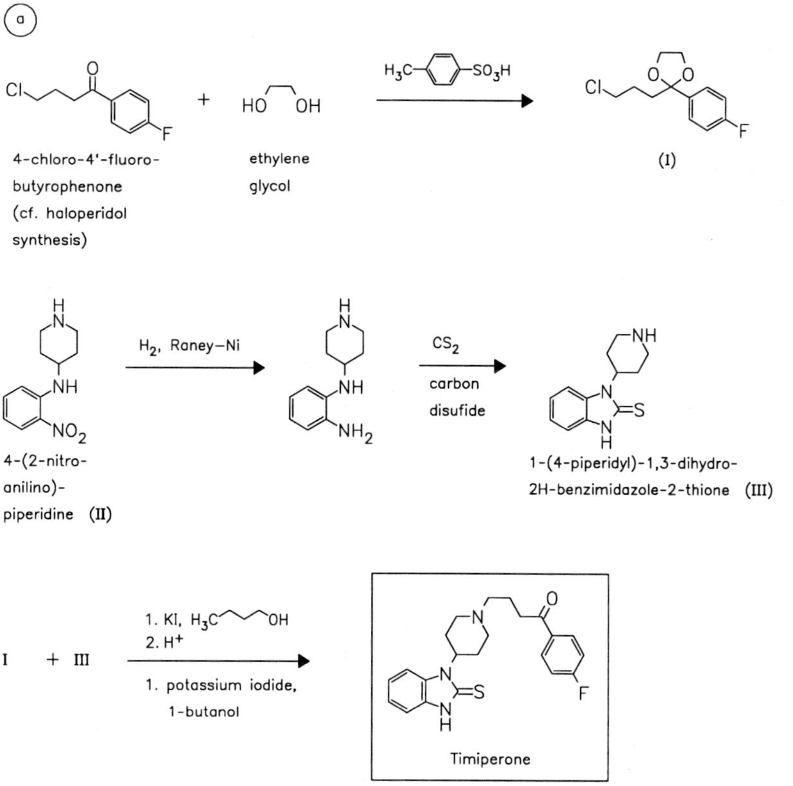

(a)

4-chloro-4'-fluoro-
butyrophenone
(cf. haloperidol
synthesis)

ethylene
glycol

(I)

4-(2-nitro-
anilino)-
piperidine (II)

H$_2$, Raney–Ni

CS$_2$
carbon
disufide

1-(4-piperidyl)-1,3-dihydro-
2H-benzimidazole-2-thione (III)

I   +   III

1. KI, H$_3$C⌒⌒OH
2. H$^+$

1. potassium iodide,
   1-butanol

Timiperone

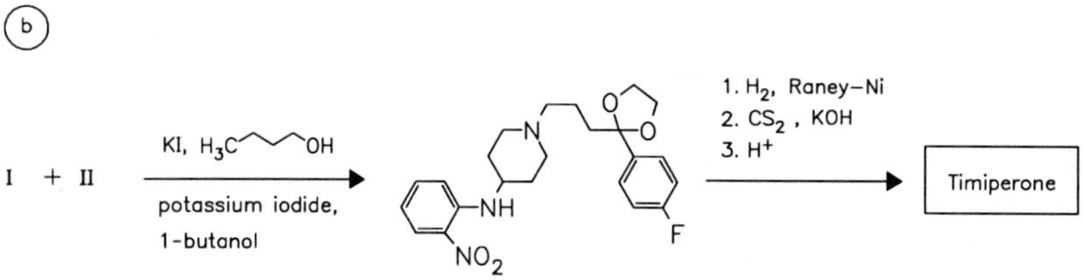

(b)

I + II

KI, H$_3$C⌒⌒OH

potassium iodide,
1-butanol

1. H$_2$, Raney–Ni
2. CS$_2$, KOH
3. H$^+$

Timiperone

Reference(s):
DOS 2 526 393 (Daiichi Seiyaku; appl. 13.6.1975).
US 3 963 727 (Daiichi Seiyaku; 15.6.1976; J.-prior. 6.6.1975).
Sato, M. et al.: J. Med. Chem. (JMCMAR) **21**, 1116 (1978).

alternative syntheses:
Sato, M.; Arimoto, M.: Chem. Pharm. Bull. (CPBTAL) **30**, 719 (1982).

Trade Name(s):
J: Tolopelon (Daiichi
      Seiyaku; 1984)

Timolol

ATC: C07AA06; C07BA06; C07DA06;
        S01ED01
Use: beta blocking agent, antiglaucoma
        agent, antianginal, antiarrhythmic

RN: 26839-75-8   MF: C$_{13}$H$_{24}$N$_4$O$_3$S   MW: 316.43   EINECS: 248-032-6
CN: (*S*)-1-[(1,1-dimethylethyl)amino]-3-[[4-(4-morpholinyl)-1,2,5-thiadiazol-3-yl]oxy]-2-propanol

maleate

RN: 26921-17-5 MF: $C_{13}H_{24}N_4O_3S \cdot C_4H_4O_4$ MW: 432.50

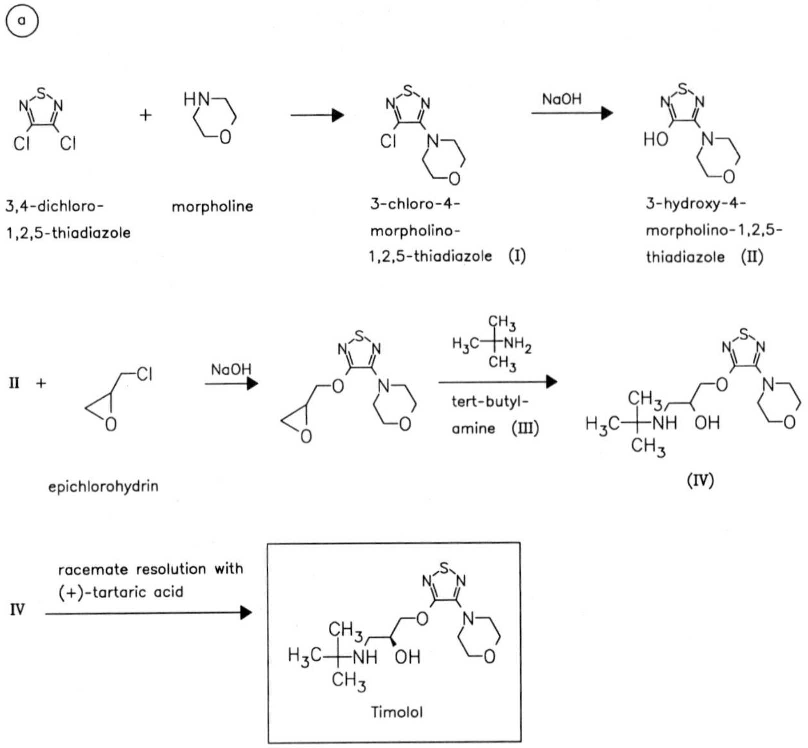
a
NaOH
3,4-dichloro-1,2,5-thiadiazole
morpholine
3-chloro-4-morpholino-1,2,5-thiadiazole (I)
3-hydroxy-4-morpholino-1,2,5-thiadiazole (II)
II +
NaOH
epichlorohydrin
tert-butylamine (III)
(IV)
IV
racemate resolution with (+)-tartaric acid
Timolol

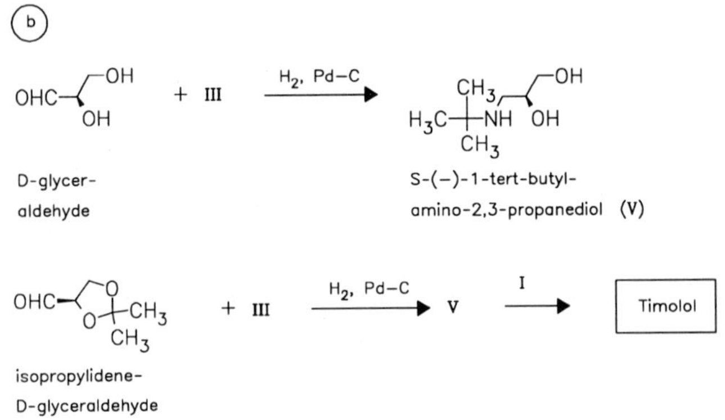
b
H2, Pd–C
+ III
D-glyceraldehyde
S-(–)-1-tert-butylamino-2,3-propanediol (V)
isopropylidene-D-glyceraldehyde
V
I
Timolol

Reference(s):

US 3 619 370 (C. E. Frosst & Co.; 9.11.1971; appl. 21.4.1969).
DOS 1 925 956 (C. E. Frosst & Co.; appl. 21.5.1969; USA-prior. 21.4.1969).
DOS 1 925 954 (C. E. Frosst & Co.; appl. 21.5.1969; USA-prior. 21.4.1969).
US 3 655 663 (C. E. Frosst & Co.; 11.4.1972; appl. 21.4.1969; prior. 22.5.1968).
DAS 1 925 956 (C. E. Frosst & Co.; appl. 21.5.1969; USA-prior. 22.5.1968, 21.4.1969).
DOS 1 925 955 (C. E. Frosst & Co.; appl. 21.5.1969; USA-prior. 21.4.1969).
US 3 657 237 (C. E. Frosst & Co.; 18.4. 1972; appl. 21.4.1969).
US 3 718 647 (C. E. Frosst & Co.; 27.2.1973; USA-prior. 21.4.1969, 16.8.1971).
US 3 729 469 (C. E. Frosst & Co.; 24.4.1973; prior. 22.5.1968, 21.4.1969, 9.9.1971).
US 3 812 182 (C. E. Frosst & Co.; 21.5.1974; prior. 21.4.1969, 16.8.1971, 18.6.1973).

alternative synthesis:
US 4 145 550 (Merck Sharp & Dohme; 20.3.1979; prior. 7.8.1975, 8.2.1977, 21.9.1977).

O-acyl-derivatives:
US 3 891 639 (Merck Sharp & Dohme; 24.6.1975; appl. 19.4.1973).
US 4 011 217 (Merck Sharp & Dohme; 8.3.1977; appl. 26.2.1975; prior. 19.4.1973).

combinations with diuretics:
US 4 178 374 (Merck & Co.; 11.12.1979; prior. 16.8.1974, 3.3.1975, 21.10.1976, 10.4.1978).
GB 1 495 034 (Merck & Co.; appl. 11.8.1975; USA-prior. 16.8.1974, 3.3.1975).

medical use for treatment of glaucoma:
GB 1 524 405 (Merck & Co.; appl. 23.9.1976; USA-prior. 26.9.1975).

Formulation(s):   eye drops 1 mg/ml, 2.5 mg/ml, 5 mg/ml, 1 mg/ml (as maleate); tabl. 5 mg, 10 mg, 20 mg (as maleate); tabl. 25 mg in comb. with hydrochlorothiazide

Trade Name(s):

D: Arutimol (Chauvin ankerpharm)
Chibro-Timoptol (Chibret; 1979)
dispatim (CIBA Vision)
duratimol (durachemie)
Moducrin (Merck Sharp & Dohme; 1978)-comb.
Timo-COMOD (Ursapharm)
Timo EDO (Mann)
Timohexal (Hexal)
Timolol-ratiopharm (ratiopharm)
Timomann (Mann)
Tim-Ophthal (Winzer)
Timosine (Chibret)
Timo-Stulln (Pharma Stulln)

F: Digaol (Leurquin)
Gaoptol (Eurphta)

Moducren (Merck Sharp & Dohme-Chibret)-comb.
Nyolol (CIBA Vision Ophthalmics)
Ophtim (Théa)
Timabak (Théa)
Timacor (Merck Sharp & Dohme-Chibret)
Timoptol (Merck Sharp & Dohme-Chibret)
numerous combination preparations

GB: Betim (Leo; as maleate)
Blocadren (Merck Sharp & Dohme; 1974)
Glaucol (Baker Norton)
Moducren (Morson)-comb.
Prestim (Leo)-comb.
Timoptol (Merck Sharp & Dohme)

I: Blocadren (Merck Sharp & Dohme)
Cusimolol (Alcon)
Droptimol (Farmigea)
Equiton (Bruschettini)-comb.
Oftimolo (Farmila)
Timicon (Merck Sharp & Dohme)-comb.
Timoptol (Merck Sharp & Dohme)

J: Timoptol (Merck-Banyu)

USA: Blocadren (Merck Sharp & Dohme; 1983)
Timolide (Merck Sharp & Dohme; 1981)
Timoptic (Merck Sharp & Dohme; 1978)
generics

Timonacic
(Thiazolidincarbonsäure)

ATC: A05
Use: liver therapeutic, choleretic

RN: 444-27-9   MF: $C_4H_7NO_2S$ MW: 133.17   EINECS: 207-146-6
LD_{50}:   400 mg/kg (M, p.o.);
875 mg/kg (R, p.o.)
CN: 4-thiazolidinecarboxylic acid

arginine salt
RN: 57631-15-9   MF: $C_4H_7NO_2S \cdot C_6H_{14}N_4O_2$ MW: 307.38

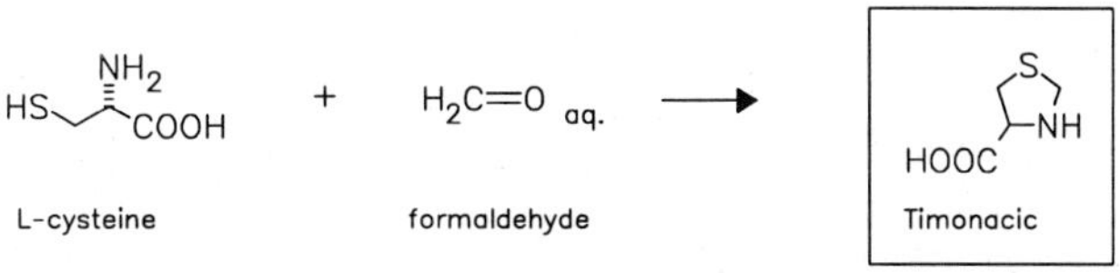

L-cysteine   formaldehyde   Timonacic

Reference(s):
FR-M 3 184 (Sogespar; appl. 4.2.1963).

Formulation(s): drinking amp. 100 mg (as arginine salt); tabl. 400 mg

Trade Name(s):

F:	Hépalidine (Riker-Mediarik)		Tiadilon (Dexo; as arginine salt)	Tiazolidin (Solvay Pharma)
	Thiobiline (Riker); wfm	I:	Sulfile (Poli)	

Tinazoline hydrochloride

ATC: R01A
Use: vasoconstrictor, nasal decongestant

RN: 55107-60-3 MF: $C_{11}H_{11}N_3S \cdot HCl$ MW: 253.76
CN: 3-[(4,5-dihydro-1*H*-imidazol-2-yl)thio]-1*H*-indole monohydrochloride

tinazoline
RN: 62882-99-9 MF: $C_{11}H_{11}N_3S$ MW: 217.30

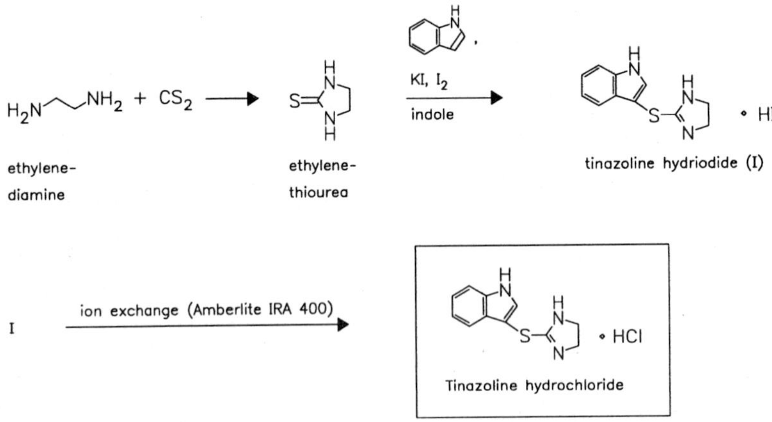

ethylene-
diamine

ethylene-
thiourea

tinazoline hydriodide (I)

Tinazoline hydrochloride

Reference(s):
DOS 2 427 207 (Ciba-Geigy; appl. 6.5.1974; CH-prior. 14.6.1973).
Nagarajan, N. et al.: Indian J. Chem. (IJOCAP) **20B**, 672 (1981).

synthesis of ethylenethiourea:
DOS 2 703 312 (Bayer, appl. 27.1.1977).

Trade Name(s):
IN: Varsyl (Ciba-Geigy; 1988)

Tinidazole

ATC: J01XD02; P01AB02
Use: chemotherapeutic (trichomonas), antiprotozoal, antiamebia

RN: 19387-91-8 MF: $C_8H_{13}N_3O_4S$ MW: 247.28 EINECS: 243-014-4
LD_{50}: >250 mg/kg (M, i.v.); 3200 mg/kg (M, p.o.);
>250 mg/kg (R, i.v.); 2710 mg/kg (R, p.o.)
CN: 1-[2-(ethylsulfonyl)ethyl]-2-methyl-5-nitro-1*H*-imidazole

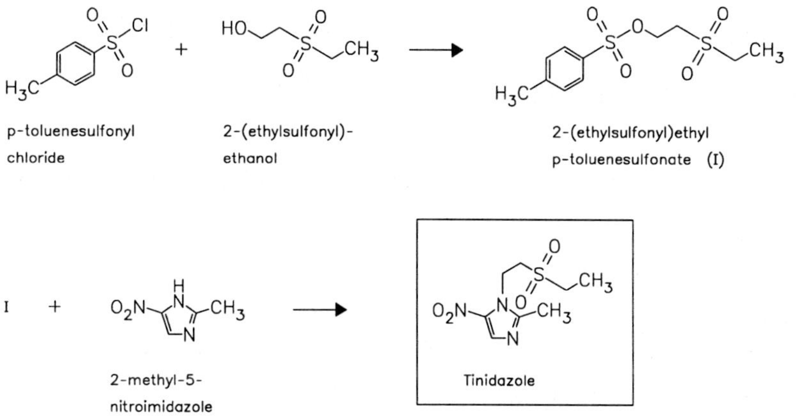

| p-toluenesulfonyl chloride | 2-(ethylsulfonyl)-ethanol | 2-(ethylsulfonyl)ethyl p-toluenesulfonate (I) |

2-methyl-5-nitroimidazole   Tinidazole

Reference(s):

US 3 376 311 (Pfizer; 2.4.1968; appl. 5.8.1966; prior. 26.10.1964).
DAS 1 745 780 (Pfizer; appl. 8.2.1967; USA-prior. 5.8.1966).
Miller, M.W. et al.: J. Med. Chem. (JMCMAR) **13**, 849 (1970).

Formulation(s):   f. c. tabl. 1 g

Trade Name(s):

D:	Simplotan (Pfizer; 1971)	I:	Fasigin N (Pfizer)	USA:	Fasigyn (Pfizer); wfm
F:	Fasigyne 500 (Pfizer)		Trimonase (Tosi-Novara)		Simplotan (Pfizer); wfm
GB:	Fasigyn (Pfizer; 1982)	J:	Fasigyn (Pfizer Taito)		

Tinoridine

ATC: M01; N02
Use: analgesic, anti-inflammatory

RN: 24237-54-5   MF: $C_{17}H_{20}N_2O_2S$ MW: 316.43   EINECS: 246-102-0
LD$_{50}$:   5.4 g/kg (M, p.o.);
>10.2 g/kg (R, p.o.)
CN: 2-amino-4,5,6,7-tetrahydro-6-(phenylmethyl)thieno[2,3-c]pyridine-3-carboxylic acid ethyl ester

monohydrochloride
RN: 25913-34-2   MF: $C_{17}H_{20}N_2O_2S \cdot HCl$ MW: 352.89   EINECS: 247-342-9
LD$_{50}$:   1601 mg/kg (M, p.o.);
1200 mg/kg (R, p.o.)

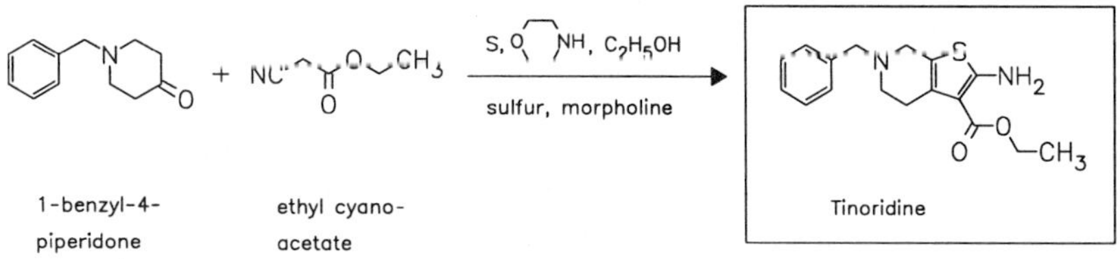

1-benzyl-4-piperidone   ethyl cyanoacetate   sulfur, morpholine   Tinoridine

Reference(s):

DE 1 812 404 (Yoshitomi; appl. 3.12.1968; J-prior. 4.12.1967).
US 3 563 997 (Yoshitomi; 16.2. 1971; J-prior. 4.12.1967).

Formulation(s):   cps. 50 mg, 100 mg (as hydrochloride)

Trade Name(s):
J: Nonflamin (Yoshitomi)

Tiocarlide
(Thiocarlide)

ATC: J04AD02
Use: tuberculostatic, leprostatic

RN: 910-86-1   MF: $C_{23}H_{32}N_2O_2S$ MW: 400.59   EINECS: 213-006-5
CN: *N,N'*-bis[4-(3-methylbutoxy)phenyl]thiourea

isopentyl bromide   +   4-nitrophenol sodium salt   →   4-isopentyloxy-1-nitrobenzene H_2, Raney–Ni → I

4-isopentyloxy-aniline (I)   + CS_2 KSCOOC$_2$H$_5$ →   Tiocarlide

Reference(s):
US 2 703 815 (Ciba; 1955; appl. 1951).

Formulation(s):   tabl. 500 mg

Trade Name(s):
GB: Isoxyl (Continental   I: Isoxyl (Lusofarmaco); wfm
      Pharma); wfm

Tioclomarol

ATC: B01AA11
Use: anticoagulant

RN: 22619-35-8   MF: $C_{22}H_{16}Cl_2O_4S$ MW: 447.34   EINECS: 245-132-1
CN: 3-[3-(4-chlorophenyl)-1-(5-chloro-2-thienyl)-3-hydroxypropyl]-4-hydroxy-2*H*-1-benzopyran-2-one

4'-chloro-acetophenone   +   2-chloro-5-thiophene-carboxaldehyde   NaOH, H$_2$O, C$_2$H$_5$OH →   4-hydroxy-coumarin   dioxane, piperidine → I

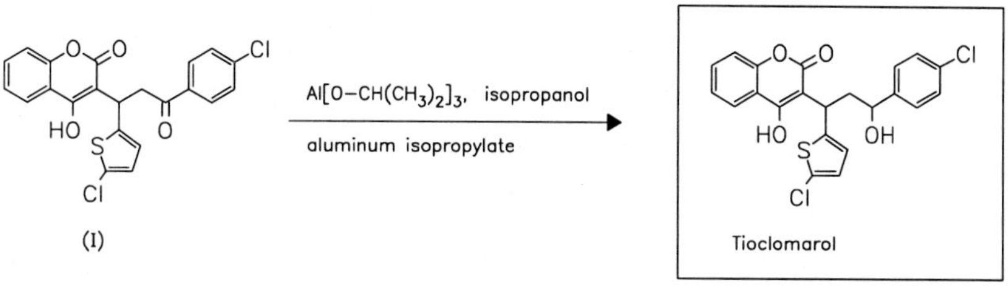

(I)

Tioclomarol

Reference(s):
ZA 6 707 267 (Lipha; appl. 7.8.1968; F-prior. 13.11.1967; 13.12.1966).

Formulation(s):   tabl. 4 mg

Trade Name(s):
F: Apegmone (Lipha Santé)

Tioconazole

ATC: D01AC07; G01AF08
Use: antimycotic, topical antifungal

RN: 65899-73-2   MF: $C_{16}H_{13}Cl_3N_2OS$ MW: 387.72   EINECS: 265-973-8
LD$_{50}$:   1870 mg/kg (M, p.o.);
770 mg/kg (R, p.o.)
CN: 1-[2-[(2-chloro-3-thienyl)methoxy]-2-(2,4-dichlorophenyl)ethyl]-1H-imidazole

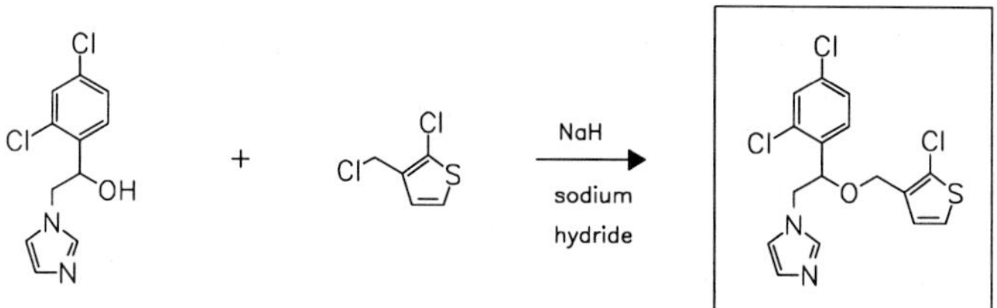

1-(2,4-dichloro-
phenyl)-2-
(1H-imidazol-1-yl)-
ethanol
(cf. miconazole
synthesis)

2-chloro-3-
(chloromethyl)-
thiophene

Tioconazole

Reference(s):
DE 2 619 381 (Pfizer; appl. 30.4.1976; GB-prior. 30.4.1975).
US 4 062 996 (Pfizer; 13.12.1977; appl. 30.4.1976; GB prior. 30.4.1975).

Formulation(s):   cream 10 mg/g; lotion 10 mg/g; ointment vaginal 6.5 %; powder 1 g/100g; spray 1 g/100g

Trade Name(s):
D: Mykontral (LAW)
Trosyl (Pfizer); wfm
F: Gyno-Trosyd (Pfizer; 1986)

GB: Trosyd (Pfizer; 1986)
Trosyl (Pfizer; 1988)
I: Trosyd (Roerig) (Irbi)

J: Trosy (Taito Pfizer; 1984)
USA: Vagistat (Bristol-Myers
Squibb)

Tioguanine
(Thioguanine)

ATC: L01BB03
Use: antineoplastic

RN: 154-42-7   MF: $C_5H_5N_5S$ MW: 167.20   EINECS: 205-827-2
LD_{50}:   160 mg/kg (M, p.o.)
CN: 2-amino-1,7-dihydro-6H-purin-6-thione

guanine $\xrightarrow[\text{phosphorus pentasulfide}]{P_2S_5}$ Tioguanine

Reference(s):
US 2 697 709 (Burroughs Wellcome; 1954; GB-prior. 1951).
US 2 884 667 (Burroughs Wellcome; 1959; prior. 1955).
US 2 800 473 (Burroughs Wellcome; 1957; appl. 1955).
US 3 019 224 (Burroughs Wellcome; 1962; appl. 1955).
US 3 132 144 (Burroughs Wellcome; 5.5.1964; appl. 10.7.1959).
Elion, G.B.; Hitchings, G.H.: J. Am. Chem. Soc. (JACSAT) **77**, 1676 (1955).

Formulation(s):   tabl. 40 mg

Trade Name(s):
D: Thioguanin-Wellcome   I: Thioguanine Wellcome   USA: Thioguanine Tabloid
      (Glaxo Wellcome)   (Glaxo Wellcome)   (Glaxo Wellcome)
GB: Lanvis (Glaxo Wellcome)

Tiomesterone
(Thiomesterone)

ATC: A14
Use: anabolic, androgen

RN: 2205-73-4   MF: $C_{24}H_{34}O_4S_2$ MW: 450.66   EINECS: 218-614-4
CN: (1α,7α,17β)-1,7-bis(acetylthio)-17-hydroxy-17-methylandrost-4-en-3-one

17β-hydroxy-17-methyl-   thioacetic   Tiomesterone
3-oxo-1,4,6-androstatriene   acid

Reference(s):
US 3 087 942 (Merck AG; 30.4.1963; D-prior. 29.10.1960).
Kramer, J.M. et al.: Chem. Ber. (CHBEAM) **96**, 2803 (1963).

starting material:
GB 854 343 (British Drug Houses; valid from 4.3.1959; prior. 13.3.1958).

Formulation(s):   15 mg, 30 mg

Trade Name(s):
D: Emdabol (Merck); wfm   Gerantabol (Merck)-comb.;
                                     wfm

Tiopronin
(Mercamidum)

ATC: R05CB12
Use: detoxicant, liver therapeutic,
        hepatoprotectant, mucolytic

RN: 1953-02-2   MF: $C_5H_9NO_3S$ MW: 163.20   EINECS: 217-778-4
LD$_{50}$: 1733 mg/kg (M, i.v.); 2330 mg/kg (M, p.o.);
        1300 mg/kg (R, p.o.)
CN: N-(2-mercapto-1-oxopropyl)glycine

monosodium salt
RN: 2015-25-0   MF: $C_5H_8NNaO_3S$ MW: 185.18
LD$_{50}$: 2100 mg/kg (M, i.v.)

2-bromo-   glycine   N-(2-bromopropionyl)-   Tiopronin
propyl   glycine
bromide

Reference(s):
FR 1 491 204 (Santen; appl. 10.8.1962; J-prior. 2.11.1961).
FR-M 3 081 (Santen; appl. 22.10.1962; J-prior. 2.11.1961).
GB 1 023 003 (Santen; appl. 14.9.1962).

use as mucolytic agent:
GB 1 482 651 (Lab. Cassenne; appl. 16.9.1974; USA-prior. 14.9.1973).
US 3 857 951 (Lab. Cassenne; 31.12.1974; appl. 14.9.1973).

against nosotoxicosa:
US 3 897 480 (Santen; 29.7.1975; J-prior. 3.10.1972, 11.5.1973).

sodium salt:
DOS 2 924 231 (P. Gargani; appl. 15.6.1979; I-prior. 16.6.1978).

Formulation(s):   amp. 100 mg, 250 mg; drg. 100 mg, 250 mg; gran. 150 mg, 350 mg; tabl. 100 mg

Trade Name(s):
D: Captimer (Fresenius)   Thiola (Coop. Farm.)   USA: Thiola (Mission)
F: Acadione (Cassenne)   Thiosol (Coop. Farm.)
I: Mucolysin (Farmila)   J: Thiola (Santen)

Tiotixene
(Thiothixene)

ATC: N05AF04
Use: neuroleptic

RN: 3313-26-6   MF: $C_{23}H_{29}N_3O_2S_2$ MW: 443.64
LD$_{50}$: 100 mg/kg (M, i.p.);
        55 mg/kg (R, i.p.)
CN: (Z)-N,N-dimethyl-9-[3-(4-methyl-1-piperazinyl)propylidene]-9H-thioxanthene-2-sulfonamide

dihydrochloride dihydrate

RN: 22189-31-7 MF: $C_{23}H_{29}N_3O_2S_2 \cdot 2HCl \cdot 2H_2O$ MW: 552.59

9H-thioxanthene → (chlorosulfonic acid, Cl-SO₃H) → 9H-thioxanthene-2-sulfonic acid → (1. thionyl chloride; 2. dimethylamine (I)) → 2-dimethylaminosulfonyl-9H-thioxanthene (II)

II → (1. butyllithium; 2. methyl acetate) → 9-acetyl-2-dimethylamino-sulfonyl-9H-thioxanthene → (formaldehyde, H₂C=O, I) → (III)

III + 1-methyl-piperazine → → (NaBH₄, sodium borohydride) → IV

(IV) → (POCl₃, phosphoryl chloride) → Tiotixene

Reference(s):
US 3 310 553 (Pfizer; 21.3.1967; appl. 26.4.1963; prior. 25.9.1962).
DE 1 470 157 (Pfizer; appl. 24.9.1963; USA-prior. 25.9.1962; 26.4.1963).
Muren, J.F.; Bloom, B.M.: J. Med. Chem. (JMCMAR) **13**, 17 (1970).

Formulation(s): cps. 1 mg, 2 mg, 4 mg, 5 mg, 10 mg; tabl. 10 mg; vial 4 mg, 10 mg (as hydrochloride)

Trade Name(s):
D: Orbinamon (Pfizer); wfm   I: Navane (Pfizer); wfm   USA: Navane (Pfizer); wfm
GB: Navane (Pfizer); wfm   J: Navane (Taito Pfizer)

Tioxolone

ATC: D10AB03
Use: antiseborrheic

RN: 4991-65-5 MF: C$_7$H$_4$O$_3$S MW: 168.17 EINECS: 225-653-0
CN: 6-hydroxy-1,3-benzoxathiol-2-one

resorcinol   ammonium rhodanide   Tioxolone

Reference(s):
US 2 332 418 (Winthrop; 1943; D-prior. 1938).

use:
US 2 886 488 (Thomae; 12.5.1959; D-prior. 2.7.1955).

Formulation(s):   sol. 200 mg/100 g in comb. with 100 mg benzoxonium chloride

Trade Name(s):
D: Loscon (Galderma)-comb.   I: Wasacne (IFI); wfm   J: Vikura (Eisai)
F: Gélacnine (Lab. du D'Furt);   Wasacne (Wassermann);
    wfm   wfm

Tipepidine

ATC: R05DB24
Use: antitussive

RN: 5169-78-8 MF: C$_{15}$H$_{17}$NS$_2$ MW: 275.44
LD$_{50}$: 55 mg/kg (M, i.v.); 867 mg/kg (M, p.o.);
    44 mg/kg (dog, i.v.)
CN: 3-(di-2-thienylmethylene)-1-methylpiperidine

4'-hydroxybenzophenone 2-carboxylate (1:1)
RN: 31139-87-4 MF: C$_{15}$H$_{17}$NS$_2$ · C$_{14}$H$_{10}$O$_4$ MW: 517.67 EINECS: 250-481-8
LD$_{50}$: 10 g/kg (M, p.o.);
    10 g/kg (R, p.o.)
citrate
RN: 5169-77-7 MF: C$_{15}$H$_{17}$NS$_2$ · xC$_6$H$_8$O$_7$ MW: unspecified

ethyl nicotinate   dimethyl sulfate   2-thienyl-magnesium bromide

(I)   →   Tipepidine

Reference(s):
ES 272 195 (A. Gallardo; appl. 20.11.1961).
(also citrate)
further literature see under citrate below

4'-hydroxybenzophenone-2-carboxylate (hibenzate):
JP 17 591 (62') (Tanabe Seiyaku; appl. 27.10.1962; prior. 19.10.1960).
GB 924 544 (Tanabe Seiyaku; valid from 7.12.1961; J-prior. 19.12.1960).

citrate:
Ponomarev, A.A.; Martemjanova, N.I.: Khim. Geterotsikl. Soedin. (KGSSAQ) **1957**, 174.
SU 176 903 (Ponomarev, Martemjanova; appl. 27.10.1962).

Formulation(s):   powder 10 %; syrup 25 mg (as hibenzate); tabl. 10 mg (as citrate)

Trade Name(s):
I: Asverin (ISF); wfm   Asverin-H (Tanabe; as   Hustopan-Syr. (Ohta)-
     Asverin (Searle); wfm   hibenzate)   comb.
J: Asverine (Tanabe Seiyaku)   Hustopan (Ohta)-comb.

Tiquizium bromide

ATC: A03
Use: antispasmodic

RN: 71731-58-3   MF: C$_{19}$H$_{24}$BrNS$_2$ MW: 410.44
LD$_{50}$:   10.3 mg/kg (M, i.v.); 578 mg/kg (M, p.o.);
             11.4 mg/kg (R, i.v.); 1177 mg/kg (R, p.o.);
             14.2 mg/kg (dog, i.v.); 662 mg/kg (dog, p.o.)
CN: trans-3-(di-2-thienylmethylene)octahydro-5-methyl-2H-quinolizinium bromide

2-piperidine-   acrylonitrile   1-(2-cyanoethyl)-   thionyl
ethanol   2-piperidineethanol   chloride

(I)   3-cyano-   (II)
                                        quinolizidine

II + BrMg—[2-thienyl] ⟶ [quinolizidine-thienyl-OH intermediate] —→ [1. HCl, 2. H₃C—Br] Tiquizium bromide

2-thienyl-
magnesium
bromide

2. methyl
bromide

Reference(s):

US 4 205 074 (Hokuriku; 27.5.1980; appl. 1.3.1979; prior. 10.5.1978).

DOS 2 820 687 (Hokuriku Pharm.; appl. 11.5.1978; J-prior. 16.5.1977, 9.11.1977, 8.12.1977, 21.12.1977, 28.2.1978).

Koshinaka, E. et al.: Chem. Pharm. Bull. (CPBTAL) **27**, 1454 (1979).

Trade Name(s):

J: Thiaton (Hokuriku; 1984)

Tiracizine

ATC: C01EB11
Use: antiarrhythmic

RN: 83275-56-3   MF: $C_{21}H_{25}N_3O_3$ MW: 367.45
CN: [5-[(dimethylamino)acetyl]-10,11-dihydro-5H-dibenz[b,f]azepin-3-yl]carbamic acid ethyl ester

monohydrochloride
RN: 78816-67-8   MF: $C_{21}H_{25}N_3O_3 \cdot HCl$ MW: 403.91
LD$_{50}$:   5.4 mg/kg (M, i.v.); 48 mg/kg (M, p.o.);
           10.9 mg/kg (R, i.v.); 78 mg/kg (R, p.o.)

10,11-dihydro-5H-
dibenz[b,f]azepine

acetyl
chloride

HNO₃, H₂SO₄

3-nitro-5-acetyl-10,11-
dihydro-5H-dibenz-
[b,f]azepine

1. Fe, NH₃
2. KOH
3. ethyl
chloroformate

I

3-carbethoxyamino-10,11-
dihydro-5H-dibenz[b,f]-
azepine (I)

chloroacetyl
chloride

Tiracizine

Reference(s):

DE 3 040 085 (VEB Arzneimittelwerk Dresden; appl. 24.10.1980; DDR-prior. 5.11.1971).

FR 2 493 314 (VEB Arzneimittelwerk Dresden; appl. 5.11.1980).

DD 258 224 (VEB Arzneimittelwerk Dresden; appl. 5.3.1987).

Skoldinov, A.P. et al.: Khim. Farm. Zh. (KHFZAN) **24**, 51 (1990).

DD 267 630 (VEB Arzneimittelwerk Dresden; appl. 25.5.1987).

alternative synthesis of 3-amino-5-acetyl-10,11-dihydro-5*H*-dibenz[*b,f*]azepine:
US 3 056 774 (Geigy; 1962; appl. 1959; CH-prior. 1958).

Formulation(s):   f. c. tabl. 50 mg, 100 mg

Trade Name(s):
D: Bonnecor
      (Arzneimittelwerk
      Dresden; 1990); wfm

Tirilazad mesilate
(U-74006)

ATC: N07XX01
Use: lipid peroxidation inhibitor

RN: 110101-67-2   MF: $C_{38}H_{52}N_6O_2 \cdot CH_4O_3S$ MW: 720.98
CN: (16α)-21-[4-(2,6-di-1-pyrrolidinyl-4-pyrimidinyl)-1-piperazinyl]-16-methylpregna-1,4,9(11)-triene-3,20-dione monomethanesulfonate

hydrate
RN: 111793-42-1   MF: $C_{38}H_{52}N_6O_2 \cdot CH_4O_3S \cdot H_2O$ MW: 739.00
tirilazad
RN: 110101-66-1   MF: $C_{38}H_{52}N_6O_2$ MW: 624.87

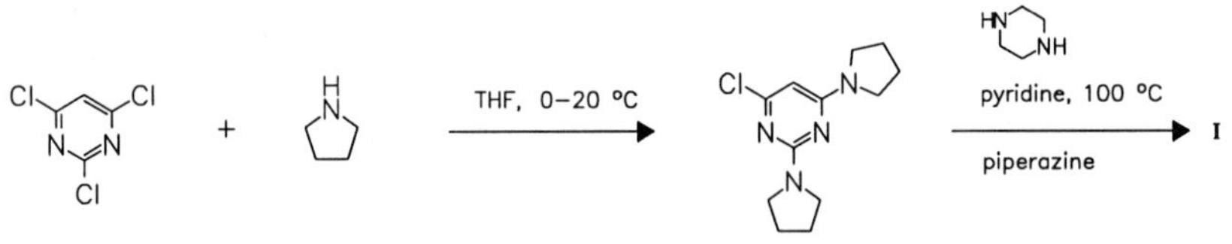

2,4,6-trichloro-   pyrrolidine   4-chloro-2,6-
pyrimidine   dipyrrolidino-
                                         pyrimidine

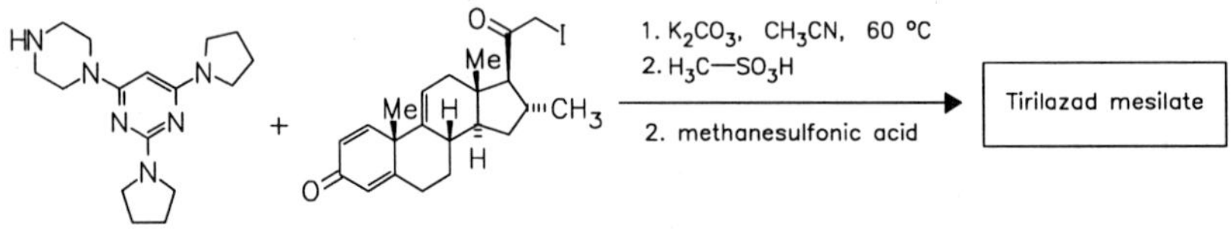

1-(2,6-dipyrrolidino-   21-iodo-16α-methyl-
4-pyrimidinyl)-   pregna-1,4,9(11)-
piperazine (I)   triene-3,20-dione

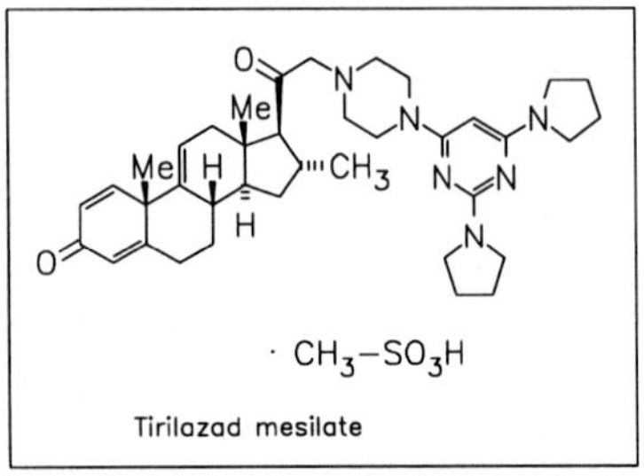

Tirilazad mesilate

Reference(s):
WO 8 701 706 (Upjohn Co.; appl. 28.8.1986; USA-prior. 29.7.1986, 12.9.1985).

use in the treatment of ischemic diseases:
WO 9 412 185 (Upjohn Co.; appl. 2.12.1993; J-prior. 3.12.1992).

use for chemotherapy:
WO 9 218 089 (Upjohn Co.; appl. 27.3.1992; USA-prior. 9.4.1991).

use for treatment ophthalmic disorders:
WO 9 119 482 (Upjohn Co.; appl. 26.12.1991; USA-prior. 12.6.1990).

Formulation(s):   amp. 45 mg/30 ml, 105 mg/70 ml; vial 45 mg, 105 mg (as hydrate)

Trade Name(s):
AU: Freedox (Pharmacia &
        Upjohn)

Tirofiban hydrochloride
(L 700462; MK 383)

ATC: B01AC17
Use: platelet aggregation inhibitor, GPIIb/
        IIIa receptor antagonist

RN: 142373-60-2   MF: $C_{22}H_{36}N_2O_5S \cdot HCl$ MW: 477.07
CN: *N*-(Butylsulfonyl)-*O*-[4-(4-piperidinyl)butyl]-L-tyrosine hydrochloride

monohydrate
RN: 150915-40-5   MF: $C_{22}H_{36}N_2O_5S \cdot HCl \cdot H_2O$ MW: 495.08
base
RN: 144494-65-5   MF: $C_{22}H_{36}N_2O_5S$ MW: 440.61

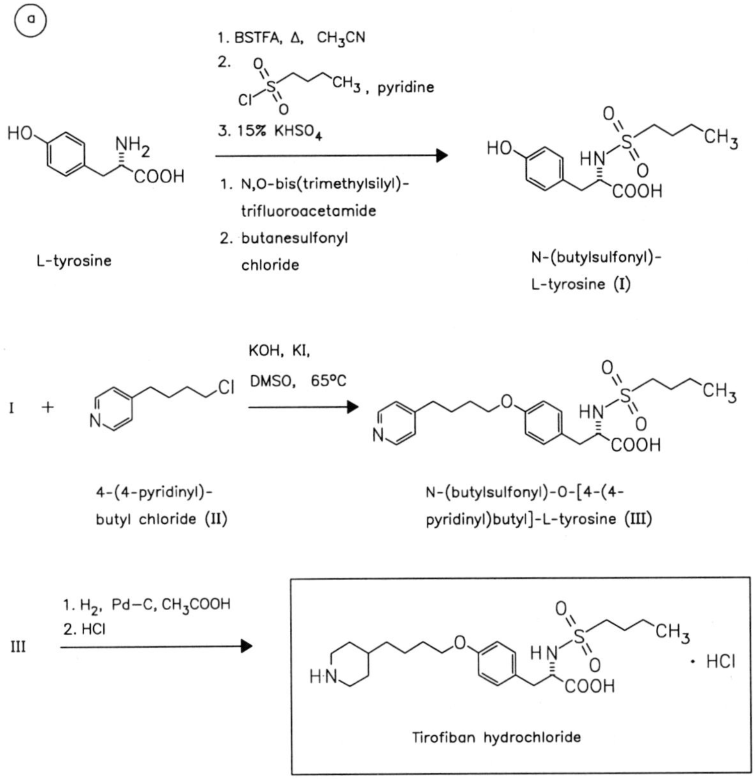

Tirofiban hydrochloride

aa) synthesis of intermediate II:

BuLi, THF

4-picoline

Br～～Cl , THF

3-bromo-1-chloro-
propane

II

b)

1. H₂, Pd–C, CH₃COOH
2. Boc–O–Boc , dioxane

4-pyridine-
acetic acid

COOH

N-(tert-butyloxy-
carbonyl)-4-pipe-
ridineacetic acid

BH₃, THF

IV

Boc:

1. (COCl)₂, DMSO
2.

N-(tert-butyloxy-
carbonyl)-4-pipe-
ridineethanol (IV)

1. oxalyl chloride
2. (methoxycarbonylmethylene)-
triphenylphosphorane

, CH₂Cl₂

methyl 4-[N-(tert-butyl-
oxycarbonyl)piperidin-4-yl]
but-2-enoate (V)

1. H₂, PdC,
ethyl acetate
2. NaOH
3. BH₃
4. PPh₃, CBr₄

V

4-[N-(tert-butyloxy-
carbonyl)piperidin-
4-yl]butyl bromide

Br

1. I
2. NaH, DMF
3. chromatography
4. HCl, ethyl acetate

Tirofiban hydrochloride

c)

4-pyridine-
butanol

OH   +   I

PPh₃, THF
(i–PrO₂CN)₂

III

1. H₂, Pd–C
2. HCl

Tirofiban hydrochloride

Reference(s):

a US 5 206 373 (Merck + Co.; 1.9.1993; USA-prior. 28.2.1992).
Chung, J.Y. et al.: Tetrahedron (TETRAB) **49** (26), 5767 (1993).
b EP 478 363 (Merck + Co.; appl. 27.9.1991; USA-prior. 30.8.1990).
Egbertson, M.S. et al.: J. Med. Chem. (JMCMAR) **37**, 2537 (1994).
c WO 9 316 994 (Merck + Co.; appl. 24.2.1993; USA-prior. 28.2.1992).

alternative synthesis:
US 5 292 756 (Merck + Co.; 8.3.1994; USA-prior. 30.8.1991, 27.9.1990).

pharmaceutical compositions:
US 5 733 919 (Merck + Co.; 31.3.1998; USA-prior. 23.10.1996).
WO 9 715 328 (Merck + Co.; appl. 23.10.1996; USA-prior. 27.10.1995).

Formulation(s): sol. for inj. 0.05 mg/ml, 0.25 mg/ml; vial 50 ml, 0,25 mg/ml

Trade Name(s):

D:	Aggrastat (Merck Sharp & Dohme; 1998)	USA:	Aggrastat (Merck Sharp & Dohme; 1998)

Tiropramide

ATC: A03AC05
Use: antispasmodic

RN: 55837-29-1 MF: $C_{28}H_{41}N_3O_3$ MW: 467.65
LD_{50}: 40.5 mg/kg (M, i.v.); 550 mg/kg (M, p.o.);
33.9 mg/kg (R, i.v.); 800 mg/kg (R, p.o.)
CN: (±)-α-(benzoylamino)-4-[2-(diethylamino)ethoxy]-*N*,*N*-dipropylbenzenepropanamide

hydrochloride
RN: 57227-16-4 MF: $C_{28}H_{41}N_3O_3 \cdot xHCl$ MW: unspecified EINECS: 260-634-0
LD_{50}: 28 mg/kg (M, i.v.); 639 mg/kg (M, p.o.);
32 mg/kg (R, i.v.); 1074 mg/kg (R, p.o.)

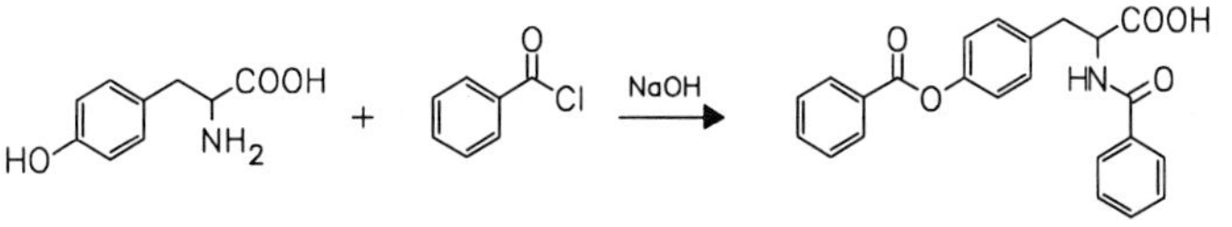
COOH
NH2
HO
O
Cl
NaOH
O
O
COOH
HN
O

DL-tyrosine benzoyl chloride (±)-O,N-dibenzoyltyrosine (I)

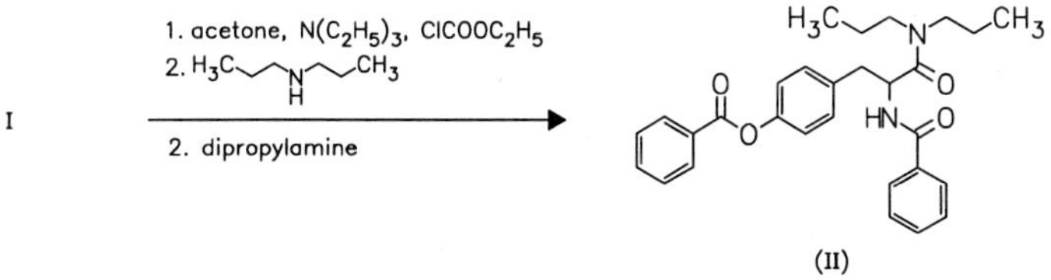
I
1. acetone, N(C2H5)3, ClCOOC2H5
2. H3C N CH3
H
2. dipropylamine
H3C N CH3
O
O
O
HN
O

(II)

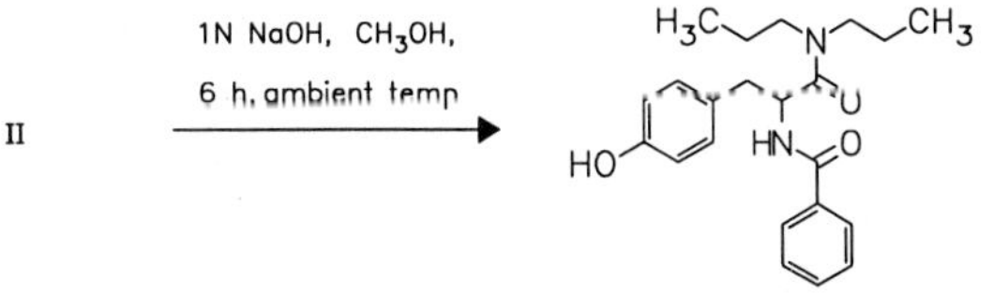
II
1N NaOH, CH3OH,
6 h, ambient temp
H3C N CH3
O
HO
HN
O

N-benzoyl-DL-tyrosine-dipropylamide (III)

III　+　2-diethylamino-ethyl chloride　→(NaOCH₃)→　Tiropramide

2-diethylamino-
ethyl chloride

Tiropramide

Reference(s):
DOS 2 503 992 (Rotta Research; appl. 31.1.1975; I-prior. 1.2.1974).
US 4 004 008 (Rotta Research; 18.1.1977; I-prior. 1.2.1974).

Formulation(s):　amp. 50 mg/3 ml; s. r. cps. 200 mg; suppos. 200 mg; tabl. 100 mg (as hydrochloride)

Trade Name(s):
D:　Alfospas (Opfermann)　　I:　Alfospas (Rottapharm)　　Maiorad (Rotta Research)

Tixocortol pivalate

(Tiocortisol pivalate; Tixocortol trimethylacetate)

ATC:　A07EA05; R01AD07
Use:　glucocorticoid

RN:　55560-96-8　MF: C₂₆H₃₈O₅S　MW: 462.65　EINECS: 259-706-4
CN:　(11β)-21-[(2,2-dimethyl-1-oxopropyl)thio]-11,17-dihydroxypregn-4-ene-3,20-dione

tixocortol
RN:　61951-99-3　MF: C₂₁H₃₀O₄S　MW: 378.53

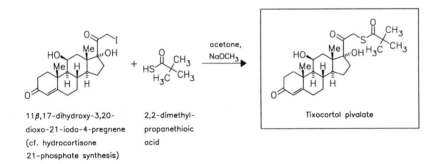

11β,17-dihydroxy-3,20-
dioxo-21-iodo-4-pregnene
(cf. hydrocortisone
21-phosphate synthesis)

2,2-dimethyl-
propanethioic
acid

Tixocortol pivalate

Reference(s):
DOS 2 357 778 (Jouveinal; appl. 20.11.1973; F-prior. 30.5.1973).

synthesis of tixocortol:
Schaub, R.E.; Weiss, M.J.: J. Org. Chem. (JOCEAH) **26**, 1223 (1961).

Formulation(s):　clysma 250 mg; nasal spray 1g/100 g; susp. 1 g/100 g

Trade Name(s):
D:　Tiovalon (Intersan; 1986);
　　wfm
F:　Dontopivalone (Jouveinal)-
　　comb.

Oropivalone-Bacitracine
(Jouveinal)-comb.
Pivalone Nasale (Jouveinal;
1978)

Pivalone Néomycine
(Jouveinal)-comb.
Rectovalone (Jouveinal)
Thiovalone (Eurorga)-
comb.

Tizanidine

ATC: M03BX02
Use: skeletal muscle relaxant

RN: 51322-75-9 MF: $C_9H_8ClN_5S$ MW: 253.72
LD$_{50}$: 235 mg/kg (M, p.o.);
        600 mg/kg (R, p.o.)
CN: 5-chloro-N-(4,5-dihydro-1H-imidazol-2-yl)-2,1,3-benzothiadiazol-4-amine

hydrochloride
RN: 64461-82-1 MF: $C_9H_8ClN_5S \cdot HCl$ MW: 290.18

4-chloro-1,2-
diaminobenzene

5-chloro-2,1,3-
benzothiadiazole

1. HNO$_3$, H$_2$SO$_4$
2. Fe, CH$_3$COOH

Cl$_2$CS
thiophosgene

5-chloro-4-
isothiocyanato-
2,1,3-benzo-
thiadiazole

ethylene-
diamine

Pb(OCOCH$_3$)$_2$
KOH

lead(II)
acetate

Tizanidine

Reference(s):
DE 2 322 880 (Sandoz; appl. 22.11.1973; prior. 7.5.1973).
US 3 843 668 (Sandoz; 22.10.1974; appl. 8.5.1973; CH-prior. 9.5.1972).
CH 579 565 (Sandoz; appl. 15.3.1973).

synthesis of 4-amino-5-chloro-2,1,3-benzothiadiazole:
Pesin, V.G.;. Khaletskil, A.M.: Zh. Obshch. Khim. (ZOKHA4) **27**, 2599 (1957).
C.A. (CHABA8) **52**, 7292.
Smith, W.T.; Chen, W.-Y.: J. Org. Chem. (JOCEAH) **27**, 676 (1962).

Formulation(s):   tabl. 2 mg, 4 mg, 6 mg (as hydrochloride)

Trade Name(s):
D: Sirdalud (Sanofi Winthrop;   GB: Zanaflex (Athena)   USA: Zanaflex (Athena)
      1985)   J: Teonelin (Sandoz)

Tobramycin

ATC: J01GB01; S01AA12
Use: antibiotic

RN: 32986-56-4 MF: $C_{18}H_{37}N_5O_9$ MW: 467.52 EINECS: 251-322-5
LD$_{50}$: 72.5 mg/kg (M, i.v.); >11500 mg/kg (M, p.o.);
        104 mg/kg (R, i.v.); >7500 mg/kg (R, p.o.)
CN: O-3-amino-3-deoxy-α-D-glucopyranosyl-(1→6)-O-[2,6-diamino-2,3,6-trideoxy-α-D-*ribo*-hexopyranosyl-
     (1→4)]-2-deoxy-D-streptamine

sulfate

RN: 49842-07-1 MF: $C_{18}H_{37}N_5O_9 \cdot xH_2SO_4$ MW: unspecified EINECS: 256-499-2

LD_{50}: 77 mg/kg (M, i.v.); >10500 mg/kg (M, p.o.);
126 mg/kg (R, i.v.)

(a) from fermentation solutions of Streptomyces tenebrarius (ATCC 17920) or (ATCC 17921)

(b)

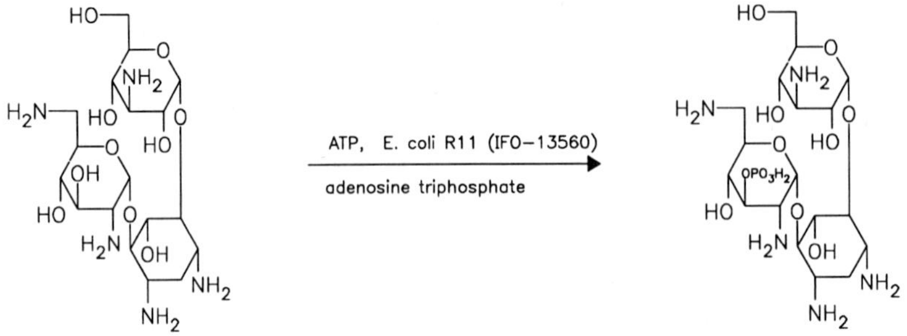
ATP, E. coli R11 (IFO-13560)
adenosine triphosphate

bekanamycin
(q. v.)

(I)

I

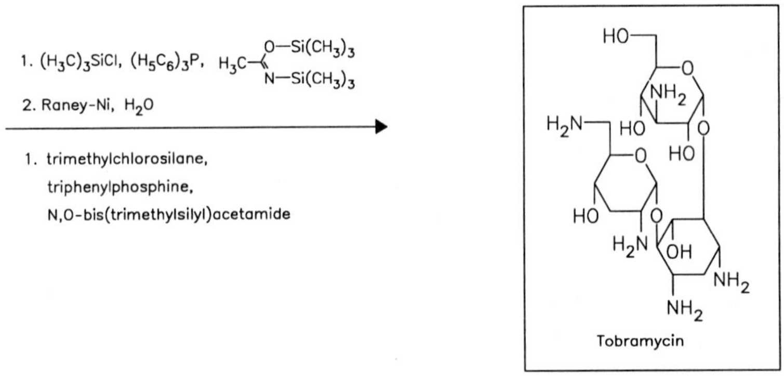
1. $(H_3C)_3SiCl$, $(H_5C_6)_3P$, $H_3C-C(=N-Si(CH_3)_3)-O-Si(CH_3)_3$
2. Raney-Ni, H_2O
1. trimethylchlorosilane,
triphenylphosphine,
N,O-bis(trimethylsilyl)acetamide
Tobramycin

Reference(s):

a US 3 691 279 (Lilly; 12.9.1972; prior. 15.4.1970, 12.2.1969, 17.9.1965).
DE 1 792 819 (Lilly).

b DOS 2 514 985 (Takeda; appl. 5.4.1975; J-prior. 10.4.1974, 25.6.1974).
Okutani, T. et al.: J. Am. Chem. Soc. (JACSAT) **99**, 1278 (1977).

alternative syntheses:

DOS 2 361 159 (Zaidan Hojin Biseibutsu Kagaku Kenkyu Kai; appl. 7.12.1973; J-prior. 8.12.1972).
DOS 2 533 985 (Meiji Seika Kaisha; appl. 30.7.1975; J-prior. 1.8.1974).
Tagaki, Y. et al.: J. Antibiot. (JANTAJ) **26**, 403 (1973).

total synthesis:

Tanabe, M. et al.: Tetrahedron Lett. (TELEAY) **1977**, 3607.

Formulation(s): amp. 40 mg, 80 mg (as sulfate); eye drops 3 mg/ml; ointment 3 mg/g; vial 20 mg, 40 mg, 80 mg (as sulfate)

D: Burlamycin (medphano)   Tobrex (Alcon)   J: Tobracin (Shionogi
      Gernebcin (Lilly; 1975)   GB: Nebcin (King)   Seiyaku)
      TOBRA-cell (cell pharm)   I: Nebicina (Lilly)   USA: Nebcin (Lilly; 1975)
      Tobramaxin (Alcon; 1982)   Tobrex (Firma)   TobraDex (Alcon)
F: Nebcine (Lilly)   Tobrex (Alcon)

Tocainide

ATC: C01BB03
Use: antiarrhythmic

RN: 41708-72-9   MF: $C_{11}H_{16}N_2O$ MW: 192.26   EINECS: 255-505-0
LD_{50}:   94 mg/kg (M, i.v.)
CN: 2-amino-N-(2,6-dimethylphenyl)propanamide

2,6-dimethyl-   2-bromo-   Tocainide
aniline   propionyl
                   bromide

Reference(s):
US 4 218 477 (Astra; 19.8.1980; prior. 28.7.1971).
US 4 237 068 (Astra; 2.12.1980; prior. 8.1.1973).
DE 2 235 745 (Astra; appl. 21.7.1972; USA-prior. 28.7.1971).

enantiomers:
DOS 2 400 540 (Astra; appl. 7.1.1974; USA-prior. 8.1.1973).
GB 1 461 602 (Astra; appl. 7.1.1974; USA-prior. 8.1.1973).

Formulation(s):   f. c. tabl. 400 mg, 600 mg (as hydrochloride)

Trade Name(s):
D: Xylotocan (Astra; 1982)   GB: Tonocard (Astra; 1981);   USA: Tonocard (Astra Merck;
                                            wfm   1984)

α-Tocopherol
(Vitamin E)

ATC: A11HA03
Use: antisterility vitamin

RN: 10191-41-0   MF: $C_{29}H_{50}O_2$ MW: 430.72   EINECS: 233-466-0
CN: 3,4 dihydro-2,5,7,8-tetramethyl-2-(4,8,12-trimethyltridecyl)-2H-1-benzopyran-6-ol

D-compound
RN: 59-02-9   MF: $C_{29}H_{50}O_2$ MW: 430.72   EINECS: 200-412-2

α-Tocopherol acetate
(Vitamin E acetate)

RN: 7695-91-2   MF: $C_{31}H_{52}O_3$ MW: 472.75   EINECS: 231-710-0
CN: 3,4-dihydro-2,5,7,8-tetramethyl-2-(4,8,12-trimethyltridecyl)-2H-1-benzopyran-6-ol acetate
D-6-acetate
RN: 58-95-7   MF: $C_{31}H_{52}O_3$ MW: 472.75   EINECS: 200-405-4

a

total synthesis

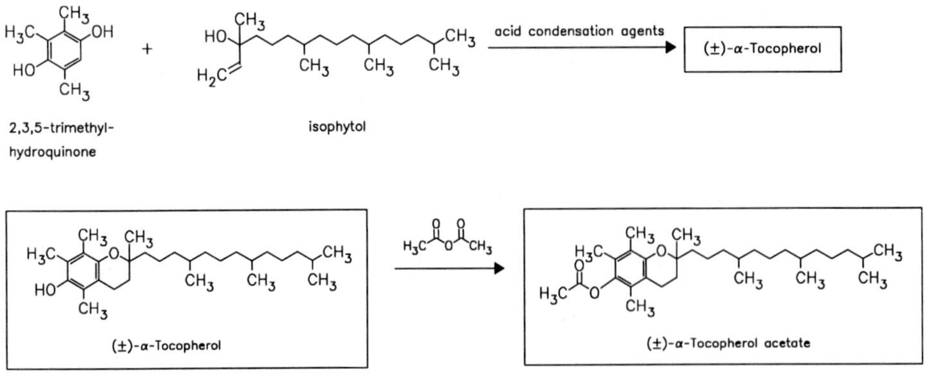

2,3,5-trimethyl-
hydroquinone

isophytol

acid condensation agents → (±)-α-Tocopherol

(±)-α-Tocopherol

(±)-α-Tocopherol acetate

b

partial synthesis
(from β-, γ-, and δ-tocopherols, occurring in vegetable oils together with
α-tocopherol), e.g. from γ-tocopherol

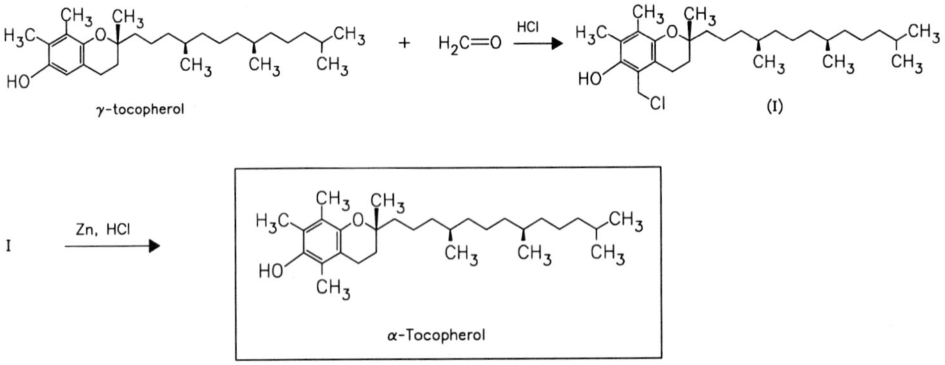

γ-tocopherol

(I)

I　Zn, HCl →

α-Tocopherol

Reference(s):

a　DRP 713 749 (Roche; appl. 1939; CH-prior. 1938).
　　DRP 731 972 (Roche; appl. 1938; CH-prior. 1938).
　　DE 960 720 (Roche; appl. 1955; USA-prior. 1954).
　　DAS 1 909 164 (Roche; appl. 24.2.1969; USA-prior. 27.2.1968, 19.11.1968).
　　DAS 2 208 795 (Diamond Shamrock; appl. 24.2.1972; USA-prior. 25.2.1971).
　　DOS 2 743 920 (Nisshin Flour Milling; appl. 29.9.1977; J-prior. 29.9.1976).
　　US 4 055 575 (SCM Corp.; 25.10.1977; prior. 20.3.1975).
　　US 4 115 466 (SCM Corp.; 19.9.1978; prior. 20.3.1975, 16.10.1975, 6.10.1977).
b　US 2 519 863 (Eastman Kodak; 1950; appl. 1949).
　　DE 909 095 (Eastman Kodak; appl. 1950; USA-prior. 1946).
　　DE 911 732 (Eastman Kodak; appl. 1950; USA-prior. 1945).
　　DE 1 056 143 (Eastman Kodak; appl. 1956; USA-prior. 1955).
　　US 2 592 531 (Eastman Kodak; 1952; appl. 1949).
　　US 2 592 628 (Eastman Kodak; 1952; appl. 1949).
　　US 2 592 630 (Eastman Kodak; 1952; appl. 1949).
　　US 4 122 094 (Lever Brothers; 24.10.1978; prior. 9.6.1976, 13.5.1977).
　　DOS 2 606 830 (BASF; appl. 20.2.1976).

Formulation(s):   amp. 100 mg/2 ml, 100 mg/ml; cps. 100 iu, 200 iu, 300 iu, 400 iu, 500 iu; drg. 100 mg (as tartrate)

Trade Name(s):

D: Biopto-E (Jenapharm)
      Equiday (Solvay
      Arzneimittel)
      Evit-Geritan (Chefaro)
      Malton-E (Sertürner)
      Optovit/-forte/fortissimum
      (Hermes)
      Pexan (Wörwag)
      Puncto E (ASTA Medica
      AWD)
      Tocorell (Sanorell)
      Vitamin E-Dragees
      (Wiedemann)
      Vit. E Stada (Stada)
      numerous combination
      preparations
F: Alvity (Solvay Pharma)-
      comb.
      Capsules Pharmaton
      (Boehringer Ing.)-comb.
      Carencyl (Riom)-comb.
      Cirkan suppositoires
      (Sinbio)-comb.
      Difrarel E (Leurquin)-
      comb.
      Hydrosol polyvitaminé
      B.O.N. (Doms-Adrian)-
      comb.

Hydrosol polyvitaminé
Roche (Roche)-comb.
Lofenalac Mead Johnson
(Bristol-Myers Squibb)-
comb.
Nutrigéne (GNR-pharma)-
comb.
Survitine (Roche
Nicholas)-comb.
Toco 500 (Pharma 2000)
Tocogestan (Théramex)-
comb.
Tocomine (Eurorga)
Uvéstérol (Crinex)-comb.
Véliten (Wyeth-Lederle)-
comb.
Vivamyne (Whitehall)-
comb.
numerous combination
preparations
GB: Ketovite (Paines & Byrne)-
      comb.
I: E-Vitum (Lipha)
      Ephynal (Roche)
      Evion (Bracco)
      Evion Forte (Bracco)
      Evitina (CT)
      Midium (Teofarma)-comb.
      Rovigon (Roche)-comb.

Salonpas (Farmila)-comb.
Tocalfa (ASTA Medica)-
comb.
J: Ephelon (Kowa)
      Ephynal (Roche)
      Eseblon (Seiko-Fuso)
      Esuverol (Sanko)
      Euvel (Nippon Chemiphar)
      Inazin (Tanabe)
      Ivet (Kuroishi-Nippon
      Shinyaku)
      Juvelux (Eisai)
      Juvevitan (Toyo Jozo)
      Kenton (Sawai)
      Magiron E (Choseido)
      Nichivita E (Nichiiko)
      Sunfull S (Maruishi)
      Takaron (Shiki)
      Tocophal (Chugai)
      Tocorol (Daigo Eiyo)
      Tokobera (Nakano)
      Tokos-E (Nippon Shoji)
      Welvin-E (Ono)
      Yurica (Kobayashi Kako)
USA: Cefol (Abbott)-comb.
      Materna (Lederle)-comb.
      Megadose (Arco)-comb.
      combination preparations
      and generics

Todralazine

(Ecarazine)

ATC: C02
Use: antihypertensive

RN: 14679-73-3   MF: $C_{11}H_{12}N_4O_2$ MW: 232.24
LD_{50}:   60 mg/kg (M, i.v.);
      110 mg/kg (R, i.v.); 318 mg/kg (R, p.o.)
CN: 2-(1-phthalazinyl)hydrazinecarboxylic acid ethyl ester

monohydrochloride
RN: 3778-76-5   MF: $C_{11}H_{12}N_4O_2 \cdot HCl$ MW: 268.70
LD_{50}:   300 mg/kg (M, i.v.), 516 mg/kg (M, p.o.);
      240 mg/kg (R, i.v.); 598 mg/kg (R, p.o.)

hydralazine   ethyl chloro-   Todralazine
(q. v.)   formate

Reference(s):
BE 647 722 (Polfa; appl. 11.5.1964; P-prior. 11.5.1963, 9.12.1963).

Formulation(s):   powder 10 % (as hydrochloride); tabl. 10 mg, 30 mg

Trade Name(s):
J: Aperdor (Tokyo Tanabe)   Dypirecohl (Daito Koeki)   Hydrapron (Isei)
     Apiracohl (Kyowa)   Ecara (Toyo Pharmar)   Marukunan (Zensei)
     Atapren (Sumitomo)   Ecarocohl (Nihon   Mohazorin (Mohan)
     Bihyst (Ohta)   Iyakuhin)   Seirof (Maruko)
     Deprezid (Ono)   Ekahain (Towa)

Tofenacin

ATC: N04; N06A
Use: antiparkinsonian, antidepressant

RN: 15301-93-6   MF: $C_{17}H_{21}NO$ MW: 255.36   EINECS: 239-338-0
CN: N-methyl-2-[(2-methylphenyl)phenylmethoxy]ethanamine

hydrochloride
RN: 10488-36-5   MF: $C_{17}H_{21}NO \cdot HCl$ MW: 291.82   EINECS: 234-011-9
LD_{50}:   32 mg/kg (M, i.v.); 182 mg/kg (M, p.o.);
       15 mg/kg (R, i.v.); 400 mg/kg (R, p.o.);
       90 mg/kg (dog, p.o.)

Reference(s):
US 3 407 258 (Brocades-Stheeman; 22.10.1968; GB-prior. 30.11.1962).

Trade Name(s):
GB: Elamol (Brocades); wfm

Tofisopam

ATC: N05BA23
Use: tranquilizer, anxiolytic

RN: 22345-47-7 MF: $C_{22}H_{26}N_2O_4$ MW: 382.46 EINECS: 244-922-3
LD_{50}: 415 mg/kg (M, i.v.); 3800 mg/kg (M, p.o.);
103 mg/kg (R, i.v.); 825 mg/kg (R, p.o.)
CN: 1-(3,4-dimethoxyphenyl)-5-ethyl-7,8-dimethoxy-4-methyl-5*H*-2,3-benzodiazepine

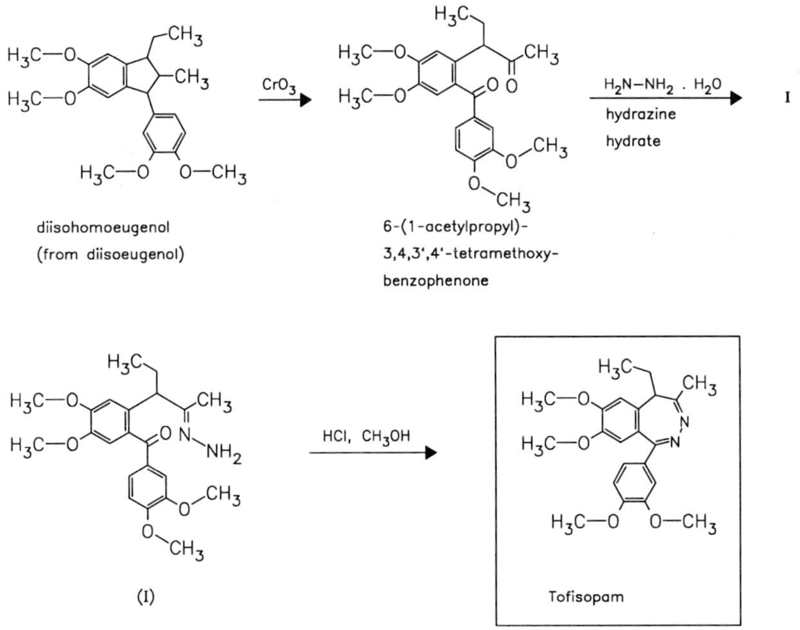
CrO3
H2N–NH2 . H2O
hydrazine
hydrate
diisohomoeugenol
(from diisoeugenol)
6-(1-acetylpropyl)-
3,4,3',4'-tetramethoxy-
benzophenone
HCl, CH3OH
(I)
Tofisopam

Reference(s):
DAS 1 670 642 (Egyt; appl. 8.12.1967; H-prior. 9.12.1966).

educt:
Doering, W. v. E.; Berson, J.A.: J. Am. Chem. Soc. (JACSAT) **72**, 1118 (1950).

Formulation(s): tabl. 50 mg

Trade Name(s):
F: Grandaxine (Ozothine); wfm
Seriel (Sinbio); wfm
J: Grandaxin (Mochida)

Tolazamide

ATC: A10BB05
Use: antidiabetic

RN: 1156-19-0 MF: $C_{14}H_{21}N_3O_3S$ MW: 311.41 EINECS: 214-588-3
LD_{50}: 1 g/kg (M, p.o.);
>5 g/kg (R, p.o.)
CN: *N*-[[(hexahydro-1*H*-azepin-1-yl)amino]carbonyl]-4-methylbenzenesulfonamide

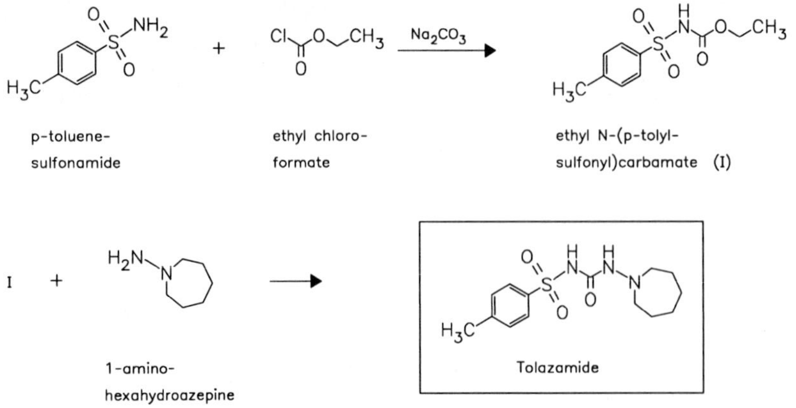

p-toluene-
sulfonamide

ethyl chloro-
formate

ethyl N-(p-tolyl-
sulfonyl)carbamate (I)

1-amino-
hexahydroazepine

Tolazamide

Reference(s):
US 3 063 903 (Upjohn; 13.11.1962; appl. 29.3.1961; prior. 9.6.1959).
GB 887 886 (Upjohn; appl. 29.9.1960).
DE 1 196 200 (Hoechst; appl. 27.12.1961).
Wright, J.B.; Willette, R.E.: J. Med. Chem. (JMCMAR) **5**, 815 (1962).

Formulation(s):　　tabl. 250 mg, 500 mg

Trade Name(s):
D:　　Norglycin (Upjohn); wfm
GB:　　Tolanase (Pharmacia & Upjohn)
I:　　Diabewas (IBI); wfm
　　Diabewas (Wassermann); wfm
J:　　Tolinase (Upjohn)
USA:　　Tolazamide (Mylan)
　　Tolinase (Upjohn); wfm

Tolazoline

ATC:　　C04AB02; M02AX02
Use:　　vasodilator, antiadrenergic

RN:　　59-98-3　MF: $C_{10}H_{12}N_2$　MW: 160.22　EINECS: 200-448-9
LD_{50}:　40 mg/kg (M, i.v.); 350 mg/kg (M, p.o.)
CN:　　4,5-dihydro-2-(phenylmethyl)-1*H*-imidazole

monohydrochloride
RN:　　59-97-2　MF: $C_{10}H_{12}N_2 \cdot HCl$　MW: 196.68　EINECS: 200-447-3
LD_{50}:　56.7 mg/kg (M, i.v.); 400 mg/kg (M, p.o.);
　　85 mg/kg (R, i.v.); 1200 mg/kg (R, p.o.)

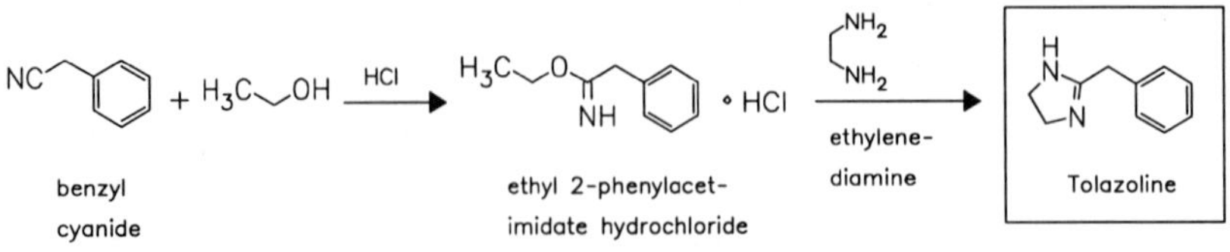

benzyl
cyanide

ethyl 2-phenylacet-
imidate hydrochloride

ethylene-
diamine

Tolazoline

Reference(s):
US 2 161 938 (Ciba; 1939; D-prior. 1934).
DRP 615 227 (A. Sonn; 1934).

alternative syntheses:
DRP 687 196 (Ciba; appl. 1938; CH-prior. 1937).
DE 842 063 (Ciba; CH-prior. 1945).

Formulation(s):   amp. 10 mg/ml

Trade Name(s):

D:	Priscol (CIBA Vision)	J:	Benzolin(Nissin)	USA: Priscoline (Ciba); wfm
GB:	Priscol (Ciba); wfm		Imidalin (Yamanouchi)	
I:	Priscofen (Ciba)-comb.;		Priscol (Ciba-Geigy-	
	wfm		Takeda)	

Tolbutamide

ATC: A10BB03; V04CA01
Use: antidiabetic

RN: 64-77-7   MF: $C_{12}H_{18}N_2O_3S$ MW: 270.35   EINECS: 200-594-3
LD_{50}:   770 mg/kg (M, i.v.); 490 mg/kg (M, p.o.);
      700 mg/kg (R, i.v.); 2490 mg/kg (R, p.o.)
CN: *N*-[(butylamino)carbonyl]-4-methylbenzenesulfonamide

p-toluenesulfonamide   butyl isocyanate   Tolbutamide
sodium salt

Reference(s):
US 2 968 158 (Hoechst; Upjohn; 17.1.1961; D-prior. 8.8.1955).
DE 974 062 (Hoechst; appl. 9.8.1955).

alternative method:
DAS 2 053 740 (Brunnengraber; appl. 2.11.1970).
Ruschig, H. et al.: Arzneim.-Forsch. (ARZNAD) **8**, 448 (1958).

Formulation(s):   tabl. 500 mg, 1 g

Trade Name(s):

D:	Artosin (Boehringer	GB:	Rastinon (Hoechst)		Nigloid (Universal)
	Mannh.)	I:	Glucosulfa (Lipha)-comb.		Rankmin (Maruishi)
	Orabet (Berlin-Chemie)	J:	Abeformin T (Maruko)		Rastinon (Hoechst)
	Rastinon (Hoechst)		Diabex-T (Funai)		Unimide 500 (Sanko)
	Tolbutamid R.A.N.		Dibetos (Kodama)		Urerubon (Seiko)
	(R.A.N.)		Insilange-D (Horita)	USA:	Tolbutamide Tablets
F:	Dolipol (Hoechst)		Mellitos D (Ono)		(Mylan)

Tolcapone

(Ro-40-7592)

ATC: N04BX01
Use: antiparkinsonian, COMT inhibitor

RN: 134308-13-7   MF: $C_{14}H_{11}NO_5$ MW: 273.24
CN: (3,4-Dihydroxy-5-nitrophenyl)(4-methylphenyl)methanone

a

4-bromotoluene + 4-benzyloxy-3-methoxy-benzaldehyde → (BuLi, THF) → 4-benzyloxy-3-methoxy-4'-methylbenzhydrol (I)

| 4-bromotoluene | 4-benzyloxy-3-methoxy-
benzaldehyde | 4-benzyloxy-3-methoxy-
4'-methylbenzhydrol (I) |

I → [1. pyridinium · ClCrO$_3$H, CH$_2$Cl$_2$; 2. HBr, CH$_3$COOH; 1. pyridinium chlorochromate] → 4-hydroxy-3-methoxy-4'-methylbenzophenone (II) → [1. HNO$_3$, CH$_3$COOH; 2. HBr, CH$_3$COOH] → Tolcapone

4-hydroxy-3-methoxy-
4'-methylbenzophenone (II)

Tolcapone

b

veratrole + p-methyl-benzoyl chloride → (AlCl$_3$, CH$_2$Cl$_2$) → II → (HNO$_3$) → III

| veratrole | p-methyl-
benzoyl chloride |

→ (AlCl$_3$, N(C$_2$H$_5$)$_3$, CH$_2$Cl$_2$) → Tolcapone

4-hydroxy-3-methoxy-4'-
methyl-5-nitrobenzophenone (III)

Reference(s):
a EP 237 929 (Hoffmann-La Roche; appl. 11.3.1987; CH-prior. 11.3.1986; 9.1.1987).
b EP 855 379 (Hoffmann-La Roche; appl. 15.1.1998; EP-prior. 22.1.1997).

process for the manufacture of a powdery preparation:
WO 9 816 204 (Hoffmann-La Roche; appl. 13.10.1997; EP-prior. 14.10.1996; CH-prior. 25.11.1996).

pharmaceutical composition for treating Parkinsons's disease:
WO 9 831 355 (Britannia Pharm.; appl. 14.1.1998; GB-prior. 16.1.1997).

Formulation(s):   tabl. 100 mg, 200 mg

Trade Name(s):
| D: | Tasmar (Hoffmann-La
Roche; 1997); wfm | GB:
I: | Tasmar (Roche); wfm
Tasmar (Roche); wfm | USA: | Tasmar (Roche; 1998);
wfm |

Tolfenamic acid

ATC: M01AG02
Use: anti-inflammatory, analgesic

RN: 13710-19-5   MF: C$_{14}$H$_{12}$ClNO$_2$ MW: 261.71   EINECS: 237-264-3
LD$_{50}$:   280 mg/kg (M, p.o.);
225 mg/kg (R, p.o.)
CN: 3-[(3-chloro-2-methylphenyl)amino]benzoic acid

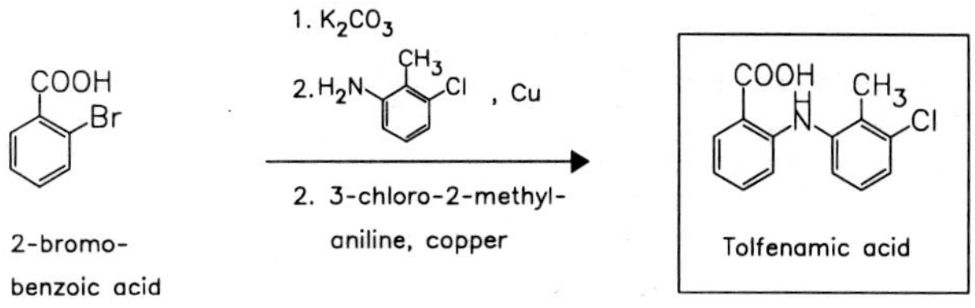

2-bromo-
benzoic acid

2. 3-chloro-2-methyl-
aniline, copper

Tolfenamic acid

Reference(s):
US 3 313 848 (Parke Davis; 11.4.1967; prior. 18.6.1964).

Formulation(s):   cps. 100 mg, 200 mg; s. r. tabl. 300 mg

Trade Name(s):
J: Clotam (Tobishi Shingaku).

Toliprolol

ATC: C07AA
Use: antiarrhythmic, antihypertensive, antianginal

RN: 2933-94-0   MF: $C_{13}H_{21}NO_2$ MW: 223.32   EINECS: 220-905-6
LD_{50}:   28.2 mg/kg (M, i.v.)
CN: 1-[(1-methylethyl)amino]-3-(3-methylphenoxy)-2-propanol

hydrochloride
RN: 306-11-6   MF: $C_{13}H_{21}NO_2 \cdot HCl$ MW: 259.78   EINECS: 206-177-2
LD_{50}:   40 mg/kg (M, i.v.)

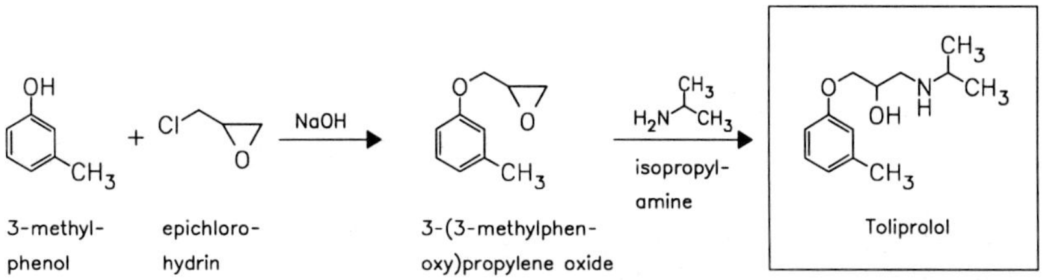

3-methyl-
phenol

epichloro-
hydrin

3-(3-methylphen-
oxy)propylene oxide

isopropyl-
amine

Toliprolol

Reference(s):
DOS 1 493 454 (Boehringer Ing.; appl. 26.8.1963).
NL-appl. 6 409 883 (Boehringer Ing.; appl. 26.8.1963).

Formulation(s):   tabl. 10 mg, 50 mg

Trade Name(s):
D: Doberol (Boehringer Ing.);
       wfm

Tolmetin

ATC: M01AB03; M02AA21
Use: anti-inflammatory

RN: 26171-23-3   MF: $C_{15}H_{15}NO_3$ MW: 257.29   EINECS: 247-497-2
LD_{50}:   680 mg/kg (M, i.v.); 914 mg/kg (M, p.o.);
       293 mg/kg (R, p.o.)
CN: 1-methyl-5-(4-methylbenzoyl)-1H-pyrrole-2-acetic acid

sodium salt

RN: 35711-34-3 MF: $C_{15}H_{14}NNaO_3$ MW: 279.27 EINECS: 252-687-3

LD_{50}: >622 mg/kg (M, i.v.); 899 mg/kg (M, p.o.);
>724 mg/kg (R, i.v.); 914 mg/kg (R, p.o.);
>800 mg/kg (dog, p.o.)

sodium salt dihydrate

RN: 64490-92-2 MF: $C_{15}H_{14}NNaO_3 \cdot 2H_2O$ MW: 315.30

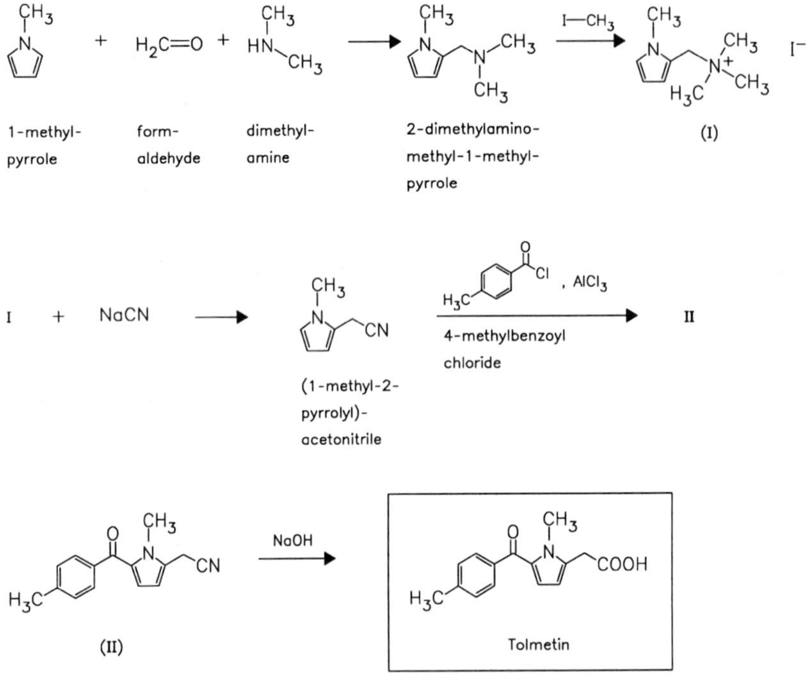

1-methyl-
pyrrole

form-
aldehyde

dimethyl-
amine

2-dimethylamino-
methyl-1-methyl-
pyrrole

(I)

(1-methyl-2-
pyrrolyl)-
acetonitrile

4-methylbenzoyl
chloride

(II)

Tolmetin

Reference(s):

US 3 752 826 (McNeil; 14.8.1973; prior. 26.7.1967, 1.7.1968).
DAS 1 770 984 (McNeil; appl. 25.7.1968; USA-prior. 26.7.1967, 1.7.1968).
Carson, J.R. et al.: J. Med. Chem. (JMCMAR) **14**, 646 (1971).
GB 1 428 272 (McNeil; appl. 12.7.1973; USA-prior. 3.8.1972).
DOS 2 102 746 (McNeil; appl. 21.1.1971; USA-prior. 26.1.1970).
DOS 2 339 140 (McNeil; appl. 2.8.1973; USA-prior. 3.8.1972).

Friedel-Crafts-synthesis without use of $AlCl_3$:
DAS 2 511 256 (Ethyl Corp.; appl. 14.3.1975; USA-prior. 18.3.1974).
GB 1 503 205 (Ethyl Corp.; appl. 19.5.1975; USA-prior. 17.6.1974).
GB 1 503 221 (Ethyl Corp.; appl. 6.3.1975; USA-prior. 18.3.1974).
GB 1 503 222 (Ethyl Corp.; appl. 6.3.1975; USA-prior. 18.3.1974).

alternative syntheses:
US 4 111 954 (McNeil; 5.9.1978; prior. 20.4.1977).
US 4 119 639 (McNeil; 10.10.1978; appl. 27.6.1977).
US 4 125 537 (McNeil; 14.11.1978; appl. 7.2.1977).
DOS 2 552 975 (Sagami; appl. 7.12.1978; J-prior. 8.12.1977).
ES 456 334 (Lab. Estedi S. L.; appl. 26.2.1977).

combination with acetaminophen or acetylsalicylic acid:
US 4 132 788 (McNeil; 2.1.1979; prior. 4.5.1976).

Formulation(s): cps. 200 mg, 400 mg; tabl. 200 mg, 600 mg (as sodium salt)

Trade Name(s):

D: Tolectin (Cilag-Chemie; 1977); wfm
GB: Tolectin (Ortho; 1979); wfm
I: Index (Edmond); wfm

Reutol (Errekappa Euroter.); wfm
Tolectin (Cilag); wfm
Tolectin (Cilag-Chemie); wfm

J: Tolmex (Biopharma); wfm
      Tolectin (Dainippon)
USA: Tolectin (Ortho-McNeil; 1976)

Tolnaftate

ATC: D01AE18
Use: antimycotic, fungicide

RN: 2398-96-1   MF: C$_{19}$H$_{17}$NOS   MW: 307.42   EINECS: 219-266-6
LD$_{50}$: 4800 mg/kg (M, i.v.); 10 g/kg (M, p.o.);
        >6 g/kg (R, p.o.);
        >14 g/kg (dog, p.o.)
CN: methyl (3-methylphenyl)carbamothioic acid O-2-naphthalenyl ester

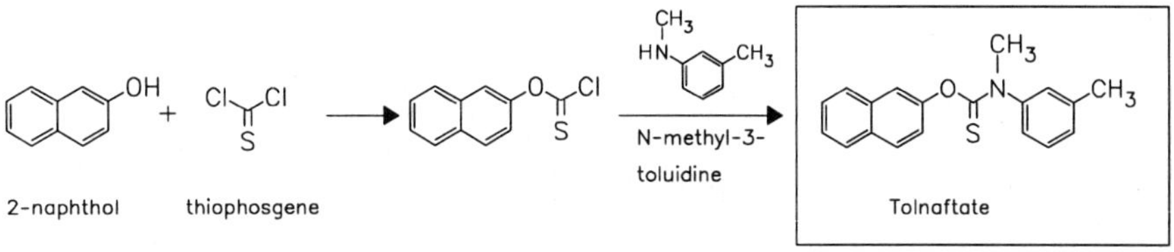

2-naphthol   thiophosgene   N-methyl-3-toluidine   Tolnaftate

Reference(s):

US 3 334 126 (Nippon Soda; 1.8.1967; J-prior. 21.6.1961, 25.8.1961, 9.4.1962, 13.4.1962).
GB 967 897 (Nippon Soda; appl. 31.5.1962; J-prior. 21.6.1961, 25.8.1961, 9.4.1962, 13.4.1962).

Formulation(s):   cream 10 mg/g; powder 5 mg/g; sol. 10 mg/ml

Trade Name(s):

D: Sorgoa (Scheurich)
      Tinatox (Brenner-Efeka)
      Tolnaftat (Pharma Wernigerode)
      Tonoftal (Essex Pharma)

F: Sporiline (Schering-Plough)
GB: Tinaderm-M (Schering-Plough)
I: Tinaderm (Schering-Plough)

J: Alarzin "Strong" (Yamanouchi)
      Hi-Alarzin (Yamanouchi)-comb.
      Separin T (Sumitomo)
USA: Tinactin (Schering); wfm

Tolonidine

ATC: C02AC04
Use: antihypertensive

RN: 4201-22-3   MF: C$_{10}$H$_{12}$ClN$_3$ MW: 209.68
CN: N-(2-chloro-4-methylphenyl)-4,5-dihydro 1H imidazol-2-amine

nitrate
RN: 4201-23-4   MF: C$_{10}$H$_{12}$ClN$_3$ · xHNO$_3$ MW: unspecified   EINECS: 224-105-8

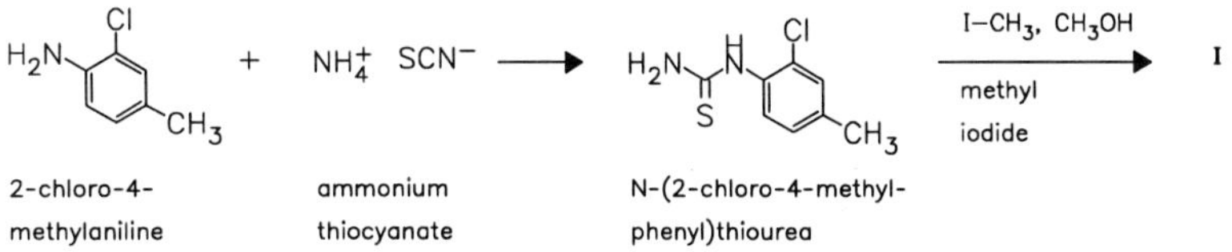

2-chloro-4-methylaniline   ammonium thiocyanate   N-(2-chloro-4-methylphenyl)thiourea

(I) + ethylene-diamine → Tolonidine

Reference(s):
GB 1 034 938 (Boehringer Ing.; valid from 28.9.1964; D-prior. 4.10.1963).
(also further methods)

Formulation(s):   vial 0.5 mg/ml (as nitrate)

Trade Name(s):
F: Euctan (Delalande); wfm

Toloxatone

ATC: N06AG03
Use: antidepressant, monoaminoxidase inhibitor

RN: 29218-27-7   MF: C$_{11}$H$_{13}$NO$_3$ MW: 207.23   EINECS: 249-522-2
LD$_{50}$:   1300 mg/kg (M, p.o.);
    1225 mg/kg (R, p.o.)
CN: 5-(hydroxymethyl)-3-(3-methylphenyl)-2-oxazolidinone

m-toluidine + glycide → 3-(m-toluidino)-1,2-propanediol (I)

I + diethyl carbonate →(NaOCH$_3$)→ Toloxatone

Reference(s):
DOS 2 011 333 (Delalande; appl. 10.3.1970; GB-prior. 18.3.1969).
DOS 2 012 120 (Delalande; appl. 13.13.1970; GB-prior. 18.3.1969).
Fauvan, C.; Douzon, C.: Chim. Ther. (CHTPBA) 3, 324 (1973).

Formulation(s):   cps. 200 mg

Trade Name(s):
F: Humoryl (Synthélabo; 1985)
I: Umoril (Synthelabo)

Tolperisone

ATC: M03BX04
Use: vasodilator, antispasmodic, skeletal
muscle relaxant

RN: 728-88-1   MF: $C_{16}H_{23}NO$ MW: 245.37   EINECS: 222-876-5
CN: 2-methyl-1-(4-methylphenyl)-3-(1-piperidinyl)-1-propanone

hydrochloride
RN: 3644-61-9   MF: $C_{16}H_{23}NO \cdot HCl$ MW: 281.83
LD_{50}:   34 mg/kg (M, i.v.); 358 mg/kg (M, p.o.);
1450 mg/kg (R, p.o.);
45 mg/kg (dog, i.v.)

4'-methylpropio-   paraform-   piperidine
phenone   aldehyde   hydrochloride

Tolperisone

Reference(s):
JP 203 90/65 (Eisai; appl. 4.11.1961).
Ruddy, A.W.; Buckley, J.S.: J. Am. Chem. Soc. (JACSAT) **72**, 718 (1950).

injection solution:
DOS 2 362 337 (Gedeon Richter; appl. 14.12.1973; H-prior. 15.1.1973).

Formulation(s):   amp. 100 mg; drg. 50 mg, 150 mg; tabl. 50 mg, 100 mg, 500 mg (as hydrochloride)

Trade Name(s):
D: Mydocalm (Strathmann)
F: Mydocalm (Richter); wfm
J: Abbsa (Sanko)
Atmosgen (Maruko)
Besnoline (Kotobuki-
Kanebo)

Kineore (Showa)
Lasmon (Tanabe)
Magnine (Toyo)
Menopatol (Nippon
Chemiphar)
Muscalm (Nippon Kayaku)

Nichiperizone (Nissin)
Roystajin (Zensei)
Sinorum (Towa)

Tolpropamine

ATC: D04AA12
Use: antihistaminic, antiallergic

RN: 5632-44-0   MF: $C_{18}H_{23}N$ MW: 253.39   EINECS: 227-071-2
CN: *N,N*,4-trimethyl-γ-phenylbenzenepropanamine

hydrochloride
RN: 3339-11-5   MF: $C_{18}H_{23}N \cdot HCl$ MW: 289.85   EINECS: 222-082-9

aceto-   paraform-   dimethyl-   3-dimethylamino-
phenone   aldehyde   amine   propiophenone

4-tolylmagnesium
bromide

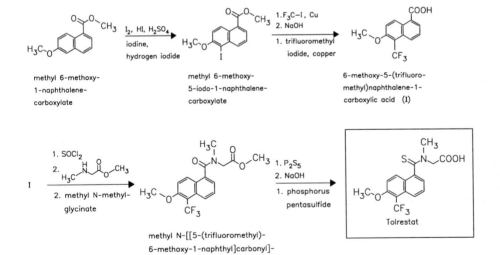

Reference(s):
DE 925 468 (Hoechst; appl. 1941).

Formulation(s):   gel 1 %

Trade Name(s):
D: Brondilat (Albert-Roussel)-   Pragman-Gelee (Albert-   Pragman Gelee (Albert-
        comb.; wfm   Roussel); wfm   Roussel); wfm
        Brondiletten (Albert-   I: Pragman Gelee (Albert-   J: Pragman Jelly (Tokyo
        Roussel)-comb.; wfm   Farma); wfm   Tanabe)

Tolrestat

(Tolrestatin)

ATC: A10XA01
Use: aldose reductase inhibitor
        (prophylaxis of diabetic neuropathy,
        retinopathy, cataract)

RN: 82964-04-3   MF: C$_{16}$H$_{14}$F$_3$NO$_3$S   MW: 357.35
CN: *N*-[[6-methoxy-5-(trifluoromethyl)-1-naphthalenyl]thioxomethyl]-*N*-methylglycine

methyl 6-methoxy-   methyl 6-methoxy-   6-methoxy-5-(trifluoro-
1-naphthalene-   5-iodo-1-naphthalene-   methyl)naphthalene-1-
carboxylate   carboxylate   carboxylic acid   (I)

methyl N-[[5-(trifluoromethyl)-
6-methoxy-1-naphthyl]carbonyl]-
N-methylglycinate

Tolrestat

Reference(s):
EP 59 596 (Ayerst; appl. 24.2.1982; CND-prior. 15.10.1981).
US 4 391 825 (Ayerst; appl. 5.7.1983; prior. 13.11.1981; CND-prior. 15.10.1981).
US 4 568 693 (Ayerst; 4.2.1986; appl. 9.9.1983; prior. 13.11.1981; CND-prior. 2.3.1981).
US 4 600 724 (Ayerst; 15.7.1986; appl. 17.7.1985; prior. 13.11.1981, 9.9.1983; CND-prior. 2.3.1981).
US 4 705 882 (Ayerst; 10.11.1987; appl. 28.3.1986; prior. 13.11.1981, 9.9.1983, 17.7.1985; CND-prior. 2.3.1981).
US 4 946 987 (Ayerst; 7.8.1990; appl. 20.6.1988; prior. 13.11.1981, 9.9.1983, 17.7.1985, 28.3.1986; CND-prior. 2.3.1981).
Sestanj, K. et al.: J. Med. Chem. (JMCMAR) **27**, 255 (1984).

synthesis of methyl 6-methoxy-1-naphthalenecarboxylate:
Price, C.C. et al.: J. Am. Chem. Soc. (JACSAT) **69**, 2261 (1947).

synthesis of 6-methoxy-5-(trifluoromethyl)naphthalene-1-carboxylic acid:
EP 245 679 (Ethyl Corp.; appl. 24.4.1987; USA-prior. 12.5.1986).
US 4 629 808 (Ethyl Corp.; 16.12.1986; appl. 20.6.1985).
US 4 590 010 (Ethyl Corp.; 20.5.1986; appl. 18.4.1985).
US 4 562 286 (Occidental Chem. Corp.; 31.12.1985; appl. 1.11.1984).
US 4 560 794 (Occidental Chem. Corp.; 24.12.1985; appl. 1.11.1984).
US 4 408 077 (Ayerst; 4.10.1983; appl. 13.11.1981).
EP 59 596 (Ayerst; appl. 24.2.1982; CND-prior. 15.10.1981, 2.3.1981).
Sestanj, K. et al.: J. Med. Chem. (JMCMAR) **27**, 255 (1984).

pharmaceutical composition for treatment of diabetic complications:
JP 61 078 725 (American Home; appl. 17.9.1985; USA-prior. 20.9.1984).

medical use to improve hearing in diabetics:
US 4 783 486 (American Home; 8.11.1988; appl. 6.11.1987).

medical use to improve wound healing:
US 4 751 243 (American Home; 14.6.1988; appl. 18.6.1986).

medical use for treatment of periodontal disease:
US 4 731 380 (American Home; 15.3.1988; appl. 26.8.1986).

medical use for stimulation of immune response:
EP 256 629 (American Home; appl. 9.6.1987; USA-prior. 12.6.1986).

medical use as antihypertensive in diabetics:
EP 245 951 (American Home; appl. 9.4.1987; USA-prior. 17.4.1986).

Formulation(s):   cps. 200 mg; tabl. 200 mg

Trade Name(s):

I:	Alredase (Wyeth; 1990); wfm	J:	Tolrestat (Wyeth-Ayerst); wfm
	Lorestat (Recordati; 1990); wfm	USA:	Alredase (Wyeth-Ayerst); wfm

Tolterodine
(Kabi 2234; PNU-200583)

ATC: G04BD07
Use: agent for urinary incontinence, muscarinic receptor antagonist

RN: 124937-51-5   MF: $C_{22}H_{31}NO$ MW: 325.50
CN: (*R*)-2-[3-[Bis(1-methylethyl)amino]-1-phenylpropyl]-4-methylphenol

tartrate
RN: 124937-52-6   MF: $C_{22}H_{31}NO \cdot C_4H_6O_6$ MW: 475.58

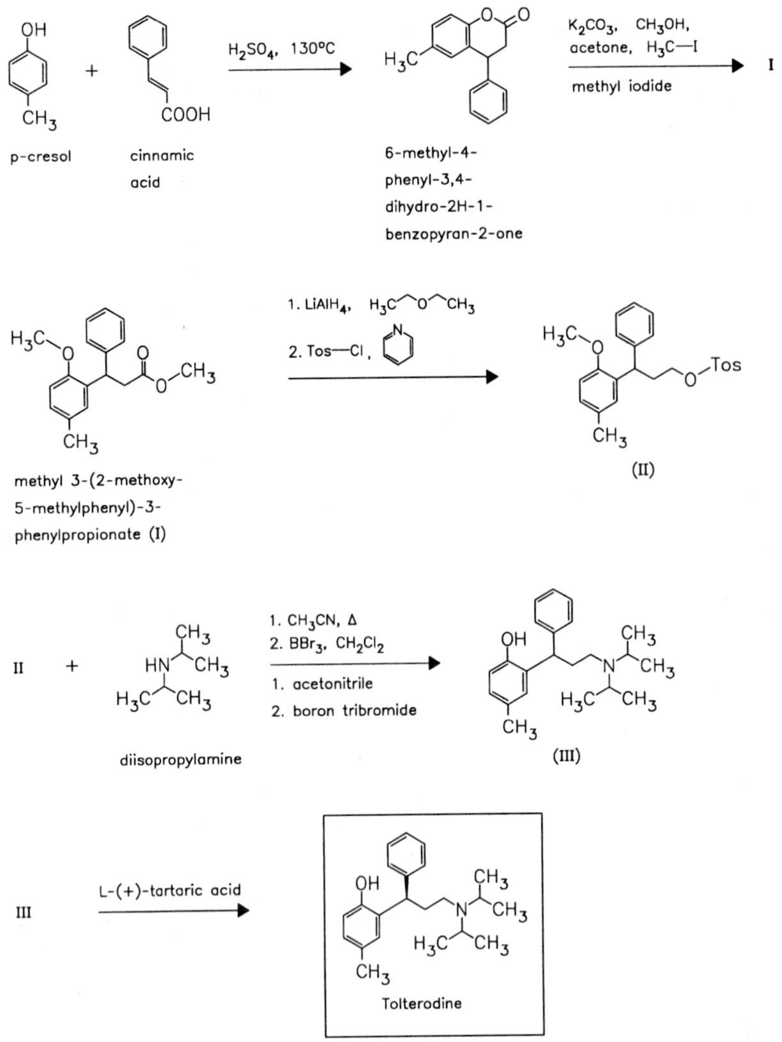

p-cresol + cinnamic acid → (H₂SO₄, 130°C) 6-methyl-4-phenyl-3,4-dihydro-2H-1-benzopyran-2-one → (K₂CO₃, CH₃OH, acetone, H₃C—I; methyl iodide) I

methyl 3-(2-methoxy-5-methylphenyl)-3-phenylpropionate (I)

1. LiAlH₄, H₃C—O—CH₃
2. Tos—Cl, (pyridine)
→ (II)

II + diisopropylamine

1. CH₃CN, Δ
2. BBr₃, CH₂Cl₂

1. acetonitrile
2. boron tribromide
→ (III)

III → (L-(+)-tartaric acid) → Tolterodine

Reference(s):
EP 325 571 (Kabi Vitrum; appl. 20.1.1989; S-prior. 22.1.1988).

pharmaceutical compositions containing anti-incontinence agents:
WO 9 811 888 (American Home Products Corp.; appl. 17.9.1997; USA-prior. 19.9.1996).

Formulation(s):　f. c. tabl. 1 mg, 2 mg (as maleate)

Trade Name(s):
D:　Detrusitol (Pharmacia & Upjohn; 1998)
F:　Detrusitol (Pharmacia & Upjohn)
GB:　Detrusitol (Pharmacia & Upjohn)
I:　Detrusitil (Pharmacia & Upjohn)
USA:　Detrol (Pharmacia & Upjohn)

Tolycaine

ATC:　N01BB
Use:　local anesthetic

RN:　3686-58-6　MF: C₁₅H₂₂N₂O₃　MW: 278.35　EINECS: 222-976-9
CN:　2-[[(diethylamino)acetyl]amino]-3-methylbenzoic acid methyl ester

monohydrochloride

RN: 7210-92-6   MF: $C_{15}H_{22}N_2O_3 \cdot HCl$ MW: 314.81   EINECS: 230-590-7

LD$_{50}$:   60 mg/kg (M, i.v.);
       44 mg/kg (R, i.v.)

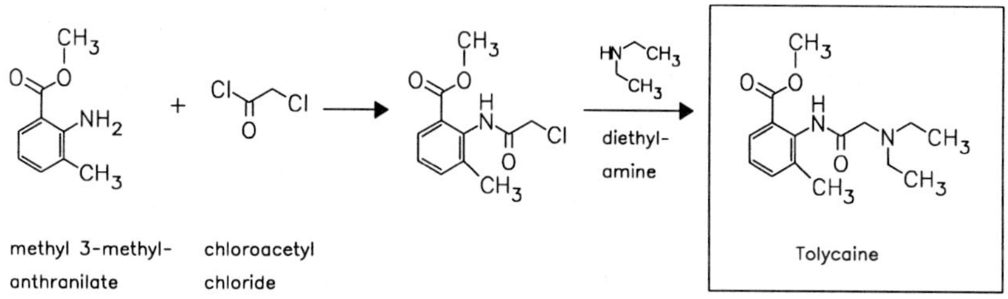

methyl 3-methyl-   chloroacetyl
anthranilate   chloride

diethyl-
amine

Tolycaine

Reference(s):

DE 1 018 070 (Bayer; appl. 26.9.1955).

Formulation(s):   vial 0.08/4 ml (as hydrochloride)

Trade Name(s):

D: Baycain (Bayer); wfm   F: Campovit (Bayer-Pharma)-   J: Baycain (Bayer)
      Tardocillin (Bayer)-comb.   comb.; wfm

Topiramate

(KW-6485; McN-4853; RWJ-17021-000)

ATC: N03AX11
Use: anticonvulsant

RN: 97240-79-4   MF: $C_{12}H_{21}NO_8S$ MW: 339.37

LD$_{50}$:   >1500 mg/kg (R, i.p.)

CN: 2,3:4,5-bis-O-(1-methylethylidene)-β-D-fructopyranose sulfamate

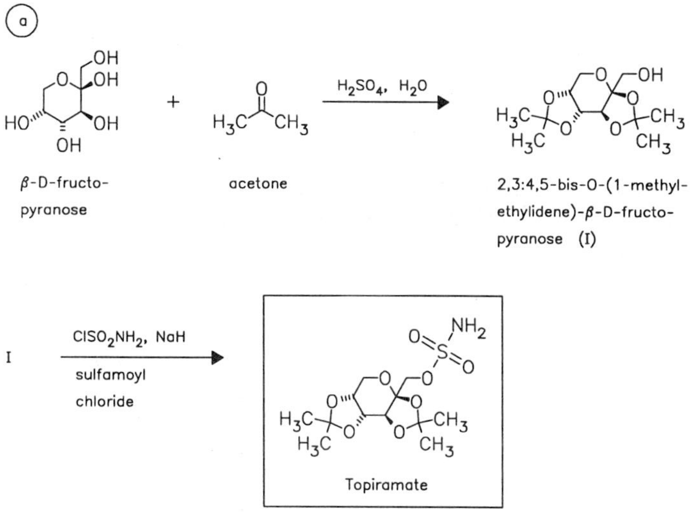

β-D-fructo-   acetone
pyranose

H_2SO_4, H_2O

2,3:4,5-bis-O-(1-methyl-
ethylidene)-β-D-fructo-
pyranose (I)

I

$ClSO_2NH_2$, NaH

sulfamoyl
chloride

Topiramate

(b)

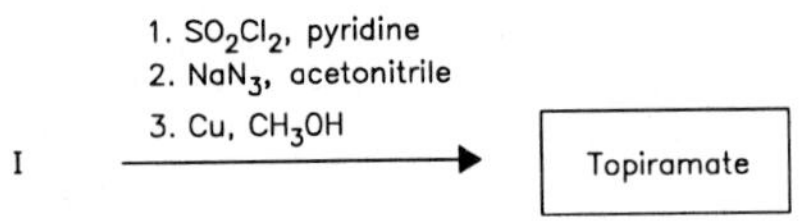

1. SO$_2$Cl$_2$, pyridine
2. NaN$_3$, acetonitrile
3. Cu, CH$_3$OH

I ──────────────→ [Topiramate]

Reference(s):
a   Maryanoff, B.E. et al.: J. Med. Chem. (JMCMAR) **30**, 880-887 (1987).
    EP 138 441 (McNeillab Inc.; appl. 25.9.1984; USA-prior. 26.9.1983, 11.2.1985).
b   EP 533 483 (McNeillab Inc.; appl. 18.9.1992; USA-prior. 19.9.1991, 5.8.1992).

Formulation(s):   tabl. 50 mg, 100 mg, 200 mg

Trade Name(s):
GB: Topamax (Janssen-Cilag)   USA: Topamax (Ortho-McNeil)

Topotecan
(NSC-609669; SK&F-S 104864-A)

ATC: L01XX17
Use: antineoplastic, topoisomerase I-
       inhibitor

RN: 123948-87-8   MF: C$_{23}$H$_{23}$N$_3$O$_5$ MW: 421.45
CN: (S)-10-[(dimethylamino)methyl]-4-ethyl-4,9-dihydroxy-1H-pyrano[3',4':6,7]indolizino[1,2-b]quinoline-
      3,14(4H,12H)-dione

monohydrochloride
RN: 119413-54-6   MF: C$_{23}$H$_{23}$N$_3$O$_5$ · HCl   MW: 457.91
acetate
RN: 123948-88-9   MF: C$_{23}$H$_{23}$N$_3$O$_5$ · C$_2$H$_4$O$_2$ MW: 481.51
dihydrochloride
RN: 123949-07-5   MF: C$_{23}$H$_{23}$N$_3$O$_5$ · 2HCl   MW: 494.38

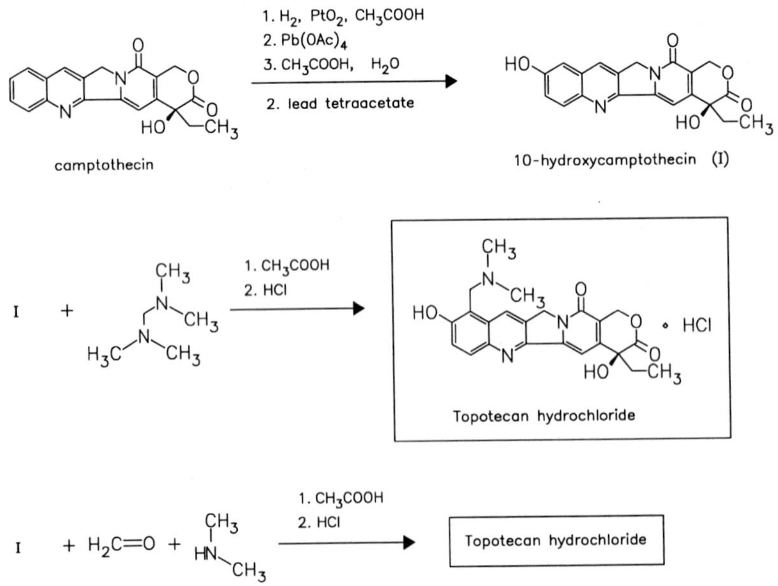

1. H$_2$, PtO$_2$, CH$_3$COOH
2. Pb(OAc)$_4$
3. CH$_3$COOH, H$_2$O

2. lead tetraacetate

camptothecin

10-hydroxycamptothecin   (I)

1. CH$_3$COOH
2. HCl

Topotecan hydrochloride

1. CH$_3$COOH
2. HCl

I   + H$_2$C=O +   (amine)   ──────────→   [Topotecan hydrochloride]

Reference(s):
Kingsbury, W.D. et al.: J. Med. Chem. (JMCMAR) **34** (1), 98 (1991).
EP 321 122 (SmithKline Beecham; appl. 30.11.1988; USA-prior. 1.12.1987).
WO 9 205 785 (SmithKline Beecham; appl. 23.9.1991; USA-prior. 28.9.1990).

Formulation(s):   vial 4 mg (as hydrochloride)

Trade Name(s):

D:	Hycamtin (SmithKline Beecham)	GB:	Hycamtin (SmithKline Beecham)	USA:	Hycamtin (SmithKline Beecham)
F:	Hycamtin (SmithKline Beecham)	I:	Hycamtin (SmithKline Beecham)		

Torasemide
(AC 4464; BM 02015)

Use: antihypertensive, loop diuretic

RN: 56211-40-6   MF: $C_{16}H_{20}N_4O_3S$ MW: 348.43
CN: *N*-[[(1-Methylethyl)amino]carbonyl]-4-[(3-methylphenyl)amino]-3-pyridinesulfonamide

sodium salt
RN: 72810-59-4   MF: $C_{16}H_{20}N_4O_3S \cdot xNa$ MW: unspecified

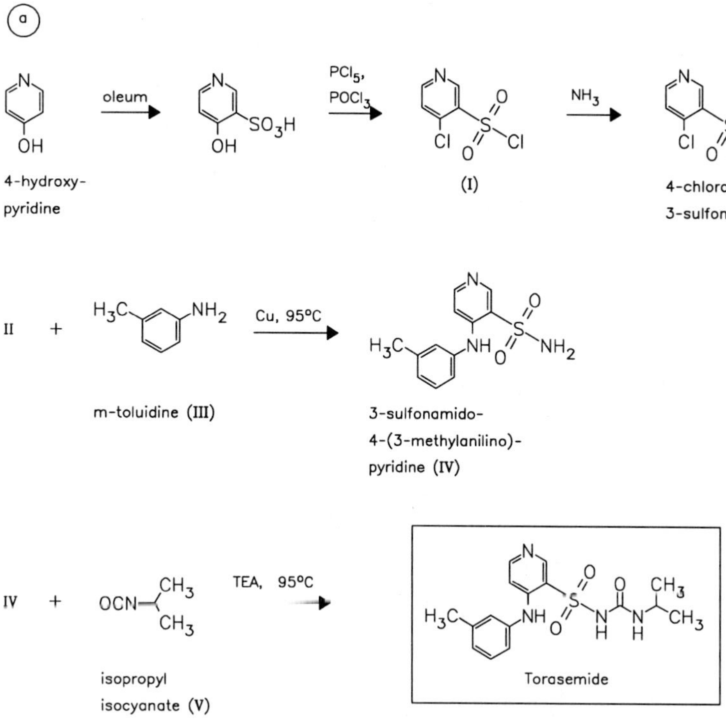

4-hydroxy-pyridine

(I)

4-chloropyridine-3-sulfonamide (II)

m-toluidine (III)

3-sulfonamido-4-(3-methylanilino)-pyridine (IV)

isopropyl isocyanate (V)

Torasemide

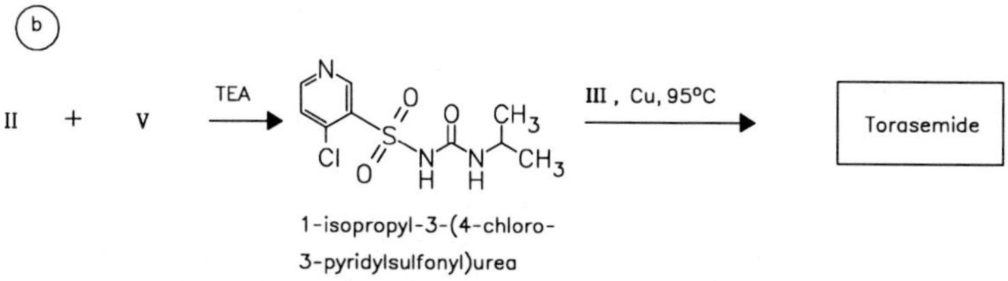

1-isopropyl-3-(4-chloro-3-pyridylsulfonyl)urea

Torasemide

Reference(s):
a,b Delarge, J.: Arzneim.-Forsch. (ARZNAD) **38** (I), 1a (1988).
   DE 2 516 025 (A. Christiaens; appl. 12.4.1975; GB-prior. 17.4.1974).

stable crystalline modification:
DE 3 623 620 (Boehringer Mannheim; appl. 17.8.1985; D-prior. 17.8.1985).

injections containing torasemide:
DE 3 623 620 (Boehringer Mannheim; D-prior. 12.7.1986).

rapidly disintegrating pellets:
WO 09 810 754 (Boehringer Mannheim; appl. 9.9.1997; D-prior. 12.9.1996).

polymorphism and control of the serum solubility of orally administered torasemide:
US 5 914 336 (Boehringer Mannheim; 22.6.1999; USA-prior. 2.6.1998).

tablets containing torasemide:
WO 9 300 097 (Boehringer Mannheim; appl. 25.6.1992; J-prior. 25.6.1991).

use for treatment of brain edema:
DE 4 113 820 (Boehringer Mannheim; D-prior. 27.4.1991).

Formulation(s):   amp. 10.631 mg/2 ml, 21.262 mg/4 ml, 212.62 mg/20 ml (as sodium salt); tabl 2.5 mg, 5mg, 10 mg

Trade Name(s):
D: Torem (Berlin-Chemie)   Unat (Roche; 1999)

Toremifene

(FC-1157a)

ATC: L02BA02
Use: antiestrogen, antineoplastic

RN: 89778-26-7   MF: $C_{26}H_{28}ClNO$ MW: 405.97
LD$_{50}$:   1700 mg/kg (R, p.o.)
CN: (Z)-2-[4-(4-chloro-1,2-diphenyl-1-butenyl)phenoxy]-*N,N*-dimethylethanamine

citrate (1:1)
RN: 89778-27-8   MF: $C_{26}H_{28}ClNO \cdot C_6H_8O_7$ MW: 598.09
LD$_{50}$:   3 g/kg (R, p.o.)

4-hydroxybenzo-
phenone

2-(dimethylamino)-
ethyl chloride

4-[2-(dimethylamino)ethoxy]-
benzophenone (I)

1. LiAlH$_4$
2. recrystallization from acetone

cinnamaldehyde

(RS,RS)-1,2-diphenyl-1-[4-
[2-(dimethylamino)ethoxy]-
phenyl]butane-1,4-diol (II)

II 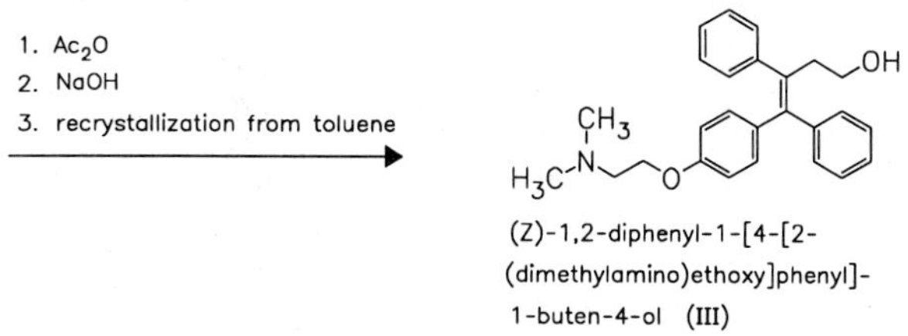
1. Ac2O
2. NaOH
3. recrystallization from toluene
CH3
H3C N O
OH
(Z)-1,2-diphenyl-1-[4-[2-(dimethylamino)ethoxy]phenyl]-1-buten-4-ol (III)

III 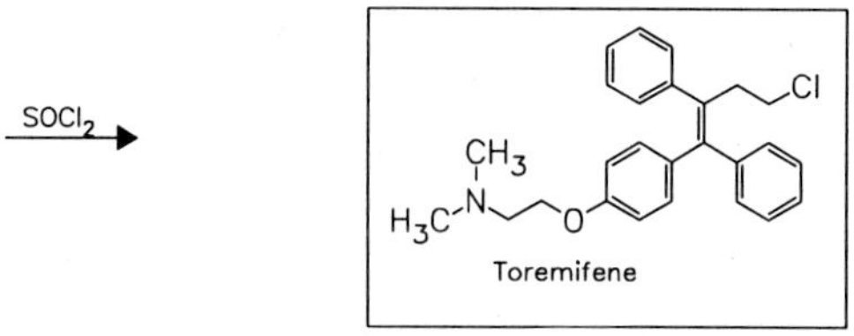
SOCl2
CH3
H3C N O
Cl
Toremifene

Reference(s):

EP 95 875 (Farmos; appl. 20.5.1983; SF-prior. 27.5.1982).
US 4 696 949 (Farmos; 29.9.1987; appl. 29.1.1986; SF-prior. 27.5.1982, 9.5.1983).

Formulation(s): tabl. 20 mg, 60 mg (as citrate)

Trade Name(s):

D:	Fareston (ASTA Medica AWD)	I:	Fareston (Schering-Plough)	USA:	Fareston (Schering-Plough)
GB:	Fareston (Orion)	J:	Fareston (Nippon Kayaku; as citrate)		

Tosufloxacin

Use: quinolone antibacterial, gyrase inhibitor

RN: 108138-46-1 MF: $C_{19}H_{15}F_3N_4O_3$ MW: 404.35
CN: (±)-7-(3-amino-1-pyrrolidinyl)-1-(2,4-difluorophenyl)-6-fluoro-1,4-dihydro-4-oxo-1,8-naphthyridine-3-carboxylic acid

monotosylate

RN: 115964-29-9 MF: $C_{19}H_{15}F_3N_4O_3 \cdot C_7H_8O_3S$ MW: 576.55
LD_{50}: 196 mg/kg (M, i.v.); >6 g/kg (M, p.o.);
270 mg/kg (R, i.v.); >6 g/kg (R, p.o.);
>3 g/kg (dog, p.o.)

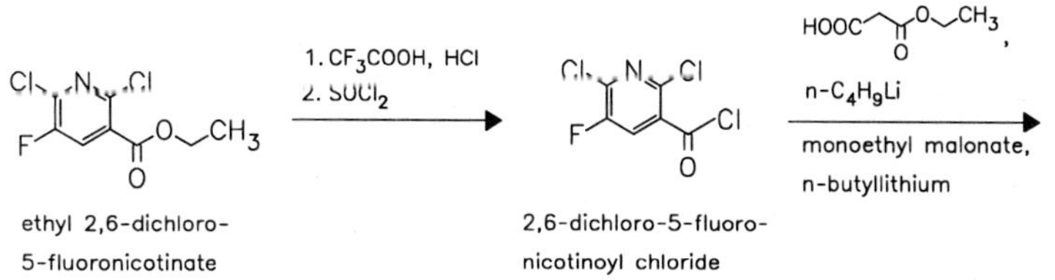 I
Cl N Cl
F
O CH3
O
ethyl 2,6-dichloro-5-fluoronicotinate
1. CF3COOH, HCl
2. SOCl2
Cl N Cl
F
Cl
O
2,6-dichloro-5-fluoronicotinoyl chloride
HOOC O CH3
O
n-C4H9Li
monoethyl malonate,
n-butyllithium

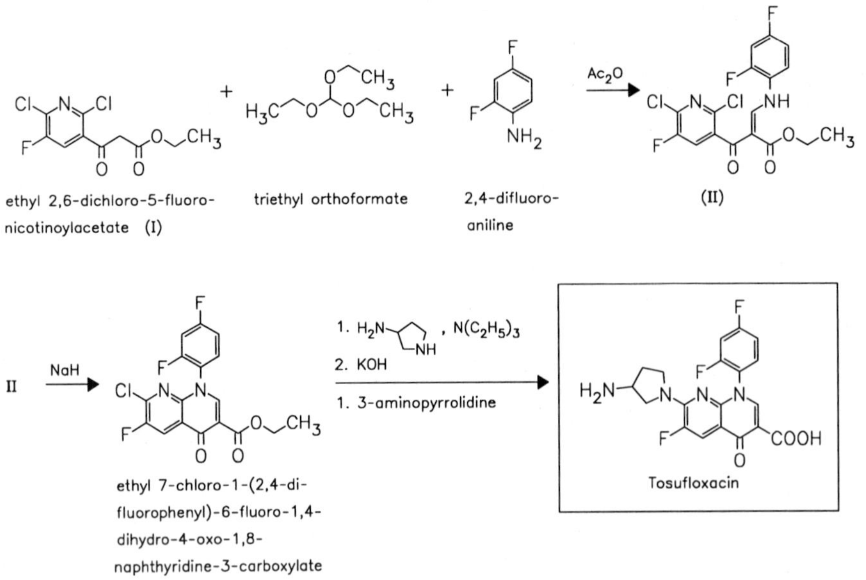
ethyl 2,6-dichloro-5-fluoro-nicotinoylacetate (I)
triethyl orthoformate
2,4-difluoro-aniline
Ac_2O
(II)
II
NaH
ethyl 7-chloro-1-(2,4-di-fluorophenyl)-6-fluoro-1,4-dihydro-4-oxo-1,8-naphthyridine-3-carboxylate
1. 3-aminopyrrolidine, $N(C_2H_5)_3$
2. KOH
1. 3-aminopyrrolidine
Tosufloxacin

Reference(s):
DE 3 514 076 (Toyama; appl. 31.10.1985; J-prior. 26.4.1984).
US 4 704 459 (Toyama; 3.11.1987; appl. 17.1.1986; J-prior. 23.1.1985, 18.2.1985, 7.3.1985, 3.4.1985, 8.5.1985, 14.6.1985).
Chu, D.T.W. et al.: J. Med. Chem. (JMCMAR) **29**, 2363 (1986).
Narita, H. et al.: Yakugaku Zasshi (YKKZAJ) **106**, 802 (1986).

synthesis of ethyl 2,6-dichloro-5-fluoronicotinate:
JP 82/72 981 (H. Matsumoto et al.; appl. 7.5.1982).

alternative synthesis:
EP 302 372 (Abbott; appl. 8.2.1989; USA-prior. 4.8.1987).
BE 904 086 (Toyama; appl. 14.6.1985; J-prior. 23.1.1985).

Formulation(s): tabl. 75 mg, 150 mg (as tosylate)

Trade Name(s):

J:	Osex (Toyama; 1990)	Tosuxacin (Dainabot; 1990)

Tralonide

ATC: H02AB; R03BA
Use: glucocorticoid

RN: 21365-49-1 MF: $C_{24}H_{28}Cl_2F_2O_4$ MW: 489.39
CN: (6α,11β,16α)-9,11-dichloro-6,21-difluoro-16,17-[(1-methylethylidene)bis(oxy)]pregna-1,4-diene-3,20-dione

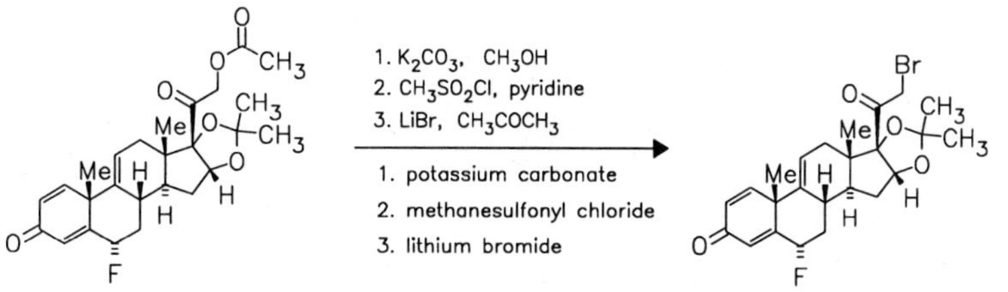

21-acetoxy-3,20-dioxo-6α-
fluoro-16α,17-isopropylidene-
dioxy-1,4,9(11)-pregnatriene
(from fludroxycortide, q. v.)

(I)

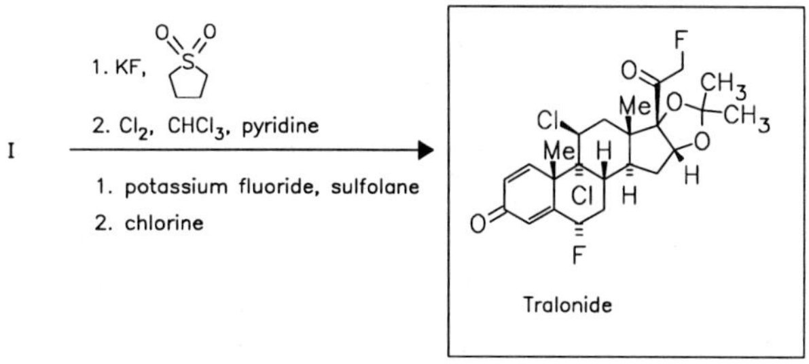

Tralonide

Reference(s):
DOS 2 225 324 (Syntex; appl. 25.5.1972; USA-prior. 26.5.1971).

starting material:
US 3 282 929 (American Cyanamid; 1.11.1966; prior. 6.7.1964).

alternative synthesis:
US 3 409 613 (Syntex; 5.11.1968; prior. 28.7.1966).
ZA 680 282 (Syntex; appl. 15.1.1968).

medical use:
US 3 934 013 (Syntex; 20.1.1976; prior. 21.2.1975).

Trade Name(s):
USA: Talidan (Lilly); wfm

Tramadol

ATC: N02AX02
Use: analgesic

RN: 27203-92-5   MF: C$_{16}$H$_{25}$NO$_2$ MW: 263.38   EINECS: 248-319-6
LD$_{50}$: 228 mg/kg (R, p.o.)
CN: cis-(±)-2-[(dimethylamino)methyl] 1 (3-methoxyphenyl)cyclohexanol

hydrochloride
RN: 36282-47-0   MF: C$_{16}$H$_{25}$NO$_2$ · HCl   MW: 299.84   EINECS: 252-950-2

3-bromo-
anisole

2-dimethylamino-
methylcyclohexanone

Tramadol

Reference(s):
GB 997 399 (Grünenthal; appl. 1.4.1964; D-prior. 2.4.1963).

Formulation(s):   amp. 50 mg/ml, 100 mg/2 ml; cps. 50 mg; drops 100 mg/ml; eff. tabl. 50 mg; s. r. tabl. 100 mg,
150 mg, 200 mg; suppos. 100 mg; tabl. 50 mg (as hydrochloride)

Trade Name(s):

D: Amadol (TAD)
      TRADOL-PUREN (Isis
      Puren)
      Trama (Kade)
      Trama AbZ (AbZ-Pharma)
      Trama beta (betapharm)
      Tramadol (ASTA Medica
      AWD; Dolorgiet;
      ratiopharm; Stada; ct-
      Arzneimittel)

Tramadura (durachemie)
Tramagetic (Azupharma)
Tramagit (Krewel
Meuselbach)
Tramal (Grünenthal)
Trama-Sanorania
(Sanorania)
Tramdolar (Hexal)
Tramedphano (medphano)
Tramundin (Mundipharma)

F: Topalgic (Hoechst Houdé)
GB: Tramake (Galen)
      Zamadol SR (ASTA
      Medica)
      Zyndol SR (Searle)
I: Contramol (Formenti)
      Fortradol (Bayer)
J: Crispin (Kowa)
USA: Ultram (Ortho-McNeil)

Tramazoline

ATC: R01AA09
Use: vasoconstrictor, rhinological
        therapeutic

RN: 1082-57-1   MF: $C_{13}H_{17}N_3$ MW: 215.30   EINECS: 214-105-6
CN: 4,5-dihydro-*N*-(5,6,7,8-tetrahydro-1-naphthalenyl)-1*H*-imidazol-2-amine

monohydrochloride
RN: 3715-90-0   MF: $C_{13}H_{17}N_3 \cdot HCl$ MW: 251.76   EINECS: 223-064-3
LD$_{50}$:   11.6 mg/kg (M, i.v.); 130 mg/kg (M, p.o.);
        190 mg/kg (R, p.o.)

5-amino-
tetralin

ammonium
rhodanide

methyl
iodide

(I)

ethylene-
diamine

Tramazoline

Reference(s):
DE 1 173 904 (Thomae; appl. 5.8.1961).
DE 1 191 381 (Thomae; appl. 24.6.1963; addition to DE 1 173 904).
DE 1 195 323 (Thomae; appl. 24.6.1963; addition to DE 1 173 904).

Formulation(s):   eye drops 0.6 mg/ml; nasal spray/drops 1.2 mg/ml

Trade Name(s):

D:	Biciron Augentropfen (Alcon)		Rhinospray (Boehringer Ing.)	I: Rinogutt Spray (Fher)
	Ellatun Nasentropfen (Alcon)	GB:	Dexa-Rhinspray (Boehringer Ing.)-comb.	J: Towk (Tanabe)

Trandolapril
(RU-44570)

ATC: C09AA10
Use: antihypertensive (ACE inhibitor)

RN: 87679-37-6   MF: $C_{24}H_{34}N_2O_5$ MW: 430.55
LD_{50}:   >2 g/kg (R, i. v.); >5 g/kg (R, p. o.);
3 g/kg (M, i. v.); 3.99 g/kg (M, p. o.);
2 g/kg (dog, p. o.)
CN: [2S-[1[R*(R*)],2α,3aα,7aβ]]-1-[2-[[1-(Ethoxycarbonyl)-3-phenylpropyl]amino]-1-oxopropyl]octahydro-1H-indole-2-carboxylic acid

hydrochloride
RN: 87725-72-2   MF: $C_{24}H_{34}N_2O_5 \cdot HCl$ MW: 467.01

indole → 1-acetyl-3aα,7aβ-octahydroindole → I

1. H_2, PtO_2, CH_3COOH
2. H_3C–CO–O–CO–CH_3 , pyridine

1. anod. oxidation, CH_3OH
2. H_3C–Si(CH_3)(CH_3)–CN , CH_2Cl_2
2. trimethylsilyl cyanide

1-acetyl-2α,3aα,7aβ-octahydroindole-2-carbonitrile (I)

HBr →

(2S,3aR,7aS)-octahydroindole-2-carboxylic acid

→ II

benzyl alcohol , $SOCl_2$

(II)   +   N-[1(S)-ethoxycarbonyl-3-phenylpropyl]-L-alanine
(cf. spirapril and imidapril syntheses)

HOBt, DCC, DMF, N-ethylmorpholine   → III

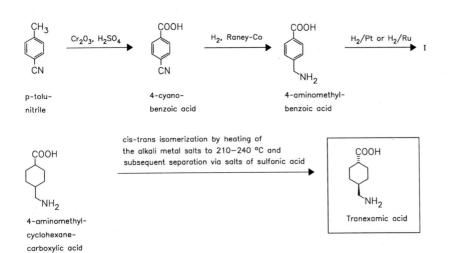

H_2, Pd-C, C_2H_5OH

(III)

Trandolapril

Reference(s):

DE 3 151 690 (Hoechst AG; appl. 29.12.1981; D-prior. 29.12.1981).

Formulation(s):   cps. 0.5 mg, 1 mg, 2 mg; tabl. 2 mg, 4 mg

Trade Name(s):

D: Gopten (Knoll)
     Tarka (Knoll)-comb. with
     verapamil hydrochloride
     Udramil (Hoechst Marion
     Roussel; Pohl-Boskamp)-
     comb. with verapamil
     hydrochloride

F: Udrik (Hoechst Marion
     Roussel; Pohl-Boskamp)
     Gopten (Ebewe, A; Knoll)
     Odrik (Roussel)

GB: Gopten (Ebewe, A; Knoll)
     Odrik (Roussel)

I: Gopten (Ebewe, A; Knoll)

J: Zeddan (Mediolanum)
     Preran (Hoechst)

USA: Mavik (Knoll Pharmac.)
     Tarka (Knoll Pharmac.)

Tranexamic acid

(Acide tranexamique)

ATC: B02AA02
Use: antifibrinolytic, hemostatic

RN: 1197-18-8   MF: $C_8H_{15}NO_2$ MW: 157.21   EINECS: 214-818-2
LD$_{50}$:   1350 mg/kg (M, i.v.); >10 g/kg (M, p.o.);
      1200 mg/kg (R, i.v.);
      1110 mg/kg (dog, i.v.); >5 g/kg (dog, p.o.)
CN: *trans*-4-(aminomethyl)cyclohexanecarboxylic acid

Cr_2O_3, H_2SO_4

p-tolu-
nitrile

4-cyano-
benzoic acid

H_2, Raney-Co

4-aminomethyl-
benzoic acid

H_2/Pt or H_2/Ru   I

cis-trans isomerization by heating of
the alkali metal salts to 210–240 °C and
subsequent separation via salts of sulfonic acid

4-aminomethyl-
cyclohexane-
carboxylic acid
cis/trans mixture   (I)

Tranexamic acid

Reference(s):
syntheses:
Einhorn, A.; Ladisch, C.: Justus Liebigs Ann. Chem. (JLACBF) **310**, 194 (1900).
Levine, M.; Sedlecky, R.: J. Org. Chem. (JOCEAH) **24**, 115 (1959).
DAS 1 443 755 (Daiichi Seiyaku; appl. 23.12.1964; J-prior. 24.12.1963).
DAS 1 793 841 (Daiichi Seiyaku; appl. 23.12.1964; 1-prior. 24.12.1963).
GB 1 202 189 (Kureha; appl. 13.6.1969; J-prior. 14.6.1968, 12.9.1968, 28.12.1968, 17.2.1969).
US 3 499 925 (Daiichi Seiyaku; 10.3.1970; J-prior. 23.3.1964, 6.7.1964).
DOS 1 568 379 (Daiichi Seiyaku; appl. 13.4.1966; J-prior. 13.4.1965).
DOS 2 227 504 (Kowa; appl. 6.6.1972).
DAS 2 344 043 (Teijin; appl. 31.8.1973; J-prior. 7.9.1972, 30.3.1973).
GB 1 409 938 (Asahi; appl. 29.11.1973; J-prior. 29.11.1972).
DAS 2 359 251 (Asahi; appl. 28.11.1973; J-prior. 29.11.1972).
GB 1 410 108 (Asahi; appl. 2.10.1973; J-prior. 2.10.1972).
DAS 2 623 130 (Kureha; appl. 22.5.1976; J-prior. 27.5.1975).

Formulation(s):   amp. 250 mg/5 ml, 500 mg/5 ml; cps. 250 mg, 500 mg; f. c. tabl. 500 mg; tabl. 250 mg

Trade Name(s):

D:	Anvitoff (Knoll)	I:	Amcacid (Bonomelli); wfm	J:	Carxamin (Sankyo Zoki)
	Cyklokapron (Pharmacia &		Amcacid (Bonomelli-		Hexatron (Nihon Shinyaku)
	Upjohn)		Hommel); wfm		Rikavarin (Toyo)
	Ugurol (Bayer)		Emorhalt (Sigurtà); wfm		Spiramin (Mitsui)
F:	Exacyl (Sanofi Winthrop)		Tranex (Malesci); wfm		Tranexamic Acid (Mohan)
	Spotof (CCD)		Transil (Malesci)-comb.;		Transamin (Daiichi)
GB:	Cyklokapron (Pharmacia &		wfm	USA:	Cyklokapron (Pharmacia &
	Upjohn)		Ugurol (Bayer); wfm		Upjohn); wfm

Tranilast

ATC: R06
Use: antiallergic

RN: 53902-12-8   MF: $C_{18}H_{17}NO_5$ MW: 327.34
LD_{50}:   680 mg/kg (M, p.o.);
1100 mg/kg (R, p.o.);
660 mg/kg (dog, p.o.)
CN: 2-[[3-(3,4-dimethoxyphenyl)-1-oxo-2-propenyl]amino]benzoic acid

anthranilic
ucid

3,4-dimethoxy-
cinnamoyl chloride

Tranilast

Reference(s):
DOS 2 402 398 (Kissei; appl. 18.1.1974; J-prior. 18.1.1973).
US 3 940 422 (Kissei; 24.2.1976; appl. 17.1.1974; J-prior. 18.1.1973).
US 4 070 484 (Kissei; 24.1.1978; prior. 18.1.1973).

Formulation(s):   cps. 100 mg, eye drops 0.5 %; gran. 10 %

Trade Name(s):
J: Rizaben (Kissei; 1982)

Tranylcypromine

ATC: N06AF04
Use: psychoanaleptic, antidepressant

RN: 155-09-9 MF: $C_9H_{11}N$ MW: 133.19 EINECS: 205-841-9
LD$_{50}$: 64 mg/kg (M, p.o.)
CN: trans-(±)-2-phenylcyclopropanamine

sulfate (2:1)
RN: 13492-01-8 MF: $C_9H_{11}N \cdot 1/2H_2SO_4$ MW: 364.47 EINECS: 236-807-1
LD$_{50}$: 37 mg/kg (M, i.v.); 38 mg/kg (M, p.o.)

styrene + ethyl diazoacetate → ethyl 2-phenyl-cyclopropane-carboxylate → (NaOH, C$_2$H$_5$OH) → trans-2-phenyl-cyclopropane-carboxylic acid (I)

I → (SOCl$_2$ thionyl chloride) → trans-2-phenyl-cyclopropane-carbonyl chloride → (1. NaN$_3$, 2. HCl / 1. sodium azide) → Tranylcypromine

Reference(s):
US 2 997 422 (Smith Kline & French; 22.8.1961; prior. 9.1.1959).
DOS 2 649 700 (Nelson Res. & Dev.; appl. 29.10.1976; USA-prior. 31.10.1975).
US 4 016 204 (Nelson Res. & Dev.; 5.4.1977; appl. 31.10.1975).
Burger, A.; Yost, W.L.: J. Am. Chem. Soc. (JACSAT) **70**, 2198 (1948).

Formulation(s):   drg. 10 mg; tabl. 10 mg (as sulfate)

Trade Name(s):
D: Jatrosom (Procter & Gamble)
F: Tylciprine (Théraplix); wfm
GB: Parnate (SmithKline Beecham)
      Parstelin (SmithKline Beecham)-comb.
I: Parmodalin (Sanofi Winthrop)-comb.
USA: Parnate (SmithKline Beecham)

Trazodone

ATC: N06AX05
Use: antidepressant, anxiolytic

RN: 19794-93-5 MF: $C_{19}H_{22}ClN_5O$ MW: 371.87 EINECS: 243-317-1
LD$_{50}$: 91 mg/kg (M, i.v.); 610 mg/kg (M, p.o.);
      91 mg/kg (R, i.v.); 690 mg/kg (R, p.o.)
CN: 2-[3-[4-(3-chlorophenyl)-1-piperazinyl]propyl]-1,2,4-triazolo[4,3-a]pyridin-3(2H)-one

monohydrochloride
RN: 25332-39-2 MF: $C_{19}H_{22}ClN_5O \cdot HCl$ MW: 408.33 EINECS: 246-855-5
LD$_{50}$: 91 mg/kg (M, i.v.); 584 mg/kg (M, p.o.);
      91 mg/kg (R, i.v.); 690 mg/kg (R, p.o.);
      >40 mg/kg (dog, i.v.); 500 mg/kg (dog, p.o.)

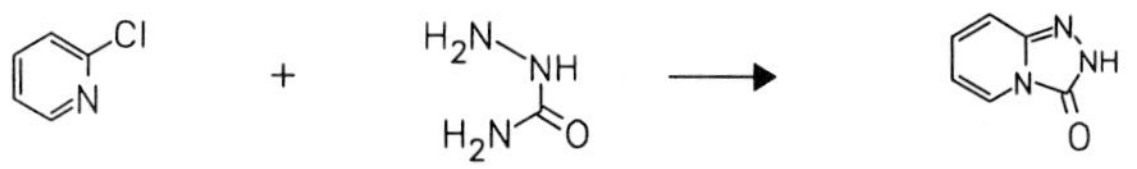

2-chloro-
pyridine

semicarbazide

1,2,4-triazolo-
[4,3-a]pyridin-
3(2H)-one (I)

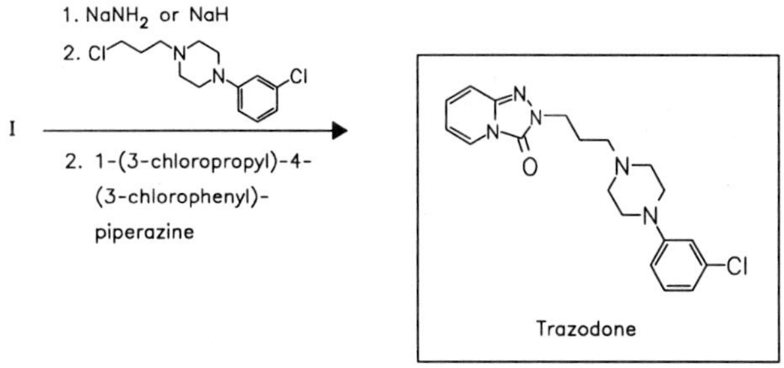

1. NaNH$_2$ or NaH

2. Cl~~~N~~~~N piperazine Cl

I

2. 1-(3-chloropropyl)-4-
   (3-chlorophenyl)-
   piperazine

Trazodone

Reference(s):
US 3 381 009 (Angelini Francesco; 30.4.1968; I-prior. 15.12.1965).
DE 1 645 947 (Angelini Francesco; appl. 13.12.1966; I-prior. 15.12.1965, 3.8.1966).

Formulation(s):   cps. 25 mg, 50 mg; f. c. tabl. 100 mg; tabl. 50 mg, 100 mg, 150 mg, 300 mg (as hydrochloride)

Trade Name(s):
D: Thombran (Boehringer   I: Trittico (Angelini)   Restin (Kanebo)
      Ing.; 1977)   J: Desyrel (Pharmacia &   USA: Desyrel (Apothecon; 1982)
F: Pragmarel (UPSA); wfm   Upjohn)

Trenbolone acetate

(Trienbolone acetate)

ATC: A14
Use: anabolic

RN: 10161-34-9   MF: C$_{20}$H$_{24}$O$_3$ MW: 312.41   EINECS: 233-432-5
CN: (17β)-17-(acetyloxy)estra-4,9,11-trien-3-one

trenbolone
RN: 10161-33-8   MF: C$_{18}$H$_{22}$O$_2$ MW: 270.37

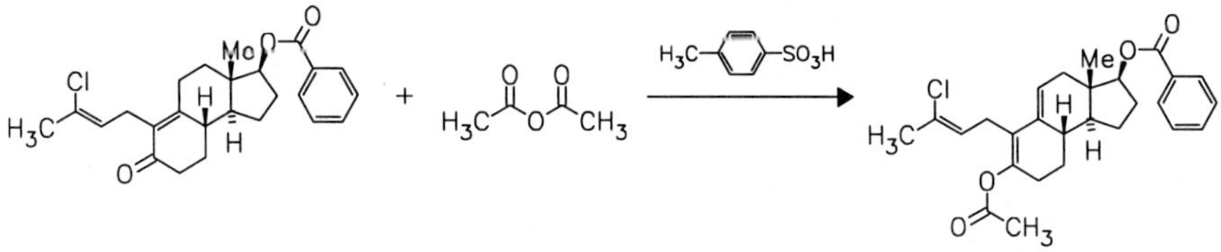

17β-benzoyloxy-3-chloro-5-oxo-   acetic   (II)
4,5-seco-2,9(10)-estradiene   anhydride (I)

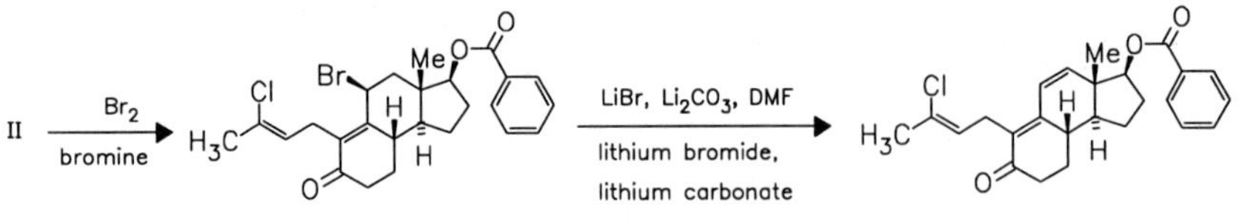

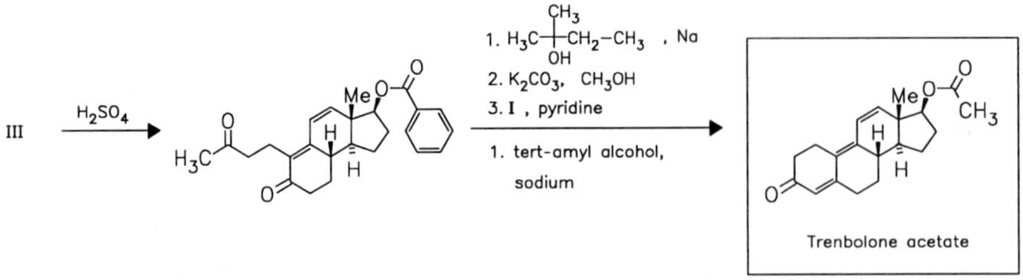

(III)

Trenbolone acetate

Reference(s):
FR-M 1 958 (Roussel-Uclaf; appl. 13.7.1962).
GB 1 035 683 (Roussel-Uclaf; valid from 19.4.1963; F-prior. 20.4.1962).
Velluz, L. et al.: C. R. Hebd. Seances Acad. Sci. (COREAF) **257**, 569 (1963).

starting material:
Velluz, L. et al.: C. R. Hebd. Seances Acad. Sci. (COREAF) **250**, 1084 (1960).

alternative syntheses:
Heker, M. et al.: Steroids (STEDAM) **10**, 211 (1967).
US 3 453 267 (Roussel-Uclaf; 1.7.1969; F-prior. 31.12.1964, 25.2.1965, 24.3.1965, 14.6.1965, 3.9.1965,
17.9.1965).

use for treatment of varicose wounds:
DOS 2 119 096 (Roussel-Uclaf; appl. 20.4.1971).

Formulation(s):   pellet 300 mg

Trade Name(s):
F: Finaject (Distrivet); wfm   Finaplix (Distrivet); wfm   Parabolan (Negma); wfm

---

Trenbolone hexahydrobenzyl carbonate

ATC: A14
Use: anabolic

RN: 23454-33-3   MF: C$_{26}$H$_{34}$O$_4$ MW: 410.55   EINECS: 245-669-1
CN: (17β)-17-[[(cyclohexylmethoxy)carbonyl]oxy]estra-4,9,11-trien-3-one

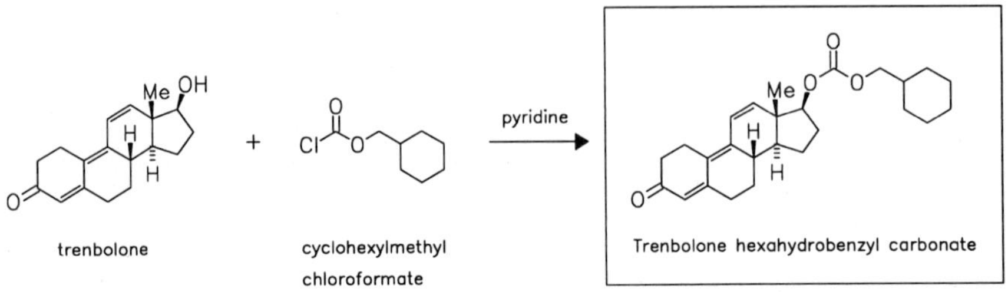

trenbolone   cyclohexylmethyl   Trenbolone hexahydrobenzyl carbonate
chloroformate

Reference(s):
FR-M 5 979 (Roussel-Uclaf; appl. 17.11.1966).

Formulation(s):   amp. 50 mg

Trade Name(s):
F: Hexabolan (Phartec); wfm   Parabolan (Negma); wfm

Trengestone

ATC: G03
Use: progestogen

RN: 5192-84-7   MF: $C_{21}H_{25}ClO_2$ MW: 344.88   EINECS: 225-978-8
CN: (9β,10α)-6-chloropregna-1,4,6-triene-3,20-dione

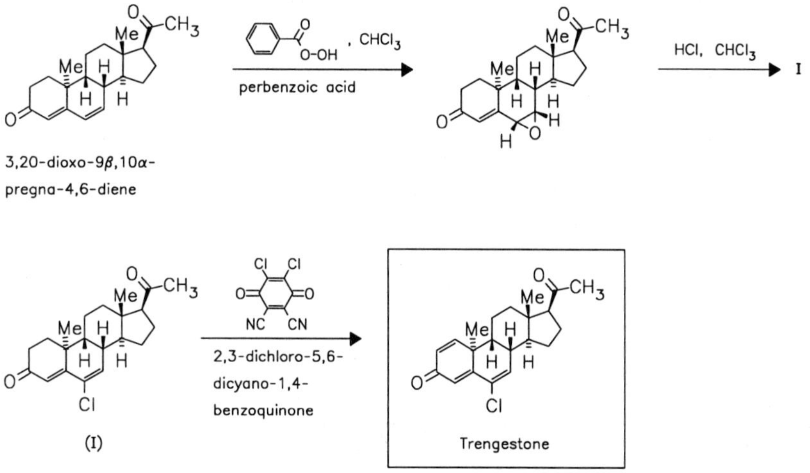

3,20-dioxo-9β,10α-
pregna-4,6-diene

(I)

Trengestone

Reference(s):
US 3 422 122 (North American Philips; 14.1.1969; prior. 7.10.1966, 25.9.1964, 12.6.1962; GB-prior. 29.6.1964).
BE 652 597 (Philips Gloeilampenfabrieken; appl. 2.12.1964; GB-prior. 29.6.1964).

Trade Name(s):
USA: Retrone (Hoffmann-La
        Roche); wfm

Tretinoin
(Retinoic acid; Vitamin-A acid)

ATC: D10AD01; L01XX14
Use: acne therapeutic, keratolytic

RN: 302-79-4   MF: $C_{20}H_{28}O_2$ MW: 300.44   EINECS: 206-129-0
LD$_{50}$:   92 mg/kg (M, i.v.); 780 mg/kg (M, p.o.);
       78 mg/kg (R, i.v.); 1960 mg/kg (R, p.o.)
CN: (all-E)-3,7-dimethyl-9-(2,6,6-trimethyl-1-cyclohexen-1-yl)-2,4,6,8-nonatetraenoic acid

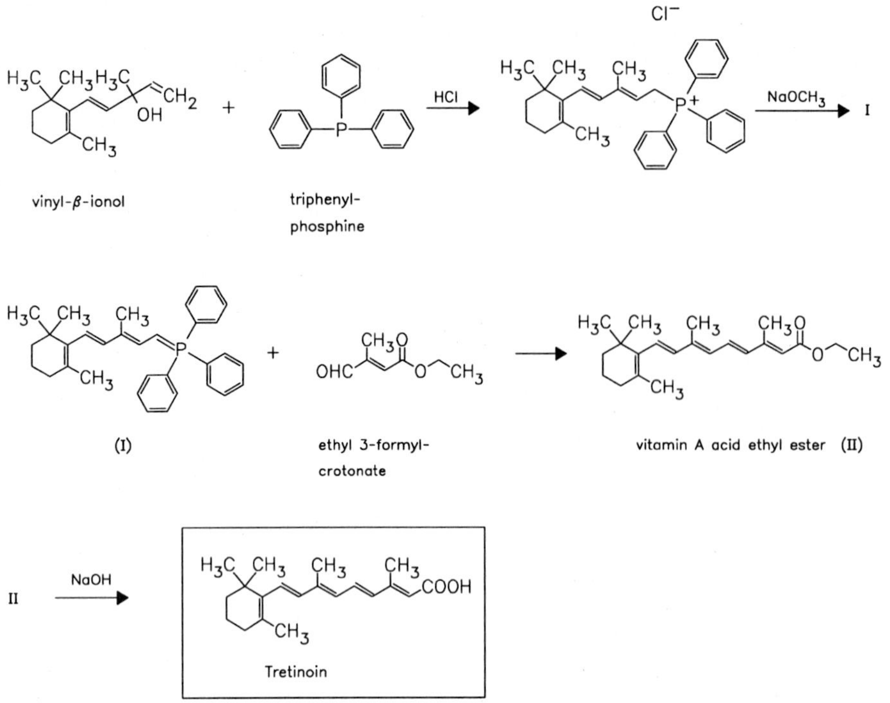

vinyl-β-ionol

triphenyl-phosphine

(I)

ethyl 3-formyl-crotonate

vitamin A acid ethyl ester (II)

Tretinoin

(cf. retinol synthesis according to BASF)

Reference(s):

DE 1 035 647 (BASF; appl. 17.1.1957).
US 3 006 939 (BASF; 31.10.1961; D-prior. 17.1.1957).
Pommer, H.: Angew. Chem. (ANCEAD) **72**, 811 (1960); **89**, 437 (1977).
König, H. et al.: Arzneim.-Forsch. (ARZNAD) **24**, 1184 (1974).

Formulation(s):　cream 25 mg/100 g, 50 mg/100g, 100 mg/100 g; cps. 10 mg; gel 25 mg/100 g, 50 mg/100 g; sol. 50 mg/100 ml, 100 mg/100 ml

Trade Name(s):

D:	Cordes VAS (Ichthyol)	Locacid (Pierre Fabre
	Epi-Aberel (Janssen-	Dermatologie)
	Chemie)	Retacnyl (Galderma)
	Eudyna (Knoll)	Retin A (Janssen-Cilag)
	Vesanoid (Roche)	Retinova (Roc)
F:	Abérel (Janssen-Cilag)	Retitop (La Roche-Posay)
	Antibio-aberel (Janssen-	Roaccutane (Roche)
	Cilag)-comb.	Trétinoïne Kéfrane (Roc)
	Effederm (CS)	Vesanoid (Roche)
	Isotrex (Stiefel)	GB: Retin-A (Janssen-Cilag)
	Kerlocal (Pierre Fabre)	Retinova (Janssen-Cilag)
	Kétrel (Biorga)	Vesanoid (Roche)

I: Airol (Roche)
Apsor (IDI)-comb.
Retin-A (Janssen-Cilag)
Tretionina (Savoma)
Vesanoid (Roche)
J: Vesanoid (Nippon Roche)
USA: Avita (Penederm)
Renova (Ortho Dermatological)
Retin-A (Ortho Dermatological)
Vesanoid (Roche)

Tretoquinol

(Trimethoquinol)

ATC: R03AC09; R03CC09
Use: bronchodilator

RN:　30418-38-3　MF: $C_{19}H_{23}NO_5$　MW: 345.40
CN:　(S)-1,2,3,4-tetrahydro-1-[(3,4,5-trimethoxyphenyl)methyl]-6,7-isoquinolinediol

hydrochloride

RN: 18559-59-6 MF: $C_{19}H_{23}NO_5 \cdot HCl$ MW: 381.86 EINECS: 242-423-5

LD_{50}: 120 mg/kg (M, i.v.); 2250 mg/kg (M, p.o.);
164 mg/kg (R, i.v.); 2 g/kg (R, p.o.);
160 mg/kg (dog, i.v.)

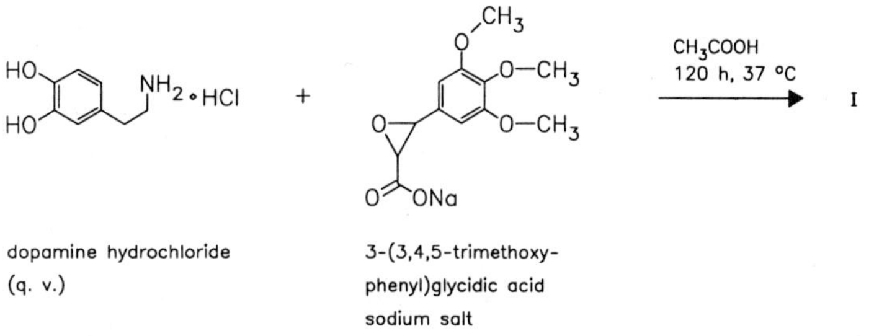
HO
HO
NH2 • HCl
+
CH3
O
O—CH3
O—CH3
O
O
ONa
CH3COOH
120 h, 37 °C
I
dopamine hydrochloride
(q. v.)
3-(3,4,5-trimethoxy-
phenyl)glycidic acid
sodium salt

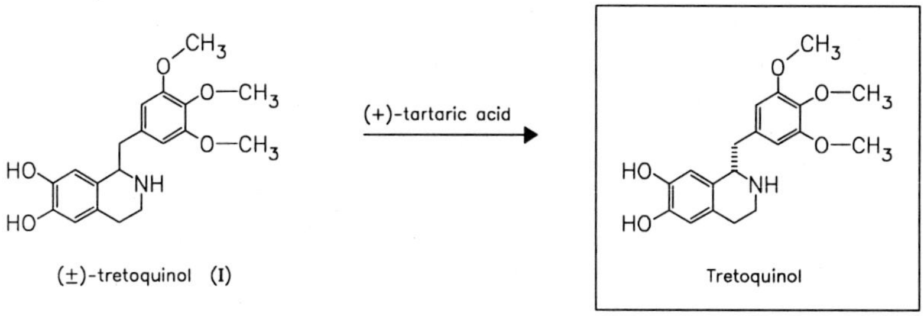
CH3
O
O—CH3
O—CH3
HO
HO
NH
(±)-tretoquinol (I)
(+)-tartaric acid
Tretoquinol

Reference(s):

GB 1 114 660 (Tanabe Seiyaku; appl. 5.12.1966; I-prior. 8.12.1965, 9.6.1966, 22.7.1966).
ZA 6 802 416 (Tanabe Seiyaku; 11.9.1968; J-prior. 27.4.1967).

Formulation(s): powder 1 %, tabl. 3 mg; vial 0.1 mg (as hydrochloride)

Trade Name(s):

I:	Vems (ISF); wfm	Vems (Searle); wfm	J:	Inolin (Tanabe)

Triamcinolone

ATC: A01AC01; D07AB09; D07BB03; D07CB01; D07XB02; H02AB08; S01BA05; S02CA04

Use: glucocorticoid

RN: 124-94-7 MF: $C_{21}H_{27}FO_6$ MW: 394.44 EINECS: 204-718-7

LD_{50}: >4 g/kg (M, s.c.);
99 mg/kg (R, s.c.)

CN: (11β,16α)-9-fluoro-11,16,17,21-tetrahydroxypregna-1,4-diene-3,20-dione

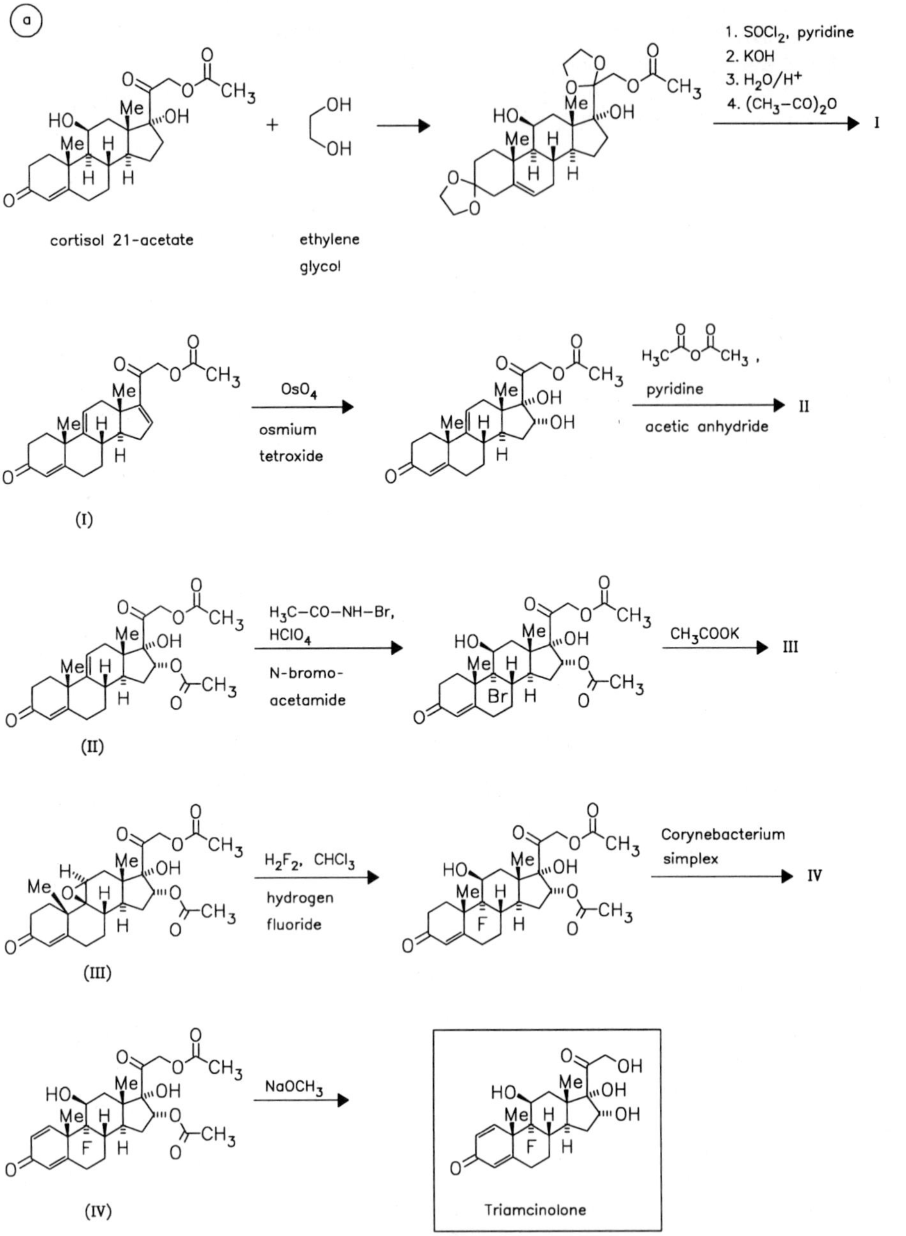

ⓐ

cortisol 21-acetate　　　ethylene
　　　　　　　　　　　glycol

1. SOCl₂, pyridine
2. KOH
3. H₂O/H⁺
4. (CH₃-CO)₂O
　　　　　　　→ I

(I)

OsO₄

osmium
tetroxide

H₃C-CO-O-CO-CH₃,

pyridine

acetic anhydride
　　　　　→ II

(II)

H₃C-CO-NH-Br,
HClO₄

N-bromo-
acetamide

CH₃COOK
　　　→ III

(III)

H₂F₂, CHCl₃

hydrogen
fluoride

Corynebacterium
simplex
　　　　→ IV

(IV)

NaOCH₃

Triamcinolone

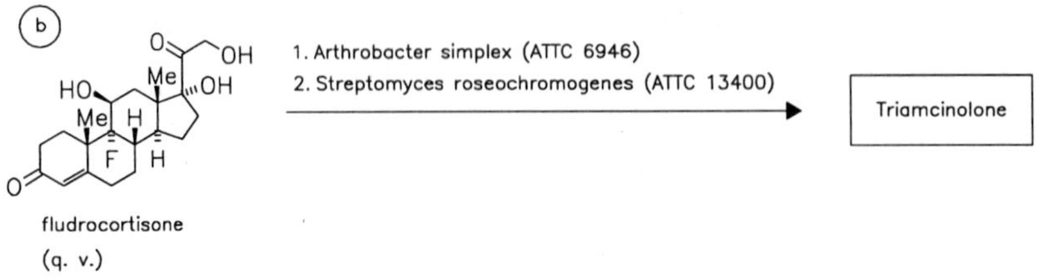

ⓑ

fludrocortisone
(q. v.)

1. Arthrobacter simplex (ATTC 6946)
2. Streptomyces roseochromogenes (ATTC 13400)
　　　　　　　　　　　　　　　→　Triamcinolone

Reference(s):

a US 2 789 118 (American Cyanamid; 16.4.1957; prior. 30.3.1956).
    Bernstein, S. et al.: J. Am. Chem. Soc. (JACSAT) **78**, 5693 (1956).
    Bernstein, S. et al.: J. Am. Chem. Soc. (JACSAT) **81**, 1689 (1959).
b US 3 536 586 (Squibb; 27.10.1970; prior. 25.1.1958).

Formulation(s):   tabl. 2 mg, 4 mg, 8 mg, 16 mg

Trade Name(s):

D:	Berlicort (Berlin-Chemie)	Ipercortis (AGIPS)	Ledercort P8 (Wyeth-
	Delphicort Tabl. (Lederle)	Kenacort-A Retard	Lederle)
	Triam-oral 4 (Sanorania)	(Bristol-Myers Squibb)	combination preparations
	Volon Tabl. (Bristol-Myers	Ledercort (Wyeth-Lederle)	J: Kenacort (Squibb-Sankyo)
	Squibb)	Ledercort A/10 (Wyeth-	Ledercort (Lederle)
GB:	Ledercort (Lederle); wfm	Lederle)	USA: Aristocort (Fujisawa)
I:	Dirahist (Teofarma)-comb.		

Triamcinolone acetonide

ATC: D07AB09
Use: glucocorticoid

RN: 76-25-5   MF: $C_{24}H_{31}FO_6$ MW: 434.50   EINECS: 200-948-7
LD_{50}:   5 g/kg (M, p.o.)
CN: (11β,16α)-9-fluoro-11,21-dihydroxy-16,17-[(1-methylethylidene)bis(oxy)]pregna-1,4-diene-3,20-dione

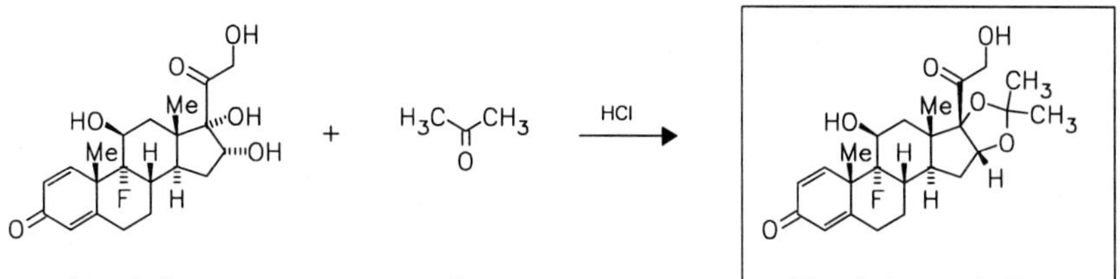

triamcinolone   +   acetone   HCl →   Triamcinolone acetonide

Reference(s):

US 2 990 401 (American Cyanamid; 27.6.1961; appl. 18.6.1958; prior. 11.3.1958).
Bernstein, S. et al.: J. Am. Chem. Soc. (JACSAT) **81**, 1689 (1959).
Heller, M. et al.: J. Org. Chem. (JOCEAH) **26**, 5044 (1961).
Fried, J. et al.: J. Am. Chem. Soc. (JACSAT) **80**, 2338 (1958).

Formulation(s):   amp. 40 mg/ml; cream 1 mg/g; ointment 1 mg/g; spray 3 mg/25 g; susp. 10 mg/ml, 40 mg/ml

Trade Name(s):

D:	Arutrin (Chauvin ankerpharm)	Triam Creme Lichtenstein (Lichtenstein)	Corticotulle Lumière (Solvay Pharma)-comb.
	Berlicort (Berlin-Chemie)	Triamgalen (Pharmagalen)	Kenacort-retard (Bristol-
	Delphicort Creme/Salbe	Triamhexal (Hexal)	Myers Squibb)
	(Lederle)	Triam-Injekt (Sanorania)	Kenalcol (Bristol-Myers
	Extracort Creme	Tri-Anemul (Medopharm)	Squibb)-comb.
	(Galderma)	Volon (Bristol-Myers	Localone (Pierre Fabre
	Kenalog (Bristol-Myers | Squibb)	Dermatologie)-comb.
	Squibb)	Volonimat (Bristol-Myers	Mycolog (Bristol-Myers
	Korticoid ratiopharm	Squibb)	Squibb)-comb.
	(ratiopharm)	combination preparations	Nasacort (Specia)
	Triamcinolon Wolff (Wolff)	F: Cidermex (Evans Medical)-	Pevisone (Janssen-Cilag)-
		comb.	comb.

GB: Adcortyl (Bristol-Myers Squibb)
Audicort (Wyeth)-comb.
Aureocort (Wyeth)-comb.
Kenalog (Bristol-Myers Squibb)
Nasacort (Rhône-Poulenc Rorer)
Nystadermal (Bristol-Myers Squibb)-comb.
Pevaryl TC (Janssen-Cilag)-comb.
Tri-adcortyl (Bristol-Myers Squibb)-comb.

I: Assocort (Bristol-Myers Squibb)-comb.
Aureocort (Wyeth-Lederle)-comb.
Kataval (Wyeth-Lederle)-comb.
Kenacort A Retard (Bristol-Myers Squibb)
Ledercort A/10 (Wyeth-Lederle)
Neo-audiocort (Wyeth-Lederle)-comb.
Pevisone (Janssen-Cilag)-comb.

J: Kenacort-A (Squibb-Sankyo)
Ledercort N (Lederle)
Rineton (Sanwa)
Tricinolon (Toko Yakuhin Osaka)

USA: Aristocort (Fujisawa)
Myco-Triacet (Teva)-comb.
Myrtrex F (Savage)
Nasacort (Rhône-Poulenc Rorer)
Tac-3 (Parnell)
Triacet (Teva)

Triamcinolone benetonide

ATC: D07AB09; D07CB01
Use: glucocorticoid

RN: 31002-79-6 MF: $C_{35}H_{42}FNO_8$ MW: 623.72 EINECS: 250-427-3
CN: (11β,16α)-21-[3-(benzoylamino)-2-methyl-1-oxopropoxy]-9-fluoro-11-hydroxy-16,17-[(1-methylethylidene)bis(oxy)]pregna-1,4-diene-3,20-dione

triamcinolone acetonide (q. v.)

β-benzoylaminoiso-butyryl chloride

Triamcinolone benetonide

Reference(s):
DOS 2 047 218 (Sigma-Tau; appl. 25.9.1970; I-prior. 31.10.1969).

Formulation(s): cream 0.075 %

Trade Name(s):
F: Tibicorten (Stiefel); wfm
I: Tibicorten F (Sigma-Tau)-comb.; wfm

Triamcinolone diacetate

ATC: A01AC01; H02AB08
Use: glucocorticoid

RN: 67-78-7 MF: $C_{25}H_{31}FO_8$ MW: 478.51 EINECS: 200-669-0
CN: (11β,16α)-16,21-bis(acetyloxy)-9-fluoro-11,17-dihydroxypregna-1,4-diene-3,20-dione

(a)

1. SeO₂, (CH₃)₃COH
   or
2. Corynebacterium simplex

1. selenium dioxide,
   tert-butanol

16α,21-diacetoxy-11β,17-
dihydroxy-3,20-dioxo-9-
fluoro-4-pregnene
(cf. triamcinolone synthesis)

Triamcinolone diacetate

(b)

H₂F₂, CHCl₃
hydrogen
fluoride

Triamcinolone diacetate

16α,21-diacetoxy-3,20-
dioxo-17-hydroxy-9β,11β-
epoxy-1,4-pregnadiene
(cf. triamcinolone synthesis)

Reference(s):
a1 DE 1 096 900 (American Cyanamid; appl. 1959; USA-prior. 1958).
   GB 835 836 (American Cyanamid; valid from 1958; USA-prior. 1957).
a2 GB 824 351 (American Cyanamid; valid from 1956; USA-prior. 1956).
b GB 851 501 (American Cyanamid; valid from 1958; USA-prior. 1957).

Formulation(s):   amp. 25 mg, 40 mg; susp.. 25 mg/ml, 40 mg/ml

Trade Name(s):
D: Delphicort (Lederle)   F: Tédarol (Specia); wfm   J: Ledercort inj. (Lederle)
      Delphimix (Lederle)-comb.   I: Ledercort (Cyanamid)   USA: Aristocorte (Fujisawa)

Triamcinolone hexacetonide

ATC: A01AC01
Use: glucocorticoid

RN: 5611-51-8   MF: C₃₀H₄₁FO₇   MW: 532.65   EINECS: 227-031-4
CN: (11β,16α)-21-(3,3-dimethyl-1-oxobutoxy)-9-fluoro-11-hydroxy-16,17-[(1-
       methylethylidene)bis(oxy)]pregna-1,4-diene-3,20-dione

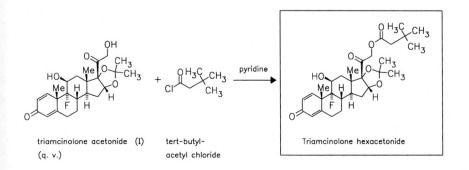

triamcinolone acetonide (I)   tert-butyl-   Triamcinolone hexacetonide
(q. v.)   acetyl chloride

I + tert-butylacetic anhydride →(pyridine)→ Triamcinolone hexacetonide

tert-butylacetic
anhydride

Reference(s):
DOS 2 317 954 (J. Zaklady Farm. "Polfa"; appl. 10.4.1973; P-prior. 21.4.1972).

injection suspension:
US 3 457 348 (American Cyanamid; 22.7.1969; prior. 27.6.1966).

review:
Zbinovsky, V.; Chrekian, G.P.: Anal. Profiles Drug Subst. (APDSB7) **6**, 579 (1977).

Formulation(s):   amp. 5 mg/ml, 20 mg/ml

Trade Name(s):
D: Lederlon 5/20 (Lederle)   F: Hexatrione longue durée   GB: Lederspan (Wyeth)
                                        (Wyeth-Lederle)   USA: Aristospan (Fujisawa)

Triamterene

ATC: C03DB02
Use: diuretic

RN: 396-01-0   MF: $C_{12}H_{11}N_7$ MW: 253.27   EINECS: 206-904-3
LD$_{50}$:   25.077 mg/kg (M, i.v.); 285 mg/kg (M, p.o.);
        400 mg/kg (R, p.o.)
CN: 6-phenyl-2,4,7-pteridinetriamine

guanidine nitrate →(1. NaOCH₃ 2. CN-CN 2. malono-nitrile)→ 2,4,6-triamino-pyrimidine →(NaNO₂, CH₃COOH)→ 5-nitroso-2,4,6-triaminopyrimidine (I)

I + benzyl cyanide →(NaOCH₃)→ Triamterene

Reference(s):
US 3 081 230 (Smith Kline & French; 12.3.1963; prior. 8.9.1960).
Spickett, R.G.W.; Timmis, G.M.: J. Chem. Soc. (JCSOA9) **1954**, 2887.
FR-M 1 014 (Smith Kline & French; appl. 5.11.1960).

5-nitroso-2,4,6-triaminopyrimidine:
Sato et al.: Nippon Kagaku Zasshi (NPKZAZ) **72**, 866 (1951).

improved method:
US 4 145 548 (Henkel; 20.3.1979; D-prior. 12.11.1976).
DOS 2 651 794 (Henkel; appl. 12.11.1976).

combination with cyclothiazide:
GB 1 547 826 (Roussel-Uclaf; appl. 31.3.1976; F-prior. 11.4.1975).

combination with verapamil:
DOS 2 658 500 (Röhm Pharma; appl. 23.12.1976).
US 4 157 394 (Röhm Pharma; 5.6.1979; D-prior. 23.12.1976).

Formulation(s):   cps. 50 mg, 100 mg; drg. 50 mg; tabl. 50 mg, 75 mg

Trade Name(s):

D: Diutensat (Azupharma)-
    comb.
    Diuretikum Verla (Verla)-
    comb.
    duradiuret (durachemie)-
    comb.
    Dytide (Procter &
    Gamble)-comb.
    Esiteren (Novartis
    Pharma)-comb.
    Hypertorr (Henning
    Berlin)-comb.
    Jatropur (Röhm Pharma)
    Jenateren (Jenapharm)-
    comb.
    Nephral (Pfleger)-comb.
    SALI-PUREN (Isis Puren)-
    comb.
    Thiazid-Wolff (Wolff)-
    comb.
    Triampur (ASTA Medica
    AWD)-comb.

    Triarese (Hexal)-comb.
    Triazid (ct-Arzneimittel)-
    comb.
    Tri-Thiazid Stada (Stada)
    Turfa-BASF (BASF
    Generics)-comb.
    numerous combination
    preparations
F: Cyclotériam (Roussel)-
    comb.
    Isobar (Jacques Logeais)-
    comb.
    Prestole (Pharmafarm)-
    comb.
GB: Dyazide (SmithKline
    Beecham)-comb.
    Dytac (Pharmark)
    Dytide (Pharmark)-comb.
    Frusene (Orion)-comb.
    Kalspare (Dominion)-
    comb.

    Triam Co (Baker Norton)-
    comb.
I: Fluss 40 (Hoechst Marion
    Roussel)-comb.
J: Amteren (Sanko)
    Diarrol (Nippon Shoji)
    Diucelpin (Eisai)
    Diurene (Hokuriku)
    Diuteren (Showa)
    Hidiurese (Nichiiko)
    Masuharmin (Fuso)
    Reviten (Tokyo Tanabe)
    Tricilone (Vangard)-comb.
    Trispan (Yamanouchi)
    Triteren (Sumitomo)
    Triurene (Kanto)
USA: Dyazide (SmithKline
    Beecham)
    Dyrenium (SmithKline
    Beecham)
    Maxzide (Bertek)
    generics

Triaziquone

ATC: L01AC02
Use: antineoplastic

RN: 68-76-8   MF: $C_{12}H_{13}N_3O_2$ MW: 231.26   EINECS: 200-692-6
LD_{50}: 500 µg/kg (R, i.v.)
CN: 2,3,5-tris(1-aziridinyl)-2,5-cyclohexadiene-1,4-dione

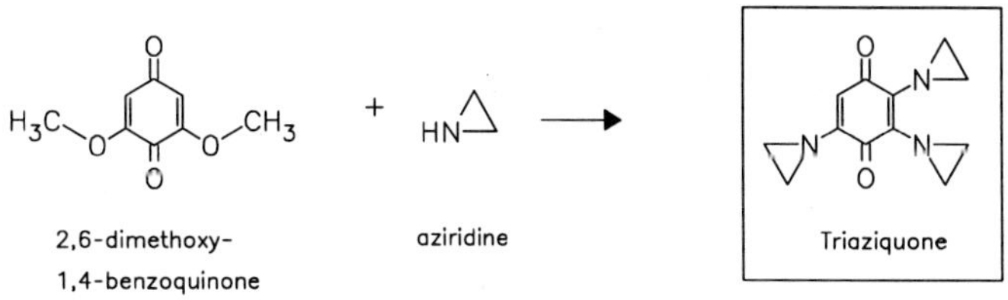

2,6-dimethoxy-   aziridine   Triaziquone
1,4-benzoquinone

Reference(s):
US 2 976 279 (Schenley Ind.; 21.3.1961; D-prior. 14.3.1957).

Trade Name(s):
D: Trenimon (Bayer); wfm   GB: Trenimon (Bayer); wfm

Triazolam

ATC: N05CD05
Use: hypnotic, sedative

RN: 28911-01-5 MF: C$_{17}$H$_{12}$Cl$_2$N$_4$ MW: 343.22 EINECS: 249-307-3
LD$_{50}$: 1080 mg/kg (M, p.o.);
>7500 mg/kg (R, p.o.)
CN: 8-chloro-6-(2-chlorophenyl)-1-methyl-4H-[1,2,4]triazolo[4,3-a][1,4]benzodiazepine

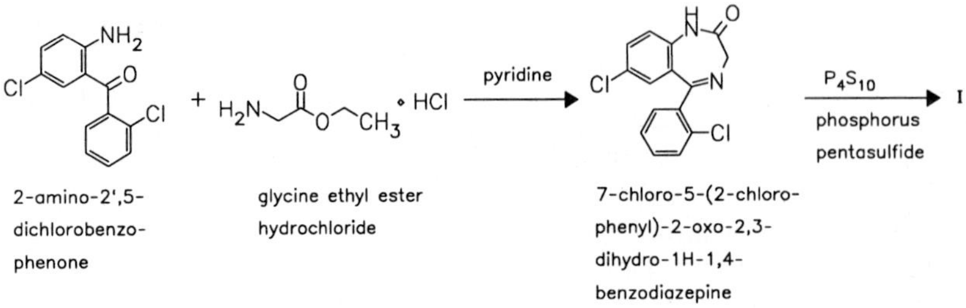

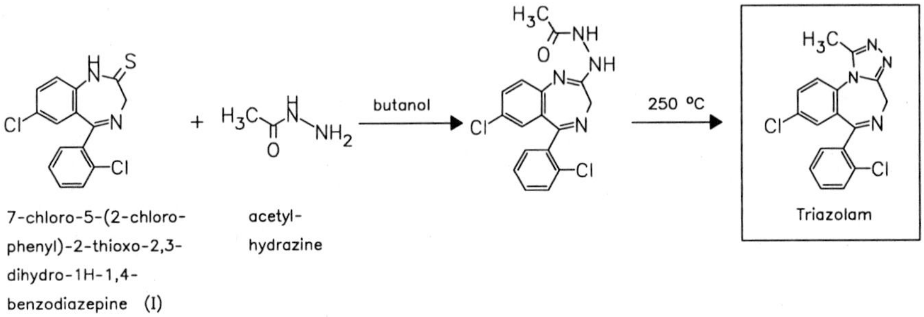

2-amino-2',5-
dichlorobenzo-
phenone

glycine ethyl ester
hydrochloride

7-chloro-5-(2-chloro-
phenyl)-2-oxo-2,3-
dihydro-1H-1,4-
benzodiazepine

7-chloro-5-(2-chloro-
phenyl)-2-thioxo-2,3-
dihydro-1H-1,4-
benzodiazepine (I)

acetyl-
hydrazine

Triazolam

Reference(s):
DOS 2 012 190 (Upjohn; appl. 14.3.1970; USA-prior. 17.3.1969, 29.10.1969).
US 3 987 052 (Upjohn; 19.10.1976; prior. 17.3.1969, 29.10.1969).
US 3 980 790 (Upjohn, 14.9.1976; appl. 4.8.1972; prior. 29.3.1971).

thiono-intermediate:
Archer, G.A.; Sternbach, L.H.: J. Org. Chem. (JOCEAH) **29**, 231 (1964).
US 3 422 091 (Roche; 14.1.1969; prior. 21.6.1962, 10.7.1962).

alternative syntheses:
DOS 2 203 782 (Upjohn; appl. 27.1.1972; USA-prior. 9.2.1971).
DOS 2 302 525 (Upjohn; appl. 19.1.1973; USA-prior. 31.1.1972).

Formulation(s): tabl. 0.125 mg, 0.25 mg

Trade Name(s):
D: Halcion (Pharmacia &
Upjohn; 1979)
F: Halcion (Pharmacia &
Upjohn; 1980)

GB: Halcion (Upjohn); wfm
I: Halcion (Pharmacia &
Upjohn)
Songar (Valeas)

J: Halcion (Upjohn-
Sumitomo)
USA: Halcion (Pharmacia &
Upjohn; 1982)

Tribenoside

ATC: C05AX05; C05CX01
Use: vein therapeutic, sclerosing agent

RN: 10310-32-4   MF: $C_{29}H_{34}O_6$ MW: 478.59   EINECS: 233-687-2
LD$_{50}$:   >30 g/kg (M, p.o.);
        >20 g/kg (R, p.o.)
CN: ethyl 3,5,6-tris-O-(phenylmethyl)-D-glucofuranoside

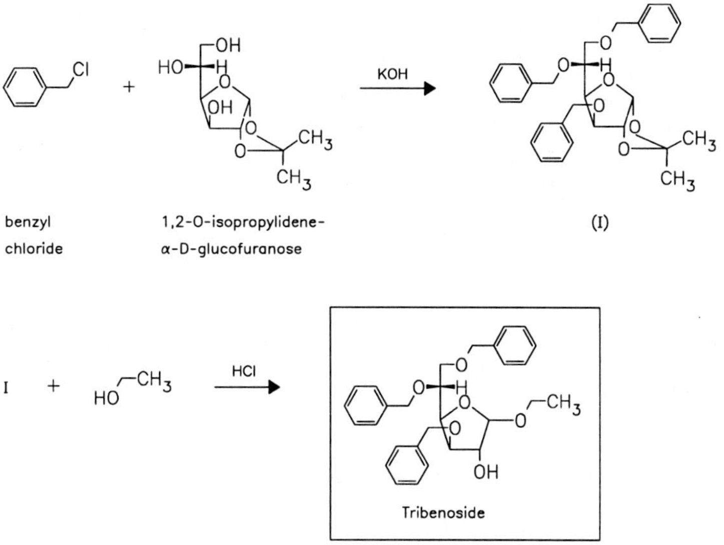

benzyl   1,2-O-isopropylidene-   (I)
chloride   α-D-glucofuranose

Tribenoside

Reference(s):
US 3 157 634 (Ciba; 17.11.1964; CH-prior. 10.1.1959, 6.11.1959, 30.11.1959).

Formulation(s):   cps. 400 mg; cream 5 %; drg. 200 mg; suppos. 400 mg

Trade Name(s):

D:	Glyvenol (Ciba); wfm	J:	Glurenol (Ciba-Geigy)
F:	Glycénol (Ciba); wfm		Hemocuron (Takeda)
I:	Venalisin (AGIPS)		

USA: Glyvenol (Ciba-Geigy); wfm

Trichlormethiazide

ATC: C03AA06
Use: diuretic, antihypertensive

RN: 133-67-5   MF: $C_8H_8Cl_3N_3O_4S_2$ MW: 380.66   EINECS: 205-118-8
LD$_{50}$:   750 mg/kg (M, i.v.); 2600 mg/kg (M, p.o.);
        920 mg/kg (R, i.v.); 5600 mg/kg (R, p.o.)
CN: 6-chloro-3-(dichloromethyl)-3,4-dihydro-2H-1,2,4-benzothiadiazine-7-sulfonamide 1,1-dioxide

4-amino-6-chloro-
1,3-benzenedi-
sulfonamide
(cf. chlorothiazide
synthesis)

dichloroacet-
aldehyde
diethyl acetal

Trichlormethiazide

Reference(s):
GB 949 373 (Scherico; appl. 2.3.1960; USA-prior. 2.3.1959, 15.7.1959).
DAS 1 147 233 (Ciba; appl. 4.10.1960; USA-prior. 8.10.1959, 16.10.1959).
BE 576 304 (Ciba; appl. 3.3.1959; USA-prior. 3.3.1958).

alternative syntheses:
US 3 264 292 (Abbott; 2.8.1966; appl. 3.11.1958).
GB 954 023 (Scherico; appl. 11.5.1960; USA-prior. 25.4.1960).
Sherlock, M.H. et al.: Experientia (EXPEAM) **16**, 184 (1960).
Stevens, G. de et al.: Experientia (EXPEAM) **16**, 113 (1960).

Formulation(s):   tabl. 2 mg, 4 mg in comb. with amiloride hydrochloride

Trade Name(s):
D: Esmalorid (Merck)-comb.
I: Fluitran (Essex); wfm
     Fluitran (Sca); wfm
     Triclordiuride (Formenti);
     wfm
J: Achletin (Toyama)
     Anatran (Tobishi)
     Anistadin (Maruko)
     Carvacron (Taiyo)

Fluitran (Shionogi)
Intromene (Teikoku)
Sanamiron (Zensei)
Tachionin (San-a)
Tolcasone (Toho)
USA: Metahydrin (Merrell Dow);
       wfm
       Metahydrin (Merrell-
       National); wfm

Metatensin (Merrell Dow)-
comb.; wfm
Metatensin (Merrell-
National)-comb.; wfm
Naqua (Schering); wfm
Naquival (Schering)-comb.;
wfm
Triazide (Legere); wfm

Triclocarban
(Trichlorcarbanilide)

ATC: D08AX
Use: bacteriostatic, cutanous antiseptic,
       germicidal agent, disinfectant

RN: 101-20-2   MF: $C_{13}H_9Cl_3N_2O$ MW: 315.59   EINECS: 202-924-1
LD_{50}: >34.6 g/kg (R, p.o.)
CN: *N*-(4-chlorophenyl)-*N'*-(3,4-dichlorophenyl)urea

4-chlorophenyl
isocyanate

3,4-dichloro-
aniline

Triclocarban

Reference(s):
US 2 818 390 (Monsanto; 1957; appl. 1954).

Formulation(s):   emulsion 250 mg/100 ml; powder 1 %

Trade Name(s):
D: Ansudor (Galderma)-comb.   Septivon (Chefaro-   GB: Cutisan (Dales); wfm
F: Cutisan (Boots Healthcare)   Ardeval)-comb.   I: Citrosil (Manetti Roberts)
        Nobacter (Boots   Solubacter (Boots   Sangen (Boots H.M. VITI)
        Healthcare)   Healthcare)

Triclofos

ATC: N05CM07
Use: hypnotic

RN: 306-52-5   MF: C$_2$H$_4$Cl$_3$O$_4$P   MW: 229.38   EINECS: 206-185-6
LD$_{50}$: 850 mg/kg (M, p.o.);
        850 mg/kg (R, p.o.)
CN: 2,2,2-trichloroethanol dihydrogen phosphate

monosodium salt
RN: 7246-20-0   MF: C$_2$H$_3$Cl$_3$NaO$_4$P   MW: 251.37   EINECS: 230-652-3
LD$_{50}$: 1400 mg/kg (M, p.o.);
        1900 mg/kg (R, p.o.)

Reference(s):
BE 623 216 (Glaxo; appl. 4.10.1962; GB-prior. 5.10.1961).

Formulation(s):   syrup 500 mg/5 ml

Trade Name(s):
GB: Tricloryl (Glaxo); wfm   USA: Triclos (Lakeside); wfm   Triclos (Merrell Dow);
J: Tricloryl (Torii)   wfm

Triclosan
(Cloxifenol)

ATC: D08AE04; D09AA06
Use: antiseptic

RN: 3380-34-5   MF: C$_{12}$H$_7$Cl$_3$O$_2$ MW: 289.55   EINECS: 222-182-2
LD$_{50}$: 4530 mg/kg (M, p.o.);
        29 mg/kg (R, i.v.); 3700 mg/kg (R, p.o.)
CN: 5-chloro-2-(2,4-dichlorophenoxy)phenol

I →[Fe, CH₃COOH] 2-amino-2',4,4'-tri-chlorodiphenyl ether →[nitrosylsulfuric acid] Triclosan

Reference(s):
US 3 506 720 (Geigy; 14.4.1970; CH-prior. 22.2.1963).

Formulation(s):   cream 10 mg/gsol. 0.1 g/100 g

Trade Name(s):
D: Rutisept (Henkel)-comb.
        Sicorten Creme (Novartis
        Pharma)-comb.
GB: Aquasept (Seton)
        Manusept (Seton)

        Oilatum Plus (Stiefel)-
        comb.
        Ster-Zac Bath Conc.
        (Seton)
I: Dopo Pik (Tipomark)
        Gampphen (Ethicon)

        Irgaman (Hoechst Marion
        Merrell)
USA: Clearasil Antibac. Soap
        (Vicks); wfm
        Sulfur-8 Shampoo
        (Plough); wfm

Tridihexethyl chloride

ATC: A03AB08
Use: anticholinergic, antispasmodic

RN: 4310-35-4   MF: $C_{21}H_{36}ClNO$ MW: 353.98   EINECS: 224-323-3
LD$_{50}$:   103 mg/kg (M, i.p.)
CN: γ-cyclohexyl-*N,N,N*-triethyl-γ-hydroxybenzenepropanaminium chloride

iodide
RN: 125-99-5   MF: $C_{21}H_{36}INO$ MW: 445.43   EINECS: 204-762-7
LD$_{50}$:   18 mg/kg (M, i.v.); 570 mg/kg (M, p.o.);
        27 mg/kg (R, i.v.); 1100 mg/kg (R, p.o.)
hydroxide
RN: 511-43-3   MF: $C_{21}H_{37}NO_2$ MW: 335.53

ⓐ   part 1 (Burroughs Wellcome):

acetophenone + paraform-aldehyde (CH₂O)ₓ + diethyl-amine → 3-diethylamino-propiophenone (I)

I + cyclohexylmagnesium bromide → 3-diethylamino-1-cyclohexyl-1-phenyl-1-propanol (II)

b part 2 (American Cyanamid):

II + ethyl iodide → tridihexethyl iodide → Tridihexethyl chloride (AgCl, silver chloride)

Reference(s):
a   US 2 698 325 (Burroughs Wellcome; 1954; prior. 1948).
b   US 2 913 494 (American Cyanamid; 17.11.1959; prior. 2.10.1957).

Formulation(s):   tabl. 25 mg (as chloride)

Trade Name(s):
I: Duoesetil (Dessy); wfm   USA: Pathibamate (Lederle)-   Pathilon (Lederle); wfm
J: Pathilon (Lederle)   comb.; wfm

Trientine
(TECZA; TETA)

ATC: V03A
Use: chelating agent for treatment of Wilson's disease

RN: 112-24-3   MF: $C_6H_{18}N_4$ MW: 146.24   EINECS: 203-950-6
LD$_{50}$:   350 mg/kg (M, i.v.); 1600 mg/kg (M, p.o.);
        2500 mg/kg (R, p.o.)
CN: N,N'-bis(2-aminoethyl)-1,2-ethanediamine

dihydrochloride
RN: 38260-01-4   MF: $C_6H_{18}N_4 \cdot 2HCl$ MW: 219.16   EINECS: 253-854-3
LD$_{50}$:   2285 mg/kg (R, p.o.)

ethylene-   1,2-dichloro-   Trientine
diamine   ethane

Reference(s):
Alphen, J. van: Recl. Trav. Chim. Pays-Bas (RTCPA3) **55**, 412 (1936).
Hoffmann, A.W. von: Chem. Ber. (CHBEAM) **23**, 3711 (1890).
Jones, G.D. et al.: J. Org. Chem. (JOCEAH) **9**, 125 (1944).

Formulation(s):   cps. 250 mg (as dihydrochloride)

Trade Name(s):
J: Metalite (Tsumura   USA: Syprine (Merck)
        Juntendo)

Trifluoperazine

ATC: N05AB06
Use: neuroleptic

RN: 117-89-5   MF: C$_{21}$H$_{24}$F$_3$N$_3$S   MW: 407.50   EINECS: 204-219-4
LD$_{50}$: 29 mg/kg (M, i.v.); 1350 mg/kg (M, p.o.)
CN: 10-[3-(4-methyl-1-piperazinyl)propyl]-2-(trifluoromethyl)-10*H*-phenothiazine

dihydrochloride
RN: 440-17-5   MF: C$_{21}$H$_{24}$F$_3$N$_3$S · 2HCl   MW: 480.43   EINECS: 207-123-0
LD$_{50}$: 82 mg/kg (M, i.v.); 424 mg/kg (M, p.o.);
         543 mg/kg (R, p.o.)

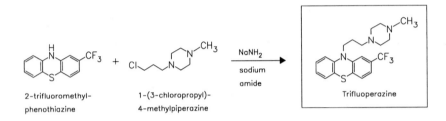

2-trifluoromethyl-   1-(3-chloropropyl)-   Trifluoperazine
phenothiazine   4-methylpiperazine

Reference(s):
US 2 921 069 (Smith Kline & French; 12.1.1960; prior. 9.4.1956).
DE 1 095 836 (Squibb; appl. 8.12.1956; USA-prior. 23.12.1955, 12.7.1956).
Craig, P.N. et al.: J. Org. Chem. (JOCEAH) **22**, 709 (1959).
DE 1 165 034 (Smith Kline & French; appl. 29.9.1956; USA-prior. 9.4.1956).

Formulation(s):   cps. 2.36 mg; f. c. tabl. 1 mg, 2 mg, 5 mg, 10 mg; vial 2 mg/ml, 10 mg/ml (as dihydrochloride)

Trade Name(s):
D: Jatroneural (Procter &   Stelazine (SmithKline   J: Normaln P (Sawai)
        Gamble)   Beecham)   Tranquis (Sumitomo)
F: Terfluzine (Spécia)   I: Modalina (Sanofi   Trifluoperazine (Yoshitomi)
GB: Parstelin (SmithKline   Winthrop)   USA: Stelazine (SmithKline
        Beecham)-comb.   Parmodalin (Sanofi   Beecham)
                                          Winthrop)-comb.

Trifluperidol

ATC: N05AD02
Use: neuroleptic

RN: 749-13-3   MF: C$_{22}$H$_{23}$F$_4$NO$_2$ MW: 409.42
LD$_{50}$: 26 mg/kg (M, i.v.); 110 mg/kg (M, p.o.);
         14 mg/kg (R, i.v.); 140 mg/kg (R, p.o.)
CN: 1-(4-fluorophenyl)-4-[4-hydroxy-4-[3-(trifluoromethyl)phenyl]-1-piperidinyl]-1-butanone

hydrochloride
RN: 2062-77-3   MF: C$_{22}$H$_{23}$F$_4$NO$_2$ · HCl   MW: 445.88   EINECS: 218-170-1
LD$_{50}$: 17.4 mg/kg (M, i.v.); 99 mg/kg (M, p.o.);
         14 mg/kg (R, i.v.)

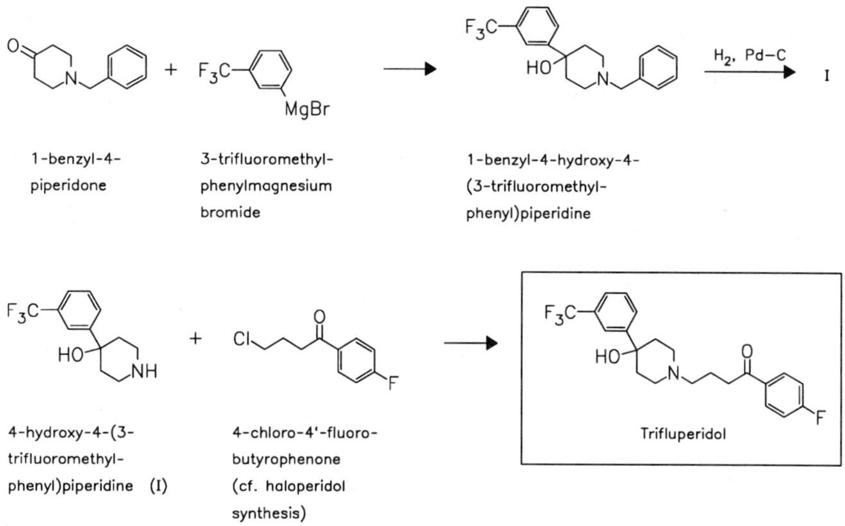

1-benzyl-4-
piperidone

3-trifluoromethyl-
phenylmagnesium
bromide

1-benzyl-4-hydroxy-4-
(3-trifluoromethyl-
phenyl)piperidine

4-hydroxy-4-(3-
trifluoromethyl-
phenyl)piperidine   (I)

4-chloro-4'-fluoro-
butyrophenone
(cf. haloperidol
synthesis)

Trifluperidol

Reference(s):
GB 895 309 (Janssen; appl. and prior. 18.11.1959; valid from 17.11.1960).

Formulation(s):   amp. 2.5 mg; drops 1 mg/ml (as hydrochloride)

Trade Name(s):
D: Triperidol (Janssen-Cilag)   I: Psicoperidol   USA: Triperidol (McNeil); wfm
F: Triperidol (Janssen-Cilag)   (Lusofarmaco)
GB: Triperidol (Janssen); wfm   J: Triperidol (Yoshitomi)

Triflupromazine

(Fluopromazine)

ATC: N05AA05
Use: neuroleptic

RN: 146-54-3   MF: $C_{18}H_{19}F_3N_2S$ MW: 352.42   EINECS: 205-673-6
LD_{50}:   34 mg/kg (M, i.v.); 245 mg/kg (M, p.o.);
         185 mg/kg (R, p.o.)
CN: N,N-dimethyl-2-(trifluoromethyl)-10H-phenothiazine-10-propanamine

monohydrochloride
RN: 1098-60-8   MF: $C_{18}H_{19}F_3N_2S \cdot HCl$ MW: 388.89   EINECS: 214-149-6
LD_{50}:   34 mg/kg (M, i.v.); 254 mg/kg (M, p.o.);
         17 mg/kg (dog, i.v.)

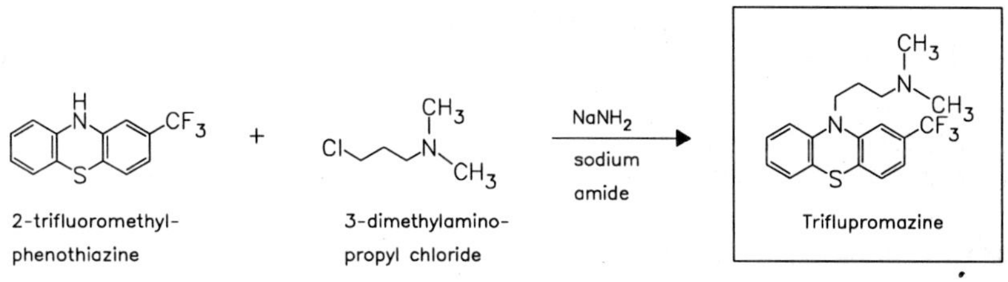

2-trifluoromethyl-
phenothiazine

3-dimethylamino-
propyl chloride

NaNH₂
sodium
amide

Triflupromazine

Reference(s):

DE 1 095 836 (Squibb; appl. 8.12.1956; USA-prior. 23.12.1955, 12.7.1956).

US 2 921 069 (Smith Kline & French; 12.1.1960; prior. 9.4.1956).

Duhm, B. et al.: Z. Naturforsch. Teil B: Anorg. Chem., Org. Chem., Biochem., Biophys., Biol. (ZENBAX) **13**, 756 (1958).

Craig, P.N. et al.: J. Org. Chem. (JOCEAH) **22**, 709 (1959).

Formulation(s):   amp. 10 mg/ml, 20 mg/ml; drg. 10 mg, 25 mg; suppos. 70 mg (as hydrochloride)

Trade Name(s):

D:	Psyquil (Sanofi Winthrop)	I:	Vesprin (Squibb); wfm	USA:	Vesprin (Squibb; as	
F:	Psyquil (Squibb); wfm	J:	Vesprin (Squibb-Showa)		hydrochloride); wfm	

Trifluridine

ATC: S01AD02
Use: antiviral

RN: 70-00-8   MF: $C_{10}H_{11}F_3N_2O_5$ MW: 296.20   EINECS: 200-722-8
LD_{50}: 3381 mg/kg (M, i.v.);
2946 mg/kg (R, i.v.)
CN: α,α,α-trifluorothymidine

5-trifluoro-
methyluracil

hexamethyl-
disilazane

chlorotrimethyl-
silane

(I)

2-deoxyribofuranosyl chloride
3,5-bis(4-nitrobenzoate)

Trifluridine

Reference(s):

US 3 531 464 (Seer. Dept. of Health Educ. and Welfare; 29.9.1970; prior. 21.10.1966).

starting material:

DD 119 423 (L. Hein, D. Cech, C. Liebenthal; appl. 17.4.1975).

US 3 201 387 (Secr. Dept. of Health Educ. and Welfare; 17.8. 1965; appl. 18.9.1963).

Formulation(s):   eye ointment 20 mg/g; eye drops 10 mg/ml, sol. 1 %

Trade Name(s):

D:	TFT Thilo 1 %		Triflumann (Mann)	I:	Triherpine (CIBA Vision)
	Augentropfen (Alcon)	F:	Virophta (Allergan)	USA:	Viroptic (Monarch)

Trihexyphenidyl

(Benzhexol)

ATC: N04AA01
Use: antiparkinsonian

RN: 144-11-6   MF: $C_{20}H_{31}NO$ MW: 301.47   EINECS: 205-614-4
LD_{50}: 41 mg/kg (M, i.v.); 335 mg/kg (M, p.o.)
CN: α-cyclohexyl-α-phenyl-1-piperidinepropanol

hydrochloride

RN: 52-49-3   MF: $C_{20}H_{31}NO \cdot HCl$ MW: 337.94   EINECS: 200-142-5
LD_{50}: 39 mg/kg (M, i.v.); 217 mg/kg (M, p.o.);
30 mg/kg (R, i.v.); 1630 mg/kg (R, p.o.)

aceto-
phenone

paraform-
aldehyde

piperidine

3-piperidino-
propiophenone (I)

cyclohexylmagnesium
bromide

Trihexyphenidyl

Reference(s):
US 2 680 115 (Winthrop-Stearns; 1954; prior. 1949).
US 2 716 121 (American Cyanamid; 1955; prior. 1946, 1949).

alternative synthesis:
US 2 682 543 (Burroughs Wellcome; 1954; appl. 1951).

Formulation(s):   amp. 10 mg/5 ml; elixir 2 mg/5 ml; tabl. 2 mg, 5 mg, 15 mg (as hydrochloride)

Trade Name(s):

D:	Artane (Lederle)	GB:	Broflex (Bioglan)	Pyramistin (Yamanouchi)
	Parkopan (Neuro Hexal)	I:	Artane (Wyeth-Lederle)	Tremin (Schering-
F:	Artane (Spécia)	J:	Artane (Lederle)	Shionogi)
	Parkinane retard (Wyeth-		Arten (Lederle-Takeda; as	Triphedionon (Toho)
	Lederle)		hydrochloride)	USA: Artane (Lederle)

Trilostane

ATC: H02CA01
Use: adrenocortical suppressant

RN: 13647-35-3   MF: $C_{20}H_{27}NO_3$ MW: 329.44   EINECS: 237-133-0
CN: (2α,4α,5α,17β)-4,5-epoxy-17-hydroxy-3-oxoandrostane-2-carbonitrile

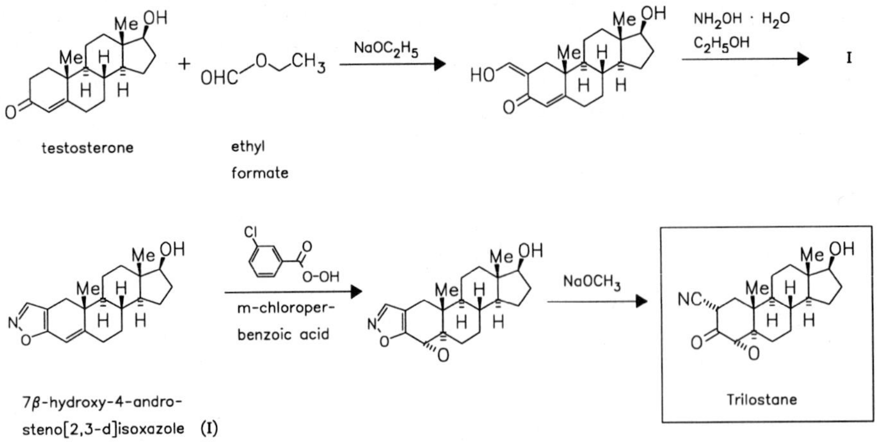

testosterone

ethyl
formate

7β-hydroxy-4-andro-
steno[2,3-d]isoxazole (I)

m-chloroper-
benzoic acid

Trilostane

Reference(s):
US 3 296 255 (Sterling Drug; 3.1.1967; USA-prior. 23.6.1958, 29.6.1960, 29.11.1963).
Neumann, H.C. et al.: J. Med. Chem. (JMCMAR) **13**, 948 (1970).

intermediates:
US 3 135 743 (Sterling Drug; 2.6.1964; appl. 29.6.1960).

Formulation(s):   cps. 60 mg; tabl. 60 mg

Trade Name(s):
GB: Modrenal (Wanskerne)   USA: Modrastane (Winthrop-
J: Desopane (Mochida)   Breon); wfm

Trimazosin

ATC: C02CA03
Use: antihypertensive

RN: 35795-16-5   MF: $C_{20}H_{29}N_5O_6$ MW: 435.48   EINECS: 252-732-7
CN: 4-(4-amino-6,7,8-trimethoxy-2-quinazolinyl)-1-piperazinecarboxylic acid 2-hydroxy-2-methylpropyl
ester

monohydrochloride monohydrate
RN: 53746-46-6   MF: $C_{20}H_{29}N_5O_6 \cdot HCl \cdot H_2O$ MW: 489.96

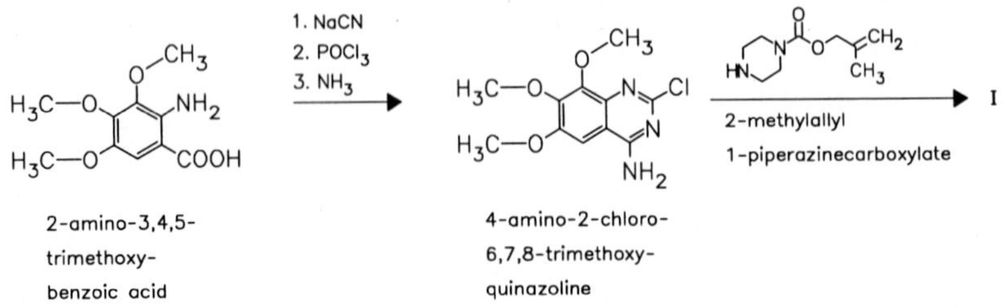

1. NaCN
2. POCl₃
3. NH₃

2-amino-3,4,5-
trimethoxy-
benzoic acid

4-amino-2-chloro-
6,7,8-trimethoxy-
quinazoline

2-methylallyl
1-piperazinecarboxylate

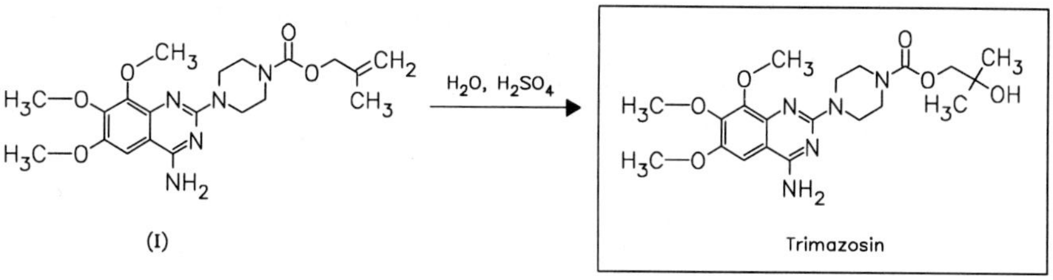

(I) → Trimazosin

Reference(s):
DOS 2 120 495 (Pfizer; appl. 27.4.1971; USA-prior. 21.5.1970).
US 3 669 968 (Pfizer; 13.6.1972; prior. 21.5.1970).

Formulation(s):   tabl. 100 mg

Trade Name(s):
D: Supres (Pfizer); wfm

Trimetazidine

ATC: C01EB15
Use: vasodilator

RN: 5011-34-7   MF: $C_{14}H_{22}N_2O_3$ MW: 266.34   EINECS: 225-690-2
CN: 1-[(2,3,4-trimethoxyphenyl)methyl]piperazine

dihydrochloride
RN: 13171-25-0   MF: $C_{14}H_{22}N_2O_3 \cdot 2HCl$ MW: 339.26   EINECS: 236-117-0
LD$_{50}$:   125 mg/kg (M, i.v.); 1550 mg/kg (M, p.o.);
         1700 mg/kg (R, p.o.)

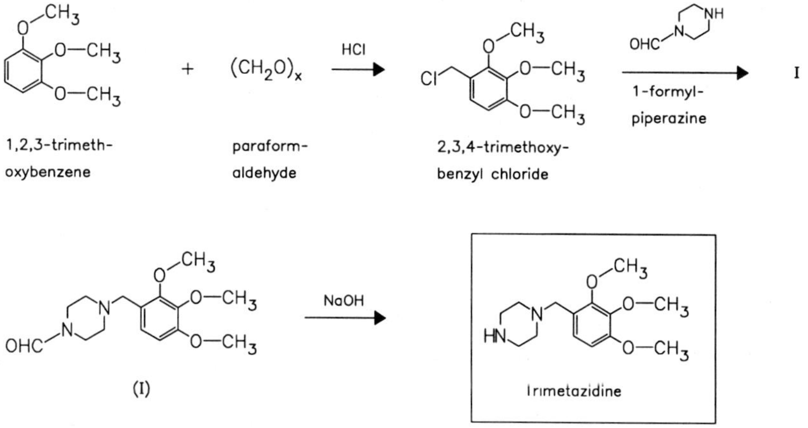

1,2,3-trimeth-
oxybenzene

paraform-
aldehyde

2,3,4-trimethoxy-
benzyl chloride

1-formyl-
piperazine

(I) → Trimetazidine

Reference(s):
FR 1 302 958 (Science Union; appl. 21.3.1961).

Formulation(s):   tabl. 3 mg, 20 mg (as hydrochloride)

Trade Name(s):
D:	Anaprel F (Servier)-comb.; wfm		Vastarel Fort (Servier); wfm	I: Vastarel (Stroder)
	Diviator (Servier)-comb.; wfm	F:	Vastarel (Biopharma)	J: Cartoma (Ohta)
		GB:	Vastarel (Servier); wfm	Coronanyl (Toho Shinyaku)
				Hiwell (Toa Eiyo)

Lubomanil (Maruko)	Vassarin-F (Taiyo)	Yosimilon (Kowa Yakuhin)
Sainosine (Chemiphar)	Vastarel (Kyoto)	
Trimeperad (Kotobuki-Kanebo)	Vastazin (Takeda-Nippon Kayaku)	

Trimethadione

(Troxidone)

ATC: N03AC02
Use: antiepileptic

RN: 127-48-0 MF: $C_6H_9NO_3$ MW: 143.14 EINECS: 204-845-8
LD_{50}: 2 g/kg (M, i.v.); 2100 mg/kg (M, p.o.);
2140 mg/kg (R, p.o.)
CN: 3,5,5-trimethyl-2,4-oxazolidinedione

ethyl α-hydroxy-isobutyrate   urea   5,5-dimethyl-2,4-oxazolidine-dione   Trimethadione

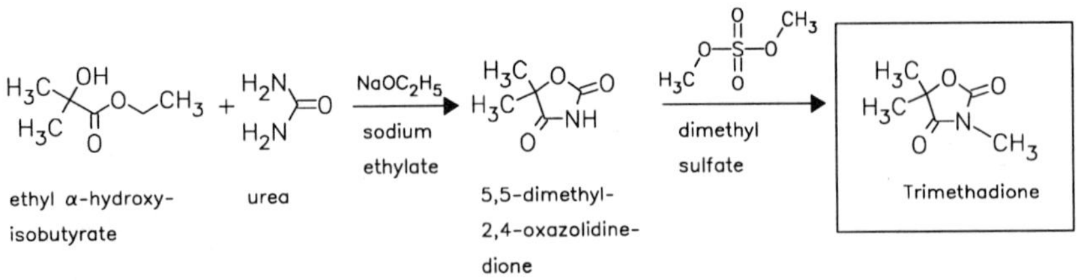

Reference(s):
US 2 559 011 (British Schering; 1951; GB-prior. 1946).
US 2 575 692 (Abbott; 1951; appl. 1947).

Formulation(s): cps. 300 mg

Trade Name(s):
D: Tridione (Abbott); wfm
F: Epidione (Roger Bellon); wfm

GB: Triméthadione Abbott (Abbott); wfm
Tridione (Abbott); wfm

J: Mino-Aleviatin (Dainippon)
Tendal (Shionogi)
USA: Tridione (Abbott); wfm

Trimethobenzamide

ATC: A04AD
Use: anti-emetic

RN: 138-56-7 MF: $C_{21}H_{28}N_2O_5$ MW: 388.46 EINECS: 205-332-1
CN: N-[[4-[2-(dimethylamino)ethoxy]phenyl]methyl]-3,4,5-trimethoxybenzamide

monohydrochloride
RN: 554-92-7 MF: $C_{21}H_{28}N_2O_5 \cdot HCl$ MW: 424.93 EINECS: 209-075-6
LD_{50}: 122 mg/kg (M, i.v.); 1600 mg/kg (M, p.o.)

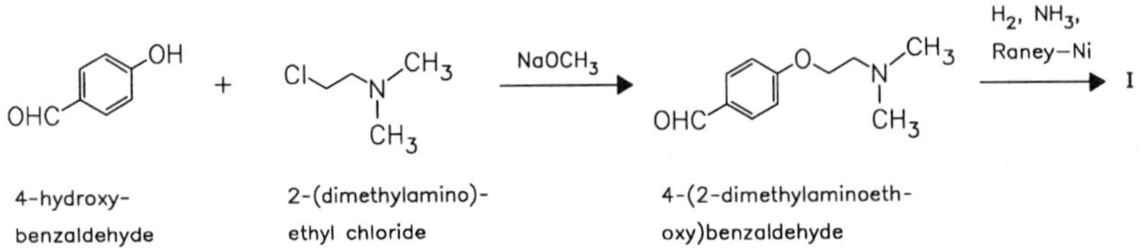

4-hydroxy-benzaldehyde   2-(dimethylamino)-ethyl chloride   4-(2-dimethylaminoeth-oxy)benzaldehyde

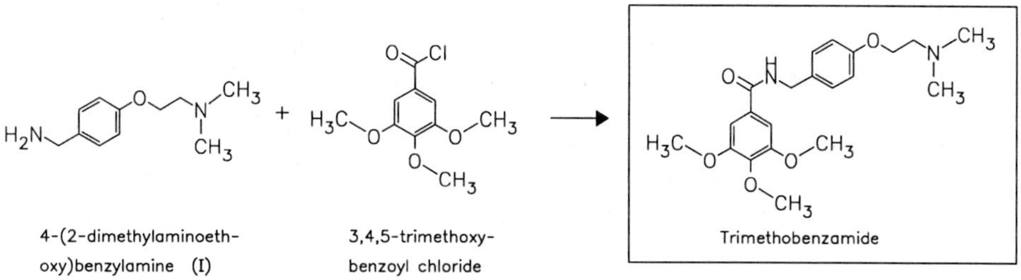

4-(2-dimethylaminoeth-   3,4,5-trimethoxy-   Trimethobenzamide
oxy)benzylamine (I)   benzoyl chloride

Reference(s):

US 2 879 293 (Hoffmann-La Roche; 24.3.1959; prior. 19.2.1957).

Formulation(s):   amp. 100 mg/ml; cps. 100 mg, 250 mg; suppos. 100 mg, 200 mg; vial 100 mg/ml (as
                      hydrochloride)

Trade Name(s):

D: Anaus (Molteni); wfm   I: Anaus (Molteni); wfm   USA: Tigan (Roberts)
       Ibikin (IBP); wfm   Ibikin (IBP); wfm

Trimethoprim

ATC: J01EA01
Use: chemotherapeutic, antibacterial

RN: 738-70-5   MF: $C_{14}H_{18}N_4O_3$ MW: 290.32   EINECS: 212-006-2
LD$_{50}$:   132 mg/kg (M, i.v.); 2764 mg/kg (M, p.o.);
        200 mg/kg (R, p.o.)
CN: 5-[(3,4,5-trimethoxyphenyl)methyl]-2,4-pyrimidinediamine

cotrimoxazole (comb. with sulfamethoxazole)
RN: 8064-90-2   MF: $C_{14}H_{18}N_4O_3 \cdot C_{10}H_{11}N_3O_3S$ MW: 543.61
LD$_{50}$:   3740 mg/kg (M, p.o.);
        5350 mg/kg (R, p.o.)
comb. with sulfamoxole
RN: 57197-43-0   MF: $C_{14}H_{18}N_4O_3 \cdot C_{11}H_{13}N_3O_3S$ MW: 557.63
LD$_{50}$:   >12 g/kg (M, p.o.);
        14 g/kg (R, p.o.);
        >1 g/kg (dog, p.o.)
comb. with sulfamerazine
RN: 54242-77-2   MF: $C_{14}H_{18}N_4O_3 \cdot C_{11}H_{12}N_4O_2S$ MW: 554.63
comb. with sulfamethoxypyridazine
RN: 54242-78-3   MF: $C_{14}H_{18}N_4O_3 \cdot C_{11}H_{12}N_4O_3S$ MW: 570.63
comb. with sulfadiazine
RN: 39474-58-3   MF: $C_{14}H_{18}N_4O_3 \cdot C_{10}H_{10}N_4O_2S$ MW: 540.61

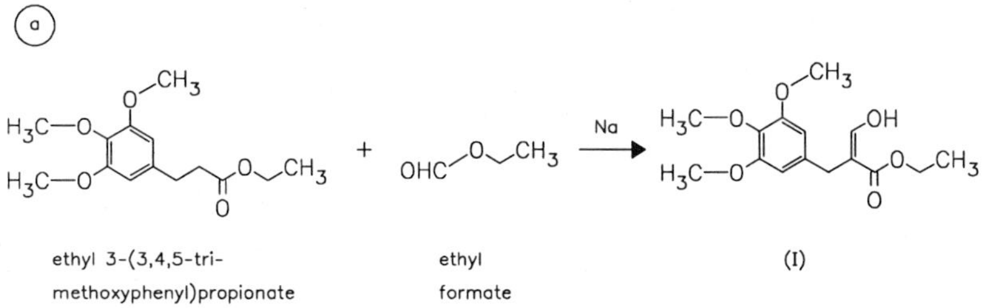

ethyl 3-(3,4,5-tri-   ethyl   (I)
methoxyphenyl)propionate   formate

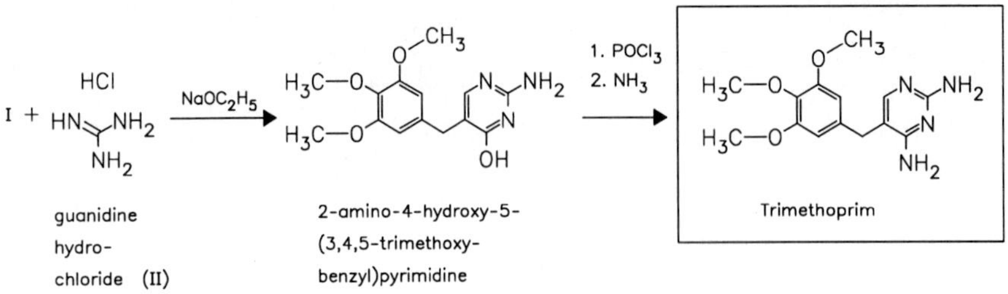
I + HCl HN NH2 NH2
NaOC2H5
1. POCl3
2. NH3
guanidine hydro-chloride (II)
2-amino-4-hydroxy-5-(3,4,5-trimethoxy-benzyl)pyrimidine
Trimethoprim

b

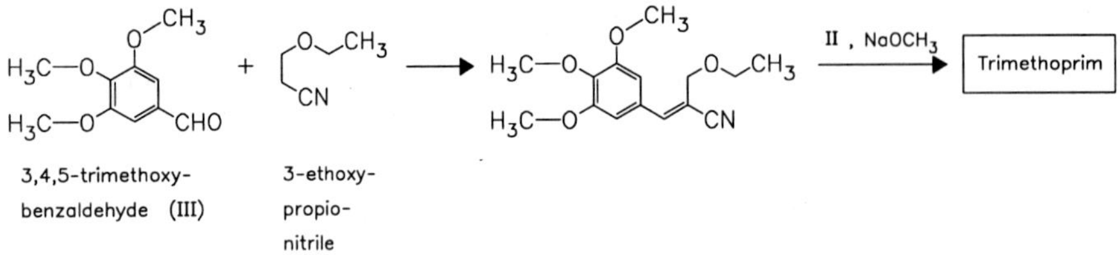
3,4,5-trimethoxy-benzaldehyde (III)
3-ethoxy-propio-nitrile
II , NaOCH3
Trimethoprim

c

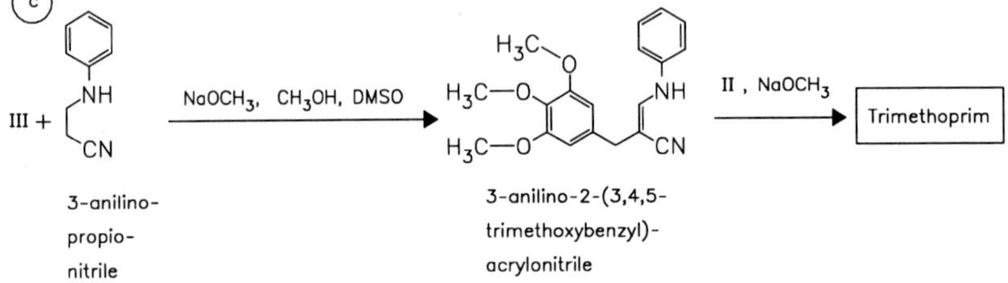
III +
NaOCH3, CH3OH, DMSO
II , NaOCH3
Trimethoprim
3-anilino-propio-nitrile
3-anilino-2-(3,4,5-trimethoxybenzyl)-acrylonitrile

d

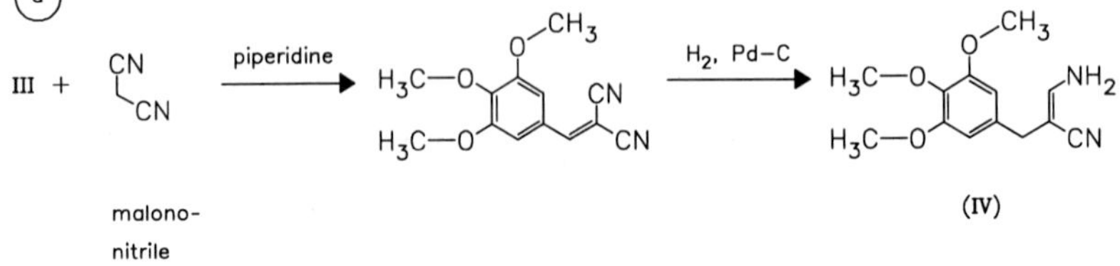
III +
piperidine
H2, Pd-C
malono-nitrile
(IV)

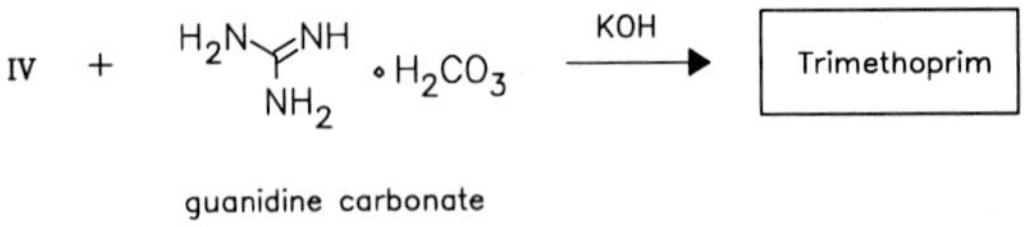
IV +
• H2CO3
KOH
Trimethoprim
guanidine carbonate

e

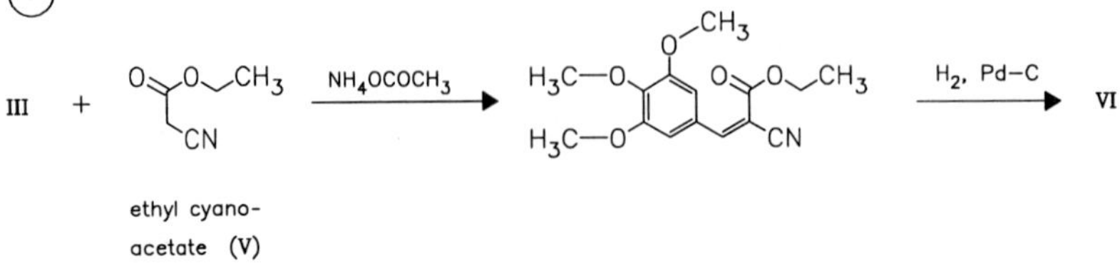
III +
NH4OCOCH3
H2, Pd-C
VI
ethyl cyano-acetate (V)

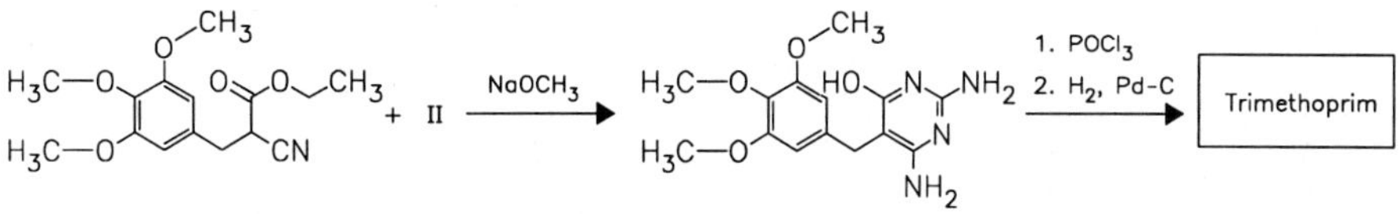

ethyl 3,4,5-trimethoxy-
benzylcyanoacetate (VI)

2,4-diamino-6-hydroxy-
5-(3,4,5-trimethoxy-
benzyl)pyrimidine (VII)

f

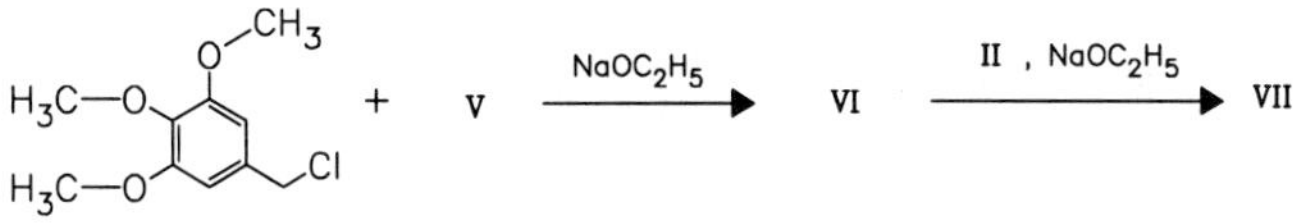

3,4,5-trimethoxy-
benzyl chloride

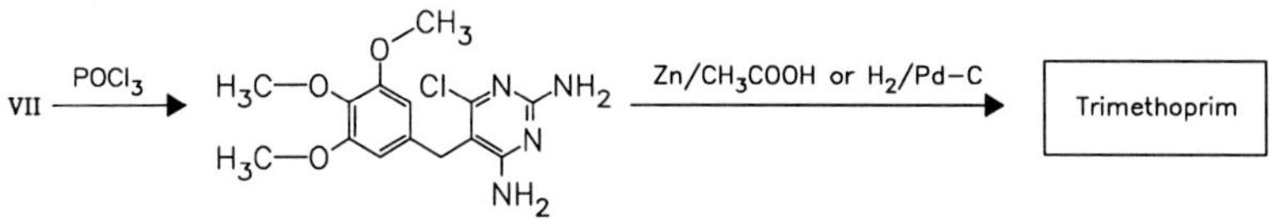

2,4-diamino-6-chloro-
5-(3,4,5-trimethoxy-
benzyl)pyrimidine

g

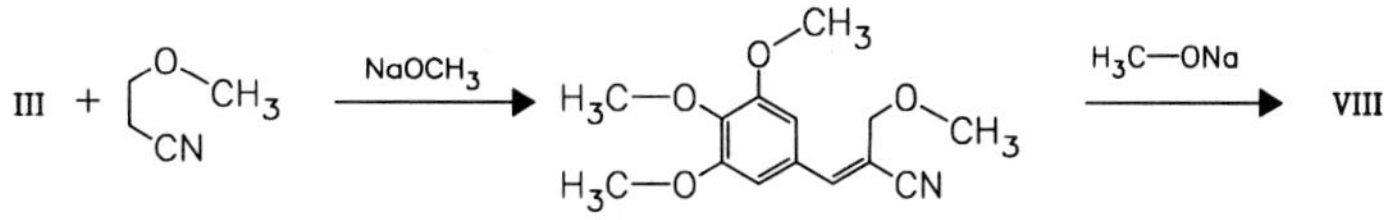

3-methoxy-
propio-
nitrile

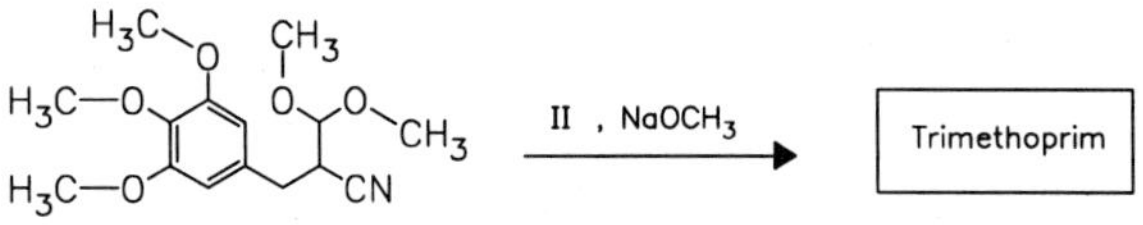

3,3-dimethoxy-2-
(3,4,5-trimethoxy-
benzyl)propionitrile (VIII)

Reference(s):
a DE 1 103 931 (Wellcome Found.; appl. 19.2.1958; GB-prior. 21.2.1957).
   US 2 909 522 (Burroughs Wellcome; 20.10.1959, GB-prior. 21.2.1957).
   GB 875 562 (Wellcome Foundation; appl. 21.2.1957; valid from 21.2.1958).
b US 3 049 544 (Burroughs Wellcome; 14.8.1962; GB-prior. 3.9.1959).
   DAS 1 303 727 (Wellcome Found.; appl. 12.8.1960; GB-prior. 3.9.1959, 20.11.1959, 11.7.1960).
   DAS 1 445 176 (Wellcome Found.; appl. 12.8.1960; GB-prior. 3.9.1959, 20.11.1959, 11.7.1960).
   DAS 1 795 586 (Wellcome Found.; appl. 12.8.1960; GB-prior. 3.9.1959, 20.11.1959, 11.7.1960).
   similar process (condensation of 3,4,5-trimethoxybenzaldehyde with 3-(methoxyethoxy)propionitrile):
   DAS 2 635 765 (Heumann; appl. 9.8.1976).

condensation with monoacetylguanidine:

GB 1 518 075 (Industria Chemica Prodotti Francis S. P. A.; appl. 3.5.1977; I-prior. 27.1.1977).

c   DAS 2 010 166 (Wellcome Found.; appl. 4.3.1970; GB-prior. 6.3.1969, 16.5.1969, 13.6.1969).

DOS 2 065 367 (Wellcome Found.; appl. 4.3.1970; GB-prior. 6.3.1969, 16.5.1969, 13.6.1969).

DAS 2 066 039 (Wellcome Found.; appl. 4.3.1970; GB-prior. 6.3.1969, 16.5.1969, 13.6.1969).

US 3 956 327 (Burroughs Wellcome; 11.5.1976; GB-prior. 6.3.1963, 16.5.1969, 13.6.1969).

analogous method:

condensation of 3,4,5-trimethoxybenzaldehyde *with* piperazine-1,4-dipropionitrile:

DOS 2 612 891 (Smith Kline, Dauelsberg; appl. 26.3.1976).

condensation of 3,4,5-trimethoxybenzaldehyde *with* 3-(1-imidazolyl)propionitrile:

DOS 2 617 967 (Nordmark-Werke; appl. 24.4.1976).

d   DAS 2 443 080 (GEA; appl. 9.9.1974; DK-prior. 10.9.1973).

GB 1 445 254 (GEA; appl. 6.9.1974; DK-prior. 10.9.1973).

e   DOS 2 165 362 (Nisshin Flour Milling; appl. 29.12.1971; J-prior. 29.12.1970).

DOS 2 258 238 (Plantex; appl. 28.11.1972; IL-prior. 1.12.1971).

modified analogous method (*reaction of* 3,4,5-trimethoxybenzylcyanoacetic acid *with* DMF *and* phosgene *and following reaction with* guanidine *directly to* trimethoprim):

DAS 2 341 214 (Nordmark-Werke; appl. 16.8.1973).

GB 1 413 459 (Nordmark-Werke; appl. 26.7.1974; D-prior. 16.8.1973).

improved method for reaction of 2,4-diamino-6-hydroxy-5-(3,4,5-trimethoxybenzyl)pyrimidine *to* trimethoprim:

DOS 2 343 419 (Grünenthal; appl. 29.8.1973).

US 3 980 649 (Grünenthal; 14.9.1976; D-prior. 29.8.1973).

f   DAS 2 003 578 (Egyt; appl. 27.1.1970; H-prior. 27.1.1969).

g   DE 1 545 966 (Roche; appl. 20.10.1965; USA-prior. 12.11.1964, 7.5.1965, 9.7.1965).

DAS 1 793 647 (Roche; appl. 20.10.1965; USA-prior. 12.11.1964, 7.5.1965, 9.7.1965).

DOS 1 620 729 (Wellcome Found.; appl. 6.7.1966; USA-prior. 8.7.1965).

similar processes:

reaction of 3,4,5-trimethoxybenzaldehyde *with* 3,3-dimethoxypropionitrile *and catalytic hydrogenation to* 3,3-dimethoxy-2-(3,4,5-trimethoxybenzyl)propionitrile:

DAS 1 593 723 (Wellcome Found.; appl. 26.10.1966; GB-prior. 28.10.1965).

DAS 1 793 767 (Wellcome Found.; appl. 26.10.1966; GB-prior. 28.10.1965).

condensation of 3,4,5-trimethoxybenzaldehyde *with* cyanoacetaldehyde *obtained by thermolysis of* isoxazole:

DOS 2 623 169 (BASF; appl. 22.5.1976).

other methods:

reaction of the Mannich-compound from 2,6-dimethoxyphenol, formaldehyde *and* dimethylamine *with* 2,4-diaminopyrimidine *and subsequent methylation of* 2,4-diamino-5-(3,5-dimethoxy-4-hydroxybenzyl)pyrimidine *with* methyl iodide:

DAS 1 720 012 (Wellcome Found.; appl. 17.2.1967; GB-prior. 19.2.1966).

DAS 1 795 635 (Wellcome Found.; appl. 17.2.1967; GB-prior. 19.2.1966).

DAS 1 795 851 (Wellcome Found.; appl. 17.2.1967; GB-Frior. 19.2.1966).

condensation of the Mannich-compound mentiored above with 2,4-diamino-6-methylthiopyrimidine *to* 2,4-diamino-5-(3,5-dimethoxy-4-hydroxybenzyl)-6-methylthiopyrimidine, *methylation with* methyl iodide *and desulfurization with Raney nickel:*

DAS 2 218 221 (Wellcome Found.; appl. 14.4.1972; GB-prior. 16.4.1971).

condensation of 3,4,5-trimethoxybenzaldehyde *with* 2,4-diamino-6-hydroxypyrimidine *to* 2,4-diamino-6-oxo-5-(3,4,5-trimethoxybenzylidene)pyrimidine, *hydrogenation with* Pd-C *to* 2,4-diamino-6-hydroxy-5-(3,4,5-trimethoxybenzyl)pyrimidine *and further reaction of the latter analogously to method* **f**:

DOS 2 546 510 (Astra; appl. 17.10.1975; S-prior. 21.10.1974).

from 3,4,5-trimethoxybenzoic acid methyl ester (*condensation with* DMSO, *reduction with* NaBH$_4$, *reaction with* 3-anilinopropionitrile *to* 3-anilino-2-(3,4,5-trimethoxybenzyl)acrylonitrile, *cf. method* c):

DOS 2 051 871 (Wellcome Found.; appl. 15.5.1970; GB-prior. 16.5.1969).

DOS 2 023 977 (Wellcome Found.; appl. 15.5.1970; GB-prior. 16.5.1969).

condensation of 3,4,5-trimethoxybenzyl chloride *with* 2,4-diamino-6-hydroxypyrimidine, *reaction with* phosphorous oxychloride *and reductive dehalogenation:*
DAS 2 530 814 (Lentia; appl. 10.7.1975).

review:
Schliemann, W.: Pharmazie (PHARAT) **31**, 140 (1976).

Formulation(s):   syrup 50 mg/5 ml, 100 mg/5 ml; tabl. 50 mg, 100 mg, 120 mg, 150 mg, 200 mg, 300 mg

Trade Name(s):

D: Bactrim forte/Sirolin
    (Roche)-cotrimoxazole-
    comb.
    Drylin (Merckle)-comb.
    with sulfamethoxazole
    Eusaprim (Wellcome)-
    comb. with
    sulfamethoxazole
    Eusaprim forte/Pyridium
    (Wellcome)-comb. with
    sulfamethoxazole
    Infectotrimet
    (Infectopharm)
    Kepinol (Pfleger)-comb.
    with sulfamethoxazole
    Microtrim (Chephasaar)-
    comb. with
    sulfamethoxazole
    Sigaprim (Siegfried)-comb.
    with sulfamethoxazole
    Sulfacet (Schwarzhaupt)-
    cotrimoxazole
    Supracombin (Grünenthal)-
    comb. with
    sulfamethoxazole
    TMP-ratiopharm
    (ratiopharm)
    TMS (TAD)-comb. with
    sulfamethoxazole
    Triglobe (Astra)-comb.
    with sulfadiazine
    Trimono (Procter &
    Gamble)

    Uretrim (TAD)
F: Antrima (Doms-Adrian)-
    comb.
    Bactrim (Roche)-comb.
    Eusaprim (Lipha Santré)-
    comb.
    Wellcoprim (Glaxo
    Wellcome)
GB: Chemotrim (Rosemont)-
    comb.
    Ipral (Squibb)
    Monotrim (Solvay)
    Polytrim (Dominion)-
    comb. with polymyxin B
    Septrin (Glaxo Wellcome)-
    comb.
    Trimopan (Berk)
I: Abacin (Benedetti)-
    cotrimoxazole
    Abaprim (Gentili)
    Bacterial (CT)-comb.
    Bactrim (Dompé)-comb.
    Chemitrim (Biomedica
    Foscama)-comb.
    Eusaprim (Glaxo
    Wellcome)-comb.
    Gantrim (Geymonat)-comb.
    Isotrim (Ghimas)-comb.
    Kelfiprim (Pharmacia &
    Upjohn)-comb. with
    sulfametopyrazine
    Kombinax (Bracco)-comb.
    with sulfadiazine

    Lidaprim (Lisapharma)-
    comb.
    Medixin (Pierrel)-comb.
    Streptoplus (Molteni)-
    comb.
    Velaten (Camillo Corvi)-
    comb. with
    sulfamethoxypyridazine
J: Bacta (Nippon Roche)-
    comb.
    Bacta (Nippon Roche)-
    cotrimoxazole
    Bactramin (Nippon
    Roche)-comb.
    Bactramin (Nippon
    Roche)-cotrimoxazole
    Baktar (Wellcome)
    Septerin (Tanabe)
    Septrim (Shionogi)-comb.
    Septrim (Shionogi)-
    cotrimoxazole
USA: Bactrim (Roche)-comb.
    Proloprim (Glaxo
    Wellcome)
    Septra (Glaxo Wellcome)-
    comb.
    Trimpex (Roche)
    combination preparations
    and generics

Trimetozine

ATC: C01AA05; C08DA01
Use: neurosedative

RN: 635-41-6   MF: $C_{14}H_{19}NO_5$ MW: 281.31   EINECS: 211-236-0
LD_{50}: 960 mg/kg (M, i.v.); 2400 mg/kg (M, p.o.);
      1800 mg/kg (R, p.o.)
CN: 4-(3,4,5-trimethoxybenzoyl)morpholine

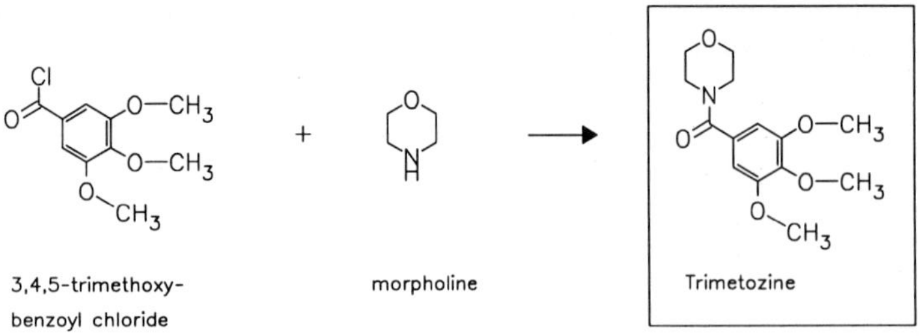

3,4,5-trimethoxy-
benzoyl chloride

morpholine

Trimetozine

Reference(s):

DE 1 164 412 (Egyesült Gyógyszer-és Tápszergyár; appl. 16.1.1960; H-prior. 23.1.1959, 2.11.1959).

Formulation(s):   drg. 150 mg

Trade Name(s):
D: Gradulon (Minden)-comb.;   F: Opalene (Théraplix)-   I: Trioxazina (Importex);
     wfm   comb.; wfm   wfm
     Seda-Miroton (Minden);   Trioxazine (Adrian-
     wfm   Marinier); wfm

Trimetrexate glucuronate
(CI-898; JB-11; NSC-249008/352122)

ATC: P01AX07
Use: antineoplastic

RN: 82952-64-5   MF: $C_{19}H_{23}N_5O_3 \cdot C_6H_{10}O_7$ MW: 563.56
CN: D-glucuronic acid compd. with 5-methyl-6-[[(3,4,5-trimethoxyphenyl)amino]methyl]-2,4-quinazolinediamine (1:1)

trimetrexate
RN: 52128-35-5   MF: $C_{19}H_{23}N_5O_3$ MW: 369.43
monoacetate
RN: 52128-36-6   MF: $C_{19}H_{23}N_5O_3 \cdot C_2H_4O$ MW: 413.48

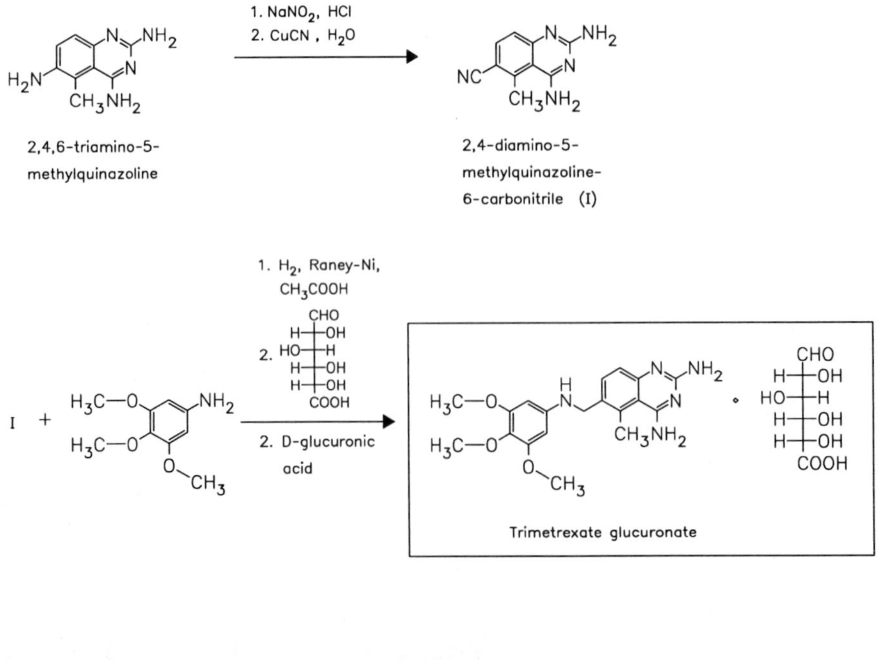

2,4,6-triamino-5-
methylquinazoline

2,4-diamino-5-
methylquinazoline-
6-carbonitrile   (I)

Trimetrexate glucuronate

Reference(s):
GB 1 345 502 (Parke Davis & Co.; appl. 6.7.1972; GB-prior. 6.7.1972).
EP 5 145 (Warner-Lambert Co.; appl. 26.10.1981; USA-prior. 29.1.1982).

lyophilic formulation:
JP 06 172 177 (Dainippon Pharm.; appl. 10.12.1992; J-prior. 10.12.1992).

Formulation(s):   vial 25 mg

Trade Name(s):

F:	Neutrexin (Ipsen/Biotech)	I:	Neutrexin (Ipsen)
GB:	Neutrexin (Speywood)	USA:	Neutrexin (US Bioscience)

Trimipramine

ATC: N06AA06
Use: antidepressant

RN: 739-71-9   MF: $C_{20}H_{26}N_2$ MW: 294.44   EINECS: 212-008-3
LD_{50}:   42 mg/kg (M, i.v.); 250 mg/kg (M, p.o.)
CN: 10,11-dihydro-N,N,β-trimethyl-5H-dibenz[b,f]azepine-5-propanamine

maleate (1:1)
RN: 521-78-8   MF: $C_{20}H_{26}N_2 \cdot C_4H_4O_4$ MW: 410.51   EINECS: 208-318-3
LD_{50}:   40 mg/kg (M, i.v.); 425 mg/kg (M, p.o.);
     38 mg/kg (R, i.v.); 800 mg/kg (R, p.o.)
monomesylate
RN: 25332-13-2   MF: $C_{20}H_{26}N_2 \cdot CH_4O_3S$ MW: 390.55   EINECS: 246-852-9

10,11-dihydro-5H-
dibenz[b,f]azepine

1. NaNH₂
2. Cl～～N～CH₃
    CH₃CH₃

1. sodium amide
2. 3-dimethylamino-
   2-methylpropyl
   chloride

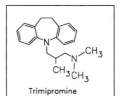

Trimipramine

Reference(s):
FR 1 172 014 (Rhône-Poulenc; appl. 14.12.1955).
Jacob, R.M.; Messer, M.: C. R. Hebd. Seances Acad. Sci. (COREAF) **252**, 2117 (1961).

Formulation(s):   amp. 25 mg/ml; cps. 25 mg, 50 mg, 100 mg; drops 5.3 g/100 ml (as monomesylate); f. c. tabl.
     25 mg; tabl. 25 mg, 100 mg (as maleate)

Trade Name(s):

D:	Hexphonal (ASTA Medica AWD)	F:	Surmontil (Specia)		Surmontil (Rhône-Poulenc Rorer)
	Stangyl (Rhône-Poulenc Rorer)	GB:	Surmontil (Rhône-Poulenc Rorer)	J:	Surmontil (Shionogi)
	Trimipramin-neuraxpharm (neuraxpharm)	I:	Surmontil (Rhône-Poulenc Rorer)	USA:	Surmontil (Wyeth-Ayerst)

Tripamide

ATC: C02
Use: antihypertensive, diuretic

RN: 73803-48-2   MF: $C_{16}H_{20}ClN_3O_3S$ MW: 369.87
LD_{50}:   >5 g/kg (M, p.o.);
    >8 g/kg (R, p.o.);
    >2 g/kg (dog, p.o.)
CN: (3aα,4α,7α,7aα)-3-(aminosulfonyl)-4-chloro-N-(octahydro-4,7-methano-2H-isoindol-2-yl)benzamide

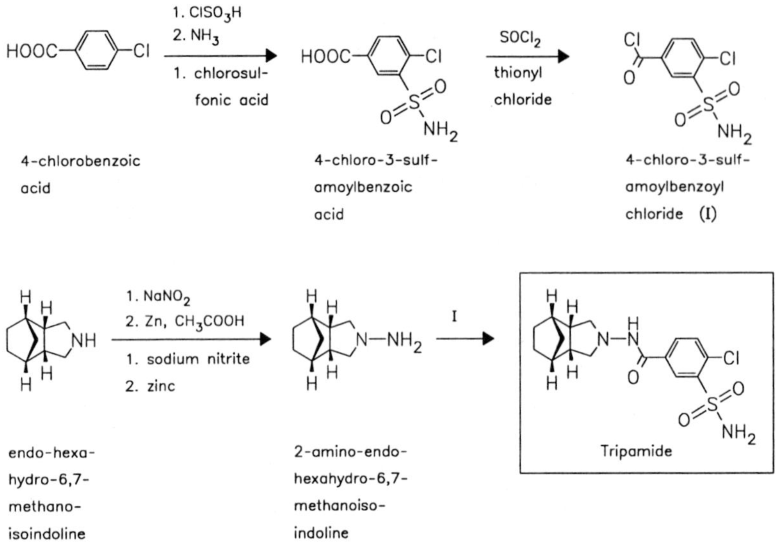

4-chlorobenzoic acid

4-chloro-3-sulfamoylbenzoic acid

4-chloro-3-sulfamoylbenzoyl chloride (I)

endo-hexahydro-6,7-methanoisoindoline

2-amino-endo-hexahydro-6,7-methanoisoindoline

Tripamide

Reference(s):
US 3 787 440 (Eisai; 22.1.1974; appl. 9.11.1971; J-prior. 9.11.1970).
DOS 2 155 660 (Eisai; appl. 9.11.1971; J-prior. 9.11.1970).
Nakamura, T. et al.: J. Labelled Compd. Radiopharm. (JLCRD4) **14**, 191 (1978).

synthesis of 2-amino-*endo*-hexahydro-4,7-methanoisoindoline:
JP 7 121 708 (Eisaei; appl. 17.8.1967).

Formulation(s):   tabl. 15 mg

Trade Name(s):
J: Normonal (Eisai; 1982)

Tripelennamine

ATC: D04AA04; R06AC04
Use: antihistaminic

RN: 91-81-6   MF: $C_{16}H_{21}N_3$ MW: 255.37   EINECS: 202-100-1
LD_{50}:   23 mg/kg (M, i.v.); 152 mg/kg (M, p.o.)
CN: N,N-dimethyl-N'-(phenylmethyl)-N'-2-pyridinyl-1,2-ethanediamine

monohydrochloride
RN: 154-69-8   MF: $C_{16}H_{21}N_3 \cdot HCl$ MW: 291.83   EINECS: 205-833-5
LD_{50}:   9 mg/kg (M, i.v.); 97 mg/kg (M, p.o.);
    12 mg/kg (R, i.v.); 469 mg/kg (R, p.o.)

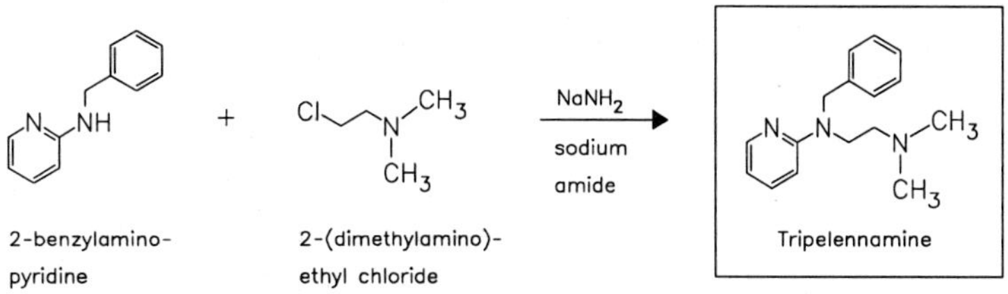

| 2-benzylamino-pyridine | 2-(dimethylamino)-ethyl chloride | | Tripelennamine |

Reference(s):
US 2 406 594 (Ciba; 1946; prior. 1943).
US 2 502 151 (Rhône-Poulenc; 1950; F-prior. 1943).

Formulation(s):   stick 115 mg/5.75 g (as hydrochloride)

Trade Name(s):
D: Azaron Stift (Chefaro)
F: Anachoc (Lipha)-comb.;
    wfm
I: Sedilene (Montefarmaco);
    wfm
J: Pyribenzamin (Ciba-Geigy-Takeda)
USA: PBZ-SR (Geigy); wfm
    Pyribenzamine (Ciba); wfm
    Tripelennamine HCl
    Tablets (Danbury); wfm

Triprolidine

ATC: R06AX07
Use: antihistaminic

RN: 486-12-4   MF: C$_{19}$H$_{22}$N$_2$ MW: 278.40   EINECS: 207-627-0
CN: (*E*)-2-[1-(4-methylphenyl)-3-(1-pyrrolidinyl)-1-propenyl]pyridine

monohydrochloride
RN: 550-70-9   MF: C$_{19}$H$_{22}$N$_2$ · HCl   MW: 314.86   EINECS: 208-985-0
LD$_{50}$:   21 mg/kg (M, i.v.); 495 mg/kg (M, p.o.);
    840 mg/kg (R, p.o.)

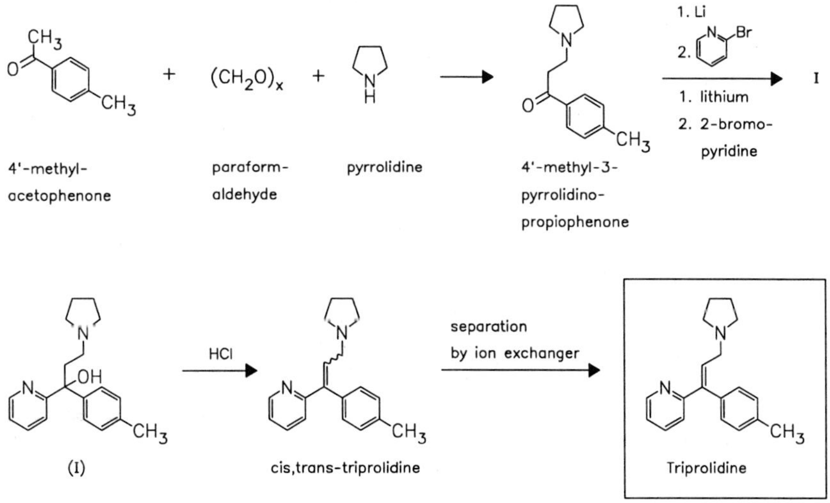

| 4'-methyl-acetophenone | paraform-aldehyde | pyrrolidine | 4'-methyl-3-pyrrolidino-propiophenone |

| (I) | cis,trans-triprolidine | Triprolidine |

Reference(s):
US 2 712 020 (Burroughs Wellcome; 1955; GB-prior. 1948).
US 2 712 023 (Burroughs Wellcome; 1955; GB-prior. 1948).

Formulation(s):   syrup 1.25 mg/5 ml; tabl. 1.25 mg, 2.5 mg (as hydrochloride)

Tritoqualine

ATC: R06AX21
Use: antiallergic

RN: 14504-73-5 MF: $C_{26}H_{32}N_2O_8$ MW: 500.55
LD$_{50}$: >15 g/kg (M, p.o.);
>15 g/kg (R, p.o.)
CN: 7-amino-4,5,6-triethoxy-3-(5,6,7,8-tetrahydro-4-methoxy-6-methyl-1,3-dioxolo[4,5-g]isoquinolin-5-yl)-1(3H)-isobenzofuranone

cotarnine + 7-nitro-4,5,6-tri-ethoxyphthalide → (I)

Tritoqualine

Reference(s):
DE 1 206 909 (M. Jeanson, Paris; appl. 14.8.1959).

Formulation(s): drops 180 mg; tabl. 100 mg

Trofosfamide
(Trophosphamide)

ATC: L01AA07
Use: antineoplastic

RN: 22089-22-1 MF: $C_9H_{18}Cl_3N_2O_2P$ MW: 323.59 EINECS: 244-770-8
LD$_{50}$: 157 mg/kg (M, i.v.); 464 mg/kg (M, p.o.);
90 mg/kg (R, i.v.); 202 mg/kg (R, p.o.)
CN: N,N,3-tris(2-chloroethyl)tetrahydro-2H-1,3,2-oxazaphosphorin-2-amine 2-oxide

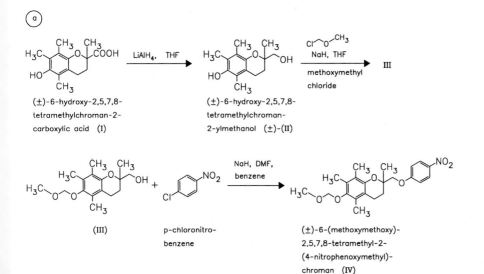

N-(2-chloroethyl)-3-
hydroxypropylamine
hydrochloride

N,N-bis(2-chloro-
ethyl)phosphoramidic
dichloride

Trofosfamide

Reference(s):
DOS 1 645 921 (ASTA-Werke; appl. 11.7.1966).
GB 1 188 159 (ASTA-Werke; appl. 11.7.1967; D-prior. 11.7.1966).
US 3 732 340 (ASTA-Werke; 8.5.1973; prior. 30.6.1967, 11.9.1970, 14.1.1971).

Formulation(s):   f. c. tabl. 50 mg

Trade Name(s):
D: Ixoten (ASTA Medica   I: Ixoten (Schering); wfm
       AWD)

Troglitazone

(CI-991; CS 045; GR-92132X)

ATC: A10BG01
Use: antidiabetic, insulin enhancer,
             antioxidant

RN: 97322-87-7   MF: $C_{24}H_{27}NO_5S$ MW: 441.55
LD_{50}: >5 g/kg (R, p.o.)
CN: 5-[[4-(3,4-dihydro-6-hydroxy-2,5,7,8-tetramethyl-2H-1-benzopyran-2-yl)methoxy]phenyl]methyl-2,4-
            thiazolidinedione

monosodium salt
RN: 97323-06-3   MF: $C_{24}H_{26}NNaO_5$ MW: 431.46

(±)-6-hydroxy-2,5,7,8-
tetramethylchroman-2-
carboxylic acid (I)

(±)-6-hydroxy-2,5,7,8-
tetramethylchroman-
2-ylmethanol (±)-(II)

methoxymethyl
chloride

(III)

p-chloronitro-
benzene

(±)-6-(methoxymethoxy)-
2,5,7,8-tetramethyl-2-
(4-nitrophenoxymethyl)-
chroman (IV)

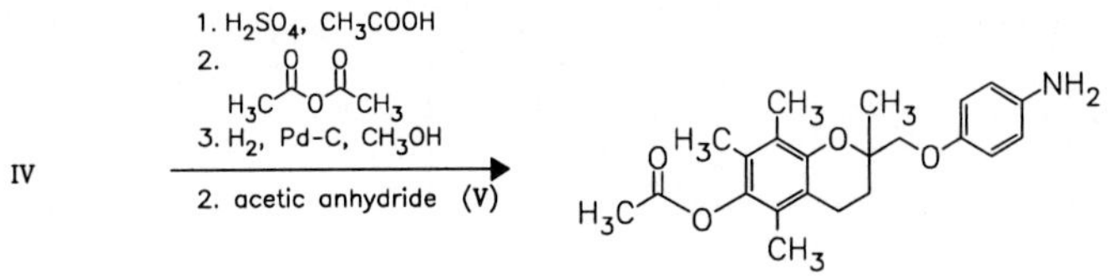

IV

1. H₂SO₄, CH₃COOH
2. H_3C — O — CH_3 (acetic anhydride)
3. H₂, Pd-C, CH₃OH

2. acetic anhydride (V)

(±)-6-acetoxy-2-(4-amino-
phenoxymethyl)-2,5,7,8-
tetramethylchroman (VI)

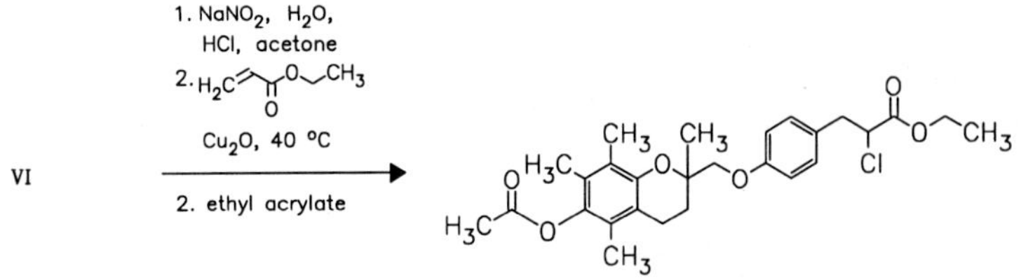

VI

1. NaNO₂, H₂O,
   HCl, acetone
2. H_2C — O — CH₃

Cu₂O, 40 °C

2. ethyl acrylate

(±)-ethyl 3-[4-[[(6-acetoxy-2,5,7,8-
tetramethylchroman-2-yl)methoxy]phenyl]-
2-chloropropionate (VII)

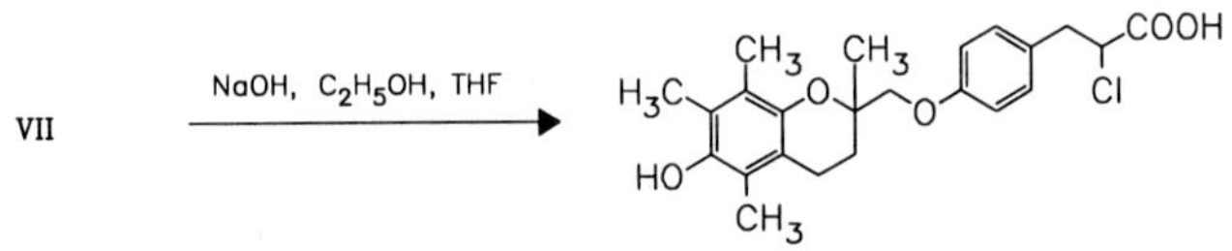

VII

NaOH, C₂H₅OH, THF

(±)-2-chloro-3-[4-[[(6-hydroxy-
2,5,7,8-tetramethylchroman-2-yl)-
methoxy]phenyl]propionic acid (VIII)

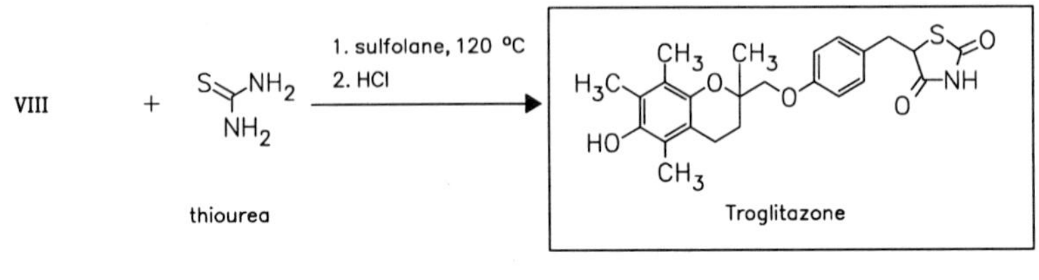

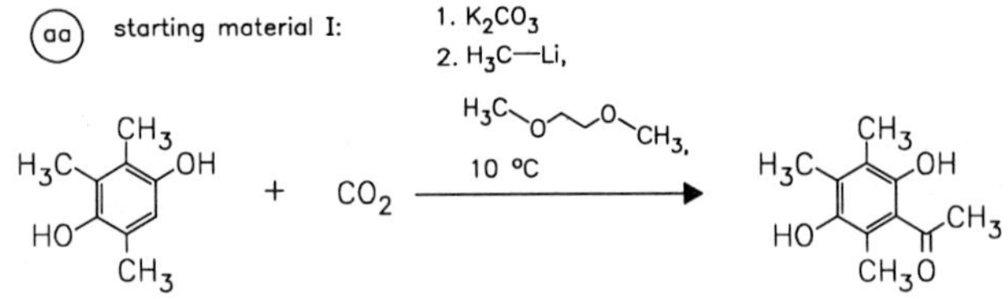

VIII   +   thiourea

1. sulfolane, 120 °C
2. HCl

Troglitazone

(aa)   starting material I:

1. K₂CO₃
2. H₃C—Li,

H₃C—O—O—CH₃,

10 °C

+   CO₂

2,3,5-trimethyl-
hydroquinone (IX)

3',4',6'-trimethyl-
2',5'-dihydroxy-
acetophenone (X)

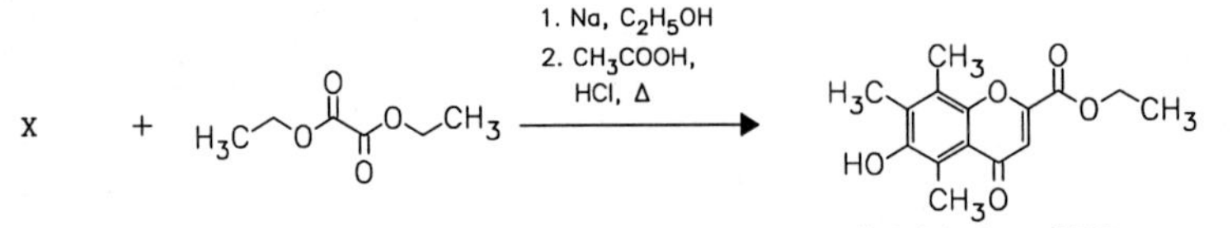

X   +   diethyl oxalate

1. Na, C₂H₅OH
2. CH₃COOH,
   HCl, Δ

ethyl 6-hydroxy-5,7,8-
trimethyl-4-oxo-4H-
chromene-2-carboxylate (XI)

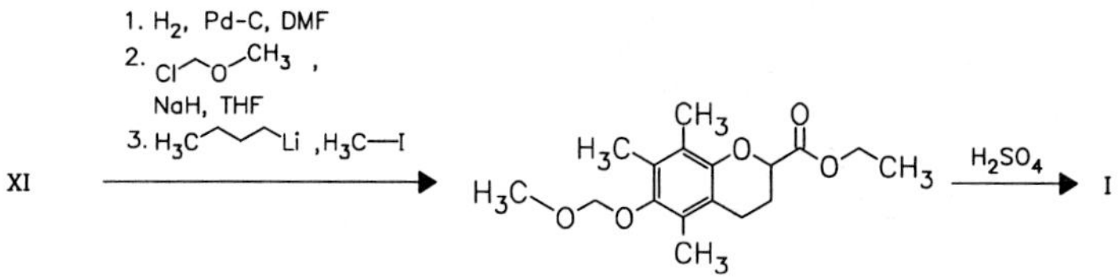

XI

1. H₂, Pd-C, DMF
2. Cl–O–CH₃ ,
   NaH, THF
3. H₃C‒‒‒Li , H₃C—I

$\xrightarrow{\qquad}$

(structure)

$\xrightarrow{H_2SO_4}$ I

(ab)

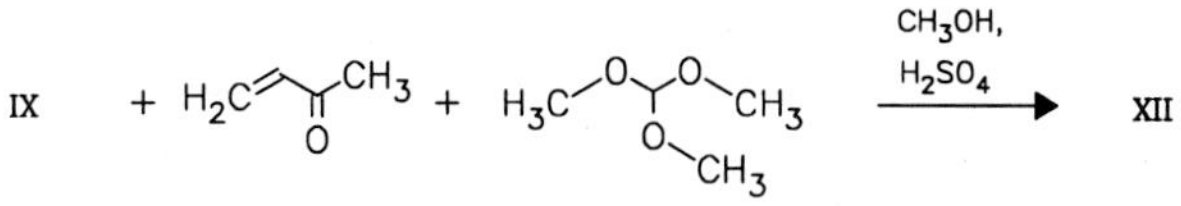

IX   +   H₂C=C(CH₃)O   +   H₃C–O–CH(OCH₃)–OCH₃

methyl vinyl
ketone

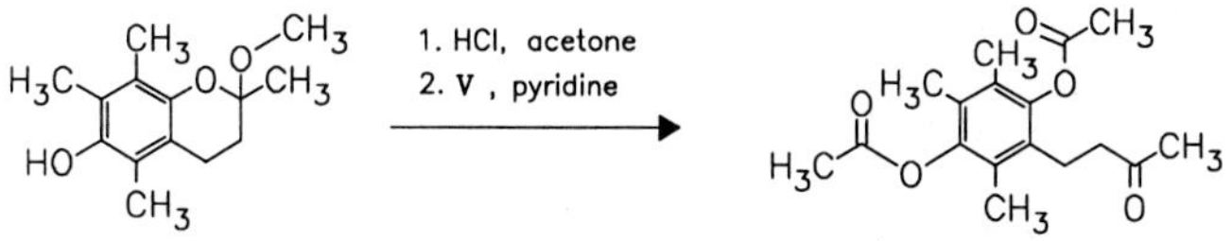

$\xrightarrow[H_2SO_4]{CH_3OH,}$ XII

(structure) 6-hydroxy-2-methoxy-
2,5,7,8-tetramethyl-
chromane (XII)

1. HCl, acetone
2. V , pyridine

$\xrightarrow{\qquad}$

(structure) 4-(2,5-diacetoxy-3,4,6-
trimethylphenyl)-
2-butanone (XIII)

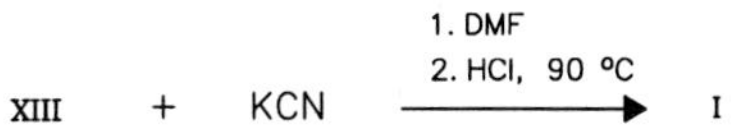

XIII   +   KCN $\xrightarrow[\text{2. HCl, 90 °C}]{\text{1. DMF}}$ I

(b)

(structure)
isoprene

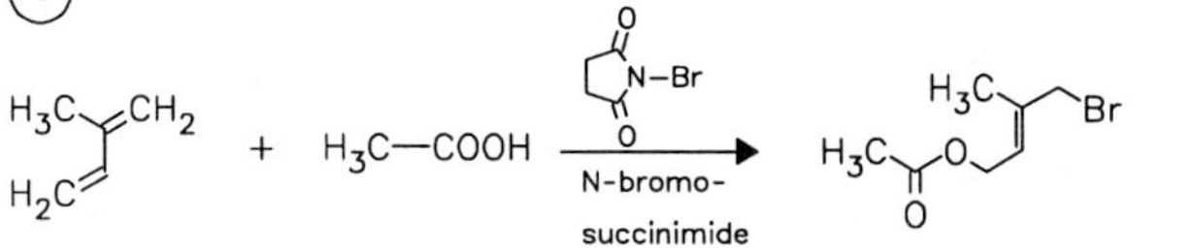

+   H₃C—COOH $\xrightarrow[\text{N-bromo-succinimide}]{\text{(N–Br)}}$ (structure)

4-bromo-3-methyl-
2-butenyl acetate (XIV)

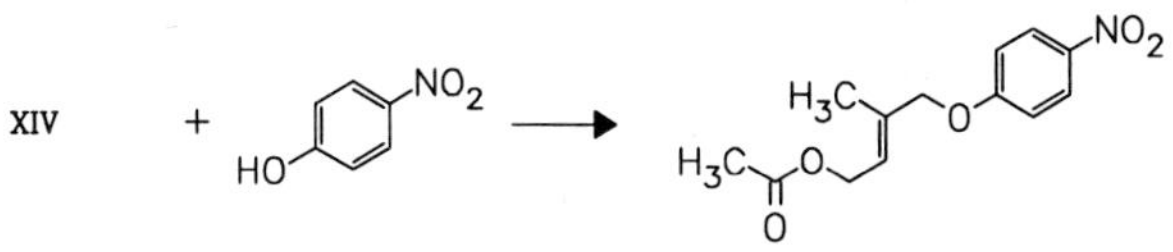

XIV   +   (HO–C₆H₄–NO₂) $\xrightarrow{\qquad}$ (structure)

4-(p-nitrophenoxy)-3-
methyl-2-butenyl acetate (XV)

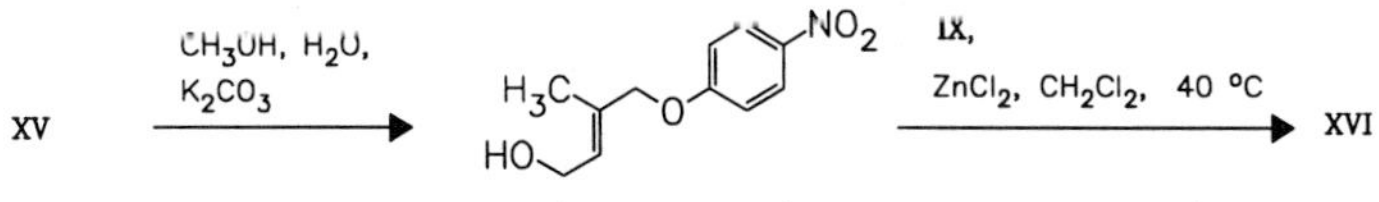

XV $\xrightarrow[\text{K}_2\text{CO}_3]{\text{CH}_3\text{OH, H}_2\text{O,}}$ (structure)

4-(p-nitrophenoxy)-
3-methyl-2-
buten-1-ol

$\xrightarrow[\text{ZnCl}_2\text{, CH}_2\text{Cl}_2\text{, 40 °C}]{\text{IX,}}$ XVI

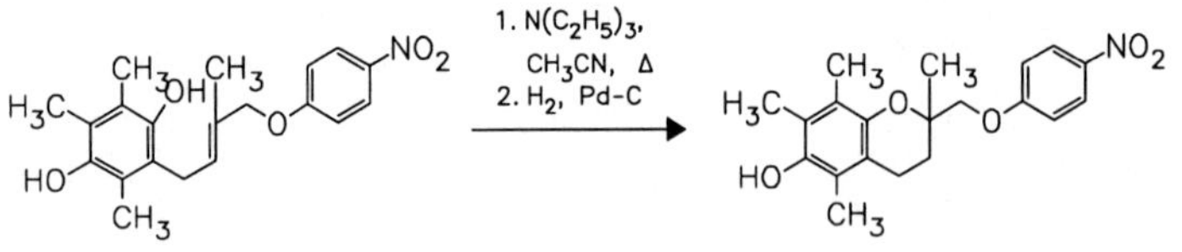
H3C
CH3
OH
CH3
NO2
HO
CH3
1. N(C2H5)3,
CH3CN, Δ
2. H2, Pd-C

2-[4-(p-nitrophenoxy)-3-methyl-2-butenyl]-3,5,6-trimethylhydroquinone (XVI)

(unprotected IV)

(c)

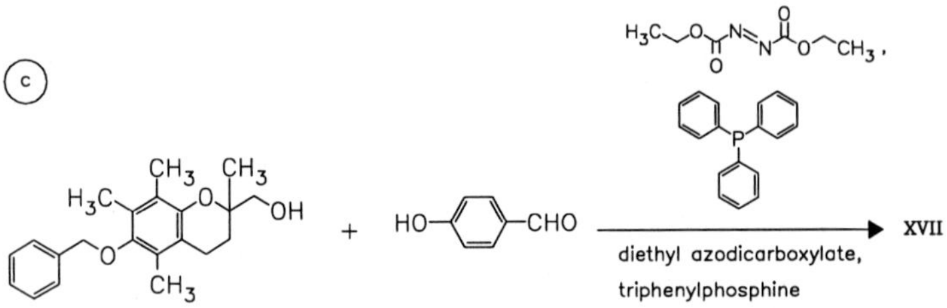
H3C
CH3
CH3
OH
O
CH3
HO
CHO
diethyl azodicarboxylate,
triphenylphosphine
XVII

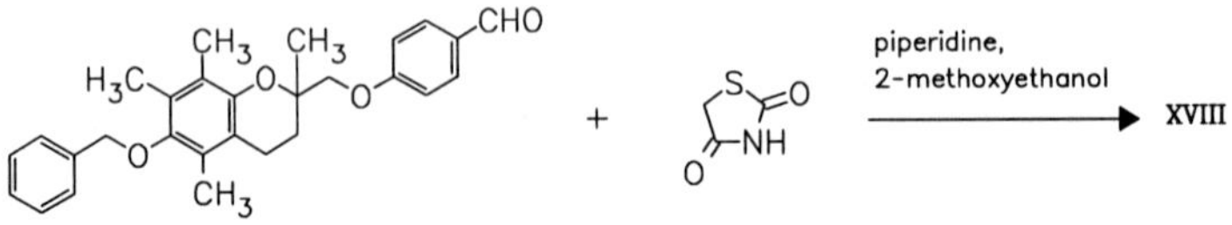
CHO
H3C
CH3
CH3
O
CH3
S
NH
O
piperidine,
2-methoxyethanol
XVIII

6-benzyloxy-2-(4-formylphenoxymethyl)-2,5,7,8-tetramethylchroman (XVII)

2,4-thiazolidinedione

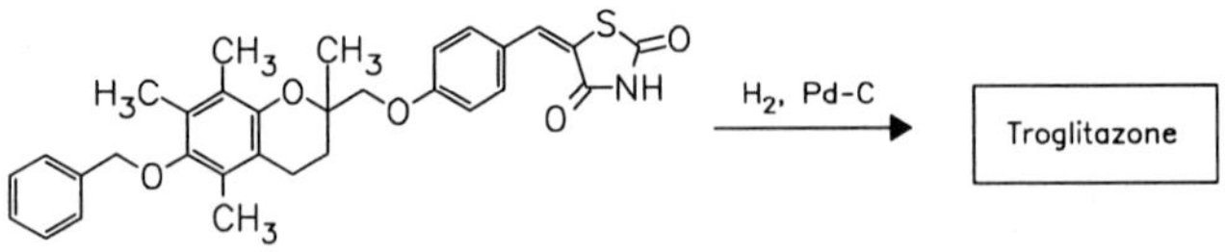
H3C
CH3
CH3
S
O
NH
CH3
H2, Pd-C
Troglitazone

5-[4-(6-benzyloxy-2,5,7,8-tetramethylchroman-2-ylmethoxy)-benzylidene]-2,4-thiazolidinedione (XVIII)

(d) alternative synthesis of VI:

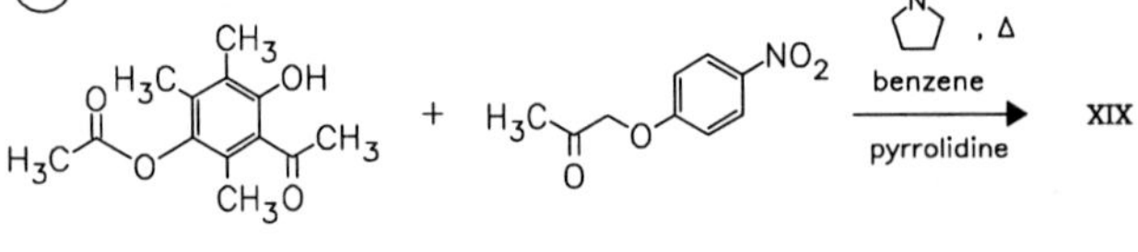
CH3
H3C
OH
H3C
CH3
CH3O
H3C
NO2
O
benzene
pyrrolidine
XIX

5'-acetoxy-2'-hydroxy-3',4',6'-trimethylacetophenone

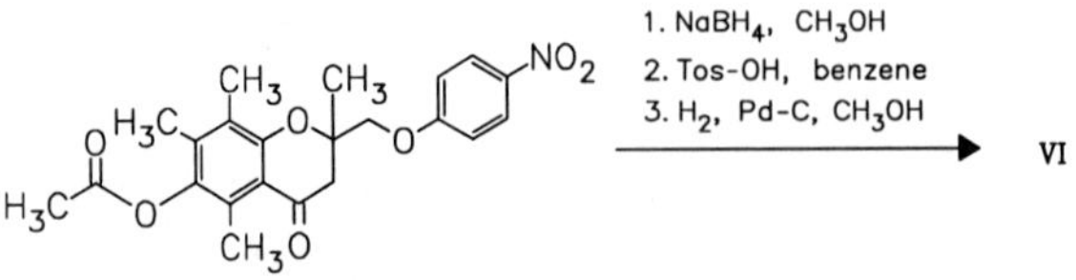
CH3
CH3
NO2
H3C
H3C
CH3O
1. NaBH4, CH3OH
2. Tos-OH, benzene
3. H2, Pd-C, CH3OH
VI

6-acetoxy-2,5,7,8-tetramethyl-2-(4-nitrophenoxymethyl)-4-chromanone (XIX)

(e) intermediate II:

(ea)

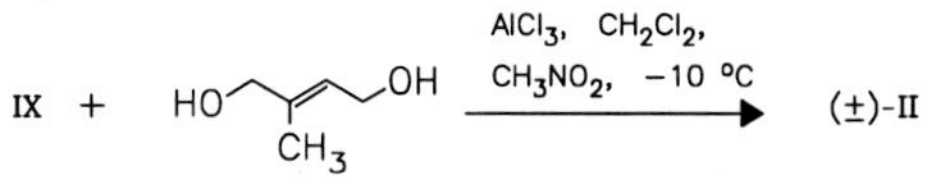

IX + HO⎯⎯⎯OH (CH₃) → (±)-II

AlCl₃, CH₂Cl₂, CH₃NO₂, −10 °C

(eb)

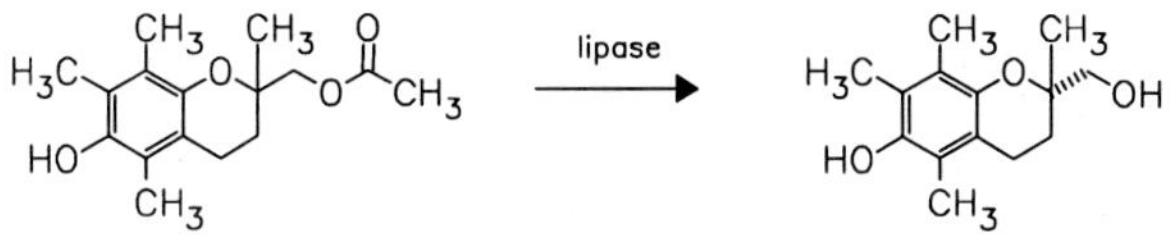

(II)

(ec)

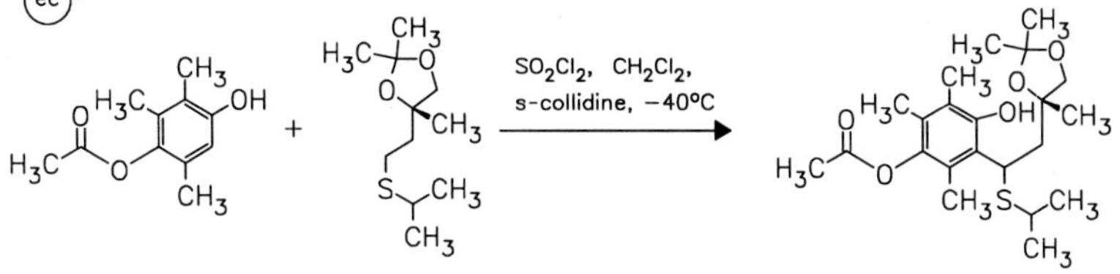

SO₂Cl₂, CH₂Cl₂, s-collidine, −40°C

(XX)

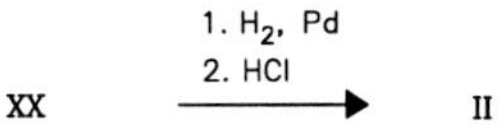

XX → II

1. H₂, Pd
2. HCl

(ed)

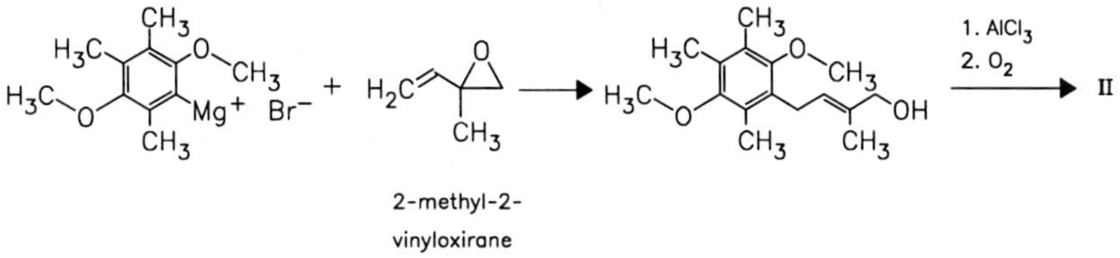

+ 2-methyl-2-vinyloxirane →   → II

1. AlCl₃
2. O₂

(ee)

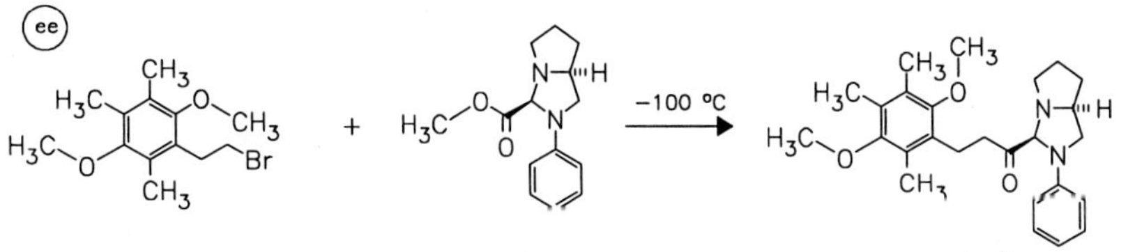

+   → (XXI)

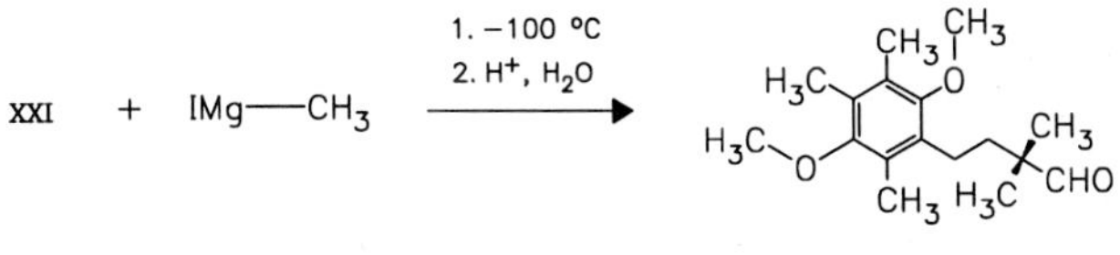

−100 °C

XXI + IMg⎯CH₃ → (XXII)

1. −100 °C
2. H⁺, H₂O

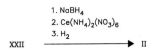

XXII → II

1. NaBH₄
2. Ce(NH₄)₂(NO₃)₆
3. H₂

Reference(s):

a Yoshioka, T. et al.: J. Med. Chem. (JMCMAR) **32**, 421 (1989).
   EP 207 581 (Sankyo Co.; appl. 26.2.1986; J-prior. 26.2.1985).
aa Witiak, D.T. et al.: J. Med. Chem. (JMCMAR) **18** (9), 934 (1975).
   EP 139 421 (Sankyo Co.; appl. 28.8.1984; prior. 30.8.1983).
   US 4 572 912 (Sankyo; 25.2.1986, J-prior. 30.8.1983).
ab Scott, J.W. et al.: J. Am. Chem. Soc. (JACSAT) **51**, 200 (1974).
b EP 670 300 (Eisai Chem. Co.; appl. 1.3.1995; J-prior. 2.3.1994).
   EP 543 346 (Lonza/Sankyo; appl. 17.11.1992; CH-prior. 20.11.1991).
c EP 454 501 (Sankyo Co.; appl. 29.4.1991; J-prior. 27.4.1990).
ea DE 3 010 504 (BASF AG; appl. 19.3.1980).
eb JP 08 119 958 (Kwaray Co.; appl. 18.10.1994).
   JP 08 119 957 (Kwaray Co.; appl. 18.10.1994).
ec JP 01 068 366 (Eisai Co.; appl. 9.9.1987).
ed Tanabe, K. et al.: Chem. Lett. (CMLTAG) **5**, 561 (1985).
ef Sakito, Y. et al.: Tetrahedron Lett. (TELEAY) **23** (47), 4953 (1982).
   EP 65 368 (Sumitomo Chem.; appl. 28.4.1982; J-prior. 30.4.1981).

kinetic resolution of intermediate II:
Hyatt, J.A.; Skelton, C.: Tetrahedron: Asymmetry (TASYE3) **8** (4), 523 (1997).

preparation of (+)-enantiomer by yeast reductase:
WO 9 310 254 (SmithKline Beecham; appl. 19.11.1992; GB-prior. 19.11.1991).

Formulation(s): tabl. 100 mg, 200 mg, 300 mg, 400 mg

Trade Name(s):
J: Noscal (Sankyo)   USA: Rezulin (Parke Davis;
                                 Warner-Lambert); wfm

Trolnitrate

ATC: C01DA09
Use: coronary vasodilator

RN: 7077-34-1 MF: $C_6H_{12}N_4O_9$ MW: 284.18 EINECS: 230-376-3
CN: 2,2',2"-nitrilotrisethanol trinitrate (ester)

diphosphate
RN: 588-42-1 MF: $C_6H_{12}N_4O_9 \cdot 2H_3PO_4$ MW: 480.17 EINECS: 209-617-1
LD₅₀: 100 mg/kg (M, i.v.); 330 mg/kg (M, p.o.);
       130 mg/kg (R, p.o.)

HO   ⌐OH
   N
HO

triethanolamine

→ HNO₃, H₂SO₄ →

O₂N—O   O—NO₂
       N
O₂N—O

Trolnitrate

Reference(s):
FR 984 523 (J. Metadier; appl. 1949).

Tromantadine

ATC: D06BB02; J05AC03
Use: antiviral

RN: 53783-83-8   MF: $C_{16}H_{28}N_2O_2$ MW: 280.41   EINECS: 258-770-0
CN: 2-[2-(dimethylamino)ethoxy]-*N*-tricyclo[3.3.1.1^{3,7}]dec-1-ylacetamide

monohydrochloride
RN: 41544-24-5   MF: $C_{16}H_{28}N_2O_2 \cdot HCl$ MW: 316.87   EINECS: 255-434-5

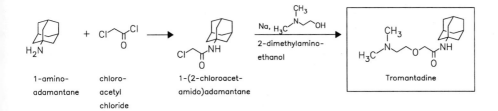

| 1-amino-adamantane | chloro-acetyl chloride | 1-(2-chloroacet-amido)adamantane | Tromantadine |

Reference(s):
DOS 1 941 218 (Merz & Co.; appl. 13.8.1969).
Peteri, D.; Sterner, W.: Arzneim.-Forsch. (ANCEAD) **23**, 577 (1973).

Formulation(s):   cream 10 mg, 100 mg/10 g; gel 10 mg, 100 mg/10 g; ointment 1 % (as monohydrochloride)

Trometamol
(Tromethamine)

ATC: B05BB03; B05XX02
Use: osmotic diuretic

RN: 77-86-1   MF: $C_4H_{11}NO_3$ MW: 121.14   EINECS: 201-064-4
CN: 2-amino-2-(hydroxymethyl)-1,3-propanediol

$$O_2N-CH_3 \ + \ HCHO \longrightarrow \quad \xrightarrow{H_2, \ Raney-Ni}$$

| nitro-methane | form-aldehyde | 2-(hydroxymethyl)-2-nitro-1,3-propanediol | Trometamol |

Reference(s):
US 2 174 242 (Purdue Res. Found.; 1939; appl. 1937).

electrolytic reduction:
US 2 485 982 (Commercial Solvents Corp.; 1949; appl. 1944).

Formulation(s):   amp. 7.3 g/20 ml, sol. 34.36 g/100 ml

Trade Name(s):
D: Elektrolyt-Konzentrat Tris   TRIS 36.34 % Braun (B/   Thamacétat (Bellon;
    (THAM) pfrimmer   Braun)   Rhône-Poulenc Rorer)
    (Pfrimmer)   F: Almide (Alcon)   I: Thamesol (Diaco)
    THAM-Köhler 3 M   Monuril (Zambon)   Ulcotris (ISF)-Comb.
    (Köhler)   J: Tham-Set (Otsuka)-comb.

Tropenziline bromide

ATC: A03; N07
Use: antispasmodic, parasympathomimetic

RN: 143-92-0   MF: $C_{24}H_{30}BrNO_4$ MW: 476.41   EINECS: 205-612-3
CN: 3-[(hydroxydiphenylacetyl)oxy]-6-methoxy-8,8-dimethyl-8-azoniabicyclo[3.2.1]octane bromide

methoxy-   methyl-   dimethyl
succinaldehyde   amine   acetonedi-
                                 carboxylate

6-methoxytropinone (I)   6-methoxytropine

ethyl benzilate

(II)   methyl   Tropenziline bromide
                  bromide

Reference(s):
CH 325 296 (Sandoz; appl. 1954).
Stoll, A. et al.: Helv. Chim. Acta (HCACAV) **37**, 495 (1954); **38**, 571 (1955).

Trade Name(s):
D: Pelerol (Sandoz)-comb.;   F: Palerol (Salvoxyl-Wander);
    wfm   wfm

Tropicamide

ATC: S01FA06
Use: parasympatholytic, mydriatic

RN: 1508-75-4   MF: $C_{17}H_{20}N_2O_2$ MW: 284.36   EINECS: 216-140-2
LD_{50}:   565 mg/kg (M, p.o.);
865 mg/kg (R, p.o.)
CN: N-ethyl-α-(hydroxymethyl)-N-(4-pyridinylmethyl)benzeneacetamide

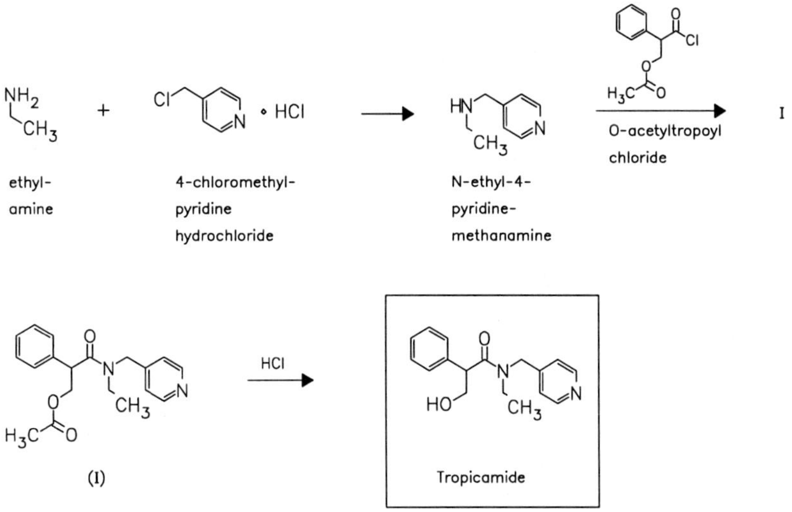

ethyl-amine
4-chloromethyl-pyridine hydrochloride
N-ethyl-4-pyridine-methanamine
O-acetyltropoyl chloride

(I)   Tropicamide

Reference(s):
US 2 726 245 (Hoffmann-La Roche; 1955; CH-prior. 1952).

Formulation(s):   eye drops 5 mg/ml, 5 mg/0.5 ml

Trade Name(s):
D: Aroclunin (Chauvin ankerpharm)
Mydriaticum Stulln (Pharma Stulln)
Mydrum (Chauvin ankerpharm)
F: Mydriaticum (Merck Sharp & Dohme-Chibret)

Tropicamide Faure (Schering)
GB: Minims Tropicamide (Chauvin)
Mydriacyl (Alcon)
I: Tropimil (Farmigea)
Visumidriatic (Pharmec)

Visumidriatic Antif. (Merck Sharp & Dohme)-comb.
Visumidriatic Fenil (Pharmec)-comb.
J: Mydrin (Santen)
USA: Tryptar (Armour); wfm

Tropisetron
(ICS-205930)

ATC: A04AA03
Use: antiemetic, antimigraine, 5-HT$_3$-antagonist

RN: 89565-68-4   MF: $C_{17}H_{20}N_2O_2$ MW: 284.36
CN: 1H-Indole-3-carboxylic acid endo-8-methyl-8-azabicyclo[3.2.1]oct-3-yl ester

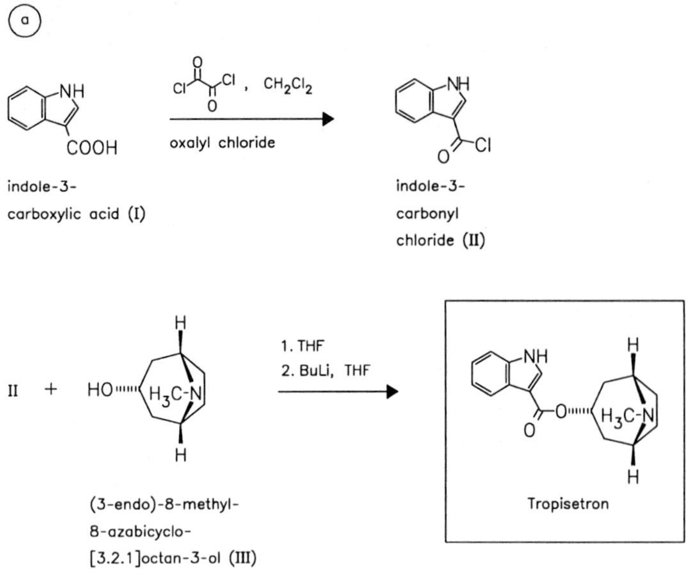

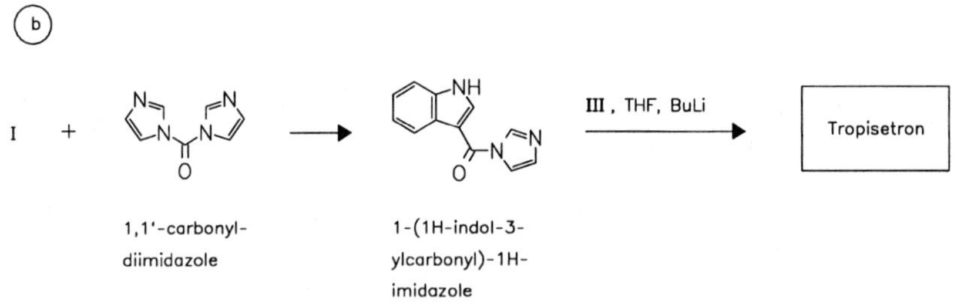

a

indole-3-
carboxylic acid (I)

oxalyl chloride

indole-3-
carbonyl
chloride (II)

II + HO······(H₃C-N)

1. THF
2. BuLi, THF

Tropisetron

(3-endo)-8-methyl-
8-azabicyclo-
[3.2.1]octan-3-ol (III)

b

I +

1,1'-carbonyl-
diimidazole

1-(1H-indol-3-
ylcarbonyl)-1H-
imidazole

III, THF, BuLi

Tropisetron

Reference(s):
a DE 3 322 574 (Novartis; appl. 23.6.1983; CH-prior. 29.6.1982).
a,b BE 901 274 (Sandoz A. G.; appl. 14.12.1984; CH-prior. 23.12.1983)
  use of serotonin-5-HT-antagonists:
  DE 3 724 059 (Sandoz-Patent GmbH; appl. 21.7.1987; D-prior. 7.8.1986).
b DE 3 445 377 (Sandoz-Patent GmbH; appl. 13.12.1984; CH-prior. 23.12.1983).
  Langlois, M. et al.: Eur. J. Med. Chem. (EJMCA5) **28**, 869 (1993).

Formulation(s): amp. 2 mg/2 ml, 5 mg/5 ml; cps. 5 mg

Trade Name(s):
D: Navoban (ASTA Medica   GB: Navoban (Novartis
   AWD; Novartis Pharma)   Pharma)
F: Navoban (Novartis   I: Navoban (Novartis
   Pharma)   Pharma)

Trospium chloride

ATC: A03AB20
Use: anticholinergic, antispasmodic

RN: 10405-02-4 MF: C₂₅H₃₀ClNO₃ MW: 427.97 EINECS: 233-875-4
LD₅₀: 11.2 mg/kg (M, i.v.); 812 mg/kg (M, p.o.);
  15.5 mg/kg (R, i.v.); 1510 mg/kg (R, p.o.)
CN: (1α,3β,5α)-3-[(hydroxydiphenylacetyl)oxy]spiro[8-azoniabicyclo[3.2.1]octane-8,1'-pyrrolidinium]
  chloride

nortropine   1,4-dibromo-
                    butane   (I)

I   +   H₂O

α-chlorodiphenyl-   Trospium chloride
acetyl chloride

Reference(s):
DE 1 194 422 (Pfleger; appl. 5.3.1963).

Formulation(s):   amp. 1.2 mg/2 ml, 2 mg/2 ml; drg. 15 mg, 20 mg, 30 mg; f. c. tabl. 5 mg; suppos. 0.75 mg, 1
                      mg

Trade Name(s):
D: Spasmex (Pfleger)   Spasmo-Urgenin
       Spasmo-Fyt (Madaus)   (Madaus)-comb.
       Spasmo-Rhoival (Byk   Trospi-forte (medac)
       Gulden/Byk Tosse)   J: Spasmex (Nikken)

Trovafloxacin mesilate
(CP-99219; CP-99219-27)

ATC: J01MA13
Use: antibacterial

RN: 147059-75-4   MF: $C_{20}H_{15}F_3N_4O_3 \cdot CH_4O_3S$ MW: 512.47
CN: (1α,5α,6α)-7-(6-Amino-3-azabicyclo[3.1.0]hex-3-yl)-1-(2,4-difluorophenyl)-6-fluoro-1,4-dihydro-4-oxo-
       1,8-naphthyridine-3-carboxylic acid

monohydrate
RN: 193478-08-9   MF: $C_{20}H_{15}F_3N_4O_3 \cdot CH_4O_3S \cdot H_2O$ MW: 530.48
base
RN: 147059-72-1   MF: $C_{20}H_{15}F_3N_4O_3$ MW: 416.36
hydrochloride
RN: 146961-34-4   MF: $C_{20}H_{15}F_3N_4O_3 \cdot HCl$ MW: 452.82

N-benzyl-   ethyl   ethyl (1α,5α,6α)-3-
maleimide (I)   diazoacetate (II)   benzyl-2,4-dioxo-3-
                                                   azabicyclo[3.1.0]hexane-
                                                   6-carboxylate (III)

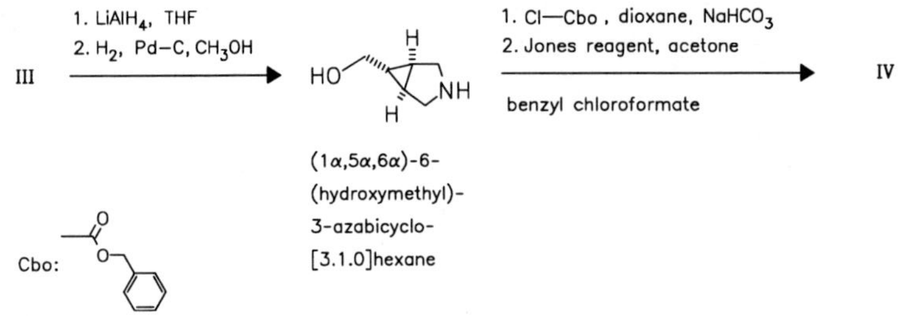

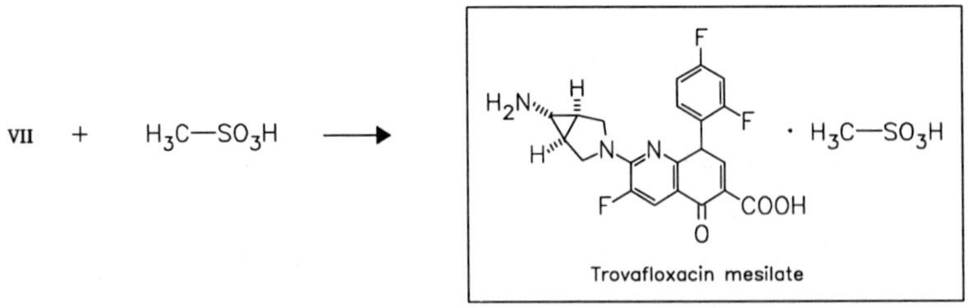

III
1. LiAlH$_4$, THF
2. H$_2$, Pd–C, CH$_3$OH
→

HO (1α,5α,6α)-6-(hydroxymethyl)-3-azabicyclo[3.1.0]hexane

1. Cl—Cbo, dioxane, NaHCO$_3$
2. Jones reagent, acetone

benzyl chloroformate
→ IV

Cbo:

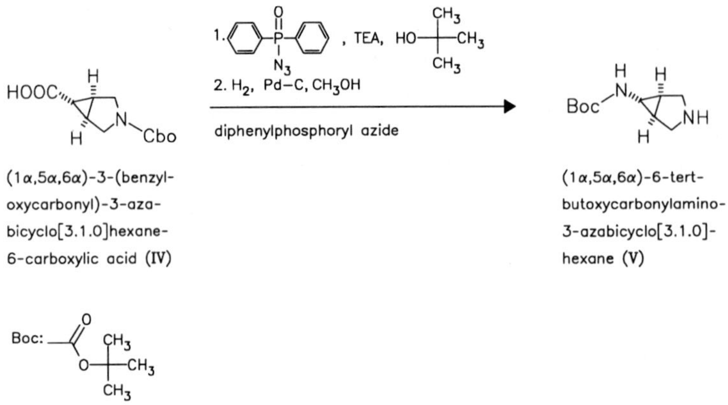

HOOC (1α,5α,6α)-3-(benzyloxycarbonyl)-3-azabicyclo[3.1.0]hexane-6-carboxylic acid (IV)

1. (diphenylphosphoryl azide), TEA, HO—CH(CH$_3$)CH$_3$
2. H$_2$, Pd–C, CH$_3$OH

diphenylphosphoryl azide

Boc—NH (1α,5α,6α)-6-tert-butoxycarbonylamino-3-azabicyclo[3.1.0]-hexane (V)

Boc:

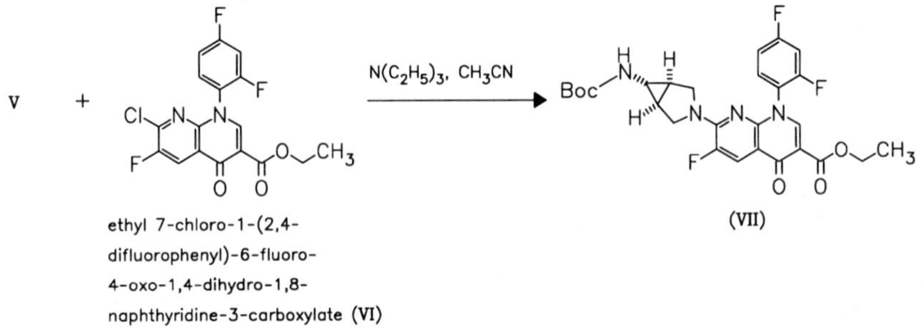

V +

ethyl 7-chloro-1-(2,4-difluorophenyl)-6-fluoro-4-oxo-1,4-dihydro-1,8-naphthyridine-3-carboxylate (VI)

N(C$_2$H$_5$)$_3$, CH$_3$CN
→

Boc—NH (VII)

VII + H$_3$C—SO$_3$H →

H$_2$N · H$_3$C—SO$_3$H

Trovafloxacin mesilate

(aa) alternative synthesis of IV

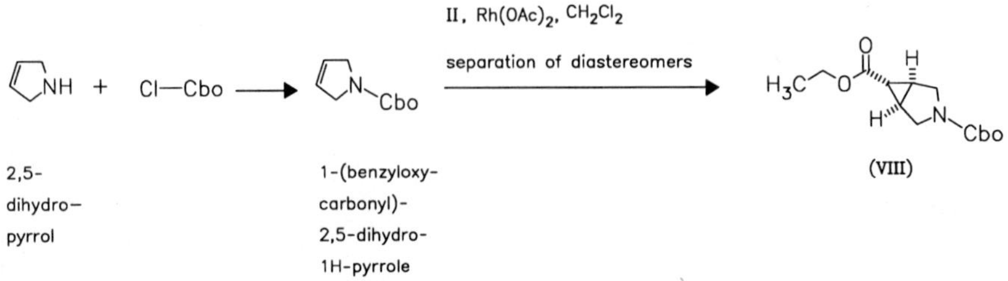

NH + Cl—Cbo →

N-Cbo

II. Rh(OAc)$_2$, CH$_2$Cl$_2$

separation of diastereomers
→

H$_3$C—O (VIII)

2,5-dihydro-pyrrol

1-(benzyloxycarbonyl)-2,5-dihydro-1H-pyrrole

VIII $\xrightarrow{\text{NaOH}}$ IV

(ab)   alternative synthesis of V

I + Br⌒NO₂ $\xrightarrow{\text{, toluene, 0°C}}$ (1α,5α,6α)-3-benzyl-6-nitro-2,4-dioxo-3-azabicyclo[3.1.0]hexane $\xrightarrow[\text{2. H}_2\text{, Pd–C}]{\text{1. BH}_3\text{, THF}}$ IX

bromonitro-methane

IX $\xrightarrow[\text{2. H}_2\text{, Pd–C, CH}_3\text{OH}]{\text{1. Boc⌒O⌒Boc , THF, TEA}}$ V   ---▸   Trovafloxacin mesilate

Reference(s):

route for trovafloxacin 6β- diastereomer:
Vilsmaier, E.; Goerz: Synthesis (SYNTBF) 739 (1998).
a   US 5 164 402 (Pfizer Inc., 17.11.1992; USA-prior. 11.7.1990).
    Brighty, K.E. et al.: Synlett (SYNLES) **1996**, 1097.
    JP 09 012 546 (Chisso Corp.; appl. 23.6.1995).
aa Braish, T.F. et al.: Synlett (SYNLES) **1996**, 1100
    Stille, J.K. et al.: J. Org. Chem. (JOCEAH) **45** (11), 2139-2145 (1980).
    ES 2 095 809 (Química Synth.; appl. 27.7.1995).
ab EP 818 445 (Pfizer Inc.; appl. 1.7.1997; USA-prior. 9.7.1996).

starting material VI:
US 4 571 396 (Warner Lambert Co.; 18.2.1986; USA-prior. 16.4.1984).
US 4 775 668 (Pfizer Inc.; 4.10.1988; USA-prior. 19.8.1986).

novel crystal forms:
WO 9 639 406 (Pfizer Inc.; USA-prior. 6.6.1995).
WO 9 707 800 (Pfizer Inc.; appl. 29.7.1996; USA-prior. 29.8.1995).

polymorphs of the prodrug:
WO 9 708 191 (Pfizer Inc.; appl. 5.7.1996; USA-prior. 29.8.1995).

suspension for oral administration:
DE 19 706 978 (U. Posanski; appl. 5.1.1998; D-prior. 21.2.1997).

use for treatment of Heliobacter pylori infections:
EP 676 199 (Pfizer Inc.; appl. 23.3.1995; USA-prior. 7.4.1994).

Formulation(s):   tabl. 100 mg, 200 mg (as mesylate); vials, 40 ml, 60 ml with 5 mg/ml

Trade Name(s):
D: Trovan (Pfizer); wfm   Turvel (Pfizer); wfm   USA: Trovan (Pfizer; 1998); wfm

Troxerutin

ATC: C05CA04
Use: vein therapeutic

RN: 7085-55-4　MF: $C_{33}H_{42}O_{19}$　MW: 742.68　EINECS: 230-389-4
LD$_{50}$: 27.16 g/kg (R, i.p.)
CN: 2-[3,4-bis(2-hydroxyethoxy)phenyl]-3-[[6-O-(6-deoxy-α-L-mannopyranosyl)-β-D-glucopyranosyl]oxy]-5-hydroxy-7-(2-hydroxyethoxy)-4H-1-benzopyran-4-one

rutoside　　2-chloroethanol　　Troxerutin

Reference(s):
DAS 1 061 327 (Zyma; appl. 30.12.1957; CH-prior. 4.7.1957).
GB 833 174 (Zyma S.A.; appl. 27.6.1958; CH-prior. 4.7.1957).

synthesis with ethylene oxide:
DAS 1 543 974 (Zyma; appl. 8.10.1966; F-prior. 25.10.1965; CH-prior. 9.3.1966).
DAS 1 793 746 (Zyma; appl. 8.10.1966; F-prior. 25.10.1965).

Formulation(s):　cps. 300 mg; eye drops 50 mg/ml; f. c. drg 300 mg; f. c. tabl. 250 mg, 300 mg; s. r. tabl. 300 mg

Trade Name(s):
D: Drisi-Ven (Sertürner)
Pherarutin (Kanoldt)
Posorutin (Ursapharm)
Troxerutin-ratiopharm (ratiopharm)
Troxeven (Kreussler)
Vastribil (Farmasan)
Veno SL 300 (Ursapharm)

numerous combination preparations
F: Ginkor (Beaufour)-comb.
Rhéobral (Niverpharm)
Rhéoflux (Niverpharm)
Veinamitol (Negma)
Vivéne (Labs. de L'Aérocid)
GB: Paroven (Zyma); wfm

I: Dermoangiopan (Abiogen Pharma)-comb.
Emorril (Poli)-comb.
Flebil (Molteni)
Premium (Synthelabo)-comb.
Venolen (Farmacologico Milanese)

Troxipide

ATC: A02BX11
Use: ulcer therapeutic

RN: 99777-81-8　MF: $C_{15}H_{22}N_2O_4$　MW: 294.35
CN: (±)-3,4,5-trimethoxy-N-3-piperidinylbenzamide

base
RN: 30751-05-4　MF: $C_{15}H_{22}N_2O_4$　MW: 294.35
LD$_{50}$: 100 mg/kg (M, i.v.); 2 g/kg (M, p.o.);
2100 mg/kg (R, p.o.)

monohydrochloride
RN: 30751-03-2   MF: $C_{15}H_{22}N_2O_4 \cdot HCl$ MW: 330.81
LD$_{50}$: 300 mg/kg (M, i.p.); 2000 mg/kg (M, p.o.); 1550 mg/kg (M, s.c.);
340 mg/kg (R, i.p.); 2100 mg/kg (R, p.o.)

| 3-amino-pyridine | 3,4,5-trimethoxy-benzoyl chloride | 3-(3,4,5-trimethoxy-benzamido)pyridine | Troxipide |

Reference(s):
DOS 1 938 512 (Kyorin; J-prior. 30.6.1969).
DOS 1 967 324 (Kyorin; J-prior. 30.6.1969).
US 3 647 805 (Kyorin; 7.3.1972; appl. 11.7.1969).
Irikura, T. et al.: J. Med. Chem. (JMCMAR), **14**, 357 (1971).

medical use for treatment of gastritis:
EP 254 068 (Kyorin; appl. 25.6.1987; J-prior. 26.6.1986).

Formulation(s):   tabl. 50 mg, 100 mg

Trade Name(s):
J: Aplace (Kyorin; 1986)

L-Tryptophan

ATC: N06AX02
Use: antidepressant, essential amino acid

RN: 73-22-3   MF: $C_{11}H_{12}N_2O_2$ MW: 204.23   EINECS: 200-795-6
LD$_{50}$: >16 g/kg (R, p.o.)
CN: L-tryptophan

| acrolein | diethyl acetamido-malonate | | phenyl-hydrazine (I) |

| (II) | | | N-acetyl-DL-tryptophan (III) |

III → L-Tryptophan (aminoacylase and racemization of N-acetyl-D-tryptophan)

b

NC—CHO + CO₂ + HCN $\xrightarrow{NH_3}$ 5-(2-cyano-ethyl)hydantoin $\xrightarrow{H_2, \text{Raney-Ni (Pb), } CH_3COOH}$ IV

3-cyano-
propion-
aldehyde

5-(2-cyano-
ethyl)hydantoin

3-(5-hydantoinyl)-
propionaldehyde (IV)

+ I → $\xrightarrow{HCl}$ 5-(3-indolylmethyl)-hydantoin $\xrightarrow{NaOH}$ V

5-(3-indolylmethyl)-
hydantoin

DL-tryptophan (V)

+ H₃C—O—CH₃ → III $\xrightarrow{aminoacylase}$ L-Tryptophan

Reference(s):
a   Warner, O.T.; Moe, O.A.: J. Am. Chem. Soc. (JACSAT) **70**, 2765 (1948).
b   Komachiya, Y. et al.: Nippon Kagaku Kaishi (NKAKB8) **86**, 856 (1965).

enzymatic racemate resolution:
Chibata, I. et al.: Bull. Agric. Chem. Soc. Jpn. (BACOAV) **21**, 58, 304 (1957).

purification:
US 5 057 615 (Mitsui Toatsu; 15.10.1991; J-prior. 27.6.1989).

combination with beta blocking agents:
US 4 161 530 (Ciba-Geigy; 17.7.1979; CH-prior. 6.1.1975).
GB 1 531 091 (Ciba-Geigy; appl. 5.1.1976; CH-prior. 6.1.1975).
Volk, W. et al.: Arzneim.-Forsch. (ANCEAD) **28** (II), 1798 (1978).

newer syntheses for DL-tryptophan:
Hengartner, M. et al.: J. Org. Chem. (JOCEAH) **44**, 3748 (1979).

Formulation(s):   f. c. tabl. 500 mg; tabl. 500 mg

Trade Name(s):
D: Ardeytropin (Ardeypharm)
      Kalma (Fresenius-Praxis)
      Lypharm (esparma)
      numerous combination
      preparations
F: Actitonic (Amido; as DL-
      form)-comb.; wfm

      Actitonic (Reygagne)-
      comb.; wfm
GB: Optimax (Merck)-comb.
J: Eltrip (Ono)
      Tryptan (Daigo Eiyo)
USA: Trofan (Upsher-Smith);
      wfm

Tryptacin (Arther); wfm
Tryptacin (Nutrition
Control Products); wfm
Tryptophane (Nature's
Bounty); wfm
Tryptophane (Solgar); wfm
Tryptoplex (Tyson); wfm

Tyson L-Tryptophan U.S.P.
(Tyson); wfm

Tuaminoheptane
(Heptylamine)

ATC: R01AA11; R01AB08
Use: sympathomimetic, vasoconstrictor

RN: 123-82-0   MF: $C_7H_{17}N$ MW: 115.22   EINECS: 204-655-5
LD$_{50}$:   60 mg/kg (M, i.p.); 115 mg/kg (M, s.c.);
130 mg/kg (R, s.c.)
CN: 2-heptanamine

sulfate (2:1)
RN: 6411-75-2   MF: $C_7H_{17}N \cdot 1/2H_2O_4S$ MW: 328.52   EINECS: 229-113-5
LD$_{50}$:   16.3 mg/kg (M, i.v.);
47.3 mg/kg (R, i.v.)

amyl methyl ketone   →   Tuaminoheptane

(reagents: NH$_3$, H$_2$, Raney–Ni)

Reference(s):
Norton, D.G. et al.: J. Org. Chem. (JOCEAH) **19**, 1054 (1954).

Formulation(s):   nasal spray 50 mg/10 ml

Trade Name(s):
D: Rinofluimucil-S (Inpharzam)-comb.
F: Rhinofluimucil (Zambon)-comb.
I: Otomicetina (Deca)-comb.
Rinofluimucil (Zambon Italia)-comb.

Tubocurarine chloride

ATC: M03AA02
Use: muscle relaxant

RN: 6989-98-6   MF: $C_{37}H_{41}ClN_2O_6 \cdot HCl \cdot 5H_2O$ MW: 771.73
LD$_{50}$:   130 µg/kg (M, i.v.); 150 mg/kg (M, p.o.)
CN: 7',12'-dihydroxy-6,6'-dimethoxy-2,2',2'-trimethyltubocuraranium chloride hydrochloride pentahydrate

anhydrous
RN: 57-94-3   MF: $C_{37}H_{41}ClN_2O_6 \cdot HCl$ MW: 681.66   EINECS: 200-356-9
LD$_{50}$:   97 µg/kg (M, i.v.); 33 mg/kg (M, p.o.),
66 µg/kg (R, i.v.); 28 mg/kg (R, p.o.)

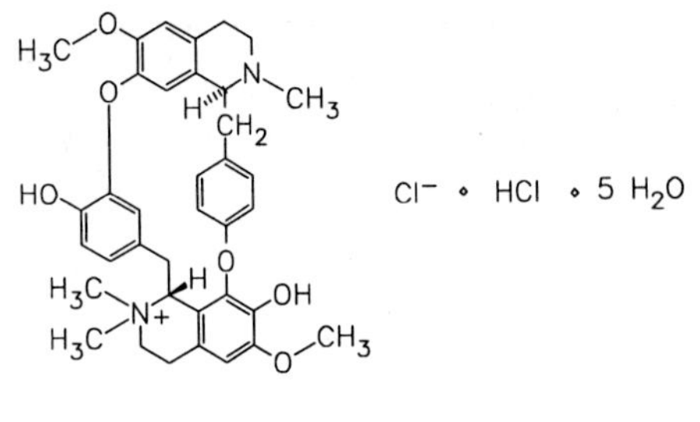

Tubocurarine chloride

By extraction from *Chondrodendron tomentosum* (Ampi Huasca) and purification via the picrate.

Reference(s):
US 2 409 241 (Squibb; 1946; prior. 1944).
US 2 600 539 (Parke Davis; 1952; appl. 1947).
Everett, A J. et al.: J. Chem. Soc. D (CCJDAO) **1970**, 1020.
Codding, P.W.; James, M.N.G.: J. Chem. Soc. D (CCJDAO) **1972**, 1.

Formulation(s):   amp. 3 mg/ml

Trade Name(s):

D:	Curarin Asta (ASTA); wfm	GB:	Jexin (Duncan, Flockhart); wfm		Tubarine (Wellcome); wfm
	Curarin HAF (Ethicon); wfm		Tubarine (Calmic); wfm	J:	Amelizol (Yoshitomi)
F:	D-Tubocurarine Abbott (Abbott); wfm	I:	Curarin (Schering); wfm	USA:	Tubocurarine Chloride (Lilly)
			Intocortrin T (Squibb); wfm		

Tulobuterol

ATC: R03AC11; R03CC11
Use: bronchodilator

RN: 41570-61-0   MF: $C_{12}H_{18}ClNO$ MW: 227.74
CN: 2-chloro-α-[[(1,1-dimethylethyl)amino]methyl]benzenemethanol

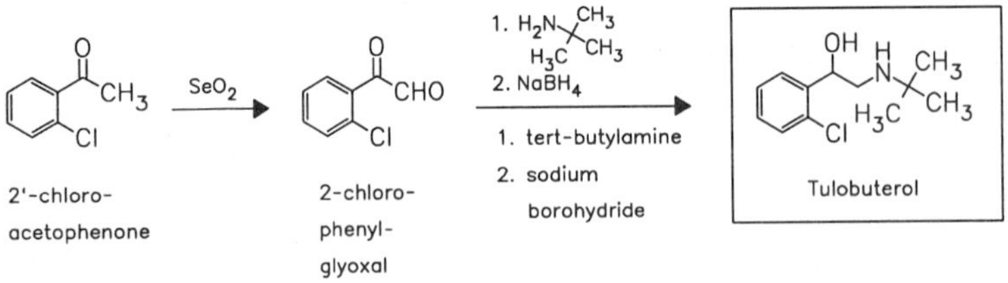

2'-chloro-
acetophenone

2-chloro-
phenyl-
glyoxal

Tulobuterol

Reference(s):
DOS 2 244 737 (Hokuriku; appl. 12.9.1972; J-prior. 13.9.1971).

Formulation(s):   sol. 1 mg/5 ml; syrup 1 mg/5 ml; tabl. 2 mg (as hydrochloride)

Trade Name(s):

D:	Atenos (UCB; 1985)	GB:	Respacal (UCB)	Hokunalin (Hokuriku)
	Brelomax (Abbott; 1985)	J:	Berachin (Tokyo Tanabe)	

Tybamate

ATC: M03
Use: tranquilizer, skeletal muscle relaxant

RN: 4268-36-4   MF: $C_{13}H_{26}N_2O_4$ MW: 274.36   EINECS: 224-254-9
LD_{50}:   254 mg/kg (M, i.v.); 800 mg/kg (M, p.o.);
1040 mg/kg (R, p.o.)
CN: butylcarbamic acid 2-[[(aminocarbonyl)oxy]methyl]-2-methylpentyl ester

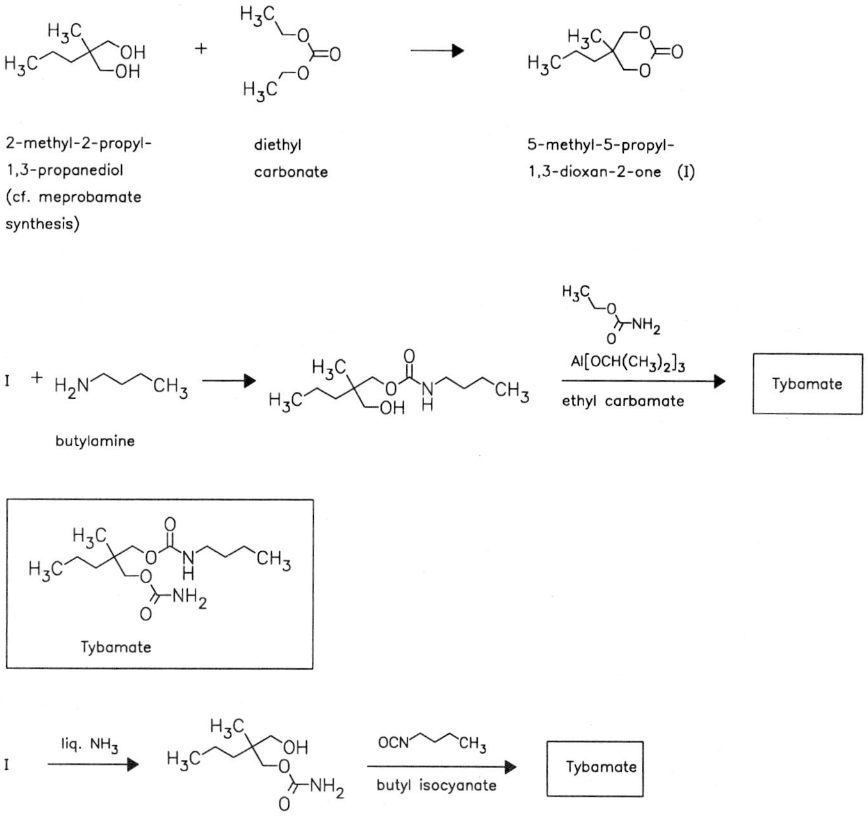

2-methyl-2-propyl-
1,3-propanediol
(cf. meprobamate
synthesis)

diethyl
carbonate

5-methyl-5-propyl-
1,3-dioxan-2-one   (I)

butylamine

ethyl carbamate

Tybamate

Tybamate

butyl isocyanate

Tybamate

Reference(s):
US 2 937 119 (Carter Products; 17.5.1960; prior. 11.6.1959).

alternative synthesis:
DE 1 196 638 (Orgamol; appl. 27.2.1962; CH-prior. 2.3.1961).

Trade Name(s):
USA: Solacen (Wallace); wfm   Tybatran (Robins); wfm

Tyloxapol

ATC: R05CA01
Use: tenside, mucolytic agent

RN: 25301-02-4   MF: $[C_{14}H_{22}O \cdot C_2H_4O \cdot CH_2O]x$ MW: unspecified
CN: formaldehyde polymer with oxirane and 4-(1,1,3-tetramethylbutyl)phenol

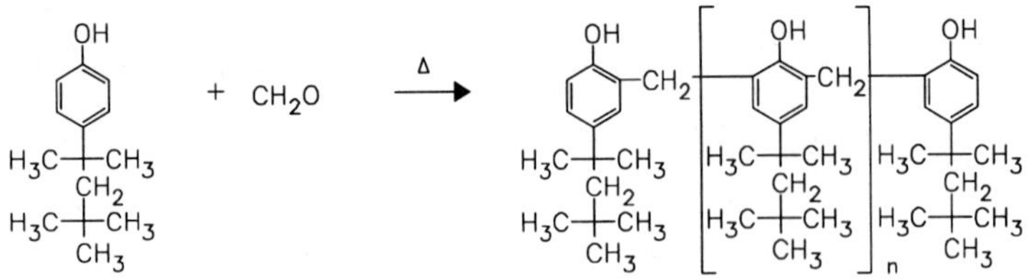

4-(1,1,3,3-tetra-
methylbutyl)-
phenol

form-
aldehyde

(I)

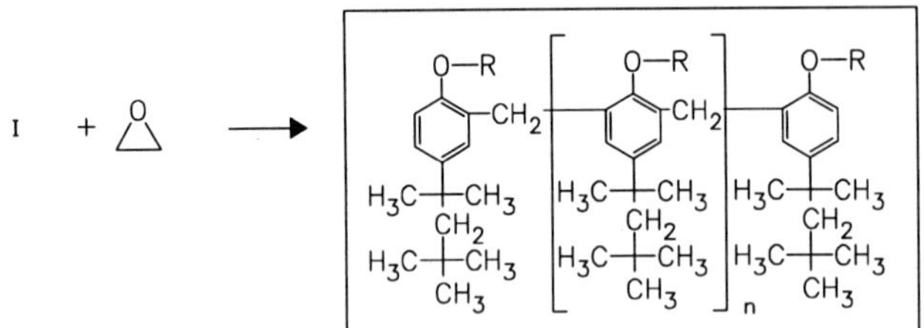

ethylene
oxide

n: c. 5
R: $-CH_2-(CH_2-O-CH_2)_m-CH_2-OH$
m: 7-9

Tyloxapol

Reference(s):
US 2 454 541 (Rohm & Haas; 1948; appl. 1944).

Formulation(s):   eye drops 2.5 mg/ml, 10 mg/ml; intratracheal susp. 8 mg/10 ml; sol. 0.25 mg/ml, 1.25 mg/ml;
vial 0.25 mg/ml

Trade Name(s):

D: Complete (Pharm-
Allergan)-comb.
Enoclen (Alcon)-comb.
Exosurf (Glaxo Wellcome)-
comb.

F: Tacholiquin (bene-
Arzneimittel)-comb.
Contactol (Merck Sharp &
Dohme-Chibret)-comb.;
wfm

GB: Alevaire (Winthrop); wfm
J: Alevaire (Nippon Shoji)
USA: Exosurf Neonatal (Glaxo
Wellcome)-comb.

L-Tyrosine

Use: non-essential proteinogenic amino
acid (for infusion solution)

RN: 60-18-4   MF: $C_9H_{11}NO_3$ MW: 181.19   EINECS: 200-460-4
LD_{50}: >1450 mg/kg (M, i.p.)
CN: L-tyrosine

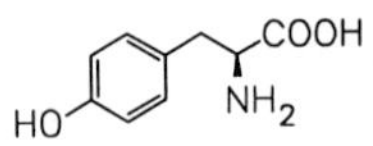

L-Tyrosine

Preparation by acidic proteine hydrolysis (e. g. of keratines) with following fractionated crystallization (obtained
in commonly with L-cystine).

Reference(s):
Ullmann's Encyclopedia of Industrial Chemistry, 5th Ed., Vol. **A2**, 74.

Formulation(s):   sol. 2.5 %, 3 %, 3.5 %, 4.5 %, 6 %, 10 %, 15 %; tabl. 30 mg

Trade Name(s):
D: numerous combination   I: Alfa Kappa (Farma-   ISI F/2/st (ISI)-comb.
       preparations   Biagini)-comb.   USA: Catemine (Tyson)-comb.

Ubidecarenone
(Coenzym Q; Ubiquinone-10)

ATC: C01EB09
Use: cardiovascular agent,
       antihypertensive

RN: 303-98-0   MF: $C_{59}H_{90}O_4$ MW: 863.37   EINECS: 206-147-9
CN: 2-(3,7,11,15,19,23,27,31,35,39-decamethyl-2,6,10,14,18,22,26,30,34,38-tetracontadecaenyl)-5,6-
      dimethoxy-3-methyl-2,5-cyclohexadiene-1,4-dione

Ubidecarenone

From culture of *Sporidiobolus johnsonii* (ATCC 20490), *Sporidiobolus ruinenii* (ATCC-20489), *Oosporidium margaritiferum* (ATCC 10676), *Rhodotorula muciladinosa* (AHM 3946), *Xanthomonas stewartii* (Pasteur-No. 1035 and 1036).

Reference(s):
US 4 070 244 (Takeda; 24.1.1978; J-prior. 27.2.1976).
DOS 2 740 614 (Kanegafuchi; appl. 9.9.1977; J-prior. 14.9.1976).
DOS 2 834 952 (Lab. Bellon; appl. 10.8.1978; GB-prior. 17.8.1977).

synthesis from 2-methyl-4,5,6-trimethoxyphenol *and* decaprenol:
US 3 068 295 (Merck & Co.; 11.12.1962; appl. 3.9.1958).
US 3 896 153 (Eisai; 22.7.1975; J-prior. 6.4.1973).
US 4 062 879 (Eisai; 13.12.1977; J-prior. 29.9.1975).

medical use as antihypertensive:
US 3 808 330 (Eisai; 30.4.1974; J-prior. 13.7.1972).

medical use for improvement of hearing:
US 4 073 883 (Eisai; 14.2.1978; J-prior. 5.3.1976).

medical use as gerontotherapeutic:
US 4 156 718 (The New England Institute; 29.5.1979; prior. 19.11.1976, 12.12.1977).

Formulation(s):   amp. 50 mg; cps. 50 mg; drg. 50 mg; tabl. 10 mg, 25 mg, 50 mg, 60 mg, 200 mg

Trade Name(s):
I: Caomet (Astra
     Farmaceutici)
     Coedieci (Mitim)
     Decafar (Lafare)
     Decorenone (Italfarmaco)
     Dymion (Pulitzer)
     Iuvacor (Scharper)
     Miodene (Bioprogress)

     Miotyn (Ibirn)
     Mitocor (Zambon Italia)
     Roburis (Ripari-Gero)
     Ubifactor (Sancarlo)
     Ubimaior (Master Pharma)
     Ubiten (Zilliken)
     generics
J: Heartcin (Ohta)

     Inokiten (Nippon Yakuhin)
     Neuquinon (Eisai)
     Yubekinon (Hishiyama)
USA: Coenzyme Q10 (Vitaline)
     Co-Q-10 (Tyson)
     Co-Q 10 (Carlson)

Ulobetasol propionate

ATC: D07A
Use: topical corticosteroid

RN: 66852-54-8   MF: $C_{25}H_{31}ClF_2O_5$ MW: 484.97
LD_{50}: >15 ml/kg (R, p.o.)
CN: (6α,11β,16β)-21-chloro-6,9-difluoro-11-hydroxy-16-methyl-17-(1-oxopropoxy)pregna-1,4-diene-3,20-dione

halobetasol
RN: 98651-66-2   MF: $C_{22}H_{27}ClF_2O_4$ MW: 428.90

21-chloro-11β-hydroxy-
16β-methyl-17-propio-
nyloxypregn-4-ene-
3,20-dione

1. CH₃SO₂Cl, pyridine
2. CH₃CONH–Br, HClO₄

2. N-bromoacetamide

21-chloro-9-bromo-11β-
hydroxy-16β-methyl-17-
propionyloxypregn-4-ene-
3,20-dione (I)

K₂CO₃

21-chloro-9β,11β-epoxy-
16β-methyl-17-propio-
nyloxypregn-4-ene-
3,20-dione

Tos–OH
triethyl
orthoformate

21-chloro-9β,11β-epoxy-3-ethoxy-
16β-methyl-17-propionyloxy-
pregna-3,5-dien-20-one (II)

ClO₃F
perchloryl
fluoride

21-chloro-9β,11β-epoxy-6α-
fluoro-16β-methyl-17-propio-
nyloxypregn-4-ene-
3,20-dione

1. HF, H₃C–CO–CH₃
2. 2,3-dichloro-
5,6-dicyano-
benzoquinone

Ulobetasol propionate

Reference(s):
CH 631 185 (Ciba-Geigy; appl. 1.1.1978).
DE 2 743 069 (Ciba-Geigy; appl. 24.9.1977; LUX-prior. 29.9.1976).
BE 849 268 (Ciba-Geigy; appl. 28.9.1977; LUX-prior. 29.9.1976).
GB 1 537 130 (Ciba-Geigy; appl. 27.9.1977; LUX-prior. 29.9.1976).

synthesis of 21-chloro-11β-hydroxy-16β-methyl-17-propionyloxypregn-4-ene-3,20-dione:
GB 898 293 (Upjohn; appl. 14.3.1960; USA-prior. 18.3.1959).

Formulation(s):   cream 0.05 %; ointment 0.05 %

Trade Name(s):
USA: Ultravate (Westwood-
       Squibb)

Undecylenic acid

(10-Undecensäure; Undecenoic acid)

ATC: D01AE04
Use: antifungal

RN: 112-38-9   MF: $C_{11}H_{20}O_2$ MW: 184.28   EINECS: 203-965-8
LD_{50}:   8150 mg/kg (M, p.o.);
       2500 mg/kg (R, p.o.)
CN: 10-undecenoic acid

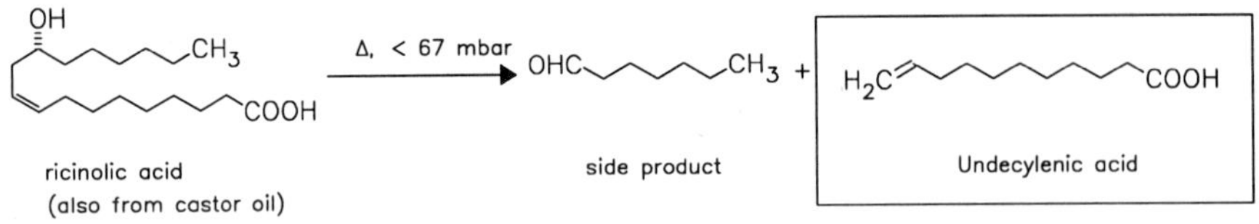

ricinolic acid   side product   Undecylenic acid
(also from castor oil)

Reference(s):
Krafft, F.: Ber. Dtsch. Chem. Ges. (BDCGAS) **10**, 2034 (1877).
Perkins, G.A.; Cruz, A.O.: J. Am. Chem. Soc. (JACSAT) **49**, 1070 (1927).

Formulation(s):   cream 43 mg; liquid 30 mg; ointment 43 mg; powder 53 mg; soap 1 g; sol. 0.1 g/100 g

Trade Name(s):
D: Skinman soft (Hentzel)   Micofoot Zeta (Zeta)-   USA: Breezee Mist Foot Powder
GB: Ceanel (Quinoderm)-comb.   comb.   (Pedinol)-comb.
I: Foot Zeta (Zeta)-comb.   J: Andecin (Fuji Seiaku)

Unoprostone isopropyl

(UF-021)

ATC: G02AD
Use: ocular antihypertensive,
       antiglaucoma, prostaglandin
       derivative

RN: 120373-24-2   MF: $C_{25}H_{44}O_5$ MW: 424.62
CN: [1*R*-[1α(Z),-2β,3α,5α]]-7-[3,5-dihydroxy-2-(3-oxodecyl)cyclopentyl]-5-heptenoic acid 1-methylethyl
      ester

unoprostone
RN: 120373-36-6   MF: $C_{22}H_{38}O_5$ MW: 382.54

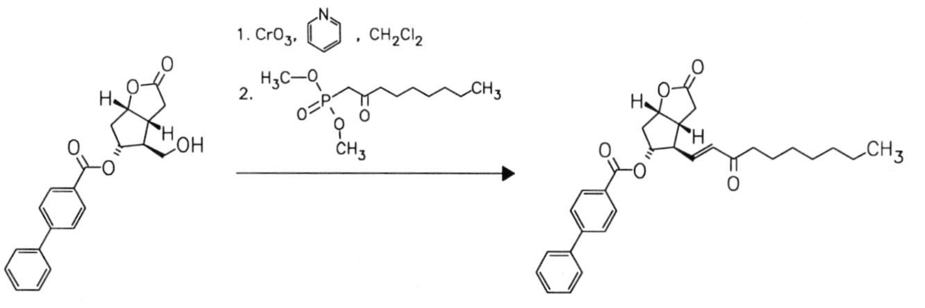

(−)-Corey lactone
(cf. dinoprost)

(I)

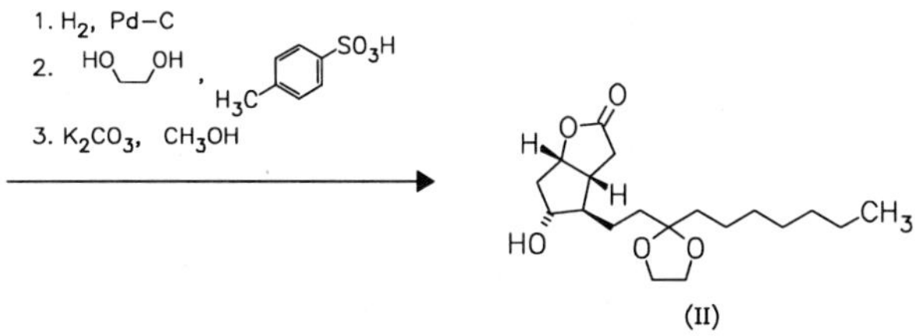

(II)

Unoprostone isopropyl

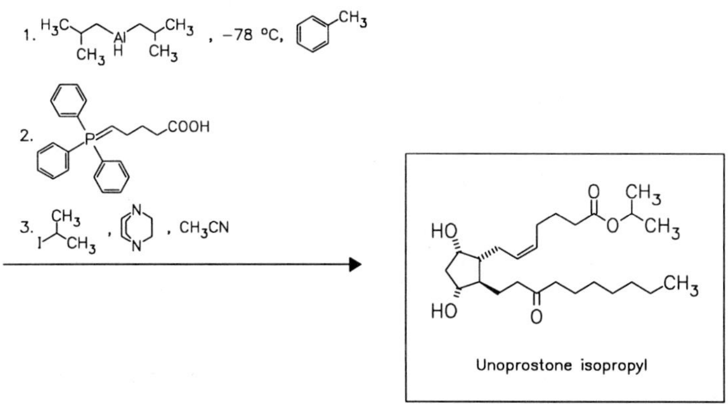

Reference(s):
Ueno, R.; Kuno, S.; Miwa, N.; Takase, M.: 7th Int. Conf. Prostagland. Relat. Compound (May 28-June 1, Florence) 1990, 28.
EP 289 349 (Kabushiki Kaisha Keno Seiyaku Oyo Kenkyusho; appl. 2.11.1988; J-prior. 30.4.1987, 18.9.1987, 29.12.1987, 30.4.1987, 17.9.1987).
EP 308 135 (Kabushiki Kaisha Keno Seiyaku Oyo Kenkyusho; appl. 8.9.1988; J-prior. 18.9.1987; 29.12.1987).

preparation of prostaglandin intermediates:
EP 532 218 (R-Tech Keno Ltd; appl. 2.9.1992; J-prior. 3.9.1991).

use of unoprostone isopropyl:
EP 308 135 (Kabushiki Kaisha Keno Seiyaku Oyo Kenkyusho; appl. 22.3.1989; J-prior. 18.9.1988, 29.12.1987).
EP 561 073 (R-Tech Keno; appl. 22.9.1993; J-prior. 19.3.1992).
EP 501 678 (Keno Seiyaku Oyo Kenkyujo; appl. 2.9.1992; J-prior. 1.3.1991).
EP 458 589 (Kabushiki Kaisha Keno Seiyaku Oyo Kenkyusho; appl. 27.11.1991; 22.5.1990).

pharmaceutical compositions:
CA 2 065 889 (R-Tech Keno; appl. 3.4.1993; J-prior. 2.10.1991).
EP 330 511 (Kabushiki Kaisha Keno Seiyaku Oyo Kenkyusho; appl. 30.8.1989; J-prior. 26.2.1989).
EP 668 076 (R-Tech Keno; appl. 15.3.1994; J-prior. 26.8.1992; EP-prior. 16.2.1994; CA-prior. 17.2.1994; USA-prior. 25.2.1994).

Formulation(s):   eye drops 6 mg/5 ml

Trade Name(s):
J: Rescula (Ueno/Fujisawa)

Uramustine
(Chlorethaminacil; Uracil-Mustard)

ATC: L01
Use: antineoplastic

RN: 66-75-1   MF: $C_8H_{11}Cl_2N_3O_2$ MW: 252.10   EINECS: 200-631-3
LD_{50}: 3550 µg/kg (R, p.o.)
CN: 5-[bis(2-chloroethyl)amino]-2,4(1H,3H)-pyrimidinedione

5-amino-   ethylene
uracil   oxide

Uramustine

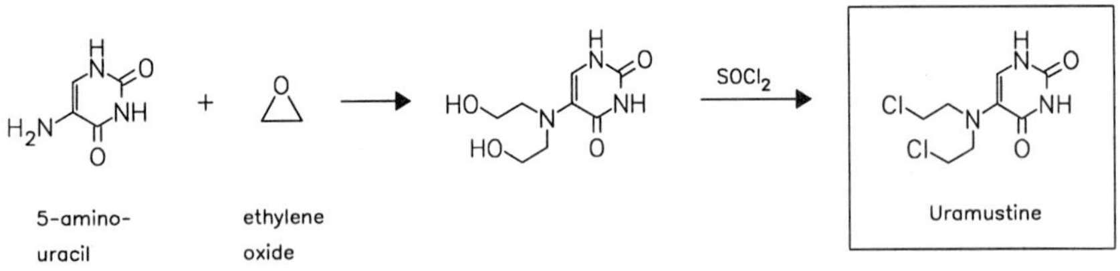

Reference(s):
US 2 969 364 (Upjohn; 24.1.1961; appl. 26.12.1957).

Formulation(s):   cps. 1 mg

Trade Name(s):
GB: Uracil Mustard (Upjohn);   USA: Uracil Mustard (Upjohn);
       wfm   wfm

Urapidil

ATC: C02CA06
Use: antihypertensive

RN: 34661-75-1   MF: $C_{20}H_{29}N_5O_3$ MW: 387.48   EINECS: 252-130-4
LD_{50}: 203 mg/kg (M, i.v.); 508 mg/kg (M, p.o.);
       140 mg/kg (R, i.v.); 520 mg/kg (R, p.o.);
       357 mg/kg (dog, p.o.)
CN: 6-[[3-[4-(2-methoxyphenyl)-1-piperazinyl]propyl]amino]-1,3-dimethyl-2,4(1H,3H)-pyrimidinedione

hydrochloride
RN: 64887-14-5   MF: $C_{20}H_{29}N_5O_3 \cdot HCl$ MW: 423.95
fumarate
RN: 102411-11-0   MF: $C_{20}H_{29}N_5O_3 \cdot xC_4H_2O_4$ MW: unspecified

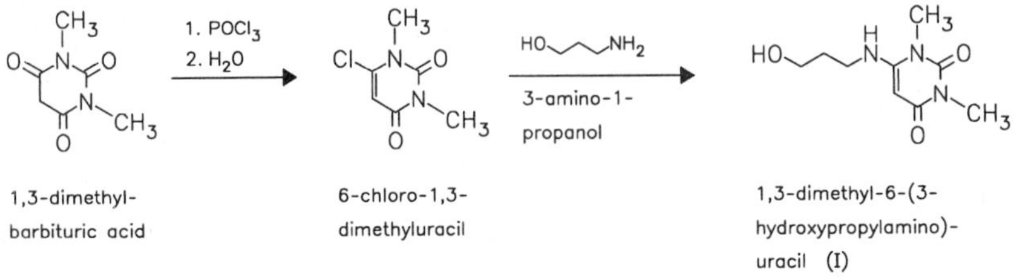

1,3-dimethyl-   6-chloro-1,3-   1,3-dimethyl-6-(3-
barbituric acid   dimethyluracil   hydroxypropylamino)-
                                             uracil (I)

1,3-dimethyl-6-(3-
chloropropylamino)-
uracil

1-(2-methoxyphenyl)-
piperazine carbonate

Urapidil

Reference(s):
DE 1 942 405 (Byk Gulden; appl. 20.8.1969).
US 3 957 786 (Byk Gulden; 18.5.1976; D-prior. 20.8.1969).
US 4 067 982 (Byk Gulden; 10.1.1978; prior. 20.8.1970, 8.4.1976).

addition compound with furosemide:
GB 1 512 771 (Byk Gulden; appl. 7.2.1977; L-prior. 9.2.1976).

Formulation(s):   amp. 27.35 mg, 54.7 mg (as hydrochloride); amp. 25 mg, 50 mg; cps. 30 mg, 60 mg (as
                      fumarate): s. r. cps. 30 mg, 60 mg, 90 mg

Trade Name(s):

D:	Alpha-Depressan (OPW)	Eupressyl gél (Byk)	I:	Ebrantil-30/-60 (Byk
	Ebrantil (Byk Gulden)	Mediatensyl gél (Débat		Gulden; as fumarate)
F:	Eupressyl (Byk; as	cardio)		Ebrantil-50 (Byk Gulden)
	hydrochloride)		J:	Ebrantil (Kaken)

Urokinase

ATC: B01AD04
Use: plasminogen activator, fibrinolytic

RN: 9039-53-6   MF: unspecified   MW: unspecified   EINECS: 232-917-9
LD$_{50}$:   >3000000 iu/kg (M, i.v.); >2.727 mg/kg (M, p.o.);
          >3000000 iu/kg (R, i.v.); >2.727 mg/kg (R, p.o.);
          >909 µg/kg (dog, i.v.)
CN: urokinase (enzyme-activating)

a   From human urine.
b   From culture of renal cells. Enrichment and purification occurs via combined adsorption and elution
    processes, e. g. on BaSO$_4$, silica gels, DEAE-cellulosis, ion-exchange resins (e. g. Amberlite-IRC-50).

Reference(s):
a   Sobal et al.: Am. J. Physiol. (AJPHAP) **171**, 768 (1952).
    US 2 961 382 (Ortho; 1960; appl. 1957).
    US 2 983 647 (Leavens; 1961; GB-prior. 1955).
    US 2 989 440 (Ortho; 1961; appl. 1959).
    US 3 081 236 (Warner-Lambert; 12.3.1963; appl. 26.4.1961).
    DAS 2 616 761 (Hitachi Chemical; appl. 15.4.1976; J-prior. 18.4.1975).
    DAS 2 629 886 (Asahi; appl. 2.7.1976; J-prior. 4.7.1975).
    DAS 2 632 212 (Hitachi Chemical; appl. 16.7.1976; J-prior. 16.7.1975).
b   DAS 2 551 017 (Abbott; appl. 13.11.1975; USA-prior. 31.3.1975).

purification:
White et al.: Biochemistry (BICHAW) **5**, 2160 (1966).
US 3 256 158 (Abbott; 14.6.1966; appl. 22.3.1963).
US 3 542 646 (Green Cross; 24.11.1970; J-prior. 22.11.1966).
DOS 2 143 815 (Mochida; appl. 1.9.1971; J-prior. 5.9.1970).
DOS 2 143 816 (Mochida; appl. 1.9.1971; J-prior. 4.9.1970).
DOS 2 246 969 (Choay; appl. 25.9.1972; F-prior. 24.9.1971, 30.6.1972).
US 3 723 251 (Mochida; 27.3.1972; J-prior. 4.9.1970).
DAS 2 502 095 (Green Cross; appl. 20.1.1975; J-prior. 22.1.1974, 28.1.1974).
GB 1 498 018 (Abbott; appl. 3.10.1975; USA-prior. 20.11.1974).
DOS 2 809 330 (Sumitomo; appl. 3.3.1978; J-prior. 10.3.1977).
DOS 2 823 353 (Sumitomo; appl. 29.5.1978; J-prior. 3.6.1977).
US 4 160 697 (Tanabe Seiyaku; 10.7.1979; J-prior. 9.4.1977, 28.4.1977, 30.9.1977).
US 4 169 764 (Ajinomoto; 2.10.1979; J-prior. 13.8.1975).

stabilization in aqueous solution:
US 3 950 223 (Ajinomoto; 13.4.1976; J-prior. 7.12.1972).

crystallized urokinase:
Lesuk et al.: Science (Washington, D.C.) (SCIEAS) **147**, 880 (1965).

Formulation(s):   vial 5000 iu/ml, 250000 iu/5 ml, 2500 iu, 50000 iu, 100000 iu, 250000 iu, 500000 iu, 600000 iu.

Trade Name(s):

D:	Actosolv (Hoechst)		Urokinase Choay (Sanofi		Persolv (Lepetit)
	Alphakinase (Alpha)		Winthrop)		Purochin (Sclavo Pharma)
	Corase (medac)	GB:	Ukidan (Serono)		Ukidan (Serono)
	Rheotromb (curasan)	I:	Actosolv (Hoechst Marion		Urochinase (Crinos; Sanofi
	Urokinase-medac (medac)		Roussel)		Winthrop)
F:	Actosolv urokinase		Alfakinasi (Alfa	J:	Urokinase (Green Cross)
	(Hoechst Houdé)		Wassermann)	USA:	Abbokinase (Abbott)
			Kisolv (Ecupharma)		

Ursodeoxycholic acid

ATC: A05AA02
Use: choleretic

RN: 128-13-2   MF: C$_{24}$H$_{40}$O$_4$ MW: 392.58   EINECS: 204-879-3
CN: (3α,5β,7β)-3,7-dihydroxycholan-24-oic acid

chenodeoxycholic acid
(q. v.)

CrO$_3$, CH$_3$COOH
chromium
trioxide

(I)

• H$_2$O

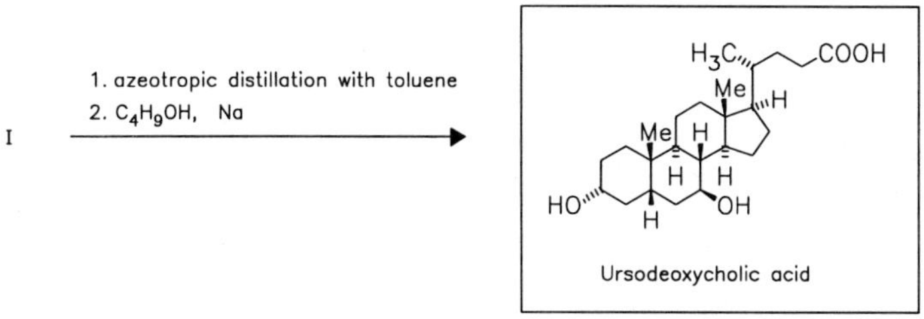

Ursodeoxycholic acid

Reference(s):
FR 1 372 109 (Tanabe; appl. 23.9.1963; J-prior. 31.10.1962).

Formulation(s):   cps. 225 mg, 250 mg, 300 mg; f. c. tabl. 250 mg, 400 mg; gran. 5 %; tabl. 150 mg

Trade Name(s):

D: Cholit-Ursan (Fresenius)
     Cholofalk (Falk)
     Peptarom (Fresenius)
     UDC (Hexal)
     Urso (Heumann)
     Ursochol (Inpharzam)
     Ursofalk (Falk)
F: Arsacol (Zambon)
     Délursan (Hoechst Houdé)
     Destolit (Marion Merrell)
     Ursolvan (Synthélabo)

GB: Combidol (CD Pharm.)-
     comb.
     Destolit (Hoechst)
     Ursofalk (Thames)
I: Biliepar (Ibirn)
     Desocol (Campugnani)
     Deursil (Sanofi Winthrop)
     Fraurs (Francia Farm.)
     Galmax (Max Farma)
     Lentorsil (Italfarmaco)
     Litoff (Caber)
     Litursol (Crinos)

     Ursacol (Zambon Italia)
     Ursilon (IBI)
     Ursobil (ABC-Torino)
     Ursoflor (So. se Pharm.)
     Ursolisin (Magis)
     generics
J: Like (SS Seiyaku)-comb.
     Urso (Tanabe)
     Urso 100 (Tanabe)
     Zeria Ichoyaku (Zeria
     Shinyaku Kogyo)-comb.
USA: Actigall (Novartis)

Valaciclovir
(BW-256U; 256 U 87)

ATC: J05AB11
Use: antiviral, prodrug of aciclovir

RN: 124832-26-4   MF: $C_{13}H_{20}N_6O_4$ MW: 324.34
CN: L-valine 2-[(2-amino-1,6-dihydro-6-oxo-9H-purin-9-yl)methoxy]ethyl ester

monohydrochloride
RN: 124832-27-5   MF: $C_{13}H_{20}N_6O_4 \cdot HCl$ MW: 360.80

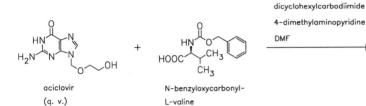

aciclovir
(q. v.)

N-benzyloxycarbonyl-
L-valine

dicyclohexylcarbodiimide
4-dimethylaminopyridine
DMF
→ I

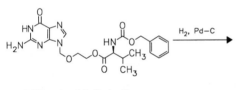

2-[(2-amino-1,6-dihydro-6-oxo-
9H-purin-9-yl)methoxy]ethyl
N-[(benzyloxy)carbonyl]-L-valinate (I)

H₂, Pd–C

Valaciclovir

Reference(s):
EP 308 065 (Wellcome Found. Ltd; appl. 12.8.1988; GB-prior. 15.8.1987, 5.11.1987).

combination with lamotrigine:
WO 9 505 179 (Wellcome Found. Ltd; appl. 17.8.1994; GB-prior. 18.8.1993).

water-dispersible tablets:
WO 9 213 527 (Wellcome Found. Ltd; appl. 29.1.1992; GB-prior. 30.1.1991, 22.11.1991, 25.11.1991).

medical use for preventing post herpetic neuralgia:
GB 2 282 759 (SmithKline Beecham; appl. 14.10.1994; GB-prior. 16.10.1993).

Formulation(s):   f. c. tabl. 500 mg; tabl. 500 mg, 1 g (as hydrochloride)

Trade Name(s):
D: Valtrex (Glaxo Wellcome)   GB: Valtrex (Glaxo Wellcome;   USA: Valtrex (Glaxo Wellcome;
F: Zélitrex (Glaxo Wellcome;   as hydrochloride)   as hydrochloride)
     as hydrochloride)

Valdetamide
(Novonal; Diethylpentenamide)

ATC: N05C
Use: hypnotic

RN: 512-48-1   MF: $C_9H_{17}NO$ MW: 155.24   EINECS: 208-143-2
LD₅₀: 400 mg/kg (R, p.o.);
        300 mg/kg (dog, p.o.)
CN: 2,2-diethyl-4-pentenamide

ethyl   ethyl   ethyl diethyl–
bromide   cyanoacetate   cyanoacetate

(I)   allyl   Valdetamide
               chloride

Reference(s):
DRP 473 329 (I. G. Farben; appl. 1925).
DRP 616 876 (I. G. Farben; appl. 1930).
DRP 622 875 (I. G. Farben; appl. 1931).
GB 253 950 (I. G. Farben; appl. 1926; D-prior. 1925).

reaction of diethylacetonitrile with allyl chloride in presence of sodium bis(trimethylsilyl)amide:
DOS 2 518 122 (Hoechst; appl. 24.4.1975).

from diethylacetaldehyde:
DOS 2 753 440 (Diamalt; appl. 30.11.1977).

Formulation(s):   drg. 50 mg; tabl. 300 mg

Trade Name(s):
D: Arantil (Hoechst)-comb.;   Insomnia (ICN); wfm   Novo-Dolestan (Much);
        wfm   Nocturetten (Starke)-   wfm
        Betadorm-N (Woelm)-   comb.; wfm
        comb.; wfm

Valethamate bromide

ATC: A03
Use: antispasmodic

RN: 90-22-2   MF: $C_{19}H_{32}BrNO_2$ MW: 386.37   EINECS: 201-977-8
LD$_{50}$:   4200 µg/kg (M, i.v.); 330 mg/kg (M, p.o.);
        4200 µg/kg (R, i.v.); 1260 mg/kg (R, p.o.)
CN: N,N-diethyl-N-methyl-2-[(3-methyl-1-oxo-2-phenylpentyl)oxy]ethanaminium bromide

benzyl   3-methyl-2-   3-methyl-2-phenyl-
cyanide   phenylvalero-   valeric acid
               nitrile

Valethamate bromide

Reference(s):
DE 969 245 (Kali-Chemie; appl. 1953).
DE 971 136 (Kali-Chemie; appl. 1953).

Formulation(s):   amp. 8 mg; drg. 10 mg; suppos. 20 mg

Trade Name(s):

D:	Epidosin (Kali-Chemie);	Epidosin (Toyo Jozo)	Shinmetane (Towa)
	wfm	Funapan (Funai)	Study (Toyo Pharmar)
I:	Epidosin (Sir); wfm	Kaichyl (Samoa)	Ulban-Q (Toho)
J:	Barespan Tab. (Hishiyama)	Letamate (Mohan)	Valate (Marishita)
	Baretaval (Shin Fuso)	Pastan (Maruko)	Valemate (Taiho)
	Beruhgen (Nissin)	Release V (Mochida)	Valemeton (Sanko)
	Cranfupan (Nichiiko)	Resitan (Grelan)	Valethalin (Hokuriku)
	Elist (Sana-Torii)	Shikitan (Shiki)	Valethamin (Sawai)

Valproic acid

ATC: N03AG01
Use: anticonvulsant, antiepileptic

RN: 99-66-1   MF: $C_8H_{16}O_2$ MW: 144.21   EINECS: 202-777-3
LD_{50}:   1098 mg/kg (M, p.o.);
        670 mg/kg (R, p.o.)
CN: 2-propylpentanoic acid

sodium salt
RN: 1069-66-5   MF: $C_8H_{15}NaO_2$ MW: 166.20   EINECS: 213-961-8
LD_{50}:   750 mg/kg (M, i.v.); 977 mg/kg (M, p.o.);
        509 mg/kg (R, i.v.); 670 mg/kg (R, p.o.);
        1420 mg/kg (dog, p.o.)
calcium salt dihydrate
RN: 138995-18-3   MF: $C_{16}H_{30}CaO_4 \cdot 2H_2O$ MW: 362.52

propyl
bromide

ethyl cyano-
acetate

ethyl dipropyl-
cyanoacetate (I)

dipropyl-
acetonitrile

Valproic acid

Reference(s):
FR-M 2 442 (H. E. J.-M. Meunier; appl. 17.10.1962).
GB 980 279 (H. E. J.-M. Meunier; appl. 14.10.1963; F-prior. 17.10.1962).
US 3 325 361 (Chemetron Corp.; 13.6.1967; F-prior. 17.10.1962).

methods:
GB 1 522 450 (Labaz; appl. 3.6.1977; F-prior. 15.3.1977).
GB 1 529 786 (Labaz; appl. 3.6.1977; F-prior. 15.3.1977).
US 4 155 929 (Labaz; 22.5.1979; prior. 25.5.1977, 10.5.1978).

Formulation(s):   amp. 300 mg/3 ml; cps. 150 mg, 300 mg, 500 mg (as free acid); sol. 300 mg/ml;
s. r. drg. 300 mg (as sodium salt); syrup 250 mg/5 ml, 300 mg/5 ml; tabl. 250 mg, 333 mg
(as calcium salt dihydrate); tabl. 150 mg, 300 mg

Trade Name(s):

D:	Convulex (Byk Gulden)		Leptilan (Geigy)	GB:	Convulex (Pharmacia &
	Convulex (Promonta)		Orfiril (Desitin)		Upjohn)
	Convulsofin (ASTA	F:	Dépakine (Sanofi	I:	Depakin (Sanofi Winthrop)
	Medica AWD; Boehringer		Winthrop)	J:	Depaken (Kyowa Hakko)
	Mannh.)		Dépakine Chrono (Sanofi	USA:	Depakene (Abbott)
	Ergenyl (Labaz)		Winthrop)		

Valsartan
(CGP-48933)

ATC: C09CA03
Use: antihypertensive, angiotensin II
blocker

RN: 137862-53-4   MF: $C_{24}H_{29}N_5O_3$ MW: 435.53
CN: *N*-(1-oxopentyl)-*N*-[[2'-(1*H*-tetrazol-5-yl)[1,1'-biphenyl]-4-yl]methyl]-L-valine

2'-cyanobiphenyl-
4-carboxaldehyde

methyl L-valinate
hydrochloride

reductive amination

I

(I)

valeryl chloride

methyl N-valeryl-
N-[(2'-cyanobiphenyl-
4-yl)methyl]-L-valinate   (II)

tributyltin azide

Valsartan

Reference(s):
US 5 399 578 (Ciba-Geigy; 21.3.1995; appl. 29.12.1992; CH-prior. 19.2.1990, 5.7.1990).
EP 443 983 (Ciba-Geigy; appl. 12.2.1991; CH-prior. 19.2.1990).
Bühlmayer, P. et al.: Bioorg. Med. Chem. Lett. (BMCLE8) **1994**, 4 (1), 29.

use for treating diabetic nephropathy:
WO 9 524 901 (Ciba-Geigy; appl. 7.3.1995; CH-prior. 17.3.1994).

use to treat post-ischaemic renal failure:
WO 9 713 513 (Novartis; appl. 24.9.1996; CH-prior. 6.10.1995).
WO 9 702 032 (MSD-Chibret; appl. 26.6.1996; GB-prior. 13.2.1996; USA-prior. 30.6.1995).

combination with aldosterone antagonists:
WO 9 640 256 (Searle; appl. 5.6.1996; USA-prior. 7.6.1995).
WO 9 640 255 (Searle; appl. 5.6.1996; USA-prior. 7.6.1995).
WO 9 640 257 (Searle; appl. 5.6.1996; USA-prior. 7.6.1995).
WO 9 640 258 (Searle; appl. 5.6.1996; USA-prior. 7.6.1995).

combination with benazepril:
WO 9 631 234 (Ciba-Geigy; appl. 2.4.1996; CH-prior. 7.4.1995).

use for treatment of glaucoma and neurodegeneration:
WO 9 521 609 (Ciba-Geigy; appl. 26.1.1995; EP-prior. 8.2.1994).

Formulation(s):   cps. 80 mg, 160 mg; tabl. 40 mg, 80 mg, 160 mg

Trade Name(s):
D: Diovan (Novartis)   GB: Diovan (Ciba)   USA: Diovan (Novartis)
F: Tareg (Novartis)   I: Tareg (Novartis Farma)

Vancomycin

ATC: A07AA09; J01XA01
Use: antibiotic

RN: 1404-90-6   MF: $C_{66}H_{75}Cl_2N_9O_{24}$ MW: 1449.27   EINECS: 215-772-6
LD$_{50}$:   430 mg/kg (M, i.v.)
CN: [3S-[3R*,6S*(S*),7S*,22S*,23R*,26R*,36S*,38aS*]]-3-(2-amino-2-oxoethyl)-44-[[2-*O*-(3-amino-2,3,6-
       trideoxy-3-*C*-methyl-α-L-*lyxo*-hexopyranosyl)-β-D-glucopyranosyl]oxy]-10,19-dichloro-
       2,3,4,5,6,7,23,24,25,26,36,37,38,38a-tetradecahydro-7,22,28,30,32-pentahydroxy-6-[[4-methyl-2-
       (methylamino)-1-oxopentyl]amino]-2,5,24,38,39-pentaoxo-22*H*-8,11:18,21-dietheno-23,36-
       (iminomethano)-13,16:31,35-dimetheno-1*H*,16*H*-[1,6,9]oxadiazacyclohexadecino[4,5-
       m][10,2,16]benzoxadiazacyclotetracosine-26-carboxylic acid

hydrochloride
RN: 1404-93-9   MF: $C_{66}H_{75}Cl_2N_9O_{24} \cdot xHCl$ MW: unspecified
LD$_{50}$:   489 mg/kg (M, i.v.); >5 g/kg (M, p.o.);
       319 mg/kg (R, i.v.); >10 g/kg (R, p.o.)

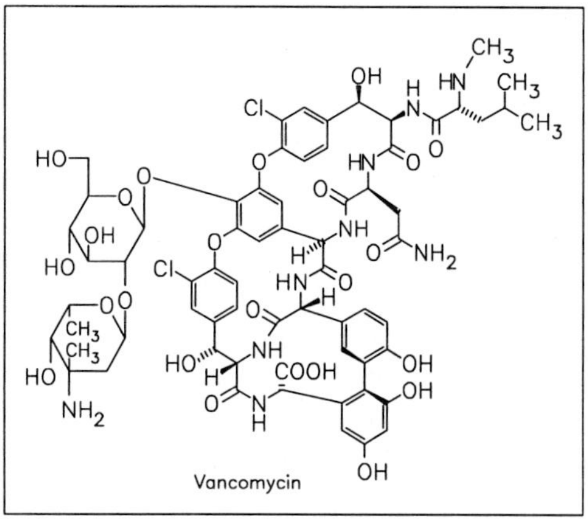

Vancomycin

Amphoteric glycopeptid antibiotic from *Nocardia orientalis* (NRRL 2450, 2451, 2452).

Reference(s):
US 3 067 099 (Eli Lilly; 4.12.1962; appl. 16.9.1955).

purification via the diphosphate:
EP 145 484 (Eli Lilly; appl. 11.12.1984; USA-prior. 12.12.1983).

structure:
Williamson, M.P.; Williams, D.H.: J. Am. Chem. Soc. (JACSAT) **103**, 6580 (1981).

Formulation(s):   cps. 250 mg; vial 500 mg/g, 500 mg/10 ml, 500 mg/15 ml, 1 g/15 ml, 10 g/100 ml (as hydrochloride)

Trade Name(s):

D:	AB-Vancomycin (Astrapin)	F:	Vancocine (Lilly)		I:	Vancocina (Lilly)
	VANCO (Reusch)		Vancomycine Dakota		J:	Vancomycin (Shionogi)
	Vancomycin CP (Lilly)		Pharm (Dakota)		USA:	Vancocin (Lilly)
	Vancomycin "Lederle"		Vancomycine Lederle			generic
	(Lederle)		(Wyeth-Lederle)			
	Vanco-saar (Chephasaar)	GB:	Vancocin (Eli Lilly)			

Vecuronium bromide

ATC: M03AC03
Use: muscle relaxant

RN: 50700-72-6   MF: $C_{34}H_{57}BrN_2O_4$ MW: 637.74   EINECS: 256-723-9
CN: 1-[(2β,3α,5α,16β,17β)-3,17-bis(acetyloxy)-2-(1-piperidinyl)androstan-16-yl]-1-methylpiperidinium bromide

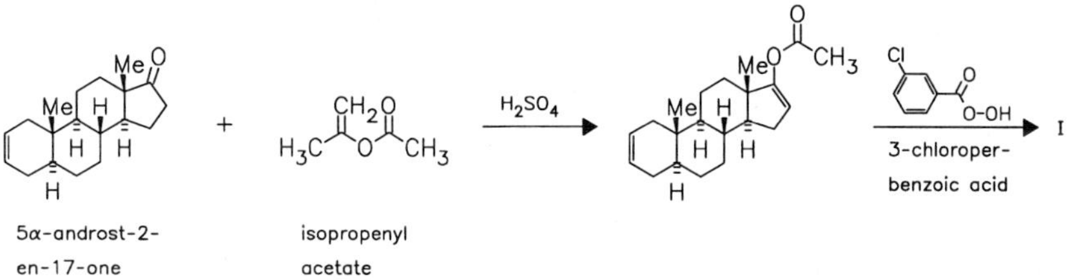

5α-androst-2-
en-17-one

isopropenyl
acetate

3-chloroper-
benzoic acid

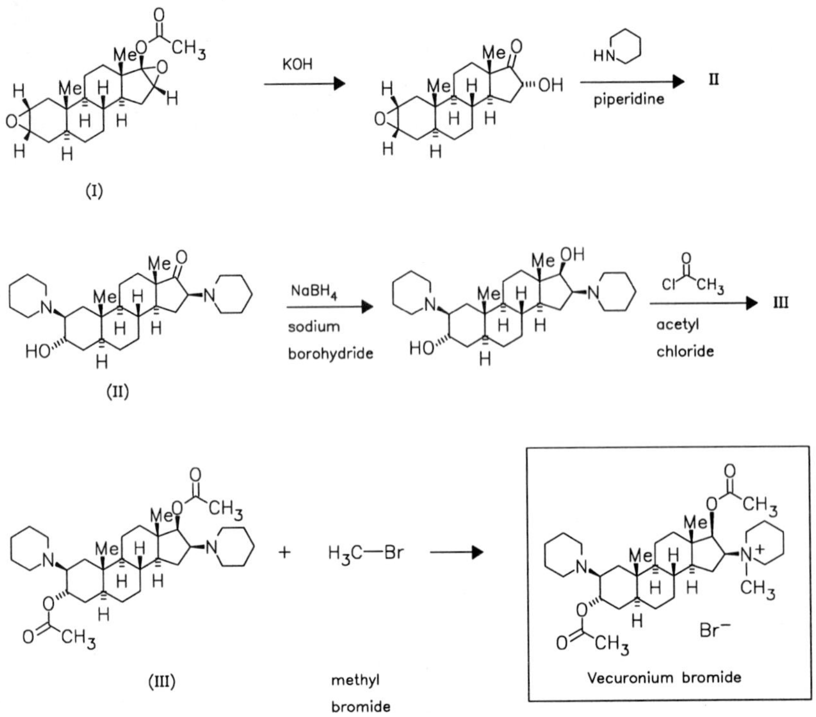

(I)

(II)

(III) + H₃C—Br → Vecuronium bromide

methyl bromide

Reference(s):
US 4 237 126 (Akzo; 2.12.1980; appl. 20.8.1979; GB-prior. 5.9.1978).
US 4 297 351 (Akzo; 2.12.1980; appl. 20.8.1979; GB-prior. 5.9.1978).
Buckett, W.R. et al.: J. Med. Chem. (JMCMAR) 16, 116 (1973).

injection solution:
EP 8 824 (Akzo; appl. 15.8.1979; GB-prior. 5.9.1978).

Formulation(s):   amp. 4 mg/ml; vial 10 mg

Trade Name(s):
D: Norcuron (Organon; 1983)   I: Norcuron (Organon
F: Norcuron (Organon); wfm   Teknika)
GB: Norcuron (Organon   J: Masculax (Organon)
        Teknika); 1983   USA: Norcuron (Organon; 1984)

Venlafaxine
(Wy-45030)

ATC: N06AA22
Use: antidepressant, norephedrine uptake inhibitor

RN: 93413-69-5   MF: $C_{17}H_{27}NO_2$ MW: 277.41
CN: (±)-1-[2-(dimethylamino)-1-(4-methoxyphenyl)ethyl]cyclohexanol

monohydrochloride
RN: 99300-78-4   MF: $C_{17}H_{27}NO_2 \cdot HCl$ MW: 313.87

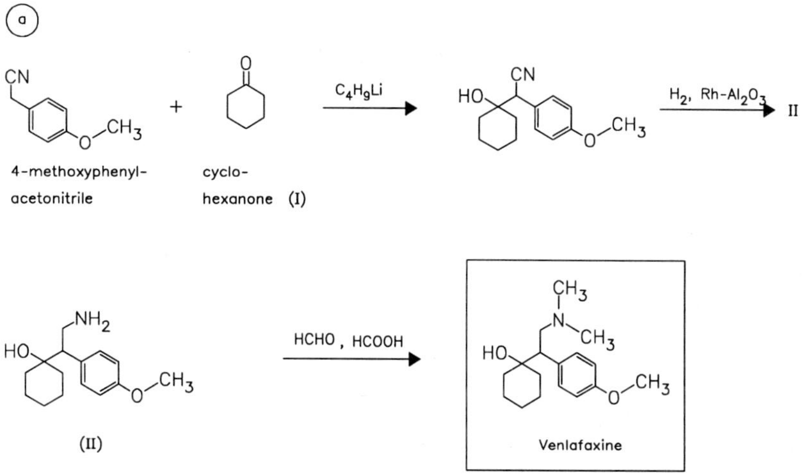
a
4-methoxyphenyl-
acetonitrile
cyclo-
hexanone (I)
C4H9Li
H2, Rh-Al2O3
II
(II)
HCHO, HCOOH
Venlafaxine

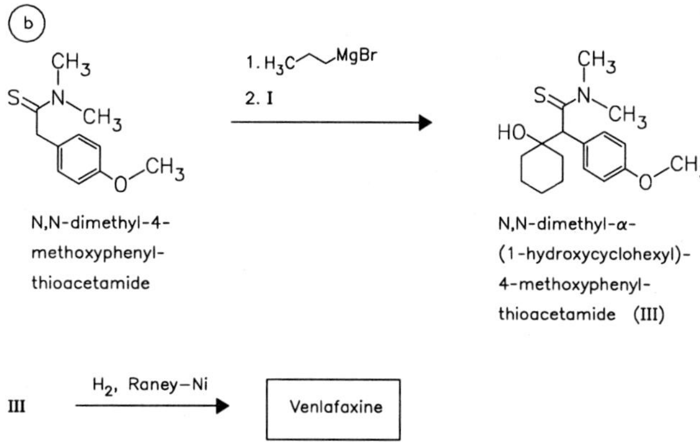
b
N,N-dimethyl-4-
methoxyphenyl-
thioacetamide
1. H3C MgBr
2. I
N,N-dimethyl-α-
(1-hydroxycyclohexyl)-
4-methoxyphenyl-
thioacetamide (III)
III
H2, Raney-Ni
Venlafaxine

Reference(s):

a EP 112 669 (American Home Products; 4.7.1984; USA-prior. 13.12.1982).

b GB 2 227 743 (Wyeth & Brother Ltd; 8.8.1990; GB-prior. 1.2.1989).

combination with opioid antagonists:
WO 9 609 047 (Du Pont Merck Pharm. Co.; 28.3.1996; USA-prior. 19.9.1994).

combination with β-blockers:
EP 687 472 (Eli Lilly & Co.; 20.2.1995; USA-prior. 19.7.1994).

controlled release formulation:
WO 9 427 589 (Alza Corp.; 8.12.1994; USA-prior. 27.5.1993).

Formulation(s): tabl. 25 mg, 37.5 mg, 50 mg, 75 mg, 100 mg (as hydrochloride)

Trade Name(s):

D:	Trevilor (Wyeth)	I:	Efexor (Wyeth-Lederle)
GB:	Efexor (Wyeth)	USA:	Effexor (Wyeth-Ayerst)

Verapamil

(Iproveratril)

ATC: C08DA01
Use: coronary vasodilator

RN: 52-53-9   MF: $C_{27}H_{38}N_2O_4$ MW: 454.61   EINECS: 200-145-1
LD_{50}: 1520 µg/kg (M, i.v.); 130 mg/kg (M, p.o.);
        7250 µg/kg (R, i.v.); 163 mg/kg (R, p.o.)
CN: α-[3-[[2-(3,4-dimethoxyphenyl)ethyl]methylamino]propyl]-3,4-dimethoxy-α-(1-methylethyl)benzeneacetonitrile

monohydrochloride

RN: 152-11-4   MF: $C_{27}H_{38}N_2O_4 \cdot HCl$ MW: 491.07   EINECS: 205-800-5
LD_{50}: 5795 µg/kg (M, i.v.); 163 mg/kg (M, p.o.);
        16 mg/kg (R, i.v.); 108 mg/kg (R, p.o.);
        >400 mg/kg (dog, p.o.)

3,4-dimethoxy-phenylacetonitrile   isopropyl chloride   2-(3,4-dimethoxyphenyl)-3-methylbutyronitrile (I)

1-bromo-3-chloropropane   N-[2-(3,4-dimethoxyphenyl)ethyl]methylamine   (II)

Verapamil

Reference(s):
DE 1 154 810 (Knoll; appl. 28.4.1961).
DE 1 158 083 (Knoll; appl. 19.12.1962).
US 3 261 859 (Knoll; 19.7.1966; D-prior. 28.4.1961).

alternative synthesis:
DAS 2 263 527 (Teikoku Hormaone Mfg.; appl. 27.12.1972; J-prior. 25.12.1971).
DAS 2 631 222 (Knoll; appl. 12.7.1976).
US 4 115 432 (Knoll; 19.9.1978; D-prior. 12.7.1976).

(–)-verapamil:
DAS 2 059 923 (Knoll; appl. 5.12.1970).

Formulation(s):   amp. 5 mg/2 ml; drg. 40 mg, 80 mg, 120 mg; f. c. tabl. 40 mg, 80 mg, 120 mg; s. r. cps.
        120 mg, 180 mg, 240 mg; s. r. tabl. 120 mg, 240 mg; vial 5 mg/2 ml (as hydrochloride)

Trade Name(s):
D: Azupamil (Azupharma)   Cardioprotect (Kytta-   Dignover (Sankyo)
                        Siegfried)   Durasoptin (durachemie)

Elthon (Knoll)-comb. with diazepam	Verasal (TAD)	Cordilox (Baker Norton)
	Vera-Sanorania (Sanorania)	Securon (Knoll)
Falicard (ASTA Medica AWD)	Veroptinstada (Stadapharm)	Tarka (Knoll)-comb. Univex (RPR)

<table>
<tr><td>Elthon (Knoll)-comb. with
diazepam
Falicard (ASTA Medica
AWD)
Isoptin (Knoll; as
hydrochloride)
Isoptin S (Knoll)-comb.
Jenapamil (Jenapharm)
Tarka (Knoll)-comb.
vera (ct-Arzneimittel)
Verabeta (betapharm)
Verahexal (Hexal)
Veramex (Sanofi Winthrop)</td>
<td>F:

GB:</td>
<td>Verasal (TAD)
Vera-Sanorania (Sanorania)
Veroptinstada
(Stadapharm)
Isoptine (Knoll)
Isoptine LP (Knoll)
Novapamyl LP (Wyeth-
Lederle)
Verapamil Bayer (Bayer
Classics)
Verapamil MSD LP (Merck
Sharp & Dohme-Chibret)
Berkatens (Berk)</td>
<td>I:

J:
USA:</td>
<td>Cordilox (Baker Norton)
Securon (Knoll)
Tarka (Knoll)-comb.
Univex (RPR)
Isoptin (Knoll)
Quasar (Ravizza)
Vasolan (Eisai)
Calan (Searle)
Isoptin (Knoll)
Tarka (Knoll)
Verelan (Lederle)
generics</td>
</tr>
</table>

Vesnarinone
(OPC-8212)

ATC: C01CX
Use: cardiotonic

RN: 81840-15-5 MF: $C_{22}H_{25}N_3O_4$ MW: 395.46
LD$_{50}$: >1200 mg/kg (M, i.p.); 56.3 mg/kg (M, i.v.); >7594 mg/kg (M, p.o.); >1200 mg/kg (M, s.c.);
>1200 mg/kg (R, i.p.); 79.3 mg/kg (R, i.v.); >7594 mg/kg (R, p.o.);
63.3 mg/kg (dog, i.v.); >3 g/kg (dog, p.o.)
CN: 1-(3,4-dimethoxybenzoyl)-4-[1,2,3,4-tetrahydro-2-oxo-6-quinolinyl]piperazine

Reference(s):
DE 3 142 982 (Otsuka; appl. 29.10.1981; J-prior. 31.10.1980).
Tominaga, M. et al.: Chem. Pharm. Bull. (CPBTAL) **32**, 2100 (1984).

alternative synthesis:
DE 3 153 260 (Otsuka; appl. 29.10.1981; J-prior. 31.10.1980).

Formulation(s): 60 mg

Trade Name(s):
J: Arkin-Z (Otsuka; 1990)   USA: Arkin (Otsuka); wfm

Vetrabutine
(Profenveramine; Revatrine)

ATC: A03
Use: uterus relaxant

RN: 3735-45-3   MF: $C_{20}H_{27}NO_2$ MW: 313.44
CN: α-(3,4-dimethoxyphenyl)-*N,N*-dimethylbenzenebutanamine

hydrochloride
RN: 5974-09-4   MF: $C_{20}H_{27}NO_2 \cdot$ HCl   MW: 349.90   EINECS: 227-771-8
LD$_{50}$: 500 mg/kg (R, p.o.)

3,4-dimethoxy-   hydrogen   dimethyl-   (3,4-dimethoxyphenyl)-
benzaldehyde   cyanide   amine   dimethylamino-
                                                           acetonitrile   (I)

3-phenylpropyl-
magnesium bromide

Vetrabutine

Reference(s):
DE 963 424 (Thomae; appl. 1954).

Formulation(s):   amp. 50 mg

Trade Name(s):
D: Monzal (Thomae); wfm

Vidarabine

ATC: J05AB03; S01AD06
Use: antiviral

RN: 5536-17-4   MF: $C_{10}H_{13}N_5O_4$ MW: 267.25   EINECS: 226-893-9
LD$_{50}$: 442 mg/kg (M, i.v.); 7800 µg/kg (M, p.o.);
           302 mg/kg (R, i.v.); >5 g/kg (R, p.o.)
CN: 9-β-D-arabinofuranosyl-9*H*-purine-6-amine

monohydrate
RN: 24356-66-9   MF: $C_{10}H_{13}N_5O_4 \cdot H_2O$ MW: 285.26
LD_{50}: >7950 µg/kg (M, p.o.)
5'-dihydrogen phosphate
RN: 29984-33-6   MF: $C_{10}H_{14}N_5O_7P$ MW: 347.22   EINECS: 249-990-8
LD_{50}: 1200 mg/kg (R, i.v.)
5'-dihydrogen phosphate disodium salt
RN: 71002-10-3   MF: $C_{10}H_{12}N_5Na_2O_7P$ MW: 391.19

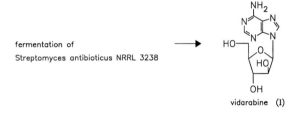

fermentation of
Streptomyces antibioticus NRRL 3238

vidarabine (I)

I

1. $POCl_3$, NaOH
2. NH_3
3. ion exchange on Dowex 1–X_2

1. phosphoryl chloride

Vidarabine phosphate

Reference(s):
fermentation:
GB 1 159 290 (Parke Davis; appl. 29.12.1967; USA-prior. 30.12.1966, 29.9.1967).

dihydrogen phosphate:
DOS 2 047 368 (Parke Davis; appl. 25.9.1970; USA-prior. 26.9.1969).
US 3 703 507 (Parke Davis; 21.11.1972; prior. 26.9.1969).

alternative synthesis from adenosine monophosphate:
Kaneka, M. et al.: Chem. Pharm. Bull. (CPBTAL) **25**, 1892 (1977).

total synthesis of vidarabine:
Lee et al.: J. Am. Chem. Soc. (JACSAT) **82**, 2648 (1960).
Reist et al.: J. Org. Chem. (JOCEAH) **27**, 3274 (1962); **29**, 3725 (1964).

Formulation(s):   ointment 3 %

Trade Name(s):
D: Vidarabin 3 % Thilo Salbe   F: Vira-MP (Pierre Fabre   J: Arasena-A (Mochida)
        (Alcon)   Dermatologie)   Vitarabine (Ajinomoto)
                                        GB: Vira-A (Parke Davis)   USA: Vira-A (Parke Davis); wfm

Vigabatrin
(γ-Vinyl-Gaba)

ATC: N03AG04
Use: anticonvulsant, irreversible inhibitor
of GABA transaminase

RN: 60643-86-9   MF: $C_6H_{11}NO_2$ MW: 129.16
LD_{50}: 3 g/kg (M, p.o.);
3 g/kg (R, p.o.)
CN: 4-amino-5-hexenoic acid

(±)-form
RN: 68506-86-5   MF: $C_6H_{11}NO_2$ MW: 129.16   EINECS: 270-929-6
LD_{50}: >2500 mg/kg (M, i.p.); >3000 mg/kg (M, p.o.);
>3000 mg/kg (R, p.o.)

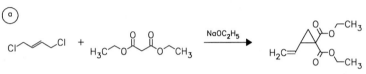

ⓐ

1,4-dichloro-
2-butene   diethyl malonate   1,1-bis(ethoxycarbonyl)-
2-vinylcyclopropane (I)

I →(NH₃) 3-carboxamido-5-
vinyl-2-pyrrolidone (II) →(HCl) Vigabatrin

ⓑ
II →(1. NaOC₂H₅ 2. HOAc, Δ) 5-vinyl-2-
pyrrolidone →(1. Br₂ 2. NaNH₂ 3. H₂, Pd–C) Vigabatrin

Reference(s):
DOS 2 607 620 (Richardson-Merrell; appl. 25.2.1976; USA-prior. 18.3.1975).
DE 2 902 438 (Merrell-Toraude; appl. 23.1.1979; USA-prior. 30.1.1978).
US 4 235 778 (Merrell-Toraude; 25.11.1980; appl. 14.1.1980; prior. 4.6.1979, 30.1.1978).
US 4 254 284 (Merrell-Toraude; 3 3.1981; appl. 14.1.1980; prior. 4.6.1979, 30.1.1978).
Wei, Z.-Y.; Knaus, E.E.: J. Org. Chem. (JOCEAH) **58**, 1586 (1993).

combination with glycine:
EP 124 091 (Merrell-Toraude; appl. 26.4.1984; GB-prior. 29.4.1983).

Formulation(s):   f. c. tabl. 500 mg; gran. 500 mg; powder 500 mg

Trade Name(s):
D: Sabril (Hoechst)
F: Sabril (Hoechst; 1990)
GB: Sabril (Hoechst)
I: Sabril (Camillo Corvi)

Viloxazine

ATC: N06AX09
Use: antidepressant, psychostimulant

RN: 46817-91-8 MF: $C_{13}H_{19}NO_3$ MW: 237.30 EINECS: 256-281-7
LD_{50}: 60 mg/kg (M, i.v.); 552 mg/kg (M, p.o.);
60 mg/kg (R, i.v.); 2 g/kg (R, p.o.)
CN: 2-[(2-ethoxyphenoxy)methyl]morpholine

hydrochloride
RN: 35604-67-2 MF: $C_{13}H_{19}NO_3 \cdot HCl$ MW: 273.76 EINECS: 252-638-6
LD_{50}: 60 mg/kg (M, i.v.); 480 mg/kg (M, p.o.);
60 mg/kg (R, i.v.); 2 g/kg (R, p.o.)

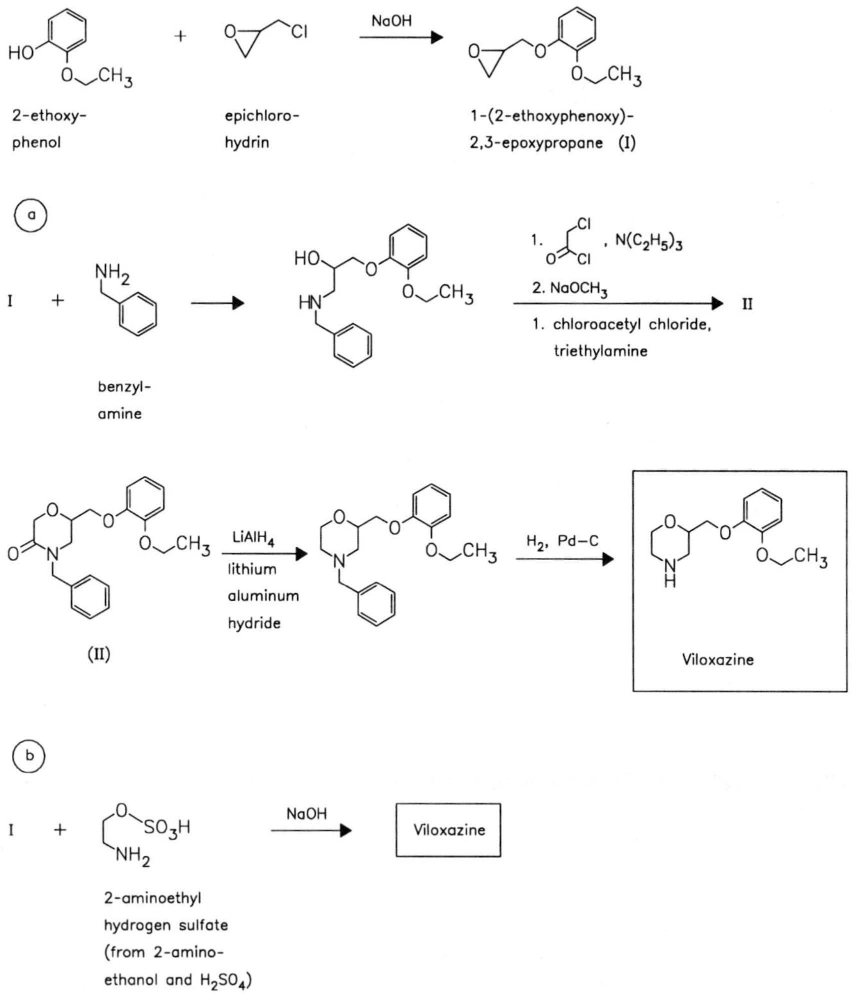
NaOH
2-ethoxyphenol
epichlorohydrin
1-(2-ethoxyphenoxy)-2,3-epoxypropane (I)
a
benzylamine
1. chloroacetyl chloride, triethylamine
2. NaOCH3
II
(II)
LiAlH4
lithium aluminum hydride
H2, Pd–C
Viloxazine
b
NaOH
Viloxazine
2-aminoethyl hydrogen sulfate (from 2-aminoethanol and H2SO4)

Reference(s):
a   GB 1 138 405 (ICI; appl. 28.12.1966; valid from 13.11.1967).
    US 3 714 161 (ICI; 30.1.1973; GB-prior. 28.12.1966).
    US 3 876 769 (ICI; 8.4.1975; prior. 24.11.1967).
    DOS 1 695 295 (ICI; appl. 24.11.1967; GB-prior. 28.12.1966).
b   US 3 857 839 (ICI; 31.12.1974; GB-prior. 20.6.1969, 13.10.1969).
    US 3 712 890 (ICI; 23.1.1973; GB-prior. 20.6.1969; 13.10.1969).
    Greenwood, D.T. et al.: J. Med. Chem. (JMCMAR) **18**, 573 (1975).

Formulation(s):   amp. 100 mg/5 ml; f. c. tabl. 100 mg; s. r. tabl. 300 mg; tabl. 50 mg, 100 mg

Trade Name(s):

D:	Vivalan (Zeneca; 1977)		Vivalan LP (Zeneca)	I:	Vicilan (ICI-Pharma)
F:	Vivalan (Zeneca; 1977)	GB:	Vivalan (Zeneca; 1974)	J:	Vicilan (Jcpharma)

Viminol
(Diviminol)

ATC: N06AX09
Use: analgesic

RN: 21363-18-8   MF: $C_{21}H_{31}ClN_2O$ MW: 362.95   EINECS: 244-347-8
LD$_{50}$:   325 mg/kg (M, p.o.)
CN: α-[[bis(1-methylpropyl)amino]methyl]-1-[(2-chlorophenyl)methyl]-1*H*-pyrrole-2-methanol

p-hydroxybenzoate (1:1)
RN: 23784-10-3   MF: $C_{21}H_{31}ClN_2O \cdot C_7H_6O_3$ MW: 501.07
LD$_{50}$:   206 mg/kg (R, i.p.)

1-(2-chloro-
benzyl)pyrrole   oxalyl
                      chloride

bis(1-methyl-
propyl)amine

Na[AlH$_2$(OCH$_2$–CH$_2$–OCH$_3$)$_2$]

sodium aluminum
bis(2-methoxyethoxy)-
dihydride

(I)

Viminol

LiAlH$_4$,   (C$_2$H$_5$)$_2$O

lithium aluminum
hydride

Viminol

Reference(s):
a   BE 790 747 (Whitefin Holding; appl. 30.10.1972; I-prior. 4.7.1972; 30.10.1971).
b   US 3 539 589 (Whitefin Holding; 10.11.1970; GB-prior. 17.5.1966).

starting material:
DAS 1 795 841 (Whitefin Holding; appl. 10.11.1970; F-prior. 12.11.1969).

review:
Chiarino, D. et al.: Arzneim.-Forsch. (ARZNAD) **28** (II), 1554 (1978).

stereoisomers:
BE 790 747 (Whitefin Holding; appl. 30.10.1972; I-prior. 30.10.1971; 4.7.1972).
DOS 2 253 149 (Whitefin Holding; appl. 30.10.1972; I-prior. 30.10.1971).

Formulation(s):   tabl. 50 mg

Trade Name(s):
D: Lenigesial (Inpharzam);   I: Dividol (Zambon Italia; as
      wfm   hydrochloride)

Vinblastine
(Vincaleukoblastine)

ATC: L01CA01
Use: antineoplastic

RN: 865-21-4   MF: $C_{46}H_{58}N_4O_9$ MW: 810.99   EINECS: 212-734-0
LD$_{50}$: 2 mg/kg (R, i.v.)
CN: [3aR-[3aα,4β,5β,5aβ,9(3R*,5S*,7R*,9S*),10bR*,13aα]]-methyl 4-(acetyloxy)-3a-ethyl-9-[5-ethyl-
      1,4,5,6,7,8,9,10-octahydro-5-hydroxy-9-(methoxycarbonyl)-2H-3,7-methanoazacycloundecino[5,4-
      b]indol-9-yl]-3a,4,5,5a,6,11,12,13a-octahydro-5-hydroxy-8-methoxy-6-methyl-1H-indolizino[8,1-
      cd]carbazole-5-carboxylate

sulfate (1:1)
RN: 143-67-9   MF: $C_{46}H_{58}N_4O_9 \cdot H_2SO_4$ MW: 909.07   EINECS: 205-606-0
LD$_{50}$: 9500 µg/kg (M, i.v.); 423 mg/kg (M, p.o.);
          37 mg/kg (R, i.v.); 305 mg/kg (R, p.o.)
sulfate monohydrate
RN: 6449-03-2   MF: $C_{46}H_{58}N_4O_9 \cdot H_2SO_4 \cdot H_2O$ MW: 927.08

Vinblastine

By extraction from leaves of *Vinca rosea.*

Reference(s):
Svoboda, G.H. et al.: J. Pharm. Sci. (JPMSAE) **51**, 707 (1962).
US 3 097 137 (CDN-P. and Dev.; 9.7.1963; appl. 19.5.1960; prior. 2.12.1958).
US 3 225 030 (Eli Lilly; 21.12.1965; appl. 15.2.1965; prior. 25.8.1958).
US 4 070 358 (Richter Gedeon; 24.1.1978; H-prior. 28.10.1975).
DOS 2 648 284 (Richter Gedeon; appl. 25.10.1976; H-prior. 28.10.1975).
DOS 2 823 461 (Richter Gedeon; appl. 30.5.1978; H-prior. 31.5.1977).

synthesis from catharanthin:
DOS 2 614 863 (Dr. Rahman; appl. 6.4.1976).

Formulation(s):   amp. 10 mg/10 ml (as sulfate); vial 10 mg (as sulfate monohydrate)

Trade Name(s):

D:	cellblastin (cell pharm)		Vinblastinesulfat-GRY	I:	Velbe (Lilly)
	Velbe (Lilly)		(Gry)	J:	Exal (Shionogi)
	Vinblastin R.P. (Rhône-	F:	Velbé (Lilly)	USA:	Velban (Lilly)
	Poulenc)	GB:	Velbe (Lilly)		

Vinburnine
(Vincamon)

ATC: C04AX17
Use: cerebral vasodilator

RN: 474-00-0   MF: C$_{19}$H$_{22}$N$_2$O   MW: 294.40   EINECS: 207-476-0
CN: eburnamenin-14(15*H*)-one

MnO₂/cellite, toluene →

cis-1-ethyl-1-(2-hydroxy-
2-ethoxycarbonylethyl)-
1,2,3,4,6,7,12,12b-octahydro—
indolo[2,3-a]quinolizine
(cf. vincamine synthesis)

Vinburnine

Reference(s):
GB 1 440 634 (Richter Gedeon; valid from 7.12.1973; H-prior. 8.12.1972).

starting material:
DOS 2 931 295 (Richter Gedeon; appl. 1.8.1979; H-prior. 1.8.1978).

alternative syntheses:
DOS 2 323 423 (Richter Gedeon; appl. 9.5.1973; H-prior. 17.5.1972).
US 3 888 865 (Richter Gedeon; 10.6.1975; appl. 14.3.1973).
FR 2 268 016 (Omnium; appl. 17.4.1974).

isolation from Hunteria eburnea:
DOS 1 932 245 (L. Olivier; appl. 25.6.1969; F-prior. 25.6.1968).

total synthesis:
Bartlett, M.F.; Taylor, W.I.: J. Am. Chem. Soc. (JACSAT) **82**, 5941 (1960).
Werkert, E.; Wickberg, B.: J. Am. Chem. Soc. (JACSAT) **87**, 1580 (1965).
BE 776 337 (Roussel-Uclaf; appl. 7.12.1971; F-prior. 6.1.1971).
BE 802 913 (Roussel-Uclaf; appl. 27.7.1973; F-prior. 31.7.1972).
Hugel, G. et al.: Tetrahedron Lett. (TELEAY) **1974**, 1597.

combination with glucose 1-phosphate:
BE 874 154 (E. Corvi Mora; appl. 14.2.1979).

quaternary ammonium salts:
DE 1 244 794 (Richter Gedeon; appl. 16.12.1963; H-prior. 19.12.1962).

Formulation(s):   amp. 15 mg/1 ml, 20 mg; cps. 20 mg, 60 mg

Trade Name(s):
F: Cervoxan (SmithKline   I: Eburnal (Chiesi)   Tensiplex (Francia Farm.)
       Beecham)   Scleramin (Ibirn)

Vincamine

ATC: C04AX07
Use: vasodilator, antihypertensive, cerebrotonic

RN: 1617-90-9   MF: $C_{21}H_{26}N_2O_3$ MW: 354.45   EINECS: 216-576-3
LD$_{50}$:   47.74 mg/kg (M, i.v.); 460 mg/kg (M, p.o.);
        1200 mg/kg (R, p.o.)
CN: (3α,14β,16α)-14,15-dihydro-14-hydroxyeburnamenine-14-carboxylic acid methyl ester

(a)   by extraction of pulverized and NH$_3$-solution treated plant material of Vinca minor L. (myrtle) with

     toluene and column chromatographic separation of numerous (c. 30 biogenetic related) by-alkaloids

     (indole alkaloids)

(b)   partial synthesis (Omnium process)

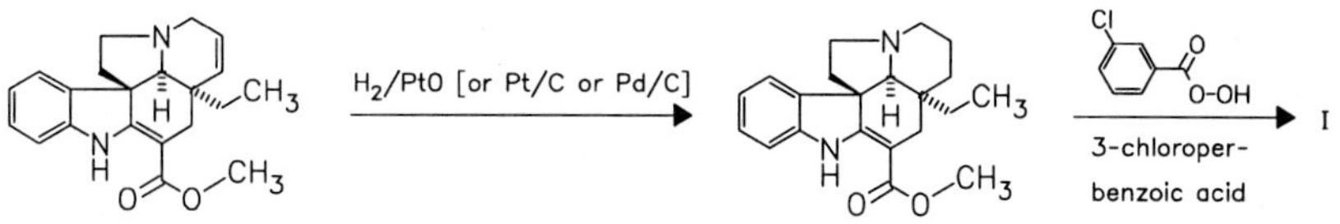

(−)-tabersonine
(from Voacanga grains)

(−)-vincadifformine

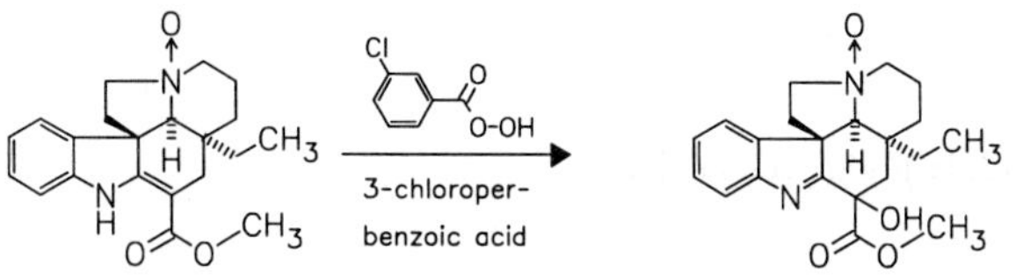

3-chloroper-
benzoic acid

I

(−)-vincadifformine
9-oxide (I)

3-chloroper-
benzoic acid

(−)-3-hydroxy-3-methoxy-
carbonyl-1,2-didehydro
aspidospermidine
9-oxide (II)

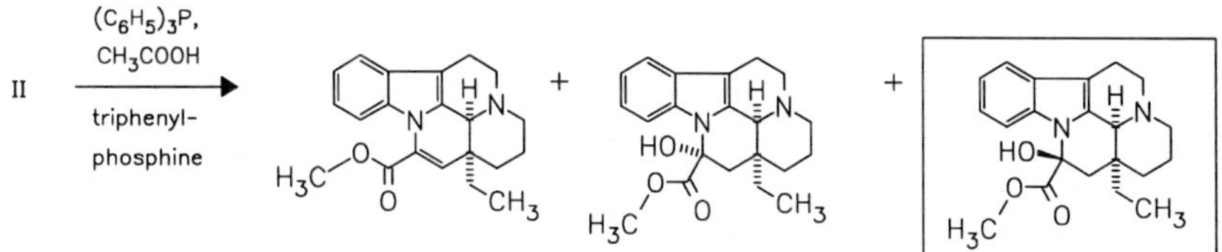

II

(C$_6$H$_5$)$_3$P,
CH$_3$COOH

triphenyl-
phosphine

apovincamine

+

(−)-14-epivincamine (III)

+

(+)-Vincamine

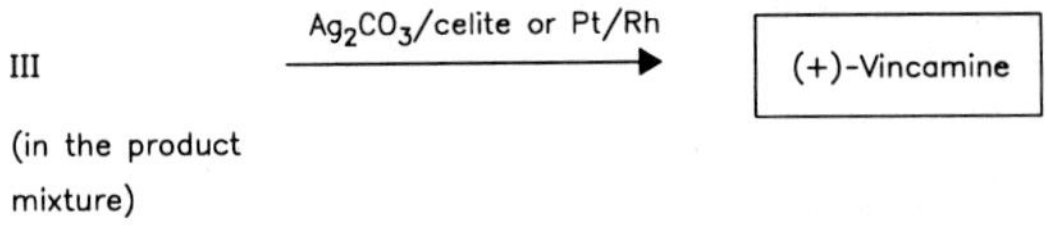

III

$\xrightarrow{\text{Ag}_2\text{CO}_3/\text{celite or Pt/Rh}}$ (+)-Vincamine

(in the product
mixture)

(c)   total synthesis

(c1)   Richter Gedeon synthesis:

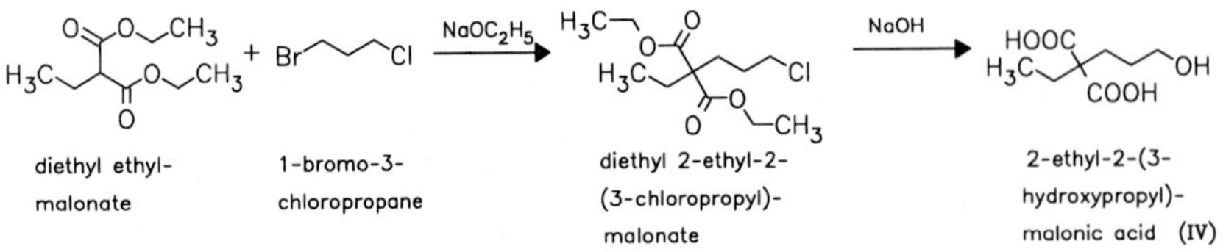

diethyl ethyl-
malonate

1-bromo-3-
chloropropane

diethyl 2-ethyl-2-
(3-chloropropyl)-
malonate

2-ethyl-2-(3-
hydroxypropyl)-
malonic acid (IV)

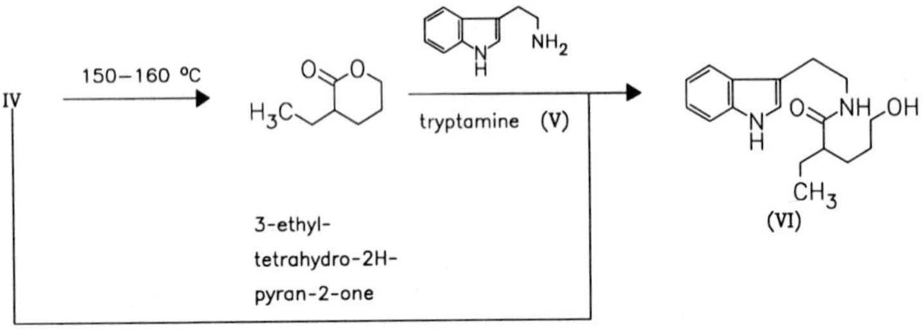

IV $\xrightarrow{150-160\ °C}$

3-ethyl-
tetrahydro-2H-
pyran-2-one

tryptamine (V)

(VI)

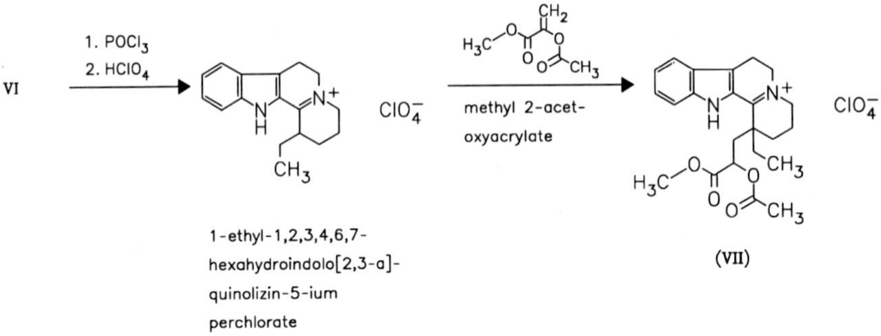

VI $\xrightarrow[\text{2. HClO}_4]{\text{1. POCl}_3}$

1-ethyl-1,2,3,4,6,7-
hexahydroindolo[2,3-a]-
quinolizin-5-ium
perchlorate

methyl 2-acet-
oxyacrylate

(VII)

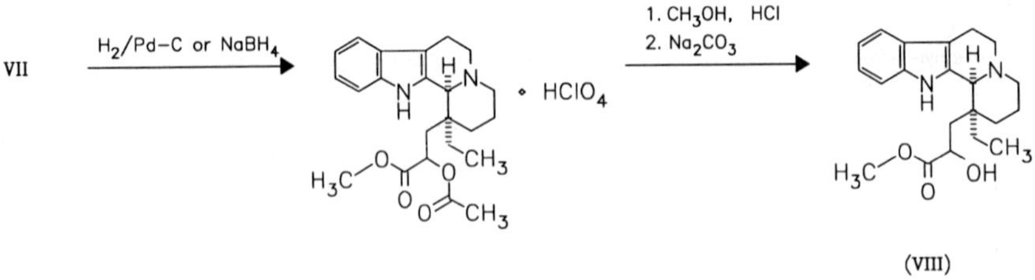

VII $\xrightarrow{\text{H}_2/\text{Pd-C or NaBH}_4}$

1. CH$_3$OH, HCl
2. Na$_2$CO$_3$

(VIII)

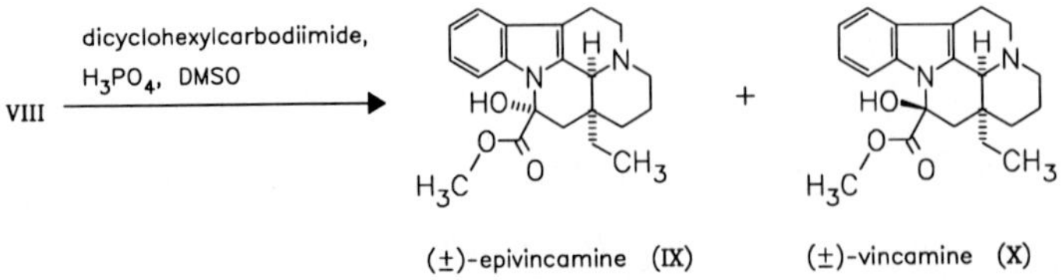

VIII $\xrightarrow[\text{H}_3\text{PO}_4,\ \text{DMSO}]{\text{dicyclohexylcarbodiimide,}}$

(±)-epivincamine (IX)

(±)-vincamine (X)

IX
(in the mixture
of racemates)

$\xrightarrow{\text{Ag}_2\text{CO}_3/\text{celite or Pt/Rh}}$ X

racemate resolution with
(+)-tartaric acid or
(+)-0,0'-dibenzoyltartaric acid or
(+)-camphorsulfonic acid

$\xrightarrow{\hspace{4cm}}$ (+)-Vincamine

(c2)   Roussel-Uclaf synthesis:

OHC∼CH₃ + [pyrrolidine structure] NH $\xrightarrow{\text{TosOH}}$ [1-pyrrolidino-1-butene structure] CH₃

1. H₃C—O—C(=O)—CH₂
2. H₂O/H⁺

$\xrightarrow{\hspace{2cm}}$ XI

1. methyl
acrylate

butyr-
aldehyde   pyrrolidine   1-pyrrolidino-
1-butene

[dimethyl 4-ethyl-4-formylpimelate structure] + V ⟶ [(±)-trans structure] + [(±)-cis structure]

dimethyl 4-ethyl-4-
formylpimelate (XI)

(±)-trans-1-ethyl-1-(2-
methoxycarbonylethyl)-
4-oxo-1,2,3,4,6,7,12,12b-
octahydroindolo[2,3-a]-
quinolizine

(±)-cis-1-ethyl-1-(2-
methoxycarbonylethyl)-
4-oxo-1,2,3,4,6,7,12,12b-
octahydroindolo[2,3-a]-
quinolizine (XII)

XII $\xrightarrow{\begin{array}{l}\text{1. NaOH}\\\text{2. (−)-ephedrine (racemate resolution)}\\\text{3. CH}_3\text{OH, H}_2\text{SO}_4\end{array}}$ [structure] $\xrightarrow[\text{phosphorus pentasulfide}]{\text{P}_2\text{S}_5\text{, THF}}$ [structure]

(XIII)

XIII $\xrightarrow{\text{Raney-Ni}}$ [(−)-1α-ethyl structure] $\xrightarrow{\text{Na tert-amylate, toluene}}$ [structure]

(−)-1α-ethyl-1-(2-
methoxycarbonylethyl)-
1,2,3,4,6,7,12,12bα-
octahydroindolo-
[2,3-a]quinolizine

(3α,16α)-14,15-di-
hydro-14-oxo-D-
homoeburnamenine (XIV)

XIV $\xrightarrow{\text{tert-butyl nitrite}}$ [structure with HO—N] $\xrightarrow{\text{CH}_2\text{O, HCl, H}_2\text{O}}$ [structure]

(3α,16α)-14,15-di-
hydro-14,15-dioxo-
D-homoeburnamenine (XV)

XV   +   H$_3$C—ONa   ⟶   (+)-Vincamine

Reference(s):
a   Schlittler, E. et al.: Helv. Chim. Acta (HCACAV) **36**, 2017 (1953).
    HU 147 282 (Richter Gedeon; appl. 30.7.1960).
    Trojanek, J. et al.: Collect. Czech. Chem. Commun. (CCCCAK) **26**, 867 (1961); **27**, 2801 (1962).
b   DAS 2 201 795 (Omnium Chimique; appl. 14.1.1972; B-prior. 15.1.1971, 3.3.1971).
    DOS 2 652 165 (Omnium Chimique; appl. 16.11.1976; F-prior. 20.11.1975).
    similar processes from (–)-vincadifformine:
    GB 1 514 337 (Buskine S.A.; appl. 22.7.1975; CH-prior. 9.8.1974).
    US 4 145 552 (Parcor; 20.3.1979; F-prior. 13.7.1976).
    DOS 2 731 480 (Parcor; appl. 12.7.1977; F-prior. 13.7.1976).
    DOS 2 745 415 (Boehringer Mannh.; appl. 8.10.1977).
    synthesis of vincadifformine:
    DOS 2 758 896 (M. E. Kuehne; appl. 30.12.1977).
c1 DAS 2 222 186 (Richter Gedeon; appl. 5.5.1972; H-prior. 7.5.1971).
    US 3 755 333 (Richter Gedeon; 28.8.1973; H-prior. 7.5.1971).
    Szántay, Cs. et al.: Tetrahedron Lett. (TELEAY) **1973**, (3), 191.
    precursors:
    DOS 2 345 068 (Richter Gedeon; appl. 6.9.1973; H-prior. 6.9.1972).
    rearrangement epi-vincamine → vincamine:
    DAS 2 203 655 (Richter Gedeon; appl. 26.1.1972; H-prior. 29.1.1971).
    DOS 2 807 912 (Boehringer Mannh.; appl. 24.2.1978).
c2 DAS 2 115 718 (Roussel-Uclaf; appl. 31.3.1971; F-prior. 31.3.1970, 10.9.1970).

further syntheses:
Kuehne, E.: J. Am. Chem. Soc. (JACSAT) **86**, 2946 (1964).
US 3 454 583 (US-Secret. of Health; 8.7.1969; prior. 19.7.1965).
Gibson, K.H.; Saxton, J.E.: Chem. Commun. (CCOMA8) **1969**, 1490.
Pfaffli, P. et al.: Helv. Chim. Acta (HCACAV) **58**, 1131 (1975).
DOS 2 314 876 (Sandoz; appl. 26.3.1973; CH-prior. 29.3.1972, 20.4.1972, 17.5.1972, 2.2.1973).
DOS 2 330 990 (Anvar; appl. 18.6.1973; F-prior. 19.6.1972).
GB 1 450 198 (Synthelabo; appl. 14.12.1973; F-prior. 15.12.1972).
US 3 925 392 (Synthelabo; 9.12.1975; F-prior. 15.12.1972).
US 4 001 251 (Synthelabo; 4.1.1977; F-prior. 15.12.1972).
DOS 2 752 776 (ELMU; appl. 25.11.1977; E-prior. 27.4.1977).

lyophilisate of vincamine *with* glycine:
FR-M 7 222 (L. O. Olivier; appl. 6.2.1968).

vincamine pamoate:
NL-appl. 7 304 654 (Merrell-Toraude; appl. 4.4.1973; F-prior. 11.4.1972).

combination with ergot alkaloids:
GB 1 494 625 (Unilever; appl. 4.2.1974; valid from 4.2.1975).

combination with rutin, hesperidin, eriodictin *or* esculoside:
DOS 2 337 202 (Centre d'Etudes pour 1'Industrie Pharmaceutique; appl. 21.7.1973; F-prior. 24.7.1972).

5-bromonicotinate of vincamine:
DOS 2 714 486 (Ferrer Internat.; appl. 31.3.1977; F-prior. 31.3.1976).

vincamine 5-pyridoxalphosphate:
DAS 2 721 171 (Soc. d'Etudes de Produits Chimiques; appl. 11.5.1977; GB-prior. 11.5.1976).

diverse salts:
US 4 122 179 (E. Corvi Mora; 24.10.1979; CH-prior. 3.6.1976).

Formulation(s):   amp. 15 mg; cps. 30 mg; s. r. cps. 30 mg, 60 mg; tabl. 10 mg

Trade Name(s):

D: Cetal (Parke Davis)
    Vincamin-retard-
    ratiopharm (ratiopharm)
F: Pervincamine (Synthélabo)
    Rhéobal (Niverpharm)
    Vinca (Substipharm)
    Vinca Retard
    (Substipharm)

I: Vincafor (Pharmafarm)
    Vincarutine (Pharbiol)
    Anasclerol (Stallergenes; as
    hydrochloride)
    Vasonett (Alfa Intes)
    Vincadar (Hoechst Marion
    Roussel)

Vincari (Alfa Intes; as
hydrochloride)
Vincatreis (Ecobi)
Vinsal (Salus Research)
Vraap (Inverni della Beffa)
generics

Vincristine
(Leurocristine)

ATC: L01CA02
Use: antineoplastic

RN: 57-22-7   MF: $C_{46}H_{56}N_4O_{10}$ MW: 824.97   EINECS: 200-318-1
LD$_{50}$: 3990 µg/kg (M, i.v.);
     1 mg/kg (R, i.v.)
CN: 22-oxovincaleukoblastine

sulfate (1:1)
RN: 2068-78-2   MF: $C_{46}H_{56}N_4O_{10} \cdot H_2SO_4$ MW: 923.05   EINECS: 218-190-0
LD$_{50}$: 1700 µg/kg (M, i.v.);
     1010 µg/kg (R, i.v.)

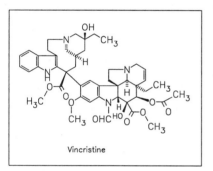

Vincristine

By extraction from leaves of *Vinca rosea*.

Reference(s):
BE 867 670 (Richter Gedeon; appl. 31.5.1978; H-prior. 31.5.1977).
FR 2 210 392 (Richter Gedeon; appl. 19.12.1972).
DOS 2 259 388 (Richter Gedeon; appl. 5.12.1972).
DOS 2 124 023 (Richter Gedeon; appl. 14.5.1971; H-prior. 27,5,1970).
DAS 1 445 689 (Eli Lilly; appl. 23.10.1962).
GB 1 382 460 (Richter Gedeon; valid from prior. 4.12.1972).

purification:
DOS 2 442 245 (Eli Lilly; appl. 4.9.1974; USA-prior. 24.10.1973).

total synthesis:
DOS 2 614 863 (A. Rahman; appl. 6.4.1976).
DOS 2 622 894 (United States Dep. of Commerce; appl. 21.5.1976; USA-prior. 30.5.1975).

semisynthetic preparation:
DOS 2 259 447 (Richter Gedeon; appl. 5.12.1972).
CA 989 829 (Richter Gedeon; appl. 4.12.1972).
BE 823 560 (Richter Gedeon; appl. 19.12.1974; H-prior. 20.12.1973).
US 3 899 493 (Richter Gedeon; 12.8.1975; prior. 22.12.1972).
FR 2 210 392 (Richter Gedeon; appl. 19.12.1972).
ZA 7 208 535 (Richter Gedeon; appl. 1.12.1972).

complex formation with tubulin *for treatment of leucemia*:
BE 854 053 (Inst. Intern. de Pathologic Cell. et Mol.; appl. 18.4.1977; F-prior. 28.4.1976).

use for treatment of psoriasis:
US 3 749 784 (Eli Lilly; 31.7.1973; prior. 26.10.1970, 3.5.1972).

Formulation(s):   vial 1 mg/ml, 1 mg/10 ml, 2 mg/ml, 5 mg/ml (as sulfate)

Trade Name(s):

D:	cellcristine (cell pharm)	Vincristin liquid Lilly	GB: Oncovin (Lilly)
	FARMISTIN (Pharmacia & Upjohn)	(Lilly)	I: Vincristina (Lilly)
		Vincristinsulfat-GRY (Gry)	Vincristina Tera (Tera)
	Vincristin (biosyn)	F: Oncovin (Lilly)	J: Oncovin (Shionogi)
	Vincristin Bristol (Bristol-Myers Squibb)	Vincristine Pierre Fabre (Pierre Fabre Oncologie)	USA: Oncovin (Lilly)

Vindesine

ATC: L01CA03
Use: antineoplastic

RN: 53643-48-4   MF: $C_{43}H_{55}N_5O_7$ MW: 753.94   EINECS: 258-682-2
LD_{50}:   13.8 mg/kg (M, i.v.)
CN: 3-(aminocarbonyl)-O^4-deacetyl-3-de(methoxycarbonyl)vincaleukoblastine

vinblastine
(q. v.)

NH₃, CH₃OH, 100 °C

Vindesine

Reference(s):
US 4 203 898 (Lilly, 20.5.1980; prior. 29.8.1977).
US 4 479 957 (Lilly; 30.10.1984; prior. 2.4.1973).
DOS 2 415 980 (Eli Lilly; appl. 2.4.1974; USA-prior. 2.4.1973).

Formulation(s):   amp. 5 mg/5 ml, 1 mg, 4 mg, 5 mg

Trade Name(s):

D:	Eldisine (Lilly; 1980)	GB:	Eldisine (Lilly; 1980)	J:	Fildesin (Shionogi; 1985)
F:	Eldisine (Lilly)	I:	Eldisine (Lilly)		

Vinorelbine

(5'-Noranhydrovinblastine; PM259)

ATC: L01CA04
Use: antineoplastic (non small cell lung cancer)

RN: 71486-22-1   MF: $C_{45}H_{54}N_4O_8$ MW: 778.95
LD$_{50}$:   26 mg/kg (M, i.p.)
CN: 3',4'-didehydro-4'-deoxy-C'-norvincaleukoblastine

hydrogen tartrate (1:1)
RN: 105661-07-2   MF: $C_{45}H_{54}N_4O_8 \cdot C_4H_6O_6$ MW: 929.03
tartrate
RN: 125317-39-7   MF: $C_{45}H_{54}N_4O_8 \cdot 2C_4H_6O_6$ MW: 1079.12

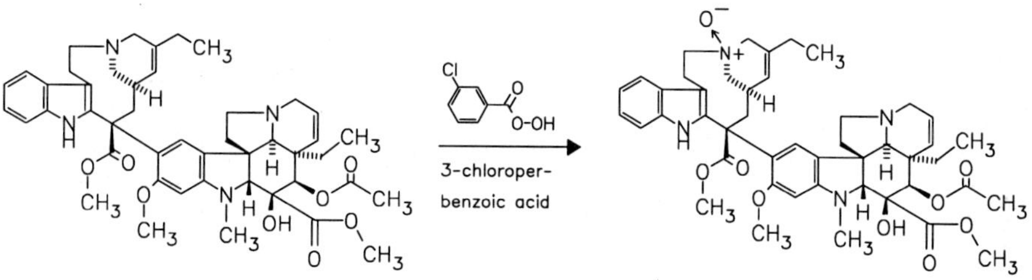

anhydrovinblastine

3-chloroper-benzoic acid

(I)

I + trifluoroacetic anhydride

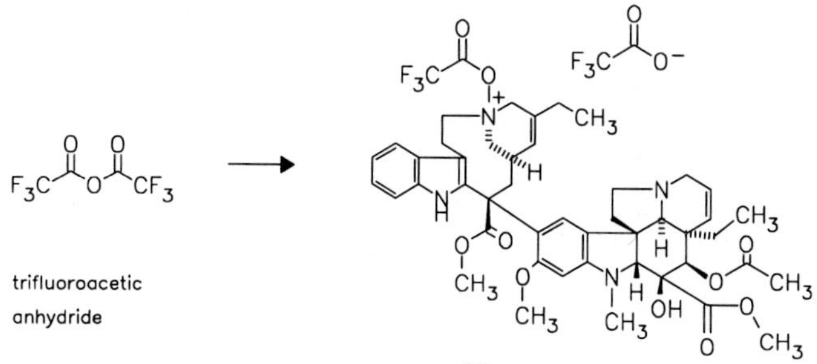

(II)

II

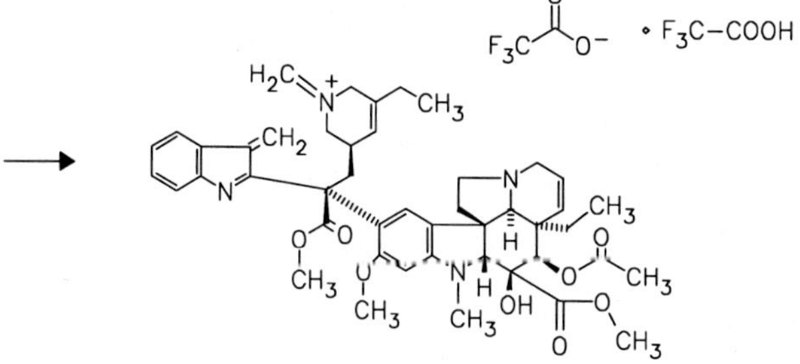

(III)

Vinorelbine

III →(THF, H₂O)

Reference(s):
EP 10 458 (ANVAR Agence Nat. Valorisation; F-prior. 24.8.1978, 6.2.1979).
Andriamialisoa, R.Z. et al.: Tetrahedron (TETRAB) **36**, 20 (1980).
Mangeney, P. et al.: Tetrahedron (TETRAB) **35**, 2175 (1979); J. Org. Chem. (JOCEAH) **44**, 3765 (1979).
Gueritte, F. et al.: Eur. J. Med. Chem. (EJMCA5) **18**, 419 (1983).
Potier, P.: Semin. Oncol. (SOLGAV) **16**, (2. Suppl. 4), 2 (1989); J. Nat. Prod. (JNPRDF) **43**, 72 (1980).

pharmaceutical formulation for parenteral administration:
EP 317 401 (PierreFabre; appl. 10.11.1988; F-prior. 13.11.1987).

synthesis of anhydrovinblastine:
EP 354 778 (Mitsui Petrochem.; appl. 9.8.1989; J-prior. 11.8.1988).
DOS 3 826 412 (Univ. of British Columbia; appl. 6.8.1988; CND-prior. 6.8.1987).
FR 2 544 319 (Pierre Fabre; appl. 14.4.1983).
HU 20 601 (Richter Gedeon; appl. 17.3.1977).
WO 8 802 002 (Mitsui Petrochem.; appl. 16.9.1987; USA-prior. 18.9.1986).
JP 63 119 690 (Mitsui Petrochem.; appl. 4.8.1987; USA-prior. 4.8.1986).
Kutney, J.P. et al.: Helv. Chim. Acta (HCACAV) **58**, 1690, 1711 (1975); **59**, 2858 (1976).
Raucher, S. et al.: J. Am. Chem. Soc. (JACSAT) **109**, 442 (1987).
Kutney, J.P. et al.: Heterocycles (HTCYAM) **27**, 621, 1845 (1988).
Goodbody, A.E. et al.: Planta Med. (PLMEAA) **54**, 136, 210 (1988).
Vokovic, J. et al.: Tetrahedron (TETRAB) **44**, 325 (1988).
Atta-Ur-Rahman, P.S.: J. Nat. Prod. (JNPRDF) **51**, 1275 (1988).
Bray, B.L.: Dissertation Univ. Washington (Seattle), Diss. Abstr. Int. B 1988, 48 (12), Pt. 1, 3567.

Formulation(s):   amp. 10 mg/ml, 50 mg/5 ml (as base); vial 10 mg/ml, 50 mg/5 ml (as tartrate)

Trade Name(s):
F: Navelbine (Pierre Fabre; 1988)

GB: Navelbine (Pierre Fabre; as tartrate)

I: Navelbine (Pierre Fabre)

USA: Navelbine (Glaxo Wellcome; as tartrate)

Vinpocetine

ATC: N06BX18
Use: vasodilator, cerebrostimulant

RN: 42971-09-5   MF: $C_{22}H_{26}N_2O_2$ MW: 350.46   EINECS: 256-028-0
LD$_{50}$:   45 mg/kg (M, i.v.); 534 mg/kg (M, p.o.);
          32 mg/kg (R, i.v.); 503 mg/kg (R, p.o.)
CN: (3α,16α)-eburnamenine-14-carboxylic acid ethyl ester

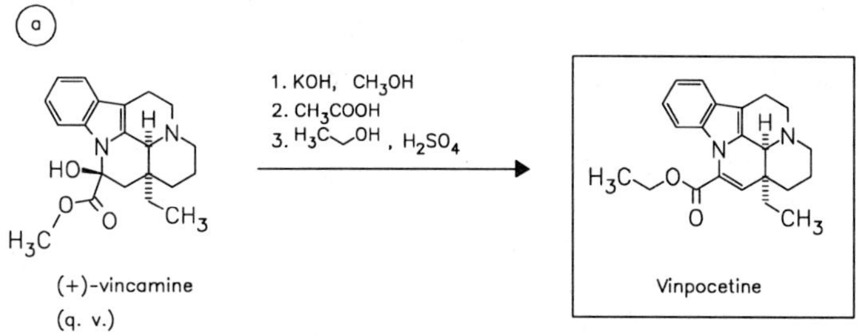

a)

1. KOH, CH₃OH
2. CH₃COOH
3. H₃C‿OH , H₂SO₄

(+)-vincamine
(q. v.)

Vinpocetine

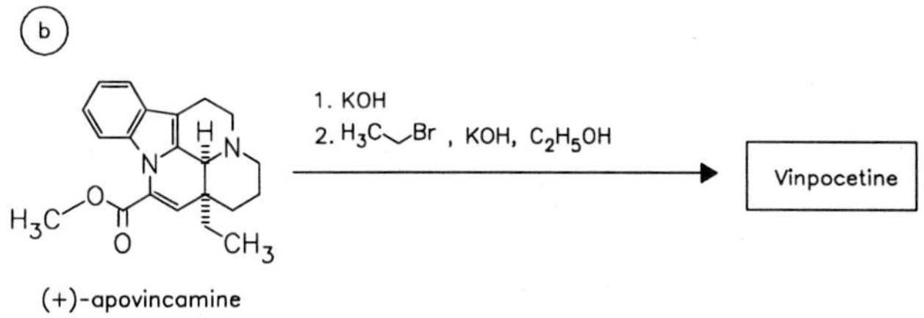

b)

1. KOH
2. H₃C‿Br , KOH, C₂H₅OH

Vinpocetine

(+)-apovincamine

Reference(s):
US 4 035 370 (Richter Gedeon; 12.7.1977; prior. 11.10.1972).
DAS 2 253 750 (Richter Gedeon; appl. 2.11.1972; H-prior. 3.11.1971).
Lörincz, C. et al.: Arzneim.-Forsch. (ARZNAD) **26**, 1907 (1976).

citrate phosphate:
EP 154 756 (Covex; appl. 21.3.1984; E-prior. 29.2.1984).

Formulation(s):   tabl. 5 mg

Trade Name(s):
D: Cavinton (Thiemann)   J: Calan (Takeda; 1984)

Vinylbital

(Butylvinal)

ATC: N05CA08
Use: hypnotic

RN: 2430-49-1   MF: $C_{11}H_{16}N_2O_3$ MW: 224.26   EINECS: 219-395-8
CN: 5-ethenyl-5-(1-methylbutyl)-2,4,6(1*H*,3*H*,5*H*)-pyrimidinetrione

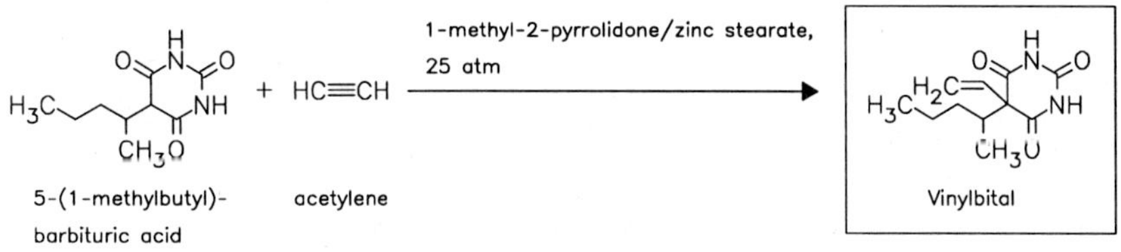

1-methyl-2-pyrrolidone/zinc stearate,
25 atm

5-(1-methylbutyl)-
barbituric acid

+ HC≡CH

acetylene

Vinylbital

Reference(s):
FR 11 825 256 (BASF; appl. 9.9.1957).
FR-M 896 (BASF; appl. 4.1.1961).

Formulation(s):   tabl. 150 mg

Viomycin

ATC: J04A
Use: antibiotic

RN: 32988-50-4 MF: $C_{25}H_{43}N_{13}O_{10}$ MW: 685.70 EINECS: 251-323-0
CN: stereoisomer of 3,6-diamino-N-[6-[[(aminocarbonyl)amino]methylene]-3-(2-amino-1,4,5,6-tetrahydro-6-hydroxy-4-pyrimidinyl)-9,12-bis(hydroxymethyl)-2,5,8,11,14-pentaoxo-1,4,7,10,13-pentaazacyclohexadec-15-yl]hexanamide

sulfate
RN: 37883-00-4 MF: $C_{25}H_{43}N_{13}O_{10} \cdot xH_2SO_4$ MW: unspecified
LD_{50}: 112 mg/kg (M, i.v.);
340 mg/kg (R, i.v.)

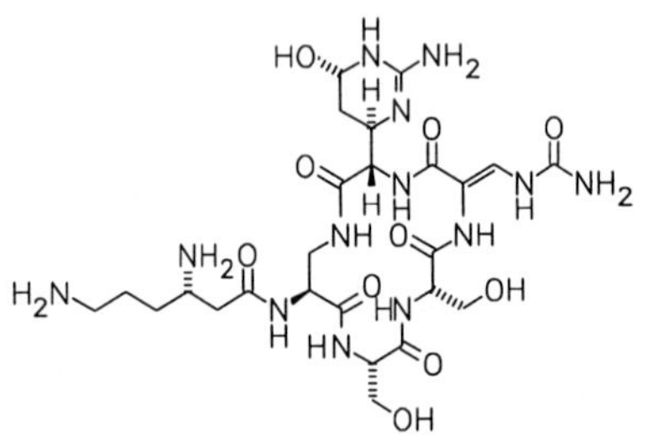

Viomycin

From fermentation solutions of *Streptomyces floridae* or *Streptomyces puniceus*.

Reference(s):
US 2 633 445 (Ciba; 1953; prior. 1947).
US 2 828 245 (Commerc Solvents; 1958; prior. 1954).

Formulation(s): amp. 1 g

Visnadine

ATC: C04AX24
Use: coronary vasodilator

RN: 477-32-7 MF: $C_{21}H_{24}O_7$ MW: 388.42 EINECS: 207-515-1
LD_{50}: 2240 mg/kg (M, p.o.);
1213 mg/kg (R, p.o.)
CN: [9R-[9α(R*),10α]]-2-methylbutanoic acid 10-(acetyloxy)-9,10-dihydro-8,8-dimethyl-2-oxo-2H,8H-benzo[1,2-b:3,4-b']dipyran-9-yl ester

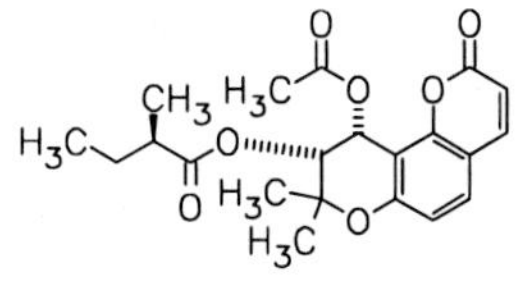

Visnadine

By extraction from *Ammi visnaga* L. (Umbelliferae) and chromatographic purification.

Reference(s):
US 2 816 118 (S. B. Penick & Co.; 10.12.1957; prior. 12.11.1953).
US 2 980 699 (S. B. Penick & Co.; 18.4.1961; prior. 20.12.1957).

Formulation(s):   cps. 70 mg

Trade Name(s):
D: Carduben (Madaus); wfm   F: Vibeline (Roger Bellon);   J: Visnamine (Chinoin)
wfm

Voglibose

ATC: A10
Use: antidiabetic, antiobesity, α-glucosidase inhibitor

RN: 83480-29-9   MF: $C_{10}H_{21}NO_7$ MW: 267.28
CN: 3,4-dideoxy-4-[[2-hydroxy-1-(hydroxymethyl)ethyl]amino]-2-*C*-(hydroxymethyl)-D-*epi*-inositol

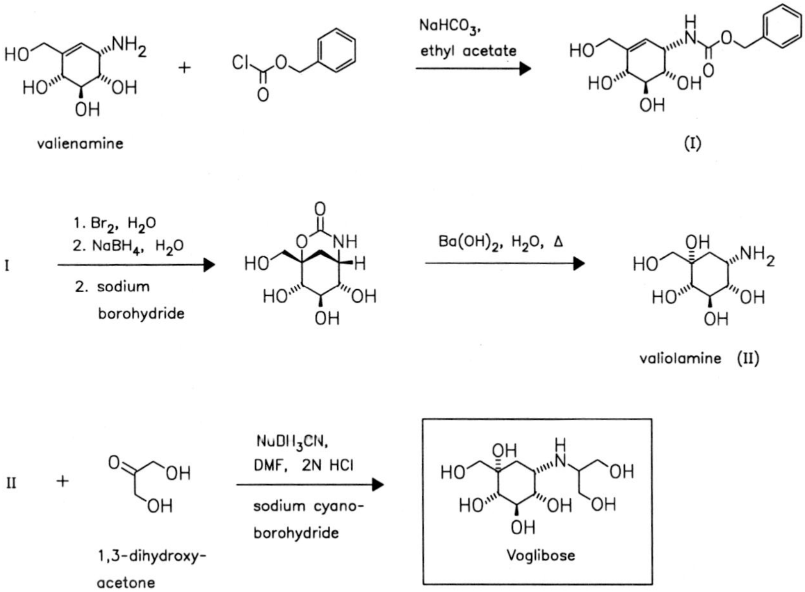

valienamine   (I)

valiolamine   (II)

1,3-dihydroxy-acetone   Voglibose

Reference(s):
EP 56 194 (Takeda Chem.; appl. 24.12.1984; J-prior. 5.1.1981, 6.10.1981).
Hori, S. et al.: J. Med. Chem. (JMCMAR) **29**, 1038 (1986).
EP 260 121 (Takeda Chem.; appl. 9.9.1987; J-prior. 9.9.1986, 5.11.1986, 6.1.1987).
EP 240 175 (Takeda Chem.; appl. 5.3.1987; J-prior. 21.5.1986, 5.3.1986, 4.3.1987).

uncoated tablets with improved resistance:
EP 610 854 (Takeda Chem.; appl. 7.2.1994; J-prior. 10.2.1993).

composition for promoting calcium absorption:
EP 364 696 (Takeda Chem.; appl. 21.8.1989; J-prior. 22.8.1988).
EP 197 661 (Takeda Chem.; appl. 10.3.1986; J-prior. 11.3.1985).
EP 194 794 (Takeda Chem.; appl. 4.3.1986; WO-prior. 8.3.1985, 30.4.1985).

combination for obesity treatment:
WO 8 605 094 (Takeda Chem.; appl. 8.3.1985; WO-prior. 8.3.1985, 30.4.1985).
EP 638 317 (Hoffmann-La Roche; appl. 22.7.1994; CH-prior. 5.8.1993).

Formulation(s):   tabl. 0.2 mg, 0.3 mg

Trade Name(s):
J: Basen (Takeda)   Glustat (Takeda)

Warfarin

ATC: B01AA03
Use: anticoagulant

RN: 81-81-2   MF: C$_{19}$H$_{16}$O$_4$ MW: 308.33   EINECS: 201-377-6
LD$_{50}$:   165 mg/kg (M, i.v.); 3 mg/kg (M, p.o.);
1600 µg/kg (R, p.o.);
3 mg/kg (dog, p.o.)
CN: 4-hydroxy-3-(3-oxo-1-phenylbutyl)-2H-1-benzopyran-2-one

sodium salt
RN: 129-06-6   MF: C$_{19}$H$_{15}$NaO$_4$ MW: 330.32   EINECS: 204-929-4
LD$_{50}$:   160 mg/kg (M, i.v.); 374 mg/kg (M, p.o.);
25 mg/kg (R, i.v.); 8700 µg/kg (R, p.o.);
200 mg/kg (dog, i.v.); 200 mg/kg (dog, p.o.)

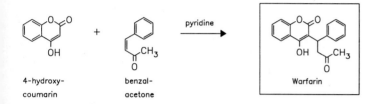

4-hydroxy-   benzal-   Warfarin
coumarin   acetone

Reference(s):
US 2 427 578 (Wisconsin Alumni Res. Found.; 1947; prior. 1945).

sodium salt:
US 2 777 859 (Wisconsin Alumni Res. Found.; 1957; prior. 1953).
US 2 765 321 (Wisconsin Alumni Res. Found.; 1956; appl. 1955).
US 3 077 481 (Wisconsin Alumni Res. Found.; 12.2.1963; appl. 21.2.1961)

Formulation(s):   amp. 2 mg/ml; tabl. 1 mg, 2 mg, 2.5 mg, 3 mg, 4 mg, 5 mg, 6 mg, 7.5 mg, 10 mg (as sodium salt)

Trade Name(s):
D: Coumadin (Du Pont)   GB: Marevan (Goldshield)   J: Warfarin (Eisai)
F: Coumadine (Du Pont)   I: Coumadin Endo (Du Pont)   USA: Coumadin (Du Pont)

Xamoterol

(ICI-118587)

ATC: C01CA; C01CX07
Use: cardiac stimulant, β-antagonist

RN: 81801-12-9   MF: $C_{16}H_{25}N_3O_5$ MW: 339.39
CN: (±)-*N*-[2-[[2-hydroxy-3-(4-hydroxyphenoxy)propyl]amino]ethyl]-4-morpholinecarboxamide

fumarate
RN: 69630-19-9   MF: $C_{16}H_{25}N_3O_5 \cdot C_4H_4O_4$ MW: 455.46
(±)-monohydrochloride
RN: 112008-18-1   MF: $C_{16}H_{25}N_3O_5 \cdot HCl$ MW: 375.85
(±)-fumarate (2:1)
RN: 90730-93-1   MF: $C_{16}H_{25}N_3O_5 \cdot 1/2C_4H_4O_4$ MW: 794.86
fumarate (2:1)
RN: 73210-73-8   MF: $C_{16}H_{25}N_3O_5 \cdot 1/2C_4H_4O_4$ MW: 794.86   EINECS: 277-319-9

4-benzyloxyphenol   epichloro-   1-(4-benzyloxyphenoxy)-   4-[N-(2-amino-
                     hydrin   2,3-epoxypropane   ethyl)carbamoyl]-
                                                              morpholine

(I)   →   Xamoterol

Reference(s):
DOS 2 822 473 (ICI; appl. 23.5.1978; GB-prior. 23.5.1977).
US 4 143 140 (ICI; 6.3.1979; GB-prior. 23.5.1977).
Barlow, J.J. et al.: J. Med. Chem. (JMCMAR) **24**, 315 (1981).

Formulation(s):   tabl. 200 mg

Trade Name(s):
GB: Corwin (Zeneca)   J: Sepan (Yamanouchi)   USA: Corwin (Zeneca)

Xantinol nicotinate

(Xanthinol-Niacinate)

ATC: C04AD02
Use: vasodilator

RN: 437-74-1   MF: $C_{13}H_{21}N_5O_4 \cdot C_6H_5NO_2$ MW: 434.45   EINECS: 207-115-7
LD$_{50}$:   673 mg/kg (M, i.v.); 17350 mg/kg (M, p.o.);
            690 mg/kg (R, i.v.); 14130 mg/kg (R, p.o.)
CN: 3-pyridinecarboxylic acid compd. with 3,7-dihydro-7-[2-hydroxy-3-[(2-
       hydroxyethyl)methylamino]propyl]-1,3-dimethyl-1*H*-purine-2,6-dione (1:1)

xanthinol (I)   nicotinic   Xantinol nicotinate
                 acid

Reference(s):
US 2 924 598 (J. A. Wülfing; 9.2.1960; D-prior. 26.10.1957).

Formulation(s):   amp. 300 mg; s. r. cps. 500 mg; s. r. tabl. 150 mg, 300 mg, 1000 mg; tabl. 150 mg, 300 mg, 1000 mg

Trade Name(s):
D: Complamin (SmithKline   Xantinol-nicotinat retard-   GB: Complamex (Gemini); wfm
      Beecham)   ratiopharm (ratiopharm)   I: Complamin (Italchimici)
      Theonikol (medpharm)   F: Complamine (Latéma);   USA: Complamin (Riker); wfm
                                     wfm

Xibenolol   Use: beta blocking agent

RN: 30187-90-7   MF: $C_{15}H_{25}NO_2$ MW: 251.37
CN: 1-[(1,1-dimethylethyl)amino]-3-(2,3-dimethylphenoxy)-2-propanol

2,3-xylenol (I)   epichloro-   (III)
                   hydrin (II)

III + tert-butyl-   Xibenolol
        amine (IV)

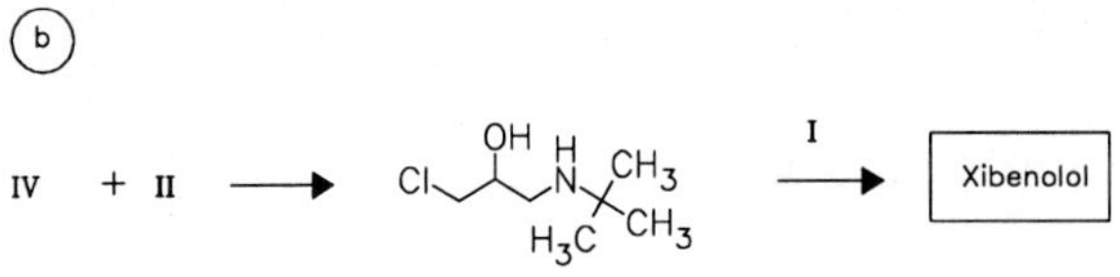

ⓑ

IV + II ⟶ [structure: CH₂Cl, OH, N-H, C(CH₃)₃ chain] →I→ [Xibenolol]

Reference(s):
JP 7 029 294 (Teikoku; appl. 17.8.1968).
JP 6 041 623 (Teikoku; appl. 17.8.1968).

alternative synthesis:
JP 4 033 185 (Teikoku; appl. 5.8.1969).
DOS 2 058 532 (Teikoku; appl. 27.11.1970; J-prior. 28.11.1969, 31.3.1970, 21.7.1970, 13.11.1970).
DOS 2 065 365 (Teikoku; appl. 27.11.1970; J-prior. 28.11.1969, 31.3.1970, 21.7.1970, 13.11.1970).

medical use:
GB 1 422 046 (Teikoku; appl. 19.1.1973).

Trade Name(s):
J: Rythminal (Teikoku)

Xibornol

ATC: J01XX02
Use: bronchochemotherapeutic

RN: 13741-18-9   MF: $C_{18}H_{26}O$ MW: 258.41   EINECS: 237-312-3
CN: exo-4,5-dimethyl-2-(1,7,7-trimethylbicyclo[2.2.1]hept-2-yl)phenol

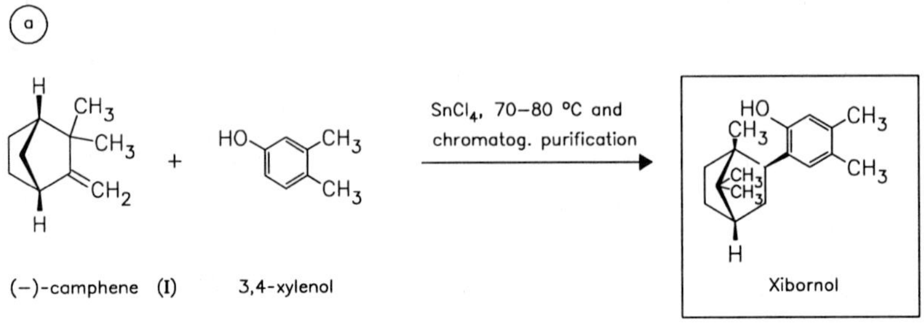

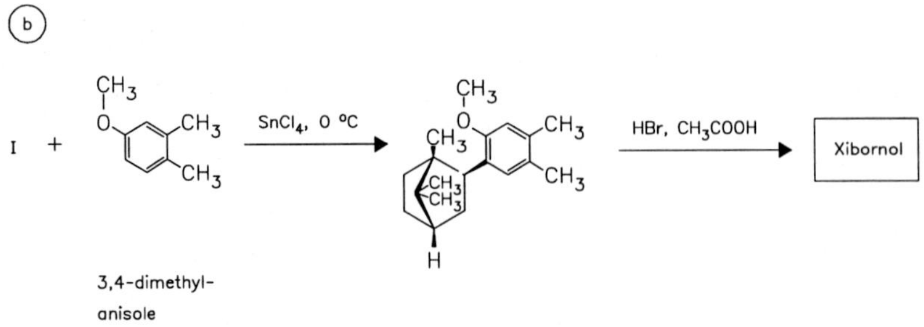

ⓐ

(−)-camphene (I)   3,4-xylenol   Xibornol

SnCl₄, 70–80 °C and
chromatog. purification

ⓑ

I + [3,4-dimethyl-anisole] →SnCl₄, 0 °C→ [intermediate] →HBr, CH₃COOH→ [Xibornol]

3,4-dimethyl-
anisole

Reference(s):
a   GB 1 206 774 (Mar-Pha; appl. 23.10.1967).
b   DOS 2 032 170 (Mar-Pha; appl. 30.6.1970; GB-prior. 4.7.1969).

alternative process:
DOS 2 912 762 (Farmatis; appl. 30.3.1979).

Formulation(s):   cps. 250 mg; spray 3 %; susp. 100 mg

Trade Name(s):
F: Nanbacine (Bellon Groupe   I: Bracen (Zyma); wfm
      Rhône-Poulenc Rorer)   Xibor (Benedetti); wfm

Xipamide

ATC: C03BA10
Use: diuretic

RN: 14293-44-8   MF: $C_{15}H_{15}ClN_2O_4S$ MW: 354.81   EINECS: 238-216-4
LD_{50}:   1810 mg/kg (M, p.o.);
      1640 mg/kg (R, p.o.);
      >50 mg/kg (dog, i.v.); >1500 mg/kg (dog, p.o.)
CN: 5-(aminosulfonyl)-4-chloro-*N*-(2,6-dimethylphenyl)-2-hydroxybenzamide

4-chloro-
salicylic acid

5-aminosulfonyl-
4-chlorosalicylic
acid (I)

2,6-dimethyl-
aniline

Xipamide

Reference(s):
US 3 567 777 (Beiersdorf; 2.3.1971; D-prior. 19.6.1965).
DE 1 270 544 (Beiersdorf; appl. 19.6.1965).

Formulation(s):   tabl. 10 mg, 20 mg, 40 mg

Trade Name(s):
D: Aquaphor (Beiersdorf-   Neotri (Beiersdorf-Lilly/   Lumitens (Solvay Pharma)
      Lilly/Lilly)   Lilly)-comb. with   GB: Diurexan (ASTA Medica)
      Durotan (Beiersdorf-Lilly)-   triamterene   I: Aquafor (ASTA Medica
      comb. with reserpine   F: Chronexan (ASTA Medica)   AWD)

Xylometazoline

ATC: R01AA07; R01AB06; S01GA03
Use: vasoconstrictor, rhinological
        therapeutic

RN: 526-36-3   MF: $C_{16}H_{24}N_2$ MW: 244.38   EINECS: 208-390-6
LD_{50}:   215 mg/kg (M, p.o.)
CN: 2-[[4-(1,1-dimethylethyl)-2,6-dimethylphenyl]methyl]-4,5-dihydro-1*H*-imidazole

monohydrochloride
RN: 1218-35-5   MF: $C_{16}H_{24}N_2 \cdot HCl$ MW: 280.84   EINECS: 214-936-4

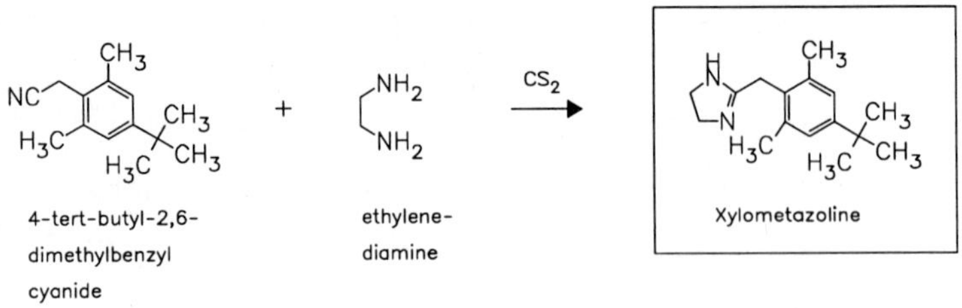

CH3
NC
H3C
CH3
H3C
CH3
4-tert-butyl-2,6-dimethylbenzyl cyanide
+
NH2
NH2
ethylenediamine
CS2
Xylometazoline

Reference(s):
US 2 868 802 (Ciba; 13.1.1959; CH-prior. 10.7.1956).
DE 1 049 387 (Ciba; appl. 3.7.1957; CH-prior. 10.7.1956).

Formulation(s): drops 0.5 mg/ml, 1 g/ml; eye drops 1 mg/ml; gel 1 mg/g; sol. 0.25 mg/ml, 0.5 mg/ml, 1 mg/ml; spray 0.5 mg/ml, 1mg/ml (as hydrochloride)

Trade Name(s):

D: Balkis (Dolorgiet)
Dorenasin (Rentschler)
Gelonasal (Pohl)
Imidin (Pharma Wernigerode)
Lomupren comp. (Fisons)-comb.
mentopin (Hermes)
Nasan (Hexal)
Nasengel-ratiopharm (ratiopharm)
Nasenspray-ratiopharm (ratiopharm)
Nasentropfen K-ratiopharm (ratiopharm)
Olynth (Warner-Lambert)
Otriven (Novartis)
Otriven (CIBA Vision)
Pertix Hommel (Hommel)
Rapako (Truw)
schnupfen endrine (Asche)
stas Nasenspray (Stada)
Xylo-COMOD (Ursapharm)
Xylo-E (ct-Arzneimittel)

GB: Otrivine (Novartis)
Otrivine-Antistin (CIBA Vision)-comb. with antazoline
Rynacrom compound (Rhône-Poulenc Rorer)

I: Neorinoleina (Synthelabo)
Otrivin (CIBA Vision)
Respiro (Byk Gulden)-comb.
Rinos (Molteni)-comb.

USA: Otrivin (Geigy); wfm

Zafirlukast
(ICI-204219)

ATC: R03DC01
Use: antiasthmatic, LTD$_4$-antagonist

RN: 107753-78-6   MF: C$_{31}$H$_{33}$N$_3$O$_6$S   MW: 575.69
CN: [3-[[2-methoxy-4-[[[(2-methylphenyl)sulfonyl]amino]carbonyl]phenyl]methyl]-1-methyl-1H-indol-5-yl]carbamic acid cyclopentyl ester

monohydrate
RN: 143052-93-1   MF: C$_{31}$H$_{33}$N$_3$O$_6$S · H$_2$O   MW: 593.70
calcium salt (2:1)
RN: 107753-86-6   MF: C$_{62}$H$_{64}$CaN$_6$O$_{12}$S$_2$ MW: 1189.43

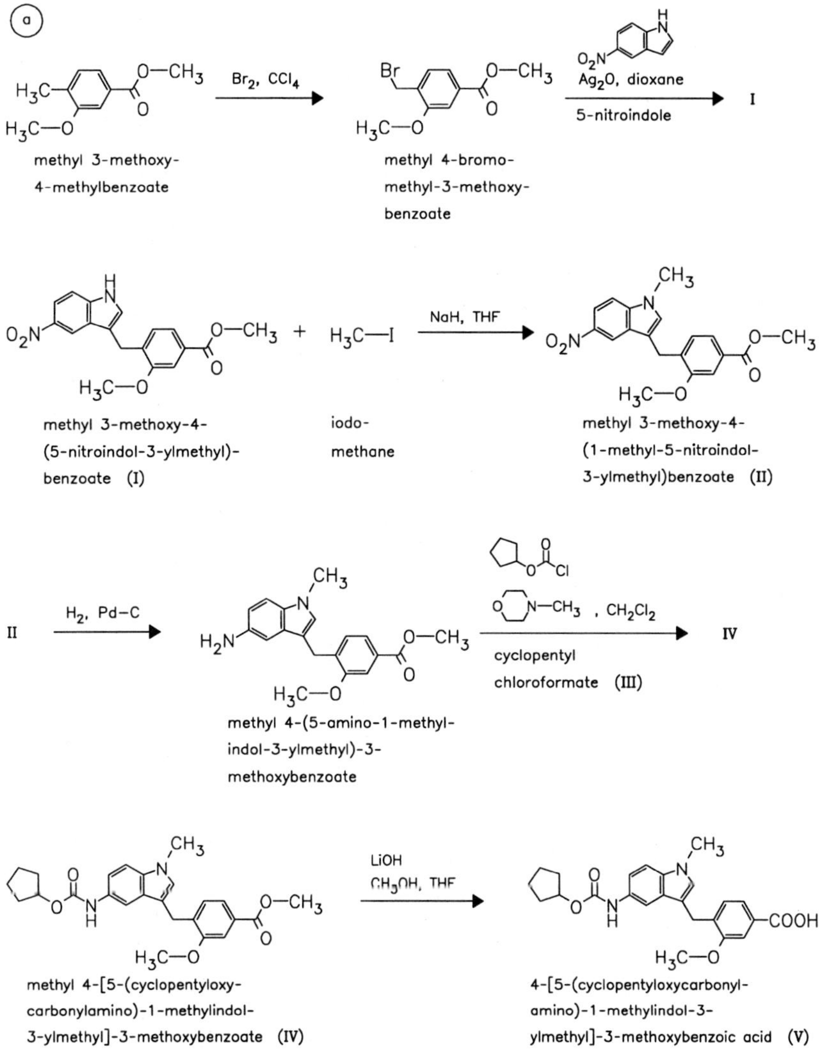

methyl 3-methoxy-
4-methylbenzoate

methyl 4-bromo-
methyl-3-methoxy-
benzoate

methyl 3-methoxy-4-
(5-nitroindol-3-ylmethyl)-
benzoate (I)

iodo-
methane

methyl 3-methoxy-4-
(1-methyl-5-nitroindol-
3-ylmethyl)benzoate (II)

methyl 4-(5-amino-1-methyl-
indol-3-ylmethyl)-3-
methoxybenzoate

cyclopentyl
chloroformate (III)

methyl 4-[5-(cyclopentyloxycarbonylamino)-1-methylindol-
3-ylmethyl]-3-methoxybenzoate (IV)

4-[5-(cyclopentyloxycarbonylamino)-1-methylindol-3-
ylmethyl]-3-methoxybenzoic acid (V)

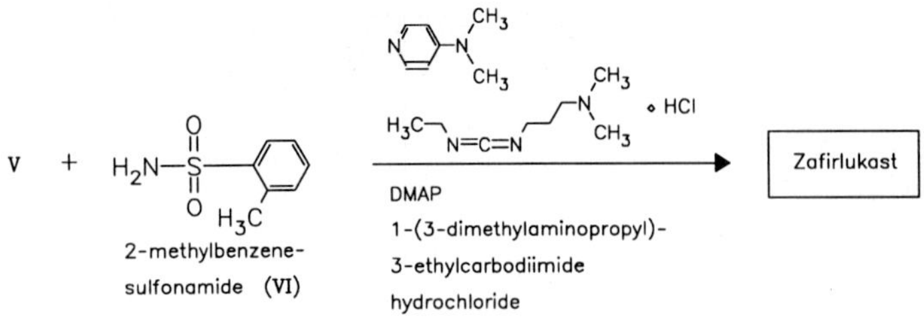

V　+　H₂N–S(=O)(=O)–（2-methylbenzene-sulfonamide **(VI)**）

2-methylbenzene-
sulfonamide　**(VI)**

DMAP

1-(3-dimethylaminopropyl)-
3-ethylcarbodiimide
hydrochloride

→　Zafirlukast

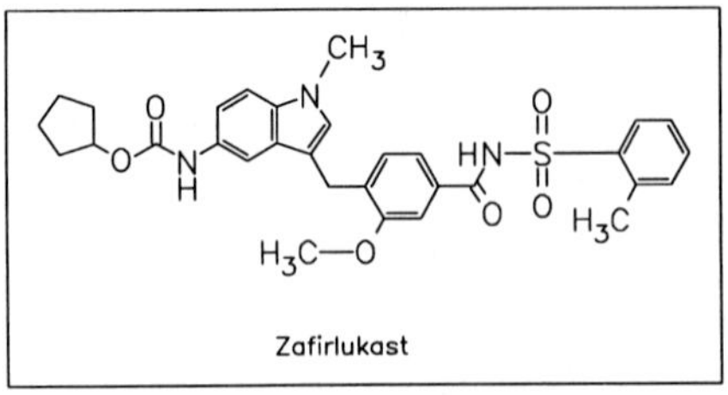

Zafirlukast

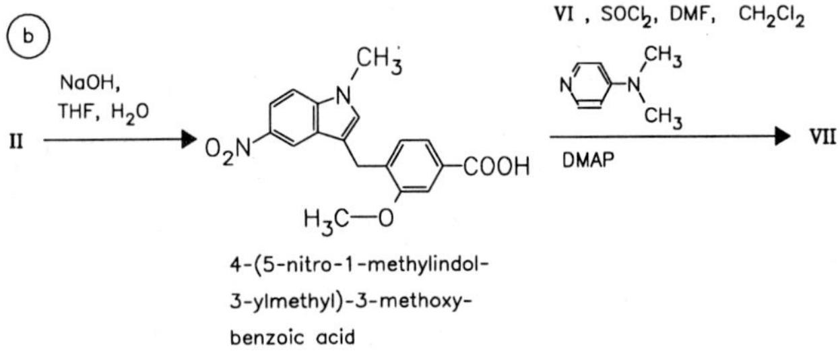

b

II　→（NaOH, THF, H₂O）→　4-(5-nitro-1-methylindol-
3-ylmethyl)-3-methoxy-
benzoic acid

VI , SOCl₂, DMF, CH₂Cl₂

DMAP

→　VII

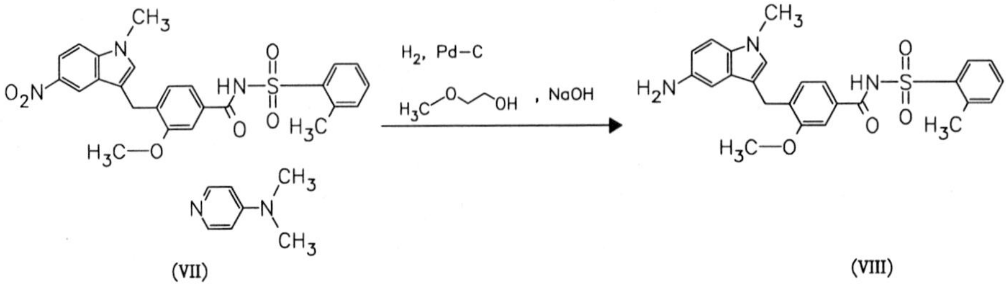

(VII)

H₂, Pd–C

H₃C–O–CH₂CH₂–OH , NaOH

→

(VIII)

VIII　+　III　→　Zafirlukast

Reference(s):

a　EP 199 543 (ICI, Zeneca; appl. 16.4.1986; GB-prior. 17.4.1985).
　　crystalline form suitable for inhalation:
b　EP 490 649 (ICI, Zeneca; 11.12.1991; GB-prior. 12.12.1990).
　　Matassa, G. et al.: J. Med. Chem. (JMCMAR) **33**, 1781 (1990).

Formulation(s):　　tabl. 20 mg

Trade Name(s):
USA:　Accolate (Zeneca)

Zalcitabine
(ddCyd; Dideoxycytidine; Ro-24-2027)

ATC: J05AF03
Use: anti-AIDS therapeutic

RN: 7481-89-2   MF: $C_9H_{13}N_3O_3$ MW: 211.22
CN: 2',3'-dideoxycytidine

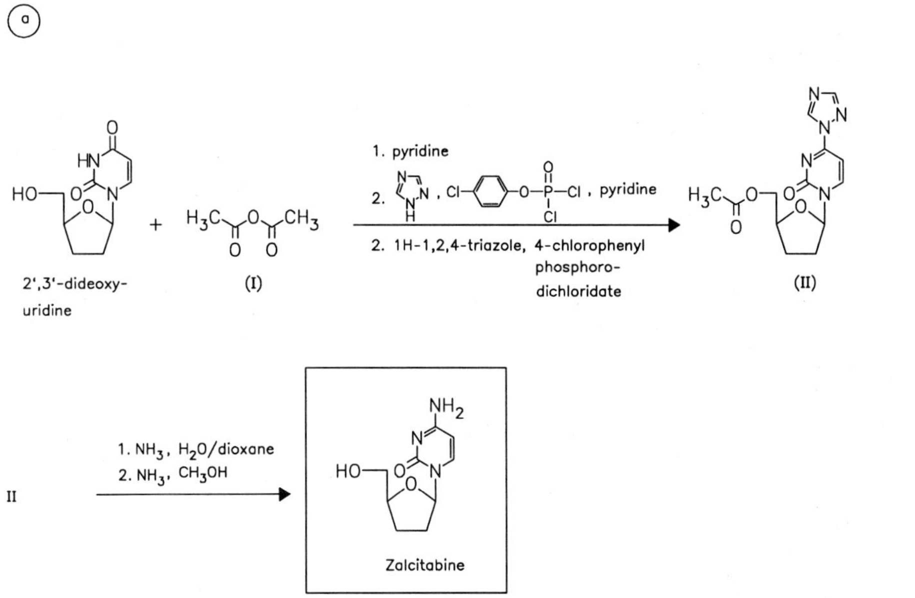

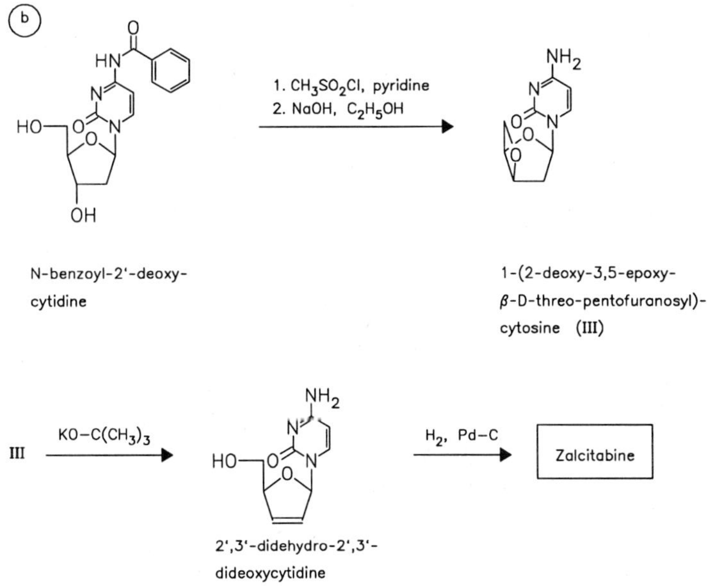

(a)

2',3'-dideoxy-
uridine   (I)

1. pyridine
2. 1H-1,2,4-triazole, 4-chlorophenyl phosphoro-dichloridate

(II)

1. NH_3, H_2O/dioxane
2. NH_3, CH_3OH

II

Zalcitabine

(b)

N-benzoyl-2'-deoxy-
cytidine

1. CH_3SO_2Cl, pyridine
2. NaOH, C_2H_5OH

1-(2-deoxy-3,5-epoxy-
β-D-threo-pentofuranosyl)-
cytosine (III)

III $KO-C(CH_3)_3$

2',3'-didehydro-2',3'-
dideoxycytidine

H_2, Pd–C

Zalcitabine

ⓒ

N-acetylcytidine

1. HBr
2. I , HOAc

(IV)

+

(V)

IV + V

1. Cu/Zn
2. Ac₂O, pyridine

N-acetyl-2',3'-didehydro-
2',3'-dideoxycytidine
5'-acetate

1. H₂, Pd—C
2. N(C₂H₅)₃, CH₃OH

Zalcitabine

Reference(s):
a   Lin, T.-S. et al.: J. Med. Chem. (JMCMAR) **30**, 440 (1987).
    synthesis of 2',3'-dideoxyuridine:
    Horwitz, J.P. et al.: J. Org. Chem. (JOCEAH) **32**, 817 (1967).
b   Horwitz, J.P. et al.: J. Org. Chem. (JOCEAH) **32**, 817 (1967).
    synthesis of N-benzoyl-2'-deoxycytidine:
    Benz, E. et al.: J. Org. Chem. (JOCEAH) **30**, 3067 (1965).
c   EP 341 704 (Hoffmann-La Roche; appl. 10.5.1989; USA-prior. 12.5.1988).

alternative synthesis:
JP 63 275 597 (Ajinomoto; appl. 7.5.1987).
JP 64 003 194 (Japan Tobacco; appl. 23.6.1987).
JP 64 003 196 (Japan Tobacco; appl. 23.6.1987).
JP 01 060 396 (Ajinomoto; appl. 28.8.1987).
EP 285 884 (Bristol-Myers; appl. 18.3.1988; USA-prior. 20.3.1987).

medical use for treatment of AIDS:
US 4 879 277 (United States Dep. of Health and Haman Services; 7.11.1989; appl. 11.8.1987; prior. 26.8.1985, 4.12.1986, 13.1.1987).

synergistic antiviral combination:
EP 361 831 (Wellcome; appl. 25.9.1989; GB-prior. 26.9.1988).

pharmaceutical tablet formulation:
EP 307 914 (Hoffmann-La Roche; appl. 15.9.1988; USA-prior. 18.9.1987).

Formulation(s):   f. c. tabl. 0.375 mg, 0.750 mg

Trade Name(s):
D:	Hivid (Roche)	GB:	Hivid (Roche)	J:	Hivid (Roche)
F:	Hivid (Roche)	I:	Hivid (Roche)	USA:	Hivid (Roche; 1992)

Zaleplon
(L-846; CL-284846; LJC 10846)

ATC: N05CF03
Use: sedative, hypnotic, GABA agonist

RN: 151319-34-5   MF: $C_{17}H_{15}N_5O$ MW: 305.34
CN: N-[3-(3-Cyanopyrazolo[1,5-a]pyrimidin-7-yl)phenyl]-N-ethylacetamide

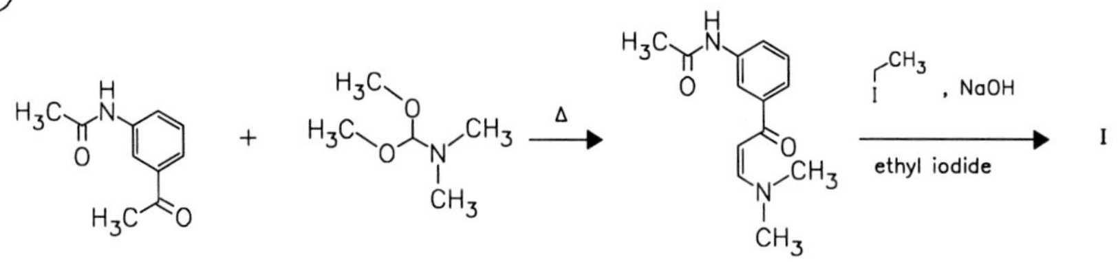

N-(3-acetylphenyl)-
acetamide

dimethylformamide
dimethyl acetal

N-[3-[3-(dimethyl-
amino)-1-oxo-2-
propenyl]phenyl]-
acetamide

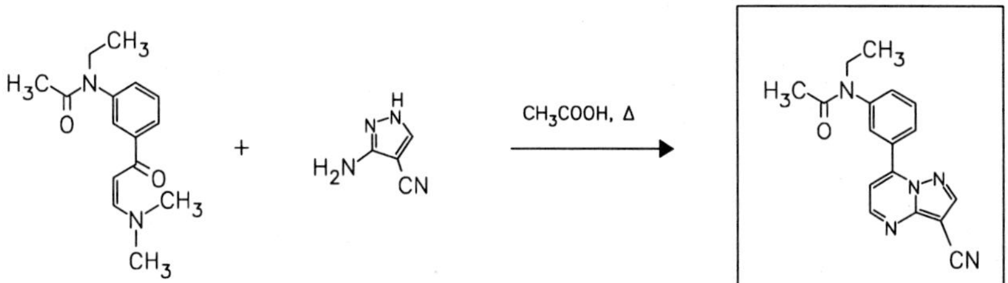

(I)

3-amino-1H-pyrazole-
4-carbonitrile (II)

Zaleplon

synthesis of 3-amino-1H-pyrazole-4-carbonitrile (II):

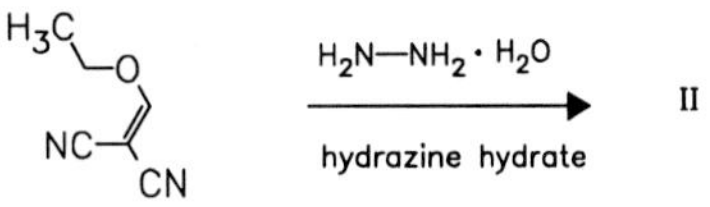

ethoxymethylene-
malononitrile

hydrazine hydrate

Reference(s):
a   US 5 714 607 (American Cyanamid; 3.2.1998; USA-prior. 1.12.1995).
    EP 776 898 (American Cyanamid; appl. 28.11.1996; USA-prior. 1.12.1995).
aa Robins: J. Am. Chem. Soc. (JACSAT) **78**, 784 (1956)

Formulation(s):   cps. 5 mg, 10 mg

Trade Name(s):
D: Sonata (Wyeth)   USA: Sonata (Wyeth Ayerst;
                   1999)

Zanamivir
(GG167; GR-121167X; 4-Guanidino-Neu5Ac2en)

ATC: J05AH01
Use: antiviral, influenza neuraminidase inhibitor

RN: 139110-80-8   MF: $C_{12}H_{20}N_4O_7$ MW: 332.31
CN: 5-(Acetylamino)-4-[(aminoiminomethyl)amino]-2,6-anhydro-3,4,5-trideoxy-D-*glycero*-D-*galacto*-non-2-enonic acid

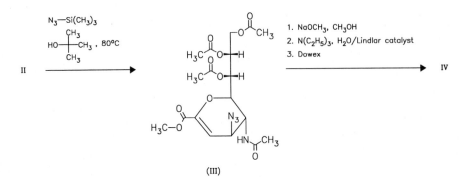

N-acetylneuraminic acid

methyl (3aR,4R,7aR)-2-methyl-
4-[(1S,2R)-1,2,3-triacetoxy-
propyl]-3a,7a-dihydro-4H-
pyrano[3,4-d]oxazole-6-
carboxylate (II)

(III)

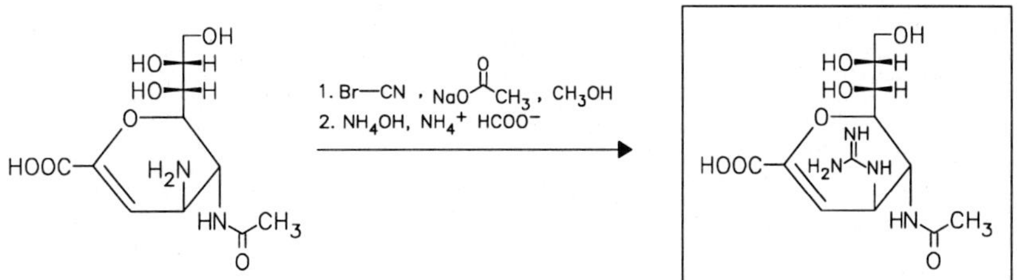

N-acetyl-4-amino-2,4-
dideoxy-2,3-didehydro-
neuraminic acid (IV)

Zanamivir

(b)

IV +

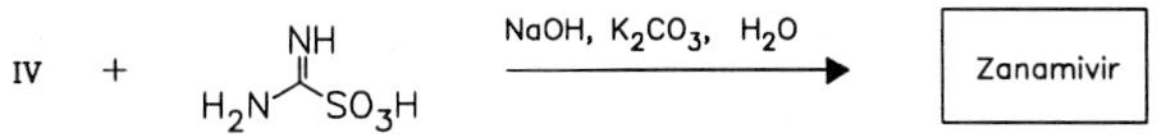

aminoimino-
methanesulfonic
acid

NaOH, K$_2$CO$_3$, H$_2$O

Zanamivir

(c)

IV +

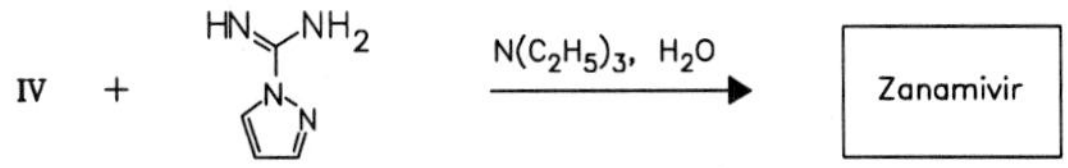

pyrazole-1-
carboxamidine

N(C$_2$H$_5$)$_3$, H$_2$O

Zanamivir

(d)

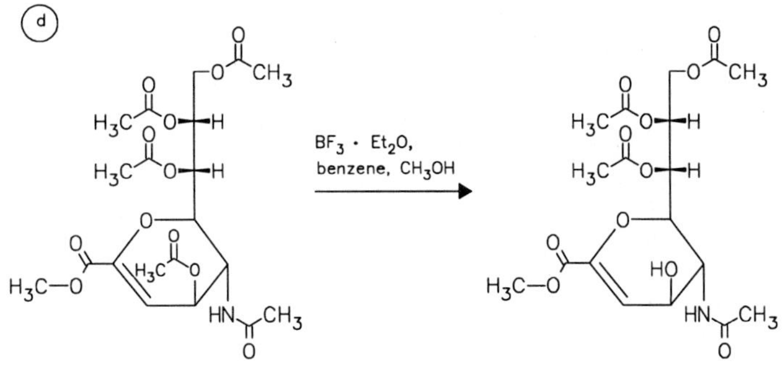

4-O,5-N,7-O,8-O,9-O-
pentaacetyl-2,3-didehydro-
2-deoxyneuraminic acid
methyl ester

BF$_3$ · Et$_2$O,
benzene, CH$_3$OH

(V)

V

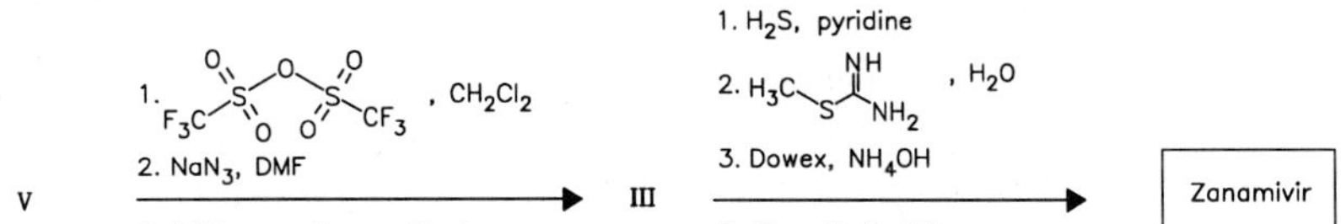

1. trifluoromethanesulfonic
   anhydride
2. sodium azide

III

1. H$_2$S, pyridine

2. S-methylisothiourea

Zanamivir

Reference(s):
a   Chandler, M. et al.: J. Chem. Soc., Perkin Trans. 1 (JCPRB4) **1995**, 1173.
    WO 9 407 885 (Glaxo; appl. 23.9.1993; GB-prior. 25.9.1992).
b   Itzstein, M. von et al.: Carbohydr. Res. (CRBRAT) **259**, 301 (1994)
c   WO 9 407 886 (Glaxo; appl. 23.9.1993; GB-prior. 25.9.1992).
d   WO 9 116 320 (Biota; appl. 24.4.1991; AU-prior. 24.4.1990).
    Scheigetz, J. et al.: Org. Prep. Proced. Int. (OPPIAK) **27**, 637 (1995).

preparation of different crystalline forms:
WO 9 516 680 (Glaxo; appl. 23.9.1993; GB-prior. 25.9.1992).

compounds and compositions for oral inhalation:
WO 9 532 712 (Glaxo; appl. 24.5.1995; GB-prior. 28.5.1994).

combination with an influenza vaccine:
GB 2 292 081 (Glaxo; appl. 1.8.1995; GB-prior. 12.8.1994).

Formulation(s):   powder for inhalation dischaler 5 mg

Trade Name(s):
D: Relenza (Glaxo Wellcome)   USA: Relenza (Glaxo Wellcome;
GB: Relenza (Glaxo Wellcome)   1999)

Zeranol

(Zearalanol)

ATC: A14
Use: estrogen

RN: 26538-44-3   MF: $C_{18}H_{26}O_5$ MW: 322.40   EINECS: 247-769-0
CN: [3S-(3R*,7S*)]-3,4,5,6,7,8,9,10,11,12-decahydro-7,14,16-trihydroxy-3-methyl-1H-2-
benzoxacyclotetradecin-1-one

zearalenone   Zeranol

Reference(s):
DE 1 543 395 (Commercial Solvents Corp.; appl. 1.2.1966; USA-prior. 15.2.1965).
US 3 239 345 (Commercial Solvents Corp.; 8.3.1966; prior. 15.2.1965).

starting material:
The Merck Index, 12th Ed., 1730 (1996).

Trade Name(s):
I: Frideron (Sandoz); wfm   Ralgro (Commercial   Ralone (Iti); wfm
                                        Solvent); wfm

Zidovudine

(Azidothymidine; AZT)

ATC: J05AB05
Use: anti-AIDS therapeutic, inhibitor of reverse transcriptase

RN: 30516-87-1   MF: $C_{10}H_{13}N_5O_4$ MW: 267.25
LD_{50}: >750 mg/kg (M, i.v.); >3000 mg/kg (M, p.o.);
>750 mg/kg (R, i.v.); >3000 mg/kg (R, p.o.)
CN: 3'-azido-3'-deoxythymidine

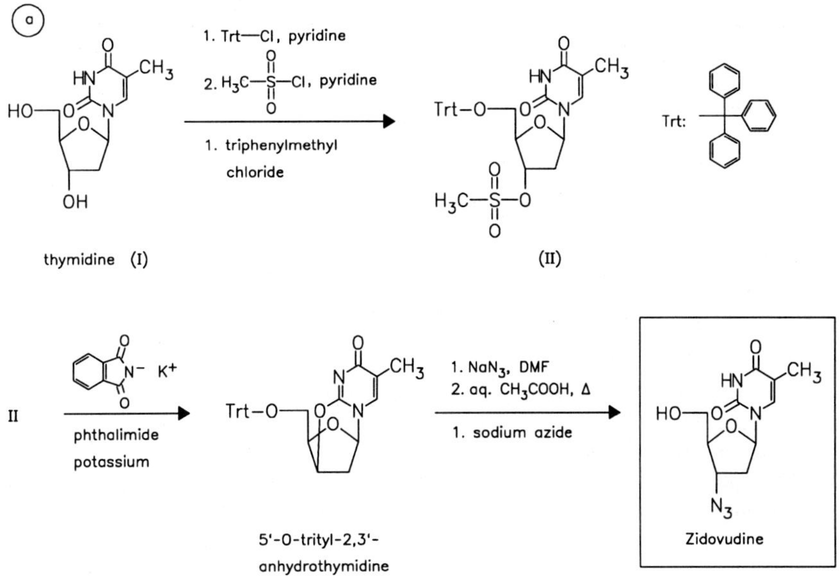

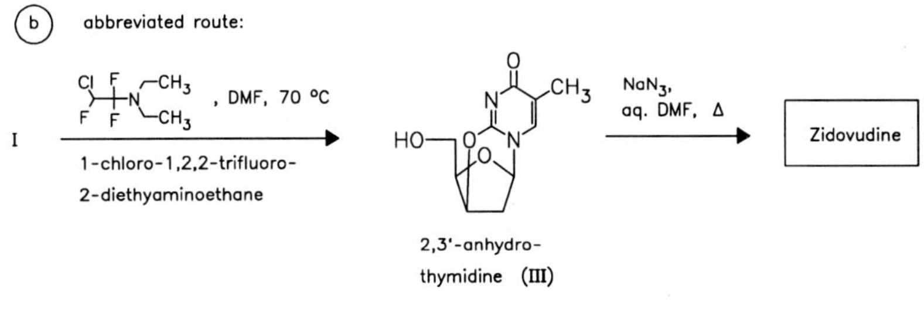

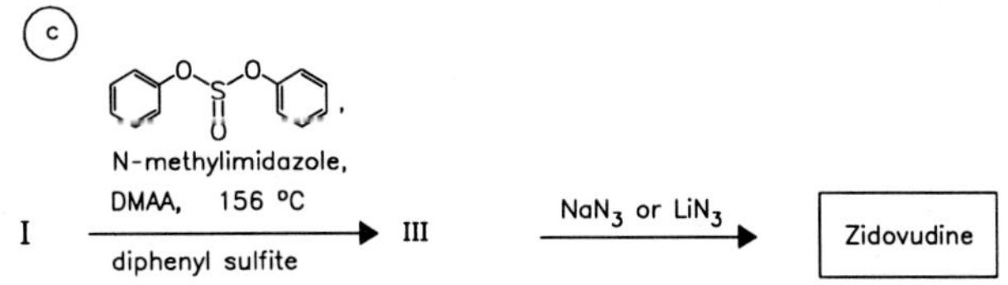

a)

1. Trt—Cl, pyridine
2. $H_3C-\overset{O}{\underset{O}{S}}-Cl$, pyridine

1. triphenylmethyl chloride

thymidine (I)

(II)

Trt:

II

phthalimide potassium

1. NaN₃, DMF
2. aq. CH₃COOH, Δ

1. sodium azide

5'-O-trityl-2,3'- anhydrothymidine

Zidovudine

b) abbreviated route:

I

1-chloro-1,2,2-trifluoro- 2-diethyaminoethane

, DMF, 70 °C

NaN₃, aq. DMF, Δ

2,3'-anhydro- thymidine (III)

Zidovudine

c)

N-methylimidazole, DMAA,   156 °C

diphenyl sulfite

I

III

NaN₃ or LiN₃

Zidovudine

Reference(s):

a   Glinski, R.P. et al.: J. Org. Chem. (JOCEAH) **38**, 4299 (1973).
    Horwitz, J.P. et al.: J. Org. Chem. (JOCEAH) **29**, 2076 (1964).
    Imazawa, M. et al.: J. Org. Chem. (JOCEAH) **43**, 3044 (1978).
b   DOS 3 608 606 (Wellcome Found.; appl. 14.3.1986; GB-prior. 16.3.1985, 9.5.1985, 27.9.1985, 12.2.1986; USA-prior. 17.9.1985).
    Czernecki, S.; Valery, J.M.: Synthesis (SYNTBF) **1991** (3), 239.
c   EP 317 207 (King's College London; appl. 11.11.1988; GB-prior. 13.11.1987).
    Rao, T.S. et al.: J. Chem. Soc., Chem. Commun. (JCCCAT) **15**, 997 (1989).

total synthesis starting with D-xylose *and* thymine:
US 4 916 218 (M. R. Almond et al.; 10.4.1990; appl. 9.6.1988).
EP 295 090 (Wellcome Found.; appl. 14.12.1988; GB-prior. 10.6.1987, 10.7.1987).
EP 292 101 (Wellcome Found.; appl. 23.11.1988; GB-prior. 25.3.1987, 23.5.1987).
Benhaddou, R.; Czernecki, S.; Valery, J.M; Belosta, V.: Bull. Soc. Chim. Fr. (BSCFAS) **1991**, 108.
US 4 921 950 (Burroughs Wellcome; 1.5.1990; appl. 9.6.1988).

alternative syntheses:
Jung, M.E.; Gardinier, J.U.: J. Org. Chem. (JOCEAH) **56** (8), 2614 (1991).
Zeidler, J.M. et al.: Nucleosides Nucleotides (NUNUD5) **9** (5), 629 (1990).
Hrebabecky, H.; Holy, A.: Carbohydr. Res. (CRBRAT) **216**, 179 (1991)
Chen, B.-C. et al.: Tetrahedron Lett. (TELEAY) **36** (44), 7961 (1995).
EP 653 437 (Bristol-Myers Squibb; appl. 3.11.1994; USA-prior. 15.11.1993).

medical use (treatment of AIDS or of other retroviral infections):
US 4 724 232 (Burroughs Wellcome; 9.2.1988; GB-prior. 16.3.1985, 9.5.1985).
US 4 828 838 (Burroughs Wellcome; 9.5.1989; GB-prior. 16.3.1985, 9.5.1985).
US 4 837 208 (Burroughs Wellcome; 6.6.1989; GB-prior. 16.3.1985, 9.5.1985).
US 4 847 244 (Burroughs Wellcome; 11.7.1989; appl. 20.10.1987; prior. 17.9.1985).
US 4 874 751 (Burroughs Wellcome; 17.10.1989; GB-prior. 16.3.1985, 9.5.1985).

controlled-release formulation:
EP 284 407 (Wellcome Found.; appl. 25.3.1988; GB-prior. 27.3.1987).
EP 232 155 (Elan; appl. 12.8.1987; IE-prior. 3.2.1986).

Formulation(s):   cps. 100 mg, 250 mg; sol. 50 mg/5 ml; syrup 50 mg/5 ml; tabl. 300 mg; vial 10 mg/ml

Trade Name(s):
D: Retrovir (Glaxo Wellcome;   GB: Retrovir (Glaxo Wellcome;   USA: Retrovir (Glaxo Wellcome;
     1987)   1987)   1987)
F: Retrovir (Glaxo Wellcome)   J: Retrovir (Wellcome; 1987)

Zileuton

(A-64077; ABT-077)

Use: anti-inflammatory, antiasthmatic, 5-lipoxigenase inhibitor

RN: 111406-87-2   MF: $C_{11}H_{12}N_2O_2S$ MW: 236.30
CN: N-(1-Benzo[b]thien-2-ylethyl)-N-hydroxyurea

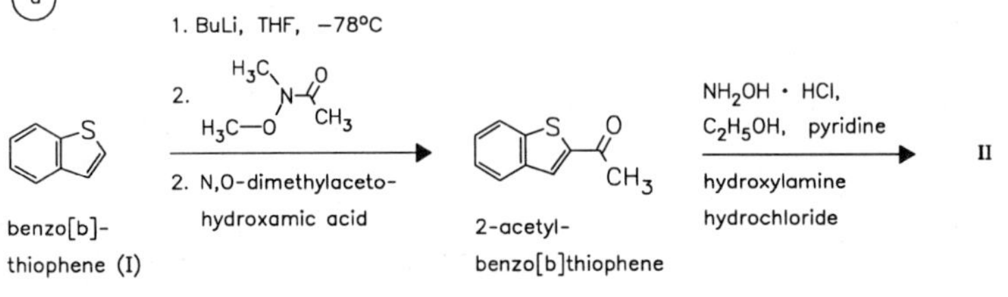

1. BuLi, THF, −78°C
2. H₃C-N(OCH₃)-C(=O)-CH₃ (N,O-dimethylaceto-hydroxamic acid)

benzo[b]-thiophene (I) → 2-acetyl-benzo[b]thiophene

$NH_2OH \cdot HCl$, C_2H_5OH, pyridine (hydroxylamine hydrochloride) → II

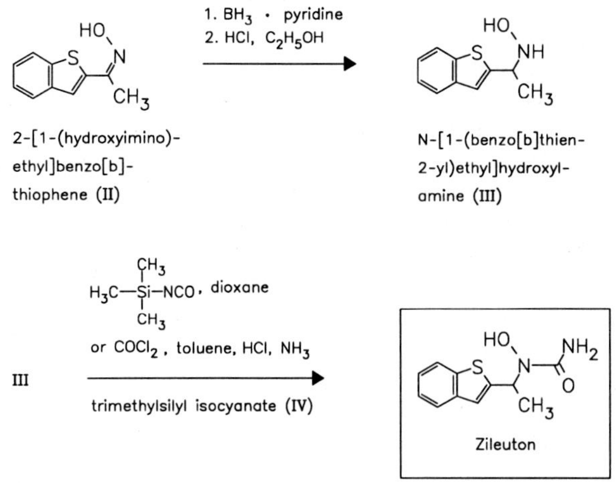
HO
N
S
CH3
1. BH3 · pyridine
2. HCl, C2H5OH
HO
NH
S
CH3
2-[1-(hydroxyimino)-ethyl]benzo[b]-thiophene (II)
N-[1-(benzo[b]thien-2-yl)ethyl]hydroxyl-amine (III)
III
H3C—Si—NCO, dioxane
CH3
CH3
or COCl2, toluene, HCl, NH3
trimethylsilyl isocyanate (IV)
HO
NH2
N
O
CH3
Zileuton

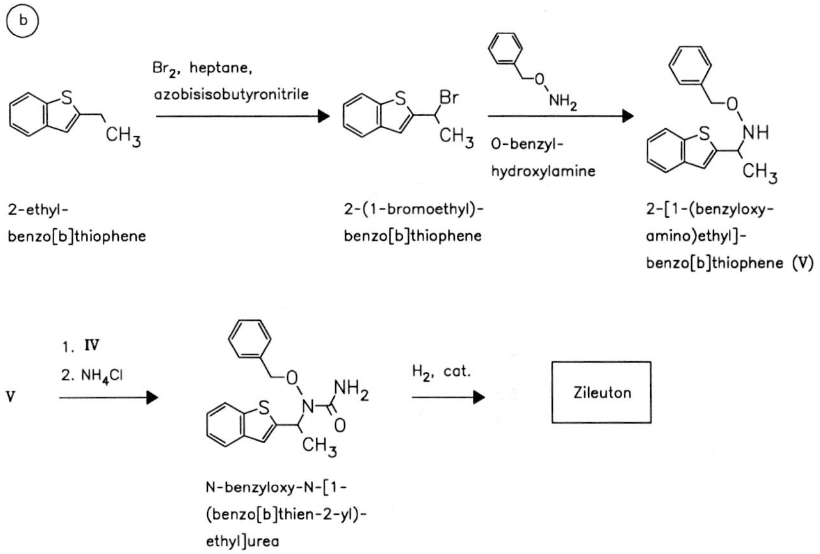
b
S
CH3
Br2, heptane,
azobisisobutyronitrile
Br
CH3
O
NH2
O-benzyl-
hydroxylamine
O
NH
CH3
2-ethyl-benzo[b]thiophene
2-(1-bromoethyl)-benzo[b]thiophene
2-[1-(benzyloxy-amino)ethyl]-benzo[b]thiophene (V)
V
1. IV
2. NH4Cl
O
NH2
N
O
CH3
N-benzyloxy-N-[1-(benzo[b]thien-2-yl)-ethyl]urea
H2, cat.
Zileuton

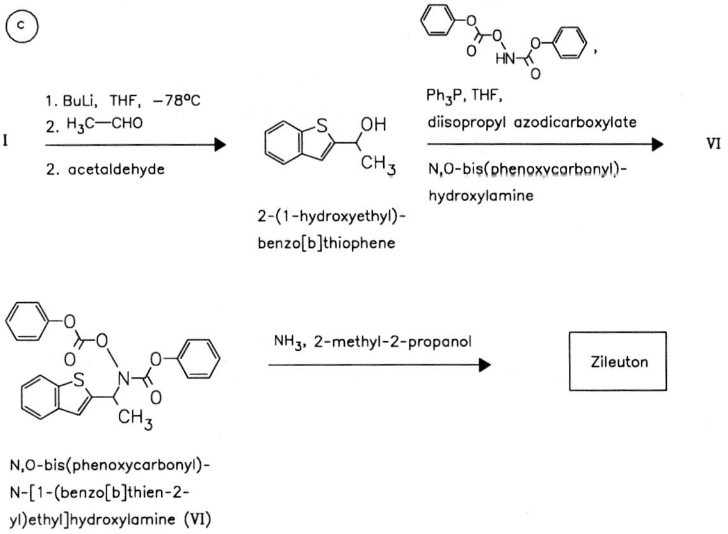
c
I
1. BuLi, THF, −78°C
2. H3C—CHO
2. acetaldehyde
OH
CH3
2-(1-hydroxyethyl)-benzo[b]thiophene
O
O
O
HN
O
O
Ph3P, THF,
diisopropyl azodicarboxylate
N,O-bis(phenoxycarbonyl)-
hydroxylamine
VI
O
O
O
N
O
O
CH3
N,O-bis(phenoxycarbonyl)-N-[1-(benzo[b]thien-2-yl)ethyl]hydroxylamine (VI)
NH3, 2-methyl-2-propanol
Zileuton

Reference(s):
a   EP 279 263 (Abbott Lab.; appl. 1.2.1988; USA-prior. 10.2.1987).
    EP 416 609 (Abbott Lab.; appl. 6.9.1990; USA-prior. 7.9.1989).
    Brooks, C.D. W. et al.: J. Med. Chem. (JMCMAR) **38**, 4768 (1995).
b   EP 589 784 (Elf Sanofi; appl. 21.9.1993; F-prior. 22.9.1992).
c   Stewart, A.O.; Brooks, D.W.: J. Org. Chem. (JOCEAH) **57**, 5020 (1992).

alternative synthesis:
Ku, Y.-Y. et al.: Tetrahedron Lett. (TELEAY) **35** (33), 6017 (1994).

preparation of trimethylsilylisocyanate:
Kijima, J. at al.: Nippon Kagaku Kaishi (NKAKB8) **7**, 1157-60 (1989),
EP 66 232 (Bayer AG; appl. 25.5.1982; D-prior. 3.6.1981).

use as anticancer agent:
WO 9 524 894 (US Dept. Health; appl. 14.3.1995; USA-prior. 14.3.1994).

use for treatment of neurodegenerative diseases:
WO 9 820 864 (Università Brescia; appl. 13.11.1997; I-prior. 13.11.1996).

combinations with COX-2-inhibitors:
WO 9 641 626 (G. D. Searle and Co.; appl. 11.6.1996; USA-prior. 12.6.1995).
WO 9 729 776 (G. D. Searle and Co.; appl. 12.2.1997; USA-prior. 13.2.1996).

Formulation(s):   tabl. 600 mg

Trade Name(s):
USA: Zyflo (Abbott; 1997)

Zimeldine

(Zimelidine)

ATC: N06AB02
Use: antidepressant

RN: 56775-88-3   MF: $C_{16}H_{17}BrN_2$ MW: 317.23
LD_{50}:   60 mg/kg (M, i.v.); 800 mg/kg (M, p.o.);
       50 mg/kg (R, i.v.); 900 mg/kg (R, p.o.)
CN: (Z)-3-(4-bromophenyl)-N,N-dimethyl-3-(3-pyridinyl)-2-propen-1-amine

dihydrochloride monohydrate
RN: 61129-30-4   MF: $C_{16}H_{17}BrN_2 \cdot 2HCl \cdot H_2O$ MW: 408.17
dihydrochloride
RN: 60525-15-7   MF: $C_{16}H_{17}BrN_2 \cdot 2HCl$ MW: 390.15

4'-bromo-   dimethyl-   3-dimethylamino-
acetophenone   amine   4'-bromopropio-
                                      phenone

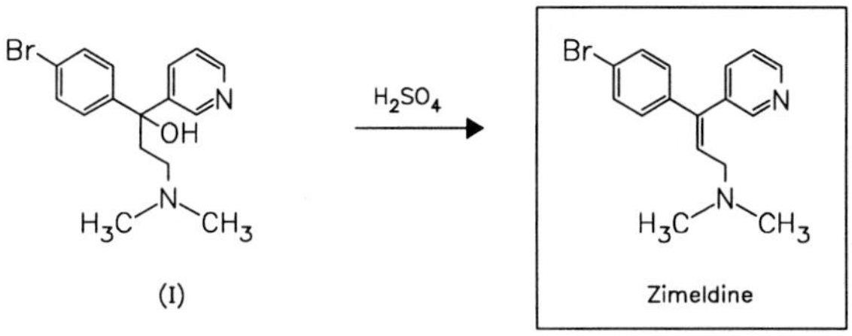

(I)   Zimeldine

Reference(s):
FR 2 134 379 (AB Hässle; appl. 12.4.1972; S-prior. 28.4.1971).

alternative syntheses:
BE 835 802 (Astra; appl. 21.11.1975; S-prior. 21.11.1974).
SU 650 501 (Pharmastra; appl. 21.5.1976).

Formulation(s):   100 mg, 200 mg (as dihydrochloride)

Trade Name(s):
D: Normud (Astra); wfm   GB: Zelmid (Astra); wfm

Zipeprol

ATC: R05DB15
Use: antitussive

RN: 34758-83-3   MF: $C_{23}H_{32}N_2O_3$ MW: 384.52   EINECS: 252-191-7
CN: 4-(2-methoxy-2-phenylethyl)-α-(methoxyphenylmethyl)-1-piperazineethanol

dihydrochloride
RN: 34758-84-4   MF: $C_{23}H_{32}N_2O_3 \cdot 2HCl$ MW: 457.44   EINECS: 252-192-2
LD$_{50}$:   44.3 mg/kg (M, i.v.); 300 mg/kg (M, p.o.);
       32.7 mg/kg (R, i.v.); 435 mg/kg (R, p.o.);
       228 mg/kg (dog, p.o.)

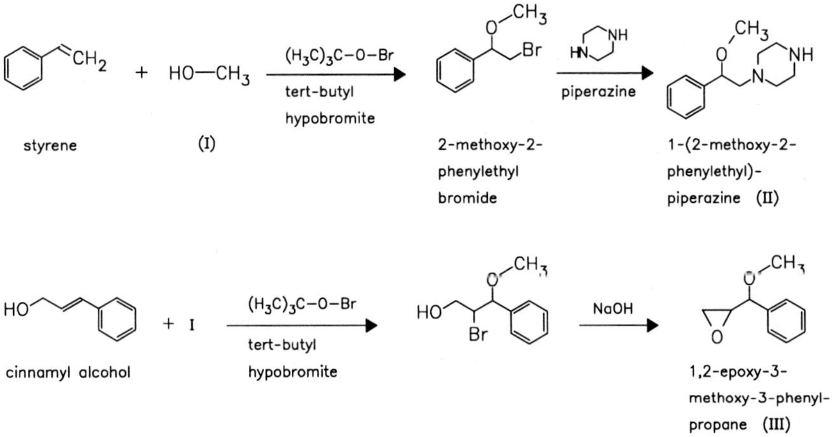

styrene   (I)   2-methoxy-2-
                  phenylethyl
                  bromide   1-(2-methoxy-2-
                                 phenylethyl)-
                                 piperazine (II)

cinnamyl alcohol   + I   1,2-epoxy-3-
                              methoxy-3-phenyl-
                              propane (III)

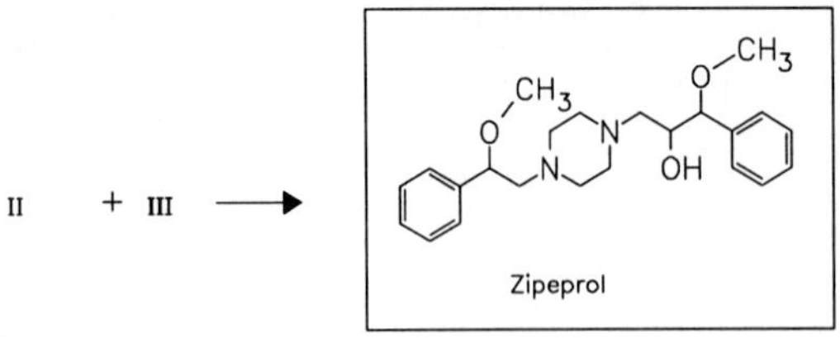

II + III ⟶

Zipeprol

Reference(s):
US 3 718 650 (Mauvernay; 27.2.1973; F-prior. 2.3.1970).
DE 2 109 366 (CERM; appl. 30.9.1971; prior. 27.2.1971).

Formulation(s):   drg. 75 mg; syrup 0.5 % (as dihydrochloride)

Trade Name(s):
F: Respilène (Winthrop; 1973)   I: Zitoxil (Italfarmaco; 1979)

Ziprasidone hydrochloride
(CP-88059-1)

Use: antipsychotic, dopamine D_2-antagonist, 5-HT_2-antagonist

RN: 138982-67-9   MF: $C_{21}H_{21}ClN_4OS \cdot HCl \cdot H_2O$ MW: 467.42
CN: 5-[2-[4-(1,2-Benzisothiazol-3-yl)-1-piperazinyl]ethyl]-6-chloro-1,3-dihydro-2H-indol-2-one hydrochloride hydrate

base
RN: 146939-27-7   MF: $C_{21}H_{21}ClN_4OS$ MW: 412.95
hydrochloride
RN: 122883-93-6   MF: $C_{21}H_{21}ClN_4OS \cdot HCl$ MW: 449.41
mesylate
RN: 185021-64-1   MF: $C_{21}H_{21}ClN_4OS \cdot CH_4O_3S$ MW: 509.05

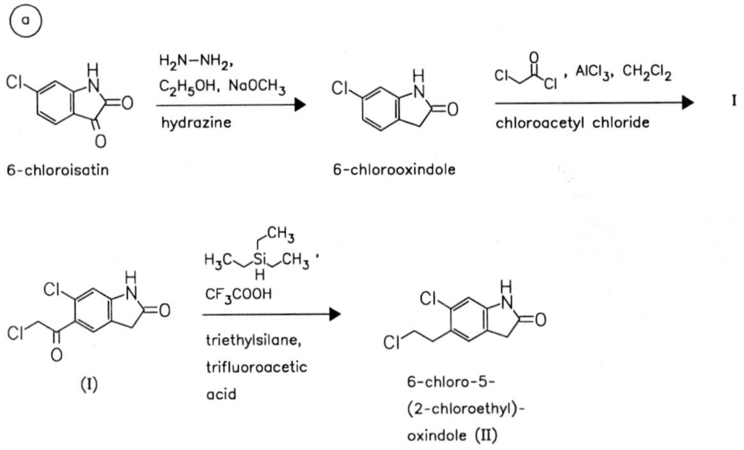

6-chloroisatin

hydrazine

6-chlorooxindole

chloroacetyl chloride

I

triethylsilane, trifluoroacetic acid

(I)

6-chloro-5-(2-chloroethyl)-oxindole (II)

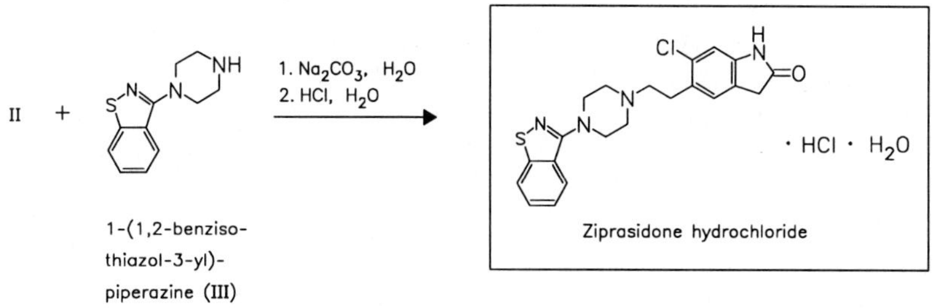

II + 1-(1,2-benziso-thiazol-3-yl)-piperazine (III)

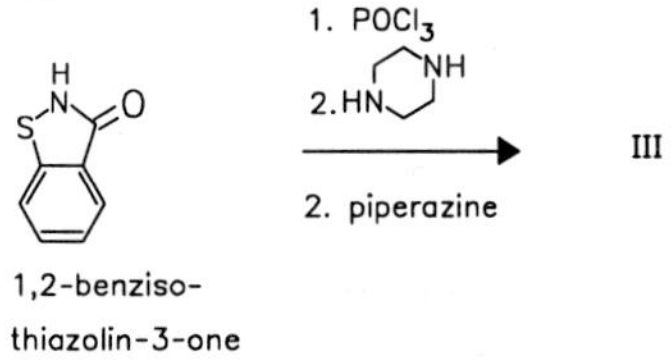

1. Na$_2$CO$_3$, H$_2$O
2. HCl, H$_2$O

Ziprasidone hydrochloride · HCl · H$_2$O

(aa)

1,2-benziso-thiazolin-3-one

1. POCl$_3$
2. HN—piperazine
2. piperazine

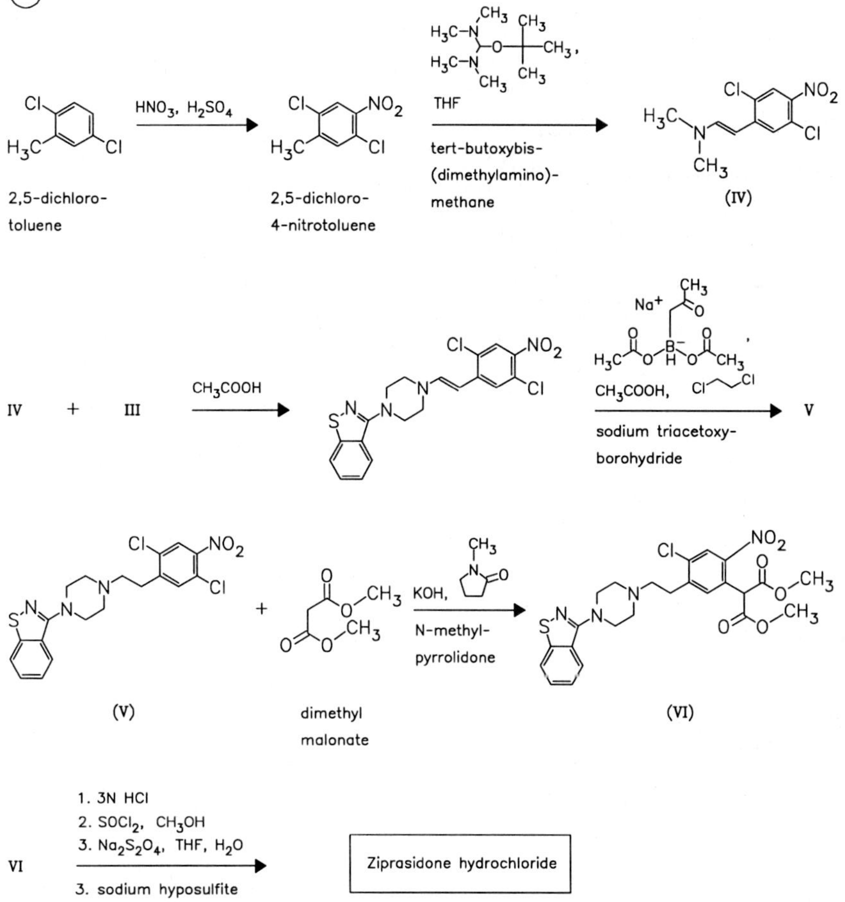

III

(b)

2,5-dichloro-toluene

HNO$_3$, H$_2$SO$_4$

2,5-dichloro-4-nitrotoluene

THF

tert-butoxybis-(dimethylamino)-methane

(IV)

IV + III

CH$_3$COOH

CH$_3$COOH, sodium triacetoxy-borohydride

V

(V) + dimethyl malonate

KOH, N-methyl-pyrrolidone

(VI)

VI

1. 3N HCl
2. SOCl$_2$, CH$_3$OH
3. Na$_2$S$_2$O$_4$, THF, H$_2$O
3. sodium hyposulfite

Ziprasidone hydrochloride

Reference(s):
a Howard, H.R. et al.: J. Labelled Compd. Radiopharm. (JLCRD4), **1994**, 51.
US 5 206 366 (Pfizer; 27.4.1993; USA-prior. 26.8.1992).
EP 281 309 (Pfizer; appl. 24.2.1988; WO-prior. 2.3.1987).
b Urban, F.J. et al: Synth. Commun. (SYNCAV) **26** (8), 1629-1638 (1996).
US 5 359 068 (Pfizer; 25.10.1994; USA-prior. 28.6.1993).

monohydrate:
EP 586 191 (Pfizer; appl. 25.8.1993; USA-prior. 1.9.1992).

mesylate dihydrate salts:
WO 9 742 191 (Pfizer; appl. 10.4.1997; USA-prior. 7.5.1996).

cyclodextrin inclusion complexes:
EP 811 386 (Pfizer; appl. 24.4.1997; USA-prior. 7.5.1996).

Formulation(s): cps. 20 mg, 40 mg, 60 mg, 80 mg

Trade Name(s):
USA: Zeldox (Pfizer)

Zolimidine

ATC: A02BX10
Use: ulcer therapeutic

RN: 1222-57-7 MF: $C_{14}H_{12}N_2O_2S$ MW: 272.33 EINECS: 214-947-4
LD_{50}: >4 g/kg (M, p.o.);
3710 mg/kg (R, p.o.)
CN: 2-[4-(methylsulfonyl)phenyl]imidazo[1,2-a]pyridine

2-amino-   2-bromo-4'-methyl-   Zolimidine
pyridine   sulfonylacetophenone

Reference(s):
GB 991 589 (Lab. Bioterapico Milanese Selvi; valid from 23.7.1963; I-prior. 30.4.1963).
Almirante, L. et al.: J. Med. Chem. (JMCMAR) **8**, 305 (1965).

Formulation(s): cps. 200 mg

Trade Name(s):
I: Solimidin (Selvi); wfm   USA: Mutil (Lakeside); wfm

Zolmitriptan
(311C90; BW-311C90)

ATC: N02CC03
Use: antimigraine agent, 5-HT$_1$D-agonist

RN: 139264-17-8 MF: $C_{16}H_{21}N_3O_2$ MW: 287.36
CN: (S)-4-[[3-[2-(dimethylamino)ethyl]-1H-indol-5-yl]methyl]-2-oxazolidinone

monohydrochloride
RN: 139264-19-0 MF: $C_{16}H_{21}N_3O_2 \cdot HCl$ MW: 323.82
racemic monohydrochloride
RN: 139346-15-9 MF: $C_{16}H_{21}N_3O_2 \cdot HCl$ MW: 323.82

synthesis of intermediate III:

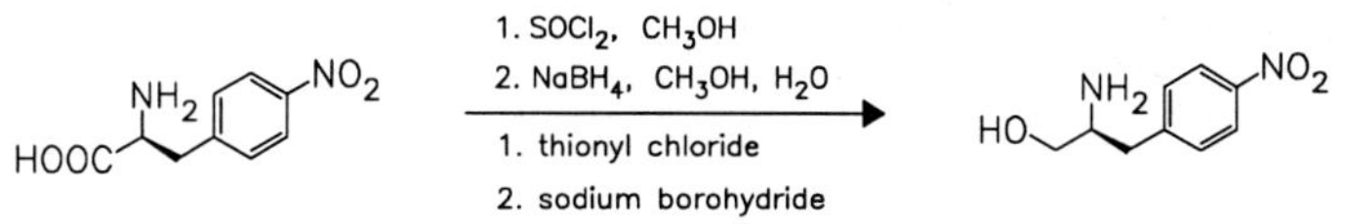

4-nitro-L-phenyl-
alanine (I)

1. SOCl$_2$, CH$_3$OH
2. NaBH$_4$, CH$_3$OH, H$_2$O

1. thionyl chloride
2. sodium borohydride

(S)-2-amino-3-
(4-nitrophenyl)-
1-propanol (II)

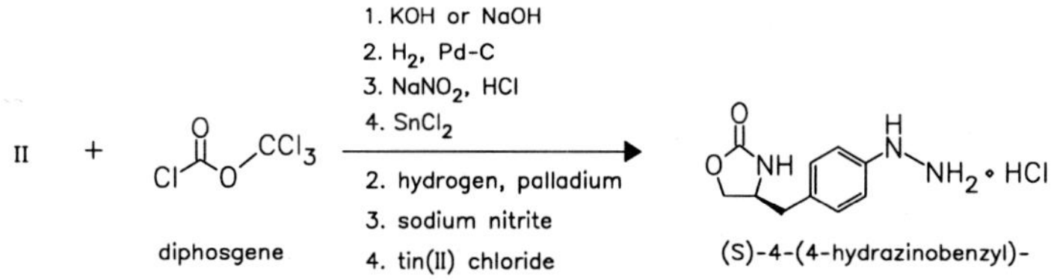

II + diphosgene

1. KOH or NaOH
2. H$_2$, Pd-C
3. NaNO$_2$, HCl
4. SnCl$_2$

2. hydrogen, palladium
3. sodium nitrite
4. tin(II) chloride

(S)-4-(4-hydrazinobenzyl)-
2-oxazolidinone
hydrochloride (III)

or:

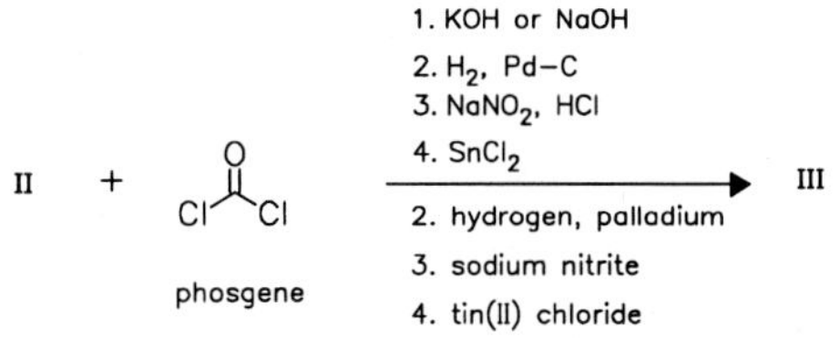

II + phosgene

1. KOH or NaOH
2. H$_2$, Pd-C
3. NaNO$_2$, HCl
4. SnCl$_2$

2. hydrogen, palladium
3. sodium nitrite
4. tin(II) chloride

III

synthesis of intermediate V:

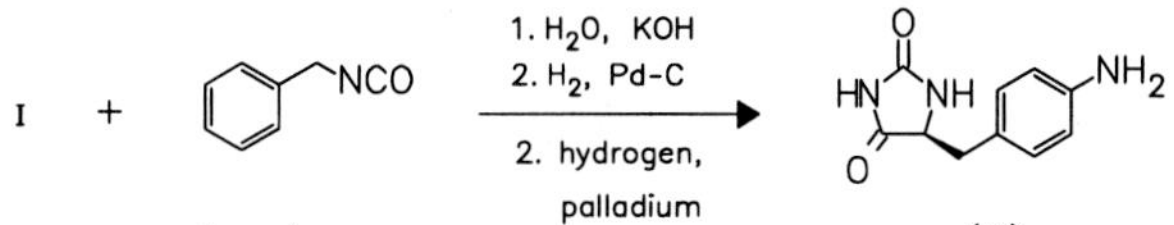

I + benzyl
isocyanate

1. H$_2$O, KOH
2. H$_2$, Pd-C

2. hydrogen,
palladium

(IV)

IV

1. NaNO$_2$, HCl
2. SnCl$_2$

1. sodium nitrite
2. tin(II) chloride

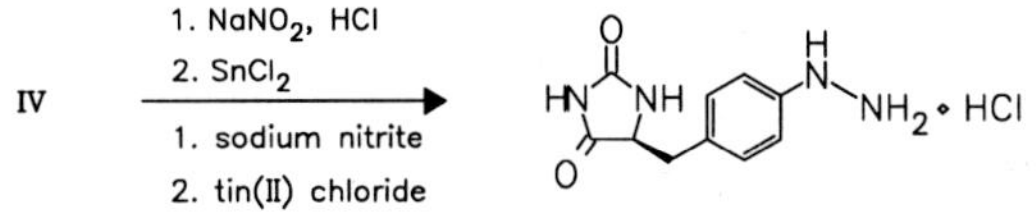

(S)-5-(4-hydrazinobenzyl)-
2,4-imidazolidinedione
hydrochloride (V)

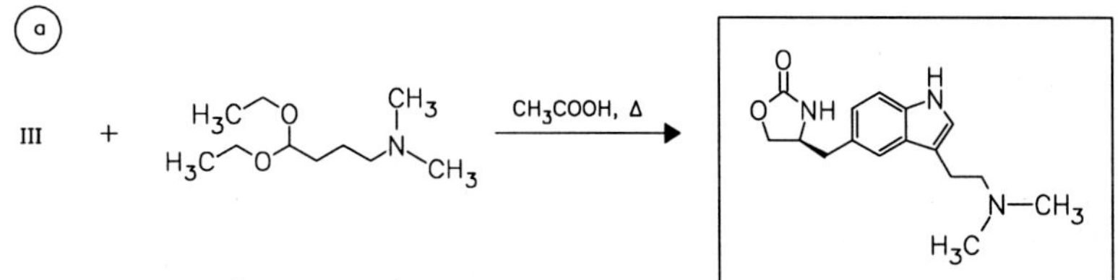

(a)

III + 4-(dimethylamino)-
butanal diethyl
acetal (VI)

CH$_3$COOH, Δ

Zolmitriptan

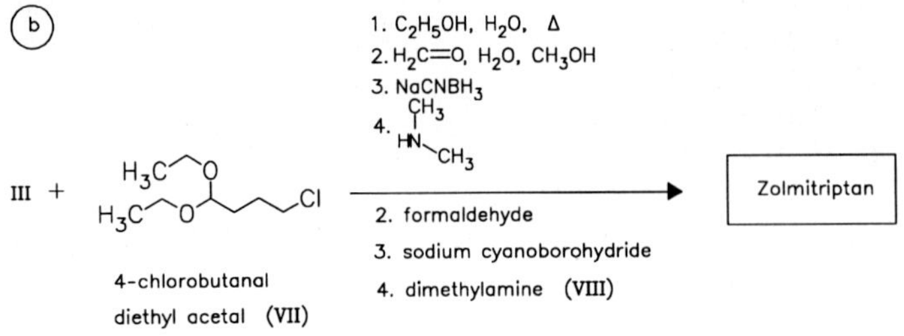

b

1. C_2H_5OH, H_2O, Δ
2. $H_2C=O$, H_2O, CH_3OH
3. $NaCNBH_3$
4.

III +

4-chlorobutanal
diethyl acetal (VII)

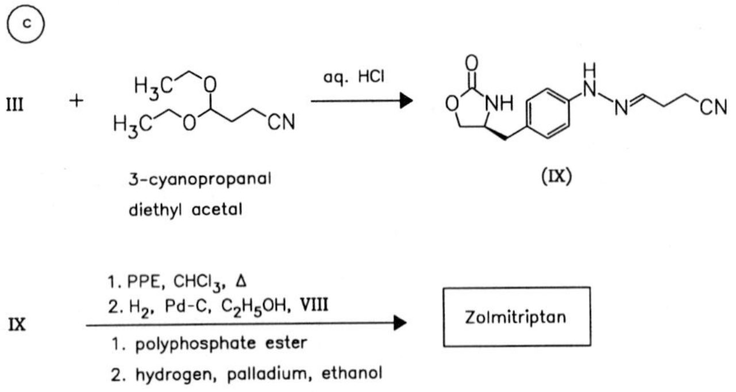

2. formaldehyde

3. sodium cyanoborohydride

4. dimethylamine (VIII)

Zolmitriptan

c

III +

aq. HCl

3-cyanopropanal
diethyl acetal

(IX)

1. PPE, $CHCl_3$, Δ
2. H_2, Pd-C, C_2H_5OH, VIII

IX

1. polyphosphate ester

2. hydrogen, palladium, ethanol

Zolmitriptan

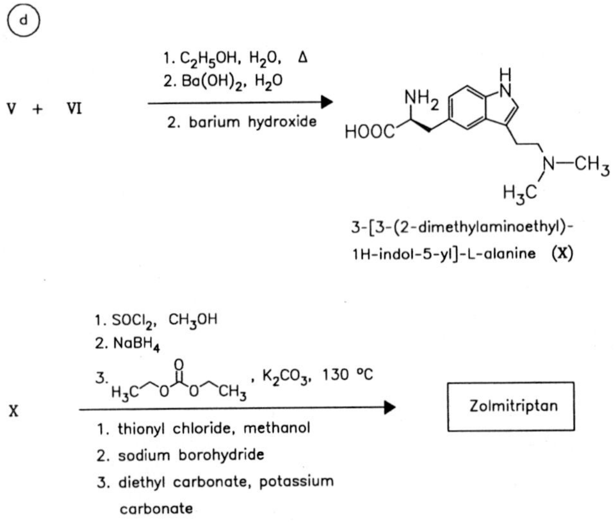

d

1. C_2H_5OH, H_2O, Δ
2. $Ba(OH)_2$, H_2O

V + VI

2. barium hydroxide

3-[3-(2-dimethylaminoethyl)-
1H-indol-5-yl]-L-alanine (X)

1. $SOCl_2$, CH_3OH
2. $NaBH_4$

3.   , K_2CO_3, 130 °C

X

1. thionyl chloride, methanol

2. sodium borohydride

3. diethyl carbonate, potassium
carbonate

Zolmitriptan

alternative synthesis of X:

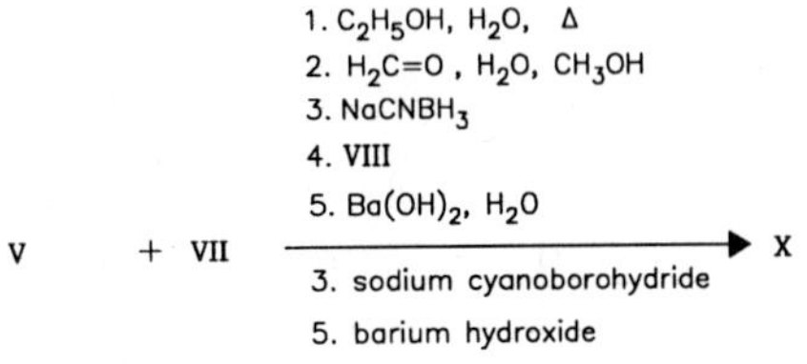

1. C_2H_5OH, H_2O, Δ
2. $H_2C=O$, H_2O, CH_3OH
3. $NaCNBH_3$
4. VIII
5. $Ba(OH)_2$, H_2O

V   + VII

3. sodium cyanoborohydride

5. barium hydroxide

X

Reference(s):
WO 9 118 897 (The Wellcome Foundation; appl. 12.12.1991; GB-prior. 7.6.1990, 1.2.1991).
Glenn, R.C. et al.: J. Med. Chem. (JMCMAR) **38**, 3566 (1995).

synthesis of 4-dimethylaminobutanal diethyl acetal:
Desaty, K.: Croat. Chem. Acta (CCACAA) **36**, 103, 107 (1964).
Somin, I.N. et al.: J. Org. Chem. (JOCEAH) **1**, 2011 (1965).
Bhattacharyya, S.: Tetrahedron Lett. (TELEAY) **35** (15), 2401 (1994).
Harries et al.: Justus Liebigs Ann. Chem. (JLACBF) **410**, 65 (1915).

synthesis of 4-chlorobutanal diethyl acetal:
Loftfield: J. Am. Chem. Soc. (JACSAT) **73**, 1365 (1951).
Anet et al.: Aust. J. Sci. Res. Ser. A (AJSRA2) **3**, 336 (1950).
Winterfeld et al.: Arch. Pharm. Ber. Dtsch. Pharm. Ges. (APBDAJ) **293**, 325 (1960).
Tamelen, Van et al.: Bioorg. Chem. (BOCMBM) **5**, 283 (1976).

Formulation(s):   f. c. tabl. 2.5 mg; tabl. 2.5 mg

Trade Name(s):
D: Asco Top (Zeneca)   GB: Zomig (Zeneca)

Zolpidem

(SL-80-0750-23N)

ATC: N05CF02
Use: hypnotic with affinity to
benzodiazepine receptor

RN: 82626-48-0   MF: $C_{19}H_{21}N_3O$ MW: 307.40
CN: *N,N*,6-trimethyl-2-(4-methylphenyl)imidazo[1,2-*a*]pyridine-3-acetamide

tartrate (2:1)
RN: 99294-93-6   MF: $C_{19}H_{21}N_3O \cdot 1/2C_4H_6O_6$ MW: 764.88
LD_{50}:   695 mg/kg (M, p.o.);
2700 mg/kg (R, p.o.)
tartrate (1:1)
RN: 103188-50-7   MF: $C_{19}H_{21}N_3O \cdot C_4H_6O_6$ MW: 457.48

2-amino-5-
methylpyridine

bromomethyl
4-methylphenyl
ketone

2-(4-methylphenyl)-6-
methylimidazo[1,2-a]-
pyridine (I)

dimethyl-
amine (II)

(III)

1. CH₃I
2. NaCN

1. methyl iodide
2. sodium cyanide

2-(4-methylphenyl)-6-methyl-
imidazo[1,2-a]pyridine-
3-acetonitrile (III)

1. HCl, CH₃COOH
2. POCl₃
3. II

2. phosphoryl
chloride

Zolpidem

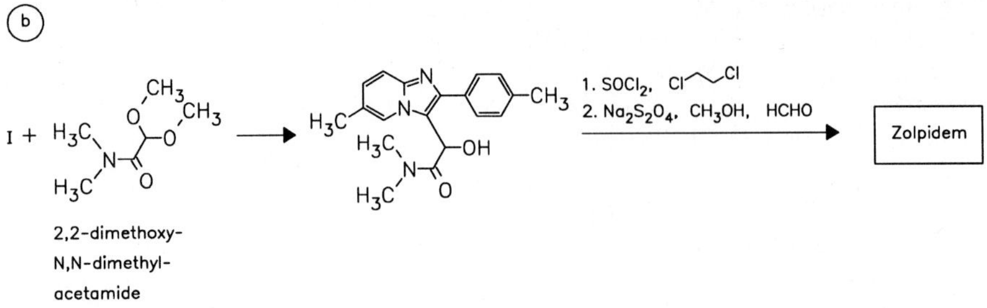

ⓑ

I + 2,2-dimethoxy-
N,N-dimethyl-
acetamide

1. SOCl₂, ClCH₂CH₂Cl
2. Na₂S₂O₄, CH₃OH, HCHO

Zolpidem

Reference(s):

a   EP 50 563 (Synthelabo; appl. 15.10.1981; F-prior. 22.10.1980).
      DE 3 163 524 (Synthelabo; appl. 15.10.1981; F-prior. 22.10.1980).
b   EP 251 859 (Synthelabo; appl. 17.6.1987; F-prior. 27.6.1986).

2,2-dimethoxy-*N,N*-dimethylacetamide:
US 3 361 757 (Du Pont; 15.11.1965).

Formulation(s):   f. c. tabl. 10 mg; tabl. 5 mg, 10 mg (as tartrate)

Trade Name(s):

D: Bikalm (Byk Gulden)		Stilnox (Synthélabo; 1988)	Stilnox (Synthelabo; 1990)
Stilnox (Synthelabo)	GB: Stilnoct (Lorex)	J: Myslee (Fujisawa)
F: Ivadal (Cipharm)	I: Niotal (Synthelabo)	USA: Ambien (Searle)

Zomepirac

ATC: M01AB04
Use: analgesic, anti-inflammatory

RN: 33369-31-2   MF: $C_{15}H_{14}ClNO_3$ MW: 291.73   EINECS: 251-474-2
CN: 5-(4-chlorobenzoyl)-1,4-dimethyl-1*H*-pyrrole-2-acetic acid

sodium salt dihydrate
RN: 64092-49-5   MF: $C_{15}H_{13}ClNNaO_3 \cdot 2H_2O$ MW: 349.75

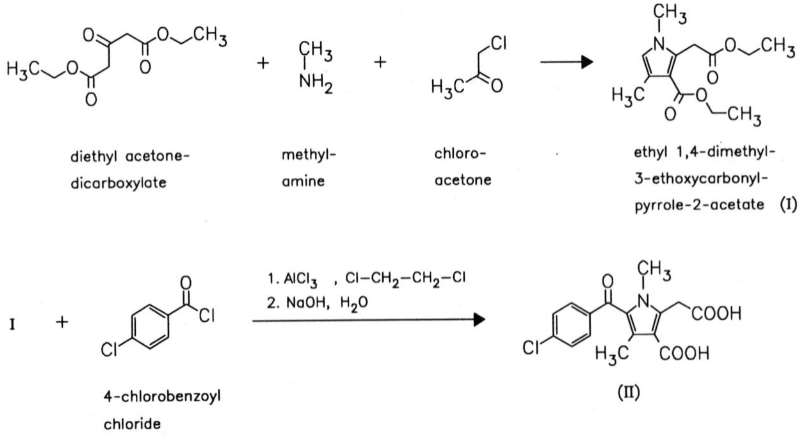

diethyl acetone-
dicarboxylate

+ methyl-
amine

+ chloro-
acetone

→ ethyl 1,4-dimethyl-
3-ethoxycarbonyl-
pyrrole-2-acetate   (I)

I +   4-chlorobenzoyl
chloride

1. AlCl₃ , Cl–CH₂–CH₂–Cl
2. NaOH, H₂O

(II)

Zomepirac

Reference(s):
DE 2 102 746 (McNeil; appl. 21.1.1971; USA-prior. 26.1.1970).
US 3 952 012 (McNeil; 20.4.1976; prior. 16.2.1973, 26.1.1970, 1.7.1968, 26.7.1967).
Carson, J.R.; Wong, S.: J. Med. Chem. (JMCMAR) **16**, 172 (1973).

alternative syntheses:
BE 762 060 (McNeil; appl. 26.1.1971; USA-prior. 26.1.1970).
DOS 2 339 140 (McNeil; appl. 2.8.1973; USA-prior. 3.8.1972).
US 3 865 840 (McNeil; 11.2.1975; prior. 16.2.1973, 26.7.1967, 1.7.1968, 26.1.1970).

Formulation(s):   tabl. 100 mg (as sodium salt dihydrate)

Trade Name(s):
D: Zomax (Cilag); wfm   F: Zomax (Cilag); wfm   USA: Zomax (McNeil); wfm

Zonisamide

(AD-810)

ATC: N03AA
Use: anticonvulsant, antiepileptic

RN: 68291-97-4   MF: $C_8H_8N_2O_3S$ MW: 212.23
LD$_{50}$:   699 mg/kg (M, i.p.); 816 mg/kg (M, i.v.); 1829 mg/kg (M, p.o.); 1009 mg/kg (M, s.c.);
        733 mg/kg (R, i.p.); 672 mg/kg (R, i.v.); 1992 mg/kg (R, p.o.); 925 mg/kg (R, s.c.);
        1 g/kg (dog, p.o.)
CN: 1,2-benzisoxazole-3-methanesulfonamide

monosodium salt
RN: 68291-98-5   MF: $C_8H_7N_2NaO_3S$ MW: 234.21

4-hydroxy-
coumarin

1,2-benzisoxazole-
3-acetic acid

3-bromomethyl-
1,2-benzisoxazole   (I)

sodium 1,2-benz-
isoxazole-3-methane-
sulfonate

Zonisamide

Reference(s):
DE 2 825 410 (Dainippon; appl. 9.6.1978).
US 4 172 896 (Dainippon; 30.10.1979; appl. 5.6.1978).
Uno, H. et al.: J. Med. Chem. (JMCMAR) **22**, 180 (1979).

synthesis of 3-bromomethyl-1,2-benzisoxazole:
Uno, H. et al.: Chem. Pharm. Bull. (CPBTAL) **24**, 632 (1976).
Giannella, M. et al.: Chim. Ther. (CHTPBA) **7**, 127 (1972).

oral formulation:
JP 63 150 220 (Dainippon; appl. 15.12.1986).

alternative synthesis:
Mohareb, R.M. et al.: Z. Naturforsch., B: Chem. Sci. (ZNBSEN) **45**, 1067 (1990).

Formulation(s):   powder 200 mg/g; tabl. 100 mg

Trade Name(s):
J: Excegran (Dainippon;
        1990)

Zopiclone
(RP-27267)

ATC: N05BX; N05CF01
Use: anxiolytic, hypnotic

RN: 43200-80-2   MF: $C_{17}H_{17}ClN_6O_3$ MW: 388.82   EINECS: 256-138-9
LD_{50}:   580 mg/kg (M, i.p.); 321 mg/kg (M, i.v.); 2174 mg/kg (M, p.o.);
        280 mg/kg (R, i.v.); 827 mg/kg (R, p.o.);
        400 mg/kg (dog, i.v.); 2500 mg/kg (dog, p.o.)
CN: 4-methyl-1-piperazinecarboxylic acid 6-(5-chloro-2-pyridinyl)-6,7-dihydro-7-oxo-5*H*-pyrrolo[3,4-
       b]pyrazin-5-yl ester

pyrazine-2,3-   2-amino-5-   3-(5-chloropyrid-2-yl-   6-(5-chloropyrid-2-yl)-
dicarboxylic   chloropyridine   carbamoyl)pyrazine-2-   5,7-dioxo-6,7-dihydro-
anhydride   carboxylic acid   5H-pyrrolo[3,4-b]pyrazine   (I)

Zopiclone

Reference(s):
DOS 2 300 491 (Rhône-Poulenc; appl. 5.1.1973; F-prior. 7.1.1972, 9.9.1972).
US 3 862 149 (Rhône-Poulenc; 21.1.1975; F-prior. 7.1.1972, 9.9.1972).

Formulation(s):   f. c. tabl. 7.5 mg

Trade Name(s):
D: Ximovan (Rhône-Poulenc   GB: Zimovane (Rhône-Poulenc   J: Amoban (Rhône-Poulenc-
        Rorer; 1991)   Rorer)   Chugai)
F: Imovane (Specia Groupe   I: Imovane (Rhône-Poulenc
        Rhône-Poulenc Rorer)   Rorer; 1989)

Zorubicin

ATC: L01DB05
Use: antineoplastic

RN: 54083-22-6   MF: $C_{34}H_{35}N_3O_{10}$ MW: 645.67
LD$_{50}$:   35 mg/kg (M, route unreported)
CN: (2S-cis)-benzoic acid [1-[4-[(3-amino-2,3,6-trideoxy-α-L-lyxo-hexopyranosyl)oxy]-1,2,3,4,6,11-hexahydro-2,5,12-trihydroxy-7-methoxy-6,11-dioxo-2-naphthacenyl]ethylidene]hydrazide

monohydrochloride
RN: 36508-71-1   MF: $C_{34}H_{35}N_3O_{10} \cdot HCl$ MW: 682.13   EINECS: 253-076-4
LD$_{50}$:   28.71 mg/kg (M, i.p.)

daunorubicin   benzoyl-   Zorubicin
(q. v.)   hydrazine

Reference(s):
DOS 2 327 211 (Rhône-Poulenc; appl. 28.5.1973).

Formulation(s):   amp. 52.8 mg (as hydrochloride)

Trade Name(s):
D: Zorubicin R. P. (Rhône-   F: Rubidazone (Rhône-
     Poulenc); wfm   Poulenc); wfm

Zotepine

ATC: N05AK
Use: neuroleptic

RN: 26615-21-4   MF: $C_{18}H_{18}ClNOS$ MW: 331.87
LD$_{50}$:   43.3 mg/kg (M, i.v.); 108 mg/kg (M, p.o.);
        36.8 mg/kg (R, i.v.); 306 mg/kg (R, p.o.);
        26.6 mg/kg (dog, i.v.); >1 g/kg (dog, p.o.)
CN: 2-[(8-chlorodibenzo[b,f]thiepin-10-yl)oxy]-N,N-dimethylethanamine

4-chloro-   2'-chloro-
thiophenol   acetophenone

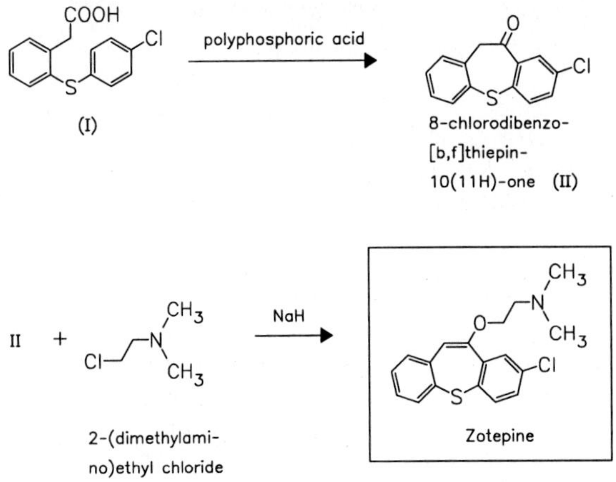
COOH
Cl
S
(I)
polyphosphoric acid
O
Cl
S
8-chlorodibenzo-
[b,f]thiepin-
10(11H)-one (II)
II +
CH3
N
Cl
CH3
2-(dimethylami-
no)ethyl chloride
NaH
CH3
O
N
CH3
Cl
S
Zotepine

Reference(s):

US 3 704 245 (Fujisawa; 28.11.1972; J-prior. 16.2.1968).
DOS 1 907 670 (Fujisawa; appl. 15.2.1969; J-prior. 16.2.1968).
GB 1 247 067 (Fujisawa; appl. 13.2.1969; J-prior. 16.2.1968).
Ueda, I. et al.: Chem. Pharm. Bull. (CPBTAL) **26**, 3058 (1978).

Formulation(s): drg. 25 mg, 50 mg, 100 mg

Trade Name(s):

D: Nipolept (Rhône-Poulenc Rorer)
J: Lodopin (Fujisawa; 1982)

A

A 313 1806
Aarane 551
Abacin 1931, 2119
Abaprim 2119
Abasin 8
Abbokinase 2152
Abboticine 772, 775
Abbsa 2075
Abcid 1922
Abedine 358
Abeformin T 2069
Abelcet 109
Abelect Injection 109
Abemide 446
Abérel 2094
Abetol 656, 1133
Abicol 1802
Abidec 767, 1806, 1809
Abilit 1945
Abiocine 651
Abiostil 434
Abirol 1272
Abmederm 210
ABOB 1367
Aboryl 1367
Abovis 35
Absorber HFV 666
AB-Vancomycin 2159
Acabel 239, 1193
Ac Acsal 29
Acadione 2051
Acardi 1638
Acarosan 215
ACC 22
Accenon 803
Accent 945
Accolate 2190
Accroibile 466
Accupaque 1085
Accupril 1772
Accuprin 1772
Accupro 1772
Accuretic 1020
Accusite 753, 898
Accutane 1111
Accuzide 1772
Ace 1292
Acecol 1984
Acecor 7
Acedicon 2007
Acediur 337, 1020
Acef 379
Ace-Line 1086
Acemin 446
Acemix 13

Acemuc 22
Aceon 1601
Aceplus 337, 1020
Acepress 337
Acepreval 1701
Acepril 337
Acequide 1020
Acequin 1772
Acerbon 1178
Acercomp 1178
Aces 221
ACES 1806
Acesal 29
ACES Antioxidant Soft
  Gels 138
Acesistem 1020
Ac Etacr 789
Acetamol 1558
Acetamox 16
Acetanol 7
Acetein 22
Acetylcholine 21
Achless 880
Achletin 2104
Achromycin 2002
Acidrine 1380
Acidylina 138
Acifugan 206
Aci-jel 1541
Acinon 1456
Acipem 1648
Aciphex 1779
Aciril 1041
Aciviran 33
Aclacinomycine 35
Aclacinon 35
Aclaplastin 35
Aclosone 51
Aclovate 51
Acneline 1342
Acnestrol 275, 1006
Acnezide 211
Acnidazil 211, 1327
Acnisal 1852
ACNU 50 1447
Acoin 2001
Acrizeal 1624
Actamin B$_{12}$ 555
Actavix 540
Acthiol J. 1220
Acticarbine 1557
Actidil 2124
Actidose 1886
Actifed 616, 678, 2124
Actifed Compound 616
Actifed Compound Linctus
  616

Actifed Jour et unit 678
Actifed Nasale 1533
Actigall 2153
Actimide 540
Actinac 64, 1024
Actino-Hermal Pflaster 898
Actiol 1220
Actiphan 1620
Actirin 1512
Actitonic 2140
Activir 33
Actocin 278
Actol 1436
Actonel 1819
Actos 1644
Actosolv 2152
Actosolv urokinase 2152
Actron 29
Acucillin 111, 536
Acuilix 1020, 1772
Acuitel 1772
Acular 1128
Acupan 1414
Acuprin 29
Acutil Fosforo 1757
Acygoxine 26
Acylanid 24
Acyvir 33
Aczen NS 1110
Adalat 1434
Adalate 1434
Adalgur 966
Adalin 349
Adancor 1430
Adcal 341
Adcortin 993
Adcortyl 2098
Addisomnol 349
Adedolon 341
Adefuronic 630
Adelfan 647
Adelphan-Esidrix 647, 1802
Ademide 540
Adenaron 341
Adenobeta 540
Adenolanat 1582
Adenoplex 540, 1757
Adenopurin Herbrand 1582
Adenovit 540
Adepal 798, 1171, 1468
Adepril 97
Aderman 1624
Aderoxin 1757
Adesipress 523
Adestan 1101
Adiazine 1921

Adiboran 542
Adiclair 1476
Adifax 612
Adinepar 928
Adipex-P 1622
Adisterolo 1806
Adiuvant 136
Adizem XL 660
Adlone 824
Adnamin 341
Adobacillin 111
Adobiol 284
Adomal 642
Adona 341
Adonamin 341
Adopilon 1912
Adopon 329
Adorm 557
Adorzon 341
Adostill-AC 341
Adozon 341
AD Pabyrn 1806
Adramycin 1269
Adrechros 341
Adremycin 435
Adrenal 753
Adrenalin 1:1000
  JENAPHARMA 753
Adrenalina Ism 753
Adrenalin Medihaler 753
Adrénalone Tétracaine
  Guillon 44
Adrenam 809
Adrenosem 341
Adrénoxyl 341
Adrenoxyl 341
Adrevil 298
Adrezon 341
Adriacin 717
Adriamycin 717
Adriblastin 717
Adriblastina 717
Adriblastine 717
Adrifane 317
Adrimedac 717
Adrin 291
Adrocaine 1712
Adronat 54
Adroyd 1534
Adumbran 1514
Advantan 1301
Adversuten 1691
Advil 1040
Adyston 1628
Aegrosan 666
Aequamen 222
Aequiton 299

Aloxidil 1343
Alpamed 1897
Alpermell 606
Alphacaïne 361
Alpha-Chymocutan 458
Alpha-Chymotrase 458
Alphachymotrypsine
  Choay 458
Alphacutanée 458
Alpha-Depressan 2151
Alphadione 58
Alphadrol 910
Alphagan 260
Alphakinase 2152
Alpha-Lipon Stada 2020
alpha-Vibolex 2020
Alphosyl 65
Alphosyle 65
Alpicort F 781
Alpress LP 1691
Alredase 2077
Alrex 1198
Alrheumun 1126
Alsanate 956
Alsogil 1558
Altace 1787
Altaflor 1102
Altat 1843
Althesin 56
Altiazem 660
Altim 548
Altimol 1452
Altocel 1187
Altocillin 1610
Altodor 792
Altosone 1359
Altramet 472
Altsamin 1912
Alupent 269, 1493
Alupir 29
Alurate 133
Alusas 497
Alvedon 1558
Alvercol 76
Al-Vite 543
Alvity 2065
Alvityl 249, 542, 555, 614,
  927, 1809
Alvo 1512
Alvonal MR 1911
Am-73 107
Amadol 2086
Amagesan 107
Amantadin 77
Amarel 970
Amaro lassat. Giuliani 1616
Amaryl 970

Amasulin 364
Ambacamp 172
Ambatrol 1438
Ambaxin 172
Ambene 1623
Ambien 2208
Ambilhar 1449
AmBisome 109
Ambisone 109
Ambodryl 267
Ambramicina 2002
Ambril 79
Ambrocef 376
Amcacid 2089
Amciderm 81
Amcill 111
Amcinil 81
Amedel 1654
Amelizol 2142
Amen 1227
Amenoren 800
Americaine 208
A-methaPred 1302
Amétycine 1347
Amias 330
Amicar 91
Amicasil 89
Amicel 729
Amico 540
Amicos 496
Amidate 816
Amidonal 133
Amiduret 90
Amikacin Sulfate 89
Amikin 89
Amiklin 89
Amilco 90
Amilit-ifi 97
Amindan 1864
Amineurin 97
Amino-Cerv 203, 1078
Aminomal 2012, 2012
Aminophyllin 2012
Aminophylline 2013
Aminophylline Lobica 2012
Aminoxidin 1565
Aminoxin 1757
Aminozim 540
Amiodar 95
Amipaque 1317
Amipenix 111
Amipres 1133
Amipress 656
Amisal 796
Amisalin 1711
Amitolen 2131

Amitript 97
Amlodin 100
Amlor 100
Amminophilline 2012
Amoban 2210
Amobarb 101
Amobronc 80
Amodex 107
Amoflux 107
Amolin 107
Amophar 107
Amoran 107
Amotril 516
Amox 107
Amoxan 105
Amoxi-Diolan 107
Amoxil 107
Amoxillat 107
Amoxina 107
Amoxine 107
Amoxipen 107
Amoxypen 107
Ampamet 128
Ampécyclal 1004
Amphicol 109
Amphocycline 109, 2002
Ampho-Moronal 109
Amphotec for Injection 109
Amphotericin B zur
  Infusion 109
Ampici 111
Ampicillina 111
Ampicilline 111
Ampiclox 111, 536
Ampilisa 111
Ampilux 111
Ampiplus Simplex 111
Amplibac 172
Amplit 1180
Amplital 111
Amplium 536
Ampliuril pH 208
Amplivix 208
Amplizer 111
Amsidine 117
Amsidyl 117
Amteren 2101
A-Mulsin 1806
Amumetazon 606
Amuno 1074
Amycor 245
Amycor onychoset 245
Amygdospray 2001
Amytal 101
Amytal Sodium 101
AN 1 108
Anabact 1318

Anabactyl 342
Anabasi 540
Anabloc 856
Anabolex 122
Anachoc 2123
Anacufen 1280
Anador 1396
Anadrol 1534
Anadur 1396
Anaestecomp 678
Anaesthesin 208
Anafluose 1205, 1935
Anafranil 521
Anagregal 2036
Anahelp 753
Ana-Kit 443
Anakit 753
Analeptone 1587
Analexin 856
Analexin-AF 856
Analgesic 2039
Analip 1554
Analock 754
Analpram-HC 1682
Anamidol 1532
Anan 251
Ananase 267
Anandron 1442
Anapazin 476
Anaphylaxie-Besteck
  Lösung Z.J. 753
Anaplex 443
Anapolon 1534
Anaprel F 1801, 2113
Anaprox 1403
Anasclerol 2175
Anaspasmin 1019
Anastil 983, 984
Anasyth 1900
Anatensol 906
Anatran 2104
Anatropin 118
Anatuss 616
Anauran 1675
Anaus 2115
Anausin Metoclopramide
  1313
Anaxeryl 687
Anaxyl 71
Ancef 379
Ancer 20 1210
Anco 1040
Ancobon 876
Ancofort 993
Ancolan 1218
Ancoloxin 1218
Ancotil 876

Aprinox 193
Aprovel 1096
Apsatan 479
Apsin VK 1619
Apsomol 1851
Apsor 1853, 2094
Apsor pomata 65
Apsor pom. derm. 228
Aptin-Duriles 73
Apurone 883
Aquafor 2187
Aqua Mephyton 1630
Aquamox 1773
Aquamycetin 426
Aquaphor 2187
Aquapred 1697
Aquareduct 1896
Aquasept 2106
Aquasol A 1806
Aquatensen 1293
Aquo B'av 1029
Aquo-Cytobion 1029
Aqupla 1410
ARA-cell 570
Aracytin 570
Aracytine 570
Aralen 439
Aramidol 856
Aramine 1274
Araminon 1274
Araminum 1274
Arane 1799
Arantil 2155
Arasemide 945
Arasena-A 2165
Arava 1149
Arbid 680
Arcasin 1619
Arcobutina 1355
Arco-Lase Plus 152, 1616
Ardefem 783
Ardesyl 1298
Ardeyceryl P 1760
Ardeydystin 1119
Ardeytropin 2140
Arduan 1647
Aredia 1552
Arelix 1663, 1786
Aremans 531
Arensin 826
Arestal 1187
Aresten 1307
Arfen 1041
Argihepar 135
Arginotri-B 1029
Argisone 1025

Argun 1185
Arhémapectine vitaminée 1241
Arhumyl 2010
Arial 1854
Aricept 705
Aricodil 616, 791
Arilin 1318
Arimidex 120
Aristamid 1940
Aristocort 2097, 2098
Aristocorte 2099
Aristospan 2100
Arithmin 129
Aritmina 45
Arkin 2164
Arkin-Z 2164
Arlef 880
Arlevert 479, 662
Arlidin 291
Arlitene 1375
Arminol 1945
Arnilose 1885
Arnipaque 1317
Aroclunin 2133
Arodoc-C 446
Arofuto 45
Aromalgyl 1284
Arovit 1806
Arovit Roche 1806
Arpha 442, 616
Arpha collutoire 15
Arpicolin 1716
Arpimycin 772
Arsacol 2153
Artane 2111
Artaxan 1383
Artegodan 1557
Artehard 516
Arten 2111
Arteoptic 361
Artex 1996
Arthaxan 1383
arthrex 630
arthro akut 1185
Arthrocine 1942
Arthrotec 1346
Artist 365
Artocoron 1387
Artosin 2069
Artotec 1346
Artracin SR 1075
Artrodar 621
Artrodol 642
Artroflog 1537
Artrolasi 1493
Artrosilene 1126

Artrotec 1346
Artroxen 1402
Artroxicam 1668
Arubendol 1851
ARUBENDOL 1992
Aruclonin 523
Arumel 898
Arusona 641
ARU Spray 535
Arutimol 2045
Arutrin 2097
Arvenum 675
Arvigol 506
Arvin 122
Arvynol 796
Arwin 122
Asacol 94, 1261
Asacolitin 1261
Asakin 230
Asamedel 790
Asasantin 684
Ascabiol 215
Ascofer 138
Ascomed 138
Ascorgil 138
Ascorvit 138
Asco Top 2207
Ascoyl 138
Asdesolon 234
Asécryl 977
Asendin 105
Asendis 105
Aseptil-Guanidina 1926
Aseptit 418
Aserbine 1852
Aslos 1593
Aslos-C 1220
Asmabec 184
Asmacortone 1301
Asmalene 254
Asmarectal 678, 2012
Asmasal 1851
Asmetil 1746
Asmidon 1851
Asorec 1926
Aspace 1557
Aspan 29
Aspar 541
Aspardolce Dolafic 140
Asparel Dietason 140
Aspartina 140
Aspégic 500 29
Aspenone 133
Aspergum 29
Aspirin 29
Aspirina 29

Aspirine Bayér 29
Aspirine duRhône 29
Aspirine pH 8 29
Aspirinetta 29
Aspirine Upsa 29
Aspirine Upsa Vitamine C 29
Aspirine Vitamine C 29
Aspirisucre 29
Aspisol 29
Aspro 29
ASS Dura 29
Assocort 2098
Assogen 531
ASS-ratiopharm 29
Assur 1367
Astat 1142
Astelin 162
Aster C 138
Asterol 661
Asterol "Roche" 661
Asthmalitan 1102
Asthma 6-N 749
Asthmo 1992
Asthmoprotect 1992
Asthone 531
Asthoxin 1922
Asthpul Sol. 1106
Astifat 1130
Astmamasit 683
Astomin 661
Astonin H 879
Astroderm 628
Asuzol 1318
Asverin 2054
Asverine 2054
Asverin-H 2054
A.T.10 652
Atabrine 1243
Atacand 330
Ataclor 450
Atalis-D 443
Atamet 344
Atapren 2066
Atapryl 1864
Atarax 1035
Atarax P 1035
Atebeta 146
Ateculon 516
Atelec 470
Ateles 516
Atem 1093
Atemarol 516
Atemur 917
Atenezol 16
Atenigron 450
Atenos 2142

Batrax 173
Baxacor 790
Baxal 1146
Baxan 369
Baxo 1669
Baycain 2079
Baycaron 1232
Baycillin 1731
Baycol 412
Baycuten 163, 605
Bayercillin 1731
Baylarmine 611
Baylotensin 1453
Baymycard 1450
Baynas 1785
Bayoline 1433
Bayotensin 1453
Baypen 1322
Baypress 1453
Bayrena 1933
Bayrogel 814
Bb-k8 89
B-Chabre 1809
Bebate 230
Beben 228
Beben crema derm. 230
Beben Sid 230
Bec 135
Becanat 1295
Bechilar 616
Becilan 1757
Beclazone 184
Beclipur 183
Becloderm 184
Becloforte 184
Beclojet 184
Beclorhinol 184
Beclosclerin 183
Becloturmant 184
Beclovent 185
Becodisks 184
Béconase 184
Beconase 184
Beconase Aquosum 184
Beconase Dosier-Spray 184
Bécotide 184
Becotide 184
Becozym 1809
Bécozyme 1809
Bécozyme injèctable 614
Bectmiran 234
Beelith 1757
Befibrate 240
Béfizal 240
Beflavine 1809
Bekunis 250

Belfène 680
Belg 184
Belivon 1822
Bella Carotin 221
Bellaserp 648
Bellatal 152, 1616, 1860
Bellergil 1616
Beloc 1316
Belsiene 1905
Bélustine 1184
Belustine 1184
Benadin Salicylate 678
Benadol 678
Benadon 1757
Benadozol 678
Benadozol-S 678
Benadryl 38, 678
Benadryl Complex 616
Benafed 616
Benambax 1585
Benamizol 892
Benanzyl 497
Benapon 678
Benasin 678
Bendaline 192
Bendigon 1232, 1802
Bendogen 235
Benecid 1710
Benemid 1710
Bénémide 1710
Bénerva 2016
Benerva 2016
Benestan 559, 566
Beneural 270
Benexol 540, 1757
Benexol B$_{12}$ 2016
Benfofen 630
Benizol 1587
Benoquin 1359
Benoral 198
Benortan 198
Benosid 281
Benoxid 211
Benoxil 1529
Benoxinat 0,4 % Thilo 1529
Benozil 911
Bentelan 228, 233
Benton 899
Bentos 185
Bentum 198
Bentyl 633
Bentyl/Phenobarbital 633
Benuride 1611
Ben-u-ron 1558
Benylin 616, 678
Benzac 211

Benzagel 211
Benzaknen 210
Benzal 203
Benzalin 1451
Benzamycin 211, 770
Benzashave 211
Benz Be 215
Benzedrex 1736
Benzerial 988
Benzidan 214
Benzil 216
Benzil B 205
Benzoderm 535
Benzofillina 791
Benzo-Gynoestryl 781
Benzoil Peros 211
Benzolin 2069
Benzomix 211
Benzoxine 235
Benzoxyl 20 Lotion 210
Benztrone 781
Benzyrin 214
Bepanten 614
Bepanthene 614
Bepanthen Roche 614
Bepricor 218
Berachin 2142
Berberil 2005
Beres 1746
Bergacef 375
Beriplast 134
Berkatens 2163
Berlicetin 163
Berlicort 2097, 2097
Berlithion 2020
Berlocid 1930
Berocca 249, 555, 1809
Berocillin 1671
Berodual 1093
Berodual Aerosol 847
Bérotec 847
Berotec 847
Berotec-Dosier-Aerosol 847
Berotec solvens 269
Bertabronc 269
Beruhgen 2156
Berzirin 214
Besacolin 237
Besnoline 2075
Bespar 296
Bestasone 892
Bestcall 387
Beston 252
Beta 228
Beta-Acetyldigoxin 27
Beta-Acetyldigoxin R.A.N. = glycotop 27

Beta-Acetyldigoxin-
  ratiopharm 0,1 mg/0,2 mg
  27
Beta-Acigoxia 28
Beta-adalat 146
Beta-Adalat 1434
Bêta-Adalate 146
Beta-Adalate 1434
Betabactyl 495, 2034
Betabion 2016
Betabioptal 228
Betacap 234
Beta-Cardone 1889
Betacef 395
Beta-Chlor 529
Betaclan 185
Betaclin 234
Betacomplesso 1809
Beta-Creme 227
Betades 1889
Betadine 174, 1675
Betadival 232
Betadorm 678
Betadorm-N 2155
Bétadran 293
Betadrenol 293
Betafluorene 228
Betagalen 227
Bétagan 1160
Betagan 1160
Betagon 1248
Betaina Manzoni 223, 224
Betaindol 235
Beta-Intensain 1035, 1435
Betalactam 1146
Betaleston 508
Betaloc 1316
Betalone 1251
Betamamallet 228
Betamann 1309
Bétamaze 1914
Betameta 228
Betameta Diprop 231
Betametha 228
Betamethason Wolff 234
Betam-Ophtal 227
Bétanol 1309
Betapace 1889
Betapar 1251
Betapred 1251
Betapressin 1574
Betapressine 1574
Beta-Prograne 1735
Betarelix 1574, 1663
Betascor 223
Bétasellen 221
Betasemid 1574

Breezee Mist Foot Powder 2148
Brelomax 2142
Brendil 476
Brentomine 476
Brepanael 476
Bres 777
Bresit 516
Brethine 1993
Breva 1093, 1851
Brevibloc 778
Brevicon 799, 1462
Brevimytal-Natrium 1286
Brevirina 436
Brevital Sodium 1286
Brevoxyl 211
Brexidol 1669
Brexin 443, 1281, 1669
Briafil 178
Briazide 190, 1020
Bricantyl 983
Bricanyl 1992
Bricanyl compound 983
Bricanyl Turbohaler 1992
Bricef 377
Briem 190
Briétal 1286
Brietal Sodium 1286
Brinacyl 1993
Brinaldix 524
Brinerdina 524, 648, 1802
Briocor 357
Briplatin 488
Brisarin 1802
Briserin 648
Briserin/mite 524
Brisporin 376
Bristacin 1834
Bristamine 1626
Bristamox 107
Bristocef 376
Bristopen 1508
Bristurin 1993
Britagel 131
Brital 501
Britane 1327
Britiazim 660
Britlofex 1181
BritLoflex 1181
Brizin 189
Brochenolo Balsamo 475
Brocillin 1731
Brocilline 1731
Brodermatin 248
Broflex 2111
Brolene 627
Bromazenil 266

Bromazepam 266
Bromazolo 2014
Bromelain 200 267
Bromfed 274
Bromfed-DM 616
Brom-Nervacit 270
Bromocodeina 541
Bromo-Kin 271
Bromrun 274
Bromural 270
Broncaid 1131
Broncal 616
Bronchalène 443, 1627
Bronchathiol 346
Bronchenolo Tosse 616
Bronchicum 541
Bronchilator 1102, 2010
Bronchisan 1516
Broncho-Abrodil 674
Bronchocux 281
Bronchocyst 346
Bronchodil 1799
Bronchodual 847, 1093
Broncho-Euphyllin 2011
Bronchokod 346
Broncholate 749
Broncholin 1204
Broncho-Noleptan 929
Bronchopront 79
Bronchoretard 2011
Bronchospasmin 1799
Bronchospray 983, 1851
Bronchovydrin Inhalationslösung 153
Broncloclar 346
Broncobeta 616
Broncoclar 22
Broncodex 616
Broncodil 500
Broncokin 269
Broncoplus 1905
Broncopulmin 1776
Broncorinol 346, 421, 1627
Broncorinol Maux de gorge 2001
Broncosedina 979
Broncospasmin 1799
Bronco-Turbinal 184
Broncovaleas 1851
Broncovanil 983
Brondilat 2076
Brondiletten 188, 2076
Bronica 1865
Bronilide 887
Bronkirex 346
Bronkometer 1102
Bronkosol 1102

Bronocon 531
Bronpax pates 806
Bronsecur 350
Brontex 541
Brontin 589
Brontina 589
Brontisol 589
Brontyl 1750
B_{12} Rotexmedica 555
Brotopon 996
Brovarin 270
Brovel 763
Brox 153
Broxil 1610
Broxol 80
Brufanic 1041
Brufen 1040
Brufen Retard 1041
Brufort 1041
Brulidine 627
Brumetidina 472
Brumeton 1918
Brumeton coll. 228
Brumixol 464
Brunac 22
Bryonon 555
B_{12}-Steigerwald 555
Buburone 1041
Bubusco-S 311
Buccastem 1715
Buccawalter 418
Bucumarol 281
Budecort 281
Budegat 281
Budeson 282
Bufal 285
Bufederm 285
Bufedil 285
Bufene 285
Bufferin 29
Buflan 285
Buflo 285
Buflocit 285
Buflofar 285
Bulentan 1624
Bulkosol 1883
Bumex 287
Bunosquin 1741
Bupap 299
Bupiforan 292
Bupivacain 292
Bupranolol Hydrochloride 293
Buprenex 294
Burinex 287
Burinex A 90, 287
Burinex K 287

Burlamycin 2063
Busala 666
Buscopan 311, 1859
Buscopan composto 311
Buscoridin 311
Buscote 311
Buspar 296
Buspimen 297
Buspon 311
Butacote 1624
Butaflogin 1537
Butaliret 1992
Butalitab 1992
Butaspirone 1537
Butazolidin 474, 1623
Butazolidine 1623
Buterazine 283
Buteridol 996
Butibatol 177
Butibol 311
Butilene 1537
Butiran 300
Butisol Sodium 1860
Butix 1256
Butix gel 678
Butobarbital Dipharma 1860
Butosin 177
Butylcain 2001
Butylenin 1041
Butylpan 311
Butymide 311
Butyn Metaphen 298
Butyn Sulfate 298
Butysco 311
B-Valet B_{12} 1029
B_6-Vicotrat 1757
B_{12}-Vicotrat 555
BVK Roche 1809
Bydolax 1539
BYK 1757

C

Cabagin 1298
Cabarol 540
Cabaser 313
CABASERIL 313
Cabermox 107
Cabral 856
Cachets Lia 1606
Cactiran 1652
Cadotussyl 346
Cadral 314
Cadraten 314
Cadrilan 314
Caelyx 717

Cebroton 490
Cebutid 912
Cecenu 1184
Ceclor 368
Ceclor CD 368
Cecon 138
Cedigossina 26
Cedilanid 1141
Cedilanid Amp. 1141
Cedilanid c. Th. 1141
Cedilanid c. Th. Amp. 1141
Cedilanid D 1141
Cédilanide 1141
Cedocard retard 1108
Cedol 375
Cedrox 368
Cedur 240
CeeNU 1184
Cefabiozim 379
Cefacet 370
Cefacidal 379
Cefadril 369
Cefadyl 376
Cefalexi 370
Cefalexina 370
Cefalo 373
Cefaloject 376
Céfalotine 373
Cefam 375
Cefamar 408
Cefamen 375
Cefamezin 379
Céfaperos 377
Cefaplus 631
Cefarin 376
Cefaseptolo 375
Cefatrexyl 376
Cefatrix 377
Cefazil 379
Cefazone 388
Cefergot 316
Cefiran 375
Cefirex 399
Cefixoral 386
Cefizox 405
Cefobid 388
Céfobis 388
Cefobis 388
Cefociclin 395
Cefogram 388
Cefol 2065, 927
Cefoneg 388
Cefoper 388
Cefoperazin 389
Cefoprim 408
Cefosint 388

Cefotan 391
Cefotax 390
Cefotrizin 377
Cefrabiotic 399
Cefro 399
Cefspan 386
Ceftim 403
Ceftix 405
Cefumax 408
Cefur 408
Cefurex 408
Cefurin 408
Cefzil 398
Celadigal 1141
Celance 1597
Celbenin 1307
Celebrex 409
Célectol 410
Celectol 410
Célestamine 227
Celestamine 611
Celestamine N 227
Celestan 227
Celestan Depot 228
Celestan depot 233
Célestàne chronodose 228
Celestan V, -"mite", -crinale 234
Celestan V mit Neomycin 234
Celestan V mit Sulmycin 234
Célestène 227, 233
Célestène Chronodose 233
Célestoderm 227, 234
Celestoderm 228
Célestoderm Relais 234
Celestoderm-V 234
Celestone 228
Celestone Ar. and im 233
Celestone Cronodose 228
Celestone Soluspan 228
Celexa 489
Celipro Lich 410
Celiptium 738
cellblastin 2170
CellCept 1378
cellcristine 2176
Cellidrin 67
Cellmustin 785
Celltop 819
Célocurine 1953
Celontin 1267
Celoslin 404
Celospor 366
Celtect 1513
Celtol 366

Cemado 375
Cemirit 29
Cemix 387
Cenomycin 395
Centrax 1689
Centyl 193
Ceolat 666
Ceoluase 1905
Ceosunin 415
Ceoxil 369
Cepacol 421
Cepaloridin-Glaxo 372
Cepan 391
Cepazine 408
Céphadol 638, 682
Céphalgan 1313
Cephalmin 2024
Cephalomax 371
Cephation 373
Cephazal 371
Céphil 796
Cephoral 386
Cephos 369
Cephradine 399
Cepidan 556
Cepol 371
Ceporan 372
Ceporex 370
Ceporexin 370
Ceporexine 370
Ceporin 372
Céporine 372
Cepotril 376
Cepovenin 373
Ceptaz 403
Cepticol 377
Cequinyl 1776
CER 372
Cerachidol 638
Ceracin 795
Cerase 1222
Cerate 1325
Cercine 623
Cerebalan 479
Cerebro 1944
Cerebroforte 1658
Cerebropan 1658
Cerebyx 940
Ceregut 490
Cerella 780
Cerepar 1658
Cernénit 540
Cernévit 249, 542, 614
Cernevit 540
Cerocral 1048

Ceropirin 376
Cerrosa 638
Cerson 885
Certobil 583
Certomycin 1421
Certonal 1371
Cerubidin 577
Cérubidine 577
Cerubidine 577
Cerucal 1313
Cerumenex 434
Cerumol 434
CERUTIL 1217
Cervevit 555
Cervex 65
Cervidil 674
Cervilane 648, 1183
Cervoxan 2171
Cesal 1104
Cesamet 1382
Cesol 1690
CET 373
Cetacaine 208, 2001
Cetal 2175
Cetapril 46
Cetavlex 418
Cétavlon 418
Cetavlon 418
Cetebe 138
Ceto sanol 1141
Cetrazil 377
Cetrotide 421
Cétylyre 421
Cevi-Bid 138
Ce-Vi-Sol 138
Cevit 138
Cevitt 138
CEX 371
Championyl 1945
Chelatran 730
Cheliboldo 942
Chemacin 89
Chemiartrol 1355
Chemicetina 426
Chemionazolo 729
Chemiovis 1935
Chemitrim 1931, 2119
Chemotrim 1931, 2119
Chemyparin 1002
Chemyterral 1918
Chendol 422
Chenix 423
Chenochol 423
Chénodex 422
Chenofalk 422
Chenossil 422

Crystapen V 1619
Crystodigin 645
C-Tard 138
Culpen 874
Culten 1593
Cumarote CD 1035
Cuplex 1852
Cuprimine 1579
Curantyl 684
Curaresin 1246
Curarin 2142
Curarin Asta 2142
Curarin HAF 2142
Curatoderm 1957
Cura-Vent/DA 443
Curoxim 408
Cusimolol 2045
Customed 269
Cutacnyl 211
Cutanum 780
Cutemol 614
Cutemol Creme 65
Cutisan 2105
Cutistad 535
Cutivate 917
Cuxabrain 1658
Cuxafenon 1727
Cyabin 251
Cyanocobalamin 555
Cycladiène 634
Cycladol 1669
Cyclaine 1014
Cyclan 556
Cyclan-Cap. 556
Cyclansato 556
Cyclapen 460
Cyclate 177
Cycleane 798
Cycleat Cap. 556
Cyclergine 556
Cyclimorph 1368
Cyclobarbitalum 557
Cyclobral 556
Cyclo-C 121
Cyclo-cell 563
Cyclocide 570
Cyclocort 81
Cycloderm 462
Cycloestrol 1009
Cycloestrol-A.H.
  Progestérone 800
Cyclogest 1718
Cyclogyl 562
Cyclomycin 564
Cyclomydril 562
Cyclonarol 561

Cyclopal 562
Cyclopan 1011
Cyclopentolat
  Augentropfen 562
Cyclo Progynova 1468
Cyclo-Progynova 783, 1468
Cycloprogynova 781
Cyclosa 597
Cyclosan 798
D-Cycloserin "Roche" 564
D-Cyclosérine Roche 564
Cycloserine Roche 564
Cyclospasmol 556
Cyclostin 563
Cyclotériam 565, 2101
Cycloviran 33
Cycluran 340
Cycnate 1079
Cycralate 556
Cydeane 597
Cyklokapron 2089
Cylert 1574
Cymavene 955
Cymerine 1788
Cymévan 955
Cymeven 955
Cymevene 955
Cynomel 1176
Cynt 1376
Cyprostat 568
Cyren A 636
Cyscholin 490
Cysticide 1690
Cystit 1454
Cystocon 20
Cysto-Conray 1089
Cystografin 86
Cysto-Myacyne O.W.G.
  1918
Cystrin 1530
Cytacon 555
Cytadren 92
Cytamen 555
Cytamid 916
Cytarbel 570
Cytéal 430
Cytellin 1880
Cytobion 555
Cytome 2002
Cytomel 1176
Cytos 513
Cytosar 570
Cytosar-U 570
Cytotec 1346
Cytovene 955
Cytoxan 563

D

Dabbeta 228
Dab M 606
Dacarbazine 571
Dacoren 650
Dacortilen Merck 1702
Dacrin 1954
Dacryne 430, 1954
Dacryoboraline 1954
Dactil 1652
Dactilase 1652
Dactil OB 1652
Dafalgan 1558
Daflon 675
Dafnegin 464
Daicoline 490
D.A. II 443
D.A.II-Tablets 1292
Daim 2040
Daiprophen 1041
Dairopeal 1897
Daisaloid 1801
Daitac 833
Daivonex 320
Daiyalose 1975
Daktacort 1024, 1327
Daktacort crema 1024, 1025
Daktar 1327
Daktarin 1327
Dalacin 503
Dalacin C 503
Dalacine 503
Dalalone 606
Dalcolax 1884
Dalet Med Balsam 984
Dalgan 621
Dalgan 621
Dalivit 767
Dalivit drops 1806
Dalivit Drops 1809
Dallergy 274, 1292
Dallergyl 443
Dalmadorm 911
Dalmane 911
Dalmate 911
Dalpan 1312
Damide 1063
Dampa D 1915
Danatrol 573
Daneral 1613
Danicon 1953
Danocrine 573
Danol 573
Dantamacrin 574
Dantrium 574
Dantrolen 574
Daonil 968

Dapotum 906
Dapson-Fatol 576
Daptazile 100 96
Daptazile Injektion 96
Daptazole 96
Daranide 631
Daraprim 1758
Darbid 1107
Dardum 388
Darebon 450, 1802
Daren 739
Daricon 1538
Daricon PB 1538
Daritran 1538
Darkene 888
Darmol 250, 1616
Darmoletten 1538
Darob 1889
Dartalan 2023
Daruma 1046
Darvocet-N 619
Darvon 316, 619
Darvon-N 619
Daskil 1992
Dasovas 581
Dasvit H 1029
Daunoblastin 577
Daunoblastina 577
Daunomycin 577
DaunoXome 577
Daunoxome 577
Davedax 1793
Davosin 1931
Daxauten 1706
Daypro 1512
DCCK 650
DCL 592
DDAVP 596
Deacura 248
Deadyn 1574
Deanase 458
Deaner 577
Deanol Riker 577
Deanxit 904, 1235
Deapril 650
Débékacyl 626
Débétrol 620
Deblaston 1648
Debridat 583
Debrum 1222
Débrumyl 1004
Decabid 1064
Decabis 590
Decaderm 606
Décadron 605
Decadron 605, 609

Desonix 598
Desopane 2112
Des Owen 598
Desoxyn 1279
de-squaman hermal 1759
Desquam-E 211
Desquam-X 211
Destolit 2153
Desulpid 1945
Désuric 206
Desuric 206
Desyrel 2091
Detantol 289
Detaril 1656
Deteclo 451, 586, 2002
Détensiel 253
Detensitral 925, 1559, 1801
Dethamedin 606
Deticene 571
Detimedac 571
DET-MS 649
Detoxergon 1757
Detoxergon Fiale 136
Detoxergon Polvere 136
Detracin 586
Detravis 586
Detrol 2078
Detrusitil 2078
Detrusitol 2078
Dettol 441
Déturgylone 848
Deturgylone 1696
Deursil 2153
Dévalène 1214
Develin retard 618
Devocin 1265
Dexa A 606
Dexa-Allvoran 605
Dexabene 609
Dexa Biciron 605, 607
Dexa-Brachialin 609
Dexacillin 750
Dexacilline 750
Dexa Effekton 609
Dexagel 605
Dexagrane 609
Dexa Loscon 605, 607
Dexaltin 606
Dexamamalet 606
Dexambutol 794
Dexambutol-INH 795, 1105
Dexame 606
Dexa-Mederma Akne 64
Dexamonozon 605
Dexamytex 605
Dexa-Philogout 605

Dexa Polyspectral 605
Dexa-Rhinaspray 607
Dexa-Rhinospray 605, 607
Dexa-Rhinspray 2087
Dexa-sine 605
Dexasone 606
Dexchlor Repeat Action
   612
Dexicam 1668
Dexium 322
Dexmy 942
Dexorat 1568
Dexpanthenol Heumann
   614
Dextophan 616
Dextrarine Phenylbutazone
   1624
DextroB Afo 616
DF-118 forte 648
D. F. P. Inj. 1104
DHC 647
DHC Contiums 648
DHC plus 648
DHCplus 316
DHE 45 649
DHE-Puren 649
DHS Sal 1853
DHS Zinc 1759
DHT 652
Diabemide 446
Diabenyl 2005
Diabeta 968
Diabetase 1277
Diabetoplex 350
Diabetoral 446
Diabetosan 1277
Diabetose B 1277
Diabe-Tuss DM 616
Diabewas 2068
Diabexan 446
Diabex-T 2069
Diabinèse 446
Diabinese 446
Diabrezide 969
Diacolon 1135
Diacon 754
Diacor 660
Diacort 640
Di-Actane 1387
Di-Ademil 1027
Diadin 1355
Diadol 65
Diafen 680
Diaflexol 1620
Diaginol 20
Diagran 1809
Dialferin 52

Dialicor 790
Diamicron 969
Diamide 447
Diamox 16
Diamox S. R. 16
Diamox Sustets 16
Dianabol 1272
Dianavit 1272
Diandrone 1686
Diane 568, 799
Diane 35 798
Dianette 568
Di-Antalvic 618
Diapatol 97, 429
Diaphal 90
Diaretyl 1187
Diarönt 544, 1000, 1629,
   1926
Diarrest 633
Diarret 1438
Diarrol 2101
Diarsed 679
Diart 169
Diasone Sodium 1941
Diaspasmyl 1739
Diastabol 1335
Diastat 623
Diaste-M 311
Dia-Tablinen 350
Diathymil 249
Diazemuls 623
Diazid 1105
Diazon 1941
Dibenyline 1618
Dibenzyline 1618
Dibenzyl-Rhenix 678
Dibenzyran 1618
Dibestil 637
Dibetos 2069
Diblocin 712
Dicefalin 399
Dichlor-Stapenor 631
Dichlotride 1020
Dichronic 630
Diclac 630
Diclex 632
diclo 630
Diclo 631
Diclocil 631
Diclocillin 632
Diclocta 632
Dicloeta 632, 1004
Diclofenamid 630
Diclofenbeta 630
Diclo KD 630
Diclomax 632
Diclo-Phlogont 630

Diclophlogont 630
Diclo-Puren 630
Diclo-rectal 630
Dicloreum 630
Diclo-saar 630
Diclo-Spondyril 630
Diclo-Tablinen 630
Diclo-Wolff 630
Dicloxapen 632
Dicodid 1021
Dicodin 648
Diconal 556
Dicortal 641
Dicton 515
Dicynene 792
Dicynone 792
Didoc 16
Didrex 211
Didrogyl 318
Didronel 808
Didrothenat 651
Diertina 648
Diethylstilbestrol 636
Dietoman aspartame 140
Dietor 1062
Diet Sucaryl 1848
Difeni 678
Difflam 214
Diffucord, -N 270
Diffumal 2012
Diflal 640
Diflor 632
Diflucan 875
Difludol 642
Difluid 648
Diflupyl 1104
Diflurex 2038
Diflusan 642
Difmecor 840
Difmedol Gel 1537
Difmetre 1075
Diforène 577
Difosfocin 490
Difosfonal 513
Difrarel E 2065
Digacin 646
Digaol 2045
Di-Genik 788
Digibaïne 1908
Digi-Baxacor 790
Digi-Complamin 26
Digicor 645
Digifar 645
Digilanid 1141
Digilanogen C 1141
Digimed 645

Diusemide 945
Diutensat 2101
Diutensen-R 1293, 1802
Diuteren 2101
Diuzol 945
Divalentyl 349
Divalvon 1760
Diviator 1708, 1801, 2113
Dividol 2169
Divimax 1559
Divina 783, 1227
Divinoctal 1282, 1862
Dixarit 523
Dixnalate 956
Dizac 623
D-Mulsin 542
Dobenam 724
Dobendan 421
Doberol 2071
Dobesifar 322
Dobetin 555, 1757, 2016
Dobica 322
Do-Bil 654
Dobren 1945
Dobutamin 689
Dobutrex 689
Doca Acetate 602
Docabolin 602, 1397
Docelan 1029
Docell 630
Docidrazin 192, 1019
Dociretic 192
Dociton 1735
Dodecatol 555, 1712
Dodécavit 1029
Dogmatil 1945
Dogmatyl 1945
Doimazin 446
Dolanaest 292
Dolantin 1604
Dolcol 1648
Dolcor aspartame 140
Dolestan 678
Dolestan forte 983
Dolevern 1029
Dolgit 1040
Dolgit-Diclo 630
Dolinac 833
Dolipol 2069
Doliprane 1558
Dolisal 642
Dolmatil 1945
Dolmen 1989
Dolo-Adamon 463
Dolo-Arthrosonex 1031
Dolobasan 630

Dolobid 642
Dolobis 642
Dolocyl 1041
Doloflex 1558
Dolo-judolor 946
Dolomo 541
Dolo-Neurobion 555
Dolophine Hydrochloride
  1278
Dolo-Phlogase 1537
Dolo-Posterine 474
Doloproct 896
Dolo Prolixan 1620
DOLO PUREN 1040
Dolormin 1040
Dolosal 1604
Dolo Visano 1246
Doloxene 316, 618
Doloxene Co. 618
Dolviran 541
Domar 1641
Domian 1940
Domicillin 111
Domin 1967
Dominal /-forte 1742
Dominans 906, 1473
Domistan 1015
Domperamol 704
Dona 975
Donalg 1853, 2001
Donamet 41
Dona-200 S 975
Donaseven 341
Donatiol 983, 1220
Donatussin 443, 616
Doncef 399
Donisolone 1695
Donjust-B 1041
Donmox 16
Donnatal 152, 1616, 1860
Donopon-GP 1313
Donormyl 720
Donray 609
Dontisolan 1694
Dontopivalone 2060
Dopacard 707
Dopaflex 1164
Dopamet 1294
Dopamin AWD 706
Dopamine 200 Lucien 706
Dopamine Nativelle 706
Dopamine Pierre Fabre 706
Dopamin Fresenius 706
Dopamin ratiopharm 706
Dopamin Solvay 706
Doparl 1165
Dopasol 1165

Dopaston 1165
Dopegyt 1294
Dopo Pik 2106
Doppelherz 1809
Dopram 711
Doral 1766
Doralese 1077
Dorbantyl 1883
Doregrippin 1558
Dorenasin 2188
Doreperol 1010
dorex-retard 1516
Doricum 892
Doricum Semplice 892
Doridamina 1186
Doriden 975
Doridéne 975
Dormalon 1451
Dormate 1214
Dormicum 1329
Dormigoa 678
Dormilfo 1860, 1862
Dormison 1298
Dormonoct 1188
Dormopan 349, 557, 1011
Dormo-Puren 1451
Dormutil 678
Dorsacaine 1529
Dortizon Oint. 1025
Doryl 338
Doryx 719
Dosberotec 847
Dossibil 767
Dostinex 313
Dosulfin 1929
Dosulfine 1929, 1937
Double Check 1459
Doven 675
Dow-Sulfisoxazole 1925
Doxans 713
Doxapril 711
Doxatet 719
Doxil 717
Doxina 719
Doxiproct-Plus 322
Doxised 720
Doxium 322
Doxycline Plantier 719
Doxygram 719
Doxylar 719
Doxylets 719
Doyle 143
Dozic 996
Draganon 128
Dramamine 662
Drapolene 203

Dravyr 33
Drenison 880
Drenison Neomicina 880
Drenison Q 880
DrenoliveR 459
Dricol 85
Drill Expectorant 346
Drimyl 813
Drisi-Ven 2138
Dristan Long Lasting Nasal
  Spray 1533
Drithocreme 687
Dritho-Scalp 687
Drix 250
Drogenil 916
Drolban 723
Droleptan 722
Dromoran 1172
Dronal 54
Droperidol 722
Dropilton 1634
Droptimol 2045
Droxar 724
Drylin 1931, 2119
D.T.I.C. 100/200 571
DTIC-DOME 571
D-Tracetten 542
D-Tubocurarine Abbott
  2142
Dubam 1031
Dufaston 725
Dulcolax 250
Duloctil 1944
Dumirox 924
Duo-C 138
Duodexa N Salbe 605
Duoesetil 2107
Duofilm 1852
Duogastral 1662
Duogastrone 343
Duogen 788
Duogynon 1718
Duoluton 1469
Duo-Ormogyn 781
Duosterone 801
Duotrate 1582
Duotrax 855
Duoventil 847, 1093
Dupéran 518
Duphalac 1135
Duphaston 725
Duplamin 1726
dura Al 300 67
dura AX 107
Durabolin 1397
Duracare 730
Durachroman 551

Elleste Deret 1463
Ellsurex 64
Elmedal 64
Elmetacin 1074
Elmitolo 1284
Elobact 408
Elocon 1359
Eloxatin 1510
Elroquil 1035
Elspar 139
Elthon 2163
Eltrip 2140
Eltroxin 1173
Eludril 430, 434, 2001
Elumonon 1955
Elvorine 928
Elyzol 1318
Elzogram 379
Emaform 504
Emasex 177
Emazian 1809
EMB-Fatol 794
Embolex 649
Emcor 253
Emcyt 785
Emdabol 2051
Emesan 678
Emeside 802
Emestid 500 775
Emete-Con 213
Emflex 13
Emgel 770
Emicholine-F 490
Emilian 490
Emirace 1419
Emko 207
EMLA 1174
Emla 1707
EMLA 1707
EMLA Creme 1707
Emlapatch 1707
Emmetip 1301
Emoantitossina 1809
Emoferrina B₁₂ o₃ 1757
Emoflux 286
Emolex 534
Emopremarin 788
Emoren 1517
Emorhalt 2089
Emorril 1025, 1437, 2138
Emovate 509
Emozide B6 1105
Empecid 535
Emulsiderm 203
Emulsione lass. Fama 1616
Enadel 537

Enantyum 613
Enapren 741
Enarax 1538
Enarmon 1998
Enarmon Depot 1999
Enarmon Susp. 2000
Enarmon Tab. 1303
Enavid 1265, 1465
Enbol 1761
Encefabol 1760
Encelin 490
Encéphabol 1760
Encephabol 1760
Encetrop 1658
Encordin 1603
Endak 361
Endal 443
Endium 675
Endobil 1083
Endocaine 1762
Endocistobil 42
Endografin 42
Endojodin 1722
Endojodo 1722
Endomirabil 1083
Endoprenovis 1697
Endoprost 1051
Endoxan 563
Endoxana 563
Endoxan ASTA 563
Endoxan-Asta 563
Enduron 1292
Enduronil 1292
Enduronyl 590, 1292
Endydol 29
Enelfa 1558
Energona 1466
Enerzer 1100
Enfluran-Pharmacia
  Inhalationsflüssigkeit 743
Enirant 650
Enirant Tropflösung 648
Enjit 1027
Enless 1367
Enlon 731
Enlon-Plus 152
Enoclen 2144
Enovid 1465
Enovid E 1465
Enoxor 744
Ensidon 1491
Ensign 490
Entair 983
Entamide 657
Entamidine 1940
Entelohl 1743
Entera-strept 651

Enterastrept 1926
Entercine 276, 651, 1017
Enterocantril 1245
Enterocura 1926
Enteromide 1928
Enteromix 1667
Entero-sediv 653
Enterosteril 1629
Enterostop 174
Enteroton 1078
Enteroton lass. 1616
Entero-Vioform 504
Entobex 1605
Entocort 281
Entocort CR 281
Entodon 1722
Entolon 1390
Entomin 358
Entra 2124
Enturen 1939
Entyderma 184
Entyfluson 508
Enuretine vit. E
  isoprapamide 1107
Envacar 989
Envarése 989
Envarèse 1676
Enzamin 214
Enzimina 1432
Enzycol 1432
Enzym-Wied 458, 267
Epa-Bon 559
Epalfen 1135
Epanutin 1627
Epaq 1851
Eparbolic 223
Epargriseovit 555, 927
Eparina 1002
Eparinovis 1002
Eparmefolin 927
Eparolo 1431
Eparsil 1876
Epecoal 1220
Epectan 1220
Epenard 748
Epeso 748
Ephed-Organidin 1281
Ephedrine "Nagai" 749
Ephedroides "3" 749
Ephelon 2065
Ephepect 749
Ephetonin 749
Ephydion 806
Ephynal 2065
Epi-Aberel 2094
Epicain Ace 724
Epiclase 1605

Epidione 2114
Epidosin 2156
Epi E-Z Pen 753
Epifoam 1682
Epileo Petitmal 802
Epi-Monistat 1327
Epinal 49, 1041
Epipen 753
EpiPen 753
Epi Pevaryl 729
Epirocain 724, 1253
Epirotin 214
Epitol 339
Epitopic 643
Epivir 1139
Epobron 1041
Epocelin 405
Epocol 1706
Epogam 954
Epokuhl 446
Epontol 1728
Eposerin 405
Eppy 753
Eppy 1 % 753
Epsilon-Aminocapronsäure
  "Roche" 91
Epsilon-Tachostypan 91
Eptadone 1278
Epuram 492
Eputes 1041
Equagesic 29, 801, 1252
Equanil 1252
Equiday 2065
Equilibrin 98
Equilid 1945
Equilium 2030
Equipar 223, 1078
Equipertine 1536
Equisil 749
Equiton 2045
Equivert 1432
Equverin 1220
Eradacin 1842
Eradocil 1842
Erbacort 1698
Erbocain 930
Erboproct 930
Ercaf 769
Ercéfuryl 1438
Ercefuryl 1438
Ercostrol 1279
Erdol 1951
Erecnos 1375
Eremfat 1812
Ergamisol 1159
Ergen 41
Ergenyl 2157

Etrynit 1729
Etynderon-DP 231
Eubetal 129, 228
Eubine 1530
Eubiol 141
Eucal 475
Eucalipt 475
Eucaliptina 984
Eucalyptine pholcodine 1627
Eucar 357
Eucardic 365
Eucardion 615, 1706
Eucarnil 357
Eucebral 815
Eucebral-N 556
Eucerin 666
Euchessina 1616
Euci 616
Eucilat 196
Euctan 2074
Eudemine 624
Eudigox 646
Euditron 1563
Eudolene 1444
Eudur 1992, 2011
Eudyna 2094
Eufibron 1738
Eufimenth 474
Eugalac 1135
Eugastran 1313
Euglucan 968
Euglucon 968
Euglucon N 968
Eugynon 799, 1468
Euhypnos 1981
Eukalasan 555
Eukodal 1530
Eukraton 187
Eulexin 916
Eulexine 916
Eulip 2026
Eulipos 620
Eu-Med 1848
Eumotol 286
Eumovate 509
Eunéphran 305
Eunerpan 1237
Eunova 1809
Eupasal sodico 94
Eupaverina 1371
Euphyllin 2011
Euphyllina 2012, 2012
Euphyllinat 1141
Euphylline L.A. 2011
Euphylong 2011
Eupnéron 763

Eupnéron xantique 763
Eupond N 583
Eupractone 665
Eupragin 770
Eupres Mite 450
Eupressyl 2151
Eupressyl gél 2151
Euralan 843
Eurason D 606
Eurax 552
Eurax Hydrocortisone 1024
Euraxil 552
Eureceptor 472
Eurex 1691
Euro-Cir 1466
Eurodin 779
Euronac 22
Eusaprim 1931, 2119
Eusaprim forte/Pyridium 2119
Eusaprine 1931
Eusedon 1726
Eusédyl aminophylline 2012
Eusod 1027
Euspirax 457
Euthyral 1173, 1176
Euthyrox 1173
Eutonyl 1563
Eutron 1563
Euvaderm 227, 230
Euvasal 1944
Euvel 2065
Euvernil 1918
Euvitol 1806
Euvitol Labra 1806
Evac-Q-Kit 1617
Evac-Q-Kwik 251
Evadene 310
Evadyne 310
Eval 1617
Evamyl 1192
Evanor 799
Evanor D 1171
Evazol 590
EVE 798
Eventin 1736
Evesin 772
Evidorm 1011
Evion 2065
Evion Forte 2065
Evipan 1011
Evipnos 1981
EVISTA 1783
Evista 1783
Evitex 1806
Evit-Geritan 2065

Evitina 2065
E-Vitum 2065
Evonton 748
Evorel 780
Evorel combi 1463
Exacin 1098
Exacor 460
Exacyl 2089
Exal 2170
Excedrin P.M. 1281
Excegran 2210
Exelderm 1916
Exelon 1826
Exiltox 687
Exirel 1661
Exluton 1202
Exlutona 1202
Exneural 1040
Exocin 1480
Exocine 1480
Exoderil 1388
Exomuc 22
Exomycol 1624
Exonal 1975
Exoseptoplix 1935
Exosurf 543, 2144
Exosurf Neonatal 543, 2144
Exosurf Neonatate 543
Exrheudon N 1623
Exrhinin 2005
Extencilline 205, 216
Extendryl 443, 1293
Extovyl 222
Extracort Creme 2097
Extramycin 1879
Extranase 267

F

Fabahistin 1214
Fadiamone 2000
Fadiamone Crème 1703
Fado 375
Fagusan 983
Faktu 474
Falicard 2163
Falithrom 1620
Falitonsin 146
Falomesin 404
Falquigut 1884
Falvin 854
Famesil 956
Famodil 827
Famvir 826
Fanasil 1924
Fansidar 1758, 1924
Fansidol 1444

Farctil 1131
Farecef 388
Faremicin 937
Fareston 2083
Faretrizin 377
Fargan 1726
Farganesse 1726
Farial 1062
Faringina 590
Farlutal 1227
Farmidone 93
Farmigea acetilcolina 21
FARMISTIN 2176
Farmitrexat 1288
Farmobion Pp 1431
Farmocillina 590
Farmodoxi 719
Farmomicin 959
Farmorubicin 755
Farmorubicina 755
Farmorubicine 755
Farmotal 2021
Farnisol 956
Farom 830
Fasax 1668
Fasdil 830
Fase 134
Fasigin 1476
Fasigin N 2047
Fasigyn 2047
Fasigyne 500 2047
Fasinorm 939
Fastin 1622
Fastjekt 753
Fastum 1126
Fasupond 1471
Fatroxid 211
Faustan 623
Faverin 924
Favistan 2014
Fazol 1101
Febichol 843
Feclobuzon-Dragees 831
Fedahist 443
Feinalmin 1054
Felacomp 583
Felbatol 833
Felden 1668
Feldène 1668
Feldene 1668
Felison 911
Felixyn 1607
Feloday 834
Felsol 749, 1441
Felunamin 881
Felviten 124

Glaucol 2045
Glauconex 185
Glaucostat 8
Glauco-Stulln 1642
Glaucotat 8
Glaucotensil 803
Glaucothil 681
Glaumid 631
Glaunorm 8
Glaupax 16
Glazidim 403
Gleiton 1026
Gliadel 355
Glianimon 199
Gliben 968
Glibénèse 971
Glibenese 971
Glibomet 968, 1277
Gliboral 968
Glicobil 223
Glifan 966
Glifanan 966
Glimicron 970
Glimidstada 968
Glistelone 1698
Glitisol 2017
Glitisone 1698
Glosso-Stérandryl 1303
Gluborid 969
Glucamide 1277
Glucazide 976
Glucidoral 350
Glucinan 1277
Glucobay 6
Glucoben 973
Glucomide 968
Gluconorm 968
Glucophage 1277
Glucor 6
Glucoreduct 968
Glucoromed 968
Glucosulfa 1277, 2069
Gluco Tablinen 968
Glucotrol 971
Glucovital 968
Gludiase 976
Glumal 11
Glurenol 2103
Glurenor 972
Glurenorm 972
Gluronazid 976
Glustat 2182
Glutacomplex 540
Glutamag Vitaminé 1809
Glutargin 135
Glution 223

Glutisal 796, 1851
Glutril 969
Glycanol 978
Glycénol 2103
Glycero-Merfen 1624
Glycolande 968
Glyconormal 978
Glycoran 1277
Glydil 508
Glynase 968
Glypolix 612
Glyset 1335
Glyvenol 2103
G-myticin 959
Gocce Antonetto 1884
Gocce Lassative Aicardi
   1884
Godamed 29
Gola 421
Golagamma 421
Golden Eye Ointment 627
Golosan 590
Gondafon 978
Gopten 2088
Gospelaze 1905
Govil 1582
Gradient 886
Gradulon 2120
Gral 648
Gramalil 2030
Gramaxin 379
Gramidil 107
Gramplus 517
Gram-Val 719
Grandaxin 2067
Grandaxine 2067
Granudoxy 719
Gravibinan 783, 1033
Gravibinon 1033
Gravistat 798
Gregoderm 1476, 1675
Grelan High S 796
Grelan Shin A 796
Gricin Creme 981
Gricin Tabl. 981
Grifulvin 981
Grifulvin V 981
Gripenin 342
Gripenin-O 351
Grippostad 442
Grisactin 981
griseco 981
Griséfuline 981
Griseofulvina 981
Grisetin 981
Grisovin 981
Grisovina Fp 981

Gris-PEG 981
Grüncef 368
Grüntin 2039
Gruntin 1393
GT 50 B 788
Guabeta 1926
Guaiacalcium Complex 722
Guanimycin 651
Gufen 983
Gumbaral 41
Guservin 981
Gutron 1332
Guttalax 1884
Guttaplast 1852
Gydrelle 786
Gynäkosid 1297
Gynäsan 786
Gynamide 992
Gynelan 513
Gynergen 769
Gynergène 769
Gynetone 2000
Gynetone Inj. 781
Gyno Canesten 535
Gyno-Canesten 535
Gyno-Daktar 1327
Gyno-Daktarin 1327
Gynodian 1686
Gynodian Depot 783, 1686
Gyno Hormetten 1686
Gynokadin 783
Gynol II 1459
Gyno-Monistat 1327
Gynomyk 306
Gyno Pevaryl 729
Gyno-Pévaryl 729
Gyno-Pevaryl 729
Gynoplix 15
Gynorest 725
Gynothérax 449
Gyno-Trosyd 2049

H

Hachimetoxin 1922
Haclan 880
Hacosan 556
Haemiton 523
HAEMO-Exhirud 64
Hämovannad 1079
Hämo-Vibolex 555
Haenal Salbe 1777
Haibrain 490
Halamid 1411
Halbmond-Tabletten 678
Halcicomp 993
Halciderm 993, 1853

Halciderm Combi 1476
Halcion 2102
Halcort 993
Haldol 996
Haldol Decanoas 996
Haldol-Janssen 996
Haldrate 1561
Haldron 1561
Haldrone 1562
Halfan 994
Halfprin 29
Haliborange 542, 1806
Halidor 191
Halivite 1806
Haloart 998
Halodrin 903
Halog 993, 1476
Halog crème 993
Halog néomycine 993
Halojust 996
Halomonth 996
Halosten 996
Halotestin 903
Halotex 999
Halothan ASID 999
Halothane 999
Hansamed 430
Hansaplast Footcare 1852
Haphryn 2010
Harmonet 798, 961
Harmonin 1252
Harmonyl 590
Harnal 1971
Harnosal 1924, 1930
Harnway 1930
Harop 666
Harpagin 206
Harzol 1880
Hasethrol 1582
Hatial 1593
Havita 249
Havlane 1188
Haymine 443
HCT-ISIS 1020
Head & Shoulders 1759
Heartcin 2146
Hébucol 559
Hectalin 793
Hedrix Plan 541
Hefasolon 1694, 1696
Heitrin 1991
Hekbilin 422
Helfergin 1217
Helidac 1318, 2003
Helmex 1751
Helmintox 1751

Hydrocortisone 1025
Hydrocortisone Roussel
  Susp. Inj. 1024
Hydrocortison Hoechst
  1024
Hydrocortison-POS 1024
Hydrocortistab 1024
Hydrocortisyl 1024
Hydrocortone 1024, 1025
Hydrocortone Phosphate
  Inj. 1026
Hydroderm 1024
HydroDIURIL 1020
Hydro-Ergoloid 650
Hydro-Ergot 650
Hydrogalen 1024
Hydro-Long-Tablinen 450
Hydromedin 789
Hydro-Merfen 1624
Hydromet 1294
Hydromox 1773
Hydronsan 976
Hydropres 1020, 1802
Hydro-Rapid-Tablinen 945
Hydrosaluric 1020
Hydrosol polyvitaminé 614
Hydrosol polyvitaminé
  B.O.N. 2065
Hydrosol polyvitaminé
  Labaz 1809
Hydrosol polyvitaminé
  Roche 2065, 1809
Hydroxo 5000 1029
Hydroxomin 1029
Hydroxystilbamide 1034
Hydroxystilbamidine
  Isethionate 1034
Hygroton 450
Hylorel 985
Hymeron 1630
Hyminal 1282
Hyoscomin 311
Hyospan 311
Hypadil 1448
Hypal 2 1859
Hypaque 86
Hypaque-Cysto 86
Hypaque-Diu 86
Hypaque Sodium 87
Hypatol 1019
Hypen 813
Hyperan 823
Hyperidyst II 1131
Hyperium 1816
Hypersin 235
Hyperstat 624
Hypertensin 126
Hypertensin CIBA 126

Hypertonalum 624
Hypertorr 2101
Hypnasmine 1860, 2011
Hypnodin 1602
Hypnomidate 816
Hypnovel 1329
Hypoca R 181
Hypocerol 516
Hypos 1019
Hypostamin 2124
Hypostamine 2124
Hypothurol 1582
Hypovase 1691
Hyprenan 1705
Hyprim 264
Hyrasedon 540
Hyrazin 2017
Hyrvalan 443
Hysron 1227
Hytakerol 652
Hytone 1024
Hytracin 1991
Hytrast 1088
Hytrin 1991
Hytrine 1991
Hyzaar 1197

I

IB-100 1041
Ibiamox 107
Ibikin 2115
Ibimicyn 111
Ibistacin 1811
Ibisterolon Iniett. 1697
Ibu 1040
Ibu Beta 1040
Ibudros 1042
Ibufug 1040
Ibuhexal 1040
Ibumerck 1040
Ibuprocin 1041
Ibustrin 1072
Icacine 626
Icalus 1975
Icavex 1375
Icaz LP 1114
Ichtho-Spasmin 1292
Icipen 1619
Idamycin 1045
Idarac 864
Idom 710
Idracemi coll. 1026
Idracemi Eparina 1002
Idracemi eparina 1026
Idrexin-Na 193
Idrilsine 40

Idro-C 138
Idrocet 1025
Idrociclin 1581
Idrocortisone Roussel 1025
Idroepar 867
Idroestril 638
Idrolone 851
Idromin 1741
Idroneomicil 1025
Idropan B 1809
Idroplurivit 1809
Idropulmina/-composta 983
Idroxoc 1029
I.D.U. 1047
Iducher 1047
Iducol 1047, 1834
Idugalen 1047
Iduridin 1047
Idustatin 1047
Iduviran 1047
Ietepar 1431
Ifenec 729
Ifex 1048
Ifomide 1048
Ifrasarl 567
Igralin 2017
Igroseles 450
Igroton 450, 1802
Igroton Lopresor 1316
Igroton-Lopresor 450
Igroton Reserpina 450
Ijilone-DP 231
Ijilone V 234
Ikaran 649
Ikelax 1883
Ikorel 1430
Ildamen 1531
Iliadin-Mini 1533
Ilidar 157
ILIO-Funktion
  Kautabletten 666
Ilomedin 1051
Ilomedine 1051
Ilopan 614
Ilopan-Choline 614
Ilosone 770, 771
Ilotycin 770
Ilotycin gluceptate 773
Ilube 22
Ilvin 274
Imakol 1527
Imap 914
Imbaral 1942
Imbretil 1008
Imbun 1040, 1041, 1537
Imdur 1109
Imeson 1451

Imet 1075
Imex 2002
Imidalin 2069
Imidazyl 1398
Imidin 2188
Imidol 1054
Imigran 1950
Imigrane 1950
Imijekt 1950
Imilanyle 1054
Imipem 468, 1053
Imipra C 1054
Imipramin 1054
Imitrex 1950
Imizol 1398
Imménoctal 1862
Immenox 1862
Immetro 1540
Immetropan 1540
Imodium 1187
Imovane 2210
Impetex 449, 641
Impletol 1712
Impresso-Puren 1019
Impromen 274
Imuran 160
Imurek 160
Imurel 160
Inadrox 1029
Inalone 184
Inamycin 1474
Inapetyl 211
Inapsine 722
Inazin 2065
Inbestan 497
Incidal 1214
Incital 1229
Incoran 1706
Incron 633
Indacin 1075
Indaflex 1063
Indamol 1063
Indanol 501
indapamid von ct 1063
Inderal 1735
Inderal LA 1735
Inderapollon 1075
Inderetic 193, 1735
Inderex 193, 1735
Inderide 1736
Index 2073
Indo 1074
Indobloc 1735
Indocid 1075
Indocin 1075
Indocollyre 1075

Isuprel 1106
Italprid 2030
Itiocide 800
Itocol 1109
Itorex 408
Itridal 557
Itrizole 1116
Itrop 1093
Iuvacor 2146
Ivadal 2208
Iversal 78
Ivet 2065
Iwalexin 371
Ixel 1337
Ixoten 2125
Ixprim 246
Ixxose 1135
Izaberizin 479

J

Jacosulfon 1926
Jadit 279
Jadit-Hydrocortisone 279
Jalonac 101
Jamylène 1883
Jasivita 1479, 1587
Jatroneural 2108
Jatropur 2101
Jatrosom 2090
Jellin 891, 1476
Jellisoft 891
Jenafenac 630
Jenamazol 535
Jenamoxazol 1931
Jenampin 111
Jenapamil 2163
Jenaprofen 1040
Jenatacin 1075
Jenateren 2101
Jenoxifen 1969
Jeorgen 1220
Jephagynon 781, 1718
Jesytryl 338
Jetrium 617
Jexin 2142
Jod-Metil-Fillina 791
Jodoibs 1284
Jodo-Muc 1014
Jodopropano 1722
Joduron 674
Jomax 285
Jonctum 1507
Josacine 1117
Josamycin 1117
Josaxin 1117
Josir 1970

judolor Dragees 946
judolor-Dragees 946
Jumex 1864
Junmycin V 2002
Justamil 1934
Justar 461
Justor 469
Juvelux 2065
Juvevitan 2065

K

Kaban 512
Kabanimat 512
Kabikinase 1905
Kadian 1368
Kadiur 305, 1677
Kadol 1624
Kafocin 372
Kaibohl 1593
Kaichyl 2156
Kalgut 588
Kalicitrine 455
Kalium-Can.-ratiopharm 1677
Kallaterol 1371
Kalma 2140
Kalspare 450, 2101
Kalten 90, 146
Kalutein 531
Kalymin 1755
Kamillosan 1014
Kamycine 1118
Kanacillin 1118
Kanacyclin 1118
Kanaderm 1118
Kanaderm 200 608
Kanafuracin 1118
Kanamicina Firma 1118
Kanamycin 1118
Kanamycin-POS 1118
Kanamytrex 1118
Kana-Ophthal 1118
Kanatrombina 1118
Kanazone 609, 1118
Kanendomycin 186
Kanendos 186
Kannasyn 1118
Kanrenol 1677
Kantec 1207
Kantrex 1118
Kapanol 1368
Kappabi 626
Kardégic 29
Kardiamed 28
Karison 508
Karvea 1096

KARVEZIDETM 1096
Katabios 1809
Katadolon 907
Katasma 683
Katasma balsamico 315
Kataval 2098
Kativ 1239, 1240
Kativ N 1630
Katoseran 479
Katovit 1722
Kattwilon 1106
Kavaform 1119
Kayeine 1630
Kaywan 1630
KC Oint. 1025
Kéal 1912
Kealain 341
Kebuzon 1121
Kedacillin 1915
Kedacillina 1915
Kefadim 403
Kefadol 375
Kefadole 375
Kefandol 375
Kefazon 388
Kefglycin 372
Keflex 370
Kéflin 373
Keflin 373
Kéflodin 372
Keflodin 372
Keforal 370
Kefox 408
Kefoxina 377
Kefral 368
Kefspor 368
Keftid 368
Kefurox 408
Kefzol 379
Keimicina 1118
K-Eine 1630
Keiperazon 381
Keipole 1630
Keldrin 1131
Kelfer 579
Kelfiprim 1927, 2119
Kelfizina 1927
Kelfizine-W 1927
Keligroll 234
Kellina 1131
Kelnac 1673
Kélocyanor 730
Kelsef 399
Kemadrin 1716
Kémadrine 1716
Kemi 1735

Kemicetine 426
Kemicetine Succinate 426
Kemodyn 490
Kenacort 2097
Kenacort-A 2098
Kenacort A Retard 2098
Kenacort-A Retard 2097
Kenacort-retard 2097
Kenalcol 203, 2097
Kendural 1809
Kennegin 1630
Kentan-S 1121
Kenton 2065
Kephton 1630
Kepinol 1931, 2119
Keracaine 1749
Kerato Biciron 325
Keratyl 1395, 1395
Kerlocal 2094
Kerlon 236
Kerlone 236
Kernit 357
Keselan 996
Kesint 408
Kessar 1969
Kest 1616
Ketaject 1121
Kétalar 1121
Ketalar 1121
Kétamine Panpharma 1121
Ketanest 1121
Ketartrium 1126
Ketas 1038
Ketaset 1121
Ketazon 1121
Ketazone 1121
Kethamed 1574
Ketobutan 1121
Ketobutane 1121
Ketobutazone 1121
Ketochol 583
Ketocid 1126
Kétoderm 1125
Ketodol 1126
Ketofen 1126
Ketonil 956
Ketophezon 1121
Ketovite 2065, 249, 1239, 1809
Kétrel 2094
Ketrizin 377
Kétum 1126
Kevatril 979
Khelline Promethazine Berthier 1131

Ledopan 1295
Lefcar 357
Légalon 1876
Legalon 1876
Legederm 51
Leios 798
Lekrica 443
Lemicut 739
Lemocin 418
Lemonvit 138
Lendormin 276
Lenen 893
Leniartril 1403
Lenident 1712
Lenigesial 2169
Lenirit 1025
Lenixil 430
Lenoxin 646
Lentaron 932
Lentinan 1151
Lentinorm 1241
Lentizol 97
Lentogest 1033
Lentorsil 2153
Lentostamin 443
Leodrine 1027
Leofungine 1571
Leostesin N 1174
Lepetan 294
Lepinal 1616
Lepinaletten 1616
Leponex 538
Leptilan 2157
Leptofen 722, 853
Leptryl 1599
Lergoban 680
Leritine 127
Lescol 924
Lesten 586
Letamate 2156
Lethidrone 1392
Letofort 1153
Leucorsan 214, 1541
Leucovorin 928
Leukase 942
Leukeran 424
Leukerin 1257
Leunase 139
Leustat 494
Leustatin 494
Leustatine 494
Levadil 656
Levanxol 1981
Levaquin 1168
Levaru 1169
Levatol 1574

Levicor 1274
Levlen 799, 1171
Levocarvit 357
Levo-Dromoran 1172
Lévoearnil 357
Levomezine 1169
Lévophta 1162
Levophta 1162
Levoprome 1169
Levospan 1296
Levostab 1162
Levothroid 1173
Levothym 1524
Lévothyrox 1173
Levotomin 1169
Lévotonine 1524
Levoxyl 1173
Lexil 1729
Lexobene 630
Lexomil Roche 266
Lexotan 266
Lexotanil 266
Lexpec 927
Lexxel 741, 834
Liberen 618
Libratar 428
Librax 429, 502
Libraxin 502
Librium 429
Licain 1174
Lidanil 1263
Lidaprim 1933, 2119
Lidex 892
Lidex E Cream 892
Lidocaine 1174
Lidocaine Hydrochloride
  1174
Lieze 534
Liféne 1621
Lifril 899
Likacin 89
Like 2153
Likuden M 981
Lilacillin 1915
Lilizin 214
Lilo 40 cioccolatini 1616
Liman 1989
Limbatril 97, 429
Limbial 1514
Limbitrol 97, 429
Limbitryl 97, 429
Limclair 731
Limican 63
Limpidon 327
Limptar 1776, 2012
Linasen 1616
Lincocin 1175

Lincocine 1175
Lindoxyl 79
Lindral 1951
Lindrax 1951
Linea Valeas 85
Linfolysin 424
Lingraine 769
Linola 1694
Linoladiol 780
Linoladiol-H 780
Linola-sept 504
Linolosal 233
Linosal 233
Linseral 1202
Linton 996
Linyl 1622
Liocarpina 1634
Liometacen 1075
Liomycin 719
Liorésal 175
Lioresal 175
Lioton 1002
Liotropina 152
Lipaderin 503
Lipanor 482
Lipanthyl 843
Lipantil Micro 843
Lipavlon 516
Lipidax 843
Lipidil 843
Lipidium 1429
Lipidium-Sedaph 1429
Lipirate 503
Lipitor 150
Lipoatox 2020
Lipobalsamo 984
Lipobay 412
Lipo-C 455
Lipoclar 843
Lipoclin 503
Lipocol 453
Lipo Cordes 64
Lipofene 843
Lipofibrate 503
Lipogeron 300 1303
Lipo-Merz 815
Liponorm 1878
Liponsäure-ratiopharm
  2020
Lipopill 1622
Liposit 843
Liposit Merz 1880
Liposolvin 1877
Lipostat 1687
Lipotalan 605
Lipotrin 559
Lipovas 1878

Lipox 240
Liprevil 1687
Liprinal 517
Liprodéne 1591
Liptan 1041
Liquamar 1620
Liquemin 1002
Liquid Pred 1700
Liquifilm 434
Lircapil 1611
Lisacef 399
Lisacol Metionina 1078
Lisacort 1700
Lisanirc 1425
Lisil 346
Lisinbiotic 1201
Lisinciclina 1201
Lisino 1190
Liskatin 1709
Lisomicina 1581
Lisomucil 346
Lisopulm 80
Lispamol 94
Listerine 1243
Listerine Antiseptic 475
Listomine 306
Listrocol 566
Litalir 1030
Litoff 2153
Litosmil 675
Litoxol 1926
Litraderm 1024
Litursol 2153
Liverin 124, 455
Livial 2033
Livocab 1162
Livostin 1162
Lixidol 1128
Lixil 287
Lizatlone 641
Llangene 1944
Lobac 1626, 1852
Lobalacid 535
Lobarthrose 1298
Lobatox 1179
Locacid 2094
Locacorten 885
Locacortène 885
Locacorten-Vioform 504
Localison 605
Localone 2097
Localyn 892
Localyn Oto 1675
Locapred 598
Locasalène 885
Locatrop 598

Mandokef 375
Mandol 375
Mandolsan 375
Mandotrilan-"forte" 133
Mandrax 1282
Mandrolax 250
Mandrolax Pico 1884
Mandros 662
Maneon 91
Manerix 1352
Manilina 770
Maninil 968
Maniol 638
Manir 1538
Manoplax 869
Manosil 1025
Mantadan 77
Mantadil 428
Mantadix 77
Manusept 2106
Manypren 1041
Maolate 444
Maon 1897
Mapro-Gry 1209
Marax 749, 1035
Marbaletten 1205
Marcain 292
Marcaina 292
Marcaina adrenalina 292
Marcaina iperbarica 292
Marcaïne 292
Marcaïne adrénaline 292
Marcain with Adrenaline 292
Marcumar 1620
Maren 714
Marevan 2183
Marezine 556
Margéryl 1990
Marienbader 250
Marinol 721
Marlyn Formula 50 1757
Marocid 770, 771
Marolderm 614
Marplan 1100
Marsilid 1095
Marsthine 498
Martigène 274
Marucyclan 556
Marukunan 2066
Marvelon 597, 798
Marygin M 1107
Marzine 556
Masblon H 1029
Maschitt 1020
Masculax 2160
Maskin 430

Masletene 498
Masnoderm 535
Masor 1905
Masterfin 1951
Masterid 723
Masterid Spritzamp. 723
Masteril 723
Masteron 723
Masterone 723
Mastisol 723
Masuharmin 2101
Matenon 1325
Materna 2065, 138, 927, 1806
Matorozin 956
Matromycin 1482
Matulane 1713
Maveral 924
Mavik 2088
Maxair 1661
MAXALT 1829
Maxalt 1829
Maxaquin 1182
Maxibolin 805
Maxicaine 1562
Maxicam 1112
Maxidex 605
Maxidol 1675
Maxifen 1671
Maxiflor 640
Maxilase Bacitracine 174
Maximed 1747
Maximum 678
Maxipen 1610
Maxitrol 606, 1675
Maxolon 1313
Maxtrex 1289
Maxzide 2101
Maycor 1108
Mayeptil 2024
Mazildene 1211
MCR 50 1109
Meaverin 1250
Mebaral 1300
Mebendazol 1212
Mebron 754
Mecain 1250
Mecalmin 638
Mecloderm 892
Meclomen 1216
Meclon 535, 1217
Meclutin 892
Mecostrin 668
Mecroeat 1217
Medaron 944
Medazepam AWD Tabletten 1222

Medemycin 1330
Mederima 64
Mederma 491
Mediabet 1277
Mediatensyl gél 2151
Mediator 195
Mediaxal 195
Médibronc 346
Medicon 616
Medigel 749, 177
Medigeron 1303
Medigesic 299
Medihaler-Ergotamine 769
Medihaler-Iso 1106
Medil 286
Medinex 678
Medinol 1558
Medinox 557, 1862
Mediobiotin 248
Mediolax 250
Mediper 388
Medipo 1878
Médiveine 675
Medixin 2119
Medocarnitin 357
Medodorm 424
Medomet 1294
Medomin 1003
Medomine 1003
Medopa 1295
Medopren 1294
Medosalgon 1298
Medoxim 408
Medozide 1020, 1294
Medramil 1228
Medrate 1301
Medrocort 1228
Médrol 1301
Medrol 1302
Medrol Loz. Antiance 1302
Medrone 1301
Medryson Faure 1228
Mefenesina 1246
Μόféκadyne 1230
Meflam 1229
Mefoxin 395
Mefoxitin 395
Mefrusal 1232
Mega 1214
Mega-B 249, 325, 555, 1029, 1078, 1431, 1757, 1809, 2016
Mégabyl 654
Megace 1233
Megacillin 216, 498
Megacillin oral 1619
Megaclor 522

Megadose 2065, 249, 1078, 1806
Megagrisevit 532
Megagrisevit N 532
Mégamag 141
Megapir 452
Megast 343
Megestat 1233
Megestil 1233
Mégimide 187
Megimide 187
Meglumine Diatrizoate 87
Megrin 1003
Meiact 382
Meilax 806
Méladinine 1290
Meladinine 1290
Melaxose 1135
Melbex 1379
Melbin 1277
Melex 1320
Melfa 1922
Méliane 798
Meliane 961
Melixeran 1235
Mellerette 2025
Melleretten 2024
Melleril 2024
Mellitos 350
Mellitos C 447
Mellitos D 2069
Melocin 1322
Melopat 222
Melval 1298
Melycin 1672
Memoq 1427
Memosprint 1757
Menabil Complex 843
Menaderm 184
Menaderm simp. 1103
Menadione Inj. 1241
Menagen 788
Menalgon 1757
Mendozal 1748
Menesit 344
Menformon 788
Menfula 1911
Meniedolin 638
Menopatol 2075
Menopax 1998
Menopax Cream 636
Menophase 1265
Menorest 780, 781
Menova 431
Menovis 781, 1718
Menrium 788
Menserene 193

Micutrin Beta 1763
Micutrin Beta crema 228
Midamor 90
Midarine 1953
Midécacine 1330
Midecin 1330
Midicel 1931
Midium 2065, 1757, 1806
Midnighton 638
Midol 478
Midone 128
Midoriamin 1333
Midorm A.R. 911
Midrid 1104
Midrin 1104
Midro 1884
Midurin 1995
Midy Vitamine C 138
Mifégyne 1334
Mifegyne 1334
Mifurol 354
Miglucan 968
Migracin 89
Migraeflux 662
Migräne-Kranit 795
Migräne-Kranit spezial 556
Migrätan 769
Migralave 279
Migralere 541
Migraleve 279
Migranet 1558
Migretamine 769
Migrexa 769, 1590
Migril 316, 556, 769
Migristène 669
Migristene 669
Migwell 556, 769
Mijal 305
Mikavir 89
Mikelan 361
Mikorten 1020
Mikroklist 1885
Milactan 479
Milfudorm 1514
Milgamma 195
Milhéparine 791
Milid 1720
Milide 1720
Milli-Anovlar 1463
Millibar 1063
Millicorten 605
Millicorten-Vioform 504, 610
Milligynon 1463
Millophyline 791
Milneuron 195
Milontin 1621

Milrila 1338
Miltex 1340
Miltown 1252
Milvane 799, 961
Milysted 1593
Mimius Proxymetacaine 1749
Minalfen 68
Minalfène 68
Mindol 1738
Mindol Merck 806
Minelcin 207
Minias 1192
Miniasal 29
Minidiab 971
Minidril 798, 1171, 1468
Miniluteolas 823
Minilyn 1202
Minims 426
Minims amethocaine 2001
Minims Benoxinate 1529
Minims Chloramphenicol 426
Minims Cyclopentolate 562
Minims Fluorescein Sodium 896
Minims gentamicin 959
Minims Homatropine Hydrobromide 1016
Minims lignocaine and fluorescein 896
Minims Pilocarpine 1634
Minims Prednisolone 1696
Minims Tropicamide 2133
Miniphase 1463
Minipress 1691
Minirin 596
Minisiston 798
Minisone 228
Minizide 1676
Mino-Aleviatin 2114
Minocin 1342
Minodiab 971
Minolip 195
Minolis 1342
Minomycin 1342
Minovital 1343
Minoximen 1343
Minprostin E_2 673
Minprostin $F_{2\alpha}$ 673
Mintal 1590
Mintezol 2026
Minulet 798, 961
Minzolum 2026
Miocamen 1331
Miocamycin 1331
Miocardin 358

Miocardina 1441
Miochol-E 21
Miocor 358
Miodar 856
Miodene 2146
Miokacin 1331
Miol Cream 444
Miolease 748
Miolene 1823
Mionevrasi 555
Mionevrasi forte 1757
Miopat 1309
Mios 338, 1712
Miotolon 943
Miotonal 358
Miotyn 2146
Miowas 1285
Miracef 377
Miraclin 719
Miradol 1945
Miradon 128
Miranova 798
Mirapex 1680
Mirapront 1622
Mirapront N 1471
Miraxid 1672
Miraxid/-K 1671, 1672
Mirciclina 586
Mirena 1171
Mirena Intrauterinpessar 1170
Miretilan 743
Mirfat 523
Mirfudorm 349
Mirfurdorm 349
Mirfusot 1516
Miridacin 1719
Mirpan 1209
Mirtilene 221
Mirtolor 1390
Mishiline 476
Misofenac 1346
Mistabronco 1262
Mistral 770
Misulban 297
Mitalon 556
Mitanoline 1707
Mitasone 606
Mitigal 1266
Mition-D 1922
Mitocor 2146
Mito-medac 1347
Mitomycin 1347
Mitomycin-C 1347
Mitoxana 1048
Mitredin 1741
Mittoval 60

Mixotone 1675
Mizollen 1350
Mnesis 1046
Moban 1357
Mobec 1236
Mobic 1236
Mobiflex 1989
Mobiforton 2004
Mobilat 1852
Mobilisin 880, 1031
Mobloc 834
Moclamine 1352
Mod 704
Modacin 403
Modacor 1531
Modalim 482
Modalina 2108
Modamide 90
Modane 325, 1617
Modane Plus 1883
Modane Soft 1883
Modatrop 1591
Modecate 906
Modenol 305, 1802
Modératan 85
Moderil 1801
Modicon 799, 1462
Modiodal 1353
Modip 834
Moditen 906
Modopar 201, 1165
Modrasone 51
Modrastane 2112
Modrenal 2112
Moducren 90, 1020, 2045
Moducrin 90, 2045
Moduret-25 90
Modurétic 90
Moduretic 90, 1020
Moduretik, -mite 90
Mofesal 1355
Mogadan Roche 1451
Mogadon 1451
Mohazorin 2066
Moisturel 666
Molevac 1764
Molidex 1024, 1025
Molin 786
Molmagen 224
Molpaque 1086
Molsicor 1358
Molsidolat 1358
Molsidomine 1358
Molsihexal 1358
Molsiton 1358
Moltanine 1220

Myolastan 2004
Myolespen 433
Myonabase 748
Myonal 748
Myoserol 1246
Myospasmal 2004
Myotenlis 1953
Myotonine 237
Myprozine 1406
Myrtrex F 2098
Myser 643
Myslee 2208
Mysoline 1709
Mysteclin 109, 2002
Mytacin 1390
Mytélase 79
Mytelase 79
Mytelase Tabletten 79
Mytrex 1476

N

Nabuser 1383
Nacom 344, 1164
Nacyl 112
Nadic 1384
Nadisan 350
Nadolol 1384
Nadrothyron-D 620
Naftazolina 1398
Nafti 1387
nafti 1387
Naftilong 1387
Naftilux 1387
Naftin 1388
Nagel-Batrafen 464
Naixan 1403
Nalcrom 551
Nalcron 551
Nalex 1626
Nalex-A 443
Nalfon 846
Nalgésic 846
Nalidicron 1390
Nalidixin 1390
Naligram 1390
Nalissina 1390
Nalline 1392
Nalone 1393
Nalorex 1394
Nalorphine Serb 1392
Naloxone Hydrochloride
  1393
Nanbacine 2187
Nandrolin 1397
Napacetin 1041
Napageln 833

Napaltan 1205
Naphcon 1398
Naphcon A 1614
Napratec 1346, 1402
Naprilene 741
Naprin 1934
Naprius 1403
Naprorex 1403
Naprosyn 1402
Naprosyne 1402
Naqua 2104
Naquival 2104
Naramig 1405
Narbel 2005
Narcan 1393
Narcan neonatal 1393
Narcanti 1393
Narcaricin 206
Narcolo 617
Narcoral 1394
Nardelzine 1610
Nardil 1610
Nardyl 101
Narigix 1390
Naropeine 1839
Naropin 1839
Naropina 1839
Narphen 1608
Narsis 1222
Nasacort 2097
Nasalcrom 551
Nasalgon 1541
Nasalide 887
Nasan 2188
Nasarel 888
Nascobal 555
Nasea 1788
Nasengel-ratiopharm 2188
Nasenspray-ratiopharm
  2188
Nasentropfen K-ratiopharm
  2188
Nasicortin 606, 606
Nasivin 1533
Nasivinetten 1533
Nasky 1079
Nasomixin 1024, 1025
Nasorex 1359
Nastenon 1533
Natabec 555, 767
Natacillin 1004
Natafucin 1406
Natarilan 498
Naticardina 1775
Natil 556
Natira U 1975
Natisedina 1775

Nativelle Digitaline 645
Natramid 1063
Natrilix 1063
Natrilix SR 1063
Natrix 1063
Natulan 1713
Natural Estrogenic
  Substance 788
Naturine 193
Nausicalm 662
Nausidol 1644
Nausilen 63
Nautamine 678
Nauzelin 704
Navane 2052
Navelbine 2178
Navidrex 561
Navidrix 561
Navispare 90, 561
Navoban 2134
Naxogin 1446
Naxogyn 1446
ND 443
Nebacetin 173
Nebcin 2063
Nebcine 2063
Nebdosator 2010
Neberk 1975
Nebicina 2063
Nebilet 1409
Nedolon 806
Nefadar 1413
Nefadol 1414
Nefam 1414
Nefluan 892
Nefrolan 530
Nefrolitin 1131
Nefrosul 1919
Nefurofan 1897
Neg-Gram 1390
NegGram 1390
Négram 1390
Negram 1390
Nehydrin 648, 650
Nelbon 1451
Nelova 799, 1265, 1462
Nembutal 1590
Nemexin 1394
Nene 1282
Neo Alinachiol 540
Neoaritmina 1678
Neoasdrin 1516
Neoasutoma 531
Neo-audiocort 2098
Neobac 173
Neobalsamocetina sosp. 772

Neobalsamocetina
  Supposte 770
Neobex 1516
Neobiphyllin-Clys 683,
  1750, 2011
Neobismocetina 770
Neoblimon 1403
Neoborocillina 616
Neocefal 375
Neocepacol 421
Neocholan 583
Neoclym 559
Neocoricidin 421, 443
Neo-Corovas 1582
Neo-cortef 1025
Neocortofen 606
Neo-Cromaciclin 586
Neocromaton 1809
Neocycline 2002
Neo-Cytamen 1029
Neocytamen 1029
NeoDecadron 942
Neo-Decadron Phosphate
  609
Neoderm 892
Neo-Diloderm Cream 628
Neodin 602
Neodopasol 201
Neodopaston 344, 1165
Neodorm 1590, 1981
Neodox 719
Neodrel 122
Neoduplamox 495
Neoepa 1078
Neoeparibiol 555
Neo-Erycinum 771
Neo-Eunomin 431, 798
Neo-Farmadol 1537
Neofepramol 1558
Neofocin 937
Neoformitrol 421
Neogama 1945
Neo Gastransil 472
Neogel 343
Neo-Gerison 1919, 1935
Neogest 1468
Neogeynevral 540, 1757
Neo-Gilurytmal 1678
Neoginon Depositum 782
Neogola 421
Neogratusminal 1741, 1862
Neogynon 798
Neoh 2 1843
Neo-Hombreol 2000
Neohydrin 432
Neoiodarsolo 136
Neoiodorsolo os 1722

Nitossil 526
Nitralfa 1109
Nitro-Crataegutt 1582
Nitrodex 1582
Nitrofurin 1454
Nitro-Novodigal 1582
Nitroret 1108
Nitro-Sandolanid 26, 1582
Nitrosorbide 1108, 1109
Nitrosorbon 1108
Nitroxolin 1455
Nitrumon 355
Nivadil 1443
Nivaquine 439
Niven 1425
Nizax 1456
Nizaxid 1456
Nizax mite 1456
Nizoral 1125
Noalcool 421
Noan 623
Nobacter 2105
Nobfelon 1041
Nobfen 1041
Nobgen 1041
N-Oblivon 1298
Nobrium 1222
Nocbin 687
Nocertone 1518
Noctadiol 101, 1862
Noctal 1728
Noctamid 1192
Noctamide 1192
Noctan 1305
Noctazepam 1514
Noctec 423
Noctenal 1728
Noctivane 1011
Noctran 14, 15
Noctran 10 682
Nocturetten 2155
Nodal 1473
Nodex 616
Nogacit 1390
Nogédal 1475
Nogram 1390
Noin 1066
Nolahist 1612
Nolamine 1612
Nolcart 234
Noleptan 929
Nolesil 956
Nolipax 843
Noludar 1305
Nolvadex 1969
Nomaze 1398

Nonflamin 2048
Non-Ovlon 798
Nootrop 1658
Nootropil 1658
Nootropyl 1658
Nopar 1597
Nopia 1836
Nopron 1425
Noracycline 1265
Noradran 983
Norakin 250
Norandrol 1397
Noravid 581
Norbalin 1397
Norbiline 1751
Norcozine 446
Norcuron 2160
Nordapanin 36
Nordaz 1460
Norden 1478
Nordette 799, 1171
Nordox 719
Norethin 799, 1265
Norethindrone and Ethinyl
    Estradiol 799
Norethisteron 1463
Norfen 1478
Norfenefrin retard forte-
    ratiopharm 1466
Norfenefrin Ziethen 1466
Norfin 1392
Norflex 1504
Norgalax 1883
Norgeric 29
Norgesic 1504
Norgeston 1171
Norglycin 2068
Noriday 1462
Norinyl 799, 1265, 1462
Norinyl-1 1265
Norisona 449
Noristerat 1464
Noritren 1473
Norkotral 1590, 1981
Norluten 1462
Norluten A 1463
Norluten D 1265, 1462
Norma 1538
Normabrain 1658
Normalene 251
Normalip 843
Normaln P 2108
Normase 1135
Normelan 1314
Normetolo 1466
Normi-Nox 1282
Normison 1981

Normix 1814
Normoc 266
Normodyne 1133
Normoglaucon 1309
Normolaxol 1471
Normonal 2122
Normoparin 1002
Normorest 1282
Normothen 712
Normotin 1004
Normotin-R rapid 791
Normoxidil 1343
Normud 2201
Noroxin 1467
Noroxine 1467
Norpace 685
Norphen 1478
Norpramin 592
Norprolac 1769
Norquinol 277
Nortestonate 1395
Nortimil 592
Nortrilen 1473
Nortussine 616, 983, 1255
Norval 1323
Norvasc 100
Norvir 1826
Norzetam 1659
Noscal 2130
Nossacin 481
Nostel 796
Notamine 443
Notens 193
Notézine 635
Notox 1516
Notul 472
Nourytan 1969
Novacef 377
Novadral 1466
Novaldin 1271
Novalgin 1271
Novalgina 1271
Novalgine 1271
Novalm 1252
Novamin 1715
Novaminsulfon 1271
Novaminsulfon-ratiopharm
    1271
Novamon 1606
Novanox/-forte 1451
Novantron 1349
Novantrone 1349
Novapamyl LP 2163
Novapen 632
Novapirina 630
Novaroc 1052
Novatropina 1017

Novazam 623
Noveril 626
Novesina 1529
Novésine 1529
Novesine 1529
Novesine Wander 1529
Novidroxin 1029
Noviform 240
Noviform-Aethylmorphin
    Dispersa Augensalbe 806
Novifort 240
Novimode 1187
Novobiocyl 388
Novocain 1712
Novo-Card-Fludilat 191
Novodigal 28
Novodigal Amp. 646
Novodil 556, 684
Novo-Dolestan 2155
Novogent 1040
Novogyn 799, 1171
Novo Heparin 1002
NovoNorm 1797
Novophyllin 2013
Novoserpina 1955
Novosulfina 1629
Noxigram 481
Noxyflex 1475
Nozinan 1169
NP 30 1706
N.T.R. 2010
Nubain 1389
Nubarène 1218
Nucofed 542
Nuctalon 779
Nuelin 2012
Nu-Iron-Plus Elixier 555
Nuital 822
Nullatuss 510
Nulogyl 1446
Numidan 1403
Numorphan 1534
Numotac 1102
Nupercain 474
Nupercainal 474
Nupercaine 474
Nuriphasic 798
Nurofen 1040
Nu-Seals Aspirin 29
Nutraflow 731
Nutrase 540
Nutrigéne 2065
Nutrigène 1809
Nycopren 1402
Nydrane 182
Nydrazid 1105
Nyolol 2045

pentox 1593
Pentoxifyllin-ratiopharm 400 1593
Pentrane 1291
Pentrex 111
Pentrexyl 111
Pentritol 1582
Pentrium 1582
Pen Vee 1619
Pepcid 827
Pepcidac 827
Pepdine 827
Pepdul 827
Pepsane 982
Peptarom 2153
Peptavlon 1583
Peracan 1099
Peracon 1099
Peracon Kali-Chemie 1099
Perandren 1303
Peraprin 1313
Perasthman 188, 2011
Perazolin 1882
Percamin 474
Perclusone 516
Percocet-5 1531
Percodan 1531
Percoffedrinol N 316
Percorten 602
Percorten M Crystals 602
Percotan 29
Percutaféine 316
Percutalgine 1851
Perdiphen 749, 680
Perdipina 1425
Perdipine 1425
Perdix 1354
Perebron 1525
Perebron /-Ciclina 1525
Peremesin 1218
Pérénan 650
Perfan 745
Perfolate 928
Perfudan 286
Pergotime 520
Perholin 1272
Periactin 567
Périactine 567
Pericardin 177
Perichron 341
Peri-Colace 1883
Peridex 431
Peridon 704
Péridys 704
Perifago 492
Perikursal 798
Periogard 431

Periplum 1446
Perisalol 1430
Perispan 1582
Perista 237
Peritol 567
Peritrast 86
Peritrate 1582
Peritrate Sincron. 1582
Perium 1585
Perivar 1004
Perketan 1122
Perkod 684
Perlatos 667
Permapen 205
Permastril 723
Permax 1597
Permiltin 684
Permitil 906
Perneuron 1230
Pernionin 1433
Pernivit 1432
Perocef 388
Peroxinorm 1493
Perphyllon 153
Persantin 684
Persantine 684
Persantin retard 684
Persedon Roche 1760
Persolv 2152
Persumbrax 684, 1514
Pertenso 192
pertenso 1019
Pertestis-Dep. 1998
Pertix 303, 1593
Pertix Hommel 2188
Pertix-Hommel 300
Pertix-Hommel Liquidum 303
Pertix-Solo-Hommel 1239
Pertofran 592
Perusid 1603
Perventil 1851
Pervetral 1535
Pervincamine 2175
Pervitin 1279
Perycit 1428
Pesiron 1905
Pesos 842
Peteha Dragees 1743
Petinutin 1267
Petnidan 802
Petylyl 592
Pevaryl 729
Pevaryl TC 2098
Pevisone 729, 2097
Pexan 2065
Pexid 1598

PFD 202
Pfizerpen 1619
Pfizerpen G 216
PFT Roche 202
Phaeva 961
Phanodorm 557
Phanurane 1677
Pharcillin 111
Pharmadose 1256
Pharmarubicin 755
Pharmatex 203
Pharmaton 555, 767
Pharmic 1975
Pharyngocin 770
Phenaemal 1616
Phenaemaletten 1616
Phencol 1620
Phénergan 1726
Phenergan 627, 1726
Phenhydan 1627
Pheniramidol 856
Phenobal 1616
Phenomet 1616
Phenoro "Roche" 332
Phénoro Roche 221
Phenoxene 445
Phenurone 1605
Phenytoin AWD 1627
Pheracor 1582
Pheramin 678
Pherarutin 2138
Philopon 1279
pHisoHex 1006
Phisohex disinf 1006
Phlébogel 291
Phlogase 1537
Phlogenzym 267
Phlogistol 1537
Phlogont 1537
Phlogont Salbe 1031
Pholcomed expect. 983
Pholcones 1627
Pholedrin liquidum 1628
Pholedrin-longo-Isis 1628
Pholtex 1626, 1627
Phortisolone 1696
Phoscortil-Klys 1697
Phospholine Iodide 729
Phospholine Jodide 729
Phospholinjodid Augentropfen 729
Phospholin Jodide 729
Phospoline Jodide 729
Phrenilin 299, 1558
Phylletten 590
Phyllocontin 2012
Phyllotemp 2012

Physeptone 1278
Physiogine 786
Physiomycine 1269
Physiostat 1202
Physiotens 1376
Phytex 1852
Piazofolina 1366
Piazoline 1366
Picolax 1884
Pierami 89
Pifazin 1631
Pilazon 1624
Pilo 1634
Pilocarpina Lux 1634
Pilocarpine Martinet 1634
Pilocarpol 1634
Pilogel 1634
Pilomann 1634
Piloral 498
Pilotonina 1634
Pilules Dupuis 251
Pilzcin 550
Pima Biciron 1405
Pimafucin 1405
Pimafucine 1405
Pimafucort 174, 1405
Pimenol 1666
Pinacetrop 1658
Pindac 1640
Pindoptan 1642
Pineroro 638
Pinimenthol 123, 474
Piniol 1398, 1516
Pinorubicin 1659
Piocaine 435
Piorin 248
Pipeacid 1648
Pipedac 1648
Pipefort 1648
Pipemid 1648
Piper 1649
Pipérilline 1651
Piperonil 1645
Pipolphen 1726
Piportil 1655
Piportil Depot 1655
Piportil L4 1655
Pipracil 1651
Pipram 1648
Pipril 1651
Piproxen 1403
Piptal 1649
Piptalin 1649
Pipurin 1648
Pirabutina 1537
Piraflogin 1537

Prednisolut 1695
Prednison "Dorsch" 1700
Prednison "Ferring" 1700
Prednison "Sanhelios" 1700
Predni-Tablinen 1700
Prednitracin 173
Predonine 1695
Predonine, water sol. 1697
Predsol 1696
Préfamone 85
Prefenid lipocrema 282
Pregaday 927
Pregnavit 767
Pregnon 798
Prelis 450, 1316
Prelone 1695
Prelu-2 1609
Preludin 1614
Prémarin 781, 788
Premarin 788
Premium 777, 2138
Prempak 788
Prempak C 1468
Premphase 1227
Prempro 1227
Prenacid 598
Prenalex 1996
Prenatal 1241
Prenisei 1698
Prenolon 1703
Prent 7
Prenylamine Lactate 1706
Prépacol 251
Pre-Par 1823
Pre-par 1823
Prepar 1823
Préparation H Veinotonic 675
Prepidil 673
Prépidil gel 673
Prepidil Gel 673
Prepidil gel 674
Prepulsid 486
Preran 2088
Pres /41
Prescal 1114
Preservex 9
Presinol 1294
Presinol pro inj. 1295
Pres i.v. 742
Presomen 1225
Pressalolo 656, 1133
Pressfall 1019
Prestim 193, 2045
Prestociclina 1581
Prestole 1020, 2101
Pretz-D 749

Prevacid 1143
Prevecillin 216
Prevex 834
Prexan 1403
Prexidine 430
Priamide 1107
Priamide-Eupharma 1107
Priatan 1590, 2014
Priaxim 890
Priftin 1813
Prigenta 960
Prilagin 1327
Prilon 1525
Prilosec 1488
Primacaine 1529
Primachina fosfato 1709
Primadol 1608
Primalan 1256
Primaquine Bayer 1709
Primaquine Phosphate 1709
Primar 78
Primaxin 468, 1053
Primaxin IV 1053
Primcor 1338
Primeral 1403
Primobolan 1276
Primobolan Depot 1276
Primobolan-Depot 1276
Primobolan Inj. 1276
Primodian 1303
Primodian Depot 1999
Primodian Inj. 2000
Primogeron 1303
Primolut Depot 1033
Primolut N 1462
Primolut-Nor 1463
Primosiston 1463
Primosiston Tab. 1462
Primoteston Depot 1999
Primoxil 1354
Primpéran 1313
Primperan 1313
Primron 1709
Primyxine 1542, 1675
Prinactizide 74, 1896
Prinalgin 49
Prinivil 1178
Prinmate 503
Prinn 788
Prinzide 1020, 1178
Priolatt 1146
Priomicina 937
Priovit 1809
Pripsen 1652
Priscofen 2069
Priscol 2069

Priscoline 2069
Privadol 966
Privin 1398
Privina 1398
ProAmatine 1332
Proampi 111, 1671
Pro-Banthine 1729
Probenecid 1710
Probenemid 1710
Probeta LA 1735
Probilin 1658
Procadil 1714
Procain 1712
Procainamid Duriles 1711
Procainamide 1711
Procainamide Durules 1711
Procaine Aguettant 1712
Procaine Hydrochloride 1712
Procaine Lavoisier 1712
Procamide 1711
Procanbid 1711
Procaptan 1601
Procardia 1434
Procardia XL 1434
Procardin 1741
Processine 479
Prochlor-Iso 1107
Prociclide 581
Procillan 1741
Proclival 291
Procorum 952
Procorum retard 952
Proctaspre 449
Proctisone 184
Proctocort 1024
Proctodon 676
Proctofoam 1025, 1682
Proctofoam HC 1682
Procto-Jellin 891
Procto Kaban 512
Procto-Kaban 474
Proctolin 892
Proctolog 1846
Proctoparf 285
Proctosedyl 474, 1025
Proctospre 680
Proculin 1398
Pro-Dafalgan 1726
Prodasone 1227
Pro-Diaban 973
Prodiol 1718
Pro-Dol 1436
Pro-Dorm 1191
Prodox 1033
Prodoxol 1526

Prodrox 1033
Prodroxan 801
Pro-effekalgan imiv 1727
Proendotel 531
Pro-Entra 2124
Profact 296
Profemin 945
Profénid 1126
Profenil 76, 1126
Proffit 540
Profollior B 781
Progehormon 1718
Progenin 1718
Progeril 650
Progeril Papaverina 650
Progesic 846
Progestab 801
Progestasert 1718
Progesteron-Depot 1033
Progestérone-Retard-Pharlon 1033
Progestogel 1718
Progestol 1718
Progestoral 801
Progestosol 1718
Proglicem 624
Proglycem 624
Prograf 1964
Progynon 781, 781
Progynon B 781
Progynon C 798
Progynon Depot 783
Progynova 783
Proherz 1741
Prohormo 1264
Pro-Iso 1107
Proketazine 352
Proladone 1530
Prolair Autohaler 184
Prolifen 520
Prolixan 158
Prolixin 906
Proloprim 2119
Proluton 1718
Proluton Depot 1033, 1033
Proluton-Depot 1033
Promac 1674
Promasone 1682
Promecon 213
Prometazina 1726
Prometazina Cloridrato 1726
Promethawern 1726
Promethazin-neuraxpharm 1726
Promexin 446
Promid 1720

Romet 1798
Romezin 1929
Romien 498
Romigal 29
Romilar 616
Rominophyllin 683
Rondec 1472, 275, 345
Rondimen 1229
Rondo-Bron 1269
Rondomycin 1269
Roniacol 1433
Ronicol 1433
Ronicol retard 1433
Ronicol-retard 1433
Ronicol Timespan 1433
Ronpacon 1318
Rontyl 1027
Ronyl 1574
Roseomix 1118
Roseramin 2017
Rosidil 1955
Rossomicina sosp. 772
Rotafuss 510
Rotilen 1269
Rovamicina 1892
Rovamycin 1892
Rovamycine 1892
Rovan 350
Rovigon 2065, 1806
Rovite Tonic 1588
Rowachol 475
Rowapraxin 1655
Rowasa 1261
Rowatinex 123, 475
Roxanol 1368
Roxene 1668
Roxenil 1668
Roxiam 1794
Roxicodone 1531
Roxiden 1668
Roximycin 719
Roxit 1843
Roystajin 2075
Rozagel 1318
Rozex 1318, 1801
Rub-All T 449
Rubex 717
Rubidazone 2211
RubieMen 662
RubieMol 1558
RubieNex 769
Rubimycin 1330
Rubitracine 771
Rubramin PC 555
Rudotel Tabletten 1222
Rufol 1930

Rugo 329
Rumicine 443
Runova 1029
Rupis 490
Rupton 1625
Rupton Chronules 274
Ruscorectal 1846
Ruscoroid 1846, 2001
Rutisept 2106
Rybutol 455
Ryegonovin 1296
Rynacrom compound 2188
Rynacrom Spray 551
Rynatan 1255
Rynaton 443
Rynatuss 749, 443, 1593
Rythminal 2186
Rythmodan 685
Rythmodul 685
Rythmol 1727
Rytmonorm 1727

S

Saal-F 881
Sabalamin 540
Sabidal 457
Sabril 2166
sab simplex 666
Saccar 1848
Sachicoron 1245
Safe Tussin 616
Sagamicin 1328
Sagittaproct 1776
Sagittol 40/80/160 1735
Sagrotan Med 203
Saiclate 556
Sainosine 2114
SalAc 1853
Sal-Acid 1853
Salactic Film 1853
Salactol 1852
Salagen 1634
Salamol Steri-Neb 1851
Salanil 956
Salarizine 479
Salazopyrin 1849
Salazopyrine 1849
Salbulair 1851
Salbumol 1851
Salbutard 1851
Salcoat 185
Salex 1079
Salflex 1854
Salf-Pas 94
Sali-Adalat 1232
Sali-Aldopur 1896

Sali-Aldopur, - forte 193
Saliamin 1852
Salibena 678
Salicol 456
Salicylic acid-Vaseline 1853
Sali-Decoderm 909
Salient 1126
Salimid 1852
Salimol 1930
Salinac 1075
Salinalon 453
Salipran 198
Sali-Prent 7, 1232
Sali-Presinol 1232, 1294
SALI-PUREN 2101
Sali-Raufuncton 213
Salistoperm 1851
Salisulf gastroprotetto 1849
Salitex 371
Salmetedur 1854
Salofalk 94, 1261
Salonair 1031
Salonpas 2065, 1031
Salpix 20
Sal-Plant 1853
Saltucin 305
Saludopin 305, 1295
Salural 193
Saluren 440
Saluric 440
Salyzoron 214
Salzone 1558
Samyr 41
Sanabronchiol 616
Sanal 214
Sanamiron 2104
Sanaprav 1687
Sanasepton 770, 771
Sanasthmax 184
Sanasthmyl 184
Sanasthmyl Dosier-Aerosol
   Rotadish 184
Sanatison 1024
Sanbetason 233
Sancyclan 556
Sandimmun 464
Sandimmune 465
Sandoin/-C 276
Sandolanid 26
Sandomigran 1673
Sandonorm 258
Sandosten-Calcium 2008
Sandosténe 2008
Sandoven 648
Sandoxin 1757
Sandrena 780
Sanflumin 1367

Sangen 2105
Saniflor 214
Sanifug 1187
Sankaira 1295
Sanmigran 1673
Sannecit 1079
Sanogyl 16
Sanoma 353
Sanomigran 1673
Sanoprostal 634
Sanoral 430
Sanorex 1211
Sanoxit 210
Sanpas Cal. 94
Sansert 1306
Sanstron 1303
Santasal 29
Santax 1187
Santemycin 1328
Santeson 606
Sapocitrosil 203
Sapratol 479
Sapresta 135
Sarenin 1859
Sargenon 141
Sargenor 135
Sargépirine 29
Saridon 1558, 1738
Saroten 97
Sarparel 1801
Sarpul 128
Satanolon 638
Satibon 456
Satolax-10 251
Satomid 540
Sausal 1436
Savamine 1723
Savarine 439, 1721
Saventrine 1106
Savitol 767
Savlodil 430
Savlol 430
Sawacillin 107
Sawasone 606
Sawatolone 641
Scabol 1266
Scandicain 1250
Scandine 1037
Schemergen 1624
Schering PC4 1468
Scheriproct 474, 498, 1695
Scherisolon Inj. 1695
Scherisolon Tab. 1695
Scherogel 210
Scheroson 547
Scheroson F 1025

Sigafenac 630
Sigamopen 107
Sigaperidol 996
Sigaprim 2119
Sigaprolol 1316
Sigasalur 945
Sigmadyn 1574
Sigmafon 1214
Sigmal 479
Sigmamycin 1482
Sigmamycine 1482
Sigmart 1430
Sijaprim 1931
Silamarin A 1741
Silbephylline 683
Silece 888
Silentan 1414
Silepar 1876
Silies 666
Silimarin B 1876
Sili-Met-San S 666
Silirex 1876
Silisan 666
Silliver 1876
Silomat 510
Silomat compositum 510
Silopentol 1516
Silvadene 1921
Silymarin 1876
Simaderm 993
Simoxil 107
Simpelate 177
Simplene 753
Simplex 1627
Simplotan 2047
Sinapsan 1658
Sinaxar 1911
Sincrivit 1809
Sinecod 300
Sinedyston 648
Sinemet 344, 1165
Sinequan 714
Sinesex 1280
Sinex Lachartre 1533
Sinfibrex 1877
Singestol 1465
Singoserp-Esidrix 1955
Singramicina 1581
Singulair 1362
Sinketol 1126
Sinkron 490
Sinnamin 158
Sinoflurol 1976
Sinografin 87
Sinomin 1931
Sinopen 436

Sinophenin 1723
Sinorum 2075
Sinosid 1565
Sinovula 798, 1463
Sinquan 714
Sinselpin 1801
Sinsurrene 602
Sinsurrene Forte 53
Sintabolin 1397
Sinteroid 516
Sinthrome 13
Sintisone 1698
Sintoclar 490
Sintodian 722
Sintopen 107
Sintosulfa 1936
Sintotrat 1024
Sintrom 13
Sinulin 443
Sinutas Sinus Allergy MS
  443
Sinvacor 1878
Siodelbate 508
Siogène 449
Siosteran 449
Siplarol 904
Siptazin 479
Sirdalud 2061
Sirenitas 188
Sirledi 1447
Siros 1116
Sirtal 339
Sisare Gel 780
Siseptin 1879
Sisolline 1879
Sisomin 1879
Sistalgin 1681
Sito-Lande 1880
Sitosterin Prostata Kapseln
  1880
Sitostérol Delalande 1880
Situalin 608
Situalin Antibiotico 608
Siutisane 1698
Sivastin 1878
Skelaxin 1275
Skelid 2041
Skenan 1368
Skiacol 562
Skilar 729
Skinman soft 2148
Skinoren 161
Sklerofibrate 240
Skleronorm 811
Skopyl 1292
SK-PETN 1582
SK-Soxazole 1925

Sloan balsamo 1031
Slo-Phyllin 2012
Slow-Fe folic 927
Slow Trasicor 1528
Slozem 660
Snel Miel 140
SNO Phenicol 426
Sno-Pilo 1634
Snup 848, 1255
Soaclens 731, 2021
Sobelin 503
Sobrepin 1881
Sodium Amytal 101
Sodium Cephalotin 373
Sodium Dehydrocholate
  583
Sodium Sulfadiazine 1921
Sodiuretic 193
Sofalead 638
Sofargen 1921
Sofarin 630
Sofmin 1169
Sofradex 606, 942
Soframycin 942
Soframycyne 1398
Sofra Tüll 942
Sofra-tulle 942
Sofra-Tulle 942
Sokaral 605
Solacen 2143
Solamin 1131, 1862
Solan 1806
Solanax 72
Solantal 2032
Solar 13
Solaskil 1159
Solaxin 453
Solcillin 111
Solcillin C 536
Solco H 1029
Solcort 609
Soldactone 1677
Soldesam 609
Soledum 216, 475
Solesorin 1019
Solfa 99
Solfomucil 346
Solgol 1384
Solimidin 2204
Solivax 1883
Solmucol 22
Solnomin 638
Solo-Decortin H 1697
Solon 1885
Solosin 2011
Solpadol 541
Solprene 1695, 1696

Soltux 515
Solubacter 2105
Solucis 346
Solucort 1696
Solu-cortef 1024
Soludacortin 1697
Soludactone 1677
Soludécadron 609
Solu-Decortin 1695
Solumedine 1929
Solu-Médrol 1301
Solu-Medrol 1302
Solu-medrol 1302
Solupen 1954
Solupred 1697
Solupsan 29, 340
Soluroid 185
Solurol 1953
Solutio Cordes 605
Solutrast 1086
Solutricine Tétracaïne 2001
Soluvit 249, 555
Solvega 508
Solvo-strept 651
Soma 353
Soma Complex 353
Somagard 594
Somagerol 1191
Somagest 98
Somanil 353
Somatoline 777
Somatoline emuls. 1173
Somatyl 223, 224
Sombulex 1011
Somelin 1000
Sominex 1726
Somnafac 1282
Somnubene 557
Somnupan C 557
Sonacon 623
Sonata 2193
Soneryl 1860
Songar 2102
Sonifilan 1881
Sonilyn 1919
Sonin 1188
Sonuctane 1862
Sonybod M Inj. 2000
Sooner 1106
Soor-Gel 590
Soorphenesin 444
Soorphenesin H 444
Sophia-A, C 1462
Sophiamin 429
Sopor 1282
Soprol 253

Stratene 417
Streptaguaine 1906
Streptase 1905
Streptocol 1906
Strepto-Fatol 1906
Streptoguanidin 651, 1629, 1912, 1926
Streptohydrazid 1907
Streptokinase 1905
Streptomagna 651
Streptomicina Morgan 651
Streptomicina Solfato 1906
Streptomycine Diamant 1906
Streptomycin-Hefa 1906
Streptomycin Sulfate 1906
Streptoniacide "LeBrun" 1907
Streptoplus 2119
Streptosil 203
Streptosil Neomicina 1938
Streptotriad 1906, 1921
Stresson 289
Striaton 344
Strocain 1517
Strodival 1908
Stromba 1900
Strombaject 1900
Stryphnasal 44
Study 2156
Stugeron 479
Styptobion 1240
Suadian 1388
Suavedol 967
Suaviter 140
Subcutin 208
Sublimaze 852
Subutex 294
Succicuran 1953
Succin 1953
Suciralin 371
Sucira N 373
Sucrabest 1912
Sucrager 1912
Sucral 1912
Sucralfate 1912
Sucralfat-ratiopharm 1912
Sucralfin 1912
Sucramal 1912
Sucraphil 1912
Sucrate 1912
Sudafed 2124
Sudocrem 215
Sufamal 65
Sufenide 1951
Sufenta 1913
Sufrexal 1122

Sugracillin 216
Suiclisin 843
Sular 1450
Sulartrene 1942
Sulen 1942
Sulfa-Adsorgan 1928
Sulfabid 1937
Sulfacet 2119
Sulfaclorazina 1919
Sulfactin Homburg 663
Sulfadiazin 1921
Sulfadiazina 1921
Sulfadiazina Sodica 1921
Sulfadimetossina 1922
Sulfalar 1925
Sulfalerm 124
Sulfalest 1936
Sulfalon 1922
Sulfamylon 1205
Sulfapadil 1936
Sulfapenta 1936
Sulfapirina 1936
Sulfarlem 124
Sulfasalazin-Heyl 1849
Sulfasuxidine 1912
Sulfa-Tardocillin 205
Sulfathalidine 1629
Sulfatreis 1936
Sulfazin 1925
Sulfenal 1937
Sulfenta 1913
Sulfenteral 1629
Sulfile 2046
Sulfixone 1936
Sulfomyl 1205
Sulfonamides Duplex 1921
Sulfonamid-Spuman 1935
Sulfopiran 1936
Sulfopirimidina 1936
Sulforal 1936
Sulfose 1921
Sulfuno 1934
Sulfur-8 Shampoo 2106
Sulic 1942
Sulinol 1942
Sulla 1933
Sulmen 1934
Sulmethon 1922
Sulmetoxyn 1922
Sulmidal 1931
Sulmycin 234, 959
Sulp 1945
Sulparex 1945
Sulperazone 1914
Sulphena 1937
Sulpirid-ratiopharm 1945

Sulpitil 1945
Sulpivert 1945
Sulplotin 1951
Sulpylon 1271
Sulpyna 1271
Sultanol 1851
Sultiréne 1931
Sultopride Panpharma 1948
Sultrin 1917, 1918, 1938
Sultroponium B 1948
Sulxin 1922
Sulzol 1938
Sumacef 369
Sumetamin 1922
Sumifon 1105
Sunbazon 748
Suncefal 396
Suncholin 490
Sundralen 2028
Sunfull S 2065
Sunfural 1976
Sunia-D Comp. 606
Sunrythm 1635
Supadol 1017
Superbolin 1397
Supero 408
Superprep/-forte 662
Superthiol 346
Suplexedil 849
Supotran 432
Supponoctal 101, 1862
Suppoptanox 2180
Supracombin 2119
Supracyclin 100/200 719
Supradyne 249
Supral 1571
Supramycin N 2002
Suprarenin 753
Supratonin 82
Suprax 386
Suprecur 296
Suprefact 296
Supres 2113
Suprexon 986
Sup-Rhinite 443
Supristol 1934
Suprol 421, 1951
Suracton 1897
Sureptil 10, 479, 1004
Surestryl 1372
Surfacaine 560
Surfacatal 80
Surfacten 1952
Surfont 1212
Surgam 2031
Surgamyl 2031

Surgestone 1724
Surheme 298
Suril 1912
Surital 2018
Surmontil 2121
Surparine 795, 1017
Survector 91
Survitine 2065, 249, 542, 1809
Suspendol 67
Sus-Phrine 753
Sustanon 2000
Sustenium 1757
Sustiva 734
SUSTIVA 734
Suvipen 1271
Suxilep 802
Suxinutin 802
S. V. C. 16
Sweetaste 1848
Sylpinale 476
Symadal 666
Symbol 1346
Symmetrel 77
Sympatocard 1587
Sympatol 1954
Synaclyn 888
Synadrin 1706
Synalar 892
Synalar C 504
Synalar Neomycin 892
Synalgo 1403
Synalgos-DC 648
Synandrol 2000
Synanthic 1519
Synapause 786, 786
Syncarpin 1419
Syncillin 163, 1610
Syncl 371
Synclotin 373
Syncorta 602
Syncortyl 602
Syncurine 578
Syndol 720
Synédil 1945
Synemol 892
Synergil 555
Synergomycin 269, 770
Synergon 788, 1718
Synerone 2000
Synflex 1402
Syngestrotabs 801
Syngynon 781
Synkavit 1240
Synkavite 1240
Synpen 436
Synpenin 111

Tensilan 1729
Tensilene 1528
Tensilon 731
Tensimic 213
Tensinase-D 809
Tensionorme 193, 1802
Tensiplex 2171
Tensitral 925, 1559, 1801
Tensobon 337
Tensodin 795
Tensoflux 193
Tensogard 939
Tensophoril 101
Tenstaten 461
Tenuate 85
Tenuate Dospan 85
Tenuate-Dospan 85
Teobid 2012
Teofilcolina 457
Teofilcolina sedativa 457
Teofilcolina Sedativo 1616
Teonelin 2061
Teonicon 1636
Teonova 2012
Teoptic 361
Teorema 974
Teoremac 974
Teostallarid 815
Teostellarid 1741
Tepam-BASF 2004
Tepanil 85
Tepilta 1517
Teprin 507
Terazol 1994
Terbul 1992
Terbutalin 1992
Terbuturmant 1992
Tercian 553
Terconal 1994
Tercospor 1994
Terfedura 1995
Terfemundin 1995
Terfium 1995
Terfluzine 2108
Terfonyl 1921
Tergynan 1318, 1476, 1697
Teridax 1087
Terion 929
Terlomexin 854
Terneurine H 5000 1029
Teronac 1211
Terpanil 956
Terpoin 983
Terracortil 1542
Terra-Cortril 1542

Terra-cortril 1542
Terramycin 1542, 1675
Terramycin/Depot 1542
Terramycine 1542
Terravenös 1542
Tersigat 1524
Tertroxin 1176
Terzolin 1125
Tesamurin 1955
Tes-Hol "Z" 1998
Teslac 1997
Tesoprel 274
Tespamin 2025
Tessalon 210
Testac 916
Testamin 616
Testaval 783
Testex 2000
Testifortan 1303
Testinon 2000
Testoderm 1998
Testodet 2000
Testo Enant 1999
Testohgen 885
Testonate 2000
Testoral 1998
Testorit-Dep. 1998
Testosteron-Depot
  Jenapharm 1999
Testosteron Depot-
  Rotexmedica 1999
Testosterone Depositum
  1998
Testostérone retard
  Théramex 1998
Testosterone Tarrico 1998
Testosteron Propionat
  "Eifelfango" 2000
Testotard 916
Testoviron 2000
Testoviron Depot 1998,
  1999
Testovis 1303, 2000
Testradiol 781
Testred 1303
Tethexal 2004
Tetocaine 2001
Tetracor 1587
Tetracycletten 1241, 1542
Tetracyclin 2002
Tétracycline Diamant 2002
Tetradek 586
Tetra-Gelomyrtol 1542
Tetragynon 798
Tetralution 2002
Tetralysal 1201
Tetramdura 2004
Tetramide 1323

Tetramil 1614, 2005
Tetranase 267, 1542
Tetra-saar 2004
Tetrasolvina 1581
Tetra-Tablinen 1542
tetrazep 2004
Tetrazol 1587
Tetrex PMT 1834
Tetrilin 2005
Teveten 762
Tevosid 2013
Texmeten 641
Texodil 392
TFT Thilo 1 %
  Augentropfen 2110
Thalamonal 722, 722, 852
Thalazole 1629
Thalitone 451
Thalomid 2007
Thamacétat 2132
Thamesol 2132
THAM-Köhler 3 M 2132
Tham-Set 2132
Thean 1750
Theelin 788
Thenfadil 2010
theo 2011
Theo-Alvonal 1911
Theocolin 457
Theodrox 2012
Theo-dur 2012
Theo-Dur 2012
Theo-Hexanicit 177
Théolair 2011
Theolair 2011
Theonikol 2185
Theophyl-Choline 457
Theophyllard 2011
Theophyllin 2011
Theophyllin-Aethylendiamin
  ratiopharm 2012
Theophyllin retard
  ratiopharm 2011
Theophyllol 2012
Théostat 2011
Theourin 683
Thephorin 1612
Théprubicine 1659
Theradia 1921
Theradiazine 1921
Thera-Gesic 1243
Théragynes 992
Théralène 62
Théralène Pectoral 62
Theralene pectoral Sirup
  806
Theramycin Z 770

Theraplix 47
Therarubicin 1659
Thevier 1173
Thiacyl 1911
Thiamazol-Henning 2014
Thiamcol 2017
Thiamilase 540
Thiancol 2017
Thianeurone 17
Thiasin 1925
Thiaton 2055
Thiaver 756
Thiazamide 1938
Thiazid-Wolff 2101
Thiazomide 1938
Thibrin 1221
Thiloadren 681
Thilocanfol 163
Thilocanfol C 426
Thilodigon 681, 986
Thilorbin 896, 1529
Thimozil 1375
Thiobal 2022
Thiobiline 2046
Thioctacid 2020
Thioctsan 2020
Thioderon 1249
Thiodrol 756
Thiofact 2017
Thiofantile 1990
Thiogamma 2020
Thioguanine Tabloid 2050
Thioguanine Wellcome
  2050
Thioguanin-Wellcome 2050
Thioinosie 1257
Thiola 2051
Thiomid 800
Thioncycline 491
Thionicol 2017
Thioniden 800
Thiopental "Hycomed"
  2021
Thioperkin 1312
Thiophénicol 2017
Thiophenicol 2017
Thiophéol 2022
Thioplex 2025
Thioridazine HCl 2025
Thioridazine-neuraxpharm
  2024
Thiosol 2051
Thiosulfil 1930
Thiotal 2017
Thio-Tepa 2025
Thiotepa "Lederle" 2025
Thiotépa Lederle 2025

Totamol 146
Totapen 111
Totifen 1130
Totocortin 609
Tovan 1374
Tovene 675
Towk 2087
Toximer 65
Toxogonin 1477
Toyomelin 447
Tozalip 150
Trabest 498
Trachiform-V 1541
Trachyl 806
Tracrium 151
Tractur 1648
Tradelia 780
Tradenal 1741
TRADOL-PUREN 2086
Tradon 1574
Trafuril 1431
Trakipearl 429
Tral 1013
Traline 1013
Traline retard 1013
Tralisin 1201
Trama 2086
Trama AbZ 2086
Trama beta 2086
Tramadol 2086
Tramadura 2086
Tramagetic 2086
Tramagit 2086
Tramake 2086
Tramal 2086
Trama-Sanorania 2086
Tramdolar 2086
Tramedphano 2086
Tramundin 2086
Trancogésic 432
Trancolon 1245
Trancopal 432, 907
Trancoprin 433
Trancrol 453
Trandate 656, 1133
Trandiur 656, 1133
Tranex 2089
Tranexamic Acid 2089
Tranquase 623
Tranquirit 623
Tranquis 2108
Tranquo-Adamon 463
Tranquo-Buscopan 311
Transamin 2089
Transanate 433
Transbilix 42

Transbronchin 346
Transcop 4 sistemi
  transderm 1859
Transcycline 1834
Transderm Scop 1860
Transene 682
Transepar 459
Transfert 358
Transil 792, 2089
Transmetil 41
Transplatin 1510
Transpulmin 475
Transpulmina gola 590
Transulose 1135
Trantoin 1454
Tranxéne 682
Tranxene 682
Tranxilium 50 682
Tranxilium N 1460
Trapanal 2021
Tra-Quilan 448
Trasacor 1528
Trasentine 42
Trasicor 1528
Trasidrex 561, 1528
Trasipressol 647, 1528
Trasitensin 450
Trasitensine 450, 1528
Trasitensin Retard 1528
Trasylol 134
Trasylol Injection 134
Traumalgyl 1246, 1624
Traumalitan 1002
Traumanase 267
Traumasenex 1031
Traumon 814
Trausabun 1235
Travelgum 662
Travist 498
Travocort 641, 1101
Travogen 1101
Travogyn 1101
Traxam 833
Trecalmo 534
Trécator 800
Trecator-SC 800
Tredalat 7
Trédémine 1428
Tredol 1912
Trédum 850
Trelidat 650
Treloc 1019, 1316
Tremaril 1312
Tremarit 1312
Tremin 2111
Tremonil 1312
Trenimon 2101

Trentadil 178
Trentadil injectable 178
Trental 1593
Trepidan 1689
Trepress 450, 1019
Tresanil 1943
Trescatyl 800
Trescazide 800
Trescillin 1731
Trest 1312
Trétinoïne Kéfrane 2094
Tretionina 2094
Treupel 541
Treupel P 1558
Trevilor 2161
Trévintix 1743
Trevintix 1743
TRH 1745
Triacet 2098
Tri-adcortyl 2098
Triadene 961
Triamcinolon Wolff 2097
Triam Co 2101
Triam Creme Lichtenstein
  2097
Triamgalen 2097
Triamhexal 2097
Triaminic 1255, 1613, 1625
Triaminic Nasale 1533
Triam-Injekt 2097
Triam-oral 4 2097
Triampur 2101
Tri-Anemul 2097
Tri-antibiotique Chibret
  451, 651
Triapten Antiviralcreme 935
Triarese 2101
Triasporin 1116
Triastonal 1880
Triatec 1787
Triatussic 1625
Triavil 97, 1603
Triaz 211
Triazid 2101
Triazide 2104
Tricandil 1244
Tricef 377
Trichocide 1318
Tricilone 2101
Tricinolon 2098
Triclordiuride 2104
Tricloryl 2105
Triclos 2105
Tricodein 541
Tricofur 944
Tricofuron 944
Tricoxidil 1343

Tridelta 542
Tridesilon 598
Tridésonit 598
Tridesonit 598
Tridione 2114
Tridodilan 195
Triella 1462
Triette 798
Triferon 1757, 2016
Triflucan 875
Triflumann 2110
Trifluoperazine 2108
Triglobe 2119
Trigoa 798
Triguilar 798
Trigynon 799, 1171
Triherpine 2110
TRI-Horm 450
Trijodina 1722
Trijodthyronin 1176
Trilafon 1603
Trilax 1707
Trileptal 1515
Tri-Levlen 799, 1171
Trilifan Retard 1603
Trilisate 456
Triludan 1995
Trimeperad 2114
Triméthadione Abbott 2114
Trimeton 443
Trimicina 651
Tri-Minulet 799
Tri-minulet 961
Triminulet 799, 961
Trimipramin-neuraxpharm
  2121
Trimonal 781
Trimonase 2047
Trimono 2119
Trimopan 2119
Trimovate 509, 1542
Trimpex 2119
Trimysten 535
Trimulin 159
Trinevrina 2016
Trinevrina B$_6$ 1757
Triniton 647, 1802
Trinordiol 798, 1171, 1468
Tri-Norinyl 799
Tri-Normin 146, 1019
TriNoum 798
Trinovum 799
TriNovum 1462
Trinovum 1462
Trinsicon 138, 555
Trinuride 1611

Ultrapoct 474
Ultraproct 474, 498, 895, 895, 896
Ultrasine 894
Ultratussin 791
Ultravate 2148
Ultrex antipelliculaire 1759
Ulup 899
Umbradil 674
Umoril 2074
Unacid 111, 1914
Unacid P Doral 1946
Unacil 719
Unacim 111, 1914
Un-Alfa 55, 318
Unaseran-D 2017
Unasyn 1914, 1946
Unat 2082
Unergol 648
Unidone 128
Uniflox 484
Unilair 2011
Unilobin 1179
Unimide 500 2069
Unipen 1386
Uniphyllin 2011
Uniphyllin Continus 2012
Uniplus 1738
Unipril 1787
Uniquin 1182
Uniretic 1354
Uniroid 474
Unisom 678
Unisom Nighttime Sleep-
  Aid 720
Unitrim 264
Univasc 1354
Univex 2163
Unixime 386
Unosyn for Injection 111
Upstène 1061
Urabon 1504
Uracil Mustard 2150
Uractone 1896
Uralgin 1390
Urbanyl 505
Urbason 1301
Urbason Retard 1302
Urecholine 237
Urecortyn 1025
Urem 1040
Urerubon 2069
Uretoin 1454
Uretrim 2119
Urex 945, 1284
Urfadyn 1440
Urfadyne 1440

Urfamicina 2017
Urgilan 1741
Urgo Hühneraugenpflaster
  1852
Uriben 1390
Uribenz 300 67
Uricemil 67
Uricillina 351
Uricodue 67, 208
Uridoz 937
Uri-Flor 1390
Urimitexan 1262
Urinorm 206
Urion 60
Uripurinol 100/300 67
Urised 152, 1284, 1304
Uriseptin 1608
Urispas 861
Uritrate 1526
Uro Berocillin 1671
Urobiotic 1608
Urobiotic-250 1542, 1930
Urocarf 351
Uro-Cephoral 386
Urochinase 2152
Urocoli 1455
Urodene 1648
Urografin 86
Urogram 1390
Urokinase 2152
Urokinase Choay 2152
Urokinase-medac 2152
Urokinon 1930
Urokizol 1930
Urolene Blue 1304
Urologin N 1390
Urolucosil 1930
Uromide 1608, 1918
Uromil 1284, 2011
Uromiro 1082
Uromitexan 1262
Uromitexan 400 1262
Uromycol 535
Uronorm 481
Urophenil 2017
Uro-Phosphate 1284
Uropimid 1648
Uropyridin 1608
Uroqid-Acid 1284
Urosan 1648
Uroseptol 793
Urosetic 1648
Urosin 67
Urosol 1930
Urospasmon 1608, 1921
Urosul 1930
Uro-Tablinen 1454

Uro-Tarivid 1480
Urotractan 1284
Urotractin 1648
Urotrate 1526
Uroval 1648
Urovison 86
Uroxacin 481
Uroxatral 60
Uroxin 1526
Uroxol 1526
Uroxol mite 1526
Ursacol 2153
Ursilon 2153
Ursinus Inlay-Tabs 340
Ursnon 897
Urso 2153
Urso 100 2153
Ursobil 2153
Ursochol 2153
Ursofalk 422, 2153
Ursoflor 2153
Ursolisin 2153
Ursolvan 2153
Urupan 614
Usevir 1888
Uskan 1514
Ustimon 1012
Utemerin 1823
Utibid 1526
Uticillin 351
Utinor 1467
Utovlan 1462
Utrogest 1718
Utrogestan 1718
Uvéline 1541
Uvéstérol 2065
Uvistat 1320
U-vit. 1298
Uzara plus 1001

V

Vacian 376
Vadilex 1048
Vagantyl 1017
Vagifem 781
Vagilen 1318
Vagilia 65
Vagi-Plex 1009
Vagistat 2049
Vagogastrin 1538
Vagogernil 956
Vagolisal 472
Vagostigmin 1419
Vahodilan 1112
Valamid 797
Valamin 797

Valate 2156
Valatux 616
Valbil 831
Valclair 623
Valdorm 911
Valeans 72
Valemate 2156
Valemeton 2156
Valergen 783
Valeriana comb. Hevert 678
Valethalin 2156
Valethamin 2156
Valette 798
Validil 1537
Valiquid 623
Valium 623
Vallergan 62
Vallestril 1279
Valmiran 565
Valocordin 270
Valoid 556
Valomerck 1393, 2039
Valontan 662
Valopride 273
Valoron 1393
Valoron N 2039
Valpin 1478
Valpinax 623, 1478
Valrelease 623
Valsera 888
Valtolmin 177
Valtomicina 1581
Valtrax 623, 1107
Valtrex 2154
Vancenase 185
Vanceril 185
VANCO 2159
Vancocin 2159
Vancocina 2159
Vancocine 2159
Vancomin 1220
Vancomycin 2159
Vancomycin "Lederle" 2159
Vancomycin CP 2159
Vancomycine Dakota
  Pharm 2159
Vancomycine Lederle 2159
Vanco-saar 2159
Vandid 791
Vanilone 565
Vanisorbyl 565
Vanitile 1990
Vanlev 1486
Vanoxide-HC 211
Vanquin 1764
Vantol 238
Vaponefrin 753

Vinblastinesulfat-GRY 2170
Vinblastin R.P. 2170
Vinca 2175
Vincadar 2175
Vincafor 2175
Vincamin-retard-
 ratiopharm 2175
Vinca Retard 2175
Vincari 2175
Vincarutine 2175
Vincatreis 2175
Vinco 251
Vinco-Abführperlen 251,
 1539
Vincristin 2176
Vincristina 2176
Vincristina Tera 2176
Vincristin Bristol 2176
Vincristine Pierre Fabre
 2176
Vincristin liquid Lilly 2176
Vincristinsulfat-GRY 2176
Vinsal 2175
Vintop 1121
Vinutro Drops 1809
Viobeta 228, 504
Viocidina 504
Viocin 2180
Vioform 504
Vioform-hydrocortisone
 504
Viomicin 2180
Viomycin Pfizer 2180
Vioxx 1833
Vira-A 2165
Viracept 1417
Viracton plus 1303
Viramid 1807
Vira-MP 2165
Viramune 1423
Virazole 1807
Virdex 769
Virgan 955
Virginiana Gocce Verdi
 1398
VIrllon 1303, 1999
Virlix 418
Virophta 2110
Viroptic 2110
Virormone 2000
Viru-"Merz" 2131
Viru-"Merz" Serol 2131
Virudin 935
Virunguent 1047
Viruserol 2131
Virusmin 1367
Virusmohin 1367

Virustat 1367
Visacor 747
Visano 1252
Visano Cor 678
VisanoCor 1582
Viscal 1313
Visceralgina 2037
Viscéralgine 2037
Visceralgine 2037
Viscéralgine comprimés 101
Visclair 1220
Viscomucil 80
Viscorin 138
Viscotiol 1153
Visderm 81
Visergil 650
Visine 2005
Viskaldix 524, 1642
Visken 1642
Visnamine 2181
Vistacarpin 1634
Vistagan 1160
Vistagan Liquifilm 1160
Vistalbalon 1398
Vista-Metasone 228
Vista-Methasone 233
Vistamycin 1811
Vistaril 1035
Vistide 467
VISTIDE 467
Vistimon 1265
Vistosan A 1255
Vistoxyn 1533
Vistrax 1538
Visuanestetico 1749
Visublefarite 1918, 2005
Visublefarite sosp. oft. 228
Visucloben 509
Visuglican 551
Visumetazone 606, 2005
Visumetazone Antib. 228
Visumicina 186, 2005
Visumidriatic 2133
Visumidriatic Antif. 2133
Visumidriatic Fenil 2133
Visustrin 2005
Visutensil 986
Vitabil Composto 1078
Vitabil composto 1431
Vita Buerlecithin 1809
Vitacimin 138
Vita-Dor 133
Vitalerina 1809
Vitalgesic 195
Vitalipid 767, 1806
Vitalipide 767, 1630

Vitamax 1809
Vita-Metrazol 1588
Vitamfenicolo 426
Vitamina C Vca 138
Vitamina C Vita 138
Vitamin A Dispersa 1806
Vitamin A Dispersa
 Baeschlin 1806
Vitamin-A-Kapseln
 "Extracta" 1806
Vitamina K Salf 1241
Vitamin-A-POS 1806
Vitamin-A-Saar 1806
Vitamin B_1 Hevert 2016
Vitamin B_1-Injektopas 2016
Vitamin B_1 JENAPHARM
 2016
Vitamin B_1 Kattwiga 2016
Vitamin B_1-ratiopharm 2016
Vitamin B_6 ratiopharm 1757
Vitamin B_{12} 555
Vitamin B 12 forte 555
Vitamin B12
 Injektionslösung 555
Vitamin-B_{12}-ratiopharm 555
Vitamin C Phytopharma
 138
Vitamine A Dulcis 1806
Vitamine A Faure 1806
Vitamine B_6 Richard 1757
Vitamine B_{12} Aguettant 555
Vitamine B_{12} Lavoisier 555
Vitamine C-B_2 Lemoine
 1809
Vitamin E-Dragees 2065
Vitamine K_1 1630
Vitanevril 195
Vitarabine 2165
Vita Schlanktropfen 1471
Vitascorbol 138
Vitaseptol 2021
Vitasol AD_3 + E 542
Vitas U 1298
Vitate 1809
Vita-thirteen 1504
Vitazell G forte 1656
Vitecaf 1834
Viteparin 1002
Viterra 1809
Vit. E Stada 2065
Vitialgin 1738
Vit-O_2 108
Vit. PP 1431
Vitron-C 138
Vittoria Lazione 203
Vivactil 1747
Vivalan 2168

Vivalan LP 2168
Vivamyne 2065, 249, 555,
 927, 1809
Vivapryl 1864
Vivelle 781
Vivéne 2138
Vividrin 551, 1995
Vividyl 1473
VM-26-Bristol 1988
Voalla 610
Vogalène 1315
Vogan 1806
Volital 1574
Volley 302
Volmac 1851
Volmax 1851
Volon 2097
Volonimat 1476, 2097
Volon Tabl. 2097
Voltaren 630
Voltaréne 630
Voltarol 630
Volumax 1851
Volutine 843
Vomacur 662
Vomex 662
Vomiles 662
Vontil 2024
Vontrol 638
Voranil 532
Vraap 2175
V-Tablopen 1619
Vumon 1988
Vytone 653

W

Wagitran 1318
Wakazepam 1514
Wallerox 648
Wandonorm 258
Wansar 638
Warfarin 2183
Wasacne 2053
Wasangor 1706
4-Way Long Acting Nasal
 Spray 1533
Wellbutrin 83
Wellcoprim 2119
Welldorm elixir 423
Welvin-E 2065
Wespuril 628
White Gol 430
White Rive 430
Wick 616
Wick Daymed 983
Wick DayMed 1625

A

abietic acid
($C_{20}H_{30}O_2$; *514-10-3*)   see: Ecabet sodium
acefylline
($C_9H_{10}N_4O_4$; *652-37-9*)   see: Acefylline
acetaldehyde
(C_2H_4O; *75-07-0*)   see: L-Alanine; *cis*-Cefprozil; Chloral hydrate; Fencamfamin; Fenfluramine; Fluroxene; Indometacin; Methohexital; Mitopodozide; Netilmicin; Zileuton
acetaldehyde dimethyl acetal
($C_4H_{10}O_2$; *534-15-6*)   see: Metolazone
acetaldehyde (4-methoxyphenyl)hydrazone
($C_9H_{12}N_2O$; *13815-71-9*)   see: Indometacin
acetaldehyde thiosemicarbazone
($C_3H_7N_3S$; *2302-95-6*)   see: Sulfamethizole
acetamide
(C_2H_5NO; *60-35-5*)   see: Sulfacetamide
acetamidine
($C_2H_6N_2$; *143-37-3*)   see: Thiamine
α-acetamido-4-acetoxy-3-methoxycinnamic acid
($C_{14}H_{15}NO_6$; *32954-41-9*)   see: Levodopa
5-acetamido-*O*-acetylsalicylic acid
($C_{11}H_{11}NO_5$; *6376-29-0*)   see: Parsalmide
5-acetamido-*O*-acetylsalicyloyl chloride
($C_{11}H_{10}ClNO_4$; *6393-86-8*)   see: Parsalmide
α-acetamido-3-amino-5-iodo-4-(*p*-methoxyphenoxy)cinnamic acid methyl ester
($C_{19}H_{19}IN_2O_5$; *98016-18-3*)   see: Dextrothyroxine
(±)-6-acetamido-2-amino-4,5,6,7-tetrahydrobenzothiazole
($C_9H_{13}N_3OS$; *104617-51-8*)   see: Pramipexole hydrochloride
α-acetamido-5-amino-*m*-toluic acid
($C_{10}H_{12}N_2O_3$; *1574-52-3*)   see: Iodamide
4-acetamidobenzenesulfinic acid sodium salt
($C_8H_8NNaO_3S$; *15898-43-8*)   see: Dapsone
4-acetamidobenzenesulfonamide
($C_8H_{10}N_2O_3S$; *121-61-9*)   see: Carbutamide; Sulfabenzamide; Sulfacarbamide; Sulfanilamide; Sulfaproxyline
4-acetamidobenzenesulfonyl chloride
($C_8H_8ClNO_3S$; *121-60-8*)   see: Sulfacitine; Sulfadiazine; Sulfadicramide; Sulfadimethoxine; Sulfadoxine; Sulfaethidole; Sulfafurazole; Sulfalene; Sulfamerazine; Sulfamethizole; Sulfamethoxazole; Sulfametoxydiazine; Sulfamoxole; Sulfanilamide; Sulfathiazole; Sulfisomidine
(4-acetamidobenzenesulfonyl)urea
($C_9H_{11}N_3O_4S$; *2828-63-9*)   see: Sulfacarbamide
4-acetamidobenzoic acid
($C_9H_9NO_3$; *556-08-1*)   see: Deanol acetamidobenzoate
2-(2-acetamidobenzoyl)pyridine
($C_{14}H_{12}N_2O_2$; *1770-89-4*)   see: Bromazepam
2-(2-acetamido-5-bromobenzoyl)pyridine
($C_{14}H_{11}BrN_2O_2$; *1770-90-7*)   see: Bromazepam
5-acetamido-*N*-butylsalicylamide
($C_{13}H_{18}N_2O_3$; *6382-44-1*)   see: Parsalmide
***trans*-4-acetamidocyclohexanol**
($C_8H_{15}NO_2$; *27489-60-7*)   see: Ambroxol
4-acetamidocyclohexanone
($C_8H_{13}NO_2$; *27514-08-5*)   see: Pramipexole hydrochloride

4-acetamido-*N*-(2-diethylaminoethyl)-2-methoxybenzamide
($C_{16}H_{25}N_3O_3$; *3614-38-8*)   see: Bromopride
1-acetamido-3,5-dimethyladamantane
($C_{14}H_{23}NO$; *19982-07-1*)   see: Memantine
α-acetamido-4-hydroxy-3-methoxycinnamic acid
($C_{12}H_{13}NO_5$; *55629-72-6*)   see: Levodopa
2-acetamido-3-hydroxy-4'-nitropropiophenone
($C_{11}H_{12}N_2O_5$; *3123-13-5*)   see: Chloramphenicol
α-acetamido-3-iodo-4-(*p*-methoxyphenoxy)-5-nitrocinnamic acid methyl ester
($C_{19}H_{17}IN_2O_7$; *94256-35-6*)   see: Dextrothyroxine
4-(acetamidomethyl)benzenesulfonamide
($C_9H_{12}N_2O_3S$; *2015-14-7*)   see: Mafenide
3-acetamido-6-methylpyridazine
($C_7H_9N_3O$; *57260-79-4*)   see: Nifurprazine
2-acetamido-4'-nitroacetophenone
($C_{10}H_{10}N_2O_4$; *1846-34-0*)   see: Chloramphenicol
4-acetamido-4'-nitrodiphenyl sulfone
($C_{14}H_{12}N_2O_5S$; *1775-37-7*)   see: Dapsone
3-acetamido-6-[2-(5-nitro-2-furyl)vinyl]pyridazine
($C_{12}H_{10}N_4O_4$; *91974-95-7*)   see: Nifurprazine
DL-*threo*-2-acetamido-1-(4-nitrophenyl)-1,3-propanediol
($C_{11}H_{14}N_2O_5$; *4618-99-9*)   see: Chloramphenicol
***p*-acetamidophenyl chloroacetate**
($C_{10}H_{10}ClNO_3$; *17321-63-0*)   see: Propacetamol
4-(4-acetamidophenyl)-4-oxobutanoic acid
($C_{12}H_{13}NO_4$; *5473-15-4*)   see: Chlorambucil
2-acetamido-4-phenylsulfinylnitrobenzene
($C_{14}H_{12}N_2O_4S$; *54029-09-3*)   see: Oxfendazole
(4-acetamidophenylsulfonyl)guanidine
($C_9H_{12}N_4O_3S$; *19077-97-5*)   see: Sulfametoxydiazine
acetamidopiperonylmalonic acid diethyl ester
($C_{17}H_{21}NO_7$; *97018-57-0*)   see: Levodopa
4-acetamidosalicylic acid
($C_9H_9NO_4$; *50-86-2*)   see: Clebopride
4-acetamidothymol
($C_{12}H_{17}NO_2$; *3383-30-0*)   see: Moxisylyte
5-acetamido-2,4,6-triiodo-*N*,*N*'-bis(2,3-dihydroxypropyl)isophthalamide
($C_{16}H_{20}I_3N_3O_7$; *31127-80-7*)   see: Iohexol
acetanilide
(C_8H_9NO; *103-84-4*)   see: Chlorambucil; Sulfanilamide
acetic acid
($C_2H_4O_2$; *64-19-7*)   see: β-Acetyldigoxin; Bromperidol; Chlormidazole; Ciclometasone; Dimetacrine; Etidronic acid; Fluocinonide; Pirbuterol; Troglitazone
acetic acid ammonium salt
($C_2H_7NO_2$; *631-61-8*)   see: Oxaprozin
acetic acid 2-[7-chloro-5-(2-chlorophenyl)-3*H*-1,4-benzodiazepin-2-yl]hydrazide
($C_{17}H_{14}Cl_2N_4O$; *41837-74-5*)   see: Triazolam
acetic acid 2-[5-(2-chlorophenyl)-7-ethyl-3*H*-thieno[2,3-*e*]-1,4-diazepin-2-yl]hydrazide
($C_{17}H_{17}ClN_4OS$; *40054-72-6*)   see: Etizolam
acetic acid cobalt(2+) salt
($C_4H_6CoO_4$; *71-48-7*)   see: Midoriamin
acetic acid diethoxymethyl ester
($C_7H_{14}O_4$; *14036-06-7*)   see: Abacavir; Imiquimod

acetic acid palladium(2+) salt

(C$_4$H$_6$O$_4$Pd; *3375-31-3*)   see: Acrivastine

acetic anhydride

(C$_4$H$_6$O$_3$; *108-24-7*)   see: Abacavir; Acecarbromal;
Aceclidine; Aceglutamide aluminum; Acenocoumarol;
Acetarsol; Acetazolamide; Acetiamine; Acetrizoic acid;
Acetylcholine chloride; Acetylcysteine; Acetylsalicylic acid;
Acetylsulfafurazole; Acexamic acid; Aciclovir; Acipimox;
Acriflavinium chloride; Actarit; Afloqualone; L-Alanine;
Alfaxalone; Amcinonide; Amidotrizoic acid; Anagestone
acetate; Auranofin; Azapetine; Benzquinamide;
Betamethasone; Biotin; Bisacodyl; Bromazepam;
Bromopride; Calcifediol; Calcitriol; Camazepam;
Canthaxanthin; Capecitabine; Cefamandole; Ceftizoxime;
Chenodeoxycholic acid; Chloramphenicol; Chlormadinone
acetate; Cinchocaine; Cinolazepam; Clebopride; Clidanac;
Cloprednol; Cortisone; Cortivazol; Cyclofenil; Cyproterone
acetate; Cytarabine; Dapsone; Deferoxamine;
Dextrothyroxine; Diacerein; Diflorasone diacetate;
Difluprednate; Diltiazem; Enoxacin; Eprosartan; Etizolam;
Etynodiol acetate; Fexofenadine hydrochloride; Fluazacort;
Fludarabine phosphate; Fludroxycortide; Flugestone acetate;
Flumetasone; Fluocinolone acetonide; Fluperolone acetate;
Fluprednidene acetate; Fluprednisolone acetate; Flutamide;
Gabapentin; Gestodene; Gitaloxin; Gitoformate; Glaziovine;
Grepafloxacin; Halopredone diacetate; Hydrocortisone;
Hydrocortisone acetate; Hydroxyprogesterone; Ibuprofen;
Idoxuridine; Imiquimod; Iocetamic acid; Iodamide; Iohexol;
Isosorbide mononitrate; Lamivudine; Leflunomide;
Levamisole; Levodopa; Levonorgestrel; Lorazepam;
Lormetazepam; Mabuterol; Medroxyprogesterone acetate;
Megestrol acetate; Melengestrol acetate; Menadiol diacetate;
Mesoridazine; Metenolone acetate; Methandriol; Methestrol
dipropionate; Metipranolol; Metoclopramide; Midazolam;
Midecamycin acetate; Montelukast sodium; Mosapride
citrate; Moxifloxacin hydrochloride; Moxisylyte; Nalorphine;
Norethisterone acetate; Omapatrilat; Omeprazole;
Oseltamivir; Oxaceprol; Oxazepam; Oxcarbazepine;
Oxfendazole; Oxyphenisatin acetate; Pancuronium bromide;
Pantoprazole sodium; Paracetamol; Paramethasone;
Paricalcitol; Pengitoxin; D-Penicillamine; Phenacetin;
Pipecuronium bromide; Prednival acetate; Pregnenolone;
Proglumide; Promegestone; Pyridinol carbamate;
Quingestanol acetate; Rabeprazole sodium; Repaglinide;
Retinol; Roxatidine acetate; Salacetamide; Salbutamol;
Spizofurone; Stavudine; Sulfacetamide; Temazepam;
Tetrazepam; Thalidomide; Thebacon; 2-Thiophenecarboxylic
acid; α-Tocopherol; Trandolapril; Trenbolone acetate;
Triamcinolone; Troglitazone; L-Tryptophan; Vesnarinone;
Zalcitabine; Zanamivir

acetoacetaldehyde dimethyl acetal

(C$_6$H$_{12}$O$_3$; *5436-21-5*)   see: Ambuside

7-acetoacetamidocephalosporanic acid

(C$_{14}$H$_{16}$N$_2$O$_7$S; *56434-32-3*)   see: Cefotiam

acetoacetic acid ethyl ester

(C$_6$H$_{10}$O$_3$; *141-97-9*)   see: Aminophenazone; Baclofen;
Cefotaxime; Ceftazidime; Chloroquine; Cloricromen;
Cloxacillin; Dipyridamole; Felodipine; Flutoprazepam;
Hymecromone; Kawain; Lacidipine; Leflunomide;
Methylthiouracil; Nevirapine; Nitrendipine; Oxacillin;
Pentoxifylline; Propyphenazone; Sulfamerazine

acetoacetic acid 4-(trifluoromethyl)anilide

(C$_{11}$H$_{10}$F$_3$NO$_2$; *351-87-1*)   see: Leflunomide

acetoacetyl chloride

(C$_4$H$_5$ClO$_2$; *39098-85-6*)   see: Rebamipide

acetohydrazide

(C$_2$H$_6$N$_2$O; *1068-57-1*)   see: Alprazolam; Muzolimine;
Triazolam

acetoin

(C$_4$H$_8$O$_2$; *513-86-0*)   see: Lenampicillin; Sulfaguanole;
Sulfamoxole

acetone

(C$_3$H$_6$O; *67-64-1*)   see: Ascorbic acid; Chlorobutanol;
Cicletanine; Ciprofibrate; Ciprofloxacin; Clofibrate;
Clortermine; Desonide; Dimethadione; Etretinate;
Fenofibrate; Fludroxycortide; Flunisolide; Fluocinolone
acetonide; Halcinonide; Hetacillin; Iproniazid; Nabumetone;
Niaprazine; D-Penicillamine; Pirisudanol; Prenalterol;
Probucol; Propyphenazone; Proquazone; Retinol;
Terconazole; Topiramate; Triamcinolone acetonide

acetone cyanohydrin

(C$_4$H$_7$NO; *75-86-5*)   see: Dimethadione

acetonedicarboxylic acid

(C$_5$H$_6$O$_5$; *542-05-2*)   see: Dolasetron mesilate; Homatropine

acetone dimethyl acetal

(C$_5$H$_{12}$O$_2$; *77-76-9*)   see: Atorvastatin calcium; Dibekacin;
Docetaxel; Doxifluridine; Epirubicin; Indinavir sulfate;
Iotrolan; Misoprostol; Oseltamivir

acetonitrile

(C$_2$H$_3$N; *75-05-8*)   see: Amantadine; Clofedanol;
Dorzolamide; Ethambutol; Gabapentin; Ritonavir

5-acetonyl-2-methoxybenzenesulfonamide

(C$_{10}$H$_{13}$NO$_4$S; *116091-63-5*)   see: Tamsulosin hydrochloride

acetophenone

(C$_8$H$_8$O; *98-86-2*)   see: Algestone acetophenide; Benmoxin;
Biperidene; Budipine; Ciclonium bromide; Cycrimine;
Eprozinol; Fendiline; Fluoxetine; Lercanidipine
hydrochloride; Mesuximide; Phenindamine; Phenoperidine;
Pridinol; Procyclidine; Pyrrobutamine; Tiemonium iodide;
Tolpropamine; Tridihexethyl chloride; Trihexyphenidyl

acetophenone benzoylhydrazone

(C$_{15}$H$_{14}$N$_2$O; *1219-41-6*)   see: Benmoxin

9-[4-acetoxy-3-(acetoxymethyl)butyl]-2-amino-6-chloro-purine

(C$_{14}$H$_{18}$ClN$_5$O$_4$; *97845-60-8*)   see: Famciclovir

3β-acetoxy-16-(5-acetoxy-4-methylpentanoyl)-5α-preg-nane-11,20-dione

(C$_{31}$H$_{46}$O$_8$)   see: Alfaxalone

2-acetoxyacetyl chloride

(C$_4$H$_5$ClO$_3$; *13831-31-7*)   see: Docetaxel; Paclitaxel

(±)-6-acetoxy-2-(4-aminophenoxymethyl)-2,5,7,8-tetrame-thylchroman

(C$_{22}$H$_{27}$NO$_4$; *107188-37-4*)   see: Troglitazone

17-acetoxy-5α-androsta-2,16-diene

(C$_{21}$H$_{30}$O$_2$; *50588-42-6*)   see: Pancuronium bromide;
Pipecuronium bromide; Vecuronium bromide

3-acetoxybenzaldehyde

(C$_9$H$_8$O$_3$; *34231-78-2*)   see: Metaraminol

2-acetoxybenzoyl chloride

(C$_9$H$_7$ClO$_3$; *5538-51-2*)   see: Benorilate; Phenprocoumon

(2-acetoxybenzoyl)(1-phenylpropyl)malonic acid diethyl ester

(C$_{25}$H$_{28}$O$_7$)   see: Phenprocoumon

[3*R*(1'*R*),4*R*]-(+)-4-acetoxy-3-[1-(*tert*-butyldimethylsilyl-oxy)ethyl]-2-azetidinone

(C$_{13}$H$_{25}$NO$_4$Si; *76855-69-1*)   see: Faropenem sodium;
Meropenem

4(*R*)-acetoxy-3(*R*)-[1(*R*)-(*tert*-butyldimethylsilyloxy)ethyl]-azetidin-2-one
see under [3*R*(1'*R*),4*R*]-(+)-4-acetoxy-3-[1-(*tert*-butyldimethylsilyloxy)ethyl]-2-azetidinone

3-acetoxy-7-chloro-5-(2-chlorophenyl)-1-methyl-1,3-dihydro-2*H*-1,4-benzodiazepin-2-one
($C_{18}H_{14}Cl_2N_2O_3$; *96576-92-0*)   see: Lormetazepam

1-acetoxy-4-chloro-3-methyl-2-butene
($C_7H_{11}ClO_2$; *38872-49-0*)   see: Retinol

3-acetoxy-7-chloro-1-methyl-5-phenyl-2-oxo-1,3-dihydro-2*H*-1,4-benzodiazepine
($C_{18}H_{15}ClN_2O_3$; *18818-64-9*)   see: Temazepam

5-acetoxy-3-chloropentan-2-one
($C_7H_{11}ClO_3$; *13051-49-5*)   see: Thiamine

1-acetoxy-3-chloro-2-propanone
($C_5H_7ClO_3$; *40235-68-5*)   see: Levofloxacin

21-acetoxy-2,4-dibromo-11α,17α-dihydroxy-16β-methyl-5β-pregnane-3,20-dione
($C_{24}H_{34}Br_2O_6$)   see: Betamethasone

17-acetoxy-2α,3α:16α,17α-diepoxy-5α-androstane
($C_{21}H_{30}O_4$; *50588-22-2*)   see: Pancuronium bromide; Pipecuronium bromide; Rocuronium bromide; Vecuronium bromide

1-acetoxy-4-diethylamino-2-butyne
($C_{10}H_{17}NO_2$; *22396-77-6*)   see: Oxybutynin

21-acetoxy-11α,17α-dihydroxy-16β-methylpregna-1,4-diene-3,20-dione
($C_{24}H_{32}O_6$; *5078-99-9*)   see: Betamethasone

21-acetoxy-11α,17α-dihydroxy-16β-methyl-5β-pregnane-3,20-dione
($C_{24}H_{36}O_6$; *5078-98-8*)   see: Betamethasone

3β-acetoxy-6,16-dimethyl-20-oxo-5,16-pregnadiene
($C_{25}H_{36}O_3$; *29147-79-3*)   see: Melengestrol acetate

21-acetoxy-3,20-dioxo-9β,11β-epoxy-17α-hydroxy-16α-methyl-1,4-pregnadiene
($C_{24}H_{30}O_6$; *2884-51-7*)   see: Dexamethasone

21-acetoxy-3,20-dioxo-9β,11β-epoxy-17-hydroxy-4-pregnene
($C_{23}H_{30}O_6$; *4383-30-6*)   see: Fludrocortisone

3α-acetoxy-11,20-dioxo-16α,17α-epoxy-5β-pregnane
($C_{23}H_{32}O_5$; *24298-90-6*)   see: Betamethasone

21-acetoxy-3,20-dioxo-9α-fluoro-11β-hydroxy-16α,17-isopropylidenedioxy-4-pregnene
($C_{26}H_{35}FO_7$; *2395-17-7*)   see: Formocortal

21-acetoxy-3,20-dioxo-6α-fluoro-17-hydroxy-16β-methyl-4,9(11)-pregnadiene
($C_{24}H_{31}FO_5$; *50763-89-8*)   see: Diflorasone diacetate

21-acetoxy-3,20-dioxo-6α-fluoro-11β-hydroxy-16α-methyl-4-pregnene
($C_{24}H_{33}FO_5$; *1176-81-4*)   see: Diflucortolone valerate

21-acetoxy-3,20-dioxo-6α-fluoro-16α,17α-isopropylidenedioxy-1,4-pregnadiene
($C_{26}H_{33}FO_6$; *25437-07-4*)   see: Flunisolide

21-acetoxy-3,20-dioxo-6α-fluoro-16α,17-isopropylidenedioxy-1,4,9(11)-pregnatriene
($C_{26}H_{31}FO_6$; *5049-89-8*)   see: Tralonide

17-acetoxy-3,20-dioxo-1,4,6-pregnatriene
($C_{23}H_{28}O_4$; *2668-75-9*)   see: Cyproterone acetate

3α-acetoxy-11,20-dioxo-16-pregnene
($C_{23}H_{32}O_4$; *67253-64-9*)   see: Dexamethasone; Meprednisone

3β-acetoxy-11,20-dioxo-16-pregnene
($C_{23}H_{32}O_4$; *2724-68-7*)   see: Alfaxalone; Fluazacort

17β-acetoxy-2,3-epoxy-5α-androstane
($C_{21}H_{32}O_3$)   see: Epitiostanol

21-acetoxy-16α,17-epoxy-3β-hydroxy-20-oxo-5-pregnene
($C_{23}H_{32}O_5$; *28444-97-5*)   see: Fludroxycortide

3β-acetoxy-5α,6α-epoxy-16α-methylpregnan-20-one
($C_{24}H_{36}O_4$)   see: Paramethasone

3α-acetoxy-16α,17α-epoxy-5β-pregnane-11,20-dione 21-ethylene acetal
($C_{25}H_{36}O_6$; *13643-92-0*)   see: Betamethasone

2-acetoxyethyl acetoxymethyl ether
($C_7H_{12}O_5$; *59278-00-1*)   see: Aciclovir

3α-acetoxy-20,20-ethylenedioxy-16α,17α-epoxy-5β-pregnan-11β-ol
($C_{25}H_{38}O_6$; *13643-94-2*)   see: Betamethasone

3α-acetoxy-20,20-ethylenedioxy-16α,17α-epoxy-5β-pregn-9(11)-ene
($C_{25}H_{36}O_5$; *13643-95-3*)   see: Betamethasone

17β-acetoxy-17-ethynyl-3-methoxy-19-nor-2,5(10)-androstadiene
($C_{23}H_{30}O_3$; *13251-69-9*)   see: Quingestanol acetate

5α-acetoxy-6β-fluoro-3β,17-dihydroxy-16α-methylpregnan-20-one
($C_{24}H_{37}FO_5$; *1525-76-4*)   see: Paramethasone

21-acetoxy-6α-fluoro-11β,17-dihydroxy-16α-methylpregn-4-ene-3,20-dione
($C_{24}H_{33}FO_6$; *1524-93-2*)   see: Flumetasone; Paramethasone

3β-acetoxy-6β-fluoro-5α-hydroxy-16α-methylpregnan-20-one
($C_{24}H_{37}FO_4$; *1994-39-4*)   see: Paramethasone

21-acetoxy-6β-fluoro-17-hydroxy-16α-methylpregn-4-ene-3,20-dione
($C_{24}H_{33}FO_5$)   see: Paramethasone

3-acetoxy-19-hydroxycholesterol
($C_{29}H_{48}O_3$; *750-59-4*)   see: Estrone

21-acetoxy-3β-hydroxy-16α-methyl-20-oxo-5-pregnene
($C_{24}H_{36}O_4$; *1173-09-7*)   see: Fluocortolone

21-acetoxy-11β-hydroxy-16-methyl-1,4-pregnadiene-3,20-dione
($C_{24}H_{32}O_5$; *1056-37-7*)   see: Desoximetasone

21-acetoxy-3α-hydroxy-16α-methylpregnane-11,20-dione
($C_{24}H_{36}O_5$; *1056-38-8*)   see: Desoximetasone

21-acetoxy-17-hydroxy-16β-methylpregna-1,4,9(11)-triene-3,20-dione
($C_{24}H_{30}O_5$; *910-99-6*)   see: Beclometasone; Betamethasone

(3β,5α,5'β)-21-acetoxy-3-hydroxy-2'-methyl-5*H*-pregn-9(11)-eno[17,16-*d*]oxazol-20-one
($C_{25}H_{35}NO_5$; *19890-70-1*)   see: Fluazacort

1α-acetoxy-25-hydroxy-10-(methylsulfonyloxy)-3,5-cyclo-19-norvitamin D$_2$ 6-methyl ether
($C_{31}H_{50}O_7S$)   see: Paricalcitol

1α-acetoxy-25-hydroxy-19-norvitamin D$_2$
($C_{29}H_{46}O_4$)   see: Paricalcitol

21-acetoxy-17-hydroxy-1,4,9(11)-pregnatrien-3,20-dione
($C_{23}H_{28}O_5$; *4380-55-6*)   see: Dichlorisone

(acetylamino)(1*H*-indol-3-ylmethyl)propanedioic acid diethyl ester
($C_{18}H_{22}N_2O_5$; *5379-97-5*)   see: L-Tryptophan

2-acetylamino-5-mercapto-1,3,4-thiadiazole
($C_4H_5N_3OS_2$; *32873-56-6*)   see: Acetazolamide

3-[(acetylamino)methyl]-5-amino-2,4,6-triiodobenzoic acid
($C_{10}H_9I_3N_2O_3$; *727-56-0*)   see: Iodamide

3-acetylamino-4-methylbenzenesulfonamide
($C_9H_{12}N_2O_3S$; *17485-44-8*)   see: Metahexamide

3-[(acetylamino)methyl]-4-chloro-5-nitrobenzoic acid
($C_{10}H_9ClN_2O_5$; *728-46-1*)   see: Iodamide

***trans*-4-[(acetylamino)methyl]cyclohexanecarbonyl chloride**
($C_{10}H_{16}ClNO_2$; *82085-98-1*)   see: Ciclometasone

4-(acetylamino)-*N*-[4-(1-methylethoxy)benzoyl]benzenesulfonamide
($C_{18}H_{20}N_2O_5S$)   see: Sulfaproxyline

(±)-2-(acetylaminomethyl)-4-(4-fluorobenzyl)morpholine
($C_{14}H_{19}FN_2O_2$; *112913-94-7*)   see: Mosapride citrate

(*S*)-2-(acetylamino)-4-(methylthio)butanoic acid 1-oxopropyl ester
($C_{10}H_{17}NO_4S$)   see: Docarpamine

(acetylamino)(3-oxopropyl)propanedioic acid diethyl ester
($C_{12}H_{19}NO_6$; *53908-65-9*)   see: Oxitriptan

(acetylamino)[3-(phenylhydrazono)propyl]propanedioic acid diethyl ester
($C_{18}H_{25}N_3O_5$; *6297-96-7*)   see: L-Tryptophan

(acetylamino)[[5-(phenylmethoxy)-1*H*-indol-3-yl]methyl]propanedioic acid diethyl ester
($C_{25}H_{28}N_2O_6$; *50469-23-3*)   see: Oxitriptan

***N*-acetyl-*N*-(*m*-aminophenyl)-2-methyl-β-alanine**
($C_{12}H_{16}N_2O_3$; *16034-74-5*)   see: Iocetamic acid

***N*-[[4-(acetylamino)phenyl]sulfonyl]acetamide**
($C_{10}H_{12}N_2O_4S$; *5626-90-4*)   see: Sulfacetamide

***N*-[[4-(acetylamino)phenyl]sulfonyl]benzamide**
($C_{15}H_{14}N_2O_4S$; *5661-33-6*)   see: Sulfabenzamide

***N*-[[4-(acetylamino)phenyl]sulfonyl]-2-ethylidenehydrazinecarbothioamide**
($C_{11}H_{14}N_4O_3S_2$; *57053-66-4*)   see: Sulfamethizole

***N*-[[4-(acetylamino)phenyl]sulfonyl]-3-methyl-2-butenamide**
($C_{13}H_{16}N_2O_4S$; *71119-41-0*)   see: Sulfadicramide

***N*-[[4-(acetylamino)phenyl]sulfonyl]-2-propylidenehydrazinecarbothioamide**
($C_{12}H_{16}N_4O_3S$)   see: Sulfaethidole

(8*S-cis*)-8-acetyl-1-amino-7,8,9,10-tetrahydro-6,8,10,11-tetrahydroxy-5,12-naphthacenedione
($C_{20}H_{17}NO_7$; *120372-33-0*)   see: Idarubicin

2-acetylamino-1,3,4-thiadiazole-5-sulfonyl chloride
($C_4H_4ClN_3O_3S_2$; *32873-57-7*)   see: Acetazolamide

***N*-acetylanthranilic acid**
($C_9H_9NO_3$; *89-52-1*)   see: Mecloqualone; Methaqualone

4-acetylbenzenesulfonamide
($C_8H_9NO_3S$; *1565-17-9*)   see: Acetohexamide

2-acetylbenzofuran
($C_{10}H_8O_2$; *1646-26-0*)   see: Benzarone

2-acetylbenzo[*b*]thiophene
($C_{10}H_8OS$; *22720-75-8*)   see: Zileuton

***N*²-acetyl-9-(2-benzoyloxyethoxymethyl)guanine**
($C_{17}H_{17}N_5O_5$; *133186-23-9*)   see: Aciclovir

***N*-acetyl-5-benzyloxy-DL-tryptophan**
($C_{20}H_{20}N_2O_4$; *53017-51-9*)   see: Oxitriptan

***N*-acetyl-*N,O*-bis(trimethylsilyl)cytosine**
($C_{12}H_{23}N_3O_2Si_2$; *18027-23-1*)   see: Gemcitabine

acetyl bromide
(C_2H_3BrO; *506-96-7*)   see: Paclitaxel

***N*-acetyl-2'-bromo-2'-deoxycytidine 3',5'-diacetate**
($C_{15}H_{18}BrN_3O_7$; *126430-12-4*)   see: Zalcitabine

***N*-acetyl-3'-bromo-3'-deoxycytidine 2',5'-diacetate**
($C_{15}H_{18}BrN_3O_7$; *126430-11-3*)   see: Zalcitabine

2-acetyl-4-butyramidophenol
($C_{12}H_{15}NO_3$; *40188-45-2*)   see: Acebutolol

***O*-acetyl-4-butyramidophenol**
($C_{12}H_{15}NO_3$; *40188-44-1*)   see: Acebutolol

2-acetylbutyrolactone
($C_6H_8O_3$; *517-23-7*)   see: Chloroquine; Risperidone

***N*-acetyl-ε-caprolactam**
($C_8H_{13}NO_2$; *1888-91-1*)   see: Acexamic acid

acetyl chloride
(C_2H_3ClO; *75-36-5*)   see: Acebutolol; Acetiamine; Acetylcholine chloride; L-Alanine; Benfurodil hemisuccinate; Chlorprothixene; Flumetasone; Ibuprofen; Iotalamic acid; Ioxitalamic acid; Levodopa; Methestrol dipropionate; Midecamycin acetate; Naproxen; Nimesulide; Paclitaxel; Paramethasone; Phensuximide; Retinol; Rocuronium bromide; Rofecoxib; Ropinirole; Tazarotene; Thiopropazate; Tiracizine; Vecuronium bromide

3-acetyl-5-chloro-2-(benzylthio)thiophene
($C_{13}H_{11}ClOS_2$; *160982-09-2*)   see: Brinzolamide

2-acetyl-10-(3-chloropropyl)phenothiazine
($C_{17}H_{16}ClNOS$; *39481-55-5*)   see: Acetophenazine; Piperacetazine

3-acetyl-5-chloro-2-thiophenesulfonamide
($C_6H_6ClNO_3S_2$; *160982-10-5*)   see: Brinzolamide

21-*O*-acetylcorticosterone
($C_{23}H_{32}O_5$; *1173-26-8*)   see: Aldosterone

21-*O*-acetylcortisone
($C_{23}H_{30}O_6$; *50-04-4*)   see: Cortisone; Hydrocortisone

acetylcyclohexane
($C_8H_{14}O$; *823-76-7*)   see: Cicrotoic acid

acetylcyclopropane
(C_5H_8O; *765-43-5*)   see: Calcipotriol

***N*-acetylcytidine**
($C_{11}H_{15}N_3O_6$; *3768-18-1*)   see: Zalcitabine

5-acetyl-10,11-dibromo-10,11-dihydro-5*H*-dibenz[*b,f*]azepine
($C_{16}H_{13}Br_2NO$; *4614-45-3*)   see: Oxcarbazepine

3-acetyl-2,5-dichlorothiophene
($C_6H_4Cl_2OS$; *36157-40-1*)   see: Brinzolamide

***N*-acetyl-2',3'-didehydro-2',3'-dideoxycytidine 5'-acetate**
($C_{13}H_{15}N_3O_5$; *62805-52-1*)   see: Zalcitabine

1-acetyl-4-(2,4-difluorobenzoyl)piperidine
($C_{14}H_{15}F_2NO_2$; *84162-82-3*)   see: Risperidone

acetyldigitoxin
($C_{43}H_{66}O_{14}$; *1111-39-3*)   see: α-Acetyldigoxin

β-acetyldigitoxin
($C_{43}H_{66}O_{14}$; *1264-51-3*)   see: Acetyldigitoxin

2-acetyl-10-methylphenothiazine
($C_{15}H_{13}NOS$; 25324-52-1)   see: Metiazinic acid

10-acetyl-2-(methylsulfinyl)-10*H*-phenothiazine
($C_{15}H_{13}NO_2S_2$; 80471-59-6)   see: Mesoridazine

10-acetyl-2-(methylthio)phenothiazine
($C_{15}H_{13}NOS_2$; 23503-69-7)   see: Mesoridazine

N^α-(*N*-acetylmuramoyl-L-alanyl-D-isoglutaminyl)-L-lysine
($C_{25}H_{44}N_6O_{12}$; 56816-17-2)   see: Romurtide

N-acetylneuraminic acid
($C_{11}H_{19}NO_9$; 114-04-5)   see: Zanamivir

N-acetyl-α-neuraminic acid methyl ester 2,4,7,8,9-penta-acetate
($C_{22}H_{31}NO_{14}$; 72690-21-2)   see: Zanamivir

4-acetyl-2-nitrobiphenyl
($C_{14}H_{11}NO_3$; 42771-77-7)   see: Flurbiprofen

21-*O*-acetyl-11-*O*-nitrosylcorticosterone
($C_{23}H_{31}NO_6$; 74220-48-7)   see: Aldosterone

2-acetyl-5-norbornene
($C_9H_{12}O$; 5063-03-6)   see: Biperidene

1-acetyl-3aα,7aβ-octahydroindole
($C_{10}H_{17}NO$)   see: Trandolapril

1-acetyl-2α,3aα,7aβ-octahydroindole-2-carbonitrile
($C_{11}H_{16}N_2O$; 89226-37-9)   see: Trandolapril

[3β,16β(*R*)]-3-(acetyloxy)-16-[[5-(acetyloxy)-4-methyl-1-oxopentyl]oxy]pregn-5-en-20-one
($C_{31}H_{46}O_7$; 58400-99-0)   see: Pregnenolone

1-[4-(acetyloxy)-3-[(acetyloxy)methyl]phenyl]-2-bromo-ethanone
($C_{13}H_{13}BrO_5$; 24085-07-2)   see: Salbutamol

1-[4-(acetyloxy)-3-[(acetyloxy)methyl]phenyl]-2-[(1,1-dimethylethyl)(phenylmethyl)amino]ethanone
($C_{24}H_{29}NO_5$; 77430-27-4)   see: Salbutamol

1-[4-(acetyloxy)-3-[(acetyloxy)methyl]phenyl]ethanone
($C_{13}H_{14}O_5$; 24085-06-1)   see: Salbutamol

N-[(3β)-3-(acetyloxy)androsta-5,16-dien-17-yl]acetamide
($C_{23}H_{33}NO_3$; 65732-71-0)   see: Prasterone

(5α,17β)-17-(acetyloxy)androstane-1,3-dione cyclic 3-(1,2-ethanediyl acetal)
($C_{23}H_{34}O_5$; 1054-83-7)   see: Metenolone acetate

N-[(3β,17β)-3-(acetyloxy)androst-5-en-17-yl]acetamide
($C_{23}H_{35}NO_3$; 4350-67-8)   see: Prasterone

[*R*-(*R**,*R**)]-α-(acetyloxy)benzeneacetic acid 1-(2-propenyl)dodecyl ester
($C_{25}H_{38}O_4$; 152906-15-5)   see: Orlistat

[*S*-(*R**,*S**)]-α-(acetyloxy)benzeneacetic acid 1-(2-propenyl)dodecyl ester
($C_{25}H_{38}O_4$; 152906-16-6)   see: Orlistat

6'-(acetyloxy)-5-bromo-2',3',8',8'a-tetrahydro-5'-methoxy-1'-methylspiro[2-cyclohexene-1,7'(1'*H*)-cyclopent[*ij*]isoquinolin]-4-one
($C_{20}H_{22}BrNO_4$; 54169-68-5)   see: Glaziovine

(*R**,*S**)-α-(acetyloxy)-β-bromobenzenepropanoic acid methyl ester
($C_{12}H_{13}BrO_4$; 132377-76-5)   see: Paclitaxel

(11β,16α)-21-(acetyloxy)-9-bromo-11,17-dihydroxy-16-methylpregn-4-ene-3,20-dione
($C_{24}H_{33}BrO_6$; 34542-57-9)   see: Dexamethasone

(3β,5α,6β,16α)-21-(acetyloxy)-5-bromo-16,17-epoxy-6-fluoro-3-hydroxypregnan-20-one
($C_{23}H_{32}BrFO_5$; 1813-08-7)   see: Fludroxycortide

(3β,5α,6β,16α)-21-(acetyloxy)-5-bromo-6-fluoro-3-hydroxy-16-methylpregnan-20-one
($C_{24}H_{36}BrFO_4$; 1176-85-8)   see: Fluocortolone

(6α,11β,16α)-21-(acetyloxy)-9-bromo-6-fluoro-11-hydroxy-16-methylpregn-4-ene-3,20-dione
($C_{24}H_{32}BrFO_5$; 2143-33-1)   see: Diflucortolone valerate

(5α,6β,16α)-21-(acetyloxy)-5-bromo-6-fluoro-16-methylpregnane-3,20-dione
($C_{24}H_{34}BrFO_4$; 22574-20-5)   see: Fluocortolone

(2α,5α,6β,11α)-21-(acetyloxy)-2-bromo-6-fluoro-5,11,17-trihydroxypregnane-3,20-dione
($C_{23}H_{32}BrFO_7$; 57781-10-9)   see: Halopredone diacetate

(4β,5β)-21-(acetyloxy)-4-bromo-17-hydroxypregnane-3,11,20-trione
($C_{23}H_{31}BrO_6$; 74243-24-6)   see: Cortisone

(1α)-17-(acetyloxy)-6-chloro-1-(chloromethyl)pregna-4,6-diene-3,20-dione
($C_{24}H_{30}Cl_2O_4$; 17183-98-1)   see: Cyproterone acetate

3-(acetyloxy)-7-chloro-5-(2-chlorophenyl)-1,3-dihydro-2*H*-1,4-benzodiazepin-2-one
($C_{17}H_{12}Cl_2N_2O_3$)   see: Lorazepam

3-(acetyloxy)-7-chloro-5-(2-fluorophenyl)-1,3-dihydro-2*H*-1,4-benzodiazepin-2-one
($C_{17}H_{12}ClFN_2O_3$; 19011-80-4)   see: Cinolazepam

(5β,16α)-21-(acetyloxy)-2,4-dibromo-16-methylpregnane-3,11,20-trione
($C_{24}H_{32}Br_2O_5$)   see: Desoximetasone

(6α,11β,16α)-21-(acetyloxy)-6,9-difluoro-11,17-dihydroxy-16-methylpregn-4-ene-3,20-dione
($C_{24}H_{32}F_2O_6$; 2358-07-8)   see: Flumetasone

(6α,11β,16α)-21-(acetyloxy)-6,9-difluoro-11-hydroxy-16-methylpregn-4-ene-3,20-dione
($C_{24}H_{32}F_2O_5$; 2664-07-5)   see: Diflucortolone valerate

(1β,2β)-17-(acetyloxy)-1,2-dihydro-3'*H*-cyclopropa[1,2]-pregna-1,4,6-triene-3,20-dione
($C_{24}H_{30}O_4$; 2701-50-0)   see: Cyproterone acetate

(2*S*-*cis*)-3-(acetyloxy)-2,3-dihydro-2-(4-methoxyphenyl)-1,5-benzothiazepin-4(5*H*)-one
($C_{18}H_{17}NO_4S$; 87447-47-0)   see: Diltiazem

(1β,2β)-17-(acetyloxy)-1,2-dihydro-3'*H*-pregna-1,4,6-trieno[1,2-*c*]pyrazol-3,20-dione
($C_{24}H_{30}N_2O_4$)   see: Cyproterone acetate

(3β,16β)-3-(acetyloxy)-5',16-dihydropregn-5-eno[17,16-*c*]-pyrazol-20-one
($C_{24}H_{34}N_2O_3$; 16137-47-6)   see: Fluprednidene acetate

(3α,16α)-14-(acetyloxy)-14,15-dihydro-1,14-seco-eburnamenine-14-carboxylic acid methyl ester perchlorate
($C_{23}H_{31}ClN_2O_8$; 40163-51-7)   see: Vincamine

(3α,16α)-21-(acetyloxy)-3,17-dihydroxy-16-methylpregnane-11,20-dione
($C_{24}H_{36}O_6$; 67253-66-1)   see: Dexamethasone

(11β,16α)-21-(acetyloxy)-11,17-dihydroxy-16-methylpregn-4-ene-3,20-dione
($C_{24}H_{34}O_6$; 41020-56-8)   see: Dexamethasone

(16α)-21-(acetyloxy)-16,17-dihydroxypregna-4,9(11)-diene-3,20-dione
($C_{23}H_{30}O_6$; 74220-43-2)   see: Triamcinolone

(6R-cis)-3-[(acetyloxy)methyl]-7-[[[(4-carboxy-2,3-dihy-dro-3-oxo-5-isothiazolyl)thio]acetyl]amino]-7-methoxy-8-oxo-5-thia-1-azabicyclo[4.2.0]oct-2-ene-2-carboxylic acid
($C_{17}H_{17}N_3O_{10}S_3$; *69713-29-7*)   see: Cefotetan

(6R-trans)-3-[(acetyloxy)methyl]-7-[[(3,5-dichloro-4-oxo-1(4H)-pyridinyl)acetyl]amino]-8-oxo-5-thia-1-azabicyclo-[4.2.0]oct-2-ene-2-carboxylic acid
($C_{17}H_{15}Cl_2N_3O_7S$; *56187-36-1*)   see: Cefazedone

[6R-[6α,7β(S*)]]-3-[(acetyloxy)methyl]-7-[[[[(1,1-dimeth-ylethoxy)carbonyl]amino]phenylacetyl]amino]-8-oxo-5-thia-1-azabicyclo[4.2.0]oct-2-ene-2-carboxylic acid
($C_{23}H_{27}N_3O_8S$; *7716-28-1*)   see: Cefalexin

α-[(acetyloxy)methyl]-N-ethyl-N-(4-pyridinylmethyl)-benzeneacetamide
($C_{19}H_{22}N_2O_3$; *87239-08-5*)   see: Tropicamide

[6R-[6α,7β(Z)]]-3-[(acetyloxy)methyl]-7-[[2-furanyl(meth-oxyimino)acetyl]amino]-8-oxo-5-thia-1-azabicyclo[4.2.0]-oct-2-ene-2-carboxylic acid diphenylmethyl ester
($C_{30}H_{27}N_3O_8S$)   see: Cefuroxime

(6R-trans)-3-[(acetyloxy)methyl]-7-[[(methoxyimino)[2-[(triphenylmethyl)amino]-4-thiazolyl]acetyl]amino]-8-oxo-5-thia-1-azabicyclo[4.2.0]oct-2-ene-2-carboxylic acid
($C_{35}H_{31}N_5O_7S_2$; *66254-46-4*)   see: Cefotaxime

[6R-[6α,7β(R*)]]-3-[(acetyloxy)methyl]-8-oxo-7-[(phenyl-sulfoacetyl)amino]-5-thia-1-azabicyclo[4.2.0]oct-2-ene-2-carboxylic acid
($C_{18}H_{18}N_2O_9S_2$; *41128-84-1*)   see: Cefsulodin

(6R-trans)-3-[(acetyloxy)methyl]-8-oxo-7-[(1H-tetrazol-1-ylacetyl)amino]-5-thia-1-azabicyclo[4.2.0]oct-2-ene-2-carboxylic acid
($C_{13}H_{14}N_6O_6S$; *32510-61-5*)   see: Cefazolin; Ceftezole

(3β,5α,16β)-3-(acetyloxy)-2'-methyl-5'H-pregnano[17,16-d]oxazol-11,20-dione-20-semicarbazone
($C_{26}H_{38}N_4O_5$)   see: Fluazacort

(3α)-3-(acetyloxy)-16-methylpregn-16-ene-11,20-dione
($C_{24}H_{34}O_4$; *14340-18-2*)   see: Meprednisone

(2R-cis)-1-[5-[(acetyloxy)methyl]tetrahydro-2-furanyl]-4-(1H-1,2,4-triazol-1-yl)-2(1H)-pyrimidinone
($C_{13}H_{15}N_5O_4$; *105784-87-0*)   see: Zalcitabine

(3β,5α)-3-(acetyloxy)-27-norcholestan-25-one
($C_{28}H_{46}O_3$; *2550-90-5*)   see: Calcifediol

5-(acetyloxy)-1,3-oxathiolane-2-carboxylic acid
($C_6H_8O_5S$)   see: Lamivudine

trans-5-(acetyloxy)-1,3-oxathiolane-2-carboxylic acid methyl ester
($C_7H_{10}O_5S$; *147027-03-0*)   see: Lamivudine

(2S)-5-(acetyloxy)-1,3-oxathiolane-2-methanol benzoate
($C_{13}H_{14}O_5S$)   see: Lamivudine

(S)-5-[[2-(acetyloxy)-1-oxopropyl]amino]-2,4,6-triiodo-1,3-benzenedicarbonyl dichloride
($C_{13}H_8Cl_2I_3NO_5$; *60166-91-8*)   see: Iopamidol

[11β,17α,17(S)]-17-[2-(acetyloxy)-1-oxopropyl]-11,17-di-hydroxyandrosta-1,4-dien-3-one
($C_{24}H_{32}O_6$; *17651-98-8*)   see: Fluperolone acetate

(3R-cis)-3-(acetyloxy)-4-phenyl-2-azetidinone
($C_{11}H_{11}NO_3$; *144790-01-2*)   see: Paclitaxel

cis-3-(acetyloxy)-4-phenyl-2-azetidinone
($C_{11}H_{11}NO_3$; *133066-59-8*)   see: Paclitaxel

17-(acetyloxy)pregna-4,6-diene-3,20-dione
($C_{23}H_{30}O_4$; *425-51-4*)   see: Cyproterone acetate

17-(acetyloxy)pregna-4,9(11)-diene-3,20-dione
($C_{23}H_{30}O_4$; *5106-48-9*)   see: Flugestone acetate

21-(acetyloxy)pregna-4,9(11),16-triene-3,20-dione
($C_{23}H_{28}O_4$; *23460-76-6*)   see: Triamcinolone

(3β,5β,6α)-3-(acetyloxy)-5,6,21-tribromo-17-hydroxy-16-methylenepregnan-20-one
($C_{24}H_{31}Br_3O_4$)   see: Prednylidene

[2S-(2R*,7Z,16Z,18E,20R*,21R*,22S*,23S*,24S*,25R*, 26S*,27R*,28E)]-25-(acetyloxy)-5,21,23-trihydroxy-27-methoxy-2,4,11,16,20,22,24,26-octamethyl-2,7-(epoxy-pentadeca[1,11,13]trienenitrilo)benzofuro[4,5-e]pyri-do[1,2-a]benzimidazole-1,6,15(2H,7H)-trione
($C_{43}H_{49}N_3O_{11}$)   see: Rifaximin

2-acetylphenothiazine
($C_{14}H_{11}NOS$; *6631-94-3*)   see: Acepromazine; Aceprometazine; Acetophenazine; Piperacetazine

(4-acetylphenoxy)acetic acid
($C_{10}H_{10}O_4$; *1878-81-5*)   see: Pifoxime

(4-acetylphenoxy)acetic acid methyl ester
($C_{11}H_{12}O_4$; *6296-28-2*)   see: Pifoxime

1-[(4-acetylphenoxy)acetyl]piperidine
($C_{15}H_{19}NO_3$; *31188-99-5*)   see: Pifoxime

N-(3-acetylphenyl)acetamide
($C_{10}H_{11}NO_2$; *7463-31-2*)   see: Zaleplon

[5-acetyl-2-(phenylmethoxy)phenyl]urea
($C_{16}H_{16}N_2O_3$; *34241-97-9*)   see: Carbuterol

(R)-N²-[N²-[N-[N-acetyl-1-O-(phenylmethyl)muramoyl]-L-alanyl]-D-α-glutaminyl]-N⁶-[(phenylmethoxy)carbonyl]-L-lysine phenylmethyl ester
($C_{47}H_{62}N_6O_{14}$)   see: Romurtide

N²-[N²-[N-[N-acetyl-1-O-(phenylmethyl)-4,6-O-(phenyl-methylene)muramoyl]-L-alanyl]-D-α-glutaminyl]-N⁶-[(phenylmethoxy)carbonyl]-L-lysine phenylmethyl ester
($C_{54}H_{66}N_6O_{14}$)   see: Romurtide

4-acetylphenylsulfonyl chloride
($C_8H_7ClO_3S$; *1788-10-9*)   see: Acetohexamide

acetylphosphonic acid diethyl ester
($C_6H_{13}O_4P$; *919-19-7*)   see: Fotemustine

acetylphosphonic acid diethyl ester oxime
($C_6H_{14}NO_4P$; *53145-08-7*)   see: Fotemustine

1-acetyl-4-piperidinecarbonyl chloride
($C_8H_{12}ClNO_2$; *59084-16-1*)   see: Risperidone

1-acetyl-4-piperidinecarboxylic acid
($C_8H_{13}NO_3$; *25503-90-6*)   see: Risperidone

6-(1-acetylpropyl)-3,4,3',4'-tetramethoxybenzophenone
($C_{22}H_{26}O_6$; *15462-91-6*)   see: Tofisopam

2-acetylpyridine
(C_7H_7NO; *1122-62-9*)   see: Doxylamine

3-acetylpyridine
(C_7H_7NO; *350-03-8*)   see: Metyrapone

5-acetylsalicylamide
($C_9H_9NO_3$; *40187-51-7*)   see: Dilevalol

acetylsalicylic acid
($C_9H_8O_4$; *50-78-2*)   see: Aloxiprin; Carbasalate calcium

O-acetylsalicyloyl chloride
see under 2-acetoxybenzoyl chloride

N-acetylserine methyl ester
($C_6H_{11}NO_4$; *55299-56-4*)   see: Ramipril

O-acetyltestosterone
($C_{21}H_{30}O_3$; *1045-69-8*)   see: Clostebol acetate

allyl alcohol

(C$_3$H$_6$O; *107-18-6*)   see: Dimercaprol

allylamine

(C$_3$H$_7$N; *107-11-9*)   see: Almitrine; Azapetine

1-allyl-2-aminomethylpyrrolidine

(C$_8$H$_{16}$N$_2$; *26116-13-2*)   see: Alizapride

2-allylaminosulfonyl-4-aminosulfonyl-5-chloroaniline

(C$_9$H$_{12}$ClN$_3$O$_4$S$_2$; *3921-09-3*)   see: Ambuside

allyl anthranilate

(C$_{10}$H$_{11}$NO$_2$; *7493-63-2*)   see: Antrafenine

allyl bromide

(C$_3$H$_5$Br; *106-95-6*)   see: Alclofenac; Alibendol;
Allobarbital; Ambuside; Aprobarbital; Azapetine; Butalbital;
Cabergoline; Clobenoside; Cyclopentobarbital; Fluoxetine;
Indinavir sulfate; Levallorphan; Methohexital; Nalorphine;
Naloxone; Nedocromil; Rocuronium bromide; Secobarbital;
Tacrolimus; Talipexole

allyl chloride

(C$_3$H$_5$Cl; *107-05-1*)   see: Valdetamide

2-allyl-6-chloro-3,4-dihydro-3-oxo-2*H*-1,2,4-benzothiadi-azine-7-sulfonamide *S,S*-dioxide

(C$_{10}$H$_{10}$ClN$_3$O$_5$S$_2$; *3921-08-2*)   see: Ambuside

9-allyl-2-chlorothioxanthen-9-ol

(C$_{16}$H$_{13}$ClOS; *33049-88-6*)   see: Chlorprothixene

6-allyl-*N*-[3-(dimethylamino)propyl]-8β-ergolinecarbox-amide

(C$_{23}$H$_{32}$N$_4$O; *85329-86-8*)   see: Cabergoline

6-allyl-8β-ergolinecarboxylic acid

(C$_{18}$H$_{20}$N$_2$O$_2$; *81409-74-7*)   see: Cabergoline

allyl glyoxylate

(C$_5$H$_6$O$_3$; *64370-42-9*)   see: Faropenem sodium

***N^b*-allylheminortoxiferine iodide**

(C$_{22}$H$_{27}$IN$_2$O$_2$; *24180-78-7*)   see: Alcuronium chloride

(–)-2-allyl-1-(4-hydroxybenzyl)-1,2,3,4,5,6,7,8-octahydro-isoquinoline

(C$_{19}$H$_{25}$NO)   see: Levallorphan

allyl iodide

(C$_3$H$_5$I; *556-56-9*)   see: Alcuronium chloride

allylmagnesium bromide

(C$_3$H$_5$BrMg; *1730-25-2*)   see: Allylestrenol;
Chlorprothixene; Flupentixol; Meglutol; Orlistat

allyl mercaptan

(C$_3$H$_6$S; *870-23-5*)   see: Altizide

allyl(1-methyl-2-pentynyl)malonic acid diethyl ester

(C$_{16}$H$_{24}$O$_4$; *101448-52-6*)   see: Methohexital

4-allyloxy-3-chlorobenzaldehyde

(C$_{10}$H$_9$ClO$_2$; *58236-91-2*)   see: Alclofenac

4-allyloxy-3-chlorobenzyl chloride

(C$_{10}$H$_{10}$Cl$_2$O; *20788-43-6*)   see: Alclofenac

4-allyloxy-3-chlorobenzyl cyanide

(C$_{11}$H$_{10}$ClNO; *20788-44-7*)   see: Alclofenac

2-allyloxyphenol

(C$_9$H$_{10}$O$_2$; *1126-20-1*)   see: Oxprenolol

3-(2-allyloxyphenoxy)-1,2-epoxypropane

(C$_{12}$H$_{14}$O$_3$; *6452-72-8*)   see: Oxprenolol

2-allylphenol

(C$_9$H$_{10}$O; *1745-81-9*)   see: Alprenolol

1-(2-allylphenoxy)-2,3-epoxypropane

(C$_{12}$H$_{14}$O$_2$; *4638-04-4*)   see: Alprenolol

(Z)-allyltributylstannane

(C$_{15}$H$_{32}$Sn; *66680-84-0*)   see: *cis*-Cefprozil

allyl *N*-(7-trifluoromethyl-4-quinolinyl)anthranilate

(C$_{20}$H$_{15}$F$_3$N$_2$O$_2$; *55300-53-3*)   see: Antrafenine

allylurea

(C$_4$H$_8$N$_2$O; *557-11-9*)   see: Chlormerodrin

***N*-allyl-Wieland-Gumlich aldehyde iodide**

see under *N^b*-allylheminortoxiferine iodide

aluminum ethylate

(C$_6$H$_{15}$AlO$_3$; *555-75-9*)   see: Alufibrate

aluminum hydroxide

(AlH$_3$O$_3$; *21645-51-2*)   see: Aluminum nicotinate

aluminum isopropylate

(C$_9$H$_{21}$AlO$_3$; *555-31-7*)   see: Aceglutamide aluminum;
Aloxiprin

aluminum tri-*tert*-butylate

(C$_{12}$H$_{27}$AlO$_3$; *556-91-2*)   see: Calusterone

1-amidino-4-butyrylhomopiperazine

(C$_{10}$H$_{20}$N$_4$O; *59775-30-3*)   see: Bunazosin

6-amidino-2-naphthol methanesulfonate

(C$_{12}$H$_{12}$N$_2$O$_3$S; *82957-06-0*)   see: Nafamostat

1-amidinothiourea

(C$_2$H$_6$N$_4$S; *2114-02-5*)   see: Ebrotidine

amidotrizoic acid

(C$_{11}$H$_9$I$_3$N$_2$O$_4$; *117-96-4*)   see: Metrizoic acid

aminoacetaldehyde diethyl acetal

(C$_6$H$_{15}$NO$_2$; *645-36-3*)   see: Thiamazole

***p*-aminoacetanilide**

(C$_8$H$_{10}$N$_2$O; *122-80-5*)   see: Vesnarinone

aminoacetonitrile

(C$_2$H$_4$N$_2$; *540-61-4*)   see: Estazolam; Orotic acid

aminoacetonitrile monohydrochloride

(C$_2$H$_5$ClN$_2$; *6011-14-9*)   see: Octopamine

3-aminoacetophenone

(C$_8$H$_9$NO; *99-03-6*)   see: Amidephrine mesilate

4-aminoacetophenone

(C$_8$H$_9$NO; *99-92-3*)   see: Acetohexamide

1-amino-5-(*N*-acetylhydroxyamino)pentane

(C$_7$H$_{16}$N$_2$O$_2$; *144108-69-0*)   see: Deferoxamine

1-aminoadamantane

(C$_{10}$H$_{17}$N; *768-94-5*)   see: Tromantadine

2-aminoadenine

(C$_5$H$_6$N$_6$; *1904-98-9*)   see: Fludarabine phosphate

7-amino-3-aminocarbonyloxymethyl-3-cephem-4-carb-oxylic acid

(C$_9$H$_{11}$N$_3$O$_5$S; *37051-07-3*)   see: Cefuroxime

(2*S-cis*)-3-amino-2-[[(aminocarbonyl)oxy]methyl]-4-oxo-1-azetidinesulfonic acid

(C$_5$H$_9$N$_3$O$_6$S; *88852-06-6*)   see: Carumonam

4-amino-5-aminomethyl-2-methylpyrimidine

(C$_6$H$_{10}$N$_4$; *95-02-3*)   see: Nimustine; Thiamine

aminoantipyrine

(C$_{11}$H$_{13}$N$_3$O; *83-07-8*)   see: Aminophenazone; Metamizole
sodium; Nifenazone

3-amino-3-azabicyclo[3.3.0]octane

(C$_7$H$_{14}$N$_2$; *54528-00-6*)   see: Gliclazide

4-aminobenzeneacetic acid ethyl ester

(C$_{10}$H$_{13}$NO$_2$; *5438-70-0*)   see: Actarit

4-aminobenzenesulfonamide monosodium salt

(C$_6$H$_7$N$_2$NaO$_2$S; *10103-15-8*)   see: Sulfadimethoxine

(3S)-3-amino-1-(carboxymethyl)-2,3,4,5-tetrahydro-1H-1-benzazepin-2-one

($C_{12}H_{14}N_2O_3$; *88372-47-8*)   see: Benazepril

7-aminocephalosporanic acid

($C_{10}H_{12}N_2O_5S$; *957-68-6*)   see: Cefacetrile; Cefaloglycin;
Cefalotin; Cefamandole; Cefapirin; Cefatrizine; Cefazedone;
Cefazolin; Cefbuperazone; Cefoperazone; Cefotaxime;
Cefoxitin; Cefsulodin; Ceftezole; Ceftriaxone

4-amino-6-chloro-1,3-benzenedisulfamide

($C_6H_8ClN_3O_4S_2$; *121-30-2*)   see: Altizide; Ambuside;
Bemetizide; Benzthiazide; Butizide; Chlorothiazide;
Cyclopenthiazide; Cyclothiazide; Epitizide; Ethiazide;
Hydrochlorothiazide; Methyclothiazide; Paraflutizide;
Teclothiazide; Trichlormethiazide

6-amino-4-chloro-1,3-benzenedisulfamide

see under 4-amino-6-chloro-1,3-benzenedisulfamide

6-amino-4-chlorobenzene-1,3-disulfonamide

see under 4-amino-6-chloro-1,3-benzenedisulfamide

4-amino-6-chloro-1,3-benzenedisulfonyl dichloride

($C_6H_4Cl_3NO_4S_2$; *671-89-6*)   see: Chlorothiazide

2-amino-5-chlorobenzoic acid

($C_7H_6ClNO_2$; *635-21-2*)   see: Tetrazepam

4-amino-2-chlorobenzoic acid

($C_7H_6ClNO_2$; *2457-76-3*)   see: Chloroprocaine

2-amino-4-chlorobenzoic acid ethyl ester

($C_9H_{10}ClNO_2$; *60064-34-8*)   see: Azosemide

2-amino-5-chlorobenzonitrile

($C_7H_5ClN_2$; *5922-60-1*)   see: Dipotassium clorazepate

2-amino-2'-chlorobenzophenone

($C_{13}H_{10}ClNO$; *2894-45-3*)   see: Clonazepam; Loprazolam

2-amino-5-chlorobenzophenone

($C_{13}H_{10}ClNO$; *719-59-5*)   see: Alprazolam;
Chlordiazepoxide; Diazepam; Estazolam; Ketazolam;
Medazepam; Nordazepam; Prazepam

2-amino-2'-(o-chlorobenzoyl)acetanilide

($C_{15}H_{13}ClN_2O_2$; *2894-47-5*)   see: Clonazepam

4-amino-2-chlorobenzoyl chloride hydrochloride

($C_7H_6Cl_3NO$; *58979-43-4*)   see: Chloroprocaine

2-amino-N-[3-(2-chlorobenzoyl)-5-ethyl-2-thienyl]acet-amide

($C_{15}H_{15}ClN_2O_2S$; *50509-09-6*)   see: Etizolam

2-amino-N-[3-(2-chlorobenzoyl)-5-ethyl-2-thienyl]-N-methylacetamide

($C_{16}H_{17}ClN_2O_2S$; *133278-83-8*)   see: Clotiazepam

2-amino-3-(2-chlorobenzoyl)-5-ethylthiophene

($C_{13}H_{12}ClNOS$; *50508-60-6*)   see: Clotiazepam; Etizolam

2-amino-3-(2-chlorobenzoyl)thiophene

($C_{11}H_8ClNOS$; *40017-58-1*)   see: Brotizolam

6-amino-5-chloro-2-cyclohexylphthalimidine

($C_{14}H_{17}ClN_2O$; *5566-71-2*)   see: Clorexolone

(αS)-2-amino-5-chloro-α-(cyclopropylethynyl)-α-(trifluoromethyl)benzenemethanol

($C_{13}H_{11}ClF_3NO$; *209414-27-7*)   see: Efavirenz

2-amino-6-chloro-1,9-dihydro-9-[2-(2-hydroxy-2-oxo-1,3,2-dioxaphosphoran-5-yl)ethyl]-9H-purine

($C_{10}H_{13}Cl_5O_4P$)   see: Penciclovir

4-amino-2-chloro-6,7-dimethoxyquinazoline

($C_{10}H_{10}ClN_3O_2$; *23680-84-4*)   see: Alfuzosin; Bunazosin;
Doxazosin; Prazosin; Terazosin

4-amino-5-chloro-2-ethoxybenzoic acid

($C_9H_{10}ClNO_3$; *108282-38-8*)   see: Mosapride citrate

2-amino-5-chloro-2'-fluorobenzophenone

($C_{13}H_9ClFNO$; *784-38-3*)   see: Cinolazepam; Doxefazepam;
Ethyl loflazepate; Flunitrazepam; Flurazepam; Flutazolam;
Midazolam; Quazepam

2-amino-N-[4-chloro-2-[(2-fluorophenyl)hydroxymethyl]phenyl]-N-[2-(diethylamino)ethyl]acetamide

($C_{21}H_{27}ClFN_3O_2$; *32566-14-6*)   see: Flurazepam

4-amino-2-chloro-5-fluoropyrimidine

($C_4H_3ClFN_3$; *155-10-2*)   see: Flucytosine

4-amino-6-chloro-5-methoxypyrimidine

($C_5H_6ClN_3O$; *5018-41-7*)   see: Sulfadoxine

3-amino-2-chloro-4-methylpyridine

($C_6H_7ClN_2$; *133627-45-9*)   see: Nevirapine

3-amino-2-chloro-4-methylthiophene

(C_5H_6ClNS)   see: Tiamenidine

2-amino-4-chloronitrobenzene

($C_6H_5ClN_2O_2$; *1635-61-6*)   see: Oxfendazole

2-amino-6-chloro-3-nitropyridine

($C_5H_4ClN_3O_2$; *27048-04-0*)   see: Flupirtine

2-amino-4-chlorophenol

(C_6H_6ClNO; *95-85-2*)   see: Chlorzoxazone

1-[2-[(2-amino-4-chlorophenyl)amino]benzoyl]-4-methylpiperazine

($C_{18}H_{21}ClN_4O$; *65514-71-8*)   see: Clozapine

1-[3-[4-[(2-amino-4-chlorophenyl)amino]-1-piperidinyl]propyl]-1,3-dihydro-2H-benzimidazol-2-one

($C_{21}H_{26}ClN_5O$; *62780-98-7*)   see: Domperidone

(2-amino-5-chlorophenyl)(2-chlorophenyl)methanone oxime

($C_{13}H_{10}Cl_2N_2O$; *13949-49-0*)   see: Lorazepam

2-amino-5-chlorophenyl cyclohexyl ketone

($C_{13}H_{16}ClNO$; *1789-30-6*)   see: Tetrazepam

(±)-2-(2-amino-5-chlorophenyl)-4-cyclopropyl-1,1,1-trifluoro-3-butyn-2-ol

($C_{13}H_{11}ClF_3NO$; *168834-43-3*)   see: Efavirenz

(2-amino-5-chlorophenyl)phenylmethanone oxime

($C_{13}H_{11}ClN_2O$; *18097-52-4*)   see: Chlordiazepoxide

4-amino-5-chloro-1-phenyl-6(1H)-pyridazinone

($C_{10}H_8ClN_3O$; *1698-60-8*)   see: Amezinium metilsulfate

2-amino-6-chloropurine

($C_5H_4ClN_5$; *10310-21-1*)   see: Abacavir; Famciclovir;
Penciclovir

(1S,4R)-4-(2-amino-6-chloro-9H-purin-9-yl)-2-cyclopentene-1-methanol

($C_{11}H_{12}ClN_5O$; *136522-33-3*)   see: Abacavir

(±)-cis-4-(2-amino-6-chloro-9H-purin-9-yl)-2-cyclopentene-1-methanol

($C_{13}H_{14}ClN_5O_2$; *118237-87-9*)   see: Abacavir

2-amino-5-chloropyridine

($C_5H_5ClN_2$; *1072-98-6*)   see: Alpidem; Zopiclone

2-amino-N-(2-chloro-3-pyridinyl)benzamide

($C_{12}H_{10}ClN_3O$; *956-30-9*)   see: Pirenzepine

2-amino-6-chloro-4(3H)-pyrimidinone

($C_4H_4ClN_3O$; *1194-21-4*)   see: Abacavir

(±)-cis-4-[(2-amino-4-chloro-6-pyrimidinyl)amino]-2-cyclopentene-1-methanol

($C_{10}H_{13}ClN_4O$; *122624-73-1*)   see: Abacavir

2-amino-4-chloro-5-sulfamoylbenzamide

($C_7H_8ClN_3O_3S$; *34121-17-0*)   see: Fenquizone;
Quinethazone

2-amino-4,5-dimethoxybenzoic acid
($C_9H_{11}NO_4$; *5653-40-7*)   see: Prazosin

2-amino-4,5-dimethoxybenzonitrile
($C_9H_{10}N_2O_2$; *26961-27-3*)   see: Bunazosin

2-amino-5-[[3,5-dimethoxy-4-(2-methoxyethoxy)phenyl]
methyl]-4(1*H***)-pyrimidinone**
($C_{16}H_{21}N_3O_5$; *55211-64-8*)   see: Tetroxoprim

2-amino-1-(3,4-dimethoxyphenyl)-1-butanol
($C_{12}H_{19}NO_3$; *1141-80-6*)   see: Moxaverine

(*S***)-2-amino-3-(3,4-dimethoxyphenyl)propanoic acid**
($C_{11}H_{15}NO_4$; *32161-30-1*)   see: Moexipril

2-amino-1-(2,5-dimethoxyphenyl)-1-propanone hydro-
chloride
($C_{11}H_{16}ClNO_3$; *103565-48-6*)   see: Methoxamine

4-amino-5,6-dimethoxypyrimidine
($C_6H_9N_3O_2$; *5018-45-1*)   see: Sulfadoxine

6-amino-2,4-dimethoxypyrimidine
($C_6H_9N_3O_2$; *3289-50-7*)   see: Sulfadimethoxine

1-(4-amino-6,7-dimethoxy-2-quinazolinyl)hexahydro-4-
formyl-1*H***-1,4-diazepine**
($C_{16}H_{21}N_5O_3$)   see: Bunazosin

(6*R***-***trans***)-7-amino-3-[[[1-[2-(dimethylamino)ethyl]-1***H***-**
tetrazol-5-yl]thio]methyl]-8-oxo-5-thia-1-azabicyclo-
[4.2.0]oct-2-ene-2-carboxylic acid
($C_{13}H_{19}N_7O_3S_2$; *61607-66-7*)   see: Cefotiam

[4*S***-(4α,4aα,5aα,12aα)]-9-amino-4-(dimethylamino)-**
1,4,4a,5,5a,6,11,12a-octahydro-3,10,12,12a-tetrahydroxy-
1,11-dioxo-2-naphthacenecarboxamide
($C_{21}H_{23}N_3O_7$; *5874-95-3*)   see: Minocycline

[4*S***-(4α,4aα,5aα,12aα)]-9-amino-4-(dimethylamino)-**
1,4,4a,5,5a,6,11,12a-octahydro-3,10,12,12a-tetrahydroxy-
7-nitro-1,11-dioxo-2-naphthacenecarboxamide
($C_{21}H_{22}N_4O_9$; *47741-18-4*)   see: Minocycline

4-amino-*N***,***N***-dimethylaniline**
($C_8H_{12}N_2$; *99-98-9*)   see: Methylthioninium chloride

4-amino-1,3-dimethylbenzene
($C_8H_{11}N$; *95-68-1*)   see: Picotamide

(5*R***,6***S***)-6-amino-2,2-dimethyl-1,3-dioxepan-5-ol acetate**
(salt)
($C_9H_{19}NO_5$; *188923-21-6*)   see: Nelfinavir mesylate

(*Z***)-2-amino-α-[[2-(1,1-dimethylethoxy)-2-oxoethoxy]imi-**
no]-4-thiazoleacetic acid
($C_{11}H_{15}N_3O_5S$; *74440-02-1*)   see: Carumonam

2-amino-α-[[2-(1,1-dimethylethoxy)-2-oxoethoxy]imino]-
4-thiazoleacetic acid ethyl ester
($C_{13}H_{19}N_3O_5S$; *149488-87-9*)   see: Carumonam

[3*S***-[2[1***R****(***R****),2***S****],3α,4aβ,8aβ]]-[3-amino-1-[[[3-[3-**
[[(1,1-dimethylethyl)amino]carbonyl]octahydro-2(1*H***)-iso-**
quinolinyl]-2-hydroxy-1-(phenylmethyl)propyl]amino]
carbonyl]-3-oxopropyl]carbamic acid phenylmethyl ester
($C_{36}H_{51}N_5O_6$; *136522-18-4*)   see: Saquinavir

5-amino-3,4-dimethylisoxazole
($C_5H_8N_2O$; *19947-75-2*)   see: Sulfafurazole

6-amino-1,3-dimethyl-5-nitroso-2,4(1*H***,3***H***)-pyrimidine-**
dione
($C_6H_8N_4O_3$; *6632-68-4*)   see: Theophylline

2-amino-4,5-dimethyloxazole
($C_5H_8N_2O$; *45529-92-8*)   see: Sulfamoxole

DL-*threo***-5-amino-2,2-dimethyl-4-phenyl-1,3-dioxane**
($C_{12}H_{17}NO_2$; *82863-88-5*)   see: Chloramphenicol

D(–)-*threo***-5-amino-2,2-dimethyl-4-phenyl-1,3-dioxane**
($C_{12}H_{17}NO_2$; *147781-29-1*)   see: Chloramphenicol

4-amino-2,3-dimethyl-1-phenyl-5-Δ³-pyrazolone
see under aminoantipyrine

1-amino-*cis***-2,6-dimethylpiperidine**
($C_7H_{16}N_2$; *61147-58-8*)   see: Clopamide

6-amino-2,4-dimethylpyrimidine
($C_6H_9N_3$; *461-98-3*)   see: Sulfisomidine

6-amino-1,3-dimethyluracil
($C_6H_9N_3O_2$; *6642-31-5*)   see: Theophylline

3-aminodiphenylamine
($C_{12}H_{12}N_2$; *5840-03-9*)   see: Moracizine

2-aminodiphenyl ether
($C_{12}H_{11}NO$; *2688-84-8*)   see: Nimesulide

2-aminodiphenylmethane
($C_{13}H_{13}N$; *28059-64-5*)   see: Perlapine

(*Z***)-2-amino-α-[[2-(diphenylmethoxy)-1,1-dimethyl-2-**
oxoethoxy]imino]-4-thiazoleacetic acid
($C_{22}H_{21}N_3O_5S$; *80542-76-3*)   see: Aztreonam

4-amino-5-ethoxymethyl-2-methylpyrimidine
($C_8H_{13}N_3O$; *73-66-5*)   see: Thiamine

9-amino-2-ethoxy-6-nitroacridine
($C_{15}H_{13}N_3O_3$; *20304-70-5*)   see: Ethacridine

4-amino-2-ethoxy-5-nitrobenzoic acid
($C_9H_{10}N_2O_5$; *86718-18-5*)   see: Cinitapride

2-[(2-aminoethyl)amino]ethanol
($C_4H_{12}N_2O$; *111-41-1*)   see: Mitoxantrone

4-amino-α-ethylbenzeneacetic acid ethyl ester
($C_{12}H_{17}NO_2$; *57960-84-6*)   see: Indobufen

4-(2-aminoethyl)benzenesulfonamide
($C_8H_{12}N_2O_2S$; *35303-76-5*)   see: Glipizide; Gliquidone;
Glisoxepide

N-(2-aminoethyl)-4-benzyloxyphenylacetamide
($C_{17}H_{20}N_2O_2$; *58027-51-3*)   see: Epanolol

4-[*N***-(2-aminoethyl)carbamoyl]morpholine**
($C_7H_{15}N_3O_2$; *69630-16-6*)   see: Xamoterol

N-(2-aminoethyl)-N'-(5-chloro-2,1,3-benzothiadiazol-4-
yl)thiourea
($C_9H_{10}ClN_5S_2$)   see: Tizanidine

α-(2-aminoethyl)-2-chloro-α-phenylbenzenemethanol
($C_{15}H_{16}ClNO$; *35173-30-9*)   see: Clofedanol

1'-(2-aminoethyl)-3',4'-dihydro-7'-methoxyspiro[cyclo-
pentane-1,2'(1'*H***)-naphthalen]-1'-ol**
($C_{17}H_{25}NO_2$; *48181-36-8*)   see: Butorphanol

4-amino-1-ethyl-5,6-dihydropyrimidin-2(1*H***)-one hydro-**
bromide
($C_6H_{12}BrN_3O$)   see: Sulfacitine

2-aminoethyl hydrogen sulfate
($C_2H_7NO_4S$; *926-39-6*)   see: Viloxazine

O-(2-aminoethyl)hydroxylamine
($C_2H_8N_2O$; *4747-18-6*)   see: Fluvoxamine

N-(2-aminoethyl)morpholine
($C_6H_{14}N_2O$; *2038-03-1*)   see: Minaprine; Moclobemide

1-(2-aminoethyl)octahydroazocine
($C_9H_{20}N_2$; *1126-67-6*)   see: Guanethidine sulfate

[*R***-(***R****,***S****)]-α-(1-aminoethyl)-3-(phenylmethoxy)benzene-**
methanol
($C_{16}H_{19}NO_2$; *47017-04-9*)   see: Metaraminol

α-aminoethylphosphonic acid diethyl ester
($C_6H_{16}NO_3P$; *54788-35-1*)   see: Fotemustine

3-(2-aminoethyl)-6,7,8,9-tetrahydro-2-methyl-4*H*-pyrido[1,2-*a*]pyrimidin-4-one
(C$_{11}$H$_{17}$N$_3$O; *181479-08-3*)   see: Risperidone

5-amino-2-ethyl-1,3,4-thiadiazole
(C$_4$H$_7$N$_3$S; *14068-53-2*)   see: Sulfaethidole

5-[[(2-aminoethyl)thio]methyl]-*N,N*-dimethyl-2-furanmethanamine
(C$_{10}$H$_{18}$N$_2$OS; *66356-53-4*)   see: Ranitidine

4-[(2-aminoethylthio)methyl]-5-methylimidazole dihydrochloride
(C$_7$H$_{15}$Cl$_2$N$_3$S; *38603-72-4*)   see: Cimetidine

[4-[[(2-aminoethyl)thio]methyl]-2-thiazolyl]guanidine
(C$_7$H$_{13}$N$_5$S$_2$; *71916-66-0*)   see: Ebrotidine

2-amino-2'-fluorobenzophenone
(C$_{13}$H$_{10}$FNO; *1581-13-1*)   see: Flunitrazepam

6-amino-3-fluoro-2-(4-ethoxycarbonyl-1-piperazinyl)-pyridine
(C$_{12}$H$_{17}$FN$_4$O$_2$; *75167-28-1*)   see: Enoxacin

4-amino-5-fluoro-2-(methylthio)pyrimidine
(C$_5$H$_6$FN$_3$S)   see: Flucytosine

α-aminoglutarimide
(C$_5$H$_8$N$_2$O$_2$; *2353-44-8*)   see: Thalidomide

aminoguanidine
(CH$_6$N$_4$; *79-17-4*)   see: Ambazone; Lamotrigine

aminoguanidine carbonate
(C$_2$H$_8$N$_4$O$_3$; *2200-97-7*)   see: Guanabenz

1-aminohexahydroazepine
(C$_6$H$_{14}$N$_2$; *5906-35-4*)   see: Glisoxepide; Tolazamide

2-amino-*endo*-hexahydro-6,7-methanoisoindoline
(C$_9$H$_{16}$N$_2$; *67505-12-8*)   see: Tripamide

1-aminohydantoin
(C$_3$H$_5$N$_3$O$_2$; *6301-02-6*)   see: Nitrofurantoin

1-aminohydantoin hydrochloride
(C$_3$H$_6$ClN$_3$O$_2$; *2827-56-7*)   see: Dantrolene

2-amino-3'-hydroxyacetophenone
(C$_8$H$_9$NO$_2$; *90005-54-2*)   see: Norfenefrine

3-amino-5-[[(2-hydroxyethyl)amino]carbonyl]benzoic acid
(C$_{10}$H$_{12}$N$_2$O$_4$; *22871-57-4*)   see: Ioxitalamic acid

1-amino-3-hydroxyguanidine
(CH$_6$N$_4$O; *36778-67-3*)   see: Guanoxabenz

(*R*)-7-amino-3-hydroxyheptanamide
(C$_7$H$_{16}$N$_2$O$_2$)   see: Gusperimus trihydrochloride

cis-4-amino-1-[2-(hydroxymethyl)-1,3-oxathiolan-5-yl]-2(1*H*)-pyrimidinone
(C$_8$H$_{11}$N$_3$O$_3$S; *136891-12-8*)   see: Lamivudine

2-amino-2-(hydroxymethyl)-1,3-propanediol
(C$_4$H$_{11}$NO$_3$; *77-86-1*)   see: Dexketoprofen trometamol

7(*R*)-[2(*R*)-amino-2-(4-hydroxyphenyl)acetamido]-3-[[(1-methyl-1*H*-tetrazol-5-yl)thio]methyl]-3-cephem-4-carboxylic acid
(C$_{18}$H$_{19}$N$_7$O$_5$S$_2$; *51929-23-8*)   see: Cefoperazone; Cefpiramide

7-[D(–)-α-amino-(4-hydroxyphenyl)acetamido]-3-(1-methyltetrazol-5-ylthiomethyl)-3-cephem-4-carboxylic acid
see under 7(*R*)-[2(*R*)-amino-2-(4-hydroxyphenyl)acetamido]-3-[[(1-methyl-1*H*-tetrazol-5-yl)thio]methyl]-3-cephem-4-carboxylic acid

[6*R*-[6α,7β(*R**)]]-7-[[amino(4-hydroxyphenyl)acetyl]-amino]-8-oxo-3-[[(trifluoromethyl)sulfonyl]oxy]-5-thia-1-azabicyclo[4.2.0]oct-2-ene-2-carboxylic acid
(C$_{16}$H$_{14}$F$_3$N$_3$O$_8$S$_2$; *133005-89-7*)   see: *cis*-Cefprozil

(3-amino-4-hydroxyphenyl)arsonic acid
(C$_6$H$_8$AsNO$_4$; *2163-77-1*)   see: Acetarsol

N-[(2*R*,3*S*)-3-amino-2-hydroxy-4-phenylbutyl]-*N*-(2-methylpropyl)-4-nitrobenzenesulfonamide
(C$_{20}$H$_{27}$N$_3$O$_5$S; *251105-80-3*)   see: Amprenavir

2-(3-amino-4-hydroxyphenyl)propionic acid
(C$_9$H$_{11}$NO$_3$; *51234-43-6*)   see: Flunoxaprofen

2-(3-amino-4-hydroxyphenyl)propionitrile
(C$_9$H$_{10}$N$_2$O; *51234-23-2*)   see: Benoxaprofen

[3*S*-[2(2*S**,3*S**),3α,4aβ,8aβ]]-2-[3-amino-2-hydroxy-4-(phenylthio)butyl]-*N*-(1,1-dimethylethyl)decahydro-3-iso-quinolinecarboxamide
(C$_{24}$H$_{39}$N$_3$O$_2$S; *159878-05-4*)   see: Nelfinavir mesylate

2-amino-4-hydroxy-5-(3,4,5-trimethoxybenzyl)pyrimidine
(C$_{14}$H$_{17}$N$_3$O$_4$; *92440-76-1*)   see: Trimethoprim

5-aminoimidazole-4-carboxamide
(C$_4$H$_6$N$_4$O; *360-97-4*)   see: Dacarbazine

4-aminoimidazole-5-carboxamide hydrochloride
(C$_4$H$_7$ClN$_4$O; *72-40-2*)   see: Orazamide

aminoiminomethanesulfonic acid
(CH$_4$N$_2$O$_3$S; *1184-90-3*)   see: Zanamivir

(*R*)-7-[(aminoiminomethyl)amino]-3-hydroxyheptanamide
(C$_8$H$_{18}$N$_4$O$_2$)   see: Gusperimus trihydrochloride

2-[(aminoiminomethyl)thio]ethanesulfonic acid
(C$_3$H$_8$N$_2$O$_3$S$_2$; *25985-57-3*)   see: Mesna

N-[5-[[(3-amino-3-iminopropyl)amino]carbonyl]-1-methyl-1*H*-pyrrol-3-yl]-1-methyl-4-[[(1-methyl-4-nitro-1*H*-pyrrol-2-yl)carbonyl]amino]-1*H*-pyrrole-2-carboxamide
(C$_{21}$H$_{25}$N$_9$O$_5$; *2573-48-0*)   see: Stallimycin

4-aminoindan
(C$_9$H$_{11}$N; *32202-61-2*)   see: Indanazoline

1-aminoindolin-2-one
(C$_8$H$_8$N$_2$O; *36149-75-4*)   see: Amfenac sodium

5-aminoisophthalic acid
(C$_8$H$_7$NO$_4$; *99-31-0*)   see: Iopamidol

2-amino-6-isopropyl-4-oxo-4*H*-1-benzopyran-3-carboxaldehyde
(C$_{13}$H$_{13}$NO$_3$; *68301-82-6*)   see: Amlexanox

2-amino-5-mercapto-1,3,4-thiadiazole
(C$_2$H$_3$N$_3$S$_2$; *2349-67-9*)   see: Acetazolamide

(6*R-cis*)-7-amino-7-methoxy-3-[[[1-[2-[[[(4-methylphenyl)methoxy]carbonyl]oxy]ethyl]-1*H*-tetrazol-5-yl]thio]-methyl]-8-oxo-5-oxa-1-azabicyclo[4.2.0]oct-2-ene-2-carboxylic acid diphenylmethyl ester
(C$_{34}$H$_{34}$N$_6$O$_8$S; *95589-11-0*)   see: Flomoxef

3-amino-2-methoxy-4-methylpyridine
(C$_7$H$_{10}$N$_2$O; *76005-99-7*)   see: Nevirapine

1-[2-amino-1-(4-methoxyphenyl)ethyl]cyclohexanol
(C$_{15}$H$_{23}$NO$_2$; *93413-77-5*)   see: Venlafaxine

N-(4-amino-3-methoxyphenyl)methanesulfonamide
(C$_8$H$_{12}$N$_2$O$_3$S; *57165-06-7*)   see: Amsacrine

3-amino-α-[[[2-(4-methoxyphenyl)-1-methylethyl]-(phenylmethyl)amino]methyl]-4-(phenylmethoxy)-benzenemethanol
(C$_{32}$H$_{36}$N$_2$O$_3$; *43229-68-1*)   see: Formoterol

3-amino-2-methoxypyrazine
(C$_5$H$_7$N$_3$O; *4774-10-1*)   see: Sulfalene

2-amino-5-methoxypyrimidine
(C$_5$H$_7$N$_3$O; *13418-77-4*)   see: Sulfametoxydiazine

8-amino-6-methoxyquinoline
(C$_{10}$H$_{10}$N$_2$O; *90-52-8*)   see: Primaquine

3-amino-4-methylacetophenone
(C$_9$H$_{11}$NO; *17071-24-8*)   see: Amosulalol

3-amino-5-[(methylamino)carbonyl]benzoic acid
(C$_9$H$_{10}$N$_2$O$_3$; *1954-96-7*)   see: Iotalamic acid

4-amino-α-methylbenzeneacetic acid methyl ester
(C$_{10}$H$_{13}$NO$_2$; *39718-97-3*)   see: Alminoprofen

α-amino-α-methylbenzenepropanenitrile monohydrochloride
(C$_{10}$H$_{13}$ClN$_2$; *56968-07-1*)   see: Metirosine

3-amino-2-methylbenzoic acid
(C$_8$H$_9$NO$_2$; *52130-17-3*)   see: Nelfinavir mesylate

4-(aminomethyl)benzoic acid
(C$_8$H$_9$NO$_2$; *56-91-7*)   see: Tranexamic acid

2-amino-4-methylbenzophenone
(C$_{14}$H$_{13}$NO; *4937-62-6*)   see: Proquazone

L-2-amino-2-methyl-3-bromopropionic acid
(C$_4$H$_8$BrNO$_2$)   see: Metirosine

2-aminomethyl-5-bromo-3-(2-pyridyl)indole dihydrochloride
(C$_{14}$H$_{14}$BrCl$_2$N$_3$; *58350-31-5*)   see: Bromazepam

3-(aminomethyl)-4-chlorobenzoic acid
(C$_8$H$_8$ClNO$_2$; *705-17-9*)   see: Iodamide

2-aminomethyl-5-chloro-1-methyl-3-phenylindole
(C$_{16}$H$_{15}$ClN$_2$; *24140-10-1*)   see: Diazepam

3-(aminomethyl)-4-chloro-5-nitrobenzoic acid
(C$_8$H$_7$ClN$_2$O$_4$; *716-30-3*)   see: Iodamide

4-(aminomethyl)cyclohexanecarboxylic acid
(C$_8$H$_{15}$NO$_2$; *701-54-2*)   see: Tranexamic acid

5-amino-2-methyl-4,6-dichloropyrimidine
(C$_5$H$_5$Cl$_2$N$_3$; *39906-04-2*)   see: Moxonidine

2-aminomethyl-2,3-dihydro-1,4-benzodioxin
(C$_9$H$_{11}$NO$_2$; *4442-59-5*)   see: Guanoxan

6-aminomethyl-6,11-dihydro-5H-dibenz[b,e]azepine
(C$_{15}$H$_{16}$N$_2$; *41218-84-2*)   see: Epinastine hydrochloride

2-aminomethyl-1,4-dioxaspiro[4.5]decane
(C$_9$H$_{17}$NO$_2$; *45982-66-9*)   see: Guanadrel

2-amino-4,5-methylenedioxyacetophenone
(C$_9$H$_9$NO$_3$; *28657-75-2*)   see: Cinoxacin

α-(aminomethylene)-3,4,5-trimethoxybenzenepropanenitrile
(C$_{13}$H$_{16}$N$_2$O$_3$; *85536-85-2*)   see: Trimethoprim

2-aminomethyl-1-ethylpyrrolidine
(C$_7$H$_{16}$N$_2$; *26116-12-1*)   see: Sulpiride; Sultopride

(±)-2-aminomethyl-4-(4-fluorobenzyl)morpholine
(C$_{12}$H$_{17}$FN$_2$O; *112914-13-3*)   see: Mosapride citrate

α^1-(aminomethyl)-4-hydroxy-1,3-benzenedimethanol
(C$_9$H$_{13}$NO$_3$; *24085-19-6*)   see: Salmeterol

(2S,3R)-2-(aminomethyl)-3-hydroxybutanoic acid hydrochloride
(C$_5$H$_{12}$ClNO$_3$; *129994-66-7*)   see: Faropenem sodium

1-amino-2-methylindoline
(C$_9$H$_{12}$N$_2$; *31529-46-1*)   see: Indapamide

3-amino-5-methylisoxazole
(C$_4$H$_6$N$_2$O; *1072-67-9*)   see: Isoxicam; Sulfamethoxazole

2-aminomethyl-1-methyl-5-nitro-3-phenylindole
(C$_{16}$H$_{15}$N$_3$O$_2$; *30008-54-9*)   see: Nimetazepam

2-aminomethyl-2-methyltetrahydrofuran
(C$_6$H$_{13}$NO; *7179-94-4*)   see: Mefruside

cis-2-(aminomethyl)-1-phenylcyclopropanecarboxylic acid
(C$_{11}$H$_{13}$NO$_2$; *69160-57-2*)   see: Milnacipran hydrochloride

4-(aminomethyl)-1-(2-phenylethyl)-4-piperidinol
(C$_{14}$H$_{22}$N$_2$O; *23808-42-6*)   see: Fenspiride

α^6-(aminomethyl)-3-(phenylmethoxy)-2,6-pyridinedimethanol
(C$_{15}$H$_{18}$N$_2$O$_3$)   see: Pirbuterol

2-amino-2-methyl-1-phenyl-1-propanol
(C$_{10}$H$_{15}$NO; *34405-42-0*)   see: Phentermine

2-amino-2-methyl-1-phenylpropyl chloride hydrochloride
(C$_{10}$H$_{15}$Cl$_2$N; *14718-27-5*)   see: Phentermine

1-amino-4-methylpiperazine
(C$_5$H$_{13}$N$_3$; *6928-85-4*)   see: Rifampicin

1-amino-3-[4-(4-methyl-1-piperazinyl)butyl]-2,4-imidazolidinedione
(C$_{12}$H$_{23}$N$_5$O$_2$)   see: Azimilide hydrochloride

2-amino-2-methyl-1-propanol
(C$_4$H$_{11}$NO; *124-68-5*)   see: Losartan potassium

α-[1-(aminomethyl)propyl]-α-phenylbenzenemethanol
(C$_{17}$H$_{21}$NO; *22101-87-7*)   see: Etifelmine

4-amino-1-methyl-3-propyl-1H-pyrazole-5-carboxamide
(C$_8$H$_{14}$N$_4$O; *139756-02-8*)   see: Sildenafil

2-amino-3-methylpyridine
(C$_6$H$_8$N$_2$; *1603-40-3*)   see: Pemirolast

2-amino-4-methylpyridine
(C$_6$H$_8$N$_2$; *695-34-1*)   see: Piketoprofen; Rifaximin

2-amino-5-methylpyridine
(C$_6$H$_8$N$_2$; *1603-41-4*)   see: Zolpidem

2-amino-6-methylpyridine
(C$_6$H$_8$N$_2$; *1824-81-3*)   see: Nalidixic acid

2-aminomethylpyridine
(C$_6$H$_8$N$_2$; *3731-51-9*)   see: Flecainide

3-(aminomethyl)pyridine
(C$_6$H$_8$N$_2$; *3731-52-0*)   see: Nicotinyl alcohol; Picotamide; Pimefylline

1-amino-2-methylpyridinium iodide
(C$_6$H$_9$IN$_2$; *7583-90-6*)   see: Ibudilast

2-amino-4-methylpyrimidine
(C$_5$H$_7$N$_3$; *108-52-1*)   see: Sulfamerazine

2-amino-6-methyl-4(1H)-pyrimidinone
(C$_5$H$_7$N$_3$O; *3977-29-5*)   see: Sulfamerazine

[(4-amino-2-methyl-5-pyrimidinyl)methyl]carbamodithioic acid 1-[2-(acetyloxy)ethyl]-2-oxopropyl ester
(C$_{14}$H$_{20}$N$_4$O$_3$S$_2$; *89285-03-0*)   see: Thiamine

N-[(4-amino-2-methyl-5-pyrimidinyl)methyl]-N'-(2-chloroethyl)urea
(C$_9$H$_{14}$ClN$_5$O; *42471-43-2*)   see: Nimustine

3-[(4-amino-2-methyl-5-pyrimidinyl)methyl]-5-(2-hydroxyethyl)-4-methyl-2(3H)-thiazolethione
(C$_{12}$H$_{16}$N$_4$OS$_2$; *299-35-4*)   see: Thiamine

N-(4-amino-2-methylpyrimidin-5-ylmethyl)-N-(4-hydroxy-1-methyl-2-mercaptobut-1-enyl)formamide
(C$_{12}$H$_{18}$N$_4$O$_2$S; *554-45-0*)   see: Acetiamine; Bentiamine; Bisbentiamine; Fursultiamine; Octotiamine

4-[[[(2-aminophenyl)amino]thioxomethyl]amino]-1-pipe-ridinecarboxylic acid ethyl ester

($C_{15}H_{22}N_4O_2S$; *73733-81-0*)   see: Astemizole

2-amino-3-phenylbicyclo[2.2.1]heptane

($C_{13}H_{17}N$; *39550-30-6*)   see: Fencamfamin

4-(4-aminophenyl)butanoic acid

($C_{10}H_{13}NO_2$; *15118-60-2*)   see: Chlorambucil

N-(2-aminophenyl)-2-chloro-N-[(4-chlorophenyl)methyl]-acetamide

($C_{15}H_{14}Cl_2N_2O$)   see: Clemizole

N-(2-aminophenyl)-N-[(4-chlorophenyl)methyl]pyrro-lidine-1-acetamide

($C_{19}H_{22}ClN_3O$)   see: Clemizole

3-(p-aminophenyl)-N-dichloroacetyl-2-methylalanine

($C_{12}H_{14}Cl_2N_2O_3$)   see: Metirosine

1-(4-aminophenyl)-2-[(1,1-dimethylethyl)amino]ethanone

($C_{12}H_{18}N_2O$; *104656-91-9*)   see: Clenbuterol

5-(4-aminophenyl)-3-(1,1-dimethylethyl)-2-oxazolidinone

($C_{13}H_{18}N_2O_2$; *41936-92-9*)   see: Clenbuterol

2-amino-1-phenylethanol

($C_8H_{11}NO$; *7568-93-6*)   see: Levamisole

2-(4-aminophenyl)ethyl bromide

($C_8H_{10}BrN$; *39232-03-6*)   see: Anileridine

(1α,5α,6α)-6-amino-3-(phenylmethyl)-3-azabicy-clo[3.1.0]hexane-2,6-dione

($C_{12}H_{12}N_2O_2$)   see: Trovafloxacin mesilate

(S)-α-[(4-aminophenyl)methyl]-1,3-dihydro-1,3-dioxo-2H-isoindole-2-acetic acid ethyl ester

($C_{19}H_{18}N_2O_4$; *74743-23-0*)   see: Melphalan

5-amino-3-phenyl-1,2,4-oxadiazole

($C_8H_7N_3O$; *3663-37-4*)   see: Butalamine; Imolamine

2-amino-1-phenylpropane

($C_9H_{13}N$; *300-62-9*)   see: Amphetaminil; Fenalcomine; Fenetylline; Racefemine

2-(4-aminophenyl)propionitrile

($C_9H_{10}N_2$; *28694-90-8*)   see: Benoxaprofen; Flunoxaprofen

3-amino-2-phenylpyrazole

($C_9H_9N_3$; *826-85-7*)   see: Sulfaphenazole

4-amino-1-phenyl-6(1H)-pyridazinone

($C_{10}H_9N_3O$; *13589-77-0*)   see: Amezinium metilsulfate

4-(3-aminophenyl)pyridine

($C_{11}H_{10}N_2$; *40034-44-4*)   see: Rosoxacin

N-(4-aminophenylsulfonyl)cyanamide

($C_7H_7N_3O_2S$; *116-47-2*)   see: Sulfamoxole

N¹-(4-aminophenylsulfonyl)-N³-cyanoguanidine

($C_8H_9N_5O_2S$; *55455-79-3*)   see: Sulfaguanole

(R*,R*)-β-[(2-aminophenyl)thio]-α-hydroxy-4-methoxy-benzenepropanoic acid

($C_{16}H_{17}NO_4S$; *42399-55-3*)   see: Diltiazem

[S-(R*,R*)]-β-[(2-aminophenyl)thio]-α-hydroxy-4-meth-oxybenzenepropanoic acid

($C_{16}H_{17}NO_4S$; *42399-48-4*)   see: Diltiazem

[S-(R*,R*)]-β-[(2-aminophenyl)thio]-α-hydroxy-4-meth-oxybenzenepropanoic acid methyl ester

($C_{17}H_{19}NO_4S$; *99109-07-6*)   see: Diltiazem

2-amino-4-phenylthionitrobenzene

($C_{12}H_{10}N_2O_2S$; *43156-47-4*)   see: Oxfendazole

(2R-cis)-4-amino-1-[2-[(phosphonooxy)methyl]-1,3-oxa-thiolan-5-yl]-2(1H)-pyrimidinone

($C_8H_{12}N_3O_6PS$; *143616-56-2*)   see: Lamivudine

(±)-2-amino-6-phthalimido-4,5,6,7-tetrahydrobenzo-thiazole

($C_{15}H_{13}N_3O_2S$; *104618-33-9*)   see: Pramipexole hydrochloride

2-amino-1,3-propanediol

($C_3H_9NO_2$; *534-03-2*)   see: Iopamidol

3-amino-1,2-propanediol

($C_3H_9NO_2$; *616-30-8*)   see: Iohexol

3-aminopropane-1-sulfonic acid

($C_3H_9NO_3S$; *3687-18-1*)   see: Acamprosate calcium

2-amino-1-propanol

(C_3H_9NO; *6168-72-5*)   see: Mexazolam

L(+)-2-amino-1-propanol

see under (S)-alaninol

3-amino-1-propanol

(C_3H_9NO; *156-87-6*)   see: Acamprosate calcium; Cyclophosphamide; Dexpanthenol; Domperidone; Gusperimus trihydrochloride; Mefenorex; Urapidil

7-amino-3-[(Z)-1-propenyl]-3-cephem-4-carboxylic acid

($C_{10}H_{12}N_2O_3S$; *106447-44-3*)   see: cis-Cefprozil

3-aminopropionaldehyde diethyl acetal

($C_7H_{17}NO_2$; *41365-75-7*)   see: Atorvastatin calcium

β-aminopropionic acid phosphite

($C_3H_{10}NO_6P$)   see: Pamidronic acid

3-aminopropionitrile

($C_3H_6N_2$; *151-18-8*)   see: Calcium pantothenate; Stallimycin

N-[4-(3-aminopropylamino)butyl]-2,2-dihydroxy-ethanamide trihydrochloride

($C_9H_{26}Cl_3N_3O_3$)   see: Gusperimus trihydrochloride

2-(3-aminopropylamino)ethyl bromide dihydrobromide

($C_5H_{15}Br_3N_2$; *23545-42-8*)   see: Amifostine

5-(3-aminopropyl)-4,6-dihydroxy-1,3,2,4,6-dioxatriphos-phorinan-5-ol 2,4,6-trioxide

($C_4H_{12}NO_8P_3$; *165043-19-6*)   see: Alendronate sodium

4-(2-aminopropyl)-1,2-dimethoxybenzene

($C_{11}H_{17}NO_2$; *120-26-3*)   see: Dimoxyline

2-aminopyrazine

($C_4H_5N_3$; *5049-61-6*)   see: Sulfalene

3-aminopyrazine-2-carboxylic acid

($C_5H_5N_3O_2$; *5424-01-1*)   see: Amiloride

3-amino-1H-pyrazole-4-carbonitrile

($C_4H_4N_4$; *16617-46-2*)   see: Zaleplon

5-aminopyrazole-4-carboxamide

($C_4H_6N_4O$; *5334-31-6*)   see: Allopurinol

2-aminopyridine

($C_5H_6N_2$; *504-29-0*)   see: Fenyramidol; Lornoxicam; Mepyramine; Piroxicam; Propiram; Risperidone; Tenoxicam; Zolimidine

3-aminopyridine

($C_5H_6N_2$; *462-08-8*)   see: Apalcillin; Troxipide

7(R)-amino-3-(1-pyridiniomethyl)-3-cephem-4-carboxylic acid chloride monohydrochloride

($C_{13}H_{15}Cl_2N_3O_3S$; *96752-43-1*)   see: Ceftazidime

2-aminopyrimidine

($C_4H_5N_3$; *109-12-6*)   see: Sulfadiazine

2-amino-4,6-pyrimidinedione

($C_4H_5N_3O_2$; *4425-67-6*)   see: Abacavir

3-aminopyrrolidine

($C_4H_{10}N_2$; *79286-79-6*)   see: Tosufloxacin

4-amino-6-trifluoromethylbenzene-1,3-disulfamide
($C_7H_8F_3N_3O_4S_2$; *654-62-6*)   see: Bendroflumethiazide;
Hydroflumethiazide

4-amino-6-trifluoromethyl-1,3-benzenedisulfochloride
($C_7H_4Cl_2F_3NO_4S_2$; *1479-95-4*)   see: Bendroflumethiazide;
Hydroflumethiazide

4-amino-3-(trifluoromethyl)benzoic acid
($C_8H_6F_3NO_2$; *400-76-0*)   see: Mabuterol

2-amino-1-(3-trifluoromethylphenyl)propane
($C_{10}H_{12}F_3N$; *1886-26-6*)   see: Benfluorex; Fenfluramine

5-amino-2,4,6-triiodo-1,3-benzenedicarbonyl dichloride
($C_8H_2Cl_2I_3NO_2$; *37441-29-5*)   see: Iopamidol

3-amino-2,4,6-triiodobenzoic acid
($C_7H_4I_3NO_2$; *3119-15-1*)   see: Acetrizoic acid; Adipiodone;
Iobenzamic acid; Iodoxamic acid; Ioglycamic acid; Iotroxic
acid

3-amino-2,4,6-triiodobenzoyl chloride
($C_7H_3ClI_3NO$; *51935-27-4*)   see: Iobenzamic acid

***N*-(3-amino-2,4,6-triiodobenzoyl)-*N*-phenyl-β-alanine
methyl ester**
($C_{17}H_{15}I_3N_2O_3$; *51934-66-8*)   see: Iobenzamic acid

**5-amino-2,4,6-triiodo-*N*,*N*'-bis(2,3-dihydroxypropyl)iso-
phthalamide**
($C_{14}H_{18}I_3N_3O_6$; *76801-93-9*)   see: Iohexol

5-amino-2,4,6-triiodoisophthalic acid
($C_8H_4I_3NO_4$; *35453-19-1*)   see: Iopamidol

2-[(3-amino-2,4,6-triiodophenyl)methylene]butanoic acid
($C_{11}H_{10}I_3NO_2$; *1215-70-9*)   see: Bunamiodyl

2-amino-3,4,5-trimethoxybenzoic acid
($C_{10}H_{13}NO_5$; *61948-85-4*)   see: Trimazosin

**4-(4-amino-6,7,8-trimethoxy-2-quinazolinyl)-1-piperazi-
necarboxylic acid 2-methyl-2-propenyl ester**
($C_{20}H_{27}N_5O_5$; *35795-15-4*)   see: Trimazosin

5-aminouracil
($C_4H_5N_3O_2$; *932-52-5*)   see: Uramustine

L-α-amino-α-vanillylpropionamide
($C_{11}H_{16}N_2O_3$; *6555-09-5*)   see: Methyldopa

DL-α-amino-α-vanillylpropionitrile
($C_{11}H_{14}N_2O_2$; *6555-27-7*)   see: Methyldopa

L-α-amino-α-vanillylpropionitrile
($C_{11}H_{14}N_2O_2$; *14818-96-3*)   see: Methyldopa

amitriptyline
($C_{20}H_{23}N$; *50-48-6*)   see: Amitriptylinoxide; Nortriptyline

amitriptyline methiodide
($C_{21}H_{26}IN$; *33445-20-4*)   see: Nortriptyline

ammonium carbonate
($CH_8N_2O_3$; *506-87-6*)   see: Clopidogrel hydrogensulfate;
Mephenytoin; Methyldopa; Metirosine; Phenytoin

ammonium dithiocarbamate
($CH_6N_2S_2$; *513-74-6*)   see: Arotinolol; Clomethiazole

ammonium formate
(CH_5NO_2; *540-69-2*)   see: Ramatroban

ammonium fumarate
($C_4H_{10}N_2O_4$; *14548-85-7*)   see: L-Aspartic acid

ammonium rhodanide
(CH_4N_2S; *1762-95-4*)   see: Acetazolamide; Benzyl mustard
oil; Brimonidine; Clonidine; Indanazoline; Thiadrine;
Tiamenidine; Tioxolone; Tolonidine; Tramazoline

ammonium thiocyanate
see under ammonium rhodanide

amoxicillin
($C_{16}H_{19}N_3O_5S$; *26787-78-0*)   see: Aspoxicillin

amoxicillin trimethylsilyl ester
($C_{19}H_{27}N_3O_5SSi$; *53512-08-6*)   see: Amoxicillin

(±)-amphetamine
see under 2-amino-1-phenylpropane

ampicillin
($C_{16}H_{19}N_3O_4S$; *69-53-4*)   see: Apalcillin; Lenampicillin;
Metampicillin; Mezlocillin; Piperacillin; Sultamicillin

ampicillin potassium salt
($C_{16}H_{18}KN_3O_4S$; *23277-71-6*)   see: Talampicillin

ampicillin sodium salt
($C_{16}H_{18}N_3NaO_4S$; *69-52-3*)   see: Hetacillin

4-*tert*-amylbenzaldehyde
($C_{12}H_{16}O$; *67468-54-6*)   see: Amorolfine

4-*tert*-amyl-α-methylcinnamaldehyde
($C_{15}H_{20}O$; *67468-55-7*)   see: Amorolfine

amyl methyl ketone
($C_7H_{14}O$; *110-43-0*)   see: Tuaminoheptane

**androsta-1,4-diene-3,17-dione cyclic 17-(1,2-ethanediyl
acetal)**
($C_{21}H_{28}O_3$; *2398-63-2*)   see: Estrone

(3β,5α,17β)-androstane-3,17-diol 17-benzoate
($C_{26}H_{36}O_3$; *6242-26-8*)   see: Mesterolone

3,17-androstanedione
($C_{19}H_{28}O_2$; *846-46-8*)   see: Androstanolone; Estrone

(3β,17β)-androst-5-ene-3,17-diol 3-acetate
($C_{21}H_{32}O_3$; *1639-43-6*)   see: Mesterolone; Testosterone

(3β,17β)-androst-5-ene-3,17-diol 3-acetate 17-benzoate
($C_{28}H_{36}O_4$; *5953-63-9*)   see: Estradiol; Mesterolone;
Testosterone

androstenediol 17-propionate
($C_{22}H_{34}O_3$; *38859-47-1*)   see: Testosterone propionate

4-androstene-3,17-dione
($C_{19}H_{26}O_2$; *63-05-8*)   see: Formestane; Penmesterol;
Spironolactone

androstenolone
($C_{19}H_{28}O_2$; *53-43-0*)   see: Androstanolone; Azacosterol;
Estrone; Ethisterone; Methyltestosterone; Prasterone
enanthate; Spironolactone

androstenolone acetate
see under 3β-acetoxy-17-oxo-5-androstene

(5α)-androst-2-en-17-one
($C_{19}H_{28}O$; *963-75-7*)   see: Pancuronium bromide;
Pipecuronium bromide; Vecuronium bromide

androsterone
($C_{19}H_{30}O_2$; *53-41-8*)   see: Mestanolone

anethole
($C_{10}H_{12}O$; *104-46-1*)   see: Anethole trithione;
Diethylstilbestrol

D-anhydro-*O*-carboxymandelic acid
($C_9H_6O_4$; *54256-33-6*)   see: Cefamandole

5,6-anhydro-1,2-*O*-isopropylidene-α-D-glucofuranose
($C_9H_{14}O_5$; *15354-69-5*)   see: Prenalterol

2,3'-anhydrothymidine
($C_{10}H_{12}N_2O_4$; *15981-92-7*)   see: Zidovudine

3',5'-anhydrothymidine
($C_{10}H_{12}N_2O_4$; *38313-48-3*)   see: Stavudine

anhydrovinblastine
($C_{46}H_{56}N_4O_8$; *38390-45-3*)   see: Vinorelbine

aniline

(C$_6$H$_7$N; *62-53-3*)   see: Alfentanil; Amsacrine; Aprindine; Bamipine; Brodimoprim; Clobazam; Fentanyl; Fluspirilene; Ibutilide fumarate; Mesalazine; Nelfinavir mesylate; Rebamipide; Sotalol; Tacrine; Thenalidine

2-anilinobenzoic acid

(C$_{13}$H$_{11}$NO$_2$; *91-40-7*)   see: Amsacrine

4-anilino-1-benzyl-4-carbamoylpiperidine

(C$_{19}$H$_{23}$N$_3$O; *1096-03-3*)   see: Fluspirilene

4-anilino-1-benzyl-4-cyanopiperidine

(C$_{19}$H$_{21}$N$_3$; *968-86-5*)   see: Alfentanil; Fluspirilene

4-anilino-1-benzylpiperidine

(C$_{18}$H$_{22}$N$_2$; *1155-56-2*)   see: Fentanyl

2-anilinoindane

(C$_{15}$H$_{15}$N; *33237-72-8*)   see: Aprindine

3-anilinopropionitrile

(C$_9$H$_{10}$N$_2$; *1075-76-9*)   see: Trimethoprim

3-anilino-2-(3,4,5-trimethoxybenzyl)acrylonitrile

(C$_{19}$H$_{20}$N$_2$O$_3$; *30078-48-9*)   see: Trimethoprim

p-anisaldehyde

(C$_8$H$_8$O$_2$; *123-11-5*)   see: Anisindione; Diltiazem; Fenoldopam mesilate; Mepyramine; Raloxifene hydrochloride

m-anisidine

(C$_7$H$_9$NO; *536-90-3*)   see: Amsacrine

anisole

(C$_7$H$_8$O; *100-66-3*)   see: Anethole; Diflunisal; Fenofibrate

4-anisoyl chloride

(C$_8$H$_7$ClO$_2$; *100-07-2*)   see: Amiodarone; Aniracetam; Benzarone; Pimobendan

anthracene

(C$_{14}$H$_{10}$; *120-12-7*)   see: Benzoctamine; Bisantrene

9-anthracenecarboxaldehyde

(C$_{15}$H$_{10}$O; *642-31-9*)   see: Benzoctamine

9,10-anthracenedicarboxaldehyde

(C$_{16}$H$_{10}$O$_2$; *7044-91-9*)   see: Bisantrene

anthranilamide

(C$_7$H$_8$N$_2$O; *88-68-6*)   see: Bromazepam; Tacrine

anthranilic acid

(C$_7$H$_7$NO$_2$; *118-92-3*)   see: Imiquimod; Lobenzarit; Tranilast

anthranilonitrile

(C$_7$H$_6$N$_2$; *1885-29-6*)   see: Bromazepam; Tacrine

1,8-anthraquinonedisulfonic acid

(C$_{14}$H$_8$O$_8$S$_2$; *82-48-4*)   see: Dithranol

anthrone

(C$_{14}$H$_{10}$O; *90-44-8*)   see: Maprotiline; Melitracen

3-(9-anthryl)propionic acid

(C$_{17}$H$_{14}$O$_2$; *41034-83-7*)   see: Maprotiline

(+)-apovincamine

(C$_{21}$H$_{24}$N$_2$O$_2$; *4880-92-6*)   see: Vincamine; Vinpocetine

apovincamine

see under (+)-apovincamine

L-arabinitol

(C$_5$H$_{12}$O$_5$; *7643-75-6*)   see: Tacrolimus

1-β-D-arabinofuranosyl-5-(chloromethyl)-2,4(1*H*,3*H*)-pyrimidinedione

(C$_{10}$H$_{13}$ClN$_2$O$_6$; *75843-06-0*)   see: Sorivudine

1-β-D-arabinofuranosyl-5-ethenyl-2,4(1*H*,3*H*)-pyrimidinedione

(C$_{11}$H$_{14}$N$_2$O$_6$; *74886-33-2*)   see: Sorivudine

(*E*)-3-(1-β-D-arabinofuranosyl-1,2,3,4-tetrahydro-2,4-dioxo-5-pyrimidinyl)-2-propenoic acid

(C$_{12}$H$_{14}$N$_2$O$_8$; *80659-43-4*)   see: Sorivudine

1-β-D-arabinofuranosyluracil

(C$_9$H$_{12}$N$_2$O$_6$; *3083-77-0*)   see: Cytarabine; Sorivudine

arecoline

(C$_8$H$_{13}$NO$_2$; *63-75-2*)   see: Paroxetine

L-arginine

(C$_6$H$_{14}$N$_4$O$_2$; *74-79-3*)   see: Arginine aspartate; Arginine pidolate; Cetrorelix

L-arginine monohydrochloride

(C$_6$H$_{15}$ClN$_4$O$_2$; *1119-34-2*)   see: Citrulline

D-Arg(Tos)-Gly-OEt

(C$_{17}$H$_{27}$N$_5$O$_5$S; *136730-95-5*)   see: Desmopressin

ascorbic acid

(C$_6$H$_8$O$_6$; *50-81-7*)   see: Carumonam

L-asparagine

(C$_4$H$_8$N$_2$O$_3$; *70-47-3*)   see: Eptifibatide

L-asparaginic acid

(C$_4$H$_7$NO$_4$; *56-84-8*)   see: L-Alanine; Arginine aspartate; Aspartame; Betaine aspartate

2-[3(*S*)-(L-asparaginylamino)-2(*R*)-hydroxy-4-phenylbutyl]-*N*-*tert*-butyldecahydro-(4a*S*,8a*S*)-isoquinoline-3(*S*)-carboxamide

(C$_{28}$H$_{45}$N$_5$O$_4$; *137431-06-2*)   see: Saquinavir

L-aspartic anhydride hydrochloride

(C$_4$H$_6$ClNO$_3$; *34029-31-7*)   see: Aspartame

atropine

(C$_{17}$H$_{23}$NO$_3$; *51-55-8*)   see: Atropine methonitrate; Sultroponium

2-azabicyclo[2.2.1]hept-5-en-3-one

(C$_6$H$_7$NO; *49805-30-3*)   see: Abacavir

3-azabicyclo[3.3.0]octane

(C$_7$H$_{13}$N; *5661-03-0*)   see: Gliclazide

(±)-*endo*,*cis*-2-azabicyclo[3.3.0]octane-3-carboxylic acid

(C$_8$H$_{13}$NO$_2$; *105307-53-7*)   see: Ramipril

azacyclonol

(C$_{18}$H$_{21}$NO; *115-46-8*)   see: Fexofenadine hydrochloride; Terfenadine

1-aza-3-oxaspiro[4.5]decane-2,4-dione

(C$_8$H$_{11}$NO$_3$; *3253-43-8*)   see: Ciclacillin

1-azaphenothiazine

(C$_{11}$H$_8$N$_2$S; *261-96-1*)   see: Isothipendyl; Oxypendyl; Pipazetate; Prothipendyl

1-azaphenothiazine-10-carbonyl chloride

(C$_{12}$H$_7$ClN$_2$OS; *94231-78-4*)   see: Pipazetate

2-azaspiro[4.5]decan-3-one

(C$_9$H$_{15}$NO; *64744-50-9*)   see: Gabapentin

azidocillin potassium

(C$_{16}$H$_{16}$KN$_5$O$_4$S; *22647-32-1*)   see: Pivampicillin

azidocillin sodium salt

(C$_{16}$H$_{16}$N$_5$NaO$_4$S; *35334-12-4*)   see: Bacampicillin

17α-azido-3β,16α-diacetoxy-5α-pregnane-11,20-dione

(C$_{25}$H$_{35}$N$_3$O$_6$; *5167-90-8*)   see: Deflazacort; Fluazacort

2-azido-*N*-[2-(2,5-dimethoxyphenyl)-2-oxoethyl]acetamide

(C$_{12}$H$_{14}$N$_4$O$_4$; *59939-34-3*)   see: Midodrine

2-azidoethanol

(C$_2$H$_5$N$_3$O; *1517-05-1*)   see: Amlodipine

6-(D-α-azidophenylacetamido)penicillanic acid 1-ethoxy-carbonyloxyethyl ester
($C_{21}H_{25}N_5O_7S$; *37661-07-7*)   see: Bacampicillin

D(−)-α-azidophenylacetic acid
($C_8H_7N_3O_2$; *29125-25-5*)   see: Azidocillin

[2S-[2α,5α,6β(S*)]]-6-[(azidophenylacetyl)amino]-3,3-di-methyl-7-oxo-4-thia-1-azabicyclo[3.2.0]heptane-2-carb-oxylic acid (2,2-dimethyl-1-oxopropoxy)methyl ester
($C_{22}H_{27}N_5O_6S$; *26255-15-2*)   see: Pivampicillin

3-azido-2,3,4,5-tetrahydro-1H-1-benzazepin-2-one
($C_{10}H_{10}N_4O$; *86499-24-3*)   see: Benazepril

azidotrimethylsilane
($C_3H_9N_3Si$; *4648-54-8*)   see: Zanamivir

aziridine
(C_2H_5N; *151-56-4*)   see: Carboquone; Levamisole; Medazepam; Quazepam; Thiotepa; Triaziquone

B

barbituric acid
($C_4H_4N_2O_3$; *67-52-7*)   see: Allobarbital; Minoxidil; Riboflavin

BCH 189 (rac.)
see under *cis*-4-amino-1-[2-(hydroxymethyl)-1,3-oxathiolan-5-yl]-2(1H)-pyrimidinone

beclometasone
($C_{22}H_{29}ClO_5$; *4419-39-0*)   see: Ciclometasone

beclometasone 21-acetate
($C_{24}H_{31}ClO_6$; *4735-64-2*)   see: Beclometasone

bekanamycin
($C_{18}H_{37}N_5O_{10}$; *4696-76-8*)   see: Dibekacin; Tobramycin

bendazolic acid chloride
($C_{16}H_{13}ClN_2O_2$; *40988-23-6*)   see: Bendacort

benzalacetone
($C_{10}H_{10}O$; *122-57-6*)   see: Warfarin

benzaldehyde
(C_7H_6O; *100-52-7*)   see: Acetorphan; Amphetaminil; Atorvastatin calcium; Azimilide hydrochloride; Benzathine benzylpenicillin; Docetaxel; L(−)-Ephedrine; Ethotoin; Fenipentol; Fenquizone; Furazolidone; Imolamine; Isocarboxazid; Metamizole sodium; Oxacillin; Paclitaxel; Phensuximide; Phentermine; Pildralazine; Propiverine

benzaldehyde [6-[(2-hydroxypropyl)methylamino]-3-py-ridazinyl]hydrazone
($C_{15}H_{19}N_5O$; *56976-47-7*)   see: Pildralazine

benzaldehyde semicarbazone
($C_8H_9N_3O$; *1574-10-3*)   see: Azimilide hydrochloride

benzaldoxime
(C_7H_7NO; *932-90-1*)   see: Imolamine; Oxacillin

6-benzamidopenicillanic acid
($C_{15}H_{16}N_2O_4S$; *6489-59-4*)   see: Latamoxef

4-benzamidopyridine
($C_{12}H_{10}N_2O$; *5221-44-3*)   see: Indoramin

benzamidoxime
($C_7H_8N_2O$; *613-92-3*)   see: Oxolamine

benzarone
($C_{17}H_{14}O_3$; *1477-19-6*)   see: Benzbromarone; Benziodarone

benzene
(C_6H_6; *71-43-2*)   see: Budipine; Clotrimazole; Fexofenadine hydrochloride; Ibuprofen; Phenylmercuric borate; Seratrodast; Sertraline

benzeneacetic acid 2-[4-(methylsulfonyl)phenyl]-2-oxo-ethyl ester
($C_{17}H_{16}O_5S$; *201737-94-2*)   see: Rofecoxib

benzenediazonium chloride
($C_6H_5ClN_2$; *100-34-5*)   see: Amsacrine; Mesalazine; Phenazopyridine; Riboflavin

benzenepropanoic acid phenyl ester
($C_{15}H_{14}O_2$; *726-26-1*)   see: Latanoprost

benzenesulfochloride
($C_6H_5ClO_2S$; *98-09-9*)   see: Clopidogrel hydrogensulfate; Dextrothyroxine; Gabapentin; Glybuzole; Orlistat

benzenesulfonic acid 4-formyl-2-iodo-6-nitrophenyl ester
($C_{13}H_8INO_6S$)   see: Dextrothyroxine

N-benzenesulfonyl-3-azaspiro[5.5]undecane-2,4-dione
($C_{16}H_{19}NO_4S$)   see: Gabapentin

benzenesulfonylguanidine
($C_7H_9N_3O_2S$; *4392-37-4*)   see: Glymidine

benzhydrol
($C_{13}H_{12}O$; *91-01-0*)   see: Adrafinil; Modafinil

benzhydroximic acid chloride
(C_7H_6ClNO; *698-16-8*)   see: Imolamine; Oxacillin

benzhydryl bromide
($C_{13}H_{11}Br$; *776-74-9*)   see: Diphenhydramine; Diphenylpyraline; Ebastine; Manidipine

benzhydryl chloride
($C_{13}H_{11}Cl$; *90-99-3*)   see: Cinnarizine; Cyclizine; Medibazine

1-benzhydrylpiperazine
($C_{17}H_{20}N_2$; *841-77-0*)   see: Cinnarizine; Oxatomide

(benzhydrylsulfinyl)acetic acid
($C_{15}H_{14}O_3S$; *63547-24-0*)   see: Adrafinil

(benzhydrylthio)acetic acid
($C_{15}H_{14}O_2S$; *63547-22-8*)   see: Adrafinil; Modafinil

benzil
($C_{14}H_{10}O_2$; *134-81-6*)   see: Phenytoin; Propiverine

benzilic acid
($C_{14}H_{12}O_3$; *76-93-7*)   see: Flutropium bromide; Mepenzolate bromide; Pipenzolate bromide; Pipoxolan; Propiverine

benzilic chloride
($C_{14}H_{11}ClO_2$; *52905-45-0*)   see: Clidinium bromide

3-benziloyloxy-1-methylpiperidine
($C_{20}H_{23}NO_3$; *3321-80-0*)   see: Mepenzolate bromide

1H-benzimidazole-2-thiol
($C_7H_6N_2S$; *134469-07-1*)   see: Rabeprazole sodium

2-benzimidazolone
($C_7H_6N_2O$; *615-16-7*)   see: Mizolastine; Oxatomide

4-(1H-benzimidazol-2-ylamino)-1-piperidinecarboxylic acid ethyl ester
($C_{15}H_{20}N_4O_2$; *73734-07-3*)   see: Astemizole

1,2-benzisothiazolin-3-one
(C_7H_5NOS; *2634-33-5*)   see: Ziprasidone hydrochloride

1-(1,2-benzisothiazol-3-yl)piperazine
($C_{11}H_{13}N_3S$; *87691-87-0*)   see: Ziprasidone hydrochloride

[5-[2-[4-(1,2-benzisothiazol-3-yl)-1-piperazinyl]ethyl]-4-chloro-2-nitrophenyl]propanedioic acid dimethyl ester
($C_{24}H_{25}ClN_4O_6S$; *160384-39-4*)   see: Ziprasidone hydrochloride

1,2-benzisoxazole-3-acetic acid
($C_9H_7NO_3$; *4865-84-3*)   see: Zonisamide

benzmorpholide

(C$_{11}$H$_{13}$NO$_2$; *1468-28-6*)   see: Ketorolac

1,4-benzodioxan-2-ylcarbonyl chloride

(C$_9$H$_7$ClO$_3$; *3663-81-8*)   see: Doxazosin

N-**(1,4-benzodioxan-2-ylcarbonyl)piperazine**

(C$_{13}$H$_{16}$N$_2$O$_3$; *70918-00-2*)   see: Doxazosin

1,3-benzodioxole-5-methanol

(C$_8$H$_8$O$_3$; *495-76-1*)   see: Levodopa

[(1,3-benzodioxol-5-ylamino)methylene]malonic acid diethyl ester

(C$_{15}$H$_{17}$NO$_6$; *17394-77-3*)   see: Oxolinic acid

2-[[2-(1,3-benzodioxol-5-yl)-1-methylethyl]amino]-1-(3,4-dihydroxyphenyl)ethanone

(C$_{18}$H$_{19}$NO$_5$)   see: Protokylol

benzofuran

(C$_8$H$_6$O; *271-89-6*)   see: Amiodarone

benzoic acid

(C$_7$H$_6$O$_2$; *65-85-0*)   see: Acetrizoic acid; Rizatriptan benzoate

benzoic acid 2-(hexahydro-1-methyl-1*H*-azepin-4-yl)-hydrazide

(C$_{14}$H$_{21}$N$_3$O; *110406-94-5*)   see: Azelastine

benzoic acid 2-(1-methyl-4-piperidinyl)hydrazide

(C$_{13}$H$_{19}$N$_3$O; *88858-10-0*)   see: Piperylone

benzoic acid (1-methyl-4-piperidylidene)hydrazide

(C$_{13}$H$_{17}$N$_3$O; *92043-04-4*)   see: Piperylone

benzoic anhydride

(C$_{14}$H$_{10}$O$_3$; *93-97-0*)   see: Bopindolol; Flavoxate; Paclitaxel

benzoin

(C$_{14}$H$_{12}$O$_2$; *119-53-9*)   see: Oxaprozin; Propiverine

benzophenone

(C$_{13}$H$_{10}$O; *119-61-9*)   see: Cibenzoline; Difenidol; Etifelmine; Perhexiline; Phenytoin; Pipradrol

5*H*-[1]benzopyrano[2,3-*b*]pyridine

(C$_{12}$H$_9$NO; *261-27-8*)   see: Pranoprofen

5*H*-[1]benzopyrano[2,3-*b*]pyridine-7-acetonitrile

(C$_{14}$H$_{10}$N$_2$O; *52549-06-1*)   see: Pranoprofen

p-**benzoquinone**

(C$_6$H$_4$O$_2$; *106-51-4*)   see: Ambazone; Calcium dobesilate; Etamsylate

1,4-benzoquinone

see under *p*-benzoquinone

p-**benzoquinone amidinohydrazone**

(C$_7$H$_8$N$_4$O; *7316-92-9*)   see: Ambazone

N-**[1-(benzo[*b*]thien-2-yl)ethyl]hydroxylamine**

(C$_{10}$H$_{11}$NOS; *118564-89-9*)   see: Zileuton

benzo[*b*]thiophene

(C$_8$H$_6$S; *95-15-8*)   see: Zileuton

2,1,3-benzoxadiazole

(C$_6$H$_4$N$_2$O; *273-09-6*)   see: Isradipine

2,1,3-benzoxadiazole-4-carboxaldehyde

(C$_7$H$_4$N$_2$O$_2$; *32863-32-4*)   see: Isradipine

α-**(benzoylamino)-4-(benzoyloxy)-*N*,*N*-dipropylbenzene-propanamide**

(C$_{29}$H$_{32}$N$_2$O$_4$; *57227-08-4*)   see: Tiropramide

(6*R*-*cis*)-7-(benzoylamino)-3-(chloromethyl)-7-methoxy-8-oxo-5-oxa-1-azabicyclo[4.2.0]oct-2-ene-2-carboxylic acid diphenylmethyl ester

(C$_{29}$H$_{25}$ClN$_2$O$_6$; *68313-94-0*)   see: Latamoxef

2-(benzoylamino)-3-(3,4-dimethoxyphenyl)-2-propenoic acid methyl ester

(C$_{19}$H$_{19}$NO$_5$; *128289-78-1*)   see: Moexipril

[6*R*-[6α,7β(*R**)]]-7-[[5-(benzoylamino)-6-(diphenyl-methoxy)-1,6-dioxohexyl]amino]-3-(chloromethyl)-8-oxo-5-thia-1-azabicyclo[4.2.0]oct-2-ene-2-carboxylic acid diphenylmethyl ester

(C$_{47}$H$_{42}$ClN$_3$O$_7$S)   see: Cefixime

[6*R*-[6α,7β(*R**)]]-7-[[5-(benzoylamino)-6-(diphenyl-methoxy)-1,6-dioxohexyl]amino]-3 -ethenyl-8-oxo-5-thia-1-azabicyclo[4.2.0]oct-2-ene-2-carboxylic acid diphenyl-methyl ester

(C$_{48}$H$_{43}$N$_3$O$_7$S)   see: Cefixime

4-(benzoylamino)-5-(dipropylamino)-5-oxopentanoic acid 3-[4-(2-hydroxyethyl)-1-piperazinyl]propyl ester

(C$_{27}$H$_{44}$N$_4$O$_5$; *59209-38-0*)   see: Proglumetacin

cis-**7-(benzoylamino)-3-[[[1-(2-hydroxyethyl)-1*H*-tetrazol-5-yl]thio]methyl]-8-oxo-5-oxa-1-azabicyclo[4.2.0]oct-2-ene-2-carboxylic acid diphenylmethyl ester**

(C$_{31}$H$_{28}$N$_6$O$_6$S; *98043-69-7*)   see: Flomoxef

4-(benzoylamino)-1-[2-(1*H*-indol-3-yl)ethyl]pyridinium bromide

(C$_{22}$H$_{20}$BrN$_3$O; *26853-15-6*)   see: Indoramin

β-**benzoylaminoisobutyryl chloride**

(C$_{11}$H$_{12}$ClNO$_2$; *49540-49-0*)   see: Triamcinolone benetonide

cis-**7-(benzoylamino)-7-methoxy-3-[[[1-[2-[[[(4-methyl-phenyl)methoxy]carbonyl]oxy]ethyl]-1*H*-tetrazol-5-yl]thio]methyl]-8-oxo-5-oxa-1-azabicyclo[4.2.0]oct-2-ene-2-carboxylic acid diphenylmethyl ester**

(C$_{41}$H$_{38}$N$_6$O$_9$S; *98043-71-1*)   see: Flomoxef

(6*R*-*cis*)-7-(benzoylamino)-7-methoxy-3-[[(1-methyl-1*H*-tetrazol-5-yl)thio]methyl]-8-oxo-5-oxa-1-azabicy-clo[4.2.0]oct-2-ene-2-carboxylic acid diphenylmethyl ester

(C$_{31}$H$_{28}$N$_6$O$_6$S; *68402-81-3*)   see: Latamoxef

[2*R*-(2α,6α,7α)]-7-(benzoylamino)-3-methylene-8-oxo-5-oxa-1-azabicyclo[4.2.0]octane-2-carboxylic acid diphenyl-methyl ester

(C$_{28}$H$_{24}$N$_2$O$_5$; *67977-91-7*)   see: Latamoxef

cis-**7-(benzoylamino)-3-[[[1-[2-[[[(4-methylphenyl)meth-oxy]carbonyl]oxy]ethyl]-1*H*-tetrazol-5-yl]thio]methyl]-8-oxo-5-oxa-1-azabicyclo[4.2.0]oct-2-ene-2-carboxylic acid diphenylmethyl ester**

(C$_{40}$H$_{36}$N$_6$O$_8$S; *98043-70-0*)   see: Flomoxef

2-benzoylbenzoic acid

(C$_{14}$H$_{10}$O$_3$; *85-52-9*)   see: Nefopam

N-**benzoyl-*N*-[2-(bromomethyl)-3-chlorophenyl]benz-amide**

(C$_{21}$H$_{15}$BrClNO$_2$; *41458-70-2*)   see: Fominoben

benzoyl chloride

(C$_7$H$_5$ClO; *98-88-4*)   see: Aciclovir; Alprazolam; Bamethan; Benfluorex; Benfotiamine; Bentiamine; Bentiromide; Benzoyl peroxide; Bifonazole; Bisbentiamine; Cefixime; Dibekacin; Dienestrol; Endralazine; Estradiol; Estradiol benzoate; Etilefrine; Fominoben; Gemcitabine; Hexylcaine; Iloprost; Indanazoline; Indinavir sulfate; Itraconazole; Ketoconazole; Latamoxef; Medazepam; (−)-Menthol; Meprylcaine; Mesterolone; Montelukast sodium; Norfenefrine; Paclitaxel; Piperocaine; Proglumide; Ropinirole; Setastine; Stavudine; Sulfabenzamide; Tacalcitol; Terconazole; Testosterone; Tiaprofenic acid; Tiropramide

2'-benzoyl-4'-chlorocyclopropanecarboxanilide

(C$_{17}$H$_{14}$ClNO$_2$; *2896-97-1*)   see: Prazepam

5-benzoyl-2-chloro-1-[3,3-di(methoxycarbonyl)propyl]-pyrrole
($C_{18}H_{18}ClNO_5$)   see: Ketorolac

N-benzoyl-N-(3-chloro-2-methylphenyl)benzamide
($C_{21}H_{16}ClNO_2$; *42313-35-9*)   see: Fominoben

N-(2-benzoyl-4-chlorophenyl)-2-chloro-N-methylacet-amide
($C_{16}H_{13}Cl_2NO_2$; *6021-21-2*)   see: Diazepam

N-(2-benzoyl-4-chlorophenyl)-N-(cyclopropylmethyl)-1,3-dihydro-1,3-dioxo-2H-isoindole-2-acetamide
($C_{27}H_{21}ClN_2O_4$; *2897-01-0*)   see: Prazepam

N-(2-benzoyl-4-chlorophenyl)-N,4-dimethylbenzene-sulfonamide
($C_{21}H_{18}ClNO_3S$; *4873-37-4*)   see: Diazepam

N-(2-benzoyl-4-chlorophenyl)-4-methylbenzene-sulfonamide
($C_{20}H_{16}ClNO_3S$; *4873-59-0*)   see: Diazepam

6-benzoyl-3-chloro-5,6,7,8-tetrahydropyrido[4,3-c]py-ridazine
($C_{14}H_{12}ClN_3O$; *39715-73-6*)   see: Endralazine

3-benzoyl-α-cyanobenzeneacetic acid ethyl ester
($C_{18}H_{15}NO_3$; *34124-51-1*)   see: Ketoprofen

3-benzoyl-α-cyano-α-methylbenzeneacetic acid ethyl ester
($C_{19}H_{17}NO_3$; *22071-25-6*)   see: Ketoprofen

N-Benzoyl-2'-deoxycytidine
($C_{16}H_{17}N_3O_5$; *4836-13-9*)   see: Zalcitabine

O-[2-O-benzoyl-3-(ethoxycarbonylamino)-3-deoxy-4,6-O-isopropylidene-α-D-glucopyranosyl-(1→6)]-O-[2,6-bis-(ethoxycarbonylamino)-2,6-dideoxy-3,4-O-isopropylidene-α-D-glucopyranosyl-(1→4)]-1,3-bis-N-(ethoxycarbonyl)-2-deoxy-D-streptamine
($C_{46}H_{69}N_5O_{11}$)   see: Dibekacin

O-[2-O-benzoyl-3-(ethoxycarbonylamino)-3-deoxy-4,6-O-isopropylidene-α-D-glucopyranosyl]-(1→6)-O-[2,6-bis-(ethoxycarbonylamino)-2,6-dideoxy-3,4-bis-O-(methane-sulfonyl)-α-D-glucopyranosyl-(1→4)]-1,3-bis-N-(ethoxy-carbonyl)-2-deoxy-D-streptamine
($C_{45}H_{69}N_5O_{15}S_2$)   see: Dibekacin

[3R-(3α,4α)]-[partial]-1-benzoyl-3-(1-ethoxyethoxy)-4-phenyl-2-azetidinone
($C_{20}H_{21}NO_4$; *201856-53-3*)   see: Paclitaxel

(2R,3S)-N-benzoyl-O-(1-ethoxyethyl)-3-phenylisoserine
($C_{20}H_{23}NO_5$; *216094-54-1*)   see: Paclitaxel

N-benzoyl-DL-glutamic acid
($C_{12}H_{13}NO_5$; *6460-81-7*)   see: Proglumide

N-benzoyl-DL-glutamic anhydride
($C_{12}H_{11}NO_4$; *91569-94-7*)   see: Proglumide

benzoylhydrazine
($C_7H_8N_2O$; *613-94-5*)   see: Azelastine; Benmoxin; Piperylone; Zorubicin

2-benzoyl-N-(2-hydroxyethyl)-N-methylbenzamide
($C_{17}H_{17}NO_3$; *24833-47-4*)   see: Nefopam

3-benzoyl-4-hydroxy-1-methyl-4-phenylpiperidine
($C_{19}H_{21}NO_2$; *5409-66-5*)   see: Phenindamine

7-benzoylindolin-2-one
($C_{15}H_{11}NO_2$; *51135-38-7*)   see: Amfenac sodium

benzoyl isocyanate
($C_8H_5NO_2$; *4461-33-0*)   see: Imiquimod

benzoyl isothiocyanate
(C_8H_5NOS; *532-55-8*)   see: Famotidine; Indanazoline

(S)-3-benzoyl-α-methylbenzeneacetic acid
($C_{16}H_{14}O_3$; *22161-81-5*)   see: Dexketoprofen trometamol

3-benzoyl-α-methylbenzeneacetyl chloride
($C_{16}H_{13}ClO_2$; *59512-44-6*)   see: Piketoprofen

4-benzoyl-1-methylpiperidine
($C_{13}H_{17}NO$; *92040-00-1*)   see: Diphemanil metilsulfate

5-benzoyl-2-(methylthio)pyrrole
($C_{12}H_{11}NOS$; *80965-00-0*)   see: Ketorolac

N-(2-benzoyl-4-nitrophenyl)-4-methylbenzenesulfonamide
($C_{20}H_{16}N_2O_5S$; *24042-91-9*)   see: Nitrazepam

(benzoyloxy)acetaldehyde
($C_9H_8O_3$; *64904-47-8*)   see: Lamivudine

3'-benzoyloxyacetophenone
($C_{15}H_{12}O_3$; *139-28-6*)   see: Etilefrine; Norfenefrine

4'-benzoyloxyacetophenone
($C_{15}H_{12}O_3$; *1523-18-8*)   see: Bamethan

(5α,17β)-17-(benzoyloxy)androstan-3-one
($C_{26}H_{34}O_3$; *1057-07-4*)   see: Mesterolone

(17β)-17-(benzoyloxy)androst-4-en-3-one
($C_{26}H_{32}O_3$; *2088-71-3*)   see: Testosterone

[3S-(3α,3aα,5α,9aα,9bβ)]-3-(benzoyloxy)-5-bromo-6-(3-chloro-2-butenyl)-1,2,3,3a,4,5,8,9,9a,9b-decahydro-3a-methyl-7H-benz[e]inden-7-one
($C_{25}H_{28}BrClO_3$)   see: Trenbolone acetate

1-benzoyloxy-2-chloromethoxyethane
($C_{10}H_{11}ClO_3$; *58305-05-8*)   see: Aciclovir

17β-benzoyloxy-3-chloro-5-oxo-4,5-seco-2,9-estradiene
($C_{25}H_{29}ClO_3$; *24156-98-7*)   see: Trenbolone acetate

[3aR-(3aα,4α,5β,6aα)]-5-(benzoyloxy)-4-[[[(1,1-dimethyl-ethyl)dimethylsilyl]oxy]methyl]hexahydro-2H-cyclopen-ta[b]furan-2-one
($C_{21}H_{30}O_5Si$; *64982-34-9*)   see: Iloprost

2-benzoyloxyethanol
($C_9H_{10}O_3$; *94-33-7*)   see: Aciclovir

9-(2-benzoyloxyethoxymethyl)guanine
($C_{15}H_{15}N_5O_4$; *59277-91-7*)   see: Aciclovir

4-[2-(benzoyloxy)ethyl]-3-chloro-1,3-dihydro-2H-indol-2-one
($C_{17}H_{14}ClNO_3$; *139122-17-1*)   see: Ropinirole

2-(2-benzoyloxyethyl)-β-nitrostyrene
($C_{17}H_{15}NO_4$; *139122-16-0*)   see: Ropinirole

[3aS-(3aα,4α,5β,6aα)]-5-(benzoyloxy)hexahydro-4-(hydr-oxymethyl)-2(1H)-pentalenone
($C_{16}H_{18}O_4$; *74842-93-6*)   see: Iloprost

[3'aS-(3'aα,4'α,5'β,6'aα)]-5'-(benzoyloxy)hexahydro-spiro[1,3-dioxolane-2,2'(1'H)-pentalene]-4'-carbox aldehyde
($C_{18}H_{20}O_5$; *74818-14-7*)   see: Iloprost

[3'aS-[3'α,4'α(1E),5'β,6'aα]]-1-[5'-(benzoyloxy)hexa-hydrospiro[1,3-dioxolane-2,2'(1'H)-pentalen]-4'-yl]-4-methyl-1-octen-6-yn-3-one
($C_{26}H_{30}O_5$)   see: Iloprost

17β-benzoyloxy-3β-hydroxy-5-androstene
($C_{26}H_{34}O_3$; *1175-12-8*)   see: Mesterolone; Testosterone

2-[1-(benzoyloxymethyl)cyclopropyl]acetonitrile
($C_{13}H_{13}NO_2$; *142148-12-7*)   see: Montelukast sodium

4-benzoyloxyphenacyl bromide
($C_{15}H_{11}BrO_3$; *5324-15-2*)   see: Bamethan

N-(4-benzoyloxyphenacyl)butylamine
($C_{19}H_{21}NO_3$)   see: Bamethan

(3-benzoylphenyl)acetonitrile
(C$_{15}$H$_{11}$NO; *21288-34-6*)   see: Ketoprofen

***N*-benzoyl-L-phenylglycinal**
(C$_{15}$H$_{13}$NO$_2$; *163010-72-8*)   see: Paclitaxel

(2*R*,3*S*)-*N*-benzoyl-3-phenylisoserine
(C$_{16}$H$_{15}$NO$_4$; *132201-33-3*)   see: Paclitaxel

(2*R*,3*S*)-*N*-benzoyl-3-phenylisoserine ethyl ester
(C$_{18}$H$_{19}$NO$_4$; *153433-80-8*)   see: Paclitaxel

2-benzoylpyridine
(C$_{12}$H$_9$NO; *91-02-1*)   see: Pirmenol hydrochloride

α-(benzoylthio)propionylglycine
(C$_{12}$H$_{13}$NO$_4$S; *6183-01-3*)   see: Stepronin

***cis*-1-benzoyl-3-(triethylsilyloxy)-4-phenyl-2-azetidinone**
(C$_{22}$H$_{27}$NO$_3$Si; *149107-83-5*)   see: Paclitaxel

***N*-benzoyl-L-tyrosine**
(C$_{16}$H$_{15}$NO$_4$; *2566-23-6*)   see: Bentiromide

***N*-benzoyl-DL-tyrosinedipropylamide**
(C$_{22}$H$_{28}$N$_2$O$_3$; *57227-09-5*)   see: Tiropramide

1-(5-*O*-benzoyl-β-D-xylofuranosyl)-5-methyl-2,4(1*H*,3*H*)-pyrimidinedione
(C$_{17}$H$_{18}$N$_2$O$_7$; *190003-80-6*)   see: Stavudine

***N*-benzylacetamide**
(C$_9$H$_{11}$NO; *588-46-5*)   see: Mafenide

(3*S*)-1-benzyl-3-(acetoacetoxy)pyrrolidine
(C$_{15}$H$_{19}$NO$_3$; *101930-01-2*)   see: Barnidipine

benzylacetone
(C$_{10}$H$_{12}$O; *2550-26-7*)   see: Buphenine; Dilevalol; Labetalol

2-benzylacrylic acid
(C$_{10}$H$_{10}$O$_2$; *5669-19-2*)   see: Acetorphan

benzyl alcohol
(C$_7$H$_8$O; *100-51-6*)   see: Fluoxetine; Gabapentin; Ganciclovir; Levocabastine; Moexipril; Nicotinic acid benzyl ester; Perindopril; Quinapril hydrochloride; Ramipril; Saquinavir; Trandolapril

benzylamine
(C$_7$H$_9$N; *100-46-9*)   see: Amosulalol; Barnidipine; Beclamide; Benperidol; Betanidine; Biotin; Cisapride; Dilevalol; Guanoxan; Moxifloxacin hydrochloride; Nebivolol; Nialamide; Reproterol; Sparfloxacin; Sulbentine; Viloxazine

benzylamine hydrochloride
(C$_7$H$_{10}$ClN; *3287-99-8*)   see: Benzyl mustard oil

2-benzylaminoethanol
(C$_9$H$_{13}$NO; *104-63-2*)   see: Indeloxacine; Phenmetrazine

7-(2-benzylaminoethyl)theophylline
(C$_{16}$H$_{19}$N$_5$O$_2$; *22680-61-1*)   see: Fenetylline; Theodrenaline

benzyl [(2*R*,3*S*)-3-amino-2-hydroxy-4-phenylbutyl](2-methylpropyl)carbamate monohydrochloride
(C$_{22}$H$_{31}$ClN$_2$O$_3$; *160232-11-1*)   see: Amprenavir

2-benzylamino-1-(4-methoxyphenyl)propane
(C$_{17}$H$_{21}$NO; *43229-65-8*)   see: Fenoterol; Formoterol

benzyl [3-[(2-aminophenyl)carbamoyl]propyl]methylcarbamate
(C$_{19}$H$_{23}$N$_3$O$_3$; *116666-61-6*)   see: Mibefradil hydrochloride

1-benzyl-4-aminopiperidine
see under 4-amino-1-benzylpiperidine

7-(3-benzylaminopropyl)theophylline
(C$_{17}$H$_{21}$N$_5$O$_2$; *24890-70-8*)   see: Reproterol

2-benzylaminopyridine
(C$_{12}$H$_{12}$N$_2$; *6935-27-9*)   see: Tripelennamine

***N*-benzylaniline**
(C$_{13}$H$_{13}$N; *103-32-2*)   see: Antazoline; Bepridil; Histapyrrodine

(3*S*)-benzyl *endo*,*cis*-2-azabicyclo[3.3.0]octane-3-carboxylate
(C$_{15}$H$_{19}$NO$_2$; *93779-31-8*)   see: Ramipril

(±)-benzyl *endo*,*cis*-2-azabicyclo[3.3.0]octane-3-carboxylate
(C$_{15}$H$_{19}$NO$_2$)   see: Ramipril

1-*O*-benzyl-4,6-*O*-benzylidene-*N*-acetylmuramic acid
(C$_{25}$H$_{29}$NO$_8$; *2862-03-5*)   see: Romurtide

***O*-benzyl-5-[*N*-benzyl-*N*-[(*R*)-1-methyl-3-phenylpropyl]glycyl]salicylamide**
(C$_{33}$H$_{34}$N$_2$O$_3$; *75615-53-1*)   see: Dilevalol

benzyl bromide
(C$_7$H$_7$Br; *100-39-0*)   see: Fosinopril; Latanoprost; Monobenzone; Orlistat; Pirbuterol; Saquinavir

benzyl bromoacetate
(C$_9$H$_9$BrO$_2$; *5437-45-6*)   see: Aceclofenac; Acemetacin; Fosinopril

8-benzyl-7-(2-bromoethyl)theophylline
(C$_{16}$H$_{17}$BrN$_4$O$_2$; *97977-40-7*)   see: Bamifylline

benzyl 2-bromopropionate
(C$_{10}$H$_{11}$BrO$_2$; *3017-53-6*)   see: Meropenem

***N*-benzyl-*tert*-butylamine**
(C$_{11}$H$_{17}$N; *3378-72-1*)   see: Bambuterol; Carbuterol; Salbutamol; Terbutaline

benzyl chloride
(C$_7$H$_7$Cl; *100-44-7*)   see: Bamipine; Benidipine; Benzalkonium chloride; Benzphetamine; Benzydamine; Benzyl alcohol; Benzyl benzoate; Bephenium hydroxynaphthoate; Betaxolol; Brinzolamide; Buphenine; Cetalkonium chloride; Dilevalol; Ifenprodil; Metaraminol; Pheniramine; Phenoxybenzamine; Tribenoside

benzyl chloroacetate
(C$_9$H$_9$ClO$_2$; *140-18-1*)   see: Acemetacin

benzyl [1-(4-chlorobenzoyl)-5-methoxy-2-methyl-3-indolylacetoxy]acetate
(C$_{28}$H$_{24}$ClNO$_6$; *53164-04-8*)   see: Acemetacin

benzyl chloroformate
(C$_8$H$_7$ClO$_2$; *501-53-1*)   see: Amprenavir; Aztreonam; Captopril; Carumonam; Deferoxamine; Fosinopril; Indalpine; Indinavir sulfate; Oxitriptan; Saquinavir; Teniposide; Trovafloxacin mesilate; Voglibose

benzyl chloromethyl ether
(C$_8$H$_9$ClO; *3587-60-8*)   see: Eprosartan

***N*-benzyl-2-(chloromethyl)morpholine**
(C$_{12}$H$_{16}$ClNO; *40987-25-5*)   see: Indeloxacine

benzyl cyanide
(C$_8$H$_7$N; *140-29-4*)   see: Azatadine; Dicycloverine; Disopyramide; Ethoheptazine; Isoaminile; Levocabastine; Mephenytoin; Methylphenidate; Methylphenobarbital; Milnacipran hydrochloride; Oxeladin; Pentapiperide; Pentoxyverine; Pethidine; Phenglutarimide; Pheniramine; Phenobarbital; Tolazoline; Triamterene; Valethamate bromide

1-benzyl-4-cyanopiperidine
(C$_{13}$H$_{16}$N$_2$; *62718-31-4*)   see: Ketanserin

1-benzyl-4-cyano-4-piperidinopiperidine
(C$_{18}$H$_{25}$N$_3$; *84254-97-7*)   see: Pipamperone

1-benzylcycloheptanol
(C$_{14}$H$_{20}$O; *4006-73-9*)   see: Bencyclane

S-benzyl-L-cysteine
($C_{10}H_{13}NO_2S$; *3054-01-1*)   see: Bucillamine

(±)-*cis*-8-benzyl-2,8-diazabicyclo[4.3.0]nonane
($C_{14}H_{20}N_2$; *161594-54-3*)   see: Moxifloxacin hydrochloride

1-benzyl-4-(5,6-dimethoxy-1-oxoindan-2-ylidene-methyl)piperidine
($C_{24}H_{27}NO_3$; *120014-07-5*)   see: Donepezil hydrochloride

benzyldimethylamine
($C_9H_{13}N$; *103-83-3*)   see: Benzethonium chloride; Cefalexin

benzyl [(2R,3S)-3-[[(1,1-dimethylethoxy)carbonyl]amino]-2-hydroxy-4-phenylbutyl](2-methylpropyl)carbamate
($C_{27}H_{38}N_2O_5$; *160232-10-0*)   see: Amprenavir

N-benzyl-N',S-dimethylisothiourea
($C_{10}H_{14}N_2S$)   see: Betanidine

O-benzyl S-(4,6-dimethyl-2-pyrimidinyl)thiocarbonate
($C_{14}H_{14}N_2O_2S$; *42116-21-2*)   see: Gusperimus trihydrochloride

benzyl 2-[N-[1(S)-ethoxycarbonyl-3-phenylpropyl]-L-alanyl]-1,2,3,4-tetrahydro-6,7-dimethoxy-3(S)-isoquinoline-carboxylate
($C_{34}H_{40}N_2O_7$; *82637-57-8*)   see: Moexipril

γ-benzyl L-glutamate
($C_{12}H_{15}NO_4$; *1676-73-9*)   see: Cilazapril

benzylhydrazine
($C_7H_{10}N_2$; *555-96-4*)   see: Isocarboxazid

α-[benzyl(2-hydroxyethyl)amino]propiophenone
($C_{18}H_{21}NO_2$; *94997-05-4*)   see: Phenmetrazine

1-benzyl-3-hydroxyimino-2-methylpyrrolidine
($C_{12}H_{16}N_2O$; *74880-17-4*)   see: Nemonapride

1-benzyl-3-hydroxy-1H-indazole
($C_{14}H_{12}N_2O$; *2215-63-6*)   see: Bendazac; Benzydamine

O-benzylhydroxylamine
(C_7H_9NO; *622-33-3*)   see: Aztreonam; Zileuton

benzyl [(2R,3S)-2-hydroxy-4-phenyl-3-[[[[(3S)-tetrahydro-3-furanyl]oxy]carbonyl]amino]butyl](2-methylpropyl)-carbamate
($C_{27}H_{36}N_2O_6$; *160232-12-2*)   see: Amprenavir

(3S)-1-benzyl-3-hydroxypyrrolidine
($C_{11}H_{15}NO$; *101385-90-4*)   see: Barnidipine

1-benzyl-4-hydroxy-4-(3-trifluoromethylphenyl)piperidine
($C_{19}H_{20}F_3NO$; *56108-27-1*)   see: Trifluperidol

4-benzylidenamino-2,3-dimethyl-1-phenyl-5-Δ³-pyrazolone
($C_{18}H_{17}N_3O$; *83-17-0*)   see: Metamizole sodium

1-(benzylidenamino)-2,4-imidazolidinedione
($C_{10}H_9N_3O_2$; *2827-57-8*)   see: Azimilide hydrochloride

1-(benzylidenamino)-3-(4-iodobutyl)-2,4-imidazolidine-dione
($C_{14}H_{16}IN_3O_2$; *92254-87-0*)   see: Azimilide hydrochloride

4-benzylidenemethylammonio-2,3-dimethyl-1-phenyl-5-Δ³-pyrazolone methyl sulfate
($C_{20}H_{23}N_3O_5S$)   see: Metamizole sodium

2-benzylidene-4-methyl-3-oxo-N-phenylpentanamide
($C_{19}H_{19}NO_2$; *125971-57-5*)   see: Atorvastatin calcium

(S)-N-benzylidene-1-phenylethylamine
($C_{15}H_{15}N$; *62696-51-9*)   see: Docetaxel; Paclitaxel

benzyl isocyanate
(C_8H_7NO; *3173-56-6*)   see: Zolmitriptan

benzyl D-isoglutaminate
($C_{12}H_{16}N_2O_3$; *71811-14-8*)   see: Romurtide

benzyl levulinoyloxyacetate
($C_{14}H_{16}O_5$; *53164-03-7*)   see: Acemetacin

benzylmagnesium chloride
(C_7H_7ClMg; *6921-34-2*)   see: Bencyclane; Clomifene; Dextropropoxyphene; Ritonavir

N-benzylmaleimide
($C_{11}H_9NO_2$; *1631-26-1*)   see: Trovafloxacin mesilate

benzylmalonic acid
($C_{10}H_{10}O_4$; *616-75-1*)   see: Acetorphan

benzyl mercaptan
(C_7H_8S; *100-53-8*)   see: Benzthiazide; Bucillamine; Thioctic acid

benzyl (5-methoxy-2-methyl-3-indolylacetoxy)acetate
($C_{21}H_{21}NO_5$; *53164-08-2*)   see: Acemetacin

benzyl [2-(4-methoxyphenylhydrazono)valeryloxy]acetate
($C_{21}H_{24}N_2O_5$; *53164-06-0*)   see: Acemetacin

N-benzylmethylamine
($C_8H_{11}N$; *103-67-3*)   see: Amidephrine mesilate; Epinastine hydrochloride; Lercanidipine hydrochloride; Oxilofrine; Pargyline

3-(benzylmethylamino)-1,1-diphenyl-1-propanol
($C_{23}H_{25}NO$; *25772-95-6*)   see: Lercanidipine hydrochloride

α-benzylmethylamino-3-methylsulfonylamino-acetophenone
($C_{17}H_{20}N_2O_3S$; *6861-18-3*)   see: Amidephrine mesilate

3-(benzylmethylamino)-1-phenylpropan-1-one
($C_{17}H_{19}NO$; *21970-65-0*)   see: Lercanidipine hydrochloride

3-(benzylmethylamino)propyl chloride
($C_{11}H_{16}ClN$; *3161-52-2*)   see: Desipramine

benzyl (4S)-1-methyl-3-[(2S)-2-[(1S)-1-ethoxycarbonyl-3-phenylpropylamino]propionyl]-2-oxoimidazolidine-4-carboxylate
($C_{27}H_{33}N_3O_6$; *89371-36-8*)   see: Imidapril

N-benzyl-N-[1-methyl-2-(4-methoxyphenyl)ethyl]amine
see under 2-benzylamino-1-(4-methoxyphenyl)propane

(±)-N-benzyl-N-[1-methyl-2-(4-methoxyphenyl)ethyl]-amine
see under 2-benzylamino-1-(4-methoxyphenyl)propane

benzyl (4S)-1-methyl-2-oxo-imidazolidine-4-carboxylate
($C_{12}H_{14}N_2O_3$; *89371-35-7*)   see: Imidapril

N-benzyl-N-(1-methyl-2-phenoxyethyl)ethanolamine
($C_{18}H_{23}NO_2$; *101-45-1*)   see: Phenoxybenzamine

benzyl (–)-3-methyl-4-phenyl-4-piperidinecarboxylate
($C_{20}H_{23}NO_2$; *104907-71-3*)   see: Levocabastine

(R)-(+)-N-benzyl-1-methyl-3-phenylpropylamine
($C_{17}H_{21}N$; *75659-06-2*)   see: Dilevalol

N-benzyl-1-methyl-3-phenylpropylamine
($C_{17}H_{21}N$; *68164-04-5*)   see: Dilevalol; Labetalol

(±)-N-benzyl-1-methyl-3-phenylpropylamine
see under N-benzyl-1-methyl-3-phenylpropylamine

1-benzyl-2-methyl-3-pyrrolidinone
($C_{12}H_{15}NO$; *69079-26-1*)   see: Nemonapride

N¹-benzyl-N²-methylthiourea
($C_9H_{12}N_2S$; *2740-94-5*)   see: Betanidine

(1α,5α,6α)-3-benzyl-6-nitro-2,4-dioxo-3-azabicyclo[3.1.0]hexane
($C_{12}H_{10}N_2O_4$; *151860-15-0*)   see: Trovafloxacin mesilate

4(S)-benzyloxazolidin-2-one
($C_{10}H_{11}NO_2$; *90719-32-7*)   see: Abacavir

(3β,5α,6β,16α)-3,5-bis(acetyloxy)-6-fluoro-17-hydroxy-16-methylpregnane-20-one
($C_{26}H_{39}FO_6$)   see: Flumetasone

(3β)-17,21-bis(acetyloxy)-3-(formyloxy)pregn-5-en-20-one
($C_{26}H_{36}O_7$; *96671-22-6*)   see: Hydrocortisone

3,4-bis(acetyloxy)-2-methylbutanal
($C_9H_{14}O_5$; *32347-78-7*)   see: Retinol

1-[3,5-bis(acetyloxy)phenyl]-2-[[2-(4-methoxyphenyl)-1-methylethyl](phenylmethyl)amino]ethanone
($C_{29}H_{31}NO_6$)   see: Fenoterol

7-[3-[[2-[3,5-bis(acetyloxy)phenyl]-2-oxoethyl](phenyl-methyl)amino]propyl]-3,7-dihydro-1,3-dimethyl-1*H*-purine-2,6-dione
($C_{29}H_{31}N_5O_7$; *62932-98-3*)   see: Reproterol

(3β,5α,11α)-3,11-bis(acetyloxy)pregn-16-en-20-one
($C_{25}H_{36}O_5$; *28507-80-4*)   see: Halopredone diacetate

3,4-bis[4-(benzoyloxy)phenyl]-3,4-hexanediol
($C_{32}H_{30}O_6$)   see: Dienestrol

1,2-bis(benzylidenamino)ethane
($C_{16}H_{16}N_2$; *104-71-2*)   see: Benzathine benzylpenicillin

4-*O*-[2,6-bis(benzyloxycarbonylamino)-3,4-di-*O*-benzyl-2,6-dideoxy-α-D-glucopyranosyl]-*N*,*N*'-bis(benzyloxycar-bonyl)-2-deoxy-D-streptamine
($C_{58}H_{62}N_4O_{14}$; *22854-78-0*)   see: Ribostamycin

(2*S*,3*R*,4*R*,5*S*)-2,5-bis[(benzyloxycarbonyl)amino]-3,4-di-hydroxy-1,6-diphenylhexane
($C_{34}H_{36}N_2O_6$; *137649-69-5*)   see: Ritonavir

(2*S*,3*R*,4*R*,5*S*)-2,5-bis[(benzyloxycarbonyl)amino]-3,4-epoxy-1,6-diphenylhexane
($C_{34}H_{34}N_2O_5$; *162849-92-5*)   see: Ritonavir

1,2-bis(benzyloxycarbonyl)-1-methylhydrazine
($C_{17}H_{18}N_2O_4$; *6002-83-1*)   see: Procarbazine

1,2-bis(2-bromoethoxy)benzene
($C_{10}H_{12}Br_2O_2$; *136383-33-0*)   see: Tamsulosin hydrochloride

bis(β-bromoethyl)amine hydrobromide
($C_4H_{10}Br_3N$; *43204-63-3*)   see: Vesnarinone

2,2'-bis(bromomethyl)biphenyl
($C_{14}H_{12}Br_2$; *38274-14-5*)   see: Azapetine

3,4-bis(bromomethyl)-5-hydroxy-6-methylpyridine hydro-bromide
($C_8H_{10}Br_3NO$; *39984-49-1*)   see: Pyritinol

3,5-bis-*O*-(*tert*-butyldimethylsilyl)-2-deoxy-2,2-difluoro-2-*O*-methanesulfonyl-D-ribofuranose
($C_{18}H_{38}F_2O_6SSi_2$; *103882-89-9*)   see: Gemcitabine

3,5-bis-*O*-(*tert*-butyldimethylsilyl)-2-deoxy-2,2-difluoro-D-ribofuranose
($C_{17}H_{36}F_2O_4Si_2$)   see: Gemcitabine

N,*O*-bis(4-chlorobenzoyl)tyramine
($C_{22}H_{17}Cl_2NO_3$; *41859-56-7*)   see: Bezafibrate

bis(2-chloroethyl)amine
($C_4H_9Cl_2N$; *334-22-5*)   see: Cyclophosphamide;
Estramustine phosphate

4-[4-[bis(2-chloroethyl)amino]phenyl]butyric anhydride
($C_{28}H_{36}Cl_4N_2O_3$; *64338-29-0*)   see: Prednimustine

bis(2-chloroethyl) ether
($C_4H_8Cl_2O$; *111-44-4*)   see: Benzethonium chloride;
Oxeladin; Risperidone

N,*N*-bis(2-chloroethyl)-*N*-methylamine
($C_5H_{11}Cl_2N$; *51-75-2*)   see: Ketobemidone; Pethidine

N,*N*-bis(2-chloroethyl)phosphoramidic dichloride
($C_4H_8Cl_4NOP$; *127-88-8*)   see: Cyclophosphamide;
Trofosfamide

N,*N*'-bis(2-chloroethyl)urea
($C_5H_{10}Cl_2N_2O$; *2214-72-4*)   see: Carmustine

bis(chloromethyl) ether
($C_2H_4Cl_2O$; *542-88-1*)   see: Obidoxime chloride

2,6-bis(chloromethyl)pyridine
($C_7H_7Cl_2N$; *3099-28-3*)   see: Pyridinol carbamate

bis(4-chlorophenyl) disulfide
($C_{12}H_8Cl_2S_2$; *1142-19-4*)   see: Tiludronate disodium

5,6-bis-*O*-[(4-chlorophenyl)methylene]-1,2-*O*-(1-methyl-ethylidene)-3-*O*-propyl-α-D-glucofuranose
($C_{26}H_{32}Cl_2O_6$; *28542-48-5*)   see: Clobenoside

1,5-bis(4-cyanophenoxy)pentane
($C_{19}H_{18}N_2O_2$; *7467-71-2*)   see: Pentamidine

N,*N*'-bis(2-diethylaminoethyl)oxamide
($C_{14}H_{30}N_4O_2$; *5432-13-3*)   see: Ambenonium chloride

1,3-bis(dimethylamino)-2-chloropropane
($C_7H_{17}ClN_2$; *40550-12-7*)   see: Aminopromazine

bis(2-dimethylaminoethyl) succinate
($C_{12}H_{24}N_2O_4$; *19249-04-8*)   see: Suxamethonium chloride

1,6-bis(dimethylamino)hexane
($C_{10}H_{24}N_2$; *111-18-2*)   see: Distigmine bromide;
Hexafluronium bromide

1,3-bis(dimethylamino)-2-propanol
($C_7H_{18}N_2O$; *5966-51-8*)   see: Prolonium iodide

3',5'-bis(dimethylcarbamoyloxy)acetophenone
($C_{14}H_{18}N_2O_5$; *81732-48-1*)   see: Bambuterol

bis(1,1-dimethylethyl) dicarbonate
($C_{10}H_{18}O_5$; *24424-99-5*)   see: Delavirdine mesilate;
Fosinopril; Indinavir sulfate; Miglitol; Nevirapine;
Temocapril; Tirofiban hydrochloride; Trovafloxacin mesilate

[1*R*-[1α[1*R**(*S**),3a*R**,4*E*,7a*R**],4α,6β]]-4-[[4,6-bis[[(1,1-dimethylethyl)dimethylsilyl]oxy]-1,3,4,5,6,7-hexahydro-2,2-dioxidobenzo[*c*]thien-1-yl]methylene]octahydro-α,7a-dimethyl-1*H*-indene-1-acetaldehyde
($C_{34}H_{60}O_5SSi_2$; *112790-51-9*)   see: Calcipotriol

(1α,3β,5*E*,7*E*)-1,3-bis[[(1,1-dimethylethyl)dimethyl-silyl]oxy]-9,10-secopregna-5,7,10(19)-triene-20-carbox-aldehyde
($C_{34}H_{60}O_3Si_2$)   see: Calcipotriol

1,2-bis(3,5-dioxopiperazin-1-yl)ethane
($C_{10}H_{14}N_4O_4$; *1506-47-4*)   see: Sobuzoxane

(11β)-3,3:17,17-bis[1,2-ethanediylbis(oxy)]-11-hydroxy-estr-5-en-18-oic acid γ-lactone
($C_{22}H_{30}O_6$; *59860-72-9*)   see: Desogestrel

3,4-bis(ethoxycarbonyloxy)phenethylamine oxalate hemi-hydrate
($C_{32}H_{44}N_2O_{21}$; *143436-67-3*)   see: Docarpamine

1,1-bis(ethoxycarbonyl)-2-vinylcyclopropane
($C_{11}H_{16}O_4$; *7686-78-4*)   see: Vigabatrin

3,3:20,20-bis(ethylenedioxy)-11β,17,21-trihydroxy-5-preg-nene
($C_{25}H_{38}O_7$; *76338-54-0*)   see: Cloprednol; Hydrocortisone;
Methylprednisolone

bis(2-ethylhexyl) fumarate
($C_{20}H_{36}O_4$; *141-02-6*)   see: Sodium dioctyl sulfosuccinate

(S)-3-[bis(phenylmethyl)amino]-1-chloro-4-phenyl-2-butanone
($C_{24}H_{24}ClNO$; *171815-94-4*) see: Saquinavir

7,10-bis(triethylsilyl)-10-deacetylbaccatin III
($C_{41}H_{64}O_{10}Si_2$; *149107-84-6*) see: Docetaxel

2',7-bis(triethylsilyl)paclitaxel
($C_{59}H_{79}NO_{14}Si_2$; *135365-62-7*) see: Paclitaxel

[bis(trifluoroacetoxy)iodo]benzene
($C_{10}H_5F_6IO_4$; *2712-78-9*) see: Tacrolimus

1,1-bis(2,2,2-trifluoroethoxy)ethane
($C_6H_8F_6O_2$; *673-67-6*) see: Fluroxene

2,8-bis(trifluoromethyl)-4-bromoquinoline
($C_{11}H_4BrF_6N$; *35853-45-3*) see: Mefloquine

2,8-bis(trifluoromethyl)-4-hydroxyquinoline
($C_{11}H_5F_6NO$; *35853-41-9*) see: Mefloquine

2,8-bis(trifluoromethyl)-4-lithioquinoline
($C_{11}H_4F_6LiN$; *112748-10-4*) see: Mefloquine

2,8-bis(trifluoromethyl)-4-quinolinecarboxylic acid
($C_{12}H_5F_6NO_2$; *35853-50-0*) see: Mefloquine

[2,8-bis(trifluoromethyl)-4-quinolinyl]-2-pyridinyl-methanone
($C_{17}H_8F_6N_2O$; *35853-55-5*) see: Mefloquine

N,O-bis(trimethylsilyl)acetamide
($C_8H_{21}NOSi_2$; *10416-59-8*) see: Cefalexin

1,3-bis(trimethylsilyl)fluorouracil
($C_{10}H_{19}FN_2O_2Si_2$; *58138-78-6*) see: Tegafur

bis(trimethylsilyl)thymine
($C_{11}H_{22}N_2O_2Si_2$; *7288-28-0*) see: Stavudine

N,O-bis(trimethylsilyl)trifluoroacetamide
($C_8H_{18}F_3NOSi_2$; *25561-30-2*) see: Tirofiban hydrochloride

N,9-bis(trimethylsilyl)-6-[(trimethylsilyl)oxy]-9H-purin-2-amine
($C_{14}H_{29}N_5OSi_3$; *18602-85-2*) see: Aciclovir

Boc-Asp(OBzl)
($C_{16}H_{21}NO_6$; *7536-58-5*) see: Ceruletide

Boc-Asp(OBzl)-Tyr-NH-NH-Z
($C_{33}H_{38}N_4O_9$; *17664-74-3*) see: Ceruletide

Boc-Gln
($C_{10}H_{18}N_2O_5$; *13726-85-7*) see: Ceruletide

Boc-Gln-Asp(OBzl)-Tyr-NH-NH-Z
($C_{38}H_{46}N_6O_{11}$; *21385-06-8*) see: Ceruletide

Boc-Gly-O-Np
($C_{13}H_{16}N_2O_6$; *3655-05-8*) see: Ceruletide

Boc-Gly-Trp-Met-Asp-Phe-NH₂
($C_{36}H_{47}N_7O_9S$; *5915-71-9*) see: Ceruletide

Boc-(S)-phenylglycinal
($C_{13}H_{17}NO_3$; *163061-19-6*) see: Docetaxel

Boc-Thr(Ac)-O-Tcp
($C_{17}H_{20}Cl_3NO_6$; *21385-12-6*) see: Ceruletide

Boc-Tyr
($C_{14}H_{19}NO_5$; *3978-80-1*) see: Ceruletide

Boc-Tyr-NH-NH-Z
($C_{22}H_{27}N_3O_6$; *17664-72-1*) see: Ceruletide

boldenone
($C_{19}H_{26}O_2$; *846-48-0*) see: Boldenone undecenylate; Estradiol

boric acid
(BH_3O_3; *10043-35-3*) see: Phenylmercuric borate

bromine azide
(BrN_3; *13973-87-0*) see: Cefoxitin

bromoacetaldehyde diethyl acetal
($C_6H_{13}BrO_2$; *2032-35-1*) see: Domiodol

bromoacetaldehyde ethylene acetal
($C_4H_7BrO_2$; *4360-63-8*) see: Carbimazole

N-bromoacetamide
(C_2H_4BrNO; *79-15-2*) see: Betamethasone; Fluazacort; Fludroxycortide; Fluperolone acetate; Halopredone diacetate; Triamcinolone; Ulobetasol propionate

7(S)-bromoacetamido-7-methoxycephalosporanic acid
($C_{13}H_{15}BrN_2O_7S$; *65871-82-1*) see: Cefotetan

bromoacetic acid
($C_2H_3BrO_2$; *79-08-3*) see: Bendazac; Tamsulosin hydrochloride

bromoacetic acid methyl ester
($C_3H_5BrO_2$; *96-32-2*) see: Sertindole

2-bromoacetophenone
(C_8H_7BrO; *70-11-1*) see: Fendosal; Hexocyclium metilsulfate; Levamisole; Nomifensine

4'-bromoacetophenone
(C_8H_7BrO; *99-90-1*) see: Zimeldine

bromoacetyl bromide
($C_2H_2Br_2O$; *598-21-0*) see: Cefapirin; Clonazepam; Flunitrazepam; Haloxazolam; Ketazolam; Sotalol

bromoacetyl chloride
(C_2H_2BrClO; *22118-09-8*) see: Cloxazolam; Flurazepam; Mexazolam; Nazasetron; Quazepam; Salbutamol

3-(bromoacetyl)-5-chloro-2-thiophenesulfonamide
($C_6H_5BrClNO_3S_2$; *160982-11-6*) see: Brinzolamide

5-(bromoacetyl)-2-hydroxybenzoic acid methyl ester
($C_{10}H_9BrO_4$; *36256-45-8*) see: Salbutamol

4-(bromoacetyl)methanesulfonanilide
($C_9H_{10}BrNO_3S$; *5577-42-4*) see: Sotalol

5-(bromoacetyl)-2-methylbenzenesulfonamide
($C_9H_{10}BrNO_3S$; *70958-71-3*) see: Amosulalol

(4S,5R)-3-(2-bromoacetyl)-4-methyl-5-phenyl-2-oxazolidinone
($C_{12}H_{12}BrNO_3$; *142722-84-7*) see: Docetaxel

[5-(bromoacetyl)-2-(phenylmethoxy)phenyl]urea
($C_{16}H_{15}BrN_2O_3$; *49639-82-9*) see: Carbuterol

5-bromoacetylsalicylamide
($C_9H_8BrNO_3$; *73866-23-6*) see: Labetalol

5-(bromoacetyl)-2-thiophenecarboxamide
($C_7H_6BrNO_2S$; *68257-90-9*) see: Arotinolol

3-(bromoacetyl)-2-thiophenesulfonamide
($C_6H_6BrNO_3S_2$; *154127-28-3*) see: Brinzolamide

1-bromoadamantane
($C_{10}H_{15}Br$; *768-90-1*) see: Amantadine

21-bromoalfaxalone
($C_{21}H_{31}BrO_3$; *32226-10-1*) see: Alfadolone acetate

2-bromoaniline
(C_6H_6BrN; *615-36-1*) see: Ondansetron

3-(2-bromoanilino)cyclohex-2-en-1-one
($C_{12}H_{12}BrNO$; *68890-19-7*) see: Ondansetron

3-bromoanisole
(C_7H_7BrO; *2398-37-0*) see: Tramadol

4-bromobenzaldehyde
(C_7H_5BrO; *1122-91-4*) see: Bromindione

bromobenzene
(C_6H_5Br; *108-86-1*)   see: Alphaprodine; Fenoprofen; Flurbiprofen

(*R*)-2-bromobenzenepropionic acid
($C_9H_9BrO_2$; *42990-55-6*)   see: Omapatrilat

4-bromobenzenesulfonamide
($C_6H_6BrNO_2S$; *701-34-8*)   see: Ebrotidine

4-bromobenzhydrol
($C_{13}H_{11}BrO$; *29334-16-5*)   see: Bromazine

4-bromobenzhydryl bromide
($C_{13}H_{10}Br_2$; *18066-89-2*)   see: Bromazine

α-bromo-1,2-benzisoxazole-3-acetic acid
($C_9H_6BrNO_3$; *37924-67-7*)   see: Zonisamide

4-(10-bromo-4*H*-benzo[4,5]cyclohepta[1,2-*b*]thien-4-ylidene)-1-methylpiperidine
($C_{19}H_{18}BrNS$; *34580-12-6*)   see: Ketotifen

4-(9-bromo-4*H*-benzo[4,5]cyclohepta[1,2-*b*]thien-4-ylidene)-1-methylpiperidine
($C_{19}H_{18}BrNS$)   see: Ketotifen

2-bromobenzoic acid
($C_7H_5BrO_2$; *88-65-3*)   see: Tolfenamic acid

2-bromobenzonitrile
(C_7H_4BrN; *2042-37-7*)   see: Losartan potassium

7-(4-bromobenzoyl)-3-(methylthio)-2,3-dihydro-1*H*-indol-2-one
($C_{16}H_{12}BrNO_2S$; *91713-90-5*)   see: Bromfenac sodium

2-bromo-3'-benzoyloxyacetophenone
($C_{15}H_{11}BrO_3$; *139-27-5*)   see: Etilefrine; Norfenefrine

***p*-bromobenzyl bromide**
($C_7H_6Br_2$; *589-15-1*)   see: Losartan potassium

4-bromobenzyl cyanide
(C_8H_6BrN; *16532-79-9*)   see: Brompheniramine

2-bromo-*N*-[4-bromo-2-(2-fluorobenzoyl)phenyl]-acetamide
($C_{15}H_{10}Br_2FNO_2$; *1647-74-1*)   see: Haloxazolam

4-bromo-1-butanol acetate
($C_6H_{11}BrO_2$; *4753-59-7*)   see: Omapatrilat

1-bromo-2-butyne
(C_4H_5Br; *3355-28-0*)   see: Iloprost

2-bromobutyric acid
($C_4H_7BrO_2$; *80-58-0*)   see: Etidocaine

α-bromo-γ-butyrolactone
($C_4H_5BrO_2$; *5061-21-2*)   see: Spizofurone

2-bromobutyryl chloride
(C_4H_6BrClO; *22118-12-3*)   see: Etidocaine; Procaterol

2-bromo-2'-chloroacetophenone
(C_8H_6BrClO; *5000-66-8*)   see: Clorprenaline

2-bromo-4'-chloroacetophenone
(C_8H_6BrClO; *536-38-9*)   see: Alpidem; Lofepramine

1-bromo-4-chlorobenzene
(C_6H_4BrCl; *106-39-8*)   see: Chlorprothixene

2-bromo-5-chlorobenzoic acid
($C_7H_4BrClO_2$; *21739-93-5*)   see: Sertindole

2-bromo-*N*-[2-(2-chlorobenzoyl)phenyl]acetamide
($C_{15}H_{11}BrClNO_2$; *2894-46-4*)   see: Clonazepam

1-bromo-4-chlorobutane
(C_4H_8BrCl; *6940-78-9*)   see: Azimilide hydrochloride

2-bromo-*N*-[4-chloro-2-(2-chlorobenzoyl)phenyl]acet-amide
($C_{15}H_{10}BrCl_2NO_2$; *5504-92-7*)   see: Cloxazolam; Mexazolam

1-bromo-2-chloroethane
(C_2H_4BrCl; *107-04-0*)   see: Alfentanil

1-bromo-2-(2-chloroethoxy)-2-(3-trifluoromethylphe-nyl)ethane
($C_{11}H_{11}BrClF_3O$; *26629-85-6*)   see: Oxaflozane

2-bromo-*N*-[4-chloro-2-(2-fluorobenzoyl)phenyl]acet-amide
($C_{15}H_{10}BrClFNO_2$; *1584-62-9*)   see: Flurazepam

bromochloromethane
(CH_2BrCl; *74-97-5*)   see: Fluticasone propionate; Saquinavir

1-bromo-3-chloro-2-methylpropane
(C_4H_8BrCl; *6974-77-2*)   see: Dixyrazine

1-bromo-2-(4-chlorophenoxy)ethane
(C_8H_8BrClO; *2033-76-3*)   see: Dodeclonium bromide; Omoconazole nitrate

7-bromo-5-(2-chlorophenyl)-1,3-dihydro-2*H*-thieno-[2,3-*e*]-1,4-diazepine-2-thione
($C_{13}H_8BrClN_2S_2$; *57801-82-8*)   see: Brotizolam

2-bromo-1-(3-chlorophenyl)-1-propanone
(C_9H_8BrClO; *34911-51-8*)   see: Amfebutamone

1-bromo-3-chloropropane
(C_3H_6BrCl; *109-70-6*)   see: Acetophenazine; Carfenazine; Cisapride; Clocapramine; Desipramine; Dilazep; Etoperidone; Gallopamil; Metopimazine; Opipramol; Oxatomide; Perphenazine; Pipamazine; Piperacetazine; Reproterol; Tirofiban hydrochloride; Verapamil; Vincamine

(1α,3β,7α)-7-bromocholest-5-ene-1,3,25-triol triacetate
($C_{33}H_{51}BrO_6$)   see: Calcitriol

3-bromocyclopentene
(C_5H_7Br; *36291-48-2*)   see: Cyclopentobarbital

(1-bromocyclopentyl)(2-chlorophenyl)methanone
($C_{12}H_{12}BrClO$; *6740-86-9*)   see: Ketamine

2-bromo-1-cyclopropylethanone
(C_5H_7BrO; *69267-75-0*)   see: Calcipotriol

2'-bromo-2'-deoxy-5-methyluridine 5'-benzoate 3'-me-thanesulfonate
($C_{18}H_{19}BrN_2O_8S$; *165047-01-8*)   see: Stavudine

2-bromo-3',5'-diacetoxyacetophenone
($C_{12}H_{11}BrO_5$; *36763-39-0*)   see: Fenoterol; Orciprenaline; Reproterol

2-bromo-2',4'-dichloroacetophenone
($C_8H_5BrCl_2O$; *2631-72-3*)   see: Isoconazole; Ketoconazole; Miconazole

(1*R*-*trans*)-2-bromo-2,3-dihydro-1*H*-inden-1-ol
(C_9H_9BrO; *79465-06-8*)   see: Indinavir sulfate

5-bromodihydroorotic acid
($C_5H_5BrN_2O_4$; *58668-21-6*)   see: Orotic acid

9-bromo-11β,21-dihydroxy-16α-methylpregna-1,4-diene-3,20-dione 21-acetate
($C_{24}H_{31}BrO_5$; *31653-81-3*)   see: Desoximetasone

4β-bromo-17α,21-dihydroxy-16β-methylpregnane-3,11,20-trione 21-acetate
($C_{24}H_{33}BrO_6$; *5078-89-7*)   see: Betamethasone

(3β,16β)-16-bromo-3,17-dihydroxypregn-5-en-20-one
($C_{21}H_{31}BrO_3$; *14072-39-0*)   see: Hydrocortisone; Hydroxyprogesterone

2-bromo-3',5'-dimethoxyacetophenone
($C_{10}H_{11}BrO_3$; *50841-50-4*)   see: Orciprenaline

4-bromo-3,5-dimethoxy-α-(anilinomethylene)hydrocinna-monitrile
($C_{18}H_{17}BrN_2O_2$; *65566-21-4*)   see: Brodimoprim

4-bromo-3,5-dimethoxybenzaldehyde
($C_9H_9BrO_3$; *31558-40-4*)   see: Brodimoprim

3-bromo-2,6-dimethoxybenzoic acid
($C_9H_9BrO_4$; *73219-89-3*)   see: Remoxipride

4-bromo-3,5-dimethoxybenzoyl chloride
($C_9H_8BrClO_3$; *56518-43-5*)   see: Brodimoprim

4-bromo-3,5-dimethoxy-α-(methoxymethyl)cinnamo-nitrile
($C_{13}H_{14}BrNO_3$; *56518-39-9*)   see: Brodimoprim

4-bromo-3,5-dimethoxy-α-(morpholinomethylene)-hydrocinnamonitrile
($C_{16}H_{19}BrN_2O_3$; *65566-19-0*)   see: Brodimoprim

bromo(2,5-dimethoxy-3,4,6-trimethylphenyl)magnesium
($C_{11}H_{15}BrMgO_2$; *73127-73-8*)   see: Troglitazone

2-bromo-N,N-dimethylacetamide
(C_4H_8BrNO; *5468-77-9*)   see: Camostat

1-bromo-3,5-dimethyladamantane
($C_{12}H_{19}Br$; *941-37-7*)   see: Memantine

(Z)-(S)-7-bromo-2-(2,2-dimethylcyclopropanecarbox-amido)-2-heptenoic acid
($C_{13}H_{20}BrNO_3$; *78834-80-7*)   see: Cilastatin

1-bromo-6,6-dimethyl-2-hepten-4-yne
($C_9H_{13}Br$; *126764-15-6*)   see: Terbinafine

2-bromo-N-(2,6-dimethylphenyl)butanamide
($C_{12}H_{16}BrNO$; *53984-81-9*)   see: Etidocaine

5-bromo-2,2-dimethyl-4-phenyl-1,3-dioxane
($C_{12}H_{15}BrO_2$; *36808-10-3*)   see: Chloramphenicol

2-bromo-N-(2,6-dimethylphenyl)propanamide
($C_{11}H_{14}BrNO$; *41708-73-0*)   see: Tocainide

3-bromo-N,N-dimethyl-1-propanamine
($C_5H_{12}BrN$; *53929-74-1*)   see: Rizatriptan benzoate

2-bromo-6-(1,3-dioxolan-2-yl)pyridine
($C_8H_8BrNO_2$; *34199-87-6*)   see: Acrivastine

4-bromo-2,2-diphenylbutyric acid
($C_{16}H_{15}BrO_2$; *37742-98-6*)   see: Loperamide

4-bromo-2,2-diphenylbutyronitrile
($C_{16}H_{14}BrN$; *39186-58-8*)   see: Diphenoxylate; Piritramide

4-bromo-2,2-diphenylbutyryl chloride
($C_{16}H_{14}BrClO$; *50650-44-7*)   see: Loperamide

(5R,6S,9α,11α,13E,15S)-5-bromo-6,9-epoxy-11,15-bis[(tetrahydro-2H-pyran-2-yl)oxy]prost-13-en-1-oic acid
($C_{30}H_{49}BrO_7$)   see: Epoprostenol

2-bromoethanesulfonic acid
($C_2H_5BrO_3S$; *26978-65-4*)   see: Mesna

2-bromoethanol
(C_2H_5BrO; *540-51-2*)   see: Doxefazepam; Miltefosine

(E)-5-(2-bromoethenyl)-1-(2,3,5-tri-O-acetyl-β-D-arabino-furanosyl)-2,4(1H,3H)-pyrimidinedione
($C_{17}H_{19}BrN_2O_9$; *87877-27-8*)   see: Sorivudine

4-(2-bromoethoxy)benzoyl chloride
($C_9H_8BrClO_2$; *51616-10-5*)   see: Raloxifene hydrochloride

(2-bromo-1-ethoxyethyl)benzene
($C_{10}H_{13}BrO$; *6589-30-6*)   see: Eprazinone

1-(2-bromoethoxy)-2-methoxybenzene
($C_9H_{11}BrO_2$; *4463-59-6*)   see: Amosulalol

[4-(2-bromoethoxy)phenyl][6-methoxy-2-(4-methoxyphe-nyl)benzo[b]thien-3-yl]methanone
($C_{25}H_{21}BrO_4S$; *170636-68-7*)   see: Raloxifene hydrochloride

1-[4-(2-bromoethoxy)phenyl]-1-propanone
($C_{11}H_{13}BrO_2$; *34645-63-1*)   see: Fenalcomine

2-bromoethyl acetate
($C_4H_7BrO_2$; *927-68-4*)   see: Fluphenazine

2-(1-bromoethyl)benzo[b]thiophene
($C_{10}H_9BrS$; *155205-54-2*)   see: Zileuton

2-(1-bromoethyl)-2-(5-bromo-6-methoxy-2-naphthalenyl)-1,3-dioxolane-4,5-dicarboxylic acid
($C_{18}H_{16}Br_2O_7$)   see: Naproxen

1-(2-bromoethyl)-2,5-dimethoxy-3,4,6-trimethylbenzene
($C_{13}H_{19}BrO_2$; *84071-98-7*)   see: Troglitazone

5-(2-bromoethyl)-2,2-dimethyl-1,3-dioxane
($C_8H_{15}BrO_2$; *97845-58-4*)   see: Penciclovir

4-(2-bromoethyl)-1-ethyl-3,3-diphenyl-2-pyrrolidinone
($C_{20}H_{22}BrNO$; *3192-92-5*)   see: Doxapram

3-(2-bromoethyl)-1H-indole
($C_{10}H_{10}BrN$; *3389-21-7*)   see: Indoramin

2-bromoethyl isothiocyanate
(C_3H_4BrNS; *1483-41-6*)   see: Levamisole

(4R,5R)-2-(1-bromoethyl)-2-(6-methoxy-2-naphthalenyl)-1,3-dioxolane-4,5-dicarboxylic acid
($C_{18}H_{17}BrO_7$)   see: Naproxen

(5-bromo-3-ethyl-4-oxo-2-thiazolidinylidene)acetic acid ethyl ester
($C_9H_{12}BrNO_3S$; *82760-32-5*)   see: Piprozolin

1-(1-bromoethyl)-3-phenoxybenzene
($C_{14}H_{13}BrO$; *32852-94-1*)   see: Fenoprofen

[4-(1-bromoethyl)phenyl]-2-thienylmethanone
($C_{13}H_{11}BrOS$; *52779-83-6*)   see: Suprofen

2-(2-bromoethyl)-1,3-propanediol diacetate
($C_9H_{15}BrO_4$; *126589-82-0*)   see: Famciclovir

2-(2-bromoethyl)pyridine
(C_7H_8BrN; *39232-04-7*)   see: Betahistine

7-(2-bromoethyl)theophylline
($C_9H_{11}BrN_4O_2$; *23146-05-6*)   see: Cafedrine; Pimefylline

9-bromofluorene
($C_{13}H_9Br$; *1940-57-4*)   see: Hexafluronium bromide

1-bromo-4-fluorobenzene
(C_6H_4BrF; *460-00-4*)   see: Paroxetine

2-bromo-N-[2-(2-fluorobenzoyl)phenyl]acetamide
($C_{15}H_{11}BrFNO_2$; *1894-70-8*)   see: Flunitrazepam

N-[4-bromo-2-(2-fluorobenzoyl)phenyl]-2-[(2-hydroxy-ethyl)amino]acetamide
($C_{17}H_{16}BrFN_2O_3$; *71980-88-6*)   see: Haloxazolam

4-bromo-2-fluorobiphenyl
($C_{12}H_8BrF$; *41604-19-7*)   see: Flurbiprofen

bromo(2-fluoro[1,1'-biphenyl]-4-yl)magnesium
($C_{12}H_8BrFMg$; *76699-46-2*)   see: Flurbiprofen

16β-bromo-6α-fluoro-17,21-dihydroxypregn-4-ene-3,20-dione diacetate
($C_{25}H_{32}BrFO_6$; *2561-13-9*)   see: Fludroxycortide

1-bromo-2-fluoroethane
(C_2H_4BrF; *762-49-2*)   see: Fleroxacin; Flutropium bromide

2-bromo-3-(1-methylethoxy)-2-propenal
($C_6H_9BrO_2$; *155272-73-4*)   see: Eprosartan

5-(2-bromomethyl)-2-hydroxy-1,3,2-dioxaphosphoran 2-oxide
($C_5H_{10}BrO_4P$)   see: Penciclovir

4-bromomethyl-5-methyl-2-oxo-1,3-dioxole
($C_5H_5BrO_3$; *80715-22-6*)   see: Lenampicillin

bromomethyl 4-methylphenyl ketone
(C_9H_9BrO; *619-41-0*)   see: Zolpidem

3-(bromomethyl)-1-methylpiperidine
($C_7H_{14}BrN$; *41886-04-8*)   see: Pecazine

[2-[3-(bromomethyl)-5-methyl-4*H***-1,2,4-triazol-4-yl]-5-chlorophenyl]phenylmethanone**
($C_{17}H_{13}BrClN_3O$; *38150-28-6*)   see: Alprazolam

α-(bromomethyl)-4-nitrobenzenemethanol
($C_8H_8BrNO_3$; *19922-82-8*)   see: Nifenalol

2-(bromomethyl)-4-[(phenylmethoxy)methyl]-1,3-dioxolane
($C_{12}H_{15}BrO_3$; *92905-04-9*)   see: Domiodol

2-bromo-*N***-(2-methylphenyl)propanamide**
($C_{10}H_{12}BrNO$; *19397-79-6*)   see: Prilocaine

9-bromo-4-(1-methyl-4-piperidinyl)-4*H***-benzo[4,5]cyclohepta[1,2-***b***]thiophene-4-ol**
($C_{19}H_{20}BrNOS$)   see: Ketotifen

10-bromo-4-(1-methyl-4-piperidinyl)-4*H***-benzo[4,5]cyclohepta[1,2-***b***]thiophene-4-ol**
($C_{19}H_{20}BrNOS$; *59776-37-3*)   see: Ketotifen

9α-bromo-16β-methylprednisolone 21-acetate
($C_{24}H_{31}BrO_6$; *4735-65-3*)   see: Betamethasone

6-(bromomethyl)-2,4-pteridinediamine monohydrobromide
($C_7H_8Br_2N_6$; *52853-40-4*)   see: Methotrexate

4-(bromomethyl)-2(1*H***)-quinolinone**
($C_{10}H_8BrNO$; *4876-10-2*)   see: Rebamipide

4-bromo-α-methylstyrene
(C_9H_9Br; *6888-79-5*)   see: Bromperidol

2-bromo-4'-(methylsulfonyl)acetophenone
($C_9H_9BrO_3S$; *50413-24-6*)   see: Rofecoxib; Zolimidine

2-bromo-4'-methylsulfonylacetophenone
see under 2-bromo-4'-(methylsulfonyl)acetophenone

α-bromo-3-methylsulfonylaminoacetophenone
($C_9H_{10}BrNO_3S$; *2065-04-5*)   see: Amidephrine mesilate

5-bromo-3-(1-methyl-1,2,3,6-tetrahydro-4-pyridinyl)-1*H***-indole**
($C_{14}H_{15}BrN_2$; *116480-53-6*)   see: Naratriptan

2-bromo-4'-methylvalerophenone
($C_{12}H_{15}BrO$)   see: Pyrovalerone

6-bromo-2-naphthol
($C_{10}H_7BrO$; *15231-91-1*)   see: Naproxen

5-bromonicotinic acid
($C_6H_4BrNO_2$; *20826-04-4*)   see: Nicergoline; Timepidium bromide

5-bromonicotinoyl chloride
($C_6H_3BrClNO$; *39620-02-5*)   see: Nicergoline

2-bromo-4'-nitroacetophenone
($C_8H_6BrNO_3$; *99-81-0*)   see: Chloramphenicol; Clenbuterol; Nifenalol

4'-bromo-3'-nitroacetophenone
($C_8H_6BrNO_3$; *18640-58-9*)   see: Flurbiprofen

2-bromo-1-nitrobenzene
($C_6H_4BrNO_2$; *577-19-5*)   see: Dibenzepine; Nimesulide

bromonitromethane
(CH_2BrNO_2; *563-70-2*)   see: Trovafloxacin mesilate

2-bromo-1-[3-nitro-4-(phenylmethoxy)phenyl]ethanone
($C_{15}H_{12}BrNO_4$; *43229-01-2*)   see: Formoterol

α-bromooctanoic acid
($C_8H_{15}BrO_2$; *2623-82-7*)   see: Orlistat

α-bromooctanoyl chloride
($C_8H_{14}BrClO$; *42768-44-5*)   see: Orlistat

9-bromo-4-oxo-4*H***-benzo[4,5]cyclohepta[1,2-***b***]thiophene**
($C_{13}H_7BrOS$; *57568-63-5*)   see: Ketotifen

10-bromo-4-oxo-4*H***-benzo[4,5]cyclohepta[1,2-***b***]thiophene**
($C_{13}H_7BrOS$; *34580-11-5*)   see: Ketotifen

5-(2-bromo-1-oxobutyl)-8-hydroxy-2(1*H***)-quinolinone**
($C_{13}H_{12}BrNO_3$; *59827-93-9*)   see: Procaterol

7-bromo-2-oxoheptanoic acid
($C_7H_{11}BrO_3$; *107872-93-5*)   see: Cilastatin

(3*R***)-3-[(2-bromo-1-oxooctyl)oxy]tetradecanoic acid methyl ester**
($C_{23}H_{43}BrO_4$)   see: Orlistat

3-[(2-bromo-1-oxopropyl)amino]-4-methyl-2-thiophene-carboxylic acid methyl ester
($C_{10}H_{12}BrNO_3S$)   see: Carticaine

10-(2-bromo-1-oxopropyl)-10*H***-phenothiazine**
($C_{15}H_{12}BrNOS$; *4091-90-1*)   see: Propyramazine bromide

5-bromopentanoic acid
($C_5H_9BrO_2$; *2067-33-6*)   see: Iloprost

1-bromo-4-pentanone
(C_5H_9BrO; *3884-71-7*)   see: Chloroquine

2-(5-bromopentyl)-1,3-dithiane-2-carboxylic acid ethyl ester
($C_{12}H_{21}BrO_2S_2$; *107871-16-9*)   see: Cilastatin

1-(5-bromopentyl)-1-methyl-7-methoxy-2-tetralone
($C_{17}H_{23}BrO_2$; *42263-81-0*)   see: Dezocine

α-bromophenylacetonitrile
(C_8H_6BrN; *5798-79-8*)   see: Amiphenazole

α-(4-bromophenyl)-α-[2-(dimethylamino)ethyl]-3-pyridinemethanol
($C_{16}H_{19}BrN_2O$; *41910-98-9*)   see: Zimeldine

2-(4-bromophenyl)-4-dimethylamino-2-(2-pyridyl)butyronitrile
($C_{17}H_{18}BrN_3$; *65676-22-4*)   see: Brompheniramine

bromo(2-phenylethyl)magnesium
(C_8H_9BrMg; *3277-89-2*)   see: Enalapril

(4-bromophenyl)hydrazine monohydrochloride
($C_6H_8BrClN_2$; *622-88-8*)   see: Bromazepam

4-(4-bromophenyl)-4-hydroxypiperidine
($C_{11}H_{14}BrNO$; *57988-58-6*)   see: Bromperidol

2-bromo-1-phenyl-1,3-propanediol
($C_9H_{11}BrO_2$; *36808-14-7*)   see: Chloramphenicol

(4-bromophenyl)(2-pyridyl)acetonitrile
($C_{13}H_9BrN_2$; *85750-24-9*)   see: Brompheniramine

4-(4-bromophenyl)-1,2,3,6-tetrahydropyridine
($C_{11}H_{12}BrN$; *91347-99-8*)   see: Bromperidol

5-(2-bromophenyl)-1*H***-tetrazole**
($C_7H_5BrN_4$; *73096-42-1*)   see: Losartan potassium

3-bromophthalide
($C_8H_5BrO_2$; *6940-49-4*)   see: Talampicillin

3-butene-1,2-diol diacetate
($C_8H_{12}O_4$; *18085-02-4*)   see: Retinol

(E)-2-butenyltriphenylstannane
($C_{22}H_{22}Sn$; *29000-09-7*)   see: Tacrolimus

4'-butoxyacetophenone
($C_{12}H_{16}O_2$; *5736-89-0*)   see: Bufexamac; Dyclonine

4-butoxybenzyl bromide
($C_{11}H_{15}BrO$; *2417-74-5*)   see: Butropium bromide

***tert*-butoxybis(dimethylamino)methane**
($C_9H_{22}N_2O$; *5815-08-7*)   see: Ziprasidone hydrochloride

***N-tert*-butoxycarbonyl-L-alanine**
($C_8H_{15}NO_4$; *15761-38-3*)   see: Enalapril; Romurtide

***N-tert*-butoxycarbonyl-L-alanyl-L-alanine**
($C_{11}H_{20}N_2O_5$; *27317-69-7*)   see: Alatrofloxacin mesilate

***tert*-butoxycarbonyl-L-alanyl-D-isoglutamine**
($C_{13}H_{23}N_3O_6$; *18814-50-1*)   see: Romurtide

(1α,5α,6α)-6-*tert*-butoxycarbonylamino-3-azabicyclo-[3.1.0]hexane
($C_{10}H_{18}N_2O_2$; *134575-17-0*)   see: Trovafloxacin mesilate

2-*tert*-butoxycarbonylamino-1-chloro-1-(2-thienyl)ethane
($C_{11}H_{16}ClNO_2S$; *102090-60-8*)   see: Temocapril

3(S)-*tert*-butoxycarbonylamino-1,2(S)-epoxy-4-phenyl-butane
($C_{15}H_{21}NO_3$; *98737-29-2*)   see: Amprenavir

3-(*tert*-butoxycarbonylamino)-2-methoxypyridine
($C_{11}H_{16}N_2O_3$; *161117-83-5*)   see: Nevirapine

(2R,3S)-3-*tert*-butoxycarbonylamino-3-phenyl-2-(2,2,2-trichloroethoxymethoxy)propionic acid
($C_{17}H_{22}Cl_3NO_6$; *145433-71-2*)   see: Docetaxel

2-*tert*-butoxycarbonylamino-1-(2-thienyl)ethanol
($C_{11}H_{17}NO_3S$; *102090-59-5*)   see: Temocapril

***S*-[2-*tert*-butoxycarbonylamino-1(S)-(2-thienyl)ethyl]-*N*-phthaloyl-L-cysteine benzhydryl ester**
($C_{35}H_{34}N_2O_6S_2$)   see: Temocapril

(2RS,6R)-6-*tert*-butoxycarbonylamino-2-(2-thienyl)-5-oxoperhydro-1,4-thiazepine
($C_{14}H_{20}N_2O_3S_2$)   see: Temocapril

***N-tert*-butoxycarbonyl-L-cysteine**
($C_8H_{15}NO_4S$; *20887-95-0*)   see: Temocapril

(4S,5R)-3-*tert*-butoxycarbonyl-2,2-dimethyl-4-phenyl-5-oxazolidinecarboxaldehyde
($C_{17}H_{23}NO_4$; *163010-82-0*)   see: Docetaxel

(4S,5R)-3-*tert*-butoxycarbonyl-2,2-dimethyl-4-phenyl-5-oxazolidinecarboxylic acid
($C_{17}H_{23}NO_5$; *143527-70-2*)   see: Docetaxel

(3R,4S)-1-*tert*-butoxycarbonyl-3-(1-ethoxyethoxy)-4-phenyl-2-azetidinone
($C_{18}H_{25}NO_5$; *201856-57-7*)   see: Docetaxel

***N-tert*-butoxycarbonyl-*trans*-4-hydroxy-L-proline**
($C_{10}H_{17}NO_5$; *13726-69-7*)   see: Fosinopril

***N*-(*N*[6]-*tert*-butoxycarbonyl-L-lysyl)-L-proline**
($C_{16}H_{29}N_3O_5$; *4583-24-8*)   see: Lisinopril

(Z)-2-(*tert*-butoxycarbonylmethoxyimino)-2-(2-form-amidothiazol-4-yl)acetic acid
($C_{12}H_{15}N_3O_6S$; *68401-68-3*)   see: Cefixime

(Z)-2-(1-*tert*-butoxycarbonyl-1-methylethoxyimino)-2-(2-tritylaminothiazol-4-yl)acetic acid
($C_{32}H_{33}N_3O_5S$; *68672-66-2*)   see: Ceftazidime

***N-tert*-butoxycarbonyl-D-α-phenylglycine**
($C_{13}H_{17}NO_4$; *33125-05-2*)   see: Cefaclor

***N-tert*-butoxycarbonylpiperidine-2(S)-carboxylic acid**
($C_{11}H_{19}NO_4$; *26250-84-0*)   see: Tacrolimus

***N-tert*-butoxycarbonyl-*trans*-4-tosyloxy-L-proline**
($C_{17}H_{23}NO_7S$; *96314-28-2*)   see: Fosinopril

3-butoxy-4-nitrobenzoic acid
($C_{11}H_{13}NO_5$; *72101-53-2*)   see: Oxybuprocaine

3-butoxy-4-nitrobenzoic acid 2-(diethylamino)ethyl ester
($C_{17}H_{26}N_2O_5$; *10367-95-0*)   see: Oxybuprocaine

3-butoxy-4-nitrobenzoic acid ethyl ester
($C_{13}H_{17}NO_5$)   see: Oxybuprocaine

3-butoxy-4-nitrobenzoyl chloride
($C_{11}H_{12}ClNO_4$; *23442-21-9*)   see: Oxybuprocaine

4-butoxyphenol
($C_{10}H_{14}O_2$; *122-94-1*)   see: Pramocaine

(4-butoxyphenoxy)acetyl chloride
($C_{12}H_{15}ClO_3$; *54022-77-4*)   see: Fenoxedil

2-(*p*-butoxyphenoxy)-2',5'-diethoxyacetanilide
($C_{22}H_{29}NO_5$; *27585-34-8*)   see: Fenoxedil

4-butoxyphenylacetic acid
($C_{12}H_{16}O_3$; *4547-57-3*)   see: Bufexamac

(4S,5R)-2-*tert*-butoxy-4-phenyl-5-(1-ethoxyethoxy)-4,5-di-hydro-1,3-oxazin-6-one
($C_{18}H_{25}NO_5$)   see: Docetaxel

4-[2-(4-butoxyphenyl)-1-thioxoethyl]morpholine
($C_{16}H_{23}NO_2S$; *55784-03-7*)   see: Bufexamac

***tert*-butylacetate**
($C_6H_{12}O_2$; *540-88-5*)   see: Atorvastatin calcium; Indinavir sulfate

***tert*-butylacetic anhydride**
($C_{12}H_{22}O_3$; *38965-26-3*)   see: Dexamethasone *tert*-butylacetate; Triamcinolone hexacetonide

***tert*-butyl acetoacetate**
($C_8H_{14}O_3$; *1694-31-1*)   see: Barnidipine; Cefixime; Fluvastatin sodium; Lercanidipine hydrochloride

***tert*-butylacetyl chloride**
($C_6H_{11}ClO$; *7065-46-5*)   see: Prednisolone tebutate; Triamcinolone hexacetonide

***tert*-butylacetylene**
(C_6H_{10}; *917-92-0*)   see: Terbinafine

***tert*-butyl alcohol**
see under *tert*-butanol

butylamine
($C_4H_{11}N$; *109-73-9*)   see: Bamethan; Buclosamide; Butanilicaine; Carbutamide; Parsalmide; Tybamate

***tert*-butylamine**
($C_4H_{11}N$; *75-64-9*)   see: Amfebutamone; Bitolterol; Dopindolol; Bucumolol; Budipine; Bufetolol; Bunitrolol; Bupranolol; Butofilolol; Carteolol; Celiprolol; Clenbuterol; Finasteride; Levobunolol; Mabuterol; Nadolol; Penbutolol; Perindopril; Saquinavir; Talinolol; Terodiline; Tertatolol; Tilisolol hydrochloride; Timolol; Tulobuterol; Xibenolol

4-(butylamino)benzoic acid
($C_{11}H_{15}NO_2$; *4740-24-3*)   see: Tetracaine

2-*tert*-butylamino-3',4'-bis(*p*-toluoyloxy)acetophenone
($C_{28}H_{29}NO_5$; *47749-96-2*)   see: Bitolterol

***N*-[4-[[[(butylamino)carbonyl]amino]sulfonyl]phenyl]-acetamide**
($C_{13}H_{19}N_3O_4S$; *6630-00-8*)   see: Carbutamide

2-*tert*-butylamino-3',4'-dihydroxyacetophenone
($C_{12}H_{17}NO_3$; *105644-17-5*)   see: Bitolterol

4'-[(2-butyl-4-oxo-1,3-diazaspiro[4.4]non-1-en-3-yl)me-thyl][1,1'-biphenyl]-2-carbonitrile
($C_{25}H_{27}N_3O$; *138401-24-8*)　see: Irbesartan

3-butyl-1-oxo-1,2-dihydroisoquinoline
($C_{13}H_{15}NO$; *132-90-1*)　see: Quinisocaine

***tert*-butyl (2*S*,6*R*)-5-oxo-6-phthalimido-2-(2-thienyl)per-hydro-1,4-thiazepine-4-acetate**
($C_{23}H_{24}N_2O_5S_2$)　see: Temocapril

***N*-(*tert*-butyloxycarbonyl)-2(*R*)-(4-hydroxyphenyl)glycine**
($C_{13}H_{17}NO_5$; *27460-85-1*)　see: *cis*-Cefprozil

***N*-(*tert*-butyloxycarbonyl)-4-piperidineacetic acid**
($C_{12}H_{21}NO_4$; *157688-46-5*)　see: Tirofiban hydrochloride

***N*-(*tert*-butyloxycarbonyl)-4-piperidineethanol**
($C_{12}H_{23}NO_3$; *89151-44-0*)　see: Tirofiban hydrochloride

4-[*N*-(*tert*-butyloxycarbonyl)piperidin-4-yl]butyl bromide
($C_{14}H_{26}BrNO_2$; *142355-81-5*)　see: Tirofiban hydrochloride

***N*-*tert*-butyloxycarbonyl-L-threonine**
($C_9H_{17}NO_5$; *2592-18-9*)　see: Aztreonam

1-(4-*tert*-butylphenyl)-4-chloro-1-butanol
($C_{14}H_{21}ClO$; *105377-23-9*)　see: Terfenadine

1-(4-*tert*-butylphenyl)-4-chloro-1-butanone
see under 4-*tert*-butyl-ω-chlorobutyrophenone

***tert*-butyl 3-phenylglycidate**
($C_{13}H_{16}O_3$; *27593-40-4*)　see: Docetaxel; Paclitaxel

1-*tert*-butyl-4-phenyl-1,2,3,6-tetrahydropyridine
($C_{15}H_{21}N$; *46713-61-5*)　see: Budipine

***N*-*tert*-butyl-4-(3-picolyl)-2(*S*)-piperazinecarboxamide**
($C_{15}H_{24}N_4O$; *183074-81-9*)　see: Indinavir sulfate

1-*tert*-butylpiperidine-4-one
($C_9H_{17}NO$; *1465-76-5*)　see: Budipine

***N*-(butylsulfonyl)-*O*-[4-(4-pyridinyl)butyl]-L-tyrosine**
($C_{22}H_{30}N_2O_5S$; *149490-61-9*)　see: Tirofiban hydrochloride

***N*-(butylsulfonyl)-L-tyrosine**
($C_{13}H_{19}NO_5S$; *149490-60-8*)　see: Tirofiban hydrochloride

***tert*-butyl β-[1,2,3,4-tetrahydro-1,1-bis(phenylthio)-2-oxo-5-methoxy-3-naphthyl]-α-methylenepropionate**
($C_{31}H_{32}O_4S_2$; *87056-68-6*)　see: Quinagolide hydrochloride

4-(butylthio)benzhydrol
($C_{17}H_{20}OS$; *94823-88-8*)　see: Captodiame

4-butylthiobenzhydryl chloride
($C_{17}H_{19}ClS$; *84245-51-2*)　see: Captodiame

4-butylthiobenzhydryl mercaptan
($C_{17}H_{20}S_2$)　see: Captodiame

4-butylthiobenzophenone
($C_{17}H_{18}OS$; *73242-21-4*)　see: Captodiame

***tert*-butyl (*S*)-*p*-toluenesulfinylacetate**
($C_{13}H_{18}O_3S$; *94404-20-3*)　see: Orlistat

1-butyne
(C_4H_6; *107-00-6*)　see: Methohexital

2-butyne-1,4-diol
($C_4H_6O_2$; *110-65-6*)　see: Amezinium metilsulfate

3-butyn-1-ol
(C_4H_6O; *927-74-2*)　see: Rizatriptan benzoate

butyraldehyde
(C_4H_8O; *123-72-8*)　see: Budesonide; Etizolam; Tetracaine; Vincamine

4-butyramidophenol
($C_{10}H_{13}NO_2$; *101-91-7*)　see: Acebutolol

butyric anhydride
($C_8H_{14}O_3$; *106-31-0*)　see: Acebutolol; Amiodarone; Bucladesine sodium; Bunamiodyl; Iopanoic acid; Iophenoic acid

butyronitrile
(C_4H_7N; *109-74-0*)　see: Etifelmine

2-butyrylbenzofuran
($C_{12}H_{12}O_2$; *85614-50-2*)　see: Amiodarone

butyryl chloride
(C_4H_7ClO; *141-75-3*)　see: Bunazosin; Butofilolol; Etacrynic acid; Telmisartan

4-butyryl-2,3-dichlorophenoxyacetic acid
($C_{12}H_{12}Cl_2O_4$; *1217-67-0*)　see: Etacrynic acid

1-butyrylhomopiperazine
($C_9H_{18}N_2O$; *61903-12-6*)　see: Bunazosin

2-butyrylphenothiazine
($C_{16}H_{15}NOS$; *25244-91-1*)　see: Butaperazine

Bzl-Mep-ONp
($C_{16}H_{15}NO_4S$; *50833-62-0*)　see: Desmopressin

Bzl-Mep-Tyr-Phe-Gln-Asn-Cys(Bzl)-Pro-D-Arg-Gly-NH$_2$
($C_{67}H_{84}N_{14}O_{14}S_3$; *16717-13-8*)　see: Desmopressin

Bzl-Mep-Tyr-Phe-NH-NH$_2$
($C_{28}H_{32}N_4O_4S$; *5254-58-0*)　see: Desmopressin

Bzl-Mep-Tyr-Phe-OMe
($C_{29}H_{32}N_2O_5S$; *5254-57-9*)　see: Desmopressin

C

caffeic acid
($C_9H_8O_4$; *331-39-5*)　see: Cynarine

caffeine
($C_8H_{10}N_4O_2$; *58-08-2*)　see: Cafaminol; Caffeine acetyltryptophanate

calcium 1,1-cyclobutanecarboxylate
($C_6H_6CaO_4$; *13799-91-2*)　see: Carboplatin

calcium D-pantothenate
($C_{18}H_{32}CaN_2O_{10}$; *137-08-6*)　see: Pantethine

camphene
($C_{10}H_{16}$; *79-92-5*)　see: Mecamylamine

(–)-camphene
($C_{10}H_{16}$; *5794-04-7*)　see: Xibornol

D-camphoric acid
($C_{10}H_{16}O_4$; *124-83-4*)　see: Carnitine; Dexfenfluramine

(1*R*,3*S*)-(+)-camphoric acid
see under D-camphoric acid

camptothecin
($C_{20}H_{16}N_2O_4$; *7689-03-4*)　see: Topotecan

canrenone
($C_{22}H_{28}O_3$; *976-71-6*)　see: Potassium canrenoate; Spironolactone

caproic anhydride
($C_{12}H_{22}O_3$; *2051-49-2*)　see: Clocortolone; Fluocortolone caproate; Gestonorone caproate; Hydroxyprogesterone caproate

ε-caprolactam
($C_6H_{11}NO$; *105-60-2*)　see: Acexamic acid; Aminocaproic acid; Pentetrazol; Setastine

carbamazepine
($C_{15}H_{12}N_2O$; *298-46-4*)　see: Oxcarbazepine

carbamimidic acid methyl ester
($C_2H_6N_2O$; *2440-60-0*)   see: Azacitidine

carbamoyl chloride
(CH_2ClNO; *463-72-9*)   see: 2-Thiophenecarboxylic acid

9-carbamoyl-9-(2-cyanoethyl)fluorene
($C_{17}H_{14}N_2O$; *79156-94-8*)   see: Indecainide

4-carbamoyl-5-diazonio-N^1-imidazolide
($C_4H_3N_5O$; *26230-33-1*)   see: Dacarbazine

N^5-carbamoyl-D-ornithine
($C_6H_{13}N_3O_3$; *13594-51-9*)   see: Cetrorelix

4-carbamoyl-4-piperidinopiperidine
($C_{11}H_{21}N_3O$; *39633-82-4*)   see: Carpipramine;
Clocapramine; Mosapramine; Pipamperone; Piritramide

carbenicillin benzyl ester
($C_{24}H_{24}N_2O_6S$; *3973-06-6*)   see: Carbenicillin

3-carbethoxyamino-10,11-dihydro-5H-dibenz[b,f]azepine
($C_{17}H_{18}N_2O_2$; *78816-40-7*)   see: Tiracizine

N-carbethoxyphthalimide
($C_{11}H_9NO_4$; *22509-74-6*)   see: Gusperimus trihydrochloride;
Thalidomide

N-carbethoxypiperazine
($C_7H_{14}N_2O_2$; *120-43-4*)   see: Amoxapine; Buclizine;
Cetirizine; Enoxacin

DL-carbidopa
($C_{10}H_{14}N_2O_4$; *302-53-4*)   see: Carbidopa

N-carbobenzyloxynortropine
($C_{15}H_{19}NO_3$; *109840-91-7*)   see: Flutropium bromide

N-carbobenzyloxynortropine benzilate
($C_{29}H_{29}NO_5$)   see: Flutropium bromide

carbon dioxide
(CO_2; *124-38-9*)   see: p-Aminosalicylic acid; Gentisic acid;
Indecainide; Lamotrigine; Salicylic acid; Troglitazone; L-
Tryptophan

carbon disulfide
(CS_2; *75-15-0*)   see: Cefotetan; Dihydralazine; Disulfiram;
Ethoxzolamide; Flomoxef; Lanoconazole; Malotilate;
Ranitidine; Sulbentine; Tibezonium iodide; Timiperone;
Tinazoline hydrochloride; Tiocarlide

**carbonic acid [2aR-(2aα,4β,4aβ,6β,9α,11α,12α,12aα,
12bα)]-12b-(acetyloxy)-12-(benzoyloxy)-2a,3,4,4a,5,6,9,10,
11,12,12a,12b-dodecahydro-9,11-dihydroxy-4a,8,13,13-
tetramethyl-5-oxo-7,11-methano-1H-cyclodeca[3,4]benz
[1,2-b]oxete-4,6-diyl bis(2,2,2-trichloroethyl) ester**
($C_{35}H_{38}Cl_6O_{14}$; *95603-44-4*)   see: Docetaxel

**carbonic acid 7-chloro-2,3-dihydro-1-methyl-2-oxo-5-phe-
nyl-1H-1,4-benzodiazepin-3-yl phenyl ester**
($C_{23}H_{17}ClN_2O_4$; *36111-95-2*)   see: Camazepam

**[5R-[5α,5aβ,8aα,9β(R^*)]]-carbonic acid 4-[9-[(2,3-di-O-
acetyl-4,6-O-ethylidene-β-D-glucopyranosyl)oxy]-5,5a,6,8,
8a,9-hexahydro-6-oxofuro[3',4':6,7]naphtho[2,3-d]-1,3-di-
oxol-5-yl]-2,6-dimethoxyphenyl phenylmethyl ester**
($C_{41}H_{42}O_{17}$; *131234-65-6*)   see: Etoposide

**[5R-(5α,5aβ,8aα,9β)]-carbonic acid 4-[5,5a,6,8,8a,9-hexa-
hydro-6-oxo-9-[(2,3,4,6-tetra-O-acetyl-β-D-glucopyrano-
syl)oxy]furo[3',4':6,7]naphtho[2,3-d]-1,3-dioxol-5-yl]-2,6-
dimethoxyphenyl phenylmethyl ester**
($C_{43}H_{44}O_{19}$; *23362-12-1*)   see: Teniposide

carbon monoxide
(CO; *630-08-0*)   see: Ibuprofen; Retinol; Rofecoxib

carbonochloridic acid (4-nitrophenyl)methyl ester
($C_8H_6ClNO_4$; *4457-32-3*)   see: Meropenem

carbonochloridothioic acid O-2-naphthalenyl ester
($C_{11}H_7ClOS$; *10506-37-3*)   see: Tolnaftate

carbonocyanidimidic acid methyl ester
($C_3H_4N_2O$; *13369-03-4*)   see: Sulfametrole

**N,N'-[carbonylbis(iminosulfonyl-4,1-phenylene)]bis[acet-
amide]**
($C_{17}H_{18}N_4O_7S_2$; *115036-71-0*)   see: Carbutamide

1,1'-carbonyldiimidazole
($C_7H_6N_4O$; *530-62-1*)   see: Tropisetron

3,4-carbonyldioxycinnamic acid
($C_{10}H_6O_5$; *5728-81-4*)   see: Cynarine

3-carboxamido-5-vinyl-2-pyrrolidone
($C_7H_{10}N_2O_2$; *71107-19-2*)   see: Vigabatrin

α-[(2-carboxy-4-acetylphenyl)oxy]-γ-butyrolactone
($C_{13}H_{12}O_6$; *72492-92-3*)   see: Spizofurone

N-carboxy-L-alanine anhydride
($C_4H_5NO_3$; *2224-52-4*)   see: Enalapril

4-carboxybenzenesulfonyl chloride
($C_7H_5ClO_4S$; *10130-89-9*)   see: Probenecid

4-carboxybutylidenetriphenylphosphorane sodium salt
($C_{23}H_{22}NaO_2P$; *41723-91-5*)   see: Iloprost

**3-carboxy-5-(4-chlorobenzoyl)-1,4-dimethyl-1H-pyrrole-
2-acetic acid**
($C_{16}H_{14}ClNO_5$; *33369-28-7*)   see: Zomepirac

2'-carboxy-4-chloro-3-nitrobenzophenone
($C_{14}H_8ClNO_5$; *85-54-1*)   see: Chlortalidone

**[6R-[6α,7β(Z)]]-1-[[2-carboxy-7-[[[[2-(1,1-dimethyl-
ethoxy)-1,1-dimethyl-2-oxoethoxy]imino][2-[(triphenylmethyl)amino]-4-thiazolyl]acetyl]amino]-8-oxo-5-thia-1-
azabicyclo[4.2.0]oct-2-en-3-yl]methyl]pyridinium inner
salt**
($C_{45}H_{44}N_6O_7S_2$; *73547-69-0*)   see: Ceftazidime

**(E)-5-[[4-[[(2-carboxyethyl)amino]carbonyl]phenyl]azo]-
2-hydroxybenzoic acid**
($C_{17}H_{15}N_3O_6$; *80573-04-2*)   see: Balsalazide sodium

DL-(1-carboxyethyl)oxamic acid diethyl ester
($C_9H_{15}NO_5$; *23460-73-3*)   see: Pyridoxine

4-carboxy-3-hydroxy-5-mercaptoisothiazole trisodium salt
($C_4NNa_3O_3S_2$; *76857-14-2*)   see: Cefotetan

**1-(N-carboxymethyl-N-cyclohexylcarbonylaminomethyl)-
1,2,3,4-tetrahydroisoquinoline**
($C_{19}H_{26}N_2O_3$; *60744-44-7*)   see: Praziquantel

8-carboxy-3-methylflavone
($C_{17}H_{12}O_4$; *3468-01-7*)   see: Flavoxate

7a-carboxymethylpyrrolizine
($C_9H_{15}NO_2$; *94794-30-6*)   see: Pilsicainide

17β-carboxy-5-oxo-A-nor-3,5-secoandrostan-3-oic acid
($C_{19}H_{28}O_5$; *76763-14-9*)   see: Finasteride

**(11β)-21-(3-carboxy-1-oxopropoxy)-11,17-dihydroxy-
pregna-1,4-diene-3,20-dione**
($C_{25}H_{32}O_8$; *2920-86-7*)   see: Prednisolone sodium succinate

**4-[[(2-carboxyphenyl)carbonyl]amino]-N-(aminocarbo-
nyl)benzenesulfonamide**
($C_{15}H_{13}N_3O_6S$)   see: Sulfaloxic acid

carbromal
($C_7H_{13}BrN_2O_2$; *77-65-6*)   see: Acecarbromal

L-carnitinamide D-camphorate
($C_{17}H_{32}N_2O_6$; *73804-72-5*)   see: Carnitine

DL-carnitinamide chloride
($C_7H_{17}ClN_2O_2$; *5261-99-4*)   see: Carnitine

2-[(chloroacetyl)amino]-α-(methoxyimino)-4-thiazole-acetic acid
($C_8H_8ClN_3O_4S$; *60846-17-5*)   see: Ceftriaxone

2-[(chloroacetyl)amino]-3-methylbenzoic acid methyl ester
($C_{11}H_{12}ClNO_3$; *77093-79-9*)   see: Tolycaine

[6R-[6α,7β(Z)]]-7-[[[2-[(chloroacetyl)amino]-4-thia-zolyl](methoxyimino)acetyl]amino]-3-[[(1-methyl-1H-tetrazol-5-yl)thio]methyl]-8-oxo-5-thia-1-azabicy-clo[4.2.0]oct-2-ene-2-carboxylic acid
($C_{18}H_{18}ClN_9O_6S_3$; *65336-94-9*)   see: Cefmenoxime

[6R-[6α,7β(Z)]]-7-[[[2-[(chloroacetyl)amino]-4-thia-zolyl](methoxyimino)acetyl]amino]-8-oxo-3-[[(1,2,5,6-tetrahydro-2-methyl-5,6-dioxo-1,2,4-triazin-3 -yl)thio]-methyl]-5-thia-1-azabicyclo[4.2.0]oct-2-ene-2-carboxylic acid
($C_{20}H_{19}ClN_8O_8S_3$; *74578-70-4*)   see: Ceftriaxone

chloroacetyl chloride
($C_2H_2Cl_2O$; *79-04-9*)   see: Butanilicaine; Carumonam; Ceftriaxone; Chlordiazepoxide; Cinolazepam; Clemizole; Diazepam; Erdosteine; Fenoverine; Fenticonazole; Fluconazole; Lidocaine; Lidoflazine; Lorazepam; Midodrine; Nefopam; Nordazepam; Oxetacaine; Pirenzepine; Piroxicam; Praziquantel; Prednisolamate; Propacetamol; Pyrrocaine; Reboxetine; Tiracizine; Tolycaine; Tromantadine; Viloxazine; Ziprasidone hydrochloride

11-(chloroacetyl)-5,11-dihydro-6H-pyrido[2,3-b][1,4]ben-zodiazepin-6-one
($C_{14}H_{10}ClN_3O_2$; *28797-48-0*)   see: Pirenzepine

10-(chloroacetyl)-10H-phenothiazine
($C_{14}H_{10}ClNOS$; *786-50-5*)   see: Fenoverine

N-[[2-(chloroacetyl)-1,2,3,4-tetrahydro-1-isoquinoli-nyl]methyl]cyclohexanecarboxamide
($C_{19}H_{25}ClN_2O_2$; *104916-35-0*)   see: Praziquantel

9-chloroacridine
($C_{13}H_8ClN$; *1207-69-8*)   see: Amsacrine

2-chloroacrylonitrile
(C_3H_2ClN; *920-37-6*)   see: Dinoprost

2-chloroadenosine
($C_{10}H_{12}ClN_5O_4$; *146-77-0*)   see: Cladribine

β-chloro-L-alanine
($C_3H_6ClNO_2$; *2731-73-9*)   see: Oxitriptan

3-chloro-D-alanine methyl ester hydrochloride
($C_4H_9Cl_2NO_2$; *112346-82-4*)   see: Cycloserine

(3β,17β)-17-(chloroamino)androst-5-en-3-ol
($C_{19}H_{30}ClNO$)   see: Prasterone

5-chloro-2-aminobenzenesulfamide
($C_6H_7ClN_2O_2S$; *5790-69-2*)   see: Diazoxide

4-chloro-β-(aminomethyl)benzenepropanoic acid ethyl ester
($C_{12}H_{16}ClNO_2$; *232597-00-1*)   see: Baclofen

2-chloro-3-aminopyridine
($C_5H_5ClN_2$; *6298-19-7*)   see: Pirenzepine

2-chloroaniline
(C_6H_6ClN; *95-51-2*)   see: Mecloqualone

3-chloroaniline
(C_6H_6ClN; *108-42-9*)   see: Chloroquine; Chlorothiazide

4-chloroaniline
(C_6H_6ClN; *106-47-8*)   see: Acetarsol; Alprazolam; Diazepam; Efavirenz; Flunitrazepam; Flutoprazepam; Medazepam; Quazepam

4-chloroaniline hydrochloride
($C_6H_7Cl_2N$; *20265-96-7*)   see: Chlorhexidine; Proguanil

8-chloroazatadine
($C_{20}H_{21}ClN_2$; *38092-89-6*)   see: Desloratadine; Loratadine

o-chlorobenzaldehyde
(C_7H_5ClO; *89-98-5*)   see: Amlodipine; Clobenzorex; Clopidogrel hydrogensulfate; Cloxacillin

4-chlorobenzaldehyde
(C_7H_5ClO; *104-88-1*)   see: Baclofen; Carbinoxamine; Chlormezanone; Chloropyramine; Nicoclonate

2-chlorobenzaldehyde oxime
(C_7H_6ClNO; *3717-28-0*)   see: Cloxacillin

chlorobenzene
(C_6H_5Cl; *108-90-7*)   see: Chlortalidone; Mitotane; Setastine

4-chlorobenzenediazonium chloride
($C_6H_4Cl_2N_2$; *2028-74-2*)   see: Abacavir; Acetarsol; Azimilide hydrochloride; Diazepam

4-chlorobenzenesulfonamide
($C_6H_6ClNO_2S$; *98-64-6*)   see: Chlorpropamide

4-chlorobenzhydrol
($C_{13}H_{11}ClO$; *119-56-2*)   see: Cloperastine

2-chlorobenzhydryl chloride
($C_{13}H_{10}Cl_2$; *56961-47-8*)   see: Chlorbenzoxamine

4-chlorobenzhydryl chloride
($C_{13}H_{10}Cl_2$; *134-83-8*)   see: Buclizine; Cetirizine; Chlorcyclizine; Clobenztropine

1-(4-chlorobenzhydryl)piperazine
($C_{17}H_{19}ClN_2$; *303-26-4*)   see: Buclizine; Cetirizine; Etodroxizine; Hydroxyzine; Meclozine

2-chlorobenzimidazole
($C_7H_5ClN_2$; *4857-06-1*)   see: Emedastine

2-chlorobenzoic acid
($C_7H_5ClO_2$; *118-91-2*)   see: Amsacrine; Diclofenac; Flufenamic acid; Thioridazine

4-chlorobenzoic acid
($C_7H_5ClO_2$; *74-11-3*)   see: Bumetanide; Clopamide; Iodamide; Progabide; Tripamide

4-chlorobenzoic acid (3-carboxy-1-methylpropylidene)(4-methoxyphenyl)hydrazide
($C_{19}H_{19}ClN_2O_4$; *69038-50-2*)   see: Indometacin

4-chlorobenzoic acid ethylidene(4-methoxyphenyl)-hydrazide
($C_{16}H_{15}ClN_2O_2$; *13815-59-3*)   see: Indometacin

4-chlorobenzoic acid 4-fluorophenyl ester
($C_{13}H_8ClFO_2$; *29558-88-1*)   see: Progabide

4-chlorobenzoic acid 1-(4-methoxyphenyl)hydrazide hy-drochloride
($C_{14}H_{14}Cl_2N_2O_2$; *16390-18-4*)   see: Indometacin

4-chlorobenzoic acid methyl ester
($C_8H_7ClO_2$; *1126-46-1*)   see: Moclobemide

2-chlorobenzoic acid potassium salt
($C_7H_4ClKO_2$; *16463-38-0*)   see: Thiethylperazine

2-chlorobenzonitrile
(C_7H_4ClN; *873-32-5*)   see: Ketamine; Repaglinide

3-chlorobenzonitrile
(C_7H_4ClN; *766-84-7*)   see: Amfebutamone

2-chlorobenzophenone
($C_{13}H_9ClO$; *5162-03-8*)   see: Clofedanol; Clotrimazole

4-chlorobutyryl chloride
($C_4H_6Cl_2O$; *4635-59-0*)   see: Bromperidol; Fexofenadine hydrochloride; Haloperidol

8-chlorocaffeine
($C_8H_9ClN_4O_2$; *4921-49-7*)   see: Cafaminol

α-(chlorocarbonyl)benzeneacetic acid
($C_9H_7ClO_3$; *41393-81-1*)   see: Carfecillin

α-(chlorocarbonyl)benzeneacetic acid phenyl ester
($C_{15}H_{11}ClO_3$; *27031-18-1*)   see: Carfecillin

α-(chlorocarbonyl)benzenemethanesulfonic acid
($C_8H_7ClO_4S$; *40125-73-3*)   see: Sulbenicillin

(S)-γ-(chlorocarbonyl)-1,3-dihydro-1,3-dioxo-2H-iso-indole-2-butanoic acid phenylmethyl ester
($C_{20}H_{16}ClNO_5$; *88767-16-2*)   see: Cilazapril

1-chlorocarbonyl-4-methylpiperazine
($C_6H_{11}ClN_2O$; *39539-66-7*)   see: Zopiclone

3-(chlorocarbonyl)-5-nitrobenzoic acid methyl ester
($C_9H_6ClNO_5$; *1955-04-0*)   see: Ioxitalamic acid

3-[(chlorocarbonyl)oxy]-3-(dimethylamino)-2-methyl-1-ethoxypropylium chloride
($C_9H_{17}Cl_2NO_3$)   see: Sulfaperin

N-[[(chlorocarbonyl)oxy]methylene]-N-methylmethan-aminium chloride
($C_4H_7Cl_2NO_2$; *53726-30-0*)   see: Sulfaperin

α-(chlorocarbonyl)-3-thiopheneacetic acid
($C_7H_5ClO_3S$; *60822-08-4*)   see: Ticarcillin

6-chloro-5-(chloroacetyl)-1,3-dihydro-2H-indol-2-one
($C_{10}H_7Cl_2NO_2$; *118307-04-3*)   see: Ziprasidone hydrochloride

N-[[1-[4-chloro-2-(2-chlorobenzoyl)phenyl]-3-[(dimethyl-amino)carbonyl]-1H-1,2,4-triazol-5-yl]methyl]-1,3-dihy-dro-1,3-dioxo-2H-isoindole-2-acetamide
($C_{29}H_{22}Cl_2N_6O_5$; *65699-00-5*)   see: Rilmazafone

7-chloro-5-(1-chlorocyclohexyl)-1,3-dihydro-2H-1,4-ben-zodiazepin-2-one
($C_{15}H_{16}Cl_2N_2O$; *10379-01-8*)   see: Tetrazepam

2-chloro-5-(1-chloro-1,3-dihydro-3-oxo-1-isobenzofura-nyl)benzenesulfonyl chloride
($C_{14}H_7Cl_3O_4S$; *68592-11-0*)   see: Chlortalidone

β-chloro-N-(2-chloroethyl)benzeneethanamine hydrochlo-ride
($C_{10}H_{14}Cl_3N$; *40371-11-7*)   see: Levamisole

β-chloro-N-(2-chloroethyl)-N-methylbenzeneethanamine
($C_{11}H_{15}Cl_2N$; *22270-22-0*)   see: Mianserin

6-chloro-5-(2-chloroethyl)oxindole
($C_{10}H_9Cl_2NO$; *118289-55-7*)   see: Ziprasidone hydrochloride

2-chloro-3-(2-chloroethyl)tetrahydro-2H-1,3,2-oxazaphos-phorine 2-oxide
($C_5H_{10}Cl_2NO_2P$; *40722-73-4*)   see: Ifosfamide

6-chloro-2-(chloromethyl)-4-(2-chlorophenyl)quinazoline 3-oxide
($C_{15}H_9Cl_3N_2O$; *13949-50-3*)   see: Lorazepam

6-chloro-3-(chloromethyl)-3,4-dihydro-2H-1,2,4-benzo-thiadiazine-7-sulfonamide 1,1-dioxide
($C_8H_9Cl_2N_3O_4S_2$; *1824-47-1*)   see: Altizide

2-chloro-N-(2-chloro-6-methylphenyl)acetamide
($C_9H_9Cl_2NO$; *6307-67-1*)   see: Butanilicaine

6-chloro-2-(chloromethyl)-4-phenylquinazoline 3-oxide
($C_{15}H_{10}Cl_2N_2O$; *5958-24-7*)   see: Camazepam; Chlordiazepoxide; Oxazepam

2-chloro-N-(2-chloro-4-methyl-3-pyridinyl)-3-pyridine-carboxamide
($C_{12}H_9Cl_2N_3O$; *133627-46-0*)   see: Nevirapine

2-chloro-3-(chloromethyl)thiophene
($C_5H_4Cl_2S$; *109459-94-1*)   see: Tioconazole

5-chloro-2-chloromethylthiophene
($C_5H_4Cl_2S$; *23784-96-5*)   see: Chloropyrilene

3-chloro-4-(3-chloro-2-nitrophenyl)-1H-pyrrole-2,5-di-carboxylic acid
($C_{12}H_6Cl_2N_2O_6$; *5875-88-7*)   see: Pyrrolnitrin

7-chloro-5-(2-chlorophenyl)-1,3-dihydro-2H-1,4-benzodi-azepin-2-one 4-oxide
($C_{15}H_{10}Cl_2N_2O_2$; *2955-37-5*)   see: Lorazepam

6-chloro-2-(4-chlorophenyl)-3-[(dimethylamino)methyl]-imidazo[1,2-a]pyridine
($C_{16}H_{15}Cl_2N_3$)   see: Alpidem

6-chloro-2-(4-chlorophenyl)imidazo[1,2-a]pyridine
($C_{13}H_8Cl_2N_2$; *88964-99-2*)   see: Alpidem

6-chloro-2-(4-chlorophenyl)imidazo[1,2-a]pyridine-3-acetic acid
($C_{15}H_{10}Cl_2N_2O_2$; *82626-74-2*)   see: Alpidem

7-chloro-5-(o-chlorophenyl)-2-(methylamino)-3H-1,4-ben-zodiazepine 4-oxide
($C_{16}H_{13}Cl_2N_3O$; *13949-51-4*)   see: Lorazepam

7-chloro-5-(2-chlorophenyl)-1-methyl-2-oxo-1,3-dihydro-2H-1,4-benzodiazepine 4-oxide
($C_{16}H_{12}Cl_2N_2O_2$; *4187-04-6*)   see: Lormetazepam

7-chloro-5-(2-chlorophenyl)-2-oxo-2,3-dihydro-1H-1,4-benzodiazepine
($C_{15}H_{10}Cl_2N_2O$; *2894-67-9*)   see: Triazolam

7-chloro-5-(2-chlorophenyl)-2-thioxo-2,3-dihydro-1H-1,4-benzodiazepine
($C_{15}H_{10}Cl_2N_2S$; *2894-71-5*)   see: Triazolam

3-chloro-5-(3-chloropropyl)-10,11-dihydro-5H-dibenz-[b,f]azepine
($C_{17}H_{17}Cl_2N$; *51551-41-8*)   see: Clocapramine

2-chloro-10-(3-chloropropyl)phenothiazine
($C_{15}H_{13}Cl_2NS$; *2765-59-5*)   see: Perphenazine; Pipamazine; Prochlorperazine

4-chloro-3-(chlorosulfonyl)benzoic acid
($C_7H_4Cl_2O_4S$; *2494-79-3*)   see: Bumetanide; Clopamide

2-[4-chloro-3-(chlorosulfonyl)benzoyl]benzoic acid
($C_{14}H_8Cl_2O_5S$; *68592-12-1*)   see: Chlortalidone

4-chloro-5-(chlorosulfonyl)-2-hydroxybenzoic acid
($C_7H_4Cl_2O_5S$; *14665-31-7*)   see: Xipamide

4-chloro-3-(chlorosulfonyl)-5-nitrobenzoic acid
($C_7H_3Cl_2NO_6S$; *22892-95-1*)   see: Bumetanide

6α-chlorocortisone
($C_{23}H_{29}ClO_6$; *16319-99-6*)   see: Chloroprednisone acetate

2'-chloro-2-cyanoacetophenone
see under 2-chlorobenzoyl-acetonitrile

2-chloro-5-cyano-4-fluorobenzenesulfonamide
($C_7H_4ClFN_2O_2S$; *27589-31-7*)   see: Azosemide

3-chloro-2-cyanopyrazine
($C_5H_2ClN_3$; *55557-52-3*)   see: Sulfalene

2-chloro-5-cyano-N^4-2-thenylsulfanilamide
($C_{12}H_{10}ClN_3O_2S_2$; *27589-57-7*)   see: Azosemide

7-chloro-1,3-dihydro-1-methyl-5-phenyl-2H-1,4-benzodiazepin-2-one 4-oxide

($C_{16}H_{13}ClN_2O_2$; *2888-64-4*)   see: Camazepam; Temazepam

8-chloro-6,11-dihydro-11-(1-methyl-4-piperidinyl)-5H-benzo[5,6]cyclohepta[1,2-b]pyridin-11-ol

($C_{20}H_{23}ClN_2O$; *38089-93-9*)   see: Loratadine

6-chloro-3,4-dihydro-3-oxo-2H-1,2,4-benzothiadiazine-7-sulfonamide S,S-dioxide

($C_7H_6ClN_3O_5S_2$; *89813-56-9*)   see: Ambuside; Methyclothiazide

2-chloro-5-(1,3-dihydro-3-oxo-1-isobenzofuranyl)benzenesulfonyl chloride

($C_{14}H_8Cl_2O_4S$; *73617-81-9*)   see: Chlortalidone

2-chloro-5-(2,3-dihydro-3-oxo-1H-isoindol-1-yl)benzenesulfonamide

($C_{14}H_{11}ClN_2O_3S$; *82875-49-8*)   see: Chlortalidone

7-chloro-2,3-dihydro-2-oxo-5-phenyl-1H-1,4-benzodiazepine-3-carboxylic acid ethyl ester

($C_{18}H_{15}ClN_2O_3$; *5606-55-3*)   see: Dipotassium clorazepate

7-chloro-2,3-dihydro-5-phenyl-1H-1,4-benzodiazepine

($C_{15}H_{13}ClN_2$; *1694-78-6*)   see: Medazepam

(Z)-7-chloro-1,3-dihydro-5-phenyl-2H-1,4-benzodiazepin-2-one hydrazone

($C_{15}H_{13}ClN_4$; *112393-62-1*)   see: Estazolam

8-chloro-6,11-dihydro-11-(4-piperidinylidene)-5H-benzo[5,6]cyclohepta[1,2-b]pyridine

($C_{19}H_{19}ClN_2$; *100643-71-8*)   see: Loratadine

(4S)-6-chloro-3,4-dihydro-2H-thieno[3,2-e]-1,2-thiazin-4-ol 1,1-dioxide

($C_6H_6ClNO_3S_2$; *160982-16-1*)   see: Brinzolamide

2-chloro-3',4'-dihydroxyacetophenone

($C_8H_7ClO_3$; *99-40-1*)   see: Adrenalone; Bitolterol; Dipivefrine; Epinephrine; Hexoprenaline; Isoprenaline; Protokylol; Theodrenaline

3-chloro-1,2-dihydroxypropane

($C_3H_7ClO_2$; *96-24-2*)   see: Chlorphenesin; Diprophylline; Doxofylline; Guaifenesin; Guanadrel; Iohexol; Iopydol; Mephenesin

2-chloro-1-(1,2-dimesyloxyethyl)benzene

($C_{10}H_{13}ClO_6S_2$; *110309-60-9*)   see: Lanoconazole

2-chloro-3,4-dimethoxybenzaldehyde

($C_9H_9ClO_3$; *5417-17-4*)   see: Fenoldopam mesilate

4'-chloro-3,5-dimethoxy-4-hydroxybenzophenone

($C_{15}H_{13}ClO_4$; *54094-08-5*)   see: Morclofone

2-chloro-3,4-dimethoxyphenylacetonitrile

($C_{10}H_{10}ClNO_2$; *7537-07-7*)   see: Fenoldopam mesilate

2-(2-chloro-3,4-dimethoxyphenyl)ethylamine

($C_{10}H_{14}ClNO_2$; *67287-36-9*)   see: Fenoldopam mesilate

α-[[[2-(2-chloro-3,4-dimethoxyphenyl)ethyl]amino]methyl]-4-methoxybenzenemethanol

($C_{19}H_{24}ClNO_4$; *71636-38-9*)   see: Fenoldopam mesilate

2-chloro-N-[2-(2,5-dimethoxyphenyl)-2-oxoethyl]acetamide

($C_{12}H_{14}ClNO_4$; *59908-77-9*)   see: Midodrine

α-chloro-2,6-dimethylacetanilide

($C_{10}H_{12}ClNO$; *1131-01-7*)   see: Lidocaine; Lidoflazine; Pyrrocaine

[1S-(1α,4aα,5β,5aα,11β,11aα,12α,12aα)]-5a-chloro-1-(dimethylamino)-1,4,4a,5,5a,6,11,11a,12,12a-decahydro-2,4a,5,7,12-pentahydroxy-11-methyl-4,6-dioxo-5,11-epoxynaphthacene-3-carboxamide

($C_{22}H_{23}ClN_2O_9$; *35689-72-6*)   see: Doxycycline

[4S-(4α,4aα,5α,5aα,11aα,12aα)]-11a-chloro-4-(dimethylamino)-1,4,4a,5,5a,6,11,11a,12,12a-decahydro-3,5,10,12a-tetrahydroxy-6-methylene-1,11,12-trioxo-2-naphthacenecarboxamide

($C_{22}H_{21}ClN_2O_8$; *31461-51-5*)   see: Doxycycline

1-chloro-3-dimethylamino-2-methylpropane

($C_6H_{14}ClN$; *23349-86-2*)   see: Alimemazine; Cyamemazine; Etymemazine; Levomepromazine; Oxomemazine; Trimipramine

2'-chloro-3-dimethylaminopropiophenone

($C_{11}H_{14}ClNO$; *91131-19-0*)   see: Clofedanol

2-chloro-9-[3-(dimethylamino)propyl]-9H-thioxanthen-9-ol

($C_{18}H_{20}ClNOS$; *4295-65-2*)   see: Chlorprothixene

[R-(R*,S*)]-β-chloro-N,α-dimethylbenzeneethanamine

($C_{10}H_{14}ClN$; *110925-64-9*)   see: Thiadrine

2-chloro-N,N-dimethylbutyramide

($C_6H_{12}ClNO$; *59843-83-3*)   see: Cropropamide; Crotetamide

6-chloro-9-[2-(2,2-dimethyl-1,3-dioxan-5-yl)ethyl]-9H-purin-2-amine

($C_{13}H_{18}ClN_5O_2$; *97845-59-5*)   see: Penciclovir

[6R-[6α,7β(R*)]]-3-chloro-7-[[[[(1,1-dimethylethoxy)carbonyl]amino]phenylacetyl]amino]-8-oxo-5-thia-1-azabicyclo[4.2.0]oct-2-ene-2-carboxylic acid (4-nitrophenyl)methyl ester

($C_{27}H_{27}ClN_4O_8S$; *53994-84-6*)   see: Cefaclor

(S)-7-chloro-2-[(E)-2-[3-[1-[[(1,1-dimethylethyl)dimethylsilyl]oxy]-3-[2-[1-methyl-1-[(tetrahydro-2H-pyran-2-yl)oxy]ethyl]phenyl]propyl]phenyl]ethenyl]quinoline

($C_{40}H_{50}ClNO_3Si$)   see: Montelukast sodium

4-chloro-2,3-dimethylpyridine N-oxide

(C_7H_8ClNO; *59886-90-7*)   see: Rabeprazole sodium

6-chloro-1,3-dimethyluracil

($C_6H_7ClN_2O_2$; *6972-27-6*)   see: Urapidil

2-chloro-1,3,2-dioxaphospholane 2-oxide

($C_2H_4ClO_3P$; *6609-64-9*)   see: Miltefosine

α-chlorodiphenylacetyl chloride

($C_{14}H_{10}Cl_2O$; *2902-98-9*)   see: Trospium chloride

1-(4-chlorodiphenylmethyl)piperazine

see under 1-(4-chlorobenzhydryl)piperazine

4-chloro-2,6-dipyrrolidinopyrimidine

($C_{12}H_{17}ClN_4$; *111669-15-9*)   see: Tirilazad mesilate

5-chloro-2,4-disulfamoylaniline

see under 4-amino-6-chloro-1,3-benzenedisulfamide

21-chloro-9β,11β-epoxy-3-ethoxy-16β-methyl-17-propionyloxypregna-3,5-dien-20-one

($C_{27}H_{37}ClO_5$; *83880-41-5*)   see: Ulobetasol propionate

21-chloro-9β,11β-epoxy-6α-fluoro-16β-methyl-17-propionyloxypregn-4-ene-3,20-dione

($C_{25}H_{32}ClFO_5$; *66852-57-1*)   see: Ulobetasol propionate

21-chloro-9β,11β-epoxy-16β-methyl-17-propionyloxypregn-4-ene-3,20-dione

($C_{25}H_{33}ClO_5$; *66852-55-9*)   see: Ulobetasol propionate

5-chloro-N-ethoxycarbonyl-2-methylaniline

($C_{10}H_{12}ClNO_2$; *35442-34-3*)   see: Metolazone

10-chloro-9-fluoro-2,3-dihydro-7-oxo-7*H*-pyrido[1,2,3-*de*]-1,4-benzothiazine-6-carboxylic acid 1-oxide
(C$_{12}$H$_7$ClFNO$_4$S; *101337-84-2*)   see: Rufloxacin hydrochloride

7-chloro-6-fluoro-1,4-dihydro-4-oxo-3-quinolinecarboxylic acid ethyl ester
(C$_{12}$H$_9$ClFNO$_3$; *75073-15-3*)   see: Norfloxacin

2-chloro-6-fluoro-*N*-hydroxybenzenecarboximidoyl chloride
(C$_7$H$_4$Cl$_2$FNO; *51088-25-6*)   see: Flucloxacillin

4-chloro-5-fluoro-2-(methylthio)pyrimidine
(C$_5$H$_4$ClFN$_2$S; *6096-45-3*)   see: Flucytosine

8-chloro-7-fluoro-3-oxo-3,4-dihydro-2*H*-1,4-benzothiazine
(C$_8$H$_5$ClFNOS; *101337-95-5*)   see: Rufloxacin hydrochloride

5-chloro-2-[(4-fluorophenyl)amino]benzoic acid methyl ester
(C$_{14}$H$_{11}$ClFNO$_2$)   see: Sertindole

[[(3-chloro-4-fluorophenyl)amino]methylene]propanedioic acid diethyl ester
(C$_{14}$H$_{15}$ClFNO$_4$; *70032-30-3*)   see: Norfloxacin; Pefloxacin

7-chloro-5-(2-fluorophenyl)-1,3-dihydro-2*H*-1,4-benzodiazepin-2-one
(C$_{15}$H$_{10}$ClFN$_2$O; *2886-65-9*)   see: Cinolazepam; Doxefazepam; Flutazolam; Flutoprazepam; Midazolam

***N*-[[7-chloro-5-(2-fluorophenyl)-2,3-dihydro-1*H*-1,4-benzodiazepin-2-yl]methyl]acetamide**
(C$_{18}$H$_{17}$ClFN$_3$O; *59467-68-4*)   see: Midazolam

7-chloro-5-(2-fluorophenyl)-1,3-dihydro-1-(2-hydroxyethyl)-2*H*-1,4-benzodiazepin-2-one 4-oxide
(C$_{17}$H$_{14}$ClFN$_2$O$_3$)   see: Doxefazepam

5-chloro-1-(4-fluorophenyl)-1,2-dihydro-3*H*-indol-3-one
(C$_{14}$H$_9$ClFNO; *170232-17-4*)   see: Sertindole

8-chloro-6-(2-fluorophenyl)-3a,4-dihydro-1-methyl-3*H*-imidazo[1,5-*a*][1,4]benzodiazepine
(C$_{18}$H$_{15}$ClFN$_3$; *59467-69-5*)   see: Midazolam

7-chloro-5-(2-fluorophenyl)-2,3-dihydro-2-(nitromethylene)-1*H*-1,4-benzodiazepine
(C$_{16}$H$_{11}$ClFN$_3$O$_2$; *59467-63-9*)   see: Midazolam

7-chloro-5-(2-fluorophenyl)-1,3-dihydro-1-(2,2,2-trifluoroethyl)-2*H*-1,4-benzodiazepin-2-one
(C$_{17}$H$_{11}$ClF$_4$N$_2$O; *49606-44-2*)   see: Quazepam

5-chloro-3-(2-fluorophenyl)-1*H*-indole-2-carbonitrile
(C$_{15}$H$_8$ClFN$_2$; *24106-94-3*)   see: Flutoprazepam

5-chloro-3-(2-fluorophenyl)indole-2-carbonyl chloride
(C$_{15}$H$_8$Cl$_2$FNO; *32502-22-0*)   see: Flutoprazepam

1-[2-[4-[5-chloro-1-(4-fluorophenyl)-1*H*-indol-3-yl]-3,6-dihydro-1(2*H*)-pyridinyl]ethyl]-2-imidazolidinone
(C$_{24}$H$_{24}$ClFN$_4$O; *106516-54-5*)   see: Sertindole

5-chloro-2-[(4-fluorophenyl)[(methoxycarbonyl)methyl]amino]benzoic acid methyl ester
(C$_{17}$H$_{15}$ClFNO$_4$)   see: Sertindole

7-chloro-5-(2-fluorophenyl)-*N*-methyl-3*H*-1,4-benzodiazepin-2-amine
(C$_{16}$H$_{13}$ClFN$_3$; *59467-61-7*)   see: Midazolam

3-(2-chloro-6-fluorophenyl)-5-methyl-4-isoxazolecarbonyl chloride
(C$_{11}$H$_6$Cl$_2$FNO$_2$; *69399-79-7*)   see: Flucloxacillin

3-(2-chloro-6-fluorophenyl)-5-methyl-4-isoxazolecarboxylic acid
(C$_{11}$H$_7$ClFNO$_3$; *3919-74-2*)   see: Flucloxacillin

3-(2-chloro-6-fluorophenyl)-5-methyl-4-isoxazolecarboxylic acid methyl ester
(C$_{12}$H$_9$ClFNO$_3$; *4415-09-2*)   see: Flucloxacillin

7-chloro-5-(2-fluorophenyl)-*N*-methyl-*N*-nitroso-3*H*-1,4-benzodiazepin-2-amine
(C$_{16}$H$_{12}$ClFN$_4$O; *59467-62-8*)   see: Midazolam

5-chloro-1-(4-fluorophenyl)-3-(1,2,3,6-tetrahydro-4-pyridinyl)-1*H*-indole
(C$_{19}$H$_{16}$ClFN$_2$; *106516-07-8*)   see: Sertindole

(11β,16α)-21-chloro-9-fluoro-11,16,17-trihydroxypregn-4-ene-3,20-dione
(C$_{21}$H$_{28}$ClFO$_5$; *982-91-2*)   see: Halcinonide

chloroform
(CHCl$_3$; *67-66-3*)   see: Chlorobutanol; Ciprofibrate; Clinofibrate; Clofibrate; Fenofibrate

chloroformic acid ethyl ester
(C$_3$H$_5$ClO$_2$; *541-41-3*)   see: Alfuzosin; Amoxapine; Amoxicillin; Ampicillin; Apalcillin; Azidocillin; Butorphanol; Carbimazole; Cefbuperazone; Cefradine; Cinitapride; Cisapride; Clebopride; Desipramine; Dibekacin; Docarpamine; Ebastine; Fluoxetine; Flupirtine; Foscarnet sodium; Ketanserin; Loratadine; Loteprednol etabonate; Loxapine; Metahexamide; Metolazone; Molsidomine; Moracizine; Nemonapride; Nipradilol; Nortriptyline; Paroxetine; Romurtide; Telmesteine; Tiracizine; Todralazine; Tolazamide

chloroformic acid isobutyl ester
(C$_5$H$_9$ClO$_2$; *543-27-1*)   see: Aspoxicillin; Cefaloglycin; Nelfinavir mesylate; Pheneticillin; Propicillin; Sobuzoxane

(1*R*-*cis*)-*N*-[4-chloro-5-(formylamino)-6-[[4-(hydroxymethyl)-2-cyclopenten-1-yl]amino]-2-pyrimidinyl]acetamide
(C$_{13}$H$_{16}$ClN$_5$O$_3$; *136522-32-2*)   see: Abacavir

***N*-chloroformyl-bis(2-chloroethyl)amine**
(C$_5$H$_8$Cl$_3$NO; *2998-56-3*)   see: Estramustine phosphate

1-chloroformylimidazolidinone
(C$_4$H$_5$ClN$_2$O$_2$; *13214-53-4*)   see: Azlocillin

3-chloroformyl-1-methanesulfonyl-2-imidazolidinone
(C$_5$H$_7$ClN$_2$O$_4$S; *41762-76-9*)   see: Mezlocillin

8-chloroformyl-3-methylflavone
(C$_{17}$H$_{11}$ClO$_3$; *51950-71-1*)   see: Flavoxate

(16α)-21-chloro-17-[(2-furanylcarbonyl)oxy]-16-methylpregna-1,4,9(11)-triene-3,20-dione
(C$_{27}$H$_{29}$ClO$_5$; *83880-65-3*)   see: Mometasone furoate

chloroglyoxylic acid ethyl ester
(C$_4$H$_5$ClO$_3$; *4755-77-5*)   see: Oxitefonium bromide; Penthienate methobromide; Tiaprofenic acid

6-chloro-2-hydrazino-4-phenylquinoline
(C$_{15}$H$_{12}$ClN$_3$; *27537-93-5*)   see: Alprazolam

6α-chlorohydrocortisone
(C$_{21}$H$_{29}$ClO$_5$; *96744-43-3*)   see: Cloprednol

6α-chlorohydrocortisone 21-acetate
(C$_{23}$H$_{31}$ClO$_6$; *112652-74-1*)   see: Cloprednol

3-chloro-4-hydroxybenzaldehyde
(C$_7$H$_5$ClO$_2$; *2420-16-8*)   see: Alclofenac

2-chloro-*N*-hydroxybenzenecarboximidoyl chloride
(C$_7$H$_5$Cl$_2$NO; *29568-74-9*)   see: Cloxacillin

2-(chloromethyl)-2,3-dihydro-1,4-benzodioxin
($C_9H_9ClO_2$; *2164-33-2*)   see: Guanoxan

4-chloromethyl-6,7-dihydroxychromen-2-one
($C_{10}H_7ClO_4$; *85029-91-0*)   see: Folescutol

2-chloromethyl-3,4-dimethoxypyridinium chloride
($C_8H_{11}Cl_2NO_2$; *72830-09-2*)   see: Pantoprazole sodium

[6R-[6α,7β(Z)]]-3-(chloromethyl)-7-[[[[2-(1,1-dimethyl-ethoxy)-2-oxoethoxy]imino][2-(formylamino)-4-thiazolyl]-acetyl]amino]-8-oxo-5-thia-1-azabicyclo[4.2.0]oct-2-ene-2-carboxylic acid diphenylmethyl ester
($C_{33}H_{32}ClN_5O_8S_2$; *79349-95-4*)   see: Cefixime

2-[5-(chloromethyl)-3-(1,1-dimethylethyl)-2-oxazolidinyl]-4-fluorophenol
($C_{14}H_{19}ClFNO_2$; *58929-09-2*)   see: Butofilolol

2-(chloromethyl)-1,4-dioxaspiro[4.5]decane
($C_9H_{15}ClO_2$; *5503-32-2*)   see: Guanadrel

3-(chloromethyl)-5,5-diphenylhydantoin
($C_{16}H_{13}ClN_2O_2$; *93360-07-7*)   see: Fosphenytoin sodium

[1R-[1α,5α,6(R*)]]-α-[1-(chloromethyl)ethenyl]-7-oxo-3-phenyl-4-oxa-2,6-diazabicyclo[3.2.0]hept-2-ene-6-acetic acid diphenylmethyl ester
($C_{28}H_{23}ClN_2O_4$; *67977-79-1*)   see: Latamoxef

1-[3-(chloromethyl)-4-hydroxyphenyl]ethanone
($C_9H_9ClO_2$; *24085-05-0*)   see: Salbutamol

2-chloromethyl-Δ²-imidazoline
($C_4H_7ClN_2$; *50342-08-0*)   see: Antazoline

2-chloromethyl-Δ²-imidazoline hydrochloride
($C_4H_8Cl_2N_2$; *13338-49-3*)   see: Phentolamine

chloromethyl iodide
(CH_2ClI; *593-71-5*)   see: Loteprednol etabonate

4-(chloromethyl)-2-isopropylthiazole hydrochloride
($C_7H_{11}Cl_2NS$; *65386-28-9*)   see: Ritonavir

1-(chloromethyl)-4-methoxybenzene
(C_8H_9ClO; *824-94-2*)   see: Meropenem

2-(chloromethyl)-4-methoxy-3,5-dimethylpyridine
($C_9H_{12}ClNO$; *84006-10-0*)   see: Omeprazole

2-(chloromethyl)-4-(3-methoxypropoxy)-3-methylpyridine
($C_{11}H_{16}ClNO_2$; *117977-20-5*)   see: Rabeprazole sodium

4-(chloromethyl)-α-methylbenzeneacetic acid ethyl ester
($C_{12}H_{15}ClO_2$; *43153-03-3*)   see: Loxoprofen

chloromethyl methyl ether
(C_2H_5ClO; *107-30-2*)   see: Cefoxitin; Troglitazone

3-(chloromethyl)-1-methylpiperidine
($C_7H_{14}ClN$; *52694-50-5*)   see: Metixene

2-chloromethyl-1-methyl-1,4,5,6-tetrahydropyrimidine
($C_6H_{11}ClN_2$)   see: Oxyphencyclimine

4-chloro-2-methyl-5-(4-morpholinyl)-3(2H)-pyridazinone
($C_9H_{12}ClN_3O_2$; *1080-85-9*)   see: Emorfazone

1-chloromethylnaphthalene
($C_{11}H_9Cl$; *86-52-2*)   see: Butenafine; Naftidrofuryl

5-chloro-1-methyl-4-nitro-1H-imidazole
($C_4H_4ClN_3O_2$; *4897-25-0*)   see: Azathioprine

6-chloro-2-methyl-4-oxo-4H-3,1-benzoxazine
($C_9H_6ClNO_2$; *7033-50-3*)   see: Tetrazepam

2-chloromethylphenethyl benzoate
($C_{16}H_{15}ClO_2$; *168476-58-2*)   see: Ropinirole

2-chloro-5-methylphenol
(C_7H_7ClO; *615-74-7*)   see: Bupranolol

5-(4-chloromethylphenoxymethyl)-3-isopropyl-2-oxazoli-dinone
($C_{14}H_{18}ClNO_3$; *87844-82-4*)   see: Bisoprolol

4-chloro-2-[(methylphenylamino)sulfonyl]benzoic acid methyl ester
($C_{15}H_{14}ClNO_4S$)   see: Tianeptine sodium

2-chloro-N-methyl-N-(phenyl-tert-butyl)acetamide
($C_{13}H_{18}ClNO$; *2293-55-2*)   see: Oxetacaine

(2-chloro-4-methylphenyl)carbamimidothioic acid methyl ester monohydroiodide
($C_9H_{12}ClIN_2S$; *52041-81-3*)   see: Tolonidine

(2-chloro-5-methylphenyl) glycidyl ether
($C_{10}H_{11}ClO_2$; *53732-26-6*)   see: Bupranolol

5-chloro-1-methyl-3-phenyl-1H-indole-2-carboxamide
($C_{16}H_{13}ClN_2O$; *21139-24-2*)   see: Diazepam

5-chloro-1-methyl-3-phenyl-1H-indole-2-carboxylic acid ethyl ester
($C_{18}H_{16}ClNO_2$; *21139-26-4*)   see: Diazepam

3-chloro-4-methyl-6-phenylpyridazine
($C_{11}H_9ClN_2$; *28657-39-8*)   see: Minaprine

N-(2-chloro-4-methylphenyl)thiourea
($C_8H_9ClN_2S$; *57005-14-8*)   see: Tolonidine

7-chloro-1-methyl-5-phenyl[1,2,4]triazolo[4,3-a]quinoline
($C_{17}H_{12}ClN_3$; *36916-18-4*)   see: Alprazolam

(chloromethyl)phosphonic dichloride
(CH_2Cl_3OP; *1983-26-2*)   see: Cidofovir

3-chloro-1-methylpiperidine
($C_6H_{12}ClN$; *22704-36-5*)   see: Mepenzolate bromide

4-chloro-1-methylpiperidine
($C_6H_{12}ClN$; *5570-77-4*)   see: Cyproheptadine; Propiverine

chloromethyl pivalate
($C_6H_{11}ClO_2$; *18997-19-8*)   see: Pivampicillin;
Pivmecillinam; Raltitrexed

1-chloro-2-methyl-2-propanol
(C_4H_9ClO; *558-42-9*)   see: Lercanidipine hydrochloride

1-chloro-2-methyl-1-propanol propanoate
($C_7H_{13}ClO_2$; *58304-65-7*)   see: Fosinopril

D-3-chloro-2-methylpropionyl chloride
($C_4H_6Cl_2O$; *80141-50-0*)   see: Captopril

N-[(2S)-3-chloro-2-methylpropionyl]-L-proline
($C_9H_{14}ClNO_3$; *80141-53-3*)   see: Captopril

N-[1-(chloromethyl)propyl]acetamide
($C_6H_{12}ClNO$; *59173-61-4*)   see: Ethambutol

4-chloro-1-(2-methylpropyl)-1H-imidazo[4,5-c]quinoline
($C_{14}H_{14}ClN_3$; *99010-64-7*)   see: Imiquimod

10-(3-chloro-2-methylpropyl)-10H-phenothiazine
($C_{16}H_{16}ClNS$; *40256-08-4*)   see: Dixyrazine

2-chloro-N⁴-(2-methylpropyl)-3,4-quinolinediamine
($C_{13}H_{16}ClN_3$; *133860-76-1*)   see: Imiquimod

2-(chloromethyl)pyridine
(C_6H_6ClN; *4377-33-7*)   see: Pimeprofen

4-(chloromethyl)pyridine hydrochloride
($C_6H_7Cl_2N$; *1822-51-1*)   see: Tropicamide

N-(2-chloro-4-methyl-3-pyridinyl)-2-(cyclopropylamino)-3-pyridinecarboxamide
($C_{15}H_{15}ClN_4O$; *133627-47-1*)   see: Nevirapine

4-chloro-6-methyl-2-pyrimidinamine
($C_5H_6ClN_3$; *5600-21-5*)   see: Sulfamerazine

3-chloromethyl-quinuclidine
($C_8H_{14}ClN$; *64099-45-2*)   see: Mequitazine

4-chloro-α-(1-oxopropyl)benzeneacetonitrile
($C_{11}H_{10}ClNO$; *55474-40-3*)   see: Pyrimethamine

(Z)-2-[[[2-chloro-2-oxo-1-[2-[(triphenylmethyl)amino]-4-thiazolyl]ethylidene]amino]oxy]-2-methylpropanoic acid 1,1-dimethylethyl ester
($C_{32}H_{32}ClN_3O_4S$; *91622-14-9*)   see: Ceftazidime

3-chloro-2-pentanol
($C_5H_{11}ClO$; *139121-35-0*)   see: Bifluranol

3-chloro-2-pentanone
(C_5H_9ClO; *13280-00-7*)   see: Bifluranol

5-chloro-2-pentanone
(C_5H_9ClO; *5891-21-4*)   see: Hydroxychloroquine

5-chloropentanoyl chloride
($C_5H_8Cl_2O$; *1575-61-7*)   see: Cilostazol

N-(5-chloropentanoyl)cyclohexylamine
($C_{11}H_{20}ClNO$; *15865-18-6*)   see: Cilostazol

1-chloro-1-penten-3-one
(C_5H_7ClO; *105-32-8*)   see: Ethchlorvynol

5-chloro-1-pentyne
(C_5H_7Cl; *14267-92-6*)   see: Efavirenz

m-chloroperbenzoic acid
($C_7H_5ClO_3$; *937-14-4*)   see: Dolasetron mesilate; Rabeprazole sodium

2-chlorophenol
(C_6H_5ClO; *95-57-8*)   see: Alclofenac; Diclofenamide

4-chlorophenol
(C_6H_5ClO; *106-48-9*)   see: Amoxapine; Chlorphenesin; Clofibrate; Dichlorophen; Dodeclonium bromide; Fenticlor

2-chlorophenothiazine
($C_{12}H_8ClNS$; *92-39-7*)   see: Chlorpromazine; Cyamemazine; Perphenazine; Pipamazine; Prochlorperazine

(4-chlorophenoxy)acetic acid
($C_8H_7ClO_3$; *122-88-3*)   see: Meclofenoxate

(4-chlorophenoxy)acetyl chloride
($C_8H_6Cl_2O_2$; *4122-68-3*)   see: Clofexamide; Fipexide

2-(4-chlorophenoxy)aniline
($C_{12}H_{10}ClNO$; *2770-11-8*)   see: Amoxapine; Loxapine

2-(4-chlorophenoxy)isobutyric acid
($C_{10}H_{11}ClO_3$; *882-09-7*)   see: Alufibrate; Clofibrate; Etofibrate; Simfibrate

2-(4-chlorophenoxy)-2-methylpropanoic acid 2-hydroxyethyl ester
($C_{12}H_{15}ClO_4$; *31637-96-4*)   see: Etofibrate

2-(4-chlorophenoxy)-2-methylpropanoic acid 3-hydroxypropyl ester
($C_{13}H_{17}ClO_4$; *14496-75-4*)   see: Ronifibrate

2-(4-chlorophenoxy)-2-methylpropionic acid
see under 2-(4-chlorophenoxy)isobutyric acid

[2-(4-chlorophenoxy)phenyl]carbamic acid ethyl ester
($C_{15}H_{14}ClNO_3$; *31879-60-4*)   see: Amoxapine; Loxapine

4-[[o-(p-chlorophenoxy)phenyl]carbamoyl]-1-piperazinecarboxylic acid ethyl ester
($C_{20}H_{22}ClN_3O_4$; *31879-61-5*)   see: Amoxapine

N-[2-(4-chlorophenoxy)phenyl]-4-methyl-1-piperazinecarboxamide
($C_{18}H_{20}ClN_3O_2$; *69478-73-5*)   see: Loxapine

3-(4-chlorophenoxy)-1,2-propanediol
($C_9H_{11}ClO_3$; *104-29-0*)   see: Chlorphenesin carbamate

2-chloro-2'-O-phenoxythiocarbonyl-3',5'-O-(tetraisopropyldisiloxanylene)adenosine
($C_{29}H_{42}ClN_5O_6SSi_2$; *149681-75-4*)   see: Cladribine

2-[(4-chlorophenyl)acetyl]benzoic acid
($C_{15}H_{11}ClO_3$; *53242-76-5*)   see: Azelastine

α-chlorophenylacetyl chloride
($C_8H_6Cl_2O$; *2912-62-1*)   see: Bietamiverine; Fenozolone

1-(chlorophenylacetyl)-3-ethylurea
($C_{11}H_{13}ClN_2O_2$; *23420-63-5*)   see: Fenozolone

4-chloro-D-phenylalanine
($C_9H_{10}ClNO_2$; *14091-08-8*)   see: Cetrorelix

2-chlorophenyl allyl ether
(C_9H_9ClO; *20788-42-5*)   see: Alclofenac

[[(3-chlorophenyl)amino]methylene]propanedioic acid diethyl ester
($C_{14}H_{16}ClNO_4$; *3412-99-5*)   see: Chloroquine

(4-chlorophenyl)arsonic acid
($C_6H_6AsClO_3$; *5440-04-0*)   see: Acetarsol

α-chloro-α-phenylbenzeneacetic acid 1-methyl-4-piperidinyl ester
($C_{20}H_{22}ClNO_2$; *118108-64-8*)   see: Propiverine

7-chloro-5-phenyl-3H-1,4-benzodiazepin-2-amine
($C_{15}H_{12}ClN_3$; *7564-07-0*)   see: Estazolam

1-(4-chlorophenyl)biguanide hydrochloride
($C_8H_{11}Cl_2N_5$; *4022-81-5*)   see: Chlorazanil

4-(4-chlorophenyl)-1-chloro-2-butanol
($C_{10}H_{12}Cl_2O$; *59363-13-2*)   see: Butoconazole

1-(3-chlorophenyl)-4-(3-chloropropyl)piperazine
($C_{13}H_{18}Cl_2N_2$; *39577-43-0*)   see: Etoperidone; Nefazodone hydrochloride; Trazodone

3-[3-(4-chlorophenyl)-1-(5-chloro-2-thienyl)-3-oxopropyl]-4-hydroxy-2H-1-benzopyran-2-one
($C_{22}H_{14}Cl_2O_4S$; *22619-37-0*)   see: Tioclomarol

1-(4-chlorophenyl)-3-(5-chloro-2-thienyl)-2-propen-1-one
($C_{13}H_8Cl_2OS$; *22619-36-9*)   see: Tioclomarol

1-(4-chlorophenyl)cyclobutyl cyanide
($C_{11}H_{10}ClN$; *28049-61-8*)   see: Sibutramine hydrochloride

1-(2-chlorophenyl)-2,2-dichloroethanol
($C_8H_7Cl_3O$; *27683-60-9*)   see: Mitotane

(4-chlorophenyl)dicyanodiamide
($C_8H_7ClN_4$; *1482-62-8*)   see: Chlorhexidine; Proguanil

5-(2-chlorophenyl)-1,3-dihydro-7-nitro-2H-1,4-benzodiazepine-2-thione
($C_{15}H_{10}ClN_3O_2S$; *35628-48-9*)   see: Loprazolam

6-(2-chlorophenyl)-2,4-dihydro-8-nitro-1H-imidazo-[1,2-a][1,4]benzodiazepin-1-one
($C_{17}H_{11}ClN_4O_3$; *61198-06-9*)   see: Loprazolam

5-(2-chlorophenyl)-1,3-dihydro-2H-thieno[2,3-e]-1,4-diazepin-2-one
($C_{13}H_9ClN_2OS$; *36811-58-2*)   see: Brotizolam

α-(4-chlorophenyl)-α-[2-(dimethylamino)ethyl]-2-pyridineacetonitrile
($C_{17}H_{18}ClN_3$; *65676-21-3*)   see: Chlorphenamine

6-(2-chlorophenyl)-2-[(dimethylamino)methylene]-2,4-dihydro-8-nitro-1H-imidazo[1,2-a][1,4]benzodiazepin-1-one
($C_{20}H_{16}ClN_5O_3$; *61197-47-5*)   see: Loprazolam

N-(4-chlorophenyl)-2,2-dimethylpropanamide
($C_{11}H_{14}ClNO$; *65854-91-3*)   see: Efavirenz

7-chloro-5-phenyl-2-oxo-2,3-dihydro-1*H*-1,4-benzodiazepine
see under 7-chloro-2-oxo-5-phenyl-2,3-dihydro-1*H*-1,4-benzodiazepine

7-chloro-5-phenyl-2-oxo-1,3-dihydro-2*H*-1,4-benzodiazepine 4-oxide
($C_{15}H_{11}ClN_2O_2$; *963-39-3*)   see: Camazepam; Oxazepam; Temazepam

1-(4-chlorophenyl)-1-phenylethanol
see under 4-chloro-α-methylbenzhydrol

2-[2-[1-(4-chlorophenyl)-1-phenylethoxy]ethyl]-1-methylpyrrolidine
($C_{21}H_{26}ClNO$; *7723-51-5*)   see: Clemastine

3-(4-chlorophenyl)-1-phenyl-1*H*-pyrazole-4-carboxaldehyde
($C_{16}H_{11}ClN_2O$; *36663-00-0*)   see: Lonazolac

3-(4-chlorophenyl)-1-phenyl-1*H*-pyrazole-4-methanol
($C_{16}H_{13}ClN_2O$; *36640-39-8*)   see: Lonazolac

3-(4-chlorophenyl)phthalide
($C_{14}H_9ClO_2$; *4889-69-4*)   see: Chlortalidone

3-(4-chlorophenyl)phthalimide
($C_{14}H_{10}ClNO$; *2224-77-3*)   see: Chlortalidone

N-(3-chlorophenyl)piperazine
($C_{10}H_{13}ClN_2$; *6640-24-0*)   see: Etoperidone

2-[3-[4-(3-chlorophenyl)-1-piperazinyl]propyl]-5-ethyl-2,4-dihydro-3*H*-1,2,4-triazol-3-one
($C_{17}H_{24}ClN_5O$; *57059-58-2*)   see: Nefazodone hydrochloride

2-(4-chlorophenyl)propene
(C_9H_9Cl; *1712-70-5*)   see: Haloperidol

(4-chlorophenyl)(2-pyridyl)acetonitrile
($C_{13}H_9ClN_2$; *5005-37-8*)   see: Chlorphenamine

(4-chlorophenyl)(2-pyridyl)carbinol
($C_{12}H_{10}ClNO$; *27652-89-7*)   see: Carbinoxamine

9b-(4-chlorophenyl)-1,2,3,9b-tetrahydro-5*H*-imidazo-[2,1-*a*]isoindol-5-one
($C_{16}H_{13}ClN_2O$; *6038-49-9*)   see: Mazindol

9b-(4-chlorophenyl)-1,2,3,9b-tetrahydro-1-[(4-methylphenyl)sulfonyl]-5*H*-imidazo[2,1-*a*]isoindol-5-one
($C_{23}H_{19}ClN_2O_3S$; *22590-16-5*)   see: Mazindol

4-(4-chlorophenyl)-1,2,3,6-tetrahydropyridine
($C_{11}H_{12}ClN$; *30005-58-4*)   see: Haloperidol

(+)-2-(2-chlorophenyl)-N-[2-(2-thienyl)ethyl]glycine methyl ester
($C_{15}H_{16}ClNO_2S$; *141109-20-8*)   see: Clopidogrel hydrogensulfate

2-[(4-chlorophenyl)thio]benzeneacetic acid
($C_{14}H_{11}ClO_2S$; *13459-62-6*)   see: Zotepine

2-[(4-chlorophenyl)thio]benzoic acid
($C_{13}H_9ClO_2S$; *6469-85-8*)   see: Chlorprothixene

2-[(4-chlorophenyl)thio]benzoyl chloride
($C_{13}H_8Cl_2OS$; *6469-86-9*)   see: Chlorprothixene

1-[2-[(4-chlorophenyl)thio]phenyl]ethanone
($C_{14}H_{11}ClOS$; *41932-35-8*)   see: Zotepine

1-[(2-chlorophenyl)thio]-2-propanone
(C_9H_9ClOS; *17514-52-2*)   see: Sertaconazole

7-chloro-5-phenyl-2-thioxo-2,3-dihydro-1*H*-1,4-benzodiazepine
($C_{15}H_{11}ClN_2S$; *4547-02-8*)   see: Alprazolam; Estazolam

N-(4-chlorophenyl)-N-(2,2,2-trifluoroethyl)-1,2-ethanediamine
($C_{10}H_{12}ClF_3N_2$; *34483-02-8*)   see: Quazepam

α-(4-chlorophenyl)-2,2,8-trimethyl-4*H*-1,3-dioxino[4,5-*c*]-pyridine-5-methanol
($C_{17}H_{18}ClNO_3$; *133545-64-9*)   see: Cicletanine

1-chlorophthalazine
($C_8H_5ClN_2$; *5784-45-2*)   see: Hydralazine

4-chlorophthalimide
($C_8H_4ClNO_2$; *7147-90-2*)   see: Clorexolone

2-chloro-1-piperidinopropane
($C_8H_{16}ClN$; *698-92-0*)   see: Propiram

chloro[3-(1-piperidinyl)propyl]magnesium
($C_8H_{16}ClMgN$; *34924-24-8*)   see: Difenidol

(9β,10α)-6-chloropregna-4,6-diene-3,20-dione
($C_{21}H_{27}ClO_2$; *4202-98-6*)   see: Trengestone

1-chloro-2,3-propanediol
see under 3-chloro-1,2-dihydroxypropane

3-chloropropane-1,2-diol
see under 3-chloro-1,2-dihydroxypropane

1-chloro-2-propanol
(C_3H_7ClO; *127-00-4*)   see: Bethanechol chloride; Proxyphylline

3-chloro-1-propanol
(C_3H_7ClO; *627-30-5*)   see: Cyclomethycaine; Piperocaine

2-chloro-9-(2-propenylidene)-9*H*-thioxanthene
($C_{16}H_{11}ClS$; *56987-24-7*)   see: Chlorprothixene

3-chloropropionaldehyde
(C_3H_5ClO; *19434-65-2*)   see: Chlorthenoxazine

3-chloropropionaldehyde diethyl acetal
($C_7H_{15}ClO_2$; *35573-93-4*)   see: Pipoxolan

β-chloropropionic acid
($C_3H_5ClO_2$; *107-94-8*)   see: Tertatolol

3-chloropropionitrile
(C_3H_4ClN; *542-76-7*)   see: Famotidine

2-chloropropionyl chloride
($C_3H_4Cl_2O$; *7623-09-8*)   see: Omoconazole nitrate

3-chloropropionyl chloride
($C_3H_4Cl_2O$; *625-36-5*)   see: Beclamide; Clidanac; Moracizine; Oxolamine; Proxazole

α-chloropropionylglycine
($C_5H_8ClNO_3$; *85038-45-5*)   see: Stepronin

3'-chloropropiophenone
(C_9H_9ClO; *34841-35-5*)   see: Amfebutamone

1-(3-chloropropoxy)-4-fluorobenzene
($C_9H_{10}ClFO$; *1716-42-3*)   see: Cisapride

1-(3-chloropropyl)-2-benzimidazolone
($C_{10}H_{11}ClN_2O$; *62780-89-6*)   see: Domperidone; Oxatomide

3-chloropropyl benzoate
($C_{10}H_{11}ClO_2$; *942-95-0*)   see: Piperocaine

5-(3-chloropropyl)-5*H*-dibenz[*b*,*f*]azepine
($C_{17}H_{16}ClN$; *51551-40-7*)   see: Opipramol

2-(3-chloropropyl)-4,5-diethyl-Δ5-1,2,4-triazolin-3-one
($C_9H_{16}ClN_3O$; *52883-44-0*)   see: Etoperidone

5-(3-chloropropyl)-10,11-dihydro-5*H*-dibenz[*b*,*f*]azepine
($C_{17}H_{18}ClN$; *16036-79-6*)   see: Desipramine

N-(3-chloropropyl)-3,4-dimethoxy-N-methylbenzeneethanamine
($C_{14}H_{22}ClNO_2$; *36770-74-8*)   see: Gallopamil; Verapamil

6β-chloro-5,11β,17,21-tetrahydroxy-5α-pregnane-3,20-dione
(C$_{21}$H$_{31}$ClO$_6$; *113113-99-8*)   see: Cloprednol

2-chloro-3',5'-O-[1,1,3,3-tetrakis(1-methylethyl)-1,3-disiloxanediyl]adenosine
(C$_{22}$H$_{38}$ClN$_5$O$_5$Si$_2$; *111556-90-2*)   see: Cladribine

8-chlorotheophylline
(C$_7$H$_7$ClN$_4$O$_2$; *85-18-7*)   see: Dimenhydrinate;
Piprinhydrinate

chlorothiazide
(C$_7$H$_6$ClN$_3$O$_4$S$_2$; *58-94-6*)   see: Hydrochlorothiazide

2-chloro-5-thiophenecarboxaldehyde
(C$_5$H$_3$ClOS; *7283-96-7*)   see: Tioclomarol

4-chlorothiophenol
(C$_6$H$_5$ClS; *106-54-7*)   see: Chlorprothixene; Zotepine

2-chlorothioxanthone
(C$_{13}$H$_7$ClOS; *86-39-5*)   see: Chlorprothixene

8-chloro-11-thioxo-10,11-dihydro-5H-dibenzo[b,e][1,4]diazepine
(C$_{13}$H$_9$ClN$_2$S; *15980-68-4*)   see: Clozapine

2-chlorotoluene
(C$_7$H$_7$Cl; *95-49-8*)   see: Clotrimazole

1-chloro-3-(m-tolyloxy)-2-propanol
(C$_{10}$H$_{13}$ClO$_2$; *42865-04-3*)   see: Bevantolol

4-chloro-1-tosylaminobenzene
(C$_{13}$H$_{12}$ClNO$_2$S; *2903-34-6*)   see: Medazepam

chloro(triethylphosphine)gold
(C$_6$H$_{15}$AuClP; *15529-90-5*)   see: Auranofin

4-chloro-2-(trifluoroacetyl)aniline hydrochloride
(C$_8$H$_6$Cl$_2$F$_3$NO; *173676-59-0*)   see: Efavirenz

1-chloro-1,2,2-trifluoro-2-diethylaminoethane
(C$_6$H$_{11}$ClF$_3$N; *357-83-5*)   see: Zidovudine

2-chloro-1,1,1-trifluoroethane
(C$_2$H$_2$ClF$_3$; *75-88-7*)   see: Halothane

[5-chloro-2-[(2,2,2-trifluoroethyl)amino]phenyl](2-fluorophenyl)methanone
(C$_{15}$H$_{10}$ClF$_4$NO; *50939-39-4*)   see: Quazepam

4-chloro-N-(2,2,2-trifluoroethyl)aniline
(C$_8$H$_7$ClF$_3$N; *22753-82-8*)   see: Quazepam

2-chloro-1,1,2-trifluoroethyl dichloromethyl ether
(C$_3$H$_2$Cl$_3$F$_3$O; *428-96-6*)   see: Enflurane

7-chloro-1-(2,2,2-trifluoroethyl)-2,3-dihydro-5-(2-fluorophenyl)-1H-1,4-benzodiazepin-2-one
(C$_{17}$H$_{13}$ClF$_4$N$_2$; *34482-99-0*)   see: Quazepam

2-chloro-1,1,2-trifluoroethyl methyl ether
(C$_3$H$_4$ClF$_3$O; *425-87-6*)   see: Enflurane

1-chloro-4-(trifluoromethyl)benzene
(C$_7$H$_4$ClF$_3$; *98-56-6*)   see: Fluoxetine

4-(4-chloro-3-trifluoromethylphenyl)-4-hydroxypiperidine
(C$_{12}$H$_{13}$ClF$_3$NO; *21928-50-7*)   see: Penfluridol

4-(4-chloro-3-trifluoromethylphenyl)-4-hydroxypiperidine-1-carboxylic acid methyl ester
(C$_{14}$H$_{15}$ClF$_3$NO$_3$)   see: Penfluridol

4-chloro-3-trifluoromethylphenylmagnesium bromide
(C$_7$H$_3$BrClF$_3$Mg; *61895-77-0*)   see: Penfluridol

4-chloro-7-(trifluoromethyl)quinoline
(C$_{10}$H$_5$ClF$_3$N; *346-55-4*)   see: Antrafenine

4-chloro-8-(trifluoromethyl)quinoline
(C$_{10}$H$_5$ClF$_3$N; *23779-97-7*)   see: Floctafenine

2-chloro-2',3',4'-trihydroxyacetophenone
(C$_8$H$_7$ClO$_4$; *17345-68-5*)   see: Methoxsalen

2-chlorotriphenylcarbinol
(C$_{19}$H$_{15}$ClO; *66774-02-5*)   see: Clotrimazole

2-chlorotriphenylmethyl chloride
(C$_{19}$H$_{14}$Cl$_2$; *42074-68-0*)   see: Clotrimazole

(±)-chlorpheniramine
(C$_{16}$H$_{19}$ClN$_2$; *132-22-9*)   see: Dexchlorpheniramine

chlorprothixen
(C$_{18}$H$_{18}$ClNS; *113-59-7*)   see: Clopenthixol

chlortetracycline
(C$_{22}$H$_{23}$ClN$_2$O$_8$; *57-62-5*)   see: Tetracycline

chlortetracycline hydrochloride
(C$_{22}$H$_{24}$Cl$_2$N$_2$O$_8$; *64-72-2*)   see: Clomocycline

(3β)-cholesta-5,7-diene-3,25-diol 3-acetate
(C$_{29}$H$_{46}$O$_3$; *24281-78-5*)   see: Calcifediol

(1α,3β)-cholesta-5,7-diene-1,3,25-triol triacetate
(C$_{33}$H$_{50}$O$_6$; *39783-16-9*)   see: Calcitriol

cholesta-1,4,6-triene-3,24-dione
(C$_{27}$H$_{38}$O$_2$; *57701-40-3*)   see: Tacalcitol

1,5,7-cholestatrien-3β-ol
(C$_{27}$H$_{42}$O; *54604-59-0*)   see: Alfacalcidol

(3β)-cholest-5-ene-3,25-diol diacetate
(C$_{31}$H$_{50}$O$_4$; *59975-17-6*)   see: Calcifediol

(1α,3β)-cholest-5-ene-1,3,24-triol
(C$_{27}$H$_{46}$O$_3$; *59780-19-7*)   see: Tacalcitol

(1α,3β)-cholest-5-ene-1,3,25-triol triacetate
(C$_{33}$H$_{52}$O$_6$; *39783-14-7*)   see: Calcitriol

(1α,3β,24R)-cholest-5-ene-1,3,24-triol tribenzoate
(C$_{48}$H$_{58}$O$_6$; *57701-50-5*)   see: Tacalcitol

cholic acid
(C$_{24}$H$_{40}$O$_5$; *81-25-4*)   see: Chenodeoxycholic acid;
Dehydrocholic acid

choline chloride
(C$_5$H$_{14}$ClNO; *67-48-1*)   see: Acetylcholine chloride; Choline
salicylate

choline hydrogen carbonate
(C$_6$H$_{15}$NO$_4$; *78-73-9*)   see: Choline theophyllinate

choline hydroxide
(C$_5$H$_{15}$NO$_2$; *123-41-1*)   see: Acetylcholine chloride; Choline
chloride; Choline dihydrogen citrate; Choline stearate

choline naphthalene-1,5-disulfonate
(C$_{20}$H$_{34}$N$_2$O$_8$S$_2$)   see: Aclatonium napadisilate

choline tosylate
(C$_{12}$H$_{21}$NO$_4$S; *55357-38-5*)   see: Miltefosine

cinnamaldehyde
(C$_9$H$_8$O; *104-55-2*)   see: Alverine; Kawain; Toremifene

cinnamic acid
(C$_9$H$_8$O$_2$; *140-10-3*)   see: Tolterodine

cinnamoyl chloride
(C$_9$H$_7$ClO; *102-92-1*)   see: Cinmetacin

cinnamyl alcohol
(C$_9$H$_{10}$O; *104-54-1*)   see: Chloramphenicol; Zipeprol

trans-cinnamyl alcohol
(C$_9$H$_{10}$O; *4407-36-7*)   see: Reboxetine

cinnamyl bromide
(C$_9$H$_9$Br; *4392-24-9*)   see: Cinnamedrine

cinnamyl chloride
(C$_9$H$_9$Cl; *2687-12-9*)   see: Cinnarizine; Naftifine

3-cyano-1,2-dihydro-2-oxo-6-propyl-4-pyridinecarboxylic acid

(C$_{10}$H$_{10}$N$_2$O$_3$)   see: Protionamide

1-cyano-2,2-diphenylcyclopropane

(C$_{16}$H$_{13}$N; *30932-41-3*)   see: Cibenzoline

γ-cyano-γ-ethylbenzenebutanoic acid methyl ester

(C$_{14}$H$_{17}$NO$_2$; *90424-96-7*)   see: Glutethimide

α-cyano-α-ethyl-1-cycloheptene-1-acetic acid methyl ester

(C$_{13}$H$_{19}$NO$_2$; *84803-64-5*)   see: Heptabarb

3-cyano-6-ethyl-1,2-dihydro-2-oxo-4-pyridinecarboxylic acid ethyl ester

(C$_{11}$H$_{12}$N$_2$O$_3$; *31718-05-5*)   see: Ethionamide

1-(2-cyanoethyl)-1-ethylurea

(C$_6$H$_{11}$N$_3$O; *28461-57-6*)   see: Sulfacitine

5-(-2-cyanoethyl)hydantoin

(C$_6$H$_7$N$_3$O$_2$; *1007-06-3*)   see: L-Tryptophan

γ-cyano-γ-ethyl-4-nitrobenzenebutanoic acid methyl ester

(C$_{14}$H$_{16}$N$_2$O$_4$; *101939-07-5*)   see: Aminoglutethimide

1-(2-cyanoethyl)-2-piperidineethanol

(C$_{10}$H$_{18}$N$_2$O)   see: Tiquizium bromide

N-[[[4-[[(2-cyanoethyl)thio]methyl]-2-thiazolyl]amino]thi-oxomethyl]benzamide

(C$_{15}$H$_{14}$N$_4$OS$_3$; *76823-90-0*)   see: Famotidine

[4-[[(2-cyanoethyl)thio]methyl]-2-thiazolyl]guanidine

(C$_8$H$_{11}$N$_5$S$_2$; *76823-93-3*)   see: Famotidine

9-cyanofluorene

(C$_{14}$H$_9$N; *1529-40-4*)   see: Indecainide

[3S-[1(cis),3α,4β]]-1-[4-cyano-4-(4-fluorophenyl)cyclo-hexyl]-3-methyl-4-phenyl-4-piperidinecarboxylic acid phenylmethyl ester

(C$_{33}$H$_{35}$FN$_2$O$_2$)   see: Levocabastine

4-cyano-4-(4-fluorophenyl)heptanedioic acid dimethyl ester

(C$_{16}$H$_{18}$FNO$_4$; *56326-92-2*)   see: Levocabastine

5-cyano-5-(4-fluorophenyl)-2-oxocyclohexanecarboxylic acid methyl ester

(C$_{15}$H$_{14}$FNO$_3$; *56326-95-5*)   see: Levocabastine

cyanogen bromide

(CBrN; *506-68-3*)   see: Anagrelide hydrochloride; Desloratadine; Epinastine hydrochloride; Fluoxetine; Nalorphine; Naloxone; Pergolide

cyanogen chloride

(CClN; *506-77-4*)   see: Oxcarbazepine

4-cyanohexahydro-1,1-dimethyl-4-phenyl-1H-azepinium bromide

(C$_{15}$H$_{21}$BrN$_2$; *7512-10-9*)   see: Ethoheptazine

2-cyano-2-hydroxyindane

(C$_{10}$H$_9$NO; *55589-21-4*)   see: Indanorex

3-cyano-4-hydroxy-6,7-methylenedioxycinnoline

(C$_{10}$H$_5$N$_3$O$_3$; *28657-78-5*)   see: Cinoxacin

3-cyano-4-imino-9-methyl-4H-pyrido[1,2-a]pyrimidine

(C$_{10}$H$_8$N$_4$; *102781-19-1*)   see: Pemirolast

5-cyano-5-(m-methoxyphenyl)heptanoic acid ethyl ester

(C$_{17}$H$_{23}$NO$_3$; *27180-88-7*)   see: Meptazinol

4-cyano-4-(3-methoxyphenyl)-1-methylpiperidine

(C$_{14}$H$_{18}$N$_2$O; *5460-79-7*)   see: Ketobemidone

2-cyano-3-methoxypyrazine

(C$_6$H$_5$N$_3$O; *75018-05-2*)   see: Sulfalene

α-cyano-α-methyl-5H-[1]benzopyrano[2,3-b]pyridine-7-acetic acid ethyl ester

(C$_{18}$H$_{16}$N$_2$O$_3$; *52549-16-3*)   see: Pranoprofen

1-cyanomethylimidazole

(C$_5$H$_5$N$_3$; *98873-55-3*)   see: Lanoconazole

N-cyano-N'-[2-[[(5-methyl-1H-imidazol-4-yl)methyl]-thio]ethyl]carbamimidothioic acid methyl ester

(C$_{10}$H$_{15}$N$_5$S$_2$; *52378-40-2*)   see: Cimetidine

2-cyano-N-methyl-N-[(methylamino)carbonyl]acetamide

(C$_6$H$_9$N$_3$O$_2$; *39615-79-7*)   see: Theophylline

5-cyano-4-methyloxazole

(C$_5$H$_4$N$_2$O; *1003-52-7*)   see: Pyridoxine

2-cyano-3-methyl-2-pentenoic acid ethyl ester

(C$_9$H$_{13}$NO$_2$; *759-51-3*)   see: Ethosuximide

4-cyano-1-methyl-4-phenylhexahydroazepine

(C$_{14}$H$_{18}$N$_2$; *6315-32-8*)   see: Ethoheptazine

cyanomethyl phenyl ketone

(C$_9$H$_7$NO; *614-16-4*)   see: Fluoxetine

4-cyano-1-methyl-4-phenylpiperidine

(C$_{13}$H$_{16}$N$_2$; *3627-62-1*)   see: Pethidine

2-cyano-3-methylpyridine

(C$_7$H$_6$N$_2$; *20970-75-6*)   see: Loratadine

2-cyano-2-methyltetrahydrofuran

(C$_6$H$_9$NO; *19679-75-5*)   see: Mefruside

2-cyano-N-methyl-N-tetrahydrofuroylethylamine

(C$_9$H$_{14}$N$_2$O$_2$; *72104-44-0*)   see: Alfuzosin

2-cyano-8-nitro-1-benzopyran-4-one

(C$_{10}$H$_4$N$_2$O$_4$; *141283-41-2*)   see: Pranlukast

5-cyano-10-nitro-5H-dibenz[b,f]azepine

(C$_{15}$H$_9$N$_3$O$_2$; *78880-63-4*)   see: Oxcarbazepine

4-cyano-2-nitrotoluene

(C$_8$H$_6$N$_2$O$_2$; *939-79-7*)   see: Hydroxystilbamidine isethionate

2-cyano-3-phenethylpyridine

(C$_{14}$H$_{12}$N$_2$; *14578-23-5*)   see: Azatadine

2-cyanophenothiazine

(C$_{13}$H$_8$N$_2$S; *38642-74-9*)   see: Cyamemazine; Periciazine

N-[2-[3-(2-cyanophenoxy)-2-hydroxypropylamino]ethyl]-4-benzyloxyphenylacetamide

(C$_{27}$H$_{29}$N$_3$O$_4$)   see: Epanolol

α-cyanophenylacetic acid ethyl ester

(C$_{11}$H$_{11}$NO$_2$; *4553-07-5*)   see: Mephenytoin; Phenobarbital

4-(2-cyanophenyl)benzyl bromide

see under 4'-(bromomethyl)biphenyl-2-carbonitrile

2-cyano-3-phenyl-2-butenoic acid methyl ester

(C$_{12}$H$_{11}$NO$_2$; *14505-27-2*)   see: Mesuximide

2-cyano-2-phenylbutyramide

(C$_{11}$H$_{12}$N$_2$O; *80544-75-8*)   see: Mephenytoin

2-cyano-2-phenylbutyric acid ethyl ester

(C$_{13}$H$_{15}$NO$_2$; *718-71-8*)   see: Phenobarbital

1-cyano-1-phenylcyclohexane

(C$_{13}$H$_{15}$N; *2201-23-2*)   see: Dicycloverine

1-cyano-1-phenylcyclopentane

(C$_{12}$H$_{13}$N; *77-57-6*)   see: Pentoxyverine

4-[2-(4-cyanophenyl)ethenyl]-3-hydroxybenzonitrile

(C$_{16}$H$_{10}$N$_2$O; *67466-66-4*)   see: Hydroxystilbamidine isethionate

(cyanophenylmethyl)urea

(C$_9$H$_9$N$_3$O; *88169-89-5*)   see: Ethotoin

α-cyclohexyl-4-methyl-α-phenyl-1-piperazineethanol
($C_{19}H_{30}N_2O$; *7556-54-9*)   see: Hexocyclium metilsulfate

6-cyclohexyl-4-methyl-2-pyrone
($C_{12}H_{16}O_2$; *14818-35-0*)   see: Ciclopirox

4-(cyclohexyloxy)benzoic acid
($C_{13}H_{16}O_3$; *139-61-7*)   see: Cyclomethycaine

3-(4-cyclohexylphenyl)dihydro-2,5-furandione
($C_{16}H_{18}O_3$; *36414-05-8*)   see: Clidanac

α-cyclohexyl-α-phenylglycolic acid
($C_{14}H_{18}O_3$; *4335-77-7*)   see: Oxyphencyclimine

α-cyclohexylphenylglycolic acid 2-diethylaminoethyl ester
($C_{18}H_{27}NO_3$; *25520-98-3*)   see: Oxyphenonium bromide

α-cyclohexylphenylglycolic acid methyl ester
($C_{15}H_{20}O_3$; *10399-13-0*)   see: Oxybutynin; Oxyphenonium bromide; Oxypyrronium bromide

α-cyclohexylphenylglycolic acid (1-methyl-2-pyrrolidinyl)methyl ester
($C_{20}H_{29}NO_3$; *94868-25-4*)   see: Oxypyrronium bromide

α-cyclohexylphenylglycolic acid propargyl ester
($C_{17}H_{20}O_3$; *81039-74-9*)   see: Oxybutynin

[(4-cyclohexylphenyl)methylene]propanedioic acid diethyl ester
($C_{20}H_{26}O_4$; *29041-00-7*)   see: Clidanac

trans-4-cyclohexyl-L-proline
($C_{11}H_{19}NO_2$; *103201-78-1*)   see: Fosinopril

cyclohexyl(3-thienyl)acetic acid
($C_{12}H_{16}O_2S$; *16199-74-9*)   see: Cetiedil

cyclohexyl(3-thienyl)glycolic acid
($C_{12}H_{16}O_3S$; *3193-02-0*)   see: Cetiedil

cyclopentadiene
(C_5H_6; *542-92-7*)   see: Abacavir; Biperidene; Bornaprine; Cyclothiazide; Fencamfamin

2,4-cyclopentadienylmethyl benzyl ether
($C_{13}H_{14}O$; *39939-07-6*)   see: Dinoprost

cyclopentaneacetonitrile
($C_7H_{11}N$; *5732-87-6*)   see: Cyclopentamine

cyclopentanone
(C_5H_8O; *120-92-3*)   see: Amcinonide; Cyclopentamine; Cyclopentolate; Irbesartan

3-cyclopentene-1-carboxylic acid
($C_6H_8O_2$; *7686-77-3*)   see: Dolasetron mesilate

cyclopentylacetaldehyde
($C_7H_{12}O$; *5623-81-4*)   see: Cyclopenthiazide

cyclopentylacetone
($C_8H_{14}O$; *1122-98-1*)   see: Cyclopentamine

cyclopentyl alcohol
($C_5H_{10}O$; *96-41-3*)   see: Penmesterol; Pentagestrone acetate; Quingestanol acetate

cyclopentyl bromide
(C_5H_9Br; *137-43-9*)   see: Quinestrol

cyclopentyl chloroformate
($C_6H_9ClO_2$; *50715-28-1*)   see: Zafirlukast

α-cyclopentyl-α-hydroxybenzeneacetic acid 1-methyl-3-pyrrolidinyl ester
($C_{18}H_{25}NO_3$; *13118-11-1*)   see: Glycopyrronium bromide

cyclopentylideneacetonitrile
(C_7H_9N; *5732-88-7*)   see: Cyclopentamine

cyclopentylmagnesium bromide
(C_5H_9BrMg; *33240-34-5*)   see: Cycrimine; Glycopyrronium bromide; Ketamine; Penthienate methobromide

4-[5-(cyclopentyloxycarbonylamino)-1-methylindol-3-yl-methyl]-3-methoxybenzoic acid
($C_{24}H_{26}N_2O_5$; *107754-20-1*)   see: Zafirlukast

3-cyclopentyloxy-17-oxo-3,5-androstadiene
($C_{24}H_{34}O_2$; *15236-92-7*)   see: Penmesterol

2-cyclopentylphenol
($C_{11}H_{14}O$; *1518-84-9*)   see: Penbutolol

3-cyclopentylpropionic acid
($C_8H_{14}O_2$; *140-77-2*)   see: Estradiol cypionate

3-cyclopentylpropionyl chloride
($C_8H_{13}ClO$; *104-97-2*)   see: Estradiol cypionate; Testosterone cypionate

cyclopentyl-2-thienylglycolic acid
($C_{11}H_{14}O_3S$; *3899-50-1*)   see: Penthienate methobromide

cyclopentyl-2-thienylglycolic acid 2-diethylaminoethyl ester
($C_{17}H_{27}NO_3S$; *15421-88-2*)   see: Penthienate methobromide

cyclopropanecarbonyl chloride
(C_4H_5ClO; *4023-34-1*)   see: Buprenorphine; Fexofenadine hydrochloride; Naltrexone; Prazepam

cyclopropanecarboxylic acid ethyl ester
($C_6H_{10}O_2$; *4606-07-9*)   see: Pimozide

1,1-cyclopropanedimethanol
($C_5H_{10}O_2$; *39590-81-3*)   see: Montelukast sodium

1,1-cyclopropanedimethanol monobenzoate
($C_{12}H_{14}O_3$; *142148-11-6*)   see: Montelukast sodium

cyclopropylacetylene
(C_5H_6; *6746-94-7*)   see: Efavirenz

cyclopropylamine
(C_3H_7N; *765-30-0*)   see: Abacavir; Ciprofloxacin; Grepafloxacin; Moxifloxacin hydrochloride; Nevirapine; Sparfloxacin

2-(cyclopropylamino)-N-(2,6-dichloro-4-methyl-3-pyridinyl)-3-pyridinecarboxamide
($C_{15}H_{14}Cl_2N_4O$; *142266-59-9*)   see: Nevirapine

2-(cyclopropylamino)-N-(2-methoxy-4-methyl-3-pyridinyl)-3-pyridinecarboxamide
($C_{16}H_{18}N_4O_2$; *162709-30-0*)   see: Nevirapine

α-[(cyclopropylamino)methylene]-2,4,5-trifluoro-3-methoxy-β-oxobenzenepropanoic acid ethyl ester
($C_{16}H_{16}F_3NO_4$; *112811-70-8*)   see: Moxifloxacin hydrochloride

(1α,3β,5E,7E,20S,22E)-24-cyclopropyl-1,3-bis[[(1,1-dimethylethyl)dimethylsilyl]oxy]-9,10-secochola-5,7,10(19),22-tetraen-24-one
($C_{39}H_{66}O_3Si_2$; *115648-68-5*)   see: Calcipotriol

(1α,3β,5E,7E,20S,22E,24S)-24-cyclopropyl-1,3-bis[[(1,1-dimethylethyl)dimethylsilyl]oxy]-9,10-secochola-5,7,10(19),22-tetraen-24-ol
($C_{39}H_{68}O_3Si_2$; *134523-61-8*)   see: Calcipotriol

(1α,3β,5Z,7E,20S,22E,24S)-24-cyclopropyl-1,3-bis[[(1,1-dimethylethyl)dimethylsilyl]oxy]-9,10-secochola-5,7,10(19),22-tetraen-24-ol
($C_{39}H_{68}O_3Si_2$; *134523-70-9*)   see: Calcipotriol

17-(cyclopropylcarbonyl)-4,5α-epoxy-3,14-dihydroxymorphinan-6-one cyclic ethylene acetal 3-cyclopropanecarboxylate
($C_{26}H_{29}NO_7$; *16676-30-5*)   see: Naltrexone

(cyclopropylcarbonylmethylene)triphenylphosphorane
($C_{23}H_{21}OP$; *7691-76-1*)   see: Calcipotriol

4-*O*-demethyldaunomycinone
($C_{20}H_{16}O_8$; *52744-22-6*)   see: Idarubicin

4'-demethylepipodophyllotoxin
($C_{21}H_{20}O_8$; *6559-91-7*)   see: Teniposide

4'-demethylpodophyllotoxin
($C_{21}H_{20}O_8$; *40505-27-9*)   see: Teniposide

6-demethyltetracycline
($C_{21}H_{22}N_2O_8$; *987-02-0*)   see: Minocycline

4-*O*-demethyl-4-*O*-(*p*-toluenesulfonyl)daunomycinone 1⁹-ethylene acetal
($C_{29}H_{26}O_{11}S$; *125310-15-8*)   see: Idarubicin

2-deoxo-9a-aza-9a-homoerythromycin A
($C_{37}H_{70}N_2O_{12}$; *76801-85-9*)   see: Azithromycin

deoxyanisoin
($C_{16}H_{16}O_3$; *120-44-5*)   see: Diethylstilbestrol; Mofezolac; Raloxifene hydrochloride

deoxyanisoin oxime
($C_{16}H_{17}NO_3$; *5471-45-4*)   see: Mofezolac

2-deoxy-3,5-bis-*O*-[(1,1-dimethylethyl)dimethylsilyl]-2,2-difluoro-D-*erythro*-pentonic acid γ-lactone
($C_{17}H_{34}F_2O_4Si_2$; *95058-78-9*)   see: Gemcitabine

2-deoxy-2,2-difluoro-4,5-*O*-(1-methylethylidene)-D-*erythro*-pentonic acid ethyl ester
($C_{10}H_{16}F_2O_5$; *95058-92-7*)   see: Gemcitabine

2-deoxy-2,2-difluoro-D-*erythro*-pentano-1,4-lactone
($C_5H_6F_2O_4$; *95058-77-8*)   see: Gemcitabine

2-deoxy-2,2-difluoro-D-ribopyranose
($C_5H_8F_2O_4$)   see: Gemcitabine

3'-deoxy-5'-*O*-[(1,1-dimethylethyl)diphenylsilyl]-5-methyl-2'-*S*-phenyl-2'-thiouridine
($C_{32}H_{36}N_2O_4SSi$; *129778-51-4*)   see: Stavudine

3-deoxy-5-*O*-[(1,1-dimethylethyl)diphenylsilyl]-2-*S*-phenyl-2-thio-D-*erythro*-pentonic acid γ-lactone
($C_{27}H_{30}O_3SSi$; *129778-50-3*)   see: Stavudine

1-deoxy-1-[[4,5-dimethyl-2-(phenylazo)phenyl]amino]-D-ribitol
($C_{19}H_{25}N_3O_4$; *21037-26-3*)   see: Riboflavin

2-deoxy-3,5-di-*O*-*p*-toluoyl-α-D-*erythro*-pentofuranosyl chloride
($C_{21}H_{21}ClO_5$; *4330-21-6*)   see: Cladribine

(+)-deoxyephedrine
($C_{10}H_{15}N$; *537-46-2*)   see: Benzphetamine

1-(2-deoxy-3,5-epoxy-β-D-*threo*-pentofuranosyl)cytosine
($C_9H_{11}N_3O_3$; *7481-87-0*)   see: Zalcitabine

5'-deoxy-5-fluorocytidine
($C_9H_{12}FN_3O_4$; *66335-38-4*)   see: Capecitabine

5'-deoxy-5-fluoro-5'-iodouridine
($C_9H_{10}FIN_2O_5$; *61787-13-1*)   see: Doxifluridine

5'-deoxy-5-fluoro-*N*-[(pentyloxy)carbonyl]cytidine 2',3'-bis(pentyl carbonate)
($C_{27}H_{42}FN_3O_{10}$; *174667-24-4*)   see: Capecitabine

5'-deoxy-5-fluoro-*N*-[(pentyloxy)carbonyl]cytidine 2',3'-diacetate
($C_{19}H_{26}FN_3O_8$; *162204-20-8*)   see: Capecitabine

1-deoxy-1-[(2-hydroxyethyl)amino]-D-glucitol
($C_8H_{19}NO_6$; *54662-27-0*)   see: Miglitol

6-deoxy-6-[(2-hydroxyethyl)amino]-L-sorbose
($C_8H_{17}NO_6$)   see: Miglitol

5'-deoxy-5'-iodoadenosine
($C_{10}H_{12}IN_5O_3$; *4099-81-4*)   see: Cobamamide

5'-deoxy-5'-iodo-2',3'-*O*-isopropylidene-5-fluorouridine
($C_{12}H_{14}FIN_2O_5$; *61787-10-8*)   see: Doxifluridine

2'-deoxy-5-iodouridine 3',5'-bis(4-methylbenzene-sulfonate)
($C_{23}H_{23}IN_2O_9S_2$)   see: Idoxuridine

5'-deoxy-2',3'-*O*-isopropylidene-5-fluorouridine
($C_{12}H_{15}FN_2O_5$; *66335-39-5*)   see: Doxifluridine

2-deoxyribofuranosyl chloride 3,5-bis(4-nitrobenzoate)
($C_{19}H_{15}ClN_2O_9$; *51841-98-6*)   see: Trifluridine

2-deoxy-D-ribose
($C_5H_{10}O_4$; *533-67-5*)   see: Idoxuridine

2'-deoxyuridine
($C_9H_{12}N_2O_5$; *951-78-0*)   see: Idoxuridine

dequalinium iodide
($C_{30}H_{40}I_2N_4$; *2019-42-3*)   see: Dequalinium chloride

desipramine
($C_{18}H_{23}ClN_2$; *58-28-6*)   see: Lofepramine

deslanoside
($C_{47}H_{74}O_{19}$; *17598-65-1*)   see: Lanatoside C

Dess-Martin periodinane
($C_{13}H_{13}IO_8$; *87413-09-0*)   see: Tacrolimus

dexamethasone
($C_{22}H_{29}FO_5$; *50-02-2*)   see: Dexamethasone *tert*-butylacetate; Dexamethasone 21-isonicotinate; Dexamethasone 21-linolate; Dexamethasone phosphate; Dexamethasone pivalate

dexamphetamine
($C_9H_{13}N$; *51-64-9*)   see: Clobenzorex

dextrin
(unspecified; *9004-53-9*)   see: Cadexomer iodine

2,6-diacetamido-9-(2,3,5-tri-*O*-benzyl-β-D-arabinofurano-syl)purine
($C_{35}H_{36}N_6O_6$; *25146-54-7*)   see: Fludarabine phosphate

diacetone-2-oxo-L-gulonic acid
($C_{12}H_{18}O_7$; *18467-77-1*)   see: Ascorbic acid

diacetone-L-sorbose
($C_{12}H_{20}O_6$; *17682-70-1*)   see: Ascorbic acid

3',5'-diacetoxyacetophenone
($C_{12}H_{12}O_5$; *35086-59-0*)   see: Fenoterol; Orciprenaline

3',5'-diacetoxy-2-bromoacetophenone
see under 2-bromo-3',5'-diacetoxyacetophenone

16α,21-diacetoxy-11β,17-dihydroxy-3,20-dioxo-9-fluoro-4-pregnene
($C_{25}H_{33}FO_8$; *426-39-1*)   see: Triamcinolone; Triamcinolone diacetate

16α,21-diacetoxy-3,20-dioxo-17-hydroxy-9β,11β-epoxy-1,4-pregnadiene
($C_{25}H_{30}O_8$; *96670-24-5*)   see: Triamcinolone diacetate

5α,21-diacetoxy-6β-fluoro-3β,17-dihydroxy-16α-methyl-pregnan-20-one
($C_{26}H_{39}FO_7$; *2707-32-6*)   see: Paramethasone

3β,26-diacetoxy-5α-furost-20(22)-en-11-one
($C_{31}H_{46}O_6$; *108248-58-4*)   see: Alfaxalone

2-diacetoxymethyl-5-nitrofuran
($C_9H_9NO_7$; *92-55-7*)   see: Nitrofurantoin

3β,17β-diacetoxy-17α-methyl-7-oxo-5-androstene
($C_{24}H_{34}O_5$; *37038-00-9*)   see: Calusterone

3α,20-diacetoxy-16β-methylpregn-17(20)-ene-11-one
($C_{26}H_{38}O_5$; *76564-00-6*)   see: Betamethasone

3,5-di-O-benzoyl-2-deoxy-2,2-difluoro-1-O-methane-sulfonyl-D-ribofuranose
($C_{20}H_{18}F_2O_8S$; *134877-43-3*)   see: Gemcitabine

N^1,N^4-dibenzoylsulfanilamide
($C_{20}H_{16}N_2O_4S$)   see: Sulfabenzamide

(±)-O,N-dibenzoyltyrosine
($C_{23}H_{19}NO_5$; *97485-13-7*)   see: Tiropramide

1,3-di-O-benzyl-2-O-(acetoxymethyl)glycerol
($C_{20}H_{24}O_5$; *84245-11-4*)   see: Ganciclovir

dibenzylamine
($C_{14}H_{15}N$; *103-49-1*)   see: Imiquimod; Labetalol

4(S)-dibenzylamino-3-oxo-5-phenylpentanenitrile
($C_{25}H_{24}N_2O$; *156732-12-6*)   see: Ritonavir

O-3,4-di-O-benzyl-2,6-bis(carboxyamino)-2,6-dideoxy-α-D-glucopyranosyl-(1→4)-O-[β-D-ribofuranosyl-(1→5)]-N,N'-dicarboxy-2-deoxystreptamine tetrabenzyl ester tribenzoate (ester)
($C_{84}H_{82}N_4O_{21}$; *34128-45-5*)   see: Ribostamycin

1,3-dibenzyl-4-(3-ethoxypropyl)-4-hydroxy-cis-perhydro-thieno[3,4-d]imidazol-2-one
($C_{24}H_{30}N_2O_3S$)   see: Biotin

1,3-dibenzyl-4-(3-ethoxypropylidene)-cis-perhydrothieno-[3,4-d]imidazol-2-one
($C_{24}H_{28}N_2O_2S$; *51591-97-0*)   see: Biotin

1,3-dibenzyl-4-(3-ethoxypropyl)-cis-perhydrothieno-[3,4-d]imidazol-2-one
($C_{24}H_{30}N_2O_2S$)   see: Biotin

N,N'-dibenzylethylenediamine
($C_{16}H_{20}N_2$; *140-28-3*)   see: Benzathine benzylpenicillin

1,3-di-O-benzylglycerol
($C_{17}H_{20}O_3$; *6972-79-8*)   see: Ganciclovir

N,N'-dibenzylhexamethylenediamine
($C_{20}H_{28}N_2$; *30070-99-6*)   see: Hexoprenaline

N^2,N^5-dibenzylideneornithine methyl ester
($C_{20}H_{22}N_2O_2$; *69955-51-7*)   see: Eflornithine

(3aS)-1,3-dibenzyl-4t-(3-methoxypropyl)-(3ar,6ac)-tetra-hydrothieno[3,4-d]imidazol-2-one
($C_{23}H_{28}N_2O_2S$)   see: Biotin

cis-1,3-dibenzyl-2-oxoimidazolidine-4,5-dicarboxylic acid
($C_{19}H_{18}N_2O_5$; *51591-75-4*)   see: Biotin

cis-1,3-dibenzyl-2-oxoimidazolidine-4,5-dicarboxylic acid monocyclohexyl ester
($C_{25}H_{28}N_2O_5$; *85610-97-5*)   see: Biotin

[3aS-(3aα,4β,6aα)]-[3-(1,3-dibenzyl-2-oxoperhydro-thieno[3,4-d]imidazol-4-yl)propyl]malonic acid diethyl ester
($C_{29}H_{36}N_2O_5S$; *101469-35-6*)   see: Biotin

1,3-dibenzyl-2-oxo-3a,8b-cis-perhydrothieno[1',2':1,2]-thieno[3,4-d]imidazolium bromide
($C_{22}H_{25}BrN_2OS$)   see: Biotin

3',5'-dibenzyloxyacetophenone
($C_{22}H_{20}O_3$; *28924-21-2*)   see: Terbutaline

3',4'-dibenzyloxybutyrophenone
($C_{24}H_{24}O_3$; *24538-59-8*)   see: Isoetarine

cis-1,3-dibenzylperhydrofuro[3,4-d]imidazole-2,4,6-trione
($C_{19}H_{16}N_2O_4$; *26339-42-4*)   see: Biotin

cis-1,3-dibenzylperhydrothieno[3,4-d]imidazole-2,4-dione
($C_{19}H_{18}N_2O_2S$; *33607-57-7*)   see: Biotin

N,N-dibenzyl-L-phenylalanine benzyl ester
($C_{30}H_{29}NO_2$; *111138-83-1*)   see: Ritonavir; Saquinavir

6,8-dibenzylthiooctanoic acid
($C_{22}H_{28}O_2S_2$; *95809-78-2*)   see: Thioctic acid

2,5-dibromoamyl acetate
($C_7H_{12}Br_2O_2$; *30727-26-5*)   see: Oxypyrronium bromide

(2α,4α,5α)-2,4-dibromoandrostane-3,17-dione
($C_{19}H_{26}Br_2O_2$; *42453-26-9*)   see: Estrone

1,4-dibromobutane
($C_4H_8Br_2$; *110-52-1*)   see: Butorphanol; Pentoxyverine; Trospium chloride

1,4-dibromo-2-butene
($C_4H_6Br_2$; *6974-12-5*)   see: Betacarotene

1,10-dibromodecane
($C_{10}H_{20}Br_2$; *4101-68-2*)   see: Decamethonium bromide; Tiadenol

9,10-dibromo-9,10-dihydro-4H-benzo[4,5]cyclohep-ta[1,2-b]thiophen-4-one
($C_{13}H_8Br_2OS$; *34580-10-4*)   see: Ketotifen

2,4-dibromo-17,21-dihydroxy-5β-pregnane-3,11,20-trione 21-acetate
($C_{23}H_{30}Br_2O_6$; *115114-29-9*)   see: Prednisone

1,3-dibromo-5,5-dimethylhydantoin
($C_5H_6Br_2N_2O_2$; *77-48-5*)   see: Calcifediol; Calcitriol; Diflucortolone valerate; Halopredone diacetate; Tacalcitol

N,N'-dibromo-5,5-dimethylhydantoin
see under 1,3-dibromo-5,5-dimethylhydantoin

1,2-dibromoethane
($C_2H_4Br_2$; *106-93-4*)   see: Amosulalol; Bamifylline; Cafedrine; Dodeclonium bromide; Fenalcomine; Guanoclor; Ketoprofen; Malotilate; Pimefylline

2',7'-dibromofluorescein
($C_{20}H_{10}Br_2O_5$; *25709-81-3*)   see: Merbromin

1,6-dibromohexane
($C_6H_{12}Br_2$; *629-03-8*)   see: Salmeterol

(2α,4α,5α,17β)-2,4-dibromo-17-hydroxyandrostan-3-one
($C_{19}H_{28}Br_2O_2$)   see: Estradiol

[S-(R*,R*)]-2,4-dibromo-3-hydroxybutanoic acid methyl ester
($C_5H_8Br_2O_3$; *88824-11-7*)   see: Carumonam

2β,4β-dibromo-17α-hydroxy-16β-methyl-5β-pregn-9(11)-ene-3,20-dione
($C_{22}H_{30}Br_2O_3$; *13656-79-6*)   see: Betamethasone

dibromomethane
(CH_2Br_2; *74-95-3*)   see: Clodronate disodium

1,6-dibromo-2-naphthol
($C_{10}H_6Br_2O$; *16239-18-2*)   see: Naproxen

6,6-dibromopenicillanic acid
($C_8H_9Br_2NO_3S$; *24158-88-1*)   see: Sulbactam

6,6-dibromopenicillanic acid S,S-dioxide
($C_8H_9Br_2NO_5S$; *76646-91-8*)   see: Sulbactam

1,5-dibromopentane
($C_5H_{10}Br_2$; *111-24-0*)   see: Cilastatin; Dezocine; Dicycloverine; Pentamidine

21,21-dibromopregn-4-ene-3,11,20-trione
($C_{21}H_{26}Br_2O_3$)   see: Hydrocortisone

1,3-dibromopropane
($C_3H_6Br_2$; *109-64-8*)   see: Brinzolamide; Carpipramine; Dibrompropamidine; Ethoheptazine; Pentoxifylline; Sibutramine hydrochloride

2,3-dibromo-1-propanol
($C_3H_6Br_2O$; *96-13-9*)   see: Dimercaprol

1,7-dichloro-5-cyclohexyl-1,3-dihydro-2H-1,4-benzodi-azepin-2-one
($C_{15}H_{16}Cl_2N_2O$; 10379-00-7)   see: Tetrazepam

2,4-dichloro-α-[(cyclopropylamino)methylene]-5-fluoro-β-oxobenzenepropanoic acid methyl ester
($C_{14}H_{12}Cl_2FNO_3$; 105392-26-5)   see: Ciprofloxacin

4-(2,2-dichlorocyclopropyl)aniline
($C_9H_9Cl_2N$; 52179-27-8)   see: Ciprofibrate

4-(2,2-dichlorocyclopropyl)phenol
($C_9H_8Cl_2O$; 52179-26-7)   see: Ciprofibrate

1,10-dichlorodecane
($C_{10}H_{20}Cl_2$; 2162-98-3)   see: Tiadenol

2,6-dichloro-9-(2-deoxy-3,5-di-O-p-toluoyl-β-D-erythro-pentofuranosyl)purine
($C_{26}H_{22}Cl_2N_4O_5$; 38925-80-3)   see: Cladribine

1,5-dichloro-1,5-dideoxy-L-arabinitol 2,4-diacetate
($C_9H_{14}Cl_2O_5$; 118227-48-8)   see: Tacrolimus

1,1-dichloro-2,2-difluoroethylene
($C_2Cl_2F_2$; 79-35-6)   see: Methoxyflurane

2,6-dichloro-α-[[(2,4-difluorophenyl)amino]methylene]-5-fluoro-β-oxo-3-pyridinepropanoic acid ethyl ester
($C_{17}H_{11}Cl_2F_3N_2O_3$; 100490-99-1)   see: Tosufloxacin

1,3-dichloro-2-(2,4-difluorophenyl)-2-propanol
($C_9H_8Cl_2F_2O$; 86386-74-5)   see: Fluconazole

8,11-dichloro-6,11-dihydro-5H-benzo[5,6]cyclohep-ta[1,2-b]pyridine
($C_{14}H_{11}Cl_2N$; 117810-66-9)   see: Loratadine

3,11-dichloro-6,11-dihydro-6-methyldibenzo[c,f][1,2]thi-azepine S,S-dioxide
($C_{14}H_{11}Cl_2NO_2S$; 26638-66-4)   see: Tianeptine sodium

2,4-dichloro-6,7-dimethoxyquinazoline
($C_{10}H_8Cl_2N_2O_2$; 27631-29-4)   see: Alfuzosin; Prazosin

2,4-dichloro-α-[(dimethylamino)methylene]-5-fluoro-β-oxobenzenepropanoic acid methyl ester
($C_{13}H_{12}Cl_2FNO_3$; 105392-19-6)   see: Ciprofloxacin

[2,3-dichloro-4-[2-[(dimethylamino)methyl]-1-oxo-butyl]phenoxy]acetic acid
($C_{15}H_{19}Cl_2NO_4$; 1160-10-7)   see: Etacrynic acid

4,5-dichloro-2,6-dimethyl-3(2H)-pyridazinone
($C_6H_6Cl_2N_2O$)   see: Emorfazone

2,6-dichlorodiphenylamine
($C_{12}H_9Cl_2N$; 15307-93-4)   see: Diclofenac

2,6-dichloro-4,8-dipiperidinopyrimido[5,4-d]pyrimidine
($C_{16}H_{20}Cl_2N_6$; 7139-02-8)   see: Dipyridamole

1,2-dichloroethane
($C_2H_4Cl_2$; 107-06-2)   see: Dofetilide; Ethambutol; Trientine

2',4'-dichloro-5'-fluoroacetophenone
($C_8H_5Cl_2FO$; 704-10-9)   see: Temafloxacin

2,4-dichloro-5-fluorobenzoyl chloride
($C_7H_2Cl_3FO$; 86393-34-2)   see: Ciprofloxacin

2,6-dichloro-5-fluoronicotinoyl chloride
(C_6HCl_3FNO; 96568-02-4)   see: Tosufloxacin

2,3-dichloro-1-fluoro-4-nitrobenzene
($C_6H_2Cl_2FNO_2$; 36556-51-1)   see: Rufloxacin hydrochloride

2,4-dichloro-5-fluoropyrimidine
($C_4HCl_2FN_2$; 2927-71-1)   see: Flucytosine

N-[4,6-dichloro-5-(formylamino)-2-pyrimidinyl]acetamide
($C_7H_6Cl_2N_4O_2$; 136470-91-2)   see: Abacavir

2,6-dichloro-N-hydroxybenzenecarboximidoyl chloride
($C_7H_4Cl_3NO$; 6579-27-7)   see: Dicloxacillin

2,3-dichloro-4-hydroxybenzoic acid
($C_7H_4Cl_2O_3$; 66584-09-6)   see: Tienilic acid

3,4-dichloro-5-hydroxy-2(5H)-furanone
($C_4H_2Cl_2O_3$; 766-40-5)   see: Amezinium metilsulfate

2,2-dichloro-N-(hydroxymethyl)acetamide
($C_3H_5Cl_2NO_2$; 1555-91-5)   see: Iodamide

(2,3-dichloro-4-hydroxyphenyl)-2-thienylmethanone
($C_{11}H_6Cl_2O_2S$; 40180-03-8)   see: Tienilic acid

2,3-dichloro-1-iodobenzene
($C_6H_3Cl_2I$; 2401-21-0)   see: Lamotrigine

6,9-dichloro-2-methoxyacridine
($C_{14}H_9Cl_2NO$; 86-38-4)   see: Mepacrine

3,4-dichloro-α-methoxybenzeneacetyl chloride
($C_9H_7Cl_3O_2$; 83833-34-5)   see: Clometocillin

2,3-dichloro-4-methoxybenzoic acid
($C_8H_6Cl_2O_3$; 55901-80-9)   see: Tienilic acid

2,3-dichloro-4-methoxybenzoyl chloride
($C_8H_5Cl_3O_2$; 76238-31-8)   see: Tienilic acid

3,4-dichloro-α-methoxyphenylacetic acid
($C_9H_8Cl_2O_3$; 13911-20-1)   see: Clometocillin

(2,3-dichloro-4-methoxyphenyl)-2-thienylmethanone
($C_{12}H_8Cl_2O_2S$; 40180-05-0)   see: Tienilic acid

4,6-dichloro-5-methoxypyrimidine
($C_5H_4Cl_2N_2O$; 5018-38-2)   see: Sulfadoxine

2-(dichloromethoxy)-1,1,1-trifluoroethane
($C_3H_3Cl_2F_3O$; 26644-86-0)   see: Isoflurane

4,6-dichloro-2-methyl-5-(1-acetyl-2-imidazolin-2-yl-amino)pyrimidine
($C_{10}H_{11}Cl_2N_5O$; 75438-54-9)   see: Moxonidine

2,6-dichloro-3-methylaniline
($C_7H_7Cl_2N$; 64063-37-2)   see: Meclofenamic acid

1,2-dichloro-3-methylbenzene
($C_7H_6Cl_2$; 32768-54-0)   see: Anagrelide hydrochloride

N-[4-(dichloromethyleneamino)-3,5-dichlorophenyl]tri-chloroacetamide
($C_9H_3Cl_7N_2O$; 86861-35-0)   see: Apraclonidine

(dichloromethylene)bisphosphonic acid tetrakis(1-methyl-ethyl) ester
($C_{13}H_{28}Cl_2O_6P_2$; 10596-22-2)   see: Clodronate disodium

dichloromethyl methyl ether
($C_2H_4Cl_2O$; 4885-02-3)   see: Clidanac

4,5-dichloro-2-methyl-3-(2H)-pyridazone
($C_5H_4Cl_2N_2O$; 933-76-6)   see: Emorfazone

2,6-dichloro-4-methyl-3-pyridinecarbonitrile
($C_7H_4Cl_2N_2$; 875-35-4)   see: Nevirapine

2,6-dichloro-4-methyl-3-pyridinecarboxamide
($C_7H_6Cl_2N_2O$; 38841-54-2)   see: Nevirapine

2,4-dichloro-6-methylpyrimidine
($C_5H_4Cl_2N_2$; 5424-21-5)   see: Epirizole

2,5-dichloro-N-methyl-3-thiophenesulfonamide
($C_5H_5Cl_2NO_2S_2$; 56946-84-0)   see: Lornoxicam

2,6-dichloro-4-nitroaniline
($C_6H_4Cl_2N_2O_2$; 99-30-9)   see: Apraclonidine

2,4-dichloro-1-nitrobenzene
($C_6H_3Cl_2NO_2$; 611-06-3)   see: Clobazam; Pirprofen

2,5-dichloro-1-nitrobenzene
($C_6H_3Cl_2NO_2$; 89-61-2)   see: Domperidone; Triclosan

2,3-dichloro-6-nitrobenzonitrile
($C_7H_2Cl_2N_2O_2$; 2112-22-3)   see: Anagrelide hydrochloride

cis-2-(2,4-dichlorophenyl)-2-(1*H*-1,2,4-triazol-1-ylmethyl)-1,3-dioxolane-4-methanol methanesulfonate
(C$_{14}$H$_{15}$Cl$_2$N$_3$O$_5$S; *67914-86-7*)   see: Itraconazole

cis-1-[4-[[2-(2,4-dichlorophenyl)-2-(1*H*-1,2,4-triazol-1-yl-methyl)-1,3-dioxolan-4-yl]methoxy]phenyl]piperazine
(C$_{23}$H$_{25}$Cl$_2$N$_5$O$_3$; *67915-50-8*)   see: Itraconazole

cis-4-[4-[4-[4-[[2-(2,4-dichlorophenyl)-2-(1*H*-1,2,4-triazol-1-ylmethyl)-1,3-dioxolan-4-yl]methoxy]phenyl]-1-piper-azinyl]phenyl]-2,4-dihydro-3*H*-1,2,4-triazol-3-one
(C$_{31}$H$_{30}$Cl$_2$N$_8$O$_4$; *89848-41-9*)   see: Itraconazole

cis-[4-[4-[4-[[2-(2,4-dichlorophenyl)-2-(1*H*-1,2,4-triazol-1-ylmethyl)-1,3-dioxolan-4-yl]methoxy]phenyl]-1-piperazi-nyl]phenyl]carbamic acid phenyl ester
(C$_{36}$H$_{34}$Cl$_2$N$_6$O$_5$; *89848-11-3*)   see: Itraconazole

2,6-dichloropurine
(C$_5$H$_2$Cl$_2$N$_4$; *5451-40-1*)   see: Aciclovir; Cladribine

2-[(2,6-dichloro-9*H*-purin-9-yl)methoxy]ethanol benzoate (ester)
(C$_{15}$H$_{12}$Cl$_2$N$_4$O$_3$; *59277-96-2*)   see: Aciclovir

3,6-dichloropyridazine
(C$_4$H$_2$Cl$_2$N$_2$; *141-30-0*)   see: Azintamide; Cadralazine; Pildralazine; Sulfachlorpyridazine

2,6-dichloropyridine
(C$_5$H$_3$Cl$_2$N; *2402-78-0*)   see: Flupirtine

3,5-dichloro-4-pyridone
(C$_5$H$_3$Cl$_2$NO; *17228-70-5*)   see: Cefazedone

4,7-dichloroquinoline
(C$_9$H$_5$Cl$_2$N; *86-98-6*)   see: Amodiaquine; Chloroquine; Glafenine; Hydroxychloroquine

3,3-dichloro-2,3,4,5-tetrahydro-1*H*-1-benzazepin-2-one
(C$_{10}$H$_9$Cl$_2$NO; *86499-22-1*)   see: Benazepril

1,3-dichloro-1,1,3,3-tetraisopropyldisiloxane
(C$_{12}$H$_{28}$Cl$_2$OSi$_2$; *69304-37-6*)   see: Cladribine

3,4-dichloro-1,2,5-thiadiazole
(C$_2$Cl$_2$N$_2$S; *5728-20-1*)   see: Timolol

[2,3-dichloro-4-(2-thienylcarbonyl)phenoxy]acetic acid ethyl ester
(C$_{15}$H$_{12}$Cl$_2$O$_4$S; *66883-42-9*)   see: Tienilic acid

2,5-dichlorothiophene
(C$_4$H$_2$Cl$_2$S; *3172-52-9*)   see: Lornoxicam

2,5-dichloro-3-thiophenesulfonyl chloride
(C$_4$HCl$_3$O$_2$S$_2$; *56946-83-9*)   see: Lornoxicam

2,6-dichlorothiophenol
(C$_6$H$_4$Cl$_2$S; *24966-39-0*)   see: Butoconazole

2,5-dichlorotoluene
(C$_7$H$_6$Cl$_2$; *19398-61-9*)   see: Ziprasidone hydrochloride

1,3-dichloro-6-(trifluoromethyl)-9-phenanthrene-carboxaldehyde
(C$_{16}$H$_7$Cl$_2$F$_3$O; *38492-84-1*)   see: Halofantrine

1,3-dichloro-6-(trifluoromethyl)-9-phenanthrene-carboxylic acid
(C$_{16}$H$_7$Cl$_2$F$_3$O$_2$; *38635-85-7*)   see: Halofantrine

diclofenac
(C$_{14}$H$_{11}$Cl$_2$NO$_2$; *15307-86-5*)   see: Aceclofenac

α,β-dicyanobenzenepropanoic acid ethyl ester
(C$_{13}$H$_{12}$N$_2$O$_2$; *5473-13-2*)   see: Phensuximide

α,α'-dicyano-1,1-cyclohexanediacetimide compd. with ammonia
(C$_{12}$H$_{16}$N$_4$O$_2$; *108669-05-2*)   see: Gabapentin

dicyanodiamide
(C$_2$H$_4$N$_4$; *461-58-5*)   see: Cyclobarbital; Hexobarbital; Metformin; Moroxydine

2,4-dicyano-3-ethyl-3-methylglutarimide
(C$_{10}$H$_{11}$N$_3$O$_2$; *1135-62-2*)   see: Bemegride

dicyanogen
(C$_2$N$_2$; *460-19-5*)   see: Sulfametrole

α,β-dicyano-β-methylhydrocinnamic acid methyl ester
(C$_{13}$H$_{12}$N$_2$O$_2$; *29840-30-0*)   see: Mesuximide

4,4'-dicyano-2-nitrostilbene
(C$_{16}$H$_9$N$_3$O$_2$; *67466-65-3*)   see: Hydroxystilbamidine isethionate

dicyclohexylamine
(C$_{12}$H$_{23}$N; *101-83-7*)   see: Cefoxitin

dicyclohexylcarbinol
(C$_{13}$H$_{24}$O; *4453-82-1*)   see: Perhexiline

***N*,*N*'-dicyclohexylcarbodiimide**
(C$_{13}$H$_{22}$N$_2$; *538-75-0*)   see: Repaglinide

dicyclohexyl ketone
(C$_{13}$H$_{22}$O; *119-60-8*)   see: Perhexiline

1,1-dicyclohexyl-2-(2-pyridyl)ethanol hydrochloride
(C$_{19}$H$_{30}$ClNO; *94439-07-3*)   see: Perhexiline

1,1-dicyclohexyl-2-(2-pyridyl)ethylene hydrochloride
(C$_{19}$H$_{28}$ClN; *6746-72-1*)   see: Perhexiline

dicyclopropylmethylamine
(C$_7$H$_{13}$N; *13375-29-6*)   see: Rilmenidine

3',4'-didehydro-4'-deoxy-6'-[(trifluoroacetyl)oxy]vinca-leukoblastinium mono(trifluoroacetate)
(C$_{50}$H$_{56}$F$_6$N$_4$O$_{12}$)   see: Vinorelbine

3',4'-didehydro-4'-deoxyvincaleukoblastine 6'-oxide
(C$_{46}$H$_{56}$N$_4$O$_9$; *60332-19-6*)   see: Vinorelbine

2',3'-didehydro-2',3'-dideoxycytidine
(C$_9$H$_{11}$N$_3$O$_3$; *7481-88-1*)   see: Zalcitabine

11,12-didehydro-7,10-dihydro-10-hydroxyretinol
(C$_{20}$H$_{30}$O$_2$; *3230-75-9*)   see: Retinol

(5α,6α)-7,8-didehydro-4,5-epoxymorphinan-3,6-diol
(C$_{16}$H$_{17}$NO$_3$; *466-97-7*)   see: Nalorphine

2',3'-dideoxyadenosine
(C$_{10}$H$_{13}$N$_5$O$_2$; *4097-22-7*)   see: Didanosine

(*S*)-2,4-dideoxy-1,3-*O*-[(4-methoxyphenyl)methylene]-4-(2-propenyl)-D-*erythro*-pentitol
(C$_{16}$H$_{22}$O$_4$; *118207-50-4*)   see: Tacrolimus

[3*R*-[3α(*S**),5β]]-2,4-dideoxy-5-*O*-[(4-methoxyphenyl)me-thyl]-2-methyl-5-*C*-[tetrahydro-5-(iodomethyl)-3-furanyl]-3-*O*-[tris(1-methylethyl)silyl]-L-*threo*-pentose
(C$_{28}$H$_{47}$IO$_5$Si; *128708-25-8*)   see: Tacrolimus

2,4-dideoxy-5-*O*-[(4-methoxyphenyl)methyl]-2-(2-prope-nyl)-L-*erythro*-pentonic acid methyl ester
(C$_{17}$H$_{24}$O$_5$; *118207-49-1*)   see: Tacrolimus

[2*R*-(2*R**,3*S**,4*R**,5*R**,8*R**,10*R**,11*R**,12*S**,13*S**,14*R**)]-13-[(2,6-dideoxy-3-*C*-methyl-3-*O*-methyl-α-L-*ribo*-hexo-pyranosyl)oxy]-2-ethyl-3,4,6,10-tetrahydroxy-3,5,8,10,12,14-hexamethyl-13-[[3,4,6-trideoxy-3-(dimethyloxido-amino)-β-D-*xylo*-hexopyranosyl]oxy]-1-oxa-6-azacy-clopentadecan-15-one
(C$_{37}$H$_{70}$N$_2$O$_{14}$; *90503-04-1*)   see: Azithromycin

4-diethylamino-2-(2-methoxycarbonylethyl)-2-phenylbu-tyronitrile
($C_{18}H_{26}N_2O_2$; *190912-70-0*)   see: Phenglutarimide

2-(diethylaminomethyl)imidazole
($C_8H_{15}N_3$; *54534-77-9*)   see: Nizofenone

2-diethylamino-4-methyl-1-pentanol
($C_{10}H_{23}NO$; *115985-81-4*)   see: Leucinocaine

N-[(diethylamino)methyl]pyrazinecarboxamide
($C_{10}H_{16}N_4O$; *1017-28-3*)   see: Morinamide

1-diethylamino-4-pentanone
($C_9H_{19}NO$; *105-14-6*)   see: Chloroquine

4-diethylamino-2-phenylbutyronitrile
($C_{14}H_{20}N_2$; *3699-29-4*)   see: Phenglutarimide

3-(diethylamino)-1-propanol
($C_7H_{17}NO$; *622-93-5*)   see: Bornaprine

3-diethylaminopropiophenone
($C_{13}H_{19}NO$; *94-38-2*)   see: Tridihexethyl chloride

3-diethylaminopropyl chloride
($C_7H_{16}ClN$; *104-77-8*)   see: Aprindine

diethylammonium hydrogen sulfite
($C_4H_{13}NO_3S$; *53690-20-3*)   see: Etamsylate

N,N-diethylaniline
($C_{10}H_{15}N$; *91-66-7*)   see: Nedocromil

diethyl benzylidenemalonate
($C_{14}H_{16}O_4$; *5292-53-5*)   see: Acetorphan

diethyl benzylmalonate
($C_{14}H_{18}O_4$; *607-81-8*)   see: Dimetindene

diethyl butylmalonate
see under butylmalonic acid diethyl ester

diethyl 2-sec-butyl-2-methylmalonate
($C_{12}H_{22}O_4$; *64770-18-9*)   see: Mebutamate

diethylcarbamodithioic acid sodium salt
($C_5H_{10}NNaS_2$; *148-18-5*)   see: Disulfiram

diethylcarbamoyl chloride
($C_5H_{10}ClNO$; *88-10-8*)   see: Celiprolol; Diethylcarbamazine

diethyl carbonate
($C_5H_{10}O_3$; *105-58-8*)   see: Ambuside; Bisoprolol;
Fenspiride; Flurbiprofen; Furazolidone; Ketoprofen;
Mephenytoin; Nifuratel; Phenobarbital; Pranoprofen;
Protizinic acid; Temafloxacin; Toloxatone; Tybamate;
Zolmitriptan

diethyl (E)-4-[2-(2-carboxyethenyl)phenyl]-1,4-dihydro-2,6-dimethyl-3,5-pyridinedicarboxylate
($C_{22}H_{25}NO_6$; *103890-71-7*)   see: Lacidipine

N,N-diethylchloroacetamide
($C_6H_{12}ClNO$; *2315-36-8*)   see: Azintamide; Propanidid

N,N-diethylcyanoacetamide
($C_7H_{12}N_2O$; *26391-06-0*)   see: Entacapone

diethyl 2-cyano-3-(4-fluorophenyl)pentanedioate
($C_{16}H_{18}FNO_4$; *198640-81-2*)   see: Paroxetine

diethyl 2-(cyclohexylamino)vinylphosphonate
($C_{12}H_{24}NO_3P$; *20061-84-1*)   see: Cerivastatin sodium

diethyl 3-cyclopentene-1,1-dicarboxylate
($C_{11}H_{16}O_4$; *21622-00-4*)   see: Dolasetron mesilate

diethyl 2-cyclopentenylmalonate
($C_{12}H_{18}O_4$; *53608-93-8*)   see: Cyclopentobarbital

diethyl cyclopropane-1,1-dicarboxylate
($C_9H_{14}O_4$; *1559-02-0*)   see: Montelukast sodium

diethyl (2,4-dichloro-5-fluorobenzoyl)malonate
($C_{14}H_{13}Cl_2FO_5$; *86483-50-3*)   see: Ciprofloxacin

diethyl diethylmalonate
($C_{11}H_{20}O_4$; *77-25-8*)   see: Barbital

diethyl [(7,8-difluoro-3-methoxymethyl-2,3-dihydro-4H-1,4-benzoxazin-4-yl)methylene]malonate
($C_{18}H_{21}F_2NO_6$; *91040-37-8*)   see: Levofloxacin

diethyl 1,4-dihydro-2,6-diisopropyl-4-(4-fluorophenyl)py-ridine-3,5-dicarboxylate
($C_{23}H_{30}FNO_4$; *124863-78-1*)   see: Cerivastatin sodium

diethyl 1,1'-(dithiodi-2,1-ethanediyl)bis[6,8-difluoro-1,4-dihydro-7-(4-methyl-1-piperazinyl)-4-oxo-3-quinoline-carboxylic acid diethyl ester]
($C_{38}H_{44}F_4N_6O_6S_2$; *165541-88-8*)   see: Rufloxacin
hydrochloride

(R*,S*)-1,1'-(1,2-diethyl-1,2-ethanediyl)bis[4-methoxy-benzene]
($C_{20}H_{26}O_2$; *28231-25-6*)   see: Hexestrol

1,1'-(1,2-diethyl-1,2-ethenediyl)bis[4-methoxybenzene]
($C_{20}H_{24}O_2$; *7773-34-4*)   see: Diethylstilbestrol

diethyl ethoxycarbonylphosphonate
($C_7H_{15}O_5P$; *1474-78-8*)   see: Foscarnet sodium

diethyl ethoxymethylenemalonate
($C_{10}H_{16}O_5$; *87-13-8*)   see: Apalcillin; Chloroquine;
Enoxacin; Floctafenine; Flumequine; Levofloxacin;
Lomefloxacin; Nalidixic acid; Norfloxacin; Ofloxacin;
Oxolinic acid; Pefloxacin; Pipemidic acid; Rosoxacin;
Rufloxacin hydrochloride

diethyl ethyl-sec-butylmalonate
($C_{13}H_{24}O_4$; *76-71-1*)   see: Secbutabarbital

diethyl 2-ethyl-2-(3-chloropropyl)malonate
($C_{12}H_{21}ClO_4$; *32821-60-6*)   see: Vincamine

diethyl 9-ethyl-6,9-dihydro-10-propyl-4,6-dioxo-4H-py-rano[3,2-g]quinoline-2,8-dicarboxylate
($C_{23}H_{25}NO_7$; *69049-72-5*)   see: Nedocromil

N,N-diethylethylenediamine
($C_6H_{16}N_2$; *100-36-7*)   see: Ambenonium chloride;
Bromopride; Cinchocaine; Clofexamide; Mefexamide;
Metoclopramide; Procainamide; Tiapride

diethyl 2-(3,3-ethylenedioxybutyl)malonate
($C_{13}H_{22}O_6$; *7796-23-8*)   see: Kebuzone

diethyl α-ethyl-α-isopentylmalonate
($C_{14}H_{26}O_4$; *77-24-7*)   see: Amobarbital

diethyl ethylmalonate
($C_9H_{16}O_4$; *133-13-1*)   see: Amobarbital; Pentobarbital;
Secbutabarbital; Thiopental; Vincamine

diethyl ethyl(1-methylbutyl)malonate
($C_{14}H_{26}O_4$; *76-72-2*)   see: Pentobarbital; Thiopental

diethyl ethylphenylmalonate
($C_{15}H_{20}O_4$; *76-67-5*)   see: Methylphenobarbital;
Phenobarbital

diethyl formamidomalonate
($C_8H_{13}NO_5$; *6326-44-9*)   see: Oxitriptan

diethyl L-glutamate hydrochloride
($C_9H_{18}ClNO_4$; *1118-89-4*)   see: Methotrexate

N,N-diethyl-1,3,4,6,7,11b-hexahydro-9,10-dimethoxy-2-oxo-2H-benzo[a]quinolizine-3-carboxamide
($C_{20}H_{28}N_2O_4$; *2214-63-3*)   see: Benzquinamide

N,N-diethyl-1,3,4,6,7,11b-hexahydro-2-hydroxy-9,10-di-methoxy-2H-benzo[a]quinolizine-3-carboxamide
($C_{20}H_{30}N_2O_4$; *53-68-9*)   see: Benzquinamide

α,β-diethyl-4-hydroxy-β-(4-hydroxyphenyl)benzene-ethanol

($C_{18}H_{22}O_3$; *2297-48-5*)   see: Diethylstilbestrol

3,3-diethyl-5-(hydroxymethylene)-2,4-piperidinedione

($C_{10}H_{15}NO_3$)   see: Methyprylon

diethyl isobutylmalonate

($C_{11}H_{20}O_4$; *10203-58-4*)   see: Butalbital

diethyl ketone

($C_5H_{10}O$; *96-22-0*)   see: Molindone; Oseltamivir

N,N-diethylleucine ethyl ester

($C_{12}H_{25}NO_2$)   see: Leucinocaine

N,N-diethylleucine 4-nitrophenyl ester

($C_{17}H_{26}N_2O_4$)   see: Leucinocaine

diethyl malonate

($C_7H_{12}O_4$; *105-53-3*)   see: Abacavir; Acetorphan; Amobarbital; Benzquinamide; Biotin; Butalbital; Ciprofloxacin; Clidanac; Cyclopentobarbital; Dolasetron mesilate; Grepafloxacin; Kebuzone; Mabuterol; Methohexital; Naftidrofuryl; Rimantadine; Risperidone; Rufloxacin hydrochloride; Secbutabarbital; Secobarbital; Vigabatrin

diethyl methoxycarbonylaminomalonate

($C_9H_{15}NO_6$; *58178-20-4*)   see: Ethyl loflazepate

diethyl methoxymalonate

($C_8H_{14}O_5$; *40924-27-4*)   see: Sulfametoxydiazine

α,β-diethyl-4-methoxy-α-(4-methoxyphenyl)benzene-ethanol

($C_{20}H_{26}O_3$; *5331-23-7*)   see: Diethylstilbestrol; Dimestrol

α,β-diethyl-4-methoxy-β-(4-methoxyphenyl)benzene-ethanol

($C_{20}H_{26}O_3$)   see: Dimestrol

diethyl N-[(4-methylamino)benzoyl]-L-glutamate

($C_{17}H_{24}N_2O_5$; *2378-95-2*)   see: Methotrexate

diethyl N-(5-methylamino-2-thenoyl)-L-glutamate

($C_{15}H_{22}N_2O_5S$; *112889-02-8*)   see: Raltitrexed

diethyl (1-methylbutyl)malonate

($C_{12}H_{22}O_4$; *117-47-5*)   see: Secobarbital

diethyl methylmalonate

($C_8H_{14}O_4$; *609-08-5*)   see: Carprofen; Iloprost; Pirprofen; Suprofen

diethyl methyl(3-oxocyclohexyl)malonate

($C_{14}H_{22}O_5$; *52263-19-1*)   see: Carprofen

diethyl methyl-2-propynylpropanedioate

($C_{11}H_{16}O_4$; *19157-51-8*)   see: Iloprost

diethyl (2-methyl-3,4,6-trifluorobenzoyl)malonate

($C_{15}H_{15}F_3O_5$; *119915-42-3*)   see: Grepafloxacin

diethyl oxalate

($C_6H_{10}O_4$; *95-92-1*)   see: Ambenonium chloride; Bromazepam; Cortisone; Cromoglicic acid; Desoxycortone acetate; Enalapril; Ethionamide; Hydrocortisone; Methylphenobarbital; Nedocromil; Phenobarbital; Piperacillin; Propiverine; Protionamide; Repirinast; Setiptiline; Sildenafil; Troglitazone

diethyl oxaloacetate

($C_8H_{12}O_5$; *108-56-5*)   see: Chloroquine

diethyl 2-(3-oxobutyl)malonate

($C_{11}H_{18}O_5$; *4761-26-6*)   see: Kebuzone

diethyl 3-oxo-2-phenylsuccinate

($C_{14}H_{16}O_5$; *7147-33-3*)   see: Methylphenobarbital; Phenobarbital

2,2-diethyl-4-pentenenitrile

($C_9H_{15}N$; *59346-54-2*)   see: Valdetamide

diethyl phenylmalonate

($C_{13}H_{16}O_4$; *83-13-6*)   see: Felbamate; Methylphenobarbital; Phenobarbital

diethyl 2-phenylthioethylmalonate

($C_{15}H_{20}O_4S$; *1558-97-0*)   see: Sulfinpyrazone

diethyl phosphite

($C_4H_{11}O_3P$; *762-04-9*)   see: Incadronic acid

diethyl phosphochloridate

($C_4H_{10}ClO_3P$; *814-49-3*)   see: Ecothiopate iodide

3,3-diethyl-2,4-piperidinedione

($C_9H_{15}NO_2$; *77-03-2*)   see: Methyprylon

diethyl propylmalonate

($C_{10}H_{18}O_4$; *2163-48-6*)   see: Azapropazone

diethyl [3-(4-pyridyl)anilinomethylene]malonate

($C_{19}H_{20}N_2O_4$; *40034-45-5*)   see: Rosoxacin

diethylstilbestrol

($C_{18}H_{20}O_2$; *56-53-1*)   see: Diethylstilbestrol dipropionate; Diethylstilbestrol disulfate; Dimestrol; Fosfestrol

diethyl succinate

($C_8H_{14}O_4$; *123-25-1*)   see: Sertraline

diethylsulfamoyl chloride

($C_4H_{10}ClNO_2S$; *20588-68-5*)   see: Quinagolide hydrochloride

diethyl sulfate

($C_4H_{10}O_4S$; *64-67-5*)   see: Ditophal; Ethenzamide; Etidocaine; Pipemidic acid; Piprozolin; Rosoxacin

diethyl tetrahydrofurfurylmalonate

($C_{12}H_{20}O_5$; *37136-39-3*)   see: Naftidrofuryl

1,8-diethyl-1,3,4,9-tetrahydropyrano[3,4-b]indole-1-acetic acid ethyl ester

($C_{19}H_{25}NO_3$; *200880-23-5*)   see: Etodolac

3,3-diethyl-1,2,3,4-tetrahydropyridine-2,4-dione

($C_9H_{13}NO_2$; *77-04-3*)   see: Methyprylon

N,N-diethylthiocarbamoyl chloride

($C_5H_{10}ClNS$; *88-11-9*)   see: Astemizole

4,5-diethyl-Δ^5-1,2,4-triazolin-3-one

($C_6H_{11}N_3O$; *52883-26-8*)   see: Etoperidone

2,4-difluoroaniline

($C_6H_5F_2N$; *367-25-9*)   see: Diflunisal; Temafloxacin; Tosufloxacin

1,3-difluorobenzene

($C_6H_4F_2$; *372-18-9*)   see: Fluconazole; Risperidone

2,4'-difluorobenzophenone

($C_{13}H_8F_2O$; *342-25-6*)   see: Flutrimazole

4-(2,4-difluorobenzoyl)piperidine hydrochloride

($C_{12}H_{14}ClF_2NO$; *106266-04-0*)   see: Risperidone

6α,9-difluoro-2-chloro-16α-methyl-11β,17-dihydroxy-21-acetoxypregna-1,4-diene-3,20-dione

($C_{24}H_{29}ClF_2O_6$; *23961-22-0*)   see: Halometasone

7,8-difluoro-3,4-dihydro-2H-1,4-benzothiazine

($C_8H_7F_2NS$; *198278-55-6*)   see: Rufloxacin hydrochloride

(–)-7,8-difluoro-2,3-dihydro-3-hydroxymethyl-4H-1,4-benzoxazine

($C_9H_9F_2NO_2$; *106939-40-6*)   see: Levofloxacin

7,8-difluoro-3,4-dihydro-3-methyl-2H-1,4-benzoxazine

($C_9H_9F_2NO$; *82419-33-8*)   see: Levofloxacin; Ofloxacin

(–)-7,8-difluoro-2,3-dihydro-3-methyl-4H-1,4-benzoxazine

($C_9H_9F_2NO$; *106939-42-8*)   see: Levofloxacin

(S)-[(7,8-difluoro-2,3-dihydro-3-methyl-4H-1,4-benzox-azin-4-yl)methylene]propanedioic acid diethyl ester
($C_{17}H_{19}F_2NO_5$; *106939-43-9*)   see: Levofloxacin

[(7,8-difluoro-2,3-dihydro-3-methyl-4H-1,4-benzoxazin-4-yl)methylene]propanedioic acid diethyl ester
($C_{17}H_{19}F_2NO_5$; *86760-99-8*)   see: Ofloxacin

[S-(R*,R*)]-7,8-difluoro-3,4-dihydro-3-methyl-4-[[1-[(4-methylphenyl)sulfonyl]-2-pyrrolidinyl]carbonyl]-2H-1,4-benzoxazine
($C_{21}H_{22}F_2N_2O_4S$; *106939-44-0*)   see: Levofloxacin

9,10-difluoro-2,3-dihydro-3-methyl-7-oxo-7H-pyri-do[1,2,3-de]-1,4-benzoxazine-6-carboxylic acid
($C_{13}H_9F_2NO_4$; *82419-35-0*)   see: Ofloxacin

(6α,11β,16α,17α)-6,9-difluoro-11,17-dihydroxy-16-methyl-3-oxoandrosta-1,4-diene-17-carboxylic acid
($C_{21}H_{26}F_2O_5$; *28416-82-2*)   see: Fluticasone propionate

(6α,11β,16α)-6,9-difluoro-11,21-dihydroxy-16-methyl-pregna-1,4-diene-3,20-dione
($C_{22}H_{28}F_2O_4$; *2607-06-9*)   see: Diflucortolone valerate; Fluticasone propionate

6α,9α-difluoro-3,20-dioxo-16β-methyl-11β,17,21-trihydr-oxy-1,4-pregnadiene
($C_{22}H_{28}F_2O_5$; *2557-49-5*)   see: Diflorasone diacetate

6,8-difluoro-1-(2-fluoroethyl)-1,4-dihydro-7-(4-methyl-1-piperazinyl)-4-oxo-3-quinolinecarbonitrile
($C_{17}H_{17}F_3N_4O$; *133369-53-6*)   see: Fleroxacin

(6α,11β)-6,9-difluoro-11-hydroxy-17,21-[(1-methoxy-butylidene)bis(oxy)]pregna-1,4-diene-3,20-dione
($C_{25}H_{34}F_2O_6$; *23640-92-8*)   see: Difluprednate

(6α,11β,16β)- 6,9-difluoro-11-hydroxy-17,21-[(1-methoxy-ethylidene)bis(oxy)]-16-methyl-pregna-1,4-diene-3,20-dione
($C_{25}H_{32}F_2O_6$; *50630-18-7*)   see: Diflorasone diacetate

(6α,11β,16α,17α)-6,9-difluoro-11-hydroxy-16-methyl-3-oxo-17-(1-oxopropoxy)androsta-1,4-diene-17-carbothioic acid
($C_{24}H_{30}F_2O_5S$; *80474-45-9*)   see: Fluticasone propionate

(6α,11β,16α,17α)-6,9-difluoro-11-hydroxy-16-methyl-3-oxo-17-(1-oxopropoxy)androsta-1,4-diene-17-carboxylic acid
($C_{24}H_{30}F_2O_6$; *65429-42-7*)   see: Fluticasone propionate

(R)-3,4-difluoro-2-(2-hydroxypropoxy)-1-nitrobenzene
($C_9H_9F_2NO_4$; *124409-94-5*)   see: Levofloxacin

4-(difluoromethoxy)aniline
($C_7H_7F_2NO$; *22236-10-8*)   see: Pantoprazole sodium

5-(difluoromethoxy)-2-[[(3,4-dimethoxy-2-pyridinyl)me-thyl]thio]-1H-benzimidazole
($C_{16}H_{15}F_2N_3O_3S$; *102625-64-9*)   see: Pantoprazole sodium

5-(difluoromethoxy)-2-mercaptobenzimidazole
($C_8H_6F_2N_2OS$; *97963-62-7*)   see: Pantoprazole sodium

4-(difluoromethoxy)-2-nitrobenzenamine
($C_7H_6F_2N_2O_3$; *97963-76-3*)   see: Pantoprazole sodium

N-[4-(difluoromethoxy)phenyl]acetamide
($C_9H_9F_2NO_2$; *22236-11-9*)   see: Pantoprazole sodium

2-(difluoromethoxy)-1,1,1-trifluoroethane
($C_3H_3F_5O$; *1885-48-9*)   see: Isoflurane

(S)-9,10-difluoro-3-methyl-7-oxo-2,3-dihydro-7H-pyri-do[1,2,3-de]-1,4-benzoxazine-6-carboxylic acid
($C_{13}H_9F_2NO_4$; *100986-89-8*)   see: Levofloxacin

[(difluoromethyl)thio]acetic acid
($C_3H_4F_2O_2S$; *83494-32-0*)   see: Flomoxef

cis-7-[[[[(difluoromethyl)thio]acetyl]amino]-7-methoxy-3-[[[1-[2-[[[(4-methylphenyl)methoxy]carbonyl]oxy]ethyl]-1H-tetrazol-5-yl]thio]methyl]-8-oxo-5-oxa-1-azabicyclo-[4.2.0]oct-2-ene-2-carboxylic acid diphenylmethyl ester
($C_{37}H_{36}F_2N_6O_9S_2$; *92823-08-0*)   see: Flomoxef

2,3-difluoro-6-nitrophenol
($C_6H_3F_2NO_3$; *82419-26-9*)   see: Levofloxacin; Ofloxacin

1-(2,3-difluoro-6-nitrophenoxy)-3-methoxy-2-propanone
($C_{10}H_9F_2NO_5$; *91040-35-6*)   see: Levofloxacin

1-(2,3-difluoro-6-nitrophenoxy)-2-propanone
($C_9H_7F_2NO_4$; *82419-32-7*)   see: Ofloxacin

2,3-difluoro-6-nitrophenyl oxiranylmethyl ether
($C_9H_7F_2NO_4$; *91040-33-4*)   see: Levofloxacin

4-(2,4-difluorophenyl)anisole
($C_{13}H_{10}F_2O$; *90101-30-7*)   see: Diflunisal

1-[2-(2,4-difluorophenyl)-2,3-epoxypropyl]-1H-1,2,4-tri-azole
($C_{11}H_9F_2N_3O$; *86386-76-7*)   see: Fluconazole

(2,4-difluorophenyl)lithium
($C_6H_3F_2Li$; *87820-35-7*)   see: Fluconazole

4-(2,4-difluorophenyl)phenol
($C_{12}H_8F_2O$; *59089-68-8*)   see: Diflunisal

(2,4-difluorophenyl)-4-piperidinylmethanone oxime
($C_{12}H_{14}F_2N_2O$; *84163-46-2*)   see: Risperidone

(2,4-difluorophenyl)(tetrahydropyran-4-yl)methanone
($C_{12}H_{12}F_2O_2$; *181479-09-4*)   see: Risperidone

(Z)-(2,4-difluorophenyl)(tetrahydro-2H-pyran-4-yl)me-thanone oxime
($C_{12}H_{13}F_2NO_2$; *181479-10-7*)   see: Risperidone

6α,9-difluoroprednisolone
($C_{21}H_{26}F_2O_5$; *806-29-1*)   see: Difluprednate

6α,9-difluoro-11β,16α,17,21-tetrahydroxypregna-1,4-di-ene-3,20-dione 16,21-diacetate
($C_{25}H_{30}F_2O_8$; *3914-23-6*)   see: Fluocinolone acetonide

1,1-difluoro-2,2,2-trichloroethane
($C_2HCl_3F_2$; *354-12-1*)   see: Methoxyflurane

digitoxin
($C_{41}H_{64}O_{13}$; *71-63-6*)   see: Acetyldigitoxin

diglycolic chloride
($C_4H_4Cl_2O_3$; *21062-20-4*)   see: Ioglycamic acid

digoxin
($C_{41}H_{64}O_{14}$; *20830-75-5*)   see: α-Acetyldigoxin; β-Acetyldigoxin; Metildigoxin

3,4-dihydro-2H-1-benzopyran-3,8-diol
($C_9H_{10}O_3$; *81486-17-1*)   see: Nipradilol

(S)-3,4-dihydro-6-chloro-4-hydroxy-2-(3-methoxypropyl)-2H-thieno[3,2-e]-1,2-thiazine 1,1-dioxide
($C_{10}H_{14}ClNO_4S_2$; *160982-13-8*)   see: Brinzolamide

1,3-dihydro-5-(2-chlorophenyl)-2H-1,4-benzodiazepin-2-one
see under 5-(2-chlorophenyl)-2-oxo-2,3-dihydro-1H-1,4-benzodiazepine

dihydrocortisone 21-acetate
($C_{23}H_{32}O_6$; *1499-59-8*)   see: Cortisone; Prednisone

6,7-dihydro-5H-dibenz[c,e]azepine
($C_{14}H_{13}N$; *6672-69-1*)   see: Azapetine

7,10-dihydro-10-hydroxyretinol 15-acetate
($C_{22}H_{34}O_3$; *95404-32-3*)   see: Retinol

(3α,16α)-14,15-dihydro-14-hydroxy-1,14-secoeburname-nine-14-carboxylic acid methyl ester
($C_{21}H_{28}N_2O_3$; *41173-96-0*)   see: Vincamine

(S)-3,4-dihydro-6-hydroxy-2,5,7,8-tetramethyl-2H-1-ben-zopyran-2-methanol
($C_{14}H_{20}O_3$; *69427-83-4*)   see: Troglitazone

3,4-dihydro-6-hydroxy-2,5,7,8-tetramethyl-2H-1-benzopy-ran-2-methanol α-acetate
($C_{16}H_{22}O_4$; *233757-09-0*)   see: Troglitazone

(±)-3,4-dihydro-4-hydroxy-2H-thieno[3,2-e]-1,2-thiazine 1,1-dioxide
($C_6H_7NO_3S_2$; *138890-97-8*)   see: Brinzolamide

dihydro-2-imino-5-methoxy-4,6(1H,5H)-pyrimidinedione
($C_5H_7N_3O_3$; *89280-05-7*)   see: Sulfametoxydiazine

2,3-dihydro-2-(1-iminopropyl)-2-[(trimethylsilyl)oxy]-1H-indene
($C_{15}H_{23}NOSi$)   see: Indanorex

(1S-cis)-2,3-dihydro-1H-indene-1,2-diol
($C_9H_{10}O_2$; *67528-22-7*)   see: Indinavir sulfate

(1aS)-1a,6a-dihydro-6H-indeno[1,2-b]oxirene
(C_9H_8O; *67528-26-1*)   see: Indinavir sulfate

(2,3-dihydro-1H-inden-4-yl)carbamimidothioic acid methyl ester monohydriodide
($C_{11}H_{15}IN_2S$; *40507-77-5*)   see: Indanazoline

2,3-dihydro-1H-indole-2-carboxylic acid ethyl ester
($C_{11}H_{13}NO_2$; *50501-07-0*)   see: Perindopril

2,3-dihydro-5-mercapto-3-oxo-4-isothiazolecarboxylic acid methyl ester, monosodium salt
($C_5H_4NaO_3S_2$)   see: Cefotetan

dihydro-5(S)-(methanesulfonyloxymethyl)-3(R)-phenyl-methyl-2(3H)-furanone
($C_{13}H_{16}O_5S$; *150323-17-4*)   see: Indinavir sulfate

4,5-dihydro-6-[4-(4-methoxybenzoylamino)-3-nitrophe-nyl]-5-methyl-3(2H)-pyridazinone
($C_{19}H_{18}N_4O_5$; *74149-73-8*)   see: Pimobendan

4-[2-(3,4-dihydro-7-methoxy-4,4-dimethyl-1,3-dioxo-2(1H)-isoquinolinyl)ethyl]benzenesulfonamide
($C_{20}H_{22}N_2O_5S$; *33456-68-7*)   see: Gliquidone

3,4-dihydro-6-(methoxymethoxy)-2,5,7,8-tetramethyl-2H-1-benzopyran-2-methanol
($C_{16}H_{24}O_4$; *107188-55-6*)   see: Troglitazone

3,4-dihydro-6-(methoxymethoxy)-5,7,8-trimethyl-2H-1-benzopyran-2-carboxylic acid ethyl ester
($C_{17}H_{24}O_5$; *107187-97-3*)   see: Troglitazone

1,2-dihydro-6-methoxy-4-methylnaphthalene
($C_{12}H_{14}O$; *30021-91-1*)   see: Dezocine

2,4-dihydro-2-(4-methoxy-6-methyl-2-pyrimidinyl)-5-methyl-3H-pyrazol-3-one
($C_{10}H_{12}N_4O_2$; *18694-45-6*)   see: Epirizole

(E)-2-[2-(3,4-dihydro-6-methoxy-1(2H)-naphthalenyli-dene)ethyl]-2-ethyl-1,3-cyclopentanedione
($C_{20}H_{24}O_3$; *62298-52-6*)   see: Levonorgestrel

[2S-[2α(E),3β]]-2-[2-(3,4-dihydro-6-methoxy-1(2H)-naph-thalenylidene)ethyl]-2-ethyl-3-hydroxycyclopentanone
($C_{20}H_{26}O_3$; *51773-47-8*)   see: Levonorgestrel

3,4-dihydro-2-(3-methoxypropyl)-4-oxo-2H-thieno[3,2-e]-1,2-thiazine-6-sulfonamide 1,1-dioxide
($C_{10}H_{14}N_2O_6S_3$; *154127-41-0*)   see: Brinzolamide

(4S)-3,4-dihydro-2-(3-methoxypropyl)-2H-thieno[3,2-e]-1,2-thiazin-4-ol 1,1-dioxide
($C_{10}H_{15}NO_4S_2$)   see: Brinzolamide

3,4-dihydro-6-methyl-2H-1-benzothiopyran-7-sulfonyl chloride 1,1-dioxide
($C_{10}H_{11}ClO_4S_2$; *1084-64-6*)   see: Meticrane

10,11-dihydro-5-methyl-5H-dibenz[b,f]azepin-10-amine
($C_{15}H_{16}N_2$; *21808-11-7*)   see: Metapramine

N-(10,11-dihydro-5-methyl-5H-dibenz[b,f]azepin-10-yl)formamide
($C_{16}H_{16}N_2O$; *21737-56-4*)   see: Metapramine

(4S-trans)-N-(5,6-dihydro-6-methyl-7,7-dioxido-4H-thieno[2,3-b]thiopyran-4-yl)acetamide
($C_{10}H_{13}NO_3S_2$; *147086-83-7*)   see: Dorzolamide

1,3-dihydro-6-methylfuro[3,4-c]pyridin-7-ol
($C_8H_9NO_2$; *5196-20-3*)   see: Pyridoxine

1,3-dihydro-4-methyl-2H-imidazol-2-one
($C_4H_6N_2O$; *1192-34-3*)   see: Enoximone

3,4-dihydro-2-methyl-4-oxo-2H-1,2-benzothiazine-3-carb-oxylic acid methyl ester 1,1-dioxide
($C_{11}H_{11}NO_5S$; *29209-30-1*)   see: Piroxicam

3-(4,7-dihydro-1-methyl-7-oxo-3-propyl-1H-pyrazo-lo[4,3-d]pyrimidin-5-yl)-4-ethoxybenzenesulfonyl chloride
($C_{17}H_{19}ClN_4O_4S$; *139756-22-2*)   see: Sildenafil

5,6-dihydro-6-methyl-4-oxo-4H-thieno[2,3-b]thiopyran
($C_8H_8OS_2$; *120279-85-8*)   see: Dorzolamide

5,6-dihydro-6-methyl-4-oxo-4H-thieno[2,3-b]thiopyran-2-sulfonamide
($C_8H_9NO_3S_3$; *120279-88-1*)   see: Dorzolamide

5,6-dihydro-6-methyl-4-oxo-4H-thieno[2,3-b]thiopyran-2-sulfonic acid
($C_8H_8O_4S_3$; *120279-86-9*)   see: Dorzolamide

1,3-dihydro-1-[(1-methyl-2-phenylethylidene)amino]-2H-indol-2-one
($C_{17}H_{16}N_2O$; *51135-33-2*)   see: Amfenac sodium

10,11-dihydro-N-methyl-N-(phenylmethyl)-5H-dibenz[b,f]azepine-5-propanamine
($C_{25}H_{28}N_2$; *3978-87-8*)   see: Desipramine

1,3-dihydro-4-[2-[[(4-methylphenyl)sulfonyl]oxy]ethyl]-2H-indol-2-one
($C_{17}H_{17}NO_4S$; *139122-20-6*)   see: Ropinirole

9,10-dihydro-4-(1-methyl-4-piperidinyl)-4H-benzo[4,5]cyclohepta[1,2-b]thiophene-4-ol
($C_{19}H_{23}NOS$; *5189-10-6*)   see: Pizotifen

4,10-dihydro-4-(1-methyl-4-piperidinylidene)-9H-benzo[4,5]cyclohepta[1,2-b]thiophen-9-one
($C_{19}H_{19}NOS$; *34580-09-1*)   see: Ketotifen

4,9-dihydro-4-(1-methyl-4-piperidinylidene)-10H-benzo[4,5]cyclohepta[1,2-b]thiophen-10-one
($C_{19}H_{19}NOS$; *34580-13-7*)   see: Ketotifen

4,5-dihydro-4-methylpyrazole
($C_4H_8N_2$; *5920-30-9*)   see: Fomepizole

(4S-trans)-5,6-dihydro-6-methyl-4H-thieno[2,3-b]thio-pyran-4-ol acetate 7,7-dioxide
($C_{10}H_{12}O_4S_2$; *147086-82-6*)   see: Dorzolamide

(4S-trans)-5,6-dihydro-6-methyl-4H-thieno[2,3-b]thio-pyran-4-ol 7,7-dioxide
($C_8H_{10}O_3S_2$; *147086-81-5*)   see: Dorzolamide

2,5-dihydroxybenzoic acid
($C_7H_6O_4$; *490-79-9*)   see: Flecainide

3,5-dihydroxybenzoic acid
($C_7H_6O_4$; *99-10-5*)   see: Brodimoprim

2,5-dihydroxybenzoic acid monopotassium salt
($C_7H_5KO_4$; *52843-95-5*)   see: Gentisic acid

1,2-dihydroxy-2-butene
($C_4H_8O_2$; *110-64-5*)   see: Iotrolan

1α,25-dihydroxycholesterol
($C_{27}H_{46}O_3$; *50392-32-0*)   see: Calcitriol

3,4-dihydroxycinnamoyl chloride cyclic carbonate
($C_{10}H_5ClO_4$; *116133-06-3*)   see: Cynarine

6,7-dihydroxycoumaranone
($C_8H_6O_4$; *6272-27-1*)   see: Methoxsalen

1α,25-dihydroxy-3,5-cyclovitamin D₂ 1-acetate 6-methyl ether
($C_{31}H_{48}O_4$)   see: Paricalcitol

6,7-dihydroxy-2,3-dihydrobenzofuran
($C_8H_8O_3$; *42484-95-7*)   see: Methoxsalen

2,4-dihydroxy-6,7-dimethoxyquinazoline
($C_{10}H_{10}N_2O_4$; *28888-44-0*)   see: Alfuzosin; Prazosin

(S)-4-[(2,4-dihydroxy-3,3-dimethyl-1-oxobutyl)amino]butanoic acid
($C_{10}H_{19}NO_5$; *49831-65-4*)   see: Calcium hopantenate

3β,5-dihydroxy-6β,17-dimethyl-5α-pregnan-20-one
($C_{23}H_{38}O_3$; *95671-00-4*)   see: Medrogestone

11β,17-dihydroxy-3,20-dioxo-9α-fluoro-21-iodo-16β-methyl-1,4-pregnadiene
($C_{22}H_{28}FIO_4$; *51548-34-6*)   see: Betamethasone adamantoate

11β,17-dihydroxy-3,20-dioxo-9α-fluoro-4-pregnene
($C_{21}H_{29}FO_4$; *337-03-1*)   see: Flugestone acetate

11β,17-dihydroxy-3,20-dioxo-21-iodo-4-pregnene
($C_{21}H_{29}IO_4$; *33767-06-5*)   see: Hydrocortisone sodium phosphate; Tixocortol pivalate

5α,17α-dihydroxy-3,20-dioxo-6β-methylpregnane
($C_{22}H_{34}O_4$; *23706-51-6*)   see: Medroxyprogesterone acetate

2,5-dihydroxy-1,3-dithiane
($C_4H_8O_2S_2$; *200396-18-5*)   see: Brotizolam

1,8-dihydroxy-3-hydroxymethylanthraquinone
($C_{15}H_{10}O_5$; *481-72-1*)   see: Diacerein

11α,17β-dihydroxy-2-(hydroxymethylene)-17-methyl-androst-4-en-3-one
($C_{21}H_{30}O_4$; *2384-26-1*)   see: Formebolone

[1R-[1α(Z),2β(R*),3α,5α]]-7-[3,5-dihydroxy-2-(3-hydroxy-5-phenylpentyl)cyclopentyl]-5-heptenoic acid
($C_{23}H_{34}O_5$; *41639-83-2*)   see: Latanoprost

3',5'-dihydroxy-2-(isopropylamino)acetophenone
($C_{11}H_{15}NO_3$; *94200-14-3*)   see: Orciprenaline

4'-[(4,6-dihydroxy-5-methoxy-2-pyrimidinyl)sulfamoyl]acetanilide
($C_{13}H_{14}N_4O_6S$; *92024-58-3*)   see: Sulfametoxydiazine

3',4'-dihydroxy-2-methylaminoacetophenone
($C_9H_{11}NO_3$; *99-45-6*)   see: Dipivefrine; Epinephrine

3β,17β-dihydroxy-17α-methyl-5-androstene
($C_{20}H_{32}O_2$; *521-10-8*)   see: Bolasterone; Methyltestosterone

(11β,17β)-11,17-dihydroxy-17-methylandrost-4-en-3-one
($C_{20}H_{30}O_3$; *1043-10-3*)   see: Fluoxymesterone

17,21-dihydroxy-16-methylenepregn-4-ene-3,20-dione
($C_{22}H_{30}O_4$; *1570-80-5*)   see: Fluprednidene acetate; Prednylidene

3β,17-dihydroxy-6-methyl-16-methylenepregn-5-en-20-one 17-acetate
($C_{25}H_{36}O_4$; *101611-22-7*)   see: Melengestrol acetate

11α,17β-dihydroxy-17-methyl-3-oxo-4-androstene
($C_{20}H_{30}O_3$; *1807-02-9*)   see: Formebolone

(11β,16α)-11,17-dihydroxy-16-methyl-21-(1-oxoprop-oxy)pregna-1,4,6-triene-3,20-dione
($C_{25}H_{32}O_6$; *69426-18-2*)   see: Alclometasone dipropionate

(3α,16α)-3,17-dihydroxy-16-methylpregnane-11,20-dione
($C_{22}H_{34}O_4$; *25324-87-2*)   see: Dexamethasone

(3α,16β)-3,17-dihydroxy-16-methylpregnane-11,20-dione
($C_{22}H_{34}O_4$; *25273-82-9*)   see: Meprednisone

3α,17α-dihydroxy-16β-methylpregnane-11,20-dione
($C_{22}H_{34}O_4$; *803-09-8*)   see: Betamethasone

5,17-dihydroxy-6β-methyl-5α-pregnane-3,20-dione cyclic bis(ethylene acetal)
($C_{26}H_{42}O_6$; *3386-01-4*)   see: Medroxyprogesterone acetate

3α,17α-dihydroxy-16β-methyl-5β-pregnane-11,20-dione 20-ethylene acetal
($C_{24}H_{38}O_5$; *5078-92-2*)   see: Betamethasone

17α,21-dihydroxy-16β-methylpregnane-3,11,20-trione 21-acetate
($C_{24}H_{34}O_6$; *1253-36-7*)   see: Betamethasone

(5α,5'β)-3β,11β-dihydroxy-2'-methyl-5'H-pregnano[17,16-d]oxazol-20-one
($C_{23}H_{35}NO_4$; *13649-86-0*)   see: Deflazacort; Fluazacort

3β,11β-dihydroxy-2'-methyl-5'βH-5α-pregnano[17,16-d]oxazol-20-one 3-acetate
($C_{25}H_{37}NO_5$; *13649-87-1*)   see: Fluazacort

17α,21-dihydroxy-16α-methyl-1,4,9(11)-pregnatriene-3,20-dione 17-(2-furoate)
($C_{27}H_{30}O_6$; *83880-62-0*)   see: Mometasone furoate

3α,17α-dihydroxy-16β-methyl-5β-pregn-9(11)-en-20-one
($C_{22}H_{34}O_3$; *13656-77-4*)   see: Betamethasone

2,4-dihydroxy-6-methylpyrimidine
($C_5H_6N_2O_2$; *626-48-2*)   see: Dipyridamole; Epirizole

(11β)-11,17-dihydroxy-21-[(methylsulfonyl)oxy]pregna-1,4-diene-3,20-dione
($C_{22}H_{30}O_7S$; *35410-28-7*)   see: Prednisolone sodium sulfobenzoate

(11β)-11,17-dihydroxy-21-[(methylsulfonyl)oxy]pregn-4-ene-3,20-dione
($C_{22}H_{32}O_7S$; *6677-96-9*)   see: Hydrocortisone sodium phosphate

3,4-dihydroxy-5-nitrobenzaldehyde
($C_7H_5NO_5$; *116313-85-0*)   see: Entacapone

11β,17α-dihydroxy-3-oxoandrosta-1,4-diene-17β-carboxylic acid
($C_{20}H_{26}O_5$; *37927-29-0*)   see: Loteprednol etabonate

1-[(11β,17α),11,17-dihydroxy-3-oxoandrosta-1,4-dien-17-yl]-1,2-propanedione
($C_{22}H_{28}O_5$; *6911-15-5*)   see: Fluperolone acetate

1α,25-dihydroxy-10-oxo-3,5-cyclo-19-norvitamin D₂ 1-acetate 6-methyl ether
($C_{30}H_{46}O_5$)   see: Paricalcitol

(3β)-3,23-dihydroxy-20-oxo-21-norchola-5,22-dien-24-oic acid ethyl ester sodium salt
($C_{25}H_{35}NaO_5$)   see: Desoxycortone acetate

2,4-dihydroxyphenyl benzyl ketone
($C_{14}H_{12}O_3$; *3669-41-8*)   see: Ipriflavone

3,4-dimethoxybenzoyl chloride
($C_9H_9ClO_3$; *3535-37-3*)   see: Itopride hydrochloride;
Mebeverine; Vesnarinone

3-[2-(3,4-dimethoxybenzoyl)-4,5-dimethoxyphenyl]-2-pentanone 2-hydrazone
($C_{22}H_{28}N_2O_5$; *37952-09-3*)   see: Tofisopam

3,4-dimethoxybenzyl chloride
($C_9H_{11}ClO_2$; *7306-46-9*)   see: Papaverine

2,6-dimethoxy-3-bromobenzoyl chloride
($C_9H_8BrClO_3$; *84225-91-2*)   see: Remoxipride

1-[3,3-(dimethoxycarbonyl)propyl]-2-(methanesulfonyl)-5-benzoylpyrrole
($C_{19}H_{21}NO_7S$; *80965-05-5*)   see: Ketorolac

3,4-dimethoxycinnamoyl chloride
($C_{11}H_{11}ClO_3$; *39856-08-1*)   see: Tranilast

2,2-dimethoxy-*N,N*-dimethylacetamide
($C_6H_{13}NO_3$; *25408-61-1*)   see: Zolpidem

3,5-dimethoxy-α,α-dimethylbenzeneacetonitrile
($C_{12}H_{15}NO_2$; *22972-63-0*)   see: Nabilone

1,2-dimethoxyethane
($C_4H_{10}O_2$; *110-71-4*)   see: Docetaxel

3,5-dimethoxy-4-ethoxycarbonyloxybenzoyl chloride
($C_{12}H_{13}ClO_6$; *18780-68-2*)   see: Syrosingopine

3,5-dimethoxy-4-hydroxybenzonitrile
($C_9H_9NO_3$; *72684-95-8*)   see: Morclofone

5,6-dimethoxy-1-indanone
($C_{11}H_{12}O_3$; *2107-69-9*)   see: Donepezil hydrochloride

3,5-dimethoxy-4-(2-methoxyethoxy)benzenepropanoic acid ethyl ester
($C_{16}H_{24}O_6$; *55211-63-7*)   see: Tetroxoprim

2,3-dimethoxy-5-methyl-6-(9-carboxynonyl)benzoquinone
($C_{19}H_{28}O_6$; *58185-99-2*)   see: Idebenone

5,6-dimethoxy-2-methyl-3-indolylacetic acid
($C_{13}H_{15}NO_4$; *71987-65-0*)   see: Oxypertine

5,6-dimethoxy-2-methyl-3-(4-phenylpiperazinocarbonyl-methyl)indole
($C_{23}H_{27}N_3O_3$; *71987-57-0*)   see: Oxypertine

3,4-dimethoxy-2-methylpyridine 1-oxide
($C_8H_{11}NO_3$; *72830-07-0*)   see: Pantoprazole sodium

6,7-dimethoxy-2-methyl-1,2,3,4-tetrahydroisoquinoline-1-acetic acid
($C_{14}H_{19}NO_4$; *54170-09-1*)   see: Glaziovine

(*E,E,E*)-1,1-dimethoxy-7-methyl-9-(2,6,6-trimethyl-1-cyclohexen-1-yl)-4,6,8-nonatrien-3-one
($C_{21}H_{32}O_3$; *82925-39-1*)   see: Retinol

(*E*)-5,5-dimethoxy-3-methyl-1-(2,6,6-trimethyl-1-cyclo-hcxcn-1-yl)-1-pentcn-3-ol
($C_{17}H_{30}O_3$; *1224-76-6*)   see: Retinol

3,5-dimethoxy-4-[2-(4-morpholinyl)ethoxy]benzonitrile
($C_{15}H_{20}N_2O_4$)   see: Morclofone

1,6-dimethoxynaphthalene
($C_{12}H_{12}O_2$; *3900-49-0*)   see: Quinagolide hydrochloride

4,5-dimethoxy-2-nitrobenzaldehyde
($C_9H_9NO_5$; *20357-25-9*)   see: Alfuzosin

4,5-dimethoxy-2-nitrobenzamide
($C_9H_{10}N_2O_5$; *4959-60-8*)   see: Alfuzosin

3,4-dimethoxyphenethylamine
($C_{10}H_{15}NO_2$; *120-20-7*)   see: Benzquinamide; Bevantolol;
Denopamine; Dobutamine; Dopamine; Dopexamine;
Papaverine

2-(3,4-dimethoxyphenethylamino)-4'-benzyloxy-acetophenone
($C_{25}H_{27}NO_4$; *64434-48-6*)   see: Denopamine

(3,4-dimethoxyphenyl)acetone
($C_{11}H_{14}O_3$; *776-99-8*)   see: Carbidopa; Dimoxyline;
Methyldopa

3,4-dimethoxyphenylacetonitrile
($C_{10}H_{11}NO_2$; *93-17-4*)   see: Methyldopa; Papaverine;
Verapamil

(3,4-dimethoxyphenyl)dimethylaminoacetonitrile
($C_{12}H_{16}N_2O_2$; *37672-97-2*)   see: Vetrabutine

α-(3,4-dimethoxyphenyl)-α-(dimethylamino)benzene-pentanenitrile
($C_{21}H_{26}N_2O_2$)   see: Vetrabutine

2-(3,4-dimethoxyphenyl)ethylamine
see under 3,4-dimethoxyphenethylamine

N-[2-(3,4-dimethoxyphenyl)ethyl]-4-methoxy-α-methyl-benzenepropanamine
($C_{21}H_{29}NO_3$; *61413-44-3*)   see: Dobutamine

N-[2-(3,4-dimethoxyphenyl)ethyl]methylamine
($C_{11}H_{17}NO_2$; *3490-06-0*)   see: Gallopamil; Verapamil

N-[2-(3,4-dimethoxyphenyl)ethyl]-N'-(2-phenyl-ethyl)hexanediamide
($C_{24}H_{32}N_2O_4$; *86480-25-3*)   see: Dopexamine

L-3-(3,4-dimethoxyphenyl)-2-hydrazino-2-methylalanine
($C_{12}H_{18}N_2O_4$; *28860-96-0*)   see: Carbidopa

N-[1-[(3,4-dimethoxyphenyl)hydroxymethyl]propyl]ben-zeneacetamide
($C_{20}H_{25}NO_4$)   see: Moxaverine

L-3-(3,4-dimethoxyphenyl)-2-methylalanine
($C_{12}H_{17}NO_4$; *39948-18-0*)   see: Carbidopa

(±)-3-(3,4-dimethoxyphenyl)-2-methylalanine
($C_{12}H_{17}NO_4$; *10128-06-0*)   see: Methyldopa

2-(3,4-dimethoxyphenyl)-3-methylbutyronitrile
($C_{13}H_{17}NO_2$; *20850-49-1*)   see: Verapamil

1-[(3,4-dimethoxyphenyl)methyl]-3,4-dihydro-6,7-dime-thoxy-2(1*H*)-isoquinolinepropanoic acid 1,5-pentanediyl ester
($C_{51}H_{66}N_2O_{12}$; *64228-77-9*)   see: Atracurium besilate

N-[2-(3,4-dimethoxyphenyl)-1-methylethyl]-4-ethoxy-3-methoxybenzeneacetamide
($C_{22}H_{29}NO_5$; *93-31-2*)   see: Dimoxyline

2-(3,5-dimethoxyphenyl)-2-methyl-3-octanone
($C_{17}H_{26}O_3$; *55048-08-3*)   see: Nabilone

1-(3,4-dimethoxyphenyl)-2-nitro-1-butanol
($C_{12}H_{17}NO_5$; *1779-85-7*)   see: Moxaverine

1-(2,5-dimethoxyphenyl)-1,2-propanedione 2-oxime
($C_{11}H_{13}NO_4$; *121347-31-7*)   see: Methoxamine

1-(3,4-dimethoxyphenyl)-2-propanone oxime
($C_{11}H_{15}NO_3$; *1454-62-2*)   see: Dimoxyline

α-(3,4-dimethoxyphenyl)-2-pyridinemethanol
($C_{14}H_{15}NO_3$; *31749-10-7*)   see: Rimiterol

3,4-dimethoxyphenyl 2-pyridinyl ketone
($C_{14}H_{13}NO_3$; *27693-42-1*)   see: Rimiterol

2',5'-dimethoxypropiophenone
($C_{11}H_{14}O_3$; *5803-30-5*)   see: Methoxamine

2,4-dimethoxypyrimidine
($C_6H_8N_2O_2$; *3551-55-1*)   see: Cytarabine

N-[4-[[(5,6-dimethoxy-4-pyrimidinyl)amino]sulfonyl]phe-nyl]acetamide
(C$_{14}$H$_{16}$N$_4$O$_5$S; *5018-54-2*)   see: Sulfadoxine

6,7-dimethoxyquinazoline-2,4-dione
see under 2,4-dihydroxy-6,7-dimethoxyquinazoline

3,3-dimethoxy-2-(3,4,5-trimethoxybenzyl)propionitrile
(C$_{15}$H$_{21}$NO$_5$; *7520-70-9*)   see: Trimethoprim

2,4-dimethoxy-6-trimethylammoniopyrimidine chloride
(C$_9$H$_{16}$ClN$_3$O$_2$; *77767-96-5*)   see: Sulfadimethoxine

(*E*)-5,5-dimethoxy-1-(2,6,6-trimethyl-1-cyclohexen-1-yl)-1-penten-3-one
(C$_{16}$H$_{26}$O$_3$; *85458-25-9*)   see: Retinol

(3*S-trans*)-3-(2,5-dimethoxy-3,4,6-trimethylphenyl)-1-(hexahydro-2-phenyl-1*H*-pyrrolo[1,2-*c*]imidazol-3-yl)-1-propanone
(C$_{26}$H$_{34}$N$_2$O$_3$)   see: Troglitazone

4-(2,5-dimethoxy-3,4,6-trimethylphenyl)-2-methyl-2-buten-1-ol
(C$_{16}$H$_{24}$O$_3$; *104679-53-0*)   see: Troglitazone

dimethylacetamide
(C$_4$H$_9$NO; *127-19-5*)   see: α-Acetyldigoxin; Iodoxamic acid

N,O-**dimethylacetohydroxamic acid**
(C$_4$H$_9$NO$_2$; *78191-00-1*)   see: Zileuton

dimethyl acetonedicarboxylate
(C$_7$H$_{10}$O$_5$; *1830-54-2*)   see: Tropenziline bromide

dimethyl acetylenedicarboxylate
(C$_6$H$_6$O$_4$; *762-42-5*)   see: Malotilate; Nedocromil

dimethyl [*N*-(4-acetyl-3-hydroxy-2-propylphenyl)-*N*-ethyl-amino]maleate
(C$_{19}$H$_{25}$NO$_6$; *77941-04-9*)   see: Nedocromil

3,3-dimethylacrylic acid
(C$_5$H$_8$O$_2$; *541-47-9*)   see: Bucillamine

1,3-dimethyladamantane
(C$_{12}$H$_{20}$; *702-79-4*)   see: Memantine

dimethylamine
(C$_2$H$_7$N; *124-40-3*)   see: Alminoprofen; Alpidem; Altretamine; Amitriptyline; Benzalkonium chloride; Camazepam; Cetalkonium chloride; Cethexonium bromide; Chlorprothixene; Ciprofloxacin; Clofedanol; Dacarbazine; Dextropropoxyphene; Dimazole; Domiphen bromide; Etacrynic acid; Fluoxetine; Loperamide; Medifoxamine; Mepindolol; Meropenem; Nelfinavir mesylate; Ondansetron; Oxitriptan; Prolonium iodide; Rizatriptan benzoate; Sumatriptan; Tilidine; Tiotixene; Tiracizine; Tolmetin; Tolpropamine; Topotecan; Vetrabutine; Zimeldine; Zolmitriptan; Zolpidem

dimethylamine hydrochloride
(C$_2$H$_8$ClN; *506-59-2*)   see: Metformin; Ranitidine

3-dimethylamino-4'-bromopropiophenone
(C$_{11}$H$_{14}$BrNO; *2138-34-3*)   see: Zimeldine

4-(dimethylamino)butanal diethyl acetal
(C$_{10}$H$_{23}$NO$_2$; *1116-77-4*)   see: Zolmitriptan

4-(dimethylamino)butanal dimethyl acetal
(C$_8$H$_{19}$NO$_2$; *19718-92-4*)   see: Rizatriptan benzoate; Sumatriptan

3-(dimethylaminocarbonyloxy)pyridine
(C$_8$H$_{10}$N$_2$O$_2$; *51581-32-9*)   see: Pyridostigmine bromide

N,N-**dimethyl-2-amino-2-[2-(2-chlorobenzoyl)-4-chloro-phenylhydrazono]acetamide**
(C$_{17}$H$_{16}$Cl$_2$N$_4$O$_2$; *65698-99-9*)   see: Rilmazafone

1-dimethylamino-2-chloropropane
(C$_5$H$_{12}$ClN; *108-14-5*)   see: Isothipendyl; Methadone; Promethazine

2-(dimethylamino)cyclohexanol
(C$_8$H$_{17}$NO; *30727-29-8*)   see: Cethexonium bromide

6-(dimethylamino)-1,2-dimethylquinolinium iodide
(C$_{13}$H$_{17}$IN$_2$)   see: Pyrvinium embonate

4-dimethylamino-2,2-diphenylbutyronitrile
(C$_{18}$H$_{20}$N$_2$; *23278-88-8*)   see: Normethadone

α-(+)-**4-dimethylamino-1,2-diphenyl-3-methyl-2-butanol**
(C$_{19}$H$_{25}$NO; *38345-66-3*)   see: Dextropropoxyphene

α-(±)-**4-dimethylamino-1,2-diphenyl-3-methyl-2-butanol**
(C$_{19}$H$_{25}$NO; *63957-11-9*)   see: Dextropropoxyphene

4-dimethylamino-2,2-diphenylvaleronitrile
(C$_{19}$H$_{22}$N$_2$; *125-79-1*)   see: Methadone

[4*S*-(4α,4aα,5α,5aα,6β,12β,12aα)]-4-(dimethylamino)-6,12-epoxy-1,4,4a,5,5a,6,11,11a,12,12a-decahydro-3,5,10,12a-tetrahydroxy-6-methyl-1,11-dioxo-12-sulfoxy-2-naphthacenecarboxamide
(C$_{22}$H$_{24}$N$_2$O$_{12}$S)   see: Metacycline

2-dimethylaminoethanol
(C$_4$H$_{11}$NO; *108-01-0*)   see: Aclatonium napadisilate; Bromazine; Chloroquine; Deanol acetamidobenzoate; Diphenhydramine; Medrylamine; Orphenadrine; Pirisudanol; Quinisocaine; Suxamethonium chloride; Tetracaine; Tromantadine

4-[2-(dimethylamino)ethoxy]benzaldehyde
(C$_{11}$H$_{15}$NO$_2$; *15182-92-0*)   see: Itopride hydrochloride; Trimethobenzamide

4-[2-(dimethylamino)ethoxy]benzophenone
(C$_{17}$H$_{19}$NO$_2$; *51777-15-2*)   see: Tamoxifen; Toremifene

4-(2-dimethylaminoethoxy)benzylamine
(C$_{11}$H$_{18}$N$_2$O; *20059-73-8*)   see: Itopride hydrochloride; Trimethobenzamide

2-[2-(dimethylamino)ethoxy]ethanol
(C$_6$H$_{15}$NO$_2$; *1704-62-7*)   see: Dimethoxanate

4-[2-(dimethylamino)ethoxy]-2-methyl-5-(1-methyl-ethyl)benzenamine
(C$_{14}$H$_{24}$N$_2$O; *83880-23-3*)   see: Moxisylyte

4-[2-(dimethylamino)ethoxy]-2-methyl-5-(1-methyl-ethyl)phenol
(C$_{14}$H$_{23}$NO$_2$; *35231-36-8*)   see: Moxisylyte

N-[4-[2-(dimethylamino)ethoxy]-2-methyl-5-(1-methyl-ethyl)phenyl]acetamide**
(C$_{16}$H$_{26}$N$_2$O$_2$; *3380-60-7*)   see: Moxisylyte

α-[4-[2-(dimethylamino)ethoxy]phenyl]-β-ethyl-α-phenyl-benzeneethanol**
(C$_{26}$H$_{31}$NO$_2$; *748-97-0*)   see: Tamoxifen

4-(2-dimethylaminoethoxy)phenylmagnesium bromide
(C$_{10}$H$_{14}$BrMgNO; *35258-27-6*)   see: Tamoxifen

2-dimethylaminoethyl 4-aminobenzoate
(C$_{11}$H$_{16}$N$_2$O$_2$; *10012-47-2*)   see: Tetracaine

2-(2-dimethylaminoethylamino)pyridine
(C$_9$H$_{15}$N$_3$; *23826-72-4*)   see: Chloropyrilene; Methapyrilene; Thenyldiamine

α-[2-(dimethylamino)ethyl]benzenemethanol**
(C$_{11}$H$_{17}$NO; *5554-64-3*)   see: Fluoxetine

2-(dimethylamino)ethyl chloride

($C_4H_{10}ClN$; *107-99-3*)   see: Bephenium hydroxynaphthoate; Binedaline; Brompheniramine; Captodiame; Carbinoxamine; Chlorphenamine; Chlorphenoxamine; Cyclopentolate; Dibenzepine; Diltiazem; Dimetindene; Doxylamine; Ethoheptazine; Itopride hydrochloride; Meclofenoxate; Mepyramine; Moxisylyte; Normethadone; Noxiptiline; Pheniramine; Phenyltoloxamine; Tamoxifen; Toremifene; Trimethobenzamide; Tripelennamine; Zotepine

2-[2-(dimethylamino)ethyl]-2,3-dihydro-1-[1-(2-pyridinyl)ethyl]-1*H*-inden-1-ol

($C_{20}H_{26}N_2O$; *70080-51-2*)   see: Dimetindene

2-(2-dimethylaminoethyl)-1-indanone

($C_{13}H_{17}NO$; *3409-21-0*)   see: Dimetindene

3-[3-(2-dimethylaminoethyl)-1*H*-indol-5-yl]-L-alanine

($C_{15}H_{21}N_3O_2$)   see: Zolmitriptan

2-dimethylaminoethyl mercaptan

($C_4H_{11}NS$; *108-02-1*)   see: Ecothiopate iodide

α-[2-(dimethylamino)ethyl]-4-methyl-α-phenylbenzenemethanol

($C_{18}H_{23}NO$; *58574-44-0*)   see: Tolpropamine

(±)-3-[1-(dimethylamino)ethyl]phenol

($C_{10}H_{15}NO$; *105601-04-5*)   see: Rivastigmine

[2-(dimethylamino)ethyl](phenylmethyl)propanedioic acid diethyl ester

($C_{18}H_{27}NO_4$; *1805-03-4*)   see: Dimetindene

(2-dimethylaminoethyl)phenyl(2-pyridyl)acetonitrile

($C_{17}H_{19}N_3$; *71486-42-5*)   see: Pheniramine

1-(2-dimethylaminoethyl)-1*H*-tetrazole-5-thiol

($C_5H_{11}N_5S$; *61607-68-9*)   see: Cefotiam

2-dimethylamino-6-hydroxybenzothiazole

($C_9H_{10}N_2OS$; *943-04-4*)   see: Dimazole

***trans*-2,2-dimethyl-5-amino-6-hydroxy-1,3-dioxepane**

($C_7H_{15}NO_3$; *79944-37-9*)   see: Iotrolan

4-(dimethylamino)-3-(imidazo[1,2-*a*]pyridin-6-yl)-3-buten-2-one

($C_{13}H_{15}N_3O$; *106730-70-5*)   see: Olprinone hydrochloride

β-dimethylaminoisobutyrophenone

($C_{12}H_{17}NO$; *91-03-2*)   see: Dextropropoxyphene

(–)-β-dimethylaminoisobutyrophenone

($C_{12}H_{17}NO$; *48141-77-1*)   see: Dextropropoxyphene

3-(dimethylamino)-2-(2-methoxyethoxy)-2-propenal

($C_8H_{15}NO_3$; *15131-88-1*)   see: Glymidine

2-(dimethylaminomethyl)-4-(2-aminoethylthiomethyl)thiazole

($C_9H_{17}N_3S_2$; *78441-62-0*)   see: Nizatidine

3-dimethylamino-7-methyl-1,2,4-benzotriazine 1-oxide

($C_{10}H_{12}N_4O$; *50632-92-3*)   see: Azapropazone

4-(dimethylamino)-3-methyl-2-butanone

($C_7H_{15}NO$; *22104-62-7*)   see: Clobutinol

2-[(dimethylamino)methyl]cyclohexanone

($C_9H_{17}NO$; *15409-60-6*)   see: Tramadol

3-dimethylamino-7-methyl-1,2-dihydro-1,2,4-benzotriazine

($C_{10}H_{14}N_4$; *43171-03-5*)   see: Azapropazone

2-dimethylamino-1-methylethyl chloride

see under 1-dimethylamino-2-chloropropane

5-(dimethylaminomethyl)furfuryl alcohol

($C_7H_{11}NO_2$; *80020-43-5*)   see: Ranitidine

2-dimethylaminomethyl-1-methylpyrrole

($C_8H_{14}N_2$; *56139-76-5*)   see: Tolmetin

α-[(dimethylamino)methyl]-4-nitrobenzeneacetic acid

($C_{11}H_{14}N_2O_4$; *71593-63-0*)   see: Alminoprofen

3-dimethylamino-2-methylpropyl chloride

see under 1-chloro-3-dimethylamino-2-methylpropane

5-[3-(dimethylamino)-2-methylpropyl]-10,11-dihydro-5*H*-dibenzo[*a,d*]cyclohepten-5-ol

($C_{21}H_{27}NO$; *2625-17-4*)   see: Butriptyline

3-dimethylamino-2-methylpropylmagnesium chloride

($C_6H_{14}ClMgN$; *36795-29-6*)   see: Butriptyline

10-(3-dimethylamino-2-methylpropyl)phenothiazine

($C_{18}H_{22}N_2S$; *84-96-8*)   see: Oxomemazine

3-[(dimethylamino)methyl]-1,2,3,9-tetrahydro-4*H*-carbazol-4-one

($C_{15}H_{18}N_2O$; *35556-30-0*)   see: Ondansetron

2-[(dimethylamino)methyl]-4-thiazolemethanol

($C_7H_{12}N_2OS$; *78441-69-7*)   see: Nizatidine

[4*S*-(4α,4aα,5α,5aα,6α,12aα)]-4-(dimethylamino)-1,4,4a,5,5a,6,11,12a-octahydro-3,5,10,12,12a-pentahydroxy-1,11-dioxo-6-[(phenylthio)methyl]-2-naphthacenecarboxamide

($C_{28}H_{28}N_2O_8S$; *146253-71-6*)   see: Doxycycline

[4*S*-(4α,4aα,5aα,12aα)]-4-(dimethylamino)-1,4,4a,5,5a,6,11,12a-octahydro-3,10,12,12a-tetrahydroxy-1,11-dioxo-2-naphthacenecarboxamide

($C_{21}H_{22}N_2O_7$; *808-26-4*)   see: Minocycline

[4*S*-(4α,4aα,5aα,12aα)]-4-(dimethylamino)-1,4,4a,5,5a,6,11,12a-octahydro-3,10,12,12a-tetrahydroxy-9-nitro-1,11-dioxo-2-naphthacenecarboxamide

($C_{21}H_{21}N_3O_9$; *4199-35-3*)   see: Minocycline

(*R*)-[2-(dimethylamino)-2-oxo-1-[(phenylthio)methyl]ethyl]carbamic acid phenylmethyl ester

($C_{19}H_{22}N_2O_3S$; *197302-34-4*)   see: Nelfinavir mesylate

***N*-[3-[3-(dimethylamino)-1-oxo-2-propenyl]phenyl]acetamide**

($C_{13}H_{16}N_2O_2$; *96605-61-7*)   see: Zaleplon

***N*-[3-[3-(dimethylamino)-1-oxo-2-propenyl]phenyl]-*N*-ethylacetamide**

($C_{15}H_{20}N_2O_2$; *96605-66-2*)   see: Zaleplon

9-[3-(dimethylamino)-1-oxopropyl]-*N,N*-dimethyl-9*H*-thioxanthene-2-sulfonamide

($C_{20}H_{24}N_2O_3S$)   see: Tiotixene

3-(dimethylamino)phenol

($C_8H_{11}NO$; *99-07-0*)   see: Edrophonium chloride; Neostigmine methylsulfate

3-dimethylaminophenol sodium salt

($C_8H_{10}NNaO$; *65161-06-0*)   see: Demecarium bromide

1-dimethylamino-2-phenoxyethane

($C_{10}H_{15}NO$; *13468-02-5*)   see: Bephenium hydroxynaphthoate; Domiphen bromide; Thenium closilate

4-dimethylamino-2-phenylbutyronitrile

($C_{12}H_{16}N_2$; *50599-78-5*)   see: Ethoheptazine

4-dimethylaminophenylmagnesium bromide

($C_8H_{10}BrMgN$; *7353-91-5*)   see: Mifepristone

[*R-(R*,*S**)]-2-(dimethylamino)-1-phenylpropyl octanoate

($C_{19}H_{31}NO_2$; *114264-02-7*)   see: Orlistat

3-(dimethylamino)-1-propanol

($C_5H_{13}NO$; *3179-63-3*)   see: Clomipramine

3-dimethylaminopropiophenone

($C_{11}H_{15}NO$; *3506-36-3*)   see: Fluoxetine; Tolpropamine

3-dimethylaminopropylamine

($C_5H_{14}N_2$; *109-55-7*)   see: Azacosterol; Cabergoline

2-dimethylaminopropyl chloride

($C_5H_{12}ClN$; *53309-35-6*)   see: Aceprometazine; Dimetotiazine; Isoaminile

3-dimethylaminopropyl chloride

($C_5H_{12}ClN$; *109-54-6*)   see: Acepromazine; Bencyclane; Benzydamine; Chlorpromazine; Citalopram; Clomipramine; Dimetacrine; Imipramine; Promazine; Prothipendyl; Triflupromazine

5-[3-(dimethylamino)propyl]-5*H*-dibenzo[*a,d*]cyclohepten-5-ol

($C_{20}H_{23}NO$; *18029-54-4*)   see: Cyclobenzaprine

5-[3-(dimethylamino)propyl]-10,11-dihydro-5*H*-dibenzo[*a,d*]cyclohepten-5-ol

($C_{20}H_{25}NO$; *1159-03-1*)   see: Amitriptyline

11-[3-(dimethylamino)propyl]-6,11-dihydrodibenzo[*b,e*]thiepin-11-ol

($C_{19}H_{23}NOS$; *1531-85-7*)   see: Dosulepin

11-[3-(dimethylamino)propyl]-6,11-dihydrodibenz[*b,e*]oxepin-11-ol

($C_{19}H_{23}NO_2$; *4504-88-5*)   see: Doxepin

9-[3-(dimethylamino)propyl]-9,10-dihydro-10,10-dimethyl-9-anthracenol

($C_{21}H_{27}NO$; *85118-29-2*)   see: Melitracen

17β-[[3-(dimethylamino)propyl]formylamino]androst-5-en-3β-ol

($C_{25}H_{42}N_2O_2$; *102399-53-1*)   see: Azacosterol

3-dimethylaminopropylmagnesium bromide

($C_5H_{12}BrMgN$; *120615-47-6*)   see: Chlorprothixene

3-dimethylaminopropylmagnesium chloride

($C_5H_{12}ClMgN$; *19070-16-7*)   see: Amitriptyline; Cyclobenzaprine; Dosulepin; Doxepin; Melitracen; Oxetorone

4-dimethylaminopyridine

($C_7H_{10}N_2$; *1122-58-3*)   see: Paclitaxel; Zafirlukast

4-dimethylamino-3-(4-pyridyl)-3-buten-2-one

($C_{11}H_{14}N_2O$; *78504-61-7*)   see: Milrinone

2-dimethylaminosulfonylphenothiazine

($C_{14}H_{14}N_2O_2S_2$; *1090-78-4*)   see: Dimetotiazine; Pipotiazine; Thioproperazine

2-dimethylaminosulfonyl-9*H*-thioxanthene

($C_{15}H_{15}NO_2S_2$; *3285-33-4*)   see: Tiotixene

dimethylaminothioacetamide

($C_4H_{10}N_2S$; *27507-28-4*)   see: Nizatidine

4-dimethylamino-1-trimethylsilyl-1-butanone

($C_9H_{21}NOSi$)   see: Rizatriptan benzoate

(3β,17β)-7,17-dimethylandrost-5-ene-3,7,17-triol

($C_{21}H_{34}O_3$; *96613-61-5*)   see: Calusterone

dimethylaniline

($C_8H_{11}N$; *121-69-7*)   see: Methylthioninium chloride; Quetiapine fumarate

***N,N*-dimethylaniline**

see under dimethylaniline

2,3-dimethylaniline

($C_8H_{11}N$; *87-59-2*)   see: Mefenamic acid; Repirinast

2,6-dimethylaniline

($C_8H_{11}N$; *87-62-7*)   see: Bupivacaine; Etidocaine; Lidocaine; Lidoflazine; Mepivacaine; Pilsicainide; Pyrrocaine; Ropivacaine hydrochloride; Tocainide; Xipamide

3,4-dimethylaniline

($C_8H_{11}N$; *95-64-7*)   see: Riboflavin

3,4-dimethylanisol

($C_9H_{12}O$; *4685-47-6*)   see: Xibornol

10,10-dimethylanthrone

($C_{16}H_{14}O$; *5447-86-9*)   see: Melitracen

1,3-dimethylbarbituric acid

($C_6H_8N_2O_3$; *769-42-6*)   see: Urapidil

***N,N*-dimethylbenzamide**

($C_9H_{11}NO$; *611-74-5*)   see: Ketorolac

α,α-dimethylbenzeneethanol acetate

($C_{12}H_{16}O_2$; *151-05-3*)   see: Fexofenadine hydrochloride

dimethyl 5-benzoyl-1,2-dihydro-3*H*-pyrrolo[1,2-*a*]pyrrole-1,1-dicarboxylate

($C_{18}H_{17}NO_5$; *80965-08-8*)   see: Ketorolac

***N,N*-dimethylbenzylamine**

see under benzyldimethylamine

2,2'-dimethylbiphenyl

($C_{14}H_{14}$; *605-39-0*)   see: Azapetine

***N,N'*-dimethyl-*N,N'*-bis(3-hydroxypropyl)ethylenediamine**

($C_{10}H_{24}N_2O_2$; *14037-75-3*)   see: Hexobendine

(11β,16α)-6,16-dimethyl-17,20:20,21-bis[methylenebis(oxy)]-2'-phenyl-2'*H*-pregna-2,4,6-trieno[3,2-*c*]pyrazol-11-ol

($C_{32}H_{38}N_2O_5$; *1110-35-6*)   see: Cortivazol

***N,N*-dimethyl-1,3-butadien-1-amine**

($C_6H_{11}N$; *1515-77-1*)   see: Tilidine

[1*S*-[1α,3α,7β,8β(2*S**,4*S**),8aβ]]-2,2-dimethylbutanoic acid 8-[2-[4-[[(1,1-dimethylethyl)dimethylsilyl]oxy]tetrahydro-6-oxo-2*H*-pyran-2-yl]ethyl]-1,2,3,7,8,8a-hexahydro-3,7-dimethyl-1-naphthalenyl ester

($C_{31}H_{52}O_5Si$; *79902-59-3*)   see: Simvastatin

***N,N*-dimethylbutyramide**

($C_6H_{13}NO$; *760-79-2*)   see: Hydrocortisone 17-butyrate

2,2-dimethylbutyryl chloride

($C_6H_{11}ClO$; *5856-77-9*)   see: Simvastatin

dimethylcarbamic acid 3-(dimethylamino)phenyl ester

($C_{11}H_{16}N_2O_2$; *16088-19-0*)   see: Neostigmine methylsulfate

dimethylcarbamic acid 5-[[(1,1-dimethylethyl)(phenylmethyl)amino]acetyl]-1,3-phenylene ester

($C_{25}H_{33}N_3O_5$; *81732-47-0*)   see: Bambuterol

dimethylcarbamoyl chloride

(C_3H_6ClNO; *79-44-7*)   see: Bambuterol; Fadrozole; Neostigmine methylsulfate; Pyridostigmine bromide

***N,N*-dimethylcarbamoylmethyl (4-hydroxyphenyl)acetate**

($C_{12}H_{15}NO_4$; *59721-16-3*)   see: Camostat

1-(dimethylcarbamoyl)-4-[3-(trimethylsiloxy)propyl]imidazole

($C_{12}H_{23}N_3O_2Si$; *102676-27-7*)   see: Fadrozole

***N,N*-dimethyl-2-chloroacetoacetamide**

($C_6H_{10}ClNO_2$; *5810-11-7*)   see: Rilmazafone

***N,N*-dimethyl-4-chlorobenzamide**

($C_9H_{10}ClNO$; *14062-80-7*)   see: Clometacin

***N,N*-dimethyl-2-chloro-2-[2-(2-chlorobenzoyl)-4-chlorophenylazo]acetoacetamide**

($C_{19}H_{16}Cl_3N_3O_3$; *85815-52-7*)   see: Rilmazafone

1,3-dimethyl-6-(3-chloropropylamino)uracil
($C_9H_{14}ClN_3O_2$; *34654-81-4*)   see: Urapidil

dimethylcyanamide
($C_3H_6N_2$; *1467-79-4*)   see: Azapropazone

dimethyl cyanocarboimidodithioate
($C_4H_6N_2S_2$; *10191-60-3*)   see: Cimetidine

dimethyl cyclohexylidenemalonate
($C_{11}H_{16}O_4$; *94286-34-7*)   see: Gabapentin

(S)-2,2-dimethylcyclopropanecarboxamide
($C_6H_{11}NO$; *75885-58-4*)   see: Cilastatin

4,4-dimethyl-3,4-dihydro-2H-1-benzothiopyran
($C_{11}H_{14}S$; *66165-06-8*)   see: Tazarotene

2,2-dimethyl-4,7-dihydro-1,3-dioxepin
($C_7H_{12}O_2$; *1003-83-4*)   see: Iotrolan; Nelfinavir mesylate; Pyridoxine

dimethyl 1,4-dihydro-4-(3-nitrophenyl)-3,5-pyridine-dicarboxylate
($C_{15}H_{14}N_2O_6$; *43113-96-8*)   see: Rosoxacin

dimethyl 2,6-dimethoxyterephthalate
($C_{12}H_{14}O_6$; *16849-68-6*)   see: Brodimoprim

6,6-dimethyl-5,7-dioxaspiro[2.5]octane-4,8-dione
($C_8H_{10}O_4$; *5617-70-9*)   see: Ketorolac

2,2-dimethyl-1,3-dioxolane-4-methanol 2-aminobenzoate
($C_{13}H_{17}NO_4$; *4934-23-0*)   see: Glafenine

2,2-dimethyl-1,3-dioxolane-4-methanol 2-nitrobenzoate
($C_{13}H_{15}NO_6$; *4601-17-6*)   see: Glafenine

6,16α-dimethyl-3,20-dioxo-11β,17,21-trihydroxy-4,6-pregnadiene
($C_{23}H_{32}O_5$; *39932-51-9*)   see: Cortivazol

N,N'-dimethyl-1,2-diphenyl-1,2-ethanediamine
($C_{16}H_{20}N_2$; *22751-68-4*)   see: Paroxetine

dimethyl(3,3-diphenyltetrahydro-2-furylidene)ammonium bromide
($C_{18}H_{20}BrNO$; *37743-18-3*)   see: Loperamide

3-O,17α-dimethylestradiol
($C_{20}H_{28}O_2$; *15236-73-4*)   see: Methylestrenolone

N-[(1,1-dimethylethoxy)carbonyl]-L-alanyl-N-[(1α,5α,6α)-3-[8-(2,4-difluorophenyl)-6-(ethoxycarbonyl)-3-fluoro-5,8-dihydro-5-oxo-1,8-naphthyridin-2-yl]-3-azabicyclo[3.1.0]hex-6-yl]-L-alaninamide
($C_{33}H_{37}F_3N_6O_7$; *186772-86-1*)   see: Alatrofloxacin mesilate

N²-[N-[(1,1-dimethylethoxy)carbonyl]-L-alanyl]-D-α-glutamine phenylmethyl ester
($C_{20}H_{29}N_3O_6$; *18814-49-8*)   see: Romurtide

N²-[N²-[N-[(1,1-dimethylethoxy)carbonyl]-L-alanyl]-D-α-glutaminyl]-N⁶-[(phenylmethoxy)carbonyl]-L-lysine phenylmethyl ester
($C_{34}H_{47}N_5O_9$; *59524-63-9*)   see: Romurtide

1-[N-[(1,1-dimethylethoxy)carbonyl]-L-alanyl]-L-proline phenylmethyl ester
($C_{20}H_{28}N_2O_5$; *35084-69-6*)   see: Enalapril

(S)-α-[[(1,1-dimethylethoxy)carbonyl]amino]benzeneacetic acid methyl ester
($C_{14}H_{19}NO_4$; *143978-88-5*)   see: Docetaxel

[2aR-[2aα,4β,4aβ,6β,9α(αR*,βS*),11α,12α,12aα,12bα]]-β-[[(1,1-dimethylethoxy)carbonyl]amino]-α-[1-(ethoxy)ethoxy]benzenepropanoic acid 12b-(acetyloxy)-12-(benzoyloxy)-4,6-bis[[(2,2,2-trichloroethoxy)carbonyl]oxy]-2a,3,4,4a,5,6,9,10,11,12,12a,12b-dodecahydro-11-hydroxy-4a,8,13,13-tetramethyl-5-oxo-7,11-methano-1H-cyclodeca[3,4]benz[1,2-b]oxet-9-yl ester
($C_{53}H_{63}Cl_3NO_{19}$)   see: Docetaxel

[2aR-[2aα,4β,4aβ,6β,9α(αR*,βS*),11α,12α,12aα,12bα]]-β-[[(1,1-dimethylethoxy)carbonyl]amino]-α-hydroxy-benzenepropanoic acid 2a,3,4,4a,5,6,9,10,11,12,12a,12b-dodecahydro-11-hydroxy-4a,8,13,13-tetramethyl-5-oxo-4,6-bis[[(2,2,2-trichloroethoxy)carbonyl]oxy]-7,11-methano-1H-cyclodeca[3,4]benz[1,2-b]oxet-9-yl ester
($C_{49}H_{55}Cl_6NO_{18}$; *114915-14-9*)   see: Docetaxel

[6R-[6α,7β(R*)]]-[[7-[[[[(1,1-dimethylethoxy)carbonyl]amino](4-hydroxyphenyl)acetyl]amino]-2-[(diphenylmethoxy)carbonyl]-8-oxo-5-thia-1-azabicyclo[4.2.0]oct-2-en-3-yl]methyl]triphenylphosphonium iodide
($C_{52}H_{49}IN_3O_7PS$; *92676-83-0*)   see: cis-Cefprozil

[6R-[6α,7β(R*)]]-7-[[[[(1,1-dimethylethoxy)carbonyl]amino]phenylacetyl]amino]-3-methyl-8-oxo-5-thia-1-azabicyclo[4.2.0]oct-2-ene-2-carboxylic acid
($C_{21}H_{25}N_3O_6S$; *28180-92-9*)   see: Cefalexin

1-[N⁶-[(1,1-dimethylethoxy)carbonyl]-N²-[(phenylmethoxy)carbonyl]-L-lysyl]-L-proline phenylmethyl ester
($C_{31}H_{41}N_3O_7$; *90826-23-6*)   see: Lisinopril

[S-(R*,R*)]-γ-[[6-[(1,1-dimethylethoxy)carbonyl]tetrahydro-1(2H)-pyridazinyl]carbonyl]-1,3-dihydro-1,3-dioxo-2H-isoindole-2-butanoic acid
($C_{22}H_{27}N_3O_7$; *88767-18-4*)   see: Cilazapril

[6R-[6α,7β(Z)]]-7-[[[[2-(1,1-dimethylethoxy)-2-oxoethoxy]imino][2-(formylamino)-4-thiazolyl]acetyl]amino]-3-ethenyl-8-oxo-5-thia-1-azabicyclo[4.2.0]oct-2-ene-2-carboxylic acid diphenylmethyl ester
($C_{34}H_{33}N_5O_8S_2$; *79350-29-1*)   see: Cefixime

[6R-[6α,7β(Z)]]-7-[[[[2-(1,1-dimethylethoxy)-2-oxoethoxy]imino][2-(formylamino)-4-thiazolyl]acetyl]amino]-3-(triphenylphosphoranidyl)-8-oxo-5-thia-1-azabicyclo-[4.2.0]oct-2-ene-2-carboxylic acid diphenylmethyl ester
($C_{51}H_{46}N_5O_8PS_2$)   see: Cefixime

(S)-3-[[(1,1-dimethylethyl)amino]carbonyl]-3,4-dihydro-2(1H)-isoquinolinecarboxylic acid phenylmethyl ester
($C_{22}H_{26}N_2O_3$; *149182-71-8*)   see: Saquinavir

5-[[(1,1-dimethylethyl)amino]carbonyl]-2,3-dihydro-1,4-pyrazinedicarboxylic acid 1-(1,1-dimethylethyl) 4-(phenylmethyl) ester
($C_{22}H_{31}N_3O_5$; *171504-92-0*)   see: Indinavir sulfate

[3S-[2(1S*,2S*),3α,4aβ,8aβ]]-[3-[3-[[(1,1-dimethylethyl)amino]carbonyl]octahydro-2(1H)-isoquinolinyl]-2-hydroxy-1-[(phenylthio)methyl]propyl]carbamic acid phenylmethyl ester
($C_{32}H_{45}N_3O_4S$; *159878-04-3*)   see: Nelfinavir mesylate

(S)-2-[[(1,1-dimethylethyl)amino]carbonyl]-1,4-piperazinedicarboxylic acid 4-(1,1-dimethylethyl) 1-(phenylmethyl) ester
($C_{22}H_{33}N_3O_5$; *150323-34-5*)   see: Indinavir sulfate

2-[3-[(1,1-dimethylethyl)amino]-2-hydroxypropoxy]-5-fluorobenzaldehyde
($C_{14}H_{20}FNO_3$; *58929-11-6*)   see: Butofilolol

[1R-[1α[E[1S*(S*),2S*,3S*,5S*,6S*]],3α,4β]]-1-(1,1-di-methylethyl)-1,2-piperidinedicarboxylic acid 2-[6-formyl-5-[(4-methoxyphenyl)methoxy]-1-[2-[3-methoxy-4-[[tris(1-methylethyl)silyl]oxy]cyclohexyl]-1-methylethe-nyl]-2-methyl-3-[[tris(1-methylethyl)silyl]oxy]-8-nonenyl] ester
($C_{58}H_{101}NO_{10}Si_2$; *128684-97-9*)   see: Tacrolimus

N-(1,1-dimethylethyl)pyrazinecarboxamide
($C_9H_{13}N_3O$; *121885-10-7*)   see: Indinavir sulfate

(1,1-dimethylethyl)[[(3β,5E,7E,22E)-9,10-secoergosta-5,7,10(19),22-tetraen-3-yl]oxy]dimethylsilane
($C_{34}H_{58}OSi$; *104846-63-1*)   see: Calcipotriol

N-(1,1-dimethylethyl)-1,4,5,6-tetrahydropyrazine-carboxamide
($C_9H_{17}N_3O$; *171504-80-6*)   see: Indinavir sulfate

dimethylformamide
(C_3H_7NO; *68-12-2*)   see: Acrivastine; Amlexanox; Amrinone; Etretinate; Fluvastatin sodium; Gitaloxin; Glymidine; Isradipine; Lonazolac; Nomegestrol acetate; Sulfaperin

dimethylformamide diethyl acetal
($C_7H_{17}NO_2$; *1188-33-6*)   see: Loprazolam; Rufloxacin hydrochloride

N,N-dimethylformamide diethyl acetal
see under dimethylformamide diethyl acetal

dimethylformamide dimethyl acetal
($C_5H_{13}NO_2$; *4637-24-5*)   see: Milrinone; Olprinone hydrochloride; Zaleplon

N,N-dimethylformamide di-tert-butyl acetal
($C_{11}H_{25}NO_2$; *36805-97-7*)   see: Lacidipine

6,6-dimethyl-1-hepten-4-yn-3-ol
($C_9H_{14}O$; *78629-20-6*)   see: Terbinafine

3-(1,1-dimethylheptyl)-7,10-dihydro-1-hydroxy-6H-diben-zo[b,d]pyran-6,9(8H)-dione
($C_{22}H_{28}O_4$; *56469-12-6*)   see: Nabilone

3-(1,1-dimethylheptyl)-7,10-dihydro-1-hydroxyspiro[9H-dibenzo[b,d]pyran-9,2'-[1,3]dioxolan]-6(8H)-one
($C_{24}H_{32}O_5$; *56469-13-7*)   see: Nabilone

5-(1,1-dimethylheptyl)resorcinol
($C_{15}H_{24}O_2$; *56469-10-4*)   see: Nabilone

3-(1,1-dimethylheptyl)-6,6a,7,8-tetrahydro-1-hydroxy-6,6-dimethyl-9H-dibenzo[b,d]pyran-9-one
($C_{24}H_{34}O_3$; *56469-14-8*)   see: Nabilone

[4aS-[4aα,6α,8aα,8bβ,10aα,11α(S*),13aβ,13bα]]-11-(1,5-dimethylhexyl)-5,6,8a,8b,10,10a,11,12,13,13a-decahydro-6-hydroxy-8a,10a-dimethyl-2-phenyl-4a,13b-etheno-1H,9H-benzo[c]cyclopenta[h][1,2,4]triazolo[1,2-a]cinno-line-1,3(2H)-dione
($C_{35}H_{47}N_3O_3$; *57102-18-8*)   see: Alfacalcidol

5,9-dimethyl-2'-hydroxybenzo-6-morphen
($C_{14}H_{19}NO$; *16808-63-2*)   see: Phenazocine

N,N-dimethyl-α-(1-hydroxycyclohexyl)-4-methoxyphenyl-thioacetamide
($C_{17}H_{25}NO_2S$; *131801-70-2*)   see: Venlafaxine

N-(1,1-dimethyl-2-hydroxyethyl)propylamine
($C_7H_{17}NO$; *55968-10-0*)   see: Meprylcaine

N,N-dimethylhydroxylamine
(C_2H_7NO; *5725-96-4*)   see: Amitriptylinoxide

2,2-dimethyl-4-hydroxymethyl-1,3-dioxolane
($C_6H_{12}O_3$; *100-79-8*)   see: Floctafenine; Glafenine

5,9-dimethyl-2'-hydroxy-2-phenylacetylbenzo-6-morphen
($C_{22}H_{25}NO_2$)   see: Phenazocine

1,3-dimethyl-6-(3-hydroxypropylamino)uracil
($C_9H_{15}N_3O_3$; *34654-80-3*)   see: Urapidil

5,5-dimethyl-2-isopropylthiazolidine-4-carbonitrile
($C_9H_{16}N_2S$; *13206-50-3*)   see: D-Penicillamine

5,5-dimethyl-2-isopropylthiazolidine-4-carboxylic acid
($C_9H_{17}NO_2S$; *13206-31-0*)   see: D-Penicillamine

5,5-dimethyl-2-isopropyl-Δ³-thiazoline
($C_8H_{15}NS$; *32899-85-7*)   see: D-Penicillamine

N-[4-[[(3,4-dimethyl-5-isoxazolyl)amino]sulfonyl]phe-nyl]acetamide
($C_{13}H_{15}N_3O_4S$; *4206-74-0*)   see: Sulfafurazole

dimethyl malonate
($C_5H_8O_4$; *108-59-8*)   see: Biotin; Dolasetron mesilate; Gabapentin; Ziprasidone hydrochloride

2,6-dimethyl-5-methoxycarbonyl-4-(3-nitrophenyl)-1,4-di-hydropyridine-3-carboxylic acid
($C_{16}H_{16}N_2O_6$; *74936-72-4*)   see: Barnidipine; Lercanidipine hydrochloride

4,4-dimethyl-7-methoxyisochroman-1,3-dione
($C_{12}H_{12}O_4$; *55974-25-9*)   see: Gliquidone

dimethyl methoxymalonate
($C_6H_{10}O_5$; *5018-30-4*)   see: Sulfadoxine

[2S-(2α,5α,6α)]-3,3-dimethyl-6-methoxy-7-oxo-6-[[3-oxo-3-phenoxy-2-(3-thienyl)-1-propenylidene]amino]-4-thia-1-azabicyclo[3.2.0]heptane-2-carboxylic acid (4-nitrophe-nyl)methyl ester
($C_{30}H_{25}N_3O_9S_2$)   see: Temocillin

4,4-dimethyl-2-(2-methoxyphenyl)-2-oxazoline
($C_{12}H_{15}NO_2$; *57598-33-1*)   see: Losartan potassium

N,N-dimethyl-4-methoxyphenylthioacetamide
($C_{11}H_{15}NOS$; *76579-52-7*)   see: Venlafaxine

2,3-dimethyl-4-methylamino-1-phenyl-5-Δ³-pyrazolone
($C_{12}H_{15}N_3O$; *519-98-2*)   see: Metamizole sodium

N,N-dimethyl-5-[[(methylamino)sulfonyl]methyl]-α-oxo-1H-indole-3-acetamide
($C_{14}H_{17}N_3O_4S$; *103628-49-5*)   see: Sumatriptan

dimethyl N-methylcarbonimidodithioate
($C_4H_9NS_2$; *18805-25-9*)   see: Ranitidine

(E)-N,N-dimethyl-3-(4-methylphenyl)-3-phenyl-2-propen-1-amine
($C_{18}H_{21}N$; *58325-63-6*)   see: Tolpropamine

dimethyl methylphosphonate
($C_3H_9O_3P$; *756-79-6*)   see: Iloprost

cis-2,6-dimethylmorpholine
($C_6H_{13}NO$; *6485-55-8*)   see: Amorolfine

dimethyl naphthalene-1,5-disulfonate
($C_{12}H_{12}O_6S_2$; *20779-13-9*)   see: Aclatonium napadisilate

dimethyl 5-nitroisophthalate
($C_{10}H_9NO_6$; *13290-96-5*)   see: Iohexol; Iotalamic acid

2,3-dimethyl-4-nitropyridine N-oxide
($C_7H_8N_2O_3$; *37699-43-7*)   see: Lansoprazole; Rabeprazole sodium

2,3-dimethyl-4-nitroso-1-phenyl-5-Δ³-pyrazolone
($C_{11}H_{11}N_3O_2$; *885-11-0*)   see: Aminophenazone

dimethyl oxalate
($C_4H_6O_4$; *553-90-2*)   see: Ceftriaxone; Misoprostol; Sulfadoxine

4'-[[1,4'-dimethyl-2'-propyl[2,6'-bi-1H-benzimidazol]-1'-yl]methyl]-[1,1'-biphenyl]-2-carboxylic acid 1,1-dimethylethyl ester
($C_{37}H_{38}N_4O_2$; *144702-26-1*)   see: Telmisartan

1,3-dimethyl-7-propylxanthine
($C_{10}H_{14}N_4O_2$; *27760-74-3*)   see: Propentofylline

2,5-dimethylpyrazine
($C_6H_8N_2$; *123-32-0*)   see: Acipimox

2,5-dimethylpyrazine 1-oxide
($C_6H_8N_2O$; *6890-37-5*)   see: Acipimox

3,5-dimethylpyrazole-1-carboxamidine nitrate
($C_6H_{11}N_5O_3$; *38184-47-3*)   see: Eptifibatide

2,3-dimethylpyridine
(C_7H_9N; *583-61-9*)   see: Rabeprazole sodium

3,4-dimethylpyridine
(C_7H_9N; *583-58-4*)   see: Pentazocine; Phenazocine

2,6-dimethylpyridine 1-oxide
(C_7H_9NO; *1073-23-0*)   see: Pyridinol carbamate

2,3-dimethylpyridine N-oxide
(C_7H_9NO; *22710-07-2*)   see: Rabeprazole sodium

N,N-dimethyl-N'-(2-pyridyl)ethylenediamine
see under 2-(2-dimethylaminoethylamino)pyridine

N-[4-[[(2,6-dimethyl-4-pyrimidinyl)amino]sulfonyl]phenyl]acetamide
($C_{14}H_{16}N_4O_3S$; *3163-31-3*)   see: Sulfisomidine

N-(2,6-dimethyl-4-pyrimidinyl)-4-nitrobenzenesulfonamide
($C_{12}H_{12}N_4O_4S$)   see: Sulfisomidine

2,6-dimethyl-4(3H)-quinazolinone
($C_{10}H_{10}N_2O$; *18731-19-6*)   see: Raltitrexed

2-dimethylsulfamoylphenothiazine
see under 2-dimethylaminosulfonylphenothiazine

dimethyl sulfate
($C_2H_6O_4S$; *77-78-1*)   see: α-Acetyldigoxin; Adrafinil; Alizapride; Amezinium metilsulfate; Aminophenazone; Azatadine; Betanidine; Bevonium metilsulfate; Brodimoprim; Bromopride; Caffeine; Camazepam; Cefotaxime; Clebopride; Clotiazepam; Diazepam; Diphemanil metilsulfate; Epimestrol; Epirizole; Etozolin; Flosequinan; Flurbiprofen; Gliquidone; Guajacol; Hexamethonium chloride; Hexobarbital; Hexocyclium metilsulfate; Isoflurane; Kawain; Ketazolam; Mecobalamin; Medazepam; Mefruside; Mephenytoin; Metamizole sodium; Methoxsalen; Metildigoxin; Metoclopramide; Metrizoic acid; Miltefosine; Nandrolone; Nemonapride; Neostigmine methylsulfate; Nimetazepam; Ondansetron; Paramethadione; Pentetrazol; Picotamide; Promestriene; Propyphenazone; Quinagolide hydrochloride; Setastine; Sildenafil; Sulpiride; Temazepam; Tienilic acid; Tilisolol hydrochloride; Timepidium bromide; Tipepidine; Trimethadione

dimethyl sulfide
(C_2H_6S; *75-18-3*)   see: Ketorolac

dimethyl sulfinyl sodium
(C_2H_5NaOS; *15590-23-5*)   see: Flosequinan; Promestriene

(R,R)-dimethyl tartrate
($C_6H_{10}O_6$; *608-68-4*)   see: Naproxen

N,N-dimethyl-2-thenylamine
($C_7H_{11}NS$; *26019-17-0*)   see: Thenium closilate

4,4-di(3-methyl-2-thienyl)-3-butenyl bromide
($C_{14}H_{15}BrS_2$; *109857-81-0*)   see: Tiagabine

di(3-methyl-2-thienyl)cyclopropylcarbinol
($C_{14}H_{16}OS_2$; *148319-26-0*)   see: Tiagabine

di(3-methyl-2-thienyl)ketone
($C_{11}H_{10}OS_2$; *30717-55-6*)   see: Tiagabine

dimethyl 2-thioxo-1,3-dithiole-4,5-dicarboxylate
($C_7H_6O_4S_3$; *7396-41-0*)   see: Malotilate

N,N-dimethyl-5-[(1H-1,2,4-triazol-1-yl)methyl]-2-trimethylsilyl-1H-indol-3-ethanamine
($C_{18}H_{27}N_5Si$)   see: Rizatriptan benzoate

2,3-dimethyl-4-(2,2,2-trifluoroethoxy)pyridine 1-oxide
($C_9H_{10}F_3NO_2$; *103577-61-3*)   see: Lansoprazole

(all-E)-[3,7-dimethyl-9-(2,6,6-trimethyl-1-cyclohexen-1-yl)-2,4,6,8-nonatetraenylidene]triphenylphosphorane
($C_{38}H_{43}P$; *51283-60-4*)   see: Betacarotene

(all-E)-[3,7-dimethyl-9-(2,6,6-trimethyl-1-cyclohexen-1-yl)-2,4,6,8-nonatetraenyl]triphenylphosphonium sulfate (1:1)
($C_{38}H_{45}O_4PS$; *62075-45-0*)   see: Betacarotene

2,2-dimethyltrimethylene acetonylphosphonate
($C_8H_{15}O_4P$; *111011-80-4*)   see: Efonidipine hydrochloride ethanol

2,2-dimethyltrimethylene 2-amino-1-propenylphosphonate
($C_8H_{16}NO_3P$; *111011-81-5*)   see: Efonidipine hydrochloride ethanol

N,N-dimethyl-2-trimethylsilyl-1,3-dithiane-2-propanamine
($C_{12}H_{27}NS_2Si$)   see: Rizatriptan benzoate

4,4-dimethyl-3,5,8-trioxabicyclo[5.1.0]octane
($C_7H_{12}O_3$; *57280-22-5*)   see: Iotrolan; Nelfinavir mesylate

N,N'-dimethylurea
($C_3H_8N_2O$; *96-31-1*)   see: Theophylline

dimorpholinophosphinic chloride
($C_8H_{16}ClN_2O_3P$; *7264-90-6*)   see: Dexamethasone phosphate; Paramethasone; Prednisolone sodium phosphate

(11β,16α)-21-[(di-4-morpholinylphosphinyl)oxy]-9-fluoro-11,17-dihydroxy-16-methylpregna-1,4-diene-3,20-dione
($C_{30}H_{44}FN_2O_8P$; *3864-50-4*)   see: Dexamethasone phosphate

dimsyl sodium
see under dimethyl sulfinyl sodium

3,5-dinitrobenzoic acid
($C_7H_4N_2O_6$; *99-34-3*)   see: Amidotrizoic acid

3,5-dinitrobenzoyl chloride
($C_7H_3ClN_2O_5$; *99-33-2*)   see: Levofloxacin

(R)-3-[[(3,5-dinitrobenzoyl)oxy]methyl]-9,10-difluoro-2,3-dihydro-7-oxo-7H-pyrido[1,2,3-de]-1,4-benzoxazine-6-carboxylic acid ethyl ester
($C_{22}H_{15}F_2N_3O_{10}$; *100993-11-1*)   see: Levofloxacin

4,4'-dinitrophenyl sulfide
($C_{12}H_8N_2O_4S$; *1223-31-0*)   see: Dapsone

4,4'-dinitrophenyl sulfone
($C_{12}H_8N_2O_6S$; *1156-50-9*)   see: Dapsone

diosgenin
($C_{27}H_{42}O_3$; *512-04-9*)   see: Pregnenolone

2-(1,4-dioxaspiro[4.5]dec-2-ylmethyl)-1H-isoindole-1,3(2H)-dione
($C_{17}H_{19}NO_4$; *22216-81-5*)   see: Guanadrel

5,7-dioxa-6-thiaspiro[2.5]octane 6-oxide
($C_5H_8O_3S$; *89729-09-9*)   see: Montelukast sodium

3,17-dioxo-1,4-androstadiene
($C_{19}H_{24}O_2$; *897-06-3*)   see: Estrone

diphenylacetic acid
($C_{14}H_{12}O_2$; *117-34-0*)   see: Adiphenine

diphenylacetic pyrrolidide
($C_{18}H_{19}NO$; *60678-46-8*)   see: Dextromoramide

1,1-diphenylacetone
($C_{15}H_{14}O$; *781-35-1*)   see: Diphenadione

diphenylacetonitrile
($C_{14}H_{11}N$; *86-29-3*)   see: Diisopromine; Diphenoxylate; Doxapram; Fenpiverinium bromide; Isopropamide iodide; Methadone; Normethadone; Prozapine

diphenylacetyl chloride
($C_{14}H_{11}ClO$; *1871-76-7*)   see: Adiphenine; Dextromoramide; Diphenadione; Piperidolate

diphenylamine
($C_{12}H_{11}N$; *122-39-4*)   see: Dimetacrine; Fencarbamide

4-(1,2-diphenyl-1-butenyl)phenol
($C_{22}H_{20}O$; *68684-63-9*)   see: Tamoxifen

1,2-diphenyl-4-butyl-4-(hydroxymethyl)pyrazolidine-3,5-dione
($C_{20}H_{22}N_2O_3$; *23111-33-3*)   see: Feclobuzone; Suxibuzone

diphenylcarbamoyl chloride
($C_{13}H_{10}ClNO$; *83-01-2*)   see: Fencarbamide

diphenyl *N*-cyanoimidocarbonate
($C_{14}H_{10}N_2O_2$; *79463-77-7*)   see: Anagrelide hydrochloride

3,3-diphenyl-3-cyanopropyl bromide
see under 4-bromo-2,2-diphenylbutyronitrile

4,4-diphenyl-2-cyclohexen-1-one
($C_{18}H_{16}O$; *4528-64-7*)   see: Pramiverine

diphenyldiazomethane
($C_{13}H_{10}N_2$; *883-40-9*)   see: Benzatropine; Cefbuperazone; Cefixime; Cefoxitin; *cis*-Cefprozil; Cibenzoline; Latamoxef

(*RS,RS*)-1,2-diphenyl-1-[4-[2-(dimethylamino)ethoxy]phenyl]butane-1,4-diol
($C_{26}H_{31}NO_3$; *141854-25-3*)   see: Toremifene

(*Z*)-1,2-diphenyl-1-[4-(2-(dimethylamino)ethoxy)phenyl]-1-buten-4-ol
($C_{26}H_{29}NO_2$; *97151-03-6*)   see: Toremifene

2-[4-(1,2-diphenylethenyl)phenoxy]-*N,N*-diethylethanamine
($C_{26}H_{29}NO$; *19957-52-9*)   see: Clomifene

(–)-*cis*-2,4-diphenyl-5-(1-ethoxyethoxy)-4,5-dihydro-1,3-oxazin-6-one
($C_{20}H_{21}NO_4$; *182072-57-7*)   see: Paclitaxel

β,β-diphenylethyl methyl ketone
($C_{16}H_{16}O$; *5409-60-9*)   see: Terodiline

1,2-diphenyl-1-(4-ethylphenyl)ethene
($C_{22}H_{20}$; *111077-74-8*)   see: Broparestrol

2,2-diphenyl-4-(hexahydro-1*H*-azepino)butyronitrile
($C_{22}H_{26}N_2$; *83898-29-7*)   see: Prozapine

diphenylmethanethiol
($C_{13}H_{12}S$; *4237-48-3*)   see: Adrafinil

[6*R*-(6α,7α)]-7-[[3-(diphenylmethoxy)-2-(4-hydroxyphenyl)-1,3-dioxopropyl]amino]-7-methoxy-3-[[(1-methyl-1*H*-tetrazol-5-yl)thio]methyl]-8-oxo-5-oxa-1-azabicyclo[4.2.0]-oct-2-ene-2-carboxylic acid diphenylmethyl ester
($C_{46}H_{40}N_6O_9S$)   see: Latamoxef

diphenylmethyl 7-aminocephalosporanate
($C_{23}H_{22}N_2O_5S$; *27266-61-1*)   see: Cefbuperazone; Cefoxitin; Cefuroxime

diphenylmethyl 7-amino-3-chloromethyl-3-cephem-4-carboxylate hydrochloride
($C_{21}H_{20}Cl_2N_2O_3S$; *107837-26-3*)   see: *cis*-Cefprozil

diphenylmethyl 7-amino-3-chloromethyl-3-cephem-4-carboxylate monohydrochloride
($C_{21}H_{20}Cl_2N_2O_3S$; *79349-53-4*)   see: Cefixime

diphenylmethyl 7-amino-7-methoxycephalosporanate
($C_{24}H_{24}N_2O_6S$; *35565-04-9*)   see: Cefoxitin

diphenylmethyl 7(*R*)-7-amino-7-methoxy-3-(1-methyl-tetrazol-5-ylthiomethyl)-1-oxa-1-dethia-3-cephem-4-carboxylate
($C_{24}H_{24}N_6O_5S$; *66510-99-4*)   see: Latamoxef

diphenylmethyl 7(*R*)-amino-3-(1-methyl-1*H*-tetrazol-5-ylthiomethyl)-3-cephem-4-carboxylate
($C_{23}H_{22}N_6O_3S_2$; *53090-86-1*)   see: Cefbuperazone

diphenylmethyl 7-amino-3-[(*Z*)-1-propenyl]-3-cephem-4-carboxylate
($C_{23}H_{22}N_2O_3S$; *106447-41-0*)   see: *cis*-Cefprozil

diphenylmethyl 7-amino-3-vinyl-3-cephem-4-carboxylate hydrochloride
($C_{22}H_{21}ClN_2O_3S$; *79349-67-0*)   see: Cefixime

diphenylmethyl 7(*S*)-azido-7-bromocephalosporanate
($C_{23}H_{19}BrN_4O_5S$; *35565-02-7*)   see: Cefoxitin

diphenylmethyl 7(*S*)-azido-7-methoxycephalosporanate
($C_{24}H_{22}N_4O_6S$; *35565-03-8*)   see: Cefoxitin

diphenylmethyl 7α-benzamido-3-chloromethyl-1-oxa-3-cephem-4-carboxylate
($C_{28}H_{23}ClN_2O_5$; *68314-04-5*)   see: Flomoxef; Latamoxef

diphenylmethyl 7-[5-benzamido-5-(diphenylmethoxy-carbonyl)pentanamido]-3-hydroxymethyl-3-cephem-4-carboxylate
($C_{47}H_{43}N_3O_8S$; *55779-09-4*)   see: Cefixime

diphenylmethyl 6-benzamidopenicillanate
($C_{28}H_{26}N_2O_4S$; *64324-01-2*)   see: Latamoxef

diphenylmethyl bromide
see under benzhydryl bromide

diphenylmethyl (6*R*,7*R*)-3-(chloromethyl)-8-oxo-7-[(phenylacetyl)amino]-5-thia-1-azabicyclo[4.2.0]oct-2-ene-2-carboxylate
($C_{29}H_{25}ClN_2O_4S$; *64308-63-0*)   see: *cis*-Cefprozil

diphenylmethyl 7-diazocephalosporanate
($C_{23}H_{19}N_3O_5S$; *35609-55-3*)   see: Cefoxitin

diphenylmethyl [6*R*-[6α,7β(*R)]]-7-[[[[(1,1-dimethyl-ethoxy)carbonyl]amino](4-hydroxyphenyl)acetyl]amino]-3-(iodomethyl)-8-oxo-5-thia-1-azabicyclo[4.2.0]oct-2-ene-2-carboxylate**
($C_{34}H_{34}IN_3O_7S$; *92676-82-9*)   see: *cis*-Cefprozil

4-(diphenylmethylene)-1-methylpiperidine
($C_{19}H_{21}N$; *6071-93-8*)   see: Diphemanil metilsulfate

diphenylmethyl 6-*epi*-benzamidopenicillanate
($C_{28}H_{26}N_2O_5S$; *69780-18-3*)   see: Latamoxef

diphenylmethyl (6*R*,7*R*)-3-(hydroxymethyl)-8-oxo-7-[(phenylacetyl)amino]-5-thia-1-azabicyclo[4.2.0]oct-2-ene-2-carboxylate
($C_{29}H_{26}N_2O_5S$; *35246-64-1*)   see: *cis*-Cefprozil

diphenylmethyl 7-methoxy-7-[2-(2-thienyl)acetamido]-cephalosporanate
($C_{30}H_{28}N_2O_7S_2$; *35565-05-0*)   see: Cefoxitin

E

edrophonium bromide
($C_{10}H_{16}BrNO$; *302-83-0*)   see: Edrophonium chloride

elliptinium iodide
($C_{18}H_{17}IN_2O$; *58447-24-8*)   see: Elliptinium acetate

embonic acid
($C_{23}H_{16}O_6$; *130-85-8*)   see: Pyrvinium embonate

enalapril
($C_{20}H_{28}N_2O_5$; *75847-73-3*)   see: Enalaprilat

enanthic anhydride
($C_{14}H_{26}O_3$; *626-27-7*)   see: Norethisterone enanthate; Prasterone enanthate; Testosterone enanthate

L-ephedrine
($C_{10}H_{15}NO$; *299-42-3*)   see: Cinnamedrine; Methamphetamine; Thiadrine

epichlorohydrin
(C_3H_5ClO; *106-89-8*)   see: Acebutolol; Alprenolol; Atenolol; Befunolol; Bepridil; Betaxolol; Bevantolol; Bisoprolol; Bopindolol; Bucumolol; Bufetolol; Bunitrolol; Bupranolol; Butoconazole; Butofilolol; Cadexomer iodine; Carazolol; Carnitine; Carteolol; Carvedilol; Celiprolol; Cromoglicic acid; Detajmium bitartrate; Esmolol; Febuprol; Ganciclovir; Guanoxan; Indeloxacine; Indenolol; Levobunolol; Levofloxacin; Mepindolol; Metipranolol; Metoprolol; Milnacipran hydrochloride; Nadolol; Nadoxolol; Naftopidil; Nifuratel; Nipradilol; Oxprenolol; Penbutolol; Pindolol; Prenalterol; Prolonium iodide; Propafenone; Propranolol; Talinolol; Tertatolol; Tilisolol hydrochloride; Timolol; Toliprolol; Viloxazine; Xamoterol; Xantinol nicotinate; Xibenolol

(±)-epichlorohydrin
see under epichlorohydrin

epinastine
($C_{16}H_{15}N_3$; *80012-43-7*)   see: Epinastine hydrochloride

DL-epinephrine
($C_9H_{13}NO_3$; *329-65-7*)   see: Epinephrine

epinephrine
($C_9H_{13}NO_3$; *51-43-4*)   see: Carbazochrome

epinine
($C_9H_{13}NO_2$; *501-15-5*)   see: Ibopamine

epithiostanol
($C_{19}H_{30}OS$; *2363-58-8*)   see: Mepitiostane

(±)-epivincamine
($C_{21}H_{26}N_2O_3$; *18210-81-6*)   see: Vincamine

(−)-14-epivincamine
($C_{21}H_{26}N_2O_3$; *6835-99-0*)   see: Vincamine

4,5-epoxyandrostane-3,17-dione
($C_{19}H_{26}O_3$; *77057-73-9*)   see: Formestane

(4α,5α,17β)-4,5-epoxyandrost-2-eno[2,3-d]isoxazol-17-ol
($C_{20}H_{27}NO_3$; *20051-76-7*)   see: Trilostane

3,4-epoxy-1-butene
(C_4H_6O; *930-22-3*)   see: Retinol

1,2-epoxy-3-(2-cyanophenoxy)propane
($C_{10}H_9NO_2$; *38465-16-6*)   see: Bunitrolol; Epanolol

1,2-epoxy-3-(2-cyclopentylphenoxy)propane
($C_{14}H_{18}O_2$; *28163-40-8*)   see: Penbutolol

(±)-1,2-epoxy-3-[p-[2-(cyclopropylmethoxy)ethyl]phenoxy]propane
($C_{15}H_{20}O_3$; *63659-17-6*)   see: Betaxolol

9β,11β-epoxy-17α,21-dihydroxy-16β-methyl-1,4-pregnadiene-3,20-dione 21-acetate
($C_{24}H_{30}O_6$; *912-38-9*)   see: Betamethasone

(5α)-4,5-epoxy-3,14-dihydroxymorphinan-6-one cyclic 1,2-ethanediyl acetal
($C_{18}H_{21}NO_5$; *16739-57-4*)   see: Naltrexone

16α,17-epoxy-3β,11α-dihydroxy-5α-pregnan-20-one
($C_{21}H_{32}O_4$; *113454-48-1*)   see: Halopredone diacetate

(5α,6α,17Z)-5,6-epoxy-3,3-[1,2-ethanediylbis(oxy)]-11-oxopregn-17(20)-en-21-oic acid methyl ester
($C_{24}H_{32}O_6$; *985-95-5*)   see: Fluprednisolone acetate

9,11β-epoxy-6α-fluoro-16α,17,21-trihydroxy-9β-pregn-4-ene-3,20-dione 16,21-diacetate
($C_{25}H_{31}FO_8$; *2265-01-2*)   see: Fluocinolone acetonide

(2α,3α,5α,16α)-2,3-epoxy-16-hydroxyandrostan-17-one
($C_{19}H_{28}O_3$)   see: Vecuronium bromide

16α,17-epoxy-3β-hydroxy-6,16-dimethylpregn-5-en-20-one acetate
($C_{25}H_{36}O_4$; *101611-21-6*)   see: Melengestrol acetate

5,6α-epoxy-3β-hydroxy-17-methyl-5α-androstane-17β-carboxylic acid methyl ester
($C_{22}H_{34}O_4$; *106598-97-4*)   see: Medrogestone

(9β,11β,17β)-9,11-epoxy-17-hydroxy-17-methylandrost-4-en-3-one
($C_{20}H_{28}O_3$; *1042-33-7*)   see: Fluoxymesterone

(5α,6α)-5,6-epoxy-17-hydroxypregnane-3,20-dione cyclic bis(1,2-ethanediyl acetal)
($C_{25}H_{38}O_6$; *3496-78-4*)   see: Medroxyprogesterone acetate

(6α,7α)-6,7-epoxy-17-hydroxypregn-4-ene-3,20-dione
($C_{21}H_{28}O_4$; *4913-88-6*)   see: Chlormadinone acetate

(3β,16α)-16,17-epoxy-3-hydroxypregn-5-en-20-one
($C_{21}H_{30}O_3$; *974-23-2*)   see: Hydrocortisone; Hydroxyprogesterone

16α,17α-epoxy-3-methoxyestra-1,3,5(10)-trien-17-ol acetate
($C_{21}H_{26}O_4$; *39057-00-6*)   see: Estriol

1,2-epoxy-3-[4-(2-methoxyethyl)phenoxy]propane
($C_{12}H_{16}O_3$; *56718-70-8*)   see: Metoprolol

1,2-epoxy-3-methoxy-3-phenylpropane
($C_{10}H_{12}O_2$; *32785-08-3*)   see: Zipeprol

2,3-epoxy-1-(1-naphthyloxy)propane
($C_{13}H_{12}O_2$; *2461-42-9*)   see: Nadoxolol; Naftopidil; Propranolol

(2R,3S)-1,2-epoxy-4-penten-3-ol
($C_5H_8O_2$; *100017-22-9*)   see: Tacrolimus

6α,7α-epoxy-9β,10α-pregn-4-ene-3,20-dione
($C_{21}H_{28}O_3$)   see: Trengestone

4-(2,3-epoxypropoxy)carbazole
($C_{15}H_{13}NO_2$; *51997-51-4*)   see: Carazolol; Carvedilol

4-(2,3-epoxypropoxy)phenylacetamide
($C_{11}H_{13}NO_3$; *29122-69-8*)   see: Atenolol

1-(2,3-epoxypropoxy)-2-(tetrahydrofurfuryloxy)benzene
($C_{14}H_{18}O_4$; *63342-69-8*)   see: Bufetolol

5-(2,3-epoxypropoxy)-1,2,3,4-tetrahydroquinolin-2-one
($C_{12}H_{13}NO_3$; *51781-14-7*)   see: Carteolol

5-(2,3-epoxypropoxy)-1-tetralone
($C_{13}H_{14}O_3$; *27562-62-5*)   see: Levobunolol

4-(2,3-epoxypropyl)-N-methylisocarbostyril
($C_{13}H_{13}NO_3$; *62775-08-0*)   see: Tilisolol hydrochloride

ethoxyacetylene
(C_4H_6O; *927-80-0*)   see: Tacrolimus

β-ethoxyacryloyl chloride
($C_5H_7ClO_2$; *6191-99-7*)   see: Vesnarinone

(3β)-3-ethoxyandrost-5-en-17-one
($C_{21}H_{32}O_2$; *62502-29-8*)   see: Methandriol

2-ethoxyaniline
($C_8H_{11}NO$; *94-70-2*)   see: Actinoquinol

4-ethoxyaniline
($C_8H_{11}NO$; *156-43-4*)   see: Ethacridine; Ethoxzolamide;
Lactylphenetidin; Phenacetin

2-(4-ethoxyanilino)-4-nitrobenzoic acid
($C_{15}H_{14}N_2O_5$; *74859-51-1*)   see: Ethacridine

2-ethoxybenzoic acid
($C_9H_{10}O_3$; *134-11-2*)   see: Sildenafil

4-ethoxybenzoic acid
($C_9H_{10}O_3$; *619-86-3*)   see: Parethoxycaine

6-ethoxybenzothiazole-2-sulfenamide
($C_9H_{10}N_2OS_2$; *5304-15-4*)   see: Ethoxzolamide

6-ethoxybenzothiazole-2-thiole
($C_9H_9NOS_2$; *120-53-6*)   see: Ethoxzolamide

4-[(2-ethoxybenzoyl)amino]-1-methyl-3-propyl-1*H*-pyrazole-5-carboxamide
($C_{17}H_{22}N_4O_3$; *139756-03-9*)   see: Sildenafil

2-ethoxybenzoyl chloride
($C_9H_9ClO_2$; *42926-52-3*)   see: Sildenafil

4-ethoxybenzoyl chloride
($C_9H_9ClO_2$; *16331-46-7*)   see: Parethoxycaine

4-(ethoxycarbonylamino)benzenesulfonyl chloride
($C_9H_{10}ClNO_4S$; *21208-62-8*)   see: Sulfaphenazole

2-[(ethoxycarbonyl)amino]benzoic acid ethyl ester
($C_{12}H_{15}NO_4$; *108890-73-9*)   see: Ketanserin

3-ethoxycarbonyl-1-benzyl-4-piperidone
($C_{15}H_{19}NO_3$; *41276-30-6*)   see: Benperidol; Droperidol

N-[(S)-1-ethoxycarbonylbutyl]-L-alanine
($C_{10}H_{19}NO_4$; *82834-12-6*)   see: Perindopril

[2S-[1[R*(R*)],2α,3aβ,7aβ]]-1-[2-[[1-(ethoxycarbonyl)bu-tyl]amino]-1-oxopropyl]octahydro-1*H*-indole-2-carboxy-lic acid phenylmethyl ester
($C_{26}H_{38}N_2O_5$; *122454-52-8*)   see: Perindopril

4-ethoxycarbonyl-1,2-cyclopentanediol
($C_8H_{14}O_4$; *115956-02-0*)   see: Dolasetron mesilate

3-ethoxycarbonyl-4-(3,4-dichlorophenyl)-4-phenylbut-3-enoic acid
($C_{19}H_{16}Cl_2O_4$; *79560-16-0*)   see: Sertraline

7-ethoxycarbonyl-9-(ethoxycarbonylmethyl)-9-azabicy-clo[3.3.1]nonan-3-one
($C_{15}H_{23}NO_5$; *115956-03-1*)   see: Dolasetron mesilate

2-[4-(ethoxycarbonyl)-3-ethoxyphenyl]acetic acid
($C_{13}H_{16}O_5$; *99469-99-5*)   see: Repaglinide

4-ethoxycarbonyl-5-(4-fluorophenyl)-2-methylpent-4-en-3-one
($C_{15}H_{17}FO_3$; *122930-45-4*)   see: Cerivastatin sodium

(±)-*trans*-3-ethoxycarbonyl-4-(4-fluorophenyl)-N-methyl-piperidine-2,6-dione
($C_{15}H_{16}FNO_4$; *109887-52-7*)   see: Paroxetine

β-ethoxycarbonylglutaraldehyde
($C_8H_{12}O_4$; *115973-49-4*)   see: Dolasetron mesilate

N-ethoxycarbonyl-14-hydroxy-3-methoxyisomorphinan
($C_{20}H_{27}NO_4$; *58115-90-5*)   see: Butorphanol

3-ethoxycarbonyl-4-hydroxy-2-methyl-2*H*-1,2-benzothia-zine 1,1-dioxide
($C_{12}H_{13}NO_5S$; *24683-26-9*)   see: Droxicam; Isoxicam

3-ethoxycarbonyl-4-hydroxy-2-methyl-2*H*-thieno[2,3-*e*]-1,2-thiazine 1,1-dioxide
($C_{10}H_{11}NO_5S_2$; *98827-42-0*)   see: Tenoxicam

3-ethoxycarbonyl-4-hydroxy-8-trifluoromethylquinoline
($C_{13}H_{10}F_3NO_3$; *23851-84-5*)   see: Floctafenine

3-ethoxycarbonyl-4-hydroxy-6,7,8-trifluoroquinoline
($C_{12}H_8F_3NO_3$; *80104-36-5*)   see: Lomefloxacin

(R)-5-ethoxycarbonyl-2-mercapto-1-(1-phenylethyl)-imidazole
($C_{14}H_{16}N_2O_2S$; *84711-26-2*)   see: Etomidate

N-ethoxycarbonyl-3-methoxy-8,14-didehydromorphinan
($C_{20}H_{25}NO_3$; *58025-69-7*)   see: Butorphanol

2'-ethoxycarbonylmethoxy-4'-(3-methyl-2-butenyloxy)-acetophenone
($C_{17}H_{22}O_5$; *64506-46-3*)   see: Sofalcone

3-ethoxycarbonyl-2-methyl-5,6-dihydro-4*H*-pyran
($C_9H_{14}O_3$)   see: Pentoxifylline

(R)-N-(ethoxycarbonylmethyl)-N-formyl-1-phenylethyl-amine
($C_{13}H_{17}NO_3$; *66514-85-0*)   see: Etomidate

(R)-N-(ethoxycarbonylmethyl)-1-phenylethylamine
($C_{12}H_{17}NO_2$; *66512-37-6*)   see: Etomidate

N^1-ethoxycarbonyl-2-methylpiperazine
($C_8H_{16}N_2O_2$; *120737-73-7*)   see: Temafloxacin

7a-ethoxycarbonylmethylpyrrolizine
($C_{11}H_{19}NO_2$; *88069-56-1*)   see: Pilsicainide

6-ethoxycarbonyl-2-methylthio-5-oxo-5,8-dihydro-pyrido[2,3-*d*]pyrimidine
($C_{11}H_{11}N_3O_3S$; *34711-92-7*)   see: Pipemidic acid

4-[[1-(ethoxycarbonyl)-2-oxocyclopentyl]methyl]-α-me-thylbenzeneacetic acid ethyl ester
($C_{20}H_{26}O_5$; *68767-26-0*)   see: Loxoprofen

(S)-N-(1-ethoxycarbonyl-3-oxo-3-phenylpropyl)-L-alanine
($C_{15}H_{19}NO_5$; *87269-99-6*)   see: Ramipril

1-[N-[1-(ethoxycarbonyl)-3-oxo-3-phenylpropyl]-L-ala-nyl]-L-proline phenylmethyl ester
($C_{27}H_{32}N_2O_6$; *105878-11-3*)   see: Enalapril

17α-(ethoxycarbonyloxy)-11β-hydroxy-3-oxoandrosta-1,4-diene-17-carboxylic acid
($C_{23}H_{30}O_7$; *133991-63-6*)   see: Loteprednol etabonate

(3β,16β,17α,18β,20α)-18-[[3-[4-[(ethoxycarbonyl)oxy]-3-methoxyphenyl]-1-oxo-2-propenyl]oxy]-11,17-dimeth-oxyyohimban-16-carboxylic acid methyl ester
($C_{36}H_{42}N_2O_{10}$; *49806-34-0*)   see: Rescimetol

N-(1-ethoxycarbonyl-3-phenylpropyl)-L-alanine
($C_{11}H_{13}NO_4$)   see: Quinapril hydrochloride

N-[1(S)-ethoxycarbonyl-3-phenylpropyl]-L-alanine
($C_{15}H_{21}NO_4$; *82717-96-2*)   see: Imidapril; Moexipril;
Quinapril hydrochloride; Spirapril; Trandolapril

N-[1(S)-ethoxycarbonyl-3-phenylpropyl]-L-alanine benzo-thiazol-2-ylthio ester
($C_{22}H_{24}N_2O_3S_2$; *124492-03-1*)   see: Spirapril

N-[1(S)-ethoxycarbonyl-3-phenylpropyl]-L-alanine benzyl ester
($C_{22}H_{27}NO_4$; *82717-95-1*)   see: Spirapril

N-(1-ethoxycarbonyl-3-phenylpropyl)-L-alanine *tert*-butylester

($C_{19}H_{29}NO_4$)   see: Quinapril hydrochloride

N-[1(*S*)-ethoxycarbonyl-3-phenylpropyl]-L-alanine *tert*-butyl ester

($C_{19}H_{29}NO_4$; *80828-38-2*)   see: Moexipril

[4*S*-[3[*R**(*R**)],4*R**]]-3-[2-[[1-(ethoxycarbonyl)-3-phenylpropyl]amino]-1-oxopropyl]-1-methyl-2-oxo-4-imidazolidinecarboxylic acid 1,1-dimethylethyl ester

($C_{24}H_{35}N_3O_6$; *89371-38-0*)   see: Imidapril

[3*S*-[2[*R**(*R**)],3*R**]]-2-[2-[[1-(ethoxycarbonyl)-3-phenylpropyl]amino]-1-oxopropyl]-1,2,3,4-tetrahydro-3-isoquinolinecarboxylic acid 1,1-dimethylethyl ester

($C_{29}H_{38}N_2O_5$; *82586-56-9*)   see: Quinapril hydrochloride

(2*S*,6*R*)-6-[[1(*S*)-ethoxycarbonyl-3-phenylpropyl]amino]-5-oxo-2-(2-thienyl)perhydro-1,4-thiazepine

($C_{21}H_{26}N_2O_3S_2$; *110143-57-2*)   see: Temocapril

(2*S*)-2-[(1*S*)-1-ethoxycarbonyl-3-phenylpropylamino]propionic acid

see under *N*-[1(*S*)-ethoxycarbonyl-3-phenylpropyl]-L-alanine

(2*S*)-2-[(1*S*)-1-ethoxycarbonyl-3-phenylpropylamino]propionic acid succiimido ester

($C_{19}H_{24}N_2O_6$; *89371-34-6*)   see: Imidapril; Spirapril

[2*S*-[2α,6β(*R**)]]-6-[[1-(ethoxycarbonyl)-3-phenylpropyl]amino]tetrahydro-5-oxo-2-(2-thienyl)-1,4-thiazepine-4(5*H*)-acetic acid 1,1-dimethylethyl ester

($C_{27}H_{36}N_2O_5S_2$; *110221-37-9*)   see: Temocapril

N^2-[(1*S*)-1-(ethoxycarbonyl)-3-phenylpropyl]-N^6-(trifluoroacetyl)-L-lysyl-L-proline

($C_{25}H_{34}F_3N_3O_6$; *103300-91-0*)   see: Lisinopril

N-ethoxycarbonylphthalimide

see under *N*-carbethoxyphthalimide

1-ethoxycarbonylpiperazine

see under *N*-carbethoxypiperazine

7-[4-(ethoxycarbonyl)-1-piperazinyl]-6-fluoro-1,4-dihydro-4-oxo-1,8-naphthyridine-3-carboxylic acid ethyl ester

($C_{18}H_{21}FN_4O_5$; *75167-04-3*)   see: Enoxacin

1-(ethoxycarbonyl)-4-piperidinone

($C_8H_{13}NO_3$; *29976-53-2*)   see: Cisapride; Endralazine; Loratadine

4-[3-(ethoxycarbonyl)propyl]-1*H*-imidazole

($C_9H_{14}N_2O_2$; *49549-65-7*)   see: Fadrozole

1-(ethoxycarbonyl)-1,2,5,6-tetrahydro-4-(1-pyrrolidinyl)-3-pyridineacetic acid ethyl ester

($C_{16}H_{26}N_2O_4$)   see: Endralazine

N-ethoxycarbonylthiopropionamide

($C_6H_{11}NO_2S$; *59812-12-3*)   see: Nefazodone hydrochloride

6-ethoxy-2-dimethylaminobenzothiazole

($C_{11}H_{14}N_2OS$; *5304-29-0*)   see: Dimazole

3-ethoxy-2,6-dimethyl-8-(2,6,6-trimethyl-1-cyclohexen-1-yl)-4,6-octadienal diethyl acetal

($C_{25}H_{44}O_3$; *114400-84-9*)   see: Betacarotene

threo-2-(1-ethoxyethoxy)-3-(*tert*-butoxycarbonylamino)-3-phenylpropionic acid

($C_{18}H_{27}NO_6$)   see: Docetaxel

4-(1-ethoxyethoxy)-3,4-dihydro-2-(3-methoxypropyl)-2*H*-thieno[3,2-*e*]-1,2-thiazine 1,1-dioxide

($C_{14}H_{23}NO_5S_2$; *165116-92-7*)   see: Brinzolamide

4-(1-ethoxyethoxy)-3,4-dihydro-2-(3-methoxypropyl)-2*H*-thieno[3,2-*e*]-1,2-thiazine-6-sulfonamide 1,1-dioxide

($C_{14}H_{24}N_2O_7S_3$)   see: Brinzolamide

3-ethoxy-2-ethoxymethylenepropionitrile

($C_8H_{13}NO_2$; *34450-87-8*)   see: Thiamine

4-(3-ethoxy-2-hydroxypropoxy)aniline

($C_{11}H_{17}NO_3$; *94056-98-1*)   see: Suplatast tosilate

N-[4-(3-ethoxy-2-hydroxypropoxy)phenyl]-3-(methylthio)propanamide

($C_{15}H_{23}NO_4S$; *94057-02-0*)   see: Suplatast tosilate

1-(4-ethoxy-3-methoxybenzyl)-3,4-dihydro-6,7-dimethoxy-3-methylisoquinoline

($C_{22}H_{27}NO_4$; *111211-22-4*)   see: Dimoxyline

4-ethoxy-3-methoxyphenylacetic acid

($C_{11}H_{14}O_4$; *120-13-8*)   see: Dimoxyline

α-(ethoxymethylene)-3,5-dimethoxy-4-(2-methoxyethoxy)benzenepropanoic acid ethyl ester

($C_{19}H_{28}O_7$)   see: Tetroxoprim

ethoxymethylenemalonic acid diethyl ester

see under diethyl ethoxymethylenemalonate

ethoxymethylenemalononitrile

($C_6H_6N_2O$; *123-06-8*)   see: Pemirolast; Thiamine; Zaleplon

2-(ethoxymethylene)-3-oxo-*N*-[4-(trifluoromethyl)phenyl]butanamide

($C_{14}H_{14}F_3NO_3$; *75706-11-5*)   see: Leflunomide

α-(ethoxymethylene)-2,4,5-trifluoro-3-methoxy-β-oxobenzenepropanoic acid ethyl ester

($C_{15}H_{15}F_3O_5$; *122375-85-3*)   see: Moxifloxacin hydrochloride

5-ethoxy-4-methyloxazole

($C_6H_9NO_2$; *5006-20-2*)   see: Pyridoxine

2-ethoxy-5-(4-methylpiperazin-1-ylsulfonyl)benzoic acid

($C_{14}H_{20}N_2O_5S$; *194602-23-8*)   see: Sildenafil

4-[[2-ethoxy-5-[(4-methyl-1-piperazinyl)sulfonyl]benzoyl]amino]-1-methyl-3-propyl-1*H*-pyrazole-5-carboxamide

($C_{22}H_{32}N_6O_5S$; *200575-15-1*)   see: Sildenafil

2-(ethoxymethyl)-3-(3,4,5-trimethoxyphenyl)-2-propenenitrile

($C_{15}H_{19}NO_4$; *50844-85-4*)   see: Trimethoprim

3-ethoxy-4-methyl-6-(2,6,6-trimethyl-1-cyclohexen-1-yl)-4-hexenal diethyl acetal

($C_{22}H_{40}O_3$; *114162-01-5*)   see: Betacarotene

2-ethoxy-1-naphthoyl chloride

($C_{13}H_{11}ClO_2$; *55150-29-3*)   see: Nafcillin

2-ethoxy-4-nitrobenzoic acid

($C_9H_9NO_5$; *2486-66-0*)   see: Cinitapride

N-(2-ethoxy-2-oxoethyl)-4-(methoxycarbonyl)pyridinium bromide

($C_{11}H_{14}BrNO_4$)   see: Clidinium bromide

3-[[(2-ethoxy-2-oxoethyl)methylamino]sulfonyl]-2-thiophenecarboxylic acid methyl ester

($C_{11}H_{15}NO_6S_2$; *59804-24-9*)   see: Tenoxicam

3-ethoxy-17-oxo-19-nor-3,5-androstadiene

($C_{20}H_{28}O_2$; *2863-88-9*)   see: Methylestrenolone; Norethisterone

4-[(3-ethoxy-3-oxopropyl)methylamino]butanoic acid ethyl ester

($C_{12}H_{23}NO_4$; *109386-70-1*)   see: Azelastine

N-(3-ethoxy-3-oxopropyl)-N-(phenylmethyl)-β-alanine ethyl ester
(C$_{17}$H$_{25}$NO$_4$; *6938-07-4*)   see: Benperidol

2-ethoxyphenol
(C$_8$H$_{10}$O$_2$; *94-71-3*)   see: Tamsulosin hydrochloride; Viloxazine

2-ethoxyphenol sodium salt
(C$_8$H$_9$NaO$_2$; *63449-45-6*)   see: Reboxetine

1-(2-ethoxyphenoxy)-2,3-epoxypropane
(C$_{11}$H$_{14}$O$_3$; *5296-35-5*)   see: Viloxazine

2-[(2-ethoxyphenoxy)methyl]-4-(phenylmethyl)morpholine
(C$_{20}$H$_{25}$NO$_3$; *47374-79-8*)   see: Viloxazine

6-[(2-ethoxyphenoxy)methyl]-4-(phenylmethyl)-3-morpholinone
(C$_{20}$H$_{23}$NO$_4$; *70154-82-4*)   see: Viloxazine

1-(2-ethoxyphenoxy)-3-[(phenylmethyl)amino]-2-propanol
(C$_{18}$H$_{23}$NO$_3$; *23184-52-3*)   see: Viloxazine

(R*,R*)-[(2-ethoxyphenoxy)phenylmethyl]oxirane
(C$_{17}$H$_{18}$O$_3$; *98769-72-3*)   see: Reboxetine

(R*,R*)-3-(2-ethoxyphenoxy)-3-phenyl-1,2-propanediol 2-methanesulfonate 1-(4-nitrobenzoate)
(C$_{25}$H$_{25}$NO$_9$S)   see: Reboxetine

5-(2-ethoxyphenyl)-1,4-dihydro-1-methyl-3-propyl-7H-pyrazolo[4,3-d]pyrimidin-7-one
(C$_{17}$H$_{20}$N$_4$O$_2$; *139756-21-1*)   see: Sildenafil

N'-(4-ethoxyphenyl)-N,N-dimethylthiourea
(C$_{11}$H$_{16}$N$_2$OS; *5304-13-2*)   see: Dimazole

1-(2-ethoxy-2-phenylethyl)piperazine
(C$_{14}$H$_{22}$N$_2$O; *6722-51-6*)   see: Eprazinone

4-ethoxyphenyl isothiocyanate
(C$_9$H$_9$NOS; *3460-49-9*)   see: Dimazole

3-ethoxypropionitrile
(C$_5$H$_9$NO; *2141-62-0*)   see: Thiamine; Trimethoprim

(11β,16α)-17,21-[(1-ethoxypropylidene)bis(oxy)]-11-hydroxy-16-methylpregna-1,4,6-triene-3,20-dione
(C$_{27}$H$_{36}$O$_6$; *67212-72-0*)   see: Alclometasone dipropionate

3-ethoxypropylmagnesium bromide
(C$_5$H$_{11}$BrMgO; *121317-16-6*)   see: Biotin

8-ethoxyquinoline
(C$_{11}$H$_{11}$NO; *1555-94-8*)   see: Actinoquinol

(3β,22E)-3-ethoxystigmasta-5,22-diene
(C$_{31}$H$_{52}$O; *63201-36-5*)   see: Methandriol

β-ethoxystyrene
(C$_{10}$H$_{12}$O; *17655-74-2*)   see: Bendroflumethiazide

(6R-trans)-3-[[(ethoxythioxomethyl)thio]methyl]-8-oxo-7-[(2-thienylacetyl)amino]-5-thia-1-azabicyclo[4.2.0]oct-2-ene-2-carboxylic acid (4-nitrophenyl)methyl ester
(C$_{24}$H$_{23}$N$_3$O$_7$S$_4$)   see: Cefaclor

4-ethoxy-N,N,N-trimethyl-2,4-dioxo-1-butanaminium chloride
(C$_9$H$_{18}$ClNO$_3$; *10485-23-1*)   see: Carnitine

ethoxytrimethylsilane
(C$_5$H$_{14}$OSi; *1825-62-3*)   see: Dimethicone

2-ethoxy-1-[2'-(1-triphenylmethyltetrazol-5-yl)biphenyl-4-ylmethyl]benzimidazole-7-carboxylic acid
(C$_{43}$H$_{34}$N$_6$O$_3$; *139481-72-4*)   see: Candesartan cilexetil

ethyl 2-acetamido-2-(ethoxycarbonyl)-3-(2-oxo-1,2-dihydroquinolin-4-yl)propionate
(C$_{19}$H$_{22}$N$_2$O$_6$; *4900-38-3*)   see: Rebamipide

ethyl acetate
(C$_4$H$_8$O$_2$; *141-78-6*)   see: Meglutol; Methyldopa; Milrinone; Mofezolac; Perindopril

ethyl acetoacetate
see under acetoacetic acid ethyl ester

(±)-ethyl 3-[4-[(6-acetoxy-2,5,7,8-tetramethylchroman-2-yl)methoxy]phenyl]-2-chloropropionate
(C$_{27}$H$_{33}$ClO$_6$; *97322-68-4*)   see: Troglitazone

ethyl (3R,4R,5S)-4-(acetylamino)-5-azido-3-(1-ethylpropoxy)-1-cyclohexene-1-carboxylate
(C$_{16}$H$_{26}$N$_4$O$_4$; *204255-06-1*)   see: Oseltamivir

ethyl acrylate
(C$_5$H$_8$O$_2$; *140-88-5*)   see: Acrivastine; Azelastine; Benperidol; Benzquinamide; Setiptiline; Troglitazone

ethyl adipoyl chloride
(C$_8$H$_{13}$ClO$_3$; *1071-71-2*)   see: Dopexamine; Thioctic acid

ethyl 5-allyl-2-hydroxy-3-methoxybenzoate
(C$_{13}$H$_{16}$O$_4$; *7152-89-8*)   see: Alibendol

ethylamine
(C$_2$H$_7$N; *75-04-7*)   see: Alverine; Brinzolamide; Cadralazine; Crotetamide; Dorzolamide; Etilefrine; Mebeverine; Piperidolate; Tropicamide

ethyl (1α,5α,6α)-7-(6-amino-3-azabicyclo[3.1.0]hex-3-yl)-1-(2,4-difluorophenyl)-6-fluoro-1,4-dihydro-4-oxo-1,8-naphthyridine-3-carboxylate
(C$_{22}$H$_{19}$F$_3$N$_4$O$_3$; *171176-56-0*)   see: Alatrofloxacin mesilate

ethyl 4-aminobenzoate
(C$_9$H$_{11}$NO$_2$; *94-09-7*)   see: Procaine; Tetracaine

L-ethyl 2-aminobutyrate hydrochloride
(C$_6$H$_{14}$ClNO$_2$; *91462-82-7*)   see: Ethambutol

ethyl N-(2-amino-6-chlorobenzyl)glycinate
(C$_{11}$H$_{15}$ClN$_2$O$_2$)   see: Anagrelide hydrochloride

ethyl (3R,4S)-rel-4-[(4-amino-5-chloro-2-methoxybenzoyl)amino]-3-methoxy-1-piperidinecarboxylate
(C$_{17}$H$_{24}$ClN$_3$O$_5$; *83863-70-1*)   see: Cisapride

α-ethyl-3-aminocinnamic acid
(C$_{11}$H$_{13}$NO$_2$; *59150-78-6*)   see: Bunamiodyl

ethyl 3-aminocrotonate
(C$_6$H$_{11}$NO$_2$; *7318-00-5*)   see: Felodipine; Lacidipine

ethyl 1-amino-1-cyclopentanecarboxylate
(C$_8$H$_{15}$NO$_2$; *1664-35-3*)   see: Irbesartan

ethyl 5-amino-1-cyclopropyl-6,7,8-trifluoro-1,4-dihydro-4-oxo-3-quinolinecarboxylate
(C$_{15}$H$_{13}$F$_3$N$_2$O$_3$; *103772-13-0*)   see: Sparfloxacin

ethyl 5-amino-2,2-diethyl-3-oxo-4-pentenoate
(C$_{11}$H$_{19}$NO$_3$; *74367-91-2*)   see: Methyprylon; Pyrithyldione

(4R-trans)-4-(ethylamino)-5,6-dihydro-6-methyl-4H-thieno[2,3-b]thiopyran-2-sulfonamide 7,7-dioxide
(C$_{10}$H$_{16}$N$_2$O$_4$S$_3$; *120279-95-0*)   see: Dorzolamide

2-(ethylamino)-N,N-dimethylbutanamide
(C$_8$H$_{18}$N$_2$O; *84803-61-2*)   see: Crotetamide

2-(ethylamino)ethanol
(C$_4$H$_{11}$NO; *110-73-6*)   see: Bamifylline; Hydroxychloroquine

ethyl β-amino-β-ethoxyacrylate
(C$_7$H$_{13}$NO$_3$; *39632-87-6*)   see: Muzolimine

ethyl 7-aminoheptanoate
(C$_9$H$_{19}$NO$_2$; *1117-66-4*)   see: Amineptine; Tianeptine sodium

ethyl 5-bromo-3-methyl-4-oxothiazolidin-2-ylideneacetate
($C_8H_{10}BrNO_3S$; *86379-70-6*)   see: Etozolin

ethyl 7-bromo-2-oxoheptanoate
($C_9H_{15}BrO_3$; *107871-17-0*)   see: Cilastatin

ethyl (±)-3-bromo-4-oxo-1-piperidinecarboxylate
($C_8H_{12}BrNO_3$; *95629-02-0*)   see: Cisapride

(±)-ethyl 2-bromo-4-phenylbutanoate
($C_{12}H_{15}BrO_2$; *82586-61-6*)   see: Moexipril; Quinapril
hydrochloride; Temocapril

ethyl 2-bromo-4-phenylbutyrate
see under (±)-ethyl 2-bromo-4-phenylbutanoate

ethyl N-[(4-bromophenyl)sulfonyl]methanimidate
($C_9H_{10}BrNO_3S$; *100981-68-8*)   see: Ebrotidine

ethyl 2-bromopropionate
($C_5H_9BrO_2$; *535-11-5*)   see: Naproxen

ethyl 5-bromo-3-(2-pyridyl)indole-2-carboxylate 1'-oxide
($C_{16}H_{13}BrN_2O_3$; *29310-54-1*)   see: Bromazepam

ethyl bromopyruvate
($C_5H_7BrO_3$; *70-23-5*)   see: Nizatidine

2-ethylbutanenitrile
($C_6H_{11}N$; *617-80-1*)   see: Valdetamide

ethyl (2R,3S)-3-tert-butoxycarbonylamino-2-hydroxy-3-phenylpropionate
($C_{16}H_{23}NO_5$; *143527-75-7*)   see: Docetaxel

ethyl 2-(tert-butoxycarbonylamino)-3-nitrobenzoate
($C_{14}H_{18}N_2O_6$; *136285-65-9*)   see: Candesartan cilexetil

ethyl (Z)-2-(1-tert-butoxycarbonyl-1-methylethoxyimino)-2-(2-tritylaminothiazol-4-yl)acetate
($C_{34}H_{37}N_3O_5S$; *68672-65-1*)   see: Ceftazidime

ethyl 4-butoxyphenylacetate
($C_{14}H_{20}O_3$; *4547-58-4*)   see: Bufexamac

ethyl 4-butylaminobenzoate
($C_{13}H_{19}NO_2$; *94-32-6*)   see: Benzonatate

2-ethylbutyric acid
($C_6H_{12}O_2$; *88-09-5*)   see: Carbromal

ethyl carbamate
($C_3H_7NO_2$; *51-79-6*)   see: Carisoprodol; Felbamate;
Mebutamate; Tybamate

ethyl carbazate
($C_3H_8N_2O_2$; *4114-31-2*)   see: Cadralazine

ethyl (S,S)-2-[(1-carboxyethyl)amino]-4-phenylbutanoate
see under N-[1(S)-ethoxycarbonyl-3-phenylpropyl]-L-alanine

ethyl chloride
(C_2H_5Cl; *75-00-3*)   see: Oxeladin; Phenacetin

ethyl 2-(2-chloroacetamido-4-thiazolyl)-2-methoxyimino-acetate
($C_{10}H_{12}ClN_3O_4S$; *60846-16-4*)   see: Ceftriaxone

ethyl chloroacetate
($C_4H_7ClO_2$; *105-39-5*)   see: Azimilide hydrochloride;
Cloricromen; Etomidate; Ibuprofen; Piracetam; Retinol;
Tiaramide; Tienilic acid

ethyl 2-chloroacetoacetate
($C_6H_9ClO_3$; *609-15-4*)   see: Cimetidine; Pyridoxine

ethyl 4-chloroacetoacetate
($C_6H_9ClO_3$; *638-07-3*)   see: Amlodipine; Carnitine;
Folescutol

ethyl α-(3-chloro-4-aminophenyl)propionate
($C_{11}H_{14}ClNO_2$; *26406-97-3*)   see: Pirprofen

ethyl 4-(4-chlorobenzhydryl)piperazine-1-carboxylate
($C_{20}H_{23}ClN_2O_2$; *80476-89-7*)   see: Buclizine; Cetirizine

7-ethyl-10-(chlorocarbonyloxy)camptothecin
($C_{23}H_{19}ClN_2O_6$; *97682-31-0*)   see: Irinotecan

ethyl 4-chlorocinnamate
($C_{11}H_{11}ClO_2$; *6048-06-2*)   see: Baclofen

ethyl 7-chloro-1-(2,4-difluorophenyl)-6-fluoro-1,4-dihy-dro-4-oxo-1,8-naphthyridine-3-carboxylate
($C_{17}H_{10}ClF_3N_2O_3$; *100491-29-0*)   see: Tosufloxacin;
Trovafloxacin mesilate

ethyl 7-chloro-1-(2,4-difluorophenyl)-6-fluoro-4-oxo-1,4-dihydro-1,8-naphthyridine-3-carboxylate
see under ethyl 7-chloro-1-(2,4-difluorophenyl)-6-fluoro-1,4-dihydro-4-oxo-1,8-naphthyridine-3-carboxylate

ethyl 2-chloro-6-ethyl-isonicotinate
($C_{10}H_{12}ClNO_2$; *4009-26-1*)   see: Ethionamide

ethyl 1-(2-chloroethyl)-4-phenyl-piperidine-4-carboxylate
($C_{16}H_{22}ClNO_2$; *76100-61-3*)   see: Diphenoxylate

ethyl 7-chloro-6-fluoro-4-hydroxyquinoline-3-carboxylate
($C_{12}H_9ClFNO_3$; *70458-93-4*)   see: Pefloxacin

ethyl 10-chloro-9-fluoro-7-oxo-2,3-dihydro-7H-pyri-do[1,2,3-de]-1,4-benzothiazine-6-carboxylate
($C_{14}H_{11}ClFNO_3S$; *101337-97-7*)   see: Rufloxacin
hydrochloride

ethyl 5-chloro-3-(2-fluorophenyl)indole-2-carboxylate
($C_{17}H_{13}ClFNO_2$; *24106-88-5*)   see: Flutoprazepam

ethyl chloroformate
see under chloroformic acid ethyl ester

ethyl 6-chloroformyl-hexanoate
($C_9H_{15}ClO_3$; *14794-32-2*)   see: Seratrodast

ethyl 2-chloroformyl-3-nitrobenzoate
($C_{10}H_8ClNO_5$; *136285-66-0*)   see: Candesartan cilexetil

ethyl 9-chloroformylnonanoate
($C_{12}H_{21}ClO_3$; *6946-46-9*)   see: Idebenone

ethyl 3-chloroformylpropionate
($C_6H_9ClO_3$; *14794-31-1*)   see: Erythromycin ethylsuccinate;
Mebeverine

ethyl 4-chloro-2-hydroxyiminoacetoacetate
($C_6H_8ClNO_4$; *50382-11-1*)   see: Ceftazidime

ethyl 5-chloro-4-hydroxy-2-quinolinecarboxylate
($C_{12}H_{10}ClNO_3$; *21640-98-2*)   see: Chloroquine

ethyl 7-chloro-4-hydroxy-2-quinolinecarboxylate
($C_{12}H_{10}ClNO_3$; *21640-97-1*)   see: Chloroquine

ethyl 7-chloro-4-hydroxy-3-quinolinecarboxylate
($C_{12}H_{10}ClNO_3$; *16600-22-9*)   see: Chloroquine

ethyl 2-chloromethylbenzoate
($C_{10}H_{11}ClO_2$; *1531-78-8*)   see: Indoprofen

ethyl 6-chloro-α-methyl-1,2,3,4-tetrahydro-9H-carbazole-2-acetate
($C_{17}H_{16}ClNO_2$; *52262-88-1*)   see: Carprofen

ethyl 6-chloronicotinate
($C_8H_8ClNO_2$; *49608-01-7*)   see: Tazarotene

α-ethyl-N-(3-chloro-1-oxopropoxy)benzeneethan-imidamide
($C_{13}H_{17}ClN_2O_2$)   see: Proxazole

ethyl 3-(4-chlorophenyl)-3-hydroxybutyrate
($C_{12}H_{15}ClO_3$; *21133-98-2*)   see: Fenpentadiol

ethyl 5-chloro-3-phenylindole-2-carboxylate
($C_{17}H_{14}ClNO_2$; *21139-32-2*)   see: Diazepam

1-ethyl-3-chloropiperidine
($C_7H_{14}ClN$; *2167-11-5*)   see: Pipenzolate bromide

ethyl (1α,5α,6α)-1-(2,4-difluorophenyl)-7-[6-[[(1,1-dimethylethoxy)carbonyl]amino]-3-azabicyclo[3.1.0]hex-3-yl]-6-fluoro-1,4-dihydro-4-oxo-1,8-naphthyridine-3-carboxylate

see under ethyl (1α,5α,6α)-1-(2,4-difluorophenyl)-7-[6-[[(1,1-dimethylethoxy)carbonyl]amino]-3-azabicyclo[3.1.0]-hex-3-yl]-6-fluoro-1,4-dihydro-4-oxo-1,8-naphthyridine-3-carboxylate

ethyl 3,4-dihydro-6,7-dimethoxy-1-isoquinolineacetate
($C_{15}H_{19}NO_4$; *21271-01-2*)   see: Benzquinamide

ethyl 3,6-dihydro-4-methoxy-1(2*H*)-pyridinecarboxylate
($C_9H_{15}NO_3$; *203984-87-6*)   see: Cisapride

3-ethyl-2,5-dihydro-4-methyl-2-oxo-*N*-(2-phenylethyl)-1*H*-pyrrole-1-carboxamide
($C_{16}H_{20}N_2O_2$; *247098-18-6*)   see: Glimepiride

6-ethyl-1,2-dihydro-2-oxo-4-pyridinecarboxylic acid
($C_8H_9NO_3$; *54881-17-3*)   see: Ethionamide

N-[4-[[(1-ethyl-1,2-dihydro-2-oxo-4-pyrimidinyl)amino]-sulfonyl]phenyl]acetamide
($C_{14}H_{16}N_4O_4S$; *25855-46-3*)   see: Sulfacitine

5-ethyl-2,4-dihydro-4-(2-phenoxyethyl)-3*H*-1,2,4-triazol-3-one
($C_{12}H_{15}N_3O_2$; *95885-13-5*)   see: Nefazodone hydrochloride

1-ethyl-1,4-dihydro-5*H*-tetrazol-5-one
($C_3H_6N_4O$; *69048-98-2*)   see: Alfentanil

ethyldiisopropylamine
($C_8H_{19}N$; *7087-68-5*)   see: Mibefradil hydrochloride; Pinacidil

ethyl 2,6-diisopropyl-4-(4-fluorophenyl)-5-hydroxymethyl-pyridine-3-carboxylate
($C_{21}H_{26}FNO_3$; *124863-80-5*)   see: Cerivastatin sodium

ethyl *N*-(3,4-dimethoxyphenethyl)malonamate
($C_{15}H_{21}NO_5$; *79641-41-1*)   see: Benzquinamide

ethyl 2-(dimethylaminomethyl)-4-thiazolecarboxylate
($C_9H_{14}N_2O_2S$; *82586-66-1*)   see: Nizatidine

N-ethyl-*N'*-[3-(dimethylamino)propyl]carbodiimide
($C_8H_{17}N_3$; *1892-57-5*)   see: Cabergoline

ethyl 1,4-dimethyl-3-ethoxycarbonylpyrrole-2-acetate
($C_{13}H_{19}NO_4$; *33369-26-5*)   see: Zomepirac

ethyl 2-[[2-[3-(1,1-dimethylethoxy)-3-oxo-1-propenyl]phe-nyl]methylene]-3-oxobutanoate
($C_{20}H_{24}O_5$; *108700-28-3*)   see: Lacidipine

[3a*R*-(2*E*,3aα,4α,5β,6aα)]-ethyl [4-[[[(1,1-dimethylethyl)-dimethylsilyl]oxy]methyl]hexahydro-5-hydroxy-2*H*-cyclo-penta[*b*]furan-2-ylidene]acetate
($C_{18}H_{32}O_5Si$; *79745-54-3*)   see: Iloprost

[3a*S*-(3aα,4α,5β,6aα)]-ethyl 4-[[[(1,1-dimethylethyl)dime-thylsilyl]oxy]methyl]octahydro-5-hydroxy-2-oxo-1-pen-talenecarboxylate
($C_{18}H_{32}O_5Si$; *79745-56-5*)   see: Iloprost

ethyl 7-(1,1-dimethylheptyl)-5-hydroxy-4-methyl-2-oxo-2*H*-1-benzopyran-3-propionate
($C_{24}H_{34}O_5$; *56469-11-5*)   see: Nabilone

ethyl 2,4-dioxoheptanoate
($C_9H_{14}O_4$; *36983-31-0*)   see: Protionamide; Sildenafil

ethyl 2,4-dioxohexanoate
($C_8H_{12}O_4$; *13246-52-1*)   see: Ethionamide

ethyl 2-[2-(1,3-dioxolan-2-yl)ethylamino]-2-(4-fluoro-phenyl)acetate
($C_{15}H_{20}FNO_4$; *110862-42-5*)   see: Atorvastatin calcium

[6*R*-[6α,7α,7(2*R**,3*S**)]]-7-[[2-[[(4-ethyl-2,3-dioxo-1-piperazinyl)carbonyl]amino]-3-hydroxy-1-oxobutyl]ami-no]-7-methoxy-3-[[(1-methyl-1*H*-tetrazol-5-yl)thio]me-thyl]-8-oxo-5-thia-1-azabicyclo[4.2.0]oct-2-ene-2-carb-oxylic acid diphenylmethyl ester
($C_{35}H_{39}N_9O_9S_2$; *76610-83-8*)   see: Cefbuperazone

[6*R*-[6α,7β(2*R**,3*S**)]]-7-[[2-[[(4-ethyl-2,3-dioxo-1-piper-azinyl)carbonyl]amino]-3-hydroxy-1-oxobutyl]amino]-3-[[(1-methyl-1*H*-tetrazol-5-yl)thio]methyl]-8-oxo-5-thia-1-azabicyclo[4.2.0]oct-2-ene-2-carboxylic acid diphenylme-thyl ester
($C_{34}H_{37}N_9O_8S_2$; *76610-82-7*)   see: Cefbuperazone

ethyl diphenylacetate
($C_{16}H_{16}O_2$; *3468-99-3*)   see: Loperamide

1-ethyl-α,α-diphenyl-3-pyrrolidineacetic acid
($C_{20}H_{23}NO_2$; *3471-97-4*)   see: Doxapram

1-ethyl-α,α-diphenyl-3-pyrrolidineacetonitrile
($C_{20}H_{22}N_2$; *3212-87-1*)   see: Doxapram

ethyl dipropylcyanoacetate
($C_{11}H_{19}NO_2$; *66546-90-5*)   see: Valproic acid

ethyl 1,3-dithiane-2-carboxylate
($C_7H_{12}O_2S_2$; *20462-00-4*)   see: Cilastatin

ethylene
(C_2H_4; *74-85-1*)   see: Maprotiline; Mibefradil hydrochloride; Thioctic acid

ethylene carbonate
($C_3H_4O_3$; *96-49-1*)   see: Hexcarbacholine bromide; Raloxifene hydrochloride

ethylene chlorohydrin
(C_2H_5ClO; *107-07-3*)   see: Acetylcholine chloride; Carbachol; Choline chloride; Etofylline; Homofenazine; Metronidazole; Oxypendyl; Tofenacin; Troxerutin

ethylenediamine
($C_2H_8N_2$; *107-15-3*)   see: Apraclonidine; Benzathine benzylpenicillin; Brimonidine; Clonidine; Edetic acid; Epanolol; Fenoxazoline; Indanazoline; Lofexidine; Mazindol; Medazepam; Naphazoline; Oxymetazoline; Tetryzoline; Theophylline ethylenediamine; Tiamenidine; Tinazoline hydrochloride; Tizanidine; Tolazoline; Tolonidine; Tramazoline; Trientine; Xylometazoline

ethylenediaminetetraacetonitrile
($C_{10}H_{12}N_6$; *5766-67-6*)   see: Edetic acid

ethylenediamine *p*-toluenesulfonate
($C_9H_{16}N_2O_3S$; *14034-59-4*)   see: Cibenzoline

20,20-ethylenedioxy-16α,17α-epoxy-5β-pregnane-3α,11β-diol
($C_{23}H_{36}O_5$; *13643-93-1*)   see: Betamethasone

3,3-(ethylenedioxy)estra-5(10),9(11)-dien-17-one
($C_{20}H_{26}O_3$; *5571-36-8*)   see: Mifepristone

3,3-ethylenedioxy-13-ethyl-17β-hydroxy-17α-ethynylgona-4,9,11-triene
($C_{23}H_{28}O_3$; *15343-94-9*)   see: Gestrinone

3,3-ethylenedioxy-13-ethyl-17-oxogona-5(10),9(11)-diene
($C_{21}H_{28}O_3$; *10109-61-2*)   see: Gestrinone

3,3-ethylenedioxy-17β-hydroxy-6-methyl-17α-(1-propy-nyl)-5-androstene
($C_{25}H_{36}O_3$)   see: Dimethisterone

3,3-ethylenedioxy-6-methyl-17-oxo-5-androstene
($C_{22}H_{32}O_3$)   see: Dimethisterone

2,2-(ethylenedioxy)-1-propanol
($C_5H_{10}O_3$; *10004-17-8*)   see: Aranidipine

(12a*S*-*cis*)-12a-ethyl-2,3,5,12,12a,12b-hexahydro-1*H*,4*H*-3a,9b-diazabenzo[*a*]naphth[2,1,8-*cde*]azulene-10,11-dione 12-oxime
($C_{20}H_{23}N_3O_2$; *35226-42-7*)   see: Vincamine

ethyl 1,3,4,6,7,11b-hexahydro-9,10-dimethoxy-2-oxo-2*H*-benzo[*a*]quinolizine-3-carboxylate
($C_{18}H_{23}NO_5$; *5911-33-1*)   see: Benzquinamide

ethyl (3a*R*,5*S*,7*R*,7a*R*)-hexahydro-5-hydroxy-2,2-dimethyl-7-[(methylsulfonyl)oxy]-1,3-benzodioxole-5-carboxylate
($C_{13}H_{22}O_8S$; *204254-81-9*)   see: Oseltamivir

1-ethyl-1,2,3,4,6,7-hexahydroindolo[2,3-*a*]quinolizin-5-ium perchlorate
($C_{17}H_{21}ClN_2O_4$; *59639-73-5*)   see: Vincamine

(13*S*-*cis*)-13-ethyl-7,11,12,13,16,17-hexahydro-3-methoxy-6*H*-cyclopenta[*a*]phenanthren-17-ol acetate
($C_{22}H_{26}O_3$; *2911-81-1*)   see: Levonorgestrel

3-ethylhexahydro-3-(3-methoxyphenyl)-1*H*-azepine
($C_{15}H_{23}NO$; *27180-90-1*)   see: Meptazinol

6-ethylhexahydro-6-(3-methoxyphenyl)-2*H*-azepin-2-one
($C_{15}H_{21}NO_2$; *27180-89-8*)   see: Meptazinol

3-ethylhexahydro-3-(3-methoxyphenyl)-1-methyl-1*H*-azepine
($C_{16}H_{25}NO$; *71556-73-5*)   see: Meptazinol

2-ethyl-1-hexanol
($C_8H_{18}O$; *104-76-7*)   see: Sodium dioctyl sulfosuccinate

2-ethylhexylamine
($C_8H_{19}N$; *104-75-6*)   see: Butoctamide; Hexetidine

N-(2-ethylhexyl)-3-oxobutanamide
($C_{12}H_{23}NO_2$; *32837-36-8*)   see: Butoctamide

13-ethyl-11β-hydroperoxy-17-hydroxy-18,19-dinor-17α-pregna-4,9-dien-20-yn-3-one
($C_{21}H_{26}O_4$; *23637-81-2*)   see: Gestrinone

ethyl 4-hydroxybenzoic acid
($C_9H_{10}O_3$; *120-47-8*)   see: Gabexate

ethyl (2-hydroxybenzylamino)acetate
($C_{11}H_{15}NO_3$; *57938-78-0*)   see: Caroxazone

7-ethyl-10-hydroxycamptothecin
($C_{22}H_{20}N_2O_5$; *86639-52-3*)   see: Irinotecan

α-ethyl-3-hydroxycinnamic acid
($C_{11}H_{12}O_3$; *59150-87-7*)   see: Iophenoic acid

ethyl 3(*R*)-hydroxy-4-cyanobutyrate
($C_7H_{11}NO_3$; *141942-85-0*)   see: Atorvastatin calcium

α-ethyl-1-hydroxycyclohexaneacetic acid ethyl ester
($C_{12}H_{22}O_3$; *51632-39-4*)   see: Cyclobutyrol

13-ethyl-17-hydroxy-18,19-dinor-17α-pregna-5(10),9(11)-dien-20-yn-3-one cyclic ethylene acetal
($C_{23}H_{30}O_3$; *23637-79-8*)   see: Gestrinone

cis-1-ethyl-1-(2-hydroxy-2-ethoxycarbonylethyl)-1,2,3,4,6,7,12,12b-octahydroindolo[2,3-*a*]quinolizine
($C_{22}H_{30}N_2O_3$; *43184-10-7*)   see: Vinburnine

5-[ethyl(2-hydroxyethyl)amino]-2-pentanone
($C_9H_{19}NO_2$; *74509-79-8*)   see: Hydroxychloroquine

7-ethyl-3-(2-hydroxyethyl)indole
($C_{12}H_{15}NO$; *41340-36-7*)   see: Etodolac

3-ethyl-5-(2-hydroxyethyl)-4-methylthiazolium
($C_8H_{14}NOS$; *45892-42-0*)   see: Atorvastatin calcium

ethyl 2-hydroxyiminoacetoacetate
($C_6H_9NO_4$; *5408-04-8*)   see: Cefotaxime; Ceftazidime

ethyl (Z)-2-hydroxyimino-2-(2-tritylaminothiazol-4-yl)-acetate
($C_{26}H_{23}N_3O_3S$; *66338-99-6*)   see: Ceftazidime

2-ethyl-5-hydroxy-N-[2-(1*H*-indol-3-yl)ethyl]pentanamide
($C_{17}H_{24}N_2O_2$; *52250-53-0*)   see: Vincamine

ethyl 2-hydroxyisobutyrate
($C_6H_{12}O_3$; *80-55-7*)   see: Dimethadione; Trimethadione

ethyl α-hydroxyisobutyrate
see under ethyl 2-hydroxyisobutyrate

ethyl hydroxymethoxyacetate
($C_5H_{10}O_4$; *19757-96-1*)   see: Retinol

ethyl 2-hydroxy-3-methoxybenzoate
($C_{10}H_{12}O_4$; *35030-98-9*)   see: Alibendol

β-ethyl-β-hydroxy-6-methoxy-α,α-dimethyl-2-naphthalenepropanoic acid ethyl ester
($C_{20}H_{26}O_4$; *85536-81-8*)   see: Methallenestril

(17β)-13-ethyl-17-hydroxy-11-methylenegon-4-en-3-one cyclic 1,2-ethanediyl mercaptole
($C_{22}H_{32}OS_2$; *54024-19-0*)   see: Desogestrel

ethyl 4-hydroxy-1,5-naphthyridine-3-carboxylate
($C_{11}H_{10}N_2O_3$; *13801-51-9*)   see: Apalcillin

(±)-17α-ethyl-17β-hydroxy-3-oxo-18-homo-5(10)-estrene
($C_{21}H_{32}O_2$; *900-88-9*)   see: Norboletone

17α-ethyl-17β-hydroxy-3-oxo-19-nor-4-androstene
($C_{20}H_{30}O_2$; *52-78-8*)   see: Ethylestrenol

ethyl 4-hydroxyphenylacetate
($C_{10}H_{12}O_3$; *17138-28-2*)   see: Betaxolol

α-ethyl-β-hydroxy-β-phenylbenzenepropanenitrile
($C_{17}H_{17}NO$; *22101-20-8*)   see: Etifelmine

ethyl (2*R*,3*S*)-2-hydroxy-3-[(*S*)-1-phenylethylamino]-3-phenylpropionate
($C_{19}H_{23}NO_3$)   see: Docetaxel

1-ethyl-3-hydroxypiperidine
($C_7H_{15}NO$; *13444-24-1*)   see: Piperidolate

N-ethyl-2-hydroxypropylamine
($C_5H_{13}NO$; *40171-86-6*)   see: Cadralazine

2-ethyl-2-(3-hydroxypropyl)malonic acid
($C_8H_{14}O_5$; *52250-47-2*)   see: Vincamine

1-ethyl-3-hydroxypyrrolidine
($C_6H_{13}NO$; *30727-14-1*)   see: Benzilonium bromide

ethyl 6-hydroxy-5,7,8-trimethyl-4-oxo-4*H*-chromene-2-carboxylate
($C_{15}H_{16}O_5$; *107188-52-3*)   see: Troglitazone

4,6-*O*-(*R*)-ethylidene-2,3-di-*O*-acetyl-β-D-glucopyranose
($C_{12}H_{18}O_8$; *118139-63-2*)   see: Etoposide

ethylidenetriphenylphosphorane
($C_{20}H_{19}P$; *1754-88-7*)   see: Promegestone

ethyl 4-(1-imidazolylmethyl)cinnamate
($C_{15}H_{16}N_2O_2$; *74002-88-3*)   see: Ozagrel

ethyl indole-2-carboxylate
($C_{11}H_{11}NO_2$; *3770-50-1*)   see: Perindopril

ethyl indole-3-glyoxylate
($C_{12}H_{11}NO_3$; *51079-10-8*)   see: Indoramin

ethyl iodide
(C_2H_5I; *75-03-6*)   see: Butibufen; Cinoxacin; Diethylstilbestrol; Enoxacin; Ethotoin; Gallamine triethiodide; Imiquimod; Lomefloxacin; Mosapride citrate; Nalidixic acid; Oxolinic acid; Pefloxacin; Pipemidic acid; Tridihexethyl chloride; Zaleplon

ethyl 4-iodobutyrate
($C_6H_{11}IO_2$; 7425-53-8) see: Meptazinol

ethyl 4-isobutylphenylacetate
($C_{14}H_{20}O_2$; 15649-02-2) see: Butibufen

ethyl isobutyrylacetate
($C_8H_{14}O_3$; 7152-15-0) see: Cerivastatin sodium

ethyl isocyanate
(C_3H_5NO; 109-90-0) see: Alfentanil; Cabergoline

ethyl isocyanatoacetate
($C_5H_7NO_3$; 2949-22-6) see: Flumazenil

ethyl isonicotinate
($C_8H_9NO_2$; 1570-45-2) see: Azacyclonol; Diphemanil metilsulfate; Isoniazid

2-ethylisonicotinonitrile
($C_8H_8N_2$; 1531-18-6) see: Ethionamide

ethyl 3,4-O-isopropylidene-5-O-(methanesulfonyl)-shikimate
($C_{13}H_{20}O_7S$; 204254-84-2) see: Oseltamivir

ethyl 3,4-O-isopropylideneshikimate
($C_{12}H_{18}O_5$; 136994-78-0) see: Oseltamivir

ethyl 2-(2-isopropylphenoxy)acetimidate hydrochloride
($C_{13}H_{20}ClNO_2$) see: Fenoxazoline

ethyl (S)-lactate
($C_5H_{10}O_3$; 687-47-8) see: Naproxen

ethyl lactimidate hydrochloride
($C_5H_{12}ClNO_2$) see: Lofexidine

ethylmagnesium bromide
(C_2H_5BrMg; 925-90-6) see: Amfebutamone; Diethylstilbestrol; Ethylestrenol; Etretinate; Fomocaine; Indanorex; Ketobemidone; Mepivacaine; Methadone; Methallenestril; Methohexital; Normethadone; Olprinone hydrochloride; Retinol

ethylmalonic acid diethyl ester
see under diethyl ethylmalonate

ethylmercaptan
(C_2H_6S; 75-08-1) see: Raloxifene hydrochloride

ethyl mercaptoacetate
($C_4H_8O_2S$; 623-51-8) see: Etozolin; Flomoxef; Letosteine

ethylmercury chloride
(C_2H_5ClHg; 107-27-7) see: Thiomersal

2-ethyl-3-(4-methoxybenzoyl)benzofuran
($C_{18}H_{16}O_3$; 3343-80-4) see: Benzarone

(–)-1α-ethyl-1-(2-methoxycarbonylethyl)-1,2,3,4,6,7,12,12bα-octahydroindolo[2,3-a]quinolizine
($C_{21}H_{28}N_2O_2$; 23944-42-5) see: Vincamine

(±)-cis-1-ethyl-1-(2-methoxycarbonylethyl)-4-oxo-1,2,3,4,6,7,12,12b-octahydroindolo[2,3-a]quinolizine
($C_{21}H_{26}N_2O_3$; 65085-43-0) see: Vincamine

(±)-trans-1-ethyl-1-(2-methoxycarbonylethyl)-4-oxo-1,2,3,4,6,7,12,12b-octahydroindolo[2,3-a]quinolizine
($C_{21}H_{26}N_2O_3$; 65085-44-1) see: Vincamine

ethyl 4-methoxycinnamate
($C_{12}H_{14}O_3$; 1929-30-2) see: Anethole trithione

(17β)-13-ethyl-3-methoxygona-2,5(10)-dien-17-ol
($C_{20}H_{30}O_2$; 14507-49-4) see: Levonorgestrel

ethyl 2-(methoxyimino)acetoacetate
($C_7H_{11}NO_4$; 60846-14-2) see: Cefotaxime

ethyl 2-(methoxyimino)-2-[2-(tritylamino)-4-thiazolyl]-acetate
($C_{27}H_{25}N_3O_3S$; 66215-70-1) see: Cefotaxime

N-ethyl-N-(p-methoxy-α-methylphenethyl)succinamic acid ethyl ester
($C_{18}H_{27}NO_4$; 109554-69-0) see: Mebeverine

(4R,5R)-2-ethyl-2-(6-methoxy-2-naphthalenyl)-1,3-dioxo-lane-4,5-dicarboxylic acid dimethyl ester
($C_{20}H_{22}O_7$; 101154-44-3) see: Naproxen

ethyl (±)-3-methoxy-4-oxo-1-piperidinecarboxylate
($C_9H_{15}NO_4$; 83863-72-3) see: Cisapride

4-[ethyl[2-(4-methoxyphenyl)-1-methylethyl]amino]-1-bu-tanol
($C_{16}H_{27}NO_2$; 14367-47-6) see: Mebeverine

β-ethyl-α-(4-methoxyphenyl)-α-phenylbenzeneethanol
($C_{23}H_{24}O_2$) see: Tamoxifen

ethyl 4-(methylamino)piperidine-1-carboxylate
($C_9H_{18}N_2O_2$; 73733-69-4) see: Mizolastine

N-ethyl-2-methylaniline
($C_9H_{13}N$; 94-68-8) see: Crotamiton

3-ethyl 5-methyl 2-[(2-azidoethoxy)methyl]-4-(2-chloro-phenyl)-1,4-dihydro-6-methyl-3,5-pyridinedicarboxylate
($C_{20}H_{23}ClN_4O_5$; 88150-46-3) see: Amlodipine

ethyl 2-methyl-2-bromobutyrate
($C_7H_{13}BrO_2$; 5398-71-0) see: Beclobrate

2-ethyl-2-methylbutanedioic acid diammonium salt
($C_7H_{18}N_2O_4$; 75315-43-4) see: Ethosuximide

ethyl 2-methylbutanoate
($C_7H_{14}O_2$; 7452-79-1) see: Beclobrate

ethyl(1-methylbutyl)malonic acid diethyl ester
see under diethyl ethyl(1-methylbutyl)malonate

(±)-N-ethyl-N-methylcarbamic acid 3-[1-(dimethylamino)-ethyl]phenyl ester
($C_{14}H_{22}N_2O_2$; 105601-20-5) see: Rivastigmine

N-ethyl-N-methylcarbamoyl chloride
(C_4H_8ClNO; 42252-34-6) see: Rivastigmine

ethyl 4-methylcinnamate
($C_{12}H_{14}O_2$; 20511-20-0) see: Ozagrel

13-ethyl-11-methylenegon-4-en-17-one
($C_{20}H_{28}O$; 54024-21-4) see: Desogestrel

3-ethyl-3-methylglutaric acid
($C_8H_{14}O_4$; 5345-01-7) see: Bemegride

3-ethyl-3-methylglutaric anhydride
($C_8H_{12}O_3$; 6970-57-6) see: Bemegride

ethyl 2-methyl-4-hexynoate
($C_9H_{14}O_2$; 116484-93-6) see: Iloprost

ethyl 5-methylimidazole-4-carboxylate
($C_7H_{10}N_2O_2$; 51605-32-4) see: Cimetidine

ethyl 5-methylisoxazole-3-carboxylate
($C_7H_9NO_3$; 3209-72-1) see: Isocarboxazid

ethyl methyl ketone
see under butanone

ethyl N-methylmalonamate
($C_6H_{11}NO_3$; 71510-95-7) see: Paroxetine

ethyl 4-methyloxazole-5-carboxylate
($C_7H_9NO_3$; 20485-39-6) see: Pyridoxine

5-ethyl-5-methyl-2,4-oxazolidinedione
($C_6H_9NO_3$; 52387-52-7) see: Paramethadione

3-ethyl-2-methyl-4-oxo-4,5,6,7-tetrahydroindol
($C_{11}H_{15}NO$; 6116-76-3) see: Molindone

ethyl 3-methyl-4-oxothiazolidin-2-ylideneacetate
($C_8H_{11}NO_3S$; 27653-75-4) see: Etozolin

ethyl 5-methyl-3-phenylisoxazole-4-carboxylate
($C_{13}H_{13}NO_3$; *1143-82-4*)   see: Oxacillin

ethyl 2-methyl-2-phenylpropionate
($C_{12}H_{16}O_2$; *2901-13-5*)   see: Fexofenadine hydrochloride

ethyl 1-methylpiperidine-2-carboxylate
($C_9H_{17}NO_2$; *30727-18-5*)   see: Mepivacaine

5-ethyl-2-methylpyridine
($C_8H_{11}N$; *104-90-5*)   see: Nicotinic acid

3-ethyl-4-methyl-δ³-pyrrolin-2-one
($C_7H_{11}NO$; *766-36-9*)   see: Glimepiride

2-ethyl-2-methylsuccinic acid
($C_7H_{12}O_4$; *631-31-2*)   see: Ethosuximide

ethyl 2-(5-methyl-1*H*-tetrazol-1-yl)benzoate
($C_{11}H_{12}N_4O_2$; *77177-26-5*)   see: Imiquimod

ethyl 2-(methylthio)acetate
($C_5H_{10}O_2S$; *4455-13-4*)   see: Bromfenac sodium

8-ethyl-2-methylthio-5-oxo-5,8-dihydropyrido[2,3-*d*]py-rimidine-6-carboxylic acid
($C_{11}H_{11}N_3O_3S$; *19572-11-3*)   see: Pipemidic acid; Piromidic acid

ethyl 2-(2-methyl-3,4,6-trifluorobenzoyl)-3-cyclopropyl-aminoacrylate
($C_{16}H_{16}F_3NO_3$; *119915-45-6*)   see: Grepafloxacin

ethyl 2-(2-methyl-3,4,6-trifluorobenzoyl)-3-ethoxyacrylate
($C_{15}H_{15}F_3O_4$; *119915-44-5*)   see: Grepafloxacin

ethyl nicotinate
($C_8H_9NO_2$; *614-18-6*)   see: Azatadine; Tipepidine

ethyl nipecotinate
($C_8H_{15}NO_2$; *5006-62-2*)   see: Tiagabine

α-ethyl-4-nitrobenzeneacetic acid
($C_{10}H_{11}NO_4$; *7463-53-8*)   see: Indobufen

ethyl 4-nitrobenzoate
($C_9H_9NO_4$; *99-77-4*)   see: Benzocaine

ethyl 3-nitro-benzylideneacetoacetate
($C_{13}H_{13}NO_5$; *39562-16-8*)   see: Nitrendipine

ethyl *N*-(2-nitro-6-chlorobenzyl)glycinate
($C_{11}H_{13}ClN_2O_4$; *50608-25-8*)   see: Anagrelide hydrochloride

α-ethyl-3-nitrocinnamic acid
($C_{11}H_{11}NO_4$; *5253-02-1*)   see: Bunamiodyl; Iopanoic acid

ethyl 1-(nitromethyl)cyclohexaneacetate
($C_{11}H_{19}NO_4$; *133938-45-1*)   see: Gabapentin

ethyl 8-nitro-4-oxo-1-benzopyran-2-carboxylate
($C_{12}H_9NO_6$; *110683-75-5*)   see: Pranlukast

ethyl 5-nitro-3-phenylindol-2-carboxylate
($C_{17}H_{14}N_2O_4$; *23515-78-8*)   see: Nimetazepam

ethyl nortriptyline-*N*-carboxylate
($C_{22}H_{25}NO_2$; *16234-88-1*)   see: Nortriptyline

ethyl L-norvalinate hydrochloride
($C_7H_{16}ClNO_2$; *40918-51-2*)   see: Perindopril

ethyl 2,3,4,4a,5,6,7,8-octahydro-3-oxo-6-pyrido[4,3-*c*]py-ridazinecarboxylate
($C_{10}H_{15}N_3O_3$; *39716-41-1*)   see: Endralazine

ethyl orthocarbonate
($C_9H_{20}O_4$; *78-09-1*)   see: Candesartan cilexetil; Prednicarbate

ethyl orthoformate
($C_7H_{16}O_3$; *122-51-0*)   see: Allopurinol; Azacitidine; Betacarotene; Ciprofloxacin; Cortivazol; Ebrotidine; Eprosartan; Flumedroxone acetate; Formocortal; Gestodene; Grepafloxacin; Imiquimod; Incadronic acid; Ipriflavone; Leflunomide; Levofloxacin; Meproscillarin; Methandriol; Methylestrenolone; Moxifloxacin hydrochloride; Norethisterone; Penmesterol; Sparfloxacin; Temafloxacin; Thiamine; Tosufloxacin; Ulobetasol propionate

2-ethyl-2-oxazoline
(C_5H_9NO; *10431-98-8*)   see: Nefazodone hydrochloride

(±)-ethyl 2-oxo-3-benzoylamino-3-phenylpropionate
($C_{18}H_{17}NO_4$; *153433-79-5*)   see: Paclitaxel

ethyl 3-oxocaproate
($C_8H_{14}O_3$; *3249-68-1*)   see: Propylthiouracil

ethyl 2-oxocyclohexanecarboxylate
($C_9H_{14}O_3$; *1655-07-8*)   see: Tacrine

ethyl 2-oxocyclopentanecarboxylate
($C_8H_{12}O_3$; *611-10-9*)   see: Loxoprofen

ethyl 6-oxo-6-[2-(3,4-dimethoxyphenyl)ethylamino]hexa-noate
($C_{18}H_{27}NO_5$; *101889-12-7*)   see: Dopexamine

ethyl 3-oxopentanoate
($C_7H_{12}O_3$; *4949-44-4*)   see: Etodolac

ethyl 2-oxo-4-phenylbutanoate
($C_{12}H_{14}O_3$; *64920-29-2*)   see: Benazepril; Cilazapril; Enalapril; Lisinopril; Spirapril

ethyl 2-oxo-4-phenylbutyrate
see under ethyl 2-oxo-4-phenylbutanoate

ethyl 4-oxo-1-piperidinecarboxylate
see under 1-(ethoxycarbonyl)-4-piperidinone

ethyl 4-oxo-1-piperidinecarboxylic acid
see under 1-(ethoxycarbonyl)-4-piperidinone

ethyl (3-oxopropylthio)acetate
($C_7H_{12}O_3S$; *94088-65-0*)   see: Letosteine

ethyl 4-oxo-7-(4-pyridyl)-1,4-dihydroquinoline-3-carb-oxylate
($C_{17}H_{14}N_2O_3$; *40034-41-1*)   see: Rosoxacin

ethyl 2-oxo-1-pyrrolidineacetate
($C_8H_{13}NO_3$; *61516-73-2*)   see: Piracetam; Pramiracetam hydrochloride

ethyl 4-oxothiazolidin-2-ylideneacetate
($C_7H_9NO_3S$; *24146-36-9*)   see: Etozolin; Piprozolin

(3-ethyl-4-oxo-2-thiazolidinylidene)acetic acid ethyl ester
($C_9H_{13}NO_3S$; *36958-87-9*)   see: Piprozolin

ethyl pentafluorobenzoylacetate
($C_{11}H_7F_5O_3$; *3516-87-8*)   see: Sparfloxacin

ethyl pentanimidate
($C_7H_{15}NO$; *999-09-7*)   see: Irbesartan

5-(1-ethylpentyl)hydantoin sodium salt
($C_{10}H_{17}N_2NaO_2$)   see: Clodantoin

2-ethyl-10*H*-phenothiazine
($C_{14}H_{13}NS$; *61852-27-5*)   see: Etymemazine

ethyl phenothiazine-2-carbamate
($C_{15}H_{14}N_2O_2S$; *37711-29-8*)   see: Moracizine

ethyl 2-phenoxymethylbenzoate
($C_{16}H_{16}O_3$; *4504-85-2*)   see: Doxepin

ethyl phenylacetate
($C_{10}H_{12}O_2$; *101-97-3*)   see: Methylphenobarbital; Phenobarbital

ethyl [3R-(Z)]-3-[(tetrahydro-2H-pyran-2-yl)oxy]-6-tetra-decenoate
($C_{21}H_{38}O_4$; 104801-91-4)   see: Orlistat

N-(5-ethyl-1,3,4-thiadiazol-2-yl)-4-nitrobenzenesulfon-amide
($C_{10}H_{10}N_4O_4S_2$; 76170-72-4)   see: Sulfaethidole

ethyl thiazole-5-carboxylate
($C_6H_7NO_2S$; 32955-22-9)   see: Ritonavir

3-ethylthioaniline
($C_8H_{11}NS$; 1783-82-0)   see: Thiethylperazine

3-ethylthiodiphenylamine
($C_{14}H_{15}NS$; 68083-49-8)   see: Thiethylperazine

2-ethylthiophenothiazine
($C_{14}H_{13}NS_2$; 46815-10-5)   see: Thiethylperazine

N-(3-ethylthiophenyl)anthranilic acid
($C_{15}H_{15}NO_2S$; 18902-94-8)   see: Thiethylperazine

ethyl 4-toluenesulfonylcarbamate
($C_{10}H_{13}NO_4S$; 5577-13-9)   see: Glibornuride; Gliclazide; Tolazamide

ethyl (E)-3-[6-(p-toluoyl)-2-pyridinyl]acrylate
($C_{18}H_{17}NO_3$; 87848-98-4)   see: Acrivastine

ethyl 3-[4-(o-tolyl)-1-piperazinyl]propionate
($C_{16}H_{24}N_2O_2$; 63853-99-6)   see: Dapiprazole

ethyl N-(p-tolylsulfonyl)carbamate
see under ethyl 4-toluenesulfonylcarbamate

ethyl trifluoroacetate
($C_4H_5F_3O_2$; 383-63-1)   see: Celecoxib; Efavirenz; Lisinopril

ethyl γ,γ,γ-trifluoroacetoacetate
($C_6H_7F_3O_3$; 372-31-6)   see: Mefloquine

1-ethyl-6,7,8-trifluoro-1,4-dihydro-4-oxo-3-quinolinecarb-oxylic acid
($C_{12}H_8F_3NO_3$; 75338-42-0)   see: Lomefloxacin

1-ethyl-6,7,8-trifluoro-1,4-dihydro-4-oxo-3-quinolinecarb-oxylic acid ethyl ester
($C_{14}H_{12}F_3NO_3$; 100501-62-0)   see: Lomefloxacin

ethyl 2-(2,4,5-trifluoro-3-methoxybenzoyl)acetate
($C_{12}H_{11}F_3O_4$; 112811-68-4)   see: Moxifloxacin hydrochloride

ethyl 2,3,5-trifluoro-4-(4-methyl-1-piperazinyl)benzoyl-acetate
($C_{16}H_{19}F_3N_2O_3$; 108860-30-6)   see: Rufloxacin hydrochloride

ethyl 2,3,5-Trifluoro-4-(4-methyl-1-piperazinyl)-α-ethoxymethylenebenzoylacetate
($C_{19}H_{23}F_3N_2O_4$)   see: Rufloxacin hydrochloride

ethyl 2(R)-trifluoromethylsulfonyloxy-4-phenylbutyrate
($C_{13}H_{15}F_3O_5S$; 88767-98-0)   see: Temocapril

ethyl 3,4,5-trimethoxybenzylcyanoacetate
($C_{15}H_{19}NO_5$; 29958-02-9)   see: Trimethoprim

ethyl 3-(3,4,5-trimethoxyphenyl)propionate
($C_{14}H_{20}O_5$; 70311-20-5)   see: Trimethoprim

ethyl (±)-3,4,4-trimethoxy-1-piperidinecarboxylate
($C_{11}H_{21}NO_5$; 83863-73-4)   see: Cisapride

ethyl (triphenylphosphoranylidene)acetate
($C_{22}H_{21}O_2P$; 1099-45-2)   see: Sorivudine

ethyl 2-(triphenylphosphoranylidene)propanoate
($C_{23}H_{23}O_2P$; 5717-37-3)   see: Sorivudine

ethyl 1-trityltetrazole-5-carboxylate
($C_{23}H_{20}N_4O_2$; 139348-78-0)   see: Pranlukast

ethyl 10-undecylenate
($C_{13}H_{24}O_2$; 692-86-4)   see: Iofendylate

ethylurea
($C_3H_8N_2O$; 625-52-5)   see: Fenozolone

ethyl vinyl ether
(C_4H_8O; 109-92-2)   see: Betacarotene; Brinzolamide; Docetaxel; Paclitaxel

ethylxanthic acid [5-hydroxy-4-(hydroxymethyl)-6-methyl-3-pyridyl]methyl ester
($C_{11}H_{15}NO_3S_2$; 92147-37-0)   see: Pyritinol

1-ethynylcyclohexanol
($C_8H_{12}O$; 78-27-3)   see: Ethinamate

17-ethynyl-3β,17β-dihydroxy-5-androstene
($C_{21}H_{30}O_2$; 3604-60-2)   see: Ethisterone; Spironolactone

6-ethynyl-4,4-dimethyl-3,4-dihydro-2H-1-benzothiopyran
($C_{13}H_{14}S$; 118292-06-1)   see: Tazarotene

17-ethynylestradiol
($C_{20}H_{24}O_2$; 57-63-6)   see: Quinestrol

17α-ethynyl-17β-hydroxy-3-oxo-4-androstene
see under ethisterone

ethynylmagnesium bromide
(C_2HBrMg; 4301-14-8)   see: Gestodene; Norgestrienone

[1R-(1α,2β,4β)]-[(4-ethynyl-2-methoxycyclohexyl)oxy]-tris(1-methylethyl)silane
($C_{18}H_{34}O_2Si$; 122948-76-9)   see: Tacrolimus

17α-ethynyl-6β-methyl-3β,5α,17β-trihydroxyandrostane
($C_{22}H_{34}O_3$; 96707-49-2)   see: Dimethisterone

etofylline
($C_9H_{12}N_4O_3$; 519-37-9)   see: Pyridofylline

etoposide
($C_{29}H_{32}O_{13}$; 33419-42-0)   see: Etopophos

etynodiol
($C_{20}H_{28}O_2$; 1231-93-2)   see: Etynodiol acetate

F

farnesylacetic acid
($C_{17}H_{28}O_2$; 6040-06-8)   see: Gefarnate

rac-fenfluramine
($C_{12}H_{16}F_3N$; 458-24-2)   see: Dexfenfluramine

fenpipramide
($C_{21}H_{26}N_2O$; 77-01-0)   see: Fenpiverinium bromide

fludrocortisone
($C_{21}H_{29}FO_5$; 127-31-1)   see: Triamcinolone

fludrocortisone 21-acetate
($C_{23}H_{31}FO_6$; 514 36 3)   see: Fludrocortisone; Isoflupredone acetate

fludroxycortide
($C_{24}H_{33}FO_6$; 1524-88-5)   see: Flunisolide

flufenamic acid potassium salt
($C_{14}H_9F_3KNO_2$; 35982-11-7)   see: Etofenamate

flumetasone acetate
($C_{24}H_{30}F_2O_6$; 2823-42-9)   see: Halometasone

fluocinolone
($C_{21}H_{26}F_2O_6$; 807-38-5)   see: Fluocinolone acetonide

fluocinolone acetonide
($C_{24}H_{30}F_2O_6$; 67-73-2)   see: Fluocinonide

N-(β-fluoroethyl)nortropine benzilate
($C_{23}H_{26}FNO_3$; *63516-27-8*)   see: Flutropium bromide

6β-fluorohydrocortisone 21-acetate
($C_{23}H_{31}FO_6$; *986-37-8*)   see: Fluprednisolone acetate

5'-fluoro-2'-hydroxybutyrophenone
($C_{10}H_{11}FO_2$; *575-67-7*)   see: Butofilolol

(Z)-6β-fluoro-5-hydroxy-3,11-dioxo-5α-pregn-17(20)-en-21-oic acid methyl ester cyclic 3-(ethylene acetal)
($C_{24}H_{33}FO_6$; *5319-18-6*)   see: Fluprednisolone acetate

9α-fluoro-16-hydroxyhydrocortisone
($C_{21}H_{29}FO_6$; *337-02-0*)   see: Halcinonide

(11β,16β)-9-fluoro-11-hydroxy-16-methyl-21-[(methylsulfonyl)oxy]-17-(1-oxobutoxy)pregna-1,4-diene-3,20-dione
($C_{27}H_{37}FO_8S$; *25092-11-9*)   see: Clobetasone butyrate

(11β,16β)-9-fluoro-11-hydroxy-16-methyl-21-[(methylsulfonyl)oxy]-17-(1-oxopropoxy)pregna-1,4-diene-3,20-dione
($C_{26}H_{35}FO_8S$; *15423-80-0*)   see: Clobetasol propionate

(6α,16α)-6-fluoro-21-hydroxy-16-methylpregn-4-ene-3,20-dione
($C_{22}H_{31}FO_3$; *1244-13-9*)   see: Fluocortolone

6β-fluoro-21-hydroxy-16α-methylpregn-4-ene-3,20-dione acetate
($C_{24}H_{33}FO_4$; *1251-27-0*)   see: Fluocortolone

2-fluoro-3-hydroxy-2-propenoic acid ethyl ester
($C_5H_7FO_3$; *185692-96-0*)   see: Fluorouracil

6-fluoro-γ-(2-iodoethyl)-1,2-benzisoxazole-3-propanol methanesulfonate (ester)
($C_{13}H_{15}FINO_4S$; *181479-14-1*)   see: Risperidone

fluoroiodomethane
(CH_2FI; *373-53-5*)   see: Fluticasone propionate

5-fluoroisatoic anhydride
($C_8H_4FNO_3$; *321-69-7*)   see: Flumazenil

1-[4-fluoro-2-(methylamino)phenyl]-2-(methylsulfinyl)-ethanone
($C_{10}H_{12}FNO_2S$; *154639-75-5*)   see: Flosequinan

4-fluoro-*N*-methylanthranilic acid
($C_8H_8FNO_2$; *128992-62-1*)   see: Flosequinan

7-fluoro-1-methyl-2*H*-3,1-benzoxazine-2,4(1*H*)-dione
($C_9H_6FNO_3$; *97927-92-9*)   see: Flosequinan

4-fluoro-α-methylcinnamic acid
($C_{10}H_9FO_2$; *22138-72-3*)   see: Sulindac

7-fluoro-4-methyl-3,4-dihydro-2*H*-1,4-benzodiazepin-2,5(1*H*)-dione
($C_{10}H_9FN_2O_2$; *78755-80-3*)   see: Flumazenil

4-fluoro-α-methyldihydrocinnamic acid
($C_{10}H_{11}FO_2$; *22138-73-4*)   see: Sulindac

5-fluoro-2',3'-*O*-(1-methylethylidene)uridine
($C_{12}H_{15}FN_2O_6$; *2797-17-3*)   see: Doxifluridine

9-fluoro-6α-methyl-hydrocortisone
($C_{22}H_{31}FO_5$; *382-51-4*)   see: Fluorometholone

5-fluoro-2-methyl-3-indanone
($C_{10}H_9FO$; *37794-19-7*)   see: Sulindac

5-fluoro-2-methyl-1*H*-indene-3-acetic acid
($C_{12}H_{11}FO_2$; *32004-66-3*)   see: Sulindac

2-(fluoromethyl)-3-(2-methylphenyl)-6-nitro-4(3*H*)-quinazolinone
($C_{16}H_{12}FN_3O_3$; *56287-73-1*)   see: Afloqualone

5-fluoro-2-methyl-1-(4-methylthiobenzylidene)indene-3-acetic acid
($C_{20}H_{17}FO_2S$; *32004-67-4*)   see: Sulindac

6β-fluoro-16α-methylpregn-17(20)-ene-3β,5α,20-triol triacetate
($C_{28}H_{41}FO_6$; *75083-51-1*)   see: Flumetasone; Paramethasone

7-fluoro-3-(methylthio)-4(1*H*)-quinolinone
($C_{10}H_8FNOS$; *76561-48-3*)   see: Flosequinan

5-fluoro-2-methylthiouracil
($C_5H_5FN_2OS$; *1480-92-8*)   see: Flucytosine; Fluorouracil

4-fluoro-1-nitrobenzene
($C_6H_4FNO_2$; *350-46-9*)   see: Nitrefazole; Pioglitazone

1-[5-fluoro-2-(oxiranylmethoxy)phenyl]-1-butanone
($C_{13}H_{15}FO_3$; *94135-58-7*)   see: Butofilolol

6-fluoro-4-oxobenzopyran-2-carboxylic acid
($C_{10}H_5FO_4$; *99199-59-4*)   see: Nebivolol

4-fluorophenol
(C_6H_5FO; *371-41-5*)   see: Butofilolol; Cisapride; Progabide

1-[3-(4-fluorophenoxy)propyl]-3-methoxy-4-piperidinamine
($C_{15}H_{23}FN_2O_2$; *108913-89-9*)   see: Cisapride

trans-1-[3-(4-fluorophenoxy)propyl]-3-methoxy-4-piperidinamine
($C_{15}H_{23}FN_2O_2$; *104860-54-0*)   see: Cisapride

(3*R*,4*S*)-*rel*-1-[3-(4-fluorophenoxy)propyl]-3-methoxy-4-piperidinamine
($C_{15}H_{23}FN_2O_2$; *104860-26-6*)   see: Cisapride

(±)-1-[3-(4-fluorophenoxy)propyl]-3-methoxy-4-piperidinone
($C_{15}H_{20}FNO_3$; *137472-67-4*)   see: Cisapride

4-fluorophenylacetonitrile
(C_8H_6FN; *459-22-3*)   see: Levocabastine

(−)-*trans*-4-(4-fluorophenyl)-3-[(1,3-benzodioxol-5-yloxy)-methyl]-1-methylpiperidine
($C_{20}H_{22}FNO_3$; *110429-36-2*)   see: Paroxetine

1-(4-fluorophenyl)-5-chloro-1*H*-indole
($C_{14}H_9ClFN$; *138900-22-8*)   see: Sertindole

1-(4-fluorophenyl)-1-cyano-4-oxo-cyclohexane
($C_{13}H_{12}FNO$; *56326-98-8*)   see: Levocabastine

5-(2-fluorophenyl)-1,3-dihydro-2*H*-1,4-benzodiazepin-2-one
($C_{15}H_{11}FN_2O$; *2648-01-3*)   see: Flunitrazepam

2-(4-fluorophenyl)-β,δ-dihydroxy-5-(1-methylethyl)-3-phenyl-4-[(phenylamino)carbonyl]-*N*-(1(*R*)-phenylethyl)-1*H*-pyrrole-1-heptanamide
($C_{41}H_{44}FN_3O_4$)   see: Atorvastatin calcium

[*R*-(*R**,*R**)]-2-(4-fluorophenyl)-β,δ-dihydroxy-5-(1-methylethyl)-3-phenyl-4-[(phenylamino)carbonyl]-1*H*-pyrrole-1-heptanoic acid 1,1-dimethylethyl ester
($C_{37}H_{43}FN_2O_5$; *134395-00-9*)   see: Atorvastatin calcium

1-[3-[2-(4-fluorophenyl)-1,3-dioxolan-2-yl]propyl]-*N*-(2-nitrophenyl)-4-piperidinamine
($C_{23}H_{28}FN_3O_4$; *60703-66-4*)   see: Timiperone

2-(4-fluorophenyl)ethanol
(C_8H_9FO; *7589-27-7*)   see: Paraflutizide

(2-fluorophenyl)-(4-fluorophenyl)-phenylchloromethane
($C_{19}H_{13}ClF_2$; *128092-75-1*)   see: Flutrimazole

2-(4-fluorophenyl)-3-hydroxy-3-methylbutyric acid
($C_{11}H_{13}FO_3$; *193673-85-7*)   see: Mibefradil hydrochloride

(*R*)-2-(4-fluorophenyl)-δ-hydroxy-5-(1-methylethyl)-β-oxo-3-phenyl-4-[(phenylamino)carbonyl]-1*H*-pyrrole-1-heptanoic acid 1,1-dimethylethyl ester
($C_{37}H_{41}FN_2O_5$; *134394-98-2*)   see: Atorvastatin calcium

6-fluoro-1,2,3,4-tetrahydro-2-methylquinoline
($C_{10}H_{12}FN$; *42835-89-2*)   see: Flumequine

6-fluoro-3-(tetrahydropyran-4-yl)-1,2-benzisoxazole
($C_{12}H_{12}FNO_2$; *181479-12-9*)   see: Risperidone

(6α,11β,16α)-6-fluoro-11,16,17,21-tetrahydroxypregna-1,4-diene-3,20-dione
($C_{21}H_{27}FO_6$; *3915-36-4*)   see: Flunisolide

6β-fluoro-5,11β,17,21-tetrahydroxy-5α-pregnane-3,20-dione 21-acetate
($C_{23}H_{33}FO_7$; *913-49-5*)   see: Fluprednisolone acetate

4-fluorothiophenol
(C_6H_5FS; *371-42-6*)   see: Bicalutamide

2-fluorotoluene
(C_7H_7F; *95-52-3*)   see: Flutoprazepam

9-fluoro-11β,17,21-trihydroxy-16-methylenepregn-4-ene-3,20-dione 21-acetate
($C_{24}H_{31}FO_6$; *2728-31-6*)   see: Fluprednidene acetate

9-fluoro-11β,17,21-trihydroxy-6α-methylpregn-4-ene-3,20-dione 21-methanesulfonate
($C_{23}H_{33}FO_7S$; *2647-52-1*)   see: Fluorometholone

6α-fluoro-16α,17,21-trihydroxypregna-4,9(11)-diene-3,20-dione 16,21-diacetate
($C_{25}H_{31}FO_7$; *2965-61-9*)   see: Fluocinolone acetonide

(6α,16α)-6-fluoro-16,17,21-trihydroxypregn-4-ene-3,20-dione
($C_{21}H_{29}FO_5$; *804-82-0*)   see: Fludroxycortide

5-fluorouracil
($C_4H_3FN_2O_2$; *51-21-8*)   see: Carmofur; Flucytosine; Tegafur

5-fluorouridine
($C_9H_{11}FN_2O_6$; *316-46-1*)   see: Doxifluridine

folic acid
($C_{19}H_{19}N_7O_6$; *59-30-3*)   see: Folinic acid

formaldehyde
(CH_2O; *50-00-0*)   see: Aciclovir; Alclofenac; Alminoprofen; Alpidem; Altretamine; Amodiaquine; Azithromycin; Bromperidol; Budipine; Calcium pantothenate; Cicloxilic acid; Clofedanol; Clomocycline; Cortivazol; Dextropropoxyphene; Dichlorophen; Domiphen bromide; Edetic acid; Eperisone; Eprozinol; Etacrynic acid; Ethambutol; Etretinate; Fenticonazole; Fluoxetine; Fosphenytoin sodium; Haloperidol; Hepronicate; Hexetidine; Hydrochlorothiazide; Ibuprofen; Lercanidipine hydrochloride; Levorphanol; Loxoprofen; Lymecycline; Meprobamate; Meptazinol; Metampicillin; Methenamine; Methotrexate; Minocycline; Moexipril; Molsidomine; Moperone; Morinamide; Nifurtoinol; Noxytiolin; Oxitriptan; Papaverine; Penimepicycline; Phenindamine; Pipebuzone; Pirbuterol; Pranoprofen; Quinapril hydrochloride; Rizatriptan benzoate; Salbutamol; Saquinavir; Setiptiline; Sobuzoxane; Sulbentine; Sulfaloxic acid; Suxibuzone; Ticlopidine; Timonacic; Tiotixene; α-Tocopherol; Tolmetin; Topotecan; Trometamol; Tyloxapol; Venlafaxine; Zimeldine; Zolmitriptan; Zolpidem

formaldehyde dimethyl mercaptal *S*-oxide
($C_3H_8OS_2$; *33577-16-1*)   see: Alclofenac

formaldehyde polymer with 4-(1,1,3,3-tetramethyl-butyl)phenol
(unspecified; *26678-93-3*)   see: Tyloxapol

formamide
(CH_3NO; *75-12-7*)   see: Allopurinol; Chlorothiazide; Cimetidine; Fludarabine phosphate; Fluspirilene; Heptaminol; Primidone; Protriptyline; Pyridoxine; Razoxane; Sulfadoxine; Theophylline

formamidine
(CH_4N_2; *463-52-5*)   see: Itraconazole

formamidine hydrochloride
(CH_5ClN_2; *6313-33-3*)   see: Allopurinol

7-formamidocephalosporanic acid
($C_{11}H_{12}N_2O_6S$; *27267-35-2*)   see: Cefamandole

2-(2-formamido-4-thiazolyl)-2-methoxyiminoacetic acid
($C_7H_7N_3O_4S$; *83594-38-1*)   see: Ceftizoxime

(2-formamidothiazol-4-yl)oxoacetic acid
($C_6H_4N_2O_4S$; *64987-06-0*)   see: Cefixime

formic acid
(CH_2O_2; *64-18-6*)   see: Abacavir; α-Acetyldigoxin; Apraclonidine; Azacosterol; Cefamandole; Chlorazanil; Cortivazol; Desoxycortone acetate; Diethylcarbamazine; Estazolam; Folinic acid; Formoterol; Gitaloxin; Gitoformate; Hydroxyprogesterone; Pioglitazone; Temocillin

***N*-formyl-DL-alanine ethyl ester**
($C_6H_{11}NO_3$; *4289-99-0*)   see: Pyridoxine

2-(formylamino)isocamphane
($C_{11}H_{19}NO$; *86351-88-4*)   see: Mecamylamine

3-formylamino-3-methyl-2-phenylbutane
($C_{12}H_{17}NO$; *22876-59-1*)   see: Pentorex

6β-formylaminopenicillanic acid benzyl ester
($C_{16}H_{18}N_2O_4S$; *53628-26-5*)   see: Temocillin

(formylamino)[[5-(phenylmethoxy)-1*H*-indol-3-yl]methyl]propanedioic acid diethyl ester
($C_{24}H_{26}N_2O_6$)   see: Oxitriptan

[6*R*-[6α,7β(*Z*)]]-7-[[[2-(formylamino)-4-thiazolyl](methoxyimino)acetyl]amino]-8-oxo-5-thia-1-azabicyclo[4.2.0]oct-2-ene-2-carboxylic acid (4-nitrophenyl)methyl ester
($C_{21}H_{18}N_6O_8S_2$; *68401-78-5*)   see: Ceftizoxime

[6*R*-[6α,7β(*Z*)]]-7-[[[2-(formylamino)-4-thiazolyl](methoxyimino)acetyl]amino]-8-oxo-5-thia-1-azabicyclo[4.2.0]oct-2-ene-2-carboxylic acid
($C_{14}H_{13}N_5O_6S_2$; *68401-79-6*)   see: Ceftizoxime

5-formyl-1-β-D-arabinofuranosyluracil
($C_{10}H_{12}N_2O_7$; *87877-24-5*)   see: Sorivudine

2-formylcinnamic acid
($C_{10}H_8O_3$; *28873-89-4*)   see: Lacidipine

(*Z*)-β-formylcrotonic acid
($C_5H_6O_3$; *70143-04-3*)   see: Isotretinoin

3-formylcrotyl acetate
($C_7H_{10}O_3$; *14918-80-0*)   see: Retinol

2-formyl-1,4-dihydro-6-methyl-4-(3-nitrophenyl)-3,5-pyridinedicarboxylic acid 3-methyl 5-(1-methylethyl) ester
($C_{19}H_{20}N_2O_7$; *75530-60-8*)   see: Nilvadipine

DL-*N*-formyl-3,5-diiodothyronine
($C_{16}H_{13}I_2NO_5$; *94298-44-9*)   see: Dextrothyroxine

L-*N*-formyl-3,5-diiodothyronine
($C_{16}H_{13}I_2NO_5$)   see: Levothyroxine

D(–)-*N*-formyl-3,5-diiodothyronine
($C_{16}H_{13}I_2NO_5$; *120408-14-2*)   see: Dextrothyroxine

***N*-formyl-1,5-dimethyl-4-hexenamine**
($C_9H_{17}NO$)   see: Heptaminol

10-formylfolic acid
($C_{20}H_{19}N_7O_7$; *134-05-4*)   see: Folinic acid

1-formyl-hexahydroazepine
($C_7H_{13}NO$; *25114-81-2*)   see: Mecillinam; Pivmecillinam

1-formyl-homopiperazine
($C_6H_{12}N_2O$; *29053-62-1*)   see: Bunazosin

L-glutamine
($C_5H_{10}N_2O_3$; *56-85-9*)   see: Aceglutamide aluminum;
Thalidomide

glutaric acid
($C_5H_8O_4$; *110-94-1*)   see: Gusperimus trihydrochloride

glutethimide
($C_{13}H_{15}NO_2$; *77-21-4*)   see: Aminoglutethimide

D-glyceraldehyde
($C_3H_6O_3$; *453-17-8*)   see: Timolol

glycerin
($C_3H_8O_3$; *56-81-5*)   see: Actinoquinol; Itraconazole;
Ketoconazole; Oxyquinoline; Phanquinone; Primaquine;
Terconazole

glycerol
see under glycerin

glycerol 1-benzyl ether
($C_{10}H_{14}O_3$; *4799-67-1*)   see: Domiodol

glycerol triricinoleate
($C_{57}H_{104}O_9$; *2540-54-7*)   see: Azelaic acid

glycide
($C_3H_6O_2$; *556-52-5*)   see: Chlorphenesin; Diperodon;
Diprophylline; Dropropizine; Guaifenesin; Iopydol;
Mephenesin; Metaxalone; Toloxatone

glycide isobutyl ether
($C_7H_{14}O_2$; *3814-55-9*)   see: Bepridil

(R)-glycidol
($C_3H_6O_2$; *57044-25-4*)   see: Cidofovir

glycidol
see under glycide

17β-glycidoyl-11β,17-dihydroxyandrosta-1,4-dien-3-one
($C_{22}H_{28}O_5$; *102084-59-3*)   see: Fluperolone acetate

glycidyl n-butyl ether
($C_7H_{14}O_2$; *2426-08-6*)   see: Febuprol

(2S)-glycidyl 3-nitrobenzenesulfonate
($C_9H_9NO_6S$; *115314-14-2*)   see: Indinavir sulfate

glycidyl phenyl ether
($C_9H_{10}O_2$; *122-60-1*)   see: Bisoprolol; Febuprol

(2S)-glycidyl tosylate
($C_{10}H_{12}O_4S$; *70987-78-9*)   see: Indinavir sulfate

glycine
($C_2H_5NO_2$; *56-40-6*)   see: Eptifibatide; Levodopa;
Loprazolam; Stepronin; Tiopronin

glycine benzyl ester tosylate
($C_{16}H_{19}NO_5S$; *1738-76-7*)   see: Acetorphan

glycine potassium salt
($C_2H_4KNO_2$; *15743-44-9*)   see: Thiamphenicol

glycolic acid
($C_2H_4O_3$; *79-14-1*)   see: Nedaplatin; Roxatidine acetate

glycyrrhetic acid
($C_{30}H_{46}O_4$; *471-53-4*)   see: Carbenoxolone

Gly-OEt.HCl
see under ethyl glycinate hydrochloride

glyoxal
($C_2H_2O_2$; *107-22-2*)   see: Amiloride; Pyrazinamide

glyoxylic acid
($C_2H_2O_3$; *298-12-4*)   see: Allantoin; Ethyl biscoumacetate;
Lamivudine; Orotic acid

gold iodide (AuI)
(AuI; *10294-31-2*)   see: Sodium aurothiomalate

guaiacol
($C_7H_8O_2$; *90-05-1*)   see: Amosulalol; Guaifenesin

guaiene
($C_{15}H_{24}$; *88-84-6*)   see: Guaiazulene

guaifenesin
($C_{10}H_{14}O_4$; *93-14-1*)   see: Methocarbamol

guaiol
($C_{15}H_{26}O$; *489-86-1*)   see: Guaiazulene

guanidine
(CH_5N_3; *113-00-8*)   see: Abacavir; Amiloride; Folic acid;
Guanfacine; Pemoline; Pyrimethamine; Sulfamerazine;
Tetroxoprim

guanidine carbonate (1:1)
($C_2H_7N_3O_3$; *124-46-9*)   see: Brodimoprim; Sulfaguanidine;
Sulfametoxydiazine; Trimethoprim

guanidine hydrochloride
(CH_6ClN_3; *50-01-1*)   see: Trimethoprim

guanidine nitrate
($CH_6N_4O_3$; *506-93-4*)   see: Triamterene

4-guanidinobenzoic acid
($C_8H_9N_3O_2$; *16060-65-4*)   see: Camostat; Nafamostat

4-guanidinobenzoyl chloride
($C_8H_8ClN_3O$; *60131-35-3*)   see: Nafamostat

4-guanidinobenzoyl chloride hydrochloride
($C_8H_9Cl_2N_3O$; *7035-79-2*)   see: Camostat

ω-guanidinocaproic acid
($C_7H_{15}N_3O_2$; *6659-35-4*)   see: Gabexate

ω-guanidinocaproyl chloride
($C_7H_{14}ClN_3O$; *41651-94-9*)   see: Gabexate

7-guanidinoheptanamide hydrochloride
($C_8H_{19}ClN_4O$; *85503-05-5*)   see: Gusperimus
trihydrochloride

trans-4-(guanidinomethyl)cyclohexanecarboxylic acid
($C_9H_{17}N_3O_2$; *38697-86-8*)   see: Benexate

guanine
($C_5H_5N_5O$; *73-40-5*)   see: Aciclovir; Tioguanine

guanosine
($C_{10}H_{13}N_5O_5$; *118-00-3*)   see: Cladribine

H

H-Asn-Arg-Val-Tyr-Val-His-Pro-Phe-O-CH₃
($C_{50}H_{72}N_{14}O_{11}$; *47917-11-3*)   see: Angiotensinamide

heptaminol
($C_8H_{19}NO$; *372-66-7*)   see: Acefylline

heptanal
($C_7H_{14}O$; *111-71-7*)   see: Undecylenic acid

[3aR-(3aα,4α,5β,6aα)]-4-[2-(2-heptyl-1,3-dioxolan-2-yl)ethyl]hexahydro-5-hydroxy-2H-cyclopenta[b]furan-2-one
($C_{19}H_{32}O_5$; *118696-65-4*)   see: Unoprostone isopropyl

hesperidin
($C_{28}H_{34}O_{15}$; *520-26-3*)   see: Diosmin

hexadecanol
($C_{16}H_{34}O$; *36653-82-4*)   see: Miltefosine

2-(hexadecylamino)cyclohexanol
($C_{22}H_{45}NO$)   see: Cethexonium bromide

2-(hexadecylamino)cyclohexanol hydrobromide
($C_{22}H_{46}BrNO$)   see: Cethexonium bromide

3-(4-hexyloxyphenyl)propionyl chloride
($C_{15}H_{21}ClO_2$)   see: Nandrolone hexyloxyphenylpropionate

(2S,3S,5R)-2-hexyl-3-(phenylmethoxy)-5-(tetrahydro-1H-pyran-2-yloxy)hexadecanoic acid
($C_{34}H_{58}O_5$)   see: Orlistat

(3S,4S)-3-hexyl-4-[(2R)-2-(phenylmethoxy)tridecyl]-2-oxetanone
($C_{29}H_{48}O_3$; 114264-05-0)   see: Orlistat

[3R-[3α,4α(R*)]]-3-hexyl-4-[2-(phenylmethoxy)tridecyl]-2-oxetanone
($C_{29}H_{48}O_3$; 125638-37-1)   see: Orlistat

3-hexyltetrahydro-4-hydroxy-6-undecyl-2H-pyran-2-one
($C_{22}H_{42}O_3$; 104801-94-7)   see: Orlistat

[3S-(3α,4α,6α)]-3-hexyltetrahydro-4-hydroxy-6-undecyl-2H-pyran-2-one
($C_{22}H_{42}O_3$; 104801-96-9)   see: Orlistat

[3S-[3α,4β(S*)]]-3-hexyl-4-[2-[(tetrahydro-2H-pyran-2-yl)oxy]tridecyl]-2-oxetanone
($C_{27}H_{50}O_4$; 112836-65-4)   see: Orlistat

3-hexyn-2-ol
($C_6H_{10}O$; 109-50-2)   see: Methohexital

H-His-OMe.2HCl
($C_7H_{13}Cl_2N_3O_2$; 7389-87-9)   see: Protirelin

homatropine
($C_{16}H_{21}NO_3$; 87-00-3)   see: Homatropine methylbromide

homoarginine
($C_7H_{16}N_4O_2$; 156-86-5)   see: Eptifibatide

homocysteine thiolactone
(C_4H_7NOS; 10593-85-8)   see: Erdosteine; Omapatrilat

homomyrtenol
($C_{11}H_{18}O$; 128-50-7)   see: Myrtecaine

homopiperazine
($C_5H_{12}N_2$; 505-66-8)   see: Fasudil

homoveratric acid
($C_{10}H_{12}O_4$; 93-40-3)   see: Papaverine

homoveratronitrile
see under 3,4-dimethoxyphenylacetonitrile

homoveratrylamine
see under 3,4-dimethoxyphenethylamine

N-homoveratrylhomoveratramide
($C_{20}H_{25}NO_5$; 139-76-4)   see: Papaverine

H-Pro-NH₂.HCl
($C_5H_{11}ClN_2O$; 42429-27-6)   see: Protirelin

H-Val-Tyr-Val-His-Pro-Phe-O-CH₃
($C_{40}H_{54}N_8O_8$; 40488-86-6)   see: Angiotensinamide

hydantoic acid nitrile
($C_3H_5N_3O$; 5962-07-2)   see: Orotic acid

hydantoin
($C_3H_4N_2O_2$; 461-72-3)   see: Levodopa

3-(5-hydantoinyl)propionaldehyde
($C_6H_8N_2O_3$; 7686-13-7)   see: L-Tryptophan

hydralazine
($C_8H_8N_4$; 86-54-4)   see: Budralazine; Todralazine

hydrallostane 21-acetate
($C_{23}H_{34}O_6$; 4004-68-6)   see: Prednisolone

hydratropic aldehyde
($C_9H_{10}O$; 93-53-8)   see: Bemetizide

hydrazine
(H_4N_2; 302-01-2)   see: Acetazolamide; Allopurinol; Brotizolam; Carbidopa; Cibenzoline; Desmopressin; Estazolam; Etizolam; Guanadrel; Isoniazid; Itraconazole; Mitopodozide; Nifuroxazide; Nifurtimox; Nitrofurantoin; Phenelzine; Primaquine; Ziprasidone hydrochloride

hydrazine-1,2-bis(thiocarboxamide)
($C_2H_6N_4S_2$; 142-46-1)   see: Acetazolamide

hydrazinecarboxylic acid phenylmethyl ester
($C_8H_{10}N_2O_2$; 5331-43-1)   see: Ceruletide

hydrazine hydrate
(H_6N_2O; 7803-57-8)   see: Alprazolam; Betazole; Dapiprazole; Dihydralazine; Endralazine; Epirizole; Flurazepam; Fomepizole; Guanoclor; Gusperimus trihydrochloride; Hydralazine; Isocarboxazid; Nefazodone hydrochloride; Nifuratel; Pantethine; Pildralazine; Pimobendan; Pramipexole hydrochloride; Propentofylline; Sildenafil; Tofisopam; Zaleplon

2-hydrazinoacetic acid
($C_2H_6N_2O_2$; 14150-64-2)   see: Nitrofurantoin

4-hydrazinobenzenesulfonamide
($C_6H_9N_3O_2S$; 4392-54-5)   see: Celecoxib

(S)-5-(4-hydrazinobenzyl)-2,4-imidazolidinedione hydrochloride
($C_{10}H_{13}ClN_4O_2$)   see: Zolmitriptan

(S)-4-(4-hydrazinobenzyl)-2-oxazolidinone hydrochloride
($C_{10}H_{14}ClN_3O_2$; 139264-57-6)   see: Zolmitriptan

α-hydrazino-3,4-dimethoxy-α-methylbenzenepropanenitrile
($C_{12}H_{17}N_3O_2$; 40248-74-6)   see: Carbidopa

2-hydrazinoethanol
($C_2H_8N_2O$; 109-84-2)   see: Furazolidone

2-hydrazino-Δ²-imidazoline
($C_3H_8N_4$; 51420-32-7)   see: Bisantrene

2-hydrazino-4-methoxy-2-methylpyrimidine
($C_6H_{10}N_4O$; 36951-92-5)   see: Epirizole

4-hydrazino-1-methylpiperidine dihydrochloride
($C_6H_{17}Cl_2N_3$; 53242-78-7)   see: Piperylone

2-(4-hydrazinophenyl)-N-methylethanesulfonamide
($C_9H_{15}N_3O_2S$)   see: Naratriptan

4-hydrazinophenyl-N-methylmethanesulfonamide
($C_8H_{13}N_3O_2S$; 139272-29-0)   see: Sumatriptan

1-[(4-hydrazinophenyl)methyl]-1H-1,2,4-triazole
($C_9H_{11}N_5$; 144035-22-3)   see: Rizatriptan benzoate

2-hydrazino-Δ¹-tetrahydroazepine
($C_6H_{13}N_3$; 31030-25-8)   see: Pentetrazol

hydrazobenzene
($C_{12}H_{12}N_2$; 122-66-7)   see: Kebuzone; Phenylbutazone; Sulfinpyrazone

hydridocobalamin
($C_{62}H_{89}CoN_{13}O_{14}P$; 18534-66-2)   see: Cobamamide; Mecobalamin

hydrocinnamoyl chloride
(C_9H_9ClO; 645-45-4)   see: Indinavir sulfate

hydrocodone
($C_{18}H_{21}NO_3$; 125-29-1)   see: Thebacon

hydrocortisone
($C_{21}H_{30}O_5$; 50-23-7)   see: Bendacort; Cloprednol; Desonide; Hydrocortisone acetate; Hydrocortisone 17-butyrate; Hydrocortisone sodium phosphate; Methylprednisolone; Prednisolone

hydrocortisone 21-acetate
see under cortisol 21-acetate

hydrogen cyanide
(CHN; 74-90-8)   see: L-Alanine; Alfentanil; Dimethadione; Edetic acid; Ibuprofen; Indanorex; Mecamylamine; Molsidomine; Nadoxolol; D-Penicillamine; Phensuximide; L-Tryptophan; Vetrabutine

hydrogen peroxide
(H_2O_2; 7722-84-1)   see: Benzoyl peroxide; Rofecoxib

hydroquinone
($C_6H_6O_2$; 123-31-9)   see: Gentisic acid; Monobenzone

hydroquinone monobenzyl ether
see under 4-benzyloxyphenol

hydroquinone monomethyl ether
($C_7H_8O_2$; 150-76-5)   see: Dextrothyroxine; Etiroxate; Mefexamide

hydroxocobalamin
($C_{62}H_{89}CoN_{13}O_{15}P$; 13422-51-0)   see: Cobamamide; Mecobalamin

4-hydroxyacetanilide
($C_8H_9NO_2$; 103-90-2)   see: Ambroxol; Benorilate; Propacetamol

hydroxyacetone
($C_3H_6O_2$; 116-09-6)   see: Enoximone

o-**hydroxyacetophenone**
($C_8H_8O_2$; 118-93-4)   see: Croconazole

3'-hydroxyacetophenone
($C_8H_8O_2$; 121-71-1)   see: Etilefrine; Fenoprofen; Norfenefrine

4'-hydroxyacetophenone
($C_8H_8O_2$; 99-93-4)   see: Bamethan; Bufexamac; Paracetamol; Pifoxime; Salbutamol

4-hydroxy-L-allothreonine monosodium salt
($C_4H_8NNaO_4$; 117095-55-3)   see: Carumonam

4'-hydroxy-2-aminoacetophenone
($C_8H_9NO_2$; 77369-38-1)   see: Octopamine

2-hydroxy-4-aminobenzoic acid sodium salt
($C_7H_7NNaO_3$; 133-10-8)   see: Nemonapride

2(*R*)-hydroxy-1(*S*)-aminoindane
($C_9H_{11}NO$; 126456-43-7)   see: Indinavir sulfate

(3β,5α)-3-hydroxyandrostan-17-one
($C_{19}H_{30}O_2$; 481-29-8)   see: Estrone

(5α,17β)-17-hydroxyandrostan-3-one
($C_{19}H_{30}O_2$; 521-18-6)   see: Drostanolone; Estradiol

7β-hydroxy-4-androsteno[2,3-*d*]isoxazole
($C_{20}H_{27}NO_2$; 60413-79-8)   see: Trilostane

N-**hydroxy-3-azaspiro[5.5]undecane-2,4-dione**
($C_{10}H_{15}NO_3$; 64744-41-8)   see: Gabapentin

3-hydroxybenzaldehyde
($C_7H_6O_2$; 100-83-4)   see: Iophenoic acid; Roxatidine acetate

4-hydroxybenzaldehyde
($C_7H_6O_2$; 123-08-0)   see: Itopride hydrochloride; Pioglitazone; Trimethobenzamide; Troglitazone

4-hydroxybenzeneacetic acid methyl ester
($C_9H_{10}O_3$; 14199-15-6)   see: Atenolol

4-hydroxybenzhydrazide
($C_7H_8N_2O_2$; 5351-23-5)   see: Nifuroxazide

2-hydroxybenzonitrile
(C_7H_5NO; 611-20-1)   see: Bunitrolol

4-hydroxybenzonitrile
(C_7H_5NO; 767-00-0)   see: Pentamidine

4-hydroxybenzophenone
($C_{13}H_{10}O_2$; 1137-42-4)   see: Clomifene; Tamoxifen; Toremifene

5-hydroxy-5*H*-[1]benzopyrano[2,3-*b*]pyridine
($C_{12}H_9NO_2$; 6722-09-4)   see: Pranoprofen

4-hydroxybenzyl alcohol
($C_7H_8O_2$; 623-05-2)   see: Bisoprolol

2-(3-hydroxybenzyl)butyric acid
($C_{11}H_{14}O_3$)   see: Iophenoic acid

4-hydroxybenzyl cyanide
(C_8H_7NO; 14191-95-8)   see: Atenolol

5-(4-hydroxybenzyl)-5-methylhydantoin
($C_{11}H_{12}N_2O_3$; 13500-25-9)   see: Etiroxate; Metirosine

(±)-1-(4-hydroxybenzyl)-1,2,3,4,5,6,7,8-octahydroiso-quinoline
($C_{16}H_{21}NO$; 74570-02-8)   see: Levallorphan

(–)-1-(4-hydroxybenzyl)-1,2,3,4,5,6,7,8-octahydroiso-quinoline
($C_{16}H_{21}NO$; 94006-09-4)   see: Levallorphan

4-hydroxybutanal
($C_4H_8O_2$; 25714-71-0)   see: Etodolac

(±)-5-(2-hydroxy-3-*tert*-butylaminopropoxy)-1-tetralone
($C_{17}H_{25}NO_3$; 27591-01-1)   see: Levobunolol

10-hydroxycamptothecin
($C_{20}H_{16}N_2O_5$; 19685-09-7)   see: Topotecan

4-hydroxycarbazole
($C_{12}H_9NO$; 52602-39-8)   see: Carazolol; Carvedilol

8-hydroxycarbostyril
($C_9H_7NO_2$; 15450-76-7)   see: Procaterol

3β-hydroxycholest-5-en-24-one
($C_{27}H_{44}O_2$; 17752-16-8)   see: Tacalcitol

25-hydroxycholesterol 3-acetate
($C_{29}H_{48}O_3$; 10525-22-1)   see: Calcifediol

14-hydroxycodeinone
($C_{18}H_{19}NO_4$; 508-54-3)   see: Oxycodone; Oxymorphone

4-hydroxycoumarin
($C_9H_6O_3$; 1076-38-6)   see: Acenocoumarol; Ethyl biscoumacetate; Tioclomarol; Warfarin; Zonisamide

α-(1-hydroxycyclohexyl)-4-methoxybenzeneacetonitrile
($C_{15}H_{19}NO_2$; 93413-76-4)   see: Venlafaxine

(4*S*)-3-[[(1*S*,2*R*)-2-hydroxy-3-cyclopenten-1-yl]carbonyl]-4-(phenylmethyl)-2-oxazolidinone
($C_{16}H_{17}NO_4$; 178327-18-9)   see: Abacavir

α-(1-hydroxycyclopentyl)phenylacetic acid
($C_{13}H_{16}O_3$; 25209-52-3)   see: Cyclopentolate

6-hydroxy-3,4-dihydrocarbostyril
($C_9H_9NO_2$; 54197-66-9)   see: Cilostazol

5-hydroxy-10,11-dihydro-5*H*-dibenzo[*a,d*]cycloheptene
($C_{15}H_{14}O$; 1210-34-0)   see: Amineptine; Deptropine

14-hydroxydihydronormorphinone
($C_{16}H_{17}NO_4$; 33522-95-1)   see: Nalbuphine; Naloxone

2'-hydroxy-4'-(2,5-dihydro-5-oxo-3-furyl)acetophenone
($C_{12}H_{10}O_4$; 3447-63-0)   see: Benfurodil hemisuccinate

O-**(4-hydroxy-3,5-diiodophenyl)-3,5-diiodo-α-methyl-tyrosine**
($C_{16}H_{13}I_4NO_4$; 3414-34-4)   see: Etiroxate

2-hydroxy-3,4-dimethoxy-6-methylbenzenedecanoic acid
($C_{19}H_{30}O_5$; 58185-85-6)   see: Idebenone

9-(2-hydroxy-3,4-dimethoxy-6-methylbenzoyl)nonanoic acid

($C_{19}H_{28}O_6$; *58185-79-8*)   see: Idebenone

(S)-α-hydroxy-2,5-dimethoxy-α,3,4,6-tetramethyl-benzenebutanal

($C_{16}H_{24}O_4$; *85148-24-9*)   see: Troglitazone

6-hydroxy-6-(3-dimethylaminopropyl)-6,12-dihydro-benzofuro[3,2-c][1]benzoxepin

($C_{21}H_{23}NO_3$; *27450-47-1*)   see: Oxetorone

2'-hydroxy-5,9-dimethylbenzo-6-morphen

($C_{14}H_{19}NO$; *25144-78-9*)   see: Pentazocine

11β-hydroxy-6,16α-dimethyl-17,20:20,21-bis(methylene-dioxy)pregna-4,6-dien-3-one

($C_{25}H_{34}O_6$; *4968-27-8*)   see: Cortivazol

D(−)-2-hydroxy-3,3-dimethylbutanolide

($C_6H_{10}O_3$; *599-04-2*)   see: Calcium pantothenate; Dexpanthenol

5-hydroxy-6β,17-dimethyl-5α-pregnane-3,20-dione

($C_{23}H_{36}O_3$; *95565-52-9*)   see: Medrogestone

3β-hydroxy-6,17-dimethylpregn-5-en-20-one

($C_{23}H_{36}O_2$; *95565-41-6*)   see: Medrogestone

15α-hydroxy-3,3-(2,2-dimethyltrimethylenedioxy)-13-ethyl-5(10)-gonen-17-one

($C_{24}H_{36}O_4$; *60919-51-9*)   see: Gestodene

15α-hydroxy-3,3-(2,2-dimethyltrimethylenedioxy)-13-ethyl-5-gonen-17-one

($C_{24}H_{36}O_4$; *60919-47-3*)   see: Gestodene

5-[(4-hydroxy-3,5-dinitrophenyl)methyl]-5-methyl-2,4-imidazolidinedione

($C_{11}H_{10}N_4O_7$; *56891-54-4*)   see: Etiroxate

3-hydroxy-2,5-dioxocyclopentaneheptanoic acid

($C_{12}H_{18}O_5$; *22935-43-9*)   see: Misoprostol

4-(hydroxydiphenylmethyl)-1-methylpyridinium methyl sulfate (salt)

($C_{20}H_{21}NO_5S$; *148302-52-7*)   see: Diphemanil metilsulfate

4-[4-[4-(hydroxydiphenylmethyl)-1-piperidinyl]-1-oxo-butyl]-α,α-dimethylbenzeneacetaldehyde

($C_{32}H_{37}NO_3$; *191155-95-0*)   see: Fexofenadine hydrochloride

4-[4-[4-(hydroxydiphenylmethyl)-1-piperidinyl]-1-oxo-butyl]-α,α-dimethylbenzeneacetic acid

($C_{32}H_{37}NO_4$; *76811-98-8*)   see: Fexofenadine hydrochloride

4-[4-[4-(hydroxydiphenylmethyl)-1-piperidinyl]-1-oxo-butyl]-α,α-dimethylbenzeneacetic acid ethyl ester

($C_{34}H_{41}NO_4$; *76812-02-7*)   see: Fexofenadine hydrochloride

3α-hydroxy-2β,16β-dipiperidino-5α-androstan-17-one

($C_{29}H_{48}N_2O_2$; *13522-14-0*)   see: Pancuronium bromide; Vecuronium bromide

9-hydroxyellipticine

($C_{17}H_{14}N_2O$; *51131-85-2*)   see: Elliptinium acetate

3-hydroxyestra-1,3,5(10),6-tetraen-17-one

($C_{18}H_{20}O_2$; *2208-12-0*)   see: Estrone

17β-hydroxy-4-estrene

($C_{18}H_{28}O$; *3646-30-8*)   see: Allylestrenol; Lynestrenol

11β-hydroxy-δ⁴-estrene-3,17-dione

($C_{18}H_{24}O_3$; *15313-96-9*)   see: Desogestrel

(11β)-11-hydroxyestr-5-ene-3,17-dione cyclic bis(1,2-ethanediyl acetal)

($C_{22}H_{32}O_5$; *59017-03-7*)   see: Desogestrel

(17β)-17-hydroxyestr-4-en-3-one cyclic 1,2-ethanediyl dithioacetal

($C_{20}H_{30}OS_2$; *74531-93-4*)   see: Allylestrenol; Ethylestrenol; Lynestrenol

2-(2-hydroxyethoxy)ethyl chloride

($C_4H_9ClO_2$; *628-89-7*)   see: Etofenamate; Hydroxyzine; Quetiapine fumarate

1-[2-(2-hydroxyethoxy)ethyl]piperazine

($C_8H_{18}N_2O_2$; *13349-82-1*)   see: Dixyrazine; Quetiapine fumarate

(5α,17β)-17-hydroxy-2-(ethoxymethylene)androstan-3-one

($C_{22}H_{34}O_3$)   see: Drostanolone

3'-hydroxy-2-ethylamino-acetophenone

($C_{10}H_{13}NO_2$; *22510-12-9*)   see: Etilefrine

3-[[(2-hydroxyethyl)amino]carbonyl]-5-nitrobenzoic acid

($C_{10}H_{10}N_2O_6$; *22871-56-3*)   see: Ioxitalamic acid

α-[[(2-hydroxyethyl)amino]methyl]benzenemethanol

($C_{10}H_{15}NO_2$; *4397-15-3*)   see: Levamisole

2-(2-hydroxyethylamino)-1-phenyl-1-propanol

($C_{11}H_{17}NO_2$; *54804-28-3*)   see: Phenmetrazine

[(3S)-(1R)]-3-(1-hydroxyethyl)-2-azetidinone

($C_5H_9NO_2$; *120236-28-4*)   see: Faropenem sodium

2-(1-hydroxyethyl)benzo[b]thiophene

($C_{10}H_{10}OS$; *51868-95-2*)   see: Zileuton

15α-hydroxy-13-ethyl-4-gonene-3,17-dione

($C_{19}H_{26}O_3$; *60919-46-2*)   see: Gestodene

1-(2-hydroxyethyl)hexahydro-1H-azepine

($C_8H_{17}NO$; *20603-00-3*)   see: Prozapine

N-(2-hydroxyethyl)-2-hydroxypropylamine

($C_5H_{13}NO_2$; *6579-55-1*)   see: Levocabastine

(2-hydroxyethyl)(2-hydroxypropyl)sulfide

($C_5H_{12}O_2S$; *6713-03-7*)   see: Nifurtimox

2-(1-hydroxyethyl)-2-imidazoline

($C_5H_{10}N_2O$; *22995-60-4*)   see: Lofexidine

3-(2-hydroxyethyl)indole

($C_{10}H_{11}NO$; *526-55-6*)   see: Indoramin

α-[[(2-hydroxyethyl)methylamino]methyl]benzene-methanol

($C_{11}H_{17}NO_2$; *23175-16-8*)   see: Mianserin

2-[[(2-hydroxyethyl)methylamino]methyl]-α-phenyl-benzenemethanol

($C_{17}H_{21}NO_2$; *60725-36-2*)   see: Nefopam

α-[N-(2-hydroxyethyl)methylamino]propiophenone

($C_{12}H_{17}NO_2$)   see: Phendimetrazine

1-(2-hydroxyethyl)-4-(2-methylbenzyl)piperazine

($C_{13}H_{20}N_2O$; *40004-66-8*)   see: Chlorbenzoxamine

[2R-[2α(R*),3β(R*)]]-3-(1-hydroxyethyl)-γ-methyl-β,4-di-oxo-2-azetidinebutanoic acid (4-nitrophenyl)methyl ester

($C_{17}H_{20}N_2O_7$; *90822-23-4*)   see: Meropenem

4-(2-hydroxyethyl)-3-methyl-2-phenylmorpholine

($C_{13}H_{19}NO_2$; *92197-26-7*)   see: Fenbutrazate

3-(2-hydroxyethyl)-2-methyl-4H-pyrido[1,2-a]pyrimidin-4-one

($C_{11}H_{12}N_2O_2$; *41078-67-5*)   see: Risperidone

5-(2-hydroxyethyl)-4-methylthiazole

(C_6H_9NOS; *137-00-8*)   see: Thiamine

N-(2-hydroxyethyl)-5-nitroisophthalamic acid methyl ester

($C_{11}H_{12}N_2O_6$; *28179-40-0*)   see: Ioxitalamic acid

(11β)-3-hydroxy-11-methoxyestra-1,3,5(10)-trien-17-one
($C_{19}H_{24}O_3$; *21375-11-1*)   see: Moxestrol

4-hydroxy-3-methoxy-4'-methylbenzophenone
($C_{15}H_{14}O_3$; *134612-39-8*)   see: Tolcapone

α-hydroxy-6-methoxy-α-methyl-2-naphthaleneacetic acid
($C_{14}H_{14}O_4$; *32721-11-2*)   see: Naproxen

4-hydroxy-3-methoxy-4'-methyl-5-nitrobenzophenone
($C_{15}H_{13}NO_5$; *134612-80-9*)   see: Tolcapone

**[S-(R*,R*)]-α-hydroxy-4-methoxy-β-[(2-nitrophenyl)-
thio]benzenepropanoic acid**
($C_{16}H_{15}NO_6S$; *42399-45-1*)   see: Diltiazem

**(R*,R*)-(±)-α-hydroxy-4-methoxy-β-[(2-nitrophenyl)-
thio]benzenepropanoic acid methyl ester**
($C_{17}H_{17}NO_6S$; *42399-43-9*)   see: Diltiazem

**3-hydroxy-2-methoxy-5-oxo-1-cyclopentene-1-heptanoic
acid methyl ester**
($C_{14}H_{22}O_5$; *32406-04-5*)   see: Misoprostol

**4-hydroxy-2-methoxy-5-oxo-1-cyclopentene-1-heptanoic
acid methyl ester**
($C_{14}H_{22}O_5$; *32561-42-5*)   see: Misoprostol

**5-[1-hydroxy-2-[[2-(2-methoxyphenoxy)ethyl](phenyl-
methyl)amino]ethyl]-2-methylbenzenesulfonamide**
($C_{25}H_{30}N_2O_5S$; *70958-78-0*)   see: Amosulalol

(4-hydroxy-3-methoxyphenyl)acetone
($C_{10}H_{12}O_3$; *2503-46-0*)   see: Methyldopa

**5-[(4-hydroxy-3-methoxyphenyl)methylene]-2,4-imidazo-
lidinedione**
($C_{11}H_{10}N_2O_4$; *52036-16-5*)   see: Levodopa

**N-[5-[1-hydroxy-2-[[2-(4-methoxyphenyl)-1-methylethyl]-
(phenylmethyl)amino]ethyl]-2-(phenylmethoxy)phenyl]-
formamide**
($C_{33}H_{36}N_2O_4$; *43229-70-5*)   see: Formoterol

**1-(4-hydroxy-3-methoxyphenyl)-1,2-propanediol 2-for-
mate**
($C_{11}H_{14}O_5$)   see: Methyldopa

17-hydroxy-20-methoxypregna-4,20-dien-3-one
($C_{22}H_{32}O_3$; *63973-94-4*)   see: Hydroxyprogesterone

6-hydroxy-5-methoxy-4(1H)-pyrimidinone
($C_5H_6N_2O_3$; *5193-84-0*)   see: Sulfadoxine

6-hydroxy-2-methoxy-2,5,7,8-tetramethylchromane
($C_{14}H_{20}O_3$; *53209-24-8*)   see: Troglitazone

4'-hydroxy-2-methylaminoacetophenone
($C_9H_{11}NO_2$; *21213-89-8*)   see: Synephrine

(17β)-17-hydroxy-17-methylandrosta-4,9(11)-dien-3-one
($C_{20}H_{28}O_2$; *1039-17-4*)   see: Fluoxymesterone

17β-hydroxy-17-methylandrosta-4,6-dien-3-one
($C_{20}H_{28}O_2$; *5585-85-3*)   see: Bolasterone

**(5α,17β)-17-hydroxy-17-methylandrostane-2,3-dione di-
oxime**
($C_{20}H_{32}N_2O_3$; *3137-81-3*)   see: Furazabol

5-(hydroxymethyl)-1-β-D-arabinofuranosyluracil
($C_{10}H_{14}N_2O_7$; *28608-82-4*)   see: Sorivudine

(1α,5α,6α)-6-(hydroxymethyl)-3-azabicyclo[3.1.0]hexane
($C_6H_{11}NO$; *134575-13-6*)   see: Trovafloxacin mesilate

**[7(S)-(1α,2β,4β,5α,7β)]-α(hydroxymethyl)benzeneacetic
acid 9-ethyl-3-oxa-9-azatricyclo[3.3.1.0²,⁴]non-7-yl ester**
($C_{18}H_{23}NO_4$; *67009-40-9*)   see: Oxitropium bromide

**[7(S)-(1α,2β,4β,5α,7β)]-α-(hydroxymethyl)benzeneacetic
acid 3-oxa-9-azatricyclo[3.3.1.0²,⁴]non-7-yl ester**
($C_{16}H_{19}NO_4$; *4684-28-0*)   see: Oxitropium bromide

3-hydroxy-2-methylbenzoic acid
($C_8H_8O_3$; *603-80-5*)   see: Nelfinavir mesylate

**(11β,16α)-11-hydroxy-16-methyl-17,21-bis(1-oxoprop-
oxy)pregna-1,4,6-triene-3,20-dione**
($C_{28}H_{36}O_7$; *67212-74-2*)   see: Alclometasone dipropionate

2'-hydroxy-4'-(3-methyl-2-butenyloxy)acetophenone
($C_{13}H_{16}O_3$; *24672-83-1*)   see: Sofalcone

2-hydroxy-2-methylbutyric acid ethyl ester
($C_7H_{14}O_3$; *77-70-3*)   see: Paramethadione

2-hydroxy-2-methylbutyronitrile
(C_5H_9NO; *4111-08-4*)   see: Paramethadione

5(R)-(hydroxymethyl)-2-cyclopenten-1(R)-ol
($C_6H_{10}O_2$; *143395-28-2*)   see: Abacavir

2-[1-(hydroxymethyl)cyclopropyl]acetonitrile
(C_6H_9NO; *152922-71-9*)   see: Montelukast sodium

**(±)-cis-2-hydroxymethyl-N,N-diethyl-1-phenylcyclo-
propanecarboxamide**
($C_{15}H_{21}NO_2$; *131091-01-5*)   see: Milnacipran hydrochloride

2-hydroxymethyl-2,3-dihydro-1,4-benzodioxin
($C_9H_{10}O_3$; *3663-82-9*)   see: Guanoxan

2-hydroxymethyl-3,4-dimethoxypyridine
($C_8H_{11}NO_3$; *72830-08-1*)   see: Pantoprazole sodium

2-(hydroxymethyl)-3,5-dimethyl-4-methoxypyridine
($C_9H_{13}NO_2$; *86604-78-6*)   see: Omeprazole

4-hydroxy-6,7-methylenedioxycinnoline
($C_9H_6N_2O_3$; *28657-76-3*)   see: Cinoxacin

**4-hydroxy-6,7-methylenedioxyquinoline-3-carboxylic acid
ethyl ester**
($C_{13}H_{11}NO_5$; *14205-65-3*)   see: Oxolinic acid

**α-(hydroxymethylene)-3,4,5-trimethoxybenzene-
propanoic acid ethyl ester**
($C_{15}H_{20}O_6$; *72830-04-7*)   see: Trimethoprim

**[1R[1α,5α,6(R*)]]-α-[1-(hydroxymethyl)ethenyl]-7-oxo-3-
phenyl-4-oxa-2,6-diazabicyclo[3.2.0]hept-2-ene-6-acetic
acid diphenylmethyl ester**
($C_{28}H_{24}N_2O_5$; *67977-88-2*)   see: Latamoxef

**8-hydroxy-5-[2-[(1-methylethyl)amino]-1-oxobutyl]-
2(1H)-quinolinone**
($C_{16}H_{20}N_2O_3$; *63235-39-2*)   see: Procaterol

4-[2-hydroxy-3-[(1-methylethyl)amino]propoxy]phenol
($C_{12}H_{19}NO_3$; *62340-37-8*)   see: Prenalterol

2-hydroxy-2-methyl-3-(4-fluorophenylthio)propionic acid
($C_{10}H_{11}FO_3S$)   see: Bicalutamide

4-hydroxy-2-methylindole
(C_9H_9NO; *35320-67-3*)   see: Bopindolol; Mepindolol

**3(S)-hydroxymethyl-7-methoxy-7-[2-(2-thienyl)acet-
amido]-3-cephem-4-carboxylic acid potassium salt**
($C_{15}H_{15}KN_2O_6S_2$; *37051-16-4*)   see: Cefoxitin

4-hydroxymethyl-5-methylimidazole hydrochloride
($C_5H_9ClN_2O$; *38585-62-5*)   see: Cimetidine

2-hydroxymethyl-1-methylpiperidine
($C_7H_{15}NO$; *20845-34-5*)   see: Bevonium metilsulfate

**α-hydroxy-α-methyl-4-(2-methylpropyl)benzene-
acetonitrile**
($C_{13}H_{17}NO$; *63367-12-4*)   see: Ibuprofen

**α-hydroxy-α-methyl-4-(2-methylpropyl)benzeneethan-
imidic acid methyl ester hydrochloride**
($C_{14}H_{22}ClNO_2$)   see: Ibuprofen

2-hydroxymethyl-5-methylpyrazine
($C_6H_8N_2O$; *61892-95-3*)   see: Acipimox

(4-hydroxy-3-nitrophenyl)arsonic acid
($C_6H_6AsNO_6$; *121-19-7*) see: Acetarsol

4-hydroxy-3-nitroquinoline
($C_9H_6N_2O_3$; *50332-66-6*) see: Imiquimod

8-hydroxy-5-nitrosoquinoline
($C_9H_6N_2O_2$; *3565-26-2*) see: Nitroxoline

4-hydroxynorephedrine
($C_9H_{13}NO_2$; *552-85-2*) see: Buphenine; Isoxsuprine

L-ε-hydroxynorleucine methyl ester
($C_7H_{15}NO_3$; *167090-40-6*) see: Omapatrilat

17β-hydroxy-19-norpregna-4,9,11-trien-20-yn-3-one oxime
($C_{20}H_{23}NO_2$; *19636-23-8*) see: Norgestrienone

17-hydroxy-19-norprogesterone
($C_{20}H_{28}O_3$; *2137-18-0*) see: Gestonorone caproate

***trans*-5-hydroxy-1,3-oxathiolane-2-carboxylic acid**
($C_4H_6O_4S$; *147027-04-1*) see: Lamivudine

17β-hydroxy-3-oxo-5α-androst-1-ene
($C_{19}H_{28}O_2$; *65-06-5*) see: Mesterolone; Metenolone acetate

3β-hydroxy-17-oxo-5-androstene
see under androstenolone

3-(17β-hydroxy-3-oxo-4-androsten-17-yl)propionic acid lactone
($C_{22}H_{30}O_3$; *976-70-5*) see: Potassium canrenoate;
Spironolactone

3-hydroxy-5-oxo-1-cyclopentene-1-heptanoic acid methyl ester
($C_{13}H_{20}O_4$; *40098-26-8*) see: Misoprostol

17β-hydroxy-3-oxo-4,9,11-estratriene
($C_{18}H_{22}O_2$; *10161-33-8*) see: Norgestrienone; Trenbolone
hexahydrobenzyl carbonate

(*S*)-2-[3-hydroxy-2-oxo-1-(phenylmethyl)propyl]-1*H*-iso-indole-1,3(2*H*)-dione
($C_{18}H_{15}NO_4$; *136465-82-2*) see: Saquinavir

[*S*-(*R**,*S**)]-[2-hydroxy-3-oxo-1-[(phenylthio)methyl]pro-pyl]carbamic acid phenylmethyl ester
($C_{18}H_{19}NO_4S$; *197302-37-7*) see: Nelfinavir mesylate

3β-hydroxy-20-oxo-5,16-pregnadiene
see under 16-dehydropregnenolone

(4*S*)-3-[(2*S*,3*R*)-3-hydroxy-1-oxo-2-(2-propenyl)-4-pente-nyl]-4-(phenylmethyl)-2-oxazolidinone
($C_{18}H_{21}NO_4$; *178327-17-8*) see: Abacavir

5-[[4-(4-hydroxyphenoxy)-3,5-diiodophenyl]methyl]-5-methyl-2,4-imidazolidinedione
($C_{17}H_{14}I_2N_2O_4$; *5165-06-0*) see: Etiroxate

4-hydroxyphenylacetamide
($C_8H_9NO_2$; *17194-82-0*) see: Atenolol

4-hydroxyphenylacetic acid
($C_8H_8O_3$; *156-38-7*) see: Atenolol; Camostat

4-hydroxyphenylacetone
($C_9H_{10}O_2$; *770-39-8*) see: Pholedrine

(–)-1-hydroxy-1-phenylacetone
($C_9H_{10}O_2$; *1798-60-3*) see: L(–)-Ephedrine

1-(4-hydroxyphenyl)-4-acetylpiperazine
($C_{12}H_{16}N_2O_2$; *67914-60-7*) see: Itraconazole; Ketoconazole

1-(4-hydroxyphenyl)-2-amino-1-propanol
see under 4-hydroxynorephedrine

(3*R*,4*S*)-3-hydroxy-4-phenyl-2-azetidinone
($C_9H_9NO_2$; *132127-34-5*) see: Paclitaxel

α-hydroxy-α-phenylbenzeneacetic acid 1-azabicyclo[2.2.2]oct-3-yl ester
($C_{21}H_{23}NO_3$; *6581-06-2*) see: Clidinium bromide

α-hydroxy-α-phenylbenzeneacetic acid 1-ethyl-3-piperidi-nyl ester
($C_{21}H_{25}NO_3$; *3567-12-2*) see: Pipenzolate bromide

3*endo*-α-hydroxy-α-phenylbenzeneacetic acid 6-methoxy-8-methyl-8-azabicyclo[3.2.1]oct-3-yl ester
($C_{23}H_{27}NO_4$) see: Tropenziline bromide

α-hydroxy-α-phenylbenzeneacetic acid 1-methyl-4-piperi-dinyl ester
($C_{20}H_{23}NO_3$; *3608-67-1*) see: Propiverine

(–)-(1*S*,2*S*)-*N*-(2-hydroxy-1-phenyl-3-butenyl)benzamide
($C_{17}H_{17}NO_2$; *136693-02-2*) see: Paclitaxel

[hydroxy(4-phenylbutyl)phosphinyl]acetic acid phenylme-thyl ester
($C_{19}H_{23}O_4P$; *87460-09-1*) see: Fosinopril

1-(4-hydroxyphenyl)ethanone oxime
($C_8H_9NO_2$; *34523-34-7*) see: Paracetamol

4-hydroxy-1-(2-phenylethyl)-4-piperidinecarbonitrile
($C_{14}H_{18}N_2O$; *23804-59-3*) see: Fenspiride

***N*-[3-(2-hydroxy-2-phenylethyl)-2-thiazolidinylidene]acet-amide**
($C_{13}H_{16}N_2O_2S$; *5028-81-9*) see: Levamisole

4-hydroxy-3-phenyl-2(5*H*)-furanone
($C_{10}H_8O_3$; *23782-85-6*) see: Rofecoxib

D-4-hydroxyphenylglycine
($C_8H_9NO_3$; *22818-40-2*) see: Aspoxicillin

DL-4-hydroxyphenylglycine
($C_8H_9NO_3$; *938-97-6*) see: Atenolol

D(–)-4-hydroxyphenylglycine sodium salt
($C_8H_8NNaO_3$; *55361-61-0*) see: Cefoperazone

D-*p*-hydroxyphenylglycyl chloride hydrochloride
($C_8H_9Cl_2NO_2$; *51431-08-4*) see: Amoxicillin; Cefatrizine;
cis-Cefprozil

D(–)-2-(4-hydroxyphenyl)glycyl chloride hydrochloride
see under D-*p*-hydroxyphenylglycyl chloride hydrochloride

7-hydroxy-7-phenylheptanoic acid
($C_{13}H_{18}O_3$; *103187-18-4*) see: Seratrodast

[*R*-(*R**,*S**)]-[2-hydroxy-1-[[(phenylmethoxy)amino]carbo-nyl]propyl]carbamic acid 1,1-dimethylethyl ester
($C_{16}H_{24}N_2O_5$; *75624-31-6*) see: Aztreonam

(*R*)-3-hydroxy-7-[[(phenylmethoxy)carbonyl]amino]hep-tanoic acid
($C_{15}H_{21}NO_5$) see: Gusperimus trihydrochloride

4-[hydroxy[5-[[(phenylmethoxy)carbonyl]amino]pen-tyl]amino]-4-oxobutanoic acid
($C_{17}H_{24}N_2O_6$; *106410-46-2*) see: Deferoxamine

D-α-(4-hydroxyphenyl)-α-(2-methoxycarbonyl-1-methyl-ethenylamino)acetic acid anhydride with monoethyl car-bonate
($C_{16}H_{19}NO_7$; *78858-51-2*) see: Amoxicillin

[1*S*-(1α,4α,5β)]-4-hydroxy-5-[(phenylmethoxy)methyl]-2-cyclopentene-1-acetic acid
($C_{15}H_{18}O_4$; *41787-51-3*) see: Dinoprost

***N*-[2-[[2-hydroxy-3-[4-(phenylmethyl)phenoxy]propyl]-amino]ethyl]-4-morpholinecarboxamide**
($C_{23}H_{31}N_3O_5$; *69630-21-3*) see: Xamoterol

hydroxystenozole

($C_{21}H_{30}N_2O$; *19120-01-5*)   see: Stanozolol

***N*-hydroxysuccinimide**

($C_4H_5NO_3$; *6066-82-6*)   see: Amprenavir; Aspoxicillin;
Cefotiam; Imidapril; Nateglinide; Ritonavir; Romurtide;
Spirapril

(*S*)-(+)-3-hydroxytetrahydrofuran

($C_4H_8O_2$; *86087-23-2*)   see: Amprenavir

2-[2(*R*)-hydroxy-3-[(tetrahydro-2*H*-pyran-2-yl)oxy]-1(*S*)-(phenylmethyl)propyl]-1*H*-isoindole-1,3(2*H*)-dione

($C_{23}H_{25}NO_5$)   see: Saquinavir

5-hydroxy-1,2,3,4-tetrahydroquinolin-2-one

($C_9H_9NO_2$; *30389-33-4*)   see: Carteolol

5-hydroxy-1-tetralone

($C_{10}H_{10}O_2$; *28315-93-7*)   see: Levobunolol

(±)-6-hydroxy-2,5,7,8-tetramethylchroman-2-carboxylic acid

($C_{14}H_{18}O_4$; *53188-07-1*)   see: Troglitazone

(±)-6-hydroxy-2,5,7,8-tetramethylchroman-2-ylmethanol

($C_{14}H_{20}O_3$; *79907-49-6*)   see: Troglitazone

8-hydroxythiochroman

($C_9H_{10}OS$; *30073-50-8*)   see: Tertatolol

α-hydroxy-2-thiopheneacetonitrile

(C_6H_5NOS; *89380-68-7*)   see: Temocapril

4-hydroxy-4-(*p*-tolyl)piperidine

($C_{12}H_{17}NO$; *57988-60-0*)   see: Moperone

6-hydroxy-2,4,5-triaminopyrimidine

($C_4H_7N_5O$; *1004-75-7*)   see: Folic acid

4-hydroxy-4-(3-trifluoromethylphenyl)piperidine

($C_{12}H_{14}F_3NO$; *2249-28-7*)   see: Trifluperidol

4-hydroxy-8-trifluoromethylquinoline

($C_{10}H_6F_3NO$; *23779-96-6*)   see: Floctafenine

4-hydroxy-8-(trifluoromethyl)-3-quinolinecarboxylic acid

($C_{11}H_6F_3NO_3$; *23779-95-5*)   see: Floctafenine

2'-hydroxy-2,5,9-trimethylbenzo-6-morphen

($C_{15}H_{21}NO$; *25144-79-0*)   see: Pentazocine

4-hydroxy-2,4,6-trimethyl-2,5-cyclohexadien-1-one

($C_9H_{12}O_2$; *16404-66-3*)   see: Metipranolol

α-hydroxy-*N*,*N*,6-trimethyl-2-(4-methylphenyl)imidazo-[1,2-*a*]pyridine-3-acetamide

($C_{19}H_{21}N_3O_2$; *118026-14-5*)   see: Zolpidem

(22*E*)-23-hydroxy-3,11,20-trioxo-21-norchola-4,22-dien-24-oic acid ethyl ester sodium salt

($C_{25}H_{31}NaO_6$; *74220-39-6*)   see: Cortisone; Hydrocortisone

(+)-(*S*)-5-hydroxy-γ-valerolactone

($C_5H_8O_3$; *32780-06-6*)   see: Stavudine

25-hydroxyvitamin D_2

($C_{28}H_{44}O_2$; *21343-40-8*)   see: Paricalcitol

L-hyoscyamine

($C_{17}H_{23}NO_3$; *101-31-5*)   see: Butropium bromide;
Fentonium bromide

hyoscyamine

see under L-hyoscyamine

hypochlorous acid sodium salt

($ClNaO$; *7681-52-9*)   see: Halazone

hypoxanthine

($C_5H_4N_4O$; *68-94-0*)   see: Mercaptopurine

I

ibuprofen

($C_{13}H_{18}O_2$; *15687-27-1*)   see: Ibuprofen lysinate; Ibuproxam;
Mabuprofen

ibuprofen methyl ester

($C_{14}H_{20}O_2$; *61566-34-5*)   see: Ibuprofen

ibuprofen sodium salt

($C_{13}H_{17}NaO_2$; *31121-93-4*)   see: Pimeprofen

imidazole

($C_3H_4N_2$; *288-32-4*)   see: Bifonazole; Butoconazole;
Clotrimazole; Eprosartan; Fenticonazole; Isoconazole;
Ketoconazole; Miconazole; Neticonazole hydrochloride;
Omoconazole nitrate; Oxiconazole; Ozagrel

1*H*-imidazole lithium salt

($C_3H_3LiN_2$; *55986-39-5*)   see: Flutrimazole

2-imidazolidinone

($C_3H_6N_2O$; *120-93-4*)   see: Azlocillin; Mezlocillin

2-[1-(1*H*-imidazol-1-yl)ethenyl]phenol

($C_{11}H_{10}N_2O$; *74204-47-0*)   see: Croconazole

1-imidazo[1,2-*a*]pyridin-6-yl-2-propanone

($C_{10}H_{10}N_2O$; *116355-08-9*)   see: Olprinone hydrochloride

2-imino-1,3-benzoxathiol-6-ol

($C_7H_5NO_2S$)   see: Tioxolone

iminodibenzyl

($C_{14}H_{13}N$; *494-19-9*)   see: Carpipramine; Desipramine;
Imipramine; Quinupramine; Tiracizine; Trimipramine

2-imino-α-phenyl-3-thiazolidineethanol

($C_{11}H_{14}N_2OS$; *10060-88-5*)   see: Levamisole

iminostilbene

($C_{14}H_{11}N$; *256-96-2*)   see: Carbamazepine; Opipramol;
Oxcarbazepine

2-iminothiazolidine

($C_3H_6N_2S$; *1779-81-3*)   see: Levamisole

2-(2-imino-3-thiazolidinyl)-1-phenylethanone

($C_{11}H_{12}N_2OS$; *6649-75-8*)   see: Levamisole

imipramine

($C_{19}H_{24}N_2$; *50-49-7*)   see: Desipramine

1,3-indanedione

($C_9H_6O_2$; *606-23-5*)   see: Diphenadione

5-indanol

($C_9H_{10}O$; *1470-94-6*)   see: Carindacillin

2-indanone

(C_9H_8O; *615-13-4*)   see: Aprindine; Indanorex

***N*-(4-indanyl)-*N'*-benzoylthiourea**

($C_{17}H_{16}N_2OS$; *40507-75-3*)   see: Indanazoline

***N*-(2-indanylidene)aniline**

($C_{15}H_{13}N$; *3201-41-0*)   see: Aprindine

2-indanyl methanesulfonate

($C_{10}H_{12}O_3S$; *777-72-0*)   see: Aprindine

(5-indanyloxycarbonyl)phenylketene

($C_{18}H_{14}O_3$; *58137-69-2*)   see: Carindacillin

indazole-3-carboxylic acid

($C_8H_6N_2O_2$; *4498-67-3*)   see: Granisetron; Lonidamine

indene

(C_9H_8; *95-13-6*)   see: Indinavir sulfate

[(1*H*-inden-4-yloxy)methyl]oxirane

($C_{12}H_{12}O_2$; *64966-57-0*)   see: Indenolol

[(1*H*-inden-7-yloxy)methyl]oxirane

($C_{12}H_{12}O_2$; *30190-85-3*)   see: Indenolol

4-isobutylbenzyl chloride
(C$_{11}$H$_{15}$Cl; 60736-79-0)   see: Ibuprofen

isobutyl bromide
(C$_4$H$_9$Br; 78-77-3)   see: Butalbital

isobutyl chloride
(C$_4$H$_9$Cl; 513-36-0)   see: Butethamine; Olprinone
hydrochloride

isobutyl chloroformate
see under chloroformic acid isobutyl ester

isobutylene
see under isobutene

isobutylene chloride
(C$_4$H$_7$Cl; 563-47-3)   see: Alminoprofen

isobutyl 2-(2-nitrobenzylidene)acetoacetate
(C$_{15}$H$_{17}$NO$_5$; 61312-59-2)   see: Nisoldipine

2-(4-isobutylphenyl)acetonitrile
(C$_{12}$H$_{15}$N; 40784-95-0)   see: Butibufen; Ibuprofen

1-(4-isobutylphenyl)ethanol
(C$_{12}$H$_{18}$O; 40150-92-3)   see: Ibuprofen

2-(4-isobutylphenyl)propionaldehyde
(C$_{13}$H$_{18}$O; 51407-46-6)   see: Ibuprofen

(RS)-2-(4-isobutylphenyl)propionyl chloride
(C$_{13}$H$_{17}$ClO; 34715-60-1)   see: Mabuprofen; Pimeprofen

2-(4-isobutylphenyl)propionyl chloride
see under (RS)-2-(4-isobutylphenyl)propionyl chloride

isobutyraldehyde
see under isobutanal

isobutyric acid
(C$_4$H$_8$O$_2$; 79-31-2)   see: Captopril

2-isobutyrylacetanilide
(C$_{12}$H$_{15}$NO$_2$; 124401-38-3)   see: Atorvastatin calcium

isobutyryl chloride
(C$_4$H$_7$ClO; 79-30-1)   see: Atorvastatin calcium; Flutamide;
Ibopamine; Mibefradil hydrochloride; Ritonavir

isochroman
(C$_9$H$_{10}$O; 493-05-0)   see: Ropinirole

2-isocyanatodiphenylmethane
(C$_{14}$H$_{11}$NO; 146446-96-0)   see: Perlapine

1-[3-isocyanato-4-(phenylmethoxy)phenyl]ethanone
(C$_{16}$H$_{13}$NO$_3$; 35037-75-3)   see: Carbuterol

6β-isocyanopenicillanic acid benzyl ester
(C$_{16}$H$_{16}$N$_2$O$_3$S; 53628-27-6)   see: Temocillin

isoeugenol
(C$_{10}$H$_{12}$O$_2$; 97-54-1)   see: Methyldopa

(+)-isoisopulegol
(C$_{10}$H$_{18}$O; 96612-21-4)   see: (–)-Menthol

D-isolysergazide
(C$_{16}$H$_{15}$N$_5$O)   see: Methylergometrine

(±)-isomenthol
(C$_{10}$H$_{20}$O; 3623-52-7)   see: (–)-Menthol

isoniazid
(C$_6$H$_7$N$_3$O; 54-85-3)   see: Glyconiazide; Iproniazid;
Nialamide; Pasiniazid; Streptoniazid

isonicotinamide
(C$_6$H$_6$N$_2$O; 1453-82-3)   see: Cefsulodin

isonicotinic acid 2-(2-carboxyethyl)hydrazide methyl ester
(C$_{10}$H$_{13}$N$_3$O$_3$; 90872-10-9)   see: Nialamide

isonicotinoyl chloride
(C$_6$H$_4$ClNO; 14254-57-0)   see: Dexamethasone 21-
isonicotinate

α-isonitrosopropiophenone
(C$_9$H$_9$NO$_2$; 119-51-7)   see: Phenylpropanolamine

isopentyl bromide
see under isoamyl bromide

4-isopentyloxyaniline
(C$_{11}$H$_{17}$NO; 5198-05-0)   see: Tiocarlide

4-isopentyloxy-1-nitrobenzene
(C$_{11}$H$_{15}$NO$_3$; 7244-79-3)   see: Tiocarlide

isophthalaldehyde
(C$_8$H$_6$O$_2$; 626-19-7)   see: Montelukast sodium

isophthaloyl chloride
(C$_8$H$_4$Cl$_2$O$_2$; 99-63-8)   see: Ditophal

isophytol
(C$_{20}$H$_{40}$O; 505-32-8)   see: α-Tocopherol

isoprene
(C$_5$H$_8$; 78-79-5)   see: Troglitazone

isoprenyl bromide
(C$_5$H$_9$Br; 870-63-3)   see: Pentazocine; Sofalcone;
Tazarotene

isopropanol
(C$_3$H$_8$O; 67-63-0)   see: Fenofibrate; Imiquimod;
Isoflurophate; Nimodipine

isopropenyl acetate
(C$_5$H$_8$O$_2$; 108-22-5)   see: Desoxycortone acetate; Estriol;
Pancuronium bromide; Pipecuronium bromide; Vecuronium
bromide

4-isopropenyltoluene
(C$_{10}$H$_{12}$; 1195-32-0)   see: Moperone

4-isopropoxybenzoyl chloride
(C$_{10}$H$_{11}$ClO$_2$; 36823-82-2)   see: Sulfaproxyline

2-isopropoxyethanol
(C$_5$H$_{12}$O$_2$; 109-59-1)   see: Bisoprolol

4-[(2-isopropoxyethoxy)methyl]phenol
(C$_{12}$H$_{18}$O$_3$; 177034-57-0)   see: Bisoprolol

**5-[4-[(2-isopropoxyethoxy)methyl]phenoxymethyl]-3-iso-
propyl-2-oxazolidinone**
(C$_{19}$H$_{29}$NO$_5$; 87844-84-6)   see: Bisoprolol

2-[[4-(2-isopropoxyethoxy)methyl]phenoxymethyl]oxirane
(C$_{15}$H$_{22}$O$_4$; 66722-57-4)   see: Bisoprolol

isopropyl acetoacetate
(C$_7$H$_{12}$O$_3$; 542-08-5)   see: Isradipine; Nilvadipine;
Nimodipine

isopropyl alcohol
see under isopropanol

isopropylamine
(C$_3$H$_9$N; 75-31-0)   see: Acebutolol; Alprenolol; Atenolol;
Befunolol; Betaxolol; Bisoprolol; Carazolol; Carisoprodol;
Clorprenaline; Esmolol; Indecainide; Indenolol; Isoetarine;
Isoprenaline; Mepindolol; Metipranolol; Metoprolol;
Nifenalol; Nipradilol; Orciprenaline; Oxaflozane; Oxprenolol;
Pindolol; Pramiverine; Prenalterol; Procarbazine; Procaterol;
Proguanil; Propranolol; Sotalol; Toliprolol

isopropyl 3-aminocrotonate
(C$_7$H$_{13}$NO$_2$; 14205-46-0)   see: Nimodipine

2-isopropylamino-3',5'-dimethoxyacetophenone
(C$_{13}$H$_{19}$NO$_3$)   see: Orciprenaline

2-isopropylamino-4-methylbenzophenone
(C$_{17}$H$_{19}$NO; 23070-81-7)   see: Proquazone

N-isopropylaniline
(C$_9$H$_{13}$N; 768-52-5)   see: Fluvastatin sodium

leucomycin V 3,4B-dipropanoate 2A,3B,9-triacetate
($C_{47}H_{73}NO_{18}$; *55881-06-6*)   see: Midecamycin acetate

leuco-1,4,5,8-tetrahydroxyanthraquinone
($C_{14}H_8O_6$; *81-60-7*)   see: Mitoxantrone

levonorgestrel acetate
($C_{23}H_{30}O_3$; *13732-69-9*)   see: Norgestimate

levulinic acid
($C_5H_8O_3$; *123-76-2*)   see: Acemetacin; Cinmetacin; Indometacin

lincomycin
($C_{18}H_{34}N_2O_6S$; *154-21-2*)   see: Clindamycin

lipstatin
($C_{29}H_{49}NO_5$; *96829-59-3*)   see: Orlistat

lithium acetylide (Li(C2H))
(C_2HLi; *1111-64-4*)   see: Levonorgestrel

lithium ethyl acetate
($C_4H_7LiO_2$; *189811-59-4*)   see: Iloprost

lithium tri-sec-butylborohydride
($C_{12}H_{28}BLi$; *38721-52-7*)   see: Rosiglitazone

loratadine
($C_{22}H_{23}ClN_2O_2$; *79794-75-5*)   see: Desloratadine

lovastatin
($C_{24}H_{36}O_5$; *75330-75-5*)   see: Simvastatin

lumazine
($C_6H_4N_4O_2$; *487-21-8*)   see: Amiloride

lumilysergol 10-methyl ether
($C_{17}H_{22}N_2O_2$; *35121-60-9*)   see: Nicergoline

lumilysergol 10-methyl ether 8-*O*-(5-bromonicotinate)
($C_{23}H_{24}BrN_3O_3$; *35264-46-1*)   see: Nicergoline

2,6-lutidine
(C_7H_9N; *108-48-5*)   see: Pyridinol carbamate; Raltitrexed

D-lysergazide
($C_{16}H_{15}N_5O$; *62074-28-6*)   see: Methylergometrine

D-lysergic acid
($C_{16}H_{16}N_2O_2$; *82-58-6*)   see: Ergometrine; Pergolide

lysergic acid
see under D-lysergic acid

lysergol
($C_{16}H_{18}N_2O$; *602-85-7*)   see: Nicergoline

L-lysine
($C_6H_{14}N_2O_2$; *56-87-1*)   see: Eptifibatide; Gusperimus trihydrochloride; Ibuprofen lysinate; Lisinopril; Lymecycline

M

magnesium monoperoxyphthalate
($C_8H_4MgO_5$; *109536-69-8*)   see: Rofecoxib

maleic acid monoureide
($C_5H_6N_2O_4$; *105-61-3*)   see: Orotic acid

maleic anhydride
($C_4H_2O_3$; *108-31-6*)   see: Azintamide

(S)-malic acid
($C_4H_6O_5$; *97-67-6*)   see: Barnidipine; Orlistat

L-malic acid
see under (S)-malic acid

malic acid
($C_4H_6O_5$; *6915-15-7*)   see: Bucumolol; Methoxsalen

malonic acid
($C_3H_4O_4$; *141-82-2*)   see: Acrivastine; Pilsicainide

malononitrile
($C_3H_2N_2$; *109-77-3*)   see: Thiamine; Triamterene; Trimethoprim

malonyl chloride
($C_3H_2Cl_2O_2$; *1663-67-8*)   see: Iotrolan

(±)-mandelic acid
($C_8H_8O_3$; *90-64-2*)   see: Cyclandelate; Fenozolone; Fenyramidol; Homatropine; Micinicate

D(–)-mandelic acid
($C_8H_8O_3$; *611-71-2*)   see: Sertraline

mandelic acid ethyl ester
($C_{10}H_{12}O_3$; *4358-88-7*)   see: Pemoline

mandelonitrile
(C_8H_7NO; *532-28-5*)   see: Ethotoin

D-mannitol
($C_6H_{14}O_6$; *69-65-8*)   see: Mitobronitol

MCPBA
see under *m*-chloroperbenzoic acid

medroxyprogesterone
see under 17-hydroxy-6α-methylprogesterone

megestrol
($C_{22}H_{30}O_3$; *3562-63-8*)   see: Megestrol acetate

melamine
($C_3H_6N_6$; *108-78-1*)   see: Altretamine

menadiol
($C_{11}H_{10}O_2$; *481-85-6*)   see: Menadiol sodium diphosphate

menadiol 1-acetate
($C_{13}H_{12}O_3$; *2211-27-0*)   see: Phytomenadione

menadiol diacetate
($C_{15}H_{14}O_4$; *573-20-6*)   see: Phytomenadione

menadione
($C_{11}H_8O_2$; *58-27-5*)   see: Menadiol diacetate; Menadiol sodium diphosphate; Menadione sodium bisulfite

(+)-*p*-mentha-2,8-dien-1-ol
($C_{10}H_{16}O$)   see: Dronabinol

(1*S*-*cis*)-*p*-menth-2-ene-1,8-diol
($C_{10}H_{18}O_2$; *15910-72-2*)   see: Dronabinol

(±)-menthol
($C_{10}H_{20}O$; *89-78-1*)   see: (–)-Menthol

(–)-menthol
($C_{10}H_{20}O$; *2216-51-5*)   see: Paroxetine

(±)-menthyl benzoate
($C_{17}H_{24}O_2$; *38649-18-2*)   see: (–)-Menthol

(±)-mepromazine
($C_{19}H_{24}N_2OS$; *51019-87-5*)   see: Levomepromazine

mercaptoacetaldehyde dimethyl acetal
($C_4H_{10}O_2S$; *89055-43-6*)   see: Epitizide; Lamivudine

3-mercaptoanisole
(C_7H_8OS; *15570-12-4*)   see: Raloxifene hydrochloride

2-mercaptobenzimidazole
($C_7H_6N_2S$; *583-39-1*)   see: Lansoprazole

2-mercapto-4-(5-carbamoyl-2-thienyl)thiazole
($C_8H_6N_2OS_3$; *52560-89-1*)   see: Arotinolol

***cis*-4-mercapto-*N,N*-dimethyl-1-(*p*-nitrobenzyloxycarbonyl)-L-prolinamide**
($C_{15}H_{19}N_3O_5S$; *96034-64-9*)   see: Meropenem

2-mercaptoethanol
(C_2H_6OS; *60-24-2*)   see: Nifurtimox; Tiadenol

(+)-mercaptolactic acid
($C_3H_6O_3S$; *30163-03-2*)   see: Lamivudine

8-methoxy-2H-1-benzopyran-3(4H)-one
($C_{10}H_{10}O_3$; *91520-00-2*)   see: Nipradilol

4-(4-methoxybenzoylamino)butyric acid
($C_{12}H_{15}NO_4$; *72432-14-5*)   see: Aniracetam

2-methoxybenzoyl chloride
($C_8H_7ClO_2$; *21615-34-9*)   see: Losartan potassium

3-methoxybenzoyl chloride
($C_8H_7ClO_2$; *1711-05-3*)   see: Nelfinavir mesylate

p-methoxybenzyl alcohol
($C_8H_{10}O_2$; *105-13-5*)   see: Efavirenz; Raloxifene
hydrochloride

4-methoxybenzylamine
($C_8H_{11}NO$; *2393-23-9*)   see: Idarubicin

2-(4-methoxybenzylamino)pyridine
($C_{13}H_{14}N_2O$; *52818-63-0*)   see: Mepyramine

4-methoxybenzyl bromide
(C_8H_9BrO; *2746-25-0*)   see: Tacrolimus

**4-methoxybenzyl 3-(chloromethyl)-7(R)-(phenylacet-
amido)-3-cephem-4-carboxylate**
($C_{24}H_{23}ClN_2O_5S$; *104146-10-3*)   see: Cefditoren pivoxil

N-(4-methoxybenzyl)-4-chloro-2-(trifluoroacetyl)aniline
($C_{16}H_{13}ClF_3NO_2$; *173676-54-5*)   see: Efavirenz

3-methoxybenzyl cyanide
(C_9H_9NO; *19924-43-7*)   see: Ketobemidone

**2-(4-methoxybenzyl)-3,4-dimethyl-1-phenethyl-1,2,5,6-
tetrahydropyridine**
($C_{23}H_{29}NO$; *1100-37-4*)   see: Phenazocine

1-(4-methoxybenzyl)-3,4,5,6,7,8-hexahydroisoquinoline
($C_{17}H_{21}NO$; *51072-35-6*)   see: Levorphanol

17,21-O-(α-methoxybenzylidene)betamethasone
($C_{30}H_{35}FO_6$; *31020-77-6*)   see: Betamethasone benzoate

4-methoxybenzylmagnesium chloride
(C_8H_9ClMgO; *38769-92-5*)   see: Chlorotrianisene;
Pentazocine; Phenazocine

5-(4-methoxybenzyl)-5-methylhydantoin
($C_{12}H_{14}N_2O_3$; *13500-24-8*)   see: Etiroxate; Metirosine

4-methoxybenzyl methyl ketone
($C_{10}H_{12}O_2$; *122-84-9*)   see: Etiroxate; Mebeverine;
Metirosine; Tamsulosin hydrochloride

**1-(4-methoxybenzyl)-2-methyl-1,2,3,4,5,6,7,8-octahydro-
isoquinoline**
($C_{18}H_{25}NO$; *38969-65-2*)   see: Levorphanol

1-(4-methoxybenzyl)-1,2,3,4,5,6,7,8-octahydroisoquinoline
($C_{17}H_{23}NO$; *51072-36-7*)   see: Levallorphan; Levorphanol

**(±)-1-(4-methoxybenzyl)-1,2,3,4,5,6,7,8-octahydro-
isoquinoline**
see under 1-(4-methoxybenzyl)-1,2,3,4,5,6,7,8-
octahydroisoquinoline

**2-(4-methoxybenzyl)-1,3,4-trimethyl-1,2,5,6-tetrahydro-
pyridine**
($C_{16}H_{23}NO$; *33216-38-5*)   see: Pentazocine

4-methoxy-α,α-bis(4-methoxyphenyl)benzeneethanol
($C_{23}H_{24}O_4$; *1817-87-4*)   see: Chlorotrianisene

3-methoxycarbazole
($C_{13}H_{11}NO$; *18992-85-3*)   see: Ramatroban

4-methoxycarbonyl-2-azaspiro[4.5]decan-3-one
($C_{11}H_{17}NO_3$; *128262-17-9*)   see: Gabapentin

2-(methoxycarbonyl)benzenediazonium chloride
($C_8H_7ClN_2O_2$; *35358-78-2*)   see: Saccharin

2-methoxycarbonylbenzenesulfonamide
($C_8H_9NO_4S$; *57683-71-3*)   see: Saccharin

1-methoxycarbonyl-3-cyclopentene oxide (cis/trans-mixt.)
($C_7H_{10}O_3$)   see: Dolasetron mesilate

8β-methoxycarbonylergoline
($C_{16}H_{18}N_2O_2$; *30341-92-5*)   see: Cabergoline; Pergolide

D-8β-methoxycarbonylergoline
see under 8β-methoxycarbonylergoline

β-methoxycarbonylglutaraldehyde
($C_7H_{10}O_4$)   see: Dolasetron mesilate

(methoxycarbonylmethylene)triphenylphosphorane
($C_{21}H_{19}O_2P$; *2605-67-6*)   see: Latanoprost; Tirofiban
hydrochloride

**N-(2-methoxycarbonyl-1-methylethenyl)-D(−)-phenylgly-
cine sodium salt**
($C_{13}H_{14}NNaO_4$; *13291-96-8*)   see: Ampicillin; Cefalexin

**3-methoxycarbonyl-4-oxo-3,4-dihydro-2H-1,2-benzo-
thiazine 1,1-dioxide**
($C_{10}H_9NO_5S$; *29209-29-8*)   see: Piroxicam

**4-methoxycarbonyl-4-[(1-oxopropyl)phenylamino]pi-
peridine**
($C_{16}H_{22}N_2O_3$; *72996-78-2*)   see: Remifentanil

4-methoxycarbonyl-1-piperidineacetic acid ethyl ester
($C_{11}H_{19}NO_4$)   see: Clidinium bromide

(1R-cis)-5-methoxy-3-cyclohexene-1-carboxylic acid
($C_8H_{12}O_3$; *118207-41-3*)   see: Tacrolimus

1-methoxycyclopentene
($C_6H_{10}O$; *1072-59-9*)   see: Mepitiostane

10-methoxy-5H-dibenz[b,f]azepine
($C_{15}H_{13}NO$; *4698-11-7*)   see: Oxcarbazepine

10-methoxy-5H-dibenz[b,f]azepine-5-carboxamide
($C_{16}H_{14}N_2O_2$; *28721-09-7*)   see: Oxcarbazepine

3-methoxy-8,14-didehydromorphinan
($C_{17}H_{21}NO$; *54313-11-0*)   see: Butorphanol

**7-methoxy-α,10-dimethylphenothiazine-2-malonic acid
ethyl methyl ester**
($C_{21}H_{23}NO_5S$; *13891-17-3*)   see: Protizinic acid

1-methoxy-4,4-dimethyl-1-phospha-2,6-dioxacyclohexane
($C_6H_{13}O_3P$; *1005-69-2*)   see: Efonidipine hydrochloride
ethanol

4-methoxy-3,5-dimethyl-2-pyridinemethanol acetate
($C_{11}H_{15}NO_3$; *91219-90-8*)   see: Omeprazole

9-methoxyellipticine
($C_{18}H_{16}N_2O$; *10371-86-5*)   see: Elliptinium acetate

(11β)-11-methoxyestra-4,9-diene-3,17-dione
($C_{19}H_{24}O_3$; *21391-55-9*)   see: Moxestrol

(17β)-3-methoxyestra-2,5(10)-dien-17-ol
($C_{19}H_{28}O_2$; *1091-93-6*)   see: Nandrolone

3-methoxyestra-1,3,5(10),16-tetraen-17-ol acetate
($C_{21}H_{26}O_3$; *6038-28-4*)   see: Estriol

(17β)-3-methoxyestra-1,3,5(10)-trien-17-ol
($C_{19}H_{26}O_2$; *1035-77-4*)   see: Nandrolone

2-methoxyethanol
($C_3H_8O_2$; *109-86-4*)   see: Nimodipine

3-methoxy-4-(ethoxycarbonyloxy)cinnamoyl chloride
($C_{13}H_{13}ClO_5$; *49806-45-3*)   see: Rescimetol

2-methoxyethyl 3-aminocrotonate
($C_7H_{13}NO_3$; *50899-10-0*)   see: Cilnidipine

3-methoxy-13-ethyl-2,5(10)-gonadien-17-one
($C_{20}H_{28}O_2$; *2322-77-2*)   see: Gestodene

(*S*)-2-(6-methoxy-2-naphthalenyl)-α,5,5-trimethyl-1,3-dioxane-2-methanol methanesulfonate
($C_{20}H_{26}O_6S$; *111197-92-3*)   see: Naproxen

2-(6-methoxy-2-naphthoyl)-2-methylpropionic acid ethyl ester
($C_{18}H_{20}O_4$; *101743-90-2*)   see: Methallenestril

6-methoxy-2-naphthylacetic acid
($C_{13}H_{12}O_3$; *23981-47-7*)   see: Naproxen

2-(6-methoxy-2-naphthyl)acrylic acid
($C_{14}H_{12}O_3$; *27602-79-5*)   see: Naproxen

4-(6-methoxy-2-naphthyl)-3-buten-2-one
($C_{15}H_{14}O_2$; *56600-90-9*)   see: Nabumetone

DL-2-(6-methoxy-2-naphthyl)propionic acid
($C_{14}H_{14}O_3$; *23981-80-8*)   see: Naproxen

2-methoxy-4-nitroaniline
($C_7H_8N_2O_3$; *97-52-9*)   see: Amsacrine

3-methoxy-4-nitroaniline
($C_7H_8N_2O_3$; *16292-88-9*)   see: Amsacrine

4-methoxy-2-nitroaniline
($C_7H_8N_2O_3$; *96-96-8*)   see: Primaquine

2-methoxy-6-nitrobenzaldehyde
($C_8H_7NO_4$; *19689-88-4*)   see: Mepindolol

4-methoxy-2-nitrobenzaldehyde
($C_8H_7NO_4$; *22996-21-0*)   see: Clometacin

2-methoxy-6-nitrobenzyl bromide
($C_8H_8BrNO_3$; *19689-86-2*)   see: Mepindolol

N-(3-methoxy-4-nitrophenyl)methanesulfonamide
($C_8H_{10}N_2O_5S$; *57165-05-6*)   see: Amsacrine

1-(2-methoxy-6-nitrophenyl)-2-nitroprop-1-ene
($C_{10}H_{10}N_2O_5$; *75595-49-2*)   see: Mepindolol

N-(2-methoxy-4-nitrophenyl)pentanamide
($C_{12}H_{16}N_2O_4$)   see: Amsacrine

6-methoxy-8-nitroquinoline
($C_{10}H_8N_2O_3$; *85-81-4*)   see: Primaquine

(17α)-3-methoxy-19-norpregna-2,5(10)-dien-20-yn-17-ol
($C_{21}H_{28}O_2$; *19357-36-9*)   see: Noretynodrel

3-methoxy-19-norpregna-1,3,5(10),17(20)-tetraene
($C_{21}H_{28}O$; *32043-13-3*)   see: Promegestone

5-methoxy-1,3-oxathiolane-2-methanol benzoate
($C_{12}H_{14}O_4S$; *139253-83-1*)   see: Lamivudine

3-(methoxyoxoacetyl)-2,4,5-trioxocyclopentaneheptanoic acid
($C_{15}H_{18}O_8$; *22935-41-7*)   see: Misoprostol

methoxyoxobutanedioic acid dimethyl ester
($C_7H_{10}O_6$; *36797-93-0*)   see: Sulfadoxine

3-methoxy-17-oxo-2,5(10)-estradiene
($C_{19}H_{26}O_2$; *17976-32-8*)   see: Noretynodrel

3-methoxy-20-oxo-19-norpregna-1,3,5(10),16-tetraene
($C_{21}H_{26}O_2$; *21321-91-5*)   see: Demegestone; Promegestone

N-[3-methoxy-4-[(1-oxopentyl)amino]phenyl]methanesulfonamide
($C_{13}H_{20}N_2O_4S$)   see: Amsacrine

α-[[(3-methoxy-3-oxopropyl)methylamino]methyl]-2-(phenylmethyl)benzeneacetic acid ethyl ester
($C_{24}H_{31}NO_4$)   see: Setiptiline

6-methoxy-3-oxo-2,4-tropanedicarboxylic acid dimethyl ester
($C_{13}H_{19}NO_6$)   see: Tropenziline bromide

4-methoxyphenacyl bromide
($C_9H_9BrO_2$; *2632-13-5*)   see: Raloxifene hydrochloride

5-methoxy-4,7-phenanthroline
($C_{13}H_{10}N_2O$; *951-06-4*)   see: Phanquinone

2-methoxyphenothiazine
($C_{13}H_{11}NOS$; *1771-18-2*)   see: Levomepromazine; Perimetazine

(4-methoxyphenoxy)acetic acid
($C_9H_{10}O_4$; *1877-75-4*)   see: Mefexamide

(4-methoxyphenoxy)acetyl chloride
($C_9H_9ClO_3$; *42082-29-1*)   see: Mefexamide

5-[[4-(4-methoxyphenoxy)-3,5-dinitrophenyl]methyl]-5-methyl-2,4-imidazolidinedione
($C_{18}H_{16}N_4O_8$; *5487-34-3*)   see: Etiroxate

2-(2-methoxyphenoxy)ethylamine
($C_9H_{13}NO_2$; *1836-62-0*)   see: Carvedilol

N-[2-(2-methoxyphenoxy)ethyl]benzylamine
($C_{16}H_{19}NO_2$; *3246-03-5*)   see: Amosulalol

5-[[*N*-[2-(2-methoxyphenoxy)ethyl]benzylamino]acetyl]-2-methylbenzenesulfonamide
($C_{25}H_{28}N_2O_5S$)   see: Amosulalol

4-methoxyphenylacetic acid
($C_9H_{10}O_3$; *104-01-8*)   see: Anisindione

(4-methoxyphenyl)acetone
see under 4-methoxybenzyl methyl ketone

4-methoxyphenylacetone
see under 4-methoxybenzyl methyl ketone

4-methoxyphenylacetonitrile
(C_9H_9NO; *104-47-2*)   see: Venlafaxine

4-methoxyphenylacetyl chloride
($C_9H_9ClO_2$; *4693-91-8*)   see: Levorphanol

3-methoxy-4-(phenylazo)benzenamine
($C_{13}H_{13}N_3O$; *80830-39-3*)   see: Amsacrine

N-[3-methoxy-4-(phenylazo)phenyl]methanesulfonamide
($C_{14}H_{15}N_3O_3S$)   see: Amsacrine

3-methoxy-*N*-phenylbenzamide
($C_{14}H_{13}NO_2$; *6833-23-4*)   see: Nelfinavir mesylate

4-(4-methoxyphenyl)-2-butanone
($C_{11}H_{14}O_2$; *104-20-1*)   see: Dobutamine

2-(3-methoxyphenyl)butyronitrile
($C_{11}H_{13}NO$; *1611-75-2*)   see: Meptazinol

5-(4-methoxyphenyl)-1,2-dithiol-3-one
($C_{10}H_8O_2S_2$; *831-30-1*)   see: Anethole trithione

4-methoxy-*o*-phenylenediamine
($C_7H_{10}N_2O$; *102-51-2*)   see: Omeprazole

[*R* (*R*,R**)] 2-methoxy-5-[2-[[(1-phenylethyl)amino]propyl]benzenesulfonamide monohydrochloride
($C_{18}H_{25}ClN_2O_3S$; *116091-64-6*)   see: Tamsulosin hydrochloride

2-methoxy-2-phenylethyl bromide
($C_9H_{11}BrO$; *13685-00-2*)   see: Eprozinol; Zipeprol

2-(4-methoxyphenyl)ethyl methanesulfonate
($C_{10}H_{14}O_4S$; *73735-36-1*)   see: Astemizole

1-(2-methoxy-2-phenylethyl)piperazine
($C_{13}H_{20}N_2O$; *6722-54-9*)   see: Eprozinol; Zipeprol

3-[4-(2-methoxy-2-phenylethyl)-1-piperazinyl]-1-phenyl-1-propanone
($C_{22}H_{28}N_2O_2$)   see: Eprozinol

4-methoxyphenylhydrazine
($C_7H_{10}N_2O$; *3471-32-7*)   see: Acemetacin; Ramatroban

4-methoxy-2,3,5-trimethylpyridine *N*-oxide
($C_9H_{13}NO_2$; *86604-80-0*)   see: Omeprazole

7-methoxy-2,4,4-trimethyl-1,2,3,4-tetrahydroisoquinoline-1,3-dione
($C_{13}H_{15}NO_3$; *191988-38-2*)   see: Gliquidone

[1*R*-(1α,3α,4β)]-3-methoxy-4-[[tris(1-methylethyl)silyl]-oxy]cyclohexanecarboxylic acid methyl ester
($C_{18}H_{36}O_4Si$; *128684-90-2*)   see: Tacrolimus

6-methoxytropine
($C_9H_{17}NO_2$)   see: Tropenziline bromide

6-methoxytropinone
($C_9H_{15}NO_2$; *112843-64-8*)   see: Tropenziline bromide

***exo*-2-(6-methoxy-3,4-xylyl)bornane**
($C_{19}H_{28}O$; *31467-21-7*)   see: Xibornol

methyl 4-acetamido-5-bromo-2-methoxybenzoate
($C_{10}H_{10}BrNO_4$; *89481-86-7*)   see: Bromopride

methyl 4-acetamido-5-chloro-2-methoxybenzoate
($C_{11}H_{12}ClNO_4$; *4093-31-6*)   see: Clebopride; Metoclopramide

methyl 2-acetamido-3-chloropropionate
($C_6H_{10}ClNO_3$; *87333-22-0*)   see: Ramipril

methyl α-acetamido-3,5-diiodo-4-(4-methoxyphenoxy)-cinnamate
($C_{19}H_{17}I_2NO_5$; *94256-36-7*)   see: Dextrothyroxine

methyl 4-acetamido-2-methoxybenzoate
($C_{11}H_{13}NO_4$; *4093-29-2*)   see: Bromopride; Metoclopramide

methyl 2-acetamido-3-(2-oxocyclopentyl)propionate
($C_{11}H_{17}NO_4$; *87269-85-0*)   see: Ramipril

methyl 4-acetamidosalicylate
($C_{10}H_{11}NO_4$; *4093-28-1*)   see: Bromopride; Metoclopramide; Mosapride citrate

methyl acetate
($C_3H_6O_2$; *79-20-9*)   see: Clopidogrel hydrogensulfate; Tiotixene

methyl acetoacetate
($C_5H_8O_3$; *105-45-3*)   see: Ampicillin; Cefradine; Cerivastatin sodium; Dicloxacillin; Epicillin; Felodipine; Flucloxacillin; Fluvastatin sodium; Nifedipine; Nitrendipine; Sultamicillin; Talampicillin

2-methylacetoacetonitrile
(C_5H_7NO; *4468-47-7*)   see: Sulfafurazole

4'-methylacetophenone
($C_9H_{10}O$; *122-00-9*)   see: Celecoxib; Moperone; Triprolidine

methyl 2-acetoxyacrylate
($C_6H_8O_4$; *686-46-4*)   see: Vincamine

16α-methyl-21-acetoxy-11β,17-α-dihydroxypregna-1,4,6-triene-3,20-dione
($C_{24}H_{30}O_6$; *13796-64-0*)   see: Alclometasone dipropionate

methyl (2*R*,3*S*)-4-acetoxy-2,3-epoxybutanoate
($C_7H_{10}O_5$; *117069-14-4*)   see: Carumonam

methyl 4-[[5-(acetoxymethyl)-2-butylimidazol-1-yl]me-thyl]benzoate
($C_{19}H_{24}N_2O_4$; *149550-86-7*)   see: Eprosartan

methyl 4-(acetylamino)-2-ethoxybenzoate
($C_{12}H_{15}NO_4$; *59-06-3*)   see: Mosapride citrate

methyl acetylenecarboxylate
($C_4H_4O_2$; *922-67-8*)   see: Rosoxacin

methyl β-(acetyloxy)-2-butyl-1-[[4-(carboxyphenyl)me-thyl]-α-(2-thienylmethyl)-1*H*-imidazole-5-propanoate
($C_{26}H_{30}N_2O_6S$)   see: Eprosartan

methyl β-(acetyloxy)-2-butyl-1-[[4-(methoxycarbonyl)phe-nyl]methyl]-α-(2-thienylmethyl)-1*H*-imidazole-5-propa-noate
($C_{27}H_{32}N_2O_6S$; *133040-05-8*)   see: Eprosartan

methyl acetylsalicylate
($C_{10}H_{10}O_4$; *580-02-9*)   see: Acenocoumarol

methyl 5-acetylsalicylate
($C_{10}H_{10}O_4$; *16475-90-4*)   see: Spizofurone

methyl 6-acetylthio-8-chlorooctanoate
($C_{11}H_{19}ClO_3S$; *923-78-4*)   see: Octotiamine

methyl 2-[1-(acetylthiomethyl)cyclopropyl]acetate
($C_9H_{14}O_3S$; *142148-14-9*)   see: Montelukast sodium

9-methylacridine
($C_{14}H_{11}N$; *611-64-3*)   see: Dimetacrine

methyl acrylate
see under acrylic acid methyl ester

2-methylallyl 1-piperazinecarboxylate
($C_9H_{16}N_2O_2$)   see: Trimazosin

methylamine
(CH_5N; *74-89-5*)   see: Adrenalone; Aspoxicillin; Benzoctamine; Betahistine; Betanidine; Butenafine; Carbimazole; Chlordiazepoxide; Chlormezanone; Cimetidine; Cyclopentamine; Deferiprone; Desipramine; Dipivefrine; L(–)-Ephedrine; Epinephrine; Flosequinan; Homatropine; Iotalamic acid; Isometheptene; Ketamine; Lorazepam; Lornoxicam; Maprotiline; Mesuximide; Midazolam; Nefopam; Nortriptyline; Oxilofrine; Oxypyrronium bromide; Phenindamine; Phensuximide; Pholedrine; Ranitidine; Ritonavir; Sertraline; Setiptiline; Tofenacin; Tropenziline bromide; Zomepirac

(methylamino)acetonitrile
($C_3H_6N_2$; *5616-32-0*)   see: Synephrine

4-(methylamino)benzoic acid
($C_8H_9NO_2$; *10541-83-0*)   see: Methotrexate

***N*-[4-(methylamino)benzoyl]-L-glutamic acid**
($C_{13}H_{16}N_2O_5$; *52980-68-4*)   see: Methotrexate

***N*-methyl-*N*-(2-aminobenzyl)-2-hydroxy-2-phenylethyl-amine**
($C_{16}H_{20}N_2O$; *65514-97-8*)   see: Nomifensine

***N*-methyl-*N*-(2-aminobenzyl)phenacylamine**
($C_{16}H_{18}N_2O$; *119810-30-9*)   see: Nomifensine

4-(methylamino)butanoic acid hydrochloride
($C_5H_{12}ClNO_2$; *6976-17-6*)   see: Azelastine

methyl 3-amino-2-butenoate
($C_5H_9NO_2$; *14205-39-1*)   see: Amlodipine; Aranidipine; Barnidipine; Benidipine; Isradipine; Lercanidipine hydrochloride; Manidipine; Nicardipine; Nisoldipine; Nitrendipine

3-[(methylamino)carbonyl]-5-nitrobenzoic acid
($C_9H_8N_2O_5$; *1954-97-8*)   see: Iotalamic acid

methyl 3-amino-5-chlorosalicylate
($C_8H_8ClNO_3$; *5043-81-2*)   see: Nazasetron

methyl 3-aminocrotonate
see under methyl 3-amino-2-butenoate

methyl 6-amino-6-deoxy-α-D-glucopyranoside
($C_7H_{15}NO_5$; *5155-47-5*)   see: Ranimustine

methyl 4-amino-3,5-dimethoxybenzoate
($C_{10}H_{13}NO_4$; *56066-25-2*)   see: Brodimoprim

methyl 3-amino-4,4-dimethoxycrotonate
($C_7H_{13}NO_4$; *85396-57-2*)   see: Nilvadipine

methyl 2-benzylaminobenzoate
($C_{15}H_{15}NO_2$; *55369-69-2*)   see: Benzydamine

2-(methylbenzylamino)ethyl acetoacetate
($C_{14}H_{19}NO_3$; *54527-65-0*)   see: Nicardipine

methyl 2-(benzylaminomethyl)-3-oxobutanoate
($C_{13}H_{17}NO_3$)   see: Faropenem sodium

p-methylbenzyl chloroformate
($C_9H_9ClO_2$; *39545-34-1*)   see: Flomoxef

1-(4-methylbenzyl)-1,2,5,6,7,8-hexahydroisoquinoline
($C_{18}H_{23}N$; *38973-15-8*)   see: Dimemorfan

4-methylbenzylmagnesium chloride
(C_8H_9ClMg; *29875-07-8*)   see: Dimemorfan

p-methylbenzylmercaptopropionic acid
($C_{11}H_{14}O_2S$; *78981-22-3*)   see: Eptifibatide

methyl 4-benzyloxyphenylacetate
($C_{16}H_{16}O_3$; *68641-16-7*)   see: Epanolol

2-(4'-methylbiphenyl-2-yl)-4,4-dimethyl-2-oxazoline
($C_{18}H_{19}NO$; *84392-32-5*)   see: Losartan potassium

5-(4'-methyl[1,1'-biphenyl]-2-yl)-1-(triphenylmethyl)-1H-tetrazole
($C_{33}H_{26}N_4$; *124750-53-4*)   see: Losartan potassium

methyl bromide
(CH_3Br; *74-83-9*)   see: Ciclonium bromide; Clidinium bromide; Demecarium bromide; Distigmine bromide; Domiphen bromide; Fenpiverinium bromide; Flutropium bromide; Glycopyrronium bromide; Heteronium bromide; Homatropine methylbromide; Ipratropium bromide; Mepenzolate bromide; Methscopolamine bromide; Methysergide; Octatropine methylbromide; Otilonium bromide; Oxitefonium bromide; Oxitropium bromide; Oxyphenonium bromide; Oxypyrronium bromide; Pancuronium bromide; Paroxetine; Penthienate methobromide; Pipecuronium bromide; Pipenzolate bromide; Propantheline bromide; Propyramazine bromide; Pyridostigmine bromide; Timepidium bromide; Tiquizium bromide; Tropenziline bromide; Valethamate bromide; Vecuronium bromide

methyl 3-(2-bromoacetylamino)-5-chlorosalicylate
($C_{10}H_9BrClNO_4$)   see: Nazasetron

methyl 2-bromobenzoate
($C_8H_7BrO_2$; *610-94-6*)   see: Montelukast sodium

methyl 4-bromo-3,5-dimethoxybenzoate
($C_{10}H_{11}BrO_4$; *26050-64-6*)   see: Brodimoprim

methyl 2-bromo-3-[4-[2-(5-ethyl-2-pyridyl)ethoxy]phenyl]propionate
($C_{19}H_{22}BrNO_3$; *105355-25-7*)   see: Pioglitazone

methyl (4-bromomethyl)benzoate
($C_9H_9BrO_2$; *2417-72-5*)   see: Eprosartan; Procarbazine

methyl 4-bromomethylbenzoate
see under methyl (4-bromomethyl)benzoate

methyl 4-bromomethyl-3-methoxybenzoate
($C_{10}H_{11}BrO_3$; *70264-94-7*)   see: Zafirlukast

2-methyl-2-butene-1,4-diol
($C_5H_{10}O_2$; *61842-14-6*)   see: Troglitazone

3-methyl-2-butenyl bromide
see under isoprenyl bromide

4-[(3-methyl-2-butenyl)oxy]benzaldehyde
($C_{12}H_{14}O_2$; *28090-12-2*)   see: Sofalcone

3-methyl-2-butenyl phenyl sulfide
($C_{11}H_{14}S$; *10276-04-7*)   see: Tazarotene

5-(1-methylbutyl)barbituric acid
($C_9H_{14}N_2O_3$; *83-29-4*)   see: Secobarbital; Vinylbital

N-methyl-4-tert-butylbenzylamine
($C_{12}H_{19}N$; *65542-26-9*)   see: Butenafine

methyl 4-[(2-butyl-4-chloro-5-formylimidazol-1-yl)methyl]benzoate
($C_{17}H_{19}ClN_2O_3$; *133040-02-5*)   see: Eprosartan

methyl (S)-4-(tert-butyldiphenylsilyloxy)-2-hydroxybutanoate
($C_{21}H_{28}O_4Si$; *153011-60-0*)   see: Orlistat

methyl 2-butyl-4-formyl-1H-imidazole-1-propanoate
($C_{12}H_{18}N_2O_3$; *212004-16-5*)   see: Eprosartan

methyl 4-[(2-butyl-5-formyl-1H-imidazol-1-yl)methyl]benzoate
($C_{17}H_{20}N_2O_3$; *133040-03-6*)   see: Eprosartan

methyl 4-[(2-butyl-5-formyl-4-iodoimidazol-1-yl)methyl]benzoate
($C_{17}H_{19}IN_2O_3$; *154371-54-7*)   see: Eprosartan

methyl (E)-α-[[2-butyl-1-[2-(4-methoxycarbonyl)ethyl]-1H-imidazol-4-yl]methylene]-2-thiophenepropanoate
($C_{20}H_{26}N_2O_4S$)   see: Eprosartan

methyl (E)-α-[[2-butyl-1-[[4-(methoxycarbonyl)phenyl]methyl]-1H-imidazol-5-yl]methylene]-2-thiophenepropanoate
($C_{25}H_{28}N_2O_4S$; *133040-06-9*)   see: Eprosartan

methyl 4-[N-(tert-butyloxycarbonyl)piperidin-4-yl]but-2-enoate
($C_{15}H_{25}NO_4$; *142355-80-4*)   see: Tirofiban hydrochloride

methyl 4-butyramido-3-methylbenzoate
($C_{13}H_{17}NO_3$)   see: Telmisartan

methyl 4-butyramido-3-methyl-5-nitrobenzoate
($C_{13}H_{16}N_2O_5$; *152628-01-8*)   see: Telmisartan

2-methylbutyric acid
($C_5H_{10}O_2$; *116-53-0*)   see: Beclobrate

methyl camphor-3-sulfonate
($C_{11}H_{18}O_4S$)   see: Camphotamide

methyl carbazate
($C_2H_6N_2O_2$; *6294-89-9*)   see: Nefazodone hydrochloride

D(–)-methyl 3-(α-carboxybenzylamino)crotonate sodium salt
see under N-(2-methoxycarbonyl-1-methylethenyl)-D(–)-phenylglycine sodium salt

methyl chloride
(CH_3Cl; *74-87-3*)   see: Atropine methonitrate; Clobazam; Dimethyltubocurarinium chloride; Methylmethionine sulfonium chloride; Naproxen; Suxamethonium chloride

methyl chloroacetate
($C_3H_5ClO_2$; *96-34-4*)   see: Cefixime; Clometacin; Diltiazem; Meloxicam; Piroxicam

methyl 4-chlorobenzenesulfonate
($C_7H_7ClO_3S$; *15481-45-5*)   see: Thenium closilate

methyl 2-chlorobenzoate
($C_8H_7ClO_2$; *610-96-8*)   see: Clozapine

methyl chloro(2-chlorophenyl)acetate
($C_9H_8Cl_2O_2$; *90055-47-3*)   see: Clopidogrel hydrogensulfate

1-methyl-3-chloro-6-(2-chlorophenyl)-1,2,3,4-tetrahydro-1,5-benzodiazocine
($C_{17}H_{16}Cl_2N_2$; *63062-27-1*)   see: Metaclazepam

methyl 6-chloro-3,5-diaminopyrazine-2-carboxylate
($C_6H_7ClN_4O_2$; *1458-01-1*)   see: Amiloride

16β-methyl-17α,21-dihydroxy-1,4,9(11)-pregnatriene-3,20-dione 21-acetate
see under 21-acetoxy-17-hydroxy-16β-methylpregna-1,4,9(11)-triene-3,20-dione

methyl *erythro*-(*E*)-7-[2,6-diisopropyl-4-(4-fluorophenyl)-5-methoxymethyl-3-pyridyl]-3,5-dihydroxy-hept-6-enoate
($C_{27}H_{36}FNO_5$; *157242-01-8*)   see: Cerivastatin sodium

4-methyl-4-(3,4-dimethoxybenzyl)hydantoin
($C_{13}H_{16}N_2O_4$; *892-02-4*)   see: Methyldopa

methyl 2-(2,4-dimethoxybenzyloxy)acetate
($C_{12}H_{16}O_5$; *128685-11-0*)   see: Tacrolimus

methyl 3-dimethylaminoacrylate
($C_6H_{11}NO_2$; *999-59-7*)   see: Ciprofloxacin

4-[2-(2-methyl-1,3-dioxolan-2-yl)ethyl]-1,2-diphenyl-3,5-pyrazolidinedione
($C_{21}H_{22}N_2O_4$; *116604-64-9*)   see: Kebuzone

1-methyl-α,α-diphenyl-4-piperidinemethanol
($C_{19}H_{23}NO$; *6071-92-7*)   see: Diphemanil metilsulfate

methyl (*S*)-1,4-dithia-7-azaspiro[4.4]nonane-8-carboxylate hydrochloride
($C_8H_{14}ClNO_2S_2$; *83552-42-5*)   see: Spirapril

methyl di(2-thienyl)glycolate
($C_{11}H_{10}O_3S_2$; *26447-85-8*)   see: Mazaticol

1-methyl-α,α-di-2-thienyl-3-piperidinemethanol
($C_{15}H_{19}NOS_2$; *5166-68-7*)   see: Tipepidine

methyldopa
($C_{10}H_{13}NO_4$; *555-30-6*)   see: Methyldopate

(±)-methyldopa
($C_{10}H_{13}NO_4$; *55-40-3*)   see: Methyldopa

3,4-methylenedioxyaniline
($C_7H_7NO_2$; *14268-66-7*)   see: Oxolinic acid

1,2-methylenedioxybenzene
($C_7H_6O_2$; *274-09-9*)   see: Oxolinic acid

1-(3,4-methylenedioxybenzyl)piperazine
($C_{12}H_{16}N_2O_2$; *32231-06-4*)   see: Fenoverine; Fipexide; Medibazine; Pifarnine; Piribedil

4,5-methylenedioxy-2-nitroacetophenone
($C_9H_7NO_5$; *56136-84-6*)   see: Cinoxacin

3,4-methylenedioxy-1-nitrobenzene
($C_7H_5NO_4$; *2620-44-2*)   see: Oxolinic acid

L-3-(3,4-methylenedioxyphenyl)alanine
($C_{10}H_{11}NO_4$; *32161-31-2*)   see: Levodopa

16-methylenehydrocortisone
($C_{22}H_{30}O_5$; *14339-90-3*)   see: Fluprednidene acetate; Prednylidene

11-methylene-18-methyl-δ⁴-estrene-3,17-dione
($C_{20}H_{26}O_2$; *54024-17-8*)   see: Desogestrel

α-methylene-4-nitrobenzeneacetic acid methyl ester
($C_{10}H_9NO_4$; *28042-27-5*)   see: Alminoprofen

α-methylene-2-(phenylmethyl)benzeneacetic acid ethyl ester
($C_{18}H_{18}O_2$)   see: Setiptiline

methylenetriphenylphosphorane
($C_{19}H_{17}P$; *3487-44-3*)   see: Desogestrel

(–)-*N*-methylephedrine
($C_{11}H_{17}NO$; *552-79-4*)   see: Orlistat

methyl 2,3-epoxy-2-methylpropionate
($C_5H_8O_3$; *58653-97-7*)   see: Bicalutamide

methyl 3-[4-(2,3-epoxypropoxy)phenyl]propionate
($C_{13}H_{16}O_4$; *81147-94-6*)   see: Esmolol

methylergometrine
($C_{20}H_{25}N_3O_2$; *113-42-8*)   see: Methysergide

(7α)-7-methylestr-5(10)-ene-3,17-dione
($C_{19}H_{26}O_2$; *105186-32-1*)   see: Tibolone

3-*O*-methylestrone
see under estrone 3-methyl ether

***N*-methyl-9,10-ethanoanthracene-9(10*H*)-propanamide**
($C_{20}H_{21}NO$; *23716-34-9*)   see: Maprotiline

[1*R*-[1α,5α,6(*R)]]-α-(1-methylethenyl)-7-oxo-3-phenyl-4-oxa-2,6-diazabicyclo[3.2.0]hept-2-ene-6-acetic acid diphenylmethyl ester**
($C_{28}H_{24}N_2O_4$; *67977-61-1*)   see: Latamoxef

***N*-[4-(1-methylethoxy)benzoyl]-4-nitrobenzenesulfonamide**
($C_{16}H_{16}N_2O_6S$)   see: Sulfaproxyline

methyl 1-ethyl-6-acetyl-7-hydroxy-4-oxo-8-propyl-4*H*-quinoline-2-carboxylate
($C_{18}H_{21}NO_5$; *69049-70-3*)   see: Nedocromil

***N*-[4-[[(1-methylethyl)amino]acetyl]phenyl]methanesulfonamide**
($C_{12}H_{18}N_2O_3S$; *60735-85-5*)   see: Sotalol

1-[(1-methylethyl)amino]-3-[4-(phenylmethoxy)phenoxy]-2-propanol
($C_{19}H_{25}NO_3$; *34380-47-7*)   see: Prenalterol

3-[(1-methylethyl)amino]propyl chloride
($C_6H_{14}ClN$)   see: Indecainide

9-[3-[(1-methylethyl)amino]propyl]-9-cyanofluorene
($C_{20}H_{22}N_2$; *74517-92-3*)   see: Indecainide

1-[3-[(1-methylethyl)amino]-2-pyridinyl]-4-[(5-nitro-1*H*-indol-2-yl)carbonyl]piperazine
($C_{21}H_{24}N_6O_3$; *136817-57-7*)   see: Delavirdine mesilate

(1-methylethyl)carbamic acid 2-(hydroxymethyl)-2-methylpentyl ester
($C_{11}H_{23}NO_3$; *25462-17-3*)   see: Carisoprodol

4-(1-methylethyl)cyclohexanecarboxylic acid
($C_{10}H_{18}O_2$; *62067-45-2*)   see: Nateglinide

***cis*-methyl 3,3-ethylenedioxy-11-oxo-5,17(20)-pregnadiene-21-carboxylate**
($C_{24}H_{32}O_5$; *3546-75-6*)   see: Fluprednisolone acetate

1,2-*O*-(1-methylethylidene)-α-D-glucofuranose 6-(4-methylbenzenesulfonate)
($C_{16}H_{22}O_8S$; *26275-20-7*)   see: Prenalterol

1,2-*O*-(1-methylethylidene)-6-*O*-[4-(phenylmethoxy)phenyl]-α-D-glucofuranose
($C_{22}H_{26}O_7$; *57528-81-1*)   see: Prenalterol

1,2-*O*-(1-methylethylidene)-3,5,6-tris-*O*-(phenylmethyl)-α-D-glucofuranose
($C_{30}H_{34}O_6$; *53928-30-6*)   see: Tribenoside

1,2-*O*-(1-methylethylidene)-α-D-xylofuranose 3-acetate 5-benzoate
($C_{17}H_{20}O_7$; *190003-74-8*)   see: Stavudine

methyl ethyl ketone
see under butanone

4-[4-(1-methylethyl)-1-piperazinyl]phenol
($C_{13}H_{20}N_2O$; *67914-97-0*)   see: Terconazole

1-[4-[(1-methylethyl)thio]phenyl]-2-(octylamino)-1-propanone
($C_{20}H_{33}NOS$; *69708-39-0*)   see: Suloctidil

methyl 3-(3-fluoroanilino)-2-(methylthio)acrylate
($C_{11}H_{12}FNO_2S$; *76561-34-7*)   see: Flosequinan

methyl (±)-(*E*)-7-[3-(4-fluorophenyl)-1-isopropylindol-2-yl]-5-hydroxy-3-oxohept-6-enoate

($C_{25}H_{26}FNO_4$; *93957-52-9*)   see: Fluvastatin sodium

methyl 4-(4-fluorophenyl)-*N*-methylnipecotate (*cis-/trans-mixt.*)

($C_{14}H_{18}FNO_2$)   see: Paroxetine

N-methylformanilide

(C_8H_9NO; *93-61-8*)   see: Benzoctamine

methyl formate

($C_2H_4O_2$; *107-31-3*)   see: Felbamate; Flosequinan; Fluphenazine; Methyprylon; Pyrithyldione; Retinol

methyl formimidate hydrochloride

(C_2H_6ClNO; *15755-09-6*)   see: Imipenem

methyl (*E*)-2-formyl-2-phenylacetate sodium salt

($C_{10}H_9NaO_3$; *246180-40-5*)   see: Felbamate

N-methylglycine

($C_3H_7NO_2$; *107-97-1*)   see: Flumazenil

methylglyoxal diethyl acetal

($C_7H_{14}O_3$; *5774-26-5*)   see: Betacarotene

4-methyl-1,6-heptadien-4-ol

($C_8H_{14}O$; *25201-40-5*)   see: Meglutol

N-methylhomopiperazine

($C_6H_{14}N_2$; *4318-37-0*)   see: Emedastine

5-methylhydantoin

($C_4H_6N_2O_2$; *616-03-5*)   see: L-Alanine

methylhydrazine

(CH_6N_2; *60-34-4*)   see: Ceftriaxone

6α-methyl-hydrocortisone

($C_{22}H_{32}O_5$; *1625-39-4*)   see: Methylprednisolone

16β-methylhydrocortisone

($C_{22}H_{32}O_5$; *18762-15-7*)   see: Betamethasone

methyl 3-hydroxyacrylate

($C_4H_6O_3$; *86761-97-9*)   see: Ciprofloxacin

methyl 4-[(hydroxyamino)carbonyl]-3,5-dimethoxybenzoate

($C_{11}H_{13}NO_6$; *65566-10-1*)   see: Brodimoprim

methyl 4-hydroxybenzoate

($C_8H_8O_3$; *99-76-3*)   see: Nifuroxazide; Raloxifene hydrochloride

methyl 4-hydroxy-2*H*-1,2-benzothiazine-3-carboxylate 1,1-dioxide

($C_{11}H_{11}NO_5S$; *35511-15-0*)   see: Meloxicam

methyl 4-(2-hydroxyethoxy)benzoate

($C_{10}H_{12}O_4$; *3204-73-7*)   see: Raloxifene hydrochloride

methyl *N*-(2-hydroxyethyl)dithiocarbamate

($C_4H_9NOS_2$; *56158-48-6*)   see: Flomoxef

N-methyl-*N*-(2-hydroxyethyl)guanidine phosphate

($C_4H_{14}N_3O_5P$; *33018-83-6*)   see: Creatinolfosfate

5-methyl-10-hydroxyimino-10,11-dihydro-5*H*-dibenz-[*b,f*]azepine

($C_{15}H_{14}N_2O$; *21737-53-1*)   see: Metapramine

N-methyl-4-hydroxyisocarbostyril

($C_{10}H_9NO_2$; *30236-50-1*)   see: Tilisolol hydrochloride

N-methylhydroxylamine

(CH_5NO; *593-77-1*)   see: Fluoxetine

O-methylhydroxylamine hydrochloride

(CH_6ClNO; *593-56-6*)   see: Cefuroxime; Quinagolide hydrochloride

methyl 3β-hydroxy-17α-methyl-androst-5-ene-17-carboxylate

($C_{22}H_{34}O_3$; *25352-87-8*)   see: Medrogestone

methyl 4-(hydroxymethyl)benzoate

($C_9H_{10}O_3$; *6908-41-4*)   see: Eprosartan

methyl 2-hydroxy-2-methyl-3-(4-fluorophenylthio)propionate

($C_{11}H_{13}FO_3S$)   see: Bicalutamide

methyl 2-hydroxy-5-[(4-methylsulfonyloxy-3-methoxy-carbonylphenyl)azo]benzoate

($C_{17}H_{16}N_2O_8S$; *80622-19-1*)   see: Olsalazine sodium

methyl 2-hydroxy-5-nitrobenzoate

($C_8H_7NO_5$; *17302-46-4*)   see: Olsalazine sodium

methyl 3-(4-hydroxyphenyl)propionate

($C_{10}H_{12}O_3$; *5597-50-2*)   see: Esmolol

N-methyl-2-hydroxypropylamine

($C_4H_{11}NO$; *16667-45-1*)   see: Pildralazine

methyl (*R*)-3-hydroxytetradecanoate

($C_{15}H_{30}O_3$; *76062-97-0*)   see: Orlistat

methyl 3-hydroxythiophene-2-carboxylate

($C_6H_6O_3S$; *5118-06-9*)   see: Tenoxicam

2-methylimidazole

($C_4H_6N_2$; *693-98-1*)   see: Metronidazole; Ondansetron; Secnidazole

3-methyl-Δ⁴-imidazol-2-thione

($C_4H_6N_2S$; *60-56-0*)   see: Carbimazole

(2-methyl-1-imidazolyl)acetone

($C_7H_{10}N_2O$; *31964-03-1*)   see: Secnidazole

β,β'-(methylimino)bis(propiophenone)

($C_{19}H_{21}NO_2$; *103756-12-3*)   see: Phenindamine

methyl 4-[[*N*-(1-iminopentyl)amino]methyl]benzoate

($C_{14}H_{20}N_2O_2$; *198065-80-4*)   see: Eprosartan

1-methylindazole-3-carbonyl chloride

($C_9H_7ClN_2O$; *106649-02-9*)   see: Granisetron

1-methylindazole-3-carboxylic acid

($C_9H_8N_2O_2$; *50890-83-0*)   see: Granisetron

1-methylindole

(C_9H_9N; *603-76-9*)   see: Ramosetron hydrochloride

N-methyl-1*H*-indole-5-methanesulfonamide

($C_{10}H_{12}N_2O_2S$; *103628-43-9*)   see: Sumatriptan

2-methylindoline

($C_9H_{11}N$; *6872-06-6*)   see: Indapamide

methyl iodide

(CH_3I; *74-88-4*)   see: Alpidem; Astemizole; Azithromycin; Betanidine; Cerivastatin sodium; Cethexonium bromide; Cisapride; Clonidine; Demegestone; Dimestrol; Dimethisterone; Dimethyltubocurarinium chloride; Dofetilide; Ecothiopate iodide; Elliptinium acetate; Emorfazone; Etretinate; Famotidine; Flomoxef; Flunitrazepam; Granisetron; Guanoxabenz; Ibuprofen; Indanazoline; Isopropamide iodide; Ketoprofen; Malotilate; Mecobalamin; Medazepam; Medrogestone; Melitracen; Meloxicam; Mepindolol; Meproscillarin; Methazolamide; Methyclothiazide; Mizolastine; Nabilone; Naproxen; Nazasetron; Nelfinavir mesylate; Nicergoline; Nortriptyline; Pentazocine; Piroxicam; Pralidoxime iodide; Pranoprofen; Prolonium iodide; Promegestone; Protizinic acid; Tacrolimus; Tetrazepam; Thenium closilate; Tiamenidine; Tibezonium iodide; Tiemonium iodide; Tolonidine; Tolterodine; Tramazoline; Zafirlukast

methyl 2-iodoacetate

($C_3H_5IO_2$; *5199-50-8*)   see: Lornoxicam

methyl isocyanate
(C_2H_3NO; *624-83-9*)   see: Pyridinol carbamate

methyl isonicotinate
($C_7H_7NO_2$; *2459-09-8*)   see: Clidinium bromide

N-[methyl(2-isopropyl-4-thiazolylmethyl)aminocarbonyl]-L-valine
($C_{14}H_{23}N_3O_3S$; *154212-61-0*)   see: Ritonavir

methyl isothiocyanate
(C_2H_3NS; *556-61-6*)   see: Betanidine; Thiamazole

S-methylisothiosemicarbazide hydriodide
($C_2H_8IN_3S$; *35600-34-1*)   see: Guanoxabenz

S-methylisothiourea
($C_2H_6N_2S$; *2986-19-8*)   see: Flubendazole; Zanamivir

S-methylisothiouronium sulfate
($C_2H_8N_2O_4S_2$; *14527-26-5*)   see: Debrisoquin

5-methylisoxazole-4-carbonyl chloride
($C_5H_4ClNO_2$; *67305-24-2*)   see: Leflunomide

5-methylisoxazole-3-carboxylic acid
($C_5H_5NO_3$; *3405-77-4*)   see: Glisoxepide; Isocarboxazid

5-methylisoxazole-4-carboxylic acid
($C_5H_5NO_3$; *42831-50-5*)   see: Leflunomide

5-methyl-3-isoxazolecarboxylic acid hydrazide
($C_5H_7N_3O_2$; *62438-03-3*)   see: Isocarboxazid

3-methyl-5-isoxazolecarboxylic acid (phenylmethylene)hydrazide
($C_{12}H_{11}N_3O_2$; *1085-33-2*)   see: Isocarboxazid

N-[4-[[(5-methyl-3-isoxazolyl)amino]sulfonyl]phenyl]acetamide
($C_{12}H_{13}N_3O_4S$; *21312-10-7*)   see: Sulfamethoxazole

[[4-[2-[[(5-methyl-3-isoxazolyl)carbonyl]amino]ethyl]phenyl]sulfonyl]carbamic acid methyl ester
($C_{15}H_{17}N_3O_6S$; *24489-02-9*)   see: Glisoxepide

methyl levulinate
($C_6H_{10}O_3$; *624-45-3*)   see: Indometacin

methyllithium
(CH_3Li; *917-54-4*)   see: Calusterone

methyl lysergate
($C_{17}H_{18}N_2O_2$; *4579-64-0*)   see: Nicergoline

methylmagnesium bromide
(CH_3BrMg; *75-16-1*)   see: Betamethasone; Binedaline; Bolasterone; Cyclopentamine; Desogestrel; Desoximetasone; Dihydroxydibutyl ether; Dimetacrine; Flumetasone; Fluoxymesterone; Gestrinone; Medrogestone; Medroxyprogesterone acetate; Mestanolone; Metenolone acetate; Methylestrenolone; Methylprednisolone; Mibolerone; Misoprostol, Montelukast sodium; Moperone; Penmesterol; Pentorex; Retinol; Setastine; Spironolactone

methylmagnesium chloride
(CH_3ClMg; *676-58-4*)   see: Chlorphenoxamine; Clemastine

methylmagnesium iodide
(CH_3IMg; *917-64-6*)   see: Calcifediol; Dexamethasone; Fenpentadiol; Indalpine; Mesterolone; Methyltestosterone; Nabilone; Paramethasone; Tiaprofenic acid; Troglitazone

methyl malonamate
($C_4H_7NO_3$; *51513-29-2*)   see: Cefotetan

methyl malonate lithium salt
($C_4H_5LiO_4$; *63460-24-2*)   see: Misoprostol

methyl mercaptane
(CH_4S; *74-93-1*)   see: Neticonazole hydrochloride; Nifuratel; Pergolide

methyl methacrylate
($C_5H_8O_2$; *80-62-6*)   see: Bicalutamide

N-methylmethanamine sodium salt
(C_2H_6NNa; *14314-59-1*)   see: Proguanil

methyl 2-methoxy-4-acetamido-5-chlorobenzoate
see under methyl 4-acetamido-5-chloro-2-methoxybenzoate

methyl methoxyacetate
($C_4H_8O_3$; *6290-49-9*)   see: Sulfadoxine

methyl 3-methoxyacrylate
($C_5H_8O_3$; *34846-90-7*)   see: Mofezolac

methyl 6-methoxybenzotriazole-5-carboxylate
($C_9H_9N_3O_3$; *59338-86-2*)   see: Alizapride

methyl 3-[4-(4-methoxybenzoylamino)-3-nitrobenzoyl]butyrate
($C_{20}H_{20}N_2O_7$; *74149-72-7*)   see: Pimobendan

methyl methoxycarbonyl disulfide
($C_3H_6O_2S_2$; *55048-60-7*)   see: Temocillin

methyl 2-[[(methoxycarbonylmethyl)methylamino]carbonyl]benzoate
($C_{13}H_{15}NO_5$; *83073-63-6*)   see: Tilisolol hydrochloride

1-methyl-2-[[4-(methoxycarbonyl)phenyl]methyl]-1,2-hydrazinedicarboxylic acid bis(phenylmethyl) ester
($C_{26}H_{26}N_2O_6$)   see: Procarbazine

5-methyl-8-methoxycoumarin
($C_{11}H_{10}O_3$; *36651-80-6*)   see: Bucumolol

methyl 6-methoxy-5-iodo-1-naphthalenecarboxylate
($C_{13}H_{11}IO_3$; *84532-68-3*)   see: Tolrestat

1-methyl-10α-methoxylumilysergol
($C_{18}H_{24}N_2O_2$; *35155-28-3*)   see: Nicergoline

(±)-methyl 4-methoxymandelate
($C_{10}H_{12}O_4$; *13305-14-1*)   see: Fenoldopam mesilate

methyl 3-methoxy-4-methylbenzoate
($C_{10}H_{12}O_3$; *3556-83-0*)   see: Zafirlukast

1-methyl-2-methoxymethyl-5-(2-chlorophenyl)-2,3-dihydro-1H-1,4-benzodiazepine
($C_{18}H_{19}ClN_2O$; *103380-39-8*)   see: Metaclazepam

methyl 5-methoxy-2-methylindole-3-acetate
($C_{13}H_{15}NO_3$; *7588-36-5*)   see: Indometacin

methyl 3-methoxy-4-(1-methyl-5-nitroindol-3-ylmethyl)benzoate
($C_{19}H_{18}N_2O_5$; *107754-15-4*)   see: Zafirlukast

methyl 3-(2-methoxy-5-methylphenyl)-3-phenylpropionate
($C_{18}H_{20}O_3$; *124937-62-8*)   see: Tolterodine

methyl 2-methoxy-4-(N-methyl-N-tosylamino)benzoate
($C_{17}H_{19}NO_5S$; *78784-42-6*)   see: Nemonapride

methyl 6-methoxy-1-naphthalenecarboxylate
($C_{13}H_{12}O_3$; *61109-48-6*)   see: Tolrestat

methyl 6-methoxy-2-naphthylacetate
($C_{14}H_{14}O_3$; *23981-48-8*)   see: Naproxen

methyl DL-2-(6-methoxy-1-naphthyl)propionate
($C_{15}H_{16}O_3$; *30012-51-2*)   see: Naproxen

methyl 3-methoxy-4-(5-nitroindol-3-ylmethyl)benzoate
($C_{18}H_{16}N_2O_5$; *107786-36-7*)   see: Zafirlukast

5α-methyl-3-methoxy-5,6,7,8,9,10,11α,12-octahydro-5,11-methanobenzocyclodecen-13-one oxime
($C_{17}H_{23}NO_2$; *42263-97-8*)   see: Dezocine

(2R,3S)-methyl 3-(4-methoxyphenyl)glycidate
($C_{11}H_{12}O_4$; *105560-93-8*)   see: Diltiazem

(±)-*trans*-methyl 3-(4-methoxyphenyl)glycidate
($C_{11}H_{12}O_4$; *96125-49-4*)   see: Diltiazem

1-methyl-7-methoxy-2-tetralone
($C_{12}H_{14}O_2$; *1204-23-5*)   see: Dezocine

α-[methyl[2-(methylamino)-1,2-diphenylethyl]amino]-3-pyridinemethanol
($C_{22}H_{25}N_3O$)   see: Paroxetine

2-methyl-2-(methylaminomethyl)tetrahydrofuran
($C_7H_{15}NO$; *7179-95-5*)   see: Mefruside

methyl *N*-methylanthranilate
($C_9H_{11}NO_2$; *85-91-6*)   see: Dibenzepine

methyl 3-methylanthranilate
($C_9H_{11}NO_2$; *22223-49-0*)   see: Tolycaine

4-methyl-6-(1-methylbenzimidazol-2-yl)-2-propylbenzimidazole
($C_{19}H_{20}N_4$; *152628-02-9*)   see: Telmisartan

methyl 4-methylbenzoate
($C_9H_{10}O_2$; *99-75-2*)   see: Procarbazine

1-methyl-5-(4-methylbenzoyl)-1*H*-pyrrole-2-acetonitrile
($C_{15}H_{14}N_2O$; *26171-22-2*)   see: Tolmetin

1-methyl-2-(3,4-methylenedioxyphenyl)ethylamine
($C_{10}H_{13}NO_2$; *4764-17-4*)   see: Protokylol

1-methyl-2-[[4-[[(1-methylethyl)amino]carbonyl]phenyl]methyl]-1,2-hydrazinedicarboxylic acid bis(phenylmethyl) ester
($C_{28}H_{31}N_3O_5$; *58914-41-3*)   see: Procarbazine

methyl 4-(1-methylethyl)cyclohexanecarboxylate
($C_{11}H_{20}O_2$; *175284-00-1*)   see: Nateglinide

methyl *N*-methylglycinate
($C_4H_9NO_2$; *5473-12-1*)   see: Tilisolol hydrochloride; Tolrestat

methyl *S*-methylisothiourea-*N*-carboxylate
($C_4H_8N_2O_2S$; *39259-32-0*)   see: Mebendazole

methyl 10-*O*-methyl-lumilysergate
($C_{18}H_{22}N_2O_3$; *23495-64-9*)   see: Nicergoline

methyl *N*-methyl-5-methoxynipecotate
($C_9H_{17}NO_3$; *35012-50-1*)   see: Timepidium bromide

3-[1-methyl-4-[1-methyl-4-(1-methyl-4-nitropyrrole-2-carboxamido)pyrrole-2-carboxamido]pyrrole-2-carboxamido]propionitrile
($C_{21}H_{22}N_8O_5$; *2522-28-3*)   see: Stallimycin

3-[1-methyl-4-(1-methyl-4-nitropyrrole-2-carboxamido)pyrrole-2-carboxamido]propionitrile
($C_{15}H_{16}N_6O_4$; *3185-94-2*)   see: Stallimycin

6-methyl-2-(4-methylphenyl)imidazo[1,2-*a*]pyridine
($C_{15}H_{14}N_2$; *88965-00-8*)   see: Zolpidem

3-methyl-1-[(4-methylphenyl)sulfonyl]-4-phenyl-4-piperidinecarbonitrile
($C_{20}H_{22}N_2O_2S$; *83863-65-4*)   see: Levocabastine

3-methyl-1-[(4-methylphenyl)sulfonyl]-4-phenyl-4-piperidinecarboxylic acid
($C_{20}H_{23}NO_4S$; *80138-94-9*)   see: Levocabastine

trans-3-methyl-1-[(4-methylphenyl)sulfonyl]-4-phenyl-4-piperidinecarboxylic acid phenylmethyl ester
($C_{27}H_{29}NO_4S$; *104907-69-9*)   see: Levocabastine

(*E*)-*N*-methyl-2-[3-(1-methyl-4-piperidinyl)-1*H*-indol-5-yl]ethenesulfonamide
($C_{17}H_{23}N_3O_2S$; *121679-24-1*)   see: Naratriptan

(α*S*)-α-methyl-*N*-[3-methyl-1-[2-(1-piperidinyl)phenyl]butylidene]benzenemethanamine
($C_{24}H_{32}N_2$; *147770-02-3*)   see: Repaglinide

α-methyl-4-(2-methylpropyl)benzeneacetaldehyde oxime
($C_{13}H_{19}NO$; *58609-72-6*)   see: Ibuprofen

α-methyl-4-(2-methylpropyl)benzeneacetamide
($C_{13}H_{19}NO$; *59512-17-3*)   see: Ibuprofen

α-methyl-4-(2-methylpropyl)benzeneacetonitrile
($C_{13}H_{17}N$; *58609-73-7*)   see: Ibuprofen

α-methyl-4-(2-methylpropyl)benzeneethanimidic acid methyl ester hydrochloride
($C_{14}H_{22}ClNO$)   see: Ibuprofen

3-methyl-3-[4-(2-methylpropyl)phenyl]oxiranecarboxylic acid ethyl ester
($C_{16}H_{22}O_3$; *58609-71-5*)   see: Ibuprofen

methyl 1-[[(methylsulfonyl)oxy]methyl]cyclopropaneacetate
($C_8H_{14}O_5S$; *170721-48-9*)   see: Montelukast sodium

methyl 2-methylsulfonyloxy-5-nitrobenzoate
($C_9H_9NO_7S$; *80430-23-5*)   see: Olsalazine sodium

(*E*)-*N*-methyl-2-[3-(1-methyl-1,2,3,6-tetrahydro-4-pyridinyl)-1*H*-indol-5-yl]vinylsulfonamide
($C_{17}H_{21}N_3O_2S$; *166306-28-1*)   see: Naratriptan

methyl (methylthio)acetate
($C_4H_8O_2S$; *16630-66-3*)   see: Flosequinan

methyl (3*R*,4*R*,7a*R*)-2-methyl-4-[(1*S*,2*R*)-1,2,3-triacetoxypropyl]-3a,7a-dihydro-4*H*-pyrano[3,4-*d*]oxazole-6-carboxylate
($C_{18}H_{23}NO_{10}$; *78850-37-0*)   see: Zanamivir

N-methylmorpholine
($C_5H_{11}NO$; *109-02-4*)   see: Nazasetron; Temocapril

N-methylmorpholine oxide
($C_5H_{11}NO_2$; *7529-22-8*)   see: Paclitaxel

2-methylnaphthalene
($C_{11}H_{10}$; *91-57-6*)   see: Menadione

N-methyl-1-naphthylmethylamine
($C_{12}H_{13}N$; *14489-75-9*)   see: Butenafine; Naftifine; Terbinafine

methyl nicotinate
($C_7H_7NO_2$; *93-60-7*)   see: Nicorandil; Paroxetine

methyl nitrate
(CH_3NO_3; *598-58-3*)   see: Atropine methonitrate

methyl nitrite
(CH_3NO_2; *624-91-9*)   see: Molindone; Phenylpropanolamine

4-methyl-2-nitroaniline
($C_7H_8N_2O_2$; *89-62-3*)   see: Azapropazone

2-methyl-3-nitroanisole
($C_8H_9NO_3$; *4837-88-1*)   see: Mepindolol

N-methyl-2-nitrobenzylamine
($C_8H_{10}N_2O_2$; *56222-08-3*)   see: Nomifensine

N-methyl-*N*-(2-nitrobenzyl)-2-hydroxy-2-phenylethylamine
($C_{16}H_{18}N_2O_3$; *85660-33-9*)   see: Nomifensine

N-methyl-*N*-(2-nitrobenzyl)phenacylamine
($C_{16}H_{16}N_2O_3$; *102436-67-9*)   see: Nomifensine

2-methyl-5-nitro-4,6-dihydroxypyrimidine
($C_5H_5N_3O_4$; *53925-27-2*)   see: Moxonidine

2-methyl-5-nitroimidazole
($C_4H_5N_3O_2$; *88054-22-2*)   see: Metronidazole; Secnidazole; Tinidazole

2-methyl-4-nitro-1*H*-imidazole sodium salt
($C_4H_4N_3NaO_2$; *74571-67-8*)   see: Nitrefazole

N-methylnitrone
(C_2H_5NO; *54125-41-6*)   see: Fluoxetine

2-methyl-*N*-(*m*-nitrophenyl)-β-alanine
($C_{10}H_{12}N_2O_4$; *16034-75-6*)   see: Iocetamic acid

N-methyl-*N*-(*o*-nitrophenyl)anthranilic acid methyl ester
($C_{15}H_{14}N_2O_4$; *16813-63-1*)   see: Dibenzepine

N-methyl-2-(4-nitrophenyl)ethylamine
($C_9H_{12}N_2O_2$; *85176-37-0*)   see: Dofetilide

N-[4-[2-[methyl[2-(4-nitrophenyl)ethyl]amino]ethoxy]phenyl]methanesulfonamide
($C_{18}H_{23}N_3O_5S$; *115256-44-5*)   see: Dofetilide

1-methyl-5-nitro-3-phenyl-1*H*-indole-2-carbonitrile
($C_{16}H_{11}N_3O_2$; *30008-52-7*)   see: Nimetazepam

1-methyl-5-nitro-3-phenyl-1*H*-indole-2-carboxylic acid
($C_{16}H_{12}N_2O_4$; *30016-53-6*)   see: Nimetazepam

2-methyl-2-nitro-1-phenyl-1-propanol
($C_{10}H_{13}NO_3$; *33687-74-0*)   see: Phentermine

*N*⁴-methyl-*N*²-(*o*-nitrophenylsulfenyl)-D-asparagine
($C_{11}H_{13}N_3O_5S$; *63329-61-3*)   see: Aspoxicillin

[2*S*-(2α,5α,6β)]-*N*-methyl-*N*²-[(2-nitrophenyl)thio]-D-asparaginyl-*N*-(2-carboxy-3,3-dimethyl-7-oxo-4-thia-1-azabicyclo[3.2.0]hept-6-yl)-D-2-(4-hydroxyphenyl)glycinamide
($C_{27}H_{30}N_6O_9S_2$; *63329-62-4*)   see: Aspoxicillin

2-methyl-2-nitropropane-1,3-diol
($C_4H_9NO_4$; *77-49-6*)   see: Hexetidine

1-methyl-4-nitro-3-propyl-1*H*-pyrazole-5-carboxamide
($C_8H_{12}N_4O_3$; *139756-01-7*)   see: Sildenafil

1-methyl-4-nitro-1*H*-pyrrole-2-carbonyl chloride
($C_6H_5ClN_2O_3$; *28494-51-1*)   see: Stallimycin

3-(1-methyl-4-nitropyrrole-2-carboxamido)propionitrile
($C_9H_{10}N_4O_3$; *3185-95-3*)   see: Stallimycin

1-methyl-4-nitro-1*H*-pyrrole-2-carboxylic acid
($C_6H_6N_2O_4$; *13138-78-8*)   see: Stallimycin

methyl 4-nitrosalicylate
($C_8H_7NO_5$; *13684-28-1*)   see: Propoxycaine

2-methyl-1-nitrosoindoline
($C_9H_{10}N_2O$; *85440-79-5*)   see: Indapamide

O-methyl-*N*-nitrosourea
($C_2H_5N_3O_2$; *85503-10-2*)   see: Gusperimus trihydrochloride

17-methyl-19-norpregn-5(10)-ene-3,20-dione
($C_{21}H_{30}O_2$; *10110-91-5*)   see: Promegestone

(±)-4-methyl-1-octyn-4-ol
($C_9H_{16}O$; *22128-43-4*)   see: Misoprostol

2-methyl-1,4-oxathiane
($C_5H_{10}OS$; *7670-56-6*)   see: Nifurtimox

2-methyl-1,4-oxathiane 4,4-dioxide
($C_5H_{10}O_3S$; *26475-39-8*)   see: Nifurtimox

4-methyloxazole
(C_4H_5NO; *693-93-6*)   see: Pyridoxine

4-methyloxazole-5-carboxamide
($C_5H_6N_2O_2$; *4866-00-6*)   see: Pyridoxine

2-methyl-4-(oxiranylmethoxy)-1*H*-indole
($C_{12}H_{13}NO_2$; *62119-47-5*)   see: Bopindolol; Mepindolol

(2*S-trans*)-(2-methyl-4-oxo-3-azetidinyl)carbamic acid 1,1-dimethylethyl ester
($C_9H_{16}N_2O_3$; *80582-03-2*)   see: Aztreonam

2-methyl-4-oxo-3,1-benzoxazine
($C_9H_7NO_2$; *525-76-8*)   see: Imiquimod

methyl 5-oxo-4,5-bis(4-methoxyphenyl)-3-pentenoate
($C_{20}H_{20}O_5$; *139475-11-9*)   see: Mofezolac

2-methyl-3-oxo-2-butanol
($C_5H_{10}O_2$; *115-22-0*)   see: Phenaglycodol

5-methyl-10-oxo-10,11-dihydro-5*H*-dibenz[*b,f*]azepine
($C_{15}H_{13}NO$; *4904-83-0*)   see: Metapramine

2-methyl-6-oxo-2-heptene
($C_8H_{14}O$; *110-93-0*)   see: Heptaminol; Isometheptene

(3-methyl-2-oxo-5-heptynyl)phosphonic acid dimethyl ester
($C_{10}H_{17}O_4P$; *70073-58-4*)   see: Iloprost

4-methyl-1-(2-oxo-2-phenylethyl)piperazine
($C_{13}H_{18}N_2O$; *41298-85-5*)   see: Hexocyclium metilsulfate

(2*S-trans*)-[2-methyl-4-oxo-1-(phenylmethoxy)-3-azetidinyl]carbamic acid 1,1-dimethylethyl ester
($C_{16}H_{22}N_2O_4$; *75659-16-4*)   see: Aztreonam

[*S*-(*R**,*R**)]-α-[[1-methyl-2-oxo-2-(phenylmethoxy)ethyl]amino]-γ-oxobenzenebutanoic acid ethyl ester
($C_{22}H_{25}NO_5$; *87269-98-5*)   see: Ramipril

N-[2-methyl-1-oxo-2-[(phenylmethyl)thio]propyl]-*S*-(phenylmethyl)-L-cysteine
($C_{21}H_{25}NO_3S_2$; *65002-16-6*)   see: Bucillamine

6α-methyl-11-oxoprogesterone
($C_{22}H_{30}O_3$; *3642-85-1*)   see: Medrysone

[[2-methyl-1-(1-oxopropoxy)propoxy](4-phenylbutyl)phosphinyl]acetic acid
($C_{19}H_{29}O_6P$; *123599-78-0*)   see: Fosinopril

[*S*-(*R**,*S**)]-[[2-methyl-1-(1-oxopropoxy)propoxy](4-phenylbutyl)phosphinyl]acetic acid
($C_{19}H_{29}O_6P$; *128948-00-5*)   see: Fosinopril

[[2-methyl-1-(1-oxopropoxy)propoxy](4-phenylbutyl)phosphinyl]acetic acid phenylmethyl ester
($C_{26}H_{35}O_6P$; *123599-80-4*)   see: Fosinopril

(6*R-trans*)-3-methyl-8-oxo-7-[(trimethylsilyl)amino]-5-thia-1-azabicyclo[4.2.0]oct-2-ene-2-carboxylic acid trimethylsilyl ester
($C_{14}H_{26}N_2O_3SSi_2$; *31461-05-9*)   see: Cefalexin

methyl palmitate
($C_{17}H_{34}O_2$; *112-39-0*)   see: Retinol

2-methylpentane-2,4-diol
($C_6H_{14}O_2$; *107-41-5*)   see: Chloralodol

4-methyl-2-pentanone
($C_6H_{12}O$; *108-10-1*)   see: Ramatroban

3-(methylpentylamino)propionic acid
($C_9H_{19}NO_2$)   see: Ibandronate sodium monohydrate

(1-methyl-2-pentynyl)propanedioic acid diethyl ester
($C_{13}H_{20}O_4$; *78800-00-7*)   see: Methohexital

3-methylphenol
(C_7H_8O; *108-39-4*)   see: Bevantolol; Toliprolol

4-[(10-methylphenothiazin-2-yl)thioacetyl]morpholine
($C_{19}H_{20}N_2OS_2$; *13611-85-3*)   see: Metiazinic acid

α-methyl-3-phenoxybenzeneacetonitrile
($C_{15}H_{13}NO$; *32852-95-2*)   see: Fenoprofen

α-methyl-3-phenoxybenzenemethanol
($C_{14}H_{14}O_2$; *32852-93-0*)   see: Fenoprofen

2-[(1-methyl-2-phenoxyethyl)amino]-1-[4-(phenylmethoxy)phenyl]-1-propanone
($C_{25}H_{27}NO_3$; *1860-67-9*)   see: Isoxsuprine

N-methyl-N-(2-phenoxyethyl)-1-dodecanamine
($C_{21}H_{37}NO$)   see: Domiphen bromide

N-(1-methyl-2-phenoxyethyl)ethanolamine
($C_{11}H_{17}NO_2$; *103-39-9*)   see: Phenoxybenzamine

N-methyl-N-(2-phenoxyethyl)-2-thiophenemethanamine
($C_{14}H_{17}NOS$)   see: Thenium closilate

3-(3-methylphenoxy)propylene oxide
see under 2,3-epoxypropyl *m*-tolyl ether

methyl phenylacetate
($C_9H_{10}O_2$; *101-41-7*)   see: Felbamate

α-methyl-DL-phenylalanine hydrochloride
($C_{10}H_{14}ClNO_2$; *14603-95-3*)   see: Metirosine

3-(methylphenylamino)acrolein
($C_{10}H_{11}NO$; *14189-82-3*)   see: Fluvastatin sodium

α-methyl-α-phenylbicyclo[2.2.1]hept-5-ene-2-methanol
($C_{15}H_{18}O$; *70772-77-9*)   see: Ciclonium bromide

2-methyl-2-phenylbutanedioic acid
($C_{11}H_{12}O_4$; *34862-03-8*)   see: Mesuximide

3-methyl-2-phenyl-3-butanol
($C_{11}H_{16}O$; *3280-08-8*)   see: Pentorex

3-methyl-2-phenylbutyronitrile
($C_{11}H_{13}N$; *5558-29-2*)   see: Isoaminile

6-methyl-4-phenyl-3,4-dihydro-2H-1-benzopyran-2-one
($C_{16}H_{14}O_2$; *40546-94-9*)   see: Tolterodine

2-methyl-9-phenyl-2,3-dihydro-1H-indeno[2,1-c]pyridine
($C_{19}H_{17}N$)   see: Phenindamine

2,2'-(5-methyl-m-phenylene)bis (2-methylpropionitrile)
($C_{15}H_{18}N_2$; *120511-72-0*)   see: Anastrozole

N-methyl-o-phenylenediamine
($C_7H_{10}N_2$; *4760-34-3*)   see: Telmisartan

1-methyl-2-phenylethylamine
see under 2-amino-1-phenylpropane

1-[4-[2-[(1-methyl-2-phenylethyl)amino]ethoxy]phenyl]-1-propanone
($C_{20}H_{25}NO_2$)   see: Fenalcomine

3-[(1-methyl-2-phenylethyl)amino]-1-propanol
($C_{12}H_{19}NO$; *4720-38-1*)   see: Mefenorex

methyl phenylglyoxylate
($C_9H_8O_3$; *15206-55-0*)   see: Glycopyrronium bromide

1-methyl-4-phenyliminopiperidine
($C_{12}H_{16}N_2$; *36796-46-0*)   see: Bamipine; Thenalidine

2-methyl-3-phenyl-1H-indole-7-acetic acid ethyl ester
($C_{19}H_{19}NO_2$; *51135-34-3*)   see: Amfenac sodium

5-methyl-3-phenyl-4-isoxazolecarbonyl chloride
($C_{11}H_8ClNO_2$; *16883-16-2*)   see: Oxacillin

5-methyl-3-phenyl-4-isoxazolecarboxylic acid
($C_{11}H_9NO_3$; *1136-45-4*)   see: Oxacillin

2-methyl-5-phenylisoxazolidine
($C_{10}H_{13}NO$; *68408-65-1*)   see: Fluoxetine

2-(4-methylphenyl)-6-methylimidazo[1,2-a]pyridine-3-acetonitrile
($C_{17}H_{15}N_3$)   see: Zolpidem

N-[3-methyl-5-[(phenylmethyl)thio]-1,3,4-thiadiazol-2(3H)-ylidene]acetamide
($C_{12}H_{13}N_3OS_2$; *95046-30-3*)   see: Methazolamide

3-methyl-2-phenylpentanenitrile
($C_{12}H_{15}N$; *5558-32-7*)   see: Pentapiperide; Valethamate bromide

3-methyl-2-phenylpentanoic acid
($C_{12}H_{16}O_2$; *7782-37-8*)   see: Pentapiperide; Valethamate bromide

3-methyl-2-phenylpentanoyl chloride
($C_{12}H_{15}ClO$; *100388-64-5*)   see: Pentapiperide

1-methyl-3-phenylpiperazine
($C_{11}H_{16}N_2$; *5271-27-2*)   see: Mirtazapine

2-(4-methyl-2-phenyl-1-piperazinyl)benzenemethanol
($C_{18}H_{22}N_2O$; *57321-32-1*)   see: Mianserin

2-(4-methyl-2-phenyl-1-piperazinyl)-3-pyridinecarbonitrile
($C_{17}H_{18}N_4$; *61337-88-0*)   see: Mirtazapine

2-methyl-2-phenyl-1-propanol
($C_{10}H_{14}O$; *100-86-7*)   see: Fexofenadine hydrochloride

2-methyl-2-phenylpropionic acid
($C_{10}H_{12}O_2$; *826-55-1*)   see: Fexofenadine hydrochloride

1-methyl-3-phenylpropylamine
($C_{10}H_{15}N$; *22374-89-6*)   see: Buphenine

3-methyl-1-phenyl-5-Δ²-pyrazolone
($C_{10}H_{10}N_2O$; *89-25-8*)   see: Propyphenazone

3-methyl-1-phenyl-5-Δ³-pyrazolone
($C_{10}H_{10}N_2O$; *19735-89-8*)   see: Aminophenazone

methyl phenyl(2-pyridyl)acetate
($C_{14}H_{13}NO_2$; *26483-64-7*)   see: Methylphenidate

α-(4-methylphenyl)-α-[2-(1-pyrrolidinyl)ethyl]-2-pyridinemethanol
($C_{19}H_{24}N_2O$; *70708-28-0*)   see: Triprolidine

N-methyl-2-phenylsuccinamic acid
($C_{11}H_{13}NO_3$; *73294-89-0*)   see: Phensuximide

(2S-trans)-4-[[(4-methylphenyl)sulfonyl]oxy]-1,2-pyrrolidinedicarboxylic acid 1-(1,1-dimethylethyl) 2-(phenylmethyl) ester
($C_{24}H_{29}NO_7S$; *96314-27-1*)   see: Fosinopril

N-methyl-4-[[2-(phenylthio)ethylidene]hydrazino]benzenemethanesulfonamide
($C_{16}H_{19}N_3O_2S_2$; *103628-42-8*)   see: Sumatriptan

3-[(4-methylphenyl)thio]propanoic acid
($C_{10}H_{12}O_2S$; *13739-35-0*)   see: Meticrane

(–)-3-methyl-4-phenyl-1-tosyl-4-piperidinecarboxylic acid
($C_{20}H_{23}NO_4S$; *83863-68-7*)   see: Levocabastine

3-methyl-2-phenylvaleric acid
see under 3-methyl-2-phenylpentanoic acid

3-methyl-2-phenylvaleronitrile
see under 3-methyl-2-phenylpentanenitrile

N-methylpiperazine
($C_5H_{12}N_2$; *109-01-3*)   see: Azimilide hydrochloride; Chlorcyclizine; Clozapine; Cyclizine; Diethylcarbamazine; Fleroxacin; Hexocyclium metilsulfate; Levofloxacin; Loprazolam; Loxapine; Ofloxacin; Olanzapine; Pefloxacin; Perlapine; Pipebuzone; Pirenzepine; Prochlorperazine; Rufloxacin hydrochloride; Sildenafil; Tiotixene

2-methylpiperazine
($C_5H_{12}N_2$; *109-07-9*)   see: Grepafloxacin; Lomefloxacin

3-[4-(4-methyl-1-piperazinyl)butyl]-1-[(phenylmethylene)amino]-2,4-imidazolidinedione
($C_{19}H_{27}N_5O_2$)   see: Azimilide hydrochloride

9-[3-(4-methyl-1-piperazinyl)-1-oxopropyl]-N,N-dimethyl-9H-thioxanthene-2-sulfonamide
($C_{23}H_{29}N_3O_3S_2$)   see: Tiotixene

2-methylpiperidine
($C_6H_{13}N$; *109-05-7*)   see: Cyclomethycaine; Piperocaine

4-methylpiperidine
($C_6H_{13}N$; *626-58-4*)   see: Melperone

1-methyl-3-piperidinecarboxylic acid ethyl ester
($C_9H_{17}NO_2$; *5166-67-6*)   see: Tipepidine

3-(2-methylpiperidino)-1-propanol
($C_9H_{19}NO$; *94-88-2*)   see: Cyclomethycaine

3-(2-methylpiperidino)propyl chloride
($C_9H_{18}ClN$; *66773-94-2*)   see: Cyclomethycaine

2-(1-methyl-4-piperidinyl)acetaldehyde
($C_8H_{15}NO$; *10333-64-9*)   see: Naratriptan

2-(methyl-4-piperidinylamino)-4(3H)-pyrimidinone
($C_{10}H_{16}N_4O$; *108612-74-4*)   see: Mizolastine

1-methyl-4-[10-(1-piperidinyl)-4H-benzo[4,5]cyclohepta-[1,2-b]thien-4-ylidene]piperidine
($C_{24}H_{28}N_2S$; *59743-86-1*)   see: Ketotifen

1-methyl-4-[9-(1-piperidinyl)-4H-benzo[4,5]cyclohepta-[1,2-b]thien-4-ylidene]piperidine
($C_{24}H_{28}N_2S$; *59743-85-0*)   see: Ketotifen

5-(1-methyl-4-piperidinyl)-5H-dibenzo[a,d]cyclohepten-5-ol
($C_{21}H_{23}NO$; *3967-32-6*)   see: Cyproheptadine

1-methylpiperidin-4-ylmagnesium chloride
($C_6H_{12}ClMgN$; *63463-36-5*)   see: Azatadine; Cyproheptadine; Ketotifen; Loratadine; Pizotifen

3-methyl-1-[2-(1-piperidinyl)phenyl]-1-butanimine
($C_{16}H_{24}N_2$; *147769-96-8*)   see: Repaglinide

3-methyl-1-[2-(1-piperidinyl)phenyl]-1-butanone
($C_{16}H_{23}NO$; *147770-03-4*)   see: Repaglinide

N-[(1E)-3-methyl-1-[2-(1-piperidinyl)phenyl]-1-butenyl]-acetamide
($C_{18}H_{26}N_2O$; *147769-95-7*)   see: Repaglinide

N-[(1Z)-3-methyl-1-[2-(1-piperidinyl)phenyl]-1-butenyl]-acetamide
($C_{18}H_{26}N_2O$; *147769-97-9*)   see: Repaglinide

(S)-3-methyl-1-[2-(1-piperidinyl)phenyl]butylamine
($C_{16}H_{26}N_2$; *147769-93-5*)   see: Repaglinide

(±)-3-methyl-1-[2-(1-piperidinyl)phenyl]butylamine
($C_{16}H_{26}N_2$; *108157-52-4*)   see: Repaglinide

(1-methyl-4-piperidinyl)[3-(2-phenylethyl)-2-pyridinyl]-methanone
($C_{20}H_{24}N_2O$; *38093-13-9*)   see: Azatadine

(αR)-α-methyl-N-[[2-(1-piperidinyl)phenyl]methylene]-benzenemethanamine
($C_{20}H_{24}N_2$; *147770-05-6*)   see: Repaglinide

1-methyl-4-piperidone
($C_6H_{11}NO$; *1445-73-4*)   see: Bamipine; Mebhydrolin; Naratriptan; Piperylone; Thenalidine

1-methyl-4-piperidylmagnesium chloride
see under 1-methylpiperidin-4-ylmagnesium chloride

(1-methyl-2-piperidylmethyl) benzilate
($C_{21}H_{25}NO_3$; *94909-90-7*)   see: Bevonium metilsulfate

16β-methylprednisolone
($C_{22}H_{30}O_5$; *2597-76-4*)   see: Betamethasone

16α-methylprednisolone 21-acetate
($C_{24}H_{32}O_6$; *13209-52-4*)   see: Alclometasone dipropionate

16β-methylprednisolone 21-acetate
($C_{24}H_{32}O_6$; *18769-24-9*)   see: Betamethasone; Betamethasone acetate

16α-methyl-1,4,9(11)-pregnatriene-17α,21-diol-3,20-dione 21-acetate
($C_{24}H_{30}O_5$; *10106-41-9*)   see: Mometasone furoate

16α-methylpregnenolone 3β-acetate
($C_{24}H_{36}O_3$; *1863-41-8*)   see: Flumetasone; Fluocortolone; Paramethasone

2-methylpropanethioamide
(C_4H_9NS; *13515-65-6*)   see: Ritonavir

2-methyl-2-propanethiol
($C_4H_{10}S$; *75-66-1*)   see: Raloxifene hydrochloride

2-methylpropanoic acid anhydride
($C_8H_{14}O_3$; *97-72-3*)   see: Ibudilast

2-methyl-2-propenal
(C_4H_6O; *78-85-3*)   see: Fomepizole

2-methyl-2-propenyl acetate
($C_6H_{10}O_2$; *820-71-3*)   see: Fexofenadine hydrochloride

6-(2-methyl-2-propenyl)imidazo[1,2-a]pyridine
($C_{11}H_{12}N_2$; *116355-20-5*)   see: Olprinone hydrochloride

(+)-(R)-β-methylpropiolactone
($C_4H_6O_2$; *32082-74-9*)   see: Dorzolamide

methyl propionate
($C_4H_8O_2$; *554-12-1*)   see: Pyrimethamine

3'-methyl-4'-propionyloxy-propiophenone
($C_{13}H_{16}O_3$; *137937-51-0*)   see: Methestrol dipropionate

4'-methylpropiophenone
($C_{10}H_{12}O$; *5337-93-9*)   see: Tolperisone

2-[(2-methylpropyl)amino]ethanol 4-nitrobenzoate (ester)
($C_{13}H_{18}N_2O_4$)   see: Butethamine

α-(1-methylpropyl)benzeneacetic acid 2-(diethylamino)-ethyl ester
($C_{18}H_{29}NO_2$; *26878-41-1*)   see: Valethamate bromide

7-methyl-2-propyl-1H-benzimidazole-5-carboxylic acid
($C_{12}H_{14}N_2O_2$; *152628-03-0*)   see: Telmisartan

1-(2-methylpropyl)-N,N-bis(phenylmethyl)-1H-imidazo-[4,5-c]quinolin-4-amine
($C_{28}H_{28}N_4$; *157875-56-4*)   see: Imiquimod

N⁴-(2-methylpropyl)-N²,N²-bis(phenylmethyl)-2,3,4-quino-linetriamine
($C_{27}H_{30}N_4$)   see: Imiquimod

5-methyl-5-propyl-1,3-dioxan-2-one
($C_8H_{14}O_3$; *7148-50-7*)   see: Tybamate

1-(2-methylpropyl)-1H-imidazo[4,5-c]quinoline 5-oxide
($C_{14}H_{15}N_3O$; *99010-63-6*)   see: Imiquimod

N-[1-(2-methylpropyl)-1H-imidazo[4,5-c]quinolin-4-yl]-benzamide
($C_{21}H_{20}N_4O$; *144660-62-8*)   see: Imiquimod

6-(2-methylpropyl)-6H-imidazo[4,5-c]tetrazolo[1,5-a]qui-noline
($C_{14}H_{14}N_6$; *201030-97-9*)   see: Imiquimod

(2-methylpropyl)magnesium bromide
(C_4H_9BrMg; *926-62-5*)   see: Repaglinide; Sibutramine hydrochloride

2-methylpropylmagnesium bromide
see under (2-methylpropyl)magnesium bromide

methyl 2-propyl-4-methylbenzimidazole-6-carboxylate
($C_{13}H_{16}N_2O_2$; *152628-00-7*)   see: Telmisartan

N-(2-methylpropyl)-4-nitrobenzenesulfonamide
($C_{10}H_{14}N_2O_4S$; *89840-80-2*)   see: Amprenavir

17α-methyltestosterone 4,5-epoxide
($C_{20}H_{30}O_3$; *51154-09-7*) see: Oxymesterone

N^1-methyl-N^2-tetrahydrofuroyltrimethylenediamine
($C_9H_{18}N_2O_2$; *81403-67-0*) see: Alfuzosin

2-methyl-5,6,7,8-tetrahydroisoquinolinium bromide
($C_{10}H_{14}BrN$) see: Dimemorfan

methyl 7-[3(RS)-tetrahydropyran-2-yloxy-5-oxocyclopent-1-en-1-yl]heptanoate
($C_{18}H_{28}O_5$; *40098-24-6*) see: Misoprostol

1-methyl-1H-tetrazole-5-thiol
($C_2H_4N_4S$; *13183-79-4*) see: Cefbuperazone; Cefmenoxime; Cefoperazone; Cefotetan

1-methyl-1H-tetrazole-5-thiol sodium salt
($C_2H_3N_4NaS$; *51138-06-8*) see: Cefamandole; Latamoxef

2-(5-methyl-1H-tetrazol-1-yl)benzoic acid
($C_9H_8N_4O_2$; *72470-51-0*) see: Imiquimod

N-methyl-2-thenylamine
(C_6H_9NS; *58255-18-8*) see: Thenium closilate

N-(5-methyl-1,3,4-thiadiazol-2-yl)-4-nitrobenzenesulfon-amide
($C_9H_8N_4O_4S_2$) see: Sulfamethizole

4-methylthiazole-5-carboxaldehyde
(C_5H_5NOS; *82294-70-0*) see: Cefditoren pivoxil

[6R-[3(Z),6α,7β]]-3-[2-(4-methyl-5-thiazolyl)ethenyl]-8-oxo-7-[(phenylacetyl)amino]-5-thia-1-azabicyclo[4.2.0]oct-2-ene-2-carboxylic acid (4-methoxyphenyl)methyl ester
($C_{29}H_{27}N_3O_5S_2$; *138514-31-5*) see: Cefditoren pivoxil

methyl[4-(2-thienylcarbonyl)phenyl]propanedioic acid diethyl ester
($C_{19}H_{20}O_5S$; *52779-57-4*) see: Suprofen

methyl 3-(2-thienyl)propionate
($C_8H_{10}O_2S$; *16862-05-8*) see: Eprosartan

4'-methylthioacetophenone
($C_9H_{10}OS$; *1778-09-2*) see: Rofecoxib

6α-methylthio-6β-aminopenicillanic acid benzyl ester
($C_{16}H_{20}N_2O_3S_2$; *40514-98-5*) see: Temocillin

3-methylthioaniline
(C_7H_9NS; *1783-81-9*) see: Thioridazine

4-(methylthio)benzaldehyde
(C_8H_8OS; *3446-89-7*) see: Sulindac

4-(methylthio)benzoyl chloride
(C_8H_7ClOS; *1442-06-4*) see: Enoximone

6-methylthiochroman
($C_{10}H_{12}S$; *71153-74-7*) see: Meticrane

6-methylthiochroman 1,1-dioxide
($C_{10}H_{12}O_2S$; *1077 61 8*) see: Meticrane

6-methyl-thiochroman-4-one
($C_{10}H_{10}OS$; *6948-34-1*) see: Meticrane

3-methylthiodiphenylamine
($C_{13}H_{13}NS$; *13313-45-6*) see: Thioridazine

2-methylthio-1,3-dithiolium iodide
($C_4H_5IS_3$; *53059-74-8*) see: Malotilate

(3-methylthio-2-hydroxypropyl)hydrazine
($C_4H_{12}N_2OS$; *14359-97-8*) see: Nifuratel

6α-methylthio-6β-isocyanopenicillanic acid benzyl ester
($C_{17}H_{18}N_2O_3S_2$; *53628-34-5*) see: Temocillin

1-(methylthio)-2-nitro-N-methylethylenamine
($C_4H_8N_2O_2S$; *61832-41-5*) see: Nizatidine; Ranitidine

α-methyl-2-thiopheneacetic acid
($C_7H_8O_2S$; *54955-39-4*) see: Tiaprofenic acid

methyl 2-thiophenepropanoate
see under methyl 3-(2-thienyl)propionate

4-methylthiophenol
(C_7H_8S; *106-45-6*) see: Meticrane

2-methylthiophenothiazine
($C_{13}H_{11}NS_2$; *7643-08-5*) see: Mesoridazine; Thioridazine

N-(3-methylthiophenyl)anthranilic acid
($C_{14}H_{13}NO_2S$; *18902-93-7*) see: Thioridazine

[4-(methylthio)phenyl]boronic acid
($C_7H_9BO_2S$; *98546-51-1*) see: Rofecoxib

4-[4-(methylthio)phenyl]-2(5H)-furanone
($C_{11}H_{10}O_2S$; *162012-28-4*) see: Rofecoxib

4-[4-(methylthio)phenyl]-3-phenyl-2(5H)-furanone
($C_{17}H_{14}O_2S$; *162012-30-8*) see: Rofecoxib

3-(methylthio)propionyl chloride
(C_4H_7ClOS; *7031-23-4*) see: Suplatast tosilate

[[[2-(methylthio)-4-pyrimidinyl]amino]methylene]pro-panedioic acid diethyl ester
($C_{13}H_{17}N_3O_4S$; *37917-93-4*) see: Pipemidic acid

2-(methylthio)pyrrole
(C_5H_7NS; *53391-61-0*) see: Ketorolac

2-S-methylthiouracil
($C_5H_6N_2OS$; *5751-20-2*) see: Mizolastine

methylthiourea
($C_2H_6N_2S$; *598-52-7*) see: Noxytiolin

S-methylthiouronium chloride
($C_2H_7ClN_2S$; *53114-57-1*) see: Benexate

S-methylthiouronium sulfate
($C_2H_8N_2O_4S_2$; *2260-00-6*) see: Fluorouracil; Guanadrel; Guanethidine sulfate; Guanoclor; Guanoxan; Mebendazole

methyl 4-toluenesulfonate
($C_8H_{10}O_3S$; *80-48-8*) see: Acriflavinium chloride; Binedaline; Suplatast tosilate

2-methyl-3-(p-toluenesulfonyloxy)propyl chloride
($C_{11}H_{15}ClO_3S$; *123094-45-1*) see: Perimetazine

N-methyl-3-toluidine
($C_8H_{11}N$; *696-44-6*) see: Tolnaftate

methyl 1-(2,3,5-tri-O-acetyl-β-D-ribofuranosyl)-1,2,4-tri-azole-3-carboxylate
($C_{15}H_{19}N_3O_9$; *39925-10-5*) see: Ribavirin

methyl 1,2,4-triazole-3-carboxylate
($C_4H_5N_3O_2$; *4928-88-5*) see: Ribavirin

methyl 2,3,6-trideoxy-3-amino-α-L-lyxo-hexopyranoside
($C_7H_{15}NO_3$; *18977-92-9*) see: Epirubicin

methyl 2,3,6-trideoxy-3-[(trifluoroacetyl)amino]-α-L-arabino-hexopyranoside
($C_9H_{14}F_3NO_4$; *56390-11-5*) see: Epirubicin

methyl 2,3,6-trideoxy-3-[(trifluoroacetyl)amino]-α-L-lyxo-hexopyranoside
($C_9H_{14}F_3NO_4$; *56390-10-4*) see: Epirubicin

methyl 2,3,6-trideoxy-3-[(trifluoroacetyl)amino]-α-L-threo-hexopyranosid-4-ulose
($C_9H_{12}F_3NO_4$; *56354-07-5*) see: Epirubicin

(±)-(E)-4-methyl-4-triethylsilyloxy-1-octenyl iodide
($C_{15}H_{31}IOSi$; *58682-78-3*) see: Misoprostol

(E)-[4-methyl-4-[(triethylsilyl)oxy]-1-octenyl]-1-pentynyl-cuprate(1-) lithium
($C_{20}H_{38}CuLiOSi$) see: Misoprostol

2-methyl-3,4,6-trifluorobenzoic acid
($C_8H_5F_3O_2$; *119916-22-2*) see: Grepafloxacin

morpholine

(C$_4$H$_9$NO; *110-91-8*)   see: Bufexamac; Citicoline;
Doxapram; Emorfazone; Fenclofenac; Folescutol;
Fomocaine; Metiazinic acid; Molindone; Moracizine;
Morinamide; Moroxydine; Naproxen; Protizinic acid;
Rocuronium bromide; Sulmetozin; Tiemonium iodide;
Timolol; Trimetozine

2-morpholinoethanol

(C$_6$H$_{13}$NO$_2$; *622-40-2*)   see: Mycophenolate mofetil

2-morpholinoethyl chloride

(C$_6$H$_{12}$ClNO; *3240-94-6*)   see: Floredil; Morclofone;
Nimorazole; Pholcodine

3-morpholinopropionitrile

(C$_7$H$_{12}$N$_2$O; *4542-47-6*)   see: Brodimoprim

3-morpholinopropyl chloride

(C$_7$H$_{14}$ClNO; *7357-67-7*)   see: Pramocaine

(4-morpholinylamino)acetonitrile

(C$_6$H$_{11}$N$_3$O; *16142-26-0*)   see: Molsidomine

(4-morpholinylnitrosoamino)acetonitrile

(C$_6$H$_{10}$N$_4$O$_2$; *26687-79-6*)   see: Molsidomine

mucochloric acid

(C$_4$H$_2$Cl$_2$O$_3$; *87-56-9*)   see: Amezinium metilsulfate

mycophenolic acid chloride

(C$_{17}$H$_{19}$ClO$_5$; *111512-13-1*)   see: Mycophenolate mofetil

N

naltrexone

(C$_{20}$H$_{23}$NO$_4$; *16590-41-3*)   see: Nalmefene

nandrolone

(C$_{18}$H$_{26}$O$_2$; *434-22-0*)   see: Allylestrenol; Ethylestrenol;
Lynestrenol; Methylestrenolone; Nandrolone decanoate;
Nandrolone hexyloxyphenylpropionate; Nandrolone
phenylpropionate; Nandrolone undecylate

naphthalene

(C$_{10}$H$_8$; *91-20-3*)   see: Perflunafene

1-naphthalenecarboxaldehyde

(C$_{11}$H$_8$O; *66-77-3*)   see: Butenafine

1-naphthalenecarboxylic acid

(C$_{11}$H$_8$O$_2$; *86-55-5*)   see: Butenafine

1,6-naphthalenediol

(C$_{10}$H$_8$O$_2$; *575-44-0*)   see: Quinagolide hydrochloride

1-naphthaleneethanimidic acid ethyl ester hydrochloride

(C$_{14}$H$_{16}$ClNO; *43002-67-1*)   see: Naphazoline

1-naphthol

(C$_{10}$H$_8$O; *90-15-3*)   see: Nadoxolol; Naftopidil; Propranolol

2-naphthol

(C$_{10}$H$_8$O; *135-19-3*)   see: Naproxen; Tolnaftate

3-(1-naphthoxy)propylene oxide

see under 2,3-epoxy-1-(1-naphthyloxy)propane

(1-naphthyl)acetonitrile

(C$_{12}$H$_9$N; *132-75-2*)   see: Naphazoline

2-naphthyl-D-alanine

(C$_{13}$H$_{13}$NO$_2$; *76985-09-6*)   see: Cetrorelix

(1-naphthylmethyl)methylamine

see under N-methyl-1-naphthylmethylamine

1-(1-naphthyloxy)-2,3-epoxypropane

see under 2,3-epoxy-1-(1-naphthyloxy)propane

2-naphthylsulfonyl chloride

(C$_{10}$H$_7$ClO$_2$S; *93-11-8*)   see: Orlistat

3-(1-naphthyl)-2-(tetrahydrofurfuryl)propanoic acid

(C$_{18}$H$_{20}$O$_3$; *25379-26-4*)   see: Naftidrofuryl

naproxen

(C$_{14}$H$_{14}$O$_3$; *22204-53-1*)   see: Piproxen

(+)-neoisoisopulegol

(C$_{10}$H$_{18}$O; *144541-38-8*)   see: (–)-Menthol

(+)-neoisopulegol

(C$_{10}$H$_{18}$O; *20549-46-6*)   see: (–)-Menthol

(±)-neomenthol

(C$_{10}$H$_{20}$O; *3623-51-6*)   see: (–)-Menthol

nicethamide

(C$_{10}$H$_{14}$N$_2$O; *59-26-7*)   see: Camphotamide

nicotinic acid

(C$_6$H$_5$NO$_2$; *59-67-6*)   see: Aluminum nicotinate; Inositol
nicotinate; Micinicate; Nicorandil; Nicotinamide; Nicotinic
acid benzyl ester; Nikethamide; Xantinol nicotinate

nicotinonitrile

(C$_6$H$_4$N$_2$; *100-54-9*)   see: Nicotinamide; Nicotinyl alcohol

nicotinoyl chloride

(C$_6$H$_4$ClNO; *10400-19-8*)   see: Etofibrate; Hepronicate;
Inositol nicotinate; Micinicate; Niaprazine; Niceritrol;
Nicoclonate; Nicotafuryl; Nifenazone; Ronifibrate

nicotinoyl chloride hydrochloride

(C$_6$H$_5$Cl$_2$NO; *20260-53-1*)   see: Nicofuranose

nitric acid

(HNO$_3$; *7697-37-2*)   see: Gallium nitrate

4'-nitroacetophenone

(C$_8$H$_7$NO$_3$; *100-19-6*)   see: Chloramphenicol; Clenbuterol

3-nitro-5-acetyl-10,11-dihydro-5H-dibenz[b,f]azepine

(C$_{16}$H$_{14}$N$_2$O$_3$; *79752-03-7*)   see: Tiracizine

p-nitroaniline

(C$_6$H$_6$N$_2$O$_2$; *100-01-6*)   see: Dantrolene; Nimetazepam;
Vesnarinone

2-nitroaniline

(C$_6$H$_6$N$_2$O$_2$; *88-74-4*)   see: Astemizole

3-nitroaniline

(C$_6$H$_6$N$_2$O$_2$; *99-09-2*)   see: Iocetamic acid

4-nitroaniline

see under p-nitroaniline

2-(2-nitroanilino)-5-methylthiophene-3-carbonitrile

(C$_{12}$H$_9$N$_3$O$_2$S; *138564-59-7*)   see: Olanzapine

4-(2-nitroanilino)piperidine

(C$_{11}$H$_{15}$N$_3$O$_2$; *57718-44-2*)   see: Timiperone

5-nitroanthranilic acid

(C$_7$H$_6$N$_2$O$_4$; *616-79-5*)   see: Afloqualone

nitro-L-arginine methyl ester hydrochloride

(C$_7$H$_{16}$ClN$_5$O$_4$; *51298-62-5*)   see: Angiotensinamide

4-nitrobenzalacetone

(C$_{10}$H$_9$NO$_3$; *3490-37-7*)   see: Acenocoumarol

2-nitrobenzaldehyde

(C$_7$H$_5$NO$_3$; *552-89-6*)   see: Aranidipine; Nifedipine;
Nisoldipine

3-nitrobenzaldehyde

(C$_7$H$_5$NO$_3$; *99-61-6*)   see: Barnidipine; Benidipine;
Efonidipine hydrochloride ethanol; Iopanoic acid;
Lercanidipine hydrochloride; Manidipine; Nicardipine;
Nilvadipine; Nimodipine; Nitrendipine; Rosoxacin

nitrobenzene

(C$_6$H$_5$NO$_2$; *98-95-3*)   see: Oxyquinoline

5-nitroorotic acid
($C_5H_3N_3O_6$; *17687-24-0*)   see: Dipyridamole

5-nitro-1-pentanamine
($C_5H_{12}N_2O_2$)   see: Deferoxamine

(5-nitropentyl)carbamic acid benzyl ester
($C_{13}H_{18}N_2O_4$; *92034-20-3*)   see: Deferoxamine

4-nitrophenethylamine hydrochloride
($C_8H_{11}ClN_2O_2$; *29968-78-3*)   see: Dofetilide

4-nitrophenetole
($C_8H_9NO_3$; *100-29-8*)   see: Phenacetin

4-nitrophenol
($C_6H_5NO_3$; *100-02-7*)   see: Paracetamol; Phenacetin; Talinolol; Troglitazone

N-[(4-nitrophenoxy)carbonyl]-L-valine methyl ester
($C_{13}H_{16}N_2O_6$; *162537-10-2*)   see: Ritonavir

(±)-1-(4-nitrophenoxy)-2-hydroxy-3-(*tert*-butylamino)-propane
($C_{13}H_{20}N_2O_4$; *133228-95-2*)   see: Talinolol

4-(*p*-nitrophenoxy)-3-methyl-2-buten-1-ol
($C_{11}H_{13}NO_4$; *171180-10-2*)   see: Troglitazone

4-(*p*-nitrophenoxy)-3-methyl-2-butenyl acetate
($C_{13}H_{15}NO_5$; *171180-09-9*)   see: Troglitazone

2-[4-(*p*-nitrophenoxy)-3-methyl-2-butenyl]-3,5,6-trimethylhydroquinone
($C_{20}H_{23}NO_5$; *171180-12-4*)   see: Troglitazone

1-(4-nitrophenoxy)-5-(4-nitrophenyl)-3-methyl-3-azapentane
($C_{17}H_{19}N_3O_5$; *115287-37-1*)   see: Dofetilide

1-(4-nitrophenoxy)-2-propanone
($C_9H_9NO_4$; *6698-72-2*)   see: Troglitazone

3-nitro-4-phenoxy-5-sulfamoylbenzoic acid
($C_{13}H_{10}N_2O_7S$; *28328-53-2*)   see: Bumetanide; Piretanide

4-nitro-L-phenylalanine
($C_9H_{10}N_2O_4$; *949-99-5*)   see: Melphalan; Zolmitriptan

4-nitro-L-phenylalanine ethyl ester monohydrochloride
($C_{11}H_{15}ClN_2O_4$; *58816-66-3*)   see: Melphalan

3-[(2-nitrophenyl)amino]-1-propanol
($C_9H_{12}N_2O_3$; *56636-93-2*)   see: Domperidone

4-[[[(2-nitrophenyl)amino]thioxomethyl]amino]-1-piperidinecarboxylic acid ethyl ester
($C_{15}H_{20}N_4O_4S$)   see: Astemizole

5-nitro-6-phenylbicyclo[2.2.1]hept-2-ene
($C_{13}H_{13}NO_2$; *92028-79-0*)   see: Fencamfamin

2-(4-nitrophenyl)butyronitrile
($C_{10}H_{10}N_2O_2$; *94814-82-1*)   see: Aminoglutethimide

4-nitrophenyl chloroformate
($C_7H_4ClNO_4$; *7693-46-1*)   see: Ritonavir

2-(4-nitrophenyl)ethyl bromide
($C_8H_8BrNO_2$; *5339-26-4*)   see: Anileridine

2-(4-nitrophenyl)-2-ethylglutarimide
($C_{13}H_{14}N_2O_4$; *38527-73-0*)   see: Aminoglutethimide

5-(4-nitrophenyl)-2-furancarboxaldehyde
($C_{11}H_7NO_4$; *7147-77-5*)   see: Dantrolene

5-nitro-3-phenyl-1*H*-indole-2-carboxylic acid
($C_{15}H_{10}N_2O_4$; *14182-37-7*)   see: Nimetazepam

2-(3-nitrophenylmethlene)butyric acid
see under α-ethyl-3-nitrocinnamic acid

4,4'-[(3-nitrophenyl)methylene]bismorpholine
($C_{15}H_{21}N_3O_4$; *40891-03-0*)   see: Efonidipine hydrochloride ethanol

2-[(3-nitrophenyl)methylene]-3-oxobutanoic acid 2-[(3,3-diphenylpropyl)methylamino]-1,1-dimethylethyl ester
($C_{31}H_{34}N_2O_5$; *210579-45-6*)   see: Lercanidipine hydrochloride

2-[(2-nitrophenyl)methylene]-3-oxobutanoic acid methyl ester
($C_{12}H_{11}NO_5$; *39562-27-1*)   see: Aranidipine

4-nitrophenyl-N-methylmethanesulfonamide
($C_8H_{10}N_2O_4S$; *85952-29-0*)   see: Sumatriptan

4-(3-nitrophenyl)pyridine
($C_{11}H_8N_2O_2$; *4282-48-8*)   see: Rosoxacin

o-nitrophenylsulfenyl chloride
($C_6H_4ClNO_2S$; *7669-54-7*)   see: Aspoxicillin

5-(3-nitrophenyl)tetrazole
($C_7H_5N_5O_2$; *21871-44-3*)   see: Tazanolast

N-[(2-nitrophenyl)thio]-D-aspartic acid 4-methyl ester
($C_{11}H_{12}N_2O_6S$; *63341-33-3*)   see: Aspoxicillin

3-nitrophthalic acid
($C_8H_5NO_6$; *603-11-2*)   see: Candesartan cilexetil

1-nitropropane
($C_3H_7NO_2$; *108-03-2*)   see: Ethambutol; Moxaverine

2-nitropropane
($C_3H_7NO_2$; *79-46-9*)   see: Phentermine

3-nitro-4-propoxybenzoic acid
($C_{10}H_{11}NO_5$; *35288-44-9*)   see: Proxymetacaine

4-nitro-2-propoxybenzoic acid
($C_{10}H_{11}NO_5$; *103204-41-7*)   see: Propoxycaine

3-nitro-4-propoxybenzoic acid 2-(diethylamino)ethyl ester
($C_{16}H_{24}N_2O_5$)   see: Proxymetacaine

4-nitro-2-propoxybenzoic acid 2-(diethylamino)ethyl ester
($C_{16}H_{24}N_2O_5$)   see: Propoxycaine

1-(3-nitro-2-pyridyl)piperazine
($C_9H_{12}N_4O_2$; *87394-48-7*)   see: Delavirdine mesilate

3-nitro-5-(4-pyridyl)-2(1*H*)-pyridinone
($C_{10}H_7N_3O_3$; *62749-33-1*)   see: Amrinone

5-nitrosalicylic acid
($C_7H_5NO_5$; *96-97-9*)   see: Mesalazine

4-nitrosothymol
($C_{10}H_{13}NO_2$; *2364-54-7*)   see: Moxisylyte

5-nitroso-2,4,6-triaminopyrimidine
($C_4H_6N_6O$; *1006-23-1*)   see: Triamterene

β-nitrostyrene
($C_8H_7NO_2$; *102-96-5*)   see: Fencamfamin

4-nitrostyrene oxide
($C_8H_7NO_3$; *6388-74-5*)   see: Nifenalol

nitrosyl chloride ((NO)Cl)
(ClNO; *2696-92-6*)   see: Aldosterone

4-nitrotetrazolo[1,5-*a*]quinolin-5-yl trifluoroacetate
($C_{11}H_4F_3N_5O_4$)   see: Imiquimod

8-nitro-2-(tetrazol-5-yl)-1-benzopyran-4-one
($C_{10}H_5N_5O_4$; *141283-42-3*)   see: Pranlukast

S-[2-nitro-1-(2-thienyl)ethyl]-N-*tert*-butoxycarbonyl-L-cysteine
($C_{14}H_{20}N_2O_6S_2$; *102090-86-8*)   see: Temocapril

5-nitro-2-thiophenecarbohydrazide
($C_5H_5N_3O_3S$; *39978-44-4*)   see: Nifurzide

2-nitrothiophenol
($C_6H_5NO_2S$; *4875-10-9*)   see: Diltiazem

olivetol
($C_{11}H_{16}O_2$; *500-66-3*)   see: Dronabinol

orthoacetic acid triethyl ester
($C_8H_{18}O_3$; *78-39-7*)   see: Acetyldigitoxin; Alprazolam;
Brotizolam; Diazoxide

orthoformic acid triethyl ester
see under ethyl orthoformate

oxalic acid
($C_2H_2O_4$; *144-62-7*)   see: Gestodene; Gestrinone;
Oxaliplatin; Pyridoxine

oxalic acid diethyl ester
see under diethyl oxalate

oxalic acid monochloride butyl ester
($C_6H_9ClO_3$; *20963-23-9*)   see: Tazanolast

oxalyl chloride
($C_2Cl_2O_2$; *79-37-8*)   see: Cefuroxime; Diclofenac;
Dorzolamide; Fexofenadine hydrochloride; Granisetron;
Gusperimus trihydrochloride; Indoramin; Maprotiline;
Micinicate; Ritonavir; Saquinavir; Sumatriptan; Tacrolimus;
Tirofiban hydrochloride; Tropisetron; Viminol

8-oxaspiro[4.5]decane-7,9-dione
($C_9H_{12}O_3$; *5662-95-3*)   see: Buspirone

1-[2-(oxiranylmethoxy)phenyl]-3-phenyl-1-propanone
($C_{18}H_{18}O_3$; *22525-95-7*)   see: Propafenone

4-[4-(oxiranylmethoxy)-1,2,5-thiadiazol-3-yl]morpholine
($C_9H_{13}N_3O_3S$; *58827-68-2*)   see: Timolol

***O*-(2-oxiranylmethyl)-2-acetyl-4-butyramidophenol**
($C_{15}H_{19}NO_4$; *28197-66-2*)   see: Acebutolol

3-oxo-4-androstene-17β-carboxylic acid
($C_{20}H_{28}O_3$; *302-97-6*)   see: Finasteride

3-oxo-4-aza-5α-androstane-17β-carboxylic acid
($C_{19}H_{29}NO_3$; *103335-55-3*)   see: Finasteride

**3-oxo-1,2-benzisothiazole-2(3*H*)-acetic acid ethyl ester
1,1-dioxide**
($C_{11}H_{11}NO_5S$; *24683-20-3*)   see: Piroxicam

5-oxo-5*H*-[1]-benzopyrano[2,3-*b*]pyridine
($C_{12}H_7NO_2$; *6537-46-8*)   see: Pranoprofen

3-oxobutanoic acid 2-methoxyethyl ester
($C_7H_{12}O_4$; *22502-03-0*)   see: Nimodipine

3-oxo-1,4,6-cholestatriene
($C_{27}H_{40}O$; *3464-60-6*)   see: Alfacalcidol

3-oxo-1,5,7-cholestatriene
($C_{27}H_{40}O$; *54604-58-9*)   see: Alfacalcidol

4-oxo-4-(4-cyclohexylphenyl)butyric acid
($C_{16}H_{20}O_3$; *35288-13-2*)   see: Bucloxic acid

9-oxodecanoic acid
($C_{10}H_{18}O_3$; *1422-26-0*)   see: Misoprostol

**4-oxo-9,10-dihydro-4*H*-benzo[4,5]cyclohepta[1,2-*b*]thio-
phene**
($C_{13}H_{10}OS$; *1622-55-5*)   see: Ketotifen; Pizotifen

6-oxo-6,12-dihydrobenzofuro[3,2-*c*][1]benzoxepin
($C_{16}H_{10}O_3$; *28763-77-1*)   see: Oxetorone

6-oxo-5,6-dihydro-11*H*-dibenz[*b,e*]azepine
($C_{14}H_{11}NO$; *1211-06-9*)   see: Perlapine

5-oxo-10,11-dihydro-5*H*-dibenzo[*a,d*]cycloheptene
see under dibenzosuberone

11-oxo-6,11-dihydrodibenzo[*b,e*]thiepin
($C_{14}H_{10}OS$; *1531-77-7*)   see: Dosulepin

11-oxo-6,11-dihydrodibenz[*b,e*]oxepin
($C_{14}H_{10}O_2$; *4504-87-4*)   see: Doxepin

3-(2-oxo-1,2-dihydroquinolin-4-yl)alanine
($C_{12}H_{12}N_2O_3$; *5162-90-3*)   see: Rebamipide

**6-oxo-6-[2-(3,4-dimethoxyphenyl)ethylamino]hexanoic
acid**
($C_{16}H_{23}NO_5$; *7574-86-9*)   see: Dopexamine

(2*S*)-3-oxo-1,4-dioxaspiro[4.5]decane-2-acetic acid
($C_{10}H_{14}O_5$; *153011-57-5*)   see: Orlistat

3-oxo-2,7-dioxa-5-thiabicyclo[2.2.1]heptane
($C_4H_4O_3S$; *161683-18-7*)   see: Lamivudine

17-oxo-4-estrene
($C_{18}H_{26}O$; *3646-28-4*)   see: Allylestrenol; Ethylestrenol;
Lynestrenol

2-oxo-L-gulonic acid
($C_6H_{10}O_7$; *526-98-7*)   see: Ascorbic acid

θ-oxo-1*H*-imidazole-1-nonanoic acid methyl ester
($C_{13}H_{20}N_2O_3$; *112497-48-0*)   see: Misoprostol

***N*-(2-oxoimidazolidinocarbonyl)-D-phenylglycine**
($C_{12}H_{13}N_3O_4$; *37091-70-6*)   see: Azlocillin

**2-(1-oxoindan-4-yloxymethyl)-4-(triphenylmethyl)mor-
pholine**
($C_{33}H_{31}NO_3$; *60929-58-0*)   see: Indeloxacine

**11-oxo-5-methyl-10,11-dihydro-5*H*-dibenzo[*b,e*][1,4]di-
azepine**
($C_{14}H_{12}N_2O$; *5026-42-6*)   see: Dibenzepine

3-oxo-17α-methyl-20-hydroxy-19-norpregn-5(10)-ene
($C_{21}H_{32}O_2$; *10110-90-4*)   see: Demegestone; Promegestone

1-oxo-3-morpholino-1-(2-thienyl)propane
($C_{11}H_{15}NO_2S$; *3339-36-4*)   see: Tiemonium iodide

(2-oxononyl)phosphonic acid dimethyl ester
($C_{11}H_{23}O_4P$; *37497-25-9*)   see: Unoprostone isopropyl

**(*S*)-4-[[4-[(2-oxo-4-oxazolidinyl)methyl]phenyl]hydrazo-
no]butanenitrile**
($C_{14}H_{16}N_4O_2$; *139264-80-5*)   see: Zolmitriptan

**(4*S*)-3-(1-oxo-4-pentenyl)-4-(phenylmethyl)-2-oxazoli-
dinone**
($C_{15}H_{17}NO_3$; *104266-88-8*)   see: Abacavir

3-oxo-*N*-phenylbutanamide
($C_{10}H_{11}NO_2$; *102-01-2*)   see: Rebamipide

3-oxo-2-phenylbutane
($C_{10}H_{12}O$; *769-59-5*)   see: Pentorex

(2-oxo-4-phenylbutyl)phosphonic acid dimethyl ester
($C_{12}H_{17}O_4P$; *41162-19-0*)   see: Latanoprost

2-oxo-4-phenylbutyric acid
($C_{10}H_{10}O_3$; *710-11-2*)   see: Lisinopril

2-oxo-5-phenyl-2,3-dihydro-1*H*-1,4-benzodiazepine
($C_{15}H_{12}N_2O$; *2898-08-0*)   see: Nitrazepam

***N*-[3-(2-oxo-2-phenylethyl)-2-thiazolidinylidene]acet-
amide**
($C_{13}H_{14}N_2O_2S$; *6649-36-1*)   see: Levamisole

**(4*S-cis*)-2-oxo-4-(phenylmethyl)-5-oxazolidinecarboxylic
acid**
($C_{11}H_{11}NO_4$; *147976-18-9*)   see: Saquinavir

(±)-2-oxo-1-phenyl-3-oxabicyclo[3.1.0]hexane
($C_{11}H_{10}O_2$; *63106-93-4*)   see: Milnacipran hydrochloride

2-oxo-1-phenylpentane
($C_{11}H_{14}O$; *6683-92-7*)   see: Prolintane

**1-(3-oxo-3-phenylpropyl)-4-phenyl-4-piperidinecarb-
oxylic acid ethyl ester**
($C_{23}H_{27}NO_3$; *4310-87-6*)   see: Phenoperidine

2-pentyl bromide
(C$_5$H$_{11}$Br; *107-81-3*)   see: Pentobarbital; Secobarbital;
Thiopental

pentyl chloroformate
(C$_6$H$_{11}$ClO$_2$; *638-41-5*)   see: Capecitabine

***n*-pentylmagnesium bromide**
(C$_5$H$_{11}$BrMg; *693-25-4*)   see: Nabilone

1-pentynylcopper(I) bis(hexamethylphosphoric triamide)
(C$_{17}$H$_{43}$CuN$_6$O$_2$P$_2$; *67840-54-4*)   see: Misoprostol

peracetic acid
(C$_2$H$_4$O$_3$; *79-21-0*)   see: Oxcarbazepine

perbenzoic acid
(C$_7$H$_6$O$_3$; *93-59-4*)   see: Pipecuronium bromide

perchloryl fluoride
(ClFO$_3$; *7616-94-6*)   see: Ulobetasol propionate

(*S*)-(–)-perillic acid
(C$_{10}$H$_{14}$O$_2$; *23635-14-5*)   see: Nateglinide

perphenazine
(C$_{21}$H$_{26}$ClN$_3$OS; *58-39-9*)   see: Thiopropazate

phenacetin
(C$_{10}$H$_{13}$NO$_2$; *62-44-2*)   see: Phenacaine

phenacyl bromide
see under 2-bromoacetophenone

1-phenacyl-2-tetralone
(C$_{18}$H$_{16}$O$_2$; *57859-83-3*)   see: Fendosal

***p*-phenetidine**
see under 4-ethoxyaniline

phenmetrazine
(C$_{11}$H$_{15}$NO; *134-49-6*)   see: Fenbutrazate

phenobarbital
(C$_{12}$H$_{12}$N$_2$O$_3$; *50-06-6*)   see: Barbexaclone

phenobarbital-4-imine
(C$_{12}$H$_{13}$N$_3$O$_2$; *58042-96-9*)   see: Phenobarbital

phenol
(C$_6$H$_6$O; *108-95-2*)   see: Beclobrate; Bisacodyl; Bisoprolol;
Carfecillin; Clinofibrate; Doxepin; Febuprol; Fenticlor;
Fomocaine; Medifoxamine; Nefazodone hydrochloride;
Normolaxol; Octopamine; Oxetorone; Oxyphenisatin acetate;
Paracetamol; Phenolphthalein; Phenoxybenzamine;
Pranoprofen; Propofol; Synephrine

phenothiazine
(C$_{12}$H$_9$NS; *92-84-2*)   see: Alimemazine; Aminopromazine;
Dimethoxanate; Dixyrazine; Fenoverine; Mequitazine;
Methdilazine; Oxomemazine; Pecazine; Perazine;
Profenamine; Promazine; Promethazine; Propyramazine
bromide

phenothiazine-10-carbonyl chloride
(C$_{13}$H$_8$ClNOS; *18956-87-1*)   see: Dimethoxanate

phenoxyacetone
(C$_9$H$_{10}$O$_2$; *621-87-4*)   see: Racefemine

3'-phenoxyacetophenone
(C$_{14}$H$_{12}$O$_2$; *32852-92-9*)   see: Fenoprofen

1-phenoxy-2-bromopropane
(C$_9$H$_{11}$BrO; *90561-10-7*)   see: Isoxsuprine

2-phenoxybutyric acid
(C$_{10}$H$_{12}$O$_3$; *13794-14-4*)   see: Propicillin

2-phenoxycarbonylaminopyridine
(C$_{12}$H$_{10}$N$_2$O$_2$; *20951-00-2*)   see: Droxicam

[1-[(2-phenoxyethyl)amino]propylidene]hydrazinecarb-
oxylic acid methyl ester
(C$_{13}$H$_{19}$N$_3$O$_3$; *99153-69-2*)   see: Nefazodone hydrochloride

2-phenoxyethyl bromide
(C$_8$H$_9$BrO; *589-10-6*)   see: Domiphen bromide; Nefazodone
hydrochloride; Thenium closilate

***N*-(2-phenoxyethyl)dimethylamine**
see under 1-dimethylamino-2-phenoxyethane

***N*-(2-phenoxyethyl)propanamide**
(C$_{11}$H$_{15}$NO$_2$; *99153-71-6*)   see: Nefazodone hydrochloride

***N*-(2-phenoxyethyl)-2-thiophenemethanamine**
(C$_{13}$H$_{15}$NOS)   see: Thenium closilate

1-phenoxy-3-isopropylamino-2-propanol
(C$_{12}$H$_{19}$NO$_2$; *7695-63-8*)   see: Bisoprolol

2'-phenoxymethanesulfonanilide
(C$_{13}$H$_{13}$NO$_3$S; *51765-51-6*)   see: Nimesulide

2-(phenoxymethyl)benzoic acid
(C$_{14}$H$_{12}$O$_3$; *724-98-1*)   see: Doxepin

4-(phenoxymethyl)benzonitrile
(C$_{14}$H$_{11}$NO; *57928-75-3*)   see: Fomocaine

3-phenoxymethylcoumarilic acid ethyl ester
(C$_{18}$H$_{16}$O$_4$)   see: Oxetorone

3-phenoxymethylcoumariloyl chloride
(C$_{16}$H$_{11}$ClO$_3$)   see: Oxetorone

5-phenoxymethyl-3-isopropyl-2-oxazolidinone
(C$_{13}$H$_{17}$NO$_3$; *39631-50-0*)   see: Bisoprolol

phenoxymethylpenicillin
(C$_{16}$H$_{18}$N$_2$O$_5$S; *87-08-1*)   see: Penimepicycline

3-(4-phenoxymethylphenyl)propyl chloride
(C$_{16}$H$_{17}$ClO; *69156-40-7*)   see: Fomocaine

4-[3-[4-(phenoxymethyl)phenyl]-1-thioxopropyl]morpho-
line
(C$_{20}$H$_{23}$NO$_2$S; *65053-11-4*)   see: Fomocaine

4'-phenoxymethylpropiophenone
(C$_{16}$H$_{16}$O$_2$; *65053-10-3*)   see: Fomocaine

2-phenoxynicotinic acid
(C$_{12}$H$_9$NO$_3$; *35620-71-4*)   see: Pranoprofen

2-phenoxy-4-nitroaniline
(C$_{12}$H$_{10}$N$_2$O$_3$; *5422-92-4*)   see: Nimesulide

***N*-(2-phenoxyphenyl)acetamide**
(C$_{14}$H$_{13}$NO$_2$; *143359-96-0*)   see: Nimesulide

1-phenoxy-2-propanol
(C$_9$H$_{12}$O$_2$; *770-35-4*)   see: Phenoxybenzamine

2-phenoxypropionic acid
(C$_9$H$_{10}$O$_3$; *940-31-8*)   see: Pheneticillin

1-phenoxy-2-propyl chloride
(C$_9$H$_{11}$ClO; *53491-30-8*)   see: Phenoxybenzamine

7-(phenylacetamido)cephalosporanic acid sodium salt
(C$_{18}$H$_{17}$N$_2$NaO$_6$S; *26382-85-4*)   see: *cis*-Cefprozil

phenylacetic acid
(C$_8$H$_8$O$_2$; *103-82-2*)   see: *cis*-Cefprozil; Deptropine;
Rofecoxib; Sulbenicillin

phenylacetic acid ethyl ester
see under ethyl phenylacetate

phenylacetic acid sodium salt
(C$_8$H$_7$NaO$_2$; *114-70-5*)   see: Cyclopentolate; Rofecoxib

phenylacetone
(C$_9$H$_{10}$O; *103-79-7*)   see: Amfenac sodium; Fenetylline;
Mefenorex; Metirosine; Prenylamine

phenylacetonitrile
see under benzyl cyanide

phenylacetylcarbinol
see under (–)-1-hydroxy-1-phenylacetone

1-(2-phenylethyl)-4-piperidone
(C$_{13}$H$_{17}$NO; *39742-60-4*)   see: Fenspiride

3-(2-phenylethyl)pyridine
(C$_{13}$H$_{13}$N; *6312-09-0*)   see: Azatadine

3-(2-phenylethyl)pyridine 1-oxide
(C$_{13}$H$_{13}$NO; *14578-22-4*)   see: Azatadine

phenyl glycidyl ether
see under glycidyl phenyl ether

(S)-phenylglycine
(C$_8$H$_9$NO$_2$; *2935-35-5*)   see: Docetaxel

D(–)-α-phenylglycine
(C$_8$H$_9$NO$_2$; *875-74-1*)   see: Azlocillin; Cefradine; Epicillin

D(–)-α-phenylglycine chloride hydrochloride
(C$_8$H$_9$Cl$_2$NO; *39878-87-0*)   see: Ampicillin

phenylglycine isopentyl ester
(C$_{13}$H$_{19}$NO$_2$; *84580-27-8*)   see: Camylofin

D(–)-phenylglycine sodium salt
(C$_8$H$_8$NNaO$_2$; *56337-83-8*)   see: Ampicillin

(+)-(S)-phenylglycinol
(C$_8$H$_{11}$NO; *20989-17-7*)   see: Cerivastatin sodium

5-phenylhydantoin
(C$_9$H$_8$N$_2$O$_2$; *89-24-7*)   see: Ethotoin

phenylhydrazine
(C$_6$H$_8$N$_2$; *100-63-0*)   see: Amezinium metilsulfate;
Aminophenazone; Cortivazol; Lonazolac; Mofebutazone; D-
Penicillamine; Propyphenazone; Sulfaphenazole; L-
Tryptophan

3-(2-phenylhydrazino)propanenitrile
(C$_9$H$_{11}$N$_3$; *26955-79-3*)   see: Sulfaphenazole

(±)-3-phenyl-3-hydroxy-1-propanamine
(C$_9$H$_{13}$NO; *5053-63-4*)   see: Fluoxetine

N-(3-phenyl-1H-indol-1-yl)acetamide
(C$_{16}$H$_{14}$N$_2$O; *57647-16-2*)   see: Binedaline

phenyl isocyanate
(C$_7$H$_5$NO; *103-71-9*)   see: Diperodon

phenyllithium
(C$_6$H$_5$Li; *591-51-5*)   see: Alphaprodine

phenylmagnesium bromide
(C$_6$H$_5$BrMg; *100-58-3*)   see: Azacyclonol; Biperidene;
Broparestrol; Budipine; Clemastine; Clofedanol;
Clotrimazole; Diphemanil metilsulfate; Dipotassium
clorazepate; Doxylamine; Flutrimazole; Fosinopril;
Hexestrol; Lercanidipine hydrochloride; Medazepam;
Oxitefonium bromide; Pridinol; Procyclidine; Propiverine;
Tiemonium iodide

phenylmalonic acid
(C$_9$H$_8$O$_4$; *2613-89-0*)   see: Carfecillin; Carindacillin

phenylmalonic acid benzyl ester chloride
(C$_{16}$H$_{13}$ClO$_3$; *35353-13-0*)   see: Carbenicillin

phenylmalonic acid diethyl ester
see under diethyl phenylmalonate

phenylmercuric acetate
(C$_8$H$_8$HgO$_2$; *62-38-4*)   see: Phenylmercuric borate

phenylmercuric hydroxide
(C$_6$H$_6$HgO; *100-57-2*)   see: Phenylmercuric borate

N-[(phenylmethoxy)carbonyl]-DL-homocysteine acetate (ester)
(C$_{14}$H$_{17}$NO$_5$S)   see: Omapatrilat

N-[(phenylmethoxy)carbonyl]-L-homocysteine acetate (ester)
(C$_{14}$H$_{17}$NO$_5$S; *167305-82-0*)   see: Omapatrilat

4-(phenylmethoxy)-1H-indole-2-acetic acid
(C$_{17}$H$_{15}$NO$_3$)   see: Mepindolol

***anti*-8-[(phenylmethoxy)methyl]-2-oxabicyclo[3.2.1]oct-6-en-3-one**
(C$_{15}$H$_{16}$O$_3$; *50889-56-0*)   see: Dinoprost

6-O-[4-(phenylmethoxy)phenyl]-α-D-glucofuranose
(C$_{19}$H$_{22}$O$_7$)   see: Prenalterol

[4-(phenylmethoxy)phenyl]hydrazine
(C$_{13}$H$_{14}$N$_2$O; *51145-58-5*)   see: Oxitriptan

5-(phenylmethoxy)-N-[(phenylmethoxy)carbonyl]-L-tryptophan
(C$_{26}$H$_{24}$N$_2$O$_5$; *3520-59-0*)   see: Oxitriptan

1-[4-(phenylmethoxy)phenyl]-2-[[2-[4-(phenylmethoxy)-phenyl]ethyl]amino]-1-propanone
(C$_{31}$H$_{31}$NO$_3$)   see: Ritodrine

1-[4-(phenylmethoxy)phenyl]-2-[4-(phenylmethyl)-1-piperidinyl]-1-propanone
(C$_{28}$H$_{31}$NO$_2$; *35133-39-2*)   see: Ifenprodil

1-[3-(phenylmethoxy)phenyl]-1,2-propanedione 2-oxime
(C$_{16}$H$_{15}$NO$_3$)   see: Metaraminol

(±)-1-phenyl-3-(methylamino)propan-1-ol
(C$_{10}$H$_{15}$NO; *42142-52-9*)   see: Fluoxetine

N-phenyl-N-methyl-N'-(2-chlorobenzoyl)-2-hydroxy-1,3-diaminopropane
(C$_{17}$H$_{19}$ClN$_2$O$_2$; *61677-60-9*)   see: Metaclazepam

(R)-phenylmethyl [3-chloro-2-oxo-1-[(phenylthio)methyl]-propyl]carbamate
(C$_{18}$H$_{18}$ClNO$_3$S; *159878-01-0*)   see: Nelfinavir mesylate

3-[(phenylmethylene)amino]-2-oxazolidinone
(C$_{10}$H$_{10}$N$_2$O$_2$; *4341-14-4*)   see: Furazolidone

3-(phenylmethylene)-1(3H)-isobenzofuranone
(C$_{15}$H$_{10}$O$_2$; *575-61-1*)   see: Deptropine

N-phenyl-N-methyl-2-hydroxy-1,3-diaminopropane
(C$_{10}$H$_{16}$N$_2$O; *63062-22-6*)   see: Metaclazepam

α,α'-[[(phenylmethyl)imino]bis(methylene)]bis[6-fluoro-3,4-dihydro-2H-1-benzopyran-2-methanol] stereoisomer
(C$_{29}$H$_{31}$F$_2$NO$_4$; *129050-28-8*)   see: Nebivolol

2-[(phenylmethyl)methylamino]-1-[4-(phenylmethoxy)-phenyl]-1-propanone
(C$_{24}$H$_{25}$NO$_2$)   see: Oxilofrine

[S-(R*,S*)]-phenylmethyl [1-oxiranyl-2-(phenylthio)-ethyl]carbamate
(C$_{18}$H$_{19}$NO$_3$S; *163462-16-6*)   see: Nelfinavir mesylate

1-(phenylmethyl)-4-piperidinone oxime
(C$_{12}$H$_{16}$N$_2$O; *949-69-9*)   see: Clebopride

N-[1-(phenylmethyl)-4-piperidinylidene]benzenamine
(C$_{18}$H$_{20}$N$_2$; *1155-57-3*)   see: Fentanyl

6-(phenylmethyl)-5H-pyrrolo[3,4-b]pyridine-5,7(6H)-dione
(C$_{14}$H$_{10}$N$_2$O$_2$; *18184-75-3*)   see: Moxifloxacin hydrochloride

1-phenyl-3-morpholino-1-propanone
(C$_{13}$H$_{17}$NO$_2$; *2298-48-8*)   see: Tiemonium iodide

phenyloxalacetic acid diethyl ester
see under diethyl 3-oxo-2-phenylsuccinate

***cis*-3-phenyloxiranecarboxylic acid methyl ester**
(C$_{10}$H$_{10}$O$_3$; *40956-18-1*)   see: Paclitaxel

(2R,3R)-rel-3-phenyloxiranemethanol
(C$_9$H$_{10}$O$_2$; *40641-81-4*)   see: Reboxetine

4-phenylphenacyl bromide
(C$_{14}$H$_{11}$BrO; *135-73-9*)   see: Fentonium bromide

phosphorothioic acid *S*-[2-(dimethylamino)ethyl] *O,O*-diethyl ester
($C_8H_{20}NO_3PS$; *3147-20-4*)   see: Ecothiopate iodide

phosphorus trichloride
(Cl_3P; *7719-12-2*)   see: Isoflurophate

phosphoryl chloride
(Cl_3OP; *10025-87-3*)   see: Cyclophosphamide; Estramustine phosphate; Etopophos; Ifosfamide; Miltefosine; Torasemide; Vidarabine

phosphorylcholine chloride
($C_5H_{15}ClNO_4P$; *107-73-3*)   see: Citicoline

phthalaldehyde
($C_8H_6O_2$; *643-79-8*)   see: Lacidipine

phthalazone
($C_8H_6N_2O$; *119-39-1*)   see: Hydralazine

phthalic anhydride
($C_8H_4O_3$; *85-44-9*)   see: Anisindione; Chlortalidone; Cilazapril; Deptropine; Fluorescein; Hydralazine; Indobufen; Indoprofen; Melphalan; Phenolphthalein; Phthalylsulfathiazole; Pizotifen; Pramipexole hydrochloride; Saquinavir; Sulfaloxic acid; Thalidomide; Tilisolol hydrochloride

phthalide
($C_8H_6O_2$; *87-41-2*)   see: Anisindione; Bromindione; Hydralazine; Indoprofen

phthalimide
($C_8H_5NO_2$; *85-41-6*)   see: Guanadrel

phthalimide potassium
($C_8H_4KNO_2$; *1074-82-4*)   see: Milnacipran hydrochloride; Zidovudine

phthalimidoacetyl chloride
($C_{10}H_6ClNO_3$; *6780-38-7*)   see: Flurazepam; Ioxaglic acid; Prazepam

4-(phthalimido)cyclohexanol
($C_{14}H_{15}NO_3$; *104618-31-7*)   see: Pramipexole hydrochloride

4-(phthalimido)cyclohexanone
($C_{14}H_{13}NO_3$; *104618-32-8*)   see: Pramipexole hydrochloride

6-(phthalimidomethyl)-11*H*-dibenz[*b,e*]azepine
($C_{23}H_{16}N_2O_2$; *74860-00-7*)   see: Epinastine hydrochloride

6-(phthalimidomethyl)-6,11-dihydro-5*H*-dibenz[*b,e*]aze-pine
($C_{23}H_{18}N_2O_2$; *143878-20-0*)   see: Epinastine hydrochloride

phthalonitrile
($C_8H_4N_2$; *91-15-6*)   see: Dihydralazine

***N*-phthaloyl-L-cysteine benzhydryl ester**
($C_{24}H_{19}NO_4S$; *102089-87-2*)   see: Temocapril

***N*-phthaloylglutamic acid**
($C_{13}H_{11}NO_6$; *6349-98-0*)   see: Thalidomide

***N*-phthaloylglutamic anhydride**
($C_{13}H_9NO_5$; *3343-28-0*)   see: Thalidomide

***N*-phthaloyl-L-glutamine**
($C_{13}H_{12}N_2O_5$; *3343-29-1*)   see: Thalidomide

***N*-phthaloylglycyl chloride**
see under phthalimidoacetyl chloride

phthalylglycylglycyl chloride
($C_{12}H_9ClN_2O_4$; *59180-28-8*)   see: Rilmazafone

phytol
($C_{20}H_{40}O$; *150-86-7*)   see: Phytomenadione

phytomenadiol 1-acetate
($C_{33}H_{50}O_3$; *50281-47-5*)   see: Phytomenadione

2-picoline
(C_6H_7N; *109-06-8*)   see: Betahistine; Bromazepam; Ibudilast; Perhexiline

4-picoline
(C_6H_7N; *108-89-4*)   see: Milrinone; Tirofiban hydrochloride

2-picoline 1-oxide
(C_6H_7NO; *931-19-1*)   see: Bromazepam

picolinic acid
($C_6H_5NO_2$; *98-98-6*)   see: Rimiterol

picolinic acid 2,6-xylidide
($C_{14}H_{14}N_2O$; *39627-98-0*)   see: Bupivacaine; Mepivacaine

2',6'-picolinoxylidide
see under picolinic acid 2,6-xylidide

3-picolylamine
see under 3-(aminomethyl)pyridine

3-picolyl chloride
(C_6H_6ClN; *3099-31-8*)   see: Indinavir sulfate

(±)-α-pinene
($C_{10}H_{16}$; *80-56-8*)   see: Sobrerol

(±)-α-pinene oxide
($C_{10}H_{16}O$; *95044-43-2*)   see: Sobrerol

L-pipecolic acid
($C_6H_{11}NO_2$; *3105-95-1*)   see: Ropivacaine hydrochloride

pipecolinic acid 2,6-xylidide
($C_{14}H_{20}N_2O$; *15883-20-2*)   see: Bupivacaine; Mepivacaine

pipecolinoyl chloride
($C_6H_{10}ClNO$; *130606-00-7*)   see: Bupivacaine

L-pipecoloyl chloride
($C_6H_{10}ClNO$)   see: Ropivacaine hydrochloride

piperazine
($C_4H_{10}N_2$; *110-85-0*)   see: Acefylline; Ciprofloxacin; Delavirdine mesilate; Doxazosin; Eprazinone; Eprozinol; Norfloxacin; Pipecuronium bromide; Pipemidic acid; Pipobroman; Piproxen; Quetiapine fumarate; Terazosin; Tirilazad mesilate; Zipeprol; Ziprasidone hydrochloride

piperazinoacetic acid pyrrolidide
($C_{10}H_{19}N_3O$; *39890-45-4*)   see: Cinepazide

11-piperazinodibenzo[*b,f*][1,4]thiazepine
($C_{17}H_{17}N_3S$; *5747-48-8*)   see: Quetiapine fumarate

6-piperazino-3,4-dihydro-2(1*H*)-quinolinone
($C_{13}H_{17}N_3O$; *87154-95-8*)   see: Vesnarinone

2-piperazinoethanol
see under 1-(2-hydroxyethyl)piperazine

10-(3-piperazinopropyl)-10*H*-pyrido[3,2-*b*][1,4]benzo-thiazine
($C_{18}H_{22}N_4S$; *42351-33-7*)   see: Oxypendyl

10-(3-piperazinopropyl)-2-trifluoromethylphenothiazine
($C_{20}H_{22}F_3N_3S$; *2804-16-2*)   see: Fluphenazine; Oxaflumazine

2-(1-piperazinyl)ethanol
see under 1-(2-hydroxyethyl)piperazine

piperidine
($C_5H_{11}N$; *110-89-4*)   see: Acrivastine; Benproperine; Bietamiverine; Biperidene; Cycrimine; Diperodon; Dipyridamole; Dyclonine; Eperisone; Etozolin; Ketotifen; Minoxidil; Pancuronium bromide; Pifoxime; Pipoxolan; Piprozolin; Pridinol; Primaperone; Pyrvinium embonate; Raloxifene hydrochloride; Repaglinide; Roxatidine acetate; Trihexyphenidyl; Vecuronium bromide

4-piperidineacetic acid
($C_7H_{13}NO_2$; *51052-78-9*)   see: Indalpine

prajmalium hydroxide (aldehyde base)
($C_{23}H_{32}N_2O_2$)   see: Prajmalium bitartrate

prasterone
see under androstenolone

precholecalciferol
($C_{27}H_{44}O$; *1173-13-3*)   see: Colecalciferol

prednisolone
($C_{21}H_{28}O_5$; *50-24-8*)   see: Loteprednol etabonate;
Prednicarbate; Prednimustine; Prednisolamate; Prednisolone
sodium phosphate; Prednisolone sodium succinate;
Prednisolone sodium sulfobenzoate; Prednisolone steaglate;
Prednisolone tebutate; Prednisolone 21-trimethylacetate;
Prednival acetate

prednisolone-21-acetate
($C_{23}H_{30}O_6$; *52-21-1*)   see: Dichlorisone

prednisolone 17,21-diethyl orthocarbonate
($C_{26}H_{36}O_7$; *26129-79-3*)   see: Prednicarbate

prednisolone 17-ethylcarbonate
($C_{24}H_{32}O_7$; *104286-02-4*)   see: Prednicarbate

prednisolone 21-phosphate (monosodium salt)
($C_{21}H_{28}NaO_8P$; *2681-16-5*)   see: Prednisolone sodium
phosphate

prednisolone 17-valerate
($C_{26}H_{36}O_6$; *15180-00-4*)   see: Prednival acetate

prednylidene
($C_{22}H_{28}O_5$; *599-33-7*)   see: Prednylidene
diethylaminoacetate

preergocalciferol
($C_{28}H_{44}O$; *21307-05-1*)   see: Ergocalciferol

(3β)-pregna-5,16,20-triene-3,20-diol 20-acetate 3-formate
($C_{24}H_{32}O_4$; *62490-12-4*)   see: Desoxycortone acetate

pregnenolone
($C_{21}H_{32}O_2$; *145-13-1*)   see: Desoxycortone acetate;
Progesterone

pregnenolone acetate
($C_{23}H_{34}O_3$; *1778-02-5*)   see: Prasterone

progesterone
($C_{21}H_{30}O_2$; *57-83-0*)   see: Alfaxalone; Cortisone;
Desoxycortone acetate; Hydrocortisone; Testolactone

proglumide
($C_{18}H_{26}N_2O_4$; *6620-60-6*)   see: Proglumetacin

L(–)-prolinamide
($C_5H_{10}N_2O$; *7531-52-4*)   see: Remoxipride

L-proline
($C_5H_9NO_2$; *147-85-3*)   see: Captopril; Cetrorelix; Enalapril;
Eptifibatide; Lisinopril

L-proline benzyl ester
($C_{12}H_{15}NO_2$; *41324-66-7*)   see: Enalapril

L-proline benzyl ester hydrochloride
($C_{12}H_{16}ClNO_2$; *16652-71-4*)   see: Lisinopril

L-proline *tert*-butyl ester
($C_9H_{17}NO_2$; *2812-46-6*)   see: Captopril

L-Pro-L-Lys(Tos)-Gly-NH₂
($C_{20}H_{31}N_5O_5S$; *6697-01-4*)   see: Felypressin

(*S*)-1,2-propanediamine
($C_3H_{10}N_2$; *15967-72-3*)   see: Dexrazoxane

propanedioic acid mono[(4-nitrophenyl)methyl] ester
magnesium salt
($C_{20}H_{16}MgN_2O_{12}$; *105995-50-4*)   see: Meropenem

(*R*)-1,2-propanediol
($C_3H_8O_2$; *4254-14-2*)   see: Levofloxacin

1,3-propanediol
($C_3H_8O_2$; *504-63-2*)   see: Simfibrate

1,3-propanedithiol
($C_3H_8S_2$; *109-80-8*)   see: Tacrolimus

4,4'-[1,3-propanediylbis(oxy)]bis[3-bromobenzonitrile]
($C_{17}H_{12}Br_2N_2O_2$; *93840-60-9*)   see: Dibrompropamidine

propane sultone
($C_3H_6O_3S$; *1120-71-4*)   see: Pyrantel; Sultroponium

propanoic anhydride
($C_6H_{10}O_3$; *123-62-6*)   see: Alclometasone dipropionate;
Alfentanil; Alphaprodine; Beclometasone;
Dextropropoxyphene; Diethylstilbestrol dipropionate;
Fentanyl; Propiram; Sulindac; Testosterone propionate

propanol
(C_3H_8O; *71-23-8*)   see: Propiverine; Propyliodone

propargyl alcohol
(C_3H_4O; *107-19-7*)   see: Spironolactone

propargyl bromide
(C_3H_3Br; *106-96-7*)   see: Haloprogin; Pargyline; Parsalmide;
Pinazepam; Selegiline

2-propenyl (3*S*,4*R*)-3-[(1*R*)-1-[[(1,1-dimethylethyl)dime-
thylsilyl]oxy]ethyl]-2-oxo-4-[(2*R*)-(tetrahydro-2-furanyl)-
carbonyl]thio]-α-hydroxy-1-azetidineacetate
($C_{21}H_{35}NO_7SSi$)   see: Faropenem sodium

[5*R*-[3(*R),5α,6α(*R**)]]-2-propenyl 6-[1-[[(1,1-dimethyl-**
ethyl)dimethylsilyl]oxy]ethyl]-7-oxo-3-(tetrahydro-2-fura-
nyl)-4-thia-1-azabicyclo[3.2.0]hept-2-ene-2-carboxylate
($C_{21}H_{33}NO_5SSi$; *120705-67-1*)   see: Faropenem sodium

[[[(1*R*)-1-(2-propenyl)dodecyl]oxy]methyl]benzene
($C_{22}H_{36}O$; *152906-18-8*)   see: Orlistat

9-(2-propenylidene)-2-(trifluoromethyl)-9*H*-thioxanthene
($C_{17}H_{11}F_3S$; *28973-34-4*)   see: Flupentixol

9-(2-propenyl)-2-(trifluoromethyl)-9*H*-thioxanthen-9-ol
($C_{17}H_{13}F_3OS$)   see: Flupentixol

Pro-Phe-O-CH₃
($C_{15}H_{20}N_2O_3$; *54793-80-5*)   see: Angiotensinamide

propionaldehyde
(C_3H_6O; *123-38-6*)   see: Amorolfine; Anethole; Ethiazide;
Pramipexole hydrochloride; Proligestone; Retinol

propionaldehyde thiosemicarbazone
($C_4H_9N_3S$; *22042-87-1*)   see: Sulfaethidole

propionic acid
($C_3H_6O_2$; *79-09-4*)   see: Imiquimod

propionic anhydride
see under propanoic anhydride

propionimidoylphloroglucinol
($C_9H_{11}NO_3$; *109817-53-0*)   see: Flopropione

propionitrile
(C_3H_5N; *107-12-0*)   see: Flopropione

propionyl chloride
(C_3H_5ClO; *79-03-8*)   see: Betamethasone butyrate
propionate; Betamethasone dipropionate; Docarpamine;
Erythromycin estolate; Erythromycin monopropionate
mercaptosuccinate; Flavoxate; Fluticasone propionate;
Naproxen; Prednicarbate; Quinethazone

2-propionyloxybenzoic acid
($C_{10}H_{10}O_4$; *6328-44-5*)   see: Flavoxate

2-propionylphenothiazine
($C_{15}H_{13}NOS$; *92-33-1*)   see: Carfenazine

3-propionylsalicylic acid
($C_{10}H_{10}O_4$; *35888-92-7*)   see: Flavoxate

(4-pyridinylmethyl)lithium
(C_6H_6LiN; *26954-25-6*)   see: Tirofiban hydrochloride

(4-pyridinylthio)acetyl chloride
(C_7H_6ClNOS; *52998-13-7*)   see: Cefapirin

4(1*H*)-pyridone
(C_5H_5NO; *108-96-3*)   see: Diodone; Propyliodone

pyridoxine
($C_8H_{11}NO_3$; *65-23-6*)   see: Cicletanine; Pyridofylline

pyridoxine hydrochloride
($C_8H_{12}ClNO_3$; *58-56-0*)   see: Pirisudanol

2-(3-pyridyl)acetic acid
($C_7H_7NO_2$; *501-81-5*)   see: Risedronate sodium

3-pyridyl-D-alanine
($C_8H_{10}N_2O_2$; *70702-47-5*)   see: Cetrorelix

α-2-pyridyl-2,8-bis(trifluoromethyl)-4-quinolinemethanol
($C_{17}H_{10}F_6N_2O$; *68496-04-8*)   see: Mefloquine

N-(2-pyridyl)chloroacetamide
($C_7H_7ClN_2O$; *5221-37-4*)   see: Piroxicam

2-(4-pyridyl)-3-dimethylaminoacrolein
($C_{10}H_{12}N_2O$; *26866-49-9*)   see: Amrinone

4-pyridyldiphenylcarbinol
($C_{18}H_{15}NO$; *1620-30-0*)   see: Azacyclonol; Diphemanil metilsulfate

2-(2-pyridyl)ethanol
(C_7H_9NO; *103-74-2*)   see: Betahistine

4-pyridyl isothiocyanate
($C_6H_4N_2S$; *76105-84-5*)   see: Pinacidil

2-pyridyllithium
(C_5H_4LiN; *17624-36-1*)   see: Mefloquine; Pirmenol hydrochloride

3-pyridyllithium
(C_5H_4LiN; *60573-68-4*)   see: Zimeldine

2-pyridylmagnesium bromide
(C_5H_4BrMgN; *21970-13-8*)   see: Mefloquine

4-pyridylmalonaldehyde
($C_8H_7NO_2$; *51076-46-1*)   see: Amrinone

1-(4-pyridyl)-2-propanone
(C_8H_9NO; *6304-16-1*)   see: Milrinone

1-(4-pyridyl)pyridinium chloride
($C_{10}H_9ClN_2$; *22752-98-3*)   see: Diodone

4-pyridylthioacetic acid
($C_7H_7NO_2S$; *10351-19-6*)   see: Cefapirin

N-(4-pyridyl)-N'-(1,2,2-trimethylpropyl)thiourea
($C_{12}H_{19}N_3S$; *67027-06-9*)   see: Pinacidil

N-[4-[(2-pyrimidinylamino)sulfonyl]phenyl]acetamide
($C_{12}H_{12}N_4O_3S$; *127 71 2*)   see: Sulfadiazine

1-(pyrimidin-2-yl)piperazine
($C_8H_{12}N_4$; *20980-22-7*)   see: Buspirone; Tandospirone

4-[4-(pyrimidin-2-yl)piperazin-1-yl]butylamine
($C_{12}H_{21}N_5$; *33386-20-8*)   see: Buspirone; Tandospirone

1-(2-pyrimidyl)-4-(4-aminobutyl)piperazine
see under 4-[4-(pyrimidin-2-yl)piperazin-1-yl]butylamine

4-(2-pyrimidyl)-1-(3-cyanopropyl)piperazine
($C_{12}H_{17}N_5$; *33386-14-0*)   see: Buspirone

1-(2-pyrimidyl)piperazine
see under 1-(pyrimidin-2-yl)piperazine

pyrocatechol
see under catechol

pyrogallol
($C_6H_6O_3$; *87-66-1*)   see: Exifone; Gallamine triethiodide; Methoxsalen

DL-pyroglutamic acid
($C_5H_7NO_3$; *149-87-1*)   see: Arginine pidolate

4*H*-pyrone
($C_5H_4O_2$; *108-97-4*)   see: Betazole

pyrrole
(C_4H_5N; *109-97-7*)   see: Ketorolac

pyrrolidine
(C_4H_9N; *123-75-1*)   see: Amixetrine; Bepridil; Buflomedil; Clemizole; Cortisone; Dextromoramide; Endralazine; Fendosal; Fluoxymesterone; Piromidic acid; Procyclidine; Prolintane; Propyramazine bromide; Pyrovalerone; Pyrrobutamine; Pyrrocaine; Ramosetron hydrochloride; Rocuronium bromide; Rolitetracycline; Tirilazad mesilate; Triprolidine; Vincamine

1-pyrrolidino-1-butene
($C_8H_{15}N$; *13937-89-8*)   see: Vincamine

4-pyrrolidinobutyronitrile
($C_8H_{14}N_2$; *35543-25-0*)   see: Buflomedil

(RS)-5-pyrrolidinocarbonyl-4,5,6,7-tetrahydro-1*H*-benz-imidazole hydrochloride
($C_{12}H_{18}ClN_3O$; *132036-42-1*)   see: Ramosetron hydrochloride

1-pyrrolidinocyclopentene
($C_9H_{15}N$; *7148-07-4*)   see: Ramipril

2-pyrrolidino-3,4-dihydronaphthalene
($C_{14}H_{17}N$; *21403-95-2*)   see: Fendosal

(2-pyrrolidinoethyl)triphenylphosphonium bromide
($C_{24}H_{27}BrNP$; *23072-03-9*)   see: Acrivastine

3-pyrrolidinomethylrifamycin SV
($C_{42}H_{56}N_2O_{12}$; *4075-42-7*)   see: Rifampicin

3-pyrrolidinopropiophenone
($C_{13}H_{17}NO$; *94-39-3*)   see: Procyclidine; Pyrrobutamine

4-pyrrolidinopyridine
($C_9H_{12}N_2$; *2456-81-7*)   see: Simvastatin

1-pyrrolidino-3-(4-tolyl)propan-3-one
see under 4'-methyl-3-pyrrolidinopropiophenone

3-(1-pyrrolidinyl)pregna-3,5,17(20)-triene-11β,21-diol
($C_{25}H_{37}NO_2$; *115486-29-8*)   see: Cortisone

2-pyrrolidone
(C_4H_7NO; *616-45-5*)   see: Aniracetam; Piracetam; Pramiracetam hydrochloride

pyruvaldehyde
($C_3H_4O_2$; *78-98-8*)   see: Folic acid

pyrvinium iodide
($C_{26}H_{28}IN_3$; *35648-29-4*)   see: Pyrvinium embonate

Q

quinaldic acid
($C_{10}H_7NO_2$; *93-10-7*)   see: Saquinavir

(–)-quinic acid
($C_7H_{12}O_6$; *77-95-2*)   see: Oseltamivir

quinic acid γ-lactone
($C_7H_{10}O_5$; *27783-00-2*)   see: Cynarine

quinine
($C_{20}H_{24}N_2O_2$; *130-95-0*)   see: Quinidine

silver dihydrogen phosphate
(AgH$_2$O$_4$P; *18725-91-2*)   see: Betamethasone phosphate

silver nitrate
(AgNO$_3$; *7761-88-8*)   see: Carboplatin

silver sulfate
(Ag$_2$O$_4$S; *10294-26-5*)   see: Carboplatin

sisomicin
(C$_{19}$H$_{37}$N$_5$O$_7$; *32385-11-8*)   see: Netilmicin

sodium acetate
(C$_2$H$_3$NaO$_2$; *127-09-3*)   see: α-Acetyldigoxin;
Dextrothyroxine; Fluazacort; Fluprednidene acetate;
Pioglitazone; Pyrrocaine

sodium acetoacetic acid ethyl ester
(C$_6$H$_9$NaO$_3$; *19232-39-4*)   see: Pentoxifylline

sodium acetylide (Na(C2H))
(C$_2$HNa; *1066-26-8*)   see: Retinol

sodium amide
(H$_2$NNa; *7782-92-5*)   see: Milnacipran hydrochloride

**sodium 5-(3-aminopropyl)-4,6-dihydroxy-1,3,2,4,6-di-
oxatriphosphorinan-5-olate 2,4,6-trioxide**
(C$_4$H$_{11}$NNaO$_8$P$_3$)   see: Alendronate sodium

sodium azide
(N$_3$Na; *26628-22-8*)   see: Alfentanil; Azosemide;
Benazepril; Docetaxel; Fluazacort; Imiquimod; Irbesartan;
Midodrine; Oseltamivir; Paclitaxel; Pemirolast; Pranlukast;
Tazanolast; Tranylcypromine; Zanamivir; Zidovudine

sodium benzenesulfinate
(C$_6$H$_5$NaO$_2$S; *873-55-2*)   see: Betacarotene; Retinol

sodium 1,2-benzisoxazole-3-methanesulfonate
(C$_8$H$_6$NNaO$_4$S; *73101-64-1*)   see: Zonisamide

sodium benzoate
(C$_7$H$_5$NaO$_2$; *532-32-1*)   see: Benzyl benzoate; Flavoxate;
Stavudine

sodium chloroacetate
(C$_2$H$_2$ClNaO$_2$; *3926-62-3*)   see: Betaine hydrate

sodium 2-(4-chlorophenoxy)-2-methylpropionate
(C$_{10}$H$_{10}$ClNaO$_3$; *7314-47-8*)   see: Ronifibrate

sodium cyanate
(CNNaO; *917-61-3*)   see: Carisoprodol; Hydroxycarbamide;
Orotic acid; Prazosin

sodium cyanide
(CNNa; *143-33-9*)   see: Alclofenac; Alpidem;
Amphetaminil; Atorvastatin calcium; Azatadine; Calcium
pantothenate; Carnitine; Clopidogrel hydrogensulfate;
Clortermine; Dexrazoxane; Diclofenac; Diloxanide; Edetic
acid; Epinastine hydrochloride; Ethosuximide; Ethotoin;
Fenoprofen; Ibuprofen; Irbesartan; Ketoprofen; Lonazolac;
Mephenytoin; Mepindolol; Montelukast sodium; Nabilone;
Oxymetazoline; Paramethadione; Pentorex; Saquinavir;
Suprofen; Thiamphenicol; Tolmetin; Trimazosin; Zolpidem

sodium cyanoborohydride
(CH$_3$BNNa; *25895-60-7*)   see: Fluoxetine; Netilmicin;
Rizatriptan benzoate

sodium 2,6-dimethylphenolate
(C$_8$H$_9$NaO; *16081-16-6*)   see: Mexiletine

sodium ethylate
(C$_2$H$_5$NaO; *141-52-6*)   see: Azelastine; Emorfazone;
Methyprylon; Oseltamivir; Pentobarbital; Promestriene;
Propallylonal; Protionamide

sodium 2-ethylhexanoate
(C$_8$H$_{15}$NaO$_2$; *19766-89-3*)   see: Faropenem sodium

sodium formaldehydesulfoxylate
(CH$_3$NaO$_3$S; *149-44-0*)   see: Sulfoxone sodium

sodium formate
(CHNaO$_2$; *141-53-7*)   see: D-Penicillamine

**sodium [2S-(2R*,3R*,5S*)]-2-hexyl-5-hydroxy-3-(phenyl-
methoxy)hexadecanoate**
(C$_{29}$H$_{49}$NaO$_4$)   see: Orlistat

sodium 3-hydroxy-2-naphthoate
(C$_{11}$H$_7$NaO$_3$; *14206-62-3*)   see: Bephenium
hydroxynaphthoate

**sodium D(–)-α-(4-hydroxyphenyl)-α-(2-methoxycarbonyl-
1-methylethenylamino)acetate**
see under DANE salt

sodium methylate
(CH$_3$NaO; *124-41-4*)   see: Atorvastatin calcium;
Brinzolamide; Ciprofloxacin; Cisapride; Dextrothyroxine;
Epirizole; Hydroxyprogesterone; Metaclazepam;
Moxifloxacin hydrochloride; Moxonidine; Oxcarbazepine;
Pantoprazole sodium; Sulfadimethoxine; Sulfalene;
Sulfamethoxypyridazine; Tacrolimus; Vincamine

sodium 3,4-(methylenedioxy)phenolate
(C$_7$H$_5$NaO$_3$; *51114-03-5*)   see: Paroxetine

sodium 4-nitrophenolate
(C$_6$H$_4$NNaO$_3$; *824-78-2*)   see: Dofetilide; Tiocarlide

sodium orotate
(C$_5$H$_3$N$_2$NaO$_4$; *154-85-8*)   see: Orazamide

sodium phenolate
(C$_6$H$_5$NaO; *139-02-6*)   see: Bephenium hydroxynaphthoate;
Bumetanide; Fomocaine; Salicylic acid

sodium phenylacetate
see under phenylacetic acid sodium salt

sodium phenylmercaptide
(C$_6$H$_5$NaS; *930-69-8*)   see: Oxfendazole

sodium phenylsulfinate
see under sodium benzenesulfinate

sodium phosphite
(HNa$_2$O$_3$P; *13708-85-5*)   see: Fosinopril

sodium pyruvate
(C$_3$H$_3$NaO$_3$; *113-24-6*)   see: Flurbiprofen

sodium salicylate
see under salicylic acid sodium salt

sodium 3-sulfobenzoate
(C$_7$H$_5$NaO$_5$S; *17625-03-5*)   see: Prednisolone sodium
sulfobenzoate

sodium S-tetrahydrofurfuryl thiosulfate
(C$_5$H$_9$NaO$_4$S$_2$; *77339-73-2*)   see: Fursultiamine

sodium 1,2,4-triazolide
(C$_2$H$_2$N$_3$Na; *41253-21-8*)   see: Anastrozole; Rizatriptan
benzoate

D-sorbitol
(C$_6$H$_{14}$O$_6$; *50-70-4*)   see: Ascorbic acid; Isosorbide dinitrate

L-sorbose
(C$_6$H$_{12}$O$_6$; *87-79-6*)   see: Ascorbic acid

stearic acid
(C$_{18}$H$_{36}$O$_2$; *57-11-4*)   see: Choline stearate

stearoyl chloride
(C$_{18}$H$_{35}$ClO; *112-76-5*)   see: Erythromycin stearate

stearoylglycoloyl chloride
(C$_{20}$H$_{37}$ClO$_3$; *7454-39-9*)   see: Prednisolone steaglate

N-(stearoyloxy)-5-norbornene-2,3-dicarboximide
(C$_{27}$H$_{43}$NO$_4$; *77290-17-6*)   see: Romurtide

sulfur trioxide-2-picoline complex
($C_6H_7NO_3S$; *18370-14-4*)   see: Carumonam

T

(–)-tabersonine
($C_{21}H_{24}N_2O_2$; *4429-63-4*)   see: Vincamine

cis,trans-**tamoxifen**
($C_{26}H_{29}NO$; *7728-73-6*)   see: Tamoxifen

L-tartaric acid
($C_4H_6O_6$; *87-69-4*)   see: Detajmium bitartrate; Prajmalium bitartrate; Selegiline

testosterone
($C_{19}H_{28}O_2$; *58-22-0*)   see: Drostanolone; Testosterone cypionate; Testosterone enanthate; Testosterone propionate; Trilostane

2,3,4,6-tetra-*O*-acetyl-β-D-glucopyranose
($C_{14}H_{20}O_{10}$; *3947-62-4*)   see: Teniposide

S-**(2,3,4,6-tetra-*O*-acetyl-β-D-glucopyranosyl)thiuronium bromide**
($C_{15}H_{23}BrN_2O_9S$; *40591-65-9*)   see: Auranofin

1,2,3,5-tetra-*O*-acetyl-β-D-ribofuranose
($C_{13}H_{18}O_9$; *13035-61-5*)   see: Azacitidine; Ribavirin

2,2',4,4'-tetraaminodiphenylmethane
($C_{13}H_{16}N_4$; *181189-62-8*)   see: Acriflavinium chloride

2,4,5,6-tetraaminopyrimidine
($C_4H_8N_6$; *1004-74-6*)   see: Fludarabine phosphate; Methotrexate

2,4,5,6-tetraaminopyrimidine dihydrobromide
($C_4H_{10}Br_2N_6$; *158754-80-4*)   see: Methotrexate

tetrabromopyrocatechol
($C_6H_2Br_4O_2$; *488-47-1*)   see: Bibrocathol

tetrabutylammonium (3*S*,4*S*)-3-(benzyloxycarbonyl-amino)-4-hydroxymethyl-2-oxoazetidine-1-sulfonate
($C_{28}H_{49}N_3O_7S$; *92973-33-6*)   see: Carumonam

tetrabutylammonium hydrogen sulfate
($C_{16}H_{37}NO_4S$; *32503-27-8*)   see: Aztreonam; Carumonam

tetrachloromethane
(CCl_4; *56-23-5*)   see: Tienilic acid

2,4,6,8-tetrachloropyrimido[5,4-*d*]pyrimidine
($C_6Cl_4N_4$; *32980-71-5*)   see: Dipyridamole

tetracycline
($C_{22}H_{24}N_2O_8$; *60-54-8*)   see: Lymecycline; Penimepicycline; Rolitetracycline

2,3,7,8-tetradeoxy-2,8-dimethyl-4,6-di-*O*-methyl-L-*glycero*-L-*manno*-nonaric acid dimethyl ester
($C_{15}H_{28}O_7$; *118299-02-8*)   see: Tacrolimus

2,3,7,8-tetradeoxy-2,8-dimethyl-4,6-di-*O*-methyl-L-*glycero*-L-*talo*-nonuronic acid δ-lactone cyclic 1-(1,3-propanediyl dithioacetal)
($C_{16}H_{28}O_4S_2$; *118227-57-9*)   see: Tacrolimus

2,3,7,8-tetradeoxy-5-[[(1,1-dimethylethyl)dimethylsilyl]-oxy]-L-*arabino*-nonanoic acid di-γ-lactone
($C_{15}H_{26}O_5Si$)   see: Tacrolimus

2,3,7,8-tetradeoxy-2,8-dimethyl-5-*O*-(phenylmethyl)-L-*glycero*-L-*manno*-nonaric acid di-γ-lactone
($C_{18}H_{22}O_5$; *118246-95-0*)   see: Tacrolimus

tetraethyl (cycloheptylamino)methylenebis(phosphonate)
($C_{16}H_{35}NO_6P_2$; *124351-81-1*)   see: Incadronic acid

tetraethylene glycol
($C_8H_{18}O_5$; *112-60-7*)   see: Iotroxic acid

tetraethyl orthocarbonate
see under ethyl orthocarbonate

2,3,4,5-tetrafluorobenzoyl chloride
(C_7HClF_4O; *94695-48-4*)   see: Levofloxacin; Rufloxacin hydrochloride

(*S*)-2,3,4,5-tetrafluoro-α-[[(2-hydroxy-1-methylethyl)amino]methylene]-β-oxobenzenepropanoic acid ethyl ester
($C_{15}H_{15}F_4NO_4$; *110548-02-2*)   see: Levofloxacin

1,2,3,4-tetrahydroacridine
($C_{13}H_{13}N$; *3295-64-5*)   see: Tacrine

1,2,3,4-tetrahydro-9-acridinecarboxamide
($C_{14}H_{14}N_2O$; *42878-53-5*)   see: Tacrine

1,2,3,4-tetrahydroacridine *N*-oxide
($C_{13}H_{13}NO$; *24403-51-8*)   see: Tacrine

1,2,3,4-tetrahydro-9-acridone
($C_{13}H_{13}NO$; *13161-85-8*)   see: Tacrine

2,3,4,5-tetrahydro-1*H*-benzazepin-2-one
($C_{10}H_{11}NO$; *4424-80-0*)   see: Benazepril

(*RS*)-4,5,6,7-tetrahydro-1*H*-benzimidazole-5-carboxylic acid
($C_8H_{10}N_2O_2$; *26751-24-6*)   see: Ramosetron hydrochloride

(3a*S*-*cis*)-tetrahydro-1,3-bis(phenylmethyl)-1*H*-furo-[3,4-*d*]imidazole-2,4-dione
($C_{19}H_{18}N_2O_3$; *28092-62-8*)   see: Biotin

1,2,4,9-tetrahydrocarbazol-3-one
($C_{12}H_{11}NO$; *51145-61-0*)   see: Ramatroban

(4a*R*-*cis*)-4,4a,5,7a-tetrahydrocyclopenta-1,3-dioxin-2-one
($C_7H_8O_3$; *159418-20-9*)   see: Abacavir

(3a*S*,8a*R*)-3,3a,8,8a-tetrahydro-2,2-dimethyl-3-[2(*S*)-benzyl-5-[4-(*tert*-butoxycarbonyl)-2(*S*)-(*tert*-butylcarbamoyl)-piperazino]-4(*R*)-hydroxyvaleryl]-2*H*-indeno[1,2-*d*]oxazole
($C_{38}H_{54}N_4O_6$; *166740-50-7*)   see: Indinavir sulfate

(3a*S*,8a*R*)-3,3a,8,8a-tetrahydro-2,2-dimethyl-3-[2(*S*)-benzyl-5-[2(*S*)-(*tert*-butylcarbamoyl)piperazino]-4(*R*)-hydroxyvaleryl]-2*H*-indeno[1,2-*d*]oxazole
($C_{33}H_{46}N_4O_4$; *182950-24-9*)   see: Indinavir sulfate

(3a*S*,8a*R*)-3,3a,8,8a-tetrahydro-2,2-dimethyl-3-[(2*S*)-2-benzyl-4-pentenoyl]-2*H*-indeno[1,2-*d*]oxazole
($C_{24}H_{27}NO_2$; *150323-06-1*)   see: Indinavir sulfate

[3a*S*-[3*S(*R***)],3aα,8aα]]-3,3a,8,8a-tetrahydro-2,2-dimethyl-3-[2-(oxiranylmethyl)-1-oxo-3-phenylpropyl]-2*H*-indeno[1,2-*d*]oxazole**
($C_{24}H_{27}NO_3$; *158512-24-4*)   see: Indinavir sulfate

(3a*S*,8a*R*)-3,3a,8,8a-tetrahydro-2,2-dimethyl-3-(3-phenylpropionyl)-2*H*-indeno[1,2-*d*]oxazole
($C_{21}H_{23}NO_2$; *141018-37-3*)   see: Indinavir sulfate

9,10,11,12-tetrahydro-9,10-[4,5][1,3]dioxoloanthracen-14-one
($C_{17}H_{12}O_3$; *5675-70-7*)   see: Bisantrene

(*R*)-(+)-tetrahydrofuran-2-carboxylic acid
($C_5H_8O_3$; *87392-05-0*)   see: Faropenem sodium

(±)-tetrahydrofuran-2-carboxylic acid
($C_5H_8O_3$; *16874-33-2*)   see: Alfuzosin; Faropenem sodium

tetrahydro-2-furancarboxylic acid anhydride with ethyl hydrogen carbonate
($C_8H_{12}O_5$; *167391-50-6*)   see: Alfuzosin

(3'aS,4'R,5'R,6'aR)-5'-[(tetrahydro-2H-pyran-2-yl)oxy]-4'-[(1E,3S)-4-methyl-3-[(tetrahydro-2H-pyran-2-yl)oxy]-1-octen-6-ynyl]-spiro[1,3-dioxolan-2,2'-[1H]pentalene]

($C_{29}H_{44}O_6$)   see: Iloprost

[3R-(3R*,6Z)]-3-[(tetrahydro-2H-pyran-2-yl)oxy]-6-tetra-decenal

($C_{19}H_{34}O_3$; 108051-90-7)   see: Orlistat

1-(1,2,3,6-tetrahydro-4-pyridyl)-2-benzimidazolinone

($C_{12}H_{13}N_3O$; 2147-83-3)   see: Droperidol

2,3,5,6-tetrahydro-1H-pyrrolizine

($C_7H_{11}N$; 20463-30-3)   see: Pilsicainide

4,6,7,8-tetrahydro-2,5(1H,3H)-quinolinedione

($C_9H_{11}NO_2$; 5057-12-5)   see: Carteolol

[8S-[8α(S*),10α]]-7,8,9,10-tetrahydro-6,8,10,11-tetrahy-droxy-1-methoxy-8-(4-methoxy-2,2-dimethyl-1,3-dioxo-lan-4-yl)-5,12-naphthacenedione

($C_{25}H_{26}O_{10}$; 56354-10-0)   see: Epirubicin

2,3,4,9-tetrahydro-N,N,N,9-tetramethyl-4-oxo-1H-carb-azole-3-methanaminium iodide

($C_{17}H_{23}IN_2O$; 99614-63-8)   see: Ondansetron

4,5,6,7-tetrahydrothieno[3,2-c]pyridine

(C_7H_9NS; 54903-50-3)   see: Clopidogrel hydrogensulfate; Ticlopidine

1,4,5,8-tetrahydroxyanthraquinone

see under leuco-1,4,5,8-tetrahydroxyanthraquinone

(5α,6β,11β)-5,11,17,21-tetrahydroxy-6-methylpregnane-3,20-dione

($C_{22}H_{34}O_6$; 76338-56-2)   see: Methylprednisolone

3β,11α,17,21-tetrahydroxy-5α-pregnan-20-one 21-acetate

($C_{23}H_{36}O_6$; 104068-20-4)   see: Halopredone diacetate

2,4,6,8-tetrahydroxypyrimido[5,4-d]pyrimidine

($C_6H_4N_4O_4$; 6713-54-8)   see: Dipyridamole

tetraisopropyl (4-chlorophenylthio)methylenediphos-phonate

($C_{19}H_{33}ClO_6P_2S$; 89987-31-5)   see: Tiludronate disodium

tetraisopropyl methylenediphosphonate

($C_{13}H_{30}O_6P_2$; 1660-95-3)   see: Clodronate disodium; Tiludronate disodium

(S)-N,N,N',N'-tetrakis(cyanomethyl)-1,2-propanediamine

($C_{11}H_{14}N_6$)   see: Dexrazoxane

2-tetralone

($C_{10}H_{10}O$; 530-93-8)   see: Fendosal

tetramethyl 2-butene-1,4-diylbisphosphonate

($C_8H_{18}O_6P_2$; 3858-16-0)   see: Betacarotene

4-(1,1,3,3-tetramethylbutyl)phenol

($C_{14}H_{22}O$; 140-66-9)   see: Benzethonium chloride; Clofoctol; Tyloxapol

2-[2-[4-(1,1,3,3-tetramethylbutyl)phenoxy]ethoxy]ethyl chloride

($C_{18}H_{29}ClO_2$; 65925-28-2)   see: Benzethonium chloride

γ,2,6,6-tetramethyl-1-cyclohexene-1-sorbaldehyde diethyl acetal

($C_{20}H_{34}O_2$; 99711-43-0)   see: Betacarotene

N,N,N',N'-tetramethylhexamethylenediamine

see under 1,6-bis(dimethylamino)hexane

N,N,N',N'-tetramethylmethanediammine

($C_5H_{14}N_2$; 51-80-9)   see: Topotecan

N,N,N,1-tetramethyl-1H-pyrrole-2-methanaminium iodide

($C_9H_{17}IN_2$; 54828-80-7)   see: Tolmetin

DL-2,2,5,5-tetramethylthiazolidine-4-carboxylic acid

($C_8H_{15}NO_2S$; 58131-62-7)   see: D-Penicillamine

4,7,10,13-tetraoxahexadecanedinitrile

($C_{12}H_{20}N_2O_4$; 57741-46-5)   see: Iodoxamic acid

4,7,10,13-tetraoxahexadecanedioyl chloride

($C_{12}H_{20}Cl_2O_6$; 31127-86-3)   see: Iodoxamic acid

tetraphosphorus hexaoxide

(O_6P_4; 12440-00-5)   see: Etidronic acid

1H-tetrazol-5-carboxylic acid 2-acetyl-6-(acetylamino)-phenyl ester

($C_{12}H_{11}N_5O_4$)   see: Pranlukast

tetrazole-1-acetic acid

($C_3H_4N_4O_2$; 21732-17-2)   see: Cefazolin; Ceftezole

tetrazolo[1,5-a]quinolin-5-ol

($C_9H_6N_4O$; 77177-27-6)   see: Imiquimod

3-(5-tetrazolyl)aniline

($C_7H_7N_5$; 73732-51-1)   see: Tazanolast

thebaine

($C_{19}H_{21}NO_3$; 115-37-7)   see: Buprenorphine; Oxymorphone

thenium iodide

($C_{15}H_{20}INOS$; 109732-56-1)   see: Thenium closilate

2-thenoyl chloride

(C_5H_3ClOS; 5271-67-0)   see: Stepronin; Suprofen; Tenonitrozole; Tienilic acid

2-(2-thenoylthio)propionic acid

($C_8H_8O_3S_2$; 81466-67-3)   see: Stepronin

2-thenylamine

(C_5H_7NS; 27757-85-3)   see: Azosemide; Thenium closilate

3-thenyl bromide

(C_5H_5BrS; 34846-44-1)   see: Thenyldiamine

2-thenyl chloride

(C_5H_5ClS; 765-50-4)   see: Methapyrilene; Thenalidine; Thenium closilate

theobromine

($C_7H_8N_4O_2$; 83-67-0)   see: Pentifylline; Protheobromine

theobromine sodium salt

($C_7H_7N_4NaO_2$; 1010-59-9)   see: Pentoxifylline

theophylline

($C_7H_8N_4O_2$; 58-55-9)   see: Acefylline; Cafedrine; Caffeine; Choline theophyllinate; Diprophylline; Doxofylline; Etamiphylline; Etofylline; Lomifylline; Pimefylline; Proxyphylline; Reproterol; Theophylline ethylenediamine; Xantinol nicotinate

theophylline-7-acetaldehyde

($C_9H_{10}N_4O_3$; 5614-53-9)   see: Doxofylline

O-[2-(7-theophyllinyl)ethyl] hydrogen sulfate

($C_9H_{12}N_4O_6S$; 55405-90-0)   see: Pyridofylline

thevetin A

($C_{42}H_{64}O_{19}$; 37933-66-7)   see: Peruvoside

thiamine

($C_{12}H_{17}ClN_4OS$; 59-43-8)   see: Acetiamine; Benfotiamine; Bentiamine; Bisbentiamine; Cocarboxylase; Fursultiamine; Midoriamin

thiamine bromide

($C_{12}H_{17}BrN_4OS$; 7019-71-8)   see: Thiamine

thiamine chloride

($C_{12}H_{18}Cl_2N_4OS$; 67-03-8)   see: Octotiamine

thiamine disulfide

($C_{24}H_{34}N_8O_4S_2$; 67-16-3)   see: Bisbentiamine

thiophosgene
(CCl$_2$S; *463-71-8*)   see: Tizanidine; Tolnaftate

thiophosphoryl chloride
(Cl$_3$PS; *3982-91-0*)   see: Thiotepa

thiosalicylic acid
(C$_7$H$_6$O$_2$S; *147-93-3*)   see: Chlorprothixene; Thiomersal

thiosemicarbazide
(CH$_5$N$_3$S; *79-19-6*)   see: Ambazone; Guanoxabenz

thiourea
(CH$_4$N$_2$S; *62-56-6*)   · see: Adrafinil; Amiphenazole;
Auranofin; Brinzolamide; Captodiame; Cefixime;
Cefmenoxime; Cefotaxime; Ceftazidime; Ceftriaxone;
Dipyridamole; Famotidine; Levamisole; Mesna;
Methylthiouracil; Modafinil; Pioglitazone; Pramipexole
hydrochloride; Propylthiouracil; Talipexole; Thiamylal;
Thiopental; Troglitazone

"thiovandid"
(C$_{12}$H$_{17}$NO$_2$S; *24115-07-9*)   see: Etamivan

thioxanthene
(C$_{13}$H$_{10}$S; *261-31-4*)   see: Metixene; Tiotixene

9*H*-thioxanthene-2-sulfonic acid
(C$_{12}$H$_{10}$O$_3$S$_2$)   see: Tiotixene

2-thioxo-1,3-dithiolane
(C$_3$H$_4$S$_3$; *822-38-8*)   see: Malotilate

2-thioxo-1,3-dithiole-4,5-dicarboxylic acid
(C$_5$H$_2$O$_4$S$_3$; *1008-62-4*)   see: Malotilate

threo-ethyl 2-hydroxy-3-amino-3-phenylpropionate
see under ethyl *threo*-3-amino-2-hydroxy-3-phenylpropionate

(±)-threo-methyl 2-hydroxy-3-(2-aminophenylthio)-3-(4-methoxyphenyl)propionate
(C$_{17}$H$_{19}$NO$_4$S; *84645-12-5*)   see: Diltiazem

DL-threo-3-(4-(methylsulfonylphenyl)serine
(C$_{10}$H$_{13}$NO$_5$S; *31925-26-5*)   see: Thiamphenicol

D$_G$-threo-3-(4-(methylsulfonylphenyl)serine ethyl ester
(C$_{12}$H$_{17}$NO$_5$S; *31925-29-8*)   see: Thiamphenicol

L-threoninamide
(C$_4$H$_{10}$N$_2$O$_2$; *49705-99-9*)   see: Aztreonam

D-threonine
(C$_4$H$_9$NO$_3$; *632-20-2*)   see: Cefbuperazone

L-threonine
(C$_4$H$_9$NO$_3$; *72-19-5*)   see: Aztreonam

L-threonine methyl ester hydrochloride
(C$_5$H$_{12}$ClNO$_3$; *39994-75-7*)   see: Aztreonam

thymidine
(C$_{10}$H$_{14}$N$_2$O$_5$; *50-89-5*)   see: Stavudine; Zidovudine

thymine
(C$_5$H$_6$N$_2$O$_2$; *65-71-4*)   see: Stavudine

thymol
(C$_{10}$H$_{14}$O; *89-83-8*)   see: (−)-Menthol; Moxisylyte

"cis,trans-tilidine"
(C$_{17}$H$_{23}$NO$_2$; *17243-69-5*)   see: Tilidine

tinazoline hydriodide
(C$_{11}$H$_{12}$IN$_3$S; *55107-59-0*)   see: Tinazoline hydrochloride

γ-tocopherol
(C$_{28}$H$_{48}$O$_2$; *54-28-4*)   see: α-Tocopherol

toluene
(C$_7$H$_8$; *108-88-3*)   see: Saccharin

p-toluenesulfamide sodium salt
(C$_7$H$_8$NNaO$_2$S; *18522-92-4*)   see: Nitrazepam; Tolbutamide

p-toluenesulfochloride
(C$_7$H$_7$ClO$_2$S; *98-59-9*)   see: Benproperine; Brinzolamide;
Carzenide; Cefoxitin; Diazepam; Flurotyl; Fosinopril;
Gusperimus trihydrochloride; Idarubicin; Idoxuridine;
Indeloxacine; Levocabastine; Mazindol; Medazepam;
Mibefradil hydrochloride; Nemonapride; Pioglitazone;
Prenalterol; Ropinirole; Tinidazole; Tolterodine

p-toluenesulfonamide
(C$_7$H$_9$NO$_2$S; *70-55-3*)   see: Carzenide; Tolazamide

2-toluenesulfonamide
(C$_7$H$_9$NO$_2$S; *88-19-7*)   see: Saccharin; Zafirlukast

p-toluenesulfonamide sodium salt
see under *p*-toluenesulfamide sodium salt

p-toluenesulfonic acid
(C$_7$H$_8$O$_3$S; *104-15-4*)   see: Cefaclor; Ganciclovir;
Perindopril

p-toluenesulfonic acid methyl ester
see under methyl 4-toluenesulfonate

p-toluenesulfonyl chloride
see under *p*-toluenesulfochloride

2-toluenesulfonyl chloride
(C$_7$H$_7$ClO$_2$S; *133-59-5*)   see: Saccharin

(2*R*)-2-(*p*-toluenesulfonyloxy)propionyl chloride
(C$_{10}$H$_{11}$ClO$_4$S; *88081-65-6*)   see: Imidapril

3-(*p*-toluenesulfonyloxy)propyl chloride
(C$_{10}$H$_{13}$ClO$_3$S; *632-02-0*)   see: Periciazine; Pipotiazine

(*S*)-*N*-(*p*-toluenesulfonyl)proline chloride
(C$_{12}$H$_{14}$ClNO$_3$S; *54731-09-8*)   see: Levofloxacin

m-toluidine
(C$_7$H$_9$N; *108-44-1*)   see: Toloxatone; Torasemide

o-toluidine
(C$_7$H$_9$N; *95-53-4*)   see: Afloqualone; Methaqualone;
Metolazone; Prilocaine

3-(*m*-toluidino)-1,2-propanediol
(C$_{10}$H$_{15}$NO$_2$; *42902-52-3*)   see: Toloxatone

p-tolunitrile
(C$_8$H$_7$N; *104-85-8*)   see: Acrivastine; Tranexamic acid

p-toluoyl chloride
see under *p*-methylbenzoyl chloride

(*E*)-3-[6-(*p*-toluoyl)-2-pyridinyl]acrylic acid
(C$_{16}$H$_{13}$NO$_3$; *94094-27-6*)   see: Acrivastine

6-[2-(*p*-tolyl)-1,3-dioxol-2-yl]pyridine-2-carboxaldehyde
(C$_{16}$H$_{15}$NO$_3$; *87848-97-3*)   see: Acrivastine

4-tolylmagnesium bromide
(C$_7$H$_7$BrMg; *4294-57-9*)   see: Losartan potassium;
Tolpropamine

S-tolylmethyl-L-cysteine
(C$_{11}$H$_{15}$NO$_2$S)   see: Eptifibatide

1-(*o*-tolyl)piperazine
(C$_{11}$H$_{16}$N$_2$; *39512-51-1*)   see: Dapiprazole

3-[4-(*o*-tolyl)-1-piperazinyl]propionic acid hydrazide
(C$_{14}$H$_{22}$N$_4$O; *72822-10-7*)   see: Dapiprazole

4-(*p*-tolyl)-1,2,3,6-tetrahydropyridine
(C$_{12}$H$_{15}$N; *59084-09-2*)   see: Moperone

Tos-Cl
see under *p*-toluenesulfochloride

O-tosyl-3-(*tert*-butoxycarbonylamino)-1-propanol
(C$_{15}$H$_{23}$NO$_5$S; *80909-96-2*)   see: Gusperimus
trihydrochloride

2,3,6-trideoxy-1,4-di-*O*-(trifluoroacetyl)-3-[(trifluoroacetyl)amino]-α-L-*arabino*-hexopyranose
($C_{12}H_{10}F_9NO_6$)   see: Epirubicin

2,3,6-trideoxy-3-trifluoroacetamido-4-*O*-trifluoroacetyl-α-L-*arabino*-hexopyranosyl chloride
($C_{10}H_{10}ClF_6NO_4$; *56354-09-7*)   see: Epirubicin

2,3,6-trideoxy-3-trifluoroacetamido-4-*O*-trifluoroacetyl-α-L-*lyxo*-hexopyranosyl chloride
($C_{10}H_{10}ClF_6NO_4$; *57785-90-7*)   see: Idarubicin

2,3,6-trideoxy-3-[(trifluoroacetyl)amino]-α-L-*arabino*-hexopyranose
($C_8H_{12}F_3NO_4$; *56354-08-6*)   see: Epirubicin

triethanolamine
($C_6H_{15}NO_3$; *102-71-6*)   see: Trolnitrate

triethoxymethane
see under ethyl orthoformate

4,5,6-triethoxy-7-nitro-3-(5,6,7,8-tetrahydro-4-methoxy-6-methyl-1,3-dioxolo[4,5-*g*]isoquinolin-5-yl)-1(3*H*)-isobenzofuranone
($C_{26}H_{30}N_2O_{10}$; *4973-70-0*)   see: Tritoqualine

triethylaluminum
($C_6H_{15}Al$; *97-93-8*)   see: Ibuprofen

triethylamine
($C_6H_{15}N$; *121-44-8*)   see: Acrivastine; Carindacillin; Docetaxel

triethylammonium acetate
($C_8H_{19}NO_2$; *5204-74-0*)   see: Deflazacort

triethylene glycol
($C_6H_{14}O_4$; *112-27-6*)   see: Iodoxamic acid

triethylene glycol monochlorohydrin
($C_6H_{13}ClO_3$; *5197-62-6*)   see: Etodroxizine

triethyl[[1-methyl-1-(2-propynyl)pentyl]oxy]silane
($C_{15}H_{30}OSi$; *58682-77-2*)   see: Misoprostol

triethyl orthoacetate
see under orthoacetic acid triethyl ester

triethyl orthoformate
see under ethyl orthoformate

triethyl orthopropionate
($C_9H_{20}O_3$; *115-80-0*)   see: Alclometasone dipropionate; Betamethasone dipropionate

triethyl phosphate
($C_6H_{15}O_4P$; *78-40-0*)   see: Fludarabine phosphate

triethyl phosphite
($C_6H_{15}O_3P$; *122-52-1*)   see: Foscarnet sodium; Gestrinone

7-*O*-triethylsilylbaccatin III
($C_{37}H_{52}O_{11}Si$; *115437-21-3*)   see: Paclitaxel

4-triethylsilyl-3-butyn-1-ol triethylsilyl ether
($C_{16}H_{34}OSi_2$; *160194-28-5*)   see: Rizatriptan benzoate

triethylsilyl chloride
($C_6H_{15}ClSi$; *994-30-9*)   see: Misoprostol; Paclitaxel; Rizatriptan benzoate

7-*O*-triethylsilyl-10-deacetylbaccatin III
($C_{35}H_{50}O_{10}Si$; *115437-18-8*)   see: Paclitaxel

[(triethylsilyl)oxy]acetic acid ethyl ester
($C_{10}H_{22}O_3Si$)   see: Paclitaxel

***cis*-3-(triethylsilyloxy)-4-phenyl-2-azetidinone**
($C_{15}H_{23}NO_2Si$)   see: Paclitaxel

trifluoroacetic anhydride
($C_4F_6O_3$; *407-25-0*)   see: Dofetilide; Dolasetron mesilate; Epirubicin; Imiquimod; Vinorelbine

1,1,1-trifluoroacetone
($C_3H_3F_3O$; *421-50-1*)   see: Mefloquine

N^6-trifluoroacetyl-N^2-carboxy-L-lysine anhydride
($C_9H_{11}F_3N_2O_4$; *42267-27-6*)   see: Lisinopril

N^6-(trifluoroacetyl)-L-lysine
($C_8H_{13}F_3N_2O_3$; *10009-20-8*)   see: Lisinopril

N^6-(trifluoroacetyl)-L-lysyl-L-proline
($C_{13}H_{20}F_3N_2O_4$; *103300-89-6*)   see: Lisinopril

2,3,4-trifluoroaniline
($C_6H_4F_3N$; *3862-73-5*)   see: Lomefloxacin

2,2,2-trifluoroethanol
($C_2H_3F_3O$; *75-89-8*)   see: Flurotyl; Fluroxene; Isoflurane; Lansoprazole

2,2,2-trifluoroethanol 4-methylbenzenesulfonate
($C_9H_9F_3O_3S$; *433-06-7*)   see: Flurotyl

2,2,2-trifluoroethanol potassium salt
($C_2H_2F_3KO$; *1652-14-8*)   see: Fluroxene

2,2,2-trifluoroethanol sodium salt
($C_2H_2F_3NaO$; *420-87-1*)   see: Flurotyl

2,2,2-trifluoroethyl 2,5-bis(2,2,2-trifluoroethoxy)benzoate
($C_{13}H_9F_9O_4$; *50778-57-9*)   see: Flecainide

2,2,2-trifluoroethyl iodide
($C_2H_2F_3I$; *353-83-3*)   see: Epitizide

(2,2,2-trifluoroethylthio)acetaldehyde dimethyl acetal
($C_6H_{11}F_3O_2S$; *84455-36-7*)   see: Epitizide; Polythiazide

2,2,2-trifluoroethyl trichloromethanesulfonate
($C_3H_2Cl_3F_3O_3S$; *23199-56-6*)   see: Quazepam

2,2,2-trifluoroethyl trifluoromethanesulfonate
($C_3H_2F_6O_3S$; *6226-25-1*)   see: Flecainide

6,7,8-trifluoro-1-(2-fluoroethyl)-1,4-dihydro-4-oxo-3-quinolinecarboxylic acid
($C_{12}H_7F_4NO_3$; *79660-52-9*)   see: Fleroxacin

6,7,8-trifluoro-4-hydroxy-3-quinolinecarboxylic acid
($C_{10}H_4F_3NO_3$; *151391-68-3*)   see: Fleroxacin

trifluoromethanesulfonic acid
(CHF_3O_3S; *1493-13-6*)   see: Loratadine; Oseltamivir

trifluoromethanesulfonic acid 4-[(2-methylpropyl)amino]-3-nitro-2-quinolinyl ester
($C_{14}H_{14}F_3N_3O_5S$; *157875-53-1*)   see: Imiquimod

trifluoromethanesulfonic acid 3-nitro-2,4-quinolinediyl ester
($C_{11}H_4F_6N_2O_8S_2$; *157875-58-6*)   see: Imiquimod

trifluoromethanesulfonic acid triethylsilyl ester
($C_7H_{15}F_3O_3SSi$; *79271-56-0*)   see: Tacrolimus

trifluoromethanesulfonic anhydride
($C_2F_6O_5S_2$; *358-23-6*)   see: Imiquimod; Zanamivir

4-trifluoromethoxyaniline
($C_7H_6F_3NO$; *461-82-5*)   see: Riluzole

2,4,5-trifluoro-3-methoxybenzenamine
($C_7H_6F_3NO$; *114214-45-8*)   see: Moxifloxacin hydrochloride

2,4,5-trifluoro-3-methoxybenzoyl chloride
($C_8H_4ClF_3O_2$; *112811-66-2*)   see: Moxifloxacin hydrochloride

1,1,1-trifluoro-2-methoxyethane
($C_3H_5F_3O$; *460-43-5*)   see: Isoflurane

3'-trifluoromethylacetanilide
($C_9H_8F_3NO$; *351-36-0*)   see: Flutamide; Nilutamide

2-trifluoromethylaniline
($C_7H_6F_3N$; *88-17-5*)   see: Floctafenine; Mabuterol; Mefloquine

triisopropyl borate

(C$_9$H$_{21}$BO$_3$; *5419-55-6*)   see: Losartan potassium; Rofecoxib

triisopropyl phosphite

(C$_9$H$_{21}$O$_3$P; *116-17-6*)   see: Clodronate disodium

(3R,4S)-3-(triisopropylsilyloxy)-4-phenyl-2-azetidinone

(C$_{18}$H$_{29}$NO$_2$Si; *132127-31-2*)   see: Docetaxel

triisopropylsilyl trifluoromethanesulfonate

(C$_{10}$H$_{21}$F$_3$O$_3$SSi; *80522-42-5*)   see: Tacrolimus

3,4,5-trimethoxybenzaldehyde

(C$_{10}$H$_{12}$O$_4$; *86-81-7*)   see: Sulmetozin; Trimethoprim

3-(3,4,5-trimethoxybenzamido)pyridine

(C$_{15}$H$_{16}$N$_2$O$_4$; *31638-96-7*)   see: Troxipide

3,4,5-trimethoxybenzenamine

(C$_9$H$_{13}$NO$_3$; *24313-88-0*)   see: Trimetrexate glucuronate

1,2,3-trimethoxybenzene

(C$_9$H$_{12}$O$_3$; *634-36-6*)   see: Trimetazidine

1,3,5-trimethoxybenzene

(C$_9$H$_{12}$O$_3$; *621-23-8*)   see: Buflomedil

3,4,5-trimethoxybenzoyl chloride

(C$_{10}$H$_{11}$ClO$_4$; *4521-61-3*)   see: Dilazep; Hexobendine; Trimethobenzamide; Trimetozine; Troxipide

2,3,4-trimethoxybenzyl chloride

(C$_{10}$H$_{13}$ClO$_3$; *1133-49-9*)   see: Trimetazidine

3,4,5-trimethoxybenzyl chloride

(C$_{10}$H$_{13}$ClO$_3$; *3840-30-0*)   see: Trimethoprim

3,4,5-trimethoxycinnamoyl chloride

(C$_{12}$H$_{13}$ClO$_4$; *10263-19-1*)   see: Cinepazet; Cinepazide

3,4,5-trimethoxyphenylacetonitrile

(C$_{11}$H$_{13}$NO$_3$; *13338-63-1*)   see: Gallopamil

3-(3,4,5-trimethoxyphenyl)glycidic acid sodium salt

(C$_{12}$H$_{13}$NaO$_6$; *39757-38-5*)   see: Tretoquinol

2-(3,4,5-trimethoxyphenyl)-3-methylbutyronitrile

(C$_{14}$H$_{19}$NO$_3$; *36622-33-0*)   see: Gallopamil

[(3,4,5-trimethoxyphenyl)methylene]propanedinitrile

(C$_{13}$H$_{12}$N$_2$O$_3$; *5688-82-4*)   see: Trimethoprim

4-[(2,3,4-trimethoxyphenyl)methyl]-1-piperazinecarbox-aldehyde

(C$_{15}$H$_{22}$N$_2$O$_4$; *92700-82-8*)   see: Trimetazidine

3,4,5-trimethoxytoluene

(C$_{10}$H$_{14}$O$_3$; *6443-69-2*)   see: Idebenone

trimethylacetyl chloride

see under pivaloyl chloride

trimethylamine

(C$_3$H$_9$N; *75-50-3*)   see: Acetylcholine chloride; Betaine hydrate; Bethanechol chloride; Carbachol; Carnitine; Cetrimonium bromide; Choline chloride; Choline hydroxide; Decamethonium bromide; Hexcarbacholine bromide; Miltefosine; Prolonium iodide

2,3,5-trimethylanisole

(C$_{10}$H$_{14}$O; *20469-61-8*)   see: Etretinate

6,6,9-trimethyl-9-azabicyclo[3.3.1]nonan-3β-ol

(C$_{11}$H$_{21}$NO; *36970-58-8*)   see: Mazaticol

trimethylchlorosilane

(C$_3$H$_9$ClSi; *75-77-4*)   see: Amoxicillin; Cefbuperazone; *cis*-Cefprozil; Fadrozole; Gestodene; Indanorex; Orlistat; Trifluridine

3,3,5-trimethylcyclohexanol

(C$_9$H$_{18}$O; *116-02-9*)   see: Cyclandelate

***cis*-3,3,5-trimethylcyclohexanol**

(C$_9$H$_{18}$O; *933-48-2*)   see: Micinicate

5-(2,6,6-trimethyl-1-cyclohexen-1-yl)-3-oxo-4-pentenal

(C$_{14}$H$_{20}$O$_2$)   see: Retinol

(1R-cis)-1,2,2-trimethyl-1,3-cyclopentanedicarboxylic acid compd. with (S)-N-ethyl-α-methyl-3-(trifluoromethyl)-benzeneethanamine (1:1)

(C$_{22}$H$_{32}$F$_3$NO$_4$; *17325-68-7*)   see: Dexfenfluramine

3',4',6'-trimethyl-2',5'-dihydroxyacetophenone

(C$_{11}$H$_{14}$O$_3$; *64794-45-2*)   see: Troglitazone

3-(2,5,5-trimethyl-1,3-dioxan-2-yl)thiophene

(C$_{11}$H$_{16}$O$_2$S; *138890-86-5*)   see: Brinzolamide

3-(2,5,5-trimethyl-1,3-dioxan-2-yl)-2-thiophenesulfon-amide

(C$_{11}$H$_{17}$NO$_4$S$_2$; *138890-87-6*)   see: Brinzolamide

3,7,11-trimethyl-2,6,10-dodecatrienol

(C$_{15}$H$_{26}$O; *4602-84-0*)   see: Indometacin farnesil

2,2,8-trimethyl-5-formyl-4H-pyrido[3,4-d]-1,3-dioxane

(C$_{11}$H$_{13}$NO$_3$; *6560-65-2*)   see: Cicletanine

2,3,5-trimethylhydroquinone

(C$_9$H$_{12}$O$_2$; *700-13-0*)   see: Seratrodast; α-Tocopherol; Troglitazone

(S)-2,2,4-trimethyl-4-[2-[(1-methylethyl)thio]ethyl]-1,3-di-oxolane

(C$_{11}$H$_{22}$O$_2$S; *123450-78-2*)   see: Troglitazone

(S)-2,3,5-trimethyl-6-[1-[(1-methylethyl)thio]-2-(2,2,4-tri-methyl-1,3-dioxolan-4-yl)ethyl]-1,4-benzenediol 4-acetate

(C$_{22}$H$_{34}$O$_5$S)   see: Troglitazone

N,N,6-trimethyl-2-(4-methylphenyl)imidazo[1,2-a]pyri-dine-3-methanamine

(C$_{18}$H$_{21}$N$_3$; *106961-33-5*)   see: Zolpidem

trimethylolpropane

(C$_6$H$_{14}$O$_3$; *77-99-6*)   see: Propatyl nitrate

trimethyl orthoacetate

(C$_5$H$_{12}$O$_3$; *1445-45-0*)   see: Brinzolamide; Diflorasone diacetate

trimethyl orthobenzoate

(C$_{10}$H$_{14}$O$_3$; *707-07-3*)   see: Betamethasone benzoate

trimethyl orthobutyrate

(C$_7$H$_{16}$O$_3$; *43083-12-1*)   see: Difluprednate

trimethyl orthoformate

(C$_4$H$_{10}$O$_3$; *149-73-5*)   see: Cisapride; Flosequinan; Lamivudine; Pyrimethamine; Troglitazone

trimethyl orthovalerate

(C$_8$H$_{18}$O$_3$; *13820-09-2*)   see: Betamethasone valerate; Prednival acetate

2,3,6-trimethyl-4-(oxiranylmethoxy)phenol acetate

(C$_{14}$H$_{18}$O$_4$; *22664-53-5*)   see: Metipranolol

2,3,5-trimethylphenol

(C$_9$H$_{12}$O; *697-82-5*)   see: Etretinate

2,4,6-trimethylphenol

(C$_9$H$_{12}$O; *527-60-6*)   see: Metipranolol

N,N,N-trimethyl-4-(phenylmethoxy)-1H-indole-2-methan-aminium iodide

(C$_{19}$H$_{23}$N$_2$O)   see: Mepindolol

trimethyl phosphate

(C$_3$H$_9$O$_4$P; *512-56-1*)   see: Lamivudine

trimethyl phosphite

(C$_3$H$_9$O$_3$P; *121-45-9*)   see: Betacarotene

1,2,2-trimethylpropylamine

(C$_6$H$_{15}$N; *3850-30-4*)   see: Pinacidil

tropine 2-propylvalerate
($C_{16}H_{29}NO_2$; *25333-49-7*)   see: Octatropine methylbromide

tropinone
($C_8H_{13}NO$; *532-24-1*)   see: Homatropine

tropinone-2,4-dicarboxylic acid
($C_{10}H_{13}NO_5$)   see: Homatropine

Trp-Met-Asp-Phe-NH₂
($C_{29}H_{36}N_6O_6S$; *1947-37-1*)   see: Ceruletide

tryptamine
($C_{10}H_{12}N_2$; *61-54-1*)   see: Vincamine

L-tryptophan
($C_{11}H_{12}N_2O_2$; *73-22-3*)   see: Eptifibatide; Oxitriptan

DL-tryptophan
($C_{11}H_{12}N_2O_2$; *54-12-6*)   see: L-Tryptophan

tyramine
($C_8H_{11}NO$; *51-67-2*)   see: Bezafibrate

Tyr-NH-NH-Z.HCl
($C_{17}H_{20}ClN_3O_4$; *17664-73-2*)   see: Ceruletide

L-tyrosine
($C_9H_{11}NO_3$; *60-18-4*)   see: Bentiromide; Cetrorelix;
Levodopa; Tirofiban hydrochloride

DL-tyrosine
($C_9H_{11}NO_3$; *556-03-6*)   see: Tiropramide

Tyr-Phe-OMe.HCl
($C_{19}H_{23}ClN_2O_4$; *65918-99-2*)   see: Desmopressin

U

undecanal
($C_{11}H_{22}O$; *112-44-7*)   see: Orlistat

undecanoyl chloride
($C_{11}H_{21}ClO$; *17746-05-3*)   see: Estradiol undecylate;
Nandrolone undecylate

10-undecenoyl chloride
($C_{11}H_{19}ClO$; *38460-95-6*)   see: Boldenone undecenylate

uracil
($C_4H_4N_2O_2$; *66-22-8*)   see: Fluorouracil

urea
(CH_4N_2O; *57-13-6*)   see: Alfuzosin; Allantoin; Amobarbital;
Barbital; Bromisoval; Butalbital; Carbasalate calcium;
Carbromal; Cyclopentobarbital; Dimethadione;
Dipyridamole; Enoximone; Ethotoin; Heptabarb; Metaxalone;
Methyclothiazide; Orotic acid; Paramethadione;
Pentobarbital; Phenacemide; Pheneturide; Phenobarbital;
Phenytoin; Proquazone; Secbutabarbital; Secobarbital;
Sulfadimethoxine; Thalidomide; Trimethadione

V

valeric anhydride
($C_{10}H_{18}O_3$; *2082-59-9*)   see: Estradiol valerate

valeronitrile
(C_5H_9N; *110-59-8*)   see: Eprosartan

valeryl chloride
(C_5H_9ClO; *638-29-9*)   see: Amsacrine; Betamethasone
divalerate; Diflucortolone valerate; Irbesartan; Valsartan

valienamine
($C_7H_{13}NO_4$; *38231-86-6*)   see: Voglibose

valiolamine
($C_7H_{15}NO_5$; *83465-22-9*)   see: Voglibose

vanillic acid
($C_8H_8O_4$; *121-34-6*)   see: Etamivan

vanillin
($C_8H_8O_3$; *121-33-5*)   see: Cyclovalone; Entacapone;
Etamivan; Levodopa

veratraldehyde
($C_9H_{10}O_3$; *120-14-9*)   see: Alfuzosin; Fenoldopam mesilate;
Moxaverine; Rimiterol; Vetrabutine

veratrole
($C_8H_{10}O_2$; *91-16-7*)   see: Papaverine; Tolcapone

vidarabine
($C_{10}H_{13}N_5O_4$; *5536-17-4*)   see: Vidarabine

vinblastine
($C_{46}H_{58}N_4O_9$; *865-21-4*)   see: Vindesine

(–)-vincadifformine
($C_{21}H_{26}N_2O_2$; *3247-10-7*)   see: Vincamine

(–)-vincadifformine 9-oxide
($C_{21}H_{26}N_2O_3$; *38199-35-8*)   see: Vincamine

(+)-vincamine
($C_{21}H_{26}N_2O_3$; *1617-90-9*)   see: Vinpocetine

(±)-vincamine
($C_{21}H_{26}N_2O_3$; *2122-39-6*)   see: Vincamine

vinylene carbonate
($C_3H_2O_3$; *872-36-6*)   see: Bisantrene

vinyl-β-ionol
($C_{15}H_{24}O$; *5208-93-5*)   see: Isotretinoin; Retinol; Tretinoin

vinylmagnesium bromide
(C_2H_3BrMg; *1826-67-1*)   see: Docetaxel; Montelukast
sodium; Paclitaxel

vinylmagnesium chloride
(C_2H_3ClMg; *3536-96-7*)   see: Levonorgestrel

5-vinyl-2-pyrrolidone
(C_6H_9NO; *7529-16-0*)   see: Vigabatrin

vitamin A acid ethyl ester
($C_{22}H_{32}O_2$; *3899-20-5*)   see: Tretinoin

vitamin D₂
($C_{28}H_{44}O$; *50-14-6*)   see: Calcipotriol

W

Wieland-Gumlich aldehyde
($C_{19}H_{22}N_2O_2$; *466-85-3*)   see: Alcuronium chloride

wintergreen oil
see under methyl salicylate

X

xanthene-9-carbonyl chloride
($C_{14}H_9ClO_2$; *26454-53-5*)   see: Propantheline bromide

xanthene-9-carboxylic acid
($C_{14}H_{10}O_3$; *82-07-5*)   see: Propantheline bromide

9*H*-xanthene-9-carboxylic acid 2-[bis(1-methylethyl)-amino]ethyl ester
($C_{22}H_{27}NO_3$; *13347-41-6*)   see: Propantheline bromide

xanthinol
($C_{13}H_{21}N_5O_4$; *2530-97-4*)   see: Xantinol nicotinate

2,3-xylenol
($C_8H_{10}O$; *526-75-0*)   see: Xibenolol

A

Acetals and Hemiacetals
see: Aldosterone; Ampiroxicam; Etopophos; Etoposide;
Medifoxamine; Mepitiostane; Teniposide
see also Acylals; Chloral hydrate derivatives; 1,3-Dioxanes;
1,3-Dioxolanes; Hemiketals; Steroid acetals; Thioacetals
Acetamides, acetylamino substituted acids and their
amides
see: Acamprosate calcium; Acetylcysteine; Acexamic acid;
Docarpamine; Oxaceprol
Acetamides, N-cyclic substituted acetamides
see: Acetazolamide; Aztreonam; Carumonam; Citiolone;
Methazolamide; Romurtide
Acetamides
see: Adrafinil; Alpidem; Azintamide; Caroxazone;
Ciclometasone; Iodamide; Modafinil; Oseltamivir;
Salacetamide; Zanamivir; Zolpidem
see also 2-Oxo-1-pyrrolidineacetamides; 1-Piperazineacet-
amides; 2-Thiopheneacetamides
Acetanilides, and derivatives
see: Acetarsol; Actarit; Benorilate; Deanol
acetamidobenzoate; Diloxanide; Diloxanide furoate;
Iocetamic acid; Iohexol; Metrizamide; Paracetamol;
Pilsicainide; Propacetamol; Zaleplon
see also Acetophenetidines; 1-Piperazineacetanilides; Pyrro-
lidineacetanilides
Acetic acid esters (acetates)
see: Aceclidine; Acetorphan; Acetylcholine chloride;
Aclatonium napadisilate; Alacepril; Benzquinamide;
Cinepazet; Diacerein; Diltiazem; Docetaxel; Escin;
Famciclovir; Josamycin; Menadiol diacetate; Midecamycin
acetate; Octotiamine; Paclitaxel; Roxatidine acetate;
Spiramycin; Thebacon; Thiopropazate; Vinblastine;
Vincristine; Vinorelbine; Visnadine
see also Rifamycins
Acetic acid esters (acetates), esters of phenols
see: Bisacodyl; Cyclofenil; Metipranolol; Moxisylyte;
Oxyphenisatin acetate
see also Acetylsalicylic acids also esters
Acetic acid esters (acetates), esters of carbohydrates
see: Acetyldigitoxin; α-Acetyldigoxin; β-Acetyldigoxin;
Auranofin; Cadexomer iodine; Lanatoside C; Pengitoxin
Acetic acid esters (acetates), Steroid 17-acetates
see: Anagestone acetate; Chlormadinone acetate; Clostebol
acetate; Cyproterone acetate; Flugestone acetate;
Flumedroxone acetate; Medroxyprogesterone acetate;
Megestrol acetate; Metenolone acetate; Nomegestrol acetate;
Norethisterone acetate; Norgestimate; Pentagestrone acetate;
Quingestanol acetate; Rocuronium bromide; Trenbolone
acetate
Acetic acid esters (acetates), Steroid acetates
see: Alfadolone acetate; Amcinonide; Betamethasone acetate;
Chloroprednisone acetate; Cortivazol; Deflazacort;
Desoxycortone acetate; Difluprednate; Fluazacort;
Fluocinonide; Fluperolone acetate; Fluprednidene acetate;
Fluprednisolone acetate; Formocortal; Hydrocortisone
acetate; Isoflupredone acetate; Melengestrol acetate;
Prednival acetate; Spironolactone
Acetic acid esters (acetates), Steroid diacetates
see: Diflorasone diacetate; Etynodiol acetate; Halopredone
diacetate; Pancuronium bromide; Pipecuronium bromide;
Tiomesterone; Triamcinolone diacetate; Vecuronium bromide
Acetic acids
see: Acefylline; Etodolac; Metiazinic acid; Mofezolac;
Montelukast sodium; Sulindac

see also Cyclohexylacetic acids; Glycolic acids; Komplexons;
Naphthylacetic acids; Phenoxyacetic acids; Phenylacetic
acids; Pyrazoleacetic acids; Pyridineacetic acids; Pyr-
roleacetic acids; Thioglycolic acids
Acetonides
see: Topiramate
see also Fluoroprednisolone acetonides; Steroid acetonides
Acetonitriles
see: Lanoconazole
see also Diphenylacetonitriles; Phenylacetonitriles
Acetophenetidines
see: Phenacetin
Acetophenones
see: Acebutolol; Acetohexamide; Adrenalone; Celiprolol;
Fentonium bromide; Lobeline; Lofepramine; Spizofurone
Acetylsalicylic acids, also esters
see: Acetylsalicylic acid; Benorilate
Acridines, also derivatives
see: Acriflavinium chloride; Amsacrine; Dimetacrine;
Ethacridine; Mepacrine
Acridines, aminotetrahydroacridines
see: Tacrine
Acrylic acids (2-Propenoic acids)
see: Acrivastine; Cicrotoic acid; Eprosartan
see also Cinnamic acids
Acylals
see: Cefditoren pivoxil; Pivampicillin; Pivmecillinam;
Sultamicillin
Adamantanes (Tricyclo[3.3.1.1^{3,7}]decanes)
see: Amantadine; Memantine; Methenamine; Rimantadine;
Tromantadine
Adamantane-1-carboxylic acid esters
see: Betamethasone adamantoate
Adenines (6-Aminopurines)
see: Abacavir; Alatrofloxacin mesilate; Fludarabine
phosphate; Vidarabine
see also Adenosines
Adenosines
see: Bucladesine sodium
Adenosines, Deoxyadenosines
see: Ademetionine; Cladribine; Cobamamide
Adrenochromes (3-Hydroxy-1-methyl-5,6-indolinediones)
see: Carbazochrome
Alanines (2-Aminopropionic acids)
see: L-Alanine; Rebamipide
see also Cysteines; Histidines; Tryptophans
Alanines, and their amides, anilides
see: Carticaine; Enalapril; Enalaprilat; Imidapril; Moexipril;
Prilocaine; Quinapril hydrochloride; Ramipril; Spirapril;
Tocainide; Trandolapril
β-Alanines (3-Aminopropionic acids)
see: Balsalazide sodium; Iobenzamic acid; Iocetamic acid
β-Alanines, and their amides and esters
see: Docetaxel; Paclitaxel; Pantethine; Perindopril;
Polaprezinc
Alcohols
see: Ajmaline; Dimercaprol; Fexofenadine hydrochloride;
Montelukast sodium; Stavudine; Tiadenol; Toloxatone;
Zeranol
see also Alkynols and Alkynol esters; Benzyl alcohols; Bromo
alcohols; Chloro alcohols; Cyclohexanols; Iodo alcohols;
Polyhydroxy compounds; Pyridinemethanols; Sugar alcohols;
2-Thiophenemethanols; Vitamin A compounds
Alcohols, alk(aryl)oxy substituted
see: Dihydroxydibutyl ether; Etofenamate; Polidocanol;
Troxerutin
see also Glycerol ethers; Phenoxypolyethoxyethanols

Aminoalkylphenols
see: Amoxicillin; Aspoxicillin; Cefadroxil; Cefatrizine;
Cefoperazone; Cefpiramide; *cis*-Cefprozil; Dobutamine;
Dopamine; Fenoterol; Ibopamine; Pholedrine; Ritodrine;
Tolterodine
***m*-Aminobenzoic acids, also amides, esters**
see: Balsalazide sodium; Bumetanide; Mesalazine; Olsalazine
sodium; Parsalmide; Piretanide; Proxymetacaine
see also 5-(p-Sulfamoylphenylazo)salicylic acids
***p*-Aminobenzoic acids, also amides, esters**
see: Balsalazide sodium; Bentiromide; Benzocaine;
Benzonatate; Butacaine; Butethamine; Camostat;
Chloroprocaine; Deanol acetamidobenzoate; Leucinocaine;
Nafamostat; Otilonium bromide; Oxybuprocaine;
Procainamide; Procaine; Tetracaine
see also p-Aminosalicylic acids; Pteridines
2-Aminoethanol salts
see: Ciclopirox
2-Aminoethyl esters
see: Trolnitrate
see also 2-Aminoethyl thioesters
2-Aminoethyl ethers
see: Amlodipine; Bepridil; Dimazole; Eprazinone;
Lercanidipine hydrochloride; Myrtecaine; Quinisocaine;
Rosiglitazone; Tromantadine; Zotepine
2-Aminoethyl ethers, quaternary β-Ammonioethyl ethers
see: Benzethonium chloride; Ciclonium bromide
2-Aminoethyl sulfides
see: Captodiame; Cimetidine; Ebrotidine; Imipenem;
Nizatidine; Ranitidine; Tibezonium iodide
2-Aminoethyl thioesters
see: Amifostine
Aminoguanidines and Amidinohydrazones (Guanylhydra-zones)
see: Ambazone; Guanabenz; Guanoclor; Guanoxabenz
Amino ketones
see: Acepromazine; Aceprometazine; Ketamine; Nizofenone
Aminophenols and Aminophenol ethers
see: Amodiaquine; Amsacrine; Dezocine; Edrophonium
chloride; Oxyphenbutazone; Phentolamine; Tiocarlide
see also Phenetidines
Aminophenols, Acylaminophenols (Hydroxyanilides)
see: Acetarsol; Diloxanide; Paracetamol; Propacetamol
***p*-Aminosalicylic acids**
see: *p*-Aminosalicylic acid
***p*-Aminosalicylic acids, amides, esters and hydrazides**
see: Bromopride; Cinitapride; Cisapride; Clebopride;
Metoclopramide; Mosapride citrate; Nemonapride;
Propoxycaine
Amino sulfonic acids
see: Acamprosate calcium
Amino thiols (Amino thioalcohols)
see: Tioguanine
Ammonium compounds (quaternary), Trialkylamine derivatives
see: Cetrimonium bromide; Cholestyramine; Neostigmine
methylsulfate; Tridihexethyl chloride
Ammonium compounds (quaternary), quaternary *N*-hete-rocyclic Systems
see: Amezinium metilsulfate; Detajmium bitartrate;
Elliptinium acetate; Prajmalium bitartrate; Tiquizium bromide
see also Isoquinolines; Morphinans; Morpholines; Phenothi-azines; Quinolines; Thiazoles
Ammonium compounds (quaternary), Antiseptics etc.
see: Cetrimonium bromide; Dodeclonium bromide;
Domiphen bromide; Methylthioninium chloride; Tibezonium
iodide

Ammonium compounds (quaternary), other
see: Benzalkonium chloride; Edrophonium chloride;
Isopropamide iodide
see also 2-Aminoethyl ethers; Benzilic acid esters; Benzylami-nes
Ammonium compounds (multiple quaternary)
see: Ambenonium chloride; Atracurium besilate;
Decamethonium bromide; Dequalinium chloride;
Dimethyltubocurarinium chloride; Gallamine triethiodide;
Hexafluronium bromide; Hexamethonium chloride;
Pancuronium bromide; Pipecuronium bromide; Prolonium
iodide; Tubocurarine chloride
Androsta-1,4-dienes
see: Boldenone undecenylate; Fluticasone propionate;
Formebolone; Loteprednol etabonate; Metandienone
Androsta-3,5-dienes
see: Penmesterol
Androstanes
see: Epitiostanol; Furazabol; Mepitiostane; Pancuronium
bromide; Pipecuronium bromide; Rocuronium bromide;
Stanozolol; Vecuronium bromide
see also Androstanolones (Dihydrotestosterones) also methyl derivatives
Androstanolones (Dihydrotestosterones), also Methyl derivatives
see: Androstanolone; Drostanolone; Mestanolone;
Mesterolone; Oxymetholone; Trilostane
Androst-1-enes
see: Metenolone acetate
Androst-4-enes
see: Fluoxymesterone; Formestane; Spironolactone;
Tiomesterone
see also Testosterones
Androst-5-enes
see: Azacosterol; Methandriol; Prasterone; Prasterone
enanthate
Anhydrides
see: Isosorbide dinitrate; Isosorbide mononitrate
Anilides
see: Adipiodone; Atorvastatin calcium; Iocarmic acid;
Leflunomide; Tazanolast
see also α-Amino acids; Carbanilides; Crotonanilides; Form-anilides; Methanesulfonanilides; Phenetidines
Anilines
see: Aminoglutethimide; Anileridine; Mifepristone;
Torasemide
*see also Aminophenols and Aminophenol ethers; Anilides;
Benzylanilines; Bromoanilines; Chloroanilines; Iodoanilines;
Nitroanilines; Phenetidines; Phenylenediamines*
Anthracenes
see: Bisantrene; Melitracen
see also Anthranols; Anthraquinones
Anthranilic acids
see: Antrafenine; Etofenamate; Floctafenine; Flufenamic
acid; Furosemide; Glafenine; Lobenzarit; Meclofenamic acid;
Mefenamic acid; Tolfenamic acid; Tolycaine; Tranilast
Anthranols
see: Dithranol
Anthraquinones
see: Diacerein; Mitoxantrone
Antibiotics
see: Cycloserine; Fosfomycin; Griseofulvin; Mupirocin;
Mycophenolic acid; Pyrrolnitrin; Spectinomycin;
Streptozocin
see also Carbapenem antibiotics; Cephamycins; Clavam anti-biotics; Erythromycins; Glycopeptide antibiotics; Leucomy-cins; Macrolide antibiotics; Mitomycins; Monobactam antibi-otics; Naphthacene antibiotics; Oligosaccharide antibiotics;

1,2-Benzisothiazoles
see: Saccharin; Ziprasidone hydrochloride
1,2-Benzisoxazoles
see: Risperidone; Zonisamide
Benzo[5,6]cyclohepta[1,2-*b*]pyridines
see: Azatadine; Desloratadine; Loratadine
Benzo[4,5]cyclohepta[1,2-*b*]thiophenes
see: Ketotifen; Pizotifen
1,4-Benzodiazepines
see: Chlordiazepoxide; Medazepam
see also Dibenzo[b,e][1,4]diazepines; [1,3]Oxazino[3,2-d]
[1,4]benzodiazepines; Pyrido[2,3-b][1,4]benzodiazepines;
[1,2,4]Triazolo[4,3-a][1,4]benzodiazepines
1,4-Benzodiazepines, bromo and fluoro derivatives
see: Bromazepam; Cinolazepam; Doxefazepam; Ethyl
loflazepate; Flunitrazepam; Flurazepam; Flutoprazepam;
Metaclazepam; Quazepam
1,4-Benzodiazepin-2-ones
see: Bromazepam; Diazepam; Ethyl loflazepate; Flurazepam;
Flutoprazepam; Nordazepam; Pinazepam; Prazepam;
Quazepam; Tetrazepam
1,4-Benzodiazepin-2-ones, 3-Hydroxy- or 7-nitro-derivatives
see: Camazepam; Cinolazepam; Clonazepam; Doxefazepam;
Flunitrazepam; Lorazepam; Lormetazepam; Nimetazepam;
Nitrazepam; Oxazepam; Temazepam
1,5-Benzodiazepines
see: Tibezonium iodide
1,5-Benzodiazepine-2,4-diones
see: Clobazam
2,3-Benzodiazepines
see: Tofisopam
1,4-Benzodioxanes (2,3-Dihydro-1,4-benzodioxines)
see: Doxazosin; Guanoxan; Silibinin
Benzo[1,2-*b*:3,4-*b*']dipyrans
see: Visnadine
Benzofurans (Coumarones)
see: Befunolol; Benfurodil hemisuccinate
Benzofurans, 2,3-Dihydro- or 3-Benzoyl-derivatives
see: Amiodarone; Benzarone; Benzbromarone; Benziodarone;
Griseofulvin; Spizofurone
Benzofuro[3,2-*c*][1]benzoxepines
see: Oxetorone
Benzoic acids
see: Cloperastine; Eprosartan; Telmisartan; Thiomersal
see also Chlorobenzoic acids also esters; Fluoresceins; Hy-
droxybenzoic acids; Salicylic acids; Sulfamoylbenzoic acids
Benzoic acids, amides (Benzamides)
see: Bentiromide; Indoramin; Nelfinavir mesylate; Paclitaxel;
Proglumetacin; Proglumide; Sulfabenzamide; Tiropramide;
Triamcinolone benetonide
Benzoic acids, amides of substituted benzoic acids
see: Procarbazine; Tripamide
see also Iodobenzoic acid amides; 3,4,5-Trimethoxybenzoic
acid amides
Benzoic acids, amides as *N*-benzoyl derivatives (also substituted) of *N*-heterocyclic Systems
see: Aniracetam; Endralazine; Proglumetacin; Sulmetozin;
Trimetozine; Vesnarinone
Benzoic acids, anilides
see: Fominoben; Iobenzamic acid
Benzoic acids, esters
see: Benfluorex; Bentiamine; Benzyl benzoate;
Betamethasone benzoate; Bisbentiamine; Bopindolol;
Docetaxel; Estradiol benzoate; Paclitaxel
Benzoic acids, esters as Local anesthetics
see: Hexylcaine; Meprylcaine; Piperocaine

Benzoic acids, esters of substituted benzoic acids
see: Bitolterol; Prednisolone sodium sulfobenzoate
see also 3,4,5-Trimethoxybenzoic acid esters
Benzoic acids, thioesters
see: Benfotiamine; Bentiamine
Benzoic acids, hydrazides
see: Benmoxin; Clopamide; Zorubicin
Benzoic acids, other derivatives
see: Benzoyl peroxide; Saccharin
see also Benzonitriles
Benzonitriles
see: Bicalutamide; Bunitrolol; Epanolol; Fadrozole; Letrozole
Benzophenones
see: Amfenac sodium; Bromfenac sodium; Cloperastine;
Dexketoprofen trometamol; Exifone; Ketoprofen; Mexenone;
Piketoprofen; Tolcapone
Benzophenones, Chlorobenzophenones
see: Fenofibrate; Morclofone; Nizofenone; Rilmazafone
[1]Benzopyrano[2,3-*b*]pyridines
see: Amlexanox; Pranoprofen
Benzo[*g*]quinolines
see: Quinagolide hydrochloride
Benzo[*a*]quinolizines
see: Benzquinamide
Benzo[*ij*]quinolizines
see: Flumequine
Benzoquinones
see: Ambazone; Idebenone; Seratrodast; Ubidecarenone
Benzoquinones, (2,5-Bis(1-aziridinyl)-1,4-benzoquinones)
see: Carboquone; Triaziquone
1,2,4-Benzothiadiazine 1,1-dioxides
see: Diazoxide
1,2,4-Benzothiadiazine 1,1-dioxides, (6-Chloro- or 6-Trifluoro-7-sulfonamides and their derivatives)
see: Altizide; Bemetizide; Bendroflumethiazide;
Benzthiazide; Butizide; Chlorothiazide; Cyclopenthiazide;
Cyclothiazide; Epitizide; Ethiazide; Hydrochlorothiazide;
Hydroflumethiazide; Methyclothiazide; Paraflutizide;
Polythiazide; Teclothiazide; Trichlormethiazide
2,1,3-Benzothiadiazoles
see: Tizanidine
1,5-Benzothiazepines
see: Diltiazem
1,2-Benzothiazine-3-carboxamide 1,1-dioxides
see: Ampiroxicam; Isoxicam; Meloxicam; Piroxicam
Benzothiazoles
see: Dimazole; Ethoxzolamide; Pramipexole hydrochloride;
Riluzole; Tiaramide
Benzo[*b*]thiophenes
see: Raloxifene hydrochloride; Sertaconazole; Zileuton
Benzotriazoles
see: Alizapride
2,1,3-Benzoxadiazoles (Benzofurazans)
see: Isradipine
Benzoxathioles
see: Tioxolone
1,3-Benzoxazines
see: Caroxazone; Chlorthenoxazine
3,1-Benzoxazines
see: Efavirenz
1,4-Benzoxazines
see: Nazasetron
see also Pyrido[1,2,3-de]-1,4-benzoxazines
2,5-Benzoxazocines
see: Nefopam
Benzoxazoles
see: Benoxaprofen; Flunoxaprofen
see also Chlorobenzoxazoles

C

Carbamic acids, esters (of substituted carbamic acids with alkanols)
see: Docetaxel; Flupirtine; Moracizine; Prednisolone steaglate; Tiracizine
Carbamic acids, esters [with alkanediols (dicarbamates)]
see: Carisoprodol; Felbamate; Mebutamate; Meprobamate; Tybamate
Carbamic acids, esters with phenols and naphthols
see: Rivastigmine
Carbamic acids, esters with furanols
see: Amprenavir
Carbamic acids, esters (with N-containing alcohols or phenols)
see: Bambuterol; Bluensomycin; Camazepam; Carboquone; Carumonam; Cefoxitin; Cefuroxime; Novobiocin; Pyridinol carbamate
see also Mitomycins
Carbamic acids, esters (with N-quaternary alcohols or phenols)
see: Bethanechol chloride; Carbachol; Demecarium bromide; Hexcarbacholine bromide; Neostigmine methylsulfate
Carbamic acids, esters (with quaternary Pyridinols)
see: Distigmine bromide; Pyridostigmine bromide
Carbamoylpiperazines
see: Cefbuperazone; Cefoperazone; Diethylcarbamazine; Piperacillin
Carbanilic acids, esters
see: Diperodon
Carbanilic acids, esters or thioesters of substituted carbanilic acids
see: Fencarbamide; Tolnaftate; Zafirlukast
Carbanilides
see: Triclocarban
see also Thiocarbanilides
Carbapenem Antibiotics
see: Imipenem; Meropenem
Carbazic acids (Hydrazinecarboxylic acids), esters
see: Cadralazine; Todralazine
Carbazoles
see: Carazolol; Carprofen; Carvedilol; Ondansetron; Ramatroban
Carbohydrates
see: Lactulose; Zanamivir
see also Polyhydroxy acids; Polysaccharides
Carbohydrates, amino derivatives
see: Acarbose; Glucametacin; D-Glucosamine; Metrizamide; Romurtide; Streptozocin; Voglibose
see also Oligosaccharide antibiotics
Carbohydrates, other derivatives
see: Auranofin; Clobenoside; Nicofuranose; Topiramate; Tribenoside
Carbonic acid esters (Carbonates)
see: Ampiroxicam; Bacampicillin; Candesartan cilexetil; Docarpamine; Loteprednol etabonate; Prednicarbate; Sobuzoxane; Syrosingopine
see also 1,3-Dioxol-2-ones
Carbonylurea derivatives
see: Cabergoline
Carboxylic acids and salts, (aliphatic monocarboxylic acids)
see: Foscarnet sodium; Gamolenic acid; Isotretinoin; Mupirocin; Mycophenolic acid; Tretinoin; Undecylenic acid; Valproic acid
see also Iodofatty acids and esters
Carboxylic acids and salts, (other monocarboxylic acids)
see: Acipimox; Orotic acid; Thioctic acid

see also Bromo carboxylic acids; Chloro carboxylic acids; Cyclohexanecarboxylic acids; Fluoro carboxylic acids; Hydroxy acids; Indancarboxylic acids; Oxo acids; Penam and Penem antibiotics; Piperidinecarboxylic acids; Thiophenecarboxylic acids
Carboxylic acids and salts, dicarboxylic acids
see: Azelaic acid; Carbocisteine; Clinofibrate; Ioglycamic acid; Lobenzarit; Nedocromil; Oxaliplatin
see also Glutaric acids
Carboxylic acids and salts, monoesters of dicarboxylic acids
see: Benazepril; Cilazapril; Fumagillin; Imidapril; Moexipril; Quinapril hydrochloride; Ramipril; Spirapril; Telmesteine; Temocapril; Trandolapril
Cardenolides
see: Gitaloxin; Peruvoside; g-Strophanthin; Thevetin A
see also Digitoxigenins; Digoxigenins; Gitoxigenins; k-Strophanthidins
Carotenes
see: Betacarotene; Canthaxanthin
Cephalosporins, 3-(acetoxymethyl) derivatives (Cephalosporanic acid derivatives)
see: Cefacetrile; Cefaloglycin; Cefalotin; Cefapirin; Cefotaxime
Cephalosporins, 7-(α-aminophenylacetamido) derivatives
see: Cefaclor; Cefadroxil; Cefalexin; Cefaloglycin; Cefatrizine; Cefoperazone; Cefpiramide; *cis*-Cefprozil
Cephalosporins, other 3-substituted derivatives
see: Cefamandole; Cefatrizine; Cefazedone; Cefazolin; Cefbuperazone; Cefmenoxime; Cefoperazone; Cefotetan; Cefotiam; Cefpiramide; Ceftezole; Flomoxef; Latamoxef
Cephalosporins, other 7-substituted derivatives
see: Cefaclor; Cefditoren pivoxil; Cefixime; Cefmenoxime; Cefotaxime; Cefotiam; Ceftazidime; Ceftizoxime; Ceftriaxone; Cefuroxime
Cephalosporins, other
see: Cefaloridine; Cefradine; Cefsulodin
see also Cephamycins; Oxacephem antibiotics
Cephamycins
see: Cefbuperazone; Cefotetan; Cefoxitin; Flomoxef
Chloral hydrate derivatives
see: Chloral hydrate; Chloralodol
Chloramphenicols and related Antibiotics
see: Azidamfenicol; Chloramphenicol; Thiamphenicol
Chlorinated hydrocarbons
see: Halothane; Mitotane
Chlorine compounds, tricyclic chlorine compounds
see: Amoxapine; Clocapramine; Clomipramine; Cloxazolam; Clozapine; Flutazolam; Ketazolam; Loratadine; Loxapine; Mexazolam; Midazolam; Mosapramine; Tianeptine sodium
see also [1,2,4]Triazolo[4,3-a][1,4]benzodiazepines
Chlorine compounds, other
see: Alpidem; Amiloride; Anagrelide hydrochloride; Azelastine; Azimilide hydrochloride; Azintamide; Brotizolam; Carbinoxamine; Chlormezanone; Chlorthenoxazine; Cladribine; Clobazam; Clotiazepam; Clotrimazole; Croconazole; Desloratadine; Diazoxide; Efavirenz; Etizolam; Guanfacine; Ketamine; Lamotrigine; Lanoconazole; Loprazolam; Montelukast sodium; Muzolimine; Pyrrobutamine; Pyrrolnitrin; Sertindole; Sertraline; Sibutramine hydrochloride; Teicoplanin; Thenium closilate; Tiamenidine; Tiaramide; Ticlopidine; Tizanidine; Viminol; Ziprasidone hydrochloride; Zopiclone
see also 1,4-Benzodiazepines; 1,4-Benzodiazepin-2-ones
Chlorine mercury compounds
see: Chlormerodrin
Chlorine platinum compounds
see: Cisplatin

Crotonamides
see: Cropropamide; Crotetamide; Sulfadicramide
Crotonanilides
see: Crotamiton
Crotonic acids (2-Butenoic acids)
see: Cicrotoic acid
Curare Alkaloids
see: Dimethyltubocurarinium chloride; Tubocurarine chloride
Curare Alkaloids of the strychnine type
see: Alcuronium chloride
Cyclobutanes
see: Butorphanol; Nalbuphine; Sibutramine hydrochloride
1,1-Cyclobutanedicarboxylic acids and derivatives
see: Carboplatin
Cycloheptanes and -heptenes
see: Bencyclane; Heptabarb; Incadronic acid
Cyclohexadienes
see: Cefradine; Epicillin; Glaziovine
see also Benzoquinones
Cyclohexanamines
see: Ambroxol; Bromhexine; Ciclacillin; Ketamine; Oxaliplatin; Pramiverine
Cyclohexanecarbonitriles
see: Levocabastine
Cyclohexanecarboxylic acids
see: Cicloxilic acid; Cynarine; Tranexamic acid
Cyclohexanecarboxylic acids, amides
see: Ciclacillin; Nateglinide; Praziquantel
Cyclohexanecarboxylic acids, esters
see: Benexate; Ciclometasone; Dicycloverine
Cyclohexanols
see: Ambroxol; Cyclobutyrol; Inositol; Tramadol; Venlafaxine
see also Alkynylcyclohexanol derivatives; Cyclohexanecarboxylic acids; Menthols; Oligosaccharide antibiotics
Cyclohexanols, esters
see: Candesartan cilexetil; Cyclandelate; Fumagillin; Micinicate
Cyclohexanols, ethers
see: Cyclomethycaine
Cyclohexanones
see: Canthaxanthin; Cyclovalone; Glaziovine; Griseofulvin; Ketamine; Nabilone; Tenylidone
Cyclohexenecarboxylic acids and their esters
see: Oseltamivir; Tilidine
Cyclohexenes
see: Alatrofloxacin mesilate; Cinitapride; Cyclobarbital; Docetaxel; Griseofulvin; Hexobarbital; Paclitaxel; Tetrazepam
Cyclohexylacetic acids
see: Cyclobutyrol; Gabapentin
Cyclohexylacetic acids, esters
see. Cetiedil
see also Benzilic acid esters (Hexahydro derivatives) also quaternary
Cyclohexylidene compounds
see: Clinofibrate; Cyclofenil; Cyclovalone; Tenylidone
3-Cyclohexylpropionic acids
see: Cicrotoic acid
Cyclooctanes
see: Docetaxel; Paclitaxel
Cyclopenta[b]furans
see: Epoprostenol
Cyclopentanes
see: Amcinonide; Cyclopentamine; Cyclopenthiazide; Cycrimine; Penbutolol; Penthienate methobromide; Rifapentine; Zafirlukast

Cyclopentanol ethers (Cyclopentyl ethers)
see: Mepitiostane; Penmesterol; Pentagestrone acetate; Quinestrol; Quingestanol acetate
Cyclopentanones and Cyclopentenones
see: Loxoprofen
Cyclopentenes and Cyclopentadienes
see: Abacavir; Cyclopentobarbital
see also Cyclopentanones and Cyclopentenones
Cyclopent[ij]isoquinolines
see: Glaziovine
3-Cyclopentylpropionic acid esters
see: Estradiol cypionate; Testosterone cypionate
Cyclopropanamines
see: Alatrofloxacin mesilate; Tranylcypromine
Cyclopropanes
see: Abacavir; Betaxolol; Calcipotriol; Cibenzoline; Cilastatin; Cimetropium bromide; Ciprofibrate; Efavirenz; Flutoprazepam; Milnacipran hydrochloride; Montelukast sodium; Nevirapine; Prazepam; Rilmenidine; Spizofurone
Cyclopropanes, N-(Cyclopropylmethyl)morphinans
see: Buprenorphine; Nalmefene; Naltrexone
Cysteines
see: Acetylcysteine; Bucillamine; Carbocisteine; Cilastatin
Cysteines, esters
see: Mecysteine hydrochloride
Cytosines (4-Amino-2(1H)-pyrimidinones)
see: Ancitabine; Citicoline; Cytarabine; Flucytosine; Gemcitabine; Lamivudine; Zalcitabine

D

Decanoic acid esters (Decanoates, Capric acid esters)
see: Nandrolone decanoate
Deoxycorticosterones (Deoxycortones)
see: Desoxycortone acetate
Dextrins and Cyclodextrins
see: Piroxicam cyclodextrin
Diamines
see: Alfuzosin; Ambroxol; Amifostine; Amiloride; Amiphenazole; Aprindine; Azacosterol; Dopexamine; Ethacridine; Hexoprenaline; Lamotrigine; Mepacrine; Oseltamivir; Phenazopyridine; Pramipexole hydrochloride
see also Ethylenediamines; Methylenediamines; Phenylenediamines; Platinum compounds; Phenazathionium compounds; Quinolinamines
p,p'-Diaminodiphenyl sulfones (p,p'-Sulfonyldianilines)
see: Acediasulfone; Dapsone; Sulfoxone sodium
1,3-Diazaspiro[4.4]nonanes
see: Irbesartan
1,4-Diazepines and perhydro-1,4-diazepines (Homopiperazines)
see: Bunazosin; Dilazep; Emedastine; Fasudil; Homofenazine
see also 1,4-Benzodiazepines; 6H-Thieno[3,2-f][1,2,4]triazolo[4,3-a][1,4]diazepines
Dibenz[b,e]azepines (Morphanthridines)
see: Perlapine
Dibenz[b,f]azepines, also aminoalkyl- or 10,10-dihydro derivatives
see: Carbamazepine; Carpipramine; Clocapramine; Clomipramine; Desipramine; Imipramine; Lofepramine; Metapramine; Mosapramine; Opipramol; Quinupramine; Tiracizine; Trimipramine
Dibenz[b,f]azepines, 10,11-dihydro derivatives
see: Oxcarbazepine

see also Oxiranes; Rifamycins

Ergolines
see: Cabergoline; Nicergoline; Pergolide
see also Lysergamides

Ergotamans
see: Bromocriptine; Dihydroergocristine; Dihydroergotamine;
Ergotamine

Erythromycins
see: Azithromycin; Erythromycin; Erythromycin estolate;
Erythromycin ethylsuccinate

Esculetins (6,7-Dihydroxycoumarins)
see: Folescutol

Esters, esters of Aminoethoxyethanols
see: Butamirate; Dimethoxanate; Oxeladin; Pentoxyverine;
Pipazetate

Esters, esters of Dialkylaminoalkanols
see: Bornaprine

Esters, esters of Trialkylammonioalkanols
see: Otilonium bromide; Oxitefonium bromide; Penthienate
methobromide; Propantheline bromide
see also Cholines also esters

Esters, bisquaternary esters of dicarboxylic acids
see: Demecarium bromide; Distigmine bromide;
Hexcarbacholine bromide; Suxamethonium chloride

Esters, other
see: Carbimazole; Ethoheptazine; Flavoxate; Gefarnate;
Malotilate; Molsidomine; Mupirocin
see also 2-Aminoethyl esters; Ethylene glycol esters; Glycerol esters

Estra-3,5-dienes
see: Quingestanol acetate

Estra-4,9-dienes
see: Mifepristone

Estra-4,15-dienes
see: Gestodene

Estradiols and their esters and ethers
see: Estradiol; Estradiol benzoate; Estradiol cypionate;
Estradiol valerate; Estradiol undecylate; Estramustine
phosphate; Promestriene

Estradiols, ethynyl- and methylestradiols
see: Ethinylestradiol; Mestranol; Moxestrol; Quinestrol

Estra-4,9,11-trienes
see: Norgestrienone; Trenbolone acetate; Trenbolone
hexahydrobenzyl carbonate

Estr-4-enes, 17α-ethynyl derivatives
see: Etynodiol acetate; Lynestrenol; Norethisterone;
Norethisterone acetate; Norethisterone enanthate

Estr-4-enes, 17α-alkyl-17β-hydroxyestr-4-en-3-ones and their esters
see: Methylestrenolone; Mibolerone; Norethandrolone;
Norethisterone; Norethisterone acetate; Norethisterone
enanthate

Estr-4-enes, 17α-alkylestr-4-ene-3β,17β-diol esters
see: Etynodiol acetate

Estr-4-enes, 17α-alkylestr-4-en-17β-ols
see: Allylestrenol; Ethylestrenol; Lynestrenol

Estr-4-enes, 17β-hydroxyestr-4-en-3-ones (Nortestosterones)
see: Nandrolone; Nandrolone decanoate; Nandrolone
hexyloxyphenylpropionate; Nandrolone phenylpropionate;
Nandrolone undecylate

Estr-4-enes, other
see: Gestonorone caproate
see also Gon-4-enes

Estr-5(10)-enes, 17α-alkyl-17β-hydroxyestr-5(10)-en-3-ones
see: Noretynodrel; Tibolone

Estriols and their esters and ethers
see: Epimestrol; Estriol; Estriol succinate

Estrols and related compounds
see: Bifluranol; Dienestrol; Hexestrol; Methestrol
dipropionate

Estrones and derivatives
see: Estrone

9,10-Ethanoanthracenes (Dibenzo[*b,e*]bicyclo-[2.2.2]octa-dienes)
see: Benzoctamine; Maprotiline

Ethers
see: Brinzolamide; Emedastine; Indeloxacine; Metaclazepam;
Obidoxime chloride; Oseltamivir; Rabeprazole sodium;
Sildenafil; Zipeprol
see also Aminoalkyl ethers; 2-Aminoethyl ethers; Chlorophenol ethers; Ethylene glycol ethers; Glycerol ethers; Halogen ethers; Phenol ethers

Ethylenediamines
see: Aminopromazine; Binedaline; Butalamine; Camylofin;
Edetic acid; Ethambutol; Hexobendine; Mitoxantrone;
Trientine

Ethylenediamines, *N*-acyl derivatives
see: Bromopride; Cinchocaine; Epanolol; Fenoxedil;
Pramiracetam hydrochloride

Ethylenediamines, Antihistaminics and Antihistaminics (chloro derivatives)
see: Chloropyramine; Chloropyrilene; Histapyrrodine;
Mepyramine; Methapyrilene; Thenyldiamine; Tripelennamine

Ethylene glycol esters
see: Etofibrate; Hydroxyethyl salicylate
see also Ethylene glycol ether esters

Ethylene glycol ethers
see: Aciclovir; Benzethonium chloride; Bisoprolol;
Glymidine; Omoconazole nitrate; Tetroxoprim
see also Phenoxypolyethoxyethanols; 1-Piperazineethoxy-ethanols

Ethylene glycol ethers, (Di-, Tri- and Polyethylene glycol ethers)
see: Benzonatate; Iodoxamic acid; Iotroxic acid; Polidocanol

Ethylene glycol ether esters
see: Benzonatate; Cilnidipine; Etofenamate; Nimodipine;
Valaciclovir

F

Flavanones
see: Silibinin

Flavans
see: Cianidanol

Flavone glycosides
see: Diosmin; Troxerutin

Flavones
see: Flavoxate
see also Flavanones

Fluoranthenes
see: Florantyrone

Fluorenes
see: Hexafluronium bromide; Indecainide

Fluoresceins
see: Fluorescein; Merbromin

Fluorinated hydrocarbons
see: Halothane; Perflunafene

G

Glycerol esters
see: Colfosceril palmitate; Floctafenine; Glafenine
see also 3-Phenoxy-1,2-propanediols
Glycerol ethers
see: Cadexomer iodine; Cromoglicic acid; Febuprol;
Ganciclovir; Suplatast tosilate
see also 3-Phenoxy-1,2-propanediols
Glycines (Aminoacetic acids)
see: Acediasulfone; Benazepril; Betaine hydrate; Temocapril;
Vancomycin
see also Komplexons
Glycines, N-acyl derivatives, amides
see: Astromicin; Cefradine; Gusperimus trihydrochloride;
Ioxaglic acid; Midodrine; Oxetacaine; Rilmazafone;
Stepronin; Tiopronin; Tiracizine; Tolrestat
Glycines, anilides
see: Butanilicaine; Lidocaine; Tolycaine
Glycines, esters
see: Acetorphan; Prednisolamate; Prednylidene
diethylaminoacetate; Propacetamol
Glycolic acids
see: Aceclofenac; Acemetacin; Bendazac; Carumonam;
Cefixime; Cetirizine
see also Phenoxyacetic acids; Thioglycolic acids
Glycolic acids, amides
see: Camostat; Gusperimus trihydrochloride; Roxatidine
acetate; Tromantadine
see also Mandelic acid amides
Glycolic acids, anilides
see: Ioglycamic acid; Iotroxic acid
Glycolic acids, esters
see: Bendacort; Mazaticol; Mibefradil hydrochloride;
Penthienate methobromide; Prednisolone steaglate
see also Benzilic acid esters
Glycolic acids, other derivatives
see: Nedaplatin
Glycopeptide Antibiotics
see: Teicoplanin; Vancomycin
Glycoproteins
see: Abciximab
Glycosides, N-glycosides
see: Pentostatin
Gold compounds
see: Auranofin; Sodium aurothiomalate
Gona-4,9,11-trienes
see: Gestrinone
Gon-4-enes
see: Levonorgestrel; Norboletone; Norgestimate; Norgestrel
Guaiacols (2-Methoxyphenols)
see: Alibendol; Diosmin; Guajacol; Rescimetol; Silibinin
Guaiacols, guaiacol ethers
see: Guaifenesin; Methocarbamol; Propanidid
see also 1,2-Dimethoxybenzenes
Guanidines[(Aminoiminomethyl)amino compounds]
see: Benexate; Betanidine; Camostat; Creatinolfosfate;
Ebrotidine; Famotidine; Gabexate; Guanadrel; Guanethidine
sulfate; Guanfacine; Guanoxan; Gusperimus trihydrochloride;
Nafamostat; Zanamivir
*see also Biguanides and N-(chlorophenyl) derivatives; Sulfa-
nilylguanidines*
Guanidines, cyanoguanidines
see: Cimetidine; Pinacidil
Guanines (2-Amino-1,9-dihydro-6H-purin-6-ones)
see: Aciclovir; Ganciclovir; Penciclovir; Valaciclovir

H

Halogen amines
see: Ketamine
see also Bromoanilines; Chloroanilines
Halogenated hydrocarbons
see: Halothane
Halogen ethers
see: Enflurane; Isoflurane; Methoxyflurane
*see also Bromophenol ethers; Chloro ethers; Chlorophenol
ethers; Fluoro ethers; Fluorophenol ethers; Iodophenol ethers*
Hemiketals
see: Amphotericin B; Natamycin
Heptanoic acid esters (Heptanoates, Enanthates)
see: Norethisterone enanthate; Prasterone enanthate;
Testosterone enanthate
Heptanoic and Heptenoic acids
see: Amineptine; Atorvastatin calcium; Cerivastatin sodium;
Cilastatin; Fluvastatin sodium; Pravastatin; Seratrodast;
Tianeptine sodium
**Hexadecanoic acid esters (Hexadecanoates, Palmitic acid
esters)**
see: Colfosceril palmitate
Hexanoic acids (Caproic acids)
see: Acexamic acid; Aminocaproic acid
Hexanoic acids, esters (Hexanoates)
see: Fluocortolone caproate; Gabexate; Gestonorone caproate;
Hydroxyprogesterone caproate
Hexenoic and Hexadienoic acids, also esters
see: Mycophenolate mofetil; Mycophenolic acid
Histidines
see: L-Histidine; Incadronic acid
Homosulfanilamides
see: Mafenide
Hydantoins (2,4-Imidazolidinediones)
see: Allantoin; Azimilide hydrochloride; Clodantoin;
Dantrolene; Ethotoin; Fosphenytoin sodium; Mephenytoin;
Nilutamide; Phenytoin
see also 1-[(5-Nitro-2-furfurylidene)amino]hydantoins
Hydrazide hydrazones
see: Nifuroxazide; Nifurzide; Zorubicin
Hydrazides
see: Benserazide; Bumadizone; Isocarboxazid; Mitopodozide
see also Isonicotinohydrazides also N²-Hydrazones (other)
Hydrazines
see: Carbidopa; Dihydralazine; Endralazine; Hydralazine;
Phenelzine; Pildralazine; Procarbazine
Hydrazones
see: Azimilide hydrochloride; Bisantrene; Budralazine
see also Hydrazide hydrazones
Hydroquinones (1,4-Benzenediols)
see: Etamsylate; Gentisic acid
Hydroquinones, monoethers (p-Alkoxyphenols)
see: Monobenzone; Prenalterol; Xamoterol
Hydroquinones, diethers
see: Fenoxedil; Flecainide; Mefexamide; Methoxamine;
Midodrine; Pramocaine
Hydroquinones, Ether esters
see: Metipranolol; Moxisylyte
Hydroxamic acids (N-Hydroxyamides)
see: Adrafinil; Bufexamac; Deferoxamine;
Hydroxycarbamide; Ibuproxam; Oxametacin

Indenes
see: Dimetindene; Indeloxacine; Indenolol; Indinavir sulfate;
Sulindac; Zolmitriptan
1-Indoleacetic acids
see: Clometacin
3-Indoleacetic acids, also amides and ester
see: Acemetacin; Cinmetacin; Glucametacin; Indometacin;
Indometacin farnesil; Oxametacin; Proglumetacin
2-Indolecarboxylic acids
see: Perindopril; Trandolapril
2(or 3)-Indolecarboxylic acids, esters
see: Dolasetron mesilate; Tropisetron
Indoles
see: Binedaline; Bopindolol; Delavirdine mesilate; Fluvastatin
sodium; Indalpine; Indoramin; Mepindolol; Molindone;
Naratriptan; Pindolol; Ramosetron hydrochloride; Rizatriptan
benzoate; Sertindole; Sumatriptan; Tinazoline hydrochloride;
Zafirlukast
see also Eburnamenines; Pyrano[3,4-b]indoles; Tryptophans
Indoles, piperazinylalkyl derivatives
see: Oxypertine
Indolines
see: Indapamide
2-Indolinones and 2,3-Indolinediones (Isatins)
see: Oxyphenisatin acetate; Ropinirole; Ziprasidone
hydrochloride
Indolo[2,3-*a*]quinolizines
see: Ajmaline; Detajmium bitartrate; Prajmalium bitartrate
see also Eburnamenines; Yohimbans
Inositol esters (Mesoinositol esters)
see: Inositol nicotinate
Inorganic compounds
see: Cisplatin; Gallium nitrate; Magaldrate
Iodine compounds
see: Cadexomer iodine; Haloprogin; Idoxuridine
Iodo alcohols
see: Domiodol; Iopydol
Iodoanilines
see: Iobenzamic acid; Iopamidol; Iotrolan
Iodobenzoic acid amides
see: Metrizamide
see also Isophthalamides
**Iodobenzoic acids and esters, (3-Amino-2,4,6-triiodoben-
zoic acids and esters)**
see: Amidotrizoic acid; Iodamide; Metrizoic acid
**Iodobenzoic acids and esters, (5-Amino-2,4,6-triiodoiso-
phthalamic acids)**
see: Iocarmic acid; Iotalamic acid; Ioxaglic acid; Ioxitalamic
acid
**Iodobenzoic acids and esters, [3,3'-(Alkylenedicarbonyl-
diimino)bis(2,4,6-triiodobenzoic acids)]**
see: Adipiodone; Iocarmic acid; Ioglycamic acid
**Iodobenzoic acids and esters, [3,3'-(Di-,Tri- and Tetra-
oxaalkylenedicarbonyldiimino)bis(2,4,6-triiodobenzoic
acids)]**
see: Iodoxamic acid; Iotroxic acid
Iodofatty acids and esters
see: Iofendylate
**Iodohydroxyphenylcarboxylic acids, Iodohydroxyphen-
oxyphenylcarboxylic acids and esters**
see: Dextrothyroxine; Etiroxate; Levothyroxine; Liothyronine
Iodophenol ethers
see: Amiodarone

Iodophenols
see: Benziodarone; Bupheniode
Iodophenylpropionic acids, Iodocinnamic acids and esters
see: Bunamiodyl; Iopanoic acid; Iophenoic acid
Iodopyridinones and Iodopyridinols
see: Diodone; Iopydol; Propyliodone
Isoalloxazines
see: Riboflavin
Isobenzofurans, dihydro derivatives (Phthalans)
see: Citalopram
Isoflavones
see: Ipriflavone
1-Isoindolinones (Phthalimidines)
see: Chlortalidone; Clorexolone; Indobufen; Indoprofen
Isonicotinamides
see: Cefsulodin
Isonicotinic acid esters
see: Dexamethasone 21-isonicotinate
Isonicotinohydrazides, also *N*²-hydrazones (other)
see: Glyconiazide; Iproniazid; Isoniazid; Nialamide;
Streptoniazid
Isonicotinothioamides
see: Ethionamide; Protionamide
Isophthalamides
see: Picotamide
Isophthalamides, 2,4,6-triiodo derivatives
see: Iohexol; Iopamidol; Iotrolan
Isophthalic acid esters
see: Ditophal
Isoquinolines
see: Fasudil; Quinisocaine
see also Aporphines; Pyrazino[2,1-a]isoquinolines
Isoquinolines, (1-Benzyl and 1-phenyl derivatives)
see: Dimoxyline; Ethaverine; Moxaverine; Papaverine
Isoquinolines, (Tetrahydroisoquinolines)
see: Debrisoquin; Gliquidone; Moexipril; Nomifensine;
Quinapril hydrochloride
see also Curare alkaloids
**Isoquinolines, [Tetrahydroisoquinolines (1-Benzyl or
1-Phthalidyl derivatives)]**
see: Atracurium besilate; Tretoquinol; Tritoqualine
Isoquinolines, (Tetrahydroisoquinolinols and -diols)
see: Tretoquinol
Isoquinolines, (Octa- and Perhydroisoquinolines)
see: Nelfinavir mesylate; Saquinavir
**Isoquinolines, [6,7-Methylenedioxyisoquinolines (1,3-
Dioxolo[4,5-*g*]isoquinolines)]**
see: Tritoqualine
Isoquinolines, Isoquinolinones
see: Tilisolol hydrochloride
Isoquinolines, 1,3-Isoquinolinediones
see: Gliquidone
Isoquinolines, quaternary
see: Atracurium besilate
Isothiocyanates (Mustard oils)
see: Benzyl mustard oil
Isoxazoles
see: Danazol; Glisoxepide; Isocarboxazid; Isoxicam;
Leflunomide; Mofezolac
Isoxazolidines
see: Cycloserine

Mitomycins
see: Mitomycin
Monobactam Antibiotics
see: Aztreonam; Carumonam
Morphinans
see: Butorphanol; Dextromethorphan; Dimemorfan;
Levallorphan; Levorphanol
Morphinans (4,5-Epoxy derivatives), Dihydromorphines, Dihydromorphinones, Morphines, Normorphines
see: Codeine; Dihydrocodeine; Ethylmorphine; Hydrocodone;
Hydromorphone; Morphine; Nalbuphine; Nalorphine;
Naltrexone; Oxycodone; Oxymorphone; Pholcodine
Morphinans (4,5-Epoxy derivatives), other
see: Buprenorphine; Nalmefene; Naloxone; Thebacon
Morpholides
see: Fominoben; Sulmetozin; Trimetozine; Xamoterol
Morpholines
see: Doxapram; Emorfazone; Folescutol; Fomocaine;
Minaprine; Moclobemide; Molindone; Molsidomine;
Moracizine; Morinamide; Moroxydine; Mosapride citrate;
Mycophenolate mofetil; Nimorazole; Rocuronium bromide;
Timolol
Morpholines, (N-[Aryl(alkyl)oxyalkyl] derivatives)
see: Floredil; Morclofone; Pholcodine; Pramocaine
Morpholines, (3,3-Diphenylpropyl derivatives)
see: Dextromoramide
Morpholines, C-substituted
see: Amorolfine; Fenbutrazate; Indeloxacine; Oxaflozane;
Phendimetrazine; Phenmetrazine; Reboxetine; Viloxazine
Morpholines, quaternary
see: Tiemonium iodide

N

Naphthacene Antibiotics
see: Aclarubicin; Daunorubicin; Doxorubicin; Epirubicin;
Idarubicin; Pirarubicin; Zorubicin
see also Tetracyclines
Naphthalenecarboxylic acids and derivatives
see: Bephenium hydroxynaphthoate; Mitopodozide; Nafcillin;
Tolrestat
Naphthalenes
see: Butenafine; Cetrorelix; Naftidrofuryl; Naftifine;
Naphazoline; Terbinafine
Naphthalenes, hydro derivatives
see: Levobunolol; Lovastatin; Mibefradil hydrochloride;
Nadolol; Perflunafene; Pravastatin; Simvastatin; Tetryzoline
Naphthalenesulfonic acids and Naphtholsulfonic acids
see: Aclatonium napadisilate
Naphthohydroquinones (1,4-Naphthalenediols) and derivatives
see: Menadiol diacetate; Menadiol sodium diphosphate
see also Rifamycins
Naphthols, esters and ethers
see: Lovastatin; Methallenestril; Nabumetone; Nadoxolol;
Nafamostat; Naftopidil; Naproxen; Pravastatin; Simvastatin;
Tolnaftate
see also Naphthoquinones
Naphthoquinones
see: Menadione; Phytomenadione
Naphthylacetic acids
see: Naproxen
Naphthylamines, tetrahydro derivatives
see: Sertraline; Tramazoline

1,5-Naphthyridines
see: Apalcillin
see also Eburnamenines
1,8-Naphthyridines, 1,4-Dihydro-4-oxo-1,8-naphthyridine-3-carboxylic acids
see: Enoxacin; Nalidixic acid; Tosufloxacin
1,8-Naphthyridines, 5,8-Dihydro-5-oxo-1,8-naphthyridine-6-carboxylic acid
see: Trovafloxacin mesilate
Nicotinic acids (also Hydro derivatives)
see: Nicotinic acid
Nicotinic acids, Anilinonicotinic acids
see: Niflumic acid
Nicotinic acids, amides
see: Cefpiramide; Niaprazine; Nicorandil; Nicotinamide;
Nifenazone; Nikethamide
Nicotinic acids, esters
see: Etofibrate; Hepronicate; Micinicate; Nicergoline;
Nicoclonate; Nicotafuryl; Nicotinic acid benzyl ester;
Ronifibrate; Tazarotene
Nicotinic acids, esters (Tetra- and Hexanicotinates of polyhydroxy compounds)
see: Inositol nicotinate; Niceritrol; Nicofuranose
Nitric acid esters (Nitrates)
see: Isosorbide dinitrate; Isosorbide mononitrate; Nicorandil;
Nipradilol; Pentaerythrityl tetranitrate; Propatyl nitrate;
Trolnitrate
Nitriles (Cyanides)
see: Anastrozole; Citalopram; Cyamemazine; Entacapone;
Milrinone; Nilvadipine; Olprinone hydrochloride;
Periciazine; Zaleplon
see also Acetonitriles; Benzonitriles; Cyclohexanecarbonitriles; Diphenylacetonitriles; Phenylacetonitriles; Propionitriles; Steroid carbonitriles
2,2',2''-Nitrilotriethanols
see: Trolnitrate
Nitroanilines
see: Flutamide; Niclosamide
see also Nitrophenol ethers
Nitrobenzoic acids, amides and anilides
see: Cinitapride
Nitro compounds
see: Acenocoumarol; Dantrolene; Efonidipine hydrochloride
ethanol; Loprazolam; Nifenalol; Nifurzide; Nilutamide;
Nitroxoline; Nizatidine; Nizofenone; Pyrrolnitrin; Ranitidine
5-Nitro-2-furaldehyde semicarbazones
see: Nitrofural
Nitrofurfurylideneamines (5-Nitro-2-furaldehyde derivatives)
see: Nifuroxazide; Nifurtimox
see also 5-Nitro-2-furaldehyde semicarbazones
1-[(5-Nitro-2-furfurylidene)amino]hydantoins
see: Nifurtoinol; Nitrofurantoin
1-[(5-Nitro-2-furfurylidene)amino]-2-oxazolidinones
see: Furazolidone; Nifuratel
3-(5-Nitro-2-furyl)allylideneamines
see: Nifurzide
5-Nitro-2-furylvinyl compounds
see: Nifurprazine
4- or 5-Nitroimidazoles
see: Azathioprine; Metronidazole; Nimorazole; Nitrefazole;
Secnidazole; Tinidazole
Nitrophenol ethers
see: Nimesulide
Nitrophenols
see: Entacapone; Tolcapone

Penicillins, Benzylpenicillins
see: Benzylpenicillin; Carbenicillin; Carfecillin; Carindacillin; Clometocillin; Sulbenicillin
Penicillins, α-Aminobenzylpenicillins and similar Penicillins
see: Amoxicillin; Ampicillin; Apalcillin; Aspoxicillin; Azidocillin; Epicillin; Metampicillin
Penicillins, α-Aminobenzylpenicillin esters
see: Bacampicillin; Lenampicillin; Pivampicillin; Sultamicillin; Talampicillin
Penicillins, α-Ureidobenzylpenicillins
see: Azlocillin; Mezlocillin; Piperacillin
Penicillins, Phenoxymethylpenicillins
see: Pheneticillin; Phenoxymethylpenicillin; Propicillin
Penicillins, Phenyl- and Naphthylpenicillins
see: Meticillin; Nafcillin
Penicillins, Isoxazolylpenicillins
see: Cloxacillin; Dicloxacillin; Flucloxacillin; Oxacillin
Penicillins, other heterocyclic substitutet Penicillins
see: Hetacillin; Temocillin; Ticarcillin
Penicillins, 6-(Alkylideneamino)penicillanic acid derivatives
see: Mecillinam; Pivmecillinam
Penicillins, 6-Malonamidopenicillanic acid derivatives
see: Carbenicillin; Carfecillin; Carindacillin; Temocillin; Ticarcillin
Penicillins, chloro, 6-methoxy derivatives, other
see: Ciclacillin; Clometocillin; Cloxacillin; Dicloxacillin; Flucloxacillin; Temocillin
Pentaerythritol esters and ethers
see: Niceritrol; Pentaerythrityl tetranitrate
Peptide Antibiotics
see: Ciclosporin; Enviomycin; Stallimycin; Viomycin
see also Glycopeptide antibiotics; Peptolide antibiotics
Peptide Hormones
see: Angiotensinamide; Buserelin; Cetrorelix; Deslorelin; Desmopressin; Eptifibatide; Felypressin; Ornipressin; Oxytocin; Saralasin acetate
see also Glycoproteins
Peptides and Polypeptides
see: Aprotinine; Ceruletide; Dornase alfa; Pentagastrin; Protirelin; Romurtide
see also Pteridines
Peptolide Antibiotics
see: Dactinomycin
Peroxides
see: Benzoyl peroxide
Phenanthrenes
see: Halofantrine
see also Aporphines; Morphinans
Phenanthrenes, Phenanthrenecarboxylic acids
see: Ecabet sodium
4,7-Phenanthrolines
see: Phanquinone
Phenazathionium compounds
see: Methylthioninium chloride
Phenethylamines
see: Amprenavir; Bevantolol; Denopamine; Dofetilide; Dopexamine; Gallopamil; Prolintane; Verapamil
see also α-Methylphenethylamines
Phenetidines
see: Lactylphenetidin; Phenacaine
see also Acetophenetidines

Phenol ethers
see: Anethole; Anethole trithione; Aniracetam; Astemizole; Benzethonium chloride; Bufexamac; Butropium bromide; Chlorotrianisene; Croconazole; Diltiazem; Etretinate; Febuprol; Fenoxazoline; Fomocaine; Ketoconazole; Metaxalone; Mofezolac; Morclofone; Nefazodone hydrochloride; Neticonazole hydrochloride; Picotamide; Pifoxime; Pimobendan; Pioglitazone; Terconazole; Tirofiban hydrochloride; Tramadol; Troglitazone; Tyloxapol; Urapidil
see also Aminophenols and Aminophenol ethers; Bromophenol ethers; Chlorophenol ethers; Curare alkaloids; 1,2-Dimethoxybenzenes; Diphenyl ethers; Fluorophenol ethers; Iodophenol ethers; Nitrophenol ethers; Phenetidines; Phloroglucinol triethers; Thiophenol ethers
Phenol ethers, Alkylenedioxydibenzenes
see: Dibrompropamidine; Pentamidine
Phenolphthalein analogous Laxatives
see: Bisacodyl; Normolaxol; Oxyphenisatin acetate; Sodium picosulfate
Phenolphthaleins
see: Phenolphthalein
Phenols
see: Dronabinol; Elliptinium acetate; Epanolol; Hydroxystilbamidine isethionate; Meptazinol; Oxymetazoline; Propofol; Quinagolide hydrochloride; Raloxifene hydrochloride; Xibornol
see also Aminoalkylphenols; Aminophenols and Aminophenol ethers; Biphenyl-x,x'-diols; Bromophenols; Chlorophenols; Flavans; Flavones; Fluorophenols; Hydroxybenzoic acids; Iodophenols; Morphinans; Phenolphthaleins
Phenols, Alkoxyphenols
see: Mexenone
Phenolsulfonic acids
see: Etamsylate
Phenones
see: Clometacin; Enoximone; Ketorolac; Mebendazole; Pyrovalerone; Raloxifene hydrochloride; Sofalcone; Tolmetin
see also Benzophenones; Butyrophenones; Chlorophenones; Propiophenones
Phenones, [(4-Fluorophenyl)-4-piperidinylmethanones]
see: Ketanserin
Phenones, other fluoro derivatives
see: Flubendazole
see also p-Fluorobutyrophenones
Phenothiazines
see: Mequitazine
see also Phenazathionium compounds
Phenothiazines, Phenothiazinecarboxylic acids and their esters
see: Dimethoxanate; Metiazinic acid; Protizinic acid
Phenothiazines, 2- and 10-acyl derivatives
see: Acepromazine; Aceprometazine; Acetophenazine; Butaperazine; Carfenazine; Fenoverine; Moracizine; Piperacetazine; Propyramazine bromide
Phenothiazines, 2-alkylthio derivatives
see: Thiethylperazine; Thioridazine
Phenothiazines, chloro derivatives
see: Chlorpromazine; Perphenazine; Pipamazine; Prochlorperazine; Thiopropazate
Phenothiazines, aminoalkyl derivatives
see: Alimemazine; Aminopromazine; Chlorpromazine; Cyamemazine; Etymemazine; Levomepromazine; Oxomemazine; Profenamine; Promazine; Promethazine; Triflupromazine
Phenothiazines, methylpiperazinylalkyl or piperazinylalkyl derivatives
see: Butaperazine; Oxaflumazine; Perazine; Prochlorperazine; Thiethylperazine; Thioproperazine; Trifluoperazine

Phosphoric acid esters, alkyl(aryl) dihydrogen phosphates or thiophosphates
see: Amifostine; Benfotiamine; Cidofovir; Creatinolfosfate; Etopophos; Fludarabine phosphate; Fosfestrol; Fosphenytoin sodium; Menadiol sodium diphosphate; Triclofos
Phosphoric acid esters, dialkyl(diaryl) hydrogen phosphates
see: Bucladesine sodium; Colfosceril palmitate; Miltefosine
Phosphoric acid esters, trialkyl(triaryl) thiophosphates
see: Ecothiopate iodide
Phosphoric acid esters, alkyl(aryl) trihydrogen and dialkyl(diaryl) dihydrogen diphosphates (acidic Pyrophosphates)
see: Citicoline; Cocarboxylase
Phosphoric acid esters, other
see: Isoflurophate
Phthalazines
see: Azelastine; Budralazine; Dihydralazine; Hydralazine; Todralazine
Phthalic acids, Imides [Phthalimides (1,3-Isoindolinediones)]
see: Tandospirone; Thalidomide
Phthalides (1-Isobenzofuranones)
see: Mycophenolate mofetil; Mycophenolic acid; Talampicillin
see also Phenolphthaleins
Phytyl derivatives
see: Phytomenadione
Piperazides
see: Delavirdine mesilate; Doxazosin; Fipexide; Ketoconazole; Pipobroman; Prazosin; Terazosin; Tiaramide; Vesnarinone
see also Carbamoylpiperazines; 3,4,5-Trimethoxycinnamoylpiperazides
1-Piperazineacetamides
see: Pirenzepine
1-Piperazineacetanilides
see: Lidoflazine
1-Piperazinealkanols
see: Dropropizine; Eprozinol; Proglumetacin
see also 1-Piperazineethanols
1-Piperazinecarboxylic acid esters
see: Trimazosin; Zopiclone
2,3-Piperazinediones
see: Cefbuperazone; Cefoperazone; Piperacillin
2,6-Piperazinediones
see: Dexrazoxane; Razoxane; Sobuzoxane
1-Piperazineethanols
see: Clopenthixol; Flupentixol; Naftopidil; Opipramol; Oxypendyl; Tiaramide; Zipeprol
1-Piperazineethanols, esters
see: Antrafenine
1-Piperazineethoxyethanols
see: Dixyrazine; Etodroxizine; Hydroxyzine; Quetiapine fumarate
Piperazines, benzhydryl derivatives
see: Almitrine; Chlorbenzoxamine; Cinnarizine; Cyclizine; Flunarizine; Manidipine; Medibazine; Oxatomide
Piperazines, chlorobenzhydryl derivatives
see: Buclizine; Cetirizine; Chlorcyclizine; Etodroxizine; Hydroxyzine; Meclozine
Piperazines, chlorophenyl derivatives
see: Etoperidone; Nefazodone hydrochloride; Trazodone
Piperazines, fluoro- and (trifluoromethyl)phenyl and -phenylalkyl derivatives
see: Almitrine; Flunarizine; Niaprazine

Piperazines, piperonyl derivatives (Methylenedioxybenzyl derivatives)
see: Fenoverine; Medibazine; Pifarnine; Piribedil
Piperazines, 1-(2-pyrimidinyl) derivatives
see: Buspirone; Tandospirone
Piperazines, without intermediate chain tricyclic substituted piperazines
see: Amoxapine; Clozapine; Levofloxacin; Loxapine; Ofloxacin; Olanzapine; Perlapine; Quetiapine fumarate; Rufloxacin hydrochloride
Piperazines, 1,4-symmetrical substituted piperazines
see: Pipobroman; Sildenafil
Piperazines, quaternary
see: Hexocyclium metilsulfate; Pipecuronium bromide
Piperazines, other
see: Azimilide hydrochloride; Dapiprazole; Enoxacin; Eprazinone; Indinavir sulfate; Itraconazole; Loprazolam; Pipebuzone; Pipemidic acid; Piperazine; Rifampicin; Rifapentine; Terconazole; Tiotixene; Tirilazad mesilate; Trimetazidine; Urapidil; Ziprasidone hydrochloride
Piperidides
see: Pifoxime
Piperidinecarboxylic acids
see: Difenoxin; Levocabastine; Tiagabine
Piperidinecarboxylic acids, amides, anilides
see: Bupivacaine; Carpipramine; Clocapramine; Mepivacaine; Metopimazine; Pipamazine; Pipamperone; Piritramide; Ropivacaine hydrochloride
Piperidinecarboxylic acids, esters of 4-Phenyl-4-piperidinecarboxylic acids
see: Anileridine; Diphenoxylate; Pethidine; Phenoperidine
Piperidinecarboxylic acids, other esters
see: Irinotecan; Loratadine; Remifentanil
2,4-Piperidinediones and Tetrahydro-2,4-pyridinediones
see: Methyprylon; Pyrithyldione
2,6-Piperidinediones (Glutarimides)
see: Aminoglutethimide; Bemegride; Buspirone; Glutethimide; Phenglutarimide; Thalidomide
Piperidines, anilino and anilinoalkyl derivatives
see: Alfentanil; Bamipine; Fentanyl; Sufentanil; Thenalidine
Piperidines, 4-benzamido derivatives
see: Cinitapride; Cisapride; Clebopride; Indoramin
Piperidines, 1,4'-bipiperidines
see: Carpipramine; Clocapramine; Irinotecan; Pipamperone; Piritramide
Piperidines, piperidinealkanols
see: Azacyclonol; Biperiden; Cycrimine; Difenidol; Fexofenadine hydrochloride; Ifenprodil; Lobeline; Mefloquine; Miglitol; Phenoperidine; Piperacetazine; Pipotiazine; Pipradrol; Pirmenol hydrochloride; Pridinol; Rimiterol; Terfenadine; Trihexyphenidyl
Piperidines, esters of piperidinealkanols
see: Cyclomethycaine; Diperodon; Flavoxate; Piperocaine
Piperidines, esters of quaternary piperidinealkanols
see: Bevonium metilsulfate
Piperidines, piperidinols
see: Bromperidol; Haloperidol; Loperamide; Miglitol; Moperone; Penfluridol; Periciazine; Perimetazine; Trifluperidol
Piperidines, esters of piperidinols
see: Benidipine; Iloprost; Pentapiperide; Piperidolate; Propiverine
Piperidines, esters of quaternary piperidinols
see: Mepenzolate bromide; Pipenzolate bromide
Piperidines, propionic acid esters of phenylpiperidinols
see: Alphaprodine

Propionic acids, 2-methylpropionic acids (Isobutyric acids)
see: Aztreonam; Bezafibrate; Ceftazidime; Ciprofibrate; Iocetamic acid

Propionic acids, amides
see: Bucillamine; Isepamicin; Nialamide; Omapatrilat; Pipobroman; Propiram; Propyramazine bromide; Stepronin; Tiopronin
see also 3-Chloropropionamides

Propionic acids, anilides
see: Alfentanil; Bicalutamide; Fentanyl; Flutamide; Iodoxamic acid; Remifentanil; Sufentanil; Suplatast tosilate

Propionic acids, esters of steroids
see: Alclometasone dipropionate; Betamethasone butyrate propionate; Betamethasone dipropionate; Clobetasol propionate; Fluticasone propionate; Prednicarbate; Testosterone propionate; Ulobetasol propionate

Propionic acids, esters of 2-methylpropionic acid (Isobutyric acid)
see: Fenofibrate; Ibopamine; Naftidrofuryl; Triamcinolone benetonide
see also 2-(p-Chlorophenoxy)-2-methylpropionic acid esters

Propionic acids, other esters
see: Atracurium besilate; Dextropropoxyphene; Diethylstilbestrol dipropionate; Erythromycin estolate; Fosinopril; Methestrol dipropionate; Midecamycin; Midecamycin acetate; Remifentanil; Spiramycin
see also 3-Cyclopentylpropionic acid esters; Tropic acid esters

Propionitriles
see: Anastrozole; Cefacetrile; Cinolazepam

Propiophenones
see: Eprazinone; Flopropione; Oxyfedrine

Propiophenones, derivatives
see: Amfebutamone; Amfepramone; Dyclonine; Eperisone; Etafenone; Propafenone; Tolperisone

2-Propynylamines (Propargylamines)
see: Pargyline; Selegiline

Prostaglandins (and related compounds)
see: Dinoprost; Dinoprostone; Epoprostenol; Iloprost

Prostaglandins, Prostaglandin esters
see: Latanoprost; Misoprostol; Unoprostone isopropyl

Pteridines
see: Triamterene
see also Isoalloxazines

Pteridines, 2,4-Diaminopteridines
see: Methotrexate

Pteridines, Pteridinylmethylaminobenzoic acid derivatives
see: Folic acid; Folinic acid; Methotrexate

Purines
see: Azathioprine; Didanosine; Famciclovir; Mercaptopurine; Tioguanine
see also Adenines (6-Aminopurines)

Pyrano[2,3-*b*][1,4]benzodioxines
see: Spectinomycin

Pyrano[3,4-*b*]indoles
see: Etodolac

Pyrano[3',4':6,7]indolizino[1,2-*b*]quinolines
see: Irinotecan; Topotecan

2-Pyranones (α-Pyrones)
see: Irinotecan; Kawain; Lovastatin; Simvastatin; Topotecan

4-Pyranones (γ-Pyrones)
see: Repirinast; Spectinomycin

Pyrano[3,2-*c*]quinolines
see: Repirinast

Pyrano[3,2-*g*]quinolines
see: Nedocromil

Pyrans and hydropyrans
see: Mupirocin; Novobiocin; Pirarubicin
see also Carbohydrates; Erythromycins; Lactones; Leucomycins; Macrolide antibiotics; Oligosaccharide antibiotics; Polyhydroxy acids

Pyrans and hydropyrans, pyrans as component of ring systems
see: Zanamivir

Pyrazinecarboxamides
see: Amiloride; Glipizide; Morinamide; Pyrazinamide

Pyrazines
see: Acipimox
see also Dibenzo[c,f]pyrazino[1,2-a]azepines; Pteridines; Sulfanilamidopyrazines

Pyrazino[2,1-*a*]isoquinolines
see: Praziquantel

Pyrazino[2,1-*a*]pyrido[2,3-*c*][2]benzazepines
see: Mirtazapine

Pyrazoleacetic acids
see: Lonazolac

Pyrazoles
see: Betazole; Celecoxib; Epirizole; Fomepizole
see also Sulfanilamidopyrazoles

Pyrazoles, (in Steroid ring systems)
see: Cortivazol; Stanozolol

3,5-Pyrazolidinediones
see: Azapropazone; Feclobuzone; Kebuzone; Mofebutazone; Oxyphenbutazone; Phenylbutazone; Pipebuzone; Sulfinpyrazone; Suxibuzone

2-Pyrazolin-5-ones
see: Muzolimine

3-Pyrazolin-5-ones (5-Pyrazolones), also derivatives
see: Aminophenazone; Metamizole sodium; Nifenazone; Piperylone; Propyphenazone

Pyrazolo[1,2-*a*][1,2,4]benzotriazines
see: Azapropazone

Pyrazolo[1,5-*a*]pyridines
see: Ibudilast

Pyrazolo[1,5-*a*]pyrimidines
see: Zaleplon

Pyrazolo[3,4-*d*]pyrimidines
see: Allopurinol

Pyrazolo[4,3-*d*]pyrimidines
see: Sildenafil

Pyridazines
see: Amezinium metilsulfate; Azintamide; Cadralazine; Minaprine; Nifurprazine; Pildralazine
see also Sulfanilamidopyridazines

Pyridazino[1,2-*a*][1,2]diazepines
see: Cilazapril

Pyridazinones
see: Emorfazone; Pimobendan

Pyridinamines
see: Ampiroxicam; Amrinone; Delavirdine mesilate; Fenyramidol; Flupirtine; Lornoxicam; Phenazopyridine; Piketoprofen; Pinacidil; Piroxicam; Propiram; Tenoxicam; Torasemide

Pyridindenes (Azafluorenes, Indenopyridines)
see: Phenindamine

Pyridineacetic acids
see: Diodone

Pyridineacetic acids, esters and amides
see: Propyliodone

Pyridinealkylamines and -alkenylamines
see: Betahistine; Picotamide; Pimefylline; Tropicamide; Zimeldine

Pyrrolizines and Pyrrolizidines
see: Ketorolac; Pilsicainide
Pyrrolo[3,4-*b*]pyrazines
see: Zopiclone
Pyrrolo[3,4-*b*]pyridins
see: Moxifloxacin hydrochloride

Q

2,4-Quinazolinediamines
see: Trimetrexate glucuronate
2,4-Quinazolinediones
see: Ketanserin
Quinazolines, 6,7-dimethoxy-4-quinazolinamines
see: Alfuzosin; Bunazosin; Doxazosin; Prazosin; Terazosin;
Trimazosin
2-Quinazolinones
see: Proquazone
4-Quinazolinones
see: Afloqualone; Methaqualone; Raltitrexed
4-Quinazolinones, chloro derivatives
see: Fenquizone; Mecloqualone; Metolazone; Quinethazone
Quinolinamines
see: Antrafenine; Floctafenine
Quinolinamines, alkoxy or chloro derivatives
see: Amodiaquine; Chloroquine; Glafenine;
Hydroxychloroquine; Primaquine
**Quinolinecarboxylic acids, 1,4-Dihydro-4-oxo-3-quinoli-
necarboxylic acids**
see: Ciprofloxacin; Grepafloxacin; Oxolinic acid; Rosoxacin
**Quinolinecarboxylic acids, 1-Cyclopropyl-1,4-dihydro-4-
oxo-3-quinolinecarboxylic acids**
see: Moxifloxacin hydrochloride; Sparfloxacin
**Quinolinecarboxylic acids, Fluoro-1,4-dihydro-4-oxo-3-
quinolinecarboxylic acids**
see: Moxifloxacin hydrochloride
**Quinolinecarboxylic acids, Fluoro-1,4-dihydro-4-oxo-7-(1-
piperazinyl)-3-quinoline carboxylic acids**
see: Ciprofloxacin; Fleroxacin; Grepafloxacin; Levofloxacin;
Lomefloxacin; Norfloxacin; Ofloxacin; Pefloxacin;
Rufloxacin hydrochloride; Sparfloxacin; Temafloxacin
Quinolinecarboxylic acids, amides
see: Cinchocaine; Saquinavir
Quinolines
see: Mefloquine; Montelukast sodium; Normolaxol
*see also Aporphines; 1,3-Dioxolo[4,5-g]quinolines; Ergoli-
nes; Lysergamides; Pyrano[3',4':6,7]indolizino[1,2-b]quino-
lines*
Quinolines, tetrahydroquinolines
see: Carteolol
Quinolines, quaternary
see: Dequalinium chloride
Quinolinesulfonic acids
see: Actinoquinol
Quinolinols (Hydroxyquinolines), also esters and ethers
see: Nitroxoline; Oxyquinoline; Procaterol
Quinolinols, Bromo, chloro and iodo derivatives
see: Broxyquinoline; Chlorquinaldol; Clioquinol;
Diiodohydroxyquinoline; Halquinol
2- and 4-Quinolinones
see: Carteolol; Cilostazol; Flosequinan; Procaterol;
Rebamipide; Vesnarinone
Quinolizines
see: Tiquizium bromide
see also Indolo[2,3-a]quinolizines

Quinones
see: Phanquinone
*see also Anthraquinones; Benzoquinones; Mitomycins; Naph-
thoquinones*
Quinoxaline 1,4-dioxides
see: Clioquinol
Quinoxalines
see: Brimonidine
Quinuclidines (1-Azabicyclo[2.2.2]octanes)
see: Aceclidine; Clidinium bromide; Mequitazine;
Nazasetron; Quinupramine
Quinuclidines, 4-quinolylmethanol derivatives
see: Quinidine; Quinine

R

Resorcinols (1,3-Benzenediols), also ethers
see: Hexylresorcinol; Sofalcone; Zeranol
Ribosides and Deoxyribosides
see: Azacitidine; Citicoline; Didanosine; Gemcitabine;
Ribavirin; Zalcitabine
see also Adenosines
Ribosides and Deoxyribosides, Antibiotics
see: Capecitabine; Mizoribine
Rifamycins
see: Rifampicin; Rifapentine; Rifaximin

S

Salicylic acids
see: Balsalazide sodium; Diflunisal; Fendosal; Mesalazine;
Olsalazine sodium; Repaglinide; Salicylic acid
*see also Acetylsalicylic acids also esters; p-Aminosalicylic ac-
ids; 5-(p-Sulfamoylphenylazo)salicylic acids*
Salicylic acids, amides and substituted amides, anilides
see: Alibendol; Bromopride; Buclosamide; Dilevalol;
Labetalol; Niclosamide; Salacetamide; Salicylamide;
Xipamide
Salicylic acids, esters
see: Hydroxyethyl salicylate; Salsalate
Salicylic acids (*O*-alkyl- and *O*-acyl derivatives)
see: Salsalate
**Salicylic acids (*O*-alkyl and *O*-acyl derivatives), amides,
anilides, esters**
see: Benexate; Ethenzamide; Exalamide; Glibenclamide;
Otilonium bromide; Parsalmide; Remoxipride; Sulpiride;
Sultopride; Tiapride
Schiff's Bases (Azomethines)
see: Progabide
9,10-Secocholestanes and -ergostanes
see: Alfacalcidol; Calcifediol; Calcipotriol; Calcitriol;
Colecalciferol; Dihydrotachysterol; Ergocalciferol;
Paricalcitol; Tacalcitol
Semicarbazones
see: Carbazochrome
see also 5-Nitro-2-furaldehyde semicarbazones
Serines, amides
see: Benserazide
Sideramines
see: Deferoxamine
Silanol ethers, polymer
see: Dimethicone

Sulfanilamides, other
see: Amprenavir
Sulfanilamidooxazoles and isoxazoles
see: Acetylsulfafurazole; Sulfafurazole; Sulfamethoxazole;
Sulfamoxole
Sulfanilamidopyrazines
see: Sulfalene
Sulfanilamidopyrazoles
see: Sulfaphenazole
Sulfanilamidopyridazines
see: Sulfachlorpyridazine; Sulfamethoxypyridazine
Sulfanilamidopyridines
see: Salazosulfapyridine
2-Sulfanilamidopyrimidines
see: Sulfadiazine; Sulfamerazine; Sulfametoxydiazine;
Sulfaperin
4(6)-Sulfanilamidopyrimidines
see: Sulfacitine; Sulfadimethoxine; Sulfadoxine;
Sulfisomidine
Sulfanilamido-1,2,5-thiadiazoles
see: Sulfametrole
Sulfanilamido-1,3,4-thiadiazoles
see: Sulfaethidole; Sulfamethizole
Sulfanilamidothiazoles and -isothiazoles
see: Phthalylsulfathiazole; Succinylsulfathiazole;
Sulfathiazole
Sulfanilylguanidines
see: Sulfaguanidine; Sulfaguanole
Sulfanilylurea and -thiourea derivatives
see: Carbutamide; Sulfacarbamide; Sulfaloxic acid
Sulfides (Thioethers)
see: Arotinolol; Azathioprine; Ceftriaxone; Docarpamine;
Enoximone; Famotidine; Meropenem; Montelukast sodium;
Nelfinavir mesylate; Neticonazole hydrochloride; Nifuratel;
Pergolide; Sulconazole; Tiadenol; Tinazoline hydrochloride
see also Disulfides; Epithio compounds; Fluoro sulfides;
Thioacetals; Thiophenol ethers
Sulfinic acids and salts
see: Sulfoxone sodium
Sulfonamides
see: Brinzolamide; Dorzolamide; Ethoxzolamide; Fasudil;
Meticrane; Mezlocillin; Naratriptan; Sildenafil; Sumatriptan;
Tiotixene; Tirofiban hydrochloride; Zonisamide
see also 1,2,4-Benzothiadiazine 1,1-dioxides; o-Chlorosulfon-
amides; Homosulfanilamides
Sulfones
see: Bicalutamide; Metopimazine; Sulforidazine; Sultopride;
Thiamphenicol; Tiapride; Tinidazole; Zolimidine
see also Dioxides (S-Dioxides)
Sulfonic acids and salts
see: Cefsulodin; Clomethiazole; Ecabet sodium; Mesna;
Sulbenicillin; Sultroponium
see also Amino sulfonic acids; Benzenesulfonic acids; Naph-
thalenesulfonic acids and Naphtholsulfonic acids; Phenolsul-
fonic acids; Quinolinesulfonic acids; Sulfosuccinic acid deriv-
atives
Sulfonic acids, esters
see: Busulfan; Improsulfan
Sulfonium compounds
see: Ademetionine; Methylmethionine sulfonium chloride;
Suplatast tosilate
see also Phenazathionium compounds
Sulfonylurea compounds, derivatives
see: Acetohexamide; Chlorpropamide; Glibenclamide;
Glibornuride; Gliclazide; Glimepiride; Glipizide; Gliquidone;
Glisoxepide; Tolazamide; Tolbutamide
Sulfonylurea compounds, other
see: Torasemide

Sulfosuccinic acid derivatives
see: Sodium dioctyl sulfosuccinate
Sulfoxides
see: Adrafinil; Flosequinan; Mesoridazine; Modafinil;
Oxfendazole; Sulfinpyrazone; Sulindac
Sulfuric acid esters [alkyl(aryl) hydrogen sulfates and
their salts]
see: Ceruletide; Diethylstilbestrol disulfate; Heparin;
Pyridofylline; Sodium picosulfate
Sulfuric diamides
see: Famotidine
Sultams
see: Sultiame; Tianeptine sodium
see also 1,2,4-Benzothiadiazine 1,1-dioxides; 1,2-Benzothiaz-
ine-3-carboxamide 1,1-dioxides
Sydnonimines
see: Molsidomine

T

Terpenes
see: Cineole; Xibornol
see also Carotenes; Vitamin A compounds
Terpenes (acyclic)
see: Gefarnate; Indometacin farnesil; Pifarnine; Plaunotol;
Ubidecarenone
see also Phytyl derivatives
Terpenes, Terpene alcohols
see: Glibornuride; Plaunotol; Sobrerol
see also Menthols
Testosterones
see: Testosterone; Testosterone cypionate; Testosterone
enanthate; Testosterone propionate
Testosterones, chlorotestosterones
see: Clostebol acetate
Testosterones, 17α-methyltestosterones
see: Bolasterone; Calusterone; Methyltestosterone;
Oxymesterone
see also Androsta-3,5-dienes
Tetracyclines
see: Doxycycline; Metacycline; Minocycline;
Oxytetracycline; Tetracycline
Tetracyclines, chloro derivatives
see: Chlortetracycline; Clomocycline; Demeclocycline
Tetracyclines, N^2-substituted
see: Clomocycline; Lymecycline; Rolitetracycline
Tetrazoles
see: Azosemide; Candesartan cilexetil; Cefazolin; Ceftezole;
Cilostazol; Irbesartan; Losartan potassium; Pemirolast;
Pranlukast; Tazanolast; Valsartan
Tetrazolines
see: Alfentanil
Tetrazolo[1,5-*a*]azepines
see: Pentetrazol
Theobromines
see: Pentifylline; Pentoxifylline; Protheobromine
Theophyllines
see: Acefylline; Bamifylline; Cafedrine; Diprophylline;
Doxofylline; Etamiphylline; Etofylline; Fenetylline;
Lomifylline; Pimefylline; Proxyphylline; Reproterol;
Theodrenaline; Theophylline; Xantinol nicotinate
Theophyllines, esters of 7-(2-hydroxyethyl)theophylline
see: Pyridofylline
1,3,5-Thiadiazines (Perhydro derivatives)
see: Sulbentine

Thymols and their esters and ethers
see: Moxisylyte
Tocopherols (Vitamin E compounds)
see: α-Tocopherol
***p*-Toluenesulfonates (4-Methylbenzenesulfonates)**
see: Ademetionine; Suplatast tosilate; Tosufloxacin
Triamines
see: Flupirtine; Gusperimus trihydrochloride; Triamterene; Trimetrexate glucuronate
1,3,8-Triazaspiro[4.5]decanes
see: Fluspirilene; Spiperone
Triazenes (Diazoamino compounds)
see: Dacarbazine
1,2,4-Triazines
see: Ceftriaxone; Lamotrigine
see also Pyrazolo[1,2-a][1,2,4]benzotriazines
1,3,5-Triazines (also hydro derivatives)
see: Azacitidine
1,3,5-Triazines (also hydro derivatives), Diamino-1,3,5-triazines
see: Almitrine; Chlorazanil
1,2,3-Triazoles
see: Cefatrizine
see also Benzotriazoles
1,2,4-Triazoles
see: Anastrozole; Etoperidone; Fluconazole; Itraconazole; Letrozole; Nefazodone hydrochloride; Ribavirin; Rilmazafone; Rizatriptan benzoate; Terconazole
see also 6H-Thieno[3,2-f][1,2,4]triazolo[4,3-a][1,4]diazepines
[1,2,4]Triazolo[4,3-a][1,4]benzodiazepines
see: Alprazolam; Estazolam; Triazolam
1,2,4-Triazolo[4,3-a]pyridines
see: Dapiprazole; Trazodone
2,2,2-Trichloroethanol esters
see: Triclofos
see also Chloral hydrate derivatives
1,2,3-Trimethoxybenzenes
see: Gallopamil; Mitopodozide; Tretoquinol; Trimetazidine; Trimethoprim; Trimetrexate glucuronate
3,4,5-Trimethoxybenzoic acid amides
see: Sulmetozin; Trimethobenzamide; Trimetozine; Troxipide
3,4,5-Trimethoxybenzoic acid esters
see: Bietaserpine; Deserpidine; Dilazep; Hexobendine; Reserpine
3,4,5-Trimethoxycinnamic acid esters
see: Rescinnamine
3,4,5-Trimethoxycinnamoylpiperazides
see: Cinepazet; Cinepazide
Trimethylacetic acid esters (2,2-Dimethylpropionic acid esters, Pivalates)
see: Cefditoren pivoxil; Dexamethasone pivalate; Dipivefrine; Fluocortolone trimethylacetate; Pivampicillin; Pivmecillinam; Prednisolone 21-trimethylacetate; Tixocortol pivalate
Triphenylmethanes
see: Clotrimazole; Flutrimazole
see also Fluoresceins; Phenolphthaleins
Tropic acid amides
see: Tropicamide
Tropic acid esters
see: Atropine; Atropine methonitrate; Butropium bromide; Butylscopolammonium bromide; Cimetropium bromide; Fentonium bromide; Ipratropium bromide; Methscopolamine bromide; Oxitropium bromide; Scopolamine; Sultroponium
Tropine esters
see: Atropine; Homatropine; Tropisetron

Tropine esters, quaternary
see: Atropine methonitrate; Butropium bromide; Fentonium bromide; Flutropium bromide; Homatropine methylbromide; Ipratropium bromide; Octatropine methylbromide; Sultroponium; Tropenziline bromide; Trospium chloride
Tropine esters (6,7-Epoxy derivatives)
see: Scopolamine
Tropine esters (6,7-Epoxy derivatives), quaternary
see: Butylscopolammonium bromide; Cimetropium bromide; Methscopolamine bromide; Oxitropium bromide
Tropine ethers
see: Benzatropine; Clobenztropine; Deptropine
Tryptophans
see: Caffeine acetyltryptophanate; Oxitriptan; L-Tryptophan
Tyrosines
see: Carbidopa; Dextrothyroxine; Levodopa; Levothyroxine; Liothyronine; Methyldopa; Metirosine; Tirofiban hydrochloride; L-Tyrosine
Tyrosines, amides and esters
see: Bentiromide; Etiroxate; Methyldopate; Tiropramide

U

Undecanoic acid esters (Undecanoates)
see: Estradiol undecylate; Iofendylate; Nandrolone undecylate
Undecenoic acid esters (Undecenoates)
see: Boldenone undecenylate
Uracils [2,4(1H,3H)-Pyrimidinediones]
see: Carmofur; Fluorouracil; Orotic acid; Sorivudine; Stavudine; Tegafur; Uramustine; Urapidil
see also Thiouracils; Uridines and Deoxyuridines
Urea derivatives
see: Allantoin; N-Carbamoyl-L-aspartic acid calcium salt; Chlormerodrin; Citrulline; Enviomycin; Viomycin
see also Biuret derivatives; Bromoacylurea derivatives; 2-Chloroethylurea derivatives; Imidazolidinones; Nitrosourea derivatives; Thiourea derivatives
Urea derivatives, hydroxyurea derivatives
see: Hydroxycarbamide; Noxytiolin; Zileuton
Urea derivatives, phenylurea derivatives
see: Carbuterol; Celiprolol; Talinolol
see also Carbanilides
Urea derivatives, N-carboxamides of nitrogen containing rings
see: Carbamazepine; Glimepiride; Oxcarbazepine; Ritonavir; Xamoterol
see also Carbamoylpiperazines
Uridines and Deoxyuridines
see: Doxifluridine; Idoxuridine; Trifluridine; Zidovudine

V

Valeric acids (Pentanoic acids)
see: Biotin; Citrulline; Eflornithine; Epoprostenol; Iloprost; Thioctic acid; Valproic acid
see also Allenolic acids
Valeric acids, amides, anilides and hydrazides
see: Indinavir sulfate; Valsartan

X

Y

Z